THE SIMON  SCHUSTER

SUPER
CROSSWORD
PUZZLE
DICTIONARY
and
REFERENCE
BOOK

A FIRESIDE BOOK

Published by Simon & Schuster

FIRESIDE
Rockefeller Center
1230 Avenue of the Americas
New York, NY 10020

FIRESIDE and colophon are registered trademarks
of Simon & Schuster Inc.

Designed by Irving Perkins Associates

Manufactured in the United States of America

10   9   8   7   6   5   4   3

Library of Congress Cataloging-in-Publication Data
The Simon & Schuster super crossword puzzle dictionary and
reference book.
p.   cm.
"A Fireside book."
1. Crossword puzzles—Glossaries, vocabularies, etc.   I. Title.
II. Title: Simon & Schuster super crossword puzzle dictionary and
reference book.
GV1507.C7G594   1999
423'.1—dc21
                                        99-10226
                                            CIP

ISBN 0-684-85696-4

Contents

Abbreviations Used in the Dictionary

abbr	abbreviation	Grk	Greek
acron	acronym	inf	infinitive
Anat	Anatomy	iron	ironic
Arch	Architecture	It	Italian
Biol	Biology	Jap	Japanese
Brit	British	Lat	Latin
Can	Canadian	Med	Medicine
Chem	Chemistry	Mus	Music
Comp	Computers	pl	plural form
fig	figurative	Russ	Russian
Fr	French	Scot	Scottish
Ger	German	Sp	Spanish
Gram	Grammar		

A: 3 amp; 5 type A; 6 ampere, group A; 8 angstrom, vitamin A; 9 excellent

a: 4 some; 7 a kind of, a sort of, a type of

A.B.: 3 tar; 4 salt; 7 jack tar; 10 able seaman

A.D.: 10 Anno Domini

a.k.a.: 5 alias; 11 also known as

A.M.: 4 morn; 5 prime; 7 morning; 8 forenoon; 12 ante meridiem, ante meridien [Lat]

A.R.: 9 anno regni [Lat]

AA: 6 ack-ack; 15 Associate in Arts

aardvark: 7 ant bear, antbear; 8 anteater

abaca: 10 Manila hemp; 11 Manilla hemp

abacist: 10 calculator; 13 arithmetician

aback: 3 aft; 5 abaft, after; 6 astern; 8 rearward

abacus: 7 suan-pan

abaft: 3 aft; 5 aback, after; 6 astern; 8 rearward

abalienation: 7 cession; 8 transfer; 9 assigning, conveying; 10 alienation, assignment, conveyance

abalone: 8 ear-shell

abampere: 5 abamp

abandon: 4 give, quit; 5 empty, let go, lurch, yield; 6 candor, desert, give up, vacate; 7 forsake, let slip; 8 abnegate, bonhomie, desolate, evacuate, wildness; 9 frankness, sincerity, surrender; 10 relinquish, wantonness; 11 leave a place; 12 unconstraint

abandoned: 4 left; 7 forlorn, given up; 8 deserted, desolate, forsaken; 9 cast aside, unpeopled; 10 disposed of, tenantless, untenanted; 11 uninhabited; 12 lost to virtue, relinquished

abandoned child: 4 waif; 9 foundling

abandoned infant: 9 foundling

abandoned ship: 8 derelict

abandonment: 8 giving up; 9 defection, desertion, forsaking, surrender; 10 abandoning, abjuration, abnegation, desolation; 12 dispensation, renunciation; 13 relinquishing

abase: 4 sink, snub; 5 abash, pitch; 6 debase, humble, reduce; 7 chagrin, mortify; 8 bring low; 9 humiliate; 10 strike dumb; 11 precipitate

abased: 4 oily; 5 soapy; 6 pliant; 7 fawning, slavish; 8 cringing; 9 groveling, sniveling; 10 dough-faced; 12 mealy-mouthed

abasement: 7 lowness; 8 humbling; 9 abjection, lowliness, servility; 10 abjectness, debasement; 11 degradation, humiliation; 12 self-contempt, subserviency

abash: 3 cow; 4 snub; 5 abase, daunt, deter; 7 overawe; 9 embarrass, terrorize; 10 discourage, intimidate, strike dumb

abashed: 6 dashed; 7 ashamed; 9 chagrined

abasic: 6 abatic

abate: 3 lay; 4 bate, calm, cool, damp, hush, lull, swag, tame; 5 allay, let up, quell, quiet, slack, slake, sober, still; 6 deaden, pacify, rebate, smooth, soothe; 7 appease, assuage, compose, die away, slacken, turn off; 8 calm down, decrease, slack off, suppress; 9 alleviate; 11 tranquilize

abatement: 6 hiatus; 7 respite; 8 discount, mark down, reprieve; 9 allowance, reduction; 10 concession, declension, suspension; 12 depreciation

abating: 9 subsiding

abatis: 6 abatis; 7 abattis

abattoir: 8 butchery, shambles; 14 slaughterhouse

abaxial: 6 dorsal; 7 abaxile

abba: 3 dad; 4 papa, sire; 6 father; 13 paterfamilias

abbe: 4 cure; 12 parish priest

abberrant: 8 abnormal

abberrantly: 10 abnormally; 11 anomalously

abbess: 8 prioress; 14 mother superior

abbey: 6 friary, priory

abbot: 5 prior; 13 archimandrite

abbreviate: 3 cut; 6 reduce, take in; 7 abridge, curtail, shorten; 8 contract; 11 foreshorten

abbreviated: 5 brief; 6 abrege [Fr]; 8 abridged; 9 shortened, truncated

abbreviation: 10 shortening; 11 curtailment

abbreviature: 10 shortening; 11 curtailment; 12 abbreviation

ABC: 4 ABCs; 6 basics; 7 grammar; 8 alphabet, elements, outlines; 9 rudiments; 10 first thing

abdal: 5 druid; 7 fanatic

abdicant: 8 retiring; 9 resigning; 10 abdicating

abdicate: 6 give up, resign; 7 lay down, throw up; 8 renounce

abdicating: 8 retiring; 9 resigning

abdication: 10 deposition, usurpation; 11 resignation; 12 dethronement, stepping down

abditory: 5 crypt; 9 oubliette

abdomen: 5 belly; 6 venter; 7 stomach

abdominal: 7 coeliac

abdominal delivery: 8 C-section, cesarean, cesarian; 9 caesarean; 16 caesarean section

abdominal nerve plexus: 11 solar plexus

abdominoscope: 11 gastroscope [Med]

abdominous: 7 paunchy; 10 potbellied

abduce: 4 cite; 6 abduct, adduce

abducens: 8 abducent; 13 abducens nerve,
abducent nerve; 14 nervus abducens
abducent: 8 abducens; 9 abducting, 13 abducens nerve, abducent nerve
abduct: 5 crimp; 6 kidnap, nobble, snatch; 7
capture
abducted: 8 kidnaped; 9 kidnapped
abductee: 3 POW; 6 detenu [Fr], inmate; 7
captive, hostage; 8 detainee, prisoner; 13
prisoner of war
abduction: 7 repulse; 8 ablation; 13 expropriation
abductor: 6 badger; 8 bunko man, kidnaper,
snatcher; 9 kidnapper; 11 cattle thief; 14
abductor muscle
abecedarian: 5 basal, basic, usher; 6 simple;
7 dominie [Fr], primary; 9 beginning, pedagogue; 10 elementary; 12 alphabetical,
schoolmaster
abecedary: 4 ABCs; 6 manual, primer; 8 alphabet; 9 rudiments, vade mecum
abele: 10 white aspen; 11 aspen poplar,
Populus alba, white poplar
Abelmoschus: 4 okra; 5 gumbo; 9 okra
plant; 11 lady's-finger; 16 genus
Abelmoschus
Aberdeen Angus: 5 Angus; 10 black
Angus
aberdevine: 6 siskin; 10 wood pigeon
aberrant: 6 errant; 7 deviant
aberration: 8 deviance; 9 aberrance, aberrancy; 10 distortion
abet: 6 second
abetment: 11 instigation
abetter: 7 abettor
abettor: 6 backer; 7 abetter; 8 advocate,
champion, partisan, seconder, upholder; 9
supporter; 11 protagonist
abeyance: 7 waiting; 8 suspense; 10 suspension; 11 interregnum
abeyant: 6 hidden, occult; 7 dormant, lurking; 8 inactive; 9 suspended
abhor: 4 hate; 6 detest, loathe; 8 execrate,
nauseate; 9 abominate
abhorrence: 4 hate; 5 odium; 6 hatred; 8
loathing; 9 antipathy; 10 execration, odi-
ousness; 11 abomination, detestation,
hatefulness; 13 execrableness, repulsiveness
abhorrent: 5 gross; 6 odious; 7 fulsome,
hateful, obscene; 9 execrable, loathsome,
repellent, repugnant, repulsive; 10 abominable, detestable; 12 insufferable
abidance: 7 abiding; 8 enduring; 9 endurance, residence, residency, suffering,
tolerance; 10 compliance, conformity, sufferance, tolerating; 11 forbearance; 12 conformation
abide: 4 bear, bide, keep, last, live, stay; 5
brook, dwell, lodge, perch, put up, roost,

stand, watch; 6 endure, nestle, pursue, remain, reside, suffer, tenant; 7 inhabit, sojourn, stomach; 8 continue, tolerate
abide by: 5 honor; 6 comply, follow, honour;
7 execute, observe, perform, respect; 10
comply with; 11 acknowledge
abiding: 7 lasting; 8 abidance, enduring; 9
endurance, suffering, tolerance; 10 continuing, sufferance, tolerating; 11 forbearance; 12 imperishable
Abies: 7 fir tree; 10 genus Abies
abigail: 9 lady's maid, soubrette; 10 confidente [Fr]
ability: 4 turn; 5 forte, parts, power; 6 talent,
virtue; 7 faculty, quality, talents; 8 capacity, efficacy, felicity, property; 9 attribute,
endowment; 10 capability, cleverness; 12
habilitation; 13 effectiveness, qualification
ability to float: 8 buoyancy
abiogenesis: 8 autogeny; 9 oogenesis; 10
biogenesis; 11 autogenesis
abiological: 5 azoic; 7 abiotic; 9 nonliving
abiotic: 5 azoic; 9 nonliving; 11 abiological
abject: 3 low; 4 base, mean, vile; 5 dirty,
lowly; 6 little, paltry, scabby, scummy,
scurvy, shabby; 7 ignoble, low-down, pitiful, scrubby; 8 beggarly, rascally, resigned,
sneaking; 9 groveling, miserable, unhopeful; 10 spiritless; 11 ignominious; 12 contemptible, pettifogging; 13 unrespectable
abjection: 6 laxity; 8 baseness, foulness,
trimming, vileness; 9 abasement, shuffling,
turpitude; 10 debasement; 11 degradation;
14 moral turpitude
abjectly: 10 resignedly
abjectness: 7 lowness; 8 meanness; 9 abasement, lowliness; 10 shabbiness; 12 self-
contempt; 13 self-abasement
abjuration: 10 abnegation, retraction; 11
abandonment, recantation; 12 renunciation
abjure: 6 forego, recant; 7 retract; 8 abnegate, disclaim, forswear, renounce
ablactation: 7 weaning
ablate: 4 file; 6 abrade, scrape
ablation: 8 ablation, excision; 9 abduction;
10 cutting out; 11 extirpation; 13 expropriation
ablaut: 9 gradation
ablaze: 5 afire; 6 aflame, aflare, alight, on
fire; 7 aroused, blazing, burning, flaming;
8 in a blaze, inflamed
able: 4 cute; 6 clever, gifted; 7 capable, endowed; 8 talented; 9 competent; 10 able-
bodied, felicitous
able-bodied: 4 able; 6 strong
ablegate: 6 remove; 8 accredit, set aside
able seaman: 2 A.B.; 3 tar; 4 salt; 6 sailor; 7
jack tar
ablism: 7 ableism; 10 able-bodism; 13 able-
bodiedism
abloom: 9 flowering; 12 efflorescent

ablude: 4 vary; **6** differ; **8** mismatch, not match; **11** be different; **12** be dissimilar

ablution: 6 laving, washup; **7** bathing

ablutionary: 9 cleansing

ably: 5 aptly; **7** capably; **11** competently

abnegate: 5 let go, yield; **6** abjure, desert, forego, give up; **7** abandon, forsake, let slip, retract; **8** disclaim, renounce; **9** surrender; **10** relinquish

abnegation: 6 denial; **7** protest; **8** negation; **9** recusancy; **10** abjuration, disclaimer, self-denial; **11** abandonment, forbearance; **12** renunciation

abnormal: 9 abberrant

abnormality: 7 anomaly, oddness; **10** abnormalcy; **12** freakishness, irregularity; **13** anomalousness, unnaturalness

abnormal mind: 11 unsound mind; **12** diseased mind

abnormity: 7 anomaly, oddness; **11** abnormality; **13** anomalousness, unnaturalness

Abo: 9 Aborigine; **10** Aboriginal; **16** native Australian

aboard: 6 afloat, on base; **7** on board, onboard; **9** alongside

abode: 4 bode, home; **5** augur; **6** typify; **7** betoken, housing, lodging, point to, portend, presage, signify; **8** domicile, dwelling, forebode, lodgment; **9** foretoken, lodgement, prefigure, residence; **10** foreshadow, habitation

aboding: 10 foreboding

abolish: 6 recall; **7** retract

abolition: 11 abolishment

abolitionist: 15 emancipationist

abomasum: 13 fourth stomach

A-bomb: 8 atom bomb; **10** atomic bomb; **11** fission bomb

abominable: 4 foul; **5** awful, nasty, reeky; **6** coarse, odious; **7** beastly, hateful, painful; **8** dreadful, terrible; **9** abhorrent, atrocious, execrable, offensive; **10** detestable; **11** unspeakable

abominable snowman: 4 yeti

abominably: 7 awfully; **8** odiously, rottenly, terribly; **9** abysmally; **10** detestably; **11** atrociously, repulsively

abominate: 4 hate; **5** abhor; **6** detest, loathe; **8** execrate, nauseate

abomination: 4 hate; **5** odium; **6** hatred; **8** aversion, loathing; **9** antipathy, bête noire; **10** abhorrence, execration; **11** detestation

a bon droit: 6 fairly, justly; **7** equably; **8** in equity, in reason; **9** in justice

abord: 7 welcome

aboriginal: 6 native, primal; **8** primeval; **9** aborigine, primaeval; **10** aborigines [pl], indigenous, primordial

Aborigine: 3 Abo; **10** Aboriginal; **16** native Australian

aborning: 7 at birth

A

abort: 4 slip, trip; **6** blow it; **7** botch it, stumble; **8** miscarry

abortion: 11 miscarriage

abortive: 5 addle; **9** stillborn; **12** unsuccessful

abound: 4 flow, rain, teem; **5** burst; **6** stream; **7** bristle; **9** exuberate

abounding: 6 galore

abounding with: 6 rich in; **8** rife with; **9** thick with

about: 3 say; **4** most, near, nigh, or so, some; **5** astir; **6** all but, almost, around, nearby, nearly; **7** close to, roughly; **8** well-nigh; **9** in the area, just about, virtually; **10** more or less; **13** thereabouts; **13** approximately

about-face: 8 reversal

about turn: 9 about-face

above: 2 up; **4** over; **5** aloft, aloof, supra; **6** high up, on high; **8** higher up, overhead

above all: 3 yea; **4** even; **7** the most; **9** a fortiori, eminently, extremely, still more, supremely, to beat all; **10** especially, peculiarly, surpassing, to crown all; **11** egregiously, exceedingly, of all things, principally, prominently; **12** particularly, preeminently

aboveboard: 4 open; **8** honestly; **9** confiding, open as day; **10** unreserved; **11** openhearted; **12** unsuspicious

above par: 4 fair; **12** considerable

above suspicion: 9 blameless

above water: 8 at anchor; **10** high and dry; **12** on sure ground

abradant: 7 abrader; **8** abrasive; **16** abrasive material

abrade: 4 file, rasp, skin, stub; **5** grate, scour; **6** ablate, abrase, rub off, scrape; **7** corrade, rub down

abraded: 4 worn; **5** filed; **7** scraped, skinned; **8** debrided, worn down

Abramis: 5 bream; **12** genus Abramis

abranchial: 8 gill-less; **11** abranchiate, abranchious

abrase: 6 abrade, rub off; **7** corrade, rub down

abrasion: 6 scrape; **7** scratch; **8** grinding; **9** attrition, corrasion, detrition; **10** rubbing off, wearing off; **11** excoriation

abrasive: 5 harsh; **8** abradant, scratchy

abreaction: 9 catharsis, katharsis

abreast: 4 arow; **5** aside; **6** beside; **9** alongside, on one side

abrege: 8 abridged; **11** abbreviated

abreption: 7 capture, seizing, seizure; **8** catching; **9** snatching; **10** prehension

abridge: 3 cut; **6** reduce, take in; **7** curtail, shorten; **8** abstract, contract; **9** epitomize, summarize; **10** abbreviate; **11** foreshorten

abridged: 6 abrege [Fr]; **11** abbreviated

abridgement: 4 note; **5** brief, draft; **6** apercu,

digest, minute, precis; **7** capsule, epitome, outline, summary; **8** abstract, analysis, synopsis; **9** concision, squeezing; **10** compacting, truncation; **10** abridgment; **12** condensation, retrenchment

abroach: 8 broached

abroad: 4 lost; **6** afield, beyond, yonder; **7** farther, further; **8** overseas

Abrocoma: 10 chinchilla; **13** genus Abrocoma

abrocome: 13 chinchilla rat, rat chinchilla

abrogate: 5 annul; **6** cancel, repeal, revoke; **7** rescind, reverse; **10** render null

abrogation: 6 repeal; **8** annuling, recision; **9** annulment, canceling; **10** abrogating, defeasance, rescinding, rescission; **12** cancellation; **13** nullification

Abronia: 7 verbena; **12** genus Abronia

abrupt: 4 rude; **5** crude, sharp; **6** sudden; **7** brusque, halting, instant, waspish; **9** immediate, momentary; **10** off-putting; **11** precipitant, precipitate, precipitous; **12** disconnected; **13** discontinuous, instantaneous

abruption: 10 disruption; **11** breaking off

abruptly: 4 dead; **5** short; **8** suddenly; **12** surprisingly, unexpectedly

abruptness: 8 curtness; **9** gruffness, shortness, steepness; **10** suddenness; **11** brusqueness; **12** precipitance, precipitancy

Abruzzi: 14 Abruzzi e Molise

abscess: 4 boil; **6** fester

abscind: 4 rend; **5** sever; **6** divide, sunder; **7** abscise, fall off; **8** dissever; **9** subdivide

abscise: 7 fall off

abscission: 8 excision, recision; **9** inscising; **10** cutting off, inscission, rescission

abscond: 4 bolt, flee; **5** go off, slope [slang]; **6** decamp, run off; **8** slip away, slope off [slang], sneak off, steal off; **9** slink away, sneak away, steal away; **12** absquatulate, make away from

absence: 4 lack, want; **10** deficiency; **12** short measure

absence of authority: 7 anarchy; **11** lawlessness

absence of error: 11 perfectness; **12** flawlessness; **13** impeccability

absence of motive: 11 aimlessness

absence of vision: 9 blindness

absence of voice: 7 aphonia [Med], no voice; **8** dumbness, muteness

absent: 6 remove, scatty, truant; **7** lacking, missing; **8** distrait; **10** abstracted, not present; **12** absentminded

absentee: 6 no-show, truant

absently: 12 abstractedly; **13** inattentively

absentminded: 6 absent, scatty; **10** abstracted

absent of meaning: 6 vacant; **9** senseless, unmeaning; **11** meaningless, nonsensical

absent without leave: 4 AWOL

absinthe: 6 old man; **7** absinth; **8** lad's love, wormwood

absinthe oil: 11 wormwood oil

absolute: 4 full, good, rank; **5** sheer, stark, total; **7** decided, perfect, plenary; **8** finished, positive, thorough; **9** arbitrary, downright, essential, ex officio, imperious, out-and-out, right-down; **10** conclusive, high-handed, imperative, inviolable, iron-handed, overruling, peremptory, sacrosanct; **11** categorical, inalienable, infrangible, unalienable, unequivocal, unqualified; **12** indefeasible, unchallenged; **13** unconditioned, unimpeachable

absolutely: 4 dead; **6** purely; **7** utterly; **9** decidedly, downright, perfectly, radically, seriously; **10** thoroughly, throughout; **11** essentially; **12** definitively, exhaustively; **13** categorically, fundamentally, unequivocally

absolute pitch: 12 perfect pitch

absolute rule: 8 iron rule, iron sway; **9** tight hand; **10** strictness, strong hand; **13** strict control

absolution: 5 grace; **6** pardon; **9** remission; **11** condonation, forgiveness

absolutism: 7 tyranny; **8** totalism; **9** autocracy, Caesarism, despotism, monocracy, shogunate; **10** one-man rule; **12** absoluteness, dictatorship, unlawful rule; **13** arbitrary rule; **15** totalitarianism

absolve: 4 free; **5** purge, remit; **6** acquit, let off, ransom, redeem, repair, shrive; **7** justify, reclaim; **8** reprieve; **9** exculpate, exonerate

absolved: 5 clear; **7** cleared; **9** acquitted; **10** exculpated, exonerated, vindicated

absonant: 9 dissonant

absorb: 4 draw, fuse, suck; **5** blend, drain, empty, merge, rivet, sop up, steep, unite; **6** embody, engage, engulf, finish, imbibe, ingest, occupy, plunge, soak up, suck up, take in, take up, tap out; **7** blend in, combine, conjoin, engross, exhaust, immerse; **8** coalesce, dissolve, intrigue, run out of, take over; **9** fascinate, mesmerize, swallow up; **10** amalgamate, assimilate, centralize, impoverish, impregnate, use up all of; **11** consolidate, incorporate

absorbed: 4 rapt; **6** intent; **7** riveted, wrapped; **9** engrossed, enwrapped, wrapped in; **10** hypnotized, mesmerized, transfixed

absorbent: 9 absorbant; **10** absorptive

absorbing: 6 crying, urgent; **7** exigent, instant; **8** gripping, pressing, riveting; **9** pervading; **10** engrossing, intriguing; **11** fascinating, mesmerizing, penetrating

absorption: 9 soaking up; **11** engrossment,

fascination; **12** assimilation, preoccupancy; **13** concentration, preoccupation

absquatulate: 4 bolt, flit; **5** go off; **6** decamp, levant, run off; **7** abscond; **9** skedaddle

abstain: 5 spare, waive; **6** desist; **7** forbear, neglect, refrain

abstainer: 7 ascetic; **9** abstinent

abstaining: 7 sparing; **9** abstinent; **10** refraining

abstemious: 5 light

abstemiously: 11 temperately

abstention: 8 inaction, not doing; **9** eschewing, not acting; **10** abstinence, forbearing, refraining; **11** forbearance, passiveness

abstentious: 9 abstinent

absterge: 4 wipe

abstergent: 9 cathartic, cleansing, purifying

abstinence: 8 inaction, not doing; **9** eschewing, not acting; **10** abstention, forbearing, refraining; **11** forbearance, passiveness

abstinence from alcohol: 11 teetotalism

abstinent: 9 abstainer; **10** abstaining; **11** abstentious

abstract: 4 hook, lift, note; **5** brief, draft, filch, pinch, snarf, sneak, swipe; **6** apercu, digest, minute, nobble, pilfer, precis; **7** abridge, cabbage, epitome, outline, purloin, summary; **8** analysis, synopsis; **9** epitomize, summarize; **10** abridgment; **11** abstraction, theoretical

abstract art: 14 abstractionism

abstract artist: 14 abstractionist

abstracted: 6 absent, scatty; **7** removed; **8** distrait; **12** absentminded

abstractedly: 8 absently; **13** in the abstract, inattentively

abstraction: 5 theft; **8** abstract, stealing, thievery, thieving; **10** extraction

abstractionism: 9 unrealism; **11** abstract art

abstractionist: 8 abstract; **12** nonobjective; **13** nonfigurative

abstract space: 6 domain

abstruse: 4 deep; **6** occult; **7** crabbed; **9** recondite

abstruseness: 9 obscurity; **10** abstrusity, profundity; **11** obscureness; **12** profoundness; **13** reconditeness

abstrusity: 10 profundity; **12** abstruseness, profoundness

absurd: 7 idiotic; **8** derisory; **9** egregious, ludicrous, senseless; **10** ridiculous; **11** incongruous, nonsensical; **12** preposterous, unreasonable

absurdity: 7 fatuity; **9** silliness; **10** absurdness; **11** fatuousness

absurdness: 9 absurdity; **14** ridiculousness

Abu Dhabi: 26 United Arab Emirates's capital

abulia: 7 aboulia

abulic: 7 aboulic**

abundance: 4 lots, over; **6** plenty; **9** amplitude, plenitude, profusion; **11** copiousness, full measure

abundant: 5 ample; **7** copious

abundantly: 6 galore; **9** copiously, profusely; **11** in abundance, plenteously, plentifully

abuse: 3 bug; **4** bait, bore; **5** beset, grind, harry, haunt, hound, shout, tease, worry; **6** badger, bother, harass, heckle, ill-use, infest, insult, misuse, molest, pester, plague, pother; **7** oppress, pervert, profane, violate; **8** bullirag, bullyrag, ill-treat, ill-usage, maltreat, mistreat; **9** contumely, desecrate, importune, invective, persecute; **10** defilement, revilement

abused: 10 ill-treated, maltreated, mistreated

abusive: 8 scornful; **9** clamorous, insulting; **10** scurrilous

abut: 4 butt, edge; **6** adjoin, border, butt on

abutment: 4 jamb; **7** meeting, mullion; **8** buttress; **10** contacting, osculation

abutting: 7 grazing, in touch; **8** adjacent, touching; **9** adjoining, bordering, in contact; **10** contiguous

abuzz: 7 buzzing, droning

aby: 4 abye, bear, bide; **5** abide, atone; **6** endure, suffer; **7** expiate, support, sustain

abye: 3 aby; **5** atone; **7** expiate

abysm: 5 abyss, chasm; **11** yawning gulf

abysmal: 7 abyssal

abysmally: 7 awfully; **8** rottenly, terribly; **10** abominably; **11** atrociously

abyss: 5 abysm, chasm, limbo; **6** trench; **7** gehenna; **9** purgatory

abyssal: 7 abysmal

Abyssinia: 8 Ethiopia, Yaltopya

Abyssinian: 13 Abyssinian cat

AC: 18 alternating current

Ac: 8 actinium

Acacia: 6 cassie; **6** gidgee; **6** mimosa; **6** wattle; **7** catechu; **8** huisache; **9** fever tree; **9** flame tree; **14** Jerusalem thorn

academia: 7 academe

academic: 7 donnish; **8** pedantic, putative; **9** doctrinal, theorized; **10** collegiate, gratuitous, scholastic, supposable; **11** academician, conjectural, presumptive, speculative, theoretical; **12** hypothesized, hypothetical; **13** faculty member

academic gown: 10 judge's robe; **12** academic robe

academician: 8 academic, gownsman; **9** schoolman; **13** faculty member

academicism: 9 academism; **13** scholasticism

academic term: 7 session; **10** school term

academism: 11 academicism; **13** scholasticism

academy: 9 alma mater; **15** honorary society**

Acanthaceae: 14 acanthus family
Acanthophis antarcticus: 10 death adder
acanthous: 7 spinous; **9** acanthoid
acanthus: 6 zigzag; **9** cartouche
acanthus family: 11 Acanthaceae
a capella: 11 alla capella [It]; **13** unaccompanied
acapnia: 10 hypocapnia
acapnic: 8 acapnial; **9** acapnotic
Acapulco: 16 Acapulco de Juarez
acaracide: 9 acaricide
acarpellous: 10 acarpelous
acarpous: 12 unproductive
acaryote: 8 akaryote; **10** akaryocyte
acaudate: 7 acaudal
acaulescent: 8 stemless
accede: 3 bow; **5** defer; **6** accept, adhere, assent, comply, give in, submit; **7** agree to, consent, receive; **9** acquiesce; **10** comply with, fall in with; **11** acknowledge, give consent
accelerate: 4 urge; **5** annoy, speed; **6** madden; **7** quicken, speed up; **8** convulse, expedite, irritate; **9** aggravate, infuriate; **10** exacerbate, exasperate, put on speed; **11** precipitate
acceleration: 4 dash, rush; **5** spurt; **7** speedup; **10** quickening; **11** forced march
accelerator: 3 gas, gun; **8** catalyst, gas pedal, throttle; **11** atom smasher
accelerator pedal: 3 gas, gun; **8** gas pedal, throttle; **11** accelerator
accelerometer: 11 seismometer
accent: 4 tone; **5** idiom, twang; **6** set off, stress; **7** dialect; **8** bring out, emphasis; **9** emphasize, punctuate; **10** accent mark, accentuate, intonation; **12** accentuation, poetic accent; **13** speech pattern
accented: 5 heavy, tonic; **6** strong
accenting: 11 emphasizing
accent mark: 6 accent
accentuate: 5 mouth; **6** accent, set off, stress; **7** deliver; **8** aspirate, bring out; **9** emphasize, enunciate, pronounce, punctuate, underline; **10** articulate, take note of; **11** lay stress on
accentuated: 6 marked; **10** emphasized
accept: 4 bear, have, take; **5** admit, go for; **6** accede, assume, insure, take on; **7** agree to, consent, endorse, indorse, receive, swallow; **8** take over, tolerate; **9** acquiesce; **10** comply with, fall in with, underwrite; **11** acknowledge, give consent, subscribe to
acceptability: 14 acceptableness
acceptable: 2 OK; **4** fair, lief, so-so; **7** average, welcome; **8** accepted, all right, bearable, mediocre, middling, ordinary, passable; **9** tolerable; **10** admissible, couci-couci, good enough; **11** indifferent
acceptance: 3 nod; **4** seal; **5** stamp; **6** assent;

7 consent; **8** adoption, credence; **9** accession, agreement, execution, signature; **10** sufferance, toleration; **11** acceptation; **12** acquiescence
accepting: 7 receipt; **9** receiving
access: 5 get at; **6** entree; **8** approach; **10** admittance; **12** memory access
accessibility: 9 handiness; **12** availability; **13** availableness; **15** approachability
accessible: 6 open to; **10** attainable, obtainable; **11** within reach; **12** approachable, easy of access
accession: 3 nod; **6** assent; **7** consent; **8** addition; **9** agreement, assenting; **10** acceptance, coronation; **11** acceptation, rise to power; **12** acquiescence, enthronement
accessories: 4 gear; **5** slops, traps; **7** harness, rigging, turn-out; **9** accessory, caparison, equipment, trappings; **12** accouterment
accessory: 4 gear; **5** extra, slops, traps; **7** adjunct, harness, rigging, turn-out; **8** additive, adjuvant, co-worker, confrere; **9** accessary, ancillary, assistant, attendant, auxiliary, caparison, equipment, increment, obbligato, trappings; **10** accomplice, cooperator, ministrant, subsidiary, supplement; **11** accessories
access road: 8 slip road
acciaccatura: 9 grace note; **12** appoggiatura
accidence: 6 praxis, syntax; **7** grammar
accident: 4 bale; **6** mishap; **7** tragedy; **8** calamity, casualty, disaster, fortuity; **9** mischance; **10** misfortune
accidental: 6 casual, chance; **8** uncaused; **9** causeless, extrinsic; **10** contingent, derivative, fortuitous, incidental; **11** inadvertent; **12** adventitious, nonessential, undetermined; **13** indeterminate
accidentally: 8 by chance; **10** by accident; **12** contingently, fortuitously, incidentally, unexpectedly
accidental property: 8 accident
accipient: 5 donee [Fr]; **6** lessee; **7** grantee; **8** releasee [Law]
Accipiter: 4 hawk; **14** genus Accipiter
acclaim: 4 clap, hail, spat; **5** eclat; **6** herald; **7** applaud, plaudit; **8** applause, plaudits; **11** acclamation
acclamate: 5 cheer; **6** encore; **7** applaud
acclamation: 5 eclat; **6** chorus; **7** acclaim, plaudit; **8** applause, plaudits; **9** consensus; **13** common consent
acclimate: 3 fit; **4** suit; **5** adapt; **11** acclimatize, accommodate
acclimatize: 3 fit; **4** suit, tame; **5** adapt; **7** break in; **9** acclimate; **11** accommodate, domesticate
acclimatized: 7 adapted; **10** acclimated
acclivitous: 6 rising, uphill
acclivity: 4 rise; **5** climb, raise, slope; **6** ascent; **7** incline, upgrade; **8** gradient
accloy: 4 cloy; **5** choke; **9** suffocate

accolade: 3 hug; 5 award, honor; 6 honour, pledge; 7 embrace, laurels, squeeze, tribute

accommodate: 3 fit; 4 hold, suit; 5 adapt, admit, lodge; 6 oblige; 9 acclimate, reconcile; 10 conciliate; 11 acclimatize

accommodating: 8 gracious, obliging; 9 indulgent; 10 complacent; 11 good-humored; 13 accommodative

accommodation: 7 advance, fitting; 10 adaptation, adjustment; 11 arrangement

accommodative: 11 cooperative, reconciling; 13 accommodating

accompaniment: 4 bass; 6 escort, second; 7 support; 11 concomitant; 12 co-occurrence

accompanist: 12 accompanyist

accompany: 6 attend, follow, go with; 7 coexist, company; 8 attach to, come with; 9 companion

accompanying: 9 attendant; 10 incidental; 11 concomitant; 12 incidental to

accomplice: 9 accessary, accessory

accomplish: 5 reach; 6 attain, fulfil; 7 achieve, compass, execute, fulfill; 8 carry out, complete; 9 hammer out; 10 consummate; 12 carry through

accomplishable: 6 doable; 10 achievable, realizable

accomplished: 4 up to; 5 crack; 6 au fait, good at; 8 at home in, complete, effected, master of, realized; 9 completed, performed; 10 carried out, discharged; 11 a good hand at, established

accomplishing: 9 achieving; 10 completing, completion; 11 achievement, fulfillment

accomplishment: 5 skill; 8 work done, 9 achieving; 10 attainment, completing, completion; 11 achievement, acquirement, acquisition, fulfillment, notable deed, realization

accompts: 7 account; 8 accounts

accord: 4 pact; 5 agree, allot, award, fit in, grant; 6 assign, concur, treaty; 7 concede, concord, consort, harmony, rapport; 8 symphony; 9 agreement, harmonize, vouchsafe; 10 accordance, be in accord, conformity, consonance; 11 be accordant, concordance, consistency

accordance: 6 accord; 8 warranty; 10 conformity; 11 consistency

accordant: 8 in accord; 9 agreeable, congruous, consonant; 10 concordant, consistent; 11 conformable, in agreement; 13 correspondent, corresponding

accordingly: 4 ergo, then, thus; 5 hence; 6 thusly, whence; 8 thence so; 9 therefore, wherefore; 12 and therefore, consequently

accordion: 7 plicate; 10 squeeze box

accordion door: 11 folding door

accost: 6 invoke; 7 address, solicit; 8 appeal to, come up to, make up to; 12 apostrophize

accouchement: 5 labor; 7 travail; 8 delivery; 10 birth-throe, childbirth; 11 confinement, parturition; 12 childbearing

accoucheur: 7 midwife; 11 accoucheuse [Fr]; 12 obstetrician

account: 4 bill, rank, tale; 5 kudos [Grk], score, story; 6 regard, report; 7 history, invoice, respect, write up; 8 accounts; 9 calculate, chronicle, narration, narrative, statement; 10 accounting, news report, popularity; 11 description, explanation; 12 appreciation

accountability: 13 answerability; 14 answerableness, responsibility

accountable: 6 liable; 8 amenable; 9 financial; 10 accounting, answerable; 11 responsible

accountancy: 10 accounting

accountant: 7 actuary, almoner, auditor, steward, trustee; 8 receiver; 10 bookkeeper, controller, liquidator; 11 bean counter, comptroller

Accountant General: 7 almoner, steward, trustee; 8 receiver; 10 accountant, liquidator

account book: 4 book; 5 books, leger; 6 ledger; 7 journal

accounter: 3 rig; 4 robe, vest; 5 array, drape, dress; 6 attire, clothe, enrobe, fit out; 7 apparel

account for: 9 answer for; 10 derive from

accounting: 7 account; 9 financial, reckoning; 11 accountable, accountancy, bookkeeping

account settled: 6 acquit, assets; 11 compte rendu [Fr], expenditure, liabilities

account statement: 7 account; 10 accounting

accouple: 4 hook, link, lock, yoke; 5 belay, brace, latch, leash; 6 couple; 7 bracket, grapple

accouplement: 5 union; 7 joinder [Law], uniting; 8 coupling; 11 conjugation, conjunction

accouter: 3 rig; 5 array, dress; 6 fettle, fledge; 7 furnish, garnish; 8 accoutre

accoutered: 9 accoutred

accouterment: 4 gear; 5 array, slops, traps; 6 outfit; 7 harness, rigging, turn-out; 8 armament; 9 accessory, caparison, equipment, trappings; 11 accessories

accoutred: 10 accoutered

accoy: 6 soften, temper; 8 mitigate, moderate

Accra: 14 capital of Ghana

accredit: 4 hire, name; 5 honor; 6 credit, engage, return; 7 appoint, bespeak, intrust; 8 nominate; 9 recognize; 11 pay regard to

accredited: 8 licenced, licensed, putative; 10 recognized; 12 commissioned

accretion: 10 concretion; 12 accumulation

accrimination: 13 incrimination, recrimination

accrual: 10 accruement; 12 accumulation

accrue: 4 fall; 11 become added

accrued: 11 accumulated

accrust: 9 crust over

accubation: 11 prostration

accueil: 12 introduction, presentation

acculturation: 7 culture; 12 assimilation; 13 socialisation, socialization

accumbent: decumbent, reclining, recumbent; 10 procumbent

accumulate: 4 fund; 5 amass, cache, hoard; 6 garner, gather, pile up, pull in; 7 collect, compile; 8 cumulate, garner up; 12 conglomerate

accumulated: 6 massed; 7 accrued, amassed, hoarded; 9 assembled, collected; 10 congregate

accumulation: 5 cache, store; 7 accrual; 9 accretion; 10 accruement, assemblage, collection; 11 aggregation; 12 stored supply

accumulative: 10 cumulative

accumulator: 8 gatherer; 9 collector; 14 storage battery

accuracy: 5 truth; 10 exactitude

accurate: 4 just; 5 exact; 6 just so, severe, strict; 7 precise

accurately: 2 so; 7 exactly; 9 precisely; 10 definitely

accurateness: 12 high accuracy

accurse: 4 damn; 5 curse; 7 swear at; 9 imprecate

accursed: 4 lost; 6 cursed, damned, doomed, undone; 7 accurst, devoted; 8 damnable, infernal, maledict, stranded; 9 atrocious, incarnate; 10 confounded, to be pitied

accusable: 9 imputable

accusation: 6 charge; 7 accusal; 10 imputation; 11 impeachment

accusative: 8 accusing, accusive; 9 objective; 10 accusatory; 13 objective case; 14 accusative case

accusatory: 8 accusing, accusive; 10 accusative

accuse: 3 tax; 6 charge, impute; 7 impeach; 9 criminate; 11 incriminate

accused: 7 charged, suspect; 9 defendant, impeached

accuser: 8 claimant; 9 plaintiff; 11 complainant

accusing: 8 accusive, charging; 10 accusative, accusatory, impeaching

accustom: 9 habituate; 11 familiarize

accustomary: 5 usual; 6 common; 7 general, regular; 8 ordinary; 9 customary; 11 established; 12 conventional

accustomed: 6 wonted; 8 habitual; 9 customary; 10 habituated; 12 familiarized

ace: 1 1, I; 3 bit, jot, one, six, ten, wiz; 4 A-one, five, four, hint, iota, jack, king, mite, nine, star, tops, trey, unit, whiz; 5 adept, crack, deuce, eight, knave, maven, queen, seven, super, trace, unity, whizz; 6 genius, morsel, single, tiptop, wizard; 7 hotshot, modicum; 8 topnotch, virtuoso; 9 first-rate, sensation

acebutolol: 7 Sectral

acedia: 5 sloth; 8 laziness

acellular: 11 noncellular

acephalous: 8 deranged

ace pitcher: 9 ace hurler

Acer: 5 maple; 8 sycamore, box elder; 9 genus Acer

Aceraceae: 11 maple family

acerate: 7 acerose; 8 acicular; 12 needle-shaped

acerate leaf: 6 needle

acerb: 4 acid; 5 acrid, sharp; 6 acetic, bitter; 7 acerbic, caustic; 8 venomous, virulent; 9 bitterish, sulfurous, vitriolic; 10 astringent, blistering, sulphurous

acerbate: 7 envenom; 8 embitter; 9 aggravate; 10 exacerbate

acerbic: 4 acid; 5 acerb, acrid, sharp; 6 bitter; 7 caustic; 8 venomous, virulent; 9 bitterish, sulfurous, vitriolic; 10 astringent, blistering

acerbity: 4 gall, huff, miff; 5 pique; 6 spleen, temper; 7 umbrage; 8 acrimony, asperity, jaundice, rankling, soreness, tartness; 9 austerity, crossness, petulance, procacity, testiness, virulence; 10 bitterness, crabbiness, protervity; 11 grouchiness; 12 captiousness, irascibility, irritability; 13 irascibleness, irritableness, querulousness

acerola: 13 surinam cherry, Surinam cherry; 14 barbados cherry

acerose: 7 acerate; 8 acicular; 12 needle-shaped

acervation: 10 cumulation

acescent: 7 sourish, subacid [Chem]

acetabular: 8 cotyloid; 10 cotyloidal

acetabulum: 14 cotyloid cavity

acetaldol: 5 aldol

acetamide: 10 ethanamide

acetaminophen: 6 Datril, Tempra; 7 Panadol, Tylenol; 9 Anacin III

acetate: 12 acetate rayon

acetic: 5 acerb

acetify: 4 sour; 7 acidify; 9 acidulate

acetone: 9 propanone

acetone body: 10 ketone body

acetonemia: 7 ketosis; 9 ketonemia

acetophenetidin: 10 phenacetin

acetose: 7 acetous; 8 vinegary

acetphenetidin: 10 phenacetin

acetylene: 6 ethyne

acetylize: 9 acetylate

acetylsalicylic acid: 5 Bayer; 7 aspirin, Empirin

achar: 8 allspice

acharne: 4 waxy

acharnement: 3 ire, pet; 4 bile, fume, tiff; 6 choler, dander, pucker, taking; 7 ferment, passion; 9 angry mood; 10 ebullition

ache: 3 yen; 4 hurt, long, pine; 5 bleed, smart, yearn; 6 aching, dolour, suffer; 8 languish

Acheron: 12 River Acheron

Acherontia atropos: 14 death's-head moth

Acheta: 7 cricket; 11 genus Acheta

achievability: 13 attainability

achievable: 6 doable; 8 feasible; 10 realizable; 11 performable, practicable

achieve: 5 reach; 6 attain; 7 compass; 8 complete; 9 hammer out; 10 accomplish, consummate

achievement: 4 feat, slab; 6 tablet; 7 exploit; 9 achieving; 10 completing, completion; 11 fulfillment, notable deed; 14 accomplishment

achiever: 6 winner; 7 success; 12 success story

achieving: 10 completing, completion; 11 achievement, fulfillment; 13 accomplishing

Achilles heel: 8 weakness; 13 vulnerability

Achilles tendon: 16 tendon of Achilles

aching: 4 ache, achy; 6 biting, in pain; 7 chafing, gnawing, hurting; 8 smarting, stinging; 9 suffering

aching heart: 10 heavy heart; 11 broken heart; 13 bleeding heart

achira: 9 arrowroot

Achras: 9 sapodilla, 11 genus Achras

achromasia: 6 pallor; 7 wanness; 8 lividity, paleness; 9 lividness, luridness; 10 pallidness

achromatic: 5 black, white; 9 colorless; 10 monochrome; 11 monochromic; 13 black and white, monochromatic

achromatic vision: 14 color blindness; 15 colour blindness

achromatism: 10 monochrome; 11 neutral tint; 13 black and white, colorlessness

achromatize: 7 tarnish; 8 tone down; 10 decolorize; 11 achromatise

achromic: 9 achromous

Achromycin: 12 tetracycline

achy: 6 aching

acicular: 7 acerate, acerose; 12 needle-shaped

acid: 3 LSD; 5 acerb, acrid; 6 bitter; 7 acerbic, caustic, searing; 8 scathing, venomous, virulent; 9 acidulous, scorching, sulfurous, vitriolic; 10 acidulated, blistering, sulphurous; 12 contumelious, vituperative

acidic: 9 acidulent, acidulous

acidify: 4 sour; 7 acetify; 9 acidulate

acidity: 4 sour; 5 low pH; 8 sourness; 13 acidulousness

acidophile: 9 acidophil

acidophilic: 8 aciduric; 12 acidophilous

acid rain: 17 acid precipitation

acid test: 4 test; 5 probe; 9 criterion; 10 diagnostic, litmus test; 11 crucial test

acidulate: 4 sour; 7 acetify, acidify

acidulous: 4 acid; 6 acidic; 9 acidulent; 10 acidulated

acidulousness: 7 acidity

aciduric: 11 acidophilic; 12 acidophilous

aciform: 8 acicular

Acinonyx: 13 genus Acinonyx

Acinonyx jubatus: 6 chetah; 7 cheetah

Acinos arvensis: 9 basil balm; 10 basil thyme; 13 mother of thyme

Acipenser: 6 beluga; 6 hausen; 8 sturgeon; 14 genus Acipenser

ack-ack: 2 AA; 4 flak; 6 pom-pom; 9 ack-ack gun; 12 antiaircraft

ackee: 4 akee

acknowledge: 3 own; 4 avow, cite, know; 5 admit, allow, grant; 6 accede, accept, agnize, comply, notice; 7 abide by, agree to, concede, confess, execute, mention, observe, perform, receipt, receive, requite, respect, satisfy; 9 acquiesce, recognize

acknowledged: 8 admitted, answered, conceded; 9 owned up to; 10 understood

acknowledging: 6 avowal; 8 owning up; 9 conceding; 10 concession; 14 acknowledgment

acknowledgment: 3 sop; 6 amends, avowal; 7 receipt, redress; 8 adhesion, owning up, requital; 9 accession, adherence, admission, atonement, conceding; 10 affirmance, concession, reparation; 11 recognition; 12 giving thanks, subscription

aclinic line: 15 magnetic equator

acme: 3 top; 4 apex, peak; 6 height, summit, vertex; 8 meridian, pinnacle; 9 elevation; 11 culmination, superlative; 12 utmost height

acned: 6 pimply; 7 pimpled; 9 pustulate

acne rosacea: 7 rosacea

acology: 12 therapeutics

acolothyst: 7 acolyte; 8 altar boy

acolyte: 8 altar boy

aconite: 7 hemlock, henbane; 9 hellebore; 10 belladonna, nightshade

Aconitum: 8 wolfbane; 9 wolfsbane, monkshood; 12 helmetflower; 13 genus Aconitum

acorn cup: 6 cupule

Acorus: 7 calamus; 8 flagroot; 9 sweet flag; 10 myrtle flag; 11 genus Acorus

acoustic: 10 acoustical

acoustical: 8 acoustic

acoustic meatus: 8 ear canal; 13 auditory canal; 14 auditory meatus

acoustic nerve: 13 auditory nerve

acoustic organs: 3 ear, lug; **7** auricle
acoustic power: 18 sound pressure level
acquaint: 7 present; **9** introduce; **11** familiarise, familiarize; **12** acquaint with
acquaintance: 3 ken; **6** friend; **7** insight; **8** intimacy; **9** informing, notifying; **10** announcing, experience, fellowship; **11** acquainting, conversance, conversancy, enunciation, familiarity, information, knowledge of
acquainted: 7 advised, alerted; **8** apprised, familiar, informed; **11** free and easy; **12** familiar with
acquainting: 9 informing, notifying; **10** announcing; **11** enunciation, information
acquest: 4 land; **5** acres, lands; **6** realty; **8** property; **9** tenements; **10** real estate; **12** real property
acquiesce: 6 accede, accept, assent, comply; **7** agree to, receive; **10** comply with, fall in with; **11** acknowledge, give consent, subscribe to
acquiescence: 3 nod; **6** assent; **7** consent; **9** accession, agreement, execution; **10** acceptance, compliance, observance; **11** acceptation, concurrence, performance
acquiescent: 6 agreed; **7** content; **8** biddable, resigned; **9** at one with, compliant; **11** acquiescing; **13** of the same mind
acquiescing: 8 resigned; **11** acquiescent
acquire: 3 get; **4** gain, grow, take; **5** adopt; **6** assume, obtain, take on; **7** develop, procure, produce
acquired: 6 gotten; **8** obtained, procured
acquired immune deficiency syndrome: 4 AIDS
acquire honor: 4 live; **6** flaunt; **7** glitter; **8** flourish; **9** gain honor
acquirement: 5 skill; **10** attainment; **11** acquisition; **14** accomplishment
acquire permission: 9 be allowed; **11** be permitted; **13** get permission
acquiring: 7 gaining, getting; **9** obtaining, obtention, procuring; **10** obtainment; **11** acquisition, procurement
acquisition: 4 gain; **5** skill; **7** gaining, getting; **8** learning; **9** acquiring, obtaining, obtention, procuring; **10** attainment, obtainment; **11** acquirement, procurement
acquisition agreement: 6 merger
acquisitive: 6 greedy; **7** craving; **8** covetous, grasping, ravenous; **9** insatiate; **10** avaricious, insatiable, quenchless; **12** recollective, unquenchable
acquit: 4 bear; **5** carry, clear, remit; **6** assets, assoil, behave, deport, exempt, remise; **7** absolve, comport, conduct, release; **9** discharge, exculpate, exonerate, quitclaim; **11** expenditure, liabilities

acquitment: 9 acquittal; **11** acquittance, exculpation, exoneration
acquittal: 9 discharge; **10** redemption; **11** acquittance, exculpation, exoneration, fulfillment, performance; **12** satisfaction
acquittance: 7 release; **9** acquittal, quittance; **11** exculpation, exoneration
acquitted: 8 absolved; **9** not guilty; **10** exculpated, exonerated
acreage: 8 land area; **11** proportions
acres: 4 land; **5** lands; **6** estate, realty; **7** demesne; **8** hectares, property; **9** tenements; **10** real estate; **11** square miles; **12** landed estate, real property
acrid: 4 acid; **5** acerb, harsh, sharp; **6** biting, bitter; **7** acerbic, caustic; **8** venomous, virulent; **9** bitterish, sulfurous, vitriolic; **10** astringent, blistering, sulphurous; **11** acrimonious
acrid fumes: 5 smoke
acridid: 22 short-horned grasshopper
acridity: 4 bite; **8** pungency; **9** acridness; **11** astringency
acridness: 8 acridity, acrimony
Acridotheres: 4 myna; **17** genus Acridotheres
acrimonious: 4 sour; **5** acrid, sharp, short, taint; **6** biting, bitter; **7** caustic, crabbed, doggish; **8** venomous, virulent; **9** envenomed, rancorous, sarcastic, trenchant; **10** mordacious; **12** contumelious
acrimoniously: 8 bitterly; **10** venomously
acrimony: 4 gall, huff, miff; **5** pique; **6** spleen; **7** umbrage; **8** acerbity, asperity, jaundice, rankling, soreness; **9** acridness, virulence; **10** bitterness
Acris: 10 genus Acris; **11** cricket frog
acritude: 8 acrimony; **9** acridness
acroama: 13 oral teachings
acroamatic: 8 profound; **12** acroamatical
acrobat: 7 gymnast, tumbler; **10** ropedancer; **13** posture master
acrobatic: 8 athletic; **9** gymnastic
acrobatic feat: 14 acrobatic stunt
acrobatics: 8 stunting, tumbling; **10** aerobatics; **11** stunt flying
acrobatic stunt: 13 acrobatic feat
acrocarp: 15 acrocarpous moss
acrocyanosis: 12 Raynaud's sign
acrogenic: 10 acrogenous
acrolein: 8 propenal
acromegalia: 10 acromegaly
acromegalic: 9 pituitary
acronym: 5 acron. [abbr]
acronymous: 9 acronymic
acropolis: 7 citadel
acrospire: 5 shoot; **6** branch, sprout; **11** olive-branch
across: 4 over; **7** crossed; **9** crossways, crosswise
across-the-board: 4 wide; **5** broad; **7** blanket;

8 panoptic; **12** all-embracing, all-inclusive, encompassing

across the country: 10 nationally, nationwide

acrostic: 8 trifling; **10** word square; **11** idle conceit

Acrostichum: 4 fern; **16** genus Acrostichum

acrylate: 10 propenoate

acrylic: 11 polyacrylic; **12** acrylic fiber, acrylic paint, acrylic resin; **13** acrylate resin

acrylic acid: 13 propenoic acid

act: 2 do; **3** bit; **4** deed, move, play, turn, work; **5** act as, event, serve, touch; **6** action, behave, number, rubric, stitch; **7** operate, perform, playact, pretend, process, routine, statute; **8** human act, overt act, roleplay; **9** be an actor, dissemble, enactment, officiate, operation, represent; **10** be in action, human event, lex scripta [Lat], regulation; **11** be operative, corpus juris [Lat], human action, physical act, transaction

act as: 3 act; **4** play

act drop: 7 curtain; **19** transformation scene

acted: 6 staged; **8** acted out; **9** performed

acted upon: 11 wrought upon

Actias: 8 Luna moth, luna moth; **11** genus Actias

acting: 4 vice; **5** doing, force; **6** action, agency; **7** playing, working; **8** function, movement; **9** deputized, effectual, efficient, operation, operative, practical, vice regal; **10** acting a lie, performing, playacting; **11** efficacious, functioning, performance; **12** representing

acting a part: 4 airs; **9** mannerism; **10** pretension; **11** affectation, pretensions [pl]; **12** affectedness

acting together: 11 cooperative; **13** cooperativity

Actinia: 12 genus Actinia

actinia: 8 actinian; **11** actiniarian

actinic ray: 16 actinic radiation

actinic rays: 8 actinism

Actinidiaceae: 4 kiwi; **10** silvervine

actinium: 2 Ac

actinometer: 10 photometer, radiometer

actinotherapy: 11 irradiation; **12** radiotherapy; **16** radiation therapy

actinozoan: 9 anthozoan

action: 3 act; **4** suit; **5** cause, doing, fight, force; **6** acting, agency, battle; **7** lawsuit, working; **8** activity, function, movement; **9** encounter, operation, suit in law; **10** activeness, engagement, litigation; **11** action at law, legal action, performance, physical act; **12** simple action; **13** natural action; **14** military action, natural process, physical action

Actitis: 9 sandpiper; **12** genus Actitis

activate: 4 trip; **5** exert, spark; **6** aerate, ex-

cite, kindle, set off, turn on; **7** actuate, trigger; **8** energize, spark off, switch on, touch off; **9** stimulate; **10** trigger off

activated: 7 excited

activated charcoal: 15 activated carbon

activating: 9 actuating, turning on; **10** activation, energizing

active: 2 on; **5** alive, brisk; **6** lively, strong; **7** dynamic, intense, running; **8** animated, bustling, fighting, forcible, physical, vigorous; **9** energetic, on the move, operating, vivacious; **11** active agent, active voice, brisk as a bee, combat-ready, functioning; **12** brisk as a lark; **13** participating

active agent: 6 active

active concealment: 7 evasion; **10** concealing; **11** concealment, suppression

activeness: 6 action; **8** activity

active service: 7 service; **11** campaigning, tented field; **12** combat action

active voice: 6 active

activist: 4 doer; **7** hustler; **8** militant; **10** activistic, politician [general]; **11** man of action

activistic: 8 activist

activity: 6 action; **9** agitation; **10** activeness; **11** body process, human action; **13** bodily process, effervescence, human activity, natural action, radioactivity; **14** bodily function, natural process

act of benevolence: 5 favor; **8** good turn; **9** good works; **11** beneficence

act of contrition: 9 atonement; **10** reparation

act of God: 8 vis major; **12** force majeure

act of grace: 5 bonus, grace

act of kindness: 5 favor; **8** good turn; **9** good works; **11** beneficence

act of spite: 7 despite

act of will: 4 will; **8** volition; **15** mental causation

act on: 6 pursue; **10** follow up on

act on instinct: 5 react; **16** react reflexively

actor: 4 doer; **5** agent; **6** player, worker; **8** affector, histrion, thespian; **9** performer; **10** role player; **11** perpetrator

actor's assistant: 7 dresser

act out: 5 enact; **7** reenact

Acts: 17 Acts of the Apostles

act together: 5 unite; **9** cooperate; **12** join together, work together

actual: 4 real; **6** extant, that is; **7** current, de facto, factual, genuine, instant, literal, present; **8** existent, existing

actual existence: 7 reality; **9** actuality; **12** sober reality; **13** real existence

actualisation: 11 realisation, realization; **13** actualization

actuality: 7 reality; **12** sober reality; **13** real existence; **15** actual existence; **17** concrete existence; **23** existence in the real world

actualization: 11 fulfillment, realisation, realization; **13** actualisation; **14** accomplishment

actualize: 7 realize; **8** engender

actually: 6 really; **9** in reality

actual thing: 6 no fake; **7** no other, no phony; **9** none other, real McCoy, real thing

actuarial calculations: 15 actuarial tables

actuary: 7 auditor; **10** accountant, bookkeeper; **11** bean counter [derogatory]; **12** statistician

actuate: 4 trip; **5** set on, spark; **6** foment, incite, set off; **7** animate, provoke, trigger; **8** activate, spark off, touch off; **9** instigate; **10** trigger off

actuating: 10 activating

actuation: 10 propulsion

acuate: 5 acute, sharp

acuity: 8 keenness; **9** acuteness, sharpness; **12** visual acuity

Acular: 7 Toradol

aculeate: 3 set; **4** barb, whet; **5** grind, point, strop; **7** sharpen

acumen: 8 sagacity; **9** shrewdness; **11** discernment, penetration; **12** perspicacity; **13** sagaciousness; **14** insightfulness

acumination: 6 acuity

acupressure: 3 G-Jo; **7** shiatsu

a cup too low: 9 ill at ease; **11** low spirited; **12** in low spirits

acupuncture: 11 stylostixis

acute: 4 ague, arch, hard, high, keen, sore, warm; **5** alive, awake, brisk, cruel, grave, harsh, quick, sharp, smart, vivid; **6** acuate, biting, lively, severe, strong; **7** caustic, cutting, intense; **8** deep-dyed, incisive, piercing; **9** knifelike, trenchant; **10** impressive; **11** acute accent, penetrating, penetrative, thin-skinned; **14** discriminating

acute accent: 4 ague; **5** acute

acute angle: 11 obtuse angle; **12** salient angle; **14** spherical angle

acute ear: 7 nice ear; **8** quick ear, sharp ear; **10** correct ear, musical ear; **11** delicate ear

acutely: 5 ultra [Lat]; **6** deeply, subtly; **9** intensely; **10** profoundly; **11** exceedingly, exquisitely

acuteness: 4 nous [Fr]; **5** parts; **6** acuity, esprit; **8** gumption, keenness, sagacity; **9** mother wit, sharpness; **10** quick parts, trenchance; **11** penetration; **12** incisiveness

acute note: 8 high note

acyclic: 9 open-chain

acyclovir: 7 Zovirax

ad: 4 TV ad, advt. [abbr]; **6** advert; **10** commercial; **11** advertising; **13** advertisement

adactylism: 8 adactyly; **9** adactylia; **13** polydactylism

adaga: 4 tuck; **8** claymore

adage: 3 saw; **6** byword, dictum, old saw, saying; **7** proverb

ad agency: 17 advertising agency

adagio: 7 andante

Adalia: 11 genus Adalia

Adalia bipunctata: 7 ladybug

Adam's apple: 10 coffee rose, Nero's crown; **12** crape jasmine, crepe jasmine; **13** crepe gardenia; **14** pinwheel flower; **16** thyroid cartilage

Adam's needle: 4 tine; **5** yucca; **9** bear grass [U.S.]; **10** needle palm; **14** spoonleaf yucca

adamance: 8 obduracy; **14** unyieldingness

adam-and-eve: 9 puttyroot

adamant: 3 oak; **4** iron; **5** bortz, steel; **7** diamond; **8** very hard; **9** carbonado; **10** adamantine, heart of oak, inexorable; **12** intransigent

adamantean: 7 adamant; **8** very hard; **10** adamantine

adamantine: 4 hard; **5** hardy, stout, valid; **6** mighty, potent, robust, strong, sturdy; **7** adamant; **8** forcible, powerful, puissant, very hard, vigorous; **10** inexorable; **12** intransigent

Adams-Stokes syndrome: 10 heart block

Adansonia: 14 genus Adansonia

Adansonia digitata: 6 baobab

Adapid: 11 Adapid group

Adapin: 7 doxepin; **8** Sinequan

adapt: 3 fit; **4** suit; **6** adjust; **7** conform, embrace, espouse, rewrite, sweep up; **9** acclimate; **10** transcribe; **11** acclimatize, accommodate

adaptable: 10 commodious

adaptation: 7 version; **10** adjustment; **13** accommodation

adapted: 7 altered; **10** acclimated; **12** acclimatized, accommodated

adapter: 7 adaptor; **8** arranger

adaption: 10 adaptation, adjustment; **13** accommodation

adapt itself to: 2 do; **3** fit; **4** meet, suit; **5** befit

adaptive: 10 adaptative

adaptor: 7 adapter

adaxial: 7 ventral

ad blitz: 10 ad campaign

ad captandum: 6 hollow; **7** canting, evasive, stilted; **8** affected, specious; **9** insincere, plausible, pretended, unnatural; **10** artificial, not natural; **11** pretentious, superficial

add: 3 sum, tot; **4** lend; **5** add up, affix, annex, bring, sum up, tally, tot up, total; **6** append, bestow, divide, impart, supply, tote up; **7** subjoin, summate; **8** multiply, subtract; **9** superpose; **10** contribute

add back: 7 put back, replace, restore

addendum: 9 adjective; **10** postscript, supplement

adder: 5 snake, viper; **7** reptile, serpent; **11** common viper, Vipera berus

adder's fern: 8 wall fern; **9** sweet fern

adder's tongue: 16 adder's tongue fern

addict: 4 hook

addicted to: 6 used to; **7** given to; **9** attuned to; **10** habituated

addiction: 9 drug habit; **10** dependence, dependency; **13** drug addiction

addictive: 12 habit-forming

addictive drug: 15 drug of addiction

adding back: 11 putting back, replacement, restoration

adding machine: 9 totaliser, totalizer

Addis Ababa: 17 capital of Ethiopia

Addison's disease: 14 hypoadrenalism; **16** Addison's syndrome

addition: 4 gain, plus; **7** adjunct; **8** additive, improver, increase; **9** accession, summation

additional: 4 else, more; **5** extra, other; **7** another, further; **12** supplemental; **13** supplementary

additionally: 6 to boot; **10** in addition; **12** as an addition

additive: 5 extra; **6** dopant, linear; **7** adjunct; **8** addition; **9** accessory, concerted; **10** collective; **11** doping agent; **12** food additive

additum: 5 affix, annex

addle: 6 muddle, puddle; **7** sketchy; **8** abortive; **9** stillborn

addled: 5 muzzy, wooly; **6** senile, woolly; **7** muddled; **9** befuddled; **11** wooly-minded; **12** woolly-headed

addle headed: 4 dull; **6** stupid; **7** witless; **8** mindless; **9** airheaded, brainless, dim-witted

add on: 5 affix; **6** append; **10** supplement

address: 4 deal, plow, work; **5** cover, craft, knack, skill, speak, treat; **6** accost, direct, handle, speech, turn to; **7** aptness, canvass, know-how, lecture, oration, oratory, speak to; **8** aptitude, come up to, facility; **9** direction, residence; **10** addressing, adroitness, allocution, apostrophe, competence; **11** destination, proficiency, savoir-faire; **12** formal speech, skillfulness; **14** legal residence

addresses: 4 suit; **6** wooing; **8** courting; **9** courtship; **10** lovemaking, making love; **11** pitching woo

addressing: 7 address; **9** direction

addressing machine: 13 Addressograph

add together: 3 add, sum, tot; **5** add up, sum up, tally, tot up, total; **6** tote up; **7** summate

adduce: 4 cite; **6** abduce

adducent: 9 adducting; **10** attractive

adduction: 9 drawing to

adductor: 14 adductor muscle

add up: 3 add, sum, tot; **4** come; **5** sum up, tally, tot up, total; **6** amount, number, tote

up; **7** summate; **9** make sense; **11** add together

add up to: 6 come to; **8** amount to

add water: 4 thin; **6** dilute; **9** water down

ade: 10 fruit drink

Adelges: 5 aphid; **12** genus Adelges

Adelie: 13 Adelie penguin

a delusion: 8 a mockery

adenoid: 16 pharyngeal tonsil

adenoidal: 5 nasal; **7** pinched

adenomyosis: 13 endometriosis

adenosis: 12 gland disease; **16** glandular disease

adenylic acid: 3 AMP; **22** adenosine monophosphate

adept: 3 ace, wiz; **4** good, star, whiz; **5** maven, whizz; **6** expert, genius, master, wizard; **7** hotshot, skilful; **8** skillful, virtuoso; **9** practiced, sensation; **10** master hand, proficient; **11** crackerjack

adeptness: 8 deftness, facility; **9** quickness; **10** adroitness

adequacy: 6 enough, withal; **8** efficacy; **10** competence, efficiency; **11** sufficiency; **12** adequateness, satisfaction

adequate: 6 decent, enough; **8** passable; **9** effective, effectual; **10** good enough, sufficient, well enough; **11** efficacious

adequately: 12 sufficiently

adequateness: 8 adequacy

adequate to: 4 up to; **7** capable, equal to

adermin: 9 pyridoxal, vitamin B6; **10** pyridoxine

ader wax: 8 earth wax; **9** ozocerite, ozokerite; **10** mineral wax

adespotic: 3 lax; **5** loose; **7** relaxed

adhere: 4 bind, bond, hold; **5** cling, stick; **6** accede, cleave, cohere, comply; **7** conform, stand by, stick by, stick to; **8** hold fast; **9** stick with; **12** hang together; **13** stick together

adherence: 3 set; **4** bond; **8** adhering, adhesion, sticking; **10** attachment, compliance, conforming, conformity, observance; **12** adhesiveness; **14** acknowledgment

adherent: believer, disciple; **9** satellite, worshiper; **10** worshipper; **11** communicant

adhering: 7 holding; **8** clinging, sticking; **9** adherence; **10** conforming, conformity

adhesion: 3 set; **4** bond; **8** sticking; **9** adherence; **10** conformity; **12** adhesiveness; **14** acknowledgment

adhesive: 5 gluey, gooey, tacky; **6** sticky

adhesive friction: 4 grip; **8** traction

adhesiveness: 4 bond; **8** adhesion, tenacity; **9** adherence

adhibit: 5 apply; **9** turn to use; **10** make useful

adhibition: 3 use; **5** using; **6** employ; **10** employment; **11** application, utilization

adhortation: 6 advice; **7** counsel; **10** suggestion; **14** recommendation

Adiantum: 13 genus Adiantum; **14** maidenhair fern

adiaphanous: 6 opaque

adieu: 3 bye; **4** ciao; **5** adios, aloha; **6** bye-bye, good-by, so long; **7** cheerio, good day, good-bye; **8** au revoir, farewell, sayonara; **10** dosvidanya [Russ]; **11** arrivederci, leave taking, valediction; **12** hasta la vista [Sp]; **14** auf wiedersehen

Adige: 10 River Adige

ad instar: 7 as usual; **12** instar omnium [Lat]

adios: 3 bye; **5** adieu; **6** bye-bye, good-by, so long; **7** cheerio, good day, good-bye; **8** au revoir, sayonara; **11** arrivederci; **14** auf wiedersehen

adipose: 3 fat; **5** fatty; **6** greasy; **9** sebaceous

adipose cell: 7 fat cell

adiposeness: 9 adiposity, fattiness

adipose tumor: 6 lipoma

adiposis: 9 stoutness; **10** corpulence, overweight

adiposity: 9 fattiness; **11** adiposeness

Adirondacks: 19 Adirondack Mountains

adit: 3 pit; **4** mine; **5** shaft; **6** avenue; **7** channel, passage; **8** approach; **12** mine entrance; **13** means of access

adjacency: 10 contiguity; **12** neighborhood; **14** contiguousness

adjacent: 4 next; **8** abutting; **9** adjoining, bordering; **10** contiguous, juxtaposed, side by side; **12** conterminous

adjection: 10 annexation; **13** superaddition, superfetation, superposition

adjective: 8 addendum; **10** adjectival, procedural

adjoin: 4 abut, butt, edge, join, meet; **5** touch; **6** abut on, border, butt on; **8** trench on; **9** march with; **11** butt against

adjoining: 7 grazing, in touch; **8** abutting, adjacent, touching; **9** bordering, in contact; **10** contiguous; **12** conterminous, in contiguity

adjourn: 5 waive; **6** recess, remand, retard, retire; **7** break up, lay over, suspend; **8** hold over, withdraw

adjournment: 4 wait; **5** pause; **7** respite; **10** suspension; **11** dissolution, prorogation, retardation; **12** postponement

adjudge: 4 hold; **7** declare; **10** adjudicate

adjudicate: 3 try; **5** judge; **7** adjudge

adjunct: 4 aide; **8** addition, additive, adjuvant; **9** accessory, ancillary, assistant, auxiliary; **10** subsidiary; **11** appurtenant

adjunction: 8 junction

adjuration: 4 oath; **8** swearing; **9** affidavit, evocation, summoning; **12** asseveration

adjure: 3 bid; **5** press; **7** beseech, conjure, entreat; **13** put to one's oath, swear a witness

adjust: 3 set; **4** trim; **5** adapt, align, aline, poise; **6** line up; **7** conform; **8** regulate; **9** methodize; **11** systematize

adjusted: 12 familiarized

adjuster: 8 adjustor; **10** claim agent; **14** claims adjuster, claims adjustor

adjusting: 10 adjustment

adjustment: 7 fitting; **9** adjusting, allowance; **10** adaptation, alteration; **11** arrangement; **12** modification, readjustment, registration; **13** accommodation

adjustor: 8 adjuster; **10** claim agent; **14** claims adjustor

adjutage: 9 discharge; **13** discharge line, discharge tube

adjutant: 4 aide; **8** adjuvant; **9** brigadier; **10** aide-de-camp; **12** adjutant bird, brigade major, staff officer; **13** adjutant stork

adjutant stork: 8 adjutant; **12** adjutant bird; **17** Leptoptilus dubius

adjuvant: 6 aiding; **7** adjunct, helpful; **8** adjutant; **9** accessory, ancillary, assisting, auxiliary; **10** subsidiary; **11** appurtenant

ad lib: 6 wing it; **7** offhand; **9** ad libitem [Lat], ad libitum, impromptu, improvise, unplanned; **10** improvised, unscripted; **11** extemporize, spontaneous, unrehearsed; **12** a limproviste [Fr]; **13** spontaneously; **14** extemporaneous

adman: 10 advertiser

administer: 3 lot; **4** deal, sway; **5** allot; **7** command, control, deal out, dish out, dole out, mete out; **8** dispense, shell out; **9** parcel out; **10** distribute; **12** administrate

administration: 5 brass; **8** disposal; **10** governance, presidency; **12** organisation, organization; **13** establishment

administrative: 8 official; **9** executive; **10** managerial; **11** directorial, supervisory; **13** authoritative

administrative official: 10 bureaucrat

administrator: 9 executive, intendant; **13** decision maker

admirability: 13 admirableness, wonderfulness

admirable: 9 estimable, excellent

admirably: 8 laudably; **11** commendable, excellently

admiral: 9 admiralty; **11** full admiral

admiralty law: 11 maritime law

Admiralty mile: 2 mi; **4** mile; **6** naut mi; **12** nautical mile

admiration: 3 awe; **6** esteem, wonder; **10** high esteem, wonderment; **12** appreciation

admire: 5 prize, value; **7** defer to; **8** look up to

admirer: 5 flame, lover; **6** adorer, friend;

7 booster; **8** champion; **9** supporter; **11** protagonist

admissibility: 9 propriety

admissible: 2 OK; **4** fair, so-so; **5** ad rem [Lat], happy; **7** average, germane, in point, on point; **8** bearable, mediocre, middling, ordinary, passable, relevant; **9** tolerable; **10** acceptable, applicable, couci-couci, felicitous; **11** indifferent

admission: 6 avowal, entree; **9** admitting, inclusion, reception; **10** admittance, affirmance, confession, membership; **11** entrance fee, subsumption; **12** admission fee; **13** comprehension, entrance money; **14** acknowledgment

admit: 3 own; **4** avow, hold, take; **5** allow, grant, let in, yield; **6** accept, embody, fess up, import, take in, take on; **7** allow in, bring in, concede, confess, contain, embrace, include, own up to, receive; **10** comprehend; **11** accommodate, acknowledge

admit of: 4 bear

admittance: 6 access, entree; **9** admission, admitting, reception

admitted: 8 conceded, received; **9** confessed, owned up to; **10** understood; **12** acknowledged; **13** self-confessed

admittedly: 4 true; **8** avowedly; **11** confessedly

admitting: 6 entree; **9** admission, receiving, reception, supposing

admixture: 3 mix; **5** alloy; **6** mixing; **7** mixture; **10** commixture

admonish: 4 warn; **5** chide; **6** rebuke; **7** caution, reprove; **9** reprehend; **10** discourage

admonished: 6 warned; **7** rebuked; **8** reproved; **9** cautioned, chastened; **10** forewarned; **11** reprimanded

admonishing: 9 reproving; **10** admonitory; **11** reproachful

admonition: 7 reproof, warning; **8** monition, reproach; **11** reprobation; **12** admonishment, remonstrance, reprehension

admonitive: 10 admonitory

adnexal: 7 annexal

ado: 4 fuss, mess, stir, to-do; **6** bother, bustle, fidget, flurry, hustle; **9** imbroglio, pottering; **11** fidgetiness

adobe: 10 adobe brick, brown stone

adolescence: 10 pubescence

adolescent: 4 teen; **6** jejune; **7** puerile, teenage; **8** juvenile, teenaged, teenager; **9** pubescent, stripling

Adolf Hitler: 6 Hitler; **9** Der Fuhrer

Adonic line: 6 Adonic

adonize: 4 bead; **5** adorn; **6** enrich; **8** beautify, decorate, ornament; **9** embellish

adopt: 4 take; **5** apply; **6** assume, borrow, follow, take in, take on, take up; **7** acquire, embrace, espouse, imitate; **8** take over; **9** dramatise, dramatize, make use of; **10** naturalize; **11** appropriate

adopted: 6 chosen; **7** elected; **8** adoptive, inspired, selected; **9** converted, justified, unearthly; **10** sanctified; **11** consecrated, regenerated

adopting: 8 choosing; **9** selecting

adoption: 6 choice; **8** choosing, election; **9** borrowing, salvation, selection; **10** acceptance, conversion; **11** decision for, inspiration; **12** regeneration; **13** beatification, justification

adorable: 6 lovely; **7** lovable; **9** endearing

adoration: 4 cult; **5** flame; **6** homage, latria; **7** passion, rapture, worship; **8** devotion, idolatry, yearning; **9** adulation, idolizing; **10** aspiration; **11** idolisation, idolization

adore: 6 aspire, revere; **7** idolize, worship

adorer: 5 flame, lover; **7** admirer

adoring: 4 fond; **6** doting; **10** worshipful

adorn: 4 bead, deck; **5** grace; **6** clothe, enrich, invest; **8** beautify, decorate, ornament; **9** embellish

adorned: 6 decked; **8** bedecked; **9** decked out, decorated; **10** beautified, ornamented; **11** embellished

adornment: 8 ornament; **10** decoration

adpressed: 9 appressed

ad rem: 5 happy; **7** germane, in point, on point; **8** relevant; **10** admissible, applicable, felicitous

adrenal: 12 adrenal gland; **15** suprarenal gland

Adrenalin: 10 adrenaline, epinephrin; **11** epinephrine

adrenaline: 9 Adrenalin; **10** epinephrin; **11** epinephrine

adrenergic: 15 sympathomimetic

adrenocorticotrophin: 4 ACTH

Adrianople: 6 Edirne; **12** Adrianopolis

Adriatic: 11 Adriatic Sea

adrift: 5 stray; **6** afloat; **7** aimless, asunder, at fault, in twain, insular; **8** drifting, isolated, planless; **10** rudderless, undirected; **13** directionless

adroit: 3 apt; **4** deft, gain; **5** civil, handy, quick, ready; **6** clever, expert, poised; **7** tactful; **9** dexterous, ingenious; **10** diplomatic

adroitly: 5 aptly; **6** deftly; **7** handily, quickly, readily; **11** dexterously

adroitness: 5 craft, knack, skill; **7** address, aptness, know-how, **8** aptitude, deftness, facility; **9** adeptness, quickness; **10** competence; **11** proficiency; **12** skillfulness

adscript: 10 adscripted

adsorbate: 10 adsorbable

adsorbent: 10 adsorptive

adsuki bean: 10 adzuki bean

adulation: 8 flattery; **9** adoration; **10** flattering; **11** idolisation, idolization

adulator: 9 flatterer

adulatory: 10 flattering; **13** complimentary

adult: 3 big; **5** grown; **6** mature; **7** grown up, grown-up, grownup; **9** full grown, full-grown

adulterate: 5 alloy, taint; **6** debase, defile, dilute, doctor, infect; **7** debased, pollute, stretch; **8** compound, doctor up; **9** water down; **10** amalgamate; **11** adulterated, contaminate; **12** sophisticate

adulterated: 7 debased; **10** adulterate, contraband; **12** contaminated, illegitimate; **13** surreptitious

adulteration: 5 alloy; **8** defiling; **9** polluting, pollution; **10** corruption, debasement, defilement; **13** contaminating, contamination

adulterous: 8 cheating; **9** two-timing; **12** extramarital

adultery: 8 cheating; **9** crim. con. [abbr]; **10** cuckolding, infidelity; **11** concubinage, fornication; **14** unfaithfulness

adulthood: 8 majority, maturity

adumbrate: 4 hint; **5** apply; **6** allude, sketch; **7** outline; **8** allude to, intimate; **9** insinuate

adumbration: 5 model, study; **7** masking; **8** allusion; **9** shadowing; **11** obscuration, occultation; **14** representation

adumbrative: 13 foreshadowing, prefigurative

aduncated: 5 bowed; **6** arched; **7** arc-like, arclike, arcuate, vaulted

aduncous: 6 beaked, hooked; **12** sickle shaped

adust: 4 arid; **5** baked, burnt; **6** burned; **7** parched; **8** scorched, sunbaked

ad valorem tax: 3 VAT; **13** value-added tax

advance: 3 run, win; **4** flow, gain, go on, pass, rise; **5** boost, get on, raise; **6** allege, broach, come on, elapse, feeler, move on, move up, pass on; **7** elevate, enhance, forward, further, headway, hold out, march on, proceed, promote, propose, shape up, upgrade; **8** advanced, approach, get ahead, get along, overture, progress, propound, set ahead, set forth, throw out; **9** advancing, come along, cultivate, encourage, enunciate, in advance, pronounce; **10** beforehand, betterment, furthering, gain ground, pay at sight, put forward, set forward; **11** advancement, furtherance, improvement, progression

advanced: 4 ripe; **6** modern; **7** advance, upfront; **9** in advance; **10** innovative; **13** paid in advance, sophisticated; **14** forward-looking

advanced age: 3 age; **6** old age; **7** oldness

advanced guard: 9 rear guard

advance guard: 3 van; **8** vanguard

advancement: 6 step up; **7** advance, headway; **8** progress; **9** advancing, elevation, promotion; **10** preferment; **11** furtherance, progression

advance payment: 10 prepayment

advance person: 10 advance man

advance work: 7 outwork; **8** horn work

advancing: 6 rising; **7** advance, forward, ongoing; **8** progress; **10** furthering, going ahead, in progress, proceeding; **11** advancement, coming ahead, furtherance, moving ahead, progressing, progression

advantage: 4 good, lead; **7** benefit, vantage; **8** whip hand; **9** dominance, good thing, upper hand; **10** ascendancy

advantaged: 7 favored

advantageous: 4 good; **6** golden, paying; **7** gainful; **8** edifying; **9** favorable, lucrative; **10** beneficial, profitable; **11** appropriate; **12** remunerative

advene: 9 supervene

advent: 5 brunt, onset; **6** coming; **7** arrival; **8** outbreak; **10** occurrence

Advent: 12 Second Advent, Second Coming

Adventism: 8 Puseyism; **9** Calvinism, Jansenism, methodism

adventitia: 5 tunic; **6** tunica

adventitious: 5 modal; **6** casual, chance; **8** uncaused; **9** causeless; **10** accidental, contingent, fortuitous, incidental; **12** undetermined; **13** indeterminate

adventure: 3 hap, hit; **4** pass, risk; **5** stake; **6** chance, crisis, gamble, hazard; **7** fortune, passage, venture; **8** casualty, escapade, fortuity, run a risk; **9** emergency, haphazard, put at risk, speculate

adventurer: 4 gent, snob; **7** gambler; **8** explorer, gamester, mushroom; **9** mercenary, novus homo [Lat]

adventures: 4 life; **7** journal; **8** fortunes; **11** confessions, experiences

adventurous: 8 cavalier, Quixotic; **10** fire eating; **12** enterprising; **13** adventuresome

adversaria: 8 jottings; **11** pigeonholes

adversary: 8 opponent; **10** antagonist, opposition; **12** adverse party

adversative: 10 oppositive

adverse: 4 loth; **6** loathe; **7** baleful, harmful, hurtful, opposed; **8** contrary, loathe to, opposing, untoward; **10** at variance, averse from; **12** antagonistic, in opposition, inauspicious

adverse luck: 7 bad luck, hard hap, hard lot, ill luck; **8** evil luck, hard luck; **11** hard fortune

adverse party: 8 opponent; **9** adversary; **10** antagonist, opposition

adversity: 7 trouble; **8** hardship; **10** difficulty

advert: 2 ad; **4** cite, hang, name; **5** refer, touch; **6** allude, attend; **7** bring up, give ear, mention, pay heed; **11** advertising; **12** pay attention; **13** advertisement

advertence: 9 alertness, attention; **10** advertency; **13** attentiveness

advertent: 7 heedful

advertently: 9 heedfully, mindfully

advertisement: 2 ad; **4** advt. [abbr]; **6** advert; **11** advertising

advertiser: 5 adman

advertising: 2 ad; **6** advert; **11** advertizing, publicizing; **13** advertisement

advertising campaign: 7 ad blitz; **10** ad campaign

advert to: 3 see; **4** look, mark, view; **6** notice, regard, remark; **7** observe; **10** take notice

advice: 4 news, word; **5** aviso [Sp]; **7** counsel, message, tidings; **10** suggestion; **11** piece of news; **12** intelligence; **14** recommendation

Advil: 6 Motrin, Nuprin; **9** ibuprofen

advisability: 12 desirability; **13** desirableness

advisable: 9 desirable

advise: 6 awaken, notify; **7** apprise, apprize, counsel, propose, suggest; **8** send word; **9** enlighten

advised: 5 meant; **7** alerted, express, studied; **8** apprised, designed, informed, intended; **10** acquainted, calculated, considered, deliberate; **11** determinate, intentional, well-advised; **12** premeditated

advisedly: 8 by choice, by design; **9** expressly, knowingly, on purpose, purposely, wittingly; **10** designedly, with design, with intent; **11** in cold blood; **12** deliberately, purposefully, with eyes open; **13** intentionally

advisement: 8 weighing; **12** deliberation

advisor: 7 adviser; **8** prompter; **10** consultant

advisory: 10 consultive; **12** consultative, consultatory; **14** recommendatory

advisory board: 13 planning board

advocacy: 6 urging; **9** promoting, promotion; **10** persuasion; **11** exhortation; **13** encouragement; **14** recommendation, representation

advocate: 4 urge; **6** backer, defend, jurist, preach, prompt, pundit; **7** abettor, counsel, suggest; **8** attorney, champion, civilian, exponent, partisan, seconder, upholder; **9** counselor, encourage, prescribe, proponent, publicist, recommend, represent, solicitor, supporter; **10** counsellor, well-wisher, wellwisher; **11** protagonist, sympathizer

advocation: 10 allegation

advoutress: 10 adulteress

advoutry: 7 crim. con. [abbr]; **8** adultery, cheating; **10** cuckolding, infidelity; **11** concubinage; **14** unfaithfulness

advt.: 2 ad; **13** advertisement

adynamic: 9 enervated, undynamic; **11** debilitated

adynamy: 6 sprain, strain; **8** cachexia [Med], delicacy; **11** decrepitude; **12** invalidation

adytum: 5 crypt; **7** sanctum; **8** abditory; **9** oubliette; **12** holy of holies, inner sanctum

adze: 3 adz

adzuki bean: 10 adsuki bean

AEC: 22 Atomic Energy Commission

Aedes: 10 genus Aedes; **13** tiger mosquito; **19** yellow-fever mosquito

aedile: 6 ranger; **7** coroner; **8** surveyor

Aegadean Isles: 12 Aegates Isles, Egadi Islands

Aegean: 9 Aegean Sea

aegir: 4 bore; **5** eager, eagre; **9** tidal bore

aegirite: 6 acmite

aegis: 4 egis; **8** auspices, **10** protection; **11** breastplate, sponsorship

Aegypius: 7 vulture; **13** genus Aegypius

Aengus: 5 Angus; **6** Oengus; **7** Angus Og

Aeolian: 6 Eolian

aeolian harp: 8 wind harp; **11** aeolian lyre

Aeolis: 6 Aeolia

aeolotropic: 10 eolotropic

aeon: 3 eon

aeonian: 6 eonian; **7** eternal, lasting; **11** everlasting

aepyornis: 12 elephant bird

aequo animo: 11 in cold blood

aerate: 8 activate

aerated: 7 charged; **10** oxygenated

aeration: 12 aerification

aere perennius: 5 great; **8** immortal; **9** deathless; **11** never fading, time honored; **12** imperishable

aerial: 4 aery, airy; **7** antenna; **8** aeriform, ethereal; **10** aeronautic; **11** forward pass

aerial ladder: 6 bucket, pumper; **9** fire truck; **13** hook and ladder

aerially: 11 via aircraft

aerial navigator: 5 flier; **6** airman; **7** aviator; **8** aeronaut

aerial perspective: 10 aerial view; **12** bird's-eye view

aerial view: 12 bird's-eye view

aerie: 4 aery, eyrie; **7** rookery; **9** bird's nest

aerification: 8 aeration

aeriform: 4 aery, airy; **6** aerial; **7** airlike; **8** ethereal

aerify: 6 gasify; **8** vaporize

aerobatics: 8 stunting; **10** acrobatics; **11** stunt flying

aerobics: 15 aerobic exercise

aerodrome: 7 airport; **8** airdrome

aerodynamics: 10 pneumatics; **13** aeromechanics, fluid dynamics

aeroembolism: 5 bends; **11** air embolism; **14** caisson disease

aerofoil: 7 airfoil, surface; 14 control surface

aerogenerator: 8 windmill; 13 wind generator

aerogram: 9 air letter; 10 aerogramme; 13 airmail letter

aerogramme: 8 aerogram; 9 air letter; 13 airmail letter

aerolite: 6 meteor; 9 meteorite, meteoroid; 11 falling star; 12 shooting star

aeromechanics: 12 aerodynamics

aeronautical engineering: 11 aeronautics

aeronaut: 5 flier, flyer; 6 airman; 7 aviator

aeronautic: 6 aerial; 12 aeronautical

aeronautics: 10 airmanship

aerophyte: 8 air plant, epiphyte; 14 epiphytic plant

aeroplane: 5 plane; 8 airplane

aeroplanist: 5 pilot; 7 birdman; 9 navigator

aeroscope: 9 barometer

aeroscopy: 8 aerology

aerosol: 3 sol; 4 mist; 8 spray can; 10 aerosol can; 11 aerosol bomb

aerospace medicine: 12 aeromedicine

aerosphere: 10 atmosphere

aerostat: 7 balloon

aerostatics: 10 airmanship; 11 aeronautics

aery: 4 airy, eyry; 5 aerie, eyrie; 6 aerial; 8 aeriform, ethereal

aesculapian: 7 medical

Aesculapius: 5 Galen; 11 Hippocrates

Aesculus: 7 buckeye; 13 horse chestnut; 13 genus Aesculus

Aesop: 7 Caliban

aesthete: 7 esthete

aesthetic: 8 artistic, esthetic, pleasing, sentient; 10 esthetical, perceptive; 11 aesthetical

aesthetical: 8 esthetic; 9 aesthetic; 10 esthetical

aesthetics: 9 esthetics

aestival: 7 estival

aether: 5 ether

aetiologist: 10 etiologist

aetiology: 8 etiology

Aetobatus: 14 genus Aetobatus

Afars and Issas: 8 Djibouti

a few: 3 any; 4 some; 5 aught; 7 several; 9 a couple of; 10 more or less; 12 quantitative

affability: 7 amenity; 8 bonhomie; 9 geniality, good humor; 10 amiability; 11 affableness, amiableness; 12 complaisance

affable: 6 genial; 7 amiable, cordial; 8 familiar, gracious; 11 good-humored

affair: 4 case; 5 amour, brush, fight, thing; 6 matter, thesis; 7 affaire, concern, episode, liaison; 8 business, intimacy, occasion; 9 collision; 11 battle royal, involvement; 14 social occasion

affaire: 5 amour; 6 affair; 7 liaison; 8 intimacy; 11 involvement

affaire d'honneur: 4 duel

affaire flambee: 10 losing game

affair of honor: 4 duel; 6 duello [It]

affairs: 16 personal business

affect: 4 lead, like, list, move, sham; 5 carry, fancy, feign, put on, smite, touch; 6 bear on, excite, impact, infect, regard, strike; 7 animate, be big on, care for, conduce, feeling, impress, inspire, involve, pretend, touch on; 8 act a part, bear upon, interest; 9 affection, dissemble, impassion, influence, put on airs; 10 affections, contribute

affectation: 4 airs, pose; 9 mannerism; 10 pretension; 11 acting a part, pretensions

affected: 4 cast; 5 moved, stiff; 6 formed, molded; 7 canting, excited, smitten, stilted, stirred, touched; 8 animated, inspired, mannered, stricken; 9 impressed, insincere, pretended, unnatural; 10 artificial, interested, not natural; 11 ad captandum, impassioned, pretentious

affectedness: 4 airs; 9 mannerism; 10 pretension; 11 acting a part, affectation, pretensions; 13 putting on airs

affected with: 9 moved with; 10 imbued with, seized with; 11 touched with; 13 impressed with

affectibility: 14 impressibility

affecting: 3 sad; 6 moving; 8 pathetic, poignant, touching; 9 evocative

affectingly: 10 poignantly, touchingly

affection: 4 love; 5 heart; 6 affect; 7 feeling; 8 feelings [pl], fondness; 10 affections, tenderness

affectionate: 4 fond, warm; 6 caring, loving, tender; 8 lovesome

affectionately: 4 dear; 6 dearly

affectionateness: 5 heart; 6 warmth; 8 fondness; 9 affection; 10 lovingness, tenderness

affections: 4 bent, bias; 6 affect; 7 feeling, leaning; 8 tendency; 9 affection, proneness; 10 proclivity, propensity; 11 disposition, inclination; 14 predisposition

affector: 5 actor; 9 performer

afferent neuron: 13 sensory neuron

affettuoso: 6 legato; 8 staccato; 9 crescendo; 10 diminuendo

affiance: 4 ally; 6 engage, plight; 7 betroth; 9 assurance, betrothal; 10 engagement; 11 betrothment

affianced: 7 engaged, fiancee, pledged; 8 bespoken; 9 betrothed

affiche: 4 bill; 6 poster; 7 placard; 9 broadside

afficionado: 3 fan; 4 buff; 5 lover; 7 devotee

affidation: 4 pact; 7 compact; 9 agreement

affidavit: 4 oath; 8 swearing; 10 adjuration, deposition; 11 attestation; 12 asseveration

affiliate: 4 join; 6 assort; 7 consort; 9 associate

affiliated: 6 agnate; 8 allied to, attached; 9 connected; 10 associated, implicated

affiliation: 3 tie; 5 tie-up; 7 joining; 8 alliance; 10 connection; 11 affiliating, association

affinity: 7 kinship; 8 alliance, homology; 11 association, homogeneity, parallelism; 17 kinship by marriage

affirm: 3 say; 4 aver, avow, swan; 5 state, swear; 6 assert; 7 confirm, declare, profess, support, sustain; 9 predicate; 11 corroborate; 12 substantiate

affirmable: 10 assertable

affirmation: 6 avowal; 9 assertion, statement; 10 affirmance

affirmative: 6 saying; 8 favoring; 9 asserting, declaring; 10 optimistic; 11 affirmatory, declaratory

affirmatively: 13 declaratively; 16 in the affirmative

affirmatory: 11 affirmative

affix: 3 add, fix; 4 bind; 5 add on, annex, twist; 6 append, attach, clinch, fasten, secure; 7 additum [Lat], stick on, subjoin; 8 make fast, saddle on; 9 superpose; 10 supplement

afflation: 9 inflation

afflict: 3 ail; 4 harm, pain; 5 smite, wrong; 6 grieve; 7 trouble; 8 distress

afflicted: 6 pained; 7 worried; 8 impaired, stricken

affliction: 3 woe; 5 grief, trial; 6 sorrow; 8 distress; 9 heartache; 10 infliction, visitation

affluence: 4 pelf; 5 lucre; 6 riches, wealth; 7 fortune; 8 opulence, richness

affluent: 4 rich; 5 flush; 6 feeder, loaded, monied; 7 moneyed, opulent, wealthy; 9 tributary, worth much

afflux: 8 approach; 13 approximation

afford: 4 cost, give, open; 5 fetch, spare, yield; 6 return; 7 bring in, sell for; 10 well afford

affordable: 7 low-cost; 9 low-priced

affranchise: 11 enfranchise

affranchisement: 15 enfranchisement

affray: 3 row; 4 fray, to-do; 5 brawl, broil, melee; 6 breeze, fracas, hubbub, pother, racket, ruffle, rumble, rumpus, squall, uproar; 7 howling, rhubarb [baseball], ruction, shindig, trouble; 8 brouhaha, scramble; 9 imbroglio, scrimmage; 10 bear garden, donnybrook, free-for-all; 11 altercation, battle royal, disturbance, embroilment piece of work [Fr]

affricate: 11 affricative; 18 affricate consonant

affriction: 8 abrasion, arrosion; 9 attrition, detrition; 10 rubbing off, wearing off

affright: 5 alarm, scare; 6 fright; 8 frighten

affront: 6 enrage, insult, offend, ruffle, vilify; 7 offense, outrage; 8 aggrieve, dishonor; 9 call names, contumely; 11 provocation; 12 vilification

affronted: 8 insulted

affuse: 4 lave, wash; 5 bathe

affusion: 7 pouring; 12 infiltration

Afghan: 5 Paxto; 6 Pashto, Pathan; 7 Afghani; 12 Afghanistani, afghanistani

afghan: 13 sheepskin coat

aficionado: 3 fan; 4 buff; 5 lover; 6 votary; 7 amateur, devotee; 10 dilettante

afield: 6 abroad, afield, at home

afire: 6 ablaze, aflame, aflare, alight, on fire; 7 blazing, burning, flaming

aflame: 3 red; 5 afire; 6 ablaze, aflare, alight, on fire; 7 aroused, blazing, burning, crimson, flaming, flushed; 8 in flames, redfaced, reddened, turned on

aflare: 5 afire; 6 ablaze, aflame, alight, flying, on fire, waving; 7 blazing, burning, flaming, flaring; 10 fluttering

Aflaxen: 5 Aleve; 7 Anaprox; 14 naproxen sodium

afloat: 4 rife; 5 afoot, awash; 6 aboard, adrift, on foot; 7 aimless, current, flooded; 8 floating, in the air, planless; 9 in the wind, inundated, prevalent; 10 going about, on the anvil, rudderless, undirected; 11 on the stocks, overflowing; 13 directionless

aflutter: 7 nervous

afoot: 6 afloat, on foot; 7 current, going on, running, walking; 8 under way, underway; 9 happening, in the fire, prevalent; 10 in progress, on the anvil; 11 on the stocks, progressing

afore: 3 ere; 11 theretofore

aforementioned: 4 said; 9 aforesaid; 14 above-mentioned

aforesaid: 4 said; 14 aforementioned

aforethought: 7 planned, plotted

a fortiori: 3 yea; 4 even; 7 the most; 8 above all; 9 eminently, extremely, still more, supremely; 10 especially, peculiarly, surpassing, to crown all; 11 egregiously, exceedingly, of all things, principally, prominently; 12 particularly, preeminently, surpassingly

afoul: 4 foul; 6 fouled

AFP: 16 alpha fetoprotein

afraid: 7 fearful; 10 frightened; 12 apprehensive

Aframomum: 14 genus Aframomum

Afrasian: 11 Afroasiatic; 13 Hamito-Semitic

afreet: 4 Loki; 8 barghast, barghest

afresh: 4 anew; 5 again, often; 6 lately; 7 just now; 8 once more; 9 over again; 10 repeatedly

African-American: 12 Afro-American

African crocodile: 13 Nile crocodile

Africanized bee: 9 killer bee

Afrikaans: 4 Taal; 7 the Taal; 9 Afrikaner; 17 South African Dutch

Afrikaner: 4 Boer; 9 Afrikaans; 10 Afrikander

Afro-American: 15 African-American

afropavo: 12 Congo peafowl

aft: 5 aback, abaft, after; 6 astern; 8 rearward

after: 3 aft; 5 aback, abaft, later; 6 astern, dorsal; 7 later on; 8 rearward; 9 afterward, following, in pursuit, posterior, 10 afterwards, subsequent, succeeding; 12 subsequently

after-age: 5 stale; 6 old hat, rococo; 7 out of it; 9 out of date; 10 antiquated; 12 behind the age, of other times, old-fashioned, out of fashion; 14 behind the times, of the old school

after all: 6 in fine; 7 finally; 10 for all that, in any event, on the whole; 11 at all events; 12 in conclusion

afterbirth: 8 placenta; 10 secundines [Med]

aftereffect: 6 sequel; 9 corollary, outgrowth; 11 development; 12 ramification

aftergrowth: 5 yield; 6 result; 7 outcome, product; 8 offshoot; 9 aftercrop, aftermath, appendage, resultant

afterlife: 9 hereafter, next world; 11 future state, world to come; 14 life after death; 15 everlasting life

aftermath: 4 wake; 5 yield; 6 result; 7 outcome, product; 8 backwash, offshoot; 9 resultant; 10 second crop; 11 consequence

afternoon: 2 P.M. [abbr], p.m. [abbr]; 12 postmeridian; 13 good afternoon

afternoon tea: 3 tea; 7 teatime

afterpart: 4 poop; 5 stern; 7 crupper

after-shave: 16 after-shave lotion

aftertaste: 4 tang

afterthought: 2 PS; 7 rethink; 10 post script; 12 after thought; 13 arriere pensee [Fr], second thought; 14 second thoughts

afterwards: 5 after, later; 7 later on; 9 afterward; 12 subsequently

Ag: 6 silver

Ag2S: 9 argentite; 12 silver glance

aga: 5 staff; 9 etat major [Fr]

agacerie: 6 luring; 8 enticing; 10 allurement, attraction, enticement, inducement, temptation; 11 beguilement, captivation

again: 4 anew; 5 often; 6 afresh; 8 once more; 9 once again, over again; 10 repeatedly

against: 3 for; 6 versus; 9 counter to

agalactia: 11 agalactosis

agamic: 7 agamous; 12 agamogenetic

agamid: 12 agamid lizard

agamist: 7 Coelebs; 8 bachelor; 11 old bachelor; 12 unmarried man

agamous: 6 agamic; 12 agamogenetic

agapanthus: 13 lily of the Nile

Agapanthus africanus: 11 African lily; 12 African tulip; 15 blue African lily

agape: 6 aghast, gaping; 7 all agog; 9 love feast; 10 breathless; 12 Ascension Day

agapemone: 11 abode of love

agar: 8 agar-agar; 12 nutrient agar

Agaricus: 8 mushroom; 13 genus Agaricus

Agastache: 6 hyssop; 14 genus Agastache

agate: 4 SiO2; 5 flint; 10 chalcedony, heliotrope

Agathis: 4 pine; 12 genus Agathis

agave family: 9 Agavaceae; 11 sisal family

agaze: 7 staring

age: 3 era; 4 fade, time; 5 epoch, get on, years; 6 mature, old age; 7 Neocene, oldness, Permian, senesce; 8 Cambrian, Cenozoic, Devonian, Jurassic, long time, maturate, Mesozoic, Silurian, Tertiary, the times, Triassic; 9 Paleogene, Paleozoic; 10 Archeozoic, Cretaceous, Ordovician, Quaternary, time of life; 11 advanced age, Precambrian, Proterozoic; 13 Mississippian, Pennsylvanian

aged: 5 cured, of age, older; 6 senior; 7 elderly, ripened

agedness: 10 senescence

ageing: 5 aging; 8 ripening; 9 mellowing, senescent

ageism: 5 agism

Agelaius: 13 genus Agelaius

Agelaius phoeniceus: 7 redwing; 18 red-winged blackbird

ageless: 7 eternal; 8 unending; 9 perpetual, unceasing; 11 everlasting

agency: 3 way; 5 force, means; 6 acting, action, bureau, office; 7 working; 8 delegacy, function; 9 authority, operation

agenda: 6 docket; 7 agendum; 8 calendar, schedule; 12 hidden agenda, hidden motive, secret motive, undercurrent; 13 arriere pensee [Fr]; 14 ulterior motive; 15 order of business

agent: 4 doer; 5 actor; 6 broker, factor; 8 delegate; 9 go-between, middleman, performer; 11 perpetrator; 12 federal agent, intermediary

Age of Fishes: 8 Devonian; 14 Devonian period

Age of Mammals: 8 Cenozoic; 11 Cenozoic era

Age of Man: 10 Quaternary

Age of Reason: 13 Enlightenment

Age of Reptiles: 8 Mesozoic; 11 Mesozoic era

age-old: 7 ancient, antique; 9 customary; 10 immemorial; 11 traditional; 12 prescriptive

ageratum: 10 mistflower

agglomerate: 9 aggregate, clustered; 12 agglomerated; 13 agglomerative

agglutinative: 9 combining; 13 polysynthetic

aggrandize: 3 pad; **4** lard, puff; **5** exalt, widen; **6** blow up, expand, extend, rarefy, spread; **7** amplify, develop, distend, elevate, inflate, magnify; **9** dramatise, dramatize, embellish, embroider, spread out

aggravate: 4 urge; **5** annoy; **6** madden, pile up, worsen; **7** amplify, magnify, provoke; **8** acerbate, convulse, embitter, heighten, irritate, pile it on; **9** infuriate, overstate; **10** accelerate, exacerbate, exaggerate, exasperate

aggravating: 7 galling; **8** annoying, stinging; **9** provoking; **10** irritating, irritation, mortifying; **11** provocation; **12** exacerbating, exasperating

aggregate: 3 sum; **4** bulk, mass; **5** total; **7** combine, complex; **8** ensemble, totality; **9** congeries; **11** agglomerate, aggregative; **14** conglomeration

aggregation: 10 assemblage, coacervate [Chem], collection; **12** accumulation

aggregative: 4 mass; **9** aggregate

aggress: 6 attack

aggression: 7 offense; **9** attacking, hostility, offensive; **14** aggressiveness

aggressive: 5 pushy; **7** pushful, pushing; **9** attacking, offensive; **11** belligerent, fast-growing; **12** enterprising

aggressiveness: 9 pugnacity; **10** aggression; **12** belligerence; **15** contentiousness, quarrelsomeness

aggressor: 8 attacker; **9** assailant

aggrieve: 5 wrong; **6** enrage, grieve, ruffle; **7** affront, oppress; **9** persecute

aggrieved: 7 injured

aggroup: 5 group, unite; **11** concentrate

aghast: 5 agape; **7** all agog, shocked; **8** appalled, dismayed; **10** breathless; **12** disconcerted

agile: 4 spry; **5** quick; **6** nimble; **11** expeditious

agilely: 6 nimbly

agility: 8 legerity, spryness; **10** nimbleness

aging: 6 ageing; **8** ripening; **9** mellowing, senescent

agio: 6 set-off; **7** premium; **8** agiotage, drawback, poundage; **10** percentage; **13** qualification

agiotage: 4 agio; **7** jobbing, premium; **11** speculation; **12** stockjobbing

agism: 6 ageism

agitate: 4 push, stir; **5** budge, fight, rouse, shake, shift; **6** charge, excite, foment, ruffle, stir up; **7** canvass, commove, crusade, discuss, disturb, fluster, perturb, provoke, raise up, shake up; **8** campaign, charge up, convulse

agitated: 7 chaotic, riotous, tossing; **8** shaken up; **9** convulsed, disturbed, in turmoil, stirred up, tremulous, turbulent; **10** disordered, disorderly, tumultuous

agitation: 6 unrest; **7** ferment, turmoil; **8** activity, disorder, disquiet, upheaval; **9** commotion; **10** excitation, excitement, hullabaloo, turbulence; **11** disturbance, stimulation; **12** fermentation, perturbation

agitative: 9 agitating, provoking

agitator: fomenter, prompter; **9** firebrand; **10** incendiary, instigator

agitprop: 12 propagandist

Agkistrodon: 10 copperhead; **11** Ancistrodon; **11** cottonmouth; **13** water moccasin; **16** genus Agkistrodon, genus Ancistrodon

agleam: 5 nitid; **8** gleaming

aglet: 6 aiglet; **8** lace doll; **10** aiguilette

aglitter: 6 fulgid; **7** sparkly; **8** glinting, glittery; **9** sparkling; **10** glistering, glittering; **11** scintillant; **13** scintillating

aglow: 5 lit up; **6** lucent; **7** glowing, lambent; **8** luminous

agnail: 8 hangnail

agnate: 7 agnatic; **8** allied to, paternal, patrikin, patrisib; **10** affiliated, associated, implicated

agnathan: 11 jawless fish

agnation: 8 alliance; **10** connection; **11** affiliation; **12** patrilineage

agnition: 9 accession; **12** subscription; **14** acknowledgment

agnize: 6 accede, accept, agnise; **7** agree to, realize, receive; **9** acquiesce, recognize; **10** comply with, fall in with; **11** acknowledge, give consent, subscribe to; **13** lend oneself to

agnostic: 7 doubter, skeptic; **9** skeptical; **10** agnostical; **12** freethinking

agnosticism: 10 pyrrhonism, scepticism, skepticism

Agnus Dei: 11 Paschal Lamb

ago: 5 agone

agone: 3 ago

agonism: 8 concours [Fr]; **12** belligerency

agonistic: 8 strained; **9** combative; **11** agonistical

agonize: 5 wring; **6** harrow; **7** agonise, torment, torture

agonizing: 7 cutting, grating, in agony, racking; **8** grinding, wretched; **9** consuming, corroding, harrowing, miserable, searching, torturing, torturous; **10** full of pain; **11** torturesome; **12** excruciating

agony: 4 pang; **5** trial; **6** ordeal; **7** anguish, torment, torture; **9** suffering

agora: 5 forum; **12** public square

agouti: 15 Dasyprocta aguti

agranulocytosis: 11 agranulosis

agraphia: 11 logagraphia; **13** anorthography

agrarian: 7 farming; **12** agricultural

agree: 3 fit; **4** gibe, jibe; **5** check, fit in,

match, tally; **6** accord, concur; **7** consort; **9** harmonize; **10** be in accord, correspond; **11** be accordant; **13** be in agreement

agreeable: 6 pliant; **8** grateful, in accord, pleasant, pleasing; **9** accordant, congenial, consonant, enjoyable; **10** concordant, gratifying, **11** conformable, in agreement, pleasurable, pleasureful

agreed: 7 carried, content

agreed upon: 11 stipulatory

agree for: 7 bargain; **8** contract, covenant

agreeing: 5 as one; **6** united; **7** suiting; **8** cemented, in accord; **9** assenting, congenial, in harmony, of one mind; **10** assentient, concordant, concurring, harmonious; **11** harmonizing, in agreement

agreement: 3 nod; **4** pact; **6** accord, assent; **7** compact, concord, consent; **9** accession; **10** acceptance; **11** acceptation, arrangement, concordance; **12** acquiescence; **13** understanding

agree to: 6 accede, accept; **7** receive; **9** acquiesce; **10** comply with, fall in with; **11** acknowledge

agrestic: 6 rustic; **8** agrarian; **12** agricultural

agricultor: 13 agriculturist

agricultural: 7 farming; **8** agrarian

agricultural agent: 11 county agent

agriculture: 7 farming, tillage; **8** agronomy, georgics; **9** husbandry; **11** cultivation; **12** agribusiness

agriculturist: 6 grower, raiser; **10** cultivator

agrimony: 9 agrimonia

Agriocharis: 6 turkey; **16** genus Agriocharis

Agrippa: 22 Marcus Vipsanius Agrippa

agrobiologic: 14 agrobiological

agrobiological: 12 agrobiologic

agrological: 9 agrologic

agronomic: 11 agronomical

agronomy: 7 farming, tillage; **8** georgics; **11** agriculture, cultivation

Agropyron: 14 genus Agropyron; **10** wheat grass

aground: 7 swamped, wrecked; **8** capsized, cast away, graveled, grounded, stranded; **9** foundered, nonplused, stuck fast; **10** high and dry, nonplussed; **11** shipwrecked

agua: 8 agua toad; **11** Bufo marinus

agua toad: 4 agua; **11** Bufo marinus

ague: 5 acute; **11** acute accent; **14** chills and fever

ague fit: 6 tremor; **7** flutter, shaking; **9** cold sweat, quivering, trembling; **11** palpitation, trepidation; **12** perturbation

ague grass: 8 ague root; **15** Aletris farinosa

agueweed: 6 arnica; **7** benzoin, calomel; **8** ague weed

aha!: 6 eureka!; **8** I've got it!

ahead: 2 on; **5** forth; **6** before, beyond, onward; **7** forward, in front, leading, onwards; **8** forrader, forwards, in the van, out front; **9** in advance, in front of, in the lead; **10** beforehand, right ahead

Ahriman: 5 Satan; **6** Belial, Samael, Zamiel; **7** Lucifer, old Nick [slang]; **8** the Devil; **9** Beelzebub; **10** the evil one, the tempter; **12** the Adversary, the arch fiend, the archenemy, the foul fiend, the wicked one; **13** the evil spirit, the old Serpent; **14** Mephistopheles

Ahura Mazda: 6 Ormazd, Ormuzd

ai: 14 three-toed sloth

aid: 4 care, help; **6** aiding, assist, succor; **7** give aid, helping, tending; **8** bring aid, lend help; **9** afford aid, assisting, attention, supply aid; **10** assistance, furnish aid; **11** furnish help

aide: 7 adjunct; **8** adjutant; **9** auxiliary; **10** aide-de-camp

aide-de-camp: 4 aide; **8** adjutant; **9** brigadier; **12** brigade major, staff officer

Aides: 5 Hades, Pluto; **8** Aidoneus

aiding: 3 aid; **4** help; **6** succor; **7** helpful, helping; **8** adjuvant; **9** assisting, auxiliary; **10** assistance

aidless: 11 defenseless

Aidoneus: 5 Aides, Hades, Pluto

aiglet: 5 aglet; **10** aiguilette

aigret: 8 aigrette

aigrette: 5 plume; **6** aigret; **7** feather, panache

aiguille: 4 crag, pike; **5** arete [Fr], crest; **8** cone peak; **9** sugar loaf

aigulet: 4 frog; **7** epaulet; **12** shoulder knot

ail: 4 have, pain; **5** bleed; **6** garlic, suffer; **7** afflict, trouble; **10** complain of, labor under

ailing: 3 ill; **4** sick; **5** ill of; **6** peaked, poorly, sickly, unwell; **8** diseased; **9** unhealthy; **10** feeling ill, indisposed; **11** in ill health

ailment: 3 ill; **6** malady; **7** disease, illness; **8** disorder, sickness; **9** complaint

aim: 3 end, get; **4** goal, take; **5** drive, place, point, train; **6** aspire, design, direct, intent, object, target; **7** bearing, heading, propose, purport, purpose, take aim; **8** end point, quo animo [Lat], shoot for; **9** calculate, intention, objective

aimed: 7 pointed; **8** directed

aimless: 6 adrift, afloat; **7** vagrant; **8** drifting, floating, planless, vagabond; **9** whimsical; **10** capricious, rudderless, undirected; **11** purposeless; **13** directionless

aimlessly: 8 by chance, randomly; **10** without aim; **12** fortuitously

ain: 3 own

aioli: 10 aioli sauce; **11** garlic sauce

air: 3 fan; **4** aura, bare, beam, cast, line, look, mien, open, port, send, tune, vent; **5** color, guise, vapor; **6** air out, airing, breeze, melody, strain, zephyr; **7** airwave, open air, recruit, thin air; **8** aviation, carriage, demeanor, outdoors, transmit; **9** air travel, air-driven, broadcast, common air, freshen up, pneumatic, publicise, publicize, ventilate; **10** atmosphere, complexion

air attack: 7 air raid

airbag: 8 seat belt; **10** safety belt

air base: 10 air station

airbed: 6 air-bed; **11** air mattress

air blower: 3 fan; **5** lungs; **7** air pump, bellows; **8** blowpipe; **10** ventilator

air cell: 6 air sac; **8** alveolus

air cleaner: 9 air filter

air current: 5 draft; **7** draught

air cushion: 9 air spring

airdock: 6 hangar; **10** repair shed

air-driven: 3 air; **9** pneumatic

airdrome: 7 airport; **9** aerodrome

air duct: 6 airway; **10** air passage

Aire: 9 River Aire

aired: 4 airy; **9** broadcast

Airedale: 15 Airedale terrier

air embolism: 5 bends; **12** aeroembolism; **14** caisson disease

airfield: 5 field; **11** flying field; **12** landing field

air filter: 10 air cleaner

airfoil: 7 surface; **8** aerofoil

air force officer: 9 commander

air gun: 5 BB gun; **6** airgun; **7** wind gun; **9** pellet gun

air hammer: 10 jack hammer, jackhammer; **15** pneumatic hammer

airhead: 4 twit

airheaded: 4 dull; **5** dizzy, giddy, silly; **6** stupid; **7** witless; **8** mindless; **9** brainless, dim-witted, dull minded, dull normal, dull witted, half witted, weak minded; **12** feeble-minded

airhole: 4 vent; **7** air vent; **8** blowhole, venthole

air hostess: 7 hostess; **10** stewardess

airily: 10 flippantly

airiness: 8 buoyancy, delicacy

air lane: 6 airway; **10** flight path

airless: 5 close; **6** stuffy; **7** unaired

air letter: 8 aerogram; **10** aerogramme; **13** airmail letter

airlike: 8 aeriform

air line: 7 beeline

airmail: 7 airpost

airmail letter: 8 aerogram; **9** air letter; **10** aerogramme

airman: 5 flier, flyer; **7** aviator; **8** aeronaut; **15** aerial navigator

airmanship: 10 seamanship; **11** aeronautics; **12** horsemanship, marksmanship

air mattress: 6 air-bed, airbed

air mile: 2 mi; **4** knot, mile; **6** naut mi; **12** nautical mile

air out: 3 air; **4** vent; **9** ventilate

air passage: 6 airway; **7** air duct

airplane maneuver: 14 flight maneuver

airplane propeller: 4 prop; **8** airscrew

air plant: 8 epiphyte; **9** aerophyte

airport: 8 airdrome; **9** aerodrome

airpost: 7 airmail

air pressure: 18 barometric pressure

air pump: 3 fan; **5** lungs; **7** bellows; **8** blowpipe; **9** air blower; **10** vacuum pump, ventilator

air raid: 9 air attack

air-raid shelter: 9 bombproof; **11** bomb shelter

airs: 4 pose; **9** mannerism, sauciness; **10** pretension; **11** acting a part, affectation, pretensions [pl]; **12** affectedness, impertinence

air sac: 7 air cell; **8** alveolus

airship: 9 dirigible

air sock: 8 wind sock; **9** air sleeve; **10** wind sleeve

air spring: 10 air cushion

airstream: 4 race, wash; **8** backwash; **10** slipstream

airstrip: 5 strip; **11** flight strip; **12** landing strip

airt: 4 work; **8** redirect; **11** make one's way, work one's way

air travel: 3 air; **8** aviation

air vent: 4 vent; **8** blowhole, venthole

airwave: 3 air

airway: 7 air duct, air lane, airline; **10** air passage, flight path

airwoman: 8 aviatrix; **9** aviatress

airy: 4 aery; **5** aired, light; **6** aerial, bright; **7** buoyant, shallow, subtile; **8** ethereal; **9** visionary; **10** debonnaire; **11** atmospheric, free and easy, impractical

airy hopes: 13 fool's paradise

aisle: 4 lane; **5** alley, glade, lobby, vista; **6** artery; **7** gangway; **8** corridor

ait: 6 island

Aix: 8 genus Aix, wood duck; **10** summer duck; **11** wood widgeon; **12** mandarin duck

Ajuga: 5 bugle; **10** genus Ajuga

ajutage: 9 discharge; **13** discharge line, discharge tube

a.k.a.: 11 also known as

Akaba: 5 Aqaba

akaryote: 10 akaryocyte

akee: 5 ackee; **8** akee tree; **13** Blighia sapida

Akha: 4 Hani

akimbo: 5 crane, fluke; **6** crutch, scythe, sickle, zigzag; **8** crinkled; **10** knock kneed

akin: 3 kin; **6** family; **7** cognate, kindred, related; **10** of the blood; **11** consanguine; **12** blood-related

akinesia: 8 akinesis

akin to: 9 related to

Aku: 6 Yoruba

akvavit: 7 aquavit
Al: 8 aluminum; **9** aluminium
Alabaman: 9 Alabamian
alabandite: 12 manganblende
alabaster: 10 onyx marble; **11** alabastrine
alacrity: 4 life; **8** despatch, dispatch, vivacity; **9** animation, briskness, readiness; **10** expedition, promptness; **11** forwardness, promptitude
alameda: 3 row; **4** road; **9** board walk, esplanade; **10** embankment
alar: 5 alary; **7** aliform; **8** axillary; **10** wing-shaped
Alar: 10 daminozide
a la mode: 6 modish; **7** in style, in vogue; **11** comme il faut [Fr]
alarm: 5 alert, appal, scare; **6** alarum, appall, dismay, fright; **7** horrify, scarify, startle; **8** affright, frighten; **10** alarm clock; **11** alarm signal, alarm system; **13** consternation, warning device, warning signal
alarming: 5 scary; **10** scarifying
alarmist: 9 pessimist
alarum: 3 cry; **4** bell; **5** alarm, alert; **6** alerts, tocsin; **9** alarm bell, hue and cry; **10** beat of drum; **11** note of alarm; **13** warning signal
alary: 4 alar; **7** aliform; **10** wing-shaped
alas: 9 unluckily; **11** regrettably; **13** unfortunately
Alaskan brown bear: 6 Kodiak
Alaskan malamute: 8 malamute, malemute
Alaskan pipeline: 20 trans-Alaska pipeline
a la tartufe: 11 insincerely; **13** uningenuously; **14** disingenuously
alated: 5 alate; **6** winged
Alauda: 11 genus Alauda
Alauda arvensis: 7 skylark
albacore: 12 long-fin tunny; **15** Thunnus alalunga
Albany: 16 capital of New York
albata: 5 paint; **6** ormolu; **10** white metal; **12** german silver
Albatrellus: 16 genus Albatrellus
Albatrellus ovinus: 13 sheep polypore
albatross: 9 millstone
albedo: 15 reflective power
albeit: 7 howbeit
alberca: 9 hog wallow [U.S.]
Albers-Schonberg disease: 13 osteopetrosis
Albert Edward: 9 Edward VII
albification: 9 whitening
albinic: 7 albinal; **9** albinotic; **10** albinistic
albite: 13 white feldspar; **14** sodium feldspar
albizzia: 7 albizia
Albizzia julibrissin: 8 silk tree; **18** Albizia julibrissin
Albright's disease: 27 polyostotic fibrous dysplasia

album: 9 portfolio; **11** record album
albumen: 7 albumin, protein; **8** egg white; **9** ovalbumin; **10** egg albumin
albuminoid: 13 scleroprotein
albuminous: 4 ropy; **6** clammy, mastic; **7** clotted, gelatin; **9** glutenous, glutinous; **10** gelatinous; **12** mucilaginous
albuterol: 8 Ventolin; **9** Proventil
alcahest: 8 alkahest; **16** universal solvent
Alcaic: 5 Ionic; **7** Sapphic; **8** Pindaric; **11** Alcaic verse
alcalescent: 11 alkalescent
Alcedo: 10 kingfisher; **11** genus Alcedo
Alces: 3 elk; **5** moose; **10** genus Alces
alchemic: 10 alchemical
Alcides: 8 Heracles, Herakles, Hercules
alcohol: 5 drink; **7** ethanol; **9** inebriant; **10** intoxicant; **12** ethyl alcohol
alcohol dependency: 10 alcoholism, dipsomania
alcoholic: 4 lush; **5** souse; **6** boozer, soaker; **11** dipsomaniac; **16** alcohol-dependent
alcoholic beverage: 5 drink; **7** alcohol, spirits; **9** inebriant; **10** intoxicant
Alcoholics Anonymous: 2 AA
alcoholism: 9 addiction, potomania; **10** dipsomania, dependency; **11** drunkenness
alcove: 3 bay; **8** cul-de-sac
Aldactone: 14 spironolactone
Aldebaran: 8 canicula
alder: 9 alder tree
alderfly: 8 alder fly; **13** Sialis lutaria
alderman: 10 councilman; **12** committeeman, councilwoman
aldol: 9 acetaldol
Aldomet: 10 methyldopa
alecost: 8 costmary; **9** bible leaf; **10** balsam herb; **12** mint geranium
Alectoris: 9 partridge; **14** genus Alectoris
alehoof: 9 field balm, ground ivy; **12** runaway robin
alembic: 5 still; **6** retort; **7** caldron; **8** crucible
alentours: 7 suburbs; **8** confines, environs, purlieus, vicinage; **10** borderland; **12** neighborhood
Alep: 6 Aleppo
aleph-zero: 9 aleph-null; **11** aleph-nought
Aleppo: 4 Alep
Aleppo boil: 9 Delhi boil; **12** oriental sore, tropical sore
alert: 5 alarm, alive, awake, ready, sharp, smart; **6** alarum; **7** qui vive; **8** alerting, open-eyed, watchful; **13** warning signal
alerted: 7 advised; **8** apprised, informed; **10** acquainted
alertness: 8 alerting, keenness; **9** a sharp eye, attention, vigilance; **10** advertence, advertency; **12** watchfulness; **13** attentiveness, particularity
alerts: 5 alarm; **6** alarum, tocsin; **9** alarm bell

Aleurites: 8 tung tree; 11 tung-oil tree; 14 genus Aleurites

Aleut: 8 Aleutian

Aleutians: 15 Aleutian Islands

Alexandria: 14 El Iskandariyah

alexandrite: 6 jasper; 7 cat's eye; 8 hematite; 9 moonstone; 10 bloodstone

alexia: 13 visual aphasia, word blindness

alexic: 9 word-blind

alfalfa: 6 banyan; 7 lucerne

alfilaria: 6 banyan, clocks; 7 alfalfa, filaree, filaria; 8 pin grass; 9 alfileria, pin clover

al fresco: 6 sub dio [Lat]; 7 outside, sub Jove [Lat]; 8 outdoors; 10 out-of-doors; 12 in the open air

algae: 4 alga

algarroba: 5 carob; 9 carob bean, carob tree, locust pod; 10 locust bean; 11 algarobilla; 12 algarrobilla; 13 algarroba bean, carob bean tree

algebraic: 8 analytic; 11 algebraical, statistical; 12 arithmetical

Algeria: 7 Algerie

algid: 5 gelid; 6 frigid

Algiers: 15 Algerian capital

alginic acid: 5 algin

algology: 10 dendrology

algometric: 12 algometrical

Algonquin: 9 Algonkian; 10 Algonquian

algorithm: 7 routine; 10 subroutine

alias: 3 a.k.a.; 9 false name; 11 also known as, assumed name

alibi: 6 excuse; 11 absenteeism; 13 nonattendance

alien: 6 assign, exotic; 7 foreign, gentile, heathen, strange, unknown; 8 alienate, estrange, stranger; 9 disaffect, extrinsic, foreigner, outlander; 10 extraneous, noncitizen, outlandish; 16 extraterrestrial

alienable: 10 negotiable

alienate: 5 alien, repel; 6 assign; 8 estrange; 9 disaffect

alienated: 6 anomic; 9 estranged; 11 disaffected, disoriented; 14 irreconcilable

alienation: 6 enmity; 7 cession; 8 coolness, transfer; 9 assigning, conveying, hostility; 10 assignment, conveyance; 12 disaffection, estrangement

alienness: 11 foreignness; 14 extraneousness

aliform: 4 alar; 5 alary; 10 wing-shaped

alight: 4 land; 5 afire, light, perch; 6 ablaze, aflame, aflare, on fire; 7 blazing, burning, flaming, get down; 8 dismount; 9 climb down

align: 5 aline, array; 6 adjust, line up; 10 coordinate

aligning: 11 positioning

alignment: 8 alliance; 9 alinement, coalition; 11 conjunction

alike: 4 like; 7 similar; 8 likewise

alikeness: 8 likeness; 10 similitude

aliment: 4 food, grub; 7 edibles, ingesta, nourish, nutrify, pabulum; 8 eatables, victuals; 9 nutriment, provender; 10 sustenance; 11 comestibles, nourishment, staff of life; 12 alimentation, sustentation

alimentary: 6 edible; 7 eatable; 8 dietetic, nutrient; 9 nutritive; 10 comestible, nourishing, nutritious

alimentary paste: 5 pasta

alimentary tract: 7 GI tract; 13 digestive tube; 14 digestive tract; 15 alimentary canal

alimentation: 4 food, grub; 7 aliment, edibles, feeding, ingesta, nurture, pabulum; 8 eatables, victuals; 9 nutriment, nutrition, provender; 10 nourishing, sustenance; 11 comestibles, nourishment, staff of life; 12 sustentation

alimony: 5 dowry; 8 palimony, pittance; 11 maintenance

alinement: 8 alliance; 9 alignment, coalition

aliphatic compound: 15 acyclic compound

aliquant: 12 aliquant part

aliquot: 5 prime; 9 divisible, sectional; 10 fractional, reciprocal; 11 aliquot part; 13 complementary

aliterate: 15 aliterate person

a little bit: 7 a wee bit

alive: 4 live; 5 acute, alert, awake, quick; 6 active, living; 8 animated

alizarine red: 3 red; 7 carmine, crimson

aljibar: 4 pond, tank; 7 cistern; 8 mill pond

alkahest: 8 alcahest; 16 universal solvent

alkalescent: 11 alcalescent

alkali: 4 base, 7 caustic; 12 lunar caustic

alkali flat: 5 llano

alkaline: 7 alkalic

alkalinity: 10 causticity

alkalize: 6 basify; 8 alkalify

alkalizer: 7 antacid; 14 gastric antacid

alkane: 8 paraffin; 12 alkane series; 13 methane series

alkanet: 7 bugloss; 18 Anchusa officinalis

alkene: 6 olefin; 7 olefine

Alkeran: 9 melphalan

all: 3 sum; 5 all of, every, total, whole; 6 wholly; 7 in a body, totally; 8 all in all, as a whole, entirely, sum total, the whole; 9 one and all, wholesale; 10 altogether, completely, everything; 11 gross amount; 12 collectively, tout ensemble

all-absorbing: 5 vital; 7 radical; 8 cardinal; 9 essential, paramount

all agog: 5 agape; 6 aghast, gaping; 10 breathless

allay: 3 lay; 4 calm, cool, damp, ease, hush, lull, swag, tame; 5 abate, quell, quiet, slake, sober, still; 6 deaden, pacify, quench, rebate, smooth, soothe; 7 appease, assuage, compose, relieve, slacken, turn off; **8** calm down, suppress; **9** alleviate; **11** tranquilize

all but: 4 most, near, nigh; **5** about; **6** almost, nearly; **7** short of; **8** not quite, well-nigh; **9** just about, virtually

all day long: 7 daylong

all decked out: 4 chic; **9** decked out, dressed up; **10** endimanche [Fr]; **12** all dressed up, in Sunday best

allegation: 8 averment; **9** assertion, complaint, statement; **10** advocation, allegement, profession; **11** declaration, predication

allege: 3 say; **4** aver; **5** plead; **6** broach; **7** advance, hold out, pretend, propose; **8** propound, set forth; **9** enunciate, pronounce

allegedly: 9 on its face; **10** apparently, ostensibly

allegiance: 6 fealty; **7** loyalty; **9** deference; **10** commitment, dedication

allegorical: 8 allusive; **9** allegoric, parabolic

allegory: 5 fable; **7** parable; **10** moral fable

allegresse: 4 life; **8** alacrity, vivacity; **9** animation

allegretto: 7 allegro

allegro: 10 allegretto

allele: 11 allelomorph

allelujah: 10 hallelujah

allemande: 14 allemande sauce

all-encompassing: 4 wide; **5** broad; **7** blanket; **8** panoptic; **12** all-embracing, all-inclusive, encompassing

allergic: 10 sensitized; **14** hypersensitive, supersensitive

allergy: 16 allergic reaction

alleviate: 3 lay; **4** calm, cool, damp, ease, hush, lull, swag, tame; **5** abate, allay, quell, quiet, sober, still; **6** deaden, pacify, rebate, smooth, soothe; **7** appease, assuage, compose, relieve, slacken, turn off; **8** calm down, mitigate, palliate, suppress; **10** facilitate; **11** tranquilize

alleviating: 6 easing; **9** relieving

alleviative: 8 lenitive; **10** mitigative, mitigatory, palliative; **11** alleviatory

alley: 4 lane; **5** aisle, glade, lobby, vista; **6** artery; **8** alleyway, corridor; **10** back street; **12** bowling alley, skittle alley

alley cat: 5 stray

All Fools' Day: 10 April Fools'; **13** April Fools' Day

all get out: 6 billyo; **7** billy-ho, billyoh

allgood: 6 fat hen; **11** wild spinach; **13** good-king-henry

Allhallows: 9 Hallowmas, November 1; **10** Hallowmass; **12** All Saints' Day

Allhallows Eve: 9 Hallowe'en, Halloween

alliaceous: 8 garlicky

alliance: 4 bond, Bund [Ger]; **6** league, Verein [Ger]; **8** affinity, homology; **9** align-

ment, alinement, coalition, syndicate; **10** connection; **11** affiliation, association, combination, homogeneity; **13** confederation

Alliaria: 13 genus Alliaria

allice: 5 allis; **9** allis shad; **10** allice shad, Alosa alosa

allied: 10 collateral; **11** confederate; **13** confederative

allied to: 6 agnate; **8** congener; **10** affiliated, associated, implicated

alligation: 7 joining; **8** junction, ligating, ligation; **9** attaching; **10** attachment, connecting

alligator: 9 crocodile

alligatored: 7 cracked

Alligatoridae: 19 family Alligatoridae

Alligator mississipiensis: 17 American alligator

alligator pear: 7 avocado; **11** avocado pear

all-important: 7 crucial; **9** essential; **12** all important, of the essence

all in all: 3 all; **7** in a body; **8** as a whole, entirely; **9** wholesale; **10** altogether, on the whole; **12** collectively, tout ensemble

all-inclusive: 4 wide; **5** broad; **7** blanket; **8** panoptic; **12** all-embracing, encompassing

allis: 6 allice; **9** allis shad; **10** allice shad, Alosa alosa

alliteration: 9 head rhyme; **12** initial rhyme; **14** beginning rhyme

alliterative: 12 antithetical

Allium: 4 leek; **5** onion; **6** garlic; **7** shallot; **8** eschalot; **8** scallion; **11** genus Allium

all kinds of: 6 divers; **7** various; **10** all sorts of; **11** all manner of, diversified

all-knowing: 7 all-wise; **9** all-seeing; **10** omniscient

all manner of: 6 divers; **7** various; **10** all kinds of, all sorts of; **11** diversified

allmouth: 5 lotte; **6** angler; **8** monkfish; **9** goosefish; **10** angler fish, anglerfish; **17** Lophius Americanus

allness: 9 wholeness; **12** completeness

allocate: 5 allot; **6** ration; **9** apportion, ration out

allocation: 3 lot; **5** share; **7** measure, portion; **9** allotment, allowance, fair share, parceling; **10** contingent, parcelling; **11** collocation; **12** apportioning

allocution: 6 speech; **7** address, lecture, oration, oratory; **12** formal speech

allodial: 6 landed; **8** freehold, manorial; **10** autonomous

all of a twitter: 7 unquiet; **8** restless; **9** in a pucker; **10** convulsive, giddy-paced

all of nature: 6 cosmos, nature; **8** creation, universe; **9** macrocosm

allopathy: 10 hydropathy [Med], osteopathy; **11** heteropathy [Med]

allopurinol: 8 Zyloprim

alloquy: 6 speech; 7 address, lecture, oration, oratory; 10 allocution; 12 formal speech

allosaurus: 8 allosaur

allot: 3 lot; 4 deal, pack; 5 grant; 6 accord, assign, ordain, ration, set out; 7 deal out, dish out, dole out, marshal, mete out, portion; 8 allocate, dispense, legalize, sanctify, shell out; 9 collocate, parcel out, prescribe, ration out; 10 administer, distribute

alloted: 5 dealt; 10 collocated; 11 distributed, parceled out

allotment: 3 lot; 5 share; 7 measure, portion, sorting; 8 alloting, division, grouping; 9 allowance, fair share, parceling; 10 allocation, assortment, contingent, parcelling; 11 classifying; 12 apportioning, dispensation, distributing, distribution; 13 apportionment, portioning out; 14 classification

all-out: 9 full-scale

all over: 4 over; 5 ended; 8 complete; 9 concluded; 10 everyplace, everywhere, terminated; 11 covered with; 12 right and left; 15 all the world over

allow: 3 let, own; 4 avow, bate, give; 5 admit, grant, leave, yield; 6 give up, permit, reduce; 7 concede, confess, earmark, reserve, take off; 8 allow for, discount, mark down, set aside; 9 price down, subscribe; 10 contribute, provide for; 11 acknowledge, appropriate, countenance; 13 make allowance, turn inside out; 15 furnish its quota, take into account

allowable: 9 permitted; 10 authorized, sanctioned; 11 permissible

allowance: 3 lot; 5 share; 6 leeway, margin; 7 measure, portion, stipend; 8 discount, mark down; 9 abatement, allotment, fair share, reduction, tolerance; 10 adjustment, allocation, concession, contingent, sufferance, toleration; 12 depreciation; 13 consideration

allowed: 9 allowable, permitted; 10 authorized, sanctioned; 11 permissible

allowed for: 7 excused; 11 glossed over

allow for: 5 allow, leave; 10 provide for

allow in: 5 admit, let in

allowing: 10 permitting

allowing of: 11 admitting of; 12 permitting of

alloy: 6 debase, infect; 7 amalgam; 8 compound; 9 admixture; 10 adulterate, amalgamate, corruption; 11 composition, tertium quid [Lat]; 12 adulteration, sophisticate; 13 contamination

alloyage: 9 matrimony; 12 intermixture

all-powerful: 8 almighty; 10 omnipotent

all right: 2 OK; 3 yes; 4 fine, okay; 7 alright, why not?; 8 very well; 9 tolerable; 10 ac-

ceptable, good enough; 11 might as well; 12 satisfactory, without doubt

all-right: 2 OK; 4 fine, okay; 8 all right

All Saints' Day: 9 Hallowmas, November 1; 10 Allhallows, Hallowmass

all-seeing: 7 all-wise; 10 all-knowing

All Souls' Day: 8 All Souls'; 9 November 2

allspice: 11 pimento tree; 12 allspice tree; 13 Pimenta dioica

all-terrain bike: 9 off-roader; 12 mountain bike

all the go: 10 all the rage

all the rage: 2 in; 6 trendy, with it; 7 current, in vogue; 9 in fashion, prevalent; 10 prevailing; 11 fashionable

all the same: 3 yet; 5 still; 6 all one, even so, withal; 7 however; 11 nonetheless; 12 nevertheless

allude: 4 hint; 5 apply, touch; 6 advert; 8 allude to, intimate; 9 adumbrate; 11 shadow forth

allude to: 4 hint; 5 apply, imply, infer; 6 allude, convey; 7 bespeak, breathe, involve, point to, suggest; 8 indicate, intimate; 9 adumbrate; 10 bear a sense; 11 shadow forth; 14 make allusion to

allure: 4 draw, lure, move; 5 tempt; 6 draw on, entice, induce; 7 attract, beguile; 9 captivate, titillate; 10 allurement; 12 temptingness; 13 take one's fancy; 14 attractiveness

allurement: 5 fancy; 6 allure, luring, magnet; 8 enticing; 9 seduction; 10 attraction, enticement, inducement, temptation; 11 beguilement, captivation, fascination; 12 solicitation, temptingness

alluring: 6 luring; 7 drawing; 8 enticing, inviting, tempting; 9 beguiling; 10 attracting, attractive

allusion: 11 adumbration, insinuation

allusive: 6 covert; 7 muffled; 10 comparable, expressive, suggestive; 11 allegorical

alluvial fan: 12 alluvial cone

alluviation: 7 deposit; 13 sedimentation

alluvium: 3 mud; 4 mire, muck, silt; 5 slosh, slush; 6 sludge; 8 quagmire

all-wise: 9 all-seeing; 10 all-knowing

all worked up: 4 wild; 5 fiery; 6 fierce, in a way, savage; 7 furious, in a fury, in a rage; 8 up in arms; 9 in a taking, infuriate; 10 infuriated

ally: 6 friend; 8 affiance; 11 confederate

allyl alcohol: 15 propenyl alcohol

Alma-Ata: 6 Almaty; 18 capital of Kazakstan

Al-Magrib: 5 Maroc; 7 Morocco; 9 Marruecos

alma mater: 7 academy

almanac: 8 calendar; 9 ephemeris; 15 farmer's calendar

almandite: 9 almandine, carbuncle; 10 Al-Fe garnet

Almaty: 7 Alma-Ata; 18 capital of Kazakstan

almightiness: 11 omnipotence

almighty: 4 holy; 6 sacred; 8 hallowed, heavenly; 9 celestial; 10 omnipotent; 11 all-powerful

Almighty: 4 Lord; 6 Divine; 7 Creator, Godhead, Jehovah; 11 God Almighty

almond: 11 sweet almond; 12 Prunus dulcis

almond cookie: 14 almond crescent

almond-shaped: 10 amygdaloid; 12 amygdaliform, amygdaloidal

almoner: 6 beadle, sexton, suisse [Fr], verger; 7 steward, trustee; 8 receiver; 9 sacristan; 10 accountant, liquidator

almost: 4 most, near, nigh; 5 about; 6 all but, nearly; 7 short of; 8 not quite, well-nigh; 9 just about, virtually; 11 just short of

alms: 6 bounty; 7 largess; 9 alms-giving

alms box: 7 mite box, poor box

almshouse: 4 home; 7 shelter; 9 poorhouse

Alnus: 5 alder; 10 genus Alnus

alocasia: 11 elephant ear; 12 elephant's ear

aloe family: 9 Aloeaceae; 15 family Aloeaceae

aloes: 3 rue; 11 bitter aloes; 15 gall and wormwood

Aloe vera: 9 burn plant

aloft: 2 up; 5 above, aloof; 6 high up, on high; 8 overhead

alogy: 8 nonsense; 13 utter nonsense

aloha: 4 ciao; 5 adieu; 7 goodbye; 8 farewell, sayonara; 10 dosvidanya [Russ]; 11 leave taking, valediction; 12 hasta la vista [Sp]; 14 auf wiedersehen [Ger]

alone: 4 lone, only, solo; 5 apart, per se; 6 lonely, singly, solely, unique; 8 by itself, entirely, solitary; 9 by oneself, on one's own, unequaled; 10 individual, unequalled; 11 exclusively; 12 individually, single-handed, unparalleled; 13 unaccompanied

aloneness: 8 solitude; 10 loneliness; 12 lonesomeness

along: 2 on; 8 at length, linearly; 10 lengthwise

alongside: 5 aside; 6 aboard, beside; 7 abreast; 9 on one side; 10 side by side

aloof: 2 up; 5 above, aloft; 6 high up, on high, remote; 7 distant; 8 detached, overhead, wide away; 14 unapproachable

aloofness: 8 coldness, coolness, distance; 9 frigidity; 10 remoteness, withdrawal; 12 lack of caring, lukewarmness; 13 lack of feeling, withdrawnness

Alopex: 3 fox; 11 genus Alopex

Alopex lagopus: 8 white fox; 9 arctic fox

Alopiidae: 15 family Alopiidae

Alopius: 8 fox shark, thrasher, thresher; 13 thresher shark; 12 genus Alopius

Alosa: 4 shad; 10 genus Alosa

a lot: 3 lot; 4 lots, much; 7 a volume; 8 very much; 9 a good deal, a quantity; 10 a great deal; 11 large amount; 13 large quantity

a lot of money: 4 pile; 6 bundle; 8 big bucks, big money; 9 much money

aloud: 4 loud; 6 loudly; 7 out loud

Alp: 4 peak, pike; 5 mount; 8 mountain

alpaca: 9 Lama pacos

alpenstock: 5 baton, staff, stick; 6 crutch

alpestrine: 9 subalpine

alpha: 7 initial

alphabet: 4 ABCs; 7 grammar; 8 elements, outlines; 9 rudiments; 10 first thing

alphabetarian: 11 abecedarian

alphabetical: 10 alphabetic; 11 abecedarian

alphabetical character: 6 letter

Alpha Centauri: 5 Rigil; 9 Rigil Kent

alpha fetoprotein: 3 AFP

Alpha Geminorum: 6 Castor

alphameric: 12 alphamerical, alphanumeric; 14 alphanumerical

alphanumeric display: 14 digital display

Alpha Orionis: 10 Betelgeuse

alpha ray: 13 alpha particle; 14 alpha radiation

alpha wave: 11 alpha rhythm

Alphitomancy: 6 by meal

Alpinia: 6 ginger; 8 galangal; 12 genus Alpinia, genus Languas; 13 genus Zerumbet

alpinism: 16 mountain climbing

alpinist: 7 climber; 11 mountaineer; 15 mountain climber

alprazolam: 5 Xanax

already: 3 yet; 10 beforehand

alright: 2 OK; 4 fine, okay; 8 all right, very well; 12 without doubt

ALS: 17 Lou Gehrig's disease

Alsace: 6 Elsass; 7 Alsatia; 14 Alsace-Lorraine

Alsatia: 6 Alsace, Elsass; 8 rapacity; 10 den of Cacus; 11 kleptomania; 12 den of thieves, thievishness

alsatian: 14 German shepherd; 15 German police dog

also: 3 and, too; 4 item; 6 as well; 7 besides, further; 8 likewise; 11 furthermore

also-ran: 5 loser

ALT: 2 EL; 8 altitude; 9 elevation

Altaic: 14 Altaic language

altar boy: 7 acolyte

altarpiece: 7 reredos

altar wine: 15 sacramental wine

alter: 3 fix; 4 spay, vary; 6 change, mutate, neuter; 7 falsify; 8 modulate; 11 interpolate

alterable: 6 mobile; 7 plastic

alteration: 6 change; 8 alterity, changing,

mutation, revision; **9** variation; **10** adjustment; **12** modification, simple change

alterative: 7 healing; **8** curative, remedial, sanative; **11** therapeutic

altercate: 6 argufy; **7** dispute, quarrel

altercation: 4 feud, spat, tiff; **5** snarl; **6** affray, fracas; **7** dispute, quarrel; **8** squabble

altered: 5 seedy; **6** varied; **7** adapted, changed; **8** battered, modified, neutered; **9** shattered; **10** pulled down

alter ego: 3 pal; **5** buddy; **8** soulmate; **9** companion, confidant; **10** fast friend; bosom friend

altering: 6 fixing; **9** neutering

alterity: 10 alteration

Alternanthera philoxeroides: 13 alligator weed; **14** alligator grass

alternate: 4 flip, jump; **6** swerve, switch; **7** sputter; exchange, flip-flop, hesitate, intermit; **9** surrogate, take turns; **10** every other, understudy; **11** alternating, alternative, every second, interchange, replacement

alternating current: 2 AC

alternation: 11 reciprocity, taking turns

alternation of generations: 11 xenogenesis; **13** heterogenesis

alternative: 5 plan B; **6** choice, option; **7** choices [pl], variant; **8** election; **9** alternate, expedient, **10** quid pro quo, substitute; **11** replacement

alternatively: 6 or else; **7** instead

alter one's course: 4 turn; **7** deviate; **10** depart from

althea: 7 althaea; **9** hollyhock

althorn: 8 alto horn

altiloquent: 6 flashy, frothy; **7** flaming

altitude: 2 EL; **3** ALT; **6** height; **7** azimuth; **9** elevation

alto: 4 hill; **5** butte [U.S.]; **9** contralto; **12** countertenor

alto clef: 9 viola clef

altocumulus: 16 altocumulus cloud

altogether: 3 all, raw; **4** buff; **5** fully, in all, quite, stark, whole; **6** in toto, wholly; **7** all told, totally, utterly; **8** all in all, entirely, outright; **10** completely, on the whole; **12** birthday suit, tout ensemble

alto horn: 7 althorn

altorilievo: 10 high relief

altostratus: 16 altostratus cloud

altostratus cloud: 11 altostratus

altruism: 8 altruism; **10** liberalism; **11** magnanimity

altruist: 7 liberal; **14** philanthropist

altruistic: 8 selfless; **9** unselfish; **13** disinterested

alula: 8 calypter; **11** bastard wing; **12** spurious wing

alum: 4 grad; **6** alumna; **7** alumnus; **8** graduate; **10** potash alum; **11** ammonia alum; **12** ammonium alum; **13** potassium alum

alumbloom: 8 alumroot

alumina: 5 argil; **13** aluminum oxide

aluminite: 10 websterite

aluminium: 2 Al; **8** aluminum

aluminous: 13 aluminiferous

aluminum foil: 7 tin foil

alumna: 4 alum, grad; **7** alumnus; **8** graduate

alumnus: 4 alum, grad; **5** eleve [Fr]; **6** alumna; **8** graduate

alumroot: 9 alumbloom

alunite: 9 alum stone

alunogenite: 8 alunogen

Alupent: 14 metaproterenol

alveary: 6 apiary

alveolar: 6 pitted; **9** alveolate; **11** honeycombed

alveolitis: 9 dry socket

alveolus: 4 dent, dint; **5** sinus; **6** air sac, dimple, lacuna; **7** air cell; **8** follicle; **11** indentation, tooth socket

always: 3 aye, e'er; **4** ever; **6** hourly; **7** for ever; **8** ever anon, evermore, steadily; **9** routinely; **10** at all times, constantly, invariably; **11** continually, day after day, day and night, incessantly, night and day, perpetually, unfailingly, without fail; **12** consistently, continuously

alyssum: 7 madwort

Alyssum: 12 genus Alyssum

Alytes: 4 toad; **11** genus Alytes

Alzheimers: 10 Alzheimer's; **17** Alzheimer's disease

Am: 9 americium

AM: 2 MA; **12** ante meridiem, Master of Arts; **14** Artium Magister; **19** amplitude modulation

amability: 7 amenity; **9** good humor; **10** affability, amiability; **12** complaisance

amadavat: 8 avadavat

amah: 4 maid; **5** biddy, bonne [Fr], nurse; **8** wet nurse; **9** housemaid; **11** maidservant

amain: 7 in a rush, in haste; **8** in a hurry; **9** hurriedly, with haste

amalgam: 5 alloy; **8** compound; **11** composition, tertium quid [Lat]; **13** dental amalgam

amalgamate: 3 mix; **4** fuse; **5** alloy, blend, fused, merge, unify, unite; **6** absorb, commix, embody, infect, mingle; **7** blend in, combine, conjoin; **8** coalesce, compound, dissolve; **9** coalesced; **10** adulterate, centralize, impregnate; **11** amalgamated, consolidate, incorporate

amalgamation: 5 union; **6** fusing, fusion, merger; **7** uniting; **8** blending; **9** synthesis; **10** coalescing, embodiment; **11** coalescence, unification; **13** incorporation

Amanita: 8 mushroom; **8** death cap, death cup; **10** death angel; **12** genus Amanita; **15** destroying angel

Amanita verna: 15 destroying angel

amanuensis: 5 clerk; 6 scribe; 9 scrivener, secretary; 12 stenographer

amaranth family: 13 Amaranthaceae; 19 family Amaranthaceae

amaranthine: 9 evergreen

Amaranthus: 8 amaranth; 10 tumbleweed; 15 genus Amaranthus

Amaryllis belladonna: 9 naked lady; 14 belladonna lily

amaryllis family: 14 Amaryllidaceae

amass: 4 fund; 5 cache, hoard; 6 embody, garner, gather, pile up; 7 collect, compile; 8 cumulate, garner up; 9 integrate; 10 accumulate; 12 conglomerate

amassed: 6 massed; 7 hoarded; 9 assembled, collected; 10 congregate; 11 accumulated

amateur: 3 fan; 4 buff, tyro; 5 lover; 6 novice, unpaid, votary; 7 devotee; 8 beginner, inexpert; 9 greenhorn, unskilled; 10 aficionado, amateurish, dilettante; 11 rank amateur; 12 recreational

amateurish: 7 amateur; 8 inexpert; 9 unskilled

amative: 7 amorous

amativeness: 7 erotism; 8 sexiness; 9 eroticism; 11 amorousness

amaze: 3 get; 4 beat; 6 baffle, gravel, puzzle; 7 astound, flummox, mystify, nonplus, perplex, stupefy, stupify, trounce; 8 astonish, bewilder; 9 dumbfound

amazed: 7 stunned; 8 astonied; 9 astounded; 10 astonished

amazement: 10 wonderment; 12 astonishment, bewilderment

amazing: 5 awful, awing; 7 awesome; 8 striking; 10 astounding; 11 astonishing; 12 awe-inspiring

amazingly: 7 awfully; 8 famously; 9 glaringly, strangely; 10 incredibly, strikingly; 11 egregiously, marvelously, prominently, wonderfully; 12 astoundingly, emphatically, stupendously, surprisingly, tremendously; 13 astonishingly, extravagantly

amazon: 6 virago

Amazon: 4 hero; 6 Hector; 7 demigod; 11 Amazon River

Amazon ant: 18 Polyergus rufescens

ambages: 4 loop; 5 twirl, twist; 7 circuit; 8 rambling; 10 digressing, digression, meandering

ambagious: 10 roundabout

amber: 4 gold; 11 yellow-brown; 14 brownish-yellow

amberjack: 9 amberfish

amber lily: 17 Anthericum torreyi

ambiance: 8 ambience; 10 atmosphere

ambidexter: 7 trimmer, waffler; 10 temporizer, time server; 11 fad follower

ambidextrous: 7 ductile; 8 trimming, two-faced; 9 deceitful, two-handed; 10 Janus-faced, neat-handed, sure-footed; 11 double-faced, duplicitous; 12 fine-fingered; 13 double-dealing, double-tongued

ambigu: 4 mess, olio; 6 medley; 7 farrago; 8 all sorts, mish-mash, pastiche; 9 patchwork, potpourri; 10 hodge-podge, hodgepodge, salmagundi; 11 gallimaufry, odds and ends; 14 conglomeration

ambiguous: 5 loose, vague; 9 equivocal; 12 undetermined

ambiguously: 11 equivocally

ambisexual: 8 bisexual

ambisexuality: 11 bisexuality

ambit: 5 lines, orbit, range, reach, scope; 7 circuit, compass, contour

ambition: 5 dream; 6 design; 10 aspiration, goal in life; 13 ambitiousness, life's ambition

ambitious: 8 aspiring, vaulting; 11 challenging, sky-aspiring; 12 high-reaching

ambitiously: 12 determinedly, with ambition

ambivalence: 11 ambivalency

ambivalency: 11 ambivalence

amble: 4 boom, dart, flit, trot; 5 bound, frisk, mosey, troll; 6 canter, gallop, prance, ramble, spring, stroll; 7 saunter; 8 caracole; 9 promenade

Ambloplites: 8 rock bass; 11 rock sunfish; 16 genus Ambloplites

amblygonite: 9 hebronite

ambo: 4 dais; 5 stump; 6 podium, pulpit; 7 lectern, rostrum, soapbox; 11 reading desk, soap box desk

amboina pine: 11 Agathis alba, amboyna pine; 14 Agathis dammara

amboyna: 6 padauk, padouk

ambrocate: 3 oil; 5 anele; 6 anoint

ambrosia: 6 nectar; 7 ragweed; 8 beebread; 10 bitterweed; 11 bonne-bouche [Fr]

Ambrosia artemisiifolia: 7 ragweed

ambrosial: 4 rich; 8 delicate, luscious; 9 ambrosian, exquisite, nectarous; 10 appetizing, delightful; 11 scrumptious

ambrosian: 9 ambrosial, nectarous

ambulance: 6 chaise

ambulant: 10 ambulatory

ambulation: 3 jog; 4 trot, turn; 5 stalk, tramp; 6 canter, ramble; 7 saunter; 9 promenade; 13 perambulation

ambulatory: 6 roving; 7 gadding, vagrant; 8 ambulant, rambling; 9 itinerant; 10 discursive; 11 peripatetic

ambuscade: 4 lurk, trap; 6 ambush, waylay; 7 scupper; 9 bushwhack, lie in wait; 11 lying in wait

ambush: 4 lurk, trap; 6 waylay; 7 scupper; 9 ambuscade, bushwhack, lie in wait, still-hunt; 11 lying in wait

ambustion: 7 burning; 10 combustion

Ambystoma: 7 axolotl; 8 mud puppy; 10 salamander; 14 genus Ambystoma

ameliorate: 5 amend; **6** better; **7** improve; **9** meliorate

ameliorating: 10 corrective, emendatory; **11** meliorative, reformatory

amelioration: 9 bettering; **10** betterment; **11** enhancement, improvement, melioration; **13** getting better

ameliorative: 10 palliative; **11** meliorative

Amen: 4 Amon

amenable: 6 liable; **7** willing; **10** answerable; **11** accountable, responsible

amenableness: 11 amenability; **15** cooperativeness

amend: 4 heal, mend; **6** better, remedy; **7** get well, improve, rectify; **9** meliorate; **10** ameliorate; **12** render better; **14** return to health

amendable: 11 correctable

amending: 6 reform; **9** amendment, reforming; **10** correcting, correction; **11** reformation

amendment: 6 reform; **8** amending; **9** reforming; **10** correcting, correction; **11** reformation

amends: 3 sop; **7** apology, damages, redress; **8** requital; **9** atonement, indemnity; **10** reparation; **11** restitution; **12** satisfaction; **14** acknowledgment

amenia: 10 amenorrhea; **11** amenorrhoea

amenities: 8 comforts; **12** conveniences; **16** creature comforts

amenity: 5 charm; **8** witchery; **9** good humor, seduction; **10** affability, amiability; **11** enchantment, fascination, winning ways; **12** complaisance; **13** agreeableness

ame no kawa: 8 milky way

amenorrhea: 6 amenia; **11** amenorrhoea

Amen-Ra: 6 Amon-Ra

ament: 6 catkin

amentaceous: 12 amentiferous

amentia: 6 idiocy

amerce: 3 tag; **4** fine; **5** mulct; **6** sconce; **10** exact a fine

amercement: 4 fine; **5** mulct

America: 2 U.S.; **3** U.S.A.; **11** the Americas; **12** United States

American bison: 7 buffalo; **10** Bison bison

American Cancer Society: 3 ACS

American Chemical Society: 3 ACS

American Civil War: 19 War between the States

American eagle: 9 bald eagle

American elk: 6 wapiti

American Federation of Labor: 3 AFL

American Federation of Labor-Congress of Industrial Organizations: 6 AFL-CIO

American Indian: 6 Indian; **10** Amerindian; **14** Native American

American Party: 16 Know-Nothing Party

American Samoa: 12 Eastern Samoa

American sign language: 3 ASL; **7** Ameslan

American Standard Code for Information Interchange: 5 ASCII [acron]; **9** ASCII code

American Stock Exchange: 4 AMEX, Curb

americium: 2 Am

Amerigo Vespucci: 8 Vespucci; **17** Americus Vespucius

Ameslan: 20 American sign language

ametabolic: 11 ametabolous

amethyst: 7 jacinth; **8** hyacinth; **9** carbuncle; **11** aniline dyes

ametropic: 6 myopic; **10** astigmatic, presbyopic; **16** visually impaired

AMEX: 4 Curb; **21** American Stock Exchange

Amharic: 17 Ethiopian language

amiability: 5 charm; **7** amenity; **8** bonhomie, witchery; **9** geniality, good humor, seduction; **10** affability, good humour, good temper, tenderness; **11** affableness, amiableness, enchantment, fascination, winning ways

amiable: 6 genial; **7** affable, cordial; **11** good-humored

amiably: 7 affably; **8** genially

Amia calva: 6 bowfin; **7** dogfish, grindle

amicability: 8 sodality; **10** fraternity; **11** brotherhood; **12** amicableness

amicable: 8 friendly; **9** favorable; **10** propitious; **12** well-disposed

amicable to: 9 helpful to; **11** favorable to; **12** propitious to

amicably: 9 cordially; **11** fraternally

amical: 8 amicable, friendly

amice: 5 scarf, stole; **8** chasuble

amicus curiae: 12 amicus curiae; **16** friend of the court

amid: 4 amid; **5** among; **6** amidst; **7** amongst

amidopyrine: 11 aminopyrine

amidship: 8 midships; **9** amidships

amidst: 4 amid; **5** among; **7** amongst

amine: 10 aminoalkane

aminic: 5 amino

amino: 6 aminic

amino acid: 17 aminoalkanoic acid

aminobenzine: 7 aniline; **10** aniline oil; **11** phenylamine

amiodarone: 9 Cordarone

amir: 4 emir; **5** ameer, emeer

amis: 3 ill; **5** wrong; **10** to one's cost

amiss: 4 awry; **5** wrong; **7** haywire; **9** the matter; **10** out of order; **11** imperfectly

amitriptyline: 6 Elavil

amity: 10 cordiality, friendship; **12** friendliness

Amman: 15 capital of Jordan

ammo: 10 ammunition

ammo belt: 9 bandolier; **14** ammunition belt

ammonoid: 8 ammonite

Ammotragus: 15 genus Ammotragus

ammunition: 4 ammo; 8 ordnance; 9 munitions
ammunition belt: 8 ammo belt; 9 bandolier
ammunition chest: 7 caisson
ammunition dump: 15 ammunition depot
amnesia: 8 blackout; 10 memory loss
amnesiac: 7 amnesic
amnesty: 6 pardon
amnion: 6 amnios
amnionic: 5 amnic; 8 amniotic
amobarbital sodium: 4 blue; 6 Amytal; 9 blue angel
amoeba: 5 ameba; 6 amebae [pl]
amok: 5 amuck; 7 berserk; 8 demoniac; 9 possessed; 10 demoniacal; 11 murderously
Amon: 4 Amen
among: 4 amid; 6 amidst; 7 amongst
Amon-Ra: 6 Amen-Ra
Amor: 5 Cupid
amoral: 7 corrupt, unmoral; 8 depraved, perverse
amoret: 4 beau; 5 swain, wooer; 6 suitor; 8 follower, young man; 9 inamorato; 10 sweetheart
amoroso: 7 captive, gallant, ingenue [Fr]; 8 Lothario, paramour; 10 jeune veuve [Fr]; 11 heavy father
amorous: 7 amative, amatory; 8 romantic
amorousness: 7 erotism; 8 sexiness; 9 eroticism; 11 amativeness; 12 enamoredness
amor patriae: 10 patriotism; 11 nationality; 13 love of country
amorphous: 8 formless; 9 shapeless; 12 unstructured; 14 uncrystallized
amortization: 12 amortisation
amortize: 8 amortise
amount: 3 sum; 4 come, cost; 5 add up, price, total; 6 charge, figure, number; 7 expense, measure, quantum; 8 quantity
amount of money: 3 sum; 6 amount; 10 sum of money
amount of time: 6 period; 10 time period; 12 period of time
amour: 4 eros [Grk]; 6 affair; 7 affaire, liaison; 8 intimacy; 11 involvement; 12 romantic love
amour propre: 6 vanity; 7 conceit, egotism; 8 self-love; 10 self-esteem; 11 self-conceit; 13 conceitedness; 14 self-admiration
amoxicillin: 6 Amoxil
Amoxil: 11 amoxicillin
Amoy: 3 Min; 6 Fukien; 9 Taiwanese; 10 Fukkianese, Hokkianese, Min dialect
AMP: 12 adenylic acid
amp: 1 A; 6 ampere
ampere: 1 A; 3 amp
ampere-second: 1 C; 7 coulomb
ampersand: 4 star

amphetamine: 5 speed, upper; 7 pep pill
Amphibia: 13 class Amphibia
amphibian: 10 amphibious
amphibious: 7 epicene; 9 amphibian; 11 heteroclite [Gram]
amphigory: 13 nonsense rhyme, nonsense verse
amphigouri: 9 amphigory; 13 nonsense rhyme, nonsense verse
amphimixis: 18 sexual reproduction
amphioxus: 8 lancelet
amphiprostyle: 9 porticoed; 11 amphistylar; 14 amphiprostylar
amphitheater: 5 forum; 7 theater; 8 coliseum; 10 auditorium; 12 amphitheatre
Amphitryon: 8 Boniface
amphiuma: 8 blind eel, congo eel; 10 congo snake
amphoteric: 11 amphiprotic
ampicillin: 12 SK-Ampicillin
ample: 4 rich, wide; 5 broad, bulky, massy, roomy, thick; 7 copious, massive, sizable; 8 abundant, sizeable, spacious; 9 capacious, expansive, extensive, plenteous, plentiful; 10 voluminous; 12 considerable
amplification: 4 gain; 8 dilating; 9 expanding; 11 elaboration; 12 augmentation
amplified: 9 magnified; 10 hyperbolic, overstated; 11 exaggerated, overwrought
amplify: 4 puff; 5 widen; 6 blow up, dilate, expand, extend, pile up, rarefy, spread; 7 descant, develop, distend, enlarge, inflate, magnify; 8 overdraw, pile it on, run out on; 9 aggravate, expatiate, overstate, spread out; 10 aggrandize, exaggerate; 11 hyperbolize
amplitude: 4 lots, over; 6 bounty, plenty; 8 latitude; 9 abundance, plenitude, profusion; 11 copiousness, full measure; 13 bountifulness, plenteousness
amplitudinous: 10 stupendous
amply: 5 fully; 6 richly
ampule: 4 vial; 5 ampul, phial; 7 ampoule
amputate: 6 cut off, garble; 8 mutilate
amrinone: 6 Inocor
Amsterdam: 12 Dutch capital
amuck: 4 amok; 7 berserk; 8 demoniac; 9 possessed; 10 demoniacal; 11 murderously
amulet: 5 charm; 6 philter; 8 talisman
Amur River: 4 Amur
amuse: 6 divert; 7 disport, enliven; 9 entertain
amusement: 3 fun; 10 recreation; 11 fun and games; 13 entertainment
amusing: 3 fun; 5 comic, funny; 6 jocose; 7 amusive, comical, jocular, risible; 8 humorous, mirthful; 9 diverting, laughable; 12 entertaining
Amygdalus: 6 almond; 14 genus Amygdalus
amylaceous: 4 ropy; 6 clammy, mastic; 7 amyloid, clotted, gelatin; 9 amyloidal,

glutenous, glutinous; **10** albuminous, gelatinous, starchlike; **12** mucilaginous

amyl alcohol: 8 fusel oil

amyloid: 9 amyloidal; **10** amylaceous, starchlike

amylum: 6 starch

amyotonia: 5 atony; **6** atonia; **9** atonicity

amyotrophic lateral sclerosis: 3 ALS; **17** Lou Gehrig's disease

amyotrophy: 11 amyotrophia

a myriad: 8 a hundred, a million; **9** a thousand; **10** a nonillion; **12** a quadrillion

Amytal: 4 blue; **9** blue angel

ana: 5 trait; **8** anecdote

anabaptism: 8 Puseyism, **9** Adventism, Calvinism, Jansenism, methodism

anabolism: 22 constructive metabolism

Anabrus: 7 cricket; **12** genus Anabrus

Anacardiaceae: 11 sumac family; **19** family Anacardiaceae

Anacardium: 15 genus Anacardium

Anacardium occidentale: 6 cashew; **10** cashew tree

anachronism: 9 misdating, mistiming; **11** prochronism; **12** metachronism, parachronism

Anacin III: 6 Datril, Tempra; **7** Panadol, Tylenol; **13** acetaminophen

anacoluthon: 5 break; **11** anacoluthia; **12** interruption; **13** discontinuity

anaconda: 7 serpent

anacrusis: 5 ictus

anaerobic: 12 anaerobiotic

anaerobic exercise: 12 bodybuilding; **14** musclebuilding

anagoge: 7 anagogy, mystery; **10** occultness

anal: 9 querulous; **12** hard to please

analcite: 8 analcime

analecta: 8 analects; **11** compilation

analectic: 8 synoptic; **11** compendious

analeptic: 5 tonic; **8** balsamic; **9** paregoric; **11** chirurgical [Med], corroborant, therapeutic

analgesic: 7 anodyne; **8** pain pill; **9** analgetic; **10** painkiller

analog: 6 linear; **8** analogue, parallel; **10** analogical

analog-digital converter: 9 digitizer

analogize: 13 draw an analogy

analogous: 13 correspondent

analogy: 10 simulation; **11** association

anal stage: 9 anal phase

analysis: 4 note; **5** brief, draft; **6** apercu, digest, minute, precis; **7** epitome, outline, summary; **8** abstract, synopsis; **9** analysing, dissecing; **10** abridgment, dissection; **11** decomposing; **13** decomposition; **14** psychoanalysis

analysis situs: 8 topology

analyst: 7 analyst; **8** analyzer, assayist; **13** psychoanalyst

analytic: 9 algebraic; **10** analytical; **11** statistical, uninflected; **12** arithmetical

analyze: 5 parse, study; **7** analyse, dissect, examine, resolve; **8** dissolve; **9** anatomize, break down, disembody, take apart; **13** psychoanalyse, psychoanalyze

analyzer: 7 analyst; **8** analyser, assayist

anamnesis: 6 recall; **11** remembrance; **12** recollection; **13** medical record; **14** medical history

anamorphosis: 10 false light; **12** virtual image; **13** malproportion

ananas: 9 pineapple

Ananas: 11 genus Ananas

Ananas comosus: 9 pineapple; **14** pineapple plant

anapest: 8 anapaest

anaplasty: 14 plastic surgery; **15** cosmetic surgery

Anaprox: 5 Aleve; **7** Aflaxen; **14** naproxen sodium

anapsid: 14 anapsid reptile

Anapurna: 7 Parvati; **9** Annapurna

anarchist: 8 nihilist; **11** syndicalist

anarchy: 9 anarchism, **11** lawlessness

Anas: 4 duck, teal; **7** mallard; **9** genus Anas

anastigmatic: 9 stigmatic

anastomose: 4 link; **6** splice; **8** dovetail

anastomosis: 7 mortise; **9** symphysis [Anat]

anatase: 11 octahedrite

anathema: 3 ban; **9** bete noire; **10** execration; **12** proscription

anathemize: 4 damn; **5** curse; **6** bedamn; **7** beshrew; **8** execrate, maledict; **9** imprecate; **12** anathematize

Anatolia: 9 Asia Minor

anatomical: 8 anatomic; **19** anatomical reference

anatomical structure: 9 structure; **13** body structure

anatomize: 5 parse; **7** analyze, dissect, resolve; **9** anatomise

anatomy: 3 bod; **4** form, soma; **5** build, flesh, frame, shape; **6** figure; **7** chassis; **8** physique; **9** human body; **12** material body, physical body

anatropous: 8 inverted

ancestor: 8 forebear; **9** forebears [pl], ascendant, ascendent; **10** antecedent; **11** forefathers [pl]

ancestral: 6 family, linear; **10** hereditary; **11** patriarchal, patrimonial

ancestry: 4 line, stem; **5** birth, blood, stock; **6** origin, stirps, strain; **7** descent, lineage, stirpes [pl]; **8** heritage, pedigree;

9 bloodline, filiation, genealogy, parentage; **10** derivation, extraction

anchor: 6 drogue, ground; **8** backbone, linchpin, lynchpin, mainstay; **9** anchorman, sea anchor; **10** cast anchor, drop anchor; **11** shee anchor; **12** anchorperson, ground tackle; **13** grappling iron

anchorage: 5 haven, roads; **7** mooring; **9** anchoring, roadstead

anchoring: 7 mooring; **9** anchorage

anchorite: 6 hermit

anchor light: 10 riding lamp; **11** riding light

anchorman: 6 anchor; **12** anchorperson

anchor ring: 4 halo, ring; **6** anulus; **7** annulus; **8** doughnut

ancient: 3 old; **4** aged; **7** antique

ancientness: 9 antiquity

ancillary: 7 adjunct; **8** adjuvant; **9** accessory, auxiliary; **10** ministrant, subsidiary; **11** appurtenant, subservient

Ancylus: 6 limpet; **12** genus Ancylus

and: 3 too; **4** also, item; **7** further; **8** as well as, likewise; **11** furthermore; **12** in addition to

Andalusia: 9 Andalucia

Andaman redwood: 7 amboyna

andante: 5 largo; **6** adagio; **9** larghetto

andantino: 5 largo; **7** andante; **9** larghetto

and eke: 7 and also

and elsewhere: 4 et al; **5** et al.

andesine: 13 feldspar group

and how: 6 you bet; **9** you said it

andiron: 3 dog; **7** dogiron, firedog

and no mistake: 4 sure; **6** certes [Lat], surely; **7** no doubt; **9** certainly, doubtless; **10** for certain

and others: 4 et al; **5** et al.

andradite: 11 black garnet; **12** common garnet

andrena: 8 andrenid; **9** mining bee

Andricus: 13 genus Andricus

androgen: 17 androgenic hormone

androgenous: 12 androgenetic

androgyne: 7 epicine; **13** epicine person, gynandromorph, hermaphrodite

androgyny: 11 bisexuality; **15** hermaphroditism

android: 8 humanoid; **13** mechanical man

and so forth: 3 etc.; **7** and so on; **8** et cetera, etcetera; **10** and the like

and so on: 3 etc.; **8** etcetera; **10** and so forth

and the like: 3 etc.; **8** et cetera; **10** and so forth

and therefore: 4 ergo, then, thus; **5** hence; **6** thusly, whence; **8** thence so; **9** therefore, wherefore; **11** accordingly; **12** consequently

anecdotal: 9 anecdotic; **11** anecdotical

anecdote: 5 trait

anecdotist: 9 raconteur

anele: 3 oil; **6** anoint; **9** ambrocate

anemia: 7 anaemia, fatigue

anemic: 7 anaemic

anemography: 12 aerodynamics

anemometer: 9 wind gauge; **11** dynamometer

anemone: 10 windflower

Anemone quinquefolia: 8 snowdrop; **11** wood anemone

anencephalous: 12 anencephalic

anesthetize: 6 put out; **8** put under; **10** put to sleep; **12** anaesthetize

anestric: 9 anestrous; **10** anoestrous

anestrum: 8 anestrus; **9** anoestrum, anoestrus

an eternity: 5 an age; **8** a century

Anethum graveolens: 4 dill

aneurin: 7 thiamin; **8** thiamine; **9** vitamin B1; **12** antiberiberi

anew: 5 again, often; **6** afresh, lately; **7** just now; **8** once more; **9** over again; **10** repeatedly

anfractuosity: 4 wave; **10** undulation

anfractuous: 7 sinuous, **8** flexuous, tortuous

angel: 4 duck, hero, idol; **5** saint; **6** backer, patron, seraph

angel dust: 3 PCP; **13** phencyclidine

angelfish: 8 monkfish; **9** spadefish; **10** angel shark

angel food cake: 9 angel cake

angelic: 5 sweet; **7** godlike, sainted, saintly; **8** beatific, cherubic, seraphic; **9** angelical, saintlike; **10** heaven-born

angelim: 8 andelmin

angel shark: 8 monkfish; **9** angelfish

angelus: 11 angelus bell

anger: 3 ira, ire; **4** gall, rile; **5** wrath; **6** choler, see red; **9** angriness, animosity; **10** cause anger, make one mad, raise anger; **11** indignation

angered: 3 mad; **5** angry, irate, wrath; **7** enraged, furious; **8** maddened; **10** infuriated

angina: 14 angina pectoris [Lat]

angiosperm: 14 flowering plant

angiospermous: 9 flowering

angiotension: 10 angiotonin; **12** Hypertension

angle: 3 tip; **4** cusp, fish, lean, tilt; **5** slant, trawl; **6** aspect

angle bracket: 7 bracket; **9** angle iron

angled loofah: 7 sing-kwa; **15** Luffa acutangula

angle iron: 12 angle bracket

anglerfish: 5 lotte; **6** angler; **8** allmouth, monkfish; **9** goosefish

angleworm: 7 dew worm, red worm, wiggler; **8** fishworm; **9** earthworm; **11** fishing worm, nightwalker; **12** nightcrawler

Anglican Church: 15 Church of England

Anglicism: 9 Briticism; 10 Britishism
anglicize: 9 anglicise
Anglo: 8 American; 13 North American
anglophile: 9 anglophil
Anglo-Saxon: 10 Old English
Angora: 9 Angora cat; 10 Angora goat; 12 Angora rabbit
angostura: 7 bitters; 13 angostura bark
angrily: 7 irately
angry: 3 mad; 4 wild; 5 irate, wrath; 6 raging; 7 angered, furious; 11 tempestuous
angry walk: 5 stalk
angstrom: 1 A; 12 angstrom unit
anguill: 7 serpent; 9 vermiform
anguish: 4 hurt, pain, pang; 5 agony; 7 torment, torture; 13 mental anguish
angular: 4 bent; 6 jagged; 7 crooked; 8 angulate, aquiline, serrated
angular motion: 8 gyration, rotation, spinning; 10 revolution; 14 circumvolution
angular vein: 13 vena angularis
Angus: 6 Aengus, Oengus; 7 Angus Og; 10 black Angus; 13 Aberdeen Angus
angustation: 5 taper; 8 tapering; 9 narrowing
anhelation: 17 shortness of breath
anil: 6 indigo; 9 indigotin
anile: 7 puerile; 8 matronly
aniline dyes: 8 amethyst
anility: 5 years; 6 dotage; 7 fatuity; 9 gray hairs
animadversion: 7 censure; 9 exception, objection, stricture; 10 reflection
animadvert: 5 opine; 7 speak up; 8 sound off
animal: 5 beast, brute, fauna, wight; 6 carnal; 7 critter [U.S. dialect], fleshly, sensual; 8 creature, zoophyte
animal doctor: 3 vet; 10 horse leech; 11 horse doctor; 12 veterinarian
animal food: 4 feed; 6 fodder; 9 provender
animalism: 9 animality, carnality; 10 sensuality; 11 physicality; 14 voluptuousness
animality: 9 animalism, animation, carnality; 10 animal life, animalness, sensuality; 12 animal nature
animal kingdom: 8 Animalia
animal magnetism: 10 bewitchery; 11 beguilement; 13 hypnotization
animal scientist: 9 zoologist
animal skin: 10 animal hide
animal stuffer: 11 taxidermist
animal trainer: 7 handler
animal with a backbone: 10 vertebrate
animal-worship: 8 zoolatry
animate: 4 move; 5 cheer, elate, exalt, liven, set on, smite, touch; 6 affect, excite, foment, incite, infect, revive, strike, vivify; 7 actuate, animize, enliven, gladden, impress, inspire, liven up, provoke, quicken; 8 inspirit, interest, recreate, revivify, sentient; 9 impassion, instigate, reanimate; 10 exhilarate, invigorate

animated: 5 alive, brisk, moved, quick; 6 active, lively; 7 excited, smitten, striken, touched; 8 affected, bustling, inspired; 9 breathing, impressed, vivacious; 10 interested; 11 impassioned
animation: 4 dash, life; 6 energy, living, spirit; 8 alacrity, vitality, vivacity; 9 aliveness, animality, vivifying; 10 animal life, animalness, excitation, excitement, liveliness; 12 invigoration, spiritedness, vivification
animosity: 5 anger; 6 animus; 8 bad blood; 11 indignation
animus: 4 bent, mind, mood, vein, view; 5 humor, spite; 7 despite, leaning, purview; 8 attitude, bad blood, penchant, proposal; 9 animosity; 10 partiality; 11 disposition, frame of mind, inclination; 12 predilection, spitefulness; 13 contemplation
anise: 7 aniseed
aniseed: 5 anise
anisometric: 13 unsymmetrical
Ankara: 14 Turkish capital; 15 capital of Turkey
ankle: 4 knee; 5 elbow, groin; 6 crotch; 7 knuckle; 10 ankle joint; 12 mortise joint
anklebone: 5 talus; 8 astragal; 10 astragalus
ankle bracelet: 6 anklet
anklet: 7 anklets; 9 bobbysock; 10 bobbysocks; 13 ankle bracelet
ankus: 4 dram, goad, spur, whet, whip; 6 fillip; 8 stimulus; 9 incentive; 10 incitement; 11 provocation
ankylosis: 9 stiffness; 10 anchylosis
anlage: 10 primordium
annalist: 9 historian; 11 chronologer; 12 chronologist
annals: 6 legend; 9 chronicle
Annam: 7 Viet Nam, Vietnam
Annamese: 8 Annamite; 10 Vietnamese
Annapolis: 17 capital of Maryland
anneal: 5 smelt; 6 temper
annelid worm: 7 annelid; 13 segmented worm
annex: 3 add; 4 wing; 5 affix; 7 additum [Lat], subjoin; 8 take over; 9 extension, superpose
annexation: 8 annexing; 13 appropriation, superaddition, superfetation, superposition
annihilate: 7 wipe out; 8 carry off, decimate; 9 eliminate, eradicate, extirpate; 10 extinguish, obliterate
annihilating: 9 withering; 11 devastating; 12 annihilative
annihilation: 10 extinction; 11 extirpation; 12 obliteration; 13 nullification; 14 disintegration, extinguishment
anniversary: 7 jubilee; 13 commemoration; 16 day of remembrance
Anno Domini: 2 A.D. [abbr]

Annona: 5 ilama; 7 soursop; 8 sweetsop; 9 cherimoya; 9 pond apple; 11 genus Annona; 12 custard-apple

Annonaceae: 16 family Annonaceae; 18 custard-apple family

anno regni: 2 A.R. [abbr]

annotate: 6 unfold; 7 expound; 8 footnote; 11 comment upon

annotation: 4 note; 7 italics; 8 notation; 9 reference; 10 annotating; 11 underlining

annotator: 9 scholiast; 11 commentator

annotto: 6 red ink

announce: 3 say; 5 utter; 6 denote, herald; 7 declare, deliver, premise, usher in; 8 foretell; 9 harbinger, pronounce; 10 annunciate, articulate

announcement: 6 notice; 8 forecast; 9 prognosis; 10 communique, prediction; 11 foretelling; 12 annunciation, notification, proclamation, promulgation; 15 prognostication

announcing: 6 saying; 8 uttering; 9 informing, notifying; 11 acquainting, enunciation, information, pronouncing; 12 acquaintance, annunciation, articulating, enlightening; 13 enlightenment

annoy: 3 bug, irk, rag, vex; 4 faze, nark, rile, tire, urge; 5 cross, devil, get at, get to, worry; 6 bother, gravel, madden, nettle; 7 disturb, mortify, perplex, trouble; 8 convulse, disquiet, irritate; 9 aggravate, disoblige, displease, incommode, infuriate; 10 accelerate, discomfort, discompose, exacerbate, exasperate; 12 lash into fury; 13 inconvenience

annoyance: 4 pain; 5 chafe, worry; 6 bother, pother; 8 annoying, nuisance, vexation; 9 grievance, troubling; 10 harassment, infliction, irritation

annoyed: 5 riled, stung, vexed; 6 peeved, pissed, roiled; 7 harried, nettled; 8 harassed, pestered, troubled; 9 irritated; 10 displeased, disquieted; 11 discomfited, discomposed

annoying: 5 pesky; 6 plaguy, vexing; 7 galling, plaguey, teasing; 8 stinging, vexation; 9 annoyance, pestering, provoking, troubling, vexatious; 10 bothersome, irritating, irritation, mortifying, nettlesome; 11 aggravating, pestiferous, provocation

annual: 6 yearly; 7 one-year; 8 yearbook

annually: 2 p.a.; 6 yearly; 7 per year; 8 each year, per annum; 9 every year

annual ring: 10 growth ring

annuity: 5 rente; 7 pension

annul: 4 lift, void; 5 avoid, quash; 6 cancel, repeal, revoke; 7 nullify, rescind, reverse; 8 abrogate, overturn; 10 invalidate, render null; 11 countermand

annular: 6 ringed; 8 annulate, circular; 9 annulated, circinate, orbicular; 10 ring-shaped

annulet: 4 hoop, ring; 6 areola, circle; 7 annulus, bandlet, circlet, roundel; 8 bandelet; 10 bandelette

annulled: 7 revoked; 8 repealed, reversed; 9 abrogated, cancelled, rescinded

annulment: 6 repeal; 8 annuling, recision; 9 canceling; 10 abrogating, abrogation, defeasance, rescinding, rescission; 12 cancellation, invalidation; 13 nullification

annulus: 4 halo, hoop, ring; 6 anulus, areola, circle; 7 circlet; 8 doughnut; 10 anchor ring

annunciate: 6 herald; 8 announce, foretell; 9 harbinger

annunciation: 9 informing, notifying; 10 announcing; 11 acquainting, enunciation, information; 12 acquaintance, announcement, enlightening, proclamation, promulgation; 13 enlightenment

Annunciation lily: 8 Lent lily; 9 white lily; 11 Madonna lily

anoa: 12 dwarf buffalo; 18 Anoa depressicornis

anodal: 6 anodic

anodyne: 4 balm, oily, soft; 5 bland; 8 lenitive, pain pill; 9 analgesic, analgetic, demulcent; 10 painkiller

anoint: 3 oil; 5 anele; 6 do over; 7 confirm; 9 ambrocate; 10 lay hands on

anointing of the sick: 9 last rites; 14 extreme unction

Anolis: 9 chameleon; 11 genus Anolis

Anomala: 6 beetle; 12 genus Anomala

anomalously: 10 abnormally; 11 abberrantly

anomaly: 7 oddness; 11 abnormality; 13 anomalousness, unnaturalness

anomic: 9 alienated; 11 disoriented

anon: 4 soon; 7 betimes, shortly; 8 sweetsop; 9 presently, right away

a nonillion: 7 a myriad

anonym: 9 pseudonym; 11 nom de guerre

anonymous: 7 unnamed; 8 nameless; 10 innominate; 12 having no name, without a name; 14 unacknowledged

anorak: 5 parka; 9 ski jacket; 11 windbreaker, windcheater

anorexic: 9 anorectic

anorthite: 12 lime feldspar

anorthography: 8 agraphia; 11 logagraphia

anosmatic: 7 anosmic

anosmia: 19 olfactory impairment

another: 5 other; 6 others [pl]; 9 different, some other; 10 additional, not the same; 11 other people [pl], someone else; 12 somebody else

anserine: 4 dopy, fool; 5 dopey, goosy; 6 goosey; 7 foolish; 9 gooselike

answer: 2 do; 3 pay; 4 plea, work; 5 avail, rebut, reply; 6 rejoin, result, retort; 7 resolve, respond, suffice; 8 demurrer, rebutter, response, solution; 9 rejoinder

answerable: 6 liable; 7 to blame; 8 amenable; 11 accountable, blameworthy, responsible

answering: 8 replying; 10 respondent, responding; 12 acknowledge

ant: 3 bee; 4 anti; 7 busy bee, pismire, termite; 8 white ant; 10 working bee

Antabuse: 10 disulfiram

antacid: 9 alkalizer

antagonism: 6 enmity; 8 opposing; 9 hostility; 10 inhibition, opposition; 13 contravention, counteraction

antagonist: 8 opponent; 9 adversary; 10 opposition; 12 adverse party

antagonistic: 7 adverse, counter, hostile, opposed; 8 clashing, opposing; 9 antipodal, repugnant; 10 antipodean, at variance, contrasted; 11 conflicting, contrasting, interfering; 12 antagonizing, antipathetic, antithetical, in opposition, incompatible; 14 antipathetical, irreconcilable

antagonize: 5 block; 6 oppose, oppugn; 7 inhibit; 10 antagonise, counteract

antarctic: 7 Austral; 8 Southern

Antarctic: 10 south-polar; 13 Antarctic Zone; 15 South Frigid Zone

ant bear: 8 aardvark, anteater, tamanoir; 13 giant anteater, great anteater

anteater: 6 numbat; 7 ant bear, echidna; 8 aardvark, pangolin; 13 scaly anteater, spiny anteater; 14 banded anteater

antebellum: 6 lapsed, no more, run out; 7 elapsed, expired, extinct, has-been; 8 exploded; 9 blown over, forgotten; 12 antediluvian; 13 irrecoverable

antecede: 6 forego; 7 precede, predate; 8 antedate

antecedence: 8 priority; 9 preceding; 10 precedence; 11 anteriority; 12 coming before, pre-existence

antecedent: 8 ancestor, anterior; 9 ascendant, ascendent, precedent, preceding, precursor; 10 derivation, forerunner; 11 determinant, predecessor

antechamber: 4 hall; 5 foyer, lobby; 8 anteroom; 9 vestibule; 12 entrance hall

antedate: 6 forego; 7 misdate, precede, predate; 8 antecede, backdate, foredate, postdate

antediluvian: 6 lapsed, no more, run out; 7 archaic, elapsed, expired, extinct, has-been; 8 exploded; 9 blown over, forgotten; 10 antebellum, antiquated; 11 that has been; 12 antediluvial; 13 irrecoverable

ante meridien: 2 A.M. [abbr]; 4 morn; 5 prime; 7 morning; 8 forenoon

antenatal: 8 prenatal

antenna: 6 aerial, feeler

antenuptial: 10 premarital, prenuptial

anterior: 4 fore; 5 front, prior; 7 frontal; 10 antecedent, front tooth

anteriority: 8 priority; 10 precedence; 11 antecedence, antecedency; 12 pre-existence

anterior nares: 8 nostrils

anteroom: 4 hall; 5 foyer, lobby; 9 vestibule; 11 antechamber; 12 entrance hall

ante up: 3 pay; 4 ante; 5 pay up

antevert: 5 avert

anthem: 4 hymn; 5 chant, motet; 6 chaunt; 8 response; 9 plain song

anthemion: 4 fret; 8 flourish; 9 arabesque; 10 coquillage [Fr], fleur-de-lis [Fr]

Anthemis: 9 chamomile; 13 genus Anthemis

antheral: 9 staminate

antherozoid: 12 spermatozoid

anthesis: 9 flowering; 10 blossoming; 13 efflorescence, inflorescence

Anthonomus: 10 boll weevil; 15 genus Anthonomus

anthophilous: 12 anthophagous

anthracite: 4 coal; 8 hard coal

anthracosis: 9 black lung

anthrax: 7 bighead; 12 splenic fever

Anthriscus: 7 chervil; 7 parsley; 15 genus Anthriscus

anthropic: 11 anthropical

anthropoid: 3 ape; 7 apelike, manlike; 12 anthropoidal

anthropophagist: 8 cannibal

Anthroposcopy: 13 by the features

Anthyllis vulneraria: 11 kidney vetch

anti: 3 ant

antiaircraft: 4 flak; 6 ack-ack, pom-pom; 9 ack-ack gun

antianxiety agent: 12 tranquilizer

antiauthoritarian: 5 balky, heady; 6 entete [Fr], unruly; 7 restive, wayward, willful; 8 contrary, perverse; 10 headstrong, rebellious, refractory, self-willed; 12 contumacious

antiballistic missile: 3 ABM

antiberiberi factor: 7 aneurin, thiamin; 8 thiamine

antibiotic drug: 10 antibiotic, wonder drug

antic: 3 rig; 4 joke, lark; 5 caper, clown, prank, spree, trick; 8 escapade; 9 fantastic, grotesque; 10 skylarking; 11 clown around, fantastical

antichrist: 7 heretic; 8 apostate

anticipate: 4 call; 5 occur; 6 expect, look to; 7 counter, foresee, look for, predict, promise; 8 forebode, foreknow, foretell, keep time; 9 forestall; 13 prognosticate

anticipated: 7 awaited; 8 expected, hoped-for; 9 looked-for

anticlimax: 6 bathos

antidiuretic hormone: 3 ADH; 11 vasopressin

Antidorcas: 9 springbok; 15 genus Antidorcas

antidote: 9 antitoxin
antielectron: 8 positron
antifertility: 12 prophylactic; 13 contraceptive
antifungal: 11 antimycotic, carminative
Antilocapra americana: 9 prongbuck, pronghorn; 16 American antelope
antilock brakes: 9 snow tires; 13 antiskid tires
antilogarithm: 4 root; 5 index, power; 7 antilog; 8 exponent; 9 logarithm
antimicrobial: 9 germicide; 12 antimicrobic, disinfectant
antimonopoly: 9 antitrust
antimycotic: 10 antifungal; 15 antifungal agent
antineoplastic: 10 cancer drug
antinomy: 8 outlawry
antipathy: 4 hate; 6 hatred; 8 aversion, distaste, loathing; 10 abhorrence; 11 abomination, detestation
antipersonnel bomb: 17 fragmentation bomb
antiphrasis: 10 corruption
antipodal: 7 opposed; 8 converse, opposing; 10 antipodean, contrasted; 11 contrasting; 12 antagonistic, antithetical
antipoison: 8 antidote; 9 antitoxin; 11 antifebrile [Med]
antiquarianism: 8 archaism; 11 medievalism; 15 Pre-Raphaelitism
antiquated: 5 stale; 6 old hat, rococo; 7 archaic, out of it; 8 after-age, time-worn; 9 out of date, venerable; 12 antediluvian, behind the age, of other times, old-fashioned, out of fashion; 14 behind the times, of the old school
antique: 5 passe; 6 age-old, demode, gaffer, old-hat, passee; 7 ancient; 8 mossback, old-timer, outmoded; 9 antiquate, old geezer; 12 old-fashioned
antiquity: 9 status quo; 11 ancientness
Antirrhinum: 10 snapdragon; 16 genus Antirrhinum
anti-Semite: 5 bigot; 6 racist
antiseptic: 10 sterilized
antithesis: 8 polarity; 9 inversion
antithetical: 5 pithy; 7 opposed, piquant, pointed, pungent; 8 opposing, poignant; 9 antipodal; 10 antipodean, antithetic, contrasted; 11 contrasting, full of point; 12 alliterative, antagonistic
antitoxin: 8 antidote
antitype: 9 archetype
Antivert: 9 meclizine
antler: 4 horn
ant lion: 7 antlion; 9 doodlebug; 10 antlion fly
Antony: 10 Mark Antony; 14 Marcus Antonius

antonym: 8 opposite; 12 opposite word
Antrozous: 3 bat; 14 genus Antrozous
Antwerp: 6 Anvers; 9 Antwerpen
anulus: 4 halo, ring; 7 annulus; 8 doughnut; 10 anchor ring
Anunnaki: 5 Enuki
anuran: 4 frog, toad; 8 toadfrog; 10 batrachian, salientian
anurous: 8 tailless
Anvers: 7 Antwerp; 9 Antwerpen
anvil: 4 prop; 5 incus, stand
anxiety: 4 care, dole, fret, load; 5 worry; 6 burden, unease; 7 concern; 8 disquiet; 10 inquietude, solicitude, uneasiness; 11 anxiousness, disquietude; 12 apprehension
anxious: 4 avid, keen; 5 dying, eager; 6 uneasy; 7 longing, nervous, unquiet, wistful, worried; 9 concerned; 12 apprehensive
anxiously: 8 uneasily; 14 apprehensively
anxiousness: 7 anxiety; 8 disquiet; 10 solicitude
any: 4 a few, some; 5 aught; 8 any one of, whatever; 10 more or less, whatsoever; 12 quantitative
anybody: 6 anyone
anyone: 7 anybody
anyplace: 8 anywhere
anything: 9 something
A-one: 3 ace; 4 tops; 5 crack, super; 6 tiptop; 8 topnotch; 9 first-rate
aortic: 6 aortal
aoudad: 4 arui; 5 audad; 10 maned sheep; 12 Barbary sheep
AP: 15 Associated Press
apace: 7 briefly, by and by, quickly, rapidly, shortly; 8 chop-chop, in a while, speedily; 9 extempore, forthwith, summarily; 11 immediately
Apalachicola: 17 Apalachicola River
apar: 20 three-banded armadillo
aparejo: 4 horn
apart: 4 free, only; 5 alone, aside, loose; 7 asunder, insular, obscure; 8 discrete, isolated, one by one, outlying, separate; 9 disparate, separated, severally, unannexed; 10 far between, individual, unattached; 11 non-touching, nonadjacent, unconnected; 12 unassociated; 13 noncontiguous
apartheid: 17 racial segregation
apartment: 4 flat, unit
apartment house: 8 tenement; 13 tenement house; 17 apartment building
apathetic: 7 neutral; 9 uncurious; 11 indifferent; 12 uninterested; 13 disinterested
apathy: 9 passivity; 10 neutrality; 12 indifference; 13 impassibility, impassiveness; 14 impassibleness, spiritlessness
apaulette: 4 frog; 7 epaulet; 12 shoulder knot
ape: 4 aper, copy, echo, mime, mock;

5 mimic; 6 monkey, parrot; 7 copycat, imitate; 8 imitator, simulate; 9 personate; 10 anthropoid, caricature; 11 impersonate, mocking bird

apelike: 5 apish; 10 anthropoid; 12 anthropoidal

ape-man: 11 missing link

aper: 3 ape; 7 copycat; 8 imitator

apercu: 4 note; 5 brief, draft; 6 digest, minute, precis; 7 epitome, outline, summary; 8 abstract, analysis, synopsis; 10 abridgment

aperient: 6 physic; 8 laxative; 9 cathartic, purgative

aperitif: 7 liqueur; 9 sweet wine

apertion: 8 puncture; 11 penetration, perforation

aperture: 4 hole; 7 opening

apery: 7 mimicry

apex: 3 top; 4 acme, peak; 6 vertex, zenith; 8 pinnacle; 9 solar apex; 16 apex of the sun's way

aphelia: 8 aphelion

aphid: 5 Aphis; 10 plant louse

Aphis: 5 aphid; 10 genus Aphis, plant louse

aphony: 7 aphonia [Med], no voice; 8 dumbness, muteness; 11 want of voice; 14 absence of voice

aphorism: 5 maxim; 8 apothegm; 10 apophthegm

aphrodisia: 4 lust; 6 libido; 8 sex drive; 11 sex instinct; 13 concupiscence

aphrodisiac: 4 sexy; 13 aphrodisiacal

Aphrodite: 5 Venus; 8 Cytherea; 11 Venus de Milo

Apia: 21 capital of Western Samoa

Apiaceae: 12 carrot family, Umbelliferae; 14 family Apiaceae

apiarian: 8 apiarist; 9 beekeeper

apiary: 8 bee house

Apicius: 3 hog, pig; 7 glutton; 8 belly god; 9 cormorant

apiculture: 10 beekeeping

apiece: 4 each; 8 one by one; 9 to each one; 10 for each one, one at a time; 11 from each one

aping: 5 apish; 9 mimicking

apish: 5 aping; 7 apelike; 9 mimicking

Apis mellifera: 8 honeybee

Apis mellifera adansonii: 9 killer bee; 14 Africanized bee

Apis mellifera scutellata: 9 killer bee; 14 Africanized bee

Apium graveolens: 6 celery

aplanatic: 9 colorless; 10 achromatic, monochrome; 11 monochromic; 13 black and white, monochromatic

aplomb: 4 cool; 5 poise; 7 ballast; 8 sobriety; 9 sang-froid; 11 assuredness; 14 self-possession

Apocalypse: 10 Revelation; 11 Revelations

apocalyptic: 10 revelatory; 13 apocalyptical

apocryphal: 5 false; 6 unreal, untrue; 8 mistaken; 9 enigmatic, erroneous; 10 fallacious, groundless, ungrounded; 11 paradoxical; 12 hypothetical; 13 devoid of truth, problematical

apodeictic: 9 apodictic, probative; 10 conclusive; 11 irrefutable, self-evident; 12 irrefragable, irresistible, unanswerable

apogee: 11 culmination

apolitical: 11 unpolitical

Apollo: 3 Sol; 6 old sol, the Sun; 7 Euterpe, Orpheus, Phoebus; 8 orb of day; 9 earth's sun; 11 Terpsichore; 13 Phoebus Apollo, the Muses Erato

Apollyon: 5 Satan; 6 Belial, Samael, Zamiel; 7 Lucifer, old Nick [slang]; 8 the Devil; 9 Beelzebub; 10 the evil one, the tempter; 12 the Adversary, the arch fiend, the archenemy, author of evil, the foul fiend, the wicked one; 13 the evil spirit, the old Serpent; 14 Mephistopheles

apologetic: 7 alleged; 8 asserted; 9 pretended; 10 ostensible

apologist: 5 flack; 9 justifier; 10 vindicator

apologize: 6 excuse, soften; 7 justify; 8 palliate; 9 apologise, beg pardon, extenuate; 11 rationalize; 16 give satisfaction

apologue: 5 fable; 7 parable; 8 allegory; 10 moral fable

apology: 5 salve, salvo; 6 amends, excuse; 8 apologia; 12 satisfaction

apoplexy: 3 CVA; 5 palsy; 6 stroke; 7 syncope; 8 collapse; 9 inanition, paralysis; 10 exhaustion; 11 prostration

apostasy: 9 defection, recusancy; 11 backsliding; 12 renunciation; 14 tergiversation

apostate: 3 rat; 7 convert, heretic, pervert; 8 deserter, recreant, renegade

apostle: 7 example, pioneer; 8 disciple, follower; 9 proselyte; 10 missionary; 12 propagandist

Apostle Paul: 4 Paul, Saul; 12 Saul of Tarsus; 14 Paul the Apostle; 20 Apostle of the Gentiles

Apostles' Creed: 11 Nicene Creed

apostolic: 5 papal, Roman; 6 Popish; 10 pontifical; 11 apostolical

Apostolic Church: 14 Catholic Church; 15 Universal Church

apostrophe: 6 appeal; 7 address, canvass; 9 monologue, soliloquy; 10 invocation, salutation; 14 interpellation

apothecary: 7 chemist; 8 druggist, pharmacy; 9 drug store; 10 pharmacist, pill pusher, pill roller

apotheosis: 5 ideal, saint; 7 nonsuch, paragon; 8 nonesuch; 9 nonpareil; 10 exaltation; 11 deification

Appalachians: 20 Appalachian Mountains

appall: 4 gnaw; **5** alarm, shock, unman; **6** dismay, offend, rankle; **7** corrode, horrify, outrage; **10** scandalize

appalling: 4 grim; **7** ghastly; **8** crushing, grimness, shocking, terrific; **9** dismaying; **10** terrifying

appanage: 3 dot; **7** apanage

apparatus: 5 setup

apparel: 3 rig, tog; **4** garb, robe, vest, wear; **5** array, drape, dress; **6** attire, clothe, enrobe, fit out; **7** clothes, garment, raiment, vesture; **8** clothing, enclothe, garments; **10** habilitate

apparent: 5 clear, plain; **6** patent; **7** evident, glaring, notable, salient, seeming, staring; **8** credible, definite, distinct, manifest; **9** prominent; **10** in full view, ostensible, presumable, reasonable, well marked

apparently: 5 plain; **7** clearly, plainly; **8** patently; **9** allegedly, evidently, glaringly, obviously, on its face, seemingly; **10** definitely, distinctly, manifestly, ostensibly; **13** conspicuously, on the face of it

apparition: 5 ghost, shade, spook; **6** shadow, spirit, vision; **7** phantom, specter, spectre; **8** revenant

apparitor: 5 crier; **6** herald; **7** marshal; **9** trumpeter; **10** flag bearer; **13** parlementaire [Fr]

appeach: 3 tax; **6** accuse, charge, impute; **7** impeach

appeal: 5 charm; **6** invoke, prayer; **7** attract; **8** entreaty; **10** apostrophe, collection, invocation, salutation; **11** ingathering; **12** appeal motion, solicitation; **13** appealingness; **14** interpellation

appealing: 7 likable; **8** likeable, pleading; **9** imploring; **11** importunate, sympathetic

appeal motion: 6 appeal

appeals court: 14 appellate court, court of appeals

appear: 4 come, look, seem, show; **5** arise, pop up; **6** cast up, crop up, show up, turn up; **7** come out; **8** spring up

appearance: 4 show, view; **5** image, scene, sight; **9** appearing, showing up

appeasable: 11 conciliable

appease: 3 lay; **4** calm, cool, damp, hush, lull, stay, swag, tame; **5** abate, allay, quell, quiet, sober, still; **6** deaden, gentle, lenify, pacify, rebate, smooth, soothe; **7** assuage, compose, gruntle, mollify, placate, slacken, turn off; **8** calm down, suppress; **9** alleviate; **10** conciliate, propitiate; **11** tranquilize

appeaser: 8 pacifier; **9** make-peace; **10** peacemaker, reconciler; **11** conciliator

appelation: 4 name; **5** title; **11** designation; **12** denomination, nomenclature

appellate: 8 claimant; **9** appellate

appellate court: 11 higher court; **12** appeals court; **13** court of appeal

appellation: 11 appellative, designation; **12** denomination

append: 3 add, tag; **4** hang; **5** add on, affix, hitch, sling, tag on; **6** hang on, hook up, suffix, supply, tack on, tack to; **7** suspend; **8** fasten to; **10** place after, supplement

appendage: 6 member; **7** process; **9** extremity, outgrowth; **12** appurtenance

appendectomy: 14 appendicectomy

appendix: 10 postscript; **14** cecal appendage; **16** vermiform process

apperception: 12 assimilation

appetize: 5 tempt; **6** allure; **7** attract; **9** titillate

appetizer: 11 hors d'oeuvre [Fr]; **12** hors d'oeuvres [Fr]

appetizing: 4 rich; **5** spicy; **7** piquant; **8** delicate, luscious; **9** ambrosial; **10** delightful; **11** scrumptious, tantalizing

applaud: 4 clap, spat; **5** cheer; **6** encore; **7** acclaim

applaudable: 8 laudable; **11** commendable; **12** praiseworthy

applause: 7 acclaim, plaudit; **8** clapping; **11** acclamation; **12** hand clapping

apple: 11 Malus pumila

apple canker: 11 apple blight

applejack: 11 apple brandy

apple of one's eye: 20 man after one's own heart

apple polisher: 6 fawner; **8** truckler; **9** groveller; **10** bootlicker

applesauce: 5 trash, tripe; **7** rubbish; **8** folderol, trumpery, wish-wash; **10** apple sauce

appliance: 3 use; **5** gizmo, using; **6** employ, gadget, widget; **10** employment; **11** application, contraption, contrivance, convenience, utilization

applicable: 3 fit, apt; **4** good; **5** ad rem [Lat], happy, valid; **6** in loco; **7** a propos [Fr], apropos, germane, in point, on point; **8** apposite, in effect, relevant, sortable, suitable; **9** effective; **10** admissible, felicitous, seasonable; **11** applicative, applicatory, appropriate

applicant: 7 applier; **8** aspirant; **9** candidate, solicitor; **10** petitioner, solicitant, supplicant

application: 3 use; **5** using; **6** employ, lotion; **7** coating, program; **8** covering; **9** diligence; **10** close study, employment; **11** utilization

applier: 9 applicant; **10** applicator

apply: 3 use; **4** give, hint, hold; **5** adopt, go for, put on; **6** allude, employ; **7** enforce, imitate, utilise, utilize; **8** allude to, intimate, practice; **9** adumbrate, implement

apply oneself: 5 study; **10** be studious; **11** hit the books

apply the torch: 4 fire; 6 kindle; 7 inflame; 8 enkindle; 9 set on fire

apply to: 5 put to; 6 call to

appoggiatura: 9 grace note; 12 acciaccatura

appoint: 3 set; 4 hire, name; 6 assign, charge, engage, return; 7 bespeak, mark out; 8 accredit, nominate; 9 prescribe; 10 constitute; 11 appropriate

appointed: 7 decreed; 8 ordained; 10 appointive, prescribed

appointment: 4 date; 6 naming, return; 7 fitting; 9 appointee; 10 assignment, engagement, nomination; 11 consignment, designation

apportion: 4 deal; 5 share; 6 divide; 7 divvy up, dole out; 8 allocate, dispense; 9 parcel out; 10 distribute, portion out

apportionment: 7 sorting; 8 alloting, division, grouping; 9 allotment, parceling; 10 allocation, assortment, parcelling; 11 classifying; 12 apportioning, dispensation, distributing, distribution; 13 portioning out; 14 classification

apposite: 3 apt, fit, pat; 6 in loco; 7 a propos [Fr], apropos; 8 sortable, suitable; 9 pertinent; 10 applicable, seasonable; 11 appropriate

apposition: 5 union; 7 contact; 9 proximity; 10 contiguity; 11 coincidence, parallelism; 13 juxtaposition, 14 contiguousness, correspondence

appositive: 12 appositional

appraise: 4 rate; 5 value; 6 assess, survey; 7 measure; 8 estimate, evaluate; 11 set a value on; 14 form an estimate

appraisement: 6 assize; 9 appraisal, valuation; 10 assessment, evaluation

appraiser: 8 valuator

appreciable: 10 detectable, noticeable; 11 perceptible

appreciate: 3 ken; 4 know, rate, scan; 5 prize, value; 6 assess, review; 7 realize, revalue; 8 estimate, treasure; 9 apprehend, be aware of; 10 comprehend, understand

appreciated: 8 pleasing; 10 gratifying, satisfying; 11 apprehended; 12 comprehended

appreciation: 4 hold; 5 grasp, kudos [Grk], taste; 6 regard; 7 account; 9 gratitude, valuation; 10 admiration, estimation, popularity; 11 discernment; 12 thankfulness; 14 perceptiveness

apprehend: 3 cop, dig, ken, nab; 4 know, nail, scan; 5 fancy, grasp, opine, savvy; 6 arrest, collar, pick up, take up; 7 compass, quail at, realize; 8 conceive; 9 be aware of; 10 appreciate, comprehend, eye askance, understand

apprehensible: 9 graspable; 11 perceivable; 12 intelligible; 14 understandable

apprehension: 4 fear; 5 catch, dread, image, pinch, savvy, worry; 6 arrest, collar, un-

ease; 7 anxiety, concern, knowing; 8 disquiet; 9 arresting, cognition, detention, misgiving; 10 cognizance, conception, impression, inquietude, perception, solicitude, uneasiness; 11 discernment, disquietude, fearfulness, mental image; 12 precognition

apprentice: 7 learner; 10 journeyman

apprenticed: 5 bound; 8 articled; 10 indentured

appressed: 9 adpressed

apprise: 4 tell; 6 advise, awaken, notify; 7 apprize; 8 instruct, send word; 9 enlighten; 10 give notice

approach: 4 come!, go up, here!, loom, near; 5 await; 6 access, attack, avenue, come on, coming, feeler, go near; 7 advance, channel, forward!, get near, go about, passage; 8 border on, come near!, draw near, overture, set about, threaten; 9 glide path; 10 come hither!, come toward, glide slope; 11 approaching, approximate, move towards; 12 approach path, approach shot; 13 approximation

approaching: 4 soon; 6 at hand, coming; 7 nearing; 8 approach, imminent, oncoming, upcoming; 11 forthcoming

approach shot: 8 approach

approbation: 8 approval, sanction; 9 attention; 10 estimation; 11 good opinion; 13 consideration

appropinquate: 4 near; 6 go near; 7 get near; 8 approach, come near, draw near; 10 come toward; 11 approximate, move towards; 12 set in towards

appropriate: 3 apt, fit; 5 adopt, allow, apply, party, seize; 6 assign, in loco, proper, suited; 7 a propos [Fr], appoint, apropos, certain, earmark, imitate, partial, private, reserve, several, special; 8 apposite, definite, especial, liberate, original, peculiar, set aside, sortable, specific, suitable, take over; 9 exclusive, make use of, pertinent; 10 applicable, commandeer, harmonious, individual, particular, plagiarize, respective, seasonable; 11 determinate, expropriate; 12 advantageous

appropriately: 5 fitly; 8 suitably; 9 fittingly; 11 befittingly

approval: 8 blessing, sanction; 9 approving, attention; 10 estimation; 11 approbation, good opinion; 12 commendation; 13 consideration

approve: 2 OK; 4 okay; 6 ratify; 7 indorse; 8 sanction; 11 countersign

approved: 6 lauded; 7 praised; 9 commended; 10 sanctioned; 12 complimented

approximate: 4 near; 5 close, gauge, guess, judge, rough; 6 go near; 7 get near, savor of, stand by; 8 approach, come near, draw near, estimate, look like, resemble; 9 come close, take after; **10** come toward; **11** move towards; **12** set in towards; **13** approximative

approximately: 4 or so, some; **5** about; **6** around, nearly; **7** close to, roughly; **9** just about; **10** more or less

approximating: 9 guesswork; **10** estimating, estimation, resembling; **11** looking like, seeming like; **13** approximation

approximation: 4 idea; **8** approach, estimate; **9** evolution, guesswork, reduction; **10** estimating, estimation, involution; **13** approximating

appulse: 4 bump; **5** clash; **7** meeting; **8** abutment, approach, congress; **9** collision, concourse, encounter; **10** concussion, confluence, contacting, osculation, percussion; **11** concurrence, convergence, convergency; **13** approximation, concentration, making contact; **14** coming together

appurtenant: 7 adjunct; **8** adjuvant; **9** accessory, ancillary, appendage; **10** supplement, auxiliary, subsidiary

apraxic: 8 apractic

April Fools': 11 All Fools' day; **13** April Fools' day

apron: 4 mask; **6** fender, panier; **8** pinafore; **11** lawn sleeves

apropos: 3 fit; **6** in loco, timely; **7** a propos [Fr]; **8** apposite, sortable, suitable; **9** well-timed; **10** applicable, seasonable, seasonably; **11** appropriate; **12** incidentally

apsis: 4 apse

apt: 3 pat; **4** deft, gain; **5** given, handy, quick, ready; **6** adroit, clever, expert, liable, minded; **7** tending; **8** apposite, disposed; **9** dexterous, pertinent; **11** appropriate

Aptenodytes: 7 penguin; **16** genus Aptenodytes

apterous: 7 apteral

apteryx: 4 kiwi

aptitude: 4 gift; **5** craft, knack, skill; **7** address, aptness, fitness, know-how, turn for; **8** facility; **10** adroitness, competence; **11** capacity for, proficiency; **12** appositeness, skillfulness, suitableness; **13** applicability

aptly: 4 ably; **6** deftly; **7** capably, handily, quickly, readily; **8** adroitly; **11** competently, dexterously

aptness: 4 gift; **5** craft, knack, skill; **7** address, fitness, know-how, turn for; **8** aptitude, facility; **10** adroitness, competence, propensity; **11** capacity for, proficiency; **12** appositeness, skillfulness, suitableness; **13** applicability

Apulia: 6 Puglia

Aqaba: 5 Akaba

aquaculture: 17 hydroponic

aqualung: 5 scuba

aquamarine: 4 aqua; **5** beryl; **7** emerald; **9**
malachite, turquoise, verdigris; **10** cobalt blue; **11** peacock blue, verd antique [Fr]; **12** greenish blue

aquanaut: 9 skin-diver

aquaphobic: 11 hydrophobic

aquarium: 8 fish tank, vivarium; **12** marine museum

Aquarius: 22 Aquarius the Water Bearer

aquatic: 6 watery; **7** aqueous

aquatic plant: 10 hydrophyte, water plant

aqua vitae: 13 ardent spirits

aqueduct: 5 canal

aqueous: 6 watery; **7** aquatic

Aquifoliaceae: 11 holly family; **19** family Aquifoliaceae

Aquila: 5 eagle; **11** genus Aquila

aquilege: 9 aquilegia, columbine

aquilegia: 8 aquilege; **9** columbine

aquiline: 4 bent; **6** hooked, jagged; **7** angular, crooked; **8** serrated

Aquinas: 11 Saint Thomas; **13** Thomas Aquinas; **18** Saint Thomas Aquinas

Aquitaine: 9 Aquitania

Ar: 5 argon

arabesque: 4 fret; **8** flourish; **10** coquillage [Fr], fleur-de-lis [Fr]

Arabian camel: 9 dromedary; **18** Camelus dromedarius

Arabic numeral: 5 digit; **6** cipher

Arab-Israeli War: 9 Six Day War; **12** Yom Kippur War

arable: 5 rural; **6** rustic; **7** country; **8** tillable; **10** cultivable; **12** cultivatable

Arab Republic of Egypt: 5 Egypt; **18** United Arab Republic

araceous: 5 aroid

Arachis: 6 peanut; **12** genus Arachis

arachnid: 9 arachnoid

Arachnida: 6 spider; **14** class Arachnida

Araliaceae: 9 ivy family; **16** family Araliaceae

Aral Sea: 8 Lake Aral

Aramaic alphabet: 14 Hebrew alphabet; **15** Hebraic alphabet

Arapaho: 8 Arapahoe

Ararat: 9 Mt. Ararat; **11** Mount Ararat

arational: 10 irrational; **11** non-rational

Arawak: 8 Arawakan

arb: 10 arbitrager; **11** arbitrageur

arbiter: 10 arbitrator

arbitrager: 3 arb; **7** scalper; **11** arbitrageur

arbitrarily: 8 at random, randomly; **10** insolently, willy-nilly; **11** haphazardly, imperiously, irregularly; **12** high-handedly, peremptorily; **13** dictatorially, every which way, magisterially

arbitrariness: 6 whimsy; **7** whimsey; **11** flightiness, intolerance, officialism; **12** absence of law, whimsicality; **13** imperiousness, inconsistency; **14** capriciousness, high-handedness, peremptoriness

arbitrary: 6 random; 7 erratic, haughty; 8 absolute, arrogant, insolent, positive; 9 imperious, irregular, whimsical; 10 capricious, high-handed, imperative, iron-handed, peremptory; 11 dictatorial, magisterial, unregulated; 12 inconsistent

arbitrate: 5 award; 6 liaise, report; 7 mediate; 9 intercede

arbitration: 9 mediation; 11 arbitrament, good offices

arbitrator: 7 arbiter; 8 mediator; 11 intercessor

arbor: 4 axle, pole; 5 bower; 6 arbour; 7 mandrel, mandril, pergola, spindle

arboreal: 8 arborary, arborous, dendroid, treelike; 9 arboreous, arborical; 10 arboresque, arboriform, dendriform, dendroidal, tree-living, tree-shaped; 11 arborescent

arboreous: 5 woody; 6 woodsy; 8 arboreal, dendroid, treelike; 10 arboresque, arboriform, dendriform, dendroidal, tree-living, tree-shaped; 11 arboraceous, arborescent

arborescent: 6 ramose; 8 arboreal, branched, treelike; 9 arboreous, branching, dendritic; 10 arboresque, dendriform, dendroidal, tree-shaped

arboretum: 6 avenue; 8 parterre; 9 shrubbery; 13 botanic garden

arboriculture: 11 tree farming

arborolatry: 11 tree-worship

arc: 3 bow, sag; 4 arch, swag, sway; 5 curve, spark, sweep; 9 discharge; 11 electric arc; 17 electric discharge

arcade: 3 bow; 4 loop, mall; 6 piazza; 8 crescent, half-moon; 9 colonnade, crane neck, horseshoe

arcade game: 9 video game

arcadian: 6 rustic; 7 bucolic; 8 pastoral

Arcadian: 4 open; 9 confiding, open as day; 10 aboveboard, unreserved; 11 open-hearted; 12 frank-hearted, unsuspicious; 13 simple-hearted, single-hearted; 15 straightforward

arcanum: 6 secret; 7 mystery

arced: 5 bowed; 6 arched; 7 arching, arcuate; 8 arciform

Arceuthobium pusillum: 9 mistletoe

arch: 3 arc, bow, top; 4 boss, head; 5 acute, chief, crass, curve, gross, vault; 7 archway, arcuate, intense; 8 arch over, mainstay, profound; 10 consummate; 11 patronising, patronizing; 13 condescending

archaean: 7 archean

Archaeozoic era: 10 Archeozoic; 11 Archaeozoic; 13 Archeozoic era

archaic: 9 primitive; 10 antiquated; 12 antediluvian

archaism: dead word; 10 archaicism; 11 black letter, medievalism; 12 monkish

Latin, obsolete word; 14 antiquarianism

archangel: 14 garden angelica; 20 Angelica Archangelica

archdeacon: 4 dean; 5 canon; 8 diocesan; 10 prebendary

archduchy: 5 duchy

archean: 8 archaean

arched: 5 arced, bowed; 7 arc-like, arching, arclike, arcuate, vaulted; 8 arciform

archegonial: 12 archegoniate

archeological remains: 6 fossil

archeologist: 13 archaeologist

archeology: 11 archaeology

Archeozoic: 14 Archaeozoic era

archer: 3 fan [U.S.]; 6 bowman

archerfish: 17 Toxotes jaculatrix

archespore: 12 archesporium

archetypal: 10 prototypal, prototypic; 12 archetypical, prototypical

archetype: 5 pilot; 8 original, paradigm

archetypical: 10 archetypal, prototypal, prototypic; 12 prototypical

archiater: 14 chief physician

Archidiskidon: 7 mammoth; 8 elephant; 18 genus Archidiskidon

archil: 6 orchil; 7 cudbear

archimandrite: 5 abbot

arching: 5 arced, bowed; 6 arched; 7 arcuate; 8 arciform

architect: 6 author; 8 designer

architectonic: 8 tectonic

architecture: 9 structure; 11 structuring; 12 organization

architeuthis: 10 giant squid

architrave: 6 frieze, sconce; 7 capital, cornice; 8 pediment; 11 coping stone

archive: 6 return, scroll; 8 archives, blue book, file away; 10 state paper

archlute: 4 lute

archness: 8 pertness; 9 perkiness, sauciness; 12 impertinence

archon: 6 warden; 7 provost; 10 lieutenant

Archosargus: 8 sea bream; 10 sheepshead; 16 genus Archosargus

archosaur: 12 archosaurian; 19 archosaurian reptile

archpriest: 7 prelate, primate; 8 hierarch; 10 high priest

arciform: 5 arced, bowed; 6 arched; 7 arching, arcuate

arc light: 7 arc lamp

arctic: 3 icy; 5 gelid, polar; 6 boreal, Boreal, frigid, frosty, galosh, golosh, rubber, wintry; 7 glacial, gumshoe; 8 freezing, Northern, Siberian; 13 septentrional

arctic moss: 12 reindeer moss; 14 reindeer lichen; 19 Cladonia rangiferina

arctics: 6 brogan

Arctictis bintourong: 7 bearcat; 9 binturong

Arctium: 7 burdock; 12 genus Arctium
Arctonyx: 6 badger; 13 genus Arctonyx
Arctostaphylos: 9 manzanita, bearberry; 19 genus Arctostaphylos
arcuate: 3 bow; 4 arch; 5 arced, bowed; 6 arched; 7 arching, arclike, vaulted; 8 arch over, arciform
Ardea: 5 heron; 10 genus Ardea
ardent: 4 fond, warm; 5 fiery, rabid; 6 enrage [Fr], fervid, red-hot, torrid; 7 burning, devoted, fervent, flaming, glowing, gushing; 8 motherly, uxorious; 9 perfervid, rapturous; 10 passionate; 11 impassioned
ardently: 9 fervently
ardor: 4 elan, fire, gush, zeal; 5 verve; 6 ardour, fervor; 7 fervour, passion; 8 fervency; 9 eagerness; 10 enthusiasm, fervidness; 11 overanxiety, zealousness
arduous: 4 hard; 5 heavy; 7 onerous; 8 grueling, toilsome; 9 gruelling, Herculean, laborious, punishing, straining, strenuous; 10 formidable, labourious; 12 backbreaking
arduously: 9 onerously; 11 laboriously
area: 3 orb; 4 soil; 5 arena, field, orbit, realm; 6 circle, domain, ground, region, sphere, square; 7 circuit, country, expanse; 8 province
area unit: 13 square measure
Arecaceae: 6 Palmae; 9 Palmaceae; 10 palm family
areca nut: 8 betel nut
arena: 4 area, bowl; 5 close, court, field, orbit; 6 domain, sphere; 7 stadium; 9 inclosure; 13 scene of action
arenaceous: 5 sandy; 6 gritty; 8 sandlike
Arenga: 6 gomuti; 9 sugar palm; 11 genus Arenga
arenose: 5 sandy; 6 gritty
areola: 4 hoop, ring; 6 circle; 7 annulus, circlet; 11 ring of color
arescent: 4 arid
arete: 4 crag, pike; 5 crest; 8 cone peak; 9 sugar loaf
aretology: 6 ethics; 8 ethology
argal: 6 argali; 9 Ovis ammon
Argand: 6 duplex; 9 moderator
argasid: 8 soft tick
argent: 6 silver; 7 silvery; 8 argentum [Lat]; 9 argentine, silverish; 11 silveryness
argentine: 6 argent; 7 silvery
argil: 7 alumina
argillaceous: 6 clayey, mellow; 9 edematous
argon: 2 Ar
Argonne: 5 Meuse; 10 Meuse River; 12 Meuse-Argonne; 13 Argonne Forest; 21 Meuse-Argonne operation
argot: 4 cant; 5 lingo, slang; 6 jargon, patois; 10 vernacular
arguable: 9 debatable; 10 disputable
argue: 4 moot; 5 fence, imply, plead; 6 debate, reason; 7 bespeak, breathe, contend, dispute, involve, wrangle; 8 indicate; 9 bandy with
arguing: 4 tilt; 8 argument; 9 reasoning; 10 contention; 11 controversy, quarrelsome; 12 contestation
argument: 4 tilt; 5 issue, point; 6 debate, reason; 7 arguing, dispute, problem; 8 question; 9 moot point, statement; 10 contention; 11 controversy, topic at hand; 12 contestation
argumentation: 4 line; 6 debate; 8 argument; 11 controversy
arguments: 4 case; 7 reasons [pl]; 11 pros and cons
Argus-eyed: 8 hawk-eyed, keen-eyed, lynx-eyed; 9 eagle-eyed
argyle: 7 argyles
Argyrotaenia: 7 tortrix; 17 genus Argyrotaenia
Arhat: 5 lohan; 6 Arhant
aria: 3 air; 4 tune; 6 melody
Arianism: 9 Origenism
Aricara: 7 Arikara
arid: 3 dry; 4 bald, dull, flat; 6 boring, jejune, mortal, barren; 7 sterile, tedious; 9 desiccate, dry as dust, infertile, unfertile, waterless; 10 desiccated, unfruitful; 11 inoperative; 13 uninteresting
Ariel: 4 Iris; 7 Mercury, mermaid, seamaid
Aries: 11 Aries the Ram
arietta: 4 aria; 9 short aria
aright: 4 well; 5 right; 9 correctly, favorably; 14 satisfactorily
ariose: 8 songlike; 9 consonant
arise: 4 go up, grow, lift, rise; 5 bob up, get up, pop up, rebel; 6 appear, cast up, come up, crop up, move up, rise up, show up, turn up; 7 develop, stand up, start up, turn out; spring up; 9 come forth, originate; 11 show its face; 13 work one's way up
arishth: 4 neem; 7 margosa, nim tree; 8 neem tree
aristate: 5 awned; 7 bearded
aristocracy: 5 elite; 6 gentry; 8 nobility; 10 great folks
aristocrat: 5 swell; 9 blue blood, patrician
aristocratic: 4 blue; 6 gentle, titled; 8 princely; 9 patrician; 10 autocratic; 11 blue-blooded; 14 aristocratical
Arithmancy: 9 by numbers
arithmetical: 8 analytic; 9 algebraic; 10 arithmetic; 11 statistical
arithmetician: 10 calculator
ark: 6 throne; 10 tabernacle; 16 ark of the covenant
Arkansan: 11 Arkansawyer
arm: 3 man; 4 arms, gird, limb, lobe, wing; 5 equip, jimmy; 6 branch, lobule, member, outfit, sleeve, weapon; 7 build up, fortify; 8 forelimb, offshoot, ordnance; 10 arm

oneself; **11** subdivision; **12** deadly weapon, ramification, weapon system
Armageddon: 13 death struggle
armament: 5 array; **6** arming, outfit; **8** armature; **9** armaments, equipment, equipping; **12** accouterment
arm band: 6 armlet
arm chair: 9 easy chair
armed force: 5 troop [pl]; **6** troops [pl], **7** sabaoth [biblical]; **8** military, soldiery; **14** military forces
armed forces: 8 military
armed robbery: 5 heist; **6** holdup; **7** stickup
Armenia: 8 Hayastan
armet: 4 helm; **5** shako; **6** casque; **8** siege cap
armful: 6 capful; **7** handful; **8** mouthful, spoonful
armiger: 5 count, laird; **11** armor-bearer
armigerous: 7 martial, warlike; **9** bellicose, combative; **11** belligerent
armillary sphere: 9 astrolabe
arming: 8 armament; **9** equipping
armistice: 5 truce; **9** cease-fire, stand-down; **12** modus vivendi [Lat]; **13** breathing time
Armistice Day: 11 Veterans' Day
armlet: 3 bay; **5** bight; **7** arm band; **8** bracelet; **9** embayment
Armoracia rusticana: 7 red cole; **11** horse-radish
armored vest: 15 bulletproof vest
armorer: 8 armourer; **9** artificer
armorial: 10 emblematic; **11** exponential
armor plated: 8 ironclad; **10** imbricated
armory: 7 armoury, arsenal; **9** inventory; **11** powder-house
armpit: 6 axilla; **13** axillary fossa; **14** axillary cavity
arms: 3 arm; **6** blazon, weapon; **8** blazonry, munition, ordnance, the sword, weaponry
arms-runner: 9 gunrunner
Armstrong gun: 12 Lancaster gun
army: 3 sea; **4** host, wing; **5** array, corps, sight, squad; **6** column, galaxy; **7** battery, brigade, company, numbers, platoon, section; **8** division, garrison, regiment, squadron; **9** a quantity, battalion; **10** detachment; **11** corps d'armee [Fr], regular army, subdivision; **12** flying column
arnica: 7 benzoin, calomel
Arno: 9 River Arno
aroid: 4 arum; **8** araceous
aroma: 4 odor; **5** odour, scent, smell; **7** perfume; **9** fragrance; **10** sweet smell
aromatic: 5 balmy, spicy; **6** savory; **7** scented; **8** fragrant, redolent; **12** sweet-scented; **13** sweet-smelling
aromatize: 7 perfume
around: 4 or so, some; **5** about, round; **6** nearby; **7** close to, roughly; **9** in the area, just about; **10** more or less; **13** approximately

around-the-clock: 7 nonstop; **11** day-and-night; **13** round-the-clock
around the corner: 4 soon; **6** at hand, coming, in hand; **7** in train; **8** imminent, in embryo, on the way, upcoming; **9** in one's eye; **10** in one's view, near at hand; **11** approaching, forthcoming
arousal: 3 rut; **4** heat; **6** estrus; **7** oestrus, rousing; **8** foreplay; **11** stimulation
arouse: 3 sex; **4** fire, stir, wake; **5** awake, brace, evoke, raise, rouse, waken; **6** awaken, elicit, excite, invoke, kindle, perk up, turn on, wake up, wind up; **7** bring up, conjure, provoke; **8** call down, energise, energize, enkindle; **9** stimulate
aroused: 5 horny, randy; **6** ablaze, aflame, roused; **7** excited, ruttish, stirred, wound up; **8** turned on; **9** emotional, stirred up; **10** stimulated
arow: 7 abreast
arpents: 4 ares
arquebus: 6 hagbut; **7** hackbut; **9** Brown Bess, flintlock, harquebus, matchlock; **11** blunderbuss
arrack: 4 arak
arraign: 6 charge
arraignment: 5 libel; **8** citation; **9** challenge
arrange: 2 do; **3** put, set; **4** coif, plan; **5** dress, fix up, frame, order, set up, stage; **6** coiffe, design, format, scheme; **7** compose, patch up; **8** coiffure, contrive, organize
arranged: 6 staged; **7** ordered, planned; **9** organized
arrangement: 5 array; **6** system; **8** grouping, ordering; **9** agreement, arranging, clearance, discharge, placement, quittance, reckoning; **10** adjustment, organizing, redemption, settlement; **11** disposition, liquidation; **12** distribution, organisation, organization, satisfaction; **13** accommodation; **14** shaking of hands; **18** musical arrangement
arranger: 7 adapter; **9** organizer
arranging: 8 ordering; **10** organizing; **11** arrangement; **12** organization
arrant: 4 base, foul, pure, vile; **5** gross, stark, utter; **7** far gone, perfect, sodding, staring; **8** complete, dreadful, flagrant, infamous; **9** downright; **10** blackguard, consummate, double-dyed; **11** everlasting, ignominious; **13** thoroughgoing
arras: 7 hanging; **8** tapestry
array: 3 rig, sea; **4** army, deck, robe, vest; **5** align, drape, dress, range, sight; **6** attire, bedeck, clothe, enrobe, fettle, finery, fit out, fledge, galaxy, lay out, outfit, set out, vector; **7** apparel, cortege, furnish, garnish, numbers, raiment, regalia, retinue; **8** accouter, armament, grouping; **9** a quantity,

cavalcade, equipment; **11** arrangement, disposition; **12** accouterment, distribution

arrayed: 4 clad; **7** attired, clothed, dressed; **8** invested; **9** panoplied

arrears: 4 debt; **7** deficit

arrest: 3 cop, get, nab; **4** halt, hold, nail, stay, stop; **5** catch, check, hitch, pinch; **6** collar, freeze, pick up, take up; **7** contain; **8** cut short, hold back, stoppage, turn back; **9** apprehend, arresting, detention; **11** lead captive, make captive, stem the tide, take captive; **12** apprehension

arresting: 6 arrest; **8** stunning; **11** sensational; **12** apprehension; **15** take into custody

arrest warrant: 12 bench warrant

arrhythmic: 5 jerky; **7** jerking; **8** unsteady; **12** arrhythmical

arriere pensee: 6 agenda; **7** evasion; **10** concealing; **11** concealment, reservation, suppression; **12** afterthought, hidden agenda, hidden motive, secret motive, undercurrent

arrival: 5 comer; **6** advent; **7** arriver; **8** reaching

arrival point: 4 goal; **8** goalpost; **11** destination, journey's end

arrive: 3 get; **4** come, hold; **5** ensue, get in, go far, issue, start; **6** make it; **13** take its course

arrivederci: 3 bye; **5** adieu, adios; **6** bye-bye, good-by, so long; **7** cheerio, good day, good-bye, **8** au revoir, sayonara; **14** auf wiedersehen

arrogance: 9 insolence; **10** lordliness; **11** haughtiness; **13** imperiousness

arrogant: 6 chesty; **7** haughty; **8** insolent; **9** arbitrary, imperious; **11** dictatorial, magisterial; **12** supercilious; **13** self-important

arrogate: 5 claim, usurp; **6** assert, assign, assume; **7** ascribe, presume, require

arrogation: 12 confiscation

arrondissement: 5 tract; **6** domain; **7** commune

arrosion: 8 abrasion; **9** attrition, detrition; **10** rubbing off, wearing off

arrow: 4 reed; **5** shaft; **7** pointer

arrowhead: 4 head; **5** point, runes; **8** arrow tip

arrowheaded: 6 barbed; **7** spurred

arrowroot: 6 achira; **10** Indian shot; **11** Canna edulis, Canna indica; **14** obedience plant

arrowroot family: 11 Marantaceae

arrow-shaped: 9 sagittate

arrow tip: 4 head; **5** point; **9** arrowhead

arroyo: 4 wadi; **5** gulch, gully; **11** dry river bed

arsenal: 6 armory; **7** armoury; **11** powderhouse

arsenic: 2 As

arsenic group: 7 cacodyl; **12** cacodyl group; **14** cacodyl radical

arson: 11 fire-raising; **12** incendiarism

arsonist: 7 fire bug [U.S.], firebug; **9** firebrand; **10** incendiary, petroleuse [Fr], pyromaniac

art: 4 opus, ruse; **7** artwork, fine art, finesse, prowess; **8** artifice, artistry, fine arts, graphics, industry; **9** work of art; **10** production; **12** ruse de guerre [Fr]; **13** manufacturing, masterfulness

Artemis: 7 Cynthia

Artemisia abrotanum: 12 southernwood

Artemisia: 4 sage; **7** mugwort; **8** tarragon, wormwood

arteria: 6 artery

arteria pulmonalis: 15 pulmonary artery

arteriola: 9 arteriole; **15** capillary artery

arteriole: 9 arteriola; **15** capillary artery

arteriosclerosis: 15 atherosclerosis; **17** arterial sclerosis; **21** coronary-artery disease; **22** hardening of the arteries

artery: 4 lane; **5** aisle, alley, lobby; **7** arteria; **8** corridor; **10** main artery

artesian: 7 flowing

artesian well: 4 well

artful: 6 crafty, shrewd; **7** cunning; **12** disingenuous

artfully: 5 slyly; **6** foxily; **8** craftily, shrewdly, trickily; **9** cunningly, elegantly, knavishly; **12** artistically; **14** disingenuously

artfulness: 4 wile; **5** craft; **7** cunning; **8** subtlety, wiliness; **10** craftiness, shrewdness

arthritic: 6 creaky; **9** rheumatic; **10** rheumatoid

arthropodal: 11 arthropodan; **12** arthropodous

artichoke: 14 artichoke plant, Cynara scolymus, globe artichoke

article: 4 ware; **6** clause; **7** product; **9** commodity; **11** merchandise; **13** review article, the literature

articled: 5 bound; **10** indentured; **11** apprenticed

articles: 6 canons, school; **8** doctrine

articular: 10 articulary

articulate: 3 say; **4** word; **5** joint, mouth, utter, voice; **6** phrase, word it; **7** deliver, enounce, express; **8** announce, aspirate, distinct, vocalize; **9** enunciate, formulate, pronounce; **10** accentuate

articulately: 10 eloquently

articulateness: 7 fluency; **10** volubility

articulatio: 5 joint; **12** articulation

articulatio coxae: 3 hip; **4** coxa; **8** hip joint

articulatio cubiti: 5 elbow; **7** cubitus; **10** elbow joint; **12** cubital joint

articulatio genus: 4 genu, knee; **9** knee joint

joint
articulation: 4 gore, join, seam; 5 hinge, joint, pivot, voice; 6 gusset; 8 junction, juncture; 11 articulatio, enunciation; 13 pronunciation
articulatio radiocarpea: 5 wrist; 6 carpus; 10 wrist joint; 16 radiocarpal joint
articulatio talocruralis: 5 ankle; 10 ankle joint; 12 mortise joint
artifact: 7 product; 8 artefact; 9 artifacts [pl]; 13 man-made object
artifacts: 8 artifact; 13 man-made object
artifice: 3 art; 4 ruse; 6 device; 7 nostrum, receipt; 9 expedient, invention; 10 production; 11 contrivance; 12 ruse de guerre [Fr]; 13 manufacturing
artificer: 5 maker; 6 wright; 7 armorer, artisan; 8 armourer, inventor; 9 craftsman; 10 discoverer, journeyman; 12 manufacturer
artificial: 5 phony, stiff; 6 ersatz [Ger], unreal; 7 canting, man-made, stilted; 8 affected, mannered; 9 contrived, insincere, pretended, unnatural; 10 not natural; 11 ad captandum, artifactual, pretentious
artificial insemination: 2 AI
artificial intelligence: 2 AI; 5 robot; 8 robotics; 14 artificial life
artificial lake: 9 reservoir
artificial lung: 8 iron lung; 19 heart and lung machine
artificially: 11 unnaturally
artificial resin: 7 polymer
artillery: 3 gun; 5 horse; 6 cannon, weapon; 7 cavalry; 8 heavy gun, ordnance; 9 voltigeur [Fr]; 10 light horse; 11 heavy weapon
artilleryman: 6 gunner; ; 9 cannoneer; 10 bombardier
artiodactyl: 8 even-toed; 14 artiodactylous
artisan: 9 artificer, craftsman; 10 journeyman
artist: 8 designer, promoter; 9 projector
artist's workroom: 7 atelier
artistic: 5 Attic; 7 correct, elegant; 8 esthetic, pleasing, polished; 9 aesthetic, classical, shipshape, technical; 10 Ciceronian, scientific, well-styled
artistically: 8 artfully; 9 elegantly
artistic style: 5 idiom
artistry: 3 art; 7 finesse, prowess; 13 masterfulness, superior skill
artless: 4 lain, naif, pure; 5 naive; 6 native, simple; 7 natural; 9 ingenuous, unspoiled; 10 unaffected, uncultured; 11 undesigning; 12 uncultivated
artlessly: 6 simply; 7 crudely, naively; 9 naturally; 10 inexpertly; 11 ingenuously; 12 unaffectedly
Artocarpus: 6 marang; 9 jackfruit; 10 breadfruit; 15 genus Artocarpus

art of memory: 9 mnemonics
art of reasoning: 5 logic; 11 formal logic
arts: 10 humanities; 11 liberal arts; 20 humanistic discipline
artwork: 3 art; 4 opus; 8 graphics; 9 work of art; 14 piece of artwork; 16 nontextual matter
arugula: 6 rocket; 8 roquette; 11 Eruca sativa, rocket salad; 12 garden rocket; 20 Eruca vesicaria sativa
arui: 5 audad; 6 aoudad; 10 maned sheep; 12 Barbary sheep
arum: 5 aroid
aruspex: 5 witch; 13 fortune teller
Aryan: 9 Indo-Aryan; 12 Indo-European
arytenoid cartilage: 9 arytenoid; 10 arytaenoid
As: 7 arsenic
as: 7 equally; 8 every bit; 11 forasmuch as
asa dulcis: 7 benzoin; 8 benjamin; 10 gum benzoin; 11 gum benjamin
as a formality: 8 pro forma; 13 perfunctorily
as a group: 6 en bloc; 7 en masse
as always: 10 invariably
asarabacca: 15 Asarum europaeum
as a rule: 7 usually; 9 generally, most often, typically; 10 ordinarily; 11 customarily; 14 for the most part, most frequently
Ascaphus: 4 toad, frog; 13 genus Ascaphus
ascend: 4 go up, rise; 5 mount; 6 uprise; 7 take off; 8 blast off, take wing; 11 take a flight
ascendancy: 7 control, mastery; 9 advantage, dominance; 10 ascendance, ascendence, ascendency
ascending: 4 rise; 6 ascent; 9 ascension
ascension: 4 rise; 6 ascent, rising; 9 ascending
Ascension: 12 Ascension Day; 18 Ascension of the Lord
ascent: 4 rise; 5 climb, raise, slope; 6 rising; 7 incline, upgrade; 8 gradient; 9 acclivity, ascending, ascension; 12 rising ground
ascertain: 3 fix, see, set; 4 find, tell; 5 check, learn, watch; 6 assure, ensure, insure, settle; 7 control, find out, see to it; 8 evidence; 9 determine, establish; 11 demonstrate
ascertainable: 12 discoverable
ascertained: 5 clear; 7 decided; 8 decisive, definite, observed, specific; 10 discovered, recognized; 11 categorical, determinate, unequivocal; 12 unmistakable
ascetic: 7 ascetic, austere, spartan; 9 abstainer, ascetical; 11 puritanical; 13 nonindulgent
Aschelminthes: 8 Nematoda; 14 phylum Nematoda; 19 phylum Aschelminthes

ASCII: 9 ASCII code
ASCII character: 11 ASCII symbol
ascititious: 10 completing; 12 supplemental;
13 complementing, supplementary, supplementing
Asclepiadaceae: 14 milkweed family
ascomycetous fungus: 10 ascomycete
ascorbic acid: 8 vitamin C
ascribable: 5 due to; 9 imputable, referable;
12 attributable
ascribe: 6 assign, impute; 8 arrogate; 9 attribute; 11 give a reason, rationalize
ascribe to: 5 blame, lay to; 7 point to, refer
to, trace to; 8 assign to, charge on, charge
to, credit to, ground on, impute to; 9 put
down to, set down to; 11 attribute to, bring
home to
ascription: 9 rationale; 11 attribution
asdic: 5 sonar; 11 echo sounder
asepsis: 9 sterility; 10 antisepsis; 11 sterile-
ness
aseptic: 7 sterile
assessor: 7 referee
asexual: 9 nonsexual
asexuality: 11 sexlessness
asexual reproduction: 12 agamogenesis
as God is my witness: 3 why; 5 marry; 6 i'
faith, indeed; 8 I must say
ash: 6 cinder; 7 ash tree; 10 incinerate; 13 reduce to ashes
ashame: 5 shame; 6 humble; 7 let down, set
down; 8 take down; 9 frown down, tread
down; 12 render humble
ashamed: 6 dashed; 7 abashed
ashcan: 6 ashbin; 7 dustbin; 8 trash bin, trash
can, wastebin; 10 garbage can; 11 trash
barrel
ashen: 3 dun, wan; 4 ashy, cold, dead, dull;
5 dingy, faint, livid, muddy, white; 6
glassy, leaden, sallow; 7 ghastly; 8
blanched; 9 bloodless; 10 cadaverous,
lackluster
ashes: 4 clay, dust; 5 earth; 7 cinders, scoriae; 11 precipitate
ashing: 12 incineration
Ashkhabad: 21 capital of Turkmenistan
ashore: 6 on land; 8 onto land; 10 toward
land
ashpan: 3 hob; 6 shovel, trivet
Ashur: 5 Ashir
ashy: 3 dun, wan; 4 cold, dead, dull; 5 ashen,
dingy, faint, muddy; 6 glassy, leaden, sallow; 7 ash-gray, ash-grey, ghastly; 10 cadaverous, lackluster
Asia Minor: 8 Anatolia
Asian: 7 Asiatic; 8 oriental
aside: 2 by; 3 cue; 4 away; 5 apart; 6 beside,
byplay; 7 abreast, sub rosa [Lat]; 8 excursus, on the sly; 9 alongside, on one side,
sotto voce [Lat]; 10 digression, divagation,

en tapinois [Fr], in a whisper; 11 parenthesis
aside from: 4 save; 6 beside, except; 7 barring, without; 8 let alone; 9 except for,
other than; 13 save and except; 18 with the
exception of
Asimina: 5 papaw; 6 papaya; 12 genus
Asimina
asinine: 4 dumb; 5 inane, silly; 6 stupid, unwise; 7 fatuous, foolish, vacuous; 8 improper, mindless; 9 ill-judged; 10
ill-advised, ill-devised; 11 ill-imagined, injudicious; 12 unreasonable; 13 without reason
ask: 4 need, pose, seek, take; 5 exact; 6 ask
for, charge, demand, expect, search; 7 call
for, enquire, inquire, involve, request, require; 11 necessitate
askance: 6 askant, squint; 7 asquint, squinty;
8 sidelong; 9 to leeward; 10 squint-eyed, to
windward
asked: 8 proposed; 9 requested; 10 asked
price, petitioned; 14 requested price
asker: 8 enquirer, inquirer; 10 questioner
askew: 3 wry; 4 awry; 5 wonky; 7 crooked; 8
cockeyed, lopsided; 10 out of shape
asking: 7 request; 9 asking for, inquiring; 10
requesting; 11 petitioning, questioning; 13
interrogative, interrogatory
ASL: 20 American sign language
aslant: 6 aslope, sloped; 7 athwart, slanted,
sloping; 8 diagonal, slanting; 9 obliquely
asleep: 4 gone, numb; 6 at rest; 7 at peace; 8
benumbed, deceased, departed, sleeping;
10 stacking z's
aslope: 6 aslant, sloped; 7 slanted, sloping; 8
diagonal, slanting
Asmodeus: 5 Titan; 6 Moloch, Shedim
asocial: 10 antisocial
asomatous: 11 disembodied, incorporeal; 12
noncorporeal
as one: 6 united; 8 agreeing, cemented, in accord, together; 9 congenial, in harmony, of
one mind; 10 concordant, harmonious; 11
harmonizing, in agreement
asp: 7 serpent
Aspalathus: 7 rooibos; 15 genus Aspalathus
aspect: 4 face, look, pose, view; 5 angle,
facet, scene, trait, vista; 7 feature, posture,
quality; 8 attitude, panorama, property,
prospect; 9 attribute; 10 expression; 11 orientation, perspective, point of view; 14
characteristic
aspergillosis: 16 brooder pneumonia
Aspergillus: 4 mold; 4 molds; 16 genus
Aspergillus
asperity: 4 gall, huff, miff; 5 pique, rigor; 6
rigour, spleen; 7 umbrage; 8 acerbity, acrimony, grimness, hardship, rankling, severity, soreness; 9 harshness, sharpness,,
virulence; 10 bitterness; 12 rigorousness
asperous: 5 crisp

asperse: 4 slur; 5 smear, sully; 6 defame, smirch; 7 slander; 8 besmirch; 9 denigrate; 10 calumniate

aspersion: 4 slur; 7 calumny, obloquy, scandal, slander; 10 backbiting, defamation, scurrility, sprinkling; 11 traducement; 12 evil-speaking, vilification; 13 disparagement

Asperula: 8 woodruff; 13 genus Asperula

asphalt: 3 tar; 6 tarmac; 7 macadam; 9 asphaltum; 10 tarmacadam; 11 macadamized; 12 mineral pitch

aspheric: 10 aspherical

asphyxiate: 5 choke; 6 stifle; 7 garrote, smother; 8 strangle, throttle; 9 suffocate

Aspidelaps: 15 genus Aspidelaps

aspidistra: 12 bar-room plant; 13 cast-iron plant

aspirant: 6 bidder, suitor; 7 hopeful, wannabe, wishful, would-be; 8 aspiring, claimant, wannabee; 9 applicant, candidate, postulant; 10 competitor, solicitant, supplicant; 12 office-seeker

aspirate: 5 mouth; 6 draw in, suck in; 7 deliver; 9 enunciate, pronounce; 10 accentuate, articulate

aspiration: 5 dream; 6 homage; 7 worship; 8 ambition, buoyancy, devotion; 9 adoration; 10 enthusiasm, goal in life; 12 heart of grace; 13 life's ambition, spiritus asper [Lat]; 14 rough breathing

aspire: 3 aim; 5 adore; 7 worship; 8 shoot for; 9 do service, pay homage

aspirin: 5 Bayer; 7 Empirin; 19 acetylsalicylic acid

Aspleniaceae: 18 family Aspleniaceae

Asplenium: 10 spleenwort; 14 genus Asplenium

asp viper: 3 asp; 11 Vipera aspis

ass: 4 rear, rump, seat, tail, tush; 5 fanny, stern; 6 behind, bottom, donkey; 7 hind end, jackass, keister, rear end, tail end, tomfool, tooshie; 8 backside, buttocks, derriere; 9 fundament, posterior

assail: 4 bite; 5 round, set on, snipe; 6 attack, impugn, snap at; 7 assault, lash out; 8 maltreat

assailable: 4 open; 10 undefended; 12 undefendable

assailant: 8 attacker, batterer; 9 aggressor, assaulter

Assamese: 7 Asamiya

Assam rubber: 11 rubber plant; 13 Ficus elastica; 14 India-rubber fig; 15 India-rubber tree; 16 India-rubber plant

assassinate: 6 murder; 7 butcher; 9 slaughter, victimize; 10 put an end to; 20 immolate, make away with

assassination: 6 murder; 8 homicide, 12 manslaughter

assault: 4 rape; 5 round, set on, snipe; 6 assail, attack, molest; 7 battery, lash out; 9 violation; 10 ravishment

assaulter: 8 batterer; 9 assailant

assay: 3 try; 4 seek, test; 5 check, essay; 6 try out; 7 attempt; 9 determine

assayist: 7 analyst; 8 analyzer; 17 analytical chemist

assemblage: 3 set; 5 group; 6 hookup; 7 cluster, meeting; 8 assembly; 9 gathering; 10 assembling, collection; 11 aggregation; 12 accumulation

assemble: 4 meet; 5 piece, set up; 6 gather, muster; 7 collect; 9 forgather, integrate; 10 foregather

assembled: 5 built; 6 made-up, massed; 7 amassed, grouped; 8 together; 9 collected; 10 congregate; 11 accumulated

assembling: 7 meeting; 8 assembly; 9 gathering; 10 assemblage, collecting, collection, converging; 11 ingathering, integrating, integration

assembly: 4 fold; 5 flock, forum, laity; 6 caucus, clique, people; 7 meeting; 8 brethren, conclave; 9 gathering; 10 assemblage, assembling, collecting, collection, conference; 11 collocation, conventicle, fabrication, ingathering, the faithful; 12 congregation

assemblyman: 13 assemblywoman [female]

assemblywoman: 11 assemblyman [male]

assent: 3 nod; 6 accede, comply; 7 consent; 9 accession, acquiesce, agreement; 10 acceptance; 11 acceptation, yield assent; 12 acquiescence

assenting: 8 agreeing; 9 accession; 10 assentient

assentment: 3 nod; 6 assent; 7 consent; 9 accession, agreement; 10 acceptance; 11 acceptation; 12 acquiescence

assert: 3 say; 4 aver, avow, swan; 5 state, swear; 6 affirm, assume, insist; 7 declare, enforce, profess, require; 8 arrogate, maintain, make good; 9 predicate, use a right; 10 asseverate, lay claim to, put forward, put in force

asserted: 7 alleged; 9 pretended; 10 apologetic, ostensible

assertion: 8 averment; 9 statement; 10 allegation, profession; 11 affirmation, declaration, predication; 12 asseveration

assertive: 5 pushy; 7 weighty; 8 emphatic; 13 self-asserting, self-assertive

assertively: 11 confidently, trenchantly; 12 dogmatically

assess: 3 tax; 4 doom [U.S.], rate; 5 value; 6 review; 7 measure; 8 appraise, estimate, evaluate; 10 appreciate; 11 set a value on; 14 form an estimate

assessment: 6 assize; 8 judgment, taxation;

9 appraisal, judgement, valuation; **10** evaluation; **12** appraisement

assessor: 5 jurat [Lat]; **11** tax assessor

asset: 4 plus; **5** means; **6** assets; **9** resources; **10** belongings; **11** item of value; **13** circumstances

asseverate: 4 avow; **5** vouch; **6** assert, assure, avouch; **7** certify, warrant; **8** maintain

asseveration: 4 oath; **8** averment, swearing; **9** affidavit, assertion; **10** adjuration

assiduous: 7 notable; **8** diligent, sedulous; **11** industrious, painstaking

assign: 3 put; **5** alien, allot, award; **6** accord, burden, charge, depute, impute, look to, oblige; **7** appoint, ascribe, consign, entrust, intrust, portion, specify; **8** alienate, arrogate, call upon, delegate, set apart; **9** attribute, designate, prescribe; **10** commission, saddle with; **11** appropriate

assignable: 10 conveyable, negotiable; **12** transferable; **13** transferrable

assigned duty: 4 care, task; **6** charge, errand; **7** mission; **10** assignment, commission, engagement; **14** responsibility

assignee: 7 devisee; **17** responsible person; **21** responsible individual

assigning: 5 trust; **7** cession; **8** transfer; **9** conveying; **10** alienation, assignment, commission, conveyance, delegating, delegation, deputation, deputizing, entrusting; **11** consignment

assignment: 4 care, task; **5** grant, trust; **6** charge, errand, naming; **7** cession, mission; **8** transfer; **9** assigning, conveying; **10** alienation, commission, conveyance, delegating, delegation, deputation, deputizing, engagement, entrusting; **11** appointment, consignment, designation; **14** responsibility

assimilate: 5 dress, level, sop up; **6** absorb, imbibe, ingest, smooth, soak up, take in; **9** bring near

assimilation: 10 absorption; **12** apperception; **13** acculturation

assist: 3 aid; **4** help; **5** serve; **6** attend, succor, wait on; **7** give aid, helping

assistance: 3 aid; **4** help; **6** aiding, assist, succor; **7** helping; **9** assisting

assistance in time of need: 6 relief, rescue

assistant: 4 help; **6** helper; **7** adjunct; **8** coworker, confrere; **9** accessory, auxiliary, supporter; **10** cooperator; **11** concomitant; **12** collaborator

assistant DA: 25 assistant district attorney

assisted: 5 aided

assisting: 3 aid; **4** help; **6** aiding, succor; **7** helpful, helping; **8** adjuvant; **9** auxiliary; **10** assistance

assize: 4 eyre; **9** valuation; **10** assessment; **12** appraisement

associate: 4 herd, link; **5** crowd, surge, tie in; **6** assort, fellow, helper, relate, stream, throng; **7** compeer, comrade, connect, consort; **8** familiar; **9** affiliate, colleague, companion; **10** consociate; **13** draw a parallel

associated: 6 agnate; **8** allied to; **9** connected; **10** affiliated, implicated

Associated Press: 2 AP

association: 3 tie; **4** link; **5** tie-up; **7** analogy, company, society; **8** affinity, alliance, homology; **9** connexion, mutuality; **10** connection; **11** affiliation, coexistence, correlation, homogeneity, institution; **12** concomitance; **13** companionship, interrelation

Association for Computational Linguistics: 3 ACL [acron]

Association for the Advancement of Retired Persons: 4 AARP

assoil: 5 clear; **6** acquit; **9** discharge, exculpate, exonerate, whitewash

assonance: 10 vowel rhyme

assonant: 8 isotonic

assort: 4 sort; **5** class, group; **7** consort, sort out; **8** classify, separate; **9** affiliate, associate; **15** divide into sorts

assorted: 3 odd; **5** mixed; **6** divers, motley, sorted, sundry, varied; **7** diverse, mingled, various; **9** different; **10** dissimilar; **11** diversified; **13** heterogeneous, miscellaneous

assortment: 6 budget, motley; **7** mixture, sorting, variety; **8** division, grouping; **9** allotment, potpourri; **10** miscellany; **11** classifying, miscellanea; **13** apportionment; **14** classification

Assouan: 5 Aswan; **6** Assuan

assuage: 3 lay; **4** calm, cool, damp, hush, lull, swag, tame; **5** abate, allay, quell, quiet, slake, sober, still; **6** deaden, gentle, lenify, pacify, quench, rebate, smooth, soothe; **7** appease, compose, gruntle, mollify, placate, relieve, slacken, turn off; **8** calm down, palliate, suppress; **9** alleviate; **10** conciliate; **11** tranquilize

assuagement: 6 relief; **9** remission; **10** mitigation, relaxation; **11** alleviation; **12** pacification

assuaging: 8 allaying

Assuan: 5 Aswan; **7** Assouan

assuasive: 7 calming; **8** allaying, soothing; **9** assuaging, pacifying

as such: 5 per se

assume: 4 bear, sham, take, wear; **5** adopt, fancy, feign, put on, usurp; **6** accept, assert, fake it, take it, take on, take up; **7** acquire, get into, presume, pretend, receive, require; **8** arrogate, feel free, make bold, make free, make good, simulate, take over; **10** lay claim to; **11** make believe

assumed: 4 sham; **5** false, put on; **6** mooted; **7** divined, fictive, guessed; **8** imagined, presumed, supposed, surmised; **9** arrogated, pretended, suspected;

conjectured, presupposed
assumed name: 5 alias; 9 false name; 12 assumed title
assuming: 7 would-be; 9 bumptious; 10 assumption, assumptive, precocious; 12 presumptuous
assumption: 6 breach; 7 premise, premiss; 8 assuming, exaction; 9 breaching, violating, violation; 10 imposition, infraction, prevention, usurpation; 11 domineering, laying claim, presumption, supposition; 12 encroachment, infringement, predilection, presentiment; 13 preconception, prepossession, transgression
Assumption of Mary: 8 August 15; 10 Assumption
assurance: 6 pledge, surety; 8 affiance, reliance, sureness; 9 authority, certainty, certitude, indenture; 10 avouchment, confidence, conviction, firm belief, profession; 11 presumption, self-respect; 12 positiveness; 13 self-assurance; 14 self-confidence
assure: 3 see; 4 avow, tell; 5 check, cheer, vouch; 6 avouch, buoy up, ensure, insure, secure; 7 certify, control, promise, satisfy, see to it, warrant; 8 embolden, reassure; 9 ascertain, encourage, guarantee, warrantee; 10 asseverate, underwrite
assured: 4 sure; 6 secure; 7 certain; 8 cocksure, positive; 9 confident, convinced, satisfied; 12 unhesitating
assuredly: 7 no doubt; 8 of course; 9 doubtless; 14 unquestionably
assuredness: 4 cool; 5 poise; 6 aplomb; 9 sang-froid; 14 self-possession
astatine: 2 At
Asteraceae: 5 aster; 10 Compositae; 11 aster family
asterisk: 4 star
astern: 3 aft; 5 aback, abaft, after; 8 rearward
asteroid: 9 planetoid; 10 star-shaped; 11 minor planet
Asterope: 7 Sterope
Asteroth: 3 Bel; 4 Baal; 5 Belus
asthenia: 6 sprain, strain; 8 cachexia [Med], delicacy; 11 decrepitude; 12 invalidation
asthenic: 8 adynamic; 9 enervated; 11 debilitated
asthenopia: 9 eyestrain
asthma: 12 asthma attack; 15 bronchial asthma
asthmatic: 6 wheezy; 8 wheezing
astigmatic: 6 myopic; 9 ametropic; 10 presbyopic; 16 visually impaired
astigmatism: 8 astigmia; 15 astigmatic sight
astir: 2 up; 5 about; 8 stirring; 9 sparkling, wrought up
as to: 5 as for; 7 vis-a-vis; 9 as regards, regarding; 10 as respects, concerning, in re-

gard to; 12 in relation to, with regard to; 13 with respect to; 15 with reference to
astomatous: 9 mouthless
astonied: 6 amazed; 7 stunned; 9 astounded; 10 astonished
astonished: 6 amazed; 7 stunned; 8 astonied; 9 astounded
astonishing: 7 amazing; 8 striking, towering; 10 astounding, incredible, prodigious, staggering, stupefying, stupendous
astonishingly: 7 awfully; 8 famously; 9 amazingly, glaringly, strangely; 10 incredibly, strikingly; 11 egregiously, marvelously, prominently, wonderfully; 12 astoundingly, emphatically, stupendously, surprisingly, tremendously; 13 extravagantly
astonishment: 9 amazement; 10 wonderment; 12 bewilderment
astound: 4 stun; 5 amaze; 7 petrify; 8 astonish; 9 electrify, galvanize; 12 give one a turn; 13 give one a shock
astounding: 7 amazing; 8 striking; 10 staggering, stupefying; 11 astonishing, dumfounding; 12 dumbfounding
astraddle: 7 astride
astragal: 4 bead; 5 talus; 6 zigzag; 7 beading; 8 acanthus, beadwork; 9 anklebone, cartouche; 10 astragalus
astragalus: 5 talus; 8 astragal; 9 anklebone
astral: 6 starry; 7 stellar; 8 sidereal
Astreus: 12 genus Astreus
astride: 9 astraddle
astringency: 4 bite; 7 stypsis; 8 acridity; 11 astringence
astringent: 5 acerb, acrid, harsh, sharp; 6 biting; 7 acerbic, styptic; 14 astringent drug
astringents: 10 sclerotics
astrologer: 11 astrologist
astrology: 9 horoscopy; 14 star divination
astronaut: 8 spaceman; 9 cosmonaut
astronautical: 11 astronautic
astronautics: 11 aeronautics; 16 orbital mechanics
astronomer: 9 stargazer; 11 uranologist
astronomical: 8 galactic; 10 astronomic; 12 cosmological
Astronomical Unit: 2 AU
astronomical year: 9 solar year; 12 tropical year; 15 equinoctial year
astronomy: 9 uranology
astute: 5 canny, leery, sharp; 6 shrewd; 7 knowing; 9 up to snuff
astutely: 8 shrewdly; 9 sapiently; 11 sagaciously
astuteness: 5 depth; 10 profundity, shrewdness; 12 perspicacity, profoundness; 17 perspicaciousness
a subtype of: 1 a; 7 a kind of, a sort of, a type of; 8 a class of

Asuncion: 17 capital of Paraguay

asunder: 4 free; **5** apart, loose; **6** adrift; **7** in twain, insular; **8** discrete, separate; **9** disparate, unannexed; **10** far between, unattached; **11** unconnected; **12** unassociated

as usual: 7 usually; **8** ad instar [Lat], commonly; **9** typically; **10** as things go; **11** as was common; **12** instar omnium [Lat]

Aswan: 6 Assuan; **7** Assouan

Aswan Dam: 7 High Dam; **12** Aswan High Dam

as well: 3 too; **4** also; **7** besides; **8** likewise; **11** on top of that

as well as: 3 and; **8** let alone; **9** including, inclusive; **12** in addition to, not to mention

as yet: 3 yet; **5** so far; **6** til now; **7** thus far, up to now; **8** hitherto, until now; **10** heretofore

asylum: 6 refuge; **7** retreat; **9** sanctuary; **10** mental home; **12** insane asylum; **13** place of asylum; **14** mental hospital

asymmetric: 10 unbalanced; **12** asymmetrical

asymmetrical: 7 crooked; **10** asymmetric

asymptomatic: 11 symptomless

asymptotic: 12 asymptotical

asynchronism: 10 asynchrony; **15** desynchronizing; **17** desynchronisation, desynchronization

asynchrony: 12 asynchronism; **15** desynchronizing; **16** difference in time

asynclitism: 9 obliquity

asynergy: 9 asynergia

asystole: 13 cardiac arrest

At: 8 astatine

Atabrine: 9 mepacrine; **10** quinacrine

Atakapa: 7 Atakapa; **8** Atakapan, Attacapa; **9** Attacapan

at all times: 6 always; **8** ever anon, steadily; **9** routinely; **10** constantly, invariably; **11** continually, day after day, day and night, incessantly, night and day, perpetually, unfailingly, without fail; **12** consistently, continuously

at any rate: 6 anyhow, anyway; **7** at least; **9** at any cost, at any risk, in any case, leastways, leastwise

ataraxic: 8 sedative; **9** ataractic; **12** ataraxic drug; **13** ataractic drug, tranquilizing

ataraxis: 5 peace; **6** repose; **8** serenity; **10** heartsease; **11** peace of mind; **12** peacefulness

at a stretch: 7 running; **8** gradatim [Lat]; **9** gradually; **10** step by step

atavism: 9 reversion, throwback

atavist: 9 throwback

ataxia: 5 ataxy

ataxic: 7 atactic

at ease: 4 easy; **6** at home, at rest; **7** relaxed;

9 in comfort; **10** at one's ease, in pleasure; **11** comfortable

Ateles: 11 genus Ateles

Ateles geoffroyi: 12 spider monkey

atelier: 6 bureau, studio

ateliosis: 10 ateleiosis

atenolol: 8 Tenormin

at every moment: 6 always; **8** ever anon, steadily; **9** routinely; **10** at all times, constantly, invariably; **11** continually, day after day, day and night, incessantly, night and day, perpetually, unfailingly, without fail; **12** consistently, continuously

Athabascan: 10 Athabaskan, Athapascan, Athapaskan; **18** Athapaskan language

athanasia: 3 aye; **8** eternity; **10** perpetuity; **11** immortality

Athanasian Creed: 11 Nicene Creed; **13** Apostles' Creed

at hand: 4 near, soon; **5** handy, ready; **7** instant; **8** imminent, tangible, upcoming; **9** available, impending; **11** approaching

at heart: 6 inside; **8** at bottom, con amore [It], deep down; **12** ab imo pectore [Lat], heart and soul

atheism: 11 godlessness

atheist: 9 atheistic; **11** atheistical

Athena: 6 Athene, Pallas; **12** Pallas Athena

Athene: 6 Athena, Pallas; **11** genus Athene; **12** Pallas Athena

Athene noctua: 9 little owl

atheneum: 9 athenaeum

Athens: 12 Greek capital; **15** capital of Greece

atherodyde: 6 ramjet; **7** athodyd

athirst: 3 dry; **6** hungry; **7** thirsty

athlete: 3 pro; **4** jock; **5** boxer, sport; **6** player; **7** bruiser; **8** pugilist, the fancy, wrestler; **9** gladiator, sportsman; **12** prize fighter

athlete's foot: 10 tinea pedis

athletic field: 5 field; **11** playing area; **12** playing field

athleticism: 5 brawn, nerve, sinew; **6** muscle; **8** physique; **11** strenuosity

athletics: 5 sport; **15** athletic contest

athletic sock: 9 sweat sock; **11** varsity sock

athletic supporter: 4 jock; **9** jockstrap, suspensory

athletic type: 10 mesomorphy

athodyd: 6 ramjet; **10** atherodyde

Athrotaxis: 4 pine; **5** cedar; **15** genus Athrotaxis

athwart: 5 cross; **6** aslant, thwart; **9** obliquely; **12** transversely

Atlanta: 15 battle of Atlanta; **16** capital of Georgia

Atlantides: 10 Hesperides

Atlantis: 6 Utopia; **9** fairyland; **10** millennium; **11** happy valley

at large: 5 loose; **7** escaped; **8** as a whole,

atlas: 7 telamon; **10** book of maps; **13** atlas vertebra, map collection
at last: 7 finally
at length: 5 along; **6** at last; **7** finally; **8** at sunset, linearly; **9** lengthily; **10** eventually, lengthwise; **14** longitudinally
at liberty: 4 free; **5** loose; **6** exempt, immune; **7** at large, escaped; **8** scot-free; **10** on the loose; **13** unconstrained
at loggerheads: 6 at feud, at odds; **7** at issue; **10** at variance; **11** at high words
atm: 10 atmosphere
ATM: 11 cash machine; **13** cash dispenser; **15** automated teller, automatic teller; **22** automated teller machine, automatic teller machine
atmometer: 12 evaporometer
atmosphere: 3 air, atm; **4** aura; **8** ambiance, ambience
atmospheric condition: 7 weather; **16** weather condition
atmospheric pressure: 11 air pressure
at odds: 6 at feud; **7** at issue; **10** at variance; **11** at high words, conflicting; **13** at loggerheads, contradictory
atoll: 4 reef; **7** breaker
atom: 4 mote; **5** speck; **8** molecule, particle; **9** corpuscle; **10** atomic unit; **15** indivisible unit
atomic: 6 minute; **7** compact, nuclear; **8** atomlike; **9** molecular, primitive, subatomic; **11** corpuscular, indivisible, microscopic; **12** indissoluble, submolecular, unanalyzable, unresolvable
atomic bomb: 5 A-bomb; **8** atom bomb; **11** fission bomb; **13** fission device, plutonium bomb
atomic energy: 11 atomic power; **12** nuclear power
Atomic Energy Commission: 3 AEC
atomic explosion: 16 nuclear explosion
atomic fission: 7 fission; **14** nuclear fission
atomic mass: 12 atomic weight
atomic physics: 14 nuclear physics
atomic pile: 4 pile; **12** chain reactor; **13** atomic reactor
atomic reactor: 4 pile; **10** atomic pile; **12** chain reactor
atomic warfare: 9 atomic war; **10** nuclear war; **14** nuclear warfare
atomic warhead: 4 nuke; **14** nuclear warhead; **20** thermonuclear warhead
atomic weight: 10 atomic mass
atomize: 3 zap; **4** nuke; **8** vaporize
atomizer: 5 spray; **7** sprayer; **8** atomiser
atomlike: 6 atomic, minute
atom smasher: 11 accelerator; **19** particle accelerator
atonal: 7 unkeyed
at once: 3 now; **7** at a time; **8** directly; **9** all

at once, at one time, forthwith, instantly, right away; **10** in real time; **11** immediately; **12** straightaway
atone: 3 aby; **4** abye; **6** repent; **7** expiate; **8** atone for, make good; **9** indemnify; **10** make amends
at one's leisure: 6 slowly; **9** leisurely; **12** deliberately
atone for: 5 atone
atonement: 3 sop; **6** amends; **7** redress; **8** judgment, requital; **9** expiation, mediation, salvation; **10** redemption, reparation; **12** intercession, propitiation, satisfaction; **14** acknowledgment; **15** act of contrition
atonic: 10 unaccented
atony: 6 atonia; **7** languor; **8** debility; **9** amyotonia, atonicity; **10** enervation, relaxation
atopic allergy: 5 atopy; **16** immediate allergy; **21** type I allergic reaction
atopy: 13 atopic allergy; **16** immediate allergy; **21** type I allergic reaction
ATP: 21 adenosine triphosphate
atrabilious: 7 bilious; **8** liverish; **9** dyspeptic, woebegone; **15** hypochondriacal
atrial auricle: 7 auricle; **13** auricula atrii
atrip: 6 aweigh
at risk: 7 at peril, in peril; **8** at hazard, in danger; **9** imperiled; **10** endangered, in jeopardy, threatened
atrium dextrum: 11 right atrium
atrium sinistrum: 10 left atrium
atrocious: 4 ugly; **5** awful; **7** heinous, painful; **8** accursed, dreadful, grievous, horrible, shocking, terrible; **9** frightful, incarnate, monstrous; **10** abominable, flagitious, horrifying; **11** unspeakable
atrociously: 7 awfully; **8** rottenly, terribly; **9** abysmally; **10** abominably; **12** outrageously
atrociousness: 8 atrocity; **9** barbarity; **11** heinousness; **13** barbarousness
atrocity: 6 infamy; **7** outrage; **8** enormity, ferocity, savagery; **9** barbarity, brutality, depravity, flagrancy; **10** inhumanity, truculence; **11** heinousness, viciousness; **13** atrociousness, barbarousness
Atropa: 11 genus Atropa
Atropa belladonna: 10 belladonna; **16** deadly nightshade
atrophic arthritis: 10 rheumatism; **19** rheumatoid arthritis
atrophied: 6 wasted; **10** diminished
atrophy: 6 blight, dry rot; **7** wasting; **8** cachexia [Med], collapse; **9** withering; **11** moth and rust, wasting away
Atrovent: 18 ipratropium bromide
at sixes and sevens: 6 at feud, at odds; **7** at issue; **10** at variance; **11** at high words; **13** at loggerheads

Attacapa: 7 Atakapa; **8** Atakapan; **9** Attacapan

attach: 3 fix; **4** bind; **5** affix, charm, seize, twist; **6** clinch, commit, enamor, endear, fasten, secure, seduce; **7** attract, bewitch, impound; **8** distrain, make fast, saddle on; **9** captivate, enrapture, fascinate, sequester; **10** confiscate; **11** turn the head

attache: 6 legate, nuncio; **11** attache case; **15** charge d'affaires [Fr]

attached: 7 sessile; **9** committed, connected; **10** affiliated

attaching: 7 joining; **8** junction, ligating, ligation; **10** attachment, connecting

attachment: 4 bond; **5** heart; **7** joining; **8** junction, ligating, ligation; **9** adherence, attaching, fastening; **10** connecting, fond regard; **12** Platonic love; **13** brotherly love

attack: 4 fire, flak; **5** blast, onset, round, set on, snipe; **6** assail, onrush; **7** aggress, assault, attempt, lash out; **8** approach; **9** onslaught; **10** visitation; **12** plan of attack; **13** tone-beginning

attack aircraft: 7 fighter; **15** fighter aircraft

attacker: 9 aggressor, assailant

attacking: 7 offense; **9** offensive; **10** aggression, aggressive, assaultive

attain: 3 hit; **4** gain, make; **5** reach; **7** achieve; **8** arrive at; **10** accomplish

attainable: 7 getable; **8** gettable; **10** accessible, come-at-able, obtainable; **11** within reach

attainder: 5 taint; **10** civil death

attainment: 5 skill; **11** acquirement, acquisition; **14** accomplishment

attaint: 5 shame; **8** disgrace, dishonor; **9** dishonour, proscribe; **10** confiscate; **11** sequestrate

attaintment: 9 attainder

attar of roses: 7 rose oil

attemper: 4 dash; **5** blend, cross, tinge; **6** season; **8** medicate, sprinkle, tincture; **10** besprinkle, infiltrate

attempt: 2 go; **3** try; **4** seek, shot; **5** assay, essay, tempt, trial; **6** attack, effort, strive; **7** venture; **8** endeavor, set about; **9** endeavour, undertake

attempted: 5 tried; **7** essayed

attend: 3 see; **4** go to, hang, look, tend; **5** serve, treat; **6** advert, assist, look on, wait on; **7** coexist, give ear, pay heed; **8** attend to, take care; **9** accompany

attendant: 5 usher; **6** fellow; **8** follower; **9** accessory, obbligato; **10** incidental; **11** concomitant; **12** accompanying, incidental to

attended: 8 tended to; **11** accompanied

attender: 6 patron; **10** frequenter

attend to: 5 serve; **6** assist, attend, wait on; **11** take to heart

attention: 3 aid; **4** care; **7** tending; **8** approval, sanction; **9** alertness, attending; **10** advertence, advertency, estimation; **11** approbation, good opinion; **13** attentiveness, consideration

attention to detail: 10 minuteness; **12** thoroughness; **13** assiduousness, particularity

attentive: 7 heedful, mindful; **9** regardful; **10** thoughtful

attentiveness: 4 heed; **6** regard; **9** alertness, attention; **10** advertence, advertency

attenuate: 5 faded, lower; **6** rarefy, weaken; **7** cut back, cut down; **8** weakened; **9** extenuate; **10** attenuated

attenuated: 5 faded; **8** barebone, rawboned, weakened; **9** attenuate, shriveled; **10** extenuated

attest: 4 cite, seal, sign; **5** quote; **7** certify, testify; **8** evidence, manifest; **11** bear witness, demonstrate, sign and seal

attestant: 7 witness

attestation: 4 hand, mark; **9** affidavit, autograph, signature; **10** autography, deposition; **11** endorsement

attested: 6 avowed; **10** attested to, documented; **13** authenticated

Attic: 7 correct, elegant; **8** artistic, polished; **9** classical; **10** Ciceronian, well-styled; **14** Classical Greek

attic: 4 bean, loft, pure; **5** witty; **6** chaste, dormer, garret, noggin, noodle; **8** cockloft, house top, top floor; **9** classical; **10** clerestory, unaffected, upper story; **11** quick-witted; **12** nimble-witted

Attila: 3 Hun

attire: 3 rig; **4** garb, robe, vest; **5** array, drape, dress, fig up, get up, prink, tog up; **6** clothe, deck up, enrobe, fig out, fit out, rig out, tog out; **7** apparel, clothes, deck out, dress up, fancy up, gussy up, trick up; **8** clothing, garments, trick out; **9** overdress; **14** wearing apparel

attitude: 4 mood, pose, vein; **5** humor; **6** animus, aspect; **7** posture; **8** position; **9** situation, viewpoint; **11** disposition, frame of mind, orientation

attollent: 7 rampant, stilted

attorney: 6 lawyer; **8** advocate; **9** solicitor; **12** legal counsel

attorney at law: 7 counsel; **10** counsellor; **15** counsellor at law

attract: 4 draw, lure, move, pull; **5** charm, fetch, tempt; **6** allure, appeal, attach, beckon, draw in, draw on, enamor, endear, entice, induce, pull in, seduce; **7** beguile, bewitch; **9** captivate, enrapture, fascinate, titillate

attracting: 6 luring; **7** drawing; **8** alluring, enticing, inviting, tempting; **10** attractive

attraction: 4 draw; **5** fancy; **6** luring, magnet; **8** enticing; **9** seduction; **10** allurement, enticement, inducement, temptation; **11** be-

nation; **12** pulling force

attractive: 6 luring; **7** drawing, winning; **8** alluring, enticing, inviting, magnetic, tempting; **9** seductive; **10** attracting; **11** interesting

attractiveness: 6 allure; **8** sexiness; **10** attraction; **12** pulling force; **14** persuasiveness

attribute: 5 trait; **6** aspect, assign, impute, virtue; **7** ability, ascribe, faculty, feature, quality; **8** property; **9** dimension, endowment; **11** give a reason, rationalize; **12** assign a cause; **13** qualification; **14** characteristic

attribute to: 5 blame, lay to; **7** point to, refer to, trace to; **8** assign to, charge on, charge to, credit to, ground on, impute to; **9** ascribe to, put down to, set down to; **11** bring home to

attrite: 6 reduce; **15** reduce the mass of

attrited: 4 worn; **5** filed; **7** abraded, scraped; **8** debrided, worn down

attrition: 8 abrasion, grinding; **9** corrasion, detrition; **10** rubbing off, wearing off; **12** contriteness

attune: 3 set; **5** prime; **13** trim one's foils; **16** sharpen one's tools

attuned: 5 keyed, tuned

attuned to: 6 used to; **7** given to; **10** addicted to, habituated

atypical: 9 irregular, untypical; **11** exceptional; **13** nonconforming, unconformable

Au: 4 gold

AU: 16 Astronomical Unit

aubergine: 7 brinjal; **8** eggplant, mad apple; **9** garden egg; **12** eggplant bush; **16** Solanum melongena

au bon droit: 6 fairly, justly; **7** equably; **8** in equity, in reason; **9** a bon droit [Fr], in justice

auburn: 3 bay; **6** dapple, russet; **8** brunette, chestnut, cinnamon, nut-brown; **12** reddish-brown

au contraire: 9 per contra; **13** on the contrary

au courant: 4 up on, up to; **6** au fait; **7** alive to; **9** abreast of, in fashion; **10** up to date on; **11** fashionable

auction: 4 roup; **6** vendue; **10** auction off, auctioneer; **11** auction sale; **12** Dutch auction; **13** auction bridge

auctorial: 9 authorial

audacious: 5 brave, sassy, saucy; **6** brassy, brazen, daring; **7** aweless; **8** fearless, impudent, insolent, intrepid; **9** barefaced, bodacious, bold-faced, dauntless, shameless, unabashed, unfearing, venturous; **11** brazen-faced, venturesome

audacity: 6 daring, hutzpa, spirit; **8** chutz-

pah, temerity; **9** gallantry, impudence; **10** high spirit; **11** intrepidity, presumption; **12** intrepidness; **13** audaciousness; **14** overconfidence

Auden: 15 Wystan Hugh Auden

au desespoir: 4 gone; **7** forlorn; **8** desolate, hopeless; **9** desperate, in despair; **10** despairing

audible: 8 hearable

audience: 7 hearing; **8** auditory; **9** interview, reception; **12** consultation; **13** conversazione [It]

audio: 5 sound; **14** audio frequency

audio CD: 16 audio compact disc

audio compact disc: 7 audio CD

audio recording: 14 sound recording

audit: 6 review; **7** inspect; **8** overhaul; **9** take stock; **10** field audit, scrutinize; **12** pass in review; **13** check the books; **14** audited account, verify accounts

audited account: 5 audit

auditing: 9 listening

audition: 6 try out, tryout; **7** hearing; **12** auscultation; **13** auditory sense; **14** sense of hearing; **16** auditory modality

auditor: 6 hearer; **7** actuary; **8** listener; **10** accountant, bookkeeper; **11** bean counter [derogatory]; **12** night student; **15** part-time student

auditorium: 3 pit; **5** boxes, forum; **6** stalls; **7** gallery, parquet, theater; **8** auditory; **11** lecture hall; **12** amphitheater

auditory aphasia: 12 word deafness; **15** acoustic aphasia

auditory canal: 8 ear canal; **14** acoustic meatus, auditory meatus; **21** external auditory canal

auditory sensation: 5 sound

auditory sense: 7 hearing; **8** audition; **14** sense of hearing; **16** auditory modality

auditory tube: 14 Eustachian tube

Audubon warbler: 15 Audubon's warbler; **17** Dendroica auduboni

au fait: 4 up on, up to; **5** crack; **6** good at; **7** alive to; **8** at home in, master of; **9** abreast of, au courant; **10** up to date on; **11** a good hand at; **12** accomplished, thoroughbred; **14** conversant with

au fond: 8 at bottom, in effect; **9** basically, in essence, in the main, virtually; **11** essentially, practically; **13** fundamentally, substantially

auf wiedersehen: 3 bye; **4** ciao; **5** adieu, adios, aloha; **6** bye-bye, good-by, so long; **7** cheerio, good day, good-bye; **8** au revoir, farewell, sayonara; **10** dosvidanya [Russ]; **11** arrivederci, leave taking, valediction; **12** hasta la vista [Sp]

Aug: 6 August

Augean stable: 3 den, sty; **4** lair; **6** pigsty; **16** sink of corruption

Augean task: 13 Herculean task

auger: borer, drill, snake; **6** gimlet, wimble; **10** screw auger; **13** plumber's snake

aught: 3 any, nil, nix, zip; **4** a few, nada, some, zero; **5** zilch; **6** cipher, cypher, naught; **7** nothing; **8** goose egg; **10** more or less; **12** quantitative

augment: 5 add to; **7** enlarge; **10** make larger; **12** augmentation, render larger

augmentation: 4 gain; **7** augment; **8** increase; **9** increment; **13** amplification

augmenting: 8 building; **12** augmentative

augur: 4 bode, omen, seer; **5** drill; **6** auspex, oil rig, typify; **7** betoken, point to, portend, predict, presage, prophet, signify; **8** forebode, forecast, foretell; **9** auspicate, foretoken, prefigure; **10** foreshadow, prophesier, soothsayer; **11** shadow forth; **13** prognosticate

augury: 4 omen, sign; **7** auspice, portent, presage; **10** prognostic

August: 3 Aug

august: 5 grand, noble, proud; **6** lordly; **7** revered, stately, sublime; **8** majestic, princely; **9** dignified, honorable, venerable; **10** worshipful

Augusta: 14 capital of Maine

Augustine: 14 Saint Augustine; **21** Saint Augustine of Hippo

Augustus: 8 Octavian; **15** Gaius Octavianus; **27** Gaius Julius Caesar Octavianus

auld lang syne: 8 lang syne, old times; **14** the good old days

Aum: 2 Om

au naturel: 4 bare, nude; **5** naked

aunt: 5 aunty; **6** auntie

aura: 3 air; **4** halo; **5** glory; **6** nimbus; **10** atmosphere; **11** titillation

aurar: 5 eyrir (plural)

aureate: 4 gilt, gold; **5** showy; **6** florid, gilded, golden; **10** flamboyant; **11** gold-colored

aurelia: 6 cocoon, orphan

aureole: 4 halo; **5** glory; **6** corona, nimbus; **7** aureola

aureolin: 11 yellow ocher

au reste: 4 more, plus; **5** extra; **10** in addition

au revoir: 3 bye; **5** adieu, adios; **6** bye-bye, good-by, so long; **7** cheerio, good day, good-bye; **8** sayonara; **11** arrivederci; **14** auf wiedersehen

auric: 6 aurous

auricle: 3 ear, lug; **5** pinna; **13** atrial auricle, auricula atrii; **14** acoustic organs

auricular: 5 close, privy; **7** in petto, private; **8** auditory; **9** inviolate; **11** clandestine

auriferous: 11 gold-bearing

auriform: 9 ear-shaped

aurist: 7 oculist

aurochs: 4 urus; **6** wisent; **12** Bison bonasus; **14** Bos primigenius

aurora: 4 dawn; **5** sunup; **7** dawning, morning, sunrise; **8** cockcrow, daybreak; **9** peep of day; **10** break of day, first light; **11** polar lights

aurora australis: 14 southern lights

aurora borealis: 14 northern lights

aurous: 5 auric

aurum: 4 gold

auscultation: 7 hearing; **8** audition

auspicate: 4 bode, omen; **5** augur; **7** betoken, portend, predict, presage; **8** forecast, foretell; **9** prefigure; **10** foreshadow; **13** prognosticate

auspice: 4 omen, sign; **6** augury; **7** fortune, portent, presage; **10** prognostic

auspices: 5 aegis; **9** patronage; **10** protection

auspicious: 4 ripe; **5** happy, lucky; **9** favorable, fortunate; **10** convenient, favourable, propitious, prosperous; **11** de bon augure [Fr], encouraging; **12** providential

Aussie: 10 Australian

austere: 5 harsh, stark, stern; **6** severe; **7** ascetic, exigent, spartan; **8** exacting, obdurate, rigorous; **9** ascetical, demanding, hard-nosed, hard-shell [U.S.], searching, unsparing; **10** hard-headed, inexorable, inflexible; **11** puritanical; **14** uncompromising

austerity: 8 acerbity; **9** hard lines; **10** asceticism, puritanism; **11** hard measure; **12** hard measures; **13** nonindulgence

Austerlitz: 18 battle of Austerlitz

Austin: 14 capital of Texas

Austral: 8 Southern; **9** antarctic

Australian: 6 Aussie; **20** Aboriginal Australian

Austral Islands: 13 Tubuai Islands

Austria: 11 Oesterreich

Austromancy: 7 by winds

autarchy: 7 autarky; **9** autocracy

autarky: 8 autarchy

authentic: 4 real, true; **7** genuine, regular; **8** bona fide, faithful, official, reliable; **9** veritable; **10** legitimate; **13** authoritative; **14** unquestionable

authenticate: 6 verify; **8** make good; **9** establish; **12** substantiate

authenticated: 8 attested; **10** documented

authentication: 6 docket; **7** voucher, warrant; **8** hallmark; **9** assay-mark; **11** certificate; **12** verification; **13** certification

authenticity: 8 validity; **9** bona fides; **10** legitimacy; **11** genuineness

author: 5 draft; **6** draw up, indite, source,

writer; **7** compose; **9** architect, authoress, formulate, generator; **11** litterateur [Fr]

author's proof: 10 press proof; **11** galley proof

authorial: 9 auctorial

authorisation: 11 empowerment; **13** authorization

authoritarian: 8 despotic, dictator; **10** autocratic, tyrannical; **11** dictatorial, overbearing

authoritarianism: 7 tyranny; **9** Caesarism, despotism, monocracy, shogunate, Stalinism; **10** absolutism, one-man rule; **12** dictatorship; **15** totalitarianism

authoritative: 8 official; **9** authentic, classical, executive, important; **10** authorized, definitive; **14** administrative

authorities: 6 regime; **8** official; **9** authority; **10** government; **14** person in charge; **17** person in authority

authority: 4 sway; **5** power, say-so; **6** agency, bureau, master, office, oracle, teller; **7** charter, delator, mastery, precept, relator; **8** exponent, luminary, official, reporter, sanction, sureness, validity, warranty; **9** assurance, dominance, informant; **10** confidence, esprit fort, mastership, mouthpiece; **11** authorities [pl]; **12** shining light; **13** applicability, authorization, self-assurance; **14** person in charge, self-confidence

authorization: 5 leave; **7** mandate; **9** authority; **10** permission, permitting; **11** authorizing, empowerment; **13** authorisation

authorize: 4 pass; **5** clear; **7** warrant; **9** authorise

authorized: 7 allowed; **8** licensed; **9** allowable, legalized, permitted; **10** sanctioned; **11** permissible; **13** authoritative

authorship: 7 penning, writing; **11** composition, publication

auto: 3 car; **7** autocar, machine; **8** motorcar; **10** automobile

autobus: 3 bus; **5** coach; **6** jitney; **7** omnibus; **8** motorbus; **9** charabanc; **10** motorcoach; **12** double-decker

autochthonous: 7 endemic; **10** indigenous; **12** autochthonal, autochthonic

autocracy: 8 autarchy, autonomy; **9** despotism; **10** absolutism, one-man rule; **12** dictatorship, unlawful rule; **13** arbitrary rule

autocrat: 6 despot, tyrant; **8** dictator; **9** strong man

autocratic: 5 bossy; **8** despotic; **10** dominating, peremptory, tyrannical; **11** dictatorial, magisterial; **12** aristocratic, autocratical; **13** authoritarian, high-and-mighty

autocue: 7 autocue; **8** prompter; **12** teleprompter

auto da fe: 9 holocaust; **10** immolation

auto driver: 8 motorist

autoeroticism: 7 onanism; **9** self-abuse; **11** autoerotism; **12** masturbation; **17** self-gratification

autogenesis: 8 autogeny; **11** abiogenesis; **21** spontaneous generation

autogenic: 10 autogenous

autogenics: 16 autogenic therapy; **17** autogenic training

autogeny: 11 abiogenesis, autogenesis; **21** spontaneous generation

autograph: 4 hand, mark; **8** inscribe; **9** signature; **10** autography; **11** attestation, endorsement, John Hancock

autogyro: 8 autogiro; **9** gryoplane

autoloading: 11 self-loading; **13** semiautomatic

Autolycus: 6 cadger, hawker, pedlar; **7** camelot [Fr], peddler; **8** huckster; **9** trickster; **10** colporteur; **12** artful dodger

automated: 13 machine-driven; **17** machine-controlled

automated teller machine: 3 ATM; **11** cash machine; **13** cash dispenser; **15** automated teller, automatic teller; **22** automatic teller machine

automatic: 5 blind; **6** reflex; **9** reflexive, robotlike; **10** mechanical; **11** instinctive, involuntary, machinelike

automatically: 12 mechanically

automatic data processing: 3 ADP

automatic drive: 21 automatic transmission

automatic rifle: 9 automatic; **10** machine gun; **12** machine rifle

automatic transmission: 14 automatic drive

automation: 8 high-tech; **13** mechanisation, mechanization; **14** high technology

automobile: 3 car; **4** auto; **7** autocar, machine; **8** motor car, motorcar

automobile mechanic: 8 mechanic; **11** car-mechanic; **12** auto-mechanic, grease monkey

automobilist: 8 motorist

automotive: 13 self-propelled

autonomous: freehold; **9** sovereign; **11** independent, self-reliant; **12** self-directed; **13** self-governing

autonomy: 7 liberty; **9** autocracy; **12** self-reliance; **13** self-direction; **14** self-government; **15** self-sufficiency

autophyte: 9 autotroph; **15** autophytic plant; **19** autotrophic organism

autophytic: 11 autotrophic

autopsy: 2 PM; **8** necropsy; **10** postmortem

autoptical: 7 evident, obvious; **8** palpable, striking; **10** pronounced; **11** indubitable, self-evident; **12** recognizable, unmistakable

autosome: 17 somatic chromosome

autosuggestion: 12 self-hypnosis; **14** self-suggestion

autotroph: 9 autophyte; **15** autophytic plant; **19** autotrophic organism

autumn: 4 fall

autumnal equinox: 11 fall equinox; **16** September equinox

aux abois: 5 at bay; **7** up a tree

auxiliary: 4 aide; **6** aiding; **7** adjunct, helpful; **8** adjuvant, co-worker, confrere; **9** accessory, ancillary, assistant, assisting, guardsman; **10** cooperator, life guards, subsidiary; **11** appurtenant, concomitant; **12** collaborator, supplemental; **13** auxiliary verb, supplementary; **14** reserve soldier, weekend soldier

avail: 2 do; **3** use; **4** help, work; **5** serve, stead; **6** answer, resort; **7** be of use, service; **8** be useful, recourse; **10** take effect; **11** be effective, be of service; **13** functionality

available: 5 handy, ready; **6** at hand, usable; **7** useable; **8** tangible; **11** uncommitted

avalanche: 7 debacle; **8** landslip, roll down; **9** landslide

avant-garde: 3 van; **6** daring; **8** vanguard

avant-propos: 5 proem; **6** prefix; **7** preface, prelude; **8** foreword, preamble, prologue; **9** prolepsis [Gram]; **11** prolegomena; **12** introduction

avarice: 5 greed; **7** avidity, craving; **8** avaritia, cupidity, grasping, rapacity; **10** greediness; **12** covetousness, ravenousness

avaricious: 5 venal; **6** grabby, greedy; **7** craving; **8** covetous, grasping, ravenous, usurious; **9** insatiate, mercenary, rapacious; **10** insatiable, prehensile, quenchless; **11** acquisitive; **12** extortionate, unquenchable

avatar: 10 embodiment; **11** incarnation

avaunt: 2 go; **4** fade, pass; **5** be off!; **6** vanish; **8** dissolve, fade away, melt away, vaporize; **9** disappear, evaporate, go your way!; **10** off with you!; **11** away with you!

ave!: 2 hi! [informal]; **4** hail!; **5** hello, howdy! [Western U.S.]; **7** welcome!, well met!; **8** greeting; **11** how do you do?

avellan: 8 avellane

Ave Maria: 8 Hail Mary; **11** the Hail Mary

Avena: 3 oat; **10** genus Avena

avenge: 7 revenge, get even; **9** retaliate, vindicate

avenger: 10 retaliator, vindicator

avenging: 8 rigorous, vengeful; **9** rancorous; **10** revengeful, vindictive; **11** retributive, retributory, vindicatory

aventail: 6 camail; **7** ventail

aventurine: 8 sunstone

avenue: 7 channel, passage; **8** approach, parterre; **9** arboretum, boulevard

aver: 3 say; **4** avow, swan; **5** state, swear; **6** affirm, allege, assert; **7** declare, profess; **9** predicate

average: 2 OK; **3** mid; **4** fair, mean, norm, so-so; **5** modal; **6** medial, median, medium, mesial [Med]; middle; **8** adequate, bearable, mediocre, middling, ordinary, passable; **9** tolerable; **10** acceptable, admissible, average out, couci-couci; **11** indifferent, take the mean; **12** intermediate; **13** reduce to a mean, take an average; **15** unobjectionable

average Joe: 9 common man; **10** average man, Joe six-pack; **12** common person; **13** average person

average person: 9 common man; **10** average Joe, average man, Joe six-pack; **12** common person; **14** man in the street

averment: 9 assertion, statement; **10** allegation, profession; **11** declaration, predication; **12** asseveration

Averrhoa: 7 bilimbi; **9** carambola; **13** genus Averrhoa

averse: 4 loth; **5** loath, shy of; **9** reluctant; **10** indisposed, not content; **11** disinclined; **12** antipathetic; **14** antipathetical

aversion: 8 distaste; **9** antipathy, bête noire; **11** abomination

avert: 5 avoid, debar; **7** deflect, fend off, head off, obviate, ward off; **8** stave off, turn away

averuncate: 6 root up, uproot; **7** root out

Aves: 9 class Aves

aves: 15 feathered tribes

Avesta: 6 Avesta; **10** Zendavesta

aviary: 6 volary; **13** bird sanctuary

aviate: 3 fly; **5** pilot

aviation: 3 air; **6** flight, flying; **8** air power; **9** air travel

aviation engineer: 20 aeronautical engineer

aviation engineering: 11 aeronautics; **24** aeronatuiical engineering

aviator: 5 flier, flyer; **6** airman; **8** aeronaut; **15** aerial navigator

aviatrix: 8 airwoman; **9** aviatress

avid: 4 keen; **5** eager, great; **6** greedy; **7** anxious, zealous; **8** esurient; **9** devouring

avidity: 5 greed; **7** avarice, craving; **8** avidness, cupidity, grasping, keenness, rapacity, venality; **9** eagerness; **10** greediness; **12** covetousness, ravenousness

avid reader: 9 book lover; **11** bibliophile

avifaunal: 12 avifaunistic

avis: 4 bird; **15** feathered friend

aviso: 4 news, word; **6** advice; **7** message, tidings; **11** piece of news; **12** intelligence

avocado: 11 avocado pear, avocado tree; **13** alligator pear; **15** Persea Americana

avocado tree: 7 avocado; **15** Persea Americana

avocation: 5 hobby; **6** by-line; **8** sideline; **17** spare-time activity; **19** spare-time occupation

avoid: 4 shun, void; **5** annul, avert, debar, quash; **7** deflect, fend off, head off, keep off, nullify, obviate, ward off; **8** keep from, stave off; **10** desist from, invalidate; **11** abstain from, forbear from, keep clear of, refrain from; **12** steer clear of

avoidable: 8 evitable

avoidance: 7 dodging; **8** shunning; **11** turning away

avoid one's duty: 5 shirk; **13** evade one's duty, shirk one's duty

avoirdupois: 3 fat; **7** fatness; **8** by weight; **9** heaviness; **17** avoirdupois weight

avow: 3 own; **4** aver, swan; **5** admit, allow, grant, swear, vouch; **6** affirm, assert, assure, avouch; **7** certify, concede, confess, warrant; **10** asseverate; **11** acknowledge

avowal: 8 owning up; **9** admission, conceding; **10** affirmance, concession; **11** affirmation; **13** acknowledging; **14** acknowledgment

avowed: 5 bared; **8** attested; **9** confessed, professed

avowedly: 4 true; **10** admittedly; **11** confessedly, professedly

a vue d'oeil: 9 before one, in one's eye

await: 4 look, loom, wait; **6** come on, expect; **8** approach, threaten; **17** stare one in the face

awaited: 8 hoped-for; **11** anticipated

awake: 4 wake; **5** acute, alert, alive, quick, waken; **6** arouse, awaken, wake up; **7** on watch, wakeful; **8** vigilant, watchful; **9** come alive, wide awake; **10** on the alert

awaken: 4 wake; **5** awake, rouse, waken; **6** advise, arouse, wake up; **7** apprise; **9** come alive, enlighten

award: 5 award, grant, honor, prize; **6** accord, assign, honour, report, trophy; **7** laurels, present, tribute; **8** accolade, awarding, estimate; **9** arbitrate; **17** bestow an award upon

awarder: 8 bestower; **9** presenter

awarding: 5 award; **10** presenting; **11** presentment; **12** presentation

aware: 7 knowing, mindful, witting; **9** cognisant, cognizant, conscious; **13** knowledgeable

awareness: 9 sentience; **10** cognizance; **11** knowingness; **13** consciousness

aware of: 7 alive to, awake to; **8** noticing; **11** cognizant of, conscious of

awash: 6 afloat; **7** flooded; **9** inundated; **11** overflowing

awash in: 10 swimming in; **14** over one's head in, up to one's ears in, up to one's eyes in, up to one's neck in

away: 2 by; **3** off, out; **4** gone; **5** aside, forth; **7** outside; **8** departed, from home; **11** nonresident

away game: 8 road game

awe: 6 dazzle, dismay, impose; **7** overawe; **9** reverence; **10** admiration, inspire awe, veneration

aweary: 5 weary

aweigh: 5 atrip

aweless: 5 sassy, saucy; **6** awless; **8** fearless, impudent; **9** audacious, dauntless, shameless, unabashed; **10** irreverent; **13** disrespectful

awestruck: 4 awed; **7** in awe of; **10** moonstruck; **11** awestricken; **12** planet-struck; **13** thunderstruck

awful: 4 awed, dire, soft; **5** awing, dread, nasty; **6** solemn; **7** amazing, awesome, awfully, direful, dreaded, fearful, painful; **8** dreadful, fearsome, horrific, terrible, terribly; **9** atrocious, deathlike; **10** abominable, horrendous; **11** frightening, frightfully, unspeakable; **12** awe-inspiring

awfully: 5 awful; **8** famously, horribly, rottenly, terribly; **9** abysmally, amazingly, glaringly, strangely; **10** abominably, dreadfully, incredibly; **11** atrociously, egregiously, frightfully, marvelously, prominently, wonderfully; **12** emphatically, stupendously, surprisingly, tremendously; **13** astonishingly, extravagantly

awkward: 4 rude; **5** gross, heavy, inapt, inept, rough; **6** clumsy, rugged, sticky, uneasy; **7** cramped, rickety, spastic, unhandy; **8** lubberly, ungainly, unwieldy; **9** graceless, ill at ease, ill-chosen, inelegant, maladroit, slouching; **10** bunglesome, cumbersome, unenviable, ungraceful, unpolished; **11** floundering, heavy-handed; **12** embarrassing; **13** uncoordinated

awkwardness: 8 delicacy, slowness; **9** gaucherie, ineptness, stiffness; **10** clumsiness, inelegance, ineptitude, want of tact; **11** lack of grace, lack of style; **12** lack of polish, unwieldiness; **13** gracelessness, inconvenience, maladroitness, nuisance value; **14** cumbersomeness

awl: 7 bradawl; **9** awl-shaped

awn: 3 bur; **4** burr; **7** bristle

awned: 7 bearded

awning: 4 tent, tilt; **7** marquee, parasol; **8** sunblind, sunshade, umbrella;

AWOL: 6 truant; **18** absent without leave

awry: 3 wry; **5** amiss, askew, wonky, wrong; **7** crooked, haywire; **8** cockeyed, lopsided; **9** the matter; **10** out of joint, out of order, out of shape

ax: 3 axe; **4** bill

axe: 2 ax; **4** rive; **5** split; **6** cleave

axeman: 8 headsman

axerophthol: 1 A; **7** retinol; **8** vitamin A; **9** vitamin A1; **16** vitamin A1 alcohol

axial: 5 axile, focal; **7** azygous; **9** umbilical; **10** concentric

axilla: 6 armpit; 13 axillary fossa; 14 axillary cavity

axillary: 4 alar

axiom: 5 maxim; 7 theorem; 11 proposition

axiomatic: 7 evident; 10 aphoristic; 11 axiomatical, self-evident; 13 postulational; 15 taken for granted

axis: 3 hub; 4 bloc, nave; 12 axis vertebra

axle: 4 pole; 5 arbor; 7 spindle; 8 axletree

axolotl: 8 mud puppy; 18 Ambystoma mexicanum

axon: 5 axone

axone: 4 axon

ay: 3 aye, yea, yes

ayah: 5 biddy, bonne [Fr], nanny, nurse; 9 catsitter, dogsitter; 10 babysitter

ayatollah: 6 mullah; 7 muezzin

aye: 2 ay; 3 yea, yes; 4 ever; 6 always; 8 eternity, evermore; 10 perpetuity; 11 immortality

Aythya: 4 duck; 5 scaup; 7 pochard; 10 canvasback; 11 genus Aythya

AZ: 7 azimuth

Azadirachta: 4 neem; 16 genus Azadirachta

azathioprine: 6 Imuran

azedarach: 9 China tree; 10 chinaberry; 12 Persian lilac, pride-of-India; 14 chinaberry tree, Melia azedarach, Melia azederach

Azerbaijan: 12 Azerbajdzhan; 19 Azerbaijani Republic

azidothymidine: 3 AZT; 10 zidovudine

azimuth: 2 AZ; 8 altitude

azoic: 7 abiotic; 9 nonliving; 11 abiological

azoimide: 2 HN; 13 hydrazoic acid

Azolla: 4 fern; 11 genus Azolla

azo radical: 8 azo group

azotaemia: 6 uremia; 7 uraemia; 8 azotemia

azote: 5 quirt; 7 rawhide

azotemia: 6 uremia; 7 uraemia; 9 azotaemia

AZT: 10 zidovudine; 14 azidothymidine

aztreonam: 7 Azactam

azure: 4 blue; 7 sky-blue; 8 blueness, cerulean, lazuline, sapphire; 10 bright blue

azygos: 7 azygous

azygous: 3 odd; 5 axial, focal; 6 azygos, unique; 8 singular; 9 umbilical; 10 concentric; 12 first and last

B

B: 1 3, 3 bel; 4 good; 5 boron, type B; 6 group B; 7 bacilli; 8 B complex, B vitamin, bacillus, vitamin B

B.A.: 14 bachelor of arts

B.C.: 12 before Christ

B.O.: 8 body odor; 9 body odour

B.S.: 17 Bachelor of Science

B.T.U.: 4 kW-hr; 12 kilowatt hour; 16 Board of Trade unit; 18 British Thermal Unit

BA: 2 AB; 14 Bachelor of Arts; 18 Artium Baccalaurens

Ba: 6 barium

baa: 3 cry; 4 blat; 5 blate, bleat; 9 ululation

Baal: 3 Bel; 5 Belus; 8 Asteroth

baba au rhum: 7 rum baba

babassu: 11 babassu palm, coco de macao; 16 Orbignya martiana, Orbignya spesiosa; 17 Orbignya phalerata

babassu oil: 9 babacu oil

babbitt: 12 Babbitt metal

babble: 3 hum; 4 blab, flow, purl, sing, talk; 5 peach, spray, spurt; 6 bubble, burble, gabble, gurgle, hot air, jabber, murmur, ripple, tattle; 7 blab out, blather, blether,

blither, breathe, smatter, sputter; 8 babbling, verbiage; 9 babble out, mere words; 11 regurgitate

babbling: 5 inept, silly; 6 babble; 7 blatant, fatuous, foolish, idiotic, prating; 8 gabbling, imbecile; 9 driveling, insensate, jabbering, prattling, senseless, twaddling; 10 blathering, blithering, chattering, irrational; 11 nonsensical

babe: 4 baby; 6 infant; 10 babe in arms

Babinski reflex: 8 Babinski; 12 Babinski sign

babirusa: 9 babirussa; 10 babiroussa; 18 Babyrousa Babyrussa

babish: 7 babyish; 8 childish; 9 child-like, infantile

babu: 5 baboo; 6 scribe; 9 secretary; 10 amanuensis; 12 stenographer

babushka: 5 snood; 8 kerchief; 19 elderly Russian woman

baby: 3 new, sop; 4 babe; 5 child, spoil, young; 6 cocker, coddle, cosset, infant, pamper, sister; 7 indulge, milksop; 8 innocent; 9 infantile; 10 babe in arms, featherbed; 11 mollycoddle

baby's room: 7 nursery

baby buggy: 4 pram [Brit]; **6** go-cart, pusher; **8** carriage, stroller; **9** pushchair; **12** baby carriage, perambulator

baby carriage: 4 pram [Brit]; **6** go-cart, pusher; **8** carriage, stroller; **9** baby buggy, pushchair; **12** perambulator

baby doctor: 10 pediatrist; **12** pediatrician; **13** paediatrician

babyhood: 7 infancy; **9** puerility; **10** simplicity; **14** early childhood

baby linen: 7 layette; **14** swaddling cloth

Babyrousa, Babyrussa: 8 babirusa; **9** babirussa; **10** babiroussa

babysitter: 5 bonne [Fr], nanny, nurse; **6** sitter; **9** catsitter, dogsitter

baby tooth: 9 milk tooth; **12** primary tooth; **14** deciduous tooth

baccalaureate: 13 baccalaureate; **15** bachelor's degree

baccarat: 11 chemin de fer

baccate: 7 berried; **9** berrylike; **11** bacciferous

bacchanal: 4 orgy, riot; **7** bacchic, debauch; **8** bacchant; **9** carousing, orgiastic; **10** debauchery, saturnalia; **11** bacchanalia; **12** bacchanalian; **14** drunken reveler, drunken revelry

Bacchanal: 7 reveler; **8** carouser; **11** thirsty soul; **12** Bacchanalian; **13** tavern haunter

Bacchanalia: 8 Dionysia

bacchic: 9 bacchanal, carousing, orgiastic; **12** bacchanalian

baccilar: 9 bacillary, rod-shaped; **10** baculiform; **11** bacilliform

bach: 8 bachelor

Bach: 19 Johann Sebastian Bach

bachelor: 4 bach; **12** unmarried man

bachelor's button: 10 bluebottle, cornflower; **13** globe amaranth; **15** Centaurea cyanus; **16** Gomphrena globosa

bachelor girl: 4 maid; **12** bachelor lady, girl-bachelor; **14** unmarried woman

bachelorhood: 10 singleness; **11** single state; **14** unmarried state

Bachelor of Arts: 2 AB, BA; **18** Artium Baccalaurens

Bachelor of Arts in Library Science: 4 ABLS

Bachelor of Arts in Nursing: 3 BAN

Bachelor of Divinity: 2 BD

Bachelor of Laws: 3 LLB

Bachelor of Literature: 5 BLitt

Bachelor of Medicine: 2 MB

Bachelor of Music: 4 BMus

Bachelor of Naval Science: 3 BNS

Bachelor of Science: 2 BS, SB

Bachelor of Science in Architecture: 6 BSArch

Bachelor of Theology: 3 ThB

bacillary: 8 baccilar, bacillar; **9** rod-shaped; **10** baculiform; **11** bacilliform

bacillary dysentery: 11 shigellosis

bacillus: 1 B; **3** rod; **7** bacilli; **18** rod-shaped bacterium

back: 4 gage, game, hind, punt, rear; **5** bet on, cover, spine, stake; **6** back up, dorsum, hinder, second; **7** binding, endorse, in reply, indorse, support; **8** back side, backbone, backrest, backward, plump for, plunk for, rearward; **9** backwards, posterior, rearwards; **11** back of torso, book binding, pay the piper; **12** spinal column, substantiate; **15** vertebral column

back and forth: 8 to and fro; **18** backward and forward

backbite: 5 brand; **6** malign

backbiter: 7 defamer, libeler; **8** maligner, satirist, traducer; **9** lampooner, slanderer; **11** calumniator

backbiting: 7 calumny, obloquy, scandal, slander; **9** aspersion; **10** defamation, scurrility; **11** traducement; **12** evil-speaking, vilification

backboard: 19 basketball backboard

backbone: 3 sap; **4** back, grit, guts, pith, sand, soul; **5** spine; **6** anchor, bottom, marrow; **8** gumption, linchpin, lynchpin, mainstay, vertebra; **9** lifeblood, umbilicus, vertebrae; **12** decisiveness, spinal column

backbreaking: 4 hard; **5** heavy; **7** arduous; **8** grueling, toilsome; **9** gruelling, laborious, punishing; **10** labourious

backchat: 6 banter; **8** raillery; **11** give-and-take

backcloth: 8 backdrop; **10** background

back country: 9 backwoods, boondocks; **10** hinterland

backdate: 7 misdate; **8** antedate, postdate

back down: 6 back up, bow out; **7** back off, pull out; **10** chicken out

backdown: 6 ceding; **7** cession; **8** giving up; **9** climb-down, surrender; **10** withdrawal; **11** resignation; **12** capitulating, capitulation, surrendering

backdrop: 9 backcloth; **10** background

back end: 4 rear; **7** rear end; **8** backside

backer: 5 angel; **6** patron; **7** abettor; **8** advocate, champion, lobbyist, partisan, seconder, upholder; **9** supporter; **11** protagonist; **13** friend at court; **14** campaign worker; backfire: **6** trench; **8** backlash; **9** boomerang, firebreak

back-geared: 12 double-geared

background: 5 scene, scope; **6** ground, milieu, offing; **7** desktop, setting; **8** backdrop, play down; **9** backcloth; **10** hinterland; **13** social setting; **16** background signal, screen background; **17** social environment

backgrounder: 17 background session

background level: 10 noise level

backhand: 8 backhand; **10** backhanded; **12** backhand shot, left-slanting; **14** backhand stroke

backhanded: 8 backhand

backhand shot: 8 backhand; **14** backhand stroke

backing: 5 mount; **7** funding, support; **9** patronage; **12** championship; **16** financial backing, financial support

backlash: 6 recoil; **7** rebound; **8** backfire; **12** repercussion

backlog: 3 log; **7** reserve; **9** stockpile

back matter: 9 end matter

backmost: 8 hindmost, rearmost; **10** hindermost

back off: 6 back up, bow out, shrink; **7** pull out; **8** back down, withdraw; **10** chicken out

back out: 7 retreat; **8** back away, crawfish, withdraw

backpack: 4 pack; **8** knapsack, rucksack; **9** haversack

backpacker: 5 hiker

backseat driver: 8 kibitzer

backset: 3 rub; **5** check, cross; **7** reverse, setback [U.S.]; **8** comedown, reversal; **11** contretemps

backslider: 8 deserter, renegade; **9** proselyte; **10** recidivist; **12** reversionist

backsliding: 5 lapse; **7** lapsing, relapse; **8** apostasy; **9** hardening, obliquity, pollution, recusancy, relapsing, reversion, reverting; **10** declension, perversion, recidivism; **11** reprobation, falling back

backspace key: 9 backspace; **10** backspacer

backstage: 4 wing; **8** offstage

back street: 5 alley; **8** alleyway

backswept: 9 sweptback

backsword: 10 broadsword; **16** single-edged sword

backtalk: 3 lip; **4** sass; **5** mouth; **7** sassing

back-to-back: 11 consecutive

backtrack: 8 turn back; **10** double back **16** take the back track

backup: 6 fill-in, relief; **7** stand-in; **9** backup man; **10** substitute; **13** traffic backup; **14** computer backup

back up: 4 back, clog, foul; **5** choke; **6** clog up, hold up; **7** back off, congest, shore up, support; **8** back down, choke off; **9** bolster up, retrocede; **10** retrograde; **11** go backwards, pay the piper; **12** substantiate

backward: 4 back, late, slow; **5** slack, tardy; **6** behind, remiss, slow to; **7** belated, laggard; **8** rearward, untimely; **9** backwards,
rearwards; **10** behindhand, retrograde, unpunctual; **12** feebleminded

backward movement: 7 regress; **10** regression; **13** counter motion, reverse motion

backwardness: 8 slowness

backwards: 4 back; **8** backward, rearward; **9** rearwards

backwards and forwards: 6 seesaw, zigzag; **7** by turns; **8** in and out, to and fro; **9** up and down, vice versa; **10** in exchange; **12** hither and yon; **14** from side to side; **15** mutatis mutandis [Lat]

backwash: 4 race, wake, wash; **9** aftermath, airstream; **10** slipstream

backwoods: 6 remote; **7** outback; **9** boondocks; **10** hinterland; **11** back country

backwoodsman: 7 settler; **8** colonist, forester, squatter, woodsman; **10** woodcutter; **11** mountain man; **12** frontiersman

Bacon: 12 Baron Verulam, Francis Bacon; **17** Viscount St. Albans

bacon-lettuce-tomato sandwich: 3 BLT

bacteremia: 11 bacteriemia; **12** bacteriaemia

bacteria: 8 bacteria; **9** bacterium

bactericide: 12 bacteriacide

bacteriological: 13 bacteriologic

bacteriological warfare: 11 germ warfare

bacteriophage: 5 phage

bacterium: 8 bacteria [pl]

bacterize: 9 bacterise

bacteroid: 10 bacterioid; **11** bacteroidal; **12** bacterioidal

Bacteroidaceae: 20 family Bacteroidaceae

Bacteroides: 16 genus Bacteroides

Bactrian camel: 17 Camelus bactrianus

bad: 3 big, ill; **4** high, poor, weak; **5** badly, fusty, risky, sorry, tough, unfit, wrong; **6** effete, forged, putrid, rancid, rotten, spoilt, strong; **7** badness, corrupt, decayed, gone bad, immoral, reeking, rotting, spoiled, tainted, touched, unsound; **8** high-risk, inferior, insecure, negative, wrongful; **9** defective, putrefied; **10** putrescent; **11** speculative; **12** putrefactive; **13** strong-scented, uncollectible

bad behavior: 9 evildoing; **10** bad conduct, wickedness, wrongdoing; **11** evil conduct, evil courses; **12** evil behavior

bad blood: 6 animus, malice; **7** cruelty, ill will; **8** ill blood; **9** animosity, cruelness, ill nature, malignity; **11** malevolence; **13** maliciousness

bad debt: 7 default; **11** defalcation

bad fairy: 3 nix; **5** nixie; **12** will-o'-the wisp

badge: 9 criterion; **11** counterfoil, countersign

badger: 3 bug, nag; **4** bait, bore; **5** abuse, beset, grind, harry, haunt, hound, tease, worry; **6** bother, harass, heckle, ill-use, infest, molest, pester, plague, pother; **7** oppress; **8** abductor, bullirag, bullyrag, bunko man, ill-treat, maltreat, mistreat; **9** beleaguer, importune, persecute

badger dog: 7 dachsie; **9** dachshund

badgered: 5 beset, bored; **6** baited; **7** harried, heckled; **8** harassed, infested, pothered; **10** importuned, persecuted

badgerer: 7 heckler

badgering: 7 torment; **8** worrying; **11** bedevilment

Badger State: 9 Wisconsin

badinage: 4 joke, quiz, twit; **5** chaff, irony, roast, tease; **6** banter, retort; **8** raillery, ready wit, repartee; **9** smartness; **10** persiflage, quid pro quo

bad language: 12 foul language; **14** strong language

badli: 5 proxy; **6** deputy; **8** delegate; **9** secondary, surrogate; **10** next friend, substitute; **11** locum tenens; **14** representative

bad luck: 6 mishap; **7** hard hap, hard lot, ill luck; **8** evil luck, hard luck; **9** mischance; **10** misfortune; **11** adverse luck, hard fortune

badly: 3 bad, ill; **6** poorly; **7** gravely; **8** severely; **9** harmfully, naughtily, seriously; **10** inexpertly; **11** injuriously, malignantly; **12** perniciously, unskillfully; **13** deleteriously, detrimentally, mischievously, prejudicially; **17** disadvantageously

bad man: 9 miscreant, wrongdoer

bad manners: 8 rudeness; **10** ill manners; **11** brusqueness, discourtesy, ill-breeding; **12** impoliteness

badminton: 7 la grace; **24** battledore and shuttlecock

bad mood: 8 bad humor, ill humor; **9** moodiness; **11** temperament; **14** bad temperament

badmouth: 6 malign; **7** traduce

bad name: 9 bad repute, discredit, disrepute, ill repute; **13** bad reputation

badness: 3 bad; **8** poorness, severity; **10** low quality; **11** balefulness, banefulness, harmfulness, naughtiness, poor quality; **13** injuriousness

bad odds: 7 poor bet; **8** long odds, long shot, poor odds; **9** fat chance [iron], off chance; **10** slim chance; **11** outside shot; **13** outside chance; **14** ghost of a chance; **15** slim possibility

bad odor: 5 fetor, stink; **6** stench; **7** ill name, ill odor, malodor; **8** bad favor, bad smell, foul odor, ill favor

bad situation: 4 pass; **6** pickle, plight; **8** bad state; **9** evil state, poor state; **11** predicament; **12** bad condition; **13** evil condition, poor condition

bad smell: 5 fetor, stink; **6** stench; **7** bad odor, malodor; **8** foul odor

bad spirits: 5 blues, dumps; **7** sadness; **8** darkness, doldrums, the blues, the dumps; **9** dejection, heaviness, tristesse [Fr]; **10**

blue devils, depression, dismalness, gloominess, low spirits, melancholy, somberness; **11** joylessness, melancholia; **12** dejectedness, heart sinking, il pensieroso [It], mournfulness

bad taste: 8 bad taste; **9** vulgarism, vulgarity; **10** mauvis gout [Fr]; **12** unsavoriness; **14** unpalatability

bad temperament: 7 bad mood; **8** bad humor, ill humor; **9** moodiness; **11** temperament

bad-tempered: 5 cross, fiery, fussy, surly, testy; **6** crabby, grumpy, tetchy, touchy; **7** crabbed, grouchy; **8** volatile; **9** irascible, irritable; **11** hot-tempered, ill-tempered

bad vision: 8 dim sight; **9** dull sight, poor sight; **10** poor vision; **12** failing sight; **14** dimsightedness

bad weather: 10 bad weather, inclemency; **13** inclementness; **16** inclement weather

baffle: 3 get; **4** beat, bilk, foil, snub; **5** amaze, cross, queer, spoil; **6** gravel, puzzle, scotch, thwart; **7** flummox, mystify, nonplus, perplex, stupefy, stupify, trounce; **8** bewilder, override, regulate; **9** dumbfound, frustrate; **10** circumvent; **11** baffle board

baffle board: 6 baffle

baffled: 4 lost; **5** at sea, mazed; **6** balked; **7** bemused, mixed-up; **8** confused; **9** befuddled; **10** bewildered, confounded, frustrated; **11** discouraged

bafflement: 10 bemusement, puzzlement; **11** obfuscation; **12** befuddlement, bewilderment; **13** mystification

baffling: 6 knotty; **8** puzzling; **9** enigmatic; **10** mystifying; **11** problematic; **13** problematical

bag: 3 nab, net, sac; **4** base, dish, grip, hook, prig, sack; **5** bulge, catch, filch, get in, purse, put up, steal, udder; **6** bagful, old bag, pilfer, pocket, secure, thieve, valise; **7** handbag, purloin, saccule; **8** cup of tea, suitcase; **9** bring home; **10** pocketbook

bagascosis: 10 bagassosis

bagatelle: 4 pool; **5** curio, fluff; **6** bauble, gewgaw, trifle; **7** bibelot, novelty, trinket, whatnot; **8** chotchke, frippery, gimcrack, kickshaw, nicknack, pingpong, pyramids, whim-wham; **9** billiards, bric-a-brac, frivolity, tchotchke; **10** knickknack; **12** bar billiards

Bagdad: 7 Baghdad; **13** capital of Iraq

bagel: 6 bublik [Russ]

baggage: 3 rig; **4** drab, jade, minx, skit, slut; **5** hussy, wench; **7** demirep, luggage, trollop; **8** harridan, slattern; **11** impedimenta

baggy: 3 lax; **5** loose, slack; **7** relaxed; **8** detached, flapping; **9** streaming; **12** loose-fitting

Baghdad: 6 Bagdad; **13** capital of Iraq
bagman: 6 bagman; **7** roadman; **9** canvasser; **15** collection agent; **17** traveling salesman
bagpiper: 5 piper
bagpipes: 7 bagpipe; **10** melody pipe; **17** union pipeschanter
baguette: 6 baguet
Bahama grass: 4 doob; **5** kweek; **9** star grass; **10** devil grass; **11** scutch
Bahamas: 13 Bahama Islands
Bahasa: 10 Indonesian; **15** Bahasa Indonesia
Bahrain: 7 Bahrain, Bahrein; **13** Bahrain Island, Bahrein Island
baht: 5 tical
bail: 4 bond; **5** billy; **6** beaker; **7** canakin; **8** bail bond
bailiff: 6 beadle, factor; **8** tipstaff; **9** catch-poll, middleman; **10** bum-bailiff
bailiwick: 8 precinct; **16** election district
bairn: 3 kid; **5** child, youth; **6** moppet; **8** children [pl], juvenile, small fry; **9** little one, youngster
bait: 3 bug, cod, rag; **4** bore, hook, lure, nosh, ride, twit, whet; **5** abuse, beset, bribe, decoy, graft, grind, harry, haunt, hound, rally, taunt, tease, worry; **6** badger, bother, come-on, harass, heckle, ill-use, infest, molest, pester, plague, pother, regale; **7** bearing, fulcrum, oppress; **8** bullirag, bullyrag, ill-treat, junk food, maltreat, mistreat; **9** importune, persecute, sweetener, tantalize
baited: 5 beset, bored; **7** harried, heckled; **8** badgered, harassed, infested, pothered; **10** importuned, persecuted
Baja California: 15 Lower California
bake: 3 fry; **5** broil, grill, parch, roast, singe, toast; **6** baking, scorch
baked: 5 adust, burnt; **6** burned; **7** parched; **8** scorched, sunbaked
baked egg: 10 shirred egg; **12** egg en cocotte
baked goods: 9 baked good
bakehouse: 8 hothouse; **10** greenhouse; **12** conservatory
bakelite: 8 Bakelite; **12** phenolic urea
baker's dozen: 2 13; **4** XIII; **8** thirteen; **9** long dozen
baker's yeast: 12 brewer's yeast; **23** Saccharomyces cerevisiae
bakery: 6 baking; **8** bakeshop
baking chocolate: 15 bitter chocolate; **16** cooking chocolate
baking soda: 9 saleratus; **17** bicarbonate of soda, sodium bicarbonate
baksheesh: 3 tip; **7** bakshis; **8** bakshish, gratuity; **10** backsheesh
bakshish: 3 tip; **7** bakshis, douceur [Fr]; **8** gratuity; **9** baksheesh, pourboire, trinkgeld [Ger]; **10** backsheesh, drink money, honorarium

Baku: 19 capital of Azerbaijan
balaclava: 15 balaclava helmet
Balaena: 5 whale; **12** genus Balaena
Balaenoptera: 7 rorqual, finback; **8** fin whale, 9 blue whale; **12** sulfur bottom; **17** genus Balaenoptera
balance: 4 trim; **5** check, demur, dress, level, pause, poise; **6** coquet, debate, equate, medium, waffle; **7** shuffle; **8** contrast, equalize, straddle, symmetry; **9** equaliser, equalizer, equipoise, fluctuate, hem and haw, hum and haw, make equal; **10** complement, neutrality, proportion; **11** equilibrate, equilibrium, equilibrize, render equal; **12** balance sheet, be on the fence, counterpoise, remain neuter; **13** counterweight
balance accounts: 14 cast up accounts, make up accounts, settle accounts, square accounts, wind up accounts
balanced: 4 even; **6** steady; **7** regular, uniform; **11** symmetrical
balance of trade: 8 trade gap; **12** trade balance; **14** visible balance
balancer: 6 halter; **7** haltere
balancing: 8 equating, equation; **12** neutralizing; **14** neutralization, reconciliation; **16** counterbalancing
Balanus: 8 barnacle; **12** genus Balanus
balarag: 3 bug; **4** bait, bore; **5** abuse, beset, grind, harry, haunt, hound, tease, worry; **6** badger, bother, harass, heckle, ill-use, infest, molest, pester, plague, pother; **7** oppress; **8** bullirag, bullyrag, ill-treat, maltreat, mistreat; **9** importune, persecute
balas: 9 balas ruby
balata: 6 balata; **8** beefwood; **9** bully tree; **10** balata tree; **11** gutta balata; **18** Manilkara bidentata
bald: 3 dry; **4** arid, bare, dull, flat, tame; **5** vapid; **6** boring, callow, feeble, jejune, meager, mortal, ragged; **7** denuded, tedious; **8** denudate, roofless; **9** bald-pated, barefaced, dry as dust; **10** bald-headed, threadbare; **13** uninteresting
baldachin: 8 credence; **12** confessional
bald eagle: 13 American eagle; **23** Haliaeetus leucocephalus
Balder: 5 Baldr
balderdash: 4 rant; **6** piffle; **7** bombast, fustian, palaver; **8** flummery; **9** baverdage, rigmarole; **11** rodomontade; **12** fiddle-faddle
bald-headed: 4 bald; **9** bald-pated
baldness: 11 phalacrosis; **12** hairlessness
baldric: 4 band, belt, girt, sash; **5** clasp; **6** fascia, fillet, girdle, wreath, zodiac; **7** garland; **8** baldrick, cincture
Bale: 5 Basel, Basle
bale: 3 jag; **4** load; **5** cargo; **6** bundle, burden, lading; **7** freight, tragedy; **8** accident, calamity, casualty, disaster, shipment; **11** catastrophe

baleen: 9 whalebone
baleen whale: 14 whalebone whale
bale-fire: 7 bonfire; 10 beacon-fire
baleful: 4 ugly; 7 adverse, baneful, harmful, hurtful, noxious, ominous; 8 menacing, minatory, sinister; 9 injurious, minacious; 10 forbidding, pernicious; 11 deleterious, detrimental, mischievous, threatening
balefulness: 7 badness; 8 mischief; 11 banefulness, harmfulness, maleficence
balibago: 5 mahoe, purau; 7 mahagua, majagua; 17 Hibiscus tiliaceus
balista: 5 sling; 8 ballista [Lat], catapult
balize: 6 beacon, pharos; 10 lighthouse
balk: 3 jib; 4 foil; 5 baulk; 6 rafter, resist, thwart, trip up; 9 frustrate; 10 disconcert; 12 blighted hope
Balkans: 11 Balkan state; 12 Balkan nation; 13 Balkan country; 15 Balkan Mountains; 19 Balkan Mountain Range
balked: 7 baffled; 10 frustrated; 11 discouraged
balkline: 9 baulk line; 10 string line
balky: 5 heady; 6 entete [Fr], unruly; 7 balking, restive, wayward, willful; 8 contrary, perverse; 10 headstrong, rebellious, refractory, self-willed; 12 contumacious
ball: 3 hal, egg, nut, orb; 4 clod, glob, lump; 5 chunk, clump, globe; 6 salute, sphere; 7 ballock, bollock; 10 musket ball
ballad: 3 lay; 4 song
balladeer: 7 crooner
ball-and-socket joint: 11 enarthrosis; 13 cotyloid joint, spheroid joint
ballast: 6 aplomb; 8 sobriety; 14 self-possession
ballast resistor: 9 barretter
ball bearing: 13 needle bearing, roller bearing
ball cartridge: 8 fireball; 9 cartouche
ballcock: 8 ball cock
ball dress: 4 gown; 7 foppery; 8 equipage, frippery; 9 full dress; 10 court dress, fancy dress; 12 evening dress
ballerina: 8 danseuse
ballet skirt: 4 tutu
ball field: 7 diamond
ball game: 8 baseball; 10 basketball
ballista: 5 sling; 8 catapult
ballistics: 7 gunnery; 18 military evolutions
ballistic trajectory: 10 ballistics
ball of fire: 6 dynamo; 7 whiz-kid; 8 fireball, go-getter, live wire, spitfire, whizz-kid; 10 powerhouse; 11 human dynamo
balloon: 6 billow; 7 inflate; 8 aerostat, Zeppelin; 9 dirigible
balloon seat: 8 bell seat
ballot: 4 poll, vote; 5 voice; 6 voting; 7 plumper; 8 election, suffrage; 9 balloting, vox populi
Ballota: 9 horehound; 12 genus Ballota

balloting: 4 vote; 6 ballot, voting
ballroom: 9 dance hall; 11 dance palace;
ball-shaped: 6 global; 7 globose, spheric; 8 globular; 9 orbicular, spherical
ball up: 4 blow, flub, muff; 5 botch, fluff, spoil; 6 bobble, bollix, bungle, foul up, fumble, mess up, muck up; 7 blunder, botch up, louse up, screw up; 8 bollix up, bollocks; 9 mishandle; 10 bollocks up
bally: 6 bloody; 7 flaming; 8 blinking, crashing
ballyhoo: 4 hype, plug; 6 hoopla
ballyhoo artist: 14 sensationalist
ballyrag: 5 bully; 6 hector; 8 browbeat, bullyrag; 9 strong-arm; 10 boss around, push around
balm: 5 myrrh, salve; 6 balsam; 7 anodyne, cordial, unguent; 8 bergamot, ointment; 9 potpourri; 12 frankincense
bal masque: 10 bal costume, masquerade; 14 masquerade ball
balmily: 6 daftly; 7 dottily, nuttily, wackily
balm of Gilead: 9 balsam fir; 12 Canada balsam; 13 Abies balsamea
balmy: 4 bats, daft, loco, mild, nuts; 5 barmy, batty, buggy, dotty, kooky, loony, loopy, nutty, spicy, wacky; 6 dreamy, fruity, kookie, savory; 7 bonkers, cracked, haywire, scented; 8 aromatic, balsamic, crackers, fragrant, redolent; 12 sweetscented; 13 sweet-smelling
balneal: 4 bath; 7 bathing
baloney: 4 bosh, bull, tosh; 5 drool; 6 humbug, muddle; 7 blarney, blunder, boloney, twaddle
balsa: 9 balsa wood; 14 Ochroma lagopus
balsam: 4 balm
balsam herb: 7 alecost; 8 costmary; 9 bible leaf; 12 mint geranium
balsamic: 5 balmy, tonic; 7 balsamy; 8 paregoric; 11 chirurgical [Med], corroborant, therapeutic
Baltic: 9 Baltic Sea; 14 Baltic language
Baltimore oriole: 8 firebird, hangbird; 13 Baltimore bird; 21 Icterus galbula galbula
baluster: 8 banister; 9 stanchion
balustrade: 4 pale, rail; 6 paling; 7 railing; 8 banister, enceinte, handrail; 9 balusters, bannister, ring fence; 10 park paling; 13 quickset hedge
Balzac: 12 Honore Balzac; 14 Honore de Balzac
bam: 8 cajolery, flattery, flimflam
bambino: 3 tot; 7 papoose, toddler; 8 yearling
bamboozle: 4 dupe, fool, gull, hoax, snow; 5 trick; 6 take in; 8 hoodwink; 9 play false; 11 hornswoggle

bamboozler: 6 hoaxer
ban: 3 bar, man [Japanese]; 4 shun, veto; 5 taboo; 6 banish, censor, enjoin, forbid, outlaw; 7 banning, cast out; 8 anathema, disallow, forefend, prohibit; 9 blackball, interdict, ostracize, proscribe; 10 execration, forbidding, inhibition; 11 forbiddance, prohibition, ten thousand; 12 disallowance, interdiction, proscription
banal: 5 stock, tired, trite; 7 trivial; 8 shopworn, timeworn, well-worn; 9 hackneyed, well known; 10 threadbare; 11 commonplace
banana: 10 banana tree; 13 Musa sapientum
banana family: 8 Musaceae; 14 family Musaceae
band: 3 bed, guy, lot, orb, set; 4 belt, crew, gang, girt, knot, list, ring, side, slip, tape, team, zone; 5 chain, clasp, cycle, group, orbit, party, spill, squad, stria, strip; 6 circle, cordon, course, fillet, girdle, picket, riband, ribbon, rundle, stripe, zodiac; 7 baldric, banding, faction; 9 dance band, striation; 11 musical band; 13 frequency band; 14 dance orchestra
bandage: 3 rib; 4 bind, lint, skid, stay; 5 shore, truss; 7 Band-Aid, plaster; 8 wrapping; 11 finger stall
bandaged: 5 bound
Band-Aid: 7 Band-Aid, bandage, bandaid
bandanna: 7 bandana
band-box: 11 portmanteau
bandeau: 3 bra; 9 brassiere
bandelet: 7 annulet, bandlet; 10 bandelette; 14 squar and rabbet
bandelette: 7 annulet, bandlet; 8 bandelet; 14 squar and rabbet
banderole: 8 old glory [U.S.]; 14 quarantine flag
bandicoot rat: 7 mole rat
bandit: 4 thug; 5 harpy, shark; 6 falcon; 7 brigand; 9 land shark; 10 freebooter
banditry: 9 marauding
bandlet: 7 annulet; 8 bandelet; 10 bandelette
band of hope: 9 abstainer; 11 Good Templar
bandolier: 8 ammo belt; 9 bandoleer; 14 ammunition belt
bandstand: 5 stand; 12 outdoor stage
band together: 10 join forces; 11 confederate; 12 draw together
bandwagon: 3 fad; 5 craze, thing, trend; 7 in thing; 8 last word; 11 latest thing
bandy: 4 flap, swap; 5 bowed, wield; 6 bowleg, switch; 7 commute, permute, shuffle; 8 brandish, flourish; 9 bowlegged, transpose; 10 kick around; 11 bandy-legged, change hands
bandy about: 8 put about; 9 buzz about,

hawk about; 10 blaze about, bruit about; 12 whisper about
bandy-legged: 5 bandy, bowed; 6 bowleg; 9 bowlegged
bandy legged: 9 bow legged
bandy legs: 6 bow leg; 7 bow legs
bandy with: 4 moot; 5 argue; 6 debate; 7 dispute, wrangle
bane: 5 curse; 7 nemesis, scourge
baneberry: 6 cohosh; 15 herb Christopher
baneful: 6 deadly; 7 baleful, harmful, hurtful, noxious; 9 injurious, pestilent; 10 pernicious; 11 deleterious, detrimental, mischievous
banefulness: 7 badness; 11 balefulness, harmfulness; 13 injuriousness
banewort: 3 pot; 4 hemp; 5 bhang, ganja, grass; 7 hashish; 9 marijuana
bang: 3 cob, eff, hit; 4 bash, beat, belt, blow, bolt, bonk, boom, clap, dash, jazz, kick, rush, slam, slap, swap, trim, warm, wham, wipe; 5 baste, blast, clack, clang, dress, flush, knock, smack, smash, spang, thump, whack; 6 blowup, charge, strike, thrill; 8 eruption, lambaste, slapdash; 9 dress down, loud noise
banger: 4 dirk; 6 dagger; 7 bayonet, cracker, dudgeon, poniard, sausage; 8 stiletto; 11 firecracker
banging: 7 booming; 8 blasting; 9 battering
Bangkok: 17 capital of Thailand
Bangladesh: 10 Bangla Desh; 12 East Pakistan
bangle: 4 gaud; 6 bauble, fallal, gewgaw; 7 novelty, trinket; 8 bracelet
bangtail: 9 race horse, racehorse
bang-up: 4 cool, keen, neat; 5 bully, dandy, great, nifty, swell; 6 groovy, not bad, peachy, slap-up; 7 corking; 8 cracking, smashing
banish: 3 ban, bar; 4 shun; 5 exile, expel; 6 maroon, outlaw; 7 cast out; 8 relegate; 9 blackball, ostracize, transport; 10 cut off from, expatriate
banished: 6 exiled; 11 expatriated
banister: 8 baluster, handrail; 9 balusters, bannister, stanchion; 10 balustrade
bank: 3 lea; 4 cant, flat, hill, mole, rely; 5 levee, mound, shelf, swear, trust; 6 camber, shoals; 7 deposit, parapet, sandbag; 8 breakers, coin bank, lee shore, money box, shallows; 9 revetment, river bank, riverbank, sunk fence; 10 embankment; 11 savings bank; 12 bank building; 14 banking company, banking concern, ironbound coast
bank bill: 4 bill, note; 8 bank note, banknote; 9 greenback; 11 banker's bill; 14 government note; 18 Federal Reserve note
bankbook: 8 passbook
bank card: 10 charge card, credit card; 11 charge plate

bank clerk: 6 teller; 7 cashier
banker: 10 cash keeper; 11 money lender
banker's check: 14 certified check, traveler's check; 15 traveller's check
bank identification number: 3 BIN; 16 ABA transit number
bank line: 4 line; 10 credit line; 12 line of credit; 18 personal credit line; 20 personal line of credit
banknote: 4 bill, note; 8 bank bill, bank note; 9 greenback; 11 banker's bill; 14 government note; 18 Federal Reserve note
bankrupt: 4 ruin, stag; 5 break; 6 debtor; 7 welsher; 8 gazetted, lame duck; 9 defaulter, insolvent; 10 man of straw; 12 in the gazette
bank vault: 5 vault; 14 safe-deposit box
banlieue: 7 suburbs; 8 confines, environs, purlieus, vicinage; 9 alentours [Fr]; 10 borderland; 12 neighborhood
banned: 6 barred; 7 tabooed; 8 enjoined, outlawed; 9 forbidden; 10 disallowed, not allowed, prohibited, proscribed
banner: 4 flag; 6 colors; 7 pennant; 8 streamer
banneret: 4 earl; 5 baron, thane; 8 viscount
banning: 3 ban; 9 enjoining; 10 forbidding; 11 forbiddance, prohibiting, proscribing
bannister: 8 banister, handrail; 9 balusters; 10 balustrade
banquet: 3 toy; 5 feast, revel, sport; 6 junket, wanton; 7 carouse, disport; 8 feed upon; 9 drown care, make merry; 10 batten upon, fatten upon
banqueting: 8 feasting
banquet song: 7 scolion
banquette: 7 bastion, curtain; 10 breastwork
banshee: fiend; 8 familiar; 10 evil genius
bantam: 4 tiny; 6 midget, petite; 10 diminutive; 11 lilliputian
banteng: 5 tsine; 7 banting; 10 Bos banteng
banter: 3 kid; 4 joke, quiz, twit; 5 chaff, irony, jolly, roast, tease; 6 retort; 8 backchat, badinage, raillery, ready wit, repartee; 9 smartness; 10 persiflage, pleasantry, quid pro quo; 11 give-and-take
bantering: 5 roast; 6 hazing; 7 teasing; 8 quizzing, roasting; 9 facetious; 13 tongue-in-cheek
Banti's syndrome: 13 Banti's disease
banting: 5 tsine; 7 banteng; 10 Bos banteng
bantling: 3 tot; 4 tyke; 5 scion; 7 toddler
Bantu: 15 Bantoid language
banzai: 4 viva!; 10 long life to!
baobab: 15 monkey-bread tree; 17 Adansonia digitata
baptism: 6 chrism; 11 christening
baptismal: 13 eucharistical
baptismal font: 4 font; 9 baptistry; 10 baptistery
baptismal name: 13 Christian name

baptize: 3 dip; 7 baptise; 8 christen, sprinkle
bar: 3 ban, lap, pub, ray, rod; 4 bolt, boom, cake, heel, lock, rest, rule, shoe, sole, stay; 5 block, debar, ingot, spoke, stile, taboo; 6 banish, enjoin, forbid, outlaw, radius, saloon, splint, stilts, streak, stripe, tavern; 7 barroom, block up, exclude, gin mill, measure, stirrup, taproom; 8 block off, blockade, deadbolt, disallow, forefend, mug house, pot house, prohibit, relegate; 9 barricade, gin palace, interdict, outrigger, proscribe; 10 police lock, prevention; 11 public house; 14 bar association, legal community
barachois: 9 hog wallow [U.S.]
baragouin: 4 rant; 7 bombast, fustian, palaver; 8 flummery; 9 baverdage, rigmarole; 10 balderdash; 11 rodomontade
bar association: 3 bar; 15 legal profession
barb: 3 cob, dig, pad, set, tit; 4 gibe, hack, jade, jibe, roan, shot, slam, spur, whet; 5 bidet, grind, point, punch, rowel, shaft, strop; 7 sharpen; 8 aculeate, roadster
barbados cherry: 7 acerola; 13 surinam cherry, Surinam cherry; 15 Malpighia glabra; 16 West Indian cherry
Barbarea: 5 cress; 10 water cress; 13 genus Barbarea
barbarian: 4 boor, Goth, hood, tike, tyke, wild, Zulu; 5 brute, bully, churl, rough, rowdy, tough, Yahoo; 6 meanie [jocular], mugger, savage, Vandal, wretch; 7 caitiff, hoodlum, peasant, pug-ugly [U.S.], ruffian; 8 barbaric, hooligan, plug-ugly; 9 barbarous, desperado, Hottentot; 10 mean mother; 11 bludgeon man, uncivilized
barbaric: 4 wild; 5 cruel; 6 brutal, savage; 7 brutish, inhuman; 8 inhumane; 9 barbarian, barbarous, malicious, malignant; 11 uncivilized; 12 semibarbaric
barbarism: 8 savagery, solecism; 9 barbarity, brutality, vandalism; 11 impropriety; 12 abuse of terms; 13 barbarousness, repulsiveness
barbarity: 7 outrage; 8 atrocity, ferocity, savagery; 9 barbarism, brutality; 10 inhumanity, truculence; 11 heinousness; 13 atrociousness, barbarousness, ferociousness, repulsiveness
Barbarossa: 10 Frederick I; 19 Frederick Barbarossa
barbarous: 4 fell, rude; 5 cruel, harsh, rough; 6 brutal, Gothic, rugged, savage; 7 brutish, inhuman, uncouth, vicious; 8 barbaric, inhumane; 9 barbarian, grotesque, malicious, malignant, roughshod; 12 semibarbaric
Barbary pirate: 7 corsair
Barbary sheep: 4 arui; 5 audad; 6 aoudad; 10 maned sheep; 16 Ammotragus lervia

barbate: 7 bearded; 8 whiskery; 9 whiskered; 11 bewhiskered
barbecue: 3 bee; 6 picnic; 7 cook out, cookout; 8 barbeque
barbecued: 7 grilled; 9 barbequed
barbed: 5 burry, spiny; 6 barded, biting, briary, briery, burred, thorny; 7 bristly, nipping, prickly, pungent, spurred; 8 bristled; 10 barbellate
barbed wire fence: 11 picket fence; 12 Cyclone fence; 13 stockade fence; 14 chain-link fence
barbel: 6 feeler
barbellate: 5 burry, spiny; 6 barbed, briary, briery, burred, thorny; 7 bristly, prickly; 8 bristled
barber: 5 foehn; 7 chinook, norther; 8 blizzard
barbital: 7 veronal; 9 barbitone; 18 diethylmalonylurea; 21 diethylbarbituric acid
barcarole: 10 barcarolle
bar chart: 8 bar graph
bar code: 20 Universal Product Code
bard: 5 scald; 7 dress up; 8 trouvere [Fr]; 9 caparison; 10 troubadour
bare: 3 air; 4 bald, mere, nude, open; 5 bleak, empty, naked, overt, sheer, spare, stark, strip; 6 barren, denude, expose, open up, patent, scanty, simple, vacant; 7 denuded, express, lay bare, lay open, literal; 8 denudate, desolate, exoteric, explicit, marginal, stripped; 9 au naturel, expressed, publicise, publicize, unadorned, untrimmed; 10 unfinished, unsheathed; 11 undisguised, ungarnished, unvarnished; 12 unornamented
bareback: 10 barebacked
barebone: 8 rawboned; 9 shriveled; 10 attenuated, extenuated
bare-breasted: 7 braless, topless
bared: 6 avowed; 9 confessed; 10 bareheaded
barefaced: 4 bald; 6 brassy, brazen; 8 insolent; 9 audacious, bodacious, boldfaced; 11 brazen-faced
barefoot: 8 shoeless; 10 barefooted
bareheaded: 5 bared; 8 decorous, honoring; 9 cap in hand, esteeming; 10 obsequious, respectful, respecting; 11 ceremonious, deferential, on one's knees, reverential
barely: 4 just; 6 hardly, scarce; 8 only just, scantily, scarcely; 10 no more than
barely adequate: 2 OK; 4 fair, so-so; 7 average; 8 bearable, mediocre, middling, ordinary, passable; 9 tolerable; 10 acceptable, admissible, couci-couci; 11 indifferent
barenness: 9 sterility
bargain: 3 buy; 4 deal; 5 steal, trade; 6 barter; 7 cut-rate; 8 agree for, contract, covenant, cut-price; 9 good value, negotiate
bargain down: 8 beat down
bargainer: 6 dealer, monger, trader
bargain-priced: 7 cut-rate; 8 cut-price
bargain rate: 7 cut rate; 8 cut price; 9 cheapness
barge: 3 hoy; 7 lighter; 8 flatboat; 11 push forward, thrust ahead
bargee: 8 bargeman; 10 lighterman
barge in: 5 crash, cut in, put in; 6 butt in; 7 break in, chime in; 9 gate-crash
bargeman: 6 bargee; 7 boatman; 8 ferryman
bar hop: 8 pub-crawl
baring: 7 husking; 9 stripping; 10 denudation, uncovering
barium: 2 Ba
bark: 4 skin; 5 clack, cluck, gnarl, growl, snarl; 6 barque, cackle, mutter
barkbound: 5 stiff; 9 hidebound; 11 straitlaced
barkeeper: 6 barman; 7 barkeep; 9 bartender; 10 mixologist
barking deer: 7 muntjac
barleycorn: 6 barley
barm: 5 yeast; 6 leaven; 7 ferment
barman: 7 barkeep; 9 barkeeper, bartender; 10 mixologist
barmy: 4 bats, daft, loco, nuts; 5 balmy, batty, buggy, dotty, kooky, loony, loopy, nutty, wacky; 6 fruity, kookie; 7 bonkers, cracked, haywire; 8 crackers
barn: 5 stall
barnacle: 8 cerriped; 9 cerripede; 13 barnacle goose; 15 Branta leucopsis
barn owl: 8 Tyto alba
barnstorm: 11 whistlestop
barnstormer: 7 trouper; 9 playactor; 10 stunt flier, stunt pilot
barnyard: 8 farmyard
barometric pressure: 11 air pressure; 19 atmospheric pressure
baron: 3 man; 4 earl, king; 5 mogul, power, thane; 6 tycoon; 7 consort, husband, magnate; 8 viscount; 12 top executive; 14 big businessman, business leader
baronage: 7 peerage
baronet: 4 bart
baronial: 5 noble; 6 lordly; 7 stately; 8 imposing
baroque: 5 gaudy; 6 rococo, tawdry; 7 strange; 10 outlandish; 11 baroqueness, out of the way; 14 churrigueresco, overornamented
bar out: 7 shut out; 8 leave out
barque: 4 bark
barrack: 4 gibe, gird, hiss, hoot, jeer, twit, urge; 5 cheer, flout, pep up, scoff, taunt; 6 deride, exhort, urge on; 7 inspire, laugh at, plafond, snigger; 8 ridicule
barracking: 8 heckling
barracoon: 6 sconce; 10 blockhouse

barrage: 7 battery; 8 shelling; 9 onslaught; 10 outpouring; 11 barrage fire, bombardment

barred: 4 fast; 6 banned, bolted, grated, locked, veined; 7 latched, secured, tabooed; 8 enjoined, outlawed, streaked, striated; 9 blockaded, forbidden; 10 barricaded, disallowed, not allowed, prohibited, proscribed; 12 not permitted

barred owl: 10 Strix varia

barrel: 3 bbl, keg; 4 cask, drum, vase; 6 bushel; 8 cut along, eyepiece, platform, puncheon; 9 barrelful, bowl along, gun barrel; 11 barrel along; 12 focusing knob; 13 objective lens

barrel cactus: 12 echinocactus

barreled: 9 barrelled

barrelhouse: 9 honky-tonk

barrel knot: 9 blood knot

barrel maker: 6 cooper

barrel organ: 9 hand organ; 10 grind organ, hurdy gurdy; 11 street organ

barren: 4 bare; 5 bleak, stark, waste; 7 sterile; 8 desolate; 9 childless, infertile, wasteland

barrenness: 7 aridity; 13 fruitlessness

barretter: 15 ballast resistor

barricade: 3 bar; 5 belay, block; 7 barrier, block up; 8 block off, blockade; 9 barricado, roadblock

Barrie: 18 James Matthew Barrie; 21 Sir James Matthew Barrie

barrier: 8 obstacle, stoppage; 9 barricade, roadblock; 11 obstruction

barring: 4 save; 5 minus; 6 beside, except; 7 without; 8 let alone; 9 aside from, blackball, except for, excepting, excluding, other than; 10 leaving out; 11 exclusive of; 13 save and except

barring out: 7 lock out, lockout, turn out; 10 locking out

barrio: 4 ward; 5 block; 6 corner, locale; 8 enceinte, environs, locality, precinct, vicinity; 9 precincts; 12 neighborhood

barrister: 2 K.C., Q.C.; 12 King's counsel; 13 Queen's counsel; 14 barrister at law

barroom: 3 bar, pub; 6 saloon, tavern; 7 gin mill, taproom; 8 mug house, pot house, pump room; 9 gin palace; 11 public house

barrow: 4 knob, pena [U.S.], tope; 5 cairn, knoll, mound; 7 hillock, hummock, tumulus; 8 cromlech, lawn cart; 9 barrowful; 10 garden cart, grave mound, hand barrow; 11 burial mound, wheel barrow, wheelbarrow

barrow-boy: 9 barrow-man; 12 costermonger

bartender: 6 barman; 7 barkeep; 9 barkeeper; 10 mixologist

barter: 4 swap; 5 trade, truck; 7 bargain, trading; 8 exchange; 10 quid pro quo

bartlett: 12 bartlett pear

baryon: 13 heavy particle

basal: 4 base; 5 basic; 7 primary, radical; 9 beginning; 11 abecedarian

bas-bleu: 12 bluestocking

base: 3 bag, low; 4 foot, foul, home, mean, post, root, send, stem, vile; 5 basal, basis, black, dirty, embed, floor, found, grave, gross, imbed, lowly, nadir, place, radix, stand, theme; 6 abject, alkali, arrant, bottom, craven, ground, humble, scurvy, shabby; 7 heinous, ignoble, immoral, modulus, pitiful, radical, scrubby, station, support; 8 baseborn, beggarly, dunghill, free-base, infamous, pedestal, recreant, root word, shameful, sinister, sneaking; 9 establish, felonious, fundament, nefarious, unethical; 10 blackguard, foundation, groundwork, of a deep dye, scandalous, villainous; 11 cornerstone, ignominious; 12 dishonorable, meanspirited, substructure; 13 dishonourable

baseball bat: 3 bat; 6 lumber

baseball club: 4 club, nine; 8 ball club

baseball diamond: 7 diamond, infield

baseball glove: 4 mitt; 5 glove; 12 baseball mitt

baseball player: 10 ballplayer

baseball swing: 3 cut; 5 swing

baseboard: 8 mopboard; 13 skirting board

baseborn: 4 base; 5 lowly; 6 humble; 7 lowborn

based: 7 founded

baseless: 4 idle; 9 in nubibus [Lat], unfounded; 10 groundless; 11 unwarranted

basely: 6 foully, meanly; 8 arrantly, scurvily

basement: 6 cellar

baseness: 6 laxity; 7 scandal; 8 foulness, trimming, vileness; 9 abjection, shuffling, turpitude; 10 debasement; 11 degradation, poltroonery; 13 despicability; 14 despicableness, moral turpitude; 15 contemptibility, ignominiousness

base on balls: 4 pass, walk

bash: 2 do; 3 bop; 4 bang, belt, bonk, sock, whap, whop; 5 brawl, knock, smash

bashaw: 3 beg; 6 pasha, despot, regent, tyrant; 7 khedive, viceroy; 8 martinet, palatine, stickler; 9 oppressor

bashful: 3 shy; 5 blate, timid; 8 blushing; 10 overmodest, shamefaced

basic: 5 basal; 6 staple; 7 canonic, primary; 9 beginning, canonical, essential; 11 abecedarian, fundamental; 12 introductory

basically: 6 au fond; 9 in essence; 11 essentially; 13 fundamentally

basic part: 4 core, gist, pith; 5 heart;

6 marrow; 9 vital part; 13 essential part, important part, intrinsic part; 15 fundamental part

basify: 8 alkalify, alkalize

basil: 10 sweet basil

basilar: 8 basilary

basilica: 4 kirk; **6** chapel, church; **7** oratory; **9** cathedral; **10** tabernacle; **11** conventicle; **12** meetinghouse basin: **3** cup; **4** bowl, dock, port, quay; **5** downs, jorum, wharf; **6** crater, harbor, trough; **8** basinful; **9** punch bowl; **10** river basin

basis: 4 base; **6** ground; **7** footing, grounds, support; **9** fundament, pro and con; **10** foundation, ground work, groundwork; **11** cornerstone, pros and cons; **13** consideration

bask: 4 pant; **5** enjoy, flush, savor, sweat; **6** relish, savour; **7** swelter

basket: 4 cran, hoop; **5** crate, creel; **6** pottle; **7** pannier; **9** basketful, field goal; **10** buckbasket, handbasket; **14** basketball hoop

basketball: 5 hoops; **14** basketball game

basketmaker: 12 basketweaver

basket rummy: 4 meld; **7** canasta

basket star: 10 basket fish

basketweaver: 11 basketmaker

bask in: 5 eat up; **6** swim in; **7** drink up; **8** wallow in

Basle: 4 Bale; **5** Basel

bas mitzvah: 10 bat mitzvah; **11** bath mitzvah

basophil: 9 basophile

bas relief: 9 low relief; **12** basso relievo, basso rilievo, bassorilievo [It]

bass: 4 bass, deep, tuna; **5** basso, trout; **6** second; **7** sardine, sea bass; **8** bass part, bass viol, basswood, mackerel, sailfish; **9** bass voice; **10** bass fiddle, bull fiddle, contrabass, double bass, muskelunge, string bass; **13** accompaniment; **14** freshwater bass

bass clarinet: 7 bassoon, serpent; **13** contrabassoon double bassoon

bass clef: 5 F clef

bass drum: 8 gran casa

basset: 7 crop out; **11** basset hound

basset horn: 4 oboe; **7** hautboy

bass fiddle: 4 bass; **8** bass viol; **10** bull fiddle, contrabass, double bass, string bass

bass horn: 4 tuba; **10** cor Anglais [Fr], sousaphone, Sousaphone; **11** English horn; **12** corno Inglese [It]

basso: 4 bass; **9** bass voice; **13** basso profondo [It]

basso continuo: 12 thorough bass

bassoon: 7 serpent, fagotto; **13** contrabassoon, double bassoon

basso profondo: 5 basso

basso relievo: 9 bas relief, low relief; **12** basso rilievo

bass viol: 4 bass; **10** bass fiddle, bull fiddle, contrabass, double bass, string bass; **12** viola da gamba

bast: 4 bast; **6** phloem; **9** bast fiber

basta!: 6 enough!

bastard: 4 fake; **5** bogus, false, phony; **6** phoney; **8** misbegot, spurious; **9** bastardly, love child; **11** misbegotten, **12** illegitimate; **14** supposititious

baste: 4 bang, beat, blow, dash, drub, slam, swap; **5** thump; **6** batter, pummel; **7** basting, belabor, clobber, leather, sandbag, tacking, trounce; **8** lambaste

bast fiber: 4 bast

bastinado: 4 cane, comb, flog, lash, lick, whip; **5** birch, strap, towel; **6** larrup, switch, thrash, thresh; **7** gantlet, scourge; **8** stick law; **9** horsewhip; **10** flagellate

basting: 5 baste; **7** tacking

bastion: 7 citadel, curtain; **9** banquette; **10** breastwork

bastioned: 9 fortified

Basuto: 7 Sesotho

Basutoland: 7 Lesotho

bat: 3 bum [U.S.]; **4** be up, bust, drub, lick, tear; **5** at-bat, punch, randy; **6** lumber, monkey, thrash; **7** be at bat, blowout [U.S.], clobber, fish fry [U.S.], flutter, hoedown, yule log; **8** jamboree; **10** cricket bat, hullabaloo; **11** baseball bat, chiropteran; **12** squash racket; **13** donation party [U.S.], squash racquet

Bataan: 10 Corregidor

batch: 3 lot, pot, wad; **4** deal, dose, heap, mass, mess, mint, pack, peck, pile, raft, slew; **5** flock, sight, spate, stack, stock; **6** clutch, hatful, mickle, muckle, plenty; **7** tidy sum; **8** good deal, whole lot; **9** great deal, whole slew

bate: 4 give; **5** abate, allow; **6** reduce; **7** take off; **8** decrease, discount, mark down, retrench; **9** price down; **13** make allowance, render smaller

bath: 3 tub; **5** bathe; **6** shower; **7** bathing, bathtub, washtub; **8** bathroom; **9** showering

Bathala: 4 Devi, Kali; **5** Brahm, Durga, oread, Ushas; **6** Brahma; **14** cloud-compeller, the Great Spirit

Bath chair: 10 sedan chair, wheelchair

bather: 7 natator, swimmer

bathetic: 5 mushy; **6** slushy; **7** maudlin, mawkish; **8** schmalzy; **9** schmaltzy; **11** sentimental

bathhouse: 6 bagnio

bathing: 4 bath; **6** laving, shower, washup; **8** ablution; **9** showering

bathing suit: 8 swimsuit, swimwear; **14** bathing costume; **15** swimming costume

bathing trunks: 6 trunks; **14** swimming trunks

batholith: 6 pluton; 9 batholite; 12 plutonic rock

bathometer: 9 depth gage

bathos: 10 anticlimax; 11 mawkishness

bathroom: 3 can, lav; 4 bath, john, head; 5 privy; 6 toilet; 8 bath room, facility, lavatory

bathroom fixture: 15 plumbing fixture

bathroom tissue: 11 toilet paper; 12 toilet tissue

bathtub: 3 tub; 4 bath; 7 washtub

bathymetry: 8 plumbing

bathyscaphe: 10 bathyscape, bathyscaph

Batidaceae: 14 saltwort family

batman: 6 feeder; 7 caterer; 8 purveyor; 9 victualer; 10 commissary; 13 quartermaster

bat mitzvah: 10 bas mitzvah; 11 bath mitzvah

baton: 5 staff, stick; 6 crutch; 10 alpenstock

Baton Rouge: 18 capital of Louisiana

batrachian: 4 frog, toad; 6 anuran; 8 toad-frog; 10 salientian

bats: 4 daft, loco, nuts; 5 balmy, barmy, batty, buggy, dotty, kooky, loony, loopy, nutty, wacky; 6 fruity, kookie; 7 bonkers, cracked, haywire; 8 crackers

batsman: 6 batter, hitter; 7 slugger

Batswana: 6 Tswana; 8 Bechuana

battalia: 4 army, host, wing; 5 corps, squad; 6 column; 7 battery, brigade, company, platoon, section; 8 division, garrison, regiment, squadron; 9 battalion; 10 detachment; 11 corps d'armee [Fr], subdivision; 12 flying column

battalion: 4 army, host, pack, wing; 5 corps, squad; 6 column, 7 battery, brigade, company, platoon, section; 8 division, garrison, regiment, squadron; 9 multitude; 10 detachment; 11 corps d'armee [Fr], large number, subdivision

batten: 4 slat; 6 secure; 10 batten down

batter: 5 baste, dinge; 6 buffet, hitter; 7 batsman, clobber, slugger; 10 knock about

batter bread: 10 spoon bread

battercake: 7 hotcake, pancake; 8 flapcake, flapjack; 11 flannelcake, griddlecake

battered: 5 seedy; 6 beat-up, beaten; 7 altered; 8 beaten-up; 9 shattered; 10 pulled down

batterer: 9 assailant, assaulter

battering: 7 banging; 9 buffeting

battery: 4 army, cell, host, park, wing; 5 corps, squad; 6 column; 7 assault, barrage, brigade, company, platoon, section; 8 basilisk, division, garrison, portable, regiment, shelling, squadron; 9 battalion; 10 detachment; 11 barrage fire, bombardment, corps d'armee [Fr], subdivision; 12 electric cell, flying column, stamp battery

battery acid: 15 electrolyte acid

batting order: 4 card; 6 lineup

battle: 5 fight; 6 action, combat; 7 wage war; 8 conflict, do battle, struggle; 9 encounter; 10 engagement, give battle; 14 engage in battle, military action

battle-axe: 6 pole-ax; 8 battle-ax; 10 Lochaber ax

Battle Born State: 6 Nevada; 11 Silver State; 14 Sagebrush State

battle cry: 6 war cry; 8 war whoop; 11 rallying cry

battle damage: 8 casualty

battle fatigue: 10 shell shock; 13 combat fatigue; 14 combat neurosis

battlefield: 5 field, front; 9 front line; 12 battleground; 13 field of battle

battlement: 5 scarp; 7 rampart; 9 embrasure; 11 crenelation; 12 crenellation

battler: 7 fighter; 8 scrapper; 9 combatant; 11 belligerent

battle royal: 3 row; 4 fray, to-do; 5 brawl, broil, brush, fight, melee; 6 affair, affray, breeze, fracas, hubbub, pother, racket, rumble, rumpus, squall, uproar; 7 howling, rhubarb [baseball], ruction, shindig, trouble; 8 brouhaha, scramble; 9 collision, imbroglio, scrimmage; 10 bear garden, donnybrook, free-for-all; 11 embroilment

battleship: 10 battleship; 11 battlewagon, dreadnaught, dreadnought; 13 ship of the line

battling: 3 war; 5 fight; 6 combat; 7 warfare, wage war; 8 conflict, fighting, 11 clash of arms, hostilities

battology: 8 pleonasm; 9 tautology; 10 exuberance, redundancy; 11 periphrasis

battue: 4 race; 5 chase; 7 carnage; 8 butchery; 9 bloodbath, bloodshed, Jacquerie, slaughter; 12 bloodletting, steeple chase

batty: 3 mad; 4 bats, daft, loco, nuts; 5 balmy, barmy, buggy, crazy, dotty, kooky, loony, loopy, nutty, wacky; 6 crazed, fruity, insane, kookie, teched [dialect]; 7 bonkers, cracked, far gone, haywire, lunatic, tetched [dialect], touched; 8 crackers, demented, deranged

bauble: 4 gaud; 5 curio; 6 bangle, fallal, gewgaw, trifle; 7 bibelot, novelty, trinket, whatnot; 8 chotchke, gimcrack, kickshaw, nicknack, whim-wham; 9 bagatelle, bric-a-brac, tchotchke; 10 knickknack

Baudelaire: 17 Charles Baudelaire; 23 Charles Pierre Baudelaire

baud rate: 4 baud

baulk: 3 jib; 4 balk; 6 rafter, resist

bavardage: 7 blabber

bawcock: 9 bon enfant [Fr]; 10 good fellow; 11 jolly fellow

bawd: 4 tart; 5 whore; 6 harlot; 7 cocotte, cyprian, trollop; 8 mackerel; 10 fancy woman, prostitute; 11 working girl

bawdiness: 8 lewdness, salacity; 9 obscenity; 13 salaciousness

bawdry: 4 smut; 5 bawdy; 8 ribaldry; 9 equivoque [Fr], obscenity

bawdy: 4 free; 5 broad, gross, loose; 6 bawdry, coarse, ribald, risque [Fr], smutty; 7 fulsome, obscene; 8 off-color; 9 equivocal; 12 pornographic

bawdyhouse: 4 stew; 7 brothel; 8 bordello, cathouse; 10 whorehouse

bawl: 4 hoop, howl, roar, wail, yawp, yell; 5 brawl, shout, whoop; 6 bellow, halloa, halloo, scream, shriek, shrill; 7 screech

bawling out: 6 earful; 9 going-over; 10 chewing out, upbraiding; 11 castigation; 12 dressing down

bawl out: 3 jaw, rag; 5 check, chide, scold; 6 berate, chew up, rebuke; 7 chew out, lambast, lecture, reproof; 8 lambaste; 9 dress down, have words, reprimand; 11 remonstrate

bay: 5 bight, quest; 6 alcove, armlet, auburn, dapple, russet; 7 bay tree; 8 chestnut, cinnamon, nut-brown; 9 bay laurel, embayment

bayberry: 8 waxberry; 10 bay-rum tree; 11 candleberry; 12 Pimenta acris, wild cinnamon; 18 Myrica pensylvanica

Bayer: 7 aspirin, Empirin

baying: 3 yap, yip; 4 howl, yawl, yipe; 5 growl, snarl

bay laurel: 3 bay; 7 bay tree; 10 true laurel

bayonet: 4 dirk, stab; 6 dagger; 7 dudgeon, poniard; 8 stiletto; 10 eviscerate, run through

bayou: 3 gut; 4 beck, burn; 5 brook, creek, crick, marsh, swamp; 6 runnel, stream

Bay State: 9 Old Colony; 13 Massachusetts

bay tree: 3 bay; 9 bay laurel; 10 true laurel

bazaar: 4 fair; 5 bazar; 6 staple

bazooka rocket: 12 bazooka shell; 14 antitank weapon

BB gun: 6 air gun; 9 pellet gun

bbl: 6 barrel

B complex: 1 B; 8 B vitamin, vitamin B

Be: 9 beryllium, glucinium

be: 2 am [1st person sing], is [3rd person sing]; 3 are [pl]; 4 cost, live, work; 5 being [gerund], equal, exist, occur; 6 embody, follow, make up; 8 comprise; 9 personify, represent; 10 constitute

beach: 6 strand

beach chair: 9 deck chair

beached: 10 high-and-dry

beach flea: 8 sand flea; 10 sandhopper

beachhead: 8 foothold; 10 bridgehead

beach wagon: 5 wagon, woody; 6 waggon, woodie; 11 beach waggon; 12 station wagon; 13 station waggon

beacon: 6 pharos; 10 beacon fire, lighthouse; 11 beacon light, radio beacon

bead: 4 drop; 5 adorn, pearl; 6 cnrich; 7 beading; 8 astragal, beadwork, beautify, decorate, ornament; 9 embellish

be a candidate: 9 volunteer; 11 come forward; 12 offer oneself

beaded: 5 beady; 6 gemmed; 7 jeweled, spangly; 8 jewelled, sequined, spangled; 9 bejeweled; 10 bejewelled, bespangled

beadle: 6 sexton, suisse [Fr], verger, warder; 7 almoner, bailiff, doorman [male]; 8 cerberus, portress [female], tipstaff; 9 catchpoll, sacristan; 10 bum-bailiff, doorkeeper

beak: 3 neb, nib; 4 bill, nose, peck, pick; 5 snoot, snout; 6 honker, hooter, nozzle, schnoz; 7 rostrum; 9 proboscis, schnozzle

beaked: 6 hooked; 12 sickle shaped

beaker: 4 bail; 5 billy; 7 canakin

beam: 3 air, ray; 4 glow, send; 5 blaze, bloom, glare, gleam, joist, shaft, shine; 6 girder, lintel, pencil, rafter, streak, stream; 7 flicker, glimmer, radiate, shimmer; 8 light ray, transmit; 9 beam scale, broadcast, light beam, radio beam, steelyard; 10 ray of light; 11 balance beam, beam of light; 12 shaft of light

beaming: 4 glad; 5 beamy; 7 radiant; 9 effulgent, refulgent

beamish: 7 smiling, twinkly

beamy: shiny; 7 beaming, lambent, radiant; 8 lustrous; 9 effulgent, refulgent

bean: 5 attic; 6 noggin, noodle; 9 bean plant; 10 edible bean

bean aphid: 8 blackfly; 10 Aphis fabae

beanball: 6 beaner

bean counter: 7 actuary, auditor; 10 accountant, bookkeeper

bean curd: 4 tofu

beano: 4 keno; 5 bingo, lotto

Beantown: 6 Boston; 16 Hub of the Universe; 22 capital of Massachusetts

bear: pay; 4 bide, bull, have, hold, port, tote [U.S.], wear; 5 abide, beast, beget, birth, brave, brook, bruin, brute, carry, lie in, put up, stand, yield; 6 accept, acquit, assume, behave, birthe, convey, deport, endure, expect, seller, suffer, ursine; 7 admit of, comport, conduct, contain, deliver, gestate, stomach, support, sustain, turn out; 8 shoulder, take over, tolerate; 9 fecundate, give birth, go through, porcupine; 10 blackguard, bring forth; 11 give birth to, short seller

bearable: 2 OK; 4 fair, so-so; 7 average; 8 mediocre, middling, ordinary, passable; 9 endurable, tolerable; 10 acceptable, admissible, couci-couci, sufferable; 11 indifferent, supportable; **12** milk and water; **14** barely adequate; **15** unobjectionable

bearberry: 8 bearwood; **9** possum haw; **11** chittamwood, chittimwood, Ilex decidua, winterberry; **16** cascara buckthorn; **17** Rhamnus purshianus

bear cat: 5 panda; **7** cat bear; **8** red panda; **11** lesser panda

bear claw: 7 bear paw

beard: 4 comb, dare, huff, shag, snub; **5** brave, brush; **6** byssus; **8** imperial, whiskers

bearded: 5 awned, bushy; **6** hispid, shaggy; **7** barbate, shagged, villous; **8** whiskery; **9** whiskered; **11** bewhiskered

beardless: 5 green, sappy, young; **6** callow, puisne; **7** budding; **8** juvenile, under age, youthful; **11** in one's teens, smooth-faced, whiskerless

bearer: 5 scout, toter; **8** conveyer; **10** pall-bearer

bear false witness: 8 forswear; **10** swear false; **14** perjure oneself

bear false witness against: 5 libel

bear grass: 4 tine; **5** yucca

bearing: 3 aim; **4** bait [U.S.], mien; **5** drift, guise, tenor; **6** charge, course, manner, vector; **7** concern, fulcrum, heading, posture; **8** carriage, carrying, coloring, demeanor, presence, relation, tendency; **9** cognation, direction; **10** connection; **11** comportment, having on one

bearish: 7 boorish; **8** churlish; **11** pessimistic

bear paw: 8 bear claw

bearskin: 5 busby, shako

bearwood: 8 bearwood; **9** bearberry; **11** chittamwood, chittimwood

beast: 4 bear, wolf; **5** bruin, brute, fauna, wight; **6** animal, savage; **7** critter [U.S. dialect], wildcat; **8** creature, zoophyte; **10** blackguard, dumb animal; **12** animate being, created being, dumb creature

beat: 3 cap, get, hit, top, wag; **4** bang, best, blow, dash, dead, drum, flap, slam, swap, tick, walk, whop; **5** all in, amaze, baste, cheat, crush, dance, dodge, lurch, march, meter, outgo, pound, pulse, range, round, shake, smite [biblical], swing, throb, thrum, thump; **6** baffle, beat up, bushed, cut out, defeat, gravel, o'er-top, outfox, outrun, outwit, puzzle, rhythm, rip off, seesaw, strike, tucker, wallop; **7** beat out, cadence, circuit, conquer, exhaust, flummox, measure, mystify, nonplus, outjump, outleap, outride, perplex, pulsate, routine, stupefy, stupify, trounce; **8** bewilder, dead beat, fatigued, lambaste, outrival, outsmart, outstrip, scramble, ticktack, ticktock, vanquish; **9** discomfit, dumbfound, go pitapat, heartbeat, overreach, palpitate, pulsation

beastliness: 8 meanness

beastly: 4 foul; **5** brute, nasty, reeky; **6** coarse; **7** bestial, brutish, hellish; **9** offensive; **10** abominable

beatable: 8 vincible; **12** vanquishable

beat about the bush: 4 trim; **5** fence; **6** ramble; **7** digress, shuffle; **8** perorate, protract; **13** procrastinate

beat back: 5 drive, repel; **7** beat off, fend off, keep off, repulse, ward off; **8** push back; **9** force back

beat down: 7 chaffer, cheapen, cut down, mow down; **8** bear down, blow down, huckster, pull down; **9** break down; **11** bargain down

beaten: 6 routed; **8** battered, overcome; **9** conquered; **10** overthrown, vanquished; **11** overwhelmed

beaten-up: 6 beat-up; **8** battered

beatic: 6 joyful, joyous; **8** beatific, blissful; **10** in paradise

beatific: 6 joyful, joyous; **7** angelic, elysian, sainted, saintly; **8** blissful, heavenly, supernal; **9** angelical, celestial, saintlike, unearthly; **10** from on high, in paradise; **12** paradisiacal

beatification: 8 adoption; **9** salvation; **10** conversion; **11** inspiration; **12** regeneration; **13** justification; **14** sanctification

beatify: 5 bless, saint; **8** canonize, enshrine, keep holy, sanctify; **10** consecrate

beating: 7 pulsing; **8** drubbing, whacking, whipping; **9** pulsating, pummeling, thrashing, threshing, trouncing; **12** flagellation

beat out: 4 beat; **5** crush; **6** tap out; **7** trounce; **8** thump out, vanquish

beats per minute: 2 M.M.; **3** bpm; **16** metronome marking

beat up: 4 beat, mash; **5** churn, rally; **6** drum up, squash; **7** thicken; **8** battered, beaten-up

be at work: 4 play, work; **7** carry on; **8** exercise, practice; **9** prosecute

beau: 3 elf, fop; **4** chap, dude; **5** blade, dandy, sheik, swain, swell, wooer; **6** amoret, fellow, gaffer, suitor, yeoman; **7** coxcomb, gallant, good man; **8** follower, macaroni [19th cent], young man; **9** boyfriend, exquisite, inamorato; **10** sweetheart; **12** clotheshorse, fashion plate

Beaufort scale: 9 wind scale

beau ideal: 4 idol; **7** paragon, phoenix; **10** perfection

beau monde: 5 court; **6** bon ton; **7** society; **8** high life, smart set; **11** drawing-room, high society

beaut: 6 beauty

beautician: 11 cosmetician

beautified: 7 adorned; **9** decorated; **10** ornamented; **11** embellished

beautiful: 4 fine; **6** lovely, pretty; **9** beauteous

beautifully: 12 attractively

beautify: 4 bead, deck; 5 adorn, grace; 6 enrich; 8 decorate, ornament, prettify; 9 embellish; 15 render beautiful

beautiless: 4 ugly; 10 uninviting, unpleasing; 11 unbeautiful; 12 unattractive; 15 unprepossessing

beauty: 4 dish, lulu; 5 beaut, peach; 6 looker; 7 mantrap, smasher, stunner; 8 knockout; 10 sweetheart; 11 le beau ideal, pretty woman

beauty parlor: 5 salon; 10 beauty shop; 11 beauty salon; 13 beauty parlour

beauty salon: 5 salon; 10 beauty shop; 12 beauty parlor; 13 beauty parlour

beaux arts: 8 fine arts

beaver: 6 castor, top hat, topper; 7 busy bee, high hat, silk hat; 8 dress hat, opera hat; 9 beaver hat, stovepipe

beaver hat: 6 beaver, castor

Beaver State: 6 Oregon

be aware of: 3 ken; 4 know, scan; 7 realize; 9 apprehend; 10 appreciate, comprehend, understand

bebop: 3 bop

becalm: 4 calm, hush, stay; 5 quell; 6 steady; 11 lull to sleep

becalmed: 5 quiet; 8 stagnant

be careless: 7 neglect; 11 be negligent; 13 be thoughtless

because: 3 for; 5 for as, since; 7 whereas; 10 ex concesso [Lat], inasmuch as, seeing that; 11 considering

bechamel: 10 white sauce

bechance: 6 befall, betide, happen

becharm: 5 catch, charm; 6 enamor, trance; 7 beguile, bewitch, capture, enamour, enchant; 8 entrance; 9 captivate, fascinate

Bechuana: 6 Tswana; 8 Batswana

beck: 3 bid, nod; 4 burn, call; 5 bayou, brook, creek, shrug; 6 behest, dictum, runnel, stream; 7 bidding

Becket: 13 Thomas a Becket; 18 Saint Thomas a Becket

becket bend: 9 sheet bend; 11 weaver's knot; 12 weaver's hitch

Beckett: 13 Samuel Beckett

beckon: 4 wave; 7 attract

become: 2 go; 3 get; 4 suit, turn; 5 befit; 6 beseem, turn to; 7 behoove; 8 turn into; 10 evolve into; 11 develop into; 15 be converted into

bedamn: 4 damn; 5 curse; 7 beshrew; 8 maledict; 9 imprecate; 10 anathemize

bedaub: 4 daub; 5 smear; 7 besmear

bedaze: 4 daze, stun

bedazzle: 4 daze; 6 dazzle; 7 radiate; 13 shoot out beams

bedbug: 6 chinch; 16 Cimex lectularius

bedchamber: 7 bedroom, chamber; 12 sleeping room

bed clothing: 7 bedding, pajamas; 9 nightgown; 10 bedclothes

bedcover: 6 spread; 9 bedspread

bedded: 10 stratified

bedder: 12 bedding plant

bedding: 6 litter; 10 bedclothes; 11 bed clothing

bedding plant: 6 bedder

bed down: 8 bunk down

bedecked: 6 decked; 7 adorned; 9 decked-out

bedevil: 3 dun, fox, rag; 5 throw; 6 fuddle, hoodoo, voodoo; 7 bewitch, confuse, crucify, torment; 8 befuddle, confound; 9 frustrate, tantalize; 14 discombobulate

bedevilment: 7 torment; 8 worrying; 9 badgering, diablerie [Fr]; 10 bewitchery; 11 enchantment

bedew: 6 sponge

bedewed: 4 dewy

bedfast: 6 bedrid, infirm; 8 sick-abed; 9 bedridden

bedfellow: 7 bedmate

bedight: 4 deck; 5 array; 6 bedeck; 10 pranked out; 11 well-groomed

bedim: 3 dim; 7 benight, obscure; 9 overcloud

bedizen: 3 dye; 4 tint, wash; 5 grain, imbue, paint, prank, stain, tinge; 7 garnish, ingrain; 8 emblazon; 10 illuminate

bedlam: 5 chaos; 10 topsy-turvy; 11 pandemonium

bedlamite: 5 crazy; 6 madcap, madman, maniac; 7 lunatic

bedmate: 9 bedfellow

bed of roses: 7 fat city, rose bed; 10 bed of downs

bedraggled: 7 unsound; 8 draggled; 10 broken-down, ramshackle, tumble-down; 11 dilapidated

bedridden: 6 bedrid, infirm, laid up; 7 bedfast; 8 confined, sick-abed; 9 invalided

bedrock: 6 basics; 7 hardpan [U.S.]; 12 fundamentals; 14 basic principle

bedroom: 7 boudoir, chamber; 9 dormitory; 10 bedchamber; 12 sleeping room

bedsheet: 5 quilt, sheet; 7 blanket; 8 coverlet; 9 comforter, tarpaulin; 11 counterpane

bedsitter: 6 bedsit; 14 bedsitting room

bedsore: 14 decubitus ulcer

bedspread: 6 spread; 8 bedcover; 11 bed covering, counterpane

bedstead: 8 bedframe; 9 shakedown

bedwarf: 5 dwarf, stunt

bed-wetting: 8 enuresis

bee: 3 ant; 7 busy bee, termite; 8 barbecue [U.S.], honeybee, white ant; 10 working bee

bee balm: 9 lemon balm, oswego tea, sweet

balm; **10** garden balm; **12** bergamot mint

beebread: 8 ambrosia

beech: 9 beech tree, beechwood

beech family: 8 Fagaceae

beef: 4 kick; **5** boeuf, gripe; **6** grouse, holler, squawk; **8** complain, grousing; **9** bellyache, complaint; **10** beef cattle; **11** bellyaching

beefalo: 7 cattalo

beef broth: 9 beef stock

beefburger: 9 hamburger

beefeater: 6 yeoman

beef jerky: 5 jerky; **8** pemmican

beef patty: 9 chopsteak; **12** chopped steak; **14** hamburger steak

beef stock: 9 beef broth

beef tea: 6 Bovril

beef tenderloin: 8 undercut; **10** tenderloin

beef up: 7 fortify; **9** reenforce, reinforce; **10** strengthen

beefwood: 6 balata; **9** bully tree; **10** balata tree

beefy: 5 burly, husky; **7** buirdly; **9** strapping

beehive: 4 hive; **10** forcing pit

Beehive State: 4 Utah; **11** Mormon State

bee house: 6 apiary

beekeeper: apiarist; **12** apiculturist

beekeeping: 10 apiculture

beeline: 7 air line

Beelzebub: 5 Devil, Satan; **6** Belial, Samael, Zamiel; **7** Lucifer, old Nick [slang]; **8** the Devil; **10** the evil one, the Tempter, the tempter; **12** the Adversary, the arch fiend, the archenemy, the foul fiend, the wicked one; **13** the evil spirit, the old Serpent; **14** Mephistopheles

bee moth: 7 wax moth; **18** Galleria mellonella

been: 3 was [sing]; **4** were [pl]

beep: 4 honk, toot; **5** blare, bleep; **6** claxon

beer: 4 brew, suds

beer barrel: 7 beer keg

beer drinker: 10 ale drinker

beer keg: 10 beer barrel

beer maker: 6 brewer

beer mug: 5 stein

beery: 3 cut; **4** high; **5** boozy, drunk, fresh, merry, tight, tipsy; **6** corned, groggy, primed; **7** drunken, fuddled; **8** elevated, overcome, top-heavy; **9** disguised, flustered, inebriate, overtaken; **10** in one's cups, inebriated; **11** intoxicated

beet: 8 beetroot; **10** common beet; **12** Beta vulgaris

Beethoven: 12 van Beethoven; **18** Ludwig van Beethoven

beetle: 4 ride; **5** bunch, mount; **6** impend; **8** beetling, bestride, hang over, overhang

beetle headed: 4 dull; **6** stupid; **7** witless; **8** mindless; **9** airheaded, brainless

B

beetling: 6 beetle; **7** hanging, soaring; **8** towering; **10** projecting; **11** jutting over, overhanging

beetroot: 4 beet

beet sugar: 7 sucrose

befall: 6 betide, happen; **8** bechance

befit: 2 do; **3** fit; **4** meet, suit; **6** become, beseem; **7** behoove; **13** adapt itself to

befitting: 3 due, fit; **4** good, meet; **5** right; **6** in loco, proper, seemly; **7** binding, correct, en regle, fitting; **8** decorous; **9** behooving; **10** obligatory

befog: 3 fog; **4** mist; **5** cloud; **7** becloud, obscure; **8** haze over, befuddle

befool: 3 cod; **4** dupe, fool, gull, hoax; **5** put on, slang, trick; **6** madden, take in; **8** stultify; **9** bamboozle, infatuate; **10** put one over

before: 5 ahead, until; **6** rather; **7** earlier, in front, prior to; **8** in the van; **9** in advance, in the lead; **12** in presence of

beforehand: 3 yet; **5** ahead; **7** advance, already; **9** in advance

before long: 4 soon; **7** ere long, shortly; **9** presently

befoul: 4 foul; **6** bemire, defile; **7** begrime, besmear, pollute; **8** maculate

befriend: 5 favor

befringed: 7 fringed

befuddle: 3 fox; **5** throw; **6** fuddle; **7** bedevil, confuse; **8** confound; **9** inebriate; **14** discombobulate

befuddled: 4 lost; **5** at sea, mazed, muzzy, wooly; **6** addled, woolly; **7** baffled, bemused, mixed-up, muddled; **8** befogged, confused; **10** bewildered, confounded; **11** wooly-minded; **12** woolly-headed

befuddlement: 10 bafflement, bemusement, puzzlement; **11** obfuscation; **12** bewilderment; **13** mystification

beg: 3 sue, tap; **4** pray; **5** crave; **6** regent; **7** implore, khedive, solicit, viceroy; **8** palatine, petition

beget: 3 get; **4** bear, sire; **5** lie in; **6** father, mother; **8** engender, generate; **9** fecundate, give birth; **10** bring forth; **11** give birth to

begetter: 6 father; **10** male parent

beggar: 4 jade; **5** scrub, tramp; **6** cadger, pauper; **7** caitiff, moocher, poor man, sponger; **8** vagabond; **9** mendicant, pauperize; **10** freeloader, panhandler, ragamuffin

beggar-ticks: 10 sticktight; **11** bur marigold; **12** beggar's-ticks, burr marigold; **14** spanish needles

begging: 7 beggary; **10** mendicancy

begild: 4 gild; **6** engild

begilt: 4 gilt, rich; **6** ornate

begin: 3 get; **4** dawn, open; **5** enter, set in, start; **6** set out; **7** lead off, start up; **8** commence, embark on, set about, start out; **9** enter upon

beginner: 6 novice; **7** amateur, founder; **8** initiate; **11** rank amateur; **14** founding father

beginning: 4 head, root; **5** basal, basic, first, start; **6** novice, offset, origin, outset, source; **7** kickoff, opening, primary; **9** inception; **10** incipience, initiation; **11** abecedarian, origination; **12** commencement, first element, starting time

begird: 3 lap; **4** gird, girt; **5** beset, bound, girth; **7** compass, embrace, enclose, environ, inclose; **8** encircle, surround; **9** encompass; **10** circumvent

beg off: 6 excuse

begone!: 5 scram!; **6** bug off!, beat it!, go away!; **7** buzz off! get lost!; **8** get along

Begoniaceae: 13 begonia family; **17** family Begoniaceae

begonia family: 11 Begoniaceae; **17** family Begoniaceae

beg pardon: 9 apologize, ask pardon; **13** implore pardon; **16** give satisfaction

begrime: 4 soil; **5** colly, dirty, grime; **6** befoul, bemire; **7** besmear; **8** maculate

begrimed: 4 dingy, grimy; **6** grubby, grungy

begrudge: 4 envy; **5** gripe, stint; **6** grudge, resent, scrimp

beguile: 4 draw, lure, move; **5** catch, charm, decoy; **6** allure, delude, disarm, draw on, enamor, entice, induce, juggle, trance; **7** attract, becharm, bewitch, capture, enamour, enchant, win over, delight; **8** entrance, hoodwink, inveigle, enthrall; **9** captivate, fascinate, reconcile; **10** conciliate, propitiate

beguiling: 8 alluring, enticing, tempting; **10** bewitching; **11** captivating, fascinating, stimulating

begum: 7 duchess; **8** princess; **11** marchioness

behalf: 4 weal; **6** behoof; **7** service; **8** interest

behave: 2 do; **3** act; **4** bear; **5** carry; **6** acquit, deport; **7** comport, conduct

behaving: 10 conducting; **17** conducting oneself

behavior: 7 conduct; **8** demeanor; **9** behaviour, demeanour; **10** deportment; **11** comportment

behavioral: 11 behavioural

behavior modification: 15 behavior therapy

behead: 3 gas; **6** gibbet; **7** turn off; **8** string up; **9** bowstring; **10** decapitate, guillotine

beheaded: 11 decapitated

behemoth: 5 giant, titan; **7** goliath, mammoth, monster; **8** colossus; **11** heavyweight

behest: 3 bid, nod; **4** beck, call; **6** dictum; **7** bidding

behind: 3 bum, can; **4** buns, butt, late, prat,

rear, rump, seat, slow, tail, tush; **5** fanny, stern, tardy; **6** bottom; **7** belated, hind end, keister, rear end, tail end, tooshie; **8** backside, backward, buttocks, derriere, in back of, trailing, untimely; **9** fundament, in arrears, posterior

behind closed doors: 10 undercover; **13** behind a screen; **14** behind one's back

behindhand: 4 late, slow; **5** tardy; **6** behind, undone; **7** belated, decayed; **8** backward, untimely; **9** in arrears; **10** unpunctual

behind in payments: 9 in arrears; **10** behindhand

behind the times: 5 stale; **6** old hat, rococo; **7** out of it; **8** after-age; **9** out of date; **10** antiquated; **12** behind the age, of other times, old-fashioned, out of fashion; **14** of the old school

behold: 3 see; **7** witness; **8** perceive; **9** lay eyes on; **11** have in sight

beholden: 7 obliged; **8** grateful, thankful; **10** indebted to; **15** under obligation

beholder: 7 witness; **8** looker-on, observer, onlooker, passer by; **9** bystander, perceiver, spectator; **10** eyewitness

behoof: 4 weal; **6** behalf, profit; **7** service; **8** interest; **10** common weal; **11** summum bonum [Lat]

behoove: 5 befit; **6** become, behove, beseem

behooving: 7 binding; **9** befitting; **10** obligatory

beige: 4 ecru

Beijing: 6 Peking; **7** Peiping; **17** capital of Red China

Beijing dialect: 8 Mandarin; **15** Mandarin Chinese, Mandarin dialect

being: 2 am [1st person sing], be [inf], is [3rd person sing]; **3** are [pl], ens [Lat], man; **4** body, esse [Lat], soul; **5** human; **6** mortal, person; **8** creature, existing, life form, organism, such a one; **9** beingness, earthling, existence, personage; **10** human being, individual, living soul

beingness: 5 being; **9** existence

be in league with: 7 collude, concert, consort; **8** conspire; **10** fraternize; **11** confederate; **12** club together, hand together, hang together, hold together, keep together, pull together

Beirut: 16 capital of Lebanon

bejeweled: 5 beady; **6** beaded, gemmed; **7** jeweled, spangly; **8** jewelled, sequined, spangled; **10** bejewelled, bespangled

Bel: 4 Baal; **5** Belus; **8** Asteroth

bel: 1 B

belabor: 4 drub, pelt; **5** baste; **6** patter, pummel; **7** leather, sandbag, trounce; **8** belabour

Belarus: 8 Byelarus; **10** Belorussia; **11** Byelorussia, White Russia

belated: 4 late, slow; **5** tardy; **6** behind; **8** backward, untaught, untimely; **9** benighted, unbookish, unlearned, untutored; **10** behindhand, uneducated, uninformed, unlettered, unpunctual, unschooled; **12** uninstructed

belaud: 4 laud; **6** praise; **7** commend; **10** compliment

belay: 4 hook, link, lock, yoke; **5** brace, latch, leash; **6** couple; **7** bracket, grapple; **9** barricade; **10** twine round

belch: 4 burp; **5** eruct, erupt; **6** bubble; **7** burping; **8** belch out, belching, eructate; **10** eructation

beldam: 3 hag; **5** crone, witch; **7** beldame, Jezebel, old lady

beleaguer: 3 bug; **5** beset [U.S.], hem in, tease; **6** badger, harass, invest, pester; **7** besiege; **8** surround; **10** circumvent

be left: 6 remain; **7** survive

Belfast: 24 capital of Northern Ireland

belfry: 9 campanile, bell tower

Belgian Congo: 5 Zaire; **28** Democratic Republic of the Congo

Belgian endive: 7 witloof; **12** French endive

Belgian sheep dog: 15 Belgian shepherd

Belgium: 8 Belgique

Belgrade: 7 Beograd; **19** capital of Yugoslavia

Belial: 5 Satan; **6** Samael, Zamiel; **7** Lucifer, old Nick [slang]; **8** the Devil; **9** Beelzebub; **10** the evil one, the tempter; **12** the Adversary, the arch fiend, the archenemy, the foul fiend, the wicked one; **13** the evil spirit, the old Serpent; **14** Mephistopheles

belie: 6 negate; **7** distort, falsify, pervert; **10** contradict; **12** give the lie to, misrepresent

belief: 5 dogma, tenet; **6** notion; **7** feeling; **10** impression

believable: 8 credible

believably: 8 credibly, probably; **9** plausibly

believe: 5 think, trust; **6** credit; **7** be godly, be pious, dare say; **8** be devout, conceive, consider; **9** have faith, speculate

believed: 7 thought

believer: 6 theist; **7** convert, devotee; **8** adherent; **9** worshiper; **10** worshipper

belittle: 5 decry; **6** pick at; **7** detract; **8** derogate, diminish, minimize; **9** denigrate, deprecate, disparage; **10** depreciate

belittled: 5 small; **10** diminished

belittling: 9 insulting, slighting; **10** derogation, derogatory, detracting, detraction, detractive, pejorative; **11** denigration, deprecating, deprecation, deprecative, deprecatory, disparaging, dyslogistic; **12** belittlement, depreciating, depreciation, depreciative, depreciatory; **13** disparagement; **15** uncomplimentary

Belize: 15 British Honduras

bell: 3 cry; **4** gong; **5** chime; **6** alarum, buzzer, cymbal; **7** campana; **8** doorbell

Bell: 13 Alexander Bell; **19** Alexander Graham Bell

belladonna: 7 aconite, hemlock, henbane; **9** hellebore; **10** nightshade; **16** Atropa belladonna, deadly nightshade

belladonna lily: 9 naked lady

bellbottoms: 18 bellbottom trousers

bellboy: 7 bellman

bell buoy: 8 gong buoy

Belleau Wood: 10 Marne River; **14** Chateau-Thierry; **16** battle of the Marne

belles lettres: 7 letters; **10** literature; **16** polite literature

bellflower family: 9 campanula; **13** Campanulaceae

bellhop: 7 bellboy, bellman

bellicose: 7 martial, warlike; **9** battleful, combative; **10** pugnacious; **11** belligerent, contentious

bellied: 5 bulgy; **7** bulbous, bulging; **8** bellying; **10** pot-bellied; **11** protuberant

belligerent: 7 battler, fighter, hostile, martial, warlike, warring; **8** fighting, militant, scrapper; **9** bellicose, combatant, combative, truculent, war-ridden; **10** aggressive; **11** contentious

bell jar: 9 bell glass

bellman: 5 crier, 6 herald; **7** bellboy, bellhop, marshal; **9** trumpeter; **10** flag bearer; **13** parlementaire [Fr]

Bellona: 4 Mars; **10** war goddess

bellow: 3 cry; **4** bawl, hoop, howl, roar, yell, yowl; **5** blare, brawl, holla, hollo, shout, whoop; **6** halloa, halloo, holler, holloa, scream, shriek, shrill; **7** roaring, screech, yowling; **8** bellows: 3 fan; 4 lung; 5 lungs; **6** blower; **7** air pump; **8** blowpipe; **9** air blower; **10** ventilator

bellows fish: 9 snipefish

bell pepper: 7 paprika, pimento; **8** pimiento; **11** green pepper, sweet pepper; **13** Jamaica pepper

bell ringing: 8 carillon; **10** canvassing

bell shape: 4 bell; **7** campana; **8** egg shape; **9** pear shape

bell-shaped curve: 11 normal curve; **13** Gaussian curve, Gaussian shape

bell tower: 9 campanile

bellwether: 11 trendsetter

bellwort: 8 wild oats; **10** merry bells

belly: 3 gut; **6** paunch, venter; **7** abdomen, stomach; **8** belly out, pot belly; **9** pork belly; **10** side of pork; **11** breadbasket

bellyache: 4 beef; **5** gripe; **6** grouse, holler, squawk; **8** complain; **10** gastralgia; **11** stomach ache

bellyacher: 6 moaner, whiner; **7** crybaby; **8** grumbler, sniveler, squawker; **10** complainer

bellybutton: 5 navel; 8 omphalos, omphalus; 9 umbilicus

belly dancer: 12 exotic dancer

bellyful: 4 fill, load; 6 bumper

bellying: 5 bulgy; 7 bellied, bulbous, bulging; 11 protuberant

belly laugh: 3 wow; 4 riot; 6 guffaw, howler, scream; 10 horse laugh; 11 hearty laugh; 12 sidesplitter, thigh-slapper

Belomancy: 8 by arrows

belong: 2 go; 3 lie; 5 dwell, lie in; 7 consist; 8 belong to; 9 pertain to

belongings: 5 asset, means; 6 assets; 7 holding; 8 property; 9 resources; 13 circumstances; 18 material possession

Belorussia: 7 Belarus; 8 Byelarus; 11 Byelorussia, White Russia

be lost: 9 be missing

beloved: 4 dear, love; 5 honey; 7 darling, dearest; 8 loved one; 11 well beloved; 13 dearly beloved

below: 5 below, infra, under; 7 beneath; 10 downstairs

belowground: 11 underground

below the mark: 8 below par, under par; 12 under the mark

belt: 3 gut, orb, rap; 4 band, bang, bash, girt, zone; 5 bayou [U.S.], clasp, creek, crick, cycle, knock, orbit, smash, swath, whack, whang; 6 cordon, girdle, rundle, zodiac; 7 baldric, belt out

beluga: 6 beluga, hausen; 10 white whale; 13 white sturgeon

Belus: 3 Bel; 4 Baal; 8 Asteroth

belvedere: 6 gazebo; 8 firebush; 11 burning bush; 13 summer cypress

bema: 7 chancel; 9 sanctuary

bemask: 4 mask; 8 disguise

bemingle: 9 commingle; 11 intermingle

bemire: 4 soil; 5 colly, dirty, grime; 6 befoul; 7 begrime, besmear; 8 maculate

bemoan: 6 bewail, grieve, lament, regret; 7 deplore

bemock: 4 mock

bemuse: 5 throw; 8 bewilder; 14 discombobulate

bemused: 4 lost, rapt; 5 at sea, mazed; 7 baffled, mixed-up; 8 confused; 9 befuddled; 10 bewildered, confounded; 11 in the clouds, preoccupied; 13 deep in thought

bemusement: 10 bafflement, puzzlement; 11 obfuscation; 12 befuddlement, bewilderment; 13 mystification

bench: 5 board, court, forum, staff; 7 cabinet, chamber, terrace; 8 tribunal; 9 judiciary, work bench, workbench; 10 court of law; 14 court of justice

bencher: 6 leader; 8 silk gown; 13 sergeant-at-law

benchmark: 9 bench mark

bench warmer: 7 reserve; 9 pine rider; 10 substitute

bench warrant: 13 arrest warrant

bend: 3 bow, dip; 4 flex, fold, fork, give, turn; 5 couch, crimp, crook, curve, relax, squat, stoop, trend, twist, verge, wheel, yield; 6 crease, crouch, deform, resign, submit; 7 bending, crinkle, defer to, deflect, flexion, flexure, incline, succumb; 8 flection, turn away; 9 bifurcate, determine, plication; 10 bend dexter, inflection

bendable: 6 pliant; 7 pliable

bend down: 9 knuckle to; 11 knuckle down; 12 knuckle under

bender: 4 bust, tear, toot; 5 binge, curve; 7 booze-up; 9 curve ball; 12 breaking ball

bending: 3 dip; 4 bend, flex; 7 curving, dipping, flexion, sagging, turning, verging; 8 flection, trending, yielding; 9 deflexion, inclining; 10 deflection, inflection

bend over: 8 hang over; 9 swell over

bends: 11 air embolism; 12 aeroembolism; 14 caisson disease; 21 decompression sickness

bendy tree: 10 portia tree; 12 seaside mahoe

beneath: 5 below; 10 underneath

Benedict: 13 Saint Benedict

benedict: 8 benedick

benediction: 5 grace; 6 praise, thanks; 7 benison, hosanna; 8 blessing, doxology; 13 glorification

benedictory: 8 praising; 9 laudatory; 10 eulogistic, uncritical; 11 benedictive, encomiastic, panegyrical; 12 commendatory; 13 complimentary

benefaction: 4 boon; 5 favor; 11 benevolence

benefactor: 6 helper, savior, patron; 10 good genius; 13 guardian angel

beneficence: 5 favor; 8 good turn; 9 good works; 13 act of kindness

beneficent: 6 humane; 8 gracious; 9 benignant; 10 benevolent; 12 eleemosynary; 13 philanthropic

beneficial: 4 good; 8 salutary; 12 advantageous

beneficiary: 5 donee, vicar; 6 curate, parson, pastor, rector; 9 mortgagor, rural dean

benefit: 4 gain, good; 6 do good, profit; 7 service, welfare; 8 usufruct; 9 advantage, good thing

benevolent: 4 good, kind; 6 kindly; 8 gracious; 10 beneficent; 11 freehearted; 12 eleemosynary; 13 philanthropic

Benghazi: 14 capital of Libya

benight: 5 bedim; 7 obscure

benighted: 4 dark; 7 belated, nighted; 8 untaught; 9 unbookish, unlearned, untutored; 10 uneducated, uninformed, unlettered, unschooled; 12 uninstructed

benign: 8 harmless, innocent; 9 benignant, innocuous, 11 uninjurious

benignant: 6 benign, humane; **8** gracious; **10** beneficent

benignity: 7 charity; **8** humanity, kindness; **9** humanness; **10** benignancy, goodliness, kindliness; **12** graciousness; **13** brotherly love; **14** charitableness, loving-kindness; **15** kind-heartedness

benign tumor: 17 nonmalignant tumor

Benin: 7 Dahomey; **8** Beninese

benison: 8 blessing; **11** benediction

benne: 5 benni, benny; **6** sesame; **14** Sesamum indicum

bennie: 5 benny; **10** Benzedrine

benolin: 7 benzene; **13** benzine benzol

benshie: 6 Ormuzd, wraith; **9** loup-garou [Fr]

bent: 3 set; **4** bias, hang, mind; **5** bowed, knack, out to; **6** animus, bended, bent on, dented, dingle [U.S.], jagged; **7** angular, crooked, dead set, leaning; **8** aquiline, crumpled, inclined, intent on, penchant, serrated, tendency; **9** bent grass, bentgrass, proneness; **10** affections, partiality, proclivity, propensity; **11** disposition, inclination; **12** predilection; **14** predisposition

bent grass: 4 bent

Benthamite: 10 eudemonist; **11** cosmopolite, eudaemonist, utilitarian; **17** citizen of the world; **19** amicus humani generis [Lat]

benthic: 7 benthal; **9** benthonic

bent on: 4 bent; **5** out to, set on; **7** dead set, set upon; **8** bent upon, dying for, intent on, mad after; **10** anxious for, intent upon

benumb: 4 dull, numb, pall, stun; **5** blunt; **6** deaden; **7** petrify, stupefy; **8** paralyze

benumbed: 4 numb; **6** asleep, dulled

Benzedrine: 5 benny; **6** bennie

benzene: 6 benzol; **7** benzine; **13** benzine benzol

benzene ring: 13 Kekule formula; **14** benzene formula, benzene nucleus

benzoate of soda: 14 sodium benzoate

benzocaine: 18 ethyl aminobenzoate

benzoin: 6 arnica; **7** calomel; **8** benjamin; **9** asa dulcis; **10** gum benzoin; **11** gum benjamin

Benzoin: 9 spicebush; **12** Benjamin bush, genus Benzoin

benzol: 7 benzene, benzine

Beograd: 8 Belgrade; **19** capital of Yugoslavia

be on the fence: 4 trim; **5** demur, pause; **6** coquet, debate, waffle; **7** balance, shuffle; **8** straddle; **9** fluctuate, hem and haw, hum and haw; **13** remain neutral

bepaint: 4 tint; **5** tinct, tinge, touch

bequeath: 4 will; **5** leave

bequeathing: 7 bequest, willing; **10** bequeathal

bequest: 6 legacy; **7** willing; **9** patrimony; **10** bequeathal; **11** bequeathing, inheritance

be quiet: 6 belt up, clam up, shut up; **7** close up, dummy up, keep mum; **8** button up

be rancid: 11 be putrefied

berate: 3 jaw, rag; **5** check, chide, scold; **6** blow, up, chew up, rebuke; **7** bawl out, chew out, lambast, lecture, reproof, upbraid; **8** lambaste; **9** dress down, have words, reprimand; **11** remonstrate

Berberidaceae: 14 barberry family

berceuse: 7 lullaby; **10** cradlesong

Bercy: 11 Bercy butter

bereaved: 5 minus; **6** bereft, cut off; **7** denuded; **8** grieving, mourning; **9** sorrowing; **13** grief-stricken

bereavement: 4 loss; **8** mourning; **9** privation

bereft: 5 minus; **6** cut off; **7** denuded; **8** bereaved, grieving, lovelorn, mourning; **9** sorrowing, unbeloved; **13** grief-stricken

berg: 7 iceberg

bergamot: 4 balm; **9** potpourri; **14** bergamot orange, Citrus bergamia

bergamot mint: 7 bee balm, beebalm; **9** lemon mint, oswego tea

berkelium: 2 Bk

Berkshires: 14 Berkshire Hills

Berlin doughnut: 7 bismark; **13** jelly doughnut

Bermuda grass: 4 doob; **5** kweek; **9** star grass; **10** devil grass; **11** Bahama grass, scutch grass

Bermuda shorts: 6 shorts, trunks; **10** short pants; **13** Jamaica shorts

Bermudian: 8 Bermudan

Berne: 4 Bern; **20** capital of Switzerland

berried: 7 baccate; **11** bacciferous

berrylike: 7 baccate

berserk: 4 amok, wild; **5** amuck, giddy, rabid; **6** doting, maniac, raving; **7** frantic, wild man; **8** demoniac, frenetic, frenzied, rambling, unhinged, wild-eyed; **9** berserker, delirious, insensate, possessed, wandering; **10** demoniacal, incoherent, reasonless; **11** dithyrambic, lightheaded, vertiginous

berserker: 6 maniac; **7** berserk, wild man

Berteroa: 6 alison; **7** alyssum; **13** genus Berteroa

berth: 3 pad; **4** bunk, digs, moor, post, slip, slot, spot; **5** place; **6** office; **7** moorage, mooring; **8** diggings, position; **9** situation; **10** built in bed, habitation, incumbency

Bertholletia: 9 brazil nut; **17** genus Bertholletia

beryl: 7 emerald; **9** malachite, verdigris; **10** aquamarine

beryllium: 2 Be; **8** glucinum; **9** glucinium

beseech: 3 bid; **5** plead, press; **6** adjure; **7** beg hard, entreat, implore; **10** supplicate

beseem: 4 suit; **5** befit; **6** become; **7** behoove

beset: 3 bug, dog, dun, lap, ply, tax; **4** bait, bore, gird, urge; **5** abuse, bored, bound, chevy, chivy, grind, harry, haunt, hound, press, stalk, tease, worry; **6** badger, baited, begird, bother, chevvy, chivvy, harass, hassle, heckle, ill-use, infest, invest, molest, pester, plague, pother, shadow; **7** besiege, compass, embrace, enclose, encrust, environ, harried, heckled, inclose, oppress, provoke, set upon; **8** badgered, bullirag, bullyrag, encircle, harassed, ill-treat, infested, maltreat, mistreat, pothered, surround; **9** beleaguer, clamor for, encompass, importune, imprecate, persecute; **10** circumvent, importuned, lay siege to, persecuted

besetting: 4 rife; **5** fixed; **6** rooted; **8** epidemic; **9** hackneyed, permanent, prevalent; **10** deep-rooted, inveterate, prevailing

beshrew: 4 damn; **5** curse, scold; **6** bedamn; **8** execrate, maledict; **9** imprecate; **10** anathemize

be sick: 3 cat; **4** barf, cast, honk, puke, sick, spew, spue; **5** chuck, heave, retch, vomit; **6** cast up; **7** bring up, chuck up, get sick, regorge, throw up, upchuck, vomit up; **8** disgorge; **11** regurgitate

beside: 4 save; **5** aside; **6** except; **7** abreast, barring, without; **8** let alone; **9** alongside, aside from, except for, on one side, other than; **10** side by side; **12** at the heels of; **13** save and except

beside oneself: 3 mad; **4** wild; **5** giddy, rabid; **6** doting, raving; **7** berserk, frantic; **8** frenetic, frenzied, rambling, unhinged, wild-eyed; **9** delirious, insensate, possessed, wandering; **10** demoniacal, distracted, distraught, hysterical, incoherent, reasonless; **11** dithyrambic, in hysterics, lightheaded, vertiginous

besides: 2 &c.; **3** too; **4** also, else; **6** as well, to boot; **8** et cetera, likewise; **9** in any case

besiege: 5 beset [U.S.], hem in; **6** invest; **8** surround; **9** beleaguer; **10** circumvent, lay siege to

besmear: 4 daub; **5** smear; **6** bedaub, befoul, bemire; **7** begrime, plaster; **8** maculate

besmirch: 4 soil; **5** smear, sully, taint; **6** defame, smirch; **7** asperse, slander, tarnish; **9** denigrate; **10** calumniate

besom: 5 broom

besot: 3 bib, sot; **4** lush, soak, swig; **5** swill; **6** guzzle; **7** carouse, stupefy, stupify

besotted: 3 wet; **5** blind, potty, stiff, tight, tipsy; **6** blotto, entete [Fr], loaded, pissed, soaked, soused, tiddly; **7** crocked, fuddled, slopped, sloshed, smashed, sozzled, squiffy, tiddley; **8** confined, dogmatic, positive; **9** conceited, fanatical, illiberal, pixilated, plastered; **10** blind drunk, infatuated, intolerant

bespatter: 6 splash, vilify; **7** blacken, spatter; **8** blow upon

bespeak: 4 hire, name, tout; **5** argue, court, imply, point, quest; **6** convey, engage, return, secure, signal; **7** appoint, betoken, breathe, call for, canvass, involve, point to, request; **8** accredit, allude to, indicate, nominate

bespectacled: 8 monocled; **10** spectacled

bespoke: 6 custom; **8** bespoken, tailored; **10** tailor-made; **11** made-to-order

bespoken: 6 custom; **7** bespoke, engaged, pledged; **8** tailored; **9** affianced, betrothed; **10** tailor-made; **11** made-to-order

besprent: 9 sprinkled

besprinkle: 4 dash; **5** blend, cross, tinge; **6** season; **8** medicate, sprinkle, tincture; **10** infiltrate

Besseya: 12 genus Besseya

best: 4 beat; **5** outdo, outgo, scoop, trump; **6** better, outrun; **7** outjump, outleap, outride; **8** outflank, outrival, outstrip

bestead: 13 be the making of; **19** stand one in good stead

bested: 7 outdone

bestial: 5 brute; **7** beastly, brutish

bestiality: 9 zooerasty; **10** zooerastia

bestialize: 10 bestialise

bestir: 5 rouse

bestow: 3 add; **4** lend; **5** bring, grant; **6** confer, impart; **10** contribute

bestower: 7 awarder; **9** presenter

bestrew: 4 shed; **6** spread; **7** diffuse, disband, scatter; **8** dispense, disperse; **10** overspread; **11** disseminate

bestride: 4 ride; **5** get on, hop on, mount; **6** beetle, impend, jump on; **7** climb on, mount up; **8** hang over, overhang

bet: 3 bet; **5** stake, wager; **6** stakes; **7** play for, risking, staking; **8** make a bet; **9** hazarding

beta-adrenergic blocking agent: 11 beta blocker

Beta Orionis: 5 Rigel

beta particle: 7 beta ray

beta ray: 12 beta particle; **13** beta radiation; **17** electron radiation

Beta recorder: 15 BetaMax recorder; **19** Sony Betamax recorder

betatron: 20 induction accelerator

Beta vulgaris: 4 beet; **10** common beet

Beta vulgaris cicla: 5 chard; **8** leaf beet; **10** chard plant, Swiss chard; **11** spinach beet

Beta vulgaris rubra: 8 beetroot

beta wave: 10 beta rhythm

betel: 10 Piper betel; **11** betel pepper

Betelgeuse: 12 Alpha Orionis

betel nut: 8 areca nut

betel palm: 12 Areca catechu

bete noire: 7 bugaboo, bugbear; **8** anathema, aversion; **9** nightmare; **11** abomination

bethel: 4 kirk; **6** chapel, church; **7** oratory;

8 basilica; 9 cathedral; 10 tabernacle; 11 conventicle; 12 meetinghouse

betide: 6 befall

betimes: 4 anon, soon; 5 early; 7 shortly; 9 presently, right away; 11 occasionally

betise: 5 folly; 9 stupidity; 10 imbecility; 11 foolishness

betoken: 4 bode, omen, show; 5 augur, point; 6 denote, evince, signal, tell of, typify; 7 bespeak, point to, portend, predict, presage, refer to, signify; 8 forebode, forecast, foretell, indicate, stand for; 9 auspicate, foretoken, prefigure, represent, symbolize; 10 be evidence, foreshadow

bet on: 4 back, gage, game, punt; 5 stake; 6 look to, rely on; 7 count on; 8 depend on, reckon on, rely upon; 9 count upon; 10 depend upon; 11 calculate on

betray: 3 rat; 4 fail, sell, shop, stag; 5 cheat, grass, peach; 6 bewray, snitch, tell on, wander; 7 cheat on, cuckold, deceive; 8 denounce, give away; 10 lead astray; 11 turn against

betrayal: 7 perfidy, treason; 9 treachery; 10 disloyalty; 13 double dealing

betrayer: 3 rat; 7 traitor; 8 informer, squealer; 11 conspirator; 12 double-dealer; 13 double-crosser

betroth: 6 engage, plight; 8 affiance; 9 betrothal; 10 engagement

betrothal: 5 troth; 7 betroth; 8 affiance, espousal; 10 engagement

betrothed: 7 engaged, fiancee, pledged; 8 bespoken; 9 affianced

better: 4 best, mend; 5 amend, break; 6 bettor, punter; 7 improve, wagerer; 8 bettered, improved; 9 better for, better off, meliorate; 10 ameliorate

better-looking: 8 handsome; 11 fine-looking, good-looking, well-favored

betterment: 7 advance; 9 bettering; 11 enhancement, improvement, melioration; 12 amelioration; 13 getting better

betting: 7 betting; 8 gambling, sporting, wagering; 10 dissipated; 11 card-playing

betting house: 6 casino; 11 gaming house; 13 gambling house

bettor: 6 better, punter; 7 wagerer

Betulaceae: 11 birch family

betweenbrain: 10 interbrain; 12 diencephalon

between: 5 'tween; 7 betwixt

between jobs: 7 jobless; 10 unemployed; 11 without a job

between the teeth: 5 aside; 9 sotto voce [Lat]; 10 in a whisper; 15 with bated breath

betwixt: 7 between

be up: 3 bat; 7 be at bat

beurre noisette: 11 brown butter

bevel: 4 cant, tilt; 6 camfer; 7 beveled, chamfer; 11 bevel square

beverage: 5 drink; 7 potable; 9 drinkable

bevue: 5 faute [Fr], lurch; 7 faux pas [Fr]

bevy: 3 fry; 4 herd, hive, nest, peck; 5 brood, cloud, covey, drove, flock, shoal, swarm; 6 bushel, farrow, flight, litter, scores; 7 draught

bewail: 5 mourn; 6 bemoan, grieve, lament, regret; 7 deplore

beware: 4 mind, ware; 7 look out!; 8 take care!, watch out!; 9 keep watch; 11 take warning

bewhiskered: 7 barbate, bearded; 8 whiskery; 9 whiskered

bewilder: 3 get; 4 beat, stun; 5 amaze, throw; 6 baffle, bemuse, bother, dazzle, gravel, molder, muddle, put out, puzzle; 7 confuse, flummox, fluster, mystify, nonplus, perplex, petrify, stagger, stupefy, stupify, trounce; 8 confound; 9 dumbfound, fascinate; 10 strike dumb; 11 flabbergast, turn the head; 12 addle the wits; 14 discombobulate

bewildered: 4 lost; 5 at sea, mazed; 7 baffled, bemused, mixed-up, stunned; 8 confused; 9 befuddled, staggered, stupefied; 10 confounded, struck dumb; 13 flabbergasted

bewildering: 11 confounding, dumfounding; 12 mind-boggling; 14 flabbergasting

bewitch: 3 hex; 4 coax, jinx, lure; 5 catch, charm, tempt, witch; 6 attach, enamor, endear, hoodoo, seduce, trance, voodoo; 7 attract, becharm, bedevil, beguile, capture, enamour, enchant, glamour, wheedle; 8 entrance; 9 captivate, carry away, enrapture, fascinate, magnetize, mesmerize, spellbind, transport; 10 conciliate

bewitched: 8 hoodooed; 9 bedeviled; 11 ensorcelled

bewitching: 8 charming, engaging; 9 beguiling; 10 enchanting, entrancing; 11 captivating, enthralling, fascinating, interesting, stimulating

be with child: 8 pregnant

bewray: 6 betray; 7 divulge

beyond: 4 more, over; 5 ahead; 6 abroad, yonder; 7 farther, further, outside

beyond all bounds: 10 infinitely; 12 immeasurably; 13 beyond measure

bezant: 6 byzant; 7 bezzant

bezique: 8 pinochle

bezoar goat: 6 pasang; 13 Capra aegagrus

bezonian: 4 jade, 5 scrub, tramp; 6 beggar, Pariah; 7 caitiff, 8 vagabond; 10 Cinderella, panhandler, ragamuffin

bhang: 3 pot; 4 hemp, weed; 5 ganja, grass; 6 reefer; 7 hashish; 9 marijuana

Bharat: 5 India

Bi: 7 bismuth

bialy: 11 bialystoker

biannual: 8 biyearly; 10 semiannual
bias: 4 bent, swag, sway, warp; 5 twist; 6 weight; 7 dispose, incline, leaning; 8 diagonal, tendency; 9 cause bias, influence, inoculate, prejudice, proneness, weigh with; 10 affections, partiality, predispose, proclivity, propensity; 11 disposition, inclination; 12 predetermine; 14 cause prejudice, predisposition
biased: 6 skewed; 7 colored, slanted; 8 lopsided, one-sided, top-heavy; 10 prejudiced
biaxial: 6 biaxal; 7 biaxate
bib: sot; 4 lush, soak, swig; 5 besot, swill; 6 guzzle, tipple, tucker; 7 carouse
bibacious: 7 drunken, sottish
bibber: 3 cry, sob, sot, tun; 4 lush, pipe, wail, weep; 5 toper; 6 soaker, sponge; 7 blubber, guzzler, tippler; 8 drunkard; 9 drop a tear, drop tears, shed a tear, shed tears; 11 hard drinker
bibelot: 5 curio; 6 bauble, gewgaw, trifle; 7 novelty, trinket, whatnot; 8 chotchke, gimcrack, kickshaw, nicknack, whim-wham; 9 bagatelle, bric-a-brac, tchotchke; 10 knick-knack
Bible: 4 Word; 5 Torah, Koran, Quran; 8 Good Book, Holy Writ, the Bible; 9 Scripture, Word of God; 13 Holy Scripture, the Scriptures
bible leaf: 7 alecost; 8 costmary; 10 balsam herb; 12 mint geranium
biblical: 6 sacred; 9 prophetic; 10 scriptural
Biblical Latin: 9 Late Latin
biblioclast: 10 book-burner
bibliographic: 15 bibliographical
bibliolatry: 10 puritanism; 11 bibliomania, book madness; 12 Bible-worship
Bibliomancy: 10 by the Bible
bibliomania: 11 book madness
bibliomaniac: 9 book lover; 10 avid reader; 11 bibliophile
bibliophile: 9 book lover, booklover; 10 avid reader
bibliothec: 9 librarian
Bibos: 10 genus Bibos
Bibos frontalis: 5 gayal; 6 mithan
Bibos gaurus: 4 gaur
bibulous: 5 boozy; 7 drunken, sottish
bicameral: 12 two-chambered
bicarbonate of soda: 4 soda; 9 saleratus; 10 baking soda; 11 bicarbonate; 17 sodium bicarbonate
bicentenary: 11 bicentenary; 12 bicentennial
bicephalous: 6 lunate; 8 crescent; 9 semilunar, two-headed; 12 double-headed; 14 crescent-shaped
bichromate: 10 dichromate
bichrome: 7 bicolor; 8 bicolour; 9 bicolored; 10 bicoloured
bicipital: 7 bivalve; 9 bilabiate

bicker: 3 nag; 4 fuss, spat, tiff; 6 jangle, niggle; 7 brabble, flicker, flitter, flutter, quibble, wrangle; 8 pettifog, squabble; 9 bickering
bickering: 4 fuss, spat, tiff; 5 words; 6 bicker, demele; 7 wrangle; 8 clashing, jangling, squabble; 9 high words, wrangling; 10 squabbling
bicolor: 8 bichrome, bicolour; 9 bicolored; 10 bicoloured
biconvex: 9 lentiform; 10 lenticular; 13 convexo-convex
bicorn: 6 bicorn; 7 bicorne; 8 bicorned; 9 bicornate, cocked hat; 10 bicornuate, bicornuous
bicuspid: 5 bifid; 8 premolar; 9 bipartite; 11 bicuspidate
bicycle: 4 bike; 5 cycle, pedal, wheel; 10 two-wheeler
bicycle built for two: 6 tandem; 16 two-person bicycle
bicycle seat: 6 saddle
bid: 3 nod; 4 beck, call, play, wish; 5 offer, press; 6 adjure, behest, charge, dictum, enjoin, invite, tender; 7 beseech, bidding, command, entreat; 8 call upon, instruct; 9 dictation
Bida: 4 Doha; 6 El Beda; 14 capital of Qatar
biddable: 9 compliant; 11 acquiescent
bidden: 7 charged; 10 called upon; 11 imposed upon
bidder: 6 suitor; 8 aspirant, claimant; 9 candidate, postulant; 10 competitor
bidding: 3 bid, nod; 4 beck, call; 6 behest, dictum; 7 command, summons; 9 dictation
bide: 4 bear, stay, wait; 5 abide, brave, brook, stand, tarry; 6 endure, suffer; 8 take time, tolerate; 9 go through
bidental: 7 bivalve; 9 bilabiate
bide one's time: 4 wait; 5 abide, watch; 8 take time; 9 lie in wait; 10 tide it over; 12 take one's time
biegnet: 13 French fritter
biennial: 7 two-year; 8 biyearly
bier: 4 pall; 6 hearse; 10 catafalque
bier patch: 5 brier; 10 brierpatch
biface: 8 bifacial
bifacial: 6 biface
biff: 4 lick, poke, blow; 5 punch, whack; 6 pommel, pummel
bifid: 8 bicuspid; 9 bipartite
bifocals: 14 reading glasses
bifurcate: 4 bend, fork; 6 forked, prongy, zigzag; 7 crinkle, pronged; 8 biramous, branched, separate; 10 bifurcated
bifurcation: 4 fork; 7 forking; 9 branching, furcation; 12 divarication, ramification
big: 3 bad; 4 high, huge; 5 adult, elder, great, grown, heavy, large, older; 6 braggy, giving, gravid; 7 crowing, grownup, liberal, swelled; 8 boastful, braggart, bragging,

enceinte, handsome; **9** bounteous, bountiful, cock-a-hoop, expectant, full-grown, momentous, prominent, with child; **10** big-hearted, boastfully, freehanded, fully grown, openhanded, vauntingly; **11** magnanimous

bigarade: 10 sour orange; **12** bitter orange; **13** Seville orange

big board: 20 New York Stock Exchange

big businessman: 4 king; **5** baron, mogul, power; **6** tycoon; **7** magnate

Big Dipper: 6 Dipper, Plough; **12** Charles's Wain

Bigfoot: 9 Sasquatch

bigger: 6 larger

biggest: 7 largest; **8** greatest

big hand: 10 minute hand

bighead: 7 anthrax

bigheaded: 4 snob; **6** snooty, snotty, uppish; **7** stuck-up; **9** snot-nosed; **11** persnickety

bighearted: 3 big; **6** giving; **8** generous

Bighorn: 12 Bighorn River

bighorn sheep: 7 bighorn; **8** cimarron

bight: 3 bay; **6** armlet; **9** embayment

big league: 6 majors; **11** major league

big leaguer: 12 major leaguer

big money: 4 pile; **6** bundle; **8** big bucks

bigmouthed: 6 blabby; **9** talkative; **12** blabbermouth

big name: 9 celebrity

bigoted: 9 fanatical; **10** intolerant

bigotry: 9 dogmatism; **11** intolerance

big shot: 3 VIP [acron]; **7** his nibs; **8** big wheel; **10** head honcho; **13** high muck-a-muck

big-sounding: 4 rich; **5** stagy, tumid; **6** florid, mouthy, ornate, turgid; **7** flowery, orotund; **8** inflated, overdone, sonorous, swelling; **9** bombastic, grandiose, high flown, overacted; **10** Johnsonian, ornamented, rhetorical, theatrical, turgescent; **11** declamatory, high flowing, overwrought; **12** high-sounding, magniloquent; **13** grandiloquent; **14** sesquipedalian

big spender: 10 high roller

big top: 8 round top; **10** circus tent

big wheel: 3 VIP [acron]; **7** big shot, his nibs; **10** head honcho; **13** high muck-a-muck

bigwig: 3 don; **7** kingpin; **8** wiseacre; **9** know-it-all, top banana

bijou: 3 gem; **4** ruby; **5** jewel, pearl; **7** diamond, jewelry; **10** bijouterie [Fr]; **13** precious stone

bike: 4 bike; **5** cycle, pedal, wheel; **7** bicycle; **10** motorcycle, two-wheeler

biker: 12 motorcyclist

bikini: 8 two-piece

bilateral: 8 two-sided

bilberry: 9 blaeberry, whinberry; **12** whortleberry; **17** European blueberry, mountain blue berry

bilbo: 5 brand; **6** rapier, stocks; **7** pillory; **8** whinyard

bile: 3 ire, pet; **4** fume, tiff; **6** choler, dander, pucker, taking; **7** ferment, passion; **9** angry mood; **10** ebullition; **11** acharnement [Fr]

bilestone: 9 gallstone

bilge: 4 gape, hold, open, yawn; **5** bulge; **8** swelling

bilharzia: 12 bilharziasis; **11** schistosome

bilious: 3 hot; **5** hasty, quick, surly; **6** livery; **7** biliary, peevish, peppery, waspish; **8** captious, choleric, liverish, shrewish, snappish; **9** dyspeptic, fractious, overhasty, querulous; **11** atrabilious

bilk: 2 do; **3** con, nab; **4** bite, foil, jilt, rook, scam; **5** cheat, cozen, cross, elude, evade, mulct, pluck, queer, spoil; **6** baffle, chouse, diddle, euchre, fleece, jockey, pigeon, scotch, sponge, thwart; **7** defraud, swindle; **9** frustrate, victimize

bilked: 7 cheated, diddled, euchred, plucked; **8** swindled; **9** defrauded; **10** victimized

bilkster: 5 fraud; **8** swindler; **10** victimizer

bill: 2 ax; **3** neb, nib; **4** beak, card, note, peak; **5** claim, flier, flyer, paper, sheet, visor, vizor; **6** charge, notice, poster; **7** account, damages, invoice, measure, placard; **8** bank bill, bank note, banknote, billhook, circular, eyeshade, handbill; **9** broadside, greenback, throwaway; **10** banker's bill

billboard: 8 hoarding; **9** signboard

billet: 3 job; **4** cast, chip, chop, mete, note; **5** check, share, tally; **6** canton, detail, letter; **7** counter, epistle, missive, quarter; **8** position; **9** duplicate

billet-doux: 5 favor; **9** valentine; **10** love letter

billeted: 6 housed, lodged; **9** quartered

billfish: 3 gar; **5** saury; **7** garfish, garpike; **10** needlefish

billfold: 6 wallet; **8** notecase

billhook: 4 bill

billiards: 4 pool; **7** snooker

billiard saloon: 12 billiard hall, billiard room; **14** billiard parlor; **15** billiard parlour

billiard table: 9 pool table; **12** snooker table

billing: 6 charge

billionth: 4 nano

bill of exchange: 4 bill; **5** draft; **14** order of payment

bill of fare: 4 card, menu; **5** carte [Fr], table; **7** cuisine; **8** ordinary; **10** table d'hote [Fr]; **11** carte du jour

bill of lading: 7 invoice, waybill

billow: 3 sea; **4** roll, wave, well; **5** heave, surge, swell; **6** wallow, well up; **7** balloon, inflate

billy: 4 bail; **5** stick; **6** beaker, he-goat;

7 canakin; **9** billy club, billy goat, truncheon; **10** billystick, nightstick
billy club: 5 billy; **10** nightstick
billycock: 9 forage cap, wideawake; **14** bearskinbonnet
billy goat: 5 billy; **6** he-goat
bimetallic: 7 bimetal; **13** bimetallistic
bimillenary: 12 bimillennium
bimonthly: 9 bimonthly; **10** bimestrial; **11** semimonthly
binary: 6 binary; **8** binomial; **10** binary star, double star
binary number: 11 octal number; **17** hexadecimal number [Comp]; **26** pure binary numeration system
binary operation: 16 boolean operation
binary star: 6 binary; **10** double star; **15** eclipsing binary
binaural: 7 biaural
binaurally: 10 in both ears, to both ears
bind: 3 cap, fix, tie, tip; **4** bond, hold; **5** affix, stick, tie up, truss, twist; **6** adhere, attach, clinch, fasten, oblige, secure; **7** bandage, stick to, tie down; **8** bind over, hold fast, make fast, saddle on; **10** constipate
binder: 7 bindery; **8** ligature; **10** ring-binder; **12** reaper binder
bindery: 6 binder
binding: 4 back; **5** cover; **8** dressing; **9** bandaging, befitting, behooving; **10** obligatory; **11** book binding, enforceable; **12** constipating, constricting
bindle stiff: 2 bo; **3** bum; **4** hobo; **5** tramp; **6** pauper; **14** homeless person
bind off: 5 tie up
bind over: 4 bind
bine: 6 flower; **7** blossom; **9** common hop; **10** common hops; **11** European hop; **14** Humulus lupulus
binge: 4 bust, glut, tear, toot; **5** gorge, spree, stuff; **6** bender, englut, pig out; **7** booze-up, engorge, overeat, satiate; **8** scarf out; **9** overgorge; **10** gormandise, gormandize; **11** gourmandize, ingurgitate, overindulge
binging: 8 bingeing
bingo: 4 keno; **5** beano, lotto
binoculars: 9 binocular; **10** field glass, opera glass; **12** field glasses, opera glasses
binomial: 6 binary
bioengineering: 10 ergonomics; **13** biotechnology
bioflavinoid: 6 citrin; **8** vitamin P
biography: 4 life; **9** life story; **11** life history; **13** autobiography
biological: 8 biologic
biological process: 14 organic process
biologist: 13 life scientist
biology: 5 biota; **13** science of life; **17** biological science

biome: 7 habitat; **16** ecological system
bionic man: 6 cyborg
bionic woman: 6 cyborg
bionomics: 7 ecology; **20** environmental science
biosynthesis: 10 biogenesis
biota: 7 biology
biotin: 6 biotin
biovular: 9 fraternal
biparous: 4 twin; **8** twinning
bipartisan: 6 two-way; **8** two-party
bipartite: 5 bifid; **6** two-way; **8** bicuspid, two-party; **8** two-part
bipartition: 9 bisection
biped: 7 bipedal; **9** two-footed
bipolar disorder: 15 manic depression
biquadratic: 7 quartic; **10** biquadrate; **11** fourth power
biquadratic equation: 11 biquadratic
biquadratic polynomial: 11 biquadratic
biramous: 6 forked, prongy; **7** pronged; **8** branched; **9** bifurcate
birch: 4 cane, comb, flog, lash, lick, whip; **5** strap, towel; **6** birken, larrup, switch, thrash, thresh; **7** birchen, scourge; **8** birch rod; **9** bastinado, birch tree, horsewhip; **10** flagellate; **12** give the stick
birch family: 10 Betulaceae; **16** family Betulaceae
bird: 3 boo; **4** avis [Lat], dame, doll, fowl, hiss, hoot; **5** chick, skirt, snort, wench; **6** birdie; **7** razzing, shuttle; **9** birdwatch, raspberry; **10** Bronx cheer; **11** shuttlecock; **15** feathered friend
bird's-eye view: 9 panoramic; **10** aerial view; **17** aerial perspective
bird's nest: 5 aerie, eyrie; **7** rookery
birdbrain: 4 loon; **9** addle-head
birdcall: 4 call, song
birder: 11 bird watcher
bird food: 8 birdseed
bird-footed dinosaur: 8 theropod; **16** theropod dinosaur
birdhouse: 8 dovecote; **11** columbarium
birdie: 4 bird; **7** shuttle; **11** shuttlecock
birdlime: 3 net; **4** lime, lute, size; **5** toils, wafer; **8** meshes
bird louse: 11 biting louse
birdman: 7 man-bird, steward; **9** navigator; **10** stewardess
bird of Jove: 5 eagle
bird of Juno: 7 peafowl
bird of Minerva: 3 owl; **11** bird of night
bird of paradise: 9 poinciana
bird of passage: 5 rover; **6** roamer; **8** wanderer
bird of prey: 5 Draco, harpy; **6** raptor; **7** vulture
bird sanctuary: 6 aviary, volary
birdseed: 8 bird food
bird shot: 8 buckshot, duck shot

birdsong: 4 call, song; 8 birdcall
bird watcher: 6 birder; 13 ornithologist
birefringence: 16 double refraction
birl: 4 spin; 5 birle, twirl, whirl
birling: 10 logrolling
birr: 4 purr, whir, whiz; 5 whirr, whizz
birth: 4 bear, have, line, rank, stem; 5 blood, order, stock; 6 hirthe, cradle, stirps, strain; 7 deliver, descent, genesis, infancy, lineage, pur sang [Fr], stirpes [pl]; 8 ancestry, birthing, heritage, nascence, nascency, nativity, nobility, pedigree; 9 genealogy, give birth, parentage; 10 extraction; 11 giving birth, high descent, parturition
birth control: 14 family planning; 15 birth prevention
birth control device: 3 IUD; 8 diaphram; 10 preventive; 12 preventative; 13 contraceptive
birth control pill: 4 pill; 13 contraceptive; 15 anovulatory drug
birthday: 8 natal day
birthday present: 12 birthday gift
birthday suit: 3 raw; 4 buff; 10 altogether
birthing: 5 birth; 7 lying-in; 11 giving birth, parturition
birthmark: 5 nevus, patch; 6 blotch, macula [Anat]; 7 freckle
birth pangs: 10 labor pains
birthplace: 4 nest, womb; 5 nidus; 6 cradle, hotbed; 7 nursery; 10 provenance
birthright: 9 patrimony
birthroot: 8 trillium
bis: 5 ditto; 6 da capo [It], de novo, encore
Bisayan: 7 Visayan
biscuit: 5 cooky; 6 cookie; 7 cracker
bise: 4 bize; 7 mistral, sirocco; 8 levanter; 9 trade wind; 10 tramontane
bisect: 5 halve, split; 6 cleave, divide; 8 cut in two 11 dichotomize
bisexual: 7 epicene; 10 ambisexual; 14 bisexual person
bisexuality: 9 androgyny; 13 ambisexuality; 15 hermaphroditism
bishop: 3 cup; 7 wassail
bishop's cap: 9 miterwort, mitrewort
bishop's hat: 10 barrenwort
bishop's throne: 8 cathedra
bishopdom: 7 prelacy; 9 bishopric; 10 episcopacy, episcopate
bishopric: 7 diocese, prelacy; 10 episcopacy, episcopate
Biskek: 6 Frunze; 18 capital of Kyrgystan
Bismarck: 11 von Bismarck; 14 Iron Chancellor; 15 Otto von Bismarck; 20 capital of North Dakota
bismark: 13 jelly doughnut; 14 Berlin doughnut
bismuth: 2 Bi
bison: 7 buffalo
Bison bison: 7 buffalo; 13 American bison; 15 American buffalo

Bison bonasus: 6 wisent; 7 aurochs
Bissau: 21 capital of Guinea-Bissau
bister: 5 ocher, sepia; 6 bistre; 12 Vandyke brown
bisulcate: 5 cleft; 6 cloven; two-grooved; 13 doubly grooved
bit: 3 ace, act, jot; 4 bite, chip, hint, hunk, iota, lump, mite, spot, turn; 5 brake, flake, fleck, piece, scrap, stung, trace; 6 bitten, bridle, minute, moment, morsel, number, second; 7 modicum, routine, snaffle; 8 drill bit, particle; 16 bit of information
bitartrate of potash: 6 arnica; 7 benzoin, calomel
bit by bit: 8 in stages, seriatim; 9 gradually, piecemeal; 10 drop by drop, foot by foot, inch by inch, step by step; 14 little by little
bite: 2 do; 3 bit, con, cut, nab, nip; 4 bilk, burn, chew, gnaw, hurt, nosh, pain, scam, wile; 5 blind, catch, chafe, champ, cheat, chomp, cozen, feint, fetch, gripe, hocus, munch, plant, pluck, prick, reach, snack, sting, trick; 6 assail, bite in, bubble, chouse, crunch, diddle, euchre, jockey, juggle, morsel, mumble, pierce, snap at; 7 chicane, defraud, munch on, swindle; 8 acridity, maltreat, pungency; 9 collation, light meal, masticate, sharpness, victimize
bite the dust: 8 drop dead, fall dead
biting: 3 dry; 4 hard, sore, sour; 5 acrid, acute, cruel, grave, harsh, sharp, short, taint; 6 aching, barbed, bitter, severe; 7 carking, caustic, chafing, crabbed, cutting, cynical, doggish, gnawing, hurting, mordant, nipping, pungent, teasing; 8 claycold, hard upon, piercing, pinching, sardonic, smarting, stinging, venomous, virulent, worrying; 9 bothering, harassing, pestering, sarcastic, satirical, trenchant, withering; 10 astringent, tormenting; 11 acrimonious, molestation; 12 contumelious
biting louse: 9 bird louse
biting midge: 5 punky; 6 punkey, punkie; 7 no-see-um
Bitis: 5 adder, viper; 10 genus Bitis
bit part: 9 minor role
bit-player: 15 supporting actor; 17 supporting actress
bits per inch: 3 bpi
bits per second: 3 bps
bitstock: 5 brace
bitt: 7 bollard
bitter: 4 acid, sour; 5 acerb, acrid, sharp, short, taint; 6 biting; 7 acerbic, caustic, crabbed, cutting, doggish; 8 bitingly, bitterly, clay-cold, piercing, pinching, venomous, virulent; 9 bitterish, envenomed, rancorous, sarcastic, sulfurous, trenchant, vitriolic; 10 bitterness, blistering,

mordacious, piercingly, sulphurous; **11** acrimonious, distasteful, unpalatable

bitterly: 5 sadly; **6** bitter, coldly, sorely; **7** cruelly, grossly; **8** bitingly, horribly, terribly, woefully; **9** fearfully, miserably, painfully, piteously; **10** dreadfully, grievously, lamentably, piercingly, shockingly, venomously; **11** frightfully; **13** acrimoniously

bitterness: 4 gall, huff, miff; **5** pique; **6** bitter, rancor, spleen; **7** rancour, umbrage; **8** acerbity, acrimony, asperity, jaundice, rankling, soreness; **9** virulence; **10** resentment; **14** unpalatability

bitter orange: 8 bigarade; **10** sour orange; **13** Seville orange

bitterroot: 15 Lewisia rediviva

bittersweet: 7 waxwork; **9** semisweet, staff vine

bitterweed: 7 bugloss, ragweed; **8** ambrosia, oxtongue; **15** bristly oxtongue, Picris echioides

bitty: 3 wee; **5** teeny, weeny; **6** bittie, teensy, weensy; **7** teentsy; **12** teensy-weensy

bitumen: 3 tar; **5** pitch

bituminous: 5 tarry; **6** pitchy

bituminous coal: 8 soft coal

bivalent: 6 double; **8** divalent

bivalve: bivalved; **9** bilabiate, pelecypod; **13** lamellibranch

bivalved: 7 bivalve

bivouac: 4 camp, hive; **5** perch, squat; **6** burrow, encamp, picket; **7** camp out, sit down; **8** campsite, se nicher [Fr]; **10** campground, cantonment, encampment; **11** camping area, camping site, get a footing; **13** camping ground

bivouacking: 7 camping, tenting; **10** encampment

biweekly: 11 fortnightly

biyearly: 8 biannual, biennial; **10** semiannual

bizarre: 3 rum; **5** flaky, outre, queer, weird; **6** freaky; **7** strange; **8** fanciful, freakish; **9** eccentric, fantastic, grotesque, repellant, repugnant, repulsive; **10** outlandish

bize: 4 bise

Bk: 9 berkelium

blab: 4 sing, talk; **5** peach, spill; **6** babble, let out, tattle; **7** blab out, divulge, let drop, let fall; **8** blurt out; **9** babble out

blabber: 5 clack, prate; **6** gabble, gibber, piffle, tattle; **7** chatter, maunder, palaver, prattle, twaddle

blabbermouth: 8 telltale, bigmouth; **10** talebearer, taleteller, tattletale

blabbermouthed: 5 leaky; **6** blabby; **8** tattling; **9** talkative; **10** bigmouthed; **11** talebearing

black: 3 dim; **4** base, dark, foul, grim, vile; **5** bleak, fatal, grave, gross; **6** scurvy; **7**

blacken, bootleg, fateful, heinous, mordant; **8** infamous, melanize, shameful, sinister, smuggled; **9** blackened, blackness, felonious, nefarious, pitch-dark; **10** achromatic, calamitous, contraband, disastrous, inglorious, of a deep dye, pitch-black, scandalous, villainous; **11** black-market, disgraceful, ignominious, opprobrious

black-and-blue: 5 livid; **7** bruised

black and white: 5 print; **9** colorless; **10** achromatic, monochrome; **11** chiaroscuro, monochromic, neutral tint; **12** clear obscure; **13** black-and-white, light and shade, monochromatic

black Angus: 5 Angus; **13** Aberdeen Angus

black art: 7 sorcery; **10** black magic

blackball: 3 ban; **4** shun, veto; **6** banish; **7** barring, cast out; **8** negative; **9** ostracize

Blackbeard: 5 Teach; **6** Thatch; **11** Edward Teach

black bile: 10 melancholy

blackbird: 4 merl; **5** merle, ousel, ouzel; **12** Turdus merula

blackboard: 5 slate; **10** chalkboard

blackbody: 12 full radiator

black book: 9 blacklist, phone book; **11** address book;

black bread: 12 pumpernickel

blackcap: 5 pewit; **9** pewit gull, chickadee; **12** laughing gull, thimbleberry; **14** black raspberry

black coat: 6 divine; **8** reverend; **9** churchman, clergyman; **12** ecclesiastic

blackcock: 4 rail; **5** snipe; **6** grouse, plover; **9** black cock

black cohosh: 7 bugbane; **9** rattletop; **14** black snakeroot

blackdamp: 9 chokedamp

Black Death: 11 black plague; **13** bubonic plague; **15** pneumonic plague

black diamond: 9 carbonado

black elder: 8 bourtree; **10** elderberry; **11** common elder; **13** European elder, Sambucus nigra

blacken: 4 char; **5** black; **6** scorch; **7** nigrify; **8** blow upon, melanize; **9** bespatter

Black English: 7 Ebonics; **22** Black English Vernacular

blackening: 9 darkening

black eye: 6 shiner

black-eyed pea: 6 cowpea; **11** cowpea plant; **13** Vigna sinensis; **16** Vigna unguiculata

black-eyed Susan: 13 bladder ketmia; **14** flower-of-an-hour, Rudbeckia hirta; **15** flowers-of-an-hour, Hibiscus trionum, Thunbergia alata; **17** Rudbeckia serotina; **18** black-eyed Susan vine

blackfish: 6 tautog; **10** black whale, pilot whale; **13** Tautoga onitis

black flag: 9 black flag; **10** Jolly Roger, pirate flag

blackfly: 9 bean aphid; **10** Aphis fabae; **11** buffalo gnat

black-footed albatross: 5 goony; **6** gooney, goonie; **10** gooney bird; **16** Diomedea nigripes

Black Forest: 11 Schwarzwald

Blackfriar: 9 Dominican

black garnet: 9 andradite

black gold: 3 oil; **8** crude oil; **9** petroleum

blackguard: 3 cad, dog, guy, rib; **4** base, bear, foul, heel, vile; **5** abuse, beast, bruin, brute, hound, rowdy, shout, sneak; **6** arrant, jest at, loafer, savage; **7** bounder, brutish, laugh at, make fun, poke fun; **8** infamous, ridicule, snobbish; **11** clapperclaw, ignominious

black gum: 7 sour gum; **10** black sally, pepperidge; **11** black mallee

blackhead: 3 zit; **6** comedo, pimple

black hickory: 6 pignut; **9** mockernut; **11** black walnut, Carya glabra; **12** brown hickory, Juglans nigra

blacking: 10 shoe polish

blackjack: 3 sap; **4** cosh; **7** jack oak, **8** pressure; **9** blackmail, twenty-one, vingt-et-un; **10** sphalerite

blackjack oak: 7 jack oak; **9** blackjack

black larch: 8 tamarack

black lead: 8 graphite, plumbago

black letter: 6 Gothic; **8** archaism, dead word

blacklist: 3 mob; **4** hiss, hoot; **6** clamor; **7** boycott; **9** black book, ostracize

black lovage: 9 Alexander; **10** Alexanders; **12** horse parsley; **17** Smyrnium

black lung: 11 anthracosis; **14** coal miner's lung; **16** black lung disease

blackmail: 8 pressure; **9** blackjack, extortion

blackmailer: 11 extortioner; **12** extortionist

Black Maria: 5 wagon; **9** police van; **10** paddy wagon; **11** patrol wagon, police wagon

black-market: 3 run; **5** black; **7** bootleg; **8** smuggled; **10** contraband

blackness: 5 black; **13** lightlessness, total darkness

black olive: 9 ripe olive

black out: 7 ink over, pass out, zonk out; **10** blacken out; **17** lose consciousness

blackout: 6 dimout; **7** amnesia; **8** brownout; **10** memory loss

black pepper: 6 pepper; **10** peppercorn; **11** Piper nigrum, white pepper; **12** common pepper

black plague: 10 Black Death

black powder: 6 powder; **9** gunpowder

Black Prince: 6 Edward

black pudding: 12 blood pudding, blood sausage

black racer: 10 blacksnake; **18** Coluber constrictor

black raspberry: 8 blackcap; **12** thimbleberry

black rhinoceros: 15 Diceros bicornis

Black Sea: 9 Euxine Sea

blacksmith: 6 forger, smithy, Vulcan

blacksnake: 5 quirt; **7** rawhide; **10** black racer; **13** black rat snake

black snakeroot: 9 rattletop; **11** black cohosh; **12** Canada ginger

blacktail: 13 blacktail deer; **15** black-tailed deer

blackthorn: 4 sloe; **7** pear haw; **12** pear hawthorn

black tie: 3 tux; **6** tuxedo; **12** dinner jacket

black-tie: 10 semiformal

blacktop: 4 pave; **6** paving; **12** blacktopping

blacktopping: 8 blacktop

black weevil: 10 rice weevil

bladder: 3 pod; **4** cyst; **5** calyx; **6** vesica; **7** capsule, utricle, vesicle; **8** cancelli; **14** urinary bladder

bladder stone: 9 cystolith

blade: 4 leaf; **7** scapula; **9** swordsman

blade edge: 4 edge; **9** knife edge; **11** cutting edge

bladelike: 8 ensiform; **9** swordlike; **11** sword shaped

blaeberry: 8 bilberry; **9** whinberry; **12** whortleberry

blah: 4 rant; **7** bombast, fustian, boring; **8** claptrap; **9** mediocre

blain: 4 bleb; **7** blister; **8** furuncle; **10** maculation

blamable: 8 blameful, culpable; **9** blameable; **10** censurable; **11** blameworthy

blame: 3 rap; **4** damn, pick; **5** fault, lay to; **6** blamed, charge, damned, darned, deuced; **7** blasted, blessed, censure, obloquy, point to, refer to, trace to; **8** assign to, charge on, charge to, credit to, ground on, impute to, infernal; **9** ascribe to, criticism, dispraise, find fault, put down to, set down to; **11** attribute to, bring home to, everlasting, inculpation; **12** depreciation, lay blame upon; **13** cast blame upon, disparagement, incrimination

blameless: 10 inculpable; **13** unimpeachable; **14** above suspicion, irreproachable

blanc fixe: 14 barium sulphate

blanch: 4 pale; **6** blench; **7** parboil; **8** etiolate; **11** become white

blanched: 4 pale; **5** ashen, livid, white; **8** bleached, etiolate; **9** bloodless, etiolated; **13** white as a sheet

blanching agent: 6 bleach; **8** whitener

bland: 3 dry; **4** cold, dull, flat, oily, soft; **5** prosy, vapid; **6** frigid, trashy; **7** anodyne, insipid, languid, prosaic; **8** lenitive, lukewarm; **9** colorless, demulcent, proposing,

savorless, tasteless; **10** flavorless; **11** flavourless, void of taste
blandiment: 12 blandishment
blandish: 6 cajole, induce; **7** flatter; **8** persuade
blandishment: 4 lure; **7** palaver; **8** cajolery; **9** lip homage, wheedling; **10** inducement, mouth honor
blandness: 7 suavity; **8** tameness, vapidity; **9** suaveness; **10** feebleness, insipidity; **11** insipidness
blank: 4 form; **5** clean, dummy, space, white; **6** hollow, lacuna; **8** negative; **10** blank sheet, blank shell, dead letter, hollowness, tabula rasa [Lat]; **13** blank document, flash in the pan; **14** blank cartridge; **15** application form
blanket: 4 wide; **5** broad, cover, quilt, sheet; **6** mantle; **8** bedsheet, coverlet, panoptic; **9** comforter, tarpaulin; **11** counterpane; **12** all-embracing, all-inclusive, encompassing; **14** across-the-board; **15** all-encompassing
blanket cloth: 11 saddle cloth
blanket flower: 9 firewheel; **10** gaillardia
blankly: 17 without expression
blankness: 14 expressionless
blank out: 5 block; **6** forget; **10** draw a blank
blank sheet: 5 blank; **13** blank document
blank shell: 5 blank, dummy
blare: 3 cry, din; **4** beep, boom, honk, peal, roar, toot; **5** blast, clang, swell; **6** bellow, clamor, claxon; **7** blaring, thunder; **9** cacophony, fulminate
Blarina: 5 shrew; **12** genus Blarina
blaring: 3 din; **5** blare; **6** clamor; **8** blasting; **9** cacophony
blarney: 4 bull, coax; **6** cajole, muddle; **7** baloney, blunder, coaxing, palaver, wheedle; **8** inveigle, soft soap; **9** sweet talk
blase: 4 bored; **6** used up; **7** worldly; **11** indifferent; **12** uninterested
blaspheme: 4 cuss; **5** curse, swear; **9** desecrate, imprecate; **15** commit sacrilege
blasphemous: 4 blue; **7** profane; **10** irreverent; **12** sacrilegious
blasphemy: 9 sacrilege; **11** desecration, profanation; **13** scoffing at God
blast: 4 bang, blow, bomb, boom, clap, fire, flak, gale, gust, nail, peal, slam, wham; **5** blare, burst, clack, clang, curse, shell, smash, swell, whack; **6** attack, blight, blow up, blowup, rocket, strafe, volley; **7** fanfare; **8** eruption, high wind; **9** discharge, explosion, half a gale, high winds [pl], loud noise; **10** detonation, strong wind
blasted: 4 damn, rent, torn; **5** blame; **6** blamed, damned, darned, deuced, ripped, ruined, wasted; **7** blessed, ravaged; **8** deso-

late, infernal; **9** desolated; **10** devastated; **11** everlasting
blastemal: 9 blastemic; **11** blastematic
blasting: 7 banging, blaring, booming, ruinous
blasting agent: 3 TNT; **9** explosive
blastocoel: 6 cavity; **14** cleavage cavity; **18** segmentation cavity
blastodermic vesicle: 8 blastula; **12** blastosphere
blastodisc: 10 blastoderm; **12** germinal area, germinal disc
blast off: 6 ascend; **7** liftoff, take off; **8** take wing; **11** take a flight
blastosphere: 8 blastula; **19** blastodermic vesicle
blastula: 12 blastosphere; **19** blastodermic vesicle
blat: 3 baa; **5** blate, bleat
blatant: 4 deep, full, open; **5** inept, silly; **7** blazing, clamant, fatuous, foolish, idiotic; **8** babbling, imbecile, powerful, strident; **9** clamorous, driveling, insensate, senseless; **10** clamourous, clangorous, irrational, vociferous; **11** conspicuous nonsensical
blate: 3 baa; **4** blat; **5** bleat, timid; **7** bashful; **8** sheepish
blather: 4 stir; **6** babble; **7** blither, smatter; **12** blatherskite
blathering: 7 prating; **8** babbling, gabbling; **9** jabbering, prattling, twaddling; **10** blithering, chattering
blatherskite: 7 blather; **8** nonsense
Blatta: 5 roach; **11** genus Blatta, blackbeetle
Blattella: 5 roach; **8** water bug; **9** Croton bug; **14** genus Blattella
blaze: 3 dot; **4** beam, fire, hell, spot; **5** flame, glare, notch, score; **7** blazing, cedilla, flicker, glimmer, hachure, shimmer; **8** blaze out; **9** blaze away; **10** brilliance; **11** bright light
blaze of glory: 4 halo; **6** nimbus; **7** aureole; **11** halo of glory; **14** blushing honors
blaze out: 5 blaze
blazer: 10 sports coat; **12** sports jacket
blazing: 4 open; **5** afire, blaze, glary; **6** ablaze, aflame, aflare, alight, on fire; **7** blatant, burning, flaming, fulgent, glaring; **8** blinding, dazzling, in a blaze, in flames, meteoric, splendid; **11** conspicuous; **14** phosphorescent
blazing star: 9 snakeroot; **10** bright star, gayfeather
blazon: 4 arms; **6** herald; **7** lionize; **8** blazonry, emblazon, enshrine, inscribe, proclaim; **10** coat of arms; **14** blow the trumpet; **15** crown with laurel
blazon forth: 5 sport; **8** brandish
blazonry: 4 arms; **6** blazon; **10** coat of arms
bleach: 5 blanch; **7** decolor, wash out;

8 whitener; **9** bleach out; **10** decolorize; **11** decolorizer, discolorize

bleached: 4 dyed; **5** faded, washy; **7** colored; **8** blanched, etiolate; **9** etiolated, washed-out

bleaching powder: 14 chloride of lime

bleak: 3 dim, raw; **4** bare, keen; **5** black, fresh, stark; **6** barren; **7** cutting, nipping; **8** desolate; **9** inclement

blear: 4 blur; **6** bleary; **9** blear-eyed; **10** bleary-eyed

blear-eyed: 5 blear; **6** bleary; **7** one-eyed; **8** moon-eyed, mope-eyed; **10** bleary-eyed, goggle-eyed; **14** gooseberry-eyed

bleary: 4 hazy; **5** blear, foggy, fuzzy, muzzy; **6** blurry; **7** blurred; **9** blear-eyed; **10** bleary-eyed

bleat: 4 blat; **5** blate

bleb: 5 bulla; **7** blister; **8** furuncle

bleed: 3 ail, run; **4** ache, hurt; **5** leech, smart; **6** extort, fleece, suffer; **9** shed blood; **10** hemorrhage, overcharge; **12** phlebotomize

bleeder: 9 hemophile; **10** haemophile; **11** hemophiliac; **12** haemophiliac

bleeder's disease: 10 hemophilia; **11** haemophilia

bleeding heart: 10 heavy heart, lyreflower; **11** aching heart, broken heart

blemish: 3 mar; **4** flaw, spot; **6** deface, defect; **8** mutilate; **9** disfigure

blemished: 6 flawed

blench: 3 shy; **4** pale; **5** blink, dodge, parry, shirk; blench; **6** blanch, flinch, whiten; **10** make way for; **11** give place to, stand aghast

blend: 2 go; **3** mix; **4** dash, fuse, meld; **5** cross, immix, merge, tinge, unite; **6** absorb, embody, season; **7** blend in, combine, conjoin; **8** blending, coalesce, conflate, dissolve, immingle, intermix, medicate, sprinkle, tincture; **9** commingle; **10** amalgamate, besprinkle, centralize, impregnate, infiltrate; **11** consolidate, incorporate, intermingle, melt into one, portmanteau

blende: 10 sphalerite, zinc blende

blender: 10 liquidizer

Blephilia: 8 wood mint **14** genus Blephilia

bless: 4 laud, sign; **6** hallow, praise; **7** beatify, glorify, magnify; **8** sanctify, say grace; **10** consecrate; **11** sing praises

blessed: 4 damn; **5** blame, blest, happy, lucky; **6** blamed, damned, darned, deuced, joyful; **7** blasted; **8** infernal; **9** beatified, fortunate; **10** endued with; **11** blessed with, everlasting

blessedness: 9 beatitude

Blessed Virgin: 4 Mary; **7** Madonna; **10** Virgin Mary; **11** Mother of God

blessing: 4 boon; **5** grace; **7** benison; **8** approval; **9** approving; **11** benediction, world of good; **12** thanksgiving

blessings: 7 godsend

blether: 5 prate; **6** babble; **7** blather, blither, prattle, smatter; **8** idle talk; **9** chin music

Bligh: 12 Captain Bligh, William Bligh

Blighia: 4 akee; **8** akee tree; **12** genus Blighia

blight: 5 blast, curse, erode; **6** dry rot, plague; **7** atrophy, corrode, eat away; **8** collapse, 11 moth and rust

blighted: 6 effete, rotten, spoilt, wasted; **7** tainted; **8** cankered; **9** crumbling, moldering

blighter: 3 lad, guy; **4** chap, cuss, gent, pest; **5** fella; **6** fellow, gadfly; **8** pesterer

Blimp: 7 airship, balloon; **12** Colonel Blimp

blind: 3 dim, wet; **4** bite, deaf, veil, wile; **5** catch, cheat, cloak, cloud, cover, feint, fetch, gloss, guise, hocus, plant, potty, reach, stiff, tight, tipsy, trick; **6** blotto, bubble, juggle, loaded, pissed, screen, soaked, soused, tiddly; **7** chicane, crocked, curtain, fuddled, slopped, sloshed, smashed, sozzled, squiffy, tiddley; **8** besotted, excecate; **9** automatic, pixilated, plastered, sightless, unsighted; **10** blind drunk, mechanical, subterfuge, visionless; **11** instinctive, involuntary, render blind, unreasoning

blind alley: 7 dead end, impasse; **8** cul de sac

blinder: 6 winker; **7** blinker

blindered: 6 masked; **11** blindfolded

blind faith: 5 dogma; **11** blind belief

blindfold: 7 blindly; **8** hoodwink; **11** blindfolded

blindfolded: 6 masked; **7** blinded, blindly; **9** blindered, blindfold

blind gut: 5 cecum; **6** caecum

blinding: 5 glary; **7** blazing, fulgent, glaring; **8** dazzling

blindman's buff: 11 hide and seek; **14** blindman's bluff

blindness: 6 cecity; **8** darkness; **11** lack of sight; **12** lack of vision; **13** sightlessness

blind spot: 9 optic disc

blind study: 13 clinical study; **16** double blind study

blindworm: 8 slowworm; **9** caecilian

blink: 3 shy; **4** wink; **5** dodge, flash, parry, shirk; **6** blench, flinch, palter, winkle; **7** nictate, shuffle, twinkle; **8** eye blink; **9** blink away, nictitate

blinker: 5 cover, shade; **6** screen, winker; **7** blinder; **10** turn signal; **11** trafficator

blink of an eye: 4 wink; **5** flash, jiffy, trice; **7** instant; **9** twinkling; **11** split second; **13** New York minute

blintze: 6 blintz

blip: 11 radar target

bliss: 8 felicity; **9** cloud nine, happiness;

B

12 blissfulness, walking on air; **13** seventh heaven

blissful: 6 joyful, joyous; **8** beatific; **10** in paradise

blissfully: 11 rapturously, with delight; **12** ecstatically

Blissus: 9 chinch bug; **12** genus Blissus

blister: 4 bleb, boil, burn, glow, whip; **5** broil, bulla; **8** furuncle

blister beetle: 6 meloid

blistering: 3 hot; **4** acid; **5** acerb, acrid; **6** bitter, red-hot; **7** acerbic, caustic; **8** blistery, venomous, virulent; **9** sulfurous, vitriolic; **10** sulphurous

blister pack: 10 bubble pack, bubble wrap

blistery: 6 blebby; **10** blistering

blithe: 6 casual; **8** heedless; **9** lightsome, unheeding, unmindful; **10** blithesome, unthinking; **11** unobservant; **12** light-hearted

blithely: 5 gayly; **7** happily, merrily; **10** jubilantly, mirthfully; **13** with happiness

blither: 6 babble; **7** blather, blether, smatter

blitz: 7 air raid; **11** safety blitz; **18** linebacker blitzing

blizzard: 5 foehn; **6** barber [Can]; **7** chinook, norther; **9** snowstorm

bloated: 3 fat; **5** puffy, tumid; **6** puffed, turgid; **7** swollen; **9** distended, dropsical, overgrown, tumescent; **11** exaggerated; **13** hypertrophied

blob: 4 blot, spot; **5** fleck, stain; **7** splotch

bloc: 4 axis

block: 3 bar, jam, lug, oaf, put, ton, tun; **4** bulk, calf, clod, colt, cord, cube, halt, knot, loaf, loon, lout, lump, mass, stop, swad, tony, ward; **5** parry, stick, stock, stuff, stymy; **6** barrio [Sp], buffer, bushel, corner, doodle, forget, freeze, hinder, impede, kibosh, locale, nugget, oppose, pulley, stymie; **7** block up, buzzard, choke up, close up, closure, deflect, dullard, occlude; **8** blank out, block off, blockade, blockage, blocking, bulkhead, enceinte, environs, locality, obstruct, precinct, stoppage, vicinity; **9** barricade, city block, embarrass, occlusion, precincts; **10** antagonize, draw a blank, heart of oak, immobilize; **11** engine block, mental block, pulley-block; **12** auction block, interference, neighborhood; **13** cylinder block; **14** beheading block, stomping ground

blockade: 3 bar; **5** block, stymy; **6** hinder, stymie; **7** block up, closure, seal off; **8** block off, blockage, obstruct; **9** barricade, embarrass, occlusion; **12** encirclement

blockage: 4 stop; **5** block; **7** closure; **8** blockade, stoppage; **9** occlusion

blocked: 7 impeded; **8** hindered, out of use; **10** obstructed

block from view: 7 obscure

blockhead: 5 dunce; **8** bonehead, bull head, lunkhead, numskull; **10** dunderhead, hammerhead, loggerhead, muttonhead, noodlehead; **11** beetlebrain, chowderhead, knucklehead

blocking: 5 block; **7** closing, closure; **8** impeding; **9** hindering; **11** obstructing, obstructive; **12** interference; **13** impedimentary

blockish: 5 blunt, heavy; **6** blocky, obtuse, stolid, stupid, unwise; **7** Boeotic, doltish; **8** ungifted; **13** unenlightened

block letter: 12 block capital

block off: 3 bar; **5** block; **7** block up, shut off; **8** blockade, close off; **9** barricade

block of metal: 5 ingot; **8** metal bar

block out: 4 mask; **6** screen; **9** hammer out

block printing: 12 type printing

blocks: 14 building blocks

blocky: 8 blockish

bloke: 3 man; **6** geezer; **6** fellow

blond: 4 fair; **6** blonde, creamy, pearly; **7** whitish; **11** light-haired; **12** light-colored

blood: 3 kin, rip; **4** buck, gore, line, rake, rank, roue; **5** birth, blade, order, stock; **6** origin; **7** descent, kindred, kinfolk [pl], kinsman, lineage, pur sang [Fr]; **8** ancestry, nobility, pedigree, relation, relative; **9** blood line, blood shed, bloodline, bloodshed, parentage; **10** connection, kith and kin [pl], profligate

bloodbath: 6 battue; **9** bloodshed; **9** slaughter; **12** bloodletting

blood cell: 9 corpuscle

blood clotting: 11 coagulation

bloodcurdling: 11 hair-raising, nightmarish

blood cyst: 10 hematocyst

blood feud: 8 vendetta

blood fluke: 11 schistosome

blood group: 9 blood type

bloodless: 5 ashen, livid, white; **7** sinless; **8** blanched, spotless; **9** faultless, stainless

bloodletting: 6 battue; **8** bleeding; **9** bloodbath, bloodshed; **10** phlebotomy; **11** venesection [Med]

bloodline: 4 line; **5** blood, stock; **6** origin; **7** descent, lineage; **8** ancestry, pedigree; **9** blood line, parentage; **13** line of descent

blood plasma: 10 blood serum

blood poisoning: 10 septicemia; **11** septicaemia

blood pudding: 12 black pudding, blood sausage

blood-red: 3 red; **4** ruby; **5** ruddy; **6** cerise, cherry; **7** carmine, crimson, reddish, ruby-red, scarlet; **9** cherry-red

blood relationship: 7 kinship; **9** family tie; **11** ties of blood; **12** relationship; **13** consanguinity

blood relative: 3 sib; **7** cognate; **13** blood relation

bloodroot: 7 puccoon, redroot; 10 tetterwort; 21 Sanguinaria canadensis

blood serum: 11 blood plasma

bloodshed: 4 gore; 5 blood; 6 battue; 8 bleeding; 9 blood shed, bloodbath

bloodstone: 6 jasper; 7 cat's eye; 8 hematite; 9 moonstone; 10 heliotrope

bloodsucker: 5 leech; 10 hirudinean

blood sugar: 7 glucose; 12 blood glucose

bloodthirstiness: 8 ferocity, savagery; 9 barbarity, brutality; 10 inhumanity; 13 barbarousness, ferociousness, murderousness

bloom: 4 beam, blow, peak; 5 blush, flush, prime, shine; 6 fatten, flower, heyday, nonage; 7 blossom; 8 blooming, flourish, fructify, minority, rosiness; 9 bear fruit, tender age; 13 efflorescence

bloomers: 5 pants; 7 bloomer, drawers; 8 knickers

blooming: 4 rosy; 5 bloom; 7 flushed; 11 in full bloom, rose-cheeked, rosy-cheeked

blooper: 4 flub; 5 boner, botch; 6 boo-boo, bungle, foul-up; 7 blunder; 8 misdoing

blossom: blow, peak; 5 bloom, flush, prime; 6 fatten, flower, heyday, unfold; 8 fructify; 9 bear fruit; 13 efflorescence

blot: 4 blob, blur, daub, flaw, miss, slip, slur, spot; 5 fault, fleck, smear, smoke, stain, taint; 6 blotch, slaver, smirch, smudge; 7 blunder, tarnish; 8 deletion, omission; 9 oversight, quiproquo; 10 defilement

blotch: 4 blot; 5 patch; 6 macula [Anat], mottle, streak; 7 freckle, splodge, splotch; 9 birthmark

blot out: 4 hide; 6 rub out; 7 obscure, take off, take out, wash out, wipe out; 8 cut short, white out; 9 sponge out, strike out; 10 obliterate, scratch out

blotted out: 10 obliterate; 11 obliterated

blotter: 7 day book; 11 charge sheet; 13 blotting paper, police blotter

blotto: 3 wet; 5 blind, drunk, potty, stiff, tight, tipsy; 6 loaded, pissed, soaked, soused, tiddly; 7 crocked, fuddled, slopped, sloshed, smashed, sozzled, squiffy, tiddley; 8 besotted; 9 pixilated, plastered; 10 blind drunk

blow: 3 gas, hit; 4 bang, beat, brag, bump, dash, drop, flub, gasp, gust, load, move, muff, pant, puff, slam, step, swap, tout, waft; 5 baste, blast, bloom, boast, botch, burst, crack, curse, drift, drive, faint, float, fluff, knock, shock, smash, split, spoil, start, swash, swoon, thump, trial, vapor, vaunt, waste; 6 ball up, blow in, blow up, bobble, bollix, breeze, bungle, burden, fatten, flower, foul up, fumble, mess up, muck up, stroke; 7 blossom, blow out, blunder, bluster, botch up, burn out, explode, louse up, measure, reverse, screw up, setback, succumb, swagger,

trouble, trumpet; 8 be adrift, bollix up, bollocks, collapse, detonate, fructify, lambaste, maneuver, reversal, shove off, squander; 9 bear fruit, explosion, gasconade, mishandle

blow dry: 7 oven dry; 9 vacuum dry

blower: 6 blower; 7 bellows, bluffer; 8 cetacean; 11 electric fan

blowfish: 6 puffer; 8 sea squab; 9 globefish

blow for blow: 9 tit for tat; 10 quid pro quo; 11 give and take

blowgun: 8 blow tube, blowpipe

blowhard: 7 boaster, vaunter; 8 braggart; 11 line-shooter

blowhole: 4 vent; 7 air vent; 8 venthole

blowing: 5 windy; 7 fanning, gusting

blow it: 4 slip, trip; 5 abort; 7 botch it, stumble; 8 miscarry; 9 make a slip; 11 get shot down; 12 make a botch of

blow off: 4 spew; 6 let out

blow-off valve: 11 safety valve

blow one's cool: 4 foam, fume, rage, roar; 5 go ape; 7 bluster; 9 go bananas; 10 hit the roof; 11 blow one's top, flip one's lid; 13 hit the ceiling

blow one's top: 4 foam, fume, rage, roar; 5 go ape; 7 bluster; 8 get angry, get upset; 9 go bananas; 10 get riled up, hit the roof; 11 become angry, flip one's lid, go ballistic; 12 blow one's cool, fly into a rage, get into a rage, get steamed up; 13 fall into a rage, get all riled up, hit the ceiling

blowout: 3 bat [U.S.], bum [U.S.]; 4 bust, fete, gala, tear; 5 randy; 7 fish fry [U.S.], hoedown, yule log; 8 festival, jamboree; 10 gala affair, hullabaloo

blow out: 4 blow, drub, rout; 5 crush, douse, snuff; 6 put out; 7 burn out; 8 roll over, snuff out; 9 good cheer, overwhelm

blow over: 4 fade, pass; 5 fleet, lapse; 7 pass off; 8 evanesce

blowpipe: 3 fan; 5 lungs; 7 air pump, bellows, blowgun; 8 blow tube; 9 air blower; 10 ventilator

blowsy: 6 blowzy, frowsy; 10 slatternly

blow tube: 7 blowgun; 8 blowpipe

blow up: 3 fly, pad; 4 blow, lard, lash, puff, trim; 5 blast, burst, flare, flash, get up, go off, widen; 6 bounce, call up, expand, extend, puff up, rarefy, rating, set off, spread, volley, wake up; 7 amplify, develop, distend, enlarge, explode, inflate, lecture, light up, magnify, puff out, raise up, thunder, trounce, wigging; 8 chastise, detonate, dressing, overhaul, scolding, summon up, trimming; 9 castigate, discharge, dramatise, dramatize, embellish, embroider, explosion

blowup: 4 bang, clap; 5 blast; 8 eruption; 9 loud noise

blow-up: 11 enlargement

blow upon: 7 blacken; 9 bespatter; 12 pull to pieces

blow valve: 11 safety valve; 12 release valve; 13 sniffing valve

blowzy: 5 puffy; 6 blowsy; 8 sluttish; 9 distended, edematous; 10 slatternly

BLT: 26 bacon-lettuce-tomato sandwich

blubber: 3 cry, sob; 4 pipe, wail, weep; 6 snivel; 7 sniffle, snuffle; 8 blubbery; 9 drop a tear, drop tears, shed a tear, shed tears

Blucher boot: 7 top boot; 8 jack boot; 11 Hessian boot; 14 Wellington boot

bludgeon: 3 hit; 4 club; 6 cudgel

blue: 3 low; 4 dark, down, gamy, grim, racy; 5 azure, gamey, juicy, solid, spicy; 6 Amytal, bluing, bluish, dismal, gentle, gloomy, risque, savant, shrewd; 7 blue air, blue sky, blueing, blueish, bookish, naughty, profane, puritan; 8 blueness, dark-blue, deep-read, downcast, profound; 9 blue angel, depressed, light-blue, patrician, puritanic; 10 depressing, dispirited, scholastic; 11 blasphemous, blue-blooded, book-learned, dispiriting, downhearted, enlightened, low-spirited, puritanical; 12 aristocratic, disconsolate

Bluebeard: 9 adulterer

bluebell: 8 harebell; 12 tulip gentian, wild hyacinth, wood hyacinth; 14 prairie gentian

bluebill: 5 scaup; 9 broadbill, scaup duck

blue-blind: 10 tritanopic

blue-blindness: 10 tritanopia

blue blood: 9 patrician; 10 aristocrat

bluebonnet: 13 buffalo clover; 15 Texas bluebonnet; 18 Lupinus subcarnosus

blue book: 6 return, scroll; 7 archive; 10 state paper

blue cheese dressing: 17 Roquefort dressing

blue chip: 13 blue-chip stock

blue-collar: 11 wage-earning; 12 property-less, working-class

blue darter: 11 Cooper's hawk

blue devils: 5 blues, dumps; 7 sadness; 8 darkness, doldrums, the blues, the dumps; 9 dejection, heaviness, tristesse [Fr]; 10 bad spirits, depression, dismalness, gloominess, low spirits, melancholy, somberness; 11 joylessness, melancholia; 12 dejectedness, heart sinking, il pensieroso [It], mournfulness; 13 cheerlessness; 14 failure of heart, lugubriousness, spiritlessness

bluefin: 7 bluefin; 11 bluefin tuna; 13 horse mackerel; 14 Thunnus thynnus

Bluegrass State: 8 Kentucky

blue-green algae: 13 cyanobacteria

blue gum: 9 fever tree; 18 Eucalyptus globulus

bluejacket: 5 jolly, middy; 6 sailor; 7 navy man; 9 sailor boy; 10 midshipman; 12 man-of-war's man

bluejack oak: 9 turkey oak; 13 Quercus incana

blue jeans: 5 jeans; 6 denims; 9 dungarees

blue-pencil: 6 delete

blue Peter: 4 jack; 7 ancient; 8 gonfalon; 9 Union Jack

blue point: 6 oyster

blueprint: 5 draft; 6 design; 7 draught, pattern

blue ribbon: 6 cordon, riband, ribbon; 10 cordon bleu

blue-ribbon: 6 select

blues: 5 dumps; 7 megrims, sadness; 8 darkness, doldrums, the blues, the dumps; 9 dejection, heaviness, tristesse [Fr]; 10 bad spirits, blue devils, depression, dismalness, gloominess, low spirits, melancholy, somberness; 11 joylessness, melancholia; 12 dejectedness, heart sinking, il pensieroso [It], mournfulness; 13 cheerlessness; 14 failure of heart, lugubriousness, spiritlessness

bluff: 3 gas; 4 bold, dull, rude, wild; 5 blunt, gruff, rough, sheer; 6 direct, fierce, hot air, obtuse, raging, rugged, savage, steeps; 7 bombast, furious, violent; 8 bluff off, bluff out, hillside, tall talk, ungentle, vaporing, vehement; 9 downright, ferocious, four flush, four-flush, outspoken; 10 blustering, boisterous, free-spoken, outrageous; 11 fine talking, plain-spoken, rodomontade; 12 matter of fact; 13 magniloquence

blunder: 3 sin; 4 blot, blow, boob, bull, flaw, flub, goof, miss, muff, slip, trip; 5 botch, fault, fluff, spoil; 6 ball up, bobble, boggle, bollix, boo-boo, bungle, foul up, foul-up, fumble, mess up, muck up, muddle, slip up, trip up; 7 baloney, blarney, blooper, botch up, louse up, screw up, stumble; 8 bollix up, bollocks, flounder, misdoing; 9 mishandle, oversight, quiproquo

blunderbuss: 8 arquebus; 9 Brown Bess, flintlock, matchlock

blunderer: 7 botcher, bumbler, bungler, butcher, fumbler, sad sack

blunder headed: 4 dull; 6 stupid; 7 witless; 8 mindless; 9 airheaded, brainless, dim-witted, fat witted, fat-headed, pig headed; 10 beef headed, dull minded, dull normal, dull witted, half witted, lean witted, weak headed, weak minded; 11 addle headed, blunt-witted, lack-brained, muddy headed, short witted, unreasoning; 12 beetle headed, feeble-minded, muddle headed, mutton headed, puzzle headed, rattle headed,

blunt: 4 calm, cool, damp, dull, flat, numb,

pall, slow, stun, tame; **5** bluff, chill, crude, frank, gruff, heavy, quiet, rough, slack, stark; **6** benumb, candid, deaden, direct, obtuse, quench, rugged, stolid, stupid, subdue, unwise; **7** Boeotic, chasten, doltish, mollify, sheathe, stupefy; **8** paralyze, sluggish, ungifted; **9** downright, outspoken; **10** forthright, free-spoken, point-blank; **11** plainspoken, render blunt; **12** matter of fact; **13** unenlightened

blunted: 6 dulled

blur: 3 dim; **4** blot, daub, fuzz, slur, spot; **5** blear, smear, smoke, speck, stain, taint; **6** slaver, smudge; **7** confuse, obscure, speckle, tarnish; **8** film over; **9** glaze over; **10** defilement

blurb: 11 endorsement

blurred: 4 hazy; **5** foggy, fuzzy, muzzy; **6** bleary, blurry; **7** clouded; **10** out of focus

blurriness: 9 fogginess, fuzziness; **11** lack of focus; **14** indefiniteness, indistinctness, poor definition

blurry: 4 hazy; **5** foggy, fuzzy, muzzy; **6** bleary; **7** blurred

blurt: 8 blurt out; **9** ejaculate; **10** blunder out

blurt out: 4 blab; **5** blurt, peach, spill; **6** let out; **7** divulge, let drop, let fall; **9** ejaculate; **10** blunder out; **13** spill the beans; **21** say what comes uppermost

blush: 5 bloom, flush, rouge; **6** mantle, redden; **7** color up, crimson, turn red; **8** blush for, blushing, lipstick, rosiness; **9** eye shadow, flesh tint, suffusion; **10** face powder, flesh color, get flushed

blusher: 5 paint, rouge; **16** Amanita rubescens, blushing mushroom

blushful: 4 rosy; **8** blushing, red-faced

blushing: 5 blush; **7** bashful, flushed; **8** blushful, red-faced; **10** overmodest, shamefaced

blush wine: 4 rose; **8** pink wine, rose wine

bluster: 3 gas; **4** blow, brag, foam, fume, rage, roar, tout; **5** boast, go ape, swash, swell, vapor, vaunt; **6** bounce; **7** bravado, look big, passion, swagger, talk big, thunder; **9** fulminate, gasconade, go bananas, hysterics, show fight; **10** blustering, hit the roof, shoot a line, swaggering; **11** blow one's top, braggadocio, flip one's lid, kick up a dust, look daggers, rodomontade, use big words; **12** blow one's cool, stare daggers; **13** hit the ceiling

blusterer: 7 vaporer; **9** loudmouth, swaggerer

blustering: 4 rude, wild; **5** bluff, gusty, rough; **6** bounce, fierce, raging, savage, stormy; **7** bluster, furious, swagger, violent; **8** blustery, ungentle, vaporing, vehement; **9** ferocious, hectoring; **10** blusterous, boisterous, outrageous, roistering, swaggering; **11** tempestuous

blustery weather: 12 windy weather

B lymphocyte: 5 B cell

BMR: 18 basal metabolic rate

BNF: 14 Backus-Naur form

bo'sun: 4 bo's'n, bos'n; **5** bosun; **9** boatswain

boa: 3 boa; **10** feather boa; **11** constrictor

boar: 3 dog, hog, pig, sow; **4** buck, cock, hart, stag; **5** drake, horse, swine; **6** gander; **7** wild pig; **8** stallion, wild boar; **9** Sus scrofa; **11** entire horse

board: 4 card, keep, room; **5** bench, get in, get on, panel, plank, staff, table; **6** bourse, embark; **7** cabinet, chamber, commons; **8** go aboard; **9** deal board, gameboard, get aboard, go on board; **10** get on board; **11** circuit card, dining table; **12** circuit board, control board, control panel, display board, display panel

boarder: 6 lodger, roomer; **11** paying guest

boarding: 9 embarking; **10** embarkment; **11** embarkation

boarding pass: 12 boarding card

board of directors: 9 directory; **11** directorate

board of education: 11 school board

boardroom: 14 council chamber

boardwalk: 3 row; **4** road; **9** esplanade; **10** embankment

boar thistle: 11 bull thistle; **12** spear thistle

boast: 3 gas; **4** blow, brag, tout; **5** sport, swash, vaunt; **7** bluster, feature; **8** boasting; **9** gasconade; **10** self-praise, shoot a line; **11** jactitation

boaster: 7 vaunter; **8** blowhard, braggart; **11** line-shooter

boastful: 3 big; **6** braggy; **7** crowing, flaming, stilted; **8** boasting, braggart, bragging; **9** cock-a-hoop, soi-disant [Fr], thrasonic; **10** swaggering; **11** gasconading; **12** magniloquent

boasting: 5 boast; **7** flaming, stilted; **8** boastful, braggart, bragging; **9** gasconade, soi-disant [Fr], thrasonic; **10** self-praise, swaggering; **11** gasconading, jactitation; **12** magniloquent, self-applause, self-flattery; **13** self-laudation

boat: 4 boat, ship; **5** craft; **6** vessel; **9** gravy boat, sauceboat, small boat; **10** sea vehicle; **12** water vehicle

boater: 6 Panama, sailor; **7** boatman, leghorn, skimmer; **8** straw hat, waterman

boating: 7 sailing; **8** yachting; **10** navigation

boatman: 6 boater; **8** bargeman, ferryman

boat race: 7 regatta; **9** yacht race

boatswain: 4 bo's'n, bos'n; **5** bo'sun, bosun

bob: 3 dip, nod, wag; **4** cork, dock, duck, reel, sway, tail, toss; **5** kneel, quake, start; **6** bobber, bounce, curtsy, foot it, quaver, quiver, shiver, tumble, waggle, writhe;

7 bobsled, bobtail, flounce, shuffle, stagger, twitter; **8** bobfloat, courtesy, shilling

bob and weave: 5 dodge; **8** sidestep

bobber: 3 bob; **4** cork; **8** bobfloat

bobbery: 6 fracas, hubbub, uproar

bobbin: 4 reel; **5** spool; **7** mandrel

bobble: 4 blow, flub, muff; **5** botch, fluff, spoil; **6** ball up, bollix, bungle, foul up, fumble, mess up, muck up; **7** blunder, botch up, louse up, screw up; **8** bollix up, bollocks; **9** mishandle; **10** bollocks up

bobby pin: 7 hairpin

bobbysocks: 6 anklet; **7** anklets

bobbysoxer: 11 bobbysocker, teeny-bopper

bobcat: 7 bay lynx; **9** Lynx rufus

bobolink: 8 reedbird, ricebird

bobsled: 3 bob; **9** bobsleigh

bobtail: 3 bob; **4** dock; **9** bobtailed; **18** Old English sheepdog

bob up: 5 arise; **6** come up

bobwhite: 5 quail; **9** partridge; **12** ruffed grouse; **13** bobwhite quail

bobwhite quail: 8 bobwhite; **9** partridge

boccie ball: 9 bocce ball, bocci ball

Boche: 3 Hun; **5** Jerry, Kraut; **9** Krauthead

bock beer: 4 bock

bod: 4 form, soma; **5** build, flesh, frame, shape; **6** figure; **7** anatomy, chassis; **8** physique; **9** human body; **12** material body, physical body

bodacious: 6 brassy, brazen; **8** insolent; **9** audacious, barefaced, bold-faced; **11** brazen-faced

bode: 4 omen; augur; **6** typify; **7** betoken, point to, portend, predict, presage, signify; **8** forebode, forecast, foretell; **9** auspicate, foretoken, prefigure; **10** foreshadow; **11** shadow forth; **13** prognosticate

Bodhisattva: 11 Boddhisatva

bodied: 8 corporal, embodied; **9** corporate, incarnate

bodiless: 8 bodyless, unbodied; **10** unembodied; **11** disembodied; **12** discorporate

bodily: 6 carnal, en bloc; **7** as a body, en masse, somatic; **8** corporal; **9** corporeal, every inch, in extenso [Lat]; **10** on the whole, throughout; **11** essentially

bodily cavity: 5 cavum; **6** cavity

boding: 10 foreboding; **11** premonition; **12** presentiment

bodkin: 7 poniard; **8** intruder; **10** interloper

Bodoni font: 6 Bodoni, modern; **10** modern font

body: 3 man, mob; **4** bulk, core, mass, soul; **5** being, crush, horde, human, press, torso, trunk; **6** corpus, mortal, person, rabble; **8** best part, creature, dead body, main part, sodality, such a one; **9** chief part, community, earthling, major part, personage, personify, principle; **10** camera body, human being, individual, living soul, solidarity, substratum; **11** consistence, consistency, greater part; **13** flesh and blood, principal part

body-build: 5 build; **8** physique

bodybuilder: 13 musclebuilder

bodybuilding: 14 musclebuilding; **17** anaerobic exercise

bodyguard: 5 guard; **6** escort; **8** champion

body politic: 4 land; **5** state; **6** nation; **7** country; **10** res publica; **12** commonwealth; **14** posse comitatus [Lat]

body snatcher: 5 ghoul; **11** graverobber

body type: 10 somatotype

Boehm: 5 Bohme; **6** Behmen, Boehme; **10** Jakob Boehm, Jakob Bohme; **11** Jakob Behmen, Jakob Boehme

Boehmeria: 5 ramee, ramie; **10** China grass; **14** genus Boehmeria; **16** Chinese silk plant

Boeotian: 4 Goth; **6** Vandal; **10** Philistine

Boeotic: 5 blunt, heavy; **6** obtuse, stolid, stupid, unwise; **7** doltish; **8** ungifted; **13** unenlightened

Boer: 9 Afrikaner; **10** Afrikander

boeuf: 4 beef

bog: 3 fen; **4** moor, moss, sink; **6** midden; **7** bog down, peat bog; **8** moorland

Bogart: 5 Bogey; **14** Humphrey Bogart; **22** Humphrey DeForest Bogart

bogbean: 8 buckbean; **9** bog myrtle; **12** marsh trefoil; **13** water shamrock; **20** Menyanthes trifoliata

bog down: 3 bog; **4** mire; **8** get stuck

Bogey: 6 Bogart; **14** Humphrey Bogart; **22** Humphrey DeForest Bogart

boggle: 4 trip; **5** hover; **6** fumble; **7** blunder, stumble; **8** bowl over, flounder, hesitate, struggle; **10** dilly-dally; **11** flabbergast

boggy: 4 miry, soft; **5** mucky, muddy; **6** marshy, quaggy, swampy; **7** sloughy

bogie: 4 bogy; **5** bogey; **8** bogeyman; **9** boogeyman

Bogota: 17 capital of Colombia

bog-trotter: 4 rube [U.S.]; **5** yokel; **7** bumpkin, hobnail

bogus: 4 fake, mock, sham; **5** phony; **6** phoney, pseudo, pseudo-; **8** so-called, spurious; **9** pretended; **10** fraudulent; **11** counterfeit, make-believe; **14** supposititious

boil: 4 burn, foam, fume, glow, moil, rage, rave, roil; **5** broil, churn, flame; **6** fester, seethe, simmer; **7** abscess, blister

boil down: 6 decoct, reduce; **8** come down, condense; **11** concentrate

boiled: 6 stewed; **7** poached

boiled egg: 10 coddled egg

boiler: 6 kettle; **11** steam boiler

boilers suit: 6 duster; **7** overall; **8** coverall; **9** coveralls, gaberdine; **10** boilersuit

boiling: 6 bubbly; **7** steamed, stewing; **8** scalding, sizzling; **9** simmering, steamed up; **11** boiling over; **12** effervescent; **17** hot under the collar

boiling hot: 6 red hot; **8** white hot; **9** piping hot; **10** burning hot, smoking hot; **13** blistering hot

boiling over: 7 boiling, flaming, flare up, steamed; **8** seething; **9** ebullient, steamed up; **13** effervescence

boiling over with enthusiasm: 5 eager; **6** gung ho; **7** zealous; **10** breathless; **12** enthusiastic; **19** eager willing and able

Boise: 14 capital of Idaho

boisterous: 4 rude, wild; **5** bluff, rough; **6** fierce, raging, savage, unruly; **7** furious, rampant, violent; **8** headlong, ungentle, vehement; **9** clamorous, ferocious, hotheaded, turbulent; **10** blustering, knockabout, outrageous, rip-roaring, robustious, uproarious; **11** precipitate, rip-snorting, rumbustious, tempestuous; **12** rambunctious

bok choy: 7 bok choi, pakchoi; **19** Chinese white cabbage; **21** Brassica rapa chinensis

Bokmal: 7 Riksmal; **13** Dano-Norwegian

bold: 4 racy; **5** bluff, fresh, sheer; **7** salient; **8** cocksure, positive; **9** prominent; **11** venturesome; **12** bold-spirited; **13** overconfident

bold-faced: 6 brassy, brazen; **8** insolent; **9** audacious, barefaced, bodacious; **11** brazen-faced

boldness: 4 face; **5** brass, cheek, nerve, valor; **6** daring; **7** bravery, courage; **8** raciness; **9** freshness, hardihood; **10** effrontery; **12** strikingness; **14** courageousness

bole: 4 hulk, hull; **5** torso, trunk; **9** tree trunk

Boleyn: 10 Anne Boleyn

bolide: 8 fireball

Bolingbroke: 7 Henry IV; **16** Henry Bolingbroke

Bolivar: 12 El Libertador, Simon Bolivar

bollard: 4 bitt

bollix: 4 blow, flub, muff; **5** botch, fluff, spoil; **6** ball up, bobble, bungle, foul up, fumble, mess up, muck up; **7** blunder, botch up, louse up, screw up; **8** bollix up, bollocks; **9** mishandle; **10** bollocks up

bollock: 3 egg, nut; **4** ball; **5** gonad; **6** testis; **7** ballock; **8** testicle

bollocks: 4 blow, flub, muff; **5** botch, fluff, spoil; **6** ball up, bobble, bollix, bungle, foul up, fumble, mess up, muck up; **7** blunder, botch up, louse up, screw up; **8** bollix up; **9** mishandle; **10** bollocks up

bolo: 4 bola; **7** bola tie, bolo tie; **9** bolo knife

boloney: 4 bosh, tosh; **5** drool; **6** humbug; **7** baloney, twaddle; **8** tommyrot; **10** bilgewater, taradiddle; **11** tarradiddle

Bolshevik: 3 red; **5** pinko; **7** Marxist; **9** bolshevik; **10** Bolshevist; **12** Bolshevistic

bolshevism: 7 Marxism; **8** Leninism; **9** Sovietism, sovietism; **12** collectivism; **15** Marxism-Leninism

bolshy: 7 stroppy

bolster: 3 pad; **4** prop; **6** hold up, uphold; **7** stand by, support, sustain; **9** bolster up; **10** long pillow

bolt: 3 bar, pin; **4** bang, dash, flit, hank, hasp, lock, nail, slap, stay; **5** catch, clamp, clasp, crimp, drive, go off, latch, rivet, screw, sling, smack; **6** decamp, devour, gobble, levant, run off, run out, winnow; **7** abscond, bolt out, rigidly, stiffly; **8** bolt down, deadbolt, gobble up, gulp down, slapdash; **9** eliminate, fulminate, pitchfork, skedaddle; **10** police lock; **11** thunderbolt

bolted: 4 fast; **6** barred, locked; **7** latched, secured

bolthead: 6 kettle; **7** capsule, matrass; **8** receiver

bolt in: 3 pen; **4** cage, coop; **5** hem in, pen in; **6** coop up, rail in, wall in; **7** impound

bolting: 7 locking

bolt out: 4 bolt; **6** run off, run out

bolt upright: 5 erect, plumb; **6** normal; **7** upright; **8** straight, vertical; **13** perpendicular

bolus: 3 sop; **6** morsel

bomb: 3 dud; **4** fail; **5** blast, flunk; **6** rocket, turkey; **7** bombard, flush it; **8** fall flat; **13** make a flat joke; **15** bomb calorimeter, drop the big one on; **17** blow to smithereens

bombard: 4 bomb, pelt; **5** shell; **6** pepper; **8** open fire; **9** bombardon

bombardier: 6 gunner; **9** cannoneer; **12** artilleryman

bombardment: 7 barrage, battery, bombing; **8** shelling; **10** bombarding

bombardon: 4 tuba; **7** bombard, helicon; **8** bass horn; **10** cor Anglais [Fr], sousaphone; **11** English horn; **12** corno Inglese [It]

bombast: 3 gas; **4** blah, rant; **5** bluff; **6** hot air; **7** fustian, palaver; **8** claptrap, flummery, richness, tall talk, vaporing; **9** baverdage, euphemism, rigmarole, turgidity; **10** balderdash, floridness, orotundity; **11** declamation, fine talking, grandiosity, prose run mad, rodomontade; **13** frills of style, magniloquence, ornamentation; **14** grandiloquence

bombastic: 4 rich; **5** large, outre, tumid; **6** florid, mouthy, ornate, turgid; **7** flowery, orotund, stilted; **8** inflated, sonorous, swelling; **9** burlesque, grandiose, high flown, monstrous; **10** Johnsonian, mock heroic, ornamented, rhetorical, turgescent; **11** big-sounding, declamatory, extravagant, high flowing; **12** high-sounding, magniloquent, preposterous; **13** grandiloquent; **14** sesquipedalian

bombastically: 8 turgidly; **11** grandiosely

Bombax: 5 simal, ceiba; **11** genus Bombax

Bombay ceiba: 5 kapok; **7** God tree; **9** ceiba tree; **14** Ceiba pentandra, silk-cotton tree; **19** white silk-cotton tree

Bombay hemp: 5 bimli, kanaf, kenaf; **9** bimli hemp; **10** deccan hemp, Indian hemp; **18** Hibiscus cannabinus

bombed: 7 smashed; **9** dead drunk; **11** high as a kite

bomber: 3 sub, zep; **4** hero; **5** hoagy, wedge; **6** hoagie; **7** grinder, poor boy, torpedo; **9** dynamiter, submarine; **12** hero sandwich

bomber crew: 13 bomber aircrew

bombilate: 4 buzz; **9** bombinate

bombilation: 4 roar; **5** noise; **7** clatter

bomb shelter: 9 bombproof; **14** air-raid shelter

bombycid moth: 8 bombycid; **12** silkworm moth

Bombycilla: 7 waxwing; **9** cedarbird; **12** cedar waxwing; **15** genus bombycilla

Bombyx: 11 genus Bombyx

Bombyx mori: 20 domestic silkworm moth

bona fide: 4 real, true; **7** genuine, regular; **9** authentic, unfeigned, veritable; **10** unaffected; **11** unfeignedly; **14** unquestionable, with no nonsense

bonanza: 4 boom; **5** bonus; **6** Potosi; **8** El Dorado [Sp], Golconda, goldmine, windfall

Bonasa: 11 genus Bonasa

Bonasa umbellus: 9 partridge; **12** ruffed grouse

bon bouche: 7 nest egg, savings; **14** money in the bank; **16** money stashed away

bond: 3 tie; **4** bail, bind, link; **5** bonds, stick; **6** adhere, fetter, hamper; **7** linkage, shackle, stick to, trammel; **8** adhesion, alliance, bail bond, covenant, enslaved, hold fast, trammels, vinculum; **9** adherence, bond paper, debenture, in bondage, indenture; **10** attachment, connection, connective, enthralled; **12** adhesiveness, chemical bond, draw together; **13** bring together

bondage: 6 thrall; **7** slavery; **8** thraldom; **9** thralldom; **10** subjection

bonded: 7 secured; **9** warranted; **10** guaranteed

bonding: 9 attaching, soldering

bond of union: 3 tie; **4** link; **6** copula, hyphen

bonds: 4 bond; **6** fetter, hamper; **7** shackle, trammel; **8** trammels

bone: 2 os; **4** cram, drum, grit, swot; **5** get up, ivory, mug up, pearl; **6** bone up, debone, swot up; **8** off-white; **9** grind away; **13** osseous tissue

bone-ash cup: 5 cupel; **13** refractory pot

boned: 7 deboned

bone-forming cell: 10 osteoblast

bonehead: 5 dunce; **8** lunkhead, numskull; **9** blockhead; **10** dunderhead, hammerhead, loggerhead, muttonhead; **11** knucklehead

boneheaded: 5 thick; **9** fatheaded; **11** blockheaded, thickheaded; **12** loggerheaded, thick-skulled, wooden-headed

bone house: 9 dead house; **12** charnel house

bonenkai: 16 New Year's Eve party

boner: 4 flub; **5** botch; **6** boo-boo, bungle, foul-up; **7** blooper, blunder; **8** misdoing

bones: 5 bones; **6** maraca; **8** castanet, clappers, dry bones, skeleton; **9** castanets; **13** finger cymbals; **15** skeletal remains

boneset: 6 arnica; **7** benzoin, calomel; **8** agueweed; **12** thoroughwort; **13** common comfrey

bone to pick: 4 crux; **6** grudge; **10** casus belli [Lat]; **11** crow to pluck, sore subject; **12** battle ground, pons asinorum [Lat]; **13** disputed point, matter at issue, vexed question

bone up: 4 bone, cram, drum, swot; **5** get up, mug up; **6** swot up; **9** grind away

boney: 4 bony

bonfire: 8 balefire

bongo: 5 bongo; **6** kettle; **7** timpani; **8** tympanum; **9** bongo drum

bonhomie: 6 candor; **7** abandon; **9** frankness, geniality, sincerity; **10** affability, amiability, tenderness; **11** affableness, amiableness

boniness: 9 gauntness; **10** emaciation, maceration

bonk: 3 bop, eff; **4** bang, bash, do it, sock, whap, whop

bonkers: 3 mad; **4** bats, daft, loco, nuts; **5** balmy, barmy, batty, buggy, crazy, dotty, kooky, loony, loopy, nutty, wacky; **6** crazed, fruity, insane, kookie, teched [dialect]; **7** cracked, far gone, haywire

bonnet: 4 hood; **10** poke bonnet

bonny: 4 fair; **5** buxom; **6** bonnie, comely, hearty; **7** winsome

bonobo: 15 pygmy chimpanzee

bon ton: 3 ton; **4** chic; **5** style, vogue; **7** fashion, society; **8** smart set; **9** beau monde; **11** high society, stylishness; **14** fashionability

bonus: 5 bonus, grace; **6** fillip, tipfee; **7** bonanza, premium; **8** windfall; **9** incentive

bon vivant: 7 epicure, gourmet, playboy; **9** epicurean; **10** gastronome; **12** man about town

bon voyage: 7 send-off

bony: 5 boney, gaunt; **6** osteal, wasted; **7** haggard, osseous, pinched, starved; **8** skeletal; **9** emaciated; **10** cadaverous

boo: 4 bird, gibe, hiss, hoot, jeer, quip, wipe; **5** fling, flout, scoff, sneer, snort, taunt;

7 razzing; **9** raspberry; **10** Bronx cheer

boob: 3 dug, pap, sin; **4** dope, goof; **5** booby, dummy; **7** blunder, pinhead; **8** dumbbell

boo-boo: 4 flub; **5** boner, botch; **6** bungle, foul-up; **7** blooper, blunder; **8** misdoing

boob tube: 2 TV; **4** tube; **5** telly, TV set; **8** idiot box; **9** goggle box; **10** television

booby: 3 owl; **4** boob, dolt, dope; **5** dummy, noddy, nonny; **6** noodle; **7** pinhead; **8** dumbbell

booby trap: 8 land mine

boogeyman: 5 bogie; **6** booger; **7** bugaboo, bugbear; **8** bogeyman

boogie-woogie: 6 boogie

book: 4 hold, post; **5** debit, enter, leger; **6** credit, ledger, record, script, volume; **7** daybook, reserve; **9** carry over; **10** playscript, recordbook

book binding: 4 back; **5** cover; **7** binding

bookdealer: 10 book seller

booked: 7 engaged; **8** set-aside; **9** given over

booker: 12 booking agent

bookie: 9 bookmaker

booking: 5 entry; **10** engagement; **11** reservation

bookish: 4 blue; **5** solid; **6** savant, shrewd; **8** deep-read, profound, studious; **10** scholastic; **11** enlightened

bookishness: 12 bibliophilia

book jacket: 7 wrapper; **9** dust cover; **10** dust jacket; **11** dust wrapper

bookkeeper: 7 actuary, auditor; **10** accountant; **11** bean counter [derogatory]

bookkeeping: 8 clerking; **9** reckoning; **10** accounting

book-learned: 4 blue; **5** solid; **6** savant, shrewd; **7** bookish; **8** deep-read, profound; **10** scholastic; **11** enlightened

bookless: 7 shallow

booklet: 6 folder; **7** leaflet; **8** brochure, pamphlet

booklover: 11 bibliophile

bookmaker: 6 bookie

bookmark: 10 bookmarker

Book of Psalms: 7 Psalter

books: 6 ledger; **7** journal; **11** account book

bookstore: 8 bookshop; **9** bookstall

bookworm: 6 pedant; **10** scholastic

Boole: 11 George Boole

Boolean algebra: 12 Boolean logic

Boolean logic: 14 Boolean algebra

boolean operation: 15 binary operation

boom: 3 bar, din, lap, rod; **4** bang, clap, dart, flit, heel, nail, peal, roar, scud, shoe, slam, sole, trot, urge, warp, wham; **5** amble, blare, blast, bound, clack, clang, drive, kedge, smash, swell, troll, whack; **6** expand, gallop, splint, spring, stilts, thrive; **7** bonanza, boom out, fanfare, prosper, roaring, stirrup, thunder; **8** flourish,

get ahead, goldmine; **9** fulminate, outrigger

boomer: 8 promoter; **10** baby boomer

boomerang: 8 backfire; **10** throw stick; **13** throwing stick

booming: 3 jog; **4** jolt, push; **5** boost [U.S.], brunt, palmy, shove, throw; **6** thrust; **7** banging, roaring, vibrant; **8** blasting, sonorous, thriving; **9** deep-toned; **10** prospering, prosperous, stentorian; **11** deep-mouthed, flourishing; **12** deep-sounding

boon: 5 favor; **8** blessing; **11** benefaction

boondocks: 6 sticks; **9** backwoods; **10** hinterland; **11** back country

Boone: 11 Daniel Boone

boorish: 6 oafish; **7** bearish, brutish, loutish, raffish, swinish; **8** churlish, clownish; **11** neanderthal

boorishness: 9 brutality, rusticity; **11** brutishness, loutishness, raffishness, uncouthness; **12** churlishness

boost: 3 jog; **4** hike, jolt, push, rise; **5** brunt, shove, throw; **6** hike up, thrust; **7** advance, booming, further, promote; **9** encourage; **11** supercharge; **13** encouragement

booster: 6 friend; **7** admirer, plugger; **8** champion, promoter; **9** supporter; **10** recall dose, shoplifter; **11** booster dose, booster shot, booster unit, protagonist; **12** booster stage; **13** booster rocket, takeoff rocket; **14** takeoff booster

booster amplifier: 8 boosters; **10** relay links; **13** relay stations

booster rocket: 7 booster; **11** booster unit; **12** booster stage; **13** takeoff rocket; **14** takeoff booster; **16** multistage rocket

boosters: 10 relay links; **13** relay stations

booster shot: 7 booster; **10** recall dose; **11** booster dose

booster stage: 7 booster; **13** booster rocket

booster stations: 8 boosters; **10** relay links; **13** relay stations

boot: 4 boot, gain, kick, pump; **5** trunk; **6** import, profit, reboot, sandal; **7** bring up, harvest, kicking, profits [pl], signify, slipper; **8** imperial, iron boot, iron heel

bootblack: 9 shoeblack

bootee: 6 bootee, bootie; **7** bootees, booties

booth: 3 cot, hut; **4** shed; **5** cabin, croft, hovel, kiosk, stall, stand; **6** chalet, dugout [U.S.], shanty; **7** cubicle

bootikin: 6 bootee, bootie

bootleg: 5 black; **7** smuggle; **8** smuggled; **10** contraband; **11** black-market

bootlegger: 10 moonshiner

bootless: 4 vain; **6** futile; **8** nugatory; **9** fruitless, pointless; **10** of no effect, profitless, sleeveless; **12** unprofitable; **13** without effect; **14** leading to no end; **15** inconsequential

bootlick: 4 fawn; **5** kotow, toady; **6** kowtow, suck up; **7** truckle

boot-licker: 4 snob, toad, tool; **5** toady; **6** flunky, sucker, yes-man; **7** flunkey, sponger; **8** courtier, hanger-on, parasite, truckler; **9** doughface [U.S.], sycophant

boot-licking: 7 fawning; **9** groveling

boot out: 4 oust; **5** eject, expel; **7** drum out, exclude, kick out, turf out, turn out; **8** chuck out, throw out

booty: 4 loot, swag; **5** prize; **7** pillage, plunder; **8** hot goods, pickings; **10** stolen item; **11** stolen goods

booze: 4 tope; **5** bouse [Fr], drink; **6** fuddle, liquor, tipple; **7** spirits; **9** booze it up, hard drink; **10** hard liquor; **11** strong drink; **12** drink too much; **14** John Barleycorn

boozer: 4 lush; **5** drunk, souse; **6** soaker; **9** alcoholic; **11** dipsomaniac

boozing: 5 drink; **6** toping; **8** drinking, guzzling, imbibing, tippling; **10** crapulence; **11** boozing it up, drunkenness

boozy: 3 cut; **4** high; **5** beery, drunk, fresh, merry, tight, tipsy; **6** corned, groggy, primed; **7** drunken, fuddled, sottish; **8** bibulous, elevated, overcome, top-heavy; **9** disguised, flustered, inebriate, overtaken; **10** in one's cups, inebriated; **11** intoxicated

bop: 4 bash, bonk, sock, whap, whop; **5** bebop

bopeep: 8 peekaboo

boracic acid: 9 boric acid

borage: 8 tailwort

Boraginaceae: 12 borage family

Borago: 11 genus Borago

Borago officinalis: 6 borage; **8** tailwort

Borassus: 4 palm; **13** genus Borassus

bordeaux blanc: 13 white bordeaux

bordello: 4 stew; **7** brothel; **8** cathouse; **10** whorehouse; **13** sporting house

border: 3 bed; **4** abut, butt, edge; **5** bound, frame, limit, skirt; **6** adjoin, bounds, butt on, edging, fringe, margin, skirts; **7** frame in, molding; **8** boundary, marginal, moulding, seed plot, skirting, surround, trapping, trimming; **9** perimeter; **10** borderline; **11** butt against

borderland: 7 suburbs; **8** confines, environs, purlieus, vicinage; **9** alentours [Fr], marchland; **12** neighborhood

borderline: 6 border; **8** marginal; **10** just enough; **12** boundary line, delimitation, just adequate

border on: 8 approach

bore: 3 bug, tap; **4** bait, drag, pill, tire; **5** abuse, aegir, beset, drill, eager, grind, harry, haunt, hound, tease, worry; **6** badger,

bother, harass, heckle, ill-use, infest, molest, pester, plague, pother; **7** caliber, calibre, dullard, oppress; **8** bore-hole, bullirag, bullyrag, ill-treat, maltreat, mistreat; **9** drill hole, importune, persecute, river bore, tidal bore; **11** buttonholer

Boreal: 6 arctic; **8** Northern; **13** septentrional

boreal: 3 icy; **6** arctic, frosty, wintry; **7** glacial; **8** freezing, Siberian; **12** circumboreal

boreas: 7 norther; **9** north wind

bore bit: 5 borer; **9** rock drill; **10** stone drill

bored: 5 beset, blase, bored; **6** baited; **7** harried, heckled; **8** badgered, harassed, infested, pothered; **10** importuned, persecuted, world-weary; **11** indifferent; **12** uninterested

boredom: 5 ennui; **6** tedium

borer: 5 auger, drill; **7** bore bit; **9** rock drill, woodborer; **10** stone drill

boric acid: 9 boric acid; **11** boracic acid; **14** orthoboric acid

boring: 3 dry; **4** arid, bald, dull, flat, slow; **5** ho-hum; **6** jejune, mortal, old-hat; **7** irksome, tedious, trivial; **8** borehole, drilling, tiresome, well-worn; **9** deadening, dry as dust, wearisome, well-known

born: 6 innate

born-again: 6 reborn; **9** converted

borne: 4 soft, weak; **5** sappy; **6** spoony; **7** shallow, wanting

Borneo: 10 Kalimantan

Bornholm disease: 6 myosis

bornite: 10 peacock ore

boron: 1 B; **13** atomic number 5

borough: 5 burgh

borrow: 5 adopt; **6** take up; **8** take over

borscht: 5 borsh; **6** borsch, borsht; **7** borshch, bortsch

bortz: 7 adamant, diamond; **9** carbonado

borzoi: 16 Russian wolfhound

boscage: 4 ceja [Sp]; **7** thicket; **8** chaparal

Boselaphus: 6 nilgai; **7** nylghai, nylghau; **15** genus Boselaphus

bosh: 4 myth, tosh; **5** drool, farce; **6** humbug; **7** baloney, boloney, eyewash, rubbish, twaddle; **8** tommyrot, wish-wash; **9** mare's nest, moonshine; **10** bilgewater, taradiddle; **11** tarradiddle; **12** fiddle-faddle

bosk: 4 ceja [Sp]; **5** copse, grove; **7** boscage, spinney; **8** chaparal; **9** greenwood

bosom: 3 hug; **4** boob, soul; **5** ghost, heart; **6** spirit; **7** embrace, squeeze; **8** inner man, intimate; **10** heart's core

bosomy: 5 buxom, curvy, sonsy; **6** sonsie; **10** curvaceous, voluptuous; **11** full-bosomed

bosque: 4 ceja [Sp]; **7** boscage; **8** chaparal

boss: 3 hub, top; **4** arch, brag, head, stud; **5** chief, hirer, rivet, stamp; **6** emboss, gaffer, honcho, hubble; **7** foreman, head man; **9** party boss; **10** embossment, head center, head honcho [informal]

boss around: 5 bully; **6** hector; **8** ballyrag, browbeat, bullyrag; **9** strong-arm; **10** push around

bossy: 6 bossed, bunchy; **7** nodular; **8** embossed; **10** autocratic, dominating, peremptory; **11** magisterial; **13** high-and-mighty

Boston: 8 Beantown; **16** Hub of the Universe; **22** capital of Massachusetts

botanical: 7 botanic

botanical garden: 9 arboretum; **13** botanic garden

botanist: 11 phytologist; **14** plant scientist

botanize: 8 botanise

botany: 9 phytology

botch: 4 blow, flub, muff, vamp; **5** boner, fluff, spoil; **6** ball up, bobble, bollix, boo-boo, bungle, cobble, foul up, foul-up, fumble, mess up, muck up, tinker; **7** blooper, blunder, botch up, louse up, retouch, screw up; **8** bollix up, bollocks, bungling, misdoing; **9** mishandle, refashion

bother: 3 ado, bug, irk, rag, vex; **4** bait, bore, faze, fuss, nark, pain, rile, stir, tire, to-do; **5** abuse, annoy, beset, cross, devil, get at, get to, grind, harry, haunt, hound, tease, worry; **6** badger, bustle, fidget, flurry, gravel, harass, hassle, heckle, ill-use, infest, molder, molest, nettle, pester, plague, pother, put out; **7** disturb, mortify, nonplus, oppress, perplex, trouble; **8** bewilder, bullirag, bullyrag, disquiet, ill-treat, irritate, maltreat, mistreat, nuisance, vexation; **9** annoyance, disoblige, displease, grievance, importune, incommode, persecute, pottering; **10** discomfort, discommode, discompose, harassment; **11** botheration, fidgetiness; **13** inconvenience, mortification

bothered: 5 fazed, tired, vexed; **6** teased; **7** daunted, plagued; **8** molested, pestered; **9** disturbed

bothersome: 5 pesky; **6** plaguy, vexing; **7** galling, plaguey, teasing; **8** annoying; **9** pestering, vexatious; **10** irritating, nettlesome; **11** pestiferous

bothy: 3 cot, hut; **4** shed; **5** booth, cabin, croft, hovel, stall; **6** chalet, dugout [U.S.], shanty

botonee: 8 botonnee

bo tree: 5 pipal, pipul; **6** peepul

botryoid: 8 boytrose; **10** botryoidal

bottle: 3 can, jar, pot, tin

bottled gas: 21 liquefied petroleum gas

bottle gourd: 8 calabash

bottle-holder: 12 candle-holder

bottleneck: 3 jam; **4** neck; **9** stricture; **10** traffic jam; **12** constriction

bottlenose: 15 bottlenose whale; **16** bottlenosed whale; **17** bottlenose dolphin; **18** bottle-nosed dolphin

bottle screw: 9 corkscrew

bottle up: 5 box up, mew up; **6** clap up, cork up, lock up, seal up, shut in, shut up; **8** button up, suppress

bottom: 3 bed, bum, can; **4** base, buns, butt, dale, dell, foot, glen, prat, rear, rump, seat, ship, tail, tush, vale; **5** embed, fanny, found, glade, grove, imbed, nadir, pluck, spine, stern; **6** behind, fathom, ground, lowest, valley, vessel; **7** hind end, keister, poorest, rear end, tail end, tooshie; **8** backbone, backside, buttocks, derriere, gameness; **9** freighter, fundament, penetrate, posterior, undermost, underside

bottomland: 10 flood plain

bottommost: 9 lowermost; **10** nethermost

botulin: 5 toxin

Botulinus toxin: 7 botulin

bouchee: 10 patty shell

boudoir: 7 bedroom; **9** dormitory

bouffant: 5 puffy

bouffe: 10 comic opera; **11** opera bouffe; **12** opera comique

bough: 4 link, limb; **5** joint, scion; **6** branch

bought: 4 hook; **5** crook; **9** purchased

bougie: 5 taper; **6** candle

bouillon: 5 broth

bouldered: 5 rocky, stony; **8** bouldery

boule: 4 buhl; **6** boulle

boulevard: 6 avenue

bounce: 3 bob, fib, fly; **4** leap; **5** bound, burst, flare, flash, go off, start, story; **6** blow up, foot it, jounce, recoil, spring; **7** bluster, crammer, explode, flounce, leaping, ousting, rebound, removal, swagger, thunder, whopper; **8** bouncing, detonate, ricochet, take a hop; **9** dismissal; **10** blustering, bounciness, spring back, swaggering

bounce back: 5 react; **6** recoil; **7** fly back, get over, get well, rebound; **9** bound back, pull round; **10** spring back

bouncing: 3 fat; **4** full; **5** lusty, obese, peppy, plump, squab, stout, zippy; **6** bounce, bouncy; **7** jolting; **8** jouncing, spirited; **9** corpulent, strapping

bouncing Bet: 8 soapwort; **9** hedge pink; **12** bouncing Bess

bouncy: 4 live; **5** peppy, zippy; **6** lively, whippy; **7** springy; **8** bouncing, spirited; **9** resilient

bound: 3 hop, lap; **4** boom, dart, edge, flit, gird, jump, leap, trot; **5** amble, beset, limit, troll, vault; **6** begird, border, bounce, bounds, gallop, jump up, recoil, spring; **7** compass, confine, embrace, enclose, environ, inclose, leaping, limited, rebound, trammel; **8** articled, as in duty, bandaged, boundary, confined, destined, encircle, enclosed, obligate, reliable, restrain, restrict, ricochet, surround, take a hop, throttle; **9** compelled, encompass; **10** circumvent, indentured; **11** apprenticed, constrained, encompassed, trustworthy

boundary: 4 edge; **5** bound, limit; **6** border, bounds; **9** perimeter

boundary line: 6 border; **10** borderline; **12** delimitation

boundedness: 8 finitude; **10** finiteness

bounder: 3 cad, dog; **4** heel; **5** hound; **6** rascal; **7** villain; **9** scoundrel; **10** blackguard

bounderish: 4 rude; **7** ill-bred, lowbred; **8** yokelish; **9** underbred

bound hand and foot: 7 hobbled; **8** fettered, manacled, pinioned; **10** handcuffed; **14** shackledgagged

boundless: 7 endless; **9** limitless, unbounded

bounds: 5 bound, limit; **6** border; **8** boundary; **9** perimeter

bound to: 5 due to; **8** tied down; **9** duty bound; **10** beholden to, indebted to

bounteous: 3 big; **4** free; **6** giving; **7** liberal; **8** generous, handsome, princely; **9** bountiful, unselfish; **10** bighearted, charitable, freehanded, full handed, munificent, openhanded

bounteousness: 6 bounty; **7** charity; **10** generosity, liberality; **11** munificence

bounty: 4 alms; **7** charity, largess, premium; **9** amplitude; **10** generosity, liberality; **11** munificence; **13** bounteousness, bountifulness

bouquet: 4 posy; **5** scent; **6** flower, wreath; **7** chaplet, corsage, essence, festoon, garland, nosegay, perfume; **9** fragrance, redolence, sweetness

bourgeois: 7 burgher, cockney, epicier [Fr]; **8** commoner, democrat, plebeian; **10** republican; **11** proletarian; **12** conservative; **13** materialistic; **14** businessperson

bourgeoisie: 11 middle class; **13** middle classes

bourgeon: 3 bud; **4** spud; **5** shoot; **6** sprout; **7** shoot up; **8** sprout up; **9** germinate, pullulate

Bourgogne: 8 Burgundy

bourn: 4 pale, term; **5** verge; **6** bourne; **7** confine, enclave; **11** reservation

bourne: 5 bourn

bourse: 5 board

bouse: 4 tope; **5** booze, bowse, drink; **6** tipple; **9** booze it up; **12** drink too much

bout: 3 say; **4** turn; **5** event, fight, fling, round, spree; **6** vagary; **7** gambade, passage; **8** echappee [Fr], rotation; **10** revolution

boutique: 4 shop; **9** small shop

bovine: 5 bovid

bow: 3 arc, bow, jib; **4** arch, bend, fore, loop, prow, star, stem; **5** couch, defer, kneel, squat, stoop; **6** accede, arcade, bowing,

cringe, crouch, curtsy, give in, salaam, submit; **7** arcuate, bow down, bowknot, rosette; **8** arch over, courtesy, crescent, half-moon; **9** crane neck, horseshoe, obeisance; **11** bend the knee, curtain call

bow and scrap: 6 kowtow, scrape

bowdlerize: 7 shorten; **9** expurgate; **10** bowdlerise

bow down: 3 bow; **9** prostrate

bowed: 4 bent; **5** arced, bandy; **6** arched, bowing, bowleg; **7** arching, arclike, arcuate, vaulted; **8** arciform, inclined; **9** bowlegged; **11** bandy-legged

bowel: 3 gut; **4** guts [pl]; **6** bowels [pl], vitals [pl]; **7** viscera [pl]; **8** entrails [pl]; **9** intestine; **10** intestines [pl]

bower: 5 arbor; **6** arbour; **7** embower, pergola, enclose

bowerbird: 7 catbird

bowfin: 7 dogfish, grindle; **9** Amia calva

bowhead: 12 bowhead whale

bowing: 3 bow; **5** bowed; **9** obeisance

bow kneed: 10 knock kneed

bowl: 4 bowl; **5** arena, basin, jorum, troll; **6** trough; **7** bowlful, stadium, trundle; **8** pipe bowl; **9** circulate, punch bowl

bowlegged: 5 bandy, bowed; **6** bowleg; **11** bandy-legged

bowler: 5 derby; **7** plug hat; **9** bowler hat

bowlful: 4 bowl

bowline: 11 bowline knot

bowl over: 5 upset; **6** boggle; **7** tip over; **8** overturn, turn over; **9** knock over; **11** flabbergast

bowman: 6 archer, bowman; **8** marksman, rifleman

bow out: 6 remove, retire; **7** back off, pull out; **8** back down, withdraw; **10** chicken out

bowse: 5 bouse

bowstring: 3 gas; **4** rope; **5** noose; **6** behead, gibbet, halter; **7** turn off; **8** string up

bow-wow: 4 yelp; **5** doggy, growl, pooch, snarl; **6** doggie; **7** belling

box: 3 pew; **4** loge; **5** cabin, lodge; **6** boxful, carton, corner; **7** box seat, boxwood, cottage, package; **9** hermitage, rus in urbe [Lat]; **10** fisticuffs; **13** exchange blows

boxberry: 8 teaberry; **9** twinberry; **10** spiceberry; **11** wintergreen

box elder: 8 box elder; **11** Acer negundo; **14** ash-leaved maple

box end wrench: 9 box wrench

boxer: 6 bagger, packer; **7** athlete, bruiser; **8** pugilist, wrestler; **9** gladiator; **12** prize fighter

boxing: 7 packing; **8** pugilism; **10** fisticuffs; **13** sweet science

boxing match: 4 spar; **5** fight, set-to

boxing ring: 4 ring; **6** canvas

box office: 11 ticket booth; **12** ticket office

box the ears: 4 cuff; 5 lay on, smack, spank, thump; 6 buffet, thwack

boxthorn: 13 matrimony vine

box up: 5 box in, mew up; 6 clap up, cork up, lock up, seal up, shut in, shut up; 8 bottle up, button up

box wrench: 12 box end wrench

boxy: 7 boxlike

boy: 3 lad, son; 5 boots, child; 7 bell boy, child, stripling; 14 whipper-snapper

boyar: 7 esquire; 8 margrave

boyfriend: 4 beau; 5 swain; 6 fellow; 8 young man

Boykinia: 13 genus Boykinia

boy wonder: 12 child prodigy

bpi: 11 bits per inch

bpm: 2 M.M.; 14 beats per minute; 16 metronome marking

BPOE: 4 Elks

bps: 13 bits per second

Br: 7 bromine

bra: 7 bandeau; 9 brassiere

brabble: 6 bicker, jangle, niggle; 7 quibble; 8 pettifog, snip-snap, squabble

brabbler: 6 Tartar

brace: 3 duo; 4 duad, duet, dyad, hook, line, link, lock, pair, span, yoke; 5 belay, deuce, latch, leash, nerve, poise, space, twain, twins; 6 arouse, braces, cheeks, couple, fillet, gallus, perk up, roller, steady, 7 bracing, bracket, couplet, distich, grapple, twosome; 8 bitstock, energise, energize; 9 doubleton, stimulate, suspender; 10 invigorate, strengthen; 12 reinvigorate

braced: 10 buttressed

bracelet: 6 armlet, bangle; 9 watchband, wristband; 10 watchstrap

bracer: 7 placebo; 8 pick-me-up; 9 faith cure

braces: 5 brace; 6 arrows; 7 slashes; 8 brackets; 11 parentheses; 12 double quotes; 13 curly brackets; 14 quotation marks

brace up: 9 undergird

Brachychiton: 9 flame tree, durrajong, currajong, kurrajong; 17 genus Brachychiton

bracing: 5 brace, brisk, fresh, tonic; 7 good for; 10 energizing, nutritious, refreshful, refreshing; 12 invigorating, invigoration

bracken: 4 fern; 5 brake; 12 pasture brake

bracket: 4 hook, link, lock, pair, yoke; 5 belay, brace, latch, leash; 6 couple; 7 grapple

bracket fungus: 11 shelf fungus

brackets: 6 arrows, braces; 7 slashes; 11 parentheses; 12 double quotes; 13 curly brackets; 14 quotation marks

brackish: 4 salt; 5 briny, salty; 6 saline

bracted: 9 bracteate

brad: 4 nail, tack

bradawl: 3 awl; 7 pricker

Bradypus: 2 ai; 13 genus Bradypus; 14 three-toed sloth

brag: 3 gas; 4 blow, boss, crow, tout; 5 boast, swash, vaunt; 7 bluster, crowing; 8 bragging, vaporing; 9 gasconade

braggadocio: 7 bluster; 8 braggart; 11 rodomontade

braggart: 3 big; 6 braggy; 7 boaster, crowing, flaming, stilted, vaunter, 8 blowhard, boastful, boasting, bragging; 9 cock-a-hoop, soi-disant [Fr], thrasonic; 10 swaggering; 11 braggadocio, gasconading, line-shooter; 12 magniloquent; 16 self-aggrandizing

bragging: 3 big; 4 brag, crow; 6 braggy; 7 crowing, flaming, stilted; 8 boastful, boasting, braggart, vaporing; 9 cock-a-hoop, gasconade, soi-disant [Fr], thrasonic; 10 self-praise, swaggering; 11 gasconading; 12 line-shooting, magniloquent, self-applause, self-flattery; 13 self-laudation

Brahma: 4 Devi, Kali; 5 Brahm, Durga, oread, Ushas; 7 Bathala, Brahman, Brahmin; 10 Bos indicus; 14 cloud-compeller, the Great Spirit

Brahmaputra: 16 Brahmaputra River

Brahms: 14 Johannes Brahms

braid: 3 mat; 4 felt, knot, lace, plat; 5 chain, cross, plait, quilt, tress, twill, twist; 6 pleach, wreath; 8 braiding; 9 embroider, gold braid; 10 cat's cradle

Braille: 11 Braille code, Braille-type; 13 Braille system; 14 Braille writing

brain: 3 wit; 4 head, mind, nous; 6 genius, psyche; 9 mentality; 10 brainpower, encephalon, mastermind

braincase: 7 cranium; 8 brainpan

brainchild: 11 inspiration

brain-dead: 10 vegetating, vegetative

brain death: 10 brain death, vegetation; 13 cerebral death; 14 vegetable state; 15 vegetative state

brain doctor: 11 neurologist

brainish: 6 madcap; 8 tearaway; 9 hot-headed, impetuous, impulsive

brainless: 4 dull; 6 stupid; 7 witless; 8 headless, mindless; 9 airheaded, dim-witted, fat witted, fat-headed, pig headed; 10 beef headed, dull minded, dull normal, dull witted, half witted, lean witted, weak headed, weak-minded

brain mushroom: 5 morel

brainpan: 5 scull, skull; 7 cranium; 9 braincase; 11 pericranium [Med]

brainpower: 3 wit; 5 brain; 9 mentality; 14 mental capacity

brainsick: 3 mad; 4 sick; 5 crazy, dizzy; 8 demented, unhinged; 9 disturbed; 10 distracted, unbalanced

brainstorm: 4 idea; 7 insight; 9 brainwave

brain sugar: 9 galactose

brain surgeon: 12 neurosurgeon

brain-teaser: 6 enigma, riddle; **9** conundrum

brainy: 4 keen; **5** sharp; **6** bright; **9** brilliant; **11** intelligent; **12** smart as a whip

brake: 3 bit; **6** bridle; **7** bracken, coppice, snaffle, thicket

brake cylinder: 14 master cylinder

brake light: 9 stoplight

braless: 7 topless; **12** bare-breasted

Brama: 10 genus Brama

Brama raii: 7 pomfret

bramble: 4 fang, tang; **5** briar, brier, sting, thorn; **6** nettle; **7** thistle

bran: 4 meal; **5** flour; **6** farina

branch: 3 arm, leg; **4** fork, limb, lobe, wing; **5** bough, shoot; **6** lobule, member, offset, ramify, sprout; **8** offshoot, separate; **9** outgrowth

branched: 6 forked, prongy, ramose; **7** pronged; **8** biramous, tree-like; **9** bifurcate, branching, dendritic; **10** dendriform

branchia: 4 gill

branching: 4 fork; **6** ramose; **7** forking; **8** branched, tree-like; **9** dendritic; **10** dendriform, tree-shaped; **11** bifurcation; **12** divarication, ramification

branchiopod: 11 branchiopod; **13** branchiopodan; **14** branchiopodous; **21** branchiopod crustacean

Branchiostomidae: 11 Amphioxidae; **17** family Amphioxidae

branchlet: 4 twig; **5** sprig

branch line: 4 spur; **9** spur track

branch off: 3 out; **7** file off; **9** glance off

branch out: 7 broaden; **9** diversify, launch out

brand: 4 fuse, link, make, mark, post, sear, slur; **5** bilbo, blade, label, stain, steel, sword, torch; **6** burn in, expose, gibbet, malign, marque, rapier, stigma; **8** backbite, denounce, fireball, flambeau, reproach, whinyard; **9** cauterize, firebrand, trade mark, trade name; **10** fire-barrel, imputation, stigmatize

branding: 14 stigmatisation, stigmatization

brandish: 4 flap, wave; **5** bandy, shake, sport, wield; **8** flourish

brandy glass: 7 snifter

brant: 5 brent; **10** brant goose, brent goose

Branta: 5 goose; **11** genus Branta

Branta canadensis: 6 honker; **11** Canada goose; **13** Canadian goose

brash: 4 weak; **5** frail, nervy; **6** cheeky; **7** fragile; **8** delicate; **9** daredevil, sensitive; **11** temerarious

brashly: 7 nervily; **8** cheekily

brashness: 4 face; **5** brass, front, glitz; **8** loudness; **9** gaudiness, hardihood, nerviness; **10** flashiness, garishness, tawdriness; **12** impertinence; **13** shamelessness

Brasilia: 15 capital of Brazil; **16** Brazilian capital

brass: 4 face; **5** cheek, front, nerve; **6** plaque; **8** boldness; **9** brashness, hardihood, nerviness; **10** effrontery, governance; **12** impertinence, organisation, organization; **13** establishment, shamelessness; **14** administration, memorial tablet

brassbound: 8 ironclad

Brassia: 12 genus Brassia, spider orchid

Brassicaceae: 4 cole, kale, napa, rape; **5** colza; **6** turnip, turnip, pe-tsai; **7** cabbage, bok choi, bok choy, mustard, pakchoi; **8** rutabaga, broccoli, kohlrabi; **10** Cruciferae; **11** cauliflower; **12** broccoli rabe; **13** mustard family; **14** Brussels sprout

brassiere: 3 bra; **7** bandeau

brassy: 4 loud; **5** cheap, flash, gaudy, tacky, tatty; **6** brazen, flashy, garish, tawdry, trashy; **8** gimcrack, insolent; **9** audacious, barefaced, bodacious, bold-faced, brasslike; **11** brazen-faced; **12** meretricious

brat: 4 chit; **6** terror, urchin; **10** holy terror; **11** spoiled brat; **12** little terror; **14** enfant terrible [Fr]

brattle: 5 clack; **7** clatter, scamper

bravado: 6 bunkum; **7** bluster

brave: 3 gay; **4** bear, bide, braw; **5** beard, brook, buxom, flush, hardy, stand; **6** endure, florid, robust, stanch, suffer; **7** staunch, venture, weather; **8** brave out, fearless, intrepid, tolerate, vigorous; **9** audacious, dauntless, go through, unfearing, withstand; **10** courageous

bravely: 12 courageously

bravery: 5 valor; **7** courage; **8** boldness; **12** fearlessness; **14** courageousness

bravo: 4 euge! [Ger], thug; **5** bully; **6** madcap, Moloch; **7** matador; **8** assassin, garroter, well done!; **9** daredevil, desperado, fire eater; **10** bravissimo!, scapegrace

bravura: 7 cantata; **8** canticle

braw: 3 gay; **5** brave

brawl: 2 do; **3** row; **4** bash, bawl, fray, hoop, howl, roar, to-do, yell; **5** broil, melee, shout, whoop; **6** affray, bellow, breeze, fracas, halloa, halloo, hubbub, pother, racket, rumble, rumpus, scream, shriek, shrill, squall, uproar; **7** howling, rhubarb [baseball], ruction, screech, shindig, trouble, wrangle; **8** brouhaha

brawler: 6 rioter; **8** renegade, runagate, wrangler

brawling: 8 fighting

brawn: 5 nerve, sinew; **6** muscle; **8** physique

brawny: 4 wiry; **5** hefty; **6** fleshy, sinewy; **8** gigantic, muscular, powerful, stalwart, well-knit; **9** strapping, well-built; **15** broadshouldered

bray: 4 mash; **5** grind; **6** crunch, hee-haw; **9** comminute

brazen: 5 nervy; **6** brassy; **8** insolent;

9 audacious, barefaced, bodacious, bold-
faced; **11** brazen-faced, impertinent
brazier: 7 brasier
Brazil: 6 Brasil
brazil nut: 6 brazil; **13** brazil-nut tree
brazilwood: 9 peach wood, peachwood; **14**
pernambuco wood
Brazos: 11 Brazos River
Brazzaville: 14 capital of Congo
breach: 3 gap; **4** rent, rift; **5** break, exact, split,
usurp; **6** offend; **7** infract, rupture, violate; **8**
disunion, division, encroach, exaction,
infringe, trench on; **9** breaching, go against,
severance, violating, violation; **10** assumption, disruption, falling out, imposition,
infraction, transgress, usurpation; **11** brouillerie [Fr], presumption; **12** encroachment,
infringement; **13** transgression
bread: 4 gelt, kale, loot, pelf; **5** dough, lucre;
6 dinero, moolah; **7** cabbage, shekels; **10**
breadstuff; **11** staff of life
bread and butter: 4 keep; **6** living; **7** support; **10** livelihood, sustenance
bread and water: 14 starvation diet
breadbasket: 3 tum; **5** belly, tummy; **6**
paunch; **7** stomach
breadbox: 8 bread-bin
bread maker: 5 baker
bread of life: 4 host
breadth: 5 width; **9** thickness; **17** comprehensiveness
break: 2 go; **3** die, gap; **4** bump, bust, chip,
damp, fail, give, part, rift, ruin, snap, stop,
tear, wear; **5** burst, check, crack, erupt,
fault, let on, pause, split; **6** better, breach,
cave in, dampen, demote, expose, fall in,
get out, hold on, impart, let out, offend,
recess, reveal, shiver, soften, sunder,
weaken; **7** break in, break up, conk out,
declare, develop, divulge, fissure, founder,
give out, give way, infract, phaeton,
respite, rupture, snap off, split up, time out,
timeout, violate, wear out; **8** bad bankrupt,
break off, break out, breakage, breaking,
breakout, bring out, collapse, delictum
[Lat], disclose, discover, fracture, give
away, good luck, infringe, intermit, relegate, separate; **9** break away, break down,
come apart, fall apart, fault line, gaolbreak,
get around, go against, interrupt, jailbreak,
open frame, severance; **10** beat a habit,
break-dance, disruption, drop a habit,
falling out, kick a habit, suspension, transgress; **11** discontinue, happy chance, prisonbreak; **12** intermission, interruption; **13**
discontinuity
breakable: 7 fragile, brittle; **9** frangible
break apart: 5 crash; **7** break up, dissect; **8**
disunify; **9** dismantle, take apart; **11** disassemble; **12** come to pieces, decentralize,
fall to pieces

break away: 3 lam, run; **4** bunk, chip; **5**
break; **6** secede; **7** chip off, come off, get
away, run away, scarper; **8** break off, break
out, slip away, splinter, turn tail
break camp: 6 decamp; **11** strike tents
break down: 2 go; **3** die; **4** fail, sink; **5** crush,
drown; **6** lose it, tumble; **7** analyse, analyze, conk out, crumble, crumple, cut
down, dissect, flat out [U.S.], founder, give
out, give way, mow down; **8** beat down,
blow down, collapse, pull down; **9** take
apart; **10** unassemble; **11** disassemble
breakdown: 4 mess; **6** scrape; **7** crack-up; **11**
dislocation; **12** partitioning
breaker: 4 reef, surf; **5** atoll; **7** trainer; **8**
breakers, ledgeman
breakers: 4 bank, flat, surf; **5** shelf; **6** shoals;
7 breaker; **8** lee shore, shallows
break in: 4 tame; **5** break, cut in, put in; **6**
butt in; **7** barge in, burst in, chime in; **9**
break into, burst into; **11** acclimatize,
domesticate
breaking: 5 break; **8** breakage; **9** violating;
10 infringing; **11** in violation; **13** transgressing
breaking away: 7 leaving; **9** breakaway; **10**
uncoupling; **11** breaking off; **13** disengagement
breaking ball: 5 curve; **6** bender; **9** curve
ball
breaking off: 7 leaving; **9** abruption; **10**
uncoupling; **13** disengagement
breaking up: 10 disruption; **11** dissolution,
liquidation
break loose: 6 escape; **7** explode, get away; **8**
break out; **9** break free; **10** burst forth
break off: 4 chip, drop, knap, quit, stop; **5**
break, leave; **6** cut off, give up; **7** chip off,
come off, snap off; **8** break way, cut short,
leave off, uncouple; **9** break away, disengage, drop out of; **10** break short; **11** break
in upon, discontinue
break of day: 4 dawn; **5** sunup; **6** aurora; **7**
dawning, morning, sunrise; **8** cockcrow,
daybreak; **9** dayspring, peep of day; **10**
first light
break one's back: 5 slave; **10** buckle down;
11 knuckle down
break one's heart: 4 damp, dash, dull, sink;
5 lower, unman; **6** deject; **9** knock down,
prostrate
break open: 5 burst, erupt, flare, split; **7** flare
up, pry open; **8** burst out; **9** force open,
prize open
breakout: 5 break, sally; **6** sortie; **8** outbreak;
9 jailbreak; **11** prisonbreak
break through: 5 break, crack, erupt; **7**
come out; **11** come through, push
through
breakthrough: 4 find; **9** discovery

break up: 3 sap; **4** mine, part, pick; **5** break, calve, crack, crash, cut up, sever, shake, split; **6** cut off, dispel, recess; **7** adjourn, crack up, crock up, disrupt, dissect, scatter, split up; **8** collapse, disperse, dissolve, fragment, separate; **9** decompose, dismantle, dissipate, fall apart, interrupt, last stage, liquidate, take apart, undermine; **10** break apart, go to pieces; **11** disassemble, fragmentize; **12** decentralize, fall to pieces, turning point

breakup: 7 breakup; **10** detachment, separation; **11** dissolution; **15** trial separation

breakwater: 4 mole, mull, spur; **5** groin, jetty; **7** bulwark, sea wall, seawall; **8** dead wall

bream: 5 bream; **8** sea bream; **15** freshwater bream

breast: 4 soul, stem; **5** bosom, front, ghost, heart; **6** spirit; **8** inner man; **9** encounter, white meat

breastbone: 7 sternum

breastfeed: 4 suck; **5** nurse; **6** suckle; **7** lactate; **8** give suck, wet-nurse

breastplate: 4 egis; **5** aegis; **7** cuirass

breastwork: 7 bastion, curtain, parapet; **9** banquette

breath: 4 coup, hint, snap; **5** burst, crack, flash, jiffy, trice; **8** breather; **9** twinkling, undertone; **10** intimation; **11** breath of air; **12** stroke of time

breathalyzer: 12 breathalyser

breathe: 3 hum, rat; **4** emit, flow, live, purl, rest, sing; **5** argue, imply, utter; **6** babble, convey, gurgle, ripple, snitch, squeal, tattle; **7** be alive, bespeak, give off, involve, let fall, pass off, point to, respire; **8** allude to, indicate, vocalize; **10** bear a sense, draw breath, give tongue, take breath

breathe in: 5 sniff, snort; **6** inhale

breathe out: 6 exhale, expire

breather: 6 breath; **7** snorkel

breathing: 5 pulse, quick; **8** animated; **9** heartbeat; **11** above ground, respiration, temperature

breathinghole: 4 vent; **7** air vent; **8** blowhole, venthole

breathing in: 8 sniffing, snorting; **10** inhalation; **11** inspiration

breathing out: 10 exhalation, expiration

breathing time: 5 truce; **6** breath; **7** time off; **8** breather; **9** armistice, stand-down; **12** modus vivendi [Lat]; **14** breathing place, breathing space, breathing spell

breathless: 5 agape, eager; **6** aghast, gung ho, urgent; **7** all agog, zealous; **8** windless, wordless; **9** inanimate, pulseless, voiceless; **10** speechless, tongueless; **11** hard pressed; **12** breathtaking, enthusiastic, undistracted

breathtaking: 10 breathless; **12** awe-inspiring

breccia: 9 composite

breech: 4 loin, rump, tail; **5** croup; **6** dorsum; **7** buttock; **10** posteriors, rear of tube

breechcloth: 7 G-string; **9** loincloth; **11** breechclout

breech delivery: 11 breech birth

breeched: 9 trousered; **11** pantalooned

breeches: 6 briefs, shorts; **8** knickers; **9** knee pants; **10** underpants; **12** knee breeches; **14** knickerbockers

breed: 3 kit; **4** line, rear, seed, spat, stem, tree; **5** brood, cover, heirs, house, issue, spawn, stock, trunk; **6** farrow, ground, litter, stirps, strain; **7** bring up, lineage, nurture, prepare, progeny, variety; **8** engender, exercise, multiply, pedigree, practice; **9** habituate, offspring, posterity

breeding: 6 comity, polish; **7** nurture, raising, rearing, suavity; **8** presence, training, urbanity; **9** education, fosterage, fostering, gentility, nurturing; **10** bringing up, refinement, upbringing; **11** genteelness, procreation; **12** reproduction

breeze: 3 air, row; **4** blow, fray, to-do; **5** brawl, broil, drift, melee; **6** affray, fracas, hubbub, pother, racket, rumble, rumpus, squall, uproar, zephyr; **7** howling, rhubarb [baseball], ruction, shindig, trouble; **8** brouhaha

breeze through: 3 ace; **10** pass easily; **11** sail through; **12** sweep through

breeziness: 9 windiness; **10** jauntiness

breezy: 5 blowy, bully, gusty, windy; **7** chipper [U.S.], squally

brent: 5 brant; **10** brant goose, brent goose

Breslau: 7 Wroclaw

Bretagne: 5 Breiz; **8** Brittany

brethren: 4 fold; **5** flock, laity; **6** people; **8** assembly; **11** the faithful; **12** congregation

breve: 5 minim; **8** crotchet; **9** semibreve [Mus]

brevet: 6 charge, errand, permit; **7** license, warrant; **9** exequatur [Lat], prescript; **12** prescription brevet rank: **3** pas; **4** rank; **5** place; **7** station; **8** position; **10** precedence

brevity: 7 brevity; **8** fugacity [Chem]; **9** briefness, terseness; **10** transience; **11** compactness, conciseness, evanescence; **12** impermanence, the soul of wit; **13** temporariness

brew: 4 beer, cook; **5** hatch, knead, steep; **6** infuse; **7** brewage

brewage: 4 brew

brewer: 9 beer maker

brewing: 7 brewing; **8** brooding; **9** preparing; **11** forthcoming

briar: 5 brier; **7** bramble, thistle; **8** catbrier; **9** briar pipe, bullbrier, eglantine, tree heath; **10** greenbrier, horsebrier, sweetbriar, sweetbrier

briary: 5 burry, spiny; 6 barbed, briery, burred, snaggy, thorny; 7 bristly, prickly, studded, thistly; 8 bristled; 9 bristling; 10 barbellate

bribable: 5 venal; 9 dishonest; 11 corruptible, purchasable

bribe: 3 buy; 4 bait; 5 graft; 6 payoff, suborn; 7 corrupt, douceur [Fr]; 10 ground bait, tamper with; 13 grease the palm

bribery: 5 graft

bric-a-brac: 5 curio; 6 bauble, gewgaw, trifle; 7 bibelot, novelty, trinket, whatnot; 8 chotchke, gimcrack, kickshaw, nicknack, whim-wham; 9 bagatelle, tchotchke; 10 knickknack

brick: 3 gem; 5 jewel, trump; 6 prince; 10 good fellow; 12 rough diamond

bricklayer: 5 mason

brickle: 7 brickly, brittle

brickyard: 10 brickfield

bridal: 6 bridal; 7 nuptial, spousal, wedding; 8 espousal, hymeneal, nuptials, spousals

bridal gown: 11 wedding gown; 12 wedding dress

bridegroom: 5 groom

bridesman: 7 best man

bride-to-be: 7 fiancee

bridge: 4 span; 5 whist; 7 isthmus; 9 nosepiece; 10 bridge deck, bridge over, bridgework; 11 bridge whist; 13 bridge circuit, stepping-stone

bridgehead: 8 foothold; 9 beachhead

bridge over: 4 span; 6 bridge, hush up; 7 arrange, patch up; 8 tide over; 9 keep going; 10 pave the way

bridge player: 4 hand

bridge whist: 5 whist; 6 bridge; 14 contract bridge

bridle: 3 bit, gag; 4 curb; 5 brake, check; 6 muzzle; 7 snaffle

bridle at: 8 bridle up; 9 bristle at, bristle up, show anger

bridle path: 9 horse road; 10 bridle road; 11 bridle track

brief: 4 note; 5 brisk, close, draft, quick, short, terse; 6 apercu, digest, little, minute, precis; 7 concise, epitome, outline, summary; 8 abstract, analysis, synopsis; 10 abridgment, legal brief; 11 abbreviated; 13 multum in parvo [Lat]; 14 extemporaneous

briefly: 5 apace; 7 by and by, in brief, in short, quickly, shortly, tersely; 8 in a while, speedily; 9 concisely, extempore, forthwith, summarily; 11 immediately; 12 in no long time; 13 at short notice, incontinently

briefness: 7 brevity; 9 terseness; 10 transience; 11 conciseness

briefs: 6 shorts; 8 breeches; 10 underpants

brier: 5 briar

brig: 3 can [slang], pen; 4 hold, jail, keep, snow, stir [slang]; 5 clink [slang], hulks, pokey [slang]; 6 chokey [slang], cooler [slang], donjon, lockup, prison; 7 slammer [slang]; 8, hoosegow, stockade; 9 calaboose [slang], guardroom, oubliette; 10 guard house

brigade: 4 army, host, wing; 5 corps, squad; 6 column; 7 battery, company, platoon, section; 8 division, garrison, regiment, squadron; 9 battalion; 10 detachment; 11 corps d'armee [Fr], subdivision; 12 flying column

brigade major: 8 adjutant; 9 brigadier; 10 aide-de-camp; 12 staff officer

brigadier: 8 adjutant; 10 aide-de-camp; 12 brigade major, staff officer; 16 brigadier general

brigand: 4 thug; 5 harpy, shark; 6 bandit, falcon; 9 land shark; 10 freebooter

bright: 4 airy, deep, keen; 5 light, sharp, shiny, smart, sunny, vivid; 6 brainy; 7 buoyant, intense, roseate, shining; 8 brightly, cheering, lustrous, sunshiny, undimmed; 9 brilliant, burnished, looking up, promising; 10 bright eyed, debonnaire; 11 brilliantly, encouraging, free and easy, inspiriting, intelligent, rose-colored

Bright's disease: 9 nephritis

bright blue: 5 azure; 7 sky-blue; 8 cerulean

bright days: 9 palmy days; 11 halcyon days

brighten: 5 clear; 7 clear up, light up, lighten; 9 lighten up

brightly: 6 bright; 11 brilliantly

brightness: 5 light; 9 luminance, smartness; 10 brilliancy, cleverness, luminosity; 11 illuminance; 12 luminousness; 14 light intensity

bright side: 9 sunny side; 12 silver lining

brilliance: 5 blaze, glare; 6 genius; 8 grandeur, splendor; 9 grandness, splendour; 10 effulgence, refulgence; 12 magnificence, resplendence

brilliancy: 6 luster, lustre; 8 radiance, splendor; 9 splendour; 10 brightness

brilliant: 3 gem; 4 rock, ruby; 5 bijou, jewel, pearl, vivid; 6 brainy, bright, superb; 7 diamond, radiant, shining; 8 glorious, splendid; 10 cut diamond; 11 illustrious, magnificent; 12 smart as a whip; 13 precious stone

brim: 3 lip, rim; 5 brink

brimstone: 7 sulphur

brindle: 5 tabby; 7 brinded; 8 brindled

brine: 5 brine; 6 pickle; 8 seawater; 9 salt water, saltwater

bring: 3 add, get; 4 land, lend, play, take, work; 5 fetch, reach, wreak; 6 bestow, convey, convoy, impart; 7 bring in, conduct, make for; 9 institute; 10 contribute

bring about: 4 give; 5 set up, stage, yield; 6 effect; 7 arrange, produce; 8 give rise; 10 effectuate, give rise to

bring back: 6 return; 7 bring to, retract; 8 take back; 9 carry back

bring down: 3 cut; 4 land, trim; 5 lower, visit; 6 impose, reduce; 7 cut back, cut down, get down, inflict, let down, put down; 8 overturn, take down, trim back, trim down; 9 overthrow

bring forth: 3 get; 4 bear, sire; 5 beget, lie in; 6 father, mother; 7 produce, trot out; 8 engender, generate; 9 fecundate, give birth; 11 give birth to

bring forward: 6 call up; 7 advance, bring on, trot out; 10 bring forth

bringing forth: 6 making; 7 forming; 8 creating, creation; 9 formation, producing; 10 generation, production

bringing up: 7 nurture, raising, rearing; 8 breeding; 9 fosterage, fostering, nurturing; 10 upbringing

bring on: 6 induce; 7 produce; 8 bring out; 12 bring forward

bring out: 5 break, educe, issue, let on; 6 accent, elicit, expose, get out, impart, let out, put out, reveal, set off, stress, unroll, unveil; 7 bring on, bring up, declare, divulge, draw out, produce, publish, release, take out, uncover; 8 disclose, discover, give away, set forth; 9 call forth, draw forth, emphasize, introduce; 10 accentuate

bring through: 4 save

bring to bear upon: 21 bring into relation with

bring to mind: 4 mind; 6 call up, recall; 7 retrace; 8 call upon, remember, summon up; 9 recollect

brinjal: 8 eggplant; 9 aubergine

brink: 3 rim; 4 brim; 5 verge; 9 threshold

briny: 4 main, salt; 5 salty; 6 saline; 8 brackish

briquette: 7 briquet

Bris: 5 Brith; 6 Berith

brisk: 4 keen; 5 acute, brief, fresh, merry, quick, sharp, tonic, vivid, zippy; 6 active, lively, severe, snappy; 7 bracing, brisk up, brisken, summary; 8 animated, bustling, deep-dyed, incisive, rattling, spanking; 9 trenchant, vivacious; 10 energizing, refreshful, refreshing

briskness: 8 alacrity; 9 quickness; 10 liveliness

brisling: 5 sprat

bristle: 5 burst; 6 abound; 8 tag thorn

bristle at: 8 bridle at, bridle up; 9 bristle up, show anger

bristled: 5 burry, spiny; 6 barbed, briary, briery, burred, thorny; 7 bristly, prickly, spicate; 8 spicular; 9 bristling, setaceous; 10 barbellate; 11 spiniferous

Brit: 6 Briton; 9 Britisher

Britain: 2 UK; 12 Great Britain; 13 United Kingdom

British Honduras: 6 Belize

British pound: 4 quid; 13 pound sterling

British shilling: 3 bob

British Thermal Unit: 3 BTU

Brittany: 5 Breiz; 8 Bretagne

brittle: 5 toffy; 6 toffee; 7 brickle, brickly; 9 breakable, frangible; 10 unannealed

broach: 3 pin; 5 found, set up, utter; 6 allege, brooch, torque; 7 advance, hold out, propose; 8 initiate, lapel pin, let blood, propound, set forth; 9 breastpin, enunciate, institute, originate, pronounce

broad: 4 flat, free, full, lake, loch, mere, pond, pool, slab, tarn, wide; 5 ample, bawdy, gross, loose, plash, round, thick; 6 coarse, marked, puddle, ribald, risque [Fr], smutty; 7 blanket, decided, fulsome, general, generic, liberal, obscene, pointed; 8 distinct, panoptic, spacious, sweeping, tolerant, unsubtle; 9 equivocal; 10 collective, peremptory, unspecific; 12 all-embracing, all-inclusive, encompassing, encyclopedic, pornographic; 13 comprehensive, encyclopaedic

broadax: 8 broadaxe

broadband: 8 wideband

broadbill: 5 scaup; 8 bluebill, boatbill, shoveler; 9 scaup duck

broadcast: 3 air, sow; 4 beam, send, sown; 5 aired; 6 spread; 7 diffuse, program; 8 disperse, transmit; 9 cast forth, circulate, programme, propagate; 10 distribute, draught off, pass around, widespread; 11 circularise, circularize, disseminate

broaden: 5 widen; 6 extend; 9 branch out, diversify

broad jump: 8 long jump

broadly: 7 loosely; 9 generally; 15 broadly speaking

broadness: 8 wideness; 9 thickness

broadsheet: 4 bill; 5 flier, flyer, paper, sheet; 8 circular, handbill; 9 broadside, throwaway

broad-shouldered: 4 wiry; 6 brawny, sinewy; 8 gigantic, muscular, stalwart, well-knit; 9 strapping, well-built

broadside: 4 bill; 5 flier, flyer; 6 poster, tirade; 7 placard; 8 circular, handbill; 9 philippic, throwaway; 10 broadsheet

broadsword: 7 cutlass; 9 backsword

broadtail: 7 caracul, karakul

Broadway: 13 Great White Way

Brobdingnagian: 5 giant; 9 cyclopean, Herculean; 10 Gargantuan, prodigious; 11 Bunyanesque

brocade: 4 lace; 7 galloon

brocaded: 6 raised; 8 embossed

brocatelle: 4 lace; 7 brocade, galloon

brochure: 6 folder; 7 booklet, leaflet; 8 pamphlet

brogan: 6 brogue; 7 arctics; 8 work shoe; 10 clodhopper

brogue: 4 lilt; 6 brogan, buskin, gaiter; 7 gambado; 8 moccasin, work shoe; 10 clodhopper

broil: 3 row; 4 bake, boil, burn, fray, glow, to-do; 5 brawl, melee; 6 affray, breeze, fracas, hubbub, pother, racket, rumble, rumpus, squall, uproar; 7 blister, howling, rhubarb [baseball], ruction, shindig, trouble; 8 broiling, brouhaha

broiled: 7 grilled

broke: 4 bust; 5 skint; 6 broken, busted; 10 broken down, out of order

broken: 3 low; 4 lame, lost; 5 broke, crazy, shaky, upset; 6 busted, rugged, ruined, shaken, undone, unkept; 7 crushed, dicousu [Fr], humbled; 8 broken in, confused, discrete, revealed, violated, wiped out, withered; 9 disclosed, infringed, shattered; 10 broken down, discovered, disordered, humiliated, out of order; 11 disjunctive, interrupted, out of action; 12 disconnected, hors de combat [Fr], impoverished, transgressed; 13 discontinuous

broken down: 5 broke; 6 broken, busted; 9 borne down, bowed down; 10 out of order, struck down

brokenhearted: 9 heartsick; 11 heartbroken

broken winded: 11 short-winded

broker: 6 agent; 7 factor; 11 stock dealer, stockbroker, underwriter

brokerage: 7 broker's; 8 wharfage; 10 freightage; 13 brokerage firm; 14 brokerage house, securities firm

brolly: 4 gamp; 8 umbrella

Bromeliaceae: 15 pineapple family

bromide: 3 saw; 6 cliche, old saw; 8 banality, chestnut; 9 platitude; 11 commonplace

bromidic: 5 corny; 12 platitudinal

bronc: 5 bronc; 6 bronco; 7 mustang

bronchi: 8 bronchia [Med], bronchus

bronchus: 7 bronchi; 8 bronchia [Med]; 13 bronchial tube

bronco: 5 bronc; 7 mustang

brontosaur: 9 apatosaur; 11 apatosaurus; 12 brontosaurus; 13 thunder lizard; 19 Apatosaurus excelsus

brontosaurus: 9 apatosaur; 10 brontosaur; 11 apatosaurus; 13 thunder lizard

Bronx cheer: 3 boo; 4 bird, hiss, hoot; 5 snort; 7 razzing; 9 raspberry

bronze: 3 tan; 6 bronzy

bronzed: 6 tanned; 7 browned; 9 suntanned

brooch: 5 clasp; 6 broach; 9 breastpin

brood: 3 fry; 4 bevy, herd, hive, loom, nest, peck, pout, seed, spat, stew, sulk; 5 breed, cloud, cover, covey, drove, dwell, flock, hatch, heirs, hover, issue, shoal, spawn, swarm, worry; 6 bushel, farrow, flight, litter, scores; 7 draught, grizzle, progeny; 8 brooding, hatching, incubate; 9 bulk large, offspring, posterity

brooder: 9 incubator

brooding: 5 brood; 6 broody, musing; 7 brewing, pensive; 8 hatching; 9 pondering; 10 incubation, meditative, reflective, ruminative; 11 pensiveness; 13 contemplative

broodmare: 8 stud mare

brood over: 4 mope; 7 con over

broody: 6 broody, musing; 7 pensive; 8 brood hen, brooding; 9 broody hen, pondering; 10 meditative, reflective, ruminative, setting hen; 13 contemplative

brook: 4 bear, beck, bide, burn; 5 abide, bayou, brave, creek, put up, stand; 6 endure, runnel, stream, suffer; 7 stomach; 8 tolerate; 9 go through

broom: 4 ling; 5 sweep; 7 heather; 12 Scots heather

broomcorn: 7 sorghum

broth: 4 soup; 5 puree, stock; 7 pottage; 8 bouillon, consomme

brothel: 4 stew; 8 bordello, cathouse; 10 whorehouse; 13 sporting house

brothel keeper: 5 madam

brother: 3 pal; 4 chum; 5 buddy, crony; 6 fellow, sister; 7 comrade, sibling; 8 sidekick; 12 blood brother

brotherhood: 5 union; 8 sodality; 10 fraternity, labor union, sisterhood, trade union; 11 amicability, trades union; 12 amicableness; 13 confraternity

brotherly: 9 fraternal; 10 neighborly; 11 brotherlike

brotherly love: 5 heart; 7 charity; 8 humanity, kindness; 9 benignity, humanness; 10 attachment, goodliness, kindliness; 12 graciousness, Platonic love

brought to light: 5 dug up; 9 unearthed

brouhaha: 3 row; 4 fray, to-do; 5 brawl, broil, melee; 6 affray, breeze, fracas, hubbub, pother, racket, rumble, rumpus, squall, uproar; 7 howling, rhubarb [baseball], ruction, shindig, trouble; 8 scramble

brouillerie: 5 split; 6 breach; 7 rupture; 8 disunion, division; 10 disruption

brow: 4 side; 5 crown, skirt; 6 flange, visage; 7 confine, eyebrow, hilltop; 8 forehead

browbeat: 5 bully; 6 hector; 7 dictate, put down, set down, swagger; 8 ballyrag, bullyrag, domineer; 9 strong-arm; 10 boss around, intimidate, push around

browbeaten: 5 cowed; 7 bullied, hangdog; 11 intimidated

brown bear: 5 bruin; 11 Ursus arctos

brown butter: 14 beurre noisette

brown coal: 7 lignite

browned: 6 tanned; 7 bronzed; 9 suntanned

Brownian motion: 7 pedesis; 16 Brownian movement

brownie: 3 elf, fay, hob, imp; 4 pixy; 5 fairy, pixie; 6 fairie

browning: 8 toasting

brownish-orange: 6 sorrel

brownish-yellow: 5 amber; 11 yellow-brown

brown-nose: 8 butter up

brownout: 6 dimout; 8 blackout

brown trout: 11 Salmo trutta, salmon trout

browse: 3 pry; 4 crop, peer, scan, shop; 5 graze, range, sound; 7 explore, pasture, ransack, rummage; 8 browsing; 9 look round; 11 reconnoiter

browser: 10 web browser

Bruce: 7 Robert I; 14 Robert the Bruce

Bruges: 13 City of Bridges

bruin: 4 bear; 5 beast, brute; 9 brown bear; 10 blackguard; 11 Ursus arctos

bruise: 4 maul; 6 buffet; 7 contuse, scratch; 9 contusion

bruised: 4 hurt; 7 wounded; 8 contused; 11 contusioned

bruiser: 5 boxer; 7 athlete; 8 plug-ugly, pugilist, the fancy, tough guy, wrestler; 9 gladiator; 12 prize fighter

bruit: 3 cry; 4 buzz, fame; 5 on dit [Fr], rumor; 6 rumour; 7 hearsay; 8 currency

brumal: 3 icy; 6 arctic, boreal, frosty, hiemal, wintry; 7 glacial; 8 freezing, Siberian

Brunhild: 8 Brynhild; 10 Brunnhilde

Brunswick: 12 Braunschweig

brunt: 3 jog; 4 jolt, push; 5 boost [U.S.], onset, shove, throw; 6 advent, thrust; 7 booming; 8 outbreak; 10 occurrence

brush: 3 fly; 4 kiss, shag, skim, tear, zoom; 5 beard, clash, copse, fight, shoot, sweep, whisk; 6 affair, swoosh; 7 coppice, cut away, thicket; 8 brushing, imperial, run a race, skirmish; 9 brushwood, collision, encounter; 10 light touch

brush aside: 6 ignore; 7 dismiss; 8 brush off, discount; 9 disregard, push aside

brushing: 7 combing

brush kangaroo: 7 wallaby

brush off: 4 snub; 5 repel; 6 ignore, rebuff; 7 dismiss, send off, turn off; 8 discount, send away, turn away, whisk off; 9 brush away, disregard, push aside, whisk away; 10 brush aside

brush up: 4 full; 5 round, rub up; 6 polish, review, vamp up, warm up; 7 dress up, refresh, touch up; 8 polish up, round off; 9 bolster up, furbish up; 10 brighten up

brushwood: 5 brush, copse; 7 coppice, thicket; 9 underwood; 10 underbrush

brusque: 4 curt; 5 brusk, short; 6 abrupt, brutal; 7 waspish

brusqueness: 8 curtness, rudeness; 9 gruff-

ness, shortness; 10 abruptness, bad manners, ill manners; 11 discourtesy; 12 impoliteness

Brussels: 14 Belgian capital; 16 capital of Belgium

brutal: 4 fell; 5 cruel, harsh; 6 savage, unkind; 7 brusque, brutish, inhuman, vicious; 8 barbaric, inhumane, rigorous; 9 barbarous, malicious, malignant, roughshod; 12 semibarbaric

brutality: 7 outrage; 8 atrocity, ferocity, savagery; 9 barbarism, barbarity; 10 brute force, inhumanity, savageness, truculence; 11 boorishness, brutishness, grossierete, loutishness, misbehavior, raffishness, viciousness; 12 churlishness; 13 barbarousness, ferociousness

brutally: 8 savagely; 9 viciously

brute: 3 dog, hag, pig; 4 bear, hood, wolf; 5 beast, bruin, bully, fauna, rough, rowdy, tough, wight, witch; 6 animal, figure, homely, meanie [jocular], mugger, savage, woofer, wretch; 7 beastly, bestial, brutish, caitiff, critter [U.S. dialect], hoodlum, pugugly [U.S.], ruffian, wildcat; 8 creature, hooligan, plug-ugly, zoophyte; 9 barbarian, desperado, ugly woman; 10 blackguard, dumb animal, mean mother; 11 bludgeon man

brutish: 5 brute, cruel, rowdy; 6 brutal, savage; 7 beastly, bestial, boorish, inhuman, loutish, piggish, raffish, swinish; 8 barbaric, churlish, clownish, inhumane, snobbish; 9 barbarous, malicious, malignant; 10 blackguard; 12 semibarbaric

Brutus: 18 Marcus Junius Brutus

Brya: 9 genus Brya

Bryaceae: 10 granadillo; 14 family Bryaceae

Bryozoa: 7 polyzoa; 13 phylum Bryozoa

bryozoan: 6 sea mat; 7 sea moss; 8 polyzoan; 10 moss animal

Bubalus: 7 water ox, tamarao, tamarau; 12 water buffalo, genus Bubalus, tribe Bubalus

bubble: 4 bite, burp, drug, purl, wile; 5 belch, blind, catch, chaff, cheat, eruct, feint, fetch, froth, hocus, plant, reach, smoke, spray, spurt, trick; 6 babble, burble, cobweb, gurgle, juggle, murmur, ripple; 7 chicane, sputter; 10 effervesce; 11 regurgitate

bubble-jet: 16 bubble-jet printer

bubble over: 8 overflow; 9 spill over

bubbler: 13 water fountain; 16 drinking fountain

bubble wrap: 10 bubble pack; 11 blister pack

bubbling: 5 foamy, spumy, sudsy; 6 bubbly, frothy; 7 foaming, sparkly, spumous; 8 frothing; 9 sparkling; 12 effervescent, effervescing; 13 effervescence, scintillating

bubbly: 5 foamy; 6 frothy; 7 boiling, foam-

Bubo: 9 genus Bubo

bubonic plague: 10 black death; **15** pneumonic plague

Bubo virginianus: 14 great horned owl

buccal: 5 cheek

buccaneer: 6 pirate; **7** corsair; **8** sea rover; **9** buccaneer

Bucephala: 6 dipper; **8** whistler; **9** goldeneye; **10** bufflehead, butterball; **14** genus Bucephala

Buchanan: 13 James Buchanan

Bucharest: 9 Bucuresti; **16** capital of Romania

Buchloe: 12 genus Buchloe, buffalo grass

buck: 3 doe, dog, roe; **4** stag, tear, wash; **5** blade, blood, drake, hitch, horse, shoot; **6** bucked, charge, dollar, gander; **7** launder, sawbuck; **8** buck jump, sawhorse, stallion; **9** go against, long horse, shoot down; **10** dollar bill; **11** entire horse; **13** one dollar bill, vaulting horse

buckbean: 7 bogbean; **9** bog myrtle

bucked up: 10 encouraged

bucket: 3 tub; **4** pail

buckeye: 6 conker; **13** horse chestnut

Buckeye: 6 Ohioan

Buckeye State: 4 Ohio

buckle: 4 warp, worm; **5** clasp, heave, helix; **6** rundle, spiral, volute; **7** crumple; **9** corkscrew

buckler: 6 shield

buckle under: 5 yield; **6** give in; **7** succumb; **12** knuckle under

buckram: 5 stiff; **7** starchy; **9** stiffness; **10** stuffiness

buckshot: 8 bird shot, duck shot

buckthorn: 7 ribwort; **8** ribgrass; **11** ripplegrass

buck up: 9 take heart

bucolic: 5 idyll; **6** rustic; **7** eclogue, peasant; **8** arcadian, pastoral; **10** provincial

Bucuresti: 9 Bucharest; **16** capital of Romania

bud: 3 bud; **4** crop, germ; **5** fruit, graft, plant, shoot; **6** sprout; **7** harvest, implant, shoot up; **8** bourgeon [Fr], sprout up; **9** germinate, handiwork

Budapest: 16 capital of Hungary, Hungarian capital

Buddha: 4 Siva; **5** Shiva; **6** Vishnu; **7** Gautama, Krishna; **9** the Buddha; **10** Juggernath, Siddhartha; **13** Gautama Buddha

budding: 5 green, sappy, young; **6** callow, puisne; **8** juvenile, underage, youthful; **9** beardless

buddy: 3 pal; **4** chum; **5** crony; **7** brother; **8** alter ego, sidekick; **9** companion, confidant

budge: 4 stir; **5** shift; **7** agitate

budget: 3 fob, net; **4** knit, poke; **5** pouch, scrip; **6** pocket, sachel, sheath, socket; **7** finance, satchel; **8** reticule, scabbard; **10** assortment; **12** money matters

budgie: 8 lovebird; **10** budgerigar, budgerygah; **11** budgereegah; **13** grass parakeet, shell parakeet

budging: 8 stirring

Buenos Aires: 18 capital of Argentina

buff: 3 fan, raw; **5** cream, flush, lover; **6** buffet, votary; **7** amateur, burnish, devotee, furbish; **9** raw sienna; **10** aficionado, altogether, dilettante; **11** afficionado; **12** birthday suit; **14** yellowish brown

buffalo: 5 bison; **10** Bison bison; **13** American bison

buffalo gourd: 11 calabazilla, wild pumpkin; **12** prairie gourd

buffer: 5 block, pilot; **6** fender, soften; **7** cushion; **8** bulkhead, polisher; **10** cowcatcher; **11** buffer store, neutralizer

Bufferin: 15 buffered aspirin

buffer state: 13 buffer country

buffet: 3 jog; **4** buff, cafe, cuff, kick, maul, whip; **5** lay on, smack, spank, thump, whack; **6** batter, bruise, hustle, joggle, jostle, jounce, stroke, thwack, wallop; **7** canteen, counter, scratch; **8** snack bar, striping; **9** buffeting, sideboard; **10** box the ears, knock about, restaurant

buffet car: 5 diner; **9** dining car; **17** dining compartment

buffeted: 11 storm-tossed, tempest-tost; **12** tempest-swept; **13** tempest-tossed

buffeting: 4 cuff, kick; **6** buffet; **8** pounding, striping; **9** battering

buffo: 7 buffoon, farceur; **8** grimacer; **9** columbine, pantaloon; **11** pantomimist

buffoon: 6 clown; **7** farceur; **8** grimacer; **9** columbine, pantaloon; **11** merry andrew, pantomimist

buffoonery: 3 gag; **5** farce, prank; **7** fooling; **8** clowning, drollery; **9** frivolity; **10** tomfoolery; **11** foolishness

Bufonidae: 10 toad family

bug: 3 bug, irk, tap, vex; **4** bait, bore, faze, flea, germ [informal], tire; **5** abuse, annoy, beset, cross, error, fault, grind, harry, haunt, hound, louse, tease, worry; **6** badger, bother, glitch, harass, heckle, ill-use, infest, molest, pester, plague, pother, vermin; **7** disturb, microbe, mortify, oppress, perplex, trouble, wiretap; **8** bullirag, bullyrag, disquiet, ill-treat, maltreat, mistreat, pathogen; **9** beleaguer, disoblige, displease, importune, incommode, intercept, persecute; **10** discomfort, discompose, hemipteran, hemipteron; **13** inconvenience; **16** programming error

bugaboo: 6 booger; **7** bugbear; **8** bogeyman;

9 bete noire [Fr], boogeyman, nightmare

bugbane: 6 cohosh

bugbear: 6 booger; **7** bugaboo, problem; **8** bogeyman; **9** bete noire [Fr], boogeyman, nightmare

bugger off: 3 get; **5** scram; **7** buzz off

buggy: 4 bats, daft, loco, nuts; **5** balmy, barmy, batty, dotty, kooky, loony, loopy, nutty, wacky; **6** fruity, kookie; **7** bonkers, cracked, haywire; **8** crackers, roadster

bug-hunter: 10 bugologist; **12** entomologist

bugle: 5 bugle; **6** cornet; **7** clarion, trumpet

bugologist: 9 bug-hunter; **12** entomologist

bug out: 3 pop; **5** bulge; **6** pop out; **7** come out; **8** bulge out, protrude

build: 3 bod; **4** form, make, rear, soma, trim; **5** erect, flesh, frame, put up, raise, run up, set up, shape; **6** figure, work up; **7** anatomy, build up, chassis; **8** physique, progress; **9** body-build, construct, establish, human body; **11** put together

builder: 7 builder; **9** developer; **11** constructor; **16** detergent builder

building: 7 edifice; **8** erecting, erection; **10** augmenting; **11** edification, heightening; **12** augmentative, constructing, construction

building block: 4 unit

build up: 3 arm; **4** gird; **5** build; **6** fill up, make up, work up; **7** fortify; **8** progress

built: 5 built; **6** made-up; **7** stacked; **9** assembled; **10** reinforced; **11** well-stacked

buirdly: 5 beefy, burly, husky; **9** strapping

Bujumbura: 8 Usumbura; **16** capital of Burundi

bulb: 3 pea; **4** clew, drop, horn, knob, pill; **6** bullet, marble, pellet, pommel; **7** globule, medulla, vesicle; **8** spherule; **9** light bulb, lightbulb; **13** electric light; **15** thermometer bulb; **16** incandescent lamp

bulbous: 5 bulgy; **7** bellied, bulging, gibbous, swollen; **8** bellying; **9** distended; **11** protuberant

bulbul: 5 mavis

bulge: 3 bag, jut, pop; **4** bulk, bump, hump, pout; **5** bilge, pouch; **6** bug out, jut out, pop out; **7** come out, poke out, project; **8** bulge out, protrude, stand out, stick out, swelling; **9** extrusion; **10** prominence, protrusion; **11** be prominent, excrescence, gibbousness; **12** protuberance

bulghur: 6 bulgur; **11** bulgur wheat

bulginess: 11 roundedness

bulging: 5 bulgy; **6** convex; **7** bellied, bulbous, gibbous, swollen; **8** bellying; **9** distended; **11** protuberant

bulgur: 7 bulghur; **11** bulgur wheat

bulk: 3 sum, ton, tun; **4** body, clod, cord, core, loaf, lump, mass, size, swad; **5** block, bulge, total; **6** bushel, nugget, volume; **7** tonnage, tunnage; **8** best part, main part, majority; **9** aggregate, chief part, dimension, magnitude, major part; **11** greater part; **13** principal part

bulk large: 4 loom; **5** brood, hover

bulky: 5 ample, massy; **7** massive; **10** voluminous; **12** considerable

bull: 3 cop, pig, rot; **4** bear, bunk, crap, fake, fuzz, guff; **5** buyer; **6** bunkum, copper, muddle, waffle; **7** baloney, blarney, blunder, bullock, hogwash; **8** bull's eye, buncombe, strapper

bull's-eye: 4 mark; **5** point; **6** target

bulla: 4 bleb; **7** blister

bullace: 4 plum; **7** bullace

bullbat: 9 nighthawk; **12** mosquito hawk

bulldog: 4 dour, lion; **5** tiger; **6** dogged; **7** bull dog, panther; **9** tenacious; **10** unyielding; **12** pertinacious; **14** English bulldog

bulldozer: 5 dozer; **6** roarer; **7** hoodlum; **8** hooligan; **10** earth mover

bullet: 3 pea; **4** bulb, clew, drop, horn, knob, pill, slug; **5** round, smoke; **6** heater, hummer, marble, pellet, pommel; **7** globule, vesicle; **8** fastball, spherule

bulletin: 5 flash; **9** fresh news, news flash; **10** news just in

bulletin board: 3 bbs; **11** notice board

bulletproof vest: 10 flak jacket; **11** armored vest

bullet wound: 4 shot

bull fiddle: 4 bass; **8** bass viol; **10** bass fiddle, contrabass, double bass, string bass

bullfight: 7 corrida

bullfighter: 8 toreador

bullied: 5 cowed; **7** hangdog; **10** browbeaten; **11** intimidated

bullion: 4 gold; **5** ingot; **6** copper, nugget, silver; **14** precious metals

bull market: 12 rising market

bullock: 4 bull; **5** steer

bullwhip: 4 lash, whip; **5** knout, strap, thong; **7** cowhide, scourge

bully: 3 yob; **4** cool, dory, hood, keen, neat, yobo; **5** bravo, brute, dandy, elect, great, nifty, rough, rowdy, swell, tough, yobbo; **6** bang-up, breezy, choice, groovy, hector, madcap, meanie [jocular], mugger, not bad, peachy, picked, savage, select, slap-up, wretch

bullying: 8 blustery, bullying; **11** domineering; **12** intimidating

bullyrag: 3 bug; **4** bait, bore; **5** abuse, beset, bully, grind, harry, haunt, hound, tease, worry; **6** badger, bother, harass, heckle, hector, ill-use, infest, molest, pester, plague, pother; **7** oppress; **8** ballyrag, browbeat, bullirag, ill-treat, maltreat, mistreat; **9** importune, persecute, strong-arm; **10** boss around, push around

bulrush: 3 fig, jot, pin, rap, sou; **4** cent, mill, rush; **5** straw; **6** button, old son; **7** feather, nailrod, red cent [U.S.]; **8** bullrush, cat's-tail, farthing, picayune, reed mace, reed-mace, soft rush; **9** halfpenny; **10** common rush, peppercorn

bulwark: 4 moat, mole, wall; **5** ditch, groin, jetty; **6** groyne; **7** rampart, seawall; **8** bulwarks; **10** breakwater; **12** entrenchment

bum: 2 bo; **3** bat [U.S.], bib, can, pig, rat, sot; **4** buns, bust, butt, drab, grub, hobo, lush, prat, puke, punk, rear, rump, seat, slut, soak, swig, tail, tear, tush; **5** besot, cadge, cheap, crumb, fanny, idler, mooch, randy, scrub, skunk, stern, sweep, swill, tinny, tramp; **6** behind, bottom, cheesy, crummy, guzzle, loafer, pauper, rotter, sleazy, sloven, sponge; **7** blowout [U.S.], carouse, chintzy, dust-man, fish fry [U.S.], hind end, hoedown, keister, lowlife, rear end, reveler, so-and-so, stinker, tail end, tooshie, toss pot, yule log; **8** backside, buttocks, carouser, derriere

bumble: 6 falter; **7** stumble

bumbler: 7 botcher, bungler, butcher, fumbler, sad sack; **9** blunderer

bump: 3 hit, jut; **4** blow, find, hump; **5** break, bulge, bunch, clash, hunch, knock; **6** chance, demote, happen; **8** dislodge, displace, relegate; **9** collision, encounter, extrusion, gibbosity; **10** concussion, percussion, prominence, protrusion; **11** excrescence, gibbousness; **12** protuberance

bumper car: 6 Dodgem

bumpkin: 4 hick, rube [U.S.]; **5** yahoo, yokel; **7** hayseed, hobnail; **9** chawbacon; **10** bog-trotter

bumpy: 5 jolty; **7** jarring, jolting

bun: 4 roll

bunch: 3 lot; **4** bump, crew, gang, hump; **5** clump, crowd, hunch; **6** beetle, bundle; **7** bunch up, cluster; **8** caboodle; **13** bunch together

bunchy: 5 bossy; **6** bossed; **7** bunched, nodular; **8** embossed; **9** clustered

bunco: 3 con, gyp; **4** rook; **5** bunko, mulct, sting; **6** diddle, hustle, nobble; **7** con game, defraud, swindle; **8** flimflam; **9** bunco game, bunko game

Bund: 6 league, Verein [Ger]; **8** alliance; **9** syndicate

bundle: 3 wad; **4** bale, pack, pile; **5** bunch, clump, sheaf, stump; **6** fascia, packet, parcel, roll up; **7** bunch up, cluster, compact, package; **8** big bucks, big money, bundle up; **9** bowl along, much money

bungalow: 4 khan; **7** cottage, hospice

Bungarus: 5 adder, krait; **13** genus Bungarus

bungee: 10 bungee cord

bungle: 4 blow, flub, muff; **5** boner, botch, fluff, spoil; **6** ball up, bobble, bollix, booboo, foul up, foul-up, fumble, mess up, muck up; **7** blooper, blunder, botch up, louse up, screw up; **8** bollix up, bollocks, misdoing; **9** mishandle

bungled: 7 botched

bungler: 7 botcher, bumbler, butcher, fumbler, sad sack; **9** blunderer

bungling: 5 botch; **6** clumsy; **8** bumbling, fumbling, handless; **9** ham-fisted, ham-handed; **10** blundering, left-handed; **11** floundering, heavy-handed, incompetent; **14** butterfingered

bunk: 3 lam, rot, run; **4** bull, crap, guff; **5** berth; **6** bunkum; **7** bunk bed, hogwash, run away, scarper; **8** buncombe, feed bunk, turn tail; **9** break away; **10** built-in bed

bunker: 4 trap; **6** dugout, screen; **8** sand trap

bunko: 3 con, gum [U.S.], gyp; **5** bunco, spoof, sting; **6** hustle; **7** con game; **8** flimflam; **9** bunco game, bunko game, four flush; **14** confidence game

bunkum: 3 rot; **4** bull, bunk, crap, guff; **7** bravado, hogwash; **8** buncombe

buns: 3 bum, can; **4** butt, prat, rear, rump, seat, tail, tush; **5** fanny, stern; **6** behind, bottom; **7** hind end, keister, rear end, tail end, tooshie; **8** backside, buttocks, derriere

bunsen burner: 4 etna; **6** bunsen

Bunyan: 10 Paul Bunyan

Bunyanesque: 9 Cyclopean, Herculean; **10** Gargantuan, prodigious; **14** Brobdingnagian

buoyancy: 8 airiness, **9** perkiness; **10** aspiration, enthusiasm, resilience, resiliency; **12** heart of grace; **14** ability to float

buoyant: 4 airy; **5** perky; **6** bright, chirpy, elated, floaty, spring; **7** elastic, flushed, springy, tensile; **8** buoyed up, exultant, flexible, floating, renitent; **9** resilient; **10** debonnaire, in a fair way; **11** free and easy, in good heart; **12** enthusiastic

buoyed up: 6 elated; **7** buoyant, flushed; **8** exultant; **11** in good heart; **12** enthusiastic

buoy up: 4 buoy; **5** cheer; **6** assure; **7** lighten; **8** embolden, reassure; **9** encourage

burble: 6 babble, bubble, guggle, gurgle, ripple

burbot: 4 cusk, ling; **7** eelpout; **8** Lota lota

Burchell's zebra: 11 common zebra

burden: 3 jag; **4** bale, blow, care, core, dole, fret, gist, load, onus; **5** cargo, curse, drone; **6** assign, charge, effect, lading, look to, oblige, saddle, stroke, weight; **7** anxiety, concern, essence, freight, loading; **8** call upon, shipment; **9** prescribe; **10** saddle with, solicitude, weight down; **11** encumbrance, impedimenta, incumbrance

burdened: 10 heavy-laden, loaded down
burdensome: 5 lumpy; 6 taxing; 7 onerous; 10 cumbersome, oppressive
burdock: 7 clotbur
bureau: 5 chest; 6 agency, office; 7 atelier, dresser; 8 chambers; 9 authority; 10 department; 11 secretariat; 13 counting-house; 14 chest of drawers; 16 government agency
bureaucracy: 13 bureaucratism
bureaucrat: 8 minister, official; 9 red-tapist; 11 functionary
bureaucratic procedure: 7 red tape
bureau de change: 15 currency counter; 16 currency exchange
burgee: 4 jack; 7 ancient; 8 gonfalon; 9 blue Peter, Union Jack
burgeon forth: 4 spud; 5 shoot; 6 sprout; 8 bourgeon; 9 germinate, pullulate
burgess: 3 cit; 7 burgher, cockney; 8 townsman
burgh: 7 borough
burgher: 3 cit; 7 burgess, cockney; 8 townsman; 9 bourgeois
burglar: 5 thief; 12 housebreaker
burglarize: 5 heist; 6 burgle
burgoo: 7 oatmeal
Burgundy: 9 Bourgogne
burial: 6 burial; 7 burying; 9 interment; 10 entombment
burial chamber: 9 sepulcher, sepulchre, sepulture
burial ground: 8 cemetery; 9 graveyard; 10 burial site, necropolis
burial mound: 6 barrow; 7 tumulus; 10 grave mound
buried: 4 sunk; 5 perdu [Fr]; 6 hidden; 7 inhumed, stifled; 8 hushed up, interred, profound; 9 covered up, smothered; 10 suppressed; 11 underground
burin: 5 style; 6 graver; 12 etching point
burke: 5 do for; 6 settle; 7 silence
burl: 4 knot, slub
burlap: 5 gunny
burlesque: 5 outre, spoof; 6 ironic, parody, send up, sendup; 7 charade, lampoon, mockery, stilted, takeoff; 8 inflated, ironical, satirize, travesty; 9 bombastic, monstrous, quizzical, sarcastic, take off on; 10 caricature, mock heroic, pasquinade; 11 extravagant, opera bouffe [Fr]; 12 preposterous
burly: 5 beefy, husky; 6 portly; 7 buirdly, well-fed; 9 full-grown, strapping
Burma: 7 Myanmar
bur marigold: 10 sticktight; 11 beggar-ticks
Burmese rosewood: 11 Burma padauk; 22 Pterocarpus macrocarpus
burn: 3 tan; 4 beck, bite, boil, fire, glow; 5 bayou, broil, brook, creek, sting; 6 be

warm, burn up, fire up, runnel, stream, suntan; 7 blister, burn off, burning, combust, explode, flame up, flare up, sunburn; 8 burn down, burn mark, take fire; 9 cauterize, get warmer; 10 incinerate
burnable: 8 burnable; 9 flammable, ignitable, ignitible; 11 combustible, inflammable
burned: 5 baked, burnt; 8 burnt-out, scorched; 9 burned-out
burn in: 4 sear; 5 brand; 9 cauterize
burning: 4 burn, warm; 5 afire, fiery, rabid; 6 ablaze, aflame, aflare, alight, ardent, fervid, on fire, red-hot, torrid; 7 blazing, fervent, flaming, glowing, gushing; 8 volatile, volcanic; 9 hot as fire, hot-headed, perfervid, simmering; 10 combustion, passionate; 11 hot as pepper, impassioned; 12 incinerating, prone to anger
burning bush: 5 wahoo; 7 dittany; 8 firebush, gas plant; 9 belvedere; 10 fraxinella; 13 Dictamnus alba, summer cypress
burning hot: 6 red hot; 8 white hot; 9 piping hot; 10 boiling hot, smoking hot; 13 blistering hot
burnish: 4 buff; 5 flush, gloss; 6 polish; 7 furbish; 10 glossiness
burnished: 5 shiny; 6 bright, glassy, glossy; 7 shining; 8 lustrous, polished
burnoose: 4 haik; 7 burnous; 8 burnouse
burn out: 4 blow; 5 go out; 6 die out; 7 blow out; 8 brown out
burn plant: 8 Aloe vera
burnt sienna: 5 sepia; 11 Venetian red; 12 reddish brown
burp: 5 belch, eruct; 6 bubble; 7 burping; 8 belching; 10 eructation
burp gun: 10 machine gun
burr: 3 awn, bur; 4 pipe; 5 clank, clink, twang; 6 jangle
burred: 5 burry, spiny; 6 barbed, briary, briery, thorny; 7 bristly, prickly; 8 bristled; 10 barbellate
burr marigold: 10 sticktight; 11 beggarticks, bur marigold; 12 beggar's-ticks
burro: 6 donkey
burr oak: 6 bur oak; 11 mossy-cup oak
burrow: 3 sap; 4 hive, mine; 5 perch, squat; 6 tunnel; 7 bivouac, sit down, stave in; 8 se nicher [Fr]; 9 undermine; 10 tunnel into
bursiform: 7 saclike; 11 pouch-shaped
burst: 3 fit, fly; 4 blow, bust, chip, coup, snap, tear; 5 blast, break, crack, erupt, flare, flash, go off, jiffy, salvo, scene, split, spurt, storm, trice; 6 abound, blow up, bounce, breath, busted, volley; 7 bristle, explode, flare-up, give way, tempest, thunder; 8 collapse, detonate, outbreak, outburst, paroxysm, ruptured; 9 break open, explosion, fusillade, twinkling; 10 break short,

burst forth: 4 open; **7** explode, leap out, rush out; **8** break out, put forth, sally out, vegetate; **9** pullulate; **10** break loose, effloresce

burst in: 7 break in; **9** break into, burst into

bursting: 9 exploding; **10** detonating

burst one's bubble: 7 deflate; **10** disenchant; **11** disillusion; **12** take down a peg

burthen: 3 jag; **4** bale, load; **5** cargo; **6** burden, lading, weight; **7** freight; **8** shipment; **10** weight down

bury: 4 sink; **5** eat up, inter; **6** encase, enfold, entomb, forget, hush up, pack up, stifle; **7** cover up, engross, immerse, smother, swallow; **8** enshrine, suppress

burying ground: 8 cemetery; **9** graveyard; **10** burial site, necropolis; **12** burial ground

bus: 3 van; **4** heap; **5** coach; **6** busbar, jalopy, jitney; **7** autobus, minibus, minivan, omnibus; **8** microbus, motorbus; **9** charabanc; **10** motorcoach; **12** double-decker

busby: 5 shako; **8** bearskin

bus depot: 10 bus station; **11** bus terminal; **12** coach station

bush: 4 wild; **5** scrub, shrub, waste; **7** outback [Australia]; **9** chaparral, pubic hair, wasteland

Bush: 10 George Bush; **23** George Herbert Walker Bush

bush baby: 6 galago

bushbuck: 4 guib; **8** antelope

bush clover: 9 lespedeza

bushed: 4 beat, dead; **5** all in, tired; **8** fatigued

bushel: 3 fix, fry, ton, tun; **4** bevy, bulk, clod, cord, herd, hive, loaf, lump, mass, mend, nest, peck, swad, vase; **5** block, brood, cloud, covey, drove, flock, shoal, swarm; **6** barrel, doctor, farrow, flight, litter, nugget, repair, scores; **7** draught, restore, touch on; **9** furbish up; **12** bushel basket

bushranger: 8 woodsman; **12** frontiersman

bushwhack: 4 lurk; **6** ambush, waylay; **7** scupper; **9** ambuscade, lie in wait

bushy: 6 hispid, shaggy; **7** bearded, shagged, villous; **9** spreading

business: 3 job; **4** firm, line, task, work; **5** chore [U.S.], firms [pl], trade; **6** affair, byplay, living, thesis, thrift [Scot]; **7** agendum, company, concern, dealing, trading, traffic; **8** commerce; **9** clientele, companies [pl], patronage, thing to do; **10** commercial, employment, enterprise, line of work, livelihood, mercantile, occupation, proceeding; **11** transaction

business district: 8 downtown

business end: 6 muzzle

business establishment: 4 shop; **8** workshop; **9** workhouse, workplace; **15** place of business

business leader: 4 king; **5** baron, mogul, power; **6** tycoon; **7** magnate; **12** top executive; **14** big businessman

businesslike: 7 earnest; **8** workaday; **9** executive, practical; **11** strategical

business organization: 4 firm; **5** firms [pl]; **7** company, concern; **8** business; **9** companies [pl]; **10** enterprise; **13** establishment

business profit: 6 profit; **7** net gain; **8** earnings, proceeds; **9** net profit

business relationship: 7 account

business suit: 10 lounge suit; **12** two-piece suit; **14** three-piece suit

buskin: 4 sock; **6** brogue, gaiter; **7** gambado, top boot; **8** half boot, moccasin; **10** chukka boot, combat boot, desert boot, dramaturgy

buss: 4 kiss; **5** smack; **8** osculate; **9** blow a kiss; **10** osculation

bust: 3 bat [U.S.], bum [U.S.]; **4** flop, raid, snap, tear, toot, wear; **5** binge, break, broke, burst, randy, skint; **6** bender, arrest; **7** blowout [U.S.], booze-up, fish fry [U.S.], hoedown, rupture, wear out, yule log; **8** jamboree; **9** fall apart; **10** hullabaloo, stone-broke, stony-broke; **13** donation party [U.S.]

busted: 5 broke, burst; **6** broken; **8** ruptured; **10** broken down, out of order; **11** out of action; **12** hors de combat [Fr]; **15** out of commission

bus terminal: 8 bus depot; **10** bus station; **12** coach station

bustle: 3 ado; **4** fuss, rout, stir, to-do; **5** drive, hurry; **6** be busy, bother, fidget, flurry, hubbub, hustle, racket; **7** flutter; **8** be active, be lively, bundle on, scramble, splutter; **9** crinoline, hoopskirt, pottering; **10** ebullition; **11** barrel along, bustle about, farthingale, fidgetiness, work quickly; **12** dart to and fro, perturbation, scuttle along; **16** flurry of activity

bustling: 5 brisk; **6** active, lively; **8** animated, eventful, stirring; **9** vivacious

busy: 5 fussy, in use; **6** occupy; **7** engaged; **8** meddling, occupied; **9** officious; **10** busybodied, meddlesome; **11** interfering

busybodied: 4 busy; **8** meddling; **9** officious; **10** meddlesome; **11** interfering

busybody: 7 meddler; **9** intriguer

busywork: 8 make-work

but: 3 yet; **4** just, only, pale, term; **5** bourn, still, verge; **6** merely, simply; **7** confine, enclave, however; **11** reservation

butanoic acid: 11 butyric acid

butanol: 7 butanol; **12** butyl alcohol

butat: 5 butut

butch: 4 dyke; **5** macho

butcher: 6 hornet, murder, urchin; **7** botcher, bumbler, bungler, fumbler, meatman, sad

sack; **8** basilisk, scorpion; **9** blunderer, cutthroat, slaughter, victimize; **10** cockatrice,
put an end to; **11** assassinate, slaughterer

butcher's broom: 15 Ruscus aculeatus

butcher block: 12 butcher board

Butea: 3 dak; **4** dhak; **5** palas; **10** genus
Butea

butene: 8 butylene

Buteo: 10 genus Buteo

Buteo buteo: 7 buzzard

Buteo jamaicensis: 7 redtail; **13** red-tailed
hawk

butler: 7 servant; **9** pantryman

but no cigar: 5 close

butt: 3 aim, bum, cag, can, end, ham, tun; **4**
abut, buns, bunt, edge, game, goal, goat,
pale, prat, rear, rump, seat, stub, tail, term,
tush; **5** bourn, fanny, stern, verge; **6** adjoin,
behind, border, bottom, butt on, jambon,
object, stooge, target; **7** butt end, cigaret,
confine, enclave, hind end, keister, rear
end, rundlet, tail end, tooshie; **8** backside,
buttocks, derriere, end point, fair game,
quo animo [Lat]; **9** butt joint, cigarette,
fundament, objective, posterior

butt against: 4 abut, butt, edge; **6** adjoin,
border, butt on; **7** run into; **8** bump into

butte: 4 alto, hill

butter: 5 court, cream; **6** slaver; **7** placebo; **8**
butter up, pander to, suck up to; **9** truckle
to

butter bean: 8 lima bean; **9** civet bean, sieva
bean; **10** butterbean

buttercup: 7 goldcup, kingcup; **8** crowfoot;
12 butterflower

butterfingered: 8 bumbling, bungling, handless; **9** ham-fisted, ham-handed; **10** left-
handed; **11** heavy-handed

butterfly bush: 8 buddleia

butterfly collector: 13 lepidopterist

buttermilk biscuit: 11 soda biscuit

butter up: 5 court; **6** butter, slaver; **8** pander
to, suck up to; **9** brown-nose, truckle to; **10**
pay court to; **14** court favor with, curry
favor with

butterweed: 7 ragwort; **9** horseweed

buttery: 4 oily; **6** larder, pantry, smarmy,
spence [Brit.]; **7** fulsome; **8** unctuous; **10**
oleaginous; **11** butyraceous

butt in: 5 cut in, put in; **7** barge in, break in,
chime in

buttocks: 3 bum, can; **4** buns, butt, prat, rear,
rump, seat, tail, tush; **5** fanny, stern; **6**
behind, bottom; **7** hind end, keister, rear
end, tail end, tooshie; **8** backside, derriere;
9 fundament, posterior; **12** hindquarters

button: 3 fig, jot, peg, pin, rap, sew, sou, tat;
4 cent, knit, lace, mill, push, rush, stud,
tack; **5** straw; **6** old son, stitch; **7** bulrush,
feather, red cent [U.S.]; **8** farthing,

picayune; **9** halfpenny; **10** peppercorn,
push button; **12** pinch of snuff; **13** brass
farthing

buttoned: 8 fastened

buttoned-down: 10 button-down; **12** conservative

buttoned up: 8 reserved, reticent; **15** uncommunicative

button fern: 17 Tectaria cicutaria; **19** Pellaea
rotundifolia

buttonhole: 5 lobby

buttonlike: 5 beady; **7** buttony; **8** beadlike

button up: 3 dam; **5** box up, dam up, mew
up; **6** belt up, clam up, clap up, cork up,
lock up, seal up, shut in, shut up; **7** be
quiet, close up, dummy up, keep mum,
stuff up; **8** bottle up

buttonwood: 5 plane; **8** sycamore

buttress: 4 jamb; **7** mullion; **8** abutment; **11**
buttressing

buttressed: 6 braced

butylene: 6 butene

butyraceous: 7 buttery

Buxaceae: 9 box family

buxom: 5 bonny, brave, curvy, flush, hardy,
plump, sonsy; **6** bosomy, chubby, florid,
hearty, robust, sonsie, stanch, zaftig, zoftig;
7 stacked, staunch, winsome; **8** vigorous; **9**
well built; **10** curvaceous, embonpoint,
voluptuous; **11** big-breasted, full-bosomed;
12 weatherproof

Buxus: 3 box; **10** genus Buxus

buy: 5 bribe, steal; **7** bargain, buy long, corrupt, procure; **8** purchase; **13** make a purchase

buy a pig in a poke: 6 raffle; **9** speculate; **10**
set on a cast; **11** try one's luck

buyback: 10 redemption, repurchase

buyer: 4 bull; **6** vendee; **9** purchaser

buy off: 6 pay off

buy out: 5 buy up; **8** take over

buy the farm: 4 conk; **5** choke, croak; **6** pop
off; **7** snuff it; **8** check out, drop dead; **11**
die suddenly; **13** kick the bucket; **15** die
unexpectedly

buzz: 3 cry, hum; **4** fame, hiss; **5** bruit, on dit
[Fr], rumor; **6** seethe; **7** hearsay; **9** bombilate, bombinate, sibilance; **11** flying rumor;
12 news stirring

buzzard: 3 oaf, put; **4** calf, colt, loon, lout,
tony; **5** block, stick, stock; **6** doodle; **7**
dullard, vulture; **10** Buteo buteo

buzz bomb: 2 V-1; **9** doodlebug, robot bomb;
10 flying bomb

buzzed: 5 flush, woozy; **6** mellow; **7** flushed

buzzer: 4 bell; **8** doorbell

buzzing: 5 abuzz; **7** droning

buzz off!: 5 scram!; **6** begone!, bug off!, go
away!, beat it!; **8** get along; **10** get you
gone!; **11** take a powder!; **12** get out of
here!

buzz saw: 11 circular saw

by: 3 bye, per; 4 away, past, side; 5 aside; 7 by way of, close by, through; 9 by means of; 10 near at hand; 11 close at hand

by all odds: 9 decidedly; 10 definitely; 12 emphatically; 14 unquestionably

by and by: 5 apace, later; 7 briefly, quickly, shortly, someday; 8 in a while, speedily; 9 extempore, forthwith, summarily; 10 eventually; 11 immediately; 12 in no long time; 13 at short notice, incontinently, sooner or later

by and large: 6 mostly; 9 generally

by chance: 5 haply; 6 by luck; 8 randomly; 9 aimlessly, perchance; 10 by accident; 12 accidentally, fortuitously, incidentally, unexpectedly

bye: 2 by; 4 pass, side; 5 adieu, adios; 6 bye-bye, good-by, so long; 7 cheerio, good day, good-bye, private, recluse, retired; 8 au revoir, sayonara, secluded; 11 arrivederci, sequestered; 14 auf wiedersehen

bye-bye: 3 bye; 5 adieu, adios; 6 good-by, so long; 7 cheerio, good day, good-bye; 8 au revoir, sayonara; 11 arrivederci; 14 auf wiedersehen

Byelorussia: 7 Belarus; 8 Byelarus; 10 Belorussia; 11 White Russia

by fits and starts: 6 by fits; 7 by jerks, by skips; 8 by spurts; 9 by catches, per saltum [Lat]; 10 by snatches; 11 at intervals; 14 intermittently; 15 discontinuously

bygone: 4 gone, over, past; 6 bypast, gone

by; 8 departed, foregone; 9 out of mind; 10 passed away; 12 unremembered

by heart: 6 by rote; 8 by memory

bylaw: 6 byelaw

by-line: 5 hobby; 8 sideline; 9 avocation; 10 credit line; 17 spare-time activity

bypass: 7 keep off; 8 go around, ring road; 9 get around; 12 short-circuit; 15 circumferential

by permission: 7 by leave, on leave; 9 with leave; 14 with permission

byplay: 3 cue; 5 aside; 8 business, dumb show; 13 stage business

by possibility: 5 haply, may be, maybe; 6 mayhap; 7 perhaps; 8 possibly; 9 perchance; 11 potentially; 12 peradventure

by-product: 7 spin-off

byre: 3 sty; 4 coop, cote; 5 hutch; 6 kennel

by right of office: 9 ex officio

byroad: 5 byway; 6 bypath; 9 crossroad

by rote: 7 by heart; 8 by memory

byssus: 5 beard

bystander: 7 witness; 8 beholder, looker-on, observer, onlooker, passerby; 9 spectator; 10 eyewitness

byway: 6 bypath, byroad; 9 crossroad

byword: 3 mot [Fr], saw, 4 word; 5 adage, motto; 7 proverb; 9 watchword

by-word: 5 sneer, spurn; 6 slight

Byzantine: 6 knotty; 7 tangled; 8 involved, tortuous; 9 intricate; 10 convoluted; 12 labyrinthine

C

C: 4 coke, fair, one C, snow; 6 carbon, cocain; 7 centred, century, cocaine, coulomb, hundred; 8 centered; 11 gentleman's C; 12 ampere-second; degree Celsius; 16 degree Centigrade

c: 7 celsius, hundred; 8 a hundred; 10 centigrade, light speed, one hundred; 12 speed of light

C.O.D.: 14 cash on delivery

C.P.U.: 9 mainframe, processor; 16 central processor; 21 central processing unit

Ca: 7 calcium; 14 atomic number 20

cab: 3 car; 4 hack, taxi; 6 hansom; 7 taxicab; 9 cabriolet, yellow cab; 10 checker cab

cabal: 4 plot; 5 junta, junto; 7 faction; 8 conspire, intrigue; 9 camarilla; 10 conspiracy; 11 machination

cabala: 6 kabala; 7 cabbala, kabbala, mystery; 8 cabbalah, kabbalah; 10 occultness

cabalistic: 4 dark; 5 weird; 6 mystic, occult, secret; 7 cryptic; 9 cryptical, recondite, sibylline; 10 talismanic; 11 incantatory

cabaret: 9 chophouse, floor show, floorshow, nightclub

cabbage: 4 chou, crib, gelt, hook, kale, lift, loot, palm, pelf; 5 bread, dough, filch, lucre, money, pinch, snarf, sneak, swipe; 6 dinero, Mammon, moolah, nobble, pilfer; 7 purloin, shekels; 8 abstract; 11 filthy lucre, legal tender

cabdriver: 4 hack; 5 cabby; 6 cabbie [informal], cabman; 7 hackman, taximan; 10 hackdriver, taxi driver

Cabernet: 17 Cabernet Sauvignon

cabin: 3 box, cot, hut; **4** shed; **5** booth, croft, hovel, lodge, stall; **6** chalet, dugout [U.S.], shanty; **7** cottage; **9** hermitage

cabin class: 11 second class

cabin cruiser: 7 cruiser; **12** pleasure boat; **13** pleasure craft

cabinet: 5 bench, board, staff; **6** closet, locker, office; **7** chamber, console, gallery; **10** canterbury; **13** storage locker

cabinetmaking: 7 joinery

cable: 3 guy; **4** line, wire; **5** chain; **7** painter; **8** moorings, telegram; **9** cablegram, telegraph; **10** hoist cable; **11** cable length, cable system; **12** cable's length; **15** cable television, electrical cable; **16** overseas telegram, transmission line

cable car: 3 car; **9** funicular; **12** cable railway

cable-drawn: 9 funicular, wire-drawn

cablegram: 5 cable; **16** overseas telegram

Cabombaceae: 17 water-shield family

caboodle: 3 lot; **5** bunch

caboose: 6 galley; **8** cabin car; **9** cookhouse; **11** ship's galley

cabriolet: 3 cab, fly; **6** growler; **10** stage wagon; **11** four-wheeler

cabstand: 9 taxistand

cacao: 9 cacao tree, cocoa bean; **13** chocolate tree

Cacatua: 7 Kakatoe; **8** cockatoo; **12** genus Cacatua, genus Kakatoe

cache: 4 fund; **5** amass, depot, hoard, stash, store; **6** garner, hive up; **7** lay away; **8** garner up; **9** repertory; **10** accumulate, depository, repository; **11** memory cache; **12** accumulation, squirrel away, stored supply

cachet: 4 seal; **14** lettre de cachet, seal of approval

cachexia: 6 sprain, strain; **7** atrophy; **8** delicacy; **11** decrepitude; **12** invalidation

cachinnation: 13 fit of laughter

cacique: 5 chief; **7** cazique; **13** grand seignior

cackle: 3 coo, yak; **4** bark, crow, honk, yack; **5** clack, cluck, on dit [Fr], prate; **6** cancan, gaggle, giggle, titter; **7** chatter, chuckle, prattle, snicker, snigger; **9** yakety-yak

cackling: 8 giggling; **9** chuckling; **10** snickering

cacodemon: 5 Eblis, demon; **7** incubus, succuba; **8** succubus; **10** cacodaemon

cacodyl: 12 arsenic group, cacodyl group; **14** cacodyl radical

cacoethes: 4 lust; **5** mania; **7** passion; **8** cupidity; **9** prurience; **13** concupiscence

cacography: 6 scrawl; **7** bad hand, scratch; **8** scribble; **11** crabbed hand, cramped hand

cacomistle: 7 coon cat; **8** civet cat, ringtail; **9**
bassarisk, cacomixle, miner's cat; **10** raccoon fox; **13** ring-tailed cat

caconym: 9 barbarism; **12** abuse of terms; **15** abuse of language

cacophonous: 6 shrill; **8** piercing; **10** cacophonic

cacophony: 3 din; **5** blare; **6** clamor; **7** blaring, discord; **10** dissonance; **11** discordance; **13** want of harmony

Cactaceae: 12 cactus family; **15** family Cactaceae

cactus family: 9 Cactaceae; **15** family Cactaceae

cacuminal: 9 retroflex

cad: 3 dog; **4** heel, snob; **5** hound; **6** rascal; **7** bounder, villain; **9** messenger, scoundrel; **10** blackguard, curmudgeon

CAD: 19 computer-aided design

cadaster: 8 cadastre

cadaver: 4 clay; **5** stiff; **6** corpse; **7** carcass, remains; **8** dead meat; **12** dead organism

cadaverous: 3 dun, wan; **4** ashy, bony, cold, dead, dull; **5** ashen, dingy, faint, gaunt, muddy; **6** glassy, leaden, sallow, wasted; **7** ghastly, haggard, pinched; **8** gruesome, skeletal; **9** emaciated; **10** corpse-like, lackluster

caddish: 9 ungallant; **12** unchivalrous

caddisworm: 9 strawworm

Caddo: 7 Caddoan; **15** Caddoan language

caddy: 6 caddie; **12** tea caddy

cadeau: 4 gift; **7** present; **8** free gift

cadence: 4 beat, gait, port; **5** meter, slump; **7** cadency, measure; **8** carriage

cadet: 5 plebe; **7** hopeful, recruit; **9** conscript, raw levies, schoolboy

cadge: 3 bum, beg; **4** grub; **5** mooch; **6** sponge; **8** scrounge

cadger: 6 beggar, hawker, pedlar; **7** camelot [Fr], moocher, peddler, sponger; **8** huckster; **9** mendicant, scrounger; **10** colporteur, freeloader, panhandler

cadmium: 2 Cd; **14** atomic number 48

cadmium sulphide: 11 greenockite

Cadra: 4 moth; **10** genus Cadra

cadre: 4 cell

caduceus: 3 rod; **4** wand; **11** divining rod, Mercury's rod; **12** Mercury's wand; **13** Mercury's staff

caducity: 7 brevity; **8** fugacity [Chem], hoary age, senility; **10** transience; **11** climacteric, decrepitude, evanescence; **12** impermanence; **13** temporariness; **14** declining years, superannuation, transitoriness

caducous: 4 shed

caecal: 5 cecal, cecum

caecilian: 9 blindworm

Caeciliidae: 17 family Caeciliidae

caecum: 5 cecum; **8** blind gut, cul-de-sac

Caesalpinia: 6 bonduc; **8** divi-divi; **9** peachwood, poinciana; **10** brazilwood;

11 Mysore thorn; 14 pernambuco, bird of paradise, flamboyant tree, paradise flower; 16 genus Caesalpinia

Caesar: 12 Julius Caesar; 17 Gaius Julius Caesar

caesarean: 8 C-section, cesarean, cesarian; 9 caesarian; 15 cesarean section, cesarian section; 16 caesarean section; 17 abdominal delivery

caesarean section: 8 C-section, cesarean, cesarian; 9 caesarean; 15 cesarean section, cesarian section; 17 abdominal delivery

caesarian: 8 cesarean, cesarian; 9 caesarean

Caesarism: 7 tyranny; 9 despotism, monocracy, shogunate, Stalinism; 10 absolutism, one-man rule; 12 dictatorship; 15 totalitarianism; 16 authoritarianism

caesium: 2 Cs; 6 cesium

caespitose: 6 tufted; 9 cespitose

caesura: 4 mesh; 6 hiatus, lacuna; 10 interstice

cafe: 4 cafe; 6 buffet; 7 canteen; 9 coffee bar; 10 coffee shop, restaurant; 11 coffeehouse

cafe noir: 9 demitasse

cafeteria: 10 dining hall

caffeine: 7 caffein

caftan: 6 kaftan, turban

cage: 3 pen; 4 coop; 5 hem in, pen in; 6 bolt in, cage in, coop up, manger, rail in, wall in; 7 impound; 9 terrarium; 11 batting cage

cager: 5 cager; 16 basketball player

cagey: 4 cagy; 5 canny, chary; 6 clever, shrewd

cahoot: 5 trust; 6 cartel, league; 7 combine [U.S.]; 9 syndicate

caiman: 6 cayman

caique: 5 sliff; 7 felucca

Cairina: 12 genus Cairina

Cairina moschata: 8 musk duck; 11 muscovy duck

cairn: 4 tope; 6 barrow; 7 tumulus; 8 cromlech; 12 cairn terrier

cairngorm: 11 smoky quartz

Cairo: 8 El Qahira; 14 capital of Egypt; 15 Egyptian capital

caisson: 3 pix, pyx; 5 chest; 6 casket, coffer, lacuna; 9 cofferdam, reliquary; 15 ammunition chest

caisson disease: 5 bends; 11 air embolism; 12 aeroembolism

caitiff: 4 hood, jade; 5 brute, bully, rough, rowdy, scrub, tough, tramp; 6 beggar, meanie [jocular], mugger, Pariah, savage, wretch; 7 hoodlum, pug-ugly [U.S.], ruffian; 8 hooligan, plug-ugly, vagabond; 9 barbarian, desperado; 10 Cinderella, mean mother, panhandler, ragamuffin; 11 bludgeon man, chiffonnier, sans culotte; 12 ugly customer

cajole: 4 coax; 6 induce; 7 blarney, flatter, palaver, wheedle; 8 blandish, inveigle, persuade; 9 sweet-talk; 10 trifle with

cajolery: 7 fawning, palaver; 8 cajoling, coquetry, flattery, flimflam; 9 wheedling; 10 inducement; 11 blandishing; 12 blandishment

cake: 3 bar, fix; 4 clot, coat, curd; 5 candy, patty, stone; 8 coagulum; 11 consolidate

calabash: 3 pan; 4 dish; 5 gourd, plate; 6 saucer; 7 platter, potager; 8 crucible, trencher; 9 porringer; 11 bottle gourd

calaboose: 3 can [slang], pen; 4 brig, gaol, hold, jail, keep, stir [slang]; 5 clink [slang], hulks, pokey [slang]; 6 chokey [slang], cooler [slang], donjon, lockup, prison; 7 dungeon, slammer [slang], the Rock; 8 Bastille, big house [slang], hoosegow, stockade; 9 guardroom, oubliette; 10 guard house, San Quentin; 11 penal colony, prison house; 12 penitentiary

calamari: 5 squid; 8 calamary

calamitous: 5 fatal; 6 tragic; 7 fateful, ruinous; 8 tragical; 10 disastrous; 12 catastrophic

calamity: 4 bale; 7 tragedy; 8 accident, casualty, disaster; 9 cataclysm; 11 catastrophe

calamus: 5 quill, shaft; 8 flagroot; 9 sweet flag; 10 myrtle flag; 12 sweet calamus

Calan: 7 Isoptin; 9 verapamil

calash: 7 caleche, vis-a-vis; 8 dormeuse [Fr], sociable; 9 calash top

calcaneus: 8 heelbone; 15 os tarsi fibulare

calcareous: 4 limy; 6 chalky

calced: 4 shod

calciferol: 1 D; 8 vitamin D; 9 vitamin D2; 14 ergocalciferol; 15 cholecarciferol

calcine: 4 char; 7 corrode; 10 incinerate

calcium: 2 Ca; 14 atomic number 20

calcium hydroxide: 4 lime; 10 slaked lime; 11 caustic lime, lime hydrate; 12 hydrated lime; 14 calcium hydrate

calculable: 10 computable

calculate: 3 aim; 6 cipher, cypher, direct, figure, reckon; 7 account, compass, compute, count on; 8 estimate, forecast

calculated: 7 advised, derived, studied; 8 designed, measured; 10 considered, deliberate; 12 premeditated

calculate on: 5 bet on; 6 look to, rely on; 7 count on; 8 depend on, reckon on, rely upon; 9 count upon; 10 depend upon

calculating: 6 shrewd; 8 scheming; 9 conniving; 10 reflecting, thoughtful; 11 calculative, long-sighted

calculation: 4 heed; 7 caution; 8 coolness, figuring, prudence; 9 reckoning; 10 discretion, steadiness; 11 computation, heedfulness; 12 cautiousness, deliberation; 13 ratiocination; 14 circumspection

calculator: figurer; 8 computer, reckoner; 9 estimator; 13 arithmetician; 18 calculating machine

calculous: 5 rocky, stony; 8 concrete
calculus: 6 tartar
caldron: 6 retort; 7 alembic; 8 cauldron, crucible
caleche: 6 calash; 7 vis-a-vis; 8 dormeuse [Fr], sociable
calefaction: 7 heating; 12 incalescence
calendar: 3 log; 5 diary; 6 agenda, docket, ledger; 7 almanac, daybook, journal; 9 chronicle, ephemeris
calendar method of birth control: 6 rhythm; 12 rhythm method; 14 calendar method
calendar year: 9 civil year
calender: 5 glaze
calendered: 6 glossy
calenture: 5 fever; 11 temperature
calf: 3 oaf, put; 4 colt, loon, lout, sura, tony; 5 block, stick, stock; 6 doodle, heifer; 7 buzzard, dullard; 8 calfskin
calf bone: 6 fibula
caliber: 4 bore; 5 depth; 7 calibre, quality; 8 solidity, subtlety; 9 scantling; 10 profundity
calibrate: 4 tune; 8 fine-tune, graduate; 11 standardize
caliche: 7 hardpan
calico bush: 6 laurel
calicular: 9 calycular
Calidris: 9 sandpiper, jacksnipe; 13 genus Calidris
California cooler: 8 spritzer; 10 wine cooler
California fern: 7 hemlock; 10 winter fern; 12 Nebraska fern; 13 poison hemlock
California laurel: 9 spice tree; 10 pepperwood; 12 Oregon myrtle; 14 mountain laurel
California redwood: 10 coast redwood; 19 Sequoia sempervirens
californium: 2 Cf; 14 atomic number 98
caliph: 4 imam; 5 calif, kalif; 6 kaliph, khalif, sultan
calk: 5 caulk; 6 calkin, careen, splice, stanch; 7 staunch; 8 stop a gap
calkin: 4 calk
call: 3 bid, cry, dub, nod; 4 beck, name, ring, song, term, yell; 5 claim, hollo, phone, shout, style, visit; 6 behest, call in, call up, charge, dictum, enjoin, holler, ordain, outcry, prefer, scream, squall; 7 bidding, call off, enforce, entitle, meeting, predict, present, promise, send for; 8 birdcall, birdsong, forebode, foretell, instruct, shout out; 9 designate, phone call, telephone, translate; 10 anticipate, call of duty, call option, consecrate, denominate, margin call; 11 sense of duty; 12 vociferation
calla lily: 8 arum lily
callant: 3 boy, lad; 7 youngun; 9 stripling; 14 whipper-snapper

call boy: 4 page; 7 bell hop; 8 prompter
called: 5 named; 6 styled, termed; 7 known as; 10 designated; 11 denominated
called upon: 6 bidden; 7 charged; 8 required; 11 imposed upon
caller: 5 guest; 6 phoner; 7 company, cooling, visitor; 10 telephoner
call for: 3 ask; 4 cite, need, take; 5 claim, exact, quest; 6 call in, demand, invite, pick up, summon; 7 bespeak, collect, involve, request, require, send for, summons; 8 call upon, gather up; 11 necessitate
call forth: 4 stir; 5 evoke, raise; 6 arouse, invoke, kick up; 7 bring up, conjure, provoke, take out; 8 bring out, call down; 9 conjure up, draw forth; 10 put forward
callidity: 6 acumen; 8 sagacity; 10 shrewdness; 11 discernment, penetration; 12 perspicacity; 13 sagaciousness
calligraphy: 10 penmanship
Callimorpha: 16 genus Callimorpha
Callimorpha jacobeae: 8 cinnabar; 12 cinnabar moth
Callinectes sapidus: 8 blue crab
calling: 4 walk; 6 career, naming; 8 vocation; 10 nomination, profession, walk of life; 11 designating; 12 denominating, nomenclature
calling together: 9 gathering; 10 assembling; 11 convocation; 16 bringing together
calliope: 8 calliope; 9 harmonium; 10 steam organ
Calliope: 4 Muse; 8 Pierides; 9 Parnassus
callipers: 7 caliper; 8 calipers, calliper
Callirhoe: 6 mallow; 14 genus Callirhoe
callithump: 3 row; 4 fray, to-do; 5 brawl, broil, melee; 6 affray, breeze, fracas, hubbub, pother, racket, rumble, rumpus, squall, uproar; 7 belling, howling, rhubarb [baseball], ruction, shindig, trouble; 8 brouhaha
Callitris: 8 sandarac; 11 Cypress pine; 14 genus Callitris
call names: 6 insult, offend, vilify; 7 affront, outrage; 12 anathematize; 13 give offense to
call off: 4 call; 6 cancel
call on: 4 go to; 6 turn to; 8 appeal to, call upon
Callorhinus: 16 genus Callorhinus
Callorhinus ursinus: 13 Alaska fur seal
callous: 8 indurate; 9 hard-nosed, unfeeling; 10 impervious; 11 hardhearted; 12 thick-skinned; 14 pachydermatous
calloused: 9 thickened
call out: 3 cry; 5 shout; 6 cry out, outcry; 7 exclaim, sing out; 9 challenge
callow: 4 bald; 5 green, naive, sappy, young; 6 puisne, ragged; 7 budding; 8 immature, juvenile, roofless, underage, youthful; 9 beardless; 10 threadbare; 11 in one's teens; 13 inexperienced; 15 unsophisticated
Calluna: 12 genus Calluna

Calluna vulgaris: 4 ling; 5 broom; 7 heather; 12 Scots heather

call up: 4 call, mind, ring; 5 get up, phone, rally, think; 6 blow up, prompt, recall, remind, wake up; 7 light up, put up to, raise up, retrace; 8 call back, mobilize, remember, retrieve, summon up; 9 recollect, telephone; 11 bring to mind

call upon: 3 bid; 4 go to; 6 assign, burden, call at, call on, charge, enjoin, look to, oblige, turn to; 7 call for; 8 appeal to, instruct; 9 prescribe

calm: 3 lay; 4 cool, damp, hush, lull, swag, tame; 5 abate, allay, blunt, chill, peace, quell, quiet, sober, still; 6 becalm, cool it, coolth, deaden, pacify, placid, quench, rebate, sedate, serene, smooth, soothe, steady; 7 appease, assuage, compose, cool off, halcyon, quieten, restful, slacken, turn off; 8 calm down, calmness, chill out, peaceful, suppress, tranquil; 9 alleviate, composure, easy-going, stillness, unruffled; 10 deliberate, equanimity, quiescence, settle down, simmer down, unagitated, untroubled; 11 tranquility, tranquilize, undisturbed; 12 tranquillize; 14 coolheadedness

calm down: 3 lay; 4 calm, cool, damp, hush, lull, swag, tame; 5 abate, allay, quell, quiet, sober, still; 6 cool it, deaden, pacify, rebate, smooth, soothe; 7 appease, assuage, compose, cool off, quieten, slacken, turn off; 8 chill out, cool down, suppress; 9 alleviate; 10 settle down, simmer down; 11 tranquilize; 12 tranquillize

calmly: 8 sedately

Calocarpum: 15 genus Calocarpum

Calocarpum zapota: 6 mammee, sapote

Calocedrus: 5 cedar; 15 genus Calocedrus

Calochortus: 4 lily; 5 tulip; 16 genus Calochortus

calomel: 6 arnica; 7 benzoin

Calophyllum: 6 calaba; 10 laurelwood; 16 genus Calophyllum

caloric: 4 heat; 7 thermal, thermic

calorie: 6 calory; 11 gram calorie; 12 small calorie

calotte: 8 skullcap; 9 zucchetto

calotype: 13 daguerreotype

Calpe: 9 Gibraltar; 15 Rock of Gibraltar

calque: 15 loan translation

Caltha: 11 genus Caltha

Caltha palustris: 7 cowslip, kingcup, May blob; 11 water dragon; 12 meadow bright; 13 marsh marigold

caltrop: 7 caltrop; 10 devil's weed; 11 starthistle; 13 water chestnut

calumet: 9 peace pipe; 11 pipe of peace

calumniate: 5 smear, sully; 6 defame, smirch; 7 asperse, slander; 8 besmirch; 9 denigrate

calumny: 7 obloquy, scandal, slander; 9 aspersion; 10 backbiting, defamation, hatchet job, scurrility; 11 traducement; 12 evil-speaking, vilification

calvary: 5 quire; 9 martyrdom; 13 choirgolgotha; 15 Easter sepulcher

Calvary: 8 Golgotha

calve: 7 break up; 9 have young

Calvin: 10 Jean Cauvin, John Calvin; 11 Jean Caulvin, Jean Chauvin

Calvins: 16 Calvin Klein jeans

calx: 4 lime; 9 burnt lime, quicklime; 11 fluxing lime; 12 calcined lime, calcium oxide, unslaked lime

Calycanthaceae: 17 calycanthus family; 20 family Calycanthaceae; 21 strawberry-shrub family

Calycanthus: 14 strawberry bush; strawberry shrub; 16 genus Calycanthus

calypso: 12 fairy-slipper; 14 Calypso bulbosa

calyx: 3 pod; 4 cyst; 7 bladder, capsule, utricle, vesicle; 8 cancelli

camaraderie: 10 friendship; 14 good fellowship

camarilla: 5 cabal, junta, junto; 7 faction

camber: 4 bank, cant; 5 swell

camboose: 7 caboose

Cambrian: 3 age; 9 Paleogene, Paleozoic

cambric: 4 wool

camellia: 7 camelia

Camellia sinensis: 3 tea

Camellia State: 7 Alabama; 12 Heart of Dixie

camelopard: 7 giraffe; 21 Giraffa camelopardalis

Camelus: 6 camels; 12 genus Camelus

Camelus bactrianus: 13 Bactrian camel

Camelus dromedarius: 9 dromedary; 12 Arabian camel

cameo appearance: 10 walk-on role

camera buff: 7 lensman; 9 cameraman; 12 photographer

camera lens: 4 lens; 11 optical lens

cameraman: 7 lensman; 10 camera buff; 12 photographer; 15 cinematographer

camfer: 4 cant; 5 bevel

camion: 3 bus; 4 dray; 5 lorry; 10 motortruck

camisado: 9 night raid

camisole: 7 doublet; 9 gabardine; 11 underbodice

camorra: 5 cabal, junto

camouflage: 7 mimicry; 8 disguise

camouflaged: 6 hidden; 9 concealed

camp: 4 pack; 5 campy, pitch; 6 clique, encamp; 7 bivouac, camp out, coterie, ingroup; 10 cantonment, encampment, summer camp; 11 inner circle

campaign: 3 run; 4 push; 5 cause, drive, fight, stump; 6 effort, safari; 7 agitate, crusade; 8 movement; 10 expedition, operations; **11** campaigning; **12** take the field; **14** electioneering; **16** military campaign

campaigner: 7 nominee, veteran; **9** candidate

campaigning: 7 service; **8** campaign; **9** candidacy; **11** candidature, tented field; **12** combat action; **13** active service; **14** electioneering

campaign worker: 6 backer; **9** supporter; **15** political worker

campana: 4 bell; **9** bell shape

campanile: 6 belfry; **9** bell tower

campaniliform: 10 bell-shaped

campanula: 8 bluebell, harebell; **10** bellflower

camp bed: 3 cot

Campephilus: 9 ivorybill; **16** genus Campephilus; **21** ivory-billed woodpecker

camper: 9 motor home; **10** camping bus

campground: 7 bivouac; **8** campsite; **10** encampment; **11** camping area, camping site

camping: 7 camping, tenting; **9** encamping; **10** encampment; **11** bivouacking

campion: 6 silene; **8** catchfly

campy: 4 camp

cam stroke: 5 throw; **6** stroke

can: 3 bum, get, lav, may, pen, pot, RIF, tin; **4** brig, buns, butt, fire, gaol, hold, jail, john, keep, prat, rear, rump, sack, seat, stir [slang], tail, tush; **5** clink [slang], fanny, hulks, might, pokey [slang], potty, privy, put up, stern, stool; **6** behind, bottle, bottom, canful, chokey [slang], cooler [slang], donjon, lockup, pickle, prison, season, throne, tin can, toilet; **7** can buoy, commode, dismiss, dungeon, fire out, hind end, keister, rear end, slammer [slang], tail end, the Rock, tooshie; **8** backside, Bastille, bathroom, be able to, big house [slang], buttocks, derriere, facility, force out, hoosegow, lavatory, send away, stockade

Canaan: 8 Holy Land; **9** Palestine

Canada goose: 6 honker; **13** Canadian goose; **16** Branta canadensis

Canadian: 6 Canuck; **13** Canadian River

canaille: 4 rout; **5** chaff, horde; **6** rabble; **8** riffraff

canal: 3 gut; **4** duct; **6** tubule, vessel; **7** channel; **8** aqueduct, canalize

canalize: 5 canal; **7** channel

canary: 4 fink; **5** sneak; **6** snitch; **7** stoolie, tattler; **8** squealer, tell-tale; **10** canary bird, tattletale; **11** stool pigeon, stoolpigeon; **12** canary yellow, canary-yellow

Canary Islands: 8 Canaries

canasta: 4 meld; **11** basket rummy

Canavalia: 4 bean; **14** genus Canavalia

Canberra: 17 Australian capital; **18** capital of Australia

cancel: 5 annul; **6** delete, offset, repeal, revoke, set off; **7** call off, natural, rescind, reverse; **8** abrogate; **10** invalidate, render null; **12** cancellation

cancellation: 6 cancel, repeal; **8** annuling, postmark, recision; **9** annulment, canceling; **10** abrogating, abrogation, defeasance, rescinding, rescission; **13** nullification

cancelli: 3 pod; **4** cyst; **5** calyx; **7** bladder, capsule, utricle, vesicle

cancellous: 10 cancellate; **11** cancellated

cancel out: 7 wipe out

Cancer: 4 crab; **11** genus Cancer; **13** Cancer the Crab

cancer of the blood: 8 leukemia; **9** leukaemia

candela: 2 cd; **6** candle; **14** standard candle

candelabra: 11 candelabrum

candent: 7 glowing, smoking; **9** ebullient; **12** incandescent

candid: 4 open; **5** blunt, frank; **6** chalky; **7** sincere; **9** downright, guileless, ingenuous, outspoken; **10** forthright, free-spoken, point-blank, unreserved; **11** open-hearted, plainspoken; **15** straightforward

Candida: 5 yeast; **15** Candida albicans

Candida albicans: 5 yeast; **7** Candida; **15** Monilia albicans

candidacy: 11 campaigning, candidature, postulation; **14** electioneering; **17** political campaign

candidate: 6 bidder, suitor; **7** hopeful, nominee; **8** aspirant, claimant, prospect; **9** applicant, postulant; **10** campaigner, competitor, solicitant, supplicant; **12** office-seeker

candidiasis: 10 moniliasis; **14** monilia disease

candidly: 7 frankly; **8** honestly; **9** sincerely; **11** guilelessly, ingenuously

candidness: 6 candor; **7** candour; **9** frankness; **14** forthrightness

candied: 5 glace; **11** crystalized, sugarcoated

candle: 2 cd; **5** taper; **6** bougie [Fr]; **7** candela; **8** wax light

candleberry: 8 bayberry, waxberry

Candlemas: 4 Feb. 2; **12** Candlemas Day; **15** the Presentation

candlenut: 11 varnish tree

candlepin bowling: 10 candlepins

candlepower unit: 21 luminous intensity unit

candor: 5 truth; **7** abandon, candour, honesty; **8** bonhomie, fairness, fidelity; **9** frankness, sincerity; **10** candidness; **13** guilelessness; **14** fair-mindedness, forthrightness

candy: 3 fix; **4** cake, clot; **5** glaze; **9** sugarcoat

candyfloss: 9 spun sugar; **11** cotton candy
candymaker: 12 confectioner
candy store: 8 tuck shop; **9** sweet shop; **13** confectionery
candystriper: 10 nurse's aide
candyweed: 13 Polygala lutea; **14** orange milkwort, yellow milkwort
cane: 4 comb, flog, lash, lick, whip; **5** birch, strap, towel; **6** larrup, switch, thrash, thresh; **7** lambast, scourge; **8** lambaste; **9** bastinado, horsewhip; **10** flagellate; **12** give the stick
canella: 8 cinnamon; **11** canella bark
canella family: 11 Canellaceae
Canella winterana: 11 Canella-alba; **12** wild cinnamon; **17** white cinnamon tree
canescent: 5 hoary
cane sugar: 7 sucrose
Canicula: 6 Sirius, Sothis; **7** Dog Star
canicular: 5 sunny; **6** steamy, torrid; **8** tropical
canicular days: 7 dog days; **8** canicule
canid: 6 canine
canine: 2 K-9 [abbr]; **5** canid; **6** cuspid; **8** dogtooth, eyetooth; **11** canine tooth
canine madness: 11 hydrophobia
canine tooth: 6 canine, cuspid; **8** dogtooth, eyetooth
caning: 6 wicker; **10** wickerwork
Canis: 10 genus Canis
Canis aureus: 6 jackal
Canis dingo: 5 dingo; **8** warragal, warrigal
Canis familiaris: 3 dog; **11** domestic dog
Canis latrans: 6 coyote; **9** brush wolf; **11** prairie wolf
Canis lupus: 8 gray wolf; **10** timber wolf
Canis lupus tundrarum: 9 white wolf; **10** Arctic wolf
Canis Major: 8 Great Dog
Canis Minor: 9 Little Dog
Canis niger: 7 red wolf; **9** maned wolf; **10** Canis rufus
Canis rufus: 7 red wolf; **9** maned wolf; **10** Canis niger
canister: 3 tin; **8** case shot, magazine; **9** cannister; **12** canister shot, film canister, film cassette
canker: 3 rot; **8** cold sore; **9** fever sore; **10** cankerworm
cankered: 6 effete, rotten, wasted; **7** tainted; **8** blighted; **9** crumbling, moldering, splenetic
cankerous: 8 ulcerous; **9** ulcerated
Cannabidaceae: 10 hemp family; **19** family Cannabidaceae
cannabis: 3 pot; **4** dope, gage, hemp, sens, sess, weed; **5** ganja, grass, skunk, smoke; **8** Mary Jane; **9** marihuana, marijuana
canned: 5 fired; **6** riffed, sacked, tinned; **7** severed; **9** dismissed; **10** terminated; **11** transcribed

cannibal: 8 cannibal, man-eater; **14** anthropophagus; **15** anthropophagite
cannister: 3 tin; **8** canister
cannon: 5 carom, shank; **8** heavy gun, ordnance; **9** artillery; **13** gun of position
cannonball: 9 round shot; **10** cannon ball; **11** bullet train; **16** lightning express
cannot: 4 can't; **6** may not
cannula: 8 catheter
cannular: 7 tubular; **9** fistulous
canny: 4 cagy; **5** cagey, leery; **6** astute, clever, shrewd; **7** knowing
canoeist: 7 paddler
canon: 4 code, dean, rule; **6** canyon; **8** diocesan; **10** archdeacon, prebendary
canonization: 10 dedication; **11** celebration; **12** canonisation, consecration, enshrinement, enthronement; **13** glorification
canonize: 5 saint; **7** beatify
canon law: 8 canon law, civil law; **17** ecclesiastical law
canorous: 5 sweet; **6** dulcet; **7** songful
cant: 4 bank, list, tilt; **5** argot, bevel, lingo, lurch, pitch, slang, slant; **6** camber, camfer, humbug, jargon, patois; **7** beveled, pietism; **8** buzzword, cant over, claptrap; **9** hypocrisy, mere words, set phrase; **10** pious fraud, vernacular; **11** insincerity
cantabile: 7 singing
cantala: 6 maguey; **10** Cebu maguey; **12** Agave cantala, manila maguey
cantaloupe: 9 cantaloup, muskmelon; **14** cantaloupe vine; **24** Cucumis melo cantalupensis
cantankerous: 5 cross, rusty; **6** cussed [U.S.], ornery; **7** froward; **9** crotchety; **11** intractable; **12** bloody-minded, deaf to reason; **15** unaccommodating
cantata: 7 bravura; **8** canticle, oratorio
cant dog: 5 peavy; **6** peavey
canted: 5 atilt; **6** tilted, tipped; **7** leaning
canteen: 3 kit; **4** cafe; **5** crock; **6** buffet, flagon; **10** restaurant
canter: 3 jog; **4** lope, trot, turn; **5** amble, frisk, stalk, tramp; **6** prance, ramble; **7** saunter; **8** caracole; **9** promenade; **13** perambulation
Canterbury tale: 3 hum; **4** fake, sell; **5** shave; **13** traveler's tale
Cantharellus: 11 chantarelle, chanterelle; **17** genus Cantharellus
cantillate: 5 chant; **6** intone; **8** intonate
canting: 5 stock; **7** stilted; **8** affected, unctuous; **9** insincere, pretended, unnatural; **10** artificial, not natural; **11** ad captandum, pharisaical, pretentious; **13** sanctimonious
cantle: 7 frustum
canton: 6 billet; **7** quarter
Cantonese: 3 Yue; **10** Yue dialect

cantonment: 4 camp; 6 colony; 7 bivouac; 10 encampment, plantation, settlement

cantor: 5 hazan; 9 precentor; 11 choir-master

canty: 6 jaunty; 8 cheerful; 9 sprightly

Canuck: 8 Canadian

canvas: 4 poll, ring, sail; 5 piece [Fr], sheet; 7 canvass, tableau; 10 boxing ring, canvas tent

canvasback: 14 canvasback duck; 17 Aythya valisineria

canvass: 4 poll, sail, tout; 5 court, sheet; 6 canvas; 7 address, agitate, bespeak, discuss; 10 apostrophe, canvas tent; 12 make interest; 17 public opinion poll

canvassing: 11 bell ringing; 14 electioneering

canzonet: 7 bravura, cantata; 8 canticle, madrigal

caoutchouc: 5 latex; 6 rubber; 10 gum elastic; 11 India rubber

cap: 3 nib, tip, top; 4 beat, bind; 5 crest, truck; 6 bung up, cork up, cut out, o'er-top, pileus; 7 capital, ceiling, closure, stopper; 8 chapiter; 9 bottlecap, crow's nest, crownwork, culminate, detonator

capability: 4 turn; 5 forte, parts; 6 talent; 7 ability, faculty, talents; 8 capacity, efficacy, felicity; 9 endowment; 10 cleverness; 11 capableness; 12 habilitation, potentiality; 13 effectiveness, qualification; 14 productiveness; 15 efficaciousness

capable: 4 able, up to; 6 open to; 7 equal to, skilled; 8 skillful; 9 competent, qualified, subject to; 10 adequate to, conversant, proficient

capably: 4 ably; 5 aptly; 11 competently

capacious: 5 ample, roomy; 7 immense; 8 spacious; 9 expansive, extensive; 13 comprehensive

capacitor: 9 condenser; 19 electrical condenser

capacity: 3 wit; 4 part, role, turn; 5 forte, parts; 6 genius, talent, volume; 7 ability, content, faculty, talents; 8 efficacy, felicity, function, judgment, keenness; 9 endowment; 10 capability, cleverness; 11 capacitance; 12 cubic measure, habilitation, intelligence; 13 comprehension, effectiveness, mental ability, qualification, understanding; 14 productiveness; 15 efficaciousness, intellectuality, quick-wittedness

capacity for: 4 gift; 7 aptness, turn for; 8 aptitude

cap-a-pie: 13 from head to toe

caparison: 4 bard, gear, perk; 5 equip, slops, traps; 7 dress up, harness, housing, rigging, turn-out; 8 housings, trapping; 9 accessory, equipment, trappings; 11 accessories; 12

accouterment, accoutrement; 13 accoutrements

cape: 4 ness; 6 mantle, tabard, tippet; 7 mantlet; 8 mantelet, mantilla; 11 point of land

caper: 3 job; 4 joke, play, romp; 5 antic, dance, prank, trick; 6 frolic, gambol

caper family: 13 Capparidaceae; 19 family Capparidaceae

capful: 6 armful; 7 handful; 8 mouthful, spoonful; 10 thimbleful

capillary: 8 hairlike

capillary artery: 9 arteriola, arteriole

capillary vein: 6 venula, venule

capilliform: 9 capillary

capital: 3 cap; 4 head, main; 5 chief, crack, great, polar, prime, stock; 6 frieze, sconce, tip-top; 7 cornice, leading, primary, supreme; 8 cardinal, chapiter, foremost, pediment, supernal, top grade, top-notch, very best; 9 exquisite, majuscule, principal, uppercase; 10 architrave, overruling, topgallant; 11 capital city, capitalized, coping stone, high-wrought; 13 most important; 14 working capital; 15 uppercase letter

capitalism: 10 free-market

capitalize: 13 take advantage

capital letter: 4 caps [abbr]; 8 capitals [pl]; 9 majuscule; 15 uppercase letter

capital punishment: 9 executing, execution; 12 death penalty

capitation: 4 poll; 6 census, muster; 8 roll call; 14 recapitulation

capitation tax: 7 head tax, poll tax

capitular: 10 capitulary, prelatical, theocratic

capitulate: 4 cede; 9 surrender; 11 come to terms

capitulation: 4 fall; 6 ceding; 7 cession; 8 backdown, giving up; 9 surrender; 11 resignation; 12 capitulating, surrendering

capitulum: 3 ear; 4 head; 5 crown, spike; 7 treetop

capote: 10 hooded coat; 11 hooded cloak

Capparidaceae: 11 caper family; 19 family Capparidaceae

Capparis: 5 caper; 13 genus Capparis

capping: 7 corking; 9 loving cup; 10 stoppering

Capra: 4 ibex, goat; 6 pasang; 7 markhor; 8 markhoor; 10 genus Capra, bezoar goat

capric acid: 12 decanoic acid

capriccio: 3 fad, fit; 5 freak, prank, quirk; 6 maggot, vagary; 7 boutade [Fr]; 8 crotchet, escapade, flimflam; 9 potpourri; 14 concerted piece, wild-goose chase

caprice: 4 whim; 5 fancy, humor; 6 vagary; 7 impulse

capricious: 6 fitful; 7 aimless, erratic; 8 freakish; 9 arbitrary, desultory, impulsive, irregular, uncertain, whimsical; 10 flickering, unpunctual; 12 inconsistent

capriciousness: 6 whimsy; **7** whimsey; **11** flightiness; **12** whimsicality; **13** arbitrariness, inconsistency; **16** unpredictability

Capricorn: 9 Capricorn; **11** Capricornus; **16** Capricorn the Goat

Caprifoliaceae: 17 honeysuckle family

caprimulgid: 8 nightjar; **10** goatsucker

caprine animal: 4 goat

caproic acid: 12 hexanoic acid

caps: 8 capitals [pl]; **9** majuscule; **13** capital letter; **15** uppercase letter

capsicum: 6 pepper; **7** cayenne; **9** red pepper; **12** chili peppers

capsid: 5 mirid; **8** mirid bug

capsize: 4 sink; **5** drown, swamp; **6** go over, invert; **8** overturn, turn over; **9** shipwreck

capsized: 7 aground, swamped, wrecked; **8** cast away, grounded, stranded; **9** foundered; **11** shipwrecked

capstan: 5 winch; **8** windlass

capstone: 9 stretcher; **11** coping stone

capsule: 3 pod; **4** cyst; **5** calyx; **6** kettle; **7** bladder, matrass, utricle, vesicle; **8** bolthead, cancelli, receiver; **10** abridgment; **11** abridgcmcnt, ejector seat; **12** condensation, ejection seat, space capsule

captain: 6 master; **7** skipper [informal]; **9** chieftain; **10** head waiter, sea captain; **11** police chicf, scnior pilot; **12** maitre d'hotel, ship's captain; **13** police captain

caption: 4 head; **6** legend, rubric; **7** capture, heading, seizing, seizure; **8** catching, subtitle; **9** snatching; **10** prehension

captious: 3 hot; **5** hasty, quick; **7** bilious, carping, peevish, peppery, waspish; **8** choleric, critical, shrewish, snappish; **9** fractious, overhasty, querulous; **10** censorious; **12** faultfinding; **13** hypercritical

captiousness: 6 temper; **8** acerbity, tartness; **9** crossness, petulance, procacity, testiness; **10** crabbiness, protervity; **11** grouchiness; **12** irascibility, irritability; **13** irascibleness, irritableness, querulousness

captivate: 4 draw, lure, move, take; **5** catch, charm; **6** allure, arrest, attach, draw on, enamor, endear, entice, induce, seduce, take up, trance; **7** attract, becharm, beguile, bewitch, capture, enamour, enchant; **8** entrance; **9** apprehend, enrapture, fascinate; **11** lead captive, make captive, take captive, turn the head; **12** make prisoner, take charge of, take prisoner

captivated: 7 charmed; **8** beguiled; **9** delighted, entranced; **10** enthralled, fascinated

captive: 3 POW; **6** detenu [Fr], inmate, jailed; **7** gallant, hostage; **8** confined, detainee, Lothario, paramour, prisoner; **10** imprisoned; **13** close prisoner, prisoner of war

captivity: 6 duress; **7** durance; **10** immurement; **11** confinement, durance vile, enslavement; **12** imprisonment; **13** incarceration

captopril: 7 Capoten

capture: 3 get; **5** catch, charm, crimp, seize; **6** abduct, enamor, kidnap, trance; **7** becharm, beguile, bewitch, conquer, enamour, enchant, seizing, seizure; **8** catching, entrance, take over; **9** captivate, fascinate, snatching; **10** prehension; **14** gaining control

capuccino: 15 coffee capuccino

capuchin: 8 ringtail

caput: 4 head; **7** chapter; **9** syndicate; **10** consistory

caquet: 11 caquetterie [Fr]

car: 3 cab; **4** auto; **7** autocar, gondola, machine, railcar; **8** cable car, motorcar; **10** automobile, railway car; **11** elevator car, railroad car

Carabidae: 15 family Carabidae

carabid beetle: 12 ground beetle

carabineer: 4 peon; **6** zouave [Fr]; **7** private, troopcr; **8** chasseur [Fr], rifleman; **9** legionary, minutemen, musketeer, subaltern; **10** carabinier, skirmisher; **11** legionnaire, rank and file; **12** cannon fodder, sharpshooter

carabiniere: 10 carabineer

caracal: 7 caracal; **10** desert lynx; **11** Lynx caracal; **12** Felis caracal

Caracas: 18 capital of Venezuela

caracole: 4 trot; **5** amble, frisk; **6** canter, curvet, prance

caracul: 7 karakul; **9** broadtail

carafe: 4 ewer; **5** cruse; **8** decanter

carambola: 9 star fruit; **13** carambola tree

caramel apple: 10 candy apple, taffy apple; **12** candied apple

caramel bun: 8 honey bun; **9** schnecken, sticky bun

caramelize: 10 caramelise

Carangidae: 16 family Carangidae

carangid fish: 8 carangid

carapace: 5 shell

Carapidae: 15 family Carapidae

Carassius: 4 carp; **8** goldfish; **14** genus Carassius

carat: 5 Karat

caravan: 3 van; **5** train; **7** cortege; **8** carriage; **9** cavalcade; **10** wagon train

caravan inn: 4 khan; **11** caravansary; **12** caravanserai

caravanserai: 4 khan; **10** caravan inn; **11** caravansary

carbamide: 4 urea

carbine: 4 rifle

carbohydrate: 5 sugar; **6** starch; **9** cellulose; **10** saccharide

carbolic acid: 6 phenol; **10** oxybenzene; **12** phenylic acid; **14** hydroxybenzene

C

carbon: 1 C; **10** carbon copy; **11** carbon paper; **13** atomic number 6
carbon-14 dating: 12 carbon dating; **17** radiocarbon dating
carbonaceous: 8 carbonic; **9** carbonous
carbonado: 5 bortz; **7** adamant, diamond; **12** black diamond
carbonated beverage: 3 pop; **4** soda; **7** soda pop; **8** minerals; **9** soda water
carbonated water: 7 seltzer; **8** club soda; **9** soda water; **14** sparkling water
carbon black: 4 smut, soot; **9** lampblack
carbon copy: 6 carbon
carbon dating: 14 carbon-14 dating; **17** radiocarbon dating
carbon dioxide: 2 CO; **15** carbonic acid gas
carbonic: 9 carbonous; **12** carbonaceous
Carboniferous: 19 Carboniferous period
carbon tetrachloride: 9 carbon tet; **16** perchloromethane; **18** tetrachloromethane
carbonyl: 10 carbonylic
carboy: 3 jug; **6** firkin; **9** kilderkin
carbuncle: 4 ruby; **5** issue; **7** jacinth; **8** amethyst, hyacinth; **9** almandite, gathering; **10** Al-Fe garnet; **12** peccant humor
carcajou: 9 skunk bear, wolverine; **10** Gulo luscus
carcase: 7 carcass
carcass: 6 corpse; **7** cadaver, carcase; **8** dead meat; **12** dead organism
Carcharhinidae: 20 family Carcharhinidae
Carcharhinus: 5 shark; **17** genus Carcharhinus
Carchariidae: 14 Odontaspididae; **18** family Carchariidae; **20** family Odontaspididae
Carcharodon carcharias: 8 man-eater; **10** white shark; **14** man-eating shark; **15** great white shark
carcinoma in situ: 17 preinvasive cancer
card: 3 wag, wit; **4** bill, menu; **5** board, carte, ravel, tease; **6** lineup, notice, poster; **7** placard, unravel; **8** postcard; **9** scorecard; **10** bill of fare, letter card, postal card; **11** calling card, carte du jour, circuit card, disentangle; **12** batting order, circuit board, identity card, visiting card
cardboard: 6 flimsy; **10** unlifelike; **16** composition board
card catalog: 13 card catalogue
cardiac arrest: 8 asystole; **12** heart failure; **13** heart stoppage
cardiac massage: 12 heart massage
cardiac monitor: 12 heart monitor
cardiac murmur: 6 murmur; **11** heart murmur
cardiac resuscitation: 3 CPR
cardiac valve: 10 heart valve
Cardigan: 18 Cardigan Welsh corgi
cardinal: 3 key; **5** crack, prime, vital; **6** poncho, primal, tip-top; **7** capital, carmine, central, radical, redbird; **8** top grade, top-notch, very best; **9** essential, exquisite, paramount; **10** high priest; **11** fundamental, high-wrought; **12** all-absorbing, cardinal bird; **14** cardinal number; **16** cardinal grosbeak
cardinal's hat: 9 shovel hat
cardinal grosbeak: 7 redbird; **8** cardinal
card index: 4 file; **8** card file
cardiogram: 3 ECG, EKG; **17** electrocardiogram
cardiograph: 3 ECG; **18** electrocardiograph
cardioid: 11 heart shaped
cardiologist: 12 heart surgeon; **15** heart specialist
cardiopathy: 12 heart disease; **14** heart condition
cardiopulmonary arrest: 8 asystole; **13** cardiac arrest
cardiopulmonary resuscitation: 3 CPR; **20** cardiac resuscitation
cardiovascular system: 17 circulatory system
Cardizem: 9 diltiazem
card-playing: 7 betting; **8** gambling, sporting; **10** dissipated
Carduelinae: 20 subfamily Carduelinae
Carduelis: 6 linnet; **7** redpoll; **9** goldfinch, red siskin; **14** genus Carduelis
Carduus: 7 thistle; **12** genus Carduus
care: 3 aid; **4** deal, dole, fear, fret, heed, keep, like, load, task, ward, wish; **5** trial, worry; **6** burden, charge, errand, handle, manage, upkeep; **7** anxiety, caution, concern, custody, mission, tending; **8** give care, tutelage; **9** attention, husbandry; **10** assignment, commission, engagement, precaution, solicitude; **11** forethought, heedfulness, maintenance, safekeeping; **12** assigned duty, guardianship, retrenchment; **14** responsibility
careen: 4 calk, keel, reel, rock, swag, sway, tilt; **5** caulk, lurch, shift; **6** splice, stanch, wobble; **7** stagger, staunch; **8** stop a gap
career: 4 walk; **7** calling; **8** vocation; **9** life's work; **10** profession, walk of life; **11** life history
care for: 4 like, list, love; **5** treat, value; **6** affect, regard; **7** be big on, cherish; **8** hold dear, treasure; **10** bear love to, set store by; **12** have a love for, set store upon
careful: 5 chary, spare; **6** frugal, saving; **7** heedful, sparing, thrifty; **8** measured; **10** deliberate, economical
careful consideration: 14 deep reflection
carefully: 9 heedfully; **10** cautiously; **12** thoughtfully
carefulness: 7 caution; **12** cautiousness
caregiver: 18 health care provider, health professional
careless: 3 lax; **5** loose; **7** inexact; **8** heedless,

mindless, slipshod, slovenly; **10** regardless; **11** thoughtless; **12** disregarding

carelessly: 8 rakishly; **9** raffishly; **10** heedlessly; **12** incautiously; **13** thoughtlessly

carelessness: 7 neglect; **9** disregard; **10** negligence; **12** mindlessness; **14** nonperformance

caress: 3 pet; **6** dandle, fondle; **7** cherish

caressing: 7 hugging, kissing, necking, petting; **8** cuddling, fondling; **9** caressive, endearing, smooching, snuggling; **10** cherishing

careworn: 4 worn; **5** drawn; **7** haggard, raddled; **9** concerned

carfare: 7 bus fare

cargo: 3 jag; **4** bale, load; **6** burden, lading; **7** freight, loading, payload; **8** shipment; **11** consignment

cargo area: 4 hold; **9** cargo deck; **11** storage area

cargo ship: 9 freighter; **11** cargo vessel, merchantman; **12** merchant ship

caribe: 6 pirana; **7** piranha

caribou: 8 reindeer

Carica: 11 genus Carica

Caricaceae: 12 papaya family; **16** family Caricaceae

caricatura: 10 caricature; **12** high coloring

caricature: 3 ape; **4** daub; **6** parody, send up; **7** distort, lampoon; **8** overdraw, satirize, travesty; **9** burlesque, imitation, take off on; **10** exaggerate; **12** high coloring, misrepresent; **13** impersonation

caricatured: 8 parodied; **10** burlesqued

caries: 6 cavity; **10** tooth decay; **12** dental caries

carillon: 11 bell ringing; **15** carillon playing

carinate: 6 keeled, ridged; **9** carinated; **10** flying bird; **12** carinate bird

carinated: 6 keeled, ridged; **8** carinate

caring: 4 fond, warm; **6** tender; **8** lovesome; **10** lovingness, protective; **12** affectionate

carious: 7 peccant; **8** purulent

carissa plum: 9 natal plum

carking: 6 biting; **7** teasing; **8** worrying, annoying; **9** bothering, harassing, pestering; **10** tormenting; **11** molestation

carle: 4 boor, lout; **5** churl; **9** underling

Carlina: 7 thistle; **12** genus Carlina

car mechanic: 8 mechanic; **12** auto mechanic, grease monkey

Carmelite: 10 White Friar

carminative: 8 laudanum, relaxant; **9** demulcent; **10** antifungal [Med]; **13** antispasmodic

carmine: 3 red; **4** lake, ruby; **5** ruddy; **6** cerise, cherry; **7** crimson, reddish, ruby-red, scarlet; **8** blood-red, cardinal; **9** cherry-red

carnage: 8 butchery; **9** slaughter

carnal: 4 sexy; **5** lusty; **6** animal, bodily, erotic, sexual; **7** fleshly, lustful, rampant,

rutting, ruttish, sensual; **8** prurient; **10** libidinous; **12** carnal-minded, concupiscent

carnality: 5 flesh; **8** salacity; **9** animalism, animality, prurience, pruriency; **10** sensuality; **14** lasciviousness, voluptuousness

carnation family: 10 pink family; **15** Caryophyllaceae; **21** family Caryophyllaceae

carnauba: 7 wax palm; **11** carnauba wax; **12** carnauba palm

Carnegie: 14 Andrew Carnegie

carnival: 4 fair; **6** circus; **7** funfair

carnivorous bat: 8 microbat

carob: 9 algarroba, carob bean, carob tree, locust pod; **10** locust bean; **11** carob powder; **13** algarroba bean, carob bean tree; **15** Saint-John's-bread

carol: 4 lilt, sing; **5** chant, chirp; **6** chaunt, intone, warble; **7** chirrup, wassail; **14** Christmas carol

caroller: 7 caroler

carom: 4 clip; **6** cannon, glance; **8** ricochet; **9** glance off, sideswipe [U.S.]; **10** sidewinder [U.S.]

carotene: 7 carotin; **11** provitamin A; **13** cryptoxanthin

carouse: 3 bib, sot, toy; **4** lush, riot, soak, swig; **5** besot, feast, revel, sport, swill; **6** guzzle, junket, wanton; **7** banquet, disport, roister; **8** carousal; **9** drink deep, drink hard, drown care, make merry

carousel: 9 whirligig; **10** roundabout; **11** minichanger; **12** merry-go-round; **15** luggage carousel

carpal: 9 wrist bone; **10** carpal bone

car park: 10 parking lot; **11** parking area

carp at: 6 peck at; **8** nibble at, complain

carpellate: 10 pistillate

carpenter's glue: 8 wood glue

carpenter's hammer: 10 claw hammer, clawhammer

carpenter's kit: 7 tool kit

carpentry: 8 woodwork; **11** woodworking

carper: 5 cynic; **6** critic

carpet: 3 rug; **8** throw rug; **9** carpeting

carpeting: 3 rug; **6** carpet

carpet pad: 6 rug pad; **8** underlay; **12** underlayment

carping: 5 cavil; **8** captious, caviling, critical; **9** quibbling; **10** censorious, nitpicking; **12** faultfinding, pettifogging; **13** hypercritical

Carpinus: 8 hornbeam; **13** genus Carpinus

Carpodacus: 5 finch; **15** genus Carpodacus

carpus: 5 wrist; **10** wrist joint

car radio: 2 CB; **8** ham radio; **10** police band; **11** police radio, two-way radio; **12** amateur radio, citizen's band, handie-talkie, walkie-talkie [military]; **13** airplane radio; **14** short-wave radio

carragheen: 8 carageen; 9 carrageen, Irish moss; 15 Chondrus crispus

carrefour: 8 crossing, crossway; 9 crossroad; 12 intersection

carrel: 5 stall; 7 carrell, cubicle

carriage: 3 air, rig, van; 4 cast, gait, look, mien, port, pram [Brit]; 5 coach, color, draft, guise; 6 manner; 7 bearing, cadence, caravan, carting, hauling, posture; 8 carrying, demeanor, equipage, shipping; 9 baby buggy, transport; 10 complexion, conveyance; 12 baby carriage, passenger car, perambulator

carriage dog: 8 coach dog; 9 dalmatian

carriage house: 10 coach house

carried out: 8 realized; 9 performed; 10 discharged; 12 accomplished

carrier: 5 toter; 6 bearer; 7 flattop, mailman, newsboy, postman; 8 conveyer; 11 carrier wave, mail carrier; 13 common carrier, letter carrier; 15 aircraft carrier

carrier bag: 4 poke, sack; 8 paper bag

carrion: 7 garbage

carrion crow: 12 black vulture; 15 Coragyps atratus

Carroll: 7 Dodgson; 12 Lewis Carroll; 14 Charles Dodgson; 15 Reverend Dodgson; 22 Charles Lutwidge Dodgson

carrom: 4 clip; 5 carom; 9 sideswipe [U.S.]

carronade: 4 park; 7 battery; 8 basilisk

carrot family: 8 Apiaceae; 12 Umbelliferae; 14 family Apiaceae

carrottop: 7 redhead; 9 redheader

carry: 3 run; 4 bear, hold, lead, pack, port, sway, take, tote [U.S.]; 5 stock; 6 acquit, affect, behave, convey, deport, expect, extend; 7 channel, comport, conduce, conduct, contain, dribble, execute, express, gestate, support, sustain; 8 overcome, persuade, shoulder, transmit; 9 stockpile, transport

carryall: 4 tote; 7 holdall, tote bag

carry away: 4 coax, lure; 5 charm, tempt; 6 seduce; 7 bear off, bewitch, take off, wheedle; 8 bear away, carry off, take away; 9 fascinate; 10 conciliate

carrying: 5 draft; 7 bearing, carting, hauling; 8 carriage, shipping; 9 transport; 10 conveyance; 11 having on one; 12 transporting; 13 having with one; 14 transportation

carrying cost: 14 carrying charge

carry on: 4 deal, go on, play, work; 6 bear on, keep up, uphold; 7 conduct, proceed; 8 be at work, carry out, continue, exercise, practice, preserve; 9 prosecute; 12 carry through; 13 put into effect; 15 carry into effect

carry out: 2 do; 4 deal; 6 effect, fulfil; 7 carry on, conduct, execute, fulfill; 8 exercise, practice, practise; 9 go through, implement; 10 accomplish, put through; 12 carry through; 13 follow through, put into effect; 15 carry into effect; 18 carry into execution

carry over: 4 book, post; 5 debit, enter; 6 credit; 8 hold over; 9 ferry over; 12 carry forward

carry the day: 9 win the day

Carson City: 15 capital of Nevada

cart: 4 drag, dray, haul; 5 wagon; 6 go-cart; 8 hand cart, handcart, pushcart; 10 streetcart

cartage: 7 carting, portage; 11 shipping fee; 13 freight charge

cart away: 7 cart off, haul off; 8 haul away, take away

carte: 4 card, menu; 10 bill of fare; 11 carte du jour

carte blanche: 8 free rein

carte du jour: 4 card, menu; 5 carte; 10 bill of fare

cartel: 5 trust; 6 cahoot; 7 combine [U.S.]; 9 challenge, syndicate

Carter: 11 Jimmy Carter; 15 James Earl Carter

carter: 7 wagoner; 9 postilion

Carthaginian: 5 Punic

Carthamus: 14 genus Carthamus

Carthamus tinctorius: 9 safflower; 12 false saffron

Carthusian: 8 Bonhomme [Fr]

cartilage: 7 gristle

cartilaginous: 7 gristly, rubbery, stringy

carting: 5 draft; 7 cartage, hauling, portage; 8 carriage, carrying, shipping; 9 transport; 10 conveyance; 12 transporting; 14 transportation

cartload: 9 wagonload

cartographer: 8 map maker

cartographic: 10 geodetical; 11 topographic; 13 topographical

cartography: 9 mapmaking

carton: 3 box; 9 cartonful

cartoon: 6 sketch; 15 animated cartoon

cartoon strip: 10 comic strip

cartouche: 6 zigzag; 8 acanthus, cartouch, fireball; 13 ball cartridge

car traffic: 17 automobile traffic

cartridge: 6 pickup; 8 magazine

cartridge clip: 4 clip; 8 magazine

cartridge holder: 4 clip; 8 magazine

cartulary: 7 diptych; 12 Domesday book

cartwheel: 12 silver dollar

Carum carvi: 7 caraway

caruncle: 6 growth; 9 caruncula; 10 proud flesh

carve: 3 cut, hew; 4 deal; 5 cut up; 6 chip at, chisel, sculpt; 9 sculpture

carven: 6 carved

carver: 6 chaser, cutter; 7 modeler; 8 sculptor, statuary; 10 sculpturer, woodcarver; 11 statue maker

carve up: 5 split; 6 divide; 7 split up; 8 dissever, separate

Carya: 5 pecan; 6 pignut; 7 hickory; 8 shagbark; 9 bitternut, shellbark; 10 genus Carya

Caryocar: 13 genus Caryocar

Caryocaraceae: 6 souari; 9 souari nut; 19 family Caryocaraceae

Caryophyllaceae: 10 pink family; 15 carnation family; 21 family Caryophyllaceae

caryopsis: 5 grain

Caryota: 5 kittul; kitul; 12 genus Caryota

casa: 5 house; 8 dwelling; 11 country seat

casaba melon: 6 casaba

Casanova: 22 Giovanni Jacopo Casanova

cascabel: 10 sleigh bell

cascade: 5 falls; 8 cataract; 9 waterfall; 11 cascade down

Cascades: 12 Cascade Range

cascara buckthorn: 8 bearwood; 9 bearberry; 11 chittamwood, chittimwood; 17 Rhamnus purshianus

cascarilla bark: 12 eleuthra bark; 13 sweetwood bark

case: 4 face, slip, suit, type; 5 causa, cause, event, shell; 6 affair, casing, encase, matter, sheath; 7 caseful, concern, example, housing, invalid, lawsuit, patient, reasons [pl], subject; 8 instance, pleading, showcase; 9 arguments [pl], character, eccentric, guinea pig, outer case, 10 pillow slip, pillowcase; 11 case in point, decided case, display case, pros and cons; 15 grammatical case

casebook: 8 textbook

case-by-case: 10 individual, item-by-item

case harden: 4 gird; 5 steel; 6 harden; 7 sustain

casehardened: 6 inured; 8 obdurate, stubborn; 9 obstinate, tenacious; 10 inflexible, unyielding

casein: 11 casein paint

case in point: 4 case; 9 precedent

case knife: 11 sheath knife

case law: 9 common law, precedent

casemate: 6 glacis; 7 barrack

casemated: 9 loopholed; 11 castellated

casement: 6 window; 9 embrasure

casern: 7 barrack

caseworker: 12 social worker; 13 welfare worker

cash: 6 cash in, specie; 8 cold cash, currency

cashable: 10 redeemable

cashbook: 7 day book; 8 pass book; 11 account book

cashbox: 4 till; 8 money box

cash cow: 10 moneymaker; 12 moneyspinner

cashew: 21 Anacardium occidentale

cashier: 6 teller; 9 bank clerk, paymaster

cash in hand: 5 funds; 8 finances; 16 monetary resource

cash in on: 8 profit by; 9 make hay of; 12 make hay out of; 13 make the most of

cash keeper: 6 banker

cash machine: 3 ATM; 13 cash dispenser; 15 automated teller, automatic teller; 22 automated teller machine, automatic teller machine

Cashmere: 7 Kashmir

cash on delivery: 3 COD

cash register: 4 till; 6 tiller; 8 register

casing: 4 case; 5 shell; 7 housing

cask: 3 keg; 4 drum; 6 barrel

casket: 3 pix, pyx; 5 chest; 6 coffer, coffin; 7 caisson; 9 reliquary

Casmerodius: 16 genus Casmerodius

Casmerodius albus: 15 great white heron

casque: 4 helm; 5 shako; 6 helmet; 8 siege cap

cassava: 6 cassava, manioc; 7 manioca

cassava starch: 6 manioc; 7 cassava, manioca

Cassia: 5 senna

cassino: 6 casino

Cassiopea: 8 Pleiades; 15 Cassiopea's chair

Cassiopea's chair: 8 Pleiades; 9 Cassiopea

Cassite: 7 Kassite

Cassius: 20 Gaius Cassius Longinus

cassock: 4 cope, gown, pall, robe; 5 frock; 7 pallium; 10 Geneva gown

cast: 3 air, cat, cut, dye, hue, put, shy; 4 damn, draw, drop, form, glow, honk, jerk, look, mete, mien, mold, port, roam, roll, rove, shed, spue, swan, tint, toss, type; 5 chuck, color, couch, drift, fling, flush, frame, guise, heave, mould, pitch, range, retch, shade, shape, share, stamp, stray, throw, tinge, vomit; 6 be sick, billet, detail, formed, hurtle, livery, molded, ramble, recast, redact, wander; 7 cast off, casting, concede, condemn, convict, project, regorge, throw up, upchuck, vomit up; 8 affected, carriage, contrive, demeanor, disgorge, organize, shake off, sprinkle, throw off, tincture, vagabond; 9 throwaway; 10 coloration, complexion, find guilty

Castanea: 7 crenata; 8 chestnut; 9 chinkapin; 10 chinquapin; 13 genus Castanea; 15 Chinese chestnut; 16 Japanese chestnut

castaneous: 3 bay; 6 auburn, dapple, russet; 8 chestnut, cinnamon, nut-brown

castanets: 5 bones; 6 maraca; 8 clappers; 13 finger cymbals

cast aside: 4 toss; 5 fling; 7 cast off, cast out, discard, dismiss, dispose, given up, put away, toss out, turn off; 8 cast away, chuck out, lay aside, put aside, set aside, throw out, toss away; 9 abandoned, fling away, pitch away, throw away; 10 cast behind, disposed of, do away with, throw aside; 12 relinquished

castaway: 6 Pariah, pariah; **7** outcast; **8** recreant, rejected; **9** defaulter; **11** shipwrecked; **17** shipwreck survivor

cast away: 4 toss; **5** fling; **7** aground, cast off, cast out, discard, dismiss, dispose, put away, swamped, toss out, turn off, wrecked; **8** capsized, chuck out, fool away, grounded, stranded, throw out, toss away; **9** cast aside, fling away, foundered, pitch away, throw away; **10** muddle away, throw aside; **11** fritter away, shipwrecked

casteless: 8 outcaste

castellan: 5 guard; **6** custos [Lat], gaoler, jailer, keeper, ranger, warder; **7** turnkey; **9** custodian, seneschal; **11** chamberlain

castellated: 7 castled; **9** loopholed; **10** crenelated; **11** crenelled; **12** battlemented

caster: 5 cruet; **6** castor

cast forth: 3 sow; **9** broadcast; **10** draught off

castigate: 4 lash, trim; **6** blow up; **7** chasten, correct, trounce; **8** chastise, chastize, overhaul; **9** objurgate, reprimand

castigation: 6 earful, rebuke; **9** going-over, reprimand; **10** bawling out, chewing out, upbraiding; **12** chastisement, dressing down

castigatory: 10 inflictive

Castile: 8 Castilla

Castilleja: 10 paintbrush, Castilleia; **15** genus Castilleia, genus Castilleja

casting: 4 cast; **7** molding

cast into prison: 4 jail; **6** immure; **8** imprison; **11** incarcerate

cast iron: 11 wrought iron

castle: 4 hall, rook; **5** court, folly, tower; **6** palace; **7** chateau, rotunda; **8** castling, pavilion; **10** manor-house

castled: 10 crenelated; **11** castellated, crenellated; **12** battlemented

castle in Spain: 6 revery; **7** reverie; **8** daydream; **9** air castle; **14** castle in the air

castle in the air: 6 revery; **7** reverie; **8** daydream; **9** air castle, pipe dream; **11** pie-in-the-sky; **12** man in the moon; **13** castle in Spain

cast light upon: 7 light up, lighten; **8** illumine; **9** enlighten, shine upon; **10** illuminate; **11** cast light in; **12** throw light in; **13** shed light upon

cast lots: 8 draw lots

cast off: 4 cast, drop, shed; **5** throw; **6** put off; **7** cast out, dismiss, put away, take off, turn off; **8** cast away, derelict, shake off, throw off; **9** cast aside, fling away, pitch away, throw away; **10** throw aside

cast-off: 5 scrap, waste; **6** junked; **9** discarded, throwaway; **10** thrown-away

castor: 6 beaver, caster; **9** beaver hat

Castor and Pollux: 6 Gemini

castor bean plant: 11 palma christ; **12** palma christi; **14** castor-oil plant

Castor canadensis: 14 New World beaver

Castor fiber: 14 Old World beaver

cast out: 3 ban; **4** shun, toss; **5** fling; **6** banish; **7** cast off, discard, dismiss, dispose, put away, toss out, turn off; **8** cast away, chuck out, throw out, toss away; **9** blackball, cast aside, fling away, ostracize, pitch away, throw away; **10** throw aside

cast overboard: 8 cast away, jettison, toss away; **9** fling away, throw away; **13** cast to the dogs, toss overboard, toss to the dogs; **14** cast to the winds, fling overboard, fling to the dogs, heave overboard, pitch overboard, throw overboard

castrate: 6 eunuch; **10** emasculate; **13** demasculinize

castrated: 7 unsexed; **11** emasculated

cast sheep's eyes upon: 4 ogle

casual: 5 loose; **6** blithe, chance; **7** cursory, fooling, natural, passing; **8** everyday, familiar, heedless, informal, uncaused; **9** causeless, easygoing, sans souci [Fr], unheeding, unmindful, unworried; **10** accidental, contingent, effortless, fortuitous, incidental, insouciant, nonchalant, occasional, phlegmatic, unthinking; **11** free-and-easy, perfunctory, unconcerned, unobservant; **12** adventitious, devil-may-care, undetermined; **13** indeterminate, unceremonious

casually: 8 casually; **9** naturally; **10** informally; **11** unwittingly; **12** nonchalantly, unthinkingly; **13** inadvertently

casualness: 11 familiarity

casualty: 3 hap, hit; **4** bale; **6** hazard, victim; **7** fortune, tragedy; **8** accident, calamity, disaster, fortuity; **9** adventure, haphazard; **11** bad accident, catastrophe; **12** chance medley, happenchance, happenstance, injured party; **13** fatal accident

Casuarius: 14 genus Casuarius

casuist: 7 casuist, sophist; **8** wrangler; **11** rationalist

casuistical: 5 moral; **7** ethical; **9** casuistic; **13** conscientious

casus belli: 6 grudge; **10** bone to pick

cat: 3 guy; **4** puss; **5** pussy; **6** big cat, feline, hombre; **7** true cat; **8** house cat, pussy cat; **11** Caterpillar; **13** cat-o'-nine-tails

CAT: 2 CT; **18** computed tomography; **23** computed axial tomography

cat's cradle: 4 knot; **5** braid, chain, cross; **6** wreath

cat's eye: 6 jasper; **8** hematite; **9** moonstone; **10** bloodstone

cat's-paw: 4 dupe, pawn, tool; **6** puppet, stooge; **9** ame damnee [Fr]; **10** instrument, running dog

cat's-tail: 7 bulrush, nailrod; 8 bullrush, reed mace, reedmace; 14 Typha latifolia

cataclysm: 5 flood, storm; 6 deluge; 7 tragedy; 8 calamity, disaster; 10 desolation, earthquake, inundation; 11 catastrophe

catafalque: 4 bier, pall; 6 hearse

Cataflam 19 diclofenac potassium

catalog: 4 list; 5 grade, index; 6 digest; 8 graduate, tabulate; 9 inventory, catalogue

catalog buying: 15 mail-order buying

catalpa: 10 Indian bean

catalysis: 10 resolution; 11 dissolution

catalyst: 11 accelerator

catamaran: 7 caravel, coracle; 9 transport

catamenia: 4 flow; 6 menses, period; 12 menstruation

catamount: 4 lynx, puma; 6 cougar; 7 painter, panther; 11 mountain cat; 12 mountain lion; 13 Felis concolor

Catananche caerula: 10 cupid's dart; 11 blue succory

cataplasm: 7 plaster; 8 liniment, poultice; 9 traumatic, vulnerary

Catapres: 9 clonidine

catapult: 5 sling; 6 onager; 7 bricole; 8 ballista [Lat], launcher; 9 slingshot

cataract: 5 falls; 6 rapids; 7 cascade, torrent; 9 waterfall; 10 white water

catastrophe: 4 bale; 7 tragedy; 8 accident, calamity, casualty, disaster; 9 cataclysm

catastrophic: 6 tragic; 7 ruinous; 8 tragical; 10 calamitous, disastrous

catatonia: 4 coma; 6 trance; 15 unconsciousness

catatonic: 4 dead [fig], numb; 7 out cold, unaware; 8 comatose; 9 senseless; 11 unconscious

catbrier: 5 briar, brier; 9 bullbrier; 10 greenbrier, horsebrier

cat burglar: 12 housebreaker

catcall: 7 whistle; 9 sibilance; 10 sibilation

catch: 3 bag, get, nab, see; 4 bite, bolt, grab, hank, hasp, haul, hook, sack, snap, stop, take, view, wile; 5 blind, charm, cheat, clasp, feint, fetch, grasp, hitch, hocus, latch, match, pinch, plant, reach, round, touch, trick, watch; 6 arrest, bubble, chorus, collar, enamor, follow, juggle, master, pick up, pocket, snatch, string, take in, trance, trip up; 7 becharm, beguile, bewitch, capture, chicane, chorale, collect, enamour, enchant, make out; 8 entrance, overhear, overtake; 9 captivate, catch up with, choral piece, fascinate, see daylight; 12 apprehension

catch a glimpse: 8 get a look

catch a likeness: 13 take a likeness

catch a whiff of: 5 scent, smoke, sniff; 9 smell a rat

catch a wink: 3 nap; 6 catnap

catcher: 5 plate; 8 receiver; 11 battery mate

catch fire: 5 erupt; 6 ignite

catching: 6 espial, spying, taking; 7 capture, seizing, seizure; 8 spotting; 9 detection, snatching; 10 contagious, infectious, prehension; 11 contracting; 12 communicable, contractable; 13 transmissable, transmissible, transmittable

catchment area: 12 drainage area; 13 drainage basin

catch on: 4 twig; 5 get it; 6 tumble; 7 get onto, latch on; 8 cotton on

catch one's breath: 4 rest; 7 breathe; 13 take a breather

cat chow: 7 cat food

catchpenny: 4 mean, vile; 5 cheap, sorry, weedy; 6 meager, scurvy, shabby, trashy; 7 scrubby; 8 beggarly, gimcrack, trumpery, wretched; 9 miserable, worthless

catchpoll: 6 beadle; 7 bailiff; 8 tipstaff

catch some Z's: 3 kip; 5 log Z's, sleep; 7 slumber

catch up with: 5 catch; 6 make up; 8 overtake

catchword: 5 motto; 6 slogan; 7 passkey; 8 password; 9 mot du guet [Fr], watchword; 10 mot de passe [Fr]

catchy: 6 tricky; 16 attention-getting

catechist: 8 examiner, inquirer; 9 inspector; 10 inquisitor; 12 investigator

catechu: 7 gambier; 12 black catechu; 13 Acacia catechu; 14 Jerusalem thorn

catechumen: 6 novice; 7 recruit; 8 neophyte; 10 raw recruit; 11 probationer

categorical: 4 flat; 5 clear; 7 crucial, decided; 8 absolute, decisive, definite, specific; 9 categoric; 11 ascertained, determinate, unequivocal; 12 unmistakable; 13 unconditional

categorize: 5 match, place; 7 make out, match up, realize; 8 classify, identify; 9 recognize; 10 stereotype; 11 distinguish; 17 assign to a category

categorized: 6 placed; 7 made out; 10 classified, identified, recognized; 13 distinguished

category: 4 kind, sort, type; 5 class; 6 family; 7 variety; 8 division

catenulate: 8 catenate; 9 chainlike

cater: 3 ply; 6 forage, purvey, supply; 7 provide, victual; 9 provision

caterer: 6 batman, feeder; 8 purveyor; 9 victualer; 10 commissary; 13 quartermaster

Caterpillar: 3 cat

caterwaul: 4 pule, yowl

cates: 6 dainty; 8 dainties, delicacy; 9 fleshpots; 10 delicacies

catfish: 6 mudcat; 8 wolffish; 14 siluriform fish

cat food: 7 cat chow

Catharanthus: 17 genus Catharanthus
Catharanthus roseus: 7 old maid; 10 periwinkle
catharsis: 9 katharsis; 10 abreaction
Cathartes: 14 genus Cathartes
Cathartes aura: 7 buzzard; 13 turkey buzzard, turkey vulture
cathartic: 6 physic; 8 aperient, evacuant, laxative; 9 cleansing, purgative, purifying, releasing
cathedra: 13 bishop's throne
cathedral: 4 kirk; 6 chapel, church; 7 oratory; 8 basilica; 10 tabernacle; 11 conventicle; 12 meetinghouse
Catherine the Great: 9 Catherine
catheter: 7 cannula
cathexis: 6 charge
cathode-ray tube: 3 CRT [acron]; 14 cathode ray tube
catholic: 6 divine; 9 Christian, inclusive; 10 scriptural; 11 evangelical; 12 monotheistic
Catholic: 5 Roman; 6 papist; 8 faithful, Romanist; 9 believing, Christian
Catholicism: 8 Romanism
catholicize: 8 latinize
catholicon: 7 panacea, cure-all
cathouse: 6 bagnio; 7 brothel; 8 bordello; 10 bawdyhouse, whorehouse; 13 sporting house; 16 house of ill repute; 19 house of prostitution
cat house: 4 stew; 7 brothel; 8 bordello; 10 whorehouse
cationic detergent: 10 invert soap
catkin: 5 ament
cat-like: 5 catty; 6 feline
catmint: 6 catnip; 13 Nepeta cataria
catnap: 3 nap; 6 snooze; 8 cat sleep; 10 catch a wink, forty winks, short sleep
catnip: 7 catmint; 13 Nepeta cataria
catoptromancy: 9 by mirrors
Catoptrophorus: 6 willet; 19 genus Catoptrophorus
Catskills: 17 Catskill Mountains
catsup: 7 cetchup, ketchup; 13 tomato ketchup
cattail family: 9 Typhaceae; 15 family Typhaceae
cattalo: 7 beefalo
cat thyme: 5 marum
cattiness: 5 spite; 9 nastiness; 12 spitefulness
cattle: 4 cows, oxen
cattleman: 6 cowboy, cowman; 7 beef man, cowhand, cowherd, cowpoke, puncher; 10 cowpuncher
cattle pen: 6 corral, cow pen
cattle plague: 5 mange; 10 rinderpest; 12 milk sickness
cattle ranch: 5 ranch; 6 spread; 10 cattle farm

cattle thief: 6 badger; 7 rustler; 8 abductor, bunko man
catty: 6 cattie, feline; 7 cat-like, cattish
catty-corner: 10 catacorner; 11 cater-corner, kitty-corner; 12 cata-cornered; 13 cater-cornered, catty-cornered, kitty-cornered
Caucasian: 5 White; 11 white person; 17 Caucasian language
caucasoid: 9 caucasian
Caucasus: 8 Caucasia, 17 Caucasus Mountains
caucus: 6 clique, confer; 8 assembly, conclave; 10 conference; 11 conventicle, hold council
caudal: 6 lumbar; 8 hindmost, taillike
caudate: 6 tailed; 7 urodele; 8 caudated
caudex: 4 stem; 5 stock
caul: 4 veil; 13 fetal membrane; 14 greater omentum; 17 embryonic membrane
cauliflower: 24 Brassica oleracea botrytis
cauline: 7 stemmed; 10 caulescent
caulk: 4 calk; 6 careen, splice, stanch; 7 staunch; 8 stop a gap; 12 bind up wounds; 13 caulking agent
caulking: 7 sealing; 8 plugging
causa: 4 case, suit; 5 cause; 7 lawsuit
causal: 8 original
causal factor: 10 determiner; 11 determinant; 13 determinative
cause: 2 do; 3 get; 4 case, have, make, suit; 5 causa, drive; 6 action, effort, induce, origin, reason, source; 7 crusade, element, grounds, lawsuit; 8 campaign, movement, occasion; 9 good cause, principle, stimulate, suit in law; 10 litigation; 11 causal agent, legal action
causeless: 6 casual, chance; 8 uncaused; 10 accidental, contingent, fortuitous, incidental, reasonless; 12 adventitious, undetermined; 13 indeterminate
cause pleasure: 5 charm; 6 please; 7 delight
causerie: 3 gab; 4 chat; 6 gossip; 7 chin-wag, gabfest; 8 chitchat, idle talk, town talk; 9 small talk, table talk; 11 chin-wagging, idle chatter, village talk; 12 tittle-tattle
cause sorrow: 4 hurt, pain; 5 wound
caustic: 4 acid, hard, racy, sore, sour; 5 acerb, acrid, acute, cruel, grave, harsh, sharp, short, taint; 6 alkali, biting, bitter, severe; 7 acerbic, crabbed, doggish, erosive, mordant, piquant, pungent; 8 poignant, venomous, virulent; 9 corrosive, envenomed, rancorous, sarcastic, stringent, sulfurous, trenchant, vitriolic; 10 blistering, irritating, mordacious, sulphurous; 11 acrimonious
caustically: 13 vitriolically
causticity: 9 virulence; 10 alkalinity
caustic remark: 5 irony; 6 satire; 7 sarcasm
cauterize: 4 burn, sear; 5 brand; 6 burn in

caution: 4 care, heed, warn; 6 caveat; 7 warning; 8 admonish, coolness, forewarn, prudence; 10 discretion, precaution, steadiness; 11 calculation, carefulness, forethought, heedfulness; 12 cautiousness, deliberation, early warning

cautionary: 7 warning; 8 monitory; 9 exemplary; 10 admonitory, cautioning, preventive; 11 premonitory; 12 prophylactic

cautious: 4 wary; 5 timid; 7 guarded; 12 conservative

cautiously: 9 carefully, guardedly, prudently; 10 discreetly; 13 circumspectly; 14 conservatively

cavalcade: 5 array; 7 caravan, cortege, retinue; 11 rank and file

cavalier: 4 pert; 5 fresh [U.S.], rider, saucy; 6 jockey; 7 cynical, forward, haughty; 8 flippant, horseman, malapert, Quixotic; 9 bumptious, chevalier, withering; 10 equestrian, fire eating, high-handed, roughrider; 11 adventurous, impertinent; 12 contumelious, supercilious

cavalierly: 12 disdainfully

cavalry: 5 horse; 10 light horse; 12 horse cavalry; 13 mounted rifles

cavalryman: 7 trooper; 12 horse soldier

cavalry sword: 5 saber, sabre

cavatina: 8 fantasia; 9 pastorale

cave: 3 den; 4 cove, lair; 6 cavern; 7 spelunk; 9 undermine

caveat: 7 caution, warning; 12 early warning

cave in: 4 fail, give; 5 break; 6 fall in, retire; 7 founder, give way; 8 collapse

caveman: 7 cave man; 10 troglodyte; 11 cave dweller

cavern: 4 cave, cove; 9 cavern out

cavernous: 6 gaping, spongy; 8 erectile, wide open

Cavia: 6 aperea; 8 wild cavy; 9 guinea pig; 10 genus Cavia

caviar: 3 roe; 7 fish roe, caviare

cavil: 4 carp; 6 refine; 7 carping, chicane, protest; 9 repudiate; 10 split hairs; 14 censoriousness

caviler: 5 cynic; 6 carper, critic; 8 frondeur; 11 word-catcher

caviling: 7 carping; 9 quibbling; 10 nitpicking; 12 pettifogging

cavitied: 6 pitted; 9 alveolate, faveolate; 11 honeycombed

cavity: 3 pit; 5 cavum; 6 caries; 10 tooth decay; 12 bodily cavity, dental caries; 13 enclosed space

cavort: 4 lark, romp; 5 frisk, sport; 6 curvet, frolic, gambol, prance; 7 disport, rollick, skylark; 9 lark about, run around

cavum: 6 cavity; 12 bodily cavity

cay: 3 key

cayenne: 8 capsicum, jalapeno; 9 red pepper; 10 long pepper; 11 chili pepper; 12 chili peppers, chilli pepper

cayman: 6 caiman

cayuse: 3 nag; 7 palfrey; 10 Indian pony; 11 saddle horse

cazique: 7 cacique

CB: 8 car radio, ham radio; 10 police band; 11 police radio, two-way radio; 12 amateur radio, citizen's band, handie-talkie, walkie-talkie [military]; 13 airplane radio; 14 short-wave radio

cc: 2 ml; 3 mil; 10 milliliter, millilitre; 15 cubic centimeter, cubic centimetre

CD: 11 compact disc, compact disk

Cd: 7 cadmium

CD-ROM: 11 compact disc; 16 compact disc drive; 25 compact disc read-only memory

Ce: 6 cerium

cease: 3 end; 4 halt, quit, stop; 6 desist, finish, give up, lay off; 9 terminate; 11 discontinue

cease-fire: 5 truce; 9 armistice

ceaseless: 8 constant; 9 incessant, perpetual, unceasing; 11 having no end, never-ending, unremitting; 12 interminable; 13 uninterrupted

ceaselessly: 9 endlessly; 10 unendingly; 11 incessantly, unceasingly; 12 continuously

Cebu maguey: 7 cantala; 12 manila maguey

cecropia: 12 cecropia moth; 18 Hyalophora cecropia

cecum: 6 caecum; 8 blind gut; 10 blind pouch

cedarbird: 12 cedar waxwing; 18 Bombycilla cedrorun

cedar of Lebanon: 12 Cedrus libani

cedar waxwing: 9 cedarbird; 18 Bombycilla cedrorum

cede: 5 grant, yield; 6 give up; 7 concede, deliver; 9 surrender; 10 capitulate; 11 come to terms

cedilla: 5 blaze; 7 hachure

ceding: 7 cession; 8 backdown, giving up; 9 surrender; 11 resignation; 12 capitulating, capitulation, surrendering

Cedrela: 5 cedar; 8 calantas, kalantas; 12 genus Cedrela

Cedrus libani: 12 Cedrus libani; 14 cedar of Lebanon

Cefobid: 12 cefoperazone

cefoperazone: 7 Cefobid

cefotaxime: 8 Claforan

ceftazidime: 6 Fortaz; 7 Tazicef

Ceftin: 7 Zinacef; 10 cefuroxime

ceftriaxone: 8 Rocephin

cefuroxime: 6 Ceftin; 7 Zinacef

Ceiba: 10 genus Ceiba

ceiba tree: 5 kapok; 7 God tree; 11 Bombay

ceiba; **14** Ceiba pentandra, silk-cotton tree; **19** white silk-cotton tree

ceiling: 3 cap

ceiling fixture: 12 ceiling light

celandine: 9 celandine, jewelweed; **10** touch-me-not; **11** swallowwort

Celebes: 8 Sulawesi

celebrant: 10 celebrater, celebrator, worshipper; **11** communicant; **12** congregation

celebrate: 4 fete, keep, mark; **7** lionize, observe; **9** signalize

celebrated: 5 famed, noted; **6** famous; **7** notable, storied; **8** far-famed, immortal, renowned, talked of; **9** historied; **11** illustrious; **13** commemorative

celebration: 9 festivity; **10** dedication; **12** canonization, consecration, enshrinement, enthronement; **13** glorification, solemnization

celebrity: 4 fame, note; **5** eclat, vogue; **6** renown; **7** big name; **9** notoriety; **10** notability, popularity; **12** famous person

celeriac: 10 celery root, knob celery, root celery

celerity: 8 rapidity; **9** fleetness, high speed, quickness, rapidness, swiftness; **10** speediness

celery cabbage: 4 napa; **6** pe-tsai; **13** Chinese celery; **14** Chinese cabbage

celery root: 8 celeriac; **10** knob celery, root celery; **18** turnip-rooted celery; **23** Apium graveolens rapaceum

celestial: 4 holy; **6** sacred; **7** elysian; **8** almighty, beatific, ethereal, hallowed, heavenly, supernal; **9** unearthly; **10** from on high; **12** paradisiacal

celestial bliss: 5 glory

celestial body: 12 heavenly body

Celestial City: 8 Holy City; **9** City of God; **12** Heavenly City

celestial equator: 11 equinoctial; **15** equinoctial line; **17** equinoctial circle

celestial latitude: 3 DEC; **11** declination

celestial longitude: 2 RA; **14** right ascension

celestial sphere: 6 sphere, welkin; **7** heavens; **8** empyrean; **9** firmament

celiac: 7 coeliac

celibacy: 8 chastity; **16** sexual abstention

cell: 4 hole; **5** cadre; **7** battery, cellule, cubicle; **8** jail cell; **9** hermitage; **10** living cell, prison cell; **11** hiding place; **12** electric cell

cellar: 8 basement; **10** root cellar, wine cellar

cellaret: 6 closet, locker; **7** commode, minibar; **8** cupboard; **12** chiffonniere

cellblock: 4 ward

cell membrane: 8 cell wall

cello: 5 cello; **11** violoncello; **12** viola da gamba [It]

cellular: 6 spongy; **10** spongiform

celluloid: 4 film; **6** cinema; **9** synthetic

cellulose nitrate: 9 celluloid; **11** nitrocotton

cell wall: 12 cell membrane

Celosia: 6 red fox; **9** cockscomb; **12** genus Celosia

Celt: 4 Kelt

Celtic: 6 Gaelic; **14** Celtic language

Celtic language: 6 Celtic; **13** Irish language

Celtis: 9 hackberry; **11** genus Celtis

cement: 3 gum; **4** lute; **5** paste; **6** mortar; **8** cementum

cemented: 5 as one; **6** united; **8** agreeing, in accord; **9** congenial, in harmony, of one mind; **10** concordant, harmonious; **11** harmonizing, in agreement

cementing: 9 spackling; **10** plastering

cement mixer: 13 concrete mixer

cementum: 6 cement

cemetery: 9 graveyard; **10** burial site, necropolis; **12** burial ground; **13** burying ground

Cenchrus: 7 sandbur; **8** sandspur; **13** genus Cenchrus

cenobite: 7 eremite; **8** monastic; **9** coenobite

cenogenesis: 11 kenogenesis; **12** caenogenesis, cainogenesis, kainogenesis

cenotaph: 6 shrine; **8** monument

Cenozoic: 3 age; **8** Tertiary; **11** Cenozoic era

Cenozoic era: 8 Cenozoic; **12** Age of Mammals

cense: 7 incense, thurify

censer: 8 thurible

censor: 3 ban; **8** censurer

censorious: 7 carping; **8** captious, critical; **13** hypercritical

censurable: 8 blamable, blameful, culpable; **9** blameable; **11** blameworthy; **13** reprehensible, uncommendable

censure: 5 blame; **6** impugn; **7** fronder [Fr], obloquy; **8** reproach; **9** criminate, criticism, dispraise, exclusion, reprimand, reprobate; **12** depreciation; **13** animadversion, disparagement, pass censure on; **15** excommunication

censured: 9 condemned

census: 4 poll; **6** muster; **8** roll call; **9** nosecount; **10** capitation

cent: 3 fig, jot, pin, rap, sou; **4** mill, rush; **5** penny, straw; **6** button, old son; **7** bulrush, centime, feather; **8** farthing, picayune; **9** halfpenny; **10** peppercorn; **11** Lincoln cent

cental: 3 cwt; **7** centner, quintal; **13** hundredweight

centare: 11 square meter, square metre

Centaur: 9 Centaurus; **10** The Centaur

Centaurea: 14 genus Centaurea

centenary: 7 century, hundred; **8** hecatomb; **10** centennial

centennial: 7 secular; **9** centenary

Centennial State: 8 Colorado

center: 3 eye, nub, sum; **4** core, gist, mall,

meat, pith, pore; **5** focus, heart, plaza, rivet; **6** centre, kernel, marrow, middle, midway; **7** essence, focus on, halfway; **8** center on, midpoint; **9** substance; **10** inwardness; **11** centerfield, concentrate, nerve center, nerve centre, nitty-gritty; **12** revolve about, shopping mall; **13** concentrate on, revolve around; **14** shopping center; **15** geometric center

centerboard: 8 drop keel; **11** centreboard, sliding keel

centered: 7 focused

centerfield: 6 center

center in: 11 center round

centering: 4 snap; **5** focus; **8** focusing

centesimal: 9 hundredth

centigrade: 1 c; **7** celsius

centiliter: 2 cl; **10** centilitre

centime: 4 cent; **5** penny

centimeter: 2 cm; **10** centimetre

centipede: 9 millipede

centner: 3 cwt; **6** cental; **7** quintal; **13** doppelzentner, hundredweight

central: 3 key; **6** primal; **8** cardinal, exchange; **11** fundamental

central body: 10 centrosome

central heating: 7 gas heat; **8** heat pump; **9** steam heat; **12** electric heat, forced hot air, hot water heat

Central Intelligence Agency: 3 CIA

centralize: 4 fuse; **5** blend, merge, unite; **6** absorb, embody; **7** blend in, combine, conjoin; **8** coalesce, dissolve; **10** amalgamate, impregnate; **11** concentrate, consolidate, incorporate, melt into one; **13** blend together, render central

central nervous system: 3 CNS

central office: 10 home office, main office; **12** headquarters

central processing unit: 3 CPU; **9** mainframe, processor; **16** central processor

Central Standard Time: 3 CST; **11** Central Time

Central Time: 3 CST; **19** Central Standard Time

Centranthus ruber: 11 red valerian

centrarchid: 7 sunfish

Centrarchidae: 19 family Centrarchidae

centred: 1 C; **3** 100; **4** one C; **7** century, focused, hundred; **8** centered; **11** centralized

centrical: 7 central, centric

centrifugal: 5 motor

centrifuge: 9 extractor, separator; **12** centrifugate

centripetal: 7 sensory; **8** unifying; **9** receptive

Centriscidae: 18 family Centriscidae

centrist: 8 moderate; **13** moderationist; **15** middle-of-the-road

centroid: 12 center of mass

Centropristis: 4 bass; **18** genus Centropristis

Centropus: 8 pheasant; **14** genus Centropus

centrosome: 11 central body

century: 1 C; **7** centred, hundred; **8** hecatomb; **9** centenary

century plant: 5 agave; **12** American aloe

CEO: 21 chief executive officer

cephalalgia: 8 headache

cephalaspid: 12 osteostracan

cephalexin: 6 Keflex, Keftab

cephalic index: 12 breadth index, cranial index

cephalosporin: 7 Mefoxin

Cephalotaxaceae: 13 plum-yew family; **21** family Cephalotaxaceae

Cepphus: 9 guillemot; **12** genus Cepphus

ceramic: 7 pottery, vitrics; **8** ceramics; **9** porcelain; **11** earthenware

ceramicist: 6 potter; **8** ceramist

ceramic ware: 7 pottery; **11** earthenware

ceramist: 6 potter; **10** ceramicist

cerastes: 9 horned asp, sand viper; **11** horned viper; **16** Cerastes cornutus

Cerastium: 8 mouse-ear; **14** genus Cerastium

cerate: 6 lotion; **8** lenitive, ointment

ceratin: 7 keratin

Ceratitis: 14 genus Ceratitis

Ceratitis capitata: 6 medfly; **21** Mediterranean fruit fly

Ceratonia: 14 genus Ceratonia

Ceratonia siliqua: 5 carob; **9** algarroba, carob tree

Ceratopetalum: 18 genus Ceratopetalum

Ceratopetalum gummiferum: 13 Christmas bush, Christmas tree

ceratopsian: 14 horned dinosaur

ceratosaur: 12 ceratosaurus

Ceratotherium: 10 rhinoceros; **18** genus Ceratotherium

cerberus: 6 beadle, warder; **7** doorman [male]; **8** portress [female]; **10** doorkeeper

Cercis: 6 redbud; **11** genus Cercis

Cercopithecus: 6 grivet, vervet; **8** talapoin; **11** green monkey; **12** vervet monkey; **18** genus Cercopithecus

cereal: 5 grain, grist; **9** food grain; **11** cereal grass

cerebral: 12 intellectual

cerebral cortex: 6 cortex; **7** pallium; **14** cerebral mantle

cerebral death: 10 brain death

cerebral mantle: 6 cortex; **7** pallium; **14** cerebral cortex

cerebrate: 5 think; **8** cogitate

cerebration: 7 thought; **8** thinking; **9** mentation; **12** intellection

cerecloth: 6 shroud; **12** winding sheet

cerement: 3 wax; **4** pall; **6** shroud; **12** winding-sheet; **14** winding-clothes

ceremonial: 4 rite; 6 ritual, solemn; 8 ceremony; 10 observance; 11 ceremonious

ceremonious: 6 ritual; 8 decorous, honoring; 9 cap in hand, esteeming; 10 bareheaded, ceremonial, obsequious, respectful, respecting; 11 deferential, on one's knees, reverential; 12 conventional

ceremony: 4 rite; 6 ritual; 10 ceremonial, observance; 18 ceremonial occasion

ceriman: 8 monstera; 17 Monstera deliciosa

cerise: 3 red; 4 ruby; 5 ruddy; 6 cherry; 7 carmine, crimson, reddish, ruby-red, scarlet; 8 blood-red; 9 cherry-red

cerium: 2 Ce

cernuous: 7 nodding; 8 drooping; 9 pendulous

cero: 7 cavalla, pintado; 8 kingfish; 12 king mackerel

cerotic acid: 16 hexacosanoic acid

cerrado: 5 finis; 6 closed

cerripede: 8 barnacle, cerriped

certain: 4 sure; 5 party; 6 proper, sealed, secure; 7 assured, partial, private, several, special; 8 cocksure, definite, especial, original, peculiar, positive, specific; 9 confident, convinced, exclusive, satisfied; 10 individual, particular, respective; 11 appropriate, determinate; 12 unhesitating; 14 characteristic

certainly: 4 sure; 5 truly; 6 indeed, surely, you bet; 7 exactly, for sure, no doubt; 9 doubtless, precisely; 10 ex concesso [Lat], for certain, sure enough; 11 that's just it; 12 and no mistake; 14 sure as shooting

certes: 4 sure; 5 truly; 6 indeed, surely, you bet; 7 exactly, no doubt; 9 certainly, doubtless, precisely; 10 ex concesso [Lat], for certain; 11 that's just it; 12 and no mistake

Certhia: 7 creeper; 12 genus Certhia

certificate: 6 docket; 7 voucher, warrant; 8 security; 10 credential; 11 credentials; 12 verification; 13 certification; 14 authentication

certificated: 10 documented; 12 credentialed

certificate of deposit: 2 CD [acron]

certification: 6 docket; 7 voucher, warrant; 10 credential; 11 certificate, credentials; 13 corroboration, documentation; 14 authentication; 15 enfranchisement

certified public accountant: 3 CPA [acron]

certify: 4 avow, seal, sign; 5 vouch; 6 assure, attest, avouch; 7 endorse, licence, license, warrant; 8 evidence, manifest; 10 asseverate; 11 demonstrate, sign and seal

certitude: 6 surety; 9 assurance, certainty; 10 conviction, firm belief; 12 cocksureness, positiveness; 14 overconfidence

cerulean: 5 azure; 7 sky-blue, sky-dyed; 8 lazuline, sapphire; 10 bright blue, sky-colored

cerumen: 6 earwax

cerussite: 12 white lead ore

Cervantes: 17 Miguel de Cervantes

cervical smear: 8 Pap smear

cervid: 4 deer

Cervidae: 14 family Cervidae

cervix: 4 neck; 13 uterine cervix

Cervus: 4 sika; 6 wapiti; 7 red deer; 11 American elk; 11 genus Cervus; 12 Japanese deer

Cervus unicolor: 6 sambar, sambur

Ceryle: 11 genus Ceryle

Ceryle alcyon: 16 belted kingfisher

cesarean: 8 C-section, cesarian; 9 caesarean, caesarian; 15 cesarean section, cesarian section; 16 caesarean section; 17 abdominal delivery

cesium: 2 Cs; 7 caesium

cess: 3 tax; 4 dues, levy; 6 tariff; 8 cesspool

cessation: 7 halting; 8 stoppage, stopping, surcease; 10 desistance; 14 discontinuance

cession: 6 ceding; 8 backdown, giving up, transfer; 9 assigning, conveying, surrender; 10 alienation, assignment, conveyance; 11 resignation; 12 capitulating, capitulation, surrendering

cesspool: 4 sink, sump; 7 cesspit

cestode: 8 tapeworm

cestus: 4 sash; 5 girth; 6 fascia, fillet, girdle, wreath; 7 baldric, garland; 8 cincture

cetacean: 6 blower; 9 cetaceous; 14 cetacean mammal

cetacean mammal: 6 blower; 8 cetacean

cetaceous: 8 cetacean

Ceylon: 8 Sri Lanka

cf: 3 see; 6 confer; 7 see also

Chablis: 13 white Burgundy

chacma: 12 chacma baboon, Papio ursinus

chador: 4 veil; 5 gauze

chaetognath: 9 arrowworm

chafe: 3 rub; 4 bite, fray, fret, fume, gall, gnaw, huff, hurt, pain, rasp, rile; 5 gripe, pique, sting, wince; 6 mantle, nettle, ruffle; 7 bear ill, provoke, scratch; 8 irritate, vexation; 9 annoyance; 10 discompose; 13 champ at the bit

chaff: 3 kid; 4 drug, husk, joke, quiz, rout, twit; 5 froth, horde, irony, jolly, roast, shuck, smoke, stalk, straw, tease; 6 banter, bubble, cobweb; 7 stubble; 8 badinage, canaille, raillery; 10 persiflage

chafing: 6 aching, biting; 7 gnawing, hurting; 8 fretting, repining, smarting, stinging

chagrin: 4 stew; 5 abase; 6 humble; 7 mortify; 8 vexation; 9 esclandre [Fr], humiliate; 11 humiliation; 13 mortification

chagrined: 5 cut up; 7 abashed; 9 horrified; 11 embarrassed

chain: 3 guy; 4 band, iron, knot, line, link,

wire; **5** braid, cable, cross, irons, range, round, suite, train; **6** chains, picket, strand, string, wreath; **7** painter; **8** moorings; **10** cat's cradle, chatelaine; **11** progression

chain armor: **4** mail; **8** ring mail; **9** chain mail, ring armor; **10** coat of mail, ring armour; **11** chain armour

chain gang: **8** road gang

chainlike: **10** catenulate

chain-link fence: **12** Cyclone fence; **13** stockade fence

chain mail: **4** mail; **8** ring mail; **9** ring armor; **10** chain armor, coat of mail, ring armour; **11** chain armour

chain pickerel: **9** chain pike, Esox niger

chain reactor: **4** pile; **10** atomic pile; **13** atomic reactor

chains: **4** iron; **5** chain, irons

chair: **4** lead; **6** induct, invest; **7** hot seat, install, preside, swear in; **8** chairman, moderate; **9** portfolio, president; **10** chairwoman, death chair, inaugurate; **11** chairperson; **13** electric chair, professorship

chair car: **9** palace car, parlor car; **10** parlour car

chairperson: **5** chair; **8** chairman; **9** president; **10** chairwoman

chaise: **6** daybed; **9** ambulance; **12** chaise longue, chaise lounge

chalcanthite: **9** blue stone; **11** blue vitriol; **12** blue copperas

chalcedony: **5** agate, flint; **9** calcedony; **10** heliotrope

chalcid: **10** chalcid fly; **11** chalcid wasp

chalcocite: **12** copper glance

chalcography: **9** engraving

chalet: **3** cot, hut; **4** shed; **5** booth, cabin, croft, hovel, stall; **6** dugout [U.S.], shanty

chalice: **3** cup; **6** goblet

chalk: **4** dash; **5** trace

chalkboard: **10** blackboard

chalkiness: **9** milkiness

chalk line: **8** snapline

chalk up: **5** run up, tally

chalky: **6** candid; **10** calcareous

challah: **6** hallah

challenge: **4** cite; **5** libel; **7** call out, dispute, gainsay; **8** citation, question; **11** arraignment, examination; **13** take exception; **16** cross-examination

challenger: **5** rival; **9** contender; **10** competitor; **11** competition

challenging: **6** daring; **7** defying; **8** defiance; **9** ambitious; **10** intriguing

Chamaecyparis: **5** cedar; **7** cypress; **18** genus Chamaecyparis

Chamaeleo: **14** genus Chamaeleo; **15** genus Chamaeleon

chamaeleon: **9** chameleon

Chamaemelum nobilis: **8** camomile; **9** chamomile

chamber: **4** room; **5** bench, board, house, staff; **7** bedroom, cabinet; **10** bedchamber; **11** compartment; **12** sleeping room

chambered nautilus: **8** nautilus; **14** pearly nautilus

chamberlain: **9** seneschal

chamber maid: **9** house maid; **10** parlor maid; **11** waiting maid; **14** femme de chambre [Fr]

chamberpot: **5** potty; **10** thunder mug

chambers: **6** bureau, office

chameleon: **10** chamaeleon

chamfer: **5** bevel, chase; **6** furrow; **7** fluting

chamfron: **8** chanfron, testiere; **10** frontstall

chamois: **6** chammy, shammy; **13** chammy leather, shammy leather; **14** chamois leather; **18** Rupicapra rupicapra

chamomile: **8** camomile; **15** Anthemis nobilis; **18** Chamaemelum nobilis

champ: **4** bite, chew, gnaw; **5** chomp, munch; **6** crunch, mumble, victor, winner; **7** munch on; **8** champion; **9** masticate; **11** prizewinner, title-holder

champ at the bit: **5** chafe, wince; **7** bear ill

champagne: **6** bubbly [informal]

champagne flute: **5** flute; **10** flute glass

champaign: **5** field, plain

champion: **4** hero; **5** champ; **6** backer, defend, friend; **7** abettor, admirer, booster, fighter, paladin; **8** advocate, partisan, seconder, upholder; **9** bodyguard, supporter; **11** protagonist, title-holder; **12** prizewinning

championship: **5** favor, title; **7** backing; **8** interest; **9** patronage; **11** countenance

champleve: **9** cloisonne

chance: **3** hap, hit; **4** bump, find, luck, risk; **6** casual, gamble, happen, hazard, turn up; **7** fortune; **8** run a risk, uncaused; **9** adventure, causeless, encounter; **10** accidental, contingent, fortuitous, incidental; **11** opportunity, probability, take a chance, take chances; **12** adventitious, undetermined, unknown cause; **13** indeterminacy, indeterminate; **14** fortuitousness

chancel: **4** bema; **6** shrine; **8** sacristy; **9** sanctuary

chancellor: **7** prefect, premier; **13** prime minister

Chancellor of the Exchequer: **17** minister of finance

chance occurrence: **8** accident, fortuity; **11** chance event; **12** happenchance, happenstance; **16** random occurrence

chance on: **6** strike; **8** come upon, discover; **9** light upon; **10** chance upon, come across, happen upon

chancery suit: **11** federal case

chances: **8** prospect; **9** prospects [pl]

chancy: **4** iffy; **5** dicey, dodgy, fluky, risky;

6 flukey; 9 chanceful; 11 speculative; 13 unforeseeable, unpredictable

chandelier: 6 luster, sconce; 7 pendant

chandler: 6 dealer, monger, trader; 8 merchant, salesman; 11 salesperson

change: 3 rap; 4 hall, mite, vary; 5 alter, shift, waver; 6 deepen, mutate, switch; 7 commute, convert, flicker, variety; 8 changing, exchange, flounder, modulate, mutation, transfer; 9 fluctuate, guildhall, petty cash, small coin, variation; 10 alteration; 11 interchange, pocket money, small change; 12 modification

change bureau: 11 money broker; 12 money changer

change course: 3 jib; 4 gybe, jibe

changed: 6 varied; 7 altered; 8 modified

changefulness: 11 inconstancy

change hands: 4 swap; 5 bandy; 6 switch

changeless: 6 steady; 8 constant; 9 immutable, invariant, unvarying; 11 unalterable

change of citizenship: 14 naturalization

change of intention: 8 reversal; 9 about-face, volte-face [Fr]; 12 change of mind

change of life: 9 menopause

change of mind: 8 flip-flop, reversal; 9 about-face, turnabout, volte-face [Fr]; 10 turnaround; 14 change of belief; 15 change of opinion, change of purpose; 16 changing one's mind

change-of-pace: 8 change-up; 13 off-speed pitch; 16 change-of-pace ball

changer: 11 auto-changer; 13 record changer

change sides: 3 rat; 6 defect, desert, go over; 10 apostatize

change-up: 12 change-of-pace; 13 off-speed pitch

changing: 6 change; 7 varying; 9 trembling; 10 alteration, flittering, fluttering; 11 fluctuating, vacillating; 12 ever-changing

changing sides: 9 defection, desertion, going over; 10 withdrawal; 14 switching sides, tergiversation

channel: 4 duct, line; 5 canal, carry, sound; 6 avenue, convey, source, strait; 7 conduct, conduit, narrows, passage; 8 approach, canalize, transfer, transmit; 9 transport

channel bass: 7 red drum, redfish

chant: 4 hymn, sing; 5 carol, chirp, motet; 6 anthem, chaunt, intone, warble; 7 chirrup; 8 intonate, response; 9 plain song; 10 cantillate

chant du cygne: 7 last act; 8 swan song [metaphorical]

chanter: 10 melody pipe

chantey: 6 chanty, shanty; 10 sea chantey

chanticleer: 7 rooster

chantlike: 7 intoned; 8 singsong

chantry: 4 kirk; 6 chapel, church; 7 oratory;

8 basilica; 9 cathedral; 10 tabernacle; 11 conventicle; 12 meetinghouse

chanty: 6 shanty; 7 chantey; 10 sea chantey

Chanukah: 7 Hanukah; 8 Hanukkah; 9 Chanukkah; 13 Feast of Lights; 16 Festival of Lights

chaos: 6 bedlam; 11 pandemonium; 13 topsy-turvydom; 14 topsy-turvyness

chaotic: 7 riotous; 8 agitated; 9 in turmoil, turbulent; 10 disordered, disorderly, tumultuous; 13 helter-skelter

chap: 3 elf, lad; 4 beau, cuss, gent, rift; 5 blade, cleft, crack, fella, swain; 6 cranny, fellow, gaffer, yeoman; 7 crevice, fissure, good man; 8 blighter

chaparajos: 5 chaps; 6 brogan; 7 arctics

chaparral: 4 bush; 5 scrub

chapati: 5 bread; 8 chapatti

chapeau: 3 hat, lid

chapel: 4 kirk; 6 church; 7 oratory; 8 basilica; 9 cathedral; 10 tabernacle; 11 conventicle; 12 meetinghouse

chaperon: 6 duenna [Sp]; 9 chaperone, custodian, preserver; 11 third person

chapfallen: 8 deflated; 11 crestfallen

chapiter: 3 cap; 7 capital

chaplet: 3 lei; 4 bays, posy; 5 crown, snood; 6 corona, flower, wreath; 7 bouquet, coronal, coronet, festoon, garland, nosegay

chapman: 6 trader; 7 peddler, higgler, merchant

chapped: 7 cracked; 9 roughened

chaps: 4 jaws; 5 chops; 6 fauces

chapter: 4 head; 5 count, synod, title, verse; 6 clause, vestry; 7 heading, section; 8 conclave; 9 paragraph, syndicate; 10 consistory; 11 convocation

chapter and verse: 3 sic; 9 literally, literatim [Lat]; 11 to the letter, word for word

char: 4 coal; 5 woman, trout; 6 scorch; 7 blacken, calcine, corrode; 9 charwoman; 10 incinerate; 12 cleaning lady; 13 cleaning woman

charabanc: 3 bus; 5 coach; 6 jitney; 7 autobus, omnibus; 8 motorbus; 10 motorcoach; 12 double-decker

characin: 8 characid; 12 characin fish

character: 3 fit, set; 4 case, mold, part, role, type; 5 fiber, fibre, kanji [Jap], mould, stamp, trait; 6 letter, manner, nature, rubric, spirit; 7 essence, persona, quality; 8 grapheme, identity, nonesuch, noumenon, original, personae [pl], quiddity; 9 eccentric, human type, lineament, qualities [pl], reference; 10 complexion, human trait, stereotype; 11 description, designation, nondescript, predicament; 12 denomination, inmost nature, inner reality, quintessence, type of person; 13 graphic symbol; 14 character trait, theatrical role, vital principle

character flaw: 4 flaw; 5 fault; 14 character fault

characteristic: 5 party, trait; 6 aspect, proper; 7 certain, feature, partial, private, quality, several, special, typical; 8 definite, especial, original, peculiar, property, specific; 9 attribute, exclusive, typifying; 10 diagnostic, individual, particular, respective; 11 appropriate, determinate, symptomatic

characterize: 6 define, depict; 7 qualify, specify; 13 particularize

characterized: 4 cast; 6 formed, molded; 8 affected, depicted

characterless: 11 nondescript

character trait: 5 trait; 9 character, qualities [pl]; 10 human trait

charade: 5 rebus, spoof; 6 enigma, parody, puzzle, riddle, sendup; 7 lampoon, mockery, takeoff; 8 travesty; 9 burlesque, conundrum; 10 nut to crack, pasquinade

Charadrii: 17 suborder Charadrii

Charadriidae: 18 family Charadriidae

Charadriiformes: 20 order Charadriiformes

Charadrius: 6 dotrel, plover; 7 kildeer; 8 killdeer, dotterel; 15 genus Charadrius

charcoal: 6 fusain; 8 wood coal; 10 oxford gray, oxford grey; 12 charcoal gray, charcoal grey, charcoal-gray, charcoal grey

chard: 8 leaf beet; 10 chard plant, Swiss chard; 11 spinach beet

Chardonnay: 15 chardonnay grape

charge: 3 ask, bid, tax; 4 bang, bill, buck, call, care, cost, file, fill, keep, kick, load, rush, send, task, tear, ward; 5 blame, exact, flush, level, lodge, onset, point, price, rouse, shoot; 6 accuse, amount, assign, brevet, burden, commit, demand, enjoin, errand, excite, figure, impugn, impute, saddle, thrill; 7 agitate, appoint, arraign, bearing, billing, burster, commove, consign, control, custody, enforce, entrust, expense, impeach, intrust, mission, require; 8 bear down, call upon, cathexis, charge up, delegate, instruct, managing, tutelage; 9 complaint, direction, directive, exequatur [Lat], onslaught, prime cost, shoot down; 10 accusation, assignment, commission, engagement, government, imputation, injunction, management; 11 controlling, impeachment, instruction, safekeeping, supervising, supervision; 12 assigned duty, guardianship

charge card: 8 bank card; 10 credit card

charged: 6 bidden; 7 accused, aerated; 9 impeached; 10 called upon; 11 imposed upon

charge d'affaires: 6 legate, nuncio; 7 attache

charge per unit: 4 rate

charger: 5 racer; 6 hunter; 7 courser; 8 destrier, war horse; 10 blood horse

charging: 8 accusing; 10 impeaching

chariness: 7 caution; 8 wariness

charioteer: 13 chariot driver

charisma: 8 charisma; 14 personal appeal; 17 personal magnetism

charitable: 4 free; 6 giving, kindly; 7 liberal; 8 generous, handsome, princely; 9 bounteous, bountiful, unselfish; 10 free handed, full handed, munificent, openhanded

charitableness: 7 charity; 8 humanity, kindness; 9 benignity, humanness; 10 goodliness, kindliness; 12 graciousness; 13 brotherly love; 14 loving-kindness; 15 kind-heartedness

charity: 4 ruth; 6 bounty; 8 humanity, kindness; 9 benignity, humanness; 10 generosity, goodliness, kindliness, liberality; 11 munificence; 12 graciousness, Jacob's ladder; 13 bounteousness, bountifulness, brotherly love, Greek valerian, long-suffering, public charity; 14 charitableness, loving-kindness; 15 kind-heartedness

charity case: 11 welfare case

charivari: 6 fracas, hubbub, quaver, racket, uproar; 7 belling, clutter; 8 chivaree, shivaree; 10 callathump, callithump

charlatan: 5 quack; 9 trumpeter; 10 mountebank; 11 jack-pudding

Charles the Great: 11 Charlemagne

Charleston: 21 capital of West Virginia

charlock: 8 chadlock; 11 wild mustard; 12 field mustard

charm: 4 coax, lure; 5 catch, spell, style, tempt; 6 amulet, appeal, attach, enamor, endear, please, seduce, trance; 7 amenity, attract, becharm, beguile, bewitch, capture, delight, enamour, enchant, philter, wheedle; 8 entrance, talisman, witchery; 9 captivate, carry away, enrapture, fascinate, influence, seduction; 10 amiability, conciliate, magic spell; 11 enchantment, fascination, put a spell on, turn the head, winning ways; 12 give pleasure, je ne sais quoi [Fr]

charmed: 7 pleased; 8 beguiled; 9 delighted, enchanted, entranced; 10 captivated, enthralled

charmer: 7 smoothy; 8 smoothie; 11 sweet talker

charming: 5 magic; 6 wizard; 7 magical; 8 engaging, witching, wizardly; 9 sorcerous; 10 bewitching, enchanting; 11 captivating, fascinating, interesting; 13 prepossessing

charnel: 7 ghastly; 10 sepulchral; 12 charnel house

charnel house: 7 charnel; 9 bone house, dead house

chart: 3 map; 4 plan, plot; 6 figure, scheme; 7 drawing, graphic; 9 flow chart, schematic

charter: 4 hire, rent, take; 5 grant, lease; 6 engage, patent; 7 empower; 8 sanction, warranty; **9** authority, privilege; **11** enfranchise

chartered: 5 hired; **6** leased, patent, vested; **8** ordained; **9** legalized; **10** prescribed; **12** enfranchised; **14** constitutional

chartless: 8 unmapped; **9** uncharted

chartreuse: 8 pea green; **10** Paris green; **11** yellow green

charwoman: 4 char; **5** woman; **10** journeyman; **12** cleaning lady; **13** cleaning woman

chary: 4 cagy; **5** cagey, shy of, spare; **6** frugal, saving; **7** careful, politic, prudent, sparing, thrifty; **8** discreet, stealthy; **10** economical; **11** circumspect

chase: 3 dog, tag; **4** fret, race, tail; **5** track, trail; **6** dispel, emboss, furrow; **7** chamfer, go after, pursuit; **8** emblazon; **9** following

chase away: 6 dispel, run off; **8** drive off, drive out, turn back; **9** drive away

chaser: 6 carver; **7** modeler, pursuer; **8** sculptor, statuary

chasm: 5 abysm, abyss; **11** yawning gulf

chasse: 6 sashay

chassepot: 9 needle gun

chasseur: 4 peon; **6** hunter, zouave [Fr]; **7** huntsman, footman, private, trooper; **8** rifleman; **9** legionary, minutemen, musketeer, subaltern; **10** skirmisher; **11** legionnaire, rank and file; **12** cannon fodder, sharpshooter

chassis: 3 bod; **4** form, soma; **5** build, flesh, frame, shape; **6** figure; **7** anatomy; **8** physique; **9** human body; **12** material body, physical body

chaste: 4 neat, pure; **5** attic, Saxon; **6** severe; **7** classic; **8** virtuous; **9** classical, continent; **10** unaffected

chasten: 4 dull, tame; **5** blunt; **6** subdue, temper; **7** correct, mollify, sheathe; **8** chastise, chastize, moderate; **9** castigate, objurgate

chastened: 7 content, rebuked, subdued; **8** reproved, resigned; **10** admonished; **11** reprimanded

chasteness: 9 restraint; **10** simplicity

chastening: 9 punishing; **10** correction, punishment; **12** chastisement

chastise: 4 lash, trim; **6** blow up; **7** chasten, correct, trounce; **8** chastize, overhaul; **9** castigate, objurgate, reprimand; **11** laver la tete [Fr]

chastisement: 9 punishing; **10** chastening, correction, punishment; **11** castigation

chastity: 6 purity, virtue; **7** undress; **8** celibacy; **14** sexual morality; **16** sexual abstention

chasuble: 5 amice, scarf, stole

chat: 3 jaw; **5** visit; **6** claver, confab, gossip, natter; **7** chaffer, chatter, palaver; **8** causerie, chitchat, idle talk, town talk; **9** small talk, table talk; **11** confabulate, idle

chatter, village talk; **12** New World chat, Old World chat; **13** confabulation; **14** shoot the breeze

chateau: 4 hall; **5** court, folly, tower; **6** castle; **7** rotunda; **8** pavilion; **10** manor-house

chatelaine: 5 chain

chatoyant: 4 shot; **6** pearly; **8** nacreous; **9** prismatic; **10** changeable, iridescent

chattels: 5 goods; **7** effects; **8** movables; **10** personalty; **14** personal estate; **15** personal effects

chatter: 3 jaw, yak; **4** chat, yack; **5** clack, click, prate, prose, visit; **6** cackle, claver, confab, gabble, gibber, gossip, jabber, natter, piffle, tattle; **7** blabber, chaffer, maunder, palaver, prattle, twaddle; **8** chitchat; **9** prattle on, yakety-yak; **10** chattering; **11** confabulate; **12** tittle-tattle

chatterbox: 9 chatterer; **12** stream orchid; **16** giant helleborine; **17** Epipactis gigantea

chattily: 7 volubly

chatty: 4 cosy; **5** gabby, newsy, talky; **7** gossipy; **9** garrulous, talkative; **10** loquacious; **14** conversational

Chaucer: 15 Geoffrey Chaucer

chauffeur: 6 driver; **11** drive around

chaulmugra: 11 chaulmoogra; **15** chaulmoogra tree; **17** Hydnocarpus kurzii; **18** Taraktagenos kurzii, Taraktogenos kurzii

chaunt: 4 hymn, sing; **5** carol, chant, chirp, motet; **6** anthem, intone, warble; **7** chirrup; **8** response; **9** plain song

chaunter: 6 singer; **7** warbler; **8** melodist, songster, vocalist

chauntress: 10 songstress

chautauqua: 14 outdoor lessons

chauvinism: 8 jingoism; **12** antifeminism; **14** male chauvinism; **15** superpatriotism; **16** ultranationalism

chauvinist: 5 jingo; **8** jingoist; **9** flag-waver

chaw: 3 cud, wad; **4** chew, plug, quid

chawbacon: 4 hick, rube; **5** yahoo, yokel; **7** bumpkin, hayseed

cheap: 3 bum, low; **4** loud, mean, punk, vile; **5** flash, gaudy, sorry, tacky, tatty, tinny, weedy; **6** brassy, cheesy, crummy, flashy, garish, meager, scurvy, shabby, shoddy, sleazy, tawdry, trashy; **7** chinchy, chintzy, scrubby; **8** beggarly, gimcrack, trumpery, wretched; **9** low priced, miserable, niggardly, worthless; **10** catchpenny; **11** cheap as dirt, inexpensive; **12** meretricious

cheapen: 7 chaffer, degrade; **8** beat down, huckster

cheap-jack: 4 tout; **6** hawker; **8** huckster

cheaply: 7 tattily; **8** stingily; **9** chintzily; **13** inexpensively

cheapness: 3 tat; **6** sleaze; **7** cut rate, poverty; **8** cut price, low price, low value, meanness, vileness; **9** tackiness; **10** meagerness, paltriness, shabbiness, shoddiness, trashiness; **11** bargain rate, pitifulness; **12** beggarliness, wretchedness; **13** miserableness, worthlessness

cheapskate: 8 tightwad

cheat: 2 do; **3** con, nab; **4** beat, bilk, bite, scam, tare, wile; **5** blind, catch, chess, cozen, feint, fetch, hocus, knave, plant, pluck, reach, rogue, shaft, trick; **6** betray, bubble, chouse, darnel, diddle, euchre, jockey, juggle, rip off, wander; **7** cheat on, cheater, chicane, cuckold, defraud, swindle; **8** cheating, deceiver; **9** sell short, trickster, victimize; **10** take a lover; **12** be unfaithful; **13** bearded darnel, keep a mistress; **14** commit adultery; **15** Bromus secalinus

cheated: 6 bilked; **7** diddled, euchred, plucked; **8** swindled; **9** defrauded; **10** victimized

cheater: 5 cheat; **8** deceiver; **9** trickster

cheating: 4 foul; **5** cheat, dirty; **8** adultery; **9** crim. con. [abbr], two-timing; **10** adulterous, cuckolding, infidelity, unsporting; **11** concubinage; **14** unfaithfulness

cheat on: 5 cheat; **6** betray, wander; **7** cuckold

cheat sheet: 9 crib sheet

check: 3 fit, jaw, let, rag, rod, rub, see, tab; **4** chip, chit, chop, curb, gibe, halt, hold, jibe, line, mark, stay, stop, test; **5** agree, assay, break, chide, chink, crack, cross, debar, draft, hitch, learn, match, scold, tally, train, watch; **6** arrest, assure, berate, billet, bridle, cheque, chew up, ensure, go over, hold in, insure, letter, rebuke, rein in, weaken; **7** balance, bawl out, checker, chequer, chew out, contain, control, counter, draw off, feel out, find out, forfend, lambast, lecture, mark off, prevent, reproof, reverse, see to it, setback [U.S.], slacken, suss out, tick off; **8** check off, check out, checkout, comedown, hold back, lambaste, look into, moderate, palliate, preclude, restrain, restrict, reversal, sound out, stoppage, telltale, turn back; **9** ascertain, bank check, check into, check mark, check over, check up on, condition, constrain, determine, dress down, duplicate, foreclose, have words, reprimand, restraint, turn aside; **10** chessboard, correspond, discipline, screw loose, touchstone; **11** contretemps, nip in the bud, remonstrate; **12** checkerboard, confirmation, grit in the oil, take the pulse, verification; **13** test the waters; **14** substantiation

checked: 6 curbed; **9** checkered, chequered

checker: 5 check; **6** streak, stripe; **7** chequer; **9** variegate

checkerberry: 11 wintergreen

checkers: 8 chequers, draughts; **9** checquers

check girl: 12 hatcheck girl

check in: 6 sign in

checkmate: 4 mate; **5** quell, trump, upset; **7** nonplus, silence; **8** confound; **9** stalemate

check off: 4 mark; **5** check; **7** mark off, tick off

check out: 3 see; **5** check; **6** cheque, go over; **7** feel out, run down, suss out; **8** look into, sound out; **9** check into, check over, check up on; **10** buy the farm; **12** take the pulse; **13** kick the bucket, test the waters

checkrein: 11 bearing rein

check the books: 5 audit; **10** field audit; **14** verify accounts

checkup: 7 medical; **11** health check, medical exam; **14** medical checkup, routine checkup

cheek: 4 face, jowl, wing; **5** brass, nerve; **6** buccal; **7** buttock; **8** boldness; **9** impudence; **10** effrontery; **12** impertinence

cheekbone: 4 mala; **9** jugal bone, malar bone; **13** os zygomaticum, zygomatic bone

cheekily: 7 brashly, nervily

cheekiness: 4 gall; **5** crust; **9** freshness, impudence, insolence; **12** impertinence

cheep: 3 coo; **4** peep, pipe; **5** chirp, trill, tweet, twirp; **6** cuckoo, warble; **7** chirrup, twitter, whistle

cheer: 4 crow, fare, urge; **5** elate, humor, nerve, pep up, rally, shout; **6** assure, buoy up, encore, exhort, gayety, hurrah, solace, urge on; **7** animate, applaud, barrack, cheer up, chirk up, comfort, console, enliven, gladden, hearten, inspire, jollity, jolly up, rejoice, spirits; **8** embolden, inspirit, l'allegro [Fr], reassure, recreate, serenade, sunshine; **9** encourage, geniality, good humor, joviality; **10** exhilarate, jolly along; **11** savoir vivre [Fr]; **12** cheerfulness; **15** raise the spirits

cheerful: 6 upbeat; **9** merriness; **10** blitheness, cheeriness; **12** cheerfulness

cheerio: 3 bye; **5** adieu, adios; **6** bye-bye, good-by, so long; **7** good day, good-bye; **8** au revoir, sayonara; **11** arrivederci; **14** auf wiedersehen

cheerless: 4 dark; **6** dismal, gloomy, somber, triste [Fr]; **7** joyless; **8** dejected, frowning; **9** saturnine; **10** lugubrious, spiritless, uncheerful; **11** comfortless; **12** heavyhearted

cheerlessness: 5 blues, dumps; **7** sadness; **8** darkness, doldrums, the blues, the dumps; **9** dejection, heaviness, tristesse [Fr]; **10** bad spirits, blue devils, depression, dismalness, gloominess, low spirits, melancholy, somberness; **11** joylessness, melancholia; **12** dejectedness, heart sinking, il pensieroso [It], mournfulness; **14** failure of heart, lugubriousness, spiritlessness

cheer up: 5 cheer; **6** bear up; **7** chirk up,

jolly up, light up; **10** brighten up, jolly along

cheese: 10 high mallow, tall mallow; **12** cheeseflower; **15** Malva sylvestris

cheesecake: 5 pin-up

cheeseparing: 4 near; **5** close; **13** penny-pinching

cheese tray: 11 cheeseboard

cheesy: 3 bum; **4** punk; **5** cheap, tinny; **6** crummy, sleazy; **7** chintzy

cheetah: 6 chetah; **15** Acinonyx jubatus

chef d'oeuvre: 2 A1; **4** pick; **5** cream, elite, prime; **6** flower; **8** nonesuch; **9** nonpareil; **11** masterpiece, tour de force; **12** coup de maitre [Fr]; **14** creme de la creme; **16** flower of the flock

chef de cuisine: 4 cook; **10** cordon bleu [Fr], expert chef

Cheilanthes: 4 fern; **16** genus Cheilanthes

Cheiranthus: 10 wall flower; **16** genus Cheiranthus

Chekhov: 6 Chekov; **20** Anton Pavlovich Chekov; **21** Anton Pavlovich Chekhov

chela: 4 claw; **6** nipper, pincer; **10** seminarian

Chelidonium: 9 celandine; **11** swallow wort; **16** genus Chelidonium

Chelonia mydas: 11 green turtle

chelonian: 16 chelonian reptile

Chelydra: 13 genus Chelydra

Chelydra serpentina: 7 snapper; **20** common snapping turtle

chemical: 6 chemic; **8** compound; **9** substance; **12** pure chemical; **16** chemical compound; **17** chemical substance; **19** composition of matter

chemical attraction: 8 affinity

chemical composition: 11 composition; **14** chemical makeup; **18** chemical components

chemical compound: 8 chemical, compound; **9** substance

chemical operations: 15 chemical warfare

chemical process: 14 chemical action, chemical change

chemical substance: 8 chemical, compound; **9** substance; **12** pure chemical; **16** chemical compound; **19** composition of matter

chemin de fer: 8 baccarat

chemise: 4 sack, slip; **5** shift, smock, teddy; **6** shimmy; **7** teddies

chemist: 8 druggist, pharmacy; **9** drug store; **10** apothecary, pharmacist, pill pusher, pill roller

chemist's shop: 8 chemist's, pharmacy; **9** drugstore; **10** dispensary; **15** apothecary's shop

Chen: 12 subgenus Chen

Chen caerulescens: 9 blue goose

chenfish: 8 kingfish; **12** white croaker; **18** Genyonemus lineatus

Chenopodiaceae: 15 goosefoot family; **20** family Chenopodiaceae

Chenopodium: 6 fat hen; **7** pigweed, all-good, sowbane; **8** wormseed; **9** goosefoot; **10** Mexican tea, Spanish tea; **11** wild spinach; **13** lamb's-quarters, good-king-henry; **16** genus Chenopodium

cheque: 5 check, draft; **8** check out; **9** bank check

cherimoya: 10 cherimolla; **13** cherimoya tree; **15** Annona cherimola

cherish: 3 hug, pet; **6** caress, dandle, fondle, foster; **7** care for, cling to; **8** hold dear, treasure

cherished: 6 petted, wanted; **7** fondled; **8** caressed, held dear, precious; **9** treasured

cherishing: 9 caressing, endearing

cherry: 3 red; **4** ruby; **5** ruddy; **6** cerise; **7** carmine, crimson, reddish, ruby-red, scarlet; **8** blood-red; **9** cherry-red; **10** cherry tree

cherrystone: 15 cherrystone clam

cherubic: 5 sweet; **7** angelic; **8** seraphic; **9** angelical

chess piece: 8 chessman

chest: 3 pix, pyx; **6** bureau, casket, coffer, pectus, thorax; **7** caisson, dresser; **9** reliquary

chest cavity: 14 thoracic cavity

chestnut: 3 bay, saw; **6** auburn, dapple, old saw, russet; **7** bromide; **8** cinnamon, nut-brown; **10** old bromide; **12** chestnut tree

chestnut blight: 14 chestnut canker; **19** chestnut-bark disease

chest of drawers: 5 chest; **6** bureau; **7** dresser

chest voice: 9 chest tone; **13** chest register

chesty: 8 arrogant; **10** big-chested; **13** self-important

chetah: 7 cheetah

cheval de bataille: 3 cue; **8** great gun; **13** stalking-horse

cheval-glass: 12 looking-glass

chevre: 10 goat cheese

chevron: 6 stripe; **7** cockade, epaulet, stripes; **13** grade insignia

chew: 3 cud, jaw, wad; **4** bite, chaw, gnaw, plug, quid; **5** champ, munch; **6** crunch, mumble; **7** chewing, munch on; **9** manducate, masticate

chewing out: 6 earful; **9** going-over; **10** bawling out, upbraiding; **11** castigation; **12** dressing down

chewink: 6 towhee; **8** cheewink

chew out: 3 jaw, rag; **5** check, chide, scold; **6** berate, chew up, rebuke; **7** bawl out, lambast, lecture, reproof; **8** lambaste; **9** dress down, have words, reprimand; **11** remonstrate

chew over: 4 mull, muse; **6** ponder; **7** reflect; **8** meditate, mull over, ruminate; **9** speculate, think over; **11** contemplate

chew up: 3 jaw, rag; **5** check, chide, scold; **6** berate, rebuke; **7** bawl out, chew out, lambast, lecture, reproof; **8** lambaste; **9** dress down, have words, reprimand; **11** remonstrate

Cheyenne: 16 capital of Wyoming

chiaroscuro: 9 grisaille [Fr]; **12** clear obscure; **13** black and white, light and shade, pepper and salt

chiasma: 6 chiasm

chic: 3 ton; **4** cool; **5** smart, style, swank, vogue; **6** modish, trendy; **7** fashion, stylish, voguish; **8** chicness; **9** decked out, dressed up, recherche, smartness; **10** endimanche [Fr], modishness; **11** stylishness; **12** all decked out, all dressed up, in Sunday best; **14** en granite tenue [Fr], fashionability

Chicago: 5 stops; **6** boodle; **8** Michigan; **9** Newmarket, Windy City

chicane: 4 bite, carp, wile; **5** blind, catch, cavil, cheat, feint, fetch, hocus, plant, reach, screw, shaft, trick; **6** bubble, chouse, jockey, juggle; **9** chicanery

chicanery: 4 wile; **5** guile; **7** chicane; **8** trickery; **10** shenanigan

chick: 4 bird, dame, doll; **5** biddy, skirt, wench

chicken: 4 wimp; **6** poulet, pullet, yellow; **7** crybaby; **8** nestling, volaille; **11** lily-livered; **12** Gallus gallus, white-livered; **13** yellow-bellied; **14** chickenhearted

chicken cacciatore: 14 hunter's chicken; **17** chicken cacciatora

chicken coop: coop; **7** hencoop; **8** henhouse

chicken feed: 11 small change

chickenhearted: 5 wimpy; **6** yellow; **7** chicken, wimpish; **11** lily-livered, lilyhearted, weak-hearted; **12** fainthearted, white-livered; **13** pigeon-hearted, yellowbellied

chicken out: 6 bow out; **7** back off, pull out; **8** back down

chickenpox: 9 varicella

chicken yard: 7 fowl run, henyard; **10** chicken run

chickpea: 8 garbanzo; **11** Egyptian pea

chickweed: 8 mouse ear

chicle: 9 chicle gum

chicness: 4 chic; **5** swank; **9** smartness; **10** modishness; **11** stylishness

chide: 3 jaw, rag; **5** check, scold; **6** berate, chew up, rebuke; **7** bawl out, chew out, lambast, lecture, reproof; **8** admonish, lambaste; **9** dress down, have words, reprehend, reprimand; **11** remonstrate

chief: 3 top; **4** arch, boss, head, main; **5** prime; **6** gaffer, honcho, top dog; **7** capital,

foreman, leading, primary; **8** foremost; **9** chieftain, principal

chief assistant: 9 man Friday; **12** right-hand man

Chief Executive: 9 President; **26** President of the United States

chief executive officer: 3 CEO; **21** chief operating officer

chiefly: 6 mainly; **7** notably; **8** signally; **9** curiously, in the main, pointedly, primarily, unusually; **10** peculiarly, remarkably, singularly, strikingly, uncommonly; **11** principally; **12** particularly

chieftain: 5 chief; **7** captain, headman; **11** tribal chief

chiffonniere: 6 closet, locker; **7** commode; **8** cellaret, cupboard

chigger: 6 chigoe, jigger, redbug; **10** chigoe flea; **11** harvest mite

chignon: 3 rug; **4** pelt; **5** front; **6** toupee

chigoe: 4 flea; **7** chigger; **10** chigoe flea

child: 3 boy, fry, kid, sop; **4** baby, girl, tike, tyke; **5** bairn [Scot], minor, youth; **6** infant, moppet, nipper, shaver; **7** milksop, tiddler; **8** children [pl], innocent, juvenile, nestling, small fry; **9** little one, youngster; **10** little girl

child's play: 4 play, snap; **5** cinch; **6** picnic; **8** duck soup, pushover, walkover; **11** kinderspiel, piece of cake

childbed: 5 labor; **6** labour; **7** lying-in, travail; **11** confinement, parturiency

childbirth: 5 labor; **7** travail; **8** delivery; **10** birth-throe; **11** confinement, parturition; **12** accouchement, childbearing, vaginal birth

childhood: 7 boyhood; **8** girlhood; **9** puerility

childhood friend: 8 playmate; **10** playfellow

childish: 4 soft; **5** green, silly; **6** simple, stupid; **7** babyish, puerile; **8** juvenile; **9** childlike, infantile

childishness: 9 puerility

childless: 6 barren

childlike: 6 simple; **7** babyish, childly; **8** childish; **9** dewey-eyed, infantile

child molester: 8 pederast; **9** paederast, pedophile

child prodigy: 10 wunderkind

child psychology: 23 developmental psychology

children: 3 kid; **5** bairn [Scot], child, youth; **6** moppet; **8** juvenile, small fry; **9** little one, youngster

chili: 5 chile; **6** chilli, chilly; **11** chili pepper; **13** chili con carne

chiliad: 1 G, K, M; **4** 1000, thou, yard; **5** grand; **8** thousand; **11** one thousand

chili pepper: 5 chile, chili; **6** chilli, chilly; **7** cayenne; **8** jalapeno; **10** long pepper;

12 chilli pepper; **13** cayenne pepper; **20** Capsicum annuum longum

chill: 4 calm, cool, damp, pall; **5** blunt, quiet; **6** chilly, quench, quiver, shiver, thrill, tingle; **7** frisson, iciness, shudder; **8** cool down, gelidity; **9** shivering

chilled: 4 cold, iced; **7** ice-cold; **9** shivering

chilling: 5 scary; **6** scarey; **7** cooling, shivery; **8** shuddery

chill out: 4 calm; **6** cool it; **7** cool off; **8** calm down; **10** settle down, simmer down

chills and fever: 4 ague

chime: 4 bell, gong, peal, toll; **9** harmonize; **12** be harmonious

chime in: 5 cut in, put in; **6** butt in; **7** barge in, break in

chime in with: 6 go with; **8** side with; **9** tally with; **10** comply with, fall in with; **11** close in with, comport with, consort with, go along with; **12** quadrate with, strike in with; **14** sympathize with

chimera: 5 dream; **6** maggot, shadow, vision; **7** conceit, figment; **8** chimaera; **23** figment of the imagination

Chimera: 8 Chimaera

chimes: 4 echo; **7** refrain; **8** repetend

chimney: 4 flue; **5** shaft; **11** lamp chimney

chimney corner: 9 ingle side, inglenook

chimneypiece: 6 mantel, mantle; **11** mantelpiece, mantlepiece

chimneysweep: 5 sweep; **14** chimneysweeper

chimpanzee: 5 chimp; **14** Pan troglodytes

chin: 6 chin up, mentum

China: 3 PRC; **6** Taiwan; **7** Formosa; **8** Red China; **13** mainland China; **14** Communist China; **15** Republic of China; **16** Nationalist China; **22** People's Republic of China

china: 9 chinaware, porcelain

chinaberry: 9 azedarach, azederach, China tree; **10** jaboncillo; **12** false dogwood, Persian lilac

china cabinet: 11 china closet

china clay: 6 kaolin; **7** kaoline; **9** terra alba; **10** china stone; **13** porcelain clay

china closet: 12 china cabinet

china stone: 6 kaolin; **7** kaoline; **9** china clay, terra alba; **13** porcelain clay

chinch: 3 bug; **4** flea; **5** louse; **6** bedbug, vermin; **9** chinch bug

chinchilla rat: 8 abrocome; **13** rat chinchilla

Chinchillidae: 19 family Chinchillidae

chine: 5 spine; **8** backbone; **12** dorsal region, lumbar region

Chinese black mushroom: 8 shiitake; **14** Lentinus edodes; **16** shiitake

Chinese cabbage: 4 napa; **6** pe-tsai; **13** celery cabbage, Chinese celery; **22** Brassica rapa pekinensis

Chinese cinnamon: 10 cassia bark

Chinese date: 6 jujube

Chinese gooseberry: 4 kiwi; **8** kiwi vine; **9** kiwi fruit; **18** Actinidia chinensis, Actinidia deliciosa

Chinese lacquer tree: 11 lacquer tree, varnish tree; **13** Japanese sumac

chinese mustard: 7 gai choi

Chinese parsley: 8 cilantro; **9** coriander

Chinese silk plant: 5 ramee, ramie; **10** China grass; **14** Boehmeria nivea

Chinese Wall: 16 Great Wall of China

Chinese white cabbage: 7 bok choi, bok choy, pakchoi

Chinese wood oil: 7 tung oil

Chingpo: 7 Jinghpo; **8** Jinghpaw

chinked: 9 stopped-up

chin music: 5 prate; **7** blether, prattle; **8** idle talk

chino: 10 chino cloth

chinook: 5 foehn; **6** barber [Can]; **7** norther; **8** blizzard; **9** snow eater; **10** king salmon; **11** chinook wind; **13** chinook salmon, quinnat salmon

chinquapin: 8 chestnut; **9** chincapin, chinkapin

chintzily: 7 cheaply; **8** stingily

chintzy: 3 bum; **4** punk; **5** cheap, tinny; **6** cheesy, crummy, sleazy; **7** chinchy

chin-wag: 3 gab; **4** chat; **6** gossip; **7** gabfest; **8** causerie, chitchat; **9** small talk; **11** chinwagging; **12** tittle-tattle, conversation

chip: 3 bit; **4** chop, knap, nick, snap, tear; **5** break, burst, check, chunk, crack, crisp, flake, fleck, scrap, shard, tally; **6** billet, cut off, letter; **7** chip off, come off, counter, cow chip, whittle; **8** break off, chip shot, chipping, fragment; **9** break away, duplicate, microchip, poker chip; **10** potato chip; **11** buffalo chip, silicon chip, splintering; **12** Saratoga chip

chipboard: 9 hardboard

chip in: 4 give; **6** kick in; **10** contribute

chip off the old block: 8 alter ego

chipper: 5 bully; **6** breezy, jaunty; **8** debonair; **9** debonaire

Chippewa: 6 Ojibwa; **7** Ojibway; **13** Chippewa tribe

Chippewyan: 9 Chipewyan; **11** Chippewaian

chipping: 4 chip; **5** chunk, shard; **8** fragment; **11** splintering

chirk up: 5 cheer; **7** cheer up

chirography: 11 handwriting

chiromancer: 7 palmist

chiromancy: 9 palmistry

chiropodist: 10 foot doctor, podiatrist

chiropody: 8 podiatry

chiropractor: 7 bone man; **10** bone doctor, bonesetter

chiropteran: 3 bat

chirp: 3 coo; **4** pipe, sing; **5** carol, chant, cheep, trill, tweet, twirp; **6** chaunt, cuckoo, intone, perk up, warble; **7** chirrup, tweedle, twitter, whistle; **9** take heart; **12** cast away care

chirpy: 5 perky; **7** buoyant

chirrup: 3 coo; **4** lilt, pipe, sing; **5** carol, chant, cheep, chirp, trill, tweet, twirp; **6** chaunt, cuckoo, intone, warble; **7** twitter, whistle

chirurgery: 7 surgery; **9** operation; **17** surgical operation

chirurgical: 5 tonic; **8** balsamic, paregoric; **11** corroborant, therapeutic

chirurgy: 7 surgery; **9** operation; **10** chirurgery [Med]; **17** surgical operation

chisel: 3 cut, hew; **5** carve, probe, rimer, scoop; **6** dibble, gimlet, lancet, sculpt, trepan, trocar [Med], warder; **7** terrier; **9** sculpture

chiseled: 4 hewn; **6** carved; **8** sculpted; **10** sculptured; **11** well-defined

chiseler: 6 gouger, sharpy; **7** sharper, sharpie; **8** swindler; **9** chiseller

Chisinau: 8 Kishinev; **16** capital of Moldova

chit: 3 tab; **4** brat; **5** child, check; **6** urchin; **11** spoiled brat; **14** enfant terrible [Fr]

chitchat: 3 gab, jaw; **4** chat; **5** visit; **6** claver, confab, gossip, natter; **7** chaffer, chatter, chin-wag, gabfest; **8** causerie, idle talk, town talk; **9** small talk, table talk; **11** chin-wagging, confabulate, idle chatter

chitlings: 8 chitlins; **12** chitterlings

chitlins: 9 chitlings; **12** chitterlings

chiton: 7 mollusk; **9** sea cradle

chitterlings: 8 chitlins; **9** chitlings

chitty: 4 chit

chivalric: 8 knightly, medieval

chivalrous: 6 heroic; **7** dashing, gallant, sublime; **8** knightly

chivalry: 7 heroism, prowess; **9** gallantry, politesse; **13** knight service

chivaree: 7 belling; **8** shivaree; **9** charivari; **10** callathump, callithump

chive: 4 cive; **6** chives [pl]; **12** schnittlaugh

chivy: 5 beset, chevy, harry; **6** chevvy, chivvy, harass, hassle, molest, plague; **7** provoke

chlordiazepoxide: 7 Librium

chloride of lime: 15 bleaching powder

chlorine: 2 Cl

chlorofluorocarbon: 3 CFC

chlorophyte: 10 green algae

chlorosis: 13 greensickness

chlorothiazide: 6 Diuril

chlorotic: 6 infirm, morbid, sickly

Chloroxylon: 9 satinwood; **16** genus Chloroxylon

chlorpheniramine maleate: 9 Coricidin

chlorpromazine: 9 Thorazine

chlortetracycline: 10 Aureomycin

choanocyte: 10 collar cell

chock: 5 wedge

chock-full: 8 chockful, cram full; **9** chokefull, chuck-full; **11** chockablock

chocolate: 3 tan; **4** fawn, foxy; **5** cocoa, tawny, umber; **6** coffee, maroon; **9** deep brown; **10** burnt umber; **11** fawn-colored; **12** hot chocolate, snuff-colored

chocolate tree: 5 cacao; **9** cacao tree; **14** Theobroma cacao

Choctow: 12 Choctow tribe

Choeronycteris mexicana: 10 hognose bat

choice: 4 fine, mind, pick, wish; **5** bully, elect, prime, prize; **6** option, picked, select; **7** choices [pl], quality; **8** adoption, choosing, decision, election, pleasure; **9** recherche, selection; **11** alternative, crackerjack, decision for, mental cause; **15** decision in favor

choir: 5 clerk, quire; **6** chorus; **7** consort; **9** chorister

choirmaster: 6 cantor; **9** precentor; **13** choir director

choke: 3 gag; **4** clog, cloy, conk, foul, fret; **5** croak, scrag; **6** back up, clog up, pop off, stifle; **7** congest, garrote, smother, snuff it; **8** choke off, drop dead, strangle, throttle; **9** choke coil, suffocate; **10** asphyxiate

choke coil: 5 choke; **7** reactor; **11** choking coil

choke off: 4 clog, foul; **5** choke; **6** back up, clog up; **7** congest; **9** choke back, choke down

choker: 4 ruff; **6** collar, ruffle; **8** neck ruff, neckband; **9** dog collar

choking: 10 smothering, strangling, throttling; **11** suffocating, suffocative; **13** strangulation

choky: 3 can [slang], pen; **4** brig, gaol, hold, jail, keep, stir [slang]; **5** clink [slang], hulks, pokey [slang]; **6** chokey [slang], cooler [slang], donjon, lockup, prison; **7** dungeon, slammer [slang], the Rock; **8** Bastille, big house [slang], hoosegow, stockade; **9** calaboose [slang], guardroom, oubliette; **10** guard house, San Quentin; **11** penal colony, prison house; **12** penitentiary

choler: 3 ire, pet; **4** bile, fume, tiff; **5** anger; **6** dander, pucker, taking; **7** ferment, passion; **9** angry mood, crossness, fussiness, petulance; **10** ebullition, yellow bile; **11** acharnement [Fr], fretfulness, peevishness; **12** irritability

choleric: 3 hot; **5** hasty, livid, quick, rabid, short; **6** fuming, raging; **7** bilious, foaming, in a rage, peevish, peppery, rageful, waspish; **8** captious, shrewish, snappish; **9** fractious, hotheaded, in a choler, irascible, overhasty, querulous, splenetic; **11** hot-tempered; **13** quick-tempered, short-tempered

Choloepus: 4 unau; 12 two-toed sloth; 14 genus Choloepus

chomp: 4 bite; 5 champ

Chondrus crispus: 8 carageen; 9 carrageen, Irish moss; 10 carragheen

choo-choo: 5 train; 13 railroad train

choose: 4 list, take, wish; 5 elect; 6 decide, opt for, prefer, select; 7 fix upon, pick out; 8 settle on; 9 determine; 10 decide upon, settle upon; 12 make choice of; 13 decide in favor

choosiness: 9 pickiness; 10 daintiness; 11 finickiness, selectivity; 14 discrimination, fastidiousness

choosing: 6 choice; 8 adopting, adoption, election; 9 selecting, selection; 11 decision for

chop: 4 chip, hack, tack, turn, veer, warp; 5 check, evert, shift, split, tally; 6 billet, chop up, crunch, cutlet, letter, shiver, sunder, swerve; 7 chopper, counter, deviate, shuffle; 8 chop shot; 9 duplicate, turn aside; 10 split apart; 11 rend asunder

chop-chop: 5 apace; 7 quickly, rapidly; 8 speedily

chopfallen: 8 deflated; 10 chapfallen; 11 crestfallen

chophouse: 7 cabaret; 10 steakhouse; 11 barrel house [U.S.]

Chopin: 22 Frederic Francois Chopin

chopines: 5 shoes; 7 chopine; 8 platform; 9 platforms

chop logic: 4 moot; 5 argue; 6 debate; 7 dispute, wrangle; 9 bandy with; 10 bandy words

chop off: 6 cut off, lop off

chopped: 6 sliced; 8 shredded

chopped steak: 9 beef patty, chopsteak; 14 hamburger steak

chopper: 4 chop; 6 copter, pearly; 7 cleaver; 9 eggbeater; 10 helicopter, whirlybird; 11 meat cleaver

choppiness: 9 roughness; 10 rough water

chopping board: 12 cutting board

chopping sea: 7 long sea; 8 cross sea, heavy sea, high seas, rough sea

chops: 4 door, jaws, lips; 5 chaps, inlet, mouth, porch; 6 fauces, portal; 7 orifice, portico

chop up: 3 cut, hew; 4 chop, hack; 5 cut up; 6 scrimp; 7 slice up; 11 cut to pieces; 13 cut into pieces

chorale: 5 catch, round; 6 choral, chorus; 11 choral piece

chore: 3 job; 4 task, work; 7 agendum, project; 8 business; 9 thing to do; 10 employment, enterprise, occupation; 11 undertaking; 12 matter in hand; 13 iron in the fire; 14 what one is about, what one is doing

choreography: 12 stage dancing

chorine: 8 showgirl; 10 chorus girl

Choriotis: 14 genus Choriotis

Choriotis australis: 11 plain turkey

chorister: 5 choir, quire

chorography: 9 geography; 10 topography

chortle: 6 giggle, titter; 7 chuckle, snicker, snigger, twitter; 11 laugh softly

chorus: 5 catch, choir, round; 6 clamor, outcry, plaint; 7 chorale, refrain; 9 consensus, hue and cry; 10 chorus line, hullabaloo; 11 acclamation, choral piece, Greek chorus

chorus girl: 7 chorine; 8 showgirl

chose: 8 property; 16 personal property

chosen: 5 elect; 7 adopted, elected; 8 selected

Choson: 5 Korea; 15 Korean Peninsula

chotchke: 5 curio; 6 bauble, gewgaw, trifle; 7 bibelot, novelty, trinket, whatnot; 8 gimcrack, kickshaw, nicknack, whim-wham; 9 bagatelle, bric-a-brac, tchotchke; 10 knickknack

chou: 7 cabbage; 9 cream puff

chouse: 2 do; 3 con, nab; 4 bilk, bite, scam; 5 cheat, cozen, pluck, shaft, trick; 6 diddle, euchre, jockey; 7 chicane, defraud, swindle; 9 victimize

chow: 4 eats, grub; 5 chuck; 8 chow chow

chowderhead: 9 blockhead

chrism: 7 baptism, chrisom, holy oil; 11 christening; 14 sacramental oil

chrisom: 6 chrism; 7 holy oil; 9 white robe; 14 sacramental oil

christ: 7 messiah

Christ: 5 Jesus; 6 Savior; 7 Saviour, The Lord; 8 Redeemer; 9 God the Son; 11 Jesus Christ, The Son of God, The Son of Man; 12 Good Shepherd; 13 The Son of David; 15 Jesus of Nazareth

christen: 7 baptise, baptize

christening: 6 chrism; 7 baptism

Christian: 6 divine; 8 Catholic, faithful; 9 believing; 10 scriptural; 11 evangelical; 12 monotheistic; 18 Christian community

Christian churches: 11 Christendom

Christian Democratic Party: 18 Christian Democrats

Christian Era: 9 Common Era

Christiania: 4 Oslo; 15 capital of Norway

Christianity: 6 church; 11 Christendom; 15 Christian church; 17 Christian religion

Christian name: 13 baptismal name

Christian year: 10 church year

Christmas: 4 Noel, Xmas, Yule; 5 Dec 25; 8 Yuletide; 12 Christmas Day, 13 Christmastide, Christmastime

Christmas berry: 5 toyon; 6 tollon

Christmas carol: 5 carol

Christmas fern: 10 dagger fern; 11 canker brake
Christmas flower: 10 poinsettia
Christmas present: 13 Christmas gift
Christmas pudding: 11 plum pudding
Christmas tree: 3 fir; 9 evergreen
chrema: 9 intensity, vividness; 10 saturation
chromatic: 7 colored; 8 measured; 9 prismatic; 10 enharmonic
chromatic color: 13 spectral color
chromaticity: 3 hue
chromatics: 6 optics; 12 spectroscopy; 16 spectrum analysis
chromato-pseudo-blepsis: 9 Daltonism; 14 color blindness
chrome: 13 chromium-plate
chromium: 2 Cr
chromosphere: 11 photosphere
chronic: 8 habitual; 9 confirmed; 10 inveterate, persistent; 12 long-standing
chronicle: 5 story; 6 annals, legend; 7 account, history; 8 calendar
chronicler: 10 journalist
chronograph: 9 stopwatch
chronographer: 10 timekeeper
chronography: 7 history
chronologer: 8 annalist; 12 chronologist
chronological record: 6 annals
chronologist: 8 annalist; 11 chronologer
chronometer: 5 clock; 9 timepiece
chronometry: 8 horology; 15 time measurement
chronoscope: 5 clock; 11 chronometer
chrysanthemum: 3 mum; 5 daisy; 7 alecost; 8 costmary, feverfew, marigold; 9 pyrethrum, bible leaf; 10 balsam herb, silverlace; 11 dusty miller; 12 mint geranium; 18 genus Chrysanthemum
chrysarobin: 7 araroba; 9 Goa powder
Chrysemys: 14 genus Chrysemys
Chrysemys picta: 13 painted turtle; 15 painted terrapin, painted tortoise
Chrysobalanus: 18 genus Chrysobalanus
Chrysobalanus icaco: 5 icaco; 8 coco plum; 9 cocoa plum; 12 coco plum tree
Chrysolepis: 9 chinkapin; 16 genus Chrysolepis
chrysolite: 4 opal; 6 garnet; 7 olivine, peridot; 8 Koh-i-noor; 9 cygne noir [Fr]; 10 tourmaline
Chrysolophus pictus: 14 golden pheasant
chrysomelid: 10 leaf beetle
Chrysophrys: 7 snapper; 10 black bream; 16 genus Chrysophrys
Chrysophyllum: 18 genus Chrysophyllum
Chrysophyllum cainito: 7 caimito; 9 star apple
Chrysophyllum oliviforme: 9 satin leaf, satinleaf; 10 caimitillo, damson plum
chrysopid: 8 stink fly; 13 green lacewing
Chrysopsis: 5 aster; 15 genus Chrysopsis

C

Chrysothamnus nauseosus: 10 rabbit bush; 11 rabbit brush
chthonic: 5 lower; 6 nether; 9 chthonian, infernal
chubby: 4 tubby; 5 buxom, plump, pudgy; 6 zaftig, zoftig; 8 roly-poly; 10 embonpoint
chub mackerel: 6 tinker; 16 Scomber japonicus
chuck: 3 cat, pat, shy; 4 barf, cast, chow, eats, grub, honk, jerk, puke, sick, spew, spue, toss; 5 ditch, fling, heave, pitch, retch, vomit; 6 be sick; 7 chuckle, discard, regorge, throw up, upchuck, vomit up; 8 chuck out, disgorge, get rid of, throw out; 9 dispose of, throw away; 11 regurgitate
chuckhole: 7 pothole
chuckle: 4 crow; 5 chuck, exult, neigh; 6 cackle, giggle, titter; 7 chortle, snicker, snigger, triumph, twitter; 8 crow over; 11 laugh softly
chucklehead: 9 blockhead; 11 chowderhead
chuck out: 4 toss; 5 chuck, eject, expel, fling, heave; 7 boot out, cast out, discard, dispose, exclude, kick out, put away, toss out, turf out, turn out; 8 cast away, get rid of, throw out, toss away; 9 cast aside, dispose of, throw away
chuck-will's-widow: 7 nightjar
chufa: 7 rush nut; 11 earth almond; 12 ground almond; 14 yellow nutgrass
chuff: 4 huff, puff, serf, tike, tyke; 6 fellah
chugalug: 6 guzzle
chukka boot: 6 buskin; 7 top boot; 8 half boot; 10 combat boot, desert boot
chum: 3 pal; 5 buddy, crony; 7 brother; 8 sidekick
chump: 3 mug; 4 dupe, fish, fool, gull, mark; 5 patsy; 6 sucker; 7 fall guy; 8 shlemiel; 9 schlemiel, soft touch
chunk: 4 ball, chip, clod, glob, lump; 5 clump, shard; 8 chipping, fragment; 9 collocate
chunky: 5 dumpy, lumpy, squat; 6 low-set, stumpy; 7 squatty
chunnel: 13 Channel Tunnel
church: 4 kirk, pope; 6 chapel, gospel; 7 oratory; 8 basilica; 9 cathedral, scripture; 10 tabernacle; 11 conventicle; 12 Christianity, meetinghouse; 13 church service; 14 church building; 15 Christian church
church bench: 3 pew
church calendar: 22 ecclesiastical calendar
church doctrine: 5 creed; 6 gospel; 17 religious doctrine
churchgoer: 12 church member
Churchill: 16 Winston Churchill; 19 Sir Winston Churchill
churchman: 6 cleric, divine; 8 reverend; 9 black coat [fig], clergyman; 12 ecclesiastic
church member: 10 churchgoer

Church of Christ Scientist: 16 Christian Science

Church of England: 14 Anglican Church; **17** Anglican Communion

Church of Jesus Christ of Latter-day Saints: 7 Mormons; **12** Mormon Church

Church of Rome: 13 Roman Catholic, Western Church; **19** Roman Catholic Church

church school: 15 parochial school, religious school

Church Slavic: 12 Old Bulgarian; **15** Old Church Slavic; **17** Old Church Slavonic

churchyard: 8 God's acre; **9** cloisters

church year: 13 Christian year

churl: 4 boor, crib, lout, tike, tyke; **5** crank, grump, harpy, hunks, miser, screw; **6** codger, grouch, scrimp, usurer; **7** grabber, peasant, scrooge; **9** barbarian, skinflint, underling; **10** crosspatch, curmudgeon

churlish: 7 bearish, boorish, brutish, loutish, raffish; **8** clownish; **9** illiberal; **10** ungenerous

churn: 4 boil, mash, moil, roil, stir; **6** beat up, squash; **7** shake up, thicken; **8** hand mill; **11** butter churn

churning: 5 roily; **6** roiled; **7** roiling, shaking; **9** churned-up, trembling, turbulent

churn up: 6 revolt, sicken; **7** disgust; **8** nauseate

churr: 5 whirr

churrigueresque: 7 baroque; **14** churrigueresco

chute: 5 slide; **9** parachute; **13** sloping trough

chutney: 12 Indian relish

chutzpah: 6 hutzpa; **8** audacity; **13** audaciousness

Ci: 5 curie

CIA: 25 Central Intelligence Agency

ciao: 5 adieu, aloha; **7** goodbye; **8** farewell, sayonara; **10** dosvidanya [Russ]; **11** leave-taking, valediction; **12** hasta la vista [Sp]; **14** auf wiedersehen [Ger]

cicada: 6 cicala

Cicadidae: 15 family Cicadidae

cicatrix: 4 scar; **9** cicatrice

cicatrize: 4 heal, scab; **8** scab over, skin over

Cicer: 8 chickpea; **11** Egyptian pea; **10** genus Cicer; **13** chickpea plant

Cicero: 5 Tully; **11** Demosthenes; **19** Marcus Tullius Cicero

cicerone: 5 guide, pilot

Ciceronian: 5 Attic; **7** correct, elegant, Tullian; **8** artistic, polished; **9** classical; **10** well-styled; **11** nuncupative

cichlid: 11 cichlid fish

Cichlidae: 15 family Cichlidae

Cichorium endivia: 6 endive; **7** witloof

Cichorium intybus: 7 chicory, succory; **12** chicory plant

cicisbeo: 5 lover 7 captive, gallant; **8** Lothario, paramour; **17** cavaliere servente [It]

Ciconia: 5 stork; **12** genus Ciconia

cider: 4 mate; **5** cyder; **9** hard cider

ci-devant: 4 late; **6** former; **7** quondam; **8** previous, pristine; **9** erstwhile

cigar: 6 stogie

cigarette: 3 fag; **4** butt, weed; **7** cigaret; **10** coffin nail

cigarette paper: 12 rolling paper

cigar-shaped: 8 fusiform; **13** spindle-shaped

cigar store: 11 tobacco shop; **12** tobacco store, tobacconists

cilantro: 9 coriander; **14** Chinese parsley, coriander plant; **17** Coriandrum sativum

cilia: 6 cilium

ciliated: 5 hairy; **6** tufted; **7** ciliate, hirsute; **10** fimbriated; **11** filamentous

cilium: 5 cilia [pl]; **7** eyelash

Cimabue: 15 Giovanni Cimabue

Cimarron: 13 Cimarron River

cimarron: 7 bighorn; **12** bighorn sheep; **14** Ovis canadensis; **18** Rocky Mountain sheep; **20** Rocky Mountain bighorn

cimetidine: 7 Tagamet

Cimex lectularius: 6 bedbug, chinch

Cimicifuga: 6 cohosh; **7** bugbane; **15** genus Cimicifuga

cinch: 4 snap; **5** girth, lasso, noose; **6** lariat, picnic; **8** duck soup, pushover, walkover; **9** surcingle, sure thing; **10** child's play

Cinclus: 10 water ouzel; **12** genus Cinclus

cincture: 4 sash; **6** fascia, fillet, girdle, wreath; **7** baldric, garland; **9** waistband; **10** waistcloth

cinder: 3 ash; **7** clinker

cine-camera: 11 movie camera; **19** motion-picture camera

cinema: 4 film; **7** the film; **9** celluloid; **10** movie house; **12** movie theater, movie theatre; **13** picture palace; **14** cinematography

cinematographer: 9 cameraman

cinematography: 6 cinema; **7** filming, the film; **11** photography; **24** motion-picture photography

cine projector: 13 film projector; **14** movie projector

cinerary: 8 mortuary; **10** sepulchral

cinerary urn: 4 bier, pall; **6** hearse; **10** catafalque

cineration: 12 incineration

cinibar: 9 vermilion; **10** Chinese-red, vermillion

cinnabar: 12 cinnabar moth; **19** Callimorpha jacobeae

Cinnamomum: 15 genus Cinnamomum

Cinnamomum camphora: 11 camphor tree

Cinnamomum cassia: 6 cassia; **14** cassia-bark tree

Cinnamomum zeylanicum: 8 cinnamon; **14** Ceylon cinnamon; **18** Ceylon cinnamon tree

cinnamon: 3 bay; **4** mace; **6** auburn, cloves, dapple, fennel, nutmeg, russet; **7** oregano; **8** chestnut, nut-brown; **12** cinnamon bark

cinnamon roll: 11 cinnamon bun

cinnamon stone: 8 essonite; **9** hessonite

cinque: 1 V; **3** fin; **4** five; **5** quint; **6** pentad; **7** quintet; **8** fivesome; **10** quintuplet

cinquefoil: 9 five-lobed; **10** five-finger; **11** five-petaled

CIO: 33 Congress of Industrial Organizations

cipher: 1 0; **3** nil, nix, zip; **4** code, nada, type, zero; **5** aught, digit, score, zilch; **6** cypher, device, encode, figure, naught, nobody, nought, number, reckon; **7** compute, encrypt, nothing, nullity, tell off; **8** encipher, goose egg, inscribe, monogram, ne'er a one, scramble; **9** calculate, never a one, nonentity; **10** secret code; **11** cryptograph, write in code; **13** Arabic numeral

ciphered: 5 coded; **7** encoded; **9** encrypted, scrambled

ciprofloxacin: 5 Cipro

Circassian walnut: 13 English walnut

Circe: 5 siren

circinate: 6 ringed, coiled; **7** annular; **8** annulate, circular; **9** annulated; **10** ring-shaped

circination: 8 orbiting; **13** orbital motion

circle: 3 lap, lot, orb, set; **4** area, band, gang, hoop, knot, ring, soil; **5** crowd, field, group, realm, round; **6** areola, clique, domain, ground, rotary, sphere; **7** annulus, circlet, circuit, coterie, environ, in-crowd; **8** encircle, province, surround; **9** circulate; **10** roundabout; **11** dress circle; **13** traffic circle

circlet: 4 hoop, ring; **6** areola, circle; **7** annulus

circuit: 3 lap, orb; **4** area, beat, loop, soil, tour; **5** ambit, field, lines, realm, round, twirl, twist; **6** circle, detour, domain, ground, sphere; **7** contour; **8** province; **10** meandering; **13** racing circuit; **15** electric circuit; **17** electrical circuit

circuitous: 5 stray; **6** zigzag; **7** devious, erratic, vagrant; **8** indirect; **10** roundabout, undirected; **11** out of the way

circuitously: 10 indirectly

circular: 4 bill; **5** flier, flyer, round; **6** ringed; **7** annular; **8** annulate, handbill, pamphlet; **9** annulated, broadside, circinate, orbicular, throwaway; **10** broadsheet, ring-shaped; **11** publication; **14** circular letter

circular file: 11 waste bucket, wastebasket

circular function: 21 trigonometric function

circularity: 9 disk shape, roundness

circularize: 6 spread; **7** diffuse; **8** disperse; **9** broadcast, circulate, propagate; **10** distribute, pass around; **11** circularise, disseminate

circular note: 14 letter of credit

circular plane: 12 compass plane

circular saw: 7 buzz saw

circulate: 4 bowl, wind; **5** troll; **6** circle, pass on, spread; **7** diffuse, meander, trundle; **8** disperse, go around, mobilize; **9** broadcast, propagate; **10** distribute, pass around, promulgate; **11** circularise, circularize, disseminate

circulating decimal: 7 decimal; **8** repetend; **16** recurring decimal, repeating decimal

circulating library: 14 lending library

circulation: 6 airing; **7** edition; **9** spreading; **13** dissemination; **14** public exposure

circulatory system: 20 cardiovascular system

circumambient: 7 girding; **8** girdling; **10** encircling; **11** surrounding; **12** circumjacent, encompassing

circumambulate: 10 walk around; **11** perambulate

circumbendibus: 4 loop; **5** twirl, twist; **7** circuit; **10** meandering; **11** indirect way

circumference: 7 outline; **9** perimeter, periphery

circumferential: 6 bypass; **8** ring road

circumfluent: 7 girding; **8** girdling; **10** encircling; **11** surrounding; **12** circumjacent, encompassing

circumfusion: 6 spread; **10** enveloping; **11** surrounding; **13** interspersion

circumjacent: 7 girding; **8** girdling; **10** encircling; **11** surrounding; **12** encompassing

circumlocution: 8 rambling; **10** digressing, digression; **11** periphrasis; **17** roundabout phrases; **18** indirect expression

circumnavigate: 7 compass; **8** go around

circumrotation: 8 gyration, rotation, spinning; **10** revolution

circumscribe: 5 limit; **7** confine, enclose, inclose; **8** restrict, withhold; **10** encincture

circumspect: 5 chary, shy of; **7** politic, prudent; **8** discreet, stealthy

circumspection: 4 heed; **7** caution; **8** coolness, prudence; **10** discretion, steadiness; **11** calculation, heedfulness; **12** cautiousness, deliberation, discreetness; **17** unadventurousness

circumstances: 3 lot; **4** fate, luck; **5** asset, means; **6** assets, estate; **7** context, destiny, fortune, portion; **9** condition, resources, situation; **10** belongings, conditions [pl]; **12** circumstance; **21** physical circumstances

circumstantial evidence: 16 indirect evidence

circumvallation: 4 pale, rail; 6 paling; 7 railing; 8 enceinte; 9 ring fence; 10 balustrade

circumvent: 3 lap; 4 beat, duck, gird, snub; 5 beset, bound, dodge, elude, evade, fudge, hedge, hem in, parry, skirt; 6 baffle, begird, double, outfox, outwit, put off; 7 besiege, compass, embrace, enclose, environ, finesse, inclose; 8 encircle, outsmart, override, sidestep, surround; 9 beleaguer, encompass, overreach, temporize

circumvolve: 4 gyre; 6 gyrate; 9 turn round; 10 spin around

circus: 6 square; 8 carnival; 10 hippodrome; 13 amphitheater

Circus: 7 harrier; 11 genus Circus

circus tent: 3 top; 6 big top; 8 round top

cirque: 3 cwm; 6 corrie, circus; 7 circlet

cirrhosis: 19 cirrhosis of the liver

cirrhus: 6 cirrus

cirrocumulus: 17 cirrocumulus cloud

cirrostratus: 12 cirrostratus; 13 cumulostratus; 17 cirrostratus cloud

cirrus: 7 cirrhus, cumulus; 11 cirrus cloud

Cirsium: 7 thistle; 12 genus Cirsium

CISC: 48 complex instruction set computer

cisco: 11 lake herring

cislunar: 8 sublunar; 9 sublunary

Cistercian: 8 Trappist

cistern: 4 pond, tank; 8 cisterna, mill pond; 9 water tank

cit: 7 burgess, burgher, cockney; 8 townsman

citadel: 7 bastion, citadel; 9 acropolis

citation: 5 libel; 6 credit; 7 mention, summons; 8 subpoena, true bill; 9 challenge, nisi prius [Lat], quotation, reference; 10 indictment; 11 arraignment, impeachment, presentment; 12 commendation

cite: 4 name; 5 quote, refer; 6 abduce, adduce, advert, attest, summon; 7 bring up, call for, mention, summons; 8 put a case; 9 challenge, exemplify, reference; 10 illustrate; 11 acknowledge; 14 quote authority, quote precedent; 17 appeal to authority

Citellus: 8 squirrel, chipmunk; 12 Spermophilus; 13 genus Citellus; 17 genus Spermophilus

cither: 6 zither; 7 cittern, zithern

citified: 8 city-born, city-bred, cityfied

citizen: 8 national

citizen's band: 2 CB; 8 car radio, ham radio; 10 police band; 11 police radio, two-way radio; 12 amateur radio, handie-talkie, walkie-talkie [military]; 13 airplane radio; 14 short-wave radio

citizen of the world: 10 Benthamite, eudemonist; 11 cosmopolite, eudaemonist, utilitarian

citizenry: 6 people; 10 population; 11 inhabitants [pl]

citric acid cycle: 10 Krebs cycle

citrin: 8 vitamin P; 12 bioflavinoid

citrine: 6 fallow

citron: 10 citron tree; 12 Citrus medica

citronwood: 8 sandarac

Citrullus: 14 genus Citrullus

Citrullus vulgaris: 10 watermelon

citrus: 7 citrous

Citrus aurantifolia: 4 lime

Citrus aurantium: 8 bigarade; 10 sour orange; 12 bitter orange; 13 Seville orange; 15 marmalade orange

Citrus bergamia: 8 bergamot; 14 bergamot orange

Citrus limetta: 9 sweet lime; 10 sweet lemon

Citrus limon: 5 lemon

Citrus maxima: 6 pomelo; 7 pummelo; 8 shaddock; 10 pomelo tree; 13 Citrus grandis; 14 Citrus decumana

Citrus medica: 6 citron

Citrus nobilis: 6 tangor; 10 king orange; 12 temple orange

Citrus paradisi: 10 grapefruit

Citrus reticulata: 8 mandarin; 14 mandarin orange

Citrus sinensis: 11 sweet orange

Citrus tangelo: 7 tangelo; 9 ugli fruit

city: 9 municipal; 10 metropolis; 11 urban center; 12 municipality

city-bred: 8 citified, city-born, cityfied

city council: 11 town council

city manager: 5 mayor

City of Bridges: 6 Bruges

City of Brotherly Love: 12 Philadelphia

City of God: 8 Holy City; 12 Heavenly City; 13 Celestial City

City of Light: 5 Paris; 13 French capital; 15 capital of France

City of the Angels: 10 Los Angeles

city planning: 12 town planning; 13 urban planning

city slicker: 7 city boy

city tax: 8 local tax

Ciudad de Mexico: 10 Mexico City; 14 Mexican capital; 15 capital of Mexico

civet: 8 civet cat

civet cat: 5 civet; 7 coon cat; 8 ringtail; 9 bassarisk, cacomixle, miner's cat; 10 cacomistle, raccoon fox; 13 ring-tailed cat; 18 Bassariscus astutus

civic: 5 civil, human; 6 mortal, public, social; 8 national, personal; 10 individual

civic center: 3 hub; 8 downtown; 15 community center, municipal center

civil: 3 lay; 5 civic; 6 adroit, laical, poised, polite; 7 profane, secular, tactful; 8 mannerly, temporal; 9 courteous; 10 diplomatic; 11 well-behaved; 12 good-mannered, well-mannered

civil action: 9 civil suit

civil death: 9 attainder

civil disorder: 7 anarchy, turmoil; 8 disorder,

disquiet; **9** agitation, commotion; **10** turbulence; **11** disturbance; **16** civil disturbance

civilian: 6 jurist, layman, pundit; **8** advocate; **9** publicist; **12** juris consult [Lat], legal adviser

civility: 8 courtesy; **10** politeness

civilization: 7 culture; **8** civility, courtesy; **10** civilizing, politeness

civilize: 5 train; **6** polish, school; **7** develop, educate; **8** humanize; **9** cultivate, modernize

civilized: 6 polite, urbane; **7** gallant, genteel, refined; **8** cultured, polished, well-bred; **10** cultivated; **11** gentlemanly; **13** gentlemanlike

civil law: 8 canon law, Roman law; **9** jus civile; **13** Justinian code

civil suit: 11 civil action

civil war: 14 internecine war

civil wrong: 4 tort

civil year: 12 calendar year

civism: 10 patriotism; **11** nationality; **13** love of country

Cl: 8 chlorine

cl: 10 centiliter, centilitre

clabber: 4 clot; **6** curdle

clack: 3 coo, jaw; **4** bang, bark, boom, clap, honk, slam, wham; **5** blast, clang, click, cluck, crack, prate, prose, whack; **6** cackle, gabble, gaggle, gibber, jabber, piffle, tattle; **7** blabber, brattle, chatter, clatter, maunder, palaver, prattle, twaddle; **9** prattle on; **10** clack valve; **12** tittle-tattle

clad: 7 arrayed, attired, clothed, dressed; **8** invested

cladding: 5 cover; **6** facing; **7** overlay

cladode: 10 cladophyll, phylloclad; **11** phylloclade

Cladonia: 13 genus Cladonia

Cladoniaceae: 18 family Cladoniaceae

Cladonia rangiferina: 10 arctic moss; **12** reindeer moss; **14** reindeer lichen

Claforan: 10 cefotaxime

claim: 4 bill, call, take; **5** exact, right, title; **6** demand, estate; **7** call for, holding, reclaim; **8** arrogate, exaction, lay claim; **10** imposition, insistence, lay claim to, pretension; **11** declaration, reclamation, requisition

claimant: 6 bidder, suitor; **7** accuser; **8** aspirant; **9** appellant, candidate, postulant; **10** competitor

clairvoyance: 3 ESP; **11** second sight

clairvoyant: 6 medium; **12** precognitive; **13** fortune teller, second-sighted

clam: 4 buck; **6** dollar; **10** dollar bill

clamant: 6 crying; **7** blatant, exigent, instant; **8** strident; **9** clamorous, insistent; **10** clamourous, vociferous

clamber: 4 ramp, shin, skin; **5** climb; **6** shinny; **7** sputter; **8** scramble, struggle, surmount

clammy: 4 dank, ropy; **6** mastic; **7** clotted,

gelatin; **9** glutenous, glutinous; **10** albuminous, gelatinous; **12** mucilaginous

clamor: 3 din, mob; **4** hiss, hoot, riot; **5** blare, croak, furor, growl, grunt; **6** chorus, murmur, mutter, outcry, plaint, tumult, uproar; **7** blaring, clamour, grizzle, grumble, maunder, rioting, tempest; **9** blacklist, cacophony, clamoring, hue and cry, ostracize; **10** clamouring, convulsion, hullabaloo; **12** vociferation

clamor for: 3 dun, ply, tax; **4** urge; **5** beset, press; **9** importune, imprecate

clamorous: 6 urgent; **7** abusive, blatant, clamant, rampant, riotous; **8** strident; **9** convulsed, turbulent; **10** boisterous, clamourous, rip-roaring, tumultuous, uproarious, vociferous; **11** importunate, rip-snorting, tempestuous; **12** condemnatory, denunciatory, vituperative

clamp: 3 pin; **4** bolt, hasp, nail; **5** clasp, crimp, rivet, screw; **6** C-clamp, U-clamp

clamp down: 8 get tough; **9** crack down

clamshell: 7 grapple

clam up: 6 belt up, shut up; **7** be quiet, close up, dummy up, keep mum; **8** button up

clan: 3 kin; **5** tribe; **7** kindred; **8** kin group; **12** kinship group

clandestine: 5 close, privy; **6** secret; **7** in petto, private; **8** hush-hush; **9** auricular, inviolate; **10** on the quiet, undercover; **11** underground; **12** hugger-mugger; **13** hole-and-corner, surreptitious; **14** cloak-and-dagger

clang: 4 bang, boom, clap, peal, roar, slam, wham; **5** blare, blast, clack, clank, clash, crash, swell, whack; **6** jangle; **7** clangor, thunder; **8** clangour; **9** fulminate

clangor: 5 clang, clank, clash, crash; **6** jangle; **8** clangour; **10** clangoring

clank: 4 burr, pipe; **5** clang, clash, clink, crash, twang; **6** jangle; **7** clangor; **8** clangour; **10** clangoring

clan member: 8 clansman; **10** clanswoman

clannish: 6 clubby, snobby; **8** cliquish, snobbish

clanship: 12 partisanship

clap: 4 bang, boom, slam, spat, wham; **5** blast, clack, clang, whack; **6** blowup; **7** acclaim, applaud; **8** eruption; **9** gonorrhea, loud noise; **10** gonorrhoea

clapboard: 12 weatherboard

clapper: 6 glossa, lingua, tongue

clapperclaw: 5 abuse, shout, scold; **6** to claw; **9** encounter, pitch into

clapping: 4 hand; **8** applause; **12** hand clapping

clap together: 6 clap up; **11** fix together, lay together, put together

claptrap: 4 blah, cant, rant; **7** bombast, fustian; **9** mere words

claqueur: 6 puffer
claret: 4 mate; 5 cider; 8 ice water; 11 red Bordeaux
clarification: 8 clearing; 11 elucidation
clarified butter: 11 drawn butter
clarify: 4 rack; 5 clear, purge; 6 refine; 7 clear up, sort out; 9 elucidate, elutriate [Chem], enlighten, expurgate; 10 illuminate; 11 crystallize, shed light on
clarion: 5 bugle; 6 cornet; 7 trumpet; 8 trombone
clarity: 8 lucidity; 9 clearness, limpidity, overtness, plainness; 10 definition; 11 perspicuity; 12 distinctness, explicitness, manifestness, pellucidness, transparence, transparency; 13 uncloudedness
clash: 3 jar; 4 bump; 5 brush, clang, clank, crash, cross, shock; 6 jangle, jostle; 7 clangor, collide, dispute, quarrel; 8 clangour, conflict, disagree, friction, skirmish; 9 collision, come amiss, encounter; 10 langoring, concussion, percussion, run counter; 12 be discordant
clashing: 7 jarring, wrangle; 8 conflict; 9 bickering, collision; 10 repugnance; 11 conflicting, interfering; 12 antagonistic
clash of arms: 3 war; 6 combat; 7 warfare; 8 battling, conflict, fighting; 11 hostilities
clasp: 3 hug, pin; 4 band, belt, bolt, girt, grab, grip, hank, hasp, hold, nail; 5 catch, clamp, crimp, grasp, latch, rivet, screw; 6 brooch, buckle, clench, clinch, clutch, girdle, zodiac; 7 baldric, cling to, embrace, grapple; 8 clutches; 9 close with; 10 fasten upon, take hold of
clasping: 7 hugging; 8 grasping, gripping; 9 embracing
clasp knife: 9 jackknife
class: 4 form, kind, sort, type, year; 5 grade, group; 6 assort, course, family, remove; 7 lecture, seminar, sort out, variety; 8 category, classify, division, separate; 11 social class; 13 affected class, course of study
class-conscious: 10 stratified
classfellow: 9 classmate
classic: 6 chaste, severe
classical: 4 pure; 5 Attic; 6 chaste; 7 correct, elegant; 8 artistic, polished; 10 Ciceronian, definitive, unaffected, wellstyled
Classical Greek: 5 Attic
classical mechanics: 18 Newtonian mechanics
classification: 5 match; 7 match-up, sorting; 8 division, grouping; 9 allotment; 10 assortment; 11 classifying, recognition; 13 apportionment; 14 categorisation, categorization, identification
classified: 6 placed; 7 made out; 10 identi-

fied, recognized; 11 categorized; 13 distinguished
classify: 4 sort; 5 class, group, match, place; 6 assort; 7 make out, match up, realize, sort out; 8 identify, separate; 9 recognize; 10 categorize; 11 distinguish
classifying: 7 sorting; 8 division, grouping; 9 allotment; 10 assortment; 12 categorizing; 13 apportionment; 14 classification
classman: 4 lion; 8 rara avis [Lat]; 9 classmate
classmate: 10 schoolmate; 11 class fellow; 12 schoolfellow
classroom: 10 schoolroom; 11 lecture room
class warfare: 8 class war; 13 class struggle
classy: 4 posh; 5 swish
clatter: 4 roar; 5 clack, noise; 7 brattle
claudication: 4 gimp, miss, slip, trip; 5 fault; 7 limping, stumble; 8 footfall, gameness, lameness, omission; 9 gimpiness, oversight
clause: 4 term; 5 count, terms, verse; 7 article, chapter; 9 condition, paragraph, provision; 10 conditions [pl]; 11 stipulation; 12 precondition
claustral: 10 cloisteral
claver: 3 jaw; 4 chat; 5 visit; 6 confab, gossip, natter; 7 chaffer, chatter; 8 chitchat; 11 confabulate
clavicle: 10 collarbone
clavier: 6 spinet; 7 Klavier; 8 dulcimer; 9 virginals; 10 Eolian harp; 11 fingerboard; 13 piano keyboard
claw: 4 hook, nail; 5 chela, talon; 6 collar, nipper, pincer, unguis; 8 throttle
clawed: 7 taloned
clawhammer: 16 carpenter's hammer
clay: 3 mud; 4 dust; 5 ashes, earth
claymore: 4 tuck; 5 sword; 8 land mine
clayware: 7 pottery
clean: 4 fair, neat, pick, plum; 5 blank, clear, fresh, light, plumb, strip, white; 6 fairly; 7 cleanly, cleanse; 8 sanitary, scavenge, sporting; 9 make clean, unclouded; 10 clean house, houseclean, uninfected; 11 clean-living; 12 clean and jerk; 13 sportsmanlike
clean-cut: 4 trig, trim; 5 clear; 8 clear-cut
cleaners: 11 dry cleaners
clean-handed: 8 innocent; 9 guiltless
clean hands: 6 purity; 15 clear conscience
cleaning lady: 4 char; 5 woman; 9 charwoman; 13 cleaning woman
cleanly: 5 clean; 10 flawlessly
clean out: 5 purge; 8 clear out, drive out; 10 clear decks
clean room: 9 white room
cleansing: 7 cleanup; 8 cleaning; 9 cathartic, purifying; 11 ablutionary
clean slate: 10 fresh start, tabula rasa
clean up: 4 tidy; 6 neaten, tidy up; 10 square away, straighten; 13 straighten out

clear: 3 net, top; **4** earn, free, gain, make, open, pass, sack, soft; **5** clean, light, plain, sunny; **6** acquit, assoil, limpid, pull in, purify, sack up, take in, unclog; **7** bring in, clarify, clear up, cleared, clearly, decided, glaring, light up, notable, realize, salient, sort out, staring, unloose; **8** absolved, apparent, brighten, clean-cut, clear out, clear-cut, decisive, defecate, definite, distinct, manifest, pellucid, readable, specific; **9** all the way, authorise, authorize, cloudless, discharge, elucidate, enlighten, exculpate, exonerate, extricate, liquidate, prominent, unclouded, unclutter, vindicate; **10** clear as day, exculpated, exonerated, illuminate, immaculate, in full view, percipient, vindicated, well-marked; **11** ascertained, categorical, conspicuous, crystallize, determinate, in plain view, shed light on, transparent, unequivocal, unmortgaged, well-defined

clearance: 7 headway, quietus; **8** clearing, headroom; **9** discharge, quittance, reckoning; **10** redemption, settlement; **11** arrangement, liquidation; **12** satisfaction; **13** deobstruction

clear as day: 10 plain as day; **12** crystal-clear

clear away: 8 clear off, clear out

clear decks: 5 purge; **8** clean out; **17** make a clean sweep of

cleared: 5 clear; **8** absolved; **10** exculpated, exonerated, vindicated

clear-eyesighted: 8 hawk-eyed, keen-eyed; **9** Argus-eyed, eagle-eyed

clearheaded: 13 clear-thinking

clearing: 5 glade; **9** clearance; **10** clarifying; **13** clarification, deobstruction

clearly: 5 clear; **6** openly; **7** lucidly, plainly; **9** glaringly; **10** apparently, definitely, distinctly, manifestly; **11** prominently; **12** intelligibly; **13** conspicuously, perspicuously, transparently; **14** understandably

clearness: 7 clarity; **8** lucidity; **9** limpidity; **11** pellucidity, perspicuity; **12** explicitness; **13** uncloudedness

clear sailing: 9 easy going

clear the throat: 4 hack, hawk; **7** sputter; **8** splutter

clear-thinking: 11 clearheaded

clear up: 5 clear, mop up; **7** clarify, light up, sort out; **8** brighten, finish up, simplify; **9** elucidate, enlighten, finish off, polish off; **10** get through, illuminate, popularize; **11** crystallize, shed light on; **13** straighten out

cleavage: 8 chopping, cleaving, layering; **12** segmentation; **14** stratification

cleave: 3 axe; **4** hold, rive; **5** cling, halve, split, stick; **6** adhere, bisect, divide; **8** cut in two, cleft; **11** dichotomize

cleaved: 5 cleft, split

cleaver: 7 chopper; **11** meat cleaver

cleft: 4 chap, rift; **5** crack, split; **6** cloven, cranny; **7** cleaved, crevice, fissure; **8** scissure

cleft lip: 7 harelip

clemency: 5 mercy; **7** quarter; **8** humanity, mildness, yearning; **10** tenderness; **11** forbearance; **12** mercifulness

clement: 7 ruthful; **11** bearing with; **13** long-suffering

clench: 3 hug; **4** grab, grip, hold; **5** clasp, grasp, gripe; **6** clinch, clutch, ratify; **7** confirm, embrace, grapple; **8** clutches; **9** subscribe; **10** fasten upon, underwrite

clenched: 8 clinched

clepe: 3 dub; **4** call, name, term; **5** style; **7** entitle; **9** designate; **10** denominate

clepsydra: 10 water clock, water glass

clerestory: 4 loft; **5** attic; **6** garret; **7** gallery; **8** cockloft; **10** clearstory

clergy: 8 ministry, the cloth; **9** clericals

clergyman: 6 divine; **8** reverend; **9** black coat [fig], churchman; **12** ecclesiastic; **13** man of the cloth

cleric: 6 divine; **9** churchman; **12** ecclesiastic

clericals: 6 clergy; **8** ministry, the cloth

clerisy: 14 intelligentsia

clerk: 5 choir, **6** notary, scribe; **7** marshal; **8** recorder; **9** scrivener, secretary, shop clerk; **10** amanuensis, salesclerk

clerking: 11 bookkeeping

Cleveland: 15 Grover Cleveland

clever: 3 apt; **4** able, cagy, cute; **5** cagey, canny; **6** adroit, gifted; **7** cunning, endowed; **8** talented; **9** ingenious; **10** felicitous

cleverness: 4 turn; **5** forte, parts; **6** talent; **7** ability, faculty, talents; **8** capacity, felicity; **9** endowment, ingenuity, smartness; **10** brightness, capability; **12** habilitation; **13** ingeniousness, inventiveness, qualification

clew: 3 cue, key, pea; **4** bulb, clue, drop, horn, knob, pill; **5** scent; **6** bullet, marble, pellet, pommel; **7** globule, vesicle; **8** spherule

clianthus: 8 glory pea

cliche: 7 bromide; **8** banality; **9** platitude; **11** commonplace

click: 3 dog; **4** dawn, pawl, snap, tick; **5** chink, clack, clink, cluck, flick; **6** detent, sink in; **7** chatter, ratchet; **8** come home; **9** get across, penetrate; **10** get through, mouse click; **11** suction stop; **13** fall into place

click beetle: 8 skipjack; **14** snapping beetle

client: 4 node; **5** guest; **6** patron; **8** customer; **9** clientele [pl]

clientele: 6 client, patron; **8** business, customer; **9** patronage

cliff: 4 drop; **7** drop-off, dropoff; **9** sheer wall

cliff-hanging: 10 suspensive; **11** suspenseful

climacteric: 8 hoary age; **9** menopause; **11** decrepitude; **12** change of life

climactic: 4 peak; **11** climactical

climate: 4 mood, zone; **5** clime

climatology: 11 meteorology

climax: 4 come; **5** pitch; **6** height, orgasm, summit; **7** maximum; **9** culminate, flood tide; **11** culmination, have a climax, ne plus ultra; **12** turning point; **13** crowning point; **16** culminating point

climb: 3 wax; **4** go up, ramp, rise; **5** mount, raise; **6** ascent; **7** clamber, climb up, upgrade; **8** climbing, mounting, scramble, surmount; **9** acclivity

climber: 7 crampon; **8** alpinist, crampoon; **11** mountaineer; **12** climbing iron; **13** social climber; **15** mountain climber

climbing iron: 7 climber, crampon; **8** crampoon

climb on: 5 get on, hop on, mount; **6** jump on; **7** mount up; **8** bestride

clime: 4 zone; **7** climate

clinch: 3 fix, hug, pun; **4** bind, grab, seal, trap; **5** affix, clasp, grasp, gripe, stamp, twist; **6** attach, clench, clutch, fasten, finish, secure, wind up, wrap up; **7** embrace, grapple; **8** make fast, make sure, saddle on; **10** fasten upon, put the seal

clinched: 8 clenched

clincher: 10 determiner; **14** decisive factor

cling: 4 hang, hold; **5** stick; **6** adhere, cleave, cohere; **8** hold fast; **10** clingstone; **12** hang together; **13** stick together

clinging: 7 holding; **8** adhering, sticking

clingstone: 5 cling

cling to: 3 hug, pet; **5** clasp; **6** clutch, hold to, take to; **7** act up to, cherish, stick to; **8** adhere to; **9** hold close, hold tight; **12** be faithful to, take a fancy to

clinical psychologist: 15 psychotherapist

clinical study: 10 blind study; **16** double blind study

clink: 3 can [slang], pen; **4** brig, burr, gaol, hold, jail, keep, pipe, ring, stir [slang], tink; **5** chink, clank, click, hulks, pokey [slang], twang; **6** chokey [slang], cooler [slang], donjon, jangle, jingle, lockup, prison, tinkle; **7** dungeon, slammer [slang], the Rock; **8** Bastille, big house [slang], hoosegow, stockade; **9** calaboose [slang], guardroom, jailhouse, oubliette; **10** guard house, San Quentin; **11** penal colony, prison house; **12** penitentiary

Clinoril: 8 sulindac

clinquant: 5 paste; **6** finery, gewgaw, tinsel; **7** spangle; **8** frippery, gimcrack, tinseled, tinselly, trickery

Clinton: 11 Bill Clinton; **23** William Jefferson Clinton

Clio: 13 Muse of history

clip: 3 jog, lop, mow, nip; **4** crop, dock, reap, snip, time, trim, trot; **5** carom, dress, prune, shave, shear; **6** nip off; **7** curtail, cut back, snip off; **8** clipping, cut short, magazine; **9** glance off, sideswipe; **10** sidewinder [U.S.]; **13** cartridge clip; **15** cartridge holder

clipped: 6 docked, pruned; **9** truncated; **12** shortenedcut

clipper: 7 limiter; **8** clippers, corvette; **11** clipper ship

clipping: 4 clip, snip, trim; **5** shave; **6** paring, shiver, sliver; **7** cutting, driblet, shaving; **8** trimming; **12** press cutting; **13** press clipping; **17** newspaper clipping

clip the wings of: 3 mar; **5** limit, spoil; **6** sprain; **7** silence; **8** restrict, withhold; **12** circumscribe

clique: 4 camp, gang, knot, pack, ring; **5** crowd, group; **6** caucus, circle; **7** coterie, in-crowd, ingroup; **8** assembly, conclave; **10** conference; **11** conventicle, inner circle

cliquish: 6 clubby, snobby; **8** clannish, snobbish

cloaca: 4 sump; **5** sewer, sough; **8** sewerage; **9** sewer pipe

cloak: 4 mask, pall, veil; **5** blind, cloud, cover; **6** mantle, screen, shroud; **7** curtain, pelisse; **9** dissemble

cloak-and-dagger: 6 secret; **8** hush-hush; **10** on the quiet, undercover; **11** clandestine, underground; **12** hugger-mugger; **13** hole-and-corner, surreptitious

cloaked: 6 draped, masked; **7** clothed, mantled, wrapped; **9** disguised

cloakroom: 8 coatroom

clobber: 3 bat; **4** drub, lick; **5** baste, stuff; **6** batter, thrash

clock in: 7 clock on, punch in

clock out: 8 clock off, punch out

clockwork: 6 steady; **7** routine; **8** constant; **9** continual, incessant, perpetual, unceasing, unfailing, wheelwork; **10** consistent, continuous, invariable, monotonous

clod: 3 oaf, ton, tun; **4** ball, bulk, clot, cord, gawk, glob, goon, loaf, lout, lump, mass, rube [U.S.], swad; **5** block, chunk, clump, klutz, yokel; **6** bushel, lubber, lummox, nugget; **8** blanc-bec; **10** clodhopper, stumblebum

clodhopper: 4 clod; **6** brogan, brogue; **8** work shoe

clog: 4 clot, foul, geta, shoe, skid; **5** choke, sabot, spoke; **6** back up, clog up, patten; **7** congest, rubbers; **8** choke off, galoshes, overload; **9** clog dance; **11** clog dancing

clogged: 6 choked; **7** clotted

clogging: 8 impeding; **9** hindering; **11** obstructive

clog up: 4 clog, foul; **5** choke; **6** back up; **7** congest; **8** choke off

cloisonne: 6 enamel; **9** champleve [Fr]

cloister: 7 convent, nunnery; **9** monastery, peristyle

cloistered: 8 monastic, secluded; **9** claustral, cloistral, reclusive; **10** conventual, monastical; **11** sequestered

cloisters: 10 churchyard

cloistral: 8 monastic; **10** cloistered, conventual, monastical

clomiphene: 6 Clomid; **17** clomiphene citrate

clone: 4 clon

clonidine: 8 Catapres

clop: 5 clump, clunk, plunk

close: 3 end, set; **4** fast, fill, firm, fold, last, mean, mews, near, nigh, plug, shut, snug, taut, yard; **5** arena, brief, court, finis, privy, rents, short, terse, tight; **6** ending, fill up, finale, finish, narrow, secure, shabby, stingy, stuffy, sultry, taught; **7** airless, closely, closing, compact, concise, contact, in petto, miserly, occlude, passage, private, scrubby, serried, unaired; **8** conclude, faithful, peddling, shut down, stifling, terminus, thickset; **9** auricular, buildings, close down, close with, confining, inclosure, inviolate, penny wise, penurious, secretive, terminate; **10** but no cigar, close as wax, conclusion, oppressive; **11** approximate, clandestine, closelipped, come to an end, make contact, neighboring, suffocating, termination, tight-lipped

close at hand: 2 by; **4** near; **5** handy; **6** at hand; **7** close by; **8** imminent; **9** impending

close call: 6 squeak; **8** squeaker; **10** close shave; **12** narrow escape

close combat: 16 hand-to-hand combat

closed: 4 shut; **6** sealed, unopen; **7** plugged; **8** closed in, occluded; **9** stopped up; **13** unsympathetic

closed book: 6 enigma, secret; **7** mystery

closed circuit: 4 loop

closed-fisted: 10 hardfisted; **11** closefisted, tightfisted

close down: 4 fold; **5** close; **8** shut down

close-fitting: 4 snug; **5** close

closelipped: 5 close; **9** secretive; **11** tightlipped; **12** closemouthed

closely: 5 close, tight; **6** nearly; **7** densely; **10** intimately; **13** close together

closeness: 8 intimacy, meanness, nearness; **9** minginess, parsimony, tightness; **11** familiarity

close quarters: 7 earshot; **11** stone's throw

closer: 4 near; **6** nearer, nigher

close shave: 6 squeak; **8** squeaker; **9** close call; **12** narrow escape

closest: 7 nearest, nighest

closet: 2 WC; **3** loo; **5** press; **6** locker, secret; **7** cabinet, commode, gallery; **8** cellaret,

cupboard, wardrobe; **11** water closet; **12** chiffonniere, confidential

close to: 4 or so, some; **5** about; **6** around; **7** roughly; **9** close upon, just about; **10** more or less; **13** approximately

close up: 3 jam; **5** block; **6** belt up, clam up, impede, shut up; **7** be quiet, dummy up, keep mum, occlude; **8** button up, obstruct; **12** at close range

closing: 3 end; **5** close, mop up; **6** ending, windup; **7** closure; **8** blocking, shutdown, shutting; **9** closedown, finishing; **10** completion, concluding, conclusion; **11** culmination, terminating

closing curtain: 5 finis; **6** finale

clostridia: 11 clostridium

closure: 3 cap; **4** halt, stop; **5** block; **7** closing, cloture, gag rule; **8** blockade, blockage, blocking, shutdown, stoppage; **9** bottlecap, closedown, occlusion; **13** making contact

clot: 3 fix; **4** cake, clod, clog, curd; **5** candy, stone; **6** curdle; **7** clabber; **8** coagulum; **9** coagulate

cloth: 6 fabric, napkin; **7** textile; **8** material

clothe: 3 rig, tog; **4** garb, robe, vest; **5** adorn, array, drape, dress; **6** attire, enrobe, fit out, invest; **7** apparel, garment, raiment; **8** enclothe; **10** habilitate

clothed: 4 clad; **6** draped; **7** arrayed, attired, cloaked, dressed, mantled, wrapped; **8** invested

clothes: 4 wear; **6** attire; **7** apparel, vesture; **8** clothing, garments; **14** wearing apparel

clothes basket: 13 clothes hamper, laundry basket

clothes designer: 8 designer; **9** couturier; **15** fashion designer

clothes hamper: 13 clothes basket, laundry basket

clotheshorse: 3 fop; **4** beau, dude; **5** dandy, sheik, swell; **7** gallant, hatrack; **12** fashion plate

clothier: 11 haberdasher

clothing: 4 wear; **6** attire; **7** apparel, clothes, vesture; **8** garments; **14** wearing apparel

clothing store: 9 men's store; **12** haberdashery; **17** haberdashery store

clotted: 4 ropy; **6** clammy, mastic; **7** clogged, gelatin; **9** glutenous, glutinous; **10** albuminous, gelatinous; **12** mucilaginous

clotted cream: 15 Devonshire cream

clotting: 8 curdling; **11** coagulation

cloture: 7 closure, gag rule

cloud: 3 fog, fry; **4** bevy, haze, herd, hive, mist, nest, peck, veil; **5** befog, blind, brood, cloak, covey, drove, flock, shoal, storm, sully, swarm, taint, vapor; **6** bushel, dapple, defile, farrow, flight, litter, mottle, scores, shower, volley; **7** becloud, corrupt, curtain, draught, ill wind, obscure; **8** haze over, overcast; **9** dark cloud; **15** gathering clouds

cloudburst: 6 deluge, soaker; **7** torrent; **8** downpour; **10** waterspout; **13** drenching rain

cloud-covered: 7 clouded, sunless; **8** overcast

clouded: 5 paned; **6** in a jam; **7** blurred, dappled, sunless; **8** overcast; **9** in a bad way, in a pickle, in trouble; **11** under a cloud

cloudiness: 8 overcast; **9** muddiness, murkiness, turbidity; **10** cloud cover

cloudland: 9 dreamland

cloudless: 5 clear; **8** painless; **9** unalloyed, unclouded; **12** without alloy

cloudlike: 7 nebular

cloud-making: 12 cloud-forming

cloud nine: 5 bliss; **12** blissfulness, walking on air; **13** seventh heaven

cloud science: 12 nephanalysis

cloudy: 4 hazy; **5** foggy, mirky, misty, muddy, murky; **6** turbid; **8** nebulose, nebulous, vaporous

clove: 9 clove tree; **11** garlic clove

cloven: 5 cleft; **9** bisulcate

cloven foot: 7 evil eye; **10** cloven hoof

clove pink: 9 carnation

clown: 4 hind; **5** antic, swain; **7** buffoon, farceur [Fr]; **11** clown around, merry andrew

clown around: 5 antic, clown

clowning: 5 prank; **6** comedy; **8** drollery; **9** frivolity, funniness; **10** buffoonery; **12** harlequinade

clownish: 4 zany; **7** boorish, brutish, loutish, raffish; **8** churlish; **9** clownlike; **10** buffoonish

cloy: 4 glut, pall; **5** choke, gorge, slake; **6** fill up, quench; **7** surfeit; **9** suffocate

cloying: 6 syrupy; **7** treacly; **10** saccharine

club: 3 hit; **4** gild, home, nine; **5** guild, lodge, order; **6** casino; **7** society; **8** ball club, bludgeon, golfclub; **9** clubhouse; **12** baseball club, headquarters

clubbable: 8 clubable, sociable; **9** convivial; **13** companionable

clubhead: 12 golfclub head

clubhouse: 4 club

club sandwich: 11 three-decker; **12** tripledecker

club soda: 7 seltzer; **9** soda water; **14** sparkling water

cluck: 3 coo; **4** bark, honk; **5** clack, click; **6** cackle, gaggle

clue: 3 cue, key; **4** clew, hint; **5** scent

clump: 4 ball, clod, clop, glob, lump, thud; **5** bunch, chunk, clomp, clunk, flock, plunk, thump; **6** bundle, pencil; **7** bunch up, cluster; **8** thumping; **11** constellate

clumsiness: 8 slowness; **9** ineptness, stiff-

ness; **10** ineptitude; **11** awkwardness; **13** gracelessness, maladroitness

clumsy: 4 rude; **5** gawky, gross, inapt, inept, rough; **6** clunky, rugged; **7** awkward, rickety, spastic, unhandy; **8** bungling, fumbling, lubberly, ungainly, unwieldy; **9** ill-chosen, maladroit, slouching; **10** bunglesome, cumbersome; **11** floundering, heavy-handed, incompetent; **13** uncoordinated

clunk: 4 clop, thud; **5** clump, plunk, thump; **8** thumping

clunker: 5 lemon; **6** jalopy

clunky: 5 gawky; **6** clumsy; **8** ungainly, unwieldy

Clupea: sprat; **7** herring; **8** brisling; **11** genus Clupea

clupeid: 11 clupeid fish

Clusiaceae: 10 Guttiferae; **16** family Clusiaceae, family Guttiferae; **17** St John's wort family

cluster: 3 set; **5** bunch, clump, flock, group, swarm; **6** bundle; **7** bunch up; **10** assemblage; **11** constellate

clustered: 6 bunchy; **7** bunched; **11** agglomerate; **12** agglomerated; **13** agglomerative

clutch: 3 hug; **4** grab, grip, hold; **5** batch, clasp, grasp, gripe, seize, swoop; **6** clench, clinch, wrench; **7** cling to, embrace, grapple, prehend; **8** clutches; **9** hold close, hold tight; **10** fasten upon; **11** clutch pedal

clutches: 4 grip, hold; **5** clasp, fangs, grasp, tongs; **6** clench, clutch, pliers, talons; **7** forceps, nippers, pincers; **8** vise grip

clutter: 6 jumble, muddle, quaver, racket, welter; **7** smother

cluttered: 8 littered

clyster: 5 enema; **6** lavage

Cm: 6 curium

cm: 10 centimeter, centimetre

Cnemidophorus: 8 whiptail; **18** genus Cnemidophorus

cnidarian: 12 coelenterate

Co: 6 cobalt

CO: 13 carbon dioxide

coacervate: 11 aggregation; **12** coacervation [Chem]

coach: 3 bus, don; **4** cram; **5** prime, train, tutor; **6** jitney; **7** autobus, handler, manager, omnibus, trainer; **8** carriage, director, motorbus; **9** charabanc, Corypheus; **10** four-in-hand, motorcoach; **12** coach-and-four, double-decker, passenger car; **17** private instructor

coach dog: 9 dalmatian

coach house: 13 carriage house

coach painter: 11 miniaturist, sign painter; **12** scene painter; **13** flower painter, marine painter; **15** portrait painter; **16** landscape painter, miniature painter; **17** historical painter

coaction: 6 duress; **8** coercion; **10** compul-

coadjutancy: **7** concert; **11** concurrence, concurrency, cooperation; **13** collaboration

coagency: **7** concert; **11** concurrence, concurrency, cooperation; **13** collaboration, cooperativity; **14** acting together; **15** working together

coagulate: **3** set; **4** clot, cure; **7** congeal, curdled, grumose, grumous; **8** concrete, take a set; **10** coagulated; **11** consolidate

coal: **4** char; **5** ember

coal black: **5** ebony, sable; **8** jet black; **9** soot black; **10** pitch black

coalesce: **3** mix; **4** fuse, meld; **5** blend, immix, merge, unite; **6** absorb, embody; **7** blend in, combine, conjoin; **8** coincide, conflate, dissolve; **9** commingle; **10** amalgamate, centralize, impregnate; **11** consolidate, incorporate, melt into one; **13** blend together

coalescence: **5** union; **6** fusing, fusion; **7** uniting; **8** blending; **9** synthesis; **10** coalescing, embodiment; **11** coalescency, coincidence, unification; **12** amalgamation; **13** incorporation

coalition: **6** fusion; **8** alliance; **9** alignment, alinement

coal miner: **6** pitman; **7** collier

coal miner's lung: **9** black lung; **11** anthracosis; **16** black lung disease

coal oil: **5** crude; **7** rock oil; **8** crude oil, kerosene; **9** fossil oil, petroleum

coapt: **12** conglutinate

coaptation: **15** fitting together

coarctate: **6** draw in, narrow; **8** contract

coarctation: **5** taper; **8** tapering; **9** narrowing, stricture; **11** restriction

coarse: **4** foul, free; **5** bawdy, broad, crude, gross, harsh, loose, nasty, reeky, rough, scaly; **6** common, earthy, ribald, risque [Fr], smutty, uneven, vulgar; **7** beastly, fulsome, obscene, rasping, unblown, uncouth; **8** scabrous, unboiled, uncooked, unformed; **9** equivocal, irregular, offensive, rough cast, rough hewn, unwrought; **10** abominable, indecorous, stertorous, unpolished; **11** unconcocted; **12** pornographic

coarse-grained: **5** mealy, sandy; **6** grainy, gritty; **8** granular; **9** granulose; **11** farinaceous

coarsely: **7** crudely, roughly

coarseness: **5** scale; **9** grossness, harshness, nubbiness, sharpness, vulgarism, vulgarity; **10** commonness, graininess, tweediness; **11** granularity; **12** irregularity

coast: **4** skim; **5** drift, glide, shore, skate, slide; **6** course, cruise; **8** seaboard, seacoast, seashore; **9** coastline

coastal: **8** littoral, riparian

coastline: **5** coast, shore; **8** seaboard, seacoast, seashore

coat: **3** fur; **4** cake; **5** plate, shell; **6** veneer; **7** coating, surface

coati: **10** coati-mondi, coati-mundi; **11** Nasua narica

coating: **4** coat; **5** shell; **6** finish; **8** covering; **9** finishing; **11** application

coat of arms: **4** arms; **6** blazon; **8** blazonry

coat of mail: **4** mail; **7** hauberk; **8** ring mail; **9** chain mail, ring armor; **10** chain armor, ring armour; **11** chain armour

coatrack: **7** hatrack

coatroom: **9** cloakroom

coauthor: **11** joint author; **12** collaborator

coax: **4** lure; **5** charm, tempt; **6** cajole, cocker, cockle, coddle, cosset, seduce; **7** bewitch, blarney, palaver, wheedle; **8** inveigle; **9** carry away, coax cable, fascinate, smile upon, sweet-talk; **10** conciliate, make much of; **12** coaxial cable

coaxial: **6** coaxal

coaxial cable: **4** coax; **9** coax cable

coaxing: **7** blarney, coaxing; **8** soft soap; **9** sweet talk; **10** cajoling; **12** ingratiatory

cobalamin: **10** vitamin B12

cobalt: **2** Co

cobalt blue: **4** aqua; **9** turquoise; **10** aquamarine; **11** peacock blue; **12** greenish blue

cobble: **4** sett, vamp; **6** tinker; **7** retouch; **9** refashion; **11** cobblestone

cobbler: **9** shoemaker; **11** deep-dish pie

cobblestone: **4** sett; **6** cobble

cobia: **12** sergeant fish

coble: **3** cog; **4** punt; **5** shell; **6** wherry; **11** cockleshell

cobnut: **3** cob; **7** filbert; **8** hazelnut

cobra: **3** asp; **4** naga, naja; **5** snake; **7** serpent

cobweb: **4** drug; **5** chaff, froth, smoke; **6** bubble; **8** gossamer; **9** spider web

cobwebby: **5** filmy, gauzy, sheer; **8** gossamer, vaporous; **10** diaphanous, see-through; **11** transparent

cocaine: **1** C; **4** coke, snow; **6** cocain

coccyx: **8** tail bone

cochineal: **15** cochineal insect

Cochlearius cochlearius: **8** boatbill; **9** broadbill; **15** boat-billed heron

cochon de lait: **8** suckling; **11** suckling pig

cock: **3** dog; **4** boar, buck, hart, stag, tool, vane; **5** drake, horse, shaft, strut; **6** gander, prance, ruffle, sashay; **7** rooster, swagger; **8** stallion, stopcock, turncock; **11** entire horse, weathercock

cockade: **7** chevron, epaulet

cock-a-hoop: **3** big; **4** awry; **6** braggy; **7** crowing; **8** boastful, braggart, bragging, exultant; **16** self-aggrandizing

cock-a-leekie: **10** cocky-leeky

cockamamy: **4** fool, zany; **5** goofy, sappy,

silly, wacky; **10** cockamamie; **12** unreasonable

cock and bull story: 10 false story; **11** absurd story, untrue story

cockatiel: 9 cockateel; **14** cockatoo parrot; **20** Nymphicus hollandicus

cockatrice: 6 hornet, urchin; **7** butcher, serpent; **8** basilisk, scorpion

cock boat: 6 tender; **7** bum boat, fly boat

cockchafer: 6 May bug; **9** May beetle

cockcrow: 4 dawn; **5** sunup; **6** aurora; **7** dawning, morning, sunrise; **8** daybreak; **9** dayspring; **10** break of day, first light

cocked hat: 7 tricorn; **8** tricorne

cocker: 4 baby, coax, curl; **5** spoil, twill; **6** cockle, coddle, cosset, pamper, rumple; **7** frizzle, indulge, wheedle; **8** cockle up; **9** smile upon; **10** featherbed, make much of; **11** mollycoddle; **13** cocker spaniel

cocker spaniel: 6 cocker

cockeyed: 4 awry; **5** askew, wonky; **8** lopsided

cockhorse: 5 hobby; **10** hobbyhorse, stick horse; **12** rocking horse

cockiness: 9 pushiness; **11** forwardness; **13** bumptiousness

cockleshell: 3 cog; **4** punt; **5** shell; **6** wherry

cockloft: 4 loft; **5** attic; **6** garret; **10** clerestory

cock of the roost: 7 rooster; **11** chanticleer; **13** cock of the walk

cockpit: 5 synod; **11** convocation, compartment

cockroach: 5 roach; **7** tarakan [Russ]; **9** cucaracha [Sp]

cockscomb: 4 comb; **7** coxcomb

cocksfoot: 8 cockspur; **12** orchard grass

cocksure: 4 bold, sure; **6** secure; **7** assured, certain; **8** positive; **9** confident, convinced, satisfied; **12** unhesitating; **13** overconfident

cockswain: 9 boatswain

cocktail: 10 mixed drink

cocky-leeky: 11 cock-a-leekie

coco: 7 coconut; **8** coco palm; **9** cocoa palm; **11** coconut palm, coconut tree; **13** Cocos nucifera

cocoa: 9 chocolate; **12** hot chocolate

cocoa bean: 5 cacao

cocoanut: 7 coconut

cocoa palm: 4 coco; **7** coconut; **8** coco palm; **11** coconut palm, coconut tree; **13** Cocos nucifera

coconut: 4 coco; **8** coco palm, cocoanut; **9** cocoa palm; **11** coconut meat, coconut palm, coconut tree; **13** Cocos nucifera

coconut oil: 8 copra oil

Cocos Islands: 14 Keeling Islands

cocotte: 4 tart; **5** whore; **6** harlot; **7** trollop; **10** prostitute; **11** working girl

cocoyam: 4 edda, eddo, taro; **6** yautia; **7** dasheen; **8** taro root

Cocytus: 4 Styx; **7** Avernus [Lat]; **8** Tartarus; **12** River Cocytus, Stygian creek

COD: 14 cash on delivery

cod: 3 pod, rag; **4** bait, dupe, fool, gull, husk, ride, twit; **5** put on, rally, slang, taunt, tease; **6** befool, take in; **7** codfish, collect; **8** seedcase; **9** tantalize; **10** put one over; **12** put one across

coda: 6 finale

coddle: 4 baby, coax; **5** spoil; **6** cocker, cockle, cosset, pamper; **7** indulge, wheedle; **9** smile upon; **10** featherbed, make much of; **11** mollycoddle

coddled: 7 spoiled; **8** pampered

coddled egg: 9 boiled egg

code: 4 rule; **5** canon; **6** cipher, cypher, encode; **7** encrypt, listing; **8** encipher, inscribe, scramble; **11** write in code; **12** codification, computer code

coded: 7 encoded; **8** ciphered; **9** encrypted, scrambled

codex: 6 manual

codger: 6 old man; **9** eccentric

codified: 7 statute

codify: 9 formulate

codling: 6 codlin

coed: 10 schoolgirl; **11** college girl; **13** coeducational

coefficiency: 7 concert; **11** concurrence, concurrency, cooperation; **13** collaboration

coelenterate: 9 cnidarian

coeliac: 6 celiac; **9** abdominal

Coeloglossum: 6 orchid; **17** genus Coeloglossum

coelom: 5 celom; **6** celoma

coenobite: 8 cenobite

coequal: 4 even; **5** level; **10** coordinate, monotonous; **11** symmetrical

coerce: 4 make; **5** drive, force; **6** compel, oblige; **7** enforce; **8** pressure; **9** constrain; **11** necessitate

coerced: 6 forced; **8** required; **9** compelled; **10** compulsory, obligatory; **11** involuntary

coetaneous: 6 coeval; **15** contemporaneous

coeval: 10 coetaneous; **12** contemporary; **15** contemporaneous

coexist: 6 attend, concur; **7** co-occur; **9** accompany

coexistence: 7 company; **9** synchrony; **11** association, coincidence, isochronism, synchronism, unity of time; **12** co-occurrence, concomitance, simultaneity

coextension: 6 parity; **8** equality

coextensive: 8 parallel; **11** coterminous

coffee: 4 java; **5** umber; **9** chocolate, deep brown; **10** burnt umber, coffee bean, coffee tree; **11** coffee berry

coffee bar: 4 cafe; **10** coffee shop; **11** coffeehouse

coffee break: 5 break; 6 recess; 7 time-out; 8 tea break

coffee grinder: 10 coffee mill

coffeehouse: 4 cafe; 9 coffee bar; 10 coffee shop

coffee house: 11 eating house

coffee mill: 13 coffee grinder

coffer: 3 pix, pyx; 5 chest; 6 casket, lacuna; 7 caisson; 8 money box; 9 reliquary, strong box; 10 money chest

cofferdam: 7 caisson

coffin: 5 shell; 6 casket; 11 sarcophagus

cog: 3 cog; 4 punt; 5 shell, spoke; 6 earwig, wherry; 7 ratchet; 8 sprocket

cogent: 5 valid; 6 potent; 7 telling, weighty; 8 powerful; 10 convincing, persuasive

cogitable: 9 thinkable; 10 ponderable; 11 conceivable

cogitate: 5 think; 9 cerebrate; 10 deliberate

cognate: 3 kin, sib; 4 akin; 7 connate; 8 relative; 10 relating to; 11 cognate word, consanguine; 12 blood-related, pertaining to; 13 blood relation, blood relative; 14 consanguineous

cognate word: 7 cognate

cognation: 7 bearing, concern, enation; 8 relation; 10 connection; 12 blood kinship, matrilineage, relationship; 13 consanguinity

cogniscenti: 8 literati, virtuoso; 10 conoscente, dilettanti, illuminati [It]

cognition: 7 knowing; 9 knowledge; 10 cognizance, conception; 12 apprehension, precognition; 13 comprehension, understanding

cognizable: 8 knowable; 10 cognisable

cognizance: 3 ken; 7 knowing; 9 awareness, cognition; 10 conception; 11 knowingness; 12 apprehension, precognition; 13 comprehension, consciousness, understanding

cogwheel: 4 gear; 9 gear wheel

cohabit: 7 shack up; 12 live together

cohere: 5 cling, stick; 6 adhere; 7 deposit; 12 hang together

coherence: 8 cohesion; 9 coherency; 12 cohesiveness

coherent: 5 lucid; 7 logical; 8 cohesive; 9 tenacious

cohesive: 8 coherent, cohering

coho: 5 cohoe; 8 blue jack; 10 coho salmon; 12 silver salmon

cohort: 6 legion; 7 phalanx

cohosh: 9 baneberry

coiffure: 2 do; 3 set; 4 coif; 5 dress; 6 coiffe, hairdo; 7 arrange; 9 hair style

coign: 4 nook; 5 niche, oriel [Arch], quoin; 6 coigne, corner, recess

coil: 4 curl, gyre, loop, roll; 5 helix, twist, whorl; 6 gyrate, scroll, spiral, volute; 7 ringlet; 8 curlicue; 9 handbuild

coin: 4 mint; 5 piece; 6 create, devise, invent,

163

strike; 9 fabricate, originate; 11 legal tender

coinage: 6 specie; 7 mintage, neology; 9 neologism; 10 metal money

coin a word: 9 coin a term, neologize

coincide: 4 meet; 5 agree, graze, merge, touch; 6 concur, go with; 7 cooccur; 8 coalesce, osculate; 11 go along with, reciprocate

coincidence: 7 contact; 9 proximity; 10 apposition, contiguity; 11 coalescence, coexistence, concurrence, conjunction; 12 co-occurrence, happenstance; 13 juxtaposition; 14 contiguousness

coinciding: 9 conducing; 10 coincident, concurrent, concurring, conjoining, conspiring; 11 cooccurring; 12 coincidental, simultaneous

coin collecting: 11 numismatics; 13 numismatology

coin collector: 11 numismatist

coin machine: 11 slot machine

coke: 1 C; 4 snow; 6 cocain; 7 cocaine; 8 Coca-Cola

Cola acuminata: 4 kola; 7 kola nut; 8 goora nut

colander: 5 sieve; 6 riddle, screen

Colaptes: 7 flicker; 13 genus Colaptes

cold: 3 dry, dun, wan; 4 ashy, cool, dead, dull; 5 ashen, bland, dingy, faint, muddy, prosy, stale; 6 frigid, glassy, leaden, sallow, trashy; 7 chilled, ghastly, inhuman, languid, prosaic; 8 coldness, lukewarm; 9 colorless, insensate, proposing; 10 cadaverous, common cold, lackluster; 11 cold-blooded, coldhearted; 13 cold sensation; 14 low temperature

cold-blooded: 4 cold; 7 inhuman; 9 insensate; 11 coldhearted, unirritable

coldcock: 4 deck, dump; 5 floor; 9 knock down

coldly: 8 bitterly; 11 in cold blood; 14 without emotion

coldness: 4 cold; 8 coolness; 9 aloofness, frigidity; 10 chilliness, remoteness, withdrawal; 12 lack of caring, lukewarmness; 13 lack of feeling; 14 low temperature

cold room: 11 cold storage

cold shoulder: 6 ignore, slight; 7 neglect; 9 disregard

cold snap: 8 cold wave; 9 cold spell; 11 cold weather

cold sore: 3 rot; 6 canker; 9 fever sore; 10 oral herpes; 12 fever blister

cold sweat: 6 tremor; 7 ague fit, flutter, shaking; 9 quivering, trembling; 10 shuddering; 11 palpitation, trepidation; 12 perturbation; 14 throbbing heart; 16 fear and trembling

cole: 4 kail, kale; 8 borecole, colewort

Coleridge: 21 Samuel Taylor Coleridge
coleslaw: 4 slaw
coleus: 11 flame nettle
colewort: 4 cole, kail, kale; 8 borecole; 24 Brassica oleracea acephala
colic: 15 intestinal colic
colicky: 5 gassy; 9 flatulent
coliseum: 9 Colosseum; 12 amphitheater, amphitheatre
collaborate: 6 concur; 9 cooperate; 10 join forces; 11 get together; 12 act in concert; 15 make common cause
collaborator: 7 pardner, partner, party to; 8 coauthor, confrere, coworker, henchman, quisling; 9 accessory, assistant, auxiliary; 10 cooperator; 11 concomitant, confederate; 14 participator in, partner in crime
collage: 6 mosaic; 7 montage; 8 pastiche; 9 composite, patchwork, potpourri; 10 hodgepodge
collapse: 3 ebb; 4 blow, drop, flop, give, pack, stow, wane, warp; 5 break, burst, crack, crash, crush, faint, lapse, palsy, smash, split, swoon, waste; 6 blight, cave in, crunch, dry rot, fall in, retire, shrink, tumble; 7 atrophy, break up, crack up, crock up, crumble, crumple, dwindle, flat out [U.S.], founder, give way, purse up, shrivel, syncope; 8 apoplexy, fainting, fall away, grow less; 9 break down, corrugate, crumple up, explosion, inanition, paralysis; 10 exhaustion
collar: 3 cop, nab; 4 claw, nail, yoke; 5 catch, pinch; 6 arrest, choker, pick up; 8 neckband, throttle; 9 apprehend, dog collar; 12 apprehension
collarbone: 8 clavicle
collar cell: 10 choanocyte
collards: 13 collard greens
collate: 4 sort; 7 collect; 8 confront
collateral: 6 allied; 7 oblique; 8 indirect; 9 verifying; 10 confirming, validating, validatory; 12 confirmative, confirmatory, pledged asset, verificatory; 13 corroborative, corroboratory; 14 substantiating, substantiative
colleague: 6 fellow; 7 compeer; 8 co-worker, confrere; 9 associate; 10 workfellow; 12 fellow worker
collect: 3 cod, see; 4 take, ween; 5 amass, catch, grasp, hoard; 6 deduce, derive, follow, garner, gather, master, muster, pick up, pile up, pull in, take in; 7 call for, collate, compile, make out; 8 assemble, gather up; 10 accumulate, congregate, see one's way; 11 get together, put together, see daylight; 12 come together, draw together, lump together, pull together; 13 bring together
collected: 6 massed, poised; 7 amassed,

grouped; 8 composed; 9 assembled; 10 congregate, equanimous; 11 accumulated; 13 self-collected, self-contained, self-possessed
collecting: 8 assembly; 9 gathering; 10 assembling, collection
collection: 6 appeal; 8 assembly; 10 assemblage, assembling, collecting, compendium; 11 aggregation
collective: 5 broad; 7 general, generic; 8 additive, sweeping; 9 concerted, corporate; 12 encyclopedic; 13 comprehensive, encyclopaedic
collective agreement: 13 labor contract; 14 labor agreement
collective bargaining: 16 labor negotiation
collectively: 3 all; 7 in a body, jointly; 8 all in all, as a whole, entirely, together; 9 wholesale; 10 conjointly; 11 put together
collectivist: 7 leftist; 10 left-winger; 13 collectivized; 14 collectivistic; 15 state-controlled
collector: 8 gatherer; 11 accumulator
college woman: 4 coed; 9 collegian
college man: 9 collegian
collegiate: 8 academic; 9 collegial; 10 scholastic
collet: 7 ferrule; 11 collet chuck
collide: 3 jar; 5 clash
collide with: 3 hit; 6 strike; 7 run into; 9 impinge on
collier: 6 pitman; 9 coal miner
colliery: 3 pit; 8 coal mine
colligate: 7 subsume; 8 assemble; 9 collocate
colligation: 8 assembly; 10 collecting, collection; 11 collocation
collimate: 8 parallel
Collinsia: 14 genus Collinsia
collision: 3 hit; 4 bump; 5 brush, clash, crash, fight, smash; 6 affair; 7 contact; 8 clashing, conflict, touching; 9 encounter; 10 concussion, percussion; 11 battle royal
collocate: 4 deal, lump, pack; 5 allot, chunk; 6 set out; 7 marshal; 9 parcel out; 10 distribute
collocation: 8 assembly; 10 allocation, collecting, collection
collocution: 4 talk; 8 colloquy, converse; 9 discourse; 13 confabulation
collogue: 3 cog; 6 confer; earwig
collop: 4 chip; 5 chunk, shard; 8 chipping, fragment
colloquial: 8 informal; 14 conversational
colloquy: 4 talk; 6 confer; 8 converse; 9 dialogue, discourse
collude: 7 concert, consort; 7 connive; 8 conspire; 10 fraternize; 11 confederate; 12 club together, hand together, hang together, hold together, keep together, pull together
collusive: 9 collusory, conniving; 14 conspiratorial

colly: 4 soil; **5** dirty, grime; **6** bemire; **7** begrime

collyrium: 7 eyewash; **8** liniment; **9** eyelotion, traumatic, vulnerary

colobus: 13 colobus monkey

Colocasia esculenta: 4 dalo, taro; **7** dasheen; **9** taro plant

Cologne: 4 Koln

cologne: 7 cologne; **12** cologne water, eau de cologne

Colombo: 17 capital of Sri Lanka

colonist: 7 settler; **8** squatter; **12** backwoodsman

colonization: 10 settlement; **12** colonisation

colonize: 11 domesticate

colonnade: 4 mall; **6** arcade, piazza

colony: 7 mandate; **8** dominion, province; **9** territory; **10** cantonment, settlement

colophony: 5 resin, rosin

color: 3 air, dye, hue; **4** cast, cook, glow, look, mien, port, tint, tone; **5** flush, gloss, guise, shade, tinge; **6** colour, livery, redden, show of; **7** color in, distort, dress up, varnish; **8** carriage, coloring, colour in, demeanor, emblazon, lividity, tincture; **9** colouring, dark color, embroider, semblance, vividness; **10** coloration, complexion

Colorado: 13 Colorado River; **15** Centennial State

Colorado beetle: 6 locust; **9** potato bug; **12** potato beetle; **20** Colorado potato beetle

Colorado spruce: 10 blue spruce

coloration: 3 dye, hue; **4** cast, glow, tint; **5** color, flush, shade, tinge; **6** livery; **8** tincture

color blindness: 9 Daltonism; **16** achromatic vision

coloring: 4 tone; **5** color, drift, tenor, value; **6** colour, strain; **7** bearing, keeping, stretch; **8** tendency; **9** colouring, food color, hyperbole; **10** food colour, local color, stretching; **12** exaggeration, food coloring, modification

coloring material: 7 pigment

colorless: 3 dry; **4** cold, dull; **5** bland, prosy; **6** frigid, trashy; **7** languid, prosaic; **8** lukewarm; **9** proposing, uncolored; **10** achromatic, colourless, monochrome, uncoloured, water-white; **11** monochromic; **12** hole-in-corner; **13** black and white, hole-and-corner, monochromatic

colorlessness: 11 achromatism

colors: 4 flag; **6** banner, ensign; **7** colours, pennant; **9** dichroism; **10** trichroism

color up: 5 blush, flush; **6** mantle, redden; **8** blush for; **10** get flushed; **11** change color

colossal: 5 giant; **7** titanic; **8** gigantic; **9** giant-like, gigantean; **10** prodigious, stupendous

Colosseum: 8 Coliseum

colossus: 5 giant, titan; **7** goliath, monster; **8** behemoth; **11** heavyweight

colostrum: 8 foremilk

colporteur: 6 cadger, hawker; **7** peddler; **8** huckster

colt: 3 oaf, put; **4** calf, foal, loon, lout, tony; **5** block, stick, stock; **6** doodle; **7** buzzard, dullard

coltish: 8 frolicky, sportive; **10** frolicsome, rollicking

Coluber: 9 blue racer, whipsnake; **10** black racer, blacksnake; **12** genus Coluber

colubrid: 13 colubrid snake

colugo: 9 flying cat; **11** flying lemur

Columba: 6 pigeon; **12** genus Columba

columbary: 6 stable; **8** dovecote; **11** columbarium

Columbia: 13 Columbia River; **22** capital of South Carolina

columbite: 7 niobite

Columbus: 13 capital of Ohio; **14** Cristobal Colon; **17** Cristoforo Colombo; **19** Christopher Colombus

columella: 5 spine; **8** backbone, vertebra; **9** vertebrae

column: 4 army, file, host, pier, post, wing; **5** corps, shaft, squad, tower; **6** pillar, rundle; **7** battery, brigade, company, obelisk, platoon, section, upright; **8** division, garrison, monolith, pilaster, regiment, squadron; **9** battalion, editorial; **10** detachment, procession, rolling-pin; **11** corps d'armee [Fr], subdivision; **12** flying column; **15** newspaper column

columnist: 12 editorialist

colza: 4 rape; **8** rapeseed

colza oil: 7 rape oil; **8** olive oil, salad oil; **10** linseed oil; **11** rapeseed oil; **12** vegetable oil

coma: 6 trance; **9** catatonia; **12** comatoseness; **15** unconsciousness

comaraderie: 9 comradery; **10** chumminess; **13** comradeliness

comatose: 4 dead [fig], numb; **7** out cold, unaware; **9** catatonic, senseless; **11** unconscious

comb: 4 cane, flog, lash, lick, rake, whip; **5** beard, birch, strap, towel; **6** larrup, switch, thrash, thresh; **7** comb out, combing, coxcomb, ransack, scourge; **9** bastinado, cockscomb, horsewhip; **10** flagellate

combat: 3 war; **5** fight; **6** battle; **7** wage war, warfare; **8** battling, conflict, do battle, fighting; **10** give battle; **11** armed combat, clash of arms, hostilities

combat action: 7 service; **11** campaigning, tented field; **13** active service

combatant: 7 battler, fighter; **8** scrapper; **11** belligerent

combat fatigue: 10 shell shock; 13 battle fatigue

combat injury: 5 wound; 6 injury

combative: 7 martial, warlike; 9 agonistic, battleful, bellicose; 10 pugnacious; 11 agonistical, belligerent, contentious

combat ship: 7 warship, carrier, cruiser; 10 battleship

combat zone: 10 tenderloin

combe: 4 dale, dell, glen, vale; 5 glade, grove; 6 bottom, dingle, valley

combination: 5 combo; 6 league, opener; 7 combine; 8 alliance, password; 9 combining, master key, syndicate; 11 compounding

combine: 3 mix; 4 fuse, meld, pool; 5 blend, immix, merge, trust, unite; 6 absorb, cahoot, cartel, embody; 7 blend in, conjoin; 8 coalesce, compound, conflate, dissolve; 9 aggregate, combining, commingle, syndicate; 10 amalgamate, centralize, impregnate; 11 combination, consolidate, incorporate, melt into one; 13 blend together

combined: 6 united; 8 conjunct; 9 concerted; 11 conjunctive, cooperative

combing: 4 comb; 8 brushing

combining weight: 2 eq; 10 equivalent; 16 equivalent weight

comb jelly: 10 ctenophore

combo: 8 jazz band; 9 jazz group; 11 combination

comb out: 4 comb; 7 weed out; 11 disentangle

comb-out: 7 teasing

combtooth blenny: 6 blenny

combust: 4 burn

combustible: 4 fuel; 6 firing; 8 burnable; 9 flammable; 11 inflammable

combustible material: 4 fuel; 11 combustible

combustion: 7 burning

come: 2 do; 3 get; 4 fall, fare, hail, here!; 5 add up, occur, total; 6 amount, appear, arrive, come in, derive, follow, number, show up; 7 descend, forward!; 8 approach!, become of, come near!, get along

come across: 3 see; 4 meet; 6 come at, strike; 7 ran into; 8 chance on, come onto, come over, come upon, discover, resonate; 9 encounter, forgather, light upon, run across; 10 chance upon, foregather, happen upon

come along: 4 go on; 5 get on; 6 appear, come on, move on, pass on, push on; 7 advance, go ahead, press on, shape up; 8 get ahead, get along, progress; 9 come ahead, go forward, move ahead, pass ahead, push ahead; 10 get forward, go for-

wards, press ahead; 11 come forward, get forwards, move forward, pass forward, push forward; 12 come forwards, move forwards, pass forwards, press forward, push forwards; 13 press forwards; 16 take steps forward

come apart: 5 break; 7 split up; 8 separate; 9 fall apart

come away: 6 detach, go away; 7 come off, get away; 8 back away, move away; 9 drift away

comeback: 6 retort, return; 7 riposte; 9 rejoinder

come back: 5 repay; 6 go back, recall, rejoin, retort, return; 7 get back, get home, put back, riposte, run back; 8 come home, draw back, fall back, hark back, turn back; 10 be restored

come before: 7 precede

comedian: 5 comic; 9 tragedian

comedie drame: 5 drame; 6 masque

comedo: 9 blackhead

come down: 4 fall; 6 go down, reduce, sicken; 7 descend; 8 boil down; 11 precipitate

comedown: 3 rub; 5 check, cross; 7 reverse, setback [U.S.]; 8 reversal; 11 contretemps

comedy: 5 farce; 8 clowning, drollery; 9 funniness

come forward: 4 go on; 6 come on, move on, pass on, push on, star it, step up; 7 be showy, come out, go ahead, press on; 8 get ahead; 9 come ahead, come along, come forth, go forward, move ahead, pass ahead, push ahead, volunteer; 10 get forward, go forwards, press ahead; 11 come in sight, get forwards, move forward, pass forward, push forward, step forward; 12 be a candidate, come forwards, come into view, move forwards, offer oneself, pass forwards, press forward, push forwards; 13 be pretentious, come to the fore, press forwards, step to the fore; 14 be ostentatious, present oneself

come in: 4 come, go in; 5 enter, get in, place, put in; 6 go into, inject; 7 come out, get into, throw in; 8 come into, move into

come loose: 6 detach; 7 come off, fall off; 8 get loose

comely: 4 fair; 5 bonny; 6 bonnie, decent, seemly; 8 becoming, decorous, handsome; 10 personable

come-on: 4 bait, hook, lure; 9 sweetener; 10 enticement

come out: 3 out, pop; 5 bulge, erupt, issue, place; 6 appear, bug out, come in, come on, emerge, pop out, show up, step up, turn up; 7 crop-out, leak out, ooze out, peep out, surface, turn out; 8 bulge out, creep out, protrude; 9 come forth; 11 come forward, come in sight, push through, step forward; 12 break through, come into view

comer: 7 arrival, arriver

comestible: 6 edible; 7 eatable, pabulum, victual; 8 victuals; 10 alimentary

comestibles: 4 food, grub; 7 aliment, edibles, ingesta, pabulum; 8 eatables, victuals; 9 nutriment, provender; 10 sustenance; 11 nourishment, staff of life; 12 alimentation, sustentation

come through: 6 make it; 7 succeed, survive

come to a close: 3 end; 5 close; 6 finish; 8 conclude; 9 terminate

come together: 4 meet; 5 close, unite; 6 concur, muster; 7 collect; 8 assemble, converge; 10 fall in with

come to pass: 4 go on; 5 occur; 6 happen; 9 take place

come to terms: 4 cede; 6 settle; 7 satisfy; 9 surrender; 10 capitulate

come to the fore: 6 step up; 7 come out; 11 come forward, step forward; 12 come foreward, step foreward

come toward: 4 near; 6 go near; 7 get near; 8 approach, come near, draw near; 11 approximate, move towards

come upon: 4 find; 6 strike; 7 pop upon; 8 chance on, discover, fall upon, luck into; 9 burst upon, enter upon, light upon, pitch upon, plump upon; 10 bounce upon, chance upon, come across, happen upon

comeuppance: 11 just deserts

come up short: 4 miss; 8 not reach; 9 come short, fall short

come up to: 6 accost, come to; 7 address; 8 amount to; 9 come close

comfit: 7 confect; 10 confection

comfort: 4 ease; 5 cheer; 6 luxury, solace, soothe; 7 console; 8 snugness; 9 set at ease; 11 consolation, lap of luxury; 13 encouragement

comfortable: 4 easy, snug; 5 comfy; 6 at ease, at rest; 7 well-off; 8 well-to-do; 9 well-fixed; 10 prosperous, well-heeled

comforter: 4 puff; 5 plaid, quilt, sheet; 7 blanket, muffler; 8 bedsheet, coverlet, pacifier

comforting: 8 cheering; 9 consoling; 10 satisfying; 11 consolatory

comfortless: 6 desole [Fr]; 7 forlorn, joyless; 8 desolate; 9 cheerless; 11 sick at heart; 12 disconsolate, inconsolable, unconsolable

comforts: 9 amenities; 12 conveniences

comfort station: 8 restroom, wash room; 11 convenience; 12 public toilet

comfrey: 7 cumfrey; 11 healing herb

comfy: 11 comfortable

comic: 5 funny; 7 amusing, comical, risible; 8 comedian, mirthful; 9 comic book, laughable

comical: 5 comic, funny; 7 amusing, risible; 8 mirthful; 9 laughable

comic opera: 6 bouffe; 11 opera bouffe; 12 opera comique

comic strip: 5 strip; 12 cartoon strip

coming: 6 advent, climax, in hand, orgasm, to come; 7 in store, in train; 8 approach, in embryo, on the way, upcoming; 9 future day, impending; 10 near at hand; 11 approaching, forthcoming, in agitation; 12 sexual climax; 13 available soon, going to happen, in preparation

coming after: 9 following; 10 succession

coming along: 7 going on; 8 coming on, moving on; 9 passing on, pushing on; 10 pressing on; 12 going forward, pushing ahead

coming and going: 11 oscillation

coming back: 6 return

coming before: 9 preceding; 10 precedence

coming days: 6 morrow; 9 after days; 14 subsequent days

coming event: 11 future event; 13 upcoming event

coming later: 9 following; 10 succession

coming together: 7 meeting, merging; 8 abutment, assembly, congress; 9 concourse, gathering; 10 assembling, collecting, confluence, contacting, converging, osculation; 11 concurrence, convergence, convergency, ingathering

coming upon: 9 encounter

comitia: 7 council; 9 committee; 12 subcommittee

comity: 6 polish; 7 suavity; 8 breeding, presence, urbanity; 9 gentility

command: 3 bid; 4 have, hold, rule, soar, sway; 5 enjoy, order, tower; 6 compel, direct, impose, occupy; 7 bidding, control, mastery, overtop, possess, require; 8 dominate, dominion, overlook; 9 dictation, statement, supremacy; 10 administer, be seized of, domination, have in hand, suzerainty; 11 instruction, program line, sovereignty

commandant: 9 commander

commandeer: 6 hijack, pirate; 8 highjack, liberate; 11 appropriate

commander: 7 manager; 8 director; 10 commandant; 15 air force officer

commanding: 5 grand, noble; 7 ranking; 8 imposing, ordering, top-level; 9 directing; 10 dominating, impressive, peremptory, top-ranking; 11 overlooking

commanding officer: 9 commander; 10 commandant

command key: 10 control key

command language: 13 query language; 14 search language

command line interface: 3 CLI

commando: 6 ranger

command post: 3 GHQ

comme il faut: 6 comely, decent, seemly; **7** a la mode, courtly, genteel; **8** becoming, decorous

Commelinaceae: 16 spiderwort family; **19** family Commelinaceae

commemorate: 4 mark; **6** record; **8** remember; **11** immortalize, memorialize

commemoration: 7 jubilee; **8** memorial; **11** remembrance

commemorative: 8 immortal; **10** celebrated

commence: 3 get; **4** dawn, open; **5** begin, enter, set in, start; **6** set out; **7** lead off, start up; **8** embark on, set about, start out

commencement: 5 first, start; **6** launch, offset, outset; **7** kickoff, opening; **9** beginning, first move, inception; **10** graduation, incipience, initiation; **11** origination; **12** starting time

commencement day: 9 degree day

commend: 4 laud; **6** praise; **8** remember; **9** recommend; **10** compliment

commendable: 8 laudable, laudably; **9** admirably; **10** creditable; **11** applaudable; **12** of estimation, praiseworthy

commendation: 4 laud; **6** praise; **8** approval, citation; **9** laudation

commensurate: 5 valid; **8** tangible; **9** competent; **12** satisfactory; **13** commensurable

comment: 5 gloss; **6** gossip, kibitz, notice, remark; **8** point out; **10** commentary, discussion; **11** scuttlebutt; **12** deliberation

commentary: 6 review; **7** comment; **8** critique; **9** criticism

commentator: 6 critic; **8** observer, reviewer; **9** annotator, scholiast

commerce: 5 trade; **7** trading, traffic; **8** business; **12** mercantilism; **13** commercialism

commercial: 2 ad; **4** TV ad; **7** trading; **8** business; **10** mercantile

commercial activity: 5 trade; **8** business

commercialism: 8 commerce; **12** mercantilism

commercialize: 6 market

commercial law: 11 law merchant; **13** mercantile law

commercial organization: 4 firm; **5** firms [pl]; **7** company, concern; **8** business; **9** companies [pl]; **10** enterprise; **13** establishment

commercial product: 7 product

commie: 9 communist

commination: 6 menace, threat; **15** excommunication

comminatory: 8 menacing, minatory; **11** threatening; **12** denunciative, denunciatory

commingle: 3 mix; **4** fuse, meld; **5** blend, immix, merge; **7** combine; **8** coalesce, conflate; **11** intermingle

comminute: 4 bray, mash; **5** grind; **6** crunch; **9** granulate, pulverize, triturate

Commiphora meccanensis: 12 balm of gilead

Commiphora myrrha: 9 myrrh tree

commiserate: 7 feel for; **8** have pity, show pity, take pity; **10** be sorry for, sympathize

commiseration: 4 pity, ruth; **6** pathos; **10** compassion, condolence

commissariat: 8 victuals; **9** provender; **10** provisions; **12** food supplies

commissary: 6 feeder; **7** caterer; **8** purveyor; **9** victualer, lunchroom; **12** commissioner; **13** quartermaster

commission: 4 care, task; **5** trust; **6** assign, charge, errand; **7** consign, entrust, intrust, mission; **8** delegacy, delegate; **9** assigning, committee, direction; **10** assignment, delegating, delegation, deputation, deputizing, engagement, entrusting; **11** consignment; **12** assigned duty

commission agent: 6 broker; **11** underwriter

commissionaire: 5 envoy; **8** emissary; **9** attendant

commissioned: 8 licenced, licensed; **10** accredited

commissioner: 4 boss; **5** chief; **10** commissary

commissioning: 5 trust; **9** assigning; **10** assignment, commission, delegating, delegation, deputation, deputizing, entrusting; **11** consignment

commissure: 4 gore, seam; **5** hinge, pivot

commit: 3 put; **4** give, pull, send; **5** place, trust, commit; **6** attach, charge, devote, invest; **7** confide, consign, entrust, inflict, intrust; **8** dedicate, distrain, imprison; **10** perpetrate; **12** give in charge, send to prison; **13** give in custody

commit adultery: 5 cheat; **10** take a lover; **12** be unfaithful

commitment: 7 loyalty; **9** committal; **10** allegiance, dedication; **11** consignment

commit sacrilege: 9 blaspheme, desecrate

committee: 7 comitia [Lat], council, nominee, trustee; **9** consignee; **10** commission; **12** subcommittee

committeeman: 8 alderman; **10** councilman; **12** councilwoman

commit to memory: 8 memorize, remember; **9** put in mind; **11** memorialize

commix: 3 mix; **5** blend, unify; **6** mingle; **8** intermix; **10** amalgamate

commode: 3 can, cap, hat, pot; **5** potty; **6** closet, locker, throne, toilet; **7** crapper; **8** cellaret, cupboard; **10** chiffonier; **12** chiffonniere

commodious: 5 roomy; **8** spacious; **9** adaptable; **10** convenient

commodity: 4 ware; **5** goods; **7** article, product; **11** merchandise

common: 3 jog, low; **4** mean, mere, park, trot; **5** green, sorry, usual, veldt; **6** coarse, mutual, normal, simple, vulgar; **7** commons, general, nominal, prairie, regular, scrubby, typical, uncouth; 8 beggarly, everyday, familiar, frequent, habitual, ordinary, plebeian, unwashed, workaday; 9 grassland, household, well-known, worldwide; 10 uneventful, vernacular; 11 commonplace, established, well-trodden; 13 garden variety

common cold: 4 cold; 10 rhinovirus

common divisor: 12 common factor; 13 common measure

commoner: 7 cockney, epicier [Fr]; 9 bourgeois, common man; 11 proletarian; 12 common person

Common Era: 12 Christian Era

common good: 10 commonweal

common knowledge: 6 truism

common land: 7 commons

common law: 6 equity; 7 case law; 9 precedent

commonly: 7 as usual, usually; 8 normally; 9 typically; 10 ordinarily; 12 unremarkably

common man: 8 commoner; 10 average Joe, average man, Joe six-pack; 12 common person

Common Market: 3 EEC

common measure: 10 common time; 11 aliquot part, common meter; 12 common factor, four-four time; 13 common divisor

common meter: 13 common measure

commonness: 7 frequency, grossness, vulgarism, vulgarity; 10 coarseness; 11 commonality; 12 everydayness, expectedness

common people: 4 folk

common person: 8 commoner; 9 common man; 10 average Joe, average man, Joe six-pack; 13 average person

commonplace: 3 jog; 4 fair, trot; 5 banal, prosy, stock, tired, trite; 6 cliche, common; 7 bromide, humdrum, prosaic, prosing, trivial, typical; 8 banality, everyday, frequent, ordinary, passable, shopworn, timeworn, well-worn; 9 hackneyed, household, platitude, pointless, tolerable, unadorned, well-known; 10 pedestrian, threadbare, ubiquitous; 11 respectable, unglamorous, unvarnished, well-trodden; 12 just passable, matter of fact, unglamourous, unornamented; 13 garden variety

common practice: 3 use; 5 usage; 6 custom; 8 practice; 10 convention, observance, prevalence

commons: 4 keep, mall, park; 5 board, green; 6 common; 10 common land, commonalty; 11 commonality, public space

common sense: 5 sense; 8 gumption; 9 good sense, mother wit; 10 horse sense [U.S.], plain sense

common shares: 11 common stock; 14 ordinary shares

common soldier: 7 private; 11 buck private

commonwealth: 4 land; 5 state; 6 nation; 7

country; 8 republic; 9 democracy; 10 commonweal, public good, res publica; 11 body politic; 13 public welfare

Commonwealth Day: 9 Empire day

Commonwealth of Australia: 9 Australia

Commonwealth of Nations: 19 British Commonwealth

commorant: 9 sojourner; 11 locum tenens

commotion: 3 din; 4 stir, to-do; 5 whirl; 6 ruckus, rumpus, tumult; 7 ruction, turmoil; 8 disorder, disquiet; 9 agitation; 10 disruption, hurly-burly, turbulence; 11 disturbance; 13 civil disorder

commove: 5 rouse; 6 charge, excite, stir up; 7 agitate, disturb, raise up, shake up; 8 charge up

communal: 5 group

commune: 5 tract; 6 domain; 11 communicate

commune with: 10 confer with; 12 commerce with; 13 discourse with

communicable: 6 taking; 8 catching; 10 contagious, infectious; 12 contractable; 13 transmissable, transmissible, transmittable

communicable disease: 9 contagion; 17 contagious disease

communicant: 8 adherent; 9 celebrant, worshiper; 10 worshipper; 11 pious person; 12 congregation; 15 religious person

communicate: 4 pass; 6 convey, impart, pass on, render; 7 commune, express, let fall, mention; 8 intimate, transmit; 9 make known, put across, represent

communicated: 4 told; 8 reported

communicating: 9 notifying; 10 intimation

communication: 6 report; 8 despatch, dispatch; 9 endowment; 10 confluence, intimation; 11 consignment; 12 dispensation

communication channel: 4 line

communications intelligence: 6 COMINT

communicative: 9 notifying; 13 communicating

communicator: 6 sender

communicatory: 9 notifying

Communion: 13 Holy Communion

communion: 6 orison, prayer; 7 sharing; 8 petition; 9 Eucharist; 11 Lord's supper; 12 denomination, the sacrament; 13 holy communion, holy sacrament

communion table: 5 altar; 9 holy table; 10 Lord's table

communique: 6 notice; 8 despatch, dispatch; 12 announcement, notification

communism: 7 statism; 9 socialism; 14 state socialism

communist: 6 commie; 11 communistic

Communist: 6 Fenian; 8 frondeur

Communist China: 3 PRC; 5 China; 8 Red China; 13 mainland China; 22 People's Republic of China

communistic: 9 communist
community: 4 body, folk; 5 world; 6 public; 7 society; 8 sodality; 10 profession, solidarity; 12 neighborhood; 15 residential area
community center: 11 civic center
communize: 10 bolshevise, bolshevize
commutable: 13 substitutable
commutation: 9 commuting; 11 composition; 12 re-sentencing; 13 intermutation
commutation ticket: 12 season ticket
commutative: 6 mutual; 10 reciprocal; 12 exchangeable
commutative group: 12 Abelian group
commute: 4 swap; 5 bandy; 6 change, redeem, switch; 7 convert, permute, shuffle; 8 compound, exchange; 9 transpose; 11 change hands, compound for; 13 commute to work
commuter: 11 suburbanite; 13 commuter train
commuter train: 8 commuter
commute to work: 7 commute
commuting: 11 commutation
commutual: 6 mutual; 10 reciprocal; 13 reciprocative
Comoro Islands: 11 Iles Comores
comose: 5 comal; 6 comate
compact: 3 wad; 4 neap, neat, pack, pact; 5 close, dense, exact, press, thick; 6 atomic, bundle, stocky; 7 serried, squeeze, summary; 8 compress, contract, covenant, heavyset, succinct, thickset; 9 agreement, concordat, constrict, corporate, primitive; 10 compact car, to the point; 11 compendious, indivisible; 12 pack together, unanalyzable; 13 powder compact
compact car: 7 compact
compact disc read-only memory: 5 CD-ROM
compact disc recordable: 3 CD-R; 4 CD-WO
compact disc: 2 CD; 5 CD-ROM; 11 compact disc
compact disc drive: 5 CD-ROM
compacted: 7 reduced; 8 squeezed; 10 compressed
compacting: 9 concision, squeezing; 10 abridgment; 12 retrenchment
compaction: 5 crush; 6 crunch; 10 concretion; 11 compression; 13 densification
compactly: 10 succinctly
compactness: 7 brevity, density; 9 denseness, small size, smallness; 10 littleness; 11 conciseness; 13 concentration
compages: 5 stuff; 7 complex; 8 ensemble; 9 aggregate
compagination: 5 union; 7 joinder [Law], uniting; 8 coupling; 11 conjugation, conjunction

companies: 4 firm; 5 firms [pl]; 7 company, concern; 8 business; 10 enterprise; 13 establishment
companion: 3 pal; 4 mate; 5 buddy; 6 fellow; 7 company, comrade; 8 alter ego, confrere, familiar, intimate; 9 accompany, associate, confidant, free lance; 10 confidante
companionable: 8 sociable; 9 clubbable, convivial
companionship: 7 company, society; 10 fellowship; 11 association, coexistence, comradeship; 12 concomitance
company: 4 army, firm, host, wing; 5 corps, firms [pl], party, squad; 6 caller, column, troupe; 7 battery, brigade, concern, coterie, platoon, section, society; 8 business, division, garrison, regiment, squadron; 9 accompany, battalion, companies [pl], companion; 10 detachment, enterprise, fellowship; 11 association, coexistence, comradeship, corps d'armee [Fr], keep company, subdivision; 12 concomitance, flying column, ship's company, social circle; 13 companionship, establishment; 14 good fellowship, theater company
comparability: 7 compare; 10 comparison; 11 equivalence
comparable: 4 like; 8 allusive; 13 corresponding
comparative grammar: 9 philology
comparatively: 10 relatively
compare: 5 liken; 6 equate; 9 compare to; 10 comparison; 11 compare with, equivalence; 13 comparability
comparing: 10 comparison; 11 contrasting
comparison: 7 compare; 8 contrast; 9 comparing; 11 contrasting, equivalence; 13 comparability
compartment: 4 room; 7 chamber; 9 partition; 10 department
compartmentalize: 5 cut up; 6 divide; 9 partition; 10 modularize; 16 compartmentalise
compass: 3 dig, lap, way; 4 gird, helm, room; 5 ambit, beset, bound, field, grasp, orbit, range, reach, savvy, scope, sweep, swing, tenor; 6 begird, needle, rudder, spread; 7 achieve, embrace, enclose, environ, inclose; 8 calipers, complete, encircle, surround; 9 apprehend, calculate, encompass, expansion, hammer out; 10 accomplish, circumvent, comprehend, consummate; 13 get the picture; 14 circumnavigate
compass about: 9 encompass
compass flower: 12 compass plant
compassion: 4 pity; 13 commiseration
compassionate: 4 pity; 7 feel for, pitying, touched; 8 have pity, show pity, take pity; 10 be sorry for, full of pity; 11 commiserate, condole with, showing pity, sympathetic

compass north: 5 north; 13 magnetic north

compass plane: 13 circular plane

compatibility: 7 rapport

compatible: 10 consistent; 11 sympathetic, well-matched; 13 IBM compatible, proportionate; 15 IBM PC-compatible

compatriot: 10 countryman; 13 fellow citizen

compeer: 4 mate, peer; 5 equal, match; 9 associate, colleague

compel: 4 make; 5 drive, force; 6 coerce, oblige; 7 command, enforce, require; 8 obligate; 9 constrain; 11 necessitate

compellation: 10 salutation

compend: 10 compendium

compendious: 7 compact, summary; 8 succinct, synoptic

compendium: 7 compend; 10 collection

compensable: 6 paying; 8 salaried; 11 stipendiary; 12 remunerative

compensate: 3 pay; 5 right; 6 even up, make up, pay off; 7 correct, even off, even out, redress; 8 make good; 9 indemnify, make up for, reimburse; 10 recompense, remunerate; 14 counterbalance

compensated: 8 salaried; 11 remunerated, stipendiary

compensation: 10 recompense; 12 compensating, remuneration

compensative: 10 offsetting; 12 compensatory; 14 countervailing

compensatory damages: 13 actual damages; 14 general damages

compensatory spending: 11 pump priming; 15 deficit spending

compense: 9 make up for; 10 compensate

compere: 5 emcee

compete: 3 vie; 4 spar; 6 square, strive; 7 contend, contest; 8 scramble, struggle; 9 square off

compete for: 6 vie for; 10 contend for, stickle for; 12 stipulate for

competence: 5 craft, knack, skill; 6 enough, withal; 7 address, aptness, know-how; 8 adequacy, aptitude, facility; 10 adroitness, competency; 11 proficiency, sufficiency; 12 satisfaction, skillfulness

competency: 10 competence

competent: 4 able; 5 valid; 7 capable, skilled; 8 skillful, tangible; 9 qualified; 10 conversant, proficient; 12 commensurate, satisfactory

compete with: 5 rival; 7 emulate; 8 cope with, race with

competing: 5 rival; 7 rivalry; 8 sparring; 10 contending, contesting

competition: 5 match, rival; 7 contest, rivalry; 8 struggle; 9 competing, contender; 10 challenger, competitor, contention

competitive: 7 emulous; 8 militant, rivaling; 11 competitory; 14 free-enterprise

competitiveness: 5 fight

competitor: 5 rival; 6 bidder, suitor; 8 aspirant, claimant; 9 candidate, contender, postulant; 10 challenger; 11 competition

competitory: 11 competitive

compilation: 4 levy; 6 digest; 9 compiling, gathering; 11 ingathering

compile: 5 amass, hoard; 6 pile up; 7 collect, compose; 10 accumulate

compiler: 13 encyclopedist

compiling program: 8 compiler

complacency: 10 easy temper, good temper, mansuetude, soft tongue; 11 complacence; 12 satisfaction

complacent: 7 content; 8 gracious, obliging; 9 contented, indulgent, satisfied; 11 complaisant, good-humored; 12 conciliatory; 13 accommodating, self-satisfied

complain: 4 beef, kick; 5 gripe, plain; 6 kvetch, quetch, squawk; 8 sound off; 9 bellyache

complainant: 7 accuser; 9 plaintiff

complainer: 6 moaner, whiner; 7 crybaby; 8 censurer, grumbler, sniveler, squawker; 10 bellyacher; 11 fault-finder

complain of: 3 ail; 4 have; 6 suffer; 10 labor under; 14 be affected with

complaint: 3 ill; 4 beef, moan, sigh; 5 gripe, groan, whine; 6 charge, malady, murmur, mutter, plaint; 7 ailment, disease, grumble, heaving, illness; 8 deep sigh, disorder, grousing, sickness; 10 allegation; 11 bellyaching, suspiration

complaisance: 7 amenity; 9 deference, good humor; 10 affability, amiability, compliance, compliancy; 12 obligingness

complaisant: 8 obliging; 10 complacent; 12 conciliatory

complection: 9 skin color; 10 complexion

complement: 7 balance; 10 difference, supplement

complemental: 10 completing; 13 complementary

complementary: 5 prime; 7 aliquot; 9 divisible; 10 completing, fractional, reciprocal; 12 complemental; 13 supplementary

complementation: 7 filling; 13 complementing, supplementing

complementing: 7 filling; 10 completing; 12 suplementing, supplemental; 13 supplementary, supplementing

complete: 4 done, nail, over, pure; 5 ended, gross, stark, utter; 6 arrant, entire, fill in, finish, settle; 7 achieve, all over, compass, fill out, make out, perfect, sodding, staring; 8 conclude, dispatch, finished; 9 completed, concluded, discharge, fulfilled, hammer out; 10 accomplish, consummate, double-dyed, terminated; 11 everlasting; 12 accomplished; 13 thoroughgoing

complete abstinence from alcohol: 11 teetotalism

complete blood count: 3 CBC; **12** blood profile

completed: 4 done, over; **8** complete, finished, realized; **9** fulfilled; **12** accomplished

completed work: 8 work done; **12** fait accompli [Fr], finished task; **14** accomplishment

completely: 3 all; **5** fully, quite, stark, whole; **6** in toto, wholly; **7** totally, utterly; **8** entirely, outright; **10** altogether, thoroughly

completely blind: 12 totally blind

completely defined: 6 formal; **8** rigorous; **11** well-defined

completeness: 9 wholeness

complete the course: 13 go the distance

completing: 5 final; **8** crowning; **9** achieving, finishing; **10** completion, concluding, conclusive; **11** achievement, fulfillment; **12** complemental, suplementing, supplemental; **13** accomplishing, complementary, complementing, supplementary; **14** accomplishment

completion: 5 mop up; **6** windup; **7** closing; **9** achieving; **10** completing; **11** achievement, culmination, fulfillment; **13** accomplishing; **14** accomplishment

complex: 6 system; **8** ensemble; **9** aggregate, complexed, composite, imaginary

complexed: 7 complex

complex fraction: 16 compound fraction

complexify: 10 complicate

complex instruction set computer: 4 CISC

complexion: 3 air, fit, set; **4** cast, look, mien, mold, port; **5** color, guise, mould, stamp; **6** nature, spirit; **8** carriage, demeanor; **9** character, skin color; **10** skin colour; **11** complection; **12** constitution; **13** skin condition

complexity: 11 complexness

complexness: 10 complexity

complex number: 11 mixed number; **15** complex quantity, imaginary number

complex quantity: 13 complex number; **15** imaginary number

complexus: 7 complex; **8** ensemble; **9** aggregate

complex voluntary human action: 8 activity

compliance: 8 abidance; **9** adherence, deference, execution; **10** compliancy, conformity, observance, submission; **11** concurrence, performance; **12** acquiescence, complaisance, conformation, oblingingness

compliancy: 9 deference; **10** compliance; **12** complaisance, obligingness

compliant: 4 meek, true; **5** loyal; **8** biddable, faithful, obedient; **9** complying, observant; **10** spiritless; **11** acquiescent

compliantly: 10 faithfully, obediently; **12** in compliance

complicate: 6 rarify, refine; **7** involve, perplex; **8** confound; **9** elaborate

complicated: 5 kinky; **6** kinked; **7** knotted, raveled, tangled; **8** involved; **9** entangled, intricate, perplexed; **12** inextricable

complicating: 12 complication

complication: 3 rub; **5** snarl; **6** tangle; **7** problem; **9** intricacy; **10** difficulty, knottiness; **11** implication; **12** complicating, ramification

compliment: 4 laud; **6** praise; **7** commend, regards [pl]; **11** compliments [pl], give regards; **12** congratulate; **14** express regards

complimentary: 4 free; **6** gratis; **8** costless, praising; **9** adulatory, laudatory; **10** eulogistic, gratuitous, uncritical; **11** encomiastic, panegyrical; **12** commendatory; **14** lavish of praise

complimented: 6 lauded; **7** praised; **8** approved; **9** commended

compliments: 4 wish; **6** regard; **7** regards [pl]; **10** compliment

complot: 4 plot; **5** cabal; **8** conspire, intrigue; **10** conspiracy; **11** machination

comply: 6 accede, adhere, assent, follow; **7** abide by, execute, observe, perform, respect; **9** acquiesce, conform to; **10** comply with; **11** acknowledge

complying: 4 true; **5** loyal; **8** faithful, obedient, obliging, yielding; **9** compliant, observant

comply with: 5 honor; **6** accede, accept, comply; **7** abide by, agree to, execute, observe, perform, receive, respect; **8** adhere to; **9** acquiesce, tally with; **10** fall in with; **11** acknowledge, chime in with, give consent, subscribe to

compo: 6 ground, stucco; **7** plaster, spackel; **11** composition

component: 4 part; **5** piece; **6** factor; **7** element, portion; **8** material; **10** ingredient; **11** constituent; **12** integral part; **13** component part, integrant

component event: 8 subevent

component material: 8 material; **9** component; **11** constituent

component part: 4 part; **5** piece; **7** element, portion; **9** component; **11** constituent; **12** integral part

components: 12 computer part; **17** computer component; **19** digital computer part

comport: 4 bear; **5** carry; **6** acquit, behave, deport; **7** conduct

comportment: 4 mien; **7** bearing, conduct; **8** behavior, presence; **10** deportment

compose: 3 lay, pen; **4** calm, cool, damp, form, hush, lull, make, swag, tame;

5 abate, allay, draft, frame, quell, quiet, sober, still, write; **6** author, deaden, draw up, indite, pacify, rebate, smooth, soothe; **7** appease, arrange, assuage, compile, outline, slacken, turn off; **8** calm down, suppress; **9** alleviate, formulate; **10** constitute, set to music; **11** tranquilize

composed: 7 drawn up; **8** authored; **9** collected; **10** formulated

Compositae: 10 Asteraceae; **11** aster family

composite: 6 hybrid, mosaic; **7** breccia, collage, complex, mongrel, montage; **8** chowchow, pastiche; **9** patchwork, potpourri; **10** hodgepodge; **11** half-and-half; **13** heterogeneous, linsey-woolsey; **14** composite plant

composite plant: 9 composite

composition: 4 opus, work; **5** alloy, compo, paper, piece, theme; **6** makeup, number, report; **7** amalgam, penning, writing; **8** compound; **9** composing, substance; **10** authorship, compromise, typography; **11** commutation, tertium quid [Lat]; **12** constitution, piece of music; **14** chemical makeup

composition board: 9 cardboard

composition of matter: 8 chemical, compound; **9** substance; **11** composition

compositor: 10 compositor, typesetter; **11** typographer

compos mentis: 4 sane; **8** rational; **10** reasonable; **11** of sound mind

composure: 4 calm; **8** calmness, coolness; **9** sangfroid [Fr]; **10** equanimity

compote: 3 mug; **7** creamer, pitcher; **9** gravy boat, punch bowl, sugar bowl; **10** butter dish; **11** chafing dish; **12** fruit compote

compound: 5 alloy; **6** deepen, infect; **7** amalgam, combine, commute; **8** chemical, colonial, heighten; **9** intensify, substance; **10** adulterate, amalgamate; **11** composition

compound arithmetic: 9 metrology

compound for: 6 redeem; **7** commute

compound fraction: 15 complex fraction

compound fracture: 12 open fracture

compounding: 9 combining; **11** combination

compound lens: 10 lens system; **12** multiple lens

compound pendulum: 16 physical pendulum

comprador: 6 grocer

comprehend: 3 dig, ken; **4** hold, know, scan; **5** admit, cover, grasp, savvy; **6** embody, take in; **7** compass, contain, embrace, realize, subsume; **8** perceive; **9** apprehend, be aware of, encompass; **10** appreciate, understand; **11** be aware that; **13** be cognizant of, be conscious of, get the picture

comprehended: 11 appreciated, apprehended

comprehendible: 14 comprehensible

comprehending: 7 knowing; **9** realizing; **12** appreciating, being aware of; **13** understanding

comprehensible: 10 fathomable; **12** intelligible; **14** comprehendible, understandable

comprehensibly: 12 intelligibly; **14** understandably

comprehension: 3 wit; **7** knowing; **8** capacity, keenness; **9** admission, cognition, inclusion, reception; **10** cognizance, comprising, conception, membership; **11** subsumption; **12** apprehension, intelligence, precognition; **13** understanding

comprehensive: 5 broad; **7** general, generic; **8** sweeping; **9** capacious; **10** collective; **12** encyclopedic; **13** encyclopaedic

comprehensiveness: 7 breadth; **8** fullness

comprehensive treatise: 8 treatise; **14** definitive work

compress: 4 cram, pack; **5** press; **7** compact, ram down, squeeze; **8** contract; **9** constrict; **12** pack together

compressed: 4 flat; **5** tight; **7** crimped, reduced; **8** squeezed; **9** compacted, condensed

compressibility: 10 sponginess; **13** contractility, squeezability

compressible: 4 fine, rare, thin; **6** flimsy, slight, subtle; **7** subtile, tenuous; **10** squeezable

compression: 10 compaction, concretion; **11** compressing, contraction; **12** condensation; **13** densification

compression bandage: 10 tourniquet

comprise: 2 be; **6** embody, make up; **7** contain; **9** consist in, consist of, represent; **10** constitute; **11** incorporate

comprising: 13 comprehension

comprobation: 5 proof; **9** probation; **10** wager of law; **13** demonstration, rigorous proof

compromise: 5 terms; **6** settle; **7** imperil; **8** endanger, via media; **9** go halfway, put at risk; **10** jeopardize, settlement; **11** composition, give and take, put in danger; **12** compromising, put into peril; **13** bring in danger, place in danger, put in harm's way, put in jeopardy; **14** expose to danger

compromised: 9 committed

compromising: 8 flexible; **10** compromise; **11** give and take; **12** conciliatory

compter: 7 counter

Comptonia: 14 genus Comptonia

Comptonia asplenifolia: 9 sweet fern

Comptonia peregrina: 9 sweet fern

comptroller: 10 accountant, controller

compulsatory: 6 forced; **7** coerced; **8** required; **9** compelled; **10** compulsory, obligatory; **11** involuntary

compulsion: 6 duress; **8** coercion; **9** obsession; **10** constraint; **11** enforcement

compulsive: 6 driven; 10 determined

compulsively: 11 obsessively; 13 obsessionally

compulsorily: 7 by force; 8 forcibly, perforce; 11 mandatorily; 12 by compulsion, obligatorily, on compulsion; 13 involuntarily

compulsory: 6 forced; 7 coerced; 8 required; 9 compelled, mandatory; 10 obligatory; 11 involuntary

compunction: 7 remorse; 9 penitence; 10 contrition, repentance; 12 self-reproach

compurgation: 7 quietus; 9 clearance, discharge; 10 wager of law

computability: 13 measurability

computable: 9 estimable; 10 calculable

computation: 8 figuring; 9 reckoning; 11 calculation

compute: 6 cipher, cypher, figure, reckon; 9 calculate

computed axial tomography: 2 CT; 3 CAT

computed tomography: 2 CT; 3 CAT

computer: 7 figurer; 8 reckoner; 9 estimator; 10 calculator; 13 data processor; 15 digital computer

computer-aided design: 3 CAD

computer backup: 6 backup

computer code: 4 code; 7 listing; 14 program listing

computer company: 13 computer maker

computer database: 14 on-line database; 18 electronic database

computer display: 14 computer screen

computer expert: 12 computer guru

computer game: 9 video game

computer guru: 14 computer expert

computerized axial tomography: 2 CT; 3 CAT

computerized axial tomography scanner: 10 CAT scanner

computer maker: 15 computer company

computer manufacturer: 13 computer maker

computer-oriented language: 15 machine language; 16 computer language

computer part: 9 component

computer peripheral: 10 peripheral; 16 peripheral device

computer program: 7 program; 8 software; 9 programme; 11 application

computer programmer: 10 programmer; 16 software engineer

computer screen: 15 computer display

computer software: 7 program; 8 software; 15 computer program

computer system: 4 ADPS; 9 ADP system; 15 computing system

comrade: 4 mate; 6 fellow; 7 brother; 8 confrere, familiar, intimate; 9 associate, companion, confidant; 10 confidante

comradeliness: 9 comradery; 10 chumminess; 11 comaraderie

comradery: 10 chumminess; 11 comaraderie; 13 comradeliness

comradeship: 7 company, society; 10 fellowship; 13 companionship; 14 good fellowship

comtation: 8 guzzling, imbibing, potation; 12 intemperance; 16 habitual drinking; 17 excessive drinking

comte de Saxe: 4 Saxe; 18 Hermann Maurice Saxe

Comte Donatien Alphonse François de Sade: 4 Sade; 6 de Sade; 13 Marquis de Sade

con: 2 do; 3 nab; 4 bilk, bite, rook, scam; 5 bunco, bunko, cheat, cozen, learn, mulct, pluck, sting; 6 chouse, diddle, euchre, hustle, inmate, jockey, nobble; 7 con game, con over, convict, defraud, swindle; 8 flimflam, gaolbird, jailbird, memorize; 9 bunco game, bunko game, victimize; 12 in opposition; 14 confidence game

conacaste: 12 elephant's ear; 22 Enterolobium cyclocarpa

Conakry: 7 Konakri; 15 capital of Guinea

Conan Doyle: 12 A. Conan Doyle; 16 Arthur Conan Doyle; 19 Sir Arthur Conan Doyle

con artist: 6 con man; 13 confidence man

concamerate: 3 bow; 4 arch; 7 arcuate; 8 arch over

concameration: 4 arch; 5 vault

concatenation: 5 chain; 10 catenation, confluence; 13 communication

concave: 9 depressed

concave lens: 13 diverging lens

concaveness: 9 concavity

concave shape: 9 concavity

concavity: 3 dip; 10 depression; 11 concaveness; 12 concave shape

concavo-concave: 9 biconcave

conceal: 4 hide; 6 hold in; 7 reserve, secrete; 8 hold back, withhold; 13 put out of sight

concealed: 6 hidden; 10 out of sight; 11 camouflaged

concealing: 6 hiding; 7 evasion; 9 secreting; 11 concealment, suppression

concealment: 5 cover; 6 covert, hiding, screen; 7 evasion, privacy, secrecy; 9 secreting; 10 concealing; 11 privateness, suppression

concede: 3 own; 4 avow, cast, cede; 5 admit, allow, grant, yield; 6 accord; 7 confess, profess; 9 vouchsafe; 11 acknowledge

conceded: 8 admitted; 9 confessed, owned up to; 12 acknowledged; 13 self-confessed

conceding: 6 avowal; 8 owning up, yielding; 10 concession, concessive; 13 acknowledging; 14 acknowledgment

conceit: 4 quip; 5 crank, dream, folly, quirk; 6 maggot, shadow, vanity, vision; 7 chimera, egotism, figment, thought; 8 quiddity, self-love, trifling; **9** frivolity, lip wisdom; **10** self-esteem; **11** amour propre [Fr], private joke, self-conceit; **12** plaisanterie [Fr], standing jest, standing joke; **13** brilliant idea, conceitedness, inconsistency, irrationality; **14** self-admiration

conceited: 4 vain; **6** entete [Fr]; **7** flushed, swollen; **8** besotted, confined, dogmatic, inflated, positive, puffed up; **9** egotistic, fanatical, high-flown, illiberal, overblown; **10** infatuated, intolerant; **11** egotistical, overweening; **12** vainglorious; **13** self-conceited, swollen-headed; **14** vain as a peacock; **15** proud as a peacock

conceitedly: 6 vainly; **11** with conceit; **15** self-conceitedly

conceitedness: 6 vanity; **7** conceit, egotism; **8** self-love; **10** self-esteem; **11** amour propre [Fr], self-conceit; **14** self-admiration

conceivable: 7 in posse; **8** credible, possible; **10** imaginable

conceive: 3 get, see; **5** fancy, opine, think; **6** ideate; **7** believe, discern, imagine; **8** consider, perceive; **9** apprehend, recognize; **10** experience; **11** be of opinion, get a sight of; **13** conceptualise, conceptualize

conceived: 6 formed; **7** created; **8** dreamt of, imagined; **10** originated

conceive of: 6 ideate; **7** imagine; **8** envisage

conceiver: 10 mastermind, originator

concenter: 5 focus

concentrate: 4 pore; **5** focus, group, rivet, unite; **6** center, centre, decoct, reduce; **8** boil down, condense, contract; **10** centralize, congregate, dressed ore; **12** conglomerate; **13** render central; **14** gather together; **15** bring into a focus

concentrated: 3 met; **6** herded; **7** crowded, flocked; **8** thronged; **9** condensed, converged, saturated; **10** boiled down; **11** congregated; **13** conglomerated

concentrated fire: 10 massed fire

concentrate on: 6 center; **7** focus on; **8** center on; **12** revolve about; **13** revolve around

concentrating: 7 meeting; **9** confluent; **10** concurrent, convergent, converging

concentration: 7 density, meeting; **8** congress; **9** assiduity, concourse, denseness; **10** absorption, confluence congestion; **11** compactness, concurrence, convergence, convergency, engrossment; **13** assiduousness; **14** coming together, specialization

concentration camp: 8 stockade

concentric: 5 axial, focal; **7** azygous; **9** umbilical; **11** homocentric; **12** concentrical

concentual: 8 assonant, isotonic

concept: 4 idea; **6** notion; **7** thought; **9** construct; **10** conception

conception: 4 idea; **6** design, notion; **7** concept, knowing, thought; **8** creation, thinking; **9** cognition, construct, invention; **10** cognizance, innovation; **11** a fine frenzy,

Vorstellung [Ger]; **12** apprehension, intellection, precognition; **13** comprehension, understanding

conceptional: 8 notional; **10** ideational

conceptualize: 6 ideate; **8** conceive; **13** conceptualise

conceptus: 6 embryo; **13** fertilized egg

concern: 4 care, case, dole, fear, firm, fret, load; **5** firms [pl], refer, touch, worry; **6** affair, bear on, burden, come to, matter, occupy, regard, relate, unease; **7** anxiety, bearing, company, dealing, pertain, touch on; **8** business, disquiet, emphasis, headache, interest, relation, vexation; **9** cognation, companies [pl], touch upon; **10** connection, enterprise, inquietude, proceeding, solicitude, uneasiness; **11** disquietude, transaction; **12** apprehension, relationship; **13** establishment

concerned: 6 uneasy; **7** anxious, worried; **8** careworn; **10** implicated, interested; **12** apprehensive

concernedly: 11 with concern

concerning: 4 as to; **7** vis-a-vis; **9** regarding; **10** in regard to; **12** in relation to, with regard to; **13** with respect to

concert: 7 collude, consort, resolve; **8** conspire; **10** fraternize, preconcert; **11** concordance, concurrence, concurrency, confederate, cooperation; **12** club together, hang together, hold together, keep together, predesignate, preestablish, pull together; **13** collaboration

concert band: 12 military band

concert dance: 6 ballet

concerted: 6 united; **8** additive, combined, conjunct; **10** collective; **11** conjunctive, cooperative

concerted music: 9 polyphony; **15** polyphonic music

concerted piece: 9 capriccio, potpourri

concert-goer: 10 music lover

concert grand: 5 grand; **12** concert piano

concert hall: 9 music hall; **11** concert room

concert piano: 5 grand; **12** concert grand

concert room: 9 music hall; **11** concert hall

concession: 5 grace, grant; **6** avowal; **7** liberty, license; **8** discount, mark down, owning up, yielding; **9** abatement, allowance, conceding, reduction; **12** depreciation; **13** acknowledging; **14** acknowledgment

concessionaire: 12 concessioner

concessive: 9 conceding

concetto: 4 quip; **5** crank, quirk; **7** conceit; **8** quiddity; **11** private joke; **12** plaisanterie [Fr], standing jest, standing joke; **13** brilliant idea

conchfish: 19 Astropogon stellatus

conchiform: 11 shell-shaped

conchoid: 8 cardioid
conchoidal: 8 serrated
conchology: 15 shell collecting
concierge: 10 coast guard, game keeper; 11 guarda costa [Sp]; 14 superintendant
conciliable: 10 appeasable
conciliate: 4 coax, lure; 5 charm, tempt; 6 disarm, gentle, lenify, make up, pacify, seduce, settle; 7 appease, assuage, beguile, bewitch, gruntle, mollify, patch up, placate, wheedle, win over; 9 carry away, fascinate, make peace, reconcile; 10 propitiate; 11 accommodate, meet halfway
conciliating: 9 pacifying; 12 conciliative, conciliatory
conciliation: 9 expiation, placation; 10 redemption; 11 appeasement, reclamation; 12 pacification, propitiation; 13 reconcilement
conciliative: 12 conciliating, conciliatory
conciliator: 8 appeaser, pacifier; 9 makepeace; 10 peacemaker, reconciler
conciliatory: 8 flexible, obliging, placable; 9 forgiving, pacifying; 10 complacent; 11 complaisant; 12 compromising, conciliating, conciliative
concinnity: 8 delicacy; 10 refinement
concise: 5 brief, close, short, terse
concisely: 7 briefly, in brief, in short, shortly, tersely; 9 summarily
conciseness: 7 brevity; 9 briefness, pithiness, terseness; 11 compactness; 12 succinctness, the soul of wit
concision: 9 squeezing; 10 abridgment, compacting; 12 retrenchment
conclave: 5 synod; 6 caucus, clique, vestry; 7 chapter; 8 assembly; 10 conference, consistory; 11 conventicle, convocation
conclude: 3 end; 4 seal; 5 close, judge; 6 finish, reason, settle; 7 resolve; 8 complete; 9 reason out, terminate
concluded: 4 over; 5 ended; 7 all over, at an end; 8 complete, finished; 10 terminated
concluding: 4 last; 5 final; 6 ending; 7 closing, judging; 8 crowning, deciding, terminal; 9 finishing; 10 completing, conclusive; 11 terminating
conclusion: 3 end; 4 last; 5 close, finis; 6 ending, finale, finish; 7 closing, finding; 8 decision, illation, judgment, terminus; 9 deduction, inference, judgement, winding up; 10 denouement, wrapping up; 11 culmination, termination; 12 consummation; 13 determination, stopping point
conclusive: 5 final; 8 absolute, crowning; 9 finishing, probative; 10 apodeictic, completing, concluding; 11 determinate, irrefutable, self-evident; 12 irrefragable, irresistible, unanswerable
conclusiveness: 8 finality; 12 decisiveness

concoct: 4 fake; 5 force, hatch; 6 cook up; 7 dream up, think of, think up, trump up
concoction: 7 mixture; 9 digestion; 10 confection; 12 intermixture
concomitance: 7 company; 11 association, coexistence, concurrence; 13 companionship
concomitant: 4 twin; 5 joint; 6 fellow; 8 coworker, confrere; 9 accessory, assistant, attendant, auxiliary; 10 coincident, concurrent, cooperator, incidental; 12 accompanying, cooccurrence, collaborator, incidental to; 13 accompaniment
concord: 6 accord; 7 harmony; 8 symphony; 9 agreement; 10 consonance; 11 concordance
Concord: 9 Lexington; 19 Lexington and Concord; 21 capital of New Hampshire
concordance: 6 accord; 7 concert, concord, harmony; 9 agreement
concordant: 5 as one; 6 united; 8 agreeing, cemented, in accord; 9 accordant, agreeable, congenial, congruous, consonant, in harmony, of one mind; 10 concurring, consistent, harmonious; 11 conformable, harmonizing, in agreement; 13 correspondent, corresponding, of the same mind
concordat: 7 compact; 8 covenant
concours: 12 belligerency
concours d'elegance: 4 show
concourse: 6 throng; 7 meeting; 8 congress; 9 multitude; 10 confluence; 11 concurrence, convergence, convergency; 12 congregation; 13 concentration
concremation: 9 cremation
concrete: 3 set; 4 cure; 5 rocky, stony; 7 congeal; 8 take a set; 9 calculous, coagulate; 10 concretion; 11 consolidate; 12 conglomerate
concrete existence: 7 reality; 9 actuality
concrete mixer: 11 cement mixer
concrete representation: 10 concretism
concretion: 7 setting; 8 concrete; 9 accretion; 10 compaction; 11 compression; 12 conglomerate; 13 densification
contraceptive method: 13 contraception
concubinage: 8 adultery, cheating; 7 crim. con. [abbr]; 10 cuckolding, infidelity; 14 unfaithfulness
concubine: 4 doxy; 8 bona roba [It], mistress, paramour; 9 chere amie [Fr], courtesan, kept woman, odalisque
concupiscence: 4 lust; 6 libido; 8 cupidity, sex drive; 9 cacoethes [Lat], prurience; 11 sex instinct; 12 sexual desire
concupiscent: 5 lusty; 6 carnal, erotic; 7 lustful, rampant, rutting, ruttish; 8 prurient; 10 libidinous; 12 carnal-minded
concur: 4 meet; 5 agree, unite; 6 accord; 7 cooccur, coexist, conduce, conjoin; 8 coincide, conspire, converge; 9 cooperate;

10 contribute, fall in with; **11** collaborate; **12** act in concert, come together, move together; **15** make common cause

concurrence: 7 concert, meeting; **8** congress; **9** concourse, execution; **10** compliance, confluence, observance; **11** coincidence, concurrency, conjunction, convergence, convergency, cooperation, performance; **12** acquiescence, cooccurrence, concomitance; **13** collaboration, concentration

concurrency: 7 concert; **11** concurrence, cooperation

concurrent: 7 meeting; **9** conducing, confluent; **10** coincident, coinciding, concurring, conjoining, conspiring, convergent, converging; **11** concomitant, cooccurring; **12** coincidental, simultaneous; **13** at the same time, concentrating

concurrently: 13 at the same time

concurring: 8 agreeing; **9** conducing; **10** coinciding, concordant, concurrent, conjoining, conspiring; **11** in agreement; **13** of the same mind

concussion: 4 bump; **5** clash, shock; **9** collision; **10** percussion

condemn: 4 cast, damn, doom; **5** decry; **7** convict; **8** sentence; **9** excoriate, objurgate; **10** find guilty; **11** bring home to

condemnable: 8 criminal; **10** deplorable; **13** reprehensible

condemnation: 5 curse; **10** conviction, execration; **14** disapprobation

condemnation to death: 12 death warrant; **13** death sentence

condemnatory: 7 abusive; **9** clamorous, damnatory; **10** condemning; **12** denunciatory

condemned: 6 doomed, guilty, seized; **8** censured; **9** convicted, taken over; **10** confiscate; **11** confiscated, found guilty; **12** appropriated

condemning: 12 condemnatory

condensate: 12 condensation

condensation: 7 capsule; **10** abridgment, condensate, condensing; **11** abridgement, boiling down, compression, contraction

condensation pump: 13 diffusion pump

condensation trail: 8 contrail

condense: 3 gel; **4** melt; **7** liquefy, thicken; **8** boil down, contract; **11** concentrate

condensed: 9 congealed; **10** compressed, evaporated; **12** concentrated

condenser: 9 capacitor; **13** condenser coil; **16** optical condenser; **19** electrical condenser

condenser coil: 9 condenser

condensing: 12 condensation

condescend: 5 deign, stoop; **7** descend; **9** patronize, vouchsafe; **12** lower oneself

condescending: 4 arch; **9** agreeable; **11** patronising, patronizing

condescendingly: 13 patronizingly

condescension: 7 disdain; **9** patronage; **14** disdainfulness; **16** superciliousness

condign: 3 due; **5** due to; **7** merited; **8** deserved; **14** richly deserved

condiment: 5 spice; **6** relish; **9** seasoning

condisciple: 13 fellow-student

condition: 4 term, trim; **5** check, hedge, shape, state, terms, train; **6** clause, status; **7** context, fitness, proviso, qualify, specify; **8** good trim, position; **9** good shape, provision, stipulate; **10** conditions [pl], discipline, sine qua non [Lat]; **11** contingency, proposition, stipulation; **12** circumstance, precondition, prerequisite; **13** circumstances [pl], consideration, good condition, specification; **14** human condition; **15** condition in life, physical fitness

conditional: 5 given, modal; **6** fenced, formal, hedged; **7** guarded; **8** hedged in; **9** dependent, qualified; **10** contingent, restricted; **11** conditioned, provisional

conditionally: 2 if; **6** in case; **8** provided; **9** admitting, supposing; **13** not absolutely; **14** with conditions

conditional relation: 11 implication; **18** logical implication

conditional response: 6 reflex

conditioned: 6 hedged; **7** learned; **9** dependent, qualified; **10** contingent, restricted; **11** conditional, in condition; **14** preconditioned

conditioned emotional response: 3 CER

conditioned upon: 9 subject to; **11** depending on; **14** contingent upon

condition in life: 9 condition

conditions: 4 term; **5** terms; **6** clause; **7** context; **9** condition; **11** stipulation; **12** circumstance, precondition; **13** circumstances [pl]; **21** physical circumstances

condo: 11 condominium

condole: 7 console; **10** sympathize; **11** condole with, express pity, testify pity

condolence: 13 commiseration

condole with: 4 pity; **7** condole, console, feel for; **10** sympathize; **11** express pity, testify pity; **13** compassionate; **14** sympathize with

condom: 4 safe; **6** rubber, safety; **12** prophylactic

condominium: 5 condo

condonation: 5 grace; **6** pardon; **10** absolution; **11** forgiveness

condone: 6 excuse; **8** overlook, pass over

condoned: 7 excused; **10** overlooked

condottiere: 8 guerilla, partisan; **9** insurgent, irregular

conduce: 4 lead; **5** carry; **6** affect, concur; **7** conjoin; **8** conspire; **10** contribute

conducement: 13 conduciveness
conducive: 9 conducing; 12 calculated to, contributing, contributive, contributory, in a fair way to; 14 working towards
conduct: 4 bear, deal, lead, take; 5 bring, carry, fetch, guide, reach; 6 acquit, behave, convey, convoy, deport, direct, govern, manage; 7 carry on, channel, comport; 8 behavior, carry out, demeanor, transmit; 9 behaviour, demeanour; 10 deportment; 11 comportment, preside over
conducted: 6 guided
conducting: 8 behaving; 10 conductive
conducting oneself: 8 behaving; 10 conducting
conduction: 12 conductivity; 17 thermal conduction
conductive: 10 conducting
conductivity: 10 conduction
conduct oneself: 11 bear oneself; 12 carry oneself; 13 acquit oneself, behave oneself, demean oneself; 14 comport oneself
conductor: 7 maestro; 8 director; 13 music director
conduct unbecoming a gentleman: 9 brutality; 11 grossierete, misbehavior
conduit: 7 channel
condyloma acuminatum: 11 genital wart; 12 venereal wart; 16 verruca acuminata
Condylura: 14 genus Condylura
Condylura cristata: 13 star-nosed mole
cone: 6 conoid; 8 cone cell, strobile; 9 cone shape, cone-shape, strobilus; 11 retinal cone
cone-bearing: 10 coniferous
cone cell: 4 cone; 11 retinal cone
cone clutch: 18 cone friction clutch
cone friction clutch: 10 cone clutch
conelike: 5 conic; 7 conical; 10 cone-shaped
conenose: 9 big bedbug; 10 kissing bug; 11 conenose bug; 12 cone-nosed bug
Conepatus: 14 genus Conepatus
cone peak: 4 crag, pike; 5 arete [Fr], crest; 9 sugar loaf
cone shape: 4 cone; 6 conoid
cone-shape: 4 cone
cone-shaped: 5 conic; 7 conical; 8 conelike; 12 funnel-shaped
conessi: 6 kurchi; 7 kurchee; 9 ivory tree
Conestoga: 12 covered wagon, prairie wagon; 14 Conestoga wagon; 15 prairie schooner
confab: 3 jaw; 4 chat; 5 visit; 6 claver, confer, gossip, natter; 7 chaffer, chatter, consult; 8 chitchat; 11 confabulate; 13 confabulation
confabulate: 3 jaw; 4 chat; 5 visit; 6 claver, confab, confer, gossip, natter; 7 chaffer,

chatter, consult, palaver; 8 chitchat; 14 shoot the breeze
confabulating: 8 chatting
confabulation: 4 chat, talk; 6 confab; 8 colloquy, converse; 9 discourse
confect: 6 comfit; 10 confection
confection: 5 sweet; 6 comfit, sweets; 7 confect; 10 concoction; 13 confectionary, confectionery
confectionary: 5 sweet; 6 sweets; 10 confection
confectioner: 10 candymaker
confectionery: 5 sweet; 8 tuck shop; 9 sweet shop; 10 candy store, confection
Confederacy: 5 Dixie, South; 9 Dixieland
confederacy: 10 conspiracy, federation; 13 confederation
confederate: 4 ally; 6 allied, friend; 7 collude, concert, consort; 8 conspire, henchman; 10 fraternize; 12 band together, club together, collaborator, hand together, hang together, hold together, keep together, pull together; 13 confederative, hunt in couples; 14 be in league with, league together, partner in crime
confederated: 5 joint; 6 united; 10 federative
Confederate flag: 12 Stars and Bars
confederate jasmine: 11 star jasmine
Confederate rose: 10 cotton rose
Confederate States of America: 5 Dixie, South; 9 Dixieland; 11 Confederacy
confederation: 8 alliance; 10 federation; 11 confederacy
confederative: 6 allied; 11 confederate
confer: 2 cf; 3 see; 5 grant; 6 bestow, call in, caucus, confab; 7 consult, discuss, refer to, see also; 11 confabulate, hold council
confer a privilege: 7 charter, empower; 9 privilege; 11 enfranchise
conferee: 13 conventioneer
conference: 5 levee; 6 caucus, clique, league, parley, powwow [U.S.]; 8 assembly, conclave, congress; 10 convention, pourparler; 11 conventicle, negotiation; 12 deliberation; 15 group discussion
conference table: 12 council board, council table
confer honor on: 14 reflect honor on
conferment: 8 bestowal; 9 conferral; 10 bestowment
confer power: 6 invest; 9 give power
conferral: 8 bestowal; 10 bestowment, conferment
conferred: 8 bestowed; 9 presented
conferring: 12 consultation
conferva: 4 moss
confer with: 7 consult; 11 commune with; 12 commerce with; 13 discourse with
confess: 3 own; 4 avow; 5 admit, allow; 6 fess up, shrive, squeal; 7 concede, own up to, profess; 11 acknowledge; 14 go to confession, receive penance

confessed: 5 bared; 6 avowed; 8 admitted, conceded; 13 self-confessed
confessedly: 4 true; 8 avowedly; 10 admittedly
confession: 9 admission; 19 auricular confession
confessional: 6 shrift; 8 credence; 9 baldachin
confessions: 4 life; 7 journal; 8 fortunes; 10 adventures; 11 experiences; 17 personal narrative
confessor: 12 penitentiary
confidant: 3 pal; 5 buddy; 8 alter ego, intimate; 9 companion
confidante: 4 mate; 7 comrade; 8 confrere, familiar, intimate; 9 companion
confide: 5 trust; 6 commit, rely on; 7 entrust, intrust; 14 put one's trust in
confide in: 9 believe in; 11 have faith in, have trust in; 14 put one's trust in
confidence: 5 troth, trust; 8 reliance, sureness; 9 assurance, authority; 11 presumption, self-respect; 12 self-reliance; 13 self-assurance; 14 self-confidence
confidence game: 3 con; 5 bunco, bunko, sting; 6 hustle; 7 con game; 8 flimflam; 9 bunco game, bunko game
confidence man: 6 con man; 9 con artist
confidence trick: 4 scam; 7 con game, swindle; 9 bunko game
confident: 4 sure; 6 formal, secure, solemn; 7 assured, certain; 8 cocksure, dogmatic, positive, sanguine; 9 convinced, satisfied, trenchant; 10 optimistic, surefooted; 11 self-reliant; 12 unhesitating
confidente: 7 abigail; 9 lady's maid, soubrette
confidential: 6 closet, secret; 7 private; 8 esoteric; 10 inviolable; 13 unmentionable
confidential information: 3 tip; 4 hint, lead, wind; 5 steer
confidently: 11 assertively, trenchantly; 12 dogmatically; 14 with confidence
confiding: 4 open; 9 open as day; 10 aboveboard, unreserved; 11 open-hearted; 12 frank-hearted, unsuspicious
confidingly: 10 trustfully, trustingly
configuration: 4 form; 5 shape; 7 contour; 12 conformation; 13 constellation
configured: 8 designed
confine: 4 brow, hold, pale, side, term; 5 bound, bourn, limit, skirt, verge; 6 detain, flange, hold in; 7 enclave, enclose, trammel; 8 restrain, restrict, throttle; 11 reservation; 12 circumscribe
confined: 5 bound; 6 entete [Fr], jailed, laid up, penned; 7 captive, limited; 8 besotted, dogmatic, enclosed, fenced in, positive; 9 bedridden, conceited, fanatical, illiberal, invalided; 10 imprisoned, in hospital, infatuated, intolerant; 11 encompassed; 13 circumscribed, on the sick list

confinement: 5 labor; 6 duress, labour; 7 durance, lying-in, travail; 8 childbed, delivery; 9 captivity, detention; 10 birth-throe, childbirth; 11 durance vile, parturiency, parturition; 12 accouchement
confines: 7 suburbs; 8 banlieue, environs, purlieus, vicinage; 9 alentours [Fr]; 10 borderland; 12 neighborhood
confining: 5 close; 8 limiting; 11 restricting; 12 constraining, constrictive
confirm: 5 prove; 6 affirm, anoint, clench, ratify; 7 support, sustain; 8 reassert; 9 subscribe; 10 lay hands on, underwrite; 11 corroborate; 12 make absolute, substantiate
confirmable: 10 verifiable
confirmation: 5 check; 7 support; 12 ratification, verification; 13 corroboration; 14 substantiation
confirmative: 9 verifying; 10 collateral, confirming, validating, validatory; 12 confirmatory, verificatory; 13 corroborative, corroboratory; 14 substantiating, substantiative
confirmed: 5 valid; 7 chronic; 8 habitual; 10 inveterate
confirmed habit: 11 innate habit; 14 intrinsic habit; 15 inveterate habit
confirming: 8 positive; 9 verifying; 10 collateral, validating, validatory; 12 confirmative, confirmatory, verificatory; 13 corroborative, corroboratory; 14 substantiating, substantiative
confiscate: 4 levy; 5 seize; 6 attach, seized; 7 attaint, forfeit, impound; 8 distrain; 9 condemned, forfeited, proscribe, sequester, taken over; 11 confiscated, sequestrate; 12 appropriated
confiscated: 6 seized; 9 condemned, taken over; 10 confiscate; 12 appropriated
confiscating: 12 confiscation
confiscation: 10 arrogation; 12 confiscating
confiture: 3 jam; 5 jelly; 8 conserve, preserve
conflagration: 7 inferno
conflate: 3 mix; 4 fuse, meld; 5 blend, immix, merge; 7 combine; 8 coalesce; 9 commingle
conflict: 3 jar, war; 5 clash, fight; 6 battle, combat, jostle; 7 dispute, quarrel, warfare; 8 battling, clashing, disagree, fighting, infringe, run afoul, struggle; 9 collision, come amiss; 10 contravene, difference, engagement; 11 clash of arms, hostilities; 12 be discordant
conflicting: 6 at odds; 8 clashing; 10 discordant, quarreling; 11 disagreeing, interfering; 12 antagonistic, inconsistent; 13 contradictory
conflicting evidence: 10 refutation
conflict with: 13 interfere with

confluence: 7 meeting, merging; 8 congress, junction; 9 concourse; 11 concurrence, convergence, convergency; 13 communication, concatenation, concentration

confluent: 7 meeting, merging; 10 concurrent, convergent, converging; 13 concentrating

conflux: 7 meeting, merging; 8 congress; 9 concourse; 10 confluence; 11 concurrence, convergence, convergency; 12 congregation; 13 concentration

conform: 5 adapt; 6 adhere, adjust; 7 stick to; 9 conform to

conformable: 8 in accord; 9 accordant, agreeable, consonant; 10 concordant; 11 in agreement

conformance: 10 conformity

conformation: 8 abidance; 10 compliance, conformity; 13 configuration

conforming: 8 adhering; 9 adherence; 10 conformist, conformity; 11 harmonizing; 14 reconciliation

conformism: 10 conformity

conformist: 10 conforming

conformity: 6 accord; 8 abidance, adhering, adhesion; 9 adherence; 10 accordance, compliance

conform to: 3 fit; 4 meet; 6 comply, follow; 7 conform, defer to; 11 subscribe to

confound: 3 fox; 4 stun; 5 quell, rebut, throw, trump, upset; 6 fuddle, refute; 7 bedevil, confuse, confute, involve, mistake, nonplus, perplex, petrify, silence, stagger, stupefy; 8 befuddle, bewilder, disprove, negative; 9 checkmate, fascinate, stalemate; 10 complicate, controvert, disconfirm, strike dumb; 11 flabbergast

confounded: 4 lost; 5 at sea, mazed; 6 cursed, damned; 7 baffled, bemused, mixed-up, refuted, stunned; 8 accursed, confused, confuted, damnable, infernal, rebutted; 9 befuddled, disproven, staggered, stupefied; 10 bewildered, struck dumb; 12 controverted, disconfirmed; 13 flabbergasted

confoundedly: 8 deucedly; 10 devilishly; 11 desperately, perplexedly

confounding: 5 mix-up; 9 confusion, confuting, rebutting; 10 disproving; 11 bewildering, dumfounding; 12 mind-boggling; 13 contradictory, controverting, disconfirming; 14 flabbergasting

confraternity: 8 sodality; 10 fraternity; 11 amicability, brotherhood; 12 amicableness

confrere: 4 mate; 6 fellow; 7 comrade; 8 co-worker, familiar, intimate; 9 accessory, assistant, auxiliary, colleague, companion; 10 confidante, cooperator; 11 concomitant; 12 collaborator

confrication: 8 abrasion; 9 attrition, detrition; 10 rubbing off, wearing off

confront: 4 face; 5 front; 6 face up; 7 collate, present; 8 cope with; 11 grapple with

confrontation: 8 showdown; 9 encounter; 10 opposition

confront danger: 10 defy danger, face danger, mock danger; 11 brave danger, front danger; 13 affront danger, despise danger

confronting: 7 braving; 8 tackling; 9 grappling; 10 coping with

confront witnesses: 16 produce witnesses

Confucius: 9 Kung Fu-Tse, Kung futzu

confuse: 3 fox; 4 blur; 5 mix up, throw; 6 dazzle, flurry, fuddle, jumble, muddle, put off, put out; 7 bedevil, fluster, mistake, obscure, perplex; 8 befuddle, bewilder, confound; 10 disconcert; 11 consternate, disorganize

confused: 4 dark, lost; 5 at sea, mazed, upset; 6 broken; 7 baffled, bemused, crabbed, garbled, jumbled, mixed-up, obscure, puzzled; 8 involved; 9 befuddled, illogical, obscurity, perplexed, scattered; 10 bewildered, confounded, discordant, disjointed, disordered, mysterious; 11 disoriented, unconnected; 12 disconnected; 14 indistinctness

confusedness: 8 disarray; 9 confusion

confusing: 8 puzzling; 10 perplexing

confusingly: 13 bewilderingly

confusion: 5 mix-up; 7 dilemma; 8 disarray; 10 perplexity; 11 confounding; 12 bewilderment, confusedness; 13 embarrassment; 15 mental confusion; 16 discombobulation

confusion of tongues: 5 Babel

confutable: 9 refutable; 10 defeasible

confutation: 8 disproof; 10 refutation; 12 invalidation

confute: 5 rebut; 6 refute; 8 confound, disprove, negative; 10 controvert, disconfirm

confuted: 7 refuted; 8 rebutted; 9 disproven; 10 confounded; 12 controverted, disconfirmed

confuting: 8 refuting; 9 rebutting; 10 disproving, falsifying; 11 confounding; 13 controverting, disconfirming, falsification

conga: 9 conga line

conga line: 5 conga

con game: 3 con; 4 scam; 5 bunco, bunko, sting; 6 hustle; 7 swindle; 8 flimflam; 9 bunco game, bunko game; 14 confidence game; 15 confidence trick

conge: 6 congee

congeal: 3 gel, set; 4 cure, jell; 8 concrete, take a set; 9 coagulate; 11 consolidate

congealed: 6 jelled; 7 jellied; 9 condensed

conge d'elire: 9 sanhedrin

congee: 5 conge

congelation: 7 setting; 8 freezing, gelation; 10 thickening

congenator: 8 congener, relative

congener: 8 allied to, relative; 10 congenator
congenerous: 10 congeneric; 13 of the same sort, of the same type; 14 of the same class
congenial: 5 as one; 6 united; 8 agreeing, cemented, in accord; 9 agreeable, fraternal, in harmony, of one mind; 10 concordant, harmonious; 11 harmonizing, in agreement
congeniality: 13 congenialness
congenialness: 12 congeniality
congenital: 6 inborn, innate; 7 genetic; 8 inherent; 9 incarnate, inherited; 10 hereditary
congenital abnormality: 11 birth defect
congenital defect: 11 birth defect
congenital disease: 14 genetic disease; 15 genetic disorder; 16 inherited disease
congenital disorder: 11 birth defect
congenite: 6 inborn; 7 genetic; 9 incarnate, inherited; 10 congenital, hereditary
conger: 9 conger eel
conger eel: 6 conger
congeries: 4 heap, pile; 9 aggregate; 14 conglomeration
congest: 4 clog, foul; 5 choke; 6 back up, clog up; 8 choke off
congested: 8 engorged
congestion: 8 overload; 11 engorgement; 12 over-crowding; 13 concentration
congius: 6 gallon; 14 Imperial gallon
conglaciation: 8 freezing
conglobate: 8 conglobe
conglobe: 10 conglobate
conglomerate: 5 amass; 6 empire, gather, pile up; 8 concrete, cumulate; 10 accumulate, concretion, congregate; 11 concentrate; 12 pudding stone; 14 conglomeration
conglomerated: 6 herded; 7 crowded, flocked; 8 thronged; 11 congregated; 12 concentrated
conglomeration: 4 mess, olio; 6 medley; 7 farrago; 8 all sorts, mish-mash, pastiche; 9 aggregate, congeries, patchwork, potpourri
conglutinate: 5 coapt; 11 agglutinate
conglutination: 13 agglomeration, agglutination
Congo: 10 Congo River; 11 French Congo; 15 Republic of Congo; 25 People's Republic of the Congo
congo copal: 8 congo gum
congo eel: 8 amphiuma, blind eel; 10 congo snake
congo gum: 10 congo copal
congoo mallee: 11 white mallee
Congo peafowl: 8 afropavo
Congo River: 5 Congo
congo snake: 8 amphiuma, blind eel, congo eel
congratulate: 5 plume, preen, pride; 10 compliment, felicitate, give one joy, wish one joy
congratulation: 12 felicitation
congratulations: 5 kudos; 6 praise

congregate: 6 gather, massed; 7 amassed, collect; 9 assembled, collected; 11 accumulated, concentrate; 12 conglomerate
congregated: 6 herded; 7 crowded, flocked; 8 thronged; 12 concentrated; 13 conglomerated
congregating: 12 congregation
congregation: 4 fold; 5 flock, laity; 6 people; 8 assembly, brethren, faithful; 9 celebrant, concourse; 10 worshipper; 11 communicant, convergence, the faithful; 12 congregating
Congregational: 17 Congregationalist
Congregationalist: 14 Congregational; 17 orthodox dissenter
congress: 4 diet; 5 levee; 6 coitus, sex act; 7 coition, meeting; 8 relation; 9 concourse; 10 conference, confluence, convention, copulation; 11 concurrence, conventicle, convergence, convergency, intercourse; 13 concentration, states-general
Congress: 20 United States Congress
congress boot: 12 congress shoe; 14 congress gaiter
congress gaiter: 12 congress boot, congress shoe
Congressional Medal of Honor: 12 Medal of Honor
congressman: 13 congresswoman; 14 representative
Congress of Industrial Organizations: 3 CIO
congress shoe: 12 congress boot; 14 congress gaiter
congresswoman: 11 congressman; 14 representative
congreve: 5 fusee, light, match, spill; 7 lucifer; 8 vesuvian
congruence: 9 congruity; 13 congruousness
congruent: 9 congruous
congruity: 10 congruence; 13 congruousness
congruous: 8 in accord; 9 accordant, congruent, consonant; 10 concordant, consistent; 13 correspondent, corresponding
congruousness: 9 congruity; 10 congruence
conic: 7 conical; 8 conelike, coniform; 10 cone-shaped; 12 conic section
conical: 5 conic; 8 conelike, coniform; 9 pyramidal; 10 cone-shaped
conical buoy: 3 nun; 7 nun buoy
conical projection: 15 conic projection
conic morel: 10 black morel
conic section: 5 conic
conic Verpa: 11 Verpa conica
conidiospore: 8 conidium
conidium: 12 conidiospore
conifer: 14 coniferous tree
Coniferales: 16 order Coniferales
coniferous: 11 cone-bearing

coniferous tree: 7 conifer
coniform: 5 conic; **7** conical; **10** cone-shaped
Conilurus: 14 genus Conilurus
Coniogramme: 16 genus Coniogramme
Coniogramme japonica: 10 bamboo fern
Conium: 11 genus Conium
Conium maculatum: 7 hemlock; **10** winter fern; **12** Nebraska fern; **13** poison hemlock, poison parsley; **14** California fern
conjectural: 8 academic, putative, supposed; **9** theorized; **10** gratuitous, supposable; **11** presumptive, speculative, theoretical; **12** hypothesized, hypothetical, suppositious; **13** suppositional; **14** supposititious
conjecturality: 5 guess; **6** theory, thesis; **7** surmise, theorem; **9** postulate; **10** conjecture, hypothesis, postulatum [Lat]; **11** postulation, supposition; **14** presupposition
conjecture: 5 guess; **6** divine, theory, thesis; **7** suppose, surmise, suspect, theorem; **8** theorise, theorize; **9** postulate, speculate; **10** hypothesis, postulatum [Lat]; **11** hypothecate, hypothesize, postulation, speculation, supposition
conjectured: 6 mooted; **7** assumed, divined, guessed; **8** imagined, presumed, supposed, surmised; **9** suspected; **10** postulated; **11** presupposed
conjecturing: 8 guessing; **9** supposing, surmising; **13** hypothesizing
conjoin: 3 wed; **4** fuse, join; **5** blend, marry, merge, unite; **6** absorb, concur, embody; **7** blend in, combine, conduce, connect, espouse; **8** coalesce, conspire, dissolve; **10** amalgamate, centralize, contribute, get married, hook up with, impregnate; **11** consolidate, incorporate
conjoined: 8 conjoint
conjoined twin: 11 Siamese twin
conjoining: 9 conducing; **10** coinciding, concurrent, concurring, conspiring
conjoint: 8 conjunct; **9** conjoined
conjointly: 7 jointly; **8** together; **11** put together; **12** collectively
conjugal: 6 wedded; **7** marital; **9** connubial; **11** matrimonial
conjugal family: 13 nuclear family
conjugally: 9 connubial
conjugate: 7 coupled; **10** conjugated
conjugated: 7 coupled; **9** conjugate
conjugated protein: 15 compound protein
conjugation: 4 yoke; **5** union; **6** mating; **7** joinder [Law], pairing, uniting; **8** coupling; **11** conjugating, conjunction
conjunct: 6 united; **8** combined, conjoint; **9** concerted; **11** conjunctive, cooperative
conjunction: 5 union; **7** joinder [Law], uniting; **8** coupling, junction; **9** alignment; **10** connective; **11** coincidence, concurrence, conjugation, conjunctive; **12** co-occurrence

conjunctive: 3 fix; **4** pass, push; **5** hitch, pinch, trial; **6** strait, united; **7** nonplus; **8** combined, conjunct, exigency, juncture, quandary, scramble; **9** concerted; **10** connective, pretty pass; **11** conjunction, cooperative, predicament
conjunctivitis: 7 pinkeye
conjuncture: 4 turn; **6** crisis; **8** juncture
conjuration: 7 conjury; **9** conjuring; **10** hocus-pocus
conjure: 4 stir; **5** raise; **6** adjure, arouse, invoke, juggle; **7** bring up; **8** call down; **9** call forth, conjure up; **10** put forward
conjure man: 8 conjurer, conjuror
conjurer: 8 conjuror, magician; **10** conjure man; **11** illusionist; **15** prestidigitator
conjure up: 4 stir; **5** raise; **6** arouse, invoke; **7** bring up, conjure; **8** call down; **9** call forth; **10** put forward
conjure up a vision: 8 envision; **9** visualize
conjuring: 7 conjury; **10** hocus-pocus; **11** conjuration
conjuring trick: 5 magic, trick; **8** illusion; **9** deception; **10** magic trick; **11** legerdemain
conjuror: 4 seer; **5** witch; **6** jockey, wizard; **7** juggler; **8** conjurer, magician; **9** trickster; **10** conjure man; **11** illusionist, necromancer; **15** prestidigitator
conjury: 9 conjuring; **11** conjuration
conk: 5 choke, croak, faint, stall, swoon; **6** pop off; **7** pass out, snuff it; **8** drop dead; **10** buy the farm; **11** die suddenly; **13** kick the bucket; **15** die unexpectedly
conker: 7 buckeye; **13** horse chestnut
conk out: 2 go; **3** die; **4** fail; **5** break; **6** run out; **7** give out, give way, poop out, run down; **8** peter out; **9** break down
con man: 9 con artist; **13** confidence man
connaitre le dessous des cartes: 13 know what's what
Connarus: 13 genus Connarus
connate: 7 cognate; **10** in the blood
connatural: 6 inborn, inbred, native; **8** allied to, congener, of a piece [Fr]; **10** consistent
connaturality: 10 uniformity; **11** consistency, homogeneity
connaturalize: 9 make alike
connaturalness: 10 uniformity; **11** consistency, homogeneity
connect: 3 tie; **4** join, link; **5** marry, tie in, unite; **6** link up, plug in, relate; **7** conjoin; **8** be linked; **9** associate, touch base; **10** get in touch; **11** be connected; **12** hook together; **13** draw a parallel; **14** be tied together
connected: 6 linked; **7** related; **8** attached; **10** affiliated, associated; **17** machine-accessible
connected chain: 11 atomic chain; **12** chain of atoms

connectedness: 4 link; 7 linkage; 9 connexion; 10 connection

connecter: 9 connector, connexion; 10 connection, connective

Connecticut: 11 Nutmeg State; 17
Constitution State

connecting: 7 joining; 8 junction, ligating,
ligation; 9 attaching, connexion; 10 attachment, connection, copulative

connection: 3 kin; 4 bond, link; 5 blood; 7
bearing, concern, joining, kindred, kinfolk
[pl], kinsman, linkage; 8 alliance, relation,
relative, vinculum; 9 cognation, connecter,
connector, connexion, mutuality; 10 connecting, connective, kith and kin [pl]; 11
affiliation, association, correlation; 12 relationship; 13 connectedness, interrelation

connection structure: 11 atomic chain; 12
chain of atoms; 14 connected chain

connective: 4 bond, link; 7 linkage; 8 vinculum; 9 connecter, connector, connexion; 10
connection; 11 conjunction, conjunctive

connector: 3 tie; 8 fastener; 9 connecter,
connexion, fastening; 10 connection, connective

connexion: 4 link; 7 joining; 9 connecter,
connector; 10 connecting, connection, connective; 11 association; 13 connectedness

connivance: 9 collusion; 12 tacit consent; 14
secret approval

connive: 6 scheme; 8 intrigue

connive at: 6 wink at

conniving: 6 shrewd; 8 scheming; 9 collusive; 11 calculating, calculative

connoisseur: 10 man of taste; 11 cognoscenti

connoisseurship: 5 vertu, virtu

connotate: 7 connote

connotation: 5 sense; 9 intension; 11 implication; 14 implied meaning; 15 implicit
meaning

connotational: 13 connotative of

connotative of: 13 connotational

connote: 5 imply; 9 predicate

connubial: 6 wedded; 7 marital; 8 conjugal;
10 conjugally; 11 matrimonial

conoid: 4 cone; 9 cone shape

Conopodium: 15 genus Conopodium

Conopodium denudatum: 8 earthnut

conoscente: 8 virtuoso; 11 cogniscenti [pl]
[It]

con over: 3 con; 8 pore over; 9 brood over,
thumb over

conquer: 4 beat, curb; 5 seize; 6 defeat, subdue; 7 capture, inhibit; 8 suppress, take
over, vanquish; 9 discomfit, stamp down

conquerable: 9 superable

conquered: 6 beaten, routed; 8 overcome; 10
overthrown, vanquished; 11 overwhelmed

conquering: 8 conquest; 10 subjection; 11
subjugation

conqueror: 10 vanquisher

conquest: 7 victory; 9 seduction; 10 conquering, subjection; 11 subjugation

consanguine: 3 kin; 4 akin; 6 agnate; 7 cognate; 12 blood-related

consanguinity: 7 kinship; 9 cognation, family tie; 11 ties of blood; 12 blood kinship,
relationship; 14 family relation; 16 family
connection

conscience: 8 scruples; 9 awareness; 10
moral sense; 13 consciousness, inward
monitor

conscienceless: 14 unconscionable

conscientious: 5 close, moral; 7 ethical; 10
principled, scrupulous; 11 casuistical,
painstaking, right-minded, straitlaced

conscientiously: 11 religiously; 12 scrupu-
lously; 13 punctiliously

conscientiousness: 7 probity; 9 integrity,
principle, propriety, punctilio, rectitude; 11
uprightness; 13 sense of ethics; 14 meticu-
lousness, scrupulousness; 15 painstaking-
ness

conscientious objector: 2 CO

conscious: 5 aware; 7 witting

consciousness: 9 awareness; 10 cognizance;
11 knowingness

conscious of: 7 aware of; 11 cognizant of

conscript: 4 levy; 5 cadet, draft, raise; 7
draftee, recruit; 9 raw levies

conscripted: 7 drafted

conscription: 5 draft; 6 muster; 8 drafting;
16 selective service

consecrate: 3 vow; 4 call; 5 bless, order; 6
devote, hallow, ordain, prefer; 7 beatify,
present; 8 dedicate, enshrine, keep holy,
sanctify; 9 dedicated, translate; 11 consecrated

consecrated: 6 sacred; 7 adopted, elected; 8
inspired; 9 converted, dedicated, justified,
unearthly; 10 consecrate, sanctified

consecration: 9 reading in; 10 dedication,
holy orders, ordination, preferment; 11 celebration, institution, translation; 12 canonization, enshrinement, enthronement,
presentation; 13 glorification

consectary: 9 deducible, following; 11 inferential; 13 consequential

consectary reasoning: 13 just reasoning; 14
sound reasoning, valid reasoning; 15
cogent reasoning

consecution: 10 succession; 15 consecutiveness

consecutive: 6 serial; 7 sequent; 8 straight;
10 back-to-back, sequential, successive; 12
sequentially

consecutiveness: 10 succession; 11 consecution

consensus: 6 chorus; 11 acclamation; 13
common consent; 16 general agreement

consent: 3 nod; 5 go for; 6 accede, accept,

assent; **9** accession, agreement; **10** acceptance; **11** acceptation, yield assent; **12** acquiescence

consentaneous: 8 in accord; **9** accordant, congruous, consonant, of one mind, unanimous; **10** concordant, consistent; **11** consentient; **13** correspondent, corresponding

consentaneousness: 10 consonance; **11** consistency

consenter: 9 permitter

consentient: 9 of one mind, unanimous; **13** consentaneous

consequence: 4 mark; **5** issue; **6** effect, import, moment, result, upshot; **7** outcome; **9** aftermath; **10** importance, prominence; **11** contingency, materiality, weightiness; **12** materialness, significance; **13** consideration

consequent: 7 ensuant, sequent; **9** resultant, resulting; **10** subsequent

consequential: 4 high; **5** blown, lofty; **6** mighty; **7** flushed, haughty, swollen; **8** eventful, puffed up; **9** deducible, following, important; **11** inferential; **12** of importance, vainglorious; **13** high and mighty, self-important

consequentially: 11 importantly, momentously

consequently: 4 ergo, then, thus; **5** hence; **6** thusly, whence; **8** of course, thence so; **9** as a result, naturally, therefore, wherefore; **10** in that case; **11** accordingly, in which case; **12** and therefore; **13** for that reason, for this reason, in consequence, in view of which, it follows that

conservancy: 10 conserving; **12** conservation

conservation: 10 conserving; **11** conservancy, maintenance; **12** preservation; **15** conservation law

conservationist: 16 environmentalist

conservation law: 12 conservation

conservatism: 7 toryism

conservative: 8 cautious; **9** bourgeois; **10** button-down; **12** buttoned-down, preservative; **13** materialistic; **14** conservativist

conservatively: 9 guardedly; **10** cautiously

conservativist: 12 conservative

conservatoire: 12 conservatory

conservator: 7 curator

conservator of the peace: 4 beak; **16** police magistrate; **27** justice of the peacemagistrate

conservatory: 8 hothouse; **10** greenhouse; **12** indoor garden; **13** conservatoire

conserve: 3 jam; **4** save; **5** jelly; **7** husband; **8** preserve; **9** conserves, economise, economize, preserves

conserves: 8 conserve, preserve; **9** preserves

conserving: 10 preserving; **11** conservancy; **12** conservation

consider: 3 see; **4** deal, moot, scan, take, view; **5** count, study, think, weigh; **6** debate, esteem, look at, ponder, reckon, regard; **7** believe, examine, think of; **8** conceive, research, turn over; **10** deliberate, scrutinize, think about; **11** contemplate, inquire into, reflect upon; **12** inquire about, meditate upon

considerable: 4 fair; **5** ample, bulky, massy; **7** massive; **8** above par; **10** voluminous

considerably: 4 well; **13** substantially

consider as: 6 deem as, hold as, take as, view as; **8** esteem as, regard as; **9** account as, set down as; **10** conceive as, look upon as

considerateness: 10 solicitude; **13** consideration; **14** thoughtfulness; **17** taking into account

consideration: 4 mark; **5** basis; **6** import, moment, return; **7** grounds, thought; **8** approval, retainer, sanction, thinking; **9** allowance, attention, condition, pro and con, sentiment; **10** cogitation, estimation, importance, meditation, prominence, quid pro quo, reflection, solicitude, toleration; **11** approbation, consequence, good opinion, materiality, observation, pros and cons, weightiness; **12** circumstance, materialness, significance; **14** thoughtfulness

considered: 4 wise; **7** advised, studied; **8** designed, reasoned; **10** calculated; **12** premeditated; **14** well thought out

considering: 3 for; **4** only; **5** for as, since; **6** enough; **7** because, whereas; **10** ex concesso [Lat], inasmuch as, seeing that; **13** for inasmuch as

consign: 6 assign, charge, pass on, vest in; **7** entrust, forward, intrust; **8** delegate, hand over, relegate; **10** commission, turn over to

consignee: 7 nominee, trustee

consigner: 9 consignor

consignificative: 10 synonymous

consignment: 4 load; **5** cargo, trust; **6** lading; **7** freight, loading, payload; **8** shipment; **9** assigning, committal, endowment; **10** assignment, commission, commitment, delegating, delegation, deputation, deputizing, entrusting; **11** appointment; **12** commisioning, dispensation; **13** communication

consignor: 9 consigner

consist: 3 lie; **5** dwell, lie in; **6** belong

consistence: 4 body; **11** consistency

consistency: 4 body; **6** accord; **10** accordance, consonance, uniformity; **11** consistence, homogeneity

consistent: 6 steady; **7** logical, ordered, orderly, routine, uniform; **8** constant, in accord, of a piece [Fr]; **9** accordant, clockwork, congruous, consonant, continual, incessant, perpetual, unceasing, unfailing; **10** compatible, concordant, continuous, invariable, monotonous; **12** reproducible;

consistently: 6 always; 8 ever anon, steadily; 9 routinely; 10 at all times, constantly, invariably; 11 continually, day after day, day and night, incessantly, night and day, perpetually, unfailingly, without fail; 12 continuously, monotonously; 13 at every moment; 14 daily and hourly, never otherwise, systematically

consist in: 5 lie in; 8 comprise; 9 consist of

consist of: 8 comprise; 9 consist in; 14 be resolved into

consistory: 5 synod; 6 vestry; 7 chapter; 8 conclave; 9 syndicate; 11 convocation

consociate: 9 associate

consolation: 6 solace; 7 comfort, unction; 8 sympathy; 10 solacement; 11 inspiration; 12 regeneration; 13 encouragement; 14 sanctification

consolatory: 8 soothing; 9 consoling; 10 comforting

console: 5 cheer; 6 solace, soothe; 7 cabinet, comfort, condole; 10 sympathize; 11 condole with, express pity, testify pity; 12 console table

console table: 7 console

Consolida ambigua: 14 rocket larkspur; 16 Delphinium ajacis

consolidate: 3 set; 4 cake, cure, fuse; 5 blend, merge, unite; 6 absorb, embody; 7 blend in, combine, congeal, conjoin; 8 coalesce, concrete, dissolve, take a set; 9 coagulate; 10 amalgamate, centralize, impregnate; 11 incorporate, melt into one; 13 blend together

consolidated: 5 fused; 9 coalesced; 10 amalgamate; 11 amalgamated

consolidation: 11 integration

consolidative: 8 unifying; 11 integrative

consoling: 10 comforting; 11 consolatory

consomme: 4 soup; 5 broth, puree; 7 pottage

consonance: 6 accord; 7 concord, harmony; 8 symphony; 11 consistency, uniformness; 14 consonant rhyme, harmoniousness

consonant: 8 harmonic, in accord; 9 accordant, agreeable, congruous, in harmony; 10 concordant, consistent, harmonical, harmonized; 11 conformable, in agreement; 13 correspondent, corresponding

consonantal: 10 nonvocalic; 11 nonsyllabic

consonantal system: 15 consonant system

consonant rhyme: 10 consonance

consort: 3 man, run; 4 mate; 5 agree, baron, choir, fit in; 6 accord, assort, spouse; 7 collude, concert, husband, partner; 8 conspire, sort with; 9 affiliate, associate, harmonize; 10 fraternize; 11 confederate

consortium: 4 pool; 9 syndicate

consortship: 11 comradeship; 13 companionship

conspectus: 8 syllabus; 10 prospectus

conspicuity: 9 plainness; 12 distinctness; 15 conspicuousness

conspicuous: 4 open; 5 clear, plain; 7 blatant, blazing, flaunty, glaring, obvious, staring; 8 apparent, definite, distinct; 10 in full view

conspicuously: 7 clearly, plainly; 9 glaringly; 10 apparently, definitely, distinctly; 11 prominently

conspicuousness: 9 plainness; 10 visibility; 12 distinctness

conspiracy: 4 plot; 5 cabal; 8 intrigue; 9 collusion; 11 confederacy, machination

conspirator: 7 plotter, traitor; 8 betrayer; 10 machinator; 13 coconspirator

conspiratorial: 9 collusive; 12 conspirative

conspire: 5 cabal; 6 concur; 7 collude, complot, concert, conduce, conjoin, consort; 10 contribute, fraternize; 11 confederate

conspiring: 9 conducing; 10 coinciding, concurrent, concurring, conjoining

constable: 3 cop; 7 officer; 8 gendarme [Fr]; 9 policeman; 13 police officer; 15 police constable

constabulary: 3 law; 6 police; 7 the cops, the fuzz [sarcastic] [U.S.]; 11 gendarmerie [Fr], police force

constancy: 6 homage; 7 loyalty, routine; 8 devotion, fidelity, monotony; 9 even tenor, stability; 10 regularity, steadiness, uniformity; 12 faithfulness; 14 continuousness

constant: 6 stable, steady; 7 routine; 8 faithful, unerring; 9 ceaseless, clockwork, continual, incessant, invariant, perpetual, steadfast, unceasing, unfailing, unvarying; 10 changeless, consistent, continuous, invariable, monotonous, unyielding; 11 never-ending, unremitting; 12 pertinacious

constantan: 6 Eureka

constant flow: 14 unbroken extent

Constantinople: 7 Stambul; 8 Istanbul, Stamboul

constantly: 6 always; 8 ever anon, steadily; 9 routinely; 10 at all times, invariably; 11 continually, day after day, day and night, incessantly, night and day, perpetually, unfailingly, without fail; 12 consistently, continuously, monotonously; 13 at every moment

constant quantity: 8 constant

constatation: 15 basic assumption; 16 self-evident truth

constellate: 3 dot; 4 stud; 5 clump, flock; 7 cluster

constellation: 3 sun; 6 galaxy; 13 configuration

consternate: 6 flurry, put off; 7 confuse; 10 disconcert

consternation: 3 awe; **5** alarm; **6** dismay
constipate: 4 bind, cram, pack; **6** stop up; **7** ram down, squeeze; **8** compress
constipated: 7 costive; **9** stopped up
constipating: 7 binding
constipation: 12 irregularity
constituent: 6 factor; **7** element, organic; **8** material; **9** component; **10** ingredient; **12** constitutive, integral part; **13** component part; **14** constitutional
constituents: 10 electorate
constitute: 2 be; **4** form, make, name; **5** found, plant, setup; **6** make up; **7** appoint, compose; **8** comprise, nominate, organize; **9** establish, institute, represent; **11** put together
constituting: 10 containing
constitution: 4 type; **6** makeup; **7** quality; **9** formation, principle, substance; **10** organic law; **11** composition; **12** organisation, organization; **13** establishment, state of health; **14** fundamental law
constitutional: 6 vested; **7** built-in, inbuilt, organic; **8** inherent, integral, ordained; **9** chartered, legalized; **10** prescribed; **11** constituent; **12** constitutive, enfranchised
Constitution State: 11 Connecticut, Nutmeg State
constitutive: 7 organic; **11** constituent; **14** constitutional
constrain: 4 curb, make; **5** check, drive, force; **6** coerce, compel, cumber, oblige; **7** control, enforce, stiffen, tighten; **8** encumber, restrain, restrict; **9** tighten up; **11** necessitate
constrained: 5 bound; **6** demure, forced, modest; **8** obligate, reserved, strained; **9** compelled, diffident; **10** controlled, restrained; **12** under control
constraining: 8 limiting; **9** confining; **11** restricting; **12** constrictive
constraint: 6 duress; **7** reserve; **8** coercion; **9** restraint; **10** compulsion, demureness, repression; **11** enforcement, suppression
constrict: 5 press, taper; **6** narrow; **7** compact, squeeze; **8** compress, contract; **10** constringe
constricted: 7 tapered; **8** narrowed, stenotic [Med], tapering; **9** narrowing
constricting: 7 binding; **9** lessening, narrowing, shrinking; **12** constrictive
constriction: 4 neck; **9** squeezing, stricture; **10** bottleneck; **13** strangulation
constrictive: 8 limiting; **9** confining, narrowing; **11** restricting; **12** constraining, constricting
constrictor: 3 boa
Constrictor constrictor: 14 boa constrictor
constringe: 6 lessen, narrow, reduce; **8** diminish; **9** constrict; **13** render smaller

construal: 10 exposition, expounding; **13** understanding; **14** interpretation
construct: 4 form, make; **5** build; **7** concept, retrace; **9** fabricate, structure; **10** conception; **11** manufacture, reconstruct; **12** construction
constructing: 8 building, erecting, erection; **11** edification; **12** construction
construction: 3 cut, set; **4** make; **5** light, sense, twist; **6** fabric; **7** lection, reading, version; **8** building, erecting, erection; **9** construct, formation, structure; **10** expression; **11** edification; **12** constructing; **15** mental synthesis
construction industry: 15 housing industry
constructive eviction: 8 eviction
constructive fraud: 10 legal fraud
constructive-metabolic: 13 energy-storing
constructive metabolism: 9 anabolism
constructor: 7 builder; **9** developer
construe: 6 define; **7** explain; **9** interpret; **10** understand; **18** put a construction on
construe with: 6 go with; **11** cooccur with; **13** collocate with
consuetudinary: 3 jog; **4** trot; **6** common; **7** typical; **8** everyday, frequent, ordinary; **9** household, well-known; **11** commonplace, well-trodden; **13** consuetudinal, garden variety
consul: 6 consul; **8** resident; **9** proconsul; **14** representative
consult: 5 refer; **6** call in, confab, confer, look up; **7** refer to; **10** confer with; **11** confabulate, take counsel
consultant: 7 adviser, advisor
consultation: 8 audience; **9** interview, reference; **10** conferring
consultative: 8 advisory; **10** consultive; **12** consultatory
consultatory: 8 advisory; **10** consultive; **12** consultative
consulting company: 14 consulting firm
consultive: 8 advisory; **12** consultative, consultatory
consult the wishes of: 6 oblige; **11** accommodate
consult together: 16 lay heads together
consume: 3 eat; **4** down, fare, feed, have, take, ware; **5** eat up, spend, use up, waste; **6** devour, expend, ingest, take in; **7** deplete, exhaust, swallow, wipe out; **8** squander; **9** go through; **10** run through
consume all of: 5 drain, empty; **6** absorb, finish, tap out; **7** exhaust; **8** run out of; **9** swallow up; **10** impoverish, use up all of
consumed: 6 used up, used-up; **7** drained; **8** depleted, expended, finished; **9** exhausted, tapped out; **11** swallowed up
consumed with curiosity: 11 overcurious; **20** burning with curiosity
consumer: 4 user; **7** end user

consumer durables: 8 durables; 12 durable goods

consumer loan: 12 personal loan

consumer price index: 3 CPI

consume time: 8 kill time, lose time, pass time; 9 spend time, waste time; 12 pass away time

consuming: 7 cutting, grating, racking; 8 grinding; 9 agonizing, corroding, searching; 12 excruciating, overwhelming

consummate: 4 arch, free, pure; 5 crass, gross, sheer, stark, utter; 6 arrant; 7 achieve, compass, intense, perfect, regular, sodding, staring; 8 complete, masterly, profound, virtuoso; 9 hammer out, masterful; 10 accomplish, double-dyed; 11 everlasting, unmitigated, unqualified; 13 thoroughgoing, unconditional

consummation: 6 finale, finish; 9 winding up; 10 conclusion, denouement, wrapping up; 11 culmination

consumption: 3 use; 6 intake, uptake, usance; 7 decline, using up; 8 phthisis; 9 depletion, ingestion; 10 emaciation; 11 attenuation, expenditure, white plague; 12 tuberculosis; 14 wasting disease

consumptive: 6 lunger

contact: 3 get; 4 link; 5 close, reach, touch; 7 liaison; 8 striking, tangency, touching; 9 close with, collision, get hold of, impinging, middleman, proximity; 10 apposition, contacting, contiguity, get in touch, get through; 11 coincidence, make contact; 12 get through to; 13 come in contact, juxtaposition, output contact; 14 contiguousness

contact arm: 5 wiper; 8 wiper arm

contacting: 7 contact, meeting; 8 abutment; 10 osculation; 13 making contact; 14 coming together

contact lenses: 10 hard lenses, soft lenses

contagion: 9 infection; 12 transmission

contagious: 6 taking; 8 catching; 10 infectious; 12 communicable, contractable; 13 transmissable, transmissible, transmittable

contagious disease: 9 contagion

contagiously: 12 infectiously

contain: 4 bear, curb, have, hold, stop, take; 5 admit, carry, check; 6 arrest, embody, hold in, take in; 7 control, embrace, include; 8 comprise, hold back, moderate, turn back; 10 comprehend; 11 incorporate

contained: 8 included; 10 restricted

container: 10 receptacle

containership: 13 container ship

container ship: 13 containership

containing: 6 having; 9 including; 12 constituting

containing air: 9 flatulent; 12 effervescent

containment: 7 embrace; 10 limitation; 11 restriction; 12 encirclement

contaminant: 5 taint; 8 impurity; 9 pollution; 13 contamination

contaminate: 4 foul; 5 taint; 6 debase, defile, poison; 7 pollute; 10 adulterate

contaminated: 5 dirty; 7 defiled, tainted; 8 infected, poisoned, polluted, vitiated; 9 corrupted; 11 adulterated

contaminating: 5 dirty; 8 debasing, defiling, tainting; 9 polluting, pollution; 10 corrupting, debasement, defilement; 12 adulteration; 13 contamination

contamination: 5 alloy, taint; 8 defiling, impurity; 9 polluting, pollution; 10 corruption, debasement, defilement; 11 contaminant; 12 adulteration; 13 contaminating

contango: 13 backwardation

conte a dormir debout: 9 heavy book

contemn: 5 scorn; 7 despise, disdain; 14 hold in contempt

contemplate: 4 mull, muse; 5 study, weigh; 6 ponder; 7 reflect; 8 chew over, consider, meditate, mull over, ruminate; 9 speculate, think over; 10 think about; 11 reflect upon; 12 meditate upon

contemplate of: 6 talk of; 7 dream of, think of; 8 meditate

contemplation: 4 mind, view; 6 animus, musing; 7 lookout, purview; 8 proposal; 9 reflexion; 10 meditation, reflection, rumination; 14 thoughtfulness

contemplative: 6 broody, musing, sedate; 7 pensive, wistful; 8 brooding, Platonic, studious; 9 pondering; 10 meditative, reflective, ruminative, thoughtful; 11 speculative; 12 deliberative; 13 introspective, philosophical

contemplativeness: 11 pensiveness, wistfulness; 12 studiousness; 14 meditativeness, thoughtfulness

contemporaneity: 9 modernism, modernity; 10 modernness

contemporaneous: 6 coeval; 10 coetaneous; 12 contemporary

contemporaneousness: 9 modernism, modernity, synchrony; 10 modernness; 11 coexistence, isochronism, synchronism, unity of time; 12 co-occurrence, simultaneity; 15 contemporaneity

contemporaries: 7 coevals; 10 generation

contemporary: 4 late; 6 coeval, modern; 7 nouveau; 8 neoteric; 10 present-day; 11 hypermodern, modernistic; 12 non-classical

contemporary world: 5 times; 11 modern times, modern world, present time

contemporation: 9 remission; 10 mitigation, relaxation; 11 assuagement; 12 pacification

contemporize: 11 synchronize

contempororary: 6 modern

contempt: 5 scorn; 7 disdain; 10 disrespect; 12 scornfulness

contemptibility: 8 baseness; 13 despicability; 14 despicableness

contemptible: 4 mean; 5 dirty; 6 abject, little, paltry, scabby, scurvy, shabby; 7 scrubby; 8 rascally, sneaking; 9 groveling; 10 despicable; 12 pettifogging; 13 unrespectable

contempt of danger: 4 dash; 9 derring-do; 16 defiance of danger

contemptuous: 8 scornful; 9 insulting; 10 disdainful

contemptuously: 10 scornfully; 12 disdainfully; 14 contumeliously; 15 showing contempt

contemptuousness: 5 scorn; 7 disdain; 8 contempt; 12 scornfulness

contend: 3 vie; 4 cope, deal, spar; 5 argue, fence, get by; 6 debate, insist, make do, manage, repugn, square, strive; 7 compete, contest, grapple, make out; 8 maintain, scramble, struggle; 9 postulate, square off; 11 lay stress on

contender: 5 rival; 10 challenger, competitor; 11 competition

contend for: 6 vie for; 8 speak for; 10 compete for, stickle for; 12 stipulate for

contend for authority: 13 vie for control

contending: 5 rival; 8 sparring; 9 competing; 10 contesting

content: 5 force, happy; 6 agreed, import; 7 meaning, message, purport, satisfy, subdued, subject; 8 capacity, resigned; 9 at one with, chastened, contented, satisfied, substance; 10 complacent; 11 acquiescent, contentment; 12 mental object, significance; 13 contentedness, of the same mind, render content, signification

contented: 7 content; 9 satisfied; 10 complacent

contentedness: 7 content; 11 contentment

contention: 4 tilt; 6 strife; 7 arguing, rivalry; 8 argument; 10 struggling; 11 competition, controversy; 12 contestation

contentious: 9 battleful, bellicose, combative, litigious, truculent; 11 belligerent, disputative, quarrelsome; 12 disputatious

contentiousness: 9 pugnacity; 12 belligerence, factiousness; 14 aggressiveness; 15 quarrelsomeness

contently: 11 contentedly; 19 to one's heart's content

contentment: 7 content; 13 contentedness

contents: 5 theme, topic; 6 matter; 7 noemata [Grk], outline, subject; 13 subject matter, what it is about; 15 table of contents

content word: 13 open-class word

conterminous: 8 abutting, adjacent, end to end; 9 adjoining, bordering; 10 contiguous, osculatory

contesseration: 9 concourse; 11 convergence; 12 congregation

contest: 3 vie; 4 spar; 5 match; 6 repugn, square, strive; 7 compete, contend; 8 scramble, struggle; 9 square off; 11 competition

contestant: 8 objector; 9 dissenter, dissident, protester

contestation: 4 tilt; 5 match; 7 arguing, contest; 8 argument, struggle; 10 contention; 11 competition, controversy

contesting: 5 rival; 8 sparring; 9 competing; 10 contending

context: 5 place, point; 9 condition; 10 conditions [pl]; 12 circumstance, context of use; 13 circumstances

contiguity: 7 contact; 9 adjacency, proximity; 10 apposition; 11 coincidence; 13 juxtaposition; 14 contiguousness

contiguous: 8 abutting, adjacent; 9 adjoining, bordering, immediate; 12 conterminous

contiguousness: 7 contact; 9 adjacency, proximity; 10 apposition, contiguity; 11 coincidence; 13 juxtaposition

continence: 5 shame; 6 virtue; 7 modesty; 10 continency

continency: 10 continence

continent: 6 chaste; 8 celibate, mainland

continental: 7 midland; 12 mid-continent

continental quilt: 5 duvet; 9 eiderdown

continental rifting: 7 rifting

continental shelf: 16 continental slope

continental slope: 11 bathyal zone; 15 bathyal district; 16 continental shelf

contingence: 11 contingency

contingency: 6 effect; 7 proviso; 8 exigency, juncture; 9 condition, provision; 10 dependence, dependency, sine qua non [Lat]; 11 consequence, contingence, eventuality, stipulation; 12 prerequisite; 13 specification

contingent: 3 lot; 5 quota, share; 6 casual, chance, detail; 7 measure, portion; 8 uncaused; 9 allotment, allowance, causeless, dependent, fair share; 10 accidental, allocation, fortuitous, incidental; 11 conditional, conditioned, dependant on, dependent on, depending on

contingently: 12 accidentally, fortuitously

continual: 6 steady; 7 routine; 8 constant; 9 clockwork, incessant, perpetual, unceasing, unfailing; 10 consistent, continuous, invariable, monotonous

continually: 6 always; 8 ever anon, steadily; 9 routinely; 10 at all times, constantly, invariably; 11 day after day, day and night, incessantly, night and day, perpetually, unfailingly, without fail; 12 consistently, continuously, monotonously; 13 at every moment

continuance: 8 duration, standing; 10 continuity; 12 continuation

continuant consonant: 10 continuant
continuation: 6 sequel; 9 extension; 10 continuity; 11 continuance
continue: 4 go on, keep, last, stay; 5 abide, stand; 6 bear on, endure, keep on, remain, retain, stay on, uphold; 7 carry on, go along, persist, proceed; 8 preserve; 9 go forward, persist in
continued: 8 unbroken, 10 continuing, continuous; 13 uninterrupted
continuing: 7 abiding, lasting; 8 enduring; 9 continued
continuity: 11 continuance, persistence; 12 continuation; 13 ceaselessness
continuous: 6 steady; 7 routine; 8 constant, unbroken; 9 clockwork, continual, continued, incessant, perpetual, unceasing, unfailing; 10 consistent, invariable, monotonous; 11 unsegmented; 13 uninterrupted
continuously: 6 always; 8 ever anon, steadily; 9 endlessly, routinely; 10 at all times, constantly, invariably, unendingly; 11 ceaselessly, continually, day after day, day and night, incessantly, night and day, perpetually, unceasingly, unfailingly, without fail; 12 consistently, monotonously
continuousness: 7 routine; 8 monotony; 9 constancy; 10 incessancy, regularity, steadiness; 13 ceaselessness, incessantness
continuous receiver watch: 14 listening watch
continuous tense: 9 imperfect; 11 progressive; 14 imperfect tense; 16 progressive tense
contort: 4 warp; 5 wring; 6 deform; 7 distort
contorted: 7 twisted, writhed, writhen; 9 distorted
contorting: 9 deforming; 10 contortion, distorting, distortion; 11 deformation
contortion: 7 torsion; 9 deforming, deformity; 10 contorting, distorting, distortion, tortuosity; 11 crookedness, deformation; 12 tortuousness
contour: 4 form; 5 ambit, lines, shape; 7 circuit, outline, profile; 9 lineament; 11 contour line; 12 cut of one's jib; 13 configuration
contour line: 7 contour
contour map: 9 relief map
contour sheet: 11 fitted sheet
contra: 9 nay rather, per contra; 10 contrarily; 12 contrariwise; 13 on the contrary
contraband: 3 hot; 5 black; 7 bootleg; 8 smuggled; 11 adulterated, black-market; 12 illegitimate; 13 surreptitious
contrabandist: 6 badger, runner; 8 abductor, bunko man, smuggler; 10 mooncurser; 11 cattle thief
contrabass: 4 bass; 8 bass viol; 10 bass fiddle, bull fiddle, double bass, double-bass, string bass

contrabasso: 4 bass; 10 double bass
contrabassoon: 7 bassoon, serpent; 12 bass clarinet; 13 contrafagotto, double bassoon
contra bonos mores: 7 lawless; 8 improper, scampish, unseemly; 10 disorderly, indecorous, unbecoming; 11 unbefitting; 12 unprincipled
contraceptive: 10 preventive; 12 birth control, preventative, prophylactic; 13 antifertility
contraceptive device: 10 preventive; 12 preventative; 13 contraceptive
contraceptive diaphragm: 7 pessary; 9 diaphragm
contraceptive pill: 4 pill; 15 anovulatory drug; 16 birth control pill
contract: 3 cut, fee, get; 4 sign, take; 5 press; 6 draw in, narrow, reduce, shrink, sign on, sign up; 7 abridge, bargain, compact, shorten, squeeze; 8 agree for, compress, condense, covenant; 9 constrict, undertake; 10 abbreviate; 11 concentrate, foreshorten; 14 contract bridge
contractable: 8 catching; 10 contagious; 12 communicable; 13 transmissible, transmittable
contract bridge: 5 whist; 6 bridge; 8 contract; 11 bridge whist
contracted: 6 agreed, shrunk; 7 reduced; 10 diminished
contractility: 15 compressibility
contracting: 8 catching; 11 contraction
contraction: 9 reduction; 10 diminution; 11 compression, contracting; 12 condensation
contract of hazard: 11 sale in gross
contractual: 10 negotiated
contradance: 11 contra danse, contredanse; 12 country-dance
contradict: 5 belie; 6 negate, oppose; 10 contravene, controvert
contradicted: 8 disputed; 11 controvened
contradiction: 7 paradox; 8 oxymoron; 13 contravention, inconsistency; 20 contradiction in terms
contradiction in terms: 7 paradox; 8 oxymoron; 13 contradiction, inconsistency
contradictory: 6 at odds; 11 conflicting, confounding; 12 inconsistent
contradictory evidence: 8 disproof; 10 refutation
contradistinction: 9 diversity; 11 discrepancy
contrafagotto: 7 bassoon, serpent; 12 bass clarinet; 13 contrabassoon, double bassoon
contraindicate: 11 warn against
contraindication: 6 lesson
contralto: 4 alto
contraposition: 10 opposition
contraption: 5 gizmo; 6 gadget, widget; 9 appliance; 11 contrivance, convenience

contrapuntal: 10 polyphonic

contrariant: 5 polar; 7 counter; 8 contrary, opposite; 11 dead against

contrariety: 8 contrast, self-will; 9 contumacy; 10 balkiness, opposition, perversity, unruliness; 11 restiveness, waywardness, willfulness; 12 contrariness, oppositeness; 14 rebelliousness, refractoriness

contrarily: 6 contra; 9 nay rather, per contra; 10 perversely; 12 contrariwise; 13 on the contrary, to the contrary

contrariness: 8 self-will; 9 contumacy; 10 balkiness, crankiness, grumpiness, perversity, unruliness; 11 contrariety, restiveness, waywardness, willfulness

contrarious: 5 polar; 7 counter; 8 contrary, opposite; 11 dead against; 12 cross-grained

contrary: 5 balky, heady, polar; 6 entete [Fr] unruly; 7 adverse, counter, restive, reverse, wayward, willful; 8 opposite, perverse; 9 obstinate; 10 headstrong, rebellious, refractory, self-willed

contrast: 4 line, tone; 7 balance; 8 tonality; 10 comparison, opposition; 11 contrariety, demarcation; 12 counterpoint, dividing line, oppositeness; 14 direct contrast

contrasted: 7 opposed; 8 opposing; 9 antipodal; 10 antipodean; 11 contrasting; 12 antagonistic, antithetical

contrasting: 7 opposed; 8 opposing; 9 antipodal, comparing; 10 antipodean, comparison, contrasted; 11 contrastive; 12 antagonistic, antithetical

contrastive: 11 contrasting, contrastive; 12 incompatible

contrast with: 6 oppose

contrate wheel: 10 crown wheel

contravallation: 8 dead wall

contravene: 6 negate; 8 conflict, infringe, run afoul, traverse; 10 contradict

contravention: 7 dispute; 8 opposing; 10 antagonism, opposition; 13 contradiction

contrecoup: 4 kick

contredanse: 11 contra danse, contradance; 12 country-dance; 14 country dancing

contribute: 3 add; 4 give, lead, lend; 5 allow, bring, carry, put up; 6 affect, bestow, chip in, concur, impart, kick in; 7 conduce, conjoin; 8 conspire; 9 subscribe; 11 subscribe to; 15 furnish its quota

contributing: 9 conducive; 12 contributive, contributory

contribution: 4 part; 5 grant, share; 8 donation

contributive: 9 conducive; 12 contributing, contributory

contributor: 5 donor; 6 poster; 10 subscriber

contributory: 9 conducive; 12 contributing, contributive

contributory cause: 22 contributory negligence

contrite: 5 sorry; 6 rueful; 8 penitent; 9 repentant, repenting; 10 remorseful

contritely: 8 ruefully; 12 remorsefully

contriteness: 9 attrition; 10 contrition

contrition: 7 remorse; 8 abrasion; 9 attrition, detrition, penitence; 10 repentance, rubbing off, wearing off; 11 compunction; 12 contriteness

contrivance: 5 dodge, gizmo; 6 device, gadget, lash-up, widget; 7 devisal, nostrum, receipt; 8 artifice; 9 appliance, expedient, invention, stratagem; 11 contraption, convenience

contrive: 4 cast, plan; 5 forge, frame, throw; 6 design, devise, invent, scheme; 7 arrange, project; 9 formulate; 10 excogitate

contrived: 7 plotted, schemed, stilted; 10 artificial

contriver: 7 deviser, planner

contrive to: 8 manage to; 9 succeed in

contriving: 9 designing; 10 intriguing; 11 maneuvering

control: 3 see; 4 curb, hold, sway; 5 check, see to; 6 assure, charge, ensure, govern, hold in, insure, master, verify; 7 command, contain, mastery, operate, see to it; 8 dominion, managing, moderate, overlook, restrain, restrict; 9 ascertain, constrain, dictation, direction, dominance, look after, restraint; 10 administer, ascendance, ascendancy, ascendence, ascendency, controller, discipline, domination, government, management, manipulate, regulation

control board: 5 board, panel; 12 control panel; 15 instrument panel

control condition: 7 control

control grid: 4 grid

control key: 10 command key

controllable: 10 governable

controlled: 10 restrained, restricted; 11 constrained; 12 under control

controller: 7 control; 10 accountant; 11 comptroller

controlling: 6 charge; 7 control; 8 managing; 9 direction; 10 government, management, prevailing; 11 supervising, supervision

controlling influence: 7 control; 8 dominion; 10 domination, regulation

control operation: 15 control function

control panel: 5 board, panel; 12 control board; 15 instrument panel

control point: 10 choke point

control stick: 5 stick; 8 joystick

control surface: 7 airfoil, surface; 8 aerofoil

controvened: 8 disputed; 12 contradicted

controversial: 7 polemic; 9 dialectic, polemical; 12 disputatious, gladiatorial; 13 argumentative

controversialist: 6 arguer; 7 debater, polemic; 9 disputant; 10 polemicist

controversially: 11 polemically

controversy: 4 tilt; **5** issue; **6** debate; **7** arguing, dispute, problem; **8** argument, question; **9** moot point; **10** contention; **11** topic at hand; **12** contestation, matter in hand; **13** argumentation, matter at issue; **14** question at hand; **15** matter in dispute

controvert: 5 rebut; **6** oppose, refute; **7** confute, gainsay; **8** confound, disprove, negative; **10** contradict, disconfirm; **12** give denial to

controverted: 7 refuted; **8** confuted, rebutted; **9** disproven; **10** confounded; **12** disconfirmed

controvertible: 9 debatable; **13** unsustainable

controverting: 9 confuting, rebutting; **10** disproving; **11** confounding; **13** disconfirming

controvertist: 6 arguer; **7** debater, polemic; **9** disputant

contumacious: 5 balky, heady; **6** entete [Fr], unruly; **7** restive, wayward, willful; **8** contrary, perverse; **10** headstrong, rebellious, refractory, self-willed; **12** incorrigible

contumaciously: 9 defiantly; **12** rebelliously

contumacy: 8 self-will; **10** balkyiness, perversity, unruliness; **11** contrariety, restiveness, waywardness, willfulness; **12** contrariness; **14** rebelliousness, refractoriness

contumelious: 4 acid, sour; **5** sharp, short, taint; **6** biting, bitter; **7** caustic, crabbed, cynical, doggish, haughty, searing; **8** cavalier, scathing, venomous, virulent; **9** bumptious, high-flown, sarcastic, scorching, trenchant, withering; **10** intolerant; **11** acrimonious, domineering, overbearing, overweening; **12** supercilious, vituperative

contumely: 5 abuse; **6** insult; **7** affront, offense; **8** dishonor; **9** hard words, invective; **10** revilement; **11** objurgation; **12** vilification, vituperation

contuse: 6 bruise

contused: 7 bruised; **11** contusioned

contusion: 6 bruise; **11** granulation, trituration [Chem]

contusioned: 7 bruised; **8** contused

conundrum: 5 rebus; **6** enigma, puzzle, riddle; **7** charade; **10** nut to crack; **11** brain-teaser

conurbation: 11 urban sprawl

convalesce: 7 recover; **10** recuperate

convalescence: 8 recovery; **12** recuperation

convalescent: 9 redivivus [Lat]; **10** recovering

convective heat: 9 solar heat

convene: 7 convoke

convenience: 5 gizmo; **6** gadget, widget; **7** leisure; **8** restroom, wash room; **9** appliance; **10** relaxation; **11** contraption, contrivance; **12** public toilet; **14** comfort station, public lavatory

conveniences: 8 comforts; **9** amenities

convenient: 4 ripe; **5** handy, happy, lucky; **9** favorable, fortunate; **10** auspicious, commodious, propitious; **11** ready to hand; **12** providential

conveniently: 7 handily

convening: 10 convention

convent: 7 nunnery; **8** cloister; **9** monastery

conventicle: 4 kirk; **5** levee; **6** caucus, chapel, church, clique; **7** oratory; **8** assembly, basilica, conclave, congress; **9** cathedral; **10** conference, convention, tabernacle; **12** meetinghouse

convention: 3 use; **4** diet, rule; **5** levee, usage; **6** custom, normal; **7** formula, pattern; **8** congress, practice; **9** convening; **10** conference, exhibition, observance, prevalence; **11** conventicle; **12** prescription; **13** states-general; **14** common practise

conventional: 5 usual; **6** formal; **9** customary, schematic; **11** ceremonious, established

conventionality: 3 use; **5** usage; **6** custom; **8** practice; **10** convention, observance, prevalence; **12** prescription; **14** common practise, wide observance; **15** conventionalism, general practise

conventionalization: 11 stylisation, stylization

conventionalize: 7 stylize; **15** conventionalise

conventionalized: 8 stylised, stylized

conventioneer: 8 conferee

conventual: 8 monastic; **9** cloistral; **10** cloistered, lay brother, monastical

converge: 4 meet; **5** unite; **6** concur; **10** fall in with; **12** come together, move together

converged: 3 met; **12** concentrated

convergence: 7 meeting, overlap; **8** congress; **9** concourse; **10** confluence, converging; **11** concurrence, convergency; **12** congregation, intersection; **13** concentration; **14** coming together

convergency: 7 meeting; **8** congress; **9** concourse; **10** confluence, converging; **11** concurrence, convergence; **13** concentration; **14** coming together

convergent: 7 meeting; **9** confluent; **10** concurrent, converging; **13** concentrating

convergent strabismus: 8 cross-eye; **10** crossed eye

converging: 7 meeting; **9** confluent, gathering; **10** assembling, concurrent, convergent; **11** convergence, convergency; **13** concentrating; **14** coming together; **15** getting together

converging lens: 10 convex lens

conversable: 4 cosy; **6** chatty; **14** conversational

conversance: 11 conversancy, familiarity; 12 acquaintance

conversancy: 11 conversance, familiarity; 12 acquaintance

conversant: 7 capable, skilled; 8 familiar, skillful; 9 competent, qualified; 10 proficient

conversant with: 4 up to; 5 crack; 6 au fait, good at; 8 at home in, master of; 11 a good hand at; 12 accomplished, familiar with, thoroughbred

conversation: 13 interlocution

conversational: 4 cosy; 6 chatty; 10 colloquial

conversationally: 10 informally; 12 colloquially

conversational partner: 12 interlocutor

conversazione: 5 levee; 6 at home; 8 audience; 9 interview, reception

converse: 4 talk; 7 reverse; 8 colloquy, reversed; 9 antipodal, discourse; 10 transposed; 12 talk together; 13 confabulation

conversing: 7 talking

conversion: 7 rebirth; 8 adoption; 9 salvation; 10 changeover, point after, transition; 11 extra points, inspiration, winning over; 12 regeneration; 13 beatification, justification; 14 sanctification, transformation

convert: 4 turn, wean; 5 edify; 6 change, theist; 7 commute, devotee, inspire, pervert, process, win over; 8 apostate, believer, convince, exchange, renegade; 9 bring over, transform; 10 bring round, change over, regenerate

converted: 6 reborn; 7 adopted, elected; 8 inspired; 9 born-again, justified, unearthly; 10 sanctified; 11 consecrated, regenerated; 13 converted into, not of the earth

converted into: 9 converted

converter: 9 convertor

convertibility: 17 practical identity; 18 interchangeability; 19 identity for a purpose, interconvertability; 20 indistinguishability

convertible: 7 sofa bed; 9 much at one; 12 exchangeable, translatable, transmutable

convertible bond: 12 callable bond

convertible security: 11 convertible

convertible sofa: 7 sofa bed; 11 convertible

convertible term: 7 synonym; 14 equivalent word

converting: 10 evangelism; 11 proselytism; 12 transforming

convert into: 4 make; 6 render; 11 process into, resolve into

convertor: 9 converter

convert to use: 5 apply; 9 turn to use; 10 make useful; 12 put to good use, render useful

convex: 5 round; 6 rotund; 7 bulging, rounded

convexity: 9 rotundity, roundness; 10 convexness; 11 convex shape

convex lens: 14 converging lens

convexness: 9 convexity

convexo-convex: 8 biconvex; 9 lentiform; 10 lenticular

convex shape: 9 convexity

convey: 3 get; 4 bear, port, take, tote [U.S.]; 5 bring, carry, fetch, imply; 6 impart; 7 bespeak, breathe, channel, conduct, express, point to; 8 allude to, indicate, transfer, transmit; 10 bear a sense; 11 communicate

conveyable: 10 assignable, negotiable; 12 transferable; 13 transferrable

conveyance: 5 draft; 7 carting, cession, hauling, vehicle; 8 carriage, carrying, shipping, transfer; 9 assigning, conveying, imparting, transport; 10 alienation, assignment; 11 impartation, transferral; 12 conveyancing, transporting; 14 transportation

conveyance of title: 9 conveying; 10 conveyance; 12 conveyancing

conveyancer: 7 pleader; 14 special pleader; 15 equity draftsman

conveyancing: 7 cession; 8 transfer; 9 assigning, conveying; 10 alienation, assignment, conveyance

convey away: 5 crimp; 8 carry off

conveyer: 6 bearer; 7 carrier; 8 conveyor; 11 transporter; 12 conveyer belt, conveyor belt

conveyer belt: 8 conveyer, conveyor; 11 transporter; 12 conveyor belt

conveying: 7 cession; 8 transfer; 9 assigning; 10 alienation, assignment, conveyance; 12 conveyancing

conveyor: 8 conveyer; 11 transporter; 12 conveyer belt, conveyor belt

conveyor belt: 8 conveyer, conveyor; 11 transporter; 12 conveyor belt

convey the knowledge of: 6 notify; 7 signify, specify

convict: 3 con; 4 cast, damn; 6 inmate; 7 condemn; 8 convince, gaolbird, jail bird, jailbird, prisoner

convicted: 9 condemned

convictfish: 15 Oxylebius pictus; 16 painted greenling

conviction: 6 surety; 7 suasion; 8 sentence; 9 assurance, certainty, certitude; 10 convincing, firm belief, persuasion; 11 firm opinion, fixed belief; 12 condemnation, positiveness, strong belief; 13 settled belief, staunch belief; 14 implicit belief, settled opinion, staunch opinion, unshaken belief

convince: 4 turn; 7 convert, win over

convinced: 4 sure; 6 secure; 7 assured, certain, won over; 8 cocksure, positive; 9 confident, persuaded, satisfied; 11 persuaded by; 12 unhesitating

convincement: 7 suasion; 10 convincing, persuasion

convince oneself: 6 clinch; 8 make sure; 11 make certain

convincible: 8 suasible; 11 persuadable, persuasible

convincing: 6 cogent; 7 suasion; 10 persuasion, persuasive

convivial: 8 good-time, sociable; 9 clubbable; 13 companionable

conviviality: 9 joviality; 11 good company, merrymaking; 13 jollification; 14 good fellowship

convocate: 7 convene, convoke

convocation: 5 synod; 6 vestry; 7 chapter, cockpit; 8 conclave; 10 consistory; 15 calling together

convoke: 7 convene

convolute: 5 twist; 7 pervert; 8 convolve; 11 twist around; 12 sophisticate

convoluted: 6 knotty; 7 tangled; 8 involved, tortuous; 9 Byzantine, intricate; 12 labyrinthine

convolution: 5 gyrus, swirl, whirl; 6 vortex; 9 windiness; 10 convolving, tortuosity

convolve: 9 convolute

convolving: 11 convolution

convoy: 5 bring, fetch, reach; 6 escort; 7 conduct

convulse: 4 fret, gall, toss, urge; 5 annoy, grate, prick, shake, slash, wring; 6 madden, pierce, thrash, thresh; 7 agitate, disturb, perturb; 8 irritate; 9 aggravate, infuriate; 10 accelerate, disconcert, exacerbate, exasperate; 11 thrash about, thresh about; 12 lash into fury; 13 break the ranks

convulsed: 7 riotous; 8 agitated, shaken up; 9 clamorous, disturbed, stirred up, tremulous; 10 tumultuous

convulsing: 9 epileptic; 10 convulsive

convulsion: 4 riot; 5 furor, spasm, throe; 6 clamor, thrill, tumult, uproar; 7 rioting, tempest; 9 revulsion

convulsive: 7 spastic, unquiet; 8 restless; 9 epileptic, explosive, spasmodic; 10 convulsing, giddy-paced; 13 all of a twitter

convulsively: 15 with convulsions

cony: 3 das; 4 pika; 5 coney, hyrax; 6 dassie, rabbit; 9 mouse hare; 10 rock rabbit

coo: 4 honk, pipe; 5 cheep, chirp, clack, cluck, trill, tweet; 6 cackle, cuckoo, gaggle, warble; 7 chirrup, twitter, whistle

co-occur: 6 concur; 7 coexist 8 coincide

co-occurrence: 9 synchrony; 11 coexistence, coincidence, concomitant, concurrence, conjunction, isochronism, synchronism, unity of time; 12 simultaneity; 13 accompaniment

cooccurring: 10 coincident, coinciding, concurrent; 12 coincidental, simultaneous

cooccur with: 6 go with; 12 construe with; 13 collocate with

cook: 3 fix; 4 brew, fake, make; 5 color,

fudge, hatch, ready; 6 wangle; 7 dress up, falsify, prepare, varnish; 9 embroider; 10 cordon bleu [Fr], manipulate; 12 misrepresent; 13 chef de cuisine

cookbook: 11 cookery book

cooked-over: 8 leftover, reheated; 10 warmed-over

cookery: 7 cooking, cuisine; 11 culinary art

cookery book: 8 cookbook

cookhouse: 6 galley; 7 caboose; 11 ship's galley

cookie: 5 cooky; 7 biscuit

cookie jar: 8 cooky jar

cooking: 7 cookery, cuisine; 11 culinary art

cooking chocolate: 15 baking chocolate, bitter chocolate

cooking implement: 8 cookware; 14 cooking utensil

cooking pot: 3 pot

cooking stove: 5 range, stove; 12 kitchen range, kitchen stove

cookout: 6 picnic; 8 barbecue

cook the books: 13 cook an account; 14 doctor the books; 15 doctor an account

cook up: 6 invent, make up; 7 concoct; 9 fabricate; 11 manufacture

cookware: 14 cooking utensil

cooky: 5 cookie; 6 cookie; 7 biscuit

cooky jar: 9 cookie jar

cool: 3 lay; 4 calm, chic, cold, damp, hush, keen, lull, neat, swag, tame; 5 abate, allay, blunt, bully, chill, dandy, great, nifty, poise, quell, quiet, sober, still, swell; 6 aplomb, bang-up, deaden, groovy, modish, not bad, pacify, peachy, quench, rebate, slap-up, smooth, soothe, steady, trendy; 7 appease, assuage, compose, cool off, corking, slacken, stylish, turn off; 8 calm down, cool down, cracking, measured, smashing, suppress; 9 alleviate, nerveless, recherche, sang-froid, temperate; 10 coolheaded, reasonable; 11 assuredness, refrigerate, tranquilize; 13 self-possessed

cool down: 4 cool; 5 chill; 7 cool off; 8 calm down; 10 become cold; 11 refrigerate

coolheaded: 4 cool; 6 demure, sedate; 9 nerveless 10 hardheaded, long-headed; 12 strong-headed

cool-headedness: 4 calm; 6 coolth; 8 calmness

Coolidge: 14 Calvin Coolidge

coolie: 5 cooly; 13 military train

cooling: 6 caller; 8 chilling; 13 cooling system, refrigeration

cool it: 4 calm; 7 cool off; 8 calm down, chill out; 10 settle down, simmer down

coolly: 11 nervelessly; 12 nonchalantly

coolness: 4 heed; 6 phlegm; 7 caution; 8 coldness, prudence; 9 aloofness, composure, frigidity, sang froid [Fr]; **10** alienation, chilliness, discretion, remoteness, steadiness, withdrawal; **11** calculation, heedfulness; **12** cautiousness, deliberation, estrangement, lack of caring, lukewarmness

cool off: 4 calm, cool; **6** cool it; **8** calm down, chill out, cool down; **10** settle down, simmer down

coolth: 4 calm; **8** calmness; **14** cool-headedness

coolwart: 10 foamflower; **14** false miterwort, false mitrewort; **18** Tiarella cordifolia

cooly: 6 coolie

coon: 3 raccoon; **8** ringtail; **12** Procyon lotor; **13** common raccoon

coon's age: 7 dog's age; **8** blue moon

coon bear: 5 panda; **9** panda bear; **10** giant panda; **21** Ailuropoda melanoleuca

coon cat: 5 coati; **8** civet cat, ringtail; **9** bassarisk, cacomixle, miner's cat; **10** cacomistle, coati-mondi, coati-mundi, raccoon fox; **11** Nasua narica; **13** ring-tailed cat; **18** Bassariscus astutus

coonskin: 11 coonskin cap

coonskin cap: 8 coonskin

coop: 3 pen, sty; **4** byre, cage, cote; **5** hem in, hutch, pen in; **6** bolt in, coop up, kennel, rail in, wall in; **7** hencoop, impound; **8** henhouse; **11** chicken coop

co-op: 11 cooperative; **12** finding store [U.S.], variety store

cooper: 11 barrel maker

Cooper's hawk: 10 blue darter; **17** Accipiter cooperii

cooperate: 5 unite; **6** concur; **10** join forces; **11** act together, collaborate, get together; **12** act in concert, join together, work together

cooperating: 11 cooperative

cooperation: 7 concert; **11** concurrence, concurrency; **13** collaboration

cooperative: 4 co-op; **6** united; **8** combined, conjunct; **9** concerted; **11** conjunctive, cooperating; **13** accommodative; **14** acting together

cooperatively: 11 hand in glove; **12** hand and glove; **15** collaboratively

cooperativeness: 11 amenability; **12** amenableness

cooperativity: 14 acting together; **15** working together

cooperator: 7 pardner, partner; **8** co-worker, confrere; **9** accessory, assistant, auxiliary; **11** concomitant; **12** collaborator

coop in: 6 coop up

co-optation: 8 co-option

cooptation: 6 choice; **8** adoption, choosing, election; **9** selection; **11** decision for

co-option: 10 co-optation

coop up: 3 pen; **4** cage, coop; **5** hem in, pen in; **6** bolt in, coop in, rail in, wall in; **7** impound

coordinate: 3 fix; **4** even; **5** align, level; **6** settle; **7** coequal; **8** organise, organize, regulate; **9** methodize; **10** monotonous; **11** symmetrical, systematize

coordinate bond: 10 dative bond

coordinated: 7 unified; **8** matching; **14** interconnected

coordinate geometry: 16 analytic geometry; **18** analytical geometry

coordinates: 20 latitude and longitude

coordinating: 12 coordinative

coordination: 10 motor skill

coordination compound: 7 complex

coordinative: 12 coordinating

co-owner: 10 joint owner

cop: 3 nab, pig; **4** bull, fuzz, glom, hook, nail; **6** arrest, collar, copper, pick up, snitch, thieve; **7** officer; **8** gendarme [Fr], knock off; **9** apprehend, constable, policeman; **13** police officer; **15** police constable

copacetic: 9 copasetic, copesetic; **10** copesettic

copaiba: 12 balsam capivi; **13** copaiba balsam

copaiba balsam: 7 copaiba; **12** balsam capivi

copal: 5 japan; **6** mastic; **7** lacquer, varnish

copaline: 8 copalite; **11** fossil copal

copalite: 8 copaline; **11** fossil copal

co-parcenary: 10 co-heirship

co-parcener: 6 co-heir

co-parceny: 10 co-heirship; **11** co-parcenary

copartner: 7 partner

copartnership: 11 partnership

copasetic: 9 copacetic, copesetic; **10** copesettic

cope: 4 deal, gown, pall, robe; **5** frock, get by; **6** coping, header, make do, manage; **7** cassock, contend, grapple, make out, pallium

copeck: 5 kopek; **6** kopeck

copepod: 17 copepod crustacean

Copernicus: 15 Mikolaj Kopernik; **18** Nicolaus Copernicus

copesetic: 9 copacetic, copasetic; **10** copesettic

cope with: 4 face, meet; **5** match, rival; **7** emulate; **8** confront, race with; **11** compete with

copied: 6 traced

copier: 10 duplicator; **14** copying machine

copier ink: 5 toner; **14** xerographic ink

coping: 4 cope; **6** header

coping-stone: 8 keystone

coping with: 7 braving; **8** tackling; **9** grappling; **11** confronting

copious: 4 rich; **5** ample, wordy; **7** diffuse, lengthy, profuse, verbose; **8** abundant; **9** expansive, extensive, exuberant, plenteous, plentiful; **10** long-winded, pleonas-tic

copiously: 6 galore [postpositive]; **9** profusely; **10** abundantly; **11** in abundance, plenteously, plentifully; **13** extravagantly

copiousness: 4 lots, over; **6** plenty; **9** abundance, amplitude, plenitude, profusion; **11** full measure; **13** plenteousness

copolymerise: 12 copolymerize

copolymerize: 12 copolymerise

cop out: 6 opt out

copper: 2 Cu; **3** cop, pig; **4** bull, fuzz, gold; **5** ingot; **6** cuprum [Lat], nugget, silver; **7** bullion; **9** large cent

copper's nark: 4 nark

copper color: 6 copper

copper colored: 7 coppery

copper-colored: 12 brass-colored, flame-colored; **14** apricot-colored

copper glance: 10 chalcocite

copper plate: 9 gold plate; **11** silver plate

copperplate engraving: 14 plate engraving, steel engraving

copperplate printing: 13 color printing, plate printing

copper pyrites: 12 chalcopyrite

copper rockfish: 18 Sebastodes caurinus

copper sulfate: 13 cupric sulfate; **14** copper sulphate, cupric sulphate

copper sulphate: 13 copper sulfate, cupric sulfate; **14** cupric sulphate

coppery: 13 copper colored

coppice: 5 brake, brush, copse; **7** thicket; **9** brushwood

copra oil: 10 coconut oil

copse: 5 brush, grove; **7** coppice, spinney, thicket; **9** brushwood, greenwood; **12** clump of trees

copter: 7 chopper; **9** eggbeater; **10** helicopter, whirlybird

copula: 6 hyphen; **10** copulative; **11** bond of union

copulate: 4 mate, pair; **6** couple

copulation: 3 sex; **6** coitus, mating, sex act; **7** coition; **8** congress, relation; **10** lovemaking; **11** intercourse

copulative: 6 copula; **10** connecting

copy: 3 ape; **4** form, pull; **5** proof, trace; **6** effigy, revise; **7** emulate, imitate, replica; **8** effigies, likeness, re-create, simulate; **9** duplicate, facsimile, imitation, replicate; **10** impression, transcript; **11** counterpart; **13** written matter

copycat: 3 ape; **4** aper; **7** copyist; **8** imitator

copyedit: 7 subedit; **8** copyread

copy editor: 10 copyreader, text editor

copying: 7 copying; **9** imitating, imitation; **11** replicating, replication; **12** transcribing

copying machine: 6 copier

copyist: 4 hack; **6** dauber, scribe; **7** copycat; **9** scrivener; **11** quill driver, transcriber

copy lease-hold: 13 free lease-hold

copy lease-holds: 14 free lease-holds

copyread: 7 subedit; **8** copyedit

copyreader: 10 copy editor, text editor

copyright: 11 copyrighted

copyrighted: 9 copyright

coquet: 3 pet, toy; **4** mash, trim; **5** dally, demur, flirt, humor, pause, spoon; **6** chat up, debate, soothe, waffle; **7** balance, romance, shuffle; **8** coquette, straddle; **9** fluctuate, hem and haw, hum and haw, philander; **10** bill and coo; **12** be on the fence, remain neuter; **13** remain neutral

coquettish: 11 flirtatious

coquettishly: 13 flirtatiously

coquet with: 9 dally with

coquillage: 4 fret; **8** flourish; **9** arabesque; **10** fleur-de-lis [Fr]

Cora: 4 Kore; **8** Despoina; **10** Persephone

coracan: 4 ragi; **5** ragee; **7** corakan; **8** kurakkan; **12** finger millet; **13** African millet; **16** Eleusine coracana

coracle: 7 caravel; **9** catamaran

corakan: 4 ragi; **5** ragee; **7** coracan; **8** kurakkan; **12** finger millet; **13** African millet; **16** Eleusine coracana

coral: 8 red coral; **13** precious coral

coral bean: 9 frijolito; **10** frijolillo, mescal bean; **19** Sophora secundiflora

Coral Sea: 19 battle of the Coral Sea

coral tree: 9 erythrina

coral vine: 16 Kennedia coccinea

coralwood: 13 Barbados pride, red sandalwood

coralwort: 9 coralroot

coram judice: 9 sub judice [Lat]

cor Anglais: 4 tuba; **8** bass horn; **10** sousaphone; **11** English horn; **12** corno Inglese [It]

cor anglais: 11 English horn

corbeille: 6 dorser, dosser, hamper, wisket; **7** whisket; **10** jardiniere

corbel: 5 truss; **6** flange

cord: 3 ton, tun; **4** bulk, clod, loaf, lump, mass, swad; **5** block; **6** bushel, nugget; **7** cordage; **8** corduroy, whipcord; **12** electric cord

cordage: 4 cord

cordate: 11 heart-shaped

cordated: 8 cardioid; **11** heart shaped

corded: 5 pique, twill; **7** twilled

cord grass: 9 cordgrass

cordgrass: 9 cord grass

cordial: 4 balm, warm; **6** balsam, genial, hearty; **7** affable, amiable, fervent, liqueur; **8** cheering, familiar, gracious; **11** good-humored, warm-hearted; **12** well-affected

cordiality: 5 amity; **8** goodwill; **9** geniality;

10 heartiness; **11** earnestness, hospitality, welcomeness; **13** hospitability

cordially: 6 warmly; **8** amicably, heartily; **11** fraternally

cordial reception: 11 hospitality

cordiform: 8 cardioid; **11** heart shaped

cordite: 7 lyddite

cordless phone: 8 cellular

Cordoba: 7 Cordova

cordon: 3 orb; **4** band, belt, door, zone; **5** cycle, hatch, orbit; **6** riband, ribbon, rundle; **10** blue ribbon

cordon bleu: 4 cook; **10** blue ribbon; **13** chef de cuisine

cordon off: 6 rope in; **7** rope off

cordon sanitaire: 10 quarantine

Cordova: 7 Cordoba

cords: 9 corduroys

corduroy: 3 log; **4** cord; **6** ribbed

corduroy road: 10 cradle hole

corduroys: 5 cords

cordwainer: 6 tailor

Cordyline australis: 9 grass tree; **11** cabbage tree

Cordyline terminalis: 2 ti

Cordylus: 13 genus Cordylus

core: 3 nub, sum; **4** body, bulk, gist, mass, meat, pith; **5** heart; **6** burden, center, effect, kernel, marrow; **7** essence, nucleus; **8** best part, main part; **9** basic part, chief part, core group, major part, substance, vital part; **10** inwardness; **11** greater part, nittygritty; **13** essential part, important part, intrinsic part, principal part; **15** fundamental part

core group: 4 core; **7** nucleus

coreid: 9 coreid bug

Coreidae: 14 family Coreidae

coreid bug: 6 coreid

corelate: 9 correlate

coreopsis: 8 tickseed, tickweed

Coreopsis gigantea: 14 giant coreopsis

Coreopsis maritima: 9 sea dahlia

Coreopsis tinctoria: 10 calliopsis

core out: 6 hollow; **9** hollow out

Corgard: 7 nadolol

corgi: 10 Welsh corgi

coriaceous: 8 leathery; **9** leathered; **11** leatherlike

coriander: 8 cilantro; **13** coriander seed; **14** Chinese parsley

Coriandrum: 15 genus Coriandrum

Coriandrum sativum: 8 cilantro; **9** coriander

corium: 5 cutis, derma; **6** dermis

Corixa: 11 genus Corixa

Corixidae: 15 family Corixidae

cork: 3 bob; **4** bung, plug; **6** bobber, cork up; **7** phellem; **8** bobfloat

corked: 5 corky

corking: 4 cool, keen, neat; **5** bully, dandy, great, nifty, swell; **6** bang-up, groovy, not bad, peachy, slap-up; **7** capping; **8** cracking, smashing; **10** stoppering

corking pin: 3 pin

cork jacket: 7 Mae West; **8** life vest; **10** life jacket, lifejacket; **13** life preserver

cork oak: 12 Quercus suber

corkscrew: 4 worm; **5** helix; **6** buckle, rundle, spiral, volute; **11** bottle screw

cork up: 3 cap; **4** cork; **5** box up, mew up; **6** bung up, clap up, lock up, seal up, shut in, shut up; **7** stopper; **8** bottle up, button up

corkwood: 12 corkwood tree; **18** Leitneria floridana

corkwood family: 13 Leitneriaceae; **19** family Leitneriaceae

corkwood tree: 8 corkwood; **18** Leitneria floridana

corky: 6 corked

cormorant: 3 hog, pig; **7** glutton; **8** belly god; **9** water bird

corn: 5 maize, wheat; **6** clavus; **7** Zea mays; **10** corn whisky, edible corn, Indian corn; **11** corn whiskey

Cornaceae: 13 dogwood family; **15** family Cornaceae

corn borer: 13 corn borer moth

corn cockle: 11 corn campion

corncrake: 4 rail; **8** Crex crex

corn dodger: 6 dodger; **7** corn dab

cornea: 4 lens

corneal graft: 12 keratoplasty

corn earworm: 9 vetchworm; **12** Heliothis zia

cornel: 7 dogwood

cornelian: 9 carnelian

corneous: 5 horny; **8** hornlike

corner: 3 box; **4** hole, nook, ward; **5** block, niche, oriel [Arch], quoin; **6** barrio [Sp], hustle, locale, recess; **8** enceinte, environs, locality, monopoly, precinct, vicinity; **9** precincts, recession; **12** neighborhood, street corner, turning point

cornered: 5 at bay, treed; **7** trapped

corner man: 6 end man; **10** cornerback

cornerstone: 4 base; **5** basis; **9** fundament; **10** foundation, groundwork

cornet: 4 horn; **5** bugle; **7** clarion, trumpet

cornetist: 9 trumpeter

cornflour: 10 cornstarch

cornflower: 10 bluebottle, corncockle; **11** strawflower; **15** bachelor's button

Cornhusker: 9 Nebraskan

Cornhusker State: 8 Nebraska

cornhusking: 8 shucking; **10** husking bee

cornice: 6 frieze, pelmet, sconce; **7** capital, valance; **8** pediment; **10** architrave; **11** coping stone

Cornish hen: 14 Rock Cornish hen

corn liquor: 9 moonshine

C

cornmeal: 4 meal
cornmeal mush: 4 mush
cornpone: 4 pone
corn-shucking: 11 corn-husking [U.S.]
cornstarch: 9 cornflour
cornucopia: 8 richness; 9 profusion; 11 profuseness; 12 horn of plenty
Cornus: 6 cornel; 7 dogwood; 10 bunchberry; 11 genus Cornus
Cornuto: 7 cuckold
corny: 8 bromidic
corollary: 5 rider; 6 sequel; 7 episode; 8 offshoot; 9 outgrowth, side issue; 11 aftereffect, development; 12 ramification
corona: 5 snood; 7 aureole, chaplet, coronet; 9 corposant; 12 electric glow, St. Elmo's fire
coronach: 5 dirge; 6 lament; 7 requiem; 8 threnody
coronal: 6 wreath; 7 chaplet, garland
coronary: 18 coronary thrombosis
coronary failure: 12 heart failure
coronate: 5 crown
coronation: 9 accession; 11 investiture; 12 enthronement; 14 enthronization
coroner: 11 pathologist; 15 medical examiner
coronet: 5 crown, snood, tiara; 6 corona, diadem; 7 chaplet
coroneted: 6 titled; 8 highborn
Coronilla varia: 6 axseed; 10 crown vetch
corp: 11 corporation
corporal: 6 bodied, bodily; 7 somatic; 8 embodied; 9 corporate, corporeal, incarnate
corporate: 6 bodied; 7 compact; 8 corporal, embodied; 9 incarnate; 10 collective; 12 incorporated
corporate executive: 3 CEO
corporation: 3 gut, pot; 4 corp; 5 belly, tummy; 8 pot belly, potbelly; 9 bay window; 12 municipality; 13 corporate body
corporeal: 4 real; 6 bodily; 7 somatic; 8 corporal, material, physical; 11 substantial, substantive
corposant: 6 corona; 12 electric glow, St. Elmo's fire; 14 Saint Elmo's fire
corps: 4 army, host, wing; 5 squad; 6 column; 7 battery, brigade, company, platoon, section; 8 division, garrison, regiment, squadron; 9 battalion; 10 detachment; 11 corps d'armee [Fr], subdivision; 12 flying column
corps de ballet: 8 ensemble
corpse: 4 clay; 5 stiff; 7 cadaver, carcass, remains; 8 dead meat; 12 dead organism
corpulence: 7 obesity; 8 adiposis; 9 stoutness; 10 overweight
corpulent: 3 fat; 4 full; 5 lusty, obese, plump, squab, stout; 6 rotund; 7 weighty; 8 bouncing; 9 strapping

corpus: 4 body; 9 principal, principle; 10 substratum; 12 principal sum
corpuscle: 4 atom; 8 molecule, particle; 9 blood cell; 14 blood corpuscle
corpus delicti affidavit: 11 bill of right, information; 12 state of facts
corpus juris: 3 act, 6 rubric, 7 statute; 10 lex scripta [Lat], regulation
corpus luteum hormone: 12 progesterone
corrade: 6 abrade, abrase, rub off; 7 rub down
corral: 6 cow pen; 9 cattle pen
corraled: 8 fenced in
correct: 3 due, fit; 4 good, meet, nice, true; 5 debug, right; 6 proper, seemly; 7 chasten, elegant, en regle, factual, fitting, redress, sort out; 8 artistic, chastise, chastize, decorous, disabuse, polished, punctual, set right; 9 befitting, castigate, classical, enlighten, objurgate, shake down, veritable; 10 Ciceronian, compensate, discipline, methodical, well-styled; 11 punctilious, put straight, set straight
correction: 6 reform; 8 amending; 9 amendment, reforming; 10 chastening, correcting, discipline; 11 fudge factor, reformation; 12 chastisement; 13 rectification
corrective: 7 healing; 10 emendatory, palliative; 11 disciplinal, reformatory, restorative
correctly: 5 right, truly; 6 aright; 7 rightly; 8 properly; 12 methodically
correctness: 7 decorum, fitness; 8 meetness, to prepon [Grk]; 9 propriety, rightness; 10 seemliness
correct style: 9 philology
Corregidor: 6 Bataan
correlated: 7 oblique; 9 correlate; 11 correlative; 12 interrelated; 14 closely related
correlation: 4 link; 9 mutuality; 10 connection; 11 association; 13 correlativity, interrelation; 14 mutual relation
correspond: 3 fit; 4 gibe, jibe; 5 agree, check, match, tally; 6 equate; 7 respond; 8 stand for; 9 represent
correspondence: 3 map; 5 union; 6 parity; 7 balance, mapping; 8 symmetry; 9 agreement; 10 apposition; 11 parallelism
correspondent: 8 in accord, pressman, reporter; 9 accordant, analogous, congruous, consonant; 10 concordant, consistent, journalist, newscaster, newswriter; 12 letter writer
corresponding: 4 like; 8 in accord; 9 accordant, congruous, consonant; 10 comparable, concordant, consistent; 13 correspondent, proportionate
correspond to: 7 fit with; 9 agree with; 10 accord with
corrida: 9 bullfight

corridor: 4 hall, lane; 5 aisle, alley, lobby; 6 artery; 7 hallway, passage

corrie: 6 cirque

corrigible: 9 reparable; 10 improvable

corrival: 5 rival; 10 competitor

corroborant: 5 tonic; 8 balsamic; 9 paregoric; therapeutic

corroborate: 6 affirm, ratify, uphold, verify; 7 bear out, confirm, indorse, support, sustain, warrant; 8 underpin, validate; 11 countersign; 12 substantiate

corroboration: 7 support; 12 confirmation, ratification; 13 certification, documentation

corrode: 3 eat, rot; 4 char, gnaw, rust; 5 erode; 6 appall, blight, rankle; 7 calcine, eat away, horrify; 8 wear away; 10 incinerate

corroding: 7 cutting, erosion, grating, racking, rotting; 8 grinding; 9 agonizing, consuming, corrosion, searching; 12 excruciating

corrosive: 5 harsh; 7 caustic, erosive, mordant; 8 virulent; 9 stringent, vitriolic; 10 irritating

corrugate: 4 pack, stow, warp; 5 crisp, crush; 6 crunch, furrow, ruffle, rumple; 7 crumple, purse up, roughen; 8 collapse; 9 crumple up, set on edge

corrupt: 3 bad, buy; 4 high, weak; 5 bribe, cloud, fusty, spoil, sully, taint, venal; 6 amoral, debase, defile, effete, putrid, rancid, rotten; 7 crooked, debauch, decayed, deprave, gone bad, pervert, profane, rotting, tainted, touched, vitiate; 8 depraved, perverse, recreant, scampish; 9 corrupted, dissolute, graceless, misdirect, putrefied, reprobate; 10 demoralize, profligate, putrescent; 12 putrefactive

corrupted: 7 corrupt, debased, defiled, tainted; 8 polluted, recreant, scampish, vitiated; 9 dissolute, graceless, reprobate; 10 profligate; 12 contaminated

corruptible: 5 venal; 8 bribable; 9 dishonest; 11 purchasable

corruption: 3 job; 5 alloy; 7 jobbery, jobbing, rotting, shuffle; 8 decaying, gangrene; 9 degrading, depravity; 10 corrupting, degeneracy, perversion, putrefying, putridness, rottenness; 11 corruptness, degradation, depravation, depravement, putrescence; 12 adulteration

corsage: 4 posy; 6 corset, girdle; 7 bouquet, nosegay; 8 corselet

corsair: 6 pirate, viking; 9 buccaneer

Corse: 7 Corsica

corse: 5 stiff; 7 dead man; 8 deceased, departed; 10 dead person

corselet: 6 corset, girdle

corset: 5 stays; 6 girdle; 8 corselet; 11 panty girdle

cortege: 4 flap; 5 array, court [pl], skirt, staff [pl], suite [pl]; 6 lappet; 7 caravan, retinue [pl]; 9 cavalcade, entourage, trappings; 10 embroidery, procession; 11 rank and file; 12 line of battle

cortex: 7 pallium; 14 cerebral cortex, cerebral mantle

Cortez: 6 Cortes; 12 Hernan Cortes, Hernan Cortez; 14 Hernando Cortes, Hernando Cortez

corticosteroid: 9 corticoid

corticotropin: 4 ACTH

cortisol: 14 hydrocortisone

coruscate: 5 flash; 7 glitter, sparkle; 11 scintillate

corvette: 7 clipper, frigate, gunboat, warship; 9 first-rate; 10 bomb vessel

Corvidae: 14 family Corvidae

Corvus: 3 daw; 4 crow, rook; 5 raven; 7 jackdaw; 11 genus Corvus

corybantic: 4 wild; 5 giddy, rabid; 6 doting, raving; 7 berserk, frantic; 8 frenetic, frenzied, rambling, unhinged, wild-eyed; 9 delirious, insensate, possessed, wandering; 10 incoherent, reasonless; 11 dithyrambic, lightheaded, vertiginous; 12 all possessed; 13 beside oneself

Corypheus: 3 don; 5 coach; 8 director

corythosaur: 13 corythosaurus

coryza: 4 cold; 5 mucus; 8 rhinitis; 10 common cold

cos: 7 romaine; 10 cos lettuce; 14 romaine lettuce

Cosa Nostra: 3 mob; 4 gang; 5 Mafia

cosh: 3 sap; 9 blackjack

cosign: 7 sponsor; 9 cosponsor; 11 countersign

cosigner: 11 cosignatory

cosmetic: 9 enhancive; 10 decorative, ornamental

cosmetician: 10 beautician

cosmetics: 6 makeup

cosmetic surgeon: 14 plastic surgeon

cosmetic surgery: 9 anaplasty; 14 plastic surgery

cosmic background radiation: 11 3K radiation

cosmic distance: 10 light-years

cosmic radiation: 9 cosmic ray

cosmonaut: 8 spaceman; 9 astronaut

cosmopolitan: 6 humane; 7 general, worldly; 9 universal, worldwide; 10 ecumenical; 11 cosmopolite, oecumenical, utilitarian; 12 humanitarian

cosmos: 5 world, order; 6 nature; 7 harmony; 8 creation, universe; 9 existence, macrocosm; 11 all of nature

cosponsor: 6 cosign; 7 sponsor; 11 countersign

cosset: 4 baby, coax, idol; 5 jewel, spoil; 6 cocker, cockle, coddle, pamper; 7 indulge, wheedle; 9 smile upon; 10 enfant gate [Fr], featherbed, make much of; 11 molly-coddle

cost: 2 be; 4 toll; 5 fetch, price, yield; 6 afford, amount, charge, figure; 7 bring in, expense, sell for; 9 deprive of, prime cost; 13 monetary value

costa: 3 rib

costermonger: 6 hawker; 9 barrow-boy, bar-row-man

costive: 4 curt; 6 stingy; 11 constipated

costless: 4 free; 6 gratis; 7 untaxed; 10 for nothing, gratuitous; 12 free of charge; 13 complimentary

costliness: 8 dearness, high cost; 9 high price; 10 fancy price; 11 famine price; 13 expensiveness

costly: 4 dear; 5 pricy; 6 pricey; 9 dearly-won, expensive; 10 high priced

cost-of-living index: 3 CPI; 18 consumer price index

costume: 10 masquerade

costume jewelry: 5 paste; 11 junk jewelry; 12 false jewelry; 15 synthetic jewels

costumer: 4 snip; 6 tailor; 7 prop man; 8 milliner; 9 costumier; 11 haberdasher, property man; 15 costume designer

cosy: 4 cozy

cot: 3 hut; 4 crib, sack, shed; 5 booth, cabin, croft, hovel, stall; 6 chalet, dugout [U.S.], shanty; 7 camp bed, hammock

cote: 3 sty; 4 byre, coop, shed; 5 hutch; 6 kennel

Cote d'Azur: 13 French Riviera

Cote d'Ivoire: 10 Ivory Coast

coterie: 4 camp, gang, knot, pack, ring; 5 crowd, group; 6 circle, clique; 7 company, in-crowd, ingroup, society; 11 inner circle; 12 social circle

cothurnus: 4 sock, boot; 6 buskin; 10 dra-maturgy

cotillion: 8 cotilion

cottage: 5 cabin, lodge; 8 bungalow; 9 her-mitage

cottage cheese: 9 pot cheese; 10 farm cheese; 13 farmer's cheese

cotton bollworm: 9 vetchworm; 11 corn ear-worm; 12 Heliothis zia

cotton candy: 9 spun sugar; 10 candyfloss

cottonmouth: 13 water moccasin

cotton on: 4 twig; 5 get it; 6 tumble; 7 catch on, get onto, latch on

cottontail: 5 bunny; 6 rabbit

cotton to: 6 take to

cottonwood: 13 white basswood

Coturnix: 5 quail; 13 genus Coturnix

cotyledon: 8 seed leaf

couch: 3 bow, lie, put; 4 bend, cast, sofa; 5

frame, squat, stoop; 6 crouch, lounge, redact; 7 recline

couchant: 5 prone; 6 supine; 9 prostrate

couch grass: 8 dog grass; 10 quack grass

couch potato: 9 vegetable

cougar: 4 puma; 7 painter, panther; 9 cata-mount; 12 mountain lion

cough: 6 sneeze; 8 coughing

cough drop: 6 pastil, troche; 7 lozenge; 8 pastille

cough out: 6 spit up; 7 cough up; 11 expec-torate

cough up: 6 pony up, spit up; 7 fork out; 8 cough out, fork over, shell out; 11 expecto-rate

could: 5 might

coulee: 4 race; 5 gully; 6 ravine

coulisse: 8 wing flat

coulisses: 9 greenroom

coulomb: 1 C; 12 ampere-second

council: 7 comitia [Lat]; 9 committee; 12 subcommittee

council board: 15 conference table

council chamber: 9 boardroom

council fire: 6 powwow [U.S.]

council table: 12 council board; 15 confer-ence table

councilman: 8 alderman; 10 councilman; 12 committeeman

counsel: 6 advice, advise; 8 advocate, guid-ance; 9 counselor, direction; 10 counseling, counsellor, give advice, suggestion; 11 give counsel; 12 impart advice; 13 attorney at law

counseling: 7 counsel; 8 guidance; 9 direc-tion

counsellor: 7 counsel; 8 advocate; 9 coun-selor; 13 attorney at law; 14 counselor-at-law; 15 counsellor at law

count: 4 tale, tell; 5 laird, tally, verse, weigh; 6 clause, matter, number, reckon, regard; 7 chapter, think of; 8 consider, counting; 9 enumerate, paragraph, reckoning; 10 numeration; 11 be important, enumeration

countenance: 3 let, mug; 5 allow, favor; 6 hold up, kisser, permit, smiler, squire, uphold, visage; 7 warrant; 8 forehead, interest, sanction; 9 patronage; 10 impri-matur; 11 endorsement

counter: 4 chip, chop, heel; 5 check, parry, polar, tally; 6 billet, buffet, letter; 7 compter [Fr], foresee; 8 contrary, opposite; 9 duplicate, forestall, sideboard, tabulator, undermine; 10 anticipate; 11 countermine, dead against, work against; 12 antagonis-tic, counterpunch

counteract: 6 oppose, weaken; 7 subvert; 8 sabotage; 9 undermine; 10 antagonise, antagonize, neutralize

counterbalance: 6 even up, offset, oppose; 7 balance, even off, even out; 9 equaliser, equalizer, equipoise; 10 compensate, counteract, neutralize; 11 countervail, cross-demand,equilibrium

counterfeit: 4 fake, mock, sham; 5 bogus, forge, fraud, phony; 6 pseudo; 7 forgery; 8 so-called, spurious; 9 imitation, imitative, pretended; 10 bogus money, fraudulent, funny money

counterfeiter: 6 forger

counterfoil: 4 stub; 5 badge; 9 check stub, criterion

counterforce: 8 reaction

countermand: 4 lift; 5 annul; 6 repeal, revoke; 7 rescind, reverse; 8 overturn; 12 counter order

countermark: 5 badge; 9 criterion

countermine: 6 weaken; 7 counter, subvert; 8 sabotage; 9 undermine; 10 counteract; 11 work against

counter motion: 7 regress; 10 regression; 13 reverse motion

counterpane: 5 quilt, sheet; 6 spread; 7 blanket; 8 bed cover, bedcover, bedsheet, coverlet; 9 bedspread, comforter, tarpaulin; 11 bed covering

counterpart: 4 copy, form, mate, pair, twin; 6 double, effigy; 7 replica, vis-a-vis; 8 effigies, likeness; 9 facsimile, imitation; 10 similitude; 13 identical twin

counterplot: 7 subplot

counterpoint: 8 contrast

counterpoise: 7 balance; 8 hold back; 9 equaliser, equalizer; 10 counteract

counterpunch: 5 parry; 7 counter

countersign: 4 word; 5 badge; 6 cosign, parole, ratify, uphold; 7 approve, bear out, indorse, sponsor, support, warrant; 8 password; 9 cosponsor, criterion, watchword; 11 corroborate

countersink: 3 set; 11 counterbore

counterspy: 4 mole

countertenor: 4 alto

counter to: 6 versus; 7 against

countervail: 5 equal, match; 6 offset, oppose; 10 counteract, neutralize; 12 counterpoise

counterweight: 7 balance; 9 equaliser, equalizer

counting: 5 count, tally; 9 reckoning; 10 numeration; 11 enumeration

countinghouse: 6 bureau, office; 7 chamber

countless: 6 myriad; 8 infinite; 9 uncounted; 10 innumerous, numberless, unnumbered; 11 innumerable, measureless, unnumerable; 12 unnumberable; 13 multitudinous

count on: 5 bet on, trust; 6 figure, look to, reckon, rely on; 8 depend on, estimate, forecast, lean upon, reckon on, rely upon,

rest upon; 9 build upon, calculate, count upon; 10 depend upon, reckon upon; 11 calculate on

countrified: 5 rural; 6 rustic; 10 provincial; 11 countryfied

country: 4 area, folk, land; 5 rural, state; 6 arable, nation, rustic; 7 a people, western; 9 hillbilly, rural area; body politic, country-bred, nationality; 12 commonwealth

country and western: 12 country music

country dance: 9 folk dance

countryman: 5 rustic; 7 peasant; 8 landsman; 10 compatriot

country store: 11 trading post; 12 general store

countrywide: 10 nationwide

counts: 5 items; 7 details; 11 particulars

count upon: 5 bet on, trust; 6 look to, rely on; 7 count on; 8 depend on, lean upon, reckon on, rely upon, rest upon; 9 build upon; 10 depend upon, reckon upon; 11 calculate on; 13 calculate upon

county: 6 parish

county agent: 10 consultant; 14 extension agent

county courthouse: 10 county seat

county seat: 10 county town, courthouse [U.S.]

coup: 4 snap; 5 burst, crack, flash, jiffy, trice; 6 breath, putsch; 8 takeover; 9 coup d'etat, twinkling

coup d'etat: 4 coup; 6 putsch; 8 takeover; 10 coup de main

coup de grace: 7 quietus; 9 deathblow; 10 last finish

coup de main: 4 coup; 9 coup d'etat [Fr]; 14 surprise attack

coup de maitre: 11 chef d'oeuvre [Fr], masterpiece, tour de force

couple: 3 duo; 4 duad, duet, dyad, hook, link, lock, mate, pair, span, twin, yoke; 5 belay, brace, deuce, latch, leash, match, mates, twain, twins; 6 cheeks; 7 bracket, couplet, distich, grapple, pair off, twosome; 8 couple on, couple up; 9 doubleton; 10 partner off

coupled: 6 joined, linked; 9 conjugate

couplet: 3 duo; 4 duad, duet, dyad, pair, span, yoke; 5 brace, twain; 6 couple; 7 distich, twosome; 9 doubleton

couple up: 6 couple; 8 couple on

couple with: 13 associate with

coupling: 4 yoke; 5 union; 6 mating; 7 coupler, joinder [Law], pairing, uniting; 11 conjugation, conjunction, sexual union

coupon: 5 order; 7 voucher, warrant; 9 debenture; 10 bond coupon; 13 exchequer bill; 14 cents-off coupon, discount coupon

courage: 5 valor; 7 bravery; 8 boldness; 14 courageousness

courageous: 5 brave; 8 fearless

courgette: 8 zucchini

courier: 6 runner; 7 showman; 8 cicerone, dragoman; 9 messenger

course: 3 bed, row, run, way; 4 band, dish, flow, flux, line, path, race, trek, walk, zone; 5 class, coast, drift, plate, route, track, trend; 6 cruise, record, stream, travel, vector; 7 bearing, journey, routine; 8 of course; 9 direction, even tenor, gradation, naturally; 12 thoroughfare

course catalog: 10 prospectus

courseness: 8 ribaldry; 9 grossness, indecorum; 11 misbehavior

course of action: 2 MO; 3 way; 4 game, mode, wise; 5 means; 6 manner, method, policy, polity; 7 fashion, process; 8 game plan, protocol; 9 mechanism, procedure, technique; 10 procedures [pl]; 13 modus operandi

course of study: 7 program; 8 syllabus; 10 curriculum

course of time: 8 time flow; 9 time lapse; 10 flow of time

courser: 5 racer; 6 hunter; 7 charger

coursing: 8 shooting

court: 3 woo; 4 hall, quad, tout, wynd [Scot]; 5 arena, bench, close, folly, forum, motel, staff [pl], suite [pl], tower; 6 butter, castle, homage, invite, slaver; 7 bespeak, canvass, chateau, cortege [pl], retinue [pl], romance, rotunda, solicit; 8 butter up, high life, motor inn, pander to, pavilion, pitch woo, suck up to, tribunal; 9 beau monde [Fr], courtroom, courtyard, inclosure, truckle to; 10 court of law, judicature

court card: 8 face card; 9 trump card; 11 picture card

court clerk: 12 stenographer

court dress: 7 foppery; 8 equipage, frippery; 9 ball dress, full dress; 10 fancy dress; 12 evening dress

courteous: 4 nice; 5 civil; 6 polite; 8 gracious, mannerly; 11 well-behaved; 12 good-mannered, well-mannered

courteously: 7 civilly; 8 politely; 12 with courtesy

courtesan: 4 doxy; 8 paramour; 9 concubine, odalisque

courtesy: 3 bob, bow, nod; 5 kneel; 6 curtsy, kowtow, salaam, scrape; 8 civility; 10 politeness; 11 good manners

courthouse: 8 city hall; 10 county seat

courtier: 4 snob, toad, tool; 5 toady; 6 flunky, sucker, yes-man; 7 flunkey, sponger; 8 hanger on, parasite, truckler; 9 flatterer, doughface [U.S.], sycophant, toad-eater; 10 boot-licker

courting: 4 suit; 6 wooing; 9 addresses, courtship; 10 lovemaking, making love; 11 pitching woo

courtly: 6 formal; 7 elegant, genteel, refined, stately; 8 politely

court of appeal: 11 court assize, higher

court; 12 court of error; 13 court of record; 14 appellate court

court of appeals: 12 appeals court; 14 appellate court

court of justice: 5 bench, court, forum; 8 tribunal; 10 court of law

court of law: 5 bench, court, forum; 8 tribunal; 14 court of justice

courtship: 4 suit; 6 wooing; 8 courting; 9 addresses; 10 lovemaking, making love; 11 pitching woo

court stenographer: 10 court clerk

court system: 9 judiciary

courtyard: 4 area; 5 court; 6 square

cousin: 7 kinsman; 8 relative

cousin-German: 11 first cousin

couth: 6 couthy; 7 couthie, refined; 8 polished

couturier: 8 designer; 15 clothes designer, fashion designer

cove: 4 cave; 5 crypt, inlet, oriel, stall; 6 cavern, recess; 10 pigeonhole

covenant: 4 bond; 7 bargain, compact; 8 agree for, contract; 9 concordat, indenture, specialty, ultimatum; 10 obligation

cover: 3 top; 4 back, deal, hide, plow, veil, ward, work; 5 blind, breed, brood, cloak, cross, flank, gloss, guise, hatch, shade, track, treat; 6 covert, extend, fill up, handle, insure, report, screen, shroud, wrap up; 7 address, binding, blanket, blinker, cover up, embrace, get over, masking, nullify; overlay, shelter; 8 covering, enshroud, incubate, pass over, traverse; 9 cut across, encompass, get across, screening; 10 comprehend, cut through, neutralize, spread over, subterfuge, underwrite; 11 book binding, concealment

coverage: 9 insurance, reportage, reporting

coverall: 6 duster; 9 coveralls, gaberdine

covered: 6 hidden, veiled; 8 obscured

covered stadium: 4 dome; 12 domed stadium

covered stand: 10 grandstand

covered up: 4 sunk; 6 buried; 7 stifled; 8 hushed up; 9 smothered; 10 suppressed

covered wagon: 9 Conestoga; 12 prairie wagon; 15 prairie schooner [U.S.]

cover girl: 5 pin-up

covering: 5 cover; 7 coating, masking; 9 screening, shielding; 10 overlaying; 11 application, overhanging; 13 overspreading

covering up: 12 whitewashing

coverlet: 5 quilt, sheet; 7 blanket; 8 bedsheet; 9 bedspread, comforter, tarpaulin

covert: 5 cover; 6 resort, screen; 7 muffled, retreat, shelter; 8 allusive; 11 concealment

cover up: 4 bury, sink; 5 cover; 6 hush up, stifle; 7 smother; 8 suppress; 9 whitewash

covet: 4 envy; 5 crave; 6 desire
coveted: 7 desired; 8 in demand; 11 sought after
covetous: 5 venal; 6 grabby, greedy; 7 craving, envious, jealous; 8 grasping, ravenous, usurious; 9 insatiate, invidious, mercenary, rapacious; 10 avaricious, insatiable, prehensile, quenchless
cow: 3 ewe; 5 abash, daunt, deter; 6 moocow; 7 overawe; 9 terrorize; 10 discourage, intimidate
coward: 5 sneak; 7 dastard, fearful; 8 cowardly, poltroon, recreant
cowardice: 9 wimpiness; 11 fearfulness; 12 cowardliness, timorousness
cow barn: 7 cowbarn, cowshed; 8 cowhouse
cowboy: 6 cowman; 7 cowhand, cowherd, cowpoke, puncher; 9 cattleman; 10 cow puncher [U.S.], cowpuncher, rodeo rider; 11 bull whacker [U.S.]
cowboy hat: 7 Stetson; 12 ten-gallon hat
cowcatcher: 5 pilot; 6 buffer, fender
cowed: 7 bullied, hangdog; 10 browbeaten; 11 intimidated
cower: 4 fawn, funk; 5 crawl, creep, sneak; 6 cringe, crouch, falter, grovel, huddle, shrink
cowhand: 6 cowboy, cowman; 7 cowherd, cowpoke, puncher; 9 cattleman; 10 cowpuncher
cowhide: 4 lash, whip; 5 knout, strap, thong; 7 cowskin, scourge; 8 bullwhip
cowl: 4 hood; 7 cowling
cowled: 6 hooded
cowling: 4 cowl, hood
cowman: 6 cowboy; 7 cowhand, cowherd, cowpoke, puncher; 9 cattleman; 10 cowpuncher
coworker: 7 party to; 12 collaborator; 14 participator in; 16 dramatis personae [Lat]; 17 particeps criminis [Lat]
co-worker: 8 confrere; 9 colleague; 10 cooperator, workfellow; 11 concomitant; 12 collaborator, fellow worker
cowpea: 12 black-eyed pea
cow pen: 6 corral; 9 cattle pen
cowpoke: 6 cowboy, cowman; 7 cowhand, cowherd, puncher; 9 cattleman; 10 cowpuncher
cowpox: 8 vaccinia
cowpuncher: 6 cowboy, cowman; 7 cowhand, cowherd, cowpoke, puncher; 9 cattleman
cowskin: 7 cowhide
cowslip: 6 paigle; 7 kingcup, May blob; 11 water dragon; 12 meadow bright, Primula veris; 13 marsh marigold
cox: 8 coxswain
coxa: 3 hip; 8 hip joint; 16 articulatio coxae

coxcomb: 4 beau, comb; 8 macaroni [19th cent]; 9 cockscomb, exquisite
coxswain: 3 cox
coy: 6 demure; 9 diffident; 10 overmodest; 12 faint-hearted
coyness: 7 prudery; 8 coquetry; 10 demureness, minauderie; 11 mock modesty; 14 sentimentalism
coyol: 9 coyol palm; 17 Acrocomia vinifera
coyote: 9 brush wolf; 11 prairie wolf; 12 Canis latrans
Coyote State: 11 South Dakota; 18 Mount Rushmore State
coypu: 6 nutria
cozen: 2 do; 3 con, nab; 4 bilk, bite, scam; 5 cheat, pluck; 6 chouse, delude, diddle, euchre, jockey, lead on; 7 deceive, defraud, swindle; 9 victimize
cozenage: 4 scam; 5 fraud; 9 collusion
cozy: 4 cosy, snug; 5 cosey, cozey, cozie; 7 tea cosy, tea cozy; 8 informal, intimate, tea cosey, tea cozey, tea cozie
cozy up: 6 play up, suck up; 7 shine up, sidle up; 8 cotton up
CPA: 25 certified public accountant
CPI: 31 cost-of-living index
CPR: 43 cardiac resuscitation
cps: 2 Hz; 5 cycle, Hertz; 13 cycles/second; 14 cycle per second
CPU: 9 mainframe, processor; 16 central processor; 21 central processing unit
CPU board: 11 mother board
Cr: 8 chromium
crab: 6 grouch; 8 crabmeat; 9 crab louse; 10 pubic louse; 12 crabby person; 14 Phthirius pubis; 15 irritable person
crabbed: 4 sour, tart; 5 cross, fiery, fussy, sharp, short, surly, taint, testy; 6 biting, bitter, crabby, crusty, grumpy, occult, tetchy, touchy; 7 caustic, doggish, grouchy, torvous; 8 abstruse, confused, involved, venomous, virulent, volatile; 9 irascible, irritable, recondite, sarcastic, trenchant; 11 acrimonious, bad-tempered, hot-tempered, ill-tempered
crabbiness: 6 temper; 8 acerbity, tartness; 9 crossness, petulance, procacity, testiness; 10 protervity; 11 crabbedness, grouchiness; 12 captiousness, irascibility, irritability; 13 irascibleness, irritableness
crabby: 5 cross, fiery, fussy, surly, testy; 6 grumpy, tetchy, touchy; 7 crabbed, grouchy; 8 volatile; 9 irascible, irritable; 11 bad-tempered, hot-tempered, ill-tempered
crabby person: 4 crab
crabgrass: 9 crab grass; 11 finger grass
crab louse: 4 crab; 10 pubic louse
crabwise: 7 oblique; 8 crab-like, flanking, sidelong, sideways, sidewise, skirting
crack: 2 go; 3 ace, gap; 4 A-one, blow, chap, chip, coup, pass, puff, quip, shot, slit, snap,

tear, tops, up to; **5** break, burst, check, clack, cleft, flash, fling, jiffy, offer, prime, sally, score, start, super, trice, vapor, vaunt, whack, whirl; **6** au fait, breath, cranny, good at, streak, tip-top, unlock; **7** break up, capital, crack up, crevice, crock up, fissure, opening, scratch, swagger, trumpet, unravel; **8** at home in, cardinal, collapse, cracking, fracture, incision, master of, scissure, top grade, top-notch, unriddle, very best; **9** crack open, exquisite, first-rate, twinkling, wisecrack; **11** a good hand at, high-wrought, spring a leak; **12** accomplished, break through, stroke of time, thoroughbred

cracked: **3** mad; **4** bats, daft, loco, nuts; **5** balmy, barmy, batty, buggy, crazy, dotty, kooky, loony, loopy, nutty, wacky; **6** crazed, fruity, insane, kookie, teched [dialect]; **7** bonkers, chapped, far gone, haywire, lunatic, tetched [dialect], touched; **8** crackers, crackled, demented, deranged, fissured, maddened, not right; **9** roughened; **10** moonstruck

cracker: **6** banger; **7** redneck, snapper; **9** feu-de-joie; **11** firecracker

cracker-barrel: **6** folksy; **8** homespun

crackerjack: **5** adept, bully, elect; **6** choice, expert, genius, master, picked, select; **8** jimdandy; **10** proficient

crackers: **4** bats, daft, loco, nuts; **5** balmy, barmy, batty, buggy, crazy, kooky, loony, loopy, nutty, wacky; **6** fruity, kookie; **7** bonkers, cracked, haywire

crack house: **7** drug den

cracking: **4** cool, keen, neat; **5** bully, crack, dandy, great, nifty, swell; **6** bang-up, groovy, not bad, peachy, slap-up; **7** corking; **8** fracture, refining, smashing

crackle: **6** crunch; **7** scranch; **8** scraunch; **9** crackling, crepitate

crackled: **6** crazed; **7** cracked

crackleware: **7** crackle; **12** crackle china

crackling: **7** crackle; **8** snapping; **11** crepitation; **13** decrepitation

crack-loo: **4** ante; **10** chuck-a-luck

crack of doom: **4** doom; **7** last day; **8** dies irae [Lat], doomsday; **10** millennium; **11** Judgment day; **12** remote future; **13** day of Judgment; **14** day of reckoning

crack open: **5** crack; **6** unlock; **7** unravel; **8** unriddle

crackpot: **3** nut; **5** crank; **7** nutcase; **9** fruitcake, screwball

crack shot: **8** dead shot, good shot, marksman; **12** sharpshooter

cracksman: **7** burglar; **11** safebreaker, safecracker

crack up: **5** crack, laugh; **7** break up, crock up; **8** collapse

crack-up: **9** breakdown

Cracow: **6** Krakau, Krakow

cradle: **4** crib, nest, rock, womb; **5** birth, nidus, nurse; **6** hotbed, suckle; **7** genesis, infancy, nursery; **8** dry nurse, nativity; **10** birthplace, first stone, provenance

cradlesong: **7** lullaby; **8** berceuse

craft: **4** boat, ship, wile; **5** guile, knack, skill, trade; **6** vessel; **7** address, aptness, cunning, know-how, mystery, slyness; **8** aptitude, facility, foxiness, subtlety, wiliness; **10** adroitness, artfulness, competence, craftiness, handicraft, sea vehicle, shrewdness; **11** proficiency, workmanship; **12** skillfulness, water vehicle

craftily: **5** slyly; **6** foxily; **8** artfully, shrewdly, trickily; **9** cunningly, knavishly

craftiness: **4** wile; **5** craft, guile; **7** cunning, slyness; **8** foxiness, subtlety, wiliness; **10** artfulness, shrewdness

craftsman: **7** artisan, crafter; **9** artificer; **10** journeyman

craftsmanship: **5** craft; **11** workmanship

crafty: **3** sly; **4** foxy, wily; **5** dodgy, slick; **6** artful, shrewd, tricky; **7** cunning, knavish, tricksy; **8** guileful

crag: **4** pike; **5** cliff, crest; **8** cone peak; **9** sugar loaf

cragged: **5** hilly; **6** craggy; **11** mountainous

craggy: **5** hilly; **6** rugged; **7** cragged; **11** mountainous

cragsman: **11** rock climber

crake: **4** blow, brag, puff, rail; **5** boast, crack, vapor, vaunt; **7** swagger, trumpet

cram: **3** jam, pad, ram, wad; **4** bone, drum, fill, pack, swot; **5** coach, get up, mug up, prime, put up, stuff, truss; **6** bone up, fill up, swot up; **7** chock up, engorge, jampack, ram down, squeeze; **8** compress; **9** grind away

crambo: **11** rhyming word

crammed: **9** saturated

cramp: **5** spasm, unfit; **6** deaden, disarm, halter, hamper, reduce, sprain, strain; **7** cramped; **9** cramp iron; **10** disqualify, invalidate; **11** tie the hands; **12** incapacitate

cramped: **5** cramp; **7** awkward; **8** confined; **9** graceless, inelegant; **10** ungraceful, unpolished

crampon: **8** crampoon; **12** climbing iron

cranberry tree: **9** crampbark; **11** guelder rose

cranch: **4** bite, chew, chop, gnaw; **5** champ, crush, grind, munch, split; **6** crunch, mumble, shiver, sunder; **7** munch on; **9** masticate; **10** split apart; **11** rend asunder

crane: **7** derrick

craniate: **10** vertebrate

cranium: **5** scull, skull; **8** brainpan; **9** braincase

crank: **3** nut; **4** quip; **5** churl, grump, quirk, tippy, winch; **6** cranky, grouch, pinion, tender, zigzag; **7** conceit, crank up, galleys, nutcase, starter; **8** crackpot, quiddity; **9** fruitcake, screwball, treadmill; **10** crosspatch; **11** private joke

crank handle: 14 starting handle

crankiness: 10 grumpiness; **12** contrariness; **13** crotchetiness

crank out: 8 grind out

cranky: 5 crank, techy, testy, tippy; **6** creaky, tender, tetchy; **7** peckish, peevish, pettish, rickety; **8** creaking, petulant; **9** fractious, irritable; **10** nettlesome

cranny: 4 chap, rift, nook; **5** cleft, crack; **7** crevice, fissure

crapper: 3 can, pot; **5** potty, stool; **6** throne, toilet; **7** commode

crappy: 4 icky; **5** lousy; **6** rotten, stinky; **8** stinking

craps: 4 dice; **8** crap game; **9** snake eyes; **12** crap shooting

crapulence: 5 drink; **7** boozing; **8** drinking; **10** free living, good living, high living, wild living; **11** drunkenness; **12** intemperance

crash: 3 ram; **4** dash, doss, fall, ruin; **5** clang, clank, clash, quell, smash, wreck; **6** freeze, go down, impact, jangle, lock up, plunge, shiver, squash; **7** barge in, break up, clangor, plummet, shatter, squelch; **8** clangour, collapse, doss down, downfall; **9** collision, crumple up, gate-crash, perdition, ruination; **10** break apart, clangoring; **11** devastation

crashing: 5 bally; **6** bloody; **7** flaming; **8** blinking

crass: 4 arch; **5** gross; **7** intense; **8** profound; **10** consummate

crassitude: 8 wideness; **9** broadness, crassness, thickness, grossness

Crataegus: 3 may, haw; **5** thorn; **8** hawthorn; **10** whitethorn, blackthorn; **14** genus Crataegus

crate: 4 cran; **5** creel; **6** basket, hurdle, pottle; **7** pannier; **8** crateful; **10** buck-basket

crater: 3 cup, pit; **4** vent, well; **5** basin, shaft; **6** hollow; **7** volcano

craunch: 6 crunch

cravat: 3 tie; **5** stock; **7** necktie

crave: 3 beg, sue; **4** lust, pray; **5** covet; **6** desire, burn to, die for, hunger, starve, thirst; **7** ache for, burn for; **8** petition, raven for; **9** hunger for, itch after, lust after; **10** crave after; **11** hanker after, hunger after, run mad after, thirst after

craved: 7 desired

craven: 4 base; **8** cowardly, dunghill, poltroon, recreant, sneaking; **11** cower before

craving: 5 greed; **6** greedy; **7** avarice, avid-

ity; **8** covetous, grasping, rapacity, ravening, ravenous, sharp-set; **9** insatiate; **10** avaricious, greediness, insatiable, quenchless; **11** acquisitive; **12** covetousness, ravenousness, unquenchable

craw: 3 maw; **4** crop; **7** gizzard

crawdad: 8 crawfish, crayfish; **9** crawdaddy, ecrevisse

crawfish: 4 scab; **5** crawl [U.S.]; **7** back out, crawdad, mugwump [U.S.], retreat; **8** back away, blackleg, crayfish, withdraw; **9** crawdaddy, ecrevisse, langouste; **11** crawfish out, rock lobster, sea crawfish; **12** spiny lobster

crawl: 4 fawn; **5** cower, creep, sneak; **6** cringe, crouch, grovel, sponge; **8** crawfish [U.S.], crawling, creeping; **9** truckle to; **10** front crawl

crawler: 5 toady; **6** lackey; **9** sycophant

crawling: 5 crawl, creep; **6** torpid; **7** languid; **8** creeping; **9** leisurely, snail-like

crayfish: 7 crawdad [regional]; **8** crawfish; **9** crawdaddy, ecrevisse, langouste; **11** rock lobster, sea crawfish; **12** spiny lobster

crayon: 9 wax crayon

craze: 3 fad; **4** cult, fury, rage; **5** furor, thing, trend; **6** frenzy, furore, madden; **7** in thing; **8** delirium, hysteria, last word; **9** bandwagon; **10** fanaticism; **11** infatuation, latest thing

crazed: 3 mad; **4** daft, loco, nuts; **5** batty, crazy, dotty, loony, nutty; **6** fruity, insane, teched [dialect]; **7** bonkers, cracked, far gone, lunatic, tetched [dialect], touched; **8** crackled, demented, deranged, maddened, not right; **10** half-crazed, moonstruck

crazily: 5 madly; **8** insanely; **10** dementedly

crazy: 3 mad; **4** daft, gaga, lame, loco, nuts, sick; **5** batty, dotty, loony, nutty, shaky; **6** broken, crazed, fruity, in love, insane, looney, madcap, madman, maniac, shaken, soft on, teched [dialect], weirdo; **7** bonkers, cracked, far gone, lunatic, smitten, tetched [dialect], touched; **8** demented, deranged, enamored, maddened, not right, unhinged, withered; **9** brainsick, disturbed, half-baked, screwball, shattered, taken with; **10** distracted, infatuated, moonstruck, soft-headed, unbalanced

crazy bone: 9 funny bone

crazy house: 6 Bedlam; **8** loony bin, madhouse, nuthouse; **9** funny farm; **10** booby hatch, funny house, sanatorium; **11** cuckoo's nest

crazyweed: 8 locoweed; **9** crazy weed

creak: 3 jar; **5** grate; **6** screak, skreak, squeak; **7** screech, skreigh, skriech, skriegh; **8** creaking

creaky: 6 cranky; **7** rickety, run-down, screaky; **8** creaking, decrepit; **9** arthritic, rheumatic

cream: 2 A1; **4** buff, pick, salt, skim; **5** elite,

prime, soupy; **6** butter, creamy, flower; **7** skim off; **8** cream off, nonesuch, ointment; **9** emollient, nonpareil; **11** chef d'oeuvre [Fr], masterpiece; **14** creme de la creme

cream off: 4 skim; **5** cream; **7** skim off

cream-of-tartar tree: 9 sour gourd

cream pitcher: 7 creamer

cream puff: 4 chou, muff; **7** cripple; **8** old woman, pussycat; **10** powder puff; **11** mollycoddle

creamy: 4 fair; **5** blond, cream, sandy, soupy, tawny; **6** pearly; **7** whitish

crease: 3 ply; **4** bend, fold, line, rake, seam; **5** crimp, crisp, graze, plait, pleat; **6** furrow, ruckle, rumple; **7** crinkle, crumple, flexure, scrunch, wrinkle; **9** plication, scrunch up

create: 4 coin, make; **6** devise, invent; **7** produce; **8** generate; **9** fabricate, originate

created: 4 made; **6** formed; **8** dreamt of, imagined, produced; **9** conceived, generated; **10** originated

create pleasure: 5 charm; **6** please; **7** delight

creating: 6 making; **7** forming, genetic; **8** creation, dreaming; **9** formation, formative, imagining, producing; **10** generating, generation, generative, production

creation: 5 start, world; **6** cosmos, making, nature; **7** forming; **8** creating, creature, founding, universe; **9** existence, formation, inception, invention, macrocosm, producing; **10** conception, foundation, generation, initiation, production; **11** all of nature, institution, origination

creative: 7 fertile; **8** original; **9** inventive; **10** productive; **11** imaginative, originative

creative person: 6 artist

creator: 8 producer; **10** originator

Creator: 3 God; **4** Lord; **6** Divine; **8** Almighty

creature: 3 man; **4** body, soul, tool; **5** beast, being, brute, fauna, human, wight; **6** animal, mortal, person, puppet; **7** critter [rural U.S.]; **8** creation, such a one, zoophyte; **9** earthling, personage; **10** dumb animal, human being, individual, living soul; **12** animate being, created being, dumb creature; **13** brute creation, flesh and blood; **14** fellow creature

creche: 7 nursery; **13** day-care center

credence: 6 credit; **8** credenza; **9** baldachin; **10** acceptance; **12** confessional

credential: 11 certificate, credentials; **13** certification

credenza: 8 credence

credible: 7 in posse; **8** apparent, reliable; **9** plausible; **10** believable, dependable, presumable, reasonable; **11** conceivable, presumptive, trustworthy, well-founded; **12** easy of belief

credibleness: 10 likelihood, likeliness; **11** credibility, probability; **13** believability

credit: 4 book, post, tick [Brit]; **5** debit, enter, merit, trust, worth; **6** desert; **7** believe, intrust, mention; **8** accredit, citation, credence, prestige; **9** carry over, patronage, quotation, reference; **10** excellence; **11** credit entry, prerogative, recognition; **12** course credit; **13** preponderance

creditable: 8 laudable; **9** estimable, plausible, reputable; **11** commendable, meritorious, respectable, up to the mark; **12** praiseworthy

credit account: 7 account; **11** open account; **13** charge account

credit card: 8 bank card; **10** charge card; **11** charge plate

credit line: 4 line; **6** by-line; **8** bank line; **12** line of credit

creditor: 6 lender

creditworthy: 11 responsible

credo: 5 creed

credulous: 8 gullible

credulously: 11 believingly

creed: 5 credo; **6** gospel, tenets

creek: 3 gut; **4** beck, burn, dike, ha-ha, leak; **5** bayou [U.S.], brook, crick; **6** runnel, stream

creel: 4 cran; **5** crate; **6** basket, pottle; **7** pannier; **10** buck-basket

creep: 4 fawn, itch; **5** cower, crawl, mouse, sneak, spook, steal, sting; **6** cringe, grovel, thrill, tingle, weirdo, weirdy; **7** weirdie; **8** crawling, creeping, grow over; **9** pussyfoot

creeping: 5 crawl, creep; **6** torpid; **7** languid; **8** crawling; **9** leisurely, snail-like

creep up: 7 sneak up

creese: 4 kris

crematorium: 9 crematory

creme de la creme: 2 A1; **4** pick; **5** cream, elite, prime; **6** flower; **8** nonesuch; **9** nonpareil; **11** chef d'oeuvre [Fr], masterpiece

creme de menthe: 8 absinthe

crenate: 9 scalloped

crenelated: 7 castled; **8** indented; **9** crenelate, embattled; **10** crenellate; **11** castellated, crenellated; **12** battlemented

crenulate: 7 scallop, serrate, vandyke; **8** serrated; **10** crenulated

creosote: 15 coal-tar creosote

creosote bush: 6 caltrop; **7** coville; **11** hediondilla

crepe: 5 crape; **7** buckled, frizzly; **10** crepe paper; **13** French pancake

crepe flower: 11 crape myrtle, crepe myrtle

crepe myrtle: 11 crape myrtle, crepe flower

crepitation: 7 crackle; **9** crackling; **13** decrepitation

crepuscular: 3 dun, dim; **5** dirty, lurid, muddy; **6** leaden; **8** overcast

crepuscule: 8 twilight
crescendo: 6 louder
crescent: 3 bow; **4** loop; **6** arcade, lunate; **8** half-moon; **9** crane neck, horseshoe, semilunar; **10** crescentic; **11** bicephalous
Crescentia: 8 calabash; **15** genus Crescentia
crescent roll: 9 croissant
crescent-shaped: 6 lunate; **8** crescent; **9** semilunar; **11** bicephalous
cresol: 12 methyl phenol
cresset: 10 fiery cross
cress plant: 5 watercress
crest: 3 cap, nib, tip, top; **4** crag, peak, pike; **5** arete [Fr], crown, plume, truck; **6** summit; **7** panache; **8** cone peak
crested: 6 plumed, tufted; **10** topknotted
crestfallen: 8 deflated; **9** jawfallen; **10** chopfallen, dispirited; **11** discouraged; **12** disheartened
crestless wave: 5 swell
Cretaceous: 3 age; **8** Mesozoic; **16** Cretaceous period
cretin: 5 idiot, moron; **7** half-wit; **8** imbecile
crevalle jack: 7 cavalla; **12** Caranx hippos, jack crevalle
crevasse: 6 ravine
crevice: 4 chap, rift; **5** cleft, crack; **6** cranny; **7** fissure; **8** scissure
crew: 4 band, gang, knot, team; **5** bunch, crowd, group, party, squad; **8** garrison; **9** work party
crew cut: 7 flattop
crewman: 6 sailor; **10** crew member
Crex: 8 land rail; **9** corncrake, genus Crex
crib: 3 hut, cot, bin; **5** steal, cheat; **6** creche; **10** plagiarism
crib death: 4 SIDS; **8** cot death
crib sheet: 10 cheat sheet
Cricetus: 7 hamster; **13** genus Cricetus
crick: 5 twist, spasm; **6** strain
crier: 6 herald, weeper; **7** marshal; **9** town crier, trumpeter; **10** flag bearer
crime: 11 law-breaking
criminal: 4 perp; **5** crook, felon, wrong; **6** outlaw, wicked; **7** culprit, immoral, lawless; **8** offender; **9** felonious; **10** deplorable, iniquitous, malefactor; **11** condemnable, perpetrator
criminal action: 11 prosecution
criminal conduct: 11 criminality, lawlessness
criminalize: 6 outlaw; **10** illegalize
criminate: 6 accuse; **7** censure, impeach; **9** reprimand; **11** incriminate
crimp: 3 pin; **4** bend, bolt, fold, hasp, kink, nail; **5** clamp, clasp, crape, crisp, decoy, frizz, pinch, rivet, screw, shill, short, wring; **6** abduct, crease, indent, kidnap, kink up, ringer, scotch; **7** capture, crimper, flexure, frizzle, scallop, scarify; **8** carry

off; **9** decoy duck, plication, splintery; **10** convey away
crimped: 8 squeezed; **10** compressed
crimson: 3 red; **4** ruby; **5** blush, flush, ruddy; **6** aflame, cerise, cherry, redden; **7** carmine, deep red, flushed, reddish, ruby-red, scarlet, violent; **8** blood-red, red-faced, reddened; **9** cherry-red
cringe: 3 bow; **4** fawn, funk; **5** cower, crawl, creep, kneel, quail, stoop, wince; **6** flinch, grovel, recoil, shrink; **7** squinch
cringing: 4 oily; **5** soapy, wormy; **6** abased, pliant; **7** fawning, slavish; **8** cowering, wormlike; **9** groveling, sniveling; **10** dough-faced, grovelling
cringle: 4 loop; **6** eyelet, gasket; **7** grommet
crinkle: 4 bend, fork, line, seam; **5** crisp; **6** crease, furrow, ruckle, rumple; **7** crumple, scrunch, wrinkle; **9** bifurcate, scrunch up
crinkled: 4 wavy; **6** akimbo; **7** crinkly, rippled; **8** wavelike; **10** knock kneed
crinoline: 6 bustle; **9** hoopskirt; **11** farthingale
crippled: 4 halt, lame; **7** halting; **8** disabled, drooping, flagging
crippling: 9 disabling; **14** incapacitating
crisis: 4 pass, turn; **7** passage; **8** juncture; **9** adventure, emergency; **11** conjuncture
crisp: 4 chip, curl, curt, firm; **5** crimp, kinky, nappy, nippy, parky, sharp, short, terse, toast, twill; **6** crease, crispy, frizzy, frosty, quaint, ruckle, ruffle, rumple, snappy; **7** crinkle, crumple, crunchy, frizzly, laconic, nipping, roughen, scrunch, wrinkle; **9** corrugate, scrunch up, set on edge, splintery
crisply: 7 sharply
crispness: 10 crispiness; **11** brittleness
crisscross: 4 mark; **5** cross; **9** hopscotch; **12** crisscrossed
criterion: 4 test; **5** badge, probe; **7** measure; **8** acid test, standard; **10** diagnostic, litmus test, touchstone
critic: 5 cynic, judge; **6** carper; **7** caviler; **8** frondeur, reviewer; **11** commentator, word-catcher
critical: 5 vital; **6** urgent; **7** carping, instant; **8** captious, decisive, delicate, pressing, ticklish; **9** difficult; **10** censorious; **11** deprecatory, disparaging, reproachful
criticality: 10 cruciality
critically: 8 urgently; **10** pressingly
critical point: 8 juncture; **10** crossroads
critical review: 6 review; **8** critique; **13** review article
critical situation: 6 crisis
criticism: 5 blame; **6** notice, report, review; **7** censure, obloquy; **8** critique; **9** dispraise; **10** commentary; **12** depreciation; **13** disparagement
criticize: 9 criticise, pick apart
critique: 6 notice, report, review; **8** judg-

critter: **5** beast, brute, wight; **6** animal; **8** creature, zoophyte

CRO: **5** scope; **12** oscilloscope

croak: **4** conk, peep; **5** choke, cronk, gnarl, growl, grunt; **6** clamor, murmur, mutter, pop off; **7** grizzle, grumble, maunder, snuff it; **8** croaking, drop dead; **10** buy the farm; **11** die suddenly; **13** kick the bucket

croaker: **7** growler; **8** grumbler; **9** dissenter, dissident, pessimist; **10** malcontent

croaking: **3** dry; **5** croak, husky; **6** croaky, hoarse, hollow; **7** raucous; **8** guttural

crochet: **4** hook

crochet needle: **11** crochet hook

crock: **3** kit; **6** flagon; **8** old fogey, old woman; **14** earthenware jar

crocked: **3** wet; **5** blind, potty, stiff, tight, tipsy; **6** blotto, loaded, pissed, soaked, soused, tiddly; **7** fuddled, slopped, sloshed, smashed, sozzled, squiffy, tiddley; **8** besotted; **9** pixilated, plastered; **10** blind drunk

crockery: **8** dishware

crocodile: **4** croc; **7** octopus; **8** mosquito; **9** alligator

Crocodile River: **7** Limpopo

crocodilian: **18** crocodilian reptile

Crocodylia: **10** Crocodilia; **15** order Crocodilia, order Crocodylia

Crocodylidae: **18** family Crocodylidae

Crocodylus: **10** Crocodilus; **15** genus Crocodilus, genus Crocodylus

crocus: **5** topaz; **7** saffron

Crocus sativus: **7** saffron; **13** saffron crocus

Crocuta: **5** hyena; **12** genus Crocuta

croft: **3** cot, hut; **4** shed; **5** booth, cabin, hovel, stall; **6** chalet, dugout [U.S.], shanty

croissant: **12** crescent roll

cromlech: **4** tope; **5** cairn; **6** barrow, dolmen; **7** tumulus

Cromwell: **14** Oliver Cromwell

crone: **3** hag; **5** witch; **6** beldam; **7** beldame; **11** grandmother

crony: **3** pal; **4** chum; **5** buddy; **7** brother; **8** old crony, sidekick

crook: **4** bend, hawk, hook, thug, turn, warp; **5** curve, felon, shift, shunt; **6** bought, hold-up [U.S.], outlaw; **8** criminal; **9** draw aside, holdup man; **10** delinquent, malefactor

crooked: **3** wry; **4** awry, bent, dark; **5** askew; **6** jagged; **7** angular, corrupt, hunched, stooped; **8** aquiline, indirect, serrated, slippery, stooping, tortuous; **9** insidious

crookedness: **5** twist; **7** torsion; **10** contortion, tortuosity; **11** deviousness

crooner: **9** balladeer

crop: **3** bud, lop, maw, mow; **4** clip, craw, cull, dock, reap, snip, trim, work; **5** dress, fruit, graze, pluck, prune, range, shave, shear; **6** browse; **7** cut back, gizzard, har-

---

C

vest, pasture; **8** cut short; **9** cultivate, handiwork

crop-dusting: **8** spraying

cropper: **12** sharecropper

crop up: **5** arise, pop up; **6** appear, cast up, show up, turn up; **7** start up; **8** spring up; **9** come forth; **11** materialize, show its face, spring forth

cross: **3** bug, irk, rub, vex; **4** bilk, dash, faze, foil, ford, knot, mark, pass, rood, span, tire; **5** annoy, blend, braid, chain, check, clash, cover, fiery, fussy, queer, rusty, spoil, surly, sweep, testy, tinge, track, worry; **6** baffle, bother, crabby, cussed [U.S.], grumpy, hybrid, resist, scotch, season, tetchy, thwart, touchy, wreath; **7** athwart, crabbed, crucial, disturb, froward, get over, grouchy, hostile, mongrel, mortify, perplex, reverse, setback [U.S.], transit, trouble; **8** comedown, crossing, crucifix, disquiet, inimical, medicate, pass over, reversal, sprinkle, tincture, traverse, volatile; **9** cruciform, cut across, disoblige, displease, frustrate, get across, incommode, intersect, irascible, irritable; **10** besprinkle, cat's cradle, crisscross, crossbreed, cut through, discomfort, discompose, infiltrate, run counter, thwartwise, transverse; **11** bad-tempered, contretemps, hot-tempered, hybridizing, ill-tempered, intractable, transversal; **12** cantankerous, deaf to reason, transversely, unpropitious

crossbred: **9** interbred

crossbreed: **5** cross; **6** hybrid; **7** mongrel; **9** hybridize; **10** interbreed

crosscurrent: **3** rip; **7** riptide, tide rip

crosscut: **6** cutoff; **8** shortcut; **9** cut across

cross-dresser: **12** transvestite

crossed: **5** irked; **6** across, dashed, hybrid; **8** crossing, unhinged; **9** interbred, perplexed; **10** frustrated; **12** disconcerted, intercrossed, intersecting

cross fire: **8** head wind; **10** raking fire

cross-grained: **11** contrarious

cross-index: **14** cross-reference

crossing: **4** ford; **5** cross; **7** crossed; **8** crossway; **9** carrefour, crossroad, crosswalk; **10** thwartwise, transverse; **11** hybridizing, transversal; **12** intersecting, intersection; **13** crossbreeding, hybridisation, hybridization, interbreeding

crossness: **6** choler, temper; **8** acerbity, tartness; **9** fussiness, petulance, procacity, testiness; **10** crabbiness, protervity; **11** crabbedness, fretfulness, grouchiness, peevishness; **12** captiousness, irascibility, irritability; **13** irascibleness, irritableness

cross off: **4** mark; **6** delete; **8** cross out; **9** strike off, strike out

crossopterygian: **7** lobefin; **10** lobe-finned

cross out: 4 mark; **6** delete; **8** cross off; **9** strike off, strike out

crosspatch: 5 churl, crank, frump, grump; **6** grouch

crosspiece: 5 trave; **8** traverse; **9** crossbeam

cross purposes: 4 blot, flaw, miss, slip; **5** fault; **7** blunder; **9** oversight; **10** quid pro quo

cross-reference: 10 cross-index

crossroad: 5 byway; **6** bypath, byroad; **8** crossing, crossway; **9** carrefour; **12** intersection

crossroads: 6 hamlet; **8** juncture; **13** critical point

crosstalk: 2 XT

crossword puzzle: 9 crossword

crotalaria: 9 rattlebox

Crotalus: 10 sidewinder, **11** diamondback; rattlesnake; **13** genus Crotalus

crotchet: 3 fad, fit; **4** hook; **5** breve, freak, hobby, minim, prank, quirk; **6** maggot, oddity, vagary; **7** brootch; **8** escapade, flimflam; **9** blind side, capriccio, queerness, semibreve [Mus]; **10** partiality, quirkiness; **11** infatuation, quarter note; **12** mote in the eye; **14** wild-goose chase

crotchetiness: 10 crankiness, grumpiness; **12** contrariness

crotchety: 5 fussy; **6** ornery; **12** cantankerous; **13** impracticable

Croton bug: 8 water bug; **15** German cockroach

crouch: 3 bow; **4** bend, fawn, funk; **5** couch, cower, crawl, sneak, squat, stoop; **6** falter, grovel, slouch, sponge, wallow; **7** scrunch; **9** scrunch up, truckle to; **10** hunker down

crouched: 5 squat; **7** huddled; **8** hunkered; **9** crouching, subjacent; **12** hunkered down

croup: 4 loin, rump, tail; **6** breech, croupe, dorsum; **7** buttock; **10** posteriors

croupier: 6 dealer

crow: 6 Corvus

crow: 3 caw; **4** brag; **5** cheer, exult, gloat, neigh, shout; **6** cackle, giggle, squawk, titter; **7** chuckle, crowbar, crowing, screech, snicker, snigger, triumph; **8** bragging, crow over, vaporing

crow's feet: 6 pucker; **8** wrinkles; **9** crow's foot, laugh line

crow's nest: 3 cap, nib; **5** crest, truck

crowbar: 3 pry; **4** crow; **6** pry bar; **11** wrecking bar

crowd: 4 crew, gang, herd, knot, push, ring; **5** bunch, group, surge, swarm; **6** circle, clique, stream, throng; **7** coterie, in-crowd; **9** associate; **12** draw together

crowded: 5 thick; **6** herded; **7** flocked, peopled, studded, teeming; **8** manifold, multiple, populous, thronged; **10** multiplied; **11** congregated; **12** concentrated

crowfoot: 7 goldcup, kingcup; **9** buttercup; **12** butterflower

crowfoot family: 13 Ranunculaceae; **15** buttercup family

crowing: 3 big; **4** brag, crow; **6** braggy; **8** boastful, braggart, bragging, cheering, shouting

crown: 3 tip, top; **4** bays, brow, pate, peak, poll; **5** crest, tiara; **6** diadem, summit; **7** chaplet, coronet, pennant, treetop; **8** coronate, crown all; **9** capitulum, culminate, major coin

crowned: 8 laureled; **9** laurelled

crown glass: 12 optical crown

crowning: 5 final; **9** finishing; **10** completing, concluding, conclusive

crowning point: 5 pitch; **6** climax, height, summit; **7** maximum; **12** turning point

crown of thorns: 5 cross; **11** Christ plant, Christ thorn

crown roast: 10 rack of lamb

crown vetch: 6 axseed

crownwork: 3 cap

crow over: 4 crow; **5** exult, neigh; **7** chuckle, triumph

crow step: 10 corbel step, corbie-step, corbiestep

crozier: 7 crosier

CRT: 14 cathode ray tube

crucial: 5 cross; **8** deciding, decisive, relevant; **9** cruciform, essential, important; **11** categorical, determinant, determining; **12** all important, all-important, of the essence; **13** determinative

cruciate: 6 secant; **7** crucify; **9** cruciform

crucible: 3 pan; **4** dish, test; **5** plate; **6** retort, saucer, ordeal; **7** alembic, caldron, platter, potager, reagent; **8** calabash, trencher; **9** porringer; **10** melting pot; **11** fiery ordeal

Cruciferae: 12 Brassicaceae; **13** mustard family; **16** family Cruciferae

cruciferous plant: 8 crucifer

crucify: 3 dun, rag; **7** bedevil, torment; **9** frustrate, tantalize; **14** nail to the cross

crude: 3 raw; **4** rude; **5** blunt, gross, rough, stark; **6** abrupt, coarse, earthy, vulgar; **7** coal oil, halting, rock oil; **8** crude oil; **9** fossil oil, petroleum, primitive, unrefined; **10** off-putting; **11** unprocessed

crudely: 7 roughly; **8** coarsely; **9** artlessly; **10** inexpertly

crudeness: 7 crudity; **8** rudeness; **9** roughness; **10** gaucheness; **11** primitivism; **13** primitiveness

crude oil: 3 oil; **5** crude; **7** coal oil, rock oil; **9** black gold, fossil oil, petroleum

cruel: 4 fell, hard, sore; **5** acute, grave, harsh, sharp; **6** biting, brutal, malign, savage, severe, unkind; **7** brutish, caustic, inhuman, vicious; **8** barbaric, inhumane, rigorous, unbenign; **9** barbarous, malicious, malignant, roughshod; **10** evil-minded, ill-natured, malevolent

cruelly: 5 sadly; **6** sorely; **7** grossly; **8** bitterly, horribly, terribly, woefully; **9** fearfully, miserably, painfully, piteously; **10** dreadfully, grievously, lamentably, shockingly, with malice; **11** frightfully, maliciously, malignantly; **12** malevolently; **13** with bad intent

cruelty: 6 malice; **7** ill will; **8** bad blood, hardness, ill blood, severity, soreness; **9** cruelness, harshness, ill nature, malignity, sharpness; **11** malevolence; **12** pitilessness, ruthlessness; **13** maliciousness, mercilessness

cruet: 6 caster, crewet

cruise: 4 sail; **5** coast, drift; **6** course, voyage; **7** passage

cruiser: 8 flagship, prowl car, squad car; **9** guard ship, patrol car, police car; **12** cabin cruiser, pleasure boat; **13** pleasure craft

cruise ship: 13 floating hotel; **14** floating palace

cruller: 7 twister; **8** doughnut

crumb: 3 bum, rat; **4** inch, puke, seed; **5** patch, scrap, skunk; **6** rotter, tatter; **7** flitter, fritter, lowlife, so-and-so, stinker; **8** fragment; **9** scantling

crumble: 4 drop, fade, fail, flag, halt, limp, rust; **5** decay, shake; **6** totter, tumble; **7** crumple, decline, give way, tremble; **8** collapse, languish; **9** break down, fall apart; **10** delapidate; **12** disintegrate

crumbled: 10 fragmented

crumbling: 5 shaky; **6** effete, rotten, wasted; **7** tainted; **8** blighted, cankered, top-heavy; **9** moldering; **10** ramshackle, tumbledown; **11** waterlogged; **12** falling apart

crumbly: 7 friable, shivery

crumhorn: 8 cromorne; **9** krummhorn

crummy: 3 bum; **4** punk; **5** cheap, tinny; **6** cheesy, sleazy; **7** chintzy

crump: 3 fly; **4** bent, thud; **5** burst, flare, flash, go off; **6** blow up, bounce, crunch; **7** brittle, crooked, explode, scrunch, thunder; **8** detonate; **9** on one side

crumple: 4 draw, knit; **5** crisp; **6** buckle, cockle, crease, pucker, ruffle, rumple, tumble; **7** crinkle, crumble, roughen, wrinkle; **8** collapse; **9** break down, corrugate, set on edge

crumpled: 4 bent; **6** dented; **7** creased, rumpled

crumple up: 4 pack, stow, warp; **5** crash, crush, quell, smash; **6** crunch, shiver, squash; **7** purse up, shatter, squelch; **8** collapse; **9** corrugate

crunch: 4 bite, bray, chew, chop, gnaw, mash, pack, stow, thud, warp; **5** champ,

crump, crush, grind, munch, split; **6** mumble, shiver, sunder; **7** crackle, munch on, purse up, scranch, scrunch; **8** collapse, scraunch; **9** comminute, corrugate, crumple up, masticate; **10** compaction, split apart; **11** rend asunder

crunchy: 4 firm; **5** crisp

crusade: 4 push; **5** cause, drive, fight; **6** effort; **7** agitate; **8** campaign, movement; **10** expedition, operations

crusader: 8 do-gooder, reformer, resister; **9** meliorist, reformist; **12** knight errant

cruse: 4 ewer; **7** caraffe; **8** decanter

crush: 3 jam, mob; **4** beat, body, drub, mash, pack, rout, stow, warp; **5** horde, press; **6** crunch, defeat, rabble, squash; **7** beat out, blow out, mortify, oppress, purse up, squeeze, squelch, trounce; **8** calf love, collapse, disgrace, roll over, suppress, vanquish; **9** break down, corrugate, crumple up, discomfit, frustrate, humiliate, overwhelm, puppy love; **10** compaction; **11** infatuation

crushed: 3 low; **6** broken, ground, packed; **7** a prey to, humbled, ill-used; **8** stricken; **10** heavy laden, humiliated, victimized

crushed rock: 6 gravel

crushing: 4 grim; **8** grimness, quelling, shocking, stifling, terrific; **9** appalling; **10** terrifying; **11** devastating, suppression

crush out: 7 stub out; **8** press out; **10** extinguish

crust: 4 gall; **9** freshness, impudence, insolence; **10** cheekiness; **11** Earth's crust, lithosphere; **12** encrustation, impertinence, incrustation

crustal plate: 13 tectonic plate

crusty: 5 gruff; **7** crabbed, crusted; **9** crustlike, encrusted; **10** ill-humored; **11** ill-humoured; **12** curmudgeonly

crutch: 5 baton, crane, fluke, staff, stick; **6** akimbo, scythe, sickle, zigzag; **10** alpenstock

crux: 5 hinge, lever, pivot; **7** fulcrum; **10** bone to pick; **12** pons asinorum [Lat], turning point

Crux Australis: 4 Crux; **13** Southern Cross

cry: 3 baa, sob; **4** bell, buzz, call, fame, hype, pipe, roar, wail, weep, yell; **5** blare, bruit, hollo, on dit [Fr], rumor, shout; **6** alarum, bellow, cry out, crying, holler, outcry, scream, squall, war cry; **7** blubber, call out, exclaim, hearsay, wailing, weeping; **8** shout out; **9** battle cry, blazon out, shed a tear, shed tears, ululation

crybaby: 4 wimp; **6** moaner, whiner; **7** chicken; **8** grumbler, sniveler, squawker; **10** bellyacher, complainer

crying: 3 cry; **4** rank, wail; **5** gross, tears; **6** outcry, urgent; **7** clamant, exigent, glaring, howling, instant, wailing, weeping, yelling; **8** flagrant, pressing, shouting; **9** absorbing, egregious, insistent, ululating, ululation, wail of woe

cry wolf: 10 false alarm

cryolite: 13 Greenland spar

cryopathy: 9 frostbite

cry out against: 7 protest; **9** deprecate; **11** expostulate, remonstrate

crypt: 4 tomb; **5** oriel, stall, vault

cryptic: 3 dim; **4** dark, deep; **5** dense, muddy; **6** opaque; **7** obscure; **8** nebulous; **9** sibylline; **10** cabalistic, clear as mud, mysterious, mystifying; **11** inscrutable

Cryptobranchus: 8 mud puppy; **10** hellbender; **19** genus Cryptobranchus

cryptogram: 11 cryptograph; **13** secret writing

cryptograph: 6 cipher, cypher; **10** cryptogram, secret code; **13** secret writing

Cryptomeria: 16 genus Cryptomeria

Cryptomeria japonica: 4 sugi; **10** Japan cedar; **13** Japanese cedar

cryptoxanthin: 8 carotene; **11** provitamin A

crystal: 6 quartz; **10** watch glass; **11** quartz glass; **12** watch crystal

crystal clear: 5 lucid; **6** limpid; **8** luculent, pellucid; **11** crystalline, perspicuous, transparent

crystal gazer: 5 witch; **13** fortune teller

crystalize: 10 effloresce; **11** crystallize

crystalized: 5 glace; **7** candied

crystalline: 5 lucid; **6** glassy, limpid; **7** hyaline; **8** pellucid, vitreous; **11** transparent; **12** crystal clear

crystallinity: 10 glassiness

crystallize: 5 clear; **7** clarify, clear up, sort out; **9** elucidate, enlighten; **10** crystalize, effloresce, illuminate; **11** shed light on; **13** straighten out

crystallized fruit: 12 candied fruit

crystal rectifier: 5 diode

crystal violet: 13 gentian violet

Cs: 6 cesium; **7** caesium

C-section: 8 cesarean, cesarian; **9** caesarean; **15** cesarean section, cesarian section; **16** caesarean section

CST: 11 Central Time; **19** Central Standard Time

CT: 3 CAT; **18** computed tomography

Ctenocephalides: 4 flea; **20** genus Ctenocephalides

ctenophore: 9 comb jelly

Cu: 6 copper

cub: 3 lad, put; **4** loon; **5** sonny; **6** gaffer, laddie, rookie; **8** sonny boy; **9** greenhorn

Cuban sandwich: 10 medionoche

cubbyhole: 4 snug; **5** cubby; **8** snuggery; **10** pigeonhole

cube: 4 dice; **5** block; **10** third power, triplicate; **11** square block

cube-shaped: 6 cuboid; **7** cubical; **8** cubelike, cubiform, cuboidal

cubic: 5 solid; **6** three-D

cubical: 6 cuboid; **8** cubelike, cubiform, cuboidal

cubic centimeter: 2 cc, ml; **3** mil; **10** milliliter, millilitre; **15** cubic centimetre

cubic content unit: 10 cubage unit, volume unit; **12** capacity unit, cubature unit, cubic measure; **15** capacity measure; **16** displacement unit

cubic decimeter: 1 l; **5** liter, litre; **14** cubic decimetre

cubic foot: 4 cu ft

cubic inch: 4 cu in

cubic kilometer: 14 cubic kilometre

cubicle: 4 cell; **5** booth, kiosk, stall; **6** byroom, carrel; **7** carrell

cubic meter: 9 kiloliter, kilolitre; **10** cubic metre

cubic millimeter: 15 cubic millimetre

cubic yard: 4 yard

cubital joint: 5 elbow; **7** cubitus; **10** elbow joint

cucaracha: 5 roach; **9** cockroach

cucking stool: 12 ducking stool

cuckold: 5 cheat; **6** betray, wander; **7** cheat on

cuckolding: 8 adultery, cheating; **9** crim. con. [abbr]; **10** infidelity; **11** concubinage; **14** unfaithfulness

cuckoo: 3 ape, coo; **4** echo, goof, mime, pipe, zany; **5** cheep, chirp, goose, trill, tweet; **6** monkey, parrot, warble; **7** chirrup, fathead, jackass, twitter, whistle; **8** imitator

cuckoo's nest: 6 Bedlam; **8** loony bin, madhouse, nuthouse; **9** funny farm; **10** booby hatch, crazy house, funny house, sanatorium

cuckoo flower: 10 lady's smock; **11** meadow cress, ragged robin

cucullate: 6 cowled, hooded

Cuculus: 6 cuckoo; **12** genus Cuculus

cucumber: 4 cuke; **14** Cucumis sativus

Cucumis: 5 melon; **8** cucumber, honeydew; **9** muskmelon, cantaloup; **10** sweet melon, cantaloupe; **11** winter melon; **12** genus Cucumis

Cucurbitaceae: 6 cushaw, squash; **7** pumpkin; **11** gourd family; **13** hubbard squash; **15** butternut squash; **19** family Cucurbitaceae

cud: 3 wad; **4** chaw, chew, plug, quid; **12** rechewed food

cuddle: 6 nestle, nuzzle; **7** snuggle; **9** draw close; **14** fold in one's arms, fold to the heart; **15** press to the bosom; **16** strain in one's arms

cuddling: 7 hugging, kissing, necking, pet-

ting; **8** fondling; **9** caressing, smooching, snuggling
cuddly: 10 cuddlesome
cuddy: 3 ass; **6** donkey; **7** jackass
cudgel: 8 bludgeon
cudweed: 6 filago; **9** white sage; **10** cotton rose; **11** genus Filago, prairie sage; **14** western mugwort
cue: 3 key; **4** clew, clue, part, role; **5** aside, scent; **6** byplay, prompt, remind; **7** pool cue; **8** capacity, cue stick, function; **9** pool stick
cue rest: 6 jigger
cue stick: 3 cue; **7** pool cue; **9** pool stick
cuff: 4 kick; **5** cuffs, lay on, smack, spank, thump, whomp; **6** buffet, sleeve, thwack, turnup; **7** manacle; **8** handcuff, handlock, striping; **9** buffeting, handcuffs, wristband; **10** box the ears
cuffed: 7 slapped
cuffs: 4 cuff; **7** manacle; **8** handcuff, handlock; **9** handcuffs
cu ft: 9 cubic foot
cu in: 9 cubic inch
cuirass: 11 breastplate
cuisine: 4 menu, food; **5** table; **7** cookery, cooking; **8** ordinary; **10** bill of fare, table d'hote [Fr]; **11** culinary art
cuke: 8 cucumber
cul: 7 deadend; **8** cul-de-sac
cul-de-sac: 6 alcove, caecum; **7** dead end, impasse; **10** blind alley; **13** dead-end street
Culex: 10 genus Culex; **14** common mosquito
culinary art: 7 cookery, cooking, cuisine
culinary implement: 14 cooking utensil
cull: 3 mug; **4** crop, fool, pick, reap, thin, weed; **5** glean, pluck; **6** reject, winnow; **7** exclude, fall guy, gudgeon; **8** decimate, get rid of, separate
cullender: 5 sieve; **6** riddle, screen; **8** colander
culling: 10 decimation; **11** elimination
culls: 7 rejects; **8** discards
cully: 2 do; **3** con, mug, nab; **4** bilk, bite, fool, scam; **5** cheat, cozen, pluck; **6** chouse, diddle, euchre, jockey; **7** deceive, defraud, fall guy, gudgeon, swindle; **9** schlemiel, victimize
culminate: 3 cap, top; **5** crown, ripen; **6** climax; **11** come to a head
culminating point: 5 pitch; **6** climax, height, summit; **7** maximum; **10** ne plus utra; **12** turning point; **13** crowning point
culmination: 4 acme; **5** mop up; **6** apogee, climax, finale, finish, windup; **7** closing; **8** meridian; **9** winding up; **10** completion, conclusion, denouement, wrapping up
culottes: 7 culotte

culpable: 6 guilty; **7** at fault, in fault, to blame; **8** blamable, blameful; **9** blameable; **10** censurable; **11** blameworthy; **13** reprehensible
culprit: 4 perp; **8** criminal, offender; **11** perpetrator
cult: 3 fad; **4** rage; **5** craze, furor; **6** furore, homage; **7** worship; **8** devotion; **9** adoration; **10** aspiration; **13** religious cult
cultivatable: 6 arable; **8** tillable; **10** cultivable
cultivate: 4 crop, grow, work; **5** raise, train, tutor; **6** school; **7** advance, educate, enhance, forward, promote, sharpen; **8** civilize; **10** naturalize; **11** domesticate
cultivated: 6 polite, tilled, urbane; **7** gallant, genteel, refined; **8** cultured, polished, wellbred; **9** civilized; **11** gentlemanly
cultivated land: 5 tilth; **7** tillage; **10** tilled land
cultivation: 7 culture, farming, tillage; **8** agronomy, georgics; **9** culturing; **11** agriculture
cultivator: 6 grower, raiser, tiller, yeoman; **13** agriculturist
cultural: 6 ethnic
culture: 9 culturing; **11** attainments, cultivation; **12** civilization; **13** acculturation
cultured: 6 polite; **7** genteel; **9** civilized; **10** cultivated
culverin: 4 park; **6** musket, cannon; **7** battery; **8** basilisk
culvert: 4 dike, moat; **5** ditch, gully; **6** trough
cumber: 4 load; **5** press, weigh; **8** encumber, restrain; **9** constrain, gravitate
Cumberland: 15 Cumberland River; **19** Cumberland Mountains
cumbersome: 5 inapt, inept, lumpy; **6** clumsy; **7** awkward; **8** cumbrous; **9** illchosen; **10** burdensome
cumbrous: 7 massive; **8** unwieldy; **10** cumbersome
Cuminum cyminum: 5 cumin
cummerbund: 10 cumberbund
cumulate: 5 amass; **6** gather, pile up; **10** accumulate; **12** conglomerate
cumulonimbus: 12 thundercloud
cumulostratus: 12 cirrostratus
cumulus: 6 cirrus; **12** cumulus cloud
cunctation: 5 delay; **8** delation, delaying; **12** shillyshally; **15** procrastination
cunctator: 9 postponer; **14** procrastinator
cuneiform: 5 Runic; **6** uncial; **8** fusiform; **11** wedge-shaped
cuneiform character: 5 Ogham, runes; **9** arrowhead
cuneus: 5 wedge; **10** wedge shape
cunner: 6 wrasse; **7** bergall; **22** Tautogolabrus adspersus

cunning: 3 sly; **4** cute, foxy, wile, wily; **5** craft, dodgy, guile, slick; **6** artful, clever, crafty, shrewd, tricky; **7** knavish, slyness, tricksy; **8** foxiness, guileful, subtlety, wiliness; **9** ingenious; **10** artfulness, craftiness, shrewdness
cunonia family: 11 Cunoniaceae; **17** family Cunoniaceae
cup: 5 basin; **6** bishop, crater, cupful, goblet, trophy; **7** chalice, wassail; **9** loving cup, punch bowl, transfuse; **10** winner's cup
cupboard: 6 closet, locker; **7** commode; **8** cellaret; **12** chiffonniere
cupel: 10 bone-ash cup
cup fungus: 11 discomycete
Cupid: 4 Amor; **5** Venus
Cupid's disease: 2 VD
cupidity: 4 lust; **7** avarice, avidity; **8** venality; **9** cacoethes [Lat], prurience; **12** covetousness
cupola: 4 dome
cuppa: 6 cupper
cupper: 5 cuppa
Cupressaceae: 13 cypress family; **18** family Cupressaceae
Cupressus: 7 cypress; **14** genus Cupressus
cur: 3 dog; **4** mutt; **5** mixed, scrub; **9** underbred
curable: 10 remediable, restorable; **11** recoverable, retrievable
curacao: 7 curacoa
curare: 12 tubocurarine
curate: 5 vicar; **6** parson, pastor, rector; **8** minister
curative: 4 cure; **6** remedy; **7** healing; **8** remedial, sanative; **10** alterative; **11** therapeutic
curator: 11 conservator, functionary
curb: 4 hold, kerb; **5** check; **6** bridle, hold in, rein in, subdue; **7** conquer, contain, control, curb bit, curtail, cut back, inhibit, slacken; **8** moderate, restrain, restrict, suppress; **9** constrain, restraint, stamp down
curbed: 7 checked
Curculionidae: 19 family Curculionidae
Curcuma: 8 turmeric, 12 genus Curcuma
curcuma paper: 11 litmus paper; **13** turmeric paper
curd: 3 pap; **4** cake, clot, pulp; **5** dough, stone; **6** curdle; **7** pudding; **8** coagulum
curdle: 4 clot, curd; **7** clabber
curdled: 7 grumose, grumous; **8** emulsive; **9** coagulate, succulent; **10** coagulated
cure: 3 set; **4** heal, salt; **6** doctor, physic, remedy; **7** congeal, healing; **8** concrete, curative, medicate, recovery, take a set; **9** coagulate; **11** consolidate, getting well, restoration; **12** recuperation
cure: 4 abbe; **12** parish priest

cure-all: 7 nostrum, panacea
cured: 4 aged; **6** corned, healed; **9** recovered; **10** vulcanized
cureless: 9 incurable; **10** remediless; **11** immedicable; **12** beyond remedy
curettage: 11 curettement
curfew: 8 eventide; **9** nightfall
curie: 2 Ci
Curie temperature: 10 Curie point
curing: 4 help; **6** remedy; **7** redress, regimen, therapy; **9** treatment
curio: 6 bauble, gewgaw, oddity, rarity, trifle; **7** bibelot, novelty, oddment, trinket, whatnot; **8** chotchke, gimcrack, kickshaw, nicknack, whim-wham; **9** bagatelle, bric-a-brac, curiosity, tchotchke; **10** knickknack; **11** peculiarity
curiosity: 5 curio, sight; **6** nicety, oddity, rarity, wonder; **7** oddment; **8** interest; **9** epicurism, exactness, friandise [Fr], spectacle; **11** curiousness, peculiarity
curious: 3 odd, rum; **4** fine, nice; **5** funny, queer, rummy; **6** strict; **7** precise, strange; **8** delicate, exacting, peculiar, singular; **9** demanding; **10** meticulous, overstrict, particular; **11** inquisitive, interesting, punctilious
curiously: 5 oddly; **6** mainly; **7** chiefly, funnily, notably; **8** signally; **9** pointedly, strangely, unusually; **10** peculiarly, remarkably, singularly, strikingly, uncommonly; **12** particularly; **13** inquisitively
curiousness: 8 interest; **9** curiosity; **11** foreignness, strangeness
curium: 2 Cm
curl: 4 coil, gyre, kink, lock, loop, roll, tuft, turn, wave; **5** crisp, curve, twill, whorl; **6** cocker, curl up, rumple, scroll; **7** frizzle, ringlet, wrinkle
curler: 6 roller; **10** hair curler
curlew: 9 sandpiper
curlicue: 4 coil, curl, gyre, roll; **5** whorl; **6** scroll; **7** ringlet; **8** squiggle
curmudgeonly: 5 gruff; **6** crusty; **10** ill-humored; **11** ill-humoured
currency: 4 cash; **5** bruit, vogue; **6** specie; **8** cold cash, hard cash; **11** currentness; **12** up-to-dateness
currency exchange: 14 bureau de change [Fr]; **15** currency counter
current: 2 in; **4** flow, rife, tide; **5** afoot, doing; **6** actual, afloat, extant, on foot, stream, that is, trendy, with it; **7** going on, in vogue, instant, present; **8** existing, floating; **9** in fashion, jet stream, prevalent; **10** all the rage, going about, prevailing, vernacular; **11** fashionable, moving water; **12** electric flow, ocean current, running water; **13** in circulation
currently: 9 presently
currentness: 8 currency; **12** up-to-dateness

current opinion: 9 vox populi [Lat]; 13 current belief, popular belief

curriculum: 7 program; 8 syllabus; 13 course of study

curriculum vitae: 6 resume

curry: 4 fray; 5 dress, groom; 13 sauce piquante [Fr]

curry favor with: 5 court, flirt; 6 butter, slaver; 8 butter up, pander to, suck up to; 9 truckle to; 10 pay court to, propitiate

curse: 3 hex; 4 bane, blow, cuss, damn, jinx, load, oath; 5 blast, swear; 6 bedamn, blight, burden, stroke; 7 beshrew, nemesis, scourge, swear at, torment; 8 maledict, swearing; 9 blaspheme, curse word, expletive, imprecate, swearword; 10 anathemize, execration; 11 imprecation, malediction; 12 condemnation; 13 excommunicate

cursed: 5 curst; 6 damned, doomed; 7 cursing, unsaved; 8 accursed, damnable, infernal; 10 confounded, unredeemed

curse word: 4 cuss, oath; 5 curse; 8 swearing; 9 expletive, swearword

cursing: 4 oath; 6 cursed; 8 ribaldry, swearing; 9 profanity; 13 foul invective

cursive: 8 longhand

cursive hand: 8 bold hand, good hand; 11 flowing hand, legible hand, running hand

cursor: 7 pointer

Cursorius: 14 genus Cursorius

cursory: 6 casual; 7 passing; 8 fleeting; 9 ephemeral; 10 evanescent, short-lived; 11 perfunctory

curst: 6 cursed

curt: 5 brusk, crisp, short, terse; 7 brusque, laconic

curtail: 4 clip, curb; 6 reduce, take in; 7 abridge, cut back, shorten; 8 cut short, restrict; 10 abbreviate

curtailment: 10 downsizing, shortening; 11 suppression; 12 abbreviation

curtain: 4 pall, veil; 5 blind, cloak, cloud, drape, shade; 6 mantle; 7 act drop, bastion, drapery, eclipse; 9 banquette; 10 breastwork

curtain call: 3 bow

curtain lecture: 6 blow up, rating; 7 lecture, wigging; 8 dressing, scolding, trimming

curtainless: 11 uncurtained

curtain raising: 7 opening; 12 opening night

curtly: 5 short; 7 shortly

curtness: 9 gruffness, shortness; 10 abruptness; 11 brusqueness, taciturnity

curtsy: 3 bob, bow, nod; 5 kneel; 6 kowtow, salaam, scrape; 7 curtsey; 8 courtesy; 13 bow submission

curule: 10 senatorial

curvaceous: 5 buxom, curvy, sonsy; 6 bosomy, sonsie; 7 shapely; 10 voluptuous; 11 full-bosomed

curvature: 5 curve; 9 roundness; 11 roundedness

curve: 3 arc, cut, sag; 4 arch, bend, curl, flex, kink, slew, slue, swag, sway, turn, veer, wind; 5 crook, sheer, sweep, trend; 6 bender, swerve; 9 curvature, curve ball; 10 curved line; 11 curved shape; 12 breaking ball

curve ball: 5 curve; 6 bender; 12 breaking ball

curved surface: 11 hypersphere

curvet: 6 cavort [U.S.], prance; 8 caracole, vaulting

curvey: 5 curvy

curvilinear motion: 7 bending, curving, turning

curving: 6 curved; 7 bending, turning

curvy: 5 buxom, sonsy; 6 bosomy, curvey, sonsie; 10 curvaceous, voluptuous; 11 full-bosomed

cushat: 6 siskin; 8 ringdove; 10 wood pigeon

cushaw: 12 winter squash

cush-cush: 16 Dioscorea trifida

cushion: 3 mat, rug; 5 shock; 6 buffer, pillow, soften; 13 shock absorber

cushioned: 6 padded; 8 cushiony

cushiony: 5 cushy, foamy, plush; 6 padded; 9 cushioned

cushy: 4 soft; 5 foamy, plush

cushy job: 8 sinecure; 9 no-show job; 10 featherbed; 14 featherbedding

cusk: 4 ling; 5 torsk; 6 burbot; 8 Lota lota; 12 Brosme brosme

cusp: 4 spit; 5 angle; 7 leaflet

cusped: 6 cusped; 7 cuspate; 8 cuspated, cuspidal; 9 cuspidate

cuspid: 6 canine; 8 dogtooth, eyetooth; 11 canine tooth

cuspidor: 8 spittoon

cuss: 3 lad; 4 chap, gent, oath, pest; 5 curse, fella, swear; 6 fellow, gadfly; 8 blighter, pesterer, swearing; 9 blaspheme, curse word, expletive, imprecate, swearword

cussed: 5 cross, rusty; 7 froward; 8 obdurate; 9 obstinate; 11 intractable, unrepentant; 12 cantankerous, deaf to reason

cussedly: 8 mulishly; 10 obdurately, stubbornly; 11 obstinately, pig-headedly

custard: 7 pudding

custard-apple family: 10 Annonaceae; 16 family Annonaceae

Custer's Last Stand: 13 Little Bighorn

custodial: 7 tutelar; 8 guardian, tutelary

custodian: 5 guard; 6 custos [Lat], duenna [Sp], gaoler, jailer, keeper, ranger, warder; 7 janitor, steward, turnkey; 8 chaperon; 9 preserver; 11 third person; 14 maintenance man [male]

custody: 4 care, hold, keep, ward; 5 hands; 6 charge, having; 7 holding; 9 detention; 11 safekeeping

custom: 3 use; 5 usage; 6 impost; 7 bespoke, customs; 8 bespoken, practice, shopping, tailored; 9 tradition; 10 convention, import duty, observance, prevalence, tailor-made; 11 customs duty, made-to-order; 12 prescription; 14 common practise, wide observance; 15 conventionalism, conventionality, general practise

customary: 5 usual; 6 age-old, wonted; 8 habitual; 10 accustomed, immemorial; 11 traditional; 12 conventional, prescriptive

custom-built: 11 made-to-order

customer: 6 client, patron; 9 clientele [pl]

customhouse: 9 tollbooth

customize: 9 customise; 10 custom-make; 11 tailor-make

custom-make: 9 customize; 10 tailor-make

customs: 6 custom, impost; 11 customs duty

customs duty: 6 custom, impost; 7 customs

customs inspector: 12 customs agent

customs officer: 6 gauger [Brit]; 8 douanier [Fr]; 9 exciseman; 15 customs official

custos: 5 guard; 6 gaoler, jailer, keeper, ranger, warder; 7 turnkey; 9 custodian

cut: 3 hew, mow, nip, rip, set; 4 bite, cast, dent, down, edit, form, gash, hack, high, hurt, make, mold, mown, nick, pass, skip, slew, slit, slue, snub, stab, thin, trim, veer; 5 beery, boozy, carve, curve, drunk, fresh, issue, knife, lunge, merry, mould, notch, prune, sheer, slash, slice, split, style, swing, tight, tipsy, trend; 6 chisel, chop up, corned, cut off, cut out, dilute, gashed, gelded, groggy, ignore, indent, pierce, primed, rasher, reduce, scrimp, sculpt, sliced, swerve, tailor, thrust; 7 abridge, boycott, cut back, cut down, cutting, drunken, edit out, fuddled, make out, shaving, shorten, slashed, stinger, thin out, thinned, trimmed, turn off, turn out, woodcut; 8 contract, deletion, elevated, incision, lacerate, overcome, top-heavy, trim back, trim down, weakened, write out; 9 bring down, cut of meat, disguised, disregard, eliminate, flustered, formation, inebriate, overtaken, sculpture, shortened, switch off; 10 abbreviate, cutting off, home thrust, in one's cups, inebriated; 11 elimination, emasculated, foreshorten, intoxicated, rationalize; 12 cold shoulder, construction; 13 baseball swing

cutaneous: 5 scaly; 6 dermal, skinny; 8 cortical, cutaneal, squamous [Anat]; 9 cuticular

cut away: 3 fly; 4 skim, tear, zoom; 5 brush, shoot, sweep, whisk; 6 cut off, cut out, swoosh; 8 run a race

cut back: 3 cut, lop; 4 clip, crop, curb, snip, trim; 5 dress, lower, prune; 6 reduce, weaken; 7 curtail, cut down; 8 restrict, trim

back, trim down; 9 attenuate, bring down, extenuate, flash back

cut capers: 3 hop; 4 ramp, skip, trip

cutch: 5 kutch; 7 cutechu

cut down: 3 cut, mow; 4 down, drop, fell, trim; 5 lower, slash; 6 cut out, reduce, weaken; 7 cut back, hew down, mow down; 8 beat down, blow down, cast down, dash down, pare down, pull down, push down, take down, trim back, trim down; 9 attenuate, break down, bring down, extenuate, fling down, knock down, throw down; 10 strike down

cute: 4 able; 5 tasty; 6 clever, gifted; 7 cunning, darling, endowed; 8 precious, talented; 10 felicitous

cuteness: 10 prettiness

cut expenses: 8 retrench

cuticle: 5 cutin; 9 epidermis

cuticular: 5 scaly; 6 dermal, skinny; 8 cortical, squamous [Anat]; 9 cutaneous, epidermal, epidermic

cut in: 5 put in; 6 butt in; 7 barge in, break in, chime in

cut-in: 6 insert

cut into: 3 dig; 5 delve; 8 turn over

cut into pieces: 5 cut up; 6 chop up; 7 slice up; 11 cut to pieces

cut in two: 5 halve, split; 6 bisect, cleave, divide; 11 dichotomize; 13 cleave in twain [archaic]

cutis: 4 skin; 6 corium, dermis; 8 tegument

cutlass: 6 cutlas; 10 broadsword

cutlery: 10 silverware

cutlet: 4 chop; 7 scallop

cutoff: 8 crosscut, shortcut

cut off: 3 cut; 4 chip, knap, part; 5 minus; 6 bereft, cut out, detach, lop off; 7 break up, chop off, cut away, denuded, disrupt, divorce, severed; 8 amputate, bereaved, break off, shortcut; 9 interrupt; 11 nip in the bud

cut out: 3 cap, cut, top; 4 beat; 6 cut off, excise, lay out, map out, o'er-top; 7 cut away, cut down, replace; 8 chalk out, supplant; 9 strike out, supersede; 10 scratch out

cut out for: 9 fitted for

cutpurse: 3 dip; 10 pickpocket

cut-rate: 7 bargain; 8 cut-price; 9 cheapness; 13 bargain-priced

cut short: 4 clip, crop; 6 arrest; 7 blot out, curtail, take off; 8 break off, retrench, truncate

cutter: 6 carver; 7 cutlery, cutters; 11 cutting tool, stone cutter

cutthroat: 6 fierce; 7 butcher; 9 bowelless, homicidal, murderous

cutting: 3 cut, dry, raw; 4 keen, slip, warm; 5 acute, bleak, edged, quick, sharp, slice, smart; 6 biting, bitter, lively, severe, strong; 7 carving, cynical, grating, racking, shaving; **8** clay-cold, clipping, grinding, hard upon, incisive, piercing, pinching, sardonic, stabbing, stinging, thinning; **9** agonizing, consuming, corroding, knifelike, sarcastic, satirical, searching, severance, sundering, trenchant, withering; **10** cutting off; **11** film editing; **12** excruciating, press cutting; **13** press clipping

cutting board: 13 chopping board

cutting edge: 4 edge; **8** vanguard; **9** blade edge, forefront, knife edge

cutting out: 8 ablation, excision; **11** extirpation

cuttings: 8 extracts; **9** gleanings

cuttlefish: 6 cuttle

cut to pieces: 5 cut up; **6** chop up; **7** cut down, slice up; **10** tear to rags; **12** cut the throat, pick to pieces, pull to pieces, tear to pieces; **13** crush to pieces, cut into pieces, shake to pieces, tear to tatters

cut to the quick: 5 cut up, wound; **8** embitter

CVA: 6 stroke; **8** apoplexy

cwm: 6 cirque, corrie

cwt: 6 cental; **7** centner, quintal; **13** hundredweight; **17** long hundredweight; **18** short hundredweight

Cyamopsis: 4 guar; **11** cluster bean; **14** genus Cyamopsis

cyanamide: 8 cyanamid

cyanide: 7 nitrile; **11** Prussic acid

Cyanocitta: 7 blue jay, jaybird; **15** genus Cyanocitta

cyanocobalamin: 9 cobalamin

cyanuramide: 8 melamine

cyberspace: 8 internet

cyborg: 9 bionic man; **11** bionic woman

Cycadaceae: 11 cycad family

cycad family: 10 Cycadaceae

Cycas: 4 palm, sago; **10** genus Cycas

Cyclades: 15 Cycladic culture

cycle: 2 Hz; **3** cps, orb; **4** band, belt, bike, rota, zone; **5** Hertz, orbit, pedal, round, wheel; **6** cordon, rhythm, rundle; **7** bicycle, routine; **9** time cycle; **10** motorcycle, two-wheeler

cycle per second: 2 Hz; **3** cps; **5** cycle, Hertz; **13** cycles/second

cycle rickshaw: 7 pedicab

cycles per second: 2 Hz; **5** hertz

cyclic: 8 cyclical

cyclically: 9 regularly; **11** recurrently; **12** periodically

cyclic disorder: 11 cyclothymia

cyclicity: 11 periodicity

cyclist: 9 bicyclist

cycloid: 9 cycloidal, ellipsoid

Cycloloma: 10 tumbleweed, **14** genus Cycloloma

cyclone cellar: 11 storm cellar; **13** tornado cellar

Cyclone fence: 11 picket fence; **13** stockade

fence; **14** chain-link fence; **15** barbed wire fence

cyclonic: 8 cyclonal; **10** cyclonical

Cyclopean: 9 Herculean; **10** Gargantuan, prodigious; **11** Bunyanesque

cyclopean: 9 Herculean; **14** Brobdingnagian

cyclopedia: 11 cyclopaedia; **12** encyclopedia; **13** encyclopaedia

Cyclopes: 7 Cyclops; **8** anteater; **13** genus Cyclopes

Cyclops: 4 flat; **8** Cyclopes; **11** simple Simon

cyclops: 9 water flea

Cyclopterus lumpus: 8 lumpfish

cyclorama: 7 diorama; **8** panorama

cyclosis: 9 streaming

cyclothymia: 14 cyclic disorder

cyder: 5 cider; **9** hard cider

Cydonia: 6 quince; **12** genus Cydonia

Cygnus: 4 swan; **11** genus Cygnus

cylinder: 13 piston chamber

cylinder block: 11 engine block

cylinder lock: 11 tumbler lock

cylindrical: 8 tubelike, vasiform; **9** cylindric; **10** tube-shaped

cylindrical lining: 7 bushing

cyma: 4 ogee; **8** cymatium

cymbal: 4 bell, gong

cymbidium: 6 cymbid

cymling: 14 pattypan squash

cymophanous: 5 paned; **7** clouded, dappled

Cymru: 5 Wales

Cynara: 7 cardoon; **9** artichoke; **11** genus Cynara

cynic: 6 carper, critic; **7** caviler, doubter, sceptic, skeptic; **8** frondeur; **10** unbeliever; **11** faultfinder, word-catcher

cynical: 3 dry; **5** sharp; **6** biting, severe; **7** acerbic, cutting, haughty, sauvage [Fr]; **8** cavalier, hard upon, sardonic; **9** bumptious, sarcastic, satirical, trenchant, withering; **11** unclubbable; **12** contumelious, inhospitable, misanthropic, supercilious

cynicism: 7 sarcasm; **8** distrust, mistrust; **10** scepticism, skepticism; **11** incredulity

cynipid wasp: 7 gallfly; **8** gall wasp

Cynodon: 4 doob; **5** kweek; **9** star grass; **10** devil grass; **11** Bahama grass, scutch grass; **12** genus Cynodon, Bermuda grass; **14** giant star grass

Cynomys: 10 prairie dog; **12** genus Cynomys

Cynoscion: 8 weakfish; **14** genus Cynoscion

cynosure: 5 guide; **6** mirror

Cynthia: 7 Artemis

cynthia moth: 12 Samia cynthia, Samia walkeri

Cyon: 4 Cuon; **9** genus Cuon, genus Cyon

Cyperaceae: 11 sedge family; 16 family Cyperaceae

Cyperus: 5 chufa; 7 papyrus, rush nut; 8 galangal, nut grass, nut sedge, nutgrass, nutsedge; 11 earth almond; 12 ground almond, genus Cyperus; 13 umbrella plant, umbrella sedge; 14 yellow nutgrass

cypher: 1 0; 3 nil, nix, zip; 4 code, nada, zero; 5 aught, zilch; 6 cipher, encode, figure, naught, nobody, nought, reckon; 7 compute, encrypt, nothing; 8 encipher, goose egg, inscribe; 9 calculate, nonentity; 10 secret code; 11 cryptograph, write in code

Cypraea: 6 cowrie; 12 genus Cypraea

Cypraeidae: 16 family Cypraeidae

cy pres: 12 rule of cy pres; 14 cy pres doctrine

cypress: 11 cypress tree

cypress family: 12 Cupressaceae; 18 family Cupressaceae

cyprian: 4 bawd, tart; 5 whore; 6 harlot; 7 cocotte, trollop; 10 prostitute; 11 working girl

cyprinid: 9 cyprinoid; 12 cyprinid fish

Cyprinidae: 16 family Cyprinidae

Cyprinus: 4 carp; 13 genus Cyprinus

Cypriot: 7 Cyprian; 8 Cypriote

Cypripedium: 11 lady slipper; 14 moccasin flower; 16 genus Cypripedium

cyproheptadine: 9 Periactin

cyrilla: 9 white titi; 11 leatherwood; 18 Cyrilla racemiflora

cyrilla family: 10 titi family; 12 Cyrilliaceae

Cyrillic: 16 Cyrillic alphabet

cyst: 3 pod; 5 calyx; 7 bladder, capsule, utricle, vesicle; 8 cancelli

cystic breast disease: 14 cystic mastitis

cystocele: 14 colpocystocele

cystolith: 12 bladder stone

Cystophora: 15 genus Cystophora

Cystophora cristata: 10 hooded seal; 11 bladdernose

Cystopteris: 4 fern; 16 genus Cystopteris

Cytesis proliferus: 9 tagasaste

Cytherea: 9 Aphrodite

Cytisus: 5 broom; 12 genus Cytisus

cytological: 9 cytologic

cytomegalovirus: 3 CMV

cytoplasm: 10 protoplasm

czar: 4 tsar [Russ], tzar

czarina: 7 tsarina, tzarina; 8 czaritza, tsaritsa

czarist: 7 tsarist, tzarist; 9 czaristic, tsaristic

czarita: 7 czarina [Russ]

Czech: 12 Chechoslovak; 15 Czechoslavakian, Czechoslovakian

D

D: 1 R; 4 poor; 8 vitamin D; 10 calciferol; 11 five hundred; 12 dextrorotary

d: 11 five hundred

D.V.: 10 Deo volente [Lat], God willing, if possible

DA: 16 district attorney

dab: 3 pat, rap, tap; 4 flap, swab, swob, whit; 6 splash, tittle; 7 soupcon; 8 splatter

dabble: 4 slop, soil; 5 stain, sully; 6 deluge, paddle, play at, potter, putter, smirch; 7 dip into, draggle, slobber, smatter; 8 dabble at, dabble in, inundate, irrigate; 10 dabble with; 12 fiddle-faddle, putter around

dabbled: 5 soggy; 7 splashy; 8 splashed; 9 spattered; 10 splattered

dabbler: 7 amateur; 9 smatterer; 10 dilettante; 11 half scholar

da capo: 8 at the top; to the top

Dacca: 5 Dhaka; 19 capital of Bangladesh

Dacelo: 10 kookaburra; 11 genus Dacelo

dacha: 11 summerhouse; 13 vacation house

dachshund: 7 dachsie; 9 badger dog

Dacridium laxifolius: 4 rimu; 12 mountain rimu

dacron: 8 Terylene

Dacrycarpus: 9 kahikatea; 16 genus Dacrycarpus

Dacrydium: 4 rimu; 7 tarwood; 14 genus Dacrydium

dactyl: 5 digit

Dactylis: 8 cockspur; 9 cocksfoot; 12 orchard grass; 13 genus Dactylis

Dactyloctenium: 13 crowfoot grass, Egyptian grass; 19 genus Dactyloctenium

dactylology: 8 pointing

Dactylopius coccus: 9 cochineal; 15 cochineal insect

Dactylorhiza: 6 orchid; 7 fuchsii; 17 genus Dactylorhiza

dad: 2 pa; 3 pop; 4 dada, papa, sire; 5 daddy, pappa, pater; 6 father, old man

Dada: 7 Dadaism

daddy longlegs: 8 crane fly; 10 harvestman
dado: 6 plinth; 8 wainscot
daedalian: 8 artistic, involved; 9 intricate, perplexed, shipshape, technical; 10 scientific; 11 complicated
daemon: 5 demon, devil, fiend; 6 daimon; 7 demigod
daft: 3 mad; 4 bats, loco, nuts; 5 balmy, barmy, batty, buggy, crazy, dotty, kooky, loony, loopy, nutty, wacky; 6 aliene, crazed, fruity, insane, kookie; 7 bonkers, cracked, far gone, haywire, lunatic, tetched, touched; 8 crackers, demented, deranged, maddened, not right; 10 moonstruck, upper story
dagger: 4 dirk; 5 knife; 7 bayonet; 8 stiletto
dagger fern: 11 canker brake; 13 Christmas fern
daguerreotype: 5 photo; 10 photograph
dah: 4 dash
Dahlia pinnata: 6 dahlia
Dahomey: 5 Benin
daikon: 14 Japanese radish
daily: 7 diurnal, each day; 8 day by day, day-to-day, every day, everyday, magazine; 9 newspaper, quotidian
daimio: 6 daimyo [Japanese]; 7 samurai [Japanese], shizoku [Japanese]
daimon: 5 demon, devil, fiend; 6 daemon
dainties: 6 dainty; 8 delicacy; 10 delicacies
daintiness: 8 delicacy, fineness; 9 pickiness; 10 choosiness; 11 finickiness, selectivity; 14 discrimination, fastidiousness
dainty: 4 fine, good, nice, prim, twee; 5 goody, picky, sweet, tasty, treat; 6 prissy, savory, tidbit; 7 finical, finicky, mincing, refined; 8 dainties, delicacy, delicate, kickshaw, overnice; 9 delicious, exquisite, palatable, squeamish; 10 delectable, delicacies, fastidious, well-tasted; 11 tasty morsel
daiquiri: 11 rum cocktail
dairy: 9 dairy farm
dairy cow: 6 milker; 7 milcher, milk cow; 8 milch cow; 11 dairy cattle
dairy farmer: 8 dairyman
dairymaid: 8 milkmaid
dais: 4 ambo; 5 divan, stump; 6 podium, pulpit, throne; 7 rostrum, soapbox
daisy chain: 6 linked; 7 festoon; 11 flower chain
daisy wheel: 15 daisy print wheel
Dakar: 17 capital of Senegala
Dalbergia: 5 sissu; 6 sisham, sissoo; 8 kingwood, cocobolo, rosewood; 9 jacaranda, blackwood; 11 caviuna wood; 14 genus Dalbergia
dale: 4 dell, glen, vale; 5 glade, grove; 6 bottom, dingle, valley
dalliance: 5 flirt; 6 toying; 7 necking, petting; 8 coquetry, dawdling, flirting, fondling, sparking, sporting, trifling; 9

making out; 10 flirtation, hanky-panky; 11 epanchement, wasting time
dallis grass: 8 paspalum
dally: 3 toy; 4 mash, play; 5 flirt, spoon, tarry; 6 chat up, coquet, linger, trifle; 7 romance; 8 coquette, kill time; 9 philander, temporize; 10 bill and coo, dilly-dally; 12 put things off; 13 procrastinate
dalmatian: 8 coach dog; 11 carriage dog
Dalmatia pyrethrum: 9 pyrethrum
dalmatic: 4 cope, gown, pall, robe; 5 frock; 7 cassock, pallium; 10 Geneva gown
Dalton: 10 John Dalton
dam: 2 up; 3 dkm; 4 dike, dyke; 5 dam up, ditch, levee, mamma; 6 mother, shut up; 7 stuff up; 8 button up; 9 decameter, decametre, dekameter, dekametre
damage: 4 harm, hurt; 5 price, terms, wrong; 6 demand, impair, injure, injury, scathe; 8 damaging, mutilate; 9 detriment, impairing, vitiation, worsening; 10 debasement, impairment, mutilating, mutilation
damaged: 7 injured, spotted, stained, sullied, tainted; 8 flyblown, impaired; 9 mutilated, tarnished; 10 besmirched; 11 discredited
damages: 4 bill; 6 amends; 7 escheat [Law], redress; 9 indemnity, premunire [Lat]; 11 restitution; 13 sequestration
damar: 5 resin; 6 dammar; 9 gum dammar
damascene: 6 damask; 10 damascened
Damascus: 14 capital of Syria
damask: 6 purple; 7 magenta; 10 grayish-red
dame: 4 bird, doll, lady, ma'am, Mrs.; 5 chick, madam, wench; 6 madame; 7 monitor; 10 schoolmarm; 11 gentlewoman
Dame's violet: 11 sweet rocket; 12 damask violet
daminozide: 4 Alar
damn: 4 cast, darn, hoot, 5 blame, curse; 6 bedamn, blamed, bloody, damn it!, damned, darned, deuced, shucks; 7 beshrew, blasted, blessed, condemn, convict, swear at; 8 all-fired, infernal, maledict; 9 imprecate; 10 anathemize, find guilty
damned: 4 damn; 5 blame; 6 blamed, cursed, darned, deuced, doomed, goddam; 7 blasted, blessed, unsaved; 8 accursed, cursedly, damnable, damnably, infernal; 9 sentenced; 10 confounded, unredeemed; 11 everlasting
damoiselle: 6 damsel; 7 damosel, damozel; 10 demoiselle
damosel: 6 damsel; 7 damozel; 10 damoiselle, demoiselle
damozel: 6 damsel; 7 damosel; 10 damoiselle, demoiselle
damp: 3 lay, wet; 4 calm, cool, dash, dull, hush, lull, mute, sink, swag, tame; 5 abate,

D

allay, blunt, break, chill, lower, moist,
quell, quiet, slack, sober, still, unman; **6**
dampen, deaden, deject, muffle, pacify,
quench, rebate, smooth, soften, soothe,
weaken; **7** appease, assuage, compose,
dampish, depress, moisten, slacken,
smother, turn off; **8** calm down, dampness,
suppress, tone down; **9** alleviate, knock
down, moistness, prostrate
dampen: 3 wet; **4** damp, dull, mute, wash; **5**
break; **6** deaden, muffle, soften, stifle,
weaken; **7** moisten; **8** tone down
damper: 6 cooler; **7** killjoy, marplot; **10** wet
blanket; **11** party pooper
damsel: 7 damosel, damozel; **10** damoiselle,
demoiselle
damselfish: 10 demoiselle
damson plum: 6 damson; **9** satin leaf, satinleaf; **10** caimitillo
dam up: 3 dam; **6** shut up; **7** stuff up; **8** button up
Danaus: 11 genus Danaus
Danaus plexippus: 7 monarch; **16** monarch
butterfly
dance: 3 jar, jog, wag; **4** beat, jerk, jolt, skip;
5 caper, dodge, lurch, shake, shock, swing;
6 quaver, quiver, seesaw; **7** dancing; **11**
terpsichore
dance hall: 8 ballroom; **11** dance palace
dance music: 13 ballroom music; **14** dance-
room music
dance of death: 12 danse macabre
dancing lady orchid: 8 oncidium; **14** butterfly plant; **15** butterfly orchid
D and C: 8 abortion
dander: 3 ire, pet; **4** bile, fume, tiff; **6** choler,
pucker, taking; **7** ferment, hackles, passion;
9 angry mood; **10** ebullition
dandified: 7 foppish
dandle: 3 pet; **6** caress, fondle, pamper; **7**
cherish
dandy: 3 fop; **4** beau, cool, dude, keen, neat;
5 bully, great, nifty, sheik, swell; **6** bang-
up, groovy, not bad, peachy, slap-up; **7**
corking, gallant; **8** cracking, smashing; **12**
clotheshorse, fashion plate
danger: 4 risk; **5** peril; **6** hazard; **7** venture; **8**
jeopardy; **10** insecurity
dangerous: 5 grave, risky; **6** severe, unsafe;
7 parlous, serious; **8** grievous, insecure,
perilous; **9** hazardous; **10** precarious
Dangla: 9 Dangaleat
dangle: 4 drop, hang, swag; **5** droop, swing;
6 depend; **19** dangle before the eyes
dangling: 7 hanging, pendant, pendent; **8**
drooping; **9** suspended; **10** suspension
Danish: 12 Danish pastry
dank: 5 humid; **6** clammy, sultry
Danmark: 7 Denmark
danse du ventre: 10 belly dance

danse macabre: 12 dance of death
danseuse: 9 ballerina
Dante: 14 Dante Alighieri
Danube: 11 Danube River
Danzig: 6 Gdansk
daphne family: 13 Thymelaeaceae
daphnia: 9 water flea
dapper: 5 natty, smart, tight; **6** goodly,
jaunty, pocket, rakish, snappy, spruce; **7**
dashing, raffish
dapple: 3 bay; **4** spot; **5** cloud, fleck, patch; **6**
auburn, mottle, russet; **7** speckle; **8** chestnut, cinnamon, nut-brown; **10** maculation
Darby and Joan: 10 wedded pair
Dardanelles: 10 Hellespont
dare: 4 defy; **5** beard; **6** daring; **7** venture; **8**
make bold; **9** presume to
daredevil: 5 brash, bravo, bully; **6** madcap; **7**
hothead, lunatic; **9** desperado, fire eater; **10**
scapegrace; **11** enfant perdu [Fr], harum-
scarum, temerarious; **12** swashbuckler
Dar es Salaam: 17 capital of Tanzania
Dari: 11 Dari Persian
daring: 4 dare; **6** spirit; **7** defying; **8** audacity, boldness, defiance; **9** audacious, gallantry, hardihood, venturous; **10**
avant-garde, high spirit; **11** challenging,
intrepidity, venturesome; **12** intrepidness;
13 audaciousness
dark: 3 dim; **4** blue, dour, ebon, glum, grim,
inky, sour; **5** black, dense, ebony, moody,
muddy, night, sable; **6** dismal, gloomy,
morose, mystic, occult, opaque, secret,
shadow, somber, sullen, triste [Fr]; **7** colored, crooked, cryptic, joyless, obscure; **8**
coloured, confused, darkling, darkness,
dejected, frowning, iniquity, nebulous, sinister, slippery, tortuous; **9** benighted, cheerless, glowering, insidious, nighttime,
recondite, saturnine; **10** cabalistic, clear as
mud, depressing, lugubrious, mysterious,
spiritless, uncheerful, wickedness; **11**
dispiriting; **12** disconsolate, heavyhearted,
Machiavelian
dark ages: 10 middle ages; **13** medieval
times
dark blue: 4 navy; **8** navy blue
dark bread: 10 brown bread, whole wheat
dark complexion: 7 swarthy
darken: 3 dim; **5** shade; **6** shadow; **7**
obscure; **8** tone down
dark glasses: 6 shades; **10** sunglasses
dark horse: 8 long shot, underdog
dark lantern: 8 bull's-eye
darkling beetle: 11 tenebrionid
darkness: 4 dark; **5** blues, dumps; **6** shadow;
7 sadness; **8** doldrums, iniquity, the blues,
the dumps; **9** blindness, dejection, duskiness, heaviness, tristesse [Fr]; **10** bad spirits, blue devils, depression, dismalness,
gloominess, low spirits, melancholy,
somberness, wickedness; **11** joylessness,

melancholia, shadowiness, swarthiness; **12** dejectedness, heart sinking, il pensieroso [It], invisibility, mournfulness; **13** cheerlessness

darling: 3 pet; **4** cute, dear, duck, idol; **5** angel, deary, ducky; **6** dearie, little, minion; **7** beloved, goddess; **8** Dulcinea, favorite, ladylove, loved one, precious

darned: 4 damn; **5** blame; **6** blamed, damned, deuced; **7** blasted, blessed; **8** infernal; **11** everlasting

darnel: 4 tare; **5** cheat

darning needle: 9 dragonfly; **11** skeeter hawk, snake doctor, snake feeder; **12** mosquito hawk, sewing needle

dart: 4 boom, dash, flit, scud, tilt, trot; **5** amble, bound, flash, fleet, lance, scoot, shoot, troll; **6** gallop, spring; **7** flutter

darter: 7 anhinga; **9** snakebird

Darvon: 12 propoxyphene

Darwin: 13 Charles Darwin; **19** Charles Robert Darwin

dash: 3 dah, sop, sup; **4** bang, beat, blow, bolt, damp, dart, dull, elan, life, line, pall, race, rush, scud, sink, slam, swap; **5** baste, blend, chalk, crash, cross, daunt, flair, flash, glitz, lower, scare, scoot, shoot, smack, smash, spice, spurt, strut, style, thump, tinge, touch, trace, unman; **6** deject, energy, hyphen, screed, season, spirit, splash, sprint, stroke; **7** glitter, globule, panache, smidgin, soupcon, splurge; **8** infusion, lambaste, medicate, scare off, sprinkle, tincture, vivacity; **9** animation, derring-do, knock down, minus sign, prostrate, scare away, seasoning; **10** besprinkle, infiltrate, sprinkling

dasheen: 4 dalo, edda, eddo, taro; **7** cocoyam; **8** taro root; **9** taro plant

dashing: 4 fast; **5** natty, showy, smart; **6** dapper, jaunty, rakish, snappy, spruce; **7** gallant, raffish; **10** chivalrous; **11** pretentious; **12** ostentatious

dassie: 3 das; **4** cony; **5** coney, hyrax

dastard: 5 sneak; **6** coward; **8** poltroon, recreant; **9** dastardly

Dasyprocta: 6 agouti; **15** genus Dasyprocta

Dasypus: 4 peba; **9** armadillo; **12** genus Dasypus

DAT: 16 digital audiotape

data: 4 fact; **5** datum, facts [pl], terms; **6** result; **7** finding, grounds, opening; **8** premises; **9** known fact, plain fact; **11** information, praecognita [Lat]; **12** matter of fact, positive fact; **13** starting point

data point: 5 datum

data processor: 8 computer

date: 3 see; **5** go out, tryst; **6** escort; **8** go steady; **9** date stamp; **10** engagement; **11** appointment, assignation; **13** day of the month

dateless: 7 endless, undated; **8** timeless

dative bond: 14 coordinate bond

datum: 4 data [pl], fact; **5** facts [pl]; **9** data point, known fact, plain fact

daub: 4 blot, blur, slur, spot; **5** smear, smoke; **6** bedaub, slaver, smirch, smudge; **7** besmear, distort, plaster, tarnish; **8** overdraw; **10** caricature, exaggerate

dauber: 4 hack; **5** stick; **6** duffer, lubber; **7** copyist, fumbler

Daucus carota: 10 wild carrot; **14** Queen Anne's lace

Daucus carota sativa: 6 carrot; **16** cultivated carrot

daughter: 4 girl

daunt: 3 cow; **4** dash, pall; **5** abash, deter, scare; **6** subdue; **7** overawe; **8** scare off; **9** scare away, terrorize; **10** discourage, intimidate; **11** frighten off; **12** frighten away

dauntless: 5 brave; **7** aweless; **8** fearless, intrepid; **9** audacious, unfearing

Davalliaceae: 4 fern; **18** family Davalliaceae

davenport: 6 day bed; **11** studio couch

Davy Jones's locker: 6 seabed; **9** sea bottom; **10** ocean floor; **11** ocean bottom

daw: 7 jackdaw

dawdle: 3 lag; **5** drawl, drone, idler, mopus; **6** linger, slouch; **8** fall back, hang back; **10** fall behind

dawdler: 5 drone; **7** laggard

dawdling: 4 poky; **5** pokey; **7** laggard; **8** dilatory, trifling; **9** dalliance

dawn: 4 open; **5** begin, click, enter, set in, start, sunup; **6** aurora, sink in; **7** dawning, morning, sunrise; **8** cockcrow, come home, commence, daybreak; **9** dayspring, enter upon, get across, peep of day, penetrate; **10** break of day, first light, get through

dawn horse: 8 eohippus

dawning: 4 dawn; **5** sunup; **6** aurora; **7** morning, sunrise; **8** cockcrow, daybreak; **9** dayspring; **10** break of day, first light

dawn redwood: 11 metasequoia

day: 7 daytime; **8** daylight, solar day

day after day: 5 daily; **6** always; **8** ever anon, steadily; **10** routinely; **10** at all times, constantly, invariably; **11** continually, day and night, day in day out, incessantly, night and day, perpetually, unfailingly, without fail; **12** consistently, continuously

daybed: 6 chaise; **8** divan bed; **12** chaise longue

day blindness: 9 nystagmus; **11** hemeralopia

daybook: 3 log; **4** book; **5** diary; **6** ledger; **7** journal; **8** calendar; **9** ephemeris

daybreak: 4 dawn; **5** sunup; **6** aurora; **7** dawning, morning, sunrise; **8** cockcrow; **9** dayspring, peep of day; **10** break of day, first light

day-care center: 6 creche; **7** nursery

D

daydream: 4 moon; **5** dream; **6** revery; **7** reverie; **8** stargaze; **9** air castle; **10** woolgather; **13** castle in Spain; **14** castle in the air

dayflower: 10 spiderwort

day laborer: 3 man; **4** hand; **9** hired hand

daylight: 3 day; **7** daytime; **8** sunlight, sunshine; **10** light of day

daylily: 9 tiger lily; **12** plantain lily

day off: 7 dies non, holiday, play day; **9** day of rest

Day of Atonement: 9 Yom Kippur

Day of Judgement: 7 Last Day; **8** Doomsday; **11** Judgment Day; **12** Judgement Day, Last Judgment

day of remembrance: 11 anniversary

day of rest: 7 Sabbath

Daypro: 9 oxaprozin

days: 5 years

days of old: 8 days past; **9** times past; **10** days gone by, days of yore, times of old; **11** times gone by, times of yore

day star: 11 morning star

daytime: 3 day; **8** daylight

daze: 3 fog; **4** haze, stun; **5** shock; **6** bedaze, dazzle, stupor; **7** radiate; **8** bedazzle

dazed: 4 logy; **5** foggy; **6** groggy, stupid; **7** stunned; **9** stupefied, stuporous

dazzle: 3 awe; **4** daze, loom; **6** impose, muddle, put out; **7** confuse, fluster, overawe, perplex, radiate, startle; **8** bedazzle, bewilder, hoodwink; **10** inspire awe

dazzled: 8 startled

dazzling: 5 glary; **6** dazing; **7** blazing, fulgent, glaring, glowing; **8** blinding, splendid; **9** fulgurant, fulgurous, sparkling, startling; **11** resplendent

dB: 2 db; **7** decibel

DC: 13 direct current; **18** District of Columbia

DD: 16 Doctor of Divinity

DDS: 21 Doctor of Dental Surgery

deactivate: 4 kill; **6** defuse; **7** turn off; **9** power down, switch off; **10** disconnect, inactivate; **13** pull the plug on

dead: 3 dun, wan; **4** ashy, beat, cold, dull, idle, numb; **5** all in, ashen, dingy, faint, muddy, short, utter; **6** bushed, deadly, glassy, leaden, sallow; **7** defunct, drained, ghastly, out cold, unaware, utterly; **8** abruptly, comatose, deadened, lifeless, stagnant, suddenly; **9** catatonic, inanimate, nonliving, perfectly, senseless; **10** absolutely, cadaverous

deadbeat: 9 defaulter

deadbolt: 3 bar; **4** bolt; **10** police lock

dead drunk: 6 bombed; **7** smashed; **11** high as a kite; **12** drunk as a lord, drunk as an owl, drunk as Chloe; **13** drunk as a piper, drunk as a skunk

deaden: 3 lay; **4** calm, cool, damp, hush, lull, mute, numb, stun, swag, tame; **5** abate, allay, blunt, cramp, quell, quiet, sober, still, unfit; **6** benumb, dampen, disarm, girdle, muffle, pacify, rebate, smooth, soothe; **7** appease, assuage, compose, slacken, stupefy, turn off; **8** calm down, paralyze, suppress, tone down; **9** alleviate; **10** disqualify, invalidate

dead end: 7 impasse; **8** cul-de-sac; **10** blind alley street

deadened: 4 dead; **12** anesthetized; **13** anaesthetized

deadening: 4 dull, slow; **5** ho-hum; **6** boring; **7** irksome, tedious; **8** tiresome; **9** wearisome; **10** impairment

deadhead: 9 free rider

dead heat: 3 tie; **4** draw, heat; **8** standoff

deadliness: 9 lethality

deadlock: 5 stand; **7** dead set, impasse, set fast; **9** stalemate; **10** standstill

deadly: 4 dead; **5** madly; **6** lethal, mortal; **7** baneful, deathly; **8** deucedly, insanely, venomous, virulent; **9** pestilent; **10** devilishly, lifelessly, pernicious

deadly nightshade: 10 belladonna; **11** bittersweet

deadly sin: 9 mortal sin

deadly weapon: 3 arm; **4** arms; **6** weapon; **8** ordnance

dead man: 5 stiff; **6** corpse; **8** deceased, departed; **10** dead person

dead march: 5 orbit; **11** muffled drum; **12** funeral march

dead meat: 6 corpse; **7** cadaver, carcass

dead on target: 4 true

deadpan: 9 impassive; **10** poker-faced; **12** unexpressive; **14** expressionless

dead person: 5 stiff; **6** corpse; **7** dead man; **8** dead soul, deceased, decedent, departed; **14** deceased person

dead reckoning: 4 shot; **5** guess; **8** guessing; **9** guesswork

dead room: 6 morgue; **8** mortuary

dead set: 4 bent; **5** out to, stand; **6** bent on; **7** set fast; **8** deadlock, intent on; **10** standstill

dead shot: 8 good shot, marksman; **9** crack shot; **12** sharpshooter

dead soul: 8 deceased, decedent, departed; **10** dead person; **14** deceased person

dead sound: 4 thud; **5** thump

deaf-aid: 10 hearing aid

deafen: 4 deaf, stun

deafening: 7 roaring; **8** thundery; **10** earrending, thunderous; **12** ear-deafening, ear-splitting; **13** loss of hearing

deal: 3 lot, pot, wad; **4** care, cope, hand, heap, load, mass, mess, mint, pack, peck, pile, plow, raft, sell, slew, take, work; **5** allot, batch, carve, cover, flock, get by, heaps, share, sight, spate, stack, trade, treat, world; **6** handle, hatful, look at, make do, manage, mickle, muckle, plenty, set out; **7** address, bargain, carry on, conduct, contend, deal out, dish out, divvy up, dole out, grapple, make out, marshal, mete out, tidy sum; **8** carry out, consider, dispense, good deal, shell out, softwood, whole lot; **9** apportion, collocate, great deal, parcel out, whole slew; **10** administer, distribute, portion out

dealer: 6 monger, trader; **8** chandler, merchant, salesman; **9** bargainer, principal; **11** salesperson, distributor

dealership: 9 franchise

deal in: 6 handle, retail; **8** dispense; **9** traffic in

dealing: 7 concern; **8** business, dealings; **10** proceeding; **11** transaction

dealings: 3 job; **6** doings; **7** dealing, traffic; **9** relations; **10** proceeding

deal out: 3 lot; **4** deal; **5** allot, issue, utter; **6** retail; **7** dish out, dole out, fork out, give out, mete out; **8** dispense, shell out; **9** parcel out; **10** administer, distribute

dealt: 7 alloted; **10** collocated; **11** distributed, parceled out

deal with: 5 treat; **6** handle; **9** trade with

dean: 5 canon, doyen; **8** diocesan; **10** archdeacon, prebendary

dear: 3 pet; **4** duck, good, lamb, love, near; **5** honey, jewel, pricy, sugar; **6** costly, dearly, devout, duckey, little, pricey; **7** beloved, darling, dearest, earnest; **8** loved one, precious; **9** expensive, heartfelt; **10** high priced; **14** affectionately

dearest: 4 dear, love; **5** honey; **7** beloved; **8** loved one

dearie: 3 pet; **5** deary, ducky; **7** darling; **8** favorite; **9** favourite

dearly: 4 dear; **14** affectionately

dearth: 6 famine; **7** paucity; **8** scarcity, shortage

death: 3 end; **4** last; **5** dying; **6** demise; **7** decease; **11** destruction, eternal rest; **12** eternal sleep, lifelessness

death's-head moth: 17 Acherontia atropos

death adder: 22 Acanthophis antarcticus

death angel: 8 death cap, death cup; **15** destroying angel; **17** Amanita phalloides

death bell: 10 death knell

deathblow: 11 coup de grace

death knell: 9 death bell

deathless: 5 great; **7** undying; **8** immortal; **12** imperishable

deathly: 6 deadly, mortal; **9** deathlike

death penalty: 9 executing, execution; **17** capital punishment

deathrate: 9 morbidity, mortality; **13** mortality rate

death rattle: 8 last gasp; **10** last breath; **11** dying breath

deb: 9 debutante

debacle: 5 havoc, smash; **6** fiasco; **8** drubbing, landslip, whipping; **9** avalanche, landslide, slaughter, thrashing, trouncing, walloping

debar: 3 bar, let; **5** avert, avoid, check; **7** deflect, draw off, exclude, fend off, head off, obviate, prevent, suspend, ward off; **8** forefend, preclude, stave off; **9** foreclose, turn aside; **11** nip in the bud

debark: 6 get off; **7** set down; **9** disembark; **10** come to land

debase: 4 sink; **5** abase, alloy, pitch, taint; **6** defile, dilute, reduce; **7** corrupt, debauch, degrade, deprave, pervert, pollute, profane, stretch, vitiate; **8** bring low; **9** misdirect, water down; **10** adulterate, demoralize; **11** contaminate, precipitate

debased: 3 low; **4** neap; **7** mongrel; **8** degraded, devalued, vitiated; **9** corrupted, denatured; **10** adulterate; **11** adulterated; **13** denaturalized

debasement: 4 harm; **6** damage, injury, laxity; **8** baseness, defiling, foulness, trimming, vileness; **9** abasement, abjection, detriment, polluting, pollution, shuffling, turpitude, vitiation, worsening; **10** defilement, depression, impairment; **11** degradation, prostration; **12** adulteration

debatable: 4 moot; **8** arguable, fallible, slippery, ticklish; **10** disputable, precarious; **11** problematic; **12** questionable

debate: 4 moot, trim; **5** argue, demur, fence, pause; **6** coquet, waffle; **7** balance, contend, dispute, shuffle, wrangle; **8** argument, consider, straddle, turn over; **9** bandy with, chop logic, fluctuate, hem and haw, hum and haw; **10** bandy words, deliberate, war of words; **11** controversy, disputation; **12** be on the fence

debater: 6 arguer; **7** polemic; **9** disputant

debauch: 4 orgy, riot; **6** debase, defile; **7** corrupt, deprave, pervert, profane, vitiate; **9** bacchanal, misdirect; **10** debauchery, demoralize, saturnalia; **11** bacchanalia, dissipation

debauched: 4 fast; **5** light; **6** wanton; **7** riotous; **8** degraded, depraved, unchaste; **9** dissolute, libertine; **10** deflowered, degenerate, dissipated, licentious, profligate

debauchee: 3 rip; **4** goat, rake; **5** satyr; **6** lecher; **7** Don Juan, fast man, gallant, seducer; **9** ladies' man

debauchery: 4 orgy, riot; **7** debauch; **9** bacchanal; **10** saturnalia; **11** bacchanalia, dissipation

debenture: 4 bond; **5** order; **6** coupon, plight; **7** warrant; **8** mortgage

debilitate: 5 drain, relax, shake; **6** weaken; **8** enervate, enfeeble; **10** eviscerate

debilitated: 5 seedy; **6** infirm; **8** adynamic, asthenic; **9** enervated, enfeebled

D

debility: 7 frailty, languor; 9 frailness, infirmity; 10 enervation, feebleness, relaxation

debit: 4 book, debt, post; 5 enter, score; 6 credit; 9 carry over, liability

debonair: 5 suave; 6 jaunty; 7 chipper; 9 debonaire; 10 debonnaire

debone: 4 bone

de bon augure: 10 auspicious

deboned: 5 boned

debouch: 5 issue, start; 6 effuse, emerge; 8 debouche, march out

debrided: 5 filed; 6 excise; 7 abraded

debris: 4 dust, junk; 5 talus; 6 rubble; 7 rubbish; 8 detritus, oddments, tailings; 10 fine powder, talus slope; 11 odds and ends

debt: 5 debit, score; 9 liability; 10 obligation

debt ceiling: 9 debt limit

debt instrument: 25 certificate of indebtedness

debtor: 4 stag; 7 welsher; 8 bankrupt, lame duck; 9 defaulter, insolvent

debug: 7 correct; 9 shake down

debunk: 6 expose

debut: 5 entry; 9 launching, unveiling; 11 embarcation [Fr]; 12 inauguration, introduction, le premier pas; 15 first appearance

debutante: 3 deb; 8 debutant

Dec: 8 December

decade: 1 X; 3 ten; 6 tenner; 9 decennary, decennium; 10 decenniumm

decadence: 10 degeneracy; 14 degenerateness

decadency: 10 degeneracy; 14 degenerateness

decadent: 6 effete

decaffeinated coffee: 5 decaf

decagram: 3 dag, dkg; 8 dekagram

decaliter: 3 dal, dkl; 9 decalitre, dekaliter, dekalitre

decalogue: 15 ten commandments; 18 The Ten Commandments

Decalogue: 15 Ten Commandments

decameter: 3 dam, dkm; 9 decametre, dekameter, dekametre

decamp: 4 bolt, skip; 5 go off; 6 run off; 7 abscond, vamoose; 9 break camp; 11 strike tents; 12 absquatulate

decampment: 7 leaving; 9 departure; 11 abscondment, embarkation

decant: 4 pour; 7 pour out; 8 draft off

decanter: 4 ewer; 5 cruse; 6 carafe; 7 caraffe

decapitate: 6 behead, gibbet; 7 turn off; 8 string up; 9 bowstring; 10 guillotine

decapod: 17 decapod crustacean

decarbonize: 6 decoke; 11 decarburize

decarbonized iron: 8 cast iron; 11 wrought iron

decarburize: 6 decoke; 11 decarbonize

decay: 3 rot; 4 fade, sink, wear; 5 go bad, go off, waste; 6 fester, molder, rankle, wither; 7 crumble, decline, degrade, ferment, putrefy; 8 decaying; 9 declining, decompose, disrepair, worsening; 10 degenerate, delapidate; 11 degradation, deteriorate; 12 degenerating, degeneration, dilapidation, disintegrate; 13 decomposition, deteriorating, deterioration, ravages of time

decayed: 3 bad; 4 high, weak, worn; 5 fusty, seedy, washy; 6 effete, putrid, rancid, rotted, rotten, undone, wasted; 7 corrupt, gone bad, laid low, rotting, tainted, touched; 8 degraded; 9 putrefied; 10 behindhand, pulled down, putrescent; 11 languishing; 12 deteriorated, putrefactive

decease: 2 go; 3 die; 4 exit; 5 death, dying; 6 demise, expire, perish; 8 pass away

deceased: 4 gone; 5 stiff; 6 asleep, at rest; 7 at peace, dead man, defunct, demised, extinct; 8 dead soul, decedent, departed; 10 dead person

deceit: 9 deception; 11 dissembling, fraudulence; 13 dissimulation

deceitful: 5 false; 8 two-faced; 9 dishonest, faithless, trothless, truthless; 10 fallacious, fraudulent, Janus-faced, mendacious; 11 double-faced, duplicitous, unveracious

deceive: 5 cozen; 6 betray, delude, lead on; 10 lead astray

deceiver: 5 cheat; 7 cheater; 9 trickster

decelerate: 4 slow; 6 retard, slow up; 8 slow down

December: 3 Dec

decency: 7 decorum, modesty; 8 delicacy

decennium: 6 decade; 9 decennary

decent: 4 nice, pure; 5 right; 6 comely, enough, modest, seemly; 8 adequate, becoming, decently, decorous, delicate, properly; 9 undefiled

decently: 5 right; 6 decent; 8 properly

decentralize: 7 break up, dissect; 10 break apart; 12 decentralise; 13 deconcentrate

deception: 5 magic, trick; 6 deceit; 8 illusion; 10 magic trick; 11 dissembling, legerdemain; 13 dissimulation

deceptive: 8 delusive, delusory; 10 misleading; 11 sophistical

decertify: 11 derecognize

decibel: 2 dB

decide: 3 try; 4 list, rule, will, wish; 6 choose, settle; 7 resolve; 9 determine, pronounce, set at rest

decided: 4 flat, over; 5 broad, clear, round, stark; 6 marked; 7 perfect, pointed, settled; 8 absolute, decisive, definite, distinct, finished, positive, specific; 9 essential, played out, set at rest; 10 definitive, peremptory;

11 ascertained, categorical, determinate, unequivocal; 12 unmistakable

decidedly: 6 purely; 9 by all odds, downright, radically, seriously; 10 absolutely, definitely; 11 essentially; 12 emphatically; 13 fundamentally, unequivocally; 14 unquestionably

deciding: 7 crucial, judging; 8 weighing; 10 concluding; 11 determinant, determining

deciduous tooth: 9 baby tooth, milk tooth; 12 primary tooth

decigram: 2 dg

deciliter: 2 dl; 9 decilitre

decimal: 5 tenth, tithe; 6 denary; 7 tenfold; 8 repetend

decimalize: 10 decimalise

decimate: 4 cull, thin; 5 prune; 7 wipe out; 8 carry off; 9 eliminate, eradicate; 10 annihilate, extinguish

decimeter: 2 dm; 9 decimetre

decipher: 6 decode, uncode; 7 decrypt, unravel; 10 unscramble; 11 disentangle

decipherable: 5 clear; 8 readable

decision: 4 mind, wish; 6 choice; 7 finding, verdict; 8 judgment, pleasure; 9 judgement; 10 conclusion, resolution; 13 determination

decisive: 5 clear; 7 crucial, decided; 8 critical, definite, specific; 11 ascertained, categorical, determinate, unequivocal; 12 unmistakable

decisive factor: 8 clincher

decisively: 10 resolutely

decisiveness: 8 backbone, decision, finality

deck: 4 dump, flag; 5 adorn, array, earth, floor, grace, lanai; 6 bedeck, carped, ground, paving; 7 bedight; 8 beautify, card deck, coldcock, decorate, pavement; 9 embellish, knock down; 10 substratum; 11 deck of cards, ground floor, pack of cards; 12 substructure

decked out: 4 chic; 6 decked; 7 adorned; 8 bedecked; 9 dressed up; 10 endimanche [Fr]; 12 all decked out, all dressed up, in Sunday best

deckled: 11 deckle-edged; 12 featheredged

declaim: 5 stump; 6 recite; 7 lecture; 8 flourish, harangue; 9 discourse, hold forth, sermonize, speechify

declamation: 7 bombast; 8 richness; 9 euphemism, turgidity; 10 floridness, orotundity; 11 grandiosity

declamatory: 4 rich; 5 large, tumid; 6 florid, mouthy, ornate, turgid; 7 flowery, orotund; 8 inflated, sonorous, swelling; 9 bombastic, grandiose, high flown; 10 ornamented, rhetorical, turgescent

declaration: 4 bill; 5 claim; 7 resolve; 8 averment; 9 assertion, statement; 10 allegation, profession, resolution

declarative: 8 fact mood; 9 asserting; 10 common mood, indicative; 11 declaratory

D

declaratory: 6 saying; 9 asserting, declaring; 10 expository; 11 affirmative, declarative

declare: 3 say; 4 aver, hold; 5 break, let on, state; 6 affirm, assert, expose, impart, let out, reveal; 7 adjudge, divulge, profess; 8 announce, bring out, disclose, discover, give away; 9 predicate

declaring: 6 saying; 9 asserting; 11 affirmative, declaratory

declasse: 8 inferior; 9 secondary; 10 second-best, second-rate

declension: 7 decline, descent; 9 abatement, declining, going down, hardening; 10 descending, perversion; 11 backsliding

declination: 3 DEC, dip; 4 fall; 7 decline, descent, refusal, regrets; 8 downhill; 9 declivity, going down

decline: 3 dip, ebb, rot, set; 4 deny, drop, fade, fail, fall, flag, halt, limp, sink, wane; 5 decay, droop, shake; 6 dodder, go down, pass up, recede, refuse, reject, totter, worsen; 7 crumble, degrade, descent, dismiss, give way, tremble; 8 decaying, downhill, languish, turn down; 9 declining, declivity, downslope, worsening; 10 degenerate, diminution, subsidence; 11 consumption, declination, degradation, deteriorate

declining: 4 down; 5 decay; 6 waning; 7 decline, failing, refusal; 8 decaying, decrepit; 9 dismissal, rejection, run to seed, worsening; 10 declension, regressing, retrograde; 11 degradation

declivitous: 8 downhill; 15 downward-sloping

declivity: 3 dip; 4 fall; 7 decline, descent; 8 downhill; 9 downslope; 11 declination

decoct: 6 reduce; 8 boil down; 11 concentrate

decode: 6 uncode; 7 decrypt; 8 decipher; 10 unscramble

decoke: 11 decarbonize, decarburize

decollation: 9 beheading; 12 decapitation

decollete: 6 low-cut; 9 low-necked

decolonization: 14 decolonisation

decolor: 6 bleach; 9 bleach out; 10 decolorize; 11 discolorize

decoloration: 6 fading; 9 bleaching; 12 decolorizing; 13 discoloration; 14 decolorization

decolorize: 6 bleach; 7 decolor, tarnish, wash out; 8 tone down; 9 bleach out; 11 achromatize, discolorize; 14 deprive of color

decolorizer: 6 bleach

decomposable: 10 analyzable

decompose: 3 rot; 5 decay; 6 molder; 7 break up, moulder; 10 decompound; 12 disintegrate

decomposing: 7 rotting; 8 analysis;

9 analysing, disseeing, moldering; **10** dissection, mouldering

decompress: 5 relax, unlax; **6** dilate, expand, rarefy, unbend, unwind; **8** loosen up, slow down; **12** depressurize

decompression sickness: 5 bends; **11** air embolism; **12** aeroembolism; **14** caisson disease

decorate: 4 bead, deck; **5** adorn, dress, grace; **6** enrich; **8** beautify, ornament; **9** embellish

decoration: 4 palm; **5** medal; **6** ribbon; **8** ornament; **9** adornment, medallion; **12** laurel wreath

decorative: 8 cosmetic; **10** ornamental

decorator: 8 designer

decorous: 3 due, fit; **4** good, meet, pure; **5** right; **6** comely, decent, modest, proper, seemly; **7** correct, en regle, fitting; **8** becoming, delicate, honoring; **9** befitting, cap in hand, esteeming, undefiled; **10** bareheaded, obsequious, respectful, respecting

decorticate: 4 flay, pare, peel, skin; **9** excoriate

decorum: 4 form; **7** decency, fitness, gravity; **8** delicacy, good form, meetness, sobriety; **9** etiquette, formality, gentility, propriety, punctilio, rightness, solemnity, staidness; **10** sedateness, seemliness; **11** correctness, earnestness, seriousness

decoy: 4 bait, lure; **5** crimp, shill; **6** delude, ringer; **7** beguile; **8** inveigle; **9** decoy duck

decrease: 4 bate, fall; **5** abate; **6** lessen, minify, reduce; **7** drop-off; **8** diminish, step-down; **9** decrement, lessening, reduction; **10** diminution

decree: 4 fiat, rule, ukaz [Russ]; **5** edict, enact, order, ukase; **6** diktat, ordain; **7** dictate, mandate, verdict; **8** rescript; **9** dictation; **10** give orders

decreed: 8 ordained; **9** appointed; **10** prescribed

decrement: 4 loss; **6** defect, reflux; **8** decrease, discount; **9** deduction; **11** defalcation; **12** depreciation

decrepit: 4 weak; **6** creaky, feeble, infirm, waning, weakly; **7** run-down, sapless; **9** declining, run to seed, woebegone; **10** fleabitten

decrepitation: 9 crackling; **11** crepitation

decrepitude: 6 sprain, strain; **8** delicacy, hoary age; **11** climacteric

decrescendo: 10 diminuendo

decriminalize: 8 legalize; **10** legitimate, legitimize; **12** legitimatize

decry: 7 condemn, detract; **8** belittle, derogate; **9** denigrate, deprecate, disparage, excoriate, objurgate; **10** depreciate

decrypt: 6 decode, uncode; **8** decipher; **10** unscramble

decubitus ulcer: 7 bedsore

decumbent: 9 reclining, recumbent

decuple: 5 tenth; **7** decimal, tenfold

decussate: 5 cross; **9** intersect

DEd: 3 EdD; **17** Doctor of Education

dedicate: 4 give; **6** commit, devote; **10** consecrate

dedication: 7 loyalty; **10** allegiance, commitment; **11** celebration; **12** canonization, consecration, enshrinement

deduce: 4 ween; **5** infer; **6** deduct, derive, gather; **7** collect; **8** subtract

deducible: 9 following; **11** inferential

deducing: 9 inferring, reasoning; **11** rationalism; **18** process of reasoning

deduct: 5 infer; **6** deduce, derive, recoup; **7** take off; **8** subtract, withhold

deduction: 4 loss; **6** defect; **8** discount, illation; **9** decrement, deducting, inference, synthesis; **10** conclusion, entailment; **11** implication, subtracting, subtraction; **12** retrenchment, tax deduction

deductions: 11 withholding

deed: 3 act; **4** feat; **5** event, title, touch; **6** effort, stitch; **7** exploit; **8** deed poll, human act, overt act; **9** title deed; **10** human event

deeds: 5 works

deem: 4 hold; **6** view as; **7** take for

deem as: 6 hold as, take as, view as; **8** esteem as, regard as; **9** account as, set down as; **10** conceive as, consider as, look upon as

deep: 3 sea; **4** bass, full, high, late, main, rich; **5** heavy, ocean, solid, sound, thick, vivid; **6** bright, deeply, strong; **7** blatant, cryptic, intense, passing, plenary; **8** abstruse, deep laid, high seas, powerful, profound; **9** cryptical, indelible, recondite; **10** clangorous, deep seated, impressive, mysterious, mystifying

deep-dish pie: 7 cobbler

deep down: 6 inside; **7** at heart; **8** at bottom

deep-dyed: 4 keen; **5** acute, brisk, sharp, vivid; **6** severe; **8** incisive; **9** trenchant

deepen: 6 change; **8** compound, heighten; **9** intensify

deepfreeze: 7 freezer

deep-fry: 9 french-fry

deeply: 4 deep; **6** subtly; **7** acutely; **10** profoundly

deepness: 5 depth; **10** profundity; **12** profoundness

deep note: 7 low note; **8** bass note

deep pockets: 9 full purse, long purse; **10** heavy purse; **14** well lined purse

deep-six: 14 throw overboard

deep sleep: 10 balmy sleep, heavy sleep, sound sleep

deer: 6 cervid

deer's-ear: 7 columbo; **9** deer's-ears; **12** pyramid plant

deer fly fever: 9 tularemia; **10** tularaemia

de-escalate: 6 weaken; **8** step down

deface: 3 mar; 6 deform; 7 blemish; 8 mutilate, truncate; 9 disfigure

de facto: 6 actual; 7 factual; 9 ipso facto

defalcation: 7 bad debt, default; 9 decrement; 10 peculation; 12 embezzlement

defamation: 7 calumny, obloquy, scandal, slander; 9 aspersion; 10 backbiting, hatchet job, scurrility; 11 traducement; 12 evil-speaking, vilification

defamatory: 8 libelous; 9 libellous, maligning, traducing, vilifying; 10 calumnious, slanderous; 11 denigrating, denigrative, denigratory

defame: 5 smear, sully; 6 smirch; 7 asperse, slander; 8 besmirch; 9 denigrate; 10 calumniate

defamer: 7 libeler; 8 maligner, satirist, traducer; 9 backbiter, lampooner, slanderer; 11 calumniator

defassa: 9 waterbuck

default: 6 laches [Law], normal; 7 bad debt, natural; 8 omission; 9 default on, default to, oversight; 10 nonpayment; 11 defalcation, nonremittal

defaulter: 4 stag; 6 debtor; 7 welsher; 8 bankrupt, castaway, deadbeat, lame duck, recreant; 9 insolvent

defeasance: 6 repeal; 8 annuling, recision; 9 annulment, canceling; 10 abrogating, abrogation, rescinding, rescission

defeasible: 9 refutable

defeat: 4 beat, kill, loss; 5 crush, parry; 6 expose; 7 conquer, licking, vote out; 8 overcome, vanquish, vote down; 9 discomfit, frustrate; 11 frustration

defeated: 6 foiled; 8 thwarted; 10 frustrated; 11 discomfited; 12 disappointed

defeatist: 10 negativist

defect: 3 rat; 4 flaw, loss; 5 fault; 6 desert, go over; 7 blemish; 8 discount; 9 decrement, deduction, weak point; 10 apostatize, deficiency

defection: 8 apostasy; 9 desertion, going over; 10 withdrawal; 11 abandonment; 12 renunciation; 13 changing sides

defective: 3 bad; 6 faulty; 7 failing, lacking, wanting; 9 deficient

defector: 7 traitor; 8 deserter, turncoat

defend: 4 fend, hold; 5 fight, guard; 6 oppose, shield; 7 fend for, forfend, protect, support; 8 advocate, champion, maintain; 9 fight back, fight down, represent

defendant: 7 accused, suspect; 10 respondent

defender: 8 guardian; 9 protector

defense: 5 reply; 6 denial; 7 defence; 8 demurrer; 9 defending; 10 protection, refutation; 11 defense team, vindication

defense attorney: 13 defense lawyer

defenseless: 5 naked; 7 unarmed; 8 harmless, sine ictu [Lat], vincible; 9 fenceless, pregnable, untenable

defensible: 6 venial; 7 tenable; 9 excusable; 10 defendable, pardonable; 11 justifiable

defensive: 10 excusatory

defer: 3 bow; 5 delay, remit, table; 6 accede, give in, put off, shelve, submit; 7 hold off, put over, set back; 8 hold over, postpone

deference: 5 honor; 6 esteem, fealty; 7 respect; 10 allegiance, compliance, compliancy, estimation, high regard

deferential: 8 decorous, deferent, honoring; 9 cap in hand, esteeming, regardful; 10 bareheaded, obsequious, respectful, respecting; 11 ceremonious, on one's knees, reverential

deferment: 8 deferral; 12 postponement

deferred: 9 postponed

defer to: 4 bend; 5 prize, value, yield; 6 admire, resign, submit; 7 succumb; 8 look up to; 9 conform to; 11 subscribe to

defiance: 6 daring; 7 defying; 11 challenging; 14 rebelliousness

defiant: 4 bold; 7 defying; 9 rebellious

deficiency: 4 flaw, lack, want; 5 fault; 6 defect; 7 absence, deficit; 9 weak point; 10 inadequacy; 11 shortcoming

deficient: 4 less; 5 lower, minor, minus; 6 lesser; 7 failing, lacking, wanting; 8 inferior; 9 defective, secondary; 11 subordinate, substandard; 12 insufficient

deficit: 7 arrears; 8 shortage; 9 shortfall; 10 deficiency; 15 deferred payment

defile: 4 foul; 5 cloud, gorge, sully, taint; 6 befoul, debase, file on; 7 corrupt, debauch, degrade, pollute, tarnish; 8 maculate; 10 adulterate; 11 contaminate

defilement: 4 blot, blur, spot; 5 abuse, stain, taint; 7 tarnish; 8 defiling; 9 polluting; 10 befoulment, debasement

define: 7 delimit, explain, specify; 8 construe; 9 delineate, interpret; 10 delimitate; 12 characterize

definite: 5 clear, party, plain, rigid; 6 proper; 7 certain, decided, defined, glaring, partial, private, several, special, staring; 8 apparent, decisive, distinct, especial, original, peculiar, rigorous, specific; 9 exclusive; 10 in full view, individual, particular, respective, well marked; 11 appropriate, ascertained, categorical, conspicuous, determinate, in plain view, unequivocal, well defined

definitely: 2 so; 7 clearly, exactly, plainly; 9 by all odds, decidedly, glaringly, precisely; 10 accurately, apparently, distinctly

definition: 7 clarity; 12 distinctness

definitive: 7 decided; 9 classical; 10 peremptory; 11 determinate

definitively: 10 absolutely; 13 categorically

deflate: 8 puncture; 10 disenchant; 11 disillusion

deflated: 11 crestfallen

deflect: 4 bend; 5 avert, avoid, block, debar, parry; 7 deviate, fend off, head off, obviate, ward off; 8 distract, draw away, stave off, turn away

deflection: 4 warp; 7 bending; 9 deflexion, deviation, diversion

defloration: 5 abuse; 10 defilement

deflower: 3 mar; 5 spoil; 6 impair; 7 vitiate

defoliate: 3 mew; 4 molt; 8 deforest; 9 disforest, exfoliate; 10 defoliated; 11 disafforest

deforest: 9 defoliate, disforest; 11 disafforest

deform: 4 bend; 5 twist, wring; 6 deface, strain; 7 contort, distort; 8 misshape, mutilate, truncate; 9 disfigure

defraud: 2 do; 3 con, gyp, nab; 4 bilk, bite, rook, scam; 5 bunco, cheat, cozen, mulct, pluck; 6 chouse, diddle, euchre, jockey, nobble; 7 swindle; 9 victimize

defrauded: 6 bilked; 7 cheated, diddled, euchred, plucked; 8 swindled; 10 victimized

defray: 3 pay; 11 make payment

defrost: 5 deice

deft: 3 apt; 4 gain; 5 handy, quick, ready; 6 adroit, expert, facile; 8 dextrous; 9 dexterous

defunct: 4 dead; 7 demised, extinct; 8 deceased, departed

defunctness: 10 extinction

defuse: 10 deactivate

defy: 4 dare, hold; 5 rebel; 6 hold up, refuse, resist; 9 withstand, challenge

degauss: 11 demagnetize

degeneracy: 9 decadence, depravity; 10 corruption

degenerate: 3 rot; 4 drop, fast; 5 decay; 6 worsen; 7 decline, degrade, deviant, deviate, fall off, pervert, riotous; 8 degraded; 9 debauched, dissolute, libertine; 10 dissipated, profligate; 11 become worse, deteriorate

degenerative: 11 progressive

degenerative arthritis: 14 osteoarthritis

deglutition: 5 drink; 7 swallow

degradation: 5 decay; 6 laxity; 7 decline; 8 baseness, decaying, foulness, trimming, vileness; 9 abasement, abjection, declining, degrading, shuffling, turpitude, worsening; 10 corrupting, corruption, debasement; 11 depravation, depravement; 12 degenerating, degeneration, demoralizing

degrade: 3 rot; 5 decay; 6 debase, defile, demean; 7 cheapen, decline, put down; 8 disgrace; 10 degenerate; 11 deteriorate

degraded: 4 fast; 7 debased, decayed, riotous; 8 devalued; 9 debauched, dissolute, libertine; 10 degenerate, dissipated, profligate

degree: 5 grade, level, point, stage; 6 extent; 8 strength; 9 arcdegree, intensity, sheepskin

dehiscence: 7 yawning; 9 splitting

dehumanized: 7 unhuman; 11 dehumanised

dehydrate: 5 dry up; 8 desicate; 9 desiccate, dessicate

deice: 7 defrost

deification: 10 apotheosis, exaltation

deify: 5 exalt; 8 enthrone; 9 signalize; 11 immortalize

deign: 7 descend; 9 vouchsafe; 10 condescend

deism: 11 free thought

Deism: 6 Theism

deity: 3 god; 7 goddess; 8 divinity, immortal, pagan god

deject: 4 damp, dash, dull, sink; 5 lower, unman; 6 dismay; 7 depress, get down; 8 cast down, dispirit; 9 knock down, prostrate; 10 demoralize

dejected: 4 dark; 6 dismal, gloomy, somber, triste [Fr]; 7 joyless; 8 frowning; 9 cheerless, saturnine; 10 lugubrious, spiritless, uncheerful

dejection: 5 blues, dumps; 7 sadness; 8 darkness, doldrums, the blues, the dumps; 9 dejection, heaviness; 10 bad spirits, blue devils, depression, dismalness, gloominess, low spirits, melancholy, somberness; 11 joylessness, melancholia

dejeuner: 5 lunch

de jure: 4 duly; 7 legally; 8 lawfully

deka: 4 deca

delapidate: 5 decay; 7 crumble

Delaware: 10 First State; 12 Diamond State; 13 Delaware River

delay: 4 hold, stay, wait; 5 defer; 6 detain, hold up, holdup, put off; 7 hold off, time lag; 8 delation, delaying, postpone; 9 detention; 10 cunctation; 12 postponement

delectability: 9 good taste, tastiness; 10 savoriness; 12 enjoyability, lusciousness, pleasantness

delectable: 4 good, nice; 5 tasty, yummy; 6 dainty, savory; 8 luscious; 9 delicious, palatable, toothsome; 10 well-tasted; 11 scrumptious

delection: 3 joy; 4 glee; 7 delight; 8 gladness; 9 enjoyment; 11 delectation

delegate: 5 agent, proxy; 6 assign, charge, depute, deputy, pass on; 7 consign, entrust, forward, intrust; 8 hand over, relegate; 9 designate, go-between, middleman, secondary, surrogate; 10 commission, next friend, substitute, turn over to

delegating: 5 trust; 9 assigning; 10 assignment, commission, delegation, deputation, deputizing, entrusting, relegating, relegation; 11 consignment; 12 commisioning

delegation: 5 trust; 7 mission; 8 delegacy; 9 assigning; 10 assignment, commission, delegating, deputation, deputizing, entrusting, relegating, relegation; **11** consignment; **12** commisioning

delete: 5 erase; **6** cancel; **10** blue-pencil

deleterious: 6 septic; **7** baleful, baneful, harmful, hurtful, noxious; **8** mephitic; **9** injurious; **10** pernicious; **11** detrimental, mischievous

deleteriously: 5 badly; **9** harmfully; **11** injuriously, malignantly; **12** perniciously

deletion: 3 cut; **4** blot; **7** elision; **8** ellipsis, omission

deli: 8 food shop; **12** delicatessen

deliberate: 4 calm, moot; **5** meant, quiet; **6** debate, wilful; **7** advised, careful, express, knowing, studied, willful; **8** cogitate, consider, intended, measured, meditate, turn over; **10** calculated; **11** determinate, intentional, undisturbed

deliberately: 6 slowly; **8** by choice, by design; **9** advisedly, expressly, gradually, knowingly, leisurely, on purpose, purposely, wittingly; **10** designedly, measuredly, with design, with intent; **11** in cold blood, unhurriedly; **12** purposefully; **13** intentionally; **14** premeditatedly

deliberation: 4 heed; **5** study; **7** caution, comment; **8** coolness, prudence, slowness, weighing; **9** pondering; **10** advisement, conference, discretion, discussion, pourparler, steadiness; **11** calculation, heedfulness, lucubration, speculation; **12** cautiousness

delicacies: 6 dainty; **8** dainties, delicacy

delicacy: 4 gust, tact; **5** demur, goody, gusto, qualm, treat; **6** dainty, nicety, sprain, strain, tidbit; **7** decency, decorum, finesse, scruple; **8** airiness, dainties, fineness, kickshaw; **9** diplomacy, fragility, punctilio; **10** daintiness, delicacies, discretion, refinement, slightness; **11** awkwardness, decrepitude, fine feeling, tasty morsel; **12** discreetness, invalidation

delicate: 4 fine, nice, pure, rich, soft, weak; **5** filmy, frail, picky, silky, spare, sweet; **6** dainty, decent, mellow, modest, pastel, pearly, satiny, tender; **7** curious, finical, finicky, fragile, refined, subtile; **8** critical, decorous, finespun, luscious, ticklish; **9** ambrosial, delicious, exquisite, gossamery, sensitive, undefiled; **10** appetizing, delightful, fastidious, harmonious, particular; **11** incapacious, scrumptious

delicatessen: 4 deli; **8** food shop

delicious: 4 good, nice; **5** tasty, yummy; **6** dainty, savory; **8** delicate, luscious; **9** palatable, toothsome; **10** delectable, delightful, well-tasted; **11** scrumptious

delight: 3 joy; **4** glee; **5** charm, enjoy, revel; **6** please, ravish; **7** enchant, enthral; **8** enthrall, gladness, pleasure; **9** enjoyment, enrapture, transport; **11** delectation; **12** give pleasure; **13** cause pleasure, offer pleasure, yield pleasure

delighted: 6 elated; **7** charmed, flushed, pleased; **8** beguiled, thrilled; **9** enchanted, entranced; **10** captivated, enraptured, enthralled; **11** tickled pink

delightful: 4 rich; **8** delicate, empyrean, luscious; **9** ambrosial, delicious, exquisite, heartfelt, rapturous, ravishing, thrilling; **10** appetizing, felicitous; **11** scrumptious

Delilah: 9 temptress; **11** enchantress, femme fatale

delimit: 6 define; **7** specify, subtend; **9** delineate, demarcate

delimitation: 6 border; **8** boundary; **10** borderline;

delimited: 7 bounded; **13** circumscribed

delineate: 4 draw, limn, line; **5** trace; **6** define; **7** delimit, outline, picture, specify; **8** describe; **9** represent; **10** delimitate, delineated

delineation: 7 limning, picture; **9** depiction, portrayal; **11** line drawing, particulars, visualizing, word picture

delinquency: 11 dereliction; **14** willful neglect; **19** juvenile delinquency

delinquent: 3 due; **4** thug; **5** crook, owing; **6** remiss, unpaid; **7** overdue, past due; **8** derelict; **10** neglectful; **11** outstanding

delirious: 3 mad; **4** wild; **5** giddy, moody, rabid; **6** doting, raving; **7** berserk, excited, frantic; **8** frenetic, frenzied, rambling, unhinged, wild-eyed; **9** insensate, possessed, wandering; **10** incoherent, reasonless

delirium: 4 fury; **5** craze; **6** frenzy, raving; **7** madness; **8** hysteria

deliver: 3 say; **4** bear, cede, give, hand, have, pass, save; **5** birth, get in, mouth, utter; **6** birthe, deport, give up, redeem, render, rescue, return, turn in; **7** present, relieve; **8** announce, aspirate, hand over, make over, pass over, turn over; **9** enunciate, extradite, extricate, give birth, pronounce, surrender; **10** accentuate, articulate; **11** deliver over

deliverance: 6 rescue, saving; **8** delivery; **9** salvation; **11** extrication

deliver a speech: 4 talk; **5** orate, speak; **7** lecture; **9** give a talk

delivered: 5 given, saved; **7** rescued; **10** extricated, handed over

deliverer: 6 savior; **7** rescuer, saviour

delivering: 6 giving; **11** handing over

delivery: 3 say; **5** labor, pitch; **6** livery, rescue, saving, sermon, speech, tirade; **7** travail; **8** bringing, harangue; **10** birth-throe, childbirth, peroration, recitation; **11** confinement, deliverance, parturition

dell: 4 dale, glen, vale; **5** glade, grove; **6** bottom, dingle, valley

Delonix: 12 genus Delonix
Delonix regia: 9 flame tree; 10 flamboyant; 13 peacock flower
Delphic: 8 Delphian, oracular
Delphic oracle: 6 Sphinx; 14 Oracle of Apollo, oracle of Delphi, Temple of Apollo
Delphinapterus: 6 beluga; 10 white whale; 19 genus Delphinapterus
Delphinus: 7 dolphin; 14 genus Delphinus
delude: 4 lure; 5 cozen, decoy; 6 lead on; 7 beguile, deceive; 8 inveigle
deluded: 6 misled; 7 misguided
deluge: 4 rush, slop; 5 flood, swamp, swash; 6 dabble, drench, soaker, splash, stream; 7 slobber, torrent; 8 downpour, flood out, flow over, inundate, irrigate, overflow, submerge; 9 cataclysm, overwhelm, surcharge; 10 cloudburst, inundation
delusion: 8 illusion; 13 hallucination
delusive: 5 false; 8 delusory; 9 deceptive
deluxe: 4 luxe; 6 gilded, luxury; 7 opulent; 8 princely; 9 luxurious, sumptuous
delve: 3 dig, hoe; 4 plow, rake; 6 dibble, harrow, plough; 7 cut into; 8 excavate, turn over
delve into: 7 dip into; 8 dive into; 9 discourse, hold forth; 10 go deep into
demagnetize: 7 degauss
demagogue: 7 demagog; 12 rabble-rouser
demand: 3 ask; 4 need, take; 5 claim, exact, right, title; 6 charge, damage, estate, insist; 7 call for, holding, involve, require; 8 exaction, question; 10 imposition, insistence; 11 necessitate, reclamation, requirement, requisition
demanding: 6 strict; 7 austere, exigent, precise; 8 exacting, obdurate, rigorous; 9 hard-nosed, hard-shell [U.S.], insistent, searching, unsparing; 10 hard-headed, inexorable, inflexible, meticulous, overstrict, particular; 11 punctilious
demarcate: 7 delimit
demarcation: 4 line; 5 limit; 8 contrast; 12 dividing line
demarche: 8 maneuver
demasculinize: 8 castrate; 10 emasculate
demean: 7 degrade, put down; 8 disgrace
demeaning: 8 humbling; 9 degrading; 10 mortifying; 11 humiliating
demeanor: 3 air; 4 cast, look, mien, port; 5 color, guise; 6 manner; 7 bearing, conduct; 8 behavior, carriage; 9 behaviour, demeanour; 10 complexion, deportment
demented: 3 mad; 4 daft, loco, nuts, sick; 5 batty, crazy, dotty, loony, nutty; 6 crazed, fruity, insane; 7 bonkers, cracked, far gone, lunatic, touched; 8 deranged, maddened, not right, unhinged; 9 brainsick, disturbed; 10 distracted, moonstruck, unbalanced,

upper story; 12 crazy as a loon, mad as a hatter; 13 of unsound mind, out of one's mind, out of one's wits
dementia: 7 madness; 8 insanity
dementia praecox: 13 schizophrenia
demerit: 5 fault; 6 defect
Demerol: 10 meperidine
demesne: 4 land, park; 5 acres, honor, manor, realm; 6 domain, estate, garden; 12 landed estate
demi-: 4 hemi-, semi-
demiglace: 9 demi-glaze
demigod: 4 hero; 5 angel; 6 daemon, seraph; 7 heroine; 8 superman
demilitarize: 6 disarm; 12 demilitarise
demirep: 3 rig; 4 drab, jade, minx, skit, slut; 5 hussy, wench; 7 baggage, trollop; 8 harridan, slattern
demised: 3 die; 7 defunct, extinct; 8 decease
demisemiquaver: 16 thirty-second note
demission: 6 bounce [U.S.]; 7 ousting, removal; 9 dismissal; 11 resignation, abdictation
demitasse: 8 cafe noir, small cup
demivolt: 8 capriole
demo: 4 show; 7 exhibit, present; 11 demonstrate; 13 demonstration
demobilize: 5 demob; 10 demobilise
democracy: 8 republic, dominion
Democratic Party: 9 Democrats
demode: 5 passe; 6 old-hat, passee; 7 antique; 8 outmoded; 12 old-fashioned
demodulator: 8 detector
demographer: 12 demographist
demography: 12 human ecology
demoiselle: 6 damsel; 7 damosel, damozel; 10 damoiselle, damselfish
demolish: 4 raze; 7 destroy; 8 tear down; 9 sacrifice, dismantle
demolishing: 6 razing; 8 leveling; 11 tearing down
demolition: 11 destruction
demon: 4 fury, ogre; 5 devil, fiend; 6 daemon, daimon; 7 monster
demoniac: 4 amok; 5 amuck; 7 berserk; 9 possessed; 10 demoniacal
demonic: 6 impish, unholy; 7 hellish, satanic; 8 diabolic, fiendish, infernal; 9 demonical; 10 demoniacal, diabolical
demonism: 8 Satanism; 9 diabolism; 10 demonology, witchcraft; 11 devil-worship
demonstrable: 7 proving, showing; 8 provable; 13 demonstrating, demonstrative
demonstrate: 4 demo, shew, show, tell; 5 march, prove; 6 attest, expose; 7 certify, exhibit, present; 8 evidence, manifest; 9 ascertain, establish; 10 illustrate
demonstrating: 7 proving, showing; 10 exposition, presenting; 11 manifesting; 12 demonstrable, illustrating, illustration
demonstration: 4 demo; 5 proof, rally; 7 showing; 9 probation; 10 exposition, pre-

senting; **11** manifesting, presentment; **12** flying colors, illustrating, illustration, logical proof, presentation, protest rally, verification

demonstrative: 4 wild; **5** clear, fiery; **6** fierce, madcap; **7** deictic, excited, furious, notable, proving, salient, showing, violent; **8** apparent, manifest, vehement; **9** prominent; **10** indicative, indicatory; **11** impassioned; **12** demonstrable, illustrative

demonstrator: 9 protester

demoralization: 9 degrading, obliquity, pollution; **10** corrupting, corruption; **11** backsliding, degradation, depravation, depravement

demoralize: 6 debase, deject, dismay; **7** corrupt, debauch, deprave, depress, get down, pervert, profane, vitiate; **8** cast down, dispirit; **9** brutalize, misdirect; **10** prostitute

demoralized: 6 amoral, done up; **7** corrupt; **8** deadbeat, depraved, perverse; **9** exhausted, shattered; **11** discouraged; **12** disheartened

demoralizing: 9 degrading; **10** corrupting, corruption; **11** degradation, depravation, depravement, dispiriting; **12** demoralising

demote: 4 bump; **5** break; **8** relegate

demulcent: 8 soothing, relaxant; **9** emollient

demur: 4 trim; **5** pause, qualm; **6** coquet, dacker, debate, except, waffle; **7** balance, dissent, scruple, shuffle; **8** delicacy, demurral, demurrer, disagree, straddle, suspense; **9** fluctuate, hem and haw, hum and haw; **10** indecision; **12** be on the fence, irresolution, remain neuter; **13** remain neutral

demure: 3 coy; **4** prim, smug; **5** pause, qualm; **6** modest, sedate; **7** prudish, scruple, stick at; **8** hesitate, priggish, reserved

den: 3 sty; **4** cave, lair; **6** pigsty; **7** hideout; **8** hideaway

denaturalized: 7 debased; **9** denatured

Dendranthema: 3 mum; **21** florist's chrysanthemum; **17** genus Dendranthema

dendriform: 8 arboreal, branched, tree-like, treelike; **9** arboreous, branching, dendritic

Dendrocalamus giganteus: 8 kyo-chiku; **11** giant bamboo

Dendroica: 7 warbler; **14** genus Dendroica

Dendroid: 8 arboreal, branched, tree-like, treelike; **9** arboreous, branching, dendritic

Dendrolagus: 16 genus Dendrolagus

dengue: 10 dandy fever; **11** dengue fever; **14** breakbone fever

Den Haag: 8 The Hague; **11** 's Gravenhage; **12** Dutch capital; **23** capital of The Netherlands

denial: 7 defense; **8** negation; **9** disavowel; **10** abnegation, self-denial

denigrate: 5 decry, smear, sully; **6** defame, smirch; **7** asperse, blacken, detract, slander; **8** belittle, besmirch, derogate, minimize; **9** deprecate, disparage; **10** calumniate, depreciate

denim: 4 jean; **8** blue jean, dungaree

Denisonia: 14 genus Denisonia

Denisonia superba: 10 copperhead

denizen: 7 dweller; **10** inhabitant

denominate: 3 dub; **4** call, name, term; **5** style; **7** entitle; **9** designate

denomination: 4 name; **5** stamp, title; **6** manner, rubric; **9** character, communion; **11** appellation, appellative, description, designation, predicament

denominational: 8 partisan; **9** sectarian

denominator: 7 divisor

denotating: 8 symbolic; **10** indicating, signifying; **12** representing

denotation: 9 extension, reference

denote: 5 refer; **6** select; **7** betoken, refer to, signify; **8** announce, indicate, point out, stand for; **9** represent, symbolize

denouement: 5 issue; **6** finale, finish, upshot; **9** end result, winding up; **10** conclusion, end product, wrapping up; **11** culmination, final result

denounce: 3 rat; **4** mark, shop, stag; **5** brand; **6** betray, snitch, tell on; **7** impeach; **8** give away; **9** fulminate, proscribe; **10** stigmatize

de novo: 4 anew; **9** over again

dense: 4 dark, dull, dumb, slow; **5** heavy, muddy, solid, thick; **6** obtuse, opaque; **7** compact, cryptic, obscure, serried; **8** nebulous; **9** difficult; **10** mysterious; **11** close-packed

densely: 6 dumbly; **7** closely, thickly; **8** obtusely

denseness: 7 density; **8** dumbness; **11** compactness

density: 7 latency; **9** denseness, obscurity; **10** difficulty; **11** compactness; **13** concentration

dent: 3 cut; **4** dint, nick, slit; **5** gouge, notch, prick, sinus, stamp; **6** dimple, indent, lacuna; **7** impress, scratch; **8** follicle, incision; **11** indentation

dental caries: 6 caries, cavity; **10** tooth decay

Dentaria: 9 coralroot, coralwort, toothwort; **10** pepper root; **11** crinkle root, crinkleroot; **13** genus Dentaria

dentate: 6 toothy; **7** toothed; **8** dentated

dented: 4 bent; **6** jagged, nicked; **7** notched; **8** crumpled, indented

denticulate: 6 toothy; **7** dentate, toothed; **8** dentated

dentifrice: 10 toothpaste

dentin: 7 dentine

denude: 4 bare; **5** strip; **8** denudate

denuded: 4 bald, bare; **5** minus; **6** bereft, cut off; **8** bereaved, denudate

denumerable: 9 countable, numerable; **10** enumerable

denunciation: 5 abuse; 11 fulmination; 12 denouncement, vilification, vituperation

denunciatory: 7 abusive; 9 clamorous, 10 imputative

deny: 6 negate, refuse, reject; 7 decline, dismiss; 8 traverse, turn down

deontology: 6 ethics; 8 ethology

deoxyribonucleic acid: 3 DNA; 15 genetic material

depart: 2 go; 4 part, quit, vary; 5 leave, start, stray; 6 go away, set off, set out; 7 deviate, digress, diverge, take off; 8 set forth, start out, straggle; 9 sidetrack, take leave

departed: 4 away, gone, lost; 5 stiff; 6 asleep, at rest, bygone, bypast; 7 at peace, dead man, defunct, demised, extinct; 8 dead soul, deceased, decedent, foregone, vanished; 9 exhausted; 10 dead person

departing: 7 leaving, outward; 8 outbound

department: 3 orb; 5 field; 6 bureau, sphere; 7 lookout, section; 8 province

department store: 8 emporium; 10 five and ten; 12 general store

departure: 4 exit, fall, loss, obit, rest; 5 going; 7 leaving, passing, quietus, release; 9 deviation, going away; 10 decampment, difference, divergence, expiration

depend: 4 hang, rely; 5 droop, swing; 6 dangle; 8 depend on

dependable: 4 good, safe, true; 6 honest, secure; 8 credible, reliable; 10 rock-steady; 11 steady-going, trustworthy

dependence: 4 need; 9 addiction; 10 dependance, dependency

dependent: 6 hooked; 7 subject; 8 addicted; 9 dependant, qualified, strung-out; 10 contingent; 11 conditional, conditioned, subordinate

depend on: 5 bet on; 6 depend, look to, rely on, ride on, turn on; 7 count on, hinge on; 8 reckon on, rely upon; 9 count upon, devolve on, hinge upon

depict: 4 draw, limn, show; 7 picture, portray; 8 describe

deplete: 3 eat; 5 drain, eat up, spend, use up; 6 expend, run out; 7 consume, exhaust, wipe out

depleted: 3 low; 6 used up; 7 drained; 8 consumed, expended, finished; 9 exhausted, tapped out

deplorable: 3 sad; 4 dire; 5 sorry; 6 rueful, woeful; 7 pitiful; 8 criminal, grievous, mournful, pitiable, wretched; 9 execrable, miserable; 10 lamentable

deplore: 6 bemoan, bewail, grieve, lament, regret

deploy: 7 arrange

depone: 3 vow; 5 swear; 6 depose; 7 testify

deponent: 9 testifier

deport: 4 bear; 5 carry, exile; 6 acquit,

behave; 7 comport, conduct, deliver; 8 relegate; 9 extradite, surrender; 10 expatriate

deportation: 5 exile; 12 expatriation

deportee: 5 exile

deportment: 7 conduct; 8 behavior, demeanor; 9 behaviour, demeanour; 11 comportment

depose: 3 vow; 5 swear; 6 depone, affirm, assert; 7 testify, witness; 8 dethrone, force out, vouch for; 11 bear witness, give witness; 12 give evidence

deposit: 3 fix; 4 bank, pose; 5 lodge, posit, stick, wedge; 6 cohere; 7 earnest, handsel, lay down, situate; 8 sediment

deposition: 7 deposal, deposit; 9 affidavit; 10 abdication, reposition, usurpation; 11 attestation

depository: 5 cache, depot, store; 7 deposit; 9 repertory; 10 repository

depot: 5 cache, store; 7 station, storage; 8 terminal, terminus; 9 repertory; 10 depository, repository, storehouse

deprave: 6 debase; 7 corrupt, debauch, degrade, pervert, profane, vitiate; 9 misdirect; 10 demoralize

depraved: 4 evil, vile; 5 wrong; 6 amoral, sinful, wicked; 7 corrupt, immoral, vicious; 8 perverse; 9 debauched, perverted, reprobate; 10 deflowered, iniquitous; 11 unrighteous

depravity: 6 infamy; 8 atrocity; 9 flagrancy, turpitude; 10 corruption, degeneracy; 11 viciousness

deprecate: 5 cut up, decry; 7 detract, protest; 8 belittle, derogate; 9 denigrate, disparage; 10 depreciate, speak ill of; 11 expostulate, remonstrate

deprecating: 9 slighting; 10 belittling

depreciate: 5 cut up, decry; 7 detract, devalue; 8 belittle, derogate; 9 denigrate, deprecate, devaluate, disparage; 10 speak ill of, undervalue; 13 find fault with; 14 not speak well of

depreciated: 9 half-price, unsalable; 12 depreciating, undervaluing; 15 underestimating

depreciation: 5 blame; 6 reflux; 7 censure, obloquy; 8 discount, mark down; 9 abatement, allowance, criticism, decrement, dispraise, reduction; 10 belittling, concession, derogation, detraction

depreciative: 9 slighting; 10 belittling; 11 deprecating, deprecative, deprecatory; 12 depreciating, depreciatory

depreciator: 7 knocker; 9 detractor; 10 disparager

depredation: 4 raid; 5 foray; 6 ravage; 7 plunder, preying; 9 predation

depredator: 7 spoiler; 8 marauder, pillager

depress: 4 damp; 5 lower; 6 deject, dismay, hollow; 7 get down, let down; 8 cast down, dispirit, take down; **9** press down; **10** demoralize

depressant: 6 downer; **8** sedative

depressed: 3 low; **4** blue, down; **7** concave; **8** downcast, indented; **10** dispirited

depressing: 4 blue, dark, grim; **6** dismal, gloomy; **8** dropping, lowering; **9** saddening; **10** depressive; **11** dispiriting; **12** disconsolate

depression: 3 dip, low; **5** blues, dumps, slump; **7** imprint, sadness; **8** darkness, doldrums, the blues, the dumps; **9** concavity, dejection, heaviness; **10** bad spirits, blue devils, debasement, dismalness, gloominess, impression, low spirits, melancholy, somberness; **11** joylessness, low pressure, melancholia, prostration

depressurize: 10 decompress

deprivation: 4 loss, want; **9** privation

deprive: 5 strip; **6** divest; **10** dispossess, impoverish

depth: 7 caliber; **8** deepness, solidity, subtlety; **10** astuteness, profundity

depth of water: 9 soundings

deputation: 5 trust; **7** mission; **8** delegacy; **9** assigning; **10** assignment, commission, delegating, delegation, deputizing, entrusting, relegating, relegating

deputize: 6 depute, step in; **7** stand in; **8** deputise; **10** substitute

deputizing: 5 trust; **9** assigning; **10** assignment, commission, delegating, delegation, deputation, entrusting; **11** consignment

deracinate: 6 pull up, uproot; **7** root out; **8** displace

derange: 5 mix up; **7** perturb; **8** disorder; **9** unbalance; **10** disarrange

deranged: 3 mad; **4** daft, loco, nuts; **5** batty, crazy, dotty, loony, nutty; **6** crazed, fruity, insane; **7** bonkers, cracked, far gone, lunatic, touched; **8** demented, maddened, not right; **10** half-crazed, moonstruck, upper story; **12** crazy as a loon, mad as a hatter

derby: 6 bowler; **7** plug hat; **9** bowler hat

derelict: 6 remiss; **7** cast off, outcast; **10** delinquent, neglectful; **13** abandoned ship

dereliction: 7 neglect; **11** delinquency

Der Fuhrer: 6 Hitler; **11** Adolf Hitler

deride: 4 gibe, gird, hiss, hoot, jeer, mock, twit; **5** taunt; **7** barrack, laugh at, snigger; **8** ridicule

derisive: 4 rude; **7** jeering, mocking; **8** derisory, gibelike, taunting; **9** sarcastic

derivation: 4 form; **7** lineage, variant; **8** ancestry, deriving, revision; **9** etymology, expansion, extension, filiation, precedent, variation; **10** antecedent

derive: 4 come, draw, gain, ween; **5** educe, infer; **6** deduce, deduct, gather; **7** collect, descend

derma: 6 corium, dermis

Dermacentor: 4 tick; **16** genus Dermacentor

dermal: 5 scaly; **6** dermic, skinny; **8** cortical, squamous [Anat]; **9** cutaneous, cuticular, epidermal, epidermic

dermatologist: 10 skin doctor

dermis: 5 cutis, derma; **6** corium

Dermochelys coriacea: 11 leatherback; **14** leathery turtle; **17** leatherback turtle

derogate: 5 decry, sneak, stoop; **6** grovel; **7** detract; **8** belittle, minimize; **9** denigrate, deprecate, disparage; **10** depreciate

derogatory: 9 degrading, insulting, slighting; **10** belittling, derogative, detracting, detractive, pejorative; **11** deprecatory, disparaging, dyslogistic

derrick: 5 crane

derriere: 4 buns, butt, prat, rear, rump, seat, tail, tush; **5** fanny, stern; **6** behind, bottom; **7** hind end, keister, rear end, tail end, tooshie; **8** backside, buttocks; **9** fundament, posterior

derris root: 8 tuba root

desalt: 10 desalinate, desalinize

descant: 5 yodel; **6** dilate, warble; **7** amplify, discant, enlarge, inflate; **8** run out on; **9** expatiate

Descartes: 13 Rene Descartes

descend: 4 come, fall; **5** deign, stoop; **6** derive, go down; **8** come down; **10** condescend

descendent: 4 heir; **5** scion; **10** descendant

descending: 7 descent; **9** going down; **10** declension; **11** declination

descent: 4 fall, line, stem; **5** birth, blood, stock; **6** origin, stirps, strain; **7** decline, lineage; **8** ancestry, heritage, pedigree; **9** bloodline, declivity, downslope, filiation, genealogy, going down, parentage; **10** declension, descending, extraction, inheriting; **11** declination, inheritance

describe: 3 key; **4** draw, line, name; **5** trace; **6** depict, key out, report; **7** outline; **8** discover, identify; **9** delineate; **11** distinguish

description: 5 stamp; **6** manner, report, rubric; **7** account; **9** character, statement; **11** designation, predicament; **12** denomination

descry: 3 ken, see, spy; **4** espy, spot; **5** sight; **6** reveal; **7** discern, make out, observe; **8** discover, perceive

desecrate: 5 abuse; **7** outrage, profane, violate; **8** dishonor; **9** blaspheme; **10** prostitute

desecration: 9 blasphemy, sacrilege; **11** profanation

desegregate: 3 mix; **9** integrate

desert: 3 rat; **4** wild; **5** elope, lurch, merit, waste, worth; **6** credit, defect, go over; **7** abandon, forsake; **8** abnegate, desolate

desert boot: 6 buskin; **7** top boot; **8** half boot; **10** chukka boot, combat boot

deserted: 4 left; **7** forlorn, given up; **8** desolate, forsaken; **9** abandoned, unpeopled; **10** tenantless, untenanted; **11** uninhabited

deserter: 4 AWOL; **8** apostate, defector, recreant, renegade

desertful: 6 worthy; **9** deserving; **11** meritorious

desertion: 9 defection, forsaking, going over; **10** withdrawal; **11** abandonment

desert lynx: 7 caracal

desert plant: 9 xerophile, xerophyte

deserve: 4 rate; **5** merit; **10** be worthy of

deserved: 3 due; **5** due to; **7** condign, merited

deserving: 5 worth; **6** worthy; **8** meriting, worthy of; **11** meritorious

desex: 3 fix; **5** unsex; **9** sterilize; **11** desexualize

desicate: 5 dry up; **9** dehydrate, dessicate

desiccant: 11 drying agent

desiccate: 4 arid; **9** dehydrate; **10** desiccated

design: 3 aim; **4** mean, plan; **5** frame; **6** figure, intend, intent, scheme; **7** arrange, pattern, project, purpose; **8** ambition, contrive; **9** blueprint, designing, intention, invention; **10** conception, innovation

designate: 3 dub; **4** call, doom, fate, name, term; **5** style; **6** assign, depute, intend; **7** destine, entitle, realize, specify; **8** delegate; **9** determine; **10** denominate, specialize

designation: 4 name; **5** stamp, title; **6** manner, naming, return, rubric; **9** character; **10** assignment, nomination; **11** appellation, appellative, appointment, description, predicament

designedly: 8 by choice, by design; **9** advisedly, expressly, knowingly, on purpose, purposely, wittingly; **10** with design, with intent; **12** purposefully

designer: 6 artist, drawer, limner; **7** painter; **8** engraver, promoter, sketcher; **9** architect, couturier, decorator, projector

designing: 6 design; **8** scheming; **10** contriving, intriguing; **11** maneuvering

desirable: 6 worthy; **8** suitable; **9** advisable

desire: 4 hope, want, wish; **5** trust

desired: 6 craved, wanted, wished; **7** coveted; **8** in demand; **11** sought after

desist: 4 halt, stop; **5** cease; **7** abstain, refrain; **11** cease acting

desk clerk: 10 hotel clerk

desktop: 10 background; **16** screen background

Des Moines: 13 capital of Iowa

desolate: 4 bare, gone, lorn; **5** bleak, lurch, stark, waste; **6** barren, desert, dreary, ravage, ruined, wasted; **7** abandon, blasted, forlorn, forsake, ravaged; **8** deserted, hopeless, lay waste; **9** abandoned, desolated,

desperate, devastate, in despair, unpeopled; **10** depopulate, despairing, devastated, lay waste to, tenantless, untenanted

desolated: 6 ruined, wasted; **7** blasted, ravaged; **8** desolate; **10** devastated

desolation: 4 ruin; **6** misery; **9** bleakness, cataclysm, withering; **10** desolating, loneliness; **11** abandonment, devastation, forlornness, tribulation

desoxyribonucleic acid: 3 DNA

despair: 11 desperation

despairing: 4 gone; **7** forlorn; **8** desolate, hopeless; **9** desperate

despatch: 6 report; **7** send off; **8** alacrity, dispatch, shipment; **10** communique, expedition, promptness

desperado: 4 hood; **5** brute, bully, rough, rowdy, tough; **6** bandit, mugger, wretch; **7** caitiff, hoodlum, pug-ugly [U.S.], ruffian; **8** criminal, hooligan, plug-ugly; **9** barbarian

desperate: 4 dire, gone, rank; **6** heroic, red-hot; **7** do-or-die, forlorn; **8** desolate, hopeless; **9** in despair

desperation: 5 burst, storm; **6** raving; **7** despair, madness; **8** delirium, paroxysm; **9** explosion; **11** distraction

despicable: 4 ugly, vile; **8** unworthy; **12** contemptible

despise: 5 scorn; **7** contemn, disdain

despised: 5 hated; **7** scorned; **8** detested; **9** disdained

despite: 5 spite; **6** animus, malice; **8** contempt; **10** act of spite

despoil: 3 gut, mar; **4** loot, rape, sack; **5** foray, reave, rifle, shear, spoil, strip, sweep, waste; **6** fleece, ravage; **7** pillage, plunder, ransack, violate

despoiler: 6 looter, raider; **7** spoiler; **8** pillager; **9** plunderer; **10** freebooter

Despoina: 4 Cora, Kore; **10** Persephone

despondency: 4 sink; **5** droop; **6** take on; **7** despond, give way; **9** lose heart

despondent: 8 overcome; **9** heartsick; **10** desponding

despot: 6 tyrant; **8** autocrat, dictator, martinet, stickler; **9** oppressor, strong man

despotic: 10 autocratic, despotical, tyrannical; **11** dictatorial; **13** authoritarian

despotism: 7 tyranny; **9** autocracy, Caesarism, monocracy, shogunate, Stalinism; **10** absolutism, one-man rule; **12** dictatorship

desquamate: 7 peel off

dessert: 5 sweet

dessicate: 8 desicate

destinate: 7 destine

destination: 4 goal; **6** object; **7** address; **8** goalpost, terminus; **9** objective; **11** journey's end; **12** arrival point

destine: 4 doom, fate; **6** devote, intend; **7** specify; **8** foredoom; **9** designate

destined: 5 bound, fated; 11 preordained; 12 foreordained

destiny: 3 lot; 4 fate, luck; 6 kismet; 7 fortune, portion

destitute: 5 needy; 8 indigent; 9 penniless; 12 impoverished

destitution: 4 lack, need, want; 6 penury; 7 poverty; 8 distress; 9 indigence, necessity, neediness, pauperism, privation

destrier: 7 charger; 8 war horse

destroy: 4 ruin; 8 demolish

destroying angel: 8 death cap, death cup; 10 death angel

destruction: 3 end; 5 death, waste; 10 demolition, destroying; 11 devastation

destructive: 7 ruinous; 10 subversive; 11 devastating

desuetude: 6 disuse

desultory: 5 loose; 6 fitful; 7 devious, epicene, sluggish; 9 irregular, spasmodic, uncertain

detach: 4 part; 6 cut off; 7 come off, divorce, fall off, peel off, pull off, tear off; 8 come away, get loose; 9 come loose

detached: 3 lax; 4 free; 5 aloof, baggy, loose, slack; 6 degage, remote; 7 relaxed; 8 flapping, isolated, set-apart; 9 disjoined, segregate, separated, streaming, withdrawn; 10 uninvolved

detachment: 4 army, host, wing; 5 corps, squad; 6 column, parcel; 7 battery, breakup, brigade, company, platoon, section; 8 division, garrison, regiment, squadron; 9 battalion, detaching; 10 insularism, insularity, insulation, separation, withdrawal; 11 segregating, segregation, subdivision

detail: 4 cast, item, mete; 5 point, share; 6 billet, factor; 10 contingent, particular

detailed: 7 graphic; 9 elaborate, well-drawn; 10 elaborated, particular

details: 5 items; 6 counts; 8 small fry; 11 particulars

detain: 4 stay; 5 delay; 6 hold up, secure; 7 confine; 9 keep close

detained: 9 in custody; 11 in detention, in the lockup

detainee: 3 POW; 6 inmate; 7 captive, hostage; 8 prisoner

detect: 4 find; 6 notice; 7 observe; 8 discover

detectable: 10 noticeable; 11 appreciable, perceptible

detected: 5 found; 8 found out; 10 discovered

detection: 4 find; 6 espial, spying; 7 sensing; 8 catching, spotting; 9 detecting, discovery, sleuthing

detective: 2 PI; 3 tec; 6 sleuth; 10 private eye; 12 investigator

detective work: 9 detecting, detection, sleuthing

detector: 6 sensor

detention: 4 hold, keep; 5 delay; 6 arrest, having, holdup; 7 custody, holding; 11 confinement; 12 apprehension

detention cell: 7 bullpen

detenu: 3 POW; 6 inmate; 7 captive, hostage; 8 abductee, detainee, prisoner

deter: 3 cow; 5 abash, daunt; 7 overawe; 8 dissuade; 9 terrorize; 10 discourage, intimidate

deterge: 4 buck, lave, wash; 6 cleanse; 7 launder

deteriorate: 3 rot; 4 drop; 5 decay; 6 worsen; 7 decline, degrade, fall off; 10 degenerate; 11 become worse

deteriorated: 4 worn; 5 seedy, washy; 6 rotten, wasted; 7 decayed, laid low; 8 worsened; 10 pulled down; 11 languishing

deterioration: 5 decay; 7 decline; 8 decaying; 9 declining, worsening; 10 impairment; 11 degradation; 12 degenerating, degeneration

determinable: 10 fathomable, ponderable

determinant: 7 crucial; 8 deciding; 9 precedent; 10 antecedent, derivation, determiner; 11 determining

determinate: 5 clear, meant, party; 6 proper; 7 advised, certain, decided, express, partial, private, several, special; 8 decisive, definite, especial, intended, original, peculiar, specific; 9 exclusive; 10 conclusive, definitive, deliberate, individual, particular, respective

determination: 4 will; 5 limit; 6 intent; 7 finding, purpose, resolve; 8 decision, judgment; 9 intention, judgement; 10 conclusion, resolution; 11 force of will; 12 resoluteness

determine: 3 dip, fix, see, set; 4 bend, find, list, wish; 5 assay, check, learn, shape, trend, verge, watch; 6 choose, decide, evolve, settle; 7 find out, incline, measure, realize, satisfy, specify; 8 diagnose, discover, estimate, pinpoint, quantify, regulate, settle on, square up; 9 ascertain, designate, enumerate, establish, influence, set at rest, square off; 10 decide upon, quantitate, settle upon, specialize; 11 resolve upon

determined: 3 set; 5 fixed; 6 driven; 7 settled; 8 dictated, resolved; 10 compulsive

determiner: 8 clincher; 11 determinant; 12 causal factor

determinist: 8 fatalist

deterrence: 9 determent; 12 disincentive, intimidation

deterrent: 8 handicap; 9 hindrance; 10 impediment

detest: 4 hate; 5 abhor; 6 loathe; 8 execrate; 9 abominate

detestable: 6 odious; 7 hateful, obscene;

9 abhorrent, execrable, repugnant, repulsive; **10** abominable
detested: 5 hated; **7** scorned; **8** despised
dethrone: 6 depose
detonate: 3 fly; **4** blow; **5** burst, flare, flash, go off; **6** blow up, bounce, set off; **7** explode, thunder; **9** discharge, fulminate
detonation: 5 blast, burst; **6** blow up, volley; **9** discharge, explosion
detonator: 3 cap; **16** detonating device
detour: 4 turn; **6** bypass; **7** circuit; **9** deviation
detract: 5 decry; **8** belittle, derogate, take away; **9** denigrate, deprecate, disparage; **10** depreciate
detracting: 9 insulting, slighting; **10** belittling, derogatory, detractive, pejorative; **11** deprecatory, disparaging
detractor: 7 knocker; **8** reprover; **10** disparager; **11** depreciator
detriment: 4 harm, hurt; **6** damage, injury; **9** vitiation, worsening; **10** debasement, impairment
detrimental: 7 baleful, baneful, harmful, hurtful, noxious; **8** damaging; **9** injurious; **10** pernicious; **11** deleterious, mischievous, prejudicial; **12** prejudicious
detrimentally: 5 badly; **9** harmfully, noxiously; **11** injuriously, malignantly
detrition: 7 rubbing; **8** abrasion, friction, grinding; **9** attrition, corrasion
detritus: 4 dust, junk; talus; **6** debris, gravel, rubble; **8** oddments, tailings
Detroit: 6 Motown; **9** Motor City
de trop: 7 too much; **8** a bit much; **11** superfluous
deuce: 3 two; **4** duet; **5** brace, devil, twins; **6** cheeks, couple; **7** dickens
deuteranopia: 9 daltonism; **14** greenblindness
deuteranopic: 10 green-blind
deuterium: 13 heavy hydrogen
deuterium oxide: 10 heavy water
Deutschmark: 4 mark; **12** Deutsche Mark
devalue: 7 revalue; **9** devaluate; **10** depreciate, undervalue
devalued: 7 debased; **8** degraded
devastate: 4 ruin; **5** waste; **6** ravage; **8** desolate, lay waste; **10** lay waste to
develop: 3 get; **4** grow, puff, rise; **5** arise, break, hatch, train, widen; **6** blow up, evolve, expand, extend, rarefy, spread; **7** acquire, amplify, bring up, distend, educate, inflate, magnify, prepare, produce; **8** civilize, make grow, spring up; **9** explicate, formulate, modernize, originate, spread out; **10** aggrandize
developed: 14 industrialized; **15** highly-developed
developer: 7 builder; **11** constructor

develop into: 6 become, turn to; **8** grow into, turn into; **10** evolve into
development: 6 growth, sequel; **7** growing; **8** ontogeny; **9** corollary, evolution, increment, outgrowth; **10** developing, maturation
devest: 6 divest; **7** uncover
deviance: 8 deviance; **9** aberrance, aberrancy, deviation; **10** aberration, perversion
deviant: 7 deviate, pervert; **8** aberrant; **10** degenerate
deviate: 4 chop, tack, turn, vary, veer, warp; **5** evert, shift; **6** depart, divert, swerve; **7** deflect, deviant, diverge, pervert, shuffle; **9** turn aside; **10** degenerate, depart from
deviation: 4 turn; **6** detour; **8** deviance; **9** deflexion, departure, diversion; **10** deflection, difference, digression, divergence, perversion
device: 4 ploy, tool, type; **5** trick, twist; **6** cipher, figure, tactic; **7** gimmick, nostrum, receipt; **8** artifice, maneuver; **9** expedient, implement, invention, stratagem, thing used; **10** instrument
device driver: 6 driver
Devil: 5 Satan; **7** Lucifer, Old Nick; **8** the Devil; **9** Beelzebub; **10** the Tempter; **16** Prince of Darkness
devil: 3 rag, vex; **4** nark, ogre, rile; **5** annoy, demon, deuce, fiend, get at, get to; **6** bother, daemon, daimon, gravel, heller, nettle; **7** dickens, hellion, monster; **8** irritate; **11** fallen angel
devilish: 7 hellish, roguish, satanic, stygian; **8** diabolic, fiendish, hell-born, infernal, rascally; **10** demoniacal, devilishly, diabolical
devilishly: 5 madly; **6** deadly; **8** deucedly, devilish, insanely; **10** fiendishly; **11** desperately; **12** confoundedly, diabolically
devil-may-care: 6 casual, rakish; **7** raffish; **8** carefree; **9** desperate, easygoing, sans souci [Fr], slaphappy, unworried; **10** insouciant, nonchalant, phlegmatic, rollicking; **11** free and easy
devil-worship: 10 demonology, diabolatry, witchcraft; **12** demon-worship
devious: 5 loose; **6** shifty; **7** cunning, oblique; **9** deceptive, desultory; **10** circuitous, roundabout
devise: 4 coin; **5** forge, get up; **6** create, invent; **7** prepare; **8** contrive, devising, organize, transmit; **9** fabricate, formulate, originate
deviser: 7 planner; **9** contriver
devising: 6 devise, making; **10** fashioning
devoir: 4 duty; **6** egards [Fr]; **7** regards; **8** respects
devolve: 4 fall, pass; **6** return; **7** succeed
devolvement: 10 devolution
Devonian: 3 age; **9** Paleozoic; **11** Age of Fishes; **14** Devonian period

Devonshire cream: 12 clotted cream

devote: 3 pay; **4** doom, give; **6** commit; **7** destine; **8** dedicate, foredoom; **10** consecrate

devoted: 4 fond, holy, lost; **5** godly, loyal, pious; **6** ardent, devout, doomed, undone; **8** accursed, faithful, motherly, reverent, stranded, uxorious; **9** pietistic, rapturous, religious, spiritual; **10** passionate

devotee: 3 fan; **4** buff; **5** lover; **6** theist, votary; **7** amateur, convert, puritan; **8** believer; **9** formalist; **10** aficionado, dilettante, enthusiast; **11** afficionado, religionist

devotion: 5 flame; **6** homage; **7** loyalty, passion, rapture, worship; **8** fidelity, idolatry, yearning; **9** adoration, constancy, idolizing; **10** aspiration, veneration; **11** devotedness, idolization

devotional: 4 pure; **6** devout, solemn; **8** reverent

devour: 3 eat, pig, sap; **4** bolt, down, fare, feed, gulp, mine, take; **5** raven; **6** guttle; **7** consume, swallow; **8** bolt down, gobble up, gulp down; **9** go through, swallow up

devout: 4 dear, holy, pure; **5** godly, pious; **6** solemn; **7** devoted, earnest; **8** reverent; **9** heartfelt, pietistic, religious, spiritual; **10** devotional, god-fearing

devoutly: 7 piously

devoutness: 13 religiousness

Dewar: 10 Dewar flask

Dewey: 9 John Dewey

dewey-eyed: 6 simple; **9** childlike

dexter: 7 offside

dexterous: 3 apt; **4** deft, gain; **5** handy, quick, ready; **6** adroit, expert; **8** dextrous

dexterously: 5 aptly; **6** deftly; **7** handily, quickly, readily; **8** adroitly; **10** dextrously

dextral: 11 right-handed

dextroamphetamine sulphate: 9 Dexedrine

dextroglucose: 8 dextrose; **10** grape sugar

dextrose: 7 glucose; **10** grape sugar; **13** dextroglucose

dg: 8 decigram

dhole: 7 wild dog

dhow: 9 wharf boat

di-: 2 bi-; **5** twice

diablerie: 7 sorcery; **10** bewitchery; **11** bedevilment, enchantment

diabolical: 6 unholy; **7** demonic, hellish, satanic, stygian; **8** devilish, fiendish, hellborn, infernal; **10** demoniacal

diabolism: 8 demonism, Satanism

diabolist: 8 Satanist

diachronic: 10 historical

diacritic: 11 diacritical; **15** diacritical mark

diadem: 5 crown, tiara; **7** coronet

diagnose: 4 name; **8** pinpoint; **9** determine, establish

diagnostic: 4 test; **5** probe; **7** symptom, typical; **8** acid test; **9** criterion, typifying; **10** litmus test; **11** crucial test, symptomatic

diagnostician: 11 pathologist

diagonal: 4 bias; **5** slash; **6** aslant, aslope, sloped, stroke; **7** slanted, sloping, solidus, virgule; **8** slanting

diagram: 4 plot; **5** parse; **9** schematic

dial: 7 sundial; **8** horologe; **9** clock dial; **13** telephone dial

dialect: 5 idiom; **6** accent, patois; **11** sublanguage; **13** local language

dialectic: 9 polemical; **11** dialectical; **13** argumentative, controversial

dialectician: 8 logician, reasoner

dialectics: 9 induction; **14** generalization

dialog: 8 dialogue, duologue

dialog box: 5 panel

diametric: 5 polar; **8** opposite; **9** diametral; **11** diametrical

diamond: 3 gem; **4** rock, ruby; **5** bijou, bortz, jewel, pearl; **7** adamant, infield, lozenge; **9** ball field, carbonado; **13** precious

diamondback rattlesnake: 11 diamondback

Diamond State: 8 Delaware; **10** First State

Diana: 4 Luna, moon; **7** Artemis; **8** Lucretia

Dianthus: 9 carnation; **10** pink family; **12** sweet William; **13** genus Dianthus

diapason: 5 range, scope; **12** diapason stop

diaper: 5 nappy; **6** napkin; **7** tracery; **9** powdering

diaper dermatitis: 10 diaper rash

diaphanous: 5 filmy, gauzy, sheer, vague; **8** cobwebby, ethereal, gossamer, vaporous; **10** see-through; **11** transparent

diaphoresis: 5 sudor, sweat, water; **8** hidrosis; **12** perspiration

diaphragm: 4 stop; **6** septum; **7** equator, midriff, pessary

diaphysis: 5 shaft; **9** bone shaft

diapsid: 14 diapsid reptile

diarchy: 7 dyarchy

diarist: 10 journalist; **11** diary keeper

diary: 3 log; **6** ledger; **7** daybook, journal; **8** calendar; **9** ephemeris

diary keeper: 7 diarist; **10** journalist

diatomaceous earth: 9 diatomite; **10** kieselguhr

diatonic: 8 measured; **9** chromatic; **10** enharmonic, rhythmical

diatribe: 6 tirade; **9** philippic; **11** fulmination

diazepam: 6 Valium

dibs: 3 rap; **4** mite; **5** claim; **6** change, rights; **9** petty cash, small coin; **11** pocket money, small change; **12** pocket change

dice: 3 die; **4** cube; **5** craps

dice cup: 7 dice box

Diceros: 10 rhinoceros; **12** genus Diceros

dicey: 5 dodgy, risky; **6** chancy; **9** chanceful; **11** speculative

dichloroethyl sulfide: 10 mustard gas
dichotomize: 5 halve, split; 6 bisect, cleave, divide; 8 cut in two
dichotomy: 11 bifurcation
dickens: 5 deuce, devil
dicker: 6 barter, haggle, higgle; 7 chaffer; 8 huckster
dickey: 10 shirtfront
dicot: 11 dicotyledon
dictate: 5 bully, edict, enact, order, ukase; 6 decree, hector, ordain; 7 mandate; 8 browbeat, domineer, instance; 9 dictation, prescribe, prompting; 10 give orders, intimidate, lord it over, push around
dictated: 3 set; 10 determined
dictator: 6 despot, tyrant; 8 autocrat; 9 potentate, strong man; 13 authoritarian
dictatorial: 7 haughty; 8 arrogant, despotic, insolent; 9 arbitrary, imperious; 10 autocratic, tyrannical; 11 magisterial, overbearing; 13 authoritarian
dictatorship: 7 tyranny; 9 autocracy, Caesarism, despotism, monocracy, shogunate, Stalinism; 10 absolutism, one-man rule
diction: 5 style; 7 wording; 8 phrasing, verbiage; 11 enunciation, phraseology
dictionary: 7 lexicon
dictum: 3 bid, nod, saw; 4 beck, call; 5 adage, say-so; 6 behest, old saw, saying; 7 bidding, proverb; 8 sentence
didactic: 10 didactical; 11 educational, instructive
diddle: 2 do; 3 con, gyp, nab, toy; 4 bilk, bite, play, rook, scam; 5 bunco, cheat, cozen, mulct, pluck; 6 chouse, euchre, fiddle, jockey, nobble; 7 defraud, swindle; 9 victimize
Didelphis: 7 opossum; 14 genus Didelphis
die: 2 go; 4 dice, exit, fail, mold, pall; 5 break, punch, stamp; 6 die out, expire, perish, run out; 7 be taken, conk out, decease, give out, give way, succumb; 8 pass away
die for: 5 crave; 6 burn to; 7 ache for, burn for; 8 raven for; 9 hunger for, itch after, lust after
die hard: 3 run; 6 endure; 7 persist, prevail; 8 stand out
dielectric: 9 insulator; 12 nonconductor
diencephalon: 10 interbrain
die out: 7 extinct
dieresis: 6 umlaut; 9 diaeresis
dieses: 12 double dagger
dies irae: 4 doom; 7 last day; 8 doomsday; 11 crack of doom, Judgment day
dies non: 6 day off; 7 holiday, play day; 9 day of rest
diet: 4 lite; 5 light; 6 low-cal; 7 dieting, regimen; 8 congress; 10 convention

diethel ether: 5 ether; 10 ethyl ether, vinyl ether; 12 divinyl ether, ethoxyethane
diethylaminoethyl cellulose: 13 DEAE cellulose
diethylbarbituric acid: 7 veronal; 8 barbital; 9 barbitone
diethylstilbestrol: 3 DES
dietician: 9 dietitian; 12 nutritionist
differ: 4 vary; 8 disagree, mismatch, not match; 9 take issue; 11 be different
difference: 7 dispute, dissent; 8 conflict; 9 departure, deviation; 10 complement, divergence
difference in time: 10 asynchrony
different: 3 odd; 5 mixed; 6 divers, unlike, varied; 7 another, diverse, mingled, unalike, various; 8 assorted, not alike; 9 differing; 10 dissimilar; 11 diversified
differentiate: 4 mark, tell; 6 secern; 8 separate; 9 secernate, tell apart; 10 severalize; 11 distinguish
differently: 9 otherwise
differing: 6 unlike; 7 unalike; 8 not alike; 9 different, divergent; 10 dissimilar, dissenting; 11 disagreeing; 15 distinguishable
difficult: 4 hard; 5 dense, tough; 7 not easy, obscure; 8 critical
difficulties: 4 lack, need, want; 6 penury; 7 poverty; 8 distress; 9 indigence, necessity, neediness, pauperism, privation; 11 destitution
difficulty: 3 rub; 7 density, problem, trouble; 8 hardness, hardship; 9 adversity, obscurity, toughness; 12 complication
diffident: 3 coy, shy; 5 timid; 6 demure, modest, unsure; 8 reserved, retiring; 10 restrained
diffuse: 4 shed; 5 imbue, rumor, wordy; 6 fan out, spread; 7 bestrew, copious, disband, lengthy, pervade, profuse, scatter, verbose; 8 dispense, disperse, permeate; 9 broadcast, circulate, expansive, exuberant, propagate, spread out; 10 distribute, long-winded, overspread, pass around, pleonastic; 11 circularize, disseminate
diffuseness: 8 pleonasm; 9 prolixity, verbosity, wordiness; 10 redundancy; 11 lengthiness, profuseness
diflunisal: 7 Dolibid
dig: 3 fag, hoe, jab; 4 barb, gibe, jibe, moil, plow, poke, prod, rake, shot, slam, stab, toil; 5 delve, grasp, grind, labor, savvy, shaft; 6 dibble, dig out, drudge, harrow, hollow, plough; 7 compass, cut into, digging, travail; 8 excavate, turn over; 9 apprehend; 10 comprehend, excavation
digest: 3 eat; 4 note; 5 brief, draft, grade, index; 6 apercu, mature, minute, pocket, precis; 7 epitome, outline, perpend, stomach, summary, swallow; 8 abstract, analysis, graduate, synopsis, tabulate;

compilation

digestive tract: 7 GI tract

digger: 5 spade; 6 shovel; 9 excavator

digging: 3 dig; 7 rummage; 10 excavating

diggings: 3 pad; 4 digs; 5 berth, place; 8 lodgings; 10 habitation

digging up: 10 exhumation; 12 disinterment

dight: 3 dab, rig; 4 deck, robe, vest, whit; 5 array, drape, dress; 6 attire, bedeck, clothe, enrobe, fit out, tittle; 7 apparel, dictate

dig in: 7 pitch in; 8 entrench

dig into: 5 probe; 8 poke into

digit: 6 cipher, dactyl, finger

digital audiotape: 3 DAT

digitalis: 8 foxglove; 9 digitalin; 18 digitalis glycoside

digital readout: 14 digital display

digital video capture: 12 video capture

Digital Video Disk: 3 DVD; 20 Digital Versatile Disk

Digitaria: 9 crabgrass; 14 genus Digitaria

digitated: 8 fingered; 10 finger-like

dignified: 5 grand, noble, proud; 6 august, lordly; 7 stately, sublime; 8 majestic, princely; 9 honorable

dignify: 7 ennoble, glorify

dignitary: 3 VIP; 6 high-up, worthy

dignity: 7 reserve; 10 lordliness, self-esteem, self-regard; 11 self-respect

dig out: 3 dig; 5 dig up; 7 unearth; 8 disinter

digraph: 6 digram

digress: 5 stray; 6 depart, ramble, wander; 8 divagate, perorate, protract, straggle; 9 sidetrack; 11 make a detour

digression: 5 aside; 8 rambling; 9 deflexion, deviation, diversion, excursion; 10 deflection, digressing, divagation

digs: 3 pad; 5 berth, place; 8 diggings, lodgings; 10 habitation; 13 domiciliation

dike: 3 dam; 4 dyke, ha-ha, leak, moat; 5 creek, ditch, gully, levee; 6 gutter, trench, trough; 7 culvert

diktat: 5 edict, order, ukase; 6 decree; 7 dictate, mandate; 9 dictation

dilapidated: 7 unsound; 10 bedraggled, broken-down, ramshackle, tumble-down

dilapidation: 4 ruin; 5 decay; 9 disrepair; 11 decrepitude

dilatable: 10 expandable

dilatation: 8 dilation; 9 expansion, inflation

dilate: 5 widen; 6 expand, rarefy, spread; 7 amplify, descant, distend, enlarge, expound, inflate; 8 flesh out, run out on; 9 elaborate, expatiate; 10 decompress

dilated: 6 spread; 9 distended, stretched

dilation: 6 growth; 8 swelling; 9 expansion, extension; 10 dilatation; 11 enlargement

dilation and curettage: 5 D and C, abort

dilatoriness: 15 procrastination

dilatory: 4 poky; 5 pokey, tardy; 6 fabian; 7 laggard; 8 dawdling, listless; 9 pottering, puttering; 11 halfhearted

dilemma: 8 quandary; 9 confusion; 10 perplexity; 12 bewilderment

dilettante: 3 fan; 4 buff; 5 lover; 6 votary; 7 amateur, dabbler, devotee; 10 aficionado

diligence: 8 industry; 10 post chaise; 11 application, painstaking

diligent: 7 notable; 8 sedulous; 9 assiduous; 11 industrious, painstaking, persevering

dill: 8 dill weed

Dillinger: 13 John Dillinger

dilly-dally: 5 dally, hover, stall; 6 boggle; 8 hesitate; 12 drag one's feet; 13 procrastinate

diltiazem: 8 Cardizem

diluent: 8 diluting

dilutant: 7 solvent, thinner; 9 dissolver, resolvent; 10 dissolvent

dilute: 3 cut; 4 thin, weak; 6 debase, reduce, watery; 7 diluted, stretch, thin out, watered; 8 add water; 9 water down; 10 adulterate, impoverish; 11 watered down

dim: 3 dip; 4 blur, dark, dull, dumb, slow, slur; 5 black, bleak, blind, dense, faint, muddy, vague, wispy; 6 darken, dimmed, obtuse, opaque; 7 cryptic, obscure, shadowy, subdued; 8 nebulous; 10 clear as mud, mysterious

dimenhydrinate: 9 Dramamine

dimension: 4 bulk, size; 8 property; 9 attribute, magnitude; 10 proportion

dimensions: 10 proportion

diminish: 4 fall; 6 lessen, reduce; 8 belittle, decrease

diminished: 5 small; 6 shrunk, wasted; 7 reduced; 8 lessened, vitiated, weakened; 9 atrophied, belittled, decreased; 10 contracted

diminuendo: 6 softer; 8 less loud; 11 decrescendo

diminution: 7 decline; 8 decrease, stepdown; 9 reduction; 11 contraction

diminutive: 4 tiny; 6 bantam, midget, minute, petite; 11 lilliputian

dimly: 6 palely; 8 pallidly; 12 indistinctly

dimness: 9 duskiness, faintness; 10 gloominess; 11 subduedness

dimout: 8 blackout, brownout

dimple: 4 dent, dint; 5 sinus; 6 lacuna; 8 follicle; 11 indentation

dimwit: 6 doofus, nitwit; 7 halfwit

dim-witted: 4 dull; 6 simple, stupid; 7 witless; 8 mindless; 9 airheaded, brainless, fat witted, fat-headed, pig headed; 10 beef headed, dull minded, dull normal, dull witted, half-witted, lean witted, weak headed, weak-minded; 11 addle headed, blunt-witted, lack-brained, muddy headed, short witted, unreasoning

din: 4 boom; 5 blare; 6 clamor, racket, ruckus, rumpus, tumult; 7 blaring, ruction; 9 cacophony, commotion

dine: 3 sup; 8 eat a meal; 9 have a meal

diner: 9 buffet car, dining car; 11 greasy spoon

dinghy: 4 dory, scow; 7 rowboat; 8 sailboat

dingle: 4 bent, dale, dell, glen, vale; 5 glade, grove; 6 bottom, valley

dingo: 3 dog; 7 wild dog; 8 warragal, warrigal; 10 Canis dingo

dingy: 3 dun, sad, wan; 4 ashy, cold, dead, drab, dull, roan; 5 ashen, dirty, drear, dusky, faint, grimy, livid, lurid, muddy, murky, sooty, sorry; 6 dismal, dreary, glassy, gloomy, grubby, grungy, leaden, pearly, pitchy, russet, sallow, somber; 7 darkish, ghastly, muddied

dining companion: 9 tablemate

dining hall: 9 cafeteria

dinner: 6 supper; 11 dinner party, evening meal

dinner bucket: 10 dinner pail

dinner dress: 10 dinner gown; 11 evening gown

dinner jacket: 3 tux; 6 tuxedo; 8 black tie

dinner pail: 12 dinner bucket

dinner service: 9 dinner set

dinnertime: 10 suppertime

dint: 3 hit; 4 bang, blow, dent, slam; 5 knock, sinus, stamp; 6 dimple, lacuna; 7 impress; 8 follicle; 11 indentation

diode: 9 rectifier

Diogenes: 5 Timon; 13 Timon of Athens

diol: 6 glycol

Diomedea nigripes: 5 goony; 6 gooney, goonie; 10 gooney bird; 20 black-footed albatross

Dionaea muscipula: 13 Venus's flytrap; 14 Venus's flytraps

Dionysia: 11 Bacchanalia

dioptric: 10 refractive

diorama: 8 panorama; 9 cyclorama

Dioscorea: 14 genus Dioscorea

Dioscoreaceae: 9 yam family

dip: 3 bob, dim; 4 bend, dive, duck, dunk, fall, sink; 5 douse, kneel, souse, trend, verge; 6 header, plunge; 7 baptize, bending, decline, dipping, immerse, incline, verging; 8 cutpurse, downhill, sprinkle, trending; 9 concavity, declivity, determine, immersion, inclining; 10 depression, pickpocket, submersion

diphenylhydantoin: 8 Dilantin

diploma: 9 sheepskin

diplomacy: 7 finesse; 8 delicacy; 10 statecraft

diplomatic: 4 wise; 5 civil; 6 adroit, poised; 7 politic, tactful; 9 strategic

Diplopoda: 9 Myriapoda; 14 class Diplopoda, class Myriapoda

Dipodomys phillipsii: 9 desert rat; 11 kangaroo rat

dipper: 5 ladle, spoon; 6 shovel, trowel; 7 spatula, thimble

dipping: 3 dip; 7 bending, verging; 8 trending; 9 inclining

Dipsacus: 6 teasel; 13 genus Dipsacus

dipsomania: 10 alcoholism

dipsomaniac: 4 lush; 5 souse; 6 boozer, soaker; 9 alcoholic

dipteran: 8 dipteron; 15 dipterous insect; 16 two-winged insects

Dipteryx: 10 Coumarouna; 13 genus Dipteryx; 15 genus Coumarouna

dire: 5 awful, dread; 7 direful, dreaded, fearful; 8 dreadful, fearsome, horrific, terrible; 9 desperate, thrilling; 10 deplorable, horrendous, tremendous; 11 frightening

direct: 3 aim; 4 even, head, lead, send, take, true; 5 bluff, blunt, guide, order, place, point, right, steer, train; 6 govern, lineal, manage, target; 7 address, command, conduct, in a line, take aim; 8 directly, engineer, maneuver, organize, straight, verbatim; 9 calculate, downright, manouevre, outspoken

direct current: 2 DC

directed: 5 aimed; 7 pointed

direct hit: 8 bull's-eye

directing: 7 guiding, heading; 8 ordering; 9 directive; 10 commanding, overseeing; 11 directional, supervising

direction: 3 way; 6 charge, course, vector; 7 address, bearing, control, counsel; 8 guidance, managing, pointing, steering; 9 directive; 10 addressing, commission, counseling, government, injunction, management; 11 controlling, instruction, supervising, supervision

directionless: 6 adrift, afloat; 7 aimless; 8 planless; 10 rudderless, undirected

directions: 12 instructions

directly: 3 now; 4 flat; 6 at once, direct; 8 straight; 9 forthwith, instantly, right away; 10 in real time; 11 immediately; 12 straightaway

director: 3 don; 5 coach; 7 manager; 9 commander, conductor; 12 film director; 13 music director, stage director

direful: 4 dire; 5 awful, dread; 7 dreaded, fearful; 8 dreadful, fearsome, horrific, terrible; 10 horrendous; 11 frightening

dirge: 6 lament; 7 requiem

dirham: 10 money table

dirigible: 7 airship; 8 zeppelin

dirk: 6 dagger; 7 bayonet; 8 stiletto

dirt: 4 crap, poop, slop, soil, turd; 5 filth, grime, stain; 6 gravel, grease; 7 scandal; 8 graveled, ungraded

dirtiness: 9 murkiness, smokiness; 10 filthiness, smuttiness; 11 uncleanness

dirt track: 11 cinder track

dirty: 3 dun, low; 4 base, foul, mean, soil, vile; 5 colly, dingy, grime, grimy, lousy, lurid, muddy, murky, smoky, thick; 6 abject, bemire, filthy, leaden, little, paltry, scabby, scurvy, shabby, soiled, sordid; 7 begrime, ignoble, muddied, pitiful, scrubby, unclean; 8 beggarly, cheating, infected, marked-up, overcast, rascally, sneaking; 9 groveling, ill-gotten; 10 obfuscated, unsporting

dirty joke: 8 blue joke; 9 blue story

Dis: 5 Orcus

dis: 12 be irreverent; 13 be disparaging; 14 be discourteous; 15 be disrespectful

disabuse: 7 correct; 8 set right

disaccord: 5 clash; 7 discord; 8 disagree; 10 dissension, dissidence, dissonance

disadvantage: 6 hamper, hinder; 8 disfavor, drawback, handicap; 9 disfavour, prejudice

disadvantaged: 8 deprived

disaffect: 5 alien; 8 alienate, estrange

disaffected: 9 alienated, estranged; 10 malcontent, rebellious; 11 ill-affected

disaffection: 8 distavor; 10 alienation; 12 estrangement, unpopularity

disaffirm: 6 disown; 7 disavow; 8 disclaim

disagree: 3 jar; 5 clash, demur; 6 differ, jostle; 7 discord, dispute, dissent, quarrel; 8 conflict; 9 come amiss, disaccord, take issue

disagreeable: 5 yucky; 9 offensive, repellant; 10 off-putting, unpleasant, unpleasing; 11 displeasing

disagreement: 7 discord, dissent; 8 mismatch, variance; 9 disparity; 10 difference, dissension, dissidence, dissonance, divergence; 11 discrepancy

disallow: 3 ban, bar; 4 veto; 5 taboo; 6 enjoin, forbid, outlaw; 8 forefend, prohibit; 9 interdict, proscribe

disannul: 6 cancel; 8 dissolve

disappear: 2 go; 4 fade, pass; 6 go away, vanish; 8 dissolve, fade away, melt away, vaporize; 9 evaporate

disappoint: 6 put out; 7 let down, mortify; 10 disconcert, dissatisfy

disappointed: 6 foiled; 8 defeated, thwarted; 10 frustrated; 11 discomfited

disapprobation: 11 disapproval; 12 condemnation

disapproval: 7 dislike; 8 disfavor; 9 disfavour

disapprove: 6 reject

disarm: 5 cramp, unarm, unfit; 6 deaden; 7 beguile, win over; 9 reconcile; 10 concili-

ate, disqualify, invalidate, propitiate; 11 tie the hands

disarmer: 8 pacifist

disarrange: 5 mix up; 7 derange; 8 disorder

disarray: 8 disorder; 9 confusion

disassemble: 7 break up; 9 break down, dismantle, take apart; 10 break apart, unassemble

disassociation: 8 disunion, disunity; 10 separation; 11 disjunction

disaster: 4 bale; 7 tragedy; 8 accident, calamity, casualty; 9 cataclysm; 11 catastrophe

disastrous: 5 fatal; 6 tragic; 7 fateful, ruinous; 8 tragical, untoward; 10 calamitous

disavow: 6 disown; 8 disclaim; 9 disaffirm

disavowal: 10 disclaimer

disband: 4 shed; 6 spread; 7 bestrew, diffuse, dismiss, scatter; 8 dispense, disperse, dissolve; 9 discharge; 10 disenthral, overspread; 11 disenthrall, disseminate

disbelief: 8 unbelief; 9 discredit, misbelief; 10 skepticism; 11 godlessness, incredulity, lack of faith, non-religion, ungodliness, want of faith

disbelieve: 8 not think; 9 discredit, lack faith

disbelieving: 9 sceptical, skeptical; 11 unbelieving

disbench: 6 disbar

disbowel: 3 gut; 10 disembowel, eviscerate

disburden: 6 unload; 8 unburden

disbursal: 6 outlay; 7 expense; 8 spending; 12 disbursement

disburse: 3 pay; 6 pay out

disbursed: 5 spent; 8 expended, payed out

disbursement: 6 outlay; 7 expense; 8 expenses, spending; 9 disbursal, outgoings; 11 expenditure

disc: 4 disk; 6 record, saucer; 7 platter; 9 recording; 11 vinyl record

discant: 7 descant

discard: 4 toss; 5 chuck, fling, heave, spurn, trash; 6 refuse; 7 cast out, dispose, garbage, nullify, protest, put away, rubbish, toss out; 8 cast away, chuck out, discards, get rid of, throw out, toss away; 9 cast aside, dispose of, repudiate, throw away

discards: 5 culls, trash; 6 refuse; 7 discard, garbage, rejects, rubbish

discern: 3 get, ken, see, spy; 4 espy; 5 sight; 6 descry; 7 make out, observe, pick out; 8 conceive, discover, perceive; 9 recognize, tell apart; 10 experience; 11 distinguish, get a sight of, have in sight

discerned: 6 unseen; 8 descried; 11 unperceived; 12 unrecognized

discernibility: 10 legibility

discernibly: 7 visibly; 9 in sight of; 11 perceptibly

discerning: 4 fine; 8 discreet, piercing; 9 observant; 10 perceptive; 11 penetrating; 12 apprehensive; 13 perspicacious

discernment: 5 savvy, taste; 6 acumen; 8 judgment, sagacity; 9 judgement; 10 discretion, shrewdness; 11 penetration

discharge: 3 arc, run, shy; 4 fire, free, keep, meet, quit, sack, shot, toss; 5 blast, clear, eject, empty, expel, fling, go off, honor, remit, salvo, shoot, spark, throw; 6 acquit, assoil, blow up, exempt, firing, redeem, remise, set off, settle, volley, waiver; 7 disband, dismiss, execute, fulfill, perform, quietus, realize, release, sacking, satisfy, venting; 8 complete, detonate, dispatch, ejecting, ejection, emission, let one go; 9 acquittal, clearance, dismissal, emanation, excretion, exculpate, exonerate, expelling, explosion, expulsion, firing off, fulminate, muster out, quitclaim, quittance, reckoning, terminate; 10 detonation, disenthral, liberation, outpouring, pushing out, redemption, settlement

discharging: 8 ejecting, ejection; 9 discharge, expelling, expulsion

disciple: 7 apostle; 8 adherent, follower, idolizer; 9 proselyte, worshiper

disciplinal: 10 corrective; 12 disciplinary

disciplinarian: 6 despot, tyrant; 8 martinet, moralist, stickler; 10 hard master, inquisitor

disciplinary: 10 corrective; 11 disciplinal

discipline: 5 check, field, study, train, trial; 7 control, correct, economy, sort out, subject; 9 condition; 10 correction, infliction, self-denial; 11 subject area

disc jockey: 2 dj; 10 disk jockey

disclaim: 6 abjure, disown, forego; 7 disavow, protest, retract; 8 abnegate, renounce; 9 disaffirm

disclaimer: 7 protest; 9 disavowal, recusancy; 10 abnegation

disclose: 5 break, let on; 6 expose, impart, let out, reveal; 7 declare, divulge; 8 bring out, discover, give away

disclosure: 4 find; 8 exposing; 9 detection, discovery, revealing; 10 revealment, revelation; 11 discovering

disco: 11 discotheque

discoid: 4 even, flat; 5 flush, plane; 7 frontal, tabular; 8 disklike; 9 discoidal

discoloration: 5 stain; 6 fading; 9 bleaching

discolored: 6 pitted; 8 freckled; 11 discoloured

discombobulate: 3 fox; 5 throw; 6 bemuse, fuddle; 7 bedevil, confuse; 8 befuddle, bewilder, confound; 11 disorganize

discombobulated: 12 disconcerted

discomfit: 4 beat, rout; 5 crush, upset; 6 defeat, thwart, untune; 7 conquer; 8 vanquish; 9 embarrass, frustrate; 10 discompose, disconcert

discomfited: 6 foiled; 7 annoyed; 8 defeated, thwarted, troubled; 10 displeased, disquieted, frustrated; 11 discomposed, embarrassed

discomfort: 3 bug, irk, vex; 4 faze, tire; 5 annoy, cross, worry; 6 bother, unease; 7 disturb, malaise, mortify, perplex, trouble; 8 disquiet, soreness; 9 disoblige, displease, incommode; 10 discompose, irritation, tenderness; 11 displeasure

discommend: 9 criticise, disparage, dispraise; 10 disapprove

discommendation: 5 blame; 7 censure, obloquy; 9 criticism, dispraise

discommode: 6 bother, put out; 7 trouble; 9 disoblige, incommode

discompose: 3 bug, irk, vex; 4 faze, fret, huff, tire; 5 annoy, chafe, cross, pique, upset, worry; 6 bother, nettle, ruffle, untune; 7 disturb, mortify, perplex, trouble; 8 disquiet, irritate; 9 discomfit, disoblige, displease, incommode; 10 discomfort, disconcert

disconcert: 4 balk, foil; 5 upset; 6 flurry, put off, put out, thwart, untune; 7 confuse, mortify; 8 convulse; 9 discomfit, frustrate; 10 disappoint, discompose, dissatisfy; 11 consternate

disconcerted: 6 aghast, dashed; 7 crossed; 8 diverted, unhinged; 10 distracted, frustrated

disconfirm: 5 rebut; 6 refute; 7 confute; 8 confound, disprove, negative; 10 controvert

disconnect: 4 kill; 5 sever; 6 unplug; 7 disjoin, turn off; 8 separate; 9 power down, switch off; 10 deactivate

disconnected: 5 split; 6 abrupt, broken; 7 garbled; 8 confused, detached, discrete, staccato; 9 disjoined, disunited, illogical, scattered, separated; 10 disjointed, disordered, fragmented; 11 disjunctive, interrupted, unconnected

disconnection: 8 disunion, disunity; 10 irrelation, separation; 11 disjunction, disjuncture, non-relation

disconsolate: 4 blue, dark, grim; 6 dismal, gloomy; 7 forlorn; 8 desolate; 10 depressing; 11 comfortless, dispiriting, sick at heart

disconsolateness: 11 despondence, despondency; 13 heartsickness

discontinue: 4 halt, quit, stop; 5 break, cease, pause; 6 give up, lay off; 7 suspend; 8 break off; 9 interrupt

discontinuity: 3 gap; 5 break, crack; 7 opening; 12 interruption

discontinuous: 6 abrupt, broken, sudden; 7 instant; 8 discrete; 9 immediate, momentary, separated; **11** disjunctive, interrupted, precipitant, precipitate, precipitous, unconnected

discord: **6** strife; **8** disagree; **9** cacophony; **10** dissension, dissidence, dissonance; **11** discordance

discordance: **7** discord; **9** cacophony; **10** dissonance

discordant: **7** jumbled, mixed up; **8** confused; **9** dissonant; **10** at variance, discrepant, inharmonic, quarreling; **11** conflicting, disagreeing

discotheque: **5** disco

discount: **4** bate, give, loss; **5** allow; **6** defect, ignore, rebate, reduce; **7** dismiss, take off; **8** brush off, mark down; **9** abatement, allowance, decrement, deduction, disregard, price down, push aside, reduction; **10** brush aside, concession

discountenance: **8** disfavor, forswear, set aside; **9** not hear of; **10** spoil sport, stand aloof

discourage: **3** cow; **4** warn; **5** abash, daunt, deter; **7** overawe; **8** admonish, dispirit; **9** terrorize; **10** dishearten, intimidate

discouraged: **6** balked; **7** baffled; **9** jawfallen; **10** dispirited, frustrated; **11** crestfallen, demoralized

discourse: **4** talk; **5** stump; **6** homily, memoir, recite, sermon; **7** declaim, discuss, lecture; **8** colloquy, converse, flourish, harangue, pastoral; **9** delve into, hold forth, preaching, sermonize, speechify, talk about, treatment; **10** discussion

discourteous: **8** impolite; **10** ill-behaved, ungracious, unmannered, unmannerly; **11** ill-mannered

discourteously: **6** rudely; **10** impolitely

discourtesy: **7** offence, offense; **8** rudeness; **10** bad manners, disrespect, ill manners; **11** brusqueness; **12** impoliteness

discover: **3** ken, key, see, spy; **4** espy, find, hear, name, view; **5** break, learn, let on, sight; **6** descry, detect, evolve, expose, impart, key out, let out, notice, pick up, reveal, strike; **7** declare, discern, divulge, find out, get wind, get word, make out, observe; **8** bring out, chance on, come upon, describe, disclose, get a line, give away, identify; **9** determine, light upon, recognize

discovered: **5** found; **6** broken; **8** detected, found out, observed, revealed; **9** disclosed; **11** ascertained

discoverer: **6** finder; **7** spotter; **8** inventor; **9** artificer

discovering: **8** exposing; **9** revealing; **10** disclosure, revealment, revelation

discovery: **4** find; **9** detection; **10** disclosure, revelation, uncovering; **11** elucidation; **12** breakthrough

discredit: **7** bad name; **8** disgrace, not think,

unbelief; **9** bad repute, disbelief, disrepute, ill repute, misbelief; **10** disbelieve

discredited: **6** shamed; **7** damaged; **9** disgraced; **10** dishonored

discreet: **5** chary, shy of; **7** politic, prudent; **8** stealthy; **10** discerning; **11** circumspect

discreetly: **9** guardedly, prudently; **10** cautiously; **13** circumspectly

discreetness: **7** finesse; **8** delicacy, prudence; **9** diplomacy; **10** discretion

discrepancy: **7** variant; **8** mismatch, variance; **9** disparity, diversity; **10** divergence

discrepant: **10** at variance, discordant; **11** disagreeing

discrete: **4** free; **5** apart, loose; **6** broken; **7** asunder, dicousu [Fr], insular; **8** distinct, separate; **9** disparate, unannexed; **10** far between, unattached; **11** disjunctive, interrupted, unconnected

discretion: **4** heed, tact; **7** caution; **8** coolness, delicacy, free will, prudence, volition; **10** steadiness; **11** calculation, discernment, heedfulness

discretionary: **8** elective, optional, unforced; **9** not forced

discriminate: **4** nice; **5** match; **8** separate; **9** know apart, single out; **11** distinguish

discriminating: **4** keen; **5** acute, sharp; **6** choosy; **8** incisive, piercing; **9** knifelike, selective; **11** penetrating, penetrative

discrimination: **9** pickiness; **10** choosiness, daintiness, favoritism; **11** distinction, favouritism, finickiness, selectivity

discriminator: **5** bigot; **6** racist

discriminatory: **9** invidious; **10** prejudiced; **12** preferential

discursive: **6** roving; **7** gadding, vagrant; **8** rambling; **9** dianoetic, excursive, itinerant

discus: **6** saucer; **11** discus throw

discuss: **6** confer; **7** agitate, canvass; **8** talk over; **9** discourse, talk about

discussant: **8** panelist

discussion: **4** word; **7** comment; **9** discourse, treatment; **11** give-and-take

disdain: **5** scorn, spurn; **6** reject; **7** contemn, despise; **8** contempt, pooh-pooh, turn down; **9** freeze off, patronage; **12** scornfulness

disdainful: **6** lordly, sniffy; **7** haughty; **8** prideful, scornful; **9** insulting; **10** swaggering

disease: **6** malady; **7** ailment, illness; **8** disorder, sickness; **9** complaint

diseased: **3** ill; **4** sick; **5** ill of; **6** ailing, morbid, unwell; **9** unhealthy; **10** pathologic

disembark: **6** debark; **7** set down; **10** come to land

disembarrass: **3** rid; **4** free; **9** extricate

disembodied: **8** bodiless, unbodied; **10** unembodied, incorporeal

disembody: 7 analyze; 8 dissolve; 9 dismember; 10 distribute; 12 spiritualize

disembowel: 3 gut; 4 draw; 10 eviscerate

disenchant: 5 repel, shock; 6 offend; 7 deflate; 10 disappoint; 11 disillusion

disencumber: 4 free; 8 untangle; 9 extricate; 11 disentangle

disencumbered: 10 unburdened; 11 disburdened; 12 unencumbered

disendowment: 7 ousting, removal; 9 dismissal

disenfranchised: 8 voteless

disengage: 4 free; 5 leave; 8 break off, break way, disunite, free from, uncouple, withdraw; 9 exonerate; 10 dissociate, emancipate; 11 disentangle

disengagement: 7 leaving, pullout; 8 disunion, disunity, fallback; 10 detachment, separation, uncoupling; 11 breaking off, disjunction, enlargement

disengaging: 9 severance; 10 disjoining, separating, separation

disentangle: 4 card, comb; 5 ravel; 6 unwind; 7 comb out, unravel, unsnarl; 8 decipher, untangle; 9 disengage, extricate; 10 cut the knot, disembroil, disinvolve; 11 disencumber

disentangled: 5 freed; 8 loosened, untwined; 9 unraveled, unsnarled, untangled; 10 extricated

disenthral: 7 disband, dismiss; 8 liberate; 9 discharge; 11 disenthrall

disentitle: 10 disqualify; 12 disfranchise

disestablish: 8 dislodge, displace

disestablishment: 7 ousting, removal; 9 dismissal

disesteem: 8 disfavor; 9 disrepute; 10 disrespect

disfavor: 7 dislike; 9 disfavour; 11 disapproval

disfigure: 5 cut up; 6 deface, deform, mangle; 7 blemish, distort; 8 mutilate, truncate

disfranchise: 10 disentitle, disqualify

disfranchised: 8 voteless; 9 forfeited

disfranchisement: 10 forfeiture; 11 loss of right

disfurnish: 6 devest, divest; 7 uncover

disgorge: 3 cat; 4 barf, cast, honk, puke, shed, sick, spew, spue; 5 chuck, repay, retch, spill, vomit; 6 be sick, refund; 7 regorge, throw up, upchuck, vomit up; 9 reimburse; 11 regurgitate

disgrace: 5 crush, shame; 6 demean; 7 attaint, degrade, mortify, put down; 8 dishonor, ignominy; 9 discredit, dishonour, humiliate; 10 put to shame

disgraceful: 8 recreant, shameful, shocking; 10 inglorious, scandalous; 11 blameworthy, ignominious, opprobrious

disgruntled: 12 dissatisfied

disguise: 4 mask; 6 bemask, garble; 7 mimicry; 9 gloss over; 10 camouflage

disguised: 4 mask; 7 conceal

disgust: 4 pall; 5 repel, shock; 6 nausea, revolt, sicken; 7 churn up, turn off; 8 loathing, nauseate; 10 repugnance

disgusted: 4 sick; 5 fed up; 6 sick of; 7 tired of

disgustful: 4 foul; 5 yucky; 6 wicked; 7 loathly; 9 loathsome, repellant, repellent, revolting; 10 disgusting; 11 distasteful

disgustingly: 11 revoltingly, sickeningly; 13 distastefully

dish: 3 bag, pan; 4 do in, lulu, undo; 5 do for, peach, plate, serve; 6 beauty, course, dish up, looker, saucer; 7 dish out, dishful, mantrap, platter, potager, serve up, smasher, stunner; 8 calabash, crucible, cup of tea, knockout, trencher; 10 dish aerial; 11 dish antenna

dish antenna: 4 dish; 6 saucer; 10 dish aerial

disharmonious: 9 dissonant; 10 discordant, inharmonic

dishcloth: 7 dishrag

dishcloth gourd: 5 luffa

dishearten: 6 put off; 8 dispirit; 10 discourage

disheartened: 9 jawfallen; 10 dispirited; 11 crestfallen, demoralized, discouraged

dishevel: 5 ravel; 6 ruffle, tangle, tousle; 8 entangle

disheveled: 7 rumpled, tousled; 8 frowzled; 9 streaming; 11 dishevelled

dishonest: 5 false, venal; 8 bribable; 9 deceitful, faithless, trothless, truthless; 10 fraudulent, mendacious; 11 corruptible, purchasable, unveracious

dishonestly: 7 falsely, venally; 11 deceitfully, truthlessly

dishonor: 4 rape; 5 shame; 6 insult, ravish; 7 affront, attaint, nullify, offense, outrage, protest, violate; 8 disgrace; 9 contumely, desecrate, dishonour, repudiate, wrongness; 10 put to shame; 11 inrectitude

dishonorable: 4 base; 7 immoral; 9 dishonest, unethical; 10 inglorious; 12 unscrupulous

dishonorably: 10 shamefully; 11 dishonestly; 12 ingloriously

dishonored: 6 shamed; 9 disgraced; 11 discredited

dish out: 3 lot; 4 deal, dish; 5 allot, serve; 6 dish up; 7 deal out, dole out, mete out, serve up; 8 dispense, shell out; 9 parcel out; 10 administer, distribute

dishrag: 9 dishcloth

dish up: 4 dish; 5 serve; 7 dish out, serve up

dishware: 8 crockery

disillusion: 7 deflate; 10 disenchant

disincentive: 10 deterrence

disinclination: 7 dislike; **8** distaste; **9** disrelish, hesitancy, loathness; **10** hesitation, reluctance

disincline: 5 repel, shake; **6** sicken; **7** stagger; **9** indispose

disinfectant: 9 germicide; **10** germicidal; **12** antimicrobic, bactericidal

disingenuous: 6 artful, **11** uningenuous; **11** calculating; **12** false-hearted

disingenuously: 8 artfully; **11** insincerely

disinherit: 6 disown

disintegrate: 5 decay; **7** crumble; **9** decompose; **12** self-destruct

disintegration: 5 decay; **9** contusion; **11** dissolution, granulation, trituration [Chem]

disinter: 5 dig up; **6** dig out, exhume; **7** unearth

disinterest: 10 neutrality; **12** indifference

disinterested: 7 neutral; **9** apathetic, uncurious, unselfish; **10** altruistic; **11** indifferent; **12** uninterested

disinterment: 9 digging up; **10** exhumation

disjoin: 8 disjoint, separate; **10** disconnect

disjunction: 8 disunion, disunity; **10** separation; **11** disjuncture

disjunctive: 6 broken; **8** discrete; **11** interrupted

disk: 4 disc; **6** harrow, record, saucer; **7** platter; **12** magnetic disc, magnetic disk

disk drive: 9 disc drive, hard drive

diskette: 6 floppy; **10** floppy disk

disk jockey: 2 dj; **10** disc jockey

disklike: 7 discoid; **9** discoidal

disk operating system: 3 DOS

dislike: 8 disfavor, distaste; **9** disfavour, disrelish; **11** disapproval

dislocate: 4 slip; **5** splay; **7** unhinge; **8** disjoint, displace

dislocation: 9 breakdown; **10** disruption

dislodge: 4 bump, free; **5** shift; **8** displace; **10** reposition

dislodged: 9 displaced; **10** transposed; **12** translocated

disloyal: 5 false; **9** faithless; **10** of bad faith, unfaithful; **11** unpatriotic

disloyalty: 8 betrayal; **9** treachery; **13** double dealing

dismal: 4 blue, dark, drab, grim; **5** dingy, drear, sorry; **6** dreary, gloomy, somber; **7** joyless; **8** dejected, frowning; **9** cheerless, saturnine; **10** depressing, lugubrious, spiritless, uncheerful; **11** dispiriting

dismantle: 4 rase, raze; **5** level, strip; **6** devest, divest; **7** break up, dismast, uncover; **8** pull down, take down, tear down; **9** take apart; **10** break apart; **11** disassemble, disorganize

dismay: 3 awe; **5** alarm, appal; **6** appall, deject; **7** depress, get down, horrify; **8** cast down, dispirit, disquiet; **10** demoralize

dismayed: 6 aghast; **7** shocked; **8** appalled

disme: 4 dime

dismember: 9 disembody, take apart; **10** distribute

dismiss: 3 can, RIF; **4** deny, drop, fire, sack; **5** expel; **6** ignore, refuse, reject; **7** cast off, cast out, decline, disband, fire out, put away, send off, turn off; **8** brush off, cast away, discount, force out, let one go, send away, throw out, turn down, usher out; **9** cast aside, discharge, disregard, fling away, pitch away, push aside, terminate; **10** brush aside, disenthral, give notice, give the axe, throw aside; **11** disenthrall, give warning, send packing

dismissal: 4 sack; **6** bounce [U.S.], firing; **7** ousting, refusal, release, removal, sacking; **9** declining, discharge, rejection, severance; **10** katatataki [Jap]

dismissed: 5 fired; **6** canned, riffed, sacked; **7** laid-off, refused, severed; **8** declined, rejected; **10** discharged, terminated, turned down; **11** pink-slipped

dismissing: 7 denying; **8** refusing; **9** rejecting; **11** turning down

dismount: 5 light; **6** alight, get off; **7** dismast, get down, unhorse

disobedient: 6 unruly; **11** uncompliant, uncomplying; **13** insubordinate

disoblige: 3 bug, irk, vex; **4** faze, tire; **5** annoy, cross, worry; **6** bother, put out; **7** disturb, mortify, perplex, trouble; **8** disquiet; **9** displease, incommode; **10** discomfort, discommode, discompose; **13** inconvenience

disorder: 5 mix up, upset; **6** malady; **7** ailment, derange, disease, illness, perturb, trouble, turmoil, unhinge; **8** disarray, disquiet, distract, sickness; **9** agitation, commotion, complaint; **10** disarrange, turbulence; **11** disturbance; **13** civil disorder

disorderly: 7 chaotic, jumbled, lawless; **8** agitated, improper, scampish, unseemly; **9** in turmoil, lawlessly, orderless, turbulent, unordered; **10** disordered, improperly, indecorous, scampishly, topsy-turvy

disorganization: 8 disorder

disorganize: 7 confuse, dismast; **9** dismantle

disorganized: 9 orderless, unordered; **10** disordered, disorderly

disorientation: 8 freak out

disoriented: 4 lost; **6** anomic; **8** confused; **9** alienated

disown: 7 disavow; **8** disclaim; **9** disaffirm; **10** disinherit

disowned: 10 repudiated

disparage: 5 decry; **6** pick at; **7** detract; **8** belittle, derogate; **9** criticise, denigrate, deprecate, dispraise; **10** depreciate

disparagement: 5 blame; 7 censure, obloquy; 9 aspersion, criticism, dispraise; 10 belittling, derogation, detraction; 11 deprecation; 12 belittlement, depreciation

disparager: 7 knocker; 9 detractor; 11 depreciator

disparaging: 8 critical; 9 insulting, slighting; 10 belittling, derogative, derogatory, detracting, detractive, pejorative; 11 deprecatory, dyslogistic, reproachful

disparate: 4 free; 5 apart, loose; 6 uneven, unlike; 7 asunder, insular, partial, unequal; 8 discrete, separate; 9 unannexed; 10 dissimilar, far between, unattached; 11 unconnected; 12 unassociated

disparity: 8 imparity, mismatch, variance; 9 diversity; 10 divergence, unevenness, unlikeness; 11 discrepancy

dispart: 4 part; 6 divide, cut off, detach; 7 divorce

dispassion: 8 coolness; 10 even temper

dispatch: 3 hit; 4 slay; 6 murder, remove, report; 7 bump off, send off; 8 alacrity, complete, despatch, shipment; 9 discharge, polish off; 10 communique, expedition, promptness; 11 promptitude; 13 communication

dispel: 5 chase; 6 run off; 7 break up, scatter; 8 disperse, dissolve, drive off, drive out, turn back; 9 chase away, dissipate, drive away

dispensable: 10 expendable

dispensation: 5 favor; 7 release; 8 alloting, division, giving up; 9 allotment, endowment, exemption, surrender; 10 abandoning, dispensing; 11 abandonment, consignment

dispense: 3 lot; 4 deal, shed; 5 allot; 6 deal in, divide, retail, spread; 7 bestrew, deal out, diffuse, disband, dish out, dole out, mete out, present, scatter; 8 disperse, give away, shell out; 9 apportion, dispose of, parcel out; 10 administer, distribute, overspread, portion out; 11 disseminate

dispeople: 10 depopulate

dispersal: 10 dispersion, divergence

disperse: 3 dot; 4 dust, shed; 6 dispel, spread; 7 bestrew, break up, diffuse, disband, diverge, scatter; 8 dispense, sprinkle; 9 broadcast, circulate, dissipate, propagate, spread out; 10 distribute, overspread, pass around; 11 circularise, circularize, disseminate

dispirit: 6 deject, dismay; 7 depress, get down; 8 cast down; 10 demoralize, discourage, dishearten

dispirited: 3 low; 4 blue, down; 8 downcast, listless; 9 depressed, jawfallen; 11 crestfallen, discouraged, downhearted, low-spirited

dispiritedly: 10 hopelessly

dispiriting: 4 blue, dark, grim; 6 dismal, gloomy; 10 depressing

displace: 4 bump, move; 6 uproot; 8 dislodge, force out, misplace; 9 dislocate

displaced: 7 removed; 9 dislodged; 10 transposed

displaced person: 2 DP; 15 stateless person

displacement: 5 shift; 6 remove; 11 supplanting, translation

displant: 6 mislay; 8 misplace, displace, supplant

display: 4 fuss, show; 6 expose, hold up, reveal; 7 exhibit, present, show off, showing; 8 exposure, flourish; 10 put forward, showing off; 12 expose to view, hold up to view, presentation

display case: 4 case; 8 showcase

displayed: 6 showed

display tube: 9 video tube

display window: 10 shopwindow, show window

displease: 3 bug, irk, vex; 4 faze, tire; 5 annoy, cross, worry; 6 bother; 7 disturb, mortify, perplex, trouble; 8 disquiet; 9 disoblige, incommode; 10 discomfort

displeasure: 7 dudgeon; 8 disquiet; 10 discomfort

displode: 3 fly; 5 burst, flare, flash, go off; 6 blow up, bounce; 7 explode, thunder; 8 detonate

disport: 3 toy; 4 lark, romp; 5 amuse, feast, frisk, revel, sport; 6 cavort, divert, frolic, gambol, junket, wanton; 7 banquet, carouse, rollick, skylark; 9 drown care, lark about, make merry, run around

disposal: 4 sale, vent; 7 selling, vending; 10 discarding; 11 disposition, electric pig, throwing out

dispose: 4 bias, form, sway, tend, toss; 5 fling, place, trend, verge; 6 bend to; 7 cast out, discard, incline, put away, qualify, toss out; 8 cast away, chuck out, throw out, toss away; 9 cast aside, influence, inoculate, throw away, weigh with; 10 predispose; 13 have a tendency

disposed: 3 apt; 4 fain; 5 given; 6 minded; 7 tending, willing; 8 inclined, prepared; 9 favorable

disposed of: 7 given up; 9 abandoned, cast aside; 12 relinquished

dispose of: 4 drop, sell, shed, vend; 5 chuck, heave, spare; 6 forego, resign; 7 discard, present; 8 chuck out, dispense, get rid of, give away, part with, renounce, throw out; 9 set at rest, throw away; 11 effect a sale

disposition: 4 bent, bias, mood, tone, turn, vein; 5 array, humor, style, tenor; 6 animus, temper; 7 leaning; 8 attitude, disposal, grouping, tendency; 9 proneness; 10 affections, proclivity, propensity; 11 arrangement, frame of mind, inclination, personality, temperament

dispossess: 5 strip; 6 divest; 7 deprive

dispossessed: 8 homeless, roofless

dispossession: 8 eviction; 11 legal ouster

dispraise: 5 blame; 7 censure, obloquy; 9 criticise, criticism, disparage;

disprize: 8 misprize, 10 undervalue

disproof: 10 refutation; 11 confutation

disprove: 5 rebut; 6 refute; 7 confute; 8 confound, negative; 10 controvert, disconfirm

disproven: 7 refuted; 8 confuted, rebutted; 10 confounded

disproving: 8 refuting; 9 confuting, rebutting; 10 falsifying; 11 confounding

disputable: 4 moot; 8 arguable, fallible, slippery, ticklish; 9 debatable; 10 precarious; 12 questionable

disputant: 5 party; 6 arguer; 7 debater, polemic; 8 partisan

disputation: 6 debate

dispute: 3 jar; 4 feud, moot, spat, tiff; 5 argue, clash, issue, snarl; 6 argufy, debate, jostle; 7 gainsay, problem, quarrel, wrangle; 8 argument, conflict, disagree, question, squabble; 9 altercate, bandy with, challenge, chop logic, come amiss, moot point; 10 bandy words, difference

disputed: 4 moot; 11 controvened; 12 contradicted

disqualification: 9 ineptness; 10 ineptitude, invalidity; 11 lack of skill, want of skill; 12 incompetence

disqualified: 5 inapt, inept, unapt; 11 disentitled, incompetent, unchartered, unqualified; 12 ill-qualified

disqualify: 5 cramp, unfit; 6 deaden, disarm; 9 indispose; 10 disentitle, invalidate

disquiet: 3 bug, irk, vex; 4 cark, faze, tire; 5 annoy, cross, worry; 6 bother, dismay, unease, unrest; 7 anxiety, concern, disturb, fidgets, mortify, perplex, perturb, trouble, turmoil, unhinge; 8 disorder, distract; 9 agitation, commotion, disoblige, displease, incommode; 10 discomfort, discompose, inquietude, solicitude, turbulence, uneasiness

disquieted: 5 upset; 7 annoyed, worried; 8 troubled; 9 disturbed; 10 displeased, distressed; 11 discomfited, discomposed

disquietude: 5 worry; 6 unease, unrest; 7 anxiety, concern, fidgets; 8 disquiet, edginess; 10 inquietude, solicitude, uneasiness

disquisition: 6 memoir; 9 discourse

disregard: 3 cut; 4 snub; 6 ignore, pass by, slight; 7 dismiss, neglect, not mind; 8 brush off, discount, misprize, overlook; 9 push aside; 10 brush aside, disrespect

disregarding: 8 careless, mindless, no matter; 10 regardless; 12 irregardless, irrespective; 13 disregardless

disrelish: 7 dislike; 8 distaste

disrepair: 5 decay; 12 dilapidation

disreputable: 11 blameworthy, disgraceful; 13 discreditable, reprehensible, uncommendable

disrepute: 7 bad name; 9 bad repute, discredit, ill repute; 13 bad reputation

disrespect: 6 pass by, slight; 8 contempt, misprize, overlook; 9 disesteem, disregard, push aside; 10 trifle with; 11 discourtesy, irreverence, set at naught

disrespected: 6 dissed; 8 insulted

disrespectful: 6 awless; 7 aweless; 10 irreverent

disrobe: 5 strip; 6 uncase; 7 discase, undress; 8 unclothe; 9 strip down

disrobing: 10 undressing

disrupt: 6 cut off; 7 break up, perturb; 9 interrupt

disruption: 3 gap; 4 stir, to-do; 5 break, split; 6 breach; 7 rupture, turmoil; 8 disunion, division; 9 commotion; 10 breaking up, hurly burly; 11 dislocation, dissolution, disturbance

disruptive: 7 riotous; 8 troubled; 9 turbulent; 10 tumultuous

dissassociate: 7 divorce; 8 disjoint, disunite; 10 dissociate

dissatisfaction: 8 disquiet; 10 discomfort; 11 displeasure; 12 discomposure

dissatisfactory: 12 unsatisfying; 13 disappointing

dissatisfied: 11 disgruntled

dissect: 5 parse; 7 analyse, analyze, break up, resolve; 9 anatomize, break down, take apart; 10 break apart

dissection: 8 analysis; 9 analysing, dissecing; 11 decomposing; 13 decomposition

dissed: 8 insulted

dissemble: 3 act; 4 mask, sham; 5 cloak, feign; 6 affect; 7 pretend; 11 dissimulate

dissembler: 5 phony; 6 fibber, phoney; 9 hypocrite

dissembling: 6 deceit; 7 evasion, fencing; 8 feigning, pretense; 9 deception, shuffling; 12 equivocation

disseminate: 4 shed; 5 graft; 6 spread; 7 bestrew, diffuse, disband, scatter; 8 dispense, disperse; 9 broadcast, circulate, evulgate, propagate; 10 distribute, overspread, pass around; 11 circularise, circularize

dissemination: 6 airing; 9 diffusion, dispersal, spreading; 10 dispersion; 11 circulation, dissipation

disseminator: 10 propagator

dissension: 7 discord; 10 dissidence, dissonance; 12 disagreement

dissent: 5 demur; 6 resist; 7 protest; 8 disagree; 9 objection; 10 difference

dissenter: 5 rebel; 7 croaker, growler, seceder; 8 grumbler, objector, recusant; 9 dissident, protester; 10 contestant, malcontent, separatist

dissentious: 8 divisive, factious

dissertation: 5 theme; 6 thesis; 8 treatise

disservice: 7 ill turn; 10 ill service

dissever: 4 rend; 5 sever, split; 6 divide, sunder; 7 carve up, split up; 8 separate; 9 subdivide

disseverance: 9 severance; 10 disjoining, separating, separation; 11 disengaging

dissidence: 7 discord; 10 dissension, dissonance

dissident: 5 rebel; 7 croaker, growler; 8 grumbler, objector; 9 dissenter, heretical, heterodox, protester; 10 contestant, dissenting, malcontent

dissimilar: 3 odd; 5 mixed; 6 divers, unlike, varied; 7 diverse, mingled, unalike, various; 8 assorted, not alike; 9 different, differing, disparate; 11 diversified

dissimulate: 9 dissemble

dissimulation: 6 deceit; 9 deception; 11 dissembling

dissipate: 4 fool; 5 shoot, waste; 6 dispel; 7 break up, fritter, scatter; 8 disperse, dissolve, fool away, melt away, squander; 9 evaporate, spread out; 10 be prodigal, be wasteful, frivol away; 11 fritter away

dissipated: 3 gay; 4 fast; 5 frail; 6 lavish, rakish; 7 gallant, profuse, riotous; 8 degraded, gambling, prodigal, wasteful; 9 debauched, dispelled, dissolute, libertine, unthrifty; 10 degenerate, profligate, thriftless; 11 extravagant, improvident, incontinent, overliberal

dissociable: 9 separable, severable

dissocial: 8 unsocial; 9 reclusive; 10 antisocial, unsociable

dissociate: 7 divorce; 8 disjoint, disunite; 9 disengage

dissociated: 11 unconnected

dissociating: 9 severance; 10 disjoining, separating, separation; 11 disengaging; 12 disseverance, dissociation; 13 disconnecting

dissolute: 4 fast; 5 light; 6 wanton; 7 corrupt, riotous; 8 degraded, recreant, scampish, unchaste; 9 corrupted, debauched, graceless, libertine, reprobate; 10 degenerate, dissipated, licentious, profligate

dissolution: 4 fall, obit, rest; 7 breakup, quietus, release; 8 solution; 9 departure; 10 breaking up, disruption, dissolving, profligacy, resolution

dissolvable: 10 dissoluble

dissolve: 2 go; 4 fade, fuse, pass; 5 blend, merge, solve, unite; 6 absorb, dispel, embody, vanish; 7 analyze, blend in, break up, combine, conjoin, disband, fade out,

resolve; 8 coalesce, disannul, fade away, melt away, vaporize; 9 disappear, disembody, dissipate, evaporate, fall apart; 10 amalgamate, centralize, impregnate; 11 consolidate, incorporate

dissolved substance: 6 solute

dissolver: 7 solvent, thinner; 8 dilutant; 9 resolvent; 10 dissolvent

dissolving: 8 solution; 11 dissolution

dissonance: 5 noise; 6 racket; 7 discord; 9 cacophony; 10 dissension, dissidence; 11 discordance; 12 disagreement

dissonant: 9 unmusical; 10 discordant, inharmonic, nonmusical, unresolved

dissuade: 5 deter

dissyllable: 10 disyllable

distaff: 6 female

distain: 5 stain; 6 befoul, bemire; 7 begrime, besmear; 8 maculate, dishonor

distal: 3 far; 6 far off, remote, wide of; 7 distant, far away

distance: 3 gap; 5 shunt, space; 6 length, remove; 8 interval, outstrip, overcome, surmount; 9 aloofness; 10 separation; 11 outdistance; 15 spatial interval

distant: 3 far; 5 aloof; 6 distal, far off, remote, wide of; 7 far away, removed

distant view: 5 vista

distaste: 7 dislike; 8 aversion; 9 antipathy, disrelish

distasteful: 4 foul; 5 yucky; 6 bitter, odious, wicked; 7 loathly; 8 unsavory; 9 loathsome, repellant, repellent, revolting, unsavoury; 10 disgustful, disgusting; 11 unpalatable

distend: 4 flex, puff; 5 swell, widen; 6 blow up, dilate, expand, extend, rarefy, spread; 7 amplify, develop, inflate, magnify, stretch, swell up; 9 be elastic, spread out; 10 aggrandize

distended: 5 puffy, tumid; 6 blowzy, puffed, spread; 7 bloated, bulbous, bulging, dilated, gibbous, swollen; 8 extended; 9 edematous, stretched, tumescent

distension: 8 diastole

distich: 3 duo; 4 duad, duet, dyad, pair, span, yoke; 5 brace, twain; 6 couple; 7 couplet, twosome; 9 doubleton

distill: 4 drip, drop; 5 plash, trill; 6 distil, purify, strain; 7 dribble, extract, trickle; 8 make pure; 9 percolate, sublimate

distillation: 6 oozing; 7 leakage; 10 distillate; 11 distillment, percolation

distillation apparatus: 5 still

distilled: 8 outlined; 10 summarized

distillery: 5 still

distinct: 4 flat; 5 broad, clear, plain, round; 6 marked; 7 decided, glaring, pointed, staring; 8 apparent, clear-cut, definite, discrete, explicit; 9 trenchant; 10 articulate, in full view, peremptory, stertorous, well marked; 11 conspicuous, in plain view, well defined

distinction: 4 mark, name, note; 6 figure; 8 eminence; 11 preeminence

distinctive: 7 typical; 11 identifying; 12 classifiable

distinctly: 7 clearly, plainly; 9 glaringly; 10 apparently, definitely

distinctness: 7 clarity; 9 otherness, plainness, severalty, sharpness; 10 definition

distinguish: 3 ken, key, spy; 4 espy, mark, name, tell, view; 5 match, place; 6 key out, secern; 7 discern, make out, match up, pick out, realize; 8 classify, describe, discover, identify, separate; 9 recognize, secernate, signalize, tell apart; 10 categorize

distinguishable: 6 unlike; 7 unalike; 8 distinct, not alike; 9 different, differing; 10 dissimilar

distinguished: 5 great, ultra; 6 placed; 7 eminent, made out; 10 classified, identified, recognized; 11 categorized

Distinguished Service Cross: 3 DSC [acron]

distort: 4 daub, warp; 5 belie, color, twist, wring; 6 deform, garble, strain; 7 contort, falsify, pervert; 8 overdraw; 9 disfigure; 10 caricature, exaggerate; 12 misrepresent

distorted: 7 garbled, twisted; 8 deformed; 9 contorted, falsified, ill-shapen, malformed, misshapen, perverted

distorter: 7 pervert; 9 falsifier

distortion: 7 torture; 8 twisting; 9 deforming, deformity, straining; 10 aberration, contorting, contortion, distorting, perversion; 11 deformation

distract: 4 cark; 6 divert; 7 deflect, perturb, trouble, unhinge; 8 disorder, disquiet, draw away

distracted: 3 mad; 4 sick; 5 crazy; 7 frantic, hyped up; 8 demented, distrait, diverted, unhinged; 9 brainsick, disturbed; 10 demoniacal, distraught, hysterical, unbalanced; 11 in hysterics; 12 disconcerted

distraction: 6 raving; 7 madness; 8 delirium; 11 beguilement, desperation

distrain: 4 levy; 6 attach, commit; 10 confiscate

distrait: 6 absent; 10 abstracted, distracted

distraught: 3 mad; 7 frantic; 10 distracted, hysterical; 11 in hysterics, overwrought

distress: 3 ill, woe; 4 hurt, lack, need, want; 5 grief, trial, worry; 6 grieve, penury, sorrow; 7 afflict, poverty, trouble; 9 distraint, heartache, indigence, necessity, neediness, pauperism, privation, suffering; 10 affliction; 11 destitution; 12 difficulties

distressed: 7 needy, upset; 7 hard put, pinched, unhappy, worried; 8 grieving, saddened, strapped, stressed; 9 disturbed, dysphoric, in a bad way, in trouble; 10 disquieted

distressfulness: 11 seriousness

distressing: 3 sad; 5 sorry; 7 pitiful; 8 worrying; 9 troubling, worrisome; 10 deplorable,

disturbing, lamentable, perturbing; 11 distressful

distressingly: 9 painfully

distribute: 3 lot; 4 deal, pack; 5 allot, stack; 6 divide, pass on, set out, spread; 7 deal out, diffuse, dish out, dole out, give out, hand out, marshal, mete out, stagger; 8 dispense, disperse, give away, shell out; 9 apportion, broadcast, circulate, collocate, disembody, dismember, parcel out, propagate; 10 administer, pass around, portion out; 11 circularise, circularize, disseminate

distributed: 5 dealt; 7 alloted; 10 collocated; 11 parceled out

distribution: 5 array; 8 alloting, division, grouping; 9 allotment; 10 dispersion; 11 arrangement, disposition; 12 apportioning, dispensation, distributing

district: 4 zone; 6 sector; 7 quarter, section; 8 division; 9 territory

district attorney: 2 DA [acron]

District of Columbia: 2 DC

distrust: 5 doubt; 7 suspect; 8 cynicism, mistrust; 9 misgiving, suspicion; 10 scepticism, skepticism; 11 incredulity

distrustful: 10 scrupulous, suspicious; 11 unconvinced

distrusting: 8 doubting

disturb: 3 bug, irk, vex; 4 faze, tire; 5 annoy, cross, shake, touch, upset, worry; 6 bother, jumble, stir up, tumble; 7 agitate, commove, embroil, mortify, perplex, perturb, raise up, shake up, startle, trouble; 8 convulse, disquiet, unsettle; 9 disoblige, displease, incommode, interrupt; 10 discomfort, discompose

disturbance: 4 fray, stir, to-do; 5 noise, upset; 6 affray, ruffle; 7 turmoil; 8 disorder, disquiet; 9 agitation, commotion; 10 disruption, hurly burly, turbulence; 12 discomposure, interference, perturbation; 13 civil disorder

disturbed: 3 mad; 4 sick; 5 crazy, tired, upset, vexed; 6 teased; 7 plagued, worried; 8 agitated, bothered, demented, molested, pestered, shaken up, unhinged; 9 convulsed, stirred up, tremulous, unsettled; 10 disquieted, distracted, distressed, unbalanced; 11 maladjusted

disulfiram: 8 Antabuse

disunion: 5 split; 6 breach; 7 rupture; 8 disunity, division; 10 disruption, separation; 11 disjunction

disunite: 4 part; 6 divide; 7 divorce, embroil; 8 disjoint, entangle, separate; 9 disengage; 10 dissociate; 13 dissassociate

disunited: 4 torn; 5 split; 10 fragmented; 12 disconnected

disusage: 6 disuse; 9 desuetude, lack of use; 12 obsolescence

disuse: 7 neglect; 8 leave off; 9 lack of use

dit: 3 dot

dita: 8 dita bark; 9 devil tree

ditch: 3 dam; 4 dike, dyke, moat; 5 chuck, gully; 6 gutter, trench, trough; 7 bulwark, culvert

dither: 4 flap, fuss; 5 tizzy; 6 pother, shiver; 7 shudder; 9 confusion; 10 excitement

dithyrambic: 4 wild; 5 giddy, rabid; 6 doting, raving; 7 berserk, frantic; 8 frenetic, frenzied, rambling, unhinged, wild-eyed; 9 delirious, insensate, possessed, wandering; 10 incoherent, reasonless; 11 lightheaded, vertiginous

ditto: 5 again; 6 de novo, encore; 8 ding-dong; 9 ditto mark

ditty bag: 8 ditty box; 10 sailor's bag

diurnal: 5 daily; 9 quotidian

diva: 10 prima donna

divagate: 5 stray; 6 wander; 7 digress, diverge

divagation: 5 aside; 8 excursus; 10 digression; 11 parenthesis

divalent: 8 bivalent

divan: 4 dais; 5 diwan

divaricate: 7 radiate, diverge

divarication: 7 forking; 9 branching; 10 divergence; 11 bifurcation

dive: 3 dip; 4 skim, wade; 5 plump, plunk; 6 diving, header, plunge, saloon [U.S.]; 8 exchange, nose dive; 9 grill room, honky-tonk

dive brake: 8 airbrake

dive in: 8 plunge in

diver: 4 loon; 7 frogman; 10 scuba diver

diverge: 4 vary; 6 depart; 7 deviate; 8 disperse

divergence: 8 mismatch, variance; 9 departure, deviation, disparity, dispersal, variation; 10 difference, dispersion

diverging lens: 11 concave lens

divers: 3 odd; 5 mixed; 6 sundry, varied; 7 diverse, mingled, not a few, several, various; 8 assorted; 9 different; 10 all kinds of, dissimilar; 11 all manner of, diversified

diverse: 3 odd; 5 mixed; 6 divers, varied; 7 mingled, various; 8 assorted, polyglot; 9 different; 10 all kinds of, dissimilar; 11 diversified, all manner of

diversify: 7 broaden; 9 branch out

diversion: 7 pastime; 9 deflexion, deviation; 10 deflection, digression, recreation

diversity: 7 variety; 9 disparity; 10 unevenness, unlikeness; 11 discrepancy, diverseness

divert: 5 amuse; 7 deviate, disport, enliven; 8 distract; 9 entertain

diverted: 6 amused; 10 distracted; 11 entertained; 12 disconcerted

divertimento: 8 serenade

diverting: 3 fun; 7 amusing, amusive; 12 entertaining

divertissement: 5 farce; 7 pastime; 9 diversion

divest: 5 strip; 6 devest; 7 deprive, uncover; 9 dismantle; 10 dispossess

divestment: 7 removal; 8 removing; 9 taking off; 10 uncovering

dividable: 11 divisible by

divide: 3 add; 4 part, rend; 5 halve, sever, split; 6 bisect, cleave, sunder; 7 carve up, dole out, split up; 8 cut in two, dispense, dissever, disunite, fraction, multiply, separate, subtract; 9 apportion, parcel out, partition, subdivide, watershed; 10 distribute, portion out; 11 dichotomize

divided: 6 shared, sliced; 7 severed; 8 dual-lane, sundered; 9 divided up, shared out; 11 partitioned

divided up: 6 shared; 7 divided; 9 shared out

divide into fifths: 11 quinquesect

divide into four parts: 7 quarter

divide into three parts: 7 trisect

dividend: 4 bonus; 9 numerator; 11 installment

divider: 9 partition

dividing line: 4 line; 8 contrast; 11 demarcation

divination: 8 prophecy; 11 foretelling, soothsaying

divine: 5 godly, guess; 6 cleric; 7 elysian, godlike, suppose, surmise, suspect; 8 canonist, catholic, inspired, prophesy, reverend, soothsay; 9 Christian, churchman, clergyman; 10 conjecture, scholastic, scriptural, superhuman, vaticinate; 11 evangelical

divined: 6 mooted; 7 assumed, guessed; 8 imagined, presumed, supposed, surmised; 9 suspected; 10 postulated

divineness: 8 divinity

divining rod: 3 rod; 4 wand; 6 dowser; 8 caduceus; 11 water finder

divinity: 3 god; 5 deity; 8 immortal, theology; 13 divinity fudge

divisible: 5 prime; 7 aliquot; 8 partible, scissile [Chem]; 9 separable; 10 fractional, reciprocal

division: 4 army, host, kind, part, sort, type, wing, zone; 5 class, corps, split, squad; 6 breach, column, sector; 7 battery, brigade, company, platoon, quarter, rupture, section, sorting, variety; 8 alloting, category, district, disunion, dividing, garrison, grouping, regiment, squadron, variance; 9 allotment, battalion, partition; 10 assortment, detachment, disruption; 11 classifying, subdivision

divisive: 8 factious; 11 dissentious

divisor: 6 factor; 11 denominator

divorce: 4 part; 6 cut off, detach; 7 split up; 8 disjoint, disunite, separate; 10 dissociate

divulge: 4 blab; 5 break, let on, peach, spill; 6 expose, impart, let out, reveal; 7 declare, let drop, let fall; 8 blurt out, bring out, disclose, discover, give away

divulged: 6 let out; 7 let slip

divvy up: 4 deal; 5 share; 9 apportion; 10 portion out

diwan: 5 divan

Dixie: 5 South; 9 Dixieland; 11 Confederacy

Dixie cup: 8 paper cup; 11 drinking cup

dizen: 5 prank; 7 bedizen, garnish

dizzily: 7 giddily; 13 light-headedly

dizziness: 7 vertigo; 8 swimming; 9 giddiness

dizzy: 5 giddy, silly, woozy; 9 airheaded; 11 empty-headed, light-headed, vertiginous, wooly-headed, woolyminded

DJ: 8 Dow Jones; 10 disk jockey

Djakarta: 7 Jakarta; 18 capital of Indonesia

Djibouti: 13 Afars and Issas; 17 capital of Djibouti

djinni: 5 genie, jinni; 6 djinny, jinnee

dkg: 3 dag; 8 decagram, dekagram

dkl: 3 dal; 9 decaliter, dekaliter

dkm: 3 dam; 9 decameter, dekameter

dl: 9 deciliter

dm: 9 decimeter, decimetre

do: 2 ut; 3 act, con, doh, fit, nab, set; 4 bash, bilk, bite, coif, come, fare, make, meet, pray, scam, suit, work; 5 avail, befit, brawl, cause, cheat, cozen, dress, pluck, serve; 6 answer, behave, chouse, coiffe, diddle, euchre, hairdo, jockey, just do, manage, please; 7 arrange, defraud, execute, make out, operate, perform, prithee, satisfy, suffice, swindle; 8 be enough, carry out, coiffure, exercise, get along, practice, practise; 9 be an actor, victimize; 10 be adequate, be in action, pass muster, take effect; 11 be effective

doable: 8 feasible; 10 achievable, realizable; 11 performable, practicable

do a job on: 5 quash; 7 put down; 8 suppress

do away with: 4 undo; 8 get rid of, set aside, shake off; 9 cast aside, eliminate

dobbin: 9 farm horse

dobson: 9 dobsonfly; 13 hellgrammiate

doc: 2 MD, Dr.; 6 doctor, medico; 8 sawbones; 9 physician

docile: 6 gentle; 9 teachable, tractable

dock: 3 bob, lop, mow; 4 clip, crop, port, quay, reap, slip, tail, yard; 5 basin, prune, shave, shear, wharf; 6 harbor, sorrel; 7 bobtail, dockage; 8 dockyard, shipyard, wharfage; 9 sour grass

dockage: 4 dock; 10 docking fee

docked: 6 lopped; 7 clipped, garbled; 9 mutilated, truncated

docker: 6 loader, lumper; 8 dockhand; 9

stevedore; 10 dock worker; 12 dock-walloper, longshoreman

docket: 3 tag; 5 entry, label; 6 agenda, ticket; 7 agendum, heading, voucher, warrant; 8 calendar, schedule; 10 memorandum, put a sign on; 11 certificate

docking: 7 mooring, tying up; 10 drop anchor

docking facility: 4 dock; 7 dockage

docking fee: 7 dockage

dock worker: 6 docker, loader, lumper; 8 dockhand; 9 stevedore; 12 dock-walloper, longshoreman

dockyard: 4 dock, slip, yard; 5 wharf; 8 shipyard

doctor: 2 MD, Dr.; 3 doc, fix; 4 cure, heal, mend; 5 nurse; 6 bushel, medico, physic, remedy, repair; 7 plaster, restore, touch on; 8 doctor up, medicate, sawbones; 9 furbish up, physician; 10 adulterate; 12 sophisticate

doctor's degree: 9 doctorate

doctoral dissertation: 14 doctoral thesis

Doctor of Arts: 5 ArtsD

Doctor of Dental Medicine: 3 DMD

Doctor of Dental Surgery: 3 DDS

Doctor of Divinity: 2 DD

Doctor of Education: 3 DEd, EdD

Doctor of Law: 2 J.D.; 11 Juris Doctor

Doctor of Laws: 3 LLD

Doctor of Medicine: 2 MD

Doctor of Music: 4 DMus, MusD

Doctor of Musical Arts: 5 AMusD

Doctor of Optometry: 2 OD

Doctor of Osteopathy: 2 DO

Doctor of Philosophy: 3 Ph.D.

Doctor of Public Health: 3 DPH

Doctor of Sacred Theology: 3 S.T.D.

Doctor of Science: 2 DS; 3 ScD

Doctor of the Church: 6 Doctor

Doctor of Theology: 3 ThD

Doctor of Veterinary Medicine: 3 DVM [acron]; 16 veterinary doctor; 17 veterinary surgeon

doctor up: 6 doctor; 10 adulterate; 12 sophisticate

doctrine: 3 ism; 5 dogma; 6 canons, school; 8 articles; 10 philosophy

docudrama: 11 documentary

document: 4 text; 6 papers; 7 writing; 8 text file

documentary: 9 docudrama; 10 documental; 12 infotainment; 15 documentary film

documentation: 7 support; 13 certification, corroboration

documented: 8 attested; 12 certificated, credentialed; 13 authenticated

dodder: 4 wane; 6 coggle, paddle, toddle, totter, waddle; 7 decline

doddering: 4 gaga; 6 senile; 7 doddery

D

dodecanoic acid: 10 lauric acid

dodge: 3 shy, wag; **4** beat, duck, hunt; **5** blink, dance, elude, evade, fudge, hedge, lurch, mouse, parry, shake, shift, shirk, skirt, swing, trace, track, trail; **6** blench, flinch, put off, scheme, seesaw; **7** dodging, finesse; **8** side blow, sidestep; **10** circumvent, make way for; **11** artful dodge, bob and weave, contrivance, give place to

Dodgem: 9 bumper car

dodger: 3 fox; **7** corn dab, shirker; **8** slyboots; **10** corn dodger

dodging: 5 dodge; **6** escape, scheme; **7** evasion; **8** shifting, shunning; **9** avoidance; **11** turning away

Dodgson: 7 Carroll; **12** Lewis Carroll; **14** Charles Dodgson; **15** Reverend Dodgson; **22** Charles Lutwidge Dodgson

dodgy: 3 sly; **4** foxy, wily; **5** dicey, risky, slick; **6** chancy, crafty, tricky; **7** cunning, knavish, tricksy; **8** guileful; **9** chanceful

dodo: 4 fogy; **5** fogey; **6** dotard, fossil; **7** extinct

doe: 3 hen, roe, sow; **4** buck, hart, mare, stag

doer: 5 actor, agent; **6** worker; **7** hustler; **8** activist; **9** performer; **11** man of action, perpetrator

doff: 7 take off

dog: 3 cad, cur, hag, pig, tag; **4** boar, buck, cock, hart, heel, pawl, stag, tail; **5** beset, brute, chase, click, drake, frump, horse, hound, stalk, track, trail, whelp; **6** detent, figure, gander, shadow, woofer; **7** andiron, bounder, dogiron, firedog, go after, mongrel, ratchet; **10** blackguard, chase after

dog collar: 6 choker, collar; **8** neckband

dog days: 6 summer; **8** canicule; **13** canicular days

dog fennel: 7 mayweed; **14** Anthemis cotula; **15** stinking mayweed; **17** stinking chamomile; **23** Eupatorium capillifolium

dogfight: 6 air war

dogged: 4 dour; **7** bulldog; **9** tenacious; **10** unyielding; **11** indomitable

doggedness: 8 tenacity; **11** persistence, persistency, pertinacity; **12** perseverence; **13** tenaciousness

doggerel: 6 Gothic, jingle; **10** heathenish, outlandish, tramontane

doggie: 5 doggy, pooch; **6** bow-wow

dogging: 10 persisting

doggo: 8 in hiding; **10** out of sight

doggy: 5 pooch; **6** bow-wow, doggie

doggy bag: 9 doggie bag

doghouse: 6 kennel

dogma: 5 tenet; **6** belief; **8** doctrine; **10** blind faith; **11** blind belief

dogmatic: 6 formal, solemn; **8** besotted, con-fined, positive; **9** conceited, confident, fanatical, illiberal, trenchant; **10** dogmatical, infatuated, intolerant

dogmatizer: 9 dogmatist, ideologue; **10** opinionist; **11** doctrinaire

do-gooder: 8 crusader, improver; **12** humanitarian, knight errant

Dog Star: 6 Sirius, Sothis; **8** Canicula

dogtooth: 6 canine, cuspid; **8** eyetooth; **11** canine tooth, houndstooth

dogwood: 6 cornel; **11** dogwood tree

dogwood family: 9 Cornaceae

Doha: 4 Bida; **6** El Beda; **14** capital of Qatar

dohickey: 5 gizmo; **6** doodad; **7** gimmick, gubbins; **8** dojigger; **9** doohickey, thingummy; **10** thingmabob, thingmajig; **11** thingamabob, thingamajig, thingumabob, thingumajig

do in: 4 dish, undo; **5** do for, waste; **8** knock off; **9** liquidate

doing: 6 acting, action; **7** current, going on; **8** movement; **9** execution, operation; **10** performing; **11** carrying out, performance

doings: 3 job; **4** life; **6** things; **8** dealings, the world

doing time: 6 in jail, jailed, sent up; **7** in limbo; **8** in chains, in charge, in prison; **10** imprisoned

doit: 6 trifle; **7** old coin

doldrums: 5 blues, dumps, sulks; **7** sadness; **8** darkness, the blues, the dumps; **9** dejection, heaviness, stagnancy; **10** bad spirits, blue devils, depression, dismalness, gloominess, low spirits, melancholy, somberness, stagnation; **11** joylessness, melancholia

dole: 4 care, fret, help, load, meed, mite, pogy; **5** pogey; **6** burden; **7** anxiety, concern; **8** oblation, pittance; **9** offertory; **10** solicitude

doled out: 8 dealt out, meted out; **11** apportioned, parceled out

doleful: 3 sad; **7** pensive; **8** mournful; **10** melancholy; **11** melancholic

dole out: 3 lot; **4** deal; **5** allot; **6** divide; **7** deal out, dish out, fork out, give out, mete out; **8** dispense, shell out; **9** apportion, parcel out; **10** administer, distribute, portion out, squeeze out

doll: 4 bird; **5** dolly; **6** puppet

dollar: 4 buck, clam; **10** dollar bill, dollar coin, dollar mark, dollar sign

dollar sign: 10 dollar mark

dolled up: 7 dressed; **9** dressed-up, spiffed up, spruced up; **11** all dolled up; **13** dressed to kill

doll up: 4 do up; **6** glam up; **8** pretty up

dolmas: 18 stuffed grape leaves

dolor: 4 pain; **6** dolour; **9** suffering; **10** infelicity, mental pain, sufferance; 11 unhappiness

dolour: 4 ache; 5 dolor

dolphin: 7 trident; 8 mahimahi, porpoise; 11 dolphinfish

dolphinfish: 8 mahimahi

dolt: 5 booby, noddy, nonny; 6 noodle, stupid; 7 dullard; 10 pudden-head; 11 pudding head; 12 stupid person

doltish: 5 blunt, heavy; 6 obtuse, stolid, stupid, unwise; 8 cloddish, ungifted

domain: 3 orb; 4 area, land, soil; 5 arena, field, honor, manor, orbit, range, realm, tract, world; 6 circle, ground, region, sphere; 7 circuit, commune, demesne; 8 province; 9 territory; 13 abstract space

dome: 6 cupola; 12 domed stadium

domed: 7 vaulted

Domesday book: 7 diptych, Red book; 8 Blue book; 9 cartulary

domestic: 4 home, tame; 6 indoor; 7 servant; 10 intramural, stay-at-home, vernacular; 11 residential

domesticate: 4 tame; 7 break in; 8 colonize; 9 cultivate; 10 naturalize; 11 acclimatize, domesticize

domesticated: 8 domestic; 10 vernacular; 11 naturalized

domesticated animal: 11 tamed animal

domestic cat: 8 house cat

domestic fowl: 4 fowl; 7 poultry

domestic help: 8 domestic; 12 house servant

domestic science: 13 home economics

domicile: 4 home; 5 abode; 7 housing, lodging; 8 dwelling; 9 lodgement, residence; 10 habitation

domiciliation: 3 pad; 4 digs; 8 diggings, lodgings

dominance: 5 reign, say-so; 7 control; 9 advantage, authority; 10 ascendance, ascendancy, ascendence, ascendency, governance, government, laterality

dominant: 7 regnant, supreme; 9 at the head, paramount; 11 in authority, predominant

dominate: 4 rule; 5 reign; 6 master; 7 command, overtop, pervade, prevail; 8 overlook; 10 run through; 11 predominate; 12 preponderate, rule the roost

dominated: 9 henpecked

dominating: 5 bossy; 9 ascendant, ascendent; 10 autocratic, commanding, invincible, peremptory, resistless; 11 indomitable, magisterial, overlooking

domination: 4 rule, sway; 7 command, control, mastery; 8 dominion; 9 supremacy; 10 regulation, suzerainty; 11 sovereignty

domineer: 5 bully; 6 hector; 7 dictate; 8 browbeat; 9 tyrannize; 10 intimidate, lord it over, push around

domineering: 8 bullying; 9 high-flown; 10

assumption, intolerant, usurpation; 11 overbearing

dominie: 5 usher; 6 domine; 7 dominee, dominus; 9 pedagogue, clergyman; 11 abecedarian; 12 schoolmaster

dominion: 4 rule, sway; 6 colony; 7 command, control, mandate; 8 province, republic; 9 supremacy, territory; 10 domination, regulation, suzerainty; 11 sovereignty; 18 democratic republic

domino: 4 mask; 5 visor; 7 eye mask; 8 half mask

dominoes: 7 dominos

dominos: 6 go bang; 8 dominoes

don: 4 wear; 5 coach, put on; 6 assume, bigwig; 7 get into; 8 director

Don: 8 Don River

donated: 7 granted; 8 bestowed; 11 given freely

donation: 5 grant; 8 donating; 12 contribution

done: 4 over; 6 done up; 7 done for, through; 8 complete, finished; 9 completed, fulfilled; 11 through with

donee: 6 lessee; 7 grantee; 9 recipient; 11 beneficiary

done for: 4 done, gone, sped, sunk; 5 kaput; 6 done up, ruined, undone; 8 washed up; 10 wrought out

donjon: 3 pen; 4 brig, gaol, hold, jail, keep, stir; 6 cooler [slang], lockup, prison; 7 dungeon, slammer, the Rock; 8 big house [slang], hoosegow, stockade; 9 calaboose [slang], guardroom, oubliette; 10 guard house, San Quentin; 11 penal colony, prison house; 12 penitentiary

Don Juan: 3 rip; 4 goat, rake; 5 satyr; 6 lecher; 7 fast man, gallant, seducer; 8 Lothario; 9 debauchee, ladies' man

donkey: 3 ass; 4 fool; 7 jackass, tomfool; 11 domestic ass, Equus asinus

donkey engine: 12 switch engine; 15 auxiliary engine

donkeywork: 5 grind; 8 drudgery, plodding

Donne: 9 John Donne

donnish: 8 academic, pedantic

donnybrook: 3 row; 4 fray, to-do; 5 brawl, broil, melee; 6 affray, breeze, fracas, hubbub, pother, racket, rumble, rumpus, squall, uproar; 7 howling, rhubarb [baseball], ruction, shindig, trouble; 8 brouhaha, scramble; 9 imbroglio, scrimmage; 10 bear garden, free-for-all; 11 battle royal, embroilment

donor: 5 giver; 9 presenter; 10 subscriber; 11 contributor

do-nothing: 3 bum; 5 idler; 6 loafer; 8 layabout

donut: 5 torus; 6 sinker, toroid; 8 doughnut

doodad: 5 gizmo; **7** gimmick, gubbins; **8** dohickey, dojigger; **9** doohickey, thingummy; **10** thingmabob, thingmajig; **11** thingamabob, thingamajig, thingumabob, thingumajig

doodle: 3 oaf, put; **4** calf, colt, loon, lout, tony; **5** block, stick, stock; **7** buzzard, dullard

doodlebug: 7 ant lion; **8** buzz bomb; **9** robot bomb; **10** flying bomb

doofus: 6 dimwit, nitwit; **7** half-wit

doohickey: 5 gizmo; **6** doodad; **7** gimmick, gubbins; **8** dohickey, dojigger; **9** thingummy; **10** thingmabob, thingmajig; **11** thingamabob, thingamajig, thingumabob, thingumajig

doom: 4 fate; **6** assess, devote; **7** condemn, destine, last day; **8** dies irae [Lat], doomsday, foredoom, sentence; **9** designate; **10** predestine; **11** crack of doom, Judgment day; **13** day of Judgment

doomed: 4 lost; **5** fated; **6** cursed, damned, undone; **7** devoted, unlucky, unsaved; **8** accursed, ill-fated, stranded; **9** condemned, ill-omened; **10** ill-starred, to be pitied, unredeemed

doomsday: 4 doom; **7** last day; **8** dies irae [Lat]; **10** millennium; **11** crack of doom, Judgment day; **12** remote future

door: 4 gate, lips; **5** chops, hatch, inlet, mouth, porch; **6** cordon, portal, wicket; **7** doorway, orifice, portico, postern; **8** trapdoor; **9** entry door, operculum, threshold; **10** room access; **11** passage door

doorbell: 4 bell; **6** buzzer

do-or-die: 9 desperate

doorframe: 8 doorcase

door guard: 6 porter; **7** doorman; **10** doorkeeper, gatekeeper, hall porter

doorhandle: 8 doorknob

door jamb: 4 jamb; **8** door post

doorkeeper: 5 usher; **6** beadle, porter, warder; **7** doorman; **9** door guard; **10** gatekeeper, hall porter

doorman: 6 beadle, porter, warder; **9** door guard; **10** doorkeeper, gatekeeper, hall porter

doormat: 8 weakling; **10** welcome mat

doorstep: 8 doorsill; **9** threshold

doorway: 4 door; **7** gangway, gateway; **8** driveway, hatchway; **9** threshold; **10** room access

dopamine: 8 Dopastat, Intropin

dopant: 8 additive; **11** doping agent

Dopastat: 8 dopamine, Intropin

dope: 3 pot; **4** cola, gage, weed; **5** dummy, dunce, ganja, grass, skunk, smoke; **6** dope up, skinny; **7** low-down; **8** cannabis, dumb-bell, Mary Jane, **9** ignoramus, marihuana, marijuana

doped: 7 drugged; **10** narcotized

dopey: 4 dopy, fool; **5** goosy; **6** goosey; **7** foolish; **8** anserine; **9** gooselike

Doppler effect: 12 Doppler shift

dork: 4 jerk

dorm: 4 hall; **9** dormitory; **13** residence hall; **16** student residence

dormancy: 8 sleeping; **10** quiescence, quiescency

dormant: 6 hidden, latent, occult, torpid; **7** abeyant, lurking; **8** inactive, sleeping; **10** smoldering; **11** hibernating, sound as a top

dormer: 5 attic; **7** lantern; **8** top floor

dormitory: 4 dorm, hall; **7** bedroom, boudoir; **8** dorm room; **13** dormitory room, residence hall; **16** student residence

dormitory room: 8 dorm room; **9** dormitory

dormouse: 6 marmot; **9** slumberer

dorm room: 9 dormitory; **13** dormitory room

dormy: 6 dormie

dorp: 3 ham; **6** hamlet; **7** village

dorsal: 5 after; **7** abaxial

dorsal region: 5 chine; **12** lumbar region

dorsum: 4 back, loin, rump, tail; **5** croup; **6** breech; **7** buttock; **10** posteriors

dory: 6 dinghy; **7** drogher, rowboat; **13** bateau battery [Can]

dosage: 4 dose

dose: 3 lot; **4** drug; **5** batch, stock; **6** dosage, potion; **7** draught; **12** prescription

do service: 5 adore; **6** aspire; **7** worship; **9** pay homage

dosimeter: 9 dosemeter

doss: 5 crash; **8** doss down

Dostoyevsky: 10 Dostoevski, Dostoevsky; **11** Dostoievski, Dostoyevski; **15** Fedor Dosoievski, Fedor Dostoevsky; **16** Fedor Dostoyevski, Fedor Dostoyevsky

dosvidanya: 4 ciao; **5** adieu, aloha; **7** goodbye; **8** farewell, sayonara; **11** leave taking, valediction; **12** hasta la vista [Sp]; **14** auf wiedersehen [Ger]

dot: 3 dit **4** dust, mote, spot, stud; **5** blaze, notch, point, score, speck; **7** scatter, stipple; **8** appanage, disperse, maculate, sprinkle; **11** constellate; **13** material point

dotage: 7 fatuity; **8** senility; **15** second childhood

dote: 4 rave; **6** drivel, ramble, trifle, wander; **8** be senile

do the best one can: 9 take pains

do time: 9 serve time; **10** be in prison; **12** be imprisoned

doting: 4 fond, wild; **5** giddy, rabid; **6** raving, senile; **7** adoring, berserk, frantic; **8** frenetic, frenzied, rambling, unhinged, wild-eyed; **9** delirious, insensate, possessed, wandering; **10** incoherent, reasonless

dot matrix printer: 10 dot printer; 11 wire printer; 13 matrix printer, stylus printer

dot product: 12 inner product; 13 scalar product

dots per inch: 3 dpi [acron]

dotted: 6 dashed; 7 flecked, specked; 8 speckled, stippled

dotty: 3 mad; 4 bats, daft, gaga, loco, nuts; 5 balmy, barmy, batty, buggy, crazy, kooky, loony, loopy, nutty, wacky; 6 crazed, fruity, in love, insane, kookie, soft on; 7 bonkers, cracked, far gone, haywire, lunatic, smitten, touched; 8 crackers, demented, deranged, enamored, maddened, not right

douanier: 6 gauger [Brit]; 9 exciseman; 14 customs officer; 15 customs official

Douay Version: 10 Douay Bible; 16 Douay-Rheims Bible, Rheims-Douay Bible; 18 Douay-Rheims Version, Rheims-Douay Version

double: 4 dual, fold, mate, pair, twin; 5 duple, image, twice, wheel; 6 doubly, duplex, forked, repeat, treble; 7 doubled, finesse, twofold; 8 bivalent, double up, doubling, redouble, stunt man, two-baser; 9 dualistic, duplicate, replicate, temporize, threefold, two-bagger; 10 circumvent, double over, stuntwoman, two-base hit; 11 counterpart, double-faced, gerrymander, reduplicate

double back: 8 turn back; 9 backtrack

double bass: 4 bass; 8 bass viol; 10 bass fiddle, bull fiddle, contrabass, string bass

double bassoon: 7 bassoon, serpent; 13 contrabassoon, contrafagotto

double blind study: 10 blind study; 13 clinical study

double boiler: 14 double saucepan

double-chinned: 5 jowly; 11 loose-jowled

double cross: 10 double deal; 13 be duplicitous

double-crosser: 7 traitor; 8 betrayer; 12 double-dealer

doubled: 6 double; 7 twofold; 10 duplicated

double dagger: 6 dieses; 13 double obelisk

double deal: 11 double cross; 13 be duplicitous

double-dealer: 7 traitor; 8 betrayer; 13 double-crosser

double-dealing: 8 two-faced; 9 deceitful, duplicity; 10 Janus-faced; 11 double-faced, duplicitous; 12 ambidextrous; 13 double-tongued

double dealing: 5 guile; 6 double; 8 betrayal, doubling; 9 duplicity, treachery; 10 disloyalty; 11 double-faced; 12 double-handed

double-decker: 3 bus; 5 coach; 6 jitney; 7 autobus, omnibus; 8 motorbus; 9 charabanc; 10 motorcoach

double down: 8 turn down; 9 down under

double entente: 4 smut; 6 bawdry; 8 ribaldry; 9 obscenity; 14 double entendre

double-faced: 6 double; 8 two-faced; 9 deceitful; 10 Janus-faced; 11 duplicitous; 12 ambidextrous; 13 double-dealing

double feature: 8 twin bill; 12 double-header

doubleheader: 8 twin bill; 13 double feature

double obelisk: 6 dieses; 12 double dagger

double over: 4 fold

double-propeller plane: 8 twin-prop; 10 double-prop; 18 twin-propeller-plane

double quick: 7 rapidly; 10 double time

double refraction: 13 birefringence

double saucepan: 12 double boiler

double sawbuck: 7 Jackson; 16 twenty-dollar bill

double star: 6 binary; 10 binary star

doublet: 8 camisole, doublets; 9 gabardine

double time: 11 double quick

doubleton: 3 duo; 4 duad, duet, dyad, pair, span, yoke; 5 brace, twain; 6 couple; 7 couplet, distich, twosome

double up: 4 lame, maim; 6 double, muzzle, parlay; 7 cripple; 8 paralyze; 9 hamstring, prostrate

doubly: 5 twice; 6 double; 9 in two ways

doubt: 5 douse; 7 dubiety, suspect; 8 distrust, question; 11 dubiousness, incertitude, uncertainty

doubter: 5 cynic; 7 sceptic, skeptic; 8 agnostic

doubtful: 7 dubious; 9 dubitable, tentative; 10 in question, suspicious

doubting: 9 sceptical, skeptical; 11 distrusting, questioning

doubtless: 4 sure; 6 certes [Lat], surely; 7 no doubt; 8 of course; 9 assuredly, certainly; 10 for certain; 11 undoubtedly; 12 and no mistake, without doubt

douceur: 4 gift; 5 bribe; 8 gratuity; 10 honorarium

dough: 3 pap; 4 curd, gelt, kale, loot, pelf, pulp; 5 bread, lucre, money; 6 dinero, moolah; 7 cabbage, pudding, shekels

doughnut: 4 halo, ring; 5 donut, torus; 6 anulus, sinker, toroid; 7 annulus; 10 anchor ring

doughty: 5 hardy; 7 valiant; 8 fearless; 12 strong-minded

doughy: 5 pasty, soggy; 6 spongy

douglas fir: 6 red fir

do up: 6 doll up, glam up, vamp up; 7 patch up, touch up; 8 pretty up; 9 plaster up

dour: 4 dark, glum, grim, hard, sour; 5 harsh, moody, rigid, stern, stiff; 6 dogged, morose, severe, strict, sullen; 7 bulldog;

D

9 glowering, saturnine, tenacious; **10** forbidding, unyielding

douse: 3 dip, sop; **4** duck, dunk, sink, soak, wipe; **5** dowse, snuff, souse, swash; **6** drench, engulf, plunge, put out, splash; **7** blow out; **8** snuff out

dove: 4 lamb; **5** squab; **6** pigeon; **8** peacenik

dovecote: 6 stable; **9** birdhouse; **11** columbarium

dovekie: 9 little auk

dove of peace: 9 white dove

Dover: 17 capital of Delaware

dovetail: 3 jam; **4** link; **5** miter, wedge; **6** rabbet, splice; **7** fit to a T, mortise; **13** dovetail joint

dovish: 10 pacifistic

dowdiness: 8 drabness; **10** homeliness

dowdy: 5 frump; **6** frumpy; **7** unkempt; **8** frumpish, pandowdy, sluttish; **13** draggletailed

dowel: 6 joggle; **8** dowel pin

dower: 5 dowry, endow; **6** dowery

do what one is told: 4 obey; **5** comply

down: 3 cut, low; **4** blue, kill, land; **6** devour, polish, refine; **7** consume, cut down, down pat, padding, toss off, wadding; **8** belt down, bolt down, downcast, downward, fine-tune, mastered, pour down, pull down, push down; **9** declining, depressed, down quark, downwards, drink down, go through, knock down, shoot down; **10** dispirited, downwardly; **11** downhearted, low-spirited

downcast: 3 low; **4** blue, down; **9** depressed; **10** dispirited

Down Easter: 6 Mainer

downer: 8 sedative; **10** depressant; **12** sedative drug

downfall: 4 fall, ruin, slip, tilt, trip; **5** crash, lurch; **6** tumble; **7** falling; **9** perdition, ruination; **11** devastation

down-fallen: 11 downtrodden

downhearted: 3 low; **4** blue, down; **8** downcast; **9** depressed; **10** dispirited; **11** low-spirited

downhill: 3 dip; **4** fall; **7** decline; **9** declivity, downwards; **11** declination, declivitous

down pat: 4 down; **8** mastered

down payment: 7 deposit, earnest

downpour: 6 deluge, soaker; **7** torrent; **10** cloudburst, waterspout

downright: 4 open, rank; **5** bluff, blunt, frank, plain, sheer; **6** arrant, candid, direct, purely; **7** far gone, sincere; **8** absolute; **9** decidedly, out-and-out, outspoken, radically, right-down, seriously

downriver: 10 downstream

downsizing: 7 cut back; **11** curtailment

downslope: 4 fall; **7** decline, descent; **9** declivity

downstairs: 5 below; **11** below stairs

downstream: 9 downriver

downswing: 8 downturn

down the drain: 6 in vain; **10** for nothing

down time: 7 off time, time off

down-to-earth: 6 earthy

downtown: 3 hub; **11** civic center

downtrodden: 5 sorry; **6** scurvy; **8** overcome, pitiable; **9** oppressed; **10** downfallen, persecuted

downturn: 9 downswing

downward-sloping: 8 downhill; **11** declivitous

downwind: 3 lee; **8** windward

downy: 4 soft; **6** flossy, fluffy, woolly; **7** flaccid, velvety; **8** downlike, soothing

do wonders: 5 outdo

dowry: 5 dower; **6** dowery; **7** alimony

dowse: 3 sop; **4** bang, beat, blow, dash, slam, soak, swap; **5** baste, douse, souse, thump; **6** drench, squash

dowser: 10 water witch; **11** divining rod, water finder, waterfinder

doxology: 5 grace; **6** praise; **7** hosanna; **11** benediction

doxy: 8 mistress, paramour; **9** concubine, courtesan, kept woman

doxycycline: 10 Vibramycin

doyen: 4 dean; **6** father

doyly: 5 doily; **6** doyley

doze: 3 nap; **6** drowse, siesta, snooze; **10** forty winks

dozen: 2 12; **3** XII, xii; **6** twelve

dozens: 4 gobs, lots, tons, wads; **5** heaps, loads, piles, rafts, scads, slews; **6** oodles, scores, stacks

doze off: 6 nod off; **7** dope off, drop off; **8** drift off, flake out; **9** drowse off; **10** fall asleep

dozer: 9 bulldozer

dpi: 11 dots per inch

Dr.: 2 MD; **3** doc; **6** doctor, Doctor, medico; **9** physician

drab: 4 dull, flat; **5** dingy, drear, livid, scrub, sober, sorry; **6** dismal, dreary, gloomy, leaden, sloven, somber, stodgy

drabble: 4 soil; **5** muddy, stain, sully; **6** dabble, smirch; **7** draggle

drachma: 4 dram; **6** drachm

Draco: 5 harpy, Minos; **7** vulture; **10** genus Draco; **11** birds of prey

Draconian: 7 Spartan; **9** stringent; **10** relentless; **11** strait-laced

draft: 4 gulp, note, swig; **5** brief, check, rough, study; **6** apercu, author, cheque, digest, draw up, enlist, indite, minute, muster, precis, sketch, tipple; **7** carting, compose, draught, drawing, epitome, hauling, outline, summary; **8** abstract, analysis, carriage, carrying, muster in, potation, shipping, skeleton, synopsis;

9 blueprint, conscript, draft copy, formulate, transport; 10 abridgment, air current, conveyance, rough draft; 11 rough sketch; 12 conscription

draft dodger: 11 draft evader
drafted: 11 conscripted
draftee: 9 conscript
draft off: 6 decant; 7 take off
drag: 3 lug, tow, tug; 4 bore, cart, draw, haul, pill, puff, pull, rake; 5 scuff, sweep, trail, train; 6 drag in, drag on, dredge, tangle; 7 drag out, embroil, sweep up; 8 hang back
dragnet: 5 trawl; 8 trawl net
dragon: 5 draco
drag one's feet: 5 stall; 10 dilly-dally; 13 procrastinate
dragon lizard: 6 Komodo; 11 giant lizard
dragoon: 6 coerce; 8 hunt down
drag out: 4 drag; 6 drag on, eke out; 7 draw out, spin out, stretch; 10 stretch out
drag through the mud: 6 malign; 7 point at, traduce; 8 badmouth
drain: 3 sap; 4 ooze; 5 empty; 6 absorb, finish, run out, strain, tap out; 7 deplete, exhaust, flow off; 8 drainage, enfeeble, flow away, run out of; 9 drainpipe, swallow up, waste pipe; 10 debilitate, impoverish
drained: 3 dry; 4 dead; 6 used up; 8 consumed, depleted, expended, finished; 9 exhausted, tapped out
drainpipe: 5 drain; 9 waste pipe
drain pit: 4 sump
drake: 8 male duck
drama: 4 play; 9 stage play
drama critic: 13 theater critic
Dramamine: 14 dimenhydrinate
dramatic: 8 striking; 10 theatrical; 11 spectacular
dramatic art: 7 theater, theatre; 9 dramatics; 10 dramaturgy
dramatic author: 9 dramatist; 10 playwright
dramatic poetry: 11 lyric poetry
dramatics: 7 theater, theatre; 10 dramaturgy; 11 dramatic art
dramatis personae: 4 cast; 10 characters
dramatist: 10 playwright
dramatize: 3 pad; 4 lard; 5 adopt; 6 blow up; 9 dramatise, embellish, embroider; 10 aggrandize
drape: 3 rig; 4 pall, pose, robe, vest; 5 array, dress; 6 attire, clothe, enrobe, fit out, mantle; 7 apparel, curtain, drapery
draped: 7 cloaked, clothed, mantled, wrapped
draught: 5 draft; 6 drafty
draughtsman: 9 draftsman; 12 draftsperson
draw: 3 get, lot, lug, tie, tow, tug; 4 cast, drag, haul, hook, knit, line, lure, make, move, puff, pull, rake, reap, suck; 5 fetch, force, sop up, trace, trail, train; 6 absorb, allure, cockle, depict, derive, draw in, draw on, entice, get out, imbibe, induce, pucker,

pull in, remove, rumple, soak up, suck up, take in, take up; 7 attract, beguile, crumple, draw out, extract, haulage, outline, pick out, pull out, take out, tear out; 8 dead heat, describe, draw play, draw upon, get money, pluck out, pull back, standoff, withdraw; 9 captivate, delineate, draw poker, draw water, drawn game, extricate, stand down, take money
draw a bead on: 5 aim at; 6 target
draw a blank: 5 block; 6 forget; 8 blank out
draw a fine line: 7 nitpick, quibble; 10 split hairs
draw and quarter: 4 hang; 7 quarter
draw an inference: 6 deduce, derive, gather
draw a parallel: 7 connect; 9 associate
draw away: 7 deflect, draw off, pull off; 8 distract
draw back: 6 go back, recede, retire; 7 get back, put back, retreat, run back; 8 come back, fall back, hang back, hark back, hold back, move back, pull away, pull back, turn back, withdraw
drawback: 6 set-off; 8 poundage; 9 objection, prejudice; 10 percentage; 12 disadvantage
drawer: 6 limner; 7 painter; 8 designer, engraver, sketcher; 9 draftsman
drawers: 5 pants, panty; 6 pantie, shorts, tights; 7 panties; 8 bloomers, knickers
draw in: 4 draw, pull, suck; 5 fetch, get in; 6 move in, narrow, pull in, suck in; 7 attract, close in, retract
drawing: 4 haul, pull; 5 chart, draft; 6 luring, scheme; 7 draught, graphic, lottery, pulling, removal; 8 alluring, drafting, enticing, inviting, removing, tempting, traction; 9 flow chart, schematic; 10 attracting, attractive, drawing off, drawing out, extracting, extraction
drawing card: 4 draw; 6 leader; 10 attraction, loss leader
drawing pin: 7 pushpin; 9 thumbtack
drawing room: 6 lounge; 8 best room; 9 state room; 11 keeping room, sitting room; 13 reception room
drawing-room car: 8 chair car; 9 parlor car
drawknife: 9 drawshave
drawl: 3 lag; 4 slug; 5 mouth; 6 dawdle, linger, loiter, slouch; 7 saunter; 8 hang back
draw lots: 8 cast lots
drawn: 4 taut, worn; 7 haggard, raddled, removed, torn out; 8 careworn, depicted, drawn out, pictured, taken out; 9 extracted, picked out, pulled out
drawn butter: 15 clarified butter
drawn out: 5 drawn; 7 haggard, removed, spun out, torn out; 8 extended, taken out; 9 extracted, lingering, picked out, prolonged,

pulled out, sustained; **10** dragged out, extricated, lengthened, protracted

drawn up: 8 authored, composed; **10** formulated

drawshave: 9 drawknife

draw to a close: 3 end; **5** close; **6** finish; **8** conclude; **9** terminate; **11** come to an end

draw together: 4 bond; **5** crowd; **6** gather, muster; **7** collect, squinch; **8** assemble; **10** join forces; **11** get together, put together

draw up: 4 form; **5** draft, frame; **6** author, fall in, haul up, indite, pull up; **7** compose, outline; **9** formulate

dray: 4 cart; **5** wagon

drayman: 6 carter; **7** wagoner

dread: 4 dire, fear; **5** awful, panic; **6** horror, terror; **7** direful, dreaded, fearful; **8** dreadful, fearsome, horrific, terrible; **10** horrendous; **11** frightening; **12** apprehension

dreadful: 4 dire; **5** awful, dread; **6** arrant; **7** direful, dreaded, fearful, painful; **8** fearsome, funereal, horrific, mournful, terrible; **9** atrocious, frightful; **10** abominable, horrendous, lamentable

dreadfully: 5 sadly; **6** sorely; **7** awfully, cruelly, grossly; **8** bitterly, dismally, horribly, terribly, woefully; **9** fearfully, miserably, painfully, piteously; **10** grievously, lamentably, shockingly; **11** frightfully

dreadless: 7 aweless; **8** fearless; **9** dauntless

dreadnaught: 5 P-coat; **6** ulster; **7** pea coat; **9** pea jacket; **10** battleship

dream: 4 muse; **6** vision; **7** chimera, conceit, figment; **8** ambition, daydream, dreaming, ruminate, stargaze; **9** pipe dream, speculate

dreamer: 8 escapist, idealist, romancer, romantic; **9** visionary; **11** romanticist

dreaming: 9 imagining

dreamlike: 7 surreal

dream up: 5 dream, hatch; **7** concoct, dream of, think of, think up

dreamworld: 9 dreamland; **14** never-never land

dreamy: 5 balmy, moony; **7** languid; **10** languorous

dreariness: 10 boringness, **11** piteousness; **12** grievousness

dreary: 4 drab, flat; **5** dingy, drear, sorry; **6** dismal, gloomy; **7** piteous; **8** desolate, grievous; **10** melancholy

dredge: 4 drag; **6** pull up, rake up

dregs: 4 lees; **7** grounds

dreidel: 3 top; **6** dreidl

Dreissena polymorpha: 11 zebra mussel

drench: 3 sop; **4** soak; **5** douse, dowse, flood, souse, swamp, swash; **6** deluge, imbrue, splash; **8** inundate, irrigate; **9** surcharge; **10** shower down

drenching: 5 souse; **7** dousing, soaking, sousing; **9** splashing

drenching rain: 8 downpour; **10** cloudburst

drepanocytic anemia: 16 sickle-cell anemia

dress: 2 do; **3** cob, lop, rig, set, tog; **4** bang, clip, coif, crop, garb, robe, snip, trim, vest, warm, wipe; **5** array, curry, drape, frock, groom, level, plume, preen, primp, prune; **6** attire, clothe, coiffe, enrobe, equate, fettle, fit out, fledge, line up, smooth; **7** apparel, arrange, balance, cut back, drapery, dress up, furnish, garment, garnish, raiment; **8** accouter, coiffure, decorate, dress out, enclothe, equalize, readjust, regulate

dress coat: 8 tail coat; **9** frock coat; **10** tuxedo coat

dress down: 3 cob, jaw, rag; **4** bang, trim, warm, wipe; **5** check, chide, dress, scold; **6** berate, chew up, rebuke; **7** bawl out, chew out, lambast, lecture, reproof; **8** lambaste; **9** have words, reprimand

dressed: 4 clad; **5** robed; **6** garbed; **7** arrayed, attired, clothed; **8** dolled up, invested, polished; **9** appareled, dressed-up, garmented, spiffed up, spruced up

dressed-up: 4 chic; **7** dressed; **8** dolled up; **9** decked out, spiffed up, spruced up; **13** dressed to kill; **17** dressed to the nines

dresser: 5 chest; **6** bureau; **14** chest of drawers; **15** actor's assistant

dressing: 6 blow up, rating; **7** binding, lecture, wigging; **8** grooming, scolding, stuffing, trimming; **9** bandaging

dressing station: 10 aid station

dressing table: 6 vanity; **11** toilet table

dressmaker: 10 seamstress

dress shop: 8 boutique

dressy clothing: 6 finery

Dreyfus: 13 Alfred Dreyfus

dribble: 4 drip, drop, gush; **5** carry, drool, plash, spout, trill; **6** drivel, filter, slaver; **7** distill, flow out, slabber, slobber, trickle; **9** dribbling, percolate

driblet: 4 drop

dried: 10 dehydrated, desiccated

dried milk: 12 powdered milk

dried-out: 10 desiccated

drift: 3 err; **4** blow, cast, roam, rove, swan, waft; **5** coast, float, range, stray, tenor, trend; **6** breeze, course, cruise, ramble, wander; **7** bearing, gallery, heading, impetus, purport; **8** be adrift, coloring, tendency, vagabond

drifter: 7 vagrant

drifting: 6 adrift; **7** aimless, vagrant; **8** floating, vagabond

drift off: 6 nod off; **7** dope off, doze off, drop off; **8** flake out; **9** drowse off; **10** fall asleep

drill: 4 bore; **5** auger, augur, borer; **6** oil rig; **8** exercise, practice, practise

drill hole: 4 bore

drilling platform: 11 offshore rig

drink: 4 have, tope; **5** booze, toast; **6** fuddle,

imbibe, pledge, salute, tipple; **7** alcohol, boozing, drink in, potable, spirits, swallow; **8** beverage, drinking; **9** booze it up, drinkable, inebriant; **10** intoxicant

drinkable: 7 potable

drinking cup: 8 Dixie cup, paper cup

drinking fountain: 7 bubbler

drinking glass: 5 glass; **7** tumbler

drink to: 5 toast; **6** pledge

drip: 4 drop; **5** plash, trill; **7** distill, dribble, trickle; **8** infusion; **9** percolate

drip-dry: 11 wash-and-wear; **14** permanent-press

drive: 3 aim, get, ram, run, tug; **4** blow, bolt, boom, make, pull, push, ride, tool, urge; **5** cause, force, jaunt, labor, motor, repel, sling; **6** airing, bustle, coerce, compel, effort, flurry, labour, oblige, outing, thrust; **7** crusade, driving, enforce, flutter, parkway, repulse; **8** beat back, campaign, driveway, movement, push back, scramble, splutter; **9** constrain, force back, fulminate, pitchfork

drive away: 5 repel; **6** dispel, rebuff, run off; **7** repulse; **8** drive off, drive out, turn back; **9** chase away, keep at bay

drivel: 4 dote; **5** drool; **6** slaver, trifle; **7** dribble, slabber, slobber; **8** nonsense

driven: 6 goaded; **8** impelled; **10** compulsive, determined, thrust upon

driver: 8 golf club; **12** device driver

driver ant: 7 army ant

driveway: 5 drive; **8** entrance; **11** private road

driving range: 9 golf range

drizzle: 4 rain; **8** sprinkle

drogue: 4 sock; **5** chute **6** anchor; **8** windsock; **9** parachute; **10** wind sleeve

droll: 4 jest; **5** sport; **6** quaint; **9** quizzical

drollery: 4 salt, whim; **5** fancy, point; **6** comedy, esprit; **7** waggery; **8** clowning; **9** funniness; **10** buffoonery, pleasantry, tomfoolery

Dromaius: 3 emu; **13** genus Dromaius

dromedary: 12 Arabian camel

drone: 5 idler; **6** burden, dawdle; **7**, dawdler, drone on, droning, laggard; **8** monotone; **9** drone pipe, insect cry; **13** sustained note; **17** pilotless aircraft, pilotless airplane

droning: 5 abuzz, drone; **7** buzzing; **8** monotone

drool: 4 bosh, tosh; **6** drivel, humbug, slaver; **7** baloney, boloney, dribble, slobber, twaddle; **8** tommyrot; **10** bilgewater

droop: 3 sag, set; **4** flag, halt, hang, loll, pine, sink, swag, wilt; **5** swing, yearn; **6** dangle, depend, repine, take on; **7** decline, despond, give way; **8** languish

drooping: 4 lame; **6** droopy; **7** halting, hanging, nodding, sagging; **8** cernuous, crippled, dangling, flagging; **9** pendulous, tottering

drop: 4 bead, blow, bulb, cast, clew, drip, fade, fail, fall, fell, flag, gasp, halt, horn, knob, limp, miss, omit, pant, pill, puff, quit, shed, sink, teem; **5** cliff, faint, pearl, plash, shake, spare, spend, swing, swoon, throw, trill, truce; **6** bullet, dangle, expend, forego, gibbet, give up, height, marble, pellet, plunge, pommel, resign, totter, unload; **7** cast off, crumble, cut down, decline, dismiss, distill, dribble, driblet, droplet, dropoff, falling, flatten, gallows, give way, globule, neglect, plummet, put down, respite, set down, succumb, tremble, trickle, vesicle; **8** break off, collapse, give away, knock off, languish, leave off, leave out, overleap, overlook, part with, renounce, scaffold, send away, shake off, spherule, throw off; **9** dispose of, not finish, percolate, throw away; **10** degenerate, strike down

drop a line: 5 write

drop by drop: 8 bit by bit

drop dead: 4 conk; **5** choke, croak; **6** pop off; **7** snuff it; **8** fall dead; **10** buy the farm; **11** bite the dust

drop in: 2 in; **5** pop in; **6** come by, drop by

droplet: 4 drop

drop off: 4 lose, slip; **5** go off; **6** nod off, pop off, recede; **7** dope off, doze off, dwindle, fall off, tail off; **8** drift off, drop away, fall away, fall back, flake out, peter out, taper off; **9** drowse off; **10** fall asleep

drop-off: 4 drop; **5** cliff, slack, slump; **7** falloff; **8** decrease; **9** lessening

drop off to sleep: 7 doze off, drop off

drop out: 4 quit; **5** leave; **6** give up; **7** throw in; **10** quit school

dropping anchor: 7 docking, mooring, tying up

droppings: 4 dung, muck

dropsical: 3 fat; **5** tumid; **6** turgid; **7** bloated, swollen; **9** edematous, overgrown

dropsy: 5 edema

drop zone: 12 dropping zone

droshky: 5 wagon; **6** drosky; **8** carriage

drosophile: 8 fruit fly

dross: 4 slag; **6** scoria; **8** impurity

drought: 6 drouth; **7** dryness; **8** shortage

drove: 4 bevy, herd; **5** brood, crowd, flock, horde, shoal, swarm; **6** litter, scores

drover: 4 cowboy, herder; **7** cowhand, grazier, vaquero [Sp]; **8** herdsman

drown: 4 duck, sink; **5** souse, swamp; **6** plunge; **7** capsize, founder; **8** submerge; **9** break down, overwhelm, shipwreck

drowse: 4 doze; **6** snooze

drowse off: 6 nod off; **7** dope off, doze off, drop off; **8** drift off; **10** fall asleep

drowsy: 4 dozy; **6** dozing; **7** napping,

D

nodding, yawning; **8** drowsing, oscitant; **9** somnolent

drub: 4 lick, rout; **5** baste, crush; **6** pummel, thrash; **7** belabor, blow out, clobber, trounce; **8** roll over; **9** overwhelm

drubbing: 7 beating, debacle; **8** whacking, whipping; **9** slaughter, thrashing, trouncing, walloping

drudge: 4 hack, moil, peon, toil; **5** grind, labor, navvy; **6** hacker, labour, strive; **7** laborer, travail, workman; **10** working man; **11** galley slave, laboring man, wade through; **12** working stiff; **13** manual laborer

drudgery: 5 grind; **8** plodding; **10** donkeywork, drudge work; **11** manual labor, routine work

drug: 4 dose, glut; **5** chaff, froth, smoke; **6** bubble, cobweb, physic; **7** nostrum, simples; **8** medicine; **10** medicament, medication

drug abuse: 5 habit; **7** drug use; **9** drug habit; **14** substance abuse

drug addict: 5 junky; **6** junkie

drug-addicted: 6 hooked; **9** dependant, dependent, strung-out

drug dependency: 9 addiction, drug habit

drugged: 5 doped; **6** stoned; **9** spaced out; **10** narcotized

drugget: 3 rug; **5** cover; **6** carpet; **8** throw rug

druggist: 7 chemist; **8** pharmacy; **9** drug store; **10** apothecary, pharmacist

drug of abuse: 10 street drug

drug peddler: 6 dealer, pusher; **7** peddler; **14** drug trafficker

drugstore: 7 chemist; **8** pharmacy; **10** dispensary

drug trafficker: 6 dealer, pusher; **7** peddler; **11** drug peddler

drum: 3 keg; **4** beat, bone, cask, cram, echo, roll, swot; **5** get up, mug up, thrum; **6** barrel, bone up, hammer, reecho, repeat, swot up, tympan; **7** iterate; **8** drumfish, harp upon, puncheon, redouble; **9** brake drum, grind away, metal drum, reiterate, reproduce

drumfire: 7 barrage; **9** cannonade

drummer: 8 traveler; **17** traveling salesman

drunk: 3 cut, sot; **4** high; **5** beery, boozy, fresh, merry, rummy, tight, tipsy; **6** corned, groggy, primed; **7** drunken, fuddled; **8** drunkard, elevated, overcome, top-heavy; **9** disguised, flustered, inebriate, overtaken; **10** in one's cups, inebriated; **11** intoxicated

drunkard: 3 sot, tun; **4** lush; **5** drunk, rummy, toper; **6** soaker, sponge; **7** guzzler, tippler; **9** inebriate; **11** hard drinker

drunken: 3 cut; **4** high; **5** beery, boozy, drunk, fresh, merry, tight, tipsy; **6** corned,

groggy, primed; **7** fuddled, sottish; **8** bibulous, elevated, overcome, top-heavy; **9** disguised, flustered, inebriate, overtaken; **10** in one's cups, inebriated; **11** intoxicated

druthers: 10 preference

dry: 3 gut, wry; **4** arid, bald, cold, dull, flat; **5** bland, husky, prosy, sharp; **6** biting, boring, dry out, formal, frigid, hoarse, hollow, ironic, jejune, mortal, severe, trashy; **7** athirst, cutting, cynical, drained, exhaust, languid, prosaic, raucous, tedious, thirsty; **8** croaking, hard upon, ironical, lukewarm, sardonic, teetotal, unvaried; **9** colorless, juiceless, proposing, sarcastic, satirical, swallow up, trenchant, withering; **10** monotonous, sepulchral; **13** uninteresting

dryad: 4 peri; **5** naiad, nymph; **6** nereid; **9** wood nymph

dry ground: 4 land; **5** earth; **6** ground; **7** dry land; **10** terra firma

drying agent: 9 desiccant

drying up: 11 dehydration, dessication, evaporation

dry land: 4 land; **5** earth; **6** ground; **9** dry ground; **10** terra firma; **11** solid ground

dryly: 11 laconically

Drymarchon: 11 gopher snake, indigo snake; **15** genus Drymarchon

dry measure: 7 dry unit

dry milk: 9 dried milk; **10** milk powder; **12** powdered milk

drynurse: 4 rear; **5** breed; **6** ground; **7** bring up, nurture, prepare; **8** exercise, practice; **9** habituate

dry out: 3 dry; **5** dry up; **6** run dry; **7** sober up; **9** become dry

dry point: 3 bur

dry river bed: 4 wadi; **6** arroyo

dry rot: 3 rot; **6** blight; **7** atrophy

dry run: 5 trial; **8** practise, trial run; **9** rehearsal; **10** run through

dry up: 6 dry out, run dry; **7** mummify; **8** desicate, melt away; **9** become dry, dehydrate, dessicate

dual: 5 duple; **6** double, treble; **7** twofold

dualism: 7 duality; **9** dichotomy

duality: 7 dualism; **9** dichotomy

dual-lane: 7 divided

dub: 4 call, name, term; **5** style; **6** knight; **7** entitle; **8** nickname; **9** designate; **10** denominate

dubiety: 5 doubt; **11** dubiousness, uncertainty

dubious: 8 doubtful; **9** dubitable; **10** in question

Dublin: 12 Irish capital

duce: 6 leader; **7** Fuehrer [Ger]

duchess: 9 duke's wife

duchy: 7 dukedom

duck: 3 bob, dip; **4** dear, dunk, idol, love; **5** angel, dodge, douse, drown, elude, evade, fudge, hedge, honey, jewel, kneel, parry, skirt, souse, sugar; **6** duckey, plunge, put off; **7** darling, goddess

duckbill: 8 platypus; **10** duck-billed, paddle-fish

duck-billed dinosaur: 9 hadrosaur; **11** hadrosaurus

ducking: 7 dousing, dunking; **9** immersion; **10** submersion

duck shot: 8 bird shot, buckshot

duck soup: 4 snap; **5** cinch; **6** picnic; **8** pushover, walkover; **10** child's play; **11** piece of cake

ducky: 3 pet; **5** deary; **6** dearie; **7** darling; **8** favorite; **9** favourite

duct: 5 canal; **7** channel

ductile: 6 pliant; **7** plastic, pliable, tensile; **8** formable, shapable, tractile, trimming, workable, yielding; **9** malleable, shapeable; **10** extendable; **11** stretchable; **12** ambidextrous

dud: 4 bomb, flop; **6** turkey; **7** misfire, washout

dude: 3 fop; **4** beau; **5** dandy, sheik, swell; **6** masher; **7** gallant; **9** greenhorn; **12** clotheshorse, fashion plate

dudeen: 8 clay pipe

dudgeon: 4 dirk, hilt; **6** dagger; **7** bayonet, poniard, offense; **8** stiletto; **11** displeasure

duds: 4 togs; **7** threads

due: 3 fit; **4** good, meet, owed; **5** due to, owing, right; **6** proper, seemly, unpaid; **7** condign, correct, en regle, fitting, merited, past due; **8** becoming, decorous, deserved, eligible; **9** befitting; **10** delinquent

duel: 6 duello [It]; **13** affair of honor

duenna: 8 chaperon, dry nurse, governor; **9** custodian, governess, preserver, protector; **11** third person

dues: 3 tax; **4** fees; **7** charges

duet: 3 duo; **4** duad, dyad, pair, span, yoke; **5** brace, deuce, twain, twins; **6** cheeks, couple, duette; **7** couplet, distich, twosome; **9** doubleton, pas de deux

dugong: 6 sea cow

dugout: 3 cot, hut; **4** shed; **5** booth, cabin, croft, hovel, stall; **6** bunker, chalet, shanty; **7** pirogue; **8** log canoe; **11** dugout canoe

dug up: 9 unearthed

dukedom: 5 duchy

dulcet: 5 sweet; **7** honeyed; **10** saccharine

dulcify: 4 dull; **5** blunt; **6** subdue; **7** chasten, mollify, sheathe, sweeten

Dulcinea: 5 angel; **7** darling, goddess; **8** ladylove; **9** mistress, inamorata; **10** sweetheart

dull: 3 dim, dry, dun, low, wan; **4** arid, ashy, bald, cold, damp, dash, dead, drab, dumb, flat, gray, grey, mute, numb, pall, sink, slow, tame; **5** ashen, bland, bluff, blunt, dense, dingy, dusky, faint, heavy, ho-hum, lower, muddy, muted, petty, proof, prosy, slack, spent, unman; **6** benumb, boring, dampen, deject, effete, frigid, glassy, jejune, leaden, mortal, muffle, obtuse, sallow, stodgy, stolid, stupid, subdue, trashy; **7** chasten, darkish, ghastly, irksome, languid, mollify, muffled, prosaic, shallow, sheathe, tedious, witless; **8** lukewarm, mindless, sluggish, softened, thudding, thumping, tiresome, tone down, ungifted; **9** airheaded, brainless, colorless, deadening, dim-witted, dry as dust, fat witted, fatheaded, knock down, pig headed, proposing, prostrate, wearisome; **10** beef headed, cadaverous, dull minded, dull normal, dull witted, half witted, lackluster, lean witted, weak headed, weak minded

dullard: 3 oaf, put; **4** bore, calf, colt, dolt, loon, lout, tony; **6** stupid; **7** buzzard; **9** numbskull

dullness: 7 dryness, dulness; **8** flatness; **9** bluntness, heaviness, inertness, stupidity; **10** incapacity, obtuseness

dumb: 3 dim; **4** dull, mute, slow; **5** dense, silly; **6** obtuse, silent, stupid, unwise; **7** asinine, foolish; **8** improper

dumbfound: 3 get; **4** beat; **5** amaze; **6** baffle, gravel, puzzle; **7** astound, flummox, mystify, nonplus, perplex, stupefy, stupify, trounce; **8** bewilder

dumbwaiter: 12 food elevator

dumdum bullet: 6 dumdum

dummy: 4 boob, dope; **5** blank, booby; **8** dolittle, dumbbell; **10** blank shell, dead letter

dumps: 5 blues, mopes, sulks; **7** sadness; **8** darkness, doldrums, the blues, the dumps; **9** dejection, heaviness; **10** bad spirits, blue devils, depression, dismalness, gloominess, low spirits, melancholy, somberness

dumpy: 5 podgy, pudgy, squab, squat, tubby; **6** chunky, low-set, stumpy; **7** squatty; **8** thickset

dun: 3 ply, rag, sad, tax, wan; **4** ashy, cold, dead, drab, dull, fawn, roan, urge; **5** ashen, beset, dingy, dirty, faint, livid, lurid, muddy, press; **6** glassy, leaden, pearly, russet, sallow, somber; **7** bedevil, crucify, ghastly, torment; **8** iron-gray, overcast

dunce: 4 dope; **8** bonehead, lunkhead, numskull; **9** blockhead, ignoramus; **10** dunderhead, hammerhead, loggerhead, muttonhead; **11** knucklehead

dunderhead: 5 dunce

dune: 5 ridge; **8** hog's back, sand dune

dungarees: 5 jeans; **6** denims; **9** blue jeans

dung beetle: 6 scarab

dungeon: 3 can [slang], pen; **4** brig, gaol, hold, jail, keep, stir [slang]; **5** clink [slang], hulks, pokey [slang]; **6** chokey [slang], cooler [slang], donjon, lockup, prison; **7** slammer [slang], the Rock; **8** Bastille, big house [slang], hoosegow, stockade; **9** calaboose [slang], guardroom

dunk: 3 dip; **4** duck; **5** douse, souse; **6** plunge; **8** dunk shot

dunking: 7 ducking; **9** immersion; **10** submersion

Dunkirk: 9 Dunkerque

dunnock: 7 sparrow

duo: 4 duad, duet, dyad, pair, span, yoke; **5** brace, twain; **6** couple, duette; **7** couplet, distich, twosome; **9** doubleton

duodecimal: 7 twelfth

duologue: 6 dialog; **8** dialogue

dupe: 4 gull, hoax, mark, tool; **5** chump, patsy, put on, slang, trick; **6** befool, puppet, stooge, sucker, take in, victim; **9** bamboozle

duplicate: 4 copy, twin; **5** check, extra, spare, tally; **6** billet, double, letter, repeat; **7** counter, twinned; **8** matching, parallel, redouble; **9** expletive, replicate; **11** duplication, on one's hands, reduplicate, replication

duplicator: 6 copier

duplicitous: 8 two-faced; **9** deceitful; **10** Janus-faced; **11** double-faced

duplicity: 5 guile; **8** doubling; **11** fraudulence

durability: 8 strength; **11** durableness, lastingness; **12** enduringness

durable: 6 stable; **7** lasting; **9** long-lived; **10** perdurable; **11** long-lasting, long-wearing

durance vile: 6 duress; **7** durance; **9** captivity; **11** confinement

duration: 6 length; **11** continuance

duress: 7 durance; **8** coercion; **9** captivity; **10** compulsion, constraint; **11** confinement, durance vile, enforcement

during: 5 while; **6** whilst; **7** pending

durum: 9 hard wheat; **10** durum wheat

Dushanbe: 7 Dusanbe; **9** Dyushambe; **19** capital of Tajikistan

dusk: 8 evenfall, gloaming, twilight; **9** nightfall

duskiness: 7 dimness; **8** darkness; **11** swarthiness

dusky: 4 dull; **5** dingy, murky, sooty, swart; **6** pitchy, somber, twilit; **7** darkish, swarthy; **8** twilight; **10** lackluster

dustbin: 6 ashbin, ashcan; **8** trash bin, trash can, wastebin; **10** garbage can; **11** trash barrel

duster: 5 smock; **7** dustrag; **8** coverall, dust coat; **9** coveralls, dustcloth, gaberdine; **11** boilers suit

dust jacket: 7 wrapper; **9** dust cover; **10** book jacket

dustman: 5 sweep; **9** scavenger; **10** garbage man

dustup: 3 row; **5** fight, run-in, words; **7** quarrel, wrangle

dusty: 5 smoky, sooty; **6** smutty

Dutch door: 8 half door

Dutch hoe: 7 scuffle; **10** scuffle hoe

duty: 4 onus; **5** shift; **6** egards, impost, office, tariff; **7** devoirs, regards; **8** respects; **9** exercises, liability; **10** obligation

duty-bound: 7 obliged

duvet: 9 comforter, eiderdown

dwarf: 3 elf; **5** elfin, gnome, stunt; **6** midget

dwarf buffalo: 4 anoa

dwarf chestnut: 10 chinquapin

dweeb: 6 flunky, stooge, yes-man; **7** flunkey

dwell: 3 lie; **4** harp, keep, live, stay; **5** abide, brood, lie in, lodge, perch, roost, shack, worry; **6** belong, nestle, people, reside, tenant; **7** consist, inhabit, sojourn; **8** maintain, populate

dweller: 7 denizen; **8** habitant, resident; **10** inhabitant

dwelling: 4 home; **5** abode; **6** living; **7** housing, lodging; **8** domicile, lodgment; **9** lodgement, residence; **10** habitation

dwindle: 3 ebb; **4** wane; **5** taper, waste; **6** shrink; **7** drop off, fall off, shrivel, tail off; **8** collapse, fall away, grow less, peter out, taper off

Dy: 10 dysprosium

dyad: 3 duo; **4** duad, duet, pair, span, yoke; **5** brace, twain; **6** couple; **7** couplet, distich, twosome

dybbuk: 6 dibbuk

dye: 3 hue; **4** cast, glow, tint, wash; **5** color, flush, grain, imbue, paint, shade, stain, tinge; **6** livery; **7** bedizen, ingrain; **8** dyestuff, emblazon, tincture; **10** coloration, illuminate

dyed in the wool: 8 inherent; **10** congenital, in the grain

dying: 5 death; **6** demise; **7** anxious, decease

dying breath: 8 last gasp; **10** last breath; **11** death rattle, last agonies

dying for: 5 set on; **6** bent on; **7** set upon; **8** bent upon, intent on, mad after; **10** anxious for, intent upon

dynamic: 6 active

dynamics: 7 statics; **8** kinetics

dynamiter: 6 bomber

dynamo: 8 go-getter, live wire, spitfire; **10** ball of fire

dysfunctional: 8 abnormal, impaired; **11** nonadaptive

dyslexic: 9 dyslectic

dyslogistic: 9 insulting, slighting; **10** belittling, derogatory

dyspepsia: 11 indigestion; **12** stomach upset, upset stomach

dysphemistic: 9 offensive

dysphoric: 7 unhappy; **10** distressed

dysprosium: 2 Dy

Dyushambe: 7 Dusanbe; **8** Dushanbe; **19** capital of Tajikistan

E

e.g.: 6 namely; 10 for example; 11 for
  instance, exemplia gratia [Lat]
each: 6 apiece; 8 one by one
each day: 5 daily
each month: 7 monthly
each other: 10 one another
each week: 6 weekly
each year: 2 p.a.; 6 yearly; 7 per year; 8
  annually, per annum; 9 every year
eager: 4 avid, bore, keen; 5 aegir, eagre,
  great; 6 gung ho; 7 anxious, forward, zealous; 9 in earnest, strenuous
eagerly: 9 thirstily; 10 desirously
eagerness: 4 zeal; 5 ardor; 7 avidity; 8 avidness, keenness; 11 overanxiety, zealousness
eagle-eyed: 8 hawk-eyed, keen-eyed, lynx-
  eyed; 9 Argus-eyed, farseeing
ear-deafening: 9 deafening; 10 ear-rending;
  12 ear-splitting
ear doctor: 9 otologist
eardrum: 8 tympanum
earful: 9 going-over; 10 bawling out, chewing out, upbraiding
earl: 5 baron, thane; 8 viscount
earlier: 6 before, sooner
early: 5 other, prime; 6 former; 7 betimes,
  early on, forward, too soon; 11 ahead of
  time
early childhood: 7 infancy; 8 babyhood
earmark: 4 note; 5 allow, stamp; 7 reserve; 8
  hallmark, set aside
earn: 4 gain, make; 5 clear; 6 garner, pull in,
  take in; 7 bring in
earnest: 4 dear; 5 grave, ready, sober, staid; 6
  devout, sedate, solemn; 7 deposit, forward,
  handsel, serious, sincere, wistful; 9 heartfelt, in earnest; 11 down payment
earnest money: 7 deposit, earnest, handsel;
  11 down payment; 12 up-front money
earnestness: 7 decorum, gravity; 8 goodwill,
  sobriety; 9 geniality, sincerity, solemnity,
  staidness; 10 cordiality, intentness, sedateness; 11 seriousness; 12 decorousness
earnings: 3 net, pay; 4 wage; 5 lucre; 6
  profit, salary; 7 net gain, profits; 8 proceeds; 9 net income, net profit; 12 remuneration
ear-nose-and-throat doctor: 6 ENT man
earphone: 5 phone; 8 earpiece; 9 headphone
ear-piercing: 9 high-toned; 11 high-pitched
ear-rending: 9 deafening; 12 ear-deafening,
  ear-splitting
ear-shaped: 8 auriform
ear-shell: 7 abalone
earshot: 5 sound; 7 hearing; 8 earreach; 11
  stone's throw; 12 hearing range; 13 close
  quarters

earsplitting: 7 roaring; 8 thundery; 9 deafening; 10 thunderous
Earth: 5 globe, terra, world; 9 wide world
earth: 4 clay, deck, dust, flag, land; 5 ashes,
  floor, world; 6 carped, ground, paving; 7
  dry land; 8 pavement; 9 dry ground; 10
  substratum, terra firma; 11 ground floor,
  solid ground
Earth's crust: 11 lithosphere
earth's sun: 3 Sol; 6 Apollo, old sol, the
  Sun; 7 Phoebus; 8 orb of day
earthborn: 7 lowborn; 8 baseborn
earthbound: 5 prosy; 7 prosaic; 10 pedestrian
earthenware: 7 ceramic, pottery, vitrics; 8
  ceramics; 9 porcelain, stoneware; 11
  ceramic ware
earthenware jar: 5 crock
earthing: 9 grounding
earthling: 3 man; 4 body, soul; 5 being,
  human; 6 mortal, person; 8 creature, earthman, such a one; 9 personage, tellurian; 10
  human being, individual, living soul
Earth longitude: 8 meridian
earthly: 7 mundane, terrene, worldly; 10
  uncultured, 11 terrestrial, unspiritual
earth mover: 9 bulldozer
earthquake: 5 quake, seism, storm; 6
  tremor; 7 temblor; 9 cataclysm
earthquake detector: 11 seismometer,
  seismograph
earthworm: 7 dew worm, red worm, wiggler; 8 fishworm; 9 angleworm; 11 fishing
  worm, nightwalker; 12 nightcrawler
earthy: 5 crude, gross; 6 coarse, vulgar; 11
  down-to-earth, terrestrial
ear trumpet: 10 hearing aid
earwax: 7 cerumen
ease: 4 mood, rest, vein; 5 allay, still; 6 luxury, relief, repose, smooth, soothe; 7 comfort, lighten, relieve; 8 easiness, facility,
  make easy, mitigate, palliate, relaxing,
  snugness; 9 alleviate, readiness, unbending; 10 facileness, facilitate, heart's ease,
  make facile, relaxation, render easy, simplicity
easement: 7 lullaby; 8 soothing; 9 softening;
  10 mitigation; 11 alleviation
ease up: 4 flag, give; 5 let up, yield; 7 ease
  off, give way; 8 move over, slack off; 10
  slacken off
easily: 4 easy, well; 8 facilely, with ease; 12
  with facility
easily excited: 4 taut; 5 tense; 8 volatile; 9
  excitable, sensitive; 10 high-strung; 13
  oversensitive
east: 1 E
East: 6 Levant, Orient

eastbound: 8 eastward
east by north: 3 EbN
east by south: 3 EbS
easterly: 6 easter; 7 eastern; 8 east wind
Eastern Orthodox: 8 Orthodox; 13 Greek Orthodox; 15 Russian Orthodox
Eastern Orthodox Church: 13 Eastern Church; 14 Orthodox Church; 22 Orthodox Catholic Church
Eastern Samoa: 13 American Samoa
Eastern Standard Time: 3 EST; 11 Eastern Time
East Indies: 16 Malay Archipelago
east northeast: 3 ENE
East Pakistan: 10 Bangladesh
east southeast: 3 ESE
easy: 4 slow, soft; 5 light, loose; 6 at ease, easily, facile, fluent, gentle, slowly, wanton; 7 flowing, lenient, natural, tardily, well-off; 8 graceful, readable, sluttish, tripping, well-to-do; 9 easygoing, leisurely
easy chair: 8 arm chair; 11 lounge chair
easy going: 12 clear sailing, plain sailing
easygoing: 4 calm, easy; 6 casual, facile, mellow, placid; 8 laid-back, peaceful, tolerant; 9 hang-loose, indulgent, leisurely, sans souci [Fr], unworried; 10 nonchalant, phlegmatic; 11 unconcerned; 12 devil-may-care
eat: 4 dine, fare, feed, rust, take; 5 drink, eat on, eat up, use up; 6 devour, digest, pocket; 7 consume, corrode, deplete, exhaust, stomach, swallow, wipe out; 10 run through
eatables: 4 food, grub; 7 aliment, edibles; 8 victuals; 9 nutriment; 10 sustenance; 11 comestibles, nourishment, staff of life; 12 alimentation, sustentation
eat away: 4 fret; 5 erode; 6 blight; 7 corrode
eaten up: 8 devoured
eat in: 6 dine in
eat one's fill: 4 cram; 5 stuff; 7 engorge; 11 over-indulge; 12 stuff oneself
eat out: 7 dine out
eat out of house and home: 5 raven, shear, strip; 6 fleece; 7 despoil
eavesdrop: 8 listen in
eavesdropper: 5 snoop; 7 snooper
ebb: 3 low; 4 wane; 5 waste; 6 ebbing, recede, reflux, shrink; 7 decline, dwindle, shrivel; 8 collapse, fall away, grow less
ebb tide: 7 low tide; 8 low point, low water, neap tide
EbN: 11 east by north
ebon: 4 dark, inky; 5 ebony, sable
Ebonics: 12 Black English
ebonite: 9 vulcanite; 10 hard rubber

ebony: 4 dark, ebon, inky; 5 sable; 6 somber; 8 jet black; 9 coal black, soot black; 10 pitch black
Ebro: 9 Ebro River
EbS: 11 east by south
ebullience: 10 enthusiasm, exuberance
ebullient: 3 hot; 5 fiery; 6 red-hot; 7 boiling, flaming, glowing, smoking; 8 seething; 9 exuberant, scorching
ebullition: 3 ire, pet; 4 bile, fume, stir, tiff; 6 bustle, choler, dander, pucker, taking; 7 ferment, passion; 8 splutter; 9 angry mood, decoction; 12 perturbation
eccentric: 3 odd; 4 case, geek, type, zany; 5 flaky, outre, wierd; 6 freaky, madcap; 7 bizarre, oddball; 8 freakish, peculiar; 9 character, egregious, exclusive, fanatical, screwball, whimsical; 10 infatuated, outlandish
ecclesiastic: 6 cleric, divine; 8 reverend; 9 churchman, clergyman
ecclesiastical attire: 8 vestment
ecclesiastical law: 8 canon law
ecclesiastical mode: 10 church mode; 12 medieval mode; 13 Gregorian mode
ecdysiast: 6 peeler; 8 stripper; 10 striptease; 11 stripteaser; 12 exotic dancer
ecdysis: 4 molt; 5 moult; 7 molting; 8 moulting
echidna: 8 anteater; 13 spiny anteater
echinate: 5 spiny; 7 spicate; 8 bristled, spicular; 9 bristling, setaceous
Echinus esculentus: 15 edible sea urchin
echo: 3 ape; 4 drum, mime, ring; 6 chimes, hammer, mirror, monkey, parrot, recall, reecho, repeat; 7 iterate, reflect, refrain, resound; 8 harp upon, imitator, redouble, repetend, resonate, ricochet; 9 reiterate, reproduce
echo chamber: 9 resonator
echoic: 8 echolike; 9 imitative; 12 onomatopoeic
echo sounder: 5 asdic, sonar
echo sounding: 12 echolocation
eclaircissement: 13 enlightenment
eclat: 4 note, pomp; 5 vogue; 6 praise; 7 acclaim, plaudit; 8 applause, plaudits; 9 celebrity, notoriety
eclipse: 5 shade; 6 occult; 7 curtain; 8 outshine; 10 overshadow
eclipsed: 8 obscured, occulted
eclipsing binary: 10 binary star
eclogue: 4 idyl; 5 idyll, lyric; 7 bucolic
ecologic: 8 bionomic, 10 bionomical, ecological
ecological niche: 11 environment
ecological system: 5 biome; 7 habitat
ecology: 9 bionomics
economical: 5 chary, spare; 6 frugal, saving, scotch; 7 careful, sparing, thrifty; 8 economic, stinting

economic crisis: 5 slump; 9 recession; 10 depression

economic expert: 9 economist

economist: 14 economic expert

economize: 4 save; 7 husband; 8 conserve; 9 economise

economy: 6 saving, thrift; 9 economics, frugality; 10 discipline; 11 thriftiness

ecrevisse: 7 crawdad; 8 crawfish, crayfish

ecru: 5 beige

ecstasis: 6 trance; 7 ecstasy

ecstasy: 4 Adam, MDMA; 6 trance; 7 rapture, repture; 9 transport; 10 exaltation, ravishment; 11 enchantment

ecstatic: 8 electric, swelling; 9 rapturous, rhapsodic, thrilling; 10 enraptured, in raptures; 11 deep-mouthed, in ecstasies; 12 soul-stirring

ECT: 12 electroshock; 19 electroshock therapy

ectoderm: 9 ectoblast

ectoparasite: 6 epizoa; 7 ectozoa, epizoon; 8 ectozoon

Ectopistes migratorius: 15 passenger pigeon

ecumenical: 7 general; 8 ecumenic; 9 universal, worldwide

edacious: 7 swinish, wolfish; 8 esurient, ravening, ravenous; 9 rapacious, voracious; 10 gluttonous, omnivorous

edacity: 8 gluttony, rapacity, voracity; 9 esurience; 12 ravenousness

eddo: 4 taro; 7 cocoyam, dasheen

eddy: 4 purl, whir; 5 swirl, twist, whirl; 6 reflux, vortex; 8 overflow; 9 Maelstrom, whirlpool; 12 undercurrent

Eddy: 13 Mary Baker Eddy

edema: 8 dropsy, oedema; 8 swelling

edematous: 5 puffy; 6 blowzy, mellow; 9 distended, dropsical, medullary [Anat]

eden: 6 heaven; 7 nirvana; 8 paradise; 9 Shangri-la

edentate: 7 edental; 9 toothless

edge: 4 abut, butt, inch, link; 5 bound, ledge, point; 6 adjoin, border, butt on, fringe, fringy, margin, skirts; 8 boundary, marginal, severity; 9 blade edge, knife edge, sharpness; 10 escarpment

edginess: 10 inquietude, uneasiness; 11 disquietude

edging: 3 hem; 4 gimp, list, welt; 5 frill; 6 border, fringe; 7 flounce, valance; 8 skirting, trapping, trimming

edgy: 5 jumpy, nervy; 7 jittery, nervous, restive, uptight; 10 high-strung, in suspense, overstrung

edibility: 10 edibleness

edible: 7 eatable, victual; 8 victuals; 10 alimentary, comestible

edibleness: 9 edibility

edibles: 4 food, grub; 7 aliment, ingesta, pabulum; 8 eatables, victuals; 9 nutriment,

provender; 10 sustenance; 11 comestibles, nourishment, staff of life; 12 alimentation, sustentation

edict: 4 fiat; 5 order; 6 decree; 7 dictate, mandate; 9 dictation

edification: 5 grace; 7 tuition, unction; 8 building, erecting, erection, teaching, tutelage, tutorage, tutoring; 11 instruction; 12 constructing, construction

edifice: 8 building

edify: 4 rear; 5 build, erect, put up, raise, run up, set up, tutor; 6 school; 7 convert, educate, inspire; 8 instruct; 9 enlighten; 10 regenerate

Edison: 12 Thomas Edison; 16 Thomas Alva Edison

edit: 3 cut; 6 delete, redact; 7 edit out

edited: 7 emended

edition: 7 version; 8 revision; 11 circulation

editor: 10 text editor

editorial: 6 column

editorialist: 9 columnist

edit out: 3 cut; 4 edit; 6 delete

educable: 9 teachable, trainable

educate: 5 edify, teach, train, tutor; 6 school; 7 develop, prepare; 8 civilize, instruct; 9 cultivate

educated: 7 erudite, knowing, learned; 8 informed, lettered; 10 instructed; 11 enlightened

education: 8 breeding, pedagogy, teaching, training; 11 instruction

educational: 8 didactic; 11 instructive; 13 instructional

educator: 5 tutor; 7 teacher; 9 pedagogue

educe: 4 evoke; 6 derive, elicit; 7 draw out, extract; 8 bring out

edulcorate: 4 rack; 5 purge; 6 refine; 7 clarify, dulcify, sweeten

Edward VII: 12 Albert Edward

Edward VIII: 13 Duke of Windsor

EEC: 12 Common Market

eelgrass family: 9 tape grass; 11 Zosteraceae

eelpout: 4 cusk, ling, pout; 6 burbot

eerie: 4 eery; 5 scary, weird; 6 spooky

efface: 4 wipe; 5 erase; 6 rub out; 7 expunge, wipe off; 8 score out; 10 obliterate

effacement: 7 erasure; 14 self-effacement

effect: 4 core, gist, pull; 5 force, issue, set up; 6 burden, result, upshot; 7 essence, outcome; 8 carry out; 9 influence; 10 bring about, effectuate, impression; 11 consequence, contingency

effected: 11 established; 12 accomplished

effective: 4 good; 5 valid; 7 in force; 8 adequate, in effect; 9 effectual, efficient; 10 applicable, felicitous, productive

effects: 5 goods, wares; 8 chattels, movables; 10 personalty; 14 personal estate; 15 personal effects

E

effectual: 6 acting; **7** working; **8** adequate; **9** effective, efficient, operative, practical; **11** efficacious, functioning

effectuate: 5 set up; **6** effect; **10** bring about

effervesce: 4 fizz, foam; **5** froth; **6** bubble, fizzle; **7** ferment, sparkle

effervescent: 2 up; **5** foamy; **6** bubbly, frothy; **7** boiling, sparkly; **8** bubbling

effete: 3 bad; **4** dull, high, weak; **5** fusty, passe, slack, spent; **6** putrid, rancid, rotten, wasted; **7** corrupt, decayed, gone bad, rotting, tainted, touched; **8** blighted, cankered, decadent

efficacious: 6 acting; **7** working; **8** adequate; **9** effective, effectual, efficient, operative, practical; **11** functioning

efficacy: 7 ability; **8** adequacy, capacity; **10** capability, efficiency; **13** effectiveness

efficiency: 8 adequacy, efficacy; **12** productivity

efficient: 6 acting; **7** working; **9** effective, effectual, operative, practical; **10** productive; **11** efficacious, functioning

efficiently: 11 effectively; **12** productively

effigy: 4 copy, form; **5** image; **7** replica; **8** effigies, likeness; **9** facsimile, imitation

effloresce: 10 burst forth, crystalize; **11** crystallize

efflorescence: 4 peak, rash; **5** bloom, flush, prime; **6** flower, heyday; **7** blossom; **8** anthesis, eruption, skin rash; **9** flowering; **10** blossoming; **12** skin eruption

effluence: 6 efflux; **7** outflow, outpour

effluvium: 4 fume, odor, reek; **5** scent, smell; **6** flatus; **7** essence

efflux: 7 outflow; **8** effusion; **9** effluence

effort: 3 try; **4** deed, feat, toil, work; **5** cause, drive, labor, sweat; **7** attempt, crusade, exploit, toiling, travail, venture, working; **8** campaign, endeavor, exertion, laboring, movement, warm; **9** endeavour; **10** enterprise; **11** elbow grease, undertaking

effrontery: 4 face; **5** brass, cheek, nerve; **8** boldness

effulgence: 5 shine; **8** radiance, radiancy, splendor; **10** brilliance, refulgence, refulgency; **12** resplendence

effulgent: 5 beamy; **7** beaming, radiant; **9** refulgent

effuse: 5 spend; **6** expend; **7** diffuse, debouch, flow out, emanate, give off, pour out

effusion: 4 gush; **6** efflux; **7** outpour; **8** outburst; **9** effluence, effluxion, secretion; **10** outpouring

eftsoons: 3 eft; **4** next; **9** close upon, soon after, thereupon

egalitarian: 9 classless; **12** equalitarian

egg: 4 eggs, ovum

eggbeater: 6 copter; **7** chopper; **8** eggwhisk; **10** helicopter, whirlybird

egg cell: 4 ovum

egg en cocotte: 8 baked egg; **10** shirred egg

egg-laying mammal: 9 monotreme

egg on: 4 prod; **5** hound; **6** incite; **7** hurry on

eggplant: 7 brinjal; **9** aubergine

egg roll: 10 spring roll

egg-shaped: 4 oval; **5** ovate, ovoid; **7** oviform, prolate; **8** elliptic; **10** elliptical

egg white: 7 albumen; **9** ovalbumin

egis: 5 aegis; **11** breastplate

eglantine: 5 briar, brier; **10** sweetbriar, sweetbrier

ego: 4 self; **7** egotism; **8** identity; **13** individuality; **14** self-importance; **16** personal identity

egocentric: 6 egoist; **10** egoistical; **11** self-centred; **12** self-centered

egoism: 7 egotism; **11** egocentrism, self-concern; **12** self-interest; **16** self-centeredness

egoist: 7 egotist; **8** nepotist; **9** swellhead; **10** egocentric, monopolist

egoistical: 9 egotistic; **10** egocentric; **11** egotistical, self-centred; **12** self-centered

egotism: 3 ego; **6** egoism, vanity; **7** conceit; **8** self-love; **10** self-esteem; **11** self-conceit, swelled head; **13** conceitedness

egotist: 6 egoist; **8** man hater, nepotist; **9** swellhead; **10** monopolist; **11** misanthrope; **13** misanthropist

egregious: 4 rank; **5** gross; **6** absurd, crying; **7** glaring; **8** fabulous, flagrant, peculiar; **9** eccentric, exclusive, senseless; **10** ridiculous; **11** extravagant, nonsensical; **12** preposterous

egregiously: 3 yea; **4** even; **7** awfully, the most; **8** above all, famously; **9** a fortiori, amazingly, eminently, extremely, glaringly, still more, strangely, supremely; **10** especially, incredibly, peculiarly, surpassing, to crown all; **11** exceedingly, marvelously, of all things, principally, prominently, wonderfully

egress: 4 exit; **5** issue; **7** exiting; **8** emersion, going out

Egretta: 5 egret, heron; **12** genus Egretta

Egyptian paper reed: 7 papyrus; **9** paper rush

Egyptian water lily: 5 lotus; **9** white lily; **10** white lotus; **13** Nymphaea lotus

Eichhornia: 11 water orchid; **13** water hyacinth; **15** genus Eichhornia

eider: 9 eider duck

eiderdown: 4 down

eidetic memory: 18 photographic memory

eidolon: 5 image; **10** impression, perception

eightfold: 7 octuple

eighth note: 6 quaver

eightsome: 5 octet; **7** octette**

Einstein: **14** Albert Einstein
einsteinium: **1** E; **2** Es
Eire: **7** Ireland
Eisenhower: **3** Ike; **16** Dwight Eisenhower; **21** Dwight David Eisenhower
Eisenhower dollar: **12** silver dollar
eject: **5** expel; **6** let out, squirt; **7** boot out, exclude, give out, kick out, push out, release, send out, turf out, turn out; **8** chuck out, force out, throw out; **9** discharge; **10** squeeze out
eke out: **7** drag out, draw out, fill out, spin out, stretch; **10** squeeze out, stretch out; **11** lengthen out
EKG: **3** ECG; **10** cardiogram
Ektachrome: **10** Kodachrome; **11** technicolor
EL: **3** ALT; **8** altitude; **9** elevation
elaborate: **5** ripen; **6** dilate, enrich, expand, fatten, mature, mellow, rarify, refine, season; **7** enlarge, expound, labored, work out; **8** detailed, flesh out, worked up; **9** expatiate, intricate, luxuriant
elaborated: **8** detailed; **9** elaborate
El Alamein: **9** Al Alamayn
elan: **4** dash, fire, zeal, zest; **5** ardor, flair, gusto, style, verve; **6** ardour, spirit; **7** panache
Elanoides: **4** hawk, kite; **14** genus Elanoides
Elapidae: **11** elapid snake
elapse: **3** run; **4** flow, go by, pass; **5** lapse; **6** slip by; **7** advance, glide by, go along, proceed, slide by; **8** slip away
elapsed: **6** lapsed, no more, run out; **7** expired, extinct, has-been; **8** exploded; **9** blown over, forgotten; **10** antebellum
elastic: **6** pliant, spring; **7** buoyant, pliable, springy, tensile; **8** flexible, renitent; **9** resilient; **10** rubber band
elasticity: **4** tone; **6** spring; **7** tension; **8** tonicity; **9** renitency; **10** resilience; **11** springiness
elate: **5** cheer; **6** elated, lift up, pick up, uplift; **7** animate, enliven, gladden, inspire; **8** inspirit; **10** exhilarate, intoxicate
elated: **5** elate; **6** joyful; **7** buoyant, flushed, gleeful, pleased; **8** buoyed up, exultant, jubilant; **9** delighted; **11** in good heart, tickled pink
E layer: **7** E region
Elbe: **9** Elbe River
elbow: **4** knee; **5** ankle, groin, joint; **6** crotch, jostle; **7** cubitus, flexion, flexure, knuckle; **8** shoulder; **10** elbow joint; **12** cubital joint
elbow grease: **5** sweat; **6** effort; **7** travail; **8** exertion
elbow room: **3** way; **4** room; **9** house room, spare room
elder: **2** sr. **3** big; **5** older; **6** elders, eldest, oldest, senior

elderly: **4** aged; **5** older; **6** senior; **9** geriatric
eldest: **5** elder, older; **6** oldest; **9** firstborn
eldritch: **5** eerie, weird; **7** uncanny; **9** unearthly
elect: **5** bully, elite; **6** choice, choose, chosen, opt for, picked, select; **7** fix upon; **8** settle on; **10** decide upon, settle upon
elected: **6** chosen; **7** adopted; **8** elective, inspired; **9** converted, justified, unearthly; **10** sanctified; **11** consecrated, regenerated
elected official: **8** official; **12** office holder; **19** occupant of a position
election: **4** poll, vote; **5** voice; **6** ballot, choice, option; **7** choices [pl], plumper; **8** adoption, choosing, fatality, foredoom, suffrage; **9** selection
election day: **10** polling day
electioneering: **8** campaign; **9** candidacy; **10** canvassing; **11** bell ringing, campaigning
elector: **5** voter
electoral district: **9** bailiwick; **16** election district
electorate: **12** constituents
electric: **5** fussy, hasty; **6** winged; **7** fidgety, hurried, unquiet; **8** ecstatic, galvanic, restless, swelling; **9** mercurial, rapturous, thrilling; **10** electrical
electrical cable: **4** line; **5** cable; **16** transmission line
electrical condenser: **9** capacitor, condenser
electrical energy: **11** electricity; **13** electric power; **15** electrical power
electrical engineering: **2** EE
Electrical Phenomenon: **8** voltaism; **9** galvanism; **11** electricity
electrical power: **7** wattage
electrical resistance: **3** ohm; **9** impedance; **10** resistance
electric cell: **4** cell; **7** battery
electric chair: **5** chair; **7** hot seat; **10** death chair
electric company: **12** light company, power company, power service
electric discharge: **3** arc; **5** spark; **9** discharge; **11** electric arc
electric glow: **6** corona; **9** corposant; **12** St. Elmo's fire
electrician: **7** lineman; **8** linesman
electricity: **8** voltaism; **9** galvanism; **13** electric power
electric outlet: **6** outlet; **8** wall plug; **10** wall socket, receptacle
electric razor: **6** shaver; **14** electric shaver
electric resistance: **3** ohm; **9** impedance; **10** resistance; **11** resistivity
electrify: **4** stun, wire; **5** shock; **7** astound, petrify, stagger; **9** galvanize
electrifying: **9** thrilling
electrocardiogram: **3** ECG, EKG; **10** cardiogram

E

electrocardiograph: 3 ECG; 11 cardiograph

electrocute: 3 fry

electroencephalogram: 3 EEG; 13 encephalogram

electroencephalograph: 3 EEG

electrolyte acid: 11 battery acid

electromagnetic unit: 3 emu

electromotive force: 3 emf; 7 voltage

electronic bulletin board: 3 bbs; 13 bulletin board

electronic data processing: 3 EDP

electronic dictionary: 3 MRD

electronic flash: 6 strobe

electronic image: 6 bitmap

electronic jamming: 3 jam; 7 jamming

electronic mail: 5 email

electronic organ: 5 organ; 12 Hammond organ; 13 electric organ

electron lens: 4 lens

electron radiation: 7 beta ray; 13 beta radiation

electron tube: 4 tube; 10 vacuum tube

electron volt: 2 eV

electrophoresis: 12 cataphoresis

Electrophorus electric: 11 electric eel

electroshock therapy: 3 ECT; 12 electroshock

electrostatic bond: 9 ionic bond

electrovalent bond: 9 ionic bond

eleemosynary: 10 beneficent, benevolent, charitable; 13 philanthropic

eleemosynary institution: 7 charity; 13 public charity

elegance: 4 form; 5 grace; 6 polish, purity; 7 euphony; 12 gracefulness

elegant: 6 formal; 7 correct, courtly, refined, stately; 8 artistic, graceful, polished; 9 classical; 10 well-styled

elegantly: 8 artfully; 12 artistically

elegiac verse: 8 elegiacs; 12 elegaic meter

elegy: 6 lament; 7 requiem

element: 5 cause; 6 factor, member, origin, reason, source; 9 component, principle, vital part; 10 groundwork, ingredient; 11 constituent, environment, group member; 12 integral part

elementary: 6 simple; 7 primary; 13 trivially easy, uncomplicated, unproblematic

elementary education: 16 primary education

elementary geometry: 17 Euclidean geometry, parabolic geometry

elementary particle: 17 subatomic particle

elementary school: 11 grade school; 13 grammar school, primary school

elephantine: 5 giant, jumbo; 7 massive, monster; 9 humongous, monstrous; 10 gargantuan

elephant seal: 11 sea elephant

Elephas maximus: 14 Indian elephant

elevate: 4 lift; 5 erect, exalt, get up, raise; 6

prefer; 7 advance, bring up, promote, upgrade; 8 heighten

elevated: 3 cut; 4 high, tall; 5 beery, boozy, drunk, fresh, great, lofty, merry, tight, tipsy; 6 corned, groggy, primed; 7 drunken, eminent, exalted, fuddled, stoical, sublime; 8 eloquent, overcome, spirited, top-heavy; 9 disguised, flustered, inebriate, overtaken

elevation: 2 EL; 3 ALT, top; 4 acme, lift, peak; 5 heave, raise; 6 height, step up, summit; 7 heights [pl], raising; 8 altitude, erection, highland, pinnacle; 9 high place, loftiness, promotion, sublimity; 10 exaltation, preferment

elf: 3 hob, imp; 4 beau, chap, pixy; 5 blade, dwarf, gnome, pixie, swain; 6 fellow, gaffer, urchin, yeoman; 7 brownie, good man, gremlin

elfin: 3 fey; 5 dwarf, elvin; 6 elfish, elvish

elicit: 5 educe, evoke, raise; 6 arouse, entail, induce, kindle; 7 draw out, extract, provoke; 8 bring out, enkindle

elicitation: 9 evocation, induction

elide: 9 strike out

eligible: 3 due; 6 proper, seemly; 8 becoming

eliminate: 3 cut; 4 bolt, pass, void, weed; 5 egest, empty, rid of; 6 reject, winnow; 7 excrete, obviate, rule out, wipe out; 8 carry off, decimate, evacuate, get rid of, shake off; 9 eradicate; 10 annihilate, do away with, extinguish

elision: 7 syncope; 8 deletion, ellipsis

El Iskandariyah: 10 Alexandria

elite: 4 pick; 5 cream, elect, prime; 6 flower; 8 nonesuch; 9 nonpareil; 11 aristocracy, masterpiece; 14 creme de la creme

elk: 5 moose; 10 Alces alces

elk nut: 6 oil nut; 10 buffalo nut

Elks: 4 BPOE

Ellice Islands: 6 Tuvalu

ellipse: 4 oval; 5 ovule

ellipsis: 7 elision; 8 deletion, eclipsis

ellipsoid: 7 cycloid; 10 spheroidal; 11 ellipsoidal, non-circular

elm: 7 elm tree, elmwood

elm family: 8 Ulmaceae

elocutionary: 8 eloquent

elongate: 6 extend, linear; 7 stretch; 8 lengthen

elope: 6 desert, run off

eloquent: 5 lofty; 6 facile, fluent, silver; 7 sublime; 8 elevated; 12 elocutionary, smooth-spoken

El Qahira: 5 Cairo; 14 capital of Egypt

Elsass: 6 Alsace; 7 Alsatia

else: 2 &c.; 6 to boot; 7 besides; 8 et cetera; 10 additional

elucidate: 5 clear, solve; 7 clarify, clear up, explain, resolve, sort out; 9 enlighten; 10 illuminate; 11 crystallize, shed light on

elude: 4 bilk, duck, fail, omit; 5 dodge, evade, fudge, hedge, parry, skirt; 6 escape, ignore, put off; **7** mystify, neglect; **8** set aside, sidestep; **9** obfuscate; **10** circumvent, equivocate

Elul: 5 Ellul

elusive: 6 subtle; **7** evasive

elutriate: 4 rack; **5** purge; **6** refine; **7** clarify

elysian: 6 divine; **8** beatific, heavenly, inspired, supernal; **9** celestial, paradisal, unearthly

Elysium: 7 Arcadia; **8** paradise, Valhalla; **11** third heaven; **13** bowers of bliss, Elysian Fields, Elysian fields

elytron: 8 wing case

emaciate: 5 waste; **8** macerate

emaciated: 4 bony; **5** gaunt; **6** wasted; **7** haggard, pinched, starved; **8** skeletal; **10** cadaverous, starveling, wasted away

e-mail: 14 electronic mail

emanate: 5 issue; **6** emerge, exhale; **9** give forth

emanation: 8 emission; **9** discharge, excretion; **10** exhalation

emancipate: 6 ransom, redeem; **7** manumit; **8** free from, liberate; **9** disengage, exonerate

emancipated: 5 freed; **7** set free; **8** released; **9** liberated

emancipation: 7 freeing; **11** manumission

emancipationist: 12 abolitionist

embalm: 5 scent; **6** lay out; **7** mummify

embankment: 3 row; **4** bank, mole, pier, quay, road; **5** jetty, mound; **7** parapet, sandbag; **9** boardwalk, esplanade, revetment, sunk fence

embargo: 5 taboo; **12** trade embargo; **13** trade stoppage

embark: 4 ship; **5** board, enter, get in, get on; **7** venture; **8** go aboard; **9** get aboard, go on board; **10** get on board

embarkation: 7 leaving; **8** boarding; **9** departure, embarking; **10** decampment, embarkment

embarrass: 4 pose; **5** abash, block, ravel, stymy; **6** enmesh, hinder, impede, put out, puzzle, stymie; **7** inhibit, perplex; **8** blockade, encumber, entangle, obstruct, restrict

embarrassed: 7 abashed; **9** chagrined, mortified; **10** humiliated; **11** discomfited

embarrassing: 6 sticky; **7** awkward; **10** mortifying, unenviable

embase: 6 debase; **7** corrupt

embassy: 7 mission; **8** legation

embayment: 3 bay; **5** bight

embed: 4 base; **5** found, imbed, plant; **6** bottom, ground; **7** engraft, implant

embellish: 3 pad; **4** bead, deck, lard; **5** adorn, grace; **6** blow up, enrich; **8** beautify, decorate, ornament, prettify; **9** dramatise, dramatize, embroider

embellished: 6 ornate, purple; **7** adorned; **9** decorated, empurpled; **10** beautified, ornamented

embellishment: 8 ornament; **9** adornment; **10** decoration

ember: 4 coal

Emberiza: 7 bunting; **13** genus Emberiza

embezzle: 8 peculate

embezzlement: 10 peculation; **11** defalcation

embezzler: 9 peculator

embitter: 4 sour; **5** wound; **7** envenom; **8** acerbate; **9** aggravate; **10** exacerbate

emblazon: 3 dye; **4** fret, tint, wash; **5** chase, color, grain, imbue, mount, paint, stain, tinge; **6** blazon, colour, emboss, set off; **7** bedizen, ingrain; **10** illuminate

emblem: 6 symbol

emblematic: 5 typic; **8** armorial, symbolic; **9** exemplary; **10** symbolical

embodied: 6 bodied; **8** corporal; **9** corporate, incarnate

embodiment: 5 shape, union; **6** avatar, fusing, fusion; **7** uniting; **8** blending; **9** synthesis; **10** coalescing; **11** coalescence, incarnation, unification

embody: 2 be; **4** fuse, hold; **5** admit, amass, blend, merge, unite; **6** absorb, take in; **7** blend in, combine, conjoin, contain, embrace; **8** coalesce, comprise, dissolve; **9** body forth, incarnate, integrate, personify

embolden: 5 cheer, nerve, rally; **6** assure, buoy up; **7** hearten; **8** inspirit, reassure, recreate; **9** encourage

embolus: 8 embolism; **10** infarction

embonpoint: 5 buxom, plump; **6** chubby, zaftig, zoftig; **7** obesity; **9** stoutness, plumpness; **10** corpulence

embosom: 7 enclose, embrace

embosomed: 6 rooted; **7** mewed up, posited, situate; **8** encysted, imbedded; **9** ensconced

emboss: 4 boss, fret; **5** chase, stamp; **8** emblazon

embouchure: 10 mouthpiece

embowel: 3 gut; **7** enclose; **10** disembowel, eviscerate

embrace: 3 hug, lap; **4** gird, grab, hold; **5** adapt, admit, adopt, beset, bosom, bound, clasp, cover; **6** begird, clench, clinch, clutch, embody, pledge, take in, take up; **7** compass, contain, enclose, environ, espouse, grapple, inclose, squeeze, sweep up; **8** accolade, encircle, surround; **9** embracing, encompass; **10** circumvent, comprehend, fasten upon, fraternize

embraced: 4 held; **6** hugged

embracing: 7 embrace, hugging; **8** clasping

embrangle: 7 embroil

embranglement: 3 row; **4** fray, to-do; **5** brawl, broil, melee; **6** affray, breeze, fracas, hubbub, pother, racket, rumble, rumpus, squall, uproar; **7** howling, rhubarb [baseball], ruction, shindig, trouble; **8** brouhaha, scramble; **9** imbroglio, scrimmage;

10 donnybrook, free-for-all; **11** battle royal, embroilment

embrasure: 4 port; **6** recess, window; **8** casement, porthole; **10** battlement

embrocation: 8 liniment

embroider: 3 pad; **4** cook, lard, work; **5** braid, color, quilt; **6** blow up; **7** broider, dress up, varnish; **9** dramatise, dramatize, embellish; **10** aggrandize

embroidery: 4 flap, yarn; **5** skirt; **6** fringe, lappet; **7** cortege; **8** tall tale; **9** fancywork, fish story, trappings

embroidery hoop: 7 tambour; **15** embroidery frame

embroil: 4 drag; **5** sweep; **6** drag in, jumble, tangle, tumble; **7** disturb, sweep up, trouble; **8** disunite, entangle, unsettle

embroilment: 3 row; **4** fray, to-do; **5** brawl, broil, melee; **6** affray, breeze, fracas, hubbub, pother, racket, rumble, rumpus, squall, uproar; **7** howling, rhubarb [baseball], ruction, shindig, trouble; **8** brouhaha, scramble; **9** imbroglio, scrimmage; **10** donnybrook, free-for-all; **11** battle royal, embroilment

embrown: 3 tan; **6** bronze, darken

embryonic membrane: 4 caul, veil; **13** fetal membrane

embryonic root: 7 radicle

emcee: 2 mc; **4** host; **18** master of ceremonies

emeer: 4 amir, emir; **5** ameer

emendation: 8 emending, revising, revision

emendatory: 10 corrective; **11** reformatory; **12** ameliorating

emerald: 5 beryl; **9** malachite, verdigris; **10** aquamarine

Emerald Isle: 7 Ireland; **8** Hibernia

emerge: 5 issue; **7** come out, emanate; **9** come forth

emergence: 5 issue; **6** egress, growth; **8** emersion; **9** egression, emergency, outgrowth

emergency: 4 pass; **5** pinch; **6** crisis; **7** passage; **8** emergent, exigency; **9** adventure

emergency exit: 10 fire escape

emergent: 7 nascent; **8** emerging

emeritus: 7 retired; **9** venerable; **10** reverenced; **11** time-honored

Emerson: 17 Ralph Waldo Emerson

emery paper: 6 sander; **9** sandpaper; **10** emery cloth

emery wheel: 13 grinding wheel

emesis: 8 vomiting

emetic: 5 vomit; **8** nauseant, vomitive; **13** vomiting agent

emeute: 6 revolt, rising; **8** outbreak, uprising; **9** rebellion; **10** insurgency

emigrant: 6 emigre; **7** emigree, outgoer

emigrate: 7 migrate

emigration: 11 immigration

emigre: 7 emigree, outgoer; **8** emigrant

eminence: 9 reverence; **11** distinction, preeminence

eminent: 4 high, tall; **5** great, lofty; **7** exalted, soaring; **8** elevated, towering; **9** prominent; **13** distinguished

emir: 4 amir, wali; **5** emeer; **6** sharif; **7** effendi

emissary: 5 envoy; **6** legate; **9** messenger

emission: 9 discharge, emanation, expelling

emit: 5 utter; **6** get out, let out, put out; **7** breathe, give off, give out, pass off, radiate; **8** let loose, put forth; **9** give forth, send forth

emit vapor: 9 transpire

emmer: 11 starch wheat

emmet: 3 ant; **7** pismire

emollient: 5 cream; **7** salving; **8** ointment

emotional: 5 gushy; **7** aroused, emotive, excited, gushing; **8** effusive

emotional response: 8 response; **11** gut reaction

emotional state: 6 spirit

emotionless: 8 soulless; **9** heartless, impassive; **10** spiritless; **11** passionless, unemotional

emotive: 9 affective, emotional; **11** affectional

empale: 5 spike; **6** impale; **8** transfix

empalement: 8 piercing; **10** puncturing; **11** penetrating, perforating

empanel: 5 panel; **7** impanel

empathetic: 4 warm; **8** empathic; **11** sympathetic; **13** understanding

empennage: 4 tail; **12** tail assembly

emperor: 7 monarch, empress [female]; **9** sovereign

emphasis: 6 accent, stress, weight; **7** concern; **9** vehemence; **10** trenchance; **12** accentuation

emphasize: 6 accent, set off, stress; **8** bring out; **9** punctuate, underline; **10** accentuate, take note of, underscore; **11** lay stress on

emphasized: 6 marked; **8** emphatic; **11** accentuated

emphatic: 7 weighty; **8** forceful, pregnant; **9** assertive, trenchant; **10** emphasized; **11** exclamatory

emphatically: 7 awfully; **8** famously; **9** amazingly, by all odds, decidedly, glaringly, strangely; **10** definitely, ex-cathedra, incredibly; **11** egregiously, marvelously, prominently, wonderfully; **12** stupendously, surprisingly, tremendously, with emphasis

empire: 12 conglomerate

Empire State: 7 New York; **12** New York State

Empire State of the South: 7 Georgia; **10** Peach State

empirically true: 6 proven; **8** verified; **13** substantiated

emplacement: 8 locating, location, position; **9** placement, situating; **11** positioning

emplane: 7 enplane

employ: 3 job, use; **4** hire; **5** apply, using; **6** engage, take on; **7** empower, utilise, utilize; **9** make use of, paying job, situation; **10** employment, occupation; **11** application, utilization

employed: 4 used; **7** working; **8** utilized; **9** made use of

employee stock ownership plan: 4 ESOP

employing: 6 hiring; **8** engaging, taking on

employment: 3 job, use; **4** hire, line, task, work; **5** usage, using; **6** employ, hiring, living; **7** agendum; **8** business, exercise; **9** paying job, situation, thing to do; **10** engagement, line of work, livelihood, occupation; **11** application, utilisation, utilization

empoison: 6 poison; **8** embitter; **11** contaminate

emporium: 4 shop; **5** store; **11** retail store; **13** establishment

empower: 4 gift; **5** endow, endue, indue; **6** employ, enable, invest; **7** charter; **9** privilege; **11** enfranchise

empressement: 4 gush, zeal; **5** ardor, verve; **6** warmth, fervor; **7** passion; **8** fervency; **9** eagerness; **10** enthusiasm

emprise: 6 effort; **7** venture; **8** endeavor; **10** enterprise; **11** undertaking

emptiness: 4 void; **6** vacuum, vanity; **7** vacancy; **8** poorness, thinness; **10** meagerness

emptor: 5 buyer; **6** vendee; **9** purchaser

empty: 4 bare, rude, void; **5** drain, green, inane; **6** absorb, finish, hollow, tap out, unread, vacant, vacate; **7** abandon, exhaust, shallow, vacuous; **8** evacuate, run out of, trifling; **9** discharge, eliminate, swallow up; **10** illiterate, impoverish, unoccupied, use up all of; **11** half-learned, superficial

empty talk: 6 hot air; **7** palaver; **8** rhetoric; **10** empty words

empyreal: 7 sublime; **9** celestial

empyrean: 7 sublime; **8** empyreal; **9** celestial, exquisite, firmament, heartfelt, rapturous, ravishing, thrilling; **10** delightful, felicitous

emulate: 3 vie; **4** copy; **5** rival; **7** imitate; **8** cope with, race with; **11** compete with

emulous: 9 rivalrous; **11** competitive

emulsive: 7 curdled; **9** succulent

Emu novaehollandiae: 3 emu

enable: 7 empower

enact: 5 put on; **6** act out, decree, ordain; **7** dictate, perform, reenact, work out; **8** transact

enactment: 3 act; **4** rule; **7** passage; **9** portrayal

enamel: 4 gild; **5** grain, japan, paint; **6** polish; **7** furbish, lacquer, smarten, varnish

enamor: 5 catch, charm; **6** attach, endear, seduce, trance; **7** attract, becharm, beguile, bewitch, capture, enamour, enchant; **8** entrance; **9** captivate, enrapture, fascinate

enamored: 4 gaga; **5** crazy, dotty; **6** in love, soft on; **7** smitten; **9** taken with; **10** infatuated

enamour: 5 catch, charm; **6** enamor, trance; **7** becharm, beguile, bewitch, capture, enchant; **8** entrance; **9** captivate, fascinate

enate: 6 enatic; **8** maternal, matrikin, matrisib

en bloc: 7 as a body, en masse; **8** as a group

encage: 3 pen; **4** cage, coop; **5** hem in, pen in; **6** bolt in, coop up, rail in, wall in; **7** impound

encamp: 4 camp; **7** bivouac, camp out

encampment: 4 camp; **7** bivouac, camping, tenting; **8** campsite; **9** encamping; **10** campground, cantonment; **11** bivouacking, camping area, camping site

encase: 4 bury, case; **6** enfold, pack up; **8** enshrine

enceinte: 4 ward; **5** block; **6** barrio [Sp]; **8** environs, locality, precinct, vicinity; **9** precincts, ring fence, with child; **10** balustrade; **12** neighborhood

encephalitis lethargica: 14 sleepy sickness

encephalogram: 3 EEG

encephalon: 5 brain

enchant: 3 hex; **4** jinx; **5** catch, charm, witch; **6** enamor, ravish, trance; **7** becharm, beguile, bewitch, capture, delight, enamour, enthral, glamour; **8** enthrall, entrance; **9** captivate, enrapture, fascinate, transport; **11** put a spell on

enchanted: 7 charmed; **8** thrilled; **9** delighted, entranced; **10** enraptured

enchantment: 5 charm, spell; **6** fervor, trance; **7** amenity, ecstasy, rapture; **8** witchery; **9** seduction, transport; **10** amiability, bewitchery, enthusiasm, ravishment; **11** bedevilment, bewitchment, captivation, fascination, infatuation

enchantress: 5 siren, witch; **7** Delilah; **9** temptress; **11** femme fatale

enchase: 3 jam; **5** inlay, miter, wedge; **6** rabbet; **7** mortise; **8** dovetail

enchiridion: 6 manual; **8** circular, handbook, pamphlet

encipher: 4 code; **6** cipher, cypher, encode; **7** encrypt; **8** inscribe

encircle: 3 lap; **4** gird, ring; **5** beset, bound, round; **6** begird, circle; **7** compass, embrace, enclose, environ, inclose; **8** surround; **9** encompass; **10** circumvent

encircled: 6 ringed; 8 wreathed; 10 surrounded

encircling: 7 girding; 8 girdling, skirting; 11 surrounding; 12 circumjacent, encompassing

enclave: 6 ghetto; 7 confine, reserve; 8 preserve; 11 reservation

enclose: 3 lap; 4 gird, wrap; 5 beset, bound, put in; 6 begird, enfold, enwrap, hold in, insert, shut in; 7 compass, confine, embrace, envelop, environ, inclose, stick in; 8 encircle, surround; 9 encompass, introduce; 10 circumvent, encincture

enclosed: 5 bound; 7 limited; 8 confined; 11 encompassed; 13 circumscribed

encode: 4 code; 6 cipher, cypher; 7 encrypt; 8 encipher, inscribe, scramble

encomiast: 8 eulogist, laudator [Lat]

encomiastic: 8 praising; 9 laudatory, panegyric; 10 eulogistic, uncritical; 12 commendatory; 13 complimentary

encomium: 4 pean; 5 paean; 6 eulogy; 7 tribute; 8 citation; 9 panegyric

encompass: 3 lap; 4 gird; 5 beset, bound, cover; 6 begird; 7 compass, embrace, enclose, environ, inclose, subsume; 8 encircle, surround

encompassed: 5 bound; 7 limited; 8 confined, enclosed; 13 circumscribed

encompassing: 4 wide; 5 broad; 7 blanket, girding; 8 girdling, panoptic; 10 encircling; 11 surrounding; 12 all-embracing, all-inclusive

encore: 7 acclaim; 8 applause; 10 repetition

encounter: 3 hit, jog, see; 4 bump, find, jolt, meet, play, stem; 5 brush, clash, enjoy, fight; 6 action, battle, breast, chance, happen, hurtle, hustle, suffer, take on; 7 meeting, ran into, receive, run into, undergo; 8 showdown, skirmish; 9 collision, forgather, go through, pitch into, run across; 10 come across, coming upon, concussion, engagement, experience, fall foul of, foregather, percussion, run a tilt at; 11 be exposed to, pass through; 13 be subjected to, confrontation

encourage: 5 boost, cheer, humor, nerve, rally; 6 assure, bear up, buoy up, prompt; 7 advance, further, promote, suggest; 8 advocate, embolden, inspirit, reassure; 9 prescribe, recommend, set at ease; 11 give comfort; 12 pat on the back

encouragement: 5 boost; 6 solace, urging; 7 comfort; 8 advocacy; 10 persuasion; 11 consolation, exhortation

encouraging: 5 lucky; 6 bright; 7 roseate; 8 cheering; 9 favorable, looking up; 10 auspicious, favourable, prosperous, supporting

encroach: 5 usurp; 6 breach, trench; 7 impinge; 8 infringe, trench on, trespass

encroacher: 7 invader

encroachment: 6 breach, impact; 8 exaction, invasion, trespass; 9 breaching, intrusion, violating, violation; 10 assumption, imposition, infraction, usurpation; 11 impingement, presumption; 12 infringement

encrypt: 4 code; 6 cipher, cypher, encode; 8 encipher, inscribe, scramble; 11 write in code

encrypted: 5 coded; 7 encoded; 8 ciphered; 9 scrambled

encumber: 5 ravel; 6 cumber, enmesh; 8 entangle, incumber, restrain; 9 constrain, embarrass

encumbrance: 4 load, onus; 5 hitch; 6 burden; 9 hindrance

encyclopedia: 10 cyclopedia; 11 cyclopaedia; 13 encyclopaedia

encyclopedical: 5 broad; 7 general, generic; 8 sweeping; 10 collective; 12 encyclopedic; 13 comprehensive, encyclopaedic

encyclopedist: 8 compiler

encysted: 8 enclosed, imbedded

end: 3 aim; 4 goal, last, tail, term; 5 cease, close, death; 6 ending, finish, object; 7 closing, oddment, remnant; 8 conclude, end point, endpoint, quo animo [Lat], terminus; 9 intention, objective, remainder, terminate; 10 conclusion

endamage: 4 harm, hurt

endanger: 5 peril; 6 expose, menace; 7 imperil, scupper; 8 threaten; 9 put at risk; 10 compromise, jeopardize

endangered: 6 at risk; 7 at peril, in peril; 8 at hazard, in danger; 9 imperiled; 10 in jeopardy, threatened

endear: 5 charm; 6 attach, enamor, seduce; 7 attract, bewitch; 9 captivate, enrapture, fascinate

endearing: 6 lovely; 8 adorable; 9 caressing; 10 cherishing

endearingly: 8 adorably

endeavor: 2 go; 3 try; 4 shot; 5 essay, tempt, trial; 6 effort, strive; 7 attempt, venture; 8 engage in; 9 endeavour, undertake; 10 enterprise; 11 undertaking

endeavoring: 11 undertaking

endeavour: 3 try; 6 effort, strive; 7 attempt; 8 endeavor; 10 enterprise

ended: 4 over; 7 all over, at an end; 8 complete, finished; 9 concluded; 10 terminated

endemic: 8 epidemic, pandemic; 9 belonging, epizootic; 10 indigenous

ending: 3 end; 5 close; 6 suffix; 7 closing; 9 finishing; 10 concluding, conclusion; 11 ending event, terminating, termination

ending time: 8 endpoint

endive: 7 witloof; 8 escarole

endless: 7 eternal, no end of; 8 dateless, unending; 9 boundless, incessant, limitless, permanent, perpetual

endlessly: 10 infinitely, unendingly, without

end; **11** ceaselessly, incessantly, unceasingly; **12** continuously, interminably

endlong: 5 along; **8** at length, linearly; **10** lengthwise

end matter: 10 back matter

endmost: 8 terminal

endoergic: 15 energy-absorbing

endogamic: 11 within-group

endogamy: 10 inmarriage; **13** intermarriage

endometriosis: 11 adenomyosis

endoparasite: 7 endozoa, entozoa; **8** endozoan, entozoan, entozoon; **12** entoparasite

endorse: 4 back; **6** second; **7** certify, indorse, support; **8** plump for, plunk for

endorsement: 4 hand, mark; **5** blurb; **6** second; **7** warrant; **8** sanction; **9** autograph, signature

endorser: 8 ratifier; **10** subscriber

endothermal: 11 endothermic; **13** heat-absorbing

endow: 4 gift; **5** dower, endue, indue; **6** invest; **7** empower; **10** settle upon

endowed: 4 able, cute; **6** clever, gifted; **8** talented; **10** felicitous

endowment: 4 gift, turn; **5** forte, parts; **6** talent, virtue; **7** ability, faculty, quality, talents; **8** capacity, felicity, property; **9** attribute; **10** capability, cleverness

endpoint: 3 end; **4** term; **8** terminus

end point: 3 aim, end; **4** goal; **6** object; **8** endpoint; **9** objective

end product: 5 issue; **6** output, upshot; **9** end result; **10** denouement; **11** final result

end run: 5 sweep

end to end: 10 osculatory; **12** conterminous

endue: 4 gift; **5** endow, indue; **6** invest; **7** empower

endurable: 8 bearable; **10** sufferable; **11** supportable

endurance: 7 abiding, stamina; **8** abidance, enduring, patience, stoicism, survival; **9** suffering, tolerance; **10** philosophy, sufferance, tolerating; **11** forbearance, persistence

endurance contest: 8 marathon

endure: 2 go; **3** run; **4** bear, bide, last, live, stay, wear; **5** abide, brave, brook, put up, stand; **6** hold up, live on, remain, suffer; **7** die hard, hold out, persist, prevail, stomach, support, survive, sustain, weather; **8** brave out, continue, tolerate; **9** go through

enduring: 7 abiding, lasting; **8** abidance; **9** endurance, suffering, tolerance; **10** continuing, persisting, sufferance, tolerating

end user: 4 user; **8** consumer

ENE: 3 ENE; **13** east northeast; **14** east northeasast

enemy: 3 foe; **6** foeman; **8** opponent; **10** opposition

energetic: 6 active, strong; **7** intense; **8** forcible, vigorous; **9** gumptious, laborious, strenuous; **11** industrious

energetically: 8 strongly; **9** intensely, with vigor; **10** vigorously; **11** intensively

energize: 5 brace, exert, nerve; **6** arouse, excite, kindle, perk up, turn on; **8** activate, energise; **9** stimulate; **10** invigorate, strengthen

energizing: 5 brisk, fresh, tonic; **7** bracing, kinetic; **10** activating, activation, energising, refreshful, refreshing

energy: 3 chi, vim; **4** dash, life, push; **5** force, might, vigor; **6** spirit, vigour; **8** vitality, vivacity; **9** animation; **10** get-up-and-go, inner force

energy-absorbing: 9 endoergic

energy-releasing: 8 exoergic

energy unit: 8 heat unit, work unit

enervate: 4 faze; **5** shake; **6** weaken; **7** unnerve; **8** enfeeble, unsettle; **10** debilitate, eviscerate

enervated: 4 weak; **5** washy, wimpy; **8** adynamic, asthenic; **10** wishy-washy; **11** debilitated

enervating: 9 weakening; **10** enfeebling; **12** debilitative

enfant terrible: 4 brat, chit; **6** urchin; **11** spoiled brat

enfeeble: 5 drain, shake; **6** weaken; **8** enervate; **10** debilitate, eviscerate

enfeebled: 5 seedy; **6** infirm; **11** debilitated

enfold: 4 bury, wrap; **6** encase, enwrap, pack up; **7** enclose, envelop; **8** enshrine

enforce: 4 call, make; **5** apply, drive, force; **6** assert, charge, coerce, compel, enjoin, impose, oblige; **8** instruct; **9** constrain, implement, use a right; **10** put in force; **11** necessitate

enforceable: 7 binding; **14** legally binding

enforced: 11 implemented

enfranchise: 7 charter, empower; **9** privilege; **11** enfranchize

enfranchised: 8 ordained; **9** chartered; **10** prescribed

enfuriate: 7 incense, outrage; **9** infuriate; **10** exasperate

engage: 4 hire, lock, mesh, name, rent, take, wage; **5** lease, set to; **6** absorb, employ, enlist, fall to, occupy, plight, pursue, retain, return, secure, take on; **7** appoint, bespeak, betroth, charter, engross, operate, procure; **8** accredit, affiance, nominate; **9** prosecute, undertake

engaged: 4 busy; **5** in use; **6** booked, meshed; **7** pledged; **8** bespoken, occupied, set-aside; **9** affianced, betrothed; **11** intermeshed

engage in: 7 venture; **8** endeavor; **9** undertake

engagement: 4 care, date, hire, mesh, task;

5 fight, troth; **6** action, battle, charge, errand, hiring; **7** betroth, booking, meshing, mission; **8** affiance, conflict; **9** betrothal, encounter; **10** assignment, commission, employment; **11** appointment, betrothment, involvement; **12** assigned duty, interlocking; **13** participation, preengagement; **14** military action, responsibility

engaging: 6 hiring; **7** piquant; **8** charming, taking on; **9** employing; **10** bewitching, enchanting; **11** captivating, fascinating, interesting

Engels: 15 Friedrich Engels

engender: 3 get; **4** sire; **5** beget, breed, spawn; **6** father, mother; **8** generate; **9** actualize; **10** bring forth; **13** call into being; **14** bring into being; **18** bring into existence

engild: 4 gild; **6** begild

engine: 5 motor; **10** locomotive; **12** vehicle motor; **16** locomotive engine; **17** railway locomotive

engine block: 5 block; **13** cylinder block

engine company: 11 fire brigade; **14** fire department

engine cooling system: 13 cooling system

engine driver: 8 engineer; **16** railroad engineer

engineer: 6 direct; **8** organize; **10** mastermind; **11** mechanician, orchestrate; **12** engine driver, technologist; **16** applied scientist, railroad engineer

engineering school: 11 polytechnic

engineering science: 10 technology

engird: 3 lap; **4** gird; **5** beset, bound; **6** begird; **7** compass, embrace, enclose, environ, inclose; **8** encircle, surround; **9** encompass

English breakfast tea: 5 congo; **6** congou; **9** congou tea

English muffin: 7 crumpet

engorge: 4 cram, glut; **5** binge, gorge, stuff; **6** englut, engulf, pig out; **7** overeat, satiate; **8** scarf out; **10** gormandise, gormandize; **11** eat one's fill, gourmandize, ingurgitate, overindulge

engraft: 4 join; **5** embed, graft, imbed, plant; **6** fasten; **7** implant, ingraft

engram: 11 memory trace

Engraulis: 7 anchovy; **4** genus Engraulis

engrave: 4 etch; **5** grave; **6** bite in, incise, scrape; **7** stipple; **8** inscribe; **10** stereotype

engraved: 6 etched, graven; **7** incised; **9** inscribed; **11** stereotyped; **12** lithographed

engraver: 6 drawer, limner; **7** painter; **8** designer, sketcher

engraving: 5 print; **7** etching; **10** impression

engross: 4 bury; **5** eat up, rivet, steep; **6** absorb, engage, engulf, occupy, plunge; **7** immerse, swallow; **8** intrigue; **9** fascinate, mesmerize, swallow up

engrossed: 4 rapt; **6** intent; **7** wrapped; **8** absorbed

engrossing: 8 gripping, riveting; **9** absorbing, iniriguing; **11** fascinating, mesmerizing

engulf: 4 fell, sink; **5** douse, steep, swamp; **6** absorb, plunge; **7** engorge, engross, immerse, scuttle; **8** submerge

engulfed: 7 flooded, swamped; **8** overcome; **9** enveloped, inundated, swallowed; **11** overpowered, overwhelmed

enhance: 5 raise; **7** advance, forward, magnify, promote; **8** heighten, redouble; **9** cultivate, intensify

enhancement: 9 bettering; **10** betterment, sweetening; **11** improvement

enharmonic: 9 chromatic

Enhydra lutris: 8 sea otter

enigma: 5 rebus; **6** puzzle, riddle, secret; **7** charade, mystery; **9** conundrum

enigmatic: 8 baffling, oracular, puzzling; **10** apocryphal, mystifying

enjoin: 3 ban, bar, bid, say; **4** call, tell; **5** exact, order, taboo; **6** charge, forbid, outlaw; **7** enforce, require; **8** call upon, disallow, forefend, instruct, prohibit; **9** interdict, proscribe

enjoy: 4 bask, have, hold, like, love; **5** revel, savor; **6** occupy, relish, riot in, savour, suffer; **7** command, delight, possess, revel in

enjoyable: 8 grateful, pleasant, pleasing; **9** agreeable; **10** gratifying

enjoyment: 3 joy, use; **4** glee; **7** delight; **8** gladness; **11** delectation

enkindle: 4 fire; **5** evoke, light, raise; **6** arouse, elicit, ignite, kindle; **7** inflame, provoke; **9** set fire to, set on fire

enlace: 4 lace; **5** twine; **7** entwine; **9** interlace; **10** intertwine

enlarge: 4 grow; **5** add to; **6** blow up, dilate, expand; **7** amplify, augment, descant, expound, inflate, magnify; **8** flesh out, increase, run out on; **9** elaborate, expatiate; **10** make larger; **12** render larger

enlarged heart: 10 megacardia

enlargement: 6 blow-up, growth; **8** dilation, swelling; **9** expansion, extension

enleague: 9 go cahoots; **10** federalize

enlighten: 5 clear, edify; **6** advise, awaken; **7** apprise, clarify, clear up, correct, light up, lighten, sort out; **8** illumine; **9** elucidate, irradiate, shine upon; **10** illuminate; **11** cast light in, crystallize, put straight, shed light on

enlightened: 4 blue; **5** solid; **6** savant, shrewd; **7** bookish, knowing, learned; **8** deep-read, educated, informed, initiate, lettered, profound, well-read; **10** scholastic; **11** book-learned; **12** well-educated; **13** knowledgeable

enlightening: 8 edifying; **9** informing, notifying; **10** announcing; **11** acquainting,

enunciation, information, informative, instructive

Enlightenment: 11 Age of Reason

enlightenment: 5 light; 9 informing, notifying; 10 announcing; 11 acquainting, enunciation, information

enlist: 5 draft; 6 engage, enroll; 7 procure; 8 muster in

enlistee: 7 recruit

enlisting: 11 recruitment

enlistment: 4 tour; 5 hitch; 8 duty tour; 10 tour of duty

enliven: 5 amuse, cheer, elate, exalt, liven; 6 divert; 7 animate, gladden, inspire, liven up; 8 inspirit; 9 entertain; 10 exhilarate, invigorate

en masse: 6 en bloc; 7 as a body; 8 as a group; 9 every inch, wholesale

enmesh: 4 mesh; 5 ravel; 7 ensnarl; 8 encumber, entangle; 9 embarrass

enmity: 7 ill will; 9 hostility; 10 alienation, antagonism; 12 estrangement

ennoble: 5 exalt; 6 gentle; 7 dignify, entitle

ennui: 6 tedium; 7 boredom

enologist: 10 oenologist; 14 fermentologist

enology: 8 oenology

enormity: 7 outrage; 8 atrocity; 9 immensity; 11 monstrosity; 14 outrageousness

enormous: 4 huge, vast; 6 mighty; 7 extreme, immense; 9 humongous; 10 tremendous

enormously: 6 hugely; 11 excessively, monstrously; 12 exorbitantly, immoderately, inordinately, outrageously, staggeringly, tremendously

enough: 4 only; 5 basta! [It]; 6 decent, plenty, richly, withal; 8 adequacy, adequate; 10 competence, sufficient; 11 considering, sufficiency, up to the mark; 12 satisfaction

enounce: 3 say; 9 enunciate, pronounce; 10 articulate

en passant: 6 awhile; 7 a propos [Fr], by the by; 8 by the way; 9 in passing; 10 in transitu [Lat]; 11 in mid course; 12 incidentally

enplane: 7 to board, emplane

enquire: 3 ask; 7 inquire

enquirer: 5 asker; 8 inquirer; 10 questioner

enquiry: 5 query; 7 inquiry; 8 question, research

enrage: 5 tease; 6 madden, ruffle; 7 affront, envenom, incense, inflame, provoke; 8 aggrieve; 9 infuriate

enrage: 5 rabid; 6 ardent; 7 burning, fervent

enraged: 7 angered, furious; 8 maddened; 10 infuriated

en rapport: 11 in touch with

enrapture: 5 charm; 6 attach, enamor, endear, ravish, seduce; 7 attract, bewitch, delight, enchant, enthral; 8 enthrall, entrance; 9 captivate, fascinate, transport

enraptured: 4 rapt; 8 ecstatic, thrilled; 9

delighted, enchanted, entranced, rapturous, rhapsodic

en regle: 3 due, fit; 4 good, meet, neat, tidy; 5 right; 6 proper, seemly; 7 correct, fitting, orderly; 8 decorous; 9 befitting; 13 well regulated

enrich: 4 bead; 5 adorn; 6 fatten, mellow; 8 beautify, decorate, ornament; 9 elaborate, embellish

enrobe: 3 rig; 4 robe, vest; 5 array, drape, dress; 6 attire, clothe, fit out; 7 apparel

enrol: 5 enter; 6 enroll; 7 recruit; 8 inscribe

enroll: 4 coat; 5 enrol, enter; 6 enlist; 7 recruit; 8 inscribe, register

en route: 8 on course, on the way, under way; 9 in transit, on the road

ensanguined: 4 gory; 6 bloody; 7 crimson

ensconce: 5 house; 6 muffle, nestle, settle; 7 smother

ensconced: 6 rooted; 7 posited, situate; 8 imbedded

ensemble: 5 get-up, whole; 6 outfit; 7 complex, integer; 8 entirety, totality; 9 aggregate

enshrine: 4 bury; 5 saint; 6 blazon, encase, enfold, pack up, shrine; 7 beatify, lionize; 8 inscribe, keep holy, sanctify; 10 consecrate

enshrinement: 10 dedication; 11 celebration; 12 canonization, consecration, enthronement; 13 glorification

enshroud: 4 hide; 5 cover; 6 shroud

ensiform: 5 spiky; 6 pointy, spiked, spikey; 7 pointed; 9 bladelike, swordlike; 11 swordshaped

ensign: 4 flag; 6 colors; 7 officer, colours, regalia; 12 national flag

ensilage: 6 silage

enslaved: 4 bond; 9 in bondage; 10 enthralled

enslavement: 7 slavery; 9 captivity, enslaving

ensnare: 4 trap; 5 frame, set up, snare; 6 entrap; 7 trammel

ensnarl: 4 mesh; 6 enmesh

ensorcelled: 9 bewitched, enchanted

ensuant: 7 sequent; 9 resultant, resulting, following; 10 consequent

ensue: 4 hold; 5 issue, occur, start; 6 arrive, follow, result

ensure: 3 see; 5 check; 6 assure, insure, secure; 7 control, see to it; 9 ascertain, guarantee

entablature: 6 frieze, sconce; 7 capital, cornice; 8 pediment; 10 architrave; 11 coping stone

entail: 4 mean; 5 evoke, imply, tie up; 6 elicit, induce, settle; 7 provoke; 9 implicate

Entandrophragma: 8 mahogany; 20 genus Entandrophragma

entangle: 3 mat; 4 mire, wind; 5 ravel, snarl, twine; 6 enmesh, ruffle, tangle, tousle; 7 embroil, ensnare, entwine, sniggle, trammel; 8 dishevel, disunite, encumber; 9 embarrass; 10 interweave

entangled: 7 knotted, raveled, tangled; 8 involved; 9 embroiled, intricate, perplexed; 11 complicated; 12 inextricable

entanglement: 3 web; 8 raveling; 10 involution; 11 involvement

entente cordiale: 7 entente; 8 alliance; 10 cordiality; 11 welcomeness; 13 rapprochement

enter: 4 book, dawn, go in, open, post; 5 begin, debit, enrol, get in, infix, set in, start; 6 come in, credit, embark, enroll, figure, go into, insert, record; 7 get into, put down, recruit; 8 commence, inscribe, move into; 9 carry over, enter upon, introduce; 11 participate

enteral: 7 enteric; 10 intestinal

entered: 8 inserted, logged in

enteric fever: 7 typhoid; 12 typhoid fever

entering: 5 entry; 7 ingoing, ingress; 8 entrance, incoming; 10 ingression

Enterobius: 7 pinworm; 10 threadworm; 15 genus Enterobius

enterprise: 4 firm; 5 chore, firms [pl]; 6 effort; 7 company, concern, go-ahead, project, venture; 8 business, endeavor; 9 companies [pl], endeavour; 10 initiative; 11 undertaking

enterpriser: 12 entrepreneur

enterprising: 5 eager, pushy; 7 forward, pushful, pushing, zealous; 9 in earnest, strenuous; 10 aggressive; 11 adventurous

entertain: 4 heed, hold, host, mind; 5 amuse, nurse, throw; 6 divert, harbor, turn to; 7 enliven, harbour, think of, toy with; 9 flirt with, pay heed to, recognize; 10 give heed to, think about

entertained: 6 amused; 8 diverted

entertainer: 7 showman; 9 performer; 10 showperson

entertainment: 3 fun; 9 amusement; 10 recreation; 11 fun and games

entertainment industry: 7 show biz; 12 show business

enter the fray: 6 join in

enthalpy: 9 total heat; 11 heat content

enthrall: 6 ravish; 7 delight, enchant, enthral; 9 enrapture, transport

enthralled: 4 bond; 7 charmed; 8 beguiled, enslaved; 9 delighted, entranced, in bondage; 10 captivated

enthralling: 10 bewitching, enchanting, entrancing; 11 captivating, fascinating

enthrone: 4 vest; 5 deify; 6 invest, throne; 9 signalize; 11 immortalize; 15 exalt to the skies

enthronement: 9 accession; 10 coronation, dedication; 11 celebration, investiture; 12 canonization, consecration, enshrinement

enthusiasm: 4 gush, zeal; 5 ardor, verve; 6 fervor; 7 passion; 8 buoyancy, fervency; 10 aspiration, ebullience, exuberance; 11 enchantment, infatuation, zealousness

enthusiast: 7 devotee, fancier; 8 partisan, partizan

enthusiastic: 5 eager; 6 elated, gung ho, lively, mobile; 7 buoyant, fanatic, flighty, flushed, utopian, zealous; 8 buoyed up, exultant, Quixotic, romantic, spirited; 9 high flown, vivacious

entice: 4 draw, lure, move; 5 tempt; 6 allure, draw on, induce; 7 attract, beguile; 9 captivate

entire: 4 full; 5 total, whole; 6 intact; 8 complete, integral, stallion; 9 immediate

entirely: 3 all; 4 only; 5 alone, fully, quite, stark, whole; 6 in toto, solely, wholly; 7 in a body, totally, utterly; 8 all in all, as a whole, outright; 9 wholesale; 10 altogether, completely; 11 exclusively

entirety: 5 whole; 7 integer; 8 ensemble, totality; 10 entireness

entitle: 3 dub; 4 call, name, term; 5 style, title; 6 gentle; 7 ennoble; 9 designate; 10 denominate

entity: 4 item; 5 thing; 6 object; 9 something

entoderm: 8 endoderm; 9 endoblast, entoblast, hypoblast

entomb: 4 bury; 5 inter; 6 in tomb; 9 lay to rest; 12 lay in the tomb

entomologist: 9 bug-hunter; 10 bugologist

entoparasite: 7 endozoa, entozoa; 8 endozoan, entozoan, entozoon

entourage: 5 suite; 7 cortege, element, retinue; 11 environment; 12 surroundings

entozoa: 7 endozoa; 8 endozoan, entozoan, entozoon; 12 endoparasite, entoparasite

entr'acte: 9 interlude; 10 intermezzo

entrails: 3 gut; 4 guts [pl]; 5 bowel; 6 bowels [pl], vitals [pl]; 7 innards, viscera [pl]; 10 intestines [pl]

entrance: 5 catch, charm, entry, way in; 6 enamor, entree, trance; 7 becharm, beguile, bewitch, capture, enamour, enchant, ingress; 8 entering, entryway, incoming; 9 captivate, enrapture, fascinate, spellbind, transport; 11 entranceway

entrance fee: 9 admission; 12 admission fee

entrance hall: 4 hall; 5 foyer, lobby; 8 anteroom; 9 vestibule; 11 antechamber

entrant: 7 starter; 8 freshman, neophyte, newcomer; 9 fledgling; 10 fledgeling

entrap: 4 trap; 5 frame, set up, snare; 7 ensnare, trammel

entreat: 3 bid; 5 plead, press; 6 adjure; 7 beg hard, beseech, implore; 10 supplicate

entreaty: 6 appeal, prayer; 8 instance; 10 invocation; 11 importunity; 12 supplication

entree: 5 entry; 6 access; 8 entrance, entryway; 9 admission, admitting, reception; 10 admittance, main course; 11 entranceway

entrench: 5 dig in, fence; 6 trench; 8 intrench

entrenchment: 4 moat; 5 ditch; 7 bulwark

entrench on: 8 encroach, infringe, trespass; 10 transgress, trench upon

entrepot: 5 depot, store; 7 storage; 9 warehouse

entrepreneur: 11 enterpriser

entropy: 5 chaos; 10 randomness; 11 information

entrust: 5 leave, trust; 6 assign, charge, commit; 7 confide, consign, intrust; 8 delegate; 10 commission

entry: 5 debut; 6 docket, entree; 7 booking, ingress; 8 entering, entrance, entryway, incoming; 9 launching, list entry, unveiling; 10 ingression, memorandum, submission; 11 entranceway, inscription, ledger

entwine: 4 knit, lace, wind; 5 ravel, twine, twist, weave; 6 enlace; 7 wreathe; 8 entangle; 9 interlace; 10 intertwine

enucleate: 5 solve; 7 resolve; 12 find the key of

enumerable: 9 countable, numerable

enumerate: 3 fix; 4 tell; 5 count, tally; 6 number, 7 itemize, measure; 8 estimate, quantify, tabulate; 9 determine; 10 quantitate

enumerated: 7 tallied; 9 tabulated

enumeration: 5 count, tally; 8 counting; 9 numbering, reckoning; 10 numeration

enunciate: 3 say; 5 mouth; 6 allege, broach; 7 advance, deliver, enounce, hold out, propose; 8 aspirate, propound, set forth, vocalize; 9 pronounce; 10 accentuate, articulate

enunciation: 7 diction; 9 informing, notifying; 10 announcing; 11 acquainting, information; 12 acquaintance, annunciation, articulation, enlightening

enured: 6 inured; 8 hardened

enuresis: 10 bed-wetting

envelop: 4 wrap; 6 enfold, enwrap; 7 enclose

enveloped: 8 engulfed; 9 swallowed

enveloping: 9 enclosing, enclosure, inclosure, shrouding; 11 envelopment

envenom: 4 rile; 6 enrage, madden, poison; 7 incense, inflame; 8 acerbate, embitter, irritate; 9 infuriate; 10 exasperate, set against

envenomed: 6 bitter; 7 caustic; 8 poisoned, venomous, virulent; 9 rancorous; 10 mordacious; 11 acrimonious

envious: 7 jealous; 8 covetous, grudging; 9 invidious; 10 begrudging

environment: 7 element; 8 environs, surround; 12 surroundings

environmentalist: 15 conservationist

Environmental Protection Agency: 3 EPA

environmental science: 7 ecology; 9 bionomics

environs: 4 ward; 5 block, haunt; 6 barrio [Sp], corner, locale; 7 suburbs; 8 banlieue [Fr], confines, enceinte, locality, precinct, purlieus, surround, vicinage, vicinity; 9 alentours [Fr], precincts; 10 borderland; 11 environment

envisage: 6 ideate; 7 imagine; 10 conceive of

envision: 3 see; 5 fancy, image; 6 figure; 7 foresee, picture, project; 9 visualize

envoi: 5 envoy

envoy: 5 envoi; 6 legate; 8 emissary; 9 messenger

envy: 5 covet; 7 invidia; 8 begrudge; 11 enviousness

enwrap: 4 wrap; 6 enfold; 7 enclose, envelop, engross

enwrapped: 4 rapt; 6 intent; 7 wrapped; 8 absorbed; 9 engrossed

Eocene: 11 Eocene epoch

eohippus: 9 dawn horse

Eolian: 7 Aeolian

eon: 4 aeon

eonian: 6 eonian; 7 aeonian, eternal, lasting; 11 everlasting

eosin: 9 bromeosin

epacris family: 12 Epacridaceae

Epacris: 5 heath

epaulet: 4 frog; 7 chevron, cockade; 9 epaulette; 12 shoulder knot

epergne: 3 urn; 5 tazza; 6 patera, salver; 7 patella

ephedra: 8 joint fir

ephemeral: 7 cursory, passing; 8 fleeting; 9 fugacious, transient; 10 evanescent, short-lived, transitory

ephemerid: 6 mayfly

ephemeris: 3 log; 5 diary; 6 ledger; 7 almanac, daybook, journal; 8 calendar

ephemeris time: 2 TT; 3 TDT

epic: 4 epos; 6 epical, heroic; 8 epic poem; 9 narrative

epicarp: 7 exocarp

epicedium: 5 elegy; 7 requiem

epicene: 11 androgynous; intersexual

epicine: 9 androgyne; 13 epicine person, hermaphrodite

epicine person: 7 epicine; 9 androgyne; 13 gynandromorph, hermaphrodite

epicure: 7 gourmet; 9 bon vivant, epicurean; 10 gastronome

epicurean: 7 epicure, gourmet, hedonic; 8 hedonist; 9 bon vivant, luxurious, sybaritic; 10 gastronome, hedonistic, sensualist

epicurism: 6 nicety; **9** exactness; **10** sybaritism; **12** epicureanism

epicyclic gear: 10 planet gear; **11** planet wheel

epidemic: 4 rife; **7** endemic; **8** pandemic; **9** besetting, epizootic, prevalent; **10** prevailing

Epidendrum: 6 orchid; **15** genus Epidendrum

epidermal: 6 dermal; **9** cuticular, epidermic

epidermis: 7 cuticle

epigenesis: 7 genesis; **10** gemination, generation, heterogamy [Biol]; **11** germination, procreation, propagation

epigram: 4 quip

epigrammatic: 5 crisp, light; **6** quaint; **8** pleasant; **9** sparkling, sprightly; **10** aphoristic

epigraph: 4 posy; **5** motto

epilate: 5 shave

epileptic: 10 convulsing, convulsive

epilogue: 6 epilog

epinephrine: 9 Adrenalin; **10** adrenaline, epinephrin

epiphyte: 8 air plant; **9** aerophyte

episcopacy: 7 prelacy; **9** bishopric; **10** episcopate

episcopalianism: 11 clericalism

episode: 4 part; **5** rider; **6** affair, matter; **7** flyleaf; **8** offshoot, sequence; **9** corollary, side issue; **11** installment

episodic: 10 incidental, occasional

epistaxis: 9 nosebleed

epistle: 4 note; **6** billet, letter; **7** missive

epithet: 4 name; **6** by-name; **8** cognomen

epitome: 4 note; **5** brief, draft, image; **6** apercu, digest, minute, precis; **7** outline, summary; **8** abstract, analysis, paradigm, synopsis; **9** microcosm, prototype; **10** embodiment

epitomize: 6 typify; **7** abridge; **8** abstract; **9** summarize

epitrochoidal engine: 12 Wankel engine

epizoa: 7 ectozoa, epizoon; **8** ectozoon; **12** ectoparasite

epoch: 3 age, era

epos: 4 epic; **8** epic poem

epoxy: 4 glue; **5** resin; **6** cement

Eptesicus: 8 brown bat; **14** genus Eptesicus

eq: 10 equivalent

equable: 4 fair, just; **5** equal; **6** placid, square; **9** equitable; **10** evenhanded, reasonable

equal: 2 be; **4** fair, just, like, mate, peer, same; **5** match, reach, rival, touch; **6** square; **7** compeer, equable; **8** equalize; **9** equitable; **10** equivalent, evenhanded, reasonable

equalitarian: 11 egalitarian

equality: 3 par; **6** parity; **11** coextension, equivalence

Equality State: 7 Wyoming

equalize: 5 dress, equal, level; **6** equate; **7** balance, get even; **9** make equal; **11** render equal

equalizer: 7 balance; **9** equaliser; **12** counterpoise; **13** counterweight; **14** counterbalance

equally: 2 as; **6** evenly; **8** every bit

equal to: 4 up to; **7** capable; **10** adequate to

Equanil: 6 Meprin; **7** Miltown; **11** meprobamate

equanimity: 4 calm; **8** calmness; **9** composure

equanimous: 6 poised; **9** collected; **13** self-collected, self-contained, self-possessed

equate: 5 dress, level, liken; **7** balance, compare; **8** equalize; **9** make equal; **10** correspond; **11** render equal

equator: 6 circle; **7** midriff; **9** diaphragm

equestrian: 5 rider; **6** jockey; **8** cavalier, horseman; **10** roughrider; **14** horseback rider

equid: 6 equine

equidistance: 9 bisection; **12** half distance

equilibrium: 7 balance; **9** equipoise

equine: 5 equid; **6** hippic, horsey; **9** horselike

equine distemper: 9 strangles

equinoctial: 7 equator

equinoctial storm: 9 line storm

equinoctial year: 9 solar year

equinox: 16 equinoctial point

equip: 3 arm, fit, man; **4** perk; **6** fit out, outfit; **7** harness; **9** caparison

equipage: 3 rig; **7** foppery, turn-out; **8** carriage, frippery, materiel; **9** ball dress, equipment, full dress; **10** court dress, fancy dress

equipment: 4 gear; **5** array, slops, traps; **6** outfit; **7** harness, rigging, turn-out; **8** armament, equipage; **9** accessory, caparison, trappings; **11** accessories; **12** accouterment

equipoise: 7 balance; **11** equilibrium

equipollence: 9 equipoise; **11** equilibrium

equipped: 6 equipt; **8** weaponed; **9** fitted out, furnished

equipping: 6 arming; **8** armament; **9** equippage; **10** outfitting

Equisetum: 9 horsetail; **14** genus Equisetum

equitable: 4 fair, just; **5** equal, right; **6** square; **7** equable; **9** impartial; **10** evenhanded, reasonable

equitableness: 6 equity; **7** justice; **8** fair play; **11** give and take, lex talionis [Lat]; **12** impartiality

equitation: 6 riding; **12** horsemanship

equity: 7 justice; **8** fair play, fairness; **9** common law; **11** give and take; **12** impartiality; **13** equitableness

equivalence: 3 par; **7** compare; **8** equality; **10** comparison; **13** comparability

equivalent: 2 eq; **4** like, same; **5** equal; **10** quid pro quo, tantamount

equivalent word: 7 synonym

equivocal: 4 free; **5** bawdy, broad, gross, loose; **6** coarse, ribald, risque [Fr], smutty; **7** fulsome, obscene; **9** ambiguous; **12** pornographic

equivocally: 11 ambiguously

equivocate: 5 elude, evade; **6** palter; **7** mystify, quibble; **9** obfuscate; **11** prevaricate

equivocater: 8 quibbler

equivocation: 7 evasion, fencing; **9** shuffling; **11** dissembling, evasiveness

equivoque: 4 smut; **7** anagram, quibble; **8** ribaldry; **9** obscenity; **14** double entendre

Equus: 3 ass; **5** horse, zebra; **6** donkey, onager, tarpan; **10** genus Equus

Er: 6 erbium

era: 3 age; **4** time; **5** epoch; **8** the times

eradicate: 6 uproot; **7** wipe out; **8** carry off, decimate; **9** eliminate, extirpate; **10** annihilate, extinguish, obliterate; **11** exterminate

eradicator: 10 terminator; **12** exterminator

erasable: 10 effaceable

erasable programmable read-only memory: 5 EPROM

erase: 6 delete, efface, rub out; **7** expunge, wipe off, wipe out

erased: 7 effaced

Erasmus: 11 Geert Geerts; **15** Gerhard Gerhards; **17** Desiderius Erasmus

erasure: 9 expunging; **10** effacement, expunction

erblum: 2 Er

ere: 6 before; **11** theretofore

Erebus: 5 Pluto

erect: 4 lift, rear; **5** build, plumb, put up, raise, run up, set up, tumid; **6** normal; **7** elevate, upright; **8** heighten, straight, vertical; **11** bolt upright, put together

erectile: 9 cavernous

erecting: 8 building, erection; **11** edification; **12** constructing, construction

erectness: 11 uprightness, verticality; **12** verticalness

E region: 6 E layer

ere long: 10 before long

eremite: 6 hermit; **8** cenobite

eremitic: 4 lone; **8** hermitic, solitary; **10** anchoritic

ere now: 7 ere then; **8** hitherto; **9** a while ago, before now, in the past

Erethizon: 9 porcupine; **14** genus Erethizon

Eretmochelys: 15 hawksbill turtle; **17** genus Eretmochelys

ergo: 4 then, thus; **5** hence; **6** thusly, whence; **8** thence so; **9** therefore, wherefore; **11** accordingly; **12** and therefore, consequently

ergocalciferol: 1 D; **8** vitamin D; **9** vitamin D2; **10** calciferol

erica: 9 true heath

Ericaceae: 11 heath family

Erigeron: 5 daisy; **8** fleabane; **13** genus Erigeron

Erinaceus: 8 hedgehog; **14** genus Erinaceus

Erinyes: 6 Furies; **9** Eumenides

Eriobotrya japonica: 6 loquat; **10** loquat tree; **12** Japanese plum

Eriocaulaceae: 14 pipewort family

eriometer: 10 photometer, radiometer

eristic: 6 arguer; **7** debater, polemic; **9** disputant

Erithacus: 14 genus Erithacus

Erithacus rubecola: 5 robin; **9** redbreast; **13** Old World robin; **14** robin redbreast

Erivan: 7 Jerevan; **16** capital of Armenia

Erlenmeyer flask: 13 Florence flask; **16** round-bottom flask

ermine: 4 pall, toga; **6** mantle, purple; **9** millinery; **12** robes of state

erne: 3 ern; **12** gray sea eagle

erode: 3 rot; **4** fret, gnaw; **5** eat at; **6** blight, gnaw at; **7** corrode, eat away; **8** wear away

eroded: 7 scoured

Erolia: 9 sandpiper; **11** genus Erolia

eros: 5 amour; **12** romantic love

erose: 5 jaggy; **6** jagged; **7** notched, toothed

erosion: 7 eroding, wearing; **9** corroding, corrosion; **10** eating away; **11** wearing away

erosive: 7 caustic; **9** corrosive, vitriolic

erotic: 4 sexy; **5** lusty; **6** carnal, sexual; **7** lustful, rampant, rutting, ruttish, sensual; **8** prurient; **10** libidinous; **11** titillating

eroticism: 7 erotism; **8** sexiness; **11** amativeness, amorousness

err: 4 slip; **5** drift, stray; **6** do evil; **7** mistake; **11** perform evil; **12** make a mistake

errand: 4 care, task; **6** brevet, charge; **7** embassy, mission; **9** exequatur [Lat]; **10** assignment, commission, engagement; **12** assigned duty; **14** responsibility

errand boy: 5 gofer, gofor; **6** gopher; **8** chore boy

errant: 6 erring; **8** aberrant, shocking; **9** notorious; **10** error-prone, outrageous

erratic: 5 stray; **6** fickle, zigzag; **7** vagrant; **8** indirect; **9** arbitrary, mercurial, planetary, wandering, whimsical; **10** capricious, circuitous, undirected; **11** quicksilver; **12** inconsistent

erratum: 4 typo; **7** literal; **8** misprint; **12** literal error

erring: 6 errant; **10** error-prone

erroneous: 5 false; **6** unreal, untrue; **8** mistaken; **10** apocryphal, fallacious, groundless, inaccurate, ungrounded

erroneously: 10 mistakenly

error: 3 bug; **5** fault; **7** fallacy, misplay, mistake; **10** wrongdoing

error correction code: 3 ECC

error-prone: 6 errant, erring

ersatz: 5 phony; 9 imitation, makeshift; 10 artificial, substitute

Erse: 6 Gaelic; 8 Goidelic

erst: 4 over; 6 whilom

erstwhile: 4 late, once; 6 ere now, former; 7 onetime, quondam; 8 hitherto, previous, pristine, sometime; 9 a while ago, before now, in the past; 10 a while back, heretofore, previously

Eruca: 10 genus Eruca

eruct: 4 burp; 5 belch; 6 bubble; 8 belch out, eructate

eructate: 5 belch, eruct; 8 belch out

erudite: 7 learned; 8 educated, lettered; 10 instructed; 13 knowledgeable

erupt: 4 ooze; 5 belch, break, burst, flare; 6 ignite; 7 come out, flare up; 8 break out, burst out, take fire; 9 break open, catch fire, spew forth; 11 push through; 12 break through

eruption: 4 bang, clap, rash, rush; 5 blast; 6 blowup; 7 torrent; 8 skin rash; 9 loud noise; 10 eructation, inclemency

eruptive: 8 erupting, plutonic, volcanic

eryngo: 6 eringo

Erysimum: 10 wall flower; 13 genus Erysimum

erythema: 11 skin redness

erythema solare: 7 sunburn

Erythrina: 6 kaffir; 8 cork tree; 9 coral tree; 11 crybaby tree; 14 genus Erythrina

erythrocyte: 12 red blood cell

Erythronium: 4 lily; 16 genus Erythronium

Erythroxylon coca: 4 coca

Es: 1 E; 11 einsteinium

escalade: 4 ramp; 5 climb; 7 clamber, scaling; 8 scramble, surmount

escalate: 6 step up; 9 intensify

escalator: 14 moving stairway; 15 moving staircase

escallop: 7 scallop

escapade: 3 fad, fit, rig; 4 lark; 5 antic, freak, prank, quirk, spree; 6 maggot, vagary; 9 adventure, capriccio, poppycock; 12 risky venture

escape: 4 fail, leak, miss; 5 elude, get by, scape; 6 flight, get off, get out; 7 dodging, evasion, get away, leakage, outflow, release; 8 escapism; 10 break loose

escape clause: 8 loop hole, loophole

escaped: 5 loose; 7 at large; 9 at liberty; 10 on the loose

escapist: 7 dreamer; 14 wishful thinker

escapologist: 12 escape expert

escargot: 5 snail

escarole: 6 endive; 15 chicory escarole

escarpment: 4 edge, flag, slab, tier; 5 ledge, scarp, stage; 6 escarp

eschalot: 7 shallot

eschew: 4 shun; 6 pass up; 8 let alone; 11 deny oneself

eschewing: 8 inaction, not doing; 9 not acting; 10 abstention, abstinence, forbearing, refraining; 11 forbearance, passiveness

escort: 4 date; 6 convoy; 7 esquire; 9 bodyguard

escritoire: 9 secretary; 10 secretaire; 12 writing table

esculent: 6 edible; 7 eatable; 10 alimentary, comestible

escutcheon: 9 scutcheon; 11 finger plate

ESE: 13 east southeast

Eskimo: 5 Inuit; 8 Esquimau

Eskimo dog: 5 husky

esophagus: 5 gorge; 6 gullet; 10 oesophagus

esoteric: 7 private; 10 inviolable; 11 specialized; 12 confidential; 13 unmentionable

Esox: 4 pike; 8 pickerel; 9 genus Esox; 11 muskellunge; 12 northern pike

ESP: 11 second sight; 12 clairvoyance

especial: 7 special

especially: 7 the most; 8 above all; 9 a fortiori, eminently, extremely, specially, still more, supremely; 11 exceedingly, of all things, principally, prominently; 12 particularly, preeminently, surpassingly

espial: 3 ken; 4 look, view; 6 gander, seeing, spying; 7 viewing; 8 catching, spotting

espieglerie: 3 fun; 4 bout; 6 vagary; 7 roguish, gambade

espionage: 5 watch; 10 espionnage; 14 reconnaissance

esplanade: 3 row; 4 road; 9 boardwalk; 10 embankment

espousal: 6 bridal; 7 wedding; 8 nuptials, spousals; 9 betrothal

espouse: 3 wed; 5 adapt, adopt, marry; 6 follow, take up; 7 conjoin, embrace, sweep up; 10 get married

esprit: 3 wit; 4 whim; 5 fancy, parts, point; 8 drollery, gumption, sagacity; 9 acuteness; 10 pleasantry

esprit de corps: 6 morale; 8 prestige; 10 team spirit

espy: 3 ken, see, spy; 4 spot, view; 5 sight; 6 descry; 7 discern, make out; 8 discover; 9 recognize; 11 distinguish

Esq: 7 Esquire

Esquimau: 5 Inuit; 6 Eskimo

Esquire: 3 Esq

esquire: 3 sir; 5 boyar; 6 escort; 8 esquired, margrave

essay: 2 go; 3 try; 4 seek, shot, test; 5 assay, prove, tempt, trial; 6 strive, try out; 7 attempt, examine, venture; 8 endeavor; 13 make an attempt

essaying: 6 trying; 10 attempting

essayist: 6 writer; 11 litterateur

essence: 3 nub, sum; 4 core, fume, gist, meat, pith, reek; 5 heart, point, scent, trail; 6 burden, center, effect, kernel, marrow, nature; 7 bouquet, perfume; 8 identity, noumenon, quiddity; 9 character, effluvium, main point, redolence, substance; 10 inwardness; 11 nitty gritty

essential: 5 basic, stark, vital; 7 crucial, decided, perfect, radical; 8 absolute, cardinal, finished, positive; 9 called for, necessary, necessity, paramount, requisite; 10 imperative; 11 fundamental, requirement, substantive, unequivocal

essentiality: 7 urgency; 9 inherence; 11 needfulness

essentially: 6 au fond, bodily, purely; 7 vitally; 9 basically, decidedly, downright, in essence, radically, seriously; 10 absolutely; 13 fundamentally, unequivocally

essonite: 9 hessonite

EST: 11 Eastern Time; 19 Eastern Standard Time

establish: 3 fix, pin, set; 4 base, give, make, root, shew, show; 5 build, found, plant, prove, set up, setup; 6 ground, instal, launch, settle, verify; 7 install, lay down; 8 diagnose, make good, organize, pinpoint, settle on; 9 ascertain, determine, institute; 10 constitute, decide upon, settle upon; 11 demonstrate

establishment: 4 firm, shop; 5 brass, firms [pl], store; 6 ecesis; 7 company, concern, fixture; 8 business, emporium, founding; 9 companies [pl], formation, setting up; 10 enterprise, governance, organizing, settlement, validation; 11 institution, retail store; 12 constitution, installation, organisation, organization

estaminet: 4 cafe; 6 buffet; 7 canteen; 10 restaurant

estate: 3 lot; 4 land; 5 acres, claim, right, title; 6 demand; 7 demesne, holding; 9 situation

estate agent: 7 realtor; 9 land agent; 10 house agent; 15 real estate agent; 16 real estate broker

esteem: 5 honor, prise, prize, value; 6 look on, regard, repute; 7 respect, think of; 8 consider, look upon, regard as, take to be; 9 deference; 10 admiration, estimation, high regard

esteemed: 7 honored; 9 honorable, respected; 11 prestigious

esthete: 8 aesthete

esthetic: 8 artistic, pleasing; 9 aesthetic; 10 esthetical; 11 aesthetical

estimable: 4 good; 6 worthy; 8 valuable; 9 admirable, honorable, plausible; 10 computable, creditable; 11 full of worth, meritorious, respectable; 13 unimpeachable

estimate: 3 fix; 4 idea, rate; 5 award, gauge, guess, judge, value; 6 assess, figure, reckon, review; 7 count on, measure; 8 appraise, evaluate, forecast, quantify; 9 appraisal, calculate, determine, enumerate; 10 appreciate, estimation, quantitate; 11 approximate

estimation: 4 idea; 5 honor; 6 esteem; 7 respect; 8 approval, estimate, sanction; 9 appraisal, attention, deference, evolution, guesswork, reduction, valuation; 10 estimating, high regard, involution; 11 approbation, good opinion; 12 appreciation

estimator: 7 figurer; 8 computer, reckoner; 10 calculator

estival: 5 sunny; 6 steamy, torrid; 8 aestival, tropical

Estonia: 8 Esthonia

estoppel: 10 injunction

estragon: 8 tarragon

estrange: 5 alien, repel; 8 alienate; 9 disaffect

estrangement: 6 enmity; 8 coolness; 9 hostility; 10 alienation; 12 disaffection

estrogen: 9 oestrogen

estrus: 3 rut; 4 heat; 7 arousal, oestrus

estuary: 5 fiord, firth, fjord, inlet

esurience: 7 edacity; 8 rapacity, voracity; 12 ravenousness; 13 rapaciousness, voraciousness

esurient: 4 avid; 6 greedy, hungry; 7 starved, wolfish; 8 edacious, famished, ravening, ravenous, sharp-set; 9 devouring, rapacious, voracious

et al: 6 et alia; 9 and others; 12 and elsewhere

etc: 2 &c.; 7 and so on; 8 et cetera, etcetera; 10 and so forth, and the like

et cetera: 2 &c., etc; 4 else; 6 to boot; 7 besides; 10 and so forth, and the like

etch: 5 grave; 6 bite in, incise, scrape; 7 engrave, stipple

etched: 6 graven; 7 incised; 8 engraved; 9 inscribed

eternal: 6 eonian; 7 aeonian, ageless, endless, lasting; 8 unending; 9 perpetual, unceasing; 11 everlasting; 12 interminable

Eternal City: 4 Roma, Rome; 14 capital of Italy

eternalize: 8 eternize; 11 immortalize

eternal life: 9 salvation; 11 life eternal; 12 eternal bliss; 13 eternal reward

eternally: 7 forever; 8 evermore; 13 everlastingly

eternal punishment: 9 damnation

eternal rest: 4 rest; 5 death, sleep; 7 quietus; 12 eternal sleep, lifelessness

eternity: 3 aye; 7 forever; 8 infinity; 10 perpetuity; 11 immortality

E

ethanamide: 9 acetamide
ethanedioic acid: 10 oxalic acid
ethanediol: 6 glycol
ethanol: 7 alcohol; 12 ethyl alcohol, grain alcohol
ethene: 8 ethylene
ether: 6 aether; 10 ethyl ether, vinyl ether; 12 diethel ether, divinyl ether, ethoxyethane, quintessence
ethereal: 4 aery, airy; 6 aerial; 8 aeriform, gossamer; 9 celestial; 10 sublimated, weightless
ethic: 11 ethical code, value-system; 14 moral principle; 16 value orientation
ethical: 5 moral; 9 honorable; 10 honourable; 11 casuistical; 13 conscientious
ethicism: 8 paganism; 10 heathenism
ethics: 6 morals; 8 ethology, morality
Ethiopia: 8 Yaltopya; 9 Abyssinia
Ethiopian language: 7 Amharic
ethnic: 8 cultural, ethnical
ethnic music: 4 folk; 9 folk music
ethological: 5 moral; 7 ethical; 11 casuistical; 13 conscientious
ethosuximide: 7 Emeside; 8 Zarontin
Ethrane: 9 enflurane
ethyl alcohol: 7 alcohol, ethanol; 12 grain alcohol; 14 neutral spirits
ethyl aminobenzoate: 10 benzocaine
ethyne: 9 acetylene
etiolate: 4 pale; 6 blanch; 8 blanched, bleached; 9 etiolated; 11 become white
etiquette: 4 form; 7 decorum; 8 good form; 9 formality, gentility, propriety
Etna: 6 Mt Etna; 9 Mount Etna
etodolac: 6 Lodine
etymology: 10 derivation
etymon: 4 root; 5 trunk; 7 nucleus, tap-root
Eu: 8 europium
Euarctos: 13 genus Euarctos
Euarctos americanus: 9 black bear; 15 Ursus americanus
eucalyptus: 8 eucalypt; 14 eucalyptus tree
Eucharist: 7 Liturgy; 9 communion; 11 Lord's supper, Lord's Supper; 12 the sacrament; 13 holy communion, Holy Sacrament
eucharistical: 9 baptismal
euchre: 2 do; 3 con, nab; 4 bilk, bite, scam; 5 cheat, cozen, pluck; 6 chouse, diddle, jockey; 7 defraud, swindle; 9 victimize; 11 five hundred
euchred: 6 bilked; 7 cheated, diddled, plucked, tricked; 8 swindled
Euclidean geometry: 17 parabolic geometry; 18 elementary geometry
eudaemon: 7 eudemon; 10 good spirit
eudemonistic: 9 eudemonic; 13 eudaemonistic; 14 eudemonistical

eudemonistical: 9 eudemonic; 12 eudemonistic; 13 eudaemonistic
Eugenia aromaticum: 5 clove; 9 clove tree
eugenics: 11 race-culture
eulogist: 9 euphemist; 10 panegyrist
eulogistic: 8 praising; 9 laudatory, panegyric; 10 uncritical; 11 encomiastic, panegyrical; 12 commendatory; 13 complimentary
eulogize: 4 puff; 5 cry up, extol
eulogy: 4 pean; 5 paean; 8 encomium, eulogium; 9 panegyric
Eumenides: 6 Furies; 7 Erinyes
Eunectes murinus: 8 anaconda
eunuch: 8 castrate
euphemism: 7 bombast; 8 richness; 9 turgidity; 10 euphonious, floridness, orotundity, rhythmical; 11 declamation, euphemistic, grandiosity, mellifluous
euphemist: 8 eulogist
euphemistic: 4 rich; 5 tumid; 6 florid, mouthy, ornate, turgid; 7 flowery, orotund; 8 inflated, sonorous, swelling; 9 bombastic, euphemism, grandiose, high flown; 10 euphonious, ornamented, rhetorical, rhythmical, turgescent
euphonium: 7 sackbut
euphonous: 10 euphonious
euphony: 5 grace, music; 6 polish, purity; 8 elegance
Euphorbiaceae: 12 spurge family
euphoric: 5 happy
Euphrates: 14 Euphrates River
euphuism: 6 purism; 7 bombast; 8 pedantry, richness; 9 euphemism, turgidity; 10 floridness, orotundity; 11 declamation, grandiosity; 12 precisianism; 13 frills of style, magniloquence, ornamentation
euphuistic: 4 rich; 5 stiff, tumid; 6 florid, mouthy, ornate, turgid; 7 flowery, orotund, stilted; 8 affected, inflated, mannered, sonorous, swelling; 9 bombastic, grandiose, high flown; 10 artificial, ornamented, rhetorical, turgescent
eureka!: 3 aha!; 8 I've got it!
European Economic Community: 3 EEC; 12 Common Market
europium: 2 Eu
eurythmics: 11 eurhythmics
Eustachian tube: 12 auditory tube
Euterpe: 9 music Muse
euthanasia: 9 sacrifice; 12 mercy killing
eutherian mammal: 9 eutherian, placental
Euxine Sea: 8 Black Sea
eV: 12 electron volt
EVA: 9 space walk; 22 extra-vehicular activity
evacuant: 9 cathartic, purgative
evacuate: 4 quit, void; 5 empty; 6 vacate; 7 abandon, exhaust; 9 eliminate, pass out of; 11 leave a place
evacuation: 7 voiding; 8 emptying, void-

ance; **9** dejection, excreting, excretion; **10** defecation; **11** elimination

evade: 4 bilk, duck, fail, omit; **5** dodge, elude, fudge, hedge, parry, skirt; **6** ignore, put off, slight; **7** mystify, neglect; **8** forswear, renounce, set aside, sidestep; **9** obfuscate, repudiate; **10** circumvent, equivocate

evaluate: 4 rate; **5** value; **6** assess; **7** measure; **8** appraise, estimate

evaluation: 6 rating; **9** appraisal, valuation; **10** assessment; **12** appraisement

evaluator: 5 judge

evanesce: 4 fade, pass; **5** fleet; **7** pass off; **8** blow over

evanescence: 7 brevity; **8** fugacity [Chem]; **10** transience; **12** ephemerality, fleetingness, impermanence

evanescent: 7 cursory; **8** fleeting; **9** ephemeral, very small; **10** impalpable, intangible, short-lived

evangelical: 6 divine; **8** catholic; **9** Christian; **10** scriptural; **12** evangelistic, monotheistic

evangelism: 10 converting; **11** proselytism

evangelist: 8 gospeler; **9** gospeller; **10** revivalist

evaporate: 2 go; **3** fly; **4** fade, flit, pass; **6** gallop, vanish; **8** dissolve, fade away, melt away, pass away, vaporize; **9** disappear, dissipate; **10** volatilize

evaporated: 9 condensed

evaporating: 6 fading, flying; **9** vanishing

evaporation: 5 vapor; **6** vapour; **8** drying up; **11** dehydration, dessication; **12** gasification, vaporisation, vaporization

evasion: 4 go by; **5** shift; **6** escape, laches [Law]; **7** dodging, elusion, failure, fencing, neglect, shuffle; **8** omission, shirking; **9** shuffling; **10** concealing, subterfuge; **11** concealment, dissembling, make-believe, suppression; **12** equivocation, inobservance

evasive: 6 feline, hollow; **7** elusive, furtive; **8** specious, stealthy; **9** plausible, secretive; **11** superficial

evasive action: 8 maneuver

eve: 7 evening

even: 3 yea, yet; **4** flat, tied, true; **5** flush, level, plane, right, still; **6** direct; **7** coequal, discoid, even out, in a line, regular, the most, uniform; **8** above all, balanced; **9** a fortiori, eminently, extremely, still more, supremely; **10** coordinate, especially, fifty-fifty, horizontal, monotonous, peculiarly, surpassing, to crown all; **11** egregiously, exceedingly, of all things, principally, prominently, symmetrical

even chance: 6 toss-up

evenhanded: 4 fair, just; **5** equal, right; **6** square; **7** equable; **9** equitable, impartial; **10** reasonable

evenhandedly: 4 fair; **6** fairly

E

evening: 3 eve; **8** eventide; **10** vespertine

evening clothes: 10 formalwear; **11** eveningwear; **12** evening dress

evening dress: 7 foppery; **8** equipage, frippery; **9** ball dress, full dress; **10** court dress, fancy dress, formalwear

evening gown: 7 tea gown; **10** dinner gown; **11** dinner dress

evening meal: 6 dinner, supper

evening party: 6 soiree

evening shift: 10 swing shift

evenly: 7 equally

evenness: 5 level; **8** monotony; **13** invariability

even out: 4 even; **5** level; **6** even up; **7** even off; **10** compensate; **14** counterbalance

even so: 3 yet; **5** still; **6** just so, withal; **7** however; **10** all the same, for all that; **11** nonetheless; **12** nevertheless

evensong: 7 vespers; **13** evening prayer

event: 3 act; **4** bout, case, deed, fact; **5** round, thing, touch; **6** stitch; **8** human act, incident, overt act; **9** happening; **10** human event, occurrence, phenomenon

even-tempered: 6 placid; **7** equable

eventful: 8 bustling, stirring; **9** momentous; **13** consequential

eventfully: 9 memorably; **10** stirringly; **13** unforgettably

eventide: 3 eve; **6** curfew; **7** evening; **9** nightfall

even-toed: 11 artiodactyl

eventuality: 4 fact; **5** event, thing; **8** incident; **9** happening; **10** occurrence, phenomenon; **11** contingency

eventually: 3 yet; **6** in time; **7** by and by, finally, some day, through; **8** at length; **10** after a time, all along of, ultimately; **11** after a while, necessarily; **13** sooner or later

eventuate: 5 prove; **6** draw on

ever: 3 aye, e'er; **6** always, ever so; **8** evermore; **9** of all time

Everest: 9 Mt. Everest; **12** Mount Everest

Everglade State: 7 Florida; **13** Sunshine State

evergreen: 7 conifer; **9** perennial

Evergreen State: 10 Washington

everlasting: 7 aeonian, ageless, blessed, eternal, lasting, perfect; **8** complete, unending; **9** incessant, perpetual, unceasing

everlasting life: 9 afterlife

everlastingly: 7 forever; **8** evermore; **9** eternally

evermore: 3 aye; **4** ever; **6** always; **7** forever; **9** eternally

eversion: 9 inversion, inside out

evert: 5 upset; **7** deviate; **9** overthrow

every: 3 all; **6** entire; **8** complete

everybody: 6 public; **8** everyone**

everyday: 3 jog; 4 trot; 5 daily, usual; 6 casual, common, normal; 7 mundane, nominal, routine, typical; 8 day-to-day, familiar, frequent, habitual, ordinary, workaday; 9 household, quotidian, well-known; 11 commonplace, day-after-day, well-trodden; 12 unremarkable

every hour: 6 hourly

every month: 7 monthly; 9 each month

every night: 7 nightly

every now and then: 7 at times; 9 sometimes; 10 now and then, on occasion; 11 not too often; 12 every so often, occasionally; 14 from time to time

everyone: 6 public; 9 everybody

every other: 9 alternate; 11 every second

everyplace: 7 all over; 10 everywhere

every quarter: 9 quarterly

everything: 3 all

every week: 6 weekly; 8 each week

everywhere: 7 all over; 10 everyplace

every year: 6 yearly; 8 annually, each year

evict: 4 oust; 8 force out

eviction: 9 extrusion; 11 exportation, legal ouster

evidence: 4 show, tell; 5 prove; 6 attest; 7 certify, grounds, testify; 8 manifest; 9 ascertain; 11 bear witness, demonstrate

evident: 5 plain; 6 patent; 7 obvious; 8 apparent, manifest, palpable, striking; 9 axiomatic; 10 observable, pronounced; 11 discernible, indubitable, self-evident; 12 unmistakable

evidently: 5 plain; 7 plainly; 8 patently; 9 obviously; 10 apparently, manifestly

evil: 3 ill; 5 wrong; 6 malign, wicked; 7 harmful, malefic, vicious; 8 bad thing, depraved, evilness, iniquity; 9 injurious; 10 immorality, malevolent, wickedness

evildoer: 6 sinner

evil-minded: 5 cruel; 6 malign; 8 unbenign; 9 malicious, malignant; 10 ill-natured, malevolent

evince: 4 show; 6 reveal, tell of; 7 betoken, express; 10 be evidence

eviscerate: 3 gut; 4 draw, stab; 5 relax, shake; 6 weaken; 7 bayonet; 8 enervate, enfeeble; 10 disembowel

evitable: 9 avoidable

evocation: 9 induction, summoning; 10 adjuration; 11 elicitation

evocative: 6 moving; 8 redolent, touching; 9 affecting, remindful; 10 redolent of; 11 reminiscent

evoke: 4 fire; 5 educe, raise; 6 arouse, elicit, entail, induce, invoke, kick up, kindle; 7 draw out, extract, provoke, suggest; 8 enkindle; 9 call forth

evoked: 8 elicited

evolution: 6 growth; 8 movement; 9 phy-

logeny, reduction, sea change; 10 estimation, involution; 11 development, elaborating, elaboration

evolve: 7 develop, find out, work out; 8 discover; 9 determine

evolve into: 6 become, turn to; 8 turn into

ewe: 5 sheep

ewer: 3 jug; 5 cruse; 7 caraffe, pitcher; 8 decanter

ex: 6 former, ex-wife; 9 ex-husband

exacerbate: 4 urge; 5 annoy; 6 madden, worsen; 8 acerbate, convulse, embitter, heighten, irritate; 9 aggravate, infuriate; 10 accelerate, exasperate; 11 render worse

exact: 3 ask, tax; 4 just, neat, take, task; 5 claim, usurp; 6 breach, charge, demand, enjoin, extort, impose, just so, severe; 7 call for, compact, precise, require, summary; 8 accurate, encroach, infringe, sostrict, succinct, trench on; 10 to the point

exacta: 8 perfecta

exacting: 5 stern; 6 strict; 7 austere, exigent, precise; 8 obdurate, rigorous; 9 demanding, hard-nosed, hard-shell [U.S.], searching, unsparing; 10 fastidious, hard-headed, inexorable, inflexible, malcontent, meticulous, overstrict, particular

exaction: 5 claim; 6 breach, demand; 9 breaching, extortion, violating, violation; 10 assumption, imposition, infraction, insistence, usurpation; 11 presumption, reclamation, requisition; 12 encroachment, infringement

exactitude: 8 accuracy; 9 exactness

exactly: 2 so; 4 just; 5 a full, all of, fully, truly; 6 indeed, on time, you bet; 8 on the dot, the sum of; 9 certainly, on the nose, precisely; 10 accurately, definitely, ex concesso [Lat], incisively, punctually

exactness: 6 nicety; 9 epicurism, precision; 10 exactitude; 11 preciseness

exaggerate: 4 daub; 6 overdo, pile up; 7 amplify, distort, magnify; 8 overdraw, pile it on; 9 aggravate, overstate; 10 caricature; 11 hyperbolize; 12 misrepresent

exaggeration: 6 strain; 7 stretch; 8 coloring; 9 hyperbole; 10 stretching

exalt: 4 laud; 5 extol, raise, swell; 6 thrill; 7 animate, elevate, enliven, glorify, inspire, magnify; 8 proclaim; 10 aggrandize

exaltation: 7 ecstasy, rapture; 9 elevation, sublimity, transport; 10 apotheosis; 11 deification, sublimation

exalted: 4 high, tall; 5 great, lofty, noble; 7 deified, eminent, stoical; 8 elevated, rarefied, rarified, spirited; 9 high-flown; 10 high-minded, idealistic; 11 noble-minded; 12 immortalized

exam: 4 test; 11 examination

examen: 11 examination

examination: 4 exam, test; 6 examen; 7 testing; 8 scrutiny; 9 challenge; 10 inspection examine: 3 try; 4 test; 5 essay, probe, prove, study; 6 try out; 7 analyse, analyze; 8 consider, research; 10 scrutinize; 11 inquire into; 12 inquire about

examinee: 6 testee

examiner: 6 tester; 8 inquirer; 9 catechist, inspector; 10 inquisitor; 12 investigator

example: 4 case, type; 5 ideal, model; 6 lesson, sample; 7 apostle, pattern, pioneer; 8 exemplar, exercise, fugleman, instance, original, paradigm, specimen, standard; 9 precedent, prototype, reference, role model, scantling; 10 file leader, missionary; 12 illustration

exanimate: 8 lifeless, soulless; 9 inanimate

ex animo: 14 de bonne volonte [Fr]

exasperate: 4 urge; 5 annoy; 6 madden, worsen; 7 envenom, incense, outrage; 8 convulse, irritate; 9 aggravate, enfuriate, infuriate; 10 accelerate, exacerbate

exasperating: 6 vexing; 9 maddening; 11 aggravating, infuriating; 12 exacerbating

excavate: 3 dig; 5 delve, dig up; 6 hollow, turn up

excavating: 9 ecavation

excavation: 3 dig, pit; 6 mining; 7 digging; 9 strip mine

excavator: 5 miner; 6 digger, sapper, shovel; 11 power shovel

exceed: 3 top; 4 pass; 5 excel, outdo, outgo; 6 go past; 7 surpass; 8 outmatch, outstrip, overstep, surmount; 12 transcend

exceedingly: 3 yea; 4 even; 7 acutely, passing, the most; 8 above all, 9 a fortiori, eminently, extremely, intensely, still more, supremely; 10 especially, surpassing, to crown all; 11 egregiously, exquisitely, of all things, principally, prominently

excel: 6 exceed; 7 surpass; 8 stand out; 9 transcend

excellence: 5 merit, worth; 6 credit, desert; 7 mastery; 9 expertise; 10 expertness, mastership

excellency: 5 grace; 8 highness

excellent: 9 admirable; 10 first-class

excellent health: 5 vigor; 8 haleness; 9 hardiness; 10 robustness

excelsior: 12 wood shavings

except: 4 omit, save; 5 demur, minus; 6 beside; 7 barring, exclude, take out, without; 8 leave off, leave out, let alone; 9 aside from, except for, excepting, other than; 11 exclusive of

except for: 4 save; 5 minus; 6 beside, except; 7 barring, without; 8 let alone; 9 aside from, excepting, other than; 11 exclusive of; 13 save and except

exception: 7 release; 8 immunity, omission; 9 exclusion, exemption, objection, privilege, rejection, stricture; 10 limitation, reflection; 11 peculiarity, restriction; 12 non-admission

exceptional: 4 rare; 7 special; 8 atypical, especial, olympian, uncommon; 9 exceeding; 10 not to be had, particular, prodigious, surpassing

excerpt: 7 extract, take out; 9 selection

excerption: 8 gleaning; 11 eclecticism

excess: 5 extra, spare; 7 surfeit, surplus; 9 redundant; 10 surplusage; 11 superfluous; 13 excessiveness, overabundance, supernumerary

excessive: 5 undue; 7 too many, too much; 8 swinging; 9 exuberant; 10 exorbitant, immoderate, inordinate, outrageous; 11 extravagant, overweening; 12 preposterous, unreasonable

excessively: 3 too; 6 overly; 7 too much; 8 to a fault; 10 enormously; 11 monstrously; 12 exorbitantly, immoderately, inordinately, outrageously, over and above

exchange: 4 hall, swap; 5 truck; 6 barter, change, switch; 7 central, commute, convert, trading; 8 swapping; 9 alternate, guildhall; 10 switch over; 11 interchange; 12 substitution

exchangeable: 6 mutual; 7 similar; 10 reciprocal; 11 commutative, convertible

exchanged: 8 permuted; 10 transposed; 12 interchanged

exchequer: 8 treasury

exchequer bill: 5 order; 6 coupon; 7 warrant; 9 debenture

excise: 6 cut out, excise, strike; 7 expunge; 9 excise tax

exciseman: 6 gauger [Brit], taxman; 8 douanier [Fr]; 12 tax collector; 14 customs officer

excision: 8 ablation, recision; 10 abscission, cutting out; 11 extirpation

excitable: 4 taut; 5 tense; 8 volatile; 9 irritable, sensitive; 10 high-strung; 13 easily excited, oversensitive

excitation: 6 praxis; 8 exercise; 9 agitation, animation, execution; 10 excitement; 12 perturbation

excitative: 8 excitant; 10 excitatory

excite: 4 lash, move, stir; 5 exert, rouse, shake, smite, touch; 6 affect, arouse, charge, foment, incite, infect, kindle, stir up, strike, turn on, wind up; 7 agitate, animate, commove, impress, inflame, inspire, quicken, shake up, sharpen; 8 activate, charge up, energize, interest; 9 impassion, stimulate

excited: 3 mad; 4 wild; 5 fiery, moved; 6 fierce, madcap; 7 aroused, frantic, furious, smitten, striken, touched, violent; 8 affected, animated, inspired, vehement; 9 activated, delirious, emotional, impressed; 10 interested; 11 impassioned; 12 unrestrained; 13 demonstrative

E

excitement: 4 heat; 5 fever, flush; 6 warmth; 7 passion, turmoil; 8 upheaval; 9 agitation, animation; 10 excitation, hullabaloo; 12 exhilaration

exciting: 7 rousing; 11 provocative, stimulating

exclaim: 3 cry; 5 shout; 6 cry out, outcry; 7 call out; 8 proclaim; 10 promulgate

exclamation: 10 exclaiming; 11 ejaculation; 12 interjection

exclamatory: 8 emphatic

exclude: 3 bar; 4 cull, omit, shut; 5 debar, eject, expel, repel; 6 except; 7 boot out, keep out, kick out, shut out, take out, turf out, turn out; 8 chuck out, get rid of, leave off, leave out, throw out

excluding: 7 barring; 10 leaving out

exclusion: 7 censure; 8 ejection, omission, riddance; 9 exception, expulsion, rejection; 11 repudiation; 12 non-admission, noninclusion

exclusive: 4 only, sole; 5 party, scoop; 6 proper, single; 7 certain, partial, private, several, special; 8 definite, especial, original, peculiar, specific; 9 eccentric, egregious, undivided; 10 individual, particular; 11 appropriate, determinate, restrictive

exclusively: 4 only; 5 alone; 6 solely; 8 entirely

exclusiveness: 12 clannishness, cliquishness

exclusive of: 4 save; 5 minus; 6 except; 7 barring, without; 9 except for, excepting

exclusive possession: 6 corner; 8 monopoly

exclusive right: 9 privilege; 10 perquisite; 11 prerogative

excogitate: 5 forge, think; 6 devise, invent; 8 cogitate, contrive; 9 formulate

excogitation: 6 devise, design; 9 invention; 10 conception, innovation

excommunicate: 5 curse, expel; 8 denounce; 9 fulminate, proscribe

excommunication: 7 censure; 9 exclusion

excoriate: 4 flay, pare, peel, skin; 5 decry, scalp; 6 abrade; 7 condemn; 9 objurgate; 11 decorticate

excoriation: 6 scrape; 7 scratch; 8 abrasion; 12 desquamation; 13 decortication

excrescence: 3 jut; 4 blot, bump, hump; 5 bulge; 9 extrusion, gibbosity; 10 prominence, protrusion; 11 gibbousness; 12 protuberance

excrete: 4 pass; 5 egest; 9 eliminate

excreted: 8 secreted

excretion: 7 excreta, voiding; 9 body waste, discharge, emanation, excrement, excreting; 10 evacuation; 11 elimination

excruciate: 4 rack; 7 torment, torture

excruciating: 7 cutting, grating, racking; 8 grinding; 9 agonizing, consuming, corroding, harrowing, searching, torturing, torturous

exculpate: 5 clear; 6 acquit, assoil; 7 absolve; 9 discharge, exonerate, vindicate

exculpation: 7 warrant; 9 acquittal; 11 acquittance, exoneration, vindication

excursion: 4 tour, trip; 5 jaunt; 6 junket, outing, sashay; 10 digression, expedition; 12 pleasure trip

excursionist: 7 tripper, tourist; 9 sightseer

excursive: 8 rambling; 10 digressive, discursive, vacationer

excursus: 5 aside; 10 digression, divagation; 11 parenthesis

excusable: 6 venial; 10 defensible, forgivable, pardonable; 11 justifiable

excuse: 4 free; 5 alibi, salve, salvo, spare; 6 beg off, exempt, let off, pardon, soften; 7 apology, condone, explain, justify, license, release, relieve; 8 overlook, palliate, pass over; 9 apologise, apologize, extenuate, franchise, indemnity, quittance; 11 exoneration, rationalize

execrable: 6 odious, woeful; 7 hateful; 8 damnable, wretched; 9 abhorrent, miserable, repellent, repulsive; 10 abominable, deplorable, detestable

execrate: 4 hate; 5 abhor, scold; 6 detest, loathe; 9 abominate

execration: 3 ban; 5 curse, odium; 8 anathema, loathing; 10 abhorrence; 11 abomination, detestation; 12 condemnation, proscription

execute: 2 do; 4 keep, make; 5 carry, stamp; 6 comply, fulfil; 7 abide by, fulfill, observe, perform, respect, satisfy; 8 carry out, transact; 9 discharge; 10 accomplish, comply with, put to death

executing: 9 execution; 12 death penalty

execution: 4 seal; 5 doing, stamp, touch; 6 praxis; 8 exercise; 9 executing, signature; 10 acceptance, compliance, excitation, expression, observance; 11 carrying out, concurrence, performance; 12 acquiescence, death penalty

executive: 8 official; 9 practical; 11 businessman

executor: 9 executrix

exegetic: 10 exegetical

exegetical: 11 explanatory

exemplar: 4 type; 5 ideal, model; 7 example, pattern; 8 original, paradigm, standard; 9 precedent, prototype, reference

exemplary: 5 model, typic; 7 warning; 8 monitory; 10 admonitory, cautionary, emblematic

exemplify: 4 cite; 5 quote; 6 embody, typify; 8 instance, put a case; 9 represent

exempli gratia: 2 e.g. [abbr]; 10 for example

exempt: 4 free; 5 remit; 6 acquit, excuse, immune, let off, remise; 7 release, relieve;

8 scot-free; **9** at liberty, discharge, quitclaim; **10** nontaxable

exemption: 5 favor; **7** freedom, liberty, release; **8** immunity; **9** exception; **10** limitation; **11** restriction; **12** dispensation

exercise: 2 do; **3** use; **4** play, rear, task, work; **5** breed, drill, exert, swing, usage; **6** ground, office, strain; **7** bring up, carry on, example, nurture, prepare, work out, workout; **8** be at work, carry out, exertion, practice, practise; **9** execution, habituate, prosecute; **10** employment, excitation, exercising, take in hand, working out

exercise bike: 9 exercycle

exercise book: 8 workbook

exercising: 7 workout; **8** exercise; **10** working out

exert: 5 wield; **6** excite, kindle, turn on; **8** activate, energize, exercise, maintain, practice; **9** stimulate

exertion: 5 sweat; **6** effort; **7** travail; **8** exercise, practise; **11** elbow grease

exhalation: 9 emanation; **10** expiration; **12** breathing out

exhale: 4 fume, reek; **5** smoke, steam; **6** expire; **7** emanate; **9** give forth; **10** breathe out

exhaust: 3 dry, eat, gut, irk, sap; **4** beat, flag, jade, tire; **5** drain, eat up, empty, fumes, use up, weary; **6** absorb, finish, run out, tap out, tucker, weaken; **7** consume, deplete, fatigue, run down, shatter, wear out, wipe out; **8** evacuate, run out of; **9** prostrate, swallow up, tucker out; **10** impoverish, run through

exhausted: 4 gone, lost; **5** spent; **6** done up, fagged, used up; **7** drained, extinct, worn out, worn-out; **8** consumed, cratered, dead beat, departed, depleted, expended, fatigued, finished, vanished; **9** played out, prostrate, shattered, tapped out, washed-out

exhaustion: 5 palsy; **7** syncope; **8** apoplexy, collapse; **9** depletion, inanition, lassitude, paralysis, tiredness; **10** enervation; **11** prostration

exhibit: 4 demo, show; **5** march; **6** expose, hold up, parade; **7** display, present, show off, showing; **10** put forward, thing shown; **11** demonstrate

exhibition: 4 expo, pomp; **7** pageant; **9** pageantry, spectacle; **10** convention, exposition, production

exhibition area: 14 exhibition hall

exhibition game: 12 practice game

exhibitionism: 9 immodesty

exhibitionist: 7 flasher, show-off

exhibitor: 6 shower; **12** exhibitioner

exhilarate: 5 cheer, elate, exalt; **6** thrill; **7** animate, enliven, gladden, inspire; **8** inspirit

exhilaration: 5 mirth; **8** hilarity; **9** merriment; **10** excitement

exhort: 4 urge; **5** cheer, pep up, press; **6** urge on; **7** barrack, inspire

exhortation: 6 urging; **8** advocacy; **10** incitement, persuasion

exhumation: 9 digging up; **12** disinterment

exhume: 7 unearth; **8** disinter

ex-husband: 2 ex

exigency: 3 fix; **4** lack, need, pass, push, want; **5** hitch, needs [pl], pinch, trial; **6** strait, stress; **7** nonplus, poverty; **8** juncture, quandary, scramble; **9** emergency, necessity

exigent: 6 crying, urgent; **7** austere, clamant, instant; **8** exacting, obdurate, pressing, rigorous; **9** absorbing, demanding, hardnosed, insistent, searching, unsparing; **10** hard-headed, inexorable

exiguity: 8 poorness; **9** scantness; **10** inadequacy, meagerness, meagreness, scantiness; **12** exiguousness

exiguous: 3 wee; **4** puny, rare, thin, tiny; **5** petit, petty; **6** petite, spotty; **9** miniature, scattered; **10** inadequate

exile: 5 expel; **6** banish, deport, maroon, outlaw; **8** deportee; **9** expulsion, transport; **10** banishment, cut off from, expatriate; **11** deportation; **12** expatriation

exist: 2 be; **4** live; **7** subsist, survive; **9** have being

existence: 5 being, world; **6** cosmos, nature; **8** creation, universe; **9** beingness, macrocosm

existent: 4 real; **6** actual

existential: 12 experiential

existing: 5 being; **6** actual, extant, that is; **7** current, instant, present; **8** existent

exit: 2 go; **3** die; **4** loss; **5** go out, going, issue, leave; **6** egress, expire, get out, outlet, perish, way out; **7** decease, exiting, passing, release; **8** going out, pass away; **9** departure

exiting: 4 exit; **5** issue; **6** egress; **8** going out

ex libris: 9 bookplate

exodus: 6 hegira, hejira

exoergic: 15 energy-releasing

ex officio: 4 duly; **6** de jure [Lat]; **8** absolute, official; **10** imperative, overruling, peremptory; **15** by right of office

exogamic: 12 outside-group

exonerate: 5 clear; **6** acquit, assoil; **7** absolve, release; **8** free from, set right; **9** discharge, disengage, exculpate; **10** emancipate

exonerative: 9 forgiving; **11** absolvitory

exorbitant: 5 steep; **8** swinging, usurious; **9** excessive; **10** immoderate, inordinate, outrageous; **11** extravagant; **12** extortionate, preposterous, unreasonable

exorcise: 8 exorcize

exorcism: 5 runes, spell; **7** cast out

exorcist: 9 exorciser

exoteric: 4 bare, open; **5** overt; **6** patent; **7** express, literal; **8** external, explicit; **9** expressed; **11** undisguised

exothermal: 10 exothermic; **13** heat-releasing

exotic: 5 alien; **7** foreign, strange, unusual

exotic dancer: 6 peeler; **8** stripper; **9** ecdysiast; **10** striptease; **11** belly dancer, stripteaser

expand: 4 boom, grow, puff; **5** widen; **6** blow up, dilate, extend, rarefy, spread, thrive; **7** amplify, be wordy, develop, distend, enlarge, expound, inflate, magnify, prosper; **8** flesh out, flourish, get ahead, increase; **9** be diffuse, be profuse, be verbose, elaborate, expatiate, spread out; **10** aggrandize, decompress

expanded: 5 grown; **7** swollen, widened; **8** enlarged, extended; **9** increased

expanse: 4 area; **5** space, sweep; **6** extent; **7** stretch; **9** extension; **11** surface area

expansion: 3 way; **4** form, room; **5** field, range, scope, sweep, swing; **6** growth, spread; **7** compass, variant; **8** dilation, revision, swelling; **9** extension, inflation, variation; **10** derivation, derivative, dilatation; **11** enlargement, rarefaction

expansive: 5 ample, grand, roomy, wordy; **7** copious, diffuse, lengthy, profuse, verbose; **8** spacious; **9** capacious, extensive, exuberant, talkative

expansiveness: 9 prolixity, verbosity, wordiness; **11** diffuseness, lengthiness, profuseness; **12** effusiveness

expatiate: 6 dilate, expand, wander; **7** amplify, descant, enlarge, expound, inflate; **8** flesh out, run out on; **9** elaborate

expatriate: 5 exile; **6** banish, deport, maroon, outlaw; **10** cut off from

expect: 3 ask; **4** bear, look, wait; **5** await, carry; **7** gestate, require; **10** anticipate

expectancy: 9 remainder, reversion; **11** possibility; **12** anticipation

expectation: 7 outlook; **8** prospect; **10** expectance, expectancy; **11** first moment; **12** anticipation

expected: 6 likely; **9** potential; **11** anticipated

expectorate: 4 spit; **6** spit up; **7** cough up; **8** cough out

expedience: 10 expediency; **11** opportunism, self-seeking, suitability; **12** self-interest

expedient: 8 artifice, suitable; **9** advisable

expedite: 5 speed; **6** foment, hasten; **7** quicken, speed up; **10** accelerate

expedition: 4 tour, trip; **5** jaunt; **6** junket,

outing, sashay; **7** crusade; **8** alacrity, campaign, despatch, dispatch; **9** excursion

expeditious: 4 spry; **5** agile, quick; **6** nimble, prompt; **7** instant; **10** timesaving

expeditiously: 7 quickly, rapidly, swiftly; **8** speedily; **11** efficiently

expel: 4 oust, rout; **5** eject, exile; **6** banish, let out; **7** boot out, dismiss, drum out, exclude, give out, kick out, push out, release, rout out, send out, turf out, turn out; **8** chuck out, throw out; **9** discharge

expelled: 6 vented; **7** ejected, emitted; **8** emitting; **9** disgorged; **10** discharged

expend: 3 use; **4** drop; **5** spend, use up; **6** effuse; **7** consume, deplete

expendable: 9 spendable; **11** dispensable

expended: 4 gone; **5** spent; **6** used up; **7** drained; **8** consumed, depleted, finished, payed out; **9** disbursed, exhausted, tapped out

expender: 7 spender; **9** disburser

expending: 8 spending; **9** paying out; **10** disbursing; **11** expenditure

expenditure: 5 outgo; **6** acquit, assets, outlay; **7** expense, using up; **8** expenses; **9** expending, outgoings; **11** compte rendu [Fr], consumption, liabilities; **12** disbursement

expense: 4 cost; **5** price; **6** amount, charge, figure, outlay; **8** expenses; **9** disbursal, outgoings, prime cost; **11** expenditure; **12** disbursement

expenses: 6 outlay; **7** expense; **9** outgoings; **11** expenditure; **12** disbursement

expensive: 4 dear; **6** costly, pricey; **10** high priced

experience: 3 get, ken, see; **4** feel, have, know, live; **5** enjoy; **6** suffer; **7** discern, insight, receive, undergo; **8** conceive, perceive; **9** encounter, go through, recognize; **11** be exposed to, familiarity

experienced: 9 hackneyed, practiced

experiences: 4 life; **7** journal; **8** fortunes; **10** adventures; **11** confessions

experiential: 11 existential

experiment: 4 test; **5** trial

experimental: 4 test; **5** model, pilot, trial; **7** wildcat; **9** data-based, empirical; **11** speculative

experimental animal: 3 rat; **5** mouse; **7** subject; **9** guinea pig

experimental data: 4 data; **6** result; **7** finding

experimentee: 7 subject

expert: 3 apt; **4** deft, gain, good; **5** adept, handy, quick, ready; **6** adroit, genius, master; **7** skilful; **8** skillful; **9** dexterous, practiced; **10** proficient; **11** crackerjack

expertise: 7 mastery; **10** excellence, expertness, mastership

expertly: 9 with skill; **10** skillfully; **11** competently; **12** proficiently

expiate: 3 aby; **4** abye; **5** atone

expiation: 9 atonement, expiation; **10** redemption; **11** reclamation; **12** conciliation, propitiation, satisfaction

expiration: 4 exit, loss; **5** going, lapse; **6** expiry; **7** passing, release; **9** departure; **10** exhalation, extinction; **11** termination

expire: 2 go; **3** die; **4** exit; **5** lapse; **6** exhale, perish, run out; **7** be taken, decease, succumb; **8** pass away

expired: 6 lapsed, no more, run out; **7** elapsed, extinct, has-been, invalid; **8** exploded; **9** blown over, forgotten; **10** antebellum

expiring: 8 moribund

explain: 6 define, excuse; **8** construe; **9** elucidate, explicate, interpret

explainer: 9 expositor, expounder; **11** interpreter

explanation: 7 account; **11** explication; **14** interpretation

expletive: 4 cuss, oath; **5** curse, spare; **7** balance; **8** swearing; **9** curse word, duplicate, swearword

explicate: 7 develop, explain; **9** formulate

explicit: 4 bare, open; **5** overt, plain; **6** patent; **7** express, literal; **8** distinct, exoteric; **9** expressed; **10** denotative; **11** undisguised

explicitness: 7 clarity; **8** lucidity; **9** clearness, lucidness, overtness, plainness

explode: 3 fly; **4** blow, burn, fire; **5** burst, flare, flash, go off; **6** blow up, bounce, fire up, go down, set off; **7** flame up, flare up, thunder; **8** detonate

exploit: 3 tap, use; **4** deed, feat; **6** effort; **7** utilize; **8** overwork; **11** achievement

exploited: 4 used; **7** ill-used, put-upon; **10** victimized

exploiter: 4 user

explore: 3 pry; **4** peer, scan; **5** sound; **6** browse, search; **7** ransack, rummage; **8** research; **9** look round; **11** reconnoiter

explorer: 10 adventurer

explosion: 3 fit; **4** blow; **5** blast, burst, scene, smash, split, storm; **6** blow up, volley; **7** plosion, tempest; **8** collapse, outbreak, outburst, paroxysm; **9** discharge; **10** detonation

explosive: 8 volatile; **9** spasmodic; **10** convulsive

expo: 10 exhibition, exposition

exponent: 4 note, root; **5** index, power, token; **6** teller; **7** delator, relator, speaker, symptom; **8** advocate, reporter; **9** authority, informant, logarithm, proponent, spokesman; **10** mouthpiece; **12** spokesperson

exponential: 8 armorial, integral; **10** emblematic; **11** logarithmic

exponentiation: 10 involution

exportation: 8 eviction; **9** exporting, extrusion

export duty: 9 export tax

expose: 4 bare, open, show; **5** brand, break, let on, parry, peril, queer; **6** debunk, defeat, gibbet, impart, let out, open up, reveal; **7** declare, display, divulge, exhibit, lay bare, lay open, present, scupper, show off, uncover; **8** bring out, disclose, discover, endanger, give away; **9** unmasking

exposed: 4 open; **9** uncovered; **10** unshielded, vulnerable; **11** unprotected

expose to danger: 4 risk; **5** stake; **6** hazard; **7** imperil, venture; **8** endanger; **10** compromise, jeopardize;

exposit: 7 expound; **8** set forth

exposition: 4 expo, pomp; **7** pageant, showing; **8** exposure; **9** construal, pageantry, spectacle; **10** exhibition, expounding, presenting

expositor: 9 explainer, expounder; **11** interpreter, commentator

ex post facto: 11 retroactive

expostulate: 7 protest; **9** deprecate; **11** recriminate, remonstrate

expostulation: 7 protest, reproof; **8** reproach; **9** mediation, objection; **10** admonition; **11** deprecation, reprobation

exposure: 5 photo; **7** display; **9** liability; **10** exposition, photograph, visibility

exposure meter: 10 light meter, photometer

expound: 6 dilate, expand, unfold; **7** enlarge; **8** annotate, flesh out; **9** elaborate, expatiate; **11** comment upon

expounder: 9 explainer, expositor; **11** interpreter

express: 4 bare, mean, open, show, word; **5** carry, meant, overt, state, utter, voice; **6** convey, evince, patent, phrase, word it; **7** advised, extract, let fall, literal, mention, signify; **8** exoteric, explicit, intended, intimate, manifest, press out; **9** expressed, make clear, make known, represent; **10** articulate, deliberate

express an emotion: 5 emote

express bus: 7 express

expressed: 4 bare, open; **5** overt; **6** patent, worded; **7** express, literal, phrased, uttered; **8** exoteric, explicit; **9** made plain; **10** manifested, verbalized; **11** articulated

expression: 4 face, look, term; **5** touch; **6** aspect, phrase, saying; **7** formula; **8** locution, presence; **9** execution, reflexion, squeezing; **10** first blush, reflection; **11** formulation, performance; **12** construction

expressionless: 7 deadpan; **9** impassive; **10** poker-faced; **12** unexpressive

expressive: 6 lively, mobile; **8** allusive, spirited; **9** vivacious; **10** mettlesome, revelatory, suggestive; **12** enthusiastic

expressly: 8 by design; **9** advisedly, knowingly, on purpose, purposely, wittingly;

10 designedly, explicitly, with design, with intent; **12** purposefully, deliberately; **13** intentionally

express mail: 7 express; **13** overnight mail; **15** next-day delivery

expressway: 4 pike; **7** freeway, thruway; **8** motorway; **10** throughway; **12** state highway, superhighway

expropriate: 6 hijack, pirate; **7** put away; **8** highjack, liberate, put aside, set aside; **10** commandeer; **11** appropriate

expropriation: 8 ablation; **9** abduction

expulsion: 5 exile; **8** ejecting, ejection, riddance; **9** discharge, exclusion, expelling, extrusion; **10** banishment, forcing out, projection, pushing out; **11** discharging, elimination

expunction: 7 erasure

expunge: 5 erase; **6** efface, excise, strike; **7** wipe out; **9** sweep away

expunged: 11 obliterated

expurgate: 4 rack; **5** purge; **6** refine; **7** clarify, shorten

exquisite: 4 beau, fine, keen, rich; **5** crack, prime; **6** dainty, tip-top; **7** capital; **8** cardinal, delicate, empyrean, luscious, top grade, top-notch, very best; **9** ambrosial, heartfelt, rapturous, ravishing, recherche, thrilling; **10** appetizing, delightful, felicitous

ex-serviceman: 3 vet; **7** veteran

exsiccate: 3 dry; **9** dehydrate, desiccate

extant: 6 actual, that is; **7** current, instant, present; **8** existing; **9** surviving

extemporaneous: 5 ad lib, ad-lib, brief, brisk, quick; **7** offhand, summary; **9** ad lib-item [Lat], extempore, impromptu, impulsive, offhanded, unplanned; **10** improvised, off-the-cuff, unscripted

extemporary: 5 ad-lib; **7** offhand; **9** extempore, offhanded; **10** off-the-cuff; **11** unrehearsed

extempore: 5 ad-lib, apace; **7** briefly, by and by, offhand, quickly, shortly; **8** in a while, speedily; **9** forthwith, offhanded, on impulse, on the spot, summarily; **10** off-the-cuff; **11** extemporary, immediately, impulsively, on the moment, unrehearsed

ex tempore: 7 off-hand

extend: 2 go; **3** run; **4** flex, lead, pass, puff; **5** carry, cover, offer, widen; **6** blow up, expand, gallop, put out, rarefy, spread, strain, unfold; **7** amplify, broaden, develop, distend, draw out, hold out, inflate, magnify, poke out, prolong, stretch; **8** be linear, elongate, lengthen, protract, reach out, stick out; **9** be elastic, spread out; **10** aggrandize, stretch out; **12** stretch forth

extended: 4 wide; **5** grown; **7** lengthy, spun out, swollen, widened; **8** drawn out, drawn-out, enlarged, expanded; **9** distended, elongated, extensive, increased, lingering, prolonged, sustained; **10** dragged out, lengthened, protracted

extend to: 4 go to; **5** get to, reach, touch; **7** reach to; **8** spread to; **9** stretch to

extensile: 8 formable; **9** malleable; **10** extensible

extension: 4 form, wing; **5** annex, space; **6** annexe, extent, growth; **7** expanse, stretch, variant; **8** dilation, revision, swelling; **9** expansion, reference, variation; **10** denotation, derivation, derivative, elongation, production; **11** enlargement, lengthiness, propagation, protraction

extensive: 4 wide; **5** ample, roomy; **7** copious; **8** extended, far-famed, spacious, sweeping; **9** capacious, expansive, worldwide; **10** widespread; **11** far-reaching

extent: 5 range, reach, scope, space; **6** degree, sphere; **7** expanse, stretch

extenuate: 5 lower; **6** excuse, soften, weaken; **7** cut back, cut down; **8** mitigate, palliate; **9** apologize, attenuate

exterior: 7 outside, surface; **8** external; **11** superficial; **12** on the surface

exterminate: 6 uproot; **7** kill off; **9** eradicate, extirpate

exterminator: 10 eradicator, terminator

external: 7 outside, surface; **8** exterior; **10** extraneous; **11** superficial; **12** on the surface

external auditory canal: 8 ear canal

external ear: 8 outer ear

externality: 11 outwardness

externally: 9 outwardly; **13** superficially

extinct: 3 out; **4** gone, lost; **6** lapsed, no more, run out; **7** defunct, demised, elapsed, expired, has-been; **8** deceased, departed, exploded, inactive, quenched, vanished, wiped out; **9** blown over, exhausted, forgotten, nonextant; **10** antebellum

extinction: 9 quenching; **10** expiration; **11** defunctness, extirpation; **12** annihilation, obliteration; **13** extermination, extinguishing, nullification

extinguish: 6 put out; **7** stub out, wipe out; **8** carry off, crush out, decimate, press out, snuff out; **9** eliminate, eradicate, extirpate; **10** annihilate, obliterate

extinguished: 3 out; **7** extinct; **8** quenched; **10** extirpated; **11** annihilated, obliterated

extirpable: 12 exterminable

extirpate: 6 dredge, pull up, uproot; **7** root out; **8** wipe out; **9** eradicate; **10** annihilate, deracinate, extinguish, obliterate; **11** exterminate

extol: 4 laud, puff; **5** cry up, exalt; **7** glorify; **8** eulogize, proclaim

extoller: 6 lauder; **8** laudator; **9** applauder

extort: 4 rack; **5** bleed, exact, gouge, wring; **6** fleece; **9** wring from; **10** overcharge

extortion: 9 shakedown

extortionate: 5 steep, venal; **6** greedy; **8** covetous, exacting, usurious; **9** excessive, mercenary, rapacious, withering; **10** avaricious, exorbitant, outrageous; **12** unreasonable

extortionist: 11 blackmailer, extortioner

extra: 4 more, mute, plus; **5** other, spare; **6** excess, walk-on; **7** special, surplus; **8** additive; **9** accessory, duplicate, redundant; **10** additional, in addition; **11** superfluous

extract: 4 draw; **5** educe, evoke; **6** distil, elicit, get out, remove; **7** distill, draw out, excerpt, express, pick out, pull out, take out, tear out; **8** infusion, pluck out, press out; **9** extricate, selection

extracted: 5 drawn; **7** removed, torn out; **8** drawn out, taken out; **9** picked out, pulled out; **10** extricated, plucked out

extraction: 4 line, stem; **5** birth, stock; **6** origin, stirps, strain; **7** descent, drawing, lineage, removal, stirpes [pl]; **8** ancestry, heritage, pedigree, removing; **9** genealogy; **10** drawing out, extracting; **11** abstraction, elimination, extrication

extractor: 9 separator; **10** centrifuge

extracurricular: 10 adulterous; **12** extramarital

extradite: 6 deport; **7** deliver; **9** surrender

extramarital: 10 adulterous; **15** extracurricular

extramundane: 9 unearthly

extraneous: 5 alien; **7** foreign, outside; **8** external; **9** extrinsic; **10** immaterial, **11** impertinent

extraordinary: 4 rare

extrapolate: 5 infer; **7** project; **10** generalise, generalize; **11** interpolate

extrasensory: 10 paranormal

extrasensory perception: 3 ESP; **11** second sight; **12** clairvoyance

extraterrestrial: 5 alien

extra time: 8 overtime

extravagance: 6 luxury; **8** drollery; **10** lavishness

extravagant: 5 outre; **6** horrid, lavish, wanton; **7** fanatic, flighty, profuse, replete, stilted, utopian; **8** fabulous, inflated, overmuch, prodigal, quixotic, romantic, swinging, wasteful; **9** bombastic, burlesque, egregious, excessive, exuberant, high flown, monstrous, quibbling, unthrifty; **10** dissipated, exorbitant, immoderate, inordinate, mock heroic, outrageous, profligate, thriftless; **11** improvident, overliberal, overweening, spendthrift, unrealistic

extravagantly: 6 richly; **7** awfully; **8** famously, lavishly; **9** amazingly, copiously, glaringly, profusely, strangely; **10** abundantly, incredibly; **11** egregiously, marvelously, prominently, wonderfully

extravasate: 4 shed; **6** effuse; **7** debouch

extra-vehicular activity: 3 EVA [acron]; **9** space walk

extreme: 4 last, vast; **6** utmost; **7** maximum, immense; **8** enormous, extremum; **9** extremity, humongous

extremely: 3 yea; **4** even; **5** super; **6** highly; **7** passing, the most; **8** above all; **9** a fortiori, eminently, still more, supremely; **10** especially, ecularily, surpassing, to crown all; **11** egregiously, exceedingly, principally, prominently

extreme unction: 9 last rites

extremist: 5 ultra; **7** radical

extremity: 4 last; **6** member; **7** extreme; **9** appendage; **11** prostration

extricable: 9 rescuable; **10** redeemable; **11** salvageable

extricate: 4 draw, save; **5** clear; **6** get out, remove, rescue; **7** deliver, draw out, extract, pick out, pull out, take out, tear out, unloose, unravel; **8** pluck out, untangle

extrication: 6 rescue; **7** drawing, removal; **8** removing; **9** salvation; **10** drawing out, extracting, extraction, unsnarling, untangling; **11** deliverance, elimination; **15** disentanglement

extrinsic: 5 alien; **7** foreign; **10** accidental, derivative, extraneous, incidental; **12** nonessential

extroverted: 8 outgoing; **9** extravert, extrovert; **11** extraverted, forthcoming; **12** extravertive, extrovertive; **13** extrospective

extrude: 10 squeeze out

extrusion: 3 jut; **4** bump, hump; **5** bulge; **8** eviction; **9** expulsion, gibbosity; **10** prominence, protrusion; **11** excrescence, exportation; **12** protuberance

exuberance: 8 pleonasm, plethora; **9** tautology; **10** ebullience, enthusiasm, oversupply, redundancy; **11** periphrasis, profuseness

exuberant: 4 lush; **5** wordy; **6** lavish, wanton; **7** copious, diffuse, lengthy, profuse, replete, riotous, verbose; **8** overmuch; **9** ebullient, excessive, expansive, luxuriant; **10** inordinate, long-winded, pleonastic; **11** extravagant, overweening; **12** high-spirited

exuberate: 4 flow, rain, teem; **6** abound, stream; **8** overflow; **10** shower down

exude: 4 ooze; **7** exudate, ooze out; **8** transude

exulcerate: 6 debase; **7** corrupt

exult: 4 crow; **5** neigh; **7** chuckle, rejoice, triumph; **8** crow over, jubilate; **9** walk on air; **10** jump for joy

exultant: 6 elated, joyful; **7** buoyant, flushed; **8** buoyed up, exulting, jubilant, prideful; **9** rejoicing, triumphal; **10** triumphant

exuviate: 4 molt, shed; **5** moult; **6** slough

eye: 4 loop; **5** heart, optic; **6** center, centre,

look at, look on, middle, oculus, peeper; **7** eyeball, glimpse; **8** look over, look upon

eyeball: 3 eye, orb

eyebrow: 4 brow; **11** supercilium

eyecup: 6 eye cup; **7** eyebath; **8** optic cup

eye doctor: 7 oculist; **11** optometrist; **15** ophthalmologist

eyeglasses: 5 specs; **7** glasses; **8** eyeglass; **9** barnacles; **10** spectacles

eye infection: 3 sty; **4** stye; **9** hordeolum

eyelash: 6 cilium

eyelet: 4 loop; **6** gasket; **7** cringle, grommet

eye-lotion: 7 eyewash; **9** collyrium

eye mask: 6 domino; **8** half mask

eyepiece: 6 barrel, ocular; **8** platform; **12** focusing knob; **13** objective lens

eyeshade: 4 bill, peak; **5** visor, vizor

eye shadow: 5 blush, rouge; **8** lipstick; **10** face powder

eyeshot: 4 view

eyesight: 5 sight; **6** seeing, vision; **11** sightedness

eye socket: 5 orbit

eyesore: 5 sight; **6** fright

eyespot: 7 ocellus

eyestrain: 10 asthenopia

eyetooth: 6 canine, cuspid; **8** dogtooth; **11** canine tooth

eyewitness: 7 witness; **8** beholder, looker-on, observer, onlooker, passer by; **9** bystander, spectator

eyewitnessing: 7 viewing; **9** beholding; **10** witnessing

eyre: 6 assize

eyrie: 4 aery; **5** aerie; **7** rookery; **9** bird's nest

eyrir: 5 aurar

F

F: 5 farad; **7** failure; **8** fluorine; **10** Fahrenheit

f: 4 Fahr, fine; **10** fahrenheit

Fabaceae: 9 pea family; **11** Leguminosae; **12** legume family

fabian: 8 dilatory, cautious

fable: 6 legend; **7** fiction, parable; **8** allegory; **9** fairy tale; **10** moral fable; **11** nursery tale

fabled: 9 legendary

fabric: 5 cloth; **7** textile; **8** material; **9** framework; **11** manufacture; **12** construction

fabricate: 4 coin; **6** cook up, create, devise, invent, make up; **9** construct, originate; **11** manufacture

fabricated: 6 forged, made-up; **7** devised, fancied; **8** fabulous, invented; **9** fictional, unfounded; **10** fictitious, improvised

fabrication: 5 fable, lying; **7** fiction, forgery; **8** assembly; **9** invention; **11** manufacture

fabricator: 6 fibber; **11** storyteller

fabulist: 4 liar; **11** fable writer

fabulous: 3 fab; **6** forged, mythic; **8** invented, mythical; **9** egregious, fantastic, fictional, imaginary, ineffable, unfounded, visionary; **10** fabricated, mythologic; **11** extravagant, unspeakable, unutterable; **12** mythological, preposterous

facade: 5 facia [Lat]; **8** frontage; **10** proscenium; **12** frontispiece

face: 3 mug [informal]; **4** case, font, guts, look, side; **5** brass, cheek, facet, fount,

front, nerve, spunk; **6** aspect, face up, facing, virtue; **7** grimace, present; **8** boldness, confront, cope with, overlook, typeface; **9** brashness, fortitude, hardihood, human face, look out on, nerviness; **10** effrontery, expression, look across

face cloth: 7 flannel, washrag; **9** washcloth

face cream: 9 cold cream; **14** vanishing cream

face lift: 12 rhytidectomy

face powder: 5 blush, rouge; **8** lipstick; **9** eye shadow

facet: 4 face; **6** aspect

facetiae: 6 levity; **14** quips and cranks

facetious: 7 waggish; **9** bantering, whimsical

face to face: 7 vis-a-vis; **10** above board, on the stage, to one's face; **11** in open court, in plain view

face up: 4 face; **8** confront

facia: 6 facade, fascia; **10** proscenium; **12** frontispiece

facial expression: 4 face, look; **6** aspect; **10** expression; **13** facial gesture

facile: 4 easy; **6** fluent, silver; **8** eloquent; **9** easy-going; **12** smooth-spoken

facilitate: 4 ease, help; **6** smooth; **7** lighten; **8** make easy; **9** alleviate; **10** make facile, render easy

facility: 3 can, lav; **4** ease, john; **5** craft, knack, privy, skill; **6** toilet; **7** address, aptness, know-how; **8** aptitude, bathroom, deftness, easiness, lavatory; **9** adeptness, quickness, readiness, technique; **10** adroitness, competence, facileness; **11** proficiency

facing: 4 face; **6** lining, veneer; **8** cladding, fronting

facsimile: 3 fax; **4** copy, form; **5** Xerox; **6** effigy; **7** replica, telefax; **8** autotype, effigies, likeness; **9** imitation; **10** mimeograph

facsimile machine: 3 fax; **9** facsimile

fact: 4 data [pl]; **5** datum, event, facts [pl], thing; **8** hard fact, incident; **9** happening, known fact, plain fact; **10** occurrence, phenomenon; **11** eventuality

faction: 4 band, sect, side; **5** cabal, junta, junto, party; **8** outbreak; **9** camarilla; **11** open rupture

factionalism: 12 partisanship

factitious: 4 sham; **6** tricky; **7** feigned, scamped; **9** trumped up; **10** fictitious

factor: 5 agent; **6** broker, detail; **7** bailiff, divisor, element; **8** factor in; **9** component, factor out; **10** ingredient; **11** constituent

factory: 4 mill; **5** plant, works; **11** manufactory

factotum: 8 croupier, shepherd; **9** majordomo, seneschal; **11** housekeeper

facts: 4 data [pl], fact; **5** datum; **7** grounds; **9** known fact, plain fact

factual: 4 true; **5** right; **6** actual; **7** correct, de facto; **9** veritable

faculty: 4 turn, walk; **5** forte, parts, staff; **6** career, module, talent, virtue; **7** ability, calling, quality, talents; **8** capacity, felicity, property, vocation; **9** attribute, endowment; **10** capability, cleverness, profession, walk of life; **12** habilitation; **13** mental faculty, qualification

faculty member: 8 academic; **11** academician

fad: 3 fit; **4** cult, rage; **5** craze, freak, furor, hobby, prank, quirk, thing, trend; **6** maggot, vagary; **7** in thing; **8** crotchet, escapade, flimflam, last word; **9** bandwagon, blind side, capriccio; **10** partiality; **11** infatuation, latest thing

faddish: 2 in; **5** faddy; **6** with it

fade: 2 go; **3** age, fly, rot; **4** drop, fail, flag, flit, halt, limp, mild, pass, weak; **5** decay, fleet, go bad, go off, shake, slice, stale, vapid; **6** gallop, molder, rankle, totter, vanish, wither; **7** crumble, decline, fade out, give way, mawkish, pass off, senesce, tremble; **8** blow over, dissolve, evanesce, fade away, languish, melt away, pass away, vaporize; **9** disappear, evaporate

faded: 5 passe, stale, washy; **6** frayed, shabby, shaken, wilted; **8** bleached, weakened; **9** attenuate, washed out, washed-out; **10** attenuated, secondhand, threadbare

fading: 6 flying, paling; **9** bleaching, vanishing; **11** attenuation, evaporating; **12** decolorizing; **13** discoloration

fading away: 9 vanishing; **12** disappearing

faerie: 5 faery, fairy; **6** sprite; **9** fairyland

Fagaceae: 11 beech family

fag end: 4 tail; **7** remnant, tail end

fag-end: 7 butt end; **8** gable end

fagged: 5 spent; **7** worn out, worn-out; **8** fatigued; **9** exhausted, played out, washed-out

Fagopyrum: 9 buckwheat; **14** genus Fagopyrum

Fagus: 5 beech; **10** genus Fagus

Fahr: 1 f; **10** fahrenheit

fahrenheit: 1 f; **4** Fahr

fail: 2 go; **3** die; **4** bomb, drop, fade, flag, halt, limp, omit; **5** break, elude, evade, flunk, shake; **6** betray, cave in, escape, ignore, run out, totter; **7** conk out, crumble, decline, flush it, give out, give way, go wrong, neglect, tremble; **8** languish, miscarry, set aside; **9** break down; **10** end in smoke, not succeed, transgress

failed: 7 failing

failing: 6 failed, losing; **7** failure, lacking, wanting; **8** tripping, weakness; **9** declining, defective, deficient; **10** regressing, retrograde; **13** deteriorating, not succeeding, retrogressive

failure: 1 F; **5** loser; **6** laches [Law]; **7** evasion, failing, neglect; **8** omission, shirking

fain: 6 as lief, freely, minded; **7** willing, wishful; **8** disposed, inclined, prepared; **9** compelled, favorable, willingly

faineance: 8 idleness

faineant: 4 lazy; **5** idler, dummy; **6** otiose; **7** work-shy; **8** do-little, indolent, slothful

faint: 3 dim, dun, wan; **4** ashy, blow, cold, conk, dead, drop, dull, gasp, pant, puff, soft; **5** ashen, dingy, light, muddy, swoon, timid, vague, wispy; **6** feeble, gentle, glassy, leaden, sallow; **7** ghastly, pass out, shadowy, succumb, syncope; **8** collapse, swooning; **10** cadaverous, lackluster; **11** light-headed; **12** fainthearted; **13** shadowed forth

fainthearted: 5 faint, timid, wimpy; **7** wimpish; **11** weak-hearted

fainting: 5 swoon; **7** syncope; **8** collapse

faintness: 7 dimness; **8** softness

fair: 1 C; **2** OK; **4** just, so-so; **5** blond, bonny, clean, equal, right; **6** bazaar, bonnie, comely, creamy, fairly, pearly, seemly, square, staple; **7** average, equable, fairish, funfair, sightly, whitish; **8** above par, bearable, carnival, handsome, mediocre, middling, ordinary, passable; **9** equitable, impartial, tolerable; **10** acceptable, admissible, couci-couci, evenhanded, personable, reasonable

fair deal: 10 square deal

fair game: 4 butt, game, prey; **6** quarry, target
fairie: 3 fay; **5** fairy; **7** brownie; **10** good genius; **14** tutelary genius
fairly: 4 fair; **5** clean; **6** justly; **7** equably; **8** in equity, in reason, middling, passably, somewhat; **9** in justice; **10** moderately, reasonably; **12** evenhandedly, within reason
fairness: 6 candor, equity; **7** candour, justice; **8** fair play, paleness; **9** blondness; **10** comeliness, loveliness; **12** impartiality
fair play: 6 equity; **7** justice; **8** fairness; **11** give and take, lex talionis [Lat]; **12** impartiality
fair share: 3 lot; **5** share; **7** measure, portion; **9** allotment, allowance; **10** allocation, contingent
fair to middling: 8 adequate, passable
fairy: 6 fairie, fearie, sprite; **7** brownie
fairy bell: 10 fingerroot; **12** fingerflower; **14** common foxglove; **17** Digitalis purpurea
fairytale: 5 fable; **10** fairy story; **11** nursery tale
fait accompli: 8 work done; **12** finished task; **13** completed work
faith: 5 piety, trust; **6** theism; **7** honesty; **8** religion; **12** spirituality; **13** religiousness
faithful: 4 fast, fold, true; **5** close, loyal, sound, valid; **7** devoted, staunch; **8** constant, lifelike, orthodox, reliable, unerring; **9** authentic, believing, compliant, complying, observant
faithfulness: 6 homage; **7** loyalty; **8** devotion, fidelity; **9** constancy
faithless: 5 false; **8** disloyal; **9** deceitful, dishonest, trothless, truthless; **10** fraudulent, mendacious, of bad faith, traitorous, unfaithful; **11** incredulous, unveracious; **12** lacking faith
fake: 3 hum; **4** bull, cook, faux, mock, sell, sham; **5** bogus, faker, false, force, forge, fraud, fudge, hatch, phony, pseud, shave; **6** phoney, pseudo, pseudo-, waffle, wangle; **7** concoct, falsify, forgery; **8** imposter, impostor, postiche, so-called, spurious; **9** imitation, pretended, pretender, simulated; **10** fraudulent, manipulate; **11** counterfeit, make-believe
faker: 4 fake, sham; **5** fraud, pseud; **6** pseudo; **8** imposter, impostor; **9** pretender
fakir: 5 faqir; **6** fakeer, faquir
falafel: 7 felafel
falchion: 7 cutlass; **10** broadsword
falciform: 6 beaked, hooked; **8** falcated; **12** sickle shaped
Falco: 4 hawk; **6** falcon; **10** genus Falco
falconer: 6 hawker
falconet: 6 falcon, cannon
Falconidae: 16 family Falconidae

Falconiformes: 18 order Falconiformes
falconry: 7 hawking
Falco peregrinus: 9 peregrine
Falco sparverius: 7 kestrel; **11** sparrow hawk
falderal: 6 frills; **8** folderol, nonsense, trumpery
Falkland Islands: 13 Islas Malvinas
fall: 3 dip, pin; **4** come, drop, dusk, flow, hang, obit, pass, rest, ruin, slip, trip; **5** crash, lapse, light, shine, spill; **6** accrue, autumn, go down, lessen, offend, plunge, return, strike, tumble; **7** decline, descend, descent, devolve, falling, plummet, quietus, release; **8** come down, decrease, diminish, downfall, downhill, drop down, evenfall, gloaming, trespass, twilight; **9** declivity, departure, downslope, nightfall, perdition, ruination, surrender; **11** declination, devastation, dissolution, precipitate, ruinousness
fallacious: 5 false; **6** unreal, untrue; **7** unsound; **8** fallible, mistaken; **9** deceitful, erroneous, incorrect
fallacy: 5 error, quirk; **7** quibble
fallal: 4 gaud; **6** bangle, bauble, gewgaw; **7** novelty, trinket
fall asleep: 6 nod off; **7** dope off, doze off, drop off; **8** drift off
fall back: 3 lag; **4** lose; **5** lapse, recur; **6** dawdle, go back, recede, resort, retire; **7** drop off, get back, put back, regress, relapse, run back; **8** come back, draw back, hark back, sink back, turn back; **9** backslide, slide back
fallen angel: 5 devil
fall flat: 4 bomb, flop; **6** go down; **7** explode, founder; **8** fall dead; **9** up in smoke
fall guy: 3 mug; **4** fish, fool, gull, mark; **5** chump, patsy; **6** sucker; **7** gudgeon; **8** shlemiel; **9** schlemiel
fallible: 4 weak; **5** frail; **8** slippery, ticklish; **9** debatable, imperfect, incorrect; **10** disputable, fallacious, precarious; **12** questionable
falling: 4 drop, fall; **8** downfall, dropping, plunging; **9** ruination; **10** plummeting; **11** ruinousness
falling star: 6 meteor; **9** meteorite, meteoroid; **12** shooting star
fall in with: 4 meet; **5** unite; **6** accede, accept, concur, go with; **7** agree to, receive; **8** converge, meet with, side with
fall off: 4 sink; **5** slump; **6** detach, worsen; **7** abscise, come off, drop off, dwindle, tail off; **8** fall away, get loose, peter out, taper off
Fallopian tube: 7 oviduct; **11** uterine tube
fall out: 7 turn out
fallout: 15 radioactive dust
fallow: 6 unsown; **7** citrine; **8** untilled
falls: 7 cascade; **8** cataract; **9** waterfall
fall short: 4 miss; **8** not reach; **9** come short, fall shy of; **10** not suffice

fall to: 5 set to; 6 engage; 9 set to work

fall to pieces: 7 break up; 9 fall apart, liquidate; 10 break apart, go to pieces

false: 4 fake, faux, sham, sour; 5 put on; 6 hollow, off-key, unreal, untrue; 7 assumed, fictive, invalid, unsound; 8 delusive, disloyal, mistaken, spurious; 9 deceitful, dishonest, erroneous, faithless, illogical, imitation, pretended, simulated, trothless, truthless; 10 apocryphal, fallacious, fictitious, fraudulent, groundless, mendacious, of bad faith, unfaithful, ungrounded

false alarm: 7 cry wolf

false doctrine: 6 heresy, schism

falsehood: 3 lie; 7 falsity, untruth

false jewelry: 5 paste; 11 junk jewelry; 14 costume jewelry

false name: 5 alias; 11 assumed name

false step: 9 wrong step

false teaching: 10 misleading; 11 misguidance

false witness: 8 perjurer

falsification: 5 gloss, lying; 8 disproof, refuting; 9 confuting, falsehood; 10 disproving, falsifying, perversion, refutation; 11 telling lies

falsify: 4 cook, fake, warp; 5 alter, belie, fudge; 6 garble, wangle; 7 distort, pervert; 8 misstate; 10 manipulate; 11 interpolate; 12 misrepresent

Falstaff: 15 Sir John Falstaff

falter: 4 flag, funk; 5 cower, waver; 6 bumble, crouch, hammer; 7 stagger, stammer, stumble, stutter, trotter; 8 flounder, hesitate; 9 faltering, vacillate; 10 hesitation, run aground; 11 be tentative, be undecided

falteringly: 10 unsteadily; 11 uncertainly

fame: 3 cry; 4 buzz; 5 bruit, rumor; 6 renown; 7 hearsay; 9 celebrity; 10 famousness; 11 flying rumor; 12 news stirring

famed: 5 noted; 6 famous; 7 notable; 8 farfamed, renowned; 10 celebrated; 11 illustrious

familial: 7 genetic; 9 inherited; 10 hereditary; 11 transmitted; 13 transmissible

familiar: 4 mate; 5 fiend, trite, usual; 6 casual, common, fellow; 7 affable, banshee, comrade, cordial, general, regular; 8 confrere, demiurge, everyday, gracious, intimate, ordinary; 9 associate, companion; 10 acquainted

familiarity: 3 ken; 7 insight, liberty; 8 intimacy; 9 closeness, indecorum; 10 casualness, experience, fellowship; 11 conversance, conversancy, impropriety, knowledge of, naturalness; 12 acquaintance

family: 3 kin; 4 akin, folk, home, sept; 5 class, house; 6 linear, menage; 7 kindred, kinfolk, phratry, related; 8 category, kinsfolk; 9 ancestral, household; 10 family

line, family unit, fellowship, kinsperson, of the blood

famine: 6 dearth; 7 drought; 8 shortage; 9 inanition; 10 starvation

famished: 7 starved; 8 esurient, ravening, ravenous, sharp-set, starving; 11 half-starved

famotidine: 6 Pepcid

famous: 5 famed, noted; 7 notable; 8 farfamed, renowned; 10 celebrated; 11 illustrious

famously: 7 awfully; 9 amazingly, glaringly, strangely; 10 incredibly; 11 egregiously, marvelously, prominently, wonderfully

famousness: 4 fame; 6 renown

famous person: 9 celebrity

fan: 3 air; 4 buff; 5 lover, lungs; 6 archer, fan out, votary, winnow; 7 air pump, amateur, bellows, devotee; 8 attic fan, blowpipe; 9 air blower, sports fan, strike out, ventilate; 10 aficionado, dilettante, ventilator; 11 aficionado

fanaloka: 10 Fossa fossa

fanatic: 5 fiend, rabid; 6 zealot; 7 flighty, utopian, zealous; 8 fanatico [Sp], quixotic, romantic; 9 fanatical, high flown; 11 extravagant, overzealous

fancied: 6 made-up; 8 invented; 9 fictional; 10 fabricated, fictitious

fancied up: 7 gussied; 9 gussied up

fancier: 10 enthusiast

fancy: 4 like, salt, whim; 5 go for, humor, image, opine, point; 6 affect, assume, esprit, figure, magnet, regard, take it, take to; 7 caprice, fantasy, imagine, picture, project; 8 conceive, drollery, envision, fanciful, fondness, illusion, notional, phantasy; 9 apprehend, seduction, visualize, whimsical; 10 allurement, attraction, partiality, pleasantry, temptation

fancywork: 10 embroidery

fane: 4 kirk; 6 chapel, church; 7 oratory; 8 basilica; 9 cathedral; 10 tabernacle; 11 conventicle; 12 meetinghouse

fanfare: 4 boom, peal; 5 blast, swell; 8 flourish; 11 ostentation; 12 trumpet blast

fangs: 5 teeth

fanlight: 7 transom; 8 skylight

Fannie Mae: 4 FNMA

fanny: 4 rear, rump, seat, tail, tush; 5 stern; 6 behind, bottom; 7 hind end, keister, rear end, tail end; 8 backside, buttocks, derriere; 9 fundament, posterior

Fanny Mae: 4 FNMA [acron]; 34 Federal National Mortgage Association [U.S.]

fan out: 3 fan; 6 spread; 7 diffuse; 9 spread out

fantan: 6 sevens; 10 parliament

fantastic: 3 rum; 5 antic, kinky [U.S.], queer, weird; 6 wanton; 7 bizarre, howling, wayward; **8** fabulous, fanciful, freakish, rattling, skittish, terrific, wondrous; **9** fictional, grotesque, imaginary, marvelous, visionary, wonderful; **10** particular, phenomenal, tremendous

fantastical: 5 antic; **8** fabulous; **9** fantastic, fictional, grotesque, imaginary, visionary

fantasy: 4 myth; **5** fancy; **7** fiction, romance; **8** illusion, phantasm, phantasy, rhapsody

fantoccini: 10 puppet show

faqir: 5 fakir; **6** fakeer, faquir

far: 6 distal, far off, remote, wide of; **7** distant, far away

farad: 1 F

Faraday: 14 Michael Faraday

farce: 4 bosh, myth; **6** comedy; **7** eyewash, fooling; **8** rhapsody, travesty; **9** forcemeat, mare's nest, moonshine; **10** buffoonery, tomfoolery

farce comedy: 5 farce; **8** travesty

farceur: 3 wag; **5** joker, clown; **7** buffoon; **8** grimacer; **9** columbine, pantaloon; **11** pantomimist

farcical: 3 odd; **5** funny, inane; **8** pour rire; **9** grotesque, laughable, ludicrous; **10** ridiculous

fardel: 4 load, onus, rick; **5** sheaf, shock, stack; **6** burden, bundle

fare: 2 do; **3** eat; **4** come, feed, menu, take; **5** cheer; **6** devour; **7** consume, make out, swallow; **8** get along

farewell: 4 ciao; **5** adieu, aloha, leave; **7** good-bye, parting; **8** sayonara; **10** dosvidanya [Russ]; **11** leave taking, leave-taking, valediction, valedictory; **12** hasta la vista [Sp]; **14** auf wiedersehen [Ger], word of farewell

farfetched: 11 implausible

far-flung: 10 widespread

farina: 4 bran, meal; **5** flour

farinaceous: 5 mealy, sandy; **6** floury, grainy, gritty; **8** granular; **9** granulose; **13** coarse-grained

farm: 4 grow, rent; **5** raise; **7** produce; **8** messuage; **9** grow crops; **10** raise crops; **11** till the soil

farm animal: 5 stock; **9** livestock; **14** barnyard animal

farmer: 7 granger; **9** sodbuster; **10** husbandman; **14** horticulturist

farmer's calendar: 7 almanac

farmer's cheese: 9 pot cheese; **10** farm cheese; **13** cottage cheese

farmer's market: 11 greenmarket

farm horse: 6 dobbin

farming: 4 land; **7** tillage; **8** agrarian, agronomy, georgics; **9** husbandry; **11** agriculture, cultivation; **12** agricultural

farm out: 3 job; **7** hire out, rent out; **11** subcontract

farm team: 8 farm club

farm worker: 8 farmhand; **9** fieldhand

farmyard: 8 barnyard

Faroes: 7 Faeroes; **12** Faroe Islands; **13** Faeroe Islands

far off: 3 far; **6** distal, remote, way off, wide of; **7** distant, far away

far-out: 5 kinky; **6** quirky, way-out; **7** offbeat

far out: 4 wild; **5** heavy; **6** way out; **10** out of sight, outtasight

farrago: 4 mess, olio; **10** hodgepodge

far-reaching: 8 sweeping; **9** extensive

farrier: 10 horse shoer, horseshoer

far-right: 11 reactionary, reactionist

Farsi: 7 Persian

farsighted: 4 long; **9** farseeing; **11** foresighted, longsighted; **12** foresightful

farther: 6 abroad, beyond, yonder; **7** further

farthest: 6 utmost; **8** furthest; **9** uttermost; **11** farthermost, furthermost

farthing: 3 fig, jot, pin, rap, sou; **4** cent, mill, rush; **5** straw; **6** button, old son; **7** bulrush, feather, red cent [U.S.]; **8** picayune; **9** halfpenny; **10** peppercorn; **12** pinch of snuff; **13** brass farthing

farthingale: 6 bustle; **9** crinoline, hoopskirt

fasces: 4 bale, mace, wand; **6** bundle; **8** fascicle

fascinate: 4 coax, grip, lure, stun, take; **5** catch, charm, rivet, tempt; **6** absorb, attach, enamor, endear, seduce, trance; **7** attract, becharm, beguile, bewitch, capture, enamour, enchant, engross, petrify, stagger, stupefy, wheedle; **8** bewilder, confound, entrance, intrigue, transfix; **9** captivate, carry away, enrapture, mesmerize, spellbind

fascinating: 8 charming, engaging, gripping, riveting; **9** absorbing, beguiling; **10** bewitching, enchanting, engrossing, entrancing, intriguing; **11** captivating, enthralling, interesting, mesmerizing, stimulating

fascination: 5 charm, fancy; **6** magnet; **7** amenity; **8** witchery; **9** seduction; **10** absorption, allurement, amiability, attraction, fanaticism, temptation; **11** captivation, enchantment, infatuation, winning ways; **12** enthrallment, entrancement, intoxication

fascine: 4 bale; **6** bundle

fash: 3 vex; **6** grieve; **7** afflict; **8** distress; **16** plunge into sorrow

fashion: 2 MO; **3** ton, way; **4** chic, form, mode, rage, wise; **5** forge, means, shape, style, vogue; **6** figure, manner, method; **7** process; **8** protocol; **9** mechanism, procedure, technique; **10** procedures [pl] sylishness; **13** modus operandi

fashionable: 2 in; **6** trendy, with it; **7** current, in vogue, stylish; **8** up to date; **9** au courant, in fashion, prevalent; **10** all the rage, prevailing; **11** popular with

fashion designer: 8 designer; 9 couturier

fashioning: 6 making; 7 forming; 8 devising; 9 formation

fashion model: 5 model; 7 manakin, manikin; 8 mannikin; 9 mannequin

fashion plate: 3 fop; 4 beau, dude; 5 dandy, sheik, swell; 7 gallant; 12 clotheshorse

fasiculus: 8 fascicle; 9 fascicule

fast: 3 set; 4 firm, taut, true, wild; 5 close, loyal, quick, rapid, swift, tight; 6 barred, bolted, firmly, flying, locked, rakish, secure, speedy, starve, taught; 7 dashing, fasting, latched, riotous, secured; 8 degraded, faithful, immobile; 9 color-fast, debauched, dissolute, libertine, stead-fast

fastball: 5 smoke; 6 bullet, heater, hummer

fast day: 9 banyan day

fasten: 3 fix; 4 bind; 5 affix, twist; 6 attach, clinch, secure; 7 tighten; 8 make fast, saddle on

fastener: 3 tie; 8 holdfast; 9 connector, fastening

fastening: 3 tie; 8 fastener, holdfast; 9 connector; 10 attachment

fasten on: 6 hook on, take up; 7 latch on, seize on

fasten to: 4 hang; 5 hitch, sling; 6 append, hook up; 7 suspend

faster: 7 quicker

fastest: 8 quickest

fast-food chef: 14 short-order cook

fastidious: 4 nice; 5 picky; 6 choosy, dainty; 7 finical, finicky; 8 delicate, exacting

fastidiously: 12 meticulously; 13 painstakingly

fastness: 4 fort, hold; 5 speed; 6 fixity; 7 redoubt; 8 fortress; 9 fixedness, swiftness; 10 secureness, stronghold

Fast of Av: 8 Fast of Ab, Tisha b'Ab, Tisha b'Av; 9 Ninth of Ab, Ninth of Av, Tishah b'Ab, Tishah b'Av

fast one: 5 trick

fat: 4 full, rich; 5 fatty, juicy, lusty, obese, plump, squab, stout, tumid; 6 fatten, greasy, turgid; 7 adipose, bloated, fatness, fertile, fill out, rounded; 8 bouncing, fatten up, flesh out, plump out; 9 corpulent, dropsical, fatten out, overgrown, sebaceous, strapping

fatal: 5 black; 6 lethal, mortal; 7 fateful; 10 calamitous, disastrous

fatal blow: 10 mortal blow

fatback: 8 salt pork, sowbelly

fat cell: 11 adipose cell

fat chance: 7 bad odds, poor bet; 8 long odds, long shot, poor odds; 9 off chance; 10 slim chance

fat city: 10 bed of roses

fate: 3 lot; 4 doom, luck; 6 kismet; 7 destine, destiny, fortune, portion; 9 designate; 13 circumstances

fated: 6 doomed; 8 destined; 11 preordained; 12 foreordained

fateful: 5 fatal; 10 calamitous, disastrous, foreboding, portentous

Fates: 6 Parcae; 8 the Fates; 10 book of fate; 12 Sisters three

fat-free: 6 nonfat; 7 fatless

Father: 5 Padre; 9 Father-God; 12 Church Father

father: 3 dad, get; 4 papa, sire; 5 beget, doyen, padre; 6 mother; 7 founder; 8 begetter, beginner, engender, generate; 10 bring forth, forefather, male parent

Father Christmas: 10 Santa Claus; 12 Kriss Kringle; 13 Saint Nicholas

fatherhood: 9 paternity

fatherland: 8 homeland; 10 motherland, native land, native soil

father upon: 5 lay at; 9 the door of; 10 invest with; 13 assign as cause

fathom: 3 ell; 4 foot, fthm, hand, inch, line, mile, nail, palm, pole, rood, yard; 5 cubit, plumb, probe, sound; 6 bottom, league; 7 furlong; 9 figure out, penetrate

fathomable: 10 ponderable; 12 determinable; 14 comprehensible

fathomless: 9 soundless; 10 bottomless; 12 unfathomable

fatigation: 9 lassitude, tiredness; 10 exhaustion

fatigue: 4 flag, jade, pall, tire, wear; 5 weary; 6 anemia, fag out; 7 anaemia, exhaust, outwear, tire out, wear out; 8 wear down, wear upon; 9 prostrate, tiredness, weariness; 11 fatigue duty

fatigued: 4 beat; 5 spent, tired; 6 bushed, fagged; 7 worn out, worn-out; 9 exhausted, played out, washed-out

fatless: 6 nonfat; 7 fat-free

fat person: 5 fatso, fatty; 8 roly-poly

fatten: 3 fat; 4 blow; 5 bloom, plump; 6 enrich, flower, mellow; 7 blossom, fill out; 8 fatten up, flesh out, fructify, plump out; 9 bear fruit, elaborate, fatten out

fatten upon: 7 banquet; 8 feed upon; 10 batten upon; 11 do justice to

fat times: 9 good times

Fat Tuesday: 9 Mardi Gras

fatty: 3 fat; 5 fatso; 6 greasy; 7 adipose; 8 roly-poly; 9 fat person, sebaceous

fatty tissue: 3 fat; 13 adipose tissue

fatuity: 6 dotage; 9 absurdity, silliness, stupidity

fatuous: 5 inane, inept, silly; 7 asinine, blatant, foolish, idiotic, vacuous; 8 babbling, imbecile, mindless; 9 driveling, insensate, senseless; 10 irrational; 11 nonsensical

fauces: 4 jaws; 5 chaps, chops

faucet: 3 tap; 5 valve; 6 spigot

Faulkner: 15 William Faulkner

fault: 3 bug; 4 blot, flaw, miss, slip, trip; 5 blame, break, error; 6 defect; 7 blunder, demerit, mistake, stumble; 8 footfall, fracture, omission; 9 fault line, oversight, quiproquo, weak point; 10 deficiency

fault-finder: 5 cynic; 8 censurer; 10 complainer

faultless: 7 perfect, sinless; 8 flawless, spotless; 9 bloodless, stainless; 10 immaculate, impeccable

fault line: 5 break, fault; 8 fracture; 15 geological fault

faun: 5 satyr

fauna: 5 beast, brute; 6 animal; 8 creature; 12 animate being

Faust: 7 Faustus

fauteuil: 5 squab; 6 settle; 7 ottoman; 8 armchair

faux: 4 fake; 5 false; 9 imitation, simulated

faux pas: 4 slip, trip; 5 gaffe, lapse, lurch; 8 intrigue, solecism; 9 gaucherie; 10 peccadillo

fava bean: 9 broad bean, horsebean

favor: 4 boon, span [U. S.]; 5 grace, honor, humor; 6 favour, honour, prefer; 7 garland, gratify, indulge, leaning, release; 8 befriend, good turn, interest, love knot; 9 exemption, good works, patronage, privilege; 10 billet-doux, favoritism, indulgence, love letter, partiality, party favor; 11 benefaction, beneficence, countenance, lean towards; 12 championship, dispensation

favorable: 4 fain, ripe; 5 happy, lucky; 6 golden, minded; 7 willing; 8 amicable, disposed, friendly, inclined, positive; 9 fortunate, opportune; 10 auspicious, convenient, favourable, propitious, prosperous; 11 encouraging; 12 advantageous, providential, well-disposed

favorably: 4 well; 6 aright; 10 favourably; 14 satisfactorily

favored: 3 pet; 6 golden; 8 favorite; 9 favourite, fortunate, preferred; 10 advantaged

favorite: 3 pet; 5 deary, ducky; 6 dearie, minion; 7 darling, favored, popular; 9 favourite, preferred; 11 front-runner

fawn: 3 dun, tan; 4 foxy; 5 cower, crawl, creep, kotow, sneak, tawny, toady; 6 cringe, crouch, grovel, kowtow, maroon, sponge

fax: 7 fax copy, telefax; 9 facsimile; 16 facsimile machine

fay: 5 fairy; 6 fairie; 7 brownie

faze: 3 bug, irk, vex; 4 tire; 5 annoy, cross, worry; 6 bother; 7 disturb, mortify, perplex, trouble, unnerve; 8 disquiet, enervate,

unsettle; 9 disoblige, displease, incommode; 10 discomfort, discompose

FBI agent: 4 G-man

F clef: 8 bass clef

FDR: 9 Roosevelt; 17 Franklin Roosevelt; 23 Franklin Delano Roosevelt

Fe: 4 iron

fealty: 6 homage; 9 deference, obeisance; 10 allegiance

fear: 4 care; 5 dread; 6 fright, revere; 7 concern, quail at; 8 venerate; 9 reverence; 11 fearfulness; 12 apprehension

fearful: 3 shy; 4 dire; 5 awful, dread; 6 afraid, coward, trepid; 7 direful, dreaded; 8 cowardly, dreadful, fearsome, horrific, terrible, timorous; 9 frightful; 10 frightened, horrendous; 11 frightening; 12 apprehensive

fearfully: 5 sadly; 6 in fear, sorely; 7 cruelly, grossly; 8 bitterly, horribly, terribly, woefully; 9 miserably, painfully, piteously; 10 dreadfully, grievously, lamentably, shockingly; 11 frightfully; 14 apprehensively

fearfulness: 4 fear; 6 fright; 9 cowardice, wimpiness; 12 apprehension, cowardliness, dreadfulness, timorousness

fearing: 7 quaking; 8 dreading

fearless: 5 brave, hardy; 7 aweless, doughty; 8 intrepid, unafraid; 9 audacious, dauntless, unfearing; 10 courageous

fearlessly: 10 intrepidly; 11 dauntlessly

fearsome: 4 dire; 5 awful, dread; 7 direful, dreaded, fearful; 8 dreadful, horrific, terrible; 10 horrendous; 11 frightening

feasible: 6 doable, viable; 8 workable; 10 achievable; 11 performable, practicable, practicably

feast: 3 toy; 4 feed, fete; 5 revel, sport; 6 fiesta, junket, regale, wanton; 7 banquet, carouse, disport; 8 feast day, festival

feast day: 5 feast; 6 fiesta [Sp]; 7 fete day; 11 festival day

Feast of Booths: 6 Succos; 7 Sukkoth; 11 Tabernacles; 18 Feast of Tabernacles

Feast of Dedication: 7 Hanukah; 8 Chanukah, Hanukkah; 16 Festival of Lights; 20 Feast of the Dedication

Feast of Lights: 8 Hanukkah; 9 Chanukkah

Feast of Lots: 5 Purim

Feast of Tabernacles: 6 Succos; 7 Sukkoth; 11 Tabernacles; 13 Feast of Booths

Feast of the Dedication: 7 Hanukah; 8 Chanukah, Hanukkah; 16 Festival of Lights; 17 Feast of Dedication

Feast of the Unleavened Bread: 5 Pesah; 6 Pesach; 8 Passover

Feast of Weeks: 7 Shavuos, Shavuot; 8 Shabuoth, Shavuoth; 9 Pentecost

feat: 4 deed; 6 effort; 7 exploit; 11 achievement

feather: 3 fig, jot, pin, rap, sou; 4 cent, mill, rush, tuft; 5 plume, straw; 6 button, fledge, fringe, kidney, old son, square, toupee; **7** bulrush, panache, plumage, red cent [U.S.]; **8** aigrette, farthing, picayune; **9** halfpenny

featherbed: 4 baby; **5** spoil; **6** cocker, coddle, cosset, pamper; **7** indulge; **8** cushy job, sinecure; **9** no-show job; **10** feather bed; **11** mollycoddle

feathered: 7 plumy; **8** feathery

feathered friend: 4 avis [Lat], bird

featheredged: 7 deckled; **11** deckle-edged

featheriness: 9 downiness; **10** fluffiness

feature: 4 have, turn; **5** boast, sport, trait; **6** aspect; **7** quality; **8** property; **9** attribute, lineament; **11** feature film, land feature; **14** characteristic

Feb: 8 February

Feb 2: 9 Candlemas

Feb 29: 7 leap day

febricity: 5 fever; **7** pyrexia; **12** feverishness

febrifuge: 11 antifebrile, antipyretic

febrile: 8 feverish; **10** hysterical

February: 3 Feb

February daphne: 8 mezereon; **14** Daphne mezereum

feckless: 5 inept

fecund: 7 fertile; **8** prolific; **9** luxuriant

fecundate: 4 bear; **5** beget, lie in; **9** give birth; **10** bring forth; **11** give birth to

federal: 8 national

Federal: 3 Fed; **5** Union

Federal Aviation Administration: 3 FAA

Federal Bureau of Investigation: 3 FBI

Federal Deposit Insurance Corporation: 4 FDIC

Federal Express: 5 FedEx

Federal Home Loan Mortgage Corporation: 5 FHLMC; **10** Freddie Mac

Federal Housing Administration: 3 FHA

federal job safety law: 4 OSHA

Federal National Mortgage Association: 4 FNMA; **9** Fannie Mae

Federal Reserve: 3 Fed

Federal Reserve note: 4 bill, note; **8** bank bill, bank note, banknote; **9** greenback

Federal Reserve System: 3 Fed; **14** Federal Reserve

federation: 5 union; **11** confederacy; **13** confederation

fedora: 6 trilby; **7** felt hat, homburg, Stetson

fed up: 4 sick; **6** sick of; **7** tired of; **9** disgusted

fee: 4 sign; **6** sign on, sign up; **7** fee tail, footing, garnish

feeble: 4 lame, poor, tame, weak; **5** faint, loose, vapid; **6** flimsy, infirm, jejune, meager, weakly; **7** sapless; **8** decrepit; **9** nerveless

feeble-minded: 4 dull, weak; **5** frail; **6** stu-

pid; **7** witless; **8** mindless; **9** airheaded, brainless

feebleness: 7 frailty, tenuity; **8** debility, tameness, vapidity; **9** blandness, frailness, infirmity

feed: 3 eat; **4** fare, give, grub, mess, prey, take; **5** feast; **6** devour, feed in, fodder, spread; **7** consume, recruit, swallow; **9** fertilize, provender; **10** animal food

feeder: 5 eater; **6** batman; **7** caterer; **8** affluent, devourer, purveyor; **9** tributary, victualer; **10** commissary, self-feeder; **13** quartermaster

feeding: 6 eating; **10** nourishing; **12** alimentation; **14** human nutrition

feeding chair: 9 high chair, highchair

feel: 3 paw; **4** find, look, tone; **5** grasp, grope, sense, smell, thumb, touch; **6** finger, flavor, fumble, handle, spirit; **7** feeling, grabble, palpate, texture; **8** perceive; **9** intuition; **10** experience

feeler: 6 barbel; **7** advance, antenna; **8** approach, overture

feeling: 4 feel, look, tone; **5** hunch, smell, touch; **6** affect, belief, flavor, notion, spirit; **8** feelings [pl], instinct, sentient; **9** affection, intuition; **10** affections, gut feeling, impression; **11** premonition, somesthesia; **12** presentiment, somaesthesia; **13** somatesthesia

feelings: 7 feeling; **9** affection; **11** sensibility, sensitivity

feel out: 3 see; **5** check; **8** check out, sound out

feeze: 4 rush; **5** alarm; **10** excitement

feign: 4 sham; **5** put on; **6** affect, assume, fake it; **7** pretend; **8** simulate; **9** dissemble; **11** make believe

feigned: 6 tricky; **7** scamped; **9** trumped up; **10** factitious

feigning: 8 pretence, pretense; **10** pretending, simulation; **11** dissembling

feisty: 6 plucky, spunky, touchy

felafel: 7 falafel

Feldene: 9 piroxicam

feldspar group: 8 andesine; **12** anorthoclase

felicitation: 14 congratulation

felicitous: 4 able, cute, neat; **5** happy; **6** clever, gifted; **7** endowed, germane, in point, on point, well put; **8** empyrean, relevant, talented; **9** effective

felicity: 4 turn; **5** bliss, forte, parts; **6** talent; **7** ability, faculty, talents; **8** capacity; **9** endowment, happiness; **10** capability, cleverness; **12** habilitation; **13** qualification

felid: 3 cat; **6** feline

feline: 3 cat; **4** puss; **5** catty, felid, pussy; **6** subtle; **7** cat-like, evasive, furtive, vulpine; **8** pussy cat, stealthy; **9** secretive

Felis: 4 lynx, puma; **5** tiger; **6** cougar, jaguar,

F

margay, ocelot, serval; **7** caracal, leopard, painter, panther, wildcat; **8** house cat; **9** catamount; **10** genus Felis; **12** mountain lion

fell: 3 fly; **4** drop, hide, sink; **5** cruel, floor, level, swamp, upset; **6** brutal, engulf, fleece, savage, vanish; **7** cut down, scuttle, subvert, untamed, vicious; **8** high moor, submerge, tameless; **9** barbarous, knock down, prostrate, roughshod, shipwreck, truculent; **10** felled seam, incendiary, strike down; **12** semibarbaric

fella: 3 lad; **4** chap, cuss, gent; **6** fellow; **8** blighter

felled: 6 downed

fellow: 3 elf, lad; **4** beau, chap, cuss, gent, twin; **5** blade, fella, joint, swain; **6** gaffer, sister, yeoman; **7** brother, comrade, good man; **8** blighter, confrere, familiar, young man; **9** associate, attendant, boyfriend, colleague, companion; **11** concomitant

fellowship: 6 family; **7** company, society; **8** intimacy; **9** tutorship; **10** readership; **11** comradeship, familiarity, knowledge of, lectureship; **12** acquaintance; **13** companionship

felo de se: 7 suicide; **8** hara-kiri [Jap]

felon: 5 crook, felon; **6** outlaw; **8** criminal

felonious: 4 base, foul, vile; **5** black, grave, gross; **6** scurvy; **7** heinous, lawless; **8** criminal, infamous, shameful, sinister; **9** nefarious; **10** of a deep dye, scandalous, villainous

felt: 3 mat; **4** lace, plat; **5** braid, mat up, plait, twill; **6** felt up, sensed; **9** perceived

felucca: 8 sailboat

female: 3 she-; **4** girl; **5** woman

female child: 4 girl; **5** child; **10** little girl

female horse: 4 mare

female monarch: 5 queen

feminate: 7 womanly; **10** effeminate

feminine: 7 womanly; **8** ladylike, maidenly, matronly

feminism: 9 women's lib

feminist: 6 libber; **8** new woman; **14** women's rightist

feminist movement: 8 feminism; **9** women's lib

femme fatale: 5 siren; **7** Delilah; **9** temptress; **11** enchantress

femoris: 5 femur; **9** thighbone

femur: 7 femoris; **9** thighbone

fen: 3 bog; **4** moor, moss; **5** marsh; **7** peat bog; **8** moorland; **9** marshland

fence: 4 trim, wall; **5** argue; **6** debate, duffer; **7** contend, fence in, fencing, shuffle; **8** entrench, palisade, surround

fenced in: 6 penned; **8** confined, corraled

fence in: 4 wall; **5** fence; **8** palisade, surround; **10** fence round, hedge round

fencer: 9 swordsman

fence rail: 9 split rail

fencing: 5 fence; **7** evasion; **9** shuffling, swordplay; **11** dissembling; **12** equivocation; **13** prevarication

fend: 5 guard; **6** defend, shield; **7** forfend, protect

fender: 4 mask, wing; **5** apron, pilot; **6** buffer; **10** cowcatcher

fend off: 5 avert, avoid, debar; **7** beat off, deflect, head off, keep off, obviate, ward off; **8** beat back, stave off

ferae naturae: 4 game, wild

feral: 6 savage

feral man: 7 wild man

ferity: 8 ferocity, savagery; **9** barbarity, brutality; **10** inhumanity

Fermat: 14 Pierre de Fermat

ferment: 3 ire, pet, rot; **4** bile, foam, fume, sour, stew, tiff, turn; **5** decay, go bad, yeast; **6** choler, dander, fester, fizzle, leaven, pother, pucker, rankle, ruffle, taking, unrest; **7** passion, putrefy, zymosis; **9** agitation, angry mood, zymolysis; **10** ebullition, effervesce

fermentation alcohol: 7 ethanol; **12** ethyl alcohol, grain alcohol

fermented: 4 hard

fermentologist: 9 enologist; **10** oenologist

Fermi: 11 Enrico Fermi

fermium: 2 Fm

ferocious: 4 rude, wild; **5** bluff, rough; **6** fierce, raging, savage; **7** furious, violent; **8** ungentle, vehement

ferocity: 4 fury, rage; **7** outrage; **8** atrocity, savagery, violence, wildness; **9** barbarity, brutality, vehemence; **10** fierceness, inhumanity, truculence; **11** furiousness

ferret out: 6 fish up, grub up; **7** fish out, hunt out, root out, worm out; **8** hunt down, trace out; **9** search out, track down

ferric: 7 ferrous

ferrum: 4 iron

ferryman: 7 boatman, **8** bargeman

fertile: 3 fat; **4** rich; **6** fecund; **8** creative, fruitful, original, prolific; **9** inventive; **10** productive; **12** fruit-bearing

fertility: 8 richness; **9** birth rate, birthrate, fecundity; **11** prolificacy; **13** fertility rate

fertility rate: 9 birth rate, birthrate, fertility

fertilization: 7 genesis; **8** dressing; **10** gemination, generation, heterogamy [Biol]; **11** fecundation, germination, procreation, propagation; **12** impregnation

fertilize: 4 feed; **8** generate; **9** procreate; **10** impregnate, inseminate

fertilized cell: 6 zygote

fertilized egg: 6 embryo; **9** conceptus

fervent: 5 fiery, rabid; **6** ardent, fervid, red-hot, torrid; **7** burning, cordial, flaming,

glowing, gushing; **9** perfervid; **10** passionate

fervid: 4 warm; **5** fiery; **6** ardent, red-hot,
torrid; **7** burning, fervent, flaming, glowing, gushing; **8** swelling, vehement; **9** perfervid; **10** passionate; **11** impassioned

fervor: 4 fire, gush, zeal; **5** ardor, verve; **6**
ardour; **7** fervour, passion; **8** fervency; **9**
vehemence; **10** enthusiasm, fervidness; **11**
enchantment, infatuation

fess: 6 fess up; **7** confess

fess up: 5 admit; **7** confess, own up to

festal: 3 fun, gay; **4** gala; **5** merry; **7** festive

fester: 3 rot; **4** boil; **5** decay, go bad; **6** rankle; **7** abscess, ferment, putrefy

festering: 3 pus; **5** ichor, pussy; **6** putrid,
sanies; **8** infected, purulent; **9** purulence

festival: 4 fete, gala; **5** feast; **6** fiesta; **7**
blowout

festival day: 6 fiesta [Sp]; **8** feast day

festive: 3 fun, gay; **4** gala; **5** merry; **6** festal;
8 cheering

festivity: 6 revels; **7** revelry; **8** reveling; **11**
celebration, merrymaking

festoon: 5 adorn; **8** decorate

fetch: 3 get; **4** bite, cost, draw, make, pull,
wile; **5** blind, bring, catch, cheat, feint,
hocus, plant, reach, trick, yield; **6** afford,
bubble, convey, convoy, draw in, juggle,
pull in; **7** attract, bring in, chicane, conduct, sell for; **8** overtake

fete: 4 gala; **5** feast; **6** fiesta; **7** blowout; **8**
festival; **9** celebrate

fete day: 8 feast day

fetich: 4 idol, juju; **6** fetish, hoodoo, voodoo;
11 graven image

fetid: 4 foul, rank; **5** funky; **6** foetid, putrid,
smelly; **7** noisome; **8** smelling, stinking; **9**
offensive; **12** foul-smelling

fetish: 4 juju; **6** fetich, hoodoo, voodoo; **9**
fetishism

fetor: 4 reek; **5** stink; **6** foetor, stench; **7** bad
odor, malodor; **8** bad smell, foul odor, malodour

fetter: 4 bond, gyve; **5** bonds, irons; **6** hamper, hobble; **7** shackle, trammel; **8** trammels

fettered: 7 hobbled, in bonds; **8** manacled,
pinioned, shackled; **9** in fetters; **10** handcuffed

feud: 4 fief, spat, tiff; **5** snarl; **7** dispute,
quarrel; **8** squabble; **10** dependency; **11**
altercation

feudal lord: 8 seigneur, seignior

fever: 4 heat; **5** flush; **7** passion, pyrexia; **9**
febricity; **10** excitement; **11** temperature

fever blister: 8 cold sore; **10** oral herpes; **14**
herpes labialis

feverish: 3 hot; **5** fussy, rabid; **6** hectic, raving, red-hot; **7** febrile, flushed; **8** feverous;
9 fanatical; **10** hysterical

fever sore: 3 rot; **6** canker; **8** cold sore

fey: 5 elfin; **7** touched

fiance: 9 groom-to-be

fiancee: 9 affianced, betrothed, bride-
to-be

fiasco: 7 debacle; **11** dead failure; **12** utter
failure

fiat: 5 edict, order; **6** decree; **8** rescript

fib: 4 tale; **5** story; **6** bounce, tussle; **7** crammer, whopper

fibber: 10 dissembler, fabricator; **11** storyteller

fiberboard: 13 particle board

fiberglass: 9 glass wool

fibril: 5 fiber; **6** strand; **8** filament

fibrous: 6 hempen, sinewy; **7** stringy; **9** fib-
rillar; **10** fibrillose, unchewable

fibula: 8 calf bone

fiche: 10 microfiche

fickle: 7 erratic; **8** shifting, unsteady, volatile,
wavering; **9** mercurial; **10** inconstant; **11**
quicksilver, vacillating

fickleness: 6 levity; **8** wavering; **9** falseness;
11 fluctuation, inconstancy, vacillation

fictile: 7 ductile, plastic, pliable; **8** formable,
moldable, shapable, workable; **9** malleable,
shapeable

fiction: 4 myth; **5** fable; **7** fantasy, forgery,
romance; **8** phantasm, phantasy, rhapsody;
9 invention; **11** fabrication

fictional: 6 made-up; **7** fancied; **8** fabulous,
invented; **9** fantastic, imaginary, visionary;
10 fabricated, fictitious

fictitious: 4 sham; **5** false, put on; **6** made-
up; **7** assumed, fancied, fictive; **8** invented;
9 fictional, pretended; **10** fabricated, factitious

fictive: 4 sham; **5** false, put on; **7** assumed; **9**
pretended; **10** fictitious

Ficus: 3 fig; **10** genus Ficus; **11** rubber plant

fiddle: 3 toy; **4** pipe, play, viol; **6** diddle, violin; **7** tweedle; **8** strike up; **11** viola
d'amore

fiddle-faddle: 4 bosh; **5** washy, putter, trashy;
7 rubbish; **8** trumpery, wish-wash; **10**
balderdash, namby-pamby, wishy-washy

fiddler: 9 violinist

fiddlesticks: 4 jest, joke; **8** mere joke

fidelity: 5 truth; **6** candor, homage; **7** honesty, loyalty; **8** devotion; **9** constancy, sincerity; **12** faithfulness

fidget: 3 ado; **4** fuss, stir, to-do; **6** bother,
bustle, flurry; **9** pottering

fidgets: 6 unrest; **8** disquiet; **10** inquietude;
11 disquietude, fidgetiness; **12** restlessness

fidgety: 5 fussy, hasty, itchy; **7** fretful, hurried, unquiet; **8** electric, galvanic, restless;
9 mercurial, pottering, tremulous

fief: 4 feud; **5** feoff

field: 3 orb, way; **4** area, room, soil; **5** arena,
orbit, plain, range, realm, scope, study,

F

sweep, swing; **6** circle, domain, ground, meadow, sphere, spread; **7** circuit, compass, lookout, subject; **8** airfield, province; **9** champaign, expansion; **10** department, discipline, force field; **11** battlefield, field of view, flying field, playing area, subject area; **12** battleground, field of force, field of study, landing field, playing field, subject field; **13** athletic field, field of battle, playing ground, scene of action; **14** domain of action, line of business

field day: 4 gala; **6** junket, outing, picnic

field general: 11 quarterback; **12** signal caller

field glasses: 9 binocular; **10** binoculars; **12** opera glasses

field goal: 6 basket

fieldhand: 8 farmhand; **10** farm worker

field mint: 8 corn mint; **14** Mentha arvensis

field of battle: 5 field; **11** battle-field, battlefield; **12** battle-ground, battleground

field of expertise: 9 specialty; **14** specialization

field piece: 8 howitzer

fiend: 4 ogre; **5** demon, devil; **6** daemon, daimon; **7** banshee, fanatic, monster; **8** familiar

fiendish: 6 unholy; **7** demonic, hellish, satanic, stygian; **8** devilish, diabolic, hellborn, infernal; **9** fiend-like; **10** demoniacal, diabolical

fiendishly: 10 devilishly; **12** diabolically

fierce: 4 rude, wild; **5** bluff, fiery, rough; **6** in a way, madcap, raging, savage; **7** excited, furious, in a fury, in a rage, tearing, violent; **8** ungentle, up in arms, vehement; **9** bowelless, cutthroat, ferocious, in a taking, infuriate; **10** blustering, boisterous, infuriated, outrageous; **11** all worked up, impassioned

fierceness: 4 fury; **8** ferocity, violence, wildness; **9** vehemence; **11** furiousness

fiery: 3 hot; **4** wild; **5** cross, surly, testy; **6** ardent, crabby, fervid, fierce, in a way, madcap, red-hot, savage, tetchy, torrid, touchy; **7** burning, crabbed, excited, fervent, flaming, furious, glowing, gushing, igneous, in a fury, in a rage, violent; **8** up in arms, vehement, volatile; **9** ebullient, in a taking, infuriate, irascible, irritable, perfervid, scorching; **10** infuriated, passionate; **11** all worked up, bad-tempered, hot-tempered, ill-tempered, impassioned

fiesta: 4 fete; **5** feast; **8** feast day, festival; **11** festival day

fife: 5 flute; **7** piccolo; **9** flageolet

fife player: 5 piper

fifer: 5 piper; **10** fife player

fifth: 3 5th; **8** one-fifth; **9** fifth part; **13** twenty percent

fifth wheel: 5 spare

fifty-cent piece: 10 half dollar

fifty-fifty: 4 even

fight: 4 bout, push, spar; **5** brush, set-to; **6** action, affair, battle, combat, defend, oppose; **7** agitate, crusade, wage war; **8** battling, campaign, conflict, do battle, fighting, struggle; **9** collision, encounter, fight back, fight down; **10** engagement, give battle; **11** battle royal, boxing match

fighter: 4 hero; **7** battler, paladin; **8** champion, scrapper; **9** combatant

fighter aircraft: 7 fighter; **14** attack aircraft

fighting: 3 war; **5** fight; **6** active, combat; **7** warfare, warring; **8** battling, brawling, conflict, militant; **9** waging war, war-ridden; **11** belligerent, clash of arms, combat-ready, hostilities

fighting cock: 8 gamecock

figment: 5 dream; **6** maggot, shadow, vision

fig moth: 10 almond moth; **13** Cadra cautella

figural: 10 figurative

figurate: 5 prime; **7** aliquot; **9** divisible; **10** fractional, reciprocal; **13** complementary

figurative: 7 figural; **9** imitative; **10** nonliteral; **12** metaphorical

figuratively: 14 metaphorically

figure: 3 bod, dog, fig, hag, pig, see; **4** cost, form, mark, name, plot, soma, type; **5** brute, build, chart, enter, fancy, flesh, frame, image, price, shape, trope, witch; **6** amount, charge, cipher, cypher, design, device, number, reckon, scheme, woofer; **7** anatomy, chassis, compute, count on, expense, fashion, pattern, picture, project; **8** envision, estimate, forecast, metaphor, physique; **9** calculate, human body, prime cost, shadow out, visualize; **10** cut a figure, figure away, shine forth; **11** distinction, shadow forth

figured: 6 formed, shaped; **9** fashioned

figurehead: 5 front; **8** front man, straw man; **11** nominal head

figure of speech: 5 image, trope; **6** figure; **8** metaphor

figure out: 4 lick, work; **5** solve; **6** fathom; **9** puzzle out

figurer: 8 computer, reckoner; **9** estimator; **10** calculator

figure skater: 9 ice skater

figurine: 9 statuette

figuring: 9 reckoning; **11** calculation, computation

filament: 5 filum; **6** fibril, strand

filamentous: 5 hairy; **6** tufted; **7** hirsute, thready; **8** ciliated

filaria: 6 clocks; **7** filaree; **8** pin grass

filbert: 3 cob; **6** cobnut; **8** hazelnut

filch: 3 bag; **4** hook, lift, prig; **5** pinch, snarf, sneak, steal, swipe; **6** nobble, pilfer, thieve; **7** purloin; **8** abstract

filcher: 5 thief; **6** rifler, robber; **8** pilferer

file: 4 rank, rasp; 5 grate, grind, guard, lodge; 6 ablate, abrade, charge, column, picket, piquet, scrape, thread; 7 rub down; 8 card file, data file, file away, file down, register, wear down; 9 card index, grind down; 10 Indian file, procession, single file; 11 file cabinet; 12 computer file; 13 filing cabinet

file a motion: 4 move

file away: 4 file; 7 archive

filed: 6 ground; 7 abraded; 8 debrided; 9 filed down; 10 ground down

filet: 6 fillet; 9 fish filet; 10 fish fillet

file transfer protocol: 3 ftp

filiation: 4 line; 7 descent, lineage; 8 alliance, ancestry; 10 connection, derivation; 11 affiliation

filibuster: 6 forage, hinder, impede, maraud; 7 inhibit; 8 restrict; 9 embarrass

filigree: 3 mat; 7 matting, tracery; 8 filagree, fretwork; 9 filagree

Filipino: 10 Philippine

fill: 3 jam, pad, wad; 4 cram, line, load, meet, sate, take; 5 close, stuff; 6 bumper, charge, fill up, fulfil, occupy; 7 filling, fulfill, incrust, pervade, replete, satiate, satisfy; 8 make full, permeate

filler: 10 makeweight

fillet: 4 band, list, sash, slip, tape; 5 brace, filet, spill, strip, tenia; 6 fascia, girdle, riband, ribbon, roller, taenia, wreath; 7 baldric, garland; 8 cincture, stopping; 9 fish filet, lemniscus; 10 fish fillet

fill-in: 6 backup, relief; 7 stand-in; 9 backup man; 10 substitute

filling: 4 fill, pick, weft, woof; 7 padding, wadding; 8 stuffing

filling station: 10 gas station; 13 petrol station

fillip: 4 dram, goad, spur, whet, whip; 5 bonus, flirt; 8 stimulus; 9 incentive; 10 incitement; 11 provocation

Fillmore: 15 Millard Fillmore

film: 4 take; 5 flick, movie, shoot; 6 cinema, ficker, movies; 7 picture; 8 membrane; 9 celluloid, movie film, movie show; 10 unused film; 11 picture show, plastic film; 13 motion picture, moving picture

film editing: 7 cutting

filming: 8 shooting; 14 cinematography

film maker: 10 movie maker; 12 film producer

film star: 9 movie star; 11 matinee idol

film writer: 12 screenwriter

filmy: 4 fine; 5 flaky, gauzy, scaly, sheer, silky; 6 satiny; 7 subtile; 8 cobwebby, delicate, gossamer, squamous [Anat], vaporous; 9 gossamery; 10 diaphanous, membranous, pellicular, see-through; 11 transparent

filter: 6 sink in, strain; 7 dribble, trickle;

8 filtrate, permeate; 9 filter out, percolate; 11 separate out

filth: 4 dirt, slop, soil; 5 grime, stain; 6 grease; 8 foulness; 9 nastiness; 10 filthiness

filthy: 4 foul, vile; 5 dirty, grimy, lousy, nasty; 6 smutty

filtrate: 6 filter, strain; 9 filter out; 11 separate out

fimbriated: 5 hairy; 6 tufted; 7 fringed, hirsute; 8 ciliated; 11 filamentous

fin: 1 V; 4 fins, five; 5 fiver, quint; 6 cinque, louver, louvre, pentad, Phoebe; 7 flipper, Lincoln, quintet, tail fin; 8 fivesome, flippers; 9 fish's tail; 10 break water, quintuplet

finagle: 6 manage, wangle

final: 3 net; 4 last; 8 crowning, terminal, ultimate; 9 final exam, finishing; 10 completing, concluding, conclusive

finale: 4 coda, last; 5 close, finis; 6 finish; 8 terminus; 9 winding up; 10 conclusion, denouement, wrapping up; 11 culmination

finally: 4 last; 6 at last, in fine, lastly; 7 for good; 8 after all, at length, in the end; 10 at long last, eventually, on the whole, ultimately; 12 in conclusion

finance: 6 budget; 12 money matters

finances: 5 funds; 7 capital; 10 cash in hand

financial: 6 fiscal; 9 sumptuary; 10 accounting; 11 accountable

financial distress: 4 lack, need, want; 6 penury; 7 poverty; 8 distress; 9 indigence, necessity, neediness, pauperism, privation; 11 destitution

financial instrument: 8 security; 10 securities [pl]

financial liability: 8 exposure

financial obligation: 9 liability; 12 indebtedness

financial officer: 9 treasurer

financial support: 7 backing, funding, subsidy, support; 9 financing

financial year: 10 fiscal year

finback: 7 rorqual; 12 finback whale

find: 3 get, hit, see; 4 bump, feel, rule; 5 incur; 6 chance, come up, detect, evolve, happen, line up, notice, obtain, regain; 7 find out, get hold, observe, receive, recover, witness; 8 come upon, discover, retrieve; 9 ascertain, detection, determine, discovery, encounter, find one in, light upon, pitch upon; 10 disclosure, revelation, uncovering

finder: 7 spotter; 10 discoverer, viewfinder

finding: 4 data; 6 result; 8 decision, judgment; 9 judgement; 10 conclusion; 13 determination

fine: 1 f.; 2 OK; 3 tag; 4 good, nice, okay,

rare, rich, thin; **5** filmy, grand, mulct, prime, prize, showy, silky; **6** amerce, choice, dainty, finely, fining, flimsy, mighty, pretty, satiny, sconce, select, slight, subtle, superb, ticket; **7** alright, curious, doing OK, quality, slender, sublime, subtile, tenuous; **8** all right, delicate, rainless, specious, towering, very well; **9** beautiful, doing well, exquisite, gossamery; **10** amercement, delicately, discerning, exact a fine, particular, purse-proud; **11** exquisitely, magnificent

fineable: 7 finable

fine arts: 3 art; **9** beaux arts

fined: 9 penalized

fine-grained: 7 powdery; **8** powdered; **10** pulverized; **12** close-grained, small-grained

fine-looking: 8 handsome; **11** good-looking, well-favored; **13** better-looking

finely: 4 fine; **10** delicately; **11** exquisitely

fineness: 8 delicacy, thinness; **10** choiceness, daintiness; **11** powderiness

finery: 5 array; **6** tinsel; **7** raiment, regalia; **8** frippery, trickery; **14** dressy clothing

finespun: 8 delicate, gossamer; **13** hairsplitting

finesse: 3 art; **4** gust, tact; **5** dodge, gusto, shift; **6** double; **8** artistry, delicacy, side blow, sidestep; **9** diplomacy, temporize; **10** circumvent, refinement; **11** artful dodge, fine feeling, gerrymander; **12** discreetness; **13** masterfulness

finest: 8 top-grade; **9** high-grade; **10** top-quality

fine-tune: 4 down; **6** polish, refine; **8** graduate; **9** calibrate

finger: 3 paw; **4** feel; **5** digit, grope, thumb, touch; **6** fumble, handle; **7** grabble

finger cymbals: 5 bones; **6** maraca; **8** clappers; **9** castanets

fingerlike: 8 digitate

fingermark: 11 fingerprint

finger plate: 9 scutcheon; **10** escutcheon

fingerpost: 8 signpost; **9** guidepost; **11** fingerboard

fingerstall: 3 cot

finical: 7 finicky

finicky: 4 nice; **5** fussy, picky; **6** dainty; **7** finical, finikin; **8** delicate; **10** fastidious, particular

finis: 3 end; **4** last; **5** close; **6** finale, finish; **8** terminus; **10** conclusion

finish: 3 end; **4** last, seal; **5** cease, close, drain, eat up, empty, end up, finis, glaze, gloss, stamp; **6** absorb, clinch, finale, tap out, wind up, wrap up; **7** coating, exhaust; **8** complete, conclude, run out of, terminus; **9** finishing, polish off, swallow up, terminate, winding up; **10** conclusion, denoue-

ment, impoverish, put the seal, use up all of, wrapping up

finished: 4 done, over; **5** stark; **6** primed, ruined, used up; **7** decided, drained, perfect, shapely, trained, well set, worn out; **8** absolute, complete, consumed, depleted, expended, positive, prepared; **9** completed, essential, exhausted, fulfilled, initiated, tapped out

finishing: 5 final; **6** ending, finish; **7** closing, coating; **8** crowning, glossing; **10** completing, concluding, conclusive; **11** terminating

finiteness: 8 finitude; **11** boundedness

fink: 5 sneak, squeal; **6** canary, snitch; **7** stoolie; **10** tattletale; **11** stoolpigeon

Finland: 5 Suomi

finnan: 12 finnan haddie; **13** finnan haddock, smoked haddock

Finnish: 5 Suomi

finocchio: 6 fennel

fins: 3 fin; **8** flippers

fin whale: 7 finback, rorqual

fiord: 5 firth, fjord, inlet; **7** estuary

fipple flute: 5 flute; **8** recorder; **10** fipple pipe; **13** vertical flute

fir: 4 pine; **7** fir tree

fire: 3 can, RIF; **4** burn, elan, flak, fuel, fume, sack, zest; **5** ardor, blast, blaze, evoke, flame, go off, gusto, light, raise, shoot, verve; **6** ardour, arouse, attack, elicit, fervor, fire up, firing, ignite, kindle, spirit; **7** dismiss, explode, fervour, fire out, flame up, flaming, flare up, inflame, passion, provoke; **8** burn down, enkindle, fervency, force out, let one go, open fire, send away, take fire; **9** discharge, set fire to, set on fire, terminate; **10** fervidness, give notice, give the axe; **12** blood boiling; **13** apply the torch

fire alarm: 10 smoke alarm; **12** heat detector; **13** smoke detector alarm

firearm: 3 gun; **5** piece; **6** weapon; **8** small-arm

fireball: 5 brand; **6** bolide; **9** cartouche; **10** ball of fire, fire-barrel, powerhouse; **11** human dynamo; **13** ball cartridge

firebrand: 5 brand; **7** fire bug [U.S.], inciter; **8** agitator, arsonist, prompter, provoker; **9** instigant; **10** incendiary, instigator, pyromaniac

firebreak: 6 trench; **8** backfire; **9** fireguard

fire brigade: 11 fire company; **13** engine company; **14** fire department

firebug: 8 arsonist; **10** incendiary, pyromaniac

fire chief: 11 fire marshal

firecracker: 6 banger; **7** cracker

fired: 6 canned, riffed, sacked; **7** laid-off, severed; **9** dismissed; **10** discharged, terminated; **11** pink-slipped

fire department: 11 fire brigade; **13** engine company

firedog: 3 dog; 7 andiron, dogiron
fire door: 8 fire wall
firedrake: 6 dragon
fire engine: 9 fire truck
fire fighter: 7 fireman; 10 extincteur [Fr]; 11 forefighter
firefly: 7 june bug; 8 glowworm; 10 fire beetle; 12 lightning bug
fireguard: 9 firebreak; 10 fire screen
firehouse: 11 fire station
fire hydrant: 4 plug; 8 fire hose, fireplug
firelock: 6 musket; 8 musketry; 9 flintlock, wheel lock
fireman: 6 stoker; 8 reliever; 9 fire eater, fire-eater; 10 extincteur [Fr]; 11 fire fighter, forefighter; 13 relief pitcher
fire marshal: 9 fire chief
Firenze: 8 Florence
fire opal: 7 girasol
fireplace: 6 hearth
fireplug: 4 plug; 11 fire hydrant
fireproof: 10 flameproof; 12 nonflammable; 13 incombustible, uninflammable
fire regulation: 8 fire code
fire-resistant: 13 fire-resisting, fire-resistive, fire-retardant
fire-retardant: 13 fire-resistant, fire-resisting, fire-resistive
fire-sale price: 13 heavy discount
fire screen: 9 fireguard
fireside: 6 hearth
fire station: 9 firehouse
fire-swallower: 9 fire-eater
fire truck: 6 bucket, pumper; 10 fire engine; 12 aerial ladder; 13 hook and ladder
fire up: 4 burn, fire, heat; 5 light; 6 ignite, stir up; 7 explode, flame up, flare up, froth up, inflame, light up; 8 bridle up, take fire
firewall: 8 fire door
firewood: 3 log; 6 faggot; 7 bobbing
firework: 12 pyrotechnics
fire-worship: 9 pyrolatry
firing: 4 fire, fuel, sack; 5 salvo; 6 volley; 7 release, sacking; 8 ignition, kindling, lighting, shooting; 9 discharge, dismissal, firing off, severance
firing mechanism: 7 gunlock
firing range: 11 target range
firkin: 6 carboy; 9 kilderkin
firm: 3 set; 4 fast, iron, taut; 5 close, crisp, firms [pl], house, loyal, rigid, solid, stiff, tight; 6 firmly, gritty [U.S.], secure, steady, strong, taught, tauten; 7 company, concern, crunchy; 8 business, immobile; 9 companies [pl], steadfast; 10 enterprise, unbendable, unshakable, unwavering; 11 established, indomitable, steadfastly, truehearted, unfaltering; 12 business firm, unwaveringly; 13 establishment, unfluctuating

firmament: 6 sphere, welkin; 7 heavens; 8 empyrean
firm hold: 8 tenacity
firmly: 4 fast, firm, hard; 8 securely; 11 steadfastly; 12 unwaveringly
firmness: 7 resolve; 8 solidity; 9 solidness, soundness; 10 resolution, solid state, steadiness; 12 resoluteness
firms: 4 firm; 7 company, concern; 8 business; 9 companies [pl]; 10 enterprise; 13 establishment; 20 business organization; 22 commercial organization
first: 3 low, top; 5 start; 6 maiden, offset, outset; 7 at first, firstly, kickoff, leading, low gear, number 1; 8 first off, foremost, imprimis [Lat]; 9 beginning, first base, first gear, inaugural, number one; 10 first of all, initiative, initiatory; 12 commencement, starting time
first and last: 3 odd; 6 unique; 7 azygous; 8 above all, singular
first appearance: 5 debut, entry; 9 launching, unveiling; 12 introduction
first balcony: 9 mezzanine
first baseman: 11 first sacker
firstborn: 6 eldest; 9 firstling
first cause: 10 prime mover; 12 primum mobile
first-class: 6 superb; 7 optimal; 9 excellent, first-rate; 11 superlative
first cousin: 6 cousin; 10 full cousin; 12 cousin-german
first estate: 6 clergy
first floor: 11 ground floor, ground level
first-growth forest: 12 virgin forest; 15 old-growth forest
first harmonic: 11 fundamental
first language: 12 mother tongue
first light: 4 dawn; 5 sunup; 6 aurora; 7 dawning, morning, sunrise; 8 cockcrow, daybreak; 9 dayspring; 10 break of day
firstling: 9 firstborn
firstly: 5 first; 7 at first; 8 first off, foremost, imprimis [Lat]; 10 first of all
first name: 8 forename; 9 given name
First of May: 6 May Day
first-rate: 3 ace; 4 A-one, tops; 5 crack, super; 6 superb, tiptop; 7 frigate, gunboat, optimal; 8 corvette, topnotch, very well; 10 bomb vessel, first-class, sloop of war; 11 superlative
First Reich: 15 Holy Roman Empire
first sacker: 12 first baseman
First State: 8 Delaware; 12 Diamond State
first stomach: 5 rumen
first team: 7 varsity
first-year: 8 freshman
firth: 5 fiord, fjord, inlet; 7 estuary
fiscal: 9 financial, sumptuary
fiscalize: 8 monetize

fish: 3 mug; 4 dupe, fool, gull, mark; 5 angle, chump, patsy; 6 go fish, sucker; 7 fall guy; 8 shlemiel; 9 schlemiel, soft touch; 10 fish around

fish's tail: 3 fin; 7 flipper

fish ball: 8 fish cake; 11 gefilte fish

fisher: 5 pekan; 8 black cat; 9 fisher cat, fisherman

fisherman's knot: 12 truelove knot

fishery: 7 piscary

fisheye lens: 13 wide-angle lens

fish farming: 12 pisciculture

fish hawk: 6 osprey; 8 sea eagle

fishing gear: 6 tackle; 13 fishing tackle

fishing pole: 10 fishing rod

fishing worm: 7 dew worm, red worm, wiggler; 8 fishworm; 9 angleworm, earthworm; 11 nightwalker; 12 nightcrawler

fishmonger: 8 fishwife

fish story: 4 yarn; 6 fringe; 8 tall tale

fish tank: 8 aquarium, vivarium; 12 marine museum

fishwife: 10 fishmonger

fish-worship: 12 ichthyolatry

fishy: 5 funny, shady; 7 suspect; 10 suspicious

fission: 13 atomic fission; 14 nuclear fission

fissionable: 7 fissile

fissionable material: 11 nuclear fuel

fission bomb: 5 A-bomb; 8 atom bomb; 10 atomic bomb

fission power: 11 atomic power; 12 nuclear power

fission reactor: 14 nuclear reactor

fissure: 4 chap; 5 break, cleft, crack, split; 6 cranny; 7 crevice; 8 fracture, scissure

fissured: 7 cracked

fistfight: 8 slugfest; 10 fisticuffs

fistful: 7 handful

fisticuffs: 6 boxing; 8 pugilism, slugfest; 9 fistfight; 12 sweet science

fistula: 5 sinus; 6 ostium

fit: 2 do, go; 3 due, fad, set; 4 gibe, good, jibe, meet, mold, suit; 5 adapt, agree, befit, burst, check, equip, freak, match, mould, prank, quirk, right, scene, stamp, tally; 6 fit out, in loco, maggot, nature, outfit, primed, proper, seemly, spirit, vagary; 7 a propos [Fr], apropos, boutade [Fr], correct, en regle, fitting, healthy, megrims, seizure, tantrum, tempest; 8 apposite, crotchet, decorous, escapade, flimflam, outbreak, outburst, paroxysm, sortable, staggers, suitable, tantrums [pl]; 9 acclimate, befitting, capriccio, character, conform to, explosion [metaphorical]; 10 applicable, complexion, correspond, seasonable; 11 acclimatize, accommodate

fitch: 7 foumart, polecat; 8 foulmart

fitful: 8 off-and-on; 9 desultory, irregular, spasmodic, uncertain; 10 capricious, flickering, hysterical, unpunctual; 11 inconsonant, interrupted

fitly: 8 suitably; 9 fittingly; 11 befittingly; 13 appropriately

fitness: 4 trim; 5 shape; 7 aptness, decorum; 8 good trim, meetness; 9 condition, good shape, propriety, rightness; 10 seemliness; 11 correctness, fittingness; 12 appositeness, suitableness

fitness center: 3 gym; 10 health club

fitted out: 8 equipped; 9 outfitted

fitted sheet: 12 contour sheet

fitting: 3 due, fit; 4 good, meet; 5 right, try-on; 6 proper, seemly; 7 correct, en regle; 8 decorous, trying on; 9 befitting; 10 adjustment; 11 appointment; 13 accommodation

fittingly: 5 fitly; 7 rightly; 8 properly, suitably; 11 befittingly; 13 appropriately

fittings: 7 harness; 9 trappings; 13 accouterments

five: 1 V; 6 cinque, pentad, Phoebe; 7 quintet; 8 fivesome; 9 quintuple; 10 quintuplet

five-dollar bill: 3 fin; 5 fiver; 7 Lincoln; 8 five-spot

fivefold: 9 quintuple

five hundred: 1 d, D; 6 euchre

five iron: 6 mashie

fix: 3 get, jam, pin, set; 4 bind, cake, clot, cook, hole, make, mend, mess, pass, pose, push, root, spay; 5 affix, alter, candy, desex, hitch, pinch, posit, ready, trial, twist, unsex; 6 attach, bushel, clinch, doctor, fasten, fixate, fixing, muddle, neuter, pay off, pickle, repair, secure, settle, strait; 7 deposit, measure, mending, nonplus, pay back, prepare, restore, situate, specify, touch on; 8 estimate, exigency, juncture, locating, location, make fast, quandary, quantify, regulate, saddle on, scramble, settle on; 9 ascertain, determine, enumerate, establish, furbish up, methodize, sterilize; 10 coordinate, decide upon, pretty pass, quantitate, reparation, settle upon; 11 conjunctive, desexualize, predicament, resolve upon, systematize

fixable: 10 repairable

fixate: 3 fix; 8 settle on

fixation: 6 fixing; 9 obsession; 10 regression

fixed: 3 set; 4 flat; 5 given, rigid; 6 frozen, intent, placed, rooted; 7 located, settled; 8 fastened, immobile, neutered, repaired; 9 besetting, hackneyed, immovable, incurable, permanent; 10 deep-rooted, determined, invariable, inveterate; 11 decided upon, established, irremovable, settled upon

fixed oil: 8 fatty oil

fixed rates: 12 exchange rate

fixing: 3 fix; 6 repair; 7 mending; 8 altering, fixation; 9 neutering; 10 reparation

fix-it shop: 10 repair shop
fixtures: 5 plant; **8** heirloom
fix up: 7 arrange
fizz: 4 foam; **5** froth; **6** fizzle; **7** sparkle; **10** effervesce
fizzle: 4 fizz; **7** ferment; **8** peter out, taper off; **9** fizzle out; **10** effervesce
fjord: 5 fiord, firth, inlet; **7** estuary
flabbergast: 4 stun; **6** boggle; **7** petrify, stagger, stupefy; **8** bewilder, bowl over, confound; **9** fascinate; **10** strike dumb; **11** turn the head
flabby: 4 limp; **6** flimsy; **7** flaccid
flaccid: 3 lax; **4** limp; **5** downy, slack; **6** flabby; **7** sapless; **10** flocculent
flag: 4 irk, pin, sag; **4** deck, drop, fade, fail, halt, iris, jade, limp, sink, slab, swag, tier, tire; **5** droop, earth, floor, shake, stage, weary; **6** banner, carped, colors, ease up, ensign, falter, ground, paving, signal, totter; **7** crumble, decline, ease off, exhaust, fatigue, give way, pennant, stagger, tremble, trotter, wear out; **8** hang fire, languish, pavement, slack off; **9** flagstone, prostrate, sword lily; **10** escarpment, fleur-de-lis, signal flag, slacken off, substratum; **11** ground floor; **12** expend itself, national flag, substructure
flagellate: 4 cane, comb, flog, lash, lick, whip; **5** birch, strap, towel; **6** larrup, switch, thrash, thresh; **7** scourge; **8** whiplike; **9** bastinado, horsewhip; **11** flagellated; **12** give the stick, mastigophore
flagellated: 8 whiplike; **10** flagellate
flagellated protozoan: 10 flagellate
flagellation: 7 beating, lashing; **8** flogging, whipping; **9** pummeling, thrashing, threshing
flageolet: 4 fife; **5** flute; **7** haricot, piccolo
flagging: 4 lame; **5** rusty; **6** used up; **7** halting, worn out; **8** crippled, drooping; **9** dulled out, life-weary; **11** weary of life
flagitious: 7 heinous; **8** flagrant, grievous; **9** atrocious, monstrous; **10** villainous
flagon: 3 kit; **5** crock; **7** canteen
flagpole: 9 flagstaff, range pole
flagrant: 4 rank; **5** gross; **6** arrant, crying; **7** glaring; **9** egregious; **10** flagitious
flags: 4 walk; **8** footpath, pavement, sidewalk
flagship: 7 cruiser; **9** guard ship
flagstaff: 4 post; **5** staff; **8** flagpole
flagstone: 4 flag
flag stop: 11 whistle stop
flag-waver: 5 jingo; **8** jingoist
flag waving: 8 jingoism
flail: 3 lam; **6** thrash, thresh
flair: 4 dash, elan; **5** style; **6** genius; **7** panache
flak: 4 fire; **5** blast; **6** ack-ack, attack, pompom; **9** ack-ack gun; **11** flak catcher; **12** antiaircraft

flake: 3 bit; **4** chip, peel; **5** fleck, scale, scrap; **7** peel off; **8** flake off; **9** snowflake
flake off: 4 peel; **5** flake, scale; **7** peel off
flakiness: 8 daftness; **9** craziness
flaky: 5 filmy, outre, scaly; **6** flakey, freaky; **7** bizarre; **8** freakish, squamous [Anat]; **9** eccentric; **10** membranous, outlandish, pellicular
flambeau: 4 link; **5** brand, torch
flamboyant: 5 showy; **6** florid; **7** aureate; **9** flame tree; **11** resplendent; **12** Delonix regia, unrestrained; **13** peacock flower
flamboyantly: 7 showily; **8** flashily
flame: 4 boil, fire, foam, fume, rage, rave; **5** blaze, flare, lover; **6** adorer, flames [pl], seethe, simmer; **7** admirer, flaming, passion, rapture; **8** devotion, idolatry, yearning; **9** adoration, idolizing; **11** idolization; **12** blood boiling; **13** tender passion
flamenco: 12 gypsy dancing
flameproof: 9 fireproof; **12** nonflammable; **13** incombustible, uninflammable; **14** flame-retardant
flame tree: 6 cassie; **8** fire tree, huisache; **9** Poinciana; **10** flamboyant, mimosa bush; **11** sweet acacia, sweet wattle
flaming: 3 hot; **4** fire; **5** afire, bally, fiery, flame; **6** ablaze, aflame, aflare, alight, ardent, bloody, fervid, flashy, frothy, on fire, red-hot; **7** blazing, burning, fervent, glowing, gushing, stilted; **8** blinking, boastful, boasting, braggart, bragging, crashing, flashing, seething; **9** ebullient, flaunting, scorching, soi-disant [Fr], thrasonic; **10** passionate, swaggering; **11** boiling over, gasconading; **12** magniloquent
flammable: 8 burnable; **9** ignitable, ignitible; **11** combustible, inflammable
flange: 3 lip, rim; **4** brow, side; **5** skirt; **6** corbel; **7** confine
flank: 3 lee; **4** side, ward, wing; **5** cover; **6** screen, shroud; **7** quarter, shelter; **8** outflank
flanking: 8 crab-like, crabwise, sidelong, sideways, sidewise, skirting
flannel: 5 tweed, white; **7** washrag; **9** face cloth, gabardine, washcloth
flap: 3 dab, pat; **4** beat, flow, fuss, wave; **5** bandy, flaps, skirt, tizzy, trail, wield; **6** dither, lappet, pother; **7** cortege, flutter; **8** brandish, flapping, flopping, flourish, undulate; **9** trappings; **10** embroidery, fluttering
flapjack: 7 hotcake, pancake; **8** flapcake; **10** battercake; **11** flannelcake, griddlecake
flapping: 3 lax; **4** flap; **5** baggy, loose, slack; **7** flutter, relaxed; **8** detached, flopping; **9** streaming; **10** fluttering
flare: 3 fly; **5** burst, erupt, flame, flash, go

off; **6** blow up, bounce, burn up; **7** blaze up, explode, flame up, flare up, thunder; **8** burst out, detonate, flare out; **9** break open; **10** solar flare

flare up: 4 burn, fire; **5** erupt, flare; **6** fire up; **7** explode, flame up, flush up, froth up; **8** bridle up, burst out, take fire; **9** break open, bristle up; **11** boiling over

flaring: 6 aflare, flared, flying, waving; **7** glaring; **10** fluttering

flash: 3 fly; **4** coup, dart, dash, loud, scud, snap, wink; **5** blink, burst, cheap, crack, flare, gaudy, glint, go off, jiffy, scoot, shoot, spark, spurt, swank, tacky, tatty, trice; **6** blow up, bounce, brassy, breath, flashy, flaunt, garish, tawdry, trashy, winkle; **7** explode, glitter, impulse, instant, show off, sparkle, thunder, twinkle; **8** bulletin, detonate, flashgun, flashing, gimcrack; **9** coruscate, flash lamp, flashbulb, fresh news, news flash, newsflash, twinkling; **10** news just in, photoflash; **11** coruscation, inspiration, scintillate, split second

flashback: 10 recurrence

flashbulb: 5 flash; **8** flashgun; **9** flash lamp; **10** photoflash

flasher: 13 exhibitionist

flash-frozen: 6 frozen; **11** quick-frozen

flashily: 7 showily; **12** flamboyantly

flashiness: 5 glitz; **8** loudness; **9** brashness, gaudiness; **10** garishness, tawdriness

flash in the pan: 5 blank, dummy; **8** collapse, hang fire; **10** dead letter; **13** come to nothing

flashlight: 5 torch [Brit]

flashy: 4 loud; **5** cheap, flash, gaudy, jazzy, showy, tacky, tatty; **6** brassy, frothy, garish, sporty, tawdry, trashy; **7** flaming; **8** gimcrack; **9** flaunting; **12** meretricious

flask: 7 flasket; **8** flaskful

flasket: 5 flask

flaskful: 5 flask

flat: 3 dry, mat; **4** arid, bald, bank, drab, dull, even, matt, muff, slow, swab, tame; **5** bland, blunt, broad, fixed, flush, heavy, inert, level, matte, plane, round, sharp, shelf, slack, vapid; **6** boring, dreary, jejune, lubber, marked, matted, mortal, shoals, stodgy, stupid, supine, torpid; **7** Cyclops, decided, discoid, flatcar, humdrum, insipid, natural, pointed, tedious; **8** breakers, directly, distinct, flat tire, lee shore, shallows, sluggish, straight, unraised; **9** apartment, categoric, dry as dust, prostrate, savorless, slow coach, tasteless, unpleated; **10** compressed, flavorless, monotonous

flatboat: 3 hoy; **4** pram; **5** barge; **7** lighter

flatcar: 4 flat

flat coat: 6 ground, primer; **9** undercoat; **11** priming coat

flatfish: 8 flounder

flatfoot: 9 patrolman, splayfoot

flat knot: 8 reef knot

flatlands: 7 lowland; **8** lowlands

flat-leaf parsley: 14 Italian parsley

flatly: 13 categorically; **15** unconditionally

flatness: 3 mat; **4** matt; **5** matte; **8** dullness; **9** heaviness, planarity, planeness

flat-nosed: 9 snub-nosed

flat note: 7 low note; **8** bass note, deep note; **9** grave note

flat solid: 5 sheet

flatten: 4 drop; **5** level; **10** flatten out, render flat

flattening: 7 planing; **8** leveling

flatter: 4 puff; **5** humor; **6** cajole, look up, tickle; **7** bid fair, indulge, promise; **8** blandish

flatterer: 8 adulator

flattering: 8 flattery; **9** adulation, adulatory

flattery: 8 cajolery, flimflam; **9** adulation

flattop: 7 carrier, crew cut; **15** aircraft carrier

flat-topped: 7 flat-top

flatulent: 5 gassy, silly; **6** frothy; **7** colicky; **12** effervescent

flatware: 6 silver

flaunt: 4 live; **5** flash, swank; **6** parade; **7** glitter, show off; **8** flourish

flautist: 7 flutist; **11** flute player

flavor: 4 feel, look, tang, tone; **5** savor, smack, smell, spice, taste, twang; **6** relish, savour, season, spirit; **7** feeling, flavour, spice up; **8** sapidity

flavorless: 4 flat; **5** bland, vapid; **7** insipid; **9** savorless

flavorous: 5 sapid; **8** saporous; **9** flavorful; **10** flavorsome, flavourful, flavourous; **11** flavoursome

flaw: 4 blot, miss, slip; **5** fault; **6** defect; **7** blemish, blunder; **8** omission; **9** oversight, weak point; **10** deficiency

flawless: 7 perfect; **8** unflawed; **9** faultless; **10** impeccable; **12** indefectible

flawlessly: 7 cleanly; **9** perfectly; **10** impeccably; **11** faultlessly

flaxen: 5 sandy

flax family: 8 Linaceae

flay: 4 pare, peel, skin; **5** scalp; **9** excoriate; **11** decorticate

F layer: 7 F region

flea: 3 bug; **5** louse; **6** chinch, vermin

flea-bitten: 6 creaky; **7** run-down, studded; **8** decrepit, freckled; **9** woebegone

fleawort: 8 psyllium

fleck: 3 bit; **4** blob, blot, chip, spot; **5** flake, patch, scrap, stain; **6** dapple; **7** speckle; **8** particle; **10** maculation

flecked: 6 dotted; **7** specked; **8** speckled, stippled

fled: 9 absconded; **10** stolen away; **11** slipped away

fledge: 3 rig; **5** array, dress; **6** fettle, flight; **7** feather, furnish, garnish; **8** accouter

fledged: 5 vaned; **6** mature

fledgling: 7 entrant, starter; **8** freshman, neophyte, newcomer; **9** unfledged; **10** fledgeling

flee: 3 fly; **7** abscond; **10** take flight

fleece: 3 rob; **4** bilk, fell, hook, rook, ruin, soak, wool; **5** bleed, mulct, pluck, plume, shear, strip; **6** extort, gazump, pigeon, sponge; **7** despoil; **9** sheepskin, surcharge; **10** impoverish, overcharge

fleecy: 6 napped; **7** brushed

fleeing: 6 flight; **7** running; **11** running away

fleer: 4 gibe, gird, hiss, hoot, jeer, twit; **5** scoff, taunt; **6** deride; **7** barrack, laugh at, snigger; **8** ridicule

fleet: 4 dart, fade, flit, pass; **5** swift; **7** flutter, pass off

fleeting: 7 cursory; **8** fugitive; **9** ephemeral, momentary; **10** evanescent, short-lived; **12** momentaneous

fleetness: 8 celerity, rapidity; **9** high speed, quickness, rapidness, swiftness; **10** speediness

flesh: 3 bod; **4** form, meat, pulp, soma; **5** build, frame, shape; **6** figure; **7** anatomy, chassis; **8** humanity, physique, salacity; **9** carnality, human body, mortality; **10** generation

flesh and blood: 3 man; **4** body, soul; **5** being, flesh, human; **6** mortal, person, plenum; **8** creature, such a one; **9** earthling, personage; **10** flow of soul, human being, individual, living soul

flesh color: 5 blush, flush; **9** flesh tint; **12** flesh-colored

flesh-eating: 10 meat-eating, zoophagous

fleshly: 6 animal, carnal; **7** sensual

flesh out: 3 fat; **5** plump; **6** dilate, expand, fatten; **7** enlarge, expound, fill out; **8** fatten up, plump out; **9** elaborate, expatiate, fatten out

flesh tint: 5 blush, flush; **10** flesh color

fleshy: 5 heavy; **6** brawny; **7** sarcoid; **8** stalwart; **10** overweight

fleur-de-lis: 4 flag, fret, iris; **8** flourish; **9** arabesque, sword lily; **10** coquillage [Fr], fleur-de-lys

flex: 4 bend; **5** curve; **6** extend; **7** bending, distend, flexion, stretch; **8** flection; **9** be elastic

flexible: 6 pliant, spring; **7** buoyant, elastic, flexile, pliable, springy, tensile; **8** renitent; **9** resilient; **12** compromising, conciliatory

flexible joint: 5 hinge

flexion: 4 bend, flex; **5** elbow, joint; **7** bending, flexing, flexure; **10** inflection

flexor: 12 flexor muscle

flexure: 4 bend, fold; **5** crimp, elbow, joint; **6** crease

flick: 4 film, flip, jerk, leaf, riff, snap; **5** click, movie, thumb; **6** movies, riffle, ruffle, strike; **7** flicker, picture; **9** movie film, movie show; **11** picture show; **13** motion picture

flicker: 4 beam, vary; **5** blaze, flick, glare, glint, shift, spark, waver; **6** bicker, change, quiver; **7** flitter, flutter, glimmer, shimmer, twinkle, twitter; **8** flounder; **9** fluctuate

flickering: 6 fitful; **8** aflicker; **9** desultory, irregular, uncertain; **10** capricious, unpunctual

flier: 4 bill; **5** flyer; **6** airman; **7** aviator; **8** aeronaut, circular, handbill; **9** broadside, throwaway; **10** broadsheet

flight: 3 fry; **4** bevy, herd, hive, nest, peck; **5** brood, cloud, covey, drove, flock, shoal, swarm; **6** bushel, escape, farrow, fledge, flying, litter, scores; **7** draught, fleeing; **8** aviation; **10** trajectory; **11** running away; **13** flight of steps; **14** flight of stairs

flight attendant: 7 steward; **10** stewardess

flight feather: 5 quill; **6** pinion

flightiness: 6 whimsy

flightless bird: 6 ratite

flight of stairs: 5 steps; **6** flight; **8** stairway; **9** staircase

flight path: 6 airway; **7** air lane

flight simulator: 7 trainer; **11** Link trainer

flight strip: 5 strip; **8** airstrip; **12** landing strip

flighty: 7 fanatic, flyaway, utopian; **8** quixotic, romantic; **9** high flown; **11** extravagant, unrealistic

flimflam: 3 con, fad, fit, gyp; **5** bunco, bunko, freak, prank, quirk, sting; **6** hustle, maggot, vagary; **7** con game; **8** cajolery, crotchet, escapade, flattery; **9** bunco game, bunko game

flimsiness: 10 shoddiness

flimsy: 4 fine, idle, limp, poor, rare, thin, weak; **5** light, loose; **6** feeble, flabby, frothy, slight, subtle; **7** fragile, slender, subtile, tenuous

flinch: 3 shy; blink, dodge, parry, quail, shirk, slink, start, wince; **6** blench, cringe, recoil, shrink, swerve, twinge, twitch, writhe; **7** shy from, squinch, wincing; **8** fight shy, turn tail; **9** back out of

flinders: 6 sliver; **8** splinter, fragment

fling: 2 go; **3** boo, shy; **4** bout, cast, gibe, hiss, hoot, jeer, jerk, pass, quip, shot, toss, wipe; **5** chuck, crack, flout, heave, offer, pitch, scoff, sneer, spree, taunt, throw, whirl; **7** cast out, discard, dispose, put away, splurge, toss out; **8** cast away, chuck out, throw out, toss away; **9** cast aside, discharge, throw away

fling overboard: 8 cast away, jettison, toss away; **9** fling away, throw away; **13** cast overboard, toss overboard

flint: 5 agate; **10** chalcedony

flint corn: 10 flint maize, Yankee corn

flintlock: 8 arquebus, firelock; **9** Brown Bess, matchlock; **10** harquebuss; **11** blunderbuss

flint maize: 9 flint corn; **10** Yankee corn; **15** Zea mays indurata

flinty: 5 stony; **8** granitic, obdurate; **10** unyielding

flip: 3 sky; **4** jerk, leaf, pass, purl, riff, toss; **5** flick, pitch, throw, thumb; **6** riffle, switch, twitch; **8** flip over, flip-flop, impudent, insolent, turn over; **9** alternate; **10** somersault

flip-flop: 4 flip; **6** switch; **8** reversal; **9** alternate, turnabout; **10** turnaround; **11** interchange; **12** change of mind

flippancy: 6 tongue; **7** flowing, fluency; **9** petulance; **10** volubility

flippant: 4 glib, pert; **5** fresh [U.S.], saucy; **6** fluent; **7** forward, voluble; **8** cavalier, malapert; **11** impertinent, light-minded

flipper: 3 fin; **4** fins; **8** flippers; **9** fish's tail

flirt: 3 toy; **4** mash, minx, play, vamp; **5** dally, spoon, tease; **6** chat up, coquet, fillip, toying, vamper; **7** romance; **8** coquetry, coquette, flirting; **9** dalliance, philander; **10** bill and coo, flirtation, propitiate

flit: 3 fly; **4** bolt, boom, dart, fade, slip, trot; **5** amble, bound, fleet, glide, shake, slide, troll; **6** gallop, levant, spring, totter, vanish; **7** flitter, flutter, shuffle, tremble; **8** flitting, pass away, take wing; **9** evaporate, migration, skedaddle, vacillate

flitch: 11 side of bacon

flitter: 4 flit, inch, seed; **5** crumb, patch, shake, waver; **6** bicker, quiver, tatter, totter; **7** flicker, flutter, fritter, shuffle, tremble; **9** scantling, vacillate

float: 4 blow, raft, swim; **5** drift, hover, plane, spire, surge; **7** pontoon; **8** be adrift; **9** be buoyant; **12** ice-cream soda, set on its legs; **13** ice-cream float

floating: 4 rife; **6** afloat; **7** aimless, buoyant, current, vagrant; **8** drifting, vagabond; **10** going about

floating bridge: 12 bateau bridge; **13** pontoon bridge

floating hotel: 10 cruise ship; **14** floating palace

floatplane: 12 pontoon plane

floaty: 7 buoyant

floc: 8 floccule

flocculent: 5 downy, dusty, wooly; **6** fluffy, woolly; **7** flaccid, velvety

flock: 3 fry, lot, pot, wad; **4** bevy, deal, fold, heap, herd, hive, mass, mess, mint, nest, peck, pile, raft, slew; **5** batch, brood, cloud, clump, covey, drove, laity, shoal, sight, spate, stack, swarm, troop; **6** bushel, farrow, flight, hatful, litter, mickle, muckle, people, plenty, scores; **7** cluster, draught, tidy sum; **8** assembly, brethren, good deal, whole lot; **9** great deal, whole slew; **11** constellate, pig together, the faithful; **12** congregation

flocked: 6 herded; **7** crowded; **8** thronged; **11** congregated; **12** concentrated

floe: 7 ice floe; **8** ice field

flog: 4 cane, comb, lash, lick, welt, whip; **5** birch, slash, strap, towel; **6** larrup, lather, switch, thrash, thresh; **7** lambast, scourge, trounce; **8** lambaste; **9** bastinado, horsewhip; **10** flagellate

flood: 4 high, rush, tide; **5** swamp; **6** deluge, drench; **7** torrent; **8** high tide, inundate, overflow; **9** cataclysm, flood lamp, surcharge; **10** floodlight, inundation, outpouring, oversupply, photoflood

flooded: 5 awash; **6** afloat; **7** swamped; **8** engulfed, overcome; **9** inundated; **11** overflowing, overpowered, overwhelmed

floodgate: 6 sluice; **8** head gate, penstock; **9** water gate; **10** sluicegate

flooding: 7 in flood, swollen; **11** overflowing; **16** implosion therapy

floodlight: 5 flood; **9** flood lamp; **10** photoflood

flood mark: 13 high water mark

flood out: 6 deluge; **9** overwhelm

flood plain: 10 bottomland

flood tide: 6 climax; **8** full tide, high tide; **9** high water; **10** rising tide

floor: 4 base, deck, dump, fell, flag, lick, stun; **5** earth, level, shock, story, worst; **6** carped, ground, paving, storey; **8** ball over, coldcock, flooring, pavement; **9** knock down, prostrate, take aback; **10** beat hollow, substratum; **11** ground floor; **12** substructure

floored: 6 struck; **13** struck with awe

floorshow: 7 cabaret

flop: 3 dud; **4** bust; **5** right; **7** flounce, founder, washout; **8** collapse, fall flat, flounder; **11** fall through

flopping: 4 flap; **7** flutter; **8** flapping; **10** fluttering

floppy: 8 diskette; **10** floppy disk; **11** floppy drive; **15** floppy disk drive

flora: 5 plant; **7** verdure; **9** plant life; **10** vegetation; **16** vegetable kingdom [pl]

floral: 8 flowered

Florence: 7 Firenze

floriculture: 9 floristry; **15** flower gardening

florid: 4 rich; **5** brave, buxom, flush, gaudy, hardy, ruddy, showy, tumid; **6** mouthy, ornate, robust, rufous, stanch, turgid;

7 aureate, flowery, orotund, staunch; **8** inflated, sanguine, sonorous, swelling, vigorous; **9** bombastic, grandiose, high flown; **10** flamboyant, ornamented, rhetorical, turgescent; **11** big-sounding, declamatory, high flowing, incarnadine

floridness: 7 bombast; **8** richness; **9** euphemism, showiness, turgidity; **10** orotundity; **11** declamation, flamboyance, grandiosity

florilegium: 7 garland; **9** anthology; **10** miscellany

florin: 6 gulden; **7** guilder

florist: 10 flower shop; **11** florist shop, flower store

florist's chrysanthemum: 3 mum

floss: 11 dental floss

flossy: 5 downy; **6** fluffy; **8** downlike

flotation device: 13 life preserver

flotilla: 5 fleet

flotsam: 6 jetsam

flounce: 3 bob, hem; **4** flop, gimp, list, welt; **5** frill, lapel, start; **6** bounce, edging, foot it, fringe, ruffle; **7** valance; **8** flounder, furbelow, selvedge, skirting, trimming

flounder: 4 flop, trip, vary; **5** shift, waver; **6** boggle, change, falter, fumble, totter; **7** blunder, flicker, flounce, stagger, stumble; **8** flatfish, hesitate, struggle; **9** fluctuate; **10** run aground

flour: 4 bran, meal; **6** farina

flourish: 4 boom, flap, fret, fuss, live, show, wave; **5** bandy, bloom, shake, strut, stump, wield; **6** expand, flaunt, hot dog, recite, thrive; **7** declaim, display, fanfare, glitter, lecture, prosper, show off; **8** brandish, get ahead, harangue; **9** arabesque, discourse, fligh high, gain honor, hold forth, sermonize, showiness, speechify; **10** be thriving, coquillage [Fr], fleur-de-lis [Fr], showing off

flourishing: 5 palmy; **7** booming, growing, roaring; **8** thriving; **10** prospering, prosperous

flout: 3 boo; **4** gibe, hiss, hoot, jeer, quip, wipe; **5** fling, scoff, scout, sneer, taunt; **7** barrack, scoff at

flow: 3 hum, run; **4** fall, flap, flux, hang, pass, purl, rain, teem; **5** trail; **6** abound, babble, course, elapse, gurgle, menses, period, ripple, stream; **7** advance, breathe, current, flowing, proceed; **8** flow rate; **9** catamenia, exuberate; **10** rate of flow, shower down

flow chart: 5 chart; **6** scheme; **7** drawing, graphic; **9** schematic; **11** flow diagram

flower: 2 A1; **4** peak, pick, pink, posy; **5** bloom, cream, elite, flush, pearl, prime; **6** fatten, heyday, wreath; **7** blossom, bouquet, chaplet, festoon, garland, nosegay; **8** fructify, nonesuch; **9** bear fruit, nonpareil; **11** masterpiece; **13** efflorescence

flower chain: 7 festoon; **10** daisy chain

flower child: 5 hippy; **6** hippie

flowered: 6 floral

flower gardening: 12 floriculture

flowering: 6 abloom; **8** anthesis; **9** unfolding; **10** blossoming

flowering plant: 10 angiosperm

flowerless: 9 bloomless

flower stalk: 5 scape

flowery: 3 gay; **4** rich; **5** smart, tumid; **6** bloomy, florid, mouthy, ornate, turgid; **7** orotund; **8** blossomy, inflated, sonorous, swelling; **9** bombastic, grandiose, high flown; **10** glittering, Johnsonian, ornamented, rhetorical, turgescent; **11** big-sounding, declamatory, high flowing; **12** high-sounding, magniloquent

flowing: 4 easy, flow; **5** fluid, loose; **6** fluent, liquid, smooth, tongue; **7** fluency, natural, passing, purling, running; **8** artesian, elapsing, graceful, readable, tripping; **9** flippancy, streaming

flowing bowl: 8 rosy wine

flow off: 5 drain; **8** flow away

flow of electricity: 7 current; **12** electric flow; **15** electric current

flow out: 4 gush, ooze; **5** spout; **6** effuse; **7** dribble

flow over: 5 swash; **6** deluge, splash, stream; **7** overrun, run over; **8** brim over, inundate, overflow, well over

flu: 4 grip; **6** grippe; **9** influenza

flub: 4 blow, muff; **5** boner, botch, fluff, spoil; **6** ball up, bobble, bollix, boo-boo, bungle, foul up, foul-up, fumble, mess up, muck up; **7** blooper, blunder, botch up, louse up, screw up; **8** misdoing; **9** mishandle

fluctuate: 4 trim, vary; **5** demur, pause, shift, waver; **6** change, coquet, debate, waffle; **7** balance, flicker, shuffle; **8** flounder, straddle; **9** hem and haw, hum and haw, vacillate

flue: 5 fluke, shaft; **7** chimney; **8** flue pipe

fluegelhorn: 10 flugelhorn

fluency: 6 tongue; **7** flowing; **9** eloquence, flippancy; **10** volubility; **14** articulateness

fluent: 4 easy, glib; **5** fluid; **6** facile, liquid, silver, smooth; **7** flowing, natural, voluble; **8** eloquent, flippant, graceful, integral, readable, tripping; **10** unaffected, articulate; **12** differential, smooth-spoken

fluff: 4 blow, flub, muff; **5** botch, spoil, tease; **6** ball up, bobble, bollix, bungle, foul up, umble, mess up, muck up, ruffle; **7** blunder, botch up, louse up, screw up; **8** bollix up, bollocks, frippery; **9** bagatelle, frivolity, mishandle; **10** bollocks up

fluffy: 5 downy; 6 flossy, woolly; 7 velvety; 8 downlike; 10 flocculent

flugelhorn: 5 bugle; 7 trumpet; 11 fluegelhorn

fluid: 5 runny; 6 fluent, liquid, mobile, smooth; 7 flowing; 8 unstable

fluid dram: 6 drachm; 8 fluidram; 11 fluid drachm

fluid drive: 14 hydraulic power

fluid dynamics: 10 pneumatics

fluidity: 9 fluidness, liquidity, runniness; 10 fluid state, liquidness

fluid mechanics: 10 hydraulics

fluidness: 8 fluidity; 9 liquidity, runniness; 10 liquidness

fluke: 4 flue; 5 crane; 6 akimbo, crutch, scythe, sickle, zigzag; 7 potluck; 8 accident, good luck; 9 trematode

fluky: 4 iffy; 6 chancy, flukey

flume: 5 gulch

flummery: 4 rant; 7 bombast, fustian, incense, mummery, palaver; 9 baverdage, rigmarole; 10 balderdash

flummox: 3 get; 4 beat; 5 amaze; 6 baffle, gravel, puzzle; 7 confuse, mystify, nonplus, perplex, stupefy, stupify, trounce; 8 bewilder; 9 dumbfound

flump: 4 plop; 5 plank, plonk, plump, plunk; 9 flump down, plump down, plunk down

flunk: 4 bomb, fail; 7 flush it

flunky: 4 toad, tool; 5 dweeb, toady; 6 lackey, menial, stooge, sucker, yes-man; 7 flunkey, footman, sponger; 8 courtier, hanger on, parasite, truckler; 9 doughface [U.S.], sycophant, toad-eater; 10 bootlicker, smell-feast, timeserver

fluor: 8 fluorite; 9 fluorspar

fluoridate: 10 fluoridize

fluoridation: 14 fluoridization

fluorine: 1 F

fluoroapatite: 7 apatite; 14 asparagus-stone

fluoxetine: 6 Prozac

flurbiprofen: 6 Ansaid

flurry: 3 ado; 4 fuss, stir, to-do; 5 drive, hurry; 6 bother, bustle, fidget, hustle, put off, quiver, ruffle, tremor; 7 confuse, fluster, flutter, heaving, twitter; 8 scramble, splutter; 9 pottering; 10 disconcert, snow flurry

flush: 3 dye, hue; 4 bang, bask, buff, cast, even, flat, glow, gush, heat, kick, pant, peak, rush, tint; 5 bloom, blush, brave, buxom, color, fever, hardy, plane, prime, rinse, scour, shade, swash, sweat, tinge, woozy; 6 buzzed, charge, florid, flower, heyday, livery, loaded, mantle, mellow, redden, robust, sluice, stanch, thrill; 7 blossom, burnish, color up, crimson, discoid, flushed, furbish, moneyed, passion, redness, staunch, swelter, turn red,

wealthy; 8 affluent, blush for, rosiness, tincture, vigorous; 9 flesh tint, suffusion; 10 coloration, excitement, flesh color

flushed: 3 hot, red; 4 high, rosy, vain; 5 blown, flush, lofty, woozy; 6 aflame, buzzed, elated, mellow, mighty, red-hot; 7 buoyant, crimson, haughty, pleased, swollen; 8 blooming, blushing, buoyed up, exultant, exulting, feverish, inflated, jubilant, puffed up, red-faced, reddened; 9 conceited, delighted, high-flown, overblown; 11 in good heart, overweening, rosecheeked, rosy-cheeked, tickled pink

flush it: 4 bomb, fail; 5 flunk

fluster: 4 fuss; 5 hurry; 6 dazzle, flurry, muddle, put out, quiver, ruffle, tremor; 7 agitate, confuse, flutter, heaving, perplex, perturb, twitter; 8 bewilder; 12 perturbation

flustered: 7 fuddled, rattled; 8 overcome; 9 disguised, overtaken, perturbed

flute: 4 fife, plow; 5 plait, pleat; 7 fluting, piccolo; 8 recorder; 9 flageolet; 10 fipple pipe, flute glass; 11 fipple flute

fluted: 6 folded, rutted; 7 grooved, pleated, plicate; 8 furrowed

flute glass: 5 flute; 14 champagne flute

flute player: 7 flutist; 8 flautist

fluting: 5 flute; 7 chamfer; 8 twilling

flutist: 8 flautist; 11 flute player

flutter: 3 bat; 4 dart, flap, flit, fuss, pant; 5 drive, fleet, heave, hurry, shake, throb, waver; 6 bicker, bustle, flurry, quiver, ruffle, thrill, tingle, totter, tremor; 7 ague fit, flicker, flitter, fluster, heaving, shaking, shudder, shuffle, tremble, twitter; 8 bundle on, flapping, flopping, scramble, splutter; 9 cold sweat, go pitapat, palpitate, quivering, trembling, vacillate; 11 barrel along, palpitation, trepidation

fluttering: 4 flap; 6 aflare, flying, waving; 7 flaring, flutter, varying; 8 changing, flapping, flopping; 9 palpitant, trembling; 10 flittering; 11 fluctuating, palpitating, vacillating

flux: 3 run; 4 flow; 5 lapse; 6 acourse, growth, stream; 7 fluxion; 8 infusion, progress

fluxion: 4 flux; 6 fluent; 8 integral; 12 differential

fly: 2 go; 4 fade, fell, flee, flit, skim, tear, wing, zoom; 5 brush, burst, flare, flash, fly by, go off, pilot, shoot, sweep, whisk; 6 aviate, blow up, bounce, gallop, spring, swoosh, vanish; 7 cut away, explode, fly ball, give way, growler, tent-fly, thunder; 8 detonate, fly front, fly sheet, pass away, run a race, tent flap

flyblown: 6 sordid; 7 damaged, maggoty, spotted, squalid, stained, sullied, tainted; 9 tarnished; 10 besmirched

fly-by-night: 5 shady

flyer: 4 bill; 5 flier, pilot; 6 airman; 7 aviator; 8 aeronaut, circular, handbill; 9 broadside, throwaway; 10 broadsheet

flying: 4 fast; 5 quick; 6 aflare, fading, flight, waving; 7 flaring; 8 aviation; 9 galloping, vanishing; 10 fast-flying, fluttering

flying bird: 8 carinate; 12 carinate bird

flying bomb: 8 buzz bomb; 9 doodlebug, robot bomb

flying carpet: 11 magic carpet

flying drainpipe: 6 ramjet; 7 athodyd; 10 atherodyde; 12 ramjet engine

flying field: 5 field; 8 airfield; 12 landing field

flying horse: 7 Pegasus

flying reptile: 9 pterosaur

flying saucer: 3 UFO

flyleaf: 7 episode; 8 endpaper

fly off the handle: 4 foam, fume, rage, roar; 5 go ape, go off; 6 fly off; 7 bluster; 8 get angry, get upset; 9 go bananas; 10 get riled up, hit the roof; 11 become angry, blow one's top, flip one's lid, go ballistic

flyover: 7 flypast; 8 overpass

fly sheet: 3 fly; 7 tent-fly; 8 tent flap

flyway: 14 migration route

Fm: 7 fermium

FNMA: 8 Fanny Mae; 9 Fannie Mae

f number: 5 speed; 10 focal ratio, stop number

fo'c'sle: 10 forecastle

foal: 4 colt

foam: 4 boil, fizz, fume, head, rage, rant, rave, roar, suds, tear; 5 flame, froth, go ape, spume, storm; 6 lather, seethe, simmer; 7 bluster, ferment, sparkle; 9 go bananas; 10 effervesce, hit the roof

foaming: 5 foamy, livid, rabid, spumy, sudsy; 6 bubbly, frothy, fuming, raging; 7 in a rage, rageful, spumous; 8 bubbling, choleric, frothing; 9 in a choler, splenetic; 12 effervescing

foaming at the mouth: 5 livid, rabid; 6 fuming, raging; 7 foaming, in a rage, rageful

foamy: 5 cushy, plush, spumy, sudsy; 6 bubbly, frothy; 7 foaming, spumous; 8 bubbling, frothing; 12 effervescing

fob: 3 fox, net; 4 knit, poke; 5 pouch, scrip, trick; 6 budget, pocket, sachel, sheath, socket; 7 satchel; 8 reticule, scabbard; 10 watch chain, watch guard; 11 watch pocket

focalization: 8 focusing

focal point: 5 focus

focal ratio: 5 speed; 7 f number; 10 stop number

focus: 4 pore; 5 nidus, rivet; 6 center, stress; 7 sharpen; 8 focusing; 9 centering, concenter, focussing, sharpness; 10 focal point; 11 concentrate

focusing knob: 6 barrel; 8 eyepiece, platform; 13 objective lens

fodder: 4 feed; 10 animal food

foe: 5 enemy; 6 foeman; 8 opponent; 10 opposition

foehn: 4 wind

Foeniculum: 6 fennel; 15 genus Foeniculum

foetid: fetid

foetus: 5 fetus

fog: 4 daze, haze, mist, murk; 5 befog, cloud, vapor; 7 becloud, obscure; 8 haze over; 9 murkiness

fogey: 4 dodo, fogy; 6 dotard, fossil; 8 old fogey

fogginess: 3 fog; 4 murk; 9 fuzziness, murkiness; 10 blurriness; 14 indistinctness

foggy: 4 hazy, logy; 5 dazed, fuzzy, misty, muzzy; 6 bleary, blurry, cloudy, fogged, groggy; 7 blurred, brumous; 8 vaporous; 9 stuporous

Foggy Bottom: 7 Potomac

foghorn: 7 fog bell

foible: 9 mannerism; 12 idiosyncrasy

foie gras: 10 goose liver

foil: 4 balk, bilk, leaf; 5 cross, sheet, spoil; 6 baffle, scotch, thwart; 8 overhead; 9 frustrate; 10 disconcert

foiled: 8 defeated, thwarted; 10 frustrated; 11 discomfited; 12 disappointed

foin: 4 prod; 5 lunge; 6 thrust

foist upon: 7 put upon; 8 palm upon, play upon; 9 palm off on; 10 impose upon

folate: 7 folacin; 8 vitamin M; 9 folic acid, vitamin Bc; 19 pteroylglutamic acid; 23 pteroylmonoglutamic acid

fold: 3 pen, ply; 4 bend; 5 close, crimp, flock, laity, pen up, plait, pleat, plica; 6 crease, double, fold up, people, turn up; 7 flexure, folding; 8 assembly, brethren, faithful, sheep pen, shut down; 9 close down, plication, sheepcote, sheepfold; 10 double over; 11 the faithful; 12 congregation

folded: 6 fluted; 7 pleated, plicate

folder: 7 booklet, leaflet; 8 brochure, pamphlet

folderol: 5 trash, tripe; 6 frills, trifle; 7 rubbish; 8 falderal, nonsense, trumpery, wishwash

folding door: 13 accordion door

fold up: 4 fold; 5 lap up; 6 turn up, wrap up; 8 muffle up

foliage: 4 leaf; 7 leafage; 9 foliation

folic acid: 6 folate; 7 folacin; 8 vitamin M; 9 vitamin Bc

folio: 4 leaf; 6 octavo, quarto; 10 page number, pagination

folk: 5 tribe, world; 6 family; 7 country, kinfolk, phratry, society, western; 8 kinsfolk; 9 community, folk music, hillbilly; 10 family line; 11 ethnic music; 12 common people

folk dance: 11 folk dancing; **12** country dance

folk music: 4 folk; **11** ethnic music

folk singer: 8 jongleur, minstrel; **10** poet-singer, troubadour

folksy: 8 homespun; **13** cracker-barrel

follicle: 4 dent, dint; **5** sinus; **6** dimple, lacuna; **11** indentation; **12** hair follicle

follow: 2 be; **3** get, see; **4** come, take, work; **5** adopt, catch, ensue, grasp, trace, watch; **6** comply, keep up, master, pursue, survey, take in; **7** abide by, be after, collect, espouse, make out, observe, stick to, succeed; **8** adhere to, postdate; **9** accompany, come after, conform to, hunt after, make after, stick with, take after, watch over; **10** prowl after, see one's way; **11** keep abreast, keep an eye on, see daylight, travel along

follow around: 5 trail

follower: 4 beau; **5** swain, wooer; **6** amoret, suitor; **7** apostle; **8** disciple, henchman, young man; **9** attendant, inamorato, proselyte; **10** sweetheart

following: 4 next; **5** after, chase, later; **7** ensuing, pursuit; **9** deducible, followers, posterior; **10** subsequent, succeeding, succession; **11** coming after, coming later, inferential; **13** consequential, postliminious

follow through: 8 carry out; **9** go through, implement; **10** put through

follow-up: 6 review; **13** reexamination

folly: 4 hall; **5** court, tower; **6** betise, castle; **7** chateau, conceit, foolery, rotunda; **8** pavilion, trifling; **9** craziness, frivolity, lip wisdom, stupidity; **10** imbecility, indulgence, manor-house, tomfoolery, unwiseness; **11** foolishness

foment: 4 heat, lash, warm; **5** set on, speed; **6** excite, foster, hasten, incite, kindle, stir up, turn on; **7** actuate, agitate, animate, inflame, provoke, quicken, sharpen; **8** expedite, poultice; **9** instigate, stimulate

fomentation: 8 mounting; **11** instigation

fond: 4 warm; **6** ardent, caring, doting, tender; **7** adoring, devoted, partial; **8** lovesome, motherly, uxorious; **9** rapturous; **10** passionate; **12** affectionate

fondle: 3 pet; **6** caress, dandle, stroke; **7** cherish

fondling: 7 hugging, kissing, necking, petting; **8** cuddling, sparking, sporting; **9** caressing, dalliance, making out, smooching, snuggling; **10** hanky-panky

fondness: 4 love; **5** fancy, heart; **6** liking, relish, warmth; **9** affection; **10** lovingness, partiality, tenderness

fondue: 5 fondu

font: 4 face, well; **5** fount; **6** spring; **8** fountain, typeface; **9** baptistry; **10** baptistery, wellspring

fontanel: 8 soft spot; **10** fontanelle

food: 4 grub; **7** aliment, edibles, ingesta, pabulum; **8** eatables, nutrient, victuals; **9** nutriment, provender; **10** sustenance; **11** comestibles, nourishment, staff of life; **12** alimentation, sustentation

Food and Agriculture Organization of the United Nations: 3 FAO

food animal: 9 livestock [pl]

food elevator: 10 dumbwaiter

food grain: 5 grain; **6** cereal

food poisoning: 8 ptomaine; **10** salmonella

food product: 9 foodstuff

food shop: 4 deli; **12** delicatessen

foodstuff: 7 grocery; **11** food product

food waste: 6 refuse, scraps; **7** garbage

fool: 3 cod, mug, sap; **4** dopy, dupe, fish, gull, hoax, jerk, mark, zany; **5** chump, dopey, goofy, goosy, patsy, put on, sappy, shoot, silly, slang, trick, wacky; **6** donkey, goosey, jester, sucker, take in; **7** fall guy, foolish, fritter, gudgeon, muggins, saphead, tomfool; **8** anserine, fool away, shlemiel; **9** bamboozle, cockamamy, dissipate, gooselike, schlemiel, soft touch; cockamamie, fool around, frivol away, nincompoop, put one over

fool's cap: 8 dunce cap; **9** dunce's cap

fool's gold: 6 pyrite; **10** iron pyrite

fool around: 3 kid; **4** fool; **9** kid around; **10** play around; **11** horse around, play the fool; **12** monkey around

foolhardy: 4 rash; **8** reckless

fooling: 5 farce; **6** casual; **10** buffoonery, tomfoolery

foolish: 4 dopy, dumb, fool, wild; **5** dopey, goosy, inept, silly; **6** goosey, stupid, unwise; **7** asinine, blatant, fatuous, idiotic; **8** anserine, babbling, imbecile, improper; **9** driveling, gooselike, ill-judged, insensate, senseless; **10** ill-advised, ill-devised, irrational; **11** ill-imagined, injudicious, nonsensical; **12** misconducted, unreasonable

foolproof: 9 goofproof, unfailing

foot: 2 ft; **3** ell; **4** base, hand, hoof, inch, line, mile, nail, palm, pick, pole, rood, yard; **5** cubit, leg it, nadir; **6** bottom, fathom, hoof it, league; **7** furlong; **8** infantry; **9** fundament, human foot; **10** animal foot, foundation, groundwork; **12** metrical foot, metrical unit, substructure

football: 7 pigskin

footballer: 12 soccer player; **14** football player

football field: 8 gridiron

football player: 10 footballer; **12** soccer player

football team: 6 eleven

foot doctor: 10 podiatrist; **11** chiropodist

footer: 6 walker; **10** pedestrian

footgear: 8 footwear

foothold: 7 footing; 9 beachhead; 10 bridge-head

footing: 3 fee; 4 post; 5 basis, range, terms; 6 ground, regime, status; 7 garnish; 8 foothold, standing; 10 ground work, stand-point

foot-lambert: 3 ft-L

footle: 4 loaf, lurk; 5 tarry; 6 linger, loiter, lounge; 8 lallygag, lollygag; 9 mess about, mill about

foot lever: 5 pedal; 7 treadle

footlights: 6 floats; 9 footlight

footling: 5 petty; 6 little; 7 trivial; 8 fiddling, niggling, picayune, piddling, piffling; 11 lilliputian

footmark: 4 step; 8 footstep; 9 footprint

footnote: 8 annotate

footpad: 10 highwayman

foot passenger: 6 walker; 10 pedestrian

footpath: 4 walk; 5 flags; 7 pathway; 8 pavement, sidewalk

foot pavement: 8 sidewalk

footprint: 4 step; 8 footstep

footrest: 7 ottoman; 9 footstool

footslog: 3 pad; 4 plod, slog; 6 trudge

footslogger: 7 marcher; 11 foot soldier, infantryman

foot soldier: 7 marcher; 8 rifleman; 11 footslogger, infantryman

footsore: 7 wayworn

footstep: 4 pace, step; 6 stride; 9 footprint

footstool: 7 hassock, ottoman; 8 footrest

footwear: 8 footgear

fop: 4 beau, dude; 5 dandy, swell; 7 gallant; 12 clotheshorse, fashion plate

foppery: 8 dandyism, equipage, frippery, puppyism; 9 ball dress, coxcombry, full dress, vainglory; 10 court dress, fancy dress; 11 foppishness

foppish: 8 dandyish; 9 dandified; 10 coxcomical

for: 5 for as, since; 7 against, because, whereas, whither; 10 inasmuch as, on behalf of, seeing that; 11 considering

forage: 5 cater, grass; 6 eatage, maraud, purvey; 7 pasture, victual; 8 foraging, scrounge; 9 pasturage, provision; 10 filibuster

foram: 11 foraminifer

Foraminifera: 17 order Foraminifera

foray: 4 loot, raid; 5 reave, rifle, strip; 7 despoil, pillage, plunder, ransack; 10 brigandage; 11 depredation

forbear: 5 relax, spare, waive; 6 relent; 7 abstain, neglect, refrain; 8 hold back, ancestor, forbears [pl], forebear, let alone, not touch, swear off; 9 do without; 11 deny oneself, forefathers [pl], give quarter; 12 dispense with

forbearance: 5 mercy; 7 abiding, quarter; 8 abidance, clemency, enduring, humanity, inaction, not doing, patience, yearning; 9 endurance, eschewing, not acting, suffering, tolerance; 10 abnegation, abstention, abstinence, forbearing, indulgence, refraining, self-denial, sufferance, tenderness, tolerating; 11 longanimity, passiveness; 12 failure to act

forbearing: 8 inaction, not doing; 9 eschewing, not acting; 10 abstention, abstinence, refraining; 11 forbearance, longanimous, passiveness

forbid: 3 ban, bar; 4 veto; 5 taboo; 6 enjoin, outlaw; 7 prevent; 8 disallow, forefend, preclude, prohibit; 9 foreclose, forestall, interdict, proscribe

forbidden: 3 out; 4 tabu; 5 taboo; 6 banned, barred; 7 tabooed; 8 enjoined, outlawed; 10 disallowed, not allowed, prohibited, proscribed; 12 not permitted

Forbidden City: 5 Lassa, Lhasa; 14 capital of Tibet

forbidding: 3 ban; 4 dour, grim, ugly; 6 odious; 7 baleful, banning, hideous, ominous, uncanny; 8 menacing, minatory, sinister; 9 enjoining, frightful, minacious, monstrous; 11 forbiddance, prohibiting, proscribing, threatening

force: 3 ram, run; 4 draw, fake, make, pull, push; 5 drive, hatch, impel, might, power, storm, vigor, wedge; 6 acting, action, agency, coerce, compel, effect, energy, import, oblige, thrust; 8 concoct, content, enforce, meaning, message, purport, squeeze, working; 8 function, pressure, strength, violence; 9 constrain, intensity, operation, personnel, puissance, substance; 10 inner force; 11 necessitate, strong point

force back: 5 drive, repel; 7 repulse; 8 beat back, push back

forced: 6 remote; 7 coerced, labored; 8 required, strained; 9 compelled, ponderous; 10 compulsory, far-fetched, obligatory, unexpected; 11 constrained, involuntary, out of the way

forced hot air: 14 central heating

force feed: 12 pressure feed

forceful: 8 emphatic

force majeure: 8 act of God, vis major; 18 inevitable accident

forcemeat: 5 farce

force of argument: 11 strong point

force open: 7 pry open; 9 break open, prize open

force out: 3 can; 4 fire, sack; 5 eject, evict, gouge, rouse; 6 depose, squirt; 7 dismiss, rout out; 8 displace, drive out, send away; 9 terminate; 10 give notice, give the axe, squeeze out

forceps: 5 tongs; 6 pliers; 7 nippers, pincers; 8 clutches, vise grip

forcible: 4 hard; 5 hardy, stout, valid;

6 active, mighty, potent, robust, strong, sturdy; **7** intense, nervous; **8** incisive, physical, powerful, puissant, vigorous; **9** energetic, strong-arm, trenchant; **10** adamantine, impressive; **18** not to be trifled with

forcible entry: 9 forcing in; **7** break-in; **11** forcing into

forcibly: 7 by force; **8** perforce; **12** by compulsion, compulsorily, on compulsion; **13** involuntarily; **15** under

Ford: 9 Henry Ford; **10** Gerald Ford; **12** Gerald R. Ford; **17** Gerald Rudolph Ford

ford: 5 cross; **7** fording; **8** crossing

fore: 3 bow; **4** prow, stem; **5** front; **7** forward, frontal; **8** anterior, frontage; **12** forepart-face

forebear: 7 forbear, refrain

forebode: 4 bode, call; **5** augur; **6** typify; **7** betoken, point to, portend, predict, presage, promise, signify; **8** foretell; **9** foretoken, prefigure; **10** anticipate, foreshadow; **11** shadow forth

foreboding: 6 boding; **7** fateful; **9** ill-boding, ill-omened; **10** portentous; **11** premonition

forecast: 4 bode, omen; **5** augur; **6** figure, reckon, sketch; **7** betoken, count on, portend, predict, presage, project; **8** estimate, foreknow, foretell; **9** auspicate, calculate, forejudge, prefigure, prognosis; **10** foreshadow, prediction; **11** foretelling; **12** announcement; **13** prognosticate

forecaster: 9 predictor; **10** soothsayer; **14** prognosticator

forecastle: 6 fo'c'sle

foreclose: 3 let; **5** check, debar; **6** forbid; **7** draw off, prevent; **8** forefend, preclude; **9** forestall, turn aside; **11** nip in the bud

foredoom: 4 doom; **6** devote; **7** destine; **8** election, fatality

forefather: 4 sire; **6** father; **7** forbear; **8** ancestor

forefend: 7 forfend

forefinger: 5 index; **11** index finger

forefront: 4 head; **8** vanguard; **11** cutting edge

foregather: 9 forgather

forego: 4 drop, shed; **5** spare; **6** abjure, resign; **7** precede, predate, retract; **8** abnegate, antecede, antedate, disclaim, give away, part with, renounce; **9** dispose of

foregoing: 6 former

foregone: 4 gone, over, past; **6** bygone, bypast, gone by; **8** departed; **10** passed away; **13** predetermined

foreground: 6 play up; **9** highlight, spotlight

forehand stroke: 8 forehand; **12** forehand shot

forehead: 4 brow; **6** visage; **8** foremost; **10** os frontale; **11** countenance, frontal bone, physiognomy

foreign: 5 alien; **6** exotic; **7** strange; **9** extrinsic; **10** extraneous

foreign body: 14 foreign element

foreign-born: 9 nonnative

foreigner: 5 alien; **8** outsider; **9** outlander; **10** noncitizen

foreign mission: 7 embassy, mission; **8** legation

forejudge: 8 forecast, foreknow, prejudge

foreknow: 7 foresee; **8** forecast; **9** forejudge; **10** anticipate

foreknowledge: 12 precognition

foreland: 8 headland; **10** promontory

forelimb: 3 arm

foreman: 4 boss; **5** chief; **6** gaffer, honcho

foremost: 3 top; **4** main; **5** chief, first, prime; **6** utmost; **7** capital, firstly, leading, primary, supreme; **8** first off, forehead, greatest; **9** frontmost, matchless, paramount, principal; **10** first of all, overruling, preeminent; **13** most important

forename: 9 first name, given name

forenoon: 2 A.M. [abbr], **4** morn; **5** prime; **7** morning; **11** morning time; **12** ante meridien [Lat]

foreordain: 9 preordain; **10** predestine; **12** predestinate

foreordained: 5 fated; **8** destined; **11** predestined, preordained; **12** predestinate

forepart: 5 front; **8** front end

foreplay: 7 arousal; **11** stimulation

forerun: 7 precede; **9** forestall; **10** anticipate

forerunner: 6 herald; **9** harbinger, precursor; **10** antecedent

foresee: 7 counter; **8** envision, foreknow; **9** forestall; **10** anticipate

foreseen: 8 foretold; **9** predicted; **12** long expected

foreshadow: 4 bode, omen; **5** augur; **6** typify; **7** betoken, point to, portend, predict, presage, signify; **8** forebode, forecast, foretell; **9** auspicate, foretoken, prefigure; **11** shadow forth; **13** prognosticate

foreshorten: 3 cut; **6** reduce; **7** abridge, shorten; **8** contract; **10** abbreviate

foresight: 9 prevision; **10** prediction; **12** anticipation

foresighted: 4 long; **9** farseeing; **10** farsighted; **11** longsighted

foreskin: 7 prepuce

forest: 4 wood; **5** woods; **6** timber; **8** afforest, woodland; **10** timberland

forestage: 10 proscenium

forestall: 6 forbid; **7** counter, foresee, prevent; **8** keep time, preclude; **9** foreclose; **10** anticipate

forester: 8 woodsman; **10** tree farmer, lumberjack, woodcutter; **12** backwoodsman

forest fire fighter: 6 ranger; **10** fire warden

forest god: 5 satyr

foreswear: 4 quit; 5 forgo, waive; 8 renounce; 10 relinquish; 12 dispense with

foretell: 4 bode, call, omen; 5 augur; 6 herald; 7 betoken, portend, predict, presage, promise; 8 announce, forebode, forecast; 9 auspicate, harbinger, prefigure; 10 annunciate, anticipate, foreshadow; 13 prognosticate

foretelling: 8 forecast; 9 prognosis; 10 divination, prediction; 11 forecasting, soothsaying; 12 announcement; 14 fortune telling

forethought: 4 care; 7 caution; 10 precaution; 13 premeditation

foretoken: 4 bode; 5 augur; 6 typify; 7 betoken, point to, portend, presage, signify; 8 forebode; 9 prefigure; 10 foreshadow; 11 shadow forth

foretold: 8 foreseen; 9 predicted

forever: 6 always; 8 eternity, evermore, infinity; 9 eternally; 13 everlastingly

forewarn: 4 warn; 7 caution; 8 admonish; 11 give warning

forewarning: 11 premonition

forewoman: 8 forelady

foreword: 5 proem; 6 prefix; 7 preface, prelude; 8 preamble, prologue; 9 prolepsis [Gram]; 11 avant-propos [Fr], prolegomena; 12 introduction

for example: 2 e.g., i.e. [abbr]; 3 viz. [abbr]; 5 id est; 6 namely; 9 videlicet; 11 for instance, that is to say; 13 exempli gratia [Lat]

forfeit: 5 be off, forgo, waive; 6 give up, palter, render; 7 retract; 9 forfeited, sacrifice; 10 confiscate, forfeiture, go back from

forfend: 4 fend; 5 guard; 6 defend, shield; 7 protect, prevent; 8 preserve

for form's sake: 8 pro forma [Lat]; 9 by the card

for free: 6 gratis; 12 free of charge

forgather: 3 see; 4 meet; 6 gather; 7 run into; 8 assemble; 9 encounter, run across; 10 come across, foregather

forge: 4 fake, form, mold; 5 mould, shape, spirt, spurt; 6 devise, hammer, invent, smithy; 7 fashion; 8 contrive; 9 formulate; 10 excogitate; 11 counterfeit; 12 fiery furnace

forged: 3 bad; 8 fabulous, invented; 9 unfounded; 10 fabricated

forger: 6 coiner, smithy, Vulcan; 10 blacksmith; 13 counterfeiter

forgery: 4 fake, sham; 5 fraud, phony; 7 fiction; 9 imitation, invention; 11 counterfeit, fabrication, make-believe

forget: 4 bury; 5 block, leave; 8 blank out, overlook; 10 draw a blank; 11 be forgetful

forgetful: 8 mindless; 9 oblivious, unmindful; 11 unretentive

forgetful person: 12 scatterbrain

forging ahead: 8 progress; 9 advancing; 10 going ahead, proceeding; 11 coming ahead, moving ahead, progressing, progression; 12 going forward; 13 forward motion, motion forward, moving forward

forgivable: 6 venial; 9 excusable

forgivably: 9 excusably; 10 pardonably

forgive: 6 pardon, excuse; 10 shake hands

forgive and forget: 6 pardon, excuse; 7 forgive; 10 shake hands

forgiven: 7 excused; 8 pardoned; 9 unavenged

forgiveness: 5 grace; 6 pardon; 10 absolution; 11 condonation

forgiving: 8 placable; 11 absolvitory, exonerative; 12 conciliatory

forgo: 5 waive; 6 give up, render; 7 forfeit; 9 foreswear; 10 relinquish; 12 dispense with

forgoing: 11 forswearing; 12 renunciation

forgotten: 4 lost; 6 lapsed, no more, run out; 7 elapsed, expired, extinct, has-been; 8 exploded; 9 blown over; 10 antebellum; 11 disregarded, that has been; 12 antediluvian

for hire: 4 free; 6 on hire; 10 disengaged

for inasmuch as: 3 for; 5 for as, since; 7 because, whereas; 10 ex concesso [Lat], inasmuch as, seeing that; 11 considering

for instance: 2 e.g.; 10 for example

fork: 3 leg; 4 bend; 5 prong; 6 branch, crotch, ramify; 7 crinkle, forking; 8 separate; 9 bifurcate, branching, pitchfork; 11 bifurcation

forked: 6 double, prongy, zigzag; 7 pronged; 8 biramous, branched; 9 bifurcate

forking: 4 fork; 9 branching, furcation; 11 bifurcation; 12 divarication, ramification

fork out: 6 lay out; 7 cough up, deal out, dole out, give out, mete out; 8 fork over, shell out; 10 squeeze out

fork over: 6 lay out; 7 cough up, fork out; 8 shell out

for lease: 5 to let; 7 for rent

forlorn: 4 gone, lorn; 6 desole [Fr]; 8 deserted, desolate, hopeless; 9 abandoned, desperate, in despair, unpeopled; 10 despairing, tenantless, untenanted; 11 au desespoir [Fr], comfortless, godforsaken, sick at heart, uninhabited; 12 disconsolate, inconsolable, unconsolable

form: 3 bod, cut, var.; 4 cast, copy, gait, kind, make, mold, rule, soma, sort, tone; 5 blank, build, class, flesh, forge, frame, grace, grade, guise, mould, place, shape; 6 draw up, effigy, fall in, figure, remove, spring, strain; 7 anatomy, chassis, compose, contour, decorum, dispose, fashion, formula, imprint, manakin, manikin, pattern, replica, seminar, variant, variety; 8 effigies, elegance, good form, likeness, mannikin, organize, physique, revision, take form, word form; **9** construct, etiquette, expansion, extension, facsimile, formalism, formality, formulary, gentility, human body, imitation, mannequin, propriety, take shape, variation; **10** bienseance [Fr], constitute, derivation, derivative, regulation, solid shape; **11** counterpart, pulchritude; **12** modification, physical body; **13** configuration

formable: 7 ductile, plastic; **8** shapable, workable; **9** extensile, malleable, shapeable

formal: 3 dry; **5** modal, stiff; **6** solemn; **7** courtly, elegant, starchy, stately; **8** dogmatic, rigorous; **9** confident, schematic, trenchant; **11** conditional, formalistic, well-defined; **12** conventional

formaldehyde: 8 methanal

formalin: 6 formol

form a line: 6 fall in

formality: 4 form; **7** decorum, formula; **8** good form; **9** etiquette, formalism, gentility, propriety, punctilio; **10** bienseance [Fr], formalness; **11** formalities

formalize: 8 validate

formally: 7 modally, stiffly; **8** solemnly; **10** officially

formal speech: 6 speech; **7** address, lecture, oration, oratory; **10** allocution

formalwear: 11 eveningwear; **12** evening dress; **14** evening clothes

form an estimate: 4 rate; **5** value; **6** assess, review; **8** appraise, estimate, evaluate; **10** appreciate; **11** set a value on

format: 7 arrange; **10** data format, formatting, initialize

formation: 3 cut, set; **4** make; **6** making; **7** forming, geology, shaping; **8** creating, creation; **9** producing; **10** fashioning, figuration, generation, production; **12** constitution, construction, organisation, organization; **13** bringing forth, establishment

formative: 6 making; **7** forming, genetic, shaping; **8** creating; **9** producing; **10** generating, generative, inchoative

formative cell: 13 embryonic cell

formative notion: 8 paradigm; **9** archetype

formatting: 6 format; **10** data format

formed: 4 cast, made; **6** molded, shaped; **7** created, defined, figured, settled; **8** affected, produced; **9** conceived, fashioned, generated

former: 4 late, once; **5** early, other; **7** one-time, quondam; **8** previous, pristine, sometime; **9** erstwhile, foregoing

formerly: 4 once; **9** at one time

Formica: 12 genus Formica

Formicarius: 3 ant; **16** genus Formicarius

formidability: 8 hardness; **9** toughness; **10** difficulty

formidable: 7 arduous, onerous; **9** Herculean, laborious, unnerving; **11** redoubtable

forming: 6 making; **7** genetic, molding, shaping; **8** creating, creation; **9** formation, formative, producing; **10** fashioning, generating, generation, generative, production; **12** productive of; **13** bringing forth

formless: 9 amorphous, shapeless

form of address: 5 title

form of life: 8 organism; **11** living being, living thing

Formosa: 5 China; **6** Taiwan; **15** Republic of China; **16** Nationalist China

formula: 4 form, rule; **6** normal, recipe; **7** pattern; **9** formality, formulary; **10** convention, expression; **15** chemical formula

formularize: 10 formulaize

formulary: 4 form; **7** formula; **13** pharmacopoeia

formulate: 4 word; **5** draft, forge; **6** author, codify, devise, draw up, indite, invent, phrase; **7** compose, develop; **8** contrive; **9** explicate; **10** articulate, excogitate

formulated: 7 drawn up; **8** authored, composed

formulation: 10 expression; **11** preparation; **13** formularising, formularizing

fornicator: 9 adulterer

for now: 12 for the moment; **13** for the interim

forrader: 5 ahead; **6** onward; **7** forward, onwards; **8** forwards

forsake: 5 lurch; **6** desert; **7** abandon; **8** abnegate, desolate; **15** leave in the lurch

forsaken: 4 left; **6** jilted; **7** given up; **8** deserted, lovelorn, rejected; **9** abandoned; **12** relinquished; **13** crossed in love

for sale: 7 salable; **8** sellable, vendible; **10** marketable; **11** in the market, on the market, purchasable; **12** merchantable

forsooth: 5 truly; **6** in fact, really; **7** in truth; **11** joking apart

for sure: 4 sure; **6** surely; **9** certainly; **10** for certain, sure enough

forswear: 4 jilt; **5** evade, unsay; **6** abjure, recant, slight; **7** neglect, retract; **8** renounce, set aside; **9** not hear of, repudiate; **10** stand aloof, swear false; **13** cast behind one; **14** discountenance, perjure oneself; **15** wash one's hands of; **16** bear false witness; **18** set one's face against; **19** have nothing to do with

forswearing: 8 forgoing; **12** renunciation

fort: 4 hold; **6** fort up; **7** fortify, redoubt; **8** fastness, fortress, garrison, stockade; **10** stronghold

forte: 4 loud, turn; **5** parts; **6** loudly, metier,

talent; **7** ability, faculty, talents; **8** capacity, felicity, long suit, strength; **9** endowment, specialty; **10** capability, cleverness, fortissimo, speciality; **11** strong point

forte-piano: 5 piano; **10** pianoforte

forth: 2 on; **3** off; **4** away; **5** ahead; **6** onward; **7** forward; **8** forwards

for that reason: 4 ergo, then, thus; **5** hence; **6** thusly, whence; **8** thence so; **9** therefore, wherefore; **11** accordingly

forthcoming: 6 coming, in hand; **7** brewing, in train; **8** in embryo, on the way, outgoing, upcoming; **9** preparing; **10** near at hand; **11** approaching

for the asking: 9 on request

for the most part: 6 mostly; **7** as a rule, largely, usually; **9** generally, in the main, most often, typically; **10** ordinarily; **11** customarily

for the sake of: 5 due to; **9** because of; **10** by reason of; **11** on account of, on the part of

for this reason: 4 ergo, then, thus; **5** hence; **6** thusly, whence; **8** thence so; **9** therefore, wherefore; **11** accordingly; **12** and therefore, consequently

forthright: 5 blunt, frank; **6** candid; **8** squarely; **9** outspoken; **10** free-spoken, point-blank; **11** plainspoken; **12** forthrightly

forthwith: 3 now; **5** apace; **6** at once; **7** briefly, by and by, quickly, shortly; **8** directly, in a while, speedily; **9** extempore, instantly, right away, summarily; **10** in real time; **11** immediately, **12** in no long time, straightaway; **13** at short notice, incontinently

fortification: 7 redoubt; **8** munition; **13** strengthening

fortified: 9 bastioned

fortify: 3 arm; **4** fort, gird, lace; **5** spike; **6** beef up; **7** build up; **9** reenforce, reinforce; **10** strengthen

fortissimo: 5 forte; **10** very loudly

fortitude: 4 face, guts; **5** spunk; **6** virtue; **9** hardihood; **19** intestinal fortitude

Fort-Lamy: 8 N'Djamena, Ndjamena; **13** capital of Chad

fortnight: 8 two weeks

fortnightly: 8 biweekly

fortress: 4 fort, hold; **7** redoubt; **8** fastness; **10** stronghold

fortuitous: 6 casual, chance; **8** not meant, uncaused, unwilled; **9** causeless, unplanned, unwitting; **10** accidental, contingent, incidental, undesigned, unintended, unpurposed; **11** inadvertent; **12** adventitious, undetermined; **13** indeterminate, unintentional

fortuitously: 7 luckily; **8** by chance, randomly; **9** aimlessly; **11** fortunately; **12** accidentally, contingently**

F

fortuity: 3 hap, hit; **6** hazard; **7** fortune; **8** accident, casualty; **9** adventure, haphazard; **11** chance event; **12** chance medley, happenchance, happenstance

fortunate: 4 ripe, rosy; **5** happy, lucky; **6** golden, in luck; **7** blessed, favored, hopeful; **9** favorable; **10** auspicious, convenient, propitious; **12** providential

fortunately: 7 luckily; **12** fortuitously; **17** as luck would have it

fortune: 3 hap, hit, lot; **4** fate, luck, pelf; **5** lucre; **6** chance, hazard, riches, wealth; **7** auspice, destiny, portion; **8** casualty, fortuity, opulence; **9** adventure, affluence, haphazard; **11** filthy lucre; **12** chance medley, happenchance, happenstance

fortunes: 4 life; **7** journal; **10** adventures; **11** confessions, experiences; **17** personal narrative

fortune teller: 5 witch; **6** medium; **10** soothsayer; **11** clairvoyant

fortune telling: 10 divination; **11** foretelling, soothsaying

forty: 2 XL; **8** two score

forty winks: 3 nap; **4** doze; **6** catnap, siesta, snooze; **8** cat sleep; **10** short sleep

forum: 5 agora, bench, court; **7** theater; **8** assembly, tribunal; **10** auditorium, court of law; **12** amphitheater, meeting place, public square

forward: 4 fore, pert; **5** ahead, eager, early, forth, fresh [U.S.], prime, ready, saucy; **6** forrad, onward, pass on, send on; **7** advance, consign, earnest, enhance, forrard, further, onwards, promote, zealous; **8** cavalier, delegate, flippant, forrader, forwards, hand over, malapert, relegate; **9** advancing, cultivate, frontward, in earnest, obtrusive, strenuous; **10** frontwards, precocious, put forward, set forward, turn over to; **11** impertinent, push forward; **12** enterprising

forwarding: 9 promotion; **11** furtherance

forward-looking: 6 modern; **8** advanced; **10** innovative

forward motion: 7 advance; **8** progress; **9** advancing; **10** going ahead, proceeding; **11** advancement, coming ahead, moving ahead, progressing, progression; **12** forging ahead, going forward, onward motion

forwardness: 8 alacrity; **9** cockiness, pushiness, readiness

forwards: 2 on; **5** ahead, forth; **6** forrad, onward; **7** forrard, forward, onwards; **8** forrader; **9** frontward; **10** frontwards

fosse: 4 dike, dyke, moat; **5** ditch; **6** kennel, trench, trough; **7** bulwark; **12** entrenchment**

fossil: 4 dodo, fogy; **5** fogey; **6** dotard; **9** Paleozoic

fossilist: 14 paleontologist; **15** palaeontologist

fossilize: 10 mineralize

fossilized: 8 ossified

fossil oil: 5 crude; **7** coal oil, rock oil; **8** crude oil; **9** petroleum

foster: 4 heat, warm; **6** foment, hazard; **7** cherish, further, nurture, possess; **9** surrogate

fosterage: 7 nurture, raising, rearing; **8** breeding; **9** fostering, nurturing; **10** bringing up, upbringing

fou: 5 drunk; **10** inebriated

foul: 4 base, clog, rank, vile; **5** afoul, black, choke, dirty, fetid, funky, grave, gross, nasty, reeky, yucky; **6** arrant, back up, befoul, clog up, coarse, defile, filthy, foetid, fouled, putrid, scurvy, smelly, smutty, wicked; **7** beastly, congest, fulsome, heinous, loathly, noisome, peccant, pollute; **8** cheating, choke off, foul ball, infamous, maculate, marked-up, shameful, sinister, stinking; **9** felonious, loathsome, nefarious, offensive, repellant, repellent, revolting; **10** abominable, blackguard, disgustful, disgusting, of a deep dye, scandalous, unsporting, villainous; **11** contaminate, distasteful

foul invective: 4 oath; **7** cursing; **8** ribaldry, swearing; **9** profanity

foulness: 5 filth; **6** laxity; **8** baseness, rankness, trimming, vileness; **9** abjection, nastiness, shuffling, turpitude; **10** debasement, filthiness, stinkiness; **11** degradation

foul odor: 5 fetor, stink; **6** stench; **7** bad odor, malodor; **8** bad smell

foul play: 5 wrong; **6** injury; **7** knavery, roguery; **8** iniquity; **9** rascality

foul shot: 9 free throw

foul-smelling: 4 foul; **5** fetid, funky; **6** foetid, putrid, smelly; **7** noisome; **8** stinking

foul up: 4 blow, flub, muff; **5** botch, fluff, spoil; **6** ball up, bobble, bollix, bungle, fumble, mess up, muck up; **7** blunder, botch up, louse up, screw up; **8** bollix up, bollocks; **9** mishandle; **10** bollocks up

found: 4 base; **5** embed, imbed, plant, set up, setup; **6** bottom, broach, ground, launch; **8** detected, found out, organize; **9** establish, institute, originate; **10** constitute, discovered; **11** put together

foundation: 4 base, foot; **5** basis; **6** ground; **7** support; **8** creation, founding; **9** fundament; **10** groundwork, initiation; **11** cornerstone, institution, origination; **12** instauration, substructure

founder: 4 flop, give, sink; **5** break, drown, mover; **6** cave in, fall in, father, wallow,

welter; **7** give way; **8** beginner, collapse, fall flat; **9** break down, generator, initiator, laminitis; **11** fall through

foundered: 7 aground, swamped, wrecked; **8** capsized, cast away, grounded, stranded; **11** shipwrecked

founding: 8 creation; **9** setting up; **10** foundation, initiation, organizing; **11** institution, origination; **12** instauration, organization; **13** establishment

founding father: 6 father; **7** founder; **8** beginner

foundling: 4 waif; **7** wastrel; **14** abandoned child

foundling hospital: 6 creche

found out: 5 found; **8** detected; **10** discovered

foundry: 7 foundry; **10** metalworks

fount: 4 face, font; **8** fountain, typeface

fountain: 3 jet; **4** font, well; **5** fount; **6** spring; **7** outflow; **10** outpouring, wellspring; **13** natural spring

fountainhead: 4 head, well; **8** wellhead; **10** headspring, spring head, wellspring

four: 2 iv, IV; **6** square; **7** quarter, quartet, quatern; **8** foursome; **10** quadruplet, quaternary, quaternion, quaternity

four and twenty: 8 two dozen; **10** twenty-four

four-centered arch: 9 Tudor arch

four-flush: 5 bluff

fourfold: 9 four times, quadruple; **13** quadruplicate

four-footed: 9 quadruped; **11** quadrupedal

four-four time: 10 common time

four-in-hand: 5 coach

four-party: 13 quadripartite

fourpence: 5 groat

fourscore: 2 80; **4** LXXX; **6** eighty

four score: 6 eighty

fourscore and ten: 6 ninety

four-sided: 13 quadrilateral

foursquare: 6 square; **8** squarely

fourth: 3 4th; **7** quarter; **8** fourthly, quartern; **9** one-fourth; **10** fourth part, quaternary; **17** twenty-five percent

fourth deck: 5 orlop; **9** orlop deck

fourth dimension: 4 time

fourth estate: 5 press; **9** news media; **10** journalism

fourthly: 6 fourth; **16** in the fourth place

fourth part: 6 fourth; **7** quarter; **8** quartern; **9** one-fourth; **17** twenty-five percent

fourth power: 7 quartic; **10** biquadrate; **11** biquadratic

fourth stomach: 8 abomasum

fourth-year: 6 senior

four-wheel drive vehicle: 4 jeep

fowl: 4 bird; **7** poultry; **8** volaille; **12** domestic fowl

fowling piece: 7 shotgun

fox: 3 fob, **5** throw, trick, vixen [female];

6 dodger, fuddle; 7 bedevil, confuse, reynard; 8 befuddle, confound, sly boots, slyboots

foxglove: 9 digitalis

foxglove family: 13 figwort family; 16 Scrophulariaceae

foxhole: 6 trench

fox hunting: 7 foxhunt; 8 the chase

foxily: 5 slyly; 8 artfully, craftily, trickily; 9 cunningly, knavishly

foxiness: 5 craft, guile; 7 cunning, slyness; 8 wiliness; 10 craftiness

foxy: 3 sly, tan; 4 fawn, wily; 5 dodgy, slick, tawny; 6 crafty, maroon, tricky; 7 cunning, knavish, tricksy; 8 guileful

foyer: 4 hall; 5 lobby; 8 anteroom; 9 vestibule; 11 antechamber; 12 entrance hall

Fr: 8 francium

fracas: 3 row; 4 fray, to-do; 5 brawl, broil, melee; 6 affray, breeze, hubbub, pother, racket, rumble, rumpus, squall, uproar; 7 howling, rhubarb [baseball], ruction, shindig, trouble; 8 brouhaha, scramble; 9 imbroglio, scrimmage; 10 bear garden, donnybrook, free-for-all; 11 altercation, battle royal, embroilment

fraction: 4 part; 6 divide; 7 portion

fractional: 5 prime; 7 aliquot; 9 divisible; 10 reciprocal; 11 fragmentary

fractious: 3 hot; 5 hasty, quick, techy, testy; 6 cranky, tetchy; 7 bilious, peckish, peevish, peppery, pettish, waspish; 8 captious, choleric, petulant, shrewish, snappish; 9 irritable, overhasty, querulous; 10 nettlesome, refractory

fractiously: 9 peevishly; 11 querulously

fracture: 5 break, crack, fault, split; 7 fissure; 8 cracking; 9 fault line; 15 geological fault

fradicin: 8 neomycin

Fragaria: 10 strawberry; 13 genus Fragaria

fragile: 4 weak; 5 brash [U.S.], frail; 6 flimsy; 8 delicate; 9 sensitive

fragility: 8 delicacy; 10 friability; 12 breakability

fragment: 4 chip; 5 chunk, shard, sherd; 7 break up; 8 chipping; 11 fragmentize

fragmentary: 10 fractional, fragmental

fragmentation: 11 atomisation, atomization

fragmentation bomb: 17 antipersonnel bomb

fragmented: 5 split; 8 crumbled; 9 disunited; 10 incomplete; 12 disconnected

fragrance: 5 aroma, scent; 7 bouquet, perfume; 9 redolence, sweetness; 10 sweet smell

fragrant: 5 balmy, spicy; 6 savory; 7 scented; 8 aromatic, redolent; 12 sweetscented; 13 sweet-smelling

frail: 3 gay, lax; 4 weak; 5 brash [U.S.]; 6 infirm, rakish; 7 fragile, gallant; 8 delicate, fallible; 9 imperfect, sensitive; 10 dissipated

frail constitution: 8 delicacy

frailness: 7 frailty; 8 debility; 9 diathesis, infirmity; 10 feebleness

frailty: 4 vice; 8 debility, weakness; 9 frailness, infirmity; 10 feebleness; 12 imperfection

frambesia: 4 yaws; 10 framboesia

framboise: 9 raspberry; 11 Rubus idaeus; 13 wild raspberry

frame: 3 bod, put; 4 cast, form, mold, plan, soma; 5 build, couch, flesh, model, set up, shape; 6 border, design, draw up, entrap, figure, inning, redact, scheme; 7 anatomy, arrange, chassis, compose, ensnare, frame in, framing, outline; 8 contrive, frame out, physique, rough hew, skeleton; 9 framework, human body, rough cast; 10 underframe

frame house: 12 shingle house; 14 wood frame house

frame in: 5 frame; 6 border

frame of mind: 4 ease, mood, vein; 5 humor; 6 animus; 8 attitude; 11 disposition, frame of soul, state of mind

frame of reference: 7 posture; 8 attitude, position; 9 viewpoint; 11 point of view

frame out: 5 frame, model; 8 rough hew; 9 rough cast

frame-up: 5 setup

framework: 5 frame, model; 6 fabric; 7 framing, outline; 8 skeleton

franchise: 6 excuse; 7 liberty, license, release; 8 immunity; 10 dealership

Francis of Assisi: 10 St. Francis; 12 Saint Francis; 20 Giovanni di Bernardone

francium: 2 Fr

Francoa ramosa: 12 bridal wreath

Francophile: 10 Francophil

frangible: 7 brittle; 9 breakable

frank: 4 open; 5 blunt; 6 candid, hot dog, weenie, wiener; 7 sincere; 8 postmark; 9 downright, guileless, ingenuous, outspoken; 10 forthright, free-spoken, point-blank, unreserved; 11 frankfurter, open-hearted, plain-spoken, plainspoken, wienerwurst; 13 Vienna sausage

Frankfort: 9 Frankfurt; 17 capital of Kentucky; 15 Frankfurt on Main

Frankfurt: 9 Frankfort; 15 Frankfurt on Main

frankfurter: 5 frank; 6 hot dog, weenie, wiener; 11 wienerwurst; 13 Vienna sausage

frankincense: 4 balm; 5 myrrh; 8 olibanum; 11 gum olibanum

frankincense pine: 10 Pinus taeda; 12 loblolly pine

Franklin stove: 9 gas burner, oil burner; 15 pot-bellied stove

frankly: 8 candidly, honestly; **9** sincerely; **11** guilelessly, ingenuously

frankness: 6 candor; **7** abandon, candour; **8** bonhomie, openness; **9** sincerity; **10** candidness; **12** truthfulness; **13** outspokenness, veraciousness

frantic: 3 mad; **4** wild; **5** giddy, rabid; **6** doting, raving; **7** berserk, excited; **8** frenetic, frenzied, rambling, unhinged, wild-eyed; **9** delirious, insensate, phrenetic, possessed, wandering; **10** demoniacal, distracted, distraught, hysterical, incoherent, reasonless; **11** dithyrambic, in hysterics, lightheaded, vertiginous; **12** all possessed, ready to burst, unrestrained

frappe: 3 ice; **5** shake; **9** milk shake

frat: 10 fraternity

Fratercula: 6 puffin; **15** genus Fratercula

fraternal: 8 biovular; **9** brotherly, congenial; **10** neighborly; **11** brotherlike

fraternity: 4 frat; **8** sodality; **11** amicability, brotherhood; **12** amicableness

fraternity house: 9 frat house; **12** chapterhouse

fraternization: 10 cordiality; **11** welcomeness; **13** rapprochement; **14** fraternisation

fraternize: 7 collude, concert, consort, embrace; **8** conspire; **11** confederate; **12** club together, hand together, hang together, hold together, keep together, make advances, pull together

fraud: 4 fake, hoax, sham; **5** faker, guile, phony, pseud, put-on; **6** dupery, pseudo; **7** forgery; **8** bilkster, imposter, impostor, swindler; **9** pretender; **10** role player, victimizer; **11** counterfeit, fraudulence, make-believe

fraudulent: 4 fake, mock, sham; **5** bogus, false; **6** pseudo; **8** so-called, spurious; **9** deceitful, dishonest, faithless, pretended, trothless, truthless; **10** fallacious, mendacious; **11** counterfeit, make-believe, unveracious

fraudulent scheme: 6 racket

fraught: 5 laden; **8** pregnant

fraught with danger: 5 risky; **6** unsafe; **7** parlous; **8** insecure, perilous; **9** dangerous, hazardous; **10** precarious

fraxinella: 8 gas plant

Fraxinus: 3 ash; **13** genus Fraxinus

fray: 3 row, rub; **4** fret, to-do; **5** brawl, broil, chafe, curry, melee; **6** affray, breeze, fracas, hubbub, pother, racket, ruffle, rumble, rumpus, squall, uproar; **7** frazzle, howling, rhubarb [baseball], ruction, scratch, shindig, trouble; **8** brouhaha, scramble; **9** imbroglio, scrimmage; **10** bear garden, donnybrook, free-for-all; **11** battle royal, disturbance, embroilment

frayed: 5 faded, passe, stale; **6** shabby, shaken, wilted; **10** secondhand, threadbare

frazzle: 4 fray

freak: 3 fad, fit; **5** prank, quirk; **6** maggot, mutant, vagary; **7** boutade [Fr], monster; **8** crotchet, escapade, flimflam, freak out, gross out; **9** capriccio; **11** lose control, monstrosity

freakish: 5 flaky, kinky [U.S.], outre; **6** freaky, wanton; **7** bizarre, wayward; **8** fanciful, skittish; **9** eccentric, fantastic; **10** capricious, outlandish, particular

freak out: 5 freak; **8** gross out; **11** lose control; **14** disorientation

freaky: 5 flaky, outre; **7** bizarre; **8** freakish; **9** eccentric; **10** outlandish

freckle: 5 patch; **6** blotch, macula [Anat]; **9** birthmark

freckled: 6 pitted; **7** studded; **10** discolored, flea-bitten

Freddie Mac: 5 FHLMC

Frederick Barbarossa: 10 Barbarossa, Frederick I

Frederick I: 10 Barbarossa; **19** Frederick Barbarossa

Frederick II: 17 Frederick the Great

Frederick the Great: 11 Frederick II

free: 3 rid; **4** open; **5** apart, bawdy, broad, clear, gross, loose, sheer, spare; **6** coarse, excuse, exempt, give up, giving, gratis, immune, let off, on hire, ribald, risque [Fr], smutty, untied; **7** absolve, asunder, for hire, fulsome, insular, justify, liberal, license, obscene, regular, release, relieve, set free, unblock, unloose, untaxed; **8** costless, detached, discrete, dislodge, freehand, generous, handsome, liberate, pass over, princely, scot-free, separate, set clear, unfreeze; **9** at liberty, bounteous, bountiful, discharge, disengage, disparate, equivocal, free as air, unannexed, unchained, unselfish; **10** charitable, consummate, disengaged, far between, for nothing, free handed, free people, freehanded, full handed, gratuitous, munificent, not charged, open handed, relinquish, render free, unattached, unfettered, unshackled; **11** disencumber, unconnected, unmitigated, unqualified; **12** disembarrass, dispense with, free of charge, pornographic, set at liberty, unassociated

free agent: 10 free spirit; **11** freewheeler

free-and-easy: 6 casual; **8** familiar

freebee: 8 giveaway, gratuity

freebooter: 4 thug; **5** harpy, shark; **6** bandit, falcon, looter, raider; **7** brigand, spoiler; **8** pillager; **9** despoiler, land shark, plunderer

freed: 7 set free; **8** exempted, released; **9** liberated; **10** extricated; **11** emancipated; **12** disentangled

freedom: 7 liberty; **9** exemption

free enterprise: 13 market economy; 12 laissez-faire

free fight: 10 hand to hand; 12 running fight,
stand up fight

free-for-all: 3 row, rub; 4 fret, to-do; 5 brawl,
broil, chafe, curry, melee; 6 affray, breeze,
fracas, hubbub, pother, racket, ruffle, rumble, rumpus, squall, uproar; 7 frazzle,
howling, rhubarb [baseball], ruction,
scratch, shindig, trouble; 8 brouhaha,
scramble; 9 imbroglio, scrimmage; 10 bear
garden, donnybrook, free-for-all; 11 battle
royal, disturbance, embroilment

freehanded: 3 big; 4 free; 6 giving; 7 liberal;
8 freehand, handsome; 9 bounteous, bountiful; 10 bighearted, openhanded

freehold: 8 free land; 10 autonomous

freeing: 10 liberating; 12 emancipating,
emancipation, emancipative

freelance: 9 mercenary; 11 independent; 12
self-employed

free land: 8 freehold

freeloader: 6 beggar, cadger; 7 moocher,
sponger; 9 mendicant; 10 panhandler

freely: 4 fain; 6 as lief; 8 givingly; 9 liberally; 10 charitably, generously; 11 bounteously, bountifully, unselfishly; 12 heart
and soul, munificently, open-handedly

free-market: 10 capitalism

Freemason: 5 Mason

free of charge: 4 free; 6 gratis; 7 for free,
untaxed; 8 costless; 10 for nothing, gratuitous, not charged; 13 without charge

free pardon: 6 pardon; 7 amnesty

free-range: 10 unenclosed

free rein: 4 play; 12 carte blanche [Fr]

free space: 9 open space

free spirit: 9 free agent; 11 freewheeler

free-spoken: 5 bluff, blunt, frank; 6 candid,
direct; 9 downright, outspoken; 10 forthright, point-blank; 11 plain-spoken; 12
matter of fact

freestanding: 8 separate

Free State: 8 Maryland; 12 Old Line
State

free-swimming: 10 unattached

freethinking: 8 agnostic; 9 skeptical; 10 infidelity, undogmatic; 11 rationalism

free thought: 5 deism

free throw: 8 foul shot

free time: 9 spare time

Freetown: 20 capital of Sierra Leone

free verse: 9 vers libre

freeway: 4 pike; 7 thruway; 8 motorway; 10
expressway, throughway; 12 state highway,
superhighway

freewheel: 5 drift

freewheeler: 9 free agent; 10 free spirit

freewheeling: 8 carefree

free will: 8 volition; 10 discretion

freeze: 4 halt, hold, stop; 5 block, crash,
frost; 6 arrest, lock up; 7 suspend; 8 freezing, glaciate, solidify, stop dead; 9 freeze
out; 10 deep-freeze, freeze down, immobilize; 11 quick-freeze

freeze-dry: 10 lyophilize

freezer: 10 deep freeze

freezing: 3 icy; 5 gelid, polar; 6 arctic,
boreal, freeze, frigid, frosty, wintry; 7
glacial; 8 Siberian, very cold

freezing temperature: 10 frigidness; 11
intense cold

free zone: 8 free port

F region: 6 F layer; 13 Appleton layer

freight: 3 jag; 4 bale, load; 5 cargo; 6 burden, lading; 7 loading, payload; 8 shipment; 10 freightage; 11 consignment,
freight rate

freightage: 7 freight; 8 wharfage; 9 brokerage; 11 freight rate

freight car: 10 baggage car, express car, luggage van

freight charge: 7 cartage; 11 shipping fee

freight elevator: 15 service elevator

freighter: 6 bottom; 9 cargo ship; 11 cargo
vessel, merchantman; 12 merchant ship

freight liner: 10 liner train

freight train: 7 rattler; 10 goods train

French: 6 Gallic

French bean: 8 snap bean; 9 green bean; 10
string bean; 11 haricot vert

French bed: 10 four poster

French endive: 7 witloof; 13 Belgian
endive

french-fried potatoes: 5 fries; 6 frites; 11
french fries

French fritter: 7 biegnet

french-fry: 7 deep-fry

French horn: 4 horn

French Oceania: 15 French Polynesia

French pancake: 5 crepe

French Polynesia: 13 French Oceania

French Riviera: 9 Cote d'Azur

frenetic: 4 wild; 5 giddy, rabid; 6 doting, raving; 7 berserk, frantic; 8 frenzied, rambling, unhinged, wild-eyed; 9 delirious,
insensate, phrenetic, possessed, wandering;
10 incoherent, reasonless; 11 dithyrambic,
lightheaded, vertiginous; 12 all possessed;
13 beside oneself

frenzied: 4 wild; 5 giddy, manic, rabid; 6
doting, raving; 7 berserk, frantic; 8 frenetic, rambling, unhinged, wild-eyed; 9
delirious, insensate, phrenetic, possessed,
wandering; 10 incoherent, reasonless; 11
dithyrambic, lightheaded, vertiginous; 12
all possessed; 13 beside oneself

frenzy: 4 fury; 5 craze, furor; 8 delirium,
hysteria; 9 hysterics

frequence: 9 frequency, oftenness
frequency: 5 pitch; 9 frequence; 10 commonness; 11 periodicity
frequency modulation: 2 FM
frequency selection: 6 tuning; 7 squelch
frequent: 3 jog; 4 shop, trot; 5 buy at, haunt, thick; 6 common, shop at; 7 not rare, sponsor, typical; 8 everyday, ordinary, resort to; 9 household, incessant, many times, patronize, well-known; 11 commonplace, well-trodden; 13 garden variety
frequenter: 6 patron
frequently: 3 oft; 5 often; 8 ofttimes; 10 oftentimes
fresh: 3 cut, new, raw; 4 bold, hale, high, keen, pert, racy, well; 5 beery, bleak, boozy, brisk, clean, drunk, frosh, green, merry, newly, novel, saucy, smart, sweet, tight, tipsy, tonic, whole; 6 corned, groggy, hearty, primed, recent, unused; 7 bracing, drunken, forward, freshet, freshly, fuddled, nipping; 8 cavalier, elevated, flippant, freshman, impudent, malapert, overbold, overcome, recently, top-heavy; 9 disguised, flustered, inclement, inebriate, overtaken, refreshed; 10 energizing, in one's cups, inebriated, refreshful, refreshing; 11 impertinent, intoxicated, invigorated; 13 reinvigorated
fresh breeze: 11 stiff breeze
freshen up: 3 air; 7 freshen, recruit, refresh; 8 renovate; 9 refreshen, refurbish
freshet: 5 fresh, spate
freshly: 3 new; 5 fresh, newly; 6 pertly; 7 saucily; 8 recently; 10 impudently; 13 impertinently
freshman: 5 fresh, frosh; 7 entrant, fresher, starter; 8 neophyte, newcomer; 9 first-year, fledgling; 10 fledgeling
freshness: 4 gall, glow; 5 crust; 7 newness, novelty, recency; 8 boldness, raciness; 9 impudence, insolence; 10 cheekiness; 12 impertinence
fresh start: 10 clean slate, tabula rasa; 12 new departure
fress: 10 gluttonize
fret: 3 gag, rub; 4 care, dole, fray, fuss, gall, huff, load, rile, stew; 5 chafe, chase, choke, erode, grate, pique, prick, sting, sweat, wince, wring; 6 burden, emboss, lather, nettle, niggle, pierce, rankle, ruffle; 7 anxiety, concern, eat away, eat into, provoke, scratch, swither; 8 convulse, emblazon, flourish, irritate
fretful: 5 itchy, whiny; 6 whiney; 7 fidgety, whining; 8 restless; 9 querulous
fretsaw: 6 jigsaw; 9 scroll saw
fretted: 8 latticed; 10 interlaced; 11 latticelike

fretwork: 3 mat; 7 lattice, matting, tracery; 8 filigree; 11 latticework
Freud: 12 Sigmund Freud
Frey: 5 Freyr
Freya: 6 Freyja
Fri: 6 Friday
friable: 5 light, sandy; 7 crumbly, fragile, shivery
friar: 4 monk; 7 brother; 9 mendicant
friar's lantern: 11 ignis fatuus; 12 jack-o'-lantern, will-o'-the-wisp
friary: 5 abbey; 6 priory; 9 monastery
fribble: 5 inane, jemmy, puppy, spark; 6 trifle; 8 farcical, popinjay; 10 ridiculous; 11 petit maitre
fricassee: 4 hash, stew; 5 mince; 6 ragout
fricative: 7 spirant; 8 sibilant
friction: 5 clash; 7 rubbing; 9 detrition
fried: 9 deep-fried
friend: 4 ally; 6 Quaker; 7 admirer, booster; 8 champion; 9 supporter; 11 confederate, protagonist; 12 acquaintance
Friend: 6 Quaker
friendless: 7 outcast; 8 homeless
friendliness: 5 amity; 10 friendship
friendly: 8 amicable; 9 favorable; 10 propitious; 12 well-disposed
Friendly Islands: 5 Tonga
friend of the court: 12 amicus curiae [Lat]
frier: 5 fryer; 6 pullet
fries: 6 frites; 11 french fries
Friesian: 8 Holstein; 16 Holstein-Friesian
frieze: 6 sconce; 7 capital, cornice; 8 pediment; 10 architrave; 11 coping stone
frigate: 7 gunboat; 8 corvette; 9 first-rate; 10 bomb vessel, sloop of war
Frigga: 5 Frigg
fright: 4 fear; 5 alarm, scare, sight; 7 eyesore, scarify, startle; 8 affright, frighten; 11 fearfulness; 12 dreadfulness
frightened: 6 afraid, scared; 7 fearful, panicky; 8 panicked; 9 terrified; 11 panic-struck; 12 apprehensive; 13 panic-stricken
frightening: 4 dire; 5 awful, dread; 6 odious; 7 direful, dreaded, fearful, hideous; 8 dreadful, fearsome, horrific, terrible; 9 atrocious, monstrous; 10 forbidding, horrendous
frightfully: 5 awful, sadly; 6 sorely; 7 awfully, cruelly, grossly; 8 bitterly, horribly, terribly, woefully; 9 fearfully, miserably, painfully, piteously; 10 dreadfully, grievously, lamentably, shockingly
frigid: 3 dry, icy; 4 cold, dull; 5 bland, gelid, polar, prosy; 6 arctic, frosty, frozen, trashy, wintry; 7 glacial, languid, prosaic; 8 freezing, lukewarm; 9 colorless, proposing
frigidity: 8 coldness, coolness; 9 aloofness; 10 frigidness, remoteness, withdrawal; 11 intense cold; 12 lack of caring, lukewarmness

Frigid Zone: 9 polar zone
frijole: 5 beans; 6 frijol; 10 kidney bean
frijoles refritos: 12 refried beans
frill: 3 hem; 4 gimp, list, welt; 6 edging, fringe, ruffle; 7 flounce, valance; 8 furbelow, selvedge, skirting, trimming
fringe: 3 hem; 4 edge, gimp, list, tuft, welt, yarn, 5 frill; 6 border, edging, fringy, toupee; 7 feather, flounce, valance; 8 furbelow, marginal, outskirt, selvedge, skirting, tall tale, trapping, trimming; 9 fish story, periphery; 10 embroidery
fringe benefit: 4 perk; 10 perquisite
fringed: 8 lacinate
frippery: 5 fluff, stuff, trash, trifle; 6 finery, gewgaw, luxury, tinsel; 7 foppery, rubbish; 8 equipage, trickery, trumpery; 9 bagatelle, ball dress, frivolity, full dress; 10 court dress, fancy dress; 12 evening dress
frisk: 4 lark, romp, trot; 5 amble, sport; 6 canter, cavort, frolic, gambol, prance, search; 7 disport, rollick, skylark; 8 caracole, frisking; 9 lark about, run around
frisky: 6 lively; 7 playful; 8 spirited, stirring; 9 kittenish; 10 frolicsome
frisson: 5 chill; 6 quiver, shiver, thrill, tingle; 7 shudder
frith: 4 holt; 5 fiord, firth, fjord, inlet; 7 estuary
fritter: 4 fool, inch, seed; 5 crumb, patch, shoot; 6 tatter; 7 flitter; 8 fool away; 9 dissipate, scantling; 10 frivol away; 11 fritter away
frivol: 6 trifle
frivolity: 5 fluff, folly, prank; 6 levity; 7 conceit; 8 clowning, frippery, trifling, zaniness; 9 bagatelle, lip wisdom; 10 buffoonery, triviality; 12 eccentricity, harlequinade
frivolous: 5 giddy, petty; 8 niggling, volatile; 9 quibbling; 10 sleeveless
frizz: 4 kink; 5 crape, crimp; 6 kink up; 7 frizzle
frizzle: 4 curl, kink; 5 crape, crimp, frizz, twill; 6 cocker, kink up, rumple; 7 recurve; 8 cockle up
frizzy: 5 crisp, kinky, nappy; 7 frizzly
frock: 4 cope, gown, pall, robe; 5 dress, habit, smock; 7 cassock, pallium; 10 Geneva gown
frock coat: 8 overcoat, tail coat; 9 dress coat; 10 tuxedo coat
frog: 4 toad; 5 frogs; 6 anuran; 7 epaulet; 8 toadfrog; 10 batrachian, salientian; 12 shoulder knot
frogman: 5 diver; 10 scuba diver
frolic: 4 lark, play, romp; 5 caper, frisk, sport; 6 cavort, gambol; 7 disport, jollity, rollick, skylark; 9 lark about, merriment, run around

frolicky: 7 coltish; 8 sportive; 10 frolicsome, rollicking
frondeur: 5 cynic, rebel; 6 carper, critic
front: 4 face, fore, look; 5 brass, stand; 7 frontal; 8 anterior, confront, forepart, front end, front man, movement, opposing, presence, straw man; 9 brashness, front line, front side, hardihood, nerviness, renitency, resisting; 10 figurehead, opposition, resistance; 11 battlefront, nominal head
frontage: 4 fore; 6 facade; 12 forepartface
frontal: 4 fore; 5 front; 6 head-on; 7 discoid; 8 anterior, frontlet
frontal bone: 8 forehead; 10 os frontale
front end: 5 front; 8 forepart
front entrance: 9 front door
frontier: 6 border; 8 terminal
frontier settlement: 7 outpost
frontiersman: 11 mountain man; 12 back woodsman
fronting: 6 facing
frontispiece: 5 facia [Lat]; 6 facade; 7 heading; 10 proscenium
front line: 5 front; 11 battlefront
front man: 5 front; 8 point man, straw man; 10 figurehead; 11 nominal head
frontmost: 8 foremost
front room: 6 parlor, 7 parlour; 10 living room; 11 sitting room
front-runner: 6 shoo-in; 8 favorite, long shot; 9 dark horse, favourite
frosh: 5 fresh; 8 freshman
Frost: 11 Robert Frost; 14 Robert Lee Frost
frost: 3 ice; 4 hoar, rime; 5 icing; 6 freeze
frostbite: 8 numbness; 9 cryopathy
frost-bitten: 4 numb; 6 frozen; 10 frostbound; 11 frost-nipped
frosted: 4 hoar, rimy; 5 hoary, rimed; 6 frosty; 8 nacreous
frostily: 8 frigidly
frostiness: 7 iciness; 9 hoariness; 10 chilliness
frosting: 3 ice; 5 icing
frosty: 3 icy; 4 hoar, rimy; 5 crisp, hoary, nippy, parky, rimed; 6 arctic, boreal, frigid, frozen, snappy, wintry; 7 frosted, glacial, nipping; 8 freezing, Siberian
froth: 4 drug, fizz, foam, head, scum, suds; 5 chaff, smoke, spume; 6 bubble, cobweb, lather; 7 sparkle; 10 effervesce
frothy: 2 up; 4 idle; 5 foamy, light; 6 bubbly, flashy, flimsy, slight; 7 flaming, foaming, slender; 8 bubbling, mousseux [Fr]
froward: 5 cross, rusty; 6 cussed [U.S.], wilful; 7 willful; 10 headstrong, self-willed; 11 intractable; 12 cantankerous
frown: 4 pout, snap; 5 gnarl, gnash, growl, lower, scowl, snarl; 6 glower; 7 grimace
frowning: 6 dismal, gloomy, somber, triste

[Fr]; **7** joyless, pouting; **8** dejected; **9** cheerless, saturnine; **10** lugubrious, spiritless, uncheerful; **12** heavy-hearted

frowsty: 5 fusty, musty

frowsy: 6 frowzy; **7** frowsty; **8** slovenly

frozen: 3 icy; **4** numb; **5** fixed; **6** frigid, frosty, rooted, wintry; **7** glacial; **10** frostbound, stock-still; **11** flash-frozen, frostbitten, frost-nipped, quick-frozen

frozen custard: 12 soft ice cream

fructification: 9 flowering; **10** sporophore; **11** pullulation

fructify: 3 set; **4** blow; **5** bloom, ripen; **6** fatten, flower, mature; **7** blossom; **9** bear fruit, pullulate

fructose: 8 levulose; **10** fruit sugar

frugal: 5 chary, sober, spare; **6** saving, scotch; **7** careful, sparing, thrifty; **8** stinting; **10** economical

fruit: 3 bud; **4** crop; **5** yield; **7** harvest, progeny; **9** handiwork, offspring

fruit bat: 7 megabat; **9** flying fox

fruitcake: 3 nut; **5** crank; **7** nutcase; **8** crackpot; **9** screwball

fruit drink: 3 ade

fruit-eating: 12 carpophagous

fruit fly: 9 pomace fly; **10** drosophile

fruitful: 7 fertile; **10** profitable ; **12** productive

fruition: 8 pleasure; **11** realisation, realization; **13** gratification

fruitless: 4 vain; **6** futile; **8** bootless; **9** pointless; **10** of no effect, profitless, sleeveless; **12** unprofitable

fruit sugar: 8 fructose, levulose; **9** laevulose

fruity: 3 mad; **4** bats, daft, loco, nuts; **5** balmy, barmy, batty, buggy, crazy, dotty, kooky, loony, loopy, nutty, wacky; **6** crazed, insane, kookie, teched [dialect]; **7** bonkers, cracked, far gone, haywire, lunatic, tetched [dialect], touched; **8** crackers, demented, deranged, maddened, not right

frump: 3 dog; **5** dowdy

frumpish: 4 drab, glum, grim; **5** dowdy, sulky; **6** frumpy, gloomy, grumpy, morose, sullen; **7** grouchy; **8** growling, scowling; **9** glowering; **10** in the dumps, in the sulks, out of sorts

frumpy: 5 dowdy; **8** frumpish

Frunze: 6 Biskek; **18** capital of Kyrgystan

frustrate: 3 dun, rag; **4** balk, bilk, foil; **5** cross, crush, queer, spoil; **6** baffle, defeat, scotch, thwart; **7** bedevil, crucify, torment; **9** discomfit, tantalize; **10** disconcert

frustrated: 6 balked, dashed, foiled; **7** baffled, crossed; **8** defeated, thwarted, unhinged; **11** discomfited, discouraged; **12** disappointed, disconcerted

frustum: 6 cantle

fruticose: 7 shrubby; **8** branched; **11** fruticulose

fry: 3 kid; **4** bake, bevy, herd, hive, nest, peck, tike, tyke; **5** brood, child, cloud, covey, drove, flock, grill, minor, parch, roast, shoal, singe, swarm, toast; **6** bushel, farrow, flight, litter, nipper, scorch, scores, shaver; **7** draught, tiddler; **8** nestling, small fry; **9** youngster; **11** electrocute

fryer: 5 frier; **6** pullet

frying: 8 sauteing

frying pan: 6 frypan; **7** skillet; **9** frying-pan

ft: 4 foot

fthm: 6 fathom

ft-L: 11 foot-lambert

fuchsia: 7 magenta

fucoid: 8 rockweed; **11** fucoid algae

fuddle: 3 fox; **5** booze, drink, throw; **7** bedevil, confuse; **8** befuddle, confound; **9** inebriate

fuddled: 3 cut, wet; **4** high; **5** beery, blind, boozy, drunk, fresh, merry, potty, stiff, tight, tipsy; **6** blotto, corned, groggy, loaded, primed, soaked, soused, tiddly; **7** crocked, drunken, slopped, sloshed, smashed, sozzled, squiffy, tiddley; **8** besotted, elevated, overcome, top-heavy; **9** disguised, flustered, inebriate, overtaken, pixilated, plastered; **10** blind drunk, in one's cups, inebriated; **11** intoxicated

fuddy-duddy: 12 stuffed shirt

fudge: 4 cook, duck, fake; **5** dodge, elude, evade, hedge, parry, skirt, trash; **6** humbug, put off, wangle; **7** falsify, garbage, inanity, twaddle, twattle; **8** sidestep; **10** circumvent, manipulate; **12** misrepresent

fudge factor: 10 correction

Fuehrer: 4 duce [It]; **6** leader, Hitler; **11** Adolf Hitler

fuel: 4 fire; **6** firing; **11** combustible

fuel oil: 10 heating oil

fugacious: 7 passing; **8** fugitive; **9** ephemeral, transient; **10** short-lived, transitory, evanescent

fugacity: 7 brevity; **10** transience; **11** evanescence; **12** impermanence

fugitive: 7 refugee, runaway; **8** fleeting, in hiding, on the lam; **9** fugacious, momentary; **12** momentaneous, wanted person

fugleman: 7 example, keynote, maestro; **9** conductor, role model; **10** file leader

Fuji: 7 Fuji-san; **6** Mt. Fuji; **8** Fujiyama

Fukien: 3 Min; **4** Amoy; **9** Taiwanese; **10** Fukkianese, Hokkianese, Min dialect

Fulani: 4 Fula; **5** Fulah

fulcrum: 4 bait [U.S.], crux; **5** hinge, lever, pivot; **7** bearing; **10** caudex; **12** turning point

fulfill: 4 fill, meet; **6** fulfil; **7** execute, perform, realize, satisfy; **8** carry out, live up to; **9** discharge; **10** accomplish; **12** carry through

fulfilled: 4 done, over; **8** complete, executed, finished; **9** completed, satisfied; **10** discharged

fulfillment: 9 achieving, acquittal, discharge; **10** completing, completion, fulfilment, redemption; **11** achievement, performance, realization; **12** satisfaction; **13** accomplishing, actualization

fulgent: 6 bright; **7** blazing, glaring, radiant, sparkly; **8** aglitter, dazzling, glinting, glittery; **9** sparkling; **10** glistering, glittering; **11** scintillant

fulgurant: 8 dazzling; **9** fulgurous

Fulica: 4 coot; **6** mud hen; **8** marsh hen, water hen; **11** genus Fulica

fuliginous: 5 dingy, dusky, murky, sooty; **6** pitchy

full: 3 fat, wax; **4** deep, good, high, wide; **5** broad, fully, heavy, lusty, obese, plump, sound, squab, stout, total; **6** entire, strong; **7** blatant, brush up, intense, passing, plenary, replete, wide-cut; **8** absolute, bouncing, powerful, thorough; **9** corpulent, strapping, to the full, undivided; **10** clangorous; **12** brimming over

full-blooded: 5 lusty; **6** hearty; **7** blooded; **8** purebred; **10** red-blooded

full-blown: 7 matured; **9** full grown, **11** full-fledged

full-bodied: 4 rich; **6** robust

full dress: 5 tails; **7** foppery; **8** equipage, frippery, tailcoat, white tie; **9** ball dress, dress suit; **10** court dress, fancy dress; **12** evening dress

full-dress rehearsal: 14 dress rehearsal

full-grown: 3 big; **5** adult, burly, grown; **6** portly; **7** grownup, well-fed; **10** fully grown

full-length: 5 uncut

full measure: 4 lots, over; **6** plenty; **9** abundance, amplitude, plenitude, profusion; **11** copiousness; **13** plenteousness

full of life: 5 vital; **6** lively, yeasty

full-scale: 6 all-out

full stop: 4 stop; **5** colon, comma, point; **6** period; **9** full point, semicolon

full treatment: 5 works; **8** whole kit; **10** whole works; **12** kit and boodle, whole shebang; **13** whole caboodle; **14** kit and caboodle

fully: 4 full; **5** a full, all of, amply, quite, stark; **6** in full, in toto, wholly; **7** exactly, totally, utterly; **8** entirely, outright, the sum of; **9** precisely, to the full; **10** altogether, completely; **11** to the tune of

fully grown: 3 big; **5** adult, grown; **7** grownup; **9** full-grown

fulminate: 4 bolt, boom, peal, rail, roar; **5** blare, clang, drive, sling, swell; **6** set off; **7** bluster, talk big, thunder; **8** denounce, det-

onate; **9** discharge, pitchfork, proscribe; **11** look daggers, use big words

fulmination: 5 abuse; **8** diatribe

fulsome: 4 foul, free, oily, rank; **5** bawdy, broad, gross, loose; **6** coarse, ribald, risque [Fr], smarmy, smutty; **7** buttery, obscene, peccant; **8** unctuous, **9** abhorrent, equivocal, loathsome, repugnant, repulsive; **10** oleaginous; **12** insufferable, pornographic

Fulton: 12 Robert Fulton

Fumariaceae: 14 fumitory family

fumble: 4 paw; **4** blow, feel, flub, muff, riot, toss, trip; **5** botch, fluff, grope, spoil, thumb, touch; **6** ball up, bobble, boggle, bollix, bungle, finger, foul up, handle, huddle, hustle, mess up, muck up, muddle; **7** blunder, botch up, grabble, louse up, screw up, stumble; **8** bollix up, bollocks, flounder; **9** mishandle

fumbler: 5 stick; **6** dauber, duffer, lubber; **7** botcher, bumbler, bungler, butcher, marplot, sad sack; **9** blunderer

fumbling: 6 clumsy; **8** bungling; **11** incompetent

fume: 3 ire, pet; **4** bile, boil, fire, foam, rage, rant, rave, reek, roar, tear, tiff; **5** chafe, flame, go ape, parch, smoke, steam, trail; **6** choler, dander, exhale, mantle, pucker, seethe, simmer, taking; **7** bluster, essence, ferment, passion; **8** fumigate; **9** angry mood, effluvium, go bananas, redolence; **10** ebullition, hit the roof

fumes: 7 exhaust; **12** exhaust fumes; **13** combustion gas

fumigate: 4 fume

fumigation: 8 steaming; **10** fumigating

fuming: 4 wild; **5** livid, rabid; **6** raging, raving; **7** foaming, in a rage, rageful

fun: 4 play; **5** sport; **6** festal; **7** amusing, amusive, festive; **8** cheering; **9** amusement, diverting, merriment; **10** recreation, titilating

funambulist: 7 acrobat; **10** rope-dancer; **15** tightrope walker

function: 2 go; **3** run, use; **4** part, role, work; **5** force, serve; **6** acting, action, agency, office; **7** operate, purpose, routine, working; **8** capacity, position, sociable [U.S.]; **9** officiate, operation, procedure; **10** subprogram, subroutine

functional: 6 usable; **7** running, useable, working; **8** official, operable; **9** operative; **11** operational

functionality: 3 use; **5** avail, stead; **7** service

functionary: 7 curator; **8** minister, official; **10** bureaucrat

functioning: 2 on; **6** acting, active; **7** running, working; **9** effectual, efficient, oper-

F

ating, operation, operative, practical; **11** efficacious, performance

fund: 5 amass, cache, hoard, stock, store; **6** garner, supply; **8** garner up, supplies; **10** accumulate; **12** monetary fund

fundament: 4 base, butt, foot, prat, rear, rump, seat, tail, tush; **5** basis, fanny, stern; **6** behind, bottom; **7** keister, rear end, tail end; **8** backside, buttocks, derriere; **9** posterior

fundamental: 3 key; **5** basic; **6** primal; **7** central; **8** cardinal, profound; **9** essential; **10** underlying; **11** rudimentary

fundamental law: 10 organic law; **12** constitution

fundamentally: 6 purely; **9** basically, decidedly, downright, in essence, radically, seriously; **10** absolutely; **11** essentially; **13** unequivocally

fundamental note: 7 key note; **11** leading note

fundamentals: 6 basics; **7** bedrock

funding: 7 backing, support; **9** financing

funds: 5 funds; **8** finances, treasure; **10** cash in hand

funeral: 11 funeral rite; **14** funeral service; **16** funeral solemnity

funeral director: 9 mortician; **10** undertaker

funeral home: 13 funeral chapel, funeral church, funeral parlor; **14** funeral parlour

funeral oration: 6 eulogy; **13** funeral sermon

funerary: 8 funereal

funereal: 8 dreadful, funerary, mournful; **10** lamentable, sepulchral

funfair: 4 fair; **8** carnival; **13** amusement park

fungal infection: 7 mycosis

Fungi: 12 kingdom Fungi; **13** fungus kingdom

fungoid: 10 funguslike

fungology: 8 mycology

fungus: 4 mold; **5** fungi [pl], mould [Brit]

fungus kingdom: 5 Fungi; **12** kingdom Fungi

funicle: 5 fiber; **6** fibril; **9** funiculus

funicular: 8 cable car; **9** wire-drawn; **10** cable-drawn; **12** cable railway

funiculus: 7 funicle

funk: 5 cower, quail, wince; **6** cringe, crouch, falter, flinch, recoil, shrink; **7** squinch; **8** blue funk; **10** abject fear

funky: 4 foul; **5** fetid; **6** foetid, putrid, smelly; **7** low-down, noisome; **8** stinking; **12** foul-smelling

funnel: 4 main; **5** gully; **11** funnel shape

funnel-shaped: 10 cone-shaped

funnily: 5 funny, oddly; **7** queerly; **9** curiously, strangely

funniness: 3 wit; **5** humor; **6** comedy; **7** odd-ness; **8** clowning, drollery; **9** wittiness; **10** comicality; **11** farcicality; **12** laughability

funny: 3 gig, odd, rum; **5** comic, fishy, oddly, rummy, shady, skiff; **6** jocose; **7** amusing, comical, curious, funnily, jocular, queerly, risible, strange, suspect; **8** farcical, humorous, mirthful, peculiar, pour rire, singular; **9** comically, grotesque, laughable, strangely; **10** suspicious

funny bone: 9 crazy bone

funny money: 10 bogus money; **11** counterfeit

fur: 4 coat, pelt; **7** fur coat

furbelow: 3 hem; **4** gimp, list, welt; **5** frill, pleat; **6** edging, fringe, ruffle; **7** flounce, valance; **8** selvedge, skirting, trimming

furbish: 4 buff, gild; **5** flush, grain, japan, paint; **6** enamel, polish; **7** burnish, lacquer, smarten, varnish; **8** renovate; **9** white-wash

furcated: 6 forked, zigzag; **9** bifurcate

furcular: 10 distichous; **11** dichotomous

Furies: 7 Erinyes; **9** Eumenides

furious: 4 rude, wild; **5** angry, bluff, fiery, rough; **6** fierce, in a way, madcap, raging, savage; **7** angered, enraged, excited, in a fury, in a rage, violent; **8** headlong, maddened, ungentle, up in arms, vehement; **9** ferocious, hotheaded, in a taking, infuriate; **10** blustering, boisterous, infuriated, outrageous; **11** all worked up, impassioned, mad with rage, precipitate, tempestuous

furl: 6 roll up

furlong: 3 ell; **4** foot, hand, inch, line, mile, nail, palm, pole, rood, yard; **5** cubit; **6** fathom, league

furlough: 5 leave; **6** lay off

furnace lining: 10 refractory

furnish: 3 rig; **4** help; **5** array, dress, equip; **6** fettle, fledge, render, supply; **7** garnish, provide; **8** accouter

furor: 3 fad; **4** cult, fury, rage, riot; **5** craze; **6** clamor, frenzy, furore, tumult, uproar; **7** rioting, tempest; **10** convulsion; **11** strong anger

furrow: 3 rut; **4** line, seam; **5** chase; **6** crease, groove, trench; **7** chamfer, crinkle, wrinkle

furrowed: 6 fluted, rutted; **7** grooved; **8** striated

further: 3 and, too; **4** also, item, more; **5** boost; **6** abroad, beyond, foster, yonder; **7** advance, farther, forward, promote; **8** likewise; **9** encourage; **10** additional, put forward, set forward; **11** furthermore

furtherance: 7 advance; **9** advancing, promotion; **10** forwarding, furthering; **11** advancement

furthermore: 3 and, too; **4** also, item; **7** further; **8** likewise, moreover; **10** in addition, what is more

furthest: **6** utmost; **8** farthest; **9** uttermost; **11** farthermost, furthermost

furtive: **5** sneak; **6** feline, sneaky; **7** evasive, lurking; **8** skulking, stealthy; **9** backstair, secretive; **10** backstairs; **13** surreptitious

furtively: **8** on the sly, secretly; **10** stealthily

furuncle: **4** boil; **7** blister

fury: **4** rage; **5** craze, demon, furor, harpy; **6** dragon, frenzy; **7** madness; **8** delirium, ferocity, hysteria, violence, wildness; **9** vehemence; **10** fierceness; **11** furiousness, strong anger; **12** intense anger

furze: **4** whin; **5** gorse

fuse: **3** mix; **4** fuze, meld; **5** blend, brand, fusee, fuzee, immix, merge, torch, unite; **6** absorb, embody, primer; **7** blend in, combine, conjoin; **8** coalesce, conflate, dissolve; **9** commingle; **10** amalgamate, centralize, impregnate; **11** consolidate, incorporate

fusel oil: **11** amyl alcohol

fusil: **6** musket

fusileer: **9** grenadier

fusillade: **5** burst, salvo; **6** volley; **8** outburst

fusing: **5** union; **6** fusion; **7** uniting; **8** blending; **9** synthesis; **10** coalescing, embodiment; **11** coalescence, unification

fusion: **5** union; **6** fusing, merger; **7** melting, uniting; **8** blending; **9** coalition, synthesis; **10** coalescing, embodiment; **11** coalescence, unification; **12** amalgamation, spinal fusion; **13** incorporation, nuclear fusion, optical fusion

fusion bomb: **5** H-bomb; **12** hydrogen bomb

fusion power: **13** thermonuclear

fuss: **3** ado; **4** flap, fret, rout, show, spat, stir, tiff, to-do; **5** hurry, tizzy; **6** bicker, bother, bustle, dither, fidget, flurry, hassle, hubbub, hustle, mother, niggle, pother, racket, ruffle; **7** display, fluster, flutter, peg away, trouble; **8** flourish, squabble; **9** bickering, pottering; **10** showing off; **11** fidgetiness, lay about one, ostentation

fussbudget: **7** fusspot, worrier; **9** worrywart, nitpicker; **13** perfectionist

fussiness: **6** choler; **9** crossness, petulance; **11** fretfulness, peevishness; **12** irritability

fusspot: **10** fussbudget

fussy: **4** busy; **5** cross, hasty; **6** crabby, grumpy; **7** crabbed, fidgety, finical, finicky, grouchy, hurried, unquiet; **8** affected, electric, feverish, galvanic, restless; **9** crotchety, mercurial, pottering; **10** particular; **11** bad-tempered, ill-tempered

fustian: **4** blah, rant; **6** jargon; **7** bombast, palaver, twaddle; **8** affected, claptrap, flummery; **9** rigmarole; **10** balderdash

fustigate: **6** cudgel; **9** criticize

fusty: **3** bad; **4** high, weak; **5** musty; **6** effete, putrid, rancid, rotten; **7** corrupt, decayed, frowsty, gone bad, rotting, tainted, touched; **8** standpat; **9** putrefied; **10** putrescent

futile: **4** vain; **6** otiose; **8** bootless, ill-spent; **9** fruitless; **10** sleeveless, unavailing; **11** ineffective, ineffectual

futilely: **10** bootlessly; **11** pointlessly

futility: **10** inefficacy

future: **4** next; **5** later; **6** to come; **8** futurity, ulterior; **9** hereafter, the future; **10** succeeding, time to come; **11** future tense

futurity: **6** future; **9** hereafter; **10** futurition, time to come

fuzz: **3** cop, pig; **4** blur, bull, dick, hair; **6** copper, smokey; **8** tomentum

fuzzy: **4** hazy; **5** foggy, muzzy; **6** bleary, blurry, fuzzed; **7** blurred; **10** out of focus

---

G

G: **1** K, M; **2** GB; **4** thou, yard; **5** grand; **7** chiliad; **8** gigabyte, thousand; **11** one thousand

g: **2** gm; **3** gee; **4** gram; **6** gramme

Ga: **7** gallium

gab: **6** gossip; **7** chin-wag, gabfest; **8** causerie, chitchat; **9** small talk; **11** chinwagging; **12** tittle-tattle

gabardine: **5** tweed, white; **7** doublet, flannel; **8** camisole

gabble: **5** clack, prate; **6** babble, gibber, jabber, piffle, tattle; **7** blabber, chatter, maunder, palaver, prattle, twaddle; **9** jabbering; **12** tittle-tattle

gabby: **5** talky; **6** chatty; **9** garrulous, talkative; **10** loquacious

gaberdine: **5** smock; **6** duster; **8** coverall, dust coat; **9** coveralls

gabfest: **3** gab; **6** gossip; **7** chin-wag, palaver; **8** causerie, chitchat; **9** small talk; **11** chinwagging; **12** tittle-tattle

gable: **8** gable end; **9** gable wall, gable roof; **10** saddle roof, saddleback

Gaborone: **17** capital of Botswana

Gabun: **5** Gabon

gadding: **6** roving; **7** vagrant; **8** rambling; **9** itinerant; **10** ambulatory, discursive; **11** peripatetic

gadfly: 4 cuss, pest; 8 blighter, pesterer

gadget: 5 gizmo; 6 widget; 9 appliance; 11 contraption, contrivance, convenience

gadolinite: 9 ytterbite

gadolinium: 2 Gd

Gadus: 3 cod; 7 whiting; 10 genus Gadus

Gaea: 2 Ge; 4 Gaia

Gaelic: 4 Erse; 6 Celtic; 8 Goidelic

gaffe: 4 slip; 7 faux pas; 8 solecism; 9 gaucherie

gaffer: 3 cub, elf, put; 4 beau, boss, chap, loon; 5 blade, chief, swain; 6 fellow, honcho, yeoman; 7 antique, foreman, good man; 8 mossback, old-timer; 9 old geezer

gag: 3 yak; 4 fret, jape, jest, joke, quip, rant; 5 choke, heave, laugh, spout; 6 bridle, muffle, muzzle, wheeze; 7 smother; 8 rehearse, suppress; 9 suffocate; 10 buffoonery, dumfounder, strike dumb

gaga: 5 crazy, dotty; 6 in love, senile, soft on; 7 doddery, smitten; 8 enamored; 9 doddering, taken with; 10 infatuated

gage: 3 pot, tie; 4 back, dope, game, punt, sens, sess, weed; 5 bet on, ganja, gauge, grass, skunk, smoke, stake; 8 cannabis, Mary Jane; 9 marihuana, marijuana

gaggle: 5 flock; 11 aggregation

gagman: 7 gagster; 8 comedian; 9 gagwriter

gag rule: 7 closure, cloture

Gaia: 2 Ge; 4 Gaea

gai choi: 11 leaf mustard

gaiety: 9 merriment; 11 playfulness

gaillard: 5 joker, spark; 6 jester; 8 jokester

gain: 3 apt, get, hit, win; 4 boot, deft, earn, make; 5 clear, handy, put on, quick, reach, ready; 6 adroit, attain, derive, expert, obtain, profit, pull in, take in; 7 acquire, advance, benefit, bring in, harvest, procure, profits [pl], realize; 8 addition, arrive at, get ahead, increase; 9 dexterous, increment; 10 gain ground; 11 acquisition, make headway

gainer: 4 dive

gainful: 4 paid; 6 paying; 9 lucrative; 10 profitable; 12 advantageous, remunerative

gainful employment: 3 job; 4 line, work; 6 living; 8 business; 10 employment, line of work, livelihood, occupation

gain ground: 3 win; 4 gain; 7 advance, go ahead; 8 get ahead

gaining: 7 getting; 9 acquiring, obtaining, obtention, procuring; 10 obtainment; 11 acquisition, procurement

gainless: 4 vain; 8 bootless, nugatory; 9 fruitless, pointless; 10 of no effect, profitless; 12 unprofitable; 13 without effect

gainsay: 7 dispute; 9 challenge; 10 controvert; 12 give denial to

Gainsborough: 18 Thomas Gainsborough

gain spurs: 10 win laurels; 11 gain laurels; 18 gain golden opinions

gain the affections: 11 win the heart

gait: 4 form, pace, port, tone; 5 guise; 7 cadence; 8 carriage

gaiter: 4 spat; 5 spats; 6 brogue, buskin; 8 overshoe

gal: 6 gallon

gala: 3 gay; 4 fete; 5 merry; 6 festal; 7 blowout, festive; 8 festival, field day, jamboree; 10 gala affair

galactic: 10 astronomic; 12 astronomical

galactopoietic hormone: 9 prolactin

galactose: 10 brain sugar

galago: 8 bush baby

Galahad: 10 Sir Galahad

galangal: 6 ginger; 7 galangl; 9 galingale

Galapagos: 16 Galapagos Islands

galavant: 9 gallivant

galax: 5 heath; 6 galaxy; 9 cold's foot; 10 beetleweed, wandflower

galaxy: 3 sea, sun; 4 army; 5 array, galax, sight; 7 numbers; 9 a quantity, cold's foot; 10 beetleweed, wandflower; 13 constellation

gale: 4 gust; 5 blast; 8 high wind; 9 high winds [pl]; 10 strong wind

Galen: 11 Hippocrates

Galeocerdo: 10 tiger shark; 15 genus Galeocerdo

Galileo: 14 Galileo Galilei

galingale: 7 galangl; 8 galangal

gall: 3 irk; 4 fret, huff, miff, rile; 5 anger, chafe, crust, grate, pique, prick, sting, venom, wring; 6 nettle, offend, pierce, rancor, spleen; 7 provoke, rancour, umbrage; 8 acerbity, acrimony, asperity, convulse, irritate, rankling, soreness, wormwood; 9 freshness, impudence, insolence, virulence; 10 bitterness, cheekiness, resentment, saddle sore; 12 impertinence

gallant: 5 brave, dandy, lofty, proud, sheik, swell; 6 rakish, squire, urbane; 7 captive, dashing, refined; 8 intrepid, knightly, majestic, paramour, polished, well-bred; 9 civilized, debauchee, ladies' man; 10 chivalrous, cultivated, dissipated; 11 gentlemanly; 12 clotheshorse, fashion plate, meretricious

gallantry: 5 valor; 6 daring, spirit, valour; 7 heroism; 8 audacity, chivalry, flirting, valiance, valiancy

galleon: 7 man-o'-war; 11 sailing ship

gallery: 3 pit; 5 boxes, drift; 6 closet, museum, stalls; 7 balcony, cabinet, heading, parquet, veranda; 8 auditory, verandah

galley: 7 caboose; 9 cookhouse; 11 ship's galley

galley proof: 10 press proof; 12 author's proof

gallfly: 8 gall gnat, gall wasp; 9 gall midge; 11 cynipid wasp

Gallic: 6 French

galligaskin: 8 breeches, leggings, trousers

gallimaufry: 4 mess, olio; 6 medley; 8 all sorts, mish-mash, pastiche; 9 patchwork, potpourri; 10 hodgepodge

Gallinago: 5 snipe; 7 Capella; 12 genus Capella; 14 genus Gallinago

galling: 5 pesky; 6 plaguy, vexing; 7 plaguey, teasing; 8 annoying, grinding, stinging, venomous; 9 pestering, provoking, vexatious; 10 bothersome, irritating, irritation, maleficent, mortifying, nettlesome; 11 aggravating

Gallinula: 7 moorhen; 8 marsh hen, swamphen, water hen; 14 genus Gallinula

gallium: 2 Ga

gallivant: 3 gad; 4 roam; 8 galavant

gallon: 3 gal; 4 pint; 5 quart; 7 congius

galloon: 4 lace; 7 brocade

gallop: 3 fly; 4 boom, dart, fade, flit, trot; 5 amble, bound

gallows: 6 gibbet; 7 gallous; 8 scaffold

gallstone: 9 bilestone

gallus: 5 brace; 9 suspender

gall wasp: 7 gallfly

galore: 6 plenty; 9 abounding, copiously, plenteous, plentiful; 10 abundantly; 11 in abundance, plenteously, plentifully

galoshes: 4 clog; 6 patten; 7 rubbers; 9 overshoes

galvanic: 5 fussy, hasty; 7 fidgety, hurried, unquiet, voltaic; 8 electric, restless; 9 mercurial; 11 galvanizing

galvanic battery: 14 voltaic battery

galvanism: 8 voltaism; 9 infection; 10 stirring up; 11 electricity, galvanizing, provocation, stimulation

galvanize: 4 stun; 7 astound, petrify, startle; 9 electrify

gambado: 5 caper; 6 brogue, buskin, gaiter; 7 legging

gambit: 4 ploy; 9 stratagem

gamble: 4 game, risk; 6 chance, hazard, wager; 7 venture; 8 run a risk

gambler: 8 gamester; 9 risk taker; 10 adventurer

gambling: 4 play; 6 gaming; 7 betting; 8 sporting, wagering; 10 dissipated; 11 cardplaying

gambling game: 12 game of chance

gambling house: 6 casino; 11 gambling den, gaming house; 12 betting house, gambling hell

gamboge: 5 lemon, maize; 11 lemon yellow, gamboge tree

gambol: 4 lark, play, romp; 5 caper, frisk, sport; 6 cavort, frolic; 7 disport, leaping, rollick, skylark; 8 skipping

gambrel: 8 curb roof; 11 mansard roof, gambrel roof

game: 3 biz; 4 back, butt, gage, gamy, play, prey, punt; 5 bet on, gamey, nerve, pluck, stake; 6 bottom, gamble, gritty, mettle, policy, polity, quarry, sports, spunky; 8 fair game, game plan, gameness, spirited; 10 game animal, mettlesome

gamecock: 12 fighting cock

gamekeeper: 10 game warden

game license: 14 hunting license

game plan: 2 MO; 4 game; 6 policy, polity; 14 course of action

game room: 8 playroom; 10 rumpus room

game show: 8 giveaway

gamester: 7 gambler, reveler; 9 sportsman; 10 adventurer

gamete: 6 gamete; 8 germ cell

gametokinetic hormone: 11 follitropin

game warden: 10 gamekeeper

gamin: 6 urchin; 6 gamine

gaming: 4 play; 8 gambling

gaming house: 6 casino; 11 gambling den; 12 betting house

gamma aminobutyric acid: 4 GABA

gamma radiation: 8 gamma ray

gammer: 6 granny, matron; 7 dowager, grandam, old lady; 8 old woman; 9 matriarch; 11 grandmother

gammon: 3 ham; 4 sell; 6 jambon; 11 side of bacon

gamp: 6 brolly; 7 umbrella

gamut: 5 range, scale

gamy: 4 blue, game, high, racy; 5 gamey, juicy, rough, sharp, spicy; 6 gritty, risque, sordid, spunky, strong; 7 corrupt, naughty, piquant; 8 spirited, stinging; 10 mettlesome

gander: 9 male goose

Gandhi: 13 Mahatma Gandhi; 24 Mohandas Karamchand Gandhi

Ganesh: 6 Ganesa; 7 Ganesha; 8 Ganapati

gang: 3 hie, mob; 4 band, crew, knot, pack, ring, team; 5 bunch, crowd, group, party, squad; 6 circle, clique, gang up; 7 coterie, in-crowd; 9 theft ring, work party

ganger: 7 foreman

Ganges: 11 Ganges River

gang fight: 6 rumble

gangland: 7 gangdom; 14 organized crime

gangly: 5 lanky, rangy; 8 gangling

gangplank: 7 gangway; 9 gangboard

gangrene: 7 mortify, necrose; 10 corruption, sphacelate; 13 mortification

gangster: 7 mobster; 9 racketeer

gangway: 5 aisle; 7 doorway, gateway; 8 driveway, hatchway; 9 gangboard, gangplank

ganja: 3 pot; 4 dope, gage, hemp, sens, sess, weed; 5 bhang, grass, skunk, smoke; 7 hashish; 8 cannabis, Mary Jane; 9 marihuana, marijuana

ganoid: 3 gar; **8** sturgeon; **10** ganoid fish
gantlet: 8 gauntlet
gantry: 7 gauntry
gaol: 3 can [slang], jug, lag, pen; **4** brig, hold, jail, keep, stir [slang]; **5** clink [slang], hulks, pokey [slang]; **6** chokey [slang], cooler [slang], donjon, immure, lockup, prison, remand; **7** dungeon, put away, slammer [slang], the Rock; **8** Bastille, big house [slang], hoosegow, imprison, stockade; **9** calaboose [slang], guardroom, jailhouse, oubliette; **10** guard house, San Quentin; **11** incarcerate, penal colony, prison house; **12** penitentiary
gaoler: 6 jailer
gap: 3 col; **4** hole, pass; **5** break, crack, notch, space; **6** breach, lacuna, spread; **7** opening, passage; **8** distance, interval; **10** disruption, separation; **11** missing part; **12** interruption, missing piece
gape: 3 yaw; **4** gawk, gawp, open, yawn; **5** bilge, stare; **6** goggle
gaping: 5 agape; **7** all agog, opening, yawning; **8** wide open; **9** cavernous
gar: 2 do; **7** garfish, garpike, operate, perform; **8** billfish; **10** needlefish
garage sale: 8 yard sale
garb: 3 tog; **5** dress; **6** attire, clothe, fit out; **7** apparel, garment, raiment; **8** enclothe; **10** habilitate
garbage: 5 fudge, trash; **6** humbug, refuse, scraps; **7** carrion, discard, inanity, rubbish, twaddle, twattle; **8** discards; **9** food waste
garbage bin: 8 waste bin
garbage can: 6 ashbin, ashcan; **7** dustbin; **8** trash bin, trash can, waste bin; **11** garbage pail, trash barrel
garbage collection: 11 trash pickup; **13** garbage pickup
garbage collector: 5 sweep; **7** dustman; **9** scavenger; **10** garbage man
garbage dump: 4 dump; **8** landfill; **9** trash dump, waste yard
garbage truck: 8 dust cart
garbanzo: 8 chickpea
garbed: 5 robed; **7** attired, dressed; **9** appareled, garmented
garble: 4 warp; **7** distort, falsify; **8** amputate, disguise, mutilate; **9** gloss over
garbled: 6 docked, lopped; **8** confused; **9** distorted, illogical, mutilated, scattered, truncated; **10** disjointed, disordered; **11** unconnected; **12** disconnected
garboard: 5 plank; **6** strake
garboil: 6 tumult, uproar; **7** turmoil
Garcinia: 10 mangosteen; **11** gamboge tree; **13** genus Garcinia
garden: 4 park; **7** demesne
garden cart: 6 barrow; **11** wheelbarrow
garden chair: 9 lawn chair

gardening: 12 horticulture
Garden State: 9 New Jersey
garden variety: 3 jog; **4** trot; **6** common; **7** typical; **8** everyday, frequent, ordinary; **9** household, well-known; **11** commonplace, well-trodden
Garfield: 13 James Garfield; **15** James A. Garfield; **20** James Abraham Garfield
gargantuan: 5 giant, jumbo; **9** Cyclopean, Herculean; **10** prodigious; **11** Bunyanesque, elephantine
gargle: 5 rinse; **9** mouthwash
gargoyle: 9 rain spout
gari: 6 manioc; **7** cassava, mandioc; **8** mandioca; **12** tapioca plant;
Garibaldi: 17 Giuseppe Garibaldi
garish: 4 loud; **5** cheap, flash, gaudy, tacky, tatty; **6** brassy, flashy, tawdry, trashy
garishness: 5 glitz; **8** loudness; **9** brashness, gaudiness; **10** flashiness, tawdriness
garland: 3 lei; **4** posy, sash; **5** favor; **6** fascia, fillet, flower, girdle, wreath; **7** baldric, bouquet, chaplet, coronal, festoon
garlic: 3 ail
garlicky: 10 alliaceous
garlic sauce: 5 aioli
garment: 3 tog; **4** garb; **5** dress; **6** clothe, fit out; **7** apparel, raiment; **8** enclothe; **10** habilitate
garmented: 5 robed; **6** garbed; **7** attired, dressed; **9** appareled; **12** habilimented
garments: 6 attire; **7** apparel, clothes; **8** clothing
garner: 4 earn, fund, stow; **5** amass, cache, hoard, store; **6** gather; **7** collect, granary; **8** garner up; **10** accumulate
garnet: 4 opal; **7** peridot; **10** chrysolite, tourmaline
garnish: 3 fee, rig; **4** trim; **5** adorn, array, dress, prank, sauce; **6** fettle, fledge, polish; **7** bedizen, footing, furnish, lacquer, varnish; **8** accouter; **9** japanning; **12** French polish
garotte: 8 garrotte
garpike: 3 gar; **7** garfish; **8** billfish
garret: 4 loft; **5** attic; **8** cockloft, house top; **10** clerestory, upper story
garrison: 4 army, crew, fort, host, wing; **5** corps, squad; **6** column, picket, piquet; **7** battery, brigade, company, platoon, section; **8** division, regiment, squadron; **9** battalion; **10** detachment
garron: 9 workhorse
garrote: 5 choke; **6** stifle; **7** garotte, smother; **8** garrotte, strangle, throttle; **9** suffocate; **10** asphyxiate, iron collar; **11** suffocation
garrulous: 5 gabby, talky; **6** chatty; **7** verbose; **9** talkative; **10** logorrheic, loquacious
Garry oak: 9 Oregon oak
garter: 6 halter; **9** supporter
gas: 3 gun; **4** blow, brag, tout; **5** bluff, boast, juice, swash, vapor, vaunt; **6** behead, hot air, petrol; **7** benzine, bluster, bombast;

8 gas pedal, gasoline, tall talk, throttle, vaporing; **9** bowstring, gasconade; **10** flatulence, flatulency, natural gas

Gascogne: 7 Gascony

gasconade: 3 gas; **4** blow, brag, tout; **5** boast, swash, vaunt; **7** bluster; **8** boasting, bragging; **10** self-praise; **12** self-applause, self-flattery; **13** self-laudation

gas cooker: 8 gas range, gas stove

gaseous: 8 vaporous

gash: 3 cut, rip; **4** hash, slit; **5** slash, slice; **6** hackle, haggle, mangle; **8** incision, scramble, slashing

gas helmet: 7 gas mask; **10** respirator

gas holder: 9 gasometer

gas jet: 9 gas burner

gasket: 4 loop; **6** eyelet; **7** cringle, grommet

gaskins: 4 hose, sock; **5** socks; **7** hosiery; **8** breeches, stocking; **9** trunk hose

gas light: 7 lantern; **9** lime light

gas line: 8 fuel line

gasoline: 3 gas; **5** juice; **6** petrol; **7** benzine; **8** gasolene

gasoline bomb: 10 petrol bomb; **15** Molotov cocktail

gasoline station: 10 gas station; **13** petrol station; **14** filling station

gasp: 4 blow, drop, pant, puff; **5** faint, heave, swoon; **6** wheeze; **7** succumb

gas pedal: 3 gas, gun; **8** throttle; **11** accelerator

gasping: 5 blown, pursy; **6** winded; **7** panting; **8** spavined; **11** out of breath, short-winded

gassification: 9 diffusion

gassing: 10 gas chamber

gassy: 7 colicky; **9** flatulent

gastralgia: 9 bellyache; **11** stomachache

gastric: 9 stomachal, stomachic

gastroenteritis: 3 flu; **10** stomach flu

gastrointestinal disorder: 8 ptomaine; **10** salmonella

gastrointestinal system: 15 digestive system

gastrointestinal tract: 7 GI tract; **13** digestive tube; **14** digestive tract

gastronome: 7 epicure, gourmet; **9** bon vivant, epicurean

gastropod: 8 univalve

gat: 3 rod; **6** pistol, roscoe; **7** handgun, side arm

gate: 4 door; **5** hatch; **6** wicket; **7** gateway, postern; **8** trapdoor

gate-crash: 5 crash; **7** barge in

gatekeeper: 6 porter; **7** doorman; **9** door guard; **10** doorkeeper, hall porter

gateway: 4 gate; **7** doorway, gangway; **8** driveway, hatchway

Gateway to the West: 8 St. Louis

gather: 3 hem; **4** meet, tuck, ween; **5** amass, infer, widen; **6** deduce, derive, garner, muster, pile up, pucker, ruffle; **7** collect; **8** assemble, cumulate; **9** forgather, gathering;

10 accumulate, congregate, foregather, understand; **11** get together, put together; **12** conglomerate

gathered: 8 deepened; **12** rendezvoused

gatherer: 9 collector; **11** accumulator

gather in: 6 take in

gathering: 4 levy; **5** issue, **6** gather; **7** meeting; **8** assembly; **9** carbuncle, compiling, deepening; **10** assemblage, assembling, collecting, converging, thickening; **11** compilation, ingathering

gather together: 4 meet; **5** unite; **8** assemble; **11** concentrate; **15** bring into a focus

gather up: 6 lift up, pick up; **7** call for, collect

gauche: 6 clumsy; **7** awkward, unhandy; **8** lubberly; **9** graceless, maladroit; **10** unpolished; **11** floundering, heavy-handed

gaucheness: 7 crudity; **9** crudeness

gaucherie: 4 slip; **5** gaffe; **7** faux pas; **8** solecism; **9** rusticity

gaud: 5 pride; **6** bangle, bauble, fallal, gewgaw; **7** novelty, trinket; **8** ornament

gaudiness: 5 glitz; **8** loudness; **9** brashness; **10** flashiness, garishness, tawdriness

gaudy: 4 loud; **5** cheap, flash, jazzy, showy, tacky, tatty; **6** brassy, flashy, florid, garish, glitzy, rococo, sporty, tawdry, trashy; **7** baroque; **8** gimcrack; **10** glittering; **12** meretricious

gauffer: 6 goffer

gauge: 4 gage; **5** guess, judge; **8** estimate; **11** approximate

gauger: 8 douanier [Fr]; **9** exciseman; **14** customs officer

gauging: 9 measuring

Gauguin: 11 Paul Gauguin

gaunt: 4 bony; **5** hulky, weedy; **6** meager, wasted; **7** haggard, hulking, lumpish, pinched; **8** lubberly, skeletal, spanking, thumping, unwieldy, whacking, whopping; **9** emaciated, walloping; **10** cadaverous, thundering

gauntlet: 9 gauntlets; **10** metal glove

Gauss: 18 Carl Friedrich Gauss

Gaussian curve: 11 normal curve

gaussmeter: 12 magnetometer

Gautama: 6 Buddha; **9** the Buddha; **10** Siddhartha; **13** Gautama Buddha

gauze: 4 veil; **6** chador, muslin; **7** netting, veiling

gauzy: 5 filmy, sheer; **8** cobwebby, gossamer, vaporous; **10** diaphanous, see-through; **11** transparent

gavel: 6 hammer

gavial: 9 crocodile

gavotte: 5 gavot

Gawain: 9 Sir Gawain**

G

gawk: 3 oaf; **4** clod, gape, gawp, goon, lout, lump; **5** klutz, stare; **6** goggle, lubber, lummox; **10** rubberneck, stumblebum

gawky: 6 clumsy, clunky; **8** ungainly, unwieldy

gawp: 4 gape, gawk; **6** goggle

gay: 4 braw, gala; **5** brave, jolly, merry, smart, sunny; **6** cheery, festal, jocund, jovial, rakish; **7** festive, flowery, gallant; **8** mirthful; **10** dissipated, glittering, homosexual

gay liberation movement: 6 gay lib

Gay-Lussac's law: 10 Charles' law; **12** law of volumes

gay woman: 7 lesbian

gaze: 5 stare; **6** regard

gazebo: 9 belvedere; **11** summerhouse

Gazella: 7 gazelle; **12** genus Gazella

gazelle hound: 6 Saluki

gazette: 7 journal; **8** magazine; **9** gazetteer

Gb: 1 G; **2** Gi; **7** gilbert; **8** gigabyte

Gc: 3 GHz; **9** gigacycle, gigahertz

G clef: 10 treble clef

Gd: 10 gadolinium

Gdansk: 6 Danzig

Ge: 4 Gaea, Gaia; **9** germanium

gear: 5 pitch, slops, traps; **7** harness, rigging, turn-out; **8** cogwheel; **9** accessory, caparison, equipment, gear wheel, trappings; **11** accessories; **12** accouterment, accoutrement; **13** accoutrements, appurtenances, gear mechanism, paraphernalia

gear case: 7 gearbox

gears: 5 train; **7** gearing; **9** gear train; **10** power train

gear up: 3 set; **5** ready, set up; **7** prepare

gear wheel: 4 gear; **8** cogwheel

gee: 1 g

geek: 7 oddball; **9** eccentric

gefilte fish: 8 fish ball

gegenschein: 11 counterglow

gehenna: 4 Hell; **5** abyss, limbo; **9** purgatory

Geiger: 10 Hans Geiger

Geiger-Muller counter: 13 Geiger counter

geisha: 10 geisha girl

geist: 4 soul; **6** genius; **11** inspiration

gel: 4 jell; **6** gluten, mousse; **7** congeal, gelatin, thicken; **8** condense; **9** semisolid

gelada: 12 gelada baboon

gelatin: 3 gel; **4** jell, ropy; **5** jelly; **6** clammy, gluten, mastic; **7** clotted; **8** gelatine; **9** glutenous, glutinous, semisolid; **10** albuminous, gelatinous; **12** mucilaginous

gelatinous: 4 ropy; **6** clammy, mastic; **7** clotted, gelatin; **9** glutenous, glutinous, jellylike; **10** albuminous; **11** gelatinlike; **12** mucilaginous

gelation: 7 gelling, setting; **10** thickening; **11** congelation; **12** inspissation

gelded: 3 cut; **11** emasculated

gelid: 3 icy; **5** polar; **6** arctic, frigid; **7** glacial; **8** freezing

gelidity: 5 chill; **7** iciness

gelignite: 5 gelly; **8** dynamite

gelling: 8 gelation; **10** thickening

gelt: 4 kale, loot, pelf; **5** bread, dough, lucre, money; **6** dinero, moolah; **7** cabbage, shekels

gem: 4 ruby; **5** bijou, brick, jewel, pearl, stone, trump; **6** muffin, prince; **7** diamond, true gem; **8** gemstone, treasure; **10** natural gem; **12** authentic gem, rough diamond; **13** precious stone

gemination: 7 genesis; **9** duplicate; **10** generation, heterogamy [Biol]; **11** germination, procreation, propagation; **13** fertilization

Gemini: 14 Gemini the Twins; **15** Castor and Pollux

gemmation: 7 budding

gemmed: 5 beady; **6** beaded; **7** jeweled, spangly; **8** jewelled, sequined, spangled; **9** bejeweled; **10** bejewelled, bespangled

Gemonil: 11 metharbital

gemote: 7 meeting; **8** assembly; **9** gathering; **10** assemblage

Gem State: 5 Idaho

gemstone: 3 gem; **5** stone; **13** precious stone

gendarme: 3 cop; **7** officer; **9** constable, policeman; **13** police officer

gender: 3 sex; **9** sexuality

genealogy: 4 line, stem; **5** birth, stock; **6** stirps, strain; **7** descent, lineage, stirpes [pl]; **8** ancestry, heritage, pedigree; **10** extraction, family tree

general: 5 broad, trite, vague; **6** common; **7** generic, regular, sketchy; **8** familiar, ordinary, sweeping; **9** universal, worldwide; **10** collective, ecumenical, vernacular; **11** established, full general, oecumenical; **12** cosmopolitan, encyclopedic; **13** comprehensive, encyclopaedic

general agreement: 6 accord; **7** concord, harmony; **8** symphony; **9** consensus; **10** consonance

General Agreement on Tariffs and Trade: 4 GATT

general assembly: 9 lawmakers; **11** legislature

general headquarters: 3 GHQ; **11** command post

generalization: 8 transfer; **9** carry-over, induction; **10** dialectics, generality; **11** abstraction

generalize: 5 infer; **10** generalise; **11** extrapolate

generalized seizure: 8 grand mal

generally: 6 mostly; **7** as a rule, broadly, loosely, usually; **9** in general, in the main,

general pardon: **7** amnesty
general practice: **3** use; **5** usage; **6** custom; **8** practice; **10** convention, observance, prevalence
general practitioner: **2** GP
general public: **6** public; **8** everyone; **9** everybody, the public
general-purpose: **10** all-purpose
general store: **10** five and ten; **11** five and dime, trading post; **12** country store
generate: **3** get; **4** give, make, sire; **5** beget, yield; **6** create, father, mother, render, return; **7** produce; **8** engender; **9** fertilize, procreate; **10** bring forth
generated: **4** made; **6** formed; **7** created; **8** produced
generation: **5** flesh; **6** making; **7** coevals, forming, genesis; **8** creating, creation, humanity; **9** formation, mortality, producing; **10** gemination, heterogamy [Biol], production; **11** germination, procreation, propagation; **13** bringing forth, fertilization
generative: **6** making; **7** forming, genetic; **8** creating; **9** formative, producing, spermatic; **10** generating, life-giving, productive; **11** procreative; **12** productive of, reproductive
generator: **5** mover; **6** author, source; **7** founder; **9** initiator
generic: **5** broad; **7** general; **8** sweeping; **10** collective; **12** encyclopedic; **13** comprehensive
generosity: **6** bounty; **7** charity; **10** liberality; **11** munificence; **12** generousness; **13** bounteousness, bountifulness, unselfishness
generous: **4** free; **6** giving; **7** liberal; **8** handsome, princely; **9** bounteous, bountiful, unselfish; **10** charitable, free handed, full handed, munificent, open handed
gene sequencing: **10** sequencing
genesis: **5** birth; **6** cradle, origin; **7** infancy; **8** nativity; **9** inception; **10** gemination, generation, heterogamy [Biol]; **11** fons et origo [Lat], germination, origination, procreation, propagation; **13** fertilization
genetic: **5** genic; **6** inborn, making; **7** forming; **8** creating, familial; **9** formative, genetical, incarnate, inherited, producing; **10** congenital, generating, generative, hereditary; **11** transmitted; **12** productive of
genetic constitution: **8** genotype
genetic endowment: **8** heredity
genetic engineering: **12** gene-splicing; **16** molecular biology
genetic material: **3** DNA
genetous: **6** inborn; **7** genetic; incarnate, inherited; **10** congenital, hereditary
Geneva: **6** Geneve
geneva: **10** Holland gin

Geneva gown: **4** cope, gown, pall, robe; **5** frock; **7** cassock, pallium
Genghis Khan: **11** Jenghis Khan, Jenghiz Khan
genial: **4** kind, mild; **6** hearty, making, mental; **7** affable, amiable, cordial, forming, genetic; **8** cheering, creating, gracious; **9** formative, producing; **10** generating, generative
geniality: **5** cheer; **6** gaiety, gayety; **7** spirits; **8** bonhomie, goodwill; **9** good humor; **10** affability, amiability, cordiality; **11** affableness, amiableness, earnestness
genic: **7** genetic
genicular vein: **9** vena genus
geniculated: **4** bent; **8** crinkled; **10** knock-kneed
genie: **3** gin; **4** jinn; **5** jinni; **6** djinni, djinny, jinnee
genital: **6** making; **7** forming, genetic; **8** creating, venereal; **9** formative, producing; **10** generating, generative; **12** productive of
genitive: **10** possessive; **12** genitive case; **14** possessive case
genitor: **10** procreator, progenitor
genito-urinary tract: **3** GUT
geniture: **5** labor; **7** travail; **8** delivery; **10** birth-throe, childbirth; **11** confinement, parturition; **12** accouchement
genius: **3** ace, wiz; **4** soul, star, whiz; **5** adept, brain, flair, maven, whizz; **6** expert, master, wizard; **7** hotshot; **8** capacity, judgment, virtuoso, wizardry; **9** genius for, ingenuity, sensation; **10** brilliance, master hand, mastermind, proficient; **11** crackerjack, inspiration
Genoa: **6** Genova
genocide: **10** race murder; **13** extermination
genre: **5** style
gens: **4** clan, name
gent: **3** cad, lad; **4** chap, cuss, snob; **5** fella; **6** fellow
genteel: **6** polite; **7** courtly; **8** cultured; **9** civilized; **10** cultivated
genteelness: **8** breeding; **9** gentility; **10** refinement
gentile: **5** alien, pagan; **7** heathen, infidel; **8** Nazarene
Gentile: **3** goy; **6** non-Jew
gentilhomme: **9** gentleman
gentility: **4** form; **6** comity, polish; **7** decorum, quality, suavity; **8** breeding, good form, presence, urbanity; **9** etiquette, formality, propriety, punctilio; **10** refinement; **11** genteelness
gentle: **4** easy, mild, soft; **5** faint; **6** docile, lenify, mellow, pacify; **7** appease, assuage, ennoble, entitle, gradual, gruntle, mollify, placate; **9** patrician; **10** conciliate; **11** blue-blooded; **12** aristocratic

G

gentleman: 3 man, sir; 5 valet; 6 master, squire; 8 laureate; 9 patrician; 11 gentilhomme [Fr]

gentlemanly: 6 urbane; 7 gallant, refined; 8 polished, well-bred; 9 civilized; 10 cultivated; 13 gentlemanlike, well-brought up

gentleness: 8 mildness; 11 gradualness; 13 temperateness

gentle wind: 3 air; 6 breeze, zephyr

gentlewoman: 4 dame, lady, ma'am; 5 madam; 6 madame

gently: 6 mildly, softly; 7 lightly

gentry: 10 gentlefolk; 11 aristocracy

genu: 4 knee; 9 knee joint

genuflect: 3 bow; 6 kowtow, scrape

genuflection: 6 homage; 8 kneeling; 9 obeisance; 11 prostration

genuine: 4 real, true; 6 actual; 7 literal, regular; 8 bona fide; 9 authentic, unfeigned; 10 legitimate

genuinely: 5 truly; 6 really; 13 authentically

genus: 15 biological genus

genu valgum: 9 knock-knee; 10 tibia valga

genu varum: 6 bowleg; 9 tibia vara

Geococcyx californianus: 10 roadrunner

geographical mile: 2 mi; 4 mile; 6 naut mi; 12 nautical mile

geographic expedition: 11 exploration

geography: 10 topography; 11 geographics

geological fault: 5 break, fault; 8 fracture; 9 fault line

geology: 9 formation

geomancer: 5 witch; 6 wizard, 13 fortune teller

geometer: 12 geometrician, statistician

geometrid: 13 geometrid moth

geomorphological: 10 structural

Geomys: 6 gopher; 11 genus Geomys

geophysical science: 10 geophysics

geophysicist: 9 geologist

geopolitical division: 9 territory

geoponics: 7 farming, tillage; 8 agronomy, georgics; 11 agriculture, cultivation

George: 11 Saint George

Geothlypis: 12 yellowthroat; 15 genus Geothlypis

Geraniaceae: 14 geranium family

geranium family: 11 Geraniaceae

gerbil: 8 gerbille

gerenuk: 8 antelope; 14 Waller's gazelle

gerfalcon: 9 gyrfalcon

geriatric: 7 elderly; 14 gerontological

geriatrician: 13 gerontologist

geriatrics: 11 gerontology

germ: 3 bud, bug; 4 seed; 6 source; 7 microbe; 8 pathogen

germane: 5 happy; 7 fitting, in point, on point, related; 8 relevant; 10 admissible, applicable, felicitous point

germanium: 2 Ge

German measles: 7 rubella

german pancake: 11 pfannkuchen

German shepherd: 8 alsatian; 15 German police dog

German silver: 12 nickel silver; 10 white metal

Germany: 11 Deutschland

germ cell: 6 gamete; 7 sex cell; 14 germinal matter

germicidal: 12 bactericidal, disinfectant

germicide: 12 antimicrobic, disinfectant; 13 antimicrobial

germinal: 7 seminal; 8 creative; 10 productive; 11 originative

germinal matter: 6 gamete; 8 germ cell

germinate: 3 bud; 4 spud; 5 shoot; 6 sprout; 7 shoot up; 8 sprout up; 9 pullulate

germination: 7 genesis; 9 sprouting; 10 gemination, generation, 11 procreation, propagation

gerontologist: 12 geriatrician

gerontology: 10 geriatrics

gerrymander: 6 double; 7 finesse; 9 temporize; 10 circumvent

gest: 6 vagary; 7 gesture, exploit; 9 adventure; 12 extravaganza

gestate: 4 bear; 5 carry; 6 expect

gestation: 5 ferry; 7 passage, sitting; 8 hatching; 9 pregnancy; 10 incubation

geste: 6 vagary; 7 gesture; 10 deportment 12 extravaganza

gesticulate: 6 motion; 7 gesture

gestural: 4 sign; 6 signed; 9 nonverbal; 12 sign language

gesture: 6 motion; 9 nonverbal; 11 gesticulate; 13 gesticulation

get: 2 go; 3 aim, can, fix, let, may, see, wax; 4 beat, come, draw, find, gain, grow, have, make, sire, take; 5 amaze, beget, begin, bring, catch, cause, drive, fetch, grasp, incur, reach, scram, start; 6 arrest, arrive, baffle, become, convey, father, follow, gravel, induce, obtain, pay off, puzzle, set out, suffer, whip in; 7 acquire, buzz off, capture, contact, develop, discern, flummox, mystify, nonplus, pay back, perplex, procure, produce, receive, stupefy, stupify, sustain, trounce, undergo; 8 bewilder, commence, conceive, contract, engender, generate, perceive, set about, start out; 9 bugger off, dumbfound, recognize, stimulate; 10 bring forth, experience, get in touch

geta: 4 clog; 5 sabot; 6 patten

getable: 8 gettable; 10 attainable, come-atable, obtainable, procurable

get aboard: 5 board; 6 embark; 10 get on board

get at: 3 rag, vex; **4** nark, rile; **5** annoy, devil, get to, trace; **6** access, bother, gravel, nettle; **8** irritate; **9** get hold of

get ahead: 3 win; **4** boom, gain, go on; **6** come on, expand, move on, pass on, push on, thrive; **7** advance, go ahead, press on, prosper; **8** flourish; **9** come ahead, come along, get before, go forward, move ahead, pass ahead, push ahead; **10** gain ground, get forward, go forward, press ahead

getaway: 3 lam; **6** pickup

get back at: 3 pay; **6** pay off; **7** pay back, get even; **11** take revenge

get by: 4 cope, deal; **6** escape, get off, get out, make do, manage; **7** contend, get away, grapple, make out

get canned: 7 be fired; **10** get the sack; **11** be dismissed

get cracking: 8 get going; **9** get moving; **10** get rolling, get started, get weaving

get down: 5 light, lower; **6** alight, deject, dismay, get off; **7** depress, let down, put down, set down, swallow, unhorse; **8** cast down, dismount, dispirit, take down; **9** bring down, write down; **10** demoralize

get going: 2 go; **5** start; **6** set out; **9** get moving; **10** get rolling, get started, get weaving, hit the road; **11** get cracking, get underway

get hitched: 3 wed; **4** join; **5** marry

get in: 3 bag, net; **4** go in, sack; **5** board, enter, get on, go far; **6** arrive, come in, draw in, embark, go into, make it, move in, pull in, render, secure, turn in; **7** deliver, get into; **8** go aboard, hand over, move into; **9** bring home, go on board

get into: 3 don; **4** go in, wear; **5** enter, get in, put on; **6** assume, come in, go into, take to; **8** move into

get in touch: 3 get; **5** reach; **7** connect, contact; **9** touch base

get married: 3 wed; **4** join; **5** marry; **7** conjoin, espouse; **10** get hitched [U.S. slang], hook up with

get on: 3 age; **4** be on; **5** board, get in, hop on, mount; **6** come on, embark, go up on, jump on; **7** advance, climb on, get up on, get upon, mount up, shape up; **8** bestride, get along, go aboard, progress

get over: 4 swim; **5** cover, cross, track; **6** master, subdue; **7** get well; **8** get about, get round, overcome, pass over, surmount, traverse; **9** cut across, get across, pull round; **10** bounce back, cut through

get religion: 7 be saved; **11** be born again, be converted

get revenge: 6 avenge; **7** revenge; **9** vindicate

get rid of: 4 cull; **5** chuck, heave; **6** remove; **7** abolish, be rid of, discard, exclude; **8** be quit of, chuck out, shake off, throw out; **9** dispose of, eliminate, get quit of, throw away

gettable: 7 getable; **10** attainable, come-at-able, obtainable, procurable

get the bugs out: 5 debug; **7** correct; **9** shake down

get the hang: 6 master

get the picture: 3 dig; **5** grasp, savvy; **7** compass; **9** apprehend; **10** comprehend

get through: 4 dawn; **5** click, mop up, reach; **6** sink in; **7** clear up, contact; **8** come home, finish up; **9** finish off, get across, get hold of, go through, penetrate, polish off, while away

get through to: 3 get; **5** reach; **7** contact; **10** get in touch

getting: 7 gaining; **9** acquiring, obtaining, obtention, procuring; **10** obtainment; **11** acquisition, procurement

getting together: 7 meeting; **9** gathering; **10** assembling, converging; **14** coming together

getting well: 4 cure; **7** healing

get to: 3 rag, vex; **4** go to, make, nark, rile; **5** annoy, devil, get at, reach; **6** bother, come to, gravel, nettle

get together: 4 join, meet; **6** fall in, gather, muster; **7** collect, meeting; **8** assemble; **9** cooperate; **10** join forces; **11** collaborate

get tough: 9 clamp down

get under way: 8 take ship, **11** weigh anchor

getup: 3 rig; **6** outfit; **8** ensemble

get up: 4 cram, drum, lift, rise, swot; **5** arise, fig up, mug up, raise, tog up; **6** attire, blow up, bone up, call up, deck up, devise, jump up, rig out, rise up, tog out, wake up, work up; **7** bring up, coach up, deck out, dress up, elevate, fancy up, gussy up, light up, prepare, raise up, stand up, start up; **8** organize, summon up; **9** grind away, overdress

get-up-and-go: 4 push; **6** energy

get well: 4 heal, mend; **5** amend; **7** get over; **8** get about, get round; **9** pull round; **10** bounce back

get word: 3 see; **4** hear; **5** learn; **6** pick up; **7** find out, get wind; **8** discover, get a line

gewgaw: 4 gaud; **5** curio, paste; **6** bangle, bauble, fallal, finery, tinsel, trifle; **7** bibelot, novelty, spangle, trinket, whatnot; **8** chotchke; **9** bagatelle, bric-a-brac, pinchbeck, tchotchke; **10** knickknack

Ghana: 9 Gold Coast

ghastly: 3 dun, wan; **4** ashy, cold, dead, dull, grim; **5** ashen, dingy, faint, muddy; **6** glassy, grisly, leaden, sallow; **7** charnel, macabre; **8** gruesome; **10** cadaverous, lackluster, sepulchral

ghee: 6 butter; **15** clarified butter

Gheg: 11 Gheg dialect

ghetto: 4 pale; **6** barrio; **7** enclave, reserve; **8** preserve; **11** reservation

ghillie: 6 gillie

ghost: 4 soul; 5 bosom, haunt, heart, manes, shade, spook, touch, trace; 6 breast, obsess, shadow, spirit, vision, wraith; 7 specter, spectre; 8 inner man, revenant; 10 apparition, ghostwrite, heart's core; 11 ghostwriter

ghost gum: 7 snow gum; 8 white ash; 18 Eucalyptus coriacea; 20 Eucalyptus pauciflora

ghostliness: 8 eeriness

ghostly: 8 spectral; 9 ghostlike, spiritual, uncarthly; 10 phantasmal; 12 apparitional, supernatural

ghost of a chance: 7 bad odds, poor bet; 8 long odds, long shot, poor odds; 9 fat chance [iron], off chance; 10 slim chance

ghoul: 6 zombie; 7 monster; 11 graverobber; 12 body snatcher

ghoulish: 6 morbid

GHQ: 11 command post; 19 general headquarters

GHz: 2 Gc; 9 gigacycle, gigahertz

Gi: 2 Gb; 7 gilbert

giant: 4 hulk; 5 jumbo, titan, whale; 7 goliath, monster, titanic; 8 behemoth, colossal, colossus, gigantic; 9 giant star, giant-like, gigantean; 10 gargantuan; 11 elephantine, heavyweight

giant anteater: 7 ant bear; 8 tamanoir; 13 great anteater

giant armadillo: 4 tatu; 5 tatou

giant bamboo: 8 kyo-chiku

giantism: 9 gigantism; 10 overgrowth

giant-like: 5 giant; 7 titanic; 8 colossal, gigantic; 9 gigantean

giant lizard: 12 dragon lizard, Komodo dragon, Komodo lizard

giant scallop: 10 sea scallop

giant sequoia: 7 big tree; 13 Sierra redwood; 15 Sequoia gigantea

giant squid: 12 architeuthis

giaour: 5 alien; 7 gentile, heathen, infidel; 8 Nazarene

gibber: 5 clack, prate; 6 gabble, jabber, piffle, tattle; 7 blabber, chatter, maunder, palaver, prattle, twaddle; 9 gibberish; 12 tittle-tattle

gibberish: 6 gibber; 8 nonsense; 10 hocus-pocus, mumbo jumbo

gibbet: 5 brand; 6 behead, expose; 7 gallous, gallows, pillory, turn off; 8 scaffold, string up; 9 bowstring; 10 stigmatize

gibbose: 7 gibbous

gibbosity: 3 jut; 4 bump, hump; 5 bilge, bulge; 8 swelling; 9 extrusion; 10 prominence, protrusion; 11 excrescence, gibbousness; 12 protuberance

gibbous: 7 bulbous, bulging, gibbose, swollen; 9 distended; 10 humpbacked

gibbousness: 3 jut; 4 bump, hump; 5 bulge; 9 extrusion, gibbosity; 10 prominence, protrusion; 11 excrescence; 12 protuberance

gibe: 3 boo, dig, fit; 4 barb, gird, hiss, hoot, jeer, jibe, quip, shot, slam, twit, wipe; 5 agree, check, fling, flout, match, scoff, shaft, sneer, tally, taunt; 6 deride; 7 barrack, laugh at, snigger; 8 ridicule; 10 correspond

Gibraltar: 5 Calpe; 15 Rock of Gibraltar

giddily: 7 dizzily; 13 light-headedly

giddiness: 7 vertigo; 9 dizziness, silliness; 15 lightheadedness

giddy: 4 wild; 5 dizzy, rabid, silly, woozy; 6 doting, raving; 7 berserk, frantic; 8 frenetic, frenzied, rambling, unhinged, volatile, wild-eyed; 9 airheaded, delirious, frivolous, insensate, possessed, wandering; 10 incoherent, reasonless, sleeveless; 11 dithyrambic, empty-headed, lightheaded, vertiginous

gift: 4 give; 5 endow, endue, indue; 6 giving, invest, talent; 7 aptness, empower, present, turn for; 8 aptitude, free gift; 9 endowment; 11 capacity for

gifted: 4 able, cute; 6 clever; 7 endowed; 8 talented; 10 felicitous

gift shop: 11 novelty shop

gig: 3 job; 5 funny, lance, skiff, spear; 6 fizgig; 7 fishgig; 8 carriage; 10 engagement

gigabyte: 1 G; 2 Gb

gigacycle: 2 Gc; 3 GHz; 9 gigahertz

gigahertz: 2 Gc; 3 GHz; 9 gigacycle

gigantean: 5 giant; 7 titanic; 8 colossal, gigantic; 9 giant-like

gigantic: 4 wiry; 5 giant; 6 brawny, sinewy; 7 mammoth, titanic; 8 colossal, muscular, stalwart, well-knit; 9 giant-like, gigantean, strapping, well-built

gigantism: 8 giantism; 10 overgrowth

giggle: 4 crow; 6 cackle, laugh, titter; 7 chortle, chuckle, snicker, snigger, twitter

gigot: 9 leg of lamb

Gila: 9 Gila River

Gilbert: 14 William Gilbert; 17 Sir William Gilbert; 21 William Schwenk Gilbert

gilbert: 2 Gb, Gi

gild: 4 club, warm; 5 grain, guild, japan, lodge, order, paint, plate; 6 begild, enamel, engild, polish; 7 furbish, lacquer, smarten, society, varnish; 9 whitewash

gilded: 4 gilt, gold; 6 deluxe, golden; 7 aureate, opulent; 8 princely, specious; 9 luxurious, sumptuous; 12 meretricious

gill: 4 rill; 6 gullet; 7 lamella, rivulet; 8 branchia

gill arch: 7 gill bar; 13 branchial arch

gill cleft: 8 gill slit; 14 branchial cleft

gilled: 10 branchiate

gill-less: 10 abranchial; 11 abranchiate, abranchious

gillyflower: 5 stock; 9 carnation, clove pink

gilt: 4 gold, rich; 6 gilded, golden, ornate; 7 aureate, gilding

gilt-edged: 4 rare; 9 priceless

gimcrack: 4 loud, mean, vile; 5 cheap, curio, flash, gaudy, paste, sorry, tacky, tatty, weedy; 6 bauble, brassy, flashy, flimsy, garish, gewgaw, meager, scurvy, shabby, tawdry, tinsel, trashy, trifle; 7 bibelot, fissile, novelty, scrubby, shivery, spangle, trinket; 8 chotchke, kickshaw, nicknack, trumpery, whim-wham, wretched; 9 bagatelle, bric-a-brac, miserable, tchotchke, worthless; 10 catchpenny, knickknack

gimlet: 5 auger, probe, rimer, scoop; 6 chisel, dibble, lancet, trepan, warder; 7 terrier; 10 screw auger

gimmick: 5 gizmo, twist; 6 device, doodad; 7 gubbins; 8 dohickey, dojigger; 9 doohickey, thingummy; 10 thingmabob, thingmajig; 11 thingamabob, thingamajig, thingumabob, thingumajig

gimp: 3 hem; 4 list, neat, tidy, trim, welt; 5 frill; 6 edging, fringe, spruce; 7 flounce, limping, valance; 8 furbelow, gameness, lameness, selvedge, skirting, trimming; 9 gimpiness

gimpiness: 4 gimp, 7 limping; 8 gameness, lameness

gin: 4 jinn, mill; 5 genie, lathe, noose, snare; 7 pitfall; 8 gin rummy; 9 cotton gin

ginger: 3 pep; 7 gingery; 8 turmeric; 9 peppiness; 10 gingerroot; 14 powdered ginger

gingerly: 8 with care

ginger up: 5 pep up; 6 jazz up; 7 juice up

gingiva: 3 gum

gingko: 6 ginkgo

ginkgo: 6 gingko; 12 Ginkgo biloba; 14 maidenhair tree

Ginkgo biloba: 6 gingko, ginkgo, gnetum; 14 maidenhair tree

ginkgo family: 11 Ginkgoaceae

gin mill: 3 bar, pub; 6 saloon, tavern; 7 barroom; 8 mug house, pothouse, taphouse; 9 gin palace; 11 public house

Ginnie Mae: 4 GNMA [acron]

gin rummy: 3 gin; 10 knock rummy

ginseng: 6 nin-sin

Gipsy: 5 Gypsy

Giraffa: 12 genus Giraffa

Giraffa camelopardalis: 7 giraffe

giraffe: 10 camelopard; 21 Giraffa camelopardalis

girandole: 6 luster, sconce; 9 girandola; 10 chandelier

girasol: 4 opal; 8 fire opal, girasole; 18 Jerusalem artichoke

gird: 3 arm, lap; 4 gibe, girt, hiss, hoot, jeer, twit; 5 beset, bound, girth, steel, taunt; 6 begird, deride, girdle, harden, swathe; 7 barrack, build up, compass, embrace,

enclose, environ, fortify, inclose, laugh at, snigger, sustain; 8 encircle, ridicule, surround; 9 encompass; 10 case harden, circumvent

girder: 4 beam; 5 joist; 6 lintel, rafter; 7 tiebeam

girdle: 4 band, belt, gird, girt, sash; 5 clasp, girth, stays; 6 corset, deaden, fascia, fillet, wreath, zodiac; 7 baldric, garland; 8 cincture, corselet; 9 waistband; 10 waistcloth

girdling: 7 girding; 10 encircling; 11 surrounding; 12 circumjacent, encompassing

girl: 4 lass, miss; 5 child, fille, missy; 6 lassie; 8 daughter; 9 young lady; 10 girlfriend, lady friend, little girl, young woman; 11 female child

girl-bachelor: 4 maid; 12 bachelor girl, bachelor lady; 14 unmarried woman

girlfriend: 4 girl; 8 mistress, paramour; 10 lady friend

girlhood: 9 childhood; 10 maidenhood

girt: 4 band, belt, gird; 5 clasp, girth; 6 begird, girdle, zodiac; 7 baldric

girth: 4 gird, girt, size; 5 cinch; 6 begird, girdle; 10 dimensions

gist: 3 nub, sum; 4 core, meat, pith; 5 heart, point; 6 burden, center, effect, kernel, marrow; 7 essence; 9 basic part, main point, substance, vital part; 10 inwardness; 11 nitty-gritty

GI tract: 13 digestive tube; 14 digestive tract; 15 alimentary canal, alimentary tract

give: 3 pay; 4 bate, bend, feed, gift, grub, hand, have, hold, make, open, pass, thaw; 5 allow, apply, break, grant, leave, reach, relax, throw, yield; 6 afford, cave in, chip in, commit, devote, ease up, fall in, give up, impart, kick in, pass on, reduce, render, return, spring; 7 abandon, deliver, founder, give way, present, take off; 8 collapse, dedicate, discount, generate, hand over, make over, mark down, move over, pass over, turn over; 9 establish, price down, sacrifice; 10 bring about, contribute; 11 deliver over, springiness

give advice: 6 advise; 7 counsel; 11 give counsel; 12 impart advice; 18 give a piece of advice [Fr]

give a hoot: 4 care; 9 care a hang

give aid: 3 aid; 4 help; 6 assist, succor; 8 bring aid, lend help

give an address: 4 talk; 5 orate, speak; 7 lecture; 9 give a talk; 11 give a speech, make a speech

give-and-take: 4 word; 6 banter; 8 backchat, raillery; 10 discussion; 11 interchange; 13 reciprocation

give and take: 5 hedge, trade; 6 equity, square; 7 justice, traffic; 8 fair play; 9 keep a shop, ply a trade, tit for tat; **10** buy and sell, compromise, quid pro quo

give an inch and take a mile: 6 assume; **7** presume; **8** arrogate, feel free, make bold, make free; **12** take a liberty

giveaway: 7 freebee; **8** game show, giveaway, gratuity

give away: 3 rat; **4** drop, shed, shop, stag; **5** break, grass, let on, peach, spare; **6** betray, expose, forego, impart, let out, resign, reveal, snitch, tell on; **7** declare, divulge, give out, hand out, present; **8** bring out, denounce, disclose, discover, dispense, part with, renounce; **9** dispose of; **10** distribute

give back: 5 repay; **6** refund, return; **7** restore; **9** restitute

give birth: 4 bear, have; **5** beget, birth, lie in; **6** birthe; **7** deliver; **9** fecundate; **10** bring forth

give consent: 6 accede, accept; **7** agree to, receive; **9** acquiesce; **10** comply with, fall in with; **11** acknowledge

give counsel: 6 advise; **7** counsel; **10** give advice; **12** impart advice

give forth: 4 emit; **6** exhale, get out, put out; **7** emanate; **8** put forth; **9** send forth

give in: 3 bow; **5** defer, yield; **6** accede, give up, submit; **7** give way, succumb; **9** give round; **11** buckle under; **12** knuckle under

give into: 6 relent; **8** come over; **9** come round

given: 3 apt; **5** fixed; **6** minded; **7** granted, tending; **8** disposed; **9** delivered; **10** handed over; **11** conditional, presumption, provisional; **12** precondition

given freely: 7 donated, granted; **8** bestowed

given name: 8 forename; **9** first name

give notice: 3 can; **4** fire, sack; **6** advise, notify; **7** apprise, apprize, dismiss; **8** force out, send away, send word, speak out; **9** terminate; **10** give the axe; **11** give warning

given up: 4 left; **8** deserted, forsaken; **9** abandoned, cast aside, given over; **10** disposed of; **12** relinquished

given warning: 6 warned; **9** cautioned; **10** admonished, forewarned

give off: 4 emit; **6** effuse; **7** breathe, give out, pass off

give one's word: 6 pledge; **7** promise

give out: 2 go; **3** die; **4** emit, fail; **5** break, eject, expel; **6** let out, run out; **7** conk out, deal out, dole out, fork out, give off, give way, hand out, mete out, push out, send out; **8** give away; **9** break down; **10** distribute, squeeze out

give quarter: 5 relax; **6** relent; **7** forbear

giver: 5 donor; **7** grantor; **9** presenter

give regards: 10 compliment

give rise: 7 produce; **10** bring about

give satisfaction: 9 apologize, beg pardon

give the axe: 3 can; **4** fire, sack; **7** dismiss; **8** force out, send away; **9** terminate; **10** give notice

give up: 4 cede, drop, free, give, quit, stop; **5** allow, cease, forgo, leave, let go, spare, waive, yield; **6** give in, lay off, render, resign, vacate; **7** abandon, deliver, drop out, forfeit, give way, lay down, let slip, release, throw in, throw up; **8** abdicate, abnegate, break off, give over, leave off, part with, renounce; **9** drop out of, give round, surrender; **10** relinquish; **11** discontinue

give way: 2 go; **3** die, fly; **4** drop, fade, fail, flag, give, halt, limp, sink; **5** break, burst, droop, shake, yield; **6** cave in, ease up, fall in, give in, give up, take on, totter; **7** conk out, crumble, decline, despond, founder, give out, tremble; **8** collapse, languish, move over; **9** break down, give round, lose heart

giving: 3 big; **4** free, gift; **7** liberal; **8** generous, handsome, princely; **9** bounteous, bountiful, unselfish; **10** bighearted, charitable, delivering, freehanded, full handed, munificent, openhanded; **11** handing over

givingly: 6 freely; **9** liberally; **10** charitably, generously; **11** bounteously, bountifully, unselfishly; **12** munificently, openhandedly

giving up: 6 ceding; **7** cession; **8** back down, yielding; **9** forsaking, surrender; **10** abandoning, falling out; **11** abandonment, dropping out, resignation; **12** capitulating, capitulation, dispensation, surrendering; **13** relinquishing

gizmo: 6 doodad, gadget, widget; **7** gimmick, gubbins; **8** dohickey, dojigger; **9** appliance, doohickey, thingummy; **10** thingmabob, thingmajig; **11** contraption, contrivance, convenience, thingamabob, thingamajig, thingumabob, thingumajig

gizzard: 3 maw; **4** craw, crop; **6** innards; **11** gastric mill, ventriculus

G-Jo: 7 shiatsu; **11** acupressure

glabrous: 4 oily; **6** glassy, smooth; **8** slippery; **9** lubricous

glace: 6 glazed; **7** candied; **11** crystalized

glacial: 3 icy; **5** gelid, polar; **6** arctic, boreal, frigid, frosty, frozen, wintry; **8** freezing, Siberian; **12** barely moving

glacial period: 6 ice age; **12** glacial epoch

glaciate: 6 freeze

glacier: 8 ice river

glacis: 6 buffer; **7** incline

glad: 4 good, lief; **5** happy, palmy; **7** beaming, halcyon

gladden: 3 joy; **5** cheer, elate; **7** animate, enliven, inspire; **8** inspirit; **10** exhilarate

gladdon: 11 gladdon iris; **12** stinking iris

glade: 4 dale, dell, glen, vale; **5** aisle, alley, grove, vista; **6** bottom, dingle, valley; **8** clearing

gladiate: 5 spiny; **7** spicate; **8** bristled, spicular; **9** bristling, setaceous spiniferous

gladiator: 5 boxer; **7** athlete, bruiser, fighter; **8** pugilist, wrestler; **12** prizefighter

gladiatorial: 7 polemic; **10** pugilistic; **12** disputatious; **13** controversial

gladiola: 9 gladiolus, sword lily

gladness: 3 joy; **4** glee; **7** delight; **9** enjoyment; **11** delectation, gladfulness

gladstone: 8 suitcase; **12** gladstone bag

glaive: 5 bilbo, brand, sword; **6** rapier; **8** whinyard; **10** broadsword

glamor: 7 glamour

glamorize: 10 glamourise; **11** romanticise, romanticize

glamour: 3 hex; **4** jinx; **5** witch; **6** glamor; **7** bewitch, enchant

glance: 4 leer, look, peek, peep, wink; **5** carom, glint, nudge, shrug; **7** glimpse

glance off: 4 clip; **5** carom; **7** file off; **9** branch off, sideswipe

glancing: 7 oblique

gland: 14 secretory organ

gland disease: 8 adenosis; **17** glandular disorder

glanders: 5 mange; **12** cattle plague, milk sickness

glandular: 8 visceral; **9** intuitive

glare: 4 beam, leer, ogle; **5** blaze; **6** glower; **7** flicker, glimmer, shimmer; **10** brilliance; **11** bright light; **13** dazzling light

glaring: 4 rank; **5** clear, glary, gross, plain; **6** crying; **7** blazing, flaring, fulgent, staring; **8** apparent, blinding, dazzling, definite, distinct, flagrant, unshaded; **9** egregious; **10** in full view, well marked; **11** conspicuous, in plain view, well defined; **12** stark staring

glaringly: 7 awfully, clearly, plainly, starkly; **8** famously; **9** amazingly, staringly, strangely; **10** apparently, definitely, distinctly, incredibly; **11** egregiously, marvelously, prominently, wonderfully; **12** emphatically, stupendously, surprisingly, tremendously; **13** astonishingly, conspicuously, extravagantly

glary: 7 blazing, fulgent, glaring; **8** blinding, dazzling

glass: 5 glaze; **7** glass in, tumbler; **8** glassful, spyglass; **9** glass over, glaze over, telescope; **10** field glass; **12** looking glass; **13** drinking glass

glasscutter: 6 glazer; **7** glazier; **11** glassworker

glassed: 6 glazed

glasses: 5 specs; **8** eyeglass; **10** eyeglasses, spectacles

glass fiber: 10 fiberglass; **12** optical fiber, optical fibre

glasshouse: 7 nursery; **10** greenhouse

glassiness: 13 crystallinity

glassless: 8 unglazed

glass over: 5 glass, glaze; **9** glaze over

glass showcase: 7 vitrine; **8** showcase

glass wool: 10 fiberglass

glasswork: 9 glassware

glassworker: 6 glazer; **7** glazier; **11** glasscutter

glassy: 3 dun, wan; **4** ashy, cold, dead, dull, oily; **5** ashen, dingy, faint, muddy; **6** glazed, glossy, leaden, sallow; **7** ghastly, hyaline; **8** glabrous, slippery, vitreous; **9** burnished, lubricous, vitrified; **10** cadaverous, lackluster; **11** crystalline

glaucoma: 10 eye disease

Glaucomys: 14 flying squirrel 14 genus Glaucomys

glaver: 4 coax; **6** cajole; **7** wheedle

glaze: 5 candy, glass, gloss; **6** finish; **7** glazing; **9** glass over, glaze over, sugarcoat

glazed: 5 shiny; **6** glassy; **7** glassed

glazier: 6 glazer; **11** glasscutter, glassworker

gleam: 3 ray; **4** beam, glow; **5** glint, shine, spark; **6** pencil, streak, stream, **7** glimmer, glisten, glitter, twinkle; **8** gleaming, lambency, light ray; **9** scintilla

glean: 4 cull, reap; **6** winnow; **7** harvest

gleaning: 10 excerption; **11** eclecticism

gleanings: 8 cuttings

glebe: 5 manse; **7** deanery, rectory; **8** vicarage; **9** parsonage; **10** presbytery

Gleditsia: 10 locust tree; **14** genus Gleditsia

glee: 3 joy; **5** gloat, mirth; **7** delight; **8** gladness, gloating, high glee, hilarity; **9** enjoyment; **11** delectation, gleefulness; **12** mirthfulness

gleeful: 6 elated, joyful; **8** jubilant

gleek: 4 gibe, gird, hiss, hoot, jeer, jibe, quip, twit, wipe; **5** sneer, taunt; **6** deride; **7** barrack, laugh at, snigger; **8** flouting, ridicule

glen: 4 dale, dell, vale; **5** glade, grove; **6** bottom, dingle, valley

glengarry: 8 glengary; **11** garrison cap, overseas cap

Glenn: 9 John Glenn

glia: 4 glia; **9** glial cell, neuroglia

glib: 3 pat; **5** slick; **6** fluent; **7** voluble; **8** flippant, slippery; **11** glib-tongued; **13** smoothtongued

glide: 4 flit, skim, slip; **5** coast, skate, slide; **7** gliding, sailing, soaring; **9** semivowel; **11** sailplaning

glide path: 8 approach; **10** glide slope; **12** approach path

glider: 9 sailplane

glider pilot: 5 pilot; **9** bush pilot, test pilot

gliding: 5 glide; 7 sailing, soaring; 11 sailplaning

gliding bacteria: 10 myxobacter; 12 myxobacteria

glimmer: 4 beam, loom; 5 blaze, glare, gleam; 7 flicker, shimmer, twinkle; 8 gleaming; 10 glimmering

glimpse: 3 eye; 4 peep; 5 glint; 6 glance; 7 inkling

glint: 4 look, peek, peep; 5 flash, gleam, shine, spark; 6 glance; 7 flicker, glimpse, glisten, glitter; 11 take a gander

glinting: 6 fulgid; 7 sparkly; 8 aglitter, glittery; 9 sparkling; 10 glistering, glittering; 11 scintillant; 13 scintillating

glisten: 5 gleam, glint, shine; 7 glister, glitter, sparkle; 13 scintillation

glister: 7 glisten, glitter, sparkle; 13 scintillation

glitch: 3 bug

glitter: 4 dash, live; 5 flash, gleam, glint, glitz, shine, strut; 6 flaunt, splash; 7 glisten, glister, shimmer, sparkle, splurge; 8 flourish; 9 coruscate, gain honor; 11 scintillate; 12 corruscation

glittery: 6 fulgid; 7 sparkly; 8 aglitter, glinting; 9 sparkling; 10 glistering, glittering; 11 scintillant

glitz: 4 dash; 5 strut; 6 splash; 7 glitter, splurge; 8 loudness; 9 brashness, gaudiness; 10 flashiness, garishness, tawdriness

glitzy: 5 gaudy; 10 glittering

gloam: 4 dark; 8 twilight

gloaming: 4 dusk, fall; 7 dewy eve; 8 cockshut, evenfall, twilight; 9 nightfall

gloat: 4 crow, glee; 6 squint; 7 triumph; 8 gloating

glob: 4 ball, clod, lump; 5 chunk, clump

global: 5 world; 7 globose, spheric; 8 globular; 9 orbicular, planetary, spherical, worldwide; 10 ball-shaped

globe: 3 orb; 4 ball; 5 Earth, terra, world; 6 sphere

globefish: 6 puffer; 8 blowfish

globegirdler: 9 buttercup; 12 globetrotter

globetrotter: 13 world traveler

Globicephala: 9 blackfish; 10 black whale, pilot whale; 17 genus Globicephala

globular: 6 global; 7 globose, spheric; 9 orbicular, spherical; 10 ball-shaped

glockenspiel: 7 marimba; 9 xylophone; 10 vibraphone

glom: 3 cop; 4 hook, take; 5 steal, sieze, catch; 6 snitch, thieve; 8 knock off

gloom: 4 murk; 8 glumness; 9 obscurity; 10 gloominess, somberness, sombreness

gloominess: 5 blues, dumps, gloom; 7 dimness, sadness; 8 darkness, doldrums, glumness, the blues, the dumps; 9 dejection,

heaviness, moodiness, sulkiness, tristesse [Fr]; 10 bad spirits, blue devils, depression, dismalness, low spirits, melancholy, somberness, sullenness; 11 joylessness, melancholia; 12 dejectedness, heart sinking, mournfulness; 13 cheerlessness

gloomy: 4 blue, dark, drab, glum, grim; 5 dingy, drear, lurid, sorry, sulky; 6 dismal, dreary, grumpy, morose, somber, sullen, triste [Fr]; 7 grouchy, joyless; 8 dejected, frowning, frumpish, gloomful, glooming, growling, scowling; 9 cheerless, glowering, long-faced, saddening, saturnine; 10 depressing, depressive

glorification: 5 glory, grace; 6 praise; 7 hosanna; 8 doxology; 10 dedication; 11 benediction, celebration; 12 canonization, consecration, enshrinement, enthronement, idealisation, idealization

glorify: 4 laud; 5 bless, exalt, extol, swell; 6 praise; 7 dignify, magnify; 8 proclaim, say grace; 10 make much of; 11 sing praises

glorious: 7 radiant; 8 splendid; 9 brilliant, respected; 11 illustrious, magnificent, redoubtable, resplendent; 13 splendiferous

Glorious Revolution: 17 English Revolution; 19 Bloodless Revolution

glory: 4 aura, halo; 5 honor, unity; 6 nimbus; 7 aureola, majesty; 8 holiness; 11 sovereignty; 12 immutability, resplendence, resplendency; 13 glorification

gloss: 5 blind, color, cover, glaze, gloss, guise; 6 finish, polish, rubric; 7 burnish, comment, varnish; 8 glossary; 10 glossiness, perversion, subterfuge; 12 whitewashing; 13 falsification

glossa: 6 lingua, tongue; 7 clapper

glossarist: 9 glossator; 10 prolocutor

glossary: 5 gloss; 10 dictionary

glossator: 12 glossologist; 13 glossographer

glossed over: 7 excused; 10 allowed for

glossina: 6 tsetse, tzetze; 9 tsetse fly, tzetze fly

glossiness: 5 gloss; 6 polish; 7 burnish

glossographer: 9 glossator; 12 glossologist, lexicologist; 13 lexicographer

gloss over: 4 slur; 5 gloze, mince; 6 garble, hush up; 7 varnish; 8 disguise, minimize, slur over; 9 gloze over, skate over, skimp over, sleek over, whitewash; 10 smooth over

glossy: 5 satin, shiny, silky, sleek, slick; 6 glassy, satiny, sheeny, silken; 7 shining; 8 lustrous, silklike; 9 burnished; 10 calendered, glistening

glottal stop: 12 glottal catch; 14 glottal plosive

glout: 4 pout; 5 frown, lower, scowl; 6 glower

glove: 4 mitt; 6 gloves; 9 gauntlet; 11 boxing glove; 12 baseball mitt; 13 baseball glove

glow: 3 dye, hue; 4 beam, boil, burn, cast,

tint, warm; **5** broil, color, flush, gleam, gusto, shade, shine, swell, tinge; **6** livery, warmth; **7** blister, glowing, radiate, unction; **8** gleaming, glowing, radiance, tincture; **9** freshness, vehemence; **10** coloration; **12** give off light, give out light, luminescence; **13** incandescence

glower: 4 pout; **5** frown, glare, lower, scowl

glowering: 4 dark, dour, glum, grim, sour; **5** moody, sulky; **6** gloomy, grumpy, morose, sullen; **7** grouchy; **8** frumpish, growling, scowling; **9** saturnine; **10** in the dumps, in the sulks, out of sorts

glowing: 3 hot; **4** glow, warm; **5** aglow, fiery, vivid; **6** ardent, fervid, lively, lucent, red-hot; **7** burning, fervent, flaming, gushing, lambent, shining, smoking; **8** dazzling, luminous, radiance, spirited, splendid, swelling; **9** ebullient, sparkling; **10** passionate; **11** resplendent

glowworm: 7 firefly, june bug; **12** lightning bug

gloze: 3 pet; **4** slur; **5** gloss, humor, mince; **6** coquet, soothe; **8** slur over; **9** gloss over

glucinium: 2 Be; **9** beryllium

glucinum: 9 beryllium

glucose: 8 dextrose

glue: 3 gum; **5** paste; **8** mucilage, adhesive

glued: 6 pasted

gluey: 5 gooey, gummy, pasty, tacky; **6** sticky, viscid; **7** viscous; **8** adhesive; **9** glutinous; **12** mucilaginous

glum: 4 dark, dour, grim, sour; **5** moody, sulky; **6** gloomy, grumpy, morose, sullen; **7** grouchy; **8** frumpish, growling, scowling; **9** glowering, long-faced, saturnine; **10** in the dumps, in the sulks, out of sorts

glume: 5 bract

glumly: 6 dourly; **8** sullenly

glut: 4 cloy, drug, glut, load, pall; **5** binge, gorge, jenny, slake, stuff, whelm; **6** englut, fill up, heddle, load up, pig out, quench; **7** can hook, engorge, overeat, satiate, surfeit; **8** scarf out; **9** overgorge; **10** gormandise, gormandize, oversupply; **11** gourmandize, ingurgitate, overindulge

gluten: 3 gel; **4** jell; **6** starch; **7** gelatin; **9** semisolid

glutenous: 4 ropy; **5** gluey, gummy, pasty; **6** clammy, mastic, sticky, viscid; **7** clotted, gelatin, viscous; **10** albuminous, gelatinous; **12** mucilaginous

gluteus: 13 gluteal muscle, gluteus muscle

glutted: 8 overfull

glutton: 3 hog, pig; **8** gourmand; **9** cormorant, wolverine

gluttonize: 5 fress

gluttony: 4 gula; **8** voracity; **10** overeating; **13** voraciousness

glyburide: 7 DiaBeta; **9** Micronase

glycerin: 8 glycerol; **9** glycerine

glycerol: 8 glycerin; **9** glycerine

Glycine: 12 genus Glycine

Glycine max: 3 soy; **4** soja, soya; **7** soybean; **8** soja bean, soya bean; **12** soybean plant

glycogen: 12 animal starch

glycol: 4 diol; **10** ethanediol; **14** ethylene glycol

Glycyrrhiza: 8 licorice; **16** genus Glycyrrhiza

glyoxaline: 9 imidazole, iminazole

glyptic art: 12 glyptography

glyptics: 13 lithoglyptics

glyptotheca: 10 art gallery

gm: 1 g; **4** gram; **6** gramme

G-man: 8 FBI agent; **13** government man

GMT: 2 UT; **3** UT1; **13** Greenwich Time, universal time; **17** Greenwich Mean Time

gnarl: 4 bark, kink, knot, pout, snap; **5** croak, frown, gnash, growl, lower, scowl, snarl; **6** murmur, mutter; **7** grumble; **11** knit the brow

gnarled: 6 gnarly, knotty; **7** knobbed, knotted, snarled

gnarly: 6 knotty; **7** gnarled, knobbed, knotted

gnash: 4 pout, snap; **5** frown, gnarl, growl, lower, scowl, snarl; **11** knit the brow

gnaw: 4 bite, chew, hurt, pain; **5** chafe, champ, eat at, erode, gripe, munch, sting; **6** appall, crunch, gnaw at, mumble, rankle; **7** corrode, horrify, munch on; **8** wear away; **9** masticate

gnawer: 6 rodent; **13** gnawing animal

gnawing: 6 aching, biting; **7** chafing, hurting; **8** pinching, smarting, stinging

gnawing mammal: 9 lagomorph

gnetum: 6 gingko; **12** Ginkgo biloba, Gnetum gnemon; **14** maidenhair tree

Gnetum gnemoninkgo: 6 gingko, gnetum; **12** Ginkgo biloba; **14** maidenhair tree

GNMA: 9 Ginnie Mae

gnome: 3 elf [fig]; **5** dwarf, maxim; **8** aphorism

Gnostic: 4 Magi; **6** Sabian; **11** Rosicrucian

GNP: 20 gross national product

gnu: 10 wildebeest

go: 3 die, fit, fly, get, run, try; **4** exit, fade, fail, last, lead, live, mode, move, pass, shot, tour, turn, work; **5** blend, break, crack, essay, fling, offer, plump, rifle, sound, spell, start, trial, whirl; **6** become, belong, depart, endure, expire, extend, go away, go game, hold up, live on, perish, recede, retire, run low, travel, vanish; **7** attempt, blend in, conk out, decease, give out, give way, hold out, operate, proceed, survive; **8** be moving, be no more, dissolve, endeavor, fade away, function, get going, locomote, melt away, move back, move from, pass away, run short, vaporize; **9** break down, disappear, evaporate

goad: 4 dram, lash, prod, spur, urge, whet, whip; **5** impel, prick; **6** fillip, incite, needle, nettle, urging; **7** goading, inspire; **8** prodding, spurring, stimulus; **9** incentive, stimulate; **10** incitement; **11** provocation

goading: 4 goad, prod, spur; **6** urging; **8** prodding, spurring

go after: 3 dog, tag; **4** be at, tail; **5** aim at, chase, go for, track, trail; **6** bid for, pursue; **7** be after, drive at, level at, point at; **8** aspire at, labor for, quest for

go against: 4 buck; **5** break; **6** breach, offend; **7** infract, violate; **10** run against, transgress; **11** beat against, grapple with

goal: 3 aim, end; **6** object; **8** end point, goalpost, quo animo [Lat]; **9** intention, objective; **11** destination

goal-directed: 9 purposive

goalie: 9 net-keeper; **10** goalkeeper, goaltender

goalpost: 4 goal; **8** uprights

goaltender: 6 goalie; **9** net-keeper; **10** goalkeeper

go ape: 4 foam, fume, rage, roar; **7** bluster; **9** go bananas; **10** hit the roof; **11** blow one's top, flip one's lid

go around: 6 bypass, rotate, spread; **7** keep off, revolve; **8** outflank; **9** circulate, get around; **12** short-circuit; **14** circumnavigate

goat: 3 rip; **4** butt, rake; **5** satyr; **6** lecher, stooge; **7** Don Juan, fast man, gallant, seducer; **9** debauchee, ladies' man, capricorn

goat cheese: 6 chevre

goatfish: 9 red mullet, surmullet

goatsucker: 8 nightjar; **11** caprimulgid

gob: 3 tar; **4** lump; **5** mouth; **6** sailor, sea dog, seaman; **7** Jack-tar, mariner, old salt; **8** seafarer

go back: 5 recur; **6** return; **7** get back, put back, recover, run back

go back on: 6 renege; **8** renege on

go bananas: 4 foam, fume, rage, roar; **5** go ape; **7** bluster; **10** hit the roof; **11** blow one's top, flip one's lid; **12** blow one's cool; **13** hit the ceiling

gobbet: 3 sop; **4** drop, inch, lump, mass, seed; **5** bolus, crumb, patch; **6** morsel, tatter; **7** flitter, fritter; **9** scantling

gobble: 4 bolt; **6** devour; **8** bolt down, gulp down, shovel in

gobbler: 3 tom; **9** tom turkey

go-between: 5 agent; **8** delegate, mediator; **9** middleman; **10** negotiator, peacemaker; **12** intermediary; **13** intermediator

Gobi: 10 Gobi Desert

goblet: 3 cup; **7** chalice

goblin: 3 hob, orc; **9** hobglobin, hobgoblin

go bonkers: 5 go mad; **6** go nuts, run mad; **7** flip out, go crazy

gobs: 4 lots, tons, wads; **5** heaps, loads, piles, rafts, scads, slews; **6** dozens, oodles, scores, stacks; **8** lashings

goby: 7 gudgeon

go by: 4 pass; **5** go off, lapse; **6** elapse, go away, go past, pass by, slip by; **7** evasion, glide by, go along, go under, pass off, slide by, surpass; **8** go beyond, pass away, slip away, travel by

go-cart: 4 cart, pram; **6** pusher, walker; **8** handcart, pushcart, stroller; **9** baby buggy, pushchair; **10** baby-walker; **12** baby carriage, perambulator

go crazy: 5 go mad; **6** go nuts, run mad; **7** flip out; **9** go bonkers

God: 5 Deity; **7** Godhead; **8** Divinity; **12** Supreme Being

god: 4 idol; **5** deity; **7** goddess; **8** divinity, immortal, pagan god; **11** graven image

God Almighty: 4 Lord; **6** Divine; **7** Creator, Godhead, Jehovah; **8** Almighty

goddess: 3 god; **4** duck, idol; **5** angel, deity; **7** darling; **8** ladylove, pagan god; **9** inamorata

go deep: 5 go far

god-fearing: 5 pious; **6** devout

godforsaken: 4 lorn, wild; **5** waste; **6** desert; **7** forlorn; **8** desolate

Godiva: 10 Lady Godiva

God knows: 8 who knows; **11** Heaven knows, nobody knows; **12** the Lord knows

godless: 6 unholy; **7** ungodly; **10** irreverent; **11** irreligious

godlessness: 7 atheism; **8** unbelief; **9** disbelief; **10** irreligion; **11** incredulity, lack of faith, non-religion

godlike: 6 divine; **7** angelic; **8** seraphic; **10** heaven-born

godly: 4 holy; **5** pious; **6** devout, divine; **7** devoted; **8** reverent; **9** pietistic, religious, spiritual; **10** worshipful; **14** heavenly-minded

go down: 3 set; **4** fall, sink, wane; **5** crash; **6** settle; **7** decline, descend, explode, go under

godsend: 5 bunce, gravy; **8** windfall; **9** blessings

Godship: 3 God; **5** Deity; **7** Godhead; **8** Divinity; **17** Judeo-Christian God

Godwin Austen: 2 K2; **7** Dapsang; **17** Mount Godwin Austen

Goeteborg: 8 Goteborg; **10** Gothenburg

Goethe: 23 Johann Wolfgang von Goethe

gofer: 6 Friday, gopher

goffer: 6 gopher; **7** gauffer

go for: 4 be at, hold, hope; **5** aim at, apply, fancy; **6** accept, bid for, take to, try for; **7** be after, consent, drive at, go after, level at, point at; **8** aspire at, labor for; **9** take aim at; **11** aspire after; **13** endeavor after

go-getter: 6 dynamo; **7** whiz-kid; **8** live wire, spitfire, whizz-kid; **10** ball of fire; **11** human dynamo

goggle: 4 gape, gawk, gawp; **5** plash

go halfway: 6 settle; **10** compromise

go halves: 7 split up; **10** divide with

Goidelic: 4 Erse; **6** Gaelic

go in: 5 enter, get in; **6** come in, go into; **7** get into; **8** move into

going: 4 exit, loss; **6** travel; **7** leaving, passing, release; **8** sledding; **9** departure, going away, traveling; **10** expiration; **11** translation; **13** translocating, translocation

going ahead: 8 progress; **9** advancing; **10** proceeding; **11** coming ahead, moving ahead, progressing, progression; **12** forging ahead, getting ahead, going forward

going away: 5 going; **7** leaving; **9** departure

going down: 7 descent; **10** declension, descending; **11** declination

going out: 4 exit; **5** issue; **6** egress; **7** exiting

going price: 9 fair price

going under: 10 foundering

goiter: 6 goitre, struma

gold: 2 Au, or; **4** gilt; **5** amber, aurum, ingot; **6** copper, gilded, golden, nugget, silver; **7** aureate, bullion; **9** gold color; **11** gold-colored; **13** precious metal

gold-backed currency: 12 gold standard; **14** silver standard

gold-bearing: 10 auriferous

goldbrick: 6 loafer; **7** goof-off, lounger, slacker; **10** ne'er-do-well; **11** goldbricker; **13** good-for-naught; **14** good-for-nothing

goldbricking: 8 shirking, slacking; **10** goofing off, soldiering

Gold Coast: 5 Ghana

gold digger: 9 gold miner; **10** gold panner; **14** gold prospector

golden: 4 gilt, gold; **6** gilded; **7** aureate, favored, halcyon; **9** favorable, fortunate; **10** prosperous; **11** gold-colored; **12** advantageous

golden anniversary: 10 fifty years; **13** golden jubilee

golden boy: 9 wonder boy

golden eagle: 16 Aquila chrysaetos

goldeneye: 8 whistler

Golden Gate: 16 Golden Gate Bridge

golden opportunity: 7 opening

Golden State: 10 California

golden syrup: 7 treacle

golden time: 9 golden age

goldfinch: 10 yellowbird; **13** Spinus tristis

gold medalist: 15 Olympic champion

gold mine: 4 boom; **7** bonanza; **15** manna from heaven

gold miner: 10 gold digger, gold panner

gold worker: 9 goldsmith

golem: 5 robot; **9** automaton

golf course: 5 links; **9** golf links

golf game: 4 golf; **9** golf match; **11** round of golf

golf range: 12 driving range

golf shot: 5 swing; **6** stroke

Golgotha: 7 Calvary; **9** mausoleum; **11** narrow house; **12** house of death

goliath: 5 giant; **7** monster; **8** behemoth, colossus

golliwog: 9 golliwogg

Gomorrah: 8 Gomorrha

gonad: 3 egg, nut; **4** ball; **6** testis; **7** ballock, bollock; **8** testicle

gondola: 3 car; **10** gondola car

gone: 4 away, late, lost, over, past; **5** kaput, spent; **6** asleep, at rest, bygone, bypast, gone by, no more; **7** at peace, done for, extinct, forlorn; **8** deceased, departed, desolate, expended, foregone, from home, hopeless, vanished; **9** desperate, exhausted, in despair; **10** despairing, passed away

go near: 4 near; **7** get near; **8** approach, come near, draw near; **10** come toward; **11** approximate, move towards

gone bad: 3 bad; **4** high, weak; **5** fusty; **6** effete, putrid, rancid, rotten; **7** corrupt, decayed, rotting, tainted, touched; **9** putrefied

gonfalon: 4 jack, flag; **6** ensign

gong: 4 bell, gong; **5** chime; **6** cymbal, tam-tam

goniometer: 10 clinometer

gonorrhea: 4 clap; **10** gonorrhoea; **16** urethritis venera

go nuts: 5 go mad; **6** run mad; **7** flip out, go crazy; **9** go bonkers; **11** flip one's lid, flip one's wig

goo: 4 gook, guck, gunk, muck, ooze; **5** slime; **6** sludge

goober: 6 peanut; **8** earthnut; **9** goober pea, groundnut, monkey nut

good: 3 due, fit; **4** dear, fine, full, glad, just, meet, near, nice, ripe, safe, well; **5** adept, happy, palmy, right, sound, tasty, valid; **6** dainty, expert, proper, savory, secure, seemly; **7** benefit, correct, en regle, fitting, halcyon, in force, plenary, serious, skilful, soundly, upright; **8** absolute, decorous, gladsome, goodness, in effect, salutary, skillful, thorough, unspoilt, virtuous; **9** advantage, befitting, delicious, effective, estimable, good thing, honorable, palatable, practiced, Saturnian, unspoiled; **10** applicable, beneficial, benevolent, delectable, dependable, proficient, thoroughly, well-tasted; **11** go-to-meeting, respectable, to one's taste; **12** advantageous

Good Book: 4 Word; **5** Bible; **8** Holy Writ;

G

9 Scripture, Word of God; **13** Holy Scripture

good-bye: 3 bye; **4** ciao; **5** adieu, adios, aloha; **6** bye-bye, good-by, so long; **7** cheerio, good day; **8** au revoir, farewell, sayonara; **10** dosvidanya [Russ]; **11** arrivederci, leave taking, valediction; **12** hasta la vista [Sp]; **14** auf wiedersehen

good condition: 4 trim; **5** shape; **7** fitness; **8** good trim; **9** condition, good shape, good state; **15** physical fitness

good enough: 2 OK; **8** adequate, all right; **9** tolerable; **10** acceptable, well enough; **11** up to the mark; **12** satisfactory

good-for-nothing: 5 sorry; **6** no-good; **7** goof-off, no-count; **9** goldbrick, meritless, no-account

good fortune: 4 luck; **5** fluke; **8** good luck

good-hearted: 4 kind; **6** kindly; **11** open-hearted

good-humored: 7 affable, amiable, cordial; **8** familiar, gracious, obliging; **9** indulgent; **10** complacent; **12** good-humoured; **13** accommodating

good judgment: 5 sense; **8** judgment; **9** good sense

good-looking: 6 pretty; **8** handsome; **9** beautiful; **11** fine-looking, well-favored

goodly: 4 tidy; **5** hefty, noble, tight; **6** dapper, mighty; **7** goodish, sizable; **8** precious, sizeable; **11** respectable; **12** considerable

good-mannered: 5 civil; **6** polite; **8** mannerly; **9** courteous; **11** well-behaved; **12** well-mannered

good morrow: 7 good day

goodness: 4 good; **5** merit, value, worth; **9** high value; **10** worthiness; **11** high quality; **12** valuableness

goods: 5 wares; **7** effects; **8** chattels, movables; **9** commodity; **10** personalty; **14** personal estate; **15** personal effects

good value: 7 bargain

good weather: 8 sunshine; **11** fair weather, fine weather; **12** clear weather, sunny weather

goodwill: 5 grace; **9** geniality; **10** cordiality; **11** earnestness

good works: 5 favor; **8** good turn; **9** well-doing; **11** beneficence, good actions; **13** act of kindness

goody: 5 treat; **6** dainty, matron; **7** dowager; **8** delicacy

gooey: 4 icky; **5** gluey, tacky; **6** sticky; **8** adhesive

goof: 3 sin; **4** boob, zany; **5** goose; **6** cuckoo; **7** blunder, fathead, jackass

go off: 3 fly, rot; **4** bolt, fade, fire, go by; **5** be off, burst, decay, flare, flash, go bad; **6** blow up, bounce, decamp, fly off, get off, go away, go over, molder, pass by, pop off, put off, rankle, run off, set off, wither; **7** abscond, come off, drop off, explode, implode, move off, pack off, pass off, thunder, whip off; **8** detonate, march off, pass away, start off; **9** discharge

goofing off: 8 shirking, slacking; **10** soldiering; **12** goldbricking

goof-off: 9 goldbrick

goofproof: 9 foolproof

goofy: 4 fool, zany; **5** sappy, silly, wacky; **9** cockamamy; **10** cockamamie; **12** unreasonable

goon: 3 oaf; **4** clod, gawk, hood, lout, lump, punk, thug; **5** klutz, tough; **6** lubber, lummox; **7** hoodlum, toughie; **10** stumblebum

goony: 6 gooney

go on a rampage: 4 rage, roar, romp; **7** rampage

gooney: 5 goony; **6** goonie; **10** gooney bird

gooney bird: 5 goony; **6** gooney, goonie; **16** Diomedea nigripes; **20** black-footed albatross

goonie: 5 goony; **6** gooney; **10** gooney bird; **16** Diomedea nigripes; **20** black-footed albatross

goosander: 9 merganser

goose: 4 goof, zany; **6** gander; **7** fathead, jackass; **9** waterfowl

gooseberry: 4 yarn; **6** fringe; **7** currant; **8** tall tale; **9** fish story; **10** embroidery; **13** traveler's tale; **14** gooseberry bush

goose bumps: 9 goose skin; **10** gooseflesh; **12** goose pimples

goose egg: 3 nil, nix, zip; **4** nada, zero; **5** aught, zilch; **6** cipher, cypher, naught; **7** nothing

goosefish: 5 lotte; **6** angler; **8** allmouth, monkfish; **10** angler fish, anglerfish

goose pimples: 9 goose skin; **10** goose bumps, gooseflesh

go over: 3 rat; **5** check, go off, sum up; **6** defect, desert, invert, review, survey; **7** capsize, come off, run over, suss out; **8** check out, fall over, look into, look over, overturn, pass over, rehearse, turn over; **9** check into, check over, check up on, go through; **10** apostatize

go over like a lead balloon: 4 bomb; **8** fall flat

GOP: 15 Republican Party

gopher: 5 gofer; **6** Friday, goffer; **9** man Friday, right hand; pouched rat; **11** spermophile; **12** gopher turtle, pocket gopher, right-hand man

gopher snake: 9 bull snake; **11** indigo snake

Gopher State: 9 Minnesota; **14** North Star State

gore: 4 seam; **5** blood, hinge, pivot; **6** gusset; **9** bloodshed; **12** articulation

gorge: 4 cloy, glut, load, pall; **5** binge, slake, stuff, whelm; **6** defile, englut, fill up, gullet, load up, pig out, quench; **7** engorge, overeat, satiate, surfeit; **8** scarf out; **9** esophagus, overgorge; **10** gormandise, gormandize, oesophagus; **11** gourmandize, ingurgitate, overindulge

gorged: 5 sated; **7** stuffed; **9** surfeited; **12** ready to burst

gorgeous: 4 rich; **8** splendid; **11** magnificent

Gorky: 5 Gorki; **6** Gorkiy; **14** Nizhni Novgorod

gormandize: 4 glut; **5** binge, gorge, stuff; **6** englut, pig out; **7** engorge, overeat, satiate; **8** scarf out; **9** overgorge; **10** gormandise; **11** gourmandize, ingurgitate, overindulge

gormless: 6 stupid

gorse: 4 whin; **5** furze; **10** Irish gorse

gory: 6 bloody; **9** butcherly; **10** sanguinary; **11** sanguineous; **12** bloodstained, slaughterous

gospel: 4 pope; **5** creed; **6** church; **9** scripture; **11** gospel truth; **14** church doctrine

gospeler: 9 gospeller; **10** evangelist, revivalist

gossamer: 5 filmy, gauzy, sheer; **6** cobweb, unreal; **7** tendril; **8** cobwebby, ethereal, illusory, vaporous; **9** gossamery; **10** diaphanous, see-through; **11** transparent

gossip: 3 gab, jaw; **4** chat; **5** visit; **6** claver, confab, natter, tattle; **7** chaffer, chatter, chin-wag, comment, gabfest, tattler; **8** causerie, chitchat, gossiper, telltale; **9** small talk; **10** newsmonger, talebearer; **11** chinwagging, confabulate, rumormonger, scuttlebutt; **12** rumourmonger, tittle-tattle

gossiper: 6 gossip; **10** newsmonger; **11** rumormonger; **12** rumourmonger

gossipy: 5 newsy; **6** chatty

Gossypium: 6 cotton; **14** genus Gossypium

go steady: 3 see; **4** date; **5** go out

go straight: 7 not turn; **10** go directly, not deviate

go the distance: 17 complete the course

Gothenburg: 8 Goteborg; **9** Goeteborg

Gothic: 4 rude; **5** rough; **6** rugged; **8** doggerel, medieval; **9** barbarous; **10** heathenish, outlandish, tramontane

gothite: 8 goethite

go through: 4 bear, bide, down, pass; **5** brave, brook, enjoy, stand; **6** devour, endure, go over, suffer; **7** consume, transit, undergo; **8** carry out, go across, look over, tolerate; **9** encounter, implement; **10** experience, get through, put through, run through

go to: 5 get to, hie to; **6** attend, call on, go at it, go to it, turn to; **7** reach to, set to it; **8** appeal to, call upon, extend to, go toward, repair to, resort to, spread to; **9** stretch to; **10** move toward

go to bed: 6 retire, turn in; **7** crawl in, kip down, sack out; **8** go to rest; **9** go to sleep, hit the hay; **10** get into bed, hit the sack, stay at home

go to pieces: 7 break up; **9** fall apart, liquidate

go to sleep: 6 retire, turn in; **7** crawl in, go to bed, kip down, sack out; **8** go to rest; **9** hit the hay; **10** get into bed, hit the sack; **12** go off to sleep; **13** settle to sleep

gotta: 4 must; **5** got to; **6** have to, need to; **9** have got to

gotten: 8 acquired, obtained, procured

Gotterdammerung: 8 Ragnarok

got to: 4 must; **5** gotta; **6** have to, need to; **9** have got to

gouache: 7 tempera

gouge: 4 dent, nick, rack, rout; **5** wring; **6** extort, groove; **8** force out, gouge out

goulash: 6 gulyas

gourd: 8 calabash; **9** gourd vine

gourmand: 7 glutton; **11** trencherman

gourmandize: 4 glut; **5** binge, gorge, stuff; **6** englut, pig out; **7** engorge, overeat, satiate; **8** scarf out; **9** overgorge; **10** gormandise, gormandize; **11** ingurgitate, overindulge

gourmet: 7 epicure; **9** bon vivant, epicurean; **10** gastronome

gout: 6 relish; **11** urarthritis; **14** gouty arthritis

govern: 4 rule; **5** order; **6** direct, manage; **7** conduct, control; **8** regulate; **10** regularize; **11** preside over

governable: 12 controllable

governance: 5 brass, reign; **9** dominance, governing; **10** government; **12** organisation, organization; **13** establishment; **14** administration

governess: 8 dry nurse

government: 5 reign; **6** charge, public, regime; **7** control; **8** managing, politics; **9** direction, dominance, governing; **10** governance, management; **11** authorities, controlling, supervising, supervision; **14** legal authority

government agency: 6 agency, bureau, office; **9** authority

government man: 4 G-man; **8** FBI agent

Government National Mortgage Association: 4 GNMA [acron]; **9** Ginnie Mae

government note: 4 bill, note; **8** bank bill, banknote; **9** greenback; **11** banker's bill

governor: 5 ruler; **6** duenna [Sp], rector; **9** protector, regulator; **10** bear leader

go with: 4 side; **8** attach to, coincide, come with, side with; **9** accompany; **10** fall in with; **11** chime in with, co-occur with, go along with, reciprocate; **12** construe with; **13** collocate with; **14** sympathize with

gown: 4 cope, pall, robe; **5** frock; **6** scrubs; **7** cassock, pallium; **10** Geneva gown; **12** surgical gown

G

gownsman: 11 academician

go wrong: 4 fail; **7** go amiss, go cross; **8** miscarry

goy: 5 goyim [pl] [Yiddish]; **6** non-Jew; **7** Gentile

grab: 4 snap; **5** catch, clasp, grasp, seize; **6** clench, clinch, clutch, snap up, snatch; **7** embrace, grapple, snaffle; **10** fasten upon, take hold of

grabble: 3 paw; **4** feel; **5** grope, thumb, touch; **6** finger, fumble, handle, sprawl

grabby: 6 greedy; **8** covetous, grasping; **10** avaricious, prehensile

grace: 4 deck, form; **5** adorn, bonus, favor, honor; **6** favour, honour, pardon, polish, praise, purity, set off; **7** euphony, hosanna, liberty, license, quarter, unction; **8** beautify, blessing, decorate, doxology, elegance, goodwill, highness, ornament, requital, response; **9** embellish, gracility; **10** absolution, act of grace, concession, excellency, seemliness; **11** benediction, condonation, edification, forgiveness, pulchritude, recognition; **12** gracefulness, state of grace, thanksgiving; **13** glorification, natural beauty

graceful: 4 easy; **6** fluent; **7** elegant, flowing, natural, refined; **8** polished, readable, tripping; **10** unaffected; **13** prepossessing

gracefulness: 5 grace; **6** polish, purity; **7** euphony; **8** elegance

graceless: 6 gauche; **7** awkward, corrupt, cramped; **8** recreant, scampish; **9** corrupted, dissolute, heartless, inelegant, reprobate, shameless; **10** profligate, relentless, ungraceful, unhallowed, unpleasing, unpolished, virtueless; **11** remorseless

grace note: 12 acciaccatura, appoggiatura

gracilariid moth: 11 gracilariid

gracile: 7 willowy; **8** graceful

gracious: 4 nice; **6** genial, hearty; **7** affable, cordial; **8** cheering, familiar, obliging; **9** benignant, courteous, indulgent; **10** beneficent, benevolent, complacent; **11** good-humored; **13** accommodating

graciousness: 7 charity; **8** humanity, kindness; **9** benignity, humanness; **10** benignancy, goodliness, kindliness; **13** brotherly love; **14** charitableness, loving-kindness; **15** kind-heartedness

grackle: 7 jackdaw, grackle; **8** hill myna; **9** blackbird

grad: 4 alum; **5** grade; **6** alumna; **7** alumnus; **8** graduate

gradation: 4 step; **5** shade; **6** ablaut, course; **10** graduation; **11** progression

grade: 4 form, grad, mark, rank, rate, tier; **5** class, index, level, order, place, range, score; **6** degree, digest, remove; **7** seminar; **8** graduate, tabulate; **9** catalogue; **11** ground level

grade crossing: 13 level crossing

graded: 6 ranked; **8** graveled; **9** graduated; **10** stratified

grade insignia: 6 stripe; **7** chevron, stripes

grade school: 13 grammar school, primary school; **16** elementary school

gradient: 4 rise; **5** slope; **6** ascent; **7** incline; **9** acclivity; **11** inclination; **12** rising ground

grad student: 12 postgraduate; **15** graduate student

gradual: 6 gentle; **10** shading off; **11** progressive

gradually: 7 running; **8** bit by bit, gradatim [Lat], inasmuch, pro tanto [It]; **9** by degrees; **10** at a stretch, step by step; **12** deliberately; **15** slowly but surely

gradualness: 10 gentleness, graduality

graduate: 4 alum, grad; **5** grade, index; **6** alumna, digest; **7** alumnus; **8** fine-tune, tabulate; **9** calibrate, catalogue; **12** postgraduate

graduated: 6 graded; **9** gradatory; **11** gradational; **12** proportional

graduated table: 5 scale; **13** ordered series

graduate nurse: 2 RN; **12** trained nurse

graduate student: 11 grad student; **12** postgraduate

graduation: 5 scale; **8** grouping, taxonomy; **9** gradation; **12** commencement

graffiti: 8 graffito

graft: 3 bud; **4** bait; **5** bribe, plant; **7** bribery, engraft, graft on, implant; **8** grafting; **9** graft onto; **10** ground bait, transplant; **11** disseminate

Graf Zeppelin: 8 zeppelin

grail: 8 Sangraal; **9** Holy Grail

grain: 3 dye, pit, web; **4** gild, tint, wash; **5** grist, humor, imbue, japan, minim, paint, stain, stone, tinge, tooth; **6** cereal, enamel, kernel, mettle, polish, tissue; **7** bedizen, furbish, ingrain, lacquer, scruple, smarten, texture, varnish; **8** emblazon; **9** food grain, granulate, whitewash; **10** illuminate

grain alcohol: 7 ethanol; **12** ethyl alcohol

graininess: 9 sandiness; **10** coarseness, grittiness; **11** granularity

grain neutral spirits: 7 alcohol, ethanol; **12** ethyl alcohol

grainy: 5 mealy, sandy; **6** gritty; **8** granular; **9** granulose; **11** farinaceous; **13** coarse-grained

gram: 1 g; **2** gm; **6** gramme

Gram's procedure: 10 Gram method; **11** Gram's method

grama: 6 gramma; **10** grama grass; **11** gramma grass

gram calorie: 6 calory; **7** calorie; **12** small calorie

Graminae family: 5 grass

Graminales: 15 order Graminales

Gramineae: 7 Poaceae; 11 Graminaceae, grass family
grammar: 4 ABCs; 6 praxis, syntax; 7 three Rs; 8 alphabet, elements, outlines; 9 accidence, rudiments
grammarian: 12 syntactician
grammar school: 11 grade school; 13 primary school; 16 elementary school
grammatical: 9 grammatic; 10 well-formed
grammatical error: 8 solecism; 10 bad grammar
gramme: 1 g; 2 gm; 4 gram
Gram method: 11 Gram's method; 14 Gram's procedure
gram molecule: 3 mol; 4 mole
gramophone: 10 phonograph
gramps: 7 grandad, grandpa; 8 granddad; 10 granddaddy; 11 grandfather
grampus: 7 dolphin; 12 whip scorpion
granadilla wood: 9 cocoswood, cocuswood
granary: 6 garner; 10 storehouse
grand: 1 G, K, M; 4 fine, rich, thou, yard; 5 noble, proud, showy; 6 august, heroic, lordly, superb; 7 chiliad, stately, sublime; 8 imposing, majestic, palatial, princely, specious, thousand; 9 dignified, expansive, honorable; 10 commanding, grand piano, impressive, millennium, worshipful; 11 magnificent, one thousand; 12 concert grand, concert piano
grandam: 6 gammer, granny; 7 old lady; 8 old woman; 9 matriarch; 11 grandmother
grandaunt: 9 great-aunt
Grand Canyon State: 7 Arizona
granddaddy: 6 gramps; 7 grandad, grandpa; 8 granddad; 11 grandfather
grandeur: 7 majesty; 8 nobility, splendor; 9 grandness, solemnity, splendour, sublimity; 10 brilliance; 12 magnificence
grandfather: 6 father, gramps; 7 grandad, grandpa; 8 granddad; 9 grandsire; 10 granddaddy
grandiloquence: 7 bombast; 8 rhetoric, richness; 9 euphemism, turgidity; 10 floridness, orotundity; 11 declamation, grandiosity; 13 frills of style, magniloquence, ornamentation
grandiose: 4 rich, tall; 5 tumid; 6 florid, mouthy, ornate, turgid; 7 flowery, orotund, pompous; 8 inflated, sonorous, swelling; 9 bombastic, grandiose, high flown, overblown; 10 ornamented, pontifical, portentous, rhetorical, turgescent; 11 declamatory
grandiosity: 7 bombast; 8 rhetoric, richness; 9 euphemism, turgidity; 10 floridness, orotundity; 11 declamation; 13, magniloquence, ornamentation; 14 grandiloquence
Grand Lama: 9 Dalai Lama
grandma: 6 granny; 7 grannie; 11 grandmother
grand mal: 8 epilepsy; 14 epilepsia major

grandmother: 6 gammer, granny; 7 grammer [Brit], grandam, grandma, grannie, old lady; 8 old woman; 9 matriarch
grandnephew: 11 great-nephew
grandness: 8 grandeur, splendor, vastness; 9 greatness, immensity, splendour; 10 brilliance, importance; 11 immenseness; 12 enormousness, magnificence, sizeableness
grandniece: 10 great-niece
grandpa: 6 gramps; 7 grandad; 8 granddad; 10 granddaddy; 11 grandfather
grandsire: 10 forefather; 11 grandfather
granduncle: 10 great-uncle
grand unified theory: 3 GUT [acron]
granger: 6 farmer; 9 sodbuster; 10 husbandman; 11 homesteader
Granite State: 12 New Hampshire
granitic: 5 stony; 6 flinty; 7 granite; 8 rocklike; 10 unyielding; 11 granitelike
granny: 6 gammer; 7 grammer [Brit], grandam, grandma, grannie, old lady; 8 old woman; 9 matriarch; 11 grandmother
Grant: 12 Ulysses Grant; 13 Ulysses S Grant
grant: 3 own; 4 avow, cede, give; 5 admit, allot, allow, award, yield; 6 accord, bestow, confer, patent; 7 charter, concede; 8 deed over, donation; 9 vouchsafe; 10 assignment, concession; 11 acknowledge; 12 contribution
granted: 5 given; 7 donated; 8 bestowed; 11 given freely
grantee: 5 donee [Fr]; 6 lessee; 7 devisee
grantor: 5 giver
gran turismo: 4 jeep; 15 off-track vehicle
granular: 5 mealy, sandy; 6 grainy, gritty; 7 powdery; 9 granulose; 10 chondritic, granulated; 11 farinaceous; 13 coarse-grained
granulate: 5 grain; 9 comminute, pulverize, triturate
grape: 9 chain shot, grape shot, grapevine
grape growing: 11 viticulture
grape louse: 10 phylloxera
grape sugar: 8 dextrose
grapevine: 5 grape; 8 pipeline; 11 word of mouth
grapevine family: 8 Vitaceae; 10 Vitidaceae
grapheme: 9 character; 13 graphic symbol
graphic: 5 chart, vivid; 6 scheme; 7 drawing; 8 detailed, lifelike; 9 flow chart, graphical, in writing, pictorial, schematic, well-drawn; 10 particular
graphical: 7 graphic; 9 in writing
graphically: 10 in pictures; 11 pictorially
graphical user interface: 3 GUI [acron]
graphic artist: 10 printmaker
graphics: 3 art; 7 artwork
graphic symbol: 8 grapheme; 9 character; 12 visual symbol
graphite: 8 plumbago; 9 black lead

G

graphitic: 12 graphite-like
graphologist: 17 handwriting expert
graphometer: 10 clinometer, goniometer
grapnel: 6 anchor; 7 grapple; 8 grappler; 13 grapnel anchor, grappling hook, grappling iron
grapple: 4 cope, deal, grab, grip, hook, link, lock, yoke; 5 belay, brace, clasp, get by, latch, leash; 6 clench, clinch, clutch, couple, make do, manage; 7 bracket, contend, embrace, grapnel, make out, wrestle; 8 grappler; 9 clamshell, grappling, wrestling
grappler: 6 matman; 7 grapnel, grapple; 8 wrestler
grasp: 3 dig, get, hug, see; 4 feel, grab, grip, hold, take; 5 catch, clasp, gripe, range, reach, savvy, stick; 6 clench, clinch, clutch, follow, hold on, master, take in; 7 collect, compass, make out; 8 clutches, iron grip; 9 apprehend, gooeyness, intuition; 10 comprehend, feeling for, get a grip on, get a hold of, get a hold on, see one's way, stickiness
grasping: 5 greed; 6 grabby, greedy; 7 avarice, avidity, craving, holding, seizing; 8 clasping, covetous, gripping, rapacity, ravenous; 9 insatiate; 10 avaricious, greediness, insatiable, prehensile, prehension, quenchless, taking hold; 11 acquisitive; 12 covetousness, ravenousness, unquenchable
grass: 3 pot, rat; 4 dope, gage, hemp, sens, sess, shop, stag, weed; 5 bhang, ganja, peach, skunk, smoke; 6 betray, eatage, forage, snitch, tell on; 7 hashish, pasture; 8 cannabis, denounce, Mary Jane; 9 grass over, marihuana, marijuana
grassland: 5 range, veldt; 6 common; 7 prairie
grass widow: 8 divorcee; 12 grass widower
grass widower: 10 grass widow; 11 divorced man
grassy: 5 turfy, 8 turf-like
grate: 3 jar; 4 file, fret, gall, rasp; 5 creak, grind, prick, wring; 6 abrade, pierce, rankle, scrape; 7 eat into, grating, rub down; 8 convulse
grateful: 7 obliged; 8 beholden, pleasant, pleasing, thankful; 9 agreeable, enjoyable; 10 gratifying, indebted to
graticule: 7 reticle; 8 reticule
gratification: 8 fruition, pleasure; 12 satisfaction
gratify: 5 favor, humor; 6 pander; 7 indulge, satisfy
gratifying: 5 sweet; 8 grateful, pleasant, pleasing; 9 agreeable, enjoyable; 10 satisfying; 11 appreciated, pleasurable
grating: 5 grate, raspy, rough; 6 gravel, grille; 7 cutting, jarring, racking, rasping; 8 creaking, gravelly, gridiron, grinding; 9

agonizing, consuming, corroding, searching; 12 excruciating
gratis: 4 free; 7 for free, untaxed; 8 costless; 10 for nothing, gratuitous, not charged; 12 free of charge; 13 complimentary, without charge
gratuitous: 4 free; 6 gratis; 7 untaxed; 8 academic, costless, hazarded, needless, putative; 9 theorized, voluntary; 10 for nothing, not charged, supposable; 11 conjectural, presumptive, speculative, spontaneous, theoretical, uncalled-for; 12 free of charge
gratuity: 3 tip; 7 bakshis, douceur [Fr], freebee; 8 giveaway; 9 baksheesh, pourboire; 10, honorarium
gratulate: 10 felicitate, give one joy, wish one joy; 12 congratulate; 24 offer one's congratulations; 25 tender one's congratulations
gratulation: 12 felicitation; 14 congratulation
grave: 3 pit, sad; 4 base, etch, foul, hard, sore, tomb, vile; 5 acute, black, cruel, gross, harsh, heavy, sharp, sober, staid; 6 biting, scrape, sculpt, scurvy, sedate, severe, solemn; 7 caustic, earnest, engrave, heinous, serious, stipple, weighty; 8 grievous, infamous, inscribe, shameful, sinister; 9 dangerous, felonious, nefarious, sculpture, sepulcher; 10 scandalous, villainous; 11 grave accent
graveclothes: 6 shroud; 9 cerecloth; 12 winding sheet
gravel: 3 get, rag, vex; 4 beat, dirt, nark, rile; 5 amaze, annoy, devil, get at, get to, raspy, rough; 6 baffle, bother, nettle, puzzle; 7 flummox, grating, mystify, nonplus, perplex, rasping, stupefy, stupify, trounce; 8 bewilder, detritus, graveled, gravelly, irritate; 9 dumbfound; 11 crushed rock
gravelly: 5 raspy, rough; 6 gravel, pebbly; 7 grating, rasping, shingly
gravely: 5 badly; 7 soberly, staidly; 8 severely, solemnly; 9 earnestly, seriously
grave mound: 6 barrow; 7 tumulus; 11 burial mound
graven: 6 etched; 7 incised; 8 engraved, sculpted; 9 inscribed; 10 sculptured
graveness: 7 gravity; 8 sobriety; 9 soberness; 10 somberness
graven image: 3 god; 4 idol; 6 fetich, fetish
grave note: 7 low note; 8 base note, bass note, deep note, flat note
graver: 5 style; 8 engraver; 9 sculpture; 12 etching point
graverobber: 5 ghoul; 12 body snatcher
Graves' disease: 6 goiter
gravestone: 9 headstone, tombstone
graveyard: 8 cemetery; 10 burial site, necropolis; 12 burial ground; 13 burying ground
graveyard shift: 10 night shift

graveyard watch: 8 midwatch; **10** night watch; **11** middle watch

gravid: 3 big; **5** great, heavy, large; **8** enceinte, pregnant; **9** expectant, with child

gravimeter: 12 gravity meter

graving dock: 7 dry dock

gravitate: 4 load; **5** press, weigh; **6** cumber

gravitate towards: 9 bid fair to, redound to; **10** lean toward

gravitational constant: 1 G

gravitational differential: 4 drop; **6** height

gravity: 7 decorum, gravity; **8** sobriety; **9** graveness, soberness, solemnity, staidness; **10** sedateness, somberness; **11** earnestness, gravitation, seriousness; **12** decorousness

gravity meter: 10 gravimeter

gravure: 12 heliogravure, photogravure

gravy: 5 bunce; **7** godsend; **8** windfall

gravy train: 9 easy money

gray: 4 dull, grey, hoar; **5** hoary; **6** leaden; **7** grayish, greyish; **8** grayness, greyness; **10** gray-haired, gray-headed, grey-haired, grey-headed; **11** neutral tint, white-haired

graybeard: 4 seer; **6** old man; **9** longbeard, patriarch; **10** bellarmine

Gray Friar: 10 Franciscan

grayish: 4 gray, grey; **7** greyish

grayish brown: 3 dun; **4** fawn; **12** greyish brown

grayish red: 6 damask

gray jay: 9 Canada jay

gray kingbird: 8 petchary

gray matter: 10 grey matter; **13** gray substance, grey substance

gray scale: 12 shades of gray

gray sea eagle: 3 ern; **4** erne

gray wolf: 10 Canis lupus, timber wolf

graze: 4 crop, meet, rake; **5** range, touch; **6** browse, crease; **7** grazing, pasture; **8** coincide, osculate

grazier: 6 drover; **7** rancher, vaquero [Sp]

grazing: 5 graze; **7** in touch, shaving; **8** abutting, skimming, touching; **9** adjoining, in contact; **12** in contiguity

grazing land: 3 lay, lea, ley; **7** pasture; **9** pasturage; **11** pastureland

grease: 3 oil; **4** dirt, lard, soap, soil, suet; **5** filth, grime, stain; **6** boodle, lather, tallow; **9** lubricate

greased: 10 lubricated

grease monkey: 8 mechanic; **11** car mechanic; **12** auto mechanic

grease pen: 6 marker; **11** magic marker; **12** grease marker; **15** glass-marking pen

grease the palm: 5 bribe; **6** suborn; **10** tamper with; **13** tickle the palm

greasy: 3 fat; **4** oily; **5** fatty; **7** adipose; **9** sebaceous; **10** oleaginous

great: 3 big; **4** avid, cool, hero, high, huge, keen, neat; **5** bully, dandy, eager, heavy, large, lofty, nifty, swell; **6** bang-up, gravid, groovy, not bad, peachy, slap-up; **7** capital,

corking, eminent, exalted, stoical, zealous; **8** cracking, elevated, enceinte, great man, immortal, smashing, spirited; **9** deathless, expectant, majuscule, with child

great anteater: 7 ant bear; **8** tamanoir; **13** giant anteater

great ape: 6 pongid

great-aunt: 9 grandaunt

Great Bear: 9 Ursa Major

Great Britain: 2 UK; **7** Britain; **13** United Kingdom

greatcoat: 7 surcoat, topcoat; **8** overcoat

great deal: 3 lot, pot, wad; **4** deal, heap, load, mass, mess, mint, peck, pile, raft, slew; **5** batch, flock, heaps, sight, spate, stack, world; **6** hatful, mickle, muckle, plenty; **7** tidy sum; **8** good deal, whole lot; **9** whole slew

Great Dog: 10 Canis Major

greater: 5 major; **6** higher; **8** superior

greater part: 4 body, bulk, core, mass; **8** best part, main part; **9** chief part, major part

greatest: 3 top; **6** utmost; **7** biggest, largest, leading, supreme; **8** foremost, sterling; **9** matchless, paramount; **10** preeminent; **11** superlative

greatest good: 11 supreme good

great folks: 5 elite; **11** aristocracy

great horned owl: 7 hoot owl; **9** horned owl; **15** Bubo virginianus

Great Lakes State: 8 Michigan; **14** Wolverine State

greatly: 12 prodigiously, stupendously

Great Mother: 6 Cybele; **9** Dindymene; **10** Magna Mater; **12** Mater Turrita

great-nephew: 11 grandnephew

greatness: 7 bigness; **8** hugeness, vastness; **9** grandness, immensity, large size, largeness, magnitude; **11** immenseness; **12** enormousness, sizeableness

great-niece: 10 grandniece

great number: 9 multitude; **11** large number; **13** large quantity

great person: 4 hero; **5** great; **8** great man, immortal; **10** great woman

great power: 5 power; **10** major power, superpower, world power

great-uncle: 10 granduncle

Great War: 8 World War; **9** World War I; **11** War to End War; **13** First World War

great white heron: 12 Egretta albus; **13** American egret

great white shark: 8 man-eater; **10** white shark

Great White Way: 8 Broadway

Grecian: 5 Greek; **8** Hellenic

greco-roman: 8 hellenic

Greece: 5 Ellas

greed: 5 greed; **7** avarice, avidity, craving;

8 avaritia, grasping, rapacity; **10** greediness; **12** covetousness, ravenousness

greediness: 5 greed; **7** avarice, avidity, craving; **8** grasping, rapacity; **11** hoggishness, piggishness; **12** covetousness, ravenousness

greedy: 4 avid; **5** venal; **6** grabby; **7** craving; **8** covetous, esurient, grasping, ravenous, usurious; **9** devouring, insatiate, mercenary, rapacious; **10** avaricious, insatiable, prehensile, quenchless

Greek Orthodox: 8 Orthodox; **15** Eastern Orthodox, Russian Orthodox

green: 3 new, raw, sod; **4** hale, lawn, park, plat, plot, rude, soft, turf, well; **5** empty, fresh, novel, sappy, silly, sward, whole, young; **6** callow, common, greens, hearty, puisne, recent, simple, stupid, unread, unripe; **7** budding, commons, shallow, uncured; **8** childish, greenish, gullible, immature, juvenile, under age, viridity, youthful; **9** beardless, dark green, greenness, unripened; **10** fleeceable, greensward, illiterate, light green; **11** half-learned, in one's teens, superficial, uninitiated; **12** putting green; **13** inexperienced

green algae: 11 chlorophyte

greenback: 4 bill, note; **8** bank bill, banknote; **10** greenbacks [pl], paper money; **11** banker's bill; **13** paper currency; **14** government note

greenbacks: 9 greenback; **8** currency; **10** paper money; **13** paper currency

green bean: 8 snap bean; **10** French bean, string bean

greenbelt: 8 greenway

green-blind: 12 deuteranopic

green-blindness: 9 daltonism; **12** deuteranopia

greenbrier: 5 briar, brier; **8** catbrier; **9** bullbrier; **10** horsebrier

greenery: 7 verdure

green-eyed: 7 jealous; **11** overjealous

green-eyed monster: 8 jealousy

green fingers: 10 green thumb

greengage: 13 greengage plum

green groceries: 7 produce; **10** green goods; **11** garden truck

greenhorn: 3 cub; **6** novice, rookie; **7** amateur

greenhouse: 7 nursery; **8** hothouse; **10** glasshouse; **12** conservatory

greening: 12 rejuvenation

greenish blue: 4 aqua; **9** turquoise; **10** aquamarine, cobalt blue; **11** peacock blue

green lacewing: 8 stink fly; **9** chrysopid

Greenland: 14 Kaballit Nunaat

Greenland spar: 8 cryolite

Greenland whale: 7 bowhead; **12** bowhead whale

green light: 7 go-ahead

greenmarket: 13 farmer's market

green mayonnaise: 10 sauce verte

Green Mountain State: 7 Vermont

greenness: 5 green; **7** verdure; **8** verdancy, viridity

green onion: 8 scallion

green pea: 9 garden pea

green pea soup: 16 potage St. Germain

green pepper: 10 bell pepper; **13** Jamaica pepper

greens: 5 green; **14** leafy vegetable

greensickness: 9 chlorosis

green soap: 8 soft soap

greensward: 3 sod; **4** lawn, plat, plot, turf; **5** green, sward

green thumb: 12 green fingers

greenway: 9 greenbelt

Greenwich Mean Time: 2 UT; **3** GMT, UT1; **13** Greenwich Time, universal time

Greenwich Village: 7 Village

greenwing: 4 teal; **10** Anas crecca; **15** green-winged teal

greet: 4 hail; **5** usher; **7** receive; **9** recognize

greeting: 6 salute; **9** reception; **10** salutation; **11** recognition

gregariously: 8 sociably

Gregorian mode: 10 church mode; **12** medieval mode

Gregory: 8 Gregory I; **11** Gregory XIII; **13** Saint Gregory I; **15** Gregory the Great

Gregory XIII: 7 Gregory; **15** Ugo Buoncompagni

gremlin: 3 elf, hob, imp; **4** pixy; **5** pixie; **7** brownie

grenade: 11 hand grenade

grenade thrower: 9 grenadier

grenadier: 7 rattail; **11** rattail fish; **14** grenade thrower

grevy's zebra: 11 Equus grevyi

grewsome: 8 gruesome; **10** cadaverous

grey: 4 gray

greybeard: 6 old man

greyish: 4 gray, grey; **7** grayish

greyish brown: 3 dun; **4** fawn; **12** grayish brown

greylag: 7 graylag; **10** Anser anser; **12** greylag goose

Grias: 10 genus Grias

Grias cauliflora: 11 anchovy pear; **15** anchovy pear tree

grid: 8 gridiron, gridwork; **9** power grid; **11** control grid, power system; **13** reference grid

griddlecake: 7 hotcake, pancake; **8** flapcake, flapjack; **9** drop scone; **10** battercake; **11** flannel cake

gridiron: 4 grid; **6** grille; **7** grating; **13** football field

gridlocked: 6 jammed; **7** snarled

grief: 3 woe; 5 trial; 6 sorrow; 8 distress; 9 heartache; 10 affliction, heartbreak

grievance: 5 score; 6 bother, grudge, pother; 8 nuisance, vexation; 9 annoyance; 10 harassment; 13 mortification; 16 worker's grievance

grieve: 6 bemoan, bewail, lament, sorrow; 7 afflict, deplore; 8 aggrieve, distress

griever: 7 mourner; 8 lamenter

grieving: 6 bereft; 7 moaning; 8 bereaved, mourning, saddened; 9 lamenting, sorrowing; 10 distressed; 13 grief-stricken

grievous: 3 sad; 5 grave, heavy; 6 dreary, severe; 7 heinous, piteous, serious, weighty; 8 wretched; 9 atrocious, dangerous, monstrous; 10 deplorable, flagitious, lamentable, melancholy; 12 heartrending; 13 heartbreaking

grievously: 5 sadly; 6 sorely; 7 cruelly, grossly; 8 bitterly, horribly, terribly, woefully; 9 fearfully, miserably, painfully, piteously; 10 dreadfully, lamentably, shockingly; 11 frightfully

griffin: 7 griffon, gryphon

griffon: 7 griffin, gryphon; 10 Gyps fulvus; 14 Belgian griffon, griffon vulture; 15 Brussels griffon

gri-gri: 6 grugru; 7 macamba; 10 grugru palm; 17 Acrocomia aculeata

grigri: 8 greegree, gres-gris, gris-gris

grill: 3 fry; 4 bake; 5 parch, roast, singe, toast; 6 grille, scorch; 9 grillroom, grillwork

grille: 5 grill; 6 wicket; 7 grating, lattice; 8 gridiron; 9 grillwork

grilled: 7 broiled; 9 barbecued

grim: 4 blue, dark, dour, glum; 5 black, stern, sulky; 6 dismal, gloomy, grisly, grumpy, morose, sullen; 7 ghastly, grouchy, macabre, mordant; 8 crushing, frumpish, growling, gruesome, scowling, shocking, terrific; 9 appalling, glowering, grim faced; 10 depressing, forbidding, in the dumps, in the sulks, inexorable, out of sorts, relentless; 11 dispiriting

grimace: 4 face; 5 frown, scowl

grime: 4 dirt, grit, soil; 5 colly, dirty, filth, stain; 6 bemire, grease; 7 begrime

griminess: 10 grubbiness

Grimm: 16 Wilhelm Karl Grimm; 20 Jakob Ludwig Karl Grimm

grimness: 5 rigor; 6 rigour; 8 asperity, crushing, hardship, severity, shocking; 9 appalling, luridness; 10 terrifying; 11 ghastliness; 12 gruesomeness, rigorousness

grimy: 5 dingy, dirty; 6 filthy, grubby, grungy; 8 begrimed

grin: 4 quip, skit; 5 smile, smirk, squib; 6 satire, simper; 7 smiling

grin and bear it: 12 grin and abide; 13 resign oneself

grind: 3 bug, dig, set; 4 bait, barb, bore, bray, file, mash, mill, moil, nerd, swot, toil, whet, wonk; 5 abuse, beset, grate, harry, haunt, hound, labor, point, strop, tease, worry; 6 badger, bother, cranch, crunch, drudge, harass, heckle, ill-use, infest, labour, pester, plague, pother; 7 craunch, oppress, rub down, sharpen, travail; 8 aculeate, bullirag, bullyrag, drudgery, file down, ill-treat, maltreat, mistreat, plodding, wear down; 9 comminute, grind down, importune, persecute

grind down: 4 file; 5 grind; 7 rub down; 8 file down, wear down; 9 tyrannize

grinder: 3 sub, zep; 4 hero, mill; 5 hoagy, molar, wedge; 6 bomber, hoagie; 7 crammer, poor boy, torpedo; 9 submarine; 12 hero sandwich

grinding: 7 cutting, galling, grating, racking; 8 abrasion, venomous; 9 agonizing, attrition, consuming, corroding, detrition, searching; 10 maleficent, oppressive, tyrannical; 12 excruciating; 13 inquisitorial

grinding wheel: 9 whetstone; 10 emery wheel, grindstone

grind organ: 9 hand organ; 10 hurdy gurdy; 11 barrel organ, street organ

grindstone: 9 whetstone; 13 grinding wheel

grip: 3 bag, flu; 4 hold; 5 clasp, grasp, gripe, stick; 6 clench, clutch, grippe, handle, hold on, valise; 7 grapple; 8 clutches, grip sack [U.S.], handgrip, iron grip, suitcase, traction, transfix; 9 fascinate, gooeyness, influenza, spellbind; 10 get a grip on, get a hold of, get a hold on, stickiness; 12 traveling bag

gripe: 3 hug; 4 beef, bite, gnaw, grip, hurt, kick, pain; 5 chafe, grasp, pinch, prick, stint; 6 clench, clinch, clutch, grouse, grudge, holler, scrimp, squawk; 8 begrudge, complain, grousing, iron grip; 9 bellyache, complaint; 11 bellyaching

grippe: 3 flu; 4 grip; 9 influenza

gripping: 7 holding; 8 clasping, grasping, riveting; 9 absorbing; 10 engrossing; 11 fascinating

grisaille: 11 chiaroscuro; 13 pepper and salt

gris-gris: 6 amulet, grigri; 8 greegree, gresgris; 11 incantation

grisly: 4 grim; 7 ghastly, macabre; 8 gruesome

grist: 5 grain; 6 cereal

grist for the mill: 9 provision

gristle: 9 cartilage

gristly: 7 rubbery, stringy; 13 cartilaginous

grit: 4 bone, guts, sand; 5 grime; 8 backbone, gritrock, gumption, true grit; 9 clear grit, gritstone

grits: 11 hominy grits

grittiness: 9 sandiness; 10 graininess; 11 granularity

G

gritty: 4 firm, game, gamy, iron; 5 gamey, mealy, proof, rough, sandy; 6 grainy, spunky; 8 granular, spirited; 9 granulose; 10 mettlesome; 11 farinaceous, indomitable; 13 coarse-grained

grizzle: 4 mewl, pule, stew, sulk, yawp; 5 brood, croak, gripe, growl, grunt, whine; 6 clamor, murmur, mutter, snivel, yammer; 7 grumble, maunder, whimper

grizzly: 8 grizzled; 9 silvertip; 11 grizzly bear

groan: 4 moan, sigh; 5 sough, whine; 6 murmur, mutter, plaint; 7 grumble, heaving; 8 deep sigh; 9 complaint; 11 suspiration

groaning: 7 moaning

groat: 6 guinea, tester; 9 fourpence

groceries: 7 grocery

grocery: 6 market; 9 foodstuff, groceries; 12 grocery store

grocery store: 6 market; 7 grocery

grog: 5 toddy; 8 hot toddy

grogginess: 6 stupor; 12 stupefaction

groggy: 3 cut; 4 high, logy; 5 beery, boozy, dazed, drunk, foggy, fresh, merry, tight, tipsy; 6 corned, primed; 7 drunken, fuddled, languid; 8 elevated, listless, overcome, top-heavy; 9 disguised, flustered, inebriate, lethargic, overtaken, stuporous; 10 in one's cups, inebriated; 11 intoxicated

groin: 6 crotch, groyne; 7 bulwark, knuckle, seawall; 10 breakwater

grommet: 4 loop; 6 eyelet, gasket; 7 cringle

groom: 5 curry, dress, train; 6 neaten, ostler; 7 equerry, hostler, prepare; 9 stableboy, stableman; 11 bridegroom

grooming: 8 dressing, training; 11 preparation; 15 personal hygiene

groom-to-be: 6 fiance

groove: 3 rut; 4 rout; 5 gouge; 6 furrow, trench

grooved: 6 fluted, rutted; 8 furrowed, striated, sulcated [Anat]; 11 well-grooved

groovy: 4 cool, keen, neat; 5 bully, dandy, great, nifty, swell; 6 bang-up, not bad, peachy, slap-up; 7 corking, swagger; 8 cracking, smashing

grope: 3 paw; 4 feel; 5 thumb, touch; 6 finger, fumble, handle; 7 grabble

Gropius: 13 Walter Gropius

grosbeak: 9 grossbeak

gross: 3 yuk; 4 arch, base, foul, free, pure, rank, rude, vile, yuck; 5 bawdy, black, broad, crass, crude, grave, loose, rough, stark, utter; 6 arrant, clumsy, coarse, crying, earthy, ribald, risque [Fr], rugged, scurvy, smutty, vulgar; 7 awkward, fulsome, glaring, heinous, intense, obscene, perfect, porcine, revenue, rickety, sodding, staring; 8 complete, flagrant, infamous, profound, receipts, shameful, sinister; 9

abhorrent, egregious, equivocal, felonious, loathsome, nefarious, repugnant, repulsive, slouching; 10 consummate, disgusting

gross amount: 3 all, sum; 5 total; 8 sum total, the whole; 9 one and all

gross domestic product: 3 GDP

grossly: 5 sadly; 6 sorely; 7 cruelly; 8 bitterly, horribly, terribly, woefully; 9 fearfully, miserably, painfully, piteously; 10 dreadfully, grievously, lamentably, shockingly; 11 frightfully

gross margin: 12 profit margin; 14 margin of profit

gross national product: 3 GNP

grossness: 8 ribaldry; 9 indecorum, vulgarism, vulgarity; 10 coarseness, commonness, courseness; 11 misbehavior; 14 indecorousness

gross out: 5 freak; 8 freak out; 11 lose control

gross profit: 6 margin

gross sales: 5 sales; 12 gross revenue

gross ton: 3 ton; 7 long ton

grot: 6 grotto

grotesque: 3 odd; 5 antic, funny, harsh; 7 bizarre, uncouth; 8 farcical, pour rire; 9 barbarous, fantastic, laughable, monstrous, repellant, repugnant, repulsive, unnatural; 11 fantastical

grotesquely: 11 monstrously

grotesqueness: 7 oddness; 9 funniness; 10 comicality; 11 farcicality, grotesquery; 12 grotesquerie, laughability

grotto: 4 grot

grouch: 4 crab; 5 churl, crank, grump, scold; 7 grumble; 10 crosspatch

grouchily: 7 crossly; 8 grumpily

grouchiness: 6 temper; 8 acerbity, tartness; 9 crossness, petulance, procacity, testiness; 10 crabbiness, protervity; 12 captiousness, irascibility, irritability; 13 irascibleness, irritableness, querulousness

grouchy: 4 glum, grim; 5 cross, fussy, sulky; 6 crabby, gloomy, grumpy, morose, sullen; 7 crabbed; 8 frumpish, growling, scowling; 9 glowering; 10 in the dumps, in the sulks, out of sorts; 11 bad-tempered, ill-tempered

ground: 3 orb; 4 area, base, deck, flag, land, rear, soil; 5 basis, breed, compo, earth, embed, field, filed, floor, found, imbed, prime, realm; 6 anchor, bottom, carped, circle, domain, motive, paving, primer, reason, sphere, stucco; 7 bring up, circuit, crushed, dry land, footing, nurture, plaster, prepare, purpose, spackel, support; 8 exercise, flat coat, pavement, practice, province; 9 dry ground, establish, filed down, habituate, reason why, undercoat; 10 background, foundation, ground down, motivation, rubbed down, run aground, substratum, take in hand, terra firma;

11 ground floor, inspiration, priming coat, solid ground; **12** substructure

ground almond: 5 chufa; **7** rush nut; **11** earth almond

ground ball: 8 grounder

ground beef: 9 hamburger; **13** hamburger meat

ground beetle: 13 carabid beetle

ground-breaking: 10 pioneering

ground cherry: 10 husk tomato

ground cloth: 11 groundsheet

groundcover: 11 undergrowth

ground down: 5 filed; **6** ground; **9** filed down; **10** rubbed down

grounded: 7 aground, swamped, wrecked; **8** capsized, castaway, stranded; **9** foundered; **10** restricted; **11** shipwrecked

grounded on: 7 based on, built on; **9** founded on

grounder: 10 ground ball

groundfish: 10 bottom fish

ground floor: 4 deck, flag; **5** earth, floor; **6** carped, ground, paving; **8** pavement; **10** first floor, substratum; **11** ground level; **12** substructure

groundhog: 9 woodchuck; **12** Marmota monax

grounding: 8 earthing

groundless: 4 idle; **5** false; **6** unreal, untrue; **8** baseless, mistaken, unproved; **9** erroneous, unfounded; **10** apocryphal, fallacious, ungrounded; **11** unwarranted; **12** inconclusive

ground level: 5 grade; **7** surface; **10** first floor; **11** ground floor; **13** ground surface

groundnut: 6 goober, peanut; **8** earthnut, wild bean; **9** goober pea, monkey nut

ground pollution: 13 soil pollution

grounds: 4 data, lees, yard; **5** basis, cause, dregs, facts; **6** reason; **8** evidence; **9** pro and con; **11** praecognita [Lat], pros and cons; **13** consideration

groundsel: 7 senecio; **13** groundsel bush, groundsel tree

groundskeeper: 10 groundsman

ground sloth: 9 megathere

ground squirrel: 11 spermophile

ground swell: 5 storm; **7** rollers, tempest; **8** heavy sea; **10** heavy swell

groundwater: 9 well water; **11** spring water; **12** mineral water

groundwater level: 10 water level, water table

groundwork: 4 base, foot; **5** basis; **6** riprap; **7** element; **9** fundament, spadework, vital part; **10** foundation, substratum, subvention; **11** cornerstone; **12** substructure, sustentation; **14** understructure

group: 3 set; **4** band, crew, gang, knot, ring, sort, team; **5** class, crowd, party, squad, unite; **6** assort, circle, clique, moiety, throng; **7** cluster, coterie, in-crowd, radical;

8 classify, communal, grouping; **10** assemblage, human group; **11** concentrate

group discussion: 10 conference

grouped: 6 sorted; **7** ordered, orderly; **9** assembled, collected, organized

grouping: 5 array, group; **7** sorting; **8** division, taxonomy; **9** allotment; **10** assortment; **11** arrangement, classifying, disposition; **12** distribution, pigeonholing; **13** apportionment; **14** classification

grouse: 4 beef, rail; **5** gripe, snipe; **6** holler, plover, squawk

grousing: 4 beef; **5** gripe; **9** complaint; **11** bellyaching

grout: 4 lees; **7** plaster

grove: 4 dale, dell, glen, vale; **5** copse, glade; **6** bottom, dingle, valley; **7** gardens, orchard, spinney, woodlet; **9** greenwood; **10** residences

grovel: 4 fawn; **5** cower, crawl, creep, sneak, stoop; **6** cringe, crouch, slouch, sponge, suck up, wallow; **8** derogate; **9** lose caste, truckle to; **10** steal along

groveling: 4 mean, oily; **5** dirty, soapy, wormy; **6** abased, abject, little, paltry, pliant, scabby, scurvy, shabby; **7** fawning, scrubby, slavish; **8** cringing, rascally, sneaking, wormlike; **9** sniveling, sucking up; **10** dough-faced, flunkeyism, grovelling, sycophancy; **11** boot-licking, slavishness

grow: 3 get, wax; **4** farm, melt, rise, turn; **5** arise, raise; **6** expand, mature, mellow; **7** acquire, develop, enlarge, produce; **8** increase, maturate, spring up; **9** cultivate, originate

grow back: 6 regrow; **10** regenerate

grow crops: 4 farm; **10** raise crops; **11** till the soil

grower: 6 farmer, raiser; **10** cultivator; **13** agriculturist

growing: 6 growth; **8** ontogeny, thriving; **10** maturation; **11** development, flourishing, ontogenesis

growl: 3 yap, yip; **4** bark, howl, pout, snap, yawl, yelp, yipe; **5** croak, frown, gnarl, gnash, grunt, lower, scowl, snarl; **6** baying, bow-wow, clamor, murmur, mutter, rumble; **7** grizzle, grumble

grown: 3 big; **5** adult; **6** raised; **7** grownup, swollen, widened; **8** enlarged, expanded, extended; **9** full-grown, increased; **10** fully grown

grownup: 3 big; **5** adult, grown; **9** fullgrown; **10** fully grown; **12** mature person

growth: 4 flux; **5** lapse; **7** growing; **8** dilation, increase, ontogeny, progress, swelling; **9** emergence, evolution, expansion, extension, increment, outgrowth; **10** maturation, proud flesh; **11** development, enlargement, ontogenesis

growth hormone: 2 GH; 12 somatotropin; 13 somatotrophin

growth hormone-releasing hormone: 4 GH-RH; 13 somatoliberin

growth regulator: 12 phytohormone, plant hormone

growth ring: 10 annual ring

grow up: 6 mature; 8 spring up

groyne: 5 groin

grub: 3 bum; 4 chow, eats, feed, food, give; 5 cadge, chuck, mooch; 6 ferret, sponge; 7 aliment, edibles, ingesta, pabulum; 8 eatables, victuals; 9 nutriment, provender; 10 sustenance; 11 comestibles, nourishment, staff of life; 12 alimentation, sustentation

grubbily: 7 dingily; 8 grungily

grubby: 5 dingy, grimy; 6 grungy; 8 begrimed

Grub-street writer: 12 literary hack

grudge: 4 stew; 5 gripe, pique, score, stint; 6 scrimp; 7 umbrage; 8 be slow to, begrudge, hang fire; 9 grievance; 10 bone to pick

grueling: 4 hard; 5 heavy; 7 arduous; 8 toilsome; 9 gruelling, laborious, punishing; 10 labourious; 12 backbreaking

gruesome: 4 grim; 6 grisly; 7 ghastly, macabre; 10 cadaverous

gruff: 5 bluff, blunt, husky, rough; 6 crusty, hoarse, rugged; 10 ill-humored

gruffness: 8 curtness; 9 huskiness, shortness; 10 abruptness, hoarseness; 11 brusqueness

grumble: 4 moan, sigh; 5 croak, gnarl, groan, growl, grunt, scold, whine; 6 clamor, grouch, murmur, mutter, plaint, rumble; 7 grizzle, heaving, maunder; 8 deep sigh, rumbling; 9 complaint, grumbling, murmuring, muttering; 11 suspiration

grumbler: 6 moaner, whiner; 7 croaker, crybaby, growler; 8 sniveler, squawker; 9 dissenter, dissident; 10 bellyacher, complainer, malcontent

grumbling: 6 murmur, mutter, rumble; 7 grumble; 8 rumbling; 9 murmuring, muttering

grump: 5 churl, crank; 6 grouch; 10 crosspatch

grumpily: 7 crossly; 9 grouchily

grumpiness: 10 crankiness; 12 contrariness; 13 crotchetiness

grumpy: 4 glum, grim; 5 cross, fussy, sulky; 6 crabby, gloomy, morose, sullen; 7 crabbed, grouchy; 8 frumpish, growling, scowling; 9 glowering; 10 in the dumps, in the sulks, out of sorts; 11 bad-tempered, ill-tempered

grungy: 5 dingy, grimy; 6 grubby; 8 begrimed

grunt: 5 croak, growl, snort; 6 clamor, murmur, mutter; 7 grizzle, grumble, maunder

gruntle: 5 grunt, snort; 6 gentle, lenify, pacify; 7 appease, assuage, mollify, placate; 10 conciliate

Grus: 9 genus Grus

Grus americana: 13 whooping crane

gryoplane: 8 autogiro, autogyro

gryphon: 7 griffin, griffon

G-string: 9 loincloth; 11 breechcloth, breechclout

G suit: 9 anti-G suit

guacharo: 7 oilbird

guaiacum: 6 guaiac; 8 guiaocum; 10 guaiac wood; 11 lignum vitae; 12 guaiacum wood

Guaira: 10 Sete Quedas; 11 Guaira Falls

guama: 11 Inga laurina

guanabana: 7 soursop

guanaco: 12 Lama guanicoe

Guangzhou: 6 Canton; 9 Kuangchou, Kwangchow

guar: 7 guar gum; 11 cluster bean

guarantee: 5 vouch; 6 assure, ensure, insure, pledge, secure; 7 warrant; 8 guaranty, warranty; 9 undertake, warrantee; 10 underwrite

guaranteed: 6 bonded; 7 secured; 9 warranted

guarantor: 6 surety; 9 warrantor

guaranty: 6 pledge; 8 warranty; 9 guarantee

guard: 4 fend, file, hold, rank, ward; 6 custos [Lat], defend, gaoler, jailer, keeper, picket, piquet, ranger, safety, sentry, shield, warder; 7 forfend, protect, turnkey; 8 sentinel, sentry go; 9 bodyguard, custodian, guard duty; 10 sentry duty

guardant: 7 gardant; 8 full-face

guard dog: 8 watchdog

guard duty: 5 guard; 8 sentry go; 10 sentry duty

guarded: 4 wary; 6 fenced; 7 on guard; 8 cautious, hedged in, shielded; 9 protected; 10 restrained; 11 conditional, on one's guard, provisional, unrevealing; 12 noncommittal

guardedly: 6 prudently; 10 cautiously, discreetly; 13 circumspectly; 14 conservatively

guard house: 3 pen; 4 brig, gaol, hold, jail, keep, stir [slang]; 5 hulks, pokey [slang]; 6 donjon, lockup, prison; 7 dungeon, slammer [slang], the Rock; 8 Bastille, big house [slang], hoosegow, stockade; 9 calaboose [slang], guardroom, oubliette; 11 prison house

guardian: 7 tutelar; 8 defender, tutelary; 9 custodial, protector

guardian angel: 6 savior; 10 benefactor

guardianship: 4 care; 6 charge; 7 keeping; 8 tutelage, wardship; 10 wardenship; 11 safekeeping

guarding: 9 defending, shielding; 10 protecting, protection

guardrail: 10 safety rail

guard ship: 6 escort; 7 cruiser; 8 flagship

guardsman: 9 auxiliary, beefeater; 10 life guards; 14 reserve soldier, weekend soldier; 15 household troops; 16 yeomen of the guard

Guatemala City: 18 capital of Guatemala

guava: 9 guava bush, true guava; 14 Psidium guajava

guck: 3 goo; 4 gook, gunk, muck, ooze; 5 slime; 6 sludge

gudgeon: 3 mug; 4 fool, goby; 5 pivot; 7 fall guy, journal; 9 schlemiel; 10 Gobio gobio

gudgeon pin: 8 wrist pin

guelder rose: 9 crampbark; 13 cranberry bush

Guenevere: 9 Guinevere

guenon: 12 guenon monkey

guerdon: 4 meed; 6 reward; 10 recompense; 12 remuneration

guerrilla: 8 guerilla; 9 insurgent, irregular; 11 underground

guess: 4 shot; 5 gauge, infer, judge, think; 6 divine, hazard, reckon, theory, thesis; 7 imagine, suppose, surmise, suspect, theorem, venture; 8 estimate, guessing; 9 guesswork, postulate; 10 conjecture, hypothesis, postulatum [Lat]; 11 approximate, postulation, speculation, supposition; 13 dead reckoning

guessed: 6 mooted; 7 assumed, divined; 8 imagined, presumed, supposed, surmised; 9 suspected; 10 postulated; 11 conjectured, presupposed

guesswork: 4 shot; 5 guess; 8 guessing; 10 estimating, estimation, rough guess; 11 speculation; 13 approximating, approximation

guest: 6 caller, client; 7 invitee, visitor; 8 visiting

guff: 3 rot; 4 bull, bunk; 6 bunkum; 7 hogwash

guffaw: 10 belly laugh; 11 laugh loudly

guggle: 3 coo; 4 honk, purl; 5 clack, cluck, spray, spurt; 6 babble, bubble, burble, cackle, gaggle, gurgle, mantle, murmur, ripple; 7 sparkle, sputter

GUI: 18 graphical interface

guidance: 7 counsel, guiding; 8 steering; 9 direction; 10 counseling, regulation

guide: 3 run; 4 head, lead, pass, take; 5 pilot, point, scout, steer, usher; 6 direct; 7 conduct, guide on, oversee, templet; 8 cicerone, cynosure, maneuver, template; 9 guidebook, manouevre, preceptor; 10 pathfinder

guidebook: 5 guide; 8 handbook, road book

guided: 9 conducted

guide dog: 12 seeing-eye dog

guideless: 8 helpless

guideline: 9 guidepost; 11 rule of thumb

guidepost: 8 signpost; 9 guideline; 11 rule of thumb; 13 directing post

guiding: 7 heading; 8 guidance, steering; 9 directing, directive; 10 overseeing; 11 directional, supervising

guiding light: 7 notable; 8 luminary; 10 notability; 12 leading light

guild: 4 club, gild; 5 lodge, order; 7 society

guilder: 6 florin, gulden

guildhall: 4 hall; 6 change; 8 exchange

guile: 4 wile; 5 craft, fraud; 7 cunning, slyness; 8 doubling, foxiness, trickery, wiliness; 9 chicanery, duplicity; 10 craftiness, shenanigan; 13 deceitfulness, double dealing

guileful: 3 sly; 4 foxy, wily; 5 dodgy, slick; 6 crafty, tricky; 7 cunning, knavish, tricksy

guileless: 4 pure; 5 frank, naive; 6 candid, honest; 7 sincere; 8 innocent; 9 ingenuous; 11 transparent

guilt: 9 guilt trip; 10 guiltiness; 11 culpability

guiltless: 8 innocent; 9 not guilty; 11 cleanhanded

guilt trip: 5 guilt; 13 guilt feelings; 16 guilty conscience

guilty: 6 shamed; 7 at fault, hangdog, in fault, to blame; 8 culpable; 9 condemned; 10 shamefaced; 11 found guilty

guilty conscience: 5 guilt; 9 guilt trip; 13 guilt feelings

guinea: 5 groat; 6 tester; 10 guinea fowl; 15 Numida meleagris

Guinea-Bissau: 11 Guine-Bissau; 16 Portuguese Guinea

guinea hen: 10 guinea fowl

guinea pig: 4 case; 7 subject; 11 Cavia cobaya

guinea T: 6 T-shirt

Guinevere: 9 Guenevere

guisard: 6 masker, mummer

guise: 3 air; 4 cast, form, gait, look, mien, port, tone, trim; 5 blind, color, cover, gloss; 6 manner, things, toilet; 7 bearing, pretext; 8 carriage, demeanor, pretence, toilette, wardrobe; 9 trousseau; 10 complexion, subterfuge

guitar player: 9 guitarist

Gujarati: 7 Gujrati; 8 Gujerati

gulch: 4 wadi; 5 flume, gully; 6 arroyo, ravine

gulden: 6 florin; 7 guilder

gull: 3 cod, mug; 4 dupe, fish, fool, hoax, mark; 5 chump, patsy, put on, slang, trick; 6 befool, sucker, take in; 7 fall guy, seagull; **8** shlemiel; **9** bamboozle, schlemiel, soft touch; **10** put one over; **11** hornswoggle; **12** put one across

gullet: 4 gill, rill; **5** gorge; **6** throat; **7** rivulet; **9** esophagus; **10** oesophagus

gullibility: 9 credulity; **13** credulousness

gullible: 5 green; **9** credulous; **10** fleeceable

gully: 4 dike, main, moat, wadi; **5** ditch, gulch; **6** arroyo, funnel, ravine, trough; **7** culvert

Gulo: 9 genus Gulo

Gulo gulo: 9 wolverine

gulosity: 8 gluttony, voracity; **10** greediness; **13** voraciousness

gulp: 3 pig; **4** swig; **5** draft, quaff, raven; **6** devour, guttle; **7** draught, gulping

gulp down: 4 bolt; **6** devour; **7** swallow; **8** bolt down, gobble up, snap down, wolf down

gulping: 4 gulp; **8** guzzling, swilling

gum: 4 glue, lute, size; **5** bunko, paste, spoof; **6** cement, mumble; **7** gingiva, gum tree, gumwood; **8** mucilage; **9** four flush; **10** chewing gum

gum acacia: 9 gum arabic

gum albanum: 8 galbanum

gum arabic: 9 gum acacia

gum benzoin: 7 benzoin; **8** benjamin; **9** asa dulcis; **11** gum benjamin

gumbo: 4 okra; **9** gumbo soil, okra plant; **11** lady's-finger

gum boot: 10 rubber boot

gum elastic: 5 latex; **6** rubber; **10** caoutchouc; **11** India rubber

gummed label: 5 label; **7** sticker

gumminess: 8 gluiness, ropiness; **9** glueyness, viscidity; **10** viscidness; **12** cohesiveness, semisolidity; **13** glutinousness; **14** gelatinousness

gummosis: 16 brown rot gummosis

gummy: 5 gluey, pasty; **6** sticky, viscid; **7** viscous; **9** glutinous; **12** mucilaginous

gum myrrh: 5 myrrh; **11** sweet cicely

gum olibanum: 8 olibanum; **12** frankincense

gum plant: 7 gumweed, tarweed; **9** rosinweed

gumption: 4 grit, guts, sand; **5** parts, sense; **6** esprit; **8** backbone, sagacity; **9** acuteness, good sense, mother wit; **10** horse sense, quick parts; **11** common sense

gumshield: 10 mouthpiece

gumshoe: 2 PI; **4** dick; **6** arctic, galosh, golosh, rubber; **8** hawkshaw; **11** private dick; **16** private detective

gumweed: 7 tarweed; **8** gum plant; **9** rosinweed

gumwood: 3 gum

gun: 3 gas; **5** piece; **6** gunman, hit man, weapon; **7** firearm, shooter, torpedo; **8** gas

pedal, hired gun, ordnance, throttle; **9** artillery, grease-gun; **10** gunslinger; **11** accelerator, heavy weapon

gunboat: 7 frigate, warship; **8** corvette, man-of-war; **9** first-rate, ship of war; **10** bomb vessel, sloop of war

guncotton: 14 nitrocellulose

gun dog: 9 retriever; **11** sporting dog

gun emplacement: 4 nest; **6** bunker; **18** weapons emplacement

gun enclosure: 6 turret; **9** gun turret

gunfight: 7 gunplay; **8** shootout

gunfighter: 8 hired gun; **10** gunslinger

gunfire: 7 gunshot

gung ho: 5 eager; **7** zealous; **10** breathless; **12** enthusiastic

gunk: 3 goo; **4** gook, guck, muck, ooze; **5** slime; **6** sludge

gunman: 3 gun; **6** hit man; **7** shooter, torpedo; **8** hired gun; **10** gunslinger

gun moll: 4 moll; **13** gangster's moll

gun muzzle: 6 muzzle; **8** gunpoint

gunnel: 6 blenny; **7** gun rest, gunwale

gunner: 9 cannoneer; **10** bombardier; **12** artilleryman; **13** machine gunner

gunnery: 10 ballistics

gunny: 6 burlap

gunnysack: 9 burlap bag

gunplay: 8 gunfight, shootout

gunpoint: 5 point; **6** muzzle; **9** gun muzzle

gunpowder: 6 powder; **11** black powder

gun rest: 6 gunnel; **7** gunwale

gunrunner: 10 arms-runner

gunshot: 7 gunfire

gunstock: 5 stock

gun trigger: 7 trigger

gun turret: 6 turret; **12** gun enclosure

gunwale: 6 gunnel; **7** gun rest

gurgle: 3 hum; **4** flow, purl; **5** spray, spurt; **6** babble, bubble, burble, mantle, murmur, ripple; **7** breathe, sparkle, sputter

gurry: 5 spawn

guru: 4 sage; **6** mentor; **7** mahatma, wise man

gush: 3 jet; **4** pour, rave, rush, zeal; **5** ardor, flush, issue, spirt, spout, spray, spurt, verve; **6** fervor, splash; **7** flow out, passion; **8** effusion, fervency, outburst; **10** enthusiasm, outpouring

gushing: 5 fiery, gushy; **6** ardent, burbly, fervid, red-hot; **7** burning, fervent, flaming, glowing, pouring; **8** burbling, effusive; **9** emotional; **10** passionate

gusset: 4 gore, seam; **5** hinge, inset, pivot

gussied: 9 fancied up, gussied up

gussy up: 6 attire, deck up, fig out, rig out, tog out; **7** deck out, dress up, fancy up; **9** overdress

gust: 4 blow, gale, tact; **5** blast, gusto, savor, whiff; **7** finesse; **8** delicacy, high wind;

9 half a gale, high winds [pl]; **10** refinement, strong wind

gustation: 5 taste; **11** degustation; **12** sense of taste

gustatory cell: 9 taste cell

gusting: 5 windy; **7** blowing

gusto: 4 elan, fire, glow, gust, tact, zest; **5** savor, verve; **6** relish, spirit, warmth; **7** finesse, unction; **8** delicacy; **9** vehemence; **10** refinement; **11** fine feeling, zestfulness

gusty: 6 breezy; **7** squally; **8** blustery; **10** blustering, blusterous

gut: 3 dry; **4** guts [pl], loot, sack; **5** bayou [U.S.], belly, bowel, canal, creek, crick, rifle, spoil, strip, sweep; **6** bowels [pl], catgut, tubule, vessel, vitals [pl]; **7** despoil, exhaust, pillage, plunder, ransack, viscera [pl]; **8** entrails [pl], pot belly; **9** intestine, swallow up; **10** deep inside, deep-seated, disembowel, eviscerate, intestines [pl]

gut feeling: 5 hunch; **7** feeling; **9** intuition

gutless: 9 spineless

guts: 3 gut; **4** face, grit, sand; **5** bowel, spunk; **6** bowels [pl], virtue, vitals [pl]; **7** viscera [pl]; **8** backbone, entrails [pl], gumption; **9** fortitude, hardihood; **10** intestines [pl]

gutsiness: 5 pluck; **10** pluckiness

gutter: 4 dike; **5** ditch; **6** trench, trough; **10** roof gutter

guttersnipe: 12 street urchin

Guttiferae: 10 Clusiaceae; **17** St. John's wort family

guttural: 4 mute; **6** croaky, dental, labial, liquid; **8** croaking

guy: 3 cat, rib; **4** band, line, wire; **5** cable, chain; **6** hombre, jest at, picket; **7** guy rope, laugh at, make fun, painter, poke fun; **8** guy cable, moorings, ridicule

guyline: 3 guy; **7** guy rope; **8** guy cable

guzzle: 3 bib, sot; **4** lush, soak, swig; **5** besot, swill; **7** carouse; **8** chugalug [slang]; **9** drink deep, drink hard

guzzler: 3 sot, tun; **4** lush; **5** toper; **6** soaker, sponge; **7** tippler; **8** drunkard; **11** hard drinker

gybe: 3 jib; **4** jibe, wear; **12** change course

gym: 9 gymnasium; **10** health club; **13** fitness center

gymnasium: 3 gym; **5** lists; **8** palestra

gymnast: 7 acrobat, tumbler

gymnastic: 8 athletic; **9** acrobatic

gymnastic apparatus: 9 exerciser

Gymnogyps: 6 condor; **14** genus Gymnogyps

gym shoe: 7 sneaker; **10** tennis shoe

gynandromorph: 7 epicine; **9** androgyne; **13** epicine person, hermaphrodite

gynecologic: 13 gynecological; **14** gynaecological

gynecologist: 12 woman's doctor; **13** gynaecologist

gynoecium: 6 pistil

gyp: 3 con; **4** rook; **5** bunco, bunko, sting; **6** bearer, diddle, hustle, nobble; **7** con game, defraud, swindle; **8** flimflam; **9** bunco game, bunko game; **14** confidence game

Gypsophila: 11 baby's breath; **15** genus Gypsophila

gypsum board: 12 plasterboard

gypsy: 3 Rom; **5** Gipsy; **6** Romani, Romany; **7** Rommany

gypsy dancing: 8 flamenco

gyrate: 4 coil, gyre, reel, spin; **5** whirl; **6** spiral, 9 turn round; **10** spin around

gyration: 4 roll; **8** rotation, spinning, whirling; **10** revolution

gyre: 4 coil, curl, roll; **5** whorl; **6** gyrate, scroll; **7** ringlet; **8** curlicue; **9** turn round; **10** spin around

gyrfalcon: 9 gerfalcon

gyro: 9 gyroscope

gyroscope: 4 gyro

gyrus: 11 convolution

gyve: 5 irons; **6** fetter; **7** shackle, trammel

H

H: 8 hydrogen

h.p.: 10 horsepower

HA: 9 hour angle

habeas corpus: 18 writ of habeas corpus

Habenaria: 6 orchid, orchis; **14** genus Habenaria

haberdasher: 4 snip; **6** tailor; **8** clothier, milliner; **9** costumier

haberdashery: 9 men's store; **13** clothing store

habiliment: 7 clothes; **8** fittings

habilimented: 5 robed; **6** garbed; **7** attired, dressed; **9** appareled, garmented

habilitate: 3 tog; **4** garb; **5** dress; **6** clothe, fit out; **7** apparel, garment, raiment; **8** enclothe

habit: 3 use, way; 4 wont; 8 habitude; 9 drug abuse; 14 substance abuse

habitant: 7 dweller; 8 resident; 10 inhabitant

habitat: 5 biome, range; 7 granger; 9 eco system; 11 homesteader

habitation: 3 pad; 4 digs, home; 5 abode, berth, place; 6 living; 8 diggings, domicile, dwelling; 11 inhabitancy; 12 inhabitation; 13 dwelling house

habit-forming: 9 addictive

habitual: 5 usual; 6 common, normal, wonted; 7 chronic, nominal, typical; 8 everyday, ordinary, workaday; 9 confirmed, customary; 10 accustomed, inveterate

habitual criminal: 8 repeater; 10 recidivist

habitually: 9 regularly, routinely; 12 as is one's wont

habituate: 4 rear; 5 breed; 6 ground; 7 bring up, nurture, prepare; 8 accustom, exercise, practice

habituated: 6 used to; 7 given to; 9 attuned to; 10 accustomed, addicted to; 12 familiarized

habitude: 3 way; 4 wont; 5 habit

habitue: 7 regular

Habsburg: 8 Hapsburg

hacek: 5 wedge; 9 diacritic

hacienda: 6 estate; 9 farmhouse; 10 plantation

hack: 3 cab, cob, cut, hew, nag, pad; 4 barb, chop, hawk, jade, plug, roan, taxi; 5 bidet, cut up, punch, slash, whoop; 6 cabbie, cabman, chop up, dauber, drudge, hack on, hacker, scrimp; 7 copyist, hackman, sputter, taxicab; 8 roadster, splutter; 9 cabdriver, potboiler; 10 hack writer, ink slinger, taxi driver, ward-heeler; 12 literary hack; 13 political hack

hackamore: 6 bridle, halter

hackdriver: 5 cabby; 6 cabman; 7 taximan; 9 cabdriver; 10 taxi driver

hacker: 4 hack; 6 drudge

hackles: 6 dander

hackmatack: 8 tamarack; 9 tacamahac; 12 balsam poplar; 18 Populus balsamifera

hackney: 12 hackney coach

hackneyed: 5 banal, fixed, stock, tired, trite; 6 rooted; 7 trivial; 8 shopworn, timeworn, well-worn; 9 besetting, permanent, practiced; 10 deep-rooted, inveterate, threadbare; 11 commonplace, experienced

hacksaw: 8 metal saw

had: 4 held; 9 possessed

Hadean: 9 Plutonian, Tartarean

Hades: 3 Hel; 4 Hell; 5 Aides, Pluto; 6 Scheol; 7 inferno; 8 Aidoneus; 10 underworld; 11 netherworld; 13 bottomless pit; 14 infernal region, place of torment

hadj: 3 haj; 4 hajj

hadji: 4 haji; 5 hajji

hadrosaur: 11 hadrosaurus; 18 duck-billed dinosaur

haem: 4 heme

haemal: 5 hemal; 7 hematal; 8 haematal

haematic: 5 hemic; 6 haemic; 7 hematic

haematite: 8 hematite

haemic: 5 hemic; 7 hematic; 8 haematic

hafnium: 2 Hf; 7 celtium

haft: 4 heft, hilt; 5 helve, shaft, shank; 6 handle

hag: 3 dog, pig; 5 brute, crone, witch; 6 beldam, figure, woofer; 7 beldame, hagfish; 9 slime eels, ugly woman

hagfish: 3 hag; 9 slime eels

haggard: 4 bony, worn; 5 drawn, gaunt, mazed; 6 wasted; 7 pinched, raddled, squalid; 8 careworn, drawn out, skeletal; 9 emaciated; 10 cadaverous

haggle: 4 gash, hash; 6 dicker, hackle, mangle; 7 chaffer, wrangle; 8 haggling, huckster, scramble; 9 wrangling

hagiolatry: 10 hierolatry; 15 worship of saints

hagridden: 6 harass; 9 tormented

haguebut: 8 arquebus; 9 Brown Bess, flintlock, matchlock; 11 blunderbuss

ha-ha: 4 dike, leak; 5 creek, fence; 6 hawhaw, hee-haw; 8 palisade, stockade; 9 sunk fence; 10 horselaugh

hahnium: 3 Unp

haik: 7 burnous; 8 burnoose

hail: 2 hi! [informal]; 3 ave! [archaic]; 4 come; 5 greet, hello, howdy! [Western U.S.], usher; 6 herald; 7 acclaim, all hail!, receive, welcome!, well met!

Haile Selassie: 9 Ras Tafari; 17 Ras Tafari Makonnen

Hail Mary: 8 Ave Maria [Lat]

hair: 4 fuzz; 8 head hair, tomentum

hair care: 12 hairdressing

hair coloring: 7 hair dye

hair curler: 6 curler, roller

hairdo: 2 do; 8 coiffure; 9 hairstyle

hairdresser: 7 stylist; 11 hairstylist

hairdressing: 7 hair oil; 8 hair care; 9 hair tonic; 10 hair grease

hair dryer: 10 hand blower

hair dye: 12 hair coloring

hairlessness: 8 baldness; 11 phalacrosis

hairlike: 9 capillary

hair oil: 9 hair tonic; 10 hair grease; 12 hairdressing

hairpiece: 3 wig; 6 toupee; 8 postiche; 9 false hair

hairpin: 8 bobby pin

hairpin curve: 10 sharp curve; 11 hairpin turn

hair-raising: 11 nightmarish; 13 bloodcurdling

hair salon: 10 beauty shop

hairsplitting: 8 finespun; **9** quibbling; **12** glossing over

hairstyle: 4 coif; **6** hairdo; **8** coiffure

hairstylist: 7 stylist; **11** hairdresser

hair tonic: 7 hair oil; **10** hair grease; **12** hair-dressing

hairy: 6 tufted; **7** hirsute; **8** ciliated; **10** fimbriated; **11** filamentous

Haiti: 10 Hispaniola

haji: 5 hadji, hajji

hajj: 3 haj; **4** hadj

halberdier: 6 lancer

halcyon: 4 calm, glad, good; **5** happy, palmy; **6** golden; **7** pacific; **8** gladsome, tranquil; **9** Saturnian; **10** prosperous, untroubled

halcyon days: 9 palmy days; **10** bright days

hale: 4 well; **5** fresh, green, whole; **6** hearty

haleness: 5 vigor; **9** hardiness, wholeness

half: 6 moiety; **7** one-half, partial

halfback: 11 running back

half-baked: 5 crazy; **9** parboiled, screwball, underdone; **10** softheaded

half boot: 6 buskin; **7** top boot; **10** chukka boot, combat boot, desert boot

half brother: 11 stepbrother

half-circle: 10 semicircle

half-clothed: 12 underclothed

half-crazed: 6 crazed; **8** deranged

half distance: 9 bisection

half dollar: 10 fifty cents

half door: 9 Dutch door

half dozen: 2 vi; **3** six; half a dozen

halfhearted: 4 tame; **8** dilatory, listless, lukewarm; **9** pottering, puttering, tentative; **10** indecisive, irresolute

halfheartedly: 8 remissly; **10** dilatorily, listlessly; **11** potteringly

half mask: 6 domino; **7** eye mask

half-moon: 3 bow; **4** loop; **6** arcade, lunula, lunule; **8** crescent; **9** crane neck, horse-shoe

half-moon-shaped: 9 semilunar; **12** semicircular

half note: 5 minim

half off: 9 half price

halfpenny: 3 fig, jot, pin, rap, sou; **4** cent, mill, rush; **5** straw; **6** button, old son; **7** bulrush, feather, ha'penny; **8** farthing, picayune; **10** peppercorn

half-pint: 4 runt; **6** peewee, shrimp

half price: 7 half off

half relief: 12 mezzo-relievo

half sister: 10 stepsister

half-slip: 9 petticoat; **10** underskirt

half-starved: 8 famished

half step: 8 semitone

half-time: 8 part-time

halftone engraving: 8 halftone

half truth: 8 white lie

halfway: 6 center, middle, midway

half-wit: 5 idiot, moron; **6** cretin, dimwit, doofus, nitwit; **8** imbecile

half witted: 4 dull; **6** stupid; **7** witless; **8** mindless; **9** airheaded, brainless, dim-witted, fat-witted, fat-headed, pig-headed; **10** beef-headed, dull-minded, dull normal, dull-witted, lean-witted, weak-headed, weak-minded; **11** addle-headed, blunt-witted, lack-brained, muddy-headed, short-witted, unreasoning; **12** beetle-headed, feeble-minded, muddle-headed, mutton-headed, puzzle-headed, rattle-headed; **13** blunder-headed, chuckle-headed, maggoty-headed, rattle-brained, shallow-minded, unintelligent

Haliaeetus: 3 ern; **4** erne; **5** eagle; **9** bald eagle; **13** American eagle; **15** genus Haliaeetus

halibut: 7 holibut

halite: 8 rock salt; **10** common salt; **14** sodium chloride

hall: 4 dorm; **5** court, folly, foyer, lobby, manse, tower; **6** castle, change; **7** chateau, hallway, mansion, passage, rotunda; **8** anteroom, corridor, exchange, pavilion; **9** dormitory, guildhall, manor hall, residence, vestibule; **10** manor-house; **11** antechamber

hallah: 7 challah

halliard: 7 halyard

hallmark: 7 earmark; **9** assay-mark, style-mark, trademark

hallow: 5 bless; **8** sanctify, venerate; **9** do honor to, solemnize; **10** consecrate

hallowed: 4 holy; **6** sacred; **8** almighty, heavenly; **9** celestial

Halloween: 12 All Saints' Eve; **13** Allhallows Eve

Hallowmas: 9 Halloween; **10** Allhallows, Hallowmass; **12** All Saints' Day

hall porter: 6 porter; **7** doorman; **9** door guard; **10** doorkeeper, gatekeeper

hallucinating: 9 delirious

hallucination: 8 delusion

hallucinogenic drug: 3 LSD; **6** peyote; **12** hallucinogen

hallway: 4 hall; **7** passage; **8** corridor

halo: 4 aura, ring; **5** glory; **6** anulus, nimbus; **7** annulus, aureola, aureole; **8** doughnut; **10** anchor ring

halobacteria: 10 halobacter; **13** halobacterium

halo blight: 8 halo spot; **10** bean blight

Haloragidaceae: 12 Haloragaceae; **18** family Haloragaceae, water-milfoil family

halt: 4 drop, fade, fail, flag, hold, lame, limp, slug, stem, stop; **5** block, cease, check, droop, hitch, shake; **6** arrest, desist, freeze, hobble, kibosh, settle, slouch, stanch, toddle, totter, waddle; **7** closure, crumble, decline, give way, halting, shamble, shuffle, staunch, traipse, tremble; **8** crippled, languish, stoppage; **10** put a stop to, put an end to; **11** cease acting, discontinue

halted: 6 paused; **7** stopped

halter: 4 rope; **5** cramp, noose; **6** garter, hamper; **7** haltere, harness; **8** balancer; **9** bowstring

haltere: 6 halter; **8** balancer; **11** stabilizers

halting: 4 halt, lame, rude; **5** crude; **6** abrupt; **8** crippled, drooping, flagging, stoppage, stopping, surcease; **9** cessation

halve: 5 split; **6** bisect, cleave, divide; **8** cut in two; **11** dichotomize

halyard: 8 halliard

ham: 4 butt; **5** kraal; **6** gammon, hamlet, jambon; **7** overact, village; **8** ham actor, overplay

hamadryad: 9 king cobra, wood nymph; **10** Naja hannah

Hamamelidaceae: 16 witch-hazel

hamburger: 6 burger; **10** beefburger, ground beef; **14** hamburger patty

hamburger bun: 13 hamburger roll

hamburger meat: 10 ground beef

hamburger place: 11 burger joint

hamburger steak: 9 beef patty, chopsteak; **12** chopped steak

ham-handed: 8 bumbling, bungling, handless; **9** ham-fisted; **10** left-handed; **11** heavy-handed

Hamito-Semitic: 8 Afrasian; **11** Afroasiatic

hamlet: 3 ham; **5** kraal; **7** village; **10** crossroads

hammer: 4 drum, echo; **5** forge, gavel, pound; **6** falter, reecho, repeat; **7** iterate, malleus; **8** harp upon, hesitate, pounding, redouble; **9** hammering, reiterate, reproduce; **11** hammer throw, power hammer

hammer and tongs: 12 heart and soul, tooth and nail

hammerhead: 5 dunce; **8** bonehead, lunkhead, numskull; **9** blockhead; **10** dunderhead, loggerhead, muttonhead; **11** knucklehead; **15** hammerhead shark

hammering: 5 pound; **6** hammer; **8** pounding

hammer out: 7 achieve, compass; **8** block out, complete; **9** thrash out; **10** accomplish, consummate

hammer together: 8 nail down; **10** hammer down; **12** nail together

hamming: 10 overacting

hammock: 3 cot; **4** sack; **5** knoll, mound; **7** hillock, hummock

Hammond organ: 5 organ; **13** electric organ

hamper: 4 bond; **5** bonds, cramp; **6** dorser, dosser, fetter, halter, hinder, wisket; **7** shackle, trammel, whisket; **8** handicap, trammels

ham radio: 2 CB; **8** car radio; **10** police band; **11** police radio, two-way radio; **12** amateur radio, citizen's band, handie-talkie, walkie-talkie [military]; **13** airplane radio; **14** shortwave radio

hamstring: 4 lame, maim; **6** muzzle; **7** cripple, disable; **8** double up, paralyze; **9** prostrate

hand: 3 ell, man, paw; **4** deal, fist, foot, give, head, hook, inch, line, mark, mile, mitt, nail, palm, pass, pole, rood, yard; **5** cubit, manus, party, reach; **6** fathom, league, mauler, pass on, script; **7** deliver, furlong; **8** clapping, hand over, hired man, make over, pass over, transmit, turn over; **9** autograph, hired hand, negotiate, signature; **10** autography, day laborer; **11** attestation, deliver over, endorsement, hand of cards, handwriting, helping hand

handbag: 3 bag; **5** purse; **10** pocketbook

handbarrow: 6 barrow; **11** wheelbarrow

handbasin: 6 lavabo; **8** washbowl; **9** washbasin

handbill: 4 bill; **5** flier, flyer; **8** circular; **9** broadside, throwaway; **10** broadsheet

hand blower: 9 hair dryer

handbook: 6 manual

hand brake: 9 emergency; **12** parking brake; **14** emergency brake

handcart: 4 cart; **6** go-cart; **8** pushcart

hand clapping: 8 applause, clapping

handclasp: 5 shake; **9** handshake; **11** handshaking

handcraft: 8 handwork; **9** handiwork; **10** handicraft

handcrafted: 8 handmade

handcuff: 4 cuff; **5** cuffs; **6** hobble; **7** manacle; **8** handlock

handcuffed: 6 gagged; **7** hobbled; **8** fettered, manacled, pinioned, shackled

handedness: 10 laterality

handed over: 5 given; **9** delivered

Handel: 20 Georg Friedrich Handel; **21** George Frederick Handel

handful: 6 armful, capful; **7** fistful, maniple; **8** mouthful, spoonful; **10** smattering, thimbleful

hand glass: 6 mirror

handgrip: 4 grip, hold; **6** handle

handgun: 3 gat; **5** piece; **6** pistol, roscoe; **7** side arm; **12** shooting iron

handicap: 6 hamper, hinder; **7** disable, invalid; **9** deterrent, hindrance; **10** disability, give points, impairment, impediment, spot points; **11** disablement; **12** disadvantage, incapacitate

handicraft: 5 craft; **8** handwork; **9** handcraft, handiwork

handily: 5 aptly; **6** deftly; **7** quickly, readily; **8** adroitly; **9** hands down; **11** dexterously; **12** conveniently

hand in hand: 7 en masse; **10** side by side

handkerchief: 5 hanky; **6** hankey, hankie; **8** kerchief

handle: 3 paw, ply; **4** care, deal, do by, feel, grip, haft, heft, hilt, hold, palm, plow, work; **5** cover, grope, shaft, shank, thumb, touch, treat, wield; **6** deal in, finger, fumble, manage; **7** address, grabble; **8** deal with, doorknob, handgrip; **9** traffic in; **10** manipulate

handlebars: 8 mustache

hand lens: 8 sunglass; **9** magnifier; **12** reading glass

handler: 5 coach; **7** manager; **13** animal trainer

handless: 6 clumsy; **8** bumbling, bungling; **9** ham-fisted, ham-handed; **10** left-handed; **11** heavy-handed

handling: 9 treatment; **12** manipulation

handmade: 11 hand-crafted

handmaid: 7 servant; **10** handmaiden

hand-me-down: 8 hand-down; **10** second-hand

hand mike: 4 mike; **10** microphone

hand mill: 5 churn; **11** butter churn

hand mirror: 9 hand glass, pier-glass; **11** cheval-glass; **12** looking-glass

hand organ: 10 grind organ, hurdy gurdy; **11** barrel organ, street organ

handout: 7 freebie, release; **8** give away; **10** distribute; **12** press release

hand over: 4 give, hand, pass; **5** get in; **6** pass on, render, turn in; **7** consign, deliver, forward; **8** delegate, make over, pass over, relegate, turn over

handrail: 8 banister; **9** balusters, bannister; **10** balustrade

hands: 3 men; **7** custody; **8** manpower; **9** workforce

handsaw: 7 back saw; **8** miter saw; **9** coping saw; **13** carpenter's saw

handsbreadth: 10 handbreath

hands down: 7 handily

handsel: 7 deposit, earnest; **11** down payment; **12** earnest money, up-front money

handsewn: 12 handstitched

handshake: 5 shake; **9** handclasp; **11** handshaking

handsome: 3 big; **4** fair, free; **5** noble; **6** comely, giving, seemly; **7** liberal; **8** generous, princely; **9** bounteous, bountiful, unselfish; **10** bighearted, charitable, free-handed, full handed, munificent, open-handed, personable; **11** broad-minded, fine-looking, good-looking

handsome man: 4 hunk

handstamp: 11 rubber stamp

handstitched: 8 handsewn

hand-to-hand combat: 11 close combat

hand-to-hand struggle: 7 grapple, wrestle; **9** grappling, wrestling

hand-to-mouth existence: 7 poverty; **8** low water

handwoven: 10 hand-loomed

handwriting: 6 script

handwriting expert: 12 graphologist

handy: 3 apt; **4** deft, gain; **5** quick, ready; **6** adroit, at hand, expert; **8** tangible; **9** available, dexterous; **10** convenient, on the table; **11** close at hand, ready to hand

handyman: 9 odd-job man; **10** roustabout; handyperson

hang: 4 bent, fall, flow; **5** cling, droop, hitch, knack, sling, swing; **6** advert, append, attend, dangle, depend, hang up, hook up; **7** give ear, pay heed, suspend; **8** fasten to

hangar: 7 airdock; **10** repair shed

hang around: 4 loaf, lurk; **5** haunt, tarry; **6** footle, linger, loiter, lounge; **8** lallygag, lollygag; **9** hang about, mess about, mill about; **10** mill around

hang back: 3 lag; **4** drag; **5** drawl, trail; **6** dawdle, slouch; **8** draw back, hold back; **9** get behind; **10** drop behind

hang by a thread: 6 teeter, totter

hangdog: 3 sad; **5** cowed; **6** guilty, shamed; **7** bullied; **8** dejected; **10** browbeaten, shamefaced; **11** intimidated

hanger on: 4 snob, toad, tool; **5** toady; **6** flunky, shadow, sucker, yes-man; **7** flunkey, sponger; **8** courtier, parasite, tagalong, truckler; **9** doughface [U.S.], satellite, sycophant, toad-eater; **10** boot licker

hang glide: 4 soar

hang in: 6 hang on, hold on; **7** persist; **9** persevere

hanging: 5 arras; **7** pendant, pendent, soaring; **8** beetling, dangling, drooping, tapestry, towering; **9** suspended; **10** suspension; **11** wall hanging

hanging over one's head: 8 imminent

hang loose: 8 be casual, laid back; **9** be natural, easygoing

hangman's rope: 4 hemp

hang on: 5 tag on; **6** append, hang in, hold on, tack on, wait on; **7** persist; **9** persevere

hang out: 6 hobnob; **8** be at home; **11** do the honors

hangout: 5 haunt; **6** repair, resort; **14** stamping ground

hang together: 4 hold; **5** cling, stick; **6** adhere, cleave, cohere; **7** collude, concert, consort; **8** conspire, hold fast; **10** fraternize

hang-up: 3 rub; **4** snag; **5** hitch; **7** problem

Hangzhou: 8 Hangchow

hank: 4 bolt, coil, loop, hasp; **5** catch, clasp, latch

hanker: 4 long; **5** yearn

hanker after: 5 crave; **6** burn to, die for; **7** ache for, burn for; **8** raven for; **9** hunger for, itch after, lust after

hankie: 5 hanky; **6** hankey; **12** handkerchief

hanky-panky: 7 necking, petting; **8** fondling, sparking, sporting, trickery; **9** dalliance, making out, slickness; **10** hocus-pocus

Hannover: 7 Hanover

Hanoi: 16 capital of Vietnam

Hansen's disease: 7 leprosy

hansom: 3 cab; **7** taxicab; **9** hansom cab, yellow cab; **10** checker cab

Hanukkah: 7 Hanukah; **8** Chanukah; **9** Chanukkah; **13** Feast of Lights; **16** Festival of Lights

hap: 3 hit; **4** go on, pass; **5** occur; **6** chance, happen, hazard, turn up; **7** fortune, pass off; **8** casualty, fortuity

haphazard: 3 hap, hit; **6** hazard, sloppy; **7** fortune; **8** casualty, fortuity, slapdash, slipshod; **9** adventure, hit or miss; **11** haphazardly; **12** chance medley, happenchance, happenstance

haphazardly: 8 at random, randomly; **9** haphazard; **10** willy-nilly; **11** arbitrarily

hapless: 4 poor; **7** piteous, pitiful, unhappy, unlucky; **8** hoodooed [U.S.], luckless, pathetic, pitiable, snakebit, wretched; **9** miserable, out of luck; **11** unfortunate

haply: 5 maybe; **6** by luck, mayhap; **7** perhaps; **8** by chance, possibly; **9** perchance

happen: 3 hap, hit; **4** bump, find, go on, pass; **5** occur; **6** befall, chance; **7** pass off; **8** bechance; **9** come about, encounter, take place; **10** come to pass; **11** materialize

happenchance: 3 hap, hit; **6** hazard; **7** fortune; **8** accident, casualty, fortuity; **9** adventure, haphazard; **11** chance event; **12** chance medley, happenstance

happening: 4 fact; **5** afoot, event, thing; **7** going on, running; **8** incident, under way; **9** occurring; **10** in progress, occurrence, phenomenon, proceeding

happenstance: 3 hap, hit; **6** hazard; **7** fortune; **8** accident, casualty, fortuity; **9** adventure, haphazard; **11** chance event, coincidence; **12** chance medley, happenchance

happen upon: 6 strike; **8** chance on, come upon, discover; **9** light upon; **10** chance upon, come across

happily: 5 gayly; **7** merrily; **8** blithely, joyfully, with glee; **10** jubilantly, mirthfully

happiness: 5 bliss; **8** felicity

happy: 4 glad, good, neat, ripe; **5** ad rem [Lat], blest, lucky, palmy; **6** joyful; **7** blessed, content, germane, halcyon, in point, on point, pleased, well put; **8** euphoric, gladsome, relevant; **9** beatified, favorable, fortunate, neatly put, Saturnian;

10 admissible, applicable, auspicious, convenient, felicitous, propitious, well-chosen

happy event: 12 blessed event

happy-go-lucky: 8 carefree

Hapsburg: 8 Habsburg

haptic: 7 tactile, tactual

hara-kiri: 7 seppuku [Japanese], suicide; **8** hari-kari

harangue: 3 say; **4** rant; **5** stump; **6** recite, sermon, tirade; **7** declaim, lecture, ranting; **8** delivery, flourish; **9** discourse, hold forth, sermonize, speechify; **10** peroration, recitation

Harare: 9 Salisbury; **17** capital of Zimbabwe

harass: 3 bug, vex; **4** bait, bore; **5** abuse, beset, chevy, chivy, grind, harry, haunt, hound, tease, worry; **6** badger, bother, chevvy, chivvy, hassle, heckle, ill-use, infest, molest, pester, plague, pother; **7** oppress, provoke; **8** bullirag, bullyrag, illtreat, maltreat, mistreat; **9** beleaguer, importune, persecute

harassing: 6 biting; **7** carking, teasing; **8** worrying; **9** bothering, pestering; **10** tormenting; **11** molestation

harassment: 6 bother, pother; **7** torment; **8** nuisance, vexation; **9** annoyance, grievance; **11** molestation, persecution

harbinger: 6 herald; **8** announce, foretell; **9** precursor; **10** annunciate, forerunner

harbor: 4 dock, hold, port, quay; **5** basin, haven, nurse, wharf; **6** shield; **7** harbour, seaport; **9** entertain

harborage: 6 harbor; **7** shelter; **10** harbourage

harbor seal: 10 common seal

harbour: 6 harbor

hard: 4 dour, sore; **5** acute, cruel, grave, hardy, harsh, heavy, rigid, rough, sharp, stern, stiff, stout, tough, valid; **6** biting, firmly, mighty, potent, robust, severe, strict, strong, sturdy; **7** arduous, caustic, heavily, not easy, styptic; **8** forcible, grueling, hardened, knockout, powerful, puissant, everely, toilsome, vigorous; **9** difficult, fermented, gruelling, laborious, punishing; **10** adamantine, labourious; **12** backbreaking

hard-and-fast: 6 strict

hardback: 9 hardbound, hardcover; **10** hardbacked

hard-bitten: 5 tough; **10** hard-boiled, pugnacious

hardboard: 9 chipboard; **10** fiberboard

hard-boiled: 8 hardened; **10** hard-bitten, pugnacious; **12** case-hardened

hardbound: 8 hardback; **9** hardcover; **10** hardbacked

hard cider: 5 cider, cyder

hard coal: 10 anthracite

hardcover: 8 hardback; **9** hardbound; **10** hardbacked

hard disk drive: 8 hard disk; 9 fixed disk, hard drive

hard drink: 5 booze; 6 liquor; 7 spirits; 10 hard liquor; 11 strong drink

hard drinker: 3 sot, tun; 4 lush; 5 toper; 6 soaker, sponge; 7 guzzler, tippler; 8 drunkard

hard drive: 9 disc drive, disk drive

hard-earned: 7 hard-won; 10 hard-fought

harden: 4 gird; 5 inure, steel; 6 season, temper; 7 stiffen, sustain; 8 indurate; 10 case harden, render hard

hardened front: 10 effrontery; 11 face of brass

hardening: 3 set; 10 declension, perversion; 11 backsliding, reprobation, solidifying

hardfisted: 11 closefisted, tightfisted

hard fortune: 7 bad luck, hard hap, hard lot, ill luck; 8 evil luck, hard luck

hard-fought: 7 hard-won; 10 hard-earned

hard hat: 6 tin hat; 9 safety hat

hardheaded: 6 mulish; 7 austere, exigent; 8 exacting, obdurate, rigorous; 9 demanding, hard-nosed, hard-shell [U.S.], practical, pragmatic, searching, unsparing; 10 coolheaded, inexorable, inflexible, longheaded; 12 strong-headed

hard-hearted: 7 callous; 8 pitiless; 9 hard-nosed, heartless, unfeeling; 10 impervious; 12 stonyhearted, thick-skinned

hard-hitting: 9 trenchant; 12 high-pressure

hardihood: 4 face, guts; 5 brass, front, spunk; 6 daring, virtue; 8 boldness; 9 brashness, fortitude, nerviness; 12 impertinence

hardiness: 5 vigor; 8 haleness; 9 lustiness; 10 robustness, rude health

Harding: 13 Warren Harding; 21 Warren Gamaliel Harding

hard knocks: 8 tug of war; 12 sharp contest

hard lines: 8 hard case; 9 austerity; 11 hard measure; 12 hard measures

hard liquor: 5 booze; 6 liquor; 7 spirits; 9 hard drink; 11 strong drink

hard luck: 7 bad luck, hard hap, hard lot, ill luck; 8 evil luck; 11 adverse luck, hard fortune

hardly: 4 just; 6 barely, scarce, seldom; 8 only just, scarcely; 10 no more than; 12 infrequently

hard master: 6 despot, tyrant; 8 martinet, stickler; 9 oppressor; 10 inquisitor; 14 disciplinarian

hard-mouthed: 8 stubborn; 9 obstinate, hidebound

hardness: 7 cruelty; 8 obduracy, rigidity, severity, soreness; 9 harshness, sharpness, stiffness, toughness; 10 difficulty, inclemency; 11 callousness

hard-nosed: 7 austere, callous, exigent; 8 exacting, obdurate, rigorous; 9 demanding,

hard-shell [U.S.], practical, pragmatic, searching, unsparing; 10 hardheaded, impervious, inexorable, inflexible; 11 hardhearted; 12 thick-skinned

hard-of-hearing: 15 hearing-impaired

hardpan: 7 bedrock, caliche

hard-pressed: 6 hard up, urgent; 7 hard put; 9 in a bad way, in trouble; 10 distressed

hard rubber: 7 ebonite; 9 vulcanite

hardscrabble: 4 poor; 8 marginal

hard set: 5 rigid, fixed; 6 hard up; 7 pinched, put to it, run hard; 10 straitened

hard-shell: 7 austere, exigent; 8 exacting, obdurate, rigorous; 9 demanding, hardnosed, searching, unsparing; 10 hardheaded, inexorable, inflexible

hard-shell clam: 6 quahog; 7 quahaug; 9 round clam

hardship: 5 rigor; 6 rigour; 7 trouble; 8 asperity, grimness, severity; 9 adversity; 10 difficulty

hardtack: 10 pilot bread, sea biscuit; 11 ship biscuit; 12 pilot biscuit

hard to believe: 10 incredible, staggering; 12 beyond belief, unbelievable; 13 inconceivable

hard to find: 4 rare; 6 scarce

hard to please: 9 querulous; 12 hard-to-please

hard up: 7 hard set, pinched, put to it, run hard; 9 penniless, penurious; 10 straitened; 11 hard-pressed

hardware: 8 ironware; 16 computer hardware

hardwareman: 10 ironmonger

hard wheat: 5 durum; 10 durum wheat

hard-won: 10 hard-earned, hard-fought

hard work: 6 teaser; 7 travail; 8 hard task, tough job; 9 tough task, tough work; 10 uphill work; 11 hard problem; 12 tough problem; 13 difficult task

hardworking: 8 tireless, untiring; 11 industrious

hardy: 4 hard; 5 brave, buxom, flush, stout, valid; 6 florid, mighty, potent, robust, stanch, strong, sturdy; 7 doughty, staunch; 8 fearless, forcible, powerful, stalwart, vigorous; 10 adamantine; 12 strong-minded, weatherproof

hare: 6 rabbit

hare and hounds: 10 paper chase

harebell: 8 bluebell

harebrained: 3 mad; 6 insane; 7 foolish

Hare Krishna: 6 ISKCON

harelip: 8 cleft lip; 13 cheiloschisis

harem: 6 hareem, serail; 8 seraglio

haricot: 9 flageolet; 10 French bean; 11 haricot vert

hari-kari: 8 hara-kiri

hark: 6 listen, hark ye!, harken; 7 hearken

hark back: 6 go back, recall, return; 7 get back, put back, run back; 8 come back, draw back, fall back, turn back

harken: 7 hearken

harlequinade: 5 prank; 8 clowning; 9 frivolity, pantomime; 10 buffoonery, shenanigan [U.S.]

Harley-Davidson: 6 Harley

harlot: 4 bawd, punk, tart; 5 whore; 7 cocotte, cyprian, trollop; 8 strumpet; 10 fancy woman, prostitute; 11 fille de joie [Fr], working girl

harm: 4 hurt; 5 wrong; 6 damage, injure, injury, scathe, trauma; 7 afflict; 9 detriment, vitiation, worsening; 10 debasement, impairment

harmful: 4 evil; 7 adverse, baleful, baneful, hurtful, noxious; 8 untoward; 9 injurious; 10 pernicious; 11 deleterious, detrimental, mischievous; 12 inauspicious; 15 disadvantageous

harmfully: 5 badly; 9 noxiously; 11 injuriously, malignantly; 12 perniciously

harmless: 4 safe; 6 benign; 7 unarmed; 8 innocent, sine ictu [Lat], unharmed, vincible; 9 innocuous, pregnable, undamaged, uninjured, unscathed, untenable; 10 weaponless; 11 defenseless, unblemished, unfortified, uninjurious; 12 indefensible, nonmalignant, not dangerous; 13 unthreatening

harmonic: 9 consonant, in harmony; 10 harmonical, harmonized; 11 sympathetic

harmonica: 4 harp; 5 organ; 9 mouth harp, reed organ; 10 mouth organ

harmonic analysis: 15 Fourier analysis

harmonious: 5 as one, sweet; 6 mellow, pastel, pearly, tender, united; 7 refined; 8 agreeing, cemented, delicate, in accord; 9 congenial, in harmony, of one mind; 10 concordant; 11 appropriate, friends with, harmonizing, in agreement, symmetrical

harmonium: 5 organ; 8 calliope; 9 reed organ; 10 steam organ

harmonize: 5 agree, chime, chord, fit in; 6 accord; 7 consort; 9 reconcile

harmonizing: 5 as one; 6 united; 8 agreeing, cemented, in accord; 9 congenial, in harmony, of one mind; 10 concordant, conforming, harmonious

harmony: 6 accord, unison; 7 concord; 8 symphony; 10 consonance; 11 concordance, condordance

harness: 4 gear, perk, rein, rule; 5 equip, slops, traps; 6 halter, rein in, traces; 7 rigging, turn-out; 8 draw rein, fittings; 9 accessory, caparison, equipment, trappings; 11 accessories; 12 accouterment

harp: 5 dwell; 9 harmonica, mouth harp; 10 mouth organ

harping: 8 unvaried; 9 iteration, iterative, recursive; 10 monotonous, recurrence, repetition; 11 reiteration

harpist: 6 harper

harpooner: 10 harpooneer

harp upon: 4 drum, echo; 6 hammer, reecho, repeat; 7 iterate; 8 redouble; 9 reiterate, reproduce

harpy: 4 crib, fury, thug; 5 churl, hunks, miser, shark, siren, vixen; 6 bandit, codger, falcon, scrimp, usurer; 7 brigand, hellcat, vulture

harquebus: 6 hagbut; 7 hackbut; 8 arquebus

harridan: 3 rig; 4 drab, jade, minx, skit; 5 shrew, hussy, wench

harried: 5 beset, bored, vexed; 6 baited; 7 annoyed, heckled; 8 badgered, harassed, infested, pestered, pothered; 10 importuned, persecuted

Harrisburg: 21 capital of Pennsylvania

Harrison: 16 Benjamin Harrison; 20 William Henry Harrison

harrow: 3 dig, hoe; 4 disk, plow, rake; 5 delve, wring; 6 dibble, plough; 7 agonize, pillage, plunder

harrowing: 7 rending; 9 agonizing, torturing, torturous

harry: 3 bug; 4 bait, bore; 5 abuse, beset, chevy, chivy, grind, haunt, hound, tease, worry; 6 badger, bother, chevvy, chivvy, harass, hassle, heckle, ill-use, infest, molest, pester, plague, pother, ravage; 7 oppress, provoke; 8 bullirag, bullyrag, illtreat, maltreat, mistreat; 9 importune, march upon, persecute

harsh: 4 dour, hard, sore; 5 acrid, acute, cruel, grave, rigid, rough, sharp, stern, stiff; 6 biting, brutal, coarse, severe, strict, unkind; 7 austere, caustic, mordant, rasping, uncouth; 8 abrasive, rigorous, virulent; 9 barbarous, corrosive, grotesque, stringent; 10 astringent, irritating, stertorous

harshly: 9 gratingly, raspingly

harshness: 5 rigor; 7 cruelty; 8 asperity, hardness, severity, soreness; 9 cruelness, raspiness, roughness, sharpness, sternness, stiffness; 10 coarseness, inclemency, stringency

hart: 4 stag

Hartford: 20 capital of Connecticut

harum-scarum: 4 wild; 6 madcap; 7 hothead, lunatic; 8 carefree, pell-mell; 9 daredevil, slaphappy

haruspical: 8 oracular; 9 prophetic

Harvard: 17 Harvard University

harvest: 3 bud; 4 boot, crop, gain, reap; 5 fruit, glean; 6 profit; 7 profits [pl]; 9 handiwork

harvester: 6 reaper

harvesting: 7 harvest, reaping; 11 harvest home

harvest mite: 6 jigger, redbug; 7 chigger

has-been: 6 lapsed, no more, run out; 7 elapsed, expired, extinct; 8 exploded; 9 blown over, forgotten; 10 antebellum, back-number

hash: 4 gash, stew; 5 mince; 6 hackle, haggle, huddle, jumble, litter, lumber, mangle, ragout, releve [Fr]; 7 hashish; 8 scramble

hashish: 3 pot; 4 hash, hemp; 5 bhang, ganja, grass; 9 marijuana

hash over: 6 rehash

hasp: 3 pin; 4 bolt, hank, nail; 5 catch, clamp, clasp, crimp, latch, rivet, screw

hassle: 4 fuss; 5 beset, chevy, chivy, harry; 6 bother, chevvy, chivvy, harass, molest, plague, tussle; 7 provoke, scuffle, trouble

hassock: 4 pouf; 6 pouffe; 7 cushion, ottoman; 9 footstool

hasta la vista: 4 ciao; 5 adieu, aloha; 7 goodbye; 8 farewell, sayonara; 10 dosvidanya [Russ]; 11 leave-taking, valediction; 14 auf wiedersehen [Ger]

haste: 4 rush; 5 hurry; 6 hasten; 7 rushing, urgency; 9 hastiness, make a dash, make haste; 10 impatience; 11 hurriedness

hasten: 3 hie; 4 post, race, rush; 5 haste, hurry, spank, speed; 6 foment, induce; 7 hotfoot, quicken, scuttle; 8 expedite

hasty: 3 hot; 5 fussy, quick; 6 rushed; 7 bilious, fidgety, hurried, peevish, peppery, unquiet, waspish; 8 captious, choleric, electric, galvanic, headlong, restless, shrewish, snappish; 9 fractious, impetuous, mercurial, overhasty, querulous; 11 precipitant, precipitate

hat: 3 cap, lid; 7 chapeau

hatch: 4 brew, cook, door, fake, gate; 5 brood, cover, force; 6 cordon, wicket; 7 bring up, concoct, develop, dream up; 8 hachure, postern, think of, think up; 8 hatching, incubate, trapdoor

hatchet: 2 ax; 8 tomahawk

hatchet job: 7 calumny, obloquy; 10 defamation; 11 traducement

hatchet man: 6 iceman; 8 enforcer, man-eater

hatching: 5 brood, hatch; 7 hachure, sitting; 8 brooding; 9 gestation; 10 crosshatch, incubation

hatchway: 7 doorway, gangway, gateway, opening, scuttle; 8 driveway

hate: 5 abhor; 6 detest, hatred, loathe; 8 execrate, loathing; 9 abominate, antipathy; 10 abhorrence; 11 abomination, detestation

hated: 7 scorned, unloved; 8 despised, detested, unvalued; 9 unbeloved; 10 uncared for, undeplored, unlamented

hateful: 4 mean; 6 odious; 8 spiteful; 9 abhorrent, execrable, repellent, repulsive; 10 abominable, detestable

hatmaker: 6 hatter; 7 modiste; 8 milliner

hatrack: 8 coatrack; 12 clotheshorse

hatred: 4 hate; 8 loathing; 9 antipathy; 10 abhorrence; 11 abomination, detestation

hat shop: 9 millinery

hatter: 7 modiste; 8 hatmaker, milliner

hauberk: 6 byrnie; 10 coat of mail

haughtiness: 7 hauteur; 9 arrogance, insolence, vainglory

haughty: 4 high; 5 blown, lofty; 6 lordly, mighty, sniffy; 7 cynical, flushed, swollen; 8 arrogant, cavalier, insolent, prideful, puffed up; 9 arbitrary, bumptious, imperious, withering; 10 disdainful, swaggering; 11 dictatorial, magisterial

haul: 3 lug, tow, tug; 4 cart, drag, draw, pull, rake, take; 5 catch, trail, train; 7 draught, drawing, haulage, pulling; 8 traction

haul away: 7 cart off, haul off; 8 cart away

hauling: 5 draft; 7 carting; 8 carriage, carrying, shipping, trucking; 9 transport; 10 conveyance; 12 transporting

haulm: 4 halm; 5 stems

haul up: 6 draw up, pull up

haunch: 3 hip; 4 loin; 6 temple; 11 hindquarter

haunt: 3 bug; 4 bait, bore; 5 abuse, beset, ghost, grind, harry, hound, stalk, tease, worry; 6 badger, bother, harass, heckle, illuse, infest, molest, obsess, pester, plague, pother, repair, resort; 7 hangout, oppress, retreat; 8 bullirag, bullyrag, environs, frequent, ill-treat, maltreat, mistreat, precinct, resort to, vicinage, vicinity; 9 hang about, importune, persecute, precincts; 10 hang around; 12 neighborhood

haunted: 7 taken up; 8 obsessed; 11 preoccupied

Hausa: 6 Haussa

hautbois: 4 oboe; 7 hautboy

haute couture: 11 high fashion

haute monde: 8 high life

hauteur: 7 arrogance, vainglory; 11 haughtiness, high notions

Havana: 11 Havana cigar; 13 capital of Cuba

have: 3 ail, get, let, own; 4 bear, give, hold, make, must, need, take; 5 birth, cause, drink, enjoy, throw; 6 accept, birthe, induce, ingest, occupy, suffer, take in; 7 command, consume, contain, deliver, feature, have got, include, possess, receive, sustain, undergo; 9 give birth, stimulate

have it out: 5 brawl

haven: 5 oasis; 6 harbor; 7 harbour, seaport; 9 anchorage

have no: 4 lack, want; 8 be void of; 9 be empty of

have-not: 4 need, want; 7 require; 10 poor person

have on: 4 wear

H

have on hand: 11 have in stock, keep in stock

haversack: 8 backpack, knapsack, rucksack

have to: 4 must; **5** got to, gotta; **6** need to; **9** have got to

having: 4 hold, keep; **7** custody, holding; **9** detention, including; **10** containing; **18** physical possession

having a screw loose: 3 mad; **4** daft, loco, nuts; **5** batty, crazy, dotty, loony, nutty; **6** crazed, fruity, insane, teched [dialect]; **7** bonkers, cracked, far gone, lunatic, tetched [dialect], touched; **8** demented, deranged, maddened, not right; **10** moonstruck, upper story

havoc: 5 smash; **6** inroad, mayhem, ravage; **7** debacle, outrage

haw: 8 hawthorn; **9** hum and haw

Hawaii: 10 Aloha State; **12** Hawaii Island

Hawaiian dancing: 4 hula; **8** hula-hula

Hawaiian guitar: 3 uke; **7** ukulele; **11** steel guitar

hawk: 4 hack, sell, vend; **5** crook, pitch; **6** hold-up [U.S.], monger, peddle; **7** sputter, war hawk; **8** huckster, splutter; **9** holdup man

hawker: 4 tout; **6** cadger, pedlar; **7** camelot [Fr], peddler; **8** falconer, huckster; **9** cheapjack

hawkeye: 8 eagle eye; **9** eagle's eye

hawk-eyed: 8 keen-eyed, lynx-eyed; **9** Argus-eyed, eagle-eyed, sharp-eyed; **11** keen-sighted; **12** quick-sighted, sharp-sighted

Hawkeye State: 4 Iowa

hawking: 7 selling, vending; **8** falconry, peddling; **9** vendition

hawksbill turtle: 8 hawkbill; **9** hawksbill

hawkshaw: 4 dick; **7** gumshoe; **9** detective

hawse: 9 hawsehole, hawsepipe

hawthorn: 3 haw

Hayastan: 7 Armenia

Haydn: 11 Joseph Haydn

Hayes: 17 Rutherford B. Hayes; **23** Rutherford Birchard Hayes

hay fever: 7 allergy; **10** pollinosis

hayfield: 6 meadow

haymaker: 7 KO punch; **11** Sunday punch; **13** knockout punch

hayrack: 6 hayrig

hayrick: 4 rick; **8** haystack

hayseed: 4 hick, rube; **5** yahoo, yokel; **6** rustic; **7** bumpkin; **8** lunkhead [U.S.]

haystack: 4 rick; **7** hayrick

haywire: 4 awry, bats, daft, loco, nuts; **5** amiss, balmy, barmy, batty, buggy, dotty, kooky, loony, loopy, nutty, wacky, wrong; **6** fruity, kookie; **7** bonkers, cracked; **8** crackers; **9** the matter; **10** out of order

hazan: 6 cantor

hazard: 3 hap, hit; **4** luck, risk; **5** guess, peril, stake; **6** chance, danger, foster, gamble; **7** fortune, pitfall, possess, venture; **8** casualty, fortuity, jeopardy, run a risk; **9** adventure, haphazard, put at risk; **10** insecurity, jeopardize

hazardous: 5 risky; **6** unsafe; **7** parlous; **8** insecure, perilous; **9** dangerous, venturous; **10** precarious; **11** venturesome

haze: 3 fog; **4** daze, mist; **5** cloud, vapor; **8** haziness

hazel: 8 hazelnut; **9** hazel tree, hazelwood; **12** hazelnut tree

hazelnut: 3 cob; **5** hazel; **6** cobnut; **7** filbert; **12** hazelnut tree

haze over: 3 fog; **4** mist; **5** befog, cloud; **7** becloud, obscure

hazing: 5 roast; **7** teasing; **8** quizzing, roasting; **9** bantering

hazy: 5 foggy, fuzzy, misty, muzzy; **6** bleary, blurry, cloudy; **7** blurred, brumous; **8** vaporous

H-bomb: 8 atom bomb; **10** fusion bomb; **12** hydrogen bomb; **17** thermonuclear bomb

he: 3 him, his, man; **4** male; **10** male person

He: 6 helium

head: 3 top; **4** arch, boss, foam, hand, lead, mind, nous, pass, pate, suds; **5** brain, caput, chief, froth, guide, jakes, order, party, point, polar, privy, spume, steer, title; **6** brains, direct, head up, herald, kitcat, lather, noggin, psyche, sconce, toilet, top dog; **7** be first, capital, caption, chapter, head man, heading, headway, latrine, oversee, section, straits, supreme, usher in; **8** arrow tip, be head of, drumhead, head word, long head, maneuver, question, supernal; **9** arrowhead, beginning, capitulum, come first, forefront, headpiece, hold a post, introduce, manouevre, principal

headache: 5 worry; **7** concern; **8** vexation

head and shoulders: 6 nicely; **8** headlong; **11** effectually

head armor: 6 helmet

headcounter: 8 pollster; **9** poll taker

head cover: 8 headgear, headwear; **9** headdress

header: 3 dip; **4** cope, dive; **6** coping, lintel, plunge

headfirst: 8 headlong

head game: 8 illusion

head gate: 8 penstock; **9** floodgate, water gate; **10** sluicegate; **11** sluice valve

headgear: 8 headwear; **9** head cover, headdress

head honcho: 4 boss, head; **7** big shot, head man; **8** big wheel; **10** head center

headhunter: 5 scout; **9** recruiter; **12** headshrinker

heading: 3 aim; **4** head; **5** drift, title; **6** docket, rubric; **7** bearing, caption, chapter, gallery, guiding, leading, section; **9** directing; **10** overseeing, precession; **11** supervising

head-in-the-clouds: 7 flighty; **14** scatterbrained

headland: 8 foreland; **10** promontory

headlight: 8 headlamp

headliner: 4 star

headlong: 5 hasty; **6** rashly; **7** furious; **9** headfirst, hotheaded; **10** boisterous, headstrong

headman: 7 foreman; **8** headsman, overseer; **9** chieftain; **11** tribal chief

head man: 4 boss, head; **10** head center, head honcho [informal]

headmaster: 6 master; **12** schoolmaster

head nurse: 6 matron

head off: 5 avert, avoid, debar; **7** deflect, fend off, obviate, ward off; **8** stave off

head of hair: 4 mane

head of state: 12 chief of state

head over heels: 8 devoutly; **10** topsy-turvy; **12** topsy-turvily

headphone: 5 phone; **8** earphone, earpiece

headpiece: 4 head, pate; **6** brains, noggin, sconce; **8** long head; **9** headstall; **10** upper story

headpin: 7 kingpin

headquarters: 2 HQ; **3** lap; **4** club, home, seat; **7** sojourn; **8** quarters; **10** home office, main office; **13** central office

head register: 8 head tone; **9** head voice

headrest: 13 head restraint

head rhyme: 12 alliteration, initial rhyme

headroom: 7 headway; **9** clearance

headshrinker: 6 shrink; **10** headhunter; **12** psychiatrist

headsman: 6 axeman; **7** headman

headspring: 4 head; **6** source; **12** fountainhead

headstone: 8 keystone; **9** tombstone; **10** gravestone

headstrong: 5 balky, heady; **6** unruly, wilful; **7** froward, restive, wayward, willful; **8** contrary, headlong, perverse; **10** rebellious, refractory, self-willed; **11** immitigable

heads-up: 9 wide-awake

head tax: 7 poll tax; **13** capitation tax

head teacher: 4 head; **9** principal; **15** school principal

head voice: 8 head tone; **12** head register

headwaiter: 7 captain; **12** maitre d'hotel

headway: 4 head; **6** leeway; **7** advance; **8** headroom, progress, sternway; **9** clearance; **11** advancement; **12** a step forward

head wind: 9 cross fire; **12** undercurrent

head word: 4 head

heady: 5 balky; **6** entete [Fr], unruly; **7** restive, wayward, willful; **8** contrary, perverse; **9** impetuous; **10** headstrong, rebellious, refractory, self-willed

367   **head-in-the-clouds / heart**

heal: 4 cure, mend; **5** amend; **6** doctor, physic, remedy; **7** get well; **8** medicate

healed: 5 cured; **9** recovered

healer: 6 doctor; **9** therapist; **12** health worker

healing: 4 cure; **8** curative, remedial, sanative; **10** alterative, corrective, palliative; **11** getting well, therapeutic

health: 6 sanity; **9** soundness; **10** good health; **11** healthiness

health care provider: 9 caregiver

health check: 7 checkup, medical; **11** medical exam

health club: 3 gym; **13** fitness center

health code: 12 sanitary code

healthful: 7 healthy; **8** salutary, sanitary; **9** wholesome; **10** salubrious

healthier: 6 fitter

healthiness: 6 health, sanity; **9** salubrity, soundness; **10** good health; **13** healthfulness, wholesomeness

health maintenance organization: 3 HMO

healthy: 3 fit; **4** well; **5** sound; **8** in health, salutary; **9** healthful, wholesome

heap: 3 bus, lot, pot, wad; **4** deal, load, mass, mess, mint, muss, peck, pile, raft, rick, slew; **5** batch, flock, heaps, mound, sight, spate, stack, world; **6** hatful, heap up, jalopy, mickle, muckle, pile on, pile up, plenty; **7** tidy sum; **8** good deal, whole lot; **9** congeries, great deal, whole slew

heaped: 5 piled

heaps: 3 pot; **4** deal, gobs, heap, load, lots, tons, wads; **5** loads, piles, rafts, scads, slews, world; **6** dozens, oodles, scores, stacks; **8** lashings; **9** great deal

hear: 3 see, try; **5** learn; **6** listen, pick up; **7** find out, get wind, get word; **8** discover, get a line, take heed

hearable: 7 audible

hear confession: 6 shrive

hearer: 7 auditor; **8** listener

hearing: 5 sound; **7** earshot; **8** audience, audition, earreach; **9** listening

hearing aid: 7 deaf-aid; **10** ear trumpet

hearing distance: 5 sound; **7** earshot, hearing; **12** hearing range

hearing-impaired: 13 hard-of-hearing

hearing impairment: 11 hearing loss

hearken: 4 hark; **6** harken

hearsay: 3 cry; **4** buzz, fame; **5** bruit, on dit [Fr], rumor; **6** rumour

hearse: 4 bier, pall; **10** catafalque

heart: 3 eye, nub, sum; **4** core, gist, meat, pith, pump, soul; **5** bosom, ghost, nerve, spunk; **6** breast, center, centre, kernel, marrow, mettle, middle, spirit, ticker; **7** essence, nucleus; **8** bull's-eye, fondness, inner man, pole axis; **9** affection, basic part, substance, vital part

heartache: 3 woe; **5** grief, trial; **6** sorrow; **8** distress; **10** affliction, heartbreak

heart and lung machine: 8 iron lung; **10** respirator; **14** artificial lung

heartbeat: 4 beat; **5** pulse; **9** breathing, pulsation

heartbreak: 5 grief; **9** heartache

heartbreaking: 8 grievous; **12** heartrending

heartburn: 6 reflux; **7** pyrosis

heart disease: 11 cardiopathy; **14** heart condition

hearten: 5 cheer; **8** embolden, recreate

heart failure: 13 cardiac arrest, heart stoppage; **15** coronary failure

heartfelt: 4 dear; **6** devout; **7** earnest; **8** deep felt, empyrean, home felt; **9** exquisite, rapturous, ravishing, thrilling; **10** deeply felt, delightful, felicitous

hearth: 8 fireside; **9** fireplace, inglenook; **11** hearthstone; **13** open fireplace

hearth fire: 8 home fire

heartily: 6 warmly; **9** cordially; **11** with feeling; **11** with passion

heartless: 8 soulless; **9** graceless, impassive, shameless; **10** spiritless, virtueless; **11** emotionless, hardhearted, passionless, unemotional

heartlessly: 11 gracelessly, shamelessly

Heart of Dixie: 7 Alabama; **13** Camellia State

heart rate: 5 pulse

heartrending: 8 grievous; **13** heartbreaking

heartsease: 5 peace; **6** repose; **8** ataraxis, serenity; **9** wild pansy; **10** field pansy; **11** peace of mind; **12** Johnny-jump-up

heart-shaped: 7 cordate; **8** cardioid

heartsick: 6 sick of; **7** tired of; **10** despondent; **11** heartbroken; **13** brokenhearted

heart specialist: 12 cardiologist, heart surgeon

heart stoppage: 12 heart failure; **13** cardiac arrest

heart surgeon: 12 cardiologist; **15** heart specialist

heartwood: 7 duramen

hearty: 4 hale, warm, well; **5** bonny, buxom, fresh, green, lusty, solid, whole; **6** genial; **7** cordial, winsome; **8** cheering, gracious; **10** red-blooded, satisfying; **11** full-blooded, substantial, warmhearted; **12** well-affected

heat: 3 rut; **4** warm; **5** fever, flush, hot up; **6** estrus, fire up, foment, foster, heat up, ignite, stir up, warmth; **7** arousal, caloric, heating, hotness, inflame, make hot, oestrus, passion; **8** dead heat; **10** excitement, heat energy; **12** heating plant; **13** heating system

heat-absorbing: 11 endothermal, endothermic

heated: 3 het; **5** het up; **6** warmed; **7** made hot; **8** heated up

heatedly: 5 hotly

heater: 5 smoke; **6** bullet, hummer, tuyere, warmer; **8** fastball, radiator; **10** heat source, warming pan

heathen: 5 alien, pagan; **7** gentile, infidel

heather: 4 ling; **5** broom, heath

heath family: 9 Ericaceae

heating: 4 heat; **7** warming; **11** calefactive, calefactory; **12** heating plant; **13** heating system

heating oil: 7 fuel oil

heating pad: 6 hot pad

heat lamp: 12 infrared lamp

heat rash: 11 prickly heat

heat-releasing: 10 exothermal, exothermic

heat unit: 8 work unit; **10** energy unit

heat wave: 8 hot spell, scorcher; **10** hot weather

heave: 3 gag, shy; **4** cast, gasp, heft, jerk, lift, pant, puff, puke, rear, spew, toss, warp; **5** chuck, fling, hoist, pitch, raise, retch, surge, throb, vomit; **6** be sick, billow, buckle, cast up, heft up, quiver, thrill, tingle; **7** bring up, discard, flutter, get sick, heave up, heaving, throw up

heaven: 4 eden; **7** nirvana; **8** paradise; **9** Shangri-la; **12** kingdom of God, promised land; **15** heavenly kingdom, kingdom of heaven

heavenly: 4 holy; **6** sacred; **7** elysian; **8** almighty, beatific, hallowed, supernal; **9** celestial, unearthly

heavenly body: 13 celestial body

Heavenly City: 8 Holy City; **9** City of God; **13** Celestial City

heavens: 3 sky; **6** sphere, welkin; **8** empyrean; **9** firmament; **13** vault of heaven

heaven-sent: 10 miraculous; **12** providential

heavenward: 7 skyward; **11** heavenwards; **12** heavenwardly

heave overboard: 8 jettison

heave to: 5 lay to; **7** bring to

heavily: 4 hard; **5** dully, heavy; **8** leadenly; **13** intemperately

heaviness: 5 blues, dumps; **7** sadness; **8** darkness, doldrums, dullness, flatness, the blues, the dumps; **9** dejection, thickness, tristesse [Fr]; **10** bad spirits, blue devils, depression, dismalness, gloominess, low spirits, melancholy, somberness; **11** joylessness, massiveness, melancholia, weightiness; **12** dejectedness

heaving: 4 moan, sigh; **5** groan, heave, vomit, whine; **6** flurry, murmur, mutter, plaint, puking, quiver, tremor; **7** fluster, flutter, grumble, panting, twitter; **8** deep sigh, vomiting; **9** complaint

Heaviside layer: 6 E layer; **7** E region; **10** ionosphere

heavy: 3 big, sad; **4** deep, dull, flat, full,

hard, high, rude, slow, tame, wild; **5** blunt, dense, grave, great, large, slack, sound, thick; **6** clayey, cloggy, far out, fleshy, gravid, leaden, obtuse, stolid, strong, stupid, sullen, unwise; **7** arduous, awkward, Boeotic, doltish, heavily, intense, labored, passing, plenary, serious, weighty; **8** accented, enceinte, grievous, grueling, laboured, lowering, profound, sluggish, sonorous, toilsome, ungifted, wakeless; **9** expectant, gruelling, laborious, lumbering, ponderous, punishing, with child; **10** labourious, out of sight, outtasight, overweight; **11** threatening, weighed down; **12** backbreaking, impenetrable

heavy gun: 6 cannon; **8** ordnance; **9** artillery; **13** gun of position

heavy-handed: 6 clumsy; **7** awkward, unhandy; **8** bumbling, bungling, handless, lubberly; **9** ham-fisted, ham-handed, maladroit, roughshod; **10** left-handed; **11** floundering; **13** uncoordinated

heavy heart: 11 aching heart, broken heart; **13** bleeding heart

heavyhearted: 4 dark; **6** dismal, gloomy, somber, triste [Fr]; **7** joyless; **8** dejected, frowning; **9** cheerless, saturnine; **10** lugubrious, spiritless, uncheerful

heavy hydrogen: 9 deuterium

heavy particle: 6 baryon

heavy sea: 5 storm; **7** long sea, tempest; **8** cross sea, high seas, rough sea; **11** chopping sea

heavyset: 5 thick; **6** stocky; **7** compact; **8** thickset

heavy water: 14 deuterium oxide

heavy weapon: 3 gun; **8** ordnance; **9** artillery

heavyweight: 4 hulk; **5** giant, power, titan, whale; **8** behemoth, colossus

hebdomad: 4 week

Hebraic: 6 Hebrew; **9** Hebraical

Hebrew: 3 Jew; **6** Jewish; **7** Hebraic; **9** Hebraical

Hebrews: 10 Israelites

Hebrides: 12 Western Isles; **14** Hebridean Isles, Western Islands; **16** Hebridean Islands

hebronite: 11 amblygonite

heckelphone: 10 basset oboe

heckle: 3 bug; **4** bait, bore; **5** abuse, beset, grind, harry, haunt, hound, tease, worry; **6** badger, bother, hackle, harass, hariff, illuse, infest, molest, pester, plague, pother; **7** oppress

heckled: 5 beset, bored; **6** baited; **7** harried; **8** badgered, harassed, infested, pothered; **10** importuned, persecuted

heckler: 8 badgerer

hectares: 5 acres; **11** square miles; **15** acres and perches, roods and perches

hectic: 8 feverish

hectogram: 2 hg

hectograph: 9 heliotype

hectoliter: 2 hl; **10** hectolitre

hectometer: 2 hm; **10** hectometre

hector: 5 bully; **7** dictate; **8** ballyrag, browbeat, bullyrag, domineer; **9** strong-arm; **10** boss around, intimidate, lord it over, push around

Hector: 4 hero

Hedera: 3 ivy; **9** common ivy; **10** English ivy; **11** genus Hedera

hedge: 4 duck, wall; **5** dodge, elude, evade, fudge, parry, skirt; **6** put off, square; **7** hedging, qualify; **8** hedgerow, sidestep; **9** condition; **10** circumvent

hedgehog: 9 porcupine

hedgerow: 4 wall; **5** hedge

hedonic: 9 epicurean; **10** hedonistic

hedonism: 10 sensuality

hedonist: 9 epicurean; **10** sensualist, voluptuary; **14** pleasure seeker

heed: 4 care, mind; **6** listen, regard; **7** caution; **8** coolness, prudence; **9** entertain, pay heed to, recognize; **10** discretion, give heed to, steadiness; **11** calculation, heedfulness, mindfulness; **12** cautiousness, deliberation, have regard to; **13** attentiveness

heedful: 7 careful; **9** advertent, attentive; **10** thoughtful

heedless: 4 wild; **6** blithe, casual, madcap, wanton; **8** careless, reckless; **9** unheeding, unmindful; **10** unthinking; **11** thoughtless, unobservant

hee-haw: 4 bray, ha-ha; **6** haw-haw; **10** horselaugh

heel: 3 bar, cad, dog, lap, rod; **4** boom, shoe, sole; **5** hound; **6** reheel, splint, stilts, swerve; **7** bear off, bounder, counter, stirrup; **9** outrigger; **10** blackguard

heelbone: 9 calcaneus

heft: 4 haft, hilt; **5** heave, shaft, shank; **6** handle, heft up; **7** heave up; **9** heftiness; **11** massiveness, ponderosity; **13** ponderousness

hefty: 4 tidy; **6** brawny, goodly; **7** goodish, sizable; **8** muscular, powerful, sizeable; **11** respectable

Hegel: 26 Georg Wilhelm Friedrich Hegel

hegira: 6 exodus, hejira

he-goat: 5 billy; **9** billy goat

heifer: 4 calf

height: 3 top; **4** acme, drop, peak; **5** pitch; **6** climax, summit; **7** heights [pl], maximum, stature; **8** altitude, highland, pinnacle, tallness; **9** elevation, high place, thickness; **10** ne plus utra; **11** superlative; **12** turning point; **13** crowning point

heighten: 4 lift, rise; **5** erect, raise; **6** deepen; **7** elevate, enhance, sharpen; **8** compound; **9** aggravate, intensify; **10** exacerbate

H

heightening: 8 building; 9 worsening; 11 aggravation

heights: 4 high; 6 height; 8 highland; 9 elevation, high place

Heimdall: 7 Heimdal; 9 Heimdallr

heinous: 4 base, foul, vile; 5 black, grave, gross; 6 scurvy; 8 grievous, infamous, shameful, shocking, sinister; 9 atrocious, felonious, monstrous, nefarious; 10 flagitious, scandalous, villainous

heir: 5 scion; 7 heiress [female], heritor, legatee; 9 inheritor, successor; 10 descendent, inheritrix [female]; 11 inheritress [female]

heirloom: 5 plant; 8 fixtures

heirs: 4 seed, spat; 5 breed, brood, issue, spawn; 6 farrow, litter; 7 progeny; 9 offspring, posterity

heist: 6 burgle, holdup, rip-off; 7 stickup; 10 burglarize; 12 armed robbery

hejira: 6 exodus, hegira

Hel: 4 Hela, Hell; 5 Hades; 6 Scheol; 10 underworld; 11 netherworld; 14 infernal region

held: 3 had; 4 kept; 8 retained, withheld; 9 possessed, preserved

held back: 7 hoarded; 8 kept back, reserved, set aside, withheld; 10 unrevealed; 11 not revealed, undisclosed; 12 not disclosed

Helena: 16 capital of Montana

heliacal: 5 solar; 6 heliac

helianthus: 9 sunflower

helical: 6 coiled, spiral, volute; 7 coiling, voluted, whorled; 9 spiraling, turbinate

helicon: 9 bombardon

helicopter: 6 copter; 7 chopper; 9 eggbeater; 10 whirlybird

heliolatry: 10 sun worship

heliotrope: 5 agate; 10 bloodstone, chalcedony

heliotype: 10 hectograph, stereotype; 13 daguerreotype

helium: 2 He

helix: 4 coil, worm; 5 whorl; 6 buckle, rundle, spiral, volute; 9 corkscrew

Helix: 5 snail; 10 genus Helix

hell: 3 sin, Hel; 5 blaze, Hades; 6 Scheol, the pit; 7 inferno, the pits; 9 perdition; 10 underworld; 11 hell on earth, netherworld; 12 nether region; 13 bottomless pit; 14 infernal region, place of torment; 15 infernal regions

hellbender: 8 mud puppy

hellcat: 5 harpy, vixen; 9 hellhound

hellebore: 10 poison herb

Hellene: 5 Greek

Hellenic: 5 Greek; 7 Grecian; 11 Hellenistic

hellenic: 10 greco-roman

heller: 5 devil, haler; 7 hellion

helleri: 9 swordtail, topminnow

Hellespont: 11 Dardanelles

hellgrammiate: 6 dobson

hellion: 5 devil; 6 heller

hellish: 6 unholy; 7 beastly, demonic, satanic, stygian; 8 devilish, diabolic, fiendish, hell-born, infernal; 10 demoniacal, diabolical

hello: 2 hi; 5 howdy, hullo; 10 how do you do

helm: 3 key; 5 blade, shako; 6 casque, needle, rudder, tiller; 7 compass, treadle, trigger; 8 siege cap

helmet: 9 head armor

helmetflower: 9 monkshood

Helmholtz: 19 Hermann von Helmholtz

helminth: 4 worm; 13 parasitic worm, segmented worm

helmsman: 9 steersman

Heloderma: 12 beaded lizard; 11 Gila monster; 14 genus Heloderma

helot: 4 serf; 5 slave

help: 3 aid; 4 dole; 5 avail, serve; 6 aiding, assist, curing, helper, remedy, succor, supply; 7 furnish, give aid, helping, redress, regimen, servant, service, therapy; 8 bring aid, helpmate, lend help, oblation; 9 afford aid, assistant, assisting, offertory, supply aid, supporter, treatment; 10 assistance, facilitate, furnish aid

helper: 4 help; 9 assistant, associate, supporter; 10 benefactor

helpful: 6 aiding; 8 adjuvant; 9 assisting, auxiliary

helpless: 4 lost; 9 paralytic, paralyzed; 13 incapacitated

helplessly: 10 impotently

help wanted ad: 5 job ad; 6 want ad

Helsinki: 11 Helsingfors; 14 Finnish capital

helter-skelter: 7 chaotic; 8 pell-mell; 11 harum-scarum

helve: 4 haft

Helvetica: 9 sans serif

hem: 4 list, tuck, welt; 5 frill; 6 edging, fringe, gather; 7 flounce, valance; 8 furbelow, selvedge, skirting, trimming

he-man: 4 stud, hunk; 8 macho-man; 12 weight lifter

hem and haw: 4 trim; 5 demur, pause; 6 coquet, debate, waffle; 7 balance, shuffle; 8 straddle; 9 fluctuate, hum and haw; 12 be on the fence, remain neuter; 13 remain neutral

hematite: 6 jasper; 7 cat's eye; 9 haematite, moonstone; 10 bloodstone

hematocyst: 9 blood cyst

hemeralopia: 9 nystagmus; 12 day blindness

hemerobiid fly: 10 hemerobiid; 13 brown lacewing

hemi-: 4 demi-, semi-

hemic: 6 haemic; 7 hematic; 8 haematic

hemicrania: 6 megrim; **8** migraine; **12** sick headache

hemicycle: 10 semicircle

hemimorphite: 8 calamine

hem in: 3 pen; **4** cage, coop; **5** pen in; **6** bolt in, coop up, rail in, wall in; **7** besiege, hedge in, impound; **8** surround; **9** beleaguer; **10** circumvent

Hemingway: 15 Ernest Hemingway

hemipteran: 3 bug; **10** hemipteron

hemisphere: 5 realm; **8** province; **18** cerebral hemisphere

hemlock: 7 aconite, henbane; **9** hellebore; **10** belladonna, nightshade, winter fern; **11** hemlock tree; **13** poison hemlock

hemming and hawing: 9 faltering; **10** hesitating, hesitation

hemophilia: 11 haemophilia; **15** bleeder's disease

hemophiliac: 7 bleeder; **9** hemophile; **10** haemophile; **12** haemophiliac

hemorrhage: 5 bleed; **8** bleeding; **9** shed blood; **11** haemorrhage

hemorrhagic cyst: 9 blood cyst; **10** hematocyst

hemorrhagic septicemia: 14 pasteurellosis

hemorrhoids: 5 piles

hemostatic: 7 styptic

hemp: 3 pot; **4** jute; **5** bhang, ganja, grass, oakum; **7** hashish; **8** cannabis; **9** marijuana; **12** hangman's rope; **13** hempen necktie; **14** Cannabis sativa, hangman's halter

hempen: 7 fibrous

hemp family: 13 Cannabidaceae

hen: 10 female bird

henbane: 7 aconite, hemlock; **9** hellebore; **10** belladonna, nightshade; **12** black henbane

hence: 4 ergo, then, thus; **6** thence, thusly, whence; **8** thence so; **9** therefore, wherefore; **11** accordingly; **12** and therefore, consequently

henceforth: 12 henceforward

henchman: 8 follower; **11** confederate; **12** collaborator

hen hawk: 11 chicken hawk

henhouse: 4 coop; **7** hen coop; **11** chicken coop

henpeck: 3 nag; **4** peck; **8** dominate

Henry Bolingbroke: 7 Henry IV; **11** Bolingbroke

Henry I: 14 Henry Beauclerc

Henry IV: 11 Bolingbroke; **16** Henry Bolingbroke

Henry Tudor: 8 Henry VII

Henry VII: 10 Henry Tudor

henyard: 7 fowl run; **10** chicken run; **11** chicken yard

hep: 3 hip; **5** hip to

hepatic: 5 liver

hepatitis: 12 liver disease

hepatitis A: 19 infectious hepatitis

hepatitis B: 14 serum hepatitis

hepatitis delta: 14 delta hepatitis

hepatoflavin: 8 vitamin G; **9** ovoflavin, vitamin B2; **10** riboflavin; **11** lactoflavin

Hephaistos: 10 Hephaestus

heptad: 3 VII; **5** seven; **6** septet; **7** sevener

heptagon: 10 seven-sided

Hera: 4 Here

Heracles: 7 Alcides; **8** Herakles, Hercules

herald: 4 hail, head; **5** crier; **6** blazon; **7** acclaim, marshal, premise, usher in; **8** announce, foretell, proclaim; **9** harbinger, introduce, precursor, trumpeter; **10** annunciate, flag bearer, forerunner

herb: 7 herbage; **15** herbaceous plant

herbaceous: 6 herbal

herbal: 10 herbaceous

herbal tea: 7 herb tea; **8** infusion

herb doctor: 9 herbalist

herbicide: 10 weed killer

Herculean: 7 arduous, onerous; **8** powerful; **9** Cyclopean, laborious; **10** formidable, Gargantuan, prodigious

Hercules: 7 Alcides; **8** Heracles, Herakles

herd: 3 fry; **4** bevy, hive, nest, peck, ruck; **5** brood, cloud, covey, crowd, drove, flock, shoal, surge, swarm; **6** bushel, farrow, flight, litter, scores, stream, throng; **7** draught; **9** associate

herded: 7 crowded, flocked; **8** thronged; **11** congregated; **12** concentrated; **13** conglomerated

herder: 6 drover; **8** herdsman

herd instinct: 12 peer pressure

herdsman: 6 drover, herder; **9** swineherd

here: 6 hither; **7** this way; **8** this-a-way

hereafter: 5 later; **6** future; **8** futurity; **9** afterlife; **10** time to come; **11** hereinafter, in the future; **13** prospectively

here and now: 6 moment; **13** present moment

here and there: 6 passim, rarely

hereditary: 6 inborn; **7** genetic; **8** familial; **9** ancestral, incarnate, inherited; **10** congenital; **11** transmitted; **13** transmissible

hereditary disease: 14 genetic disease; **16** inherited disease

heredity: 11 inheritance; **16** genetic endowment

Hereford: 9 whiteface

heresy: 6 schism; **10** heterodoxy; **11** unorthodoxy; **13** false doctrine

heretic: 8 apostate; **11** misbeliever

heretical: 9 dissident, heterodox; **10** unorthodox

heretofore: 3 yet; **5** as yet, so far; **6** ere now, til now; **7** as far as, thus far, up to now; **8** hereunto, hitherto, until now; **9** a while ago, before now, in the past; **10** a while back, by that time, previously

H

hereunto: 3 yet; **5** so far; **7** as far as; **10** by that time, heretofore; **11** prior to this

heritable: 10 hereditary; **11** inheritable

heritage: 4 line, stem; **5** birth, stock; **6** stirps, strain; **7** descent, lineage, stirpes [pl]; **8** ancestry, pedigree; **9** genealogy, reversion; **10** extraction; **11** inheritance

heritor: 4 heir; **7** heiress [female], legatee; **9** inheritor; **10** inheritrix [female]; **11** inheritress [female]

hermaphrodite: 7 epicine; **9** androgyne; **13** epicine person, gynandromorph; **14** hermaphroditic

hermaphroditism: 9 androgyny; **11** bisexuality

hermit: 7 recluse; **9** anchorite; **10** troglodyte

hermitage: 3 box; **4** cell; **5** cabin, lodge; **7** cottage

hernia: 7 rupture; **10** herniation

herniated disc: 11 slipped disc

hero: 3 sub, zep; **5** angel, great, hoagy, wedge; **6** Amazon, bomber, Hector, hoagie, seraph; **7** demigod, fighter, grinder, heroine, paladin, poor boy, torpedo; **8** champion, great man, immortal; **9** submarine; **11** great person

heroic: 4 epic; **5** grand; **6** sacred, solemn; **7** sublime; **8** heroical, imposing, majestic; **9** desperate; **10** chivalrous, heaven-born

heroin: 1 H; **4** junk, scag; **5** horse, smack; **16** diacetyl morphine

heroine: 4 hero; **5** angel; **6** seraph; **7** demigod

heroism: 5 valor; **6** valour; **7** prowess; **8** chivalry, valiance, valiancy; **9** gallantry

hero sandwich: 3 sub, zep; **4** hero; **5** hoagy, wedge; **6** bomber, hoagie; **7** grinder, poor boy, torpedo; **9** submarine

hero worship: 6 homage, revere; **7** idolize, worship

herpes labialis: 8 cold sore; **10** oral herpes; **12** fever blister

Herpestes: 8 mongoose; **9** ichneumon; **14** genus Herpestes

herpes virus: 6 herpes

herpes zoster: 6 zoster; **8** shingles

Herrenvolk: 10 master race

Hertz: 2 Hz; **3** cps; **5** cycle; **15** cycles per second

herz hormone: 12 heart hormone; **14** cardiac hormone

hesitant: 7 groping; **10** hesitating, irresolute

hesitate: 5 hover, pause, waver; **6** boggle, demure, falter, hammer, swiver; **7** scruple, sputter, stick at; **8** flounder, intermit; **9** alternate; **10** dilly-dally; **12** stop and start

hesitater: 7 waverer; **9** hesitator; **10** vacillator

hesitation: 5 waver; **6** falter; **8** suspense, wavering; **9** faltering, hesitancy; **10** hesitating, reluctance; **11** vacillation; **13** indisposition

hesitator: 7 waverer; **9** hesitater; **10** vacillator

Hesperian: 7 Western; **10** occidental

Hesperides: 10 Atlantides

Hessian boot: 7 hessian, top boot; **8** jackboot

hessonite: 8 essonite; **12** grossularite; **13** cinnamon stone

heteroclite: 7 epicene; **10** amphibious

heterodox: 9 dissident, heretical; **10** unorthodox

heterodoxy: 6 heresy; **11** unorthodoxy

heterodyne receiver: 8 superhet

heterogamy: 7 genesis; **10** gemination, generation; **11** germination, procreation, propagation

heterogeneous: 3 odd; **5** mixed; **6** divers, hybrid, varied; **7** diverse, mingled, mongrel, various; **8** assorted, chow-chow, polyglot; **9** composite, different; **10** dissimilar; **11** diversified, half-and-half; **12** heterogenous, multifarious

heterogenous: 13 heterogeneous

heterograft: 9 homograft

heterologous: 11 heterologic; **13** heterological

heterosexual: 8 straight; **14** straight person

het up: 3 het; **5** upset; **6** heated; **8** heated up

hew: 3 cut; **4** hack; **5** carve, slash; **6** chisel, chop up, hew out, scrimp

hewn: 6 carved; **8** chiseled, hand-hewn

hex: 4 jinx; **5** curse, witch; **7** bewitch, enchant, glamour; **11** hexadecimal

hexacosanoic acid: 11 cerotic acid

hexad: 2 VI; **3** six; **4** sise; **5** sixer; **6** sestet, sextet; **9** sextuplet; **10** half a dozen

hexagon: 8 six-sided

hexanoic acid: 11 caproic acid

Hexapoda: 7 Insecta; **12** class Insecta; **13** class Hexapoda

hexed: 6 jinxed

heyday: 4 peak; **5** bloom, flush, prime; **6** flower; **7** blossom

Hf: 7 hafnium

HF: 13 high frequency

hg: 9 hectogram

Hg: 7 mercury; **11** quicksilver

Hi: 3 ave [archaic]; **4** hail; **5** hello, howdy; **7** welcome, well met; **11** how do you do?

hiatus: 7 caesura, respite; **8** reprieve; **9** abatement; **10** suspension

hibernal: 3 icy; **6** arctic, boreal, brumal, frosty, hiemal, wintry; **7** glacial; **8** freezing, Siberian

hibernate: 6 hole up

hibernating: 6 torpid; **7** dormant

Hibernia: 7 Ireland; **11** Emerald Isle

Hibernian: 8 Irishman

Hibiscus esculentus: 4 okra; **5** gumbo

Hibiscus heterophyllus: 10 sorrel tree

Hibiscus sabdariffa: 6 sorrel; 7 roselle, rozelle; 9 red sorrel; 13 Jamaica sorrel

hiccup: 8 hiccough; 9 singultus

hick: 4 rube; 5 yahoo, yokel; 6 rustic; 7 bumpkin, hayseed

hidalgo: 7 grandee; 8 nobility

hidden: 6 buried, occult, secret, veiled; 7 abeyant, covered, dormant, lurking, obscure; 8 obscured; 9 concealed; 10 out of sight; 11 camouflaged

hidden agenda: 6 agenda; 12 hidden motive, secret motive, undercurrent; 14 ulterior motive

hide: 4 fell, pelt, skin; 5 cover; 6 occult, shroud; 7 blot out, conceal, hide out, obscure, secrete; 8 enshroud; 10 obliterate

hideaway: 3 den; 7 hideout, retreat

hidebound: 5 stiff; 6 sordid; 11 hard-mouthed, straitlaced

hideous: 6 horrid, odious; 7 uncanny; 8 horrific; 9 frightful, monstrous, repulsive; 10 forbidding, outrageous

hideout: 3 den; 8 hideaway

hidrosis: 5 sudor, sweat, water; 11 diaphoresis; 12 perspiration

hie: 4 gang, post, race, rush; 5 spank, speed; 6 hasten; 7 hotfoot, scuttle

hierarch: 7 prelate, primate; 10 archpriest, high priest

hierarchical menu: 7 submenu; 13 cascading menu

hierarchy: 12 pecking order; 14 power structure

hicratic: 8 priestly; 10 hieratical, sacerdotal; 14 hieratic script

hieroglyphical: 5 Runic; 6 uncial; 9 cuneiform; 12 hieroglyphic

hifalutin: 6 la-di-da; 9 grandiose; 10 hoity-toity; 11 highfalutin; 12 highfaluting

hi-fi: 12 high fidelity

higgle: 6 dicker, haggle; 7 chaffer; 8 huckster

high: 3 bad, big, cut; 4 deep, full, gamy, tall, weak; 5 acute, beery, blown, boozy, drunk, flood, fresh, fusty, gamey, great, heavy, lofty, merry, sharp, sound, steep, tight, tipsy; 6 corned, effete, groggy, high up, mellow, mighty, primed, putrid, rancid, richly, rotten, strong; 7 corrupt, decayed, drunken, eminent, exalted, flushed, fuddled, gone bad, haughty, heights, intense, passing, plenary, reeking, rotting, stoical, swollen, tainted, touched; 8 elevated, high gear, overcome, piercing, puffed up, spirited, top-heavy; 9 disguised, flustered, inebriate, overtaken, putrefied, secondary

high and dry: 7 aground, beached; 8 at anchor, stranded; 9 stuck fast; 10 above water

high and mighty: 4 high; 5 blown, bossy, lofty; 6 mighty; 7 flushed, haughty, swollen; 8 puffed up; 10 high-handed, autocratic, dominating, peremptory; 12

vainglorious; 13 consequential, self-important

high art: 11 portraiture; 13 the grand style

high blood pressure: 12 hypertension

highborn: 6 titled; 8 well-born; 9 coroneted

highbrow: 7 thinker; 8 longhair; 10 high-browed; 12 intellectual

high chair: 12 feeding chair

high class: 8 top-notch

high cost: 8 dearness; 9 high price; 10 costliness, fancy price; 11 famine price; 13 expensiveness

high court: 12 supreme court

high-density lipoprotein: 3 HDL

higher: 5 major; 7 greater; 8 superior

higher court: 13 court of appeal; 14 appellate court

higher rank: 9 seniority; 12 higher status, senior status

higher-ranking: 7 ranking; 8 superior

highest: 4 peak; 7 tallest; 9 most lofty; 12 most elevated

high fashion: 12 haute couture

high fidelity: 4 hi-fi

highflier: 4 seer; 8 proud man; 9 highflyer

high-flown: 4 rich, vain; 5 lofty, tumid; 6 florid, mouthy, ornate, turgid; 7 exalted, fanatic, flighty, flowery, flushed, orotund, utopian; 8 inflated, puffed up, quixotic, rarefied, rarified, romantic, sonorous, swelling; 9 bombastic, conceited, grandiose, high-toned, overblown; 10 high-flying, high-handed, high-minded, high-plumed, high-souled, idealistic, intolerant, ornamented, rhetorical, turgescent; 11 big-sounding, declamatory, domineering, extravagant, high-flowing, noble-minded, overbearing, overweening, pretentious, unrealistic

highflyer: 9 highflier

high frequency: 2 HF; 9 high pitch

high-handed: 8 absolute, cavalier, insolent, positive; 9 arbitrary, high-flown, high-toned, imperious; 10 high-minded, high-plumed, high-souled, imperative, iron-handed, peremptory

highjack: 6 hijack

highjacker: 8 hijacker

highland: 6 height, upland; 7 heights [pl]; 9 elevation, high place

highlight: 6 play up; 8 high spot; 9 spotlight; 10 foreground; 12 highlighting

high living: 10 free living, good living, wild living; 12 intemperance

highly educated: 12 well educated; 14 college educated

high mass: 12 missa cantata [Lat]

high-minded: 5 lofty; 7 exalted; 8 rarefied, rarified; 9 high-flown, high-toned; 10 high-handed, high-plumed, high-souled, idealistic

high muck-a-muck: 3 VIP [acron]; **7** big shot, his nibs; **8** big wheel

highness: 5 grace; **9** loftiness; **10** excellency

high noon: 4 noon; **6** midday; **7** noonday; **8** noontide; **10** twelve noon

high-octane: 9 high-power; **11** high-powered, high-voltage

high price: 4 dear; **5** pricy; **6** costly, pricey; **8** dearness, high cost; **10** costliness, fancy price; **11** famine price; **13** expensiveness

high priest: 6 Levite, priest; **7** prelate, primate, prophet; **8** cardinal, hierarch; **10** archpriest

high probability: 6 odds on; **8** good odds; **10** good chance, main chance

high quality: 7 upscale; **8** goodness; **11** superiority

high-reaching: 8 aspiring, vaulting; **9** ambitious

high regard: 5 honor; **6** esteem; **7** respect; **9** deference; **10** estimation

high-rise: 5 tower; **10** skyscraper

high risk: 3 bad; **5** risky; **8** insecure; **11** speculative

high roller: 10 big spender

high school: 4 high; **10** senior high

high seas: 3 sea; **4** deep, main; **5** ocean; **7** long sea; **8** cross sea, heavy sea

high society: 7 society; **8** smart set; **9** beau monde

high-sounding: 4 rich; **5** tumid; **6** florid, mouthy, ornate, turgid; **7** flowery, orotund, pompous; **8** inflated, sonorous, swelling; **9** bombastic, grandiose, high-flown; **10** high-flying, ornamented, rhetorical, turgescent; **11** big-sounding, declamatory

high speed: 8 celerity, rapidity; **9** fleetness, quickness, rapidness, swiftness; **10** great speed, speediness

high spirit: 6 daring, spirit; **8** audacity; **9** gallantry; **11** intrepidity; **12** intrepidness

high-strung: 4 edgy, taut; **5** jumpy, nervy, tense; **7** jittery, nervous, restive, uptight; **8** volatile; **9** excitable, sensitive

high technology: 8 high-tech; **10** automation; **13** mechanisation, mechanization

high tide: 4 tide; **5** flood; **8** full tide; **9** flood tide, high water

high-toned: 7 pompous; **11** pretentious

high-up: 3 VIP; **9** dignitary

high water: 8 high tide

high water mark: 9 flood mark

highway: 7 thruway; **8** main road, motorway, turnpike

highwayman: 5 thief; **6** robber

high wind: 4 gale, gust; **5** blast; **9** half a gale, high winds [pl]; **10** strong wind

high yield bond: 8 junk bond

hijack: 6 pirate; **8** highjack; **10** commandeer; **11** expropriate

hijacker: 9 road agent; **10** highjacker, highwayman

hike: 4 rise; **5** boost, raise, tramp; **6** hike up

hiker: 10 backpacker

hilarious: 5 funny; **7** risible; **8** rattling; **9** screaming, very funny; **10** uproarious; **13** side-splitting

hilarity: 4 glee; **5** mirth; **9** merriment; **11** gleefulness; **12** exhilaration, mirthfulness

hill: 4 alto, bank; **5** butte [U.S.], mound; **13** pitcher's mound

hillbilly: 4 folk; **7** country, western

hillock: 4 knob, pena [U.S.]; **5** knoll, mound; **6** barrow; **7** hammock, hummock

hillside: 5 bluff; **6** steeps

hilltop: 4 brow

hilly: 6 craggy, knobby [U.S.]; **7** cragged; **11** mountainous

hilt: 4 haft, heft; **5** shaft, shank; **6** handle

Himalayas: 17 Himalaya Mountains

hind: 4 back; **5** clown, swain; **6** hinder; **8** hindmost

hinder: 4 back, hind; **5** block, stymy; **6** hamper, impede, stymie; **7** inhibit; **8** blockade, handicap, hindmost, obstruct, restrict; **9** embarrass; **10** filibuster [U.S.]; **12** disadvantage

Hindi: 5 Hindu

hindmost: 4 hind; **6** caudal, hinder; **8** backmost, rearmost; **10** hindermost

hindrance: 5 hitch; **8** handicap, impeding; **9** deterrent, hindering, stricture; **10** impediment, inhibition, preventive; **11** encumbrance, incumbrance, interfering, restriction; **12** interference, preventative

Hindu: 5 Hindi; **6** Hindoo; **10** Hindustani

Hindu Kush Mountains: 9 Hindu Kush

hinge: 4 crux, gore, seam; **5** lever, pivot; **6** gusset; **7** fulcrum; **12** articulation, turning point

hinge joint: 9 ginglymus; **12** knuckle joint

hinge on: 6 ride on, turn on; **8** depend on; **9** devolve on, hinge upon; **10** depend upon

hint: 3 ace, bit, jot, tip; **4** clue, iota, lead, mite, wind; **5** apply, pinch, speck, steer, touch, trace; **6** allude, breath, morsel; **7** hinting, modicum, soupcon, suggest; **8** allude to, intimate, proposal, reminder; **9** adumbrate; **10** intimation, suggestion

hinterland: 9 backwoods, boondocks; **10** background; **11** back country

hinting: 4 hint; **9** prompting, reminding

hip: 2 in; **3** hep; **4** coxa, loin; **5** hip to; **6** haunch, pelvis; **8** hip joint, parietes [Lat]

hip bath: 8 sitz bath

hip boots: 6 waders; **7** hip boot; **9** thigh boot; **10** thigh boots

hipflask: 11 pocket flask
hip joint: 3 hip; 4 coxa
hippie: 5 hippy; 11 flower child
hippo: 10 river horse; 12 hippopotamus
Hippobosca: 8 louse fly, horsefly; 9 horse tick; 15 genus Hippobosca
Hippocastanaceae: 19 horse-chestnut family
hippodrome: 6 circus, 12 amphitheater
Hippoglossus: 7 halibut; 17 genus Hippoglossus
hippopotamus: 5 hippo; 10 river horse;
hippy: 6 hippie; 11 flower child
hire: 4 name, rent, take; 5 lease; 6 employ, engage, hiring, return, take on; 7 appoint, bespeak, charter; 8 accredit, nominate; 10 employment, engagement
hired: 6 leased; 7 taken on; 9 chartered, recruited
hired gun: 3 gun; 6 gunman, hit man; 7 shooter, torpedo, 8 hireling; 9 mercenary; 10 gunfighter, gunslinger
hired hand: 3 man; 4 hand; 8 hired man; 10 day laborer
hire out: 7 farm out, rent out
hiring: 4 hire; 8 engaging, taking on; 9 employing; 10 employment, engagement
hirsute: 5 hairy; 6 tufted; 8 ciliated; 10 fimbriated; 11 filamentous
hirudinean: 5 leech; 11 bloodsucker
Hirudo: 5 leech; 11 genus Hirudo
Hirundo: 6 martin; 7 swallow; 12 genus Hirundo
Hispanic American: 6 Latino; 8 Hispanic; 15 Spanish American
Hispaniola: 5 Haiti; 17 Dominican Republic
hispid: 5 bushy, spiny; 6 shaggy; 7 bearded, shagged, villous
hiss: 3 boo, hum, mob; 4 bird, buzz, gibe, gird, hoot, jeer, quip, siss, sizz, twit, wipe; 5 fling, flout, scoff, scout, sneer, snort, taunt; 6 clamor, deride, whoosh; 7 barrack, hissing, laugh at, razzing, scoff at, snigger; 8 ridicule, sibilate; 9 blacklist, ostracize, raspberry, sibilance; 10 Bronx cheer
historian: 8 annalist
historical: 8 historic; 10 diachronic
historic Muse: 4 Clio
historied: 7 storied; 10 celebrated
history: 4 gone; 5 story; 7 account; 9 chronicle
histrion: 5 actor; 6 player; 8 thespian; 10 role player
histrionic: 8 dramatic; 10 theatrical; 12 melodramatic
hit: 3 hap, pip; 4 bang, beat, blow, bump, club, find, gain, make, slam, slap, slay, whop; 5 knock, reach, score, shoot, smash, smite [biblical], tally; 6 attain, chance, come to, happen, hazard, murder, rack up, remove, strike, wallop; 7 bump off, fortune, hitting, run into, stumble; 8 arrive at, bludgeon, casualty, dispatch, fortuity, striking; 9 adventure, collision, encounter, haphazard, impinge on, polish off
hitch: 3 fix, rub; 4 buck, halt, hang, jerk, jolt, lash, limp, pass, push, snag, stay, stop, toss, tour; 5 catch, check, pinch, sling, thumb, trial, truss, whisk; 6 append, arrest, hang-up, hobble, hook up, strait, tumble; 7 nonplus, suspend; 8 duty tour, exigency, fasten to, juncture, quandary, scramble, stoppage; 9 hindrance, hitchhike; 10 enlistment, pretty pass, preventive, screw loose, tour of duty; 11 conjunctive, contretemps, encumbrance, incumbrance, predicament
hitched: 3 wed; 7 married
hitchhike: 5 hitch, thumb
hitchrack: 11 hitching bar
hither: 4 here; 7 this way; 8 this-a-way
hitherto: 3 yet; 5 as yet, so far; 6 ere now, til now; 7 thus far, up to now; 8 until now; 9 a while ago, before now, in the past
hit home: 10 strike home; 12 strike a chord
Hitler: 9 Der Fuhrer; 11 Adolf Hitler
hit man: 3 gun; 6 gunman; 7 shooter, soldier, torpedo; 8 hired gun; 10 gunslinger
hit-or-miss: 9 haphazard
hitter: 6 batter; 7 batsman, slugger
hit the books: 5 study; 10 be studious; 12 apply oneself
hit the ceiling: 4 foam, fume, rage, roar; 5 go ape; 7 bluster; 9 go bananas; 10 hit the roof; 11 blow one's top, flip one's lid; 12 blow one's cool
hit the hay: 6 retire, turn in; 7 crawl in, go to bed, kip down, sack out; 9 go to sleep; 10 get into bed
hit the road: 6 set out; 8 get going; 11 get underway
hit the roof: 4 foam, fume, rage, roar; 5 go ape; 7 bluster; 8 get angry, get upset; 9 go bananas; 10 get riled up; 11 become angry, blow one's top, flip one's lid, go ballistic; 12 blow one's cool, fly into a rage, get into a rage, get steamed up
hit the sack: 6 retire, turn in; 7 crawl in, go to bed, kip down, sack out; 9 go to sleep, hit the hay; 10 get into bed
HIV: 4 AIDS; 9 AIDS virus
hive: 3 fry; 4 bevy, herd, nest, peck; 5 brood, cloud, covey, drove, flock, perch, shoal, squat, swarm; 6 burrow, bushel, farrow, flight, litter, scores; 7 beehive, bivouac, draught, sit down
hives: 9 urticaria; 10 nettle rash, urtication
hl: 10 hectoliter, hectolitre
hm: 10 hectometer, hectometre
HN: 8 azoimide; 13 hydrazoic acid
Ho: 7 holmium
hoagie: 3 sub, zep; 4 hero; 5 hoagy, wedge; 6 bomber; 7 grinder, poor boy, torpedo; 9 submarine; 12 hero sandwich

hoagy: 6 hoagie

hoar: 4 gray, grey, rime; 5 frost, hoary; 6 frosty; 7 frosted; 9 hoarfrost; 10 gray-haired, gray-headed, grey-haired, grey-headed; 11 white-haired

hoard: 4 fund; 5 amass, cache, stash; 6 garner, hive up, pile up; 7 collect, compile, lay away; 8 garner up; 10 accumulate; 12 squirrel away

hoarded: 7 amassed; 8 held back, kept back, reserved, set aside; 11 accumulated

hoarfrost: 4 hoar, rime; 5 frost; 10 white frost

hoariness: 10 frostiness

hoarse: 3 dry; 5 gruff, husky; 6 hollow; 7 raucous; 8 croaking; 10 sepulchral

hoarseness: 9 gruffness, huskiness

hoary: 4 gray, grey, hoar; 5 rusty; 6 frosty; 7 frosted; 9 canescent; 10 gray-haired, gray-headed, grey-haired, grey-headed; 11 white-haired

hoatzin: 8 hoactzin; 9 stinkbird

hoax: 4 dupe, fool, gull; 5 fraud, put-on, spoof, trick; 6 dupery, take in; 9 bamboozle, imposture; 11 fraudulence, hornswoggle

hoaxer: 9 prankster, trickster; 10 bamboozler; 14 practical joker

hob: 3 elf, imp; 4 pixy; 5 pixie; 6 ashpan, goblin, shovel, trivet; 7 brownie, gremlin; 9 hobgoblin

hobble: 4 halt, limp, slug; 5 hitch; 6 fetter, scrape, slouch, slough, toddle, waddle; 7 manacle, shamble, shuffle, traipse; 8 handcuff, quagmire

hobby: 3 fad; 5 quirk; 6 by-line; 8 crotchet, sideline; 9 avocation

hobbyhorse: 5 hobby; 9 cockhorse; 10 stick horse; 12 rocking horse

hobgoblin: 3 hob; 6 goblin

hobnob: 7 hang out

hobo: 2 bo; 3 bum; 4 drab; 5 scrub, sweep, tramp; 6 pauper; 7 dust-man, vagrant

hoc genus omne: 11 rank and file

Ho Chi Minh City: 6 Saigon

hock: 4 pawn, soak; 8 rhennish; 9 Rhine wine

hockey: 9 ice hockey; 10 hockey game; 11 field hockey

hocus: 4 bite, wile, dope, drug; 5 blind, catch, cheat, feint, fetch, plant, reach, trick; 6 bubble, juggle; 7 chicane, deceive

hocus-pocus: 8 nonsense, trickery; 9 conjuring, gibberish, slickness; 10 hanky panky, mumbo jumbo; 11 conjuration, skulduggery; 12 skullduggery

hod: 4 tray; 6 trough

hodgepodge: 4 mess, olio; 6 jumble, medley, mosaic, ragbag; 7 collage, farrago, melange, montage; 8 all sorts, mishmash, oddments, pastiche; 9 composite, patchwork, potpourri; 10 hotchpotch; 11 odds and ends

hoe: 3 dig; 4 rake; 6 harrow, plough; 7 backhoe

hoedown: 5 dance; 11 square dance

hog: 3 pig, sow; 4 boar, hogg; 5 swine; 6 hogget; 7 glutton; 8 belly god; 9 cormorant

hognose snake: 9 puff adder, sand viper

hogwash: 3 rot; 4 bull, bunk, guff; 6 bunkum; 8 buncombe

Hohenzollern empire: 11 Second Reich

ho-hum: 4 dull, slow; 6 boring; 7 irksome, tedious; 8 tiresome; 9 deadening, wearisome

hoi polloi: 3 low; 4 mass; 5 demos [Grk]; 6 common, masses, people; 9 multitude

hoist: 4 lift, rear, wind; 5 heave, run up

Hokkaido: 3 Ezo; 4 Yezo

Hokkianese: 3 Min; 4 Amoy; 6 Fukien; 9 Taiwanese; 10 Fukkianese, Min dialect

hold: 3 can [slang], pen; 4 bear, bind, book, brig, curb, deem, defy, fort, gaol, give, grip, halt, have, jail, keep, make, stir [slang], stop, take, wait; 5 admit, apply, bilge, carry, check, clasp, cling, clink [slang], delay, enjoy, ensue, go for, grasp, guard, hulks, issue, nurse, pokey [slang], spare, start, stick, think, throw, vault; 6 adhere, arrest, arrive, cleave, clench, clutch, cooler [slang], defend, donjon, embody, freeze, handle, harbor, having, hold in, hold on, hold up, lockup, oblige, obtain, occupy, prison, pull up, retain, view as; 7 adjudge, command, confine, contain, control, custody, declare, dungeon, embrace, harbour, have got, holding, possess, prevail, redoubt, eserve, slammer [slang], support, sustain, take for, the Rock, time lag; 8 clutches, fastness, fortress, handgrip, hold back, hold fast, hoosegow, keep back, maintain, moderate, preserve, restrain, shoulder, stockade, take hold; 9 cargo area, cargo deck, detention, entertain, guardroom, oubliette, stop short, withstand; 10 be seized of, comprehend, guard house, have in hand, San Quentin, stronghold, take care of; 11 accommodate

hold back: 4 hold, keep, stop, wait; 5 check; 6 arrest, hold in, keep in, retain; 7 conceal, contain, hold off, repress, reserve; 8 draw back, hang back, hold from, keep back, keep from, restrain, shift off, stave off, tide over, turn back, withhold; 11 hold in check, keep in check

hold close: 6 clutch; 7 cling to; 9 hold tight

hold dear: 5 prize; 7 care for, cherish; 8 treasure

holder: 9 possessor

holdfast: 4 lock; 8 fastener; 9 fastening

hold fast: 4 bind, bond, hold; 5 cling, stick;

6 adhere, cleave; 7 stick to; 9 stick fast; 12 hang together; 13 stick together

hold forth: 5 stump; 6 recite; 7 declaim, lecture; 8 flourish, harangue; 9 delve into, discourse, sermonize, speechify

hold in: 4 curb, hold; 5 check; 6 keep in; 7 conceal, confine, contain, control, enclose; 8 hold back, hold from, keep back, keep from, moderate

holding: 4 hold, keep; 5 claim, right, title; 6 demand, estate, having; 7 custody, keeping; 8 adhering, clinging, grasping, gripping, property, sticking; 9 detention, retaining, retention; 10 belongings, preserving

hold in esteem: 5 honor; 6 esteem, regard; 7 respect

hold off: 4 wait; 5 defer, delay; 6 put off; 8 hold back, keep from, postpone, stand off; 9 hold aloof; 10 stand aloof

hold on: 4 go on, grip, hold, keep, stop; 5 break, grasp, jog on, run on; 6 hang in, hang on, keep on; 7 hold out, persist; 9 persevere

hold one's tongue: 5 be mum; 6 be mute; 7 keep mum, not talk; 8 be silent, not speak

hold onto: 4 keep; 6 retain; 8 withhold

hold out: 2 go; 4 last, live, wear; 6 allege, broach, endure, extend, hold on, hold up, invite, live on, put out, resist; 7 advance, propose, survive; 8 hold firm, propound, set forth; 9 enunciate, pronounce, stand firm, withstand

hold out the olive branch: 7 placate; 9 make peace, reconcile; 10 conciliate, propitiate

hold over: 5 defer, remit, table, waive; 6 put off, remand, retard, shelve; 7 adjourn, lay over, put over, set back, suspend; 8 postpone; 9 carry over

hold the line: 6 hang on, hold on

hold tight: 6 clutch; 7 cling to; 9 hold close

hold together: 7 collude, concert, consort; 8 conspire; 10 fraternize; 11 confederate

holdup: 4 hawk; 5 crook, delay, heist; 7 mugging, robbery, stickup; 9 detention, holdup man; 12 armed robbery

hold up: 2 go; 4 defy, hold, last, live, prop; 5 delay; 6 back up, bail up, be fine, bear up, detain, endure, keep up, live on, uphold; 7 bolster, display, exhibit, hold out, shore up, stand by, stand up, stick up, support, survive, sustain; 8 sanction; 9 bolster up, withstand

hold up one's hand: 4 poll, vote

hold water: 8 hold good, hold true

hole: 3 fix, gap, jam, maw, yap; 4 cell, mess, nook, trap; 5 niche; 6 corner, hollow, lacuna, muddle, pickle, recess; 7 hole out, opening; 8 aperture

hole up: 9 hibernate

holey: 6 porous

holiday: 6 day off; 7 dies non, play day; 8 vacation; 9 day of rest

holiletic: 7 preachy; 11 homiletical

holiness: 5 glory, unity; 7 majesty; 8 sanctity; 11 saintliness, sovereignty

Holland: 11 Netherlands; 14 The Netherlands

Hollander: 8 Dutchman; 12 Netherlander

holler: 3 cry; 4 beef, call, roar, yell, yowl; 5 gripe, holla, hollo, shout; 6 bellow, grouse, holloa, hollow, scream, squall, squawk; 7 roaring, yowling; 8 shout out; 9 bellowing, bellyache

Hollerith card: 9 punch card; 11 punched card

hollo: 3 cry; 4 call, roar, yell, yowl; 5 holla, shout; 6 bellow, holler, holloa, scream, squall; 7 roaring, yowling; 8 shout out; 9 bellowing, hollering

hollow: 3 dig, dry, pit; 4 hole, lame, well; 5 blank, empty, false, husky, shaft; 6 crater, hoarse, holler, meager; 7 core out, depress, evasive, raucous, sketchy, stove in, vacuous; 8 croaking, excavate, specious; 9 hollow out, insincere, plausible; 10 sepulchral

holloware: 8 flatware; 10 hollowware

hollow-eyed: 8 deep-eyed; 10 sunken-eyed

hollowness: 5 blank; 6 hollow

holly family: 13 Aquifoliaceae

hollyhock: 6 althea; 7 althaea

Holmes: 14 Sherlock Holmes

holmium: 2 Ho

Holocaust: 4 Shoa; 12 the Holocaust [1934–1945]

holocaust: 8 auto da fe, hecatomb; 9 sacrifice; 10 immolation

Holocene epoch: 8 Holocene; 11 Recent epoch

holograph: 10 manuscript; 11 holographic; 13 holographical

holonym: 9 whole name

holothurian: 11 sea cucumber

holotype: 12 type specimen

Holstein-Friesian: 8 Friesian, Holstein

holy: 5 godly, pious; 6 devout, sacred, solemn; 7 devoted, sanctum; 8 almighty, hallowed, heavenly, reverent; 9 celestial, holy place, pietistic, religious, spiritual

Holy City: 9 City of God; 12 Heavenly City; 13 Celestial City

holy communion: 9 communion, Eucharist; 11 Lord's supper; 12 the sacrament; 13 holy sacrament

Holy Father: 4 pope; 7 pontiff; 13 Vicar of Christ

Holy Ghost: 10 Holy Spirit

Holy Grail: 5 grail

Holy Joe: 5 padre; 8 sky pilot, chaplain

Holy Land: 6 Canaan, Israel; 9 Palestine

holy of holies: 6 adytum; 7 sanctum;

H

12 inner sanctum; 16 innermost sanctum, sanctum sanctorum

holy oil: 6 chrism; 7 chrisom; 14 sacramental oil

holy orders: 9 reading in; 10 ordination, preferment; 11 institution, translation; 12 consecration, presentation

holy person: 5 angel, saint; 7 prophet

holy place: 4 holy; 7 sanctum; 10 house of God; 13 house of prayer

Holy Roman Empire: 10 First Reich

Holy Sacrament: 7 Liturgy; 9 Eucharist; 11 Lord's Supper; 18 Eucharistic liturgy

Holy Scripture: 4 Word; 5 Bible; 8 Good Book, Holy Writ; 9 Scripture, Word of God

holy table: 10 Lord's table; 14 communion table

holy terror: 4 brat; 6 terror; 12 little terror

Holy Thursday: 12 Ascension Day; 14 Maundy Thursday

Holy Week: 11 Passion Week

Holy Writ: 4 Word; 5 Bible; 8 Good Book; 9 Scripture, Word of God; 13 Holy Scripture; 14 Holy Scriptures

homage: 5 court; 6 fealty; 7 loyalty, worship; 8 devotion, fidelity, kneeling; 9 adoration, constancy, obeisance; 10 aspiration; 11 hero worship; 12 faithfulness, genuflection

homard: 7 lobster

Homaridae: 7 lobster; 15 family Homaridae

Homarus: 7 lobster; 12 genus Homarus

hombre: 3 cat, guy; 6 fellow

home: 4 base, club; 5 abode, house, place, plate; 6 family, indoor, menage; 7 housing, lodging; 8 domestic, domicile, dwelling, interior, internal, intimate, lodgment, national, rest home; 9 home plate, household, lodgement, poorhouse, residence; 10 habitation, intramural, vernacular; 11 nursing home; 12 headquarters

homebody: 10 stay-at-home

homebound: 6 shut-in; 10 housebound

home bred: 6 homely; 8 homespun

homecoming: 6 return; 10 return home

home fire: 10 hearth fire

homegrown: 5 local

home improvement center: 10 lumber yard; 11 lumber store

home in: 6 zero in; 7 range in

homeland: 10 fatherland, motherland, native land, native soil

homelike: 4 homy; 5 homey; 6 homely

homeliness: 7 lowness; 8 drabness; 9 dowdiness, plainness

homely: 4 homy; 5 brute, homey, plain; 6 simple; 8 home bred, homelike, homespun

home office: 10 main office; 12 headquarters; 13 central office

homeopathic: 9 very small; 10 evanescent; 13 inappreciable, infinitesimal

homer: 7 home run; 12 homing pigeon

home reserve: 13 National Guard

home run: 5 homer

homesick: 9 nostalgic

homespun: 5 nubby; 6 folksy, homely, nubbly, tweedy; 7 slubbed; 8 home bred; 13 cracker-barrel

homesteader: 6 nester; 7 granger; 8 squatter

home territory: 9 home range

homework: 4 prep; 7 studies; 10 assignment; 11 preparation

homey: 4 homy; 6 homely; 8 homelike

homicidal: 9 cutthroat, murderous

homicide: 6 murder; 7 slaying; 12 manslaughter; 13 assassination

homiletic: 7 preachy; 11 homiletical

homily: 6 sermon; 7 lecture; 8 pastoral; 9 discourse; 10 preachment; 11 predication

homing pigeon: 5 homer

hominid: 8 hominian

hominy grits: 5 grits

homogeneity: 6 purity; 8 affinity, alliance, homology; 10 uniformity; 11 association, consistency

homogeneous: 4 neat, pure; 5 sheer; 6 simple, single; 7 uniform; 8 of a piece

homogenize: 13 render uniform

homograft: 9 allograft

homology: 8 affinity, alliance; 11 association, homogeneity

homophony: 6 unison

homopterous insect: 10 homopteran

Homo sapiens neanderthalensis: 11 Neanderthal

Homo sapiens sapiens: 9 modern man; 11 Homo sapiens

homosexual: 3 gay

homosexuality: 7 gayness

honcho: 4 boss; 5 chief; 6 gaffer; 7 foreman

Hondo: 6 Honshu

hone: 5 strop; 7 perfect; 9 sharpener

honest: 4 true; 8 Platonic, reliable, virtuous; 9 guileless, honorable, veracious; 10 dependable, scrupulous; 11 trustworthy

honestly: 7 frankly; 8 candidly; 10 aboveboard

honest-to-goodness: 3 old; 10 sure-enough; 11 honest-to-god

honesty: 5 faith, truth; 6 candor; 8 fidelity, satinpod; 9 sincerity; 10 honestness

honey: 4 dear, duck, love; 5 jewel, sugar; 6 duckey; 7 beloved, dearest; 8 loved one

honeybee: 3 bee; 13 Apis mellifera

honeycomb: 5 wreck; 6 sponge, weaken; 7 subvert

honeycombed: 6 pitted, spongy; 8 alveolar, cavitied; 9 alveolate, faveolate

honeycreeper: 6 oscine; 20 Hawaiian honeycreeper

honeydew melon: 8 honeydew; 11 winter melon; 12 Persian melon vine

honeyed: 5 sweet; 6 dulcet, honied, smooth, syrupy

honey gland: 7 nectary

honeymooner: 8 newlywed

honey-mouthed: 6 smooth; 7 honeyed; 12 honey-tongued, mealy-mouthed

honeysuckle family: 14 Caprifoliaceae

honey-tongued: 6 smooth; 7 honeyed; 12 honey-mouthed, mealy-mouthed

honied: 6 syrupy; 7 candied, honeyed

honk: 4 beep, toot; 5 blare, cluck

honker: 4 beak; 5 snoot, snout; 6 hooter, nozzle; 9 schnozzle; 11 Canada goose

honky-tonk: 4 dive; 11 barrelhouse

Honolulu: 15 Hawaiian capital

honor: 4 quit; 5 award, favor, glory, grace, manor; 6 domain, esteem, favour, honour, purity, redeem, regard, reward, settle; 7 abide by, demesne, laurels, observe, respect, satisfy; 8 accolade, accredit, adhere to; 9 deference, discharge; 10 comply with, estimation, high regard; 11 pay regard to, think much of; 12 hold in esteem, honorability

honorable: 4 good; 5 grand, moral, noble, proud; 6 august, honest, lordly; 7 ethical, honored, stately; 8 esteemed, princely; 9 dignified, estimable, respected; 10 honourable, worshipful; 11 respectable

honorably: 9 uprightly; 10 honourably

honorarium: 5 bonus; 6 tipfee; 7 douceur [Fr], premium; 8 gratuity

honorary: 6 unpaid; 8 unbought

honorary society: 7 academy

honored: 8 esteemed, honoured; 9 honorable, respected; 11 prestigious

honoring: 8 decorous; 9 cap in hand, esteeming; 10 bareheaded, obsequious, observance, respectful, respecting; 11 ceremonious, deferential, on one's knees, reverential

Honshu: 5 Hondo

hooch: 6 hootch; 8 dwelling

hood: 4 cowl, goon, punk, thug; 5 brute, bully, rough, rowdy, tough; 6 bonnet, meanie [jocular], mugger, savage, wretch; 7 caitiff, cowling, hoodlum, ruffian, toughie; 8 hooligan, plug-ugly; 9 barbarian, desperado

hooded: 6 cowled

hooded cloak: 6 capote

hooded coat: 6 capote

hooded seal: 11 bladdernose

hooded sheldrake: 15 hooded merganser

hoodlum: 4 goon, hood, punk, thug; 5 brute, bully, rough, rowdy, tough; 6 meanie [jocular], mugger, roarer, savage, wretch; 7 caitiff, ruffian, toughie; 8 hooligan, plug-ugly; 9 barbarian, bulldozer [U.S.], desperado

hoodoo: 4 juju; 6 fetich, fetish, voodoo; 7 bedevil, bewitch

hoodooed: 7 hapless, unhappy, unlucky; 8 luckless, snakebit; 9 bedeviled, bewitched, out of luck; 11 unfortunate

hoodwink: 4 snow; 6 dazzle, juggle; 7 beguile; 9 bamboozle, blindfold, play false

hooey: 5 stuff; 9 poppycock; 16 stuff and nonsense

hoof: 3 toe; 4 foot, keel, root, sole; 5 leg it

hoofed: 6 hooved; 8 ungulate; 9 ungulated

hoofed mammal: 8 ungulate

hoofer: 9 tap dancer

hoofprint: 8 hoofmark

hook: 3 bag, cop, nab, paw, rob; 4 bait, claw, draw, glom, hand, lift, link, lock, lure, mitt, sack, soak, yoke; 5 belay, brace, catch, crook, filch, latch, leash, manus, pinch, pluck, plume, snarf, sneak, swipe; 6 addict, bought, come-on, couple, fleece, gazump, mauler, nobble, pilfer, pocket, snitch, thieve; 7 bracket, cabbage, crochet, grapple, purloin; 8 abstract, crotchet, hook shot, knock off; 9 surcharge, sweetener; 10 overcharge

hookah: 6 kalian; 8 narghile; 9 water pipe; 12 hubble-bubble

hook and ladder: 9 fire truck; 12 aerial ladder

hooked: 6 beaked; 8 aquiline; 9 dependant, dependent, strung-out; 12 drug-addicted, sickle shaped

hooker: 6 floozy; 7 floozie, hustler; 8 slattern; 10 prostitute, street girl; 12 streetwalker

hook shot: 4 hook

hookup: 10 assemblage

hook up: 4 hang; 5 hitch, sling; 6 append; 7 suspend; 8 fasten to

hook up with: 3 wed; 5 marry; 7 conjoin, espouse; 10 get married

hook wrench: 11 hook spanner

hooky: 7 truancy

hooky player: 6 truant

hooligan: 3 yob; 4 hood, yobo; 5 brute, bully, rough, rowdy, tough, yobbo; 6 meanie [jocular], mugger, roarer, savage, wretch; 7 caitiff, hoodlum, ruffian; 9 barbarian, bulldozer [U.S.], desperado, roughneck

hooliganism: 9 vandalism

hoop: 4 bawl, howl, ring, roar, yell; 5 brawl, shout, whoop; 6 areola, basket, bellow, circle, halloa, halloo, scream, shriek, shrill, wicket; 7 annulus, circlet, screech

hoopla: 4 hype, plug; 8 ballyhoo

hoopoe: 6 hoopoo

hoops: 10 basketball

hoopskirt: 6 bustle; 9 crinoline

hoosegow: 3 can [slang], pen; 4 brig, gaol, hold, jail, keep, stir [slang]; 5 clink [slang], hulks, pokey [slang]; **6** chokey [slang], cooler [slang], donjon, lockup, prison; **7** dungeon, hoosgow, slammer [slang], the Rock; **8** Bastille, big house [slang], stockade; **9** calaboose [slang], guardroom, oubliette; **10** guard house, San Quentin; **11** penal colony, prison house; **12** penitentiary

Hoosier: 8 Indianan

Hoosier State: 7 Indiana

hoot: 3 boo, hoo, mob; **4** bird, damn, darn, gibe, gird, hiss, jeer, quip, twit, wipe; **5** fling, flout, noose, scoff, scout, sneer, snort, taunt; **6** clamor, deride, shucks; **7** barrack, laugh at, razzing, scoff at, snigger; **8** ridicule; **9** blacklist, ostracize, raspberry; **10** Bronx cheer

hootch: 5 hooch

hooter: 4 beak; **5** snoot, snout; **6** honker, nozzle; **9** schnozzle

hoot owl: 9 horned owl; **14** great horned owl

hooved: 6 hoofed; **8** ungulate; **9** ungulated

hoover: 6 vacuum

Hoover: 13 Herbert Hoover; **18** Herbert Clark Hoover

hop: 4 hops, jump, leap, ramp, skip, trip; **5** bound, vault; **6** spring; **7** hop-skip

hop clover: 8 shamrock

hope: 5 go for, hopes, trust; **6** desire; **7** promise

hope chest: 12 wedding chest

hope for: 4 long; **6** cry for; **7** gape for, gasp for, pant for, pine for, sigh for; **8** yearn for

hopeful: 4 rosy; **5** cadet; **6** hoping, likely; **7** wannabe; **8** aspirant, probable, wannabee; **9** candidate, fortunate, schoolboy

hopeless: 4 gone; **7** forlorn; **8** desolate; **9** desperate, in despair

hopelessly: 12 dispiritedly

Hopi tribe: 4 Hopi

hop on: 5 get on, mount; **6** jump on; **7** climb on, mount up; **8** bestride

hopped-up: 6 stoned

hopscotch: 10 crisscross

hop skip and jump: 8 leapfrog

hora: 5 horah

horah: 4 hora

horde: 3 mob; **4** body, host, rout; **5** chaff, crush, drove, press, swarm; **6** legion, rabble; **7** phalanx

hordeolum: 3 sty; **4** stye; **12** eye infection

Hordeum: 6 barley; **12** genus Hordeum

horizon: 4 view; **5** vista; **7** purview, skyline; **8** prospect; **11** perspective

horizontal: 4 even; **5** level, plane

horizontal bar: 7 high bar

horizontality: 9 levelness

hormone: 17 internal secretion

horn: 3 pea; **4** bulb, clew, drop, knob, pill, tusk; **6** antler, bullet, cornet, marble, pellet, pommel, rummer; **7** car horn, globule,

trumpet, vesicle; **8** spherule; **9** motor horn; **10** French horn

horn book: 8 text book

horned asp: 8 cerastes; **9** sand viper; **11** horned viper

horned dinosaur: 11 ceratopsian

horned lizard: 10 horned toad

horned owl: 7 hoot owl; **14** great horned owl

horned rattlesnake: 10 sidewinder

horned viper: 8 cerastes; **9** horned asp, sand viper

hornet: 4 wasp

hornet's nest: 8 hot water; **9** wasp's nest

horn in: 8 poke into; **10** meddle with; **11** intrude into

hornlike: 5 horny; **8** corneous

horn of Amalthaea: 12 horn of plenty

hornpipe: 7 pibgorn; **9** stockhorn

horn poppy: 8 sea poppy

horns: 4 hots; **13** sexual arousal

hornstone: 8 hornfels

hornswoggle: 4 dupe, fool, gull, hoax; **5** trick; **6** take in; **9** bamboozle

hornswoggler: 11 flimflam man; **14** flimflam artist

horny: 3 hot; **5** randy; **7** aroused, rutting, ruttish; **8** corneous, hornlike, turned on

horny layer: 7 corneum

horologe: 4 dial; **7** sundial

horologer: 10 horologist, watchmaker

horology: 11 chronometry

horoscope: 8 nativity, forecast

horoscopy: 9 astrology

horrendous: 4 dire; **5** awful, dread; **7** direful, dreaded, fearful; **8** dreadful, fearsome, horrific, terrible; **11** frightening

horrible: 4 ugly; **6** horrid; **8** horrific; **9** atrocious, frightful; **10** horrifying

horribly: 5 sadly; **6** sorely; **7** awfully, cruelly, grossly; **8** bitterly, terribly, woefully; **9** fearfully, miserably, painfully, piteously; **10** dreadfully, grievously, lamentably, shockingly; **11** frightfully

horrid: 5 awful; **7** hideous; **8** horrible, horrific; **9** monstrous; **10** horrifying, outrageous

horrific: 4 dire; **5** awful, dread; **6** horrid; **7** direful, dreaded, fearful, hideous; **8** dreadful, fearsome, horrible, terrible; **10** horrendous, horrifying, outrageous; **11** frightening

horrified: 5 cut up; **9** chagrined, petrified, terrified

horrify: 4 gnaw; **5** alarm, appal; **6** appall, dismay, rankle; **7** corrode

horror: 5 dread, panic; **6** terror; **9** repulsion, revulsion; **10** repugnance

hors d'oeuvre: 9 appetizer; **12** hors d'oeuvres

hors de combat: 5 all in, broke; **6** broken, busted; **8** disabled; **11** out of action

horse: 1 H [slang]; **3** dog; **4** colt, mare;

5 drake, filly, smack; **6** heroin; **7** cavalry, sawbuck; **8** sawhorse, stallion

horse around: 4 fool; **10** fool around

horseback rider: 8 horseman; **10** equestrian

horseback riding: 6 riding; **10** equitation

horse balm: 8 richweed; **9** horseweed, stone root, stoneroot

horse barn: 6 stable, stalls

horsebean: 8 fava bean; **9** broad bean; **14** Jerusalem acorn

horse blanket: 10 saddlecoth; **13** saddle blanket

horse chestnut: 6 conker; **7** buckeye

horse doctor: 3 vet; **12** animal doctor, veterinarian

horse-drawn carriage: 3 rig; **7** turn-out; **8** equipage

horse fancier: 8 horseman

horseflesh: 9 horsemeat

horsefly: 4 cleg; **5** clegg; **8** horse fly

horse gentian: 9 feverroot

horselaugh: 4 ha-ha; **6** haw-haw, hee-haw; **10** belly laugh; **11** hearty laugh

horseman: 5 rider; **6** jockey; **8** cavalier; **10** equestrian, roughrider

horsemanship: 6 manege [Fr], riding; **10** equitation

horsemeat: 10 horseflesh

horsemint: 9 lemon mint; **7** monarda

horse opera: 7 Western

horsepower: 2 hp

horse racing: 6 racing; **7** the turf; **8** the track; **9** the horses, the ponies; **12** the racetrack

horse road: 10 bridle path, bridle road; **11** bridle track

horse sense: 5 sense; **8** gumption; **9** good sense, mother wit; **10** plain sense; **11** common sense

horseshoe: 3 bow; **4** loop, shoe; **5** quoit; **6** arcade; **8** crescent, half-moon

horseshoe arch: 11 Moorish arch

horseshoer: 7 farrier

horseshoes: 6 quoits

horse soldier: 10 cavalryman

horsetail family: 12 Equisetaceae

horseweed: 8 fleabane, richweed; **9** horse balm, stone root, stoneroot

horsewhip: 4 cane, comb, flog, lash, lick, whip; **5** birch, strap, towel; **6** larrup, switch, thrash, thresh

horsey: 5 horsy; **6** equine, hippic; **9** horselike

hortative: 8 advisory; **9** hortatory; **11** exhortative, exhortatory

horticulture: 9 gardening; **11** agriculture

horticulturist: 6 farmer; **8** gardener; **10** husbandman

hosanna: 5 grace; **6** praise; **8** doxology, hosannah; **11** benediction; **13** glorification

hose: 4 sock; **5** socks; **6** tights, tubing; **7** hosiery; **8** hose down, hosepipe, stocking; **9** trunk hose

hosiery: 4 hose, sock; **5** socks; **8** stocking; **9** trunk hose

hospitability: 10 cordiality, heartiness; **11** hospitality

hospitable: 6 open to

hospital: 9 infirmary; **13** medical center

hospital attendant: 7 orderly

hospitality: 10 cordiality, heartiness

host: 2 MC; **4** army, wing; **5** corps, emcee, horde, squad, throw; **6** column, legion, server; **7** battery, brigade, company, hostess [female], platoon, section; **8** division, garrison, regiment, squadron; **9** battalion, entertain, innkeeper

hostage: 3 POW; **6** detenu [Fr], inmate, surety; **7** captive; **8** detainee, prisoner

hostel: 3 inn; **5** lodge; **8** hostelry; **11** youth hostel; **14** student lodging

hosteller: 8 hotelier, hotelman; **11** hotelkeeper; **12** hotel manager

hostile: 5 cross; **8** inimical; **9** repugnant; **10** unfriendly; **11** uncongenial; **12** antagonistic, incompatible, unpropitious

hostilities: 3 war; **6** combat; **7** warfare; **8** battling, conflict, fighting; **11** clash of arms

hostility: 6 enmity; **7** ill will; **10** aggression, alienation, antagonism; **12** belligerency, estrangement

hostler: 5 groom; **6** jockey, ostler; **9** stableboy, stableman

hot: 4 live, warm; **5** fiery, hasty, horny, quick, randy, spicy; **6** raging, red-hot, stolen; **7** bilious, flaming, flushed, gingery, glowing, peevish, peppery, rutting, waspish; **8** captious, choleric, feverish, shrewish, snappish; **9** ebullient, fractious, overhasty, purloined, querulous, scorching; **10** blistering, contraband

hot air: 3 gas; **5** bluff; **6** babble, jabber; **7** bombast, palaver; **8** rhetoric, tall talk, vaporing, verbiage; **9** empty talk, mere words; **10** empty words

hot and bothered: 7 rattled; **9** flustered, perturbed

hotbed: 4 nest, womb; **5** nidus; **6** cradle; **7** nursery; **8** hothouse; **10** birthplace

hot-blooded: 5 lusty; **9** hotheaded; **10** libidinous, passionate

hotcake: 7 pancake; **8** flapcake, flapjack; **10** battercake; **11** flannelcake, griddlecake

hot chocolate: 5 cocoa; **9** chocolate

hotchpotch: 6 ragbag; **7** farrago, melange; **8** oddments; **10** hodgepodge; **11** odds and ends

hot dog: 5 frank; **6** weenie, wiener; **7** showoff; **11** frankfurter, wienerwurst

hotdog: 5 strut; **6** red hot; **7** show off; **8** flourish

hotdogging: 7 heroics; **9** strutting; **10** showing off

H

hotei-chiku: 10 gosan-chiku; 14 fishpole bamboo

hotel clerk: 9 desk clerk; 14 hotel desk clerk

hotel detective: 9 house dick; 14 house detective

hotelkeeper: 8 hotelier, hotelman; 9 hosteller, innkeeper; 12 hotel manager

hotfoot: 3 hie; 4 race, rush; 5 speed; 6 hasten; 9 belt along, pelt along, rush along

hot goods: 4 loot, swag; 5 booty; 8 pickings; 10 stolen item; 11 stolen goods

hothead: 6 madcap; 7 lunatic; 9 daredevil, fire-eater; 11 harum-scarum; 12 swashbuckler

hotheaded: 5 short; 6 madcap; 7 furious; 8 brainish, choleric, headlong, tearaway; 9 impetuous, impulsive, irascible; 10 boisterous, hot-blooded; 11 hot-tempered

hot-headed: 7 burning; 8 volatile, volcanic; 9 simmering

hothouse: 6 hotbed; 10 greenhouse; 12 conservatory, indoor garden

hotly: 8 heatedly

hot pad: 10 heating pad

hot pants: 7 hotness, aroused; 9 horniness

hot pepper: capsicum

hot rod: 5 racer; 8 stock car; 9 racing car; 11 souped-up car

hot seat: 5 chair; 10 death chair; 13 electric chair

hotshot: 3 ace, wiz; 4 star, whiz; 5 adept, maven, whizz; 6 genius, wizard; 8 virtuoso; 9 sensation

hot spell: 8 heat wave; 10 hot weather

hot spring: 6 geyser; 13 thermal spring

hot toddy: 4 grog; 5 toddy

hot water heat: 7 gas heat; 8 heat pump; 9 steam heat; 12 electric heat, forced hot air; 14 central heating

hot-water heater: 11 water heater

hot weather: 8 heat wave, hot spell

Houdini: 12 Harry Houdini

hound: 3 bug, cad, cur, dog; 4 bait, bore, heel, hunt; 5 abuse, beset, egg on, grind, harry, haunt, stalk, tease, trace, worry; 6 badger, bother, harass, heckle, ill-use, infest, molest, pester, plague, pother, shadow; 7 bounder, hurry on, oppress

hound's-tongue: 6 borage

hour: 2 hr; 9 time of day

hour angle: 2 HA

hourglass: 4 neck; 9 sandglass

hour hand: 10 little hand

houri: 5 nymph

hourly: 6 always, annual; 9 by the hour, every hour

house: 4 firm, home, line, sign, stem, tree; 5 breed, put up, stock, trunk; 6 family, menage, nestle, stirps, strain; 7 chamber, lineage, mansion, theater, theatre; 8

ensconce, pedigree; 9 household; 12 business firm

house agent: 7 realtor; 9 land agent; 11 estate agent; 15 real estate agent

housebound: 6 shut-in; 9 homebound

housebreaker: 5 thief; 7 burglar; 10 cat burglar; 12 housewrecker

housebreaking: 5 theft; 7 break-in

housebroken: 12 house-trained

house cat: 3 cat; 10 Felis catus; 11 domestic cat

housed: 6 lodged; 8 billeted; 9 quartered

house decorator: 8 designer; 9 decorator; 13 room decorator

house detective: 9 house dick; 14 hotel detective

household: 4 home; 5 house; 6 common, family, menage; 7 typical; 8 everyday, frequent, ordinary; 9 well-known; 11 commonplace, well-trodden

household linen: 10 white goods

housekeeping: 9 housework

housemaid: 10 parlor maid; 11 chamber maid, waiting maid

house of cards: 9 cardhouse; 10 cardcastle; 12 house of glass

house of correction: 3 can [slang], pen; 4 brig, gaol, hold, jail, keep, stir [slang]; 5 clink [slang], hulks, pokey [slang]; 6 chokey [slang], cooler [slang], lockup, prison; 7 slammer [slang]; 8 big house [slang], hoosegow; 9 calaboose [slang]; 10 guard house, San Quentin; 11 penal colony, prison house; 12 penitentiary

house of God: 9 holy place; 13 house of prayer; 14 house of worship, place of worship

house of peers: 5 lords; 12 House of Lords

House of Representatives: 5 House [U.S.]; 12 lower chamber

house of worship: 10 house of God; 13 house of prayer; 14 place of worship

house physician: 8 resident

house raising: 11 barn raising

house servant: 8 domestic; 12 domestic help

house top: 4 loft; 5 attic; 6 garret; 10 upper story

house-to-house: 10 door-to-door

house trailer: 7 trailer; 10 mobile home; 13 camper trailer

house-trained: 11 housebroken

housework: 12 housekeeping

housing: 4 case, home; 5 abode; 6 casing; 7 lodging; 8 domicile, dwelling, housings, lodgment, trapping; 9 caparison, lodgement, residence

Housing and Urban Development: 3 HUD

hovel: 3 cot, hut; 4 shed; 5 booth, cabin, croft, hutch, shack, stall; 6 chalet, dugout [U.S.], shanty

hover: 4 loom; 5 brood, float, plane, spire,

surge; **6** boggle, linger; **8** hesitate, levitate, straggle; **9** bulk large, hover over, vacillate; **10** dilly-dally

howbeit: 6 albeit; **8** although

how come: 3 why; **9** wherefore

however: 3 but, how, yet; **5** still; **6** even so, withal; **9** howsoever, per contra [Lat], quand meme [Fr]; **10** all the same; **11** nonetheless; **12** nevertheless

howitzer: 6 mortar, cannon; **10** field piece; **9** artillery

howl: 3 yap, yip; **4** bawl, hoop, roar, wail, yawl, yell, yipe, yowl; **5** brawl, growl, shout, snarl, whoop, wrawl; **6** baying, bellow, halloa, halloo, scream, shriek, shrill, yammer; **7** howling, screech, ululate; **9** ululation

howler: 3 wow; **4** riot; **6** scream; **10** belly laugh; **12** howler monkey, sidesplitter, thigh-slapper

howling: 3 row; **4** fray, howl, to-do; **5** brawl, broil, melee; **6** affray, breeze, crying, fracas, hubbub, pother, racket, rumble, rumpus, squall, uproar; **7** rhubarb [baseball], roaring, ruction, shindig, trouble, yelling; **8** brouhaha, rattling, scramble, shouting, whooping, wondrous; **9** bellowing, fantastic, imbroglio, marvelous, screaming, scrimmage, shrieking, ululation, wonderful

hoy: 5 barge; **7** lighter; **8** flatboat

hp: 10 horsepower

HQ: 12 headquarters

hr: 4 hour; **12** sixty minutes

HS1: 14 herpes simplex 1

HS2: 14 herpes simplex 2

Hsian: 4 Sian, Xian; **6** Singan; **7** Changan

Hsuan Chiao: 6 Taoism

huaraches: 7 sandals

hub: 4 axis, boss, nave; **6** hubble; **8** down town; **10** embossment; **11** civic center

hubble-bubble: 6 hookah, kalian; **8** narghile; **9** water pipe; **9** commotion

hubbub: 3 row; **4** fray, fuss, rout, to-do; **5** brawl, broil, melee; **6** affray, breeze, bustle, fracas, pother, racket, rumble, rumpus, squall, uproar; **7** howling, rhubarb [baseball], ruction, shindig, trouble; **8** brouhaha, scramble; **9** imbroglio

hubby: 7 husband; **10** club shaped, married man

Hub of the Universe: 6 Boston; **8** Beantown; **22** capital of Massachusetts

huck: 9 huckaback

huckster: 4 hawk, tout, vend; **5** pitch; **6** cadger, dicker, haggle, hawker, higgle, monger, peddle, pedlar; **7** camelot [Fr], chaffer, cheapen, peddler

huddle: 4 hash, riot, toss; **5** cower; **6** fumble, hustle, jumble, litter, lumber, muddle, powwow

huddled: 8 crouched, hunkered; **9** crouching; **12** hunkered down

Hudson: 11 Hudson River

hue: 3 dye; **4** cast, glow, tint; **5** color, flush, imbue, shade, tinge; **6** livery; **8** tincture; **10** coloration; **12** chromaticity

huff: 4 fret, gall, miff, puff, snub; **5** beard, chafe, chuff, pique, snort; **6** nettle, ruffle, spleen; **7** umbrage; **8** acerbity, acrimony, asperity, irritate, rankling, soreness; **9** seeing red, virulence; **10** bitterness, discompose

huffing: 5 puffy; **7** puffing; **8** snorting

huffy: 3 mad; **4** sore; **6** touchy; **7** pettish; **8** petulant; **11** thin-skinned

hug: 3 pet; **5** clasp, grasp, gripe; **6** clench, clinch, clutch, pledge; **7** cherish, cling to, embrace, squeeze; **8** accolade; **9** close with; **10** take hold of

huge: 3 big; **4** vast; **5** great, large; **6** mighty; **7** immense; **8** enormous

hugely: 10 enormously; **12** staggeringly, tremendously

hugger-mugger: 6 secret; **7** jumbled; **8** hush-hush; **10** disorderly, mumbo jumbo, on the quiet, topsy-turvy, undercover; **11** clandestine, underground

hugging: 7 kissing, necking, petting; **8** clasping, cuddling, fondling; **9** caressing, embracing, smooching, snuggling

Hugo: 10 Victor Hugo; **15** Victor Marie Hugo

huisache: 6 acacia, cassie; **9** flame tree; **10** mimosa bush; **11** sweet acacia, sweet wattle

huitre: 6 oyster

hula: 8 hula-hula; **15** Hawaiian dancing

hulk: 4 bole, hull, loom; **5** giant, torso, tower, trunk, whale; **11** heavyweight

hulking: 5 gaunt, hulky; **7** lumpish; **8** lubberly, spanking, thumping, unwieldy, whacking, whopping; **9** walloping; **10** thundering

hulks: 10 prison ship

hulky: 5 gaunt; **7** hulking, lumpish; **8** lubberly, spanking, thumping, unwieldy, whacking, whopping; **9** lumbering, walloping; **10** thundering

hull: 4 bole, hulk; **5** torso, trunk

hullabaloo: 3 bat [U.S.], bum [U.S.]; **4** bust, tear; **5** randy; **6** chorus, clamor, outcry, plaint; **7** blowout [U.S.], fish fry [U.S.], hoedown, turmoil, yule log; **8** jamboree, upheaval; **9** agitation, hue and cry; **10** excitement; **12** vociferation

hum: 4 buzz, fake, flow, hiss, purl, sell; **5** shake, shave, thrum, trill; **6** babble, gurgle, humbug, ripple, seethe; **7** breathe, humming; **9** sibilance

human: 3 man; **4** body, homo, soul; **5** being, civic; **6** mortal, person, public, social; **7** someone; **8** creature, national, personal, somebody, such a one; **9** earthling, personage; **10** human being, individual, living soul

human being: 3 man; **4** body, homo, soul; **5** being, human, woman; **6** mortal, person; **9** earthling, personage; **10** individual, living soul

human beings: 3 man; **5** woman, world; **6** humans; **7** mankind; **8** humanity; **9** human race, humankind

human body: 3 bod; **4** form, soma; **5** build, flesh, frame, shape; **6** figure; **7** anatomy; **8** physique; **12** material body, physical body

human-centered: 8 humanist; **10** humanistic; **12** humanitarian

hum and haw: 3 haw; **4** trim; **5** demur, pause; **6** coquet, debate, waffle; **7** balance, shuffle; **8** straddle; **9** fluctuate, hem and haw; **12** be on the fence, remain neuter; **13** remain neutral

humane: 8 humanist; **9** benignant; **10** beneficent, humanistic; **11** utilitarian

human ecology: 10 demography

human event: 3 act; **4** deed; **5** event, touch; **6** stitch; **8** human act, overt act; **11** transaction

human growth hormone: 12 somatotropin

human immunodeficiency virus: 3 HIV

humanist: 6 humane; **10** humanistic; **12** humanitarian; **13** human-centered

humanitarian: 6 humane; **8** do-gooder, humanist, improver; **10** humanistic; **11** utilitarian; **13** human-centered, philanthropic; **14** public-spirited

humanities: 4 arts; **11** liberal arts

humanity: 3 man; **5** flesh, mercy, world; **6** humans; **7** charity, mankind; **8** clemency, kindness, yearning; **9** benignity, human race, humankind, humanness, mortality; **10** generation, goodliness, kindliness, tenderness; **11** forbearance, human beings; **12** graciousness, philanthropy; **13** brotherly love

humanize: 6 polish; **8** civilize, humanise

humankind: 3 man; **5** world; **6** humans; **8** humanity; **9** human race; **11** human beings

human language: 5 lingo; **6** tongue; **8** language

humanness: 7 charity; **8** humanity, kindness; **9** benignity; **10** goodliness, kindliness; **12** graciousness; **13** brotherly love

humanoid: 5 robot; **7** android; **13** mechanical man

human race: 3 man; **5** world, woman; **6** humans; **7** mankind; **8** humanity; **9** human kind, humankind; **11** human beings, human nature; **12** human species

human trait: 5 trait; **9** character, qualities [pl]; **14** character trait

humble: 3 low; **4** base, pure; **5** abase, lowly, shame, small; **6** menial, modest; **7** chagrin, let down, mortify, set down; **8** baseborn, take down; **9** frown down, humiliate, tread down; **11** sober-minded

humblebee: 9 bumblebee

humbled: 3 low; **6** broken; **7** crushed; **9** bowed down; **10** humiliated

humbling: 9 abasement, demeaning; **10** mortifying; **11** humiliating, humiliation

humbly: 6 meanly, meekly

humbug: 3 hum; **4** bosh, cant, tosh; **5** drool, fudge, trash; **7** baloney, boloney, empiric, garbage, inanity, twaddle, twattle; **8** tommyrot; **9** hypocrisy

humdrum: 4 flat, slow; **5** vapid; **6** stupid; **7** insipid, prosaic, routine; **10** monotonous; **11** commonplace, unglamorous; **12** unglamourous

humid: 3 wet; **4** dank; **5** moist; **6** sultry

humidify: 10 moisturize

humidity: 9 humidness

humiliate: 5 abase, crush; **6** humble; **7** chagrin, mortify; **8** disgrace

humiliation: 5 shame; **7** chagrin; **8** humbling, kneeling; **9** abasement; **11** prostration; **12** genuflection; **13** mortification

humility: 7 modesty; **10** humbleness

hummer: 5 smoke; **6** bullet, heater; **7** live man [U.S.], rustler [U.S.]; **8** fastball; **11** hummingbird

hummock: 4 knob, pena [U.S.]; **5** knoll, mound; **6** barrow; **7** hammock, hillock

humongous: 4 vast; **5** jumbo; **7** extreme, immense, monster; **8** enormous, thumping, whopping; **9** monstrous, walloping; **11** elephantine

humor: 3 pet, wit; **4** mood, vein, whim; **5** cheer, fancy, favor, grain; **6** animus, coquet, humour, mettle, soothe, temper, tickle; **7** caprice, flatter, gratify, indulge; **8** attitude; **9** encourage, witticism, wittiness

humoring: 8 pleasing; **9** indulging, pampering; **10** indulgence

humorist: 3 wag, wit; **8** comedian; **9** humourist

humorous: 5 funny; **6** jocose; **7** amusing, jocular; **9** humourous

humour: 3 wit; **4** mood; **5** humor; **6** temper; **9** witticism, wittiness; **12** sense of humor; **13** sense of humour

humpbacked: 6 humped; **9** crookback, hunchback; **11** crookbacked, hunchbacked

humpback whale: 6 baleen; **8** humpback

Humulus: 3 hop; **4** hops; **12** genus Humulus

Hun: Attila

hunch: 4 bump, hump; **5** bunch; **7** feeling; **8** instinct; **9** hunch over, intuition, suspicion; **10** gut feeling; **11** premonition

hunchback: 6 humped; **8** humpback, kyphosis; **9** crookback; **10** humpbacked; **11** crookbacked, hunchbacked

hunched: 7 crooked, stooped; 8 stooping; 11 round-backed

hundred: 1 C; 4 one C; 5 lathe; 6 riding; 7 century, tithing; 8 a hundred, hecatomb; 9 centenary; 10 one hundred

hundred-dollar bill: 5 C-note

hundred-percenter: 5 jingo; 8 jingoist; 9 flag-waver; 10 chauvinist

hundredth: 7 secular; 10 centesimal, one percent; 12 one-hundredth

hundredweight: 3 cwt; 6 cental; 7 centner

Hungarian: 6 Magyar

Hungarian goulash: 6 gulyas; 7 goulash

Hungarian pointer: 5 vizla

Hungary: 12 Magyarorszag

hunger: 4 lust; 5 crave, twist; 6 starve, thirst; 7 stomach; 8 be hungry, keenness; 10 be famished, be ravenous, hungriness; 13 sharp appetite

hungrily: 10 ravenously

hungry: 7 craving; 8 appetite, famished, starving; 10 lack of food

hunk: 3 bit; 4 lump, stud; 6 morsel; 8 particle; 11 handsome man

hunker down: 5 squat; 6 crouch; 7 scrunch; 9 scrunch up

hunkered down: 7 huddled; 8 crouched, hunkered; 9 crouching

hunt: 3 run; 5 dodge, hound, mouse, quest, shoot, trace, track, trail; 6 search, venery; 7 hunting, pursuit; 8 hunt club, hunt down; 9 searching, track down

hunter: 8 huntsman

hunting: 4 hunt; 6 search, venery; 9 searching

hunting crop: 10 riding crop

hunting expedition: 6 safari; 8 campaign

huntsman: 6 hunter

hurdle: 5 crate, vault; 7 barrier; 8 obstacle

hurdy gurdy: 9 hand organ; 10 grind organ; 11 barrel organ, street organ

hurl: 4 cast; 5 lunge, throw; 6 hurtle, thrust; 7 project

hurler: 7 pitcher, twirler

hurling: 8 throwing; 10 projection

hurly burly: 4 stir, to-do; 7 turmoil; 9 commotion; 10 disruption; 11 disturbance

hurrah: 5 cheer

hurricane lantern: 9 storm lamp; 12 storm lantern; 13 hurricane lamp

hurried: 5 fussy, hasty; 6 rushed; 7 fidgety, unquiet; 8 electric, galvanic, restless; 9 impetuous, mercurial

hurriedly: 7 hastily, in a rush, in haste; 8 in a hurry; 9 with haste

hurry: 3 zip; 4 fuss, rush; 5 haste, speed; 6 bustle, flurry, hasten, ruffle; 7 fluster, flutter, rushing, urgency; 8 bundle on, scramble; 9 hastiness

hurt: 3 cut; 4 ache, bite, gnaw, harm, pain, sore; 5 bleed, chafe, gripe, smart, spite,

sting, wound; 6 damage, injure, injury, offend, scathe, suffer, trauma; 7 anguish, bruised, wounded; 8 cause woe, distress, give pain, weakened; 9 bring pain, cause pain, detriment, indignant, suffering; 10 cause grief, create pain, induce pain, inflict woe; 11 cause sorrow, inflict pain, produce pain

hurtful: 7 adverse, baleful, baneful, harmful, hurting, noxious, painful; 9 injurious; 10 pernicious; 11 causing pain, deleterious, detrimental, mischievous

hurting: 4 pain; 6 aching, biting; 7 chafing, gnawing, hurtful, painful; 8 smarting, stinging; 11 causing pain

hurtle: 3 jog; 4 cast, hurl, jolt; 5 fling, lunge; 6 hustle, thrust; 9 encounter

husband: 3 man; 5 baron, hubby; 6 spouse; 7 consort, steward; 8 conserve, overseer; 9 economise, economize; 10 married man

husbandman: 6 farmer; 7 granger; 9 sodbuster; 14 horticulturist

husbandry: 4 care; 7 farming; 11 agriculture; 12 retrenchment; 15 animal husbandry

hush: 3 lay, mum!; 4 calm, cool, damp, lull, soft!, stay, swag, tame, tush!; 5 abate, allay, peace, quell, quiet, sober, still, whist!; 6 becalm, deaden, hush up, pacify, rebate, shut up, smooth, soothe; 7 appease, assuage, compose, quiesce, quieten, silence!, slacken, turn off; 8 calm down, pipe down, suppress; 9 alleviate, quiet down, stillness; 11 lull to sleep, tranquilize

hush-hush: 6 secret; 10 on the quiet, undercover; 11 clandestine, underground

husk: 3 cod, pod; 5 chaff, shuck, stalk, straw; 7 stubble

huskily: 8 hoarsely

huskiness: 9 gruffness, toughness; 10 hoarseness, ruggedness

husking: 6 baring; 9 stripping; 10 denudation, husking-bee [U.S.], uncovering

husking bee: 7 husking; 11 cornhusking

husk tomato: 9 tomatillo

husky: 3 dry; 5 beefy, burly, gruff; 6 hoarse, hollow; 7 buirdly, raucous; 8 croaking; 9 Eskimo dog, strapping; 10 sepulchral

hussy: 3 rig; 4 drab, jade, minx, skit; 5 wench; 7 baggage, demirep, trollop; 8 strumpet; 10 adulteress

hustings: 5 stump; 7 tribune

hustle: 3 ado, con, jog; 4 fuss, jolt, riot, roll, stir, toss, whip; 5 bunco, bunko, pluck, sting; 6 be busy, buffet, bustle, corner, flurry, fumble, huddle, hurtle, joggle, jostle, jounce, muddle, wallop; 7 con game; 8 be active, be lively, flimflam; 9 bunco game

hustler: 4 doer; 6 hooker; 8 activist,

operator; **11** man of action; **12** streetwalker; **13** wheeler dealer

hut: 3 cot; **4** shed; **5** booth, cabin, croft,
hovel, hutch, shack, stall; **6** chalet, dugout
[U.S.], shanty

hutch: 3 hut, sty; **4** byre, coop, cote; **5** hovel,
shack; **6** kennel, shanty

hutzpa: 8 audacity, chutzpah; **13** audaciousness

Huxley: 12 Thomas Huxley; **17** Thomas
Henry Huxley

Hwang Ho: 12 Hwang Ho River

hyacinth: 6 jargon, zircon; **7** jacinth; **8**
amethyst; **9** carbuncle

Hyacinthaceae: 19 family Hyacinthaceae

hyaena: 5 hyena

Hyaenidae: 5 hyena; **6** hyaena; **15** family
Hyaenidae

hyaline: 6 glassy, hyalin; **8** vitreous; **11** crystalline

Hyalophora cecropia: 8 cecropia; **12**
cecropia moth

hybrid: 5 cross; **6** zygote; **7** crossed, mongrel; **8** chow-chow; **9** composite, interbred,
loanblend; **10** crossbreed, merozygote; **11**
half-and-half; **12** intercrossed; **13** heterogeneous

Hydra: 5 snake; **11** snake-headed

hydrangea family: 13 Hydrangeaceae

hydrant: 3 tap; **6** spigot; **8** water tap; **11**
water faucet

hydrargyrum: 7 mercury; **11** quicksilver

Hydrastis: 10 golden seal, goldenseal, yellow root; **12** turmeric root; **14** genus
Hydrastis

hydrated: 7 hydrous; **13** reconstituted

hydrated lime: 4 lime; **10** slaked lime; **11**
caustic lime, lime hydrate; **14** calcium
hydrate

hydrated oxide: 9 hydroxide

hydraulic brake cylinder: 13 brake cylinder; **14** master cylinder

hydraulic power: 10 fluid drive

hydraulics: 14 fluid mechanics

hydrazoic acid: 2 HN; **8** azoimide

Hydrocharidaceae: 13 frogbit family; **14**
frog's-bit family

Hydrocharis: 7 frogbit; **8** frog's-bit

hydrochloric acid: 12 muriatic acid

hydrocortisone: 8 cortisol

hydrocyanic acid: 7 cyanide; **11** prussic
acid

hydrodynamics: 9 hydrology; **12** hydrostatics; **13** hydrokinetics

hydroelectric power: 10 water power

hydrofoil: 10 hydroplane

hydrogen: 1 H

hydrogen-3: 7 tritium

hydrogen bomb: 5 H-bomb; **10** fusion
bomb; **17** thermonuclear bomb

hydrogen carbonate: 11 bicarbonate

hydrogen peroxide: 8 peroxide

hydrography: 13 marine science

hydroid: 9 hydrozoan

hydrokinetics: 13 hydrodynamics

hydrolith: 4 calcium hydride

hydrology: 12 hydrostatics; **13** hydrodynamics

hydrolyze: 9 hydrolize, hydrolise, hydrolyse

Hydromantes: 10 salamander; **16** genus
Hydromantes

hydrometer: 10 gravimeter

hydrophobia: 6 rabies; **13** canine madness

hydrophobic: 10 aquaphobic

hydrophytic plant: 10 hydrophyte, water
plant; **12** aquatic plant

hydroplane: 8 seaplane; **9** hydrofoil

hydroponic: 12 aquacultural, aquicultural

hydroponic farming: 11 aquaculture, aqui-
culture, hydroponics

hydrostatics: 9 hydrology; **13** hydrodynamics

hydrotherapy: 10 hydropathy

hydrous: 8 hydrated

hydroxybenzene: 6 phenol; **10** oxybenzene;
12 carbolic acid, phenylic acid

hydroxyzine hydrochloride: 6 Atarax

hydrozoan: 7 hydroid

hyena: 6 hyaena

hygiene: 9 hygienics, **10** hygienical

hygienize: 8 sanitize

Hylobates lar: 6 gibbon

Hylocichla: 5 veery; **6** thrush; **15** genus
Hylocichla

hymen: 10 maidenhead

hymeneal: 6 bridal; **7** nuptial, spousal

hymn: 5 chant, motet; **6** anthem, chaunt; **8**
response; **9** plain song

hymnal: 7 hymnary; **8** hymnbook

hymnody: 8 psalmody

hyoscine: 11 scopolamine

Hyoscyamus: 7 henbane; **15** genus
Hyoscyamus

hype: 3 cry; **4** plug; **6** hoopla; **8** ballyhoo

hyped up: 8 agitated; **10** distracted, distraught

hyperactive: 10 overactive

hyperbole: 6 strain; **7** stretch; **8** coloring; **10**
stretching; **12** exaggeration

hyperbolic: 8 inflated; **9** amplified, magnified; **10** overstated; **11** exaggerated, overwrought

hyperbolize: 6 pile up; **7** amplify, magnify; **8**
overdraw, pile it on; **9** aggravate, overstate;
10 exaggerate

hypercapnia: 11 hypercarbia

hypercritical: 7 carping, exigent; **8** captious,
critical, exacting; **9** difficult; **10** censorious,
malcontent; **12** malcontented, overcritical

hypercriticism: 6 nicety; **9** epicurism, exactness

hyperemia: 10 hyperaemia

Hypericum: 11 St. John's wort; **12** St. Peter's wort; **14** genus Hypericum

hypermetropia: 9 hyperopia; **12** hypermetropy; **14** farsightedness; **15** longsightedness

hypermetropic: 9 hyperopic

Hyperoodon ampullatus: 10 bottlenose; **15** bottlenose whale

hyperopia: 12 hypermetropy; **13** hypermetropia; **14** farsightedness; **15** longsightedness

hypersensitive: 8 allergic; **10** sensitized; **14** supersensitive

hypersphere: 13 curved surface

hypertension: 17 high blood pressure

hypertext markup language: 4 HTML

hypertext transfer protocol: 4 HTTP

hyperthermia: 9 high fever; **11** hyperthermy

hypertrophied: 3 fat; **5** tumid; **6** turgid; **7** bloated; **8** enlarged; **9** dropsical, overgrown; **11** exaggerated

hype up: 7 psych up

hyphen: 4 dash; **6** copula; **9** hyphenate, minus sign

hyphenation: 12 word division

hypnotic: 8 mesmeric, relaxant; **9** soporific; **11** mesmerizing; **12** spellbinding

hypnotic state: 8 hypnosis; **14** hypnotic trance

hypnotism: 9 mesmerism; **10** suggestion

hypnotist: 9 mesmerist; **10** hypnotizer

hypnotize: 9 mesmerize

hypnotized: 4 rapt; **7** riveted; **8** absorbed; **9** wrapped in; **10** fascinated, hypnotised, mesmerised, mesmerized, spellbound, transfixed

hypo: 9 injection; **10** hypodermic; **17** hypodermic syringe; **18** sodium thiosulphate

hypoactive: 11 underactive

hypoblast: 8 endoderm, entoderm; **9** endoblast, entoblast

hypochondria: 15 hypochondriasis

hypochondriacal: 9 woebegone; **13** hypochondriac

hypochondriasis: 6 spleen, vapors; **7** horrors, megrims; **9** pessimism; **12** hypochondria

hypocrisy: 4 cant; **6** humbug; **10** lip service; **11** insincerity

hypocrite: 5 phony; **6** phoney; **10** dissembler

hypodermic needle: 6 needle; **7** syringe; **10** hypodermic; **17** hypodermic syringe

hypodermic syringe: 4 hypo; **6** needle; **7** syringe; **10** hypodermic; **16** hypodermic needle

hypophyseal: 11 hypophysial

hypophysis: 9 pituitary; **13** pituitary body; **14** pituitary gland

hypostasis: 9 epistasis, substance; **11** materiality; **14** substantiality

hypotension: 16 low blood pressure

hypothecate: 4 pawn; **5** spout; **7** suppose; **8** mortgage, theorise, theorize; **9** speculate; **10** conjecture; **11** hypothesize

hypothesis: 5 guess; **6** theory, thesis; **7** surmise, theorem; **9** postulate; **10** conjecture, postulatum [Lat]; **11** possibility, postulation, speculation, supposition; **14** presupposition

hypothesize: 7 suppose; **8** theorise, theorize; **9** speculate; **10** conjecture; **11** hypothecate

hypothesized: 8 academic, putative; **9** theorized; **10** gratuitous, supposable; **11** conjectural, presumptive, speculative, theoretical; **12** hypothetical

hyrax: 3 das; **4** cony; **5** coney; **6** dassie

hyssop: 19 Hyssopus officinalis

Hyssopus: 6 hyssop; **13** genus Hyssopus

hysteria: 4 fury; **5** craze; **6** frenzy; **8** delirium

hysterical: 3 mad; **5** rabid; **6** fitful, raving; **7** febrile, frantic, telling; **8** feverish, hysteric; **9** fanatical; **10** demoniacal, distracted, distraught; **11** in hysterics, sensational

hysterics: 6 frenzy; **7** bluster, passion

Hz: 3 cps; **5** cycle, hertz; **12** cycles/second; **14** cycle per second; **15** cycles per second

I

I: 2 me [dative]; **3** ace, one; **5** iodin, unity; **6** iodine, myself [reflexive], single

i.e.: 2 e.g. [abbr]; **3** viz. [abbr]; **5** id est; **6** namely, that is

I.O.U.: 14 promissory note

i.v.: 11 intravenous

I/O: 11 input-output

iamb: 6 iambus

ib.: 4 ibid.; **6** ibidem

Iberian Peninsula: 6 Iberia

Iberis: 11 genus Iberis

ibex: 9 Capra ibex

ibid.: 2 ib.; **6** ibidem

Ibis ibis: 8 wood ibis; **9** wood stork

IBM PC-compatible: 3 IBM; **10** compatible; **13** IBM compatible

IBRD: 9 World Bank
Ibsen: 11 Henrik Ibsen
ibuprofen: 5 Advil; **6** Motrin, Nuprin
icaco: 8 coco plum; **9** cocoa plum; **12** coco plum tree; **18** Chrysobalanus icaco
ICBM: 7 missile
ice: 5 frost, icing; **6** frappe; **7** ice rink; **8** frosting, water ice; **11** frozen water
ice age: 12 glacial epoch; **13** glacial period
ice ax: 6 ice axe
ice bag: 7 ice pack
ice bear: 9 polar bear
ice berg: 4 berg; **7** ice floe; **8** floe berg
iceboat: 8 ice canoe, ice yacht; **10** ice-breaker
icebox: 12 refrigerator
icebox cake: 12 ice-cream cake
icebreaker: 7 iceboat
ice chest: 6 cooler, icebag; **7** icepail
ice-cold: 4 iced; **7** chilled
ice-cream cake: 10 icebox cake
ice-cream float: 5 float; **12** ice-cream soda
ice-cream soda: 5 float; **13** ice-cream float
ice crystal: 7 poudrin; **8** snow mist; **9** frost mist, frost snow, ice needle; **11** diamond dust
ice cube maker: 8 ice maker; **10** ice machine
iced: 7 chilled, ice-cold
ice floe: 4 floe; **7** ice berg; **8** ice field
Iceland moss: 13 Iceland lichen
Iceland poppy: 11 arctic poppy
ice maker: 10 ice machine; **12** ice cube maker
ice pack: 6 ice bag
ice rink: 3 ice; **4** rink; **11** skating rink
ice river: 5 nevee; **7** glacier
ice skater: 6 skater; **12** figure skater
ichor: 3 pus; **6** sanies; **9** festering, purulence; **11** suppuration
ichthyolatry: 11 fish-worship
iciness: 5 chill; **8** gelidity; **10** chilliness, frostiness
icing: 3 ice; **5** frost; **8** frosting; **12** icing the puck
icky: 5 gooey, lousy; **6** crappy, rotten, stinky; **8** stinking
icon: 4 ikon; **5** image; **7** picture
iconoclast: 12 image breaker
iconoclastic: 8 recusant; **10** schismatic
iconography: 7 imagery; **9** picturing; **11** portraiture
ICSH: 2 LH; **8** lutropin
Ictalurus: 10 channel cat; **14** channel catfish; **14** genus Ictalurus
icterus: 8 jaundice
Icterus: 6 oriole
icy: 5 gelid, polar; **6** arctic, boreal, frigid, frosty, frozen, wintry; **7** glacial; **8** freezing

ID: 14 identification
idea: 4 look, mind; **5** theme; **6** notion; **7** concept, thought; **8** estimate; **10** conception, estimation; **12** melodic theme, musical theme; **13** approximation
ideal: 4 mock, type; **5** limit, model, saint; **6** unreal; **7** example, nonsuch, paragon, pattern; **8** exemplar, nonesuch, original, paradigm, standard; **9** nonpareil, precedent, prototype, reference, scantling; **10** apotheosis, idealistic
idealism: 8 ideality; **14** high-mindedness; **15** noble-mindedness
idealist: 7 dreamer; **8** romancer, romantic; **9** visionary; **11** romanticist
idealistic: 5 ideal, lofty; **7** exalted; **8** rarefied, rarified; **9** high-flown; **10** high-minded; **11** noble-minded
idealization: 12 idealisation; **13** glorification
idealize: 7 realize; **8** idealise
ideate: 7 imagine; **8** conceive, envisage; **10** conceive of; **13** conceptualise, conceptualize
idee fixe: 9 fixed idea
identical: 3 one; **4** same, very; **8** selfsame; **9** duplicate, monovular; **12** superposable; **13** one and the same
identical twin: 4 mate, pair, twin; **6** double; **11** counterpart; **14** monozygous twin
identification: 5 match; **7** match-up; **11** designation, recognition; **14** categorization, classification
identified: 6 placed; **7** made out; **10** classified, recognized; **11** categorized; **13** distinguished
identify: 3 key; **4** name; **5** match, place; **6** key out; **7** make out, match up, realize; **8** classify, describe, discover, parallel; **9** recognize; **10** categorize; **11** distinguish
identifying: 8 matching; **11** distinctive, recognizing; **14** distinguishing
identity: 3 ego; **4** self; **6** nature; **7** essence, oneness; **8** noumenon, quiddity, sameness; **9** character; **12** inmost nature, inner reality, quintessence, selfsameness; **13** identicalness, individuality
identity matrix: 10 unit matrix
ideogram: 8 logogram; **9** ideograph; **10** pictograph
ideograph: 8 ideogram; **10** pictograph
ideological: 9 ideologic
ideologue: 9 dogmatist; **10** dogmatizer, ideologist, opinionist; **11** doctrinaire
ideology: 15 political theory
id est: 2 i.e. [abbr]
idiocy: 6 stupid; **7** foolish, amentia
idiom: 6 accent, phrase; **7** dialect; **8** parlance; **9** set phrase; **10** expression; **12** phrasal idiom, turn of phrase; **13** artistic style
idiomatic: 7 typical; **11** idiomatical, idiotypical
idiomatic expression: 5 idiom; **6** phrase;

9 set phrase; 12 phrasal idiom; 15 non-standard word

idiosyncrasy: 6 foible, oddity; 9 mannerism; 11 originality, peculiarity; 13 individuality

idiosyncratic: 8 peculiar

idiot: 5 moron; 7 half-wit; 8 imbecile

idiot box: 2 TV; 5 telly, TV set; 8 boob tube; 9 goggle box; 10 television; 13 television set

idiotic: 5 inept, silly; 6 absurd; 7 blatant, fatuous, foolish, moronic; 8 babbling, imbecile; 9 driveling, imbecilic, insensate, senseless; 10 irrational, ridiculous; 11 non-sensical

idle: 4 dead, laze; 5 inert, light, loose; 6 flimsy, frothy, slight, unused; 7 jobless, slender; 8 baseless, inactive, stagnate; 9 out of work, run at idle, unfounded; 10 groundless; 11 unwarranted

idleness: 6 idling; 7 loafing; 9 faineance; 10 remissness

idler: 3 bum; 5 drone; 6 dawdle, loafer; 8 layabout; 9 do-nothing

idler pulley: 9 idle wheel; 10 idle pulley

idling: 7 loafing; 8 idleness

idly: 6 lazily

idocrase: 8 vesuvian; 11 vesuvianite

idol: 3 god; 4 duck; 5 angel, jewel; 6 cosset, fetich; 7 darling, goddess, paragon; 8 ladylove, megastar; 9 beau ideal, inamorata, superstar; 10 enfant gate [Fr], perfection; 11 graven image

idolatry: 5 flame; 7 passion, rapture; 8 devotion, yearning; 9 adoration, idolizing; 10 veneration; 11 idol worship, idolization

idolize: 5 adore; 6 revere; 7 worship; 11 hero-worship

idolizer: 8 disciple; 9 worshiper

idol worship: 8 idolatry

idol worshiper: 8 idolater

idyl: 5 lyric; 7 eclogue

idyll: 7 bucolic, eclogue; 8 pastoral; 9 pastorale

idyllic: 8 pastoral

i.e.: 5 id est; 6 that is

if: 6 in case; 8 provided; 13 conditionally

iffy: 5 fluky; 6 chancy, flukey

Ig: 14 immunoglobulin

igloo: 8 ice house; 9 snow house

igneous: 5 fiery; 8 plutonic, volcanic; 9 pyrogenic

ignitable: 8 burnable; 9 flammable, ignitible; 11 inflammable

ignite: 4 fire, heat; 5 erupt, light; 6 fire up, kindle, stir up; 7 inflame; 8 enkindle, take fire; 9 catch fire, set fire to, set on fire

ignited: 7 kindled; 9 enkindled

ignitible: 8 burnable; 9 flammable, ignitable; 11 inflammable

ignition: 6 firing; 8 kindling, lighting; 14 ignition system

ignoble: 3 low; 4 base, mean, vile; 5 dirty; 6

abject, shabby; 7 pitiful, scrubby; 8 beggarly, ungentle, untitled; 11 ignominious

ignominy: 5 odium, shame; 7 obloquy; 8 disgrace; 10 opprobrium

ignoramus: 4 dope; 5 dunce; 11 know nothing; 16 uneducated person

ignorance: 9 nescience; 13 unfamiliarity

ignorant: 7 unaware; 8 innocent, nescient, unversed; 9 unknowing, unlearned, unwitting; 10 illiterate, uninformed, unlettered; 13 inexperienced, unenlightened

ignorantly: 10 unknowingly; 11 benightedly

ignore: 3 cut; 4 fail, omit, snub; 5 elude, evade, quash; 6 slight; 7 dismiss, neglect, nullify; 8 brush off, discount, set aside; 9 be blind to, disregard, hold aloof, push aside, repudiate; 10 brush aside; 12 cold-shoulder, refuse to hear

ignored: 8 unheeded; 9 neglected

iguana: 12 common iguana, Iguana iguana

Iguanidae: 7 Iguania

ii: 3 two; 5 deuce

iii: 4 trey, trio; 5 leash, three, triad, trine; 6 tercet, tierce, troika; 7 ternary, ternion, trinity, triplet; 8 deuce-ace, terzetto; 9 threesome

Ike: 10 Eisenhower; 16 Dwight Eisenhower; 18 Dwight D. Eisenhower; 21 Dwight David Eisenhower

ikon: 4 icon; 5 image; 7 picture

Il Duce: 9 Mussolini; 15 Benito Mussolini

Iles Comores: 13 Comoro Islands

Iles Marquises: 16 Marquesas Islands

Iliamna: 9 hollyhock; 12 genus Iliamna

Ilium: 4 Troy; 5 Ilion

ill: 3 bad; 4 amis [Fr], evil, sick; 5 badly, ill of, wrong; 6 ailing, poorly, unwell; 7 ailment, ominous, trouble; 8 bad thing, diseased, distress, negative; 9 complaint, unhealthy

ill-advised: 4 dumb; 5 silly; 6 stupid, unwise; 7 asinine, foolish; 8 improper; 9 ill-judged, unadvised; 10 ill-devised, misadvised; 11 ill-imagined, injudicious; 12 ill-contrived, unreasonable; 13 without reason

illation: 9 deduction, inference; 10 conclusion

illative: 11 inferential

ill-behaved: 8 impolite; 10 unmannered, unmannerly; 11 ill-mannered; 12 discourteous

ill-bred: 4 rude; 7 lowbred; 8 yokelish; 9 underbred; 10 bounderish; 14 ill-conditioned

ill-conceived: 9 misguided

illegal: 7 illicit; 8 unlawful; 12 illegitimate

illegal act: 5 crime; 6 felony; 11 breach of law; 13 illegal action; 14 violation of law

illegalize: 6 outlaw; 11 criminalize

illegally: 9 illicitly, lawlessly; 10 unlawfully

illegal money: 8 hot money
illegible: 10 unreadable
illegitimacy: 8 bastardy; **9** falseness; **11** bar sinister; **12** spuriousness
illegitimate: 5 false; **6** by-blow, outlaw; **7** bastard, illegal, illicit; **8** outlawed, spurious, unlawful; **9** love child; **10** contraband; **11** adulterated; **13** surreptitious
illegitimate child: 6 by-blow; **7** bastard; **9** love child; **12** illegitimate
illegitimate enterprise: 6 racket
ill fame: 9 notoriety
ill-famed: 8 infamous; **9** notorious
ill-fated: 6 doomed; **7** unlucky; **9** ill-omened; **10** ill-starred
ill-gotten: 5 dirty
ill health: 7 illness; **8** sickness; **10** poor health, sickliness; **12** lack of health, loss of health; **13** health problem, unhealthiness
ill humor: 7 bad mood; **8** bad humor; **9** ill humour, moodiness; **11** temperament
illiberal: 4 mean; **6** entete [Fr], stingy; **7** bigoted; **8** besotted, churlish, confined, dogmatic, positive; **9** conceited, fanatical; **10** infatuated, intolerant, ungenerous; **12** narrow-minded
illicit: 6 outlaw; **7** illegal; **8** outlawed, unlawful; **12** illegitimate
illicit sex: 8 adultery
Illicium: 5 anise; **9** star anise; **12** Chinese anise; **13** genus Illicium
illiterate: 4 rude; **5** empty, green; **6** unread; **7** shallow; **8** ignorant; **11** half-learned, superficial; **12** analphabetic
ill-mannered: 4 rude; **8** impolite; **10** ill-behaved, unmannered, unmannerly; **12** discourteous
illness: 6 malady; **7** ailment, disease; **8** disorder, sickness; **9** complaint, ill health
illogical: 5 false; **7** garbled, invalid, unsound; **8** confused; **9** scattered, unlogical; **10** disjointed, disordered; **11** unconnected; **12** disconnected, unreasonable
ill repute: 7 bad name; **9** bad repute, discredit, disrepute
ill-spent: 6 futile; **10** unavailing; **11** ineffective, ineffectual, uncalled for; **13** inefficacious
ill-starred: 6 doomed; **7** unlucky; **8** ill-fated; **9** ill-omened
ill-tempered: 5 cross, fiery, fussy, moody, surly, testy; **6** crabby, grumpy, tetchy, touchy; **7** crabbed, grouchy; **8** volatile; **9** irascible, irritable; **10** ill-humored, in a bad mood
ill timed: 5 wrong; **8** untimely; **12** unseasonable
ill-treated: 6 abused; **10** maltreated, mistreated

ill-treatment: 5 abuse; **8** ill-usage; **11** molestation; **12** maltreatment
illume: 5 light; **7** light up, lighten; **8** illumine; **9** enlighten, shine upon; **10** illuminate
illuminance: 10 brightness; **12** illumination
illuminate: 3 dye; **4** tint, wash; **5** clear, grain, imbue, light, paint, stain, tinge; **6** illume; **7** bedizen, clarify, clear up, ingrain, light up, lighten, sort out; **8** emblazon, illumine; **9** elucidate, enlighten, shine upon; **11** cast light in, crystallize, shed light on
illuminated: 3 lit; **7** lighted; **11** well-lighted
illuminati: 8 literati; **10** dilettanti; **11** cogniscenti [It], litterateur [Fr]
illuminating: 12 enlightening
illuminator: 11 light source
illumine: illuminate
ill-usage: 5 abuse; **12** ill-treatment, maltreatment
ill-use: 3 bug; **4** bait, bore; **5** abuse, beset, grind, harry, haunt, hound, tease, worry; **6** badger, bother, harass, heckle, infest, molest, pester, plague, pother; **7** oppress; **8** bullirag, bullyrag, ill-treat, maltreat, mistreat; **9** importune, persecute
illusion: 5 fancy, magic, trick; **7** fantasy; **8** delusion, head game, phantasy; **9** deception, semblance; **10** magic trick
illusionary: 10 illusional
illusionist: 4 seer; **8** conjurer, conjuror, magician; **9** visionary; **13** stage magician; **15** prestidigitator
illusory: 6 unreal; **8** gossamer, illusive; **9** gossamery; **13** insubstantial
illustrate: 4 cite, show; **5** quote; **6** expose; **7** present; **8** instance, put a case; **9** exemplify, symbolize; **11** demonstrate; **14** quote authority, quote precedent
illustration: 7 example, showing; **8** instance; **9** visual aid; **10** exposition, presenting; **11** delineation, manifesting, visualizing
illustrative: 7 in point; **12** exemplifying; **13** demonstrative
illustrious: 5 famed, noted; **6** famous; **7** notable, radiant; **8** far-famed, glorious, renowned, splendid; **9** brilliant, respected; **10** celebrated; **11** redoubtable
ill will: 6 enmity, malice; **7** cruelty; **8** bad blood, ill blood; **9** cruelness, hostility, ill nature, malignity; **11** malevolence; **13** maliciousness
ill wind: 5 cloud; **8** evil star; **9** dark cloud; **15** gathering clouds
image: 3 see; **4** icon, ikon, view; **5** fancy, scene, sight, trope; **6** double, effigy, figure; **7** epitome, imagery, persona, picture, project; **8** envision, paradigm; **9** prototype, visualize; **10** appearance, impression, perception, simulacrum, what is seen; **11** field of view, mental image, public image, what one sees; **12** apprehension; **13** visualization

imagery: **5** image; **7** imaging; **9** picturing; **11**
iconography, imagination, portraiture; **13**
mental imagery

imaginable: **8** possible; **11** conceivable

imaginary: **7** complex; **8** fabulous, fanciful,
imagined, notional; **9** fantastic, fictional,
visionary

imaginary number: **13** complex number; **15**
complex quantity

imagination: **6** vision; **7** imagery, imaging; **8**
resource; **9** imagining, inventing, invention; **11** inspiration; **13** mental imagery

imaginative: **8** creative; **9** ingenious, inventive

imagine: **5** fancy, guess, think; **6** ideate,
reckon; **7** suppose; **8** conceive, envisage;
10 conceive of

imagined: **6** mooted; **7** assumed, created,
divined, guessed; **8** dreamt of, fanciful,
notional, presumed, supposed, surmised; **9**
conceived, imaginary, suspected; **10** originated, postulated; **11** conjectured, presupposed

imaging: **7** imagery; **10** tomography; **11**
imagination; **13** mental imagery

imagining: **8** creating, dreaming; **9** inventing, invention; **11** imagination, inspiration

imam: **5** imaum

Imavate: **10** imipramine

imbalance: **9** asymmetry, unbalance; **11**
instability

imbecile: **5** idiot, inept, moron, silly; **7** blatant, fatuous, foolish, half-wit, idiotic; **8**
babbling; **9** driveling, imbecilic, insensate,
senseless; **10** changeling, irrational; **11**
nonsensical

imbecilic: **7** idiotic, moronic; **8** imbecile

imbed: **4** base; **5** embed, found, plant; **6** bottom, ground; **7** engraft, implant

imbedded: **6** rooted; **7** mewed up, posited,
situate; **8** encysted; **9** ensconced

imbibe: **4** draw, suck; **5** drink, sop up; **6**
absorb, soak up, suck up, take in, take up;
10 assimilate

imbiber: **5** toper; **7** drinker

imbibing: **6** toping; **7** boozing; **8** drinking,
guzzling, potation, tippling; **10** imbibition

imbricate: **7** lapping, overlap; **11** overlapping

imbricated: **8** ironclad; **9** imbricate; **11**
armor plated

imbroglio: **3** ado, row; **4** fray, mash, mess,
muss [U.S.], to-do; **5** brawl, broil, melee; **6**
affray, breeze, fracas, hubbub, muddle,
pother, racket, rumble, rumpus, squall,
uproar; **7** howling, rhubarb [baseball], ruction, shindig, trouble; **8** brouhaha, scramble; **9** scrimmage; **10** bear garden,
donnybrook

imbrue: **5** stain; **6** drench, infuse; **7** instill; **8**
saturate; **9** inoculate; **10** impregnate, infiltrate

imbue: **3** dye, hue; **4** soak, tint, wash; **5**
grain, paint, stain, tinge; **6** infuse; **7** bedizen, diffuse, implant, ingrain, instill, pervade; **8** emblazon, permeate, saturate; **9**
inoculate; **10** illuminate, impregnate, infiltrate

imidazole: **9** iminazole; **10** glyoxaline

iminazole: **9** imidazole; **10** glyoxaline

imipramine: **7** Imavate

imitate: **3** ape; **4** copy; **5** adopt, apply; **8** simulate; **9** make use of, replicate; **11** appropriate

imitating: **7** copying; **9** imitation; **11** replicating, replication

imitation: **4** copy, fake, faux, form; **5** false; **6**
effigy, ersatz; **7** copying, forgery, replica; **8**
effigies, likeness; **9** facsimile, imitating,
simulated; **10** caricature, substitute; **11**
counterfeit, counterpart, replicating, replication; **13** impersonation

imitative: **6** echoic; **10** derivative, figurative,
unoriginal; **11** counterfeit; **12** onomatopoeic

imitator: **3** ape; **4** aper, echo, mime; **6** monkey, parrot; **7** copycat; **11** mocking bird; **12**
impersonator

immaculate: **4** spic; **5** clear, spick; **8** spotless, unsoiled; **9** faultless, speckless, undefiled, unspotted, unstained, unsullied; **10**
impeccable; **11** spic-and-span; **12** spick-
and-span

immanence: **9** immanency, inherence

immaterial: **10** extraneous; **11** impertinent,
incorporeal, indifferent, non-physical, nonmaterial

immateriality: **10** triviality; **11** nothingness;
12 incorporeity, unimportance

immature: **3** raw; **5** green, young; **6** callow,
unripe, yeasty; **8** unformed; **9** unfledged,
unripened, unsettled

immeasurable: **9** unplumbed; **11** illimitable,
inestimable, innumerable; **12** immensurable, incalculable, incomputable, interminable, unfathomable

immeasurably: **10** infinitely; **11** boundlessly; **13** beyond measure; **15** beyond all
bounds

immediate: **5** quick; **6** abrupt, entire, prompt,
sudden; **7** instant; **9** momentary; **10** contiguous; **11** recipitant, precipitate, precipitous; **12** straightaway; **13** discontinuous,
instantaneous

immediate danger: **13** imminent peril; **14**
immediate peril, imminent danger

immediately: **3** now; **5** apace; **6** at once; **7**
briefly, by and by, quickly, shortly; **8**
directly, in a while, speedily; **9** extempore,
forthwith, instantly, right away, summarily

immediate memory: **3** STM; **15** short-term
memory

I

immedicable: 8 cureless; 9 incurable; 10 remediless; 12 beyond remedy

immemorial: 6 age-old; 9 customary; 11 traditional; 12 prescriptive

immense: 4 huge, vast; 5 roomy; 6 mighty; 7 extreme; 8 enormous, spacious; 9 capacious, humongous

immensely: 6 vastly

immenseness: 8 vastness; 9 grandness, greatness, immensity; 12 enormousness, sizeableness

immensurable: 12 immeasurable, unmeasurable

immerge: 5 merge; 7 immerse; 8 submerge

immerse: 3 dip; 4 bury; 5 eat up, merge, steep; 6 absorb, engulf, plunge; 7 engross, immerge, swallow; 8 submerge, submerse; 9 swallow up

immersed in: 8 buried in

immersion: 3 dip; 6 plunge; 7 dousing, ducking, dunking, soaking; 9 immersing; 10 submerging, submersion; 11 submergence

immigrant: 8 newcomer

immigration: 10 emigration; 11 in-migration

imminence: 9 imminency; 10 impendence, impendency

imminent: 4 soon; 6 at hand; 8 upcoming; 9 impending; 11 approaching, close at hand, over hanging, forthcoming

imminent peril: 14 immediate peril, imminent danger; 15 immediate danger

immingle: 5 blend; 8 intermix; 11 intermingle

immiscible: 9 unmixable

immitigable: 10 headstrong; 12 unappeasable, ungovernable

immix: 3 mix; 4 fuse, meld; 5 blend, merge; 6 commix; 7 combine; 8 coalesce, conflate, intermix; 9 commingle

immobile: 4 fast, firm; 5 fixed; 8 immotile; 9 immovable; 11 irremovable

immobility: 6 fixity; 9 fixedness; 14 stationariness

immobilization: 12 immobilizing; 14 immobilisation

immobilize: 3 pin; 4 trap; 5 block; 6 freeze

immoderate: 8 swinging; 9 excessive; 10 exorbitant, inordinate, outrageous; 11 extravagant

immodest: 9 shameless

immodesty: 9 indecency; 10 indelicacy; 13 exhibitionism

immolate: 9 burn alive, sacrifice

immolation: 8 auto da fe; 9 holocaust, sacrifice

immoral: 3 bad; 4 base, vile; 5 wrong; 6 sinful, wicked; 8 criminal, depraved, perverse; 9 perverted, reprobate, unethical; 10 iniquitous; 11 unrighteous; 12 dishonorable, unprincipled

immorality: 4 evil; 7 scandal; 8 iniquity; 9 indecorum; 10 wickedness; 11 impropriety

immortal: 3 god; 4 hero; 5 deity, great; 7 undying; 8 divinity, great man; 9 deathless; 10 celebrated; 11 great person, never fading, time honored; 12 imperishable; 13 commemorative

immortality: 3 aye; 8 eternity; 10 perpetuity; 12 immortal name

immortalize: 5 deify; 6 record; 8 enthrone, eternize; 9 signalize; 10 eternalize; 11 commemorate, memorialize

immotile: 8 immobile; 9 nonmotile

immovability: 8 obduracy; 9 obstinacy; 10 cussedness [U.S.], mulishness; 12 stubbornness; 13 immovableness, inflexibility, obstinateness

immovable: 5 fixed; 7 stabile; 8 immobile; 9 unmovable; 10 immoveable, unshakable; 11 irremovable

immune: 4 free; 6 exempt; 8 scot-free; 9 at liberty, resistant

immunity: 7 liberty, license, release; 9 exception, exemption, franchise, privilege

immunization: 4 shot; 11 inoculation, vaccination; 12 immunisation

immunize: 9 inoculate, vaccinate; 10 innoculate

immunizing: 12 preventative, prophylactic

immunochemistry: 10 immunology

immunoglobulin: 2 Ig

immunological: 11 immunologic

immunologic response: 14 immune reaction, immune response

immunologist: 10 serologist

immure: 3 jug, lag; 4 gaol, jail; 6 remand; 7 put away; 8 imprison; 11 incarcerate

immurement: 9 captivity; 12 imprisonment; 13 incarceration

immutable: 10 changeless; 11 unalterable; 12 unchangeable

imp: 3 elf, hob; 4 pixy; 5 pixie, scamp; 6 monkey, rascal; 7 brownie, gremlin; 8 scalawag; 9 scallywag

impact: 3 set; 5 crash, shock, touch; 6 affect, bear on, solder; 7 touch on; 8 bear upon; 11 impingement; 12 encroachment

impacted: 6 wedged

impaction: 11 impingement; 13 impacted tooth

impair: 3 mar; 5 spoil; 6 damage, scathe; 7 vitiate; 8 deflower, mutilate

impairment: 4 harm; 6 damage, injury; 8 damaging, handicap; 9 deadening, detriment, impairing, vitiation, worsening; 10 debasement, disability, mutilating, mutilation; 11 disablement; 13 deterioration

impale: 5 spear, spike, stake; 6 empale; 8 enfilade, transfix

impalpable: 10 evanescent, intangible

impanel: 5 panel; 7 empanel
imparity: 9 disparity; 10 unevenness, inequality
impart: 3 add; 4 give, lend; 5 break, bring, leave, let on; 6 bestow, convey, expose, let out, pass on, render, reveal; 7 declare, divulge; 8 bring out, disclose, discover, give away, impart to, 10 contribute; 11 communicate
impartation: 9 imparting; 10 conveyance
impartial: 4 fair, just; 5 right; 6 square; 9 equitable; 10 evenhanded; 12 unprejudiced
impartiality: 6 equity; 7 justice; 8 fair play, fairness; 11 give and take, lex talionis [Lat]; 13 equitableness; 14 even-handedness
imparting: 10 conveyance; 11 impartation
impassable: 10 impervious, unpassable; 12 inextricable
impasse: 7 dead end, 8 cul de sac, deadlock; 9 stalemate; 10 blind alley, standstill
impassibility: 6 apathy; 9 passivity; 13 impassiveness, lack of emotion
impassion: 4 move; 5 smite, touch; 6 affect, excite, infect, strike; 7 animate, impress, inspire; 8 interest
impassioned: 4 wild; 5 fiery, moved; 6 ardent, fervid, fierce, madcap, torrid; 7 burning, excited, fervent, furious, smitten, striken, touched, violent; 8 affected, animated, inspired, vehement; 9 fanatical, impressed, perfervid; 10 interested; 13 demonstrative
impassive: 6 stolid; 7 deadpan; 8 soulless; 9 heartless; 10 poker-faced, spiritless; 11 emotionless, passionless, unemotional; 12 unexpressive
impassiveness: 6 apathy, phlegm; 9 passivity, stolidity; 11 impassivity; 12 indifference; 13 impassibility, lack of emotion
impassivity: 9 stolidity; 12 indifference; 13 impassiveness
impatience: 5 haste; 7 urgency; 11 intolerance; 12 restlessness
impeach: 3 tax; 6 accuse, charge, impute, indict; 8 denounce; 9 criminate; 11 incriminate
impeachment: 6 charge; 8 citation, true bill; 10 accusation, imputation, indictment; 11 presentment
impeccable: 7 perfect; 8 flawless, 9 faultless; 10 immaculate; 12 indefectible
impecuniosity: 4 lack, need, want; 6 penury; 7 poverty; 8 distress; 9 indigence, necessity, neediness, pauperism, privation; 11 destitution; 12 difficulties
impecunious: 6 hard up; 7 pinched; 9 out of cash, penniless, penurious; 10 out of money; 11 short of cash
impedance: 10 resistance; 11 resistivity; 15 ohmic resistance
impede: 3 jam; 5 block; 6 hinder; 7 close up,

inhibit, occlude; 8 obstruct, restrict; 9 embarrass; 10 filibuster [U.S.]
impediment: 8 handicap; 9 deterrent, hindrance, stricture; 11 impedimenta, obstruction, restriction
impeding: 8 blocking, clogging; 9 hindering, hindrance; 10 inhibition, precluding; 11 obstructing, obstruction, obstructive; 12 interference, preventative; 13 impedimentary
impel: 4 goad, push, spur; 5 drive, force, shove; 6 incite, propel; 7 inspire; 9 give a push, stimulate
impend: 5 hover; 6 menace
impending: 6 at hand, coming; 8 imminent, upcoming; 11 close at hand, forthcoming
impenetrable: 5 dense, heavy; 9 nonporous; 11 impermeable; 12 unassailable, unattackable
impenitent: 8 obdurate; 10 uncontrite; 11 unrepentant; 12 unremorseful
imperative: 8 absolute, positive; 9 arbitrary, called for, essential, ex officio, imperious; 10 high-handed, iron-handed, overruling, peremptory; 11 jussive mood; 12 prerequisite; 13 indispensable
imperator: 7 emperor
imperceptible: 7 trivial; 9 invisible; 10 insensible; 13 inappreciable, insignificant, unperceivable
imperceptibly: 8 minutely; 9 invisibly; 10 observably; 12 unnoticeably
imperfect: 3 lax; 4 weak; 5 frail; 6 flawed, infirm; 8 fallible; 10 suboptimal; 11 progressive; 14 imperfect tense
imperfection: 7 frailty; 8 weakness; 13 imperfectness
imperforate: 5 solid; 9 nonporous
imperial: 4 boot, shag; 5 beard, brush, regal, royal; 6 purple; 8 majestic; 13 Imperial beard
imperil: 5 peril; 6 menace; 8 endanger, threaten; 9 put at risk; 10 compromise, jeopardize
imperious: 7 haughty; 8 absolute, arrogant, insolent, positive; 9 arbitrary, masterful; 10 high-handed, imperative, iron-handed, peremptory; 11 dictatorial, magisterial
imperishable: 5 great; 7 abiding, undying; 8 enduring, immortal; 9 deathless; 11 never fading, time honored; 13 incorruptible; 14 indestructible
impermanence: 7 brevity; 8 fugacity [Chem]; 10 transience; 11 evanescence; 12 impermanency
impermanent: 7 passing; 8 temporal; 9 temporary, transient; 10 transitive, transitory
impermeable: 9 nonporous; 10 impervious; 12 impenetrable

impersonal: 7 neutral; 9 objective; 11 unspecified

impersonate: 3 ape; 4 mock, pose; 5 mimic; 6 pose as; 7 portray; 8 simulate; 9 personate, personify

impersonation: 9 imitation, imposture; 10 caricature; 11 personation

impersonator: 8 imitator

impertinence: 4 airs, face, gall; 5 brass, cheek, crust, front; 8 archness, pertness; 9 brashness, freshness, hardihood, impudence, insolence, nerviness, perkiness, sauciness; 10 cheekiness

impertinent: 4 pert, rude; 5 fresh [U.S.], nervy, saucy, smart; 6 brazen; 7 forward; 8 cavalier, flippant, impudent, malapert, overbold; 10 extraneous, immaterial, inapposite, irreverent

imperturbable: 11 unexcitable, unflappable

impervious: 7 callous; 9 hard-nosed; 10 impassable; 11 hardhearted, impermeable, imperviable; 12 inextricable, thick-skinned; 13 impracticable

impetuous: 5 hasty; 6 madcap, rushed; 7 hurried; 8 brainish, tearaway; 9 hotheaded, impulsive; 10 passionate

impetus: 5 drift; 7 impulse; 9 impulsion

impiety: 11 impiousness, irreverence

impinge: 6 trench; 8 encroach, infringe

impingement: 6 impact; 9 impaction; 12 encroachment

impious: 6 unholy; 7 ungodly; 9 undutiful; 11 irreligious

impish: 7 demonic, implike, puckish; 8 prankish; 9 demonical, pixilated; 10 demoniacal; 11 mischievous

implacability: 6 rancor; 14 vindictiveness

implacable: 10 inexorable; 12 stony-hearted

implant: 3 bud; 5 embed, graft, imbed, imbue, plant; 7 engraft; 10 impregnate

implantation: 9 inserting, insertion; 12 introduction

implausible: 10 farfetched

implausibly: 10 improbably, incredibly; 12 unbelievably

implement: 4 tool; 5 apply; 6 device; 7 enforce, utilize; 8 carry out; 9 go through; 10 instrument, put through; 13 follow through

implementation: 9 execution; 11 carrying out; 12 effectuation

implicate: 6 entail; 7 involve; 9 inculpate

implicated: 6 agnate; 8 allied to; 9 concerned; 10 affiliated, associated

implication: 6 import; 9 deduction, intricacy; 10 entailment; 11 connotation, implicating; 12 complication, significance

implicit: 5 tacit; 6 latent; 7 implied; 10 inexplicit, understood; 13 unquestioning

implicit meaning: 11 connotation, implication; 14 implied meaning

implied: 5 tacit; 6 latent, silent; 8 implicit; 10 understood

implike: 6 impish; 7 puckish; 8 prankish; 9 pixilated; 11 mischievous

implode: 5 go off

implore: 3 beg; 4 pray; 5 plead; 6 appeal; 7 beg hard, beseech, entreat; 10 supplicate

imply: 4 mean; 5 argue, infer; 6 convey, entail; 7 bespeak, breathe, connote, involve, point to; 8 allude to, indicate; 9 inculpate; 10 bear a sense; 11 incriminate

impolite: 10 ill-behaved, unmannered, unmannerly; 11 ill-mannered; 12 discourteous

impolitely: 6 rudely; 14 discourteously

impoliteness: 8 rudeness; 10 bad manners, ill manners; 11 brusqueness, discourtesy

impolitic: 9 untactful; 12 undiplomatic

import: 4 boot, mark; 5 admit, force, jam in, let in, run in, spell; 6 edge in, moment, plow in, work in, worm in; 7 bring in, content, foist in, imports, meaning, message, purport, receive, signify, throw in, wedge in; 9 interject, interpose, introduce; 10 be an object, importance, prominence, put between; 11 consequence, implication, intercalate, interpolate, materiality, weightiness; 12 infiltration, materialness, significance

importance: 4 mark; 6 import, moment; 9 grandness; 10 prominence; 11 consequence, materiality, weightiness; 12 materialness, significance; 13 consideration

important: 7 crucial; 8 of import; 11 significant; 12 of importance; 13 authoritative, consequential

importation: 8 infusion; 9 importing

import barrier: 12 trade barrier

import duty: 6 custom; 12 import tariff

importunate: 6 urgent; 8 pleading; 9 appealing, clamorous, imploring

importune: 3 bug, dun, ply, tax; 4 bait, bore, urge; 5 abuse, beset, grind, harry, haunt, hound, press, tease, worry; 6 badger, bother, harass, heckle, ill-use, infest, insist, molest, pester, plague, pother; 7 oppress; 8 bullirag, bullyrag, ill-treat, maltreat, mistreat; 9 clamor for, imprecate, persecute

importunity: 8 entreaty, instance; 10 invocation; 12 supplication; 14 interpellation

impose: 3 awe, tax; 4 levy, task; 5 exact, visit; 6 dazzle; 7 enforce, inflict, overawe

imposed: 9 commanded

imposing: 5 grand, noble; 6 heroic, sacred, solemn; 7 stately, sublime; 8 baronial, majestic; 10 commanding, heaven-born, impressive; 11 distracting, magisterial; 12 transcendent; 13 distinguished

imposition: 5 claim; 6 breach, deceit, demand; 8 exaction; 9 breaching, deception, violating, violation; **10** assumption, infliction, infraction, insistence, usurpation; **11** presumption, reclamation, requisition; **12** encroachment, infringement; **13** transgression

impossibility: **8** no chance; **12** what cannot be

impossible: **9** ungranted; **12** insufferable, unacceptable, unimaginable, unsufferable; **13** inconceivable

impost: **4** duty; **6** custom; **7** customs; **8** springer; **11** customs duty

imposter: **4** fake, sham; **5** faker, fraud, pseud; **6** pseudo; **8** impostor; **9** pretender; **10** role player

imposture: **4** fake, hoax, sham; **5** fraud, spoof; **13** impersonation

impotence: **7** sterile; **9** impotency, inability; **10** disability, incapacity

impotent: **7** sterile; **8** helpless; **9** powerless

impound: **3** pen; **4** cage, coop; **5** hem in, pen in, seize; **6** attach, bolt in, coop up, rail in, wall in; **9** sequester; **10** confiscate

impounding: **8** poundage; **10** internment; **11** impoundment

impoverish: **5** drain, empty, shear, strip; **6** absorb, dilute, finish, fleece, reduce, tap out; **7** deprive, despoil, exhaust; **8** run out of; **9** pauperize, swallow up; **10** render poor

impoverished: **4** poor; **5** needy; **6** broken, slight; **7** sketchy; **8** indigent, wiped out; **9** destitute

impracticable: **5** fussy; **9** crotchety; **10** impervious, infeasible, unfeasible, unworkable; **12** unachievable

impractical: **4** airy; **9** visionary

imprecate: **3** dun, ply, tax; **4** cuss, damn, urge; **5** beset, curse, press, swear; **6** bedamn; **7** beshrew, swear at; **8** maledict; **9** blaspheme, clamor for, importune; **10** anathemize

imprecation: **5** curse; **11** malediction

imprecisely: **9** inexactly

impregnable: **6** secure, strong; **10** inviolable; **12** inexpugnable, proof against, unassailable, unattackable

impregnate: **4** fuse; **5** blend, imbue, merge, unite; **6** absorb, embody, imbrue, infuse; **7** blend in, combine, conjoin, implant, instill, prang up; **8** coalesce, dissolve, generate, saturate, tincture; **9** fertilize, inoculate, procreate; **10** amalgamate, centralize; **11** consolidate, incorporate

impregnated: **10** fertilised, fertilized, inoculated; **11** inseminated

impregnation: **7** seeding; **9** pervasion, suffusion; **10** permeation, saturation; **11** fecundation; **13** fertilization

impresario: **7** showman; **8** producer, promoter

impress: **4** dent, dint, move; **5** print, smite,

stamp, touch; **6** affect, excite, infect, strike; **7** animate, imprint, ingrain, inspire, instill, yarn-dye; **8** interest, shanghai; **9** impassion; **10** impression

impressed: **5** moved; **7** excited, printed, smitten, striken, touched; **8** affected, animated, inspired; **9** imprinted; **10** interested, shanghaied; **11** impassioned

impression: **4** copy, pull; **5** image, print, proof, stamp; **6** belief, effect, notion, revise; **7** feeling, impress, imprint, inkling, picture; **8** printing; **9** engraving, sensation, suspicion; **10** depression, perception, weak belief; **11** inspiration, mental image; **12** apprehension; **13** mental picture

impressionable: **6** pliant; **7** pliable; **11** impressible

impressive: **4** deep, keen; **5** acute, grand, noble, sharp, vivid; **6** lively; **7** nervous, telling; **8** forcible, imposing, incisive, powerful, profound, vigorous; **9** indelible, trenchant; **10** commanding, persuasive; **11** distracting, thin-skinned

impressiveness: **7** unction; **8** piquance, piquancy; **9** grandness; **12** magnificence

imprimatur: **7** warrant; **8** sanction; **8** approval; **11** countenance, endorsement

imprimis: **5** first; **7** at first, firstly

imprint: **4** form; **7** impress; **8** printing; **10** depression, embossment, impression

imprison: **3** jug, lag; **4** gaol, jail; **6** commit, immure, remand, send up; **7** put away; **11** incarcerate

imprisoned: **6** jailed; **7** captive, in limbo; **8** confined, in chains, in charge, in prison; **9** doing time

improbable: **4** tall; **8** unlikely; **9** marvelous; **10** marvellous; **12** just possible, unbelievable, unconvincing

impromptu: **5** ad lib; **7** offhand; **9** ad libitum, impulsive; **11** spontaneous; **13** improvisation, spontaneously

improper: **4** dumb; **5** inapt, silly, unapt, unfit, wrong; **6** stupid, unmeet, unwise; **7** asinine, foolish, lawless; **8** scampish, unlawful, unseemly; **9** ill-judged; **10** disorderly, ill-advised

improperness: **11** impropriety

impropriety: **7** liberty, scandal; **8** solecism; **9** barbarism, indecency, indecorum; **10** immorality, inaptitude; **11** familiarity; **12** improperness

improvable: **10** corrigible

improve: **4** mend; **5** amend; **6** better; **9** meliorate; **10** ameliorate

improvement: **7** advance; **9** bettering; **10** betterment; **11** enhancement

improvident: **6** lavish; **7** profuse; **8** prodigal, wasteful; **9** ill-judged, imprudent, shiftless, unguarded, unthrifty; **10** dissipated, profligate, thriftless; **11** extravagant, overliberal, temerarious, thoughtless; **12** shortsighted; **13** ill-considered

improving: 2 up; **9** bettering; **11** progressive

improvisation: 5 ad-lib; **9** impromptu

improvise: 5 ad lib; **6** wing it; **9** unplanned; **10** improvised, off-the-cuff; **11** extemporise, extemporize

improvised: 5 ad lib; **7** devised; **8** invented; **9** ad libitem [Latin], improvise, makeshift, unplanned; **10** fabricated, jury-rigged, off-the-cuff, unscripted; **11** spontaneous, unmeditated, unrehearsed

imprudence: 8 rashness, temerity; **9** incaution; **12** indiscretion

imprudent: 8 reckless; **11** improvident, temerarious

impudence: 4 gall; **5** cheek, crust; **8** audacity, pertness; **9** freshness, insolence, petulence; **10** cheekiness; **12** impertinence

impudent: 4 flip, rude; **5** fresh, sassy, saucy, smart; **7** aweless; **8** insolent, overbold; **9** audacious, shameless, unabashed; **11** impertinent, snotty-nosed

impugn: 5 rebut; **6** assail, charge; **7** censure; **8** reproach, traverse; **9** reprobate

impuissance: 8 weakness; **9** impotence, inability; **10** disability, incapacity; **12** helplessness, incapability

impulse: 4 urge, whim; **5** flash, pulse, spurt; **6** vagary; **7** caprice, impetus, pulsing; **8** momentum; **9** impulsion, pulsation; **11** inspiration

impulsion: 5 drift; **7** impetus, impulse

impulsive: 6 madcap; **7** driving; **8** brainish, tearaway; **9** hotheaded, impetuous, impromptu, whimsical; **10** capricious, passionate, unprompted; **11** precipitate, spontaneous

impunity: 9 exemption

impure: 7 unclean

impurity: 5 dross, taint; **9** pollution; **10** impureness; **11** contaminant; **13** contamination

imputable: 5 due to; **9** accusable, referable; **10** ascribable

imputation: 4 slur; **5** brand; **6** charge, stigma; **8** reproach; **10** accusation; **11** impeachment

impute: 3 tax; **6** accuse, assign, charge; **7** ascribe, impeach; **9** attribute

in: 3 hip; **4** inch; **5** pop in, press, put in, ram in; **6** drop in, inside, inward, trendy, tuck in, whip in, with it; **7** current, drive in, faddish, in favor, in vogue, inwards, popular, stick in, stuff in; **8** inside of, thrust in; **9** in fashion, prevalent; **10** prevailing; **11** fashionable

In: 6 indium

inability: 9 impotence, unfitness; **10** disabil-

ity, incapacity, infelicity; **11** impuissance; **12** incapability

in accord: 5 as one; **6** united; **8** agreeing, cemented, in unison; **9** accordant, agreeable, congenial, congruous, consonant, in harmony, of one mind; **10** concordant, consistent, harmonious; **11** conformable, harmonizing, in agreement

inaccurate: 7 inexact; **9** erroneous

inaction: 7 latency; **8** not doing; **9** eschewing, not acting; **10** abstention, abstinence, forbearing, inactivity, refraining; **11** forbearance, passiveness; **12** failure to act, inactiveness

inactivate: 7 disable; **10** deactivate

inactive: 3 off; **4** idle; **5** inert, still; **6** at rest, static; **7** abeyant, dormant, extinct, passive, reserve, stopped; **9** suspended; **10** in abeyance, motionless

inactivity: 6 torpor; **7** inertia, languor; **8** inaction; **12** inactiveness

in addition: 4 more, plus; **5** extra; **6** to boot; **11** furthermore; **12** additionally

in addition to: 3 and; **8** as well as

inadequacy: 8 exiguity; **10** deficiency, scantiness; **12** exiguousness; **13** insufficiency

inadequate: 4 poor; **5** short; **9** not enough, too little; **12** insufficient; **13** not sufficient

inadmissible: 5 inapt; **8** ill-timed; **10** ineligible, mal a propos [Fr]; **12** unseasonable

in advance: 5 ahead; **6** before; **7** advance, in front; **8** advanced, in the van; **9** in the lead; **10** beforehand

inadvertent: 8 not meant, unwilled; **9** unplanned, unwitting; **10** accidental, fortuitous, undesigned, unintended, unpurposed; **13** unintentional

inadvertently: 8 casually; **11** unknowingly, unwittingly; **12** unthinkingly; **13** inattentively; **14** absent-mindedly

inadvisable: 11 unadvisable

inadvisably: 11 expediently

in a flash: 8 outright; **9** instantly; **15** instantaneously

in agony: 6 in pain; **8** wretched; **9** agonizing, miserable

in agreement: 5 as one; **6** agreed, united; **8** agreeing, cemented, in accord, together; **9** accordant, agreeable, congenial, consonant, in concert, in harmony, of one mind; **10** concordant, concurring, harmonious

inalienable: 8 absolute; **10** inviolable, sacrosanct; **11** unalienable; **12** indefeasible, unchallenged; **13** unforfeitable, unimpeachable

inalterable: 11 unalterable

in a manner of speaking: 8 as it were

inamorata: 4 idol; **5** angel; **7** darling, goddess; **8** ladylove

inane: 5 empty; **7** asinine, fatuous, vacuous; **8** farcical, mindless, trifling; **10** ridiculous

inanely: 9 fatuously**

inanimate: 4 dead; 8 lifeless; 9 inorganic, nonliving, pulseless; 10 breathless

inanity: 5 fudge, trash; 6 humbug, vanity; 7 garbage, twaddle, twattle, vacuity; 9 emptiness; 12 mindlessness

in any event: 6 anyhow, anyway; 8 after all; 9 at any rate, in any case

inapplicable: 10 irrelevant, unsuitable

inapposite: 10 out of place; 11 impertinent

inappositeness: 9 inaptness

inappreciable: 4 so-so; 7 trivial; 9 invisible, very small; 10 evanescent, negligible

inappreciably: 8 minutely; 9 invisibly; 13 imperceptibly; 15 microscopically

inappropriate: 5 inapt, unapt, wrong; 8 improper; 9 incorrect, unfitting; 12 incompatible, out of keeping

inappropriately: 10 unsuitably; 11 not suitably

inapt: 5 inept, unapt; 6 clumsy; 7 awkward; 8 improper, inhabile [Fr]; 9 ill-chosen; 10 cumbersome, ineligible; 11 incompetent, unqualified

inaptitude: 9 inaptness; 10 ineptitude; 11 impropriety; 12 incompetence

in arrears: 3 due; 5 owing; 6 behind, unpaid; 7 past due; 9 in default; 10 behindhand, delinquent; 11 outstanding

inarticulate: 9 inaudible; 12 unarticulate

inartistic: 8 ordinary; 10 unartistic

inasmuch as: 3 for; 5 for as, since; 7 because, whereas; 10 seeing that; 11 considering

inattentive: 6 deaf to; 9 unheeding; 10 neglectful, unvigilant, unwatchful; 11 unlistening, unobservant

inattentively: 8 absently; 12 abstractedly; 13 inadvertently

inaudible: 10 unhearable; 12 inarticulate, out of hearing

inaugural: 5 first; 6 maiden; 9 prefatory; 10 initiative, initiatory; 11 preliminary; 12 inauguration, introductory

inaugurate: 5 chair; 6 induct, invest, launch; 7 install, kick off, swear in, usher in; 8 initiate; 9 introduce

inauguration: 5 debut; 7 startup; 9 inaugural, induction; 11 embarcation [Fr]; 12 installation

inauspicious: 3 ill; 7 adverse, harmful, ominous, unlucky; 8 untoward; 9 ill-omened; 10 mal a propos [Fr]; 11 clouded over, threatening, unbefitting, unfavorable

inauthentic: 8 spurious; 11 unauthentic

in authority: 7 supreme; 8 dominant; 9 at the head, paramount; 11 predominant

in a while: 5 apace; 7 briefly, by and by, quickly, shortly; 8 speedily; 9 extempore, forthwith, summarily

in back of: 6 behind

in-between: 6 middle; 7 mediate

in black and white: 7 written; 9 in writing

inborn: 6 inbred, innate, native; 7 genetic; 9 incarnate, ingrained, inherited; 10 congenital, connatural, hereditary

inbound: 6 inward; 8 arriving

in breadth: 7 in width

inbred: 6 inborn, native; 9 ingrained; 10 connatural

inbuilt: 7 built-in; 8 inherent, integral

incalculable: 11 illimitable, innumerable; 12 immeasurable, interminable, unfathomable

incandescence: 4 glow

incandescent lamp: 4 bulb; 9 lightbulb; 13 electric light

incantation: 10 magic words

incantatory: 5 weird; 6 mystic; 10 cabalistic, talismanic

incapability: 9 impotence, inability; 10 disability, incapacity, 11 impuissance

incapable: 6 unable; 9 unequal to; 11 incompetent, unqualified

incapacitate: 5 cramp, unfit; 6 deaden, disarm; 7 disable, invalid; 8 handicap; 9 disenable; 10 disqualify, invalidate

incapacitated: 8 disabled, helpless; 11 handicapped

incapacity: 8 dullness; 9 impotence, inability, stupidity; 10 disability, infelicity; 11 impuissance; 12 incapability, incompetence

incarcerate: 3 jug, lag; 4 gaol, jail; 6 immure, remand; 7 put away; 8 imprison

incarceration: 7 jailing; 9 captivity; 10 immurement; 12 imprisonment

incarnadine: 5 ruddy; 6 florid, rufous; 8 sanguine; 9 render red, rubricate

incarnate: 6 bodied, embody, inborn; 7 genetic; 8 accursed, corporal, embodied

incarnation: 6 avatar; 10 embodiment

in case: 2 if; 8 provided; 10 just in case; 12 in the event of; 13 conditionally

incased: 5 cased; 7 encased

incaution: 8 rashness, temerity; 10 imprudence; 12 indiscretion; 14 incautiousness

incautious: 4 rash; 9 unguarded; 10 indiscreet

incendiarism: 5 arson; 11 fire-raising

incendiary: 4 fell; 7 fire bug [U.S.], untamed; 8 agitator, arsonist, incitive, prompter, tameless; 9 firebrand, seditious, truculent; 10 instigator, petroleuse [Fr], pyromaniac

incense: 4 rile; 5 cense; 6 enrage, madden; 7 envenom, inflame, outrage, thurify; 8 flummery, irritate; 9 enfuriate, infuriate; 10 exasperate, set against

incensed: 8 outraged; 9 indignant; 10 umbrageous

incentive: 4 dram, goad, spur, whet, whip;

I

5 bonus; **6** fillip; **8** stimulus; **10** incitement, inducement; **11** provocation

inception: 5 start; **6** origin, outset; **7** genesis, opening; **8** creation; **9** beginning; **10** incipience, initiation; **11** origination; **12** commencement

inceptive: 9 incipient; **12** introductory

incertain: 6 unsure; **9** uncertain

incertitude: 5 doubt; **7** dubiety; **11** dubiousness, uncertainty; **12** doubtfulness

incessant: 6 steady; **7** endless, routine; **8** constant, frequent, unending; **9** ceaseless, clockwork, continual, perpetual, unceasing, unfailing; **10** consistent, continuous, invariable, monotonous; **11** everlasting, having no end, never-ending, unremitting

incessantly: 6 always; **8** ever anon, steadily; **9** endlessly, routinely; **10** at all times, constantly, invariably, unendingly; **11** ceaselessly, continually, perpetually, unceasingly, unfailingly, without fail; **12** consistently, continuously

inch: 2 in; **3** ell; **4** edge, foot, hand, line, mile, nail, palm, pole, rood, seed, yard; **5** crumb, cubit, patch; **6** fathom, league, tatter; **7** flitter, fritter, furlong; **9** scantling; **10** column inch

inchoate: 4 rise; **5** arise; **8** formless; **9** incipient, originate; **11** provisional

inchworm: 6 looper

incident: 4 fact; **5** event, thing; **9** happening; **10** incidental, occurrence, phenomenon; **11** eventuality

incidental: 6 casual, chance; **8** episodic, incident, uncaused; **9** attendant, causeless, extrinsic; **10** accidental, contingent, derivative, fortuitous; **11** concomitant

incidentally: 7 apropos, by the by; **8** by chance, by the bye, by the way; **9** en passant [Fr]; **12** accidentally

incinerate: 3 ash; **4** burn, char; **7** calcine, corrode; **13** reduce to ashes

incipience: 6 outset; **7** opening; **9** beginning, inception; **10** incipiency, initiation; **11** origination; **12** commencement

incipient: 8 inchoate; **9** inceptive; **12** introductory

incise: 4 etch; **6** bite in; **7** engrave

incised: 6 etched, graven; **8** engraved; **9** inscribed

incision: 3 cut, rip; **4** dent, gash, slit; **5** crack, notch, prick, score, slice; **7** scratch, section

incisive: 4 keen, warm; **5** acute, brisk, quick, sharp, smart, vivid; **6** lively, severe, strong; **7** cutting, nervous; **8** deep-dyed, forcible, piercing, powerful, vigorous; **9** knifelike, trenchant; **10** impressive; **11** penetrating, penetrative

incisiveness: 8 keenness; **9** acuteness, sharpness; **10** trenchance, trenchancy

incite: 4 goad, lash, move, prod, spur; **5** egg on, impel, set on; **6** excite, foment, kindle, prompt, propel, set off, stir up, turn on; **7** actuate, animate, inflame, inspire, provoke, quicken, sharpen; **8** motivate; **9** instigate, stimulate

incitement: 4 dram, goad, spur, whet, whip; **6** fillip; **8** stimulus; **9** incentive; **10** incitation; **11** exhortation, provocation

inciter: 8 provoker; **9** firebrand, instigant; **10** instigator

incitive: 9 seditious; **10** incendiary; **11** instigative; **12** inflammatory

incivism: 11 misanthropy

inclemency: 4 rush; **7** torrent; **8** eruption, hardness, severity; **9** harshness, stiffness; **10** bad weather

inclement: 3 raw; **4** keen; **5** bleak, fresh; **7** nipping; **9** unpitying; **10** unmerciful

inclement weather: 10 bad weather

inclination: 3 dip; **4** bent, bias, lean, list, mind, tilt; **5** slant, slope; **6** animus; **7** leaning, sloping; **8** penchant, slanting, tendency, velleity; **9** inclining, proneness; **10** affections, angle of dip, partiality, proclivity, propensity; **11** disposition, magnetic dip; **12** predilection

incline: 3 dip, run; **4** bend, bias, lean, mind, ramp, rise, side, sway, tend, tilt; **5** pitch, slope, trend, verge; **6** ascent, bend to, lean to; **7** dispose, propend, recline; **8** gradient; **9** acclivity, determine, influence, inoculate, weigh with; **10** predispose

inclinometer: 9 dip circle; **10** clinometer

inclose: 3 lap; **4** gird; **5** beset, bound, put in; **6** begird, insert, shut in; **7** compass, embrace, enclose, environ, stick in; **8** encircle, surround; **9** encompass, introduce; **10** circumvent, encincture; **12** circumscribe

inclosure: 5 arena, close, court; **6** inside; **8** envelope, interior; **9** enclosing, enclosure; **10** enveloping; **11** envelopment; **12** enclosed area; **14** circumscribing; **15** circumscription

include: 4 have; **5** admit, let in; **7** contain; **11** number among

included: 9 contained

inclusion: 9 admission, reception; **10** membership; **11** subsumption; **13** comprehension

inclusive: 8 as well as, catholic, let alone; **9** including; **12** not to mention

incognizable: 11 inscrutable; **12** inexplicable; **13** incognoscible

incognizant: 7 unaware; **11** unconscious

incoherence: 6 raving; **7** ranting; **11** incoherency, noncohesion

incoherent: 4 wild; **5** giddy, rabid; **6** doting, raving; **7** berserk, frantic; **8** frenetic, frenzied, rambling, unhinged, wild-eyed; **9** delirious, insensate, possessed, wandering;

10 reasonless, tongue-tied; **11** dithyrambic, lightheaded, unconnected, vertiginous

in cold blood: 6 coldly; **9** advisedly; **10** with design; **12** deliberately

incombustible: 9 fireproof; **10** flameproof; **12** nonflammable; **13** uninflammable; **14** noncombustible

income: 6 influx; **7** revenue; **8** entrance; **9** incomings

income tax bracket: 10 tax bracket; **13** income bracket

income tax return: 6 return; **9** tax return

incoming: 5 entry; **7** ingress; **8** entering, entrance

incommensurable: 11 irreducible; **13** not comparable; **14** incommensurate

incommode: 3 bug, irk, vex; **4** faze, tire; **5** annoy, cross, worry; **6** bother, put out; **7** disturb, mortify, perplex, trouble; **8** disquiet; **9** disoblige, displease; **10** discomfort, discommode, discompose; **13** inconvenience

incommunicable: 11 inalienable, undefinable; **13** inexpressible

incomparable: 9 sovereign; **11** ne plus ultra [Lat], superlative; **12** uncomparable

incompatible: 7 hostile; **8** mismated, unsuited; **9** ill-sorted, repugnant, unfitting; **10** discrepant; **11** contrastive, uncongenial; **12** antagonistic, inharmonious, out of keeping; **13** inappropriate

incompetence: 8 dullness; **9** ineptness, stupidity; **10** inaptitude, incapacity, ineptitude; **11** lack of skill, want of skill; **12** incompetency; **13** dim-wittedness

incompetent: 5 inapt, inept, unapt; **6** clumsy, unable; **8** bungling, fumbling, inhabile [Fr]; **9** incapable, simpleton, unequal to, unskilled; **11** unqualified; **12** disqualified, ill-qualified; **15** mental defective

incomplete: 10 fragmented, uncomplete; **11** uncompleted

in compliance: 10 obediently; **11** compliantly

incomprehensible: 12 inexplicable

incomputable: 11 inestimable; **12** immeasurable

inconceivable: 9 unheard-of; **10** impossible, incredible, staggering; **11** unthinkable; **12** beyond belief, unbelievable, unimaginable; **13** hard to believe

inconceivably: 10 incredibly

in concert: 6 in tune; **8** in league, together; **11** in agreement; **13** in cooperation

in conclusion: 4 last; **6** in fine, lastly; **7** finally; **8** after all

inconclusive: 8 unproved; **10** groundless

in condition: 6 in trim; **7** in shape; **11** conditioned; **13** physically fit

incongruous: 6 absurd; **9** intrusive; **10** solecistic; **12** unreasonable; **13** ungrammatical

in conjunction: 5 as one; **8** together

inconsequential: 4 vain; **8** bootless, nugatory; **9** fruitless, pointless; **10** of no effect, profitless; **12** inconsequent, unprofitable; **13** without effect

inconsiderable: 4 so-so; **6** paltry; **7** trivial; **9** invisible; **10** negligible; **12** undetectable

inconsiderate: 6 vacant; **7** no-brain, vacuous; **8** mindless; **10** unoccupied, unthinking; **11** thoughtless; **12** unconsidered

inconsistency: 5 folly; **7** conceit, paradox; **8** oxymoron, trifling; **9** frivolity, lip wisdom; **13** arbitrariness, contradiction

inconsistent: 7 erratic; **9** arbitrary, whimsical; **10** capricious, discrepant, irrational; **11** conflicting

inconsolable: 6 desole [Fr]; **7** forlorn; **8** desolate; **11** comfortless, sick at heart; **12** disconsolate

inconsonant: 6 fitful; **9** spasmodic; **10** discordant

inconspicuous: 9 unnoticed, invisible

inconstant: 6 fickle; **8** shifting, unstable, unsteady, wavering; **11** vacillating

in contact: 7 grazing, in touch; **8** abutting, touching; **9** adjoining

in contempt: 9 in spite of; **10** in defiance

incontestable: 11 indubitable; **12** indisputable, undisputable

incontrovertible: 8 positive; **11** indubitable, irrefutable, stereotyped; **12** demonstrable, indisputable

inconvenience: 3 bug, irk, vex; **4** faze, tire; **5** annoy, cross, worry; **6** bother, put out; **7** disturb, mortify, perplex, trouble; **8** disquiet; **9** disoblige, displease, incommode, worriment; **10** discomfort, discommode, discompose; **11** awkwardness

incorporate: 4 fuse; **5** blend, merge, unite; **6** absorb, embody, merged; **7** blend in, combine, conjoin, contain, unified; **8** coalesce, comprise, dissolve; **9** integrate; **10** amalgamate, centralize, impregnate, integrated; **11** consolidate, disembodied, incorporeal

incorporated: 6 merged; **7** unified; **9** corporate; **10** integrated; **11** incorporate

incorporation: 5 union; **6** fusing, fusion; **7** uniting; **8** blending; **9** synthesis; **10** coalescing, embodiment; **11** coalescence, unification; **12** amalgamation

incorporeal: 6 unreal; **10** immaterial; **11** disembodied; **12** noncorporeal

incorrect: 5 wrong; **7** naughty; **8** fallible; **9** undutiful; **10** fallacious; **13** inappropriate

incorrectly: 5 wrong; **7** falsely, naughty, wrongly

incorrigible: 4 lost; **5** fixed; **6** unruly; **8** obdurate; **9** incurable, reprobate; **10** delinquent, invariable, inveterate; **12** contumacious, deaf to advice, ineradicable, ungovernable

incorruption: 9 innocence; 13 impeccability, incorruptness

increase: 4 gain, grow; 6 expand, growth, step-up; 7 enlarge; 8 addition; 9 increment; 12 augmentation, become larger

increased: 5 grown; 7 swollen, widened; 8 enlarged, expanded, extended

incredibility: 8 cynicism, distrust, mistrust; 10 scepticism, skepticism; 11 incredulity

incredible: 8 towering; 10 prodigious, staggering, stupendous; 11 astonishing; 12 beyond belief, unbelievable; 13 hard to believe, inconceivable

incredibly: 7 awfully; 8 famously; 9 amazingly, glaringly, strangely; 10 improbably; 11 egregiously, implausibly, marvelously, prominently, wonderfully; 12 emphatically, stupendously, surprisingly, tremendously, unbelievably

incredulity: 8 cynicism, distrust, mistrust, unbelief; 9 disbelief; 10 irreligion, scepticism, skepticism; 11 lack of faith

incredulous: 9 faithless, sceptical, skeptical; 11 unbelieving; 12 lacking faith

increment: 4 gain; 6 growth; 8 increase; 9 accessory; 10 supplement; 11 development, pullulation; 12 augmentation

incriminate: 5 imply; 6 accuse; 7 impeach; 9 criminate, inculpate

in-crowd: 4 gang, knot, ring; 5 crowd, group; 6 circle, clique

incrust: 3 pad, wad; 4 fill, line; 5 stuff; 7 encrust

incubate: 5 brood, cover, hatch; 10 be pregnant

incubation: 7 sitting; 8 brooding, hatching; 9 gestation

incubator: 7 brooder

incubus: 5 Eblis; 7 succuba; 8 succubus; 9 nightmare

inculcate: 5 infix; 6 infuse; 7 implant, instill; 9 catechize, inoculate; 10 infiltrate

inculpable: 9 blameless; 13 unimpeachable; 14 irreproachable

inculpate: 5 imply; 9 implicate; 11 incriminate

incumbency: 4 post; 5 berth, place; 6 tenure; 8 position; 12 term of office

incumbent: 9 overlying; 11 householder, supernatant; 12 officeholder, superimposed; 13 public servant; 14 public official

incumber: 8 encumber

incumbrance: 4 load, onus; 5 hitch; 6 burden; 9 hindrance; 10 preventive; 11 encumbrance; 12 interference, preventative

incur: 3 get; 4 find; 6 obtain; 7 receive

incurable: 5 fixed; 8 cureless; 10 invariable,

remediless; 11 immedicable; 12 beyond remedy, incorrigible

incurious: 11 indifferent; 12 uninterested; 13 uninquisitive

incursion: 6 influx, inroad; 8 invasion; 9 intrusion, irruption; 11 penetration

incursive: 8 invading, invasive

incurvate: 4 bend, flex; 5 curve; 8 incurved

incus: 5 anvil

in danger: 6 at risk; 7 at peril, in peril; 8 at hazard; 9 imperiled, in a bad way, prostrate; 10 endangered, in jeopardy, threatened

indebted: 6 in debt

indebtedness: 9 liability

indebted to: 5 due to; 7 bound to, obliged; 8 beholden, grateful, thankful, tied down; 9 duty bound; 10 beholden to

indecency: 9 immodesty; 10 indelicacy; 11 impropriety

indecent: 8 uncomely, unseemly, untoward; 10 indecorous, indelicate, unbecoming

indecent exposure: 12 public nudity

indecipherable: 7 unclear; 10 unreadable

indecision: 5 demur; 8 suspense; 12 irresolution; 14 indecisiveness; 15 indetermination

indecisive: 9 tentative; 10 irresolute; 11 half-hearted; 12 double-minded

indecisiveness: 5 demur; 8 suspense; 10 indecision; 12 irresolution

indecorous: 5 gross; 6 coarse, ribald; 7 lawless; 8 improper, indecent, scampish, uncomely, unseemly, untoward; 10 disorderly, indelicate, unbecoming

indecorously: 9 lawlessly; 10 disorderly, improperly, scampishly; 12 unbecomingly

indecorum: 7 liberty, scandal; 8 ribaldry; 9 grossness; 10 courseness, immorality; 11 familiarity, impropriety, misbehavior

indeed: 2 so; 3 why; 4 most, much, well; 5 a deal, marry, truly; 6 i' faith, really, verily, you bet; 7 exactly, no end of; 8 I must say; 9 certainly, in reality, precisely

indefatigable: 8 tireless, untiring; 9 unwearied; 10 unflagging, unwearying; 11 never tiring

indefeasible: 8 absolute; 10 inviolable, sacrosanct; 11 inalienable, unalienable; 12 unchallenged

indefectible: 7 perfect; 8 flawless; 9 faultless; 10 impeccable; 20 free from imperfection

indefensible: 7 unarmed; 8 harmless, sine ictu [Lat], vincible; 9 pregnable, untenable; 10 weaponless; 11 defenseless, inexcusable, unfortified, unwarranted; 13 insupportable, unjustifiable

indefinable: 9 ineffable; 10 untellable; 11 undefinable, unspeakable, unutterable; 13 indescribable

indefinite: 7 shadowy; 9 undefined; 11 exhaustless; 13 indeterminate

indelible: 4 deep; 8 profound; 10 impressive, unerasable

indelicacy: 9 immodesty, indecency

indelicate: 8 indecent; 10 indecorous

in demand: 7 coveted, desired; 8 demanded; 9 mandatory; 10 marketable; 11 sought after

indemnification: 6 amends; 7 damages, redress; 9 indemnity, quittance; 10 making good; 11 restitution; 13 reimbursement

indemnify: 5 atone; 8 make good; 9 make whole, reimburse; 10 compensate, make amends, recompense; 12 hold harmless

indemnity: 6 amends, excuse; 7 damages, redress, release; 9 insurance, quittance; 10 making good; 11 exoneration, restitution; 13 reimbursement; 15 indemnification

indent: 3 cut; 4 dent, nick; 5 crape, crimp, notch, wring; 7 scallop; 9 indenture; 11 indentation

indentation: 4 dent, dint; 5 sinus; 6 dimple, indent, lacuna; 7 pitting; 8 follicle; 9 indenture, roughness

indented: 6 dented, jagged, nicked; 7 notched; 9 crenelate, depressed, embattled; 10 crenelated, crenellate; 11 crenellated

indenture: 4 bond; 6 indent; 8 covenant; 9 assurance; 11 indentation

indentured: 5 bound; 8 articled; 11 apprenticed

independence: 10 irrelation; 11 non-relation; 12 dissociation, independency; 13 disconnection, unrelatedness

Independence Day: 12 Fourth of July

independent: 4 main; 5 loose; 7 at large, mugwump; 8 scot-free, separate, unallied; 9 freelance, sovereign; 10 autonomous; 12 out of harness; 13 self-governing, unconditional, uncoordinated

independently: 9 severally; 10 separately

independent variable: 8 argument

Inderal: 11 propranolol

indescribable: 8 fabulous; 9 ineffable; 10 untellable; 11 indefinable, unspeakable, unutterable; 13 inexpressible

in despair: 4 gone; 7 forlorn; 8 desolate, hopeless; 9 desperate; 10 despairing

indestructible: 7 durable, undying; 10 perdurable; 12 imperishable

indeterminate: 5 vague; 6 casual, chance; 7 obscure; 8 uncaused; 9 causeless; 10 accidental, contingent, fortuitous, incidental, indefinite; 11 enigmatical; 12 adventitious, undetermined

indetermination: 5 demur; 6 chance; 8 suspense; 10 indecision, indefinity; 12 irresolution, unknown cause; 13 indeterminacy

index: 4 root; 5 grade, power; 6 digest; 8 exponent, graduate, indicant, tabulate; 9 catalogue, indicator, logarithm; 10 forefinger; 11 index finger, index number

index finger: 5 index; 10 forefinger

India: 6 Bharat

Indian: 10 Amerindian, East Indian; 14 American Indian, Native American

Indianan: 7 Hoosier

Indianapolis: 16 capital of Indiana

Indianapolis 500: 7 Indy 500

Indian cobra: 8 Naja naja

Indian meal: 8 cornmeal

Indian relish: 7 chutney

Indian rice: 8 wild rice

India rubber: 5 latex; 6 rubber

Indic: 9 Indo-Aryan

indicant: 5 index; 9 indicator; 11 index number

indicate: 4 show; 5 argue, imply, point; 6 convey, denote, select, signal; 7 bespeak, betoken, breathe, point to, refer to, signify, suggest; 8 allude to, point out, stand for; 9 represent, symbolize

indicating: 8 symbolic; 10 denoting, denotative, indication, signifying; 11 symbolizing; 12 representing; 13 symbolization; 14 representative

indication: 4 sign; 6 symbol; 9 selection; 10 indicating; 13 specification; 14 representation

indicative: 7 deictic; 8 fact mood; 10 common mood, indicatory, suggestive; 11 declarative; 13 demonstrative, significative

indicative mood: 8 fact mood; 10 common mood, indicative; 11 declarative

indicator: 5 index; 7 pointer, readout, witness; 8 indicant; 9 testifier; 11 index number

indicatory: 7 deictic; 10 indicative; 13 demonstrative

indict: 6 accuse; 7 impeach; 9 criticize

indictable: 10 chargeable; 11 impeachable

indictment: 8 citation, true bill; 11 impeachment, presentment

indifference: 6 apathy, phlegm; 9 stolidity, unconcern; 10 neutrality; 11 impassivity, nonchalance; 13 impassiveness

indifferent: 2 OK; 4 deaf, fair, so-so; 5 blase, bored, inert; 7 average, neutral; 8 bearable, mediocre, middling, ordinary, passable, unbiased; 9 apathetic, incurious, tolerable, unbiassed, uncurious; 10 acceptable, admissible, immaterial; 12 uninterested; 13 disinterested, uninquisitive

indigence: 4 lack, need, want; 6 penury; 7 poverty; 8 distress; 9 necessity, neediness, pauperism, privation; 11 destitution; 12 difficulties

indigene: 6 native; 16 native inhabitant

indigenous: 6 native; 7 endemic; 10 aboriginal; 12 autochthonal, autochthonic

indigenousness: 8 endemism; 11 autochthony

indigent: 4 poor; 5 needy; 6 ill off; 8 badly

off; **9** destitute, poorly off; **11** necessitous; **12** impoverished; **15** poverty-stricken

indigestible: 8 ungenial

indigestion: 9 dyspepsia; **12** stomach upset, upset stomach

indignant: 4 hurt, sore; **8** incensed, outraged; **10** umbrageous

indignation: 5 anger; **7** outrage; **9** animosity

indignity: 6 slight; **7** neglect

indigo: 4 anil; **9** indigotin; **11** indigo plant

indigo snake: 11 gopher snake

indirect: 5 stray; **6** zigzag; **7** crooked, erratic, oblique, vagrant; **10** circuitous, collateral, roundabout, undirected; **11** inferential, out of the way

indirectly: 12 circuitously

indiscernible: 10 insensible; **12** undetectable

indiscipline: 12 undiscipline

indiscreet: 4 rash; **10** incautious

indiscretion: 8 rashness, temerity; **9** incaution; **10** imprudence, peccadillo; **14** incautiousness

indiscriminate: 6 random; **7** epicene; **9** desultory; **11** promiscuous; **13** miscellaneous

indiscriminately: 8 at random, randomly; **10** willy-nilly; **11** arbitrarily, haphazardly

indispensable: 9 called for, essential; **10** imperative; **12** prerequisite

indispose: 5 shake, unfit; **7** stagger; **10** disincline, disqualify

indisposed: 4 loth; **5** loath, seedy, shy of; **6** ailing, averse, peaked, poorly, sickly, unwell; **9** reluctant, squeamish; **10** not content; **11** disinclined

indisposition: 9 hesitancy, infirmity, loathness; **10** hesitation, reluctance; **13** unwillingness

indisputable: 4 sure; **11** indubitable; **12** undisputable; **13** incontestable

indissoluble: 9 permanent

indistinctly: 5 dimly

indistinctness: 8 confused; **9** fogginess, fuzziness, obscurity; **10** blurriness

indistinguishable: 9 identical; **10** indistinct; **11** convertible; **15** interchangeable

indite: 3 pen; **5** draft, write; **6** author, draw up, make up; **7** compose; **9** formulate

indium: 2 In

individual: 3 ace, man, one; **4** body, lone, soul, unit; **5** alone, apart, being, civic, human, party; **6** mortal, person, proper, public, single, social; **7** certain, partial, private, several, someone, special; **8** creature, definite, especial, national, original, peculiar, personal, separate, somebody, specific, such a one; **9** earthling, exclusive, personage; **10** case-by-case, human being, item-by-item, living soul, particular, respective

individualism: 12 laissez faire; **13** individuality

individuality: 3 ego; **4** self; **5** unity; **7** oneness; **8** identity; **9** mannerism; **10** speciality, uniqueness; **11** originality, peculiarity, personality, singularity, specialness, specificity; **12** idiosyncrasy

individualize: 7 realize, specify; **9** designate, determine; **10** specialize; **11** personalize

individually: 4 solo; **5** alone, per se; **6** singly; **8** by itself, one by one; **9** by oneself, on one's own, severally; **10** separately

individual retirement account: 3 IRA

indocile: 6 unruly; **11** intractable; **12** ungovernable

Indocin: 12 indomethacin

indoctrinate: 11 proselytize; **12** propagandize

Indo-European: 5 Aryan; **9** Indo-Aryan; **11** Indo-Hittite; **12** Indo-Germanic

indoleacetic acid: 3 IAA

indolence: 5 sloth; **8** laziness

indolent: 4 lazy; **5** slack; **6** otiose, remiss, supine, torpid; **7** languid, work-shy; **8** faineant, slothful, sluggish

indomethacin: 7 Indocin

indomitable: 4 firm, iron; **6** dogged, gritty [U.S.]; **10** dominating, invincible, resistless; **11** never-say-die, unsubduable; **13** unconquerable

Indonesian: 6 Bahasa; **15** Bahasa Indonesia

Indonesian Borneo: 10 Kalimantan

indoor: 4 home; **6** inside; **8** domestic; **10** intramural, vernacular

indoor garden: 8 hothouse; **10** greenhouse; **12** conservatory

indoors: 6 inside

indorse: 4 back; **6** accept, insure, ratify, second, uphold; **7** approve, bear out, endorse, support, warrant; **10** underwrite; **11** corroborate, countersign

indrawn: 5 aloof; **8** reserved; **9** withdrawn

indri: 5 lemur; **6** indris; **10** Indri indri

indubitable: 7 evident, obvious; **8** palpable, striking; **10** pronounced; **11** beyond doubt, self-evident; **12** indisputable, unmistakable; **13** incontestable

induce: 3 get; **4** draw, have, lure, make, move, rush; **5** cause, evoke; **6** allure, cajole, draw on, elicit, entail, entice, hasten; **7** attract, beguile, bring on, provoke; **8** blandish, motivate, persuade; **9** captivate, stimulate

inducement: 4 lure; **6** luring; **8** cajolery, enticing, inducing; **9** incentive; **10** allurement, attraction, enticement, temptation; **11** beguilement, blandishing, captivation

inducive: 9 inductive

induct: 4 seat; **5** chair; **6** invest; **7** install, swear in; **8** initiate; **10** inaugurate

induction: 7 trigger; **8** prologue; **9** evocation; **10** dialectics, inductance, initiation;

11 elicitation; **12** inauguration, installation, introduction, presentation
induction accelerator: 8 betatron
induction furnace: 13 muffle furnace
inductive: 8 inducive; **12** introductory
inductive reasoning: 9 induction; **14** generalization
indue: 4 gift; **5** endow, enduc; **6** invest; **7** empower
indulge: 4 baby; **5** favor, humor, spoil; **6** cocker, coddle, cosset, pamper, pander, tickle; **7** flatter, gratify; **8** live high, live it up, live well; **9** luxuriate; **10** featherbed; **11** mollycoddle, overindulge
indulgence: 5 favor, folly; **7** foolery; **8** humoring, lenience, leniency, pleasing; **9** indulging, pampering; **10** tomfoolery; **11** forbearance
indulgent: 3 lax; **4** soft; **7** lenient; **8** gracious, obliging, tolerant; **9** easy-going; **10** complacent, permissive; **11** good-humored; **13** accommodating
indurate: 6 harden; **7** callous, stiffen; **9** indurated; **10** render hard; **12** thick-skinned
induration: 8 obduracy; **9** sclerosis; **12** petrifaction
Indus: 10 Indus River
industrial: 13 manufacturing
industrialize: 7 develop; **8** urbanize
industrialized: 9 developed, urbanized
industrialized nation: 14 advanced nation; **15** developed nation
industrial watercourse: 4 race; **7** millrun; **8** head race, millrace, tail race
industrious: 7 notable; **8** diligent, sedulous, tireless, untiring; **9** assiduous, energetic, gumptious; **11** hardworking, painstaking, up-and-coming
industry: 3 art; **8** business; **9** assiduity, diligence; **11** manufacture; **13** manufacturing
Indy 500: 15 Indianapolis 500
inebriant: 5 drink; **7** alcohol; **10** intoxicant
inebriate: 3 cut, sot; **4** high, soak; **5** beery, boozy, drunk, fresh, merry, rummy, souse, tight, tipsy; **6** corned, fuddle, groggy, primed; **7** drunken, fuddled, hit it up; **8** befuddle, drunkard, elevated, overcome, top-heavy; **9** disguised, flustered, overtaken; **10** in one's cups, inebriated, intoxicate; **11** intoxicated
inedible: 9 uneatable
ineducable: 11 unteachable
ineffable: 8 fabulous; **10** unnameable, untellable; **11** indefinable, unspeakable, unutterable
ineffaceable: 10 deep-rooted, inveterate
in effect: 4 good; **5** valid; **6** au fond; **7** in force; **8** at bottom; **9** effective, in the main, virtually; **10** applicable; **11** effectively, practically
ineffective: 6 effete, futile, unable; **8** ill-

spent; **10** unavailing; **11** ineffectual, inefficient, uncalled for, uneffective; **13** inefficacious
ineffectual: 6 effete, futile, otiose, unable; **8** ill-spent; **10** unavailing; **11** ineffective, uncalled for, uneffective; **13** inefficacious
inefficacy: 8 futility
inefficiency: 12 wastefulness
inefficient: 11 ineffective
inelasticity: 6 laxity; **8** limpness; **10** flaccidity
inelegant: 7 awkward, cramped; **9** graceless; **10** ungraceful, unpolished
ineligible: 5 inapt; **12** inadmissible
ineluctable: 10 inevitable; **11** inescapable, unavoidable
in embryo: 5 in ovo [Lat]; **6** coming, embryo, in hand, unborn; **7** in train; **8** in the bud, on the way; **9** embryonic, embryotic; **10** near at hand; **11** forthcoming
inept: 5 inapt, silly, unapt; **6** clumsy; **7** awkward, blatant, fatuous, foolish, idiotic; **8** babbling, feckless, imbecile, inhabile [Fr], tactless; **9** driveling, ill-chosen, insensate, senseless; **10** cumbersome, irrational; **11** incompetent, nonsensical, unqualified; **12** disqualified, ill-qualified
ineptitude: 8 slowness; **9** inaptness, ineptness; **10** clumsiness, inaptitude; **11** awkwardness, lack of skill; **12** incompetence
inequality: 10 unfairness; **13** dissimilitude
inequitable: 6 unfair, unjust
inequity: 9 injustice; **10** unfairness
in equity: 6 fairly, justly; **7** equably; **8** in reason
ineradicable: 5 fixed; **9** incurable; **10** deep-rooted, invariable; **12** incorrigible
inerrant: 8 unerring; **9** inerrable
in error: 8 mistaken; **12** under an error; **15** under an illusion
inert: 4 flat, idle; **6** supine, torpid; **7** neutral, passive; **8** inactive, sluggish; **10** unreactive; **11** indifferent
inert gas: 7 argonon; **8** noble gas
inertia: 9 inertness; **10** inactivity; **12** inactiveness
inertness: 7 inertia; **8** dullness
inescapable: 11 ineluctable, unavoidable
in essence: 8 in theory; **9** basically; **11** essentially, in principle, substantial, substantive; **13** fundamentally
inessential: 11 unessential; **12** nonessential
inestimable: 9 priceless; **10** invaluable; **12** immeasurable, incomputable
inevitable: 10 inexorable; **11** irrevocable, unavoidable; **12** irresistible; **14** uncontrollable
inevitable accident: 8 act of God, vis major; **12** force majeure
inevitably: 5 needs; **10** inexorably;

11 ineluctably, inescapably, necessarily, of necessity, unavoidably

inexact: 3 lax; **5** loose; **8** careless, slipshod, slovenly; **10** inaccurate

inexactitude: 11 inexactness

in excess: 7 to spare

inexcusable: 12 indefensible, unforgivable

inexhaustible: 9 unlimited; **11** exhaustless, illimitable, innumerable; **12** immeasurable, incalculable, interminable, unfathomable

inexhaustibly: 10 tirelessly; **13** indefatigably

inexorable: 4 grim; **5** stern; **7** adamant, austere, exigent; **8** exacting, obdurate, rigorous; **9** demanding, hard-nosed, hard-shell [U.S.], searching, unsparing; **10** adamantine, hard-headed, implacable, inevitable, inflexible, relentless; **11** irrevocable, unavoidable, unforgiving, unrelenting; **12** intransigent, irresistible, stony-hearted, unappeasable

inexpedient: 6 unwise

inexpensive: 3 low; **5** cheap; **9** low priced

inexperienced: 3 raw; **5** green, naive; **6** callow; **8** ignorant; **11** uninitiated

inexperienced person: 8 innocent

inexpert: 7 amateur; **9** unskilled; **10** amateurish, unskillful

inexpertly: 5 badly; **6** poorly; **7** crudely; **9** artlessly; **12** unskillfully

inexpiable: 12 unpardonable

inexplicit: 8 implicit

inexpressible: 8 fabulous; **9** ineffable; **11** undefinable, unspeakable, unutterable; **13** indescribable, unexpressible

inexpressive: 12 unexpressive

inexpugnable: 11 impregnable

in extenso: 6 en bloc; **7** as a body, at large, en masse; **9** every inch; **10** on the whole, throughout

inextinguishable: 8 ravening, tameless; **11** irreducible; **12** ungovernable, unquenchable; **13** irrepressible

inextricable: 5 kinky; **6** kinked; **7** knotted, raveled, tangled; **8** involved; **9** entangled, intricate, perplexed; **10** impassable, impervious; **11** complicated, inseparable

infallibility: 11 reliability

infallible: 8 unerring

infamous: 4 base, foul, vile; **5** grave, gross; **6** arrant, scurvy, too bad; **7** heinous; **8** ill-famed, shameful, sinister; **9** felonious, nefarious, notorious; **10** scandalous, villainous; **11** ignominious; **13** unmentionable

infamy: 8 atrocity, villainy; **9** depravity, flagrancy; **10** opprobrium; **11** viciousness

infancy: 5 birth; **6** cradle; **7** genesis; **8** babyhood, nativity; **14** early childhood

infant: 3 sop; **4** babe, baby; **5** child; **7** milk-

sop; **8** innocent; **9** infantile; **10** babe in arms

infant deathrate: 15 infant mortality; **19** infant mortality rate

infantile: 4 baby; **6** infant; **7** babyish; **8** childish; **9** child-like

infantile amaurotic idiocy: 8 Tay-Sachs; **15** Tay-Sachs disease

infantile fixation: 8 fixation; **10** regression

infantile paralysis: 5 polio; **13** poliomyelitis

infant mortality rate: 15 infant deathrate, infant mortality

infantry: 4 foot; **12** foot soldiers

infantryman: 7 marcher; **8** rifleman; **11** foot soldier, footslogger

infant school: 9 pre-school; **13** nursery school

infarction: 7 embolus, infarct; **8** embolism

in fashion: 2 in; **6** trendy, with it; **7** current, in vogue; **8** up to date; **9** au courant, prevalent; **10** all the rage, prevailing; **11** fashionable

infatuated: 3 odd; **4** gaga; **5** crazy, dotty; **6** entete [Fr], in love, soft on; **7** smitten; **8** besotted, confined, dogmatic, enamored, positive; **9** conceited, eccentric, fanatical, illiberal, induced by, seduced by, taken with; **10** inspired by, intolerant, spellbound; **11** smitten with

infatuation: 3 fad; **5** craze, crush, hobby, quirk; **6** fervor; **8** calf love, crotchet; **9** blind side, puppy love; **10** enthusiasm, fanaticism, partiality; **11** enchantment, fascination

infeasible: 10 unfeasible, unworkable; **12** unachievable; **13** impracticable

infect: 4 move; **5** alloy, smite, taint, touch; **6** affect, excite, strike; **7** animate, impress, inspire; **8** compound, interest; **9** impassion; **10** adulterate, amalgamate; **12** sophisticate

infected: 5 dirty, pussy; **6** putrid; **8** purulent; **9** festering; **12** contaminated

infection: 9 contagion, galvanism; **10** stirring up; **11** provocation, stimulation

infectious: 6 taking; **8** catching; **9** infective, vitiating; **10** contagious; **12** communicable; **13** transmissable

infectious hepatitis: 10 hepatitis A

infectiously: 12 contagiously

infective: 8 morbific, striking; **10** infectious, pathogenic

infelicitous: 4 poor; **7** unhappy, unlucky; **8** untoward; **9** woe-begone

infelicity: 4 pain; **5** dolor; **9** inability, suffering; **10** incapacity, mental pain, sufferance; **11** unhappiness

infer: 5 guess, imply; **6** deduce, deduct, derive, gather; **7** involve; **8** allude to; **10** generalise, generalize, understand; **11** extrapolate

inference: 8 illation; **9** deduction; **10** conclusion

inferential: 7 crooked; **8** illative, indirect; **9** deducible, following

inferior: 3 bad; 4 poor; 5 lower, lowly, petty; 7 smaller; 8 declasse; 9 deficient, secondary, subaltern, subscript; 10 second-best, second-rate; 11 junior-grade, subordinate, substandard; 12 lower-ranking

infernal: 4 damn; 5 blame; 6 blamed, cursed, damned, darned, deuced, unholy; 7 blasted, blessed, demonic, hellish, satanic, stygian; 8 accursed, damnable, devilish, diabolic, fiendish, hell-born; 10 confounded, demoniacal, diabolical

infernal regions: 4 hell; 5 Hades; 7 inferno; 13 bottomless pit

inferno: 4 hell; 5 Hades; 6 the pit; 7 the pits; 11 hell on earth; 12 nether region; 13 bottomless pit, conflagration; 14 place of torment; 15 infernal regions

inferring: 8 deducing; 9 reasoning; 11 rationalism

infertile: 4 arid, 6 barren; 7 sterile; 9 unfertile; 10 unfruitful; 11 inoperative

infertility: 9 sterility

infest: 3 bug; 4 bait, bore; 5 abuse, beset, grind, harry, haunt, hound, tease, worry; 6 badger, bother, harass, heckle, ill-use, molest, pester, plague, pother; 7 oppress, overrun; 8 bullirag, bullyrag, ill-treat, maltreat, mistreat; 9 importune, persecute

infested: 5 beset, bored; 6 baited; 7 harried, heckled, overrun, plagued; 8 badgered, harassed, pothered; 10 importuned, persecuted

in fetters: 7 in bonds; 8 fettered, shackled

infidel: 5 deist, pagan; 7 gentile, heathen; 10 pyrrhonist, unbeliever

infidelity: 8 adultery, cheating; 10 cuckolding; 11 concubinage, rationalism; 12 freethinking; 13 faithlessness; 14 unfaithfulness

infield: 7 diamond; 15 baseball diamond

in file: 6 in line, on line; 8 in column; 10 single file

infiltrate: 4 dash; 5 blend, cross, imbue, infix, tinge; 6 imbrue, infuse, season; 7 ingrain, instill; 8 medicate, saturate, sprinkle, tincture; 9 inculcate, inoculate; 10 besprinkle; 11 pass through

infiltration: 6 import; 12 transudation

infinite: 6 myriad; 9 countless, non-finite, uncounted; 10 innumerous, numberless, unnumbered; 11 innumerable, unnumerable; 12 unfathomable, unnumberable; 13 multitudinous

infinitely: 9 endlessly; 11 boundlessly; 12 immeasurably

infiniteness: 8 infinity; 10 infinitude; 13 boundlessness, limitlessness, unboundedness

infinite power: 11 omnipotence

infinitesimal: 6 minute; 9 very small; 10 evanescent; 11 homeopathic, microscopic; 13 inappreciable

infinite wisdom: 11 omniscience

infinitive: 11 uninflected

infinity: 7 forever; 8 eternity; 10 infinitude; 12 infiniteness

infirm: 3 lax; 4 poor, weak; 5 frail, seedy; 6 bedrid, feeble, morbid, sickly, weakly; 7 bedfast, languid, sapless; 8 decrepit, sickabed; 9 bedridden, enfeebled, imperfect; 11 debilitated

infirmary: 8 hospital

infirmity: 7 frailty; 8 debility; 9 frailness; 10 feebleness

inflame: 4 fire, heat, lash; 5 light; 6 enrage, excite, fire up, foment, ignite, incite, kindle, madden, stir up, turn on; 7 envenom, incense, quicken, sharpen; 8 enkindle; 9 infuriate, set fire to, set on fire, stimulate

inflamed: 6 ablaze; 7 fired up; 8 reddened; 9 enkindled

in flames: 6 aflame; 7 blazing; 8 in a blaze

inflammable: 8 burnable; 9 flammable, ignitable, ignitible; 11 combustible

inflammation: 5 flush; 7 redness; 9 inflaming; 13 conflagration

inflammatory: 8 incitive; 9 provoking, seditious; 10 incendiary; 11 instigative, provocative; 13 rabble-rousing

inflatable cushion: 10 air cushion

inflate: 4 puff; 5 widen; 6 billow, blow up, dilate, expand, extend, puff up, rarefy, spread, turn up; 7 amplify, balloon, descant, develop, distend, enlarge, magnify; 8 run out on; 9 expatiate, spread out; 10 aggrandize

inflated: 4 rich, vain; 5 outre, tumid; 6 florid, mouthy, ornate, raised, turgid; 7 flowery, flushed, orotund, stilted; 8 puffed up, sonorous, swelling; 9 bombastic, burlesque, conceited, grandiose, high flown, monstrous, overblown; 10 high-flying, hyperbolic, mock heroic, ornamented, rhetorical, turgescent; 11 big-sounding, declamatory, exaggerated, extravagant, high flowing, overweening; 12 high-sounding, magniloquent, preposterous, vainglorious; 13 grandiloquent

inflation: 9 expansion; 10 dilatation, pretension; 11 rarefaction; 12 rising prices

inflect: 8 modulate

inflected: 6 tensed; 12 inflectional

inflection: 4 bend, flex; 7 bending, flexion, prosody; 8 flection; 9 inflexion

inflexibility: 8 hardness, obduracy, rigidity; 9 obstinacy, stiffness; 10 cussedness [U.S.], mulishness; 12 immovability, stubbornness

inflexible: 5 rigid; 7 austere, exigent; 8 exacting, obdurate, rigorous, stubborn; 9 demanding, hard-nosed, hard-shell [U.S.], obstinate, searching, tenacious, unbending, unsparing; **10** hard-headed, inexorable, unyielding

inflexion: 4 mood; **10** inflection

inflict: 5 visit, wreak; **6** commit, impose; **9** bring down, tyrannize; **10** perpetrate

inflorescence: 8 anthesis; **9** flowering; **10** blossoming; **13** efflorescence

inflow: 6 influx

inflowing: 8 influent

influence: 4 bias, pull, sway; **5** charm, shape, tempt; **6** affect, effect; **7** act upon, dispose, incline; **8** regulate; **9** determine, inoculate, weigh with; **10** predispose

influential: 9 effective

influenza: 3 flu; **4** grip; **6** grippe

influx: 6 inflow, inroad; **8** invasion; **9** incursion, intrusion, irruption

info: 11 information

infold: 6 enfold; **10** envelope

in force: 4 good; **6** in play; **8** in action, in effect; **9** effective; **10** in exercise; **11** in operation

inform: 6 notify; **7** apprise; **8** acquaint

informal: 4 cozy; **5** loose, stray; **6** casual, wanton; **7** lawless, natural, wayward; **8** intimate; **9** wandering; **10** colloquial, unofficial; **12** unauthorized; **13** unceremonious

informality: 4 ease; **6** laxity; **12** unlawfulness; **13** unofficiality

informal language: 13 colloquialism; **14** informal speech

informant: 6 source, teller; **7** delator, relator, witness; **8** exponent, reporter; **9** authority; **10** mouthpiece

information: 4 data, info, lore; **6** wisdom; **7** entropy; **8** learning; **9** informing, knowledge, notifying; **10** announcing; **11** acquainting, bill of right, enunciation; **12** acquaintance, annunciation, enlightening, state of facts; **13** enlightenment

information processing system: 8 computer; **13** data processor

information system: 10 data system

informative: 9 informing; **11** informatory, instructive; **12** enlightening; **13** informational

informatively: 13 instructively

informatory: 11 informative

informed: 7 advised, alerted, knowing; **8** apprised, educated; **10** acquainted; **11** enlightened; **13** knowledgeable

informer: 3 rat; **7** relator; **8** betrayer, squealer

informing: 7 ratting; **9** notifying; **10** announcing; **11** acquainting, enunciation, information, informative, making known; **12** acquaintance, annunciation, enlightening

infotainment: 9 docudrama; **11** documentary

infra: 5 below

infract: 5 break; **6** breach, offend; **7** violate; **9** go against; **10** transgress

infraction: 6 breach; **7** offence, offense; **8** exaction; **9** breaching, violating, violation; **10** assumption, imposition, usurpation; **11** misdemeanor, presumption; **12** encroachment, infringement, misdemeanour

infrangible: 8 absolute; **10** inviolable; **11** indivisible, inseparable; **12** inextricable

infrared lamp: 8 heat lamp

Infrared spectrometer: 4 FTIR

infrastructure: 4 base

infrequency: 6 rarity; **8** rareness; **12** uncommonness

infrequently: 6 hardly, seldom; **8** scarcely

infringe: 5 break, exact, usurp; **6** breach; **7** impinge, violate; **8** conflict, encroach, run afoul, trench on, trespass; **10** contravene, entrench on, not observe, transgress, trench upon; **11** not adhere to

infringement: 6 breach; **7** offence, offense; **8** exaction; **9** breaching, violating, violation; **10** assumption, imposition, infraction, usurpation; **11** misdemeanor, presumption; **12** encroachment, misdemeanour; **13** noncompliance, nonobservance, transgression

in front: 5 ahead; **6** before; **8** in the van; **9** in advance

in front of: 5 ahead

infundibular: 10 cone-shaped; **12** funnel-shaped

infuriate: 4 urge, wild; **5** annoy, fiery; **6** enrage, fierce, in a way, madden, savage; **7** envenom, furious, in a fury, in a rage, incense, inflame, outrage; **8** convulse, irritate, up in arms; **9** aggravate, enfuriate, in a taking; **10** accelerate, exacerbate, exasperate, infuriated

infuriated: 4 wild; **5** fiery; **6** fierce, in a way, savage; **7** angered, enraged, furious, in a fury, in a rage; **8** maddened, up in arms; **9** in a taking, infuriate

infuse: 4 brew; **5** imbue, infix, steep; **6** imbrue; **7** instill, suffuse; **8** tincture; **9** inculcate, inoculate, transfuse; **10** impregnate, infiltrate

infused: 9 implanted, instilled; **10** inculcated

infusion: 4 dash, drip, flux; **5** smack, spice, tinge, touch; **7** extract, soupcon; **8** tincture; **9** seasoning; **10** sprinkling; **11** importation

ingathering: 4 levy; **6** appeal; **8** assembly; **9** compiling, gathering; **10** assembling, collecting, collection; **11** compilation

in general: 7 at large; **8** as a whole; **9** generally, in the main

ingenious: 6 adroit, clever; **7** cunning; **8** masterly; **9** inventive, masterful; **11** imaginative

ingenue: 4 naif; **5** naive; **10** jeune veuve [Fr]

ingenuity: 6 genius; **9** genius for; **10** cleverness; **13** ingeniousness, inventiveness

ingenuous: 5 frank; 6 candid; 7 artless, sincere; 8 innocent; 9 guileless, outspoken

ingest: 4 have, take; 6 absorb, take in; 7 consume; 10 assimilate

ingesta: 4 food, grub; 7 aliment, edibles, pabulum; 8 eatables, victuals; 9 nutriment, provender; 10 sustenance; 11 comestibles, nourishment; 12 alimentation, sustentation

ingle: 5 angle; 6 corner; 9 fireplace

inglenook: 6 hearth; 9 ingle side; 13 chimney corner

inglorious: 8 recreant, shameful; 11 disgraceful, ignominious, opprobrious; 12 dishonorable

ingoing: 8 entering

ingot: 3 bar; 4 gold; 6 copper, nugget, silver; 7 bullion; 8 metal bar

ingrain: 3 dye; 4 tint, wash; 5 grain, imbue, paint, stain, tinge; 7 bedizen, impress, instill; 8 emblazon; 10 illuminate, infiltrate

ingrained: 6 inborn, inbred, innate; 7 planted; 9 implanted, inwrought; 10 deep-rooted, deep-seated

ingraining: 10 instilling; 11 inculcation

ingrate: 9 thankless

ingratiating: 7 winning; 12 ingratiatory

ingredient: 6 factor, leaven; 7 element; 9 component; 11 constituent; 12 subcomponent

ingress: 5 entry; 8 entering, entrance, incoming; 10 ingression

ingroup: 4 camp, pack; 6 clique; 7 coterie; 11 inner circle

ingrowing: 7 ingrown

ingrown: 9 ingrowing, withdrawn

ingurgitate: 4 glut; 5 binge, gorge, stuff; 6 englut, guzzle, pig out; 7 engorge, overeat, satiate, snuff up, swallow; 8 scarf out; 9 overgorge; 10 gormandise, gormandize; 11 gourmandize, overindulge

inhabit: 4 live, stay; 5 abide, dwell, lodge, perch, roost, shack; 6 nestle, occupy, people, reside, tenant; 7 sojourn; 8 populate

inhabitant: 7 denizen, dweller; 8 habitant, resident

inhabitants: 9 citizenry; 10 population

inhabited: 7 peopled; 8 populous; 9 populated

inhalation: 8 sniffing, snorting; 11 breathing in, inspiration

inhale: 4 nose; 5 sniff, snort; 9 breathe in

inhaler: 9 inhalator

in hand: 5 by one; 6 coming, on hand; 7 at issue, in train; 8 in embryo, on the way; 9 in dispute; 10 in progress, in question, near at hand; 11 forthcoming, in agitation, in one's hands; 12 under control

in handwriting: 6 by hand

inharmonic: 9 dissonant; 10 discordant

inharmonious: 9 unmatched, unrelated; 10 discordant; 12 incompatible, unharmonious

in harmony: 5 as one; 6 united; 8 agreeing,

cemented, harmonic, in accord; 9 congenial, consonant, of one mind; 10 concordant, harmonical, harmonious, harmonized; 11 harmonizing, in agreement; 12 harmoniously

inherent: 7 built-in, inbuilt; 8 integral; 9 intrinsic; 10 congenital, implicit in, in the grain, underlying

inherit: 8 come into; 15 receive a bequest

inheritable: 9 heritable

inheritance: 6 legacy; 7 bequest, descent; 8 heredity, heritage; 9 patrimony, reversion

inheritance tax: 8 death tax; 9 death duty, estate tax

inherited: 6 inborn; 7 genetic; 8 familial; 9 incarnate; 10 congenital, hereditary; 11 transmitted; 13 transmissible

inheritor: 4 heir; 7 heiress [female], heritor, legatee; 10 inheritrix [female]; 11 inheritress [female]

inhibit: 4 curb; 6 hinder, impede, subdue; 7 conquer; 8 restrict, suppress; 9 embarrass, stamp down; 10 antagonize, filibuster [U.S.]

inhibited: 7 impeded; 8 hindered; 10 obstructed, restricted

inhibiting: 10 inhibitory, repressing, repressive

inhibition: 3 ban; 8 impeding; 9 hindering, hindrance, renitency; 10 antagonism, resistance; 11 prohibition, suppression; 12 disallowance, interdiction, interference, proscription

in hiding: 7 runaway; 8 fugitive, in ambush, on the lam; 10 in disguise, out of sight

inhomogeneous: 10 nonuniform

inhuman: 4 cold; 5 cruel; 6 brutal, savage; 7 brutish; 8 barbaric, inhumane; 9 barbarous, insensate, malicious, malignant; 11 cold-blooded; 12 semibarbaric

inhumanity: 8 atrocity, ferocity, savagery; 9 barbarity, brutality; 12 inhumaneness

inhuman treatment: 7 cruelty

inhumation: 6 burial; 9 interment, sepulture; 10 entombment

inhume: 4 bury; 5 inter

inimical: 5 cross; 7 hostile; 10 unfriendly; 12 unpropitious

inimitable: 9 matchless; 11 unparagoned; 12 unparalleled

iniquitous: 4 vile; 5 wrong; 6 sinful, wicked; 7 immoral, ungodly, vicious; 8 criminal, depraved; 11 unrighteous; 12 unprincipled

iniquity: 3 sin; 4 dark, evil; 8 darkness, foul play; 9 injustice; 10 immorality, unfairness, wickedness

initial: 5 first, alpha; 9 incipient; 10 initiative, initiatory

initialize: 6 format

initially: 7 at first; 8 ab initio; 10 at the start

initial public offering: 3 IPO

initiate: 5 start; **6** broach, induct, launch, lead up, novice, pundit, savant; **7** pioneer; **8** beginner; **9** initiated, originate; **10** inaugurate; **11** enlightened

initiated: 6 primed; **7** trained; **8** finished, initiate, prepared

initiation: 6 outset; **7** grammar, opening, three Rs, trigger; **8** creation, founding; **9** beginning, inception, induction; **10** foundation, incipience; **11** institution, origination; **12** commencement, installation

initiative: 4 move; **5** first; **6** maiden, recall; **7** go-ahead, initial, opening; **9** first move, first step, inaugural; **10** enterprise, initiatory, plebiscite, referendum

initiator: 5 mover; **7** founder; **9** generator; **10** instigator

initiatory: 5 first; **6** maiden; **7** initial; **9** inaugural; **10** initiative

inject: 5 prick, put in, shoot, stick; **6** come in; **7** throw in; **9** interject, interpose

injecting drugs: 10 shooting up

injection: 4 shot; **9** injectant, injecting

in jeopardy: 6 at risk; **7** at peril, in peril; **8** at hazard, in danger; **9** imperiled; **10** endangered, threatened

injudicious: 4 dumb; **5** silly; **6** stupid, unwise; **7** asinine, foolish; **8** improper; **9** ill-judged; **10** ill-advised, ill-devised; **11** ill-imagined; **12** unreasonable

injudiciously: 8 unwisely; **9** foolishly; **12** unreasonably

injunction: 6 charge; **8** estoppel [Law]; **9** direction, directive, enjoining; **10** enjoinment; **11** instruction

injure: 4 harm, hurt; **5** spite, wound; **6** damage, offend; **8** do harm to; **11** cause harm to

injured: 7 damaged; **9** aggrieved

injured party: 8 casualty

injurious: 4 evil; **7** baleful, baneful, harmful, hurtful, noxious; **8** tortious [Law]; **10** pernicious; **11** deleterious, detrimental, mischievous

injury: 4 harm, hurt; **5** wound, wrong; **6** damage, trauma; **8** foul play; **9** detriment, vitiation, worsening; **10** debasement, impairment

injustice: 8 inequity, iniquity; **10** unfairness, unjustness

ink: 4 sign; **6** pastel

inkberry: 8 pokeweed

ink bottle: 6 ink pot, inkpot; **7** ink horn, ink well; **8** ink stand

inking pad: 3 pad; **6** inkpad; **8** stamp pad

ink-jet printer: 6 ink-jet

inkling: 6 notion; **7** glimpse, longing; **9** hankering, suspicion; **10** impression, intimation

inkpad: 3 pad; **8** stamp pad; **9** inking pad

ink slinger: 4 hack; **9** potboiler; **10** hack writer; **11** penny a liner

inky: 4 dark, ebon, sable; **6** somber; **8** ink-black; **9** inky-black

inland sea: 5 sound

inlay: 6 veneer

inlet: 4 cove, door, lips; **5** chops, fiord, firth, fjord, mouth, porch; **6** portal, recess; **7** estuary, orifice, portico

in lieu of: 9 in place of

in love: 4 gaga; **5** crazy, dotty; **6** soft on; **7** smitten; **8** enamored; **9** taken with; **10** infatuated

inmate: 3 con, POW; **6** detenu [Fr]; **7** captive, convict, hostage; **8** detainee, gaolbird, jail bird, jailbird, prisoner; **9** incumbent, inpatient

inmost: 9 innermost

in motion: 6 moving; **9** traveling

inn: 5 hotel, lodge; **6** hostel, tavern; **8** hostelry

innards: 7 viscera; **8** entrails

innate: 4 born; **6** inborn; **9** ingrained, inwrought, unlearned; **10** congenital

inner: 6 inside, inward; **8** interior, internal, intimate

inner circle: 4 camp, pack; **6** clique; **7** coterie, ingroup

inner coating: 6 lining

inner ear: 9 labyrinth; **11** internal ear

inner force: 5 force; **6** energy

innermost: 6 inmost

innersole: 6 insole

inning: 5 frame

innings: 6 income; **7** revenue; **8** pickings, winnings; **9** incomings

innkeeper: 4 host; **11** hotel keeper

innocent: 2 OK; **3** sop; **4** baby, okay; **5** child; **6** benign, infant; **7** milksop, neutral, sinless; **8** harmless, ignorant; **9** guiltless, impeccant, ingenuous, innocuous, not guilty; **11** clean-handed, inoffensive, uninjurious

innoculate: 8 immunize; **9** inoculate, vaccinate

innocuous: 2 OK; **4** okay; **6** benign; **7** neutral; **8** harmless, innocent; **11** inoffensive, uninjurious

innominate: 7 unnamed; **8** nameless; **9** anonymous

innominate bone: 7 hipbone

innovate: 9 introduce

innovation: 6 design; **9** invention; **10** conception; **12** excogitation

innovative: 6 modern; **8** advanced

innovator: 7 pioneer

in no way: 5 nohow

innuendo: 4 hint; **7** sarcasm; **11** insinuation

innumerable: 6 myriad; **8** infinite; **9** countless, uncounted; **10** innumerous, numberless, unnumbered; **11** illimitable, unnumerable; **12** immeasurable, incalculable, interminable, unfathomable, unnumberable

inobservance: 6 laches [Law]; **7** evasion, failure, neglect; **8** omission

Inocor: 8 amrinone

inoculate: 4 bias, sway; **5** imbue, infix; **6** imbrue, infuse; **7** dispose, incline, instill; **8** immunize; **9** inculcate, influence, vaccinate, weigh with; **10** impregnate, infiltrate, innoculate, predispose

inoculating: 11 vaccinating

inoculation: 4 shot; **11** inculcation, vaccination; **12** immunization

inodorous: 8 odorless; **9** onodorate

inoffensive: 2 OK; **4** okay; **6** savory; **7** neutral, savoury; **8** innocent; **9** innocuous; **11** euphemistic, unoffending

in one ear: 8 to one ear; **10** monaurally

inoperable: 8 unusable

inopportune: 8 timeless; **9** intrusive

in order: 2 so; **6** in trim; **9** called for

inordinate: 5 undue; **6** lavish, wanton; **7** profuse, replete; **8** overmuch, swinging; **9** excessive, exuberant; **10** exorbitant, immoderate, outrageous; **11** extravagant; **12** preposterous, unreasonable

inorganic: 9 inanimate

inosculation: 7 joining, uniting, mortise; **11** anastomosis

in ovo: 8 in embryo

in pain: 6 aching; **7** in agony; **8** smarting; **9** suffering

in part: 6 partly; **9** partially

inpatient: 6 inmate

in peril: 6 at risk; **7** at peril; **8** at hazard, in danger; **9** imperiled; **10** endangered, in jeopardy, threatened

in person: 10 in the flesh, personally

in petto: 5 close, privy; **7** private; **8** secretly; **9** auricular, inviolate; **11** clandestine

in place: 6 in situ; **10** in position

in plain view: 5 clear, plain; **7** glaring, staring; **8** apparent, definite, distinct; **10** above board, face to face, in full view, on the stage, to one's face, well marked; **11** conspicuous, in open court, well defined

in poor taste: 9 tasteless

inpour: 6 inrush; **9** inpouring

in principle: 8 in theory; **9** in essence

in progress: 5 afoot; **6** in hand; **7** going on, ongoing, running; **8** under way; **9** advancing, happening

in propria persona: 10 personally

in public: 6 openly; **8** publicly; **9** in the open; **10** publically

input: 8 stimulus; **9** stimulant; **11** input signal, stimulation

input-output board: 8 I/O board

inquest: 11 inquisition

inquietude: 5 worry; **6** unease, unrest; **7** anxiety, concern, fidgets; **8** disquiet, edginess;

10 solicitude, uneasiness; **11** disquietude; **12** apprehension, restlessness

inquire: 3 ask; **4** seek; **6** search, wonder; **7** enquire; **11** make inquiry

inquirer: 5 asker; **8** enquirer, examiner; **9** catechist, inspector; **10** inquisitor, questioner; **12** investigator

inquiry: 5 query; **7** enquiry; **8** question, research; **13** investigation

inquisition: 7 inquest

inquisitive: 7 curious; **9** wondering; **11** questioning, speculative

inquisitor: 6 despot, tyrant; **8** examiner, inquirer, martinet, stickler; **9** catechist, inspector, oppressor; **12** interrogator, investigator

inquisitory: 7 probing; **9** searching; **13** inquisitorial

in quod: 6 jailed; **7** in limbo; **8** in chains, in charge, in prison; **9** doing time; **10** imprisoned

in regard to: 4 as to; **7** vis-a-vis; **9** regarding; **10** concerning

in relief: 6 raised; **7** jutting; **8** repousse; **10** jutting out, projecting, protruding, sticking up; **11** protuberant, standing out, sticking out

in remission: 8 arrested

in reply: 4 back

in request: 9 requested

in response: 8 in answer; **12** responsively

inroad: 5 havoc; **6** influx, ravage; **7** outrage; **8** invasion; **9** incursion, intrusion, irruption

inrush: 6 inpour; **8** crowding; **9** inpouring

insalubrious: 9 unhealthy; **11** unhealthful, unwholesome

insane: 3 mad; **4** daft, loco, nuts; **5** batty, crazy, dotty, loony, nutty; **6** crazed, fruity, teched [dialect]; **7** bonkers, cracked, far gone, lunatic, tetched [dialect], touched; **8** demented, deranged, maddened, not right; **10** moonstruck, upper story; **11** harebrained

insane asylum: 6 asylum; **10** mental home; **14** mental hospital

insanely: 5 madly; **6** deadly; **7** crazily; **8** deucedly; **10** dementedly, devilishly

insanitary: 10 unsanitary; **11** unhealthful; **12** contaminated

insanity: 6 lunacy

insatiable: 6 greedy; **7** craving; **8** covetous, grasping, ravenous; **9** insatiate; **10** avaricious, quenchless, unsatiable; **11** acquisitive; **12** unquenchable

inscising: 10 abscission, inscission, rescission

inscribe: 4 code; **5** enrol, enter, grave; **6** blazon, cipher, cypher, encode, enroll; **7** dash

off, encrypt, engrave, lionize, recruit; **8**
encipher, enshrine; **9** autograph
inscribed: 6 etched, graven; **7** incised; **8**
engraved
inscription: 5 entry; **6** docket; **9** lettering; **10**
memorandum
inscrutable: 4 deep; **7** cryptic; **9** cryptical;
10 mysterious, mystifying; **12** inexplicable
insect: 3 bug
Insecta: 8 Hexapoda; **12** class Insecta; **13**
class Hexapoda
insect bite: 4 bite; **5** sting
insect cry: 5 drone
insect-eater: 11 insectivore
insect repellent: 11 insectifuge; **15** insect
repellant
insecure: 3 bad; **5** risky; **6** unsafe; **7** parlous;
8 high-risk, perilous, unstable; **9** dangerous, hazardous; **10** precarious; **11** speculative
insecurity: 4 risk; **5** peril; **6** danger, hazard; **7**
venture; **8** jeopardy; **9** self-doubt
inseminate: 3 sow; **5** sow in; **9** fertilize
insensate: 4 cold, wild; **5** giddy, inept, rabid,
silly; **6** brutal, doting, raving; **7** berserk,
blatant, fatuous, foolish, frantic, idiotic,
inhuman; **8** babbling, frenetic, frenzied,
imbecile, rambling, unhinged, wild-eyed; **9**
delirious, driveling, possessed, senseless,
wandering; **10** incoherent, insentient, irrational, reasonless
insensible: 9 senseless, unfeeling; **10** unaffected; **12** undetectable
insensitive: 6 obtuse
insentient: 9 insensate
inseparable: 9 severable; **12** indissoluble,
inextricable
in series: 6 in a row; **7** in a line, lined up; **8**
serially, seriatim
insert: 4 post, tuck; **5** cut-in, enter, infix,
inset, put in; **6** post up, slip in; **7** enclose,
inclose, sneak in, stick in; **9** introduce
inserted: 5 put in; **7** entered, put into; **8**
logged in; **10** introduced, placed into
inset: 6 gusset, insert
in shape: 6 in trim; **11** in condition; **13** physically fit
inshore: 7 onshore, seaward
in short: 7 briefly, in a word, in brief,
shortly; **9** concisely, in epitome
inside: 2 in; **5** inner; **6** indoor, inward,
within; **7** at heart, indoors; **8** at bottom,
deep down, inside of, interior, inwardly; **9**
inclosure
insidious: 4 dark; **6** subtle, tricky; **7** crooked,
elusive; **8** slippery, tortuous; **10** pernicious;
11 underhanded
in sight: 6 in view; **7** visible; **10** in full view,
in prospect; **11** discernible, perceivable,
perceptible

insight: 3 ken; **9** brainwave; **10** brainstorm,
experience, sixth sense; **11** familiarity, penetration; **12** acquaintance, perceptivity
insightfulness: 6 acumen
insignia: 7 insigne
insignificant: 4 so-so; **5** small; **6** little,
peanut; **7** trivial; **9** invisible, unmeaning;
10 negligible; **11** unimportant; **12** undetectable
insincere: 6 hollow; **7** canting, stilted; **8**
affected; **9** pretended, unnatural; **10** artificial, not natural
insincerity: 4 cant; **6** humbug; **9** falseness,
hypocrisy
insinuate: 7 suggest; **9** introduce
insinuation: 7 sarcasm; **8** allusion, innuendo;
9 intrusion, obtrusion
insipid: 4 flat, slow; **5** bland, vapid; **6** jejune,
stupid; **7** humdrum; **9** savorless, tasteless;
10 flavorless, monotonous; **11** flavourless
insist: 6 assert, demand; **7** contend; **9** importune; **11** lay stress on; **14** take a firm stand
insistence: 5 claim, press; **6** demand; **8** exaction, instancy, pressure; **9** insisting; **10**
imposition, insistency; **11** reclamation, requisition
insistent: 6 crying; **7** clamant, exigent,
instant; **9** demanding; **10** repetitive
insist upon: 7 dwell on; **8** insist on; **9** stipulate
in situ: 6 in loco; **7** unmoved, in place
insobriety: 11 drunkenness, inebriation; **12**
intoxication
insolation: 8 siriasis; **9** sunstroke; **12** thermic
fever
insolence: 4 gall; **5** crust; **9** arrogance, freshness, impudence; **10** cheekiness; **11** haughtiness; **12** impertinence
insolent: 4 flip; **6** brassy, brazen; **7** haughty;
8 arrogant, impudent; **9** arbitrary, audacious, barefaced, bodacious, bold-faced,
imperious
insoluble: 9 infusible; **12** indissoluble
insolvable: 9 insoluble, unsoluble; **10**
unsolvable; **12** unresolvable
insolvency: 10 bankruptcy
insolvent: 4 stag; **6** debtor; **8** bankrupt,
gazetted, lame duck; **9** defaulter
insomniac: 8 watchful; **9** sleepless
insouciance: 9 unconcern; **11** nonchalance;
12 carefreeness
insouciant: 6 casual; **9** easygoing, sans
souci [Fr], unworried; **10** nonchalant,
phlegmatic; **11** unconcerned; **12** devil-
may-care
inspect: 4 scan; **5** audit, visit; **6** review, survey; **10** scrutinize
inspection: 6 review; **8** scrutiny; **11** examination
inspector: 8 examiner, inquirer; **9** catechist;
10 inquisitor; **12** investigator
inspiration: 5 flash, geist [Ger], spurt;

6 genius, ground, motive, reason; 7 impulse, purpose, unction; 8 adoption, afflatus, stirring; 9 imagining, inventing, invention, reason why, salvation; 10 brainchild, conversion, impression, inhalation, motivation, revelation of action

inspire: 4 goad, move, spur, urge; 5 cheer, edify, elate, exalt, impel, pep up, smite, touch; 6 affect, excite, exhort, incite, infect, prompt, strike, urge on; 7 animate, barrack, convert, enliven, gladden, impress; 8 inspirit, interest, spirit up; 9 impassion, instigate, stimulate; 10 exhilarate, invigorate, regenerate

inspired: 5 moved; 6 divine; 7 adopted, elected, elysian, excited, smitten, striken, touched; 8 affected, animated; 9 converted, impressed, justified, unearthly; 10 interested, sanctified; 11 consecrated, impassioned, regenerated

inspirit: 5 cheer, elate, nerve, rally; 6 spirit; 7 animate, enliven, gladden, inspire; 8 embolden, reassure, spirit up; 9 encourage; 10 exhilarate, invigorate

inspirited: 6 piqued; 7 stirred; 8 worked up; 9 stirred up

inspissation: 7 setting; 8 gelation; 10 thickening; 11 congelation

in sport: 6 at play, in jest, in joke, in play; 8 jocosely, jokingly; 9 jestingly

inst: 7 instant

instability: 9 imbalance, unbalance; 12 unstableness

in stages: 7 in steps; 8 bit by bit, stepwise; 9 piecemeal

install: 4 post, seat; 5 chair, put in, set up; 6 induct, instal, invest; 7 station, swear in; 9 establish; 10 inaugurate

installation: 8 facility; 9 induction; 10 initiation, installing, settlement; 11 installment; 12 inauguration, presentation; 13 establishment

installment: 7 episode; 8 dividend; 10 installing, instalment; 12 installation; 15 periodic payment

installment buying: 8 time plan; 12 hire-purchase; 15 installment plan

installment rate: 11 payment rate; 13 rate of payment, repayment rate

instance: 4 case; 6 sample; 7 dictate, example; 8 entreaty, specimen; 9 exemplify, prompting; 10 illustrate, invocation; 11 importunity; 12 illustration

instancy: 9 immediacy; 10 insistence, insistency

instant: 4 inst, near, spry, wink; 5 flash, jiffy, quick, trice; 6 abrupt, actual, at hand, crying, extant, minute, moment, prompt, second, sudden, that is, urgent; 7 clamant, current, exigent, present; 8 critical, existing, pressing; 9 absorbing, immediate, insistent, momentary, twinkling; 11 expe-

ditious, precipitant, precipitate, precipitous, split second

instantaneous: 6 abrupt, sudden; 7 instant; 9 immediate, momentary; 11 precipitant, precipitate, precipitous

instanter: 6 presto; 8 in a trice, suddenly; 9 at a stroke

instantly: 3 now; 6 at once; 8 directly, in a flash, outright; 9 forthwith, right away; 10 in real time; 11 immediately; 12 straightaway

instant photo: 8 Polaroid; 13 Polaroid photo

instate: 5 endow; 6 invest, bestow, confer; 7 install

instauration: 8 creation, founding; 10 foundation, initiation; 11 institution, origination, restoration

instead: 6 or else, rather

instigate: 5 set on; 6 foment, incite, prompt, set off, stir up; 7 actuate, animate, inspire, provoke

instigative: 8 incitive; 9 seditious; 10 incendiary; 12 inflammatory

instigator: 7 inciter; 8 agitator, prompter, provoker; 9 firebrand, initiator, instigant; 10 incendiary

instill: 5 imbue, infix; 6 imbrue, infuse, instil; 7 impress, ingrain; 8 tincture, 9 inculcate, inoculate; 10 impregnate, infiltrate

instinct: 5 hunch; 6 imbued; 7 feeling; 9 intuition; 11 premonition; 12 blind impulse, presentiment

instinctive: 5 blind; 9 automatic, intuitive, reflexive; 10 mechanical; 11 instinctual, involuntary

institute: 5 bring, found, plant, set up; 6 broach; 8 organize; 9 establish, originate; 10 constitute

institution: 8 creation, founding; 9 institute, ordinance, reading in; 10 foundation, holy orders, initiation, ordination, preferment, regulation; 11 association, origination, translation

institution not for profit: 9 non-profit

in stock: 7 in store

in store: 6 coming, to come; 7 in stock; 8 upcoming; 9 in reserve; 10 in ordinary

instruct: 3 bid; 4 call; 5 edify, learn, teach, tutor; 6 charge, enjoin, school; 7 apprise, apprize, educate, enforce

instructed: 6 taught; 7 erudite, learned, trained, tutored; 8 educated, lettered, schooled

instructee: 7 student

instruction: 6 charge; 7 command, tuition; 8 pedagogy, teaching, tutelage, tutorage, tutoring; 9 direction, directive, education, statement; 10 injunction; 11 edification

instruction manual: 12 instructions

instructions: 10 directions
instructive: 8 didactic; 11 educational, informative; 12 enlightening; 13 instructional
instructor: 7 teacher, trainer
instrument: 4 tool; 6 device; 9 implement; 13 legal document
instrumentalist: 6 player; 8 musician
instrument panel: 5 board, panel; 12 control board, control panel
insubordinate: 9 resistant, resistive; 11 disobedient, uncompliant, uncomplying
insubstantial: 6 flimsy, jejune, unreal; 7 shadowy; 8 gimcrack, gossamer, illusory
in succession: 6 in turn
insufferable: 5 gross; 7 fulsome; 9 abhorrent, loathsome, repugnant, repulsive; 10 impossible; 11 intolerable; 12 unacceptable, unsufferable
insufficient: 9 deficient, not enough, too little; 10 inadequate
insular: 4 free; 5 apart, loose; 6 adrift; 7 asunder, seagirt; 8 discrete, isolated, separate; 9 disparate, parochial, unannexed; 10 far between, unattached; 11 unconnected; 12 unassociated
insulate: 7 isolate; 8 set apart; 9 keep apart, segregate
insulating material: 8 insulant; 10 insulation
insulating tape: 12 friction tape
insulin reaction: 12 insulin shock
insult: 5 abuse, wound; 6 offend, vilify; 7 affront, offense, outrage; 8 dishonor; 9 call names, contumely; 10 revilement
insulted: 6 dissed; 9 affronted; 11 disregarded; 12 disrespected
insulting: 7 abusive; 8 scornful; 9 provoking, slighting, vilifying; 10 affronting, belittling, derogatory, detracting, detractive, disdainful, irritating, pejorative, scurrilous; 11 deprecatory, disparaging
insupportable: 11 intolerable, unwarranted; 12 indefensible, insufferable
insurance: 6 policy; 8 coverage; 9 indemnity
insurance agent: 5 agent; 6 broker
insurance company: 7 insurer
insurance policy: 6 policy; 9 insurance
insure: 3 see; 5 check, cover; 6 accept, assure, ensure, secure; 7 control, indorse, see to it; 9 ascertain, guarantee; 10 underwrite
insurgency: 6 emeute [Fr], revolt, rising; 8 outbreak, uprising; 9 rebellion; 12 insurrection
insurgent: 5 rebel; 7 riotous; 8 guerilla, mutineer, mutinous, partisan; 9 guerrilla, irregular, seditions, seditious; 10 subversive
insurrection: 6 revolt, rising; 8 outbreak, uprising; 9 rebellion; 10 insurgency

insurrectionist: 5 rebel; 8 mutineer; 9 insurgent; 13 revolutionary
in suspense: 4 edgy; 5 jumpy, nervy; 7 jittery, nervous, restive, uptight; 10 highstrung, in abeyance, overstrung
intact: 5 sound, uncut; 6 entire; 7 unshorn; 8 integral, unbroken; 9 inviolate, uncropped, undivided
intaglio: 4 seal; 5 punch; 8 diaglyph
intake: 6 uptake; 9 air intake, ingestion; 11 consumption
intangible: 10 evanescent, impalpable; 11 nonphysical
in tears: 9 lacrymose; 10 lachrymose
integer: 5 whole; 8 ensemble, entirety, totality; 11 whole number
integral: 5 total, whole; 6 entire, fluent, intact; 7 built-in, inbuilt; 8 inherent; 11 exponential, logarithmic
integral part: 7 element; 9 component; 11 constituent
integrate: 3 mix; 5 amass; 6 embody; 8 assemble; 11 desegregate, incorporate, put together
integrated: 5 mixed; 6 merged; 7 unified; 10 structured; 11 amalgamated, incorporate; 12 incorporated, intermingled
integrated circuit: 12 microcircuit
integrated data processing: 3 IDP
integrator: 10 planimeter
integrity: 5 unity; 7 probity; 9 principle, propriety, rectitude, wholeness; 11 uprightness
intellect: 3 wit; 4 mind, wits; 6 reason; 12 intellectual; 13 understanding
intellection: 7 thought; 8 thinking; 9 mentation, reasoning; 10 conception; 11 cerebration
intellectual: 6 mental; 7 thinker; 8 cerebral, rational; 9 intellect; 10 learned man
intelligence: 3 wit; 4 news, word; 6 advice; 7 message, tidings; 8 capacity, keenness; 11 piece of news; 13 comprehension, understanding
intelligence agent: 3 spy; 9 operative; 11 secret agent
intelligence quotient: 2 IQ [acron]
intelligence test: 6 IQ test
intelligent: 4 keen; 5 sharp, sound; 6 brainy, bright; 7 healthy; 8 thinking; 9 reasoning; 11 levelheaded; 12 well-informed
intelligible: 9 graspable; 11 perceivable; 13 apprehensible; 14 comprehensible, understandable
intelligibly: 7 clearly
intemperance: 8 guzzling, imbibing, potation; 10 free living, good living, high living, wild living
intemperately: 4 hard; 7 heavily
intend: 4 mean; 5 think; 6 design; 7 destine, purpose, signify, specify; 8 stand for; 9 designate

intended: 5 meant; 7 advised, express; 10 deliberate; 11 determinate, intentional

intense: 4 arch, deep, full, high; 5 acute, crass, gross, heavy, sound, vivid; 6 active, bright, strong; 7 passing, plenary; 8 forcible, profound, vigorous; 9 energetic; 10 consummate

intensely: 5 ultra [Lat]; 7 acutely; 8 strongly; 9 with vigor; 10 vigorously; 11 exceedingly, exquisitely, intensively

intensify: 6 deepen, step up; 7 enhance, magnify, sharpen; 8 compound, escalate, heighten, redouble

intension: 5 sense; 11 connotation

intensity: 5 force, might, vigor; 6 chroma, degree, extent, volume; 8 fullness, loudness, strength; 9 vividness; 10 saturation

intensively: 8 strongly; 9 intensely, with vigor; 10 vigorously

intent: 3 aim; 4 rapt; 5 fixed; 6 design, spirit; 7 purport, purpose, resolve, wrapped; 8 absorbed; 9 engrossed, enwrapped, intention

intention: 3 aim, end; 4 goal; 6 design, intent, object; 7 purpose, resolve; 9 objective

intentional: 5 meant; 6 wilful; 7 advised, express, knowing, willful; 8 designed, intended; 10 deliberate; 11 determinate

intentionally: 8 by choice, by design; 9 advisedly, expressly, knowingly, on purpose, purposely, wittingly; 10 designedly, with design, with intent; 11 puposefully

inter: 4 bury; 6 entomb; 9 lay to rest

interactive: 11 synergistic

interbred: 6 hybrid; 7 crossed; 9 crossbred; 12 intercrossed

intercalary year: 8 leap year

intercede: 6 liaise; 7 mediate; 9 arbitrate, interfere, interpose, intervene

intercept: 3 bug, tap; 4 stop; 7 wiretap; 9 interrupt

intercession: 6 orison, prayer; 7 protest; 8 judgment, rogation; 9 atonement, mediation, salvation; 10 invocation, redemption; 11 deprecation; 12 interference, intervention

intercessor: 8 mediator; 10 arbitrator

interchange: 4 flip, swap; 6 change, switch; 8 exchange, flip-flop, swapping; 9 alternate, transpose

interchangeable: 6 mutual; 7 similar; 10 reciprocal; 11 commutative, convertible; 12 exchangeable, standardized

intercom speaker: 8 squawker; 9 squawk box

interconnect: 9 interlink

intercontinental ballistic missile: 4 ICBM

interdenominational: 11 interchurch

interdict: 3 ban, bar; 4 veto; 5 taboo; 6 enjoin, forbid, outlaw; 8 disallow, forefend, prohibit; 9 proscribe

interdiction: 3 ban; 9 interdict; 10 inhibition; 11 prohibition

interdigitate: 5 fit in; 9 interlace, interline, interlink, intersect, squeeze in; 10 intertwine

interest: 4 move, sake, weal; 5 favor, share, smite, stake, touch, worry; 6 affect, behalf, behoof, excite, infect, occupy, strike; 7 animate, concern, impress, inspire, pastime, service; 8 matter to; 9 curiosity, impassion, patronage; 10 common weal; 11 countenance, curiousness, involvement

interested: 5 moved; 7 excited, smitten, striken, touched; 8 affected, animated, inspired; 9 concerned, impressed; 11 impassioned

interesting: 7 curious; 8 charming, engaging; 10 attractive, bewitching, enchanting; 11 captivating, fascinating

interface: 4 port; 13 user interface

interfere: 6 step in; 7 intrude; 9 come amiss, intercede, interpose, intervene

interference: 5 block, hitch, noise; 8 blocking, impeding; 9 hindering, hindrance, intrusion, renitency; 10 inhibition, preventive, resistance; 11 disturbance, encumbrance, incumbrance, interfering; 12 intercession, intervention, preventative

interfering: 4 busy; 8 clashing, meddling; 9 hindrance, officious; 10 busybodied, meddlesome; 11 conflicting

interim: 3 lag; 5 while; 12 intervention

interior: 4 home; 5 inner; 6 inside; 7 midland; 8 internal, national; 9 inclosure, upcountry; 12 enclosed area

interior decoration: 5 decor; 14 interior design

interior decorator: 8 designer; 9 decorator

Interior Department: 8 Interior

interior designer: 8 designer; 9 decorator

interject: 5 jam in, put in, run in; 6 come in, edge in, import, inject, plow in, work in, worm in; 7 foist in, throw in, wedge in; 9 interpose, introduce

interjection: 11 ejaculation, exclamation

interlace: 4 lace, lock; 5 twine; 6 enlace; 7 entwine; 9 interlink, interlock, intersect; 10 intertwine, interweave

interlaced: 7 fretted; 8 latticed; 10 interwoven; 11 latticelike; 12 interlinked, interlocked

interlard: 10 interweave; 11 intersperse

interline: 5 fit in; 9 squeeze in; 10 sandwich in

interlock: 4 lock, mesh; 7 meshing; 9 interlace; 12 interlocking

interlocutor: 9 middleman; 10 prolocutor

interloper: 8 intruder, newcomer; 10 trespasser

interlude: 8 entr'acte; 10 intermezzo

I

intermeddler: 7 meddler; **8** busybody; **9** intriguer

intermediary: 5 agent; **8** delegate, mediator; **9** go-between, middleman; **10** permeating; **11** intercalary, intervening, penetrating

intermediate: 4 mean; **6** medium, middle; **7** average

intermediate range ballistic missile: 4 IRBM

intermediator: 8 mediator; **9** go-between; **12** intermediary

interment: 6 burial; **9** sepulture; **10** entombment, inhumation

intermeshed: 6 meshed; **7** engaged; **8** enmeshed

intermezzo: 8 entr'acte; **9** interlude

interminable: 7 endless, eternal, no end of; **9** ceaseless, incessant, unceasing; **11** having no end, illimitable, innumerable; **12** immeasurable, incalculable, unfathomable

intermingle: 5 blend; **8** immingle, intermix; **9** commingle

intermingled: 5 mixed; **10** integrated; **11** amalgamated

intermission: 4 drop; **5** break, pause, truce; **7** respite; **10** suspension; **12** interruption

intermit: 5 break, pause, remit; **7** sputter; **8** hesitate; **9** alternate

intermix: 5 blend; **6** commix; **8** immingle; **11** intermingle

intermixture: 7 mixture; **9** matrimony; **10** concoction

intern: 9 internist; **13** medical intern

internal: 4 home; **5** inner; **7** organic; **8** interior, intimate, national; **10** intragroup

internal combustion engine: 12 piston engine

internal ear: 8 inner ear; **9** labyrinth

internally: 6 within; **8** inwardly

internal medicine: 15 general medicine

internal organization: 9 structure; **11** structuring; **12** architecture, organization

internal revenue agent: 6 taxman; **9** exciseman; **12** tax collector

Internal Revenue Service: 3 IRS

internal secretion: 7 hormone

international: 7 outside; **8** external

international affairs: 12 world affairs

International Atomic Energy Agency: 4 IAEA

International Bank for Reconstruction and Development: 4 IBRD; **9** World Bank

international boundary: 6 border; **8** frontier

International Business Machines Corporation: 3 IBM

International Civil Aviation Organization: 4 ICAO

International Court of Justice: 10 World Court

International Date Line: 8 date line

International Development Association: 3 IDA

International Finance Corporation: 3 IFC

International Labor Organization: 3 ILO

international logistic support: 9 mutual aid

International Maritime Organization: 3 IMO

International Monetary Fund: 3 IMF

international Morse code: 5 Morse; **9** Morse code

international nautical mile: 2 mi; **4** knot, mile; **6** naut mi; **7** air mile; **12** nautical mile

international pitch: 12 concert pitch

International Society for Krishna Consciousness: 6 ISKCON; **11** Hare Krishna

International System: 2 SI

internecine feud: 7 faction; **8** outbreak; **11** open rupture

internecine war: 8 civil war

internet: 3 net; **10** cyberspace

internist: 6 intern; **7** interne; **8** houseman; **13** medical intern

internment: 8 poundage; **10** impounding; **11** impoundment; **12** imprisonment

internment camp: 7 POW camp; **10** prison camp

interpellation: 6 appeal; **7** summons; **8** citation, entreaty, instance, subpoena; **10** apostrophe, invocation, salutation; **11** importunity; **12** supplication

interpenetrate: 7 slide in; **8** permeate; **9** intervene

interpolate: 5 alter, jam in, run in; **6** edge in, import, plow in, work in, worm in; **7** falsify, foist in, throw in, wedge in; **9** interject, interpose, introduce

interpose: 5 jam in, put in, run in; **6** come in, edge in, import, inject, plow in, step in, work in, worm in; **7** foist in, throw in, wedge in; **9** intercede, interfere, interject, intervene, introduce; **10** put between; **11** intercalate, intermeddle, interpolate

interpret: 4 read; **6** define, render; **7** explain; **8** construe; **9** represent, translate; **10** understand

interpretation: 7 reading, version; **9** construal, rendering, rendition; **11** explanation, explication; **12** interpreting; **13** understanding

interpreter: 5 voice; **9** explainer, expositor, expounder; **10** translator; **12** spokesperson

interpreting: 9 rendering, rendition

interpretive: 10 expository; **11** explanatory

interracial: 5 mixed

interred: 6 buried; **7** inhumed

interregnum: 8 abeyance

interrelated: 10 correlated; **11** correlative

interrelation: 4 link; **9** mutuality; **10** connection; **11** association, correlation

interrogate: 8 question

interrogation: 8 question; 11 examination
interrogation point: 12 question mark
interrogative: 6 asking; 8 question; 11 questioning; 13 interrogation
interrogator: 10 inquisitor
interrupt: 5 break, pause; 6 cut off; 7 break up, disrupt, disturb, perturb, suspend; 8 intromit; 9 intercept; 11 discontinue
interscholastic: 11 interschool
intersect: 5 cross; 9 interlace, interlink; 10 intertwine, interweave
intersection: 7 overlap, product; 8 crossing, crossway; 9 carrefour, crossroad; 11 convergence
intersperse: 9 interlard; 10 interleave
interspersion: 6 spread
interstellar travel: 11 space travel
interstital cell-stimulating hormone: 2 LH; 4 ICSH; 8 lutropin
interstitial: 10 permeating; 11 intercalary, intervening, penetrating
intertwine: 3 tat; 4 lace, loop; 5 twine; 6 enlace; 7 entwine; 9 interlace, interlink, intersect; 10 interweave
interval: 3 gap; 4 span, time; 5 space; 6 period, remove; 8 distance; 10 separation
intervene: 6 step in; 7 mediate, slide in; 8 minister; 9 intercede, interfere, interpose
intervening time: 5 while; 7 interim; 12 intervention
intervention: 5 while; 7 interim; 9 mediation; 12 intercession, interference
interview: 8 audience, question; 9 reception; 12 consultation
interweave: 5 weave; 9 interlace, interlard, interlink, intersect; 10 intertwine
interwoven: 6 matted; 7 twisted; 11 interlacing; 12 interlinking, interlocking
intestinal: 7 enteral, enteric; 9 intestine
intestinal bacterium: 12 enterobacter
intestinal fortitude: 4 face, guts; 5 spunk; 6 virtue; 9 fortitude, hardihood
intestinal gas: 3 gas; 6 flatus
intestine: 3 gut; 5 bowel, tripe; 7 stomach; 10 intestinal
in the black: 7 solvent; 9 out of debt; 11 all straight
in the buff: 3 raw; 6 peeled; 8 in the raw; 10 stark naked
in the cards: 9 in reserve, in the wind, on the dice; 10 in the cards
in the dumps: 4 glum, grim; 5 sulky; 6 gloomy, grumpy, morose, sullen; 7 grouchy, in a fume; 8 growling, scowling; 9 glowering
in the end: 6 at last; 7 finally; 10 at long last, ultimately
in the final analysis: 10 ultimately
in the flesh: 6 in life; 8 in person
in the future: 5 later; 9 hereafter
in the lead: 5 ahead; 6 before; 7 leading; 8 in the van, out front; 9 in advance

in the near future: 4 anon, soon; 7 betimes, shortly; 9 presently, right away
in the open: 6 openly; 8 in public, publicly; 12 out in the open
in theory: 7 on paper; 9 in essence; 11 in principle; 13 theoretically
in the same boat: 7 en masse; 10 hand in hand, side by side
in the twinkling of an eye: 6 presto; 8 in a trice, suddenly
in the vicinity: 5 about; 6 around, nearby; 9 in the area
in the wind: 8 in the air; 10 in the cards
in thing: 3 fad; 5 craze, thing, trend; 8 last word; 9 bandwagon; 11 latest thing
in this: 6 in that; 7 therein
intimacy: 5 amour; 6 affair; 7 affaire, liaison; 9 closeness; 10 fellowship
intimate: 4 cozy, hint, home, mate; 5 apply, bosom, inner, thick; 6 allude, sexual; 7 comrade, express, let fall, mention, suggest; 8 allude to, confrere, familiar, informal, internal; 9 adumbrate, companion, confidant, insinuate, make known, represent
intimately: 4 well; 6 nearly; 7 closely
intimation: 4 hint; 6 breath; 7 inkling; 10 suggestion
in time: 3 yet; 6 on time, prompt, timely; 8 punctual; 10 eventually, seasonable, soon enough, the long run
intimidate: 3 cow; 5 abash, bully, daunt, deter; 6 hector; 7 dictate, overawe; 8 browbeat, domineer, restrain; 9 terrorize; 10 discourage, lord it over, push around
intimidation: 8 bullying; 9 determent; 10 deterrence
intolerable: 12 insufferable
intolerant: 6 entete [Fr]; 7 bigoted; 8 besotted, confined, dogmatic, positive; 9 conceited, fanatical, high-flown, illiberal, impatient; 10 infatuated; 11 domineering, overbearing
intonation: 4 tone; 5 pitch, twang; 6 accent, timbre; 8 chanting; 11 tone of voice
intone: 4 sing; 5 carol, chant, chirp; 6 chaunt, warble; 7 chirrup; 8 intonate; 10 cantillate
intoned: 8 singsong; 9 chantlike
into the wind: 6 upwind; 14 against the wind
in toto: 5 fully, quite, stark; 6 wholly; 7 totally, utterly; 8 entirely, outright; 10 altogether, completely
in touch: 7 grazing; 8 abutting, touching; 9 adjoining, in contact
intoxicant: 5 drink; 7 alcohol; 9 inebriant; 12 intoxicating
intoxicate: 4 soak; 5 elate; 6 lift up, pick up, uplift; 9 inebriate
intoxicated: 3 cut; 4 high; 5 beery, boozy,

drunk, fresh, merry, tight, tipsy; **6** corned, groggy, primed; **7** drunken, fuddled; **8** elevated, overcome, top-heavy; **9** disguised, flustered, inebriate, overtaken; **10** in one's cups, inebriated

intractable: 5 cross, rusty; **6** cussed [U.S.]; **7** froward; **10** refractory; **12** cantankerous, unmanageable

intragroup: 8 internal

intramural: 4 home; **6** indoor; **8** domestic; **10** vernacular

intransigent: 7 adamant; **10** adamantine, inexorable

in transit: 7 en route; **8** on course, under way; **9** on the road, on the wing

intravenous: 2 i.v. [abbr]

in-tray: 8 in-basket

intrench: 5 fence; **8** entrench

intrenchment: 4 moat; **5** ditch; **7** bulwark; **12** entrenchment

intrepid: 5 brave; **7** gallant; **8** fearless; **9** audacious, dauntless, unfearing

intrepidity: 6 daring, spirit; **8** audacity; **9** gallantry; **10** high spirit

intricacy: 7 meander; **11** elaboration, implication

intricate: 5 kinky; **6** kinked, knotty; **7** knotted, raveled, tangled; **8** involved, tortuous; **9** Byzantine, elaborate, entangled, luxuriant, perplexed; **10** convoluted; **11** complicated

intricately: 11 elaborately

intrigue: 4 plot; **5** cabal, rivet; **6** absorb, scheme; **7** connive, engross, faux pas [Fr]; **9** fascinate, mesmerize; **10** conspiracy

intriguing: 9 designing; **10** contriving; **11** challenging, maneuvering

in trim: 7 in order, in shape; **11** in condition

intrinsic: 8 inherent; **11** intrinsical

intrinsically: 5 per se; **6** as such

intrinsic part: 4 core, gist, pith; **5** heart; **6** marrow; **9** basic part, vital part

intrinsic value: 5 value, worth

introduce: 4 head, lead; **5** enter, infix, jam in, put in, run in; **6** edge in, herald, import, insert, plow in, work in, worm in; **7** be first, bring in, enclose, foist in, inclose, preface, premise, present, stick in, throw in, usher in, wedge in; **8** acquaint, bring out, innovate, intromit; **9** come first, interject, interpose; **10** inaugurate

introduced: 5 put in; **7** put into; **8** inserted; **10** placed into

introduction: 5 debut, entry, intro, proem; **6** prefix; **7** preface, prelude; **8** foreword, preamble, prologue; **9** induction, inserting, insertion, launching, prolepsis [Gram], unveiling

introductory: 5 basic; **9** inaugural, inceptive, incipient, prefatory

intromission: 9 insertion; **11** penetration; **12** introduction

Intropin: 8 dopamine, Dopastat

introspection: 5 study

introspective: 6 sedate; **7** pensive, wistful; **8** Platonic, studious; **10** meditative, reflective, thoughtful; **11** introverted, speculative

introvert: 3 shy; **6** invert; **7** subvert; **8** reserved

intrude: 6 invade, irrupt; **7** obtrude; **8** trespass; **9** come amiss, interfere

intruder: 8 newcomer; **9** novus homo [Lat]; **10** interloper, trespasser

intrusion: 6 influx, inroad; **8** invasion, trespass; **9** incursion, irruption, obtrusion, violation; **11** insinuation; **12** encroachment, interference

intrusive: 8 timeless; **11** incongruous, inopportune

intrust: 7 entrust

in truth: 5 truly; **6** really; **8** forsooth, of a truth; **9** in earnest

intuition: 4 feel; **5** grasp, hunch; **7** feeling; **8** instinct; **9** suspicion; **10** feeling for, gut feeling; **11** premonition

intumescence: 8 swelling; **11** tumefaction; **12** intumescency

in turmoil: 7 chaotic; **8** agitated; **9** turbulent; **10** disordered, disorderly

in turn: 9 in its turn; **10** in rotation; **12** in succession, successively

Inuit: 6 Eskimo

inunction: 7 unction; **9** anointing

inundate: 4 slop; **5** flood, swamp, swash; **6** dabble, deluge, drench, splash, stream; **7** slobber; **8** flow over, irrigate, overflow, submerge; **9** surcharge; **13** supersaturate

inundated: 5 awash; **6** afloat; **7** flooded, swamped; **8** engulfed, overcome; **11** overflowing, overpowered, overwhelmed

in unison: 8 in accord, in chorus

inure: 6 harden, season; **10** caseharden

in usable condition: 7 working

in use: 4 busy; **7** engaged; **9** being used

inutile: 7 of no use, useless; **9** of no avail; **12** unprofitable

invade: 6 occupy; **7** intrude; **8** trespass; **9** intrude on; **11** obtrude upon; **12** encroach upon

invader: 10 encroacher

invading: 8 invasive; **9** incursive

invaginate: 9 introvert

in vain: 6 vainly; **10** for nothing; **11** fruitlessly; **12** down the drain, unprofitably

invalid: 4 case; **5** false; **6** shut-in; **7** disable, expired, patient, unsound; **8** handicap; **9** illogical; **12** incapacitate, unreasonable

invalidate: 4 void; **5** annul, avoid, cramp, quash, unfit; **6** cancel, deaden, disarm; **7** explode, nullify, vitiate; **9** overthrow; **10** disqualify

invalidation: 6 sprain, strain; 8 delicacy, disproof; 9 annulment; 10 refutation

invaluable: 9 priceless; 10 above price; 11 beyond price, inestimable

invariable: 5 fixed; 6 steady; 7 routine; 8 constant; 9 clockwork, continual, incessant, incurable, invariant, perpetual, unceasing, unfailing, unvarying; 10 consistent, continuous, monotonous; 11 undeviating

invariably: 6 always; 8 as always, ever anon, steadily; 9 routinely; 10 at all times, constantly; 11 continually, day after day, day and night, incessantly, night and day, perpetually, unfailingly, without fail; 12 consistently, continuously, monotonously

invariant: 6 steady; 8 constant; 9 unvarying; 10 changeless, invariable

invasion: 6 influx, inroad; 9 incursion, intrusion, irruption; 12 encroachment

invasive: 8 invading; 9 incursive; 11 encroaching, trespassing

invective: 5 abuse; 7 vitriol; 9 contumely; 11 objurgation

inveigh: 4 rail

invent: 4 coin; 5 forge; 6 cook up, create, devise, make up; 8 contrive; 9 fabricate, formulate, originate; 10 excogitate; 11 manufacture

invented: 6 forged, made-up; 7 devised, fancied; 8 fabulous; 9 fictional, unfounded; 10 ben trovato [It], fabricated, fictitious, improvised

inventing: 9 imagining, invention; 11 imagination, inspiration

invention: 6 design, device; 7 fiction, forgery, nostrum, receipt; 8 artifice, creation; 9 expedient, imagining, inventing; 10 conception, innovation; 11 contrivance, fabrication, imagination, inspiration

inventive: 7 fertile; 8 creative, original; 9 ingenious; 11 imaginative

inventiveness: 9 ingenuity; 10 cleverness, creativity; 11 originality; 12 creativeness

inventor: 9 artificer; 10 discoverer

inventory: 4 list; 5 stock; 6 armory; 7 armoury, catalog; 9 catalogue, stock list; 11 stocktaking

inverse: 6 invert; 7 reverse; 8 opposite, reversal; 10 reciprocal; 12 retroversion

inversely: 12 reciprocally

inversion: 8 eversion, everting, upending; 9 inverting, reversion; 10 anastrophe, antithesis

invert: 6 go over; 7 capsize, inverse, reverse, subvert; 8 overturn, reversal, turn over

inverted: 8 reversed; 10 anatropous, overturned, upside down; 11 wrong side up; 12 turned around

invest: 3 put; 4 gift, seat, vest; 5 adorn, beset [U.S.], chair, endow, endue, indue, place; 6 clothe, commit, induct; 7 besiege,

empower, install, intrust, swear in; 8 enthrone; 9 give power, sink money; 10 inaugurate, lay siege to, make up a sum, settle upon; 11 confer power, invest money

investigate: 6 look at; 8 look into

investigation: 5 probe; 7 probing; 8 scrutiny; 11 examination

investigative: 11 fact-finding

investigator: 2 PI; 3 tec; 8 examiner, inquirer; 9 catechist, detective, inspector; 10 inquisitor, researcher

investiture: 10 coronation, investment, swearing-in; 12 enthronement

investment: 5 siege; 6 attire; 7 apparel, clothes; 8 clothing, garments; 9 investing; 11 envelopment, investiture

investment banker: 11 underwriter

investment company: 4 fund

investment manager: 11 fund manager

investor: 8 operator; 10 speculator

inveterate: 5 fixed; 6 rooted; 7 chronic; 8 habitual; 9 besetting, confirmed, hackneyed, permanent

inveterately: 11 chronically

invidious: 7 envious; 8 covetous, spiteful; 9 vexatious

in view: 7 in sight, visible; 10 in prospect; 11 discernible, perceivable, perceptible

invigilate: 7 proctor, monitor; 9 supervise

invigorate: 5 brace, exalt, liven, nerve; 7 animate, enliven, inspire, liven up, quicken; 8 energize, inspirit; 10 strengthen; 12 reinvigorate

invincible: 10 dominating, resistless, unbeatable; 11 indomitable

inviolable: 6 secure, strong; 7 private; 8 absolute, esoteric; 9 inviolate; 10 sacrosanct; 11 impregnable, inalienable, infrangible, unalienable; 12 confidential, indefeasible, unassailable, unattackable, unchallenged

inviolate: 5 close, privy; 6 intact; 7 in petto, private; 9 auricular; 10 inviolable, sacrosanct; 11 clandestine

invisible: 7 trivial; 9 unseeable; 13 imperceptible, inconspicuous

invitation: 6 motion; 9 incentive; 10 inducement; 12 invitational

invite: 3 bid, woo; 5 ask in, court, tempt; 6 ask for, pay for, take in; 7 ask over, call for, hold out, receive, solicit

invitee: 5 guest

invite out: 6 ask out; 7 take out

inviting: 6 luring; 7 drawing; 8 alluring, enticing, tempting; 10 attracting, attractive

invocation: 6 appeal, orison, prayer; 8 entreaty, instance, rogation; 10 apostrophe, salutation; 11 importunity

in vogue: 2 in; 6 modish, trendy, with it; 7 a la mode, current, in style; 9 in fashion, prevalent; **10** all the rage, prevailing; **11** fashionable

invoice: 4 bill; **7** account; **12** bill of lading

invoke: 4 pray, stir; **5** evoke, raise; **6** accost, appeal, arouse; **7** bring up, conjure; **8** appeal to, call down, make up to; **9** call forth, conjure up; **10** put forward, supplicate

involuntarily: 7 by force; **8** forcibly, perforce; **11** reluctantly, unwillingly

involuntary: 5 blind; **6** forced; **7** coerced; **8** required; **9** automatic, compelled; **10** compulsory, mechanical, obligatory

involuntary servitude: 7 slavery; **11** enslavement

involute: 5 curve; **6** rolled

involve: 3 ask, lap; **4** need, take; **5** argue, imply, infer; **6** affect, demand, regard; **7** bespeak, call for, perplex, require; **8** allude to, confound, envelope; **9** implicate; **10** complicate; **11** necessitate

involved: 5 kinky, mired; **6** kinked, knotty; **7** crabbed, knotted, raveled, tangled; **8** confused, tortuous; **9** Byzantine, entangled, intricate, perplexed; **10** convoluted, incumbered; **11** complicated

involvement: 6 affair; **7** affaire, liaison; **8** interest, intimacy; **10** engagement; **12** entanglement; **13** participation

invulnerable: 11 impregnable

inward: 2 in; **5** inner; **6** inside; **7** inbound, inwards; **8** arriving

inwardness: 3 nub, sum; **4** core, gist, meat, pith; **5** heart; **6** center, kernel, marrow; **7** essence; **9** substance; **11** nitty-gritty

inwards: 2 in; **6** inward

in working order: 6 usable; **7** useable; **8** operable; **10** functional; **11** operational

in writing: 7 graphic, on paper, written; **9** graphical

inwrought: 6 innate; **9** ingrained; **10** ornamented

iodine: 1 I; **5** iodin

iodize: 6 iodise

ionic: 7 ionized

ionized: 5 ionic

iota: 3 ace, bit, jot; **4** hint, mite, whit; **5** shred, trace; **6** morsel, smidge, tittle; **7** modicum, smidgen, smidgin; **8** smidgeon; **9** scintilla

IOU: 14 promissory note

Ioway: 4 Iowa

ipecac: 11 ipecacuanha

Ipomoea: 7 manroot; **8** scammony; **9** starglory; **10** moonflower; **11** sweet potato; **12** morning glory, genus Ipomoea

Ir: 7 iridium

Iran: 6 Persia

Iranian: 5 Irani; **7** Persian; **15** Iranian language

Iraq: 4 Irak; **6** Al-Iraq

Iraqi: 5 Iraki

irascibility: 6 spleen, temper; **8** acerbity, tartness; **9** crossness, petulance, procacity, testiness; **10** crabbiness, protervity; **11** grouchiness, quick temper, short temper; **12** captiousness, irritability

irascible: 5 cross, fiery, short, surly, testy; **6** crabby, tetchy, touchy; **7** crabbed; **8** choleric, volatile; **9** hotheaded, irritable; **11** bad-tempered, hot-tempered, ill-tempered

irate: 3 mad; **5** angry, wrath; **6** ireful; **7** angered

ire: 3 ira, pet; **4** bile, fume, tiff; **5** anger, wrath; **6** choler, dander, pucker, taking; **7** ferment, passion; **9** angry mood

Ireland: 4 Eire; **8** Hibernia; **11** Emerald Isle; **13** Irish Republic

Irelander: 11 Irish person

Iridaceae: 10 iris family

iridescence: 6 striae; **10** maculation, polychrome, spottiness; **11** opalescence

iridescent: 7 opaline; **8** nacreous; **9** chatoyant; **10** changeable, opalescent; **11** pearlescent

iridium: 2 Ir

Iridoprocne: 7 swallow; **16** genus Iridoprocne

Iris: 7 Mercury

iris family: 9 Iridaceae

Irish: 8 the Irish; **11** Irish Gaelic, Irish people, Irish whisky; **12** Irish whiskey

Irish language: 14 Celtic language

Irishman: 9 Hibernian

Irish moss: 8 carageen; **9** carrageen; **10** carragheen

irk: 3 bug, vex; **4** faze, flag, gall, jade, tire; **5** annoy, cross, weary, worry; **6** bother; **7** disturb, exhaust, fatigue, mortify, perplex, trouble, wear out; **8** disquiet; **9** disoblige, displease

irksome: 4 dull, slow; **5** ho-hum; **6** boring, stupid; **7** tedious; **8** tiresome, toilsome; **9** deadening, wearisome; **11** troublesome

iron: 2 Fe; **4** firm; **5** chain, irons, steel; **6** chains, ferrum, gritty [U.S.], mangle; **7** adamant, iron out; **8** cast-iron, hot-press; **11** indomitable; **12** branding iron

Iron Chancellor: 8 Bismarck; **11** von Bismarck; **21** Otto von Bismarck

ironclad: 3 ram; **7** monitor; **10** brassbound, imbricated, iron-plated, turret ship, unshakable, watertight; **11** armor plated

iron collar: 7 garotte, garrote; **8** garrotte

iron-handed: 8 absolute, positive; **9** arbitrary, imperious; **10** high-handed, imperative, peremptory

iron horse: 11 steam engine; **15** steam locomotive

ironic: 3 dry, wry; **8** ironical; **9** burlesque, quizzical, sarcastic

ironing: 8 pressing

ironist: 8 satirist
iron lung: 10 respirator; 14 artificial lung
ironmonger: 11 hardwareman
ironmongery: 13 hardware store
iron out: 4 iron; 8 put right; 13 straighten out
iron-plated: 8 ironclad
iron pyrite: 6 pyrite; 9 fool's gold
irons: 4 iron; 5 chain; 6 chains, fetter; 7 shackle, trammel
ironware: 8 hardware; 9 ironwares
irony: 5 chaff; 6 banter, satire; 7 sarcasm; 8 badinage, raillery; 10 persiflage; 13 caustic remark
Iroquois: 9 Iroquoian
irradiate: 3 ray; 9 enlighten
irradiation: 12 radiotherapy
irrational: 5 inept, silly; 7 blatant, fatuous, foolish, idiotic; 8 babbling, imbecile; 9 driveling, insensate, senseless; 11 nonrational, nonsensical; 12 inconsistent
irreality: 9 unreality
irreclaimable: 4 lost; 8 obdurate; 9 reprobate; 11 irreparable, irrevocable; 12 incorrigible, irredeemable, irremediable, irreversible, unredeemable
irreconcilable: 7 hostile; 9 alienated, estranged, repugnant; 11 disaffected
irrecoverable: 6 lapsed, no more, run out; 7 elapsed, expired, extinct, has-been; 8 exploded; 9 blown over, forgotten; 10 antebellum; 11 irreparable, irrevocable; 12 antediluvian, irredeemable, irremediable, irreversible
irrefragable: 9 probative; 10 apodeictic, conclusive; 11 irrefutable, self-evident, unbreakable; 12 unanswerable
irrefutable: 8 positive; 9 probative; 10 apodeictic, conclusive; 11 self-evident; 12 irrefragable, irresistible
irregular: 5 scaly; 6 coarse, fitful, second, uneven, varied; 8 atypical, guerilla, maverick, partisan, scabrous; 9 arbitrary, desultory, guerrilla, insurgent, temporary, uncertain; 10 capricious, nonuniform, unorthodox, unpunctual
irregularity: 5 scale; 9 diversity; 10 coarseness, unevenness; 11 abnormality, uncertainty
irrelevant: 12 inapplicable
irreligion: 8 unbelief; 9 disbelief; 11 godlessness, incredulity, lack of faith, non-religion
irremediable: 9 incurable; 11 irreparable, irrevocable; 12 irreversible
irremovable: 5 fixed; 8 immobile; 9 immovable
irrepressibility: 8 buoyancy; 10 resilience, resiliency
irreproachable: 9 blameless; 10 inculpable
irresistible: 9 probative; 10 apodeictic, conclusive, inevitable, inexorable, resistless;

11 irrefutable, irrevocable, self-evident, unavoidable
irresolute: 8 hesitant; 9 tentative; 10 hesitating, indecisive; 11 half-hearted
irrespective: 8 no matter; 10 regardless; 12 disregarding
irreverent: 4 pert; 5 saucy; 7 aweless, godless, profane; 11 blasphemous, impertinent; 12 sacrilegious
irreversible: 11 irreparable, irrevocable; 12 irredeemable, irremediable
irrevocable: 10 inevitable, inexorable; 11 irreparable, irrevokable, unavoidable
irrigate: 4 slop; 5 water; 6 dabble, deluge, drench; 7 slobber; 8 inundate; 10 shower down
irritability: 6 choler, temper; 8 acerbity, tartness; 9 crossness, fussiness, petulance, procacity, surliness, testiness; 10 crabbiness, protervity; 11 biliousness, fretfulness, grouchiness, peevishness, pettishness
irritable: 5 cross, fiery, surly, techy, testy; 6 crabby, cranky, tetchy, touchy; 7 crabbed, peckish, peevish, pettish; 8 petulant, volatile; 9 excitable, fractious, irascible; 10 nettlesome; 11 bad-tempered, hot-tempered, ill-tempered
irritate: 3 rag, vex; 4 fret, gall, huff, nark, rile, urge; 5 annoy, chafe, devil, get at, get to, pique, sting; 6 bother, gravel, madden, nettle, ruffle; 7 envenom, incense, provoke; 8 convulse; 9 aggravate, infuriate; 10 accelerate, discompose, exacerbate, exasperate
irritated: 5 riled, stung; 6 peeved, pissed, roiled; 7 annoyed, nettled
irritating: 5 harsh, pesky; 6 plaguy, vexing; 7 caustic, galling, mordant, painful, plaguey, teasing; 8 annoying, stinging, virulent; 9 corrosive, insulting, pestering, provoking, stringent, vexatious; 10 bothersome, irritative, mortifying, nettlesome; 11 aggravating
irrupt: 7 intrude
irruption: 6 influx, inroad; 8 invasion; 9 incursion, intrusion
Irtish: 6 Irtysh; 11 Irtish River, Irtysh River
Irvingia: 4 dika; 9 wild mango; 13 genus Irvingia
is: 2 am [1st person sing], be [inf]; 3 are [pl]; 5 being [gerund]
Isere: 10 Isere River
isinglass: 4 mica
Isis: 2 Ra; 6 Osiris
ISKCON: 11 Hare Krishna
Islam: 8 Islamism; 9 Muslim
Islamabad: 17 capital of Pakistan
Islamic: 6 Moslem, Muslim
island: 4 isle
island-dweller: 8 islander

Islas Malvinas: 9 Falklands; **15** Falkland
   Islands
isle: 5 islet; **6** island
ism: 8 doctrine; **10** philosophy
isochronism: 9 synchrony; **11** coexistence,
   synchronism, unity of time; **12** co-
   occurrence, simultaneity;
isochronous: 10 isochronal
isocyclic: 10 homocyclic; **11** carbocyclic
Isoetaceae: 15 quillwort family
isogonal line: 7 isogone; **12** isogonic line
isolate: 8 insulate, set apart; **9** keep apart,
   segregate, sequester; **11** sequestrate
isolated: 5 apart, stray; **6** adrift, single; **7**
   insular, obscure; **8** detached, disjunct,
   marooned, set apart, solitary, stranded; **9**
   insulated, kept apart, scattered, separated;
   10 segregated; **11** quarantined
isolation: 7 privacy; **8** solitude; **9** reclusion,
   seclusion; **10** closing off, quarantine, separation; **11** segregation
isopropyl alcohol: 11 isopropanol
Isoptin: 5 Calan; **9** verapamil
isotonic: 8 assonant; **9** isosmotic
Israel: 4 Zion; **7** Yisrael
Israelites: 7 Hebrews
issue: 3 cut, jet; **4** exit, gush, hold, pour,
   seed, spat, take; **5** breed, brood, ensue,
   heirs, spawn, spout, start, topic, utter,
   yield; **6** arrive, effect, egress, emerge, farrow, litter, matter, number, outlet, payoff,
   put out, result, retail, return, stream, supply, upshot, way out; **7** come out, deal out,
   debouch, dispute, emanate, exiting, issu-
   ing, make out, outcome, problem, progeny,
   publish, release, subject, takings; **8** argument, bring out, going out, issuance, march
   out, proceeds, question, write out; **9** come
   forth, emergence, end result, gathering,
   moot point, offspring, posterity; **10**
   denouement, end product; **11** consequence,
   controversy, final result, publication, topic
   at hand
Istanbul: 7 Stambul; **8** Stamboul; **14**
   Constantinople
isthmus: 6 bridge; **10** neck of land; **13** stepping-stone
Istiophoridae: 19 family Istiophoridae
Istiophorus: 8 sailfish; **16** genus Istiophorus
Isuridae: 14 family Isuridae

Isurus: 4 mako; **11** bonito shark, genus
   Isurus
Italia: 5 Italy
Italian rice: 7 risotto
Italian sandwich: 3 sub, zep; **4** hero; **5**
   hoagy, wedge; **6** bomber, hoagie; **7** grinder,
   torpedo; **9** submarine
italics: 9 reference; **10** annotation; **11** underlining
Italy: 6 Italia
itch: 3 rub; **4** urge; **5** creep, sting; **6** thrill, tingle; **7** itching, scabies, scratch
itching: 4 itch; **8** pruritis [Med]
itch mite: 9 sarcoptid
itchy: 7 fidgety, fretful; **8** restless
item: 3 and, too; **4** also; **5** point, thing, token;
   6 detail, entity, object, sucker; **7** further; **8**
   likewise; **10** particular
itemization: 5 tally; **7** listing; **11** itemisation
itemize: 4 list; **9** enumerate
items: 6 counts; **7** details; **11** particulars
iterate: 4 drum, echo; **6** hammer, reecho,
   repeat, retell; **7** restate; **8** harp upon, redouble; **9** reiterate, reproduce
iteration: 7 harping; **10** recurrence, repetition; **11** reiteration
it follows that: 4 then; **8** of course; **9** as a
   result, naturally; **10** in that case; **11** in
   which case
itinerant: 4 road; **6** roving; **7** gadding, touring, vagrant, voyager; **8** rambling, traveler,
   wayfarer; **9** traveling; **10** ambulatory, discursive; **11** peripatetic
itinerary: 4 plan; **10** travel plan
IV: 4 four; **6** tetrad; **7** quartet, quatern; **8**
   foursome; **10** quadruplet, quaternary,
   quaternion, quaternity
ivied: 8 academic; **10** ivy-covered
ivory: 4 bone, tusk; **5** pearl; **8** off-white; **9**
   like ivory; **12** white as ivory
ivory-billed woodpecker: 9 ivorybill
ivory black: 9 blue-black, lampblack
Ivory Coast: 11 Cote d'Ivoire
ivy: 9 common ivy; **10** English ivy; **11**
   Hedera helix
ivy family: 10 Araliaceae
Iwo Jima: 3 Iwo; **13** invasion of Iwo
IX: 4 nine; **5** niner
Ixodes: 4 tick; **11** genus Ixodes
Ixodes dammini: 8 deer tick
ixodid: 8 hard tick
Iyar: 5 Iyyar

J

J: 5 joule; 10 watt second
J.D.: 11 Doctor of Law, Juris Doctor
jab: 3 dig; 4 plug, poke, prod, slap, stab; 5 smack; 6 poking, thrust; 7 jabbing; 9 thrusting
jabber: 3 jaw; 4 rant, rave; 5 clack, prate, prose, spout; 6 babble, gabble, gibber, hot air; 7 chatter, palaver, prattle; 8 mouth off, rabbit on, verbiage; 9 jabbering, mere words, prattle on
jabberer: 9 driveller
jabbing: 3 jab; 4 poke; 6 poking, thrust; 9 thrusting
jabiru: 5 stork; 10 saddlebill
Jabiru mycteria: 6 jabiru
jaboticaba tree: 10 jaboticaba
jacana: 9 lotusbird
jacinth: 8 amethyst, hyacinth; 9 carbuncle
jackal: 4 dupe, tool; 6 puppet, stooge; 7 cat's-paw; 9 ame damnee [Fr]; 10 running dog; 11 Canis aureus
jackanapes: 4 minx; 5 saucy; 8 impudent, malapert; 9 conceited; 10 jackadandy
jackass: 3 ass; 4 goof, jack, zany; 5 cuddy, goose; 6 cuckoo, donkey; 7 fat-head
jack bean: 10 wonder bean
jackdaw: 3 daw; 7 grackle
jacket: 4 coat; 6 casing; 8 covering; 9 waistcoat, 11 jacket crown
jackfruit tree: 9 jackfruit
jackhammer: 9 air hammer; 15 pneumatic hammer
jackknife: 10 clasp knife; 11 pocket knife
jackknife clam: 9 razor clam
jack-o'-lantern: 6 fungus; 11 ignis fatuus; 13 friar's lantern
jack of all trades: 8 handyman; 9 odd-job man
jackpot: 3 pot; 5 kitty
Jackson: 10 Old Hickory; 13 Andrew Jackson, double sawbuck; 16 twenty-dollar bill; 20 capital of Mississippi
jackstones: 5 jacks; 7 marbles; 12 knucklebones
jackstraw: 9 spillikin
jack tar: 2 AB; 3 gob, tar; 4 salt; 6 sea dog, sailor; 7 mariner, old salt; 8 seafarer; 10 able seaman
jack up: 4 jack; 5 raise
Jacob's ladder: 8 valerian; 12 marine ladder
Jacobin: 9 Dominican
Jacobinic: 11 Jacobinical
Jacquerie: 6 revolt; 12 levee en masse [Fr]
jactitation: 7 jerking; 9 twitching
jade: 3 out; 4 wear, tire, dull; 7 jadeite; 8 nephrite; 9 jadestone, jade-green
jaded: 7 wearied

Jaffa: 4 Yafo; 5 Joppa
jag: 4 bale, barb, load; 5 cargo, prick, spree; 6 burden, lading, thrust; 7 freight; 8 shipment
jaggary: 7 jaggery; 8 jagghery
jagged: 4 bent; 5 erose, jaggy; 6 dented, nicked, ragged; 7 angular, crooked, notched, scraggy, toothed; 8 aquiline, indented, serrated
jaggery: 7 jaggary; 8 jagghery
jaggery palm: 5 kitul; 6 kittul
jaggy: 5 erose; 6 jagged; 7 notched, scraggy, toothed
jaguar: 7 panther; 9 Felis onca; 12 Panthera onca
jaguarundi cat: 4 eyra; 10 jaguarondi, jaguarundi
Jahweh: 2 El; 4 Lord; 5 Yahve, Yahwe; 6 Heaven [metonymically], Jahvey, Wahvey, Yahveh, Yahweh; 7 Jehovah; 9 Ens Entium [Lat]; 10 Providence, The All-holy, The All-wise, The Eternal; 11 Omnipotence, The Almighty, The Infinite; 13 The First Cause, the Prime Mover; 14 The All-merciful, The All-powerful; 15 The Supreme Being
jai alai: 6 pelota
jail: 3 can [slang], jug, lag, pen; 4 brig, gaol, hold, keep, stir [slang]; 5 clink, hulks, pokey [slang]; 6 chokey [slang], cooler [slang], donjon, immure, lockup, prison, remand, send up; 7 put away, slammer [slang]; 8 big house [slang], hoosegow, imprison, stockade; 9 calaboose [slang], guardroom, jailhouse; 10 guard house; 11 incarcerate, penal colony, prison house; 12 penitentiary
jailbird: 3 con; 6 inmate; 7 convict; 8 prisoner
jailbreak: 5 break; 6 escape; 8 breakout; 11 prisonbreak
jail cell: 4 cell; 10 prison cell
jailed: 6 in quod [Lat]; 7 captive, in limbo; 8 confined, in chains, in charge, in prison, locked up; 9 doing time; 10 imprisoned
jailer: 5 guard, screw; 6 custos [Lat], gaoler, keeper, ranger, warder; 7 turnkey; 9 custodian; 11 prison guard
jailing: 12 imprisonment; 13 incarceration
jak: 4 jack; 9 jackfruit
Jakarta: 8 Djakarta; 18 capital of Indonesia
jakes: 2 WC; 3 loo [Brit]; 4 head, john; 5 privy; 6 toilet; 7 latrine; 8 outhouse; 9 necessary; 11 water-closet
jalapeno: 5 chili; 8 capsicum; 11 chili pepper; 12 chilli pepper
jalopy: 3 bus; 4 bomb; 5 lemon; 7 clunker

jalousie: 6 louvre; 14 louvered window, Venetian blinds

jam: 3 fix, ram, wad; 4 cram, fill, hole, mess, pack, pile; 5 block, crush, jelly, miter, press, stuff, wedge; 6 fill up, impede, muddle, pickle, rabbet, throng; 7 chock up, close up, jamming, jampack, mortise, occlude; 8 conserve, dovetail, obstruct, preserve; 10 bottleneck, traffic jam

Jamaican cherry: 8 calabura, silkwood

Jamaica pepper: 10 bell pepper; 11 green pepper

Jamaica sorrel: 6 sorrel; 7 roselle, rozelle; 8 hibiscus; 9 red sorrel

jamb: 7 mullion; 8 abutment, buttress, door jamb, door post

jambeau: 5 armor; 6 greave; 7 greaves

jambon: 3 ham; 4 butt; 6 gammon

jamboree: 4 gala; 7 blowout [U.S.], fish fry [U.S.], hoedown; 8 assembly; 9 gathering; 10 gala affair, hullabaloo

James: 7 St James; 10 Henry James, James River, Saint James; 12 William James; 20 Saint James the Apostle

jammed: 5 stuck; 6 packed; 7 snarled; 9 jam-packed; 10 gridlocked

jamming: 3 jam; 11 improvising; 17 electronic jamming

jampack: 3 jam, ram, wad; 4 cram, pack; 7 chock up

jam-packed: 6 jammed, packed

Jan: 7 January

jangle: 4 burr, pipe; 5 clang, clank, clash, clink, crash, twang; 6 bicker, jingle; 7 clangor, wrangle; 8 clangour, snip-snap, squabble; 10 clangoring

Jansen: 14 Cornelis Jansen; 18 Cornelius Jansenius

Jansenism: 8 Puseyism; 9 Adventism, Calvinism, methodism

Janus-faced: 8 two-faced; 9 deceitful; 11 double-faced, duplicitous; 12 ambidextrous

Japan: 5 Nihon; 6 Nippon

japan: 4 gild; 5 grain, paint; 6 enamel, mastic, polish; 7 furbish, lacquer, smarten, varnish

Japan current: 8 Kuroshio

Japanese: 9 Nipponese

Japanese alphabet: 4 kana

Japanese apricot: 3 mei

Japanese cedar: 4 sugi

Japanese deer: 4 sika

Japanese plum: 6 loquat

Japanese radish: 6 daikon

jape: 3 gag, yak; 4 jest, jibe, joke; 5 laugh; 6 wheeze

japonica: 6 quince; 14 Japanese quince

jar: 3 jog; 4 jerk, jolt; 5 clash, creak, dance, grate, shock; 6 bottle, jarful, jostle, jounce, quaver, quiver; 7 collide, dispute, quarrel, shake up; 8 conflict, disagree

jardiniere: 5 stand; 6 dorser, dosser, hamper, wisket; 7 garnish, whisket; 9 corbeille

jargon: 4 cant; 5 argot, lingo, slang; 6 patois, zircon; 7 fustian, jargoon, twaddle; 8 hyacinth; 10 vernacular

jarring: 5 bumpy, jolty; 7 grating, jolting; 8 clashing, creaking, jostling

Jarvik artificial heart: 11 Jarvik heart

Jasminum: 7 jasmine; 13 genus Jasminum

jasper: 7 cat's eye; 8 hematite; 9 moonstone; 10 bloodstone

jaundice: 7 icterus; 8 acerbity, acrimony; 10 bitterness; 12 yellowed skin

jaundiced: 6 yellow

jaunt: 4 ride, trip; 5 drive; 6 airing, junket, outing, sashay, travel; 9 excursion; 10 expedition; 12 pleasure trip

jaunty: 5 natty, smart; 6 dapper, rakish, snappy, spruce; 7 chipper, dashing, raffish; 8 debonair; 9 debonaire; 11 free and easy

java: 6 coffee

Java man: 9 Trinil man

Java olives: 9 kalumpang; 16 Sterculia foetida

javelina: 7 peccary

Javelle water: 6 bleach; 10 Javel water; 12 disinfectant, eau de Javelle

jaw: 3 rag; 4 chat, chew, jaws, yack; 5 check, chide, clack, prate, prose, scold, visit; 6 berate, chew up, claver, confab, gossip, jabber, natter, rebuke; 7 bawl out, chaffer, chatter, chew out, lambast, lecture, palaver, prattle, reproof, yap away; 8 chitchat, lambaste, rattle on, yack away; 9 dress down, have words, manducate, masticate, prattle on, reprimand

jawbone: 4 jowl; 7 shmooze; 8 lower jaw, mandible; 9 mandibula; 10 submaxilla

jawless vertebrate: 8 agnathan; 11 jawless fish

jaws: 3 jaw; 5 chaps, chops; 6 fauces

jaws of death: 11 hand of death

jay: 4 bird, poll; 5 dandy; 7 bluejay; 9 greenhorn

jazz group: 5 combo; 8 jazz band

jazz musician: 7 jazzman

jazz up: 5 pep up; 7 juice up, spice up; 8 ginger up

jazzy: 5 gaudy, showy; 6 flashy, sporty

jealous: 7 envious; 8 covetous; 9 green-eyed; 11 overjealous

jealousy: 11 jealousness; 16 green-eyed monster

jeans: 6 denims; 9 blue jeans, dungarees

jeep: 9 landrover; 14 off-road vehicle

jeer: 3 boo; 4 gibe, gird, hiss, hoot, quip, twit, wipe; 5 fling, flout, scoff, sneer, taunt; 6 deride; 7 barrack, jeering, laugh at, mockery, snigger; 8 derision, ridicule, scoffing

Jefferson City: 17 capital of Missouri
Jeffrey pine: 9 black pine
jehad: 5 jihad
Jehovah: 2 El; 4 Lord; 5 Yahve, Yahwe; 6
Divine, Heaven [metonymically], Jahvey,
Jahweh, Wahvey, Yahveh, Yahweh; 7
Creator, Godhead; 8 Almighty; 9 Ens
Entium [Lat]; 10 Providence, The All-holy,
The All-wise, The Eternal; 11 God
Almighty, Omnipotence, The Almighty,
The Infinite; 13 The First Cause, the Prime
Mover; 14 The All-merciful, The All-
powerful; 15 The Supreme Being
Jehu: 4 whip; 8 coachman
jejune: 3 dry; 4 arid, bald, dull, flat, tame; 5
vapid; 6 boring, feeble, meager, mortal; 7
insipid, puerile, tedious; 8 immature, juvenile; 9 dry as dust; 10 adolescent
jell: 3 gel, set; 6 gluten; 7 congeal, gelatin; 9
semisolid
jelly: 3 jam; 7 gelatin, jellify; 8 conserve,
preserve
jelly doughnut: 7 bismark
jellyfish: 6 medusa; 7 medusan; 8 man-of-
war; 18 Portuguese man-of-war
jemmy: jimmy
je ne sais quoi: 5 charm, style; 6 oddity; 7
whatsit; 9 curiosity
Jenghis Khan: 11 Genghis Khan, Jenghiz
Khan
jennet: 5 jenny, hinny; 8 jenny ass
jenny: 4 glut, wren; 6 jennet; 7 can hook; 8
jenny ass
jeopardize: 5 peril, stake; 6 hazard, menace;
7 imperil, venture; 8 endanger, threaten; 9
adventure, put at risk; 10 compromise; 11
put in danger
jeopardy: 4 risk; 5 peril; 6 danger, hazard; 7
venture; 10 insecurity
jeremiad: 8 harangue; 9 jeremiade
jerk: 3 jar, jog, shy, tug; 4 buck, cast, dork,
flip, fool, jolt, toss, yank; 5 chuck, dance,
flick, fling, heave, hitch, pitch, shock, start,
whisk; 6 quaver, quiver, tumble, twitch,
wrench; 7 jerking; 10 nincompoop
jerked meat: 5 jerky
jerkily: 13 spasmodically
jerkiness: 10 fitfulness
jerking: 4 jerk, jolt; 5 jerky; 8 unsteady; 10
arrhythmic; 13 uncoordinated
jerkwater: 7 trivial
jerky: 7 jerking; 8 pemmican, unsteady; 9
beef jerky; 10 arrhythmic, jerked meat; 13
uncoordinated
jerry-built: 6 shoddy
jersey: 6 T-shirt; 7 sweater; 8 tee shirt
Jersey pine: 9 scrub pine; 12 Virginia pine
Jerusalem: 15 capital of Israel
Jerusalem artichoke: 7 girasol; 8 sunchoke
jest: 3 gag, yak; 4 jape, jibe, joke; 5 laugh; 6
wheeze; 8 cut jokes, mere joke; 9 make a

joke; 10 jocularity; 11 fiddlestick; 12 fiddlesticks
jest book: 8 joke book
jester: 4 fool; 5 joker, spark; 8 jokester
jesting: 6 jocose, joking; 7 jocular
Jesus: 6 Christ, Savior; 7 Saviour, The Lord;
8 Redeemer; 9 God the Son; 11 Jesus
Christ, The Son of God, The Son of Man;
12 Good Shepherd; 13 The Son of David;
15 Jesus of Nazareth
jet: 4 gush, pour; 5 issue, shoot, sooty, spirt,
spout, spray, spurt; 6 pitchy, squirt; 7 jet
d'eau [Fr]; 8 fountain, jet plane, jet-black,
shoot out, waterjet; 9 coal-black; 10 waterspout; 11 jet airplane
jet black: 5 ebony, sable; 9 coal black, soot
black; 10 pitch black
jet fuel: 8 kerosene
jet liner: 7 prop-jet; 8 jet plane, turbojet
jetsam: 7 flotsam
jet stream: 6 stream; 7 current
jetting: 8 spouting, spurting; 9 squirting
jettison: 13 cast overboard
jetty: 4 mole, mull, pier, quay, spur; 5 groin;
6 groyne; 7 bulwark, seawall; 8 jet-black; 9
coal-black; 10 breakwater, embankment
jeu de mots: 8 word-play; 11 play of words,
play on words
jeune fille: 4 lass; 6 lassie; 9 young girl
jeune veuve: 7 ingenue [Fr]; 11 heavy father
jewel: 3 gem; 4 dear, duck, idol, love, ruby; 5
bijou, brick, honey, pearl, sugar, trump; 6
cosset, duckey, prince; 7 diamond,
jewelry
jeweled: 5 beady; 6 beaded, gemmed; 7
spangly; 8 jewelled, sequined, spangled; 9
bejeweled; 10 bejewelled, bespangled
jeweler's loupe: 5 loupe
jewelry dealer: 12 jewelry store
jewelry maker: 7 jeweler; 8 jeweller
jewelweed: 9 celandine; 10 touch-me-not; 12
orange balsam
Jewish: 6 Judaic
Jewish calendar: 14 Hebrew calendar
Jewish New Year: 11 Rosh Hashana, Rosh
Hashona; 12 Rosh Hashanah, Rosh
Hashonah
Jewish religion: 7 Judaism
jib: 3 bow, shy; 4 balk, gybe, jibe, prow,
stem; 5 baulk; 6 resist, shrink
jibe: 3 dig, fit, jib; 4 barb, gibe, gybe, jape,
jest, joke, quip, shot, slam, wipe; 5 agree,
check, match, shaft, sneer, tally, taunt; 8
flouting; 10 correspond; 12 change course
jiffy: 4 coup, snap, wink; 5 burst, crack,
flash, trice; 6 breath; 7 instant; 9 twinkling;
11 split second
jig: 8 Irish jig
jigger: 4 pony; 6 redbug; 7 chigger, cue rest;
9 shot glass

J

jiggery-pokery: 8 trickery; 9 slickness; 10 hanky panky, hocus-pocus
jiggle: 6 joggle, wiggle
jigsaw: 7 fretsaw; 9 scroll saw
jihad: 5 jehad; 7 holy war
jillions: 8 billions, millions, zillions; 9 trillions
jilt: 4 bilk; 8 forswear
jilted: 7 spurned; 8 forsaken, lovelorn, rejected
Jim Crow: 8 color bar; 9 color line; 8 race laws
jimdandy: 9 jimhickey; 11 crackerjack
jimmies: 9 sprinkles
jimmy: 3 arm, pry; 4 limb, wing; 5 jemmy, lever, prise, prize; 7 crowbar
jimsonweed: 10 thorn apple
jingle: 4 ring; 5 chink, clink; 6 jangle; 8 doggerel; 12 jinglejangle
jingo: 8 jingoist; 9 flag-waver; 10 chauvinist
jingoism: 10 chauvinism, flag waving; 15 superpatriotism
jingoist: 5 jingo; 9 flag-waver; 10 chauvinist
jingoistic: 10 flag-waving; 12 chauvinistic; 13 nationalistic; 14 superpatriotic
jinks: 7 hijinks; 9 high jinks
jinni: 5 genie; 6 djinni, djinny, jinnee
jinrikisha: 7 ricksha; 8 rickshaw
jinx: 3 hex; 5 curse, jonah, witch; 7 bewitch, enchant, glamour
jitney: 3 bus; 5 coach; 7 autobus, omnibus; 8 motorbus; 9 charabanc; 10 motorcoach; 12 double-decker
jitters: 6 nerves; 9 jumpiness; 11 nervousness; 16 screaming meemies
jittery: 4 edgy; 5 jumpy, nervy, shaky; 7 nervous, restive, uptight; 9 tremulous; 10 high-strung, in suspense, overstrung
jiujitsu: 7 jujitsu
jive: 5 swing; 10 swing music
Jnr: 2 Jr; 6 Junior
job: 4 line, task, work; 5 caper, chore; 6 doings, employ, living, thrift [Scot]; 7 agendum, farm out, jobbery, jobbing, problem, shuffle; 8 business, dealings; 9 paying job, situation, speculate, thing to do; 10 corruption, employment, line of work, livelihood, occupation
job ad: 6 want ad; 12 help wanted ad
jobber: 9 middleman, worldling; 10 wholesaler
jobbery: 3 job; 7 jobbing, shuffle; 10 corruption
jobbing: 3 job; 7 jobbery, shuffle; 10 corruption; 11 speculation; 12 stockjobbing
jobless: 4 idle; 9 out of work; 10 unemployed
joblessness: 12 unemployment
jock: 3 pro; 5 sport; 6 player; 7 athlete; 9 jockstrap, sportsman, supporter

jockey: 2 do; 3 con, nab; 4 bilk, bite, scam; 5 cheat, cozen, pluck, rider, screw, shaft; 6 chouse, diddle, euchre; 7 chicane, defraud, hostler, juggler, swindle; 8 cavalier, conjuror, horseman; 9 trickster, victimize; 10 equestrian, roughrider
jockey shorts: 6 shorts; 7 drawers
jock itch: 11 tinea cruris
jockstrap: 4 jock; 9 suspensor, supporter
jocose: 5 funny; 6 joking; 7 amusing, jesting, jocular, waggish; 8 humorous
jocund: 3 gay; 5 jolly, merry; 6 jovial, joyful, joyous; 7 roguish; 8 mirthful
jodphur: 14 riding breeches
Joe Blow: 7 John Doe; 14 man in the street
Joe six-pack: 9 common man; 10 average Joe, average man; 12 common person; 13 average person; 14 man in the street
jog: 3 jar; 4 clip, jerk, jolt, lope, push, trot, turn, whip; 5 boost [U.S.], brunt, dance, shock, shove, stalk, throw, tramp; 6 buffet, canter, common, even up, hurtle, hustle, joggle, jostle, jounce, quaver, quiver, ramble, thrust, wallop; 7 booming, saunter, typical; 8 everyday, frequent, ordinary, ramble on, square up; 9 encounter, household, promenade, well-known; 11 commonplace, well-trodden
joggle: 3 jog; 4 whip; 5 dowel; 6 buffet, hustle, jiggle, jostle, jounce, wallop, wiggle; 8 dowel pin
jog the memory: 6 prompt, remind; 7 suggest
John: 6 St John; 9 Saint John
john: 3 can, lav, loo [Brit]; 4 head; 5 jakes, privy; 6 toilet; 7 latrine; 8 bathroom, facility, lavatory; 9 necessary; 10 powder room
John Barleycorn: 5 booze; 6 liquor; 7 spirits; 9 hard drink; 10 hard liquor; 11 strong drink
John Bull: 5 limey
John Doe: 7 Joe Blow; 14 man in the street
johnnycake: 10 johnny cake; 11 journey cake
Johnny-jump-up: 9 wild pansy; 10 heartsease, wood violet; 11 pansy violet
Johnny Reb: 3 Reb; 5 Rebel; 6 Johnny; 8 grayback
Johnson: 13 Andrew Johnson, Lyndon Johnson; 19 Lyndon Baines Johnson
Johnsonian: 4 rich; 5 tumid; 6 florid, mouthy, ornate, turgid; 7 flowery, orotund; 8 inflated, sonorous, swelling; 9 bombastic, grandiose, high flown; 10 ornamented, rhetorical
join: 3 sum, wed; 4 link, meet; 5 joint, marry, union, unite; 6 abut on, adjoin, fall in, rejoin; 7 conjoin, connect; 8 junction, juncture; 9 affiliate, march with; 10 get hitched [U.S. slang], get married; 11 get together; 12 articulation

joinder: 5 union; 7 uniting; 8 coupling; 11 conjugation, conjunction
joined: 6 linked, united; 7 coupled
joinery: 13 cabinetmaking
join forces: 9 cooperate; 11 collaborate
joining: 8 junction, ligating, ligation; 9 attaching, connexion; 10 attachment, connecting, connection; 11 affiliating, affiliation
joining point: 5 joint; 8 juncture
joint: 4 join, link, twin; 5 bough, elbow, roast, scion, stick; 6 fellow, reefer, united; 7 flexion, flexure; 8 junction, juncture; 9 body joint; 10 articulate, crack house, federative; 11 articulatio, concomitant; 12 articulation, confederated
joint author: 8 coauthor
joint effort: 10 team effort
jointer: 5 plane
joint fir: 7 ephedra
join the priesthood: 10 take orders
jointly: 8 together; 10 conjointly; 11 put together; 12 collectively
join together: 5 unite; 9 cooperate; 11 act together; 12 work together
joint owner: 7 co-owner
joint stock: 11 common stock
joint-stock company: 12 joint concern
joint tenant: 8 co-tenant
jointworm: 9 strawworm
joist: 4 beam; 6 girder, lintel, rafter
joke: 3 gag, yak; 4 jape, jest, jibe, quiz, twit; 5 antic, caper, chaff, laugh, prank, roast, tease, trick; 6 banter, wheeze; 8 badinage, cut jokes, mere joke; 9 make a joke; 10 jocularity
joke book: 8 jest book
joker: 5 spark; 6 jester, turkey; 8 jokester
joking: 6 jocose; 7 jesting, jocular, kidding, puckish
jokingly: 6 in jest, in joke, in play; 7 in sport; 8 jocosely; 9 jestingly; 11 facetiously; 13 tongue-in-cheek
jollification: 11 merrymaking; 12 conviviality
jollity: 5 cheer; 6 frolic; 9 jocundity, joviality, merriment
jolly: 5 merry, middy; 6 banter, jocund, jovial, pretty; 7 roguish; 8 chopping, mirthful
jolly boat: 4 yawl; 5 jolly
Jolly Roger: 9 black flag; 10 pirate flag
jolt: 3 jar, jog; 4 jerk, push, toss; 5 boost [U.S.], brunt, dance, hitch, shock, shove, throw, whisk; 6 hurtle, hustle, jounce, quaver, quiver, thrust, tumble; 7 booming, jerking; 9 encounter
jolted: 6 shaken
jolting: 5 bumpy, jolty; 7 jarring; 8 bouncing, jouncing
jonah: 4 jinx
jongleur: 7 juggler; 8 minstrel; 10 folk singer, poet-singer, troubadour

Joppa: 4 Yafo; 5 Jaffa
Jordan: 11 Jordan River
jorum: 4 bowl; 5 basin; 9 punch bowl
Joshua tree: 5 yucca
jostle: 3 jar, jog; 4 whip; 5 clash, elbow, shove; 6 buffet, hustle, joggle, jounce, wallop; 7 dispute, quarrel; 8 conflict, disagree, jostling, shoulder; 9 come amiss; 12 be discordant
jot: 3 ace, bit, fig, pin, rap, sou; 4 cent, hint, iota, mill, mite, rush; 5 pinch, speck, straw, touch, trace; 6 button, morsel, old son; 7 bulrush, feather, jot down, jotting, modicum, red cent [U.S.], soupcon; 8 farthing, picayune
jot down: 3 jot; 7 put down, set down; 8 note down, take down; 9 write down
Jotun: 6 Jotunn
joule: 1 J; 10 watt second
jounce: 3 jar, jog; 4 jolt, whip; 6 bounce, buffet, hustle, joggle, jostle, wallop
journal: 3 log; 4 life; 5 books, diary; 6 ledger; 7 daybook, gazette; 8 calendar, fortunes, magazine; 9 ephemeris; 10 adventures; 11 account book, confessions, experiences
journalism: 5 media; 9 news media, reporting; 12 fourth estate
journalist: 7 diarist, newsman; 8 reporter; 9 newswoman; 10 chronicler, newscaster; 11 diary keeper; 13 correspondent
journey: 6 course, travel; 10 journeying
journey cake: 10 johnny cake, johnnycake
journeyer: 8 wayfarer
journeying: 7 journey; 9 traveling
journeyman: 7 artisan; 9 artificer, charwoman, craftsman; 10 apprentice
joust: 4 list, tilt
Jove: 7 Jupiter
jovial: 5 jolly, merry; 6 jocund, joyful, joyous; 7 roguish; 8 mirthful
joviality: 5 cheer; 7 jollity; 9 jocundity; 12 conviviality
Jovian planet: 7 Jupiter
jowl: 4 wing; 5 cheek; 7 jawbone; 8 lower jaw, mandible; 9 mandibula; 10 submaxilla
jowly: 10 double-chin
joy: 4 glee; 7 delight, gladden, rejoice; 8 gladness, pleasure; 9 enjoyment
joyful: 5 blest, happy; 6 elated, jocund, jovial, joyous; 7 blessed, gleeful; 8 beatific, blissful, exultant, exulting, jubilant; 9 beatified, rejoicing
joyless: 4 dark; 6 dismal, gloomy, somber, triste [Fr]; 8 dejected, frowning; 9 cheerless, saturnine; 10 lugubrious, spiritless, uncheerful; 11 comfortless
joyous: 6 jocund, jovial, joyful; 8 beatific, blissful; 10 in paradise
joystick: 5 stick; 12 control stick

J

J particle: 11 psi particle
Jr: 3 Jnr; 6 Junior
jr.: 7 younger
Juarez: 12 Ciudad Juarez
jubilant: 6 elated, joyful; 7 flushed, gleeful; 8 exultant, exulting, prideful; 9 rejoicing, triumphal; 10 triumphant
jubilate: 5 exult; 7 rejoice, triumph
jubilee: 11 anniversary; 13 commemoration
Judaic: 6 Jewish; 8 Judaical
Judaical: 6 Judaic
Judas: 7 traitor; 8 Quisling; 13 Judas Iscariot
Judas tree: 8 love tree
judder: 5 shake
judge: 3 try; 5 gauge, guess, label; 6 critic, jurist; 7 justice; 8 conclude, estimate; 9 evaluator, pronounce, protector; 10 adjudicate, judge of law, magistrate; 11 approximate
judgement: 4 mind; 7 finding, judging, opinion; 8 decision, judgment, sagacity; 10 assessment, conclusion; 11 discernment; 12 perspicacity; 13 determination
Judgement Day: 7 Last Day; 8 Doomsday; 11 Judgment Day; 12 Last Judgment
judge of law: 5 judge; 7 justice
judging: 8 deciding, judgment, weighing; 9 judgement; 10 concluding; 11 determining
judgment: 4 mind; 5 sense; 6 genius; 7 finding, judging, opinion, verdict; 8 capacity, critique, decision, sagacity; 9 atonement, good sense, judgement, mediation, salvation; 10 assessment, conclusion, due sense of, redemption; 11 discernment; 12 good judgment, intercession, perspicacity, propitiation; 13 determination
Judgment Day: 7 Last Day; 8 Doomsday; 12 Judgement Day, Last Judgment
judicial: 7 juridic; 9 judiciary, juridical; 14 discriminative
judicial decision: 8 judgment; 9 judgement
judicial sale: 10 forced sale; 12 sheriff's sale
judicial system: 9 judiciary; 10 judicatory, judicature
judiciary: 5 bench
judicious: 4 wise; 8 sensible; 10 reasonable; 12 strong-minded
judiciousness: 6 reason, wisdom; 8 sagacity, sapience; 11 rationality
jug: 3 lag; 4 gaol, jail; 6 immure, jugful, pipkin, remand; 7 pitcher, put away; 8 imprison; 11 incarcerate
Juggernaut: 9 Jagannath, Jagganath; 10 Jagannatha
juggle: 4 bite, wile; 5 blind, catch, cheat, feint, fetch, hocus, plant, reach, trick; 6 bubble; 7 beguile, chicane, conjure; 8 hoodwink, juggling
Juglans: 6 walnut; 7 hickory; 9 butternut; 12 genus Juglans

Jugoslav: 8 Yugoslav; 11 Jugoslavian, Yugoslavian
Jugoslavia: 10 Yugoslavia
jugular vein: 7 jugular; 13 vena jugularis
juice: 3 gas; 6 petrol, succus; 7 benzine; 8 gasoline
juiceless: 3 dry; 7 sapless
juicer: 6 reamer
juiciness: 10 succulence
juicy: 3 fat; 4 blue, gamy, racy; 5 gamey, sappy, spicy; 6 liquid, red-hot, risque, serous; 7 naughty; 8 luscious; 9 succulent; 10 voluptuous
jujitsu: 8 jiujitsu
juju: 6 fetich, fetish, hoodoo, voodoo
jujutsu: 8 jiujitsu
julep: 9 mint julep
Julian calendar: 8 Old Style
Julius Caesar: 6 Caesar; 17 Gaius Julius Caesar
July 1: 11 Dominion Day
July 14: 11 Bastille Day
July 4: 12 Fourth of July; 15 Independence Day
jumble: 4 hash; 5 mix up; 6 huddle, jumbal, litter, lumber, mingle, muddle, tumble, welter; 7 clutter, confuse, disturb, embroil, smother, trouble; 8 scramble, unsettle; 9 mare's nest, patchwork; 10 hodgepodge
jumbled: 7 mixed up; 8 confused; 10 discordant, disorderly, topsy-turvy
jumbo: 5 giant; 7 monster; 9 humongous, monstrous; 10 gargantuan; 11 elephantine
jump: 3 hop; 4 leap, miss, omit, rise, sink, skip; 5 bound, start, vault; 6 derail, plunge, shelve, spring; 7 climb up, jump out, jumping, leap out, startle; 8 pass over, skip over, stand out; 9 alternate, jumpstart, parachute
jumper: 4 sled; 5 pinny; 6 sledge, sleigh; 8 jump shot, pinafore
jumper cable: 4 lead; 10 jumper lead
jump for joy: 5 exult; 11 jumping bean; 18 Mexican jumping bean
jump on: 5 get on, hop on, mount; 7 climb on, mount up; 8 bestride
jump rope: 8 skip rope; 12 skipping rope
jump shot: 6 jumper
jumpy: 4 edgy; 5 nervy; 7 jittery, nervous, restive, uptight; 10 high-strung, in suspense, overstrung
Juncaceae: 10 rush family
junco: 5 finch; 8 snowbird
junction: 4 join; 5 joint; 7 joining, meeting; 8 juncture, ligating, ligation; 9 attaching; 10 adjunction, attachment, confluence, connecting; 11 conjunction; 12 articulation
junction rectifier: 5 diode
juncture: 3 fix; 4 join, pass, push, turn; 5 hitch, joint, pinch, trial; 6 crisis, strait; 7 nonplus; 8 exigency, junction, occasion, quandary, scramble; 10 crossroads, pretty pass; 11 conjunctive, conjuncture, contin-

gency, predicament; **12** articulation, joining point; **13** critical point

Juncus: 4 rush; **8** bullrush; **11** genus Juncus

June 14: 7 Flag Day

June 21: 9 midsummer; **14** summer solstice

June 23: 10 St John's Eve; **12** Midsummer Eve

June 24: 10 St John's Day; **12** Midsummer Day; **13** Midsummer's Day

Juneau: 15 capital of Alaska

June beetle: 6 May bug; **7** June bug; **9** May beetle

juneberry: 8 shadblow, shadbush; **11** service tree; **12** serviceberry

June bug: 6 May bug; **9** May beetle; **10** June beetle

Jung: 8 Carl Jung; **14** Carl Gustav Jung

jungle: 10 rain forest, wilderness

jungle cat: 10 Felis chaus

Junior: 2 Jr; **3** Jnr

junior: 7 younger; **9** third-year; **10** next-to-last

junior-grade: 5 lower, lowly, petty; **8** inferior; **9** secondary, subaltern; **11** subordinate

juniper: 5 retem

Juniperus: 5 cedar; **7** juniper; **14** genus Juniperus

junk: 1 H; **4** dust, scag; **5** horse, scrap, smack, trash; **6** debris, heroin, rubble; **8** detritus; **11** odds and ends

junked: 5 scrap, waste; **7** cast-off; **9** discarded

junket: 3 toy; **5** feast, jaunt, revel, sport; **6** outing, sashay, wanton; **7** banquet, carouse, disport; **8** field day; **9** drown care, excursion, make merry; **10** expedition; **12** pleasure trip

junk food: 4 bait, nosh, whet

junkie: 5 junky; **10** drug addict

junk jewelry: 5 paste; **12** false jewelry; **14** costume jewelry; **15** synthetic jewels

junky: 6 junkie; **10** drug addict

Junoesque: 10 statuesque

junta: 5 cabal, junto; **7** faction; **9** camarilla; **13** military power

Jupiter: 4 Jove

jural: 8 juristic

Jurassic: 3 age; **8** Mesozoic; **14** Jurassic period

jurat: 8 assessor

juris consult: 6 jurist, pundit; **8** advocate, civilian; **9** publicist; **12** legal adviser

jurisdiction: 10 judicature, legal power

Juris Doctor: 2 J.D.; **11** Doctor of Law

jurisprudence: 3 law

jurist: 5 judge; **6** pundit; **7** justice; **8** advocate, civilian; **9** publicist; **10** magistrate; **11** legal expert; **12** juris consult [Lat], legal adviser

juror: 7 juryman; **9** jurywoman

jury: 5 panel

juryman: 5 juror; **8** talesman; **9** jurywoman

jury-rigged: 9 makeshift; **10** improvised

jury-rigging: 5 shift; **7** stopgap; **8** jury mast; **9** makeshift

jurywoman: 5 juror; **7** juryman

jus civile: 8 civil law, Roman law; **13** Justinian code

jus gentium: 12 law of nations; **16** international law

jussive mood: 10 imperative; **14** imperative mood

just: 3 but; **4** fair, good, only; **5** equal, exact, right; **6** barely, hardly, just so, merely, scarce, severe, simply, square, strict; **7** equable, exactly, just now, precise, upright; **8** accurate, scarcely, virtuous; **9** equitable, impartial, precisely; **10** evenhanded, reasonable

just about: 4 most, near, nigh, or so, some; **5** about; **6** all but, almost, around, nearly; **7** close to, roughly; **8** well-nigh; **9** virtually; **10** more or less; **13** approximately

just adequate: 10 borderline

just around the corner: 4 soon; **6** at hand; **8** imminent, upcoming; **9** in one's eye; **10** in one's view; **11** approaching, close at hand

just deserts: 7 deserts; **9** what is due; **11** comeuppance; **13** poetic justice

justice: 5 judge; **6** equity, jurist; **8** fair play, fairness, justness; **10** judge of law, judicature, magistrate; **11** give and take, lex talionis [Lat]; **12** impartiality; **13** equitableness; **14** even-handedness

justifiable: 6 venial; **8** rightful; **9** excusable; **10** defensible, legitimate, pardonable

justifiably: 10 with reason

justification: 7 warrant; **8** adoption, linotype, logotype; **9** rationale, salvation; **10** conversion, live matter; **11** exculpation, exoneration, inspiration, vindication

justificative: 9 defensive; **10** excusatory; **11** vindicatory

justified: 7 adopted, elected; **8** inspired; **9** converted, unearthly; **10** sanctified; **11** consecrated, regenerated

justifiedly: 6 justly; **7** rightly

justifier: 9 apologist; **10** vindicator

justify: 4 free; **6** excuse; **7** absolve, warrant; **9** apologise, apologize, vindicate; **11** rationalize

Justinian code: 8 civil law, Roman law; **9** jus civile

justly: 5 right; **6** fairly; **7** equably, rightly; **8** in equity, in reason; **9** a bon droit [Fr], in justice; **10** au bon droit [Fr]; **11** justifiedly

just out: 6 latest; **7** fire-new, span-new; **8** brand-new

just right: 4 to a T; **11** to the letter; **12** to perfection

just so: 4 just; **5** exact; **6** even so, severe, strict; **7** precise; **8** accurate

jut: 4 bump, hump; **5** bulge; **7** jutting; **9** extrusion, gibbosity; **10** projection, prominence, protrusion; **11** excrescence, gibbousness; **12** protuberance

jute: 4 hemp; **5** oakum

Jutish: 7 Kentish

jut out: 4 pout; **5** bulge; **7** poke out, project; **8** protrude, stand out, stick out; **11** be prominent

jutting: 3 jut; **6** raised; **8** in relief, repousse, sticking; **9** projected; **10** jutting out, pro-jecting, projection, protruding, protrusion, sticking up; **11** protuberant

juvenile: 3 kid; **5** bairn [Scot], child, green, sappy, young, youth; **6** callow, jejune, moppet, puisne; **7** budding, puerile; **8** childish, children [pl], small fry, under age, youthful; **9** beardless, little one, youngster; **10** adolescent

juvenility: 5 youth; **10** callowness, jejuneness; **12** youthfulness

juxtaposed: 8 adjacent

juxtaposition: 7 contact; **9** proximity; **10** apposition, contiguity; **11** coincidence

K

K: 1 G, M; **2** KB; **4** thou, yard; **5** grand; **6** kelvin; **7** chiliad; **8** kilobyte, Kilobyte, thousand; **9** potassium; **11** one thousand

K2: 7 Dapsang; **12** Godwin Austen; **17** Mount Godwin Austen

K-9: 6 canine

Kaballit Nunaat: 9 Greenland

kabbala: 6 cabala, kabala; **7** cabbala; **8** cabbalah, kabbalah

kabob: 5 kebab; **10** shish kebab

Kabul: 20 capital of Afghanistan

Kadai language: 5 Kadai; **6** Kam-Tai

kaffir: 5 kafir; **6** caffer, caffre; **9** kafir corn; **10** kaffir corn; **11** great millet

Kafka: 10 Franz Kafka

kaftan: 6 caftan

Kakatoe: 7 Cacatua; **8** cockatoo; **12** genus Cacatua, genus Kakatoe

kala-azar: 10 Assam fever; **11** dumdum fever

Kalahari: 14 Kalahari Desert

kale: 4 cole, gelt, kail, loot, pelf; **5** bread, dough, lucre; **6** dinero, moolah; **7** cabbage, shekels; **8** borecole, colewort

kalian: 6 hookah; **8** narghile; **9** water pipe; **12** hubble-bubble

Kalimantan: 6 Borneo; **16** Indonesian Borneo

Kampala: 15 capital of Uganda

kampong: 6 hamlet; **7** village, campong

Kampuchea: 8 Cambodia

kana: 16 Japanese alphabet

Kanarese: 7 Kannada

Kanawha: 12 Kanawha River

kanji: 9 character; **16** Chinese character

Kannada: 8 Kanarese

Kansas: 5 Kansa; **8** Kaw River; **11** Kansas River; **14** Sunflower State

Kant: 12 Immanuel Kant

kaolin: 7 kaoline; **9** china clay, terra alba; **10** china stone; **13** porcelain clay

kaon: 6 k-meson; **9** K particle; **10** kappa-meson

kapok: 9 ceiba tree; **10** silk cotton

kappa-meson: 4 kaon; **6** k-meson; **9** K particle

kaput: 4 gone; **7** done for

karabiner: 8 snap ring; **9** carabiner

Karakoram: 7 Mustagh; **12** Mustagh Range; **14** Karakoram Range, Karakorum Range

karakul: 7 caracul; **9** broadtail

Karat: 5 carat

Kashmir: 8 Cashmere

katharsis: 9 catharsis; **10** abreaction

Katmandu: 9 Kathmandu; **14** capital of Nepal

Kauai: 11 Kauai Island

kayak: 4 boat

kayo: 8 knock out; **9** knock cold

kayoed: 3 KO'd; **7** stunned; **10** knocked out

Kazak: 6 Kazakh; **9** Kazakstan; **10** Kazakhstan

kb: 1 K; **8** kilobyte

kc: 3 kHz; **9** kilocycle, kilohertz

kebab: 5 kabob; **10** shish kebab

kedge: 4 boom, scud, warp

keel: 3 toe; **4** hoof, reel, root, sole, swag; **5** lurch; **6** careen; **7** stagger

keeled: 6 ridged; **8** carinate; **9** carinated

keen: 3 raw; **4** avid, cool, neat; **5** acute, bleak, brisk, bully, dandy, eager, fresh, great, nifty, sharp, swell, vivid; **6** bang-up, brainy, bright, groovy, lament, lively, not bad, peachy, severe, slap-up; **7** anxious, corking, cutting, nipping, pointed; **8** cracking, deep-dyed, incisive, piercing, smashing, stabbing, well read; **9** exquisite,

keep: 3 can [slang], pen; **4** brig, care, gaol, go on, hold, jail, mark, save, stir [slang], tend, ward; **5** abide, board, clink [slang], dwell, hulks, pokey [slang]; **6** charge, chokey [slang], cooler [slang], donjon, having, hold on, keep on, living, lockup, prison, pursue, retain; **7** commons, custody, dungeon, execute, go along, holding, observe, perform, prevent, proceed, satisfy, slammer [slang], support, sustain, the Rock; **8** big house [slang], continue, hold back, hold onto, hold open, hoosegow, keep back, keep open, maintain, preserve, restrain, stockade, withhold; **9** calaboose [slang], celebrate, detention, discharge, guardroom, keep by one, oubliette, signalize, stay fresh; **10** guard house, keep on foot, keep on hand, livelihood, sustenance, take care of; **11** penal colony, prison house, safekeeping

keep an eye on: 5 watch; **6** follow; **7** observe; **9** look after, watch over

keeper: 5 guard; **6** custos [Lat], gaoler, jailer, ranger, warder; **7** steward, turnkey; **9** custodian

keep from: 5 avoid; **6** hold in, keep in; **7** hold off; **8** hold back, hold from, keep back, stand off; **9** hold aloof; **10** desist from, stand aloof; **11** abstain from, forbear from, hold in check, keep in check, refrain

keeping: 4 tone; **5** value; **7** holding, marking; **8** coloring; **9** retaining, retention; **10** local color, preserving; **11** celebrating, safekeeping

keep off: 5 avoid; **6** bypass; **7** beat off, fend off, ward off; **8** beat back, go around, hands off!, keep away, stand off, stave off, stay away; **9** get around, keep aloof, stand away

keep out: 4 shut; **7** exclude, shut out

keepsake: 5 relic, token; **7** memento; **8** souvenir; **11** memorabilia

keep silence: 5 be mum; **6** be mute; **7** keep mum, not talk; **8** be silent, not speak

keep together: 7 collude, concert, consort; **8** conspire; **10** fraternize; **11** confederate

keep to oneself: 5 stand; **8** keep back; **9** keep aloof; **10** be secluded; **11** be reclusive; **12** live secluded

keep up: 5 sit up; **6** bear up, follow, hold up, stay up; **7** carry on, prolong, sustain; **8** maintain, preserve

Keflex: 6 Keftab; **10** cephalexin

keg: 4 cask, drum; **6** barrel

keister: 3 bum, can; **4** arse, buns, butt, prat, rear, rump, seat, tail, tush; **5** fanny, stern; **6** behind, bottom; **7** hind end, rear end, tail end, tooshie; **8** backside, buttocks, derriere; **9** fundament, posterior; **12** hindquarters

kelpie: 6 sprite

Kelt: 4 Celt

kelvin: 1 K

kempt: 4 tidy, trim; **8** tidied up; **9** spruced up

ken: 3 spy; **4** espy, know, look, scan, view; **5** sight; **6** descry, gander; **7** discern, insight, make out, realize; **8** discover; **9** apprehend, be aware of, recognize; **10** appreciate, cognizance, comprehend, experience, understand; **11** be aware that, distinguish, familiarity; **12** acquaintance

kenaf: 5 bimli, kanaf; **9** bimli hemp

Kennedy: 11 Jack Kennedy; **21** John Fitzgerald Kennedy

kennel: 3 sty; **4** byre, coop, cote; **5** hutch; **6** trench, trough; **8** dog house, doghouse

keno: 5 beano, bingo, lotto

kentan: 9 devil lily, tiger lily

Kentish: 6 Jutish

Kentucky bluegrass: 9 June grass; **12** Kentucky blue

Kentucky coffee tree: 6 bonduc, chicot

Kentucky Fried Chicken: 3 KFC

kepi: 9 peaked cap; **10** service cap; **11** yachting cap

Kepler: 11 Johan Kepler; **14** Johannes Kepler

Kepler's law of planetary motion: 10 Kepler's law

Kepler's second law: 10 law of areas; **15** law of equal areas

Kepler's third law: 11 harmonic law

kept: 4 held; **8** retained, unbroken, withheld; **9** preserved

kept apart: 8 isolated, set apart; **9** insulated; **10** segregated

kept back: 7 hoarded; **8** held back, reserved, set aside

kept up: 8 well-kept; **10** maintained

kept woman: 8 mistress; **9** concubine

keratin: 7 ceratin

keratoplasty: 11 corneal gaft

kerb: 4 curb

kerchief: 11 neckerchief

kernel: 3 nub, pit, sum; **4** core, gist, meat, pith; **5** grain, heart, stone; **6** center, marrow; **7** essence, nucleus; **9** substance; **10** inwardness; **11** nitty-gritty

kerosene: 7 jet fuel; **8** kerosine

kerosene heater: 8 oilstove; **9** oil heater; **14** kerosine heater

kerosene lamp: 7 oil lamp; **12** kerosine lamp

kerugma: 7 kerygma

kestrel: 11 sparrow hawk

ketchup: 6 catsup; **7** cetchup; **13** tomato ketchup

ketoacidosis prone diabetes: 13 Type I diabetes; **16** juvenile diabetes

ketone body: 11 acetone body

ketosis: 9 ketonemia; **10** acetonemia

kettle: 6 boiler; **7** capsule, matrass, timpani,

K

tympani; **8** bolthead, receiver, tympanum; **9** kettleful; **10** kettle drum, kettledrum

kettle of fish: 3 fix, jam; **4** hole, mess; **6** muddle, pickle

key: 2 kg; **3** cay, cue; **4** clew, clue, helm, kilo, name, tone; **5** blade, scent; **6** key out, primal, signet, tiller, winder; **7** central, treadle, trigger; **8** cardinal, describe, discover, identify, kilogram, tonality; **9** operative; **11** distinguish, Florida keys, fundamental; **13** typewriter key

keyed: 5 tuned; **7** attuned

Keynes: 17 John Maynard Keynes

keynote: 5 model, tonic; **8** keystone, standard

keynote speech: 14 keynote address

key out: 3 key; **4** name; **8** describe, discover, identify; **11** distinguish

key signature: 9 signature

keystone: 7 keynote; **9** headstone; **10** main motive, mainspring; **11** coping-stone

Keystone State: 12 Pennsylvania

KFC: 20 Kentucky Fried Chicken

kg: 3 key; **4** kilo; **8** kilogram

Khalkha: 5 Kalka; **6** Khalka

khan: 10 caravan inn; **12** caravanserai

Khartoum: 14 capital of Sudan

khedive: 6 regent; **7** viceroy; **8** palatine

kHz: 2 kc; **9** kilocycle, kilohertz

kibitz: 7 comment, kibbitz

kibitzer: 14 backseat driver

kibosh: 4 halt, stop; **5** block

kick: 4 bang, beef, boot, cuff, rush; **5** flush, gripe, plain, punch, spurn; **6** buffet, charge, kvetch, quetch, recoil, squawk, strike, thrill; **7** kicking; **8** complain, kick back, sound off, striping; **9** buffeting

kick a habit: 5 break; **10** beat a habit, drop a habit; **11** break a habit

kick around: 5 bandy

kick back: 4 kick; **6** recoil

kick downstairs: 4 bump; **5** break; **6** demote; **8** relegate

kicking: 4 boot, kick; **5** front, stand; **8** opposing; **9** renitency, resisting; **10** opposition, resistance

kickoff: 5 first, start; **6** offset, outset; **7** send-off; **8** start-off; **9** beginning; **10** inaugurate; **12** commencement, starting time

kick out: 4 oust; **5** eject, expel; **7** boot out, drum out, exclude, turf out, turn out; **8** chuck out, throw out

kick out of school: 5 expel; **7** dismiss

kickshaw: 5 curio, goody, treat; **6** bauble, dainty, gewgaw, trifle; **7** bibelot, novelty, trinket, whatnot; **8** chotchke, delicacy, gimcrack, nicknack, whim-wham; **9** bagatelle, bric-a-brac, tchotchke; **10** knickknack

kick the bucket: 3 die; **4** conk; **5** choke, croak; **6** pop off; **7** snuff it; **8** check out,

drop dead; **10** buy the farm; **11** die suddenly

kick up: 5 evoke; **7** provoke; **9** call forth

kick upstairs: 5 raise; **7** advance, elevate, promote, upgrade

kid: 3 fry; **4** tike, tyke; **5** bairn [Scot], chaff, child, jolly, minor, youth; **6** banter, moppet, nipper, shaver; **7** kidskin, tiddler; **8** children [pl], juvenile, nestling, small fry; **9** kid around, little one, youngster

Kidd: 11 Captain Kidd, William Kidd

kiddie car: 8 pedal car

kidding: 6 joking; **7** puckish

kid glove: 10 suede glove

kidnap: 5 crimp; **6** abduct, nobble, snatch; **7** capture

kidnapped: 8 abducted, kidnaped

kidnapper: 8 abductor, kidnaper, snatcher

kidney bean: 6 frijol; **7** frijole

kidney failure: 12 renal failure

kidney-shaped: 8 reniform

kidney stone: 10 nephrolith; **13** renal calculus

kieselguhr: 9 diatomite

Kiev: 19 capital of the Ukraine

Kigali: 15 capital of Rwanda

Kiggelaria: 15 genus Kiggelaria

Kiggelaria africana: 9 wild peach

kilderkin: 4 cask; **6** carboy, firkin

Kilimanjaro: 16 Mount Kilimanjaro

kill: 4 down, slay; **6** defeat; **7** killing, toss off, turn off, vote out, wipe out; **8** belt down, bolt down, pour down, stamp out, vote down; **9** drink down, power down, shed blood, switch off; **10** deactivate, disconnect, obliterate, put to death

killdeer: 6 plover; **7** kildeer

killer: 6 slayer

killer whale: 4 orca; **6** killer; **7** grampus, sea wolf; **11** Orcinus orca

killing: 4 kill; **6** taking; **7** cleanup, slaying; **8** draining, windfall; **10** exhausting; **12** violent death; **13** sidesplitting

killjoy: 6 damper; **7** marplot; **10** spoilsport, wet blanket; **11** party pooper

kill off: 11 exterminate

kill time: 5 dally

kilo: 2 kg; **3** key; **8** kilogram

kilobyte: 1 K; **2** kB; **8** Kilobyte

kilocalorie: 7 calorie; **8** frigorie

kilocycle: 2 kc; **3** kHz; **9** kilohertz

kilocycle per second: 2 kc; **3** kHz; **9** kilocycle, kilohertz

kilogram: 2 kg; **3** key; **4** kilo

kilogram calorie: 7 calorie; **8** frigorie; **11** kilocalorie; **12** large calorie

kilohertz: 2 kc; **3** kHz; **9** kilocycle

kiloliter: 9 kilolitre; **10** cubic meter, cubic metre

kilometer: 2 km; **5** klick; **9** kilometre

kilometers per hour: 3 kph, km/h; **4** kmph
kilovolt: 2 kV
kilowatt: 2 kW
kilowatt hour: 3 B.T.U.**4** kW-hr
kilt: 13 Scotsman's kilt
kin: 4 akin, clan; **5** blood, tribe; **6** family; **7** cognate, kindred, kinfolk [pl], kinsman; **8** kin group, relation, relative; **10** connection, kinsperson, kith and kin [pl]; **11** consanguine; **12** blood-related
kind: 4 form, sort, type; **5** class; **6** genial, kindly; **7** variety; **8** category, division, merciful, tolerant; **10** benevolent, thoughtful; **11** good-hearted, openhearted
kinda: 6 kind of, rather, sort of
kinderspiel: 5 cinch [U.S.]; **10** child's play
kindle: 4 fire, lash; **5** evoke, exert, light, raise; **6** arouse, elicit, excite, fly out, foment, ignite, incite, stir up, turn on; **7** inflame, provoke, quicken, sharpen; **8** activate, energize, enkindle, take fire; **9** set fire to, set on fire
kindling: 4 punk; **5** spunk; **6** firing, tinder; **8** ignition, lighting; **9** touchwood
kindly: 4 kind; **10** benevolent, charitable; **11** good-hearted, openhearted, sympathetic
kindness: 7 charity; **8** humanity; **9** benignity, humanness; **10** goodliness, kindliness; **12** graciousness; **13** brotherly love, forgivingness
kind of: 5 kinda; **6** rather, sort of
kindred: 3 kin; **4** akin, clan; **5** blood, tribe; **6** family; **7** kinfolk [pl], kinsman, related; **8** kin group, relation, relative; **10** connection, kith and kin [pl], of the blood
kine: 4 cows, oxen; **6** cattle
kinescope: 11 picture tube; **14** television tube
kinesthesia: 11 kinesthesis, muscle sense; **12** kinaesthesia, kinaesthesis, kinesthetics; **15** sense of movement
kinetic: 10 energising, energizing
kinetics: 8 dynamics
kinfolk: 3 kin; **4** folk, sept; **5** blood; **6** family; **7** kindred, kinsman, phratry; **8** kinsfolk, relation, relative; **10** connection, family line
King: 16 Martin Luther King
king: 5 baron, knave, mogul, power; **6** tycoon; **7** magnate, majesty; **9** imperator [Lat]; **11** crowned head, male monarch, world-beater; **12** anointed king [male], top executive; **14** big businessman, business leader
King's counsel: 2 Q.C.; **9** barrister
King's English: 13 Queen's English
king's evil: 6 struma; **8** scrofula
King's highway: 12 broad highway; **13** Queen's highway
kingbolt: 7 kingpin; **9** swivel pin

king cobra: 9 hamadryad; **10** Naja hannah
kingcup: 7 cowslip, goldcup; **13** marsh marigold
King Death: 13 King of terrors
kingdom: 4 land; **5** realm
kingdom Animalia: 13 animal kingdom
kingdom Fungi: 13 fungus kingdom
kingdom of God: 6 heaven; **15** heavenly kingdom, kingdom of heaven
kingdom Plantae: 12 plant kingdom
kingfish: 4 cero; **7** pintado; **8** chenfish; **12** white croaker, king mackerel
King James Version: 17 Authorized Version
kingly: 8 kinglike; **11** monarchical
king of beasts: 4 lion; **11** Panthera leo
kingpin: 6 bigwig; **7** headpin; **8** kingbolt; **9** swivel pin, top banana
king post: 9 crown post
king salmon: 7 chinook; **13** chinook salmon, quinnat salmon
Kingston: 15 Jamaican capital; **16** capital of Jamaica
kink: 4 curl; **5** crape, crimp, curve, frizz, gnarl, twirl, twist; **6** kink up; **7** frizzle
kinky: 5 crisp, nappy; **6** far-out, frizzy, kinked, quirky, wanton, way-out; **7** frizzly, knotted, offbeat, raveled, tangled, wayward; **8** fanciful, freakish, involved, skittish; **9** entangled, fantastic, intricate, perplexed, perverted; **10** particular; **11** complicated; **12** inextricable
kinsfolk: 4 folk, sept; **6** family; **7** kinfolk, phratry; **10** family line
Kinshasa: 12 Leopoldville; **14** capital of Zaire
kinship: 8 affinity; **9** family tie; **11** ties of blood; **12** relationship; **13** consanguinity; **14** family relation
kinship by marriage: 8 affinity
kinship group: 3 kin; **4** clan; **5** tribe; **7** kindred; **8** kin group
kinsman: 3 kin; **5** blood; **7** kindred, kinfolk [pl]; **8** relation, relative; **10** connection, kith and kin [pl]
kiosk: 5 booth, stall, stand; **7** cubicle
kip: 5 log Z's, sleep; **7** slumber; **11** catch some Z's
Kipling: 14 Rudyard Kipling
kippered herring: 6 kipper
Kirghiz: 6 Kirgiz; **8** Khirghiz, Kirgizia; **9** Kirghizia, Kyrgystan; **10** Kirgizstan; **11** Kirghizstan
kirk: 6 chapel, church; **7** oratory; **8** basilica; **9** cathedral; **10** tabernacle; **11** conventicle; **12** meetinghouse
Kishinev: 8 Chisinau; **16** capital of Moldova
kishke: 12 stuffed derma
kismet: 4 fate; **6** kismat; **7** destiny, portion
kiss: 4 buss; **5** brush, smack; **8** osculate

K

kisser: 3 mug; 6 smiler, visage; 9 osculator; 11 countenance, physiognomy

kissing: 7 hugging, necking, petting; 8 cuddling, fondling; 9 caressing, smooching, snuggling

kissing bug: 8 conenose

kissing disease: 4 mono; 14 glandular fever

kiss of peace: 3 pax

kiss the hem of one's garment: 4 fawn; 5 cower, crawl, sneak; 6 crouch, grovel, sponge, suck up; 9 truckle to

kit: 5 breed, crock, kit up; 6 flagon, kit out, outfit; 7 canteen

kit and caboodle: 5 works; 8 whole kit; 10 whole works

kitchen maid: 8 scullion; 12 scullery maid

kitchen stove: 5 range, stove; 12 cooking stove, kitchen range

kit fox: 10 prairie fox

kitsch: 11 pretentious; 12 ostentatious

kitten: 3 cat; 5 kitty

kittenish: 6 frisky; 7 babyish

kitty: 3 pot; 4 pool, puss; 5 pussy; 6 kitten, pet cat; 7 jackpot; 8 kitty cat, pussy cat

kitty cat: 4 puss; 5 kitty, pussy; 6 pet cat; 8 pussycat

kitty-corner: 10 catacorner; 11 catercorner, catty-corner; 12 cata-cornered; 13 catercornered, catty-cornered, kitty-cornered

kiwi: 7 apteryx

KKK: 4 Klan; 10 Ku Klux Klan

Klan: 3 KKK; 10 Ku Klux Klan

Klavier: 7 clavier

kleptomania: 8 rapacity

klick: 2 km; 9 kilometer, kilometre

klutz: 3 oaf; 4 clod, gawk, goon, lout, lump; 6 lubber, lummox; 10 stumblebum

km: 5 klick; 9 kilometer, kilometre

k-meson: 4 kaon; 9 K particle; 10 kappa-meson

knack: 4 bent, hang; 5 craft, skill; 7 address, aptness, know-how; 8 aptitude, facility; 10 adroitness, competence; 11 proficiency; 12 skillfulness

knap: 3 rap; 4 chip, knob, pena [U.S.]; 5 knoll, mound; 6 barrow, cut off; 7 hillock, hummock; 8 break off

knapsack: 8 backpack, rucksack; 9 haversack

knave: 5 cheat, rogue; 6 rascal, varlet; 8 scalawag; 9 scallywag; 11 rapscallion

knavery: 7 roguery; 8 foul play; 9 rascality; 10 dishonesty

knavish: 3 sly; 4 foxy, wily; 5 dodgy, slick; 6 crafty, tricky; 7 cunning, tricksy; 8 guileful

knawe: 6 knawel; 17 Scleranthus annuus

knead: 4 brew, mash, work; 6 squash; 7 massage, rub down; 10 work up into

knee: 4 genu; 9 knee joint

knee breeches: 8 breeches, knickers; 9 knee pants; 14 knickerbockers

kneecap: 7 kneepan, patella

knee deep: 8 skin deep; 9 ankle deep

knee-jerk reflex: 8 knee jerk; 14 patellar reflex

kneel: 3 bob, bow, dip; 4 duck; 5 stoop; 6 cringe, curtsy, kowtow; 8 courtesy, kneeling

kneeling: 5 kneel; 6 homage; 9 obeisance; 11 prostration; 12 genuflection

knee pants: 8 breeches, knickers; 12 knee breeches; 14 knickerbockers

knell: 4 ring

Knesset: 8 Knesseth

knickerbockers: 8 breeches, knickers; 9 knee pants; 12 knee breeches

knickers: 5 pants; 7 drawers; 8 bloomers, breeches; 9 knee pants; 12 knee breeches; 14 knickerbockers

knickknack: 5 curio; 6 bauble, gewgaw, trifle; 7 bibelot, novelty, trinket, whatnot; 8 chotchke, gimcrack, kickshaw, nicknack, whim-wham; 9 bagatelle, bric-a-brac, tchotchke; 13 knickknackery

knife: 3 cut; 4 stab; 5 slash; 6 tongue

knifelike: 4 keen; 5 acute, sharp; 7 cutting; 8 incisive, piercing, stabbing; 11 penetrating, penetrative

knife thrust: 4 stab

knight: 3 dub; 5 horse; 10 knighthood

knight's service: 8 chivalry

knight errant: 8 crusader, do-gooder

knight errantry: 8 chivalry; 9 quixotism

knightly: 7 gallant; 8 medieval; 9 chivalric; 10 chivalrous

knit: 3 fob, net, sew, tat; 4 draw, lace, poke, tack; 5 plain, pouch, scrip; 6 budget, button, cockle, pocket, pucker, rumple, sachel, sheath, socket, stitch; 7 crumple, entwine, satchel; 8 knitting, knitwork, reticule, scabbard; 10 knit stitch; 11 plain stitch

knit the brow: 4 pout, snap; 5 frown, gnarl, gnash, growl, lower, scowl, snarl

knob: 3 pea; 4 bulb, clew, drop, horn, node, pena [U.S.], pill; 5 knoll, mound; 6 barrow, bullet, marble, pellet, pommel; 7 globule, hillock, hummock, vesicle; 8 spherule

knobbed: 6 gnarly, knobby, knotty; 7 gnarled, knotted; 9 papillary, papillose

knob celery: 8 celeriac; 10 celery root, root celery

knock: 3 hit, rap, tap; 4 bang, bash, belt, blow, bump, ping, pink, slam; 5 roast, smash, whack, whang; 6 strike; 8 knocking; 10 strike hard

knock against: 7 run into; 8 bump into; 10 jar against; 11 butt against

knock cold: 2 KO; 4 kayo; 8 knock out

knock down: 4 dash, deck, down, dull, dump, fell, sink; 5 floor, lower, unman; 6 deject, topple; 7 cut down, hew down;

8 cast down, coldcock, dash down, pull down, push down, take down; **9** fling down, knockover
knocker: 9 detractor; **10** disparager; **11** depreciator, doorknocker
knocking: 5 knock; **7** rapping, tapping
knock-knee: 10 genu valgum, tibia valga
knock off: 3 cop; **4** do in, drop, glom, hook; **5** shave, waste; **6** snitch, thieve; **7** dash off, toss off; **8** fling off; **9** finish off, liquidate, polish off
knockout: 2 KO; **4** dish, hard, lulu; **5** peach; **6** beauty, looker, severe; **7** mantrap, smasher, stunner; **10** sweetheart; **11** pretty woman; **14** beautiful woman
knockout drops: 10 Mickey Finn
knockout punch: 7 KO punch; **8** haymaker; **11** Sunday punch
knockover: 6 topple; **9** knock down
knock up: 3 irk; **4** flag, jade, tire; **5** weary; **7** exhaust, fatigue, prang up, wear out; **9** prostrate
knockwurst: 10 knackwurst
knoll: 4 knob, pena [U.S.]; **5** mound; **6** barrow; **7** hammock, hillock, hummock
knot: 2 mi; **3** let, net; **4** band, burl, crew, gang, lump, mass, mile, ring, slub, team; **5** block, braid, chain, cross, crowd, gnarl, group, party, ravel, snarl, squad, twist; **6** circle, clique, naut mi, tangle, tassel, wreath; **7** air mile, coterie, in-crowd; **8** grayback; **10** cat's cradle; **11** Gordian knot; **12** nautical mile
knotted: 5 kinky; **6** gnarly, kinked, knotty, snarly; **7** gnarled, knobbed, raveled, snarled, tangled; **8** involved; **9** entangled, intricate, perplexed; **11** complicated; **12** inextricable
knout: 4 lash, whip; **5** strap, thong; **7** cowhide, scourge; **8** bullwhip
know: 3 scan; **7** cognize, realize; **9** apprehend, be aware of, recognize; **10** appreciate, comprehend, experience, understand; **11** acknowledge, be aware that, be cognizant; **12** be acquainted
know by rote: 11 know by heart
know-how: 5 craft, knack, skill; **7** address, aptness; **8** aptitude, facility; **10** adroitness, competence; **11** proficiency; **12** skillfulness
knowing: 4 wise; **5** aware, canny, leery; **6** astute, wilful, wise to; **7** learned, willful; **8** educated, informed, lettered, well-read; **9** cognition, realizing, up to snuff; **10** cognizance, conception, deliberate; **11** enlightened, intentional; **12** appreciating, apprehension, being aware of, precognition, well-educated
knowingly: 8 by design; **9** advisedly, expressly, on purpose, purposely, wittingly; **10** designedly, with design, with intent; **11** puposefully; **12** deliberately; **13** intentionally

know-it-all: 6 bigwig; **7** know-all; **8** wiseacre
knowledge: 4 lore; **6** wisdom; **8** learning; **9** cognition; **11** information
knowledgeable: 5 aware; **6** versed; **7** erudite, knowing, learned; **8** educated, informed, intimate, lettered, well-read; **10** instructed; **11** enlightened; **12** intimate with, well-educated
known as: 6 called; **7** ycleped
known fact: 4 data, fact; **5** datum, facts
know nothing: 9 ignoramus; **16** uneducated person
Know-Nothing Party: 13 American Party
knuckle: 4 knee; **5** ankle, elbow, groin, joint; **6** crotch; **12** knuckle joint
knuckleball: 8 knuckler
knucklebones: 5 jacks; **10** jackstones
knuckle down: 5 slave; **8** bend down
knuckle duster: 6 knucks; **8** knuckles; **11** brass knucks; **13** brass knuckles
knucklehead: 5 dunce; **8** bonehead, lunkhead, numskull; **9** blockhead; **10** dunderhead, hammerhead, loggerhead, muttonhead
knuckle joint: 7 knuckle; **10** hinge joint
knuckler: 11 knuckleball
knuckle under: 5 yield; **6** give in; **7** succumb; **8** bend down; **9** knuckle to; **11** buckle under, knuckle down
knucks: 8 knuckles; **11** brass knucks; **13** brass knuckles, knuckle duster
KO: 8 knockout, haymaker; **11** Sunday punch; **13** knockout punch
KO'd: 3 out; **6** kayoed; **7** stunned; **10** knocked out
koala bear: 5 koala
Kobenhavn: 10 Copenhagen; **13** Danish capital
Kodachrome: 10 Ektachrome; **11** technicolor
Kodiak: 10 Kodiak bear; **16** Alaskan brown bear
Kogia: 10 genus Kogia; **15** pygmy sperm whale, dwarf sperm whale
Koh-i-noor: 9 cygne noir [Fr]; **10** chrysolite
kohlrabi: 13 turnip cabbage
koine: 12 lingua franca
kok-saghyz: 8 kok-sagyz; **16** Russian dandelion
kola nut: 4 kola; **7** cola nut; **8** goora nut
Koln: 7 Cologne
Komodo dragon: 11 giant lizard; **12** dragon lizard, Komodo lizard
Konakri: 7 Conakry; **15** capital of Guinea
Kon Tiki: 9 balsa raft
koodoo: 4 kudu; **6** koudou
kook: 5 crazy; **6** weirdo; **7** offbeat; **9** screwball
kookaburra: 15 laughing jackass
kooky: 4 bats, daft, loco, nuts; **5** balmy,

K

barmy, batty, buggy, dotty, loony, loopy, nutty, wacky; **6** fruity, kookie; **7** bonkers, cracked, haywire; **8** crackers
kopek: 6 copeck, kopeck
Koran: 5 Quran
Kore: 4 Cora; **8** Despoina; **10** Persephone
Korea: 6 Choson; **15** Korean Peninsula
Korinthos: 7 Corinth
Koweit: 6 Kuwait; **15** capital of Kuwait
kowtow: 4 fawn; **5** kneel, kotow, toady; **6** curtsy, scrape, suck up; **7** truckle; **8** bootlick, courtesy; **9** genuflect, kowtowing, obeisance; **11** prostration; **13** bow submission
K particle: 4 kaon; **6** k-meson; **10** kappa-meson
Kr: 7 krypton
kraal: 3 ham; **6** hamlet; **7** village
Krakatoa: 8 Krakatao, Krakatau
Krakow: 6 Cracow, Krakau
Krebs cycle: 15 citric acid cycle
kriegspiel: 8 war games
Krishna: 4 Siva; **5** Shiva; **6** Buddha, Vishnu; **10** Juggernath
Kriss Kringle: 10 Santa Claus; **13** Saint Nicholas; **15** Father Christmas
krona: 12 Swedish krona; **14** Icelandic krona
krone: 11 Danish krone; **14** Norwegian krone

krummhorn: 8 cromorne, crumhorn
krypton: 2 Kr
Ku: 2 Rf; **3** Unq; **10** element 104; **12** kurchatovium, unnilquadium; **13** rutherfordium
Kuala Lumpur: 17 capital of Malaysia
Kuangchou: 6 Canton; **9** Guangzhou, Kwangchow
kudos: 6 praise, regard; **7** account; **10** popularity; **12** appreciation; **15** congratulations
kudu: 6 koodoo, koudou
kudzu vine: 5 kudzu; **14** Pueraria lobata
Ku Klux Klan: 3 KKK; **4** Klan
kumquat tree: 7 cumquat, kumquat
Kung Fu-Tse: 9 Confucius
Kunlun Mountains: 6 Kunlun; **7** Kuenlun; **16** Kuenlun Mountains
Kura: 9 Kura River
kurchatovium: 2 Ku, Rf; **3** Unq; **12** unnilquadium; **13** rutherfordium
Kurile Islands: 7 Kuriles
Kuroshio: 12 Japan current
Kuwait: 6 Koweit; **15** capital of Kuwait
kV: 8 kilovolt
kvetch: 4 kick; **5** plain; **6** quetch; **8** complain, sound off
kW: 8 kilowatt
kwai: 4 yuan
Kwanzaa: 6 Kwanza
kW-hr: 3 B.T.U.; **12** kilowatt hour
kyo-chiku: 11 giant bamboo
kyphosis: 8 humpback; **9** hunchback

L

L: 5 fifty, liter, litre; **7** lambert; **14** cubic decimeter, cubic decimetre
La: 9 lanthanum
la: 3 lah
lab: 10 laboratory, science lab; **11** research lab
labdanum: 7 ladanum; **11** gum labdanum
label: 3 tag; **4** mark; **5** brand, judge; **6** docket, marque, ticket; **7** sticker; **9** pronounce, trade name
labial: 4 mute; **6** dental, liquid; **8** guttural
Labiatae: 9 Lamiaceae; **10** mint family
labiate: 7 liplike
Labor: 10 Labor Party; **11** Labour Party
labor: 3 dig, tug; **4** moil, push, task, toil, work; **5** drive, grind; **6** drudge, effort, labour; **7** lying-in, project, toiling, travail, working; **8** childbed, delivery, laboring; **10** birth-throe, childbirth; **11** confinement, parturiency, parturition, proletariat, undertaking; **12** accouchement, working class; **13** labor movement

laboratory: 3 lab; **10** science lab; **11** research lab; **14** research center
laboratory animal: 3 rat; **9** guinea pig
labor contract: 14 labor agreement
laborer: 6 drudge, worker; **7** workman; **9** demiurgus; **10** working man, workingman; **11** laboring man; **12** working stiff; **13** manual laborer, working person
labor force: 9 labor pool
laborious: 4 hard; **5** heavy; **7** arduous, onerous; **8** grueling, toilsome; **9** energetic, gruelling, Herculean, punishing, strenuous; **10** formidable, labourious; **12** backbreaking
labor movement: 5 labor; **13** union movement
labor of love: 7 pastime; **9** diversion
labor pains: 10 birth pangs
labor pool: 10 labor force
labor union: 5 union; **10** trade union; **11** brotherhood, trades union
labrocyte: 8 mast cell; **9** mastocyte

labyrinth: 4 maze, mazy; 7 network; 8 inner ear; 11 internal ear

labyrinthine: 4 mazy; 6 knotty; 7 tangled; 8 involved, tortuous; 9 Byzantine, intricate, labyrinth; 10 convoluted; 12 labyrinthian

labyrinthitis: 13 otitis interna

lace: 3 sew, tat; 4 felt, knit, tack; 5 braid, plait, spike, twine; 6 button, enlace, lace up, lacing, stitch; 8 brocade, entwine, fortify, galloon; 9 interlace; 10 intertwine

lacerate: 3 cut; 4 slit, torn; 5 slice; 7 mangled; 9 lacerated

lacewing fly: 8 lacewing

laches: 7 default, evasion, failure, neglect; 8 omission; 9 oversight; 12 inobservance

lachrymal: 8 lacrimal

lachrymose: 7 in tears, tearful, weeping; 8 dolorous; 9 dolourous, lacrymose

lack: 4 miss, need, want; 6 be poor, have no, penury; 7 absence, poverty, require; 8 be void of, distress, exigency; 9 be empty of, indigence, necessity, neediness, pauperism, privation; 10 be indigent, deficiency; 11 destitution; 12 difficulties, short measure

lackadaisical: 6 dreamy; 7 languid; 8 dilatory, listless; 9 pottering, puttering; 10 languorous; 11 half-hearted

lackey: 5 toady; 6 flunky, menial; 7 crawler, flunkey, footman; 9 sycophant

lack faith: 10 disbelieve

lacking: 6 absent, void of; 7 empty of, failing, missing, needing, wanting; 9 defective, deficient; 11 nonexistent

lackluster: 3 dun, wan; 4 ashy, cold, dead, dull; 5 ashen, dingy, dusky, faint, muddy; 6 glassy, leaden, sallow; 7 darkish, ghastly; 10 cadaverous

lack of feeling: 8 coldness, coolness; 9 aloofness, frigidity; 10 remoteness, withdrawal

lack of form: 9 amorphism

laconic: 4 curt; 5 crisp, terse

laconically: 5 dryly

laconism: 7 brevity; 9 briefness, terseness; 10 laconicism; 11 conciseness

la cosa nostra: 5 mafia; 6 the mob; 12 the syndicate; 14 organized crime

lacquer: 4 gild; 5 grain, japan, paint; 6 enamel, mastic, polish; 7 furbish, garnish, smarten, varnish; 9 japanning, whitewash; 12 French polish

lacquering: 6 waxing; 7 priming; 8 painting; 11 shellacking

lacrimal: 9 lachrymal

lacrimal gland: 9 tear gland

lacrimation: 7 tearing; 8 watering; 11 fit of crying; 12 flood of tears, lachrymation

lacrymose: 7 in tears; 10 lachrymose

lactate: 4 suck; 5 nurse; 6 suckle; 8 wetnurse; 10 breastfeed

lactating: 3 wet

lacteal: 5 milky

lactoflavin: 8 vitamin G; 9 ovoflavin, vitamin B2; 10 riboflavin; 12 hepatoflavin

lactose: 9 milk sugar

Lactuca: 7 lettuce; 12 genus Lactuca

lacuna: 3 gap; 4 dent, dint, hole, mesh; 5 blank, sinus; 6 coffer, dimple; 7 caesura, caisson; 8 follicle; 10 interstice; 11 indentation, missing part

lacy: 5 webby; 6 netted, webbed; 7 netlike, weblike; 8 lacelike

lad: 3 boy, cub; 4 chap, cuss, gent; 5 fella, sonny; 6 fellow, laddie; 7 youngun; 8 blighter, sonny boy; 9 stripling; 14 whipper-snapper

ladanum: 8 labdanum

ladder: 3 run; 5 ravel, stile

ladder truck: 13 hook and ladder

laddie: 3 cub, lad; 5 sonny; 8 sonny boy

lade: 4 load, pack; 5 laden, ladle; 6 load up

laden: 4 lade, load; 5 ladle; 6 load up, loaded; 7 fraught, ladened; 9 oppressed

la-di-da: 9 grandiose, hifalutin; 10 hoity-toity; 11 highfalutin; 12 highfaluting

ladies' man: 3 rip; 4 goat, rake; 5 satyr; 6 lecher; 7 Don Juan, fast man, gallant, seducer; 8 Lothario; 10 lady killer

ladies' room: 8 lavatory, rest room; 10 powder room

ladies' slipper: 11 lady-slipper; 12 lady's slipper; 13 slipper orchid

lading: 3 jag; 4 bale, load; 5 cargo; 6 burden; 7 freight, loading, payload; 8 shipment; 11 consignment

ladle: 3 hod, hoe; 4 lade; 5 laden, spool, spoon; 6 dipper, shovel, trowel; 7 spatula, thimble; 8 spoon off

Ladrone Islands: 8 Marianas

lady: 4 dame, ma'am; 5 madam; 6 madame; 7 peeress; 10 noblewoman; 11 gentlewoman

lady's slipper: slipper orchid

ladybug: 8 ladybird; 10 lady beetle, ladybeetle; 14 ladybird beetle

Lady Day: 12 Annunciation

lady friend: 4 girl; 10 girlfriend

lady killer: 7 seducer; 9 ladies' man

lag: 3 jug; 4 gaol, jail, slug; 5 drawl, stave; 6 dawdle, immure, linger, loiter, remand, slouch; 7 interim, put away, saunter; 8 fall back, hang back, imprison, slowdown, slugabed, sluggard; 10 fall behind; 11 incarcerate

lag bolt: 8 lag screw

lager beer: 4 lite; 8 bock beer, heavy wet; 9 light beer; 10 malt liquor; 12 Pilsener beer

laggard: 4 poky; 5 drone, pokey, slack; 6 remiss, slow to; 7 dawdler; 8 backward, dawdling, dilatory

lagomorph: 13 gnawing mammal

Lagos: 16 capital of Nigeria

L

lah: 2 la

laical: 3 lay; 5 civil; 7 profane, secular; 8 temporal

laid: 3 set

laid-back: 6 mellow; 9 easygoing

laid low: 4 worn; 5 seedy, washy; 6 rotten, wasted; 7 decayed; 8 stricken; 10 pulled down; 11 languishing; 12 deteriorated

laid-off: 5 fired; 9 dismissed; 10 discharged; 11 pink-slipped

laid up: 8 confined; 9 bedridden, invalided; 10 in hospital; 13 on the sick list

lair: 3 den, sty; 4 cave; 6 pigsty

laird: 5 count; 12 landed gentry

laissez faire: 13 individualism

laissez-faire economy: 13 market economy; 14 free enterprise

laissez passer: 4 pass

laity: 4 fold; 5 flock; 6 people; 8 assembly, brethren; 10 temporalty; 11 the faithful; 12 congregation

lake: 4 loch, mere, pond, pool, slab, tarn; 5 broad, plash; 6 puddle; 7 carmine

Lake Aral: 7 Aral Sea

lake bed: 10 lake bottom

lake duck: 11 lesser scaup

lake herring: 5 cisco

lakeshore: 8 lakeside

lake trout: 11 salmon trout

lakh: 15 hundred thousand

Lallans: 5 Scots

lallygag: 4 loaf, lurk; 5 tarry; 6 footle, linger, loiter, lounge; 8 lollygag; 9 mess about, mill about; 10 hang around, mill around

lam: 3 run; 4 bunk; 5 flail; 6 thrash, thresh; 7 getaway, run away, scarper; 8 turn tail; 9 break away

Lama: 5 llama; 6 alpaca; 7 guanaco

Lamaze method of childbirth: 12 Lamaze method

lamb: 4 dear, dove

lambast: 3 jaw, rag; 4 cane, flog; 5 check, chide, scold; 6 berate, chew up, rebuke; 7 bawl out, chew out, lecture, reproof; 8 lambaste; 9 dress down, have words, reprimand; 11 remonstrate

lambda hyperon: 14 lambda particle

lambent: 5 aglow, shiny; 6 lucent; 7 glowing, radiant; 8 luminous, lustrous

lambert: 1 L

lambskin: 9 sheepskin

lame: 4 halt, maim; 5 crazy, shaky; 6 broken, feeble, hollow, meager, muzzle, shaken; 7 cripple, halting, sketchy; 8 crippled, double up, drooping, flagging, paralyze, spavined, withered; 9 hamstring, prostrate, shattered; 11 half-and-half, perfunctory

lame duck: 4 stag; 6 debtor; 7 welsher; 8 bankrupt; 9 defaulter, insolvent

lamella: 4 gill; 6 lamina

lamellibranch: 7 bivalve; 9 pelecypod; 12 pelecypodous

lameness: 7 limping

lament: 4 keen, wail; 5 dirge, elegy; 6 bemoan, bewail, grieve, plaint, regret; 7 deplore, requiem; 8 coronach, threnody; 11 lamentation

lamentable: 3 sad; 5 sorry; 6 rueful, woeful; 7 pitiful; 8 dreadful, funereal, grievous, mournful, pitiable, wretched; 10 deplorable; 11 distressing

lamented: 4 rued; 7 mourned; 8 bewailed; 9 regretted

lamenter: 7 griever, mourner

Lamiaceae: 8 Labiatae; 10 mint family

laminated glass: 11 safety glass; 17 shatterproof glass

laminitis: 7 founder

lammergeyer: 11 lammergeier; 14 bearded vulture

lamp: 5 light

lampblack: 4 smut, soot; 9 blue-black; 10 ivory black; 11 carbon black

lampoon: 4 skit; 5 libel, spoof; 6 parody, send up, sendup; 7 charade, mockery, takeoff, traduce; 8 satirize, travesty; 9 burlesque, take off on; 10 caricature

lampooner: 7 defamer, libeler; 8 parodist, satirist

lamprey: 9 lamper eel; 10 lamprey eel

Lampropeltis: 9 kingsnake, milk adder, milk snake; 17 genus Lampropeltis

lampshell: 10 brachiopod

LAN: 16 local area network

Lanai: 11 Lanai Island

lanai: 4 deck; 5 porch; 7 veranda

lance: 3 gig; 4 dart, pink, tilt; 5 shaft, spear; 6 fizgig, lancet, riddle; 7 fishgig; 8 puncture

lancelet: 9 amphioxus

Lancelot: 11 Sir Lancelot

lanceolate: 9 lancelike, lanciform; 11 lanceshaped

lancet: 5 lance, probe; 10 lancet arch

Lanchou: 7 Lanchow, Lanzhou

land: 4 down, soil; 5 acres, bring, earth, lands, realm, shore, state; 6 alight, domain, estate, ground, nation, realty; 7 a people, country, demesne, dry land, farming, kingdom, put down, set down; 8 go ashore, property; 9 bring down, dry ground, set ashore, shoot down, tenements; 10 real estate, res publica, terra firma; 11 body politic, nationality, solid ground, terrestrial; 12 commonwealth

land agent: 7 realtor; 10 house agent; 11 estate agent; 15 real estate agent

land area: 7 acreage

landed: 8 manorial; 11 territorial

landed gentry: 5 laird; 11 squirearchy

landholder: 9 landowner; 13 property owner

landing deck: 10 flight deck

landing field: 5 field; 8 airfield; 11 flying field

landing strip: 5 strip; 8 airstrip; 11 flight strip

land mile: 2 mi; 4 mile; 6 stat mi; 11 statute mile

land mine: 9 booby trap

Land of Enchantment: 9 New Mexico

Land of Lincoln: 8 Illinois, 12 Prairie State

Land of Opportunity: 8 Arkansas

landowner: 10 landholder

landrover: 4 jeep

lands: 4 land; 5 acres; 6 realty; 8 property; 9 tenements; 10 real estate

landscape: 7 scenery

land shark: 4 thug; 5 harpy, shark; 6 bandit, falcon; 7 brigand; 10 freebooter

landslide: 7 debacle; 8 landslip; 9 avalanche

Landsmal: 7 Nynorsk; 12 New Norwegian

landsman: 6 lubber; 7 landman; 10 compatriot, countryman, landlubber, 13 fellow citizen

land tax: 11 property tax

lane: 5 aisle, alley, lobby; 6 artery; 8 corridor

Langobard: 7 Lombard

langouste: 8 crawfish, crayfish; 11 rock lobster, sea crawfish; 12 spiny lobster

langoustine: 6 scampo; 16 Norwegian lobster

lang syne: 7 long ago; 8 old times; 9 long since; 12 auld lang syne; 14 the good old days

language: 5 lingo, lyric, words; 6 speech, tongue; 11 terminology; 12 nomenclature

languid: 3 dry; 4 cold, dull, lazy, poor; 5 bland, prosy, slack; 6 dreamy, frigid, groggy, infirm, otiose, remiss, supine, torpid, trashy; 7 prosaic; 8 crawling, creeping, indolent, listless, lukewarm, slothful, sluggish; 9 colorless, leisurely, lethargic, proposing, snail-like

languidly: 6 lazily; 7 slackly; 8 torpidly; 10 indolently, slothfully, sluggishly

languish: 3 yen; 4 ache, drop, fade, fail, flag, halt, limp, long, pine, sink; 5 droop, shake, waste, yearn; 6 repine, run low, totter; 7 crumble, decline, give way, tremble; 8 hang fire, pine away

languishing: 4 worn; 5 seedy, washy; 6 rotten, wasted; 7 decayed, laid low; 10 pulled down; 12 deteriorated

Laniidae: 6 shrike; 14 family Laniidae

lank: 5 lanky; 7 spindly

lanky: 4 lank; 5 rangy; 6 gangly; 8 gangling

lanolin: 7 wool fat; 10 wool grease

Lansing: 17 capital of Michigan

lantern: 6 dormer; 8 gas light; 9 lime light

lantern image: 10 slide image

lantern pinion: 10 gear pinion; 12 lantern wheel

lanthanide: 9 lanthanon, rare earth; 16 rare-earth element

lanthanon: 9 rare earth; 10 lanthanide; 16 rare-earth element

lanthanum: 2 La

Lanzhou: 7 Lanchou, Lanchow

Lao-Tzu: 5 Laozi; 6 Lao-Tse

lap: 3 bar, rod; 4 boom, gird, heel, lick, seat, shoe, sole; 5 beset, bound, lap up, swish, swosh; 6 begird, circle, splint, stilts; 7 circuit, compass, embrace, enclose, environ, inclose, involve, overlap, sojourn, stirrup; 8 encircle, envelope, quarters, surround; 9 encompass, outrigger; 10 circumvent

lapdog: 6 toy dog

lapel: 7 flounce

lapel pin: 3 pin; 6 broach, torque

lapidary: 8 lapidist; 10 lapidarian, lapidarist

lapin: 6 rabbit

lapis lazuli: 5 lapis

lap joint: 6 splice

lap-jointed: 11 overlapping

La Plata: 10 Plata River; 12 Rio de la Plata

lap of luxury: 4 ease; 6 luxury; 7 comfort; 13 lap of pleasure, luxuriousness

Lapp: 4 Sami; 10 Lapplander

lappet: 4 flap

lapping: 11 imbrication, overlapping

Lapplander: 4 Lapp

lapse: 4 fall, flux, go by, pass, sink, slip, trip; 5 shift; 6 come to, elapse, expire, growth, offend, slip by; 7 faux pas [Fr], glide by, go along, lapsing, regress, relapse, slide by, turn out; 8 blow over, collapse, fall back, progress, slip away, trespass; 9 backslide, oversight, relapsing, reversion, reverting; 10 expiration, peccadillo, recidivate, recidivism, regression, retrogress; 11 backsliding

lapsed: 6 no more, run out; 7 elapsed, expired, extinct, has-been; 8 exploded; 9 blown over, forgotten; 10 antebellum; 11 that has been; 12 antediluvian

lap-strake: 12 clinker-built

lapsus linguae: 13 clerical error

lapsus linouae: 12 slip of the lip; 15 slip of the tongue

laptop computer: 6 laptop

lapwing: 5 pewit; 6 peewit; 11 green plover

larboard: 4 left, port

larcener: 9 larcenist

larcenous: 12 thievishness

larceny: 5 theft; 8 stealing, thievery, thieving; 12 grand larceny, petty larceny

larch: 9 larch tree

lard: 3 pad; 4 suet; 6 blow up, grease, tallow; 9 dramatise, dramatize, embellish, embroider; 10 aggrandize

larder: 6 pantry, spence [Brit.]; 7 buttery

lares et penates: 10 golden calf; 13 household gods

large: 3 big; 4 huge; 5 great, heavy, tumid; 6 gravid, turgid; 7 orotund; 8 enceinte;

L

9 bombastic, expectant, prominent, with child; **10** boastfully, vauntingly; **11** declamatory, macroscopic, magnanimous

large amount: 3 lot; **4** a lot, lots; **7** a volume; **9** a quantity; **13** large quantity

large calorie: 7 Calorie; **8** frigorie; **11** kilocalorie

large cent: 6 copper

large group: 8 quantity

largely: 6 mostly

largeness: 7 bigness; **8** hugeness; **9** greatness, large size, magnitude

large number: 4 pack; **9** battalion, multitude; **11** great number; **13** large quantity

large order: 9 tall order

larger: 6 bigger

larger-than-life: 4 epic; **6** heroic

large-scale: 4 mass

large size: 7 bigness; **8** hugeness; **9** greatness, largeness

largesse: 7 largess; **6** bounty; **10** generosity; **11** magnanimity, munificence; **14** openhandedness

largest: 7 biggest, outside; **8** greatest

largest part: 8 majority

larghetto: 5 largo; **7** andante

largish: 7 biggish

largo: 7 andante; **9** larghetto

lariat: 5 cinch, lasso, noose

Larix: 5 larch; **8** tamarack; **10** genus Larix

lark: 3 rig; **4** romp; **5** antic, frisk, pipit, prank, sport, spree; **6** cavort, frolic, gambol; **7** disport, rollick, skylark, titlark; **8** escapade; **9** lark about, run around; **10** meadowlark, skylarking

larrup: 4 cane, comb, flog, lash, lick, whip; **5** birch, spank, strap, towel; **6** paddle, switch, thrash, thresh; **7** scourge; **9** bastinado, horsewhip; **10** flagellate; **12** give the stick

Larus: 3 cob, mew; **4** gull; **5** pewit; **6** sea mew; **7** mew gull; **10** genus Larus

larynx: 8 voice box

lasagna: 7 lasagne

lascivious: 4 lewd; **7** lustful; **9** lecherous, salacious; **10** libidinous

lasciviousness: 7 lechery; **8** lewdness; **9** carnality, lubricity, prurience, pruriency

lash: 4 cane, comb, flog, goad, lick, spur, trim, urge, welt, whip; **5** birch, hitch, knout, prick, slash, strap, thong, towel, truss; **6** blow up, excite, foment, incite, kindle, larrup, lather, stir up, switch, thrash, thresh, turn on; **7** cowhide, inflame, quicken, scourge, sharpen, trounce; **8** bullwhip, chastise, overhaul, whiplash; **9** bastinado, castigate, horsewhip, reprimand, stimulate; **10** flagellate

lashing: 8 flogging, whipping; **12** flagellation

lashings: 4 gobs, lots, tons, wads; **5** heaps, loads, piles, rafts, scads, slews; **6** dozens, oodles, scores, stacks

lash out: 5 round, snipe; **6** assail, attack; **7** assault

lass: 4 girl; **6** lassie; **9** young girl; **10** jeune fille

Lassa: 5 Lhasa; **13** Forbidden City; **14** capital of Tibet

lassie: 4 girl, lass; **9** young girl; **10** jeune fille

lassitude: 7 languor; **8** lethargy; **9** inanition, tiredness; **10** exhaustion; **12** listlessness, sluggishness

lasso: 5 cinch, noose, riata; **6** lariat; **9** surcingle

last: 2 go; **3** end, net; **4** go on, live, stay; **5** abide, close, death, final, finis, later; **6** endure, finale, finish, hold up, lastly, latest, latter, live on, lowest, matrix, newest, remain, utmost; **7** extreme, finally, hold out, persist, survive; **8** continue, terminal, terminus, ultimate, up-to-date; **9** extremity, last-place; **10** concluding, conclusion

last act: 8 swan song; **12** chant du cygne [Fr]

last but one: 11 penultimate

last day: 4 doom; **8** dies irae [Lat], doomsday; **11** crack of doom, Judgment day; **13** day of Judgment; **14** day of reckoning

last finish: 11 coup de grace

Last Frontier: 6 Alaska

last half: 10 second half

lasting: 6 eonian; **7** abiding, aeonian, durable, eternal; **8** enduring; **9** long-lived, permanent; **10** continuing, persistent; **11** everlasting, long-lasting

lastingness: 8 strength; **10** durability; **11** endlessness; **12** enduringness

lastly: 4 last; **7** finally; **12** in conclusion

last name: 7 surname; **8** cognomen; **10** family name

last-place: 4 last; **6** lowest

last rites: 14 extreme unction

Last Supper: 11 Lord's Supper

last word: 3 fad; **5** craze, thing, trend; **7** in thing; **9** bandwagon; **11** latest thing

lat: 14 latisimus dorsi

latch: 4 bolt, hank, hasp, hook, link, lock, yoke; **5** belay, brace, catch, clasp, leash; **6** couple; **7** bracket, grapple

latched: 4 fast; **6** barred, bolted, locked; **7** secured

latchkey: 7 passkey; **9** master key

latch on: 4 twig; **5** get it; **6** hook on, take up, tumble; **7** catch on, get onto, seize on; **8** cotton on, fasten on

late: 4 deep, gone, slow; **5** later, tardy; **6** behind, former, lately, modern, no more, of late, recent; **7** belated, nouveau, quondam, tardily; **8** backward, ci-devant [Fr], latterly, neoteric, previous, pristine, recently, untimely; **9** belatedly, erstwhile;

10 behindhand, unpunctual; 11 hypermodern, modernistic; 12 contemporary, nonclassical
lateen: 10 lateen sail; 12 lateen-rigged
Late Latin: 13 Biblical Latin
lately: 4 anew, late; 6 afresh, of late; 7 just now; 8 latterly, nowadays, recently; 9 these days
latency: 7 density; 8 inaction; 9 obscurity; 12 latent period
latency period: 12 latency phase, latency stage
lateness: 9 tardiness; 12 untimeliness; 13 unpunctuality
latent: 5 tacit; 7 dormant, implied; 8 implicit; 10 smoldering, understood
later: 4 last, late; 5 after; 6 future, latter; 7 by and by, later on; 8 ulterior; 9 afterward, following, hereafter, posterior; 10 afterwards, subsequent, succeeding; 11 in the future; 12 subsequently; 13 prospectively
lateral: 8 sidelong; 11 lateral pass
laterality: 9 dominance; 10 handedness
later on: 5 after, later; 9 afterward; 10 afterwards; 12 subsequently
latest: 4 last; 6 newest; 7 fire-new, just out, span-new; 8 brand-new, up-to-date; 10 most recent
latest thing: 3 fad; 5 craze, thing, trend; 7 in thing; 8 last word; 9 bandwagon
latex: 10 caoutchouc, gum elastic, latex paint; 11 India rubber
lather: 3 oil; 4 flog, foam, fret, head, lash, soap, stew, suds, welt, whip; 5 froth, slash, spume, strap, sweat; 6 grease; 7 swither, trounce; 8 soapsuds
Lathyrus: 3 pea; 13 genus Lathyrus
Latimeria: coelacanth; 14 genus Latimeria
Latin: 7 Romance
Latin American: 15 Spanish American
Latino: 8 Hispanic; 15 Spanish American
Latin Quarter: 8 Left Bank
latisimus dorsi: 3 lat
latitude: 4 play; 5 range, scope; 6 leeway; 8 parallel, purchase; 9 amplitude, tolerance; 14 line of latitude
latitude and longitude: 11 coordinates
latitudinarian: 5 Deist; 6 theist; 9 espri fort [Fr], Unitarian; 10 undogmatic; 11 freethinker, rationalist; 12 free-thinking, undogmatical
latke: 13 potato pancake
latria: 6 vigils; 9 adoration
latrine: 4 head, john; 5 jakes, privy; 6 toilet
Latrodectus: 16 genus Latrodectus
Latrodectus mactans: 10 black widow
latter: 4 last; 5 later
Latter-day Saint: 6 Mormon
latterly: 4 late; 6 lately, of late; 8 recently; 9 these days
lattice: 6 grille, wicket; 8 fretwork; 11 latticework

Latvian: 4 Lett; 7 Lettish
laud: 5 bless, exalt, extol; 6 praise; 7 commend, glorify, magnify; 8 proclaim, say grace; 9 laudation; 10 compliment; 11 sing praises; 12 commendation
laudably: 9 admirably; 10 creditably; 11 commendable, commendably; 14 praiseworthily
laudanum: 8 relaxant; 9 demulcent; 11 carminative; 13 antispasmodic
laudatory: 8 praising; 9 praiseful; 10 eulogistic, uncritical; 11 encomiastic, panegyrical; 12 commendatory; 13 complimentary
lauder: 8 extoller, laudator; 9 applauder
laugh: 3 gag, yak; 4 jape, jest, joke; 6 wheeze; 8 laughter; 10 express joy; 12 express mirth
laughable: 3 odd; 5 comic, funny; 7 amusing, comical, risible; 8 farcical, mirthful, pour rire; 9 grotesque
laugher: 4 romp; 6 shoo-in; 7 runaway; 8 walkaway
laughing: 5 riant
laughing gas: 12 nitrous oxide
laughing hyena: 12 spotted hyena
laughing jackass: 10 kookaburra
laughingstock: 4 butt, goat; 6 stooge
laugh line: 7 gag line, tag line; 9 punch line
laugh softly: 7 chortle, chuckle
launce: 7 sand eel; 9 sandlance
launch: 4 send; 5 found, mount, set up; 6 let fly, let off, plunge; 7 fire off, pinnace, release, send off; 8 initiate; 9 establish, first move, launching, send forth; 10 inaugurate; 11 set in motion; 12 commencement
launch area: 3 pad; 9 launch pad, launchpad; 12 launching pad
launcher: 8 catapult; 14 rocket launcher
launching: 5 debut, entry; 6 launch; 9 unveiling; 12 introduction
launch into: 6 tackle, take up; 8 embark in, embark on; 10 plunge into, take in hand
launder: 4 buck, lave, wash; 12 launder money
laundress: 9 washwoman; 10 laundryman; 11 washerwoman; 12 laundrywoman
laundry: 4 wash; 8 lavatory; 9 washables; 11 laundry room
laundry basket: 13 clothes basket, clothes hamper
Lauraceae: 12 laurel family; 15 family Lauraceae
laureate: 6 squire; 9 gentleman, patrician
laureled: 7 crowned
laurel family: 9 Lauraceae; 15 family Lauraceae
laurels: 5 award, honor; 6 honour, trophy; 8 accolade; 9 bay wreath; 12 laurel wreath
laurel wreath: 4 palm; 5 medal; 6 ribbon,

L

wreath; **7** garland, laurels; **9** bay wreath, medallion; **10** decoration

Laurus: 3 bay; **7** bay tree; **9** bay laurel; **11** genus Laurus

lav: 3 can; **4** john; **5** privy; **6** toilet; **8** bathroom, facility, lavatory

lavabo: 8 washbowl; **9** handbasin, washbasin

lavage: 5 enema; **7** washing

lavaliere: 7 pendant; **8** lavalier; **10** lavalliere

Lavandula: 8 lavender; **14** genus Lavandula

lavation: 6 laving; **7** bathing, washing; **8** ablution; **9** cleansing

lavatory: 3 can, lav; **4** john; **5** privy; **6** toilet; **7** laundry; **8** bathroom, facility, men's room, rest room, washbowl; **9** washbasin, washstand; **10** ladies' room; **11** flush toilet

lave: 4 buck, wash; **5** bathe; **7** launder, residue

lavender: 5 lilac, mauve; **11** plum-colored

lavish: 4 lush; **5** plush; **6** plushy, pour on, shower, wanton; **7** profuse, replete; **8** lucullan, overmuch, prodigal, wasteful; **9** exuberant, unsparing, unstinted, unthrifty; **10** dissipated, inordinate, munificent, profligate, thriftless, thrust upon, unstinting; **11** extravagant, improvident, overliberal, too-generous; **12** overgenerous; **13** superabundant

law: 4 rule; **6** police; **7** statute; **10** natural law; **11** law of nature, legislation, physical law, police force; **12** constabulary, law of physics; **13** jurisprudence

law-abiding: 8 peaceful; **9** observant

lawbreaker: 8 violator

law-breaking: 5 crime

lawful: 4 true; **5** legal, licit; **7** orderly; **8** rightful; **10** legitimate; **12** rule-governed

lawfully: 6 de jure; **7** legally, licitly; **10** wrongfully; **12** legitimately

lawgiver: 8 lawmaker; **10** legislator, politician

lawless: 4 open; **5** stray; **6** outlaw, wanton; **7** wayward; **8** anarchic, criminal, improper, informal, scampish, unlawful, unseemly, wide-open; **9** felonious, wandering; **10** anarchical, disorderly, indecorous; **12** unprincipled

lawless behavior: 11 criminality

lawlessly: 8 wantonly; **9** illegally, illicitly; **10** disorderly, improperly, informally, scampishly; **12** indecorously

lawlessness: 7 anarchy; **8** outlawry; **11** criminality

law-makers: 11 legislature

lawmaking: 11 legislating, legislation

lawman: 10 law officer; **12** peace officer

lawn: 3 sod; **4** plat, plot, turf; **5** green

lawn cart: 6 barrow; **10** garden cart; **11** wheelbarrow

lawn party: 11 garden party

law officer: 6 lawman; **12** peace officer

law of gravitation: 10 Newton's law

law of large numbers: 13 Bernoulli's law, law of averages

law of motion: 10 Newton's law

law of multiple proportions: 10 Dalton's law

law of partial pressures: 10 Dalton's law

law of volumes: 10 Charles' law; **13** Gay-Lussac's law

lawrencium: 2 Lw

Laws: 5 Torah; **10** Pentateuch

Laws of Moses: 9 Mosaic law

lawsuit: 4 case, suit; **5** causa, cause; **6** action; **9** suit in law; **10** litigation; **11** legal action

lawyer: 8 attorney; **12** legal counsel

lax: 4 limp, soft, weak; **5** baggy, frail, loose, slack; **6** infirm; **7** flaccid, inexact, lenient, relaxed; **8** careless, detached, flapping, slipshod, slovenly; **9** imperfect, indulgent, streaming

laxative: 6 physic; **8** aperient; **9** cathartic, purgative

laxity: 7 laxness; **8** baseness, foulness, limpness, quietism, trimming, vileness; **9** abjection, shuffling, turpitude; **10** debasement, flaccidity, remissness; **11** degradation, informality

lay: 3 lea, ley, put, set; **4** calm, cool, damp, hush, laic, lull, pose, song, swag, tame; **5** abate, allay, civil, place, quell, quiet, sober, still, whelp; **6** ballad, deaden, evolve, laical, pacify, rebate, repose, smooth, soothe; **7** appease, assuage, compose, profane, put down, secular, slacken, turn off; **8** calm down, overload, position, suppress, temporal; **9** alleviate, lay a wager, pasturage; **11** grazing land, tranquilize

layabout: 3 bum; **5** idler; **6** loafer; **9** do-nothing

lay away: 6 cache, hoard, stash; **6** hive up; **12** squirrel away

lay claim to: 5 claim; **6** assert, assume; **7** reclaim, require; **8** arrogate

layered: 12 superimposed

layette: 9 baby linen; **14** swaddling cloth

lay eyes on: 6 behold

laying the groundwork: 8 readying; **9** preparing; **11** preparation

laying waste: 4 ruin; **7** ruining; **8** wrecking; **9** ruination

lay in ruins: 10 lay in ashes

lay into: 7 lam into; **8** lace into, tear into; **9** pitch into

lay it on thick: 10 overpraise

layman: 8 civilian; **9** layperson

lay off: 4 quit, stop; **5** cease; **6** give up; **8** furlough; **11** discontinue

lay on the line: 4 risk

lay open: 4 bare, open; **6** expose, open up; **7** lay bare, pop open, unclose, uncover; **8** pull open; **9** throw open; **12** bring to light

lay out: 5 array, range, set up; 6 cut out,
embalm, map out, set out; 7 fork out, lay
down, mummify, present; 8 chalk out, fork
over, shell out
layover: 4 stop; 8 stopover
layperson: 6 layman
lay the foundation of: 5 found, set up; 6
broach; 9 institute, originate
lay to rest: 4 bury; 5 inter; 6 entomb
lay waste: 6 ravage; 8 desolate; 9 devastate
lazar: 5 leper
laze: 4 idle; 8 stagnate
lazily: 4 idly; 7 slackly; 8 torpidly; 9 languidly; 10 indolently, slothfully, sluggishly
laziness: 5 sloth; 6 acedia
lazuline: 5 azure; 7 sky-blue; 8 cerulean,
sapphire
lazy: 5 slack; 6 otiose, remiss, supine, torpid;
7 languid, work-shy; 8 indolent, slothful,
sluggish
lazy Susan: 9 turntable
Ld.: 3 Ltd.; 14 limited company
LE: 3 SLE; 4 lupus
lea: 3 lay, ley; 7 pasture; 9 pasturage; 11 pastureland
leach: 5 strip; 8 leaching; 9 percolate
lead: 2 go, Pb; 3 run, tip; 4 head, hint, pass,
star, take, wind; 5 carry, chair, guide, leash,
leave, steer, track, trail; 6 affect, direct,
extend, lead in, result, tether; 7 be first,
conduce, conduct, leading, oversee,
plumbum, precede, usher in; 8 moderate,
whip hand; 9 advantage, come first, introduce, lead story, principal, upper hand; 10
contribute
lead carbonate: 9 white lead
leaden: 3 dun, sad, wan; 4 ashy, cold, dead,
drab, dull, gray, grey, roan; 5 ashen, dingy,
dirty, faint, heavy, livid, lurid, muddy; 6
glassy, pearly, russet, sallow, somber; 7
ghastly; 8 iron-gray, overcast, plodding,
weighted; 10 cadaverous, lackluster; 11
crepuscular
leader: 5 guide; 7 example; 9 conductor, role
model
leaders: 10 leadership
lead-free: 9 nonleaded
leading: 4 lead, main, star; 5 ahead, chief,
first, prima, prime; 7 capital, heading, primary, stellar; 8 foremost, greatest, starring;
9 in the lead, precedent, principal; 10 leadership, overruling, precession, preeminent
leading tone: 8 subtonic
lead into error: 10 lead astray
lead line: 12 sounding line
lead off: 5 begin, start; 8 commence
lead on: 5 cozen; 6 delude; 7 deceive
lead-pipe cinch: 5 cinch; 9 sure thing
lead the way: 4 head, lead; 7 be first, lead
off, usher in; 9 come first, introduce
leaf: 4 flip, foil, page, riff; 5 flick, folio,
thumb; 6 riffle; 7 foliage, leafage, leaflet

441 **lay out / leaseholder**

leafage: 4 leaf; 7 foliage
leaf beetle: 11 chrysomelid
leaf fat: 8 leaf lard
leaflet: 4 cusp, leaf; 6 folder; 7 booklet; 8
brochure, pamphlet
leaf mustard: 7 gai choi, mustard
leafstalk: 7 petiole
league: 3 ell; 4 Bund [Ger]; 5 class, cubit; 6
fathom; 8 alliance, category; 9 syndicate;
10 conference; 11 combination
leak: 6 escape; 7 leak out, leakage, outflow;
10 out through, run through
leakage: 4 leak; 6 escape, oozing; 7 outflow;
11 percolation; 12 distillation
Leakey: 11 Louis Leakey; 24 Louis Seymour
Bazett Leakey
leakproof: 10 watertight
lean: 4 list, tend, thin, tilt; 5 angle, slant,
slope; 6 skimpy, skinny; 7 incline, leaning;
11 inclination
lean back: 7 recline
leaning: 4 bent, bias, lean, list, mind, tilt; 5
atilt, favor; 6 animus, canted, tilted, tipped;
7 tending; 8 penchant, tendency, trending;
9 inclining, proneness; 10 affections,
favoritism, partiality, proclivity, propensity;
11 disposition, inclination; 12 predilection;
14 predisposition
leanness: 8 thinness
lean towards: 5 favor
lean upon: 5 trust
leap: 3 hop; 4 jump; 5 bound, vault; 6
bounce, jump up, plunge, spring
leap day: 13 bissextile day
leapfrog: 14 hop skip and jump
leap year: 14 bissextile year; 15 intercalary
year
learn: 4 hear, larn, read, take; 5 check, study,
teach, watch; 6 pick up; 7 find out, get
wind, get word; 8 discover, instruct, memorize; 9 ascertain, determine
learned: 7 erudite, knowing; 8 educated, lettered, well-read; 10 instructed; 11 conditioned, enlightened; 12 well-educated; 13
knowledgeable
learned person: 12 intellectual
learned writing: 5 theme; 6 thesis; 8 treatise;
12 dissertation
learner: 5 pupil; 7 scholar, student; 8 prentice; 10 apprentice
learning: 4 lore; 6 wisdom; 9 erudition,
knowledge; 11 acquisition, eruditeness,
information, learnedness, scholarship
lease: 3 let; 4 hire, rent, take, term; 6 demise,
engage, rental; 7 charter, letting; 8 under-
let; 10 leasing out, limitation, renting out,
settlement
leased: 3 let; 5 hired; 9 chartered
lease giver: 6 lessor
leaseholder: 6 lessee

leash: 4 hook, lead, link, lock, rope, trey, trio, yoke; **5** belay, brace, latch, three, tie up, triad, trine; **6** couple, pinion, tercet, tether

least: 6 lowest; **8** littlest, smallest

least common multiple: 3 lcm

leather: 4 drub, skin; **5** baste; **6** pummel; **7** belabor, sandbag, trounce

leatherback turtle: 11 leatherback

leatherette: 16 imitation leather

leatherneck: 6 Marine

leather soap: 10 saddle soap

leave: 3 let; **4** exit, give, lead, quit, will; **5** allow, go out; **6** depart, forget, get out, give up, go away, impart, pass on, result; **7** drop out, entrust, go forth, parting, throw in; **8** allow for, bequeath, break off, break way, farewell, separate, uncouple; **9** disengage; **10** permission, permitting, provide for; **11** authorizing; **13** authorization

leave a place: 4 quit; **6** vacate; **7** abandon; **8** evacuate

leave in the lurch: 6 desert; **7** abandon, forsake; **8** abnegate

leave it: 4 stet

leaven: 5 alloy, prove, raise, yeast; **6** season, temper; **7** ferment; **8** denature, imoderate; **9** leavening; **10** adulterate, corruption, ingredient

leave off: 4 drop, omit, quit; **6** disuse, except, give up; **7** exclude, take out; **8** break off

leave out: 4 drop, miss, omit; **6** bar out, except; **7** exclude, neglect, shut out, take out; **8** overlook

leave-taking: 5 leave; **7** parting; **8** farewell; **9** departure

leaving: 5 going; **9** departing, departure; **10** decampment, uncoupling; **11** embarkation; **13** disengagement

leavings: 7 stubble, residue; **8** remnants

lebensraum: 11 living space

Lebistes: 5 guppy; **11** rainbow fish; **13** genus Lebistes

lech: 4 lust

lecher: 3 rip; **4** goat, rake; **5** satyr; **7** Don Juan, fast man, gallant, seducer; **8** Lothario; **9** debauchee, ladies' man

lecherous: 4 lewd; **9** salacious; **10** lascivious

lechwe: 8 antelope

lectern: 6 pulpit

lection: 5 light, sense; **7** reading, version

lector: 6 reader; **8** lecturer

lecture: 3 jaw, rag; **4** talk; **5** check, chide, class, orate, scold, speak, stump; **6** berate, blow up, chew up, homily, lesson, preach, recite, sermon, speech; **7** address, declaim, lambast, oration, oratory, reproof, reprove, seminar, wigging; **8** dressing, flourish, harangue, lambaste, pastoral, scolding, trimming; **9** discourse, dress down, hold forth, lecturing, predicate, reprimand, sermonize, speechify

lecture hall: 10 auditorium

lecturer: 6 lector, orator, reader; **7** speaker; **8** preacher; **9** professor; **10** prolocutor

lecture room: 9 classroom

ledge: 4 edge; **5** shelf; **7** plateau; **10** escarpment

ledger: 3 log; **4** book; **5** books, diary, leger; **7** daybook, journal; **8** calendar

Lee: 10 Robert E. Lee; **15** Robert Edward Lee

lee: 4 side; **5** flank; **7** lee side, leeward, quarter; **8** downwind

leech: 5 bleed; **8** parasite; **11** bloodsucker; **12** phlebotomize

leek: 8 scallion

leer: 4 ogle, wink; **5** glare, nudge, shrug, sneer; **6** glance; **8** sneering

leery: 4 wary; **5** canny; **6** astute; **7** knowing; **10** suspicious, untrusting; **11** mistrustful

lees: 5 dregs; **7** grounds

lee shore: 4 bank, flat; **5** shelf; **6** shoals; **8** breakers, shallows; **14** ironbound coast

lee side: 3 lee; **7** leeward

leeward: 3 lee; **6** upwind; **7** lee side

leeway: 4 play; **6** margin; **7** headway; **8** latitude, purchase, sternway; **9** allowance, tolerance

left: 3 odd; **4** port; **7** given up; **8** deserted, forsaken, larboard, left hand, left over, left side, left wing, left-hand, leftover; **9** abandoned, leftfield, remaining; **10** unexpended; **12** relinquished

Left Bank: 12 Latin Quarter

left behind: 8 left over, residual; **9** residuary, surviving

left brain: 14 left hemisphere

left-handed: 6 clumsy; **7** awkward, unhandy; **8** bumbling, bungling, handless, lubberly; **9** ham-fisted, ham-handed, maladroit

left-handed pitcher: 5 lefty; **8** southpaw; **10** left-hander

left hemisphere: 9 left brain

leftist: 7 liberal; **8** left-wing; **10** left-winger; **12** collectivist, left-of-center

left-of-center: 7 leftist; **8** left-wing

leftover: 3 odd; **4** left; **7** remnant; **8** left over, reheated; **9** remaining; **10** cooked-over, unexpended

left-winger: 7 leftist; **12** collectivist

lefty: 8 southpaw; **10** left-hander

leg: 4 fork, rook; **5** shank, stage; **6** branch

legacy: 7 bequest; **9** patrimony; **11** inheritance

legal: 5 licit, sound; **6** lawful; **10** legitimate

legal action: 4 suit; **5** cause; **6** action; **7** lawsuit

legal age: 8 majority

legal assistant: 9 paralegal

legal authority: 10 government

legal community: 3 bar

legal counsel: 6 lawyer; **8** attorney

legal document: 10 instrument
legal estate: 15 equitable estate
legal expert: 6 jurist
legal guardian: 7 trustee
legal injury: 4 tort; 5 wrong; 6 damage
legalize: 5 allot; 6 ordain; 8 sanctify; 9 prescribe; 10 legitimate, legitimize; 12 legitimatize; 13 decriminalize
legalized: 6 vested; 9 chartered; 10 authorized; 14 constitutional
legally: 6 de jure; 7 licitly; 8 lawfully; 10 wrongfully; 12 legitimately
legally binding: 11 enforceable
legal ouster: 8 eviction; 13 dispossession
legal philosophy: 3 law; 13 jurisprudence
legal power: 12 jurisdiction
legal profession: 3 bar
legate: 5 envoy; 7 attache; 8 emissary; 9 messenger
legatee: 4 heir; 7 heiress [female], heritor; 9 inheritor
legation: 7 embassy, mission; 10 legateship
legato: 6 smooth
leg covering: 5 legin; 7 legging
legend: 5 fable; 6 annals; 7 caption; 9 chronicle, tradition
leger: 4 book; 6 ledger; 11 account book
legerdemain: 5 magic, trick; 8 illusion; 9 deception
legerity: 7 agility, 10 nimbleness; 13 lightsomeness
legging: 5 legin; 8 leggings; 11 leg covering
leggy: 7 spindly
legibility: 11 readability; 14 discernability
legible: 8 readable; 12 recognizable
legion: 4 host; 5 horde; 6 cohort; 7 phalanx
legislate: 4 pass; 8 pass a law
legislating: 9 lawmaking; 11 legislation
legislation: 3 law; 7 statute; 9 lawmaking; 11 legislating
legislator: 8 lawgiver; 10 politician
legitimacy: 11 genuineness; 12 authenticity; 14 legitimateness
legitimate: 5 legal, licit; 6 lawful; 7 genuine, logical; 8 legalize, rightful; 9 authentic; 10 legitimize; 11 justifiable
leg of lamb: 5 gigot
legume: 4 bean; 5 pulse; 9 vegetable
legume family: 8 Fabaceae; 9 pea family; 11 Leguminosae
lei: 6 wreath; 7 chaplet, coronal, garland
Leibnitz: 7 Leibniz; 23 Gottfried Wilhelm Leibniz; 24 Gottfried Wilhelm Leibnitz
Leicestershire: 9 Leicester
leisure: 8 leisured; 10 relaxation; 11 convenience
leisurely: 4 easy; 6 slowly, torpid; 7 languid; 8 crawling, creeping; 9 at leisure, easygoing
leisure time: 9 spare time
leitmotif: 9 leitmotiv
Leitneria: 8 corkwood; 14 genus Leitneria
LEM: 11 lunar lander, lunar module

Lemmus: 7 lemming; 11 genus lemmus
Lemna: 8 duckweed; 10 genus Lemna
lemniscus: 6 fibers
lemon: 4 lime; 5 maize; 6 citrus, citron, jalopy; 7 clunker
lemon butter: 14 Meuniere butter
lemon-colored: 5 amber; 6 citron; 11 lemon yellow
lemonlike: 4 tart; 5 tangy; 6 lemony; 7 sourish
lemon peel: 9 lemon rind
lemon sole: 11 English sole; 14 winter flounder
lemony: 4 tart; 5 tangy; 7 sourish; 9 lemonlike
Lena: 9 Lena River
lend: 3 add; 4 loan; 5 bring; 6 bestow, impart; 10 contribute
lend assistance: 3 aid; 4 help; 6 assist, succor
lender: 6 loaner; 8 creditor
lending: 4 loan; 7 loaning
lending library: 13 public library
length: 8 distance, duration
lengthen: 6 extend; 8 elongate
lengthiness: 8 longness; 9 extension, prolixity, verbosity, wordiness; 11 diffuseness, protuseness, protraction; 12 prolongation; 13 expansiveness
length of service: 9 longevity
lengthwise: 5 along; 8 at length, linearly, longways, longwise; 10 lengthways; 14 longitudinally
lengthy: 4 long; 5 wordy; 7 copious, diffuse, profuse, verbose; 8 drawn-out, extended; 9 expansive, exuberant, prolonged; 10 longwinded, protracted
leniency: 6 lenity; 8 lenience, mildness; 9 tolerance; 10 indulgence, toleration
lenient: 3 lax; 4 easy, soft; 9 indulgent
Lenin: 12 Nikolai Lenin; 13 Vladimir Lenin; 21 Vladimir Ilyich Ulyanov
Leningrad: 9 Peterburg, Petrograd; 13 St. Petersburg; 15 Saint Petersburg
Leninism: 7 Marxism; 9 communism, Sovietism, sovietism; 10 bolshevism; 12 collectivism
lenitive: 8 soothing
lenity: 8 clemency, lenience, leniency, mildness; 9 tolerance; 10 moderation, toleration
Lenni Lenape tribe: 8 Delaware; 12 Lenni Lenapes
lens: 6 cornea; 8 meniscus; 10 camera lens, lens system; 12 electron lens
lens cap: 9 lens cover
Lens culinaris: 6 lentil; 11 lentil plant
lens maker: 8 optician
lensman: 9 cameraman; 10 camera buff; 12 photographer
lens-shaped: 10 lenticular

L

lent: 6 loaned
lenten: 6 meager; **7** paschal
Lententide: 4 Lent
lenticular: 8 biconvex; **9** lentiform; **10** lens shaped, lens-shaped; **13** convexo-convex
lentil: 11 lentil plant; **13** Lens culinaris
Lentinus: 8 shiitake; **13** genus Lentinus
lento: 6 slowly
Leo: 10 Leo the Lion
Leontopodium: 9 edelweiss; **17** genus Leontopodium
leopard: 7 panther
Leopoldville: 8 Kinshasa; **14** capital of Zaire
Leo the Lion: 3 Leo
le pas: 7 the head, the lead
leper: 5 lazar
Lepidochelys: 6 ridley; **17** genus Lepidochelys
lepidopterist: 18 butterfly collector
lepidopterous insect: 12 lepidopteran, lepidopteron
lepidote: 5 scaly; **6** scurfy; **7** leprose; **8** scabrous
Lepidothamnus: 4 rimu; **18** genus Lepidothamnus
Lepisma: 10 silverfish; **12** genus Lepisma
Lepisosteus: 3 gar; **7** garfish; **8** billfish; **16** genus Lepisosteus
Lepomis: sunfish; **8** bluegill; **11** pumpkinseed; **12** genus Lepomis
leprous: 5 scaly; **6** scurfy; **8** lepidote, scabrous
leprosy: 14 Hansen's disease
leptospirosis: 10 swamp fever
lepus: 4 hare; **6** rabbit; **10** genus Lepus
lesbian: 7 sapphic; **8** gay woman
lese majesty: 7 treason; **11** high treason
lesion: 5 wound
Lesotho: 10 Basutoland
lespedeza: 10 bush clover
less: 5 lower, minor, minus; **6** lesser; **9** deficient, secondary; **11** subordinate
lessee: 5 donee [Fr]; **6** renter; **7** grantee; **8** releasee [Law]; **11** leaseholder
lessen: 4 fall; **6** minify, reduce, shrink; **7** subside; **8** decrease, diminish
lessened: 8 vitiated, weakened; **9** decreased; **10** diminished
lessening: 7 drop-off; **8** decrease, reducing; **9** shrinking; **10** decreasing; **12** constricting
lesser: 4 less; **5** lower, minor, minus; **9** deficient, secondary; **11** subordinate
lesser celandine: 8 pilewort
lesson: 5 moral; **7** example, lecture; **9** reprimand
lessor: 9 mortgagee; **10** lease giver
let: 4 rent; **5** allow, lease, leave; **6** leased, permit; **7** rent out
let be: 4 stet [copy editing]
let down: 5 lower, shame; **6** humble; **7**

depress, get down, set down; **8** take down; **9** bring down, frown down, tread down; **10** disappoint
letdown: 14 disappointment
let fly: 4 send; **6** fly off, launch, let off; **7** fire off, release, send off; **8** let drive, loose off; **9** send forth
let go: 5 loose, yield; **6** give up, let out; **7** abandon, let go of, let slip, release; **8** abnegate, let loose, unclutch; **9** surrender; **10** relinquish
lethal: 5 fatal; **6** deadly, mortal
lethargic: 6 groggy; **7** languid; **8** listless; **11** unenergetic
lethargic encephalitis: 16 sleeping sickness
lethargy: 6 torpor; **7** languor; **9** inanition, lassitude, torpidity; **10** supineness; **12** sluggishness
Lethe: 10 River Lethe
lethe: 8 oblivion; **10** forgetting; **13** forgetfulness, obliviousness
lethean: 8 mindless; **9** forgetful, oblivious
let in: 5 admit; **6** hook in, import; **7** allow in, bring in, include, receive
let it be: 4 stet [copy editing]
let loose: 4 emit; **5** let go, loose, utter; **6** let out; **7** let slip, unleash
let off: 4 free, send; **5** remit, spare; **6** excuse, exempt, launch, let fly; **7** absolve, fire off, license, release, relieve, send off; **8** pass over, reprieve
let on: 5 break; **6** expose, impart, let out, reveal; **7** declare, divulge; **8** bring out, disclose, discover
let one go: 4 fire; **7** dismiss; **9** discharge, terminate
let out: 4 blab, emit, spew; **5** break, eject, expel, let go, let on, loose, peach, spill, utter, widen; **6** expose, impart, reveal; **7** blow off, declare, divulge, prolong; **8** disclose, discover, divulged
Lett: 7 Latvian
letter: 4 note; **7** epistle, missive; **9** character, duplicate; **13** varsity letter
letter box: 3 POB; **7** call box, mailbox, postbox
letter card: 4 card; **8** postcard; **10** postal card
letter carrier: 7 carrier, mailman, postman
lettered: 7 erudite, knowing, learned; **8** educated, well-read; **10** instructed; **11** enlightened; **12** well-educated; **13** knowledgeable
lettering: 11 inscription
letter opener: 10 paperknife
letter paper: 10 stationery
letters: 10 literature; **13** belles lettres [Fr]
letter writer: 13 correspondent
letting: 5 lease; **6** rental; **10** leasing out, renting out
letting down: 8 lowering
Lettish: 7 Latvian
lettuce: 5 salad; **6** greens; **10** rabbit food

let up: 5 abate, slack; 6 ease up
letup: 4 lull
Leuciscus: 4 chub, dace; 14 genus Leuciscus
leukemia: 9 leukaemia; 11 blood cancer
leukocyte: 9 leucocyte, white cell; 14 white blood cell, white corpuscle
Levant: 4 East; 6 Orient
levant: 4 bolt, flit; 9 skedaddle
levee: 3 dam, lea; 4 bank, dike; 6 at home; 8 congress; 9 reception, river bank; 10 conference, convention
level: 4 even, fell, flat, rase, raze, roll, tier; 5 dress, floor, grade, plane, point, stage, story, upset; 6 charge, degree, equate, smooth, storey; 7 balance, coequal, even out, flatten, subvert; 8 equalize, evenness, level off, monotony, pull down, take down, tear down; 9 dead level, dismantle, make equal, prostrate; 10 assimilate, coordinate, horizontal, monotonous, unwavering
level best: 6 utmost; 7 maximum; 9 uttermost
level crossing: 13 grade crossing
levelheaded: 5 sound; 7 healthy; 11 intelligent
leveling: 6 razing; 7 grading, planing, rolling; 10 flattening; 11 demolishing, tearing down; 12 equalization, equilisation
lever: 3 pry; 4 crux; 5 hinge, jimmy, pivot, prise, prize; 7 fulcrum
leverage: 4 play; 5 power; 8 purchase; 10 leveraging; 13 effectiveness
Levi's: 5 jeans; 6 denims; 9 blue jeans
leviathan: 5 whale; 8 cachalot, elephant, porpoise; 12 hippopotamus
levitate: 5 hover
Levite: 6 priest; 7 prophet; 10 high priest
levity: 9 frivolity, lightness; 10 fickleness, triviality; 11 fluctuation, inconstancy, vacillation
levorotatory: 10 left-handed, levorotary
levulose: 8 fructose; 9 laevulose; 10 fruit sugar
levy: 3 tax; 4 dues; 5 raise; 6 impose, tariff; 7 draught, recruit; 8 distrain; 9 compiling, conscript, gathering; 10 confiscate; 11 compilation, ingathering
lewd: 7 lustful, obscene; 9 lecherous, salacious; 10 lascivious, libidinous
lewdness: 7 lechery; 8 salacity; 9 bawdiness, lubricity, obscenity; 13 salaciousness; 14 lasciviousness
lexicographer: 12 lexicologist; 13 glossographer
lexicologist: 13 glossographer, lexicographer
lexicon: 10 dictionary, vocabulary
ley: 3 lay, lea; 7 pasture; 9 pasturage; 11 grazing land, pastureland
Leyte: 11 Leyte Island; 13 Leyte invasion
LF: 12 low frequency
Lhasa: 5 Lassa; 9 Lhasa apso; 13 Forbidden City; 14 capital of Tibet
Li: 7 lithium

liabilities: 5 debts; 6 acquit, losses; 11 expenditures
liability: 4 debt, duty, onus; 5 debit, score; 8 exposure; 10 obligation; 11 sensitivity; 12 indebtedness; 13 sensitiveness, vulnerability
liable: 3 apt; 4 open; 6 open to; 7 subject; 8 amenable; 9 exposed to, nonimmune; 10 answerable, chargeable; 11 accountable, responsible, susceptible
liaise: 7 mediate; 9 arbitrate, intercede
liaison: 4 link; 5 amour; 6 affair; 7 affaire, contact; 8 intimacy; 11 involvement
liar: 6 fibber; 12 prevaricater, prevaricator
libation: 7 draught; 8 oblation, potation; 9 sacrifice
libber: 8 feminist
libel: 4 skit; 6 malign; 7 lampoon; 8 citation; 9 challenge; 10 defamation
libeler: 7 defamer; 8 maligner, satirist, traducer; 9 backbiter, lampooner, slanderer
liberal: 3 big; 4 free; 5 broad, loose; 6 giving; 8 altruist, generous, handsome, princely, tolerant
liberal arts: 4 arts; 10 humanities
liberalism: 7 whigism; 8 altruism; 11 magnanimity; 13 progressivism, unselfishness
liberalization: 10 relaxation
liberally: 6 freely; 8 givingly; 10 charitably, generously; 11 bounteously, bountifully, unselfishly; 12 munificently
liberate: 4 free; 5 loose; 7 release, set free, unloose; 10 commandeer, emancipate, render free; 11 appropriate, expropriate
liberated: 5 freed; 7 set free; 8 released; 11 emancipated
libertine: 8 freedman; 11 freethinker
liberty: 5 grace; 7 freedom, license; 8 autonomy, immunity; 9 exemption, franchise, indecorum; 10 concession, shore leave
libidinous: 4 lewd; 5 lusty; 6 carnal, erotic; 7 lustful, rampant, rutting, ruttish; 8 prurient; 10 hot-blooded, lascivious, passionate
libido: 4 lust; 8 sex drive; 11 sex instinct; 13 concupiscence
Libra: 14 Libra the Scales; 15 Libra the Balance
libratory: 10 undulatory
Libreville: 14 capital of Gabon
license: 4 free; 5 grace, spare; 6 brevet, excuse, let off, permit; 7 certify, liberty, licence, warrant; 8 immunity, pass over; 9 franchise; 10 concession, permission
licensed: 8 licenced; 10 accredited, authorized; 12 commissioned
licensed practical nurse: 3 LPN
license tax: 12 licensing fee
licentious: 5 light; 6 wanton; 8 unchaste; 9 debauched, dissolute

L

lichee: 5 lichi; 6 litchi, lychee; 7 leechee, litchee
lichgate: 8 lychgate
licit: 5 legal; 6 lawful; 10 legitimate
lick: 3 bat, lap; 4 biff, cane, comb, drub, flog, lash, peck, pick, poke, whip, work; 5 birch, floor, punch, solve, strap, towel, worst; 6 larrup, switch, thrash, thresh; 7 clobber, scourge; 8 salt lick; 9 bastinado, figure out, horsewhip, puzzle out; 10 flagellate
licking: 6 defeat
lickspittle: 4 snob, toad, tool; 5 toady; 6 flunky, sucker, yes-man; 7 flunkey, sponger; 8 courtier, hanger on, parasite, truckler; 9 doughface [U.S.], sycophant, toad-eater; 10 boot-licker
licorice stick: 8 clarinet
lid: 3 cap, hat, top; 5 check; 6 eyelid; 7 chapeau; 9 restraint
lidocaine: 9 Xylocaine
lie: 4 rest; 5 couch, dwell, lie in, stand; 6 belong; 7 consist, lie down, recline, untruth; 9 falsehood
lieder: 4 lied [Ger], song
lief: 4 glad; 6 gladly; 7 welcome; 10 acceptable
liege: 6 vassal; 8 liegeman; 9 feudatory, liege lord
lie in wait: 4 lurk, wait; 6 ambush, waylay; 9 ambuscade, bushwhack
lien: 6 spleen
Lietuva: 9 Lithuania
lieu: 4 spot; 5 place, point, stead; 8 location, position
lieutenant: 6 archon, deputy, warden; 7 provost; 9 assistant
life: 4 dash; 6 doings, energy, living, spirit, things; 7 journal; 8 alacrity, fortunes, lifespan, lifetime, the world, vitality, vivacity; 9 aliveness, animation, biography, life story, viability; 10 adventures, liveliness; 11 confessions, experiences
life's ambition: 4 goal; 5 dream; 10 aspiration
life's work: 6 career
life after death: 9 afterlife
life belt: 8 life buoy, life ring; 9 life saver; 10 safety belt
life beyond the grave: 9 afterlife
lifeblood: 3 sap; 4 soul; 8 backbone
life form: 5 being; 8 organism
life history: 4 life; 6 career; 9 biography, life story
lifejacket: 8 life vest; 13 life preserver
lifeless: 4 dead; 8 deceased; 9 exanimate
lifelike: 5 vivid; 7 graphic, natural; 8 faithful; 9 pictorial
life scientist: 9 biologist
lifespan: 4 life; 8 lifetime
lift: 4 go up, hook, rear, rise, wind; 5 annul, arise, erect, filch, get up, heave, hoist, pinch, raise, snarf, sneak, swipe; 6 come up, move up, nobble, pick up, pilfer, repeal, revoke, rustle, ski tow; 7 airlift, bring up, elevate, purloin, raising, rescind, reverse, ski lift, support; 8 abstract, elevator, face-lift, heighten, overturn; 9 elevation
lift bridge: 10 drawbridge
lifted: 8 upraised
lifter: 12 weightlifter
liftman: 11 elevator man
liftoff: 7 take off; 8 blast off
lift the veil: 6 unfold, unseal, unveil; 7 uncover
lift up: 5 elate; 6 pick up, uplift; 8 gather up; 10 intoxicate
ligation: 7 joining; 8 junction, ligating; 9 attaching; 10 attachment, connecting
ligature: 6 binder; 8 ligament
light: 4 airy, diet, easy, fall, fire, idle, lamp, lite, thin, weak; 5 clean, clear, faint, fusee, loose, match, perch, sandy, scant, sense, short, spark, spill; 6 alight, bright, fire up, flimsy, frothy, get off, ignite, illume, kindle, low-cal, scanty, slight, wanton; 7 friable, get down, igniter, ignitor, inflame, lection, light up, lighter, lightly, limited, reading, slender, sparkle, subtile, unhorse, version, wakeful; 8 dismount, enkindle, illumine, lighting, pleasant, sluttish, swooning, tripping, unchaste, vesuvian; 9 lightness, lightsome, luminance, set fire to, set on fire, sparkling, sprightly, unclouded; 10 abstemious, brightness, illuminate, luminosity, unaccented
light and shade: 11 chiaroscuro; 13 black and white
light beam: 3 ray; 4 beam; 5 shaft
light beer: 4 lite
light-colored: 4 fair; 5 blond
light comedy: 9 low comedy
light company: 12 power company, power service; 15 electric company
lighted: 3 lit; 11 illuminated, well-lighted
light emitter: 8 luminary
light-emitting diode: 3 LED
lighten: 4 ease; 6 buoy up, smooth; 7 light up; 8 brighten, illumine, make easy; 9 enlighten, lighten up, shine upon; 10 facilitate, illuminate
lighter: 5 barge, light; 7 igniter, ignitor; 8 flatboat
lighterman: 6 bargee; 7 boatman; 8 bargeman, ferryman
light-haired: 5 blond; 6 blonde
lightheaded: 4 wild; 5 dizzy, faint, silly, giddy, rabid; 6 doting, raving; 7 berserk, frantic; 8 frenetic, frenzied, rambling, unhinged, wild-eyed; 9 delirious, insensate, possessed, wandering; 10 incoherent, reasonless; 11 dithyrambic, vertiginous

lighthearted: 6 blithe; 9 lightsome; 10 blithesome
lighthouse: 6 beacon, pharos
lighting: 5 light; 6 firing; 8 ignition, kindling
light intensity: 10 brightness; 11 illuminance
lightless: 5 unlit; 7 sunless; 9 unlighted; 13 unilluminated
lightly: 5 light; 6 gently, softly, thinly
light meal: 4 bite; 5 snack
light meter: 10 photometer
lightness: 5 light; 6 levity
lightning arrester: 13 spike arrester; 14 surge protector
lightning bolt: 9 lightning; 14 lightning flash
lightning bug: 7 firefly, june bug; 8 glowworm
lightning conductor: 12 lightning rod
light of day: 8 daylight, sunlight, sunshine
light opera: 8 operetta
light pipe: 11 fiber optics
light ray: 3 ray; 4 beam; 5 gleam; 6 pencil, streak, stream
light-sensitive: 14 photosensitive
light source: 5 light; 8 luminary; 11 illuminator
lights-out: 4 taps
light speed: 1 c
light touch: 5 brush
ligneous plant: 10 woody plant
lignified: 5 woody
lignite: 8 wood coal; 9 brown coal
Ligustrum: 6 privet; 14 genus Ligustrum
likable: 8 likeable; 9 appealing; 11 sympathetic
like: 4 care, list, same, wish; 5 alike, enjoy, equal, fancy; 6 affect, relish; 7 be big on, care for, similar; 10 comparable, equivalent; 12 smack the lips; 13 corresponding
likeable: 7 likable; 9 appealing; 11 sympathetic
likelihood: 4 odds; 10 likeliness; 11 probability
likely: 6 belike; 7 hopeful; 8 expected, probable, probably; 9 plausible, potential
liken: 6 equate; 7 compare
likeness: 4 copy, form; 6 effigy; 7 replica; 8 effigies; 9 alikeness, facsimile, imitation, semblance; 10 similarity, similitude; 11 counterpart, resemblance
likewise: 3 and, too; 4 also, item; 5 alike; 6 as well; 7 besides, further; 9 similarly; 11 furthermore
liking: 4 love; 6 relish; 8 fondness
Liliaceae: 10 lily family
Lilium: 4 lily; 11 genus Lilium
Lilium longiflorum: 10 Easter lily
lilliputian: 4 tiny; 5 petty; 6 bantam, little, midget, petite; 7 trivial; 8 picayune; 10 diminutive
lilt: 4 purl; 5 carol, shake, swing, trill; 6 brogue, quaver; 7 chirrup, twitter
lilting: 6 swingy; 8 swinging, tripping

lily family: 9 Liliaceae
lily-livered: 6 yellow; 7 chicken
lily-white: 5 white
Lima: 13 capital of Peru
lima bean: 9 sieva bean; 10 butter bean
limb: 3 arm; 4 lobe, wing; 5 jimmy; 6 branch, lobule, member; 8 offshoot; 12 ramification
limbed: 7 boughed
limber: 6 lissom, supple; 7 plastic, pontoon, tumbrel; 8 limber up
limber up: 6 limber, warm up; 8 loosen up
limbo: 4 quod [Lat]; 5 abyss; 6 stocks; 7 bilboes, gehenna; 8 oblivion; 9 purgatory
lime: 4 calx; 6 linden; 8 basswood, birdlime, lime tree; 9 burnt lime, quicklime; 10 linden tree
lime hydrate: 4 lime; 10 slaked lime; 11 caustic lime; 12 hydrated lime
limelight: 9 public eye, spotlight
limen: 9 threshold
Limenitis: 7 viceroy; 12 white admiral; 14 genus Limenitis
lime tree: 4 lime; 6 linden; 8 basswood
limey: 8 John Bull; 10 Englishman
limit: 5 bound, ideal; 6 border, bounds, modify; 7 confine, trammel; 8 boundary, restrain, restrict, throttle, withhold; 9 perimeter; 10 limit point, limitation; 11 demarcation; 12 circumscribe
limitation: 4 term; 5 lease, limit; 6 demise; 8 monopoly; 9 exception, exemption; 10 protection, settlement; 11 containment, restriction
limited company: 2 Ld.; 3 Ltd.
limiting: 9 confining; 10 qualifying; 11 restricting; 12 constraining, constrictive, modification
limitless: 7 endless; 9 boundless, unbounded, unlimited; 10 unmeasured; 11 illimitable, measureless
limn: 6 depict, pencil, sketch; 7 outline, portray; 8 describe; 9 delineate
Limnocryptes: 5 snipe; 17 genus Limnocryptes
limousine: 4 limo
limp: 3 lax; 4 drop, fade, fail, flag, halt, slug; 5 hitch, shake, slack; 6 flabby, flimsy, hobble, slouch, toddle, totter, waddle, wilted
limpid: 5 clear, lucid; 6 liquid; 8 luculent, pellucid; 11 crystalline, perspicuous, transparent
limping: 4 gimp; 8 gameness, lameness
limpness: 6 laxity; 10 flabbiness, flaccidity; 12 inelasticity
Limulus: 8 king crab; 13 horseshoe crab; 12 genus Limulus
limy: 10 calcareous
Linaceae: 10 flax family

L

linchpin: 6 anchor; 8 backbone, lynchpin, mainstay
Lincoln: 3 fin; 5 fiver; 14 Abraham Lincoln, five-dollar bill; 17 capital of Nebraska
Lincoln cent: 4 cent; 5 penny
linden: 4 lime; 8 basswood, lime tree; 10 linden tree
linden family: 9 Tiliaceae
linden tree: 4 lime; 6 linden; 8 basswood, lime tree
lindy: 8 lindy hop
line: 3 air, ell, guy, job, pad, rod, wad; 4 dash, draw, fill, foot, hand, inch, mile, nail, note, palm, pole, rood, seam, stem, team, tier, tree, tune, wire, work, yard; 5 birth, blood, brace, breed, cable, chain, check, cubit, house, range, space, stock, stuff, trace, trunk; 6 course, crease, fathom, furrow, league, living, melody, origin, stirps, strain, string, stroke, thread, thrift [Scot]; 7 channel, crinkle, descent, furlong, incrust, lineage, outline, painter, railway, wrinkle; 8 ancestry, bank line, business, contrast, describe, heritage, moorings, pedigree, pipeline, railroad, run along; 9 agate line, blood line, bloodline, delineate, genealogy, parentage, phone line; 10 credit line, employment, extraction, line of text, line of work, livelihood, occupation; 11 demarcation, line of verse, melodic line, product line, railway line, short letter
lineage: 4 line, stem, tree; 5 birth, blood, breed, house, stock, trunk; 6 linage, origin, stirps, strain; 7 descent, stirpes [pl]; 8 ancestry, heritage, pedigree; 9 blood line, bloodline, filiation, genealogy, parentage; 10 derivation, extraction
lineal: 6 direct, linear
lineament: 4 turn; 5 lines, trait; 7 contour, feature, outline, profile, quality; 9 character
linear: 6 analog, family, lineal; 7 running; 8 additive, analogue, elongate, straight; 9 ancestral
linear accelerator: 5 linac
linear dimension: 6 length
linear order: 5 order; 10 sequential
linecut: 9 line block; 13 line engraving
lined: 6 seamed
line drawing: 7 limning; 9 depiction; 11 delineation
lined up: 6 in a row; 7 in a line; 8 in series
line engraving: 7 linecut; 9 line block, mezzotint
lineman: 8 linesman; 11 electrician
line of battle: 5 array; 7 cortege, retinue; 9 cavalcade; 11 rank and file
line of business: 4 line; 5 field
line of collimation: 7 azimuth

line of credit: 4 line; 8 bank line; 10 credit line
line of merchandise: 4 line; 11 product line
line of work: 3 job; 4 line, work; 6 living, thrift [Scot]; 8 business; 10 employment, livelihood, occupation
liner: 6 lining; 9 line drive; 10 ocean liner
lines: 5 ambit; 7 circuit, contour, outline, profile, ribbons; 9 headstall, lineament
linesman: 7 lineman; 11 electrician
lineup: 4 card; 12 batting order
ling: 3 cod; 4 cusk, hake; 6 burbot; 7 lingcod
linger: 3 lag; 4 loaf, lurk, slug; 5 dally, drawl, hover, tarry; 6 dawdle, footle, loiter, lounge; 7 saunter; 8 lallygag, lollygag
lingerer: 8 loiterer
lingo: 4 cant; 5 argot, slang; 6 jargon, patois, tongue; 8 language; 10 vernacular
lingua: 6 glossa, tongue
lingua franca: 5 koine
lingual: 4 oral; 8 phonetic; 9 outspoken, unwritten; 10 linguistic
linguine: 8 linguini
linguist: 8 polyglot
linguistic atlas: 12 dialect atlas
linguistic communication: 8 language
linguistics: 9 philology
linguistic scientist: 8 linguist
linguistic symbol: 6 letter; 9 character
liniment: 7 unguent; 8 ointment; 9 traumatic, vulnerary; 11 embrocation
lining: 5 liner; 6 facing; 12 inner coating
link: 3 peg, tie; 4 bond, edge, hook, join, lock, rung, yoke; 5 belay, bough, brace, brand, chain, joint, latch, leash, nexus, notch, scion, tie in, tie-in, torch, unite; 6 couple, link up, linkup, relate, splice; 7 bracket, connect, contact, grapple, liaison, linkage; 8 data link, dovetail, flambeau, vinculum; 9 associate, connexion, mutuality, radio link; 10 anastomose [Med], connection, connective; 11 association, correlation; 13 connectedness, interrelation
links: 9 golf links; 10 golf course
linksman: 6 golfer
Link trainer: 7 trainer; 15 flight simulator
linkup: 3 tie; 5 tie-in
Linnaean System: 8 binomial
linnet: 10 house finch
linoleum: 4 lino
linotype: 8 logotype; 13 justification
linseed: 8 flaxseed
linseed oil: 11 flaxseed oil
linsey-woolsey: 6 hybrid; 7 mongrel; 9 composite
linskman: 6 golfer; 7 golf pro; 10 golf player
lint: 4 fuzz
lintel: 4 beam; 5 joist; 6 girder, header, rafter
lion: 3 leo; 6 cougar; 12 king of beasts
lion's share: 8 majority
lioness: 10 female lion

lion-hearted: 5 stout, brave; 8 fearless; 9 dauntless
lionize: 6 blazon; 8 enshrine, inscribe; 9 celebrate
Lions Clubs International: 5 Lions
lip: 3 rim; 4 brim, sass; 5 mouth; 6 flange, muzzle; 7 sassing; 8 backtalk
lipid-mobilizing hormone: 10 lipotropin
liplike: 7 labiate
lipophilic: 10 lipotropic
Liposcelis: 9 booklouse; 15 genus Liposcelis
lip rouge: 8 lipstick
lips: 4 door; 5 chops, inlet, mouth, porch; 6 portal; 7 orifice, portico
lip service: 9 hypocrisy, lip homage
lipstick: 5 blush, rouge; 8 lip rouge
lip synchronization: 7 lip sync; 8 lip synch, mouthing
lip wisdom: 5 folly; 7 conceit; 8 trifling; 9 frivolity; 13 inconsistency, irrationality
liquefied: 6 molten; 9 liquified
liquefied petroleum gas: 10 bottled gas
liquefy: 3 run; 4 melt, thaw; 7 liquify; 8 condense; 9 liquidise, liquidize
liquescent: 7 melting
liqueur: 7 cordial; 8 aperitif; 9 sweet wine
liquid: 4 mute; 5 fluid, juicy, sappy; 6 dental, fluent, labial, limpid, melted, serous, smooth, watery; 7 flowing; 8 guttural, swimming; 9 liquidity, liquified, succulent; 10 liquidness
liquidambar: 6 storax; 8 sweet gum
liquidate: 4 do in; 5 clear, waste; 6 pay off; 7 break up, realize; 8 knock off; 9 fall apart
liquidation: 9 clearance, discharge, quittance, reckoning; 10 breaking up, disruption, redemption, settlement; 11 arrangement, dissolution, elimination; 12 satisfaction; 13 extermination
liquidator: 7 almoner, steward, trustee; 8 murderer, receiver; 10 accountant
liquid crystal display: 3 LCD
liquidity: 6 liquid; 8 fluidity; 9 fluidness, runniness; 10 liquidness
liquidity crisis: 12 credit crunch
liquidize: 6 sell up; 7 liquefy, liquify, sell out; 9 liquidise
liquid oxygen: 3 LOX
liquid propellant: 10 liquid fuel
liquified: 6 liquid, melted, molten; 9 liquefied
liquor: 5 booze; 7 spirits; 10 hard liquor
liquorice: 8 licorice
Liriodendron: 9 tulip tree; 17 genus Liriodendron
Lisbon: 6 Lisboa; 17 capital of Portugal
lisinopril: 7 Zestril
lissom: 5 lithe; 6 limber, nimble, supple, svelte; 7 lissome, plastic, slender; 9 lithesome, sylphlike
list: 3 hem; 4 band, cant, gimp, lean, like, name, slip, tape, tilt, welt, wish; 5 frill, joust, lurch, spill, strip; 6 affect, choose,

decide, edging, fillet, fringe, listen, number, riband, ribbon; 7 catalog, flounce, itemize, leaning, listing, tilting, valance; 8 furbelow, selvedge, skirting, trimming; 9 catalogue, determine, inventory; 11 inclination
listed: 8 enrolled
listen: 4 hear, heed, list, mind
listener: 6 hearer; 7 auditor
listener-in: 12 eavesdropper
listen in: 9 eavesdrop
listening: 7 hearing; 8 auditing
listen with both ears: 9 be all ears
Listera: 9 twayblade; 12 genus Listera
listing: 4 code, list; 5 tally; 11 itemisation, itemization
listless: 6 groggy; 7 languid; 8 dilatory, mindless; 9 lethargic, pottering, puttering; 10 dispirited, regardless; 11 half-hearted; 13 lackadaisical
listlessly: 8 remissly; 10 dilatorily; 11 potteringly, putteringly; 13 half-heartedly; 15 lackadaisically
listlessness: 6 torpor; 7 languor; 9 lassitude, torpidity; 10 torpidness
list-processing language: 4 LISP
lit: 7 lighted; 11 illuminated, well-lighted
litchee: 5 lichi; 6 lichee, litchi, lychee; 7 leechee; 9 litchi nut
lite: 4 diet; 5 light; 6 low-cal; 9 light beer
literal: 4 bare, open, real, typo; 5 overt, plain; 6 actual, patent, verbal; 7 erratum, express, genuine; 8 exoteric, explicit, misprint; 9 expressed; 11 undisguised, word-for-word; 12 literal error; 13 unembellished
literal error: 4 typo; 7 erratum, literal; 8 misprint
literally: 3 sic; 7 mot a mot [Fr]; 8 verbatim; 9 literatim [Lat], virtually
literary: 11 well-written
literary critic: 8 reviewer
literary man: 12 intellectual
literary pirate: 10 plagiarist
literati: 10 dilettanti, illuminati [It]; 11 cogniscenti [It], litterateur [Fr]
literatim: 3 sic; 7 mot a mot [Fr]; 8 verbatim; 9 literally; 11 to the letter, word for word
literature: 7 letters; 13 belles lettres [Fr]
lithe: 6 lissom, supple, svelte; 7 lissome, slender; 9 lithesome, sylphlike
lithic: 5 rocky, stone, stony; 8 concrete; 9 calculous
lithium: 2 Li
lithium carbonate: 7 Lithane; 9 Lithonate
Lithocarpus: 3 oak; 16 genus Lithocarpus
lithoglyptics: 8 glyptics
lithographed: 6 etched; 8 engraved
lithograph machine: 10 lithograph

L

lithosphere: 5 crust; 9 geosphere
Lithuania: 7 Lietuva
litigant: 6 suitor; 9 litigator, litigious
litigate: 3 sue; 7 process
litigation: 4 suit; 5 cause; 6 action; 7 lawsuit
litigator: 8 litigant
litigious: 8 litigant; 11 contentious, disputative; 12 disputatious
litmus test: 4 test; 5 probe; 8 acid test; 9 criterion; 10 diagnostic
litre: 5 liter
litter: 3 fry; 4 bevy, hash, herd, hive, nest, peck, seed, spat; 5 breed, brood, cloud, covey, drove, flock, heirs, issue, shoal, spawn, swarm, trash; 6 bushel, farrow, flight, huddle, jumble, lumber, refuse, scores; 7 bedding, draught, progeny, rubbish, scatter; 9 offspring, posterity, stretcher
litterateur: 6 author, writer; 8 essayist, literati; 9 authoress; 10 dilettanti, illuminati [It]; 11 cogniscenti [It]
litterer: 9 litterbug; 10 litter lout
little: 3 pet; 4 dear, mean; 5 brief, dirty, mingy, petty, small, tight; 6 abject, paltry, peanut, scabby, scurvy, shabby; 7 darling, miserly, scrubby, trivial, younger; 8 fiddling, footling, picayune, piddling, piffling, precious, rascally, sneaking; 9 groveling, minuscule; 11 lilliputian, small-minded; 12 contemptible, pettifogging; 13 insignificant, unrespectable
Little Bear: 9 Ursa Minor
Little Bighorn: 6 Custer [Last Stand]
little by little: 8 bit by bit, by inches, in stages, seriatim; 9 piecemeal
Little Dog: 10 Canis Minor
little finger: 5 pinky; 6 pinkie
little hand: 8 hour hand
littleneck: 14 littleneck clam
little one: 3 kid; 5 bairn [Scot], child, youth; 6 moppet; 8 children [pl], juvenile, small fry; 9 youngster
littler: 7 smaller
Little Rock: 17 capital of Arkansas
littlest: 5 least; 8 smallest
littoral: 5 sands; 7 coastal, litoral; 8 riparian
lit up: 5 aglow
live: 2 be, go; 3 hot; 4 know, last, stay; 5 abide, alive, dwell, exist, lodge, perch, roost, shack; 6 bouncy, endure, flaunt, hold up, live on, lively, living, nestle, people, reside, tenant, whippy; 7 be alive, breathe, glitter, go-ahead, hold out, inhabit, outlive, sojourn, springy, subsist, survive; 8 flourish, populate; 9 gain honor, on-the-spot, resilient; 10 experience, unrecorded
live from hand to mouth: 4 lack, want; 6 be poor
live high: 7 indulge

live it up: 7 indulge; 8 live high, live well; 11 overindulge
livelihood: 3 job; 4 keep, line, work; 6 living, thrift [Scot]; 7 support; 8 business; 9 provision; 10 employment, line of work, occupation, sustenance
liveliness: 4 life; 6 spirit; 9 animation, briskness, quickness; 13 sprightliness
live load: 9 superload
livelong: 5 orpin; 6 orpine; 8 lifelong; 11 live-forever; 14 Sedum telephium
lively: 4 keen, live, racy, warm; 5 acute, brisk, merry, quick, sharp, smart, vital, vivid, zippy; 6 active, bouncy, mobile, snappy, strong, whippy; 7 cutting, glowing, springy; 8 animated, bustling, incisive, piercing, rattling, spanking, spirited; 9 resilient, sparkling, vivacious
liven: 7 animate, enliven, liven up; 10 invigorate
liveness: 9 aliveness; 11 animateness
live on: 2 go; 4 last, live; 6 endure, hold up, live by; 7 survive
live over: 6 relive
live performance: 9 spectacle; 11 mise en scene [Fr], performance; 12 jeu de theatre [Fr], presentation
liver disease: 9 hepatitis
liverish: 6 livery; 7 bilious; 9 dyspeptic; 11 atrabilious
liverleaf: 8 hepatica
liver sausage: 10 liverwurst
livery: 3 dye, hue; 4 cast, glow, tint; 5 color, flush, shade, tinge; 7 bilious, uniform; 8 delivery, liverish, tincture; 10 coloration
livestock: 5 stock, sheep; 6 cattle
live up to: 6 fulfil; 7 fulfill, satisfy
live well: 7 indulge
live wire: 6 dynamo, sharpy; 7 sharpie; 8 go-getter, spitfire
livid: 3 dun, sad; 4 drab, roan; 5 ashen, dingy, rabid, white; 6 fuming, leaden, pearly, raging, russet, somber; 7 foaming, rageful; 8 blanched, choleric, iron-gray; 9 bloodless, splenetic
lividity: 4 tone; 5 color; 6 pallor; 7 wanness; 8 paleness; 9 dark color, lividness, luridness; 10 achromasia, pallidness
living: 3 job; 4 keep, life, line, live, work; 5 alive; 6 thrift [Scot]; 7 support; 8 business, dwelling, vitality; 9 aliveness, animation, surviving, viability; 10 employment, habitation, line of work, livelihood, occupation, sustenance
living being: 8 organism
living room: 6 parlor; 7 parlour; 9 front room
living soul: 3 man; 4 body, soul; 5 being, human; 6 mortal, person; 8 creature; 9 earthling, personage; 10 individual
living space: 10 lebensraum
living stone: 7 lithops; 9 stoneface

living substance: 10 protoplasm
living thing: 5 being; **8** organism
living together: 12 cohabitation
lizard: 7 reptile; **8** dinosaur
llano: 5 plain
lm: 5 lumen
load: 3 jag, lot, pot; **4** bale, blow, care, deal, dole, fill, fret, glut, heap, lade, lode, lump, onus, pack, stow; **5** cargo, curse, gorge, heaps, laden, press, weigh, whelm, world; **6** bumper, burden, charge, cumber, lading, load up, stroke; **7** anxiety, concern, freight, loading, payload, warhead; **8** pressure, shipment; **9** gravitate, great deal; **10** solicitude; **11** consignment, encumbrance, impedimenta, incumbrance
load-bearing: 10 supporting
load down: 4 pack
loaded: 3 wet; **5** blind, flush, laden, potty, stiff, tight, tipsy; **6** blotto, pissed, soaked, soused, tiddly; **7** crocked, fuddled, ladened, moneyed, slopped, sloshed, smashed, sozzled, squiffy, tiddley, wealthy; **8** affluent, besotted; **9** pixilated, plastered
loaded down: 8 burdened; **12** overburdened
loader: 6 docker, lumper; **8** dockhand; **9** stevedore; **10** dock worker; **12** longshoreman
loading: 4 load; **5** cargo; **6** burden, lading; **7** freight, payload; **8** shipment; **11** consignment
loading area: 11 loading zone
load line: 8 Plimsoll, **12** Plimsoll line, Plimsoll mark
loads: 4 gobs, lots, tons, wads; **5** heaps, piles, rafts, scads, slews; **6** dozens, oodles, scores, stacks; **8** lashings
loadstar: 8 lode star, pole star
loadstone: 6 magnet; **8** lodestar; **9** lodestone
load the dice: 3 cog
load up: 4 glut, lade, load, pack; **5** gorge, laden, whelm
loaf: 3 ton, tun; **4** bulk, clod, cord, loll, lump, lurk, mass, poke, swad; **5** block, tarry; **6** bushel, footle, linger, loiter, lounge, nugget; **8** lallygag, lollygag
loafer: 3 bum; **5** idler, sneak; **7** lounger; **8** layabout; **9** do-nothing, goldbrick
loaf sugar: 9 sugarloaf
loam: 4 marl
loan: 4 lend; **6** loaner; **7** lending, loaning; **8** loanword
loaned: 4 lent
loaner: 4 loan; **6** lender
loan shark: 5 shark; **6** usurer; **11** moneylender
loath: 4 loth; **5** shy of; **6** averse; **9** reluctant; **10** indisposed; **11** disinclined; **12** antipathetic; **14** antipathetical
loathe: 4 hate, loth; **5** abhor; **6** detest; **7** adverse; **8** execrate, nauseate; **9** abominate
loathsome: 4 foul, vile; **5** gross, yucky; **6** wicked; **7** fulsome, loathly, noisome; **8** nauseous; **9** abhorrent, offensive, repellant, repellent, repugnant, repulsive, revolting, sickening; **10** disgustful, disgusting, nauseating; **11** distasteful; **12** insufferable
lobby: 3 PAC; **4** hall, lane; **5** aisle, alley, foyer; **6** artery; **8** anteroom, corridor; **9** vestibule; **10** buttonhole, third house; **11** antechamber; **13** pressure group
lobe: 3 arm; **4** limb, wing; **6** branch, lobule, member; **8** offshoot; **12** ramification
lobefin: 15 crossopterygian
lobscouse: 6 scouse
lobster: 6 homard [Fr]
lobule: 3 arm; **4** limb, lobe, wing; **6** branch, member; **8** offshoot; **12** ramification
local: 7 topical; **8** regional; **9** homegrown, parochial; **10** provincial; **11** territorial
local area network: 3 LAN
local color: 4 tone; **5** value; **7** keeping; **8** coloring
local death: 8 necrosis
locale: 4 ward; **5** block, locus, place, venue; **6** barrio [Sp], corner; **8** enceinte, environs, locality, location, position, precinct, vicinity; **9** precincts; **12** neighborhood; **14** stomping ground
locality: 4 ward; **5** block, place; **6** barrio [Sp], corner, locale; **8** enceinte, environs, location, position, precinct, vicinity; **9** precincts; **12** neighborhood
localization: 3 fix; **7** placing, putting; **8** locating, location; **11** positioning
localize: 3 put, set; **5** place; **6** locate; **7** situate; **8** localise, position
localized: 6 placed; **7** located
local language: 6 patois; **7** dialect; **11** sublanguage
local road: 6 street
local tax: 7 city tax
locate: 3 put; **4** site; **5** place; **6** settle, turn up; **7** situate; **8** localize, position, relocate
located: 3 set; **5** fixed; **6** placed; **7** situate; **8** situated; **9** localized
locating: 3 fix; **7** placing, putting; **8** location, position; **9** placement, situating; **11** emplacement, positioning; **12** localisation, localization
location: 3 fix; **4** lieu, spot; **5** place, point; **6** locale; **7** placing, putting; **8** locality, locating, position; **9** placement, situating; **11** emplacement, positioning; **12** localization
loch: 4 lake, mere, pond, pool, slab, tarn; **5** broad, lough, plash; **6** puddle
Loch Ness monster: 6 Nessie
lock: 3 bar; **4** bolt, curl, hook, link, mesh, stay, tuft, yoke; **5** belay, brace, latch, leash, whorl; **6** couple, engage, lock in, lock up, shut up, sluice; **7** bracket, grapple, operate,

L

put away, ringlet; **8** lock away, shut away; **9** interlace, interlock; **11** lock chamber; **12** ignition lock

Locke: 9 John Locke

locked: 4 fast; **6** barred, bolted; **7** latched, secured

locker: 6 closet; **7** cabinet, commode; **8** cellaret, cupboard; **10** footlocker

lockjaw: 7 tetanus

lockman: 10 lockkeeper, lockmaster

lockup: 3 can [slang], pen; **4** brig, gaol, hold, jail, keep, stir [slang]; **5** clink [slang], hulks, pokey [slang]; **6** chokey [slang], cooler [slang], prison; **7** dungeon, locking, slammer [slang], the Rock; **8** Bastille, big house [slang], hoosegow, stockade; **9** calaboose [slang], guardroom; **12** penitentiary

lock washer: 8 lockring

loco: 3 mad; **4** bats, daft, nuts; **5** balmy, barmy, batty, buggy, crazy, dotty, kooky, loony, loopy, nutty, wacky; **6** crazed, fruity, insane, kookie, teched [dialect]; **7** bonkers, cracked, far gone, haywire, lunatic, tetched [dialect], touched; **8** crackers, demented, deranged, maddened

locomote: 2 go; **4** move; **6** travel

locomotion: 6 travel

locomotive: 6 engine

locoweed: 9 crazyweed

locum tenens: 5 locum, proxy, shift; **6** deputy; **7** stopgap; **8** delegate, jury mast, pis aller [Fr]; **9** makeshift, secondary, sojourner, surrogate

locus: 5 venue; **6** locale

locust: 7 wastrel; **8** prodigal

locust bean: 5 carob

locution: 4 talk; **6** saying, speech; **7** talking; **8** parlance, speaking; **10** expression

lode: 4 load, mine, vein; **6** quarry

lodestar: 8 loadstar, polestar; **9** loadstone, lodestone

lodestone: 8 lodestar; **9** loadstone

lodge: 3 box, inn; **4** club, file, gild, live, stay; **5** abide, cabin, dwell, guild, order, perch, roost, stick, wedge; **6** charge, hostel, nestle, reside, tenant; **7** cottage, deposit, inhabit, quarter, shelter, society, sojourn; **8** hostelry; **9** hermitage; **11** accommodate

lodgement: 4 home; **5** abode; **7** housing, lodging; **8** domicile, dwelling, lodgment; **9** residence

lodger: 6 roomer; **7** boarder

lodging: 4 home; **5** abode; **7** housing; **8** domicile, dwelling, lodgment; **9** lodgement, residence

lodgings: 3 pad; **4** digs; **8** diggings; **13** domiciliation

loft: 5 attic; **6** garret; **8** cockloft, house top; **10** clerestory

loftiness: 7 majesty; **8** highness; **9** elevation, sublimity; **11** stateliness

lofty: 4 high, tall; **5** blown, great, proud; **6** mighty; **7** eminent, exalted, flushed, gallant, haughty, soaring, stoical, sublime, swollen; **8** elevated, eloquent, majestic, puffed up, rarefied, rarified, spirited, towering; **9** high-flown; **10** high-minded, idealistic; **11** noble-minded; **12** vainglorious

log: 5 diary; **6** ledger, lumber; **7** backlog, bobbing, daybook, journal; **8** calendar, corduroy, firewood; **9** ephemeris, logarithm

logarithm: 3 log; **4** root; **5** index, power; **8** exponent

logarithmic: 8 integral; **11** exponential; **12** differential, proportional

log cabin: 8 log house

log canoe: 6 dugout; **11** dugout canoe

loge: 3 box; **5** booth

logged in: 7 entered; **8** inserted

loggerhead: 5 dunce; **8** bonehead, bull head, lunkhead, numskull; **9** blockhead; **10** dunderhead, hammerhead, muttonhead, noodlehead; **11** beetlebrain, knucklehead

loggerhead turtle: 10 loggerhead

loggia: 5 porch; **6** piazza; **7** gallery, portico, veranda

logical: 5 lucid; **7** ordered, orderly; **8** coherent; **10** consistent, legitimate

logical thinking: 9 reasoning

logician: 8 reasoner; **11** logistician

logistician: 8 logician

log off: 6 log out

logomania: 9 logorrhea

logorrhea: 9 logomania, loquacity

logorrheic: 7 verbose; **9** garrulous, talkative; **10** loquacious

Logos: 3 Son; **4** Word

logotype: 4 logo; **8** linotype; **13** justification

log out: 6 log off

logrolling: 7 birling

log up: 7 clock up

logy: 5 dazed, foggy; **6** groggy; **7** unfunny; **9** stuporous

loin: 3 hip; **4** rump, tail; **5** croup, loins; **6** breech, dorsum, haunch; **7** buttock; **10** posteriors

loincloth: 7 G-string; **11** breechcloth, breechclout

loins: 4 loin; **5** pubes

Loire: 10 Loire River

loiter: 3 lag; **4** loaf, lurk, poke, slug; **5** drawl, tarry; **6** footle, linger, lounge; **7** saunter; **8** lallygag, lollygag

loiterer: 8 lingerer

loll: 4 loaf; **5** droop; **6** sprawl

lolling: 8 lounging

lollipop: 5 lolly; **6** sucker

lollygag: 4 loaf, lurk; **5** tarry; **6** footle, linger, loiter, lounge

Lombard: 9 Langobard

Lombardy: 9 Lombardia

Lome: 13 capital of Togo

London: 13 Greater London; 14 British capital

lone: 4 only, sole; 5 alone; 6 lonely; 8 eremitic, lonesome, solitary; 10 individual

loneliness: 8 solitude; 9 aloneness; 10 desolation; 11 forlornness; 12 lonesomeness, solitariness

lonely: 4 lone; 5 alone; 8 lonesome, solitary; 12 unfrequented

lonesome: 4 lone, only, sole; 6 lonely; 8 solitary

Lone-Star State: 5 Texas

long: 3 yen; 4 ache, pine; 5 yearn; 6 cry for, hanker; 7 gape for, gasp for, hope for, lengthy, pant for, pine for, sigh for; 8 languish; 9 farseeing, tenacious; 10 farsighted; 11 foresighted, longsighted; 12 foresightful

long ago: 8 lang syne; 9 anciently

longanimity: 8 patience; 11 forbearance, placability

long-distance lens: 9 telephoto

long-distance runner: 10 marathoner, road runner

long dozen: 8 thirteen; 11 baker's dozen

longevity: 8 long life; 9 seniority

long expected: 8 foreseen

long-faced: 3 wan; 4 glum; 6 gloomy, rueful

long-familiar: 9 well-known

Longfellow: 24 Henry Wadsworth Longfellow

longhair: 7 thinker; 8 highbrow; 12 intellectual

longhand: 7 cursive

long-horned beetle: 9 longicorn

long-horned grasshopper: 11 tettigoniid

long horse: 4 buck

long hundredweight: 3 cwt

longing: 7 anxious, inkling, wistful; 8 yearning; 9 hankering

long in the tooth: 3 old; 8 wrinkled

longitude: 4 span; 8 longness, meridian

longitudinally: 5 along; 8 at length, linearly, longways, longwise; 10 lengthways, lengthwise

long jump: 9 broad jump

long-lasting: 7 durable, lasting; 9 long-lived

long-legged: 5 leggy

longlegs: 5 stilt; 9 stiltbird

long life: 9 longevity

long life to!: 4 viva!; 6 banzai! [Jap]

long-lived: 7 durable, lasting; 11 long-lasting

long-neck clam: 7 steamer

longness: 4 span; 9 longitude; 11 great length, lengthiness

long odds: 7 bad odds, poor bet; 8 long shot, poor odds; 9 fat chance [iron]

long plane: 7 jointer

long-run: 8 long-term

long run: 8 long haul

longshoreman: 6 docker, loader, lumper; 8 dockhand; 9 stevedore; 10 dock worker

longsightedness: 9 hyperopia; 12 hypermetropy; 13 hypermetropia; 14 farsightedness

long sleeve chair: 9 long chair; 11 morris chair

long-standing: 7 chronic; 10 persistent

long-standing custom: 9 tradition

long suit: 5 forte; 6 metier; 8 strength; 9 specialty; 10 speciality

long-term disability: 3 LTD [acron]

long-term memory: 3 LTM

long ton: 3 ton; 8 gross ton

long underwear: 9 union suit

longways: 8 longwise; 10 lengthways, lengthwise

long-wearing: 7 durable

long-winded: 5 windy, wordy; 6 prolix; 7 copious, diffuse, lengthy, profuse, tedious, verbose; 9 expansive

longwise: 8 longways; 10 lengthways, lengthwise; 14 longitudinally

Lonicera: 8 woodbine; 11 honeysuckle; 13 genus Lonicera

Loniten: 7 Rogaine; 9 minoxidil

loo: 2 W.C.; 4 john; 5 jakes; 6 closet, toilet

loofah: 5 loofa, luffa; 6 sponge

look: 3 air, ken, see; 4 cast, face, feel, idea, mark, mien, peep, port, seem, show, tone, view, wait; 5 await, color, front, glint, guise, smell; 6 appear, aspect, attend, expect, flavor, gander, glance, notice, regard, remark, search, spirit; 7 feeling, look you, looking, observe, thought; 8 advert to, carriage, demeanor, look here, look to it!, take care; 9 coup d'oeil [Fr], looking at; 10 complexion, expression

look across: 4 face; 8 overlook

look at: 3 eye; 4 deal, take, view; 6 look on, look to; 8 consider; 11 investigate

look back: 6 review; 10 retrospect

look downcast: 4 pout; 5 frown, lower

looker-on: 7 witness; 8 beholder, observer, onlooker, passer by; 9 bystander, spectator; 10 eyewitness

look for: 4 seek; 6 search

looking: 4 look; 6 seeing; 7 viewing; 8 sounding; 9 looking at, observing; 10 looking for; 11 observation

looking like: 10 resembling; 13 approximating

looking up: 6 bright; 7 roseate; 8 cheering; 11 encouraging, inspiriting, rose-colored

look into: 5 check; 11 investigate

look on: 3 eye; 5 watch; 6 attend, esteem, look at, repute

look out: 4 ware!; 5 vigil, watch; 6 beware!; 8 take care!, watch out

lookout: 3 orb; 5 field, scout, watch;

L

6 picket, sentry, sphere; **7** outlook; **8** province, sentinel

lookout station: 7 lookout; **11** observatory

lookup: 5 refer; **6** search

loom: 4 hulk; **5** await, brood, hover, lower, tower; **6** come on, dazzle; **7** glimmer; **8** approach, threaten

loon: 3 oaf; **6** doodle, gaffer; **7** buzzard, dullard, outcast; **9** birdbrain

loony: 3 mad; **4** bats, daft, loco, nuts; **5** balmy, barmy, batty, buggy, crazy, dotty, kooky, loopy, nutty, wacky; **6** crazed, fruity, insane, kookie, looney, teched [dialect], weirdo; **7** bonkers, cracked, far gone, haywire, lunatic, tetched [dialect], touched; **8** crackers, demented, deranged, maddened

loop: 3 bow, eye; **4** coil, curl; **6** arcade, eyelet, gasket; **7** circuit, cringle, grommet; **8** crescent, half-moon; **9** crane neck, horseshoe; **10** intertwine

looped: 7 whorled

loophole: 5 salvo; **7** come off; **8** peephole; **9** mousehole; **10** pigeonhole; **11** escape hatch, keyhole view, pinhole view, way of escape; **12** escape clause

loopy: 4 bats, daft, loco, nuts; **5** balmy, barmy, batty, buggy, dotty, kooky, loony, nutty, wacky; **6** fruity, kookie; **7** bonkers, cracked, haywire; **8** crackers

loose: 3 lax; **4** easy, free, idle, open, poor, weak; **5** apart, baggy, bawdy, broad, gross, let go, light, relax, slack, vague; **6** casual, coarse, feeble, flimsy, let out, loosen, ribald, risque [Fr], smutty, wanton; **7** asunder, at large, devious, escaped, flowing, fulsome, inexact, insular, let slip, liberal, natural, obscene, relaxed, release, unleash, unloose; **8** careless, detached, discrete, flapping, informal, let loose, liberate, scotfree, separate, slipshod, slovenly, sluttish; **9** ambiguous

loose-fitting: 5 baggy

loose-jowled: 5 jowly; **13** double-chinned

loosely: 7 broadly, slackly; **9** generally

loosen: 5 loose, relax, tease; **7** slacken

loosen control: 5 relax

loosened: 9 unsnarled; **12** disentangled

looseness: 4 play

looseness of morals: 6 laxity

loosen up: 5 relax, unlax; **6** unbend, unwind, warm up; **7** unstuff; **8** limber up, slow down, unstrain; **10** decompress

loose thread: 4 blot, flaw, miss, slip; **5** fault; **7** blunder; **9** oversight

loot: 3 gut; **4** gelt, kale, pelf, sack, swag; **5** booty, bread, dough, foray, lucre, prize, reave, rifle, spoil, strip, sweep; **6** dinero, moolah; **7** cabbage, despoil, pillage, plun-

der, ransack, shekels; **8** hot goods, pickings

looted: 8 pilfered, pillaged; **9** plundered, purloined, ransacked

looter: 6 raider; **7** spoiler; **8** pillager; **9** despoiler, plunderer; **10** freebooter

looting: 4 sack; **6** rapine; **7** pillage, plunder, robbery; **10** spoliation; **12** despoliation

lop: 3 mow; **4** clip, crop, dock, reap, snip, trim; **5** dress, prune, sever, shave, shear

lope: 3 jog; **4** trot; **6** canter

Lophius: 5 lotte; **6** angler; **8** allmouth, monkfish; **9** goosefish; **10** anglerfish; **12** genus Lophius

Lopholatilus: 8 tilefish; **17** genus Lopholatilus

Lophophora: 6 mescal, mezcal, peyote; **15** genus Lophophora

lopped: 6 docked; **7** garbled; **9** lopped off, mutilated, truncated

lopsided: 4 awry; **5** askew, wonky; **6** biased, skewed; **7** crooked; **8** cockeyed, one-sided, top-heavy

loquacious: 5 gabby, talky; **6** chatty; **7** verbose; **9** garrulous, talkative; **10** logorrheic

Loranthaceae: 15 mistletoe family

Loranthus: 9 mistletoe; **14** genus Loranthus

lord: 5 noble; **6** master; **8** mistress, nobleman, overlord

Lord's supper: 9 communion, Eucharist; **12** the sacrament; **13** holy communion

lord it over: 5 bully; **6** hector; **7** dictate; **8** browbeat, domineer

lordless: 10 masterless

lordly: 5 grand, noble, proud; **6** august, sniffy; **7** haughty, stately; **8** baronial, prideful, princely; **9** dignified, honorable; **10** disdainful, swaggering, worshipful; **12** supercilious

lordosis: 10 hollow-back

lordotic: 6 dipped; **8** swayback; **10** swaybacked

lore: 6 wisdom; **8** learning; **9** knowledge; **11** information

Lorisidae: 5 loris; **15** family Lorisidae

lorn: 7 forlorn; **8** desolate, forsaken

Lorraine: 10 Lothringen

lorry: 5 truck; **6** camion

Los Angeles: 15 City of the Angels

lose: 4 miss; **6** mislay, recede; **8** misplace

lose consciousness: 7 pass out, zonk out; **8** black out

lose heart: 4 sink; **5** droop; **6** take on; **7** despond, give way

lose one's marbles: 5 go mad; **6** go nuts, run mad; **7** flip out, go crazy

loser: 7 also-ran, failure

lose weight: 4 slim, thin; **6** reduce; **8** slim down

losing: 4 loss; **7** failing

losings: 6 losses

loss: 4 exit; **5** going; **6** defeat, defect, losing;

7 passing, release; **8** discount; **9** decrement, deduction, departure; **10** expiration; **11** bereavement, deprivation

loss of hearing: 8 deafness

lost: 4 gone; **5** at sea, mazed; **6** abroad, broken, doomed, missed, ruined, undone; **7** baffled, bemused, devoted, extinct, missing, mixed-up; **8** accursed, confused, departed, helpless, stranded, vanished; **9** befuddled, exhausted, forgotten; **10** bewildered, confounded; **11** disoriented, preoccupied; **12** absent-minded, incorrigible

lost sheep: 10 black sheep

lot: 3 pot, set, wad; **4** a lot, band, deal, dose, draw, fate, heap, load, lots, luck, mass, mess, mint, pack, peck, pile, plot, raft, slew; **5** allot, batch, bunch, flock, patch, share, sight, spate, stack, stock, tract; **6** circle, estate, hatful, mickle, muckle, parcel, plenty; **7** a volume, deal out, destiny, dish out, dole out, fortune, measure, mete out, portion, tidy sum; **8** caboodle, dispense; **9** a quantity, allotment, allowance, situation

Lota: 4 cusk, ling; **6** burbot; **7** eelpout; **9** genus Lota

loth: 5 loath, shy of; **6** averse, loathe; **7** adverse; **8** loathe to; **9** reluctant

lothario: 3 rip; **4** goat, rake; **5** satyr; **6** lecher; **7** captive, Don Juan, fast man, gallant, seducer; **8** paramour; **9** debauchee, ladies' man

Lothringen: 8 Lorraine

lotion: 6 cerate; **8** dilution, lenitive, ointment; **10** maceration; **11** application

lots: 3 lot; **4** a lot, gobs, over, tons, wads; **5** heaps, loads, piles, rafts, scads, slews; **6** dozens, oodles, plenty, scores, stacks; **7** a volume; **8** lashings; **9** a quantity, abundance, amplitude, plenitude, profusion

lotte: 6 angler; **8** allmouth, monkfish; **9** goosefish; **10** anglerfish

lottery: 7 drawing

lotto: 4 keno; **5** beano, bingo

lotus: 11 sweet clover

lotus eater: 7 dreamer; **9** stargazer

louche: 5 shady

loud: 5 aloud, cheap, flash, forte, gaudy, noisy, tacky, tatty; **6** brassy, flashy, garish, loudly, tawdry, trashy; **8** gimcrack, sonorous

loud-hailer: 8 bullhorn

loudly: 4 loud; **5** aloud, forte; **7** noisily; **11** clamorously

loudmouth: 9 blusterer

loudness: 5 glitz, power; **6** volume; **9** brashness, gaudiness, intensity, noisiness; **10** flashiness, garishness, tawdriness

loufah sponge: 5 loofa, luffa; **6** loofah

Lou Gehrig's disease: 3 ALS

lough: 4 lake, loch, mere, pond, pool, slab, tarn; **5** broad, plash; **6** puddle

Louis XIV: 7 Sun King; **13** Louis the Great

lounge: 4 loaf, lurk, poke, sofa; **5** couch, tarry; **6** footle, linger, loiter; **8** best room, lallygag, lollygag

lounge chair: 9 easy chair

lounger: 4 mope; **6** loafer; **7** dallier; **8** recliner; **9** goldbrick, lazzarone [It]

loupe: 4 lens; **9** magnifier

loup-garou: 8 werewolf

lour: 5 lower; **6** lowery

louse: 3 bug; **4** heel; **6** insect, vermin; **8** dirt ball

louse up: 4 blow, flub, muff; **5** botch, fluff, spoil; **6** ball up, bobble, bungle, foul up, fumble, mess up, muck up; **7** blunder, screw up; **8** bollocks; **9** mishandle

lousiness: 11 pediculosis

lousy: 4 icky; **5** dirty; **6** crappy, filthy, rotten, stinky; **8** stinking

lout: 3 oaf, put; **4** boor, calf, clod, colt, gawk, goon, loon, lump; **5** block, churl, klutz, stick, stock; **6** doodle, lubber, lummox; **7** buzzard, dullard; **9** underling; **10** stumblebum

loutish: 6 oafish; **7** boorish, brutish, raffish, swinish; **8** churlish, clownish; **11** neanderthal

louvered window: 8 jalousie

louvre: 3 fin; **6** louver; **8** jalousie

Louvre Museum: 6 Louvre

lovable: 8 adorable

love: 4 dear; **5** enjoy, honey, jewel, sugar; **6** duckey, liking, regard, relish; **7** beloved, dearest, passion; **8** fondness, loved one, make love, true love; **9** affection; **10** be intimate, bear love to, lovemaking, making love, tenderness

love affair: 6 affair; **7** romance

love apple: 6 tomato

love child: 7 bastard; **12** illegitimate

loved one: 4 dear, love; **5** honey; **7** beloved, darling, dearest

love letter: 9 valentine

love line: 9 heart line; **10** mensal line; **11** line of heart

lovelorn: 6 bereft, jilted; **8** forsaken, rejected; **9** unbeloved

lovely: 5 sweet; **6** pretty; **8** adorable; **9** beauteous, beautiful, endearing

lovemaking: 3 sex; **4** love, suit; **6** coitus, mating, wooing; **8** courting; **9** courtship

love of country: 10 patriotism

lover: 3 fan; **4** buff; **5** flame; **6** adorer, votary; **7** admirer, amateur, devotee; **10** aficionado, dilettante; **11** afficionado

love seat: 6 settee; **7** vis-a-vis; **9** tete-a-tete

lovesome: 4 fond, warm; **6** caring, tender; **7** amorous; **12** affectionate

love story: 7 romance

loving cup: 3 cup; **6** trophy

low: 3 ebb, moo; **4** base, blue, down, dull,

mean, neap, so-so, vile; **5** cheap, dirty, first, lowly, small, sorry; **6** abject, broken, common, humble, modest, scummy, scurvy, shabby; **7** crushed, debased, humbled, ignoble, low gear, low-down, pitiful, scrubby; **8** beggarly, depleted, downcast, low-toned, middling; **9** depressed, first gear, low priced, miserable, tolerable; **10** depression, dispirited, humiliated, low-pitched; **11** downhearted, ignominious, inexpensive

lowball: 13 underestimate
low blood pressure: 11 hypotension
lowborn: 8 baseborn
lowbred: 4 rude; **7** ill-bred; **8** yokelish
lowbrow: 10 philistine; **12** uncultivated
low-cal: 4 diet, lite; **5** light
low-carbon steel: 9 mild steel; **13** soft-cast steel
low-cost: 9 low-priced; **10** affordable
low-cut: 9 decollete, low-necked
low density: 6 rarity; **7** tenuity
low-density lipoprotein: 3 LDL
low-down: 3 low; **4** dope, poop; **5** funky; **6** abject, scummy, scurvy, skinny; **9** miserable
low earned run average: 6 low ERA
lower: 4 damp, dash, dull, less, loom, lour, pout, sink, snap; **5** frown, gnarl, gnash, growl, lowly, minor, minus, petty, scowl, snarl, unman; **6** deject, glower, lesser, nether, weaken; **7** cut back, cut down, depress, get down, let down; **8** inferior, take down, tone down, turn down; **9** attenuate, deficient, extenuate, prostrate, secondary, subaltern
lower atmosphere: 11 troposphere
Lower California: 4 Baja
lower case: 11 small letter; **15** lower-case letter
lowerclassman: 13 underclassman
lower court: 10 trial court
lowering: 5 heavy; **6** sullen; **8** dropping; **10** depressing; **11** letting down, threatening
lower jaw: 4 jowl; **7** jawbone; **8** mandible; **9** mandibula
lower limit: 7 minimum
lowermost: 10 bottommost, nethermost
lower oneself: 5 stoop; **10** condescend
lower-ranking: 5 lower, lowly, petty; **8** inferior; **9** secondary, subaltern; **11** junior-grade, subordinate
lowest: 4 last; **5** least; **6** bottom; **8** smallest; **9** last-place
lowest common multiple: 3 lcm
low frequency: 2 LF; **8** low pitch
Low German: 12 Plattdeutsch
low-key: 7 subdued
lowlands: 9 flatlands
low-level formatting: 14 initialization

lowlife: 3 bum, rat; **4** puke; **5** crumb, skunk
lowliness: 7 lowness; **9** abasement; **10** abjectness
lowly: 3 low; **4** base; **5** lower, petty, small; **6** abject, humble, menial, modest; **8** baseborn, inferior; **9** secondary, subaltern; **10** spiritless; **11** junior-grade, subordinate
low-necked: 6 low-cut; **9** decollete
low note: 8 base note, bass note, deep note, flat note; **9** grave note
low pH: 7 acidity
low point: 7 ebb tide
low priced: 3 low; **5** cheap; **10** affordable; **11** inexpensive
low quality: 7 badness; **8** poorness; **11** inferiority
low relief: 9 bas relief [Fr]; **12** basso relievo
low-salt diet: 12 salt-free diet; **13** low-sodium diet
low spirits: 5 blues, dumps; **7** sadness; **8** darkness, doldrums, the blues, the dumps; **9** dejection, heaviness, tristesse [Fr]; **10** bad spirits, blue devils, depression, dismalness, gloominess, melancholy, somberness; **11** joylessness, melancholia; **12** dejectedness, mournfulness
low temperature: 4 cold; **8** coldness
low tide: 7 ebb tide
low-voltage: 10 low-tension
low-water mark: 5 nadir
lox: 6 salmon; **12** liquid oxygen
Loxodonta: 8 elephant; **14** genus Loxodonta
loxodrome: 5 rhumb; **9** rhumb line
loyal: 4 fast, firm, true; **7** devoted, staunch; **8** faithful; **9** compliant, complying, observant, patriotic; **11** truehearted
loyalist: 8 stalwart
loyalty: 6 homage; **8** devotion, fidelity; **9** constancy; **10** allegiance, commitment, dedication; **12** faithfulness
lozenge: 4 pill; **6** tablet; **7** diamond
LPN: 14 practical nurse
LSD: 4 acid
LTD: 10 disability
Ltd.: 2 Ld.; **14** limited company
LTM: 14 long-term memory
Lu: 8 lutecium, lutetium
Luanda: 14 Angolan capital
lubber: 3 oaf; **4** clod, flat, gawk, goon, lout, lump, muff, swab; **5** klutz, stick; **6** dauber, duffer, lummox; **7** fumbler, marplot; **10** landlubber, stumblebum
lubricate: 3 oil; **4** lube; **6** grease
lubricating substance: 3 oil; **6** grease; **9** lubricant; **10** lubricator; **11** lubrication
lubricious: 7 lustful; **8** prurient; **9** salacious
lubricity: 7 lechery; **8** lewdness; **11** lubrication; **14** lasciviousness
lucent: 5 aglow, lucid; **7** glowing, lambent; **8** luminous; **10** luciferous
lucerne: 7 alfalfa
lucid: 6 limpid, lucent; **7** logical; **8** coherent,

luculent, pellucid; **10** luciferous; **11** crystalline, perspicuous, transparent

lucidity: 7 clarity; **8** sobriety; **9** clearness, limpidity, lucidness; **10** brightness, luminosity; **11** rationality

lucifer: 5 fusee, light, match, spill; **7** matches; **8** vesuvian

Lucifer: 5 Devil, Satan; **6** Belial, Samael, Zamiel; **7** Old Nick [slang]; **8** the Devil; **9** Beelzebub; **10** the evil one, the Tempter; **12** the Adversary, the arch fiend, the archenemy, the foul fiend, the wicked one; **13** the evil spirit, the old Serpent; **14** Mephistopheles; **16** Prince of Darkness

luck: 3 lot; **4** fate; **6** chance, hazard; **7** destiny, fortune, portion; **8** good luck; **10** random luck; **11** good fortune; **13** circumstances

luckily: 11 fortunately; **12** fortuitously

luckless: 7 hapless, unhappy, unlucky; **8** hoodooed [U.S.], snakebit; **11** unfortunate

lucky: 4 ripe; **5** happy; **6** in luck; **7** blessed; **9** favorable, fortunate; **10** auspicious, convenient, favourable, propitious, prosperous; **11** encouraging; **12** providential

lucrative: 6 paying; **7** gainful; **10** profitable; **11** moneymaking; **12** advantageous, remunerative

lucre: 4 gelt, loot; **5** bread, dough, money; **6** dinero, moolah, profit, riches, wealth; **7,** fortune, profits, shekels; **8** earnings, opulence; **9** affluence

lucubration: 5 study; **9** pondering; **11** speculation; **12** deliberation

luculent: 5 lucid

lucullan: 4 lush; **5** plush; **6** lavish, plushy

ludicrous: 6 absurd; **8** derisory, farcical; **10** ridiculous; **11** nonsensical; **12** preposterous

ludicrously: 9 laughably; **12** ridiculously; **14** preposterously

luffa: 5 loofa; **6** loofah

lug: 3 ear, tow, tug; **4** drag, draw, haul, pull, rake, tote; **5** block, stuff, trail

luge: 4 sled; **8** toboggan

luger: 6 slider

luggage: 7 baggage

luggage compartment: 5 trunk

luggage rack: 8 roof rack

lugubrious: 4 dark; **6** dismal, gloomy, somber, triste [Fr]; **7** joyless; **8** dejected, frowning; **9** cheerless, saturnine; **10** spiritless, uncheerful

lugworm: 3 lug; **7** lobworm

lukewarm: 4 cold, dull, warm; **5** bland, prosy, tepid; **6** frigid, trashy; **7** languid, prosaic; **9** colorless, proposing; **11** halfhearted

lull: 3 lay; **4** calm, cool, damp, hush, rest, swag, tame; **5** abate, allay, letup, pause, peace, quell, quiet, sober, still; **6** deaden, pacify, rebate, smooth, soothe; **7** appease,

assuage, compose, quieten, slacken, turn off; **8** calm down, suppress; **9** alleviate; **11** tranquilize

lullaby: 8 berceuse, easement, soothing; **9** soft music, softening; **10** cradlesong

lull to sleep: 4 hush, stay; **5** quell; **6** becalm

lumbar puncture: 9 spinal tap

lumber: 3 bat, log; **4** hash, pack, plod, wood; **5** pound; **6** huddle, jumble, litter, timber, trudge; **7** trammel

lumbering: 5 heavy; **8** unwieldy; **9** ponderous

lumberjack: 9 lumberman, timberman

lumbermill: 7 sawmill

lumber store: 10 lumber yard

lumen: 2 lm

luminance: 5 light; **10** brightness, luminosity; **12** luminousness

luminary: 6 oracle; **7** notable; **9** authority; **10** esprit fort, notability; **11** light source

luminescence: 4 glow

luminous: 5 aglow; **6** lucent; **7** glowing, lambent; **11** transparent

luminous intensity unit: 11 candlepower

lummox: 3 oaf; **4** clod, gawk, goon, lout, lump, rube [U.S.]; **5** klutz; **6** lubber; **10** stumblebum

lump: 3 bit, oaf, ton, tun; **4** ball, bulk, clod, cord, gawk, glob, goon, hunk, knot, load, loaf, lout, mass, swad; **5** block, chunk, clump, klutz; **6** bushel, lubber, lummox, morsel, nugget; **8** particle, swelling; **9** collocate, puffiness; **10** stumblebum

lumpen: 7 lumpish; **10** unthinking

lumper: 6 docker, loader; **8** dockhand, handyman; **9** stevedore; **10** dock worker, roustabout; **12** dock-walloper, longshoreman

lumpish: 4 dull; **5** gaunt, heavy, hulky, lumpy; **6** leaden, lumpen; **7** hulking, lumping, massive; **8** lubberly, spanking, thumping, unwieldy, whacking, whopping; **9** walloping; **10** burdensome, cumbersome, thundering, unthinking; **11** substantial

lump together: 6 gather, muster; **7** collect; **8** assemble

lumpy: 6 chunky; **10** burdensome, cumbersome

Luna: 4 moon

lunacy: 7 madness; **8** insanity; **10** insaneness

lunar excursion module: 3 LEM

lunar month: 4 moon; **8** lunation; **12** synodic month

lunar time period: 4 tide

lunate: 8 crescent; **9** semilunar; **10** crescentic; **11** bicephalous; **14** crescent-shaped

lunatic: 3 mad; **4** daft, loco, nuts; **5** batty, crazy, dotty, loony, nutty; **6** crazed, fruity, insane, madcap, madman, maniac, teched [dialect]; **7** bonkers, cracked, far gone,

L

hothead, tetched [dialect], touched; **8**
demented, deranged, maddened, not right;
9 daredevil; **10** moonstruck
lunation: 4 moon; **10** lunar month; **12** synodic month
lunch: 8 dejeuner, luncheon
lunette: 10 fenestra
lung: 5 lungs [pl]; **7** bellows [pl]; **10** respirator
lunge: 3 cut; **4** hurl; **5** lurch; **6** hurtle, poke at, thrust
lunger: 10 tubercular
lungs: 3 fan; **4** lung; **7** air pump, bellows; **8** blowpipe; **9** air blower; **10** ventilator
lunkhead: 5 dunce; **6** rustic; **7** hayseed; **8** bonehead, numskull; **9** blockhead; **10** dunderhead, hammerhead, loggerhead, muttonhead; **11** knucklehead
lupine: 5 lupin; **7** wolfish; **9** rapacious, raptorial
Lupinus: 6 lupine; **12** genus Lupinus
lupus erythematosus: 2 LE; **3** SLE
lurch: 3 wag; **4** beat, cant, keel, list, reel, slip, swag, tilt, trip; **5** bevue [Fr], dance, dodge, faute [Fr], lunge, pitch, prowl, shake, shift, skunk, swing; **6** careen, desert, seesaw, tumble; **7** abandon, faux pas [Fr], forsake, stagger, stumble; **8** desolate, downfall, pitching
lure: 4 bait, coax, draw, hook, move; **5** charm, decoy, tempt; **6** allure, come-on, delude, draw on, entice, induce, seduce; **7** attract, beguile, bewitch, wheedle; **8** inveigle; **9** captivate, carry away, fascinate, sweetener; **10** conciliate, enticement, inducement; **12** blandishment
lurid: 3 dun; **5** dingy, dirty, muddy; **6** gloomy, leaden; **8** overcast, shocking, stammell; **11** crepuscular
luridness: 6 pallor; **7** wanness; **8** grimness, lividity, paleness; **9** lividness; **10** achromasia, pallidness; **11** ghastliness; **12** gruesomeness; **14** sensationalism
luring: 7 drawing; **8** alluring, enticing, inviting, tempting; **10** allurement, attracting, attraction, attractive, enticement, inducement, temptation; **11** beguilement, captivation
lurk: 4 loaf; **5** prowl, skulk, slink, sneak, tarry; **6** ambush, footle, linger, loiter, lounge, waylay; **7** scupper, smolder; **8** lallygag, lollygag, underlie; **9** ambuscade, bushwhack, lie in wait
lurker: 7 lurcher, skulker
Lusaka: 15 capital of Zambia
Luscinia: 11 nightingale; **13** genus Luscinia
luscious: 4 lush, rich; **5** juicy, yummy; **6** redhot; **8** delicate; **9** ambrosial, delicious, exquisite, toothsome; **10** appetizing, delectable, delightful, voluptuous; **11** scrumptious

lush: 3 bib, sot, tun; **4** rank, soak, swig; **5** besot, plush, souse, swill, toper; **6** boozer, guzzle, lavish, plushy, soaker, sponge; **7** carouse, guzzler, profuse, riotous, tippler; **8** drunkard, lucullan, luscious; **9** alcoholic, drink deep, drink hard, exuberant, luxuriant, succulent you
lust: 5 crave; **6** hunger, libido, starve, thirst; **7** luxuria; **8** cupidity, sex drive; **9** cacoethes [Lat], prurience; **11** lustfulness; **13** concupiscence, lecherousness
luster: 5 sheen; **6** lustre, sconce; **8** radiance, splendor; **9** shininess, splendour; **10** brilliancy
lustful: 4 lewd; **5** lusty; **6** carnal, erotic; **7** rampant, rutting, ruttish; **8** prurient; **9** salacious; **10** lascivious, libidinous, lubricious; **12** carnal-minded, concupiscent
lustrous: 5 shiny; **6** bright, glossy, sheeny; **7** lambent, radiant, shining; **9** burnished; **10** glistening
lusty: 3 fat; **4** full; **5,** stout, verry; **6** joyous, robust, hearty; **7** lustful, rampant, rutting, ruttish; **8** bouncing, prurient, vigorous; **9** strapping
lutanist: 6 lutist; **8** lutenist
lute: 3 gum; **4** size; **5** paste, wafer; **6** cement, luting; **8** birdlime
lutecium: 2 Lu; **8** lutetium
lutein: 10 xanthophyl; **11** xanthophyll
luteinizing hormone: 2 LH; **4** ICSH; **8** lutropin
lutetium: 2 Lu; **8** lutecium
Luther: 12 Martin Luther
lutist: 8 lutanist, lutenist
Lutjanus: 10 red snapper; **11** gray snapper; **13** genus Lutjanus; **15** mangrove snapper
Lutra: 5 otter; **10** genus Lutra
lutropin: 2 LH; **4** ICSH
lux: 2 lx
luxe: 6 deluxe, luxury
Luxembourg City: 9 Luxemburg; **10** Luxembourg; **19** capital of Luxembourg
Luxemburg: 10 Luxembourg; **14** Luxembourg City; **19** capital of Luxembourg
Luxemburger: 12 Luxembourger
luxuriant: 4 lush; **6** fecund; **7** profuse, riotous; **9** elaborate, exuberant, intricate
luxuriate: 6 wanton; **7** indulge
luxurious: 6 deluxe, gilded; **7** opulent; **8** pleasing, princely; **9** epicurean, sumptuous, sybaritic; **10** voluptuary, voluptuous
luxuriousness: 4 ease; **6** luxury; **7** comfort; **8** opulence
luxury: 4 ease, luxe; **6** deluxe; **7** comfort; **8** opulence; **10** lavishness; **11** sumptuosity; **12** extravagance
luxury sedan: 8 four-door
Lw: 10 lawrencium
lx: 3 lux; **5** sixty; **10** threescore
LX: 5 sixty

LXXX: 6 eighty; **9** fourscore
lycanthrope: 7 wolfman; **8** werewolf
lycee: 6 lyceum; **9** gymnasium; **12** middle school; **15** secondary school
lychee: 5 lichi; **6** lichee, litchi; **7** leechee, litchee; **9** litchi nut
lychgate: 8 lichgate
Lycopersicon: 6 tomato; **9** love apple; **10** plum tomato; **12** cherry tomato, Lycopersicum; **17** genus Lycopersicon, genus Lycopersicum
lycopod: 8 clubmoss
Lycosa: 9 tarantula; **10** wolf spider
lyddite: 7 cordite
lying: 7 sitting; **9** reclining; **10** mendacious; **11** fabrication, telling lies; **13** falsification, prevarication
lying-in: 5 labor; **7** travail; **8** birthing, childbed; **11** confinement
lying in wait: 4 trap; **6** ambush; **7** lurking; **8** skulking; **9** ambuscade

lying under oath: 7 perjury
Lymantria: 9 gypsy moth; **14** genus Lymantria
lymph cell: 10 lymphocyte
lymph gland: 4 node; **9** lymph node
lynch law: 7 anarchy; **6** mob law
lynchpin: 6 anchor; **8** backbone, linchpin, mainstay
lynx: 6 bobcat; **9** catamount
lynx-eyed: 8 hawk-eyed, keen-eyed; **9** Argus-eyed, eagle-eyed, sharp-eyed
lyophilize: 9 freeze-dry
lyric: 4 idyl; **5** words; **7** eclogue, lyrical, tuneful; **8** language; **9** lyric poem
lyrical: 5 lyric; **7** tuneful
lysergic acid diethylamide: 3 LSD [abbr]; **4** acid

M

M: 1 G, K; **4** thou, yard; **5** grand; **7** chiliad; **8** molarity, thousand
m: 1 k; **5** meter, metre; **8** thousand; **9** a thousand
M.: 8 monsieur [Fr]
M.M.: 3 bpm; **14** beats per minute
M-1 rifle: 6 Garand; **11** Garand rifle
ma: 3 mom, mum; **4** mama; **5** mamma, mammy, mater, momma, mommy, mummy
mA: 11 milliampere
ma'am: 4 dame, lady; **5** madam; **6** madame; **11** gentlewoman
macabre: 4 grim; **6** grisly; **7** ghastly; **8** gruesome
Macaca: 6 rhesus; **7** macaque; **12** rhesus monkey; **11** genus Macaca
macadam: 6 tarmac; **7** asphalt; **10** tarmacadam
macadamia nut: 9 macadamia
macadamized: 6 tarmac; **7** asphalt, macadam; **10** tarmacadam
Macao: 5 Macau
macaroni: 3 fop; **4** beau; **5** pasta; **7** coxcomb; **9** exquisite
maccaroni wheat: 5 durum; **9** hard wheat
mace: 4 wand; **5** macer, sprig, staff; **6** nutmeg; **7** oregano; **9** truncheon; **10** macebearer; **12** chemical mace
mace bearer: 8 huissier [Fr]
Macedonia: 7 Macedon

macer: 4 mace; **10** macebearer
macerate: 4 soak; **5** steep, waste; **6** pickle; **8** emaciate
Machaeranthera: 5 aster; **19** genus Machaeranthera
machete: 5 panga; knife; **7** matchet
Machiavellian: 7 crooked; **8** slippery, tortuous; **9** insidious
Machiavelli: 18 Niccolo Machiavelli
machination: 4 plot, ploy; **5** cabal, trick; **6** device, tactic; **8** intrigue, maneuver; **9** stratagem; **10** conspiracy
machinator: 7 plotter; **10** strategist; **11** conspirator; **13** coconspirator
machine: 3 car; **4** auto; **8** motorcar; **10** automobile; **13** simple machine; **16** political machine
machine action: 9 operation; **11** functioning
machine-controlled: 9 automated
machine gun: 14 automatic rifle
machine language: 4 code; **11** machine code
machinelike: 9 automatic, robotlike; **13** automatonlike
machine politician: 4 hack; **10** ward-heeler
machine readable dictionary: 3 MRD
machinery: 9 mechanism
machinist: 8 mechanic
macho: 8 machismo
macho-man: 4 stud; **5** he-man

macintosh: 3 mac; **4** mack; **8** raincoat; **10** mackintosh

Mackenzie: 14 Mackenzie River

mackerel: fish

mackinaw: 8 wool, coat, boat; **7** blanket

macon: 4 wine [Fr]; maconnais

Macrocheira: 9 giant crab; **16** genus Macrocheira

macrocosm: 5 world; **6** cosmos, nature; **8** creation, universe; **9** existence

macromolecule: 13 supermolecule

Macropus: 7 wallaby, **13** giant kangaroo, genus Macropus

macroscopic: 5 large

Macrotis: 5 bilby; **9** bandicoot; **13** genus Macrotis

macula: 5 patch; **6** blotch, macule; **7** freckle, sunspot; **9** birthmark

macula lutea: 6 macula; **10** yellow spot

maculate: 3 dot; **4** foul; **5** sully; **6** befoul, bemire, defile; **7** begrime, besmear, defiled, stipple, tarnish

maculation: 4 spot; **5** fleck, patch; **6** dapple, striae; **7** speckle; **8** spotting, staining; **10** polychrome, spottiness

mad: 4 daft, loco, nuts, sick, sore; **5** angry, batty, crazy, dotty, huffy, irate, loony, moody, nutty, wrath; **6** crazed, fruity, insane, teched [dialect]; **7** angered, bonkers, cracked, excited, far gone, frantic, lunatic, tetched [dialect], touched; **8** demented, deranged, maddened, not right, unhinged; **9** delirious, disturbed; **10** demoniacal, distracted, distraught, hysterical, moonstruck, unbalanced

Madagascar periwinkle: 10 periwinkle

madam: 4 dame, lady, ma'am, Mrs.; **6** madame; **11** gentlewoman; **13** brothel keeper

madame: 4 dame, lady, ma'am, Mrs.; **5** madam; **11** gentlewoman

madcap: 4 wild, zany; **5** bravo, bully, crazy, fiery, wierd; **6** fierce, madman, maniac, wanton; **7** beldame, excited, furious, hothead, lunatic, violent; **8** brainish, heedless, reckless, tearaway, vehement; **9** daredevil, desperado, eccentric, hotheaded, impetuous, impulsive, screwball

madden: 4 urge; **5** annoy, craze; **6** enrage; **7** envenom, incense, inflame; **8** convulse, irritate; **9** aggravate, infatuate, infuriate; **10** accelerate, exacerbate, exasperate

maddening: 6 vexing; **11** infuriating; **12** exasperating

made: 6 formed; **7** created; **8** produced; **9** generated

Madeira: 4 wine; **12** Madeira River

made-to-order: 6 custom; **7** bespoke; **8** bespoken, tailored

made-up: 5 built; **7** fancied; **8** invented; **9**

assembled, fictional; **10** fabricated, fictitious

Madia: 5 madia; **6** melosa; **10** genus Madia

Madison: 12 James Madison; **18** capital of Wisconsin

madly: 6 deadly; **7** crazily; **8** deucedly, insanely; **10** dementedly, devilishly

madman: 5 crazy; **6** madcap, maniac; **7** lunatic

madness: 4 fury, rage; **6** lunacy, rabies, raving; **8** delirium; **10** insaneness; **11** desperation, distraction, hydrophobia

Madonna: 4 Mary; **5** Saint; **7** Our Lady; **9** good woman, Notre Dame [Fr], the Virgin; **10** Virgin Mary

Madonna lily: 8 Lent lily; **9** white lily

madrepore: 10 stony coral

Madrid: 14 capital of Spain

madwort: 7 alyssum

maelstrom: 4 eddy; **6** vortex; **9** whirlpool; **12** undercurrent

maestro: 6 master; **9** conductor

Mae West: 8 life vest; **9** air jacket; **10** cork jacket, lifejacket; **13** life preserver

mafia: 6 the mob; **12** la cosa nostra [It], the syndicate; **13** Sicilian Mafia; **14** organized crime

Mafioso: 7 Mafiosi [pl]

mag: 8 magazine

magazine: 3 mag; **4** clip; **5** daily, lager; **7** gazette, journal; **8** canister; **9** cartridge, newspaper

Magellan: 17 Ferdinand Magellan

Magen David: 10 Mogen David; **11** Star of David

magenta: 6 damask, purple; **7** fuchsia

maggot: 3 fad, fit; **4** whim; **5** dream, freak, prank, quirk; **6** shadow, vagary, vision; **7** figment; **8** crotchet, escapade, flimflam

Magi: 7 Wise Men

magic: 5 trick; **6** wizard; **7** magical; **8** charming, illusion, witching, wizardly; **9** deception, sorcerous; **10** necromancy

magic carpet: 12 flying carpet

magic eye: 9 photocell; **11** electric eye

magician: 6 wizard; **8** conjurer, conjuror, sorcerer; **11** illusionist, necromancer; **15** prestidigitator

magic lantern: 14 phantasmagoria

magic marker: 6 marker

magic spell: 5 charm, spell

magic trick: 5 magic, trick; **8** illusion; **9** deception

magic words: 11 incantation

magisterial: 5 bossy; **7** haughty; **8** arrogant, imposing, insolent; **9** arbitrary, imperious; **10** autocratic, dominating, peremptory; **11** dictatorial; **13** distinguished, high-and-mighty

magisterially: 10 insolently; **11** arbitrarily, imperiously; **12** high-handedly; **13** dictatorially, **14** autocratically

magistrate: 5 judge; 6 jurist; 7 justice

magma: dregs; 7 melange; 8 sediment; 10 miscellany

Magna Carta: 11 Magna Charta; 12 great charter

magnanimity: 7 largess; 8 altruism, largesse; 10 liberalism; 11 munificence; 13 unselfishness; 14 openhandedness

magnanimous: 3 big; 5 large; 7 liberal; 12 greathearted

magnate: 3 CEO; 4 king; 5 baron, mogul, power; 6 tycoon

magnesium: 2 Mg

magnesium oxide: 8 magnesia; 9 periclase

magnet: 5 fancy; 8 siderite; 9 loadstone, magnetite, seduction; 10 allurement, attraction, temptation; 11 fascination

magnetic: 10 attractive, magnetized; 11 charismatic

magnetic field: 4 flux

magnetic iron-ore: 9 magnetite

magnetic north: 5 north; 12 compass north

magnetic personality: 8 charisma

magnetic resonance imaging: 3 MRI

magnetics: 9 magnetism

magnetoelectric machine: 7 magneto

magnetometer: 10 gaussmeter

magnification: 11 enlargement; 12 exaggeration; 13 overstatement

magnificence: 8 grandeur, splendor; 9 grandness, splendour; 10 brilliance; 12 gorgeousness; 14 impressiveness

magnificent: 4 fine, rich; 5 grand, showy; 6 mighty, superb; 7 sublime; 8 glorious, gorgeous, specious, splendid, towering; 9 brilliant, sumptuous; 11 outstanding

magnifico: 7 grandee, hidalgo; 8 nobleman

magnified: 8 enlarged; 9 amplified; 10 hyperbolic, overstated; 11 exaggerated, overwrought

magnify: 4 laud, puff; 5 bless, exalt, swell, widen; 6 blow up, expand, extend, pile up, praise, rarefy, spread, strain; 7 amplify, develop, distend, enhance, enlarge, glorify, inflate; 8 overdraw, pile it on, redouble, say grace; 9 aggravate, intensify, overstate, spread out; 10 aggrandize, exaggerate

magnifying glass: 8 hand lens, sunglass; 9 hand glass, magnifier; 12 reading glass

magniloquence: 3 gas; 5 bluff; 6 hot air; 7 bombast; 8 rhetoric, richness, tall talk, vaporing; 9 euphemism, turgidity; 10 floridness, orotundity; 11 declamation, grandiosity, rodomontade; 13 ornamentation

magniloquent: 4 rich, tall; 5 tumid; 6 florid, mouthy, ornate, turgid; 7 flaming, flowery, orotund, stilted; 8 boastful, boasting, braggart, bragging, inflated, sonorous, swelling; 9 bombastic, grandiose, high flown; 10 ornamented, rhetorical, swaggering, turgescent; 11 big-sounding, declama-tory, gasconading, high-flowing; 12 high-sounding; 13 grandiloquent

magnitude: 4 bulk, size; 9 dimension, greatness, largeness

magnolia family: 12 Magnoliaceae

Magnolia State: 11 Mississippi

magnum: 6 bottle; 15 forty-four magnum

magpie: 3 jay; 9 scavenger

maguey: 7 cantala

Magyar: 9 Hungarian

Magyarorszag: 7 Hungary

Mahabharata: 12 Mahabharatam, Mahabharatum

mahagua: 5 mahoe, purau; 7 majagua; 8 balibago; 9 blue mahoe, Cuban bast; 14 Hibiscus elatus; 17 Hibiscus tiliaceus

maharaja: 9 maharajah; 11 Hindu prince

maharani: 9 maharanee; 13 Hindu princess

mahatma: 4 guru, sage

Mahican: 7 Mohican

mahimahi: 11 dolphinfish

mahlstick: 9 maulstick

mahoe: 8 hibiscus

mahogany family: 9 Meliaceae

mahuang: 13 Ephedra sinica

maid: 6 maiden; 9 housemaid; 11 maidservant; 12 bachelor lady; 14 unmarried woman

maiden: 4 maid; 5 first; 9 inaugural; 10 initiative, initiatory

maidenhair fern: 10 maidenhair

maidenhair tree: 6 gingko, ginkgo; 12 Ginkgo biloba

maidenhood: 8 girlhood, maidhood

mail: 4 post, send; 6 get off; 7 mail car, mail van; 8 ring mail; 9 chain mail, ring armor; 10 chain armor, coat of mail, ring armour; 11 chain armour; 12 mail delivery; 13 postal service

mail advertising: 10 direct mail

mailbag: 7 postbag; 9 mail pouch

mail boat: 6 packet; 10 packet boat

mailbox: 7 postbox; 9 letter box

mail carrier: 7 carrier, mailman, postman; 13 letter carrier

mail clerk: 11 postal clerk

maillot: 6 jersey, tights; 8 tank suit

mailman: 7 carrier, postman; 11 mail carrier; 13 letter carrier

mail-order buying: 13 catalog buying

maim: 4 lame; 6 muzzle; 7 cripple; 8 double up, paralyze; 9 hamstring, prostrate

maimed: 7 wounded; 9 mutilated

maiming: 10 mutilation

main: 3 sea; 4 deep; 5 briny, chief, gully, ocean, prime; 6 funnel; 7 capital, leading, primary; 8 foremost, high seas; 9 principal; 10 overruling; 11 independent

main board: 11 motherboard

M

main course: 6 entree
Mainer: 10 Down Easter
mainframe: 3 CPU; 9 processor
mainland: 9 continent
mainland China: 3 PRC; 5 China; 8 Red
China; 14 Communist China
mainly: 7 chiefly, notably; 8 signally; 9 curiously, in the main, pointedly, primarily, unusually; 10 peculiarly, remarkably, singularly, strikingly, uncommonly; 11 principally; 12 particularly
main motive: 8 keystone; 10 mainspring
main office: 10 home office; 12 headquarters
main point: 4 gist; 5 point; 7 essence; 9 substance
main road: 7 highway
mainstay: 4 arch; 6 anchor, pillar; 8 backbone, linchpin, lynchpin
maintain: 4 hold, keep, play; 5 dwell, exert, wield; 6 assert, defend, keep up, strain, strike, uphold; 7 contend, observe, perform, quicken, support, sustain; 8 preserve
maintained: 6 kept up; 8 repaired, retained, serviced, well-kept
maintain its course: 4 keep; 5 abide; 6 pursue
maintenance: 4 care, play, work; 5 swing; 6 office, strain, upkeep; 7 alimony; 8 exercise; 9 provision; 10 livelihood, sustenance; 11 safe-keeping, sustainment; 12 conservation, preservation, sustentation
maintenance person: 8 repairer; 9 custodian
maitre d'hotel: 7 captain, maitre d'; 10 headwaiter
maize: 4 corn; 6 yellow
majestic: 5 grand, lofty, proud, regal, royal; 6 august, heroic, purple, sacred, solemn; 7 gallant, stately, sublime; 8 imperial, imposing, olympian; 9 dignified
majesty: 4 king [male]; 5 glory, queen [female], unity; 8 grandeur, holiness, nobility, splendor; 9 imperator [Lat], loftiness, solemnity, sublimity; 11 crowned head, sovereignty, stateliness; 12 anointed king [male], immutability
major: 6 higher; 7 greater; 8 superior
Majorana: 8 marjoram; 13 genus Majorana
major diatonic scale: 10 major scale
major-domo: 6 butler; 7 steward; 8 croupier, factotum, shepherd; 11 chamberlain, housekeeper
majority: 4 bulk; 8 legal age; 9 adulthood
major league: 6 majors; 9 big league
major part: 4 body, bulk, core, mass
major power: 5 power; 10 superpower
majors: 9 big league; 11 major league
majuscule: 4 caps [abbr]; 5 great; 7 capital; 8 capitals [pl]; 9 uppercase; 13 capital letter
Makaira: 6 marlin; 12 genus Makaira
make: 2 do; 3 cut, fix, get, hit; 4 cook, draw,

earn, form, gain, give, have, hold, name, take; 5 brand, build, cause, clear, drive, fetch, force, get to, reach, ready, score, throw; 6 attain, coerce, compel, create, induce, oblige, render; 7 compose, enforce, execute, prepare, produce, realize, shuffle; 8 arrive at, generate, nominate, overtake; 9 constrain, construct, establish, formation, shuffling, stimulate; 10 constitute; 11 manufacture, necessitate; 12 construction
make a case: 5 argue, plead
make amends: 5 atone; 8 make good; 9 indemnify
make a mess of: 5 botch; 6 bungle; 7 screw up
make believe: 5 feign, put on; 6 assume, fake it; 7 pretend
make-believe: 4 fake, mock, play, sham; 5 bogus, fraud, shift; 6 pseudo; 7 evasion, forgery, pretend, shuffle; 8 pretense, so-called, spurious; 9 pretended; 10 fraudulent, subterfuge; 11 counterfeit; 14 supposititious
make certain: 6 clinch
make certain of: 6 verify
make clear: 7 express; 8 manifest
make do: 4 cope, deal; 5 get by; 6 manage; 7 contend, grapple, make out
make easy: 4 ease; 6 smooth; 7 lighten; 10 facilitate
make fast: 3 fix; 4 bind; 5 affix, twist; 6 attach, clinch, fasten, secure
make fun: 3 guy, rib; 6 jest at; 7 laugh at, poke fun; 8 ridicule
make good: 5 atone; 6 assert, assume, make up, verify; 7 require; 8 arrogate, make sure; 9 establish, indemnify, reimburse, replenish; 10 compensate
make hot: 4 heat, warm
make merry: 3 toy; 5 feast, revel, sport; 6 junket, racket, wanton; 7 banquet, carouse, disport, wassail
make one mad: 4 gall, rile; 5 anger; 10 cause anger, raise anger
maker: 6 shaper, wright; 9 artificer; 12 manufacturer
makeshift: 5 shift; 6 ersatz; 7 stopgap; 8 jury mast; 10 improvised, jury-rigged, substitute
make sure: 6 clinch
makeup: 9 cosmetics; 11 composition; 12 constitution
make up for: 10 compensate; 16 make compensation
makeweight: 6 filler; 13 counterweight
make whoopie: 5 revel
make-work: 8 busywork
making: 7 forming, genetic; 8 creating, creation, devising; 9 formation, formative, producing; 10 fashioning, generating, generation, generative, production

making love: 4 love, suit; 6 wooing; 8 courting; 9 addresses, courtship; 10 lovemaking
mako: 9 mako shark
mako shark: 4 mako
malacca: 11 malacca cane
malachite: 6 copper
maladjusted: 9 disturbed
maladroit: 6 clumsy; 7 awkward, unhandy; 8
lubberly; 11 floundering, heavy handed; 13
uncoordinated
malady: 7 ailment, disease, illness; 8 disorder, sickness; 9 complaint
mala fide: 10 in bad faith
malaise: 6 unease; 10 discomfort, uneasiness
malamute: 8 malemute; 15 Alaskan malamute
malapert: 4 minx, pert; 5 fresh [U.S.], saucy;
7 forward; 8 cavalier, flippant; 10 jackanapes; 11 impertinent
malapropos: 7 unlucky; 8 ill-timed, untoward; 11 unbefitting, unfavorable, unfortunate; 12 inadmissible, inauspicious,
infelicitous, unpropitious, unseasonable
malaria parasite: 10 plasmodium
Malawi: 9 Nyasaland
Malay: 7 Malayan
Malay Archipelago: 10 East Indies
Malaysian capital: 11 Kuala Lumpur; 17
capital of Malaysia
Malcolm X: 13 Malcolm Little
malcontent: 7 croaker, exigent, growler; 8
exacting, grumbler, nonjuror; 9 dissenter,
dissident; 10 noncontent, rebellious; 11
disaffected, ill-affected; 12 malcontented;
13 hypercritical
malcontented: 7 exigent; 8 exacting; 10 malcontent; 13 hypercritical
mal de mer: 9 naupathia; 11 seasickness
male: 2 he; 3 him, man; 5 manly; 6 manful,
virile; 7 manlike; 9 masculine; 10 male
animal, male person
male chauvinism: 12 antifeminism
male chauvinist: 6 sexist
male child: 3 boy
maledict: 4 damn; 5 curse; 6 bedamn; 7
accurst, beshrew; 8 accursed, execrate; 9
imprecate; 10 anathemize
malediction: 5 curse; 11 imprecation
malefaction: 5 crime
malefactor: 5 crook, felon; 6 outlaw; 8 criminal, evil doer, evildoer
malefic: 4 evil; 6 malign; 7 baleful; 9 malicious, malignant; 10 malevolent
maleficence: 8 mischief; 9 malignity; 10
malignance; 11 balefulness, noxiousness
maleficent: 7 galling; 8 grinding, venomous
male monarch: 4 king
maleness: 9 manliness; 11 masculinity
male parent: 6 father
male person: 2 he; 3 him, man; 4 male
malevolence: 6 malice; 7 cruelty; 9 cruelness, malignity; 11 malevolency; 13 maliciousness

malevolent: 4 evil; 5 cruel; 6 malign; 7
malefic; 8 unbenign; 9 malicious, malignant
malfeasance: 11 malefaction, malpractice
malformed: 7 ill-made; 8 deformed; 9 distorted, ill-shapen, misshapen; 11 misbegotten
malfunction: 11 misfunction
malfunctioning: 13 nonfunctional
malice: 5 spite, venom; 7 cruelty, ill will; 8
bad blood, ill blood; 9 cruelness, ill nature,
malignity; 11 malevolence, malevolency;
12 spitefulness; 13 maliciousness
malicious: 5 cruel; 6 brutal, malign, savage;
7 brutish, inhuman; 8 barbaric, inhumane,
unbenign; 9 barbarous, malignant; 10 evil-
minded, ill-natured, malevolent; 11 ill-
disposed; 12 evil-disposed, ill-contrived,
semibarbaric, unbenevolent
malign: 4 evil; 5 brand, cruel; 7 malefic, traduce; 8 backbite, badmouth, unbenign; 9
malicious, malignant; 10 evil-minded, ill-
natured, malevolent; 11 ill-disposed; 12
evil-disposed
malignant: 5 cruel; 6 brutal, malign, savage;
7 brutish, inhuman, malefic; 8 barbaric,
inhumane, unbenign; 9 barbarous, malicious; 10 evil-minded, ill-natured, malevolent
maligned: 7 reviled
maligner: 7 defamer, libeler; 8 traducer; 9
backbiter, slanderer
malinger: 5 skulk
mall: 4 maul; 5 plaza; 6 arcade, center, mallet, piazza; 7 commons; 9 colonnade,
promenade
mallard: 4 duck
malleability: 7 pliancy; 8 softness, weakness; 9 ductility; 10 plasticity, pliability; 11
pliableness
malleable: 6 pliant; 7 ductile, plastic, pliable,
tensile; 8 formable, shapable, tractile,
workable; 9 extensile, shapeable
mallet: 4 mall, maul
malleus: 6 hammer [ear]
mallow family: 9 Malvaceae
malodor: 4 reek; 5 fetor, stink; 6 foetor,
stench
malposition: 12 misplacement
malpractice: 11 malfeasance
malt: 6 malted; 10 malt liquor, malted milk
malted milk: 4 malt; 6 malted
Malthus: 13 Thomas Malthus; 19 Thomas
Robert Malthus
maltreat: 3 bug; 4 bait, bite, bore; 5 abuse,
beset, grind, harry, haunt, hound, tease,
worry; 6 assail, badger, bother, harass,
heckle, ill-use, infest, molest, pester,
plague, pother, snap at; 7 oppress; 8 mistreat; 9 importune, persecute

M

malt sugar: 7 maltose
malt whiskey: 6 Scotch; 10 single-malt
Malus: 5 apple; 9 crab apple; 10 genus Malus
Malvaceae: 12 mallow family
malversation: 11 malefaction, malfeasance
mamma: 2 ma; 3 dam, mom, mum; 4 mama; 5 mammy, mater, momma, mommy, mummy; 6 mother
Mammalia: 13 class Mammalia
Mammea: 5 mamey; 6 mammee; 11 genus Mammea
mammon: 5 dough, lucre, money; 6 riches, wealth; 7 fortune; 8 opulence; 9 affluence
mammoth: 7 monster; 8 behemoth, gigantic; 13 woolly mammoth
Mammut: 11 genus Mammut; 13 genus Mastodon
mammy: 2 ma; 3 mom, mum; 4 mama; 5 mamma, mater, momma, mommy, mummy
man: 2 he; 3 arm, ban [Japanese], him; 4 body, hand, homo, male, soul; 5 baron, being, equip, human, piece, valet, world; 6 humans, mortal, outfit, person; 7 consort, husband, mankind; 8 creature, humanity, such a one; 9 adult male, earthling, gentleman, hired hand, human race, humankind
Man: 9 Isle of Man
man about town: 7 fast man, playboy; 9 bon vivant
manacle: 4 cuff; 5 cuffs; 6 hobble; 8 handcuff, handlock; 9 handcuffs
manacled: 7 hobbled; 8 fettered, pinioned; 10 handcuffed
manage: 2 do; 4 care, cope, deal; 5 get by; 6 direct, govern, handle, make do, wangle; 7 conduct, contend, finagle, grapple, make out, oversee, pull off; 9 supervise; 11 superintend
manageability: 4 ease; 8 easiness, facility; 10 facileness; 12 tractability
manageable: 6 wieldy
management: 6 charge; 7 control; 8 managing; 9 direction; 10 government; 11 controlling, supervising, supervision
manager: 5 coach; 7 handler; 8 director; 9 commander
Managua: 18 capital of Nicaragua
Manama: 16 capital of Bahrain
man and wife: 8 marriage
man at arms: 11 fighting man
manatee: 6 sea cow
mandamus: 4 writ
mandate: 5 edict, ukase; 6 colony, decree; 7 dictate; 8 dominion, province; 9 dictation, territory; 13 authorization
mandatory: 8 demanded, in demand, required; 9 mandatary; 10 compulsory
mandible: 4 jowl; 7 jawbone; 8 lower jaw; 9 mandibula; 10 submaxilla
mandioca: 4 gari; 6 manioc; 7 mandioc

Mandragora: 8 mandrake, may apple; 12 mandrake root; 15 genus Mandragora
mandrel: 5 arbor; 6 bobbin; 7 mandril, spindle
Mandrillus: 8 mandrill; 15 genus Mandrillus
mane: 10 head of hair
man-eater: 8 cannibal; 10 white shark
maned wolf: 7 red wolf; 10 Canis niger, Canis rufus
manege: 6 riding; 10 equitation; 12 horsemanship
manes: 5 ghost, shade
maneuver: 4 blow, head, move, play, ploy, step; 5 guide, point, steer, trick; 6 device, direct, stroke, tactic; 7 measure, operate; 9 manoeuvre, stratagem; 11 machination
manful: 4 male; 5 manly; 6 virile; 7 manlike, manlike
manganese: 2 Mn
mange: 12 cattle plague, milk sickness
mangel-wurzel: 6 mangel; 7 mangold
manger: 4 cage; 6 trough
Mangifera: 5 mango; 14 genus Mangifera
manginess: 9 seediness; 10 shabbiness
mangle: 4 gash, hash, iron, maul; 5 cut up; 6 hackle, haggle, murder; 8 hot-press, mutilate, scramble; 9 disfigure
mangled: 4 torn; 8 lacerate; 9 lacerated, mutilated
mango: 15 Mangifera indica
mangold: 12 mangel-wurzel; 13 mangold-wurzel
mangrove family: 14 Rhizophoraceae
mangy: 6 mangey
Manhattan: 15 Manhattan Island
manhood: 8 virility; 9 manliness
mania: 4 rage; 7 passion; 9 cacoethes
maniac: 5 crazy; 6 madcap, madman; 7 berserk, lunatic; 8 maniacal; 9 berserker
manic: 8 frenzied
manic depression: 15 bipolar disorder
manic disorder: 5 mania
manicure: 4 trim
manifest: 5 clear, plain; 6 attest, patent; 7 certify, evident, express, notable, salient; 8 apparent, evidence; 9 prominent; 11 demonstrate; 13 demonstrative
manifestation: 9 reflexion; 10 expression, reflection
manifesting: 7 showing; 10 exposition, presenting; 12 illustrating, illustration; 13 demonstrating, demonstration
manifesto: 13 pronouncement
manifold: 5 thick; 7 crowded, peopled, studded, teeming; 8 multiple, multiply, populous; 9 many-sided, multiplex; 10 multiplied; 12 multinominal; 13 multitudinous
Manihot: 4 gari; 6 manioc; 7 cassava, mandioc; 8 mandioca; 12 tapioca plant, genus Manihot

manikin: 4 form; 5 model; 7 manakin; 8 mannikin; 9 lay-figure, mannequin

Manila: 23 capital of the Philippines

Manila bean: 7 goa bean; 9 winged pea; 10 winged bean

manila paper: 6 manila; 7 manilla; 12 manilla paper

Manilkara: 9 sapodilla; 14 genus Manilkara

manioc: 4 gari; 7 cassava, mandioc, manioca; 8 mandioca; 12 tapioca plant

manioca: 6 manioc

manipulate: 3 ply, rig; 4 cook, fake, work; 5 fudge, wield; 6 handle, wangle; 7 control, falsify; 12 misrepresent

manipulation: 3 use; 8 handling

manipulator: 8 operator

manitou: 6 manitu, spirit

manliness: 5 vigor; 6 energy; 7 manhood; 8 maleness, virility; 10 manfulness; 11 masculinity

manly: 4 male; 6 manful, virile; 7 manlike; 8 manfully

man-made: 9 synthetic; 10 artificial; 11 artifactual; 12 manufactured; 13 semisynthetic

man-made fiber: 9 synthetic

mannequin: 4 form; 5 model; 7 manakin, manikin; 8 mannikin; 9 lay-figure; 12 fashion model

manner: 2 MO; 3 way; 4 mode, wise; 5 guise, means, stamp, style; 6 method, rubric, strain; 7 bearing, fashion, process; 8 carriage, demeanor, protocol; 9 character, mechanism, procedure, technique; 10 procedures [pl]; 11 description, designation, predicament; 12 denomination

mannered: 5 stiff; 7 stilted; 8 affected; 10 artificial

mannerism: 4 airs, pose; 6 foible; 10 pretension; 11 acting a part, affectation, originality, peculiarity, personality, pretensions [pl]; 12 affectedness, idiosyncrasy; 13 individuality

mannerly: 5 civil; 6 polite; 9 courteous; 11 well-behaved

mannikin: 4 form; 5 model; 7 manakin, manikin; 9 lay-figure, mannequin; 12 fashion model

man of action: 4 doer; 7 hustler; 8 activist

man of affairs: 11 businessman

man-of-war: 7 gunboat, warship; 9 jellyfish

manor: 5 honor; 6 domain

manor-house: 4 hall; 5 court, folly, tower; 6 castle; 7 chateau, rotunda; 8 pavilion

manorial: 6 landed

manpower: 3 men; 5 hands; 9 workforce

manque: 7 would-be

mansard roof: 7 mansard; 8 curb roof; 11 gambrel roof

manse: 4 hall; 5 glebe; 7 deanery, mansion, rectory; 8 vicarage; 9 parsonage, residence; 10 presbytery

mansion house: 4 hall; 5 manse; 7 mansion; 9 residence

manslaughter: 6 murder; 8 homicide

mansuetude: 8 tameness, meekness; 10 easy temper, good temper, soft tongue; 11 complacency

manta ray: 5 manta; 9 devilfish

mantel: 6 mantle; 11 mantelpiece, mantlepiece; 12 chimneypiece

mantelpiece: 6 mantel, mantle; 11 mantlepiece; 12 chimneypiece

mantic: 5 vatic; 7 vatical; 8 sibyllic; 9 prophetic, sibylline; 10 divinatory

mantid: 6 mantis

mantilla: 4 cape; 5 cloak; 6 tabard, tippet; 7 mantlet; 8 mantelet

mantis: 6 mantid

Mantis religioso: 13 praying mantid, praying mantis

mantle: 3 wax; 4 cape, fume, pall, toga; 5 blush, chafe, cloak, drape, flush; 6 ermine, gurgle, mantel, purple; 7 blanket, color up, curtain, drapery, pallium, pelisse, sparkle, turn red; 11 mantelpiece, mantlepiece; 12 chimneypiece

mantlepiece: 6 mantel, mantle; 11 mantelpiece; 12 chimneypiece

man-to-man: 8 one-on-one

manual: 5 codex; 6 primer; 9 rudiments, vade mecum

manual alphabet: 14 finger alphabet

manual dexterity: 7 sleight; 9 dexterity, handiness; 13 dexterousness

manual labor: 8 drudgery; 11 routine work

manual laborer: 7 laborer, workman; 10 workingman; 11 laboring man

manufactory: 4 mill; 5 plant, works; 7 factory

manufacture: 4 make; 6 fabric, invent, make up; 7 produce; 8 industry; 9 construct, fabricate; 11 fabrication

manufactured: 7 man-made

manufacturer: 5 maker; 6 wright; 8 producer; 9 artificer business

manufacturing plant: 4 mill; 7 factory; 11 manufactory

manumission: 12 emancipation

manumit: 10 emancipate

manumitter: 11 emancipator

manure: 4 muck; fertilizer

manus: 3 paw; 4 hand, hook, mitt; 6 mauler

manuscript: 2 ms; 9 holograph

many: 8 numerous

Mao Zedong: 3 Mao; 10 Mao Tsetung

map: 4 plan; 5 chart; 6 map out; 7 mapping; 9 represent; 14 correspondence

map collection: 5 atlas

maple family: 9 Aceraceae

map maker: 12 cartographer

M

mapmaking: 11 cartography
mapper: 7 plotter
Maputo: 19 capital of Mozambique
mar: 5 spoil; 6 impair; 7 blemish, despoil, vitiate; 8 deflower, mutilate
Mar: 5 March
marabou stork: 7 marabou; 8 marabout
maraca: 5 gourd; 6 rattle
Marantaceae: 15 arrowroot family
maraschino cherry: 7 marasca; 10 maraschino
marathon: 8 footrace; 12 long-distance
marathon runner: 10 marathoner, road runner
maraud: 4 raid; 5 foray; 6 forage; 10 filibuster
marauder: 7 spoiler, vulture; 8 pillager, predator; 10 depredator
marble: 3 pea; 4 bulb, clew, drop, horn, knob, pill; 5 table; 6 bullet, pellet, pillar, pommel, tablet; 7 globule, vesicle; 8 deadness, spherule
marbled: 7 mottled
march: 4 beat [of police], pace, plod, step, walk, wend; 5 range, tread; 6 foot it, hoof it, parade, stride; 7 exhibit, process; 8 marching; 11 demonstrate; 12 martial music
March: 3 Mar
March equinox: 13 spring equinox, vernal equinox
marcher: 7 parader; 11 foot soldier, infantryman
marchioness: 8 marquise
marchland: 10 borderland
marchpane: 8 marzipan
Marcus Antonius: 6 Antony; 10 Mark Antony
Mardi Gras: 10 Fat Tuesday; 13 Shrove Tuesday
mare: 11 female horse
mare's nest: 4 bosh, myth; 5 farce
mare's tail: 9 horseweed
margarine: 4 oleo; 5 marge; 8 margarin; 13 oleomargarine
margay cat: 6 margay; 10 Felis wiedi
marge: 4 oleo; 8 margarin; 9 margarine; 13 oleomargarine
margin: 4 edge, rope; 5 swing; 6 border, leeway; 7 stowage; 9 allowance, elbowroom, perimeter, tolerance; 11 gross profit
marginal: 4 bare, edge; 6 border, fringe, fringy; 8 skirting; 10 borderline; 12 hardscrabble
marginally possible: 10 improbable; 12 just possible; 14 barely possible
margrave: 5 boyar; 7 esquire
marguerite: 5 daisy
maria: 4 mare
Marianas: 14 Ladrone Islands, Mariana Islands

marijuana: 3 pot; 4 dope, gage, hemp, sens, sess, weed; 5 bhang, ganja, grass, skunk, smoke; 7 hashish; 8 cannabis, Mary Jane; 9 marihuana; 14 Cannabis sativa
marijuana cigarette: 5 joint, stick; 6 reefer
marimba: 9 xylophone; 10 vibraphone; 12 glockenspiel
Marine: 8 devil dog; 11 leatherneck
marine: 4 navy; 7 oceanic; 8 maritime, nautical; 9 saltwater man
marine museum: 8 aquarium, fish tank, vivarium
marine mussel: 7 mytilid
marine painting: 8 seascape; 10 waterscape
mariner: 3 gob, tar; 6 sailor, sea dog, seaman; 7 Jack-tar, old salt; 8 seafarer; 9 navigator
marine science: 11 hydrography
marine turtle: 9 sea turtle
marionette: 6 puppet
marital: 6 wedded; 7 married; 8 conjugal; 9 connubial; 11 matrimonial
maritime: 5 naval; 6 marine; 7 oceanic; 8 nautical; 9 seafaring
maritime law: 12 admiralty law
Maritime Provinces: 9 Maritimes
mark: 3 mug, pas, pit, see, set, tag; 4 dupe, fish, fool, gull, hand, keep, look, name, nock, note, pock, scar, sign, view; 5 brand, check, chump, cross, grade, label, patsy, pitch, place, point, score, stain; 6 figure, import, marker, moment, notice, period, regard, remark, scrape, stigma, sucker, target; 7 marking, observe, scratch; 8 advert to, bull's-eye, check off, cross off, cross out, denounce, shlemiel; 9 autograph, celebrate, punctuate, schlemiel, signalize, signature, soft touch, strike off, strike out; 10 autography, bell ringer, crisscross, importance, prominence, stigmatize; 11 attestation, commemorate, consequence, Deutschmark, distinction, distinguish, endorsement, materiality, weightiness
Mark Antony: 6 Antony; 14 Marcus Antonius
mark down: 4 bate, give; 5 allow; 6 reduce; 7 take off; 8 discount; 9 abatement, allowance, reduction; 10 concession; 12 depreciation
marker: 4 mark; 7 marking; 9 grease pen; 11 magic marker
market: 4 mart; 7 grocery; 9 quotation; 11 marketplace; 12 grocery store
marketable: 7 salable; 8 sellable, vendable, vendible
market economy: 12 laissez-faire; 14 free enterprise
market garden: 9 truck farm
marketing: 7 selling; 13 merchandising

market keeper: 9 tradesman; **10** shopkeeper; **11** storekeeper

marketplace: 4 mart; **5** place, plaza; **6** market

market price: 6 market; **9** quotation

marking: 4 mark; **6** marker; **7** keeping; **11** celebrating

marking down: 11 discounting

marking time: 6 static; **9** not moving; **10** motionless, stationary

mark into evidence: 6 adduce

mark off: 4 mark; **5** check; **7** mark out, tick off; **8** check off

mark of recognition: 3 nod

marksman: 6 bowman; **8** dead shot, good shot, rifleman; **9** crack shot; **12** sharpshooter

mark twain: 9 mark twine

marl: 4 loam

marmalade orange: 8 bigarade; **10** sour orange; **12** bitter orange; **13** Seville orange

marmalade plum: 6 mammee, sapote

Marmota: 6 marmot; **9** groundhog, woodchuck; **12** genus Marmota

Maroc: 7 Morocco; **8** Al-Magrib, Moroccan; **9** Marruecos

maroon: 5 exile, tawny; **6** banish, outlaw, strand; **7** dark red; **10** expatriate

marooned: 8 isolated, stranded

marplot: 5 stick; **6** damper, dauber, duffer, lubber, medler; **7** fumbler, killjoy

marque: 5 brand, label; **9** trade name

marquee: 4 tent, tilt; **6** awning; **7** parasol; **8** marquise, pavilion, sunshade, umbrella

marquetry: 9 parquetry; **11** marqueterie

marquise: 7 marquee; **11** marchioness

marred: 7 defaced, scarred

marriage: 5 match, union; **7** wedding, wedlock; **9** matrimony; **10** nuptial tie

marriageable: 6 nubile

marriage broker: 10 matchmaker

marriage ceremony: 6 bridal; **7** wedding; **8** espousal, marriage, nuptials, spousals

marriage offer: 8 proposal

married: 3 wed; **7** hitched [slang], marital; **11** matrimonial

married man: 5 hubby; **7** husband

married person: 4 mate; **6** spouse; **7** partner

married woman: 4 wife

marrow: 3 nub, sum; **4** core, gist, meat, pith; **5** heart; **6** center, kernel; **7** essence; **8** backbone; **9** substance, umbilicus; **10** bone marrow, inwardness

marry: 3 tie, wed, why; **4** join; **6** indeed; **7** conjoin, connect, espouse; **10** get hitched [U.S. slang], hook up

Mars: 4 Aries; **9** Red Planet

marsh: 3 fen; **5** swamp; **6** marshy, morass; **7** wetland; **9** marshland

marshal: 4 deal, pack; **5** allot, clerk, crier; **6** herald, set out, summon; **8** marshall, mobi-

lize; **9** collocate, parcel out, secretary, trumpeter; **10** distribute, flag bearer

marshaling: 12 mobilization

Marshall: 12 John Marshall; **16** Thurgood Marshall

marsh elder: 3 iva

marsh gas: 7 methane

marsh hawk: 10 hen harrier; **15** northern harrier

marsh hen: 7 bittern

marshland: 3 fen; **5** marsh, swamp; **7** wetland

marsh marigold: 7 cowslip, kingcup

marshy: 4 miry; **5** boggy, marsh, mucky, muddy; **6** quaggy, swampy; **7** sloughy

Marsilea: 5 nardo; **6** nardoo; **11** water clover; **13** genus Marsilea

marsupial: 13 pouched mammal; **15** marsupial mammal

mart: 6 market; **11** marketplace

Martes: 6 marten; **11** genus Martes

martial: 7 warlike; **9** bellicose, combative, soldierly; **11** belligerent, soldierlike, warriorlike

martial law: 11 military law

martial music: 5 march

martyr: 7 torture; **8** sufferer

martyrdom: 7 torture; **10** affliction

marvel: 6 wonder; **7** miracle

marvelous: 8 terrific, wondrous; **9** fantastic, wonderful; **10** marvellous, miraculous, prodigious, stupendous, tremendous

marvelously: 8 famously, superbly, wondrous; **9** amazingly, glaringly; **10** incredibly, wondrously; **11** egregiously, prominently, wonderfully

Marx: 8 Karl Marx

Marxism: 8 Leninism; **9** communism, Sovietism; **10** bolshevism; **12** collectivism

Marxist: 3 red; **5** pinko; **9** Bolshevik, communist

Mary: 7 Madonna; **9** the Virgin; **10** Virgin Mary; **11** Mother of God; **13** Blessed Virgin

marzipan: 9 marchpane

masculine: 4 male; **6** virile

masculinity: 8 maleness; **9** manliness

Maseru: 16 capital of Lesotho

mash: 4 bray, mess, muss [U.S.], work; **5** churn, crush, dally, flirt, grind, knead; **6** beat up, crunch, muddle, squash

masher: 4 dude, wolf; **11** skirt chaser, woman chaser

mask: 5 apron, cloak, visor; **6** bemask, domino, fender, masque; **8** block out, disguise

masked: 7 cloaked; **9** blindered, disguised; **11** blindfolded

masked ball: 14 masquerade ball

M

masking: 5 cover; 8 covering; 9 screening, shadowing; 11 adumbration, obscuration

masking tape: 8 duct tape

mask of pregnancy: 7 melasma; 8 chloasma

masochism: 13 sado-masochism

Mason: 9 Freemason

mason: 10 bricklayer, stonemason; 11 stone-cutter

Masons: 10 Freemasons

Masqat: 6 Muscat; 13 capital of Oman

masque: 4 mask; 5 drame; 6 mummer; 10 masquerade

masquerade: 4 mask, pose; 6 masque; 7 costume, mummery; 9 bal masque

masquerade dress: 4 mask; 5 visor; 6 domino

mass: 3 lot, pot, ton, tun, wad; 4 body, bulk, clod, cord, core, deal, heap, knot, loaf, lump, mess, mint, peck, pile, raft, slew, swad; 5 batch, block, flock, sight, spate, stack; 6 bushel, hatful, masses, mickle, muckle, nugget, people, pile on, pile up, plenty, volume

massacre: 7 mow down; 9 slaughter; 10 mass murder

massage: 5 knead; 7 rub down

massasauga: 11 rattlesnake

massed: 7 amassed; 9 assembled, collected; 10 congregate; 11 accumulated

masses: 4 mass; 6 people; 9 multitude

massive: 5 ample, bulky, massy; 8 cumbrous, unwieldy; 10 monolithic, monumental, voluminous; 11 substantial; 12 considerable

massiveness: 4 heft; 9 bulkiness, heaviness, heftiness; 11 ponderosity, weightiness

mass meeting: 5 rally

mass murder: 8 massacre

mast cell: 9 labrocyte, mastocyte

master: 3 see, sir; 4 lord, swim, take; 5 adept, catch, grasp, tutor; 6 expert, follow, genius, subdue, take in, victor; 7 captain, collect, control, get over, maestro, make out, skipper; 8 dominate, original, overcome, overlord, superior, surmount; 9 authority, gentleman; 10 headmaster, institutor, master copy, proficient

master's dissertation: 6 thesis

master copy: 6 master; 8 original

mastered: 4 down; 7 down pat

masterful: 8 masterly, virtuoso; 9 imperious, ingenious; 10 consummate

master hand: 5 adept; 6 expert, genius, master; 10 proficient; 11 crackerjack

Master in Business: 3 MBA

master key: 6 opener; 7 passkey; 8 latchkey, password; 11 combination

mastermind: 5 brain; 6 direct, genius; 8 engineer, organize; 9 conceiver; 10 master head, originator; 11 orchestrate

Master of Architecture: 5 MArch

Master of Arts: 2 AM, MA; 14 Artium Magister

Master of Arts in Library Science: 4 MALS

Master of Arts in Teaching: 3 MAT

Master of Business Administration: 3 MBA

master of ceremonies: 2 MC; 4 host; 5 emcee

Master of Divinity: 4 MDiv

Master of Education: 3 MEd

Master of Fine Arts: 3 MFA

Master of Laws: 3 LLM

Master of Library Science: 3 MLS

Master of Literature: 5 MLitt

Master of Science: 2 MS, SM

master of the house: 7 maitre d'; 12 maitre d'hotel

Master of Theology: 3 ThM

masterpiece: 4 pick; 5 cream, elite, prime; 6 flower; 8 nonesuch; 9 nonpareil

master race: 10 Herrenvolk

mastery: 7 command, control; 9 authority, expertise, supremacy; 10 ascendancy, domination, excellence, expertness, mastership; 13 subordination

mastic: 4 ropy; 5 japan; 6 clammy; 7 clotted, gelatin, lacquer, varnish; 9 glutenous, glutinous; 10 albuminous, gelatinous; 12 mucilaginous

masticate: 3 jaw; 4 bite, chew, gnaw; 5 champ, munch; 6 crunch, mumble; 7 munch on; 9 manducate

mastication: 4 chew; 7 chewing

Masticophis: 9 coachwhip, whipsnake; 12 striped racer; 16 genus Masticophis

mastocyte: 8 mast cell; 9 labrocyte

mastodon: 9 mastodont

mat: 3 rug; 4 felt, flat, matt, plat; 5 braid, mat up, matte, plait, snarl, twill; 6 felt up, matted, tangle; 7 cushion, matting, tracery; 8 entangle, filigree, flatness, fretwork, place mat

matador: 11 bullfighter

Mata Hari: 21 Margarete Gertrud Zelle

match: 3 fit, pit; 4 gibe, jibe, mate, meet, pair, peer, twin; 5 agree, catch, check, equal, fusee, light, mates, place, reach, rival, spill, tally, touch, union; 6 couple, oppose; 7 compeer, contest, lucifer, match-up, matches, pendant, realize, wedlock; 8 classify, identify, marriage, parallel, struggle, vesuvian; 9 matrimony, recognize, rhyme with; 10 categorize, correspond; 11 competition, distinguish, recognition; 12 discriminate; 14 categorization, classification, identification

matches: 5 match; 7 lucifer

matching: 4 twin; 7 twinned; 9 duplicate; 11 coordinated, identifying, recognizing

matchless: 3 one; 6 utmost; 7 supreme;

8 foremost, greatest, peerless; **9** nonpareil, paramount, unmatched, unrivaled; **10** preeminent, unrivalled; **11** unmatchable

matchlock: 8 arquebus; **9** Brown Bess, flintlock; **11** blunderbuss

match-up: 5 match; **11** recognition

mate: 4 pair, peer, twin; **5** equal, match; **6** couple, double, spouse; **7** comrade, consort, partner; **8** confrere, copulate, familiar, ice water, intimate, teammate; **9** checkmate, companion, first mate; **10** confidante; **11** counterpart

mated: 6 paired

mater: 2 ma; **3** mom, mum; **4** mama; **5** mamma, mammy, momma, mommy, mummy; **6** mother

material: 4 real; **5** cloth, stock, stuff; **6** fabric, matter, staple; **7** textile; **8** physical; **9** component, corporeal, momentous, substance; **10** substratum; **11** constituent, substantial, substantive

material body: 3 bod; **4** form, soma; **5** build, flesh, frame, shape; **6** figure; **7** anatomy, chassis; **8** physique

material evidence: 7 exhibit

materialism: 10 empiricism, positivism; **11** physicalism, worldliness; **12** philistinism; **13** phenomenalism

materialistic: 6 neuter; **7** earthly, worldly; **9** bourgeois, mercenary; **10** uncultured; **11** unspiritual; **12** conservative; **13** earthly-minded, worldly-minded

materialize: 5 pop up; **6** appear, crop up, happen; **8** spring up; **11** spring forth

materially: 7 notably; **9** saliently; **11** prominently

material object: 4 item; **5** thing; **6** object

material point: 3 dot; **4** mote; **5** point, speck

material possession: 7 holding; **8** property; **10** belongings

material witness: 10 earwitness, eyewitness

maternal: 5 enate; **6** enatic; **8** parental, paternal

maternally: 8 motherly

maternity: 10 motherhood

mates: 5 match; **6** couple

matey: 5 pally; **6** chummy; **10** palsy-walsy

math: 5 maths; **11** mathematics

mathematical: 9 numerical

mathematical function: 8 function; **9** operation

mathematical precision: 5 rigor

matin: 7 morning

matinee idol: 4 idol; **8** film star; **9** movie star

mating: 3 sex; **5** union; **6** coitus; **10** copulation, lovemaking; **11** conjugation

mating behavior: 12 mating ritual

matman: 8 grappler, wrestler

Matoaka: 10 Pocahontas; **12** Rebecca Rolfe

matriarch: 6 granny; **7** grandam, old lady; **8** old woman; **11** grandmother

Matricaria: 9 chamomile; **15** genus Matricaria

matriculation: 6 matric; **9** novitiate

matrimonial: 6 wedded; **7** marital, married; **8** conjugal; **9** connubial

matrimonial agent: 10 matchmaker

matrimony: 3 bed; **5** match, union; **7** wedlock; **8** marriage; **10** nuptial tie

matrix printer: 10 dot printer

matron: 5 goody; **7** dowager; **9** head nurse, matronage

matronage: 6 matron

matronymic: 10 metronymic

matte: 3 mat; **4** flat, matt; **6** matted; **8** flatness; **14** lusterlessness

matted: 3 mat; **4** flat, matt; **5** matte; **7** twisted; **10** interwoven

matter: 4 case; **5** count, issue, theme, thing, topic, weigh; **6** affair, makeup, matrix, slough; **7** concern, episode, subject; **8** contents, material; **9** substance

matter-of-fact: 5 plain; **6** severe, simple; **7** natural, prosaic; **9** pragmatic; **11** pragmatical

matter to: 8 interest

Matthew: 9 St. Matthew; **12** Saint Matthew

matting: 3 mat; **7** tracery; **8** filigree, fretwork

maturate: 3 age, **4** grow; **5** ripen; **6** mature; **7** perfect

maturation: 6 growth; **7** growing; **8** maturing, ontogeny, ripening; **9** nurturing, seasoning; **10** maturement; **11** development, ontogenesis

mature: 3 age; **4** grow, melt, ripe; **5** adult, ripen; **6** digest, grow up, mellow, season; **7** fledged, grown up, matured, perfect; **8** fructify, maturate; **9** elaborate

maturity: 7 due date; **8** ripeness; **9** adulthood; **10** matureness, mellowness

matzoh: 5 matzo; **6** matzah; **15** unleavened bread

maudlin: 4 flat; **5** inert, mushy; **6** slushy, supine, torpid; **7** mawkish, muddled, screwed, sewed up; **8** bathetic, schmalzy, sluggish, whittled; **9** schmaltzy; **10** obfuscated; **11** sentimental

Maui: 10 Maui Island

maul: 4 mall; **6** bruise, buffet, mallet, mangle, sledge; **7** scratch; **12** sledgehammer

mauler: 3 paw; **4** hand, hook, mitt; **5** manus

maunder: 5 clack, croak, growl, grunt, prate, prose; **6** clamor, gabble, gibber, maffle, mumble, murmur, mutter, piffle, tattle; **7** blabber, chatter, grizzle, grumble, palaver, prattle, twaddle; **9** mussitate; **12** tittle-tattle; **14** make a fuss about

Mauritania: 10 Mauritanie, Muritaniya

mausoleum: 4 tomb; **5** vault

mauvais gout: 8 bad taste

mauve: 5 lilac; **6** purple, violet; **8** lavender

M

maven: 3 ace, wiz; **4** star, whiz; **5** adept, whizz; **6** genius, wizard; **7** hotshot; **8** virtuoso; **9** sensation

maverick: 5 rebel; **9** irregular; **10** unorthodox

mavis: 10 song thrush

maw: 3 yap; **4** craw, crop, hole, trap; **6** gullet; **7** gizzard, stomach

mawkish: 4 fade, mild, weak; **5** mushy, stale, vapid; **6** slushy; **7** maudlin; **8** bathetic, schmalzy; **9** schmaltzy; **10** wishy-washy; **11** sentimental

maxim: 5 axiom; **8** aphorism

maximal: 7 maximum

maximum: 5 pitch; **6** climax, height, summit, utmost; **7** maximal; **9** level best, uttermost; **10** upper limit; **11** ne plus ultra

maxwell: 2 Mx

may: 3 can, get; **5** might

May 1: 6 May Day; **10** First of May

Maya: 5 Mayan; **13** Mayan language

maybe: 7 perhaps; **8** possibly; **9** perchance; **11** potentially; **12** peradventure

mayfly: 6 dayfly; **7** shadfly; **9** ephemerid

mayhap: 5 haply, may be, maybe; **7** perhaps; **8** possibly; **9** perchance; **11** potentially; **12** peradventure

mayhem: 5 havoc

mayor: 11 city manager

maze: 4 daze; **7** perplex, stupefy; **8** bewilder; **9** labyrinth

MB: 8 megabyte

Mbabane: 18 capital of Swaziland

Mc: 3 MHz; **9** megacycle, megahertz

mcg: 9 microgram

McKinley: 11 Mt. McKinley; **13** Mount McKinley; **15** William McKinley

MD: 2 Dr.; **3** doc [informal]; **6** doctor, medico; **8** sawbones; **9** physician

Md: 2 Mv; **11** mendelevium

me: 1 I; **6** myself [reflexive]; **7** I myself

mead: 6 meadow; **11** honeysuckle

meadow: 4 mead; **5** field; **8** hayfield

meadowgrass: 9 bluegrass; **11** meadow grass

meadowlark: 4 lark

meadow mouse: 10 meadow vole

meadow mushroom: 13 field mushroom

meadow saffron: 12 autumn crocus

meadow vole: 11 meadow mouse

meager: 4 lame, mean, poor, tame, thin, vile; **5** cheap, gaunt, sorry, spare, vapid; **6** feeble, hollow, jejune, scrimp; **7** scrimpy, scrubby, sketchy, sparing, stinted

meal: 4 bran; **5** flour; **6** farina, repast; **8** cornmeal

mealy: 5 sandy; **6** floury, grainy, gritty; **8** granular; **9** granulose; **11** farinaceous; **13** coarse-grained

mealy-mouthed: 4 oily; **5** soapy; **6** abased, pliant, smooth; **7** devious, fawning, hon-

eyed, slavish; **8** cringing; **9** groveling, sniveling; **10** dough-faced

mean: 3 low, mid; **4** base, near, vile; **5** cheap, close, dirty, imply, midst, mingy, small, sorry, think, tight, weedy; **6** abject, common, design, entail, intend, little, meager, medial, median, middle, paltry, scabby, scurvy, shabby, stingy, trashy; **7** average, express, hateful, ignoble, miserly, pitiful, purpose, scrubby, signify, think of; **8** beggarly, gimcrack, peddling, rascally, sneaking, spiteful, stand for, trumpery, wretched; **9** groveling, illiberal, miserable, pennywise, penurious, worthless; **10** have in mind, ungenerous; **11** ignominious; **12** contemptible

meander: 4 wave, wind; **5** twist, weave; **6** thread; **8** undulate; **9** circulate, intricacy

meandering: 5 twirl, twist; **7** circuit, winding; **8** rambling; **9** wandering

meanie: 4 hood; **5** brute, bully, meany, rough, rowdy, tough; **6** mugger, savage, wretch; **7** caitiff, hoodlum, ruffian; **8** hooligan; **9** barbarian, desperado

meaning: 5 force, sense; **6** import; **7** content, message, purport; **8** pregnant; **9** substance; **10** meaningful; **11** significant; **12** significance; **13** signification

meaningless: 6 vacant; **9** senseless, unmeaning; **11** nonsensical

meanly: 6 basely, humbly; **7** nastily; **8** scurvily

meanness: 8 vileness; **9** cheapness, closeness, minginess, parsimony, tightness; **10** abjectness, meagerness, paltriness, shabbiness, trashiness; **11** beastliness, pitifulness; **12** beggarliness, wretchedness

means: 2 MO; **3** way; **4** mode, wise; **5** asset; **6** agency, assets, manner, method; **7** fashion, process; **8** protocol, resource; **9** mechanism, procedure, resources, substance, technique; **10** belongings, procedures [pl]; **11** wealthiness, wherewithal; **13** circumstances, modus operandi

meanspirited: 4 base, mean; **10** ungenerous

meant: 7 advised, express; **8** intended; **10** deliberate; **11** determinate, intentional

meanwhile: 8 meantime

meany: 6 meanie; **12** unkind person

measles: 7 rubeola, rubella [German measles]; **8** morbilli

measly: 6 paltry; **9** miserable

measurability: 13 computability; **15** quantifiability

measurable: 10 mensurable

measure: 3 bar, fix, lot; **4** beat, bill, blow, mete, move, step; **5** meter, share, value; **6** amount, assess, rhythm, stroke; **7** cadence, portion, quantum; **8** appraise, estimate, evaluate, maneuver, quantify, quantity, standard; **9** allotment, allowance, criterion, determine, enumerate, fair share, measuring; **10** allocation, contingent, measure out, quantitate, touchstone; **11** measurement, mensuration

measured: 4 cool; **5** sober; **6** metric; **7** careful; **8** metrical; **9** chromatic, temperate; **10** calculated, deliberate, reasonable, rhythmical

measure for measure: 6 equity; **7** justice; **8** fair play

measureless: 9 countless, limitless; **10** numberless, unmeasured; **11** illimitable

measurement: 5 value; **7** measure; **9** measuring; **11** mensuration

measure up: 7 qualify

measuring: 7 gauging, measure; **11** measurement, mensuration

measuring stick: 7 measure; **12** measuring rod

measuring worm: 6 looper; **8** inchworm

meat: 3 nub, sum; **4** core, gist, pith; **5** flesh, heart; **6** center, kernel, marrow; **7** essence; **9** substance; **10** inwardness; **11** nitty-gritty

meat cleaver: 7 chopper, cleaver

meat-eating: 10 zoophagous; **11** flesh-eating

meat house: 10 smokehouse; **11** butchershop

meatman: 7 butcher

meat packing plant: 8 abattoir, shambles; **14** slaughterhouse

mechanic: 9 machinist, operative; **11** car-mechanic; **12** grease monkey

mechanical: 5 blind; **9** automatic; **11** instinctive, involuntary

mechanical drawing: 8 drafting

mechanical man: 5 robot; **7** android; **8** humanoid

mechanical piano: 7 Pianola; **11** player piano

mechanician: 8 mechanic, engineer; **9** machinist

mechanism: 2 MO; **3** way; **4** mode, wise; **5** means; **6** manner, method; **7** fashion, process; **8** protocol; **9** machinery, mechanics, procedure, technique; **10** procedures [pl]

mechanization: 8 high-tech; **10** automation

mechanize: 8 motorize

meclizine: 8 Antivert

Meconopsis: 5 poppy; **15** genus Meconopsis

medal: 4 palm; **6** ribbon; **9** medallion; **10** decoration

medallion: 4 palm; **5** medal; **6** ribbon; **10** decoration

medal play: 10 stroke play

medal winner: 8 medalist; **9** medallist

meddle: 4 moil; **6** tamper

meddler: 8 busybody; **9** intriguer; **12** inter-meddler

meddling: 4 busy; **5** pushy; **7** pushing; **8** dabbling; **9** officious, tampering; **10** busy-bodied, meddlesome; **11** interfering

medfly: 8 fruit fly

media: 6 medium; **9** mass media, news media; **10** journalism

media consultant: 9 media guru

medial: 3 mid; **4** mean; **6** median, middle; **7** average

median: 3 mid; **4** mean; **6** medial, middle; **7** average

mediate: 6 liaise, middle; **8** minister; **9** arbitrate, in-between, intercede, intervene

mediation: arbitration; **12** intercession, intervention

mediator: 9 go-between; **10** arbitrator; **11** intercessor; **12** intermediary; **13** intermediator

medic: 6 medick; **7** trefoil; **8** corpsman; **14** medical officer

Medicago: 6 clover, medick; **7** alfalfa, lucerne, trefoil; **13** genus Medicago

medical: 7 checkup; **9** medicinal; **11** aesculapian, health check, medical exam

medical aid: 4 care

medical examiner: 7 coroner

medical history: 6 record; **9** anamnesis

medical officer: 5 medic; **8** corpsman

medical practitioner: 2 MD; **6** doctor, healer; **10** medical man; **12** health worker

medical prognosis: 8 prospect; **9** prognosis

medical social worker: 7 almoner

medical treatment: 4 help; **6** curing, remedy; **7** redress, regimen, therapy; **9** treatment

medicament: 4 drug; **6** physic; **7** nostrum, simples; **8** medicine; **10** medication

medicate: 4 cure, dash, heal; **5** blend, cross, tinge; **6** doctor, physic, remedy, season; **8** medicine, sprinkle, tincture; **10** besprinkle, infiltrate

medication: 4 drug; **6** physic; **7** nostrum, simples; **8** medicine; **10** medicament, medicating; **14** pharmaceutical

medicine: 4 drug; **5** music; **6** physic; **7** nostrum, simples; **8** medicate; **10** medicament, medication; **14** pharmaceutical

medick: 5 medic; **7** trefoil

medico: 2 Dr., MD; **3** doc; **6** doctor; **9** physician

medieval: 6 gothic; **8** knightly; **9** chivalric, mediaeval

medievalism: 8 archaism; **14** antiquarianism

medieval mode: 10 church mode; **13** Gregorian mode

mediocre: 2 OK; **4** fair, poor, so-so; **7** average; **8** bearable, middling, ordinary, passable; **9** tolerable; **10** acceptable, admissible, second-rate; **11** indifferent

mediocrity: 10 moderation; **11** averageness, second-rater

meditate: 4 mull, muse; **5** study; **6** ponder, talk of; **7** dream of, reflect, think of;

M

8 ruminate; 9 speculate; 10 deliberate; 11 contemplate

meditation: 6 musing; 7 thought; 8 thinking; 9 reflexion; 10 cogitation, reflection, rumination; 13 consideration, contemplation; 14 thoughtfulness

meditative: 6 broody, musing, sedate; 7 pensive, wistful; 8 brooding, Platonic, studious; 9 pondering; 10 reflective, ruminative, thoughtful; 11 speculative; 12 deliberative; 13 contemplative, introspective, philosophical

Mediterranean fruit fly: 6 medfly

Mediterranean Sea: 13 Mediterranean

medium: 6 metier; 7 average, balance, vehicle; 10 middle term; 11 clairvoyant; 12 intermediate, spiritualist; 13 fortune teller

medium frequency: 2 MF

medium of exchange: 4 pelf; 5 bread, dough, lucre, money; 6 Mammon; 11 filthy lucre, legal tender

medley: 4 mess, olio; 7 farrago; 8 all sorts, mishmash, pastiche; 9 patchwork, potpourri; 10 hodgepodge

medroxyprogesterone: 7 Provera

medulla: 4 bulb; 6 myelin; 7 myeline; 16 medulla oblongata

medulla oblongata: 4 bulb; 7 medulla

medullary sheath: 12 myelin

medulla spinalis: 10 spinal cord

medusa: 7 medusan; 9 jellyfish

meed: 4 dole; 6 reward; 8 pittance; 12 remuneration

meek: 4 mild, tame; 6 modest; 9 compliant; 10 spiritless, unaspiring, unassuming; 11 unobtrusive; 13 unpretentious; 14 unostentatious

meekly: 6 humbly

meerschaum: 9 sepiolite

meet: 2 do; 3 due, fit, see; 4 fill, good, join, play, suit; 5 befit, graze, match, right, touch, unite; 6 adjoin, concur, fulfil, gather, proper, rejoin, seemly, suffer, take on; 7 correct, en regle, fitting, fulfill, ran into, receive, satisfy; 8 assemble, coincide, converge, cope with, decorous, osculate; 9 befitting, conform to, discharge, encounter, forgather

meet halfway: 7 placate; 9 make peace, reconcile; 10 conciliate, propitiate

meeting: 4 call; 5 visit; 7 merging, palaver, reunion, session, sitting; 8 abutment, assembly, congress, junction; 9 concourse, confluent, encounter, gathering; 10 assemblage, assembling, concurrent, confluence, contacting, convergent, converging, osculation, pourparler; 11 concurrence, convergence, convergency; 13 concentrating, concentration

meetinghouse: 4 kirk; 6 chapel, church; 7

oratory; 8 basilica; 9 cathedral; 10 tabernacle; 11 conventicle

meeting place: 5 forum; 8 assembly

meeting room: 11 meeting hall

meetness: 7 decorum, fitness; 9 propriety, rightness; 10 seemliness; 11 correctness

mefenamic acid: 7 Ponstel

meg: 7 million

megabat: 8 fruit bat

megabyte: 2 MB [acron]; 8 Megabyte

megacycle: 2 Mc; 3 MHz; 9 megahertz

megahertz: 2 Mc; 3 MHz; 9 megacycle

megalithic structure: 8 megalith

megaphone: 8 bullhorn

Megaptera: 8 humpback; 13 humpback whale; 14 genus Megaptera

megascopic: 5 gross

megastar: 4 idol; 9 superstar

megatonnage: 5 power

megrim: 7 vertigo; 8 migraine; 9 dizziness; 10 hemicrania

meiosis: 7 litotes; 14 understatement

meistersinger: 12 mastersinger

Mekong: 11 Mekong River, Mekong Delta

melamine: 11 cyanuramide

melancholia: 5 blues, dumps; 7 sadness; 8 darkness, doldrums; 9 dejection, heaviness, tristesse [Fr]; 10 depression, dismalness, gloominess, melancholy, somberness

melancholic: 3 sad; 7 doleful, pensive; 10 melancholy

melancholy: 3 sad; 5 blues, dumps; 6 dreary; 7 doleful, pensive, piteous, sadness; 8 darkness, doldrums, grievous; 9 depression, dismalness, gloominess, somberness; 11 joylessness, melancholia, melancholic; 12 dejectedness

Melanerpes: 7 redhead; 15 genus Melanerpes; 19 redheaded woodpecker

melange: 5 magma; 6 ragbag; 7 farrago; 8 oddments; 10 hodgepodge, hotchpotch, miscellany

melanize: 5 black; 7 blacken

melanocyte-stimulating hormone: 3 MSH; 12 melanotropin

Melanogrammus: 7 haddock; 18 genus Melanogrammus

melanoma: 5 tumor; 9 malignant

melanotropin: 3 MSH

meld: 3 mix; 4 fuse; 5 blend, immix, merge; 7 canasta, combine; 8 coalesce, conflate; 9 commingle

Meleagris: 6 turkey; 14 genus Meleagris

Meleagris gallopavo: 6 turkey

melee: 3 row; 4 fray, to-do; 5 brawl, broil; 6 affray, breeze, fracas, hubbub, pother, racket, rumble, rumpus, squall, uproar; 7 trouble; 8 brouhaha

Meliaceae: 14 mahogany family

melilot: 9 melilotus; 11 sweet clover

meliorate: 5 amend; 6 better; 7 improve; 10 ameliorate

melioration: 9 bettering; 10 betterment; 11 enhancement, improvement; 12 amelioration

meliorist: 8 crusader, reformer, resister; 9 reformist

Melissa: 4 balm; 12 genus Melissa

mellifluous: 5 sweet; 6 dulcet, mellow; 7 honeyed; 9 euphemism; 10 euphonious, rhythmical; 11 euphemistic, mellisonant

mellow: 4 grow, high, melt, mild, ripe; 5 flush, relax, ripen, sweet, woozy; 6 buzzed, enrich, fatten, gentle, mature, pastel, pearly, season, temper, tender; 7 flushed, mollify, refined; 8 delicate, laid-back, mellowed, mellowly; 9 easygoing, edematous, elaborate, medullary [Anat], mellowing; 10 harmonious

mellowing: 5 aging; 6 ageing, mellow; 8 relaxing, ripening; 9 softening; 10 mollifying

mellowness: 8 fullness, maturity, richness, ripeness

melodic: 7 musical; 9 melodious

melodic line: 3 air; 4 line, tune; 6 melody, strain; 13 melodic phrase

melodic theme: 4 idea; 5 theme; 12 musical theme

melodious: 7 melodic, musical, tuneful

melodist: 6 singer; 7 warbler; 8 songster, vocalist

melodramatic: 10 histrionic

melody: 3 air; 4 line, tune; 6 strain

Melolontha: 6 May bug; 9 May beetle; 10 cockchafer; 15 genus Melolontha

Melopsittacus: 6 budgie; 8 lovebird; 18 genus Melopsittacus

Melospiza: 7 sparrow; 14 genus Melospiza

melphalan: 7 Alkeran

melt: 3 run; 4 grow, thaw, weep; 6 mature, mellow, unthaw; 7 liquefy, melting, thawing; 8 condense, melt down, unfreeze

melt away: 2 go; 4 fade, pass; 5 dry up; 6 run dry, vanish; 7 die away; 8 dissolve, fade away, vaporize; 9 disappear, dissipate, evaporate

melt down: 3 run; 4 melt

melted: 6 liquid; 9 liquified

melting: 4 melt, thaw; 6 fusion; 7 thawing, warming; 10 liquescent

Melursus: 9 sloth bear; 13 genus Melursus

Melville: 14 Herman Melville

member: 3 arm; 4 limb, lobe, wing; 5 penis; 6 branch, lobule; 7 element, phallus; 8 offshoot; 9 appendage, extremity; 11 class member, group member; 12 ramification

member of parliament: 2 MP

member of the clergy: 6 priest, divine; pastor; 8 reverend; 9 black coat [fig], churchman, clergyman; 12 ecclesiastic

membership: 4 rank; 9 admission, inclusion;

reception; 11 subsumption; 12 affilitation; 13 comprehension

membrane: 4 film; 11 tissue layer; 12 cell membrane

membrane-forming: 10 membranous

membranous: 5 filmy, flaky, scaly; 8 squamous [Anat]; 10 pellicular

memento: 5 relic; 8 keepsake, souvenir; 11 memorabilia

memo: 9 memoranda; 10 memorandum

memo book: 8 notebook; 10 pocketbook; 14 memorandum book

memoir: 6 report; 9 biography, discourse, memorials; 12 disquisition; 13 autobiography

memorabilia: 5 relic; 7 memento; 8 keepsake, souvenir

memorable: 6 signal; 9 momentous; 13 unforgettable

memorably: 10 eventfully, stirringly; 13 unforgettably

memorandum: 4 memo; 5 entry; 6 docket; 9 memoranda; 11 inscription

memorandum book: 8 memo book, notebook; 10 pocketbook

memorial: 8 monument; 11 remembrance; 13 commemoration

memorialize: 6 record; 8 memorize, remember; 11 commemorate, immortalize

memorials: 6 memoir

memorial tablet: 5 brass; 6 plaque

memorization: 9 retention; 10 memorizing; 11 remembering

memorize: 5 learn; 8 remember; 11 memorialize

memorizing: 9 retention; 11 remembering; 12 memorization

memory: 5 store; 6 recall; 7 storage; 9 recalling, retention; 10 retrospect; 11 remembering, remembrance; 13 retentiveness, retrospection

memory board: 5 store; 6 memory; 7 storage

memory loss: 7 amnesia; 8 blackout

memory trace: 6 engram

men: 5 hands; 8 manpower; 9 workforce

men's furnishings: 12 haberdashery

men's room: 8 bathroom, lavatory, rest room

men's store: 12 haberdashery

menace: 5 peril; 6 threat; 7 imperil; 8 endanger, threaten; 10 jeopardize

menacing: 4 ugly; 7 baleful, ominous; 8 minatory, sinister; 9 minacious; 10 forbidding; 11 threatening

menadione: 9 vitamin K

menage: 4 home; 5 house; 6 family; 9 household

menagerie: 3 zoo; 6 museum; 8 vivarium

mend: 3 fix; 4 heal; 5 amend, patch; 6 better,

M

bushel, doctor, repair; **7** get well, improve, restore

mendacious: 5 false, lying; **9** deceitful, dishonest, faithless, trothless, truthless; **10** fraudulent; **11** unveracious

mendacity: 7 perjury

Mendel: 12 Gregor Mendel; **18** Gregor Johann Mendel

mendelevium: 2 Md, Mv

Mendeleyev: 9 Mendeleev; **25** Dmitri Ivanovich Mendeleyev

mender: 6 tinker

mendicancy: 7 beggary, begging

mendicant: 4 monk; **5** friar; **6** beggar; **7** moocher, poor man; **10** panhandler

mending: 3 fix; **6** fixing, repair; **10** reparation

menial: 5 lowly; **6** humble, lackey; **7** footman; **9** underling

meninx: 8 meninges

Menippe: 9 stone crab; **12** genus Menippe

meniscus: 4 lens

Menispermaceae: 14 moonseed family

menopause: 11 climacteric; **12** change of life

Menopon: 10 shaft louse; **12** chicken louse; **12** genus Menopon

menses: 4 flow; **6** period; **7** courses; **9** catamenia; **12** menstruation

menstrual: 7 monthly

menstruate: 4 flow

menstruation: 4 flow; **6** menses, period; **9** catamenia

mensurable: 10 measurable

mensuration: 7 measure; **9** measuring; **11** measurement

mental: 6 genial; **8** rational; **12** intellectual

mental ability: 8 capacity

mental anguish: 4 pang; **5** agony; **7** anguish

mental capacity: 3 wit; **4** mind; **5** brain; **9** mentality; **10** brainpower

mental condition: 11 mental state

mental disease: 13 mental illness

mental hygiene: 13 psychotherapy

mental image: 5 image; **10** impression, perception; **12** apprehension

mentally: 10 rationally; **14** intellectually

mentally ill: 7 unsound; **8** unstable; **10** unbalanced

mental picture: 10 impression

mental pressure: 4 load; **6** stress; **7** urgency; **8** pressure

mental telepathist: 10 mind reader

mental unsoundness: 9 unbalance; **11** derangement

mentation: 7 thought; **8** thinking; **11** cerebration; **12** intellection

Mentha: 4 mint; **9** spearmint; **10** peppermint; **11** genus Mentha

Menticirrhus: 7 whiting; **7** genus Menticirrhus

mention: 4 cite, name, note; **5** refer; **6** advert, credit, remark; **7** bring up, express, let fall, observe; **8** citation, intimate; **9** make known, quotation, reference, represent; **11** acknowledge, communicate

mentor: 4 guru; **6** Nestor; **7** monitor, senator, wise man

mentum: 4 chin

menu: 4 card, fare; **5** carte [Fr], table; **7** cuisine; **8** ordinary

Menyanthaceae: 14 buckbean family

meow: 3 mew

Mephistopheles: 5 Satan; **6** Belial, Samael, Zamiel; **7** Lucifer, Old Nick [slang]; **8** the Devil; **9** Beelzebub; **10** the evil one, the tempter; **12** the Adversary, the arch fiend, the archenemy, the foul fiend, the wicked one; **13** the evil spirit, the old Serpent; **16** Prince of Darkness

mephistophelian: 7 hellish, satanic, stygian; **8** devilish, diabolic, fiendish, hell-born, infernal; **10** demoniacal

mephitic: 4 foul; **6** septic; **7** miasmic; **11** deleterious, suffocating

Mephitis: 5 skunk; **13** genus Mephitis

meprobamate: 6 Meprin; **7** Equanil, Miltown

mercantile: 7 trading; **8** business; **9** mercenary; **10** commercial; **11** moneymaking

mercantile establishment: 6 outlet; **11** retail store, sales outlet

mercantile law: 11 law merchant; **13** commercial law

mercantilism: 8 commerce; **13** commercialism

mercaptopurine: 10 Purinethol

Mercenaria: 4 clam; **6** quahog; **7** quahaug; **9** round clam; **13** hard-shell clam; **5** genus Mercenaria

mercenary: 5 venal; **6** greedy; **8** covetous, hireling, usurious; **9** freelance, rapacious; **10** adventurer, avaricious, mercantile; **11** moneymaking; **12** extortionate; **13** materialistic

mercer: 6 draper

merchandise: 4 ware; **5** trade, wares; **7** article, product; **9** commodity

merchandiser: 8 merchant

merchandising: 7 selling; **9** marketing

merchant: 6 dealer, monger, trader; **8** chandler, salesman; **11** salesperson; **12** merchandiser

merchant bank: 8 acquirer

merchant marine: 8 shipping; **10** cargo ships

merchant ship: 6 bottom; **9** cargo ship, freighter; **11** cargo vessel, merchantman

merciful: 4 kind

merciless: 8 pitiless, ruthless; **9** bowelless; **10** unmerciful

mercurial: 5 fussy, hasty; **6** fickle, mobile, winged; **7** erratic, fidgety, hurried, movable, unquiet; **8** electric, galvanic, restless, shifting; **11** eagle winged, quicksilver, telegraphic

mercurous chloride: 7 calomel, jonquil

mercury: 2 Hg; **11** hydrargyrum [Lat], quicksilver

Mercury: 6 Hermes

Mercury's rod: 8 caduceus

mercy: 7 quarter; **8** clemency, humanity, yearning; **10** tenderness; **11** forbearance; **12** mercifulness

mercy killing: 10 euthanasia

mere: 4 bare, lake, loch, pond, pool, slab, tarn; **5** broad, plash, sheer, stark; **6** common, puddle, simple; **10** uneventful

merely: 3 but; **4** just, only; **6** purely, simply

meretricious: 3 gay; **4** loud; **5** cheap, flash, frail, gaudy, tacky, tatty; **6** brassy, flashy, garish, gilded, plated, rakish, tawdry, tinsel, trashy; **7** gallant; **8** gimcrack, specious; **9** pinchbeck; **10** dissipated; **11** incontinent

meretriciously: 8 flashily

meretriciousness: 5 glitz; **8** loudness; **9** brashness, gaudiness; **10** flashiness, garishness, tawdriness; **12** speciousness

merganser: 7 sawbill; **8** fish duck; **9** sheldrake

merge: 3 mix; **4** fuse, meld; **5** blend, immix, unify, unite; **6** absorb, embody; **7** blend in, combine, conjoin, immerge, immerse; **8** coalesce, coincide, conflate, dissolve, submerge; **9** commingle; **10** amalgamate, centralize, impregnate; **11** consolidate, incorporate

merged: 7 unified; **10** integrated; **11** incorporate; **12** incorporated

merger: 6 fusion; **7** uniting; **11** unification; **12** amalgamation

merging: 7 conflux, meeting; **8** blending, mingling; **9** confluent; **10** confluence

Mergus: 4 smew; **9** goosander, merganser; **11** genus Mergus

meridian: 4 acme; **5** prime, sunny; **6** orient; **8** noontide; **9** longitude; **11** culmination

merino sheep: 6 merino

merit: 4 rate; **5** value, worth; **6** credit, desert, virtue; **7** deserve; **8** goodness; **9** high value; **10** be worthy of, excellence, worthiness; **12** valuableness

merited: 3 due; **5** due to; **7** condign; **8** deserved

meriting: 5 worth; **8** worthy of; **9** deserving

meritorious: 6 worthy; **9** deserving, estimable, meritable, plausible; **10** creditable; **13** unimpeachable

merl: 5 merle

Merlangus: 7 whiting; **14** genus Merlangus

merle: 4 merl; **5** ousel, ouzel; **9** blackbird; **12** Turdus merula; **17** European blackbird

merlin: 4 hawk

Merluccius: 7 whiting; **10** silver hake; **15** genus Merluccius

mermaid: 6 merman [male]; **7** merfolk [pl], seamaid

merrily: 5 gayly; **7** happily; **8** blithely; **10** jubilantly, mirthfully

merriment: 3 fun; **5** mirth; **6** frolic, gaiety; **7** jollity; **8** hilarity; **11** playfulness; **12** exhilaration

merry: 3 cut, gay; **4** gala, high; **5** beery, boozy, brisk, drunk, fresh, jolly, tight, tipsy, zippy; **6** corned, festal, groggy, jocund, jovial, lively, primed, snappy; **7** drunken, festive, fuddled; **8** elevated, mirthful

merry andrew: 5 clown; **7** buffoon

merry-go-round: 8 carousel; **9** whirligig; **10** roundabout

merrymaker: 7 reveler; **8** reveller

merrymaking: 6 revels; **7** revelry; **8** reveling; **9** festivity; **12** conviviality

Merthiolate: 10 thimerosal

mesa: 5 table

mescal: 6 mezcal, peyote

mescaline: 6 peyote

mesencephalon: 8 midbrain

mesh: 3 net, web; **4** lock; **6** engage, enmesh, lacuna, plexus, riddle; **7** caesura, ensnarl, meshing, network, operate; **8** meshwork; **9** interlock; **10** engagement, interstice; **12** interlocking, reticulation

meshing: 4 mesh; **9** interlock; **10** engagement; **12** interlocking

mesial: 3 mid; **4** mean; **6** medial, median, middle; **7** average

mesmeric: 8 hypnotic; **11** mesmerizing; **12** spellbinding

mesmerism: 9 hypnotism; **10** suggestion

mesmerist: 9 hypnotist; **10** hypnotizer

mesmerize: 5 rivet; **6** absorb; **7** bewitch, engross; **8** intrigue; **9** fascinate, hypnotize, magnetize, spellbind

mesmerized: 4 rapt; **7** riveted; **8** absorbed; **9** wrapped in; **10** fascinated, hypnotised, hypnotized, mesmerised, spellbound, transfixed

mesomorphic: 5 husky; **8** athletic, muscular

Mesozoic era: 8 Mesozoic; **13** Age of Reptiles

mesquite: 7 mesquit

mess: 3 ado, fix, jam, lot, pot, wad; **4** deal, feed, heap, hole, mash, mass, mint, muss [U.S.], olio, peck, pile, raft, slew; **5** batch, flock, quota, ratio, sight, spate, stack; **6** hatful, medley, mess up, mickle, muckle, muddle, pickle, plenty, scrape, spread; **7** farrago, modicum, tidy sum; **8** mess hall, mishmash, pastiche, whole lot; **9** break-

M

down, imbroglio, messiness, mussiness, patchwork, potpourri

message: 4 news, word; 5 force; 6 advice, import; 7 content, meaning, purport, tidings; 9 substance; 11 piece of news; 12 intelligence, significance; 13 signification

mess around: 6 monkey, potter, putter, tinker

messenger: 3 cad; 4 rack, scud; 5 envoy; 6 herald, legate, nimbus; 7 courier; 8 emissary; 10 forerunner

messenger boy: 9 errand boy

messenger RNA: 4 mRNA

mess hall: 4 mess

messiah: 6 savior

messily: 8 untidily

messiness: 4 mess, muss; 9 mussiness; 10 untidiness; 12 slovenliness

messuage: 7 premise

mess up: 4 blow, flub, mess, muff; 5 botch, fluff, spoil; 6 ball up, bobble, bollix, bungle, foul up, fumble, muck up, ruffle, rumple; 7 blunder, botch up, louse up, screw up; 9 mishandle

messy: 5 mussy; 6 untidy; 8 slovenly; 9 uncleanly

met: 9 converged; 12 concentrated

metabolic process: 10 metabolism, metastasis

metabolism: 10 metastasis; 13 metamorphosis

metacarpophalangeal joint: 7 knuckle

metal: 8 metallic

metal bar: 5 ingot

metal glove: 8 gauntlet

metallic: 5 metal

metallurgical engineer: 12 metallurgist

metal money: 6 specie; 7 coinage, mintage

metal saw: 7 hacksaw

metalworker: 5 smith

metalworks: 7 foundry

metamere: 6 somite

metameric: 9 segmental, segmented

metamorphose: 9 transform; 11 transfigure

metamorphosis: 6 change; 14 transformation

metaphor: 5 trope; 6 figure; 14 figure of speech

metaphorical: 10 figurative, metaphoric, nonliteral

metaphysics: 8 ontology

metaproterenol: 7 Alupent

metastasis: 10 metabolism; 13 transposition

metastatic tumor: 14 malignant tumor

mete: 4 cast; 5 share; 6 billet, detail; 7 measure

meted out: 8 dealt out, doled out; 11 apportioned, parceled out

metempsychosis: 7 rebirth; 14 transmigration

meteor: 9 meteorite, meteoroid; 11 falling star; 12 shooting star

meteoric: 6 ablaze; 7 blazing; 8 splendid, volcanic; 12 meteorologic

meteorite: 6 meteor; 9 meteoroid; 11 falling star; 12 shooting star

meteoroid: 6 meteor; 9 meteorite; 11 falling star; 12 shooting star

meteorologic: 8 meteoric; 14 meteorological

meteorology: 11 climatology; 15 weather forecast

meteor shower: 12 meteor stream

mete out: 3 lot; 4 deal; 5 allot; 8 dispense; 9 parcel out; 10 administer, distribute

meter: 1 m; 4 beat, time; 5 metre; 6 rhythm; 7 cadence, measure

metes and bounds: 12 property line

meth: 10 Methedrine; 15 methamphetamine

methacholine: 8 Mecholyl

methadone: 8 methadon

methamphetamine: 4 meth; 10 Methedrine

methamphetamine hydrochloride: 4 meth; 10 Methedrine; 14 deoxyephedrine; 15 methamphetamine

methanal: 12 formaldehyde

methane: 8 marsh gas

methane series: 6 alkane; 8 paraffin

methanol: 10 wood spirit; 11 wood alcohol; 13 methyl alcohol

methaqualone: 8 Quaalude

metharbital: 7 Gemonil

Methedrine: 4 meth; 15 methamphetamine

method: 2 MO; 3 way; 4 mode, wise; 5 means; 6 manner; 7 fashion, process; 8 protocol; 9 mechanism, procedure, technique; 10 procedures [pl]; 13 modus operandi

methodical: 7 correct, orderly, regular; 10 systematic

Methodist: 8 Wesleyan

methodize: 3 fix; 6 adjust, settle; 8 regulate; 10 coordinate; 11 systematize

methyl alcohol: 8 methanol; 10 wood spirit; 11 wood alcohol

methylbenzene: 7 toluene

methylphenidate: 7 Ritalin

methyl phenol: 6 cresol

methyl salicylate: 8 birch oil

meticulous: 6 strict; 7 precise; 8 exacting; 9 demanding; 10 overstrict, particular; 11 punctilious

meticulously: 12 fastidiously

metier: 5 forte; 6 medium; 8 long suit, strength; 9 specialty; 10 speciality

metre: 5 meter

metric: 8 measured, metrical

metric hundredweight: 7 centner; 13 doppelzentner, hundredweight

metric ton: 2 MT; 5 tonne

metritis: 12 endometritis

metro: 4 tube; 6 subway; 11 underground; 12 metropolitan metronome marking: 2 MM; 3 bpm; 14 beats per minute

metropolis: 4 city; 11 urban center; 12 municipality

metropolitan: 5 urban

mettle: 4 game; 5 grain, heart, humor, nerve, pluck, spunk

mettlesome: 4 game, gamy; 5 gamey; 6 gritty, lively, mobile, plucky, spunky; 8 skittish, spirited; 9 vivacious; 10 expressive; 12 enthusiastic

meuniere butter: 11 lemon butter

Meuse: 7 Argonne; 10 Meuse River; 12 Meuse-Argonne; 13 Argonne Forest

Mevacor: 10 lovastatin

mew: 4 meow, mewl, molt; 5 miaou, miaow; 6 sea mew; 7 confine, mew gull; 9 defoliate, exfoliate

mew gull: 3 mew; 6 sea mew; 10 Larus canus

mewl: 3 mew; 4 pule, wail; 5 whine; 6 snivel; 7 grizzle, whimper

mews: 4 yard; 5 close, rents; 7 passage; 9 buildings

Mexican husk tomato: 9 tomatillo

Mexican jumping bean: 11 jumping bean

Mexico City: 14 Ciudad de Mexico; 15 capital of Mexico

mezcal: 6 mescal, peyote

mezereon family: 13 Thymelaeaceae

mezuzah: 6 mezuza

mezzanine: 12 first balcony

mezzanine floor: 4 trap; 9 mezzanine

mezzo: 4 half; 6 middle; 8 moderate; 12 mezzo-soprano

mezzo-relievo: 10 half relief; 12 mezzo-rilievo

Mg: 9 magnesium

mg: 9 milligram

mho: 7 siemens

MHz: 2 Mc; 9 megacycle, megahertz

miasmal: 7 miasmic; 8 vaporous

Micawber: 11 Mr. Micawber

Michaelis constant: 2 Km

Michigander: 9 Wolverine

mickle: 3 lot, pot, wad; 4 deal, heap, mass, mess, mint, much, peck, pile, raft, slew; 5 batch, flock, sight, spate, stack; 6 muckle, plenty

micro: 11 microscopic; 13 microcomputer; 14 microprocessor

microbe: 3 bug; 4 germ; 13 microorganism

microbial: 8 microbic

microbus: 3 bus, van; 7 minibus, minivan

microchip: 4 chip; 11 silicon chip

microcircuit: 10 integrated

microcomputer: 2 PC; 5 micro; 16 personal computer

microcosm: 7 epitome; 14 Elzevir edition

microgram: 3 mcg

microliter: 6 lambda

Micromeria: 6 savor; 10 yerba buena; 15 genus Micromeria

micrometer: 6 micron

micrometermillimeter: 2 mm; 6 micron

micromicron: 9 picometer, picometre

micromillimeter: 9 nanometer, nanometre; 11 millimicron; 15 micromillimetre

micron: 2 mm

microorganism: 7 microbe

microphone: 4 mike

microprocessor chip: 14 microprocessor

Micropterus: 10 smallmouth, largemouth; 14 smallmouth bass, largemouth bass; 16 genus Micropterus

microscopic: 5 small; 6 atomic, minute; 9 molecular, subatomic; 11 corpuscular; 13 infinitesimal, microscopical

microscopically: 8 minutely; 9 invisibly; 13 imperceptibly, inappreciably

microseism: 6 tremor; 11 earth tremor

Microsoft disk operating system: 5 MS-DOS

Microstomus: 9 lemon sole; 16 genus Microstomus

Microtus: 4 vole; 13 genus Microtus

microwave oven: 3 zap; 4 nuke; 9 microwave; 13 microwave oven

Micruroides: 10 coral snake; 16 genus Micruroides

Micteria: 8 wood ibis; 9 wood stork; 13 genus Micteria

mid: 4 mean; 5 midst; 6 medial, median, middle; 7 average

mid-continent: 7 midland; 11 continental

midday: 4 noon; 7 noonday; 8 high noon, noontide; 10 twelve noon

midden: 3 bog; 4 sink; 8 dunghill, muckheap, muckhill

middle: 3 eye, mid; 4 mean; 5 heart, midst, waist; 6 center, centre, medial, median, midway; 7 average, halfway, mediate, midriff; 9 in-between, waistline; 10 midsection; 12 intermediate

middle ages: 8 dark ages; 13 medieval times

middle class: 11 bourgeoisie

middle ear: 8 tympanum

Middle East: 8 Near East

middleman: 5 agent; 6 jobber; 7 bailiff, contact; 8 delegate; 9 go-between; 10 wholesaler; 12 interlocutor, intermediary

middlemost: 7 midmost

middle-of-the-road: 8 centrist

middle of the roader: 8 centrist, moderate; 13 moderationist

middling: 2 OK; 3 low; 4 fair, so-so; 6 fairly; 7 average; 8 bearable, mediocre, ordinary, passable, passably, somewhat; 9 tolerable; 10 acceptable, admissible, couci-couci, moderately, reasonably; 11 indifferent

middy: 6 blouse; 10 bluejacket, midshipman

M

middy blouse: 5 middy

midget: 4 tiny; **5** dwarf, elfin, pygmy; **6** bantam, petite; **7** dwarfed; **8** dwarfish; **10** diminutive, Liliputian, undersized; **11** lilliputian

midland: 8 interior; **9** upcountry; **11** continental; **12** mid-continent

midnight: 12 witching hour

midpoint: 6 center, centre

midriff: 5 waist; **6** middle; **7** equator; **9** diaphragm, waistline; **10** midsection

midsection: 6 middle; **7** midriff

midshipman: 5 jolly, middy; **10** bluejacket

midships: 8 amidship; **9** amidships

midst: 3 mid; **4** mean; **5** thick; **6** middle

midsummer: 6 summer; **14** summer solstice

midterm examination: 7 midterm; **11** midterm exam

Midway: 14 battle of Midway

midway: 6 center, middle; **7** halfway

Midwest: 10 Middle West

midwifery: 10 obstetrics

mien: 3 air; **4** cast, look, port; **5** color, guise; **7** bearing; **8** carriage, demeanor, presence; **10** complexion; **11** comportment

miff: 4 gall, huff; **5** pique; **6** spleen; **7** umbrage; **8** acerbity, acrimony, asperity, rankling, soreness; **9** seeing red, virulence; **10** bitterness

might: 3 can, may; **5** could, force, power; **6** energy; **8** fullness, strength; **9** intensity, puissance; **10** mightiness

mightily: 6 mighty; **10** powerfully

mightiness: 5 might, power

mighty: 4 fine, hard, high, huge; **5** blown, hardy, lofty, noble, right, stout, valid; **6** goodly, potent, robust, strong, sturdy; **7** flushed, haughty, immense, swollen; **8** enormous, forcible, mightily, powerful, precious, puissant, towering, vigorous; **10** adamantine, powerfully; **11** magnificent

mignonette: 11 sweet reseda

mignonette family: 10 Resedaceae

migraine: 6 megrim; **8** headache; **10** hemicrania

migrant: 9 migratory

migrate: 8 emigrate

migration: 6 roving; **9** wandering

migration route: 6 flyway

migratory: 7 migrant

mikado: 5 tenno [Jap]; **7** emperor

mike: 10 microphone

mil: 2 cc, ml; **10** milliliter, millilitre

Milan: 6 Milano

mild: 4 fade, meek, weak; **5** balmy, stale, vapid; **6** genial, gentle, mellow, modest; **7** mawkish

mildew: 5 fungi; **6** fungus

mildewed: 5 moldy, musty, rusty, seedy; **7** spotted; **8** time-worn; **9** moss-grown, moth-eaten

mildly: 6 gently

mildness: 6 lenity; **8** clemency, lenience, leniency; **10** gentleness

mild steel: 14 low-carbon steel

mile: 2 mi; **6** naut mi, stat mi; **7** air mile, sea mile; **8** land mile, mile race; **11** statute mile; **12** nautical mile

Mile-High City: 6 Denver; **17** capital of Colorado

mileometer: 8 odometer

milepost: 9 milestone

miles per gallon: 7 mileage

miles per hour: 3 mph [acron]

milestone: 8 milepost

milfoil: 6 yarrow

milieu: 5 scene; **10** background; **12** surroundings

militance: 9 militancy; **13** combativeness

militant: 7 warring; **8** activist, fighting, military; **9** soldierly, war-ridden; **11** belligerent, competitive, soldier-like

militarist: 9 warmonger

militarization: 12 mobilization

military: 5 troop [pl]; **6** troops [pl]; **8** militant, soldiery; **9** soldierly; **10** armed force; **11** armed forces, soldier-like

military academy: 14 military school

military action: 5 fight; **6** action, battle; **9** encounter; **10** engagement

military blockade: 5 siege; **9** besieging; **12** beleaguering

military chaplain: 5 padre; **7** Holy Joe; **8** sky pilot

military control: 10 occupation

military engagement: 5 fight; **6** action, battle; **8** skirmish; **9** encounter, fire-fight; **10** engagement

military government: 5 junta

military greeting: 6 salute

military headquarters: 2 HQ

military leader: 7 warlord

military personnel: 3 man; **6** troops; **8** soldiery; **10** serviceman

military policeman: 2 MP

military rank: 8 paygrade

military submarine: 5 U-boat; **9** submarine

militia: 8 reserves

milium: 9 whitehead

milk: 5 milky; **6** suckle; **7** exploit; **9** lactation

milk cow: 6 milker; **7** milcher; **8** dairy cow, milch cow

milkiness: 10 chalkiness; **11** opalescence

milk leg: 8 white leg

milkmaid: 9 dairymaid

milk powder: 7 dry milk; **9** dried milk; **12** powdered milk

milkshake: 5 shake; **6** frappe

milk sickness: 8 trembles

milksop: 3 sop; **4** baby; **5** child, pansy, sissy; **6** infant; **8** innocent; **9** lily liver; **10** panty-

waist, smock-faced, white liver; **11**
Milquetoast, mollycoddle
milk sugar: 7 lactose
milk tooth: 14 deciduous tooth
milkweed family: 14 Asclepiadaceae
milk-white: 9 snow-white
milkwort family: 12 Polygalaceae
milky: 4 milk; **6** pearly; **7** lacteal, whitish; **8**
milklike
milky way: 14 Milky Way galaxy
mill: 3 fig, gin, jot, pin, rap, sou; **4** cent, rush,
spar; **5** fight, grind, lathe, set-to, straw; **6**
button; **7** bulrush, factory, feather, grinder;
8 farthing, picayune; **10** mill around, peppercorn; **11** manufactory; **13** pulverization
mill about: 4 loaf, lurk, mill; **5** tarry; **6** footle, linger, loiter, lounge; **8** lallygag, lollygag
milled: 8 polished
millennium: 13 thousand years
miller: 14 milling machine
mill-hand: 13 factory worker
milliampere: 2 mA
milliard: 7 billion
milliequivalent: 3 meq
milligram: 2 mg
milliliter: ml; **3** mil
millimeter: 2 mm
milliner: 4 snip; **6** hatter, tailor; **7** modiste; **8**
hatmaker; **9** costumier; **11** haberdasher
millinery: 7 hat shop
milling: 9 shuffling
milling machine: 6 miller
million: 3 meg
millionaire: 4 rich; **6** tycoon; **7** wealthy
millipede: 8 milliped; **9** centipede, millepede
millisecond: 4 msec
millivolt: 2 mV
mill pond: 4 pond, tank; **7** cistern; **8** fish
pond
millrun: 4 race; **8** head race, millrace
millstone: 9 albatross
Milquetoast: 4 meek; **5** timid; **11** unassertive
milt: 7 soft roe
mime: 3 ape; **4** echo; **5** mimer; **6** monkey,
mummer, parrot; **8** imitator; **9** pantomime;
10 pantomimer; **11** pantomimist
mimeograph: 4 copy; **5** mimeo, xerox; **9** facsimile; **10** duplicator
mimer: 4 mime; **6** mummer; **10** pantomimer;
11 pantomimist
mimic: 3 ape; **4** mock; **8** mimicker, simulate;
9 personate; **11** impersonate
mimicker: 5 mimic
mimicry: 5 apery; **7** mockery; **8** disguise; **10**
camouflage
Mimosaceae: 6 mimosa
Mimus: 6 mocker; **11** mockingbird; **10** genus
Mimus
min: 6 minute
minatory: 4 ugly; **7** baleful, ominous; **8**

menacing, sinister; **9** minacious; **10** forbidding; **11** threatening
mince: 4 hash, slur, stew; **6** ragout, releve
[Fr], simper, soften; **8** moderate; **9** fricassee
mincing: 4 prim, twee; **6** dainty; **9** simpering, **10** namby-pamby; **11** sentimental
mind: 4 head, heed, idea, view, wish; **5** brain,
worry; **6** animus, beware, call up, choice,
lean to, listen, psyche, recall; **7** incline,
leaning, opinion, propend, purview,
retrace, thinker; **8** decision, judgment,
object to, penchant, pleasure, proposal,
remember; **9** entertain, intellect, judgement, recognize, recollect
minded: 3 apt; **4** fain; **5** given; **7** tending,
willing; **8** disposed, inclined; **9** favorable,
intending
mindful: 5 aware; **9** attentive, regardful
mindfully: 9 heedfully; **11** advertently
mindless: 4 dull; **5** inane; **6** stupid, vacant; **7**
asinine, fatuous, no-brain, vacuous, wit-
less; **8** careless, listless, retarded; **9** airheaded, brainless, dim-witted, forgetful,
oblivious, senseless, unmindful; **10** dull-
witted, half-witted, reasonless, regardless,
unoccupied, unthinking, weak-minded; **11**
thoughtless, unreasoning; **13** inconsiderate,
unintelligent; **14** unintellectual
mind reader: 11 telepathist
mine: 3 pit, sap; **4** lode, vein; **5** shaft, shake;
6 burrow, devour, quarry, tunnel; **7** break
up; **9** undermine
minelaying: 6 mining
miner: 9 excavator; **10** mineworker
mineralize: 9 fossilize
mineralized: 9 petrified
mineral pitch: 7 asphalt
mineral wax: 7 ader wax; **8** earth wax; **9**
ozocerite, ozokerite
mineral wool: 8 rock wool
mineral world: 14 mineral kingdom
minestrone: 13 vegetable soup
mineworker: 5 miner
mingle: 3 mix; **5** mix in, unify; **6** commix,
jumble; **10** amalgamate
mingled: 3 odd; **5** mixed; **6** divers, varied; **7**
diverse, various; **8** assorted; **9** different; **10**
dissimilar; **11** diversified; **13** heterogeneous
mingling: 7 merging; **8** blending
mingy: 4 mean; **5** small, tight; **6** little, stingy;
7 miserly
miniature: 3 toy, wee; **4** puny, tiny; **5** petit,
petty; **6** petite; **8** exiguous
minibike: 9 motorbike
minibus: 3 bus, van; **7** minivan; **8** microbus
minichanger: 7 carousel
minify: 6 lessen; **8** decrease
minim: 8 half note

M

minimal: 7 minimum
minimize: 8 belittle, derogate; **9** denigrate, gloss over; **10** understate
minimum: 7 minimal; **10** lower limit
mining: 10 excavation, minelaying
minion: 3 pet; **4** idol; **5** leech; **6** sponge; **7** darling; **8** favorite, parasite
minister: 6 curate, parson, pastor, rector, vizier; **7** mediate; **8** official; **9** intervene, officiate; **10** bureaucrat; **11** functionary; **14** perform service
ministerial: 8 pastoral, priestly; **10** sacerdotal; **11** subservient
ministering: 9 attending; **10** ministrant
minister plenipotentiary: 5 envoy
ministration: 6 relief, succor; **7** succour; **8** ministry
ministry: 6 clergy; **8** the cloth; **9** clericals; **10** priesthood; **12** ministration
minivan: 3 bus, van; **7** minibus; **8** microbus
Minnneapolis and Saint Paul: 10 Twin Cities
Minnesota: 11 Gopher State; **14** North Star State
minnow: 4 bait
minor: 3 fry, kid; **4** less, tike, tyke; **5** child, lower, minus, small; **6** lesser, modest, nipper, shaver, venial; **7** nonaged, tiddler; **8** nestling, small fry, underage; **9** deficient, secondary, youngster
minor details: 8 minutiae
minor expense: 10 incidental
Minorites: 10 Franciscan
minority: 5 bloom; **6** nonage; **9** tender age; **11** inferiority, subordinacy
minor planet: 8 asteroid; **9** planetoid
minor role: 7 bit part
minoxidil: 7 Loniten, Rogaine
Minsk: 20 capital of Byelorussia
minstrel: 8 jongleur; **10** folk singer, poet-singer, troubadour
mint: 3 lot, pot, wad; **4** coin, deal, heap, mass, mess, peck, pile, raft, slew; **5** batch, flock, sight, spate, stack; **6** hatful, mickle, muckle, plenty, strike; **7** tidy sum; **8** good deal, whole lot
mintage: 6 specie; **7** coinage; **10** metal money
mint family: 8 Labiatae; **9** Lamiaceae
minus: 4 less, save; **5** lower, minor; **6** bereft, cut off, except, lesser; **7** barring, denuded, nowhere, without; **8** bereaved, negative; **9** deficient, except for, excepting, secondary
minuscule: 5 small; **6** little; **10** minuscular
minus sign: 4 dash; **6** hyphen
minute: 3 bit, min; **4** note; **5** brief; **6** atomic, digest, moment, narrow, precis, second; **7** epitome, instant, minutes, outline, summary; **8** abstract, analysis, atomlike, synopsis; **9** arcminute; **10** abridgment, diminutive; **11** microscopic
minute hand: 7 big hand
minutely: 9 invisibly; **13** imperceptibly, inappreciably
minutes: 4 note; **6** minute; **11** proceedings; **12** transactions
minutiae: 7 details; **8** small fry; **12** minor details
minx: 4 pert
Mirabilis: 9 maravilla; **14** genus Mirabilis
miracle: 6 marvel, wonder; **7** prodigy
miracle play: 7 mystery
miracle-worship: 13 thaumatolatry
miraculous: 9 marvelous; **10** heaven-sent; **12** providential
miraculous food: 5 manna
mirasol: 9 sunflower
mire: 3 mud; **4** muck, silt, sump, wash; **5** slosh, slush; **6** morass, muck up, slough, sludge; **7** bog down; **8** alluvium, entangle, quagmire
mired: 8 involved
mirky: 5 muddy, murky; **6** cloudy, turbid
mirror: 4 echo; **5** model; **7** pattern, reflect; **8** cynosure, speculum, standard; **9** reflector
mirror image: 9 reflexion; **10** reflection
mirrorlike: 8 specular
mirror symmetry: 6 parity
mirth: 4 glee; **8** hilarity; **9** merriment; **11** gleefulness; **12** exhilaration, mirthfulness
mirthful: 3 gay; **5** comic, funny, jolly, merry; **6** jocund, jovial; **7** amusing, comical, risible; **9** laughable; **10** rollicking
mirthless: 8 unamused
misadventure: 6 mishap; **8** accident; **9** mischance; **10** misfortune
misanthropic: 7 cynical; **10** antisocial
misappropriated: 9 embezzled
misappropriation: 6 misuse; **8** misusage
misbegotten: 7 bastard, ill-made, natural; **8** misbegot, spurious; **9** bastardly, malformed, misshapen
misbehaving: 7 sinning; **13** transgressing
misbehavior: 7 misdeed; **8** misdoing, ribaldry; **9** brutality, grossness, indecorum; **10** courseness, misconduct
miscarry: 4 fail, slip, trip; **5** abort
miscellaneous: 5 mixed; **6** motley, sundry; **8** assorted
miscellany: 5 magma; **6** motley; **7** garland, melange, mixture, variety; **9** potpourri; **10** assortment
mischief: 7 devilry, roguery; **8** deviltry, nuisance; **9** devilment, rascality; **10** shenanigan; **11** balefulness, maleficence, roguishness
mischievous: 6 impish; **7** baleful, baneful, harmful, hurtful, implike, naughty, noxious, puckish; **8** prankish; **9** injurious, pixilated; **10** pernicious; **11** deleterious, detrimental

misconception: 14 miscalculation

misconduct: 7 misdeed, missend; 8 misapply, misdoing; 9 misdirect, mishandle, mismanage; 10 wrongdoing; 11 misbehavior, misfeasance; 12 misdirection

miscreant: 6 bad man; 9 reprobate, wrongdoer

miscue: 4 slip; 6 slipup

misdemeanor: 7 offence, offense; 9 violation; 10 infraction, misprision; 11 misfeasance; 12 infringement

misdirect: 6 debase; 7 corrupt, debauch, deprave, mislead, missend, pervert, profane, vitiate; 8 misapply, misguide; 9 misinform, mismanage; 10 demoralize, misconduct

mise en scene: 6 milieu; 7 display, setting, context; 10 background; 11 environment

miser: 6 scrimp, usurer; 9 skinflint; 10 cheapskate

miserable: 3 low; 4 mean, poor, vile; 5 cheap, sorry, weedy; 6 abject, meager, measly, paltry, scummy, scurvy, shabby, trashy, woeful; 7 hapless, in agony, lowdown, piteous, pitiful, scrubby; 8 beggarly, gimcrack, pathetic, pitiable, trumpery, wretched; 9 agonizing, execrable, suffering, worthless; 10 deplorable

miserably: 5 sadly; 6 sorely; 7 cruelly, grossly; 8 bitterly, horribly, terribly, woefully; 9 fearfully, painfully, piteously; 10 dreadfully, grievously, lamentably, shockingly, wretchedly; 11 frightfully

miserly: 4 mean, near; 5 close, mingy, small, tight; 6 little, shabby, stingy; 7 scrubby; 8 peddling; 9 penny wise

misery: 10 desolation; 11 tribulation; 12 wretchedness

misfire: 3 dud

misfortune: 6 mishap; 7 bad luck, ill luck; 8 accident; 9 mischance; 12 misadventure

misgiving: 5 qualm; 6 demure, qualms [pl]; 7 scruple; 8 distrust, mistrust; 9 suspicion; 11 trepidation; 12 apprehension

misguided: 6 misled; 7 deluded; 8 mistaken, unguided, unversed; 10 uninformed; 11 uninitiated; 12 ill-conceived, uncultivated; 13 unenlightened

mishap: 7 bad luck; 8 accident; 9 mischance; 10 misfortune; 12 misadventure

mishmash: 4 mess, olio; 6 medley; 7 farrago; 8 all sorts, pastiche; 9 patchwork, potpourri; 10 hodgepodge

Mishna: 7 Mishnah

misinformed: 6 misled; 9 mistaught, misguided; 11 misdirected

misjudge: 11 misconceive, misestimate

misleading: 8 deluding; 9 deceptive; 10 misguiding; 11 misguidance; 12 misdirecting, misdirection, misinforming; 14 misinformation

misled: 7 deluded; 9 misguided, mistaught; 11 misdirected, misinformed

mismatch: 4 vary; 6 differ; 8 not match, variance; 9 disparity; 10 divergence; discrepancy; 12 disagreement

mismatched: 6 uneven; 9 misplaced, unendowed; 13 misclassified

misogamist: 10 misogynist, woman hater

misogynism: 8 misogyny

misplace: 4 lose; 6 mislay; 8 displace

misplaced: 7 mislaid; 10 mismatched, out of place; 13 misclassified

misprint: 4 typo; 7 erratum, literal; 12 literal error

misrepresent: 4 cook, daub, fake; 5 belie, fudge; 6 wangle; 7 distort, falsify, pervert; 8 misquote, misstate, overdraw; 9 misreport; 10 caricature, exaggerate, manipulate

misrepresentation: 6 deceit; 9 deception, falsehood; 10 distortion, perversion; 12 misstatement; 13 falsification

miss: 4 blot, drop, flaw, girl, jump, lack, lose, need, omit, sink, skip, slip, trip, want; 5 fault, fille, missy; 6 escape, shelve; 7 blunder, misfire, neglect, stumble; 8 leave out, not reach, omission, overleap, overlook; 9 come short, fall short, miss stays, oversight, push aside, young lady

missa cantata: 8 high mass

missed: 4 lost; 8 passed by; 10 passed over

Misses: 3 Mrs. [abbr]

misshape: 6 deform

misshapen: 7 ill-made; 8 deformed; 9 distorted, ill-shaped, ill-shapen, malformed; 10 bad-looking, ill-looking; 11 hard visaged, misbegotten

missile: 6 rocket

missing: 4 lost; 6 absent; 7 lacking, wanting; 11 nonexistent

mission: 4 care, task; 6 charge, errand; 7 embassy; 8 delegacy, legation; 10 assignment, commission, delegation, deputation, engagement; 12 assigned duty; 14 responsibility

missionary: 7 apostle, example, pioneer; 9 missioner; 10 revivalist

missionary work: 7 mission

Mississippi: 16 Mississippi River

missive: 4 note; 6 billet, letter; 7 epistle

Missouri: 11 Show Me State; 13 Missouri River

misstate: 7 falsify, pervert; 8 misquote; 9 misreport; 12 misrepresent

misstep: 4 trip; 7 stumble

missy: 4 girl, miss; 5 fille; 9 young lady; 10 young woman

mist: 3 fog; 4 haze; 5 befog, cloud, vapor; 7 aerosol, becloud, obscure

mistake: 3 err; 4 slip; 5 error, fault; 7 confuse; 8 confound; 11 misidentify

M

mistaken: 5 false; 6 unreal, untrue; 7 in error; 9 erroneous, misguided; 10 apocryphal, fallacious, groundless, ungrounded

mistakenly: 11 erroneously

mister: 2 Mr.; 5 spray; 9 vaporizer

mistimed: 8 ill-timed

mistiness: 8 haziness

mistletoe family: 9 Viscaceae; 12 Loranthaceae

mistral: 7 sirocco; 8 levanter; 9 trade wind

mistreat: 3 bug; 4 bait, bore; 5 abuse, beset, grind, harry, haunt, hound, tease, worry; 6 badger, bother, harass, heckle, ill-use, infest, molest, pester, plague, pother; 7 oppress; 8 bullirag, bullyrag, ill-treat, maltreat; 9 importune, persecute

mistress: 6 master; 9 concubine; 10 fancy woman, schoolmarm; 14 schoolmistress

mistrust: 7 suspect; 8 cynicism, distrust; 9 misgiving, suspicion; 10 scepticism, skepticism; 11 incredulity

mistrustful: 4 wary; 5 leery; 10 suspicious, untrusting

misty: 4 hazy; 5 foggy; 6 cloudy; 7 brumous; 8 vaporous

misunderstand: 8 misapply, misspell; 11 misconceive, misconstrue; 12 misapprehend, misinterpret, mistranslate

misunderstanding: 7 mistake, wrangle; 8 clashing; 9 bickering, mistaking; 13 misconception; 14 misapplication; 15 misapprehension

misuse: 5 abuse; 7 pervert; 8 misapply, misusage; 9 misemploy

mite: 3 bit, jot, rap; 4 dole, hint, iota; 5 pinch, speck, touch, trace; 6 change, morsel; 7 modicum, soupcon; 8 pittance

miter: 3 jam; 5 mitre, tiara, wedge; 6 rabbet; 7 mortise; 8 dovetail; 11 triple crown

mitigate: 4 ease; 6 soften, soothe, temper; 7 relieve; 8 moderate, palliate; 9 alleviate, extenuate

mitt: 3 paw; 4 hand, hook; 5 glove, manus; 6 mauler; 12 baseball mitt; 13 baseball glove

mix: 4 fuse, meld; 5 admix, blend, immix, merge, mix in, unify; 6 commix, mingle, mixing, premix, ruffle; 7 combine, mixture, shuffle; 8 coalesce, conflate; 9 admixture, commingle, integrate; 10 amalgamate, commixture; 11 desegregate

mixed: 3 cur, odd; 5 scrub; 6 divers, motley, sundry, varied; 7 diverse, mingled, mongrel, various; 8 assorted; 9 different, underbred; 10 dissimilar, integrated; 11 amalgamated, diversified, interracial; 12 intermingled; 13 heterogeneous, miscellaneous

mixed drink: 8 cocktail

mixed number: 13 complex number

mixed up: 4 lost; 5 at sea, mazed; 7 baffled, bemused, jumbled; 8 confused; 9 befuddled; 10 bewildered, confounded

mixer: 6 social; 8 sociable

mix in: 3 mix; 6 mingle; 7 blend in; 9 mix up with

mixing: 3 mix; 7 mixture; 9 admixture; 10 commixture

mixing up: 9 shuffling

mixologist: 6 barman; 7 barkeep; 9 barkeeper, bartender

mixture: 3 mix; 6 mixing, motley; 7 variety; 9 admixture, potpourri; 10 assortment, commixture, concoction, miscellany; 11 miscellanea; 12 intermixture

mix up: 5 stump; 6 jumble; 7 confuse, derange; 8 disorder; 10 disarrange

mizzen: 5 mizen; 9 mizenmast; 10 mizzenmast

mizzle: 7 drizzle

ml: 2 cc; 3 mil; 10 milliliter, millilitre

mm: 6 micron; 10 millimeter, millimetre

mm Hg: 4 torr

Mn: 9 manganese

mnemonics: 11 art of memory; 15 memoria technica [Lat]

Mo: 10 molybdenum

MO: 3 way; 4 mode, ways, wise; 5 means; 6 manner, method; 7 fashion, process; 8 practice, protocol; 9 mechanism, procedure, technique; 10 procedures [pl]; 13 modus operandi

moan: 4 sigh; 5 groan, sough, whine; 6 murmur, mutter, plaint; 7 grumble, heaving; 8 deep sigh; 9 complaint; 11 suspiration

moaner: 6 whiner; 7 crybaby; 8 grumbler, sniveler, squawker; 10 bellyacher, complainer

moat: 4 dike; 5 ditch, fosse, gully; 6 trough; 7 bulwark, culvert; 12 entrenchment

mob: 3 jam; 4 body, gang, hiss, hoot, pack, pile, ring, rout; 5 crush, horde, press; 6 clamor, rabble, throng; 7 mobbish, moblike; 9 blacklist, ostracize, syndicate

Mobile: 11 Mobile River

mobile: 5 fluid; 6 lively, roving; 7 movable, nomadic, plastic, unquiet; 8 shifting, spirited; 9 alterable, mercurial, peregrine, vivacious, wandering

mobile home: 7 trailer; 9 Airstream; 12 house trailer

mobile telephone: 11 mobile phone

mobility: 11 movableness, versatility

mobilization: 10 marshaling; 12 mobilisation

mobilize: 5 rally; 6 call up, summon; 7 marshal; 9 circulate

mob law: 7 club law; 8 lynch law; 11 vigilantism

mobster: 8 gangster

Mocambique: 10 Mozambique

mocassin: 8 moccasin; 9 moccasins

mock: 3 ape; 4 fake, sham; 5 bogus, ideal,

mimic, taunt; **6** bemock, deride, pseudo; **7** mocking; **8** ridicule, simulate, so-called, spurious; **9** personate, pretended; **10** fraudulent, simulating; **11** counterfeit, impersonate

mocker: 7 scoffer; **11** mockingbird

mockery: 4 jeer; **5** scoff, spoof; **6** parody, sendup; **7** charade, jeering, lampoon, mimicry, sarcasm, takeoff; **8** derision, ridicule, scoffing, travesty; **9** burlesque; **10** pasquinade

mocking: 4 mock; **7** chiming, jeering, teasing; **8** derisive, gibelike, taunting

mockingbird: 6 mocker

mockingly: 8 gibingly; **9** jeeringly; **10** derisively, derisorily, scoffingly

mock orange: 7 syringa; **12** philadelphus

mock-up: 5 model

mod: 6 modern; **8** up-to-date

modal: 6 formal; **7** average; **11** conditional; **12** adventitious

modality: 4 mode, mood

mode: 2 go, MO; **3** way; **4** mood, rage, wise; **5** means, style, vogue; **6** manner, method; **7** fashion, process; **8** modality, protocol; **9** mechanism, procedure, technique; **10** modishness, procedures [pl]; **11** musical mode, savoir faire [Fr]; **13** modus operandi

model: 3 sit; **4** mold, pose, test, type; **5** frame, ideal, mould, pilot, poser, study, trial; **6** mirror, mock up; **7** example, keynote, manakin, manikin, paragon, pattern, posture, reenact; **8** exemplar, frame out, mannikin, modeling, original, paradigm, rough hew, simulate, standard; **9** exemplary, framework, mannequin, modelling, precedent, prototype, reference, role model, rough cast; **10** simulation

modeler: 6 carver, chaser; **8** modeller, sculptor, statuary

modeling: 4 mold; **5** model, mould; **7** molding; **8** moulding; **9** modelling; **13** clay sculpture

mode of expression: 5 style; **7** diction, wording; **11** phraseology

moderate: 4 curb, hold, lead; **5** chair, check, mince; **6** hold in, leaven, modest, rein in, season, soften, temper; **7** chasten, contain, control, slacken; **8** centrist, mitigate; **9** temperate; **10** reasonable, restrained; **13** moderationist

moderately: 6 fairly, pretty; **7** passing; **8** middling, passably, somewhat; **10** reasonably

moderation: 6 easing, lenity, relief; **10** mediocrity, temperance

moderator: 6 duplex; **7** monitor; **10** taskmaster

modern: 3 mod; **4** late; **7** nouveau; **8** advanced, neoteric, up-to-date; **10** innova-

tive; **11** hypermodern, modernistic; **12** contemporary, non-classical

modern: 3 new

modernistic: 4 late; **6** modern; **7** nouveau; **8** neoteric; **11** hypermodern; **12** contemporary, non-classical

modernize: 7 develop; **8** civilize, overhaul

modest: 3 low; **4** meek, mild, pure; **5** lowly, minor, plain, small; **6** decent, demure, humble, simple; **8** decorous, delicate, moderate, reserved; **9** diffident, undefiled; **10** restrained, small-scale; **11** sober-minded; **12** humble-minded; **14** unostentatious

modesty: 5 shame; **6** virtue; **7** decency, reserve; **8** humility; **10** continence, humbleness

modicum: 3 bit, jot; **4** hint, iota, mess, mite; **5** quota, ratio, trace; **6** morsel; **10** proportion

modification: 4 form; **6** change; **7** variant; **8** coloring, limiting, revision; **9** expansion, extension, variation; **10** adjustment, alteration, derivation, derivative, modulation

modified: 6 varied; **7** altered, changed, limited

modifier: 9 qualifier

modify: 4 vamp; **5** limit; **7** qualify; **8** restrict; **11** superinduce

modish: 4 chic, cool; **6** trendy; **7** a la mode, in style, in vogue, stylish; **9** recherche

modishness: 2 go; **4** chic, mode; **5** swank; **8** chicness; **9** smartness; **11** savoir faire [Fr], stylishness

modiste: 6 hatter; **8** hatmaker, milliner

modulate: 4 vary; **5** alter; **6** change, mutate; **7** inflect; **8** regulate

modulation: 10 transition; **12** modification

module: 7 faculty; **10** protoplast

modulus: 4 base

modus operandi: 2 MO; **3** way; **4** mode, ways, wise; **5** means; **6** manner, method; **7** fashion, process, routine; **8** practice, protocol; **9** mechanism, procedure, technique; **10** procedures [pl]

modus ponens: 9 syllogism

modus vivendi: 5 truce; **9** armistice, lifestyle, stand-down

Moehringia: 8 sandwort; **15** genus Moehringia

Mogadiscio: 16 capital of Somalia

Mogen David: 10 Magen David; **11** Star of David

Mogul: 6 Moghul

mogul: 4 king; **5** baron, power; **6** tycoon; **7** magnate; **10** great mogul; **9** executive

Mohammed: 7 Mahomet, Mahound; **8** Mohammad, Muhammad

Mohammedanism: 5 Islam; **8** Islamism; **9** Muslimism; **13** Mohammedanism

Mohammedan: 6 Moslem, Muslim;

M

9 Mussulman; **10** Muhammadan, Muhammedan
Mohawk tribe: 6 Mohawk
Mohican: 7 Mahican
moiety: 4 half; **5** group; **7** mediety, radical
moil: 3 dig; **4** boil, roil, toil; **5** churn, grind, labor; **6** drudge, labour, meddle, strive; **7** travail
moire: 7 watered; **11** watered-silk
moist: 3 wet; **4** damp; **7** dampish
moisten: 3 wet; **4** wash; **6** dampen; **7** drizzle
moisture: 3 wet
moisturize: 8 humidify
Mojave: 6 Mohave; **12** Mojave Desert
molar: 5 molal; **7** grinder
molar concentration: 1 M; **8** molarity
molasses: 7 treacle
mold: 3 cut, die, fit, set; **4** cast, form, must; **5** forge, frame, fungi [pl], model, mould, shape, stamp; **6** fungus, mildew, molder, nature, spirit; **7** molding; **8** modeling, moulding; **9** character; **10** complexion
moldable: 7 fictile, plastic
Moldavia: 7 Moldova
molded: 4 cast; **6** formed, shaped; **7** wrought; **8** affected; **13** characterized
molder: 3 rot; **4** fade, mold; **5** decay; **6** bother, rankle, wither; **7** moulder; **8** bewilder; **9** decompose; **12** disintegrate
moldering: 6 effete, rotten, wasted; **7** rotting, tainted; **8** blighted, cankered; **9** crumbling; **10** mouldering; **11** decomposing
moldiness: 9 mustiness; **10** rottenness
molding: 4 mold; **5** mould; **6** border; **7** casting, forming, shaping; **8** modeling, moulding, stamping; **9** mildewing
moldy: 5 musty, rusty, seedy; **6** mouldy; **7** spotted; **8** mildewed, time-worn; **9** moss-grown, moth-eaten
mole: 3 mol, zit [slang]; **4** bank, mull, spur; **5** nevus, jetty; **6** pimple; **7** bulwark, parapet, sandbag, seawall; **8** tunneler; **9** revetment; **10** breakwater, counterspy, embankment; **12** gram molecule
molecular: 6 atomic; **9** subatomic; **11** corpuscular, microscopic
molecule: 4 atom, mote; **5** speck; **8** particle; **9** corpuscle
mole-eyed: 7 dim-eyed; **8** cock-eyed
molest: 3 bug; **4** bait, bore; **5** abuse, beset, chevy, chivy, grind, harry, haunt, hound, tease, worry; **6** badger, bother, chevvy, chivvy, harass, hassle, heckle, ill-use, infest, pester, plague, pother; **7** oppress, provoke; **8** ill-treat, maltreat, mistreat; **9** importune, persecute
molested: 5 raped, tired, vexed; **6** teased; **7** plagued; **8** bothered, pestered; **9** assaulted, disturbed
moll: 7 gun moll; **13** gangster's moll

mollification: 8 relaxing; **9** mellowing, softening; **10** mollifying; **12** pacification
mollify: 4 dull; **5** blunt, relax; **6** gentle, lenify, mellow, pacify, subdue, temper; **7** appease, assuage, chasten, gruntle, placate
Mollusca: 14 phylum Mollusca
mollusk: 7 mollusc; **9** shellfish
mollycoddle: 4 baby, muff; **5** betty, sissy, spoil; **6** cocker, coddle, cosset, pamper; **7** cripple, indulge; **8** old woman, pussycat; **9** creampuff; **10** featherbed, powder puff
Molokai: 13 Molokai Island
Molotov cocktail: 10 petrol bomb; **12** gasoline bomb
molt: 3 mew; **4** shed; **5** moult; **6** slough; **7** ecdysis, molting; **8** exuviate, moulting; **9** defoliate, exfoliate
molten: 9 liquefied, liquified
molting: 4 molt; **5** moult; **7** ecdysis; **8** moulting
molybdenum: 2 Mo
mom: 2 ma; **3** mum; **4** mama; **5** mamma, mammy, mater, momma, mommy, mummy
moment: 3 bit; **4** mark; **6** import, minute, second; **7** instant; **10** here and now, importance, prominence; **11** consequence, materiality, weightiness; **12** materialness, significance; **13** consideration
momentary: 6 abrupt, sudden; **7** instant; **8** fleeting, fugitive; **9** immediate; **11** precipitant, precipitate, precipitous; **12** momentaneous; **13** discontinuous, instantaneous
momentous: 3 big; **6** signal; **8** material; **9** memorable
momentum: 7 impulse
momma: 2 ma; **3** mom, mum; **4** mama; **5** mamma, mammy, mater, mommy, mummy; **6** mother
mommy: 2 ma; **3** mom, mum; **4** mama; **5** mamma, mammy, mater, momma, mummy; **6** mother
Mon: 6 Monday
monad: 3 one; **4** unit, atom; **5** monas
monarch: 4 king; **5** queen, ruler; **9** sovereign; **11** butterfly
monarchist: 8 royalist
monastery: 7 convent, nunnery; **8** cloister
monastic: 4 monk; **7** monkish; **8** cenobite; **9** cloistral; **10** cloistered, conventual, monastical; **11** monasterial
monaurally: 6 one ear
Monday: 3 Mon
monetary: 9 pecuniary
monetary compensation: 3 pay; **4** wage; **5** wages; **6** salary, income
monetary value: 4 cost; **5** price, value, worth; **14** intrinsic value
money: 5 bread, dough, lucre; **11** legal tender
money box: 4 bank, till; **6** coffer; **7** cashbox; **8** coin bank; **9** strong box
money changer: 9 exchanger; **11** money broker; **12** change bureau

money chest: 6 coffer; 8 money box; 9 strong box

moneyed: 4 rich; 5 flush; 6 loaded, monied; 7 opulent, wealthy; 8 affluent

moneyed class: 5 money; 10 rich person, upperclass, uppercrust

money going out: 6 outlay; 7 expense; 8 expenses; 9 outgoings; 11 expenditure; 12 disbursement

money income: 3 pay; 4 wage; 5 wages; 6 salary

money in the bank: 7 nest egg, savings

money lender: 5 shark; 6 banker, usurer; 9 loan shark

money lent: 9 principal

moneymaker: 7 cash cow

moneymaking: 9 lucrative, mercenary; 10 mercantile; 12 remunerative

moneyman: 9 financier

money stashed away: 5 cache, stash; 7 nest egg, savings

monger: 4 hawk, vend; 5 pitch; 6 dealer, peddle, trader; 8 chandler, huckster, merchant, salesman; 9 bargainer; 11 salesperson

Mongol: 9 Mongolian

Mongolia: 13 Outer Mongolia; 24 Mongolian People's Republic

mongolism: 12 Down syndrome

Mongol Tatar: 5 Tatar; 6 Tartar

mongrel: 3 cur, dog; 4 mutt; 5 cross, mixed, scrub, whelp; 6 hybrid; 7 debased; 8 chowchow; 9 composite, underbred; 10 crossbreed; 11 half-and-half; 13 heterogeneous, linsey-woolsey

monied: 4 rich; 7 moneyed, opulent, wealthy; 8 affluent; 9 worth much

moniker: 8 cognomen, nickname; 9 sobriquet

Monilia albicans: 15 Candida albicans

moniliasis: 11 candidiasis; 14 monilia disease, yeast infection

monition: 7 caution, warning

monitor: 3 VDT; 4 dame, tend; 5 varan, watch; 6 mentor, patrol, tend to; 7 proctor, senator, surveil; 8 ironclad, reminder, terminal; 9 moderator, supervise; 10 admonisher, schoolmarm, taskmaster, turret ship; 11 guard camera; 12 pupil teacher, stormy petrel, warning voice

monitoring: 7 tending; 8 watching; 12 surveillance

monitor lizard: 5 varan; 7 monitor

monitory: 7 warning; 9 exemplary; 10 admonitory, cautionary, cautioning; 11 premonitory

monk: 5 friar; 8 monastic; 9 mendicant

monkey: 3 ape, bat, imp; 4 echo, mime; 5 punch, scamp; 6 parrot, potter, putter, rascal, tamper, tinker; 8 imitator

monkey jacket: 10 mess jacket; 11 shell jacket

monkeypod: 8 rain tree

monkfish: 5 lotte; goosefish; 10 angel shark

monkish: 8 monastic

monkshood: 12 helmetflower

mono: 10 monophonic; 13 mononucleosis, single-channel

monoamine oxidase: 3 MAO [acron]

monoamine oxidase inhibitor: 4 MAOI

monochromatic: 9 colorless; 10 achromatic, monochrome; 11 monochromic; 12 monochromous; 13 black and white

monochrome: 9 colorless; 10 achromatic, polychrome; 11 monochromic, neutral tint; 12 monochromous; 13 black and white

monocle: 8 eyeglass

monocot: 13 monocotyledon

monocot family: 15 liliopsid family

monocracy: 7 tyranny; 9 Caesarism, despotism, shogunate, Stalinism; 10 absolutism, one-man rule; 12 dictatorship; 15 totalitarianism; 16 authoritarianism

monocycle: 8 unicycle

Monodon: 6 narwal; 7 narwhal; 8 narwhale; 12 genus Monodon

monody: 8 one voice

monogram: 6 cipher; 7 anagram

monograph: 5 tract

monolith: 6 column, pillar; 7 obelisk

monolithic: 7 massive; 10 monumental

monologue: 9 monodrama, soliloquy

monomania: 8 fixation; 10 possession

mononucleosis: 4 mono

monophonic: 4 mono; 13 single-channel

monophonic music: 6 monody

monoploid: 7 haploid

monopolist: 6 egoist; 7 egotist; 8 nepotist; 11 monopolizer

monopolize: 7 engross; 13 have a corner on

monopolizer: 10 monopolist

monopoly: 6 corner; 10 limitation, protection; 11 restriction

monosodium glutamate: 3 MSG

monotheistic: 6 one God

monotone: 5 drone; 7 droning; 9 monotonic; 10 monotonous

monotonous: 3 dry; 4 even, flat, slow; 5 level, vapid; 6 steady, stupid; 7 coequal, harping, humdrum, insipid, routine; 8 constant, monotone, unvaried; 9 clockwork, continual, incessant, iterative, monotonic, perpetual, recursive, unceasing, unfailing; 10 consistent, continuous, coordinate, invariable; 11 symmetrical

monotonously: 6 always; 8 steadily; 9 routinely; 10 constantly, invariably; 11 continually, incessantly, perpetually, unfailingly; 12 consistently, continuously

monotony: 5 level; 6 tedium; 7 routine; 8 dull work, evenness, sameness;

M

9 constancy; **10** regularity, steadiness, tautophony; **14** continuousness

monotreme: 15 egg-laying mammal

monovalent: 9 univalent

monovular: 9 identical; **11** monozygotic

Monroe: 11 James Monroe

Monrovia: 16 capital of Liberia

monsieur: 2 M. [abbr]

monster: 4 ogre; **5** demon, devil, fiend, freak, giant, jumbo; **7** goliath, mammoth; **8** behemoth, colossus; **9** humongous, monstrous; **11** elephantine, monstrosity

Monstera deliciosa: 7 ceriman

monstrosity: 5 freak; **7** monster; **8** enormity; **9** immensity

monstrous: 5 jumbo, outre; **6** horrid, odious; **7** heinous, hideous, monster, stilted, uncanny; **8** grievous, inflated; **9** atrocious, bombastic, burlesque, frightful, grotesque, humongous, marvelous, overgrown, unnatural; **10** flagitious, forbidding, mock heroic, prodigious, stupendous; **11** elephantine, extravagant; **12** preposterous

montage: 7 collage

monte: 13 four-card monte; **14** three-card monte

Montevideo: 16 capital of Uruguay

Montgomery: 16 capital of Alabama

Montpelier: 16 capital of Vermont

monument: 6 shrine; **8** cenotaph, memorial; **10** repository

monumental: 7 massive; **10** monolithic

mooch: 3 bum; **4** grub; **5** cadge; **6** sponge

moocher: 6 beggar, cadger; **7** sponger; **9** mendicant, scrounger; **10** freeloader, panhandler

mood: 4 ease, mode, vein; **5** humor; **6** animus, humour, temper; **7** climate; **8** attitude, modality; **9** inflexion; **11** disposition

moodiness: 7 bad mood; **9** sulkiness; **10** gloominess, sullenness; **11** temperament

moody: 3 mad; **4** dark, dour, glum, sour; **6** morose, sullen; **9** delirious, glowering, saturnine; **13** temperamental

moolah: 4 gelt, kale, loot, pelf; **5** bread, dough, lucre, money; **6** dinero; **7** cabbage, shekels

moon: 4 Luna; **6** moon on; **8** daydream, lunation; **9** moonlight, moonshine, satellite; **10** Earth's moon, lunar month, moon around, orb of night; **12** synodic month

moonbeam: 7 moonray

moon blindness: 7 mooneye

mooncalf: 9 simpleton

moon-faced: 10 round-faced

moonfish: 4 opah; **5** platy

moonless: 8 starless; **10** pitch-black

moonlight: 4 moon; **9** moonshine

moonlit: 5 moony

moonray: 8 moonbeam

moonshine: 4 bosh, moon, myth; **5** farce, hooch; **6** put off; **7** eyewash, rubbish; **8** wish-wash; **9** moonlight; **10** corn liquor

moonshiner: 10 bootlegger

moonstruck: 3 mad; **4** daft, loco, nuts; **5** batty, crazy, dotty, loony, nutty; **6** crazed, fruity, insane, teched [dialect]; **7** bonkers, cracked, lunatic, tetched [dialect], touched; **8** demented, deranged, maddened, not right; **9** awestruck

moon-worship: 11 selenolatry

moony: 6 dreamy; **7** moonlit

Moor: Berber

moor: 3 bog, fen; **4** moss; **5** berth; **6** picket, tether; **7** peat bog; **8** moorland

moorage: 4 slip; **5** berth; **7** mooring

moored: 7 on a rock; **8** anchored, at anchor, tethered; **9** rock solid

mooring: 4 slip; **5** berth; **7** docking, moorage, tying up; **9** anchorage, anchoring

moorings: 3 guy; **4** line, wire; **5** cable, chain; **7** painter

Moorish: 8 Moresque

Moorish arch: 13 horseshoe arch

moose: 10 Alces alces

moot: 5 argue; **6** debate; **7** dispute, wrangle; **8** consider, disputed, proposed, turn over; **9** bandy with, debatable, sub judice [Lat]; **10** deliberate, disputable

mooted: 7 assumed, divined, guessed; **8** imagined, presumed, supposed, surmised; **9** suspected; **10** postulated; **11** conjectured, presupposed

moot point: 5 issue; **7** dispute, problem; **8** argument, question; **11** controversy

mop: 3 mow; **4** pout, swab, swob; **5** mop up; **6** wipe up

mope: 4 mope; **7** dallier, lounger

moppet: 3 kid; **4** idol; **5** bairn [Scot], child, jewel, youth; **6** cosset; **8** children [pl], juvenile, small fry; **9** little one, youngster

mopping: 8 swabbing

mop up: 3 mop, pip; **4** whip; **5** worst; **6** rack up, windup, wipe up; **7** clear up, closing; **8** finish up; **9** finish off, polish off; **10** completion, get through; **11** culmination

moral: 6 lesson; **7** ethical; **9** honorable; **10** honourable, philosophy; **11** casuistical; **13** conscientious

morale: 10 team spirit; **13** esprit de corps

moralist: 14 disciplinarian

morality: 6 ethics, morals; **9** rightness; **13** ethical motive, righteousness

moralize: 6 preach; **8** moralise; **9** preachify, sermonize

morally: 4 well; **5** nobly; **10** virtuously; **11** righteously

moral obligation: 4 duty, onus; **9** liability; **10** obligation

moral philosophy: 6 ethics; **8** ethology, psychics

morals: 6 ethics; **8** morality

moral sense: 8 scruples; 10 conscience
morass: 4 mire; 5 marsh, swamp; 7 wetland; 8 quagmire
moratorium: 8 holdover
moray: 8 moray eel
morbid: 6 infirm, sickly; 8 diseased, ghoulish; 9 chlorotic [Med]; 10 deathly ill, pathologic; 12 pathological
morbidity: 9 deathrate, mortality; 10 morbidness
morbilli: 7 measles, rubeola
Morchella: 5 morel; 14 genus Morchella
mordant: 4 grim; 5 black, harsh; 6 biting; 7 caustic; 8 virulent; 9 corrosive, stringent; 10 irritating
more: 4 over, plus; 5 extra; 6 beyond; 7 further; 8 more than; 10 additional
more and more: 12 increasingly; 13 progressively
more or less: 3 any; 4 a few, or so, some; 5 about, aught; 6 around; 7 close to, roughly; 9 just about; 12 quantitative; 13 approximately
moreover: 11 furthermore
Moresque: 7 Moorish, Morisco, tooling; 8 moresque; 9 frost work
Morgan: 8 J. P. Morgan, Sir Henry; 11 Henry Morgan; 12 Daniel Morgan; 16 Thomas Hunt Morgan; 18 John Pierpont Morgan
morgue: 8 dead room, mortuary
moribund: 8 expiring, stagnant
morion: 4 helm; 5 shako; 6 casque; 8 cabasset, siege cap
Morisco: 7 tooling; 8 Moresque [Lat]
Mormon: 14 Latter-day Saint
Mormon Church: 7 Mormons
Mormon State: 4 Utah; 12 Beehive State
morning: 2 A.M. [abbr]; 4 dawn, morn; 5 matin, prime, sunup; 6 aurora; 7 dawning, sunrise; 8 cockcrow, daybreak, forenoon; 9 dayspring; 10 break of day, first light; 12 ante meridien [Lat]
morning star: 7 day star
Moroccan: 5 Maroc
Morocco: 5 Maroc; 8 Al-Magrib; 9 Marruecos
moron: 5 idiot; 7 half-wit; 8 imbecile
moronic: 7 idiotic; 9 imbecilic
Moro reflex: 13 startle reflex
morose: 4 dark, dour, glum, grim, sour; 5 moody, sulky; 6 gloomy, grumpy, sullen; 7 grouchy; 8 frumpish, growling, scowling
morphine: 7 morphia
morphologic: 10 structural
morphological change: 10 inflection
morphology: 4 form; 9 structure
morrow: 7 morning; 8 tomorrow
Morse: 9 Morse code
morsel: 3 ace, bit, jot, sop; 4 bite, hint, hunk, iota, lump, mite; 5 bolus, trace; 7 modicum; 8 particle
mortal: 3 dry, man; 4 arid, bald, body, dull,

flat, soul; 5 being, civic, fatal, human; 6 boring, deadly, jejune, lethal, person, public, social; 7 deathly, someone, tedious; 8 creature, national, personal, somebody; 9 earthling, personage; 10 human being, individual, living soul; 13 uninteresting
mortal blow: 9 fatal blow
mortality: 5 flesh; 8 humanity; 9 deathrate, morbidity; 10 generation; 13 eventual death
mortality rate: 9 deathrate, morbidity, mortality
mortal sin: 9 deadly sin
mortar: 6 cement; 8 howitzer
mortgage: 4 pawn; 5 spout; 6 pledge, plight; 9 debenture; 11 hypothecate; 13 hypothecation
mortgagee: 6 lessor
mortgagor: 11 beneficiary
mortician: 10 undertaker; 15 funeral director
mortification: 4 stew; 6 bother, pother; 7 chagrin; 8 gangrene, nuisance, vexation; 9 annoyance, grievance; 10 corruption, harassment, maceration; 11 humiliation
mortify: 3 bug, irk, vex; 4 faze, tire; 5 abase, annoy, cross, crush, worry; 6 bother, humble, put out, subdue; 7 chagrin, disturb, necrose, perplex, trouble; 8 disgrace, disquiet, gangrene; 9 disoblige, displease, humiliate, incommode; 10 disappoint, discomfort, discompose, disconcert, dissatisfy, sphacelate; 13 inconvenience
mortifying: 7 galling; 8 annoying, humbling, stinging; 9 demeaning, provoking; 10 irritating, irritation; 11 aggravating, humiliating, provocation; 12 embarrassing
mortise: 3 jam; 5 miter, wedge; 6 rabbet, splice; 7 mortice; 8 dovetail
mortuary: 4 mute; 6 morgue; 8 dead room; 10 sepulchral, undertaker
Morus: 8 mulberry; 10 genus Morus
mosaic: 6 motley; 7 collage, montage; 8 pastiche; 9 composite, patchwork, potpourri; 10 hodgepodge, variegated
Mosaic law: 11 Laws of Moses
Moscow: 14 Russian capital
mosey: 5 amble
Moslem: 6 Muslim; 7 Islamic; 9 Mussulman; 10 Mohammedan, Muhammadan, Muhammedan
mosque: 6 masjid, musjid
mosquito boat: 6 PT boat
mosquito hawk: 9 dragonfly
moss: 3 bog, fen; 4 moor; 7 peat bog; 8 moorland
moss animal: 6 sea mat; 7 sea moss; 8 bryozoan, polyzoan
mossback: 4 fogy; 6 gaffer; 7 antique; 8 old-timer; 9 old geezer

M

mossy: 6 stodgy; 7 fogyish; 8 mosslike; 9 moss-grown; 13 stick-in-the-mud

most: 4 much, near, nigh, well; 5 about; 6 all but, almost, indeed, most of, nearly; 8 well-nigh; 9 almost all, just about, nearly all, virtually

most important: 4 main; 5 chief, prime; 7 capital, leading, primary; 8 foremost; 9 principal; 10 overruling

mostly: 7 largely; 9 generally; 10 by and large

most often: 7 as a rule, usually; 9 generally, typically; 10 ordinarily; 11 customarily

most valuable player: 3 MVP

mot: 4 word; 5 motto; 6 bon mot, byword; 9 watchword

mot a mot: 3 sic; 8 verbatim; 9 literally, literatim [Lat]; 11 to the letter, word for word

mote: 3 dot; 4 atom; 5 point, speck; 8 molecule, particle

motel: 5 court; 8 motor inn; 10 motor hotel, motor lodge

motet: 4 hymn; 5 chant; 6 anthem, chaunt; 8 response

mothball: 11 camphor ball

moth-eaten: 3 old; 5 moldy, musty, ratty, rusty, stale, tatty; 6 shabby; 8 mildewed; 9 worm-eaten

mother: 2 ma; 3 dam, get, mom, mum; 4 fuss, mama, sire; 5 beget, mamma, mammy, mater, momma, mummy; 7 cinders, produce, scoriae; 8 engender, generate; 10 bring forth; 11 overprotect, precipitate; 12 female parent; 13 materfamilias [Lat]

mother's boy: 8 mama's boy; 9 mamma's boy

mother board: 8 CPU board

motherhood: 9 maternity

motherland: 8 homeland; 10 fatherland, native land; 13 mother country; 15 country of origin

motherly: 4 fond; 6 ardent; 7 devoted; 8 uxorious; 9 rapturous; 10 maternally, passionate

mother superior: 6 abbess; 8 prioress

mother wit: 5 parts, sense; 6 esprit; 8 gumption, sagacity; 9 acuteness, good sense; 10 horse sense, quick parts; 11 common sense

motif: 5 theme; 6 motive

motion: 4 move; 6 moving; 7 gesture; 8 movement, question; 10 invitation, resolution; 11 gesticulate; 13 gesticulation

motionless: 5 still; 6 at rest, static; 8 inactive, moveless; 9 not moving, quiescent; 10 stationary

motion picture: 4 film; 5 flick, movie; 6 movies; 7 picture; 8 flickers [pl]

motion-picture fan: 9 moviegoer

motivate: 4 move; 6 incite, induce, prompt, propel

motivation: 4 need; 6 ground, motive, reason; 7 purpose; 9 reason why; 11 inspiration

motive: 4 need; 5 motif, motor; 6 ground, moving, reason; 7 purpose; 9 reason why; 10 motivating, motivation, motivative; 11 inspiration

motiveless: 6 wanton; 10 unprovoked

motley: 4 pied, vary; 5 mixed; 6 mosaic, sundry; 7 mixture, painted, variety; 8 assorted; 9 potpourri, variegate; 10 assortment, miscellany, multicolor, parti-color, variegated

motor: 5 drive; 6 engine, motive; 11 centrifugal

motorbike: 8 minibike; 10 motorcycle

motorboat: 9 powerboat

motorbus: 3 bus; 5 coach; 6 jitney; 7 autobus, omnibus; 9 charabanc; 10 motorcoach

motorcar: 3 car; 4 auto; 10 automobile

Motor City: 6 Motown; 7 Detroit

motor coil: 5 rotor; 6 stator

motorcycle: 4 bike; 5 cycle; 9 motor bike

motorcyclist: 5 biker

motor home: 2 RV; 6 camper

motor hotel: 5 court, motel; 8 motor inn; 10 motor lodge

motoring: 7 driving

motorist: 6 driver; 12 automobilist

motorize: 9 mechanize

motorless: 11 unmotorized

motor memory: 12 muscle memory

motor mower: 10 power mower

motor paralysis: 5 palsy; 9 paralysis

motor scooter: 7 scooter

motor skill: 11 motor skills [pl]; 12 coordination

motor vehicle: 3 car; 4 auto; 7 vehicle; 10 automobile; 17 automotive vehicle

motorway: 4 pike; 7 freeway, highway, thruway; 10 expressway, throughway; 12 state highway, superhighway

Motown: 7 Detroit; 9 Motor City

Motrin: 5 Advil; 6 Nuprin; 9 ibuprofen

mottle: 5 cloud; 6 blotch, dapple, streak

mottled: 7 dappled, marbled

motto: 3 mot [Fr]; 4 posy, word; 6 byword, slogan; 8 epigraph; 9 catchword, watchword

moue: 4 pout

moujik: 5 mujik; 6 muzhik, muzjik

mould: 4 mold

moult: 4 molt

mound: 4 bank, heap, hill, knob, mole, pena [U.S.], pile; 5 knoll; 6 barrow; 7 hammock, hillock, hummock, parapet, sandbag; 8 mountain; 9 revetment, sunk fence; 10 embankment; 13 pitcher's mound

mount: 3 Alp, wax; 4 go up, peak, pike, ride, rise; 5 climb, get on, hop on, put on;

6 ascend, beetle, go up on, impend, jump on, launch, proner [Fr], set off; **7** backing, climb on, climb up, get up on, get upon, mount up, setting; **8** bestride, emblazon, hang over, mountain, overhang

mountain: 3 Alp; **4** mass, peak, pike; **5** mound, mount

mountain bike: 9 off-roader; **14** all-terrain bike

mountain cat: 9 catamount

mountain chain: 5 chain, range; **13** mountain range

mountain climber: 7 climber; **8** alpinist; **11** mountaineer

mountain cranberry: 11 lingonberry

mountaineer: 7 climber; **8** alpinist; **15** mountain climber

mountain fever: 9 tick fever

mountain-flax: 9 earth-flax

mountain lion: 4 puma; **6** cougar; **7** panther; **9** catamount

mountain man: 12 backwoodsman, frontiersman

mountainous: 5 hilly; **6** alpine, craggy; **7** cragged; **9** subalpine

mountain pass: 4 pass; **5** notch

mountain range: 5 chain, range

Mountain Standard Time: 3 MST; **12** Mountain Time

Mountain State: 12 West Virginia

Mountain Time: 3 MST

mountebank: 5 quack; **9** charlatan

mounted rifles: 7 cavalry

mounties: 4 RCMP; **26** Royal Canadian Mounted Police

mounting: 5 climb; **8** climbing; **11** fomentation, instigation

mount up: 5 get on, hop on, mount; **6** jump on; **7** climb on; **8** bestride

mourned: 8 bewailed, lamented

mourner: 7 griever; **8** lamenter

mournful: 6 rueful, woeful; **7** doleful, tearful; **8** dreadful, funereal, pitiable; **9** plaintive; **10** deplorable, lamentable

mourning: 6 bereft; **8** bereaved, grieving; **9** sorrowing; **10** in mourning; **11** bereavement

mouse: 4 hunt; **6** rodent; **8** black eye; **13** computer mouse

mousse: 3 gel; **10** hair mousse

mousseux: 2 up; **6** frothy; **9** sparkling; **12** effervescent

moustache: 8 mustache

mousy: 6 mousey; **9** mouselike; **12** mouse-colored

mouth: 3 lip; **4** door, lips, sass, talk; **5** chops, drawl, inlet, porch, speak, utter; **6** portal; **7** deliver, orifice, portico, sassing; **8** aspirate, backtalk; **9** enunciate, pronounce, verbalize; **10** accentuate, articulate, mouthpiece, oral cavity, river mouth

mouthful: 5 taste; **6** armful, capful; **7** handful; **8** spoonful; **10** thimbleful

mouthless: 10 astomatous

mouth off: 4 rant, rave; **5** spout; **6** jabber

mouth organ: 4 harp; **9** harmonica, mouth harp

mouthpiece: 5 mouth; **6** teller; **7** delator, relator, speaker; **8** exponent, reporter; **9** authority, gumshield, informant, spokesman; **10** embouchure; **12** spokesperson

mouthwash: 6 gargle

mouth-watering: 5 tasty; **6** drouth, savory

mouthy: 4 rich; **5** tumid; **6** florid, ornate, turgid; **7** flowery, orotund; **8** inflated, sonorous, swelling; **9** bombastic, grandiose; **10** ornamented, rhetorical, turgescent; **11** big-sounding, declamatory; **12** high-sounding, magniloquent; **13** grandiloquent

mouton: 6 mutton

movable: 6 mobile; **7** unquiet; **8** moveable, shifting; **9** mercurial; **12** transferable; **13** transferrable, transportable

move: 2 go; **3** act, run; **4** blow, draw, lure, step; **5** smite, start, touch; **6** affect, allure, draw on, entice, excite, incite, induce, infect, motion, prompt, propel, strike, stroke, submit, travel; **7** animate, attract, beguile, bring to, impress, inspire, measure, proceed; **8** displace, interest, locomote, maneuver, motivate, movement, persuade, put a case; **9** captivate, first move, impassion

moveable: 7 movable; **12** transferable; **13** transferrable, transportable

move back: 2 go; **6** recede, retire; **7** retreat; **8** withdraw

move backward: 7 retreat; **12** step backward

moved: 7 excited, smitten, touched; **8** affected, animated, inspired, stricken; **9** impressed; **10** interested; **11** impassioned

move into: 4 go in; **5** enter

movement: 4 move; **5** cause, doing, drive, front; **6** acting, action, effort, motion, moving; **7** crusade; **8** campaign; **9** operation; **11** performance

mover: 7 founder; **8** proposer; **9** generator, initiator; **10** prime mover; **11** public mover, removal firm; **13** moving company

move towards: 4 near; **8** approach

move up: 4 go up, lift, rise; **5** arise; **6** come up; **7** advance

movie actor: 9 film actor; **11** screen actor

movie house: 6 cinema; **12** movie theater

movie industry: 9 Hollywood; **12** film industry

movie maker: 9 film maker; **12** film producer

movies: 4 film; **5** flick, movie

M

movie star: 4 star; **8** film star; **11** matinee idol

movie studio: 10 film studio

moving: 6 motion, motive; **8** in motion, movement, touching; **9** affecting, evocative, traveling; **10** motivating, relocation

moving apart: 7 parting; **10** separating, separation

moving company: 5 mover

moving in: 9 occupying; **10** occupation

moving staircase: 9 escalator

moving van: 3 van

moving water: 4 flow; **7** current

mow: 3 cut, lop, mop; **4** clip, crop, dock, pout, reap; **5** prune, shave, shear; **7** cut down, hayloft

mower: 9 lawnmower

mown: 3 cut

Mozambique: 10 Mocambique

Mozart: 21 Wolfgang Amadeus Mozart

mph: 12 miles per hour

Mr: 6 mister

Mrs.: 4 dame; **5** madam; **6** madame, Misses

MS: 2 SM; **10** manuscript; **15** Master of Science; **17** multiple sclerosis

msec: 11 millisecond

MSG: 19 monosodium glutamate

MST: 12 Mountain Time; **20** Mountain Standard Time

MT: 5 tonne; **9** metric ton

much: 3 rag, tag; **4** a lot, most, well; **5** a deal, often, scrap, shred; **6** indeed; **7** no end of; **8** splinter, very much; **11** practically

mucilage: 3 gum; **4** glue; **5** paste

mucilaginous: 4 ropy; **5** gluey, gummy, pasty; **6** clammy, mastic, sticky, viscid; **7** clotted, gelatin, viscous; **9** glutenous, glutinous; **10** albuminous, gelatinous

muck: 3 goo, mud; **4** dung, gook, guck, gunk, mire, ooze, silt; **5** slime, slosh, slush; **6** manure, muck up, sludge; **8** alluvium, quagmire; **9** droppings

muckraker: 10 mudslinger

muck up: 3 mud; **4** blow, flub, mire, muck, muff; **5** botch, fluff, spoil; **6** ball up, bobble, bollix, bungle, foul up, fumble, mess up; **7** blunder, botch up, louse up, screw up; **9** mishandle

mucky: 4 miry; **5** boggy, muddy; **6** marshy, quaggy, swampy; **7** sloughy

mucous: 5 slimy; **6** mucoid; **7** phlegmy

mucous membrane: 6 mucosa

mucous secretion: 5 mucus

mucus: 6 phlegm; **15** mucous secretion

mud: 4 clay, mire, muck, ooze, silt; **5** slime, slosh, slush; **6** muck up, sludge, squash; **8** alluvium, quagmire

muddied: 5 dingy, dirty, muddy

muddle: 3 fix, jam; **4** bull, hole, mash, mess, muss [U.S.], riot, toss; **5** addle; **6** dazzle,

fumble, huddle, hustle, jumble, pickle, puddle, put out, welter; **7** baloney, blarney, blunder, clutter, confuse, fluster, perplex, smother; **8** bewilder

muddy: 3 dim, dun, wan; **4** ashy, cold, dark, dead, dull, miry; **5** ashen, boggy, dense, dingy, dirty, faint, lurid, mirky, mucky, murky, thick; **6** cloudy, glassy, leaden, marshy, opaque, quaggy, sallow, sloppy, swampy, turbid; **7** cryptic, ghastly, muddied, muddy up, obscure, sloughy, squashy; **8** nebulous, overcast; **10** cadaverous, clear as mud, lackluster, mysterious, obfuscated

mudguard: 11 splashguard

mud puppy: 7 axolotl; **10** hellbender

mudslinger: 9 muckraker

Muenchen: 6 Munich

muezzin: 6 mullah; **7** muazzin; **9** ayatollah, mu'adhdhin

muff: 4 blow, flat, flub, swab; **5** betty, botch, fluff, spoil; **6** ball up, bobble, bollix, bungle, foul up, fumble, lubber, mess up, muck up; **7** blunder, botch up, louse up, screw up

muffin pan: 9 muffin tin

muffle: 3 gag; **4** damp, dull, mute, stop; **6** dampen, deaden, muzzle, stifle; **7** smother; **8** ensconce, suppress

muffled: 4 dull; **5** muted; **6** covert; **7** stifled; **8** allusive, dampened, softened

muffler: 5 plaid; **8** silencer; **9** comforter

mufti: 6 civies; **15** civilian clothes

mug: 3 rob; **4** face, fish, fool, gull, mark; **5** chump, patsy; **6** kisser, mugful, smiler, sucker, visage; **7** compote, creamer, fall guy, gudgeon, pitcher; **8** shlemiel; **9** schlemiel; **11** countenance, physiognomy

mugger: 4 hood; **5** brute, bully, rough, rowdy, thief, tough; **6** robber, savage, wretch; **7** hoodlum, ruffian; **8** hooligan

mugging: 6 holdup [U.S.]; **7** robbery

muggy: 6 steamy, sticky

mugho pine: 8 mugo pine

Mugil: 6 mullet; **10** genus Mugil

mugwump: 11 independent

Muhammad: 7 Mahomet, Mahound; **8** Mohammed

Muhammadan: 6 Moslem, Muslim; **10** Mohammedan, Muhammedan

Muhammadanism: 5 Islam; **8** Islamism; **9** Muslimism; **13** Mohammedanism

mujik: 6 moujik, muzhik, muzjik

mulatto: 10 mixed-blood

mulberry family: 8 Moraceae

mulct: 3 con, tag; **4** bilk, fine, rook; **5** bunco, pluck; **6** amerce, diddle, fleece, nobble, pigeon, sconce, sponge; **7** defraud, swindle

mule: 8 smuggler, stubborn

mule deer: 5 scuff; **9** burro deer

mule skinner: 8 muleteer; **10** mule driver

mulish: 9 pig-headed, obstinate; **10** hard-headed

mulishly: 8 cussedly; **10** obdurately, stubbornly; **11** obstinately, pig-headedly
mull: 4 mole, muse, spur; **5** jetty; **6** ponder; **7** reflect; **8** chew over, meditate, mull over, ruminate; **9** pulverize, speculate, think over; **10** breakwater; **11** contemplate
mullah: 7 muezzin; **9** ayatollah
mulligan stew: 8 mulligan; **11** Irish burgoo
mullion: 4 jamb; **8** abutment, buttress
mull over: 4 mull, muse; **6** ponder; **7** reflect; **8** chew over, meditate, ruminate; **9** speculate, think over; **11** contemplate
multicolor: 4 pied; **6** motley; **7** painted, piebald; **11** varicolored; **12** multicolored, particolored
multifaceted: 9 many-sided; **12** multifarious
multifarious: 7 diverse; **8** polyglot; **9** many-sided, multifold, multiform, multiplex; **12** multifaceted, polymorphous; **13** heterogeneous
multifold: 4 many; **8** numerous; **9** multiform, multiplex; **12** multifarious, polymorphous
multiform: 9 multifold, multiplex; **12** multifarious, polymorphous
multihued: 14 rainbow-colored
multilateral: 9 many-sided
multinominal: 10 polynomial
multiple: 5 thick; **6** plural; **7** crowded, peopled, product, studded, teeming; **8** manifold, populous; **9** upwards of; **10** multiplied; **12** multinominal; **13** multitudinous
multiple lens: 10 lens system; **12** compound lens
multiple personality: 16 split personality
multiple sclerosis: 2 MS
multiplex: 8 manifold; **9** multifold, multiform; **12** multifarious, polymorphous
multiplication: 5 times; **10** generation; **11** propagation
multiplicity: 9 plurality; **10** numerosity; **12** numerousness
multiplied: 5 thick; **7** crowded, peopled, studded, teeming; **8** manifold, multiple, populous; **12** multinominal; **13** multitudinous
multiply: 4 teem; **5** breed; **6** divide, repeat; **8** manifold; **9** outnumber, procreate, propagate, reproduce
multiprocessing: 8 parallel
multistage rocket: 7 booster
multitude: 4 mass, pack; **6** masses, people, throng
multitudinous: 5 thick; **6** myriad; **7** crowded, peopled, studded, teeming; **8** infinite, manifold, multiple, populous; **9** countless, uncounted; **10** innumerous, multiplied, numberless, unnumbered; **11** innumerable, unnumerable; **12** multinominal, unnumberable
multivalent: 10 polyvalent; **11** multivalued
mum: 2 ma; **3** mom; **4** hush!, mama, mute; **5** mamma, mammy, mater, momma, mommy, mummy; **6** silent; **7** silence!; **13** chrysanthemum
mumble: 3 gum; **4** bite, chew, gnaw; **5** champ, munch; **6** crunch, maffle, mutter; **7** maunder, munch on; **9** masticate, mussitate
mumbler: 8 mutterer
mumblety-peg: 6 shinny; **7** shinney; **8** pushball; **12** mumble-the-peg
mumbo jumbo: 8 nonsense; **9** gibberish; **10** hocus-pocus; **12** hugger-mugger
mummer: 4 mime; **5** mimer; **6** masque; **10** pantomimer; **11** pantomimist
mummery: 6 vagary; **8** escapade, flummery; **9** poppycock; **10** masquerade, tomfoolery
mummichog: 9 killifish
mummify: 5 dry up; **6** embalm
mummy: 2 ma; **3** mom, mum; **4** mama; **5** mamma, mammy, mater, momma, mommy
mumps: 9 parotitis
munch: 4 bite, chew, gnaw; **5** champ; **6** crunch, mumble, nibble; **7** munch on; **9** masticate
mundane: 7 earthly, routine, terrene, worldly; **8** everyday, workaday; **9** quotidian; **11** terrestrial, worldly-wise; **12** unremarkable
mung bean: 4 mung; **9** green gram; **10** golden gram
Munich: 8 Muenchen
municipal: 4 city
municipal center: 3 hub; **8** downtown; **11** civic center
municipality: 4 city; **10** metropolis; **11** corporation
munificence: 6 bounty; **7** charity, largess; **8** largesse; **10** generosity, liberality; **11** magnanimity
munificent: 4 free; **6** giving, lavish; **7** liberal; **8** generous, handsome, princely, prodigal; **9** bounteous, bountiful, unselfish, unsparing, unstinted; **10** charitable
munition: 4 arms; **8** weaponry, ordnance; **10** ammunition
mural: 12 wall painting
murder: 3 hit; **4** kill, slay; **6** mangle, remove, whack; **7** bump off, butcher, slaying; **8** dispatch, homicide, mutilate; **9** polish off, slaughter, victimize; **11** assassinate; **12** manslaughter
murderer: 6 killer, hit man; **9** terrorist; **10** liquidator
murderous: 9 cutthroat, homicidal; **12** slaughterous
murk: 3 fog; **5** gloom; **9** fogginess, murkiness, obscurity
murkiness: 3 fog; **4** murk; **9** dirtiness, fogginess, muddiness, smokiness; **10** cloudiness
murky: 5 dingy, dirty, dusky, mirky, muddy,

M

smoky, sooty, thick; **6** cloudy, pitchy, turbid; **10** obfuscated

murmur: 4 moan, purl, sigh; **5** croak, gnarl, groan, growl, grunt, spray, spurt, whine; **6** babble, bubble, clamor, gurgle, mutter, plaint; **7** grizzle, grumble, heaving, maunder, sputter; **8** deep sigh; **9** complaint, grumbling, murmuring, muttering; **11** heart murmur

murrain: 3 pox; **6** plague; **10** pestilence

Musa: 6 banana; **9** genus Musa

Musales: 6 banana; **8** plantain

muscadine: 9 ambrosial

Musca domestica: 8 housefly

muscae volitantes: 7 floater

Muscari: 8 hyacinth; **12** genus Muscari

Muscat: 6 Masqat; **13** capital of Oman

muscat grape: 6 muscat, muskat; **8** muscadel, muscatel; **10** muscadelle

muscle: 5 brawn, nerve, sinew; **8** musculus, physique

musclebuilder: 11 bodybuilder

muscle memory: 11 motor memory

muscle sense: 11 kinesthesia, kinesthesis

muscle system: 11 musculature

muscovy duck: 8 musk duck

muscular: 4 wiry; **5** hefty; **6** brawny, sinewy; **8** gigantic, powerful, stalwart, well-knit; **9** strapping, well-built; **11** mesomorphic; **15** broad-shouldered

muscular structure: 11 musculature

musculus: 6 muscle

muse: 4 mull; **5** dream; **6** ponder; **7** reflect; **8** chew over, meditate, mull over, ruminate; **9** speculate, think over; **11** contemplate

museum: 7 gallery

mush: 12 cornmeal mush

mushiness: 7 schmalz; **8** schmaltz; **9** pulpiness

mushroom: 4 grow; **5** fungus; **7** upstart; **9** toadstool; **13** mushroom cloud

mushy: 5 pulpy; **6** slushy; **7** maudlin, mawkish; **8** bathetic, schmalzy; **9** schmaltzy; **11** sentimental

music: 4 tune; **7** euphony; **10** sheet music

musical: 7 melodic; **9** melodious

musical comedy: 7 musical; **14** musical theater

musical composition: 4 opus, work; **5** piece; **6** number; **11** composition

musical instrument digital interface: 4 MIDI

musical performer: 6 player

musical rhythm: 4 beat

musical theater: 7 musical; **13** musical comedy

musical theme: 4 idea; **5** theme

music director: 9 conductor

music hall: 10 vaudeville; **11** concert hall

musician: 6 player; **7** artiste; **9** performer; **15** instrumentalist

music lover: 11 concert-goer

music paper: 10 score paper

music rack: 10 music stand

musing: 6 broody; **7** pensive; **8** brooding; **9** pondering, reflexion; **10** meditation, meditative, reflection, reflective, rumination, ruminative; **13** contemplation, contemplative; **14** thoughtfulness

musjid: 6 masjid, mosque

musk duck: 11 muscovy duck

musket: 9 flintlock

musketeer: 8 rifleman

muskmelon: 9 cantaloup; **10** cantaloupe

muskrat: 8 musquash

musk turtle: 8 stinkpot

Muslim: 6 Moslem; **7** Islamic; **10** Mohammedan, Muhammadan, Muhammedan

muslin: 5 gauze

Mus musculus: 10 house mouse

musquash: 7 muskrat

muss: 4 heap, mash, mess; **6** muddle, tussle

Mussolini: 6 Il Duce; **15** Benito Mussolini

mussy: 5 messy

must: 4 have, mold, need; **5** got to, gotta, musty, ought; **6** have to, mildew, need to, should

mustache: 9 moustache

mustachio: 10 handlebars, moustachio

mustang: 5 bronc; **6** bronco

mustard family: 10 Cruciferae; **12** Brassicaceae

mustard gas: 7 mustard; **13** sulfur mustard

Mustela: 4 mink; **6** ermine, ferret, weasel; **7** polecat; **12** genus Mustela

muster: 4 poll; **5** draft, rally; **6** census, come up, gather, recite, summon; **7** collect; **8** assemble, muster up, roll call; **10** capitation

muster in: 5 draft; **6** enlist

muster out: 9 discharge

mustiness: 9 moldiness

musty: 4 must; **5** fusty, moldy, rusty; **6** mouldy; **8** mildewed; **9** moth-eaten

mutable: 8 variable; **9** checkered; **10** changeable; **12** ever changing

mutant: 5 freak, sport; **6** change; **8** mutation

mutate: 4 vary; **5** alter; **6** change; **8** modulate

mutation: 5 sport; **6** change, mutant; **9** variation; **10** alteration

mute: 3 mum; **4** damp, dull; **5** dummy, extra; **6** dampen, deaden, dental, labial, liquid, muffle, silent

muted: 4 dull; **5** quiet; **6** hushed; **7** muffled, subdued; **8** softened

mutilate: 3 mar; **5** cut up; **6** damage, deface, deform, garble, impair, mangle, murder; **7** blemish; **8** amputate, truncate; **9** disfigure

mutilated: 6 docked, lopped, maimed;

7 damaged, garbled, mangled; **8** impaired; **9** truncated

mutilation: 6 damage; **7** maiming; **8** damaging; **9** impairing; **10** impairment

mutineer: 5 rebel; **8** revolter; **9** insurgent; **15** insurrectionist

muting: 9 silencing

mutinous: 7 riotous; **9** insurgent, seditions

mutiny: 5 rebel; **9** rebellion; **10** revolution

mutt: 3 cur; **7** mongrel

mutter: 4 moan, sigh; **5** croak, gnarl, groan, growl, grunt, snarl, whine; **6** clamor, maffle, mumble, murmur, plaint; **7** grizzle, grumble, heaving, maunder; **9** complaint, grumbling, murmuring, muttering

mutton chop: 8 burnside, sideburn; **12** sidewhiskers

muttonhead: 5 dunce; **8** bonehead, bull head, lunkhead, numskull; **9** blockhead; **10** dunderhead, hammerhead, loggerhead, noodlehead; **11** beetlebrain, knucklehead

mutual: 6 common; **10** reciprocal; **11** commutative; **12** exchangeable; **13** reciprocative; **15** interchangeable

mutual fund: 11 open-end fund

mutuality: 4 link; **10** connection, mutualness; **11** association, correlation; **13** interrelation

mutually: 12 reciprocally

muzhik: 5 mujik; **6** moujik, muzjik

muzzle: 3 gag, lip; **4** lame, maim; **5** snout; **6** bridle, muffle; **7** cripple, smother; **8** double up, gunpoint, paralyze, suppress; **9** gun muzzle, hamstring, prostrate

muzzy: 4 hazy; **5** dizzy, foggy, fuzzy, wooly; **6** addled, bleary, blurry, woolly; **7** blurred, maudlin, muddled, screwed, sewed up; **8** whittled; **9** befuddled, **10** obfuscated

mV: 9 millivolt

Mv: 2 Md; **11** mendelevium

Mx: 7 maxwell

Mya: clam; 8 genus Mya

Myanmar: 5 Burma

Mycostatin: 8 nystatin

myelin: 7 medulla, myeline

mynah: 4 mina, myna; **5** minah; **8** myna bird; **9** mynah bird

myocardial inflammation: 11 myocarditis

myopia: 15 nearsightedness

myopic: 9 ametropic; **10** astigmatic, presbyopic; **12** shortsighted; **16** visually impaired

myriad: 8 infinite; **9** countless, uncounted; **10** innumerous, numberless, unnumbered;

11 innumerable, unnumerable; **12** unnumberable; **13** multitudinous

Myricaceae: 15 wax-myrtle family

Myristica: 6 nutmeg; **14** genus Myristica

Myristicaceae: 12 nutmeg family

Myrmecobius: 6 numbat; **8** anteater; **16** genus Myrmecobius

myrrh: 4 balm

Myrrhis: 5 myrrh; **12** genus Myrrhis

Myrsinaceae: 13 myrsine family

myrsine family: 11 Myrsinaceae

Myrtaceae: 12 myrtle family

myrtle family: 9 Myrtaceae

Myrtus: 12 common myrtle; **11** genus Myrtus

mysterious: 3 dim; **4** dark, deep; **5** dense, muddy; **6** mystic, occult, opaque, secret; **7** cryptic, obscure; **8** confused, mystical, nebulous; **9** cryptical; **10** mystifying; **11** inscrutable

mystery: 5 craft; **6** enigma, puzzle, riddle, secret; **8** whodunit; **10** closed book, handicraft, occultness; **11** miracle play

mystic: 4 dark; **5** weird; **6** occult, secret; **8** mystical, oracular; **9** recondite; **10** cabalistic, mysterious, talismanic; **11** incantatory

mystical: 6 mystic, occult, secret; **10** mysterious

mysticism: 9 occult art; **13** mystification, pseudoscience

mystification: 9 mysticism; **10** bafflement, bemusement, puzzlement; **11** obfuscation; **12** befuddlement, bewilderment; **13** pseudoscience

mystify: 5 amaze, elude, evade; **6** baffle, gravel, puzzle; **7** flummox, nonplus, perplex, stupefy, stupify, trounce; **8** bewilder; **9** dumbfound, obfuscate; **10** equivocate

mystifying: 4 deep; **7** cryptic; **8** baffling, puzzling; **9** cryptical, enigmatic; **10** mysterious; **11** inscrutable

myth: 5 fable; **6** legend; **7** parable, allegory

mythic: 8 fabulous, mythical; **10** mythologic; **12** mythological

mythologic: 6 mythic; **8** fabulous, mythical; **12** mythological

Mytilidae: 15 family Mytilidae

Mytilus: 12 edible mussel, genus Mytilus

myxobacter: 12 myxobacteria; **13** myxobacterium, slime bacteria; **15** gliding bacteria

M

N: 5 north; **6** newton; **8** due north, nitrogen

N'Djamena: 8 Fort-Lamy; **13** capital of Chad

N.B.: 8 nota bene [Lat], note well

Na: 6 sodium

nab: 2 do; **3** bag, con, cop; **4** bilk, bite, hook, nail, sack, scam; **5** catch, cheat, cozen, pluck; **6** arrest, chouse, collar, diddle, euchre, jockey, pick up, pocket; **7** defraud, swindle; **9** apprehend, victimize

nabob: 9 maharajah [India]

nacre: 4 mica; **13** mother-of-pearl

nacreous: 4 shot; **6** pearly; **7** frosted, opaline; **9** prismatic; **10** iridescent, opalescent; **11** pearlescent

nada: 3 nil, nix, zip; **4** zero; **5** aught, zilch; **6** cipher, cypher, naught; **7** nothing; **8** goose egg

nadir: 4 base, foot; **6** bottom; **12** low-water mark

nag: 4 hack, jade, peck, plug; **5** horse, scold, skate [U.S.]; **6** badger, bicker, cayuse [U.S.], jangle, nagger; **7** hen-peck, palfrey, scolder, wrangle; **8** squabble

nagger: 3 nag; **5** scold; **7** scolder

nagging: 8 shrewish

naiad: 4 peri; **5** dryad, nymph; **6** nereid; **10** water nymph

naiant: 8 swimming

naif: 4 lain, pure; **5** naive; **6** native, simple; **7** artless, ingenue, natural; **9** unspoiled; **10** unaffected; **11** undesigning

nail: 3 cop, ell, nab, peg, pin; **4** bolt, boom, brad, claw, hasp, line, mile, palm, pass, pole, rood, rope, tack, yard; **5** blast, clamp, clasp, crimp, cubit, rivet, screw, smash, talon; **6** arrest, collar, fathom, league, make it, pick up; **7** furlong; **8** complete, nail down; **9** apprehend; **10** fingernail

nail to the cross: 7 crucify

Nairobi: 14 capital of Kenya

naive: 4 lain, naif, pure; **6** callow, native, simple; **7** artless, natural; **9** unspoiled; **10** unaffected; **11** undesigning; **13** inexperienced; **15** unsophisticated

Naja: 3 asp; **9** genus Naja, hamadryad, king cobra; **13** spitting cobra, Egyptian cobra

naked: 3 raw; **4** bare, nude; **7** unaided; **9** au naturel; **11** defenseless

nakedness: 6 nudity; **8** bareness, nudeness

namby-pamby: 7 mincing; **9** simpering, spineless; **10** wishy-washy; **11** sentimental

name: 3 dub, key; **4** call, cite, gens, hire, list, make, mark, term; **5** refer, style, title; **6** advert, engage, figure, key out, return; **7** appoint, bespeak, bring up, entitle, epithet, mention; **8** accredit, describe, diagnose, discover, identify, nominate; **9** designate;

10 constitute, denominate; **11** designation, distinction, distinguish; **12** denomination, nomenclature

named: 6 called, styled, termed; **10** designated; **11** denominated

nameless: 7 unknown, unnamed; **9** anonymous; **10** innominate; **12** unidentified; **14** unacknowledged

namelessness: 9 anonymity

namely: 2 e.g. [abbr], i.e. [abbr]; **3** viz. [abbr]; **5** id est, to wit; **9** videlicet; **10** for example; **14** exemplia gratia [Lat]

name part: 9 title role

naming: 7 calling; **10** assignment, nomination; **11** appellative, appointment, designating, designation; **12** denominating, nomenclature

Nanking: 7 Nanjing

nanny: 5 nurse; **7** she-goat; **9** nanny-goat, nursemaid; **10** babysitter

nano-: 9 billionth

nanometer: 2 nm

nanosecond: 10 picosecond; **11** femtosecond

Nantua: 11 shrimp sauce

nap: 4 doze; **5** sleep; **6** catnap, siesta, snooze

napa: 6 pe-tsai; **14** Chinese cabbage

nape: 6 scruff

napery: 10 table linen

naphthoquinone: 8 vitamin K

Napier: 10 John Napier

Napier's bones: 11 Napier's rods

Napierian logarithm: 16 natural logarithm

napkin: 5 cloth, nappy; **6** diaper; **9** serviette

Napoleon Bonaparte: 8 Napoleon; **9** Napoleon I

napped: 6 fleecy; **7** brushed

napping: 4 dozy; **6** dozing, drowsy; **7** nodding; **8** drowsing

nappy: 2 up; **5** crisp, kinky; **6** diaper, frizzy, frothy, napkin; **7** frizzly, maudlin, muddled, screwed, sewed up; **8** mousseux [Fr], whittled; **9** sparkling; **10** obfuscated; **12** effervescent

naproxen sodium: 5 Aleve; **7** Aflaxen, Anaprox

narc: 4 nark; **14** narcotics agent

narcissism: 7 narcism; **8** self-love

narcissistic: 9 egotistic; **10** self-loving; **11** egotistical

narcotic: 9 soporific; **11** narcotizing; **12** soporiferous

narcotics agent: 4 narc, nark

narcotized: 5 doped; **7** drugged

nard: 9 spikenard

narghile: 6 hookah, kalian; **9** water pipe

nark: 3 rag, vex; **4** narc, rile; **5** annoy, devil, get at, get to; **6** bother, gravel, nettle; **8** irritate; **11** copper's nark; **14** narcotics agent

narrate: 4 spin, tell; 6 recite, relate; 7 recount

narration: 4 tale, yarn; 5 story; 7 account, recital; 9 narrative

narrative: 4 epic, tale, yarn; 5 story; 7 account, recital; 9 narration

narrator: 6 teller; 7 relator; 9 raconteur; 11 storyteller

narrow: 4 thin, 5 close, taper; 6 draw in, minute, temper; 7 peg down, pin down, specify; 8 contract, nail down; 9 constrict; 10 constringe

narrow down: 6 narrow; 7 peg down, pin down, specify; 8 nail down; 10 specialize

narrowed: 7 tapered; 8 stenotic [Med], tapering; 9 narrowing; 11 constricted

narrowing: 5 taper; 7 tapered; 8 narrowed, tapering; 11 constricted; 12 constricting, constrictive

narrow-minded: 4 mean; 6 narrow; 9 illiberal, shockable; 10 ungenerous

narrow-mindedly: 13 small-mindedly

narrows: 6 strait; 7 channel

narwhal: 6 narwal; 8 narwhale; 16 Monodon monoceros

nasal: 6 rhinal; 7 pinched; 8 os nasale; 9 adenoidal, nasal bone

nasal bone: 5 nasal; 8 os nasale

nasal tone: 11 nasal accent

nascence: 5 birth; 8 nascency, nativity

nascent: 5 natal; 7 newborn; 8 emergent, emerging, neonatal [Med]; 10 new-fledged

NASDAQ: 11 NASDAQ index; 14 over-the-counter

Nashville: 18 capital of Tennessee

Nassau: 19 capital of the Bahamas

Nasser: 16 Gamal Abdel Nasser

Nast: 10 Thomas Nast

nastily: 6 meanly

nastiness: 5 filth, spite; 8 foulness; 9 cattiness; 10 filthiness; 12 spitefulness

nasty: 4 foul, vile; 5 awful, reeky, tight; 6 coarse, filthy, smutty; 7 beastly; 9 offensive, repulsive; 10 abominable

Nasua: 5 coati; 7 coon cat; 10 coati-mondi, coati-mundi, genus Nasua

natal: 6 native; 7 nascent

natal day: 8 birthday

natator: 6 bather; 7 swimmer

natatorium: 12 swimming bath, swimming pool

nation: 4 land, race; 5 state, stock; 7 a people, country; 11 body politic, nationality; 12 commonwealth

national: 4 home; 5 civic, human; 6 mortal, public, social; 7 citizen, federal, subject; 8 interior, internal, personal; 10 individual

National Aeronautics and Space Administration: 4 NASA

National Guard: 11 home reserve

national holiday: 12 legal holiday

National Institutes of Health: 3 NIH

nationalism: 10 patriotism

Nationalist China: 5 China; 6 Taiwan; 7 Formosa; 15 Republic of China

nationalistic: 10 flag-waving, jingoistic; 11 nationalist; 12 chauvinistic; 14 superpatriotic

nationality: 4 land; 6 nation; 7 a people, country; 10 patriotism; 11 citizenship

National Labor Relations Board: 4 NLRB [acron] [U.S.]

national leader: 5 solon; 9 statesman

nationally: 10 nationwide

national socialism: 6 Nazism

national socialist: 4 Nazi

nationwide: 10 nationally; 11 countrywide

native: 4 lain, naif, pure; 5 naive, natal; 6 inborn, inbred, simple; 7 artless, natural; 8 indigene; 9 unspoiled; 10 aboriginal, connatural, indigenous, unaffected; 11 undesigning

Native American: 10 Amerindian; 14 American Indian

native Australian: 3 Abo; 9 Aborigine; 10 Aboriginal

native country: 8 homeland; 10 fatherland

native inhabitant: 6 native; 8 indigene

native intelligence: 3 wit; 8 capacity, keenness; 12 intelligence; 13 comprehension, understanding; 15 intellectuality, quick-wittedness

native land: 8 homeland; 10 fatherland, motherland, native soil

Nativity: 11 Virgin Birth

nativity: 5 birth; 6 cradle; 7 genesis, infancy; 8 nascence, nascency; 9 horoscope

natrium: 6 sodium

natter: 3 jaw; 4 chat; 5 visit; 6 claver, confab, gossip; 7 chaffer, chatter; 8 chitchat; 11 confabulate

natty: 4 neat, tidy, trig, trim; 5 smart; 6 dapper, jaunty, quaint, rakish, snappy, spruce; 7 dashing, raffish

natural: 3 raw; 4 easy, flat, lain, naif, pure, rude, wild; 5 loose, naive, plain, sharp, sound; 6 cancel, casual, fluent, native, normal, severe, simple; 7 artless, default, flowing; 8 graceful, informal

naturalism: 7 realism

naturalize: 5 adopt; 9 cultivate; 11 domesticate

naturally: 4 then; 5 natch; 6 course, simply; 7 naively; 8 by nature, casually, normally, of course; 9 artlessly, as a result; 10 as expected, in that case, informally; 12 consequently, unaffectedly

natural mother: 11 birth mother

naturalness: 8 severity; 9 innocence, plainness; 10 simplicity; 11 artlessness, familiarity; 13 ingenuousness

natural number: 15 positive integer

N

natural selection: 8 survival
natural spring: 6 spring; 7 outflow; 8 fountain
natural state: 4 wild; 6 nature
nature: 3 fit, set; 4 mold, rule, wild; 5 stamp, world; 6 cosmos, spirit; 7 essence, naivete, quality; 8 creation, identity, universe; 9 character, existence, macrocosm; 10 complexion, simplicity
naught: 3 nil, nix, nul, zip; 4 nada, null, void, zero; 5 aught, zilch; 6 cipher, cypher, nought; 7 nothing, nullity; 8 goose egg
naughtily: 5 badly; 13 mischievously
naughty: 4 blue, gamy, racy; 5 gamey, juicy, spicy; 6 risque; 9 incorrect, undutiful; 11 incorrectly, mischievous
nausea: 7 disgust; 8 loathing, sickness; 10 repugnance
nauseate: 4 pall; 5 abhor, shock; 6 loathe, revolt, sicken; 7 churn up, disgust; 9 abominate
nauseated: 4 sick; 6 queasy; 7 sickish
nauseating: 4 vile; 7 noisome; 8 nauseous; 9 loathsome, offensive, sickening; 10 disgusting; 14 stomach-turning
nauseous: 4 vile; 7 noisome; 9 loathsome, offensive, sickening; 10 disgusting, nauseating
nautical: 5 naval; 6 marine; 8 maritime; 9 seafaring
nautical mile: 2 mi; 4 knot, mile; 6 naut mi
nautical signal flag: 8 code flag
Nautilidae: 8 nautilus; 16 family Nautilidae
naut mi: 12 nautical mile
Navajo: 6 Navaho
naval: 8 maritime, nautical; 9 seafaring
naval chart: 10 pilot chart
naval engagement: 8 sea fight
naval engineer: 14 marine engineer
naval school: 12 naval academy
nave: 3 hub; 4 axis; 5 navel
navel: 4 nave; 8 omphalos, omphalus; 9 umbilicus; 11 bellybutton
navicular: 12 scaphoid bone
navigate: 4 sail; 5 pilot; 6 voyage
navigation: 7 boating, sailing; 8 pilotage, piloting; 9 seafaring
navigator: 6 sailor; 7 birdman, mariner
navvy: 7 laborer, workman; 10 workingman; 11 laboring man; 13 manual laborer
navy: 6 marine; 8 dark blue, navy blue
navy bean: 7 pea bean; 9 white bean
navy blue: 4 navy; 8 dark blue
navy man: 6 sailor; 10 bluejacket
nay: 2 no
Naziism: 6 Nazism; 17 national socialism
Nb: 7 niobium
NbE: 11 north by east
NbW: 11 north by west
N by E: 2 NE; 9 northeast

Nd: 9 neodymium
Ndjamena: 8 Fort-Lamy; 13 capital of Chad
NE: 4 N by E; 7 nor'-east; 9 northeast
Ne: 4 neon
ne'er: 5 never
ne'er a one: 3 nil; 4 zero; 6 cipher, naught; 7 nothing, nullity
ne'er-do-well: 3 rip; 5 scamp; 7 goof-off; 8 runagate, scalawag; 9 goldbrick, reprobate, scallawag
neanderthal: 6 oafish; 7 boorish, loutish, swinish
neap: 3 low; 7 compact, debased
neap tide: 4 neap; 7 ebb tide, low tide; 8 low water
near: 4 most, next, nigh; 5 about, close; 6 almost, at hand, closer, come on, go near, nearby, nearly; 8 approach, come near, draw near, well-nigh; 9 just about, virtually; 11 approximate
nearby: 4 near, nigh; 5 about; 6 around; 9 in the area; 13 in the vicinity
Near East: 10 Middle East
nearer: 6 closer, nigher
nearest: 7 closest, nighest
nearing: 11 approaching
nearly: 3 say; 4 most, near, nigh; 5 about; 6 all but, almost; 7 closely, short of; 8 not quite, well-nigh; 9 just about, virtually; 10 intimately; 11 thereabouts; 13 approximately
nearly all: 4 most
nearness: 9 closeness
nearsighted: 12 shortsighted
nearsightedness: 6 myopia
neat: 4 cool, keen, pure, tidy, trig, trim; 5 bully, clean, dandy, exact, great, happy, natty, nifty, sheer, smart, swell; 6 bang-up, groovy, not bad, peachy, quaint, simple, single, slap-up, spruce; 7 compact, orderly, refined, summary, uniform, well put; 8 cracking, straight, succinct, tasteful
neaten: 4 tidy; 5 groom; 6 tidy up; 7 clean up; 10 square away, straighten
neb: 3 nib; 4 beak, bill, nose; 5 snout; 6 nozzle, schnoz; 9 proboscis
Nebraskan: 10 Cornhusker
nebular: 8 nebulous; 9 cloudlike
nebulous: 3 dim; 4 dark; 5 dense, muddy; 6 cloudy, opaque; 7 cryptic, nebular, obscure, unfixed; 8 nebulose, overcast; 10 mysterious
NE by N: 3 NNE
necessary: 6 needed; 7 needful; 8 required; 9 essential, necessity, requisite; 11 requirement
necessitate: 3 ask; 4 make, need, take; 5 drive, force; 6 coerce, compel, demand, oblige; 7 enforce, involve, require; 9 constrain
necessities: 5 needs [pl]; 7 needful; 8 exi-

requirement

necessity: 4 lack, need, want; **5** needs [pl]; **7** needful, poverty; **8** distress, exigency; **9** essential, indigence, necessary, neediness, privation, requisite; **11** destitution, necessities [pl], requirement

neck: 7 make out; **9** hourglass, stricture; **10** bottleneck; **12** constriction

neckband: 6 choker, collar; **9** dog collar

neckcloth: 5 stock; **8** kerchief; **11** neckerchief

necking: 7 hugging, kissing, petting; **8** cuddling, fondling, sparking, sporting; **9** caressing, dalliance, making out, smooching, snuggling

necktie: 3 tie; **5** stock; **6** cravat

necrology: 4 obit; **8** obituary

necromancer: 4 seer; **5** witch; **6** wizard; **8** conjuror, magician, sorcerer

necromancy: 5 magic

necropolis: 8 cemetery; **9** graveyard; **10** burial site; **12** burial ground

necropsy: 2 PM; **7** autopsy; **10** postmortem

necrose: 7 mortify; **8** gangrene

necrosis: 10 local death

nectar: 8 ambrosia

nectarous: 9 ambrosial, ambrosian

need: 3 ask; **4** have, lack, miss, must, take, want; **5** needs [pl], ought; **6** demand, motive, penury, should; **7** call for, have got, involve, poverty, require; **8** distress, exigency; **9** indigence, necessity, neediness, privation; **10** motivation; **11** destitution, necessitate, necessities [pl], requirement

needed: 7 needful; **8** required; **9** necessary, requisite

neediness: 4 lack, need, want; **6** penury; **7** poverty; **8** distress; **9** indigence, necessity, pauperism, privation; **11** destitution

needle: 4 goad, helm; **5** spine; **6** nettle, rudder; **7** compass, pointer, syringe; **10** hypodermic

needlecraft: 10 needlework

needlefish: 3 gar; **8** billfish, pipefish

needlepoint: 9 point lace

needless: 10 gratuitous; **11** superfluous, uncalled for, unnecessary

needs: 4 need; **8** exigency; **9** necessity; **10** inevitably; **11** necessarily, necessities [pl], requirement

needy: 7 pinched; **8** indigent, strapped; **9** destitute; **10** distressed, straitened; **11** necessitous; **12** impoverished

nefarious: 4 base, foul, vile; **5** grave, gross; **6** scurvy; **7** heinous; **8** infamous, shameful, sinister; **9** felonious; **10** scandalous, villainous

negate: 4 deny; **5** belie; **10** contradict, contravene

negative: 3 bad, ill; **4** deny, nill, veto; **5** blank, minus, rebut; **6** negate, refute; **7** confute; **8** confound, damaging, disprove, negatory, positive; **9** blackball; **10** controvert, disconfirm

negative stimulation: 7 turnoff

negativism: 10 negativity

negativist: 9 defeatist

Negev Desert: 5 Negev

neglect: 4 drop, fail, miss, omit; **5** elude, evade, spare, waive; **6** disuse, ignore, laches [Law], slight; **7** abstain, evasion, failure, forbear; **8** forswear, omission, overleap, overlook, renounce, set aside; **9** disregard, do without, indignity, repudiate; **10** be careless, negligence; **12** carelessness, cold-shoulder, inobservance

neglected: 7 disused, ignored; **8** unheeded; **10** overlooked, unattended; **11** disregarded

neglectful: 6 remiss; **8** derelict; **9** negligent, unmindful; **10** delinquent; **11** inattentive

negligee: 7 neglige, pajamas, wrapper; **8** peignoir; **9** housecoat, nightgown

negligence: 7 neglect; **12** carelessness

negligent: 9 unmindful; **10** neglectful

negligible: 4 so-so; **6** paltry; **8** trifling; **12** undetectable; **13** inappreciable, insignificant

negotiable: 9 alienable; **10** assignable, conveyable; **12** transferable; **13** transferrable

negotiant: 10 negotiator

negotiate: 4 hand, pass; **5** treat; **6** step in; **7** bargain; **8** complete, transmit; **9** make terms, negociate, stipulate, talk terms; **10** accomplish

negotiating: 9 parleying; **10** bargaining; **11** negotiation

negotiation: 5 talks; **6** parley; **9** parleying; **10** bargaining, conference; **11** negotiating

negotiator: 9 go-between, negotiant; **10** peacemaker

Nehru: 15 Jawaharlal Nehru

neigh: 6 whinny

neighborhood: 4 ward; **5** block, haunt; **6** barrio [Sp], corner, locale, region; **7** suburbs; **8** confines, enceinte, environs, locality, precinct, vicinity; **9** precincts

neighboring: 5 close; **8** neighbor

neighborly: 6 social; **9** brotherly, fraternal

neither: 9 not either

neither here nor there: 6 forced, remote; **10** far-fetched

Nelumbo: 5 lotus; **11** Indian lotus, sacred lotus; **12** genus Nelumbo

Nematoda: 13 Aschelminthes

nematode: 9 roundworm

Nembutal: 12 yellow jacket; **13** pentobarbital; **19** pentobarbital sodium

nem con: 11 unanimously

nemertean: 9 nemertine; **10** ribbon worm

nemesis: 4 bane; **5** curse; **7** scourge; **9** archenemy

N

neocortex: 10 neopallium
neodymium: 2 Nd
neo jazz: 7 new jazz; **10** modern jazz
Neo-Latin: 8 New Latin
neologism: 7 coinage, neology
neologize: 9 coin a term, coin a word
neomycin: 8 fradicin
Neomys: 10 water shrew; **11** genus Neomys
neon: 2 Ne
neonatal: 7 nascent, newborn; **10** new-
  fledged
neonate: 7 newborn; **11** newborn baby
neophyte: 6 novice; **7** entrant, recruit, starter;
  8 freshman, newcomer; **9** fledgling
neoplasm: 5 tumor
neoplastic disease: 5 tumor; **8** neoplasm
neoteric: 4 late; **6** modern; **7** nouveau; **11**
  hypermodern, modernistic; **12** contemporary, non-classical
Neotoma: 7 woodrat, packrat; **11** genus
  Neotoma
Nepalese: 6 Nepali
Nepeta: 6 catnip; **7** catmint; **11** genus Nepeta
nephanalysis: 12 cloud science
Nephelium: 6 lichee, litchi, longan; **7**
  pulasan; **8** rambotan, rambutan; **14** genus
  Nephelium
nephritic: 5 renal
Nephrolepis: 4 fern; **10** Boston fern; **16**
  genus Nephrolepis
ne plus ultra: 4 acme; **5** ideal, limit, pitch; **6**
  climax, height, summit; **7** maximum; **9**
  sovereign; **10** perfection; **11** superlative; **12**
  flawlessness, incomparable
Neptune: 8 Poseidon
neptunium: 2 Np
nerd: 4 swot, wonk; **5** grind; **6** wombat
nereid: 5 dryad, naiad, nymph; **8** sea
  nymph
nerve: 5 brace, brass, brawn, cheek, cheer,
  heart, pluck, rally, sinew, spunk, steel; **6**
  mettle, muscle, nervus, neuron; **8** boldness,
  embolden, energize, inspirit; **9** encourage,
  nerve cell; **10** effrontery, invigorate,
  strengthen
nerve cell: 6 neuron
nerveless: 4 cool; **6** feeble; **10** coolheaded
nerve pathway: 5 tract
nerve-racking: 6 trying; **9** stressful
nerves: 7 jitters; **11** nervousness
nerve tract: 7 pathway
nervous: 3 shy; **4** edgy; **5** jumpy, nervy,
  shaky; **6** neural, spooky, uneasy; **7** anxious,
  jittery, restive, unquiet, uptight; **8** aflutter,
  forcible, incisive, powerful, sheepish, skittish, vigorous; **9** tremulous, trenchant; **10**
  high-strung, impressive, in suspense, overstrung
nervure: 4 vein
nervus ischiadicus: 12 sciatic nerve

nervus opticus: 10 optic nerve, optic tract;
  18 second cranial nerve
nervy: 4 edgy; **5** brash, jumpy; **6** brazen,
  cheeky; **7** jittery, nervous, restive, uptight;
  10 high-strung, in suspense, overstrung; **11**
  impertinent
nescience: 9 ignorance, unknowing
nescient: 8 ignorant; **9** unlearned; **10** unlettered; **11** unbelieving; **13** unenlightened
ness: 4 cape; **10** promontory
Nessie: 15 Loch Ness monster
nest: 3 fry; **4** bevy, herd, hive, peck, womb; **5**
  brood, cloud, covey, drove, flock, nidus,
  shoal, swarm; **6** bushel, cradle, farrow,
  flight, litter, scores; **7** draught, nursery; **10**
  birthplace
nest egg: 7 savings
nester: 8 squatter; **11** homesteader
nesting: 8 roosting
nestle: 4 live, stay; **5** abide, dwell, house,
  lodge, perch, roost; **6** cuddle, nuzzle,
  reside, tenant; **7** inhabit, snuggle, sojourn;
  8 ensconce
net: 3 bag, web; **4** knit, knot, last, mesh; **5**
  clear, final, get in, lucre, pouch, scrip,
  sieve, toils; **6** budget, meshes, plexus,
  pocket, profit, sachel, sack up, screen,
  secure, sheath, socket; **7** network, profits,
  satchel, webbing; **8** earnings, meshwork,
  reticule, scabbard, seine net; **9** bring home,
  net income, net profit
net gain: 6 profit; **8** earnings, proceeds; **9** net
  profit
nether: 5 lower, under; **8** chthonic; **9** chthonian; **10** nethermost
Netherlander: 8 Dutchman; **9** Hollander
Netherlands: 7 Holland; **14** The Netherlands
nethermost: 6 bottom; **9** lowermost, undermost; **10** bottommost
nether region: 4 Hell; **6** the pit; **7** Inferno; **9**
  perdition
netherworld: 3 Hel; **4** Hell; **5** Hades; **6**
  Scheol; **10** underworld; **14** infernal region
net income: 3 net; **5** lucre; **6** profit; **7** profits;
  8 earnings; **9** net profit
netkeeper: 6 goalie; **10** goalkeeper, goaltender
netmail: 5 e-mail
net profit: 3 net; **5** lucre; **6** profit; **7** net gain,
  profits; **8** earnings, proceeds; **9** net income
nett: 3 net
netting: 5 gauze; **6** tissue; **7** veiling
nettle: 3 rag, vex; **4** fang, fret, gall, goad,
  huff, nark, rile, tang; **5** annoy, brier, chafe,
  devil, get at, get to, pique, sting, thorn; **6**
  bother, gravel, needle, ruffle; **7** bramble,
  provoke; **8** irritate; **10** discompose
nettled: 5 riled, stung; **6** peeved, pissed,
  roiled; **7** annoyed; **9** irritated
nettle family: 10 Urticaceae
nettle rash: 5 hives; **9** urticaria
nettlesome: 5 pesky, techy, testy; **6** cranky,

plaguy, tetchy, vexing; **7** galling, peckish, peevish, pettish, plaguey, teasing; **8** annoying, petulant; **9** fractious, irritable, pestering, vexatious; **10** bothersome, irritating

network: 3 net, web; **4** mesh; **8** meshwork; **9** labyrinth; **12** reticulation

neural: 6 dorsal; **7** nervous; **8** neuronal, neuronic

neuralgia: 7 lumbago

neuroglia: 4 glia

neurologist: 11 brain doctor

neuron: 5 nerve; **9** nerve cell

neurosurgeon: 12 brain surgeon

Neurotrichus: 9 shrew mole; **17** genus Neurotrichus

neuter: 3 fix; **4** spay; **5** alter; **7** neutral, sexless; **8** castrate

neutered: 5 fixed; **7** altered; **9** castrated

neutral: 2 OK; **4** okay; **5** inert; **6** neuter; **8** innocent; **9** apathetic, innocuous, uncharged, uncurious; **10** impersonal; **11** indifferent, inoffensive; **12** uninterested; **13** disinterested

neutrality: 6 apathy; **7** balance; **11** disinterest; **12** indifference

neutralization: 8 equating, equation; **9** balancing; **12** neutralizing; **13** counteraction

neutralize: 4 undo; **5** cover; **6** fill up; **7** nullify; **10** counteract; **11** countervail; **14** counterbalance

neutralizer: 6 buffer

neutral spirits: 12 ethyl alcohol

nevee: 7 glacier; **8** ice river

never: 4 ne'er; **7** not ever

never again: 9 nevermore

never-ending: 8 constant; **9** ceaseless, incessant, perpetual, unceasing; **10** never-dying; **11** unremitting

never married: 5 unwed; **9** unmarried

never-never land: 9 dreamland; **10** dreamworld

nevertheless: 3 yet; **5** still; **6** even so, withal; **7** however; **10** all the same; **11**, nonetheless; **15** notwithstanding

nevus: 9 birthmark

new: 3 raw; **4** baby; **5** fresh, green, new to, newly, novel, young; **6** recent; **7** freshly; **8** original, recently; **10** newfangled, unexampled

newborn: 7 neonate, nascent; **8** neonatal [Med]; **9** new-sprung, unfledged; **10** new-fledged

Newcastle-upon-Tyne: 9 Newcastle

newcomer: 7 entrant, starter; **8** freshman, intruder, neophyte; **9** fledgling, immigrant, novus homo [Lat]; **10** fledgeling, interloper

New Delhi: 14 capital of India

new edition: 7 reprint

newel post: 5 newel

New Englander: 4 Yank; **6** Yankee

newest: 4 last; **6** latest; **8** up-to-date

newfangled: 3 new; **12** new-fashioned

New Guinea: 5 Papua

New Hebrides: 7 Vanuatu

new jazz: 7 neo jazz; **10** modern jazz

New Latin: 8 Neo-Latin

newly: 3 new; **5** fresh; **7** freshly; **8** recently

newlywed: 11 honeymooner

new model: 6 recast, reform; **7** remodel; **10** reorganize

new money: 12 nouveau riche

new moon: 17 new phase of the moon

newness: 7 novelty, recency; **9** freshness; **11** originality

New Norwegian: 7 Nynorsk; **8** Landsmal

new phase of the moon: 7 new moon

new printing: 7 reprint

news: 4 word; **6** advice; **7** message, tidings; **8** news show; **10** public news; **11** news program; **12** intelligence; **14** newsworthiness

news agency: 11 press agency, wire service

newsagent: 10 newsdealer, newsvendor

newsboy: 7 carrier

news bulletin: 5 flash; **9** newsflash

newscaster: 8 reporter; **10** journalist; **12** anchorperson; **13** correspondent

news department: 8 news team

news flash: 5 flash; **8** bulletin; **9** fresh news; **10** news just in

newsletter: 9 newssheet

news media: 5 media; **10** journalism; **12** fourth estate

newspaper: 5 daily, paper; **8** magazine; **9** newsprint

newspaper clipping: 7 cutting; **8** clipping

newspaperman: 8 pressman; **10** newswriter; **13** correspondent; **14** newspaperwoman

news report: 5 story; **6** report; **7** account, write up

news reporting: 9 reporting; **10** journalism

news secretary: 10 press agent; **14** press secretary

newsstand operator: 10 newsdealer, newsvendor

New Style: 17 Gregorian calendar

newswire: 6 ticker

newsy: 6 chatty; **7** gossipy

Newton: 8 Sir Isaac; **11** Isaac Newton; **14** Sir Isaac Newton

new to the field: 3 raw; **5** green; **11** uninitiated; **13** inexperienced

New Wave: 13 Nouvelle Vague

new woman: 8 feminist

New World: 8 occident; **17** western hemisphere

New Year's Eve party: 8 bonenkai [Jap]

New York: 11 Empire State, New York City; **12** New York State

New York minute: 4 wink; **5** flash, jiffy, trice; **7** instant; **9** twinkling; **11** split second

N

New York Stock Exchange: 8 big board
next: 4 near; 6 future; 8 adjacent; 9 following, thereupon, upon which; 10 subsequent, succeeding
next-day delivery: 11 express mail; 13 overnight mail
next generation: 2 F1; 15 first generation
next-to-last: 6 junior; 9 third-year; 11 penultimate
nexus: 4 link; 5 focus; 6 center; 10 connection
Ni: 6 nickel
niacin: 13 nicotinic acid
Niagara: 12 Niagara Falls, Niagara River
Niamey: 14 capital of Niger
nib: 3 cap, neb, nip, tip; 4 beak, bill, snip, tusk; 5 crest, point, tooth, truck; 6 pen nib; 9 crow's nest
nibble: 4 pick; 5 munch, piece
nibbling: 8 munching
nice: 4 fine, good; 5 picky, sweet, tasty; 6 dainty, decent, prissy, savory; 7 correct, curious, finical, finicky; 8 delicate, gracious, overnice, punctual, skillful; 9 courteous, delicious, palatable, squeamish; 10 delectable, fastidious, particular
Nicene Creed: 13 Apostles' Creed
nicety: 5 shade; 6 nuance; 8 delicacy, justness, subtlety; 9 epicurism, exactness, rightness; 10 refinement
niche: 4 hole, nook; 6 corner, recess; 9 recession
nick: 3 cut; 4 chip, dent; 5 gouge, notch, score, snick; 6 indent
nicked: 6 dented, jagged; 7 notched; 8 indented
nickel: 2 Ni
nickel-and-dime: 9 small-time
nickel-cadmium accumulator: 5 nicad
nickelodeon: 7 jukebox
nickel silver: 12 German silver
nicker: 5 neigh; 6 whinny; 7 whicker
nicknack: 5 curio; 6 bauble, gewgaw, trifle; 7 bibelot, novelty, trinket, whatnot; 8 chotchke, gimcrack, kickshaw, whimwham; 9 bagatelle, bric-a-brac, tchotchke; 10 knickknack
nickname: 3 dub; 6 by-name; 7 moniker, pet name; 8 cognomen; 9 sobriquet
Nicosia: 15 capital of Cyprus
Nicotiana: 7 tobacco; 14 genus Nicotiana
nicotinic acid: 6 niacin
nictitate: 4 wink; 5 blink; 7 nictate
nidus: 4 nest, womb; 5 focus; 6 cradle, hotbed; 7 nursery; 10 birthplace
nifty: 4 cool, keen, neat; 5 dandy, great, swell; 6 bang-up, groovy, peachy, slap-up; 7 corking; 8 cracking, smashing
Niger: 10 Niger River
niggard: 4 crib; 5 churl, harpy, hunks, miser, screw; 6 codger, scrimp, usurer; 7 grabber, scrooge; 9 skinflint; 10 curmudgeon
niggardly: 4 mean, near, vile; 5 cheap, close, sorry, weedy; 6 meager, scrimy, scurvy, shabby, stingy, trashy; 7 miserly, scrubby; 8 gimcrack, grudging, peddling, trumpery, wretched; 9 miserable, penny wise, worthless
niggle: 4 carp, fret, fuss, gibe, gird, hiss, hoot, jeer, twit; 5 taunt, trifle; 6 bicker, deride; 7 quibble, snigger; 8 pettifog, ridicule, squabble
niggling: 5 petty; 6 little; 7 trivial; 8 fiddling, picayune, piddling, piffling; 9 frivolous
nigh: 4 most, near; 5 about, close; 6 all but, almost, nearby, nearly; 8 well-nigh; 9 just about, virtually
night: 4 dark; 7 evening; 9 nighttime, nightfall
night and day: 6 always; 8 ever anon, steadily; 9 routinely; 10 constantly, invariably; 11 continually, incessantly, perpetually, unfailingly, without fail; 12 consistently, continuously, monotonously
night blindness: 10 nyctalopia
nightclothes: 9 nightwear
nightclub: 7 cabaret
nightcrawler: 7 dew worm, red worm, wiggler; 8 fishworm; 9 angleworm, earthworm; 11 fishing worm, nightwalker
nighted: 9 benighted
nightfall: 4 dusk, fall; 6 curfew; 8 evenfall, eventide, gloaming, twilight
nightgown: 7 nightie, pajamas; 8 negligee; 10 night shirt; 12 dressing gown
nightie: 9 night-robe, nightgown; 10 nightdress
Nightingale: 19 Florence Nightingale
nightingale: 6 thrush; 20 Luscinia megarhynchos
nightjar: 10 goatsucker
nightlong: 9 overnight
nightmare: 7 bugaboo, bugbear, incubus; 8 bad dream
nightmarish: 11 hair-raising; 13 bloodcurdling
nightshade: 10 belladonna
night shift: 9 graveyard
nightstick: 5 billy, stick; 9 billy club, truncheon; 10 billystick
night student: 7 auditor; 15 part-time student
nighttime: 4 dark; 5 night
night walker: 11 sleepwalker; 12 somnambulist
nihilist: 9 anarchist; 11 syndicalist
nil: 3 nix, zip; 4 nada, zero; 5 aught, nihil, zilch; 6 cipher, cypher, naught; 7 nothing, nullity; 8 goose egg, ne'er a one
Nile: 9 Nile River
nill: 6 refuse; 8 negative
nimble: 4 spry; 5 agile, quick; 11 expeditious

nimbleness: 7 agility; 8 legerity, spryness

nimble-witted: 5 attic, witty; 11 quick-witted; 12 needle-witted

nimbly: 7 agilely

nimbus: 4 aura, halo, rack, scud; 5 glory; 7 aureola, aureole; 9 messenger, rain cloud; 11 nimbus cloud

nimbus cloud: 6 nimbus; 9 rain cloud; 11 thunderhead

nimiety: 6 excess; 7 surfeit, surplus; 8 overplus, plethora; 11 superfluity

Nimrod: 6 hunter; 9 sportsman

nincompoop: 4 fool, jerk, poop, zany; 5 ninny

nine: 2 IX

ninepin: 7 skittle; 10 skittle pin

ninepins: 5 bowls; 8 skittles

niner: 2 IX; 4 nine; 6 ennead

nineteen: 3 XIX

nine times: 8 ninefold

ninety: 2 XC; 15 fourscore and ten

ninny: 4 poop; 10 nincompoop

ninth: 8 ninefold, one-ninth

Ninth of Ab: 8 Fast of Ab, Fast of Av, Tisha b'Ab, Tisha b'Av; 9 Ninth of Av, Tishah b'Ab, Tishah b'Av

niobium: 2 Nb

nip: 3 cut, nib, sip; 4 bite, clip, shot, snip, tang, zest; 5 pinch, stunt, tweet; 6 nip off, pierce, twinge, twitch; 7 snip off, squeeze; 8 piquance, piquancy; 9 tanginess, vellicate; 11 nip in the bud; 16 check the growth of, chill to the marrow; 20 make one's teeth chatter

nip in the bud: 3 nip; 5 check, debar, stunt; 6 cut off; 7 draw off, prevent; 8 forefend, preclude; 9 foreclose

nipper: 3 fry, kid; 4 tike, tyke; 5 child, minor; 6 pincer, shaver; 7 tiddler; 8 nestling, small fry; 9 youngster

nippers: 5 tongs; 6 pliers; 7 forceps, pincers; 8 vise grip

nipping: 3 raw; 4 keen; 5 bleak, crisp, fresh, nippy, parky, sharp; 6 barbed, biting, frosty, snappy; 7 pungent; 8 chilling; 9 inclement

nipple: 3 pap, tit; 4 teat; 7 mamilla, papilla; 8 mammilla

Nippon: 5 Japan, Nihon

Nipponese: 8 Japanese

nippy: 5 crisp, parky; 6 frosty, snappy; 7 nipping

nirvana: 6 heaven; 8 paradise; 9 Shangri-la; 12 promised land

nisi prius: 4 writ; 7 summons; 8 citation, subpoena

Nissen hut: 10 Quonset hut

nisus: 5 pains; 6 strain; 8 striving

niter: 5 nitre; 9 saltpeter, saltpetre; 16 potassium nitrate

nitid: 5 shiny; 6 agleam, bright; 7 lambent, radiant; 8 gleaming, lustrous

nitpick: 7 quibble; 10 split hairs

nitpicker: 10 fussbudget; 13 perfectionist

nitpicking: 7 carping; 8 caviling; 9 quibbling; 12 pettifogging

nitric: 6 azotic; 7 nitrous

nitrile: 7 cyanide

nitrogen: 1 N

nitrous: 6 azotic, nitric

nitrous oxide: 11 laughing gas

nitty-gritty: 3 nub, sum; 4 core, gist, meat, pith; 5 heart; 6 center, kernel, marrow; 7 essence; 9 substance; 10 inwardness

nitwit: 6 dimwit, doofus; 7 half-wit

nitwitted: 7 witless; 9 senseless; 10 soft-witted

nix: 3 nil, zip; 4 nada, zero; 5 aught, nixie, zilch; 6 cipher, cypher, naught; 7 nothing; 8 bad fairy, goose egg

Nixon: 19 Richard Milhous Nixon

Nizhni Novgorod: 5 Gorki, Gorky

nm: 9 nanometer; 11 millimicron

no: 3 nay; 6 no more, none of

No: 6 nobelium

no.: 7 ordinal; 13 ordinal number

no-account: 5 sorry; 6 no-good; 7 no-count; 9 meritless

nob: 4 head, pate, toff

nobble: 3 con; 4 hook, lift, rook; 5 cheat, steal, catch, bunco, filch, mulct, pinch, snarf, sneak, swipe; 6 abduct, diddle, kidnap, pilfer, snatch; 7 cabbage, defraud, purloin, swindle; 8 abstract

nobelium: 2 No

Nobel Laureate: 8 Nobelist

nobility: 4 rank; 5 birth, blood, order; 7 majesty; 8 grandeur, noblesse, splendor; 9 solemnity, sublimity; 11 aristocracy

noble: 4 lord, pure; 5 grand, proud, solid; 6 august, goodly, lordly, mighty, worthy; 7 exalted, stately; 8 baronial, handsome, imposing, nobleman, precious, princely, sterling; 9 dignified, honorable; 10 commanding, impressive, upstanding, worshipful

noble gas: 7 argonon; 8 inert gas

nobleman: 4 lord, peer; 5 noble

noble-minded: 5 lofty; 7 exalted; 8 rarefied, rarified; 9 high-flown; 10 high-minded, idealistic

noblesse: 8 nobility

noblewoman: 4 lady; 7 peeress

nobly: 4 well; 7 morally; 10 virtuously; 11 righteously

nobody: 4 none; 5 no one; 6 cipher, cypher; 8 not a soul; 9 nonentity

no-brain: 6 vacant; 7 vacuous; 8 mindless; 10 unoccupied, unthinking; 11 thoughtless; 13 inconsiderate; 14 unintellectual

no-count: 5 sorry; 6 no-good; 9 meritless, no-account

N

noctambulatory: 12 mundivagrant, sleep-walking

noctambulism: 12 sleepwalking, somnambulism

noctambulist: 11 sleepwalker; **12** somnambulist

noctuid: 9 owlet moth; **11** noctuid moth

nocuous: 7 harmful

nod: 3 bid, bob; **4** beck, call, sway, yawn; **5** shrug; **6** assent, behest, curtsy, dictum; **7** bidding, consent; **8** courtesy, get sleep, nutation; **9** accession, agreement; **10** acceptance; **11** acceptation; **12** acquiescence

nodding: 4 dozy; **6** dozing, drowsy; **7** napping; **8** cernuous, drooping, drowsing; **9** pendulous

noddy: 4 dolt; **5** booby, inept; **6** stupid

node: 4 knob; **5** guest; **6** client, vertex; **9** lymph node; **10** lymph gland

no doubt: 4 sure; **6** surely; **8** of course, to be sure; **9** assuredly, certainly, doubtless; **14** unquestionably

nodule: 8 tubercle

Noel: 4 Yule; **8** Yuletide; **9** Christmas; **13** Christmastide, Christmastime

nog: 6 eggnog

noggin: 4 bean, head, pate; **5** attic, stoup; **6** noodle, sconce; **9** headpiece

no-good: 5 sorry; **7** no-count; **9** meritless, no-account

no great shakes: 3 low; **4** so-so; **8** middling; **9** tolerable

no-hit game: 8 no-hitter

noise: 4 roar; **6** racket; **7** clatter, resound; **9** make noise; **10** dissonance; **11** disturbance; **12** interference

noiseless: 5 quiet; **9** soundless

noise pollution: 14 sound pollution

noisily: 6 loudly

noisome: 4 foul, rank, vile; **5** fetid, funky; **6** foetid, putrid, smelly; **7** nocuous, noxious; **8** nauseous, smelling, stinking; **9** loathsome, offensive, sickening; **10** nauseating; **12** foul-smelling

noisy: 4 loud; **8** sonorous

no laughing matter: 6 no joke

no longer: 6 no more

nomadic: 6 mobile, roving; **9** peregrine, wandering

nom de guerre: 6 anonym; **7** war name; **9** pseudonym

nom de plume: 7 pen name

nom de theatre: 11 theater name

nomenclature: 4 name; **5** title; **6** naming; **7** calling; **8** language; **10** nomination; **11** designating, designation, terminology; **12** denominating, denomination

nominal: 5 token, usual; **6** common, normal; **7** titular, typical; **8** everyday, habitual, ordinary, tokenish, workaday; **10** nominative; **11** nuncupative

nominal head: 5 front; **8** front man, straw man; **10** figurehead

nominal value: 8 par value; **9** face value

nominate: 4 hire, make, name; **5** put up; **6** engage, return; **7** appoint, bespeak, propose; **8** accredit; **10** constitute

nomination: 6 naming, return; **7** calling; **10** nominating; **11** appointment, designating, designation; **12** denominating, nomenclature

nominative: 7 nominal; **9** nominated; **11** subject case; **14** nominative case

nominee: 7 trustee; **9** candidate, consignee; **10** campaigner

no more: 2 no; **4** gone, late; **6** lapsed, run out; **7** elapsed, expired, extinct, has-been; **8** no longer; **9** forgotten; **10** antebellum

nonacceptance: 8 turndown

nonadjacent: 5 apart; **9** separated

non-admission: 8 omission; **9** exception, exclusion, rejection

nonage: 5 bloom; **8** minority

nonaged: 5 minor; **8** underage

nonagon: 9 nine-sided

nonalcoholic: 4 soft

nonattendance: 5 alibi; **11** absenteeism

nonattender: 6 no-show, truant

nonautomatic: 12 hand-operated

nonce: 9 time being

nonchalance: 9 unconcern; **11** insouciance; **12** indifference

nonchalant: 6 casual; **9** easygoing, sans souci [Fr], unworried; **10** insouciant, phlegmatic; **11** unconcerned

nonchalantly: 6 coolly; **8** casually

nonchurchgoing: 6 lapsed

noncitizen: 5 alien; **9** foreigner, outlander

non-classical: 4 late; **6** modern; **7** nouveau; **8** neoteric; **11** hypermodern, modernistic; **12** contemporary

noncombustible material: 10 insulation

noncommissioned officer: 6 noncom

noncommittal: 7 guarded; **11** unrevealing

noncommunicable: 13 noncontagious

noncompliance: 9 violation; **10** infraction; **12** disobedience, infringement, non-execution; **13** nonobservance, transgression

noncompliant: 12 nonobservant

nonconducting: 10 insulating

nonconductor: 9 insulator; **10** dielectric

nonconforming: 8 atypical; **11** exceptional; **13** nonconformist, unconformable

nonconformist: 6 weirdo; **8** non-juror, recusant; **10** malcontent, non-content

non-content: 10 malcontent

noncontiguous: 5 apart; **9** separated; **11** nontouching, nonadjacent

noncorporeal: 11 disembodied, incorporeal

nondescript: 8 nonesuch, original; **9** charac-

ter; **10** sui generis [Lat]; **13** characterless
nondisposable: 8 reusable
none: 5 no one; **6** nobody; **8** not a soul
noneffervescent: 5 still
nonentity: 3 nil; **6** cipher, cypher, nobody;
12 nominis umbra [Lat]
none of: 2 no
nonessential: 9 extrinsic; **10** accidental,
derivative, incidental; **11** inessential,
unessential
nonesuch: 4 pick; **5** cream, elite, ideal,
prime, saint; **6** flower; **7** nonsuch, paragon;
8 original; **9** character, nonpareil; **10**
apotheosis; **11** masterpiece, nondescript
nonetheless: 3 yet; **5** still; **6** even so, withal;
7 however; **12** nevertheless
nonexempt: 7 taxable
nonexistence: 8 non-being
nonexistent: 7 lacking, missing, wanting; **9**
not extant; **11** not existing
nonextant: 7 extinct
nonfat: 7 fat-free, fatless
nonfigurative: 8 abstract; **12** nonobjective;
14 abstractionist
nonflammable: 9 fireproof; **10** flameproof;
13 incombustible, uninflammable
nonflowering plant: 12 pteridophyte
non-functional: 10 inoperable; **13** unservice-
able
non-Jew: 3 goy; **7** Gentile
nonkosher: 4 tref; **7** terefah
nonleaded: 8 lead-free
nonlegal: 10 extralegal
non-linguistic: 8 symbolic; **9** nonverbal
non-linguistic symbol: 6 emblem, symbol
non-literal: 10 figurative; **12** metaphorical
nonliving: 4 dead; **5** azoic; **7** abiotic; **9** inanimate
nonmalignant: 8 harmless
non-numerical: 8 symbolic
nonobjective: 8 abstract, personal; **10** subjective; **13** nonfigurative; **14** abstractionist
nonobservance: 9 disregard, violation; **10**
infraction; **12** inadvertence, inadvertency,
infringement, nonexecution; **13** noncompliance, transgression
nonobservant: 12 noncompliant
nonparallel: 6 serial
nonpareil: 3 one; **4** pick; **5** cream, elite,
ideal, prime, saint; **6** flower; **7** nonsuch,
paragon; **8** nonesuch, peerless; **9** matchless, unmatched, unrivaled; **10** apotheosis, unrivalled; **11** masterpiece, unmatchable
nonpayment: 7 default; **11** nonremittal
nonperformance: 7 neglect; **10** negligence;
12 carelessness, nonexecution
non-performance: 7 neglect
nonphysical: 10 intangible

non-physical: 10 immaterial; **11** nonmaterial
nonplus: 5 hitch, pinch, quell, trial; **6** baffle,
bother, puzzle, strait; **7** flummox, mystify,
perplex, silence, stupefy, stupify, trounce; **8**
bewilder, confound, exigency, juncture,
quandary, scramble; **9** checkmate, dumbfound, stalemate; **11** conjunctive, predicament
nonplussed: 7 aground, at a loss, puzzled; **8**
graveled, stranded
nonpoisonous: 8 nontoxic
nonporous: 5 solid; **11** imperforate, impermeable; **12** impenetrable
nonprescription: 14 over-the-counter
nonprofit: 12 not for profit
non prosequitur: 7 non pros
nonrapid eye movement sleep: 9 NREM
sleep
nonrational: 9 intuitive
nonrecreational: 4 paid
nonresonant: 4 dead; **13** unreverberant
nonsense: 6 frills; **8** trumpery; **9** gibberish,
gimcracks; **10** hocus-pocus, mumbo
jumbo; **11** gimcrackery, nonsensical
nonsensical: 5 inept, silly; **6** absurd, vacant;
7 blatant, fatuous, foolish, idiotic; **8** babbling, derisory, imbecile, nonsense; **9** driveling, egregious, insensate, ludicrous,
senseless, unmeaning; **10** irrational, ridiculous
non sequitur: 9 untenable; **11** unwarranted;
12 not following
nonsexual: 7 asexual
nonstop flight: 7 nonstop
nonsubjective: 9 objective; **10** impersonal
nonsuch: 5 ideal, saint; **7** paragon; **8** nonesuch, original; **9** character, nonpareil; **10**
apotheosis; **11** nondescript
nontaxable: 6 exempt
nontoxic: 6 atoxic; **12** nonpoisonous
nonuniform: 6 uneven, varied; **9** irregular;
11 diversified
nonunionized: 11 unorganized
nonuple: 8 ninefold
nonverbal: 8 gestural, symbolic; **13** non-linguistic
nonviolent: 8 peaceful, unbloody
noodles: 5 pasta; **8** linguine; **9** spaghetti, fet-
tucini
nook: 4 hole; **5** niche; **6** corner, recess
noon: 6 midday; **7** noonday; **8** high noon,
noontide; **10** twelve noon
no one: 4 none; **6** nobody
noose: 3 gin; **4** hoot, rope; **5** cinch, lasso,
snare; **6** halter, lariat; **9** bowstring, slip
noose
nor'-east: 2 NE; **9** northeast
nor'-nor'-east: 3 NNE
nor'-nor'-west: 3 NNW
nor'-west: 2 NW; **9** northwest

Nordic: 5 Norse; **12** Scandinavian; **13** North Germanic
noreaster: 11 northeaster
Norge: 5 Noreg; **6** Norway
norm: 7 average, precept; **8** standard
normal: 4 rule; **5** erect, plumb, usual; **6** common; **7** default, formula, natural, nominal, pattern, typical, upright; **8** everyday, habitual, ordinary, straight, vertical, workaday; **10** convention; **13** unexceptional
normal curve: 8 Gaussian
normalcy: 9 normality
normalize: 11 standardize
normally: 7 usually; **8** commonly; **9** naturally; **10** ordinarily; **12** unremarkably
Normandy: 9 Normandie
normative: 12 prescriptive
Norse: 6 Nordic; **8** Norseman, Northman; **9** Norwegian; **12** Scandinavian
Norseman: 5 Norse; **6** Viking; **9** Norwegian
North: 5 Union; **8** Northern; **9** northerly, Northerly, northland, northward
north: 8 due north; **9** northerly, northward; **10** in the north, northwards, to the north; **12** compass north; **13** magnetic north
North American Indian: 14 Native American, American Indian
North Atlantic Treaty Organization: 4 NATO
northbound: 9 northward
north by east: 3 NbE
north by west: 3 NbW
northeast: 2 NE; **4** N by E; **7** nor'-east; **12** northeastern; **13** northeasterly
northeast by east: 4 NEbE
northeast by north: 4 NEbN
northeaster: 9 noreaster
Northern: 5 North; **6** arctic, Boreal; **9** Northerly; **13** septentrional
northern: 9 northerly
Northerner: 4 Yank; **6** Yankee
northern harrier: 9 marsh hawk
northern lights: 14 aurora borealis
northern porgy: 4 scup
North Frigid Zone: 6 Arctic; **10** Arctic Zone
northmost: 12 northernmost
north northeast: 3 NNE
north northwest: 3 NNW
north-polar: 6 Arctic
North Star: 7 Polaris; **8** polestar; **9** polar star
North Star State: 9 Minnesota; **11** Gopher State
northward: 5 north, North; **9** northerly; **10** in the north, northbound, northwards
northwest: 2 NW; **7** nor'-west; **12** northwestern; **13** northwesterly
northwest by north: 4 NWbN
northwest by west: 4 NWbW
northwest wind: 11 northwester

north wind: 6 boreas; **7** norther
Norway: 5 Noreg, Norge
nose: 3 neb, pry; **4** beak, poke, wind; **5** aroma, scent, sniff, snout; **6** inhale, nozzle, nuzzle, schnoz; **7** bouquet; **9** olfaction, proboscis
nosebag: 7 feedbag
nosebleed: 9 epistaxis
nosecount: 6 census
no-see-um: 5 punky; **6** punkey, punkie; **11** biting midge
nosegay: 4 posy; **6** flower, wreath; **7** bouquet, chaplet, corsage, festoon, garland
nose job: 11 rhinoplasty
nose out: 8 scent out, smell out, sniff out
nosepiece: 6 bridge
nosh: 4 bait, bite, whet; **5** snack; **8** junk food; **9** collation
no-show: 6 truant; **8** absentee; **11** nonattender
no-show job: 8 cushy job; **10** featherbed
nosiness: 6 prying; **10** snoopiness
nosology: 8 etiology; **9** pathology; **11** diagnostics
nostalgia: 12 homesickness
nostalgic: 8 homesick
nostrum: 4 drug; **6** device, physic; **7** cure-all, panacea, receipt, simples; **8** artifice, medicine; **9** expedient, invention; **10** medicament, medication; **11** contrivance; **14** pharmaceutical
nosy: 5 nosey; **6** prying, snoopy; **7** peering
nota bene: 2 N.B.; **8** note well
notability: 4 note; **5** eclat, vogue; **7** notable; **8** luminary, notables [pl], somebody; **9** celebrity, notoriety, personage; **10** popularity
notable: 5 clear, famed, noted; **6** famous, of note, signal; **7** salient; **8** apparent, diligent, far-famed, luminary, manifest, notables [pl], renowned, sedulous, somebody; **9** assiduous, personage, prominent; **10** celebrated, notability, noteworthy; **11** illustrious
not able: 6 unable
notably: 6 mainly; **7** chiefly; **8** signally; **9** curiously, pointedly, saliently, unusually; **10** materially, peculiarly, remarkably, singularly, strikingly; **11** prominently; **12** particularly
not adopted: 6 reject
not alike: 6 unlike; **9** different, differing; **10** dissimilar
not a little: 4 most, much, well; **5** a deal; **6** indeed; **7** no end of
not allowed: 6 banned, barred; **7** tabooed; **8** enjoined, outlawed; **9** forbidden; **10** disallowed, prohibited, proscribed
notary: 5 clerk; **8** recorder; **12** notary public
not a soul: 4 none; **5** no one; **6** nobody
notation: 4 note; **10** annotation
not bad: 4 cool, keen, neat; **5** bully, dandy,

great, nifty, swell; **6** bang-up, groovy, peachy, slap-up; **7** corking; **8** cracking, smashing

notch: 3 cut, dot, gap, peg; **4** dent, link, nick, pass, rung, slit, spot; **5** blaze, prick, score, snick; **6** indent; **7** passage, scratch; **8** incision

not charged: 4 free; **6** gratis; **7** untaxed; **8** costless; **10** gratuitous

notched: 5 erose, jaggy; **6** dented, jagged, nicked; **7** serrate, toothed; **8** indented, serrated; **10** saw-toothed

not chosen: 6 reject

not comply with: 7 violate; **8** infringe; **10** not observe, transgress

not compulsory: 8 elective, optional, unforced; **9** not forced; **12** discretional; **13** discretionary

not content: 4 loth; **5** loath, shy of; **6** averse; **9** reluctant; **10** indisposed; **11** disinclined

not dangerous: 4 safe; **8** harmless; **13** unthreatening

not disclosed: 8 withheld; **10** unrevealed; **11** undisclosed

not doing: 8 inaction; **9** eschewing; **10** abstention, abstinence, forbearing, refraining; **11** forbearance, passiveness

note: 4 bill, line, mark, tone; **5** brief, draft, eclat, stamp, token, vogue; **6** aperçu, billet, digest, letter, minute, notice, precis, remark; **7** earmark, epistle, epitome, mention, minutes, missive, observe, outline, summary, symptom; **8** abstract, analysis, bank bill, banknote, eminence, exponent, notation, synopsis, take down, take note; **9** celebrity, greenback, notoriety; **10** abridgment, annotation, notability, popularity; **11** banker's bill, distinction, musical note, pre-eminence, short letter

not easy: 4 hard; **5** tough; **9** difficult

notebook: 8 memo book; **10** pocketbook; **14** memorandum book

notebook computer: 6 laptop; **8** notebook

noted: 5 famed; **6** famous, of note; **7** notable, noticed; **8** far-famed, observed, received, renowned; **9** notorious, well-known; **10** celebrated; **11** illustrious, widely known

not enough: 10 inadequate; **12** insufficient

notepaper: 10 stationery

note well: 2 N.B.; **8** nota bene [Lat]

noteworthy: 7 notable; **10** remarkable

not expressed: 6 untold; **9** unexposed, unwritten; **10** unreported; **11** unexpressed, unpublished

not far: 7 shortly

not following: 9 untenable; **11** non sequitur [Lat], unwarranted

not forced: 8 elective, optional, unforced; **12** discretional; **13** discretionary

not give: 8 withhold

not guilty: 8 innocent; **9** acquitted, guiltless

nothing: 3 nil, nix, zip; **4** nada, zero; **5** aught, zilch; **6** cipher, cypher, naught, trifle; **7** nullity; **8** goose egg

notice: 3 see; **4** bill, card, find, look, mark, note, view; **6** detect, poster, regard, remark, report, review; **7** comment, observe, placard; **8** advert to, critique, discover, point out; **9** criticism; **10** communique, observance; **11** acknowledge, observation; **12** announcement, notification

noticeable: 9 obtrusive; **10** detectable; **11** appreciable, perceptible

noticeably: 11 perceptibly

noticed: 5 noted; **8** observed

notification: 6 notice; **7** telling; **8** appraisal; **9** notifying; **10** communique; **11** presentment; **12** announcement

notify: 6 advise; **7** apprise, apprize, signify, specify

notifying: 7 telling; **8** appraisal; **9** informing; **10** announcing

not including: 9 excepting

notion: 4 idea, whim; **6** belief, whimsy; **7** concept, feeling, inkling, notions, thought, whimsey; **9** suspicion; **10** conception, impression

not match: 4 vary; **6** differ; **8** mismatch; **9** different; **10** dissimilar

not mind: 6 slight; **7** not care; **9** disregard

not moving: 6 static; **10** motionless, stationary

notoriety: 4 note; **5** eclat, vogue; **7** ill fame

notorious: 5 noted; **6** errant; **8** ill-famed, infamous, received, shocking; **9** well-known; **10** outrageous

Notoryctus: 4 mole; **11** pouched mole; **13** marsupial mole; **15** genus Notoryctus

not paying: 9 non-paying; **13** non-performing

not permitted: 6 banned, barred; **7** tabooed; **8** enjoined, outlawed; **9** forbidden; **10** disallowed, not allowed, prohibited, proscribed

not possess: 7 not have; **9** be without

not present: 6 absent

not quite: 6 all but, almost, nearly; **7** short of; **8** well-nigh

not reach: 4 miss; **9** come short, fall short

Notre Dame: 5 Saint; **7** Madonna, Our Lady

not revealed: 8 held back, withheld; **10** unrevealed; **11** undisclosed

not speaking: 7 silence; **8** muteness

not too often: 7 at times; **9** sometimes; **12** occasionally

not used: 6 unused; **9** unapplied; **10** unemployed

notwithstanding: 3 but, yet; **5** still; **6** even so, withal; **7** however; **11** nonetheless; **12** nevertheless

not written: 4 oral; 7 lingual; 8 phonetic; 9 outspoken, unwritten

nought: 3 nul; 4 null, void, zero; 6 cipher, cypher, naught

nourish: 7 aliment, nurture, nutrify, sustain

nourished: 8 fostered

nourishing: 7 feeding; 8 nutrient; 9 nutritive; 10 alimentary, nutritious; 12 alimentation

nourishment: 4 food, grub; 7 aliment, edibles, ingesta, nurture; 8 eatables, victuals; 9 nutriment, nutrition, provender; 10 sustenance; 11 comestibles; 12 alimentation, sustentation

nous: 4 head, mind; 5 brain, parts; 6 esprit, psyche, reason; 8 gumption, sagacity; 9 acuteness, alertness

nouveau: 3 new; 4 late; 6 modern; 8 neoteric; 11 hypermodern, modernistic; 12 contemporary, non-classical

nouveau riche: 7 parvenu, upstart; 8 new money

Nouvelle Vague: 7 New Wave

nova: 9 supernova

novel: 3 new; 5 fresh, green; 6 recent; 7 romance; 8 original; 10 refreshing

novelty: 4 gaud; 5 curio; 6 bangle, bauble, fallal, gewgaw, trifle; 7 bibelot, newness, recency, trinket, whatnot; 8 a novelty, chotchke, gimcrack, kickshaw, nicknack, whim-wham; 9 bagatelle, bric-a-brac, freshness, tchotchke; 10 knickknack

novelty shop: 8 gift shop

November: 3 Nov

November 1: 9 Hallowmas; 10 Allhallows, Hallowmass; 12 All Saints' Day

November 11: 9 Martinmas; 11 Veterans' Day; 12 Armistice Day, St Martin's Day

November 2: 11 All Souls' Day

novice: 3 nun; 7 amateur, recruit; 8 beginner, initiate, neophyte; 9 beginning, greenhorn

novitiate: 9 noviciate; 13 matriculation

now: 5 today; 6 at once; 8 directly, nowadays, right now; 9 forthwith, instantly; 11 immediately; 12 straightaway

noxious: 7 baleful, baneful, harmful, hurtful, noisome; 9 injurious; 10 pernicious; 11 deleterious, detrimental, mischievous

noxiously: 9 harmfully; 13 detrimentally

nozzle: 4 beak, nose; 5 snoot, snout; 6 honker, hooter, schnoz; 9 proboscis, schnozzle

Np: 9 neptunium

nuance: 5 shade; 6 nicety; 8 subtlety; 10 refinement

nub: 3 sum; 4 core, gist, meat, pith, stub; 5 heart; 6 center, kernel, marrow; 7 essence; 9 substance; 10 inwardness; 11 nitty-gritty

nubby: 6 nubbly, tweedy; 7 slubbed; 8 homespun

nubile: 10 attractive; 12 marriageable

Nucifraga: 10 nutcracker; 14 genus Nucifraga

nuclear: 6 atomic

nuclear family: 14 conjugal family

nuclear magnetic resonance spectrometer: 3 NMR [acron]; 10 NMR machine

nuclear power: 6 fusion; 7 fission; 11 atomic power; 12 atomic energy

nuclear-powered submarine: 8 nautilus

nuclear weapon: 4 nuke

nucleon number: 10 mass number

nucleoplasm: 10 nuclear sap, karyoplasm

nucleus: 4 core, root; 5 heart, trunk; 6 etymon, kernel; 7 tap-root; 9 core group, nucleolus

nude: 4 bare; 5 naked; 9 au naturel

nudeness: 6 nudity; 9 nakedness

nudge: 4 leer, prod, wink; 5 shrug, touch; 6 glance, poke at

nudism: 8 naturism

nudist: 8 naturist; 10 naturistic

nugatory: 4 null, vain, void; 8 bootless; 9 fruitless, pointless; 10 of no effect, profitless; 11 inoperative, null and void; 12 unprofitable

nugget: 4 lump, mass; 5 block, ingot; 7 bullion

nuisance: 4 pain; 6 bother, pother; 8 mischief, vexation; 9 annoyance, grievance; 10 harassment; 11 botheration

nuke: 3 zap; 7 atomize; 8 atom-bomb; 9 micro-cook, microwave; 13 atomic warhead, nuclear weapon; 14 nuclear warhead

null: 3 nul; 4 void; 6 naught, nought; 8 nugatory

null and void: 8 nugatory; 10 of no effect; 11 inoperative

nullification: 6 repeal; 8 annuling, recision; 9 annulment, canceling; 10 abrogating, abrogation, defeasance, extinction, rescinding, rescission, retraction

nullified: 11 invalidated

nullify: 4 void; 5 annul, avoid, cover, quash; 6 fill up, ignore; 7 discard, protest; 8 dishonor; 9 repudiate; 10 invalidate, neutralize

numb: 4 dead [fig], dull, stun; 5 blunt; 6 asleep, benumb, deaden, frozen; 7 out cold, stupefy, unaware; 8 benumbed, comatose, paralyze; 9 catatonic, petrified, senseless; 10 frost-bound; 11 frost-bitten, frost-nipped, unconscious

number: 3 act, bit; 4 come, list, opus, tell, turn, work; 5 add up, count, issue, piece, tally, total; 6 amount, cipher, figure; 7 numeral, routine; 9 enumerate; 11 composition, phone number

number among: 7 include

numbering: 11 enumeration

numberless: 6 myriad; 8 infinite; 9 countless, uncounted; 10 innumerous, unnum-

bered; **11** innumerable, measureless, unnumerable
number one: 5 first
number one wood: 6 driver
numbers: 3 sea; **4** army; **5** array, sight; **6**
galaxy, strain; **9** a quantity; **11** numbers
game, numbers pool; **13** numbers racket
numbly: 10 insensibly
Numenius: 6 curlew; **13** genus Numenius
numerable: 9 countable; **10** enumerable; **11**
denumerable
numeral: 6 number; **7** numeric; **9** numerical
numeration: 5 count, tally; **8** counting; **9**
reckoning; **11** enumeration
numerator: 8 dividend
numerical: 7 numeral, numeric; **12** mathematical
numerous: 4 many
Numida: 6 guinea; **10** guinea fowl; **11** genus
Numida
numismatics: 13 numismatology; **14** coin
collecting
numismatist: 13 coin collector
nun: 6 novice, sister; **7** nun buoy; **9** postulant; **10** religieuse [Fr]; **11** conical buoy
Nunc dimittis: 16 Canticle of Simeon
nuncio: 6 legate; **7** attache
nuncupative: 4 oral; **9** unwritten
nunnery: 7 convent; **8** cloister; **9** monastery
Nuprin: 5 Advil; **6** Motrin; **9** ibuprofen
nuptial: 6 bridal; **7** spousal; **8** hymeneal
nuptials: 6 bridal; **7** wedding; **8** espousal,
spousals
Nuremburg: 8 Nurnberg; **9** Nuernberg
nurse: 2 RN; **4** hold, suck; **5** biddy, nanny; **6**
cradle, doctor, harbor, physic, suckle; **7**
harbour, lactate, plaster; **8** dry nurse, wet-
nurse; **9** catsitter, dogsitter, entertain,
nursemaid; **10** babysitter, breastfeed
nurse's aide: 12 candystriper
nursed: 7 suckled
nursemaid: 5 nanny, nurse; **11** nursery maid
nursery: 4 nest, womb; **6** cradle, creche; **10**
birthplace, glasshouse, greenhouse, schoolroom; **11** seed nursery; **13** day-care center
nurseryman: 8 gardener
nursery tale: 5 fable; **9** fairy tale
nursing home: 4 home; **8** rest home
nurture: 4 rear; **5** breed, raise; **6** foster,
ground, parent; **7** bring up, nourish, prepare, raising, rearing, sustain; **8** breeding,
exercise, practice; **9** fosterage, fostering,
habituate, nurturing, nutrition; **10** bringing
up, upbringing; **11** nourishment; **12** alimentation
nurturing: 7 nurture, raising, rearing; **8**
breeding, maturing, ripening; **9** fosterage,
fostering, seasoning; **10** maturation,
upbringing

nut: 4 core; **5** crank, heart; **7** nutcase; **8**
crackpot; **9** fruitcake, screwball; **10** enthusiast
nutation: 3 nod; **6** wobble
nut-brown: 3 bay; **6** auburn, dapple, russet;
8 chestnut, cinnamon
nutcase: 3 nut; **5** crank; **8** crackpot; **9** fruitcake, screwball
nutlike: 5 nutty
nutmeg: 4 mace
nutmeg family: 13 Myristicaceae
Nutmeg State: 11 Connecticut; **17**
Constitution State
nut pine: 5 pinon; **6** pinyon
nutrient: 4 food; **9** nutritive; **10** alimentary,
nourishing, nutritious
nutrition: 7 nurture; **11** nourishment; **12** alimentation, sustentation
nutritionist: 9 dietician, dietitian
nuts: 3 mad; **4** bats, daft, loco; **5** balmy,
barmy, batty, buggy, crazy, dotty, kooky,
loony, loopy, nutty, wacky; **6** crazed, fruity,
insane, kookie, teched [dialect]; **7** bonkers,
cracked, far gone, haywire, lunatic, tetched
[dialect], touched; **8** crackers, demented,
deranged, maddened, not right; **10** moonstruck
nutsedge: 8 nutgrass
nuttily: 6 daftly; **7** balmily, dottily, wackily
nut to crack: 5 rebus; **6** enigma, puzzle, riddle; **7** charade; **9** conundrum
Nuytsia: 8 fire tree; **9** flame tree; **12** genus
Nuytsia
nuzzle: 4 nose; **6** cuddle, nestle; **7** snuggle; **9**
draw close
NW: 7 nor'-west; **9** northwest
Nyasaland: 6 Malawi
nylons: 6 rayons; **12** silk stocking; **13** nylon
stocking, rayon stocking
nymph: 4 peri; **5** dryad, houri, naiad; **6**
nereid
Nymphaea: 5 lotus; **8** pond lily; **9** blue lotus,
water lily, white lily; **10** white lotus, water
nymph; **13** genus Nymphaea
Nymphaeaceae: 15 water-lily family
Nymphicus: 9 cockateel, cockatiel; **14** cockatoo parrot; **14** genus Nymphicus
nymphomaniac: 6 nympho
Nynorsk: 8 Landsmal; **12** New Norwegian
NYSE: 8 big board
Nyssa: 7 sour gum; **8** black gum; **8** water
gum; **10** genus Nyssa
Nyssaceae: 12 tupelo family; **13** sour-gum
family
nystagmus: 12 day blindness
nystatin: 10 Mycostatin

N

O

O: 5 type O; **6** group O, oxygen
o'er: 4 over
o.d.: 8 overdose
o.k.: 4 fine, okay; **8** all right
oaf: 3 put; **4** calf, clod, colt, gawk, goon, loon, lout, lump, tony; **5** block, klutz, stick, stock; **6** doodle, lubber, lummox; **7** buzzard, dullard
oafish: 7 boorish, loutish, swinish; **11** neanderthal
Oahu: 10 Oahu Island
oak: 4 iron; **5** oaken, steel; **7** adamant, oak tree; **10** heart of oak
oaken: 3 oak
oakum: 4 hemp, jute
oarfish: 10 ribbonfish
oarlock: 3 peg, pin; **5** thole; **7** rowlock; **8** tholepin
oarsman: 3 oar; **5** rower
oasis: 5 haven
oath: 3 vow; **4** cuss; **5** curse; **7** cursing; **8** ribaldry, swearing; **9** affidavit, curse word, expletive, profanity, swearword; **10** adjuration; **12** asseveration
oatmeal: 10 rolled oats
Oaxaca de Juarez: 6 Oaxaca
Ob: 7 Ob River
obbligato: 8 obligato; **9** accessory, attendant
obduracy: 8 adamance, hardness, rigidity; **9** obstinacy, stiffness
obdurate: 5 stony; **6** cussed, flinty; **7** austere, exigent; **8** exacting, rigorous, stubborn; **9** demanding, hard-nosed, obstinate, reprobate, searching, tenacious, unsparing
obeah: 3 obi; **5** magic; **6** voodoo
obedience: 7 respect; **10** compliance
obedient: 9 compliant, complying
obeisance: 3 bow; **6** bowing, fealty, homage, kowtow
obelisk: 6 column, dagger, pillar; **7** pyramid; **8** monolith
obese: 3 fat; **4** full; **5** lusty, plump, squab, stout; **6** rotund; **7** weighty; **8** bouncing; **9** corpulent
obey: 6 comply, behave; **7** conform
obfuscate: 5 elude, evade; **7** mystify; **10** equivocate
obfuscated: 5 dirty, muddy, murky; **7** baffled, muddled; **8** confused
obit: 4 fall, rest; **7** quietus, release; **8** obituary; **9** departure, necrology
obiter dictum: 6 dictum; **13** parenthetical
obituary: 4 obit; **9** necrology
object: 3 aim, end; **4** goal, item; **5** thing; **6** entity, target; **8** end point, quo animo [Lat]; **9** intention, objective; **11** destination
objection: 7 dissent, protest; **8** demurral, drawback; **9** cavilling, exception

objectionable: 9 obnoxious; **10** unpleasant
objective: 3 aim, end; **4** goal; **6** object, target; **8** end point, quo animo [Lat]; **9** intention; **10** accusative, impersonal; **11** destination
objective evidence: 7 exhibit
objective lens: 6 barrel; **8** eyepiece, platform; **12** focusing knob
objectiveness: 6 non ego; **11** objectivity
object lesson: 7 example
object of affection: 3 pet; **6** minion; **7** darling; **8** favorite
objector: 9 dissenter, dissident, protester
objet d'art: 5 curio, objet
objurgation: 5 abuse; **7** chiding; **8** scolding; **9** contumely, invective
oblate: 11 elliptical; **13** pumpkin-shaped
oblate spheroid: 7 pigskin; **8** football
oblation: 4 dole, help; **8** libation, offering; **9** offertory, sacrifice
obligate: 5 bound; **6** compel, oblige; **9** compelled; **11** constrained
obligation: 4 debt, duty, onus; **5** debit, score; **8** covenant; **9** liability
obligatory: 6 forced; **7** binding, coerced; **8** required; **9** compelled; **10** compulsory; **11** involuntary
oblige: 4 bind, hold, make; **5** drive, force; **6** assign, burden, coerce, compel, look to; **7** enforce; **8** call upon, obligate; **9** constrain, prescribe; **11** accommodate
obliging: 8 gracious, yielding; **9** complying, indulgent; **10** complacent; **11** complaisant, good-humored; **12** conciliatory; **13** accommodating
oblique: 7 devious; **8** crabwise, glancing, indirect, sideways; **10** collateral, correlated
obliquely: 6 aslant; **7** athwart; **8** sidelong, sideways
obliterate: 4 kill, wipe; **6** efface; **7** blot out, obscure, wipe out; **9** extirpate; **10** annihilate, extinguish; **11** obliterated
obliteration: 10 extinction; **11** eradication
oblivion: 5 lethe, limbo; **10** forgetting; **11** nothingness
oblivious: 8 mindless; **9** forgetful, unmindful
obloquy: 5 blame, odium; **7** calumny, censure, scandal, slander; **8** ignominy; **9** aspersion, criticism, dispraise; **10** backbiting, defamation
obnoxious: 6 odious; **9** offensive, repulsive; **10** unpleasant; **13** objectionable
oboe: 7 hautboy; **8** hautbois; **10** basset horn
Ob River: 2 Ob
obscene: 4 lewd; **5** bawdy, broad, gross, loose; **6** coarse, ribald, risque [Fr], smutty, vulgar; **7** fulsome; **9** abhorrent, equivocal, repugnant, repulsive, salacious; **10** detestable; **12** pornographic

obscenely: 6 lewdly

obscenity: 4 smut; 8 lewdness, ribaldry, salacity; 9 bawdiness, equivoque [Fr], vulgarism

obscure: 3 dim, fog; 4 blur, dark, hide, mist; 5 apart, befog, cloud, dense, muddy, shade, vague; 6 darken, hidden, opaque, unsung; 7 benight, blot out, confuse, cryptic, unclear; 8 confused, haze over, isolated, nebulous, untitled; 9 difficult

obscured: 6 hidden, veiled; 7 covered; 8 eclipsed, occulted

obscurely: 9 unclearly

obscurity: 4 murk; 5 gloom; 7 density, latency; 8 confused; 9 muddiness, vagueness

obsequious: 7 fawning, servile; 8 decorous, honoring, toadyish; 9 esteeming, pandering

observable: 7 evident; 11 discernible

observance: 4 rite; 5 usage; 6 custom, notice, ritual; 8 ceremony, honoring, practice, watching; 9 adherence, execution, observing; 10 ceremonial, compliance, convention, prevalence; 11 concurrence, observation, performance

observant: 4 true; 5 loyal; 8 faithful, noticing, piercing; 9 compliant, complying, observing; 10 discerning, law-abiding, perceptive

observation: 6 notice, remark, result, seeing; 7 looking, viewing; 8 watching; 9 observing, reflexion, sentiment; 10 observance, reflection; 13 consideration, something seen

observational: 9 data-based

observation post: 7 lookout

observation tower: 7 lookout; 11 observatory

observatory: 7 lookout

observe: 3 see; 4 find, keep, look, mark, note, view; 5 honor, sight, watch; 6 comply, descry, detect, follow, honour, notice, regard, remark; 7 abide by, discern, execute, mention, perform, respect; 8 adhere to, advert to, discover, maintain, perceive, take note; 9 celebrate

observed: 4 seen; 5 noted; 7 noticed; 10 discovered; 11 ascertained

observer: 7 witness; 8 beholder, onlooker, passerby; 9 bystander, perceiver, spectator; 10 eyewitness; 11 commentator

observing: 6 seeing; 7 looking, viewing; 8 noticing

obsess: 5 ghost, haunt

obsessed: 7 haunted, taken up; 9 possessed; 11 preoccupied

obsession: 5 siege; 8 fixation; 10 compulsion, investment

obsessive: 10 compulsive

obsolete: 3 old; 7 disused; 8 outdated; 9 out-of-date; 13 superannuated; 12 old-fashioned

obstacle: 7 barrier; 8 stoppage; 11 obstruction

obstetrics: 10 gynecology

obstinacy: 8 obduracy, self-will; 10 obstinance; 12 immovability, stubbornness; 13 inflexibility

obstinance: 8 self-will; 9 obstinacy; 12 stubbornness

obstinate: 6 cussed; 7 wayward; 8 contrary, obdurate, perverse, stubborn; 9 tenacious; 10 inflexible, unyielding; 11 unrepentant

obstreperous: 6 ornery, unruly; 7 rackety; 10 uproarious

obstreperously: 6 loudly; 11 clamorously

obstruct: 3 jam; 4 stop; 5 block, stymy; 6 hinder, impede, stymie; 7 close up, occlude; 8 blockade

obstructing: 8 blocking, impeding; 9 hindering; 10 precluding; 11 obstruction, obstructive; 12 preventative

obstruction: 7 barrier; 8 impeding, obstacle, stoppage; 10 impediment

obstructionist: 10 filibuster [U.S.]

obstructive: 8 blocking, clogging, impeding; 9 hindering; 10 precluding; 11 obstructing; 12 preventative; 13 impedimentary, oppositionist

obtain: 3 get; 4 find, gain, hold; 5 incur, stand; 7 acquire, prevail, procure, receive

obtainable: 7 getable; 8 gettable; 10 accessible, attainable, procurable

obtained: 6 gotten; 8 acquired, procured

obtrude: 7 intrude, push out; 9 thrust out

obtrude upon: 6 invade; 9 intrude on; 12 encroach upon

obtrusive: 4 pert; 5 saucy; 7 forward; 10 noticeable, precocious; 11 impertinent

obtuse: 3 dim; 4 dull, dumb, slow; 5 bluff, blunt, dense, heavy, proof; 6 stolid, stupid, unwise; 7 doltish; 8 ungifted; 11 insensitive; 13 unenlightened

obviate: 5 avert, avoid, debar, rid of; 7 deflect, fend off, head off, ward off; 8 stave off; 9 eliminate

obviation: 10 preclusion; 12 forestalling

obvious: 7 evident, visible; 8 palpable, striking; 10 pronounced; 11 conspicuous, indubitable, perceptible, self-evident

obviously: 5 plain; 7 plainly; 8 patently; 9 evidently

occasion: 4 room, time; 5 cause; 6 affair; 7 opening; 8 juncture; 9 rationale, right time; 10 occurrence; 11 opportunity

occasional: 6 casual; 8 episodic

occasionally: 7 at times; 9 sometimes; 10 now and then

occident: 4 West; 8 New World

occidental: 7 Western

Occitan: 9 Provencal

occlude: 3 jam; 4 plug; 5 block, close; 6 impede; 7 close up; 8 obstruct

occlusion: 4 stop; 5 block; 7 closure; 8 blockade, blockage, stoppage

occult: 4 dark, hide; 6 hidden, mystic, secret; 7 eclipse, lurking; 8 abstruse, mystical; 9 recondite; 10 cabalistic

occult art: 9 mysticism; 14 occult sciences

occultation: 6 hiding; 7 eclipse, masking; 9 shadowing

occulted: 8 eclipsed, obscured

occupancy: 7 tenancy; 10 occupation

occupant: 8 resident

occupation: 3 job; 4 line, task, work; 6 employ, living; 7 agendum; 8 business, moving in, vocation; 9 occupancy, occupying, situation; 10 employment, livelihood

occupational safety and health act: 4 OSHA

occupied: 4 busy; 7 engaged; 8 tenanted

occupy: 4 busy, fill, have, hold, take; 5 enjoy, use up, worry; 6 absorb, engage, invade, reside; 7 command, concern, engross, inhabit, possess; 8 interest

occupying: 8 moving in; 10 inhabiting, occupation

occur: 2 be; 3 hap; 4 come, go on, pass; 5 ensue; 6 happen

occurrence: 4 fact; 5 brunt, event, onset, thing; 6 advent; 7 going on; 8 incident, occasion, outbreak; 9 happening, occurring; 10 phenomenon

ocean: 3 sea; 4 deep, main; 8 high seas

ocean bottom: 6 seabed; 9 Davy Jones, sea bottom; 10 ocean floor; 16 Davy Jones's locker

oceangoing: 8 seagoing; 9 seafaring

oceanic: 6 marine; 8 maritime

oceanic abyss: 4 deep

oceanic bird: 7 pelagic

Oceanid: 8 sea nymph

Ocean State: 11 Little Rhody, Rhode Island

ocean trench: 5 abyss; 6 trench

ocean trip: 6 voyage

ocellus: eyespot

ocelot: 7 wildcat, panther

ocher: 5 ochre, sepia; 12 Vandyke brown

Ochroma: 5 balsa; 12 genus Ochroma

Ocimum: 10 sweet basil; 11 common basil; 11 genus Ocimum

Oct: 7 October

octad: 4 VIII; 5 eight, octet; 7 eighter; 8 octonary

octagon: 10 eight-sided

octangular: 9 octagonal

Octavian: 8 Augustus; 15 Gaius Octavianus; 27 Gaius Julius Caesar Octavianus

octet: 4 VIII; 5 eight, octad; 7 eighter, octette; 8 octonary; 9 eightsome

October: 3 Oct

ocular: 5 optic; 6 visual; 7 optical; 8 eyepiece; 10 ophthalmic

ocular muscle: 9 eye muscle

oculist: 9 eye doctor; 11 optometrist; 15 ophthalmologist

Ocyurus: 10 yellowtail; 12 genus Ocyurus

OD: 8 overdose

odalisque: 4 doxy; 8 paramour; 9 concubine, courtesan

odd: 3 rum; 4 left, over; 5 funny, mixed, queer, rummy; 6 divers, unique, varied; 7 azygous, curious, diverse, mingled, strange, unmated, various; 8 assorted, farcical, leftover, peculiar, singular, unpaired; 9 different, eccentric, fanatical, grotesque, laughable, remaining, unmatched; 10 dissimilar

oddball: 9 eccentric

oddity: 5 curio, quirk; 6 rarity; 7 oddment, oddness; 8 crotchet, original; 9 curiosity, queerness

odd-job man: 8 handyman

oddly: 5 funny; 7 funnily, queerly; 9 curiously, strangely; 10 peculiarly

oddment: 3 end; 5 curio, scrap; 6 oddity, rarity; 7 remnant; 9 curiosity

oddness: 6 oddity; 7 anomaly

odds: 7 chances

odds and ends: 4 junk, mess; 5 talus; 6 debris, medley, ragbag; 7 farrago, melange; 8 detritus, mishmash, oddments, pastiche; 9 patchwork, potpourri

Oder: 9 Oder River

odious: 7 hateful, hideous, uncanny; 9 abhorrent, execrable, frightful, monstrous, obnoxious, offensive, repellent, repulsive; 10 abominable, detestable, forbidding

odium: 7 obloquy; 8 ignominy, loathing

Odobenus: 6 walrus; 13 genus Odobenus

Odocoileus: 4 deer; 8 mule deer; 9 burro deer; 13 whitetail deer, blacktail deer; 15 genus Odocoileus

odometer: 9 milometer; 10 mileometer

odor: 5 aroma, odour, scent, smell; 9 effluvium

odoriferous: 5 sweet; 7 odorous, scented; 8 perfumed

odorize: 5 scent

odorous: 5 sweet; 7 scented; 8 perfumed; 11 odoriferous

Odysseus: 7 Ulysses

oecumenic: 8 ecumenic

oedema: 5 edema; 6 dropsy

Oedipus: 11 King Oedipus

Oengus: 5 Angus; 6 Aengus; 7 Angus Og

oenology: 7 enology

oenophile: 9 wine lover; 11 oenophilist

oesophagus: 9 esophagus

Oesterreich: 7 Austria

oestrogen: 8 estrogen

oestrus: 3 rut; 4 heat; 6 estrus; 7 arousal

oeuvre: 4 opus, work; 5 works

of course: 4 then; 6 be it so, course, so be it; 7 no doubt; 9 assuredly, doubtless, naturally

off: 4 away, sour; 5 forth; 6 turned; 7 off duty, off-duty, stopped; 8 inactive; 9 cancelled

off-and-on: 6 fitful; 11 interrupted

offbeat: 5 kinky; 6 far-out, quirky, way-out

off-color: 5 bawdy; 6 ribald

offence: 7 offense

offend: 4 fall, hurt; 5 appal, break, lapse, pique, repel, shock, spite, wound; 6 appall, breach, injure, insult, vilify; 7 affront, infract, outrage, violate; 10 disenchant

offended: 5 riled; 6 galled, pained; 9 resentful

offender: 4 perp; 7 culprit; 8 criminal; 9 wrongdoer; 11 perpetrator

offense: 6 insult; 7 affront, offence, umbrage; 8 dishonor, trespass; 9 attacking, contumely, offensive, violation

offensive: 4 foul, rank, vile; 5 fetid, nasty, reeky, yucky; 6 coarse, odious; 7 beastly, noisome, offence, offense; 8 nauseous, smelling, stinking, unsavory; 9 attacking, loathsome, obnoxious, repellant, repulsive, sickening, unsavoury, violative; 10 aggressive, nauseating; 12 disagreeable

offer: 3 bid; 4 pass; 5 crack, fling, put up, whirl; 6 extend, tender; 7 offer up, present, proffer, propose, provide; 8 offering, overture, proposal; 9 volunteer; 11 proposition

offering: 5 offer; 8 oblation; 9 proposing

offertory: 4 dole, help; 8 oblation

off-guard: 7 napping

offhand: 5 ad-lib; 9 extempore, impromptu; 10 off-the-cuff; 11 extemporary

office: 4 duty, part, play, post, role, slot, spot, work; 5 berth, place, power, swing; 6 agency, bureau, strain; 7 cabinet; 8 chambers, exercise, function, position

office holder: 7 officer; 8 official; 9 incumbent

Office of Management and Budget: 3 OMB

officer: 3 cop; 8 gendarme [Fr]; 9 constable, policeman; 12 officeholder

officer of the day: 2 OD

office-seeker: 7 hopeful; 8 aspirant; 9 candidate

official: 8 minister; 9 authentic, authority, ex officio, executive; 10 bureaucrat

official emissary: 6 legate

officially: 8 formally

officiate: 3 act; 5 serve; 6 do duty; 8 function, minister

officiating: 8 umpirage, umpiring; 10 refereeing

officiator: 8 presider

officious: 4 busy; 5 pushy; 7 pushing; 8 meddling; 10 busybodied, meddlesome; 11 interfering

off-key: 4 sour; 5 false

off-limits: 11 out-of-bounds

offload: 6 unlade, unload, unpack, unship

offset: 5 first, start; 6 branch, cancel, outset, runner, set off, stolon; 7 kickoff, set back; 8 offshoot; 9 beginning, outgrowth; 11 countervail; 12 commencement

offset printing: 6 offset

offshoot: 3 arm; 4 limb, lobe, wing; 5 rider, yield; 6 branch, lobule, member, offset, result; 7 episode, outcome, product; 9 aftermath, corollary, outgrowth, resultant

off-speed pitch: 8 change-up

offspring: 4 seed, spat; 5 breed, brood, heirs, issue, spawn, young; 6 farrow, litter; 7 progeny

offstage: 4 wing; 9 backstage

off-the-cuff: 5 ad-lib; 7 offhand; 9 extempore, improvise, offhanded, unplanned; 10 improvised; 11 extemporary, unmeditated, unrehearsed

off-the-shelf: 5 stock; 7 vanilla; 10 off-the-rack, unmodified; 11 ready-to-wear

off time: 7 time off; 8 down time

off-track vehicle: 4 jeep

off-white: 4 bone; 5 ivory, pearl; 7 whitish

of late: 4 late; 6 lately; 8 latterly, recently; 9 these days

of note: 5 noted; 7 notable

oft: 5 often; 8 ofttimes; 10 frequently, oftentimes

often: 3 oft; 4 anew, much; 5 again; 6 afresh; 8 once more; 9 over again; 10 a great deal, frequently, oftentimes, repeatedly

oftentimes: 3 oft; 5 often; 8 ofttimes; 10 frequently

of use: 6 usable, useful; 7 useable; 9 of service; 11 serviceable

of value: 6 useful; 8 valuable

of vital importance: 4 main; 5 chief, prime; 7 capital, leading, primary; 8 foremost; 9 principal

of yore: 5 of old

Ogalala: 6 Oglala

ogee arch: 8 keel arch

Ogham: 5 runes

ogive: 4 ogee; 8 nose cone

Oglala: 7 Ogalala

ogle: 4 leer; 5 glare

ogre: 5 demon, devil, fiend; 7 monster

Ohio: 9 Ohio River; 12 Buckeye State

Ohioan: 7 Buckeye

Ohm: 13 Georg Simon Ohm; 14 George Simon Ohm

oil: 4 lube; 5 anele; 6 anoint, grease, lather; 8 crude oil, oil color; 9 ambrocate, black gold, lubricate, petroleum; 11 oil painting

oilbird: 8 guacharo

oil color: 3 oil; 4 oils; 5 paint; 8 oil paint

oil heater: 8 oilstove

oiliness: 7 unction; 10 greasiness, smarminess; 11 fulsomeness

oil production: 6 boring; 8 drilling

oil rig: 5 augur, drill; 8 drill rig; 11 drilling rig

oilskin: 7 slicker

oil tanker: 5 oiler; 6 tanker; 8 tank ship

oily: 6 abased, glassy, greasy, pliant, smarmy; 7 anodyne, buttery, fawning, fulsome, slavish; 8 cringing, glabrous, lenitive, slippery, specious, unctuous

oink: 6 squeal

ointment: 4 balm; 5 cream, salve; 6 cerate, lotion; 7 unguent; 8 lenitive, liniment; 9 emollient

Ojibwa: 7 Ojibway; 8 Chippewa

OK: 3 yes; 4 fair, fine, okay, okeh, okey, so-so; 7 alright, average, neutral; 8 all right, bearable, innocent, mediocre, middling, ordinary, passable, very well; 9 innocuous, tolerable; 10 acceptable

oka: 3 oca

okay: 2 OK; 4 fine, okeh, okey; 7 alright, approve, neutral; 8 all right, innocent, sanction; 9 innocuous; 11 inoffensive

okeh: 2 OK; 4 okay, okey

okey: 2 OK; 4 okay, okeh

Oklahoma City: 17 capital of Oklahoma

okra: 5 gumbo; 9 okra plant; 11 lady's-finger

old: 4 aged, worn; 5 older, stale; 7 antique, ancient, archaic; 8 obsolete, previous; 9 venerable

old age: 3 age; 5 years; 7 oldness; 11 advanced age

old clothes: 4 rags; 7 tatters

Old Colony: 8 Bay State; 13 Massachusetts

old custom: 9 tradition

Old Dominion State: 8 Virginia; 11 Old Dominion

Old English: 10 Anglo-Saxon

Old English sheepdog: 7 bobtail

older: 2 sr.; 3 big, old; 4 aged; 5 elder; 6 eldest, oldest, senior; 7 elderly

oldest: 5 elder, older; 6 eldest

old-fashioned: 5 passe, stale; 6 demode, old hat, passee, rococo; 7 antique; 8 after-age, outmoded; 10 antiquated

Old Glory: 6 U.S. flag; 15 Stars and Stripes

old growth: 12 virgin forest

old hand: 3 vet; 7 veteran; 8 old-timer, warhorse

old hat: 5 passe, stale; 6 boring, demode, passee, rococo; 7 antique, trivial; 8 outmoded, well-worn; 9 well-known; 12 old-fashioned

Old Hickory: 7 Jackson; 13 Andrew Jackson

old lady: 5 crone

Old Line State: 8 Maryland; 9 Free State

old maid: 6 zinnia; 8 spinster; 10 periwinkle

old man: 2 pa; 3 dad, pop; 4 dada, papa, seer; 5 daddy, pappa, pater; 6 old boy; 8 absinthe; 9 graybeard, greybeard, patriarch

Old Nick: 5 Devil, Satan; 7 Lucifer; 8 the Devil; 9 Beelzebub

Old North State: 12 Tar Heel State; 13 North Carolina

old salt: 3 gob, tar; 6 sea dog, seaman; 7 Jack-tar, mariner; 8 seafarer

old saw: 3 saw; 5 adage; 6 dictum, saying; 7 bromide, proverb

old sol: 3 sun, Sol; 6 Apollo, the Sun; 9 earth's sun

Old Style: 14 Julian calendar

old-time: 6 quaint

old timer: 6 gaffer; 7 antique, old hand, veteran; 8 mossback, warhorse; 9 old geezer, old stager

old times: 8 langsyne; 11 former times; 12 auld langsyne

Olea: olive; 9 genus Olea

Oleaceae: 11 olive family

oleaginous: 4 oily; 6 greasy, smarmy; 7 buttery, fulsome; 8 unctuous; 9 sebaceous

Oleandra: 12 oleander fern; 13 genus Oleandra

oleaster family: 12 Elaeagnaceae

olefin: 6 alkene; 7 olefine

oleomargarine: 4 oleo; 9 margarine

olfaction: 5 smell

olfactory impairment: 7 anosmia

olfactory organ: 4 nose

olfactory perception: 4 odor; 5 smell

oligarchy: 8 demagogy

Oligocene epoch: 9 Oligocene

Olimbos: 7 Olympus; 10 Mt. Olympus; 12 Mount Olympus

olio: 4 mess; 6 medley; 7 farrago; 8 mishmash, pastiche; 9 patchwork, potpourri; 10 hodgepodge

olive: 9 dull green

olive branch: 13 peace offering

olive family: 8 Oleaceae

olive oil: 11 extra-virgin

Olympia: 19 capital of Washington

Olympiad: 8 Olympics; 12 Olympic Games

olympian: 8 majestic; 9 exceeding; 10 prodigious, surpassing; 11 exceptional

Olympian: 7 Olympic; 10 Olympic god

Olympic: 8 Olympian

Olympic athlete: 8 Olympian

Olympic champion: 12 gold medalist

Olympic Games: 8 Olympiad, Olympics; 13 Olympian Games

Olympic god: 8 Olympian

Olympics: 8 Olympiad; 12 Olympic Games

Olympus: 7 Olimbos; 10 Mt. Olympus; 12 Mount Olympus

omelette: 6 omelet

omen: 4 bode, sign; 5 augur; 6 augury; 7 auspice, betoken, portend, portent, predict, presage; 8 forecast, foretell; 9 auspicate, prefigure; 10 foreshadow

ominous: 3 ill; 4 ugly; 7 augural, baleful; 8 augurial, menacing, minatory, sinister; 9 ill-omened, minacious; 10 forbidding

omission: 4 blot, flaw, miss, skip, slip, trip; 5 fault; 6 laches [Law]; 7 default, evasion, failure, neglect, stumble; 8 deletion, footfall; 9 exception, exclusion, oversight

omit: 4 drop, fail, jump, miss, sink, skip; 5 elude, evade; 6 except, ignore, shelve; 7 exclude, neglect, take out; 8 leave off, leave out, overleap, overlook

omnibus: 3 bus; 5 coach; 6 jitney; 7 autobus; 8 motorbus; 10 motorcoach; 12 double-decker

omnipotent: 8 almighty; 11 all-powerful

omnipresence: 8 ubiquity

omniscient: 10 all-knowing

omnium gatherum: 4 mess, olio; 6 medley; 7 farrago; 8 all sorts, mishmash, pastiche; 9 patchwork, potpourri; 10 congestion, hodgepodge

omnivorous: 7 swinish; 10 gluttonous

omphalos: 3 hub; focus; 10 focal point

omphalus: 5 navel; 9 umbilicus; 11 bellybutton

on: 5 ahead, along, forth; 6 active, on duty; 7 on top of, running; 8 forwards; 9 operating

on account: 8 on credit

onager: 7 bricole; 8 catapult

on a higher floor: 8 upstairs

on a lower floor: 5 below; 10 downstairs

on a razor's edge: 4 taut; 5 tense

on a rock: 6 moored; 8 anchored, at anchor, tethered

once: 4 when; 6 former, one day; 7 one time, quondam; 8 formerly, only once, sometime

once and for all: 12 conclusively

once in a while: 7 at times; 10 now and then, on occasion, time to time; 11 now and again; 12 occasionally

once more: 4 anew; 5 again, often; 6 afresh

once-over: 8 look-over

Onchorynchus: 4 coho; 6 salmon; 7 chinook, sockeye; 9 red salmon; 10 king salmon; 12 silver salmon; 13 salmon; 17 genus Onchorynchus

oncoming: 5 onset; 11 approaching

Ondatra: 7 muskrat; 12 genus Ondatra

on dit: 3 cry; 4 buzz, fame; 5 rumor; 6 cackle; 7 hearsay

on duty: 2 on; 6 at work, on-duty; 7 working

one: 3 ace; 4 only, same, sole, unit; 5 unity; 6 single; 7 someone, unitary; 8 peerless, selfsame, solitary, somebody

one and all: 3 all, sum; 5 total

one and the same: 3 one; 4 same, self, very; 8 selfsame, very same; 9 identical

one another: 9 each other

one-armed bandit: 4 slot

one by one: 4 each; 5 apart; 6 apiece, singly

one-dimensional: 6 linear

one dollar bill: 4 buck, clam; 6 single dollar; 10 dollar bill

one-fifth: 5 fifth; 9 fifth part; 13 twenty percent

one-fourth: 6 fourth; 7 quarter

one-horse: 4 poky; 5 pokey; 9 jerkwater

one hundred and forty-four: 5 gross

one-hundredth: 9 hundredth; 10 one percent

one in a million: 4 rare

one iron: 11 driving iron

one-man rule: 7 tyranny; 9 autocracy, despotism, monocracy, shogunate; 10 absolutism; 12 dictatorship

one-member: 10 uninominal

on end: 2 up

oneness: 5 unity; 8 identity, sameness; 11 singularity

one-of-a-kind: 6 unique; 8 singular

one of these days: 3 yet; 6 in time; 10 eventually

one percent: 9 hundredth; 12 one-hundredth

onerous: 6 taxing; 7 arduous; 9 laborious; 10 burdensome, formidable, oppressive

one-seventh: 7 seventh

one shot: 5 round

one-sided: 6 biased, unfair; 7 colored, partial, slanted, unequal; 8 lopsided

one-sixth: 5 sixth

one step at a time: 10 step by step

one-tenth: 5 tenth; 9 tenth part; 10 ten percent

one third: 5 third; 6 a third; 9 third part

one thousand: 4 thou; 5 grand; 8 thousand

one thousand thousand: 3 meg

onetime: 6 former; 7 quondam; 8 sometime

one-year: 6 annual

on fire: 5 afire; 6 ablaze, aflame, aflare, alight; 7 blazing, burning, flaming

ongoing: 9 advancing; 10 in progress, proceeding; 11 progressing

on high: 2 up; 5 above, aloft, aloof; 6 high up; 8 overhead

onion: 10 Allium cepa, onion plant

onionskin: 6 flimsy

on-key: 4 true

on land: 6 ashore

onlooker: 7 witness; 8 beholder, observer; 9 bystander, spectator; 10 eyewitness

only: 3 but, one; 4 just, lone, sole; 5 alone, apart; 6 enough, merely, only if, purely, simply, single, solely; 7 unitary; 8 entirely, lonesome, only when, solitary; **9** exclusive; **11** considering, exclusively

Onoclea: 8 bead fern; **10** fiddlehead; **13** sensitive fern; **12** genus Onoclea

on-off switch: 6 toggle

onomatopoeia: 6 echoic; **9** imitative

on one's head: 10 topsy-turvy

on one's own: 4 solo; **5** alone; **6** singly

on one side: 5 aside; **6** beside; **7** abreast; **9** alongside

Ononis: 10 restharrow; **11** genus Ononis

Onopordon: 7 thistle; **9** Onopordum; **14** genus Onopordon, genus Onopordum

on paper: 8 in theory; **9** in writing; **13** theoretically

on purpose: 9 advisedly, expressly, knowingly, purposely, wittingly; **10** designedly

onrush: 5 onset; **6** attack; **9** onslaught

onslaught: 5 onset; **6** attack, charge, onrush; **7** barrage; **10** outpouring

on the alert: 5 awake; **7** on watch, wakeful; **8** on the job, vigilant, watchful; **9** wide awake

on the ball: 5 sharp; **6** shrewd

on the basis of: 4 from

on the button: 7 exactly; **8** on the dot; **9** precisely

on the contrary: 6 contra, rather; **10** contrarily

on the decline: 9 on the wane

on the dot: 7 exactly; **9** precisely

on the far side: 6 beyond

on the fence: 9 undecided

on the job: 7 working

on the lam: 7 runaway; **8** fugitive, in hiding

on the lookout: 5 awake; **7** on watch, wakeful; **8** vigilant, watchful

on the loose: 5 loose; **7** at large, escaped; **9** at liberty

on the market: 7 for sale, salable; **8** sellable, vendible; **10** marketable

on the move: 6 active

on the nose: 7 exactly; **8** on the dot; **9** precisely

on the other hand: 7 but then, however; **9** then again

on the QT: 8 in secret, secretly

on the road: 6 on tour; **7** en route; **8** on course, on the way, underway

on the sly: 5 aside, slyly; **9** furtively, sotto voce [Lat]; **10** stealthily

on the surface: 7 surface; **8** exterior, external; **11** superficial

on the table: 5 handy; **7** offered; **8** proposed

on the way: 6 coming, in hand; **7** en route

on the whole: 6 en bloc, in fine; **7** as a body, en masse, finally; **8** after all, all in all; **10** altogether

on time: 6 in time, prompt, timely; **7** exactly,

not late; **8** punctual; **9** precisely; **10** punctually

ontogenesis: 6 growth; **7** growing; **8** ontogeny; **10** maturation; **11** development

ontogeny: 6 growth; **7** growing; **10** maturation; **11** development, ontogenesis

onto land: 6 ashore

ontology: 11 metaphysics

on tour: 9 on the road

onus: 4 duty, load; **6** burden; **9** liability; **10** obligation

onus probandi: 13 burden of proof

onward: 5 ahead, forth; **7** forward, onwards; **8** forwards

on watch: 5 awake; **7** wakeful; **8** vigilant, watchful

onychophoran: 9 peripatus

oodles: 4 gobs, lots, tons, wads; **5** heaps, loads, piles, rafts, scads, slews; **6** dozens, scores, stacks; **8** lashings

oogenesis: 10 biogenesis

oomph: 4 zing; **6** pizzaz; **7** pizzazz; **8** dynamism

oophorectomy: 11 ovariectomy

ooze: 3 goo, mud; **4** gook, guck, gunk, muck, seep; **5** drain, erupt, exude, slime, slush; **6** oozing, sludge, squash; **7** exudate, seepage

opacity: 10 opaqueness

opah: 8 moonfish

opal: 3 gem

opalescence: 11 iridescence

opalescent: 7 opaline; **10** iridescent

opaline: 10 iridescent, opalescent

opaque: 3 dim; **4** dark; **5** dense, muddy; **7** cryptic, obscure; **8** nebulous; **10** mysterious

opaqueness: 7 opacity

open: 3 air, out; **4** bare, free; **5** clear, enter, frank, loose, overt, start; **6** afford, candid, deploy, expose, liable, open to, open up, opened, patent, public, spread, unfold; **7** blatant, blazing, exposed, express, lawless, lay bare, lay open, literal, open air, pop open, sincere, subject, surface, unclose, uncover; **8** commence, exoteric, explicit, outdoors, pull open, put forth, unfenced, vegetate, wide open, wide-open; **9** confiding, downright, enter upon, exposed to, expressed, open as day, pullulate, spread out, throw open, undecided, undivided, unstopped; **10** aboveboard, assailable, burst forth, out-of-doors, undefended, unenclosed, unfastened, unreserved, unresolved; **11** conspicuous, open-hearted, plain-spoken, susceptible, undisguised

open-air: 8 alfresco, outdoors

opencast mining: 11 strip mining

open-chain: 7 acyclic

opencut: 5 strip; **8** opencast

open-end fund: 10 mutual fund

open-end wrench: 12 tappet wrench

opener: 8 password; 9 master key; 11 combination
open-eyed: 5 alert; 7 wakeful; 8 vigilant,
watchful
open fire: 4 fire; 5 shell; 6 pepper; 7 bombard
open fireplace: 6 hearth; 9 fireplace
open fracture: 16 compound fracture
open handed: 4 free; 6 giving; 7 liberal; 8
generous, handsome, princely; 9 bounteous, bountiful, unselfish; 10 charitable,
free handed, full handed, munificent
open-hearted: 4 kind, open; 5 frank; 6 candid, kindly; 9 confiding; 11 good-hearted
opening: 3 gap; 4 data, hole, room; 5 crack,
terms; 6 gaping, outset; 7 orifice, scuttle,
yawning; 8 aperture, hatchway, occasion,
premises; 9 beginning, first step, inception,
opening up; 10 incipience, initiation, initiative, timeliness; 11 opportunity
opening in the woods: 5 glade; 8 clearing
opening night: 5 debut; 7 opening
openly: 7 clearly, plainly; 8 in public, publicly
openness: 9 frankness; 11 receptivity; 12
truthfulness
open sore: 5 wound
open space: 9 free space
open to: 4 open; 6 liable; 7 capable, subject;
9 exposed to, subject to; 10 accessible,
hospitable; 11 susceptible
opera: 4 opus; 7 musical; 10 opera house
operable: 6 usable; 7 useable; 10 functional;
11 operational
opera bouffe: 6 bouffe; 9 burlesque; 10
comic opera; 12 opera comique
opera glasses: 9 binocular; 10 binoculars; 12
field glasses
opera hat: 6 top hat, topper; 7 high hat, silk
hat; 8 dress hat; 9 stovepipe
opera house: 5 opera; 7 theater
operant: 6 at work
operate: 2 do, go; 3 act, run; 4 lock, mesh,
work; 6 engage; 7 control, perform, procure; 8 function, maneuver
operate on batteries: 6 mobile; 8 portable
operating: 2 on; 6 active; 7 running; 9 operation; 11 functioning
operating cost: 8 overhead
operating room: 7 surgery; 7 theater
operating surgeon: 7 surgeon; 8 sawbones
operating system: 2 OS
operating theater: 7 surgery; 13 operating
room
operation: 3 act; 5 doing, force; 6 acting,
action, agency; 7 process, running, surgery,
working; 8 function, movement; 9 operating, procedure; 11 functioning, performance
operational: 6 usable; 7 useable; 8 operable;
9 operating; 10 functional

515   opener / opposite

operations: 7 crusade; 8 campaign; 10 expedition
operative: 2 PI; 3 key; 6 acting; 7 running,
working; 8 mechanic, sherlock, surgical; 9
effectual, efficient, practical; 10 functional,
private eye; 11 efficacious, functioning,
secret agent
operator: 7 hustler, sharpie; 8 investor,
shrewdie; 10 speculator; 11 manipulator;
13 wheeler dealer
operculum: 3 lid; 4 door; 5 cover
operetta: 7 musical; 10 light opera
Ophidia: 9 Serpentes; 15 suborder Ophidia;
17 suborder Serpentes
ophidian: 5 snake; 7 serpent
Ophidiidae: 16 family Ophidiidae
Ophiodon: 7 lingcod; 13 genus Ophiodon
ophiolatry: 14 serpent-worship
Ophiophagus: 9 hamadryad, king cobra; 10
Naja hannah; 16 genus Ophiophagus
Ophrys: 9 fly orchid, bee orchid; 11 genus
Ophrys
ophthalmologist: 7 oculist; 9 eye doctor
opiate: 5 opium, poppy; 8 narcotic
opine: 7 speak up; 8 conceive, sound off
opinion: 4 mind, view; 5 stand; 6 ruling; 7
thought; 8 judgment, position; 9 judgement, sentiment, vox populi; 10 persuasion; 13 public opinion
opinionate: 9 opinioned
opinion poll: 4 poll; 6 survey
opium: 5 poppy; 6 opiate; 8 narcotic
opium addict: 10 opium taker
opium eater: 10 lotus eater
opossum: 6 possum; 9 phalanger
Oppenheimer: 17 Robert Oppenheimer
opponent: 3 foe; 5 enemy; 6 foeman; 8
opposing, opposite; 9 adversary; 10 antagonist, opposition
opportune: 6 timely; 9 favorable, well-
timed; 10 seasonable
opportunism: 10 expedience; 11 self-
seeking; 12 self-interest
opportunist: 10 self-seeker
opportunity: 4 room; 6 chance; 7 opening; 8
good time, occasion; 9 right time; 10 timeliness
oppose: 3 pit; 5 block, fight, match, react; 6
defend, reluct, resist; 9 fight back; 10
antagonize, contradict, controvert, counteract
opposed: 7 adverse; 8 opposing; 9 antipodal;
10 antipodean, at variance, contrasted; 11
contrasting; 12 antagonistic
opposing: 5 front, stand; 7 adverse, opposed;
8 opponent; 9 antipodal, renitency, resisting; 10 antagonism, antipodean, at variance, contrasted, opposition, resistance
opposite: 5 polar; 6 paired; 7 antonym,

counter, inverse, reverse; **8** contrary, opponent; **9** diametric; **10** opposition

opposite number: 11 counterpart

opposite word: 7 antonym; **8** opposite

opposition: 3 foe; **5** enemy, front, stand; **8** contrast, opponent, opposing, opposite; **9** adversary, renitency, resisting; **10** antagonism, antagonist, resistance

oppress: 3 bug; **4** bait, bore; **5** abuse, beset, crush, grind, harry, haunt, hound, tease, worry, wrong; **6** badger, bother, harass, heckle, ill-use, infest, molest, pester, plague, pother; **8** aggrieve, bullirag, bullyrag, ill-treat, maltreat, mistreat, override, suppress; **9** importune, persecute

oppression: 7 outrage; **11** persecution, subjugation

oppressive: 5 close; **6** stuffy, sultry; **7** onerous; **8** grinding, stifling; **9** tyrannous; **10** burdensome, tyrannical; **11** suffocating

oppressor: 6 despot, tyrant

opprobrious: 7 abusive; **8** scornful, shameful; **9** insulting

opprobrium: 5 odium; **6** infamy; **7** obloquy; **8** ignominy

oppugn: 8 question; **10** antagonize

optative: 4 fain; **7** wishful

opt for: 5 elect; **6** choose, prefer, select

optic: 3 eye; **6** ocular, oculus, peeper, visual; **7** optical; **10** ophthalmic

optical lens: 10 camera lens

optic cup: 6 eyecup

optic disc: 9 blind spot

optician: 9 lens maker

optimal: 6 superb; **7** optimum; **9** first-rate; **10** first-class; **11** superlative

optimist: 8 laudator [Lat]; **9** encomiast; **11** whitewasher

optimistic: 8 sanguine; **9** confident; **11** affirmative

optimum: 7 optimal

option: 6 choice; **7** choices [pl]; **8** election; **11** alternative

optional: 8 elective, unforced; **9** not forced; **12** discretional

optometrist: 7 oculist; **9** eye doctor

opt out: 6 cop out

opulence: 6 luxury, riches, wealth; **7** fortune; **9** affluence, abundance, profusion

opulent: 4 rich; **6** deluxe, gilded, monied; **7** moneyed, wealthy; **8** affluent, princely; **9** luxurious, sumptuous

Opuntia: 4 tuna; **5** nopal; **6** cholla

opus: 3 art; **4** work; **5** piece, works; **6** number; **7** artwork; **9** work of art; **11** composition

OPV: 4 TOPV; **12** Sabin vaccine; **12** polio vaccine

or: 4 gold; **9** gold color

oracle: 7 prophet; **8** luminary; **9** authority

Oracle of Apollo: 13 Delphic oracle; **14** oracle of Delphi, Temple of Apollo

oracular: 6 mystic; **7** Delphic; **9** enigmatic

oral: 5 vocal; **7** lingual; **8** oral exam, phonetic, viva voce; **9** outspoken

oral cavity: 5 mouth

oral communication: 4 talk; **6** speech; **7** talking; **8** commerce, language, locution, parlance, speaking

oral contraceptive: 4 pill

oral examination: 4 oral; **8** oral exam, viva voce

oral herpes: 8 cold sore; **12** fever blister

oral ingestion: 10 swallowing

oral poliovirus vaccine: 3 OPV; **4** TOPV; **12** Sabin vaccine

orang: 9 orangutan; **10** orangutang

orange: 8 orangish; **10** orange tree, orangeness; **12** red and yellow

orange peel: 4 rind

orange pekoe tea: 5 pekoe

orange red: 7 scarlet; **9** vermilion

orange rind: 4 peel

orange yellow: 7 saffron

orangutan: 5 orang; **10** orangutang

orate: 4 talk; **5** speak; **7** lecture, expound

oration: 6 speech; **7** address, lecture, oratory

orator: 7 speaker; **8** lecturer; **11** rhetorician, speechmaker; **13** public speaker

oratorical: 10 rhetorical

oratorio: 10 choral work

oratory: 4 kirk; **6** chapel, church, speech; **7** address, lecture, oration; **8** basilica; **9** cathedral; **10** allocution, tabernacle

orb: 4 area, ball, band, belt, soil, zone; **5** cycle, field, globe, orbit, realm; **6** circle, cordon, domain, ground, sphere; **7** circuit, eyeball

orbicular: 6 global; **7** annular, globose, spheric; **8** circular, globular; **9** spherical; **10** ball-shaped, orbiculate

orbit: 3 orb; **4** area, band, belt, zone; **5** ambit, arena, cycle, field, range, reach, scope; **6** cordon, domain, rundle, sphere; **7** compass, revolve; **9** eye socket

orbital cavity: 5 orbit; **9** eye socket

orbital mechanics: 12 astronautics

orbital motion: 8 orbiting

orbiter: 7 sputnik [Russ]; **9** satellite

orb of day: 3 Sol; **6** old sol, the Sun; **9** earth's sun

orb of night: 4 Luna, moon

orbs: 3 eye

orc: 6 goblin; **9** hobglobin

orca: 6 killer; **7** grampus, sea wolf; **11** killer whale, Orcinus orca

orchard: 5 grove; **7** woodlet; **10** plantation

orchestra pit: 3 pit

orchestrate: 6 direct; **8** engineer, organize; **10** mastermind

Orchidaceae: 12 orchid family

orchidaceous plant: 6 orchid
Orchidales: 15 order Orchidales
orchid cactus: 10 epiphyllum
orchid family: 11 Orchidaceae
Orcinus orca: 4 orca; 6 killer; 7 grampus, sea wolf; 11 killer whale
ordain: 4 call; 5 allot, enact, order; 6 decree, prefer; 7 dictate, present; 8 legalize, sanctify; 9 prescribe, translate; 10 consecrate, give orders
ordained: 7 decreed; 8 in orders; 9 appointed, chartered
ordaining: 10 ordination
ordeal: 5 agony, trial
order: 3 put, say; 4 club, fiat, head, rank, rate, tell; 5 edict, grade, guild, lodge, place, range, set up; 6 coupon, decree, direct, enjoin, govern, ordain; 7 arrange, command, dictate, section, society, warrant; 8 nobility, ordering, organize, regulate, rescript; 9 debenture, prescribe; 10 consecrate, regularity, regularize, uniformity; 11 orderliness
ordered: 7 grouped, logical, orderly; 8 arranged; 9 organized, regulated; 10 consistent
ordered sequence: 6 series; 8 sequence; 10 succession
ordering: 5 order; 9 arranging, directing; 10 commanding; 12 organization
orderless: 9 unordered; 10 disordered, disorderly; 12 disorganized
orderly: 4 neat, tidy; 6 lawful, 7 grouped, logical, ordered, regular; 9 organized, regulated; 10 consistent, methodical, systematic
order of business: 6 agenda, docket; 7 agendum
order of payment: 5 draft
ordinance: 10 regulation; 11 institution
ordinarily: 7 usually; 8 commonly, normally; 9 generally, typically; 11 customarily
ordinary: 2 OK; 4 fair; 5 table, usual; 6 common, normal; 7 average, general, nominal, regular, typical; 8 bearable, everyday, familiar, frequent, habitual, mediocre, middling, passable, workaday; 9 household, tolerable, well-known; 10 acceptable; 11 commonplace, established
ordinary shares: 11 common stock; 12 common shares
ordnance: 3 arm, gun; 4 arms; 6 cannon, weapon; 8 heavy gun; 9 artillery, munitions; 10 ammunition; 11 heavy weapon; 12 deadly weapon
Ordovician period: 10 Ordovician
ordure: 4 dung; 5 feces, offal, stool; 9 dejection, excrement
Oreamnos: 12 mountain goat; 13 genus Oreamnos
oregano: 12 wild marjoram

Oregon pine: 6 red fir; 9 Oregon fir; 10 douglas fir
or else: 7 instead; 13 alternatively
organ: 5 offal; 7 utensil; 9 body organ, harmonica, harmonium, organ meat, pipe organ, reed organ; 11 variety meat; 12 Hammond organ; 13 electric organ
organdy: 8 organdie
organelle: 9 cell organ
organic: 8 internal; 9 organized; 10 structural; 11 constituent; 12 constitutive
organic world: 4 life
organization: 5 brass; 6 system; 8 founding, ordering; 9 arranging, formation, setting up, structure; 10 governance, organizing; 11 arrangement, structuring
organizational: 10 structural
organization not for profit: 9 non profit
Organization of American States: 3 OAS
Organization of Petroleum-Exporting Countries: 4 OPEC
organize: 4 cast, form; 5 found, get up, order, setup; 6 devise, direct, recast; 7 arrange, prepare; 8 engineer; 9 establish, institute; 10 constitute, coordinate, mastermind; 11 orchestrate, systematize
organized: 7 grouped, ordered, orderly, organic; 8 arranged; 9 unionized
organized body of knowledge: 7 science
organized crime: 5 mafia; 6 the mob; 7 gangdom; 8 gangland; 12 la cosa nostra, the syndicate
organized nature: 4 life; 12 organic world
organizer: 8 arranger
organizing: 8 founding, ordering; 9 arranging, setting up; 11 arrangement
organ meat: 5 offal, organ; 11 variety meat
organ of thought: 5 brain
organ pipe: 4 pipe; 8 pipework
organs: 11 variety meat
orgasm: 6 climax
orgiastic: 7 bacchic; 9 bacchanal, carousing; 12 bacchanalian
orgy: 4 riot; 7 debauch; 9 bacchanal; 10 debauchery, saturnalia; 11 bacchanalia
oriel window: 4 cove, nook; 5 niche, oriel; 6 corner, recess
orient: 4 East; 5 point, sunny; 8 meridian, oriental, reorient; 9 orientate; 17 change orientation, eastern hemisphere
Orient: 4 East
oriental: 5 Asian; 6 orient; 7 Asiatic
Oriental black mushroom: 8 shiitake
orientation: 4 pose; 6 aspect; 7 posture; 8 attitude
orifice: 4 door, lips; 5 chops, inlet, mouth, porch; 6 portal; 7 opening, portico
oriflamme: 5 eagle; 8 standard, streamer
origami: 12 paper folding

Origanum majorana: 13 sweet marjoram
Origanum vulgare: 7 oregano; 8 marjoram
origin: 4 line, root; 5 blood, cause, stock; 6 reason, source; 7 descent, element, genesis, lineage; 8 ancestry, pedigree; 9 beginning, bloodline, inception, parentage, principle; 10 extraction; 11 origination
original: 3 new; 4 type; 5 ideal, model, novel, pilot; 6 causal, master, oddity, proper; 7 certain, example, fertile, partial, pattern, private, several, special; 8 creative, definite, especial, exemplar, nonesuch, paradigm, peculiar, specific, standard; 9 archetype, character, exclusive, inventive, precedent, prototype, reference, scantling, unheard of; 10 individual, master copy, particular, respective, unfamiliar
originality: 7 newness, novelty; 9 mannerism; 10 creativity; 11 peculiarity, spontaneity; 12 creativeness, idiosyncrasy, nonimitation; 13 individuality
originally: 7 earlier
originate: 4 coin, grow, rise; 5 arise, found, set up, start; 6 broach, create, devise, invent; 7 develop; 8 inchoate, initiate, spring up; 9 fabricate, institute
origination: 6 origin, outset; 7 genesis, opening; 8 creation, founding; 9 beginning, inception; 10 foundation, incipience, initiation; 11 institution; 12 commencement
originator: 7 creator; 8 producer; 9 conceiver; 10 mastermind
origin of species: 10 speciation
Orinoco: 12 Orinoco River
oriole: 14 American oriole, New World oriole, Old World oriole
Oriolidae: 15 family Oriolidae
Oriolus: 6 oriole; 12 genus Oriolus
Orion: 9 The Hunter
orison: 6 prayer; 8 petition; 9 communion; 10 invocation
orlop deck: 5 orlop; 10 fourth deck
Ormosia: 8 bead tree; 9 jumby bead; 12 genus Ormosia
Ormuzd: 10 Ahura Mazda
ornament: 4 bead; 5 adorn, grace; 6 enrich; 8 beautify, decorate; 9 adornment, embellish; 10 decoration, overcharge; 13 embellishment
ornamental: 8 cosmetic; 10 decorative
ornamentalist: 9 decorator
ornamentation: 7 bombast; 8 ornament, richness; 9 adornment, euphemism, turgidity; 10 decoration, floridness, orotundity; 11 declamation, grandiosity; 13 embellishment
ornamented: 4 rich; 5 tumid; 6 florid, mouthy, ornate, turgid; 7 adorned, flowery, orotund; 8 inflated, sonorous, swelling; 9 bombastic, decorated, grandiose, high-

flown; 10 beautified, rhetorical, turgescent; 11 big-sounding, declamatory
ornate: 4 gilt, rich; 5 tumid; 6 florid, mouthy, turgid; 7 flowery; 9 elaborate
ornery: 6 unruly; 9 crotchety; 12 cantankerous
ornithischian dinosaur: 13 ornithischian
ornithologist: 11 bird watcher
ornithopod dinosaur: 10 ornithopod
Ornithorhynchus: 8 duckbill, platypus; 20 genus Ornithorhynchus
Orobanchaceae: 15 broomrape family
orogenesis: 7 orogeny; 16 mountain-building
orotund: 4 rich; 5 large, round, tumid; 6 florid, mouthy, ornate, rotund, turgid; 7 flowery; 8 inflated, sonorous, swelling; 9 bombastic, grandiose, high-flown; 10 Johnsonian, ornamented, rhetorical, turgescent; 11 big-sounding, declamatory
orphan: 8 orphaned; 10 parentless
orphans' asylum: 9 orphanage
orpine: 5 sedum, orpin; 8 livelong; 11 liveforever
orrisroot: 5 orris
orthoboric acid: 9 boric acid
orthodontics: 11 orthodontia
orthodox: 5 sound; 8 faithful; 9 canonical
Orthodox: 13 Greek Orthodox; 14 Jewish-Orthodox; 15 Eastern Orthodox, Russian Orthodox
orthodoxy: 9 true faith; 14 religious truth
orthogonal: 11 rectangular; 13 perpendicular
orthography: 8 spelling; 13 writing system
orthopaedic: 10 orthopedic
orthopedic: 11 orthopaedic; 12 orthopedical
ortolan bunting: 7 ortolan
Orycteropus: 7 ant bear; 8 aardvark, anteater; 16 genus Orycteropus
oryx: 7 gemsbok; 8 antelope, gemsbuck
Oryza: 4 rice; 10 genus Oryza
Oryza sativa: 14 cultivated rice
Os: 6 osmium
os: 4 bone
Osage: 10 Osage River
oscillate: 7 vibrate
oscilloscope: 3 CRO
oscine bird: 6 oscine
Oscines: 8 Passeres; 15 suborder Oscines; 16 suborder Passeres
osculate: 4 kiss
osculator: 6 kisser
os frontale: 8 forehead
Oslo: 11 Christiania; 15 capital of Norway
Osmitrol: 8 mannitol
osmium: 2 Os
Osmundaceae: 14 fiddlehead fern; 17 family Osmundaceae
os nasale: 9 nasal bone
osprey: 8 fish hawk
osseous: 4 bony; 6 osteal
ossicle: 7 bonelet; 9 ossiculum
ossified: 10 fossilized

osteal: 4 bony; 7 osseous
ostensible: 7 alleged, seeming; 8 apparent, asserted; 9 colorable, ostensive, plausible, pretended
ostentation: 4 fuss, show; 7 display, fanfare; 8 flourish; 9 pomposity; 10 showing off; 11 pompousness, splashiness
ostentatious: 5 showy; 6 kitsch; 7 dashing; 11 pretentious
osteopathist: 9 osteopath
ostler: 7 hostler
ostracism: 10 banishment
ostracize: 3 ban, mob; 4 hiss, hoot, shun; 6 banish, clamor; 7 cast out; 9 blackball, blacklist
oswego tea: 7 bee balm; 12 bergamot mint
otalgia: 7 earache
other: 4 them, they; 5 early, extra; 6 former, others [pl]; 7 another; 8 outsider; 9 different; 10 additional
others: 5 other; 7 another
other than: 4 save; 6 beside, except; 7 barring, without
otherwise: 11 differently
otiose: 4 idle, lazy; 5 slack; 6 futile, remiss, supine, torpid, wasted; 7 languid, workshy; 8 faineant, indolent, slothful, sluggish; 9 pointless
otolaryngologist: 3 ENT
otologist: 9 ear doctor
Ottawa: 15 Canadian capital, capital of Canada
ottoman: 4 seat; 5 couch; 8 footrest; 9 footstool
Otus: 3 owl; 10 screech owl; 9 genus Otus
Ouachita: 13 Ouachita River
oubliette: 7 dungeon
ouch: 2 ow
ought: 4 must, need; 6 should
Ouija: 10 Ouija board
ounce: 9 troy ounce; 11 snow leopard
Our Father: 11 Lord's prayer
Our Lady: 5 Saint; 7 Madonna; 9 Notre Dame [Fr]
ousel: 4 merl; 5 merle, ouzel; 9 blackbird; 12 Turdus merula
oust: 5 evict, expel; 7 boot out, drum out, kick out; 8 throw out
ousting: 6 bounce [U.S.], ouster; 7 removal; 9 dismissal
out: 3 KO'd; 4 away, open, oust, over, tabu; 5 eject, taboo; 6 absent, kayoed, public, uncool; 7 come out, extinct, retired, stunned, without; 8 outwards, quenched, finished
out-and-out: 4 rank; 5 sheer; 8 absolute; 9 downright, right-down
outback: 4 bush, wild; 6 remote; 9 backwoods
outbalance: 5 outdo; 7 outrank; 8 outweigh

outbound: 7 outward; 9 departing; 12 outward-bound
outbreak: 3 fit; 5 brunt, burst, onset, sally, scene; 6 advent, revolt, rising, sortie; 7 faction, tempest; 8 breakout, outburst, uprising; 9 rebellion; 10 insurgency, occurrence
outburst: 3 fit; 4 gush; 5 burst, scene; 6 strain; 7 flare-up, tempest; 8 effusion, outbreak
outcast: 5 exile; 6 pariah; 8 castaway, derelict
out cold: 4 dead [fig], numb; 7 unaware; 8 comatose; 9 catatonic, senseless; 11 unconscious
outcome: 5 issue, yield; 6 effect, output, result, upshot; 7 product; 8 offshoot; 9 aftermath, resultant; 11 consequence
outcry: 3 cry; 4 call, wail, yell; 5 shout; 6 chorus, clamor, cry out, crying, plaint; 7 call out, exclaim, wailing
outdated: 8 obsolete; 9 out-of-date
outdistance: 8 distance, outstrip, overcome, surmount
outdo: 4 best; 5 outgo, scoop, trump; 6 exceed, outwit; 7 outrank, surpass; 8 outflank, outmatch, outrival, outstrip
outdone: 6 bested
outdoor: 7 outside; 9 out-of-door
outdoor lessons: 10 chautauqua
outdoors: 3 air; 4 open; 7 open air, outside; 8 alfresco
outdoor stage: 5 stand; 9 bandstand
outer boundary: 6 fringe; 9 periphery
outer ear: 11 external car
outer garment: 11 overgarment
Outer Mongolia: 8 Mongolia; 24 Mongolian People's Republic
outer space: 5 space
outerwear: 11 overclothes
outface: 7 outlook; 8 outstare
outfit: 3 arm, fit, kit, man, rig; 5 array, equip, getup; 6 fit out; 8 armament, ensemble; 9 equipment; 12 accouterment
outfitted: 9 fitted out
outfitting: 9 equippage, equipping
outflank: 4 best; 5 flank, outdo, scoop, trump; 6 outwit
outflow: 4 leak; 6 efflux, escape, spring; 7 leakage
outflowing: 8 effluent
outfox: 4 beat; 6 outwit; 8 outsmart; 9 overreach; 10 circumvent
out front: 5 ahead; 9 in the lead
outgo: 4 beat, best; 5 outdo; 6 exceed, outlay, outrun; 7 outjump, outleap, outride, surpass; 8 outmatch, outrival, outstrip, surmount; 10 beat hollow; 11 expenditure
outgoer: 6 emigre; 7 emigree; 8 emigrant
outgoing: 11 extroverted, forthcoming

outgoings: 6 outlay; **7** expense; **8** expenses; **11** expenditure

outgrowth: 6 branch, growth, offset, sequel; **7** process; **8** offshoot; **9** appendage, corollary, emergence; **11** aftereffect, development

outguess: 11 secondguess

outhouse: 5 privy; **11** outbuilding

outing: 4 ride; **5** drive, jaunt; **6** airing, junket, picnic, sashay; **8** field day; **9** excursion; **10** expedition; **12** pleasure trip

outjump: 7 outleap

outlander: 5 alien; **9** foreigner; **10** noncitizen

outlandish: 5 alien, flaky; **6** exotic, freaky; **7** bizarre, foreign, strange; **8** freakish; **9** eccentric

outlandishly: 10 exotically

outlast: 7 outlive, survive

outlaw: 3 ban, bar; **5** crook, exile, felon, taboo; **6** banish, enjoin, forbid; **7** illicit, lawless; **8** criminal, disallow, forefend, outlawed, prohibit, unlawful; **9** interdict, proscribe; **10** expatriate, illegalize

outlawed: 6 banned, barred, outlaw; **7** illicit, tabooed; **8** enjoined, unlawful; **9** forbidden; **10** disallowed, not allowed, prohibited

outlay: 5 outgo; **7** expense; **8** expenses, spending; **9** disbursal, outgoings; **11** expenditure; **12** disbursement

outlet: 4 exit; **5** issue; **6** way out; **7** release; **8** wall plug; **10** wall socket; **11** retail store, sales outlet; **14** electric outlet

out like a light: 4 dead [fig], numb; **7** out cold, unaware; **8** comatose; **9** catatonic, senseless; **11** unconscious

outline: 4 draw, limn, line, note; **5** brief, draft, frame, lines, rough, study, trace; **6** apercu, digest, draw up, minute, precis, schema, scheme, sketch; **7** compose, contour, epitome, profile, summary; **8** abstract, analysis, contents, describe, skeleton, synopsis; **9** delineate, framework, lineament, perimeter, periphery; **10** abridgment, paraphrase, rough draft

outlive: 4 live; **7** outlast, subsist, survive

outlook: 7 lookout, outface; **8** outstare, prospect; **9** mentality, world view; **11** expectation

out loud: 5 aloud

outlying: 5 apart; **7** outside, outward; **11** outstanding

outmaneuver: 5 outdo; **6** outwit; **8** outflank, outreach, outsmart

outmatch: 5 outdo, outgo; **6** exceed; **7** surpass; **8** outstrip, surmount

out-migration: 10 emigration

outmoded: 5 passe; **6** demode, old-hat, passee; **7** antique; **12** old-fashioned

outmost: 9 outermost

out of action: 5 broke; **6** broken, busted; **8** disabled; **10** broken down, inoperable, out of order

out of-bounds: 8 sideline; **9** off-limits

out of breath: 6 winded; **7** gasping, panting

out of commission: 5 broke; **6** broken, busted; **10** broken down, out of order

out of date: 5 stale; **6** old hat, rococo; **7** out of it; **8** obsolete, outdated; **10** antiquated; **12** old-fashioned

out of fashion: 5 stale; **6** old hat, rococo; **7** out of it; **8** obsolete, outdated; **10** antiquated; **12** old-fashioned

out of it: 3 out; **5** stale; **6** old hat, rococo, uncool; **8** after-age, unversed; **9** misguided, out of date, unstylish; **10** antiquated

out of one's mind: 3 mad; **4** daft, loco, nuts; **5** batty, crazy, dotty, loony, nutty; **6** crazed, insane, teched [dialect]; **7** bonkers, cracked, far gone, lunatic, tetched [dialect], touched; **8** demented, deranged

out of order: 4 awry; **5** amiss, broke, wrong; **6** broken, busted; **7** haywire

out of place: 7 mislaid; **9** misplaced

out of practice: 5 rusty

out of service: 7 retired; **10** inoperable

out of the ordinary: 4 rare; **11** exceptional; **13** extraordinary

out of the question: 5 unfit; **6** unmeet; **8** improper; **9** ungranted; **10** impossible, out of reach; **12** unimaginable

out of this world: 12 otherworldly

out of work: 4 idle; **7** jobless; **10** unemployed

outperform: 7 outjump, surpass; **8** outrival, outshine

outpour: 8 effusion; **9** effluence, effluxion; **10** outpouring

outpouring: 3 run; **4** gush, tide; **5** flood, flush; **6** spring; **7** barrage, outflow, outpour; **8** effusion, fountain, overflow; **9** discharge, effluence

output: 5 yield; **7** outcome, outturn, turnout; **8** printout; **10** end product

outrage: 5 appal, havoc, shock; **6** appall, inroad, insult, offend, ravage, ravish, vilify; **7** affront, ill turn, incense, profane, scandal, violate; **8** atrocity, dishonor, enormity, ferocity, savagery; **9** barbarity, brutality, desecrate, infuriate

outrageous: 4 rude, wild; **5** bluff, rough, steep; **6** errant, fierce, horrid, raging, savage; **7** furious, hideous, violent; **8** horrific, shocking, ungentle, usurious, vehement; **9** excessive

outrank: 4 rank; **5** outdo; **8** outrival, outweigh

outre: 5 flaky; **6** freaky; **7** bizarre, stilted; **8** fabulous, freakish

outreach: 6 exceed; **8** reach out

outride: 4 beat, best; **8** outstrip

outrigger: 3 bar, rod; **4** boom

outright: 5 fully, quite, stark; **6** wholly;

7 totally, utterly; **8** entirely; **9** instantly, unlimited; **10** altogether, completely

outrun: 4 beat, best; **8** outstrip

outset: 5 first, start; **7** kickoff, opening; **9** beginning, inception; **10** incipience, initiation; **11** origination; **12** commencement

outshine: 7 eclipse, outjump, surpass; **8** outrival; **10** outperform

outside: 4 away; **6** beyond, remote; **7** outdoor, outward, surface; **8** alfresco, exterior, external, outdoors, outlying; **10** extraneous

outside-group: 8 exogamic

outside marriage: 12 out of wedlock

outsider: 4 them, they; **5** other; **9** foreigner

outsized: 7 outsize; **8** oversize, too large; **9** oversized

outskirt: 6 fringe; **7** outpost

outsmart: 4 beat; **6** outfox, outwit; **9** overreach; **10** circumvent; **11** outmaneuver

outspoken: 4 oral; **5** bluff, blunt, frank, vocal; **6** candid, direct; **7** lingual; **8** phonetic; **9** downright, ingenuous, unwritten; **10** forthright, free-spoken

outstanding: 3 due; **4** owed; **5** great, owing; **6** unpaid; **7** past due, salient; **8** outlying, striking; **9** prominent; **10** delinquent; **11** magnificent, spectacular

outstay: 8 overstay

outstretched: 8 extended; **9** elongated, outspread; **10** lengthened

outstrip: 4 beat, best; **5** outdo, outgo; **6** exceed, outrun; **7** outride, surpass; **8** distance, outmatch, outrival, surmount

outtasight: 4 wild; **5** heavy; **6** far out; **10** out of sight

outturn: 6 output; **7** turnout

outward: 7 outside; **8** outbound, outlying, outwards; **9** departing; **12** outward-bound

outwardly: 10 externally

outwards: 3 out; **4** over; **7** ab extra, outward, without; **10** out of doors

outwear: 3 fag; **4** jade, tire, wear; **5** weary; **6** fag out; **7** exhaust, fatigue, tire out, wear out

outwit: 4 beat; **5** outdo; **6** outfox; **8** outflank, outreach, outsmart

ouzel: 4 merl; **5** merle, ousel; **9** blackbird

oval: 5 ovate, ovoid, ovule; **7** ellipse, oviform, prolate; **8** elliptic; **9** egg-shaped; **10** elliptical

ovalbumin: 7 albumen; **8** egg white

ovate: 4 oval; **5** ovoid; **7** oviform, prolate; **8** elliptic; **9** egg-shaped; **10** elliptical

ovation: 5 paean; **7** acclaim, triumph; **8** applause

oven stuffer: 7 roaster

over: 3 o'er, odd, out; **4** done, gone, lots, more, past; **5** above, ended; **6** across, beyond, bygone, gone by, plenty; **7** all over, decided, settled, upwards, without; **8** complete, finished, foregone, outwards; **9**

abundance, amplitude, completed, concluded, fulfilled, played out, plenitude, profusion; **10** terminated; **11** copiousness

overabundance: 6 excess; **7** surfeit, too many, too much; **8** overmuch; **10** saturation

overabundant: 4 rife; **9** plethoric

overachiever: 10 workaholic

overact: 3 ham; **6** overdo; **8** overplay

overacted: 5 stagy; **8** overdone; **10** theatrical

overactive: 11 hyperactive

over again: 4 anew; **5** again, often; **6** afresh; **8** once more; **9** once again; **10** repeatedly

overall: 5 total

overalls: 5 pants; **8** trousers

over and above: 3 too; **6** overly; **8** moreover; **9** exceeding

overawe: 3 awe, cow; **5** abash, daunt, deter; **6** dazzle, impose

overbalance: 7 overtop; **8** outweigh, overpass, override; **9** overmatch, overweigh

overbearing: 9 high-flown; **10** intolerant; **11** dictatorial, domineering, overweening; **12** supercilious

overbearingly: 9 haughtily; **10** arrogantly

overbid: 8 overcall

overblown: 4 vain; **7** flushed, pompous; **8** inflated, puffed up; **9** conceited, high-flown; **10** portentous; **11** overweening; **12** vainglorious

overburden: 6 overdo; **7** overtax; **8** overload, overtask, overwork

overburdened: 9 bowed down; **10** loaded down

overcast: 3 dun; **5** cloud, dirty, lurid, muddy; **6** leaden; **7** clouded, sunless; **8** nebulous; **10** cloud cover, cloudiness, overshadow

overcharge: 3 rob; **4** hook, soak; **5** bleed, pluck, plume; **6** extort, fleece

overclothe: 9 overdress

overclothes: 9 outerwear

overcoat: 7 surcoat, topcoat; **9** great coat, greatcoat; **11** overcoating

overcome: 3 cut; **4** high, swim; **5** beery, boozy, carry, drunk, fresh, merry, tight, tipsy, whelm; **6** beaten, corned, defeat, groggy, master, primed, routed, subdue; **7** drunken, flooded, fuddled, get over, swamped; **8** distance, elevated, engulfed, override, overtake, surmount; **9** conquered, disguised, flustered, inebriate, inundated, overmatch, overpower, overreach, overtaken, overthrow, overwhelm; **10** despondent, desponding, overmaster, overthrown, vanquished

overcome a habit: 4 kick, beat, drop; **5** break

overcompensate: 11 overcorrect

overconfidence: 8 audacity; **9** certitude; **11** presumption

overconfident: 4 bold; 5 cocky; 8 cocksure, positive

overcritical: 8 critical; 9 difficult; 13 hypercritical

overcrowding: 10 congestion

overdo: 7 overact; 10 exaggerate

overdone: 5 hammy, stagy; 9 overacted; 10 overstated, theatrical; 11 big-sounding, exaggerated, overwrought

overdose: 2 o.d.

overdraw: 4 daub; 6 strain; 7 amplify, distort, magnify, overlay, stretch; 9 overstate; 10 caricature, exaggerate

overdue: 6 remiss; 7 past due; 9 excessive; 10 delinquent

overeat: 4 glut; 5 binge, gorge, stuff; 6 englut, pig out; 7 engorge, satiate; 8 scarf out; 9 overgorge

overeating: 8 gluttony

overemphasize: 10 overstress

overestimate: 8 overrate; 9 overvalue, overweigh; 10 overrating

overflow: 4 eddy; 5 flood, swash; 6 deluge, reflux, runoff, splash, stream, vortex; 7 overrun, run over; 8 brim over, flow over, inundate, well over; 9 overspill, spill over

overflowing: 5 awash; 6 afloat, runoff; 7 flooded, in flood, swollen; 8 flooding

overfull: 7 glutted

overgarment: 12 outer garment

overgenerous: 6 lavish; 8 prodigal; 9 unsparing, unstinted; 10 munificent, unstinting

overgrow: 7 outgrow; 8 grow over

overgrown: 3 fat; 5 tumid; 6 turgid; 7 bloated; 9 dropsical, monstrous; 11 exaggerated

overgrowth: 8 giantism; 9 gigantism

overhang: 4 ride; 5 mount; 6 beetle, impend; 8 bestride, hang over

overhasty: 3 hot; 5 hasty, quick; 7 bilious, peevish, peppery, waspish; 8 captious, shrewish, snappish

overhaul: 4 pass, trim; 5 audit; 6 blow up, revise; 7 service, trounce; 8 chastise, overtake, pore over; 9 modernize

overhauling: 7 service; 8 overhaul

overhead: 2 up; 4 foil; 5 above, aloft

overhead railway: 2 el

overhear: 5 catch; 6 take in

overindulge: 4 glut; 5 binge, gorge, stuff; 6 englut, pig out; 7 engorge, indulge, overeat, satiate; 8 live high, live it up, live well, scarf out; 9 overgorge

overindulgence: 6 excess

overladen: 10 overloaded

overlap: 3 lap; 8 overleap, overpass, override, overstep; 9 overreach; 11 convergence; 12 intersection

overlay: 5 cover; 9 overlayer, sheathing

overload: 3 lay; 4 clog; 6 overdo; 9 surcharge; 10 congestion, overburden

overlook: 4 drop, face, miss, omit; 5 see to; 6 excuse, pass by, slight; 7 command, condone, control, neglect, overtop; 8 dominate, leave out, overleap, pass over; 9 disregard

overlooked: 7 excused, unnoted; 8 condoned, unmarked; 9 neglected; 11 disregarded

overly: 3 too; 11 excessively

overlying: 9 incumbent; 12 superimposed

overnight: 9 nightlong

overnight mail: 11 express mail; 15 next-day delivery

over one's head in: 7 awash in; 10 swimming in

overornamented: 5 gaudy; 6 rococo, tawdry; 7 baroque

overpass: 7 flyover, flypast, overtop, overlap; 10 cloverleaf

overplay: 3 ham; 7 overact

overpower: 5 whelm; 8 overcome, override, overtake; 9 overmatch, overreach, overthrow

overpowered: 7 flooded, swamped; 8 engulfed, overcome; 9 inundated; 11 overwhelmed

overprize: 8 overrate; 9 overvalue

overprotect: 4 fuss; 6 mother

overrate: 9 overprize, overvalue; 12 overestimate

overreach: 4 beat; 6 outfox, outwit; 7 overlap; 8 outsmart, overcome

override: 4 snub; 6 baffle; 7 reverse; 8 overrule, overturn; 9 overthrow; 10 circumvent

overriding: 9 paramount; 11 predominant, predominate

overrule: 7 reverse; 8 override, overturn; 9 overthrow

overrun: 4 rout; 6 infest; 7 plagued, run over; 8 brim over, flow over, infested, overflow

overseas: 6 abroad

oversee: 4 head, lead; 5 guide, watch; 6 manage, survey; 9 supervise; 11 superintend

overseeing: 7 guiding, heading; 9 directing; 11 supervising

overseer: 10 supervisor; 14 superintendent

oversensitive: 4 taut; 5 tense; 8 volatile; 9 excitable, sensitive; 10 high-strung

overshadow: 5 dwarf; 6 shadow; 7 eclipse; 8 overcast

overshoot: 7 wave-off; 6 overdo; 8 go-around, pass over

oversight: 4 blot, flaw, miss, slip, trip; 5 fault, lapse; 6 laches [Law]; 7 blunder, default, stumble; 8 footfall, omission; 9 quiproquo; 11 loose thread, supervising, supervision; 12 inadvertence, surveillance; 13 cross purposes; 15 superintendence

oversize: 7 outsize; 8 outsized, too large; 9 oversized
overspill: 6 runoff
overstate: 6 pile up; 7 amplify, magnify; 8 overdraw, pile it on; 9 aggravate; 10 exaggerate; 11 hyperbolize
overstatement: 12 exaggeration
overstep: 3 top, 4 pass; 6 exceed, go past; 7 overlap; 8 overleap, overpass, override, trespass; 9 overreach, transcend; 10 transgress
overstress: 9 emphasize; 13 overemphasize
overstuffed chair: 9 easy chair; 11 lounge chair
oversupply: 4 glut; 5 flood; 7 surfeit; 8 plethora; 9 abundance
overt: 4 bare, open; 6 patent; 7 express, literal; 8 exoteric, explicit; 9 expressed; 11 undisguised
overtake: 4 make, pass; 5 catch, fetch, whelm; 8 overcome, overhaul; 9 overpower, overwhelm
overtaken: 6 caught; 7 catch up; 8 passed by
overtax: 8 overtask, overwork; 10 overburden, overstrain
over-the-counter: 15 nonprescription
over the counter stock: 8 OTC stock; 13 unlisted stock
over the sea: 6 abroad; 8 overseas
overthrow: 4 rout; 5 upset; 6 rebuff; 7 repulse, reverse; 8 overcome, override, overrule, overturn; 9 bring down, overmatch, overpower
overtime: 9 extra time
overtness: 7 clarity; 9 plainness; 12 explicitness, manifestness
overture: 5 offer; 6 feeler; 7 advance, prelude, proffer; 8 approach, proposal, symphony; 11 preliminary, proposition; 12 presentation
overturn: 4 lift; 5 annul, upset; 6 go over, invert, repeal, revoke; 7 capsize, rescind, reverse, tip over; 8 override, overrule, turn over; 9 bring down, knock over, overthrow, overwhelm; 11 countermand
overutilized: 8 overused
overvalue: 8 overrate; 9 overprize; 10 overstrain; 12 overestimate
overweening: 4 vain; 6 uppity; 7 flushed; 8 inflated, puffed up; 9 conceited, excessive, exuberant, high-flown, overblown; 10 intolerant; 11 domineering, extravagant, overbearing
overweight: 3 fat; 5 heavy; 6 fleshy; 9 stoutness; 10 corpulence
overwhelm: 4 drub, rout; 5 crush, drown, whelm; 6 engulf, deluge; 7 blow out, conquer, consume; 8 flood out, overcome, overtake, overturn; 9 overpower, overthrow
overwork: 7 exploit, overtax; 8 overtask; 10 overburden, overstrain; 11 overworking
overwrought: 5 stagy, tense; 6 taught; 8 overdone; 9 amplified, magnified, over-

acted; 10 distraught, hyperbolic, overstated, theatrical; 11 exaggerated
overzealous: 5 rabid; 7 fanatic; 9 fanatical; 12 enthusiastic
Ovibos: 6 musk ox; 9 musk sheep; 11 genus Ovibos
oviduct: 11 uterine tube; 13 Fallopian tube
oviform: 4 oval; 5 ovate, ovoid; 7 prolate; 8 elliptic; 9 egg-shaped; 10 elliptical
Ovis: 5 sheep, argal; 7 bighorn, mouflon; 8 cimarron; 9 genus Ovis
ovoflavin: 8 vitamin G; 9 vitamin B2
ovoid: 4 oval; 5 ovate; 7 oviform, prolate; 8 elliptic; 9 egg-shaped; 10 elliptical
ovolo: 12 quarter round
ovule: 4 oval; 7 ellipse
ovum: 3 egg; 7 egg cell
owing: 3 due; 4 owed; 6 unpaid; 7 past due; 10 delinquent; 11 outstanding; 12 undischarged
own: 4 avow, have; 5 admit, allow, grant; 7 concede, confess, possess; 11 acknowledge
owned up to: 8 admitted, conceded; 12 acknowledged
owner: 9 possessor; 10 proprietor
ownerless: 7 unowned
ownership: 10 possession; 14 proprietorship
owning up: 6 avowal; 9 conceding; 10 concession; 13 acknowledging; 14 acknowledgment
own jointly: 5 share; 7 partake; 11 participate
own up to: 5 admit; 6 fess up; 7 confess
Oxalidaceae: 16 wood-sorrel family
oxalis: 6 sorrel; 10 wood sorrel
oxaprozin: 6 Daypro
oxazepam: 5 Serax
oxen: 2 ox; 6 bovine, cattle; 9 livestock
oxeye: 5 daisy; 9 heliopsis
oxford gray: 8 charcoal
Oxford University: 6 Oxford
oxheart cherry: 7 oxheart; 11 heart cherry
oxidant: 8 oxidizer
oxidation-reduction: 5 redox
oxidize: 7 oxidise
oxidizing agent: 7 oxidant; 8 oxidizer
oxlip: 6 paigle
oxybenzene: 6 phenol; 12 carbolic acid
oxygenated: 7 aerated
oxymoron: 7 paradox; 13 contradiction, inconsistency
Oxytropis: 10 purple loco; 14 purple locoweed; 14 genus Oxytropis
oyez: 4 o yes
oyster: 6 huitre
oyster bed: 10 oyster bank, oyster park
oyster dressing: 14 oyster stuffing
oyster plant: 7 salsify
oyster stuffing: 14 oyster dressing
Ozarks: 14 Ozark Mountains
ozokerite: 7 ader wax; 10 mineral wax

O

P: 10 phosphorus
p.a.: 7 per year; 8 annually, each year, per annum
p.m.: 9 afternoon; 12 post meridiem, postmeridian
p.o.: 5 per os
PA: 8 PA system; 19 public address system
pa: 3 dad, pop; 4 dada, papa; 5 daddy, pappa, pater; 6 old man
Pa: 6 pascal; 12 protactinium; 13 protoactinium
Pabir: 4 Bura
pablum: 3 pap; 8 soft diet; 9 spoon food
pabulum: 4 food, grub; 6 edible; 7 aliment, eatable, edibles, ingesta, victual; 8 eatables, victuals; 9 nutriment, provender; 10 comestible, sustenance; 11 comestibles, nourishment, staff of life; 12 alimentation, sustentation
pace: 4 gait, plod, rate, step, wend, yard; 5 march, tempo, tread; 6 stride; 8 footstep, velocity
pacemaker: 5 pacer; 6 SA node; 10 pacesetter; 14 sinoatrial node
pacer: 9 pacemaker; 10 pacesetter
pacesetter: 5 pacer; 9 pacemaker
pace step: 4 span
pace up and down: 4 roam, rove; 5 prowl, range; 6 patrol; 8 traverse
pachyderm: 3 pig; 8 elephant; 11 rhinocerous
pachydermatous: 7 callous; 9 hard-nosed; 10 impervious; 11 hardhearted; 12 thickskinned
pacific: 7 halcyon; 8 peaceful; 9 peaceable
Pacific: 12 Pacific Ocean
pacifically: 9 peaceably
pacification: 9 placating, remission; 10 mitigation, mollifying, relaxation; 11 assuagement; 12 conciliation; 13 mollification
pacificist: 8 disarmer, pacifist
Pacific Standard Time: 3 PST; 11 Pacific Time
pacifier: 8 appeaser; 9 comforter, makepeace; 10 peacemaker, reconciler; 11 conciliator; 12 teething ring
pacifist: 8 disarmer; 10 pacificist, pacifistic
pacifistic: 6 dovish
pacify: 3 lay; 4 calm, cool, damp, hush, lull, swag, tame; 5 abate, allay, quell, quiet, sober, still; 6 deaden, gentle, lenify, rebate, smooth, soothe; 7 appease, assuage, compose, gruntle, mollify, placate, slacken, turn off; 8 calm down, suppress; 9 alleviate; 10 conciliate
pacing: 5 tempo
pack: 3 jam, lot, ram, wad; 4 camp, cram, deal, lade, load, pile, ring, stow, take, tamp,

warp; 5 allot, batch, carry, crush, put up, truss; 6 bundle, clique, crunch, load up, lumber, set out, throng, tuck in; 7 chock up, compact, coterie, ingroup, jampack, marshal, package, ram down, squeeze; 8 backpack
package: 3 box; 4 pack; 6 bundle, packet, parcel
package store: 10 off-license; 11 liquor store
packaging: 7 packing; 9 packing up
packed: 6 jammed; 7 crushed, encased; 8 packed up; 9 jam-packed
packer: 5 boxer; 6 bagger
packet: 6 bundle, parcel; 7 package
packing: 6 boxing; 7 wadding; 8 stuffing; 9 packaging, packing up; 11 backpacking
packinghouse: 12 packing plant
packing up: 7 packing; 9 packaging
pack rat: 6 magpie; 9 scavenger
pack tent: 15 backpacking tent
packthread: 5 twine; 6 string
pack together: 7 compact; 8 compress
pact: 6 accord, treaty; 7 compact; 9 agreement
pad: 3 cob, tit, wad; 4 barb, cram, digs, fill, hack, jade, lard, line, plod, roan, slog; 5 berth, bidet, place, punch, stuff; 6 blow up, inkpad, tablet, trudge; 7 bolster, fill out, incrust; 8 diggings, footslog, lodgings, roadster, stamp pad; 9 dramatize, embellish, embroider, inking pad, launchpad; 10 aggrandize, habitation
padded: 8 cushiony; 9 cushioned
padding: 4 down; 7 filling, wadding; 8 stopping, stuffing; 10 cushioning
paddle: 3 oar, row; 5 spank
paddleboat: 9 steamboat
paddler: 7 kayaker; 8 canoeist
paddle steamer: 10 paddleboat; 13 paddle wheeler
paddock: 5 pound
paddy: 4 padi; 9 rice paddy; 10 paddy field
paddy wagon: 5 wagon; 9 police van; 11 patrol wagon
padi: 5 paddy
pad of paper: 3 pad; 6 tablet; 7 notepad
Padova: 5 Padua; 8 Patavium
padre: 6 priest, father; 7 Holy Joe; 8 sky pilot
Padua: 6 Padova; 8 Patavium
paean: 4 pean; 6 eulogy; 7 ovation, triumph
paediatric: 9 pediatric
Paeonia: 5 peony; 12 genus Paeonia
Paeoniaceae: 11 peony family
paeony: 5 peony
pagan: 7 gentile, heathen, infidel; 10 heathenish
pagan religion: 8 paganism; 10 heathenism

page: 4 leaf; 5 folio; 6 squire, varlet; 7 page-boy; 8 paginate

pageant: 4 pomp; 9 pageantry, spectacle; 10 exhibition, exposition

pageboy: 4 page

page number: 5 folio; 10 pagination

pagination: 5 folio; 6 paging; 10 page number

Pago Pago: 10 Pango Pango

Pagophilus: 8 harp seal; 15 genus Pagophilus

paid: 6 paying; 7 gainful, paid off

paid employment: 3 job; 6 employ; 9 paying job, situation; 10 employment, occupation

paid in advance: 7 prepaid, up-front; 8 advanced

paigle: 5 oxlip; 7 cowslip

pail: 3 tub; 6 bucket; 7 pailful

paillasse: 8 trimming

pain: 3 ail; 4 bite, gnaw, hurt; 5 chafe, dolor, grief, gripe, sting, wound; 6 bother; 7 afflict, anguish, hurting

pained: 7 worried; 8 offended; 9 afflicted

painful: 4 sore; 5 awful; 7 hurtful, hurting; 8 dreadful, terrible; 9 atrocious; 10 abominable, afflictive, irritating

painfully: 5 sadly; 6 sorely; 7 cruelly, grossly; 8 bitterly, horribly, terribly, woefully; 9 fearfully, miserably, piteously; 10 dreadfully, grievously, lamentably, shockingly; 11 frightfully; 13 distressingly

painfully slow: 7 glacial

pain in the neck: 4 pain; 6 bother; 8 nuisance; 9 annoyance

painkiller: 7 anodyne; 8 pain pill; 9 analgesic

painstaking: 7 notable; 8 diligent, sedulous; 9 assiduous, diligence; 10 scrupulous; 11 hard-working, industrious; 13 conscientious

painstakingly: 12 fastidiously

paint: 3 dye; 4 gild, oils, tint, wash; 5 grain, imbue, japan, rouge, stain, tinge; 6 enamel, ormolu, polish; 7 bedizen, blusher, furbish, ingrain, lacquer, smarten, varnish; 8 emblazon, oil color, oil paint; 9 oil paints, whitewash; 10 illuminate, white metal; 12 german silver; 14 Britannia metal

painted: 4 pied; 6 motley; 10 multicolor; 12 multicolored

painted cup: 16 Indian paintbrush

painted daisy: 9 pyrethrum

painted leaf: 10 poinsettia

painter: 3 guy; 4 line, puma, wire; 5 cable, chain; 6 artist, cougar, drawer, limner; 7 panther; 8 designer, engraver, moorings, sketcher; 9 catamount

painter's colic: 9 lead colic

painting: 6 waxing; 7 picture, priming; 10 lacquering; 11 shellacking

painting style: 5 genre, style

pair: 3 duo; 4 duad, duet, dyad, mate, span, twin, yoke; 5 brace, deuce, match, twain, twins; 6 couple, double; 7 bracket, couplet, distich, pair off, twosome

paired: 5 mated; 8 opposite

pairing: 5 union; 6 mating; 8 coupling; 11 conjugation

pair off: 4 pair; 6 couple; 10 partner off

Paiute: 5 Piute

pajamas: 6 pajama, pyjama; 7 pyjamas; 8 negligee; 9 nightgown; 10 night shirt; 12 dressing gown

pakchoi: 7 bok choi, bok choy

pal: 4 chum; 5 buddy, crony, pal up; 8 alter ego, sidekick; 9 companion, confidant

palace: 6 castle

palace car: 8 chair car; 9 parlor car

paladin: 4 hero; 7 fighter; 8 champion

palatable: 4 good, nice; 5 tasty; 6 dainty, savory; 9 delicious; 10 delectable, well-tasted

palate: 14 roof of the mouth

palatial: 5 grand

palatine: 8 palatial

palaver: 3 jaw; 4 chat, coax, rant; 5 clack, prate, prose; 6 cajole, gabble, gibber, hot air, jabber, piffle, tattle; 7 blabber, bombast, chatter, gabfest, meeting, prattle, session, sitting, twaddle, wheedle; 8 cajolery, flummery, inveigle, rhetoric

pale: 3 wan; 4 rail, term; 5 bourn, faint, verge; 6 blanch, blench, feeble, ghetto, paling, pallid, picket; 7 confine, enclave, railing, reserve; 8 blanched, etiolate, preserve, turn pale

palely: 5 dimly; 8 pallidly

paleness: 6 pallor; 7 wanness; 8 fairness, lividity

Paleocene epoch: 9 Paleocene

paleography: 11 archaeology

paleolithic: 8 stone age; 11 paleologist; 13 archaeologist; 14 paleontologist

paleology: 11 archaeology, paleography; 12 paleontology

paleontologist: 9 fossilist; 11 paleologist; 13 archaeologist

paleontology: 11 archaeology, fossilology

Paleozoic era: 9 Paleozoic

paleozoolical: 6 fossil; 9 Paleozoic

Palestine: 6 Canaan; 8 Holy Land

palette: 6 pallet; 8 pallette

palfrey: 3 nag; 6 cayuse [U.S.]; 11 saddle horse

palimony: 7 alimony

paling: 4 pale, rail; 6 fading; 7 railing; 8 enceinte, palisade; 9 ring fence; 10 balustrade; 11 picket fence

palingenesis: 12 reappearance, reconversion, resurrection; 14 metempsychosis

palinode: 10 retraction; 11 recantation

P

palisade: 4 wall; 5 fence; 6 cliffs, paling; 7 fence in; 8 stockade, surround

pall: 3 die; 4 bier, cloy, cope, dash, dull, glut, gown, jade, robe, stun, tire, toga; 5 blunt, chill, cloak, daunt, drape, frock, gorge, scare, slake, weary; 6 benumb, hearse, mantle, purple, quench, shroud, sicken; 7 curtain, disgust, drapery, fatigue, pallium, satiate, surfeit; 8 cerement, nauseate

palladium: 2 Pd; 9 safeguard

Pallas: 6 Athena, Athene; 12 Pallas Athena

pallbearer: 6 bearer

pallet: 7 palette

palliasse: 13 straw mattress

palliate: 4 ease; 5 abate, check; 6 excuse, soften, soothe; 7 assuage, relieve; 8 mitigate; 9 alleviate, apologize, extenuate

palliation: 7 lullaby; 8 easement, soothing; 9 softening; 10 mitigation, palliative; 11 alleviation, extenuation

palliative: 7 healing; 8 lenitive; 9 softening; 10 corrective, mitigation, mitigative, mitigatory, palliating, palliation; 11 alleviative, alleviatory, extenuation, meliorative; 12 ameliorative

pallid: 3 wan; 4 pale

pallidness: 6 pallor; 7 wanness; 8 lividity, paleness; 9 lividness, luridness

pallium: 4 cope, gown, pall, robe; 5 frock; 6 cortex, mantle; 7 cassock

pallor: 7 wanness; 8 lividity, paleness; 9 lividness, luridness, pallidity; 10 achromasia, pallidness

pally: 5 matey; 6 chummy; 10 palsy-walsy

palm: 5 medal; 6 handle, ribbon; 8 palm tree; 9 medallion; 10 decoration; 12 laurel wreath

Palmaceae: 6 Palmae; 9 Arecaceae; 10 palm family; 12 family Palmae

Palmae: 9 Arecaceae, Palmaceae; 10 palm family; 12 family Palmae

palmer: 7 pilgrim

Palmetto State: 13 South Carolina

palm family: 6 Palmae; 9 Arecaceae, Palmaceae

palmist: 11 chiromancer

palmistry: 10 chiromancy

palm kernel: 7 palm nut

palm off: 7 pass off

palm-shaped: 7 palmate

palm tree: 4 palm

palmy: 4 glad, good; 5 happy, sunny; 7 booming, halcyon, roaring; 8 gladsome, thriving; 10 prospering, prosperous; 11 flourishing

palooka: 3 oaf; 4 lout; 5 boxer; 10 stumblebum

palpable: 7 evident, obvious; 8 sensible, striking, tangible; 10 ponderable, pro-

nounced; 11 indubitable, self-evident; 12 recognizable, unmistakable

palpate: 4 feel

palpitant: 10 fluttering; 11 palpitating

palpitate: 4 beat, pant; 5 heave, throb; 6 quiver, thrill, tingle; 7 flutter, pulsate, tremble, twitter; 9 go pitapat

palpitation: 5 throb; 6 quiver, tremor; 7 ague fit, flutter, panting, shaking; 9 cold sweat, pulsation, quivering, shakiness, trembling, vibration; 11 trepidation; 12 perturbation

palsgrave: 8 palatine

palsy: 7 syncope; 8 apoplexy, collapse; 9 paralysis

palsy-walsy: 5 matey, pally; 6 chummy

palter: 3 lie; 6 haggle; 7 chaffer; 10 equivocate

paltry: 4 mean, poor; 5 dirty; 6 abject, little, measly, scabby, scurvy, shabby; 7 pitiful, scrubby; 8 rascally, sneaking, trifling; 9 groveling, miserable; 10 negligible

pampas: 5 pampa; 7 prairie

pamper: 4 baby; 5 spoil; 6 coddle; 7 indulge; 11 mollycoddle

pamphlet: 5 tract; 6 folder; 7 booklet, leaflet; 8 brochure, circular; 11 publication

pan: 4 dish; 5 plate, trash; 6 pan off, pan out, saucer; 7 platter, potager; 8 calabash, crucible, trencher

Pan: 7 goat god; 8 genus Pan

panacea: 7 cure-all, nostrum

panache: 4 dash, elan; 5 crest, flair, plume, style; 7 feather

Panadol: 6 Datril, Tempra; 7 Tylenol; 9 Anacin III; 13 acetaminophen

panama: 6 boater, sailor; 7 leghorn, skimmer; 8 straw hat

Panama City: 15 capital of Panama

panatela: 5 cigar; 8 panetela; 9 panetella

Panax: 4 sang; 6 nin-sin; 7 ginseng; 10 genus Panax

pancake: 7 hotcake; 8 flapcake, flapjack; 10 battercake; 11 flannelcake, griddlecake

pancake day: 9 Mardi Gras

pancreatic gland: 8 pancreas

panda: 7 bear cat, cat bear; 8 coon bear, red panda; 9 panda bear; 10 giant panda; 11 lesser panda

Pandanaceae: 15 screw-pine family

pandanus: 9 screw pine

Pandean pipes: 6 syrinx; 7 panpipe; 10 pipes of Pan

pandemic: 7 endemic; 8 epidemic

pandemonium: 5 chaos; 6 bedlam

pander: 4 pimp; 5 ponce; 6 pandar; 7 gratify, indulge; 8 panderer, procurer

panderer: 4 pimp; 5 ponce; 6 pandar, pander; 8 procurer

pandering: 7 servile; 10 obsequious; 11 sycophantic

pander to: 5 court; **6** butter, slaver; **8** butter up, suck up to

Pandion: 6 osprey; **8** fish hawk, sea eagle; **9** fish eagle; **12** genus Pandion

Pandionidae: 17 family Pandionidae

pandowdy: 5 dowdy

pandurate: 11 panduriform; **12** fiddle-shaped

pane: 8 paneling; **9** panelling; **11** pane of glass

panegyric: 4 pean; **5** paean; **6** eulogy; **8** encomium; **10** eulogistic; **11** encomiastic, panegyrical

panegyrical: 8 praising; **9** laudatory, panegyric; **10** eulogistic, uncritical

panegyrist: 8 eulogist

panel: 4 jury; **5** board; **6** roster; **8** jury list; **9** dialog box; **11** room divider; **12** control board, control panel

paneled: 10 wainscoted

panelist: 10 discussant

panelling: 4 pane; **8** paneling

panel truck: 11 delivery van; **13** delivery truck

pane of glass: 4 pane

panetela: 5 cigar; **8** panatela; **9** panetella

pang: 5 agony, sting; **6** twinge; **7** anguish; **13** mental anguish

panga: 7 machete

Pangea: 7 Pangaea

pangolin: 8 anteater; **13** scaly anteater

Pango Pango: 8 Pago Pago

panhandler: 4 jade; **5** scrub, tramp; **6** beggar, cadger; **7** moocher, sponger; **8** vagabond; **9** mendicant; **10** freeloader, ragamuffin

panic: 5 dread, scare; **6** horror, terror

panicked: 7 panicky; **9** panicking, terrified; **10** frightened; **11** panic-struck, scared stiff

Panicum: 6 millet; **10** goose grass, witchgrass; **11** switch grass; **12** genus Panicum

panier: 5 apron

panjandrum: 3 VIP; **6** high-up; **9** dignitary

pannier: 4 cran; **5** crate, creel, skirt; **6** basket

pan off: 3 pan; **6** pan out

Panonychus: 13 red spider mite; **15** genus Panonychus

panoplied: 7 armored, arrayed

panoply: 5 array, armor

panoptic: 4 wide; **5** broad; **7** blanket; **9** panoramic; **10** panoptical

panorama: 4 view; **5** scene, vista; **6** aspect; **7** diorama

panoramic: 8 bird's-eye

pan out: 3 pan; **6** pan off; **7** work out

Pan paniscus: 6 bonobo; **15** pygmy chimpanzee

panpipe: 6 syrinx; **10** pipes of Pan

pansy violet: 10 wood violet

pant: 4 gasp, puff; **5** faint, flush, heave, sweat, swoon, throb; **7** flutter, succumb

pantaloon: 5 pants; **7** buffoon, farceur; **8** breeches, grimacer, trousers; **9** columbine, harlequin; **11** pantomimist

pantheist: 10 polytheist; **11** pantheistic

panther: 4 lion, puma; **5** tiger; **6** cougar, jaguar; **7** bulldog, painter; **9** catamount; **12** mountain lion

Panthera: 13 genus Panthera

Panthera leo: 4 lion; **12** king of beasts

Panthera onca: 6 jaguar; **7** panther; **9** Felis onca

Panthera pardus: 7 leopard

Panthera tigris: 5 tiger

Panthera uncia: 5 ounce; **11** snow leopard

panther cat: 6 ocelot; **13** Felis pardalis

pantie: 5 panty; **6** scanty, step-in, tights; **7** drawers, panties; **8** scanties; **14** unmentionables

panting: 5 blown, pursy; **6** winded; **7** gasping, heaving; **9** pulsation; **10** trousering; **11** out of breath, palpitation, short-winded

pantomime: 4 mime

pantomimist: 4 mime; **5** mimer; **6** mummer; **7** buffoon, farceur; **8** grimacer; **9** columbine, pantaloon; **10** pantomimer

pantothenic acid: 9 pantothen

Pantotheria: 10 chimpanzee; **19** subclass Pantotheria

pantry: 6 larder, spence [Brit.]; **7** buttery; **8** scullery

pantryman: 6 butler

pants: 7 drawers; **8** bloomers, knickers, overalls, trousers

panty: 6 pantie, scanty, step-in, tights; **7** drawers, panties; **8** scanties; **14** unmentionables

panty girdle: 5 stays; **6** corset, girdle

pantywaist: 5 pansy, sissy; **7** milksop; **11** Milquetoast

pap: 4 curd, pulp, teat; **5** dough; **6** mammae, nipple, pablum; **7** mamilla, pudding; **8** mammilla, soft diet; **9** spoon food

Papa: 4 Pope; **7** pontiff

papa: 2 pa; **3** dad, pop; **4** dada, sire; **5** daddy, pappa, pater; **6** father, old man; **13** paterfamilias

papacy: 7 primacy; **11** pontificate

papal: 9 apostolic; **10** pontifical

Papanicolaou test: 7 Pap test

Papaver: 5 poppy; **12** genus Papaver

Papaveraceae: 11 poppy family

Papaverales: 10 Rhoeadales; **15** order Rhoeadales; **16** order Papaverales

Papaver somniferum: 10 opium poppy

papaw: 6 papaya, pawpaw

papaya: 5 papaw; **6** papaia, pawpaw; **9** melon tree; **10** papaya tree

papaya family: 10 Caricaceae

paper: 4 bill; **5** sheet, theme; **6** report;

7 project; 9 newspaper, parchment, term paper, wallpaper; 10 settlement; 11 composition

paperback: 8 softback; 9 soft-cover; 11 paperbacked

paper bag: 4 poke, sack

paper birch: 10 canoe birch

paperboard: 11 posterboard

paper chase: 13 hare and hounds

paper cup: 8 Dixie cup

paperer: 11 paperhanger

paper folding: 7 origami [Jap]

paperhanger: 7 paperer

paperhanging: 8 papering

paperlike: 6 papery; 11 chartaceous

paper money: 5 notes, bills; 9 greenback; 10 greenbacks [pl], paper money; 12 folding money

paper rush: 7 papyrus

papers: 8 document

paperwork: 10 office work

Paphian: 6 wanton

papilla: 6 nipple

papillary: 6 knobby; 7 knobbed; 9 papillose; 10 nipple-like

papillary tumor: 9 papilloma

papillose: 6 knobby; 7 knobbed; 9 papillary; 10 nipple-like

Papio: 5 drill; 6 baboon, gelada, chacma; 8 mandrill; 10 genus Papio

papoose: 4 baby; 5 child; 6 infant

pappa: 2 pa; 3 dad, pop; 4 dada, papa; 5 daddy, pater; 6 old man

pappiloma: 4 wart

paprika: 7 pimento; 8 pimiento; 10 bell pepper; 11 sweet pepper

paprika sauce: 14 Hungarian sauce

Pap smear: 13 cervical smear

Pap test: 16 Papanicolaou test

Papua: 9 New Guinea

papule: 3 wen; 5 wheel; 6 papula [Med]; 7 pustule

papyrus: 9 paper rush

par: 6 normal; 8 equality; 11 equivalence

para: 6 beside; 7 related; 9 accessory, alongside; 10 subsidiary

para-aminobenzoic acid: 4 PABA

parable: 5 fable; 8 allegory, apologue; 10 moral fable

parabolic: 11 allegorical, parabolical

parabolic geometry: 9 Euclidean

parachute: 4 jump; 5 chute; 7 sky dive

parachute jumper: 8 skydiver; 11 paratrooper, parachutist

parachute jumping: 9 sky diving; 11 parachuting

Paraclete: 10 Holy Spirit

parade: 5 march, troop; 6 flaunt, review; 7 exhibit; 9 march past, promenade; 10 procession

parader: 7 marcher

paradiddle: 4 roll; 8 drum roll; 8 rudiment

paradigm: 4 type; 5 ideal, image, model; 7 epitome, example, pattern; 8 exemplar, original, standard; 9 archetype, precedent, prototype

paradisal: 7 elysian; 10 paradisaic, paradisiac, paradisial; 12 paradisaical, paradisiacal

paradise: 4 eden; 6 heaven; 7 Elysium, nirvana; 8 Valhalla; 9 Shangri-la; 12 promised land; 13 Elysian Fields

paradisiacal: 7 elysian; 8 beatific, heavenly, supernal; 9 celestial, paradisal, unearthly; 10 paradisaic, paradisiac, paradisial; 12 paradisaical

paradox: 8 oxymoron; 13 contradiction, inconsistency

paradoxical: 9 enigmatic; 10 apocryphal; 11 unexplained

paradoxical sleep: 8 REM sleep

paraesthesia: 11 paresthesia

paraffin: 3 wax; 6 alkane; 11 paraffin oil

paraffin scale: 8 scale wax

paragon: 4 idol; 5 ideal, model, saint; 7 nonsuch, phoenix; 8 nonesuch; 9 nonpareil; 10 apotheosis, perfection

paragraph: 5 count, verse; 6 clause

Paraguay tea: 4 mate

parakeet: 8 paraquet, paroquet, parroket; 9 parrakeet, parroquet

paralegal: 14 legal assistant

Paralichthys: 8 flounder; 17 genus Paralichthys

paralinguistic communication: 12 paralanguage

Paralithodes: 15 Alaskan king crab; 17 genus Paralithodes

parallel: 4 twin; 5 match; 6 analog, do like; 8 analogue, identify, latitude; 9 duplicate; 11 coextensive, counterpart

parallel interface: 12 parallel port

parallelism: 5 union; 8 affinity; 10 apposition

paralysis agitans: 10 Parkinson's

paralyze: 4 lame, maim, numb, stun; 5 blunt; 6 benumb, deaden, muzzle; 7 cripple, stupefy; 9 hamstring, prostrate

Paramaribo: 17 capital of Suriname

paramecia: 9 protozoan; 10 paramecium

paramount: 5 vital; 6 utmost; 7 radical, supreme; 8 cardinal, dominant, foremost, greatest; 9 at the head, essential, matchless; 10 overriding, preeminent; 11 in authority, predominant, predominate

paramour: 4 doxy; 8 mistress; 9 concubine, courtesan

Parana: 11 Parana River

paranoia: 8 distrust; 9 psychosis

paranoid: 9 paranoiac

paranormal: 12 extrasensory

parapet: 4 bank, mole; 5 mound; 7 sandbag;

paraphernalia: **4** gear; **5** traps; **6** things; **13** appurtenances

paraphrase: **6** digest, reword; **7** outline, summary; **8** rephrase, synopsis

parasite: **4** snob, toad, tool; **5** leech, toady; **6** flunky, minion, sponge, sucker, yes-man; **7** sponger; **8** hanger-on, truckler; **9** sycophant

parasitic: **9** leechlike; **11** parasitical; **12** bloodsucking

parasitic worm: **8** helminth

parasol: **8** sunshade, umbrella

parathyroid hormone: **3** PTH; **10** parathyrin; **12** parathormone

paratrooper: **8** airborne; **11** parachutist

parboil: **6** blanch

Parcae: **4** Fate

parcel: **3** lot; **4** plot; **5** patch, share, tract; **6** bundle, packet; **7** package, portion; **10** detachment

parceled out: **5** dealt; **7** alloted; **8** dealt out, doled out, meted out; **11** apportioned, distributed

parcel out: **3** lot; **4** deal, pack; **5** allot; **6** divide, set out; **7** deal out, dish out, dole out, marshal, mete out; **8** dispense, shell out; **9** apportion, collocate; **10** administer, distribute

parch: **3** dry, fry; **4** bake, fume, sear; **5** grill, roast, singe, toast; **6** scorch

parched: **5** baked; **8** scorched, sunbaked

parched with thirst: **3** dry; **7** thirsty

parchment: **5** paper; **6** vellum; **8** lambskin; **9** sheepskin; **10** settlement

pardner: **7** partner; **10** cooperator; **12** collaborator

pardon: **5** grace; **6** excuse; **7** amnesty, forgive; **10** absolution, free pardon, shake hands; **11** condonation, forgiveness

pardonable: **6** venial; **9** excusable; **10** defensible; **11** justifiable

pardoned: **8** forgiven; **9** unavenged

pare: **4** flay, peel, skin, trim; **5** scalp, shave, slice; **7** cut down, whittle; **8** pare down; **9** excoriate

parent: **4** rear; **5** raise; **7** bring up, nurture

parentage: **4** line; **5** birth, blood, stock; **6** origin; **7** descent, lineage; **8** ancestry, pedigree; **9** bloodline; **10** parenthood

parenthesis: **5** aside; **8** excursus, interval; **9** interlude; **10** digression, divagation; **16** hysteron proteron [Grk]

parenthetical: **8** episodic; **10** incidental

parenthood: **9** parentage

parentless: **8** orphaned

parer: **11** paring knife

paresthesia: **8** tingling, pricking

par excellence: **7** the most; **8** above all; **9** eminently, extremely, supremely; **10** especially, surpassing; **11** egregiously, exceed-

ingly, of all things, principally, prominently; **12** particularly, preeminently, surpassingly; **13** superlatively

parget: **7** plaster; **9** whitewash

parhelic circle: **9** solar halo; **12** parhelic ring

parhelion: **6** sundog; **7** mock sun

pariah: **7** outcast; **8** castaway

paring: **5** shave; **6** shiver, sliver; **7** driblet, parings, shaving; **8** clipping

paring knife: **5** parer

pari passu: **8** equal rate, equal pace

Paris: **10** genus Paris; **11** City of Light; **15** capital of France

Paris green: **8** pea green; **11** yellow green; **14** yellowish green

parish: **6** county, region; **7** quarter

parish priest: **4** abbe, cure

parity: **8** equality

park: **5** green; **6** common, garden; **7** battery, commons; **8** ballpark, basilisk

parka: **6** anorak; **9** ski jacket; **11** windbreaker, windcheater

parking area: **7** car park; **10** parking lot

parking brake: **9** emergency, hand brake; **14** emergency brake

Parkinson: **20** C. Northcote Parkinson; **23** Cyril Northcote Parkinson

Parkinson's disease: **10** Parkinson's; **12** Parkinsonism, shaking palsy; **16** paralysis agitans

parkway: **5** drive

parlance: **4** talk; **5** idiom; **6** speech; **7** talking; **8** locution, speaking

parlay: **8** double up

parley: **6** powwow [U.S.]; **10** conference; **11** negotiation

parleying: **10** bargaining; **11** negotiating, negotiation

parliament: **15** legislative body

Parliamentarian: **2** MP

parliamentary procedure: **5** order; **12** rules of order; **16** parliamentary law

parlor: **5** salon; **6** saloon; **7** parlour; **9** front room; **10** living room, livingroom; **11** sitting room

parlor car: **8** chair car; **9** palace car; **14** drawing-room car

parlor grand: **9** baby grand

parlour: **6** parlor

parlous: **5** risky; **6** unsafe; **8** insecure, perilous; **9** dangerous, hazardous; **10** precarious, touch-and-go

parochial: **5** local; **6** narrow; **7** insular; **8** regional; **10** provincial; **11** territorial

parochial school: **12** church school; **15** religious school

parodist: **9** lampooner

parody: **5** spoof; **6** sendup; **7** charade, lampoon, mockery, takeoff; **8** ridicule,

P

satirize, travesty; **9** burlesque; **10** caricature

parole: 3 vow; **4** word; **5** troth; **6** plight; **8** password; **9** watchword; **11** countersign

parolee: 11 probationer

paronomasia: 3 pun; **11** play on words

Parophrys: 9 lemon sole; **11** English sole; **14** genus Parophrys

paroxysm: 3 fit; **5** burst, scene, storm; **7** tempest; **8** outbreak, outburst

parquet: 3 pit; **5** boxes; **6** stalls; **7** gallery; **10** auditorium; **12** parquet floor

parquet circle: 8 parterre

parrakeet: 8 parakeet

parrot: 3 ape, jay; **4** echo, mime, poll; **6** magpie, monkey; **8** imitator; **10** pollparrot; **11** mockingbird

parrot fever: 11 psittacosis

parry: 4 duck; **5** blink, block, dodge, elude, evade, fudge, hedge, repel, shirk, skirt; **6** blench, defeat, expose, flinch; **7** counter, deflect; **8** sidestep; **10** circumvent

parse: 7 analyze, diagram, dissect, resolve; **9** anatomize

Parsee: 5 Parsi

Parsi: 6 Parsee

parsimonious: 6 stingy; **7** miserly; **8** peddling; **9** penny wise

parsimony: 6 penury, thrift; **8** meanness; **9** tightness; **10** stinginess; **11** miserliness

parslane family: 13 Portulacaceae

parsley: 4 herb; **7** garnish

parson: 5 vicar; **6** curate, pastor, rector; **8** minister; **9** rural dean

parsonage: 5 glebe, manse; **7** deanery, rectory; **8** vicarage; **10** presbytery

part: 4 role; **5** break, piece, share, split, start, voice; **6** cut off, depart, detach, divide, office, partly, region, set off, set out; **7** break up, divorce, episode, persona, portion, section, split up, take off; **8** capacity, disunite, division, fraction, function, move away, separate; **9** character, component, move apart, partially

partake: 5 share, touch; **11** participate

partaker: 6 sharer

part by part: 9 piecemeal

part company with: 4 part; **9** break with; **16** break squares with

parterre: 13 parquet circle

Parthenocissus: 8 woodbine; **9** Boston ivy; **11** American ivy; **19** genus Parthenocissus

partial: 4 fond; **5** party; **6** proper, uneven, unfair; **7** certain, private, several, special, unequal; **8** definite, especial, one-sided, original, peculiar, specific; **9** disparate, exclusive; **10** individual, particular, respective; **11** appropriate, determinate, superficial; **14** characteristic

partiality: 3 fad; **4** bent, bias, mind; **5** fancy, favor, hobby, quirk; **6** animus, weight; **7** leaning; **8** crotchet, fondness, penchant; **9** blind side; **10** favoritism, prevalence; **11** inclination, infatuation

partially: 4 part; **6** in part, partly; **10** one-sidedly

partially ordered set: 5 poset

partible: 8 scissile [Chem]; **9** divisible, separable

participant: 5 party; **6** player

participate: 5 enter, share; **7** partake

participating: 6 active

participation: 10 engagement, taking part; **11** involvement

participator: 6 sharer

particle: 3 bit; **4** atom, hunk, lump, mote; **5** speck; **6** morsel; **8** molecule

particle accelerator: 11 accelerator, atom smasher

particle board: 10 fiberboard

particolored: 4 pied; **6** motley; **7** painted, piebald; **10** multicolor

particular: 4 fine, item, nice; **5** fussy; **6** detail, proper, strict, wanton; **7** certain, curious, finical, finicky, graphic, partial, precise, private, several, special, wayward; **8** definite, delicate, detailed, especial, exacting, fanciful, freakish, original, peculiar, skittish, specific; **9** demanding, exclusive, fantastic, well-drawn; **10** individual, meticulous, overstrict, respective; **11** appropriate, determinate, exceptional

particularly: 4 even; **6** mainly; **7** chiefly, notably, the most; **8** above all, signally; **9** a fortiori, curiously, eminently, extremely, pointedly, specially, supremely, unusually; **10** especially, peculiarly, remarkably, singularly, strikingly, surpassing, uncommonly; **11** exceedingly, principally, prominently

particulars: 5 items; **6** counts; **7** details; **9** depiction; **11** delineation

particular time: 4 time; **8** occasion

parting: 5 leave; **8** farewell; **10** separating, separation

part interest: 5 share; **8** interest

partisan: 5 party; **6** backer, zealot; **7** abettor; **8** advocate, champion, guerilla, upholder; **9** disputant, insurgent, irregular, political, supporter; **10** enthusiast; **11** protagonist, sympathizer

partisanship: 8 prestige; **10** partiality; **11** party spirit; **12** clannishness, factionalism

partition: 4 zone; **6** divide, region; **7** divider; **8** division, separate, subspace; **9** subdivide; **11** compartment, repartition, subdivision

partitive: 10 separative

partly: 4 part; **6** in part; **9** partially

partner: 4 mate; **6** spouse; **7** consort, pardner; **9** copartner; **10** cooperator; **12** collaborator

partner in crime: 8 henchman; 11 confederate; 12 collaborator

part of speech: 9 form class, word class

partridge: 8 bobwhite; 12 ruffed grouse

part-time: 8 half-time

part-time student: 7 auditor; 12 night student

parturient: 5 labor; 8 childbed

parturition: 5 birth, labor; 8 birthing, delivery; 10 birth-throe, childbirth; 11 confinement, giving birth

party: 4 band, crew, gang, hand, head, knot, side, team; 5 group, squad; 6 proper; 7 certain, company, faction, partial, private, several, special; 8 definite, especial, original, partisan, peculiar, specific

party crasher: 10 interloper

party hack: 10 ward heeler

party line: 7 program; 8 platform

party of the first part: 8 proposer

party of the second part: 7 aggreer

par value: 9 face value; 12 nominal value

parvenu: 7 upstart; 8 parvenue; 12 nouveau riche

parvo: 10 parvovirus

pas: 4 mark, rank; 5 pitch, place, point; 6 period; 7 station; 8 position; 10 precedence

pascal: 2 Pa

Pascal: 12 Blaise Pascal

Pasch: 6 Pascha, Easter; 8 Passover

paschal: 6 lenten

Paschal Lamb: 8 Agnus Dei

Pas-de-Calais: 14 Strait of Calais, Straits of Dover

pas de deux: 4 duet

paseo: 4 walk; 7 walkway

Pashto: 5 Paxto; 6 Afghan, Pathan; 7 Afghani; 12 Afghanistani

pasquinade: 4 skit; 5 libel, spoof; 6 parody, sendup; 7 charade, lampoon, mockery, takeoff; 8 travesty; 9 burlesque

pass: 2 go; 3 bye, cut, fix, gap, hap, run, top; 4 fade, fall, flip, flow, give, go by, go on, hand, head, lead, nail, push, sink, toss, walk; 5 clear, crack, cross, egest, fleet, fling, guide, hitch, lapse, lunge, notch, occur, offer, pinch, reach, spend, trial, whirl; 6 crisis, elapse, exceed, extend, go past, happen, make it, pass by, pass on, return, slip by, strait, thrust, vanish; 7 advance, deliver, devolve, excrete, glide by, go along, nonplus, pass off, passage, passing, proceed, slide by, straits, surpass, transit; 8 blow over, dissolve, evanesce, exigency, hand over, juncture, make pass, overhaul, overstep, overtake, passport, scramble, transmit; 9 authorise, authorize, disappear, eliminate, emergency, evaporate, go through, legislate

passable: 2 OK; 4 fair, so-so; 7 average; 8 adequate, bearable, mediocre, middling, ordinary; 9 tolerable; 10 acceptable, admissible, couci-couci; 11 commonplace, respectable

passage: 3 gap; 4 bout, hall, mews, pass, sail, yard; 5 notch, rents; 6 avenue, crisis, cruise, voyage; 7 hallway, passing, transit; 8 approach, corridor; 9 adventure, enactment; 10 passageway, transition; 14 musical passage

pass a law: 9 legislate

pass around: 6 pass on, spread; 7 diffuse; 8 disperse; 9 circulate, propagate; 10 distribute

pass away: 2 go; 3 die, fly; 4 exit, fade, flit, go by; 5 go off; 6 expire

passbook: 8 bankbook

pass catcher: 8 receiver

passe: 5 faded, stale; 6 demode, frayed, old-hat, passee, run out, shabby, shaken, wilted; 7 antique; 8 outmoded; 10 secondhand, threadbare; 12 old-fashioned

passementerie: 4 trim; 8 trimming

passenger: 5 rider

passe-partout: 6 opener; 7 passkey; 8 passport, password; 9 master key

passer: 11 quarterback

passerby: 7 witness; 8 beholder, looker-on, observer, onlooker; 9 bystander, spectator; 10 eyewitness

Passer domesticus: 12 house sparrow; 14 English sparrow

Passeres: 7 Oscines; 15 suborder Oscines; 16 suborder Passeres

Passeridae: 16 family Passeridae

passeriform bird: 9 passerine

passetemps: 7 pastime; 9 diversion; 14 divertissement

Passifloraceae: 19 passionflower family

passim: 10 throughout; 12 here and there

passing: 4 deep, exit, full, high, loss, pass; 5 going, heavy, sound; 6 casual, pretty, strong; 7 cursory, flowing, intense, passage, plenary, release, running, transit; 8 elapsing, temporal; 9 departure, ephemeral, extremely, fugacious, temporary, transient; 10 expiration, moderately, overtaking, qualifying, short-lived, transitive, transitory; 11 exceedingly, impermanent, passing game, passing play, perfunctory

passing play: 4 pass; 7 passing; 11 passing game

passion: 3 ire; 4 bile, fire, fume, gush, heat, love, rage, tiff, woes, zeal; 5 ardor, fever, flame, flush, mania, verve; 6 fervor, pucker, taking, trials, warmth; 7 bluster, ferment, rapture; 8 devotion, fervency, idolatry, yearning; 9 adoration, hysterics, idolizing, vehemence; 10 ebullition, enthusiasm, excitement

passionate: 4 fond; 5 fiery, lusty; 6 ardent, fervid, red-hot; 7 burning, devoted, fervent, flaming, glowing, gushing; **9** impetuous, impulsive, rapturous; **10** hot-blooded, libidinous

passionless: 8 soulless; **9** heartless, impassive; **10** spiritless; **11** emotionless, unemotional

Passion Week: 8 Holy Week

passive: 5 inert; **8** inactive, peaceful, resigned; **12** passive voice

passiveness: 8 inaction, not doing; **9** eschewing, not acting, passivity; **10** abstention, abstinence, forbearing, refraining

passive resistance: 11 nonviolence

passivism: 8 pacifism

pass judgment: 8 sentence

passkey: 8 latchkey; **9** master key; **11** skeleton key

pass on: 4 give, go on, hand, pass; **5** leave, reach; **6** come on, impart, move on, push on, submit; **7** advance, consign, forward, go ahead, march on, press on; **8** delegate, get ahead, hand over, progress, relegate, turn over; **9** circulate; **10** distribute

pass out: 4 conk; **5** faint, swoon; **7** zonk out; **8** black out

Passover: 6 Pesach

Passover supper: 5 Seder

passport: 4 pass; **8** password; **11** safe-conduct; **12** passe-partout

pass the time: 8 kill time, vegetate

pass up: 6 eschew, refuse, reject; **7** decline

pass with flying colors: 3 ace; **6** breeze; **10** pass easily; **11** sail through; **12** sweep through; **13** breeze through

password: 4 word; **6** opener, parole; **8** passport; **9** catchword; **10** mot de passe [Fr], pass-parole; **11** countersign, safe-conduct; **12** passe-partout

past: 2 by; **4** gone, over, yore; **6** bygone, gone by; **8** foregone, retiring; **9** past tense, past times, preceding; **10** passed away, yesteryear

pasta: 5 paste; **7** noodles; **15** alimentary paste

past due: 3 due; **5** owing; **6** unpaid; **7** overdue; **10** delinquent; **11** outstanding

paste: 3 gum; **4** glue, lute; **5** pasta; **6** cement, gewgaw, spread, tinsel; **7** noodles, spangle; **8** gimcrack, mucilage; **11** junk jewelry

pasted: 5 glued

pastel color: 9 soft color

pastern: 10 fetter bone

Pasteur: 12 Louis Pasteur

pasteurize: 9 sterilize

pastiche: 4 mess, olio; **6** medley, mosaic; **7** collage, montage; **8** all sorts, mishmash; **9** composite, patchwork, potpourri; **10** hodgepodge

pastille: 6 pastil, troche; **9** cough drop

pastime: 8 interest; **9** diversion

Pastinaca: 7 parsnip; **14** genus Pastinaca

past one's prime: 6 waning; **8** decrepit; **9** declining, run to seed

pastor: 5 vicar; **6** curate, parson, rector; **8** minister; **9** rural dean

pastoral: 5 idyll; **6** homily, rustic, sermon; **7** bucolic, idyllic, lecture; **8** arcadian, priestly; **9** discourse, pastorale; **10** sacerdotal; **11** ministerial, predication

pastorale: 5 idyll; **8** fantasia, pastoral

past times: 4 past, yore; **10** yesteryear

pasturage: 3 lay, lea, ley; **5** grass; **6** eatage, forage; **7** herbage, pasture; **11** grazing land

pasture: 3 lea, ley; **4** crop; **5** grass, graze, range; **6** browse, eatage, forage; **9** pasturage; **11** grazing land, pastureland

pastureland: 3 lea, ley; **7** pasture; **11** grazing land

pasty: 3 pie; **5** gluey, gummy, patty; **6** sticky, viscid; **7** viscous; **8** turnover; **9** glutinous, pastelike; **12** mucilaginous

PA system: 2 PA

pat: 3 apt, dab, rap, tap; **4** flap, glib; **5** chuck, slick; **8** apposite; **9** pertinent

Patavium: 5 Padua; **6** Padova

patch: 3 lot; **4** inch, mend, plot, seed, spot; **5** crumb, fleck, piece, tract; **6** blotch, dapple, parcel, tatter; **7** flitter, freckle, fritter, patch up, speckle; **8** eyepatch; **9** birthmark, scantling; **10** maculation; **12** plot of ground

patchboard: 9 plugboard; **11** switchboard

patched: 7 spotted

patch up: 4 do up; **5** patch; **6** make up, settle, vamp up; **7** arrange, touch up; **9** plaster up, reconcile; **10** conciliate

patchwork: 4 mess, olio; **6** jumble, medley, mosaic; **7** collage, farrago, montage; **8** all sorts, mishmash, pastiche; **9** composite, potpourri; **10** hodgepodge

pate: 4 head, poll; **5** crown; **6** noggin, sconce; **9** headpiece

pate a choux: 9 pouf paste; **10** puff batter

pate de foie gras: 8 foie gras

pate feuillete: 9 puff paste

patella: 3 urn; **5** tazza; **6** patera, salver; **7** kneecap, kneepan

Patella: 6 limpet; **12** genus Patella

patellar reflex: 8 knee jerk

patent: 4 bare, open; **5** grant, overt, plain; **7** charter, evident, express, literal; **8** apparent, exoteric, explicit, manifest; **9** chartered, expressed; **11** undisguised

patently: 5 plain; **7** plainly; **9** evidently, obviously; **10** apparently, manifestly

pater: 2 pa; **3** dad, pop; **4** dada, papa; **5** daddy, pappa; **6** old man

patera: 3 urn; **5** tazza; **6** salver; **7** epergne, patella

paterfamilias: 3 dad; **4** papa, sire; **6** father; **9** patriarch; **15** head of household

paternal: 6 agnate; **7** agnatic; **8** maternal, parental

paternity: 10 fatherhood
paternoster: 9 Our Father; **11** Lord's prayer
path: 3 way; **5** route, track; **6** course; **9** way of life; **12** thoroughfare
Pathan: 6 Afghan, Pashto; **12** Afghanistani
pathetic: 3 sad; **4** poor; **5** silly; **7** hapless, piteous, pitiful; **8** pitiable, touching, wretched; **9** affecting, miserable; **10** ridiculous; **12** misfortunate
pathetically: 8 pitiably
pathfinder: 5 guide, scout
pathless: 6 untrod; **8** roadless; **9** trackless, untracked, untrodden
pathogen: 3 bug; **4** germ; **5** virus; **8** bacteria
pathogenic: 9 infective
pathologic: 6 morbid; **8** diseased; **12** pathological
pathologist: 13 diagnostician
pathology: 8 etiology
pathos: 4 pity, ruth; **9** deep sense, poignancy; **13** commiseration
pathway: 5 tract; **7** roadway; **8** footpath; **10** nerve tract; **12** nerve pathway
patience: 9 endurance, solitaire, tolerance; **11** forbearance
patient: 4 case; **7** invalid
patio: 7 terrace
patois: 4 cant; **5** argot, lingo, slang; **6** jargon; **7** dialect; **10** vernacular; **11** sublanguage; **13** local language
patriarch: 4 seer; **6** old man; **9** graybeard; **13** paterfamilias; **15** head of household
patriarchal: 6 family, linear; **9** ancestral
patrician: 4 blue; **6** gentle, squire, titled; **8** laureate, princely; **9** blue blood, gentleman; **10** aristocrat; **11** blue-blooded; **12** aristocratic
Patrick: 10 St. Patrick; **12** Saint Patrick
patrilineal kin: 6 agnate; **8** patrikin, patrisib; **14** patrilineal sib
patrimonial: 9 ancestral; **10** hereditary
patrimony: 6 legacy; **7** bequest; **10** birthright; **11** inheritance
patriot: 11 nationalist
patriotic: 5 loyal
patriotism: 11 amor patriae [Lat], nationalism, nationality; **13** love of country
patrol: 4 roam, rove; **5** prowl, range, watch; **6** police; **7** monitor; **8** traverse; **9** patrolman; **10** mount guard, patrolling
patrol car: 7 cruiser; **8** prowl car, squad car; **9** police car
patrolman: 3 cop; **6** patrol; **8** flatfoot
patrol torpedo boat: 6 PT boat; **11** torpedo boat
patrol wagon: 5 wagon; **9** police van; **10** paddy wagon; **11** police wagon
patron: 5 angel; **6** backer, client; **7** favorer, sponsor; **8** attender, customer; **9** clientele, supporter; **10** frequenter
patronage: 5 favor, trade; **6** credit; **7** backing, disdain, support; **8** auspices, business,

interest, prestige; **9** clientele, patronize; **10** protection
patronize: 4 shop; **5** buy at; **6** shop at; **7** sponsor, support; **8** frequent; **9** patronage; **10** condescend
patronless: 12 unpatronized
patronymic: 9 otchestvo [Russian]
patsy: 3 mug; **4** dupe, fish, fool, gull, mark; **5** chump; **6** sucker; **7** fall guy; **8** shlemiel; **9** schlemiel, soft touch
patten: 4 clog, geta; **5** sabot; **6** sandal; **7** rubbers; **8** galoshes, overshoe
patter: 5 spiel; **7** belabor, spatter; **8** sprinkle; **9** line of gab; **12** pitter-patter
pattern: 4 form, rule, type; **5** ideal, model, shape; **6** design, figure, mirror, normal; **7** example, formula; **8** exemplar, original, paradigm, practice, standard; **9** blueprint, precedent, prototype, reference, scantling; **10** convention
patty: 4 cake; **7** meat pie; **8** turnover
pattypan squash: 7 cymling
patty shell: 7 bouchee
paucity: 6 dearth; **11** small number
Paul the Apostle: 4 Paul, Saul; **11** Apostle Paul; **12** Saul of Tarsus; **20** Apostle of the Gentiles
paunch: 5 belly; **7** stomach; **8** potbelly; **11** breadbasket
paunchy: 10 abdominous, potbellied
pauper: 4 hobo; **5** tramp; **6** beggar; **7** poor man
pauperism: 4 lack, need, want; **6** penury; **7** poverty; **8** distress; **9** indigence, necessity, neediness, privation; **11** destitution; **12** difficulties
pauperize: 6 beggar, reduce; **10** impoverish
pause: 4 lull, rest, trim, wait; **5** break, demur; **6** coquet, debate, demure, waffle; **7** balance, respite, scruple, shuffle, stick at; **8** hesitate, intermit, straddle; **9** fluctuate, interrupt; **10** suspension; **11** adjournment, discontinue, prorogation, retardation; **12** intermission, interruption, postponement
paused: 6 halted; **7** stopped; **9** suspended; **11** interrupted
pavement: 4 deck, flag, walk; **5** earth, flags, floor; **6** ground, paving; **8** footpath, sidewalk; **10** substratum; **11** ground floor; **12** substructure
pavilion: 4 hall; **5** court, tower; **6** castle; **7** chateau; **10** manor-house
paving: 4 deck, flag; **5** earth, floor; **6** ground; **8** pavement; **10** substratum; **11** ground floor; **12** substructure
pavior: 7 paviour; **13** paving machine
Pavlov: 10 Ivan Pavlov; **19** Ivan Petrovich Pavlov
Pavo: peafowl; **9** genus Pavo
paw: 4 feel, hand, hook, mitt; **5** grope,

P

manus, thumb, touch; **6** finger, fumble, handle, mauler; **7** grabble

pawl: 4 bolt; **6** tongue

pawn: 7 consign, hostage; **8** mortgage; **9** guarantee; **10** instrument, pawn ticket

pawnbroker's shop: 8 pawnshop; **10** loan office

pawpaw: 6 papaya

pax: 3 pyx; **5** peace; **11** kiss of peace

pay: 4 bear, give, wage; **5** pay up, wages, yield; **6** answer, ante up, defray, devote, make up, pay off, salary; **7** bring in, pay back; **8** disburse, earnings; **10** compensate

pay as you earn: 4 PAYE

pay attention: 4 hang, list; **6** advert, attend, listen; **7** give ear, pay heed

payback: 6 retort; **8** reprisal; **11** retaliation

pay back: 3 fix, get, pay; **5** repay; **6** pay off, reward; **9** get back at

paycheck: 12 payroll check

pay claim: 9 wage claim

payed out: 5 spent; **8** expended; **9** disbursed

payer: 11 remunerator

paygrade: 6 rating; **12** military rank

pay homage: 5 adore; **6** aspire; **7** worship; **9** do service

paying: 4 paid; **7** gainful, payment; **8** defrayal, salaried; **9** lucrative; **10** defrayment, profitable; **11** compensable, stipendiary; **12** advantageous, remunerative

pay in advance: 6 prepay; **7** advance

paying back: 6 return; **8** repaying; **9** repayment; **11** getting even

paying guest: 6 lodger; **7** boarder

paying out: 8 spending; **9** expending; **10** disbursing

payload: 4 load; **5** cargo; **6** lading; **7** freight, loading, warhead; **8** shipment; **11** consignment

paymaster: 6 teller; **7** cashier

payment in advance: 10 prepayment; **14** advance payment

pay off: 3 fix, get, pay; **6** buy off, make up, redeem; **7** pay back; **9** get back at, liquidate; **10** compensate

payoff: 4 take; **5** bribe, issue, wages, yield; **6** return, reward; **7** takings; **8** proceeds; **12** final payment

pay one's respects: 5 visit; **8** wait upon; **9** pay a visit

pay out: 8 disburse, serve out

payroll: 8 paysheet

payroll check: 8 paycheck

pay telephone: 8 pay phone

pay too much: 7 overpay

pay up: 3 pay; **6** ante up; **11** pay old debts

Pb: 4 lead

P-coat: 6 ulster; **7** pea coat; **9** pea jacket; **11** dreadnaught, dreadnought

PCP: 9 angel dust

pct: 7 percent; **9** per centum; **10** percentage

Pd: 9 palladium

pdl: 7 poundal

pea: 4 bulb, clew, drop, horn, knob, pill; **6** bullet, marble, pellet, pommel; **7** globule, vesicle; **8** pea plant, spherule

pea bean: 8 navy bean; **9** white bean

peace: 4 calm, hush, lull; **6** repose; **8** ataraxis, serenity; **10** heartsease; **11** peace of mind, peace treaty, tranquility

peaceable: 7 pacific; **8** peaceful; **11** peaceloving

peaceful: 4 calm; **6** placid; **7** pacific, passive; **9** easygoing, peaceable; **10** law-abiding

Peace Garden State: 11 North Dakota

peacemaker: 8 appeaser, pacifier; **9** gobetween, make-peace; **10** negotiator, reconciler; **11** conciliator

peacenik: 4 dove

peace offering: 7 handsel; **11** olive branch

peace officer: 6 lawman; **10** law officer

peace of mind: 4 ease; **5** peace; **6** repose; **8** ataraxis, serenity

peace pipe: 7 calumet

peach: 3 rat; **4** blab, shop, sing, stag, talk; **5** grass, spill; **6** babble, beauty, betray, let out, looker, snitch, tattle, tell on; **7** apricot, blab out, divulge, smasher, stunner; **8** blurt out, denounce; **9** peach tree; **10** salmon pink, sweetheart

peach-colored: 13 salmon-colored

Peach State: 7 Georgia; **21** Empire State of the South

peach tree: 5 peach; **13** Prunus persica

peachy: 4 cool, keen, neat; **5** bully, dandy, great, nifty, swell; **6** bang-up, groovy, not bad

pea coat: 5 P-coat; **6** ulster; **9** pea jacket; **11** dreadnaught, dreadnought

peacock: 9 Inachis io; **16** peacock butterfly

peacock blue: 4 aqua; **9** turquoise; **10** aquamarine, cobalt blue; **12** greenish blue

peacock flower: 9 flame tree; **14** royal poinciana

pea family: 8 Fabaceae; **11** Leguminosae; **12** legume family

pea green: 10 chartreuse, Paris green; **11** yellow green; **14** yellowish green

pea jacket: 5 P-coat; **6** ulster; **7** pea coat; **11** dreadnaught, dreadnought

peak: 3 Alp, tip, top; **4** acme, apex, bill, pike, pine; **5** bloom, crest, crown, flush, mount, point, prime, visor, vizor; **6** flower, height, heyday, summit, vertex, zenith; **7** blossom, highest; **8** mountain, pinnacle; **9** climactic

peaked: 6 ailing, poorly, sickly, unwell; **7** salient; **10** indisposed

peaked cap: 4 kepi; **10** service cap; **11** yachting cap

peaky: 5 spiky

peal: 4 boom, ring, roar, roll, toll; **5** blare,

blast, chime, clang, swell; **7** fanfare, pealing, rolling, thunder

pean: 5 paean; **6** eulogy; **8** encomium; **9** panegyric

peanut: 5 small; **6** goober, little; **8** earthnut; **9** goober pea, groundnut; **13** insignificant; **15** Arachis hypogaea

pear: 8 pear tree; **13** Pyrus communis

pearl: 3 gem; **4** bead, bone; **5** jewel; **8** off-white; **10** pearl white

pearl diver: 7 pearler

pearlescent: 7 opaline; **8** nacreous; **10** iridescent, opalescent

pearly: 3 dun, sad; **4** drab, fair, roan, shot; **5** blond, livid, milky; **6** creamy, mellow, pastel, tender; **7** whitish; **8** delicate; **9** prismatic; **10** harmonious; **11** pearly-white

peasant: 4 serf; **6** farmer; **7** laborer; **10** provincial

peat: 4 turf

peat bog: 3 bog, fen; **4** moor, moss; **8** moorland

peat moss: 7 bog moss; **8** sphagnum; **12** sphagnum moss

peavey: 5 peavy; **8** cant hook

pebbly: 7 shingly; **8** gravelly

pecan: 3 nut

peccadillo: 4 slip, trip; **5** lapse; **7** faux pas [Fr]; **12** indiscretion

peccant: 4 foul, rank; **6** faulty; **7** carious, fulsome, sinning, tainted; **8** peccable, purulent, vitiated

peccary: 7 musk hog

peck: 3 fry, lot, nag, pot, wad; **4** beak, bevy, deal, heap, herd, hive, lick, mass, mess, mint, nest, pick, pile, raft, slew; **5** batch, brood, cloud, covey, drove, flock, shoal, sight, smack, spate, stack, swarm; **6** bushel, farrow, flight, hatful, litter, mickle, muckle, peck at, pick at, pick up, plenty, scores

peck at: 4 peck; **6** carp at, pick at; **8** nibble at

pecking order: 9 hierarchy; **14** power structure

Pecos: 10 Pecos River

Pecten irradians: 10 bay scallop

Pecten magellanicus: 10 sea scallop; **12** giant scallop

pectoral: 4 pecs; **8** thoracic; **10** pectoralis; **14** pectoral muscle

pectus: 5 chest; **6** thorax

peculate: 8 embezzle; **14** misappropriate

peculator: 8 swindler; **9** embezzler

peculiar: 3 odd, rum; **5** funny, party, queer, rummy; **6** proper; **7** certain, curious, several, special; **8** definite, especial, original

peculiarity: 5 curio; **6** oddity, rarity; **7** oddment; **9** curiosity, exception, mannerism, specialty; **10** speciality; **11** originality, specialness; **12** idiosyncrasy

pecuniary: 8 monetary

pecuniary obligation: 9 liability; **12** indebtedness

pecuniary resource: 5 funds; **8** finances; **10** cash in hand

pedagogue: 5 usher; **6** pedant; **7** dominie [Fr]; **8** educator; **11** abecedarian; **12** schoolmaster

pedagogy: 8 teaching; **9** education; **11** instruction

pedal: 4 bike; **5** cycle, wheel; **7** bicycle, treadle; **9** foot lever

Pedaliaceae: 12 sesame family

pedal pusher: 12 toreador pant

pedant: 8 bookworm; **9** pedagogue; **10** scholastic; **11** doctrinaire

pedantic: 6 stodgy; **7** pompous, stilted; **8** academic

peddle: 4 hawk, vend; **5** pitch; **6** monger, piddle; **8** huckster

peddler: 6 cadger, hawker, pedlar, pusher; **7** camelot [Fr]; **8** huckster; **10** colporteur; **11** drug peddler; **14** drug trafficker

pederast: 13 child molester

pedestal: 4 base; **5** stand

pedestrian: 5 prosy; **6** footer, stodgy, walker; **7** prosaic, prosing; **8** pedantic

pedestrian bridge: 10 footbridge; **12** overcrossing

pedestrian mall: 4 mall; **7** commons; **12** suburban mall

pedestrian traffic: 11 foot traffic

pediatrician: 10 baby doctor, pediatrist

pediculosis: 9 lousiness

Pediculus: 5 louse; **9** body louse, head louse; **14** genus Pediculus

pedigree: 4 line, stem, tree; **5** birth, blood, breed, house, stock; **6** origin, stirps, strain; **7** descent, lineage; **8** ancestry, heritage; **9** bloodline, genealogy, parentage, pedigreed, pureblood; **10** extraction

pediment: 6 frieze, sconce; **7** capital, cornice, pedicle; **10** architrave; **11** coping stone

pedlar: 6 cadger, hawker; **7** peddler; **8** huckster

pedunculate: 6 tailed; **7** caudate, stalked

peek: 4 peep; **5** glint; **6** glance

peel: 4 flay, pare, rind, skin; **5** flake, scale, scalp, shave, slice; **7** peel off; **8** flake off; **9** excoriate

peeled: 3 raw; **9** uncovered

peep: 3 pry; **4** look, peek, peer; **5** cheep, croak, glint; **6** glance; **7** glimpse

peeper: 3 eye; **5** optic; **6** oculus, voyeur

peephole: 7 spyhole; **8** loophole; **9** mousehole; **10** pigeonhole

Peeping Tom: 6 peeper, voyeur

peer: 3 pry; **4** mate, peep, scan; **5** equal, match, sound; **6** browse; **7** compeer, explore, peerage, ransack, rummage

peeress: 4 lady; **10** noblewoman

peering: 4 nosy; **6** prying, snoopy

P

peerless: 3 one; 9 matchless, nonpareil, unmatched, unrivaled; 10 one and only, unrivalled; 11 unmatchable

peeved: 5 riled, stung; 6 pissed, roiled; 7 annoyed, nettled; 9 irritated

peevish: 3 hot; 5 hasty, quick, testy; 6 cranky, tetchy; 7 bilious, peckish, peppery, pettish, waspish; 8 captious, petulant, shrewish, snappish; 9 fractious, irritable, overhasty, querulous; 10 nettlesome

peewee: 4 runt; 5 pewee, pewit; 6 peewit, shrimp; 8 half-pint

peg: 3 pin; 4 plug; 5 throw, attach; 8 identify, restrict

Pegasus: 11 flying horse

pegleg: 3 leg, peg; 9 wooden leg

peignoir: 7 neglige; 8 negligee; 9 housecoat

pejorative: 9 insulting, slighting; 10 belittling, derogatory, detracting, detractive; 11 deprecatory, disparaging

Peke: 8 Pekinese; 9 Pekingese

Pekinese: 4 Peke; 9 Pekingese

Peking: 7 Beijing, Peiping; 17 capital of Red China

pekoe: 3 tea; 11 orange pekoe

pelagic: 7 oceanic; 8 pelagian

Pelargonium: 8 geranium; 16 genus Pelargonium

Pelecanus: 7 pelican; 14 genus Pelecanus

pelf: 5 money; 6 riches

Pelican State: 9 Louisiana

pelisse: 4 pall; 5 cloak; 6 mantle

Pellaea: 4 fern; 12 genus Pellaea

pellet: 3 pea; 4 bulb, clew, drop, horn, knob, pill, shot; 6 bullet, marble, pommel, tablet; 7 globule, vesicle; 8 spherule

pellet gun: 5 BB gun; 6 air gun

pellicular: 5 filmy, flaky, scaly; 8 squamous [Anat]; 10 membranous

pell-mell: 8 disorder; 9 confusion; 11 harum-scarum; 13 helter-skelter

pellucid: 5 clear, lucid; 6 limpid; 8 luculent; 11 crystalline, transparent

pellucidity: 7 clarity; 8 lucidity; 9 clearness, limpidity; 12 pellucidness, transparence, transparency

pelmet: 7 cornice, valance

pelota: 7 jai alai

pelt: 3 fur, rug; 4 hide, plug, pour, rock, skin; 5 front, punch, stone, thump; 6 patter, pepper, stream

pelting: 4 rain

pelvis: 3 hip

pemmican: 5 jerky; 9 beef jerky

pen: 4 coop; 5 quill; 6 shut in, writer; 7 bullpen, enclose; 9 ballpoint, enclosure; 12 penitentiary

penal: 8 punitive; 9 punishing; 10 punishable

penalization: 7 penalty; 10 punishment

penalize: 6 punish

penalized: 5 fined

penal servitude: 9 hard labor

penalty: 8 sentence; 10 punishment

penance: 9 penitence; 10 repentance; 13 self-abasement

penchant: 4 bent, mind; 5 taste; 6 animus; 7 leaning; 10 partiality, preference; 11 inclination

pencil: 3 ray; 4 beam, limn; 5 clump, gleam, stump; 6 sketch, streak, stream; 8 light ray

pencil eraser: 6 rubber; 12 rubber eraser

pencil in: 6 draw in

pendant: 5 match; 6 pennon; 7 hanging, pendent; 8 dangling; 9 suspended; 10 chandelier

pending: 5 while; 6 during, whilst

pendulous: 7 nodding; 8 cernuous, drooping

penetralia: 8 recesses

penetrate: 4 dawn; 5 click; 6 bottom, fathom, pierce, seep in, sink in; 8 come home, permeate, puncture; 9 get across, perforate

penetrating: 4 keen; 5 acute, sharp; 8 incisive, piercing; 9 absorbing, knifelike, observant, pervading; 10 discerning, perceptive, permeating

penetration: 6 acumen; 7 insight; 8 puncture, sagacity; 9 acuteness, incursion; 10 shrewdness; 11 discernment, perforation

pen-friend: 6 pen pal

pen in: 3 pen; 4 cage, coop; 5 hem in; 6 bolt in, coop up, rail in, wall in; 7 impound

peninsula: 12 tongue of land

penitence: 7 penance, remorse; 10 contrition, repentance; 11 compunction

penitent: 5 sorry; 8 contrite; 9 repentant, repenting

penitentiary: 3 can [slang], pen; 4 stir [slang]; 6 lockup, prison; 7 slammer [slang], the Rock; 8 big house [slang]; 10 San Quentin

penknife: 7 whittle; 11 pocketknife

penman: 6 author, scribe, writer; 9 scribbler

penmanship: 7 penning; 11 calligraphy

pen name: 10 nom de plume

pennant: 4 flag, waft; 6 banner, colors; 8 streamer

penned: 8 confined, fenced in

penniless: 6 hard up; 7 pinched; 9 destitute, penurious; 11 impecunious

Pennisetum: 11 pearl millet; 13 fountain grass; 15 genus Pennisetum

pennon: 4 waft, wing; 6 pinion; 7 pendant, pennant; 8 streamer, penoncel; 9 pennoncel

penny: 4 cent; 7 centime; 11 Lincoln cent

penny a liner: 4 hack; 9 potboiler; 10 hack writer, ink slinger

penny ante: 9 low stakes

penny bank: 9 piggy bank

penny dreadful: 9 dime novel

penny-pinching: 4 near; 5 close; 6 thrift; 9 parsimony

pennywhistle: 7 whistle; **10** tin whistle
penny wise: 4 mean, near; **5** close; **6** shabby, stingy; **7** miserly, scrubby; **8** peddling; **9** penurious; **12** parsimonious
penny wise and pound foolish: 8 wasteful
penocha: 7 penuche
pen pal: 9 pen-friend
pension: 7 annuity, nest egg
pensionary: 8 hireling; **9** pensioner
pensioned: 11 stipendiary; **12** under pension
pensive: 3 sad; **6** broody, musing, sedate; **7** doleful, wistful; **8** brooding; **9** pondering; **10** meditative, melancholy, reflective, ruminative, thoughtful
Penstemon: 9 penstemon; **14** genus Penstemon
penstock: 4 weir; **6** sluice; **8** head gate; **9** floodgate, sluiceway, water gate; **10** sluicegate; **11** sluice valve
pent: 6 shut up
pentacle: 9 pentagram
pentad: 3 fin; **4** five; **5** quint; **6** cinque; **7** quintet; **8** fivesome; **10** quintuplet
pentagon: 9 five-sided
pentagonal: 11 pentangular
pentagram: 8 pentacle
pentangular: 10 pentagonal
Pentateuch: 4 Laws; **5** Torah
pentavalent: 12 quinqevalent
Pentecost: 7 Shavous, Shavuot; **8** Shabuoth, Shavuoth; **10** Whitsunday; **12** Feast of Weeks
Pentecostal: 14 Pentecostalist
pentobarbital: 8 Nembutal; **12** yellow jacket
pent-up: 9 repressed
penuche: 5 fudge; **7** penocha
penult: 9 penultima; **11** penultimate
penultimate: 6 penult; **9** penultima; **10** definitive, last but one, next-to-last
penumbra: 6 fringe; **13** partial shadow
pen up: 4 fold
penurious: 4 mean, near; **5** close; **6** hard up, shabby, stingy; **7** miserly, pinched, scrubby; **8** peddling; **9** penniless, penny wise; **11** impecunious; **12** parsimonious
penury: 4 lack, need, want; **7** poverty; **8** distress; **9** indigence, necessity, neediness, parsimony, pauperism, privation; **10** stinginess; **11** destitution, miserliness
peon: 4 serf; **5** menial; **6** drudge; **7** peasant; **11** infantryman
peony family: 11 Paeoniaceae
people: 4 fold, live, mass; **5** dwell, flock, laity, shack; **6** masses, reside; **7** inhabit, persons; **8** assembly, brethren, populate; **9** citizenry, multitude; **12** congregation
People's Republic of China: 3 PRC; **5** China; **8** Red China; **13** mainland China; **14** Communist China
People's Republic of Kampuchea: 8 Cambodia; **9** Kampuchea

People's Republic of the Congo: 5 Congo; **11** French Congo; **15** Republic of Congo
peopled: 5 thick; **7** crowded, studded, teeming; **8** manifold, multiple, populous; **9** inhabited, populated; **10** multiplied; **12** multinominal; **13** multitudinous
pep: 5 peppy; **6** energy; **11** high spirits
pepper: 4 pelt; **5** shell; **7** bombard; **8** capsicum, open fire; **10** peppercorn; **11** black pepper, white pepper
pepper and salt: 11 chiaroscuro
peppercorn: 8 capsicum; **11** black pepper, white pepper
peppered steak: 11 pepper steak; **13** steak au poivre
pepper family: 10 Piperaceae
pepper grass: 11 garden cress
pepper grinder: 10 pepper mill
peppermint candy: 10 peppermint
pepper sauce: 8 Poivrade
pepper tree: 5 molle; **12** Schinus molle
peppery: 3 hot; **5** hasty, quick, spicy; **7** bilious, gingery, peevish, waspish; **8** captious, shrewish, snappish; **9** fractious, overhasty
pep pill: 5 speed, upper; **11** amphetamine
peppy: 5 zippy; **6** bouncy; **8** bouncing, spirited
Pepsi Cola: 5 Pepsi
peptidase: 8 protease; **10** proteinase
per: 2 by; **7** through
peradventure: 5 haply, may be, maybe; **6** mayhap; **7** perhaps; **8** possibly; **9** perchance
perambulate: 9 walk about; **10** walk around
perambulation: 3 jog; **4** trot, turn; **5** amble, stalk, tramp; **6** canter, ramble, stroll; **7** saunter; **9** promenade
perambulator: 4 pram [Brit]; **6** go-cart, pusher; **8** carriage, stroller; **9** baby buggy, pedometer, pushchair; **12** baby carriage
per annum: 2 p.a.; **7** per year; **8** annually, each year
Perca: perch; **10** genus Perca
perceivable: 6 in view; **7** in sight, visible; **9** graspable; **11** discernible, perceptible
perceive: 3 get, see; **4** feel; **5** sight; **6** behold, descry; **7** discern, observe; **8** conceive; **9** recognize; **10** comprehend, experience
perceived: 4 felt; **6** sensed
perceiver: 8 beholder, observer
perceiving: 7 sensing; **10** perception
percent: 3 pct; **9** per centum; **10** percentage
percentage: 3 pct; **4** part; **5** share; **6** setoff; **7** percent, portion; **8** drawback, poundage; **9** per centum
percentage point: 12 decimal point
percentage sign: 11 percent sign
per centum: 3 pct; **7** percent; **10** percentage
percept: 10 perception
perceptible: 6 in view; **7** in sight, obvious,

P

visible; **10** detectable, noticeable; **11** appreciable, discernible, perceivable

perception: 5 image; **7** percept, sensing; **9** sensation; **10** impression, perceiving; **11** mental image

perceptive: 8 piercing, sentient; **9** aesthetic, observant; **10** discerning

perceptual faculties: 5 sense; **6** senses

perch: 3 rod; **4** hive, live, pole, rest, seat, stay; **5** abide, dwell, light, lodge, roost, squat; **6** alight, burrow, nestle, reside, tenant; **7** bivouac, inhabit, sit down, sojourn; **8** surmount; **11** get a footing

perchance: 5 haply, may be, maybe; **6** mayhap; **7** perhaps; **8** by chance, possibly

perched: 6 perked; **8** perked up

perchloromethane: 9 carbon tet

percipient: 5 clear

percolate: 4 drip, drop, perk; **5** leach, plash, trill; **6** filter, perk up, pick up, sink in; **7** distill, dribble, trickle; **8** permeate

percolation: 6 oozing; **7** leakage; **12** distillation

per contra: 6 contra; **7** however; **9** nay rather; **10** contrarily; **11** au contraire [Fr]

percussion: 4 bump; **5** clash; **8** drumming; **9** collision, encounter; **10** concussion

percutaneous: 9 diadermic; **11** transdermic

per diem: 8 by the day

perdition: 4 fall, Hell, loss, ruin; **5** crash; **6** losing, the pit; **7** Inferno; **8** downfall; **9** ruination; **11** devastation; **12** nether region; **14** infernal region

perdu: 6 unseen, hidden

perdurable: 7 durable

peregrine: 6 falcon, mobile, roving; **7** nomadic; **9** wandering

peregrine falcon: 9 peregrine; **15** Falco peregrinus

peremptory: 4 flat; **5** bossy, broad, round; **6** marked; **7** decided, haughty, pointed; **8** absolute, distinct, positive; **9** arbitrary, ex officio, imperious, stringent; **10** autocratic, commanding, definitive, dominating, high-handed, imperative, ironhanded

perennial: 8 biennial, repeated; **9** evergreen, recurrent

perfect: 4 pure; **5** stark, utter; **6** arrant, mature; **8** absolute, complete, finished, flawless, maturate, positive; **9** essential, faultless; **10** consummate, impeccable

perfecta: 6 exacta

perfection: 4 idol; **7** paragon; **12** flawlessness

perfectionist: 9 nitpicker; **10** fussbudget

perfectly: 7 utterly; **10** absolutely, flawlessly, impeccably; **11** faultlessly

perfect memory: 11 total recall

perfect pitch: 13 absolute pitch

perfervid: 5 fiery; **6** ardent, fervid, torrid; **7** burning, fervent; **11** impassioned

perfidious: 5 punic; **8** perjured; **11** treacherous

perfidy: 7 treason; **8** betrayal; **9** treachery

perforate: 5 punch; **6** pierce; **7** pierced; **8** puncture; **9** penetrate, punctured; **10** perforated

perforation: 8 puncture; **11** penetration

perform: 2 do; **3** act; **4** keep, play; **5** enact, put on; **6** comply, strain, strike; **7** abide by, execute, fulfill, observe, operate, quicken, realize, respect, satisfy, support, sustain; **8** maintain

performable: 6 doable; **8** feasible; **10** achievable; **11** practicable

performance: 5 doing, touch; **6** acting, action; **8** movement; **9** acquittal, discharge, execution, operation, spectacle; **10** compliance, expression, observance, redemption; **11** carrying out, concurrence, fulfillment, functioning; **12** presentation

performance artist: 7 showman; **10** showperson; **11** entertainer

performed: 5 acted; **6** staged; **8** acted out, realized; **10** carried out, discharged; **12** accomplished

performer: 4 doer; **5** actor, agent; **6** player, stager

performing: 5 doing; **6** acting; **7** playing; **10** playacting

perform surgery: 7 operate

perfume: 5 aroma, scent; **6** embalm; **7** bouquet, essence; **9** aromatize, fragrance, redolence

perfumed: 5 sweet; **7** odorous, scented; **11** odoriferous; **12** sweet-scented; **13** sweetsmelling

perfunctorily: 8 pro forma, remissly

perfunctory: 4 lame; **6** casual, hollow, meager, remiss; **7** cursory, passing, sketchy; **8** pro forma

perfuse: 7 suffuse

pergola: 5 arbor, bower; **6** arbour; **7** trellis

perhaps: 5 haply, may be, maybe; **6** mayhap; **8** possibly; **9** perchance; **11** potentially

pericarp: 10 seed vessel

periclase: 8 magnesia

pericranium: 5 scull, skull; **7** cranium

peridot: 3 gem; **7** olivine

peril: 4 risk; **5** queer; **6** danger, expose, hazard, menace; **7** imperil, scupper, venture; **8** endanger, jeopardy, threaten; **9** riskiness

perilous: 5 risky; **6** unsafe; **7** parlous; **8** insecure; **9** dangerous, hazardous; **10** precarious

perimeter: 5 limit; **6** border, bounds, margin; **7** outline; **8** boundary; **9** periphery

period: 3 pas; **4** flow, mark, span, stop, time; **5** phase, pitch, place, point, space, stage; **6** menses; **8** full stop, interval

periodical: 6 serial; **8** periodic

periodically: 9 regularly; **10** cyclically; **11** recurrently; **12** sporadically

periodicity: 9 cyclicity, frequency; **13** intermittence

periodic law: 13 Mendeleev's law

periodic payment: 11 installment

period of enlistment: 5 hitch; **10** enlistment

periodontal disease: 13 periodontitis

peripatetic: 6 roving; **7** gadding, vagrant; **8** rambling; **9** itinerant, wayfaring; **10** ambulatory, discursive

peripatus: 10 velvet worm; **12** onychophoran

peripheral: 8 auxilary; **13** supplementary

peripheral device: 10 peripheral

periphery: 6 fringe; **7** outline; **9** perimeter

Periplaneta: 9 cockroach; **16** genus Periplaneta

perirhinal: 9 perinatal

perish: 3 die; **4** exit; **6** expire; **7** be taken, decease, succumb; **8** pass away

perishables: 10 spoilables

Perisoreus: 7 gray jay; **9** Canada jay; **15** genus Perisoreus

peristyle: 8 cloister; **9** colonnade

periwig: 6 peruke

periwinkle: 5 snail; **6** winkle; **7** mollusk

perjured: 10 perfidious; **11** treacherous

perjure oneself: 3 lie; **8** forswear; **10** swear false

perjurer: 12 false witness

perjury: 9 mendacity; **12** lie under oath; **13** false swearing

perk: 5 equip; **6** perk up, pick up; **7** harness; **9** caparison, gain vigor, percolate; **10** perquisite; **13** fringe benefit

perkiness: 8 archness, buoyancy, pertness; **9** sauciness

perks: 11 perquisites

perky: 6 chirpy; **7** buoyant

perm: 6 hairdo; **9** permanent

permanent: 4 perm; **5** fixed; **6** rooted; **7** endless, lasting; **9** besetting, hackneyed; **10** deep-rooted, inveterate

permanently: 7 for good

permanent magnet: 6 magnet; **8** siderite; **9** magnetite

permanent-press fabric: 6 no-iron; **7** drip-dry; **12** durable press

permanent residence: 7 address; **9** residence

permanent wave: 4 perm; **9** permanent

permeabiity vitamin: 6 citrin; **8** vitamin P

permeable: 6 porous; **8** pervious

permeate: 4 fill; **5** imbue; **6** filter, seep in, sink in, thread; **7** diffuse, pervade; **9** penetrate, percolate

permeating: 8 permeant; **9** pervasive; **10** permeative; **11** intercalary, intervening, penetrating; **12** intermediary, intermediate, interstitial

Permian period: 7 Permian

permissible: 7 allowed; **9** allowable, permitted; **10** authorized, sanctioned

permission: 5 leave; **6** permit; **7** license; **10** permitting; **11** authorizing; **13** authorization

permissive: 9 indulgent

permissiveness: 9 tolerance

permit: 3 let; **5** allow; **6** brevet; **7** license, warrant; **10** permission

permitted: 7 allowed; **9** allowable; **10** authorized, sanctioned; **11** permissible

permitter: 9 consenter

permitting: 5 leave; **8** allowing; **10** permission; **11** authorizing; **13** authorization

permutation: 6 switch; **11** replacement; **12** substitution; **13** transposition

permute: 4 swap; **5** bandy; **6** switch; **7** commute, shuffle; **9** transpose; **11** change hands

Pernambuco: 6 Recife

pernicious: 6 deadly, subtle; **7** baleful, baneful, harmful, hurtful, noxious; **9** injurious, insidious, pestilent; **11** deleterious, detrimental, mischievous

Peromyscus: 5 mouse; **15** genus Peromyscus

Peronospora: 6 mildew; **16** genus Peronospora

perorate: 6 ramble; **7** digress; **8** protract

peroration: 3 say; **6** sermon, tirade; **8** delivery, harangue; **10** recitation

per os: 2 p.o. [abbr]

perp: 7 culprit; **8** criminal, offender; **11** perpetrator

perpend: 6 digest, ponder; **7** reflect

perpendicular: 5 erect, plumb; **6** normal; **7** upright; **8** straight, vertical; **9** plumb line

perpendicularly: 5 sheer

perpetrate: 4 pull; **6** commit; **7** inflict

perpetrator: 4 doer, perp; **5** actor, agent; **7** culprit; **8** criminal, offender; **9** performer

perpetual: 6 steady; **7** ageless, endless, eternal, routine; **8** constant, unending; **9** ceaseless, clockwork, continual, incessant, unceasing, unfailing; **10** consistent, continuous, invariable, monotonous; **11** everlasting, unremitting

perpetually: 6 always; **8** ever anon, steadily; **9** routinely; **10** at all times, constantly, invariably; **11** continually, incessantly, unfailingly, without fail; **12** consistently, continuously

perpetuity: 3 aye; **8** eternity; **11** immortality

perplex: 3 bug, get, irk, vex; **4** beat, faze, pose, tire; **5** amaze, annoy, cross, worry; **6** baffle, bother, dazzle, gravel, muddle, put out, puzzle; **7** confuse, disturb, flummox, fluster, involve, mortify, mystify, nonplus, stupefy, stupify, trouble, trounce; **8** bewilder, confound, disquiet; **9** disoblige, displease, dumbfound

perplexity: 7 dilemma; 9 confusion

perquisite: 4 perk; 9 privilege; 11 prerogative; 13 fringe benefit

perquisites: 5 perks

per se: 4 solo; 5 alone; 6 as such, singly; 8 by itself; 12 individually

Persea: 7 avocado; 11 genus Persea

persecute: 3 bug; 4 bait, bore; 5 abuse, beset, grind, harry, haunt, hound, tease, worry, wrong; 6 badger, bother, harass, heckle, ill-use, infest, molest, pester, plague, pother; 7 oppress; 8 aggrieve, ill-treat, maltreat, mistreat

persecuted: 5 beset, bored; 6 baited; 7 harried, heckled; 8 badgered, harassed, infested, pothered; 9 oppressed; 10 importuned; 11 downtrodden

persecution: 7 outrage; 10 harassment, oppression

persecutor: 9 tormentor

perseverance: 8 tenacity; 11 persistence

persevere: 6 hang in, hang on, hold on; 7 persist

perseverence: 8 tenacity; 10 doggedness; 11 persistence

persevering: 8 diligent; 10 persistent, persisting

Persia: 4 Iran; 13 Persian Empire

Persian: 5 Farsi, Irani; 7 Iranian

persiflage: 5 chaff, irony; 6 banter; 8 badinage, raillery

persist: 3 run; 4 go on, last, stay; 6 endure, hang in, hang on, hold on, remain; 7 die hard, prevail; 8 continue; 9 persevere

persistence: 8 tenacity; 9 endurance; 10 continuity

persistency: 8 tenacity; 10 doggedness; 11 persistence

persistent: 7 chronic, lasting; 8 haunting; 10 persisting, relentless; 11 persevering, unrelenting

persisting: 7 dogging; 8 enduring; 10 persistent; 11 persevering

persnickety: 6 snooty, snotty, uppish; 7 stuck-up; 9 bigheaded, snot-nosed

person: 3 man; 4 body, soul; 5 being, human, woman; 6 mortal; 7 someone; 8 creature, somebody, such a one; 9 earthling, personage; 10 human being, individual

persona: 4 part, role; 5 image; 8 personae [pl]; 9 character; 11 public image

personable: 4 fair; 6 comely, seemly; 8 handsome

personae: 4 part, role; 7 persona; 9 character

personage: 3 man; 4 body, soul; 5 being, human, woman; 6 mortal, person; 7 notable; 8 creature, notables [pl], somebody; 9 earthling; 10 human being, individual

personal: 5 civic, human; 6 mortal, public, social; 8 national; 10 individual, subjective; 12 nonobjective

personal appeal: 8 charisma

personal business: 7 affairs

personal computer: 2 PC; 13 microcomputer

personal credit line: 4 line; 8 bank line; 10 credit line; 12 line of credit

personal effects: 5 goods; 7 effects; 8 chattels, movables

personal hygeine: 8 grooming

personal identity: 3 ego; 4 self; 8 identity

personality: 4 tone, turn; 5 style, tenor; 6 temper; 9 mannerism; 11 disposition, temperament; 13 individuality

personally: 8 in person

personal magnetism: 5 charm; 8 charisma

personal narrative: 3 bio; 4 life; 7 journal; 8 fortunes; 10 adventures; 11 confessions, experiences

persona non grata: 15 unwelcome person

personate: 3 ape; 4 mock, pose; 5 mimic; 6 pose as; 8 simulate; 9 personify; 11 impersonate

personify: 2 be; 4 body; 6 embody, pose as; 9 personate; 11 impersonate

personnel: 5 force

personnel casualty: 4 loss

persons: 6 people

person-to-person: 8 one-on-one

perspective: 4 view; 5 angle, vista; 6 aspect; 7 horizon; 8 position, prospect; 9 viewpoint; 11 point of view

perspicacious: 4 keen; 6 shrewd; 7 sapient; 8 piercing; 9 clear-eyed, observant, sagacious

perspicuous: 5 lucid; 6 limpid; 8 lucidity

perspiration: 5 sudor, sweat, water; 8 hidrosis, sweating; 10 perspiring

perspire: 5 sweat

persuade: 4 move, sway, urge; 5 carry; 6 cajole, induce; 7 bring to; 8 blandish, convince

persuaded: 7 seduced, won over; 9 convinced

persuasion: 4 view; 6 urging; 7 opinion, suasion, thought; 8 advocacy; 9 sentiment; 10 convincing

persuasive: 6 cogent; 10 convincing, impressive

pert: 5 fresh [U.S.], saucy; 7 forward; 8 cavalier, flippant; 9 obtrusive; 10 irreverent, precocious; 11 impertinent

pertain: 5 refer, touch; 6 bear on, come to, relate; 7 concern, touch on; 9 appertain

pertinacious: 6 dogged, steady; 8 constant; 9 steadfast, tenacious; 10 unyielding

pertinence: 9 relevancy

pertinent: 3 apt, pat; 8 apposite; 10 to the point; 11 appropriate

pertly: 7 freshly, saucily; 10 impudently; 13 impertinently

perturb: 6 ruffle; 7 agitate, disrupt, disturb,

fluster, trouble, unhinge; **8** convulse, disorder, disquiet, distract; **9** interrupt

perturbation: 4 fuss, stir; **5** hurry, upset; **6** bustle, flurry, ruffle, tremor; **7** fluster, flutter, shaking; **8** splutter; **9** agitation, quivering, trembling; **10** disruption; **11** disturbance

perturbing: 8 worrying; **9** troubling, worrisome; **10** disturbing

pertussis: 13 whooping cough

peruke: 7 periwig

perusal: 8 perusing, scanning, studying; **10** poring over

peruse: 4 scan; **5** spell

pervade: 4 fill; **5** imbue; **7** diffuse, prevail; **8** dominate, permeate; **10** run through; **11** predominate

pervading: 9 absorbing, pervasive; **11** penetrating

pervasive: 8 permeant; **10** permeating, permeative

perverse: 5 balky, heady; **6** amoral, rugged, thorny, trying, unruly; **7** corrupt, immoral, restive, wayward, willful; **8** contrary, depraved

perversion: 5 abuse, gloss; **8** deviance; **9** casuistry, deviation, hardening, sophistry; **10** corruption, declension, distortion; **11** profanation

pervert: 5 abuse, belie, twist; **6** debase, misuse; **7** convert, corrupt, debauch, deprave, deviant, deviate, distort, falsify, profane, quibble, vitiate; **8** apostate, misstate, renegade; **9** brutalize, convolute, distorter, falsifier, misdirect

perverted: 5 kinky; **7** immoral, twisted; **8** depraved, hardened, perverse; **9** distorted

pervious: 6 porous; **9** permeable

per year: 2 p.a.; **8** annually, each year, per annum

Pesach: 5 Pesah; **8** Passover

pes cavus: 8 clawfoot

pesky: 6 plaguy, vexing; **7** galling, plaguey, teasing; **8** annoying; **9** pestering, vexatious; **10** bothersome, irritating, nettlesome; **11** pestiferous

peso: 9 Cuban peso; **11** Chilean peso, Mexican peso; **13** Colombian peso, Dominican peso, Uruguayan peso; **14** Philippine peso; **16** Guinea-Bissau peso

pessary: 9 diaphragm

pessimism: 6 gloomy; **7** cynical

pessimist: 8 alarmist

pest: 6 gadfly, plague, vermin; **7** varmint [Western U.S.]; **8** blighter

pester: 3 bug; **4** bait, bore; **5** abuse, beset, grind, harry, haunt, hound, tease, worry; **6** badger, bother, harass, heckle, ill-use, infest, molest, plague, pother; **7** oppress

pestered: 5 tired, vexed; **6** teased; **7** annoyed, harried, plagued; **8** bothered, harassed, molested; **9** disturbed

pesthouse: 7 lazaret; **9** lazarette, lazaretto; **10** lazar house

pestilence: 3 pox; **6** plague; **7** murrain

pestilent: 6 deadly; **7** baneful; **10** pernicious, plaguelike

pestle: 5 stamp

pet: 3 hug; **4** dear, fume, tiff; **5** deary, ducky, humor; **6** caress, choler, coquet, dander, dandle, dearie, fondle, little, minion, pucker, soothe, taking; **7** cherish, cling to, darling, favored, ferment, passion; **8** favorite, precious; **9** pet animal, preferred

pet cat: 4 puss; **5** kitty, pussy; **8** kitty cat, pussycat

Peter: 7 St. Peter; **10** Saint Peter; **20** Saint Peter the Apostle

Peterburg: 9 Leningrad, Petrograd; **13** St. Petersburg; **15** Saint Petersburg

peter out: 6 fizzle, run out; **7** conk out, drop off, dwindle, fall off, poop out, run down, tail off; **8** taper off

petiole: 9 leafstalk

petit: 3 wee; **4** puny, tiny; **5** petty; **6** petite; **8** exiguous; **9** miniature

petit dejeuner: 9 breakfast

petite: 3 wee; **4** puny, tiny; **5** petit, petty; **6** bantam, midget; **8** exiguous; **9** miniature; **10** diminutive; **11** lilliputian

petite marmite: 10 minestrone; **13** vegetable soup

petition: 3 beg, sue; **4** pray, suit; **5** crave; **6** orison, prayer; **7** request; **9** communion

petitioned: 5 asked; **8** proposed; **9** requested

petitioner: 9 applicant, solicitor, suppliant; **10** supplicant

petit jury: 9 petty jury

petit larceny: 12 petty larceny

petit maitre: 3 fop; **5** dandy

petit mal: 14 epilepsia minor

petit point: 10 tent stitch

pet name: 6 by-name; **8** nickname; **9** sobriquet

Petrarch: 8 Petrarca; **17** Francesco Petrarca

petrified: 4 numb; **9** horrified, terrified; **11** mineralized

petrify: 4 stun; **6** benumb; **7** astound, stagger, stupefy, terrify; **8** bewilder, confound, lapidify; **9** electrify, fascinate, galvanize; **10** strike dumb

Petrograd: 9 Leningrad, Peterburg; **13** St. Petersburg; **15** Saint Petersburg

petrol: 3 gas; **5** juice; **7** benzine; **8** gasolene, gasoline

petrolatum: 12 mineral jelly; **14** petroleum jelly

petrol bomb: 12 gasoline bomb; **15** Molotov cocktail

petroleum: 3 oil; **5** crude; **7** coal oil, rock oil; **8** crude oil; **9** black gold, fossil oil

P

petroleum jelly: 10 petrolatum; 12 mineral jelly

Petromyzon: 10 sea lamprey; 15 genus Petromyzon

Petroselinum: 7 parsley; 17 genus Petroselinum

Petroselinum crispum: 7 parsley

petrous: 9 stonelike

pe-tsai: 4 napa; 13 celery cabbage; 14 Chinese cabbage

petted: 7 fondled; 8 caressed; 9 cherished

petticoat: 5 woman; 6 female; 8 half-slip; 10 underskirt

pettifogger: 7 shyster

petting: 7 hugging, kissing, necking; 8 cuddling, fondling, sparking, sporting; 9 caressing, dalliance, making out, smooching, snuggling; 10 hanky-panky

pettish: 5 huffy, techy, testy; 6 cranky, tetchy; 7 peckish, peevish; 8 petulant; 9 fractious, irritable; 10 nettlesome

petty: 3 wee; 4 dull, puny, tiny; 5 lower, lowly, petit, small; 6 little, petite, stolid; 7 shallow, trivial; 8 exiguous, fiddling, footling, inferior, picayune, piddling; 9 frivolous

petty cash: 3 rap; 4 mite; 6 change; 9 small coin; 11 pocket money, small change; 12 pocket change

petty jury: 9 petit jury

petty larceny: 7 larceny; 12 grand larceny, petit larceny

petulance: 6 choler, temper; 8 acerbity, tartness; 9 crossness, flippancy, fussiness, procacity, testiness; 10 crabbiness, protervity; 11 fretfulness, grouchiness, peevishness

petulant: 5 huffy, techy, testy; 6 cranky; 7 peckish, peevish, pettish; 9 fractious, irritable; 10 nettlesome

petulantly: 7 testily; 9 irritably, pettishly

pew: 3 box; 5 stall; 11 church bench

pewee: 6 peewit; 10 flycatcher

pewit: 5 pewee; 6 peewee, peewit

peyote: 6 mescal, mezcal; 9 mescaline

pfannkuchen: 13 german pancake

pH: 7 pH scale

phaeton: 5 break; 6 tourer; 10 touring car

phage: 13 bacteriophage

Phalacrocorax: 9 cormorant; 18 genus Phalacrocorax

phalacrosis: 8 baldness

phalanger: 9 marsupial

Phalangium: 10 harvestman; 13 daddy longlegs; 15 genus Phalangium

phalanx: 5 horde; 6 cohort, legion

Phalaris: 11 canary grass; 12 Harding grass; 13 birdseed grass; 13 genus Phalaris

phallic: 7 priapic

phanerogam: 9 seed plant

phantasm: 4 myth; 7 fantasy, fiction, phantom, romance; 8 phantasy, rhapsody

phantasmagoria: 12 magic lantern

phantasmagoric: 7 surreal

phantasmal: 7 ghostly; 8 spectral; 9 ghostlike, spiritual; 12 apparitional

phantasy: 4 myth; 5 fancy; 7 fantasy, fiction, romance; 8 illusion, phantasm, rhapsody

phantom: 6 shadow; 7 specter, spectre; 8 phantasm; 10 apparition

pharisaical: 7 canting; 8 unctuous; 9 pharisaic, pietistic

pharmaceutical: 4 drug; 8 medicine; 10 medicament, medication; 12 pharmaceutic

pharmaceutical chemist: 14 pharmacologist

pharmaceutical company: 11 drug company

pharmaceutics: 8 pharmacy; 12 pharmacology

pharmacist: 7 chemist; 8 druggist; 10 apothecary

pharmacopoeia: 9 formulary

pharmacy: 7 chemist; 8 chemist's, druggist; 9 drugstore; 10 apothecary, dispensary; 12 chemist's shop

pharos: 6 beacon; 10 lighthouse; 11 beacon light

pharyngeal tonsil: 7 adenoid

pharyngitis: 9 raw throat; 10 sore throat

pharynx: 6 throat

Phascolarctos: 5 koala; 9 koala bear; 10 native bear; 12 kangaroo bear; 18 genus Phascolarctos

phase: 5 stage; 6 period; 10 phase angle

phase modulation: 2 PM

Phaseolus: 8 mung bean, lima bean; 10 adsuki bean, adzuki bean, runner bean, butter bean; 14 genus Phaseolus

Phasianus colchicus: 18 ring-necked pheasant

phasmid: 13 phasmid insect

phasmid insect: 7 phasmid

phellem: 4 cork

Phellodendron: 4 cork; 18 genus Phellodendron

Phellodendron amurense: 8 cork tree

phencyclidine: 3 PCP; 9 angel dust

Phenicia: 9 Phoenicia

phenobarbital: 7 Luminal

phenomenal: 9 fantastic

phenomenon: 4 fact; 5 event, thing; 6 wonder; 7 prodigy, species; 8 incident; 9 happening; 10 occurrence, wonderment

phial: 4 vial; 5 ampul; 6 ampule; 7 ampoule

Philadelphia: 19 City of Brotherly Love

philander: 4 mash; 5 dally, flirt; 6 chat up, coquet; 7 romance; 8 womanize

philanderer: 9 womaniser, womanizer

philanthropic: 6 humane; 10 beneficent, benevolent; 11 utilitarian; 12 humanitarian

philanthropist: 8 altruist

philatelist: 14 stamp collector

philately: 15 stamp collecting, stamp collection
Philippi: 16 battle of Philippi
philippic: 6 tirade; 8 diatribe; 9 broadside
Philippine: 8 Filipino
Philippines: 17 Philippine Islands; 24 Republic of the Philippines
philistine: 7 lowbrow
philistinism: 11 materialism, worldliness
philologist: 10 philologue
philology: 11 linguistics
philosophic: 5 staid; 6 stayed; 7 stoical; 8 Platonic; 13 philosophical
philosophical: 6 sedate; 7 pensive, wistful; 8 Platonic, studious; 10 meditative, reflective, thoughtful
philosophy: 6 ethics; 8 doctrine, stoicism
philosphy of being: 8 ontology; 11 metaphysics
philter: 5 charm; 6 amulet; 7 philtre; 8 talisman; 10 love-potion; 11 aphrodisiac
phlebogram: 8 venogram
phlebotomize: 5 bleed, leech
phlebotomus: 12 sandfly fever
Phlebotomus: 7 sandfly; 16 genus Phlebotomus
phlebotomy: 8 bleeding; 12 bloodletting
phlegm: 5 mucus; 6 sputum; 8 coolness
phlegmatic: 6 casual; 9 easygoing, sans souci [Fr], unworried; 10 insouciant, nonchalant; 11 unconcerned
phlegmy: 6 mucoid, mucous
phloem: 4 bast
phlox family: 13 Polemoniaceae
Phnom Penh: 16 Cambodian capital
phobia: 4 fear; 8 aversion
Phoca: 10 common seal, harbor seal; 10 genus Phoca
Phoebus Apollo: 6 Apollo; 7 Phoebus
Phoenicia: 8 Phenicia
Phoenix: 6 Phenix; 12 genus Phoenix; 16 capital of Arizona
phoenix: 7 paragon
phone: 4 call, ring; 5 sound; 6 call up; 8 earphone, earpiece; 9 headphone, telephone
phonebook: 9 directory
phoner: 6 caller; 10 telephoner
phonetic: 4 oral; 5 vocal; 7 lingual; 9 outspoken, unwritten
phonetics: 7 phonics; 9 phonology
phoney: 4 fake; 5 bogus, phony; 7 bastard; 9 hypocrite; 10 dissembler
phonics: 9 phonetics, phonology
phonograph: 12 record player
phonograph album: 11 record album
phonograph needle: 6 needle, pickup, stylus
phonograph record: 4 disc, disk; 6 record; 7 platter; 9 recording; 11 vinyl record
phonograph recording disk: 11 acetate disk
phonology: 7 phonics; 9 phonemics, phonetics
phony: 4 fake, sham; 5 bogus, fraud; 6 ersatz

[German], phoney; 7 bastard, forgery; 9 hypocrite, trumped up; 10 artificial, dissembler; 11 counterfeit
phony reason: 7 pretext; 8 pretense; 10 pretension
l'horadendron: 9 mistletoe; 17 genus Phoradendron
phosphate buffer solution: 3 PBS
phosphorescent: 6 ablaze; 7 blazing; 8 in a blaze, meteoric, splendid
photo: 7 picture; 8 exposure; 10 photograph
photocell: 8 magic eye; 11 electric eye
photocopy: 5 xerox; 6 run off
photoelectric cell: 8 magic eye; 9 photocell; 11 electric eye
photoengraving: 8 halftone
photoflash: 5 flash; 8 flashgun; 9 flash lamp, flashbulb
photoflood: 5 flood; 9 flood lamp; 10 floodlight
photograph: 4 snap; 5 photo, shoot; 7 picture; 8 exposure; 13 daguerreotype
photographer: 7 lensman; 9 cameraman; 10 camera buff
photographic memory: 11 exact memory
photography: 13 photographing, picture taking; 14 cinematography
photogravure: 7 gravure; 11 rotogravure; 12 heliogravure
photometer: 10 light meter, radiometer; 13 exposure meter
photon: 7 quantum, wavicle
photosensitive: 14 light-sensitive
photovoltaic cell: 9 solar cell
Phoxinus: 6 minnow; 13 genus Phoxinus
phrasal idiom: 5 idiom; 6 phrase; 9 set phrase
phrase: 4 word; 5 idiom, voice; 7 express; 9 formulate, set phrase; 10 articulate, expression
phrased: 5 style; 6 worded; 9 expressed; 11 articulated
phraseology: 5 style; 7 diction, wording; 8 phrasing, verbiage
phrase structure: 6 syntax
phrasing: 7 diction, wording; 8 verbiage; 11 phraseology
phratry: 4 folk; 6 family; 7 kinfolk; 8 kinsfolk; 10 family line
phrenetic: 7 frantic; 8 frenetic, frenzied
pH scale: 2 pH
Phthirius pubis: 4 crab; 9 crab louse; 10 pubic louse
phthisis: 7 wasting; 11 consumption
Phylloxera vitifoleae: 10 grape louse
phylogenesis: 9 evolution, phylogeny
phylogenetic relation: 8 affinity
phys ed: 13 physical drill; 17 physical education

P

Physeter: 8 cachalot; 10 black whale, sperm whale; 13 genus Physeter

physiatrics: 13 physiotherapy; 15 physical therapy

physic: 4 cure, drug, heal; 5 nurse; 6 doctor, remedy; 7 nostrum, plaster, simples; 8 aperient, laxative, medicate, medicine; 9 cathartic, purgative; 10 medicament, medication

physical: 4 real; 6 active; 8 forcible, material, tangible; 9 corporeal, touchable; 11 substantial, substantive

physical body: 3 bod; 4 form, soma; 5 build, flesh, frame, shape; 6 figure; 7 anatomy, chassis; 8 physique; 9 human body; 12 material body

physical condition: 4 trim; 5 shape; 7 fitness; 9 condition

physical education: 6 phys ed; 13 physical drill

physical exercise: 7 workout; 8 exercise; 10 exercising, working out

physical fitness: 4 trim; 5 shape; 7 fitness; 8 good trim; 9 condition, good shape

physical harm: 4 hurt; 6 injury, trauma

physical law: 3 law; 4 rule; 12 law of physics

physically fit: 6 in trim; 7 in shape; 11 in condition

physicalness: 11 materiality; 12 corporeality

physical object: 4 item; 5 thing; 6 object

physical rehabilitation: 7 therapy

physical science: 7 physics; 12 hard sciences

physical separation: 3 gap; 5 space; 8 distance, interval; 10 separation

physical therapy: 11 physiatrics; 13 physiotherapy

physician: 2 Dr., MD; 3 doc; 6 doctor, medico; 8 sawbones

physics: 15 physical science

physics laboratory: 10 physics lab

physiological reaction: 6 reflex

physiology: 16 animal physiology

physiotherapist: 17 physical therapist

physiotherapy: 11 physiatrics; 15 physical therapy

physique: 3 bod; 4 form, soma, trim; 5 brawn, build, flesh, frame, shape, sinew; 6 figure, muscle; 7 anatomy, chassis; 9 bodybuild

Phytolaccaceae: 14 pokeweed family

phytologist: 8 botanist

phytology: 6 botany

phytophagic: 11 plant-eating

PI: 8 sherlock; 9 detective, operative; 10 private eye

Piaget: 10 Jean Piaget

pianissimo: 5 piano; 10 very softly

pianist: 11 piano player

piano: 4 soft; 6 softly; 10 pianissimo, pianoforte

pianoforte: 5 piano

piano keyboard: 7 clavier; 11 fingerboard

Pianola: 11 player piano

piano player: 7 pianist

piazza: 4 mall; 5 place, plaza, porch; 6 arcade, loggia; 7 portico, veranda; 9 colonnade

pica: 2 em; 6 pica em

Picardy: 8 Picardie

Picasso: 12 Pablo Picasso

picayune: 5 petty; 6 little; 7 trivial; 8 piddling; 11 lilliputian

piccolo: 4 fife; 5 flute; 9 flageolet

Picea: 6 spruce; 10 genus Picea

pick: 4 cull, sift; 5 blame, clean, cream, elite, piece, pluck, plunk, prime; 6 choice, pickax, winnow; 7 break up, pickaxe, picking; 8 nonesuch, plectrum; 9 nonpareil, selection

pickax: 4 pick; 7 pickaxe

pick by hand: 8 hand-pick

picked out: 5 drawn; 7 removed, torn out; 8 drawn out, taken out; 9 extracted

picket: 3 guy; 4 band, file, moor, pale, rank; 5 chain, guard, scout, watch; 6 piquet, sentry, tether; 7 bivouac, lookout; 8 garrison, sentinel; 9 picketing; 10 lookout man

picket fence: 6 paling; 13 stockade fence

picketing: 6 picket

pickiness: 10 choosiness, daintiness; 11 finickiness, selectivity

picking up: 7 lifting

pickle: 3 can, fix, jam, pot, tin; 4 hole, mess, pass, soak, stew; 5 brine, steep; 6 plight, season; 8 macerate; 11 predicament

picklepuss: 8 sourpuss

pick-me-up: 5 tonic; 6 bracer, pickup; 9 stimulant

pick out: 4 draw, take; 6 choose, get out, remove, select; 7 discern, draw out, extract, make out, pull out, take out, tear out; 8 pluck out; 9 extricate, recognize, single out, tell apart; 11 distinguish

pickpocket: 8 cutpurse

pickup: 6 stylus; 7 getaway, tone arm; 8 pick-me-up; 9 cartridge, pickup arm; 11 pickup truck

pick up: 3 cop, nab, see; 4 hear, lift, nail, peck, perk; 5 catch, elate, learn, rally; 6 arrest, collar, lift up, perk up, uplift; 7 collect, receive

pickup truck: 6 pickup

picky: 7 finicky; 10 fastidious

picnic: 4 snap; 5 cinch; 6 outing; 7 cookout; 8 barbecue, field day, pushover, walkover; 10 child's play; 11 piece of cake

pico: 13 one trillionth

picornavirus: 11 rhabdovirus

picosecond: 10 nanosecond

Picrasma: 10 bitterwood; 13 genus Picrasma

pictograph: 8 ideogram; 9 ideograph
pictorial: 5 vivid; 7 graphic; 8 lifelike, pictural; 11 picturesque
pictorially: 10 in pictures; 11 graphically
pictorial matter: 7 picture
picture: 3 see; 4 film, icon, show; 5 fancy, flick, image, movie, photo, scene, video; 6 depict, figure; 7 project, tableau; 8 envision, painting; 9 delineate, depiction, represent, visualize; 10 impression, photograph; 11 delineation
pictured: 5 drawn; 8 depicted; 9 portrayed; 10 envisioned, visualized
picture element: 3 pel; 5 pixel
picture gallery: 7 exhibit, gallery; 10 art gallery
picture palace: 6 cinema; 10 movie house; 12 movie theater, movie theatre
picturephone: 10 videophone
picture show: 4 film; 5 flick, movie; 7 picture; 13 motion picture
picturesque: 9 pictorial
picture taking: 11 photography
picture tube: 9 kinescope; 14 television tube
picturing: 7 imagery; 11 envisioning, iconography, portraiture
piddle away: 6 piddle, trifle, wanton
piddling: 5 petty; 6 little; 7 trivial
pidgin: 13 pigeon English
pie: 2 pi; 5 pasty; 6 pastry
piebald: 4 pied; 6 motley; 7 painted; 8 blotched; 10 multicolor
piece: 3 bit, gun, man; 4 coin, miss, opus, part, pick, play, work; 5 drama, patch, set up, slice, spell, while; 6 canvas, number, weapon; 7 firearm, tableau; 8 assemble, small-arm; 9 component, game piece, stage play; 11 composition
piece de resistance: 9 showpiece
piece goods: 9 yard goods
piecemeal: 8 bit by bit, in stages, stepwise; 10 part by part, step-by-step
piece of cake: 4 snap; 5 cinch; 6 picnic; 8 duck soup, pushover, walkover; 10 child's play
piece of land: 5 tract; 6 parcel; 12 parcel of land; 13 piece of ground
piece of music: 4 opus, work; 5 piece; 6 number; 11 composition
piece of paper: 5 sheet
piece of property: 4 land; 5 acres, lands; 6 realty; 8 property; 9 tenements; 10 real estate
piece of rock: 4 rock; 5 stone
piece of work: 3 row; 4 fray, work; 5 brawl, broil, melee; 6 affray, breeze, fracas, hubbub, pother, racket, rumble, rumpus, squall, uproar
pie crust: 8 pie shell
pied: 6 motley; 7 painted, piebald; 10 multicolor; 12 multicolored
Piedmont: 8 Piemonte

pie-in-the-sky: 9 pipe dream
Piemonte: 8 Piedmont
pie plant: 7 rhubarb
pier: 4 quay; 5 jetty; 6 column, pillar; 7 upright; 10 embankment
pierce: 3 cut, nip; 4 stab; 5 prick; 8 puncture; 9 penetrate, perforate
Pierce: 14 Franklin Pierce
pierced: 9 perforate, punctured; 10 perforated
piercing: 4 high, keen, warm; 5 acute, quick, sharp, smart; 6 biting, bitter, lively, shrill, strong; 7 cutting; 8 clay-cold, incisive, pinching, pricking, stabbing, stinging; 9 knifelike, observant; 10 discerning, perceptive, puncturing; 11 cacophonous, penetrating
piercing object: 7 piercer
pier-glass: 10 pier mirror
Pierian spring: 5 Muses; 8 Calliope, Pierides; 9 Parnassus
pier mirror: 9 pier glass
Pierre: 20 capital of South Dakota
pie shell: 8 pie crust
pietistic: 4 holy; 5 godly, pious; 6 devout; 7 devoted; 8 reverent; 9 pharisaic, religious, spiritual; 11 pharisaical, pietistical
piety: 5 faith; 6 theism; 8 religion; 9 piousness; 12 spirituality; 13 religiousness
piffle: 5 clack, prate; 6 gabble, gibber, tattle; 7 blabber, chatter, prattle; 8 nonsense; 10 balderdash
pig: 3 bum, hog, sow; 4 boar, drab, gulp, hobo, slob; 5 brute, pig it, swine; 6 devour; 7 glutton
pig's knuckles: 8 pig's feet
pig-a-back: 9 piggyback
pigeon: 4 bilk, dove, rook; 5 pluck, squab; 6 fleece, sucker, victim
pigeon English: 13 pidgin English
pigeon hawk: 6 merlin
pigeonhole: 4 cove, jump, miss, omit, sink, skip; 5 stall, stamp; 6 shelve; 8 loophole, peephole; 9 cubbyhole
pigeonholing: 8 grouping
piggish: 5 piggy; 7 brutish, hoggish, porcine, swinish
piggishness: 10 greediness; 11 hoggishness
piggy: 5 shoat; 6 piglet; 7 hoggish, piggish, porcine, swinish
piggy bank: 9 penny bank
pigheaded: 8 stubborn; 9 obstinate
piglet: 5 piggy, shoat
pigman: 9 swineherd
pigment: 5 color
pigmy: 5 dwarf, pygmy
pignolia: 7 pine nut; 8 pinon nut
pig out: 4 glut; 5 binge, gorge, stuff; 6 englut; 7 engorge, overeat, satiate; 8 scarf out
pigpen: 3 sty; 6 pigsty

P

pigskin: 8 football
pigsty: 3 den, sty; 4 lair; 6 pigpen
pigswill: 4 slop; 5 slops, swill; 7 pigwash
pika: 4 cony; 5 coney
pike: 3 Alp; 4 crag, peak; 5 crest, mount; 7 freeway, thruway; 8 cone peak, motorway, mountain, turnpike; 9 sugar loaf; 10 expressway, throughway; 12 state highway, superhighway
pilaf: 5 pilau, pilaw; 6 pilaff
pilaster: 4 post; 5 shaft; 6 column, pillar
pilau: 5 pilaf, pilaw; 6 pilaff
pilchard: 7 sardine
pile: 3 jam, lot, mob, pot, wad; 4 deal, heap, mass, mess, mint, moss, pack, peck, raft, rock, slew; 5 batch, flock, mound, sight, spate, spile, stack, stilt; 6 bundle, hatful, pile on, pile up, piling, plenty, throng; 8 good deal; 9 great deal; 10 atomic pile, hemorrhoid
piled: 6 heaped; 8 heaped-up
pile on: 4 heap, mass, pile; 6 heap up, pile up
piles: 4 gobs, lots, tons, wads; 5 heaps, loads, rafts, scads, slews; 6 dozens, oodles, scores, stacks; 8 lashings; 11 hemorrhoids
pile up: 4 heap, mass, pile; 5 amass, hoard; 6 gather, heap up, pile on; 7 amplify, collect, compile, magnify, stack up; 8 cumulate; 10 accumulate
pileus: 3 cap
pilewort: 15 lesser celandine
pilfer: 3 bag; 4 lift; 5 filch, pinch, sneak, steal, swipe; 6, thieve; 7 purloin
pilfered: 6 looted; 9 plundered, purloined
pilferer: 5 thief; 6 rifler, robber
pilgrim: 6 palmer
pilgrim's journey: 10 pilgrimage
pill: 3 pea; 4 bore, bulb, drag, drop, knob; 6 bullet, marble, pellet, pommel, tablet; 7 globule, lozenge, vesicle; 8 spherule; 13 contraceptive
pillage: 3 gut; 4 loot, sack, swag; 5 booty, foray, prize, reave, rifle, spoil, strip, sweep; 6 rapine; 7 despoil, looting, plunder, ransack; 9 pillaging; 10 plundering, spoliation
pillaged: 5 raped; 6 looted, sacked; 7 ravaged; 9 despoiled, plundered, ransacked
pillager: 6 looter, raider; 7 spoiler; 8 marauder; 9 despoiler, plunderer; 10 depredator, freebooter
pillar: 4 pier, post; 5 shaft, table, tower; 6 column, marble, tablet; 7 obelisk, upright; 8 mainstay, monolith, pilaster
pillion: 6 saddle
pillow: 4 rest; 7 cushion; 9 bed pillow
pillowcase: 4 case, slip; 10 pillow slip
pillow lace: 10 bobbin lace
pillow slip: 4 case, slip; 10 pillowcase
pilot: 3 fly; 4 test; 5 guide, model, trial; 6 aviate, buffer, fender; 8 navigate, original; 9 archetype, bush pilot, pilot film, steersman, test pilot
pilotage: 8 piloting, steerage; 10 navigation
pilot biscuit: 8 hardtack; 10 pilot bread, sea biscuit; 11 ship biscuit
pilot burner: 10 pilot light
pilothouse: 10 wheelhouse
piloting: 8 pilotage; 10 navigation
pilot jacket: 12 bomber jacket
pilot ladder: 10 jack ladder; 12 Jacob's ladder
pilot lamp: 10 pilot light; 13 indicator lamp
pilotless aircraft: 5 drone
pilot light: 9 pilot lamp; 11 pilot burner; 13 indicator lamp
pilot whale: 9 blackfish
pilous: 5 bushy; 6 hispid, pilose, shaggy; 7 bearded, shagged, villous
pilsener: 7 pilsner
Pilsener beer: 9 lager
Piltdown hoax: 11 Piltdown man
Pimenta: 8 bayberry; 10 bay-rum tree; 11 pimento tree; 12 allspice tree, genus Pimenta
pimento tree: 8 allspice
pi-meson: 4 pion
pimiento: 10 bell pepper; 11 sweet pepper
pimp: 5 ponce; 6 pandar, pander; 8 panderer, procurer
Pimpinella: 5 anise; 15 genus Pimpinella
pimple: 3 zit [slang]; 4 mole
pimply: 5 acned; 7 pimpled; 9 pustulate
pin: 3 peg; 4 bolt, hasp, mill, nail, trap; 5 clasp, pin up, pivot, rivet, stick; 6 broach; 7 oarlock, pin down, rowlock; 8 lapel pin
Pinaceae: 10 pine family
pinafore: 5 apron, pinny; 6 jumper, panier
pincer: 4 claw; 6 nipper; 7 tweezer
pincers: 5 tongs; 6 pliers; 7 forceps, nippers; 8 vise grip
pinch: 3 fix, jot, nip, top; 4 hint, hook, lift, mite, pass, push; 5 catch, crimp, filch, gripe, hitch, prick, snarf, sneak, speck, swipe, touch, trial, tweak, tweet; 6 arrest, benumb, collar, nobble, pilfer, strait, stress, twinge, twitch; 7 cabbage, nonplus, petrify, purloin, soupcon, squeeze; 8 abstract, exigency, juncture, quandary, scramble; 9 emergency
pinchbeck: 5 paste; 6 gewgaw, plated, tinsel; 7 spangle
pinching: 6 biting, bitter; 7 cutting, gnawing; 8 clay-cold, piercing; 10 tightening
Pinctada: 11 pearl oyster; 13 genus Pinctada
pine: 3 fir, yen; 4 ache, long, peak, sink; 5 droop, yearn; 6 repine, sicken; 8 languish, pine away, pine tree, true pine
pineapple: 6 ananas; 13 Ananas comosus
pineapple family: 12 Bromeliaceae
pineapple guava: 6 feijoa
pineapple plant: 9 pineapple; 13 Ananas comosus

pine away: 4 pine; 5 waste; 8 languish
pine family: 8 Pinaceae
pine nut: 8 pignolia, pinon nut
pine rider: 7 reserve; 10 substitute; 11 bench warmer
pine tree: 4 pine; 8 true pine
Pine Tree State: 5 Maine
ping: 5 knock
ping-pong: 11 table tennis
Pinguinus: 8 great auk; 14 genus Pinguinus
pinhole view: 8 loophole; 11 keyhole view
pinion: 4 wing; 5 crank, leash, quill, tie up, winch; 6 pennon, tether; 7 pin down, shackle, tie down; 12 quill feather; 13 flight feather
pinioned: 7 hobbled; 8 fettered, manacled; 10 handcuffed
pink: 3 rap, tap; 5 knock, lance, lunge, pearl; 6 flower, poke at, riddle; 7 paragon, phoenix, pinkish; 8 puncture
pinkeye: 14 conjunctivitis
pink family: 15 carnation family
pinkie: 5 pinky; 11 small finger; 12 little finger
pinko: 3 red; 7 Marxist; 9 Bolshevik, communist
pink-slipped: 5 fired; 6 sacked; 7 laid-off; 9 dismissed; 10 discharged
pink wine: 4 rose; 8 rose wine; 9 blush wine
pinky: 6 pinkie; 12 little finger
pinna: 3 ear; 7 auricle, pinnule
pinnace: 6 launch, tender; 9 ship's boat
pinnacle: 3 top; 4 acme, apex, peak; 6 height, summit, vertex, zenith; 9 elevation; 11 superlative
pinned: 7 stapled
pinny: 6 jumper; 8 pinafore
pinon: 6 pinyon; 7 nut pine
Pinot: 10 Pinot grape
pinpoint: 5 speck; 8 diagnose; 9 determine, establish
pins and needles: 8 tingling; 11 paresthesia
pintado: 4 cero; 8 kingfish
pin-tailed duck: 7 pintail
pint-sized: 5 runty; 8 pint-size, sawed-off
pin-up: 9 cover girl
Pinus: 3 fir; 4 pine; 5 pinon; 6 pinyon; 10 genus Pinus
pinworm: 8 parasite
pinyon: 5 pinon; 7 nut pine
pion: 7 pi meson, pi-meson
pioneer: 6 open up; 7 apostle, example; 8 initiate, preparer; 9 innovator; 10 missionary; 11 trailblazer
pious: 4 holy; 5 godly; 6 devout; 7 devoted; 8 reverent; 9 pietistic, religious, spiritual; 10 god-fearing
piously: 8 devoutly
piousness: 5 piety
pious person: 8 adherent; 9 worshiper; 10 worshipper; 11 communicant
pipage: 4 pipe; 6 piping

pipe: 3 coo, cry, sob, yap; 4 burr, play, pule, tube, wail, weep; 5 cheep, chirp, clank, clink, trill, twang, tweet, whine; 6 pipage, pipe up, piping, shriek, shrill, squall, squeak, squeal, warble; 7 whistle; 8 pipework
pipe clamp: 8 pipe vise
pipeclay: 9 terra alba
pipe down: 4 hush; 5 quiet; 7 quiesce, quieten; 9 quiet down
pipe dream: 5 dream; 11 pie-in-the-sky
pipe fitter: 7 plumber
pipeline: 4 line; 9 grapevine; 11 word of mouth
pipe of peace: 7 calumet; 9 peace pipe
pipe organ: 5 organ
piper: 8 bagpiper; 10 fife player
Piperaceae: 12 pepper family
Piper nigrum: 11 black pepper, white pepper; 12 common pepper
pipes: 7 bagpipe
pipes of Pan: 6 syrinx; 7 panpipe
pipe up: 4 pipe; 6 shriek, shrill; 7 screech
pipe vise: 9 pipe clamp
pipewort family: 13 Eriocaulaceae
piping hot: 6 red hot; 8 white hot; 10 boiling hot, burning hot
pipit: 4 lark; 7 titlark
pipkin: 3 jug; 7 pitcher
pippin: 5 apple
pip-squeak: 6 squirt; 8 small fry
piquance: 5 spicy, tasty; 7 pungent
piquancy: 4 tang, zest; 5 twang; 8 piquance, pungency; 9 pithiness, poignance, spiciness, tanginess
piquant: 4 gamy, racy; 5 pithy, rough, salty, sharp, spicy, zesty; 6 savory; 7 caustic, pointed, pungent, savoury; 8 engaging, poignant, stinging; 9 trenchant; 10 appetizing
pique: 4 fret, gall, huff, miff, rile, stir; 5 chafe, sting, twill; 6 corded, grudge, nettle, offend, ruffle, spleen, stir up, temper, work up; 7 provoke, umbrage; 8 acerbity, acrimony, asperity, irritate, rankling, soreness; 9 virulence; 10 bitterness, discompose, irritation
piqued: 7 stirred; 8 worked up; 9 stirred up; 10 inspirited
piracy: 12 buccaneering; 14 plagiarisation, plagiarization
Piranga: 7 redbird, tanager; 12 genus Piranga
piranha: 6 caribe
pirate: 6 hijack, viking; 7 corsair; 8 highjack, sea rover; 9 buccaneer, sea robber; 10 commandeer, pirate ship, plagiarist
pirate flag: 9 black flag; 10 Jolly Roger
pirogi: 8 piroshki, pirozhki
pirogue: 6 dugout; 11 dugout canoe

P

pis aller: 5 shift; **7** stopgap; **8** jury mast; **9** makeshift, expedient
piscatory: 5 fishy; **11** piscatorial
Pisces the Fishes: 6 Pisces
pisciculture: 11 fish farming
pismire: 3 ant; **5** emmet
pistachio: 12 pistachio nut
Pistacia: 9 pistachio; **13** genus Pistacia
Pistacia vera: 9 pistachio; **13** pistachio tree
pistia: 12 water cabbage
pistillate: 10 carpellate
pistol: 5 piece; **6** roscoe; **7** handgun, sidearm
piston: 7 plunger
piston chamber: 8 cylinder
Pisum: 8 field pea; **9** common pea, garden pea; **10** genus Pisum; **12** edible-pod pea
pit: 4 mark, mine, pock, scar, tomb, well; **5** boxes, fossa, grain, grave, match, shaft, stone; **6** cavity, crater, hollow, kernel, oppose, quarry, stalls; **7** gallery, parquet, pitfall; **8** auditory, colliery, stone pit; **9** sepulcher, strip mine; **10** auditorium, excavation; **12** orchestra pit
pita: 11 pocket bread
pitch: 3 tar; **4** camp, cant, cast, flip, gear, hawk, jerk, mark, rake, sink, swag, tilt, toss, trip, vend; **5** abase, chuck, fling, heave, lurch, place, point, set up, shift, slant, slope; **6** climax, debase, height, monger, peddle, period, reduce, summit, tumble; **7** bitumen, incline, maximum, stumble; **8** bring low, cant over, delivery, eminence, huckster, pitching; **9** frequency, pitch shot, sales talk
pitch-black: 5 black; **8** moonless, starless
pitchblende: 9 uraninite
pitch contour: 10 intonation
pitcher: 3 jug, mug; **4** ewer; **5** mound; **6** hurler, pipkin; **7** compote, creamer, twirler; **9** gravy boat
pitcher's mound: 4 hill; **5** mound
pitcher-plant family: 14 Sarraceniaceae
pitch in: 5 dig in
pitching: 5 lurch, pitch
pitching woo: 4 suit; **6** wooing; **8** courting; **9** addresses, courtship; **10** lovemaking, making love
pitch overboard: 8 jettison; **13** cast overboard
pitch pine: 11 Georgia pine
pitch shot: 5 pitch
pitchy: 3 jet; **5** dingy, dusky, murky, sooty, tarry; **6** resiny
piteous: 4 poor; **6** dreary; **7** hapless, pitiful; **8** grievous, pathetic, pitiable, wretched
piteously: 5 sadly; **6** sorely; **7** cruelly, grossly; **8** bitterly, horribly, terribly, woefully; **9** fearfully, miserably, painfully; **10** dreadfully
pitfall: 6 hazard

pith: 3 nub, sum; **4** core, gist, meat; **5** heart; **6** center, kernel, marrow; **7** essence; **8** backbone; **9** basic part, pithiness, substance, umbilicus, vital part
pith helmet: 4 topi; **5** topee; **7** pith hat; **9** sun helmet
pithiness: 4 pith; **8** piquance, piquancy, pungency; **9** poignance
pithy: 7 piquant, pointed, pungent; **8** poignant, pregnant; **9** trenchant
pitiable: 4 poor; **5** sorry; **6** rueful, scurvy, woeful; **7** hapless, piteous, pitiful; **8** mournful, pathetic, wretched; **9** miserable; **10** deplorable
pitiful: 3 low, sad; **4** base, mean, poor, vile; **5** dirty, sorry; **6** abject, paltry, shabby; **7** hapless, ignoble, piteous, pitying, scrubby, touched; **8** beggarly, pathetic, pitiable, wretched; **9** miserable; **10** deplorable, full of pity, lamentable; **11** distressing, ignominious, showing pity, sympathetic; **12** misfortunate; **13** compassionate
pitiless: 6 unkind; **8** ruthless; **9** bowelless, merciless, unpitying; **11** hard-hearted, remorseless
pitman: 7 collier; **9** coal miner
pittance: 4 dole, meed, mite; **6** meager
pitted: 8 alveolar, cavitied, freckled; **9** alveolate
pitting: 9 roughness; **11** indentation
Pittsburgh of the South: 10 Birmingham
pituitary gland: 9 pituitary; **10** hypophysis; **13** pituitary body
Pituophis melanoleucus: 11 gopher snake
pity: 4 ruth; **5** shame; **6** pathos; **7** feel for; **10** compassion
pitying: 5 sorry; **7** touched; **8** sorry for; **10** full of pity; **11** showing pity, sympathetic; **13** compassionate
Pityrogramma: 4 fern; **17** genus Pityrogramma
Piute: 6 Paiute
pivot: 3 pin; **4** crux, gore, seam; **5** hinge, lever; **6** gusset, swivel; **7** fulcrum; **8** pivot man, trunnion; **10** pivot point
pivotal: 7 crucial
pivot point: 5 pivot; **6** swivel
pix: 5 films; **6** photos; **11** photographs; **13** motion picture
pixel: 3 pel
pixie: 3 elf, hob, imp; **4** pixy; **5** pyxie; **7** brownie, gremlin
pixy: 3 elf, hob, imp; **5** pixie, pyxie; **7** brownie, gremlin
pizza: 8 pizza pie
pizza parlor: 8 pizzeria; **9** pizza shop
pizzaz: 4 zing; **5** oomph; **7** pizzazz; **8** dynamism
pizzeria: 9 pizza shop; **11** pizza parlor
placable: 9 forgiving; **12** conciliatory
placard: 4 bill, card; **6** notice, poster; **9** broadside

placate: 6 gentle, pacify; 7 appease, assuage, mollify; 9 make peace, reconcile; 10 conciliate, propitiate; 11 meet halfway

place: 3 aim, lay, pad, put, set; 4 base, digs, form, home, lieu, mark, pose, post, rank, rate, seat, send, site, slot, spot; 5 berth, grade, match, order, pitch, plaza, point, range, shoes, space, stead; 6 come in, commit, direct, invest, locale, locate, period, piazza, target; 7 come out, context, dispose, make out, match up, realize, situate, station; 8 classify, diggings, identify, locality, localize, location, position, property; 9 recognize, situation

place after: 6 append, suffix

placebo: 9 faith cure

placed: 3 set; 5 fixed; 7 located, made out; 8 situated; 9 localized; 10 classified

placed into: 5 put in; 7 put into; 8 inserted; 10 introduced

place in danger: 7 imperil; 8 endanger; 9 put at risk; 10 compromise, jeopardize

place in order: 5 order; 7 arrange; 8 organize

placement: 8 locating, location, position; 9 situating; 11 arrangement, emplacement, positioning

place name: 7 toponym

placenta: 10 afterbirth

placental growth hormone: 3 HCS

place of birth: 10 birthplace

place of business: 4 shop; 8 workshop; 9 workhouse, workplace

place of origin: 10 birthplace, provenance

placid: 4 calm; 5 quiet, still; 7 equable; 8 peaceful, tranquil; 9 easygoing, unruffled; 12 even-tempered, good-tempered

placidity: 5 quiet; 6 repose; 8 serenity; 10 placidness; 11 tranquility

placing: 7 putting; 8 locating, location; 11 positioning; 12 localization

placoid: 9 platelike

plagiarist: 6 pirate; 14 literary pirate

plagiarize: 4 lift; 10 plagiarise; 11 appropriate

plague: 3 bug, pox; 4 bait, bore, pest; 5 abuse, beset, grind, haunt, hound, tease, worry; 6 badger, blight, bother, harass, hassle, heckle, ill-use, infest, molest, pester; 7 oppress, provoke; 8 ill-treat, maltreat, mistreat; 9 importune, persecute; 10 pestilence

plagued: 5 tired, vexed; 6 teased; 7 overrun; 8 bothered, infested, molested, pestered; 9 disturbed

plaguy: 5 pesky; 6 rugged, thorny, trying, vexing; 7 galling, plaguey, teasing; 8 annoying, perverse, plaguing; 9 pestering, vexatious; 10 bothersome, irritating

plaid: 6 tartan

plain: 4 kick, knit; 5 clear, field, sheer; 6 homely, kvetch, modest, patent, severe,

simple; 7 evident, glaring, literal, natural, plainly, popular, staring, unmixed; 8 apparent, complain, definite, distinct, explicit, manifest, patently, sound off; 9 evidently, obviously, unmingled; 10 apparently, in full view, knit stitch, manifestly, well marked; 11 conspicuous, in plain view, plain stitch, unpatterned; 12 matter-of-fact, unornamented

plainchant: 9 plainsong

plain dealing: 9 bona fides [Lat]

plainly: 5 plain; 6 openly, simply; 7 clearly; 8 patently; 9 evidently, glaringly, obviously; 10 apparently, definitely, distinctly, manifestly; 11 prominently; 13 conspicuously

plain sense: 10 horse sense [U.S.]; 11 common sense

plain song: 4 hymn; 5 chant, motet; 6 anthem, chaunt; 8 response

plainsong: 10 plainchant

plain-spoken: 4 open; 5 bluff, blunt, frank; 6 candid, direct; 7 sincere; 9 downright, outspoken; 10 free-spoken, unreserved; 12 matter of fact

plaint: 4 moan, sigh, wail; 5 groan, whine; 6 chorus, clamor, lament, murmur, mutter, outcry; 7 grumble, heaving; 8 deep sigh; 9 complaint, hue and cry; 11 lamentation

plaintiff: 7 accuser; 11 complainant

plaintiff in error: 9 appellant

plaintive: 8 mournful

plain weave: 12 taffeta weave

plait: 3 mat, ply; 4 felt, fold, lace, plat; 5 braid, flute, pleat, tress, twill, twist; 6 crease, wattle; 7 reticle, trellis

plan: 3 map; 5 chart, frame, plans; 6 design, scheme; 7 arrange, be after, program

planar board: 9 main board; 11 motherboard

planate: 9 flattened

plan B: 7 variant; 9 expedient; 11 alternative

planchet: 9 coin blank

plane: 4 even, flat, skim, swim; 5 float, flush, hover, level, shave, sheet, spire, surge; 6 planer; 7 discoid; 8 airplane; 9 aeroplane; 10 horizontal

planeness: 8 flatness; 9 planarity

planer: 5 plane; 14 planing machine

planet: 9 satellite

planetary: 5 world; 6 global; 8 planetal; 9 wandering, worldwide; 11 terrestrial

planetary house: 4 sign; 5 house; 7 mansion

planetoid: 8 asteroid; 11 minor planet

plane-tree family: 11 Platanaceae

planet wheel: 10 planet gear

plangency: 7 ringing; 8 sonority, vibrancy; 9 resonance; 12 reverberance, sonorousness

planimeter: 10 integrator

planing: 8 leveling; 10 flattening

P

planing machine: 5 plane; **6** planer
plank: 4 plop; **5** board, flump, plonk, plump, plunk, slate [U.S.]; **6** ticket [U.S.]; **8** platform
planless: 6 adrift, afloat; **7** aimless; **10** rudderless, undirected; **13** directionless
planned: 7 plotted; **8** arranged; **12** aforethought
planner: 7 deviser, schemer; **9** contriver
planning: 9 provision; **11** preparation
planning board: 13 advisory board
plant: 3 bud, set, sow; **4** bite, wile; **5** blind, catch, cheat, embed, feint, fetch, flora, found, graft, hocus, imbed, reach, trick, works; **6** bubble, juggle; **7** chicane, engraft, factory, implant; **8** fixtures, heirloom, materiel; **9** establish, institute, plant life, vegetable; **10** constitute; **11** manufactory; **15** industrial plant
Plantae: 12 plant kingdom; **14** kingdom Plantae
plantain family: 8 plantain; **14** Plantaginaceae
plantation: 6 colony; **7** orchard; **10** cantonment, settlement
plantation owner: 7 planter
plant-eating: 11 phytophagic; **12** phytophagous, phytophilous
planted: 9 implanted, ingrained; **10** deep-rooted, deep-seated
plant hormone: 12 phytohormone
planting: 6 sowing; **7** seeding
plant kingdom: 7 Plantae; **14** kingdom Plantae
plant life: 5 flora, plant; **7** verdure
plant louse: 5 aphid, Aphis, louse
plant scientist: 8 botanist; **11** phytologist
plaque: 5 brass; **14** memorial tablet
plash: 6 splash; **7** spatter
plasm: 4 last; **5** serum; **6** matrix, plasma
plasma: 4 onyx; **5** plasm, serum; **10** protoplasm
plasma membrane: 8 cell wall; **12** cell membrane
plasmin: 9 fibrinase
plaster: 4 daub, lint; **6** doctor, ground, stucco; **7** bandage, spackel, stick on; **8** poultice, wrapping; **9** cataplasm; **11** plaster over; **14** plaster of Paris
plasterboard: 11 gypsum board
plastered: 5 drunk; **10** inebriated
plastering: 7 daubing; **9** cementing, spackling
plaster of Paris: 7 plaster
plastic: 6 limber, lissom, mobile, pliant; **7** ductile, fictile; **8** formable, moldable, shapable, workable; **9** alterable, malleable, shapeable
plastic explosive: 9 plastique
plastic surgeon: 15 cosmetic surgeon

plastic surgery: 9 anaplasty
plat: 3 mat, sod; **4** felt, lawn, plot, turf; **5** braid, green, plait, twill; **6** survey
Platalea: 9 spoonbill; **13** genus Platalea
Platanaceae: 15 plane-tree family
Platanthera: 6 orchid; **16** genus Platanthera
Plata River: 7 La Plata; **12** Rio de la Plata
plate: 3 pan; **4** coat, dish, gild, home, slab; **5** scale, shell; **6** course, saucer, veneer; **7** plating, platter, potager; **8** calabash, crucible, plateful, trencher; **9** home plate, porringer; **10** rigid sheet
plateau: 5 ledge; **9** tableland
plated: 6 tinsel; **9** pinchbeck; **12** meretricious
platelet: 11 thrombocyte
platelike: 7 placoid
plate tectonics: 9 tectonics
platform: 5 plank, slate [U.S.], stage; **6** barrel, ticket [U.S.]; **7** chopine, program, rostrum; **8** eyepiece; **9** party line, platforms
platforms: 7 chopine; **8** chopines, platform
platinum: 2 Pt
platitude: 6 cliche; **7** bromide; **8** banality; **11** commonplace
Platonic: 5 staid; **6** honest, sedate, stayed; **7** pensive, stoical, wistful; **8** studious, virtuous; **10** meditative, reflective, thoughtful; **11** philosophic, speculative; **12** deliberative; **13** contemplative, introspective, philosophical
Platonism: 7 realism
platoon: 6 squads
platoon fire: 8 file fire
Plattdeutsch: 9 Low German
Platte: 11 Platte River
platter: 3 pan; **4** disc, dish, disk, slab; **5** plate; **6** record, saucer; **7** potager; **8** crucible, trencher; **9** porringer, recording; **10** rigid sheet; **11** vinyl record
platyhelminth: 8 flatworm
platypus: 8 duckbill
platyrhine: 10 broadnosed
plaudit: 5 eclat; **7** acclaim; **8** applause, plaudits; **11** acclamation
plaudits: 5 eclat; **7** acclaim, plaudit; **11** acclamation
plausible: 6 likely; **8** credible, probable; **9** estimable; **10** creditable
plausibly: 8 credibly, probably; **10** believably
play: 3 act, bid, fun, run, toy; **4** game, meet, pipe, romp, turn, work; **5** act as, bring, caper, dally, drama, flirt, piece [Fr], range, scope, spiel, sport, swing, wreak; **6** diddle, fiddle, frolic, gambol, gaming, leeway, office, play on, render, strain, strike, take on, trifle; **7** carry on, make for, perform, play off, playact, playing, pretend, quicken, shimmer, support, sustain, tweedle; **8** be at work, exercise, free rein, gambling, latitude, leverage, maintain, maneuver, practice, purchase, recreate, roleplay, strike up;

9 encounter, looseness, play a role, prosecute, represent, stage play, tolerance
playact: 3 act; **4** play; **8** roleplay
playacting: 6 acting; **7** playing; **10** performing
playactor: 7 trouper; **11** barnstormer
play back: 6 replay
playboy: 9 bon vivant; **10** Corinthian; **12** man about town, man-about-town
play dead: 10 play possum
play down: 9 soft-pedal
player: 3 pro; **4** jock; **5** actor; **7** athlete; **8** musician, thespian; **9** performer; **10** game player, role player; **11** participant; **15** instrumentalist
player piano: 7 Pianola
playfellow: 8 playmate
playful: 8 sportive
playgoer: 11 theatergoer
playground: 6 resort; **12** vacation spot; **13** archery ground, cricketground, croquet ground, holiday resort, hunting ground; **14** pleasure ground
play hooky: 6 truant
playing: 4 play; **6** acting; **10** performing, playacting; **12** playing music
playing area: 5 field; **12** playing field
playing on words: 7 punning
play on words: 3 pun; **8** word-play
play possum: 8 play dead
playroom: 8 game room; **10** rumpus room
playschool: 9 play group
play second fiddle: 10 be upstaged
play the field: 11 sleep around
play the lead: 4 star
plaything: 3 toy
playwright: 9 dramatist; **10** play writer
plaza: 4 mall; **5** place; **6** center, piazza; **11** market place
plea: 5 reply; **6** answer; **7** pretext; **8** demurrer, pretense, rebutter; **9** rejoinder; **10** pretension; **11** replication; **12** supplication
plea bargain: 11 strike a deal
pleach: 5 braid, plash, plait; **9** interlace
plead: 5 argue; **6** allege; **7** beg hard, beseech, entreat, implore, pretend; **9** make a case; **10** supplicate
pleading: 4 case; **9** appealing, imploring, pleadings; **11** importunate
plead one's cause: 6 defend; **8** advocate
pleasant: 5 light; **6** grateful, pleasing; **9** agreeable, enjoyable, sparkling, sprightly; **10** gratifying
pleasantly: 7 sunnily; **8** cheerily; **9** agreeably, enjoyably
please: 2 do; **4** pray; **5** charm; **7** delight, prithee; **12** give pleasure
pleased: 5 happy; **6** elated; **7** charmed, flushed, proud of; **9** delighted
pleasing: 8 artistic, esthetic, grateful, humoring, pleasant; **9** aesthetic, agreeable, enjoy-

able, indulging, luxurious, pampering; **10** gratifying, indulgence, satisfying
pleasurable: 8 grateful, pleasant, pleasing; **9** agreeable, enjoyable; **10** gratifying
pleasure: 3 joy; **4** mind, wish; **6** choice; **7** delight; **8** decision, fruition; **9** pleasance; **11** mental cause; **13** gratification; **15** sensual pleasure; **16** physical pleasure, sensuous pleasure
pleasure boat: 7 cruiser; **10** cruise ship; **12** cabin cruiser; **13** pleasure craft
pleasure craft: 7 cruiser; **12** cabin cruiser, pleasure boat
pleasure seeker: 8 hedonist
pleasure trip: 5 jaunt; **6** junket, outing, sashay; **9** excursion; **10** expedition
pleat: 3 ply; **4** fold; **5** flute, plait; **6** crease, ruffle; **9** plication
pleb: 8 plebeian
plebe: 5 cadet
plebeian: 4 pleb; **6** common; **8** commoner
plebiscite: 5 voice; **6** recall; **10** initiative, referendum
plebiscitum: 6 recall; **10** initiative, plebiscite, referendum
Plectrophenax: 8 snowbird; **9** snowflake; **11** snow bunting; **18** genus Plectrophenax
plectrum: 4 pick; **8** plectron
pledge: 3 hug; **4** word; **5** drink, toast; **6** plight, salute; **7** embrace, promise, squeeze; **8** accolade, guaranty, warranty; **9** assurance, guarantee
pledged: 5 sworn; **7** engaged; **8** bespoken, promised; **9** affianced, betrothed
pledged asset: 10 collateral
Pleiades: 9 Cassiopea
Pleistocene epoch: 11 Pleistocene; **12** Glacial epoch
plenary: 4 deep, full, good, high; **5** heavy, sound; **6** strong; **7** intense, passing; **8** absolute, thorough
plenitude: 4 lots, over; **6** plenty; **9** abundance, amplitude, profusion; **10** plentitude; **11** copiousness
plentiful: 4 rich; **5** ample; **6** galore, plenty; **7** copious; **9** bountiful, plenteous
plenty: 3 lot, pot, wad; **4** deal, heap, lots, mass, mess, mint, over, peck, pile, raft, slew; **5** batch, flock, sight, spate, stack; **6** enough, galore, hatful, mickle, muckle; **7** tidy sum; **8** good deal, whole lot; **9** abundance, amplitude, great deal, plenitude, plenteous, plentiful, profusion
pleonasm: 9 tautology; **10** exuberance, redundancy; **11** diffuseness, periphrasis
pleonastic: 5 wordy; **7** copious, diffuse, lengthy, profuse, verbose; **9** expansive, exuberant, redundant; **10** long-winded
Plethodon: 10 salamander; **14** genus Plethodon
plethodont: 18 lungless salamander

P

plethora: 10 oversupply; 11 profuseness

plethoric: 4 rife; 6 turgid; 9 dropsical; 12 overabundant

Pleurotus: 14 oyster mushroom; 14 genus Pleurotus

plexus: 3 net, web; 4 mesh; 8 meshwork

pliable: 6 pliant; 7 ductile, elastic, fictile, tensile; 8 bendable, flexible, tractile; 9 malleable

pliancy: 8 softness, weakness; 10 pliability, pliantness, suppleness; 11 flexibility, pliableness; 12 malleability

pliant: 4 oily; 5 soapy; 6 abased; 7 ductile, elastic, fawning, plastic, pliable, slavish, tensile; 8 bendable, cringing, flexible, tractile; 9 agreeable, groveling, malleable, sniveling

plicate: 4 fold; 6 double, fluted, folded; 7 pleated; 9 accordion; 10 double over

plication: 3 ply; 4 bend, fold; 5 crimp, plait, pleat; 6 crease; 7 flexure, folding; 8 pleating

pliers: 5 tongs; 6 plyers; 7 forceps, pincers; 8 vise grip

plight: 3 vow; 4 pass; 5 troth; 6 engage, parole, pickle, pledge; 7 betroth; 8 affiance, mortgage, quandary; 9 debenture; 11 predicament

Plimsoll: 8 load line; 12 Plimsoll line, Plimsoll mark

Pliocene epoch: 8 Pliocene

plod: 3 pad; 4 pace, slog, step, wend; 5 march, tread; 6 foot it, hoof it, lumber, trudge

plodding: 5 grind; 6 leaden; 8 drudgery, slogging

plosive: 4 stop

plot: 3 lot, sod; 4 lawn, plat, turf; 5 cabal, chart, green, patch, sward, tract; 6 figure, parcel, scheme, survey; 7 diagram; 8 intrigue; 10 conspiracy, greensward, land survey, secret plan; 11 machination

plot line: 9 storyline

plot of ground: 4 plot; 5 patch

plotted: 7 planned, schemed; 9 contrived; 12 aforethought

plotter: 6 mapper; 7 schemer; 10 machinator; 11 conspirator

plough: 3 dig, hoe; 4 plow, rake, turn; 5 delve; 6 dibble, harrow

ploughman: 7 plowman

plover: 4 rail; 5 snipe; 6 grouse

plow: 3 dig, hoe; 4 deal, rake, turn, work; 5 cover, delve, flute, treat; 6 dibble, handle, harrow, plough; 7 address; 9 plowshare

plowing: 7 tilling; 9 ploughing

plowman: 9 ploughman

ploy: 5 trick; 6 device, gambit, tactic; 8 maneuver; 9 stratagem; 11 machination

pluck: 2 do; 3 con, nab, rob; 4 bilk, bite, crop, cull, game, hook, pick, pull, reap, roll, rook, scam, soak, spin, tear; 5 cheat, mulct, nerve, plume, plunk, tweak; 6 fleece, hustle, jockey, mettle, pigeon, sponge; 7 defraud, deplume, pick off, pull off, swindle; 8 gameness

plucked: 6 bilked, plowed; 7 cheated, diddled; 8 ploughed, swindled; 9 defrauded; 10 victimized

pluck out: 4 draw; 6 get out, remove; 7 draw out, extract, pick out, pull out, take out, tear out; 9 extricate

plucky: 6 feisty, spunky; 10 mettlesome

plug: 3 cud, jab, nag, wad; 4 bung, chaw, chew, cork, hack, hype, jade, pelt, quid, seal; 5 close, punch, skate [U.S.], thump; 6 secure, stop up; 7 occlude, stopper, stopple; 8 ballyhoo, fireplug, male plug, plug away; 9 spark plug; 11 fire hydrant; 12 electric plug, sparking plug

plugged: 6 closed, sealed; 8 occluded; 9 stopped up

plug in: 7 connect

plum: 5 prune

plumage: 5 plume; 7 feather

plumb: 5 clean, erect, probe, sound; 6 fathom, normal; 7 plummet, upright; 8 plumb bob, straight, vertical

Plumbaginaceae: 14 leadwort family; 17 sea-lavender family

plumbago: 8 graphite; 9 black lead

plumb bob: 5 plumb

plumbed: 7 sounded

plumber: 10 pipe fitter

plumber's snake: 5 auger, snake

plumbism: 9 saturnism; 13 lead poisoning

plum-colored: 5 lilac, mauve; 8 lavender

plume: 5 crest, dress, pluck, preen, pride, primp; 6 fleece, gazump; 7 feather, panache, plumage; 8 aigrette; 9 surcharge; 10 overcharge; 12 congratulate

plumed: 5 plumy; 7 crested, plumate, plumose

Plumeria: 10 pagoda tree; 8 Plumiera; 13 genus Plumeria

plummet: 4 drop, fall; 5 crash, plumb, plump, probe, sound; 6 plunge; 8 plumb bob; 9 plumb line

plump: 3 fat; 4 full, plop, slap; 5 buxom, flump, obese, squab, stout; 6 chubby, fatten, zaftig, zoftig; 7 fill out, plummet; 8 bouncing, fatten up, plump out, unawares; 9 corpulent

plum pudding: 16 Christmas pudding

plum tomato: 12 cherry tomato

plunder: 4 loot, rape, sack, swag; 5 booty, foray, prize, reave, rifle, spoil, strip, sweep; 6 rapine; 7 despoil, looting, pillage, ransack, violate

plunderer: 6 looter, raider; 7 spoiler; 8 pillager; 9 despoiler; 10 freebooter

plundering: 7 pillage; 9 pillaging

plunge: 3 dip; 4 dive, drop, duck, dump, dunk, fall, jump, leap; 5 crash, douse, drown, plunk, souse, steep; 6 absorb, engulf, header, launch; 7 engross, immerse, plummet; 9 immersion

plunger: 6 piston

plunging: 7 falling; 8 dropping; 10 plummeting

plunk: 4 clop, dive, pick, plop; 5 clump, clunk, flump, plank, plonk, pluck, plump; 6 plunge

pluperfect: 11 past perfect

plural: 8 multiple; 9 upwards of; 10 plural form; 11 more than one

plus: 4 more; 5 asset, extra; 8 addition, positive; 9 summation

plush: 4 lush; 5 cushy, foamy; 6 lavish, plushy

Pluteus: 12 genus Pluteus, roof mushroom

Pluto: Hades

Plutonian: 6 Hadean; 9 Tartarean

plutonic: 7 igneous; 8 eruptive, volcanic; 9 irruptive

plutonium: 2 Pu

plutonium bomb: 5 A-bomb; 8 atom bomb; 10 atomic bomb; 11 fission bomb

pluvial: 5 rainy; 7 showery

ply: 3 dun, run, tax, tug; 4 fold, pull, urge, work; 5 beset, cater, plait, pleat, press, wield; 6 crease, handle, supply; 7 provide; 9 clamor for, importune, imprecate, plication; 10 manipulate

PM: 7 autopsy, premier; 8 necropsy; 10 postmortem; 12 post meridiem; 13 Prime Minister

Pm: 10 promethium

pneumatic: 3 air; 9 air-driven

pneumatic hammer: 9 air hammer; 10 jack hammer, jackhammer

pneumatic power: 8 air power

pneumatics: 12 aerodynamics; 13 fluid dynamics

pneumogastric nerve: 5 vagus

pneumonia: 14 lobar pneumonia

pneumonic: 8 pulmonic, rachitic; 9 pulmonary

pneumonic plague: 10 black death; 13 bubonic plague

Po: 7 Po River; 8 polonium

Poaceae: 9 Gramineae; 11 Graminaceae, grass family

poached: 6 boiled, stewed

poacher: 8 sea poker, smuggler; 10 sea poacher

poaching: 9 smuggling

POB: 7 call box; 9 letter box; 13 post-office box

Pocahontas: 7 Matoaka; 12 Rebecca Rolfe

pock: 3 pit; 4 mark, scar

pocked: 8 potholed; 10 pockmarked

pocket: 3 bag, fob, nab, net, sac; 4 hook, knit, poke, sack; 5 catch, pouch, put up,

scoop, scrip; 6 budget, digest, sachel, sheath, socket; 7 satchel, stomach, swallow; 8 reticule, scabbard

pocket billiards: 4 pool

pocketbook: 3 bag; 5 purse; 7 handbag; 8 memo book, notebook; 14 memorandum book

pocket bread: 4 pita

pocket flask: 8 hipflask

pocket handkerchief: 6 hankie

pocket money: 6 change; 8 pin money; 9 petty cash, small coin; 11 small change; 12 pocket change; 13 spending money

pod: 3 cod; 4 cyst, husk; 5 calyx, shell; 7 bladder, capsule, fuel pod, seed pod, seedpod, utricle, vesicle; 8 seed case, seedcase

podgy: 5 dumpy, pudgy, tubby

podiatrist: 10 foot doctor; 11 chiropodist

podiatry: 9 chiropody

Podiceps: 5 grebe; 13 genus Podiceps

podium: 4 dais; 5 stump; 6 pulpit; 7 rostrum, soapbox

poem: 5 verse; 6 poetry

poesy: 5 verse; 6 poetry; 7 poetics

poet: 9 versifier; 12 poet laureate

poetical: 6 poetic

poetic justice: 11 just deserts

poetic rhythm: 7 prosody

poetics: 5 poesy, verse; 6 poetry

poetize: 4 scan, sing; 5 rhyme, verse; 7 versify; 9 poeticize

poetry: 4 poem; 5 poesy, verse; 7 poetics

poet-singer: 8 jongleur, minstrel; 10 troubadour

pogge: 8 bullhead

pogonophoran: 9 beard worm

Pogostemon: 8 pachouli; 9 patchouli, patchouly; 15 genus Pogostemon

pogy: 5 pogey; 8 menhaden

poignance: 8 piquance, piquancy, pungency; 9 pithiness, poignancy; 11 pointedness

poignancy: 6 pathos; 9 poignance

poignant: 4 racy; 5 pithy; 7 caustic, piquant, pointed, pungent, rousing; 8 touching; 9 affecting, trenchant; 12 antithetical

Poinciana: 9 flame tree; 14 bird of paradise; 17 subgenus Poinciana

point: 3 aim, dot, nib, pas, set, tip; 4 barb, edge, gist, head, item, lieu, luff, mark, mote, peak, salt, show, spot, stop, whet, whim; 5 fancy, grind, guide, level, pitch, place, speck, stage, steer, strop, taper; 6 charge, degree, detail, direct, esprit, orient, period, points, reason, signal, target; 7 bespeak, betoken, context, essence, point to, repoint, sharpen; 8 aculeate, argument, arrow tip, bull's-eye, drollery, full stop, gunpoint, indicate, location, maneuver, position, severity; 9 arrowhead, full point, main point, manouevre, point size, substance; **10** pleasantry, power point; **11** pointedness; **12** breaker point, circumstance

point after: 10 conversion

point-blank: 5 blunt, frank; **6** candid; **9** outspoken; **10** forthright, free-spoken; **11** plainspoken

pointed: 4 keen; **5** aimed, pithy, sharp, spiky; **6** marked, of mark, pointy, spiked, spikey; **7** decided, piquant, pungent, veriest; **8** directed, distinct, poignant; **9** trenchant; **10** peremptory, remarkable; **12** antithetical

pointedly: 6 mainly; **7** chiefly, notably; **8** signally; **9** curiously, unusually; **10** peculiarly, remarkably, singularly, strikingly, studiously, uncommonly; **12** particularly

pointer: 5 arrow; **6** cursor, needle; **9** indicator

pointing: 9 direction

point lace: 11 needlepoint

pointless: 4 vain; **5** prosy; **6** otiose, wasted; **7** prosaic, prosing; **8** bootless, nugatory; **9** fruitless, senseless, unpointed; **10** of no effect, pedestrian, profitless; **11** commonplace, purposeless, superfluous; **12** matter of fact, unprofitable

point of no return: 7 Rubicon; **12** turning point

point of view: 5 angle, stand; **6** aspect; **7** posture; **8** attitude, position; **9** viewpoint; **10** standpoint; **11** perspective

point out: 6 denote, notice, remark, select; **7** comment, point at, point to; **8** indicate; **9** signalize; **11** remonstrate

point to: 4 bode; **5** augur, blame, imply, lay to, point; **6** convey, typify; **7** bespeak, betoken, breathe, point at, portend, presage, refer to, signify

pointy: 5 spiky; **6** spiked, spikey; **7** pointed

poise: 4 cool, trim; **5** brace, weigh; **6** adjust, aplomb; **7** balance; **8** symmetry; **9** sangfroid; **11** assuredness; **14** self-possession

poised: 5 civil; **6** adroit; **7** tactful; **9** collected; **10** diplomatic, equanimous

poison: 5 toxin; **7** envenom; **11** contaminate

poisoned: 9 envenomed; **12** contaminated

poisonous: 5 toxic; **7** vicious; **8** toxicant, venomous

poisonous substance: 5 toxin; **6** poison

Poitou-Charentes: 6 Poitou

poke: 3 dig, jab, pry; **4** biff, knit, lick, loaf, nose, prod, sack, stab; **5** pouch, pound, punch, scoke, scrip, thump; **6** budget, garget, loiter, lounge, pocket, poking, sachel, sheath, socket, thrust

poke along: 4 plod; **6** lumber, trudge

poke at: 4 pink, prod; **5** lunge, nudge

poke fun: 3 guy, rib; **6** jest at; **7** laugh at, make fun; **8** ridicule

poker: 8 fire hook; **9** poker game; **10** salamander, stove poker

poker-faced: 7 deadpan; **9** impassive; **12** unexpressive; **14** expressionless

pokey: 3 can [slang], pen; **4** brig, gaol, hold, jail, keep, poky, stir [slang]; **5** clink [slang], hulks; **6** chokey [slang], cooler [slang], donjon, lockup, prison; **7** dungeon, laggard, slammer [slang], the Rock; **8** big house [slang], dawdling, dilatory, hoosegow, one-horse, stockade; **9** calaboose [slang], guardroom, jerkwater; **10** guard house; **11** penal colony, prison house; **12** penitentiary

poking: 3 jab; **4** poke; **6** thrust; **7** jabbing; **9** thrusting

pol: 8 politico; **10** politician

Poland: 6 Polska

polar: 3 icy; **4** head; **5** gelid; **6** arctic, frigid; **7** bipolar, capital, counter, glacial, pivotal, supreme; **8** contrary, freezing, opposite, supernal; **9** diametric; **11** diametrical

polar bear: 7 ice bear

polar front: 9 cold front

polar hare: 10 Arctic hare

Polaris: 8 polestar; **9** North Star, polar star

polarity: 4 sign; **10** antithesis, bipolarity

polar lights: 6 aurora

Polaroid photo: 8 Polaroid; **12** instant photo

polar star: 7 Polaris; **8** polestar; **9** North Star

pole: 3 ell, rod, sky; **4** axle, foot, hand, inch, line, mile, nail, palm, punt, rood, yard; **5** arbor, cubit, perch; **6** fathom, league; **7** furlong, spindle; **8** terminal; **12** magnetic pole

pole-ax: 8 battle-ax

pole axis: 5 heart; **8** bull's eye

polecat: 5 fitch, skunk; **7** foumart; **8** foulmart

polemic: 6 arguer; **7** debater; **9** disputant, polemical; **10** polemicist

polestar: 7 Polaris; **8** lodestar; **9** North Star, polar star

pole vault: 8 pole jump; **11** pole jumping

pole vaulter: 7 vaulter; **10** pole jumper

police: 3 law; **6** patrol; **7** the cops, the fuzz [sarcastic] [U.S.]; **11** gendarmerie [Fr], police force; **12** constabulary

police blotter: 7 blotter, day book; **11** charge sheet

police car: 7 cruiser; **8** prowl car, squad car; **9** patrol car

police detective: 3 tec; **9** detective; **12** investigator

police headquarters: 12 police office, station house; **13** police station

police investigation: 9 detecting, detection, sleuthing; **13** detective work

police lock: 3 bar; **4** bolt; **8** deadbolt

policeman: 3 cop; **7** officer; **8** gendarme [Fr]; **9** constable

police station: 12 police office, station house; **18** police headquarters

police wagon: 5 wagon; **9** police van; **10** paddy wagon; **11** patrol wagon

policy: 4 game; 6 polity; 8 game plan; 9 insurance

policy change: 8 reversal; 9 about-face, volte-face

policy study group: 9 think tank

poliomyelitis: 5 polio

polish: 4 down, gild; 5 gloss, grace, grain, japan, paint, round, scour, shine; 6 comity, enamel, purity, refine, smooth; 7 brush up, burnish, euphony, furbish, garnish, lacquer, smarten, suavity, varnish; 8 breeding, civilize, elegance, fine-tune, humanize, polish up, presence, round off, smoothen, urbanity; 9 gentility, japanning, whitewash; 10 glossiness, refinement, shoe polish

polished: 5 suave; 6 milled, smooth, svelte, urbane; 7 correct, courtly, dressed, elegant, gallant, refined, scoured; 8 artistic, graceful, well-bred; 9 burnished, civilized, classical; 10 cultivated, well-styled; 11 gentlemanly; 12 thoroughbred

polished rice: 9 white rice

polisher: 6 buffer

polishing: 7 shining

polish off: 3 hit; 4 slay; 5 eat up, mop up; 6 finish, murder, remove; 7 bump off, clear up; 8 dispatch, finish up, knock off; 9 finish off

polite: 5 civil; 7 genteel; 8 cultured, mannerly; 9 civilized, courteous; 10 cultivated; 11 well-behaved; 12 good-mannered, well-mannered

politely: 7 civilly; 11 courteously

politeness: 8 civility, courtesy, niceness

politic: 5 chary, shy of, suave; 6 smooth; 7 prudent, tactful; 8 discreet, stealthy; 9 strategic; 10 diplomatic; 11 circumspect

political: 8 partisan

political action committee: 3 PAC

political boss: 4 boss; 9 party boss

political campaign: 8 campaign; 9 candidacy; 11 campaigning

political contribution: 12 contribution

political district: 9 bailiwick

political hack: 4 hack; 10 ward-heeler

political leader: 3 pol; 8 politico; 10 politician

politically correct: 2 PC [acron]

political maneuver: 8 demarche

political orientation: 8 ideology

political program: 8 platform

political theory: 8 ideology

political worker: 6 backer; 9 supporter; 14 campaign worker

politician: 3 pol; 8 activist, lawgiver, politico; 9 tactician; 10 legislator, strategist

politico: 3 pol; 10 politician

politics: 10 government; 16 political science

polity: 4 game; 6 policy; 8 game plan; 10 civil order

Polk: 9 James Polk; 13 James Knox Polk

poll: 4 vote; 5 voice; 6 ballot, canvas, census, muster, parrot, recite, survey; 7 canvass, plumper, pollard; 8 election, roll call, suffrage; 9 vox populi; 10 capitation, poll parrot; 11 opinion poll; 12 recapitulate

Pollachius: 7 pollack, pollock; 15 genus Pollachius

pollard: 8 truncate

pollex: 5 thumb

polling day: 11 election day

pollinosis: 8 hay fever

polliwog: 7 tadpole; 8 pollywog

pollock: 7 pollack

pollster: 9 poll taker; 11 headcounter

poll tax: 7 head tax; 13 capitation tax

pollute: 4 foul; 5 taint; 6 debase, defile; 10 adulterate; 11 contaminate

polluted: 7 defiled, tainted; 8 vitiated; 9 corrupted; 12 contaminated

polluting: 8 debasing, defiling, tainting; 9 pollution; 10 corrupting, debasement, defilement; 12 adulteration; 13 contaminating, contamination

pollution: 4 blot, blur, spot; 5 stain, taint; 7 tarnish; 8 defiling, impurity; 9 obliquity, polluting; 10 befoulment, debasement, defilement; 11 backsliding, contaminant; 12 adulteration; 13 contaminating, contamination

pollyannaish: 6 upbeat; 8 cheerful

pollyfish: 10 parrotfish

pollywog: 7 tadpole; 8 polliwog

Polo: 9 Marco Polo

polonium: 2 Po

polo shirt: 10 sport shirt

polo stick: 6 mallet

Polska: 6 Poland

poltroon: 6 coward

polychete worm: 9 polychete; 10 polychaete

polychrome: 6 striae; 10 maculation, monochrome, spottiness; 11 iridescence, polychromic; 12 multicolored, polychromize; 13 polychromatic

Polyergus: 9 Amazon ant; 14 genus Polyergus

Polygala: 8 milkwort; 13 genus Polygala

Polygalaceae: 14 milkwort family

polygamy: 8 polygyny

polyglot: 6 diglot; 7 diverse; 8 linguist; 10 translator; 12 multifarious; 13 heterogeneous

Polygonaceae: 15 buckwheat family

Polygonum: 9 buckwheat; 14 genus Polygonum

polygyny: 8 polygamy

polymer: 5 resin

polymerase chain reaction: 3 PCR [acron]

polymorphous: 9 multifold, multiform, multiplex; 11 polymorphic; 12 multifarious

Polyodon: 8 duckbill; 10 paddlefish; 13 genus Polyodon

P

polyoma virus: 7 polyoma
polyp: 7 polypus
polyphonic: 11 polyphonous; 12 contrapuntal
polyphonic letter: 9 polyphone
polyphonic music: 9 polyphony
polyplacophore: 6 chiton; 9 sea cradle
Polypodium: 4 fern; 15 genus Polypodium
Polypodium vulgare: 8 wall fern; 9 sweet fern; 10 adder's fern
polypore: 10 pore fungus; 11 pore mushrum
polypropylene: 11 polypropene
polypus: 4 bleb; 5 polyp; 7 blister; 8 furuncle
polysaccharide: 7 polyose
polysemous word: 13 ambiguous word
Polystichum: 4 fern; 16 genus Polystichum
polysyllabic word: 12 polysyllable
polysynthetic: 9 combining; 13 agglutinative
polytechnic institute: 11 polytechnic
polytetrafluoroethylene: 4 PTFE; 6 teflon
polytheism: 9 pantheism
polytheist: 9 pantheist
polyurethane cooler: 6 cooler, damper
polyurethane foam: 8 polyfoam
polyvalent: 11 multivalent
polyvinyl acetate: 3 PVA
polyvinyl chloride: 3 PVC
polyvinyl resin: 10 vinyl resin; 12 vinyl polymer
polyzoan: 6 sea mat; 7 sea moss; 8 bryozoan; 10 moss animal
pomade: 7 pomatum; 8 ointment; 12 hair dressing
Pomatomus: 8 bluefish; 14 genus Pomatomus
pomatum: 6 pomade
pomegranate: 14 Punica granatum
pomelo: 7 pummelo; 8 shaddock
pomfret: 9 Brama raii
pommel: 6 pummel
pommel horse: 9 side horse
Pomolobus: 7 alewife; 14 genus Pomolobus
Pomoxis: 7 crappie; 12 genus Pomoxis
pomp: 5 eclat; 7 pageant; 9 pageantry, spectacle; 10 exhibition, exposition
Pompey: 14 Pompey the Great; 20 Gnaeus Pompeius Magnus
pom-pom: 4 flak, tuft; 6 ack-ack, pompon; 9 ack-ack gun; 12 antiaircraft; 15 antiaircraft gun
pomposity: 8 pedantry; 11 ostentation, pompousness, splashiness; 15 pretentiousness
pompous: 7 stilted; 8 pedantic; 9 overblown; 10 pontifical, portentous; 12 high-sounding; 13 grandiloquent
ponce: 4 pimp; 6 pander; 8 panderer, procurer
poncho: 8 raincoat, raingear
pond: 4 lake, loch, mere, pool, slab, tank,

tarn; 5 broad, plash; 6 puddle; 7 cistern; 8 fish pond, mill pond
ponder: 4 mull, muse; 5 study, weigh; 7 reflect; 8 chew over, consider, meditate, mull over, ruminate; 9 speculate
ponderable: 8 palpable, sensible, tangible; 9 cogitable, ponderous; 10 fathomable; 12 determinable
pondering: 5 study; 6 broody, musing; 7 pensive; 8 brooding; 10 meditative, reflective, ruminative; 11 lucubration, speculation; 12 deliberation; 13 contemplative
ponderosa pine: 8 bull pine; 9 ponderosa
ponderous: 5 heavy; 6 forced; 7 labored; 9 lumbering; 10 ponderable
pond lily: 9 water lily
pone: 8 cornpone
pongid: 8 great ape
Pongo: 5 orang; 9 orang-utan, orangutan; 10 genus Pongo
poniard: 6 dagger
pontiff: 4 Papa, Pope, pope; 10 Holy Father
pontifical: 5 papal, Roman; 6 Popish; 7 pompous; 9 apostolic; 10 portentous; 13 grandiloquent
pontificate: 6 papacy; 7 primacy
pontoon: 4 raft; 5 float
pontoon bridge: 12 bateau bridge; 14 floating bridge
pontoon plane: 10 floatplane
pony: 4 crib, trot [U.S.]; 6 jigger; 9 shot glass, racehorse
pony up: 6 spit up; 7 cough up
pooch: 3 dog; 5 doggy; 6 bow-wow, doggie; 8 pooch out
pooh-pooh: 4 pooh; 5 scorn, spurn; 6 reject; 7 disdain, sneer at
pool: 3 pot; 4 lake, loch, mere, pond, slab, tarn; 5 broad, kitty, plash; 6 puddle; 7 combine; 8 pingpong, pyramids; 9 bagatelle, billiards, syndicate; 10 consortium
pool cue: 3 cue; 8 cue stick; 9 pool stick
pool table: 12 snooker table; 13 billiard table
poop out: 6 run out; 7 conk out, run down; 8 peter out
poor: 1 l, D; 3 bad; 4 thin, weak; 5 loose, short, spare; 6 feeble, flimsy, ill off, infirm, meager, paltry, scrimp, slight; 7 hapless, languid, piteous, pitiful, sketchy, sparing, stinted, unhappy; 8 indigent, inferior, mediocre, pathetic, pitiable, wretched; 9 miserable; 10 inadequate, second-rate; 12 hardscrabble, impoverished, infelicitous, misfortunate
poor box: 7 alms box, mite box
poor boy: 3 sub, zep; 4 hero; 5 hoagy, wedge; 6 bomber, hoagie; 7 grinder, torpedo; 9 submarine; 12 hero sandwich
poor definition: 9 fuzziness, unfocused; 10 blurriness; 14 indefiniteness
poor devil: 6 wretch
poor health: 9 ill health; 10 sickliness

poorhouse: 4 home; **7** shelter

poorly: 3 ill; **5** badly, seedy; **6** ailing, peaked, sickly, unwell; **9** squeamish; **10** indisposed, inexpertly; **12** unskillfully

poor man: 6 beggar, pauper

poorness: 7 poverty; **8** exiguity, thinness; **9** emptiness, scantness; **10** low quality, meagerness, meagreness, scantiness; **14** impoverishment

poor quality: 7 badness; **8** poorness; **10** low quality

poor shape: 5 unfit

poor timing: 9 bad timing

pop: 2 pa; **3** dad; **4** dada, papa, soda; **5** bulge, daddy, pappa, pater, plump, tonic; **6** bug out, old man, pop out, turn up; **7** come out, popping, popular, skin pop, soda pop; **8** bulge out, minerals, pop music, protrude, unawares; **9** soda water, soft drink

pop bottle: 10 soda bottle

Pope: 4 Papa; **7** pontiff

pope: 6 church, gospel; **7** pontiff; **9** scripture; **10** Holy Father; **13** Vicar of Christ

popeyed: 10 goggle-eyed; **11** openmouthed

popgun: 6 toy gun

Popillia japonica: 14 Japanese beetle

poppet: 4 dear, doll; **5** valve; **10** marionette

poppy: 5 opium; **6** opiate

poppycock: 5 hooey, stuff; **6** vagary; **7** boutade [Fr], mummery; **8** escapade; **10** tomfoolery

poppy family: 12 Papaveraceae

pop the question: 5 offer; **7** propose

populace: 5 world; **6** public

popular: 2 in; **3** pop; **5** plain; **7** in favor; **8** favorite; **10** democratic

popularity: 4 note; **5** eclat, kudos [Grk], vogue; **6** regard; **7** account; **9** celebrity, notoriety; **10** notability; **12** appreciation

popularity poll: 11 opinion poll

popular opinion: 7 opinion; **9** vox populi

popular with: 11 fashionable

populate: 4 live; **5** dwell, shack; **6** people, reside; **7** inhabit

populated: 7 peopled; **8** populous; **9** inhabited

population: 8 universe; **9** citizenry; **10** populating; **11** inhabitants [pl]

population scientist: 11 demographer; **12** demographist

populous: 5 thick; **7** crowded, peopled, studded, teeming; **8** manifold, multiple, swarming; **9** inhabited, populated; **10** multiplied

Populus: 5 aspen; **6** poplar; **12** genus Populus

pop up: 5 arise; **6** appear, cast up, crop up, jump up, show up, turn up; **8** spring up; **9** come forth; **11** materialize

porcelain: 5 china; **7** ceramic, pottery, vitrics; **8** ceramics; **11** earthenware

porcelain clay: 6 kaolin; **7** kaoline; **9** china clay, terra alba

porch: 5 inlet, mouth; **6** loggia, piazza, portal; **7** orifice, portico, veranda

porcine: 5 gross, piggy; **7** hoggish, piggish, swinish

porcupine: 8 hedgehog

pore: 5 focus, rivet, spout, stoma; **6** center, centre; **11** concentrate

porgy: 4 scup

poring over: 7 perusal; **8** perusing, studying

Po: 7 Po River

pork barrel: 14 appropriations

pork belly: 5 belly; **10** side of pork

porkpie hat: 7 porkpie

porn: 11 pornography

porn merchant: 12 pornographer

porno: 4 porn; **11** pornography

pornographic: 4 free; **5** bawdy, broad, gross, loose; **6** coarse, ribald, risque [Fr], smutty; **7** fulsome, obscene; **9** equivocal

pornographic film: 9 skin flick; **10** X-rated film

pornography: 4 porn; **5** porno

porosity: 10 porousness, sponginess

porous: 5 holey; **8** pervious; **9** permeable; **10** poriferous

porousness: 8 porosity

porpoise: 5 whale; **7** dolphin

porringer: 3 pan; **4** bowl, dish

port: 3 air; **4** bear, cast, dock, gait, left, look, mien, quay, tote [U.S.]; **5** basin, carry, color, guise, wharf; **6** convey, harbor; **7** cadence; **8** carriage, demeanor, larboard, port wine, porthole; **9** embrasure, interface; **10** complexion

portable: 14 battery-powered

portage: 7 cartage, carting

portal: 4 door; **5** inlet, mouth, porch; **7** orifice, portico

Port-au-Prince: 14 Haitian capital

portend: 4 bode, omen; **5** augur; **6** typify; **7** betoken, point to, predict, presage, signify; **8** forebode, forecast, foretell; **9** auspicate, foretoken, prefigure; **10** foreshadow

portent: 4 omen, sign; **6** augury; **7** auspice, presage; **10** prognostic

portentous: 7 augural, fateful, ominous, pompous; **8** augurial; **9** ill-boding, ill-omened, overblown; **10** foreboding, pontifical, prodigious; **13** grandiloquent

porter: 6 redcap; **7** doorman; **9** door guard; **10** doorkeeper, gatekeeper

porterhouse steak: 11 porterhouse

portfolio: 5 album, chair

porthole: 4 port; **9** embrasure

portico: 4 door; **5** inlet, mouth, porch; **6** loggia, piazza, portal; **7** orifice, veranda; **9** colonnade

portion: 3 lot; **4** fate, luck, part; **5** allot, share; **6** assign, kismet, parcel; **7** destiny, fortune, helping, measure, serving;

P

8 fraction; **9** allotment, allowance, component, fair share; **10** allocation, contingent, percentage

portion out: 4 deal; **5** share; **6** divide; **7** divvy up, dole out; **8** dispense; **9** apportion, parcel out; **10** distribute

portly: 5 burly, stout; **7** well-fed; **9** full-grown

portmanteau: 5 blend

Port Moresby: 23 capital of Papua New Guinea

Port-of-Spain: 26 capital of Trinidad and Tobago

Porto Novo: 14 capital of Benin

portrait: 9 portrayal

portray: 4 limn; **6** depict; **7** present; **11** impersonate

portrayal: 8 portrait; **9** depicting, depiction, enactment; **10** portraying; **11** delineation

portress: 6 beadle, warder; **7** doorman [male]; **8** cerberus; **9** charwoman; **10** doorkeeper

Portuguese man-of-war: 9 jellyfish

Portulacaceae: 14 parslane family

port wine: 4 port

pose: 3 ask, fix, lay, put, set, sit; **4** airs; **5** drape, model, place, posit; **6** aspect, put out, puzzle; **7** deposit, perplex, posture, present, situate; **8** attitude, position; **9** embarrass, mannerism, personate; **10** masquerade; **11** affectation, impersonate, orientation

pose as: 9 personate, personify; **11** impersonate

Poseidon: 7 Neptune

poser: 5 model; **6** poseur; **7** stumper, toughie

poseur: 5 poser

posh: 6 classy

posing: 7 sitting

posit: 3 fix; **4** pose; **7** deposit, situate; **9** postulate

position: 3 lay, put, set; **4** lieu, pose, post, rank, side, slot, spot, view; **5** berth, place, point, stand, stead; **6** locale, locate, office, status; **7** opinion, posture, situate, station; **8** attitude, function, locality, localize, locating, location; **9** condition, placement, situating, situation, viewpoint; **10** brevet rank, incumbency, precedence; **11** emplacement, perspective, point of view, positioning, proposition

positioning: 7 placing, putting; **8** aligning, locating, location, position; **9** placement, situating; **11** emplacement; **12** localization

position in society: 12 social status

position of responsibility: 4 post; **5** berth, place; **8** position; **10** incumbency

positive: 4 bold, plus, sure; **5** rigid, sound, stark; **6** secure; **7** assured, certain, decided, perfect; **8** absolute, besotted, cocksure,

confined, finished; **9** arbitrary, conceited, confident, convinced, essential, favorable, satisfied; **10** confirming, imperative, peremptory, positivist, prescribed; **11** irrefutable, unequivocal; **12** positivistic, unhesitating; **13** overconfident

positive integer: 13 natural number

positron emission tomography: 3 PET

posse comitatus: 5 posse; **11** body politic

possess: 3 own; **4** have, hold; **5** enjoy; **6** foster, hazard, occupy; **7** command

possessed: 3 had; **4** amok, held, wild; **5** amuck, giddy, rabid; **6** doting, raving; **7** berserk, frantic; **8** demoniac, frenetic, frenzied, obsessed, rambling, unhinged, wild-eyed; **9** delirious, insensate, wandering; **10** demoniacal, incoherent, reasonless

possession: 5 chose [Law]; **6** seisin [Law], seizin [Law]; **8** property; **9** monomania, ownership

possessive: 8 genitive

possessor: 5 owner; **6** holder

possibility: 6 theory; **7** opening; **9** remainder, reversion; **10** expectancy, hypothesis

possible: 9 potential; **10** imaginable; **11** conceivable

possibly: 5 haply, may be, maybe; **6** mayhap; **7** perhaps; **9** perchance; **11** potentially

possum: 7 opossum; **9** phalanger

post: 3 hie; **4** base, book, mail, seat, send, slot, spot; **5** berth, brand, debit, enter, place, put up, shaft, spank, staff, stake; **6** column, credit, hasten, insert, office, pillar, post up; **7** footing, install, scuttle, station; **8** pilaster, position, standing; **9** carry over, flagstaff, situation; **10** incumbency, standpoint, stigmatize; **12** mail delivery, military post; **13** postal service

postage: 5 stamp

postal clerk: 9 mail clerk

postal code: 7 zip code

postal service: 4 mail, post

postbag: 7 mailbag

postbox: 7 mailbox; **9** letter box

postdate: 6 follow; **7** misdate; **8** antedate, backdate

post-doctoral student: 7 post-doc

poster: 4 bill, card; **6** notice; **7** placard; **9** broadside, post horse; **11** contributor

posterboard: 10 paperboard

poster color: 7 tempera

posterior: 4 back, butt, prat, rear, rump, seat, tail, tush; **5** after, fanny, later, stern; **6** behind, bottom; **7** hind end, keister, postern, rear end, tail end, tooshie; **8** back side, backside, buttocks, derriere; **9** following, fundament; **10** subsequent, succeeding; **12** hindquarters

posterity: 4 seed, spat; **5** breed, brood, heirs, issue, spawn; **6** farrow, litter; **7** progeny; **9** offspring; **11** descendants

postern: 4 door, gate; 5 hatch; 6 wicket; 8 trapdoor; 9 posterior, threshold, vestibule
postfix: 6 suffix
post-free: 8 post-paid
postgraduate: 8 graduate; 11 grad student
post haste: 6 speedy; 9 immediate
postiche: 3 wig; 4 fake, sham; 6 toupee; 9 false hair, hairpiece
postilion: 6 carter; 7 wagoner; 10 postillion
posting: 7 mailing
postman: 7 carrier, mailman; 11 mail carrier; 13 letter carrier
postmark: 5 frank; 12 cancellation
postmeridian: 2 P.M. [abbr]; 9 afternoon
postmortem: 2 PM; 7 autopsy; 8 necropsy; 10 postmortal
post-office box: 3 POB
Post Office order: 10 money order
post-paid: 7 prepaid; 8 post-free
postpone: 4 stay; 5 defer, delay, remit, table; 6 put off, shelve; 7 hold off, put over, set back; 8 hold over
postponement: 4 hold, stay, wait; 5 delay, pause; 7 respite, time lag; 8 deferral; 9 deferment; 10 suspension; 11 adjournment, prorogation, retardation
postponer: 14 procrastinator
postprandial: 11 after-dinner
postscript: 2 PS; 8 addendum, appendix; 10 supplement; 12 afterthought
posttraumatic stress disorder: 4 PTSD
postulant: 3 nun; 6 bidder, novice, suitor; 8 aspirant, claimant; 9 candidate
postulate: 5 guess, posit; 6 theory, thesis, 7 contend, surmise, theorem; 10 conjecture, hypothesis, postulatum [Lat]; 11 postulation, supposition; 14 presupposition
postulated: 6 mooted; 7 assumed, divined, guessed; 8 imagined, presumed, supposed, surmised; 9 suspected; 11 conjectured, presupposed
postulation: 5 guess; 6 theory, thesis; 7 surmise, theorem; 9 candidacy, postulate; 10 conjecture, hypothesis, postulatum [Lat]; 11 predication, supposition
post up: 4 post; 6 insert; 13 make an entry of
posture: 3 sit; 4 pose; 5 model; 6 aspect; 7 bearing; 8 attitude, carriage, position; 9 situation, viewpoint; 11 orientation, point of view; 14 mental attitude
posy: 5 motto; 6 flower, wreath; 7 bouquet, chaplet, corsage, festoon, garland, nosegay; 8 epigraph
pot: 3 can, lot, mug, tin, wad; 4 deal, dope, gage, heap, hemp, load, mass, mess, mint, peck, pile, pool, raft, sens, sess, slew, weed; 5 batch, bhang, flock, ganja, grass, heaps, kitty, potty, sight, skunk, smoke, spate, stack, stool, tummy, world; 6 bottle, hatful, mickle, muckle, pickle, plenty, potful, season, throne, toilet; 7 commode, hashish, jackpot, tidy sum; 8 cannabis,

good deal, Mary Jane, potbelly; 9 bay window, flowerpot, great deal, marihuana, marijuana
potable: 5 drink; 8 beverage; 9 drinkable
potager: 3 pan; 4 dish; 5 plate; 6 saucer; 7 platter; 8 calabash, crucible, trencher; 9 porringer
potage St. Germain: 7 pea soup
potassium: 1 K; 6 kalium
potassium alum: 4 alum
potassium hydrogen tartrate: 6 tartar; 13 cream of tartar
potassium hydroxide: 6 potash
potassium nitrate: 5 niter; 9 saltpeter
potation: 5 draft; 6 tipple; 7 draught; 8 guzzling, imbibing, libation; 12 intemperance
potato: 4 spud; 5 tater
potato chip: 4 chip
potato family: 10 Solanaceae
potato pancake: 5 latke
potato skin: 4 peel
potbellied: 7 paunchy; 10 abdominous
pot-bellied stove: 13 Franklin stove
potbelly: 3 gut, pot; 5 belly, tummy; 6 paunch
potboiler: 4 hack; 10 hack writer, ink slinger
potbound: 9 rootbound
pot cheese: 13 cottage cheese
potency: 5 power; 8 strength; 9 potential; 12 potentiality, powerfulness; 13 effectiveness
potent: 4 hard; 5 hardy, stout, valid; 6 cogent, mighty, robust, strong, sturdy, virile; 8 forcible, powerful, puissant, vigorous; 10 adamantine
potentate: 8 dictator
potential: 6 likely, unreal; 7 potency, virtual; 8 expected, possible; 12 potentiality
potential energy: 13 dynamic energy
potentially: 5 haply, may be, maybe; 6 mayhap; 7 perhaps; 8 possibly; 9 perchance
potentiometer: 3 pot
potently: 10 powerfully
pother: 3 bug, row; 4 bait, bore, flap, fray, fuss, stew, to-do; 5 abuse, beset, brawl, broil, grind, harry, haunt, hound, melee, tease, tizzy, worry; 6 affray, badger, bother, breeze, dither, fracas, harass, heckle, hubbub, ill-use, infest, molest, pester, plague, racket, ruffle, rumble, rumpus, squall, uproar; 7 ferment, howling, oppress, rhubarb [baseball], ruction, shindig, trouble; 8 brouhaha, bullirag, bullyrag, ill-treat, maltreat, mistreat, nuisance, scramble, vexation; 9 annoyance, grievance, imbroglio, importune, persecute, scrimmage; 10 donnybrook, free-for-all, harassment; 11 battle royal, embroilment
pothered: 5 beset, bored; 6 baited; 7 harried, heckled; 8 badgered, harassed, infested; 10 importuned, persecuted

pothole: 9 chuckhole
potholed: 6 pocked; 10 pockmarked
pothouse: 3 pub; 6 saloon; 7 gin mill; 8 taphouse; 11 public house
potion: 4 dose; 7 draught; 12 prescription
Potomac: 11 Foggy Bottom; 12 Potomac River
potpourri: 4 balm, mess, olio; 6 medley, mosaic, motley; 7 collage, farrago, mixture, montage, variety; 8 all sorts, bergamot, mishmash, pastiche; 9 capriccio, composite, patchwork; 10 assortment, hodgepodge, miscellany
pottage: 4 soup; 5 broth, puree; 8 consomme
potter: 6 dabble, monkey, putter, tinker; 8 ceramist; 10 ceramicist
pottery: 7 ceramic, vitrics; 8 ceramics, clayware; 9 porcelain; 11 ceramic ware, earthenware
pouch: 3 fob, net, sac; 4 knit, poke, sack; 5 bulge, scrip; 6 budget, pocket, sachel, sheath, socket; 7 satchel; 8 protrude, reticule, scabbard
pouched mammal: 9 marsupial
pouch-shaped: 7 saclike; 9 bursiform
poulet: 7 chicken
poulterer: 10 poultryman
poultice: 6 foment; 7 plaster; 9 cataplasm
poultry: 4 fowl
poultryman: 9 poulterer
pounce: 5 swoop
pound: 2 lb; 3 lbf., ram; 4 beat, poke, punt, quid; 5 throb, thump; 6 hammer, lumber; 7 paddock; 8 dog pound, pounding; 9 hammering
poundal: 3 pdl
pounding: 5 pound, throb; 6 hammer; 9 buffeting, hammering, throbbing
pounds per square inch: 3 psi
pounds shillings and pence: 3 L.s.d.
pound sterling: 4 quid; 5 pound
pour: 3 jet; 4 gush, rain; 5 issue, spout, swarm; 6 decant, pour in, run out, stream; 7 pour out, trickle
pourboire: 3 tip; 8 gratuity
pouring: 7 gushing; 8 affusion
pour on: 6 lavish
pourparler: 7 meeting, palaver, session, sitting; 10 conference; 12 deliberation
pout: 3 mop, mow; 4 moue, snap, sulk; 5 brood, bulge, frown, gnarl, gnash, growl, lower, scowl, snarl; 6 glower; 7 eelpout, poke out, project, wry face; 8 hornpout, protrude
Pouteria: 6 mammee, sapote; 13 genus Pouteria
poverty: 4 lack, need, want; 6 penury; 8 distress, exigency, meanness, poorness, vileness; 9 indigence, necessity, neediness, pauperism, privation; 10 meagerness, paltriness, shabbiness, trashiness; 11 destitu-

tion, pitifulness; 12 beggarliness, difficulties, wretchedness; 13 impecuniosity, miserableness
poverty-stricken: 4 poor; 5 needy; 6 ill off; 8 badly off, indigent; 9 destitute, poorly off; 11 necessitous; 12 impoverished
pow: 4 wham; 5 whack
POW: 6 detenu [Fr], inmate; 7 captive, hostage; 8 detainee, prisoner
POW camp: 10 prison camp; 14 internment camp
powder: 4 dust; 7 shingle, spangle; 9 bespangle, gunpowder, powderize, pulverize; 11 black powder, suppository
powdered: 6 spotty; 7 powdery, spotted; 8 speckled; 10 pulverized; 11 fine-grained; 12 small-grained
powdered milk: 7 dry milk; 9 dried milk; 10 milk powder
powder horn: 11 powder flask
powder-house: 6 armory; 7 arsenal
powderiness: 8 fineness
powderize: 6 powder; 9 pulverize
powder puff: 4 muff, puff; 7 cripple; 8 pussycat; 9 creampuff; 11 mollycoddle
powder store: 8 magazine
powdery: 8 granular, powdered; 10 pulverized; 11 fine-grained, pulverulent; 12 small-grained
power: 4 king, root; 5 baron, force, index, might, mogul, sight [dialect], vigor; 6 office, tycoon; 7 ability, magnate, potency, powered; 8 exponent, loudness; 9 authority, logarithm, noisiness; 10 mightiness, superpower, world power; 11 heavyweight; 12 powerfulness
powerboat: 9 motorboat
power cable: 9 power line
power company: 12 light company, power service; 15 electric company
power down: 4 kill; 7 turn off; 9 switch off; 10 deactivate, disconnect
powerful: 4 deep, full, hard; 5 hardy, hefty, right, stout, valid; 6 brawny, cogent, mighty, potent, robust, strong, sturdy; 7 blatant, nervous; 8 forcible, incisive, muscular, puissant, vigorous; 9 herculean, knock-down, trenchant; 10 adamantine, clangorous, impressive
powerfully: 6 mighty; 8 mightily, potently, strongly
power generator: 11 power source; 12 energy source
powerhouse: 8 fireball
power hunger: 13 status seeking
powerless: 4 weak; 8 impotent
power plant: 10 powerhouse; 12 power station
power shovel: 6 digger, shovel; 9 excavator
power structure: 9 hierarchy
power system: 4 grid

power train: 5 gears, train; 7 gearing; 9 geartrain

Powhatan: 13 Wahunsonacock

powwow: 6 huddle, parley; 10 conference; 11 council fire

pox: 4 syph; 6 cowpox, plague; 7 murrain; 8 smallpox, syphilis; 10 pestilence

Pr: 12 praseodymium

practicable: 6 doable, viable; 8 feasible, operable, workable; 10 achievable; 11 performable

practical: 6 acting; 7 virtual, working; 9 effectual, efficient, executive, hard-nosed, operative, pragmatic; 10 hardheaded; 11 efficacious, functioning, strategical; 12 businesslike

practicality: 11 feasibility

practical joker: 6 hoaxer; 9 prankster, trickster

practically: 4 much; 9 virtually; 13 substantially

practical nurse: 3 LPN

practice: 2 do, MO; 3 use; 4 play, rear, ways, work; 5 apply, breed, drill, exert, usage; 6 custom, ground; 7 bring up, carry on, nurture, pattern, prepare, process; 8 exercise, practise, rehearse; 9 habituate, procedure, prosecute; 10 convention, observance, prevalence

practiced: 4 good; 5 adept; 6 expert; 7 skilful; 8 skillful; 9 practised; 10 proficient; 11 experienced

practice game: 10 exhibition

practice session: 5 drill; 8 exercise, practice

practise: 2 do; 5 drill, trial; 6 dry run; 8 carry out, exercise, exertion, practice, rehearse, trial run; 9 rehearsal

practitioner: 6 stager, worker; 10 practician

praenomen: 9 first name [U.S.]

praesidium: 9 presidium

pragmatic: 9 hard-nosed, practical; 10 hardheaded; 11 pragmatical; 12 matter-of-fact

Prague: 4 Prag; 5 Praha; 23 capital of Czechoslovakia

Praha: 4 Prag; 6 Prague; 23 capital of Czechoslovakia

Praia: 18 capital of Cape Verde

prairie: 5 veldt; 6 common; 9 grassland

prairie marmot: 10 prairie dog

prairie rattler: 11 rattlesnake

prairie schooner: 9 Conestoga; 12 covered wagon

Prairie State: 8 Illinois; 13 Land of Lincoln

prairie wolf: 6 coyote

praise: 4 laud; 5 bless, grace, kudos; 6 thanks; 7 commend, glorify, hosanna, magnify; 8 doxology; 9 laudation; 10 compliment; 11 benediction; 12 commendation; 13 glorification; 15 congratulations

praised: 6 lauded; 8 approved; 9 commended; 12 complimented

praiseworthy: 8 laudable; 10 creditable; 11 applaudable, commendable

praising: 9 laudatory, praiseful; 10 eulogistic, uncritical; 11 encomiastic, panegyrical; 12 commendatory

pram: 6 go-cart, pusher; 8 carriage, flatboat, stroller; 9 baby buggy, pushchair; 12 baby carriage, perambulator; 16 flat-bottomed boat

prance: 4 cock, trot; 5 amble, frisk, strut; 6 canter, cavort [U.S.], curvet, ruffle, sashay; 7 swagger

prank: 3 fad, fit, rig; 4 joke, lark; 5 antic, caper, freak, quirk, spree, trick; 6 maggot, vagary; 8 clowning, escapade, flimflam

prankish: 6 impish; 7 implike, puckish; 9 pixilated; 11 mischievous

prankishness: 9 rascality; 11 roguishness

prankster: 6 hoaxer; 9 trickster; 14 practical joker

praseodymium: 2 Pr

prat: posterior

prattle: 3 jaw; 5 clack, prate, prose; 6 cackle, gabble, gibber, jabber, parole, piffle, tattle; 7 blabber, blether, chatter

prawn: 6 shrimp

praxis: 6 syntax; 7 grammar; 8 exercise; 9 accidence, execution; 10 excitation

pray: 2 do; 3 beg, sue; 5 crave; 6 invoke, please; 7 implore, prithee; 8 petition; 10 supplicate

prayer: 4 suit; 6 appeal, orison; 8 entreaty, petition, rogation; 9 communion; 10 invocation, supplicant; 12 intercession, supplication

prayer beads: 6 rosary

prayer machine: 11 prayer wheel

prayer mat: 9 prayer rug

prayer shawl: 7 tallith

praying mantis: 6 mantis; 13 praying mantid

PRC: 5 China; 8 Red China; 13 mainland China; 14 Communist China; 22 People's Republic of China

preach: 7 lecture; 8 advocate, moralize, prophesy; 9 predicate, sermonize

preacher: 6 reader; 8 lecturer; 10 sermonizer; 11 preacher man

preaching: 6 sermon; 9 discourse; 10 preachment

preachment: 6 homily, sermon; 9 preaching; 15 preachification [informal]

preachy: 8 didactic

preadolescent: 11 prepubertal; 12 prepubescent

preamble: 6 prefix; 7 preface, prelude; 8 foreword, prologue; 12 introduction

preassemble: 12 prefabricate

prebendary: 4 dean; 5 canon; 8 diocesan; 10 archdeacon

Precambrian period: 11 Precambrian

P

precarious: 5 risky, shaky; 6 unsafe; 7 parlous; 8 fallible, insecure, perilous, slippery, ticklish, unstable; 9 dangerous, debatable, hazardous; 10 disputable, touch-and-go; 12 questionable

precaution: 4 care; 7 caution; 9 safeguard; 11 forethought; 12 watchfulness

precautionary: 9 provident; 12 precautional

precede: 4 lead; 6 forego; 7 forerun, predate; 8 antecede, antedate

precedence: 4 rank; 5 place; 7 station; 8 position, priority; 9 preceding; 10 precedency, precession; 11 antecedence, antecedency, anteriority

precedent: 4 type; 5 ideal, model; 7 case law, example, leading, pattern; 8 exemplar, original, paradigm, standard; 9 common law, preceding, precursor, prototype, reference, scantling; 10 antecedent, derivation; 11 determinant, predecessor

preceding: 4 past; 8 retiring; 9 precedent; 10 antecedent, precedence; 11 antecedence

precentor: 5 choir, clerk; 6 cantor; 8 director; 11 choirmaster

precept: 4 norm, rule; 8 sanction, teaching; 9 authority, principle

preceptor: 3 don; 5 guide, tutor; 7 teacher

precinct: 4 ward; 5 block, haunt; 6 barrio [Sp], corner, locale; 7 marches, station; 8 enceinte, environs, locality, premises, vicinage, vicinity; 9 bailiwick, precincts; 12 neighborhood

precious: 3 pet; 4 cute, dear; 5 noble; 6 goodly, little, mighty, wanted; 7 darling; 9 cherished, treasured

precious metals: 4 gold; 5 ingot; 6 copper, nugget, silver; 7 bullion; 8 platinum

preciousness: 12 valuableness; 13 pricelessness; 14 invaluableness

precious object: 8 treasure

precious stone: 3 gem; 4 ruby; 5 bijou, jewel, pearl; 7 diamond; 8 gemstone, sapphire

precipitant: 5 hasty; 6 abrupt, sudden; 7 instant; 9 immediate, momentary, overhasty; 11 precipitate, precipitous; 13 discontinuous, instantaneous

precipitate: 4 fall, sink; 5 abase, ashes, hasty, pitch; 6 abrupt, debase, reduce, sudden; 7 cinders, deposit, furious, instant, quicken, scoriae, speed up; 8 expedite, headlong; 9 hotheaded, immediate, impulsive, momentary, overhasty, premature; 10 accelerate, boisterous; 11 precipitant, precipitous; 13 discontinuous, instantaneous

precipitated: 9 deposited; 10 coagulated

precipitation: 4 hail, mist, rain, snow; 5 sleet; 8 downfall; 9 precocity; 10 subversion; 11 prematurity, prostration; 12 precipitancy

precipitous: 5 sharp; 6 abrupt, sudden; 7 instant; 9 immediate, momentary; 11 precipitant, precipitate; 13 discontinuous, instantaneous

precis: 4 note; 5 brief, draft; 6 apercu, digest, minute; 7 epitome, outline, summary; 8 abstract, analysis, synopsis; 10 abridgment

precise: 4 just; 5 exact; 6 just so, severe, strict; 8 accurate, exacting; 9 demanding; 10 meticulous, overstrict, particular; 11 punctilious

precisely: 2 so; 4 just; 5 a full, all of, fully, truly; 6 indeed, on time; 7 exactly; 8 on the dot, the sum of; 9 certainly, on the nose; 10 accurately, definitely, ex concesso [Lat], incisively, punctually

preciseness: 9 exactness, precision; 12 clearcutness; 13 high precision

precision: 9 exactness; 11 preciseness

preclude: 3 let; 5 check, debar; 6 forbid; 7 prevent, rule out; 8 close out, forefend; 9 foreclose, forestall

precluded: 9 prevented

precocious: 4 pert; 5 saucy; 7 forward, would-be; 8 assuming; 9 bumptious, obtrusive, premature

precognition: 7 knowing; 9 cognition; 10 cognizance, conception, prescience; 12 apprehension, presentiment; 13 comprehension, foreknowledge, understanding

preconception: 10 assumption, prevention; 11 presumption; 12 predilection, presentiment; 13 prepossession

precondition: 4 term; 5 given, terms; 6 clause; 9 condition; 10 conditions [pl]; 11 presumption, stipulation

precursor: 6 herald; 9 harbinger, precedent; 10 antecedent, forerunner; 11 predecessor

predaceous: 9 predatory, rapacious; 10 predacious

predate: 6 forego; 7 precede; 8 antecede, antedate, foredate

predation: 7 preying; 11 depredation

predator: 7 vulture; 8 marauder

predatory: 7 raiding; 8 ravening; 9 marauding, rapacious, raptorial, vulturine, vulturous; 10 predaceous, predacious

predatory animal: 8 predator

predecessor: 9 precedent, precursor; 10 antecedent

predestinate: 9 preordain; 10 foreordain, predestine; 11 predestined; 12 foreordained

predestination: 8 election, fatality, foredoom; 13 preordination

predestine: 4 doom; 9 preordain; 10 foreordain; 12 predestinate

predestined: 12 foreordained, predestinate

predetermination: 13 preordination

predetermine: 4 bias

predetermined: 6 preset; 8 foregone

predicament: 3 fix; 4 pass, push; 5 hitch, pinch, stamp, trial; 6 manner, pickle, plight, rubric, strait; **7** nonplus; **8** exigency, juncture, quandary, scramble

predicate: 3 say; **4** aver; **5** state; **6** affirm, assert, preach; **7** connote, declare, lecture, profess; **8** proclaim; **9** sermonize; **10** verb phrase; **11** predicative

predication: 6 homily, sermon; **7** lecture; **8** averment, pastoral; **9** assertion, discourse, statement; **10** allegation, profession; **11** declaration, postulation

predict: 4 bode, call, omen; **5** augur; **7** betoken, portend, presage, promise; **8** forebode, forecast, foretell; **9** auspicate, prefigure; **10** anticipate, foreshadow; **13** prognosticate

predicted: 8 foreseen, foretold

prediction: 8 forecast; **9** foresight, prognosis; **11** forecasting, foretelling

predictor: 10 forecaster, soothsayer; **14** prognosticator

predilection: 4 bent, mind, tone, turn; **5** taste; **6** animus; **7** leaning; **8** penchant; **9** sentiment; **10** assumption

predispose: 4 bias, sway; **7** dispose, incline; **8** dig a mine; **9** influence, inoculate

predisposed: 5 prone; **7** tending; **8** inclined

predisposition: 4 bent, bias; **7** leaning; **8** tendency; **9** proneness; **10** affections, proclivity, propensity; **11** disposition, inclination, sensitivity

predominant: 7 regnant, supreme; **8** dominant; **9** paramount; **10** overriding, prevailing; **11** in authority, predominate; **12** preponderant

predominate: 4 rule; **5** reign; **7** pervade, prevail, **8** dominate; **9** paramount; **10** overriding; **11** predominant; **12** preponderant, preponderate

preemie: 6 premie; **13** premature baby

preeminence: 4 note; **8** eminence; **9** supremacy; **11** distinction

preeminent: 6 utmost; **7** leading, supreme; **8** foremost, greatest; **9** matchless, paramount

preen: 5 dress, plume, pride, primp; **12** congratulate

prefabricate: 11 preassemble

prefabricated: 6 prefab

preface: 6 prefix; **7** prelude, premise; **8** foreword, preamble, prologue; **9** introduce; **12** introduction

prefatory: 9 inaugural; **11** prefatorial, preliminary; **12** introductory

prefect: 10 chancellor

prefer: 4 call; **5** favor; **6** choose, favour, opt for, ordain; **7** elevate, present, promote

preferable: 9 preferred

preference: 5 taste; **8** druthers, penchant; **12** predilection

preferred: 3 pet; **7** favored; **8** favorite; **10** preferable

prefigure: 4 bode, omen; **5** augur; **6** typify; **7** betoken, point to, portend, predict, presage, signify; **8** forebode, forecast, foretell; **9**

auspicate, foretoken; **10** foreshadow; **13** prognosticate

prefix: 7 preface, prelude; **8** foreword, preamble, prologue; **12** introduction

pregnable: 7 unarmed; **8** harmless, sine ictu [Lat], vincible; **9** untenable; **10** weaponless; **11** defenseless, unfortified; **12** indefensible

pregnancy: 9 gestation

pregnant: 5 pithy; **6** gravid; **7** fraught, meaning, pointed; **8** emphatic; **9** trenchant; **11** significant

prehensile: 8 grasping

prehension: 7 capture, seizing, seizure; **8** catching, grasping; **9** snatching

prejudgment: 9 prejudice

prejudice: 4 bias, warp; **8** drawback; **9** cause bias; **10** prepossess; **11** prejudgment; **12** disadvantage

prejudiced: 6 biased; **14** discriminatory

prejudicial: 8 damaging; **11** detrimental; **12** prejudicious

prelacy: 9 bishopric, prelature; **10** episcopacy, episcopate

prelate: 7 primate; **8** hierarch; **10** high priest

prelature: 7 prelacy

prelim: 11 preliminary

preliminary: 6 prelim; **7** prelude; **8** overture; **9** inaugural, prefatory; **11** preparative, preparatory; **12** introductory

preliminary sketch: 5 draft, study; **6** sketch; **7** drought, outline; **10** rough draft; **11** rough sketch; **12** rough drawing

preliterate: 11 nonliterate

prelude: 6 prefix; **7** preface, premise; **8** foreword, nocturne, notturno [It], overture, preamble, prologue; **11** preliminary; **12** introduction

premarital: 10 prenuptial; **11** antenuptial

premature: 8 previous, untimely; **10** precocious; **11** precipitate

premature baby: 6 premie; **7** preemie

premeditated: 7 advised, studied; **8** designed; **10** calculated, considered

premeditatedly: 9 advisedly; **10** with design; **11** in cold blood; **12** deliberately

premeditation: 11 forethought

premenstrual syndrome: 3 PMS

premier: 2 PM; **5** first, prime; **8** earliest, premiere; **10** chancellor; **13** prime minister

premiere: 7 premier

premise: 6 herald; **7** preface, prelude, premiss, usher in; **8** announce; **9** introduce; **10** assumption

premises: 4 data; **5** terms; **7** opening, station; **8** precinct

premium: 4 agio; **5** bonus; **6** bounty, tipfee; **7** payment; **8** agiotage; **9** first-rate; **10** honorarium

premium price: 9 top dollar**

premolar: 8 bicuspid
premonition: 5 hunch; 6 boding; 7 feeling; 8 instinct; 9 intuition; 10 foreboding; 11 forewarning
premonitory: 7 warning; 8 monitory; 10 cautionary, cautioning, precursory
prentice: 7 learner; 10 apprentice, journeyman
prenuptial: 10 premarital; 11 antenuptial
preoccupation: 10 absorption; 11 distraction, engrossment; 12 preoccupancy
preoccupied: 4 lost; 7 bemused, haunted, taken up; 8 obsessed
preordained: 5 fated; 8 destined; 12 foreordained
prep: 8 homework; 11 preparation
prepackaged: 9 prepacked
prepaid: 8 postpaid
preparation: 4 prep; 8 grooming, homework, planning, readying, training; 9 preparing, provision; 11 formulation
preparatory: 11 preliminary
preparatory school: 10 prep school
prepare: 3 fix, set; 4 cook, make, rear; 5 breed, get up, groom, ready, set up, train; 6 devise, gear up, ground; 7 bring up, develop, educate, nurture; 8 exercise, organize, practice; 9 habituate
prepared: 4 fain; 5 ready; 6 primed; 7 readied, trained; 8 disposed, finished, inclined; 9 initiated
preparedness: 9 readiness
preparing: 7 brewing; 8 readying; 11 forthcoming, preparation
preponderance: 4 sway; 6 credit; 8 prestige; 9 patronage; 10 prevalence
prepossess: 9 prejudice
prepossessed: 10 infatuated
prepossessing: 7 elegant; 8 charming, engaging, graceful
preposterous: 6 absurd; 7 stilted, would-be; 8 derisory, fabulous, inflated, swinging; 9 bombastic, burlesque, egregious, excessive, ludicrous, monstrous, senseless; 10 exorbitant, immoderate, inordinate, outrageous, ridiculous; 11 extravagant, nonsensical, pretentious
prepubescent: 11 prepubertal; 13 preadolescent
prepuce: 8 foreskin
Pre-Raphaelite: 11 medievalist
Pre-Raphaelitism: 8 archaism; 11 medievalism
prerequisite: 7 proviso; 9 condition, essential, provision; 10 imperative, sine qua non [Lat]; 11 contingency, requirement, stipulation; 13 indispensable, specification
prerogative: 5 right, title; 6 credit; 8 prestige; 9 patronage, privilege
presage: 4 bode, omen, sign; 5 augur;

6 augury, typify; 7 auspice, betoken, portend, portent, predict, signify; 8 forebode, forecast, foretell; 9 auspicate, foretoken, prefigure; 10 foreshadow, prognostic; 13 prognosticate
presbyter: 8 shepherd
presbytery: 5 glebe, manse; 7 deanery, rectory; 8 vicarage; 9 parsonage
preschool: 12 infant school; 13 nursery school
prescience: 9 foresight, prevision; 12 precognition, presentiment
prescribe: 3 set; 5 allot, order; 6 assign, burden, look to, oblige, ordain, prompt; 7 appoint, dictate, mark out, suggest; 8 advocate, legalize, sanctify; 9 encourage, recommend
prescribed: 7 decreed; 8 official, ordained, positive; 9 appointed, chartered
prescript: 4 rule; 6 brevet; 12 prescription
prescription: 3 use; 4 dose; 5 right, title, usage; 6 brevet, custom, potion; 7 draught; 8 practice; 9 prescript, privilege; 10 convention, observance, prevalence
prescriptive: 6 age-old; 9 customary, normative; 10 immemorial; 11 presumptive, traditional
presence: 4 mien; 5 front; 6 comity, polish; 7 bearing, suavity; 8 breeding, urbanity; 9 gentility; 10 expression, first blush; 11 comportment
present: 4 call, demo, face, gift, give, pose, show; 5 award, offer, stage; 6 actual, expose, extant, lay out, ordain, prefer, salute, submit, that is; 7 current, deliver, display, exhibit, instant, portray, proffer, propose, show off; 8 acquaint, confront, dispense, existing, free gift, give away, nowadays; 9 dispose of, introduce, translate; 10 consecrate, illustrate
presentation: 4 show; 5 intro, offer; 7 display, proffer; 8 awarding, overture, proposal; 9 induction, reading in, spectacle; 10 ordination, preferment, presenting; 11 institution, performance, presentment, proposition; 12 consecration, inauguration, installation, introduction; 13 demonstration
present-day: 8 up-to-date; 12 contemporary
presented: 8 bestowed; 9 conferred
presenter: 5 donor, giver; 7 awarder; 8 bestower
presenting: 7 showing; 8 awarding; 10 exposition, round robin; 11 manifesting, presentment; 12 illustrating, illustration, presentation; 13 demonstrating, demonstration
presently: 4 anon, soon; 7 betimes, shortly; 9 currently
preservation: 6 saving, upkeep; 8 creation; 10 preserving; 11 maintenance, safe-keeping; 12 conservation
preservative: 9 preserver

preserve: 3 jam; **4** hold, keep, pale, save; **5** jelly; **6** bear on, keep up, uphold; **7** carry on, enclave, reserve; **8** conserve, continue, maintain; **9** conserves, preserves; **11** reservation

preserved: 4 held, kept

preserving: 6 saving; **7** holding, keeping; **10** conserving; **12** preservation

preset: 13 predetermined

preside: 5 chair

President: 14 Chief Executive

president: 5 chair; **11** chairperson

presidential term: 10 presidency; **14** administration

President of the United States: 9 President; **14** Chief Executive

preside over: 4 lead; **6** direct, govern, manage; **7** conduct

press: 2 in; **3** bid, dun, jam, mob, ply, tax; **4** body, load, push, urge; **5** beset, crush, horde, pop in, put in, ram in, weigh; **6** adjure, closet, cumber, drop in, exhort, rabble, tuck in, urge on, whip in; **7** beseech, compact, drive in, entreat, squeeze, stick in, stuff in; **8** compress, contract, press out, pressing, pressure; **9** clamor for, constrict, force upon, gravitate, importune, imprecate; **10** insistence, insistency, weightlift; **11** impressment, instigation; **12** clothespress, fourth estate

press agency: 10 news agency; **11** wire service

press agent: 5 PR man; **12** publicity man; **13** news secretary; **14** press secretary

press clipping: 7 cutting; **8** clipping

press conference: 14 news conference

press down: 7 depress

pressing: 5 press; **6** crying, urgent; **7** exigent, instant, ironing; **8** critical, pressure, stamping; **9** absorbing

pressman: 7 printer; **10** newswriter; **13** correspondent

press release: 7 handout, release

press run: 8 print run

press secretary: 10 press agent

press the flesh: 10 shake hands

pressure: 4 load, push; **5** force, press; **6** coerce, stress, weight; **7** squeeze, tension, urgency; **8** pressing, push into; **9** blackjack, blackmail; **10** insistence

pressured: 8 stressed

pressure group: 5 lobby

prestidigitation: 5 magic; **12** slight of hand; **13** sleight of hand

prestidigitator: 8 conjurer, conjuror, magician; **9** trickster; **11** illusionist

prestige: 6 credit; **9** patronage; **11** party spirit, prerogative; **12** clannishness, partisanship

prestigious: 7 honored; **8** esteemed

presto: 8 suddenly

presumable: 8 apparent, credible; **10** reasonable, supposable, surmisable; **11** presumptive, well-founded

presume: 5 strut; **6** assume; **7** receive, swagger; **8** arrogate, feel free, make bold, make free; **10** presuppose

presumed: 6 mooted; **7** assumed, divined, guessed; **8** imagined, supposed, surmised; **9** suspected; **10** postulated; **11** conjectured, presupposed

presumption: 5 given; **6** breach; **8** audacity, exaction, reliance; **9** assurance, breaching, violating, violation; **10** assumption, confidence, imposition, infraction, prevention, usurpation; **12** encroachment, infringement, precondition

presumptuous: 8 assuming; **10** assumptive

presuppose: 7 presume

presupposed: 6 mooted; **7** assumed, divined, guessed; **8** imagined, presumed, supposed, surmised; **9** suspected; **10** postulated; **11** conjectured

pretence: 5 guise; **7** pretext; **8** feigning, pretense; **10** pretending, pretension, simulation

pretend: 3 act; **4** play, sham; **5** feign, plead, put on; **6** affect, allege, assume, fake it

pretended: 4 fake, mock, sham; **5** bogus, false, put on; **6** pseudo; **7** alleged, assumed, canting, fictive, stilted; **8** affected, asserted, so-called, spurious; **9** insincere, unnatural; **10** apologetic, artificial, fictitious, fraudulent

pretender: 4 fake, sham; **5** faker, fraud, pseud; **6** pseudo; **7** usurper; **8** imposter, impostor

pretending: 8 feigning, pretence, pretense; **10** pretension, simulation

pretense: 7 pretext; **8** feigning, pretence; **10** pretending, pretension, simulation; **11** dissembling, make-believe

pretentious: 5 showy; **6** kitsch; **7** canting, dashing, stilted, would-be; **8** affected, insincere, pretended, unnatural; **10** artificial, not natural; **12** ostentatious, preposterous

preterite: 6 bygone, former; **8** preterit

preternatural: 6 exotic; **10** nonnatural, outlandish; **12** otherworldly

pretext: 5 guise; **8** pretense; **10** pretension

Pretoria: 20 capital of South Africa

prettiness: 8 cuteness

pretty: 4 fine; **5** jolly; **6** lovely; **7** passing; **9** beauteous, beautiful

prevail: 3 run; **4** hold, rule; **5** reign; **6** endure, obtain; **7** die hard, persist, pervade, triumph; **8** dominate; **9** have place; **10** run through; **11** predominate

prevailing: 2 in; **4** rife; **6** trendy, with it; **7** current, in vogue; **8** epidemic; **9** besetting, in fashion, prevalent

prevalence: 3 run, use; **4** sway; **5** usage;

6 custom; **8** practice; **10** convention, observance, partiality; **12** prescription; **13** preponderance

prevalent: 2 in; **4** rife; **5** afoot; **6** afloat, on foot, trendy, with it; **7** current, in vogue, rampant; **8** epidemic; **9** besetting, in fashion

prevaricate: 3 lie; **6** palter; **7** quibble; **10** equivocate; **12** tergiversate

prevaricator: 4 liar

prevent: 3 let; **4** keep; **5** check, debar; **6** forbid; **7** draw off; **8** forefend, preclude; **9** foreclose, forestall, turn aside

preventative: 5 hitch; **8** impeding; **9** hindering, hindrance; **10** immunizing, precluding, preventive; **11** encumbrance, incumbrance, obstructing, obstructive; **12** interference, prophylactic

prevented: 9 precluded

prevention: 3 bar; **10** assumption, preclusion

previous: 3 old; **4** late; **5** prior; **6** former

previously: 6 ere now; **8** hitherto

prevision: 9 foresight; **10** prescience

prey: 4 feed, game; **5** raven; **6** quarry, target, victim; **8** fair game

preying: 9 predation; **11** depredation

price: 4 cost, toll; **5** terms; **6** amount, charge, damage, figure; **7** expense

price competition: 8 price war

priceless: 4 rare; **10** invaluable

price reduction: 8 discount; **9** deduction

pricey: 4 dear; **5** pricy; **6** costly; **9** expensive; **10** high priced, high-priced

prick: 4 bite, dent, fret, gall, goad, lash, slit, spur, urge, whip; **5** grate, gripe, notch, pinch, sting, wring; **6** inject, pierce, twinge; **7** prick up, prickle, scratch; **8** convulse, incision

prickling: 6 tingle; **8** stinging, tingling

prickly: 5 burry, spiny; **6** barbed, briary, briery, burred, snaggy, thorny; **7** bristly, studded, thistly, waspish; **8** bristled; **9** bristling, splenetic; **10** barbellate

prickly heat: 8 heat rash

prick one's balloon: 7 deflate; **10** disenchant; **11** disillusion

pricy: 4 dear; **6** costly, pricey; **10** high-priced

pride: 4 gaud; **5** plume, preen; **8** superbia; **12** congratulate, pridefulness

prideful: 6 lordly, sniffy; **7** haughty; **8** exultant, exulting, jubilant; **9** rejoicing, triumphal; **10** disdainful, swaggering, triumphant; **12** supercilious

priesthood: 8 ministry

prig: 3 bag; **4** snob, snot; **5** filch, jemmy, prude, puppy, spark, steal; **6** pilfer, purist, thieve; **7** fribble, puritan, purloin; **8** popinjay

prim: 4 smug, twee; **6** dainty, demure, prim up, prissy; **7** mincing, prim out, prudish; **8**

priggish; **9** quakerish, victorian; **11** pragmatical, puritanical, straitlaced

prima: 4 star; **7** leading, stellar; **8** starring

primacy: 6 papacy; **11** pontificate

prima donna: 4 diva

prima facie: 8 apparent; **9** seemingly; **10** ostensibly; **11** self-evident

primal: 3 key; **7** central; **8** cardinal, primeval; **9** primaeval; **10** aboriginal, primordial; **11** fundamental

primarily: 6 mainly; **7** chiefly; **9** in the main; **11** principally

primary: 4 main; **5** basal, basic, chief, prime; **7** capital, leading; **8** foremost; **9** beginning, primitive, principal; **10** elementary, overruling, primordial

primary school: 11 grade school; **13** grammar school

primary tooth: 9 baby tooth, milk tooth

primate: 6 leader; **7** prelate; **8** hierarch; **10** archpriest, high priest

Primates: 13 order Primates

prime: 2 A.M. [abbr]; **4** cram, fine, main, morn, peak, pick; **5** bloom, chief, coach, crack, cream, early, elite, flush, prize; **6** attune, choice, flower, ground, heyday, select, tip-top; **7** aliquot, blossom, capital, forward, leading, morning, premier, primary, quality; **8** cardinal, foremost, forenoon, meridian, nonesuch, noontide, top grade, top-notch, very best; **9** divisible, exquisite, nonpareil, principal, undercoat; **10** fractional, overruling, reciprocal; **11** high-wrought, masterpiece, prime number

prime coat: 6 primer

Prime Minister: 2 PM; **7** premier; **10** chancellor

primer: 4 fuse, fuze; **6** ground, manual; **7** priming; **8** flat coat; **9** prime coat, rudiments, undercoat, vade mecum

primeval: 6 primal; **9** primaeval, primitive; **10** aboriginal, primordial

priming: 6 primer, waxing; **8** painting; **10** lacquering; **11** shellacking

primitive: 4 rude; **5** crude; **6** atomic; **7** archaic, compact, primary; **8** primeval; **9** elemental; **10** primordial; **11** indivisible; **12** unanalyzable

primly: 8 prissily

primness: 7 prudery

primogeniture: 4 line; **7** lineage

primordial: 6 primal; **7** primary; **8** primeval; **9** primaeval, primitive; **10** aboriginal

primp: 5 dress, plume, preen

primrose family: 11 Primulaceae

Primulaceae: 14 primrose family

primum mobile: 8 keystone; **10** first cause, main motive, mainspring, occasioner, prime mover

primus inter pares: 7 paragon; **9** nonpareil; **13** nulli secundus [Lat]

prince: 3 gem; **4** duke; **5** brick, jewel, trump; **10** good fellow

princely: 4 free; **5** grand, noble, proud; **6** august, deluxe, gilded, giving, lordly, titled; **7** liberal, opulent, stately; **8** generous, handsome; **9** bounteous, bountiful, dignified, honorable, luxurious, patrician, sumptuous, unselfish; **10** charitable, free handed, full handed, munificent, open handed, worshipful; **12** aristocratic

Prince of Darkness: 5 Devil, Satan; **7** Lucifer, Old Nick; **8** the Devil; **9** Beelzebub; **10** the Tempter

prince of the church: 8 cardinal; **10** high priest

Princeton: 19 Princeton University

princewood: 5 cypre; **8** salmwood; **10** Spanish elm; **13** Ecuador laurel; **15** Cordia alliodora; **18** Cordia gerascanthus

principal: 4 head, lead, main, star; **5** chief, prime; **6** corpus, dealer; **7** capital, leading, primary; **8** foremost, venturer; **9** money lent; **10** overruling; **11** head teacher; **12** principal sum; **13** most important; **15** school principal

principal investigator: 2 PI

principally: 4 even; **6** mainly; **7** chiefly, the most; **8** above all; **9** a fortiori, eminently, extremely, in the main, primarily, still more, supremely; **10** especially, surpassing; **11** egregiously, exceedingly

principal sum: 6 corpus; **9** principal

principia: 9 principle

principle: 4 body, rule, type; **5** cause, tenet; **6** corpus, nature, origin, reason, source; **7** element, precept, probity, quality; **9** integrity, principia [Lat], propriety, rationale, rectitude

prink: 5 primp

print: 7 impress, printed, publish; **8** print out; **9** engraving; **10** impression

printable character: 6 letter

printed: 5 print; **9** impressed, imprinted

printed document: 4 text; **8** printing

printer: 8 pressman

printer's ink: 8 India ink

printer ink: 5 toner

printing: 4 text; **7** imprint; **10** impression

printmaker: 13 graphic artist

printout: 6 output

print run: 8 press run

prior: 5 abbot; **8** anterior, previous

prioress: 6 abbess; **14** mother superior

priority: 10 precedence, precedency; **11** antecedence

prior occurence: 9 precedent

prior to: 6 before

priory: 5 abbey; **6** friary

prise: 3 pry; **5** jimmy, lever, prize, value; **6** esteem; **7** respect

prison: 3 can [slang], pen; **4** brig, gaol, hold, jail, keep, stir [slang]; **5** clink [slang],

hulks, pokey [slang]; **6** chokey [slang], cooler [slang], donjon, lockup; **7** dungeon, slammer [slang]; **8** big house [slang]; **10** San Quentin; **11** penal colony, prison house; **12** penitentiary

prisonbreak: 5 break; **8** breakout; **9** jailbreak

prison camp: 7 POW camp; **8** work camp; **10** prison farm; **14** internment camp

prisoner: 3 POW; **6** inmate; **7** captive, convict, hostage; **8** detainee, jail bird; **13** prisoner of war

prisoner of war: 3 POW; **6** detenu [Fr], inmate; **7** captive, hostage; **8** detainee, prisoner

prison farm: 8 work camp; **10** prison camp

prison guard: 5 screw; **6** jailer; **7** turnkey

prison term: 4 time; **8** sentence

prissily: 6 primly

prissy: 4 nice, prim; **6** dainty; **7** prudish; **8** overnice, priggish; **9** squeamish, victorian; **10** square-toed, tight-laced; **11** puritanical, straitlaced

pristine: 4 late; **6** former

prithee: 2 do; **4** pray; **6** please

privacy: 7 secrecy; **8** solitude; **9** isolation, reclusion, seclusion; **11** concealment, privateness

private: 3 bye; **4** peon; **5** close, party, privy; **6** proper, secret; **7** certain, partial, recluse, retired, several, special, trooper; **8** definite, esoteric, especial, original, peculiar, rifleman, secluded, specific; **9** auricular, exclusive, inviolate; **10** individual, inviolable, particular, respective; **11** appropriate, buck private, clandestine, determinate, rank and file, sequestered; **12** confidential

private detective: 2 PI; **7** gumshoe; **8** sherlock; **9** operative; **10** private eye; **11** private dick

private-enterprise: 11 competitive; **14** free-enterprise

privateer: 5 rover; **6** ranger; **13** privateersman

private eye: 2 PI; **8** sherlock; **9** operative; **16** private detective

private investigator: 2 PI; **8** sherlock; **9** operative; **10** private eye

privation: 4 lack, need, want; **6** penury; **7** poverty; **8** distress; **9** indigence, necessity, neediness, pauperism; **11** bereavement, deprivation, destitution

privilege: 5 favor, right, title; **6** favour; **7** charter, empower, release; **8** immunity; **9** exception; **10** perquisite; **11** enfranchise, prerogative

privy: 6 toilet; **7** latrine; **8** bathroom, facility, lavatory

prix fixe: 10 table d'hote

prize: 5 award, booty, jimmy, lever, prime, prise, rifle, spoil, value; **6** admire, choice,

P

esteem, select, trophy; **7** defer to, pillage, plunder, quality, respect; **8** treasure, winnings; **10** appreciate

prizefighter: **5** boxer; **7** athlete, bruiser; **8** pugilist; **9** gladiator

prizewinner: **5** champ; **6** victor, winner

prizewinning: **8** champion

PR man: **10** press agent

pro: **4** jock; **6** player; **7** athlete; **12** professional

probability: **6** chance; **10** likelihood, likeliness

probability theory: **10** statistics

probable: **6** likely; **7** hopeful; **9** plausible

probably: **6** belike, likely; **8** credibly; **9** plausibly; **10** believably

probation: **5** proof; **12** verification; **13** demonstration

probationer: **6** novice; **7** parolee, recruit; **8** neophyte

probe: **4** test; **5** plumb, rimer, scoop, sound; **6** chisel, dibble, fathom, gimlet, lancet, trepan, warder; **7** examine

probing: **5** probe; **9** searching; **11** inquisitory; **13** investigation

problem: **3** job, rub; **5** issue; **7** dispute, trouble; **8** argument, question; **9** moot point; **10** difficulty; **11** controversy; **12** complication

problematic: **6** knotty; **8** baffling; **9** debatable

proboscis: **3** neb; **4** beak, nose; **5** snout, trunk; **6** nozzle, schnoz

procaine hydrochloride: **9** novocaine

procedural: **9** adjective

procedure: **2** MO; **3** way; **4** mode, ways, wise; **5** means; **6** manner, method; **7** fashion, process, routine; **8** function, practice, protocol; **9** mechanism, operation, technique; **10** procedures [pl], subprogram, subroutine; **13** modus operandi

proceed: **2** go; **3** run; **4** flow, go on, keep, move, pass; **6** elapse, keep on; **7** advance, carry on, go along; **8** continue, progress

proceedings: **7** minutes; **10** proceeding; **12** transactions

proceeds: **4** take; **5** issue, yield; **6** payoff, profit, return; **7** net gain, takings; **8** earnings

process: **2** MO; **3** act, sue, way; **4** mode, ways, wise, work; **5** march, means, serve, treat; **6** manner, method, work on; **7** convert, fashion, summons; **8** litigate, practice, protocol, swear out; **9** appendage, mechanism, operation, outgrowth, procedure, technique, transform; **10** procedures [pl]; **12** human process; **13** modus operandi

processed: **7** refined

procession: **4** file; **6** column, parade, review; **9** promenade

processive: **8** stepwise; **10** processing

process of reasoning: **8** deducing; **9** inferring, reasoning; **11** rationalism

processor: **3** CPU; **9** mainframe

proces verbal: **10** deposition

proclaim: **4** laud; **5** exalt, extol; **6** blazon, herald; **7** exclaim, glorify; **9** predicate; **10** promulgate

proclaimed: **9** announced

proclamation: **11** propagation; **12** announcement, annunciation

proclivity: **4** bent, bias; **7** leaning; **8** tendency; **9** proneness; **10** affections, propensity; **11** disposition, inclination

procrastinate: **5** dally, stall; **9** temporize; **10** dilly-dally

procrastinator: **9** cunctator, postponer

procreate: **6** repeat; **8** generate, multiply; **9** fertilize, propagate, reproduce; **10** impregnate

procreation: **7** genesis; **8** breeding; **10** gemination, generation

procreator: **7** genitor; **10** progenitor

Procrustean: **5** rigid, sound; **6** strict; **8** positive; **14** uncompromising

proctor: **7** monitor; **9** solicitor; **10** invigilate, procurator

procurable: **7** getable; **8** gettable; **10** obtainable

procurator: **5** proxy; **7** proctor

procure: **3** buy, get; **4** gain; **6** engage, enlist, obtain, secure; **7** acquire

procured: **6** gotten; **8** acquired, obtained

procurement: **7** gaining, getting; **8** procural; **9** acquiring, obtaining, obtention, procuring; **10** obtainment, procurance; **11** acquisition

procurer: **4** pimp; **5** ponce; **6** pander; **8** panderer

Procyon lotor: **4** coon; **8** ringtail; **13** common raccoon

prod: **3** dig, jab; **4** goad, poke, spur, stab; **5** egg on, nudge; **6** incite, poke at, thrust, urging; **7** goading; **8** prodding, spurring

prodding: **4** goad, prod, spur; **6** urging; **7** goading; **8** spurring

prodigal: **6** lavish; **7** profuse, wastrel; **8** wasteful; **9** unsparing, unstinted, unthrifty; **10** dissipated, munificent, profligate, squanderer, thriftless, unstinting; **11** extravagant, improvident, overliberal, spendthrift

prodigious: **8** colossal, olympian, towering; **9** Cyclopean, exceeding, Herculean, marvelous, monstrous; **10** Gargantuan, incredible, portentous, stupendous, surpassing; **11** astonishing, Bunyanesque, exceptional

prodigy: **6** wonder; **7** miracle; **10** phenomenon, wonderment; **11** wonder child

produce: **3** get; **4** farm, grow, make, work; **5** raise, yield; **6** create, profit; **7** acquire, bring on, develop, product; **8** bring out, generate, give rise, protract; **10** bring about, bring forth, green goods, production; **11** garden truck, manufacture; **14** green groceries

produced: 4 made; **6** formed; **7** created; **9** generated

producer: 7 creator; **10** impresario, originator; **12** manufacturer

producing: 6 making; **7** forming, genetic; **8** creating, creation; **9** formation, formative; **10** generating, generation, generative, production

product: 4 ware; **5** wares, yield; **6** profit, result; **7** article, outcome, produce; **8** artifact, multiple, offshoot; **9** aftermath, commodity, resultant; **10** production; **11** merchandise

production: 3 art; **4** work; **6** making; **7** forming, produce, product; **8** artifice, creating, creation; **9** extension, formation, producing; **10** exhibition, generation

production line: 4 line; **12** assembly line

productive: 3 fat; **4** rich; **7** fertile; **8** creative; **9** effective, efficient; **10** generative

productively: 10 fruitfully, profitably; **11** effectively, efficiently

proem: 6 prefix; **7** preface, prelude; **8** foreword, preamble, prologue; **12** introduction

profanation: 5 abuse; **9** blasphemy, profanity, sacrilege; **10** perversion; **11** desecration

profane: 3 lay; **4** blue; **5** abuse, civil, scoff; **6** debase, laical, revile; **7** corrupt, debauch, deprave, outrage, pervert, secular, violate, vitiate; **8** temporal; **9** desecrate, misdirect; **10** demoralize, irreverent; **11** blasphemous; **12** sacrilegious

profaned: 8 violated

profanity: 4 oath; **7** cursing; **8** ribaldry, swearing

profess: 3 say; **4** aver; **5** state; **6** affirm, assert; **7** concede, confess, declare; **9** predicate

professed: 6 avowed

profession: 4 walk; **6** career; **7** calling; **8** averment, vocation; **9** assertion, assurance, community, statement; **10** allegation, avouchment, empty words, professing, walk of life; **11** declaration

professional: 3 pro; **6** master; **11** white collar

professional athlete: 3 pro; **4** jock; **6** player; **7** athlete

professor: 6 reader; **8** lecturer; **10** prolocutor

professorship: 5 chair; **9** tutorship; **10** fellowship, readership; **11** lectureship

proffer: 5 offer; **7** present, propose; **8** overture, proposal; **10** suggestion; **11** proposition; **12** presentation

proficiency: 5 craft, knack, skill; **7** address, aptness, know-how; **8** aptitude, facility; **9** technique; **10** adroitness, competence; **12** skillfulness

proficient: 4 good; **5** adept; **6** expert, genius,

master; **7** capable, skilful, skilled; **8** skillful; **9** competent, practiced, qualified

profile: 5 lines; **7** contour, outline; **9** lineament; **10** projection, silhouette

profit: 3 net; **4** boot, gain; **5** lucre; **7** benefit, harvest, net gain, produce, product, profits [pl]; **8** earnings, proceeds

profitable: 6 paying; **7** gainful; **8** edifying, fruitful; **9** lucrative; **12** advantageous, remunerative

profitably: 10 fruitfully; **12** productively

profitless: 4 vain; **8** bootless, nugatory; **9** fruitless, pointless

profits: 3 net, win; **4** boot, gain; **5** lucre; **6** profit; **7** harvest; **8** earnings, winnings; **9** net income, net profit

profligate: 3 rip; **4** fast, rake, roue; **5** blood; **6** lavish; **7** corrupt, profuse, riotous, wastrel; **8** degraded, prodigal, recreant, scampish, wasteful; **9** corrupted, debauched, dissolute, graceless, libertine, reprobate, unthrifty; **10** degenerate, dissipated, squanderer, thriftless; **11** extravagant, improvident, overliberal, spendthrift

pro forma: 11 perfunctory

profound: 4 arch, blue, deep, sunk; **5** crass, gross, heavy, solid, sound; **6** buried, savant, shrewd; **7** bookish, intense; **8** deep laid, deep-read, wakeless; **9** indelible, unplumbed, unsounded; **10** consummate, impressive, scholastic

profoundly: 6 deeply, subtly; **7** acutely

profundity: 5 depth; **7** caliber; **8** deepness, solidity, subtlety; **10** abstrusity, astuteness

profuse: 4 lush; **5** wordy; **6** lavish, wanton; **7** copious, diffuse, lengthy, replete, riotous, verbose; **8** overmuch, prodigal, wasteful; **9** expansive, exuberant, luxuriant, unthrifty; **10** dissipated, inordinate, long-winded, pleonastic, profligate, thriftless; **11** extravagant, improvident

profusely: 9 copiously; **10** abundantly; **13** extravagantly

progenitor: 7 genitor; **10** procreator

progeny: 4 seed, spat; **5** breed, brood, heirs, issue, spawn; **6** farrow, litter; **9** offspring, posterity

prognosis: 8 forecast, prospect; **10** prediction; **11** foretelling; **12** announcement

prognosticate: 4 bode, call, omen; **5** augur; **7** betoken, portend, predict, presage, promise; **8** forebode, forecast, foretell; **9** auspicate, prefigure; **10** anticipate, foreshadow

prognostication: 8 forecast, prophecy; **9** prognosis; **10** prediction; **11** foretelling

program: 4 plan; **8** platform, software, syllabus; **9** broadcast, party line, programme; **10** curriculum; **13** course of study; **14** television show; **15** computer program;

P

16 computer software, political program; **17** computer programme, political platform, television program

program line: 7 command; 9 statement; 11 instruction

program listing: 4 code; 7 listing

programmer: 16 software engineer

programming: 10 scheduling

programming error: 3 bug

progress: 4 flux, go on; 5 build, get on, lapse; 6 come on, growth, move on, pass on, work up; 7 advance, build up, headway, march on, proceed, shape up; 8 get along; 9 advancing, come along; 10 going ahead, proceeding; 11 advancement, progressing, progression

progressing: 5 afoot; 7 going on, ongoing, running; 8 progress, under way; 9 advancing, happening; 10 going ahead, in progress, proceeding; 11 coming ahead, moving ahead, progression

progression: 5 chain, round, suite, train; 7 advance; 8 progress; 9 advancing, gradation; 10 going ahead, proceeding; 11 advancement

progressive: 7 gradual, liberal; 9 bettering, imperfect, improving, reformist

Progressive Party: 11 Bull Moose

progressivism: 10 liberalism

prohibit: 3 ban, bar; 4 veto; 5 taboo; 6 enjoin, forbid, outlaw; 8 disallow, forefend; 9 interdict, proscribe

prohibited: 3 out; 4 tabu; 5 taboo; 6 banned, barred; 7 tabooed; 8 enjoined, outlawed; 9 forbidden; 10 disallowed

prohibition: 3 ban; 10 inhibition, preclusion; 12 disallowance, interdiction, proscription; 14 prohibition era

prohibitionist: 3 dry

project: 3 see; 4 cast, hurl, plan, pout, task; 5 bulge, chore, fancy, image, labor, paper, theme, throw; 6 design, figure, jut out, scheme, sketch; 7 picture, poke out, propose, send off; 8 contrive, envision, forecast, protrude, stand out, stick out; 9 term paper, visualize; 10 enterprise, projection; 11 be prominent, externalize, extrapolate, undertaking

projectile: 4 shot; 7 missile; 10 propulsive; 11 projectiles [pl]

projecting: 6 raised; 7 jutting; 8 beetling, in relief, repousse, sticking; 9 projected; 10 jutting out, protruding

projection: 3 jut; 7 hurling, jutting, profile, project; 8 ejection, throwing; 9 expulsion; 10 forcing out, prominence, protrusion; 12 protuberance; 13 extrapolation

projector: 6 artist; 8 designer, promoter

prolate: 4 oval; 5 ovate, ovoid, utter; 7 breathe, oviform; 8 elliptic, vocalize; 9 egg-shaped

proletarian: 5 prole; 6 worker

prolific: 6 fecund; 7 fertile

prolix: 5 windy; 7 prosing, spun out; 10 long-winded, maundering, protracted

prolixity: 9 verbosity, wordiness

prolocutor: 6 reader; 8 lecturer; 9 professor; 12 interlocutor

prologue: 5 proem; 6 prefix; 7 preface, prelude; 8 foreword, preamble; 12 introduction

prolong: 6 extend, keep up, let out; 7 draw out, sustain; 8 protract

prolonged: 7 lengthy, spun out; 8 drawn out, drawn-out, extended; 9 elongated, lingering, sustained

prom: 9 promenade

promenade: 3 jog; 4 mall, prom, trot, turn; 5 amble, stalk, tramp, troop; 6 canter, parade, ramble, review, stroll; 7 saunter; 9 march past; 10 procession

promethium: 2 Pm

prominence: 3 jut; 4 bump, hump, mark; 5 bulge; 6 import, moment; 9 extrusion, gibbosity; 10 importance, projection, protrusion; 11 consequence, excrescence, gibbousness, materiality, weightiness; 12 materialness, protuberance, significance

prominent: 3 big; 4 bold; 5 clear, large; 6 signal; 7 eminent, notable, salient; 8 apparent, manifest, striking; 11 outstanding, spectacular

prominently: 3 yea; 4 even; 6 openly; 7 awfully, clearly, notably, plainly, the most; 8 above all, famously; 9 a fortiori, amazingly, eminently, extremely, glaringly, saliently, still more, strangely, supremely; 10 especially, incredibly, manifestly, materially, peculiarly, surpassing, to crown all; 11 egregiously, exceedingly, marvelously, principally, wonderfully; 12 emphatically, particularly, preeminently, stupendously, surpassingly, surprisingly, tremendously

promiscuous: 4 easy; 5 light, loose; 6 random, wanton; 8 sluttish; 13 miscellaneous; 14 indiscriminate

promiscuously: 8 wantonly

promise: 4 call, hope, word; 6 assure, look up, pledge; 7 bid fair, flatter, predict; 8 forebode, foretell; 10 anticipate

promised: 7 pledged

promised land: 4 eden; 6 heaven; 7 nirvana; 8 paradise; 9 Shangri-la

promising: 6 bright; 8 pledging; 10 propitious

promissory note: 3 IOU

promontory: 8 foreland, headland

promote: 4 push; 5 boost, raise; 6 prefer; 7 advance, elevate, enhance, forward, further, upgrade; 9 advertize, cultivate, encourage

promoter: 7 booster, plugger, showman; 8 designer; 9 projector; 10 impresario
promoting: 8 advocacy; 9 promotion
promotion: 6 step up; 8 advocacy; 9 elevation, promoting, publicity; 10 forwarding, preferment; 11 advancement, furtherance
prompt: 3 cue; 4 move, spry; 5 quick; 6 call up, in time, incite, on time, propel, remind, timely; 7 inspire, instant, put up to, suggest; 8 advocate, motivate, punctual; 9 encourage, give a clue, immediate, instigate, prescribe, recommend
prompter: 7 adviser, advisor, autocue, call boy; 8 agitator; 9 firebrand; 10 incendiary, instigator; 12 teleprompter
prompting: 7 dictate, hinting; 8 instance; 9 reminding; 10 suggestion
promptly: 5 quick; 6 pronto; 7 quickly
promptness: 8 alacrity, despatch, dispatch; 10 expedition; 11 promptitude, punctuality
promulgate: 7 exclaim; 8 proclaim; 9 circulate, propagate
prone: 6 supine; 7 tending; 8 couchant, inclined; 9 prostrate; 11 predisposed
proneness: 4 bent, bias; 7 leaning; 8 tendency; 10 affections, proclivity, propensity; 11 disposition, inclination; 14 predisposition
prong: 4 fork
prongbuck: 8 antelope; 9 pronghorn
pronged: 5 tined; 6 forked, prongy; 8 biramous, branched; 9 bifurcate
pronghorn antelope: 9 prongbuck
pronounce: 3 say, try; 4 rule; 5 judge, label, mouth, utter; 6 allege, broach, decide; 7 advance, deliver, enounce, hold out, propose; 8 announce, aspirate, propound, set forth; 9 enunciate; 10 accentuate, articulate
pronounced: 6 marked, spoken; 7 evident, obvious, uttered; 8 palpable, striking; 11 articulated, indubitable, self-evident; 12 unmistakable
pronouncing: 6 saying; 8 uttering; 10 announcing; 12 articulating
pronto: 8 promptly; 12 without delay
pronunciation: 12 articulation
proof: 4 copy, dull, pull; 6 gritty, obtuse, revise; 7 proving; 8 test copy; 9 probation, proofread; 10 impression, validating, validation; 12 verification
proofread: 5 proof
propagandize: 12 indoctrinate
propagate: 6 repeat, spread; 7 diffuse; 8 disperse, multiply; 9 broadcast, circulate, procreate, reproduce; 10 distribute, pass around, promulgate
propagation: 7 genesis; 9 extension; 10 gemination, generation
propanol: 13 propyl alcohol
propanone: 7 acetone
propel: 4 move; 5 impel; 6 incite, prompt; 8 motivate

propeller: 9 propellor
propeller plane: 7 prop-jet
propelling: 10 propellant, propellent, propulsive
propend: 4 mind; 6 lean to; 7 incline; 10 be disposed, be inclined
propensity: 4 bent, bias; 7 aptness, leaning; 8 tendency; 9 proneness; 10 affections, proclivity; 11 disposition, inclination
proper: 3 due, fit; 4 good, meet; 5 party, right; 6 seemly; 7 certain, correct, en regle, fitting, partial, private, several, special, upright; 8 becoming, decorous, definite, eligible, especial, original, peculiar, specific, suitable; 9 befitting, exclusive; 10 individual, particular, respective; 11 appropriate
properly: 5 right; 6 decent; 7 rightly; 8 by rights, decently; 9 correctly, fittingly
proper name: 10 proper noun
properness: 9 propriety; 12 correctitude
property: 4 land, prop; 5 acres, chose [Law], lands, place, trait; 6 aspect, realty, virtue; 7 ability, faculty, feature, holding, quality; 9 attribute, dimension, endowment, tenements; 10 belongings, possession, real estate
property owner: 9 landowner; 10 landholder
property tax: 7 land tax
prophecy: 10 divination
prophesy: 6 divine, preach; 8 foreshow, soothsay; 10 vaticinate
prophet: 4 seer; 5 augur; 6 oracle, priest; 10 high priest, prophesier, soothsayer
prophetic: 6 sacred; 8 biblical; 10 predictive, scriptural; 11 prophetical
prophylactic: 4 safe; 6 condom, rubber, safety; 10 cautionary, immunizing, preventive; 12 preventative; 13 antifertility, contraceptive
propitiate: 4 fast; 5 flirt; 6 disarm; 7 appease, beguile, placate, win over; 9 makepeace, reconcile; 10 conciliate
propitiated: 10 reconciled; 11 conciliated
propitious: 4 ripe; 5 happy, lucky; 8 amicable, friendly; 9 favorable, fortunate, promising; 10 auspicious
prop man: 9 costumier; 11 property man
proponent: 8 advocate, exponent
proportion: 4 mess; 5 quota, ratio; 7 balance, modicum; 8 quotient, symmetry; 9 dimension; 10 dimensions
proportions: 10 dimensions, proportion
proposal: 4 hint, mind, view; 5 offer; 6 animus; 7 proffer, purview; 8 overture; 10 suggestion; 11 proposition; 12 presentation; 13 contemplation, marriage offer
propose: 3 aim; 5 offer; 6 advise, allege, broach; 7 advance, hold out, present, prof-

P

fer, project, purport, purpose, suggest; **8** nominate, propound, set forth; **9** enunciate, pronounce

proposition: 5 axiom, offer; **7** proffer, theorem; **8** overture, position, proposal; **9** condition; **10** suggestion; **12** presentation

propranolol: 7 Inderal

proprietor: 5 owner

proprietorship: 9 ownership; **11** proprietary

propriety: 4 form; **7** decorum, fitness, probity; **8** good form, meetness; **9** etiquette, formality, gentility, integrity, principle

prop up: 4 prop; **7** shore up

propyl alcohol: 8 propanol

prosaic: 3 dry; **4** cold, dull; **5** bland, prosy; **7** humdrum, languid, prosing; **8** lukewarm; **9** colorless, pointless, proposing, unadorned; **10** earthbound, pedestrian; **11** commonplace, unglamorous

proscenium: 5 facia [Lat]; **6** facade; **9** forestage; **12** frontispiece

proscribe: 3 ban, bar; **4** veto; **5** taboo; **6** enjoin, forbid, outlaw; **7** attaint; **8** denounce, disallow, forefend, prohibit; **9** fulminate, interdict; **10** confiscate

prose: 3 jaw; **5** clack, prate; **6** jabber; **7** chatter, maunder, palaver, prattle; **9** prattle on; **12** matter of fact; **13** take au serieux [Fr]; **15** be caught napping

prosecution: 5 quest; **7** pursuit; **8** pursuing; **9** pursuance; **12** criminal suit

proselyte: 7 apostle; **8** deserter, disciple, follower, renegade; **10** backslider, recidivist

prosing: 5 prosy; **6** prolix; **7** prosaic, spun out; **9** pointless; **10** maundering, pedestrian, protracted; **11** commonplace

prosody: 10 inflection

Prosopium: 9 whitefish; **14** genus Prosopium

prospect: 4 view; **5** scene, vista; **6** aspect; **7** chances, horizon, outlook; **8** good view, panorama; **9** candidate, prognosis, prospects [pl]; **11** distant view, expectation, perspective

prospectively: 5 later; **9** hereafter; **11** in the future

prospects: 7 chances; **8** prospect

prospectus: 8 syllabus; **10** conspectus

prosper: 4 boom; **6** expand, thrive; **8** flourish

prospering: 7 booming, roaring; **8** thriving; **10** prosperous; **11** flourishing

prosperity: 7 welfare; **9** well-being

prosperous: 4 easy; **5** lucky, palmy; **6** golden; **7** booming, halcyon, roaring, well-off; **8** thriving, well-to-do; **9** favorable, well-fixed; **10** auspicious, favourable, prospering, well-heeled; **11** comfortable, encouraging, flourishing

prostrate: 3 irk; **4** damp, dash, dull, fell, flag, flat, jade, lame, maim, sink, tire; **5**

floor, level, lower, prone, spent, unman, upset, weary; **6** deject, muzzle, supine; **7** bow down, cripple, exhaust, fatigue, subvert, wear out; **8** couchant, double up, in danger, paralyze; **9** exhausted

prosy: 3 dry; **4** cold, dull; **5** bland; **6** frigid, trashy; **7** languid, prosaic, prosing; **8** lukewarm; **9** colorless, pointless, proposing; **10** earthbound, pedestrian; **11** commonplace

protactinium: 2 Pa; **13** protoactinium

protagonist: 6 backer, friend; **7** abettor, admirer, booster; **8** advocate, champion, partisan, seconder, upholder; **9** supporter

pro tanto: 7 thus far; **8** inasmuch; **9** by degrees, gradually

protease: 9 peptidase; **10** proteinase

protect: 4 fend; **5** guard; **6** defend, shield; **7** forfend

protected: 5 saved; **6** secure; **7** guarded; **8** shielded

protection: 5 aegis; **7** defense, shelter, tribute; **8** auspices, guarding, monopoly, security; **9** defending, patronage, shielding; **10** limitation, protecting; **11** restriction

protective: 6 caring; **10** protecting

protective goggles: 13 safety glasses, safety goggles

protector: 8 defender, governor, guardian

protege: 4 ward

proteinase: 8 protease; **9** peptidase

pro tempore: 6 pro tem

protest: 5 cavil; **6** resist; **7** discard, dissent, nullify; **8** demurral, disclaim, dishonor; **9** cavilling, deprecate, mediation, objection, recusancy, repudiate; **10** abnegation, disclaimer; **11** deprecation, expostulate, remonstrate; **12** intercession, protestation

Protestant: 16 Protestant Church

protest demonstration: 5 rally; **12** protest rally; **13** demonstration

protester: 8 objector; **9** dissenter, dissident; **10** contestant; **12** demonstrator

protoactinium: 2 Pa; **12** protactinium

protocol: 2 MO; **3** way; **4** mode, wise; **5** means; **6** manner, method; **7** fashion, process; **9** mechanism, procedure, technique

protomammal: 9 therapsid

protoplasm: 9 cytoplasm

protoplast: 6 module; **7** energid

prototype: 4 type; **5** ideal, image, model; **7** epitome, example, pattern; **8** exemplar, original, paradigm, standard; **9** precedent, reference, scantling

protozoa: 9 protozoan

protract: 6 extend, ramble; **7** digress, draw out, produce, prolong

protracted: 6 prolix; **7** lengthy, prosing, spun out; **8** drawn out, drawn-out, extended; **9** lingering, prolonged, sustained

protrude: 3 pop; **4** pout; **5** bulge, pouch; **6** bug out, jut out, pop out; **7** come out, poke out, project; **8** bulge out, stand out, stick out

protruding: **6** raised; **7** jutting; **8** in relief, repousse, sticking; **9** projected

protrusion: **3** jut; **4** bump, hump; **5** bulge; **7** jutting; **9** extrusion, gibbosity; **10** projection, prominence

proud: **5** grand, lofty, noble; **6** august, lordly; **7** gallant, stately; **8** majestic, princely; **9** dignified, honorable; **10** worshipful

Proust: **12** Marcel Proust

provable: **12** demonstrable

prove: **3** try; **4** rise, shew, show, test; **5** essay, raise, taste, touch; **6** draw on, leaven, try out, verify; **7** confirm, examine, testify, turn out; **8** evidence; **9** establish

proven: **5** shown; **6** proved; **8** verified; **11** established; **12** demonstrated; **13** substantiated

provender: **4** feed, food, grub; **6** fodder, viands; **7** aliment, edibles, ingesta, pabulum; **8** eatables, victuals; **9** nutriment; **10** animal food, provisions, sustenance

proverb: **3** saw; **5** adage; **6** byword, dictum, old saw, saying

proverbial: **6** gnomic; **10** aphoristic

provide: **3** ply; **5** cater, offer, put up; **6** render, supply; **7** furnish

Providence: **20** capital of Rhode Island

providential: **4** ripe; **5** happy, lucky; **6** divine; **9** favorable, fortunate

provider: **8** supplier

providing: **6** supply; **9** provision, supplying; **10** providence

province: **3** orb; **4** area, soil; **5** field, realm, state; **6** circle, colony, domain, ground, sphere; **7** circuit, lookout, mandate; **8** dominion; **9** territory; **10** department, provincial; **14** responsibility

provincial: **5** local, rural; **6** rustic; **7** bucolic, peasant; **8** province, regional; **9** parochial; **11** countrified, territorial

proving: **5** proof; **7** showing; **10** validating, validation; **12** demonstrable; **13** demonstrating, demonstrative

provision: **5** cater; **6** forage, purvey, ration, supply; **7** proviso, rations, victual; **8** planning; **9** condition, providing, supplying; **10** livelihood, providence, provisions; **11** contingency, maintenance, preparation, stipulation, supplygrist; **12** prerequisite

provisional: **5** given; **6** fenced; **7** guarded; **8** hedged in, inchoate; **9** probative, provisory, tentative; **11** conditional

provisions: **6** ration, stores, viands; **7** clauses, rations; **8** supplies, victuals

proviso: **9** condition, provision; **10** sine qua non [Lat]; **11** contingency, stipulation; **12** prerequisite

provitamin A: **7** carotin; **8** carotene

provocation: **4** dram, goad, spur, whet, whip; **6** fillip; **7** affront, galling, offense; **8** annoy-

ing, stimulus, stinging; **9** galvanism, heavy news, incentive, infection; **10** incitement, irritation, mortifying, stirring up; **11** aggravating, aggravation

provocative: **8** exciting; **9** provoking; **12** inflammatory

provoke: **4** fire, fret, gall, rile; **5** beset, chafe, chevy, chivy, evoke, harry, pique, raise, set on, sting, tease; **6** arouse, chevvy, chivvy, elicit, enrage, entail, foment, harass, hassle, incite, induce

provoking: **7** galling; **8** annoying, stinging; **9** agitating, agitative, insulting; **10** irritating, mortifying; **11** aggravating, provocative; **12** inflammatory

provost: **6** archon, warden; **10** lieutenant

prow: **3** bow, jib; **4** fore, stem

prowess: **3** art; **7** heroism; **8** artistry

prowl: **4** lurk, roam, rove; **5** lurch, range, skulk, slink, sneak; **6** patrol

prowl car: **7** cruiser; **8** squad car; **9** patrol car, police car

prowler: **5** sneak, thief; **7** burglar

proximity: **7** contact; **10** apposition, contiguity

proxy: **6** deputy; **8** delegate; **9** secondary, surrogate; **10** procurator, substitute

Prozac: **10** fluoxetine

prude: **4** prig; **7** puritan

prudence: **4** heed, tact; **7** caution; **8** coolness; **10** discretion, steadiness; **11** calculation, heedfulness; **12** cautiousness, deliberation, discreetness

prudent: **7** politic; **8** discreet, stealthy; **11** circumspect

prudery: **7** coyness; **8** coquetry, primness

prudish: **4** prim, smug; **6** demure, prissy; **8** priggish; **9** quakerish, victorian; **10** squaretoed, tight-laced; **11** pragmatical, puritanical, straitlaced

prune: **3** cut, lop, mow; **4** clip, crop, dock, reap, snip, thin, trim; **5** dress, shave, shear; **8** decimate; **9** lop and top; **11** rationalize

pruned: **7** clipped; **9** truncated; **12** shortenedcut

pruning hook: **6** pruner

Prunus: **4** plum; **5** peach; **6** almond, cherry; **7** apricot; **9** nectarine; **11** sweet almond; **11** genus Prunus, chokecherry

prurience: **4** lust; **8** cupidity; **9** cacoethes [Lat], carnality, pruriency; **13** concupiscence; **14** lasciviousness

prurient: **5** lusty; **6** carnal, erotic; **7** lustful, rampant, rutting, ruttish; **9** salacious; **10** libidinous

pruritis: **7** itching

Prussia: **8** Preussen

Prussic acid: **7** cyanide

pry: **4** nose, peep, peer, poke, scan; **5** jimmy, lever, prise, prize, sound; **6** browse, pry

P

bar; **7** crowbar, explore, ransack, rummage; **9** look round, take a peep; **11** reconnoiter, wrecking bar

prying: 4 nosy; **5** nosey; **6** snoopy; **7** peering; **8** nosiness; **10** snoopiness

PS: 10 post script, postscript; **12** afterthought

psalm: 8 psalmody

Psalter: 12 Book of Psalms

Psetta: 6 turbot; **11** genus Psetta

pseud: 4 fake, sham; **5** faker, fraud; **6** pseudo; **8** imposter, impostor; **9** pretender

pseudo: 4 fake, mock, sham; **5** bogus, faker, fraud, pseud; **8** imposter, impostor, so-called, spurious; **9** pretended, pretender; **10** fraudulent, role player, simulating; **11** counterfeit, make-believe

pseudonym: 6 anonym; **10** pseudonymy; **11** nom de guerre

pseudoscience: 9 mysticism

Psidium: 5 guava; **12** genus Psidium

psilocybin: 8 psilocin

PST: 11 Pacific Time; **19** Pacific Standard Time

psyche: 4 head, mind, nous, soul; **5** brain

psychedelic drug: 12 hallucinogen

psychiatric hospital: 6 asylum

psychiatrist: 6 shrink; **12** head shrinker, head-shrinker

psychic phenomena: 14 parapsychology

psycho: 9 psychotic

psychoanalysis: 8 analysis

psychoanalyst: 7 analyst

psychokinesis: 11 telekinesis

psychological medicine: 10 psychiatry

psychological science: 10 psychology

psychopath: 9 sociopath

psychotherapeutic: 9 cathartic

psychotic: 6 psycho

psychotic belief: 8 delusion

psychotic person: 6 psycho; **9** psychotic

psych up: 6 hype up

Pt: 8 platinum

PT boat: 11 torpedo boat; **12** mosquito boat

pteroylglutamic acid: 6 folate; **7** folacin; **8** vitamin M; **9** folic acid

PTFE: 6 Teflon, teflon

Ptolemy: 18 Claudius Ptolemaeus

ptomaine: 7 ptomain; **13** food poisoning

ptyalize: 4 spew, spit, spue

Pu: 9 plutonium

pub: 3 bar; **6** saloon, tavern; **7** bar room, gin mill; **8** mug house, pot house, pothouse, taphouse

pub-crawl: 6 bar hop

puberty: 10 pubescence

pubescence: 7 puberty; **11** adolescence

public: 3 out; **4** open; **5** civic, human, world; **6** mortal, social; **8** everyone, national, personal, populace; **9** community, everybody

public address system: 2 PA; **8** PA system

publication: 5 issue; **8** circular, pamphlet; **10** authorship, publishing

public eye: 9 limelight, spotlight

public house: 3 bar, pub; **6** saloon, tavern

public image: 5 image; **7** persona

publicise: 3 air; **4** bare; **9** publicize

publicity: 9 promotion

publicity man: 5 PR man; **10** press agent

publicize: 3 air; **4** bare; **9** advertise, advertize, publicise

publicly: 6 openly; **8** in public; **9** in the open

public official: 9 incumbent; **13** public servant

public opinion: 7 opinion; **9** vox populi

public opinion poll: 4 poll; **7** canvass

public park: 8 city park; **9** state park; **10** county park; **12** national park; **14** national forest

public-service corporation: 7 utility

public space: 7 commons

public speaker: 6 orator; **11** rhetorician, speechmaker

public square: 5 agora, forum; **6** square

public telephone: 8 pay phone; **12** pay telephone

publish: 5 issue, print, write; **6** put out; **7** release

published: 7 in print

publishing company: 9 publisher; **14** publishing firm; **15** publishing house

puce: 5 lilac, mauve; **8** lavender; **11** plum-colored

puck: 10 hockey puck

Puck: 15 Robin Goodfellow

pucker: 3 ire, pet; **4** bile, draw, fume, knit, ruck, tiff, tuck; **6** choler, cockle, dander, gather, ruck up, rumple, taking; **7** crumple

puckish: 6 impish, joking; **7** implike, kidding; **8** prankish; **9** pixilated; **11** mischievous

pudden-head: 4 dolt; **6** stupid; **7** dullard; **8** poor fish; **11** pudding head; **12** stupid person

puddle: 4 pool

pudginess: 9 tubbiness; **10** chubbiness; **12** rolypoliness

pudgy: 5 dumpy, podgy, tubby

puerile: 5 anile; **6** jejune; **8** childish, juvenile; **10** adolescent

puerility: 8 babyhood; **9** childhood; **10** simplicity; **12** childishness

Puerto Rico: 9 Porto Rico

puff: 4 blow, drag, draw, drop, gasp, huff, pant, pull; **5** chuff, crack, cry up, extol, faint, heave, quilt, swoon, vapor, vaunt, whiff, widen; **6** blow up, expand, extend

puffed: 4 puff; **5** puffy, tumid; **7** bloated, swollen; **9** distended, tumescent

puffer: 8 blowfish

puffiness: 4 lump; **7** puffing; **8** swelling

puff of air: 4 puff; **5** whiff

puff paste: 13 pate feuillete

puffy: 5 tumid; 6 blowzy, puffed; 7 bloated, huffing, puffing, swollen; 8 bouffant; 9 distended, edematous, tumescent

pug: 6 pug-dog, stumpy; 8 thickset

pugilism: 6 boxing; 10 fisticuffs

pugilist: 5 boxer; 7 athlete, bruiser; 9 gladiator; 12 prize fighter

Puglia: 6 Apulia

pugnacious: 5 rough; 9 bellicose, combative; 10 hard-bitten, hard-boiled

puissance: 5 force, might; 6 energy

puissant: 4 hard; 5 hardy, stout, valid; 6 mighty, potent, robust, strong, sturdy; 8 forcible, powerful, vigorous; 10 adamantine

puke: 5 heave, retch, vomit; 6 be sick; 8 disgorge; 11 regurgitate

pulchritude: 4 form; 5 grace; 8 elegance

pule: 3 yap; 4 mewl, pipe, wail; 5 whine; 6 snivel, squall, squeak, squeal; 7 grizzle, whimper; 9 caterwaul

pull: 3 lug, ply, rip, tow, tug; 4 copy, drag, draw, haul, puff, punt, rake, rend, rive, tear; 5 drive, fetch, force, pluck, proof, scull, trail, train, twist; 6 commit, draw in, effect, get out, pull in, revise, strain, wrench; 7 attract, deplume, draught, drawing, pull out, pulling, take out; 8 displume, traction; 9 deplumate, influence; 10 impression, perpetrate; 11 overstretch

pullet: 5 frier, fryer; 7 chicken; 8 nestling

pulley: 5 block; 11 pulley-block

pulling: 4 haul, pull; 7 draught, drawing; 8 traction

Pullman car: 7 Pullman, sleeper; 8 wagon-lit; 11 sleeping car

Pullman porter: 6 porter, redcap

pull off: 5 pluck, tweak; 6 detach, manage; 7 draw off, peel off, pick off, tear off; 8 bring off, carry off, draw away

pullout: 8 fallback; 13 disengagement

pullover: 8 slipover; 10 turtleneck

pull the leg of: 3 kid

pull through: 4 save; 6 make it; 7 survive

pull together: 6 garner, gather; 7 collect, collude, concert, consort; 8 conspire; 10 fraternize; 11 confederate

pulmonary: 8 pulmonic; 9 pneumonic

pulmonary tuberculosis: 8 phthisis; 11 consumption

pulp: 3 pap; 4 curd; 5 dough, flesh, nerve; 7 pudding; 12 pulp magazine

pulpit: 4 ambo, dais; 5 stump; 6 podium; 7 lectern, rostrum, soapbox

pulsate: 4 beat; 5 pulse, throb; 9 palpitate

pulsating: 7 beating, pulsing

pulse: 4 beat; 5 throb; 6 legume; 7 impulse, pulsate, pulsing; 9 breathing, heart rate, heartbeat, pulsation

pulsing: 5 pulse; 7 beating, impulse; 9 pulsating, pulsation

pulverization: 4 mill; 5 grind

pulverize: 6 powder; 9 comminute, granulate, powderize, triturate

pulverized: 7 powdery; 8 powdered; 11 fine-grained; 12 small-grained

puma: 6 cougar; 7 panther; 9 catamount; 12 mountain lion

pumice stone: 6 pumice

pummel: 4 biff, drub; 5 baste; 6 pommel; 7 belabor, leather, sandbag, trounce

pummeling: 7 beating; 9 thrashing, threshing; 12 flagellation

pummelo: 6 pomelo; 8 shaddock

pump: 4 boot; 5 heart, pumps; 6 sandal, ticker; 7 slipper

pumped up: 5 wired; 8 pumped-up

pumper: 6 bucket; 9 fire truck

pumpernickel: 10 black bread

pun: 5 rhyme; 7 punning; 8 wordplay; 11 paronomasia

punch: 3 hit; 4 barb, biff, hack, kick, lick, pelt, plug, poke; 9 perforate

Punch and Judy: 11 marionettes

punch bowl: 4 bowl; 5 basin; 7 pitcher

punch-drunk: 5 silly; 9 slaphappy

puncheon: 3 keg; 4 cask, drum; 5 punch; 6 barrel; 7 puncher

puncher: 5 punch; 6 cowboy, cowman; 7 cowhand, cowherd, cowpoke; 8 puncheon; 9 cattleman; 10 cowpuncher

punch in: 7 clock in, clock on

punch line: 7 gag line, tag line; 9 laugh line

punch out: 5 punch; 8 clock off, clock out

punctilio: 4 form; 6 nicety; 7 decorum; 8 delicacy, good form; 9 etiquette, formality, gentility, propriety

punctual: 6 in time, on time, prompt, steady, timely

punctuality: 10 promptness; 13 immediateness

punctually: 4 duly; 6 on time; 7 exactly; 9 precisely

punctuate: 4 mark; 6 accent, stress; 9 emphasize; 10 accentuate

puncture: 5 lance, wound; 6 pierce, riddle; 7 deflate; 9 penetrate, perforate; 10 puncturing; 11 penetration, perforation

punctured: 7 pierced; 9 perforate; 10 perforated

pundit: 6 jurist, savant; 8 advocate, civilian, initiate; 9 publicist

pungency: 4 bite, race; 5 twang; 8 acridity, piquance, piquancy; 9 pithiness, poignance, sharpness, spiciness; 11 pointedness

pungent: 4 racy; 5 pithy; 6 barbed, biting, strong; 7 caustic, nipping, piquant, pointed; 8 poignant, redolent

Punic: 12 Carthaginian

punic: 10 perfidious; 11 treacherous

P

Punica fides: 8 bad faith; **9** mala fides [Lat]; **10** Punic faith

puniness: 9 runtiness; **11** stuntedness

punish: 8 penalize

punishable: 5 penal

punishing: 4 hard; **5** heavy, penal; **7** arduous; **8** grueling, punitive, toilsome; **9** gruelling, laborious; **10** chastening, labourious, punishment; **12** backbreaking, chastisement

punishment: 7 penalty; **9** punishing; **10** chastening; **12** chastisement, penalization

punitive: 5 penal; **8** punitory; **9** punishing

punk: 3 bum; **4** goon, hood, thug; **5** cheap, spunk, tinny, tough; **6** cheesy, crummy, sleazy, smudge [U.S.], tinder; **7** chintzy, hoodlum, toughie; **8** kindling, punk rock

punkie: 5 punky; **6** punkey; **7** no-see-um; **11** biting midge

punning: 3 pun; **8** wordplay

punt: 3 cog; **4** back, gage, game, pole, pull; **5** bet on, pound, scull, shell, stake; **6** wherry; **7** punting

punter: 6 better, bettor, kicker; **7** wagerer

puny: 3 wee; **4** tiny; **5** petit, petty, runty; **6** petite; **7** shrimpy; **8** exiguous; **9** miniature

pup: 5 puppy, whelp

pupil: 4 iris; **7** learner, scholar, student; **8** educatee; **11** schoolchild

puppet: 4 doll, dupe, tool; **6** stooge

puppet play: 10 puppet show

puppy: 3 pup

puppy love: 5 crush; **9** young love; **11** infatuation

purblind: 6 obtuse

purchasable: 5 venal; **7** for sale; **8** bribable; **9** dishonest; **11** corruptible

purchase: 3 buy; **4** play; **6** buying, leeway; **7** procure; **8** latitude, leverage

purchased: 6 bought

purchase money: 5 price

purchaser: 5 buyer; **6** emptor, vendee

purchasing: 6 buying

pure: 4 naif, neat; **5** attic, gross, naive, noble, sheer, sound, stark, utter; **6** arrant, chaste, decent, devout, humble, modest, native, simple, single, solemn, vestal, virgin; **7** artless, natural, perfect, sodding, staring, uniform, unmixed; **8** complete, decorous, delicate, of a piece, reverent, sterling, virginal, virtuous; **9** classical, guileless, saturated, stainless, undefiled, undiluted, unspoiled, untainted

pureblood: 8 pedigree, purebred

puree: 4 soup; **5** broth; **7** pottage

purely: 4 only; **6** merely, simply; **8** strictly; **9** decidedly, downright, radically, seriously; **10** absolutely; **11** essentially

purgative: 5 physic; **8** aperient, evacuant, laxative; **9** cathartic

purgatory: 5 abyss, limbo; **7** gehenna

purge: 4 rack; **6** ransom, redeem, refine, repair, shrive; **7** absolve, clarify, purging, reclaim; **8** clean out

purified: 7 refined; **9** sublimate

purify: 5 clear; **7** distill; **8** defecate, make pure, sanctify; **9** sublimate

puritan: 4 blue, prig; **5** prude, saint [ironically]; **7** devotee

puritanical: 4 blue, prim, smug; **6** demure, prissy; **7** ascetic, austere, prudish, puritan; **8** priggish; **9** victorian

puritanism: 9 austerity; **10** asceticism

purity: 5 grace, honor; **6** honour, polish; **7** euphony; **8** chastity, elegance, pureness; **9** innocence; **10** clean hands; **11** homogeneity, sinlessness; **12** gracefulness

purl: 4 eddy, flip, flow, lilt; **5** gurge, shake, spray, spurt, swirl, trill, whirl; **6** babble, bubble, gurgle, murmur, quaver, ripple; **7** breathe, sputter

purlieus: 7 suburbs; **8** confines, environs, vicinage; **9** outskirts; **10** borderland; **12** neighborhood

purloin: 3 bag; **4** hook, lift, prig; **5** filch, pinch, snarf, sneak, steal, swipe; **6** nobble, pilfer, thieve

purloined: 3 hot; **6** looted, stolen; **8** pilfered; **9** plundered

purple: 4 pall, toga; **5** regal, royal; **6** violet; **7** magenta; **8** empurple, imperial, majestic, purplish; **10** purpleness; **11** embellished, ultraviolet

purport: 3 aim; **5** drift, force; **6** import, intent, spirit; **7** content, meaning, message, propose, purpose

purported: 7 reputed; **8** putative, supposed

purpose: 3 aim, use; **4** mean, role; **6** design, ground, intend, intent, motive, reason; **7** propose, purport, resolve; **8** function; **9** intention, reason why; **10** motivation; **11** inspiration; **13** determination

purposefully: 8 by design; **9** advisedly, expressly, knowingly, on purpose, purposely, wittingly

purposeless: 7 aimless; **9** pointless, senseless

purposely: 9 advisedly, expressly, knowingly, on purpose, wittingly; **10** designedly

purpura: 8 peliosis

purr: 4 birr, whir, whiz; **5** whirr, whizz

purse: 3 bag; **7** handbag, wrinkle; **10** pocketbook

purslane family: 13 Portulacaceae

pursuance: 5 quest; **7** pursuit; **8** pursuing

pursue: 4 keep; **5** abide, act on; **6** engage, follow; **7** go after; **8** quest for; **9** prosecute

pursued: 6 chased

pursuer: 6 chaser

pursuit: 4 hunt; **5** chase, quest; **8** pursuing; **9** following, pursuance

pursy: 5 blown, puffy; **6** blowzy, winded; **7** gasping, panting; **9** distended, edematous; **11** short-winded

purulence: 3 pus; 5 ichor; 6 sanies; 9 festering, purulency; 11 suppuration

purulent: 6 putrid; 7 carious, peccant; 8 infected; 9 festering

purvey: 5 cater; 6 forage; 7 victual; 9 provision

purveyor: 6 feeder; 7 caterer; 9 victualer; 10 commissary; 13 quartermaster

purview: 4 mind, view; 6 animus; 7 horizon; 8 proposal; 13 contemplation

pus: 5 ichor; 6 matter, sanies, slough; 9 festering, purulence; 11 suppuration

Puseyism: 13 Tractarianism

push: 3 fix, jog, tug; 4 jolt, pass; 5 boost [U.S.], brunt, crowd, drive, fight, force, hitch, impel, labor, pinch, press, shove, throw, trial; 6 bear on, button, energy, labour, strait, thrust; 7 agitate, booming, crusade, nonplus, promote, pushing, squeeze; 8 campaign, exigency, juncture, pressure

push around: 5 bully; 6 hector; 7 dictate; 8 ballyrag, browbeat, bullyrag, domineer; 9 strong-arm; 10 boss around, intimidate

push back: 5 drive, repel; 7 repulse; 8 beat back, rollback

pushcart: 4 cart; 8 handcart

pushchair: 4 pram; 6 go-cart, pusher; 8 stroller; 9 baby buggy; 12 baby carriage, perambulator

pusher: 4 pram, zori; 6 go-cart; 7 peddler; 8 stroller, thruster; 9 baby buggy, pushchair; 10 drug dealer; 11 drug peddler; 12 baby carriage, perambulator

pushiness: 9 cockiness; 11 forwardness; 13 assertiveness, bumptiousness

pushing: 4 push; 5 pushy; 7 pushful; 8 meddling; 9 officious; 10 aggressive, meddlesome; 12 enterprising

pushover: 4 snap; 5 cinch; 6 picnic; 8 duck soup, walkover; 10 child's play; 11 piece of cake

pushpin: 9 thumbtack

push through: 5 erupt

pushy: 8 meddling; 9 assertive, officious; 10 aggressive, meddlesome; 12 enterprising

pussycat: 4 cat; 4 muff, puss; 5 kitty, pussy; 6 pet cat, feline; 8 kitty cat, old woman; 9 creampuff; 10 powder puff; 11 mollycoddle

pussyfoot: 5 creep, mouse, sneak, steal

pustule: 3 wen; 5 wheal; 6 papula [Med], papule

put: 3 lay, set; 5 block, frame, order, place, set up, stick, stock; 6 assign, commit, invest; 7 arrange, situate; 8 localize, position

put a stop to: 4 halt, stop

putative: 7 reputed; 8 academic, supposed; 9 purported, theorized; 10 accredited, gratuitous, supposable; 11 conjectural, presumptive, speculative, theoretical; 12 hypothesized, hypothetical

put down: 3 lay; 4 drop, land, snub; 5 enter, quash; 6 demean, record, repose, unload; 7 degrade; 8 browbeat, disgrace, suppress

put-on: 4 hoax; 5 fraud; 6 dupery; 11 fraudulence

put on airs: 6 affect

put out: 4 emit, pose; 5 douse, issue; 6 bother, dazzle, extend, get out, muddle, puzzle, retire; 7 blow out, confuse, fluster, hold out, mortify, perplex, publish, release, smother, trouble, turn out; 8 bewilder, snuff out, stamp out; 9 disoblige, embarrass, give forth, incommode

putrefaction: 3 rot; 7 rotting; 8 decaying; 10 corruption, putrefying; 11 putrescence; 13 decomposition

putrefied: 3 bad; 4 high, weak; 5 fusty; 6 effete, putrid, rancid, rotten; 7 corrupt, decayed, rotting, tainted, touched; 9 putrified

putrefy: 3 rot; 5 decay, go bad; 6 fester, rankle; 7 ferment

putrescent: 3 bad; 4 high, weak; 5 fusty; 6 effete, putrid, rancid, rotten; 7 corrupt, decayed, gone bad, rotting, tainted, touched; 9 putrefied

putrid: 3 bad; 4 foul, high, weak; 5 fetid, funky, fusty, pussy; 6 effete, foetid, rancid, rotten, smelly; 7 corrupt, decayed, gone bad, noisome, rotting, tainted, touched; 8 infected, purulent, stinking; 9 festering, putrefied, putrified; 10 putrescent

putsch: 4 coup; 8 takeover; 9 coup d'etat

put straight: 7 correct; 9 enlighten

putter: 6 dabble, monkey, potter, tinker

puttering: 8 dilatory, listless; 9 pottering; 11 half-hearted

put things off: 5 dally; 9 temporize; 13 procrastinate

putting: 4 putt; 7 placing; 8 locating, location; 11 positioning; 12 localization

putting iron: 6 putter

put to good use: 5 apply

put to sea: 7 set sail

puzzle: 3 get; 4 beat, pose; 5 amaze, rebus; 6 baffle, enigma, gravel, riddle; 7 charade, flummox, mystery, mystify, nonplus, perplex, puzzler, stupefy, stupify, trounce; 8 bewilder; 9 conundrum, dumbfound

puzzled: 8 confused; 9 nonplused, perplexed; 10 nonplussed

puzzling: 8 baffling; 9 confusing, enigmatic; 10 mystifying, perplexing; 11 enigmatical

pygmy: 5 dwarf

Pyongyang: 19 capital of North Korea

pyramid: 5 spire; 7 obelisk

Pyramids of Egypt: 12 Great Pyramid

pyre: 11 funeral pyre

pyrexia: 5 fever
pyridoxine: 7 adermin; **9** pyridoxal, vitamin B6; **12** pyridoxamine
pyrite: 9 fool's gold; **10** iron pyrite
pyrogenic: 7 igneous
pyrola: 11 wintergreen
Pyrolaceae: 17 wintergreen family
pyrolatry: 11 fire-worship
pyromaniac: 7 fire bug [U.S.]; **8** arsonist; **9** firebrand; **10** incendiary

Pyrophorus: 7 firefly; **10** fire beetle
pyrosis: 9 heartburn
pyrotechnics: 8 firework; **10** pyrotechny
pyrrhic: 7 dibrach
pyrrhonism: 10 scepticism, skepticism
pyrrhonist: 5 deist; **7** infidel; **11** misbeliever
Pyrus: 4 pear; **10** genus Pyrus
Pythonidae: 12 python family
Pythoninae: 6 python; **19** subfamily Pythoninae
pyx: 3 pax [Lat], pix; **5** chest; **6** coffer; **7** caisson

Q

Q.C.: 9 barrister
Qatar: 5 Katar
qintar: 8 qindarka
Quaalude: 12 methaqualone
quack: 9 charlatan
quad: 4 wynd [Scot]; **5** court, space, therm; **10** quadrangle, quadriceps, quadruplet; **17** quadriceps femoris; **25** musculus quadriceps femoris
quadrant: 10 right angle; **13** quarter-circle
quadrate: 6 square
quadriceps: 4 quad
quadrilateral: 9 four-sided
quadruped: 10 four-footed; **11** quadrupedal
quadruple: 8 fourfold
quadruplet: 2 IV; **4** four, quad; **7** quartet, quatern; **8** foursome; **9** quartette; **10** quadrature, quadrifoil, quadriform, quaternary, quaternion, quaternity
quaff: 4 gulp, swig
quaggy: 4 miry, soft; **5** boggy, mucky, muddy; **6** marshy, swampy; **7** sloughy
quagmire: 3 mud; **4** mire, muck, silt, sump, wash; **5** slosh, slush; **6** hobble, morass, scrape, slough, sludge; **8** alluvium
quahog: 4 clam; **7** quahaug; **9** round clam; **13** hard-shell clam
quail: 4 funk; **5** quake, wince; **6** cringe, flinch, quaver, quiver, recoil, shrink; **7** squinch; **8** bobwhite
quaint: 4 neat, tidy, trig, trim; **5** crisp, droll, natty, smart; **6** spruce; **7** old-time
quake: 4 reel, sway, toss; **5** quail, seism, shake; **6** quaver, quiver, shiver, starve, tremor, tumble, waggle, writhe; **7** shudder, shuffle, stagger, temblor, tremble, twitter, vibrate; **10** earthquake
Quaker: 6 Friend
quaking: 5 shaky; **7** fearing, shaking; **8** dreading; **9** quivering, shivering, trembling
qualification: 4 turn; **5** forte, parts; **6** set-off, talent, virtue; **7** ability, faculty, quality, talents; **8** capacity, drawback, felicity, poundage, property; **9** attribute, endowment; **10** capability
qualified: 7 capable, skilled; **8** skillful; **9** certified, competent, dependant, dependent, moderated; **10** conversant, proficient
qualify: 6 modify; **7** specify; **8** restrict; **9** condition, measure up, stipulate; **12** characterize
qualifying: 4 pass; **7** passing; **8** limiting; **12** modification
qualities: 5 trait; **9** character
quality: 4 fine, tone, type; **5** prime, prize, trait; **6** aspect, choice, nature, select, timber, timbre, virtue; **7** ability, caliber, calibre, faculty, feature; **8** property; **9** attribute, character, endowment
qualm: 5 demur; **6** demure, qualms [pl]; **7** scruple; **8** delicacy; **9** misgiving; **10** queasiness; **11** trepidation
qualms: 5 qualm; **9** misgiving; **11** trepidation
quandary: 3 fix; **4** pass, push; **5** hitch, pinch, trial; **6** plight, strait; **7** dilemma
quantify: 3 fix; **7** measure; **8** estimate; **9** determine, enumerate
quantitative: 3 any; **4** a few, some
quantity: 6 amount; **7** measure, quantum
quantum: 6 amount, photon, ration; **7** measure, wavicle; **8** quantity
quantum jump: 11 quantum leap
quantum sufficit: 2 Q.S.
quarantine: 9 isolation; **10** separation; **11** segregation
quarantined: 8 isolated
quarrel: 3 jar, row; **4** feud, spat, tiff; **5** clash, run-in, snarl, words; **6** argufy, dustup, jostle; **7** dispute, wrangle; **8** conflict, disagree, squabble; **9** altercate; **11** altercation
quarreling: 10 discordant; **11** conflicting, disagreeing

quarrelsome: 7 arguing; **11** contentious; **12** disputatious

quarry: 3 pit; **4** game, lode, mine, prey, vein; **6** target; **8** fair game, stone pit

quarryman: 8 quarrier

quarter: 3 lee; **4** four, poop, side, tail, zone; **5** flank, grace, lodge, mercy, stern; **6** billet, canton, fourth, parish, region, sector, square, tetrad; **7** quartet, section, shelter, two bits; **8** clemency, district, division, quartern; **9** one-fourth

quarterback: 12 field general, signal caller

quarter-circle: 8 quadrant

quartered: 6 housed, lodged; **8** billeted

quartermaster: 6 feeder; **7** caterer; **8** purveyor; **9** victualer; **10** commissary

quartern: 6 fourth; **7** quarter; **9** one-fourth; **10** fourth part

quarter note: 8 crotchet

quarters: 3 lap; **4** seat; **7** sojourn; **12** headquarters

quartet: 2 IV; **4** four; **6** square, tetrad; **7** quarter, quatern; **8** foursome; **9** quartette; **10** quadruplet, quaternary, quaternion, quaternity

quartette: 7 quartet; **8** foursome

quartz: 7 crystal

quash: 4 void; **5** annul, avoid; **6** ignore, reduce, subdue; **7** nullify, put down, repress; **8** suppress

quasi: 4 as if; **6** just as; **8** provided

quasi-stellar radio source: 6 quasar

quassia: 3 rue; **5** aloes; **10** bitterwood

quassia family: 13 Simaroubaceae

quaternary: 2 IV; **3** 4th; **4** four; **6** fourth, tetrad; **7** quartet, quatern; **8** foursome; **10** quadruplet, quaternate, quaternion, quaternity

quaver: 3 bob, jar, jog, wag; **4** jerk, jolt, lilt, purl, reel, sway, toss; **5** dance, quail, quake, shake, shock, trill, waver; **6** quiver, racket, shiver, tumble, waggle, warble, writhe; **7** clutter, shuffle, stagger, twitter, vibrate; **10** eighth note

quay: 4 dock, pier, port; **5** basin, jetty, wharf; **6** harbor; **10** embankment

queasy: 4 sick; **7** sickish; **9** nauseated, squeamish

queen: 7 majesty; **8** queen bee; **9** imperator [Lat]; **11** crowned head; **13** female monarch

Queen Anne's lace: 10 wild carrot

queer: 3 odd, rum; **4** bilk, foil; **5** cross, fishy, funny, peril, shady, spoil, weird; **6** baffle, expose; **7** bizarre, curious, suspect

quell: 3 lay; **4** calm, cool, damp, hush, lull, stay, swag, tame; **5** abate, allay, crash, quiet, smash, sober, still, trump, upset; **6** becalm, deaden, pacify, rebate, shiver, smooth, soothe, squash; **7** appease, assuage, compose, nonplus, shatter, silence, slacken, squelch; **8** suppress; **9**

alleviate, checkmate, stalemate; **11** tranquilize

quench: 4 calm, cloy, cool, damp, glut, pall; **5** allay, blunt, chill, gorge, quiet, slack, slake; **6** fill up; **7** assuage, satiate, smother, surfeit

quenched: 3 out; **6** slaked; **7** extinct, quelled; **9** satisfied, squelched; **12** extinguished

Quercus: 3 oak; **12** genus Quercus

querulous: 3 hot; **5** hasty, quick, whiny; **6** whiney; **7** bilious, fretful, peevish, peppery, waspish, whining

query: 7 enquiry, inquiry; **8** question

quest: 3 bay; **4** hunt; **7** bespeak, call for, pursuit, request, seeking; **8** pursuing; **9** pursuance

question: 4 head; **5** doubt, issue, query; **6** demand, motion, oppugn, wonder; **7** dispute, enquiry, inquiry, problem; **8** argument; **9** challenge, interview, moot point; **11** controversy, dubiousness, interrogate; **12** doubtfulness; **13** interrogation, interrogative

questionable: 8 fallible, slippery, ticklish; **9** debatable, refutable; **10** disputable, precarious

questioner: 5 asker; **8** enquirer, inquirer

questioning: 6 asking; **8** doubting; **9** inquiring, quizzical, sceptical, skeptical, wondering; **11** inquisitive, speculative; **13** interrogative

quetzal bird: 7 quetzal

queue: 4 rear, tail, wake; **5** trail, train; **6** line up

quibble: 5 quirk; **6** bicker, niggle; **7** anagram, brabble, fallacy, nitpick, pervert, twaddle; **8** pettifog, squabble, subtlety; **10** equivocate

quibbling: 7 carping; **8** caviling, trumpery, waffling; **9** frivolous, twaddling; **10** nitpicking; **11** extravagant; **12** fiddle-faddle, glossing over; **13** hairsplitting

quick: 3 apt, hot; **4** deft, fast, gain, spry, warm; **5** acute, agile, alive, awake, brief, brisk, handy, hasty, rapid, ready, sharp, smart, swift; **6** adroit, expert, flying, lively, nimble, prompt, speedy, strong; **7** bilious, cutting, instant, peevish, peppery, quickly, summary, waspish; **8** animated, captious, incisive, piercing, promptly, snappish; **9** dexterous, fractious, immediate

quicken: 4 lash, play, whet; **5** speed; **6** excite, foment, hasten, incite, kindle, revive, stir up, strain, strike, turn on, vivify; **7** animate, inflame, perform, sharpen, speed up, support, sustain; **8** expedite, maintain, recreate, revivify; **9** stimulate; **10** accelerate, invigorate

quicker: 6 faster

quickest: 7 fastest

quick fix: 6 quicky; **7** band aid

quick-freeze: 6 freeze; 10 deep-freeze; 11 flash-freeze

quick-frozen: 11 flash-frozen

quicklime: 4 calx, lime

quickly: 5 apace, aptly, quick; 6 deftly; 7 briefly, by and by, handily, rapidly, readily, shortly, swiftly; 8 adroitly, chop-chop, in a while, promptly, speedily; 9 cursorily, extempore, forthwith, summarily; 11 dexterously, immediately; 13 expeditiously

quick meal: 8 fast food

quicksilver: 2 Hg; 6 fickle; 7 erratic, mercury; 9 mercurial

quick-tempered: 5 short; 9 hotheaded, irascible; 11 hot-tempered; 13 short-tempered

quid: 3 cud, wad; 4 chaw, chew, plug; 5 pound; 12 British pound; 13 pound sterling

quiddity: 4 quip; 5 crank, quirk; 6 nature; 7 conceit, essence; 9 character

quid pro quo: 4 swap, swop; 5 trade; 6 barter, return; 9 tit for tat; 10 equivalent, substitute; 11 alternative

quiesce: 4 hush; 5 quiet; 7 quieten

quiescence: 4 calm; 5 quiet; 8 dormancy, sleeping; 9 stillness

quiet: 3 lay; 4 calm, cool, damp, hush, lull, swag, tame; 5 abate, allay, blunt, chill, muted, quell, sober, still; 6 deaden, hushed, pacify, placid, quench, rebate, repose, smooth, soothe; 7 appease, assuage, compose, quiesce, quieten, quietly, silence, slacken, subdued, turn off; 8 becalmed, quietude, serenity, stagnant, suppress, tranquil; 9 alleviate, placidity, stillness, unruffled; 10 deliberate, quiescence, restrained

quiet down: 4 hush; 5 quiet; 8 pipe down

quietly: 5 quiet; 6 softly; 9 privately, restfully

quietus: 4 fall, obit, rest; 5 sleep; 7 release; 9 clearance, deathblow, departure, discharge

quill: 3 pen; 5 shaft; 6 pinion; 7 calamus; 8 quill pen; 10 goose quill

quillwort family: 10 Isoetaceae

quilt: 4 puff; 5 braid, sheet; 7 blanket; 8 bedsheet, coverlet; 9 comforter, embroider, tarpaulin

quinine water: 5 tonic; 10 tonic water

quint: 10 quintuplet

quintain: 4 mark; 5 point; 6 target; 8 bull's-eye

quintal: 3 cwt; 6 cental; 7 centner; 13 hundredweight

quintessence: 5 ether; 6 nature; 7 essence

quintet: 3 fin; 4 five; 5 quint; 6 cinque, pentad; 8 fivesome; 9 quintette; 10 quintuplet

quintuple: 4 five; 8 fivefold

quintuplet: 3 fin; 4 five, quin; 5 quint; 6 cinque, pentad; 7 quintet; 8 fivesome

quip: 3 boo, gag; 4 gibe, grin, hiss, hoot, jeer, jibe, skit, wipe; 5 crack, crank, fling, flout, quirk, sally, scoff, sneer, squib, taunt; 6 satire; 7 conceit, epigram; 8 flouting, quiddity; 9 wisecrack

quirk: 3 fad, fit; 4 quip; 5 crank, freak, hobby, prank; 6 oddity, vagary; 7 conceit, fallacy, quibble; 8 crotchet, escapade, flimflam, quiddity, subtlety; 9 capriccio, queerness

quirkiness: 5 quirk; 6 oddity; 8 crotchet; 9 queerness

quirky: 5 kinky; 6 far-out, way-out; 7 offbeat

quirt: 4 whip, lash; 7 rawhide

Quiscalus: 7 grackle; 14 genus Quiscalus

quisling: 7 traitor; 12 collaborator

quit: 3 rid; 4 drop, stop; 5 cease, honor, leave; 6 depart, give up, lay off, redeem, settle, vacate; 7 abandon, drop out, satisfy, throw in; 8 break off, evacuate, renounce, step down; 9 discharge, foreswear, take leave; 10 relinquish; 11 discontinue

quitclaim: 5 remit; 6 acquit, exempt, remise; 7 release; 9 discharge

quite: 5 fully, stark; 6 in toto, quite a, rather, wholly; 7 totally, utterly; 8 entirely, outright; 10 altogether, completely

Quito: 16 capital of Ecuador

quit school: 7 drop out

quittance: 5 quits; 6 excuse; 7 release; 9 clearance, discharge, indemnity, reckoning, repayment; 10 making good, redemption, settlement; 11 acquittance, arrangement, exoneration, liquidation, restitution; 12 satisfaction; 13 reimbursement; 15 indemnification; 17 making restitution

quiver: 3 bob, jar, jog, wag; 4 jerk, jolt, pant, reel, sway, toss; 5 chill, dance, heave, quail, quake, shake, shock, throb, waver; 6 flurry, quaver, shiver, starve, thrill, tingle, tremor, tumble, waggle, writhe; 7 flicker, flitter, fluster, flutter, frisson, heaving, shaking, shudder, shuffle, stagger, tremble, twitter, vibrate; 9 palpitate, quivering, shakiness, trembling, vibration; 11 palpitation

qui vive: 5 alert; 7 lookout

quixotic: 8 romantic, wild-eyed

quiz: 4 joke, mock, test, twit; 5 chaff, roast, tease; 6 banter, hazing; 7 teasing; 8 badinage, quizzing, roasting; 9 bantering

quizzical: 5 droll; 6 ironic, quaint; 7 mocking, teasing; 8 ironical; 9 burlesque, sarcastic; 11 questioning

quod: 5 limbo; 6 prison

quondam: 4 late, once; 6 former; 7 onetime; 8 previous, sometime; 9 erstwhile

Quonset hut: 9 Nissen hut

quota: 4 mess; 5 ratio; 7 modicum; 10 contingent, proportion

quotable: 10 repeatable

quotation: 5 quote; 6 credit, market; 7 mention; 8 citation; 9 reference; 11 market price

quote: 4 cite; 6 attest; 9 exemplify, quotation
quotidian: 5 daily; 6 common; 7 mundane, routine; 8 everyday, workaday; 12 unremarkable

quotient: 5 ratio; 10 proportion
Quran: 5 Koran

R

r: 6 radius
R: 8 roentgen
R.N.: 15 Registered Nurse
Ra: 2 Re; 6 radium
Rabat: 16 capital of Morocco
rabbet: 3 jam; 5 miter, wedge; 6 rebate; 7 mortise; 8 dovetail
Rabbi: 5 Rebbe, Rabbin
rabbit: 4 cony, hare; 5 bunny, coney, lapin
rabbit burrow: 10 rabbit hole
rabbit fever: 9 tularemia
rabbit food: 6 vegies; 10 vegetables
rabble: 3 mob; 4 body, rout; 5 crush, horde, press; 8 riffraff
rabble-rouser: 7 demagog; 9 demagogue
rabble-rousing: 8 incitive; 9 seditious; 10 incendiary; 11 instigative; 12 inflammatory
Rabelais: 16 Francois Rabelais
rabid: 4 wild; 5 giddy, livid; 6 ardent, doting, fuming, raging, raving; 7 berserk, burning, fanatic, fervent, foaming, frantic, in a rage, rageful; 8 feverish, frenetic, frenzied, rambling, unhinged, wild-eyed; 9 delirious, fanatical, insensate, possessed, splenetic, wandering; 10 hysterical, incoherent, reasonless; 11 dithyrambic, lightheaded, overzealous
rabies: 7 madness; 11 hydrophobia
raccoon: 4 coon
race: 3 run; 4 beat, dash, rush, walk, wash; 5 chase, round, speed, spurt, stock, twang; 6 coulee, course, hasten, nation, record; 7 hotfoot, millrun, raceway, routine; 8 millrace, marathon
racecourse: 5 track; 7 raceway; 9 racetrack
race-culture: 8 eugenics
racehorse: 12 thoroughbred
race murder: 8 genocide
racer: 6 hot rod, hunter; 7 charger, race car; 8 stock car; 9 racing car; 10 blood horse, racing bike; 11 souped-up car
racetrack: 5 track; 7 raceway; 10 racecourse
rachet: 5 ratch; 7 ratchet
rachitic: 7 rickety
rachitis: 7 rickets
racial segregation: 9 apartheid
Racine: 10 Jean Racine
raciness: 8 boldness, gaminess, ribaldry; 9 freshness, spiciness

racing bike: 5 racer
racing car: 5 racer; 6 hot rod; 7 race car; 8 stock car; 11 souped-up car
racing skiff: 11 single shell
racism: 9 racialism
racist: 9 racialist
rack: 5 gouge, purge, stand, wheel, wrack, wring; 6 extort, refine; 7 clarify, torment, torture; 9 expurgate, messenger; 10 excruciate
racket: 3 din, row; 4 fray, fuss, rout, to-do; 5 brawl, broil, melee, noise, revel; 6 bustle, fracas, hubbub, pother, quaver, rumble, rumpus, squall, uproar; 7 howling
racking: 7 cutting, grating; 8 grinding; 9 agonizing, consuming, corroding, searching, wrenching; 12 excruciating
rack up: 3 hit, pip; 4 whip; 5 mop up, score, tally, worst
racon: 11 radar beacon
raconteur: 6 teller; 7 relator; 8 narrator; 10 anecdotist
racquet: 6 racket
racy: 4 blue, bold, gamy; 5 fresh, gamey, juicy, rough, sharp, spicy; 6 lively, risque; 7 caustic, naughty, piquant, pungent; 8 poignant, stinging; 9 trenchant
rad: 4 cool; 6 radian; 7 radical
radar beacon: 5 racon
radar speed meter: 8 radar gun
radar target: 4 blip
raddle: 6 ruddle; 10 interweave
raddled: 4 worn; 5 drawn; 7 haggard, maudlin, muddled, screwed, sewed up, worn-out
radial: 8 stellate; 10 radial tire
radial engine: 12 rotary engine
radial ply tire: 6 radial; 10 radial tire
radian: 3 rad
radiance: 4 glow; 5 shine; 6 luster; 7 glowing; 8 radiancy; 10 brilliancy, effulgence, refulgence, refulgency
radiant: 5 beamy, shiny; 7 beaming, lambent; 8 glorious, lustrous, splendid; 9 brilliant, divergent, effulgent, refulgent; 11 illustrious
radiate: 3 ray; 4 beam, daze, glow; 5 shine; 6 dazzle; 8 bedazzle; 9 emit light, sterilize; 10 divaricate, pasteurize

R

radical: 4 base, real, root, stem, surd; **5** basal, group, radix, theme, ultra, vital; **6** moiety; **8** cardinal, immanent, root word, rudiment, sweeping; **9** essential, extremist, paramount; **10** exhaustive; **11** free radical, radical sign; **12** all-absorbing; **13** revolutionary, revolutionist, thorough-going

radically: 6 purely; **7** vitally; **9** decidedly, downright, seriously; **10** absolutely; **11** essentially; **13** fundamentally, unequivocally

radicle: 9 hypocotyl

radio: 5 tuner; **8** radio set, receiver, wireless

radioactive decay: 5 decay; **8** half-life; **14** disintegration

radioactive dust: 7 fallout

radio aerial: 12 radio antenna

radiocarbon: 8 carbon

radiocarpal joint: 5 wrist; **6** carpus

radio-controlled aircraft: 5 drone

radio detection and ranging: 5 radar

radio emission: 9 radio wave

radiogram: 10 radiograph

radio receiver: 5 radio, tuner; **8** radio set, receiver, wireless

radiotelephone: 8 wireless; **10** radiophone

radiotherapist: 11 radiologist

radiotherapy: 11 irradiation

radium: 2 Ra

radius: 1 r; **3** bar, ray; **4** rule; **5** spoke; **6** streak, stripe

radix: 4 base; **7** radical; **8** rudiment

radon: 2 Rn; **5** niton

Radyera: 8 hibiscus; **12** genus Radyera

RAF: 13 Royal Air Force

raffish: 5 natty, smart; **6** dapper, jaunty, rakish, snappy, spruce; **7** boorish, brutish, dashing, loutish; **8** churlish

raffishly: 8 rakishly; **10** carelessly

raft: 3 lot, pot, wad; **4** deal, heap, mass, mess, mint, peck, pile, slew; **5** batch, float, flock, sight, spate, stack; **6** hatful, mickle, muckle, plenty; **7** pontoon, tidy sum; **8** good deal, whole lot; **9** great deal

rafter: 4 balk, beam; **5** baulk, joist; **6** girder, lintel

rag: 3 cod, dun, jaw, tag, vex; **4** bait, much, nark, ride, rile, twit; **5** annoy, check, chide, devil, get at, get to, rally, scold, scrap, sheet, shred, taunt, tease; **6** berate, bother, chew up, gravel, nettle, rebuke, tag end, tatter; **7** bawl out, bedevil, chew out, crucify, lambast, lecture, ragtime, reproof, tabloid, torment; **8** irritate, lambaste, splinter; **9** dress down, frustrate, have words, reprimand, tantalize; **11** remonstrate

ragamuffin: 5 scrub, tramp; **6** beggar; **8** vagabond

rage: 3 fad; **4** boil, cult, foam, fume, fury, mode, ramp, rant, rave, roar, romp, tear; **5** craze, flame, furor, go ape, mania, storm, vogue; **6** furore, seethe, simmer; **7** bluster, fashion, madness, passion, rampage

rageful: 5 livid, rabid; **6** fuming, raging; **7** foaming

ragged: 4 bald; **6** callow; **8** roofless; **10** threadbare

raggedly: 8 jaggedly, unevenly; **12** stragglingly

raging: 3 hot; **4** rude, wild; **5** angry, bluff, livid, rabid, rough; **6** fierce, fuming, raving, savage; **7** foaming, furious, in a rage, rageful, violent; **8** choleric, ungentle, vehement; **9** ferocious

Ragnarok: 15 Gotterdammerung

ragout: 4 hash, stew; **5** mince; **9** fricassee

rags: 7 tatters

ragtag: 6 rabble; **8** riffraff

ragtime: 3 rag

raid: 4 bust; **5** foray; **6** maraud

raider: 6 looter; **7** spoiler; **8** pillager; **9** despoiler, plunderer; **10** freebooter

raiding: 9 marauding, predatory

rail: 4 pale; **5** rails, snipe, track; **6** grouse, paling, plover, rail at, revile, vilify; **7** inveigh, railing; **8** enceinte; **9** fulminate, ring fence

railing: 4 pale, rail; **6** paling; **8** enceinte; **9** ring fence; **10** balustrade, park paling; **13** quickset hedge

raillery: 4 jest; **5** chaff, irony; **6** banter; **8** backchat

railroad: 4 line; **7** railway; **11** railway line; **12** railroad line

railroad station: 5 depot; **8** terminal

railroad tie: 3 tie; **8** crosstie

rails: 4 rail; **5** track

railway: 4 line; **8** railroad; **11** railway line; **12** railroad line

railway locomotive: 6 engine

railway station: 5 depot [U.S.]; **7** station; **8** terminal

raiment: 3 tog; **4** garb; **5** array, dress; **6** clothe, finery, fit out; **7** apparel, drapery, garment, regalia; **8** enclothe; **10** habilitate

rain: 4 flow, pour, teem; **6** abound, shower, stream; **7** drizzle, pelting; **8** rain down, rainfall; **9** exuberate, rainwater

rainbow-colored: 9 multihued

rain buckets: 4 pelt, pour; **6** stream

rain cloud: 6 nimbus

raincoat: 8 raingear; **10** waterproof

rain forest: 6 jungle

rainless: 7 drought

rain out: 7 wash out

rainproof: 10 waterproof

raise: 4 farm, fire, grow, hike, levy, lift, rear, rise, stir; **5** build, climb, erect, evoke, exalt, get up, heave, prove, put up, run up, set up; **6** arouse, ascent, elicit, invoke, kindle, leaven, parent; **7** advance, bring up, conjure, elevate, enhance, nurture, produce, promote, provoke, recruit, upgrade, upraise; **8** call down, enkindle, heighten; **9** acclivity, call forth, conjure up, conscript, cultivate, elevation, resurrect

raise crops: 4 farm

raised: 5 grown; **7** jutting; **8** brocaded, embossed, in relief, inflated; **10** jutting out, projecting, protruding, sticking up; **11** protuberant

raiser: 6 grower; **10** cultivator; **13** agriculturist

raise the spirits: 5 cheer, elate; **7** animate, enliven, gladden, inspire; **8** inspirit; **10** exhilarate

raise the veil: 6 unfold, unseal, unveil; **7** uncover

raising: 4 lift; **7** nurture, rearing; **8** breeding; **9** elevation, fosterage, fostering, nurturing; **10** bringing up, upbringing

rajah: 4 raja; **8** maharaja

rake: 3 dig, hoe, lug, rip, tow, tug; **4** comb, drag, draw, goat, haul, plow, pull, scan, skim; **5** blood, delve, graze, pitch, satyr, slant, trail, train; **6** crease, dibble, harrow, lecher, plough; **7** Don Juan, gallant, seducer

raking fire: 9 cross fire

rakishly: 9 raffishly; **10** carelessly

Raleigh: 22 capital of North Carolina

rallentando: 10 ritardando

rally: 5 cheer; **6** banter, embolden, inspirit, mobilize, muster up, rallying, reassure

rallying cry: 3 cry; **6** war cry; **8** war whoop; **9** battle cry

ram: 3 jam, run, tup, wad; **4** cram, pack; **5** crash, drive, force, pound; **6** ramrod

ramble: 3 jog; **4** cast, roam, rove, trot, turn; **5** amble, drift, range, stalk, stray, tramp; **6** canter, stroll, wander; **7** saunter

rambler: 5 rover; **8** wanderer; **9** straggler

rambling: 4 wild; **5** giddy, rabid; **6** doting, raving, roving; **7** berserk, frantic, gadding, vagrant, winding; **8** frenetic, frenzied, unhinged, wild-eyed; **9** delirious, possessed

rambunctious: 6 unruly; **10** boisterous, robustious; **11** rumbustious

ramekin: 8 ramequin

ramification: 3 arm; **4** fork, limb, lobe, wing; **6** branch, lobule, member, sequel; **7** forking; **8** offshoot; **9** branching, corollary, outgrowth; **11** aftereffect, bifurcation, development; **12** complication, divarication

ramjet: 7 athodyd; **10** atherodyde

ramose: 8 branched, tree-like; **9** branching, dendritic; **10** dendriform

ramp: 3 hop; **4** rage, skip, trip; **5** climb, storm; **7** clamber, incline; **8** scramble, surmount, wild leek; **9** cut capers; **15** Allium tricoccum

rampage: 4 rage, roar, romp

rampantly: 4 wild

rampart: 4 wall; **5** scarp; **7** bulwark; **10** battlement

ramshackle: 5 shaky; **7** unsound; **8** topheavy; **9** crumbling; **10** bedraggled, broken-down, tumble-down, tumbledown; **11** dilapidated, waterlogged

Rana: 4 frog; **8** bullfrog; **9** genus Rana

ranch: 6 spread; **10** cattle farm; **11** cattle ranch

rancid: 3 bad; **4** high, sour, weak; **5** fusty; **6** effete, putrid, rotten; **7** corrupt, decayed, gone bad, rotting, tainted, touched; **9** putrefied; **10** putrescent; **12** putrefactive

rancor: 4 gall; **5** venom; **7** rancour; **8** rankling; **9** virulence; **10** bitterness, resentment

rancorous: 6 bitter; **7** caustic; **8** avenging, rigorous, vengeful, virulent; **9** envenomed; **10** mordacious, rancourous, revengeful, vindictive; **11** acrimonious

random: 9 arbitrary, unordered; **11** promiscuous, statistical; **14** indiscriminate

random access memory: 3 RAM

randomly: 8 by chance; **9** aimlessly; **10** willy-nilly; **11** arbitrarily, haphazardly; **12** fortuitously

random occurrence: 8 accident, fortuity; **12** happenchance

random sample: 9 spot check

randy: 7 lustful; **9** lecherous

range: 3 run, way; **4** beat [of police], cast, crop, line, play, rank, rate, roam, room, rove, sift, size, swan, team, tier, walk; **5** ambit, array, chain, drift, field, grade, grasp, graze, march, orbit, order, place, prowl, reach, scope, stove, stray, sweep, swing; **6** browse, domain, extent, lay out, patrol, ramble, riddle, set out, sphere, spread, string, thread, wander; **7** compass, footing, habitat, pasture; **8** latitude, straddle, traverse, vagabond; **9** expansion, grassland, territory

range of mountains: 5 chain, range

Ranger: 11 Texas Ranger

Rangifer: 7 caribou; **8** reindeer; **13** genus Rangifer

rangy: 5 lanky; **6** gangly; **8** gangling

ranitidine: 6 Zantac

rank: 3 pas, row; **4** file, foul, lush, rate, sift, size; **5** birth, blood, fetid, grade, gross, guard, order, place, range, sheer; **6** crying, picket, piquet, red-hot, riddle; **7** account, fulsome, glaring, noisome, outrank, peccant, station; **8** absolute, flagrant, nobility, position, smelling, stinking; **9** desperate, downright, egregious, offensive; **10** membership, precedence, social rank; **11** high descent, rank and file, uninitiated

R

rank and file: 4 peon, rank; 7 cortege, private, retinue, trooper; 8 rifleman; 9 legionary, minutemen, musketeer, subaltern; 10 skirmisher; 11 legionnaire; 12 cannon fodder, sharpshooter

ranked: 5 sized; 6 graded; 10 stratified

ranking: 6 sizing; 8 superior, top-level; 10 commanding, top-ranking

rankle: 3 rot; 4 fade, fret, gnaw; 5 decay, go bad, go off, grate; 6 appall, fester, molder, wither; 7 corrode, eat into, ferment, horrify, putrefy

rankness: 8 foulness; 10 stinkiness; 14 malodorousness

ransack: 3 gut, pry; 4 comb, loot, peer, sack, scan; 5 foray, reave, rifle, sound, spoil, strip, sweep; 6 browse; 7 despoil, explore, pillage, plunder, rummage; 11 reconnoiter

ransacked: 6 looted; 8 pillaged; 9 plundered

ransom: 5 purge; 6 redeem, repair, shrive; 7 absolve, reclaim, salvage; 10 emancipate

rant: 3 gag; 4 blah, foam, fume, rage, rave, tear; 5 spout; 6 jabber; 7 bombast, fustian, palaver, ranting; 8 claptrap, flummery, harangue, mouth off

ranting: 4 rant; 6 raving; 8 harangue; 9 jabbering; 11 incoherence

Ranunculaceae: 14 crowfoot family; 15 buttercup family; 19 family Ranunculaceae

Ranunculus: 8 crowfoot; 9 buttercup; 15 genus Ranunculus

rap: 3 dab, fig, jot, pat, pin, sou, tap; 4 belt, cent, knap, mill, mite, pink, rush, slap; 5 blame, knock, straw, whack, whang; 6 button, change, old son, strike; 7 bulrush, feather; 8 farthing, picayune, rap music

rapacious: 5 venal; 6 greedy, lupine; 7 wolfish; 8 covetous, edacious, esurient, ravening, ravenous, usurious; 9 mercenary, predatory, raptorial, voracious, vulturine, vulturous; 10 avaricious; 12 extortionate

rapacity: 5 greed; 7 avarice, avidity, craving, edacity; 8 avaritia, grasping, voracity

rape: 5 colza; 6 rapine, ravage, ravish; 7 assault, despoil, outrage, plunder, violate; 8 dishonor; 9 dishonour, violation; 10 ravishment; 13 Brassica napus

rape oil: 11 rapeseed oil

raper: 6 rapist

Raphanus: 5 runch; 6 daikon, radish; 13 genus Raphanus

raphia: 6 raffia

Raphus: 4 dodo; 11 genus Raphus

rapid: 4 fast; 5 quick, swift; 6 speedy

rapid eye movement sleep: 8 REM sleep

rapid growth: 4 zoom

rapidity: 8 celerity; 9 fleetness, high speed, quickness, rapidness, swiftness; 10 speediness

rapidly: 5 apace; 7 quickly, swiftly; 8 chop-chop, speedily; 13 expeditiously

rapids: 7 torrent; 8 cataract; 10 white water

rapid transit: 11 mass transit

rapier: 5 sword, bilbo, brand; 8 whinyard

rapine: 4 rape, sack; 7 looting, pillage, plunder; 12 despoliation

rapist: 5 raper; 8 ravisher, molester

rappel: 7 descend

rapping: 7 tapping; 8 knocking

rapport: 6 accord; 13 compatibility

rapprochement: 10 cordiality; 11 welcomeness; 14 fraternization, reconciliation

rapscallion: 3 imp; 5 knave, rogue, scamp; 6 monkey, rascal, varlet; 8 scalawag; 9 scallywag

rapt: 6 intent; 7 bemused, riveted, wrapped; 8 absorbed; 9 engrossed, enwrapped, wrapped in; 10 enraptured, hypnotized, mesmerized, transfixed

raptor: 10 bird of prey

Raptores: 13 order Raptores

raptorial bird: 6 raptor; 10 bird of prey

rapture: 5 flame; 7 ecstasy, passion; 8 devotion, idolatry, yearning; 9 adoration, idolizing, transport; 10 exaltation, ravishment; 11 enchantment, idolization

rapturous: 4 fond; 6 ardent; 7 devoted; 8 ecstatic, electric, empyrean, motherly, swelling, uxorious; 9 exquisite, heartfelt, ravishing, rhapsodic, thrilling; 10 delightful, enraptured, felicitous, passionate; 11 deep-mouthed; 12 soul-stirring; 14 heart-expanding

rara avis: 6 rarity; 8 rare bird

rare: 4 fine, thin; 6 flimsy, scarce, slight, spotty, subtle; 7 subtile, tenuous; 8 exiguous, rarefied, rarified, uncommon; 9 gilt-edged, priceless, scattered; 10 unexampled; 11 exceptional; 12 compressible; 13 extraordinary

rarebit: 11 Welsh rabbit; 12 Welsh rarebit

raree-show: 8 peepshow

rarefaction: 9 expansion, inflation; 10 dilatation

rarefied: 4 rare; 5 lofty; 7 exalted; 8 rarified; 9 high-flown; 10 high-minded, idealistic; 11 noble-minded

rarely: 6 seldom; 10 hardly ever

rarified: 4 rare; 5 lofty; 7 exalted; 8 rarefied; 9 high-flown; 10 high-minded, idealistic; 11 noble-minded

rarity: 5 curio; 6 oddity; 7 oddment, tenuity; 8 rareness; 9 curiosity; 11 infrequency, peculiarity, tenuousness

rascal: 3 cad, imp; 5 knave, rogue, scamp; 6 monkey, varlet; 7 bounder, villain; 8 scalawag; 9 scallywag, scoundrel; 11 rapscallion

rase: 4 raze; 5 erase

rash: 8 eruption, reckless, skin rash; 9 foolhardy; **10** incautious, indiscreet; **11** breaking out; **12** skin eruption; **13** efflorescence

rasher: 3 cut; **5** slice; **7** shaving

rashly: 8 headlong; **11** imprudently; **12** incautiously, indiscreetly

rashness: 8 temerity; **9** incaution; **10** imprudence; **12** heedlessness, indiscretion, mindlessness, recklessness

rasp: 4 file; **5** chafe, grate; **6** abrade, scrape; **7** rasping, rub down

raspberry: 3 boo; **4** bird, hiss, hoot; **5** snort; **7** razzing

rasping: 4 rasp; **5** harsh, raspy, rough; **6** coarse, gravel; **7** grating; **8** gravelly; **10** stertorous

raspy: 5 rough; **6** gravel; **7** grating, rasping; **8** gravelly

rassle: 7 wrestle

Ras Tafari: 13 Haile Selassie

rat: 4 sing; **5** utter; **6** betray, defect, desert, go over, rotter, snitch, squeal, tattle, tell on; **7** breathe, lowlife, so-and-so, stinker; **8** apostate, betrayer, denounce, give away, informer, squealer; **10** apostatize; **13** strikebreaker

ratchet: 3 cog; **4** pawl; **5** click, ratch, spoke; **6** detent, rachet; **8** rachet up; **11** ratchet down

rat chinchilla: 8 abrocome

rate: 4 pace, rank; **5** grade, merit, order, place, range, scold, value; **6** assess, review; **7** deserve, upbraid; **8** appraise, estimate, evaluate, velocity; **9** appraisal, objurgate, valuation; **10** appreciate, assessment, evaluation; **12** appraisement

rate of sales: 6 volume; **8** turnover

ratepayer: 8 taxpayer

rather: 5 kinda, quite; **6** before, kind of, sooner, sort of; **7** instead; **8** somewhat; **9** tolerably; **10** preferably

ratification: 7 signing; **10** settlement; **12** confirmation; **13** corroboration

ratified: 10 sanctioned

ratifier: 8 endorser; **10** subscriber

ratify: 4 sign; **6** clench, uphold; **7** approve, bear out, confirm, indorse, support, warrant; **9** subscribe; **10** underwrite; **11** corroborate, countersign

rating: valuation; **10** evaluation

ratio: 4 mess; **5** quota; **7** modicum; **8** quotient; **10** proportion

ratiocination: 6 reason; **9** reckoning; **11** calculation

ration: 5 allot; **7** quantum, rations; **8** allocate; **9** provision, ration out; **10** provisions

rational: 4 sane; **5** sound; **6** mental; **8** sensible; **10** irrational, reasonable

rationale: 8 occasion; **9** principle; **10** ascription; **11** attribution; **13** justification

rationality: 6 reason, wisdom; **8** lucidity, sapience, sobriety

rationalize: 6 excuse; **7** ascribe, justify; **9** apologise, apologize, attribute

rationally: 8 mentally; **10** reasonably; **14** intellectually

rational number: 8 fraction

ration out: 5 allot; **6** ration; **8** allocate

rations: 6 ration; **9** provision; **10** provisions

rattail: 9 grenadier

rattan cane: 6 rattan; **10** rattan palm; **13** Calamus rotang

ratting: 9 informing

rattle: 7 twaddle, twattle; **8** rattle on, rattling; **13** sounding-board

rattled: 9 flustered, perturbed

rattlesnake: 7 rattler, serpent

rattletraps: 5 traps; **6** things; **13** paraphernalia

rattling: 4 real, very; **5** brisk, merry, zippy; **6** lively, rattle, really, snappy; **7** howling; **8** spanking, terrific, wondrous; **9** fantastic, hilarious, marvelous, wonderful; **10** clattering, tremendous

Rattus: 3 rat; **8** brown rat, wharf rat; **9** Norway rat; **11** genus Rattus

ratty: 5 tatty; **6** shabby; **9** moth-eaten

raucous: 3 dry; **5** husky, rowdy; **6** hoarse, hollow; **8** croaking, strident

raucously: 7 rowdily

ravage: 4 rape; **5** harry, havoc, waste; **6** inroad; **7** outrage; **8** desolate, lay waste; **9** devastate

ravaged: 5 raped; **6** ruined, sacked, wasted; **7** blasted; **8** desolate, pillaged; **9** desolated, despoiled; **10** devastated

rave: 4 boil, dote, foam, fume, gush, rage, rant, tear; **5** flame, spout; **6** jabber, ramble, raving, seethe, simmer

ravel: 3 run; **4** card, knot, wind; **5** twine; **6** enmesh, ladder, ruffle, tangle, tousle; **7** entwine, unravel; **8** dishevel, encumber, entangle

raveled: 5 kinky; **6** kinked; **7** knotted, tangled; **8** involved; **9** entangled, intricate, perplexed; **11** complicated; **12** inextricable

raven: 4 gulp, prey; **6** devour, guttle

ravenous: 6 greedy; **7** craving, starved, wolfish; **8** covetous, edacious, esurient, famished, grasping, ravening, sharp-set; **9** insatiate, rapacious, voracious; **10** avaricious, insatiable, quenchless

raver: 5 crazy; **6** madcap, madman, maniac, ranter; **7** lunatic

ravine: 8 crevasse

raving: 4 rave, wild; **5** giddy, rabid; **6** doting, fuming, raging; **7** berserk, frantic, madness, ranting; **8** delirium, feverish, frenetic, frenzied, rambling, ravingly, unhinged, wild-eyed; **9** delirious, fanatical, insensate, possessed, wandering

ravish: 4 rape; **7** delight, enchant, enthral,

outrage, violate; **8** dishonor, enthrall; **9** dishonour, enrapture, transport

ravisher: 6 rapist; **8** violator; **9** debaucher

ravishing: 8 empyrean; **9** exquisite, heartfelt, rapturous, thrilling; **10** delightful, felicitous

raw: 3 new; **4** buff, keen, rude, sore; **5** bleak, crude, fresh, green, naked, rough; **6** peeled, yeasty; **7** bare-ass, cutting, natural, nipping; **8** immature, in the raw, unsanded; **9** in the buff, inclement, unsettled; **10** altogether; **11** uninitiated, unprocessed

rawhide: 5 quirt; **8** untanned

raw material: 5 stock, stuff; **6** staple; **8** material

rawness: 7 crudity; **9** roughness

raw sienna: 4 buff; **14** yellowish brown

ray: 4 beam, rule; **5** gleam, shaft, spoke; **6** pencil, radius, streak, stream, stripe; **7** radiate; **9** irradiate

rayons: 6 nylons; **12** silk stocking; **13** nylon stocking, rayon stocking

rayon stocking: 6 nylons, rayons; **12** silk stocking

raze: 4 rase; **5** erase, level; **6** efface; **7** expunge, wipe out; **8** demolish; **9** dismantle

razing: 8 leveling, wrecking; **11** demolishing, tearing down

razorback hog: 9 razorback; **14** razorbacked hog

razzing: 3 boo; **4** bird, hiss, hoot; **5** snort; **9** raspberry; **10** Bronx cheer

Rb: 8 rubidium

rbi: 11 run batted in

Re: 2 Ra; **7** rhenium

re: 3 ray

reach: 3 get; **4** gain, give, hand, make, pass, span, sway, wile; **5** ambit, blind, bring, catch, cheat, equal, feint, fetch, get to, grasp, hocus, match, orbit, plant, range, scope, touch, trick; **6** attain, bubble, convoy, extent, juggle, pass on, sphere, strain, stride, strive; **7** achieve, chicane, compass, conduct, contact, stretch

reach out: 5 reach; **6** extend

react: 6 oppose, recoil; **7** fly back, rebound, respond; **9** bound back; **10** bounce back, spring back

reactant: 7 reagent

reacting: 8 renitent; **9** resisting; **10** responding; **11** reactionary; **12** recalcitrant, repercussive

reaction: 6 solace; **8** response; **10** relaxation; **11** retroaction; **12** counterforce

reactionary: 8 far-right, reacting, renitent; **9** resisting, revulsive; **10** regressive; **11** reactionist

reaction time: 7 latency

read: 3 say; **4** scan, show, take; **5** learn,

study; **6** record; **8** register; **9** interpret, translate; **10** understand

read/write memory: 3 RAM; **12** random memory

readability: 10 legibility

readable: 4 easy; **5** clear; **6** fluent; **7** flowing, legible, natural; **8** graceful, tripping; **10** unaffected; **12** decipherable, recognizable

reader: 6 lector; **8** lecturer, preacher; **9** professor; **10** prolocutor, subscriber

readied: 5 ready; **8** prepared

readily: 5 aptly; **6** deftly; **7** handily, quickly; **8** adroitly, smoothly; **10** swimmingly; **11** dexterously

readiness: 3 set; **4** ease; **6** memory, recall; **8** alacrity, deftness, facility; **9** quickness; **11** forwardness; **12** preparedness

reading: 5 light, sense; **7** lection, recital, version; **10** recitation

reading desk: 5 stand; **6** pulpit; **7** lectern; **9** secretary

reading glasses: 8 bifocals; **9** trifocals

readjust: 5 dress, reset; **7** readapt; **8** regulate

read-only memory: 3 ROM

readout: 9 indicator

ready: 3 apt, fix, set; **4** deft, gain, make; **5** alert, handy, quick, set up, sharp, smart; **6** adroit, at hand, expert, gear up; **7** earnest, forward, prepare, readied; **8** prepared, tangible; **9** available, dexterous

reaffirm: 8 reassert

Reagan: 12 Ronald Reagan; **18** Ronald Wilson Reagan

reagent: 8 crucible, reactant

real: 4 surd, true, very; **6** actual, really; **7** genuine, literal, radical, regular; **8** bona fide, existent, material, physical, rattling, tangible; **9** authentic, corporeal, veridical; **10** real number; **11** substantial, substantive; **14** unquestionable

real estate: 4 land; **5** acres, lands; **6** realty; **8** property; **9** tenements

real estate agent: 6 broker; **7** realtor

realism: 7 reality; **8** realness; **9** Platonism; **10** naturalism; **12** naive realism

reality: 7 realism; **8** realness; **9** actuality

realization: 8 fruition; **11** fulfillment, realisation, recognition

realize: 3 ken, see; **4** earn, gain, know, make, scan; **5** clear, match, place; **6** agnise, agnize, pull in, take in; **7** bring in, fulfill, make out, match up, perform, specify; **8** classify, idealize, identify; **9** actualize, apprehend, be aware of, designate, determine, discharge, liquidate, recognize; **10** appreciate, categorize, comprehend, specialize, understand

reallocate: 11 reapportion

really: 4 real, very; **5** truly; **6** indeed, verily; **7** in truth; **8** actually, forsooth, rattling; **9** genuinely; **13** authentically; **14** unquestionably

realm: 3 orb; **4** area, land, soil; **5** field, state;

6 circle, domain, ground, region, sphere; **7** circuit, kingdom; **8** province

real McCoy: 4 real; **7** genuine

realtor: 6 broker

realty: 4 land; **5** acres, lands; **8** property; **9** tenements

ream: 5 cheat; **9** victimize, reprimand

reamer: 6 juicer

reanimate: 6 revive, vivify; **7** animate, quicken; **8** recreate, revivify; **10** regenerate; **11** resuscitate

reap: 3 lop, mow; **4** clip, crop, cull, dock, draw; **5** glean, pluck, prune, shave, shear; **7** harvest

reaping hook: 6 sickle

reappear: 5 recur; **6** resume, return, revert; **8** re-emerge

reappearance: 12 resurrection

reappraisal: 6 review

reappraise: 8 reassess; **10** reevaluate

rear: 4 back, butt, lift, prat, rise, rump, seat, tail, tush, wake; **5** breed, build, erect, fanny, heave, hoist, put up, queue, raise, run up, set up, stern, trail, train; **6** behind, bottom, ground, parent

rearing: 7 nurture, raising, rampant; **8** breeding; **9** fosterage, fostering, nurturing; **10** upbringing

rearrange: 9 recombine

reason: 3 wit; **4** wits; **5** argue, cause, point, **6** ground, motive, origin, source, wisdom; **7** element, grounds, purpose; **8** argument, conclude, sapience; **9** intellect, principle, reason out, reason why; **10** motivation; **11** inspiration, rationality

reasonable: 4 cool, fair, just, sane; **5** equal, sober, sound; **6** square; **7** equable, fairish; **8** apparent, credible, measured, moderate, rational, sensible; **9** equitable, judicious, temperate; **10** evenhanded, presumable; **11** presumptive, well-founded

reasonably: 6 fairly, sanely; **8** middling, passably, sensibly, somewhat; **10** moderately, rationally

reasoned: 5 sound; **10** considered

reasoner: 8 logician

reasoning: 7 arguing; **8** deducing, thinking; **9** inferring; **11** intelligent, rationalism

reasonless: 4 wild; **5** giddy, rabid; **6** doting, raving; **7** berserk, frantic; **8** frenetic, frenzied, mindless, rambling, unhinged, wild-eyed; **9** causeless, delirious, insensate, possessed, senseless, wandering; **10** incoherent

reassembly: 8 remaking; **11** reformation; **13** refabrication

reassert: 7 confirm; **8** reaffirm

reassess: 10 reappraise, reevaluate

reassessment: 6 review

reassign: 8 transfer

reassure: 5 cheer, nerve, rally; **6** assure, buoy up; **8** embolden, inspirit; **9** encourage

reave: 4 loot; **5** foray, rifle, seize, strip; **6** snatch; **7** despoil, pillage, plunder, ransack

Reb: 5 Rebel; **6** Johnny; **8** grayback; **9** Johnny Reb

rebate: 3 lay; **4** calm, cool, damp, hush, lull, swag, tame; **5** abate, allay, quell, quiet, sober, still; **6** deaden, pacify, rabbet, smooth, soothe; **7** appease, assuage, compose, slacken, turn off; **8** calm down, discount, suppress; **9** alleviate; **11** tranquilize

Rebbe: 5 Rabbi; **6** Rabbin

Rebecca Rolfe: 7 Matoaka; **10** Pocahontas

Rebel: 3 Reb; **6** Johnny; **8** grayback; **9** Johnny Reb

rebel: 4 rise; **5** arise; **6** mutiny, rise up; **8** maverick, mutineer, renegade, revolter; **9** insurgent, rebelling; **10** rebellious; **13** revolutionary

rebellion: 6 mutiny, revolt, rising; **8** outbreak, uprising; **10** insurgency, revolution; **12** insurrection

rebellious: 5 balky, heady, rebel; **6** unruly; **7** restive, wayward, willful; **8** contrary, perverse; **9** rebelling; **10** headstrong, malcontent, refractory, self-willed; **11** disaffected

rebirth: 7 revival; **10** conversion, renascence; **11** reanimation, renaissance

reboot: 4 boot; **7** bring up

reborn: 9 born-again, converted, reclaimed

rebound: 5 bound, rally, react; **6** bounce, recoil, spring; **7** fly back; **8** backlash, ricochet, take a hop; **9** bound back; **10** bounce back, spring back; **12** repercussion

rebroadcast: 5 rerun

rebuff: 4 rout, snub; **5** repel; **6** slight; **7** repulse

rebuild: 11 reconstruct

rebuilt: 9 remodeled

rebuke: 3 jaw, rag; **5** check, chide, scold; **6** berate, chew up; **7** bawl out, chew out, lambast, lecture, reproof; **8** admonish, lambaste, reproval; **9** dress down, have words, reprehend, reprimand; **11** castigation, remonstrate

rebus: 6 enigma, puzzle, riddle; **7** charade; **9** conundrum

rebut: 5 reply; **6** answer, impugn, refute, rejoin, retort; **7** confute, respond; **8** confound, disprove, negative, traverse; **10** controvert, disconfirm

rebuttal: 6 retort; **7** riposte; **8** rebutter; **9** rejoinder

rebutting: 9 confuting; **10** disproving; **11** confounding

recall: 4 echo, mind; **5** think; **6** call in, call up, memory, remind, return; **7** abolish, retrace, retract; **8** remember, retrieve, summon up, withdraw; **9** namnesis, recollect; **10** initiative, plebiscite, referendum

recant: 6 abjure; **7** retract; **8** forswear**

R

recap: 6 review; 7 retread; 12 recapitulate; 14 recapitulation

recapitulate: 4 poll, skim; 5 recap, sum up; 6 go over, muster, recite, repeat, resume, review, reword; 7 reprise, run over; 8 rehearse

recapture: 6 retake; 8 retaking

recast: 4 cast; 6 remold; 7 reforge, remodel

recasting: 9 rewording; 10 rephrasing

recede: 3 ebb; 4 lose, wane; 6 retire, return, revert; 7 decline, drop off, regrade, retreat

receding: 6 ebbing; 7 fadeout; 8 retiring; 9 recession, reverting; 10 retreating

receipt: 6 device, recipe; 7 nostrum; 8 artifice, receipts; 9 accepting, expedient, invention, receiving, reception; 11 acknowledge, contrivance; 13 money coming in, value received; 14 acknowledgment, receiving money

receive: 3 get; 4 find, hail, have, meet; 5 admit, greet, incur, let in, usher; 6 accede, accept, assume, import, invite, obtain, pick up, take in; 7 agree to, bring in, presume, undergo, welcome; 9 acquiesce, encounter

received: 3 set; 5 noted, stock; 8 accepted, admitted, standard; 9 notorious, receiving, well-known; 11 established, stereotyped, traditional

receiver: 5 radio; 6 kettle; 7 capsule, steward, trustee; 8 bolthead, wireless; 9 recipient; 10 accountant, liquidator

receiver of stolen goods: 5 fence

receiving: 7 receipt; 8 received; 9 accepting, admitting, reception, recipient

recent: 3 new; 4 late; 5 fresh, green, novel; 9 the latest

receptacle: 9 container

reception: 5 levee; 6 at home, entree; 7 receipt, welcome; 8 audience, greeting, response; 9 admission, admitting, inclusion, interview, receiving; 10 admittance, membership, salutation; 11 recognition

reception room: 6 lounge

receptiveness: 8 openness

recess: 4 cove, hole, nook; 5 break, inlet, niche; 6 corner; 7 adjourn, break up, respite, time out, timeout; 8 deferral; 9 recession, seclusion; 10 retirement

recessed: 6 sunken; 7 deep-set

recession: 5 niche; 6 corner, ebbing, recess; 8 receding; 10 retirement, withdrawal

recharge: 6 reload

recherche: 4 chic, cool; 6 choice, modish, picked, select, trendy; 7 stylish; 9 exquisite; 11 crackerjack

rechewed food: 3 cud

recidivate: 5 lapse; 7 regress, relapse; 8 fall back; 10 retrogress

recidivism: 5 lapse; 7 lapsing, relapse; 9 relapsing, reversion, reverting; 11 backsliding

recidivist: 8 deserter, renegade, repeater; 9 proselyte; 10 backslider; 12 reversionist

Recife: 10 Pernambuco

recipe: 7 formula, receipt

recipient: 8 receiver; 9 receiving; 11 reservatory

reciprocal: 5 prime; 6 mutual; 7 aliquot, inverse; 9 divisible; 10 fractional; 11 commutative; 12 exchangeable; 13 complementary

recision: 6 repeal; 8 annuling, excision; 9 annulment, canceling; 10 abrogating, abrogation, abscission, defeasance, rescinding, rescission; 12 cancellation; 13 nullification

recital: 4 tale, yarn; 5 story; 7 reading; 9 narration, narrative; 10 recitation

recitation: 3 say; 6 sermon, tirade; 7 reading, recital; 8 delivery; 10 peroration

recite: 4 poll, spin, tell; 5 stump; 6 muster, relate, retell; 7 declaim, lecture, narrate, recount; 8 flourish, harangue; 9 discourse, sermonize, speechify

reckless: 4 rash, wild; 6 madcap, wanton; 8 heedless; 9 foolhardy, imprudent

reckon: 3 see; 4 view; 5 count, guess, think; 6 cipher, cypher, figure, regard; 7 compute, count on, imagine, suppose; 8 consider, estimate, forecast; 9 calculate

reckoner: 7 figurer; 8 computer; 9 estimator; 10 calculator

reckoning: 5 count, score, tally; 8 counting, figuring; 9 clearance, discharge, quittance; 10 accounting, numeration, redemption, settlement; 11 arrangement, bookkeeping, calculation, computation, enumeration

reclaim: 5 claim, purge; 6 ransom, redeem, repair, shrive; 7 absolve, recover, recycle; 8 retrieve; 9 repossess

reclamation: 5 claim; 6 demand; 7 redress, renewal, revival; 8 exaction; 9 expiation, retrieval; 10 imposition, insistence, redemption; 11 reformation, requisition; 12 conciliation, propitiation; 14 rehabilitation

recline: 3 lie; 4 tilt; 5 couch; 6 repose; 7 incline; 8 lean back

reclining: 5 lying; 7 sitting, tilting; 9 accumbent, decumbent, inclining, recumbent

reclining chair: 7 lounger; 8 recliner

recluse: 6 hermit; 7 private, retired; 8 secluded; 9 reclusive, withdrawn; 10 troglodyte; 11 sequestered

reclusion: 7 privacy; 8 solitude; 9 isolation, seclusion

reclusive: 7 recluse; 8 secluded, unsocial; 9 withdrawn; 10 antisocial, cloistered, unsociable; 11 sequestered

recognition: 5 grace, match; 6 credit; 7 match-up; 8 greeting, requital, response; 9 reception; 10 preferment, salutation

recognize: 3 get, ken, see, spy; 4 espy, heed,

know, mind, view; **5** greet, match, place; **6** agnise, agnize, suffer; **7** discern, make out, match up, pick out, realize; **8** accredit, bear with, classify, conceive, discover, identify, perceive, tolerate; **9** entertain; **10** categorize, experience; **11** acknowledge, distinguish

recognizing: 11 identifying

recoil: 4 kick; **5** bound, quail, react, wince; **6** bounce, cringe, flinch, shrink, spring, swerve; **7** fly back, rebound, squinch; **8** backlash, kick back, ricochet; **9** revulsion, shrinking; **10** bounce back, reluctance, spring back; **12** repercussion

recollect: 4 mind; **5** think; **6** call up, recall, remind; **7** retrace; **8** call back, remember, retrieve, summon up

recollection: 6 recall; **9** anamnesis; **11** remembrance; **12** reminiscence

recombinant DNA technology: 12 gene-splicing

recombine: 9 rearrange

recommence: 6 resume

recommend: 4 urge; **6** prompt; **7** commend, suggest; **8** advocate; **9** encourage, prescribe

recommendation: 6 advice, urging; **7** counsel; **8** advocacy; **10** persuasion, suggestion; **11** exhortation, testimonial; **13** encouragement

recommended: 9 suggested

recompense: 5 repay; **7** requite; **9** indemnify; **10** compensate, remunerate

reconcile: 6 make up, resign, settle, square, submit; **7** patch up, placate, win over; **9** harmonize; **10** conciliate, propitiate; **11** accommodate

reconciler: 8 appeaser, pacifier; **9** makepeace; **10** peacemaker; **11** conciliator

recondite: 4 dark, deep; **6** mystic, occult, secret; **7** crabbed; **8** abstruse; **9** concealed

reconditioned: 5 fixed; **8** repaired

reconnaissance: 5 watch; **9** espionage

reconnoiter: 3 pry; **4** peer, scan; **5** scout, sound; **6** browse; **7** explore, ransack, rummage

reconnoitering: 8 scouting

reconsider: 6 review; **7** revisit

reconstitute: 6 remake; **10** reorganize

reconstruct: 4 redo; **7** rebuild, remodel, retrace; **9** construct

record: 4 book, disc, disk, race, read, show, tape, walk; **5** enter; **6** course; **7** platter; **8** register; **9** recording; **10** recordbook; **11** commemorate, immortalize, memorialize, vinyl record; **14** criminal record

recorder: 5 clerk, flute; **6** notary; **9** registrar

record hop: 3 hop

recording machine: 8 recorder

record-keeper: 8 recorder; **9** registrar

record player: 10 phonograph

record sleeve: 5 cover; **6** jacket

recount: 4 spin, tell; **6** recite, relate; **7** narrate

recoup: 6 deduct, redeem, regain; **7** get back, recover; **8** retrieve, withhold; **9** reimburse

recourse: 5 avail; **6** refuge, resort

recover: 4 find; **6** go back, recoup, redeem, regain; **7** get back, reclaim; **8** retrieve; **10** convalesce, recuperate

recoverable: 7 curable; **10** remediable, restorable; **11** retrievable

recovered: 5 cured; **6** healed

recovery: 4 cure; **6** regain; **9** retrieval; **11** restoration; **12** recuperation

recreant: 4 base; **5** sneak; **6** coward, craven, truant; **7** corrupt, dastard; **8** apostate, castaway, deserter, renegade, scampish, sneaking; **9** corrupted, defaulter, dissolute, graceless, reprobate

recreate: 4 play; **5** cheer; **6** revive, solace, vivify; **7** animate, hearten, quicken, rejoice; **8** embolden, revivify; **9** reanimate

recreation: 3 fun; **9** amusement, diversion; **13** entertainment

recreational: 6 unpaid; **7** amateur; **10** recreative

recreational vehicle: 2 RV; **9** motor home

recreation room: 7 rec room

recruit: 3 air; **4** feed, levy; **5** cadet, enrol, enter, raise, refit; **6** enroll, novice; **7** refresh, relieve; **8** enlistee, inscribe, neophyte; **9** conscript

recruited: 5 hired; **7** taken on

recruitment: 9 enlisting

rectangular: 6 square; **10** orthogonal; **12** multilateral

rectifiable: 9 reparable

rectification: 10 correcting, correction

rectify: 5 amend; **6** remedy; **8** set right; **10** straighten

rectifying tube: 5 diode

rectitude: 7 probity; **9** integrity, principle, propriety

rector: 5 vicar; **6** curate, parson, pastor; **8** governor, minister

rectory: 5 glebe, manse; **7** deanery; **8** vicarage; **9** parsonage; **10** presbytery

recumbent: 9 reclining

recuperate: 7 recover; **10** convalesce

recuperated: 8 restored; **9** refreshed, unwearied

recuperation: 4 cure; **6** regain; **8** recovery; **9** retrieval; **11** restoration

recur: 6 repeat, resort, return, revert

recurrence: 6 return; **7** harping; **9** flashback, iteration; **10** repetition

recurrent: 8 repeated; **9** perennial, recurring

recyclable: 8 reusable; **11** reclaimable

recycle: 5 reuse; **7** reclaim; **9** reprocess

red: 4 ruby; **5** pinko, ruddy; **6** aflame, cerise, cherry; **7** carmine, crimson, flushed, Marxist, reddish, redness, ruby-red, scarlet,

R

violent; **8** blood-red, red-faced, reddened; **9** Bolshevik, cherry-red

Red: 8 Red River

redact: 3 put; **4** cast, edit; **5** couch, frame

redactor: 7 reviser; **8** rewriter

red blood cell: 11 erythrocyte

red-blooded: 5 lusty; **6** hearty; **11** full-blooded

redbreast: 5 robin

redbug: 7 chigger

redcap: 6 porter; **13** Pullman porter

red cent: 5 penny

Red China: 3 PRC; **5** China; **13** mainland China; **14** Communist China

redden: 5 blush, color, flush; **7** color up, crimson

reddened: 3 red; **6** ablaze, aflame; **7** crimson, flushed; **8** inflamed, red-faced

red devil: 7 Seconal; **12** secobarbital

reddish: 3 red; **4** ruby; **5** ruddy; **6** cerise, cherry; **7** carmine, crimson, ruby-red, scarlet; **8** blood-red; **9** cherry-red

reddish blue: 6 violet

reddish brown: 5 sepia

reddish-brown: 6 auburn

reddishness: 8 erythema; **9** ruddiness

red drum: 7 redfish

redeem: 4 quit, save; **5** honor, purge; **6** pay off, ransom, recoup, regain, repair, settle, shrive; **7** absolve, commute, deliver, reclaim, recover, satisfy; **8** retrieve; **9** discharge; **10** emancipate

redeemed: 8 ransomed

redeeming: 6 saving; **10** redemptive

redemption: 7 buyback, salvage; **8** judgment; **9** acquittal, atonement, clearance, discharge, expiation, mediation, quittance, reckoning, salvation; **10** repurchase, settlement; **11** arrangement, fulfillment, liquidation, performance, reclamation

redemptive: 6 saving; **9** redeeming; **10** redemptory; **12** redemptional

redevelop: 11 reformulate

red-faced: 3 red; **6** aflame; **7** crimson, flushed; **8** blushful, blushing, reddened

red fir: 10 douglas fir

redfish: 7 red drum

red gram: 4 dahl, dhal

red gum: 8 sweet gum

redhead: 9 carrottop

redheaded woodpecker: 7 redhead

red herring: 13 smoked herring

red-hot: 3 hot; **5** fiery, juicy; **6** ardent, fervid; **7** burning, fervent, flaming, flushed, glowing, gushing; **8** feverish, luscious, sizzling; **9** desperate, ebullient, scorching; **10** blistering, passionate, voluptuous

redisposition: 12 redeployment

red-letter day: 6 day off; **7** dies non, holiday, play day; **9** day of rest

red light: 12 warning light

red mullet: 8 goatfish

redneck: 7 cracker

redness: 3 red; **5** flush; **12** inflammation

redo: 6 remake; **7** remodel; **8** make over; **9** refashion; **11** reconstruct

redolence: 4 fume; **5** scent, trail; **7** bouquet, essence, perfume; **9** fragrance, sweetness

redolent: 5 balmy, spicy; **6** savory; **7** pungent, scented; **8** aromatic, fragrant, smelling; **9** evocative, remindful; **10** redolent of; **11** reminiscent; **12** sweet-scented

red onion: 11 purple onion

redouble: 4 drum, echo; **6** double, hammer, reecho, repeat; **7** enhance, iterate, magnify; **8** harp upon; **9** duplicate, intensify, reiterate, reproduce; **11** reduplicate

redoubt: 4 fort, hold; **6** sconce; **8** fastness, fortress; **10** stronghold

redoubtable: 8 glorious; **9** respected, unnerving; **10** formidable; **11** illustrious

red pepper: 5 chili; **7** cayenne, tabasco; **8** capsicum

Red Planet: 4 Mars

red region: 8 hellfire

redress: 3 sop; **4** help; **5** right; **6** amends, curing, remedy; **7** correct, damages, regimen, therapy; **8** requital; **9** atonement, indemnity, retrieval, treatment; **10** compensate, reparation; **11** reclamation, remediation

red salmon: 7 sockeye

red setter: 11 Irish setter

red snapper: 11 huachinango

red sorrel: 8 hibiscus; **13** Jamaica sorrel

red spider mite: 9 red spider

red-tailed hawk: 7 redtail

reduce: 3 cut; **4** bate, give, sink, slim, thin, trim; **5** abase, allow, cramp, pitch, quash; **6** debase, decoct, dilute, lessen, shrink, sprain, strain, subdue, take in; **7** abridge, curtail, cut back, cut down, melt off, repress, shorten, take off, thin out, tighten; **8** boil down, bring low, come down, contract, diminish, discount, keep down, mark down, simplify; **9** bring down, deoxidise, deoxidize, subjugate; **10** abbreviate, impoverish, lose weight, slenderize

reduced: 6 shrunk; **8** squeezed; **9** compacted, decreased; **10** compressed, contracted, diminished

reduced instruction set computer: 4 RISC

reductio ad absurdum: 7 dilemma

reduction: 8 decrease, discount, mark down, reducing, step-down; **9** abatement, allowance, evolution; **10** concession, diminution, estimation, involution, loss of mass, resolution; **11** contraction; **12** depreciation

reduction by one-tenth: 10 decimation

reduction of temperature: 7 cooling; **13** refrigeration

redundance: 10 redundancy; 11 duplication, superfluity; 15 superfluousness

redundant: 5 extra, spare, wordy; 6 excess; 7 surplus; 10 pleonastic, tautologic; 11 superfluous

reduviid: 11 assassin bug

red-winged blackbird: 7 redwing

redwood: 7 sequoia

redwood family: 11 Taxodiaceae

red worm: 7 dew worm, wiggler; 8 fishworm; 9 angleworm, earthworm; 11 fishing worm, nightwalker; 12 nightcrawler

reed: 4 cane; 5 arrow, shaft

Reed: 10 Walter Reed

reed organ: 5 organ; 9 harmonica, harmonium

reedy: 6 twiggy, wheezy; 8 twiglike

reef: 5 atoll, snags; 7 breaker

reefer: 5 joint, stick; 6 doobie

reef knot: 8 flat knot

reefy: 5 shoal; 6 shelfy, shelvy, shoaly

reek: 4 fume, stew; 5 fetor, smack, smell, smoke, steam, stink; 6 exhale, flatus, foetor, reek of, seethe, simmer, stench; 7 essence, malodor; 8 malodour, smell bad; 9 effluvium; 13 have a bad smell

reeking: 3 bad; 4 high, soft; 6 sloppy, sodden, strong, watery; 7 soaking; 8 dripping; 13 strong-scented; 14 strong-smelling

reeky: 4 foul; 5 nasty; 6 coarse; 7 beastly; 9 offensive; 10 abominable

reel: 3 bob, wag; 4 keel, spin, swag, sway, toss; 5 lurch, quake, spool, whirl; 6 bobbin, careen, gyrate, quaver, quiver, shiver, tumble, waggle, wamble, writhe; 7 shuffle, stagger, twitter; 10 spin around; 12 Scottish reel, Virginia reel

reelect: 6 return

re-emerge: 8 reappear

reenact: 5 enact, model; 6 act out; 8 simulate

reenforce: 6 beef up; 7 fortify, recruit; 9 reinforce; 10 strengthen

reestablish: 6 reseat; 7 replace, restore; 9 reinstall, reinstate; 12 rehabilitate

reevaluate: 8 reassess; 10 reappraise

reexamination: 6 review; 8 follow-up

reexamine: 6 review

ref: 7 referee

refabrication: 8 remaking; 10 reassembly; 11 reformation

refashion: 4 redo, vamp; 6 cobble, remake, tinker; 7 retouch; 8 make over

refer: 4 cite, name; 5 touch; 6 advert, bear on, come to, denote, look up, relate; 7 bring up, concern, consult, mention, pertain, touch on

referable: 5 due to; 9 imputable; 10 ascribable

referee: 3 ref; 6 umpire; 8 assessor, reviewer

refereeing: 8 umpirage, umpiring; 11 officiating, officiation

reference: 4 cite, type; 5 ideal, model; 6 credit, source; 7 example, italics, mention, pattern; 8 citation, exemplar, original, paradigm, standard; 9 character, extension, precedent, prototype, quotation, scantling; 10 annotation, denotation; 11 underlining; 12 consultation

referendum: 6 recall; 10 initiative, plebiscite

refill: 9 replenish

refine: 4 down, rack; 5 cavil, purge; 6 polish, rarify; 7 clarify; 8 fine-tune; 9 elaborate

refined: 4 neat; 5 sweet; 6 dainty, mellow, pastel, pearly, svelte, tender, urbane; 7 courtly, elegant, gallant; 8 delicate, graceful, polished, purified, tasteful, well-bred; 9 civilized, processed, sublimate; 10 cultivated, harmonious; 11 gentlemanly; 12 thoroughbred; 13 gentlemanlike

refinement: 4 gust, tact; 5 gusto, shade; 6 nicety, nuance, polish; 7 finesse; 8 breeding, delicacy, refining, subtlety; 9 gentility; 11 elaboration, fine feeling, genteelness

refining industry: 11 oil business, oil industry

refinisher: 8 restorer; 9 preserver, renovator

refit: 7 recruit

reflect: 4 echo, mull, muse; 5 shine; 6 mirror, ponder, reecho; 8 chew over, meditate, mull over, ruminate; 9 speculate, think over; 11 contemplate

reflection: 6 musing, reflex, reflux; 7 thought; 8 thinking; 9 exception, objection, reflexion [Brit], sentiment, stricture; 10 cogitation, expression, meditation, reflecting, resilience, rumination; 11 mirror image, observation; 12 reflectivity; 13 consideration, contemplation

reflective: 6 broody, musing, sedate; 7 pensive, wistful; 8 brooding, Platonic, studious; 9 pondering; 10 meditative, ruminative, thoughtful; 11 speculative; 12 deliberative

reflector: 6 mirror

reflex: 8 reaction

reflux: 3 ebb; 4 eddy; 6 reflex, vortex; 8 overflow

reforge: 6 recast; 7 remodel

reform: 7 remodel; 8 amending, new model; 9 amendment, reforming; 10 correcting, correction, regenerate, reorganize

reformer: 8 crusader, resister

reforming: 6 reform; 8 amending; 9 amendment; 10 correcting, correction; 11 reformation

reform school: 11 reformatory

refraction: 4 warp; 9 deflexion; 10 deflection

refractory: 5 balky, heady; 6 unruly; 7 restive, wayward, willful; 8 contrary, perverse, recusant, stubborn; 9 fractious;

R

10 headstrong, rebellious, self-willed; **11** intractable; **12** contumacious, recalcitrant, unmanageable

refrain: 4 echo; **5** spare; **6** chimes, chorus, desist; **7** abstain, forbear; **8** forebear

refrain from: 5 avoid

refresh: 6 regale, review; **7** brush up, freshen, recruit, relieve, restore; **9** freshen up, refreshen; **12** reinvigorate; **18** infuse new blood into

refreshing: 5 brisk, fresh, novel, tonic; **7** bracing; **10** energizing, refreshful; **11** restorative; **12** recuperative

refried beans: 8 frijoles

refrigerate: 4 cool

refrigerator: 6 icebox

refuge: 6 asylum, resort, safety; **8** recourse; **9** sanctuary

refugee: 8 fugitive

refulgence: 5 shine; **8** radiance, radiancy, splendor; **10** brilliance

refulgent: 5 beamy; **7** beaming, radiant; **9** effulgent

refund: 5 repay; **6** return; **8** disgorge, give back; **9** reimburse, repayment

refurbish: 8 renovate; **9** freshen up

refusal: 7 regrets; **9** declining, dismissal, rejection; **10** preemption; **11** declination

refuse: 4 defy, deny; **5** trash; **6** litter, pass up, reject, resist, scraps; **7** decline, discard, dismiss, garbage, rubbish; **8** discards

refuse collector: 7 dustman; **8** trashman; **10** garbage man

refuse heap: 4 dump; **9** wasteyard

refutable: 10 defeasible; **12** questionable

refutation: 7 defence, defense; **8** disproof; **11** confutation; **12** invalidation

refute: 5 rebut; **7** confute; **8** confound, disprove, negative; **10** controvert, disconfirm

regain: 4 find; **6** recoup, redeem; **7** recover; **8** recovery, retrieve; **9** retrieval

regaining: 6 return; **11** restitution, restoration

regal: 5 royal; **6** purple; **7** regnant; **8** imperial, majestic; **9** sovereign

regale: 5 feast, treat; **7** refresh; **9** symposium

regalia: 5 array; **6** ensign, finery; **7** raiment

regard: 3 see; **4** gaze, heed, look, love, mark, view, wish; **5** count, fancy, honor, kudos [Grk], touch; **6** affect, esteem, notice, reckon, remark; **7** account, care for, concern, involve, observe, respect, think of; **8** advert to, consider

regarding: 4 as to; **7** vis-a-vis; **10** concerning

regardless: 8 careless, listless, mindless, no matter; **11** thoughtless; **12** disregarding, irregardless, irrespective; **13** disregardless

regards: 4 duty; **6** devoir, egards; **7** devoirs; **8** respects; **10** compliment; **11** compliments [pl]; **12** remembrances

regatta: 8 boat race; **9** yacht race

regenerate: 5 edify, renew; **6** reform, regrow, revive; **7** convert, inspire, restore; **8** revivify; **9** reanimate; **10** revitalize; **11** resuscitate

regent: 3 beg; **5** vicar; **7** trustee, viceroy; **8** palatine

regime: 5 reign; **6** status; **7** footing, regimen; **8** standing; **10** government; **11** authorities

regimen: 4 diet, help; **6** curing, regime, remedy; **7** redress, therapy; **9** treatment

regiment: 4 army, host, wing; **5** corps; **6** column; **7** section; **10** detachment

region: 4 area, part; **5** realm; **6** domain, parish; **7** quarter; **8** subspace; **9** partition; **12** neighborhood

regional: 5 local; **9** parochial; **10** provincial; **11** territorial

regionalism: 8 localism

register: 4 file, read, show; **6** enroll, record

registered nurse: 2 RN; **5** nurse

registrar: 8 recorder, register; **12** record-keeper

registration: 10 enrollment

regnant: 5 regal; **6** ruling; **8** dominant, reigning; **9** sovereign; **11** predominant; **14** in the ascendant

regorge: 5 vomit; **6** be sick; **7** throw up; **8** disgorge; **11** regurgitate

regress: 5 lapse; **6** return, revert; **7** relapse; **8** fall back

regressive: 6 reflex; **9** relapsing, resilient, revulsive; **10** recidivous; **11** reactionary

regret: 3 rue; **6** bemoan, bewail, lament, repent, sorrow; **7** deplore

regrets: 7 refusal; **11** declination

regrettable: 6 too bad; **11** unfortunate

regrettably: 4 alas

regretted: 4 rued; **8** lamented

regroup: 10 reorganize

regrowth: 7 renewal; **12** regeneration

regular: 4 even, free, real, true; **5** sheer, trite; **6** common, steady; **7** general, genuine, habitue, orderly, uniform; **8** balanced, bona fide, familiar, ordinary, punctual, unvaried; **9** authentic, unchanged, veritable; **10** consummate, methodical, systematic, unchanging, vernacular; **11** established

regular as clockwork: 6 steady; **7** regular; **8** punctual

regularity: 5 order; **7** routine; **8** monotony; **9** constancy; **10** steadiness, uniformity

regulate: 3 fix; **5** dress, order, shape; **6** adjust, baffle, govern, settle; **8** modulate, readjust; **9** determine, influence, methodize; **10** coordinate, regularize; **11** systematize

regulation: 3 act; **4** form, rule; **6** rubric; **7** control, statute; **8** dominion, guidance; **9** ordinance

Regulus: 7 kinglet; **12** genus Regulus

regurgitate: 4 puke, purl, sick, spew, spue; 5 chuck, heave, retch, vomit; 7 bring up, get sick, regorge, sputter, throw up, upchuck, vomit up; 8 disgorge

rehabilitation: 4 cure; 7 renewal, revival; 8 recovery; 10 renovation; 11 reclamation, restoration; 12 recuperation

rehear: 5 retry

rehearsal: 5 trial; 6 dry run; 8 practise, relation, trial run

rehearse: 8 practice

reheated: 8 leftover; 10 cooked-over, warmed-over

reign: 4 rule; 6 regime; 7 prevail; 8 dominate; 9 dominance; 10 governance, government; 11 be sovereign, predominate, sovereignty

reign of terror: 9 terrorism; 10 oppression

reimburse: 5 repay; 6 recoup, refund; 8 disgorge, make good; 9 indemnify; 10 compensate

rein: 4 rule; 5 reins; 6 rein in; 7 harness, shackle

reincarnation: 7 rebirth

reindeer: 7 caribou

reinforce: 6 beef up, reward; 7 fortify, recruit; 9 reenforce; 10 strengthen

reinforced: 5 built; 12 strengthened

reinforced concrete: 13 ferroconcrete

reinforcement: 6 reward; 7 support; 9 accession, accessory, increment; 10 reinforcer; 12 strengthener

rein in: 4 curb, rein; 5 check; 6 pull in; 7 harness

reinstall: 6 reseat; 7 replace; 9 reinstate; 11 reestablish

reinstate: 6 reseat, revest; 7 replace, restore; 8 reinvest; 9 reinstall; 11 reestablish

reinvigorate: 5 brace; 7 refresh; 10 invigorate

reissue: 7 reprint

reiterate: 4 drum, echo; 6 hammer, reecho, repeat, retell; 7 iterate, restate; 8 redouble; 9 reproduce

reject: 4 cull, deny; 5 scorn, spurn; 6 pass up, refuse; 7 decline, disdain, dismiss, rule out; 8 pooh-pooh, turn away, turn down; 9 eliminate, freeze off, not chosen; 10 disapprove, not adopted; 11 not selected

rejected: 6 jilted; 7 refused, spurned; 8 castaway, declined, forsaken, lovelorn; 9 dismissed; 10 repudiated, turned down

rejection: 7 refusal; 8 omission; 9 declining, dismissal, exception, exclusion

rejects: 5 culls; 8 discards

rejoice: 3 joy; 5 cheer, exult, revel; 6 solace, wallow; 7 triumph; 8 jubilate, recreate

rejoin: 4 join, meet; 5 rebut, repay, reply, unite; 6 answer, retort, return; 7 respond, riposte; 8 come back

rejoinder: 4 plea; 5 reply; 6 answer, retort, return; 7 riposte; 8 comeback, demurrer, rebuttal, rebutter; 11 replication

rejuvenation: 8 greening

rekindle: 6 revive; 8 reignite

relapse: 5 lapse; 7 lapsing, regress; 8 fall back, get worse; 9 relapsing, reversion, reverting; 10 recidivate, recidivism, regression, retrogress; 11 backsliding

relate: 3 say; 4 link, tell; 5 refer, tie in, touch; 6 bear on, come to, recite; 7 concern, connect, narrate, pertain, recount, touch on; 9 associate

related: 4 akin; 6 family; 7 germane, kindred; 9 connected

relation: 3 kin; 5 blood; 7 bearing, concern, kindred, kinfolk [pl], kinsman, telling; 8 relative; 9 cognation, rehearsal; 10 connection

relations: 8 dealings

relationship: 7 bearing, concern, kinship; 8 relation; 9 cognation, family tie; 10 connection

relative: 3 kin; 5 blood; 7 cognate, kindred, kinfolk [pl], kinsman; 8 congener, relation; 10 congenator, connection, kith and kin [pl]

relax: 4 bend, give, rest; 5 loose, shake, unlax, yield; 6 loosen, mellow, relent, repose, retard, temper, unbend, unwind, weaken; 7 forbear, mollify, slacken; 8 enervate, enfeeble, loosen up

relaxation: 4 ease, rest; 6 repose, solace; 7 languor, leisure; 8 debility, easiness, reaction, relaxing; 9 loosening

relaxed: 3 lax; 5 baggy, loose, slack; 6 at ease; 8 detached, flapping, unnerved; 9 streaming

release: 4 exit, fall, free, loss, obit, rest, sack, send, turn; 5 eject, expel, favor, going, issue, let go, loose, remit, spill; 6 acquit, escape, excuse, exempt, firing, give up, launch, let fly, let off, outlet, put out, remise, waiver; 7 handout, passing, publish, sacking, secrete, send off, unblock, unloose; 8 bring out, immunity, liberate, spillage, unfreeze; 9 departure, discharge, dismissal, exception, exemption, exonerate, franchise, indemnity, privilege, quitclaim, quittance; 10 expiration, liberation, relinquish

release valve: 9 blow valve; 11 safety valve

releasing: 9 cathartic

relegate: 3 bar; 4 bump; 5 break; 6 banish, demote, deport, pass on, submit; 7 consign

relent: 5 relax, remit, yield; 6 soften; 7 forbear; 8 come over, give into

relentless: 4 grim; 5 stern; 7 Spartan; 9 Draconian, graceless, stringent; 10 inexorable, persistent; 11 remorseless, straitlaced, unforgiving, unrelenting

R

relevant: 7 crucial, germane, in point, on point; 10 admissible, applicable

reliable: 4 true; 5 bound; 6 honest; 8 credible, faithful; 9 authentic; 10 dependable; 11 trustworthy

reliably: 10 dependably, faithfully

reliance: 5 trust; 9 assurance; 10 confidence; 11 presumption

relic: 5 token; 6 relics; 7 memento, remains, remnant; 8 keepsake, remanent, souvenir; 11 memorabilia

relief: 4 ease, rest; 6 backup, easing, fill-in, rescue, succor; 7 relieve, relievo [It], respite, rilievo, stand-in, succour; 9 backup man; 10 embossment, moderation, rest period, substitute; 11 alleviation

relief map: 10 contour map

relief pitcher: 7 fireman; 8 reliever

relieve: 4 ease, free, save; 5 allay, salve, spell, still; 6 excuse, exempt, let off, relief, remedy, rescue, soothe; 7 assuage, deliver, recruit, refresh

religieuse: 3 nun; 6 novice; 9 postulant

religion: 5 faith, piety; 6 theism; 12 spirituality

religionist: 5 saint, 7 devotee

religiosity: 7 pietism

religious: 4 holy; 5 godly, pious; 6 devout, strict; 7 devoted; 8 reverent; 9 pietistic, spiritual

religious doctrine: 5 creed; 6 gospel; 8 doctrine

religious order: 4 sect

religious outcast: 7 heretic; 11 misbeliever

religious person: 8 adherent; 9 worshiper; 10 worshipper

religious residence: 8 cloister

religious school: 9 parochial

Religious Society of Friends: 7 Quakers

relinquish: 4 free, quit; 5 forgo, let go, waive, yield; 6 give up; 7 abandon, let slip, release; 8 abnegate, renounce; 9 foreswear, surrender

reliquary: 3 pix, pyx; 5 chest; 6 casket, coffer; 7 caisson

relish: 4 bask, like, love, tang, zest; 5 enjoy, gusto, savor, smack, spice; 6 flavor, liking, riot in, savour; 7 revel in; 8 fondness, sapidity; 9 condiment, seasoning

reload: 8 recharge

relocate: 6 settle

relocation: 6 moving; 12 resettlement

reluctance: 6 recoil; 9 hesitancy, shrinking; 10 hesitation

reluctant: 4 loth; 5 loath, shy of; 6 averse; 10 indisposed

rely: 4 bank; 5 swear, trust

remain: 4 last, rest, stay; 5 abide, stand; 6 be left, endure, stay on; 7 persist, survive; 8 continue

remainder: 3 end; 4 rest; 5 scrap; 7 oddment, remnant, residue; 8 residual; 9 reversion; 10 expectancy

remaining: 3 odd; 4 left; 8 left over, leftover, survival; 9 surviving; 10 unexpended

remains: 4 clay; 5 relic, stiff, trace; 6 corpse; 7 cadaver, remnant, vestige; 8 remanent

remake: 4 redo; 8 make over; 9 refashion; 10 reorganize; 12 reconstitute

remanent: 5 relic; 7 remains, remnant

remark: 3 see; 4 look, mark, note, view; 6 notice, regard; 7 comment, mention, observe; 11 observation

remarkable: 6 marked, of mark; 7 pointed, veriest; 8 singular; 10 noteworthy

remarkably: 4 unco; 6 mainly; 7 chiefly, notably; 8 signally; 9 curiously, pointedly, unusually; 10 peculiarly, singularly, strikingly, uncommonly; 12 noteworthily, particularly, unmistakably; 13 outstandingly

rematch: 6 replay

Rembrandt: 15 Rembrandt van Ryn; 16 Rembrandt van Rijn; 24 Rembrandt Harmensz van Rijn

remedial: 7 healing; 8 curative, sanative; 10 alterative; 11 therapeutic

remediation: 6 remedy; 7 redress

remedy: 4 cure, heal, help; 5 amend; 6 curing, doctor, physic; 7 rectify, redress, regimen, relieve, therapy; 8 curative, medicate; 9 treatment; 11 remediation

remember: 4 mind; 5 think; 6 call up, recall, remind, reward; 7 commend, retrace, think of; 8 memorize, retrieve, summon up; 9 put in mind, recollect

remembering: 6 memory; 9 recalling, retention; 10 memorizing, retrospect

remind: 3 cue; 5 think; 6 call up, prompt, recall; 7 suggest; 8 call back, remember, retrieve; 9 recollect

reminder: 4 hint

reminiscent of: 8 redolent; 9 evocative, remindful

remise: 5 remit; 6 acquit, exempt; 7 release; 9 discharge, quitclaim

remiss: 4 lazy; 5 slack; 6 otiose, slow to, supine, torpid; 7 laggard, languid; 8 backward, derelict, indolent, slothful, sluggish; 10 delinquent, neglectful; 11 perfunctory

remission: 8 remittal; 10 absolution, mitigation, relaxation, remittance, subsidence; 11 assuagement

remit: 5 defer, table; 6 acquit, exempt, let off, put off, relent, remand, remise, shelve; 7 absolve, put over, release, set back, slacken; 8 intermit, postpone, reprieve; 9 discharge, quitclaim

remnant: 3 end; 5 relic, scrap; 7 oddment, remains; 8 leftover, remanent; 9 remainder

remodel: 4 redo; 6 recast, reform; 7 reforge; 8 new model; 10 reorganize; 11 reconstruct

remodeled: 7 rebuilt

remold: 6 recast; 7 remould, reshape, retread

remonstrance: 7 protest, reproof; 8 reproach; 9 mediation, objection; 10 admonition; 11 deprecation, reprobation; 12 intercession

remonstrate: 3 jaw, rag; 5 check, chide, scold; 6 berate, chew up, rebuke; 7 bawl out, chew out, lambast, lecture, protest, reproof; 8 lambaste, point out; 9 deprecate, reprimand

remora: 10 suckerfish

remorse: 9 penitence; 10 contrition, repentance; 11 compunction; 12 self-reproach

remorseful: 5 sorry; 6 rueful; 8 contrite

remote: 3 far; 5 aloof; 6 distal, far off, forced, wide of; 7 distant, far away, outback, outside, removed; 8 detached; 9 backwoods, withdrawn; 10 far-fetched

remote-controlled: 8 unmanned

removal: 6 bounce [U.S.]; 7 drawing, ousting; 8 remotion, removing; 9 dismissal; 10 divestment, extracting, extraction, uncovering, withdrawal; 11 elimination, extrication

remove: 4 draw, form, slay, take; 5 shunt; 6 absent, bow out, get out, murder, retire; 7 bump off, draw out, extract, move out, pick out, pull out, seminar, take out, tear out; 8 dispatch, distance, transfer, withdraw; 9 extricate

remove from office: 7 dismiss

remove the veil: 6 unfold, unseal, unveil; 7 uncover

removing: 7 drawing, removal; 9 taking off; 10 divestment, drawing out, extracting, extraction, taking away, uncovering, withdrawal; 11 elimination, extrication

remuneration: 3 pay; 4 meed, wage; 6 reward, salary; 8 earnings; 12 compensation

remunerator: 5 payer

renaissance: 7 rebirth; 10 renascence

Renaissance man: 10 generalist

renal: 9 nephritic

renal calculus: 11 kidney stone

renascence: 7 rebirth; 11 renaissance

renascent: 9 resurgent; 11 reappearing

rend: 3 rip; 4 pull, rive; 5 sever; 6 divide, sunder; 8 dissever; 9 subdivide

render: 3 try; 4 give, make, play; 5 forgo, get in, spiel, waive, yield; 6 give up, impart, return, submit, supply, turn in; 7 deliver, forfeit, furnish, provide; 8 generate; 9 interpret; 11 communicate

render equal: 5 dress, level; 6 equate; 7 balance; 8 equalize; 9 make equal

rendering: 7 version; 9 depiction, rendition; 11 translation; 12 interpreting

rendezvous: 4 meet; 5 tryst; 6 resort, gather

rending: 7 ripping; 9 harrowing, splitting

rendition: 7 version; 9 rendering; 11 translation; 12 interpreting

renegade: 5 rebel; 6 rioter; 7 brawler, convert, pervert, traitor; 8 apostate, deserter, recreant, runagate, turncoat; 9 proselyte; 10 backslider, recidivist

renege: 6 revoke

renew: 8 renovate; 10 regenerate

renewal: 6 repair; 7 revival; 8 regrowth, restoral; 9 refilling; 10 renovation, reparation; 11 reclamation, replacement, restoration

renitent: 6 spring; 7 buoyant, elastic, springy, tensile; 8 flexible, reacting; 9 resilient, resisting

rennin: 8 chymosin

renounce: 4 drop, quit, shed; 5 evade, spare; 6 abjure, forego, give up, resign, slight, vacate; 7 neglect, retract; 8 abdicate, abnegate, disclaim, forswear, give away, part with; 9 dispose of, foreswear, repudiate; 10 relinquish; 15 wash one's hands of

renovate: 5 renew; 6 revamp, update; 9 freshen up, refurbish, restitute

renovator: 8 restorer; 9 preserver; 10 refinisher

renown: 4 fame; 9 celebrity; 10 famousness

renowned: 5 famed, noted; 6 famous; 7 notable; 8 far-famed, talked of; 10 celebrated; 11 illustrious

rent: 3 let, rip; 4 hire, take, tear, torn; 5 lease, split; 6 breach, engage, rental, ripped

rental: 4 rent; 5 lease; 7 letting, renting

renter: 6 lessee, tenant

rent out: 3 let; 4 rent, 7 farm out, hire out

renunciant: 11 self-denying; 12 renunciative

renunciation: 8 apostasy, forgoing; 9 defection; 10 abjuration, abnegation; 11 abandonment, forswearing, repudiation; 12 renouncement

reorganize: 6 reform, remake; 7 regroup, remodel, shake up; 8 new model; 12 reconstitute

repair: 3 fix; 4 mend; 5 haunt, purge; 6 bushel, doctor, fixing, ransom, redeem, resort, shrive; 7 absolve, hangout, mending, reclaim, renewal, restore, touch on; 8 restoral; 9 furbish up, refection; 10 reparation; 11 refreshment, restoration

repairable: 7 fixable; 10 restorable

repaired: 5 fixed; 8 serviced; 10 maintained; 13 reconditioned

repairer: 8 handyman; 9 repairman

reparation: 3 fix, sop; 6 amends, fixing, repair; 7 mending, redress, renewal; 8 requital, restoral; 9 atonement; 11 restoration

repartee: 6 banter, retort

repast: 4 meal

repay: 6 refund, rejoin, retort, return, reward; 7 pay back, requite, riposte; 8 come back, disgorge, give back; 9 reimburse; 10 recompense

R

repayment: 6 refund; 8 repaying; 9 quittance; 13 reimbursement

repeal: 4 lift; 5 annul; 6 cancel, revoke; 7 rescind, reverse; 8 abrogate, annuling, overturn, recision; 9 annulment, canceling; 10 abrogating, abrogation, defeasance, render null, rescinding, rescission; 11 countermand; 12 cancellation; 13 nullification

repeat: 4 drum, echo; 5 recur; 6 double, hammer, reecho, retell; 7 iterate, reprise, restate; 8 harp upon, multiply, redouble; 9 duplicate, reiterate, replicate, reproduce; 10 repetition; 12 recapitulate

repeatedly: 4 anew; 5 again, often

repel: 4 snub; 5 drive, parry, shock; 6 offend, rebuff, revolt, sicken; 7 disgust, exclude, repulse, turn off; 8 alienate, beat back, brush off, drive off, estrange; 10 disenchant, disincline

repellent: 4 foul; 5 yucky; 6 odious, wicked; 7 hateful, loathly; 9 abhorrent, execrable, loathsome, repellant, repulsive, resistant, revolting; 10 disgustful, disgusting; 11 distasteful, rebarbative

repent: 3 rue; 5 atone; 6 regret; 10 be contrite, be penitent; 11 be repentant

repercussion: 6 recoil; 7 rebound; 8 backlash

repertory: 5 cache, depot, store; 10 depository, repertoire, repository

repetition: 6 repeat; 7 harping; 9 iteration, repeating; 10 recurrence; 11 duplication, reiteration; 13 reduplication

repetitious: 9 iterative; 10 repetitive; 11 reiterative

repetitive: 9 insistent, iterative; 11 reiterative, repetitious

rephrase: 6 reword; 10 paraphrase

replace: 6 cut out, reseat; 7 restore; 8 supplant; 9 reinstall, reinstate, supersede; 10 substitute

replacement: 6 switch; 7 renewal; 9 alternate, refilling, replacing, successor, surrogate; 10 substitute; 11 alternative, permutation, restoration; 12 substitution

replay: 7 rematch; 8 play back; 12 action replay

replenish: 6 refill; 8 make good; 9 fill again

replete: 4 fill, full, sate; 6 lavish, wanton; 7 profuse, satiate; 8 overmuch; 9 exuberant; 10 inordinate; 11 extravagant

replica: 4 copy, form; 6 effigy; 8 likeness; 9 facsimile, imitation; 11 counterpart; 12 reproduction

replicate: 4 copy; 5 rerun; 6 double, repeat; 7 imitate; 9 duplicate

replication: 4 plea; 5 reply; 6 answer; 7 copying; 8 demurrer, rebutter; 9 duplicate, imitating, imitation, rejoinder; 11 replicating; 12 reproduction

reply: 4 plea; 5 rebut; 6 answer, rejoin,

retort; 7 defense, respond; 8 demurrer, rebutter, response; 9 rejoinder; 11 replication

report: 5 award, cover, paper, story, study, theme; 6 notice, review, turn in; 7 account, write up; 8 critique, describe, despatch, dispatch; 9 arbitrate, criticism, statement

reported: 4 told; 12 communicated

reporter: 6 teller; 7 delator, newsman, relator; 8 exponent; 9 authority, informant, newswoman; 10 journalist, mouthpiece, newscaster, newsperson; 13 correspondent

reporting: 8 coverage; 9 reportage; 10 journalism

repose: 3 lay; 4 ease, rest; 5 peace, quiet, relax; 6 reside; 7 put down, recline, resting; 8 ataraxis, reposing, serenity; 9 placidity; 10 relaxation

repositing: 5 store; 7 storing; 10 reposition; 11 warehousing

repository: 5 cache, depot, store; 7 deposit; 8 monument; 9 repertory, secretary; 10 depository

repossess: 7 reclaim; 8 take back

reprehend: 5 chide; 6 rebuke; 8 admonish

reprehensible: 8 criminal, culpable; 10 answerable, censurable, deplorable; 11 blameworthy, condemnable, disgraceful; 12 disreputable; 13 discreditable, uncommendable

reprehension: 6 rebuke; 7 reproof; 8 reproach, reproval; 9 reprimand; 10 admonition

represent: 2 be; 3 act, map; 4 play; 6 defend, denote, make up, typify; 7 betoken, express, let fall, mention, picture, refer to, signify; 8 advocate, comprise, indicate, intimate, stand for; 9 delineate, exemplify, interpret, symbolize; 10 constitute, correspond

representation: 4 sign; 5 model, study; 6 agency, symbol; 8 advocacy, delegacy; 9 depiction, rendering

representative: 5 proxy, voice; 6 consul, deputy; 7 example; 8 delegate, instance, resident, symbolic; 9 secondary, surrogate; 10 denotating, denotative, indicating, next friend, signifying, substitute; 11 congressman, interpreter

repress: 5 quash; 6 reduce, subdue; 8 suppress; 9 subjugate

reprieve: 5 remit; 6 hiatus, let off; 7 absolve, respite; 9 abatement; 10 suspension

reprimand: 3 jaw, rag; 4 lash, trim; 5 check, chide, scold; 6 berate, blow up, chew up, rebuke; 7 bawl out, censure, chew out, lambast, lecture, reproof, trounce; 8 chastise, lambaste, overhaul, reproval; 9 castigate, criminate, dress down

reprinting: 7 reissue, reprint

reprisal: 6 retort; 7 payback, reprise; 11 retaliation

reprise: 6 repeat; 8 reprisal; 12 recapitulate

reproach: 4 slur, twit; 5 brand; 6 impugn, stigma; 7 censure, reproof, upbraid; 9 reprobate; 10 admonition, imputation

reprobate: 3 rip; 5 scamp; 6 impugn; 7 censure, corrupt, fronder [Fr], immoral; 8 depraved, hardened, obdurate, perverse, recreant, reproach, runagate, scalawag, scampish; 9 corrupted, dissolute, graceless, miscreant, perverted, scallawag; 10 ne'er-do-well, profligate, scapegrace

reprocess: 5 reuse; 7 recycle

reproduce: 6 repeat; 7 iterate; 8 multiply, redouble; 9 procreate, propagate, reiterate

reproduction: 7 replica; 8 breeding; 9 duplicate; 11 procreation, propagation

reproductive cell: 7 sex cell; 8 germ cell

reprove: 7 lecture; 8 admonish

reproved: 7 rebuked; 9 chastened; 10 admonished; 11 reprimanded

reprover: 9 detractor

reptile: 9 reptilian

Reptilia: 13 class Reptilia

republic: 8 dominion; 9 democracy; 12 commonwealth

Republican Party: 3 GOP; 11 Republicans

Republic of China: 5 China; 6 Taiwan; 7 Formosa; 16 Nationalist China

repudiate: 5 quash, scout; 6 ignore, slight; 7 discard, neglect, nullify, protest; 8 dishonor, forswear, renounce

repudiated: 8 disowned, rejected

repugn: 6 oppose, reluct, resist; 7 contend, contest

repugnance: 6 horror, nausea; 7 disgust; 8 clashing, loathing; 9 repulsion, revulsion

repugnant: 5 gross; 7 bizarre, fulsome, hostile, obscene; 9 abhorrent, grotesque, loathsome, repellant, repulsive; 10 detestable

repulse: 4 rout, snub; 5 drive, repel; 6 rebuff

repulsion: 6 horror; 8 standoff; 9 repelling, revulsion; 10 repugnance

repulsive: 5 gross, nasty; 6 odious; 7 bizarre, fulsome, hateful, hideous, obscene; 9 abhorrent, execrable, grotesque, loathsome, obnoxious, offensive, repellant, repellent, repugnant; 10 detestable

repurchase: 7 buyback; 10 redemption

reputable: 10 creditable; 11 respectable

repute: 6 esteem

reputed: 8 putative, supposed; 9 purported

request: 3 ask; 5 quest; 6 ask for, asking; 7 bespeak, call for; 8 petition; 11 requisition

requiem: 5 dirge, elegy; 6 lament

require: 3 ask, tax; 4 lack, need, take, want; 5 exact; 6 assert, assume, charge, compel, demand, enjoin, expect; 7 command, involve; 8 arrogate, make good; 11 necessitate

required: 6 forced, needed; 7 coerced, needful; 9 compelled, mandatory, necessary, requisite; 10 compulsory, obligatory; 11 involuntary

requirement: 4 need; 5 needs [pl]; 6 demand; 8 exigency; 9 essential, necessary, necessity, requisite; 11 necessities [pl]; 12 prerequisite

requisite: 6 needed; 7 needful; 8 required; 9 essential, necessary, necessity; 11 requirement

requisition: 5 claim; 6 demand; 7 request; 8 exaction; 10 imposition

requital: 3 sop; 5 grace; 6 amends; 7 redress; 8 response; 9 atonement

requite: 5 repay; 10 recompense; 11 acknowledge

rerun: 9 replicate; 11 rebroadcast

rescind: 4 lift, part; 5 annul; 6 cancel, cut off, detach, repeal, revoke; 7 divorce, reverse; 8 abrogate, overturn; 11 countermand

rescinded: 7 revoked; 8 annulled, repealed, reversed; 9 abrogated, cancelled

rescript: 4 fiat; 5 edict, order; 6 decree, revise; 7 revisal, rewrite; 8 revision; 10 transcript

rescue: 4 save; 6 relief, saving; 7 deliver, relieve; 8 delivery; 9 extricate, salvation; 11 deliverance, extrication

rescuer: 5 saver; 6 savior; 9 deliverer, recoverer

research: 5 study; 6 search; 7 enquiry, examine, explore, inquiry; 8 consider; 10 scrutinize

researcher: 12 investigator

research lab: 3 lab; 10 laboratory

resemblance: 8 likeness; 9 semblance; 10 similarity, similitude

resent: 8 begrudge

resentful: 5 riled; 6 galled; 8 offended

resentment: 4 gall; 6 rancor; 7 rancour; 10 bitterness

reservation: 4 pale, term; 5 bourn, verge; 6 ghetto; 7 booking, confine, enclave, reserve; 8 preserve; 9 reticence; 11 withholding

reserve: 4 book, hold, pale; 5 allow, spare; 6 ghetto, retain; 7 backlog, conceal, dignity, earmark, enclave, modesty; 8 hold back, inactive, keep back, preserve, set aside, withhold; 9 pine rider, restraint, reticence, stockpile; 10 demureness, substitute; 11 appropriate, bench warmer, reservation, withholding

reserved: 6 demure, modest; 7 hoarded; 8 reticent, set aside; 9 diffident; 10 buttoned up, restrained; 11 unemotional

Reserve Officers Training Corps: 4 ROTC

reserves: 7 militia

reserve soldier: 9 auxiliary

reset: 8 readjust

resettled: 9 relocated

R

reshape: 6 remold

reside: 4 live, rest, stay; **5** abide, dwell, lodge, perch, roost, shack; **6** nestle, occupy, people, repose, tenant; **7** inhabit, lodge in, sojourn; **8** populate

residence: 4 hall, home; **5** abode, manse; **7** address, housing, lodging, mansion; **8** abidance, domicile, dwelling, lodgment; **9** lodgement, residency

residence hall: 4 dorm, hall; **9** dormitory

resident: 7 dweller; **8** habitant, occupant; **10** inhabitant, inhabiting

residential: 8 domestic

residual: 4 rest; **7** residue; **9** remainder, surviving

residue: 3 tar; **4** rest; **8** residual; **9** remainder

resign: 4 bend, drop, shed; **5** spare, yield; **6** forego, give up, submit, vacate; **7** succumb; **8** abdicate, renounce; **9** reconcile, surrender

resignation: 6 ceding; **7** cession; **8** backdown, giving up; **9** surrender; **10** abdication

resigned: 6 abject; **7** content, passive, subdued; **9** chastened, crouching, unhopeful; **10** submissive; **11** acquiescent, acquiescing

resilient: 4 live; **6** bouncy, lively, reflex, spring, whippy; **7** buoyant, elastic, springy, tensile; **8** flexible; **10** recidivous, regressive

resin: 5 rosin; **9** colophony

resist: 3 jib; **4** balk, defy; **5** baulk, cross, stand; **6** oppose, refuse, reluct; **7** dissent, hold out, protest; **9** stand firm, withstand

resistance: 5 front, stand; **7** kicking; **8** opposing, resistor; **9** impedance, resisting; **10** inhibition, opposition; **11** resistivity, underground

resistant: 6 immune, strong; **9** repellent, resisting, resistive

resister: 8 crusader, reformer

resisting: 5 front, stand; **6** strong; **7** kicking; **8** opposing, reacting, renitent; **9** resistant; **10** opposition, resistance; **11** reactionary

res judicata: 7 settled

resolute: 12 strong-minded, strong-willed, unhesitating

resolutely: 10 decisively; **12** determinedly; **14** strong-mindedly

resoluteness: 4 will; **7** resolve; **8** firmness; **10** resolution

resolution: 4 will; **6** answer, motion, result; **7** resolve, solving; **8** decision, firmness, solution; **9** reduction, resolving; **10** settlement; **11** declaration, dissolution

resolve: 4 will; **5** parse, solve; **6** answer, decide, intent, settle; **7** analyze, concert, dissect, purpose; **8** conclude, dissolve, firmness; **9** anatomize, elucidate, enucleate, intention; **10** resolution

resonance: 7 ringing; **8** sonority, vibrancy; **12** reverberance, sonorousness

resonant: 7 rolling; **10** resonating, resounding; **11** reverberant

resonate: 4 echo; **6** reecho; **7** resound; **11** reverberate

resonator: 11 echo chamber

resort: 5 avail, haunt, recur; **6** covert, refuge, repair; **7** hangout, retreat; **8** recourse

resort hotel: 3 spa

resources: 5 asset, means; **6** assets; **8** resource; **9** substance; **10** belongings; **11** wealthiness, wherewithal

respect: 5 honor, prise, prize, value; **6** comply, esteem, honour, regard; **7** abide by, account, execute, observe, perform; **9** deference, obedience; **10** comply with, estimation

respectable: 4 good, tidy; **5** hefty; **6** goodly; **7** goodish, sizable; **8** passable, sizeable; **9** estimable, honorable, reputable, tolerable; **10** creditable

respected: 7 honored; **8** esteemed, glorious; **9** honorable; **11** illustrious, redoubtable

respectful: 8 decorous, honoring; **9** esteeming; **10** venerating

respective: 5 party; **6** proper; **7** certain, partial, private, several, special, various; **8** definite, especial, original, peculiar, specific; **9** exclusive; **10** individual, particular; **11** appropriate, determinate; **14** characteristic

respects: 4 duty; **6** devoir, egards; **7** devoirs, regards; **12** remembrances

respiration: 4 wind; **9** breathing

respirator: 7 gasmask; **8** iron lung; **9** gas helmet

respire: 7 breathe

respite: 4 drop, rest, wait; **5** break, pause, truce; **6** hiatus, recess, relief; **7** time out; **8** reprieve; **9** abatement; **10** suspension

resplendence: 5 glory; **8** splendor; **10** brilliance

resplendent: 7 glowing; **8** dazzling, glorious, splendid; **9** sparkling; **10** flamboyant

respond: 5 react, rebut, reply, tally; **6** answer, rejoin, retort; **10** correspond

respondent: 8 answerer; **9** answering, defendant, responder

responding: 8 reacting, replying; **9** answering

response: 5 reply; **6** answer; **8** reaction

response time: 7 latency

responsibility: 4 care, duty, onus, task; **6** charge, errand; **7** mission; **8** province; **9** liability; **10** assignment, commission, engagement, obligation

responsible: 6 liable; **8** amenable; **10** answerable; **11** accountable

res publica: 4 land; **5** state; **6** nation; **7** country; **11** body politic; **12** commonwealth

rest: 3 bar, lie; **4** ease, fall, lull, obit, stay; **5** pause, perch, relax, roost, sleep, tarry;

6 pillow, relief, remain, repose, reside; **7** breathe, quietus, release, residue, respite, resting; **8** reposing, residual; **9** departure, remainder; **10** relaxation

restart: 6 resume

restate: 6 repeat, retell; **7** iterate; **9** reiterate

restaurant: 4 cafe; **6** buffet; **7** canteen

restful: 4 calm; **8** relaxing; **9** reposeful

rest home: 11 nursing home

resting: 4 rest; **6** repose; **8** relaxing, reposing

restitute: 6 return; **7** restore; **8** give back, renovate

restitution: 6 amends, return; **7** damages, redress; **9** indemnity, quittance, regaining; **11** restoration

restive: 4 edgy; **5** balky, heady, jumpy, nervy; **6** unruly; **7** jittery, nervous, uptight, wayward, willful; **8** contrary, perverse; **10** headstrong, overstrung, rebellious, refractory

restless: 5 fussy, hasty, itchy; **6** uneasy; **7** fidgety, fretful, hurried, unquiet; **8** electric, galvanic; **9** mercurial, perturbed; **10** convulsive; **11** ungratified, unsatisfied

restlessness: 6 fidget, unrest; **7** fidgets; **8** disquiet; **10** impatience, inquietude, uneasiness; **11** disquietude, fidgetiness, nervousness

restoration: 4 cure; **6** repair, return; **7** renewal; **8** recovery, restoral; **9** regaining, restoring; **10** renovation, reparation; **11** replacement, restitution; **12** recuperation

restorative: 5 tonic; **8** renewing, reviving; **9** restoring, returning; **10** corrective, refreshing; **12** recuperative, revitalizing

restore: 3 fix; **4** mend; **6** repair, return; **7** refresh, replace; **9** reinstate, restitute; **10** regenerate; **11** reestablish

restorer: 9 preserver, renovator; **10** refinisher

restrain: 4 curb, hold, keep; **5** bound, check, limit; **6** cumber; **7** confine, control, trammel; **8** encumber, restrict; **9** constrain; **10** intimidate

restrained: 5 quiet; **6** demure, modest; **7** guarded; **8** moderate, reserved, reticent; **9** diffident; **10** controlled; **11** constrained, unemotional

restraint: 4 curb; **5** check; **7** control, reserve; **10** chasteness, constraint, demureness, simplicity

restrict: 4 curb; **5** bound, check, limit; **6** hinder, impede, modify; **7** confine, control, curtail, cut back, inhibit, qualify, trammel; **8** restrain, throttle, withhold; **9** constrain

restricted: 6 hedged; **7** impeded; **8** hindered; **9** contained, inhibited, qualified; **10** controlled, obstructed; **11** conditional, conditioned

restricting: 8 limiting; **9** confining; **12** constraining, constrictive

restriction: 8 monopoly; **9** exception, exemption, hindrance, stricture; **10** impedi-

ment, limitation, protection; **11** containment

restroom: 8 lavatory, bathroom, washroom

result: 4 data, lead; **5** ensue, issue, leave, yield; **6** answer, effect, upshot; **7** finding, outcome, product, stubble; **8** offshoot, solution; **9** aftermath, resultant; **10** resolution

resultant: 5 yield; **6** result; **7** ensuant, outcome, product, sequent; **8** end point, offshoot; **9** aftermath, resulting; **10** consequent

resume: 5 sum up; **6** pass to, retake, review, reword, sketch, survey, take up; **7** restart; **8** reappear, return to; **9** summarize; **10** recommence

resurgence: 7 revival

resurrect: 5 raise; **7** upraise

resuscitate: 6 revive; **8** revivify; **9** reanimate; **10** regenerate

retail: 5 issue, relay, utter; **6** deal in, retell; **7** deal out; **8** dispense

retail merchant: 8 retailer

retail store: 4 shop; **5** store; **6** outlet; **8** emporium

retain: 4 hold, keep; **6** engage, keep on; **7** reserve; **8** continue, withhold

retake: 6 resume; **7** reshoot; **9** recapture

retaliate: 6 avenge, retort; **7** revenge

retaliation: 6 retort; **7** payback, revenge; **8** reprisal

retard: 4 slow; **5** check, relax, waive; **6** remand, slow up; **7** adjourn, lay over, slacken, suspend; **8** hold over, slow down; **10** decelerate

retardation: 3 lag; **4** wait; **5** pause; **7** respite, slowing; **8** slowdown, slowness; **10** suspension

retch: 3 cat; **4** puke, sick, spew; **5** vomit; **6** be sick, vomit up; **8** disgorge; **11** regurgitate

retell: 5 relay; **6** recite, repeat, retail; **7** iterate, restate; **9** reiterate

retention: 6 memory; **7** holding, keeping; **9** retaining; **10** memorizing; **11** remembering, retentivity; **12** memorization

reticent: 8 reserved; **10** buttoned up, restrained; **11** unemotional

reticle: 5 plait; **6** wattle; **7** trellis; **8** reticule; **9** graticule; **10** cross-hairs

reticulation: 3 net; **4** mesh; **7** network; **8** meshwork

retinol: 8 vitamin A

retinue: 5 array, court [pl], staff [pl], suite [pl]; **7** cortege; **9** cavalcade, entourage

retire: 2 go; **6** recede, remove, turn in; **7** adjourn, retreat, sack out; **8** collapse, withdraw

retired: 3 bye, out; **7** private, recluse; **8** emeritus, secluded; **11** sequestered

R

retired person: 7 retiree
retirement: 6 recess; 7 retreat; 9 recession, seclusion; 10 withdrawal
retirement benefit: 7 pension
retiring: 4 past; 8 receding; 9 diffident, preceding, resigning; 10 abdicating, unassuming; 11 unassertive
retort: 5 rebut, repay, reply, still; 6 answer, banter, rejoin, return; 7 alembic, payback, respond, riposte; 8 badinage, come back, comeback, crucible, rebuttal, repartee, reprisal, turn upon; 9 rejoinder, retaliate, smartness; 10 quid-pro-quo; 11 retaliation
retouch: 4 vamp; 6 cobble, tinker; 7 touch up; 9 refashion
retrace: 4 mind; 5 trace; 6 call up, recall; 8 remember, summon up; 9 construct, recollect; 11 reconstruct
retract: 6 abjure, draw in, forego, palter, recall, recant; 7 abolish, forfeit; 8 disclaim, forswear, renounce
retread: 5 recap; 6 remold, rework; 8 make over
retreat: 5 haunt; 6 asylum, covert, recede, resort, retire, return, revert; 7 back out, regrade; 8 back away, hideaway, move back, pull away, pull back, withdraw; 9 sanctuary; 10 retirement, retrograde
retrenchment: 4 care; 9 concision, deducting, deduction, husbandry, squeezing; 10 abridgment, compacting, downsizing; 11 curtailment, subtracting, subtraction
retribution: 7 revenge; 9 repayment, requittal, vengeance
retrieval: 6 regain; 7 redress; 8 recovery; 11 reclamation
retrieve: 4 find; 5 think; 6 call up, recall, recoup, redeem, regain, remind; 7 reclaim, recover; 8 call back, remember; 9 recollect
retrograde: 6 back up, rehash, retral; 7 failing, regress, retreat; 8 backward; 9 declining, retrocede; 10 regressing, retrogress
retrospect: 6 memory, review; 8 look back; 9 recalling; 11 remembering, remembrance
return: 4 fall, give, hire, name, pass, take; 5 issue, recur, repay, yield; 6 afford, engage, go back, payoff, recall, recede, refund, rejoin, render, retort, revert, scroll; 7 appoint, archive, bespeak, deliver, devolve, get back, reelect, regrade, regress, restore, retreat, revolve, riposte, takings; 8 accredit, blue book, come back, comeback, generate, give back, hark back, nominate, proceeds, reappear, replevin [Law], take back, trip back, turn back; 9 bring back, regaining, rejoinder, restitute, return key, reversion, tax return; 10 homecoming, nomination, quid pro quo, recurrence
return home: 10 homecoming
return ticket: 9 round-trip

reunification: 7 reunion
reuse: 7 recycle; 9 reprocess
rev: 3 rpm; 5 rev up
reveal: 4 show; 5 break, let on; 6 expose, impart, let out, unveil; 7 declare, display, divulge, uncover; 8 disclose, discover
revealing: 7 telling; 8 exposing, telltale; 10 disclosure, revealment, revelation; 11 discovering
reveille: 6 wake-up
revel: 3 toy; 5 enjoy, feast, sport; 6 junket, racket, wallow, wanton; 7 banquet, carouse, delight, disport, rejoice, revelry, triumph, wassail
revelation: 4 find; 8 exposing; 9 detection, discovery, revealing; 10 disclosure, revealment; 11 discovering, inspiration
Revelations: 10 Apocalypse
reveler: 8 carouser, gamester, reveller; 10 merrymaker
revelry: 5 revel; 6 revels; 8 reveling; 9 festivity; 11 merrymaking
revenant: 5 ghost, shade, spook; 6 shadow, vision; 7 specter; 10 apparition
revenge: 6 avenge; 9 retaliate, vengeance, vindicate; 11 retaliation, retribution
revenue: 5 gross; 6 income; 7 innings; 8 receipts, taxation; 9 incomings
reverberance: 7 ringing; 8 sonority, vibrancy; 9 plangency, resonance
reverberate: 4 echo, ring; 6 reecho; 7 resound; 8 resonate
reverberating: 7 rolling; 8 resonant; 10 resonating, resounding
revere: 5 adore; 7 idolize, worship; 8 venerate; 9 reverence
reverence: 3 awe; 4 fear; 6 revere; 8 eminence, reverend, venerate; 10 veneration
reverend: 6 divine; 7 revered, sublime; 9 black coat [fig], churchman, clergyman, reverence, venerated; 10 reverenced; 12 ecclesiastic
reverent: 4 holy, pure; 5 godly, pious; 6 devout, solemn; 7 devoted; 9 pietistic, religious, spiritual; 10 devotional, worshipful
reverie: 6 revery, trance; 8 daydream
reversal: 5 check, cross; 6 invert; 7 inverse, reverse, setback; 8 comedown, flip-flop; 9 about-face, reversion, turnabout; 10 turnaround
reverse: 4 lift, turn; 5 annul, check, cross, tails, verso; 6 cancel, invert, repeal, revoke; 7 inverse, rescind, setback [U.S.]; 8 abrogate, comedown, contrary, converse, opposite, override, overrule, overturn, rearward, reversal; 9 overthrow, reversion, turnabout
revert: 5 recur; 6 recede, return, revest; 7 regrade, regress, retreat; 8 reappear, turn back
review: 4 rate; 5 audit, recap, revue, sum up, value; 6 assess, go over, notice, parade, report, resume, revise, survey; 7 brush up,

brushup, inspect, refresh, revisit, run over; **8** critique, estimate, follow-up, look back; **9** criticism, march past, promenade, reexamine; **10** appreciate, commentary, inspection, procession, reconsider, retrospect; **11** reappraisal, revaluation

reviewer: 6 critic; **7** referee; **11** commentator

revile: 4 rail; **5** scoff; **6** vilify; **7** profane

reviled: 8 maligned

revise: 4 copy, pull; **5** proof; **6** retool, review; **7** revisal; **8** overhaul, pore over, rescript, revision; **10** impression

revision: 4 form; **6** revise; **7** edition, revisal, rewrite, variant, version; **8** emending, rescript, revising; **9** expansion, extension, variation; **10** alteration, derivation, derivative, emendation; **12** modification

revisit: 6 review; **10** reconsider

revitalization: 7 revival; **10** resurgence; **14** revitalisation, revivification

revitalizing: 8 renewing, reviving; **11** restorative

revival: 7 rebirth, renewal; **10** resurgence; **11** reanimation, reclamation

revivalist: 8 gospeler; **9** gospeller; **10** evangelist, missionary

revive: 5 rally; **6** come to, vivify; **7** animate, quicken; **8** recreate, rekindle, revivify; **9** reanimate; **10** regenerate; **11** resuscitate

revoke: 4 lift; **5** annul; **6** cancel, renege, repeal; **7** rescind, reverse; **8** abrogate, overturn; **11** countermand

revolt: 5 repel, shock; **6** rising, sicken; **7** churn up, disgust, turn off; **8** nauseate, outbreak, uprising; **9** rebellion; **10** insurgency, scandalize; **12** insurrection

revolter: 5 rebel; **8** mutineer

revolting: 4 foul; **5** yucky; **6** wicked; **7** loathly; **9** loathsome, repellant, repellent, sickening; **10** disgustful, disgusting; **11** distasteful

revolution: 4 bout, roll, turn; **5** round; **6** mutiny; **8** gyration, rotation, spinning; **9** rebellion

revolutionary: 5 rebel; **7** radical; **9** insurgent, subverter; **10** subversive

revolutionize: 6 infect; **7** inspire; **8** overturn

revolutions per minute: 3 rev, rpm

revolve: 4 roll, spin, turn; **5** orbit; **6** return, rotate

revolver: 6 six-gun; **8** repeater; **10** six-shooter

revulsion: 5 spasm, throe; **6** horror, recoil; **9** repulsion; **10** convulsion, repugnance

reward: 4 meed; **5** honor, repay, wages; **6** payoff; **7** pay back; **8** remember; **9** reinforce; **12** remuneration; **13** reinforcement

reword: 6 resume; **8** rephrase, return to; **10** paraphrase; **12** recapitulate

rework: 7 retread; **8** make over

rewrite: 5 adapt; **8** rescript, revision

Reykjavik: 16 capital of Iceland

601

---

reynard: 3 fox; **5** vixen [female]; **8** sly boots

Rf: 2 Ku; **3** Unq; **12** kurchatovium, unnilquadium; **13** rutherfordium

Rh: 7 rhodium; **8** Rh factor; **12** rhesus factor

Rhamnaceae: 15 buckthorn family

Rhamnus: 9 buckthorn; **12** genus Rhamnus

rhapsodic: 8 ecstatic; **9** rapturous; **10** enraptured

rhapsodical: 8 rambling

rhapsody: 4 myth; **5** farce; **6** mosaic; **7** collage, ecstasy, fantasy, fiction, montage, rapture, romance; **8** pastiche, phantasm, phantasy; **9** composite, patchwork, potpourri; **10** hodgepodge

Rheims-Douay Version: 10 Douay Bible; **12** Douay Version

Rhein: 5 Rhine; **10** Rhine River

Rheinland: 9 Rhineland

rhenium: 2 Re

rhennish: 4 hock; **9** Rhine wine

rhesus factor: 2 Rh; **8** Rh factor

rhesus monkey: 6 rhesus

rhetoric: 6 hot air; **7** palaver; **9** empty talk; **10** empty words; **11** grandiosity; **13** magniloquence; **14** grandiloquence

rhetorical: 4 rich; **5** tumid; **6** florid, mouthy, ornate, turgid; **7** flowery, orotund; **8** inflated, sonorous, swelling; **9** bombastic, grandiose, high flown; **10** oratorical, ornamented, turgescent; **11** big-sounding, declamatory

rhetorician: 6 orator; **11** speechmaker

rheum: 4 spit; **5** tears; **6** saliva; **7** spittle

rheumatic: 6 creaky; **9** arthritic; **10** rheumatoid

Rheum: 7 rhubarb; **10** genus Rheum

Rh factor: 2 Rh; **12** rhesus factor

rhinal: 5 nasal

Rhine: 5 Rhein; **10** Rhine River

Rhineland: 9 Rheinland

Rhine wine: 4 hock; **8** rhennish

rhinitis: 10 common cold

rhinoceros: 5 rhino

rhinoceros family: 14 Rhinocerotidae

rhinolaryngologist: 3 ENT

rhinoplasty: 7 nose job

rhizome: 9 rootstalk, rootstock

Rhizophoraceae: 14 mangrove family

Rhizopus nigricans: 9 bread mold

Rhodesia: 8 Zimbabwe

rhodium: 2 Rh

rhodopsin: 12 visual purple

rhomb: 7 rhombus; **8** rhomboid

rhonchus: 5 snore

Rhone: 10 Rhone River

rhubarb: 3 row; **4** fray, to-do; **5** brawl, broil, melee; **6** affray, breeze, fracas, hubbub, pother, racket, rumble, rumpus, squall, uproar; **7** howling, ruction, shindig, trouble; **8** brouhaha, pieplant, scramble;

R

9 imbroglio, scrimmage; **10** bear garden, donnybrook, free-for-all

rhumba: 5 rumba

rhumb line: 5 rhumb; **9** loxodrome

Rhus: 5 sumac; **9** genus Rhus, poison ash, poison oak, poison ivy; **11** lacquer tree, varnish tree, poison sumac; **13** poison dogwood

rhyme: 3 pun; **4** rime, scan, sing; **5** verse; **7** poetize, rhyming, versify

rhythm: 4 beat; **5** cycle, meter, round; **7** measure

rhythmical: 8 measured, rhythmic; **9** chromatic, euphemism; **10** euphonious; **11** euphemistic, mellifluous

rhythmic pattern: 7 prosody

rhytidoplasty: 8 face lift

riant: 3 gay; **8** mirthful, laughing

riata: 5 lasso; **6** lariat

rib: 3 kid; **4** joke; **6** parody

ribald: 5 bawdy, broad, crude, gross, loose; **6** coarse, risque [Fr], smutty; **7** fulsome, obscene; **8** off-color

ribbed: 7 costate; **8** corduroy

ribbon: 4 band, list, palm, slip, tape; **5** medal, spill, strip; **6** cordon, fillet, riband, thread; **9** medallion; **10** blue ribbon, decoration

ribbon worm: 9 nemertean

Ribes: 7 currant; **10** gooseberry, red currant; **12** black currant; **10** genus Ribes

ribgrass: 8 plantain

riboflavin: 8 vitamin G; **9** vitamin B2

ribonuclease: 5 RNase

ribonucleic acid: 3 RNA

ribwort: 8 ribgrass

rich: 4 deep, fine, gilt; **5** ample, grand, showy, tumid; **6** florid, monied, mouthy, ornate, robust, superb, turgid; **7** copious, fertile, flowery, moneyed, opulent, orotund, sublime, wealthy; **8** affluent, delicate, gorgeous, inflated, luscious, sonorous, specious, swelling; **9** ambrosial, bombastic, exquisite, grandiose, high flown, plenteous, plentiful, worth much; **10** appetizing, delightful, full-bodied, Johnsonian, ornamented, productive, rhetorical, turgescent; **11** big-sounding, declamatory, magnificent, scrumptious

Richard the Lion-Hearted: 8 Richard I

Richelieu: 17 Cardinal Richelieu; **19** Armand Jean du Plessis

richly: 4 high; **5** amply; **6** enough; **8** lavishly; **11** luxuriously; **13** extravagantly

Richmond: 17 capital of Virginia

Richmondena Cardinalis: 7 redbird; **8** cardinal

rich person: 4 have; **5** money; **11** billionaire, millionaire; **12** moneyed class

rick: 4 heap, turn; **5** crick, sheaf, shock, stack, twist, wrick; **6** sprain, wrench

rickety: 4 rude; **5** gross, rough, shaky, wonky; **6** clumsy, cranky, creaky, rugged, wobbly; **7** awkward; **8** creaking; **9** slouching

ricksha: 8 rickshaw; **10** jinrikisha

ricochet: 4 echo; **5** bound, carom; **6** bounce, recoil, spring; **7** rebound

rid: 4 free, quit; **12** disembarrass

riddance: 8 ejection; **9** exclusion, expulsion; **11** elimination

riddle: 4 mesh, pink, rank, sift, size; **5** lance, range, rebus, sieve; **6** enigma, puzzle, screen; **7** charade, mystery; **8** colander, puncture; **9** conundrum

ride: 4 bait; **5** drive, jaunt, mount, rally, taunt, tease; **6** impend, outing

ride herd on: 7 monitor; **9** supervise

ride out: 4 stay; **7** last out, outride

rider: 6 jockey; **7** episode; **8** cavalier, horseman, offshoot; **9** corollary, passenger; **10** equestrian, roughrider

ridge: 4 dune; **8** hog's back, rooftree; **9** ridgepole

ridged: 6 keeled

ridicule: 3 rib; **4** gibe, gird, hiss, hoot, jeer, mock, twit; **5** taunt; **6** deride, jest at; **7** barrack, laugh at, make fun, mockery, poke fun, snigger; **8** derision

ridiculous: 5 inane, silly; **6** absurd; **7** idiotic; **8** derisory, farcical, pathetic; **9** egregious, ludicrous, senseless; **11** nonsensical; **12** preposterous

riding: 8 equitation; **12** horsemanship

riding breeches: 7 jodhpur; **8** jodhpurs

rid of: 9 eliminate

rife: 6 afloat; **7** current, rampant; **8** epidemic, floating; **9** besetting, plethoric, prevalent; **10** prevailing; **12** overabundant

riff: 3 bit; **4** skim; **6** riffle; **7** routine

riffle: 4 flip, leaf, riff; **5** flick, thumb; **6** cockle, ripple, ruffle; **7** rollers, wavelet; **8** rippling, undulate

riffraff: 6 rabble, ragtag, vermin

rifle: 2 go; **3** gut; **4** loot, sack; **5** foray, prize, reave, spoil, strip, sweep; **7** carbine, despoil, pillage, plunder, ransack

rifleman: 6 sniper; **8** marksman; **12** sharpshooter

rifler: 5 thief; **6** robber; **8** pilferer

rifling: 8 grooving

rift: 5 break, cleft; **6** breach, cranny; **7** crevice, rupture; **9** severance

rig: 5 dress, equip; **6** clothe, adjust; **7** arrange; **9** construct; **10** manipulate

Riga: 15 capital of Latvia

Rigel: 11 Beta Orionis

rigging: 3 rig; **4** gear; **5** slops, traps; **6** tackle; **7** harness, turn-out; **8** tackling; **9** accessory, caparison, equipment, trappings; **11** accessories; **12** accouterment

right: 3 due, fit; **4** even, fair, flop, good, just, meet, ripe, true; **5** claim, title; **6** aright,

decent, demand, direct, estate, justly, mighty, proper, seemly, square; **7** correct, en regle, factual, fitting, holding, in a line, redress, right on; **8** decently, decorous, powerful, properly, suitable; **9** befitting, correctly, equitable, impartial, privilege, righteous, right hand, right side, right wing, starboard, veritable; **10** compensate, evenhanded, right thing, rightfield

right angle: 8 quadrant

right away: 3 now; **4** anon, soon; **6** at once; **7** betimes, shortly; **8** directly, promptly; **9** forthwith, instantly, presently; **11** immediately

righteously: 4 well; **5** nobly; **7** morally; **10** virtuously

rightfield: 5 right

rightful: 4 true; **6** lawful; **10** legitimate; **11** justifiable

rightful owner: 5 owner; **10** legal owner, right owner

right-hand: 5 gofer; **6** gopher

right-handed: 7 dextral

right hemisphere: 10 right brain

rightist: 9 right-wing; **11** right-winger

rightly: 6 justly; **8** properly; **9** correctly, fittingly; **11** justifiedly

right of first publication: 9 copyright

right of possession: 6 seisin [Law], seizin [Law]

right time: 4 room; **7** opening; **8** good time, occasion, true time; **9** exact time; **10** proper time, timeliness; **11** correct time, opportunity

right to vote: 4 vote; **8** suffrage

rigid: 3 set; **4** dour, firm, hard; **5** fixed, harsh, sound, stern, stiff; **6** severe, strict; **8** definite, positive, rigorous; **9** unbending; **10** inflexible

rigidity: 8 hardness, obduracy; **9** renitency, rigidness, stiffness; **13** inflexibility

Rigil Kent: 5 Rigil; **13** Alpha Centauri

rigor: 6 rigour; **7** cogency; **8** asperity, grimness, hardship, severity, validity; **9** harshness, sternness; **10** stringency

rigorous: 5 harsh, rigid, tight; **6** brutal, formal, strict; **7** austere, exigent; **8** avenging, definite, exacting, obdurate, vengeful; **9** demanding, hard-nosed, rancorous, searching, stringent, unsparing

Riksmal: 6 Bokmal

rile: 3 rag, vex; **4** fret, gall, nark, roil; **5** anger, annoy, chafe, devil, get at, get to, pique, sting; **6** bother, gravel, nettle; **7** envenom, incense, provoke; **8** irritate

rill: 3 run; **4** gill; **5** brook; **6** gullet, runnel; **7** rivulet; **9** streamlet

rim: 3 lip; **4** brim; **5** brink; **6** flange

rime: 4 hoar; **5** chink, frost, rhyme; **9** hoarfrost

rimy: 5 rimed; **6** frosty; **7** frosted

rind: 4 peel, skin

rinderpest: 12 cattle plague

ring: 4 band, call, echo, gang, halo, hoop, knot, pack, peal; **5** chink, clink, crowd, group, knell, phone, round; **6** anulus, areola, call up, canvas, circle, clique, jingle; **7** annulus, circlet, coterie, environ, incrowd, resound, ringing; **8** doughnut, encircle, surround; **9** telephone; **10** anchor ring, boxing ring; **11** closed chain, reverberate

ring armor: 4 mail; **8** ring mail; **9** chain mail; **10** chain armor, coat of mail

ringed: 7 annular; **8** annulate, circular, wreathed; **9** annulated, circinate, encircled; **10** ring-shaped

ringer: 4 fake; **8** imposter

ringing: 4 ring; **8** sonority, vibrancy; **9** plangency, resonance; **11** reverberant

ringlet: 4 coil, curl, gyre, lock, roll, tuft; **5** whorl; **6** scroll; **8** curlicue

ring of color: 6 areola

ringside seat: 8 ringside

ringtail: 4 coon; **7** coon cat; **8** civet cat, raccoon

ringworm: 5 tinea; **9** roundworm

rink: 3 ice; **10** hockey rink; **11** croquet lawn, skating rink

rinse: 4 wash; **5** flush, swash, wring; **6** gargle; **7** rinsing; **8** rinse off

Rio: 12 Rio de Janeiro

riot: 5 furor; **6** clamor, muddle, tumult, uproar; **7** carouse, debauch, rioting, roister, tempest; **9** bacchanal; **10** debauchery, saturnalia; **11** bacchanalia

rioter: 7 brawler; **8** renegade, runagate

rioting: 4 riot; **5** furor; **6** clamor, tumult, uproar; **7** tempest; **10** convulsion

riotous: 4 fast, lush; **7** chaotic, profuse; **8** agitated, degraded, mutinous, troubled; **9** clamorous, convulsed, debauched, dissolute, exuberant, insurgent, libertine, luxuriant, seditious, turbulent; **10** degenerate, disruptive, dissipated, profligate, tumultuous

rip: 3 cut; **4** gash, pull, rake, rend, rent, rive, slit, tear; **5** slice, split; **7** riptide; **8** incision

riparian: 7 coastal; **8** littoral

ripe: 4 good; **5** happy, lucky, right; **6** mature, mellow; **8** advanced; **9** favorable, fortunate; **10** auspicious, convenient, propitious; **12** providential

ripen: 6 mature, mellow, season; **7** perfect; **8** fructify, maturate

ripeness: 8 maturity; **10** mellowness

ripening: 5 aging; **6** ageing; **8** maturing; **9** mellowing, nurturing, seasoning; **10** maturation, maturement

ripe olive: 10 black olive

rip off: 3 rob; **4** beat; **5** cheat, heist, steal; **9** sell short

riposte: 5 repay; 6 rejoin, retort, return; 8 comeback, rebuttal; 9 rejoinder

ripple: 3 hum; 4 flow, purl; 6 babble, bubble, burble, cockle, guggle, gurgle, riffle, ruffle; 7 breathe, wavelet; 8 rippling, undulate

riprap: 10 groundwork, substratum, subvention; 12 sustentation

rip-roaring: 7 rackety, rampant; 9 clamorous, turbulent; 10 boisterous

ripsaw: 8 splitsaw

rip-snorting: 7 rampant; 9 clamorous, turbulent; 10 boisterous, rip-roaring, uproarious; 11 tempestuous

riptide: 3 rip; 7 tide rip; 10 rip current; 12 crosscurrent

rip up: 5 shred; 6 rake up, tear up

rise: 4 grow, hike, jump, lift, rear; 5 arise, boost, climb, get up, mount, prove, raise, rebel, slope; 6 ascend, ascent, come up, move up, rise up, rising, source, uprise; 7 advance, be about, climb up, develop, incline, stand up, surface, turn out, upgrade; 8 gradient, heighten, inchoate, spring up; 9 acclivity, ascending, ascension

rise to power: 9 accession

rise up: 4 rear, rise; 5 arise

risible: 5 comic, funny; 7 amusing, comical; 8 mirthful; 9 hilarious, laughable, very funny; 10 uproarious; 13 side-splitting

rising: 4 rise; 6 ascent, revolt, uphill; 8 emerging, outbreak, uprising; 9 advancing, ascension, rebellion; 10 insurgency; 11 acclivitous; 12 insurrection

rising market: 10 bull market

rising of the curtain: 5 debut

rising prices: 9 inflation

rising slope: 4 rise; 7 upgrade

rising tide: 9 flood tide

risk: 5 peril, stake; 6 chance, danger, gamble, hazard; 7 venture; 8 jeopardy; 9 adventure; 10 insecurity

risk capital: 14 venture capital

risk-free: 8 riskless; 11 unhazardous

riskiness: 5 peril

risking: 3 bet; 5 wager; 7 staking; 9 hazarding

risk taker: 7 gambler

risky: 3 bad; 5 dicey; 6 chancy, unsafe; 7 parlous; 8 high-risk, insecure, perilous; 9 dangerous, hazardous, venturous; 10 precarious; 11 speculative, venturesome

risotto: 11 Italian rice

risque: 4 blue, free, gamy, racy; 5 bawdy, broad, gamey, gross, juicy, loose, spicy; 6 coarse, ribald, smutty; 7 fulsome, naughty, obscene; 9 equivocal; 12 pornographic

ritardando: 8 ritenuto; 11 rallentando

rite: 6 ritual; 8 ceremony; 10 ceremonial, observance

ritenuto: 10 ritardando; 11 rallentando

ritual: 4 rite; 8 ceremony; 10 ceremonial, observance; 11 ceremonious

ritual killing: 9 sacrifice

rival: 3 vie; 5 equal, match, touch; 7 emulate; 8 sparring; 9 competing, contender; 10 challenger, competitor

rivalry: 9 competing; 10 contention; 11 competition

rive: 3 axe, rip; 4 pull, rend; 5 split; 6 cleave

river: 6 stream; 11 watercourse

riverbank: 3 lea; 4 bank; 5 levee; 9 river bank, riverside

riverbed: 6 bottom

river bottom: 8 riverbed

riverside: 9 riverbank

rivet: 3 pin; 4 bolt, boss, hasp, nail, pore, stud; 5 clamp, clasp, crimp, focus, screw; 6 absorb, center, centre; 7 engross; 8 intrigue; 9 fascinate, mesmerize; 11 concentrate

riveted: 4 rapt; 6 rooted; 8 absorbed; 9 wrapped in; 10 hypnotized, mesmerized, transfixed

rivulet: 3 run; 5 brook; 4 gill, rill; 6 gullet, runnel; 9 streamlet

Riyadh: 20 capital of Saudi Arabia

Rn: 5 radon

RN: 5 nurse; 15 registered nurse

roach: 9 cockroach, cucaracha [Sp]

road: 3 row; 5 route; 7 roadway, touring; 9 boardwalk, esplanade, itinerant, traveling; 10 embankment

roadblock: 7 barrier; 9 barricade

road book: 8 handbook; 9 guidebook

road game: 8 away game

road gang: 9 chain gang

road map: 9 street map

road runner: 10 marathoner

roadside: 7 wayside

roadster: 3 cob, pad, tit; 4 barb, hack, jade, roan; 5 bidet, buggy, punch; 6 wheels; 8 runabout; 9 sports car, two-seater

road-test: 9 test drive

roadway: 4 road; 7 pathway

roam: 4 cast, rove, swan; 5 drift, prowl, range, stray; 6 patrol, ramble, wander; 8 traverse, vagabond

roamer: 5 rover; 8 wanderer

roar: 3 cry; 4 bawl, boom, fume, hoop, howl, peal, rage, romp, wail, yawl, yell, yowl; 5 blare, noise, shout, split, swell, whoop; 6 bellow, scream, shriek, shrill; 7 bluster, clatter, rampage, roaring, screech, ululate, yowling; 9 bellowing, fulminate, hollering

roast: 3 fry; 4 bake, joke, quiz, twit; 5 chaff, grill, joint, knock, parch, singe, tease, toast; 6 banter, hazing, scorch; 7 roasted, teasing; 8 quizzing, roasting; 9 bantering

roasting: 5 roast; **6** hazing; **7** teasing; **8** quizzing; **9** bantering

rob: 3 mug; **4** hook, soak; **5** pluck, plume; **6** fleece, gazump, ripoff; **8** poultice; **9** surcharge; **10** overcharge

robber: 5 thief; **6** mugger, rifler; **8** pilferer

robbery: 6 hold-up [U.S.]; **7** looting, mugging

robe: 3 rig; **4** gown, vest; **5** array, drape, dress, frock; **6** attire, clothe, enrobe, fit out; **7** apparel, cassock

robed: 6 garbed; **7** attired, dressed, mantled; **9** appareled, garmented

Robert the Bruce: 5 Bruce; **7** Robert I

robin: 9 redbreast

Robin Goodfellow: 4 Puck

Robinia: 6 locust; **11** black locust; **12** yellow locust; **12** genus Robinia

robot: 7 android; **8** robotics; **9** automaton

robot bomb: 8 buzz bomb; **9** doodlebug

robust: 4 hard, rich; **5** brave, buxom, flush, hardy, stout, valid; **6** florid, mighty, potent, stanch, strong, sturdy; **7** staunch; **8** forcible, powerful, vigorous

robustness: 5 vigor; **8** haleness; **9** hardiness, lustiness

Roccus: 7 striper; **8** rockfish; **11** striped bass; **11** genus Roccus

rock: 4 pile, sway, tilt; **5** shake, stone, swing; **6** careen, cradle; **7** diamond; **9** brilliant, rock candy

rock and roll: 4 rock; **9** rock 'n' roll, rock music

rock-bottom: 7 reduced

rock climber: 8 cragsman

rocker arm: 11 valve rocker

rocket: 4 bomb; **5** blast; **7** arugula, missile; **9** skyrocket

rocket fuel: 10 propellant, propellent

rockfish: 7 striper; **11** striped bass

Rockies: 14 Rocky Mountains

rocking chair: 6 rocker

rocking horse: 5 hobby; **9** cockhorse; **10** hobbyhorse

rocklike: 5 stony

rock lobster: 12 spiny lobster

rock maple: 10 sugar maple

Rock of Gibraltar: 5 Calpe; **9** Gibraltar

rock oil: 5 crude; **7** coal oil; **8** crude oil; **9** fossil oil, petroleum

rock pigeon: 8 rock dove

rock-ribbed: 7 die-hard; **9** rockbound

rockrose family: 9 Cistaceae

rock solid: 6 moored; **8** anchored, tethered

rock-steady: 10 dependable

rock wool: 11 mineral wool

rocky: 5 rough, stony; **8** bouldery, concrete; **9** bouldered, calculous

Rocky Mountain sheep: 7 bighorn; **8** cimarron

Rocky Mountain spotted fever: 9 tick fever; **13** mountain fever

rococo: 5 gaudy, stale; **6** old hat, tawdry; **7** baroque, out of it, strange; **8** after-age; **9** out of date; **10** antiquated, outlandish; **11** baroqueness; **12** old-fashioned

rod: 3 gun, bar; **4** pole, wand; **5** osier, perch; **7** handgun, scepter; **8** bacillus; **10** punishment

rodent: 6 gnawer

Rodentia: 13 order Rodentia

rodeo rider: 6 cowboy

rodomontade: 3 gas; **4** rant; **5** bluff; **6** hot air; **7** bluster, bombast, fustian, palaver; **8** flummery, vaporing; **9** baverdage, rigmarole; **10** balderdash; **11** braggadocio

rod-shaped: 7 rodlike; **8** bacillar; **9** bacillary

rod-shaped bacterium: 3 rod; **8** bacillus

roe: 3 doe; **6** caviar; **8** fish eggs

roentgenogram: 4 X ray

roentgen ray: 4 X ray; **10** X-radiation

Rogaine: 7 Loniten; **9** minoxidil

rogation: 6 litany, orison, prayer; **10** invocation; **12** intercession, supplication

rogue: 5 cheat, knave; **6** rascal, varlet; **8** scalawag; **9** scallywag

roil: 4 boil, moil, rile; **5** churn

roiled: 5 riled, roily, stung; **6** peeved, pissed; **7** annoyed, nettled, roiling; **8** churning; **9** irritated, turbulent

roister: 4 riot; **7** carouse

Rolando's area: 9 motor area; **11** motor cortex, motor region

role: 3 use; **4** part; **6** office; **7** persona, purpose; **8** capacity, function, personae [pl]; **9** character

role model: 5 model; **7** example

roleplay: 3 act; **4** play; **7** playact

role player: 4 fake, sham; **5** actor, faker, fraud, pseud; **6** player, pseudo; **8** histrion, imposter, impostor, thespian; **9** pretender

roll: 3 bun; **4** cast, coil, curl, drum, lath, peal, well, wind, wrap; **5** level, pluck, swell, wheel, whorl; **6** billow, hustle, roll on, roll up, roller, roster, scroll, seethe, well up; **7** pealing, revolve, ringlet, roll out, rolling; **8** bankroll, curlicue, drum roll, gyration, rotation, turn over, undulate; **9** roll along; **10** paradiddle

rollback: 8 push back

roll call: 4 poll; **6** census, muster; **10** capitation

rolled: 6 furled; **7** rolling, trilled; **8** involute, rolled-up

rolled oats: 7 oatmeal

roller: 4 roll; **5** brace; **6** curler, fillet; **7** tumbler

roller skates: 12 rollerblades

rollick: 4 lark, romp; **5** frisk, sport; **6** cavort, frolic; **7** disport, skylark

rolling: 4 peal, roll; **6** rolled; **7** pealing,

trilled; **8** drumming, leveling, resonant, tumbling, wheeling

roll of dough: 3 wad

roll over: 4 drub, rout; **5** crush; **7** blow out; **9** overwhelm

roll up: 4 furl, roll; **6** bundle

roly-poly: 3 fat; **5** fatso, fatty

Roma: 4 Rome; **11** Eternal City; **14** capital of Italy

romaine lettuce: 3 cos; **7** romaine

Roman: 5 Latin

romance: 3 woo; **4** mash, myth; **5** court, dally, flirt, novel; **7** fantasy, fiction, solicit; **8** coquette, phantasm, phantasy, rhapsody; **9** love story, philander

Romance: 5 Latin

romancer: 7 dreamer; **8** idealist, romantic; **9** visionary; **11** romanticist

Roman collar: 14 clerical collar

Romani: 5 Gypsy; **6** Romany

Roman law: 8 civil law; **9** jus civile; **13** Justinian code

Romanoff: 7 Romanov

romantic: 4 soft; **7** amatory, amorous, dreamer, fanatic, flighty, utopian; **8** idealist, quixotic, romancer, wild-eyed; **9** high flown, visionary; **11** romanticist, sentimental, unrealistic

romanticist: 7 dreamer; **8** idealist, romancer, romantic; **9** visionary

romanticize: 9 glamorize

romantic love: 5 amour

Romany: 5 Gypsy; **6** Romani

Rome: 4 Roma; **11** Eternal City; **14** capital of Italy

Rommel: 11 Erwin Rommel; **9** Desert Fox

romp: 4 lark, play, rage, roar; **5** caper, frisk, sport; **6** cavort, frolic, gambol, hoyden, shoo-in; **7** disport, laugher, rampage, rollick, runaway, skylark

rondeau: 5 rondo; **6** rondel

rood: 5 cross; **8** crucifix, rood-tree

roof: 3 hip; **7** gambrel, mansard; **9** household

roofing paper: 8 tar paper

roof of the mouth: 6 palate

roof rack: 11 luggage rack

rooftree: 5 ridge; **9** ridgepole

rook: 3 con; **4** bilk; **5** bunco, mulct, pluck; **6** fleece, nobble, pigeon, sponge; **7** defraud, swindle

rookery: 4 slum; **5** aerie, eyrie; **9** bird's nest

rookie: 3 cub; **9** greenhorn

room: 3 way; **5** board, chance, field, place, range, scope, stead, sweep, swing; **6** spread; **7** chamber, opening; **8** occasion; **9** elbow room, expansion; **10** timeliness; **11** compartment

room decorator: 8 designer; **9** decorator

room divider: 5 panel

roomer: 6 lodger; **7** boarder

room for maneuver: 4 play; **6** leeway; **8** latitude, purchase; **9** tolerance

roomily: 10 spaciously

rooming house: 12 lodging house

rooms: 5 suite

roomy: 5 ample; **7** immense; **8** spacious; **9** capacious, expansive, extensive

Roosevelt: 3 FDR; **16** Eleanor Roosevelt; **17** Franklin Roosevelt, Theodore Roosevelt; **20** Anna Eleanor Roosevelt; **23** Franklin Delano Roosevelt

roost: 4 live, rest, stay; **5** abide, dwell, lodge, perch; **6** nestle, reside, tenant; **7** inhabit, sojourn

rooster: 4 cock; **11** chanticleer

roosting: 7 nesting

root: 3 fix, pin, toe; **4** base, hoof, keel, rout, side, sole, stem; **5** index, power, theme, trunk; **6** etymon, origin, rootle, source; **7** nucleus, radical, tap-root; **8** exponent, hair root, root word, solution; **9** beginning, establish, logarithm

rootbound: 8 potbound

root celery: 8 celeriac

rooted: 5 fixed; **6** frozen; **7** posited, riveted, situate; **8** imbedded; **9** besetting, ensconced, permanent

rootless: 8 vagabond

rootstock: 7 rhizome; **9** rootstalk

root word: 4 base, root, stem; **5** theme

rope: 4 nail; **5** leash, noose, swing; **6** halter, margin; **9** bowstring, elbowroom

ropedancer: 10 ropewalker

rope off: 6 cordon

ropewalker: 10 ropedancer

ropeway: 4 tram; **7** tramway; **8** cable car

ropy: 4 wiry; **5** ropey; **6** clammy, mastic; **7** clotted, gelatin, stringy, thready

Rosa: 4 rose; **9** genus Rosa

rosacea: 11 acne rosacea

Rosaceae: 10 rose family

rosaceous: 4 rose; **7** roseate

rosary beads: 6 rosary

roscoe: 3 gat; **6** pistol; **7** handgun, side arm

rose: 7 roseate; **8** pink wine, rose wine; **9** blush wine, rosaceous

roseate: 4 rose; **6** bright; **8** cheering; **9** looking up, rosaceous; **11** encouraging, inspiriting

rosebay: 8 fireweed

rose-cheeked: 4 rosy; **7** flushed; **8** blooming

rose-colored: 4 rosy; **6** bright; **7** roseate; **8** cheering; **9** looking up; **11** encouraging, inspiriting

rose family: 8 Rosaceae

rosefish: 7 redfish

rosette: 3 bow; **4** star

rose wine: 4 rose; **9** blush wine

Rosh Chodesh: 10 Rosh Hodesh

Rosh Hashanah: 7 New Year; **11** Rosh Hashana, Rosh Hashona; **12** Rosh Hashonah; **13** Jewish New Year

rosin: 5 resin; 8 rosining

rosiness: 5 bloom, blush, flush; 9 ruddiness

Rosmarinus: 8 rosemary; 15 genus Rosmarinus

Ross: 9 Betsy Ross; 16 Betsy Griscom Ross

Rossetti: 20 Dante Gabriel Rossetti

Rossini: 24 Gioacchino Antonio Rossini

roster: 4 roll; 5 panel; 8 jury list

Rostov: 11 Rostov on Don; 12 Rostov na Donu

rostrum: 4 ambo, beak, dais; 5 snout, stump; 6 podium, pulpit; 7 soapbox; 8 platform

rosy: 5 ruddy; 7 flushed, hopeful; 8 blooming, blushful; 9 fortunate

rosy-cheeked: 4 rosy; 7 flushed; 8 blooming

rot: 4 bull, bunk, fade, guff; 5 decay, erode, go bad, go off, waste; 6 bunkum, canker, dry rot, fester, molder, rankle, wither; 7 corrode, decline, degrade, ferment, hogwash, moulder, putrefy, rotting; 9 decompose; 10 degenerate; 11 deteriorate; 12 putrefaction; 13 decomposition

rota: 5 cycle; 7 routine

rotary: 6 circle; 8 rotating, spinning; 10 roundabout

rotary engine: 12 radial engine

Rotary International: 10 Rotary Club

rotary press: 11 letterpress

rotate: 4 spin, turn; 7 revolve; 8 go around

rotating: 6 rotary; 7 turning; 8 spinning, wheeling; 9 revolving

rotation: 4 roll, turn; 5 round; 8 gyration, spinning; 10 revolution

rote: 11 brute memory; 12 rote learning

rotor: 5 blade; 6 stator; 9 motor coil, rotor coil

rotted: 6 rotten; 7 decayed

rotten: 3 bad; 4 icky, weak, worn; 5 lousy, seedy, washy; 6 crappy, putrid, rancid, rotted, stinky, wasted; 7 corrupt, decayed, gone bad, laid low, rotting, tainted, touched; 8 blighted, cankered, stinking; 9 crumbling, moldering, putrefied; 10 putrescent; 11 languishing; 12 deteriorated

rotund: 5 obese, round; 6 convex; 7 orotund, rounded, weighty; 9 corpulent

rotunda: 4 hall; 5 court; 8 pavilion

rouble: 5 ruble

roue: 3 rip; 4 rake

rouge: 5 blush, paint; 7 blusher; 8 lipstick; 9 eye shadow; 10 face powder

rough: 3 raw; 4 gamy, hard, hood, racy, rude, wild; 5 bluff, blunt, brute, bully, crude, draft, gross, gruff, harsh, raspy, rocky, rowdy, sharp, tough, uncut; 6 clumsy, coarse, fierce, gravel, gritty, meanie [jocular], mugger, raging, rugged, savage, wretch; 7 awkward, caitiff, furious, grating, hoodlum, outline, rasping, rickety, rough in, roughly, ruffian, styptic, violent; 8 gravelly, hooligan, plug-ugly, rough out,

stinging, ungentle, unsmooth, vehement; 9 barbarian, barbarous, desperado, ferocious, roughneck, slouching; 10 blustering, boisterous

rough-and-tumble: 6 hassle, tussle; 7 scuffle

rough breathing: 10 aspiration

roughcast: 5 frame, model; 6 coarse; 7 unblown; 8 frame out, rough hew, unformed; 9 rough hewn, unwrought; 10 rough draft, unpolished

rough draft: 5 draft, study; 6 sketch; 7 draught, outline

roughen: 5 crisp; 6 ruffle, rumple; 7 crumple; 9 corrugate

roughened: 7 chapped, cracked

rough guess: 9 guesswork; 11 speculation

rough-hewn: 6 coarse; 7 unblown; 8 unformed; 9 rough cast, unwrought; 10 unpolished

rough it: 5 slave, sweat; 8 work hard

roughly: 4 or so, some; 5 about, rough; 6 around; 7 crudely; 8 coarsely; 9 just about; 10 more or less; 13 approximately

roughneck: 3 yob; 4 yobo; 5 bully, rough, rowdy, tough, yobbo; 7 ruffian; 8 hooligan

roughness: 7 crudity, rawness; 8 rowdyism; 9 crudeness, harshness, raspiness, rowdiness; 10 choppiness, unevenness

roughrider: 5 rider; 6 jockey; 8 horseman; 10 equestrian

roughshod: 4 fell; 5 cruel; 6 brutal, savage; 7 vicious; 9 barbarous; 11 heavy-handed

rough sketch: 5 draft, study; 6 sketch; 7 draught, outline

rough water: 9 roughness; 10 choppiness

Roumania: 7 Romania, Rumania

round: 4 beat, bout, flat, ring, rung, sill, slug, step, turn; 5 broad, catch, chain, cycle, event, snipe, stave, suite, train; 6 around, assail, attack, bullet, chorus, circle, convex, marked, polish, rhythm, rotund; 7 assault, brush up, chorale, circuit, decided, environ, fill out, lash out, one shot, orotund, pointed, round up, rounded, routine; 8 circular, distinct, encircle, polish up, rotation

roundabout: 6 circle, rotary; 7 devious; 8 carousel, indirect; 9 whirligig; 10 circuitous

round clam: 6 quahog

rounded: 5 round; 6 convex, rotund

roundelay: 5 rondo; 7 rondeau [Fr]

round-eyed: 4 wide; 10 saucer-eyed

round-faced: 9 moon-faced

round house: 4 blow; 5 punch; 6 lockup

roundly: 6 widely; 7 bluffly, bluntly, flat out; 9 brusquely

round off: 5 round; 6 polish

round of applause: 7 acclaim, plaudit; 8 applause; 11 acclamation

R

round robin: 10 presenting; **11** presentment; **12** presentation

round-shouldered: 7 crooked, hunched, stooped; **8** stooping

round-the-clock: 7 nonstop

roundworm: 5 tinea; **8** nematode, ringworm

roundworms: 9 heartworm

rouse: 5 waken; **6** arouse, awaken, bestir, charge, excite, wake up; **7** agitate; **9** stimulate

rousing: 5 brisk; **6** lively; **7** arousal; **8** exciting, poignant, stirring; **11** stimulating

Rousseau: 19 Jean-Jacques Rousseau

roustabout: 8 deckhand, handyman; **12** longshoreman

rout: 3 mob; **4** drub, fuss, root; **5** chaff, crush, expel, gouge, horde; **6** bustle, groove, hubbub, rabble, racket, rebuff, rootle, throng; **7** blow out, overrun, repulse, rout out; **9** discomfit, overthrow, overwhelm

route: 3 way; **4** path, road; **6** course; **12** thoroughfare

routed: 6 beaten; **8** overcome; **9** conquered; **10** overthrown, vanquished; **11** overwhelmed

routine: 3 act, bit; **4** beat, rota, rule, turn; **5** cycle, round; **6** course, number, steady; **7** humdrum, mundane; **8** constant, everyday, function, monotony, workaday; **9** clockwork, constancy, continual, incessant, perpetual, procedure, quotidian, time cycle, unceasing, unfailing; **10** consistent, continuous, invariable, monotonous, regularity, steadiness

routinely: 6 always; **8** ever anon, steadily; **10** at all times, constantly, habitually, invariably; **11** continually, incessantly, perpetually, unfailingly; **12** consistently, continuously, monotonously

rout out: 4 rout; **5** expel, rouse

rove: 4 cast, roam; **5** drift, prowl, range, stray; **6** patrol, ramble, wander; **8** traverse, vagabond

rover: 6 ranger, roamer; **7** rambler; **8** wanderer; **9** privateer, straggler

row: 4 fray, rank, road, to-do; **5** brawl, broil, melee, run-in, words; **6** affray, breeze, course, dustup, fracas, hubbub, paddle, pother, racket, rowing, rumble, rumpus, squall, uproar; **7** howling, quarrel, rhubarb [baseball], ruction, trouble, wrangle; **8** brouhaha, scramble; **9** esplanade, imbroglio, scrimmage; **10** donnybrook, embankment, free-for-all

rowboat: 4 dory; **6** dinghy

rowdy: 3 yob; **4** hood, yobo; **5** brute, bully, rough, tough, yobbo; **6** meanie [jocular], mugger, savage, wretch; **7** brutish, hoodlum, raucous, ruffian; **8** hooligan, plug-

ugly, snobbish; **9** barbarian, desperado, roughneck

rowel: 3 vex; **7** trouble

rower: 7 oarsman

row house: 9 town house

rowlock: 3 peg, pin; **5** pivot, thole; **7** oarlock

royal: 5 regal; **6** purple; **8** imperial, majestic, royalist

Royal Air Force: 3 RAF

Royal Canadian Mounted Police: 4 RCMP; **8** mounties

royal family: 6 royals; **7** royalty; **9** royal line; **10** royal house

royalist: 5 royal; **10** monarchist

royal line: 7 royalty; **10** royal house; **11** royal family

royal poinciana: 9 flame tree; **10** flamboyant; **13** peacock flower

royal road: 8 highroad, main road; **9** coach road; **12** thoroughfare

royalty: 8 regality

Roystonea: 4 palm; **14** genus Roystonea

rpm: 3 rev

Ru: 9 ruthenium

Ruanda: 6 Rwanda

rub: 4 fray, fret, itch, snag, wipe; **5** chafe, check, cross, hitch, slide; **6** hang-up; **7** problem, reverse, scratch, setback [U.S.]; **8** comedown, reversal

rubber: 5 latex; **10** caoutchouc; **11** India rubber

rubber band: 7 elastic

rubberneck: 4 gawk; **5** stare; **6** rubber; **7** tripper; **9** sightseer; **12** excursionist

rubber-necking: 11 sightseeing

rubbers: 8 galoshes

rubbing: 8 friction; **9** detrition

rubbing off: 7 wear off; **8** abrasion; **9** attrition, detrition

rubbish: 4 bosh; **5** stuff, trash, tripe; **6** litter, refuse; **7** discard, garbage; **8** discards

rubbish dump: 4 dump; **9** trash dump, wasteyard; **10** refuse heap; **11** garbage dump

rubbishy: 6 trashy

rubble: 4 dust, junk; **5** ruins; **6** debris; **8** detritus

rube: 4 clod, hick; **5** yahoo, yokel; **6** lummox; **7** bumpkin, hayseed

rubella: 13 German measles

rubeola: 7 measles; **8** morbilli

Rubiaceae: 12 madder family

rubicund: 5 ruddy; **8** sanguine

rubidium: 2 Rb

ruble: 6 rouble

rub off: 6 abrade, abrase

rub out: 4 kill; **5** erase; **6** efface

rubric: 3 act; **5** gloss, stamp; **6** manner; **7** caption, heading, statute; **9** character; **10** lex scripta [Lat], regulation; **11** corpus juris [Lat], description, designation; **12** denomination

Rubus: 8 dewberry; 9 framboise, raspberry; 10 genus Rubus, loganberry; 11 salmonberry

ruby: 3 gem, red; 5 bijou, jewel, ruddy; 6 cerise, cherry; 7 carmine, crimson, deep red, reddish, ruby-red, scarlet; 8 blood-red

ruck: 3 hem; 4 herd, tuck; 6 gather, pucker, ruck up; 7 crinkle, wrinkle

rucksack: 8 backpack, knapsack; 9 haversack

ruckus: 3 din; 6 rumpus, tumult; 7 ruction; 9 commotion

ruction: 3 din, row; 4 fray, to-do; 5 brawl, broil, melee; 6 affray, breeze, fracas, hubbub, pother, racket, ruckus, rumble, rumpus, squall, tumult, uproar; 7 howling, rhubarb, shindig, trouble; 8 brouhaha, scramble; 9 commotion, imbroglio, scrimmage; 10, donnybrook, free-for-all

Rudbeckia: 9 hortensia; 14 black-eyed Susan, genus Rudbeckia

rudderless: 6 adrift, afloat; 7 aimless; 8 planless; 10 undirected; 11 water-logged

ruddy: 3 red; 4 rosy, ruby; 6 cerise, cherry, florid, rufous; 7 carmine, crimson, reddish, ruby-red, scarlet; 8 blood-red, rubicund, sanguine; 9 cherry-red; 11 incarnadine

rude: 3 raw; 4 wild; 5 bluff, crude, empty, green, gross, heavy, rough, saucy; 6 abrupt, clumsy, fierce, raging, rugged, savage, unread; 7 awkward, furious, halting, natural, rickety, shallow, uncivil; 8 derisive, impolite, impudent, ungentle, vehement, yokelish; 9 barbarous, ferocious, primitive, sarcastic, slouching; 10 blustering, boisterous, bounderish, off-putting, outrageous, unmannered, unmannerly

rudiment: 5 basic; 9 beginning

rudimentary: 5 basic; 9 embryonic, vestigial; 10 rudimental, underlying; 11 fundamental

rudiments: 3 ABC; 4 ABCs; 6 basics, manual, primer; 7 grammar; 8 alphabet, elements, outlines; 9 vade mecum; 10 first thing

rue: 5 aloes; 6 regret, repent

rued: 8 lamented; 9 regretted

rue family: 8 Rutaceae

rueful: 3 wan; 5 sorry; 6 woeful; 8 contrite, mournful, pitiable; 9 long-faced, regretful; 10 deplorable, lamentable, remorseful

ruff: 5 trump; 6 choker, ruffle; 8 trumping

ruffian: 3 yob; 4 hood, yobo; 5 brute, bully, rough, rowdy, tough, yobbo; 6 meanie [jocular], mugger, savage, wretch; 7 hoodlum; 8 hooligan; 9 barbarian, desperado, roughneck

ruffle: 3 mix; 4 fray, fret, fuss, huff, ruff, stew, tuck; 5 chafe, crisp, flick, fluff, frill, hurry, pique, pleat, ravel, strut; 6 affray, choker, enrage, flurry, gather, mess up, net-

tle, pother, prance, riffle, ripple, rumple, sashay, tangle, tousle; 7 affront, agitate, crumple, ferment, flounce, fluster, flutter, perturb, roughen, shuffle, swagger; 8 aggrieve, dishevel, entangle, irritate, neck ruff, ruffle up, undulate; 9 corrugate; 10 discompose; 11 disturbance

rufous: 5 ruddy; 6 florid; 7 reddish; 8 sanguine

rug: 3 mat; 4 pelt; 5 front; 6 carpet, toupee; 7 cushion; 8 throw rug; 9 carpeting

rugby football: 5 rugby; 6 rugger

rugged: 4 rude; 5 bluff, blunt, gross, gruff, rough, tough; 6 broken, clumsy, craggy, thorny, trying; 7 awkward, rickety

rugger: 5 rugby; 13 rugby football

rug pad: 8 underlay; 9 carpet pad; 12 underlayment

Ruhr: 9 Ruhr River; 10 Ruhr Valley

ruin: 4 fall; 5 break, crash, ruins, wreck; 6 fleece; 7 destroy, ruining; 8 bankrupt, downfall, wrecking; 9 perdition, ruination; 10 desolation; 11 devastation; 12 dilapidation

ruination: 4 fall, ruin; 5 crash; 7 falling, ruining; 8 downfall, wrecking; 9 perdition; 11 devastation, ruinousness

ruined: 4 lost, sunk; 6 broken, undone, wasted; 7 blasted, done for, ravaged; 8 desolate, finished, washed-up; 9 desolated, destroyed; 10 devastated

ruing: 8 repining; 10 regretting

ruinous: 6 tragic; 8 blasting, tragical; 10 calamitous, disastrous, subversive; 11 destructive, devastating; 12 catastrophic

ruins: 4 ruin; 6 rubble

rule: 3 bar, law, ray, try; 4 code, find, form, rein, sway; 5 canon, reign, ruler, spoke; 6 decide, decree, govern, nature, normal, radius, streak, stripe; 7 command, formula, harness, pattern, precept, prevail, routine; 8 dominate, dominion, standard; 9 enactment, prescript, principle, pronounce, supremacy; 10 convention, domination, regulation, suzerainty; 11 physical law, predominate, sovereignty

rule of thumb: 9 guideline, guidepost; 10 empiricism

rule out: 6 reject; 8 preclude; 9 eliminate

ruler: 4 rule; 8 governor, standard

rule the roost: 8 dominate

rule with an iron hand: 7 dictate

ruling: 7 opinion, regnant; 8 reigning; 9 governing

rum: 3 odd; 5 funny, queer, rummy, weird; 7 bizarre, curious; 8 fanciful, peculiar, singular; 9 fantastic

Rumania: 7 Romania; 8 Roumania

rumba: 6 rhumba

rumble: 3 row; 4 fray, to-do; 5 brawl, broil,

growl, melee; **6** affray, breeze, fracas, hubbub, racket, rumpus, squall, uproar; **7**
grumble, rhubarb [baseball], ruction, trouble; **8** brouhaha, rumbling, scramble; **9**
gang fight, grumbling, imbroglio, scrimmage; **10** donnybrook, free-for-all
rum cocktail: 8 daiquiri
rumen: 12 first stomach
Rumex: sorrel; **10** genus Rumex
ruminate: 4 mull, muse; **5** dream; **6** ponder;
7 reflect; **8** chew over, meditate, mull over;
9 speculate; **11** contemplate
ruminative: 6 broody, musing; **7** pensive; **8**
brooding; **9** pondering; **10** meditative,
reflective; **13** contemplative
rummage: 3 pry; **4** peer, scan; **5** sound; **6**
browse; **7** digging, explore, ransack; **9** look
round; **10** ransacking; **11** reconnoiter
rummage sale: 8 yard sale
rummy: 3 odd, rum, sot; **5** drunk, funny,
queer; **7** curious; **8** drunkard, peculiar, singular; **9** inebriate
rumor: 3 cry; **4** buzz, fame; **6** rumour; **7** diffuse, hearsay
rumormonger: 6 gossip; **8** gossiper; **10**
newsmonger
rump: 4 butt, loin, prat, rear, seat, tail, tush;
5 croup, fanny, stern, stump, thump,
whump; **6** behind, bottom, breech, croupe,
dorsum; **7** buttock; **8** backside, buttocks,
derriere; **9** posterior
rumple: 4 curl, draw, knit; **5** crisp, twill; **6**
cocker, cockle, crease, mess up, pucker,
ruffle; **7** crinkle, crumple, frizzle, roughen,
wrinkle
rumpled: 7 creased, tousled; **8** crumpled
rumpus: 3 din, row; **4** fray, to-do; **5** brawl,
broil, melee; **6** affray, breeze, fracas, hubbub, pother, racket, ruckus, rumble, squall,
tumult, uproar; **7** howling, rhubarb [base-
ball], ruction, shindig, trouble; **8** brouhaha,
scramble; **9** commotion, imbroglio, scrimmage; **10** donnybrook, free-for-all
run: 2 go; **3** lam, ply, ram; **4** bunk, flow, flux,
hunt, lead, lean, melt, move, pass, play,
race, rill, tend, test, work; **5** bleed, carry,
drive, force, guide, range, ravel, tally, trial;
6 course, dog run, elapse, endure, extend,
ladder, run for, runnel, series, streak,
stream; **7** advance, bank run, be afoot, consort, incline, operate, persist, prevail, proceed, rivulet, run away, running, scarper,
smuggle, unravel
runabout: 8 roadster
run abreast: 5 equal, match, reach; **12** keep
pace with
run across: 3 see; **4** meet; **7** run into; **9**
encounter, forgather
run afoul: 8 conflict, infringe; **10** contravene

runagate: 3 rip; **5** scamp; **6** rioter; **7** brawler,
runaway; **8** renegade
run aground: 6 falter, ground; **8** flounder
run a risk: 4 risk; **6** chance, gamble, hazard;
9 adventure
run away: 3 lam, run
runaway: 4 romp; **6** shoo-in; **7** laugher; **8**
fugitive
run batted in: 3 RBI
rundle: 4 rung
rundlet: 3 keg; **6** barrel
run down: 3 sap; **5** use up; **6** creaky, run out;
7 exhaust, poop out; **8** decrepit
Rundstedt: 12 von Rundstedt; **26** Karl
Rudolf Gerd von Rundstedt
runes: 9 cuneiform
rung: 3 peg; **4** link, sill, step; **5** notch, round,
spoke, stave; **6** rundle
Runic: 6 uncial; **9** cuneiform
runic letter: 4 rune
run-in: 3 row; **5** words; **7** quarrel, wrangle
run into: 3 hit; **6** strike; **8** bump into; **9**
encounter
runnel: 3 run; **4** beck, burn, rill; **5** bayou,
brook, creek; **6** stream; **7** rivulet; **9** streamlet
runner: 4 tout; **5** flume; **6** offset; **7** courier; **8**
smuggler; **9** messenger; **10** base runner,
mooncurser
running: 2 on; **3** run; **5** afoot, track; **6** active,
linear; **7** fleeing, flowing, going on, pass-
ing, working; **8** elapsing, gradatim [Lat]; **9**
gradually, happening, operating, operation,
operative; **10** functional
running away: 6 flight; **7** fleeing
running back: 8 fullback, halfback, tailback
running dog: 4 dupe, tool; **6** lackey, puppet,
stooge
running head: 8 headline
running shoe: 7 sneaker; **9** track shoe
running title: 4 head; **5** title; **7** chapter, heading, section
running water: 4 flow; **7** current
runny: 5 fluid
runoff: 8 overflow; **9** overspill; **11** overflowing
run off: 4 bolt; **5** elope, go off, waste, xerox;
6 decamp, dispel, run out; **7** abscond; **9**
photocopy
run off the rails: 4 jump; **6** derail
run out: 3 die; **4** bolt, fail, pour; **5** drain,
passe, spill; **6** expire, lapsed, no more, run
off; **7** bolt out, conk out, deplete, elapsed,
exhaust, expired, extinct, give out, has-
been, poop out
runt: 4 puny; **6** peewee, shrimp; **8** half-pint,
pint-size, sawed-off
run through: 3 eat; **4** leak; **5** drain, eat up,
use up; **6** dry run, run out; **7** bayonet, consume, deplete, exhaust, pervade, prevail,
wipe out; **8** dominate; **9** go through,
rehearsal

run up: 3 sew; 4 rear; 5 build, erect, hoist, put up, raise, set up; 6 stitch

run upon: 5 run on

Rupert: 12 Prince Rupert

Rupicapra: 7 chamois; 14 genus Rupicapra

rupture: 4 bust, rent, rift, snap, tear; 5 break, split; 6 breach, hernia, wrench; 7 shatter; 8 disunion, division; 9 severance; 10 disruption

ruptured: 5 burst; 6 busted

rural: 6 arable, rustic; 7 country; 10 provincial

rural area: 7 country

ruse: trick

rush: 4 dash, gush, mill, race, tear; 5 flood, flush, haste, hurry, sedge, spate, speed, spray, spurt, straw, surge; 6 charge, deluge, hasten, rushed, splash, thrill; 7 bulrush, rushing, torrent, upsurge; 8 eruption; 9 stimulate

rush candle: 9 rushlight

rushed: 4 rush; 5 hasty; 7 hurried; 9 impetuous

rush family: 9 Juncaceae

rushlight: 10 rush candle

Rushmore: 11 Mt. Rushmore; 13 Mount Rushmore

rusk: 8 zwieback

Russell: 15 Bertrand Russell; 28 Bertrand Arthur William Russell

russet: 5 brown, Idaho; 12 reddish-brown

Russian alphabet: 8 Cyrillic

Russian capital: 6 Moscow

Russian Orthodox: 8 Orthodox; 13 Greek Orthodox; 15 Eastern Orthodox

Russian wolfhound: 6 borzoi

rust: 3 eat; 5 rusty, shake; 7 corrode, crumble, rust-red, rusting; 8 iron mold; 9 plant rust, rustiness; 10 rust fungus; 28 fall into the sear and yellow leaf

rustic: 4 hick; 5 rural; 6 arable; 7 bucolic, country, hayseed; 8 agrestic, arcadian, pastoral; 9 bumpkinly; 10 provincial; 11 countrified, countryfied

rustle: 4 lift; 7 whisper; 8 rustling; 10 whispering, 11 steal cattle

rustler: 8 kidnaper; 11 cattle thief

rustling: 6 rustle; 7 whisper; 9 murmurous, susurrous; 10 whispering

rusty: 4 rust; 5 cross, hoary, moldy, musty, seedy; 6 hoarse; 7 grating; 8 flagging, mildewed, outmoded, time-worn; 11 intractable; 12 cantankerous, deaf to reason; 13 out of practice

rut: 4 heat; 6 furrow, groove; 7 channel

Rutaceae: 9 rue family

Ruth: 8 Babe Ruth; 12 Sultan of Swat; 16 George Herman Ruth

ruth: 4 pity; 6 pathos, sorrow; 7 charity; 10 compassion

ruthenium: 2 Ru

rutherfordium: 2 Ku, Rf; 3 Unq; 12 kurchatovium, unnilquadium

ruthful: 6 woeful, tender; 7 clement

ruthless: 8 pitiless; 9 merciless, unpitying; 11 remorseless

ruthlessness: 7 cruelty; 10 inclemency

Rutilus: 5 roach; 12 genus Rutilus

rutted: 5 rutty; 6 fluted; 7 grooved; 8 furrowed

rutting: 3 hot; 5 horny, lusty, randy; 6 carnal, erotic; 7 lustful, rampant, ruttish; 8 prurient; 10 libidinous

RV: 9 motor home

Rwanda: 6 Ruanda

rya: 3 rug

rye: 8 rye bread; 10 rye whiskey

S

S

---

s: 3 sec; 6 second

S: 3 mho; 5 south; 6 sulfur; 7 siemens, sulphur

s.c.: 9 subdermal; 12 subcutaneous

Sabah: 11 North Borneo

sabayon: 10 zabaglione

sabbat: 14 witches' Sabbath

sabbatical leave: 10 sabbatical

saber: 5 sabre, sword

saber-toothed tiger: 10 sabertooth

Sabine: 11 Sabine River

Sabin vaccine: 3 OPV; 4 TOPV; 12 polio vaccine

sable: 4 dark, inky; 5 black, ebony; 6 somber

sabot: 4 clog, geta; 6 patten

sabotage: 6 weaken; 7 subvert; 9 undermine; 10 counteract; 11 countermine

saboteur: 7 wrecker; 12 diversionist

sabre: 5 saber

sac: 3 bag; 4 sack; 5 pouch, theca; 6 pocket; 7 saccule

saccarify: 5 sugar

saccharide: 5 sugar; 12 carbohydrate

saccharine: 5 sweet; 6 dulcet, syrupy; 7 cloying, treacly

Saccharomyces: 11 baker's yeast; 15 winemaker's yeast; 18 genus Saccharomyces

saccharose: 7 sucrose

Saccharum: 9 sugarcane; 14 genus Saccharum

saccule: 3 bag, sac; 4 sack; 8 sacculus

sacerdotal: 8 hieratic, pastoral, priestly; 10 hieratical; 11 ministerial

sachel: 3 fob, net; 4 knit, poke; 5 pouch, scrip; 6 budget, pocket, sheath, socket; 7 satchel; 8 reticule, scabbard

sachet: 6 packet; 9 potpourri

Sachs disease: 8 Tay-Sachs; 15 Tay-Sachs disease

sack: 3 bag, can, cot, gut, nab, net, RIF, sac; 4 fire, hook, loot, poke; 5 catch, clear, get in, pouch, rifle, shift, spoil, strip, sweep; 6 firing, pocket, rapine, sack up, sacque, secure; 7 chemise, despoil, dismiss, fire out, hammock, looting, pillage, plunder, ransack, release, saccule, sackful, sacking; 8 force out, paper bag, pink slip; 9 discharge, dismissal, terminate

sackcloth and ashes: 8 mourning; 10 maceration; 12 flagellation; 13 mortification

sacked: 5 fired, raped; 6 canned, riffed; 7 ravaged, severed; 8 pillaged; 9 despoiled, dismissed; 10 terminated

sacking: 4 sack; 6 firing; 7 bagging, release; 9 discharge, dismissal; 10 liberation

sack out: 5 sleep; 6 retire, turn in; 7 crawl in, go to bed, kip down; 9 go to sleep, hit the hay; 10 hit the sack

saclike: 9 bursiform; 11 pouch-shaped

sacramental oil: 6 chrism; 7 chrisom, holy oil

sacramental wine: 9 altar wine

Sacramento: 19 capital of California

sacrament of the Eucharist: 7 Liturgy; 9 Eucharist; 11 Lord's Supper; 13 Holy Sacrament

sacred: 4 holy; 6 heroic, solemn; 7 sublime; 8 almighty, biblical, hallowed, heavenly, imposing, majestic; 9 celestial, prophetic; 10 heaven-born, sanctified, scriptural; 11 consecrated; 12 transcendent

sacredly: 11 religiously

sacrifice: 4 give; 7 forfeit; 8 demolish, immolate, libation, oblation; 9 scapegoat; 10 euthanasia, forfeiture, immolation

sacrificed: 10 victimized

sacrilege: 9 blasphemy; 11 desecration, profanation

sacrilegious: 7 profane; 10 irreverent; 11 blasphemous

sacristan: 6 beadle, sexton

sacristy: 6 shrine, vestry; 7 chancel; 9 sanctuary

sacrosanct: 8 absolute; 9 inviolate; 10 inviolable; 11 inalienable, unalienable; 12 indefeasible, unchallenged

sad: 3 dun; 4 drab, roan; 5 dingy, grave, heavy, livid, sorry; 6 leaden, pearly, russet, sadden, somber; 7 doleful, pensive, pitiful, serious, unhappy; 8 grievous, pathetic, touching, wretched; 9 affecting; 10 deplorable, lamentable, melancholy; 11 distressing, melancholic

saddened: 8 grieving; 10 distressed

saddening: 6 gloomy; 10 depressing, depressive

saddle: 6 burden, charge; 7 pillion; 10 saddleback; 11 bicycle seat

saddleback roof: 9 gable roof; 10 saddle roof, saddleback

saddle blanket: 10 saddlecoth; 12 horse blanket

saddle horse: 3 nag; 5 mount; 6 cayuse [U.S.]

saddle shoe: 6 oxford

saddle soap: 11 leather soap

saddle sore: 4 gall

Sade: 6 de Sade; 13 Marquis de Sade

sadly: 6 sorely; 8 bitterly, horribly, terribly, woefully; 9 fearfully, miserably, painfully, piteously, seriously, unhappily; 10 deplorably, dreadfully, grievously, lamentably

sadness: 5 blues, dumps; 6 sorrow; 8 darkness, doldrums, the blues, the dumps; 9 dejection, heaviness, tristesse [Fr]; 10 depression, dismalness, gloominess, melancholy, somberness; 11 joylessness, melancholia, unhappiness; 12 dejectedness

sado-masochism: 9 masochism

sad sack: 7 botcher, bumbler, bungler, butcher, fumbler; 9 blunderer

safari: 4 hunt; 7 journey; 8 campaign; 10 expedition

safe: 4 good, sure; 6 safety, secure, unhurt; 8 harmless; 10 dependable; 12 not dangerous, prophylactic

safe-conduct: 8 passport, password

safecracker: 9 cracksman; 11 safebreaker

safe-deposit box: 7 lockbox; 9 bank vault; 10 deposit box

safeguard: 9 palladium; 10 precaution

safekeeping: 4 care, keep, ward; 6 charge; 7 custody, keeping; 12 guardianship

safe to drink: 7 potable; 9 drinkable

safety: 4 safe; 5 guard; 6 bingle, condom, refuge, rubber, surety; 7 base hit; 8 security; 12 prophylactic

safety belt: 6 airbag; 8 life belt, seat belt

safety blitz: 5 blitz; 8 pass rush

safety glass: 9 laminated; 12 shatterproof

safety glasses: 13 safety goggles

safety hat: 7 hard hat

safety match: 11 book matches

safety rail: 9 guardrail

safety valve: 6 escape; 9 blow valve; 10 escape cock; 11 escape valve, relief valve; 12 blow-off valve

saffron: 5 topaz; 6 crocus; 12 orange yellow

sag: 3 arc; 4 flag, swag, sway; 5 curve, droop, slump, sweep; 7 sag down

sagacious: 4 sage, wise; 6 shrewd; 7 sapient; 13 perspicacious

sagacity: 6 acumen, esprit; 8 gumption, judgment; 9 acuteness, judgement; 10 quick parts, shrewdness; 11 discernment

sage: 4 guru, wise; 6 salvia, 7 mahatma, sapient, wise man; 9 sagacious, sage-green

Sagebrush State: 6 Nevada; 11 Silver State; 15 Battle Born State

sagely: 6 wisely

sagging: 6 droopy; 7 bending; 8 drooping, yielding

Sagittariidae: 19 family Sagittariidae

Sagittarius the Archer: 11 Sagittarius

sagittate: 11 arrow-shaped, sagittiform

Sahaptin: 10 Shahaptian

Sahara: 12 Sahara Desert

said: 9 aforesaid; 14 aforementioned

Saigon: 13 Ho Chi Minh City

sail: 4 ship; 5 sheet, sweep; 6 canvas, cruise, sailer, voyage; 7 canvass, passage; 8 navigate, take ship, tall ship; 10 windjammer; 11 sailing ship

sailfish: 8 billfish

sailing: 5 at sea, glide; 7 boating, gliding, soaring; 9 seafaring; 10 navigation; 11 sailplaning

sailing master: 7 captain; 9 navigator

sailing-race: 9 yacht race

sailing ship: 4 sail, ship; 6 sailer; 8 schooner, tall ship; 10 windjammer; 13 sailing vessel

sailor: 6 boater, panama; 7 crewman, leghorn, mariner, navy man, skimmer; 9 navigator, sailor boy

sailplane: 4 soar; 6 glider

sailplaning: 5 glide; 7 gliding, sailing, soaring

sail through: 3 ace; 10 pass easily

saint: 5 angel, ideal; 7 beatify, devotee, holy man, nonsuch, paragon, puritan; 8 canonize, enshrine, nonesuch; 9 formalist, nonpareil; 10 apotheosis, holy person; 11 religionist

sainted: 7 angelic, saintly; 8 beatific; 9 angelical, saintlike

saintlike: 7 saintly

saintly: 7 angelic, sainted; 8 beatific; 9 angelical, saintlike

Saint Monday: 10 Whit Monday; 12 Easter Monday

Saint Nicholas: 10 Santa Claus; 12 Kriss Kringle; 15 Father Christmas

Saintpaulia: 13 African violet; 16 genus Saintpaulia

sake: 4 saki; 8 interest

saki: 4 sake

Sakti: 6 Shakti

salaam: 3 bow; 6 curtsy; 7 deep bow; 8 courtesy

salable: 7 for sale; 8 saleable, sellable, vendible; 10 marketable

salacious: 4 lewd; 7 lustful, obscene; 8 prurient; 9 lecherous; 10 lascivious, lubricious

salacity: 5 flesh; 8 lewdness; 9 bawdiness, carnality, obscenity

salamander: 5 poker; 6 heater, tuyere; 8 fire hook; 10 stove poker, warming pan

Salamandra: 10 salamander; 15 genus Salamandra

sal ammoniac: 13 smelling salts

salaried: 6 paying; 11 compensable, compensated, remunerated, stipendiary; 12 remunerative

salary: 3 pay; 4 wage; 5 wages; 6 income; 8 earnings; 12 remuneration

sale: 4 vent; 7 selling, vending; 8 disposal

Salem: 15 capital of Oregon

saleroom: 8 showroom; 9 salesroom

sales booth: 5 stall, stand

sales clerk: 11 salesperson

sales department: 10 sales force

salesperson: 6 dealer, monger, trader; 8 chandler, merchant; 10 sales clerk, store clerk

salesroom: 8 saleroom, showroom

sales talk: 5 pitch

Salicaceae: 12 willow family

salience: 8 saliency; 9 highlight; 12 strikingness

salient: 4 bold; 5 clear; 6 peaked, signal; 7 notable; 8 apparent, manifest, striking; 9 prominent; 11 outstanding, spectacular; 13 demonstrative

saliently: 7 notably; 10 materially; 11 prominently

saline: 4 salt; 5 briny, salty; 8 brackish

salinity: 4 salt; 9 brininess, saltiness

Salisbury: 6 Harare; 17 capital of Zimbabwe

saliva: 4 spit; 5 rheum; 7 spittle

Salix: 6 willow; 10 genus Salix; 13 weeping willow

salle-a-manger: 10 dining room

sallet: 6 helmet; 7 sallade

sallow: 3 dun, wan; 4 ashy, cold, dead, dull; 5 ashen, dingy, faint, muddy; 6 glassy, leaden, sickly; 7 ghastly; 10 cadaverous, lackluster

sally: 4 quip; 5 crack; 6 sortie; 8 breakout, outbreak; 9 wisecrack

sally forth: 7 go forth

sally port: 4 gate; 7 passage

salmagundi: 4 mess, olio; 6 medley; 7 farrago; 8 all sorts, mishmash, pastiche; 9 patchwork, potpourri; 10 hodgepodge

Salmo: 10 genus Salmo, brown trout; 11 salmon trout; 12 rainbow trout; 14 Atlantic salmon

Salmon: 11 Salmon River

S

salmon-colored: 5 peach
salmon pink: 5 peach; 7 apricot
salmon trout: 8 sea trout; 9 lake trout; 10 brown trout
salon: 6 parlor, saloon; 10 beauty shop; 11 beauty salon; 12 beauty parlor
Salonika: 12 Thessalonika
saloon: 3 bar, pub; 4 dive [U.S.]; 5 salon; 6 parlor, tavern; 7 barroom, gin mill, taproom; 8 exchange, pothouse, taphouse
salsify: 11 oyster plant; 15 vegetable oyster
sal soda: 4 soda; 7 soda ash; 11 washing soda
Salsola: 10 tumbleweed; 12 genus Salsola
salt: 2 A.B.; 3 tar; 4 cure, whim; 5 briny, cream, fancy, point, salty; 6 esprit, saline, salted; 7 jack tar; 8 brackish, drollery, salinity; 9 salt-cured, saltiness, table salt
salt-cured: 6 salted
saltiness: 4 salt; 8 salinity
Salt Lake City: 13 capital of Utah
salt pork: 7 fatback; 8 sowbelly
saltwater: 5 brine; 6 marine; 8 seawater
salt water: 5 brine
saltwort family: 10 Batidaceae
salubrious: 7 healthy; 8 salutary; 9 healthful, wholesome
Saluki: 12 gazelle hound
salutary: 4 good; 7 healthy; 9 healthful, wholesome; 10 beneficial, salubrious
salutation: 6 appeal, salute; 8 greeting; 9 reception; 10 apostrophe, invocation; 11 recognition
salutatory speaker: 12 salutatorian
salute: 4 ball; 5 drink, toast; 6 pledge; 7 present; 8 greeting; 10 salutation
Salvador: 10 El Salvador
salvage: 4 save; 5 salve; 6 ransom; 7 relieve; 8 scavenge; 10 redemption
salvation: 6 rescue; 8 adoption, judgment; 9 atonement, mediation; 10 conversion, redemption; 11 deliverance, extrication
salve: 4 balm, save; 5 salvo; 6 excuse; 7 apology, relieve, salvage, unguent; 8 ointment
Salvelinus: 9 lake trout; 10 Arctic char, brook trout; 11 salmon trout; 13 speckled trout; 15 genus Salvelinus
salvia: 4 sage
salvo: 5 burst, salve; 6 excuse, firing, volley; 7 apology, come off; 8 loophole; 9 discharge, fusillade
samara: 8 key fruit
samarium: 2 Sm
Samarkand: 9 Samarcand
samba: 5 dance
sambar: 6 sambur
Sambucus: 5 elder; 10 elderberry; 13 genus Sambucus

same: 3 one; 4 like; 5 equal; 8 selfsame; 9 identical; 10 equivalent
sameness: 7 oneness; 8 identity, monotony; 12 selfsameness
Sami: 4 Lapp
Samolus: 9 brookweed; 12 genus Samolus
Samoyed: 8 Samoyede; 11 Siberian dog
samphire: 9 glasswort
sample: 3 try; 5 taste; 6 try out; 7 example; 8 instance, specimen
samurai: 7 warrior
sanative: 7 healing; 8 curative, remedial; 10 alterative, reparative; 11 therapeutic
sanctified: 6 sacred; 7 adopted, elected; 8 inspired; 9 converted, justified, unearthly; 11 consecrated, regenerated
sanctify: 5 allot, bless; 6 hallow, ordain, purify; 7 beatify; 8 enshrine, keep holy, legalize; 9 prescribe; 10 consecrate
sanctimonious: 7 canting; 8 unctuous; 9 pharisaic, pietistic; 11 pharisaical
sanction: 2 OK; 4 okay; 6 hold up, uphold; 7 approve, charter, precept, warrant; 8 approval, warranty; 9 attention, authority; 10 estimation, imprimatur; 11 approbation, countenance, endorsement
sanctioned: 7 allowed, canonic; 8 approved, ratified; 9 allowable, canonical, permitted; 10 authorized; 11 permissible
sanctity: 8 holiness; 11 saintliness
sanctuary: 4 bema; 6 asylum, refuge, shrine; 7 chancel, retreat
sanctum: 4 holy; 9 holy place; 12 holy of holies, inner sanctum
sand: 4 grit, guts; 5 beach; 8 backbone, gumption; 9 sandpaper
sandal: 4 boot, pump; 7 slipper
sandalwood family: 11 Santalaceae
sandbag: 4 bank, drub, mole, stun; 5 baste, mound; 6 pummel; 7 belabor, leather, parapet, trounce; 9 revetment, sunk fence; 10 embankment
sand-blind: 8 purblind
sandbox: 8 sandpile
sand bucket: 10 fire bucket
sandbur: 8 sandspur
sander: 8 smoother; 9 sandpaper
sandfly fever: 11 phlebotomus
sandglass: 9 hourglass
sandiness: 10 graininess, grittiness; 11 granularity
sand lance: 6 launce; 7 sand eel; 10 sand launce
sandpaper: 4 sand; 10 emery paper
sands of time: 10 Father Time
sandspur: 7 sandbur
sandstorm: 7 sirocco; 9 dust storm
sand trap: 4 trap; 6 bunker
Sandwich Islands: 15 Hawaiian Islands
sandy: 5 light, mealy, tawny; 6 creamy, flaxen, grainy, gritty; 7 friable; 8 granular, sandlike; 9 granulose

sane: 8 rational; 10 reasonable
sanely: 8 sensibly; 10 reasonably
saneness: 6 sanity
sangaree: 7 sangria
sangfroid: 4 cool; 5 poise; 6 aplomb; 8 coolness; 9 composure, frigidity; 11 assuredness
Sangraal: 5 grail; 9 Holy Grail
sangria: 8 sangaree
sanguinary: 4 gory; 6 bloody; 9 butcherly
sanguine: 5 ruddy; 6 florid, rufous; 8 rubicund; 9 confident; 10 optimistic; 11 incarnadine
sanicle: 9 snakeroot
sanitary: 5 clean; 9 healthful
sanitize: 9 hygienize
sanity: 6 health; 8 saneness; 9 soundness; 10 good health; 11 healthiness
San Jose: 18 capital of Costa Rica
San Marino: 18 capital of San Marino
San Salvador: 17 Salvadoran capital
sans pareil: 8 none such
sans serif: 9 Helvetica
sans souci: 6 casual; 8 sine cura [Lat]; 9 easygoing, unworried; 10 insouciant, nonchalant, phlegmatic; 11 unconcerned
Santa Claus: 12 Kriss Kringle; 13 Saint Nicholas; 15 Father Christmas
Santa Fe: 18 capital of New Mexico
Santalaceae: 16 sandalwood family
Santalum: 10 sandalwood; 13 genus Santalum
Santee Sioux: 6 Santee; 12 Eastern Sioux, Santee Dakota
Santiago: 14 capital of Chile, Santiago de Cuba
Santiago de Cuba: 8 Santiago
Santo Domingo: 29 capital of the Dominican Republic
Saone: 10 Saone River
sap: 4 fool, mine, tire; 5 drain, shake, use up; 6 burrow, devour, tunnel, weaken; 7 break up, exhaust, run down, saphead; 8 backbone, bludgeon; 9 blackjack, lifeblood, undermine
sapid: 8 saporous; 9 flavorful, flavorous; 10 flavorsome, flavourful, flavourous; 11 flavoursome
sapience: 6 reason, wisdom; 8 sagacity; 11 rationality
sapient: 4 sage, wise; 9 sagacious
Sapindus: 9 China tree; 10 chinaberry, 13 genus Sapindus
sapodilla: 6 sapota
sapodilla family: 10 Sapotaceae
saponaceous: 5 soapy
sapota: 9 sapodilla
Sapotaceae: 15 sapodilla family
sapote: 6 mammee
sapper: 5 miner; 9 excavator
sapphic: 7 lesbian
sapphire: 4 blue; 5 azure

sapphism: 10 lesbianism
sappy: 5 silly; 11 sentimental
Saragossa: 8 Zaragoza
sarape: 6 serape
sarcasm: 5 irony; 6 satire; 7 mockery; 8 cynicism, innuendo; 11 insinuation
sarcastic: 6 ironic; 7 satiric; 8 sardonic
sarcoid: 6 fleshy
sarcophagus: 4 tomb; 6 coffin
Sarcorhamphus: 11 king vulture; 18 genus Sarcorhamphus
Sarda: 6 bonito; 8 skipjack; 10 genus Sarda
Sardegna: 8 Sardinia
Sardina: 7 sardine; 8 pilchard; 12 genus Sardina; 13 genus Sardina
Sardinia: 8 Sardegna
Sardinops: 14 Pacific sardine, genus Sardinops
sardius: 4 sard; 7 sardine
sardonic: 3 dry, wry; 5 sharp; 6 biting, severe; 7 cutting, cynical; 8 hard upon; 9 sarcastic, satirical, trenchant, withering
saree: 4 sari
sargasso: 8 gulfweed; 9 sargassum
sari: 5 saree
sartor: 6 tailor
sash: 6 fascia, fillet, girdle, wreath; 7 baldric, garland; 8 cincture; 9 waistband; 10 waistcloth, window sash
sashay: 5 jaunt, sidle, strut; 6 prance, ruffle; 7 swagger; 9 excursion; 10 expedition
Sasquatch: 7 Bigfoot
sass: 3 lip; 5 mouth; 7 sassing; 8 backtalk
sassy: 5 saucy; 7 aweless; 8 impudent; 9 audacious, shameless, unabashed
Sat: 8 Saturday
Satan: 5 Devil; 6 Belial, Samael, Zamiel; 7 Lucifer, Old Nick; 8 the Devil; 9 Beelzebub; 10 the evil one, the Tempter; 12 the Adversary, the arch fiend, the archenemy, the foul fiend, the wicked one; 13 the evil spirit, the old Serpent; 14 Mephistopheles; 16 Prince of Darkness
satanic: 6 unholy; 7 demonic, hellish, stygian; 8 devilish, diabolic, fiendish, hellborn, infernal; 10 demoniacal, diabolical; 15 Mephistophelian
Satanism: 8 demonism; 9 diabolism
Satanist: 9 diabolist
satchel: 3 bag; 5 pouch; 6 sachel
sate: 4 fill; 7 replete, satiate, satisfy; 8 saturate
sated: 6 gorged; 9 surfeited
satellite: 4 moon; 6 planet; 7 orbiter, sputnik [Russ]
satiate: 4 fill, glut, sate; 5 binge, gorge, slake, stuff; 6 pig out, quench; 7 engorge, overeat, replete, satisfy; 8 satiated, saturate, scarf out; 9 overgorge; 10 gorman-

S

dise, gormandize; **11** gourmandize, overindulge

satin: 5 silky, sleek, slick; **6** glossy, satiny, silken; **8** silklike

satiny: 4 fine; **5** filmy, satin, silky, sleek, slick; **6** glossy, silken; **7** subtile; **8** delicate, silklike

satire: 4 grin, quip, skit; **5** irony, squib; **7** sarcasm

satirical: 3 dry; **5** sharp; **6** biting, severe; **7** cutting, cynical, satiric; **8** sardonic; **9** sarcastic, trenchant, withering

satirist: 7 ironist; **9** lampooner

satirize: 6 parody, send up; **7** lampoon, traduce; **8** travesty; **9** burlesque, take off on; **10** caricature

satisfaction: 6 amends, enough, withal; **7** apology, satiety; **8** adequacy; **9** acquittal, atonement, clearance, discharge, expiation, quittance, reckoning, repletion; **10** competence, redemption, satisfying, settlement; **11** fulfillment, performance, sufficiency; **13** gratification

satisfactory: 2 OK; **5** valid; **8** all right, tangible; **9** competent, tolerable; **10** acceptable

satisfied: 4 sure; **6** secure, slaked; **7** assured, certain, content; **8** cocksure, executed, positive, quenched, satiated; **9** confident, contented, convinced, fulfilled; **10** complacent

satisfy: 2 do; **4** fill, keep, meet, quit, sate; **5** honor; **6** assure, fulfil, just do, redeem, settle; **7** content, execute, fulfill, gratify, perform, satiate, suffice; **8** saturate; **9** determine, discharge

satisfying: 5 solid; **6** hearty; **8** cheering, pleasing; **10** comforting, gratifying; **11** appreciated, substantial; **12** satisfaction

saturate: 4 sate, soak; **5** imbue; **6** imbrue; **7** satiate, satisfy; **10** infiltrate

saturated: 4 pure; **5** soppy; **6** soaked, sodden; **7** crammed, soaking, sopping; **8** drenched; **12** concentrated

saturation: 6 chroma; **7** satiety, too many, too much; **9** intensity, pervasion, repletion, suffusion, vividness; **10** permeation

Saturday: 3 Sat

Satureja: 8 calamint, Satureia; **9** basil balm, wild basil, field balm; **10** yerba buena; **12** summer savory, winter savory; **13** genus Satureia, genus Satureja

Saturn: 12 ringed planet

saturnalia: 4 orgy, riot; **6** excess; **7** debauch; **9** bacchanal; **10** debauchery; **11** bacchanalia; **12** extravagance

saturnine: 4 dark, dour, glum, sour; **5** moody; **6** dismal, gloomy, morose, somber, sullen; **7** joyless; **8** dejected, frowning; **9** cheerless, glowering

satyr: 4 faun, goat, rake; **6** lecher; **7** Don

Juan, fast man, gallant, seducer; **8** Lothario; **9** debauchee, forest god, ladies' man, loose fish; **11** whoremonger

saucer: 3 UFO; **4** disc, dish, disk; **5** plate; **6** discus; **7** platter; **9** porringer; **10** dish aerial; **11** dish antenna

saucily: 6 pertly; **7** freshly, perkily; **10** impudently; **13** impertinently

saucy: 4 pert, rude; **5** fresh [U.S.], sassy, smart; **7** aweless, forward; **8** flippant, impudent; **9** audacious, obtrusive, shameless, unabashed; **10** irreverent, precocious; **11** impertinent

Saudi: 12 Saudi Arabian

Saul: 4 Paul; **11** Apostle Paul; **12** Saul of Tarsus; **14** Paul the Apostle; **20** Apostle of the Gentiles

sauna: 8 warm bath; **9** steam bath, sweat room, vapor bath

saunter: 5 amble; **6** ramble, stroll; **9** promenade

saunterer: 8 stroller

saurel: 12 jack mackerel

sausage: 4 link; **5** patty; **6** banger

saute: 3 fry

savage: 4 wild; **5** beast, brute; **6** brutal, fierce, raging; **7** brutish, untamed; **8** barbaric; **9** barbarian, barbarous, ferocious, malicious; **11** uncivilized

savagery: 7 outrage; **8** atrocity, ferocity; **9** barbarism, barbarity, brutality; **10** inhumanity

savannah: 7 savanna

Savannah: 13 Savannah River

savant: 6 pundit, shrewd; **7** bookish, scholar; **8** profound; **10** scholastic; **11** book-learned, enlightened

save: 4 keep, stow; **5** minus, salve, spare, store; **6** beside, except, redeem, rescue, save up; **7** barring, deliver, relieve, salvage, without; **8** conserve, preserve

saved: 6 stored; **7** rescued; **9** delivered, protected; **10** extricated

saving: 5 chary, spare; **6** frugal, rescue; **7** careful, economy, sparing, storing, thrifty; **8** delivery; **9** redeeming; **10** economical, preserving, redemptive; **11** deliverance; **12** preservation

savings: 7 nest egg

savior: 7 rescuer; **9** deliverer; **10** benefactor; **13** good Samaritan, guardian angel, tutelary saint

savor: 4 bask, gust, tang; **5** enjoy, gusto, smack, taste, twang; **6** flavor, relish

savory: 5 tasty, zesty; **6** dainty; **7** piquant, scented; **8** aromatic, fragrant, redolent; **9** delicious, palatable; **10** delectable

savoy: 7 cabbage

savvy: 3 dig; **4** take; **5** grasp; **7** compass; **9** apprehend; **10** comprehend; **11** discernment; **12** apprehension; **13** get the picture, understanding

saw: 3 cut; **5** adage; **6** byword, dictum, saying; **7** proverb; **8** power saw

sawbones: 2 MD; **3** doc [informal]; **6** doctor; **7** surgeon; **9** physician

sawbuck: 4 buck; **5** horse; **8** sawhorse; **13** ten-dollar bill

sawed-off: 5 runty; **8** pint-size; **9** pint-sized, shortened

sawhorse: 4 buck; **5** horse; **7** sawbuck

saw logs: 5 snore; **7** saw wood

sawmill: 10 lumbermill

saw-toothed: 7 notched, serrate, toothed; **8** serrated

saw wood: 5 snore; **7** saw logs

sawyer beetle: 6 sawyer

sax: 9 saxophone

Saxony: 4 Saxe; **7** Sachsen

saxophone: 3 sax

say: 4 aver, bout, read, tell, turn; **5** about, state, utter; **6** affirm, allege, assert, enjoin, nearly; **7** declare, deliver, enounce, profess; **8** announce, delivery, harangue, rotation; **9** enunciate, pronounce; **10** articulate

saying: 3 saw; **5** adage; **6** dictum; **7** proverb; **8** locution, sentence, uttering; **9** asserting, declaring; **10** announcing, expression; **11** affirmative, declaratory, pronouncing; **12** articulating

sayonara: 3 bye; **4** ciao; **5** adieu, adios, aloha; **6** bye-bye, good-by, so long; **7** cheerio, good day, good-bye; **8** au revoir, farewell; **10** dosvidanya [Russ]; **11** arrivederci, leave taking, valediction; **12** hasta la vista [Sp]; **14** auf wiedersehen

say-so: 6 dictum; **9** authority, dominance; **13** pronouncement

Sb: 8 antimony

SbE: 11 south by east

SbW: 11 south by west

Sc: 8 scandium

scab: 9 cicatrize; **13** strikebreaker

scabbard: 6 sheath

scabby: 4 mean; **5** dirty; **6** abject, paltry, scurvy, shabby; **7** scrubby; **8** rascally, sneaking; **9** groveling

scabies: 4 itch

scabrous: 5 scaly; **6** coarse, scurfy, uneven; **7** leprose; **8** lepidote; **9** irregular

scads: 4 gobs, lots, tons, wads; **5** heaps, loads, piles, rafts, slews; **6** dozens, oodles, scores, stacks; **8** lashings

scaffold: 6 gibbet; **7** gallows

scalawag: 5 knave, rogue, scamp; **6** rascal, varlet; **9** reprobate, scallawag, scallywag

scald: 4 burn; **6** scorch

scalding: 7 boiling; **8** scathing

scale: 4 peel, slug; **5** flake, gamut, plate, scrap, scurf, serif, shank, shell; **6** scales; **7** descale, peel off; **8** flake off, shoulder, surmount, underlay; **10** coarseness, graduation

scale down: 6 reduce

scales: 5 scale; **15** weighing machine; **18** weighing instrument

scaling: 7 grading

scallawag: 5 scamp; **8** runagate, scalawag; **9** reprobate; **10** ne'er-do-well, scapegrace

scallion: 4 leek; **10** green onion

scallop: 5 crape, crimp, wring; **6** indent; **7** scollop, vandyke

scallywag: 3 imp; **5** knave, rogue, scamp; **6** monkey, rascal, varlet; **8** scalawag

scalp: 4 flay, pare, peel, skin; **9** excoriate

scaly: 5 flaky; **6** coarse, dermal, scaled, scaley, scurfy; **7** leprose; **8** cortical, lepidote, scabrous, squamous [Anat]; **9** cutaneous, cuticular, irregular; **10** membranous, pellicular

scam: 3 con; **4** bilk, bite; **5** cheat, pluck; **7** con game, defraud, swindle; **9** bunko game, victimize

scamp: 3 imp; **5** rogue; **6** rascal; **8** scalawag; **9** reprobate, scallawag, scallywag

scamper: 6 scurry; **7** scuttle, skitter; **8** scramble

scampish: 8 improper; **9** corrupted, dissolute, graceless, reprobate; **10** indecorous, profligate; **12** unprincipled

scan: 3 ken, pry; **4** know, peer, rake, read, skim; **6** browse, peruse, survey; **7** explore, inspect; **8** consider; **10** glance over, scrutinize

scandal: 4 dirt; **6** defame; **7** slander; **8** baseness; **9** aspersion, indecorum; **10** backbiting, defamation, immorality, scurrility; **11** impropriety

scandalize: 5 shock; **6** appall, offend, revolt; **7** outrage

scandalous: 4 base, foul, vile; **5** grave, gross; **7** heinous; **8** infamous, shameful, shocking; **11** disgraceful

scandent: 8 climbing

Scandinavian: 5 Norse; **6** Nordic

scandium: 2 Sc

scanning: 7 perusal

scanning electron microscope: 3 SEM

scant: 5 light, short, skimp, stint; **6** scanty, slight; **7** limited, scraggy, scrubby, slender

scanties: 5 panty; **7** drawers, panties

scantily: 6 barely

scanty: 4 bare; **5** light, panty, scant, spare; **6** meager, pantie, slight, step-in; **7** limited, slender

scape: 6 escape; **11** flower stalk

scapegoat: 9 sacrifice; **11** whipping boy

scapegrace: 5 scamp; **6** madcap, rascal; **8** scalawag

Scaphiopus: 9 spadefoot; **15** genus Scaphiopus

scaphoid bone: 9 navicular

scapula: 12 shoulder bone; **13** shoulder blade

scapulary: 4 cope, gown, pall, robe; **5** frock;

S

7 cassock, pallium; **8** scapular; **10** Geneva gown

scar: 3 pit; **4** mark, pock; **6** scrape; **7** scratch; **8** cicatrix; **9** cicatrice

scarab beetle: 6 scarab; **10** dung beetle

scarce: 4 rare; **6** barely, hardly; **8** scarcely, uncommon

scarcely: 4 just; **6** barely, hardly, scarce, seldom; **8** only just; **10** no more than; **12** infrequently

scarcely ever: 6 rarely

scarcity: 6 dearth; **10** scarceness

scare: 5 alarm, daunt, panic; **6** fright; **7** scarify, startle; **8** affright, frighten

scarecrow: 8 strawman

scared: 8 panicked; **9** panicking; **10** frightened

scaremonger: 7 stirrer

scare off: 4 dash, pall; **5** daunt, scare; **9** scare away

scarf: 5 amice, scoff, stole; **6** mantle, runner, tippet; **8** chasuble

scarf out: 4 glut; **5** binge, gorge, stuff; **6** englut, pig out; **7** engorge, overeat, satiate; **9** overgorge; **10** gormandize; **11** ingurgitate, overindulge

scarfpin: 6 tiepin; **7** tie tack

scarify: 5 alarm, crimp, scare; **6** fright, scotch; **7** startle; **8** frighten

scarlatina: 12 scarlet fever

scarlet: 3 red; **4** ruby; **5** ruddy; **6** cerise, cherry; **7** carmine, crimson, reddish, ruby-red; **8** blood-red; **9** cherry-red

scarp: 6 escarp; **7** rampart; **10** battlement, escarpment

scarper: 3 lam, run; **4** bunk, flee; **5** leave; **6** depart; **7** run away; **8** turn tail; **9** break away

scarred: 6 marred

scary: 6 scarey; **7** shivery; **8** alarming, chilling, shuddery; **10** scarifying; **11** frightening

scat: 11 scat singing

scathe: 4 harm, hurt, sear; **6** damage, impair, scorch

scathing: 4 acid; **7** searing; **9** scorching

scat singing: 4 scat

scatter: 3 dot; **4** dust, shed; **6** dispel, litter, spread; **7** bestrew, break up, diffuse, disband; **8** dispense, disperse, sprinkle, strewing; **9** dissipate, spread out; **10** overspread, scattering; **11** disseminate

scatterbrain: 9 forgetful

scattered: 4 rare, shed, thin; **5** stray; **6** spotty, spread, strewn; **7** garbled; **8** bestrewn, confused, diffused, isolated; **9** disbanded, dispensed, dispersed, illogical; **10** disjointed, disordered

scattergun: 7 shotgun

scattering: 7 scatter; **8** sprinkle, strewing; **9**

diffusing, diffusive, spreading; **10** dispersion, dispersive, sprinkling

scatter rug: 8 throw rug

scatty: 5 crazy; **6** absent; **10** abstracted; **12** absentminded

scaup duck: 5 scaup; **8** bluebill; **9** broadbill

scavenge: 5 glean; **7** salvage

scavenger: 5 sweep; **6** magpie; **7** pack rat, vulture; **10** garbage man

scend: 5 surge

scene: 3 fit; **4** view; **5** image, sight, vista; **6** aspect, milieu; **7** picture, scenery, setting, tableau, tantrum, tempest; **8** outbreak, outburst, panorama, prospect; **10** appearance, background

scene painting: 4 view; **5** scene; **8** panorama

scenery: 5 scene; **9** landscape

scent: 3 cue, key; **4** clue, nose, odor, wind; **5** aroma, smell, smoke, sniff, spoor; **7** bouquet, essence, odorize, perfume; **9** effluvium, fragrance, redolence, smell a rat, suspicion

scented: 5 balmy, spicy, sweet; **6** savory; **7** odorous; **8** aromatic, fragrant, perfumed, redolent; **11** odoriferous

scepter: 4 wand; **5** baton, staff, verge; **11** sovereignty

sceptic: 5 cynic; **7** doubter, skeptic; **10** unbeliever

sceptical: 8 doubting; **9** skeptical; **11** incredulous, questioning, unbelieving; **12** disbelieving

scepticism: 8 cynicism, distrust, mistrust; **10** skepticism; **11** agnosticism, incredulity

schadenfreude: 4 glee; **5** gloat; **8** gloating

schedule: 6 agenda, docket

scheduling: 11 programming

Schefflera: 12 umbrella tree; **15** genus Schefflera

schema: 7 outline

schematic drawing: 5 chart; **6** scheme; **7** graphic; **8** diagram; **9** schematic

schematization: 11 diagramming

scheme: 4 plan, plot; **5** chart, dodge, frame; **6** design, figure; **7** arrange, connive, drawing, graphic, outline, project; **8** contrive, intrigue, strategy; **9** flow chart, schematic

schemed: 7 plotted; **9** contrived

schemer: 7 planner, plotter

scheming: 6 shrewd; **9** conniving, designing; **11** calculating

Scheol: 3 Hel; **4** Hell; **5** Hades; **10** underworld; **11** netherworld

schism: 5 split; **6** heresy; **13** false doctrine

schistorrhachis: 11 spina bifida

schistosome: 10 blood fluke

schistosomiasis: 9 bilharzia

schizoid: 13 schizophrenic

schizophrenia: 8 paranoia; **15** dementia praecox

schizophrenic: 8 schizoid

schlemiel: 4 fool, mark; **5** chump, patsy; **6** sucker; **7** fall guy; **8** shlemiel
schlep: 9 pull along
schlock: 6 shlock
Schlumbergera: 6 cactus; **18** genus Schlumbergera
schmaltz: 3 fat; **7** schmalz; **9** mushiness; **11** sentimental
schmaltzy: 5 mushy; **6** slushy; **7** maudlin, mawkish; **8** bathctic, schmalzy; **11** sentimental
schmear: 6 shmear; **7** schmeer
schmuck: 4 jerk; **5** creep; **6** weirdo
schnapps: 7 schnaps
schnitzel: 15 Wiener schnitzel
schnorkel: 7 snorkel; **8** breather; **10** schnorchel
schnoz: 4 beak, nose; **5** snout; **6** nozzle; **9** proboscis
schnozzle: 4 beak; **5** snoot, snout; **6** honker, hooter, nozzle
scholar: 5 pupil; **6** savant; **7** learner, student
scholarly: 10 scholastic
scholarly writing: 5 theme; **6** thesis; **8** treatise; **12** dissertation
scholarship: 8 learning; **9** erudition; **11** eruditeness, learnedness
scholastic: 4 blue; **5** solid; **6** divine, pedant, savant, shrewd; **7** bookish; **8** academic, bookworm, canonist, deep-read, profound; **9** doctrinal, scholarly; **10** collegiate; **11** book-learned, enlightened
scholasticism: 9 academism; **11** academicism
scholiast: 9 annotator; **11** commentator
school: 5 edify, train, tutor; **7** educate; **8** articles, civilize, doctrine, instruct; **9** cultivate, schooling
schoolbook: 4 text; **8** textbook
schoolboy: 5 cadet; **7** hopeful
schoolchild: 5 pupil
schooled: 6 taught; **7** tutored; **10** instructed
schoolfellow: 9 classmate; **10** schoolmate
schoolgirl: 4 coed
schoolmate: 9 classmate
school of medicine: 13 medical school
school of music: 12 conservatory
school of thought: 3 ism; **8** doctrine; **10** philosophy
school pal: 10 schoolmate
school principal: 4 head; **9** principal; **10** headmaster; **11** head teacher; **12** headmistress
schoolroom: 7 nursery; **9** classroom
school term: 7 session; **8** semester; **12** academic term
school text: 4 text; **8** textbook
schooner: 4 boat, ship; **8** sailboat; **7** terrine
schrod: 3 cod; **5** scrod
Schwarzwald: 11 Black Forest
Schweiz: 6 Suisse; **8** Svizzera; **11** Switzerland

Sciaenops: 7 red drum, redfish; **14** genus Sciaenops
science: 5 skill; **6** system; **9** knowledge
science lab: 3 lab; **10** laboratory
science of agriculture: 12 horticulture
science of being: 8 ontology; **11** metaphysics
science of life: 7 biology
scientific agriculture: 8 agronomy
scientific literature: 7 article; **13** review article, the literature
scimitar: 5 saber, sword
scincid lizard: 5 skink; **7** scincid
Scindapsus: 11 genus Pothos
scintilla: 4 iota, whit; **5** gleam, shred, spark; **6** smidge; **7** smidgen, smidgin; **8** smidgeon
scintillate: 5 flash; **6** winkle; **7** glitter, sparkle, twinkle
scintillating: 6 fulgid; **7** sparkly; **8** aglitter, bubbling, glinting, glittery; **9** sparkling; **10** glistering, glittering; **11** scintillant; **12** effervescent
scintillation: 5 flash, spark; **7** glisten, glister, glitter, sparkle, twinkle; **9** sparkling
scion: 4 heir, link; **5** bough, joint; **8** bantling; **10** descendant
scissile: 8 partible; **9** divisible, separable
scissors: 6 shears
scissure: 4 rime, **5** chink, cleft, crack; **7** crevice, fissure
Sciurus: 8 squirrel; **11** red squirrel, fox squirrel; **12** gray squirrel, genus Sciurus
scleroprotein: 10 albuminoid
sclerosed: 8 hardened; **9** sclerotic
sclerosis: 6 harden; **9** hardening; **10** induration
scoff: 3 boo; **4** gibe, hiss, hoot, jeer, quip, wipe; **5** fling, flout, sneer, taunt; **6** revile; **7** barrack, jeering, mockery, profane; **8** derision, scoffing
scoffer: 6 mocker; **10** blasphemer
scoffing: 4 jeer; **5** scoff; **7** jeering, mockery; **8** derision
scold: 3 jaw, nag, rag; **4** rate; **5** check, chide, shrew, vixen; **6** berate, chew up, grouch, nagger, rebuke; **7** bawl out, chew out, grumble, lambast, lecture, reproof, scolder, upbraid; **8** lambaste; **9** dress down, reprimand; **11** remonstrate
scollop: 7 scallop
Scolytus: 13 genus Scolytus; **14** Dutch-elm beetle
Scomberomorus: 4 cero; **6** shiner, sierra; **7** cavalla; **8** kingfish, mackerel; **12** king mackerel; **18** genus Scomberomorus
sconce: 7 cornice; **8** pediment; **9** headpiece; **10** chandelier
scoop: 3 dig, dip; **5** outdo, probe; **6** shovel; **7** lift out; **8** outflank; **9** exclusive
scoop up: 5 scoop; **6** take up; **7** lift out; **8** scoop out

S

scoot: 4 dart, dash, scud; 5 flash, shoot
scooter: 6 scoter; 9 motorbike; 10 motorcycle; 12 motor scooter
scope: 3 way; 5 ambit, field, orbit, range, reach, sweep, swing; 6 extent, sphere, object, spread; 7 compass, setting; 8 latitude; 9 intention, telescope; 10 background
scopolamine: 8 hyoscine
scorch: 3 fry; 4 bake, char, sear; 5 grill, parch, roast, singe, toast; 6 swinge; 7 blacken
scorched: 5 adust, baked, burnt; 6 burned; 7 parched; 8 sunbaked
scorching: 3 hot; 4 acid; 5 fiery; 6 red-hot; 7 flaming, searing; 8 scathing
score: 2 xx; 3 dot, hit; 4 debt, make, mark, nick, nock, slit, spot; 5 blaze, crack, debit, grade, notch, tally; 6 cipher, grudge, rack up, seduce, streak, twenty; 7 account, scratch; 8 incision; 9 grievance, liability, reckoning; 10 obligation; 12 musical score
scorekeeper: 6 scorer
scoreless: 7 hitless; 8 goalless
scorer: 11 scorekeeper
scores: 3 fry; 4 bevy, gobs, herd, hive, lots, peck, tons, wads; 5 brood, covey, drove, flock, heaps, loads, piles, rafts, scads, shoal, slews, swarm; 6 bushel, dozens, farrow, flight, litter, oodles, stacks
scoria: 4 slag
scoriae: 4 slag; 5 ashes; 7 cinders; 11 precipitate
scorn: 5 spurn; 6 reject; 7 despise, disdain; 8 contempt, turn down
scornful: 7 abusive; 9 insulting; 10 disdainful, scurrilous; 12 contemptuous
Scorpaena: 12 scorpionfish; 14 genus Scorpaena
scorpaenid fish: 10 scorpaenid
Scorpio: 8 Scorpius; 18 Scorpio the Scorpion
scorpion: arachnid
Scorpio the Scorpion: 7 Scorpio
Scot: 8 Scotsman; 9 Scotchman
scotch: 4 foil; 5 cross; 6 thwart; 9 frustrate
Scotch: 5 Scots; 8 Scottish; 11 malt whiskey; 13 Scotch whiskey
Scotch fir: 10 Scotch pine
Scotchman: 4 Scot; 8 Scotsman
Scotch pine: 9 Scotch fir, Scots pine
Scotch terrier: 7 Scottie
Scotch whiskey: 6 Scotch; 11 malt whiskey
scot-free: 4 free; 5 loose; 6 exempt, immune
Scots: 6 Scotch; 8 Scottish
Scots heather: 4 ling; 5 broom; 7 heather
Scotsman: 4 Scot; 9 Scotchman
Scottie: 13 Scotch terrier; 15 Scottish terrier
Scottish: 5 Scots; 6 Scotch
Scottish terrier: 7 Scottie; 13 Scotch terrier
scoundrel: 3 cad; 6 rascal; 7 bounder, villain
scour: 5 flush, scrub; 6 abrade, polish

scoured: 6 eroded; 8 polished
scourge: 4 bane, cane, comb, flog, lash, lick, whip; 5 birch, curse, knout, strap, thong, towel; 6 switch, thrash, threat, thresh; 7 cowhide, nemesis; 8 bullwhip; 9 bastinado, horsewhip; 10 flagellate
Scourge God: 6 Attila
scouring: 5 scrub; 9 scrubbing
scouse: 8 lobscuse; 9 lobscouse
scout: 5 guide, watch; 6 bearer, picket, sentry; 7 lookout; 8 boy scout, sentinel; 9 girl scout; 10 pathfinder; 11 reconnoiter, talent scout
scout group: 5 troop; 10 scout troop
scouting: 14 reconnoitering; 17 exploratory survey
scow: 6 dinghy
scowl: 4 pout; 5 frown, gnarl, gnash, growl, lower, snarl; 6 glower; 7 grimace
scowling: 4 glum, grim; 5 sulky; 6 gloomy, grumpy, morose, sullen; 7 grouchy; 8 frumpish, growling; 9 glowering
scrabble: 6 scrawl; 7 scratch; 8 grope for, scribble
scrag: 4 slip; 5 choke, snack; 6 snatch; 7 garotte; 8 garrotte, scrag end
scraggy: 5 jaggy, scant, weedy; 6 jagged, skinny; 7 scrawny, scrubby; 11 underweight
scram: 3 get; 7 buzz off; 9 bugger off
scramble: 3 vie; 4 code, push; 5 climb, hurry; 6 bustle, cipher, encode, jostle, strive, scurry; 7 clamber, scamper, scatter; 8 struggle
scrambled: 5 coded; 7 encoded; 8 ciphered; 9 encrypted
scrambling: 6 coding; 8 encoding; 9 ciphering; 10 encrypting
scranch: 6 crunch; 7 crackle, crumble; 8 scraunch; 12 disintegrate
scrap: 3 bit, end, rag, tag; 4 chip, junk, much; 5 flake, fleck, scale, shred, trash, waste; 6 junked; 7 cast-off, oddment, remnant; 8 splinter; 9 discarded, remainder
scrape: 4 etch, file, mark, mess, rasp, scar, skin, stub; 5 grate, grave, scrub; 6 ablate, abrade, come up, curtsy, hobble, kowtow, slough; 7 engrave, rub down, scratch, stipple; 8 abrasion, courtesy, quagmire, scrape up, scraping; 9 breakdown, genuflect, kowtowing, scratch up; 10 scratching; 11 excoriation
scrape by: 8 rub along, squeak by
scraped: 4 worn; 7 abraded, skinned; 8 attrited, worn down; 9 scratched
scrape together: 6 gather, muster; 7 collect; 8 assemble
scrapheap: 8 junk heap, junk pile; 9 trash heap, trash pile; 11 garbage heap, rubbish heap
scraping: 6 scrape; 7 scratch; 10 scratching

scrapper: 7 battler, fighter; 9 combatant; 11 belligerent

scraps: 6 refuse; 7 garbage; 9 food waste

scratch: 3 rub; 4 dent, fray, fret, itch, mark, maul, scar, slit; 5 chafe, crack, notch, prick, score, scrub; 6 bruise, scrape, scrawl, streak; 8 abrasion, incision, scrabble, scraping, scribble

scratch awl: 7 scriber

scratched: 7 scraped

scratching: 6 scrape, scrawl; 7 scratch; 8 scraping

scratch pad: 7 notepad

scratchy: 8 abrasive

scraunch: 6 crunch; 7 crackle

scrawl: 7 scratch; 8 scrabble, scribble; 10 cacography, scratching, scribbling

scrawled: 9 scribbled

scrawny: 5 weedy; 6 skinny; 7 scraggy, scrubby, stunted; 11 underweight

screak: 4 bawl, hoop, howl, roar, yell; 5 brawl, creak, shout, whoop; 6 bellow, halloa, halloo, scream, shriek, shrill, skreak, squawk, squeak; 7 screech

screaky: 6 creaky; 7 squeaky; 8 creaking, screechy; 9 squeaking, squealing

scream: 3 cry, wow; 4 bawl, call, hoop, howl, riot, roar, yell; 5 brawl, hollo, shout, whoop; 6 bellow, halloa, halloo, holler, howler, shriek, shrill, squall; 7 screech; 8 shout out; 9 screaming, shrieking, shrieking; 10 belly laugh, screeching

screaming: 6 scream, shriek; 7 howling, roaring, screech, 8 shouting, whooping; 9 bellowing, hilarious, shreiking, shrieking

screaming meemies: 6 nerves; 7 jitters; 11 nervousness

scree: 5 talus

screech: 3 caw; 4 bawl, crow, hoop, howl, pipe, roar, yell; 5 brawl, creak, shout, whoop; 6 bellow, halloa, halloo, pipe up, screak, scream, shriek, shrill, skreak, squawk, squeak; 9 screaming, shreiking, shrieking; 10 screeching

screechy: 7 screaky, squeaky; 9 squeaking, squealing

screed: 5 shred; 6 speech; 7 lecture; 8 fragment

screen: 3 net; 4 sort, test, veil, ward, wing; 5 blind, cloak, cover, flank, shade, sieve; 6 bunker, covert, riddle, shield, shroud; 7 blinker, shelter; 8 block out, colander; 9 CRT screen, screen out, side scene; 10 screen door; 11 concealment; 12 silver screen, window screen

screen actor: 9 film actor; 10 movie actor

screen background: 7 desktop; 10 background

screen font: 10 raster font

screening: 5 cover; 7 masking, showing, viewing; 8 covering

screenwriter: 10 film writer

screw: 4 coil; 6 spiral; 7 turnkey; 8 begrudge, fastener; 9 propeller, skinflint; 10 curmudgeon; 11 prison guard

screwball: 3 nut; 4 zany; 5 crank, crazy, weird; 6 madcap; 7 nutcase; 8 crackpot; 9 eccentric, fruitcake, half-baked

screwbean mesquite: 9 screwbean

screwdriver: 9 turnscrew

screw jack: 9 jackscrew

screw-like motion: 7 coiling

screw-loose: 6 screwy

screw pine: 8 pandanus

screw-pine family: 11 Pandanaceae

screwy: 10 screw-loose

scribble: 6 scrawl; 7 scratch; 8 scrabble; 10 cacography, scratching

scribbler: 3 pen; 6 penman, scribe

scribe: 5 clerk; 6 penman; 7 copyist; 9 scribbler, scrivener, secretary; 12 stenographer

scriber: 3 awl

scrimmage: 7 scuffle; 8 skirmish

scrimp: 5 miser; 6 stingy, frugal

scrimpy: 6 meager

scrip: 3 bag; 5 purse, token; 6 wallet

script: 4 book, text, hand; 10 playscript; 11 handwriting

scripted: 7 written

scriptural: 6 divine, sacred; 8 biblical

scripture: 4 Word; 5 Bible; 8 Good Book; 9 Word of God; 13 Holy Scripture

scrivener: 5 clerk; 6 scribe; 7 copyist; 9 secretary

scrod: 3 cod; 6 schrod; 7 haddock

scroll: 3 roll; 4 coil, curl, list, roll; 5 whorl; 6 return; 7 archive

scroll saw: 6 jigsaw; 7 fretsaw

scrooge: 5 miser; 9 skinflint; 10 cheapskate

Scrophulariaceae: 13 figwort family; 14 foxglove family

scrounge: 5 cadge; 6 forage

scrounger: 6 cadger; 7 moocher, sponger

scrub: 4 bush; 5 scour; 8 scouring

scrubby: 6 paltry, shabby

scrubs: 4 gown; 12 surgical gown

scruff: 4 nape

scruffy: 5 seedy; 7 unkempt

scrum: 6 huddle; 9 scrummage

scrumptious: 4 rich; 5 yummy; 8 delicate, luscious; 9 ambrosial, delicious, exquisite

scrunch: 5 crush, hunch; 6 crunch, crouch; 7 crumple

scruple: 4 iota; 5 pause, qualm; 8 hesitate; 9 misgiving

scruples: 10 conscience

scrupulous: 6 honest; 7 upright, careful

scrutineer: 9 canvasser

scrutinize: 4 scan; 5 audit, study; 6 size up; 7 examine, inspect

scrutiny: 10 inspection; 11 examination

scuba: 8 aqualung

S

scud: 4 dart, dash, gust, rush, warp; 5 flash

scuff: 4 drag, mule; 5 mules

scuffle: 4 cuff; 6 hassle, tussle; 7 shamble, shuffle

scull: 3 row; 4 pull

scullery: 6 pantry

sculpt: 3 cut; 5 carve, grave; 6 chisel; 9 sculpture

sculptor: 6 carver, chaser; 7 modeler; 8 statuary; 11 statue maker

sculpture: 3 cut; 5 carve, grave; 6 chisel, sculpt; 7 carving

scum: 5 froth, trash; 6 refuse

scummy: 3 low; 6 abject, scurvy; 7 lowdown; 9 miserable

scup: 5 porgy

scurf: 5 scale; 8 dandruff

scurfy: 5 scaly; 6 scurvy

scurrilous: 7 abusive; 8 scornful, scurrile; 9 insulting

scurry: 7 scamper, scuttle, skitter; 8 scramble

scurvy: 3 low; 4 base, foul, mean, vile

scutcheon: 10 escutcheon

Scutigera: 9 centipede; 14 genus Scutigera

scuttle: 3 hie; 4 fell, post, sink; 5 swamp; 6 engulf, hasten, scurry; 7 opening, scamper, skitter, utensil; 8 hatchway, submerge; 9 shipwreck

scuttlebutt: 6 gossip

scythe: 6 sickle

SE: 9 southeast

Se: 8 selenium

sea: 4 main, wave; 5 ocean; 6 marine

seabed: 5 floor; 6 bottom; 9 Davy Jones

sea biscuit: 8 hardtack; 10 pilot bread; 11 ship biscuit

seaboard: 5 coast, shore; 7 seaside; 8 seacoast, seashore; 9 coastline

sea captain: 6 master; 7 captain, skipper

sea change: 9 evolution

sea chantey: 6 chanty, shanty; 7 chantey

seacoast: 5 coast, shore; 8 seaboard, seashore; 9 coastline

sea cow: 8 sirenian

sea cucumber: 11 holothurian

sea dog: 3 gob, tar; 6 seaman; 7 Jack-tar, mariner, old salt; 8 seafarer

sea eagle: 6 osprey; 8 fish hawk; 9 fish eagle

sea-ear: 5 ormer

seafarer: 3 gob, tar; 6 sea dog, seaman; 7 Jack-tar, mariner, old salt; 12 seafaring man

seafaring: 5 naval; 7 sailing; 8 maritime, nautical, seagoing; 10 navigation, oceangoing

seafood sauce: 13 cocktail sauce

seagull: 4 gull; 11 frigate bird; 15 frigate bird gull

sea horse: 6 walrus; 8 seahorse

seal: 4 plug, sign, stop; 5 stamp; 6 clinch, finish, signet; 7 certify, varnish; 8 conclude, sealskin; 9 execution, signature

sea lane: 6 seaway; 9 ship route; 10 trade route

sealant: 6 sealer

sealed: 6 closed; 7 certain, plugged; 9 stopped up

sea lettuce: 5 laver

sea-lettuce family: 8 Ulvaceae

sealing: 8 caulking, plugging; 13 waterproofing

seal off: 4 seal, stop; 8 blockade

seal of approval: 2 OK; 4 okay

seal ring: 10 signet ring

sealskin tent: 5 tupek, tupik

Sealyham terrier: 8 Sealyham

seam: 4 line; 6 crease, furrow; 7 crinkle, wrinkle

seamaid: 7 mermaid

seaman: 3 gob, tar; 6 sea dog; 7 Jack-tar, mariner, old salt; 8 seafarer

seamed: 5 lined

sea mew: 3 mew; 7 mew gull

seamless: 7 unlined; 8 unseamed

seamstress: 6 tailor; 10 dressmaker

seamy: 5 seedy; 6 sleazy, sordid

seance: 7 session, sitting

sea nymph: 5 siren; 6 Nereid; 7 Oceanid

sea onion: 6 squill

seaport: 4 snug; 5 haven; 6 harbor

sea puss: 8 undertow

sear: 4 sere; 5 brand, parch; 6 burn in, scorch; 7 dried-up, shrivel; 8 withered; 9 cauterize

search: 4 hunt, look, seek; 5 probe; 6 lookup; 7 explore, hunting, inquire, look for, seeking; 8 research

searcher: 6 seeker

sea robber: 6 pirate; 8 sea rover; 9 buccaneer

sea robin: 7 gurnard

sea rover: 6 pirate

seascape: 10 waterscape; 14 marine painting

sea scorpion: 7 sculpin; 10 eurypterid

seashore: 5 coast, shore; 8 seacoast; 9 coastline

seasickness: 8 mal de mer, scrofula; 9 naupathia

sea slug: 10 nudibranch

season: 5 blend, cross, inure, ripen, spice, tinge; 6 flavor, harden, leaven, temper; 7 spice up

seasonable: 3 fit; 6 in loco, in time, on time, prompt, timely; 7 apropos; 8 punctual, suitable; 9 opportune

seasoned: 6 inured; 7 veteran; 8 flavored, hardened

seasoning: 5 spice; 8 flavorer, maturing, ripening, seasoner; 9 condiment, flavoring

sea spray: 4 surf

sea star: 8 starfish

seat: 3 sit; 5 place, stern, venue; 6 induct, invest; 7 install; 8 buttocks; 9 posterior

seat belt: 10 safety belt

seated: 7 sitting

seat of authority: 12 headquarters

sea trout: 8 weakfish

sea turtle: 6 ridley; 9 hawksbill; 10 loggerhead; 11 leatherback

sea vehicle: 4 boat, ship; 5 craft; 6 vessel

seawall: 4 mole; 5 groin, jetty; 6 groyne; 7 bulwark; 10 breakwater

seawater: 5 brine; 9 saltwater

seaway: 7 sea lane

sea wolf: 4 orca; 6 killer; 7 grampus; 11 killer whale

seaworthy: 3 fit; 4 snug

sebaceous: 3 fat; 4 oily; 5 fatty; 6 greasy

sebaceous cyst: 3 wen

Sebastodes: 10 ocean perch; 11 red rockfish; 15 genus Sebastodes

sec: 1 s; 6 second

Secale cereale: 3 rye

secede: 8 splinter, withdraw; 9 break away

secern: 11 distinguish

secession: 10 withdrawal

seckel pear: 6 seckel

secluded: 3 bye; 5 privy; 6 secret; 7 private, recluse, retired; 9 reclusive; 10 cloistered; 11 sequestered

seclusion: 6 recess; 7 privacy; 8 solitude; 9 isolation, reclusion; 10 retirement; 11 privateness

secobarbital: 7 Seconal; 8 red devil

second: 3 sec; 4 abet, back; 6 minute, moment; 7 endorse, instant

Second Advent: 6 Advent; 12 Second Coming

secondary: 4 less; 5 proxy; 6 deputy, lesser; 9 surrogate; 10 substitute

secondary school: 5 lycee; 10 high school

second baseman: 12 second sacker

second best: 8 runner-up

second class: 8 inferior

Second Coming: 6 Advent; 12 Second Advent

secondguess: 8 outguess

secondhand: 4 used; 5 faded, passe, stale; 6 frayed, shabby

second-hand store: 10 thriftshop

second nature: 12 prescriptive

second power: 6 square

second-rate: 4 poor; 8 inferior, mediocre; 9 secondary

second sight: 3 ESP; 12 clairvoyance

second stomach: 9 reticulum

second-string: 10 substitute

second thought: 7 rethink; 10 reconsider

second-year: 9 sophomore

secrecy: 7 privacy, silence; 11 concealment

secret: 4 dark; 5 privy; 6 covert, enigma, hidden; 7 furtive, mystery, private; 8 hush-

hush, mystical, stealthy; 10 mysterious, undercover; 11 clandestine

secret agent: 3 spy; 4 mole; 9 operative

secretariat: 6 bureau; 10 department

secretary: 5 clerk; 6 scribe

secret code: 6 cipher, cypher; 11 cryptograph

secrete: 7 give off

secreting: 6 hiding; 10 concealing; 11 concealment

secretion: 8 effusion

secretive: 7 evasive, furtive; 8 stealthy

secretory organ: 5 gland

secret plan: 4 plot

secret writing: 10 cryptogram; 11 cryptograph

sect: 5 party; 7 faction

sectarian: 9 parochial

section: 4 area, part; 5 group; 6 carpel, member, region; 7 segment; 8 division; 9 component; 11 subdivision

sector: 4 zone; 6 sphere; 7 quarter, section; 8 district, division

secular: 3 lay; 4 laic; 5 civil; 6 laical; 8 temporal

secure: 3 bag, fix, net, set; 4 bind, fast, firm, good, plug, sack, safe, sure, taut; 5 affix, close, get in, tight, twist; 6 assure, attach, batten, clinch, detain, engage, ensure, fasten, insure, stop up, strong, taught; 7 assured, bespeak, certain, procure, warrant; 8 positive, unafraid; 9 bring home, confident

securities firm: 9 brokerage

securities market: 11 stock market; 13 stock exchange

security: 6 safety, surety; 10 protection, secureness, securities [pl]

security deposit: 6 margin

security guard: 8 watchman

sedan chair: 5 sedan

sedate: 4 calm; 5 sober, staid; 6 demure, solemn; 7 earnest, pensive, serious; 8 Platonic, studious; 10 cool-headed

sedation: 8 drugging

sedative drug: 6 downer; 8 sedative; 10 depressant

sedentary: 7 sitting, settled

Seder: 14 Passover supper

sedge: 4 rush

sediment: 7 deposit

sedition: 7 treason

seditious: 7 riotous; 8 incitive, mutinous; 9 insurgent; 10 incendiary, subversive; 11 instigative

seduce: 4 coax, lure; 5 charm, score, tempt; 6 attach, enamor, endear; 7 attract, bewitch; 9 captivate, fascinate

seduced: 8 violated; 9 persuaded

seduction: 8 conquest; 10 allurement, temptation

S

sedulous: 7 notable; **8** diligent; **9** assiduous; **10** solicitous; **11** industrious

see: 4 find, look, meet, view; **5** sight, visit, watch; **6** behold, notice; **7** diocese, discern, observe, picture, project, run into, realize, witness; **8** envision; **9** visualize

see action: 5 serve

seed: 3 sow; **4** germ; **5** breed, brood, heirs, semen, sough, spawn; **7** progeny; **9** offspring

seed case: 3 pod; **7** seed pod

seed coat: 5 testa; **8** episperm

seeded: 4 sown

seed fern: 12 pteridosperm

seediness: 9 manginess; **10** shabbiness

seeding: 6 sowing; **8** planting; **12** impregnation

seed leaf: 9 cotyledon

seedless raisin: 7 sultana

seed pod: 3 pod; **8** seed case

seedy: 4 worn; **5** moldy, seamy; **6** rotten, sleazy, sordid, wasted; **7** decayed, scruffy, squalid; **8** time-worn

seeing-eye dog: 8 guide dog

seeing red: 4 huff, miff; **5** angry

seek: 3 ask, try; **6** search; **7** attempt, inquire, look for

seem: 4 look, show; **6** appear

seeming: 8 apparent; **10** ostensible

seemly: 3 due, fit; **4** good; **5** right; **6** comely, decent, proper; **7** correct, fitting; **8** becoming, decorous, eligible, handsome; **9** befitting; **10** personable

seen: 8 observed

seep: 4 ooze

seep in: 8 permeate; **9** penetrate

seer: 7 prophet; **9** visionary; **10** soothsayer

see red: 5 anger

seesaw: 6 teeter, totter, zigzag; **8** to and fro; **9** up and down

seethe: 4 boil, fume, rage, rave, stew; **6** simmer

see to it: 3 see; **5** check; **6** assure, ensure, insure

segment: 7 section

segmentation: 8 cleavage, division; **9** partition

segmented worm: 7 annelid; **8** helminth

segregate: 7 isolate; **8** detached, insulate, relegate, set apart; **9** keep apart

seigneur: 10 feudal lord

seigneury: 7 signory; **8** seignory

Seine: 10 Seine River

seine net: 3 net

seismic disturbance: 5 shock, quake; **10** earthquake

seismosaur: 12 ground-shaker

seize: 4 grab; **6** clutch, snatch; **7** capture, conquer, impound; **8** take over; **9** sequester; **10** confiscate; **11** appropriate

seizing: 7 capture, seizure; **8** catching, grasping; **9** snatching

seizure: 3 fit; **5** ictus

seldom: 6 hardly, rarely; **8** scarcely; **12** infrequently

select: 4 fine, take; **5** bully, elect, prime, prize; **6** choice, choose, denote, opt for, picked; **7** fix upon, pick out, quality; **8** indicate, point out

selection: 4 pick; **6** choice; **7** excerpt, extract; **8** adoption, choosing, election, survival

selective service: 5 draft; **6** muster; **12** conscription

selenium: 2 Se

self: 3 ego, one; **4** same; **8** identity, selfsame; **9** identical; **13** individuality

self-abasement: 7 lowness, penance; **9** abasement, lowliness, servility; **10** abjectness; **12** self-contempt

self-admiration: 6 vanity; **7** conceit, egotism

self-assurance: 10 confidence

self-centered: 7 selfish; **10** egocentric, egoistical

self-confessed: 8 admitted, conceded

self-confidence: 8 sureness; **9** assurance, authority; **10** confidence

self-control: 8 self-will; **9** willpower

self-destruct: 12 disintegrate

self-destruction: 7 suicide

self-destructive: 8 suicidal

self-determination: 8 self-rule

self-doubt: 10 diffidence, insecurity

self-effacing: 8 reticent

self-employed: 9 freelance

self-employed person: 10 freelancer; **11** independent

self-esteem: 10 confidence

self-evident: 7 obvious

self-governing: 9 sovereign; **10** autonomous; **11** independent

self-importance: 3 ego; **7** egotism

self-important: 7 haughty; **8** arrogant

self-indulgent: 7 selfish

self-interest: 6 egoism; **8** self-love; **10** expedience; **11** egocentrism

selfish: 7 piggish; **12** self-centered; **13** self-indulgent

selfless: 10 altruistic

selflessness: 8 altruism; **13** self-sacrifice

self-loading: 13 semiautomatic

self-love: 6 vanity; **7** conceit, egotism, narcism; **10** narcissism

self-possessed: 4 calm, cool; **6** poised, steady; **9** collected

self-praise: 8 boasting, bragging

self-propelled: 10 automotive

self-propelled motion: 10 locomotion

self-regard: 7 dignity; **10** self-esteem

self-reliance: 8 autonomy

self-reliant: 9 confident; **10** autonomous

self-respect: 7 dignity; **9** assurance; **10** confidence, self-esteem, self-regard

self-righteous: 9 pharisaic, pietistic; 11 pharisaical, pietistical; 13 sanctimonious; 14 holier-than-thou
self-sacrifice: 10 self-denial
selfsame: 3 one; 4 same, very; 9 identical; 13 one and the same
self-seeker: 11 opportunist
self-seeking: 7 selfish; 10 expedience; 11 opportunism, self-serving
self-suggestion: 12 self-hypnosis
sell: 4 deal, vend; 5 trade; 6 betray; 9 dispose of
seller: 4 bear; 6 vender, vendor; 10 trafficker
sell for: 4 cost; 5 fetch, yield; 6 afford; 7 bring in
selling: 4 sale, vent; 7 vending; 8 disposal; 9 marketing; 13 merchandising
seltzer: 8 club soda; 9 soda water; 14 sparkling water
selvedge: 3 hem; 5 frill; 6 edging, fringe
semblance: 5 color; 6 show of; 8 illusion, likeness; 10 similarity; 11 resemblance
semen: 4 seed; 5 sperm
semi: 6 half of; 9 semifinal; 11 semitrailer
semiannual: 8 biannual, biyearly
semiautomatic: 11 autoloading, self-loading
semibreve: 9 whole note
semicircle: 8 half-moon; 10 half-circle
semicircular arch: 9 Roman arch
semiconsciousness: 6 stupor, 10 grogginess; 12 stupefaction
semidetached house: 6 duplex
semifinal: 4 semi
semilunar: 6 lunate; 8 crescent
semimonthly: 9 bimonthly
seminal: 8 creative, original
seminar: 5 class; 6 course, remove; 7 lecture, meeting
semiopacity: 8 lucidity
semipermanent: 7 long-run; 8 long-term
semiprofessional: 7 semipro
semiquaver: 13 sixteenth note
semisolid: 3 gel; 4 jell; 6 gluten; 7 gelatin
semisweet: 11 bittersweet
semitone: 8 half step
semitrailer: 4 semi
semitropical: 9 subtropic
sempiternal: 7 endless; 8 dateless; 9 continual
sempstress: 10 seamstress
send: 3 air; 4 base, beam, mail, post, ship; 5 place; 6 charge, commit, direct, get off, launch, let fly, let off; 7 fire off, release; 8 transmit; 9 broadcast, transport
send away: 3 can; 4 drop, fire, sack; 7 dismiss, send off; 9 terminate
send back: 5 remit
sender: 11 transmitter
send for: 4 call; 7 call for
send-off: 7 kickoff; 8 start-off; 9 bon voyage
send packing: 4 drop; 7 dismiss, send off; 8 send away

send up: 4 jail; 6 parody; 7 lampoon; 8 imprison, satirize
sendup: 5 spoof; 6 parody; 7 lampoon, mockery, takeoff
send up the river: 4 jail; 6 send up; 8 imprison
send word: 6 advise, notify; 7 apprise
Seneca: 19 Lucius Annaeus Seneca
seneka snakeroot: 6 senega
senescence: 8 agedness
senescent: 5 aging; 6 ageing
seneschal: 5 agent; 7 steward
senile dementia: 8 senility
senior: 4 aged; 5 elder, older; 7 elderly; 8 superior
senior citizen: 7 oldster; 9 old person
senior high: 4 high; 10 highschool
seniority: 9 eldership, longevity; 10 higher rank; 12 higher status
sensation: 3 ace, wiz; 4 star, whiz; 5 adept, maven, sense, whizz; 6 genius, wizard; 7 hotshot; 8 virtuoso
sensational: 8 stunning
sensation drama: 9 melodrama
sense: 4 feel; 5 light; 6 import, senses [pl]; 7 meaning, version; 8 gumption, judgment, perceive; 9 good sense, intention, sensation, sentience, sentiency, substance; 10 horse sense; 11 common sense
senseless: 4 dead [fig], numb; 5 inept, silly; 6 absurd, vacant; 7 blatant, fatuous, foolish, idiotic, out cold, unaware, witless; 8 comatose, mindless; 9 pointless, unfeeling, unmeaning; 10 insensible, irrational
sense of balance: 11 equilibrium
sense of ethics: 7 probity; 9 integrity, principle, propriety, rectitude
sense of right and wrong: 8 scruples; 10 conscience
sense of smell: 9 olfaction
sense of urgency: 6 stress; 8 pressure
sense organ: 8 receptor
sensibility: 8 feelings; 11 sensitivity
sensible: 4 wise; 5 sound; 8 palpable, rational, tangible; 9 judicious
sensibly: 6 sanely; 10 reasonably
sensing: 9 detection; 10 perceiving, perception
sensitive: 4 sore, taut, weak; 5 frail, tense; 6 tender; 7 fragile; 8 delicate, volatile; 9 excitable; 10 high-strung
sensitivity: 8 feelings; 9 liability
sensor: 8 detector; 10 transducer
sensory: 9 receptive
sensory hair: 7 whisker; 8 vibrissa
sensual: 4 sexy; 6 animal, carnal, erotic, sexual, sultry; 7 fleshly; 10 voluptuous
sensualist: 8 hedonist; 9 epicurean
sent: 11 transmitted
sentence: 4 doom, time; 6 dictum, saying; 7 condemn, penalty

S

sentenced to death: 6 doomed; **9** condemned

sentence structure: 6 syntax

sententious: 5 pithy; **10** moralizing

sentience: 5 sense; **9** awareness, sensation, sentiency; **14** sensory faculty

sentient: 5 aware; **7** animate, feeling; **9** aesthetic; **10** perceptive

sentiment: 4 tone, turn, view; **7** opinion, thought

sentimental: 4 soft; **5** mushy; **6** slushy; **7** maudlin, mawkish, mincing; **8** romantic, schmalzy; **9** schmaltzy, simpering

sentinel: 5 guard, scout, watch; **6** picket, sentry; **7** lookout

sentry: 5 guard, scout, watch; **6** picket; **7** lookout; **8** sentinel

sent up: 6 in jail; **8** in prison; **9** doing time

Seoul: 19 capital of South Korea

Sep: 4 Sept; **9** September

separable: 8 partible, scissile [Chem]; **9** divisible, severable; **11** dissociable

separate: 4 cull, fork, free, part, sort; **5** apart, break, loose, split; **6** branch, divide; **7** asunder, break up, carve up, disjoin, divorce, insular, split up; **8** disunite; **9** bifurcate, disjoined, disparate; **10** disconnect

separated: 5 apart; **6** spaced; **8** detached, isolated, separate, set-apart; **9** disjoined; **10** disjointed, dislocated; **11** nontouching, nonadjacent; **12** disconnected

separately: 6 singly; **8** one by one; **9** severally; **12** individually; **13** independently

separation: 3 gap; **5** space; **6** remove; **7** breakup, parting; **8** distance, disunion, disunity, interval; **9** isolation, severance; **10** detachment, disjoining, quarantine, separating

sepia: 5 ocher

sepiolite: 10 meerschaum

seppuku: 8 hara-kiri

sept: 3 kin; **4** clan, folk; **5** tribe; **6** family; **7** kinfolk

September: 3 Sep; **4** Sept

September equinox: 3 fall; **8** autumnal

septentrion: 5 north

septentrional: 8 northern

septet: 3 VII; **5** seven; **6** heptad; **7** sevener; **8** septette; **9** sevensome

septic: 8 mephitic; **11** deleterious

septicemia: 11 septicaemia; **14** blood poisoning

septum: 9 diaphragm

septuple: 9 sevenfold

sepulcher: 4 tomb; **5** grave; **9** sepulchre, sepulture

sepulchral: 7 charnel; **8** funereal, mortuary

sepulture: 6 burial; **9** interment, sepulcher, sepulchre; **10** entombment

sequel: 6 result, suffix; **9** corollary, out-

growth, successor; **11** aftereffect, development, subsequence; **12** continuation

sequence: 6 series; **7** episode; **10** succession

sequent: 6 serial; **7** ensuant; **9** resultant, resulting; **10** consequent, sequential, successive

sequester: 5 seize; **6** attach; **7** impound, isolate, seclude; **8** set apart; **10** confiscate

sequestered: 7 private, recluse, retired; **8** secluded; **9** reclusive; **10** cloistered

sequin: 7 spangle

sequined: 5 beady; **6** beaded, gemmed; **7** jeweled, spangly; **8** jewelled, spangled

sequoia: 7 redwood

Sequoiadendron: 7 redwood, sequoia; **19** genus Sequoiadendron

seraglio: 5 harem

serape: 5 shawl; **6** sarape

seraph: 4 hero; **5** angel; **7** demigod, heroine

seraphic: 7 angelic, godlike; **8** cherubic; **9** angelical

Serbia: 6 Srbija

Serbian: 4 Serb

Serbo-Croatian: 10 Serbo-Croat

sere: 4 sear; **7** dried-up; **8** withered; **9** shriveled; **10** shrivelled, threadbare

serenade: 5 cheer; **12** divertimento

serene: 4 calm; **8** tranquil

serenity: 5 peace, quiet; **6** repose; **9** placidity; **10** heartsease; **11** tranquility

Serenoa: 11 saw palmetto; **12** genus Serenoa

serf: 6 vassal; **7** peasant

sergeant: 8 serjeant

sergeant first class: 13 first sergeant

serial: 6 series; **7** sequent; **10** periodical, sequential, successive

serial music: 9 serialism

serial publication: 6 serial, series

seriatim: 8 bit by bit, in series, serially, stepwise

sericeous: 5 downy

series: 3 run; **6** serial; **8** sequence, TV series; **10** succession

Series: 11 World Series

Serinus: 12 common canary, genus Serinus

seriocomic: 10 tragicomic

Seriola: 8 kingfish; **10** rudderfish, yellowtail; **12** genus Seriola

serious: 5 grave, heavy, sober, staid; **6** sedate, severe, solemn; **7** earnest; **8** grievous

serious matter: 6 no joke

seriousness: 7 decorum, gravity; **8** sobriety; **9** sincerity, solemnity, staidness; **10** sedateness

sermon: 3 say; **6** homily, tirade; **7** lecture; **8** delivery, harangue, pastoral; **9** discourse, preaching; **10** recitation

sermonize: 5 stump; **6** preach, recite;

sermonizer: 8 preacher
serologist: 12 immunologist
serous: 4 thin; 6 watery, liquid
serous membrane: 6 serosa
serpent: 3 asp; 5 adder, cobra, snake, viper; 7 bassoon; 11 rattlesnake
Serpentes: 7 Ophidia
serpentine: 5 snaky; 8 circling; 9 snake-like
serpent-worship: 10 ophiolatry
serrate: 6 jagged; 7 notched, toothed; 8 serrated; 9 crenulate; 10 saw-toothed
serried: 5 close, dense; 7 compact
serum: 4 whey; 5 plasm; 6 plasma
serum hepatitis: 10 hepatitis B
serval cat: 6 serval
servant: 4 help; 8 handmaid, retainer; 10 handmaiden
serve: 2 do; 3 act; 4 dish, help; 5 avail; 6 assist, attend, wait on; 7 process, serve up, service; 8 attend to
server: 4 host; 6 waiter
service: 3 use; 4 help, weal; 5 avail, serve, stead; 6 behalf; 7 benefit, serving; 8 interest, overhaul, services [pl]; 9 servicing; 11 campaigning
serviceable: 5 of use; 6 usable, useful; 7 useable; 9 of service
service cap: 4 kepi; 9 peaked cap; 11 yachting cap
serviced: 8 repaired; 10 maintained
serviceman: 3 man; 7 soldier; 8 repairer; 9 repairman
service stripe: 8 hashmark
serviette: 6 napkin
servile: 6 abject; 9 pandering; 11 subservient
servility: 9 abasement
serving: 7 helping, portion, service
serving cart: 7 teacart
servitor: 8 retainer
sesame family: 11 Pedaliaceae
sesame seed: 9 benniseed
sesquipedalian: 6 florid; 7 flowery; 8 inflated; 9 bombastic
sessile: 8 attached; 9 stalkless
session: 4 term; 6 seance; 7 meeting, sitting; 8 semester
sestet: 6 stanza; 8 six lines
set: 2 do; 3 cut, fit, fix, lay, lot, put, sic; 4 coif, fast, firm, jell, laid, make, mark; 5 fixed, group, prime, ready, rigid; 6 adjust, attune, coiffe, placed, secure; 7 arrange, congeal, prepare, specify
Set: 4 Seth
set about: 5 begin, start; 6 set out; 7 attempt; 8 commence
setaceous: 5 spiny; 7 spicate; 8 bristled
set aflame: 8 set afire; 9 set ablaze, set on fire
set ahead: 7 advance

set apart: 7 isolate, specify; 8 insulate, isolated; 9 segregate, sequester
set-apart: 8 detached, isolated; 9 separated
set ashore: 4 land
set aside: 7 earmark, reserve; 8 lay aside, put aside, sock away
set at ease: 7 comfort; 9 encourage
set a trap: 8 lay a trap
set back: 5 defer, remit, table; 6 offset, put off, shelve
setback: 3 rub; 4 blow; 5 check, cross; 7 reverse; 8 comedown, reversal
set chisel: 10 cold chisel
set down: 4 drop, land; 5 shame; 6 debark, humble, unload
set fire to: 4 fire; 5 light; 6 ignite, kindle
set forth: 4 part; 5 start; 6 allege, broach, depart, set off, set out
Seth: 3 Set
set in motion: 4 move; 6 launch; 9 set to work; 11 put in motion
set in order: 7 arrange; 8 organize
set off: 4 part, trip; 5 be off, go off, start; 6 accent, depart, incite, offset, put off, set out, stir up, stress; 7 actuate, trigger; 8 activate, bring out, detonate, touch off; 9 emphasize; 10 accentuate
set on: 6 assail, attack, bent on, foment, incite; 7 assault
set on fire: 4 fire; 5 light; 6 ignite, kindle; 7 inflame
set out: 3 get; 4 deal, pack, part; 5 allot, array, begin, range, start; 6 depart, set off; 8 commence, get going, set about, set forth, start out
set phrase: 5 idiom
set right: 7 correct, rectify; 8 disabuse; 9 exonerate
settee: 8 love seat
setting: 5 mount, scene, scope; 10 background, thickening
setting up: 8 founding; 10 organizing
settle: 3 fix, set; 6 decide, locate, make up; 7 patch up, resolve; 8 complete, finalize, relocate; 9 ascertain, determine, reconcile; 10 compromise, conciliate
settled: 4 over; 5 fixed; 6 formed; 7 decided, defined; 9 colonized; 10 determined
settle down: 4 calm; 6 cool it, settle; 7 cool off; 8 calm down, chill out
settlement: 6 colony; 7 village; 9 clearance, reckoning; 10 compromise, resolution; 11 arrangement, liquidation; 12 colonization, satisfaction
settler: 8 colonist, squatter
set to music: 7 arrange, compose
set up: 5 build, erect, frame, put up, raise, ready; 6 entrap; 7 arrange, ensnare, install; 8 assemble; 9 establish
seven: 3 vii; 6 heptad, septet; 7 sevener

S

sevenfold: 8 septuple
seventeen: 4 xvii
seventeen-year locust: 6 cicada
seventh heaven: 5 bliss; **9** cloud nine
seventy: 3 lxx
sever: 3 lop; **4** rend; **6** divide, sunder
several: 4 a few, some; **5** party; **6** divers, sundry; **7** certain
severally: 5 apart; **6** singly; **8** in detail, one by one; **10** separately; **12** individually
severance: 4 rift; **5** break; **6** breach, firing; **7** cutting, rupture; **8** severing; **9** dismissal, sundering
severe: 3 dry; **4** hard, keen, sore; **5** acute, cruel, exact, rave, harsh, rigid, sharp, stark, stern, vivid; **6** biting, strict; **7** austere, caustic, cutting, precise, serious, spartan; **8** grievous, incisive, sardonic, terrible
severed: 5 fired; **6** canned, cut off, riffed, sacked, sliced; **7** divided; **8** sundered; **9** dismissed; **10** terminated
Seville orange: 10 sour orange; **12** bitter orange
sew: 4 knit, lace, tack; **6** stitch, tailor
sewer: 6 tailor; **9** waste pipe; **10** seamstress
sewer line: 9 sewer main
sewer water: 8 effluent; **10** wastewater
sewing: 9 stitchery, stitching
sewn: 5 sewed; **8** stitched
sew up: 6 stitch, suture
sex: 6 arouse, excite, gender, mating; **9** sexuality; **10** copulation, lovemaking
sex drive: 4 lust; **6** libido
sexiness: 7 erotism; **9** eroticism
sexist: 14 male chauvinist
sexless: 6 neuter; **7** asexual
sextet: 2 VI; **3** six; **4** sise; **5** hexad, sixer; **6** sestet; **7** sixsome; **8** sextette; **9** sextuplet; **10** half a dozen
sexton: 6 beadle
sextuple: 7 sixfold
sextuplet: 2 VI; **3** six; **4** sise; **5** hexad, sixer; **6** sestet; **7** sixsome; **8** sextette; **10** half a dozen
sexual: 4 sexy; **6** carnal, erotic; **7** sensual; **8** intimate
sexual abnormality: 8 deviance; **10** perversion
sexual abstention: 8 celibacy, chastity
sexual arousal: 4 hots; **5** horns, horny
sexual assault: 4 rape
sexual climax: 6 orgasm
sexual conquest: 5 score
sexually transmitted disease: 2 VD; **3** HIV
sexual partner: 4 mate
sexual reproduction: 10 amphimixis
Seymour: 11 Jane Seymour
shabby: 5 cheap, dirty; **6** frayed, trashy; **7** pitiful, scrubby; **8** beggarly; **9** miserable
shack: 3 hut; **5** hovel, hutch; **6** shanty

shackle: 4 bond; **5** bonds, irons; **6** fetter
shack up: 7 cohabit
shadberry: 8 shadblow, shadbush; **12** serviceberry
shaddock: 6 pomelo; **7** pummelo
shade: 3 hue; **4** cast, glow, tint, tone; **5** color, cover, flush, ghost, manes, spook; **6** darken, nicety, nuance, screen, shadow; **7** curtain, eclipse, obscure, specter; **8** subtlety, tincture; **9** gradation; **10** apparition, coloration
shades: 10 sunglasses; **11** dark glasses
shadow: 3 dog; **4** dark, tail; **5** beset, dream, ghost, hound, shade, spook, stalk; **6** darken, vision; **7** figment, phantom; **8** darkness, hanger on, revenant, shade off; **10** apparition
shadowgraph: 10 shadowplay
shadowy: 3 dim; **5** faint, shady, vague, wispy; **8** shadowed, spectral; **9** undefined, visionary; **10** indefinite
shady: 5 fishy, funny, queer; **7** shadowy, suspect; **8** shadowed; **10** fly-by-night, suspicious
shaft: 3 dig, pit, ray; **4** barb, beam, flue, gibe, haft, heft, hilt, jibe, mine, post, reed, shot; **5** arrow, cheat, lance, quill, shank, spear; **6** column, pillar
shag: 5 beard, brush
shagbark hickory: 8 shagbark
shaggy: 5 bushy; **7** bearded, shagged
shake: 3 hum, sap, wag; **4** beat, drop, fade, rock; **5** lurch, quake, relax, shock, swing, trill; **6** excite, frappe, quaver, shiver, totter, tremor, weaken; **7** agitate, break up, crumble, decline, disturb, flutter, perturb, shake up, shudder, stagger, tremble, twitter, vibrate; **8** brandish, flourish; **9** handclasp, handshake, milkshake; **11** handshaking
shakedown: 9 extortion
shake off: 4 cast, drop, shed; **5** shake, throw; **7** cast off; **8** get rid of
Shakespeare: 16 William Shakspere; **18** William Shakespeare
shake up: 3 jar; **4** stir; **6** excite, stir up; **7** agitate, disturb; **9** stimulate
shakiness: 6 quiver, tremor; **7** shaking; **9** quivering, trembling, vibration; **11** palpitation
shaking palsy: 10 Parkinson's
shaky: 6 shaken, wobbly; **7** jittery, nervous, quaking, rickety, shaking; **9** quivering, shivering, trembling; **10** precarious
shall: 4 will
shallot: 8 eschalot
shallow: 4 airy, dull, rude, soft, weak; **5** borne, empty, green, petty, sappy, shoal; **6** spoony, stolid, unread; **7** wanting
shallows: 4 bank, flat; **5** shelf; **6** shoals; **8** breakers, lee shore; **14** ironbound coast
sham: 4 fake, mock; **5** bogus, faker, false,

feign, fraud, phony, pseud, put on; **6** affect, assume, pseudo; **7** assumed, forgery, pretend; **8** imposter, impostor, so-called, spurious; **9** pretended, pretender; **10** fictitious, fraudulent

shaman: 11 witch doctor; high priest

shambles: 8 wreckage; **14** slaughterhouse

shame: 8 disgrace, dishonor, ignominy; **11** humiliation

shameful: 4 base, foul, vile; **5** grave, gross; **6** scurvy; **7** heinous; **8** infamous, shocking, sinister; **9** nefarious; **10** scandalous, villainous; **11** disgraceful

shameless: 5 sassy, saucy; **7** aweless; **8** immodest, impudent; **9** audacious, graceless, heartless, unabashed; **10** unblushing, virtueless

shammy leather: 6 chammy, shammy; **7** chamois

shamrock: 7 trefoil; **10** wood sorrel; **11** white clover

shandygaff: 6 shandy

shanghai: 7 impress

Shanghai dialect: 2 Wu; **9** Wu dialect

shanghaier: 9 kidnapper

Shangri-la: 4 eden; **6** heaven; **7** nirvana; **8** paradise

shank: 3 leg; **4** haft, heft, hilt, stem; **5** scale, serif, shaft; **6** handle

shanty: 3 hut; **4** shed; **5** cabin, croft, hovel, hutch, shack; **6** chalet, chanty

shape: 3 bod; **4** cast, form, mold, soma, trim; **5** build, flesh, forge, frame, state; **6** figure, status; **7** anatomy, chassis, contour, fashion, fitness, pattern; **8** physique, regulate; **9** condition, determine, human body, influence; **10** embodiment

shapeless: 8 formless; **9** amorphous

shaping: 7 forming, molding; **8** defining; **9** formation, formative

shard: 4 chip; **5** chunk, sherd; **8** fragment

share: 3 lot; **4** cast, deal, mete, part; **6** billet, divide, detail, parcel; **7** divvy up, measure, partake, portion, share in; **8** interest; **9** allotment, allowance, apportion

sharecrop farmer: 7 cropper; **12** sharecropper

shark: 4 thug; **6** usurer; **9** land shark, loan shark; **11** moneylender

sharp: 3 dry; **4** hard, high, keen, sour, tart; **5** acute, alert, brisk, crisp, harsh, quick, short, smart, vivid; **6** astute, biting, brainy, bright, shreed; **7** cutting, cynical, piquant, pointed, sharply; **8** incisive, piercing, sardonic; **9** knifelike, sarcastic, satirical

sharp curve: 11 hairpin turn

sharpen: 3 set; **4** barb, lash, whet; **5** focus, grind, point, strop, taper; **6** excite, foment, incite, kindle, stir up, turn on; **7** inflame, quicken; **8** aculeate, heighten; **9** cultivate, intensify, stimulate

sharpener: 4 hone; **5** strop

sharpshooter: 8 dead shot, good shot, marksman, rifleman; **9** crack shot

shatter: 5 crash, quell, smash; **6** batter, shiver, squash, weaken; **8** splinter

shatterproof glass: 9 laminated; **11** safety glass

shave: 3 lop, mow; **4** clip, crop, dock, trim; **5** plane, prune, shear, slice; **6** paring, shiver, sliver; **7** shaving, whittle; **8** clipping

shaver: 3 fry, kid; **4** tike, tyke; **5** child, minor; **6** nipper; **7** tiddler; **8** nestling, small fry; **9** youngster; **13** electric razor; **14** electric shaver

shaving soap: 12 shaving cream

Shavuoth: 7 Shavuos, Shavuot; **8** Shabuoth; **9** Pentecost; **12** Feast of Weeks

Shaw: 6 G. B. Shaw; **17** George Bernard Shaw

sheaf: 4 rick; **5** shock, stack; **6** bundle

shear: 3 lop, mow; **4** clip, crop, reap; **5** prune, shave, strip; **6** fleece

sheared: 5 shorn

shears: 8 scissors

sheath: 4 case, knit, poke; **5** dress, pouch; **6** swathe; **7** satchel, swaddle; **8** reticule, roll up in, scabbard

sheathing: 6 sheath; **7** overlay; **9** overlayer

shebang: 5 whole; **10** everything

shed: 3 cot, hut; **4** cast, drop, molt; **5** booth, cabin, croft, hovel, spare, spill, stall, throw; **6** chalet, forego, resign, shanty, slough, spread; **7** cast off, diffuse, disband, scatter; **8** caducous, diffused, disgorge, dispense, disperse, exuviate, part with, renounce, shake off, throw off

shed a tear: 3 cry, sob; **4** pipe, wail, weep

shed blood: 4 kill, slay; **5** bleed; **10** hemorrhage

shed light on: 5 clear; **7** clarify, clear up, sort out; **9** elucidate, enlighten; **10** illuminate

sheen: 6 luster; **9** shininess

sheep's eye: 6 sheepcote: **4** fold; **9** sheepfold

sheep farm: 7 station

sheepfold: 4 fold; **8** sheep pen; **9** sheepcote

sheepherder: 8 shepherd

sheepish: 3 shy; **7** nervous; **8** skittish; **9** sheeplike; **10** shamefaced

sheep ked: 9 sheep tick

sheep laurel: 8 lambkill

sheep pen: 4 fold; **9** sheepcote, sheepfold

sheepskin: 6 fleece; **7** diploma; **8** lambskin; **9** parchment

sheepskin coat: 6 afghan

sheep station: 9 sheep farm

sheep tick: 8 sheep ked

sheepwalk: 5 range; **7** pasture; **8** sheeprun

sheer: 3 cut; **4** bare, bold, free, neat, pure, slew, veer; **5** bluff, plain, stark; **6** swerve; **7** regular, uniform, unmixed; **8** absolute,

S

vaporous; **9** unmingled; **10** see-through; **11** homogeneous, transparent

sheer wall: 5 cliff

sheet: 4 foil, pane, sail, tack; **5** paper, plane; **6** canvas, shroud; **7** tabloid; **8** bedsheet, coverlet; **9** mainsheet, tarpaulin

sheet anchor: 6 anchor; **8** mainstay; **11** waist anchor

sheet bend: 4 knot; **5** hitch

sheet of glass: 10 plate glass

she-goat: 5 nanny; **6** tabita; **9** nanny-goat

sheik: 4 beau, dude; **6** sheikh; **7** gallant; **9** Arab chief; **12** clotheshorse, fashion plate

shekels: 4 gelt, kale, loot, pelf; **5** bread, dough, lucre, money; **6** dinero, moolah

sheldrake: 7 sawbill; **8** fish duck, shel duck; **9** merganser

shelf: 4 bank, flat; **5** ledge; **6** shoals; **8** breakers, lee shore, shallows, shelving

shelf fungus: 13 bracket fungus

shell: 3 pod; **4** case, coat; **5** blast, plate, scale; **6** casing, coffin, pepper, strafe; **7** bombard, coating; **8** egg shell, nutshell; **9** cannonade; **11** cannon shell, cockleshell, racing shell

shellacking: 6 waxing; **7** priming; **8** painting; **10** lacquering

shellbark hickory: 8 shagbark

shell collecting: 10 conchology

shellfish: 7 mollusk; **10** crustacean

shell jacket: 10 mess jacket

shell out: 3 lot; **4** deal; **5** allot; **6** lay out; **7** cough up, deal out, dish out, dole out, fork out, mete out; **8** dispense

shellproof: 9 bombproof

shell shock: 13 battle fatigue, combat fatigue

shelter: 4 ward; **5** cover, flank, lodge; **6** covert, screen, shroud; **7** quarter; **9** sanctuary; **10** protection, tax shelter

shelterbelt: 9 windbreak

sheltie: 6 shelty; **12** Shetland pony; **16** Shetland sheepdog

shelve: 4 miss, omit, skip; **5** defer, remit, table; **6** put off; **7** put over, set back; **8** hold over, postpone; **9** push aside; **10** pigeonhole

shenanigan: 4 wile; **5** guile; **7** devilry, roguery; **8** deviltry, mischief, trickery

Shepard: 11 Alan Shepard

shepherd: 6 pastor; **8** sheepman; **9** presbyter

shepherd's dog: 8 sheep dog

sherbet: 6 sorbet; **8** sherbert

sherd: 5 shard; **8** fragment

sheriff: 10 shire reeve

sheriff's sale: 7 auction; **10** forced sale

sherlock: 2 PI; **9** operative, detective; **10** private eye

Sherlock Holmes: 6 Holmes

Shetland: 7 Zetland; **15** Shetland Islands; **16** Shetland sheepdog

Shetland pony: 6 shelty; **7** sheltie

shew: 4 show

Shiite Muslim: 6 Shiite

shiatsu: 3 G-Jo; **11** acupressure

shibboleth: 5 motto; **6** slogan, truism; **9** catchword

shield: 4 fend; **5** guard; **6** defend, harbor, screen; **7** buckler, forfend, protect; **10** supporters

shift: 4 duty, slip, tack, tilt, turn, vary, veer, warp; **5** budge, dodge, evert, lapse, lurch, smock, stint; **6** careen, change, swerve, switch; **7** chemise, deviate, evasion, finesse; **8** shifting, sidestep, transfer

shifting: 5 shift; **6** fickle, mobile, unfirm; **7** dodging, movable, unquiet; **8** slippery, unsteady, wavering; **9** mercurial; **10** inconstant; **11** vacillating

shifty: 7 devious

Shiite: 5 Shiah; Shiite Muslim

shikari: 5 guide; **9** sportsman

shiksa: 6 shikse; **12** female non-Jew

shill: 8 pitchman, promoter; **12** spokesperson

shillelagh: 6 cudgel; **9** shillalah

shilling: 3 bob

shimmer: 4 beam, play; **5** blaze, glare; **7** flicker, glimmer, glitter

shimmy: 4 slip; **5** shift, teddy; **6** wobble; **7** chemise, teddies

shin: 4 skin; **5** tibia; **6** shinny; **7** clamber; **8** scramble, shinbone, struggle

shindig: 5 party; **6** fracas, shindy, uproar

shine: 4 beam, fall, glow; **5** bloom, excel, gleam, glint; **6** polish, smooth, strike; **7** glisten, glitter, radiate, reflect; **8** radiance, radiancy, smoothen

shiner: 8 black eye, mackerel

shingle: 4 dust, tile; **5** shake; **6** powder

shingles: 6 zoster; **12** herpes zoster

shin guard: 7 shin pad

shining: 5 shiny, sunny, vivid; **6** bright, glossy; **7** glowing; **8** lustrous, sunshiny; **9** brilliant, burnished, polishing; **10** glistening

shinny: 4 shin; **6** hockey; **7** shinney

Shinto: 9 Shintoism, Shintoist; **11** Shintoistic

shiny: 5 sunny; **6** bright, glazed, glossy, sheeny; **7** lambent, radiant, shining; **8** lustrous, sunshiny; **9** burnished; **10** glistening

ship: 4 boat, sail, send; **5** craft; **6** bottom, embark, sailer, tanker vessel; **8** tall ship; **9** transport; **10** windjammer; **11** supertanker

ship's boat: 6 tender; **7** pinnace

ship's captain: 7 skipper [informal]

ship's galley: 7 kitchen

ship biscuit: 8 hardtack

shipboard soldier: 6 Marine; **8** devil dog; **11** leatherneck

shipload: 8 boatload

shipment: 4 bale, load; **5** cargo; **6** burden,

lading; **7** freight, loading, payload; **11** consignment

ship of the line: 8 man-of-war; **10** battleship; **11** battle wagon, dreadnaught

ship of war: 7 gunboat, warship; **8** man-of-war

shipping: 7 carting, hauling; **8** carrying; **9** transport; **10** cargo ships, conveyance; **12** transporting

shipping fee: 7 cartage; **13** freight charge

ship route: 6 seaway; **7** sea lane; **10** trade route

shipshape: 4 trim; **7** uniform; **8** artistic, well-kept

shipworm: 9 teredinid

shipwrecked: 7 aground, swamped, wrecked; **8** capsized, cast away, grounded, stranded; **9** foundered

shipwreck survivor: 8 castaway

shipyard: 4 dock, slip, yard; **5** wharf; **7** drydock; **8** dockyard

shire horse: 5 shire

shire reeve: 7 sheriff

shire town: 10 county town

shirk: 3 shy; **4** ware; **5** avoid, blink, dodge, parry; **6** blench, flinch

shirker: 6 dodger; **7** slacker; **9** goldbrick

shirking: 7 evasion, failure; **8** slacking; **10** goofing off, soldiering; **12** goldbricking

shirred egg: 8 baked egg

shirtfront: 5 dicky; **6** dickey, dickie

shirty: 5 angry; **9** irritated

shish kebab: 5 kabob, kebab

Shiva: 4 Siva

shivah: 5 shiva; **8** mourning

shivaree: 8 chivaree; **9** charivari

shiver: 5 chill, quake, quell, shake, throb; **6** quaver, quiver, sunder, thrill, tingle; **7** shudder, tremble, twitter

shlemiel: 4 fool, mark; **5** chump, patsy; **6** sucker; **7** fall guy; **9** schlemiel, soft touch

shlep: 6 schlep; **7** traipse; **9** pull along

shlock: 7 schlock

shmear: 7 schmear, schmeer

shmooze: 7 jawbone

shoal: 3 fry; **4** bevy; **5** brood, cloud, covey, drove, reefy, swarm; **6** litter, school, scores, shelfy, shelvy, shoaly; **7** draught, shallow

shoals: 4 bank, flat; **5** shelf; **8** breakers, shallows

shoat: 5 piggy; **6** piglet

shock: 3 jar, jog; **4** daze, jolt, stun, turn; **5** appal, floor, repel, shake; **6** appall, impact, offend, quaver, quiver, revolt, strain, stupor, thrill; **7** cushion, disgust, outrage, stagger, trouble; **8** nauseate, tingling; **10** concussion, scandalize, traumatize

shock absorber: 5 shock; **7** cushion

shocked: 6 aghast; **8** appalled, dismayed; **11** scandalized

shocking: 4 grim; **5** lurid; **6** errant; **7** heinous; **8** crushing, grimness, shameful,

terrific; **9** appalling, atrocious, notorious; **10** outrageous, scandalous, terrifying; **11** disgraceful

shod: 5 shoed; **6** calced; **7** shodden

shoddy: 5 cheap; **6** tawdry, trashy, flimsy

shoe: 4 clog, heel, skid, sole; **9** brake shoe, horseshoe

shoelace: 10 shoestring

shoeless: 8 barefoot

shoemaker: 7 cobbler

shoemaking: 8 cobbling

shoe polish: 6 polish; **8** blacking

shoe repairing: 8 cobbling; **10** shoemaking

shoestring: 8 shoelace

shofar: 7 shophar; **7** ram horn

shogun: 6 general [Japan]

shoo-in: 4 romp; **7** laugher, runaway; **8** walkaway

shoot: 3 bud; **4** dart, film, fire; **5** spout, spray; **6** charge, inject, sprout; **7** fritter, shoot up; **8** shoot out, shooting, sprout up; **9** discharge, dissipate, germinate; **10** photograph

shooter: 6 gunman, hit man; **7** torpedo; **8** hired gun; **10** gunslinger

shoot for: 3 aim; **6** aspire

shooting: 4 shot; **5** shoot; **6** firing; **7** filming; **8** coursing

shooting gallery: 5 joint; **10** crack house; **13** shooting range

shooting iron: 6 pistol; **7** handgun, shooter, sidearm

shooting star: 6 meteor; **9** meteorite, meteoroid; **11** falling star

shooting up: 14 injecting drugs

shootout: 7 gunplay; **8** gunfight

shoot up: 3 bud; **5** run up, shoot; **6** sprout; **7** start up, stick up; **9** germinate

shop: 5 buy at, store; **6** betray, browse; **7** sponsor; **8** emporium, workshop; **9** patronize, workplace

shop clerk: 10 salesclerk

shopfront: 10 storefront

shophar: 6 shofar; **7** ram horn

shopkeeper: 11 storekeeper

shopping center: 4 mall; **5** plaza

shopworn: 5 banal, stock, tired, trite; **8** timeworn, well-worn; **9** hackneyed; **10** threadbare; **11** commonplace

shore: 4 land, skid, stay; **5** coast, truss; **8** seaboard, seacoast, seashore; **9** coastline

shore leave: 7 liberty

shore up: 4 prop; **6** back up, hold up, prop up; **7** bolster

shorn: 7 sheared

short: 4 curt; **5** brief, brusk, close, crisp, scant, terse; **6** curtly; **7** brusque, concise; **8** abruptly, shortest, suddenly; **9** hotheaded

S

shortage: 6 dearth, famine; 7 deficit; 9 short-fall

short aria: 7 arietta

short bone: 7 os breve

short-circuit: 5 short; 6 bypass; 8 go around

shortcoming: 6 defect; 10 deficiency

shortcut: 6 cutoff; 8 crosscut; 10 circumvent

short document: 4 note

shorten: 3 cut; 6 reduce, take in; 7 abridge, curtail; 8 contract; 9 expurgate; 10 abbreviate

shortened: 3 cut; 8 sawed-off; 9 truncated; 11 abbreviated

shortfall: 7 deficit; 8 shortage

shorthand: 11 stenography

short-handed: 11 undermanned; 12 short-staffed, understaffed

shorthand typist: 12 stenographer

shorthorn: 6 Durham

short-horned grasshopper: 7 acridid

short hundredweight: 3 cwt; 6 cental; 7 centner, quintal; 13 hundredweight

shortly: 4 anon, soon; 5 apace, short; 6 curtly, not far; 7 briefly, by and by, not long, quickly; 9 forthwith, presently, right away, summarily; 11 immediately

shortness: 8 curtness; 9 gruffness; 10 abruptness

shorts: 6 boxers, briefs, trunks; 7 drawers; 8 breeches; 10 short pants, underpants; 12 jockey shorts; 13 Bermuda shorts

short seller: 4 bear

shortsighted: 5 short; 6 myopic; 8 purblind; 9 ill-judged; 11 improvident, nearsighted

shortsightedness: 6 myopia

short sleep: 3 nap; 6 catnap, snooze; 10 forty winks

shortstop: 5 short

short-tempered: 5 short; 9 hotheaded, irascible

short ton: 3 ton; 6 net ton

short-wave radio: 8 ham radio

Shoshone: 8 Shoshoni

shot: 3 dig, try; 4 barb, gibe, jibe, toss; 5 crack, fling, guess, scene, throw; 6 pellet, report; 7 attempt; 8 blastoff, endeavor, guessing, shooting, snapshot; 9 discharge, guesswork, injection

shot glass: 4 pony; 6 jigger

shotgun: 10 scattergun

shot in the dark: 9 guess

should: 4 must, need; 5 ought

shoulder: 4 bear, hold; 5 carry; 7 support, sustain; 8 underlay; 9 sheet work, signature

shoulder blade: 7 scapula

shout: 3 cry; 4 bawl, call, crow, hoop, howl, roar, yell; 5 abuse, brawl, cheer, whoop; 6 bellow, cry out, holler, outcry, scream, shriek, shrill, squall; 7 call out, exclaim, screech

shove: 3 jog; 4 push; 5 impel, stuff, throw; 6 jostle, thrust

shovel: 3 dig; 5 ladle, scoop, spade, spoon; 6 digger; 8 spadeful; 9 excavator

shoveler: 9 broadbill

shovel hat: 12 cardinal's hat

shove off: 7 get lost; 9 move along

show: 4 demo, fuss, look, read, seem, shew; 5 point, prove, usher; 6 appear, depict, evince, expose, record, reveal; 7 display, exhibit, express, picture, present; 8 evidence, flourish, indicate, register; 9 establish, spectacle; 10 appearance, illustrate

show bill: 8 playbill

show business: 7 show biz

showcase: 4 case; 7 vitrine; 10 show window; 11 display case

showdown: 9 encounter; 13 confrontation

shower: 4 bath, scud; 5 cloud, storm; 6 lavish, volley; 7 bathing; 9 exhibitor, showering; 10 rain shower, shower bath

showery: 5 rainy; 7 pluvial

showgirl: 7 chorine; 10 chorus girl

showing beforehand: 7 preview

showing off: 4 fuss, show; 7 display, heroics; 8 flourish; 9 strutting; 10 hotdogging

showman: promoter; 10 impresario, showperson; 11 entertainer

Show Me State: 8 Missouri

shown: 6 proven; 11 established; 12 demonstrated

show off: 5 flash, strut, swank; 6 expose, flaunt, hot dog; 7 display, exhibit; 13 exhibitionist

showroom: 8 saleroom; 9 salesroom

show up: 4 come, show; 5 arise, pop up; 6 appear, crop up, turn up; 7 surface; 8 spring up

show window: 8 showcase; 10 shopwindow; 13 display window

showy: 4 fine, rich; 5 gaudy, grand, jazzy; 6 flashy, florid, sporty, superb; 7 aureate, dashing, splashy, sublime; 8 specious; 9 flaunting

shrapnel: 4 flak

shred: 3 rag, tag; 4 iota, much, tear, whit; 5 rip up, scrap; 6 sliver, smidge, tag end, tatter; 7 smidgen, smidgin; 8 smidgeon, splinter; 9 scintilla

shredded: 6 sliced; 7 chopped

shrew: 5 scold, vixen; 6 dragon

shrewd: 5 canny; 6 crafty; 7 cunning; 8 profound, scheming; 9 conniving; 10 scholastic; 11 calculating

shrewdness: 4 wile; 5 craft; 6 acumen; 7 cunning; 8 sagacity, subtlety, wiliness; 10 artfulness, astuteness, craftiness

shrewish: 3 hot; 5 hasty, quick; 7 bilious, nagging, peevish, peppery, waspish

shriek: 4 bawl, hoop, howl, pipe, roar, yell;

5 brawl, shout, whoop; 6 bellow, scream, shrill; 7 screech; 9 screaming, shreiking, shrieking; 10 screeching

shrift: 10 white sheet; 12 confessional

shrill: 4 bawl, hoop, howl, pipe, roar, yell; 5 brawl, sharp, shout, whoop; 6 bellow, scream, shriek; 7 screech; 8 piercing; 11 cacophonous

shrimp: 4 runt; 5 prawn; 6 peewee; 8 half-pint

shrimp sauce: 6 Nantua

shrine: 7 chancel; 8 enshrine, monument, sacristy; 9 sanctuary

shrink: 3 ebb, jib, shy; 4 funk, wane; 5 cower, quail, start, waste, wince; 6 cringe, flinch, recoil, reduce, wither; 7 back off, dwindle, shrivel, squinch; 8 collapse, contract, withdraw; 12 psychiatrist

shrink from: 5 shirk; 6 recoil

shrinking: 6 recoil, 9 lessening, shrinkage, 10 reluctance; 12 constricting

shrinking violet: 9 shy

shrive: 5 purge; 6 ransom, redeem, repair; 7 absolve, confess, reclaim

shrivel: 3 ebb; 4 wane; 5 waste; 6 shrink, wither; 7 dwindle

shroud: 4 hide, pall, tack, veil, ward; 5 cloak, cover, sheet; 6 screen; 7 shelter; 8 enshroud; 12 winding sheet

Shrove Tuesday: 9 Mardi Gras

shrub: 4 bush

shrug: 3 nod

shrunk: 7 reduced; 8 shrunken; 10 contracted, diminished

shuck: 4 husk; 5 chaff, stalk, straw; 7 stubble

shudder: 5 chill, quake, shake, throb; 6 quiver, shiver, starve, thrill, tingle, tremor; 7 flutter, tremble

shuddery: 5 scary; 6 scarey; 7 shivery; 8 chilling

shuffle: 5 shift; 6 jumble

shuffleboard: 11 shovelboard

shun: 3 ban; 5 avoid; 6 banish, eschew; 7 cast out; 9 blackball, ostracize

shunt: 4 warp; 5 shift; 8 distance

shut: 5 close; 6 closed, unopen; 7 exclude, keep out, shut out

shut down: 4 fold; 5 close; 9 close down

shut-in: 7 invalid; 9 homebound; 10 housebound; 12 introvertish

shut out: 4 shut; 6 bar out; 7 exclude, keep out; 8 leave out

shutting: 7 closing

shuttle: 4 bird; 6 birdie; 11 shuttlecock; 10 shuttle bus; 12 space shuttle

shut up: 3 dam; 4 hush, lock, pent; 5 still; 6 clam up, clap up, hush up; 7 be quiet, silence

shy: 3 jib; 4 cast, jerk, shot, toss; 5 blink, chuck, dodge, fling, timid, wince; 6 flinch, shrink, unsure; 7 bashful, fearful, nervous; 8 sheepish, skittish; 9 diffident

shyster: 11 pettifogger

si: 2 ti

Si: 7 silicon

Siam: 8 Thailand

Siamese: 3 Tai; 4 Thai; 10 Siamese cat

Siamese cat: 7 Siamese

Siamese twin: 13 conjoined twin

Sian: 4 Xian; 5 Hsian; 6 Singan

sib: 7 cognate, sibling

sibilance: 3 hum; 4 buzz, hiss; 7 catcall, hissing; 10 sibilation

sibilate: 4 hiss, siss, sizz

sibling: 3 sib

sibylline: 5 vatic; 6 mantic; 7 cryptic, vatical; 8 oracular, sibyllic; 9 prophetic

sic: 3 set; 7 mot a mot [Fr]; 8 verbatim; 9 literally, literatim [Lat]; 11 to the letter, word for word

Sichuan: 8 Szechuan, Szechwan

Sicily: 7 Sicilia

sick: 3 ill; 6 ailing, queasy, unwell; 7 sickish; 8 demented, diseased, unhinged; 9 disturbed, nauseated, unhealthy; 10 unbalanced

sickbay: 9 infirmary

sicken: 4 pall, peak, pine; 5 repel; 6 revolt; 7 churn up, disgust; 8 come down, nauseate; 10 disincline

sickening: 4 vile; 7 noisome; 8 nauseous; 9 loathsome, offensive, revolting; 10 disgusting, nauseating

sickle: 6 scythe; 8 reap hook; 11 reaping hook

sickle-cell anemia: 10 sickle-cell

sickle-shaped: 6 beaked, hooked; 7 falcate

sickly: 6 ailing, infirm, morbid, peaked, poorly, unwell

sickness: 6 malady, nausea; 7 ailment, disease, illness; 8 disorder; 9 complaint, ill health

sick of: 5 fed up; 7 tired of; 9 disgusted

Siddhartha: 6 Buddha; 7 Gautama

side: 3 lee; 4 band, face, wall; 5 flank, party, slope; 7 faction, incline, quarter

side arm: 5 piece; 6 pistol, roscoe; 7 handgun; 12 shooting iron

sideburn: 10 mutton chop

side by side: 4 next; 6 beside; 8 adjacent; 9 alongside

side effect: 8 reaction

side horse: 11 pommel horse

sidekick: 3 pal; 4 chum; 5 buddy, crony

sideline: 5 hobby; 6 by-line; 9 avocation; 11 out-of-bounds

sidelong: 8 sideways, skirting; 9 obliquely

side of pork: 5 belly

side reaction: 10 side effect

sidereal: 6 astral, starry; 7 stellar

sides: 4 wall

S

side-splitting: 5 funny; 9 hilarious; 10 uproarious

sidestep: 4 duck; 5 dodge, elude, evade, fudge, hedge, parry, shift, skirt; 6 put off; 7 finesse; 10 circumvent

sideswipe: 4 clip; 5 carom; 9 glance off

sidetrack: 5 stray; 6 depart, siding; 7 digress

sidewalk: 8 pavement

sideways: 7 oblique, sideway

side-whiskers: 8 sideburn; 10 mutton chop

sidewinder: 11 rattlesnake

siding: 9 sheathing

sidle: 6 sashay

sidle up: 6 cozy up, play up, suck up

SIDS: 9 crib death

siege: 9 besieging

siege cap: 4 helm; 5 shako; 6 casque

siemens: 3 ohm

Sierra Nevada: 21 Sierra Nevada Mountains

Sierra redwood: 7 big tree; 12 giant sequoia

siesta: 3 nap; 4 doze; 6 snooze; 10 forty winks

sieva bean: 8 lima bean; 10 butter bean

sieve: 3 net; 4 sift, sort; 6 riddle, screen, strain; 8 colander

sift: 4 pick, rank, size, weed; 5 range, sieve; 6 riddle, strain, winnow

sigh: 4 moan; 5 groan, whine; 6 murmur, mutter, plaint; 7 grumble, heaving; 8 deep sigh; 9 complaint; 11 suspiration

sight: 3 ken, lot, pot, sea, see, spy, wad; 4 army, deal, espy, heap, mass, mess, mint, peck, pile, raft, slew, view; 5 image, scene; 6 seeing, survey, vision; 7 discern, eyesore, observe; 8 eyesight, perceive; 10 appearance

sightless: 5 blind; 7 eyeless; 8 viewless; 10 visionless

sightly: 4 fair

sightseeing: 7 touring

sightseer: 7 tripper; 10 rubberneck; 12 excursionist

sigil: 4 seal; 6 signet; 11 hand and seal [Law]

sign: 4 mark, omen, seal; 6 attest, ratify, sign on, sign up, signal, signed, symbol; 7 auspice, certify, portent, presage; 9 signaling, subscribe; 10 indication

signal: 4 flag, sign; 5 point; 7 notable, salient; 8 indicate; 9 watchword; 10 indication

signal caller: 10 point guard; 11 quarterback

signalize: 4 keep, mark, sign; 5 deify; 6 signal; 8 enthrone, indicate, point out; 9 celebrate; 11 distinguish, immortalize

signally: 6 mainly; 7 chiefly, notably

signals intelligence: 6 SIGINT

signatory: 6 signer

signature: 4 mark, seal; 5 scale, serif, stamp; 9 autograph, execution, theme song; 10 acceptance; 11 endorsement

signature tune: 9 theme song

signboard: 9 billboard

signer: 9 signatory

signet: 3 key; 4 seal; 5 sigil [Lat]

signet ring: 8 seal ring

significance: 4 mark; 5 force; 6 import, moment; 7 content, meaning, message, purport; 10 importance, prominence

significant: 7 meaning, telling; 8 pregnant; 9 important; 11 substantial

significant other: 5 lover

signify: 4 bode, mean; 5 augur; 6 denote; 7 portend, presage, refer to, specify; 8 forebode, indicate, stand for; 9 represent, symbolize

sign in: 7 check in

signing: 12 ratification, sign language

sign-language: 4 sign; 6 signed; 8 gestural

sign of the zodiac: 4 sign; 5 house

sign on: 4 sign; 6 sign up; 8 contract

signor: 7 signior

sign over: 8 sign away

sign up: 4 sign; 6 sign on; 8 contract

sika: 12 Japanese deer

silence: 4 hush; 5 quell, quiet; 6 hush up, shut up; 7 secrecy; 8 muteness

silencer: 7 muffler

silencing: 6 muting

silent: 3 mum; 4 mute; 5 still, tacit; 9 soundless, unsounded

silhouette: 5 shade; 6 shadow; 7 profile

silicon: 2 Si

silicon chip: 4 chip; 9 microchip

silicon dioxide: 6 silica

silk cotton: 5 kapok

silken: 5 satin, silky, sleek, slick; 6 glossy, satiny; 8 silklike

silk hat: 6 top hat, topper; 7 high hat; 8 dress hat, opera hat; 9 stovepipe; 12 stovepipe hat

silk-screen: 9 serograph

silk stocking: 6 nylons, rayons

silkweed: 8 milkweed

silkworm moth: 8 bombycid

silky: 4 fine; 5 filmy, satin, sleek, slick; 6 glossy, satiny, silken; 7 subtile; 8 delicate

silky terrier: 11 Sydney silky

sill: 9 threshold

sillabub: 8 syllabub

silly: 4 dumb, fool, zany; 5 dizzy, goofy, inept, sappy, wacky; 6 simple, stupid, unwise; 7 asinine, blatant, fatuous, foolish, idiotic; 8 babbling, childish, imbecile; 10 cockamamie, irrational, ridiculous

silt: 3 mud; 4 mire, muck; 5 slosh, slush; 6 silt up, sludge

Silurian period: 8 Silurian

Siluriformes: 7 catfish; 17 order Siluriformes

silvan: 5 woody; 6 sylvan, wooded, woodsy

silver: 2 Ag; 8 flatware; 9 tableware

silver anniversary: 13 silver jubilee

silver glance: **9** argentite
silver gray: **6** silver; **7** ash gray, ash grey; **10** silver grey
silver hake: **7** whiting
silverish: **6** argent, silver; **7** silvery
silver lining: **10** bright side
silver salmon: **4** coho
silver screen: **14** motion pictures
Silver State: **6** Nevada; **14** Sagebrush State; **15** Battle Born State
silver-tongued: **6** facile, fluent, silver; **8** eloquent
silverworker: **11** silversmith
silvery: **6** argent, silver; **7** silvern; **8** silvered; **9** argentine, silverish
Simchas Torah: **11** Simhat Torah; **12** Simchat Torah, Simhath Torah
similar: **4** like; **5** alike; **12** exchangeable, standardized; **15** interchangeable
similarity: **8** likeness; **9** semblance; **10** similitude; **11** resemblance
simmer: **4** boil, foam, fume, rage, rave, reek, stew; **5** flame, smoke; **6** seethe
simmer down: **4** calm; **6** cool it; **7** cool off; **8** calm down, chill out
simmering: **7** boiling, burning, stewing; **8** volatile, volcanic; **9** hot-headed
simoom: **6** samiel, simoon; **7** hot wind
simper: **4** grin; **5** mince, smile, smirk
simpering: **7** mincing; **10** namby-pamby; **11** sentimental
simple: **4** mere, naif, pure; **5** naive, plain, stark; **6** common, homely, modest, stupid; **8** childish; **9** childlike, dim-witted, simpleton, unspoiled; **10** elementary, unaffected
simple fraction: **14** common fraction
simple fracture: **14** closed fracture
simple-minded: **6** simple; **9** dim-witted, untutored; **10** half-witted; **12** single-minded
simpleton: **6** simple; **11** incompetent
simplicity: **4** ease; **5** folly; **6** candor; **7** clarity, naivete; **8** easiness, severity; **9** naiveness, innocence; **10** chasteness, simpleness; **12** inexperience
simplify: **6** reduce; **7** clear up; **10** popularize, streamline; **12** uncomplicate
simply: **3** but; **4** just, only; **6** easily, merely, purely; **7** naively, plainly; **9** naturally
Simpson: **11** Mrs. Simpson; **21** Wallis Warfield Simpson
simulacrum: **5** image; **6** effigy
simulate: **3** ape; **4** copy, mock, sham; **5** feign, mimic, model; **6** assume; **7** imitate, reenact; **11** impersonate
simulated: **4** fake, faux; **5** false; **9** imitation
simulated military operation: **8** maneuver
simulation: **5** model; **7** analogy
simultaneous: **10** coexistent, coexisting, coincident, coinciding, concurrent
sin: **5** fault; **7** blunder, offense; **8** iniquity; **10** transgress, wickedness

Sinai: **10** Mount Sinai; **11** Sinai Desert; **14** Sinai Peninsula
since: **3** for; **5** for as; **7** because, whereas; **10** inasmuch as, thereafter
sincere: **4** open, true; **5** frank; **6** candid, solemn; **7** earnest, wistful; **9** downright, guileless, in earnest, ingenuous; **10** unreserved; **11** plain-spoken
sincerity: **5** truth; **6** candor; **7** abandon, honesty; **8** fidelity; **9** frankness
sinecure: **8** cushy job; **9** no-show job; **10** featherbed
sine curve: **8** sinusoid
sine die: **11** without date; **12** indefinitely
sine qua non: **9** essential; **13** indispensable
sinew: **5** brawn, nerve, power; **6** muscle, tendon; **8** physique
sinewy: **4** wiry; **6** brawny; **7** fibrous, stringy; **8** muscular
sinful: **4** vile; **5** wrong; **6** unholy, wicked; **7** immoral, ungodly; **8** depraved; **10** iniquitous; **11** unrighteous; **12** unprincipled
sing: **3** rat; **4** blab, scan, talk; **5** carol, chant, chirp, peach, rhyme, utter; **6** babble, intone, snitch, squeal, tattle, warble
Singapore: **18** capital of Singapore
singe: **4** burn; **5** grill, parch, roast, toast; **6** scorch, swinge
singer: **7** warbler; **8** melodist, songster, vocalist
Singhalese: **7** Sinhala; **9** Sinhalese
singing: **10** vocalizing
single: **3** ace, one; **4** neat, only, pure, sole; **5** sheer, unity; **6** simple; **7** uniform, unitary; **8** isolated, separate, solitary; **9** exclusive, undivided, unmarried; **10** individual
single-channel: **4** mono; **10** monophonic
single crochet: **12** single stitch
single-handed: **5** alone
single out: **7** pick out; **8** separate
singlet: **10** undershirt
singly: **4** solo; **5** alone
sing praises: **4** laud; **5** bless; **6** praise; **7** glorify, magnify
singsong: monotonous
singular: **3** odd, rum; **5** funny, queer, rummy; **6** unique; **7** curious; **8** peculiar; **10** one-of-a-kind, remarkable
singularity: **5** unity; **7** oneness; **10** uniqueness
singularly: **6** mainly; **7** chiefly, notably; **8** signally, uniquely
Sinhalese: **7** Sinhala; **10** Singhalese
sinister: **4** base, foul, ugly, vile; **7** heinous, ominous; **8** infamous, menacing, shameful; **9** nefarious; **10** forbidding, scandalous, villainous; **11** threatening
sinistral: **10** left-handed
sink: **3** bog, dip, set; **4** bury, damp, drop, dull, fell; **5** drown, swamp, yearn; **6** engulf;

S

7 capsize, decline, founder, go under; **8** submerge; **9** shipwreck

sinker: 5 donut; **8** doughnut; **10** sinker ball

sink money: 6 invest

sinless: 8 innocent, spotless; **9** bloodless, faultless, impeccant, stainless

sinner: 8 evildoer

sinoatrial node: 6 SA node; **9** pacemaker

sinuous: 6 wiggly; **7** complex, sinuate, winding; **8** flexuous; **9** intricate

sinus: 6 cavity, hollow

SiO2: 5 agate, flint; **10** chalcedony

SiO2.xH20: 4 opal

Sioux: 6 Siouan; **10** Sioux tribe

sip: 3 nip

sipping: 7 tasting

sir: 5 senor; **6** master; **7** esquire; **8** monsieur; **9** gentleman; **12** mastersignor

Siracusa: 8 Syracuse

sire: 3 dad, get; **4** papa; **5** beget; **6** father, mother; **8** engender, generate; **10** forefather; **13** paterfamilias

siren: 8 sea nymph; **9** temptress; **11** enchantress, femme fatale

Sirenia: 6 sea cow; **12** order Sirenia

sirenian mammal: 6 sea cow; **8** sirenian

siriasis: 9 sunstroke

Sirius: 7 Dog Star; **8** Canicula

sirocco: 7 mistral; **9** dust storm, sandstorm, trade wind

sirup: 5 syrup

sis: 6 sister

sisal: 9 sisal hemp

sisal family: 9 Agavaceae; **11** agave family

sise: 2 VI; **3** six; **5** hexad, sixer; **6** sestet, sextet; **9** sextuplet; **10** half a dozen

sissy: 10 effeminate

sister: 3 sis; **7** sibling

sisterlike: 7 sororal; **8** sisterly

Sisters three: 5 Fates

Sistrurus: 10 massasauga; **13** ground rattler; **14** genus Sistrurus

sit: 3 lie; **4** pose, rest, seat; **5** perch, roost, brood, dwell; **7** baby-sit, posture, repress, squelch, sit down

site: 4 seat; **5** place, venue; **6** locate; **8** land site; **9** situation; **11** whereabouts

Sitophylus: 10 rice weevil; **11** black weevil; **15** genus Sitophylus

Sitsang: 5 Tibet; **6** Thibet

Sitta: 8 nuthatch; **10** genus Sitta

sitter: 10 babysitter

sitting duck: 6 target; **8** easy mark

sitting room: 6 lounge, parlor; **9** front room, state room; **10** living room

situate: 3 fix, put; **4** pose; **5** place, posit; **6** locate, rooted; **7** deposit, located, posited; **8** imbedded, localize, position, situated; **9** ensconced

situation: 3 job, lot; **4** post, site, slot, spot; **5** berth, place, state; **6** employ, estate, office, status; **7** posture; **8** attitude, position; **13** circumstances

sitz bath: 7 hip bath

Siva: 5 Shiva

six: 2 vi; **5** sixer; **6** sestet, sextet; **9** half dozen, sextuplet; **10** half a dozen

Six Day War: 14 Arab-Israeli War

sixfold: 8 sextuple, six times

six-shooter: 6 six-gun; **8** revolver

sixteen: 3 xvi

sixteenth note: 10 semiquaver

sixth: 8 one-sixth

sixth sense: 7 insight

sixty: 2 lx; **10** threescore

sixty-fourth note: 18 hemidemisemiquaver

sizable: 4 tidy; **5** ample, hefty; **6** goodly; **7** goodish; **8** sizeable; **11** respectable

size: 4 bulk, rank; **5** range; **6** sizing; **7** bigness; **8** font size; **9** dimension, magnitude

sized: 6 ranked

size up: 9 take stock; **10** scrutinize

sizzling: 6 red-hot

skate: 3 nag; **5** coast, glide, slide; **6** skates; **11** roller skate

skater: 9 ice skater; **12** rollerblader, rollerskater

skates: 5 skate; **12** roller skates

skedaddle: 4 bolt

skeet: 12 trapshooting; **13** skeet shooting

skeletal: 4 bony; **5** gaunt; **6** wasted; **7** haggard, pinched; **9** emaciated; **10** cadaverous

skeletal remains: 5 bones; **8** dry bones, skeleton

skeleton: 5 bones, draft, frame; **6** sketch; **7** draught, outline, remains; **8** dry bones; **9** framework; **10** underframe

skeptic: 5 cynic; **7** doubter, sceptic; **8** agnostic; **10** unbeliever

skeptical: 8 agnostic, doubting; **9** sceptical; **11** incredulous, questioning

skepticism: 8 cynicism, distrust, mistrust; **9** disbelief

sketch: 4 limn; **5** draft, study; **6** survey; **7** cartoon, outline, project; **8** skeleton; **10** rough draft; **11** rough sketch; **12** rough drawing

sketchbook: 9 sketch pad; **11** sketchblock

sketcher: 6 drawer, limner; **7** painter; **8** designer

sketch pad: 10 sketchbook; **11** sketchblock

sketchy: 4 lame, poor; **5** addle, vague; **6** hollow, meager, slight; **7** general

skew: 5 slant

skewed: 4 skew; **6** biased; **8** lopsided, top-heavy

skewer: 4 spit

skiagram: 10 radiograph

ski cap: 11 stocking cap

skid: 4 slip; **5** slide; **6** pallet; **8** sideslip

skiff: 7 rowboat**

skiing race: 6 slalom; 8 downhill

ski jacket: 5 parka; 6 anorak; 11 windbreaker

ski lift: 4 lift; 6 ski tow

skill: 5 craft, knack; 7 address, aptness,
know-how, science; 8 aptitude, facility; 10
adroitness, attainment, competence; 11
proficiency

skilled: 7 capable; 8 skillful; 9 competent,
qualified; 10 proficient

skillet: 6 frypan; 9 frying pan

skillet bread: 8 fry bread

skillful: 5 adept; 6 expert; 7 capable, skilled;
9 competent, practiced, qualified; 10 proficient

skim: 4 scan, skip; 5 coast, glide, plane,
skate; 6 review; 7 skim off, skimmed, skitter; 10 glance over

skimp: 5 scant, stint; 6 scrimp

skimpy: 4 lean

skin: 4 bark, flay, hide, pare, peel, pelt, rind,
shin, stub; 5 cutis, scalp; 6 abrade, scrape,
shinny; 9 excoriate

skin condition: 10 complexion

skin-deep: 7 surface; 11 superficial

skin-dive: 10 skin diving

skin-diver: 8 aquanaut; 9 snorkeler

skin doctor: 13 dermatologist

skin eruption: 4 rash

skin flick: 10 X-rated film; 16 porno film

skinflint: 5 miser; 6 scrimp, usurer; 7 niggard, scrooge; 10 cheapskate

skink: 7 scincid

Skinner: 9 B. F. Skinner; 22 Burrhus
Frederic Skinner

skinny: 4 dope, lean, poop; 5 scaly, weedy; 6
dermal; 7 low-down, scraggy, scrawny; 8
cortical, squamous [Anat]; 9 cutaneous,
cuticular; 11 underweight

skin rash: 8 eruption

skint: 4 bust; 5 broke; 9 penniless; 10 stone-
broke, stony-broke

skip: 3 cut, hop; 4 jump, miss, omit, ramp,
sink, skim, trip; 5 dance; 6 shelve; 7 hop-
skip, skitter, vamoose

skipjack: 12 skipjack tuna

skip over: 4 jump, skip; 8 jump over, pass
over

skipper: 6 master; 7 captain; 10 sea captain

skipping rope: 8 jump rope, skip rope

skirmish: 5 brush, clash; 9 encounter

skirt: 4 duck, side; 5 dodge, elude, evade,
hedge; 6 border, flange; 10 circumvent

skirt chaser: 4 wolf; 6 masher; 11 woman
chaser

skirting: 3 hem; 4 list, welt; 5 frill; 6 border,
edging, fringe; 8 trimming

skit: 5 sketch; 6 satire; 7 lampoon

ski tow: 4 lift; 7 ski lift

skitter: 4 skim, skip; 6 scurry; 7 scamper,
scuttle

skittish: 3 shy; 7 nervous; 8 sheepish

skittle: 7 ninepin; 10 skittle pin

skittle alley: 5 alley; 12 bowling alley

skittles: 5 bowls; 8 ninepins

skulduggery: 8 trickery; 10 hanky panky,
hocus-pocus

skulk: 4 lurk; 5 prowl, slink, sneak; 8
malinger

skulker: 6 lurker; 7 lurcher; 10 malingerer

skulking: 5 sneak; 6 sneaky; 7 furtive, lurking; 8 stealthy

skull: 7 cranium

skullcap: 7 calotte; 8 calvaria, yarmelke,
yarmulka, yarmulke

skunk: 5 cheat; 6 defeat; 7 polecat, stinker

sky: 4 flip, toss; 5 pitch; 7 heavens; 8
empyrean

sky-blue: 5 azure

sky dive: 9 parachute

skydiver: 11 parachutist; 15 parachute
jumper

skylark: 4 lark, romp; 5 frisk, sport; 6 cavort,
frolic, gambol; 7 disport, rollick

skylarking: 4 lark; 5 antic, prank, spree; 8
escapade

skylight: 8 fanlight

skyline: 7 horizon

sky pilot: 5 padre; 7 Holy Joe; 16 military
chaplain

slab: 5 thick; 7 viscous; 8 pavement; 10
foundation

slabber: 5 drool; 6 drivel, slaver; 7 dribble,
slobber

slack: 3 lax; 4 damp, dull, lazy, limp; 5 abate,
blunt, heavy, let up, loose, slake, slump,
spent; 6 quench, remiss; 7 flaccid, laggard,
languid, relaxed, slacken; 8 slack off,
slothful, sluggish; 9 negligent, slackness

slacker: 7 shirker

slacking: 8 shirking; 10 goofing off, soldiering; 12 goldbricking

slack off: 4 flag; 5 abate, let up, slack; 6 ease
up; 7 die away, ease off; 10 slacken off

slag: 5 dross; 6 scoria; 7 scoriae

slake: 5 abate, slack; 6 fill up, quench; 7
assuage, crumble, hydrate, satiate, satisfy,
surfeit

slaked: 8 quenched; 9 satisfied

slaked lime: 4 lime; 11 caustic lime, lime
hydrate

slake one's thirst: 5 swill

slam: 4 bang, blow, mosh, shot, wham; 5
knock, thump, whack; 6 thrash; 8 lambaste

slam dance: 4 mosh, slam; 6 thrash; 11 slam
dancing

slammer: 4 jail; 6 prison

slander: 5 smear, sully; 6 defame; 7 scandal;
9 aspersion, denigrate; 10 backbiting,
defamation

slanderer: 7 defamer, libeler; 8 maligner,
satirist; 9 backbiter, lampooner

S

slang: 4 cant; 5 argot, lingo; 6 jargon, patois; 10 vernacular

slant: 3 tip; 4 cant, lean, rake, tilt; 5 angle, pitch, slope; 7 sloping; 8 slanting; 9 inclining; 11 inclination

slap: 3 hit; 5 smack; 8 slapdash, smacking

slap in the face: 3 boo; 4 gibe, hiss, hoot, jeer, quip, slap; 5 fling, flout, scoff, sneer, taunt; 6 buffet

slapped: 6 cuffed

slash: 3 cut, hew; 4 gash; 5 knife, slice

slat: 6 batten, spline

slate: 5 plank; 6 ticket [U.S.]; 7 slating; 8 platform; 10 blackboard

slater: 9 woodlouse

slates: 6 tiling; 7 slating, tablets

slattern: 4 slut; 6 hooker; 7 trollop; 10 prostitute

slaughter: 6 murder; 7 butcher, carnage, debacle, mow down; 8 butchery, drubbing, massacre, whipping; 9 thrashing, trouncing

slaughterer: 7 butcher

slaughterhouse: 8 abattoir, butchery; 12 packing plant

slave: 5 sweat; 6 drudge, toiler; 7 rough it, striver; 8 work hard; 10 buckle down

slave dealer: 6 slaver; 11 slave trader

slaveholder: 6 slaver, master

slaver: 5 drool

slavery: 7 bondage; 11 enslavement

slave trader: 6 slaver; 11 slave dealer

slavey: 6 drudge; 6 skivvy

Slavic: 8 Slavonic; 14 Slavic language; 16 Slavonic language

slavish: 4 oily; 5 soapy; 6 abased, pliant; 7 fawning; 8 cringing; 9 groveling, sniveling; 10 submissive; 11 subservient

Slavonic: 6 Slavic; 14 Slavic language; 16 Slavonic language

slaw: 8 coleslaw

slay: 3 hit; 4 kill; 6 murder, remove; 7 bump off; 8 dispatch; 9 polish off

slayer: 6 killer

slaying: 6 murder; 7 killing; 8 homicide

SLE: 2 LE; 5 lupus

sleaze: 9 cheapness, tackiness

sleazy: 5 cheap, seamy, seedy, tinny; 6 cheesy, crummy, sordid; 7 chintzy, squalid

sled: 6 jumper, sledge, sleigh; 8 toboggan

sledge: 4 maul, sled; 6 jumper, sleigh; 12 sledgehammer

sleek: 5 satin, silky, slick; 6 glossy, satiny, silken; 8 silklike

sleep: 3 nap; 4 coma, rest; 5 death, log Z's; 6 trance; 7 quietus, slumber; 8 be asleep; eternal rest

sleeper: 3 tie; 4 mole; 8 crosstie; 9 slumberer; 10 Pullman car; 11 railroad tie, sleeper goby, sleeping car, stringpiece

sleep in: 6 live in; 9 sleep late

sleepiness: 5 tired; 10 drowsiness, somnolence

sleeping: 6 asleep; 7 dormant; 8 dormancy; 10 quiescence, quiescency, slumbering

sleeping around: 11 promiscuity

sleeping car: 7 sleeper; 8 wagon-lit; 10 Pullman car

sleeping room: 7 bedroom, chamber; 10 bedchamber

sleeping together: 3 sex; 6 mating; 10 lovemaking

sleep late: 7 sleep in

sleepless person: 9 insomniac

sleep talking: 10 somniloquy; 12 somniloquism

sleepwalk: 12 somnambulate

sleepwalker: 11 night walker; 12 noctambulist, somnambulist

sleeve: 4 cuff; 5 skein, twill; 9 wristband

sleigh: 4 sled; 6 jumper, sledge

sleigh bell: 8 cascabel

sleight: 5 skill, trick; 9 dexterity, slickness

sleight of hand: 11 legerdemain; 16 prestidigitation

slender: 4 fine, slim, thin; 5 light, lithe, scant; 6 flimsy, lissom, scanty, slight, supple, svelte; 7 limited, lissome; 9 lithesome, sylphlike

slenderize: 4 slim, thin; 6 reduce; 7 melt off; 8 slim down; 10 lose weight

sleuth: 2 PI; 9 detective; 11 sleuthhound

sleuthing: 9 detecting, detection

slew: 3 cut, lot, pot, wad; 4 deal, heap, mass, mess, mint, peck, pile, raft, skid, slip, slue, veer; 5 batch; 6 plenty

slice: 3 cut, rip; 4 gash, pare, peel, slit; 5 piece, shave, slash; 6 rasher; 7 cutting, shaving, slice up; 8 incision, lacerate

slick: 3 pat, sly; 4 foxy, glib, slip, wily; 5 dodgy, satin, silky, sleek, smart; 6 crafty, glossy, satiny, silken, tricky; 7 cunning, knavish, tricksy; 8 guileful, silklike, slippery

slicked: 9 plastered

slicker: 7 oilskin

slickly: 6 glibly

slide: 3 rub; 4 flit, skid, skim, slew, slip, slue; 5 chute, coast, glide, skate, swoop; 7 slither; 10 cover glass, slide glass, slide photo; 12 lantern slide, transparency; 13 sloping trough; 15 counting chamber

slide action: 10 pump action

slide fastener: 3 zip; 6 zipper

slide photo: 5 slide; 12 transparency

slide valve: 5 valve; 6 spigot

sliding keel: 8 drop keel; 11 centerboard

sliding panel: 8 trapdoor

slight: 4 slim, thin; 5 evade, light, scant, sneer, spurn; 6 flimsy, ignore, pass by, rebuff, scanty, subtle; 7 limited, neglect, sketchy, slender, tenuous; 8 forswear, overlook; 9 disregard, indignity, repudiate; 10 disrespect

slightly: 6 slimly; 8 somewhat; 9 slenderly

slightness: 8 delicacy, slimness; 9 pettiness; 10 triviality; 11 slenderness

slim: 3 sly; 4 thin, wily; 5 taper; 6 reduce, slight; 7 melt off, slender; 8 slim down, stealthy; 10 lose weight, slenderize, slight-made

slim down: 4 slim, thin; 6 reduce; 7 melt off; 10 lose weight, slenderize

slime: 3 goo, mud; 4 gook, gunk, muck, ooze; 5 slush; 6 sludge

slime eels: 3 hag; 7 hagfish

sling: 4 bolt, hang; 5 drive, hitch; 6 append, hook up; 7 suspend; 8 catapult, fasten to; 9 fulminate, slingshot

slingshot: 5 sling

slink: 4 lurk; 5 prowl, skulk, sneak

slink away: 7 abscond; 8 slip away, sneak off, steal off; 9 sneak away, steal away

slip: 3 err; 4 blot, case, dock, fall, flaw, flit, list, miss, skid, slew, slue, tape, tilt, trip, yard; 5 abort, berth, fault, gaffe, glide, lapse, lurch, shift, slick, slide, snack, sneak, spill, splay, steal, strip, teddy, wharf; 6 blow it, fillet, miscue, offend, riband, ribbon, shimmy, slipup, snatch, tumble; 7 blunder, botch it, chemise, cutting, eluding, elusion, faux pas, mistake, moorage, mooring, stumble, teddies; 8 dockyard, downfall, miscarry, omission; 9 oversight

slipover: 8 pullover

slipped disc: 9 herniated

slippery: 4 glib, oily; 5 slick; 6, slippy, tricky; 7 crooked; 8 fallible, glabrous, shifting; 9 debatable, insidious, lubricous; 10 disputable, precarious; 12 questionable; 13 Machiavellian, untrustworthy

slipping: 10 slithering

slippy: 8 slippery

slipshod: 3 lax; 5 loose; 6 sloppy; 7 inexact; 8 careless, slovenly; 9 haphazard

slipstream: 8 backwash; 9 airstream

slipup: 4 slip; 6 miscue

slit: 3 cut, rip; 4 gash; 5 score, slice; 7 scratch, slitted; 8 incision, lacerate

slither: 5 slide

sliver: 5 shave, shred; 6 paring, shiver; 7 shaving; 8 clipping, splinter

slob: 3 pig; 6 slovenly

slobber: 4 slop; 5 drool

sloe: 10 blackthorn

slog: 4 plod, slug; 6 trudge; 7 peg away; 8 footslog, plug away

slogan: 5 motto; 9 catchword; 10 shibboleth

slogger: 7 plodder, slugger

slop: 5 filth, slops, slosh, spill, swill; 6 deluge, splash; 7 pigwash, slobber, squelch; 8 pigswill

slope: 4 lean, rise, side, wall; 5 chink, pitch,

slant; 6 ascent; 7 abscond, incline, sloping; 8 gradient, slanting, slip away, slope off [slang], sneak off, steal off; 9 inclining

sloping: 5 slant, slope; 6 aslant, aslope, sloped; 7 slanted; 8 diagonal, slanting; 9 inclining; 11 inclination

sloppy: 5 messy; 8 slipshod, slovenly, careless; 9 haphazard

slosh: 3 mud; 4 mire, muck, slop; 5 slush; 6 sludge, splash, splosh, squish

sloshed: 5 drunk; 10 inebriated

slot: 4 post, spot; 5 berth, place; 8 position, time slot; 9 situation; 13 expansion slot; 14 one-armed bandit

sloth: 8 laziness; 9 indolence, tree sloth

slothful: 4 lazy; 5 slack; 6 otiose, remiss, supine, torpid; 7 languid, work-shy; 8 indolent, sluggish

slouch: 4 lout; 5 droop

slouched: 7 slumped; 9 slouching

slouch hat: 11 cavalier hat

slough: 4 molt, plod, shed, slog; 5 swamp; 7 discard, cast off; 9 backwater

sloven: 3 bum, pig; 4 slob; 5 scrub

slovenly: 3 lax; 5 messy; 6 frowsy, untidy; 7 inexact; 8 careless, slipshod; 9 uncleanly

slow: 3 dim; 4 dull, dumb; 5 blunt, delay, dense, heavy, slack, tardy; 6 retard, slow up, slowly, stupid; 7 belated, gradual, tardily; 8 backward, slow down, sluggish, tiresome, untimely; 10 decelerate, monotonous

slow down: 4 slow; 5 relax, slack; 6 retard, slow up, unbend, unwind; 7 slacken; 8 loosen up; 10 decelerate

slowly: 4 easy, slow; 5 lento; 7 tardily; 9 leisurely

slow-moving: 8 sluggish

slowpoke: 7 plodder

slow-witted: 10 half-witted; 12 feebleminded

slub: 4 burl, knot

slubbed: 5 nubby; 6 nubbly, tweedy; 8 homespun

sludge: 3 goo, mud; 4 gook, guck, gunk, mire, muck, ooze, silt; 5 slime, slosh, slush; 8 quagmire

slue: 3 cut; 4 skid, slew, slip, veer; 5 curve, sheer, slide; 6 swerve

slug: 3 lag, wad; 4 blow, slog, swig; 6 bullet; 8 sluggard

slugabed: 8 sluggard

slugfest: 5 fight; 9 fistfight; 10 fisticuffs

slugger: 6 batter, hitter; 7 batsman, slogger

sluggish: 4 dull, flat, lazy, slow, tame; 5 blunt, heavy, inert, slack, tardy; 6 torpid; 7 languid; 8 indolent, slothful

sluice: 4 lock; 5 flush; 8 penstock; 9 floodgate, sluiceway

slum: 6 ghetto

S

slumber: 3 nap; 5 sleep; 6 torpor; 8 lethargy

slumberous: 6 sleepy; 8 slumbery; 9 somnolent

slump: 3 sag; 4 sink; 5 slack; 6 slouch; 7 cadence, drop-off, fall off; 9 recession, slide down; 10 depression

slur: 4 blot, blur, daub, spot; 5 smear; 6 smirch, smudge, stigma; 7 asperse; 8 reproach, slur over; 9 aspersion; 10 imputation, stigmatize

slush: 3 mud; 4 mire, muck, ooze, silt; 5 slime, slosh; 6 sludge, splash, splosh, squash; 8 quagmire

slushy: 5 mushy; 7 maudlin, mawkish; 8 bathetic, schmalzy; 9 schmaltzy; 11 sentimental

sly: 4 foxy, slim, wily; 5 dodgy, slick; 6 crafty, tricky; 7 cunning, knavish, tricksy; 8 guileful, stealthy

sly boots: 3 fox; 7 reynard

slyness: 5 craft, guile; 7 cunning, stealth; 8 foxiness, wiliness

Sm: 8 samarium

smack: 4 cuff, junk, kiss, peck, scag, slap, tang; 5 savor, spank, taste, thump, tinge, touch, twang; 6 flavor, heroin, relish

small: 3 low; 4 mean, tiny; 5 lowly, minor, petty; 6 humble, little, minute, modest, peanut; minuscule; 7 trivial; 9 lowercase, miniature; 10 diminutive; 11 microscopic; 13 insignificant

small change: 3 rap; 4 mite; 6 change; 9 petty cash, small coin; 11 chickenfeed, pocket money; 12 pocket change

small computer system interface: 4 SCSI

smaller: 7 littler

smallest: 5 least; 6 lowest; 8 littlest

small finger: 6 pinkie

small fry: 3 fry, kid; 4 tike; 5 child, minor, youth; 6 moppet, nipper, shaver, squirt; 8 juvenile

small letter: 9 lower case

small-minded: 5 petty

smallmouth: 4 bass

small number: 7 paucity

small person: 5 dwarf

smallpox: 7 variola

small talk: 3 gab; 4 chat; 6 gossip; 8 chitchat

small-time: 13 nickel-and-dime

small town: 7 village; 10 settlement

smarmy: 4 oily; 7 buttery, fulsome; 8 unctuous; 10 oleaginous

smart: 4 ache, hurt, neat, tidy; 5 acute, alert, natty, quick, ready, saucy, sharp, slick; 6 bright, dapper, jaunty, lively, quaint, snappy; 7 cutting, dashing

smart aleck: 7 wise guy; 8 wiseacre; 11 wisenheimer; 12 weisenheimer

smart as a whip: 6 brainy; 9 brilliant

smarting: 5 smart; 6 aching, biting, in pain;

7 chafing, gnawing, hurting; 8 stinging; 9 suffering

smart set: 7 society; 11 high society

smash: 3 hit; 4 bang, bash, belt, blow, boom, dash, nail; 5 blast, crash, havoc, knock, quell, split; 6 bang up, shiver, squash, strike; 7 debacle, shatter, smash up, squelch; 8 collapse, overhead; 9 collision, crumple up, explosion; 10 eboulement [Fr], smashingly; 11 delabrement [Fr]

smashed: 5 drunk; 10 inebriated

smashing: 4 cool, keen, neat; 5 great, swell; 6 groovy, peachy

smattering: 7 handful

smear: 4 slur; 5 stain, sully; 6 defame, smudge; 7 asperse, slander, tarnish; 9 denigrate

smell: 4 odor, reek; 5 aroma, scent, stink; 7 feeling; 8 smell bad, smelling; 9 effluvium, olfaction

smell bad: 4 reek; 5 smell, stink

smelling: 4 rank; 5 fetid, smell; 7 noisome; 8 redolent, stinking; 9 offensive

smell up: 7 stink up; 8 stink out

smelly: 4 foul; 5 fetid, funky; 6 putrid; 7 noisome; 8 stinking; 12 foul-smelling

smelt: 6 anneal, refine, reduce, temper

smidgen: 4 iota, whit; 5 shred; 6 smidge, tittle; 7 smidgin; 8 smidgeon; 9 scintilla

Smilax: 5 briar, brier; 10 greenbrier; 11 genus Smilax

smile: 4 grin; 5 smirk

smirch: 4 blot, daub, slur, soil, spot; 5 smear, stain, sully; 6 defame, smudge; 7 slander; 9 denigrate

smirched: 6 smudgy; 7 smeared, smudged

smirk: 4 grin; 5 smile; 6 simper

smite: 3 hit; 4 beat, move, whop; 5 touch; 6 affect, excite, infect, strike, wallop; 7 afflict, animate, impress, inspire; 8 interest; 9 impassion

smith: 11 metalworker

smithy: 5 forge; 6 forger, Vulcan; 10 blacksmith

smitten: 4 gaga; 5 crazy, dotty, moved; 6 bitten, in love, soft on, struck; 7 excited, touched; 8 affected, animated, enamored, inspired, stricken; 9 impressed, taken with; 10 infatuated, interested; 11 impassioned

smock: 5 shift; 6 duster; 7 chemise; 8 dust coat; 9 gaberdine

smoke: 4 cure, fume, reek, stew; 5 steam; 6 heater, smudge; 7 smoking; 8 fumigate

smoke alarm: 9 fire alarm

smoked: 10 smoke-cured, smoke-dried

smoked haddock: 6 finnan; 12 finnan haddie

smoked herring: 10 red herring

smoker: 10 smoking car; 11 smoker-party, tobacco user

smokestack: 5 stack

smokey: 4 police
smokiness: 9 dirtiness, murkiness
smoky: 5 dirty, dusty, murky, sooty; 6 smutty
smoky quartz: 9 cairngorm
smoldering: 6 latent; 7 dormant
smooch: 4 kiss, snog; 5 smack, smear, spoon; 6 smudge
smooching: 7 hugging, kissing, necking, petting; 8 cuddling, fondling; 9 caressing, snuggling
smooth: 3 lay; 4 calm, cool, damp, ease, hush, lull, tame; 5 abate, allay, fluid, level, quell, quiet, shine, still, suave; 6 fluent, pacify, polish, soothe; 7 appease, assuage, lighten; 8 polished, smoothen; 9 alleviate, smooth out; 10 untroubled, unwrinkled
smoothbore: 8 unrifled
smoothie: 7 charmer, smoothy; 11 sweet talker
smooth-spoken: 6 facile, fluent, silver; 8 eloquent
smooth-tongued: 4 glib; 6 smooth; 7 honeyed
smoothy: 7 charmer; 8 smoothie; 11 sweet talker
smother: 3 gag; 4 bury; 5 choke; 6 hush up, muddle, muffle, stifle; 8 strangle, suppress; 9 suffocate; 10 asphyxiate
smothered: 6 buried; 7 stifled; 8 hushed up; 9 covered up, strangled
smudge: 4 blot, blur, daub, slur, spot; 5 smear, smoke, stain; 7 tarnish
smug: 4 prim; 6 demure; 7 prudish; 8 priggish
smuggle: 3 run; 7 bootleg
smuggled: 7 bootleg; 10 contraband; 11 black-market
smuggler: 6 runner; 7 poacher; 10 mooncurser; 13 contrabandist
smut: 4 soot; 8 ribaldry; 9 obscenity; 10 smut fungus
smutty: 4 foul, free; 5 bawdy, broad, dusty, gross, loose, nasty, smoky, sooty; 6 coarse, filthy, ribald, risque [Fr]; 7 fulsome, obscene; 9 equivocal; 12 pornographic
Sn: 3 tin
snack: 4 bite, nosh
snaffle: 3 bit
snag: 3 rub; 5 hitch; 6 hang-up
snaggy: 6 thorny; 7 prickly, studded, thistly; 9 bristling
snail: 8 escargot [Fr]
snakebird: 7 anhinga
snakebit: 7 hapless, unhappy, unlucky; 8 hoodooed [U.S.], luckless
snake doctor: 9 dragonfly
snake eyes: 5 craps
snake fence: 9 worm fence
snake in the grass: 7 traitor
snaky: 8 circling; 9 snake-like; 10 serpentine
snap: 5 cinch, click, crack, flash, frown, gnarl, gnash, growl, jiffy, shoot, snarl; 6 breath, picnic, sunder; 7 rupture; 8 pushover, walkover
snap bean: 9 green bean; 10 French bean, string bean
snapline: 9 chalk line
snap off: 5 break; 8 break off
snap pea: 12 sugar snap pea
snapper: 14 snapping turtle
snapping: 9 crackling
snappish: 3 hot; 5 hasty, quick; 6 snappy; 7 bilious, peevish, waspish
snappy: 5 brisk, crisp, merry, natty, nippy, smart, zippy; 6 lively
snap ring: 9 carabiner
snapshot: 4 shot; 5 still; 10 still photo
snap up: 4 grab
snare: 3 gin; 4 trap; 5 noose; 6 entrap; 7 ensnare, trammel; 9 snare drum
snarl: 4 feud, howl, knot, spat, tiff; 5 frown, gnarl, gnash, growl, scowl; 6 tangle; 7 dispute, quarrel, snarl up; 8 entangle, squabble; 9 embrangle
snarled: 6 jammed, snarly; 7 gnarled, knotted; 10 gridlocked
snarl-up: 10 traffic jam
snatch: 4 grab, slip, snap; 5 catch, seize, snack; 6 abduct, kidnap
snatcher: 8 abductor; 9 kidnapper
sneak: 4 lift, lurk, slip; 5 creep, filch, pinch, prowl, skulk, slink, steal, swipe; 6 coward, pilfer; 7 furtive, prowler, purloin; 8 recreant, skulking, stealthy
sneaker: 7 gym shoe; 9 track shoe; 10 tennis shoe; 11 running shoe
sneaking suspicion: 6 notion; 7 inkling; 9 suspicion; 10 impression
sneaky: 5 sneak; 7 furtive, lurking; 8 skulking, stealthy; 9 underhand; 11 underhanded; 13 surreptitious
sneer: 4 gibe, jeer, jibe, quip; 5 flout, scoff, spurn, taunt; 6 slight
snick: 4 nick
snicker: 4 crow; 5 snort; 6 cackle, giggle, titter; 7 chortle, chuckle, snigger
snickersnee: 10 knife fight
snide: 8 sneering; 12 supercilious
sniff: 4 nose; 5 scent, snort, snuff, whiff; 6 inhale; 7 sniffle
sniffy: 7 haughty; 8 prideful; 10 disdainful, swaggering; 12 supercilious
snifter: 11 brandy glass
snigger: 5 taunt; 6 deride, titter; 7 chortle, chuckle, laugh at, snicker, twitter; 8 ridicule
snip: 3 bit, cut, lop, nip; 4 clip, crop, trim; 7 snippet; 8 clipping, fragment, snipping
snipe: 4 rail; 5 round; 6 assail, attack, grouse, plover; 7 assault, lash out; 10 sharpshoot
snippet: 4 snip
snips: 8 tinsnips

S

snitch: 3 rat; **4** fink, sing; **6** betray, canary, squeal, tattle, tell on; **7** stoolie; **8** denounce; **10** tattletale; **11** stool pigeon

snivel: 5 whine; **7** blubber, sniffle, snuffle, whimper; **9** sniveling

sniveler: 6 moaner, whiner; **7** crybaby; **8** grumbler, squawker; **10** bellyacher, complainer

snobbish: 6 clubby, snobby, snooty; **7** brutish, stuck-up; **8** clannish, cliquish

snood: 7 hair net

snooker: 4 pool; **8** hoodwink; **9** billiards

snoop: 3 pry, spy; **4** nosy; **7** snooper; **9** eavesdrop

snoot: 4 beak, nose; **5** snout; **6** honker, hooter, nozzle; **9** schnozzle

snooty: 6 snotty; **7** stuck-up; **9** bigheaded

snooze: 3 nap; **4** doze; **5** sleep; **6** catnap, drowse, siesta; **8** cat sleep; **10** forty winks

snore: 5 snort; **7** saw logs, saw wood, snoring; **8** rhonchus

snorkel: 8 breather; **9** schnorkel; **10** schnorchel

snort: 4 huff; **5** grunt, sniff, snore; **6** inhale

snorting: 7 huffing; **8** puffing, sniffing; **9** guffawing; **10** inhalation

snot: 4 prig, snob

snot-nosed: 6 snooty, snotty, uppish; **7** stuck-up; **9** bigheaded

snout: 3 neb; **4** beak, nose; **5** snoot; **6** honker, hooter, muzzle, nozzle, schnoz; **7** rostrum; **9** proboscis, schnozzle

snow: 7 cocaine, snowing; **8** blizzard, hoodwink, snowfall; **9** bamboozle, be snowing, play false; **10** fall of snow

snow bank: 5 drift

snowbird: 5 junco; **9** fieldfare

snow chains: 10 tire chains

snow-covered: 5 snowy; **8** snow-clad

snowflake: 5 flake; **7** crystal; **8** snowbird

snowing: 4 snow; **8** snowfall

snow pea: 8 sugar pea

snowshoe hare: 11 varying hare; **14** snowshoe rabbit

snowstorm: 8 blizzard

snow thrower: 10 snow blower

snowy: 5 white; **8** snow-clad; **9** snow-white; **11** snow-covered

snowy egret: 10 snowy heron

snub: 4 huff; **5** repel; **6** ignore, rebuff; **7** put down, repulse; **8** brush off, override; **9** disregard; **10** circumvent; **12** cold shoulder

snub-nosed: 7 pug-nose; **8** pug-nosed; **9** flat-nosed

snuff: 5 douse, scent, smell, sniff; **7** blow out, snuff up, snuffle; **8** snuff out

snuffle: 5 snuff, whine; **6** snivel, wheeze; **7** blubber, sniffle

snuff out: 5 douse, snuff; **6** put out; **7** blow out; **8** stamp out; **10** extinguish

snug: 4 cosy, cozy; **5** close, cubby, tight; **6** at rest; **8** domestic, snuggery; **9** cubbyhole, seaworthy; **11** comfortable

snuggery: 4 nest, snug; **5** cubby; **9** cubbyhole

snuggle: 6 cuddle, nestle, nuzzle; **9** draw close

snugness: 4 ease; **7** comfort; **8** cosiness, coziness; **11** domesticity

so: 3 soh, sol; **4** then, thus; **5** and so; **6** indeed, such as, thusly; **7** and then, exactly, in order; **8** truthful; **9** in this way, precisely

soak: 3 bib, rob, sop, sot; **4** lush; **5** bathe, douse, imbue, soppy, souse, steep, swill; **6** drench, fleece, guzzle, pickle; **7** immerse, soaking; **8** macerate, saturate; **9** inebriate; **10** intoxicate, overcharge

soaking wet: 11 wringing wet

soak up: 4 draw; **5** sop up; **6** absorb, imbibe, take in, take up; **10** assimilate

soap: 4 suds; **6** lather

soapberry family: 11 Sapindaceae

soapbox: 4 dais; **5** stump; **6** podium, pulpit; **7** rostrum

soap box desk: 6 pulpit; **7** lectern

soaping: 9 lathering

soapstone: 8 soaprock, steatite

soapy: 4 oily; **6** pliant; **7** fawning, slavish; **8** cringing, specious, unctuous

soar: 4 zoom; **5** glide, surge, tower; **6** soar up; **7** command, run high, take off; **9** hang glide, sailplane, transcend

soaring: 5 glide, lofty; **7** eminent, gliding, sailing

sob: 3 cry; **4** wail, weep; **7** blubber, sobbing, whimper; **9** shed tears; **10** whimpering

sober: 4 calm, cool, drab, tame; **5** grave, quiet, solid, staid; **6** sedate, solemn, somber; **7** earnest, serious; **9** temperate

soberly: 7 gravely, staidly; **8** solemnly; **9** earnestly, seriously

sobriquet: 6 by-name, handle; **7** moniker, pet name; **8** nickname

so-called: 4 fake, mock, sham; **5** bogus; **6** pseudo; **7** alleged; **8** spurious, supposed; **9** pretended; **10** fraudulent; **11** counterfeit

soccer: 8 football

soccer game: 5 match

sociable: 5 mixer; **6** calash, social; **8** gracious; **9** convivial

social: 5 civic, human, mixer; **6** formal, public; **8** sociable, societal

social circle: 7 company, coterie, society

social disease: 2 VD

social drinker: 7 tippler

social occasion: 6 affair

social rank: 4 rank; **12** social status

social science: 9 sociology

social service: 10 social work; **11** welfare work

social worker: 10 caseworker; **13** welfare worker

societal: 6 social
societal pressure: 12 peer pressure
society: 4 club; **5** guild, lodge, order, world; **7** company, coterie; **8** smart set; **9** community; **12** organization
Society of Friends: 7 Quakers
socio-economic class: 11 social class
sociology: 13 social science
sociopath: 10 psychopath
sock: 3 bop, hit; **4** bash, bonk, hose, whap, whop; **5** socks; **7** hosiery; **8** stocking, windsock
sock away: 8 lay aside, put aside, set aside, tuck away; **12** squirrel away
sockeye salmon: 7 sockeye; **8** blueback; **9** red salmon
socks: 4 hose, sock; **7** hosiery; **8** stocking; **9** trunk hose
sod: 4 lawn, turf; **5** green; **6** bugger; **8** sodomist
soda: 3 pop; **5** tonic; **7** soda ash, soda pop; **8** minerals; **9** soda water; **11** bicarbonate, washing soda
sodality: 4 body; **9** community; **10** fraternity, solidarity
sodbuster: 4 plow; **6** farmer
sodden: 4 soft; **5** soppy; **6** sloppy, soaked; **7** soaking, sopping; **8** drenched, dripping; **9** saturated
sodium: 2 Na; **7** natrium
sodium bicarbonate: 4 soda; **10** baking soda; **11** bicarbonate
sodium chloride: 4 salt; **6** halite; **8** rock salt; **9** table salt
sodium hydroxide: 11 caustic soda
sofa: 5 couch; **6** lounge
sofa bed: 11 convertible
so far: 3 yet; **5** as yet; **7** till now; **8** hereunto, hitherto
Sofia: 16 Bulgarian capital
soft: 4 easy, kind, slow, weak; **5** cushy, faint, piano; **6** feeble, gentle, low-key, tender; **7** anodyne, subdued; **8** delicate; **9** compliant
soft coal: 10 bituminous
soft color: 6 pastel
soft-cover: 9 paperback
soft diet: 3 pap; **6** pablum
soften: 4 damp, dull, mute; **5** yield; **6** buffer, dampen, muffle, relent, temper, weaken; **7** cushion, diffuse; **8** mitigate, moderate
soft goods: 8 drygoods
soft ice cream: 13 frozen custard
soft lenses: 8 contacts; **13** contact lenses
softly: 5 piano; **6** gently; **7** lightly, quietly
softness: 7 pliancy; **8** weakness; **9** faintness; **10** pliability, tenderness
soft palate: 5 velum
soft-pedal: 8 play down
soft soap: 7 blarney, coaxing

software: 7 program; **11** application
software engineer: 6 hacker; **10** programmer
soggy: 3 wet; **6** soaked; **11** waterlogged
soi-disant: 8 so-called; **9** pretender; **10** self-styled
soigne: 5 sleek; **7** soignee; **11** well-groomed
soil: 4 dirt, dung, land; **5** dirty, earth, filth, grime, realm, stain, sully; **6** domain, ground, refuse, sewage; **7** country, corrupt, pollute, soilage; **9** excrement; **10** corruption
soiree: 12 evening party
sojourn: 4 stay; **5** abide, lodge; **6** reside, tenant; **7** inhabit
Sol: 3 sun; **6** Apollo, old sol; **7** Phoebus; **9** earth's sun
solace: 5 cheer; **6** soothe; **7** comfort, console, rejoice
Solanaceae: 12 potato family
Solanum: 6 potato; **7** brinjal; **8** eggplant; **9** aubergine; **12** genus Solanum
solar energy: 10 solar power
solar halo: 12 parhelic ring
solarium: 7 sunroom
solar trap: 7 suntrap
solder: 3 set; **5** unite
soldering: 7 bonding
soldier: 2 GI; **5** grunt; **7** warrior
soldierlike: 7 martial; **8** militant, military
soldier of fortune: 9 mercenary; **10** adventurer
sole: 3 one; **4** lone, only, shoe; **6** single; **7** unitary; **8** lonesome, solitary; **9** exclusive
Solea: 4 sole; **10** genus Solea
solecism: 4 slip; **5** gaffe; **7** faux pas, sophism; **9** barbarism, gaucherie; **10** bad grammar; **11** impropriety
solely: 4 only; **5** alone; **8** entirely; **11** exclusively
solemn: 4 holy, pure; **5** grave, sober; **6** devout, heroic, sacred, sedate; **7** earnest, serious, sincere, stately, sublime; **8** reverent; **10** devotional; **12** transcendent
solemnize: 6 hallow
solemnly: 7 gravely, soberly; **8** formally; **9** earnestly, seriously
solicit: 4 urge, lure; **6** entice; **7** entreat; **9** importune
solicitor: 7 proctor; **8** advocate, attorney; **9** applicant; **10** petitioner
solicitous: 5 eager; **8** sedulous; **12** apprehensive
solicitude: 4 care, dole, fret, load; **5** worry; **6** burden, unease; **7** anxiety, concern
solid: 2 3-D; **4** firm; **5** cubic, dense; **6** hearty, stanch, strong, sturdy, three-D, worthy; **7** staunch; **8** tangible; **9** nonporous, solid

S

body, solidness, unanimous; **10** up-standing
Solidago: 9 goldenrod; **13** genus Solidago
solidarity: 5 unity; **8** solidity; **9** community
solidification: 3 set; **9** hardening
solidified: 8 hardened; **10** coagulated
solidify: 6 freeze
solidity: 8 firmness
solid shape: 4 form; **5** shape
solid state: 8 firmness, solidity; **9** solidness
solidus: 8 diagonal
soliloquy: 9 monologue
solitary: 3 one; **4** lone, only, sole; **5** alone; **6** single; **7** unitary; **8** isolated, lonesome; **9** nonsocial
solitude: 7 privacy; **9** aloneness, isolation, reclusion, seclusion
solo: 5 alone; **6** singly
solon: 9 statesman
so long: 3 bye; **5** adieu, adios; **6** bye-bye, good-by; **7** cheerio, good day, good-bye; **8** au revoir, sayonara; **11** arrivederci; **14** auf wiedersehen
solus: 5 alone
solution: 6 answer, result; **10** dissolving, resolution
solve: 4 lick, work; **7** resolve; **8** dissolve; **9** elucidate, figure out, puzzle out
solvent: 7 thinner; **8** dilutant; **9** dissolver, out of debt, resolvent; **10** dissolvent, in the black
soma: 4 body, form; **5** build, frame, shape; **6** figure; **7** anatomy
Somali: 8 Somalian
somatic: 6 bodily; **8** corporal; **9** corporeal
somatic chromosome: 8 autosome
somatotype: 8 body type
somber: 3 sad; **5** sober; **6** dismal, gloomy, triste [Fr]; **7** joyless; **8** dejected, frowning; **9** cheerless
some: 3 any; **4** a few, or so; **5** about; **6** around; **7** roughly, several
somebody: 3 one; **4** soul; **5** human; **6** person; **7** someone
somehow: 7 someway
someone: 3 one; **4** soul; **5** human; **6** person; **7** some one; **8** somebody; **10** individual
someplace: 9 somewhere
somersault: 4 flip; **5** vault
something: 6 entity; **8** anything, somewhat
something new: 7 novelty
sometime: 4 once; **6** former; **7** onetime
someway: 7 somehow
somewhat: 6 fairly, rather, sort of; **8** in a sense
somewhere: 9 someplace
somite: 8 metamere
Somme: 10 Somme River; **16** battle of the Somme
sommelier: 10 wine waiter; **11** wine steward

somnambulate: 9 sleepwalk
somnambulist: 11 night walker, sleepwalker; **12** noctambulist
somnolence: 10 drowsiness, sleepiness
somnolent: 6 drowsy; **8** slumbery; **9** slumbrous; **10** slumberous
son: 3 boy
sonant: 6 voiced; **8** syllabic
sonar: 11 echo sounder
Sonchus oleraceus: 8 milkweed
song: 4 tune; **6** ballad, lieder [Ger] [pl], melody, strain; **7** singing
songful: 9 melodious
songfulness: 8 lyricism
songster: 6 singer; **7** warbler; **8** melodist, songbird, vocalist; **10** songwriter
song thrush: 5 mavis; **8** throstle
songwriter: 8 songster
sonic barrier: 12 sound barrier
sonic depth finder: 10 fathometer
sonneteer: 4 poet; **9** versifier
sonny: 3 cub, lad; **6** laddie; **8** sonny boy
sonority: 7 ringing; **8** vibrancy; **9** resonance; **12** reverberance
sonorous: 4 loud, rich; **5** heavy, noisy; **7** booming, vibrant
sonsie: 5 buxom, curvy, sonsy; **6** bosomy; **10** curvaceous, voluptuous
sonsy: 5 buxom, curvy; **6** bosomy, sonsie; **10** curvaceous, voluptuous; **11** full-bosomed
soon: 4 anon; **6** at hand; **7** shortly; **8** imminent, upcoming; **9** presently
sooner: 7 earlier; **10** preferably
sooner or later: 3 yet; **6** in time; **7** by and by, some day; **10** eventually, ultimately
Sooner State: 8 Oklahoma
soonest: 8 earliest
soot: 4 smut; **9** lampblack; **11** carbon black
soothe: 4 calm, ease, hush, lull, tame; **5** abate, allay, quell, quiet; **6** pacify, smooth, solace; **7** appease, assuage, comfort, compose
soothsay: 6 divine; **8** prophesy
soothsayer: 4 seer; **5** augur; **7** prophet; **9** predictor; **10** forecaster, prophesier; **14** prognosticator
sooty: 5 dingy, dusky, dusty, murky, smoky; **6** pitchy, smutty
sop: 4 soak, sops; **5** child, douse, dowse, souse; **6** amends, drench, morsel; **7** milksop, redress; **9** atonement; **10** reparation
sophist: 7 casuist, thinker; **11** philosopher
sophistical: 9 deceptive, sophistic
sophisticate: 5 alloy, twist; **6** doctor, infect; **7** pervert; **8** compound, doctor up; **9** convolute, prejudice; **10** adulterate, amalgamate
sophisticated: 6 urbane; **8** advanced
sophistication: 11 edification, worldliness; **12** adulteration
sophistry: 7 sophism; **9** casuistry; **10** perversion; **14** false reasoning
sophomore: 10 second-year

soporiferous: 8 narcotic, somnific; 9 soporific; 11 somniferous

soporific: 4 slow; 8 hypnotic, narcotic, somnific; 11 somniferous; 12 soporiferous

sopping: 5 soppy; 6 soaked, sodden; 7 soaking; 8 drenched, dripping; 9 saturated

soprano: 6 treble

sorb: 6 take up

sorbet: 7 sherbet; 8 sherbert

sorcerer: 6 wizard; 8 magician; 11 necromancer

sorcery: 5 magic; 7 magical

sordid: 5 dirty, seamy, seedy; 6 sleazy; 7 squalid

sordino: 4 mute; 8 sourdine

sore: 3 mad; 4 hard, hurt; 5 acute, cruel, harsh, sharp, ulcer; 6 biting, severe, soured, tender; 7 caustic, painful; 8 soreness; 9 indignant, sensitive

sorely: 5 sadly; 7 cruelly, grossly; 8 bitterly, horribly, terribly, woefully; 9 fearfully, miserably, painfully

soreness: 4 gall, huff, miff, sore; 5 pique; 6 spleen; 7 cruelty, umbrage; 8 acerbity, acrimony, asperity, hardness, rankling, severity; 9 harshness, sharpness, virulence; 10 bitterness, discomfort, irritation, tenderness

sore throat: 9 raw throat; 11 pharyngitis

Sorex: 5 shrew; 10 genus Sorex

sorgho: 5 sorgo; 12 sugar sorghum, sweet sorghum

sorghum molasses: 7 sorghum

sorgo: 6 sorgho; 12 sugar sorghum, sweet sorghum

sororal: 8 sisterly; 10 sisterlike

sorrel: 4 dock; 6 oxalis; 7 roselle, rozelle; 9 red sorrel, sour grass; 10 wood sorrel; 12 common sorrel; 13 Jamaica sorrel

sorrel tree: 8 sourwood

sorrow: 3 woe; 5 grief, trial; 6 grieve, regret; 7 sadness; 8 distress; 9 heartache; 10 affliction, ruefulness

sorrowfulness: 6 sorrow; 7 sadness; 11 ruthfulness; 12 mournfulness

sorry: 3 bad, low, sad; 4 drab, mean, vile; 6 common, dismal, meager, no-good, rueful; 7 no-count, pitiful, pitying, scrubby; 8 contrite, penitent, pitiable, wretched; 9 miserable, regretful, repentant, repenting, sorrowful, sorrowing, worthless

sort: 4 form, kind, type; 5 class, group, sieve; 6 assort, screen; 7 collate, sort out, sorting, variety; 8 category, classify, division, separate

sortie: 5 sally; 8 breakout, outbreak

sortition: 11 casting lots, drawing lots

sort out: 4 sort; 5 class, clear; 6 assort; 7 clarify, clear up, correct; 8 classify, separate; 9 elucidate, enlighten; 10 discipline, illuminate

so-so: 2 OK; 3 low; 4 fair; 7 average; 8 bearable, mediocre, middling, ordinary, pass-

able; 9 tolerable, tolerably; 10 acceptable, acceptably, admissible, couci-couci, negligible; 11 indifferent

sot: 4 lush, soak, swig; 5 drunk, swill; 6 guzzle; 7 carouse, guzzler, tippler; 8 drunkard; 9 inebriate

Sothis: 6 Sirius; 7 Dog Star; 8 Canicula

sotto voce: 5 aside; 10 in a whisper

soubriquet: 9 sobriquet

sough: 4 moan, sigh; 5 groan

sought after: 7 coveted, desired; 8 in demand

soul: 3 man; 4 body; 5 being, geist [Ger], human; 6 mortal, person, psyche, spirit; 7 someone; 8 creature, somebody; 9 earthling, lifeblood, personage; 10 human being, individual; 11 inspiration

soul kiss: 8 deep kiss; 10 French kiss

soulmate: 8 alter ego

sound: 4 deep, good, well; 5 audio, plumb, voice; 6 fathom, intact, strong; 7 explore, healthy, soundly; 8 positive, profound, rational, reasoned, sensible, vocalize

sound barrier: 12 sonic barrier

sounded: 7 plumbed

sounding line: 8 lead line

soundings: 5 water; 10 submersion; 12 depth of water

soundless: 5 still; 6 silent; 9 noiseless; 10 bottomless, fathomless

soundly: 4 good; 5 sound; 10 thoroughly

sound mind: 6 senses; 8 mens sana [Lat]; 9 right mind

soundness: 6 health, sanity, wisdom; 8 firmness, vitality, wiseness; 10 good health, strictness; 11 healthiness

soundness of mind: 6 sanity

sound off: 4 kick; 5 opine, plain; 6 kvetch, quetch; 7 speak up; 8 complain

sound out: 3 see; 5 check; 7 feel out

sound reflection: 4 echo; 13 reverberation

sound structure: 10 morphology

sound system: 11 audio system

soup: 5 broth, puree; 7 pottage; 8 consomme

soupcon: 3 dab, jot; 4 dash, hint, mite, whit; 5 pinch, speck

souped-up car: 5 racer; 6 hot rod; 8 stock car; 9 racing car

soup to nuts: 8 full meal

soup up: 5 hop up

sour: 3 off; 4 dark, dour, glum, turn; 5 false, moody, sharp, short, taint; 6 biting, bitter, morose, rancid, sullen, turned; 7 acetify, acidify, acidity, caustic, ferment; 8 embitter, sourness, tartness; 9 acidulate; 11 acrimonious

source: 4 germ, rise, root, seed; 5 cause; 6 author, origin, reason; 7 element; 9 informant, reference

sourdine: 4 mute; 7 sordino

S

sour grapes: 9 false plea
sour grass: 6 sorrel
sour gum: 8 black gum
sour-gum family: 9 Nyssaceae; 12 tupelo
  family
sourish: 4 tart; 5 tangy; 6 lemony
sour mash whiskey: 8 sour mash
sourness: 4 sour; 7 acidity; 8 tartness; 9 sulkiness; 10 moroseness, sullenness
sour orange: 8 bigarade; 12 bitter orange; 13
  Seville orange
sourpuss: 6 grouch; 7 killjoy
soursop: 9 guanabana apple
sourwood: 10 sorrel tree
Sousa: 15 John Philip Sousa
sousaphone: 4 tuba
souse: 3 dip, sop; 4 duck, dunk, lush, soak; 5
  douse, dowse, drown; 6 boozer, drench,
  plunge, soaker
soused: 5 drunk; 10 inebriated
south: 8 due south
South: 5 Dixie; 11 Confederacy
South American bullfrog: 7 crapaud
south by east: 3 SbE
south by west: 3 SbW
South Carolina: 13 Palmetto State
South Dakota: 11 Coyote State; 18 Mount
  Rushmore State
southeast: 2 SE
southeast by east: 4 SEbE
southeast by south: 4 SEbS
southern arrow wood: 9 arrow wood
southern beech: 14 evergreen beech
southern beech fern: 14 broad beech fern
southern blue flag: 13 Iris virginica
southern buckthorn: 7 shittim; 10 mock
  orange; 11 shittimwood
Southern crab apple: 13 flowering crab
Southern Cross: 13 Crux Australis
southern cypress: 11 bald cypress; 12
  swamp cypress
southern magnolia: 7 bull bay
southern maidenhair: 9 Venushair; 13
  Venus'-hair fern
southern porgy: 4 scup; 12 southern scup
southern red oak: 9 turkey oak; 11 swamp
  red oak
Southern Rhodesia: 8 Zimbabwe
southern white cedar: 12 white cypress
southern yellow pine: 9 pitch pine; 11
  Georgia pine; 12 longleaf pine
South Frigid Zone: 9 Antarctic
South Korea: 15 Republic of Korea
southpaw: 5 lefty
south-polar: 9 Antarctic
south southeast: 3 SSE
southwest: 2 SW
southwest by south: 4 SWbS
southwest by west: 4 SWbW
south wind: 7 souther

souvenir: 5 relic, token; 7 memento; 8 keepsake; 11 memorabilia
sovereign: 5 regal; 7 monarch
sovereignty: 4 rule; 5 reign; 8 autonomy
sovietism: 7 Marxism; 8 Leninism; 9 communism; 10 bolshevism
Soviet Union: 4 USSR
sow: 3 pig; 4 seed; 5 plant
sowbane: 12 red goosefoot
sowbelly: 8 salt pork
sow one's wild oats: 8 live hard
sow thistle: 11 milk thistle
soy: 4 soya; 7 soybean
sozzled: 6 splash
spa: 6 hot tub; 11 resort hotel
space: 3 gap; 4 area, span, time; 5 blank; 6
  volume; 7 expanse, separate
spacecraft clock time: 4 SCLK
spacecraft event time: 4 SCET
spaceman: 9 astronaut, cosmonaut
space vehicle: 9 spaceship; 10 spacecraft
space walk: 3 EVA
spacious: 4 wide; 5 ample, roomy
spackle: 6 cement; 7 plaster
spade: 6 shovel
spadefish: 9 angelfish
spades: 4 suit
Spain: 6 Espana
span: 6 bridge; 7 measure; 8 distance
spangle: 7 sparkle
spaniel: 6 lapdog
Spanish American: 6 Latino; 8 Hispanic
Spanish broom: 12 Spanish gorse, weaver's
  broom
Spanish burgoo: 11 olla podrida
Spanish elm: 5 cypre; 8 salmwood; 10
  princewood
Spanish garlic: 8 sand leek; 9 rocambole
Spanish lime: 5 genip, ginep; 10 honey
  berry, mamoncillo
Spanish mackerel: 6 saurel
spanish needles: 11 beggar-ticks
Spanish psyllium: 8 fleawort
Spanish tea: 8 wormseed
spank: 5 smack; 6 strike
spanking pace: 9 swift pace
spanner: 6 wrench
span of time: 6 period; 8 interval
spar: 3 box; 7 compete
Sparaxis tricolor: 10 wandflower
spare: 5 extra, waive, avoid; 6 afford, let off,
  meager
spareribs: 8 pork ribs
spare time: 8 free time; 11 leisure time
spare-time activity: 5 hobby
sparing of words: 8 taciturn
spark: 5 flash; 6 ignite; 7 flicker
sparkle: 4 glow; 5 flash, light; 7 glitter
sparkling water: 7 seltzer; 8 club soda; 9
  soda water
spark off: 4 trip; 7 trigger; 8 activate
sparrow: 7 dunnock

sparrow hawk: 7 kestrel
sparse: 4 thin
spartan: 7 ascetic, austere
Spartina pectinmata: 11 slough grass
Spartium junceum: 12 Spanish broom,
    weaver's broom
spasm: 5 cramp; 10 convulsion
spasmodic: 6 fitful
spasmodic laryngitis: 5 croup
spastic: 9 spasmodic
spat: 4 spit, tiff; 6 bicker; 7 quarrel
spate: 4 rush, slew; 5 flood, surge
spathe flower: 9 peace lily; 13 spathiphyllum
spatterdock: 7 cow lily
spatula: 5 spool; 7 epaulet
spavined: 8 swelling
spawn: 4 seed; 7 product; 8 generate; 9 offspring
spay: 5 alter; 6 neuter
speak: 4 talk; 5 orate, utter; 7 address, lec-
    ture; 9 verbalize
speak daggers: 10 vituperate
speaker: 8 exponent
speak ill of: 9 deprecate
speaking: 8 locution, parlance
speak one's mind: 7 be frank; 8 be candid,
    speak out
speak volumes: 4 tell
spear: 6 weapon, impale
spearfish: 6 marlin
special: 5 extra; 7 certain; 8 especial, spe-
    cific; 10 particular, individual
special effect: 10 stage trick
specialty: 5 forte; 8 strength; 9 expertise; 11
    strong point
species: 7 variety
specific: 5 clear; 7 certain; 9 exclusive; 10
    individual, particular
specification: 4 spec; 9 condition, provision,
    selection
specific gravity: 7 density
specify: 6 define; 7 signify; 9 explicate
specimen: 6 sample; 7 example; 8 instance
specious: 5 showy; 9 plausible
speck: 3 bit, dot; 5 pinch; 8 particle
speckle: 5 fleck
speckled trout: 10 brook trout
spectacle: 4 pomp, show; 5 sight; 7 pageant
spectacled: 8 monocled
spectacles: 8 eyeglass
spectacular: 8 dramatic, striking; 10 theatri-
    cal; 11 outstanding
spectator: 6 viewer; 7 watcher, witness; 8
    observer, onlooker; 9 bystander
specter: 5 ghost; 6 spirit; 7 phantom
spectrogram: 8 spectrum
spectrometer: 13 monochrometer
spectroscopy: 6 optics; 10 chromatics
specular: 10 mirrorlike
speculate: 5 think; 6 wonder, ponder; 7
    reflect
speculation: 5 guess; 7 surmise
speculative: 11 theoretical

speech: 4 talk; 5 words; 7 address, lecture,
    dialect; 8 language
speechless: 4 dumb; 6 silent
speed: 4 fast; 5 haste, swift; 7 rapidly
speed indicator: 11 speedometer
speed up: 7 quicken; 8 expedite; 10 accelerate
speedwell: 8 veronica
spelaeologist: 9 spelunker
spell: 4 term, tour, turn, word; 5 charm; 6
    trance
spellbind: 9 fascinate; hypnotize
spelling: 11 orthography
spelunk: 4 cave
spence: 6 pantry; 7 buttery
spend: 5 use up; 6 outlay; 7 deplete
spendthrift: 10 squanderer
spent: 8 consumed; 9 exhausted
Spergula arvensis: 10 corn spurry
Spergularia rubra: 9 sea spurry; 10 sand
    spurry
sperm: 5 semen; 12 spermatozoan
spermatophyte: 9 seed plant; 10
    phanerogam
spermophile: 6 gopher
Spermophilus: 8 Citellus; 13 genus Citellus;
    17 genus Spermophilus
sperm whale: 8 cachalot; 10 black whale
spew: 4 ooze; 5 erupt, exude, vomit
sphacele calycina: 11 pitcher sage
Sphacelotheca reiliana: 8 head smut
sphagnum: 7 bog moss; 8 peat moss
sphalerite: 10 zinc blend
Spheniscus demersus: 14 jackass penguin
Sphenodon punctatum: 7 tuatara
sphere: 3 orb; 4 ball; 5 globe, orbit; 6 planet
sphingid: 8 hawk moth; 10 sphinx moth
Sphyrna tiburo: 10 bonnethead, shovelhead;
    11 bonnet shark
spicate: 5 spike
spice: 4 dash, zest; 6 flavor, relish, season; 7
    piquant
spiceberry: 8 boxberry, teaberry; 10 coral-
    berry; 11 wintergreen; 12 checkerberry
spice tree: 10 pepperwood; 12 Oregon myr-
    tle; 14 mountain laurel
spick-and-span: 8 spotless
spider: 4 lota, toby; 6 chatti, mussuk, urceus;
    7 terrine; 8 schooner [U.S.]; 9 arachnoid
spider fern: 10 ribbon fern; 11 spider brake
spiderflower: 6 cleome
spider mite: 11 tetranychid
spider web: 6 cobweb
spiderwort: 9 dayflower
spiel: 5 pitch; 9 line of gab
spiff up: 6 spruce
spigot: 3 tap; 5 valve; 6 faucet
spike: 5 laced; 6 impale; 7 fortify
spike heel: 12 stiletto heel
spiky: 6 pointy
spile: 4 bung, pile, plug

S

spill: 4 fall, slip, pour; 6 tumble; 7 divulge
spillikin: 9 jackstraw
spill the beans: 4 blab
Spilogale putorius: 12 spotted skunk
spin: 4 reel, turn; 5 twirl, twist, whirl; 6 gyrate, rotate
spinach beet: 5 chard; 8 leaf beet
spinach mustard: 11 tendergreen
spinal column: 4 back; 5 spine; 8 backbone
spin a long yarn: 6 ramble
spindle: 4 axle, pole
spindle horn: 10 forest goat
spindly: 4 lank
spindrift: 5 spray; 8 sea spray
spine: 4 back; 7 spicule [Biol]; 8 backbone, vertebra
spineless: 7 gutless
spinet: 4 harp; 5 piano
spin-off: 9 by-product
spinster: 7 old maid
Spinus pinus: 9 pine finch; 10 pine siskin
Spinus tristis: 9 goldfinch; 10 yellowbird
spiny: 6 thorny
spiny anteater: 7 echidna; 8 anteater
spiracle: 4 vent
Spiraea prunifolia: 12 bridal wreath
spiral: 4 coil, worm; 5 helix, whorl
spirant: 9 fricative
spire: 7 steeple
spirit: 4 soul, mood; 5 ghost
spirited: 5 peppy, zippy; 6 bouncy, lively, spunky
spiritless: 4 dark; 6 dismal, gloomy, somber; 7 joyless; 8 dejected
spirit of the times: 9 zeitgeist [Ger]
spirits: 5 cheer, drink; 9 good humor
spiritual: 4 holy; 6 devout
spiritualist: 6 medium
spirituality: 5 faith; 6 clergy
Spirodela polyrrhiza: 13 great duckweed, water flaxseed
spit: 6 saliva, skewer; 11 expectorate
spite: 4 hurt; 6 malice
spiteful: 4 mean; 7 hateful; 10 vindictive
spitfire: 6 dynamo
spitting snake: 8 ringhals, rinkhals
spittoon: 8 cuspidor
Spizella arborea: 11 tree sparrow
Spizella pusilla: 12 field sparrow
splanchnic: 8 visceral
splash: 5 douse, spray; 6 deluge, drench
splashy: 5 showy; 9 pomposity; 11 ostentation
splatter: 6 splash; 7 spatter
splay: 5 slope, slant
splayfoot: 8 flatfoot
spleen: 6 malice; 10 melanchoy
splendid: 7 blazing, glowing, radiant; 8 dazzling, glorious
splendor: 4 pomp; 6 luster, bright; 9 brilliant

splenetic: 5 spite; 6 fuming, raging
splenic fever: 7 anthrax
splice: 4 link; 5 unite
splint: 3 rod, set
splinter: 5 shred; 6 sliver; 7 shatter
split: 3 axe, cut; 4 tear; 6 divide
split hairs: 7 nitpick, quibble
split second: 4 wink; 5 flash, jiffy; 7 instant
split the difference: 11 give and take
splitworm: 10 potato moth
splotch: 6 blotch; 7 splodge
splurge: 5 glitz; 7 indulge; 11 extravagant
splutter: 7 stammer
Spodoptera frugiperda: 12 fall armyworm
spoil: 4 baby, foil, loot, harm, ruin; 5 botch, prize, decay
spoiler: 6 raider
spoilsport: 7 killjoy
spoke: 3 cog, bar
spoken: 5 vocal; 7 uttered; 11 articulated
spokesperson: 5 voice
Spondias mombin: 7 hog plum; 12 yellow mombin
sponge: 4 bilk, wipe; 5 luffa; 8 parasite
sponginess: 8 porosity
sponsor: 6 patron; 9 supporter
spontaneous: 5 ad lib; 7 natural; 9 impromptu, impulsive
spontaneous generation: 11 abiogenesis
spoof: 4 hoax; 6 parody; 7 mockery, takeoff
spook: 5 creep, ghost
spooky: 5 eerie; 8 skittish
spool: 4 reel; 6 bobbin
spoon: 5 ladle; 6 dipper
spoonbill catfish: 6 goujon, mudcat
spoonflower: 6 tannia, yautia; 7 malanga
spoonful: 6 capful; 8 mouthful
sporadic: 6 sparse; 12 periodically
Sporobolus cryptandrus: 12 sand dropseed
Sporobolus poiretii: 9 blackseed, smut grass; 11 carpet grass
sport: 3 fun; 4 game; 5 boast; 7 athlete, feature, contest; 8 mutation
sportive: 6 ardent; 7 playful
sports car: 6 wheels; 8 roadster
sports coat: 6 blazer; jacket
sportsman: 4 jock; 7 athlete
sportsmanlike: 5 clean
spot: 3 dot; 4 blot; 5 smear, stain; 7 blemish; 8 location, position
spotless: 5 clean; 8 unsoiled
spotted bat: 10 jackass bat
spotted cranesbill: 12 wild geranium
spotter: 6 finder; 9 keep watch
spotty: 4 thin; 6 uneven
spouse: 4 mate; 7 partner; 13 married person
spout: 4 gush; 5 spurt
Spraguea umbellatum: 8 pussy-paw
sprain: 4 turn; 5 twist
sprawl: 10 stretch out
spray: 3 jet; 4 gush; 5 splash; 8 atomizer
spray can: 7 aerosol

spread: 3 gap; 5 ranch, range, scope, sweep, widen; 6 expand, unfold
spread-eagle: 6 sprawl
spread like wildfire: 7 overrun; 15 run like wildfire; 18 disperse themselves
spread out: 6 unfold; 7 develop
spree: 4 lark; 5 binge, fling; 8 escapade
sprig: 4 twig; 6 branch
sprightly: 5 light; 8 pleasant
spring: 3 fly, hop; 4 flit, jump, leap; 5 amble, vault; 6 bounce
spring a leak: 5 crack
spring back: 7 rebound
Springfield: 17 capital of Illinois
springiness: 4 give; 6 spring; 10 elasticity
springlike: 6 vernal
spring squill: 8 sea onion
spring up: 4 grow, rise; 6 appear
sprinkle: 4 dust
sprinkling: 4 dash; 5 tinge, touch
sprint: 4 dash
spritzer: 10 wine cooler
sprocket: 3 cog
sprout: 3 bud; 5 shoot; 6 branch
spruced up: 8 tidied up; 9 dressed-up
spruce pine: 9 lodgepole, shore pine; 11 black spruce
sprung: 5 leaky
spry: 5 agile, quick; 6 nimble
spud: 5 tater; 6 potato
spunk: 4 guts; 5 heart, nerve; 6 mettle; 9 fortitude
spur: 4 prod; 6 motive
spuriousness: 9 falseness
spurn: 4 kick, jilt; 6 reject, slight; 7 discard
spur-of-the-moment: 9 impromptu
spurt: 5 spout; 6 squirt
sputnik: 9 satellite
sputter: 5 spray, spurt; 7 spatter
sputum: 6 phlegm
spy: 5 watch, snoop
squab: 3 fat; 5 plump; 7 cushion
squabble: 4 feud, fuss, spat, tiff; 6 bicker
squad: 4 unit, band, crew, team; 5 group
squadron: 8 division; 12 flying column
squalid: 5 dirty; 6 sordid
squall: 4 yell; 6 scream, storm
squamous cell carcinoma: 8 cancroid
squander: 5 waste; 7 scatter; 8 disperse
square: 4 area, fair, four, just; 5 equal
square block: 4 cube
square miles: 5 acres
square off: 3 vie; 4 spar; 6 settle; 7 compete, contest; 9 reconcile
squash: 4 mash; 5 crush, smash; 7 squelch
squash racket: 3 bat
squat: 6 crouch
Squatina squatina: 8 monkfish; 9 angelfish; 10 angel shark
squatter: 6 nester; 7 settler
squawk: 4 moan; 5 gripe; 7 screech; 8 complain; 9 bellyache

squeak: 3 yap; 6 squeal, escape
squeal: 3 rat, yap; 4 oink
squealer: 6 canary; 7 tattler; 8 betrayer, informer
squeamish: 6 queasy; 11 thin-skinned
squeeze: 3 hug; 5 crush; 7 embrace, squelch; 8 compress
squeeze box: 9 accordion
squeeze out: 5 eject; 6 eke out, squirt
squelch: 5 crush, quell
squid: 8 calamari, calamary
squiggle: 8 curlicue
squill: 6 scilla
squinch: 6 flinch
squint: 7 askance
squire: 4 page
squirm: 4 worm; 6 wiggle, writhe
squirrel away: 5 cache, hoard, stash
squirrelfish: 7 pinfish
squirreltail grass: 13 foxtail barley
squirt: 5 eject, spout, spurt; 9 pip-squeak
squish: 7 squelch
sr.: 5 elder, older
St. Augustine grass: 12 buffalo grass
St. Elmo's fire: 6 corona; 9 corposant; 12 electric glow
St. George's: 16 capital of Grenada
St. Lawrence: 16 St. Lawrence River
St. Louis: 16 Gateway to the West
stab: 3 cut, dig, jab; 4 poke, prod; 5 knife, slash; 6 pierce
stable: 6 stalls, static; 7 durable; 8 constant, dovecote; 9 horse barn; 10 unchanging
stableboy: 5 groom
staccato: 6 abrupt; 10 disjointed
Stachys sylvatica: 10 dead nettle; 11 hedge nettle
stack: 3 lot, pot, wad; 4 heap, mass, pile; 5 batch
stadium: 4 bowl; 5 arena
staff: 4 club; 5 baton, stick, shaft; 7 faculty; 9 personnel
staff of life: 5 bread
staff vine: 7 waxwork; 11 bittersweet
stag: 3 spy; 7 go alone
stage: 4 tier; 5 level, phase, acted; 7 arrange
stagger: 4 stun, sway; 5 waver; 6 careen, totter; 7 stumble; 8 bewilder
staghorn moss: 11 ground cedar
stagnant: 4 idle, calm, dead; 5 quiet; 8 doldrums
stag party: 6 smoker
staid: 5 grave, sober; 7 serious
stain: 3 dye; 4 tint, soil; 5 paint, smear, taint; 7 varnish
stair: 4 step
stake: 3 bet; 4 post, risk; 5 wager
stale: 3 old; 4 fade; 5 passe, weary; 9 tasteless
stalemate: 7 impasse

S

Stalin: 12 Joseph Stalin
Stalinism: 7 tyranny; **12** dictatorship
stalk: 3 dog; **4** hunt; **5** hound; **6** shadow, follow
stall: 3 pew; **4** barn; **5** delay, booth, stand; **7** cubicle
stallion: 5 horse
stalwart: 5 hardy; **6** strong
stamina: 9 endurance, toughness; **12** staying power
stammer: 6 falter; **7** stutter
stamp: 4 seal, type; **6** emboss; **7** postage; **10** acceptance
stamp collecting: 9 philately
stamp out: 6 put out; **8** snuff; **10** trample out
stanch: 4 stem; **5** allay; **10** extinguish
stand: 4 post, base, bear; **5** abide, booth; **6** endure; **7** opinion; **8** position
standard: 4 norm; **5** gauge; **9** criterion; **10** touchstone
standardized: 7 similar
standard operating procedure: 3 SOP
standard transmission: 10 stick shift
stand by: 4 hold; **7** support
stand corrected: 9 take blame
stand-down: 10 suspension
stand firm: 6 resist; **7** hold out
stand for: 4 mean; **6** intend; **7** signify; **8** indicate
stand in: 10 substitute
standing: 8 stagnant
stand in awe of: 4 fear
standing for: 6 symbol
standoff: 3 tie; **4** draw; **8** dead heat
standoffish: 5 aloof
stand out: 5 bulge, excel; **8** protrude
stand pat: 8 hold firm
standpoint: 9 viewpoint
stand shoulder to shoulder: 7 collude; **8** conspire; **10** fraternize
stand to reason: 9 be certain
standup comedian: 6 gagman
stand up to: 9 withstand
Stanleya pinnata: 11 desert plume; **12** prince's-plume
stannic sulfide: 10 mosaic gold
stapelia: 13 carrion flower; **14** starfish flower
stapes: 7 stirrup
staple: 5 stock; **6** secure
star: 3 ace, sun, wiz; **4** lead, whiz; **10** preeminent
star apple: 7 caimito
starboard: 5 right
starch: 6 amylum, gluten
starched: 5 stiff
starch wheat: 5 emmer; **13** two-grain spelt
stare: 4 gaze
stare down: 7 outface
starfish flower: 8 stapelia; **13** carrion flower
starflower: 10 sleepy dick; **15** summer snowflake

star fruit: 9 carambola
stargaze: 5 dream
stargazer: 10 astronomer, lotus eater; **11** uranologist
star-glory: 10 Indian pink; **11** cypress vine
star grass: 9 colic root; **10** devil grass; **11** Bahama grass, scutch grass, unicorn root; **13** windmill grass
stark: 4 bare; **5** bleak; **6** barren; **7** austere
stark raving mad: 4 wild; **7** berserk, frantic; **8** frenetic; **9** possessed
starring: 5 prima; **7** leading
Stars and Stripes: 8 Old Glory
star-shaped: 8 asteroid
Star-Spangled Banner: 8 Old Glory
start: 2 go; **4** move; **5** begin; **6** embark; **8** commence
star-thistle: 7 caltrop
starting point: 6 origin; **9** beginning
startle: 4 jump; **5** alarm, scare; **7** disturb; **8** frighten, surprise
starvation: 6 famine; **7** drought
starve: 4 fast; **5** crave; **8** famished; **9** emaciated
stash: 5 hoard
stasis: 10 stagnation
state: 3 say; **4** aver, land, tell, term; **5** shape; **6** affirm, assert, status; **7** declare, express; **8** condition
state's evidence: 10 eyewitness
stately: 5 grand, noble, proud; **6** formal; **8** imposing, majestic
statement: 6 report; **7** account; **9** assertion; **11** affirmation, declaration
stateroom: 5 cabin
statesman: 8 diplomat; **10** politician
static: 5 still; **6** stable; **8** inactive; **10** motionless
statice: 11 sea lavender; **13** marsh rosemary
statics: 8 dynamics
station: 4 base, post, rank, site; **5** depot [U.S.]; **8** position, terminal
stationary: 6 static
statism: 9 communism
statistical: 6 random
statistician: 7 actuary
statistics: 11 probability
stator: 5 rotor
statue: 8 figurine; **9** sculpture
statue maker: 8 sculptor
stature: 6 height
status: 5 state; **8** position; **9** condition
status quo: 8 standing
statute: 3 act, law
staunch: 5 sound, solid; **8** faithful; **9** steadfast
stave: 4 rung
stave off: 5 avert, avoid; **7** deflect
stay: 4 rest; **5** pause, lodge; **6** detain
stay-at-home: 8 domestic
staying power: 7 stamina
stay of execution: 8 reprieve

stay on: 6 remain; **8** continue
stead: 4 lieu; **5** place; **8** position
steadfast: 4 firm; **6** steady; **7** staunch; **10** conviction, unbendable, unshakable
steady: 4 even, calm; **6** stable, 7 uniform; **8** constant
steak au poivre: 11 pepper steak
steal: 3 bag, **5** sneak; **6** pilfer, thieve; **7** bargain, purloin
stealth: 7 slyness; **10** sneakiness; **13** imperceptable
steam: 4 fume; **5** smoke; **6** exhale
steam bath: 5 sauna; **6** hot tub
steamed: 7 boiling
steam organ: 8 calliope
steamy: 5 muggy; **6** sticky; **8** tropical
stearin: 6 elaine [Chem]
steatite: 9 soapstone
steatocystoma: 3 wen; **9** pilar cyst; **13** sebaceous cyst
Steatornis caripensis: 7 oilbird; **8** guacharo
steel: 4 gird, iron; **5** blade, nerve, sword
steel oneself for: 7 prepare
steel-plated: 9 armor-clad
steep: 4 brew, high, soak
steeple: 5 spire
steeple chase: 4 race
steer: 4 bull; **5** guide; **6** direct; **8** maneuver
steer clear of: 4 shun; **5** avoid
stein: 7 beer mug
stellar: 4 star; **5** prima; **7** leading
Stellaria holostea: 8 starwort; **10** stitchwort
Stellaria media: 15 common chickweed
stem: 3 jib; **4** halt, root; **5** stalk
stem canker: 7 rosette; **10** russet scab; **12** little potato
stemless: 11 acaulescent
stemmed: 7 cauline
stench: 4 reek; **5** stink; **7** malodor
Stenocarpus salignus: 8 beefwood
Stenocarpus sinuatus: 9 wheel tree; **13** firewheel tree
stenography: 6 scribe, typist; **9** shorthand
Stenotaphrum secundatum: 12 buffalo grass
stenotic: 8 narrowed; **11** constricted
Stenotomus aculeatus: 4 scup; **12** southern scup; **13** southern porgy
stentorian: 7 booming
step: 4 move, pace; **5** march, stair; **6** stride, stroke
step by step: 9 gradually
step dancing: 7 hoofing
step down: 4 quit; **8** abdicate; **11** leave office
Stephanotis floribunda: 9 waxflower; **17** Madagascar jasmine
step in: 9 interfere; **10** substitute
stepping-stone: 6 bridge
step up: 8 escalate
Stercorarius parasiticus: 10 arctic skua
Sterculia acerifolia: 9 flame tree
Sterculia apetala: 10 Panama tree

Sterculia foetida: 9 kalumpang; **10** Java olives
stereo: 10 two-channel
stereotype: 4 type; **5** stamp; **10** categorize, pigeonhole
sterile: 4 arid; **6** barren; **7** aseptic; **9** infertile
sterling: 4 pure; **5** noble
stern: 4 rear; **5** harsh, rigid; **6** strict, severe
Sterna hirundo: 10 sea swallow
sternum: 10 breastbone
sternutation: 6 sneeze
stertor: 5 snore
stet: 5 let be; **7** leave it
Stetson: 6 fedora
stevedore: 8 dockhand
stew: 4 sulk; **5** brood; **6** grudge, seethe, simmer
steward: 6 manager
stewardess: 6 manager
stewed: 6 boiled
Sticherus flabellatus: 7 fan fern; **12** umbrella fern
stick: 4 stay; **5** baton, cling; **6** adhere, crutch; **7** stay put
sticker: 5 label
sticking out: 7 jutting; **8** protruding
stick-in-the-mud: 6 stodgy; **8** slowpoke
stickle: 7 scruple
stickler: 5 poser
stick on: 5 affix
stick one's neck out: 8 run a risk
stick-to-itiveness: 8 tenacity; **11** persistence
stick to one's guns: 9 stand firm
stickup: 5 heist
sticky: 5 gluey, clammy, gooey; **7** awkward
Stictopelia cuneata: 10 turtledove
stiff: 4 firm, hard; **5** rigid, stern
stiff gentian: 8 ague weed
stifle: 4 bury, stop; **5** choke; **6** muffle; **7** smother; **8** suppress
stigma: 4 mark; **5** brand
stile: 5 stair
stiletto: 6 dagger
still: 3 but, yet; **4** calm, hush, lull; **5** allay, quiet; **6** silent; **8** tranquil; **11** nonetheless
still photo: 8 snapshot
stilt: 4 pile; **8** longlegs
stilted: 5 lofty; **7** pompous
stimulate: 4 rush, stir; **6** arouse, excite, incite
sting: 3 con, gyp; **4** bite, itch, pain
stingaree-bush: 12 chaparral pea
stingy: 4 mean; **7** miserly; **10** ungenerous
stink: 4 reek; **5** smell; **6** stench; **7** malodor
stinker: 3 bum; **5** crumb
stink fly: 9 chrysopid; **13** green lacewing
stinking cedar: 10 Torrey tree; **11** stinking yew
stinking chamomile: 7 mayweed; **9** dog fennel

S

stinking gladwyn: 7 gladdon; 11 gladdon
  iris; 12 stinking iris
stinking hellebore: 9 bear's foot; 10 setter-
  wort
stinking nightshade: 7 henbane
stinking wattle: 6 gidgee
stinking weed: 11 coffee senna, styptic
  weed; 12 mogdad coffee
stinkpot: 10 musk turtle
stinky: 5 lousy; 6 rotten
stint: 4 task; 5 shift
stipendiary: 8 salaried; 11 compensated
stipple: 3 dot; 4 etch; 6 scrape
stipulate: 5 terms; 6 clause; 7 qualify, specify; 9 condition
stir: 3 ado; 4 fuss; 5 churn; 6 bustle, flurry,
  arouse; 7 agitate; 9 commotion
stirpes: 5 birth, stock; 7 lineage; 8 heritage,
  pedigree
stirrup: 6 stapes
stitch: 3 sew; 4 tack; 5 crick; 6 twinge
Stizostedion vitreum: 7 walleye; 10 jack
  salmon
stock: 3 lot; 4 fund; 5 breed, trunk; 6 supply;
  7 lineage; 9 inventory, livestock
stockade: 3 pen
stock car: 5 racer; 6 hot rod
stock dealer: 6 broker
stockholder: 10 shareowner
Stockholm: 15 capital of Sweden
stocking: 5 socks; 7 hosiery
stocky: 5 thick; 7 compact; 8 heavyset
stodgy: 4 drab, dull; 5 mossy; 6 stuffy; 8
  pedantic
stoical: 5 great, lofty; 7 exalted
stokehold: 10 boiler room
stole: 4 robe; 5 scarf
stolid: 9 impassive
stomach: 4 bear; 5 belly, stand, tummy; 7
  abdomen, gastric
stomach upset: 9 dyspepsia; 11 indigestion
stone: 3 gem; 4 clot, rock
stonecutter: 5 mason
stone mimicry plant: 10 living rock; 13 living granite
stone root: 8 richweed; 9 horse balm
stooge: 4 dupe; 5 dweeb; 6 flunky, puppet
stoolpigeon: 4 fink; 5 sneak; 6 canary, snitch
stoop: 3 bow; 4 bend; 6 crouch
stop: 4 quit, halt; 5 cease; 6 desist
stopgap: 9 makeshift
stopper: 3 cap; 4 plug
store: 4 shop, save, stow; 5 cache, depot,
  stock
storm: 4 rage; 5 force; 6 attack, squall; 7
  paroxysm
story: 4 tale, yarn; 5 floor, level; 7 account; 9
  narration
stout: 3 fat; 5 hardy, plump; 6 portly, sturdy
stove: 5 range

stow: 4 load, pack; 5 store
straddle: 4 span, trim; 9 astride on
strafe: 5 blast, shell
straggle: 4 rove; 5 stray; 6 ramble
straight: 5 erect; 6 direct, linear, unbent
straightaway: 3 now; 5 quick; 6 at once,
  prompt
straighten out: 4 tidy; 5 clear; 6 neaten,
  reform; 7 clarify,
straightforward: 4 open; 5 frank; 6 candid
straightlaced: 4 prim; 7 prudish
strain: 3 tax; 4 pull; 6 extend, stress, sprain;
  7 distort, lineage; 8 ancestry
strainer vine: 5 luffa; 8 rag gourd; 11 sponge
  gourd
strait: 4 pass; 8 juncture; 9 difficult
strand: 5 chain; 6 string
stranded: 4 lost; 7 isolated, marooned
strand wolf: 10 brown hyena
strange: 3 odd; 5 alien; 6 exotic; 7 bizarre,
  curious, unusual; 8 uncommon
stranger: 5 alien
strangle: 5 choke; 6 stifle; 7 smother, throttle
strap: 3 tie; 4 lash, whip, bind; 9 constrict
strapped: 5 needy
strapping: 5 beefy, burly, husky; 6 brawny; 8
  muscular
strategy: 4 plan; 6 scheme
stratified: 6 graded, ranked
Stravinsky: 21 Fyodorovich Stravinsky
straw: 4 husk; 5 chaff, stalk
straw man: 8 front man
stray: 4 roam; 5 drift; 6 depart, wander; 7
  vagrant
streak: 3 ray; 5 gleam, strip; 6 trace
stream: 4 pour; 5 brook, creek, surge
streamer: 6 banner; 7 pennant
stream orchid: 10 chatterbox
streetcar: 4 tram; 7 trolley
strength: 5 force, might; 6 degree, extent,
  metier; 7 potency; 8 vitality
strengthen: 4 tone; 7 fortify; 8 energize
strenuous: 7 arduous
stress: 6 strain; 7 tension; 8 emphasis, pressure
stretch: 4 flex; 5 spell; 6 extend, elastic; 7
  distend, expanse
strewn: 9 scattered
striation: 4 band; 5 stria; 6 streak, striae
stricken: 7 touched; 8 affected
strict: 4 hard; 5 harsh, rigid, stern; 6 severe;
  9 demanding
strictly: 6 purely
stricture: 11 restriction; 12 constriction
stride: 4 pace, step; 5 tread; 8 footfall, footstep
strident: 4 loud; 7 blatant; 9 clamorous; 10
  vociferous
strife: 7 discord
strike: 3 hit; 6 delete, cancel, attain; 7 inflict;
  12 disadvantage
strike out: 3 fan; 6 retire
strike up: 4 pipe, play; 5 start

striking: 7 amazing; 8 dramatic 10 notice-able

string: 3 tie; 4 line; 5 twine; 6 thread

stringent: 5 harsh; 6 strict; 8 rigorous

strings attached: 5 catch

string up: 4 hang

stringy: 4 wiry; 5 ropey; 6 sinewy

strip: 3 gut; 4 bare, slip; 5 piece, shear; 6 remove; 7 relieve, undress

stripe: 4 band, rule; 6 design, streak

striped dogwood: 9 moosewood; 12 striped maple; 14 goosefoot maple; 18 Acer pennsylvanicum

striped killifish: 7 mayfish

striped squirrel: 6 hackee; 14 ground squirrel

striper: 8 rockfish; 11 striped bass

stripes: 7 chevron

stripling: 5 youth

strip mine: 3 pit; 10 excavation

striptease: 8 stripper

strive: 3 try, vie; 5 reach; 6 strain; 7 attempt

Strix aluco: 8 tawny owl

Strix nebulosa: 12 great gray owl

Strix varia: 9 barred owl

strobe: 5 flash

stroke: 3 pet, row; 4 dash, line; 5 slash; 8 apoplexy

stroll: 5 amble; 7 saunter; 9 promenade

stroller: 12 baby carriage

stromateid: 10 butterfish

Strombus gigas: 10 giant conch

strong: 5 stout, tough; 6 sturdy; 7 intense

strong-arm: 5 bully

stronghold: 4 fort, hold

strong point: 5 forte; 8 strength; 9 specialty

strong-willed: 8 resolute

Strongylodon macrobotrys: 8 jade vine; 14 emerald creeper

strontium: 2 Sr

struck dumb: 7 stunned; 9 stupefied

structure: 11 composition; 12 architecture, organization

struggle: 5 fight, match; 6 battle; 7 compete, contest

strut: 6, prance, sashay; 7 show off, swagger

Struthio camelus: 7 ostrich

strychnine: 8 nicotine

stub: 3 nub; 5 stump; 6 scrape

stubble: 5 stalk, straw; 10 extinguish

stubborn: 9 obstinate, tenacious; 10 inflexible

stucco: 5 compo; 6 ground; 7 plaster, spackel

stuck-up: 9 conceited

stud: 4 hunk; 5 rivet

student: 5 pupil

studious: 8 diligent

study: 4 read, work; 5 learn; 6 ponder, survey; 7 analyze, examine; 8 consider

stuff: 3 jam; 4 cram; 5 gorge, shove; 6 things

stuffed grape leaves: 6 dolmas

stuffed shirt: 10 fuddy-duddy

stuffy: 6 stodgy; 8 stifling; 10 oppressive

stumble: 4 slip, trip; 6 falter; 8 bewilder, confound

stump: 4 stub; 5 stomp; 6 podium; 8 bewilder, confound

stun: 4 daze, numb; 7 astound

stunning: 9 arresting; 10 staggering

stunt: 3 nip; 5 dwarf; 6 limit

stunt man: 6 double

stupefy: 4 stun; 5 amaze

stupendous: 8 colossal

stupid: 4 dolt, dumb, slow; 6 simple

stupor: 4 daze; 5 shock

sturdy: 5 hardy, solid; 6 strong; 7 staunch

Sturt pea: 9 desert pea

stutter: 6 falter; 7 stammer

sty: 3 den; 6 pigpen; 12 eye infection

style: 3 way; 4 chic; 5 genre, trend; 6 manner

stylish: 4 chic, cool; 6 modish, trendy

Stylophorum diphyllum: 9 wood poppy

stymie: 5 block

Styphelia humifusum: 11 groundberry; 14 cranberry heath; 15 native cranberry

styptic: 10 astringent

styptic weed: 11 coffee senna; 12 mogdad coffee, stinking weed

Styrax obassia: 8 snowbell

suasible: 9 easy-going; 11 convincible, persuadable

suave: 6 smooth; 8 debonair, polished

sub: 4 hero; 5 hoagy, U-boat, wedge; 6 hoagie; 7 grinder

subconscious: 10 subliminal

subcontract: 7 farm out

subdue: 4 curb, tame, hush; 5 quiet; 7 conquer

subject: 4 case, open; 5 field, issue, theme, topic; 6 expose, matter; 7 content

subjugate: 7 conquer

sublime: 4 fine, rich; 5 grand, lofty; 9 dignified

submarine: 3 sub; 4 hero; 5 hoagy, U-boat, wedge; 6 hoagie; 7 grinder

submaxilla: 4 jowl; 7 jawbone

submerge: 4 sink; 6 engulf; 7 immerse

submission: 8 yielding; 10 compliance

submit: 3 bow; 5 enter, put in; 7 present

suboptimal: 9 imperfect

subordinate: 4 less; 5 lower; 8 inferior; 9 underling

suborn: 5 bribe; 6 induce

subpoena: 4 writ; 7 summons; 8 citation

subscribe: 4 sign; 6 assent; 7 support, receive

subscriber: 6 reader

subsequent: 4 next; 5 after, later; 9 following

subservient: 7 slavish; 10 submissive

subside: 6 lessen, settle

subsidiary: 7 adjunct; 9 auxillary

subsidization: 5 grant

substance: 4 core, meat; 5 heart, means; 7 content, essence, meaning; 10 usefulness

S

substantial: 6 hearty; **7** massive

substantiate: 6 affirm, verify; **7** confirm, support

substantive: 4 real; **5** meaty

substitute: 5 proxy; **6** backup, relief; **7** stand in

substratum: 10 foundation

subterfuge: 9 deception

subtle: 4 fine; **6** slight; **12** unnoticeable

subtract: 6 deduct

suburbanite: 8 commuter

suburbs: 8 environs

subvert: 7 ruinous; **9** undermine

subway: 4 tube; **5** metro; **11** underground

succeed: 6 follow

succeed in: 8 manage to

success: 6 winner; **8** achiever

succession: 6 series; **8** sequence

successor: 4 heir

succinct: 4 neat; **5** exact; **7** compact

succor: 3 aid; **4** help; **6** assist, relief

succulent: 4 lush; **5** juicy

succumb: 3 die; **5** yield

suck: 4 draw; **5** nurse; **6** absorb

sucker: 4 dupe, fool; **8** lollipop, parasite

sucking fish: 6 remora

sucking up: 9 groveling

sucrose: 9 beet sugar, cane sugar

sudden: 6 abrupt; **7** instant; **9** immediate

suds: 4 beer, foam, head; **5** froth; **6** lather

sue: 3 woo; **5** plead; **8** litigate

suffer: 4 ache, bide, hurt, meet; **6** endure; **7** sustain

sufferer: 6 martyr

suffice: 2 do; **7** satisfy; **8** be enough

suffix: 4 tail; **6** append, ending

suffocate: 3 gag; **5** choke; **6** stifle; **7** smother; **10** asphyxiate

suffrage: 4 poll, vote; **5** voice; **6** ballot

suffuse: 6 infuse

sugar: 4 dear, love; **5** honey; **10** saccharide

sugar apple: 4 anon

sugarcoat: 5 candy, glaze

suggest: 4 hint; **5** evoke; **6** advise, prompt, remind; **7** propose

suit: 2 do; **3** fit; **4** case; **5** adapt, befit

suitable: 6 proper, worthy

suitcase: 3 bag; **6** valise

suite: 5 rooms

suitor: 4 beau

sulfur bottom: 9 blue whale

sulfurous: 4 acid; **5** acerb, acrid; **6** bitter

sulk: 4 pout; **5** brood

sullen: 4 dour, glum, grim; **5** moody, sulky

Sullivan: 14 Arthur Sullivan

sully: 4 soil; **5** stain; **6** defile

sultan: 4 king

sultry: 5 close, humid; **6** stuffy; **7** sensual

sum: 3 add, all; **5** tally, total; **6** amount

summary: 7 concise

summer cypress: 8 firebush; **9** belvedere; **11** burning bush

summer sweet: 10 pepper bush, white alder

summit: 3 tip, top; **4** apex, peak; **5** crown; **8** pinnacle; **9** elevation

summon: 4 cite; **5** rally; **6** muster

summons: 4 cite, writ; **8** citation, subpoena

sump: 4 mire, sink, wash; **8** cesspool

sumptuary: 6 fiscal; **9** financial

sumptuous: 6 deluxe; **7** opulent; **8** splendid; **9** luxurious; **11** magnificent

sun: 4 star

sunburn: 3 tan

sunder: 5 split; **8** separate

sundial lupine: 10 Indian beet

sundry: 7 various; **13** miscellaneous

sunfish: 4 mola

Sunflower State: 6 Kansas

sunglasses: 6 shades

sunk: 6 buried, ruined; **7** done for; **10** suppressed

sunny: 3 gay; **5** clear, palmy, shiny; **6** bright, cheery; **8** sunshine

sunrise: 4 dawn

sunset: 4 dusk; **7** sundown

Sunshine State: 7 Florida

sun spurge: 8 wartweed, wartwort; **10** devil's milk

sunstone: 6 jasper; **7** cat's eye; **8** hematite; **9** moonstone; **10** aventurine, bloodstone

super: 3 ace; **4** tops; **6** tiptop

superb: 4 fine, rich; **5** grand, showy; **7** optimal; **11** magnificent

supercilious: 5 proud

superficial: 5 empty; **7** evasive, shallow, surface; **8** external

superfluous: 8 needless; **9** pointless; **11** unnecessary

superimpose: 7 overlay

superior: 5 major; **6** higher, master; **7** greater; **8** higher-up

superlative: 7 supreme; **9** excellent, excessive

supernal: 8 ethereal, heavenly

supernatural: 6 occult

supersede: 7 replace; **8** supplant

superstar: 4 idol

superstition: 6 belief

supervise: 6 manage; **7** monitor, oversee

supine: 5 inert, prone; **8** inactive

supper: 6 dinner; **11** evening meal

supplant: 6 cut out; **7** replace; **9** supersede

supple: 4 soft; **5** lithe

supplement: 6 append; **8** addendum; **10** complement

supply: 4 fund, help; **5** cater, issue; **7** provide

support: 4 back, base, bear, hold; **6** uphold; **8** advocate

supporter: 6 backer, friend, patron

suppose: 3 say; **5** guess, think; **7** imagine, surmise; **8** theorize; **9** speculate

supposititious: 10 fictitious; **11** conjectural; **12** hypothetical

suppress: **5** check, arrest, stunt; **6** stifle
suppression: **10** constraint, inhibition
supreme: **4** head; **6** utmost; **8** dominant, foremost, greatest
surcharge: **3** fee
surd: **9** voiceless; **10** irrational
sure: **4** safe; **6** secure; **7** assured, certain
surf: **5** waves
surface: **4** coat; **8** exterior
surfeit: **6** excess; **7** satiate
surge: **4** rush; **5** swell
surgery: **9** operation
surgical dressing: **5** gauze
surgical seam: **6** suture
surinam cherry: **7** acerola
surly: **4** ugly; **5** cross, testy; **6** crabby, touchy; **8** volatile; **9** irascible
surmise: **5** guess; **6** theory; **7** suppose, suspect; **9** postulate; **10** conjecture
surmount: **5** excel; **8** overcome
surpass: **5** excel, outdo, outgo; **6** exceed
surplus: **5** extra, spare; **6** excess
surprise: **7** startle
surreal: **9** dreamlike
surrender: **4** cede, fall; **5** yield; **6** give up, resign
surreptitious: **6** secret; **8** stealthy; **11** clandestine
surrogate: **5** proxy; **6** deputy, foster; **9** alternate
surround: **6** border, circle; **7** enclose
surveil: **7** monitor
survey: **7** inspect; **11** opinion poll
survive: **4** last, live; **5** exist; **6** endure; **7** outlast, outlive
susceptible: **4** open; **6** liable; **7** subject
suspect: **5** guess; **7** accused, suppose, surmise; **10** suspicious
suspend: **4** hang; **5** defer, waive; **6** freeze
suspense: **7** waiting; **8** abeyance; **10** indecision
suspicion: **5** hunch; **6** notion; **7** inkling; **9** intuition
sustain: **6** suffer, uphold; **7** nourish, prolong
sustenance: **4** food; **11** nourishment
susurrous: **10** whispering
sutler: **11** provisioner
suture: **5** sew up; **6** stitch; **12** surgical seam
svelte: **5** lithe; **6** supple; **7** slender
swab: **3** mop; **4** wipe; **6** sponge
swaddle: **4** wrap; **6** swathe
swag: **3** arc; **5** curve, droop; **6** dangle; **10** stolen item
swagger: **5** strut; **7** bravado, haughty; **8** arrogant; **9** conceited
swain: **6** suitor; **7** servant
swallow: **3** eat; **5** drink; **6** devour; **7** consume
swallow wort: **9** celandine
swamp: **4** sink; **5** flood, marsh; **7** wetland
swamp cottonwood: **11** downy poplar
swamp hare: **10** canecutter
swamp hickory: **9** bitternut

swamp laurel: **8** swamp bay; **9** bog kalmia, bog laurel
swampy: **5** mucky, muddy; **6** marshy
swan: **4** roam; **5** dally; **7** declare
swank: **4** chic
swan song: **7** last act
swap: **6** barter, switch; **8** exchange
swarm: **4** teem; **5** throng, crowd
swarthy: **4** dark
swash: **7** bluster, swagger
swashbuckler: **10** adventurer
swat: **5** whack; **6** thwack
swathe: **4** gird; **6** sheath; **7** swaddle
sway: **5** swing; **8** persuade; **9** influence
swear: **3** vow; **4** aver, avow, cuss, oath; **5** curse; **6** affirm
sweat: **4** fret, pant; **5** flush, sudor, water; **6** effort; **7** swelter; **8** perspire
sweater: **6** jersey
sweep: **3** arc; **5** erase, broom, brush, field, range; **7** wipe out
sweeping: **5** broad
sweet: **4** nice; **5** fresh; **6** tender; **7** dessert, sugared
sweet acacia: **6** cassie; **8** huisache; **9** flame tree; **10** mimosa bush; **11** sweet wattle
sweetbread: **8** pancreas
sweet cicely: **5** myrrh
sweet clover: **7** melilot
sweet cup: **9** bell apple; **10** water lemon; **16** yellow granadilla
sweet flag: **7** calamus; **8** flagroot; **10** myrtle flag
sweetheart: **4** beau; **6** darling
sweetmeat: **4** plum
sweet pepper: **7** paprika, pimento
sweet potato: **3** yam; **7** ocarina
sweet-scented: **5** aroma, spicy, sweet; **6** savory; **7** odorous; **9** fragrance
sweet-talk: **4** coax; **5** charm; **6** cajole
sweet wattle: **6** cassie; **8** huisache; **9** flame tree; **10** mimosa bush; **11** sweet acacia
swell: **6** peachy, expand; **8** excellent
swelter: **5** flush, sweat; **6** steamy
Swertia speciosa: **12** green gentian
swerve: **4** turn, veer, warp; **5** curve; **7** deviate
Swift: **13** Jonathan Swift
swift: **4** fast; **5** fleet, quick, rapid; **6** speedy
swig: **4** gulp, slug, soak; **5** swill, drink
swill: **4** swig, wash; **5** drink; **6** guzzle
swim: **5** float
swimmer: **6** bather
swimmingly: **8** smoothly
swimming pool: **10** natatorium
swindle: **3** con, gyp; **4** bilk, scam; **5** cheat
swine: **3** hog, pig, sow; **4** boar
swing: **4** sway, wave; **5** waver; **8** brandish
swipe: **4** lift; **5** steal; **6** pilfer
swirl: **4** purl; **5** twirl, whirl
switch: **4** swap; **8** exchange; **9** transpose

S

switch-ivy: 9 dog hobble, dog laurel
swivel: 5 pivot
swollen: 5 puffy; **7** bloated; **8** expanded; **9** distended
swollen-headed: 4 vain; **7** swollen; **9** conceited, egotistic
swoon: 5 faint; droop; **7** rapture
swoop: 6 pounce
sword: 5 blade, brand, steel
sword lily: 4 flag, iris; **8** gladiola
swordsman: 6 fencer
swordtail: 7 helleri; **9** topminnow
sworn: 7 pledged
sycamore: 6 platan; **8** lacewood; **9** plane tree; **10** buttonwood
sycophant: 8 parasite
syllabus: 7 program; **10** curriculum
sylvan: 6 wooded
Sylvia communis: 11 whitethroat
Sylvilagus aquaticus: 9 swamp hare; **10** canecutter; **11** swamp rabbit
Sylvilagus floridanus: 17 eastern cottontail
Sylvilagus palustris: 9 marsh hare; **11** swamp rabbit
symbol: 4 sign; **6** emblem; **10** indication
symbolic: 9 nonverbal
symbolize: 6 denote; **7** betoken, signify; **8** indicate
symmetrical: 4 even; **7** uniform; **8** balanced

sympathize: 7 console; **9** empathize; **10** understand; **11** commiserate
sympathy: 6 warmth; **8** response; **11** consolation
symphony: 9 orchestra
Symphoricarpos alba: 8 waxberry; **9** snowberry
Symphoricarpos orbiculatus: 10 coralberry; **13** Indian currant
Symplocarpus foetidus: 11 polecat weed; **12** foetid pothos, skunk cabbage
symptom: 4 sign
symptomatic: 7 typical
synagogue: 6 temple
Synanceja verrucosa: 9 stonefish
synchronic: 11 descriptive
synchronize: 7 coexist
syncopated: 11 abbreviated
syncope: 5 faint; **8** collapse
syndicate: 6 cartel; **8** alliance
synonym: 10 equivalent
synonym finder: 9 thesaurus
synopsis: 5 brief; **7** summary; **8** abstract
syntax: 7 grammar
synthesis: 5 union; **6** fusion; **7** uniting, combine; **8** blending
synthetic: 7 man-made
Syringa vulgaris: 11 common lilac
syringe: 6 needle; **10** hypodermic
syrupy: 5 thick; **6** sticky
system: 5 order; **11** arrangement; **12** organization
Syzygium aromaticum: 5 clove; **9** clove tree

T

T: 2 tb, MT; **5** tonne; **8** terabyte; **9** metric ton
T.B: 12 tuberculosis
TV ad: 2 ad; **10** commercial
Ta: 8 tantalum
Taal: 7 the Taal; **9** Afrikaans
tab: 4 chit; **5** check; **6** tab key
tabard: 4 cape; **6** tippet; **7** mantlet; **8** mantelet, mantilla
tabasco pepper: 9 hot pepper; **9** red pepper
tabbouleh: 7 tabooli
tabby: 5 queen; **7** brinded, brindle; **8** brindled, tabby cat
tabernacle: 3 ark; **4** kirk
Tabernacles: 6 Succos; **7** Sukkoth
tabes: 7 wasting
tabita: 7 she goat; **9** Nanny goat
table: 4 menu, mesa; **5** board, defer, remit; **6** marble, pillar, put off, shelve, tablet; **7** cuisine, set back; **8** postpone

tableau: 5 piece [Fr], scene; **6** canvas; **7** picture
table d'hote: 4 menu; **5** table; **7** cuisine, potluck; **8** ordinary, prix fixe
tableland: 7 plateau
table napkin: 9 serviette
table of contents: 7 outline
tablespoon: 5 ladle, spoon; **6** dipper, shovel, trowel
tablet: 3 pad; **4** pill, slab; **5** table; **6** marble, pellet, pillar; **7** lozenge
table talk: 4 chat; **8** chitchat
table tennis: 8 ping-pong
tabloid: 3 rag; **5** sheet
taboo: 3 ban, bar, out; **4** tabu; **6** enjoin, forbid, outlaw; **7** embargo; **8** disallow, forefend, prohibit; **9** forbidden, interdict, proscribe; **10** prohibited
tabooli: 9 tabbouleh
tabulate: 5 grade, index, tally; **6** digest;

8 graduate; **9** catalogue, enumerate; **10** tabularise, tabularize

tabulator key: 3 tab; **6** tab key

tacamahac: 10 hackmatack; **12** balsam poplar

tachometer: 4 tach

Tachyglossidae: 7 echidna

tacit: 6 latent, silent; **7** implied; **8** implicit; **10** understood

taciturnity: 7 reserve; **8** curtness; **9** reticence

tack: 3 sew, tat; **4** brad, chop, knit, lace, nail, turn, veer, warp; **5** evert, sheet, shift; **6** button, shroud, stitch, swerve; **7** deviate, shuffle, tacking; **8** saddlery; **9** mainsheet, turn aside; **10** stable gear; **12** weather sheet

tackiness: 3 tat; **6** sleaze; **9** cheapness

tacking: 4 tack; **5** baste; **7** basting

tackle: 3 rig; **6** take on, take up; **7** rigging; **8** embark in, embark on, tackling; **9** undertake; **11** fishing gear

tack on: 5 tag on; **6** append, hang on

tacky: 4 loud; **5** cheap, flash, gaudy, gluey, gooey, tatty; **6** brassy, flashy, garish, sticky, tawdry, trashy; **8** adhesive, gimcrack; **12** meretricious

tact: 4 gust; **5** gusto; **7** finesse; **8** delicacy, prudence; **9** tactility; **10** discretion, refinement; **11** tactfulness

tactful: 5 civil; **6** adroit, poised; **7** politic; **9** strategic; **10** diplomatic

tactic: 4 ploy; **5** trick; **6** device; **8** maneuver; **9** stratagem; **11** machination

tactician: 10 politician, strategist

tactile: 5 touch; **6** haptic; **7** tactual, feeling

tactless: 5 inept; **9** untactful; **12** undiplomatic

Tadarida: 8 guano bat; **3** genus Tadarida

Tadjik: 5 Tajik; **7** Tadzhik; **10** Tajikistan

tadpole: 8 polliwog, pollywog

taenia: 5 tenia; **6** fillet

taffeta weave: 10 plain weave

taffrail log: 8 screw log; **9** patent log

taffy: 5 candy

taffy apple: 10 candy apple; **12** candied apple, caramel apple

Taft: 17 William Howard Taft

tag: 3 dog, rag; **4** fine, mark, much, tail; **5** chase, label, mulct, scrap, shred, tag on, track, trail; **6** amerce, append, docket, sconce, tack to, tag end, tatter, ticket; **7** go after, tag line; **8** splinter

tagalong: 8 hanger-on

Tagamet: 10 cimetidine

tag end: 3 rag, tag; **5** shred; **6** tatter

Tagetes erecta: 11 big marigold; **12** genus Tagetes

tag line: 3 tag; **7** gag line; **9** laugh line, punch line

tag thorn: 7 bristle

taguan: 9 flying cat; **12** flying marmot

Tagus: 10 Tagus River

Tai: 4 Thai; **7** Siamese

Tai Dam: 8 Black Tai

tail assembly: 4 tail; **9** empennage

tailboard: 8 tailgate

tail bone: 6 coccyx

tailcoat: 5 tails; **8** white tie; **9** dress suit, full dress; **10** tuxedo coat

tailed: 7 caudate

tail fin: 3 fin; **9** caudal fin; **11** vertical fin

tailflower: 9 anthurium

tailing: 6 debris; **8** detritus; **9** shadowing; **10** fine powder, talus slope

tail lamp: 8 rear lamp; **9** rear light, taillight

taillike: 6 caudal

tail off: 7 drop off, dwindle, fall off; **8** peter out, taper off

Tai Long: 4 Shan

tailor: 3 cut, sew; **4** snip, trim; **5** style; **6** sartor; **7** bespoke; **8** milliner, shoehorn, bespoken; **9** costumier, customize, millinery; **10** tailor-make, custom-make; **11** haberdasher

tailorbird: 18 Orthotomus sutorius

tailpiece: 8 vignette; **9** head piece [Fr]

tail race: 4 race; **7** millrun; **8** head race, millrace

tailspin: 4 spin

taint: 4 blot, blur, sour, spot; **5** cloud, sharp, short, stain, sully; **6** biting, bitter, debase, defile, infect; **7** caustic, corrupt, crabbed, doggish, pollute, tarnish; **8** impurity, venomous, virulent; **9** attainder, blot sully, pollution, sarcastic, trenchant; **10** adulterate, defilement

tainted: 3 bad; **4** high, weak; **5** fusty; **6** effete, faulty, flawed, putrid, rancid, rotten, wasted; **7** corrupt, damaged, decayed, defiled, gone bad, peccant, rotting, spotted, stained, sullied, touched, unsound; **8** blighted, cankered, flyblown, polluted, vitiated

Taipei: 25 capital of Nationalist China

taira: 5 tayra

Taiwan: 5 China; **7** Formosa; **15** Republic of China; **16** Nationalist China

Taiwanese: 3 Min; **4** Amoy; **7** Chinese; **8** Formosan

takahe: 8 notornis

take: 3 aim, ask, eat, get, see; **4** deal, fare, feed, fill, film, haul, have, hire, hold, lead, make, need, pack, read, rent, tell; **5** admit, adopt, bring, carry, catch, claim, exact, grasp, guide, issue, learn, lease, savvy [U.S.], shoot, study, train, trust, use up; **6** accept, assume, choose, convey, demand, devour, direct, engage, follow, ingest, look at, master, occupy, payoff, remove, return, select, submit, take in, take it, take on, take up; **7** acquire, call for, charter, collect, conduct, consume, contain, involve, make out, pick out, require, swallow, take aim, takings, undergo; **8** consider, contract, proceeds, take away, work well; **9** bear fruit, captivate, fascinate, subscribe

T

take "for better or for worse": 3 wed; 5 marry; 7 espouse

take aback: 4 stun; 5 floor, shock; 7 startle; 8 ball over, surprise

take advantage of: 4 dupe, fool, gull, hoax; 5 trick; 6 take in; 8 cash in on, profit by; 9 bamboozle; 10 capitalize

take after: 6 follow

take a breather: 4 rest; 7 breathe, respire

take a bullet: 6 be shot; 7 get shot

take a chance: 4 risk; 6 chance, gamble, hazard; 8 run a risk; 9 adventure

take a firm stand: 6 insist

take a gander: 4 look, peep; 5 glint; 6 glance

take a liking to: 6 take to; 8 cotton to

take a peep: 3 pry; 4 peep, peer

take a powder: 8 skip town

take away: 4 take; 6 remove; 7 bear off, detract

take away one's breath: 4 stun; 7 petrify, stagger, stupefy; 8 bewilder; 9 electrify, fascinate; 10 strike dumb; 11 flabbergast

take back: 5 unsay; 6 return; 7 retract, swallow; 8 withdraw; 9 repossess

take by assault: 11 take by storm

take captive: 6 arrest, take up; 9 apprehend

take care: 3 see; 4 look, mind, hold, keep; 6 attend; 8 take heed, maintain, preserve; 9 be heedful, be prudent

take charge of: 6 arrest, take up; 8 take hold; 9 apprehend

take comfort: 9 take heart

take command: 8 take hold; 10 take charge; 11 take control; 12 take the reins

take counsel: 7 consult

take down: 4 note, rase, raze; 5 level, lower, shame; 6 humble

take effect: 4 play, work; 5 avail; 6 answer, strain, strike; 7 perform, quicken, support, sustain; 8 maintain; 9 play a role; 11 be effective

take exception: 8 object to; 9 challenge

take fire: 4 burn, fire; 5 erupt; 6 fire up, fly out, ignite, kindle; 7 explode, flame up, flare up; 9 catch fire

take flight: 3 fly; 4 flee

take for: 4 deem, hold; 6 view as

take form: 4 form; 6 spring; 9 take shape

take for a spin: 8 road-test; 9 test drive

take for granted: 6 assume; 7 believe, dare say, presume; 9 speculate

take forty winks: 8 take a nap

take fright: 9 take alarm

take hold: 3 hug; 4 hold, grab; 5 catch, clasp; 7 possess; 8 take root; 9 close with, get hold of; 10 take charge; 11 take control, catch hold of

take home: 9 bring home

take in: 3 cod, see; 4 draw, dupe, earn, fool, gain, have, hoax, hold, make, suck, take, view; 5 admit, adopt, catch, clear, grasp, slang, sop up, touch, trick, watch; 6 absorb, embody, follow, imbibe, ingest, invite, master, reduce; 7 abridge, collect, consume, contain, curtail, embrace, realize, receive, shorten; 8 overhear; 9 bamboozle; 10 abbreviate, comprehend

take in hand: 4 rear; 5 breed; 6 ground, tackle, take up; 7 bring up, nurture, prepare

take into account: 5 allow; 7 involve

take in water: 5 bilge

take issue: 6 differ; 8 disagree

take it easy: 4 rest; 5 relax; 6 repose; 7 sit back

take it from the top: 6 resume; 10 recommence

take its course: 4 hold, keep; 5 abide, ensue, issue, start; 6 arrive, pursue

take leave: 4 quit; 6 depart

take liberties: 5 usurp; 6 assume; 7 presume; 8 arrogate, feel free

take money: 4 draw

taken: 8 ingested; 11 interpreted

taken aback: 8 startled; 9 surprised

take on: 5 hired; 9 recruited

take note of: 9 emphasize, underline; 10 accentuate

take notice: 3 see; 4 look, mark, view; 6 notice, regard, remark; 7 observe

taken out: 5 drawn; 7 removed; 9 extracted; 10 extricated

taken over: 6 seized; 9 condemned; 10 confiscate; 11 confiscated; 12 appropriated

taken up: 7 haunted; 8 obsessed; 9 engaged in; 11 preoccupied

taken with: 4 gaga; 5 crazy, dotty; 6 in love, soft on; 7 smitten; 8 enamored; 10 infatuated

takeoff: 5 spoof; 6 parody, sendup; 7 charade, lampoon, mockery; 8 travesty; 9 burlesque

take off: 4 bate, doff, give, part, soar; 5 allow, start, tower; 6 ascend, deduct, depart, reduce

take on: 4 hire, meet, play, sink, take; 5 admit, adopt, droop; 6 accept, assume, employ, engage, tackle; 7 acquire, despond; 9 encounter, undertake

take one's stand: 6 assert, assume, insist; 7 require, contend; 8 arrogate

take one's time: 3 lag; 5 drawl; 6 dawdle, slouch; 8 hang back

take out: 4 draw, omit, pull; 6 ask out, except, get out, remove, rub out, unpack; 7 excerpt, exclude, extract

takeover: 4 coup; 6 putsch; 9 coup d'etat

take over: 4 bear; 5 adopt, annex, buy up, seize, usurp; 6 absorb, accept, assume, borrow, repeat; 7 capture, conquer, relieve; 8 arrogate; 11 appropriate

take pity: 7 feel for; 8 have pity, show pity; 11 commiserate

take place: 3 hap; 4 go on, pass; 5 occur; 6 happen

take precautions: 12 guard against

take precedence: 7 precede; 9 come first

take root: 6 settle

take shape: 4 form; 6 spring

take soundings: 5 plumb, sound; 6 fathom

take stock: 5 audit; 6 size up; 8 overhaul; 10 scrutinize

take the field: 8 campaign

take the lead: 4 head, lead; 6 herald

take the place of: 7 replace; 8 supplant; 9 supersede

take the plunge: 6 dare it, risk it

take the pulse: 3 see; 5 check; 7 feel out; 8 check out, sound out; 13 test the waters

take the stand: 6 attest; 7 testify, witness

take the sun: 8 sunbathe

take the wind out of one's sails: 9 undermine

take time: 4 bide, stay, wait; 5 tarry

take time off: 5 relax; 6 unbend; 7 slacken

take to: 5 fancy

take turns: 9 alternate

take up: 4 draw, sorb, suck, take; 5 adopt, scoop, sop up, start; 6 absorb, arrest, assume, borrow, resume

take warning: 4 ware; 6 beware; 9 keep watch

take wing: 4 flit; 6 ascend

takin: 7 gnu goat

taking exception: 7 protest; 8 demurral; 9 cavilling, objection

taking hold: 7 seizing; 8 grasping; 10 prehension

taking into account: 10 solicitude; 13 consideration

taking into one's hand: 8 clasping, grasping, gripping

taking over: 10 succession

taking part: 13 participation

taking possession: 9 occupancy; 10 occupation

talapoin: 5 druid

talcum: 4 talc

tale: 3 fib; 4 yarn; 5 count, story, tally; 7 account, recital; 9 narration, narrative

talebearer: 6 gossip; 7 tattler; 8 telltale; 10 taleteller, tattletale; 12 blabbermouth

talent: 4 gift, turn, able, cute; 5 forte, parts; 6 clever, gifted; 7 ability, faculty, talents, endowed; 8 capacity, felicity; 9 endowment; 10 capability, cleverness, felicitous; 12 habilitation; 13 qualification

talesman: 7 juryman

Talinum: 8 rock pink; 12 genus Talinum, pigmy talinum

talipes: 8 clubfoot

talipot: 11 talipot palm

talisman: 5 charm; 6 amulet; 7 philter

talismanic: 5 weird; 6 mystic; 10 cabalistic; 11 incantatory

talk: 4 blab, sing; 5 mouth, orate, peach, speak, utter; 6 babble, speech, tattle; 7 lecture, talking, discuss; 8 colloquy, converse, locution, parlance, speaking; 9 discourse, verbalize; 11 negotiation; 13 confabulation

talkative: 5 gabby, talky; 6 blabby, chatty; 7 verbose; 9 expansive, garrulous; 10 bigmouthed, logorrheic, loquacious

talked of: 8 renowned; 10 celebrated

talking picture: 6 talkie

talk of the town: 4 talk; 8 prestige

talk over: 7 discuss

talk with one in private: 9 tete-a-tete

tall: 4 high; 5 lofty; 7 eminent, exalted, highest; 8 elevated; 9 marvelous, most lofty; 10 improbable, marvellous

Tallahassee: 16 capital of Florida

tallboy: 7 highboy

tall buttercup: 12 tall crowfoot

tallied: 9 tabulated; 10 enumerated

Tallinn: 16 capital of Estonia

tallith: 11 prayer shawl

tall mallow: 6 cheese; 10 high mallow; 12 cheeseflower

tall meadow grass: 8 false oat; 9 French rye; 12 tall oat grass

tallow: 4 lard, suet; 6 grease

tall ship: 4 sail [sing & pl], ship; 6 sailer; 10 windjammer

tall talk: 3 gas; 5 bluff; 7 bombast; 8 vaporing; rodomontade; 13 magniloquence

tally: 3 add, fit, hit, run, sum; 4 chip, chop, gibe, jibe, tale, tell; 5 add up, agree, check, count, match, score; 6 billet, letter, number; 7 counter, listing, respond, summate; 8 tabulate; 9 duplicate, enumerate, reckoning; 10 correspond, numeration; 11 enumeration, itemization

talon: 4 claw, nail; 5 fangs; 8 clutches

talus: 6 debris; 8 astragal, detritus, oddments; 9 anklebone; 10 astragalus

tam: 5 tammy; 11 tam-o'-shanter

tamandu: 8 tamandua

tamanoir: 7 ant bear; 13 giant anteater, great anteater

tamarack: 10 black larch

tamarao: 7 tamarau

tamarillo: 10 tree tomato

tamarin: 8 leoncita; 10 lion monkey; 12 lion marmoset

tamarind: 9 tamarindo

tambour: 10 tambourine

Tamburlaine: 5 Timur; 9 Tamerlane

tame: 3 lay; 4 bald, calm, cool, damp, dull, flat, hush, lull, meek, slow, swag; 5 abate, allay, blunt, heavy, quell, quiet, slack, sober, still, tamed, vapid; 6 deaden, feeble, jejune, meager, pacify, rebate, smooth, soothe, subdue; 7 appease, assuage, break

T

in, chasten, compose, slacken; **8** domestic,
sluggish, suppress; **9** alleviate; **11** acclimatize, domesticate, tranquilize

tameless: 4 fell; **7** untamed; **8** ravening; **9**
truculent; **10** incendiary; **12** semibarbaric

Tamias: 6 hackee; **11** genus Tamias

Tammuz: 6 Dumuzi; **7** Thammuz

tamp: 4 pack; **6** tamper

tamper: 4 tamp, moil; **5** bribe; **6** meddle,
monkey, suborn; **7** qualify

tamphitheater: 6 circus; **10** hippodrome

tam-tam: 4 gong

Tamus: 10 genus Tamus; **11** black bryony;
13 black bindweed

tan: 4 burn, fawn, foxy; **5** tawny, topaz; **6**
bronze, maroon, suntan; **7** sunburn; **9**
chocolate

tang: 3 nip; **4** fang, zest; **5** brier, savor,
smack, sting, thorn; **6** flavor, nettle, relish,
savour; **7** bramble; **8** piquance, sapidity; **9**
sharpness, tanginess; **10** aftertaste; **12** blad-
derwrack

tangelo: 4 ugli; **9** ugli fruit

tangency: 7 contact

tangential: 10 digressive

tangible: 4 real; **5** handy, ready, solid, valid;
8 palpable, physical, sensible; **9** available,
competent, touchable; **10** ponderable; **11**
substantial; **12** commensurate, satisfactory

Tangier peavine: 10 Tangier pea

tangle: 3 mat; **4** drag, knot; **5** ravel, snarl,
sweep, kinky; **6** ruffle, tousle; **7** embroil; **8**
dishevel, entangle, involved, tortuous; **10**
convoluted; **12** complication

tanglebush: 11 desert olive

tangor: 10 king orange; **12** temple orange

tangy: 4 tart; **6** lemony; **7** sourish; **9** lemonlike

tank: 4 pond; **5** oiler; **6** cooler, tanker; **7** cistern, tankful

tank suit: 7 maillot

tanner: 8 sixpence

tanner's cassia: 6 avaram

tannia: 6 yautia; **7** malanga; **11** spoonflower

tannic acid: 6 tannin

tansy: 7 benweed, ragweed, ragwort

tantalize: 3 cod, dun, rag; **4** bait, ride, twit; **5**
rally, taunt, tease, spicy; **7** bedevil, crucify,
torment, annoyer, piquant; **8** tempting; **9**
frustrate; **10** appetizing

tantamount: 10 equivalent

Tantric: 7 Tantrik

tantrum: 3 fit; **5** scene

Taoism: 3 Tao; **6** Daoism

tap: 3 beg, bug, dab, pat, rap; **4** bore, pink,
slap; **5** knock, spill; **6** faucet, spigot, strike;
7 exploit, hydrant, solicit, wiretap; **8** tap-
dance; **9** intercept

tap dancer: 6 hoofer

tape: 4 band, list, slip; **5** spill, strip; **6** fillet,

record, riband, ribbon, taping; **8** tapeline; **9**
videotape

tape drive: 9 transport

tape grass: 8 eelgrass; **10** wild celery

taper: 4 slim, wick; **5** point; **6** candle, narrow; **7** sharpen; **8** tapering; **9** constrict, narrowing

taper off: 6 fizzle; **7** drop off, dwindle

tapestry: 5 arras, tapis; **7** hanging

tapestry moth: 10 carpet moth

tapeworm: 7 cestode

tapioca plant: 4 gari; **6** manioc; **7** mandioc;
8 mandioca; **13** bitter cassava

Tapirus indicus: 11 Indian tapir; **12** Malayan
tapir

tap out: 5 drain, empty; **6** absorb, finish; **7**
exhaust, drained, depleted, expended; **9**
exhausted

tap-root: 4 root; **5** trunk; **6** etymon; **7**
nucleus

taps: 9 lights-out

tar: 3 gob; **4** salt; **5** pitch; **6** seaman; **7**
asphalt, bitumen, mariner, old salt, residue;
8 seafarer

taradiddle: 3 fib; **4** bosh, tale, tosh; **5** drool,
story; **6** bounce, humbug; **7** baloney,
boloney, crammer, twaddle, whopper; **8**
tommyrot; **10** bilgewater

tarakan: 5 roach; **9** cockroach, cucaracha
[Sp]

tarantula: 18 European wolf spider

tardy: 4 late, slow; **6** behind; **7** belated; **8**
backward, sluggish, untimely; **10** behind-
hand, unpunctual

tare: 5 cheat; **6** darnel

tares: 5 weeds

target: 3 aim; **4** butt, mark, prey; **5** aim at,
place, point; **6** direct, object, quarry; **9**
objective

Tar Heel State: 13 North Carolina, Old
North State

tariff: 3 tax; **4** dues, duty, levy

tarmac: 7 asphalt, macadam; **10**
macadamize, tarmacadam; **11**
macadamized

tarn: 4 lake, loch, mere, pond, pool, slab; **5**
broad, plash; **6** puddle

tarnish: 4 blot, blur, daub, spot; **5** smear,
smoke, stain, sully, taint; **6** defile, slaver,
smudge; **7** damaged, spotted, stained, sullied, tainted; **8** flyblown, maculate; **10**
decolorize, besmirched, defilement; **11**
achromatize

taro: 4 dalo, edda, eddo; **7** cocoyam,
dasheen

tarpaulin: 4 tarp; **5** quilt, sheet; **7** blanket; **8**
bedsheet, coverlet; **9** comforter; **11** counterpane

tarragon: 8 estragon

tarriance: 9 lingering

Tarrietia: 10 silver tree; **14** genus Tarrietia

tart: 4 bawd; **5** sharp, tangy; **6** lemony;

7 cocotte, cyprian, sourish, trollop; **9** lemonlike
tartan: 5 plaid
tartar: 6 dragon; **8** calculus
Tartar: 5 Tatar; **11** Mongol Tatar
Tartarean: 6 Hadean; **9** Plutonian
tartar steak: 13 cannibal mound
Tartarus: 4 Styx; **7** Cocytus, Gehenna; **12** Stygian creek
tartness: 4 sour; **6** temper; **8** acerbity, sourness; **9** crossness, petulance, procacity, testiness; **10** crabbiness, protervity; **11** grouchiness; **12** captiousness, irascibility, irritability
tarweed: 7 gumweed; **8** gum plant; **9** rosinweed
Tashkent: 7 Taskent; **14** capital of Uzbek
task: 3 job, tax; **4** care, wear, work; **5** chore [U.S.], exact, labor; **6** charge, errand, impose, strain, **7** agendum, mission, project; **8** business, exercise; **10** assignment, commission, employment, engagement, occupation; **11** undertaking
taskmaster: 7 monitor; **9** moderator
tassel: 4 knot
taste: 3 try; **5** prove, savor, smack; **6** flavor, sample, try out; **7** tasting, sipping; **8** mouthful, penchant; **9** gustation, relishing; **10** preference; **11** discernment; **12** appreciation, predilection
tasteful: 4 neat; **7** refined; **10** savoriness; **12** pleasingness
tasty: 4 cute, good, nice; **6** dainty, savory; **9** delicious, palatable; **10** delectable
tat: 3 sew; **4** knit, lace, tack; **6** button, sleaze, stitch; **9** cheapness, tackiness; **10** intertwine
tater: 4 spud; **6** potato; **11** white potato
tatou: 4 tatu
tatouay: 9 cabassous
tatter: 3 rag, tag; **4** inch, seed; **5** crumb, patch, shred; **6** tag end; **7** flitter, fritter; **9** scantling
tattily: 7 cheaply; **13** inexpensively
tattle: 3 rat; **4** blab, sing, talk; **5** clack, peach, prate, utter; **6** babble, gabble, gibber, gossip, piffle, snitch, squeal; **7** breathe, chatter, singing, telling, twaddle
tattoo: 8 drumming, drumroll; **10** beat of drum
tatty: 4 loud; **5** cheap, flash, gaudy, ratty, tacky; **6** brassy, flashy, garish, shabby, tawdry, trashy; **8** gimcrack; **12** meretricious
taught: 3 set; **4** fast, firm, taut; **5** close, tense, tight; **6** secure; **7** trained, tutored; **8** schooled; **10** instructed; **11** overwrought
taunt: 3 boo, cod, rag; **4** bait, gibe, gird, hiss, hoot, jeer, jibe, mock, quip, ride, twit, wipe; **5** fling, rally, scoff, sneer, tease; **6** deride; **7** barrack, snigger; **8** flouting, ridicule, taunting, twitting; **9** tantalize
Taurus: 13 Taurus the Bull

tautog: 9 blackfish
Tautoga onitis: 6 tautog; **9** blackfish
tautologic: 9 redundant, battology; **10** pleonastic
tautophony: 8 monotony
tavern: 3 bar, pub
taw: 7 shooter
tawny: 3 tan; **4** fawn, foxy; **5** sandy; **6** creamy, maroon; **9** chocolate
tax: 3 dun, ply; **4** dues, levy, task, urge, wear; **5** beset, exact, press; **6** accuse, assess, charge, impose, impute, strain, tariff; **7** impeach, require; **8** taxation
taxa: 5 taxon
Taxaceae: 9 yew family; **14** family Taxaceae
taxi: 3 cab; **4** hack; **6** hansom; **7** taxicab; **9** yellow cab; **10** checker cab
taxidermist: 13 animal stuffer
taxing: 7 onerous; **10** burdensome
Taxodiaceae: 13 redwood family; **20** subfamily Taxodiaceae
Taxodium ascendens: 11 bald cypress, pond cypress
taxonomy: 8 grouping
Taxus baccata: 10 English yew; **11** Old World yew
Taxus brevifolia: 10 Pacific yew, western yew; **13** California yew
Taxus cuspidata: 11 Japanese yew
Taxus floridana: 10 Florida yew
Tayassu angulatus: 8 javelina
Taylor: 13 Zachary Taylor
tayra: 5 taira; **11** Eira barbara
Tazicef: 6 Fortaz; **11** ceftazidime
tazza: 3 urn; **6** patera, salver; **7** epergne, patella
TB: 8 terabyte; **12** tuberculosis
Tbilisi: 6 Tiflis; **16** capital of Georgia
Tc: 10 technetium
T cell: 11 T lymphocyte
tchotchke: 5 curio; **6** bauble, gewgaw, trifle; **7** bibelot, novelty, trinket, whatnot; **8** chotchke, gimcrack, kickshaw, nicknack; **9** bagatelle, bric-a-brac; **10** knickknack
Te: 9 tellurium
teaberry: 8 boxberry; **10** spiceberry; **11** groundberry, wintergreen; **12** checkerberry
Teach: 11 Edward Teach
teachable: 6 docile; **8** educable; **9** trainable
teacher: 7 trainer; **10** instructor
teaching: 5 learn; **7** precept, tuition; **8** pedagogy, tutelage, tutorage, tutoring, instruct; **9** educating, education; **11** edification, instructing, instruction
tea family: 8 Theaceae; **14** family Theaceae
teal: 8 teal duck; **11** bluish green
team: 4 band, crew, gang, knot, line, tier; **5** group, party, range, squad; **6** string, thread
team spirit: 6 morale
teamster: 7 trucker

T

tear: 3 bat [U.S.], bum [U.S.], fly, rip; 4 buck, bust, chip, foam, fume, pull, rage, rant, rave, rent, rush, skim, snap, toot, zoom; 5 binge, break, brush, burst, crack, pluck, randy, shoot, split, sweep, whisk; 6 bender, charge; 7 blowout [U.S.], hoedown, rupture; 8 jamboree; 10 hullabaloo

tear apart: 3 pan; 5 trash

tearaway: 6 madcap; 8 brainish; 9 hotheaded, impetuous, impulsive

tear down: 4 rase, raze; 5 level; 9 dismantle

tearful: 7 weeping; 8 dolorous, mournful; 9 dolourous; 10 lachrymose

tear gas: 10 lacrimator

tear gland: 13 lacrimal gland

tearing: 6 fierce; 7 violent; 8 vehement, watering; 11 lacrimation; 12 lachrymation

tearless: 7 dry-eyed

tear off: 6 detach

tear out: 4 draw; 6 remove; 7 extract; 9 extricate

tear sac: 10 dacryocyst; 11 lacrimal sac

tease: 3 bug, cod, rag; 4 bait, bore, card, joke, minx, quiz, ride, twit, vamp; 5 abuse, annoy, beset, chaff, flirt, haunt, hound, rally, roast, taunt, worry, tired, vexed; 6 badger, banter, bother, enrage, harass, heckle, infest, loosen, molest, pester, plague, pother, vamper, biting, hazing; 7 oppress, provoke; 8 mistreat; 9 beleaguer, importune, persecute, tantalize; 10 tantalizer

teat: 3 dug, pap, tit; 6 mammae, nipple; 7 mamilla; 8 mammilla

tec: 9 detective; 12 investigator

teched: 3 mad; 4 daft, loco, nuts; 5 batty, crazy, dotty, loony, nutty; 6 crazed, fruity, insane; 7 bonkers, cracked, lunatic, touched; 8 demented, deranged, maddened; 10 moonstruck

techie: 10 technician

technical: 8 artistic; 9 shipshape; 10 scientific

technical competence: 5 craft, knack, skill; 7 address, aptness, know-how; 8 aptitude, facility; 10 adroitness, competence; 11 proficiency; 12 skillfulness

technical knockout: 3 TKO

technicolor: 10 Ektachrome, Kodachrome

technique: 3 way; 4 mode, wise; 5 means; 6 manner, method; 7 fashion, process; 8 facility, protocol; 9 mechanism, procedure; 11 proficiency

technology: 11 engineering

techy: 5 cross, fiery, surly, testy; 6 crabby, cranky, tetchy, touchy; 7 crabbed, peevish, pettish; 8 petulant, volatile; 9 fractious, irascible, irritable; 10 nettlesome

Tectaria cicutaria: 10 button fern

Tectona grandis: 4 teak

teddies: 4 slip; 5 shift, teddy; 6 shimmy; 7 chemise

Te Deum: 6 thanks

tedious: 3 dry; 4 arid, bald, dull, flat, slow; 5 ho-hum, windy, wordy; 6 boring, jejune, mortal; 7 irksome, verbose; 8 tiresome; 9 deadening, wearisome; 13 uninteresting

teed off: 6 ticked; 9 ticked off

teem: 4 drop, flow, rain; 5 swarm; 6 abound, stream; 8 multiply; 9 exuberate

teeming: 5 thick; 7 crowded, peopled, studded; 8 manifold, multiple, populous, swarming; 10 multiplied; 12 multinominal; 13 multitudinous

teensy: 3 wee; 5 bitty, teeny, weeny; 6 bittie, weensy

teenybopper: 10 bobbysoxer

teepee: 4 tipi

tee shirt: 6 jersey

teeterboard: 6 seesaw

teeth: 5 fangs

teething ring: 8 pacifier; 9 comforter

teetotal: 3 dry

teff: 9 teff grass

teflon: 4 PTFE

Tegucigalpa: 15 Honduran capital

tegument: 4 skin; 5 cutis; 10 integument

Teheran: 13 capital of Iran

telamon: 5 atlas

telecast: 5 video

telefax: 3 fax; 9 facsimile

telegram: 4 wire; 5 cable

telegraphic: 6 winged; 7 tersely; 8 electric; 9 mercurial; 11 eagle winged

telekinesis: 13 psychokinesis

telemeter: 9 rheometer

telepathist: 10 mind reader; 13 thought-reader

telephone: 4 call, ring; 5 phone; 6 call up

telephone directory: 9 phonebook

telephone exchange: 7 central

telephone solicitation: 13 telemarketing

telephoto lens: 8 zoom lens

teleprinter: 5 telex; 12 telex machine

teleprompter: 7 autocue; 8 prompter

telescope: 5 glass; 9 shortened

television: 4 tube; 5 telly, TV set, video

television advertisement: 10 commercial

television newscaster: 8 reporter

television program: 6 TV show

telingo potato: 9 pungapung; 11 elephant yam

Tell: 11 William Tell

tell: 3 say; 4 spin, take; 5 count, order, state, tally, weigh; 6 assure, enjoin, number, recite, relate; 7 narrate, recount, discern; 8 evidence, separate; 9 ascertain, enumerate, secernate; 10 severalize; 11 demonstrate, distinguish; 13 differentiate

teller: 7 cashier, delator, relator; 8 exponent, narrator, reporter; 9 authority, informant, paymaster, raconteur; 10 mouthpiece

tell fortunes: 6 divine; **8** prophesy, soothsay; **10** vaticinate

telling: 6 cogent, tattle; **7** singing, weighty; **8** appraisal, relation, telltale; **9** notifying, revealing; **10** hysterical, impressive, recounting; **11** sensational, significant; **12** notification

tell of: 4 show; **6** evince; **7** betoken

tell off: 5 score; **6** cipher

tell on: 3 rat; **4** shop, stag; **5** grass, peach; **6** betray, snitch; **8** denounce

tellurian: 7 terrene; **8** earthman, telluric; **9** earthling; **11** terrestrial

Telopea: 7 waratah; **12** genus Telopea

temblor: 5 quake, seism; **6** tremor; **10** earthquake; **11** ground quake

temerarious: 5 brash; **9** daredevil, imprudent; **11** improvident

temerity: 8 audacity, rashness; **9** incaution; **10** imprudence; **12** indiscretion; **13** audaciousness; **14** incautiousness

temper: 4 mood, tone, turn; **5** humor, pique, relax, smelt, style, tenor; **6** anneal, harden, leaven, mellow, narrow, season, soften; **7** chasten, mollify; **8** acerbity, mitigate, moderate, tartness; **9** crossness, petulance, procacity, surliness, testiness, toughness; **10** crabbiness, irritation

tempera: 7 gouache; **11** poster color, poster paint

temperamental: 5 moody; **7** erratic

temperance: 8 sobriety; **10** moderation

temperate: 4 cool; **5** sober; **8** measured, moderate; **10** reasonable; **12** abstemiously

temperateness: 8 sunshine; **10** gentleness

temperature: 5 fever, pulse; **9** breathing, heartbeat

temperature reduction: 7 cooling; **8** chilling

tempered: 7 treated; **8** hardened; **9** toughened, annealing

tempest: 3 fit; **4** riot; **5** burst, furor, scene, storm; **6** clamor, squall, tumult, uproar; **7** rioting; **8** outbreak, outburst; **9** explosion [metaphorical]; **10** convulsion

tempest-tossed: 4 lost; **8** buffeted

tempestuous: 4 wild; **5** angry; **6** raging, stormy; **7** furious, rampant; **9** clamorous, turbulent; **10** blustering, boisterous, uproarious

Templar: 13 Knight Templar

template: 5 guide; **7** templet

temple: 3 hip; **4** loin; **6** haunch; **9** synagogue

Temple of Apollo: 13 Delphic oracle

temple orange: 6 tangor; **10** king orange

Templetonia retusa: 9 coral bush, flame bush

temple tree: 10 pagoda tree

tempo: 4 pace; **6** pacing

temporal: 3 lay; **5** civil; **6** laical; **7** passing, profane, secular, worldly; **9** temporary, transient; **10** transitive, transitory; **11** impermanent

temporalty: 5 laity

temporariness: 7 brevity; **8** fugacity [Chem]; **10** transience; **11** evanescence; **12** impermanence

temporary: 7 passing; **8** temporal; **9** irregular, transient; **10** transitive, transitory; **11** impermanent

temporary expedient: 5 shift; **7** stopgap; **8** jury mast; **9** makeshift; **13** improvisation

temporary hookup: 5 patch

temporary removal: 10 suspension

temporize: 5 dally; **6** double; **7** finesse; **10** circumvent; **11** gerrymander; **12** put things off; **13** procrastinate

temporizer: 7 trimmer, waffler

tempt: 3 try; **4** coax, lure; **5** charm, essay; **6** allure, entice, invite, seduce, strive; **7** attempt, attract, bewitch, venture, wheedle; **8** endeavor; **9** fascinate, influence, titillate; **10** conciliate

temptation: 5 fancy; **6** luring, magnet; **8** enticing; **9** seduction; **10** allurement, attraction, enticement, inducement; **11** beguilement, captivation, fascination

tempt fortune: 9 adventure, speculate

temptress: 5 siren; **7** Delilah; **11** enchantress

ten: 3 ace, six; **4** five, four, jack, king, nine, trey; **5** deuce, eight, knave, queen, seven; **6** decade, tenner

tenable: 10 defensible

tenacious: 4 dour, long; **5** tough; **6** dogged; **7** bulldog; **8** coherent, obdurate, stubborn; **9** obstinate, retentive; **10** inflexible, unyielding; **11** persistence; **12** casehardened, pertinacious

tenacity: 6 memory, recall; **8** firm hold; **10** doggedness; **11** persistence, persistency, pertinacity; **12** adhesiveness, illiberality, perseverance, persqverence; **13** retentiveness, tenaciousness

tenaculum: 8 tentacle

tenancy: 6 tenure; **9** occupancy

tenant: 4 live, stay; **5** abide, dwell, lodge, perch, roost; **6** nestle, renter, reside; **7** inhabit, sojourn

tenantless: 7 forlorn; **8** deserted, desolate; **9** abandoned, unpeopled; **10** untenanted; **11** uninhabited

tench: 10 Tinca tinca

Ten Commandments: 9 Decalogue

tend: 3 run; **4** keep, lean; **5** trend, verge, watch; **6** attend, squire; **7** dispose, incline, monitor

ten-day fern: 11 leather fern

tendency: 4 bent, bias; **5** drift, tenor, trend; **7** bearing, leaning; **8** coloring; **9** proneness; **10** affections, proclivity, propensity; **11** disposition, inclination

tender: 3 bid; **4** fond, soft, sore, warm; **5** crank, offer, sweet, tippy; **6** caring, cranky,

T

mellow, pastel, pearly, subtle, supple; **7** pinnace, refined; **8** delicate, lovesome; **9** sensitive, tenderize, transport; **10** harmonious, vulnerable; **11** untoughened; **12** affectionate
tenderfoot: 8 Dutchman; **9** Easterner [U.S.]
tendergreen: 14 spinach mustard
tender hearted: 6 tender; **8** bonhomie
tenderloin: 8 undercut
tender loving care: 3 TLC
tenderness: 4 love; **5** heart, mercy; **8** bonhomie, clemency, fondness, humanity, softness, soreness, yearning; **9** affection, litheness; **10** amiability, discomfort, irritation, suppleness; **11** forbearance
ten-dollar bill: 7 sawbuck
tendon: 5 sinew; **7** tendril; **8** gossamer
tenebrious: 7 obscure; **9** tenebrous; **10** tenebrific
tenements: 4 land; **5** acres, lands; **6** realty; **8** property
tenet: 5 dogma, creed; **6** belief; **9** principle
tenfold: 5 tenth; **6** denary; **7** decimal
ten-gallon hat: 9 cowboy hat
tenia: 6 fillet, taenia
tenner: 3 ten; **6** decade
Tennessee: 14 Tennessee River, Volunteer State
Tennessee walker: 12 Walking horse
tenno: 6 mikado
tenor: 4 tone, turn; **5** drift, style; **6** strain, temper; **7** bearing, compass, cremona; **8** coloring, tendency; **11** disposition, personality, temperament, violoncello
tenor drum: 6 tom-tom, tomtom
Tenormin: 8 atenolol
ten percent: 5 tenth; **8** one-tenth; **9** tenth part
tenpounder: 8 ladyfish; **11** Elops saurus
tense: 4 taut; **6** strain, taught, stress; **8** volatile; **9** excitable, sensitive, tautness; **11** overwrought
tensile: 6 pliant, spring; **7** buoyant, ductile, elastic, pliable, springy; **8** flexible, renitent, tractile; **9** malleable, resilient
tension: 4 tone; **6** spring, stress; **7** tensity; **8** pressure, tautness, tonicity; **9** tenseness; **10** elasticity
tent: 4 tilt; **6** awning; **7** marquee, parasol; **8** sunshade, umbrella
tentative: 8 doubtful; **9** empirical; **10** indecisive, irresolute; **11** provisional; **12** probationary, provisionary
tented field: 7 service; **11** campaigning
tent stitch: 10 petit point
tenuous: 4 fine, rare, thin; **6** flimsy, slight, subtle; **7** subtile; **9** planarity; **10** feebleness; **11** slenderness; **12** compressible
tenure: 7 tenancy; **10** incumbency, land tenure; **12** term of office
tepee: 4 tipi; **6** wigwam

tepid: 4 warm; **8** lukewarm
Tera: 7 Yamaltu; **8** Pidlimdi
tercet: 3 III; **4** trey, trio; **5** leash, three, triad, trine; **9** threesome
teredinid: 8 shipworm
terefah: 4 tref; **9** nonkosher
tergiversation: 8 apostasy; **9** defection, desertion; **10** withdrawal; **12** equivocation
term: 3 dub, end; **4** call, name, pale, word; **5** lease, spell, state, style, terms, verge; **6** clause; **7** confine, enclave, entitle; **8** endpoint; **9** condition, designate; **10** conditions [pl], denominate, expression, limitation, settlement; **11** reservation, stipulation; **12** precondition
termagant: 5 scold, shrew, vixen
terminal: 3 VDT; **4** last, pole; **5** depot, final; **7** endmost, monitor, station; **8** frontier, ultimate; **10** concluding
terminal node: 4 leaf
terminate: 3 can, end, RIF; **4** fire, sack, stop, over; **5** cease, close; **6** finish, riffed; **7** dismiss, severed; **8** conclude; **9** discharge
terminator: 10 eradicator; **12** exterminator
terminology: 8 language; **12** nomenclature
termite: 3 ant, bee; **7** busy bee; **8** white ant; **10** working bee
term of office: 6 tenure; **10** incumbency
term paper: 5 theme; **7** project
terms: 4 data; **5** price; **6** clause, damage; **7** footing, opening; **8** premises; **9** condition; **10** compromise, conditions [pl]; **11** stipulation; **12** precondition
terpsichore: 5 dance; **7** dancing
terra: 5 Earth, globe, world
terra alba: 6 kaolin; **7** kaoline; **8** pipeclay; **9** china clay; **10** china stone; **13** porcelain clay
terrace: 5 bench, patio; **8** terrasse
terra firma: 4 land; **5** earth; **6** ground; **7** dry land; **9** dry ground; **11** solid ground
terrarium: 4 cage
terrestrial: 4 land; **6** earthy; **7** earthly, mundane, terrene, worldly; **8** sublunar, telluric; **9** planetary, sublunary, tellurian
terrible: 4 dire; **5** awful, dread, sadly; **6** severe, wicked, sorely; **7** direful, dreaded, fearful, painful, cruelly, grossly; **8** dreadful, fearsome, horrific, terrific, horribly, rottenly, woefully; **9** atrocious, frightful; **10** abominable, horrendous, terrifying, dreadfully, grievously, lamentably, shockingly; **11** atrociously, frightfully, frightening, unspeakable
terrier: 5 probe, rimer, scoop; **6** chisel, dibble, gimlet, lancet, trepan, warder
terrific: 4 grim; **7** howling; **8** superbly, crushing, rattling, shocking, terrible, wondrous; **9** appalling, fantastic, marvelous, wonderful; **10** terrifying, tremendous
terrified: 7 panicky; **8** panicked; **9** horrified, petrified; **10** frightened

terrine: 4 lota, toby; 6 chatti, mussuk, spider, urceus; 8 schooner [U.S.]

territorial: 5 local; 6 landed; 8 regional; 9 parochial; 10 provincial

territory: 5 range; 6 colony, domain; 7 mandate; 8 district, dominion, province

terror: 4 brat; 5 dread, panic; 6 horror, threat; 7 scourge

terrorisation: 11 frightening

terrorism: 13 reign of terror

terrorist: 8 alarmist, murderer; 9 pessimist

terrorize: 3 cow; 5 abash, daunt, deter; 7 overawe, terrify; 10 discourage, intimidate

terse: 4 curt; 5 brief, close, crisp, short; 7 concise, laconic

Tertiary: 14 Tertiary period

tertiary: 5 third

tertium quid: 5 alloy, magma; 7 amalgam, melange; 8 compound; 10 miscellany; 11 composition

Terylene: 6 Dacron

tesselated: 6 mosaic; 9 festooned

test: 3 run, try; 4 exam, quiz; 5 assay, check, essay, model, pilot, probe, prove, touch, trial; 6 screen, tryout, verify; 7 examine; 9 criterion; 10 diagnostic; 11 examination; 12 experimental

testa: 8 episperm, seed coat

testament: 4 will

test drive: 8 road-test; 12 take for a spin

tester: 5 groat; 6 guinea, pallet; 8 examiner

testes: 6 oyster, stones

testifier: 7 witness; 8 deponent; 9 indicator

testify: 4 show; 5 prove; 6 attest, depose; 7 witness; 8 evidence

testimonial: 7 tribute

testing: 11 examination

test the waters: 3 see; 5 check

testy: 5 cross, fiery, surly, techy; 6 crabby, cranky, tetchy, touchy; 7 crabbed, peckish, peevish, pettish; 8 petulant, volatile; 9 fractious, irascible, irritable; 10 nettlesome

tetanus: 7 lockjaw

tetched: 3 mad; 4 daft, loco, nuts; 5 batty, crazy, dotty, loony, nutty; 6 crazed, fruity, insane, teched [dialect]; 7 bonkers, cracked, lunatic, touched; 8 demented, deranged, maddened; 10 moonstruck

tether: 4 lead, moor; 5 leash; 6 picket, pinion

tetrad: 4 four; 6 square; 7 quarter, quartet, quatern; 8 foursome; 10 tetragonal

tetragon: 9 rectangle; 10 quadrangle; 13 quadrilateral

tetrode: 5 diode; 6 triode; 7 pentode

tetterwort: 7 puccoon, redroot; 9 bloodroot

Teucrium scorodonia: 8 wood sage

Teutonic: 6 German

Tevere: 5 Tiber

Texas: 13 Lone-Star State

Texas armadillo: 4 peba

Texas bluebonnet: 10 bluebonnet; 13 buffalo clover

Texas Independence Day: 6 March 2

Texas millet: 10 goose grass

text: 7 writing; 8 document, printing; 10 schoolbook

text file: 8 document

textile: 5 cloth; 6 fabric; 8 material

textile screw pine: 7 lauhala; 17 Pandanus tectorius

texture: 4 feel; 5 grain, tooth

Th: 7 thorium; 8 Thursday

Thai: 3 Tai; 7 Siamese; 11 Central Thai

Thailand: 4 Siam

Thais: 4 Lais; 6 Phryne; 7 Delilah, Jezebel; 9 Messalina; 10 petite dame

Thalarctos maritimus: 7 ice bear; 9 polar bear

thalmencephalon: 10 interbrain; 12 diencephalon; 13 betweeenbrain

Thames: 11 Thames River

thane: 4 earl; 5 baron; 8 viscount

thankful: 7 obliged; 8 beholden, grateful

thankfulness: 9 gratitude; 12 appreciation, gratefulness

thankless: 7 ingrate; 9 unpopular; 10 ungrateful, unthankful; 12 unacceptable, ungratifying; 13 unappreciated

thanks: 6 praise; 11 benediction, recognition

Thanksgiving cactus: 10 crab cactus

that's just it: 5 truly; 6 indeed; 7 exactly; 9 certainly, precisely

that-a-way: 5 there

that being so: 5 since

thatch tree: 9 broom palm; 10 thatch palm; 12 silver thatch

that has been: 6 lapsed; 7 elapsed, expired, extinct; 8 exploded; 9 forgotten

that is: 6 actual, extant; 7 current, instant, present; 8 existing

that is to say: 6 namely

thaw: 3 run; 4 give, melt, weep; 6 unthaw; 7 liquefy, melting, thawing, warming; 8 unfreeze

the Absolute: 6 psyche

Theaceae: 9 tea family; 14 family Theaceae

the almighty dollar: 9 greenback

the antithesis: 9 opposites [pl]

the army: 6 rifles; 8 regulars, reserves, yeomanry; 10 volunteers; 11 auxiliaries

theater: 5 forum, house; 7 theatre; 9 dramatics; 10 auditorium, dramaturgy; 12 amphitheater

theater in the round: 6 circus; 10 hippodrome

theater of action: 5 arena, field

theatric: 5 stagy

thee: 3 you; 4 thou

theft ring: 4 gang

The Hague: 7 Den Haag; 11 Gravenhage; 12 Dutch capital; 23 capital of The Netherlands

The Hunter: 5 Orion

T

theism: 5 faith, piety; 8 religion; 12 spirituality; 13 religiousness

theme: 4 base, idea, root, stem; 5 motif, paper, topic; 6 matter, report, thesis; 7 project, radical, subject; 8 contents, treatise; 11 composition; 12 dissertation

theme song: 9 signature

then: 4 ergo, thus, upon; 5 and so, hence; 6 thusly, whence; 9 naturally, therefore, wherefore; 11 accordingly

thence so: 4 ergo, then, thus; 5 hence; 6 thusly, whence; 9 therefore, wherefore; 11 accordingly

The Netherlands: 7 Holland; 11 Netherlands

The New York Times News Service: 3 NYT [abbr]

theology: 8 divinity

theorem: 5 axiom, guess; 6 theory, thesis; 7 surmise; 9 postulate; 10 conjecture, hypothesis; 11 postulation, proposition, supposition

theoretical: 8 abstract, academic, putative; 9 theoretic, theorized; 10 gratuitous, supposable; 11 conjectural, presumptive, speculative; 12 hypothesized

theoretical account: 5 model; 8 paradigm; 9 framework

theory: 5 guess; 6 thesis; 7 surmise, theorem; 9 postulate; 10 conjecture

theory of beauty: 10 aesthetics

theory of chances: 10 statistics

theory of knowledge: 12 epistemology

the other way around: 9 vice versa

therapeutic: 5 tonic; 7 healing; 8 balsamic, curative, remedial, sanative; 10 alterative

therapist: 6 healer

therapsid: 11 protomammal

therapy: 4 help; 6 curing, remedy; 7 redress, regimen; 9 treatment

there: 7 that way, thither

thereafter: 5 since; 11 thenceforth

therefore: 4 ergo, then, thus; 5 hence; 6 thence, thusly, whence; 8 thence so; 9 wherefore; 11 accordingly

therefrom: 6 thence; 7 thereof

therein: 6 in that, in this

theretofore: 3 ere

thereupon: 4 next; 8 hereupon

therm: 4 quad

thermal: 7 caloric, thermic

Thermobia domestica: 8 firebrat

thermonuclear power: 11 fusion power

thermonuclear warhead: 4 nuke

thesaurus: 8 treasure; 13 synonym finder

these days: 6 lately, of late; 8 latterly, nowadays, recently

thesis: 5 guess, theme; 6 affair, theory; 7 surmise, theorem; 8 business, treatise; 9 postulate; 10 conjecture, hypothesis

thiamin: 7 aneurin; 8 thiamine

thick: 4 deep, wide; 5 ample, broad, dense, dirty, heavy, midst, muddy, murky; 6 chummy, stocky, stuffy; 7 compact, crowded, peopled, slurred, studded, teeming, thickly, viscous; 8 frequent, heavyset, intimate, multiple, populous, thickset

thicken: 3 gel; 4 mash; 5 churn, widen; 8 condense

thickened: 9 calloused

thicket: 5 brake, brush, copse; 7 coppice; 9 brushwood

thickly settled: 8 populous

thickness: 5 width; 6 height; 7 breadth; 8 wideness; 9 broadness, heaviness

thick-ribbed: 8 stubborn

thickset: 3 pug; 5 close, dumpy, squab, squat, thick; 6 stocky, stumpy; 7 compact; 8 heavyset

thick-skinned: 7 callous; 8 indurate

thief: 6 rifler, robber; 8 pilferer

thievery: 5 theft; 7 larceny; 8 stealing

thighbone: 5 femur; 7 femoris

thigh-slapper: 3 wow; 4 riot; 6 howler, scream

thimble: 5 ladle, spoon; 6 dipper, shovel, trowel, capful; 7 spatula; 10 tablespoon

thimblerig: 9 shell game

thin: 3 cut; 4 cull, fine, lean, poor, rare, slim, weak; 5 light, prune, spare; 6 dilute, flimsy, meager, narrow, reduce, scrimp, slight, sparse, spotty, subtle, watery; 7 diluted, melt off, slender, sparing, stinted, subtile, tenuous, watered

thin air: 5 vapor

thine: 5 yours

thing: 3 fad; 4 fact, item; 5 craze, event, trend; 6 affair, entity, matter, object, sucker; 7 in thing; 8 incident

thingamabob: 5 gizmo; 6 doodad; 7 gimmick; 8 dohickey; 11 thingamajig

thing-in-itself: 8 noumenon

think: 4 hold, mean; 5 guess; 6 intend, recall, reckon, remind; 7 believe, imagine, suppose, thought; 8 cogitate, conceive, consider, remember, retrieve; 9 cerebrate, recollect

think about: 5 study, weigh; 6 ponder

think ahead: 11 premeditate

think aloud: 7 be frank; 8 be candid

think back: 8 remember

think better of it: 6 flinch, swerve

think highly of: 5 honor; 6 esteem, regard; 7 respect

thinner: 7 solvent; 8 dilutant; 9 dissolver, resolvent; 10 dissolvent

thinness: 7 tenuity; 8 fineness, leanness, poorness, slimness; 9 emptiness,

thin-skinned: 4 keen; 5 acute, huffy, sharp, vivid; 6 lively, queasy, touchy; 9 squeamish

third person: 8 chaperon; 9 custodian, preserver

third power: 4 cube

third-year: 6 junior

thirst: **4** lust; **5** crave; **6** hunger, starve
thirsty: **3** dry
thirteen: **11** baker's dozen
this-a-way: **4** here; **6** hither
thistle: **5** briar, brier; **7** bramble
thistly: **6** snaggy, thorny; **7** prickly
thole: **3** peg, pin; **4** bear; **6** endure, suffer; **7** support, sustain
Thompson automatic rifle: 8 Tommy gun; **13** submachine gun
thong: **4** lash, whip; **5** knout, strap; **7** cowhide, scourge; **8** bullwhip
thoracic: **8** pectoral
thorax: **5** chest; **6** pectus
Thoreau: 17 Henry David Thoreau
thorn: **4** fang, tang; **5** brier, spine, sting; **6** nettle; **7** bramble, prickle; **8** irritant
thorny: **5** burry, spiny; **6** barbed, briary, rugged, snaggy; **7** bristly, prickly, studded, thistly
thorough: **4** full, good; **7** plenary; **8** absolute; **10** exhaustive, completely
thoroughbred: **4** up to; **5** crack; **7** courtly, refined; **8** pedigree, polished, purebred
thoroughfare: **3** way; **4** path; **5** route; **6** course
thoroughwort: **7** boneset; **8** agueweed
thou: **3** you; **4** thee
thought: **4** idea, look, view; **6** notion; **7** conceit, concept, opinion; **8** believed; **9** mentation, sentiment
thoughtful: **4** kind; **6** sedate; **7** heedful, pensive, wistful; **8** Platonic, sensible; **9** attentive; **10** meditative
thoughtless: **6** vacant; **7** vacuous; **8** careless, heedless, mindless, uncaring
thought-provoking: **11** challenging
thousand: **5** grand
thrall: **7** bondage, slavery
thrash: **3** bat, lam; **4** cane, comb, flog, lash, lick, mosh, slam, toss, whip; **5** flail, slash, strap
thread: **4** file, line, reed, team, tier, wind, yarn; **5** range, weave; **6** ribbon, string
threadbare: **4** bald; **5** banal, faded, passe, stale, tired, trite; **6** frayed, ragged
thread maker: **7** spinner; **8** spinster
threads: **4** duds, togs
threadworm: **7** pinworm
threat: **6** menace, terror; **7** scourge
threaten: **4** loom; **5** await, peril; **6** menace, at risk; **7** imperil
threatening: **4** ugly; **5** heavy; **6** sullen; **7** baleful, ominous; **8** lowering, menacing
three: **4** trey, trio; **5** triad; **6** tercet
three-base hit: **6** triple; **11** three-bagger
three-day measles: **7** rubella; **13** German measles; **15** epidemic rubeola
three-decker: **12** club sandwich
three-dimensional: **5** cubic, solid
threefold: **6** triple; **10** triplicate
three-sided: **10** triangular, trilateral

threnody: **5** dirge; **6** lament, monody; **7** requiem
threshold: **4** door; **5** brink, verge; **6** wicket; **7** doorway; **8** doorsill, doorstep; **9** vestibule; **10** room access
thrice: **7** thirdly
thrift: **3** job; **4** line, work; **6** living; **7** economy; **8** business; **9** frugality
thrill: **4** bang, itch, kick, pant, rush; **5** chill, exalt, flush, shock, sting, throb; **6** charge, quiver, shiver, tickle, tingle
thrilling: **4** dire; **8** ecstatic, electric
Thrinax keyensis: 7 key palm; **12** silver thatch
thrive: **4** boom; **6** expand; **7** prosper; **8** flourish
throat: **6** gullet; **7** pharynx
throb: **4** beat, pant; **5** heave, pound, pulse; **6** quiver, shiver, thrill, tingle, tremor; **7** flutter, pulsate, shudder, tremble, twitter
throe: **5** spasm
thrombocyte: **8** platelet; **13** blood platelet
thrombolytic: **10** clot buster
throne: **3** ark, can, pot; **4** dais; **5** divan, potty, stool; **6** toilet; **7** commode
throng: **3** jam, mob; **4** herd, pack, pile; **5** crowd, group, surge; **6** stream
throstle: **5** mavis; **10** song thrush
throttle: **3** gas, gun; **4** claw; **5** bound, choke, limit; **6** collar, stifle
through: **3** per, via; **4** done
throughway: **4** pike; **7** freeway, thruway; **8** motorway; **10** expressway
throw: **3** fox, jog, shy; **4** cast, drop, flip, give, have, hold, host, hurl, jolt, toss; **5** fling
throwing out: **8** disposal
throw in the towel: **4** quit; **5** leave; **6** give up
throw overboard: **5** forgo, waive
throw the voice: **13** ventriloquize
throw up: **3** cat; **4** barf, cast, honk, puke, sick, spew, spue; **5** chuck, heave, retch, vomit
thrum: **3** hum; **4** beat, drum; **5** strum
thrust: **3** cut, jab, jog; **4** hurl, jolt, pass, poke, prod, push, stab; **5** boost [U.S.], brunt, drive, force, lunge, shove, stuff, throw, barge; **6** hurtle
thud: **5** clump, clunk, crump, thump
thug: **4** goon, hood, punk; **5** bravo, crook, harpy, shark, tough; **6** bandit
Thuja occidentalis: 10 white cedar
thumb: **3** paw; **4** feel, flip, leaf, riff; **5** flick, grope, hitch, touch; **6** finger
thump: **4** bang, beat, blow, pelt, plug, poke, rump, slam, swap, thud; **5** baste, clunk, pound, punch, smack, spank, whump
thunder: **3** fly; **4** boom, peal, roar; **5** blare, burst, clang
thundercloud: **12** cumulonimbus
thundering: **5** gaunt, hulky; **7** hulking

T

thunder lizard: 9 apatosaur; 10 brontosaur; 19 Apatosaurus excelsus

thunder snake: 9 worm snake

thunderstruck: 9 awestruck, stupefied; 10 dumfounded, moonstruck

Thunnus alalunga: 8 albacore

Thunnus albacares: 9 yellowfin

Thunnus thynnus: 7 bluefin

thurible: 6 censer

thus: 4 ergo, then; 5 hence; 6 thence, thusly, whence

thus far: 3 yet

thwack: 4 cuff, swat; 5 smack, spank, thump, whack; 6 buffet, stroke

thwart: 4 balk, bilk, foil; 5 cross, queer, spoil; 6 baffle

thylacine: 13 Tasmanian wolf; 14 Tasmanian tiger

thyme: 4 sage; 7 parsley; 8 marjoram, rosemary

thyme camphor: 6 thymol; 10 thymic acid

thymus: 10 sweetbread

thyroid cartilage: 10 Adam's apple

thyroid-stimulating hormone: 3 TSH; 11 thyrotropin

ti: 2 si, te

Ti: 8 titanium

tiang: 4 topi; 6 hirola; 7 sassaby; 8 korrigum; 15 Hunter's antelope

tiara: 5 crown, miter; 6 diadem; 7 coronet

tibia: 4 shin

tical: 4 baht

tichodrome: 11 wall creeper

tick: 4 beat; 5 click, trust

ticked: 7 teed off

ticker: 4 pump; 5 heart, watch

ticket: 3 tag; 4 fine; 5 label, plank, slate; 6 docket; 8 platform

ticket booth: 9 box office

tickle: 5 humor; 6 thrill; 7 flatter, indulge; 9 titillate

tickled pink: 6 elated; 7 flushed, pleased; 9 delighted

tickle the palm: 5 bribe

ticklish: 8 critical, delicate, fallible, slippery; 9 debatable; 10 disputable, precarious; 12 questionable

tick off: 4 mark; 5 check

ticktack: 4 beat, tick; 8 ticktock

tick trefoil: 10 beggar lice; 11 beggar's lice

tickweed: 8 tickseed; 9 coreopsis

tidal wave: 7 tsunami

tidbit: 6 dainty, titbit; 8 delicacy, treasure

tiddly: 3 wet; 5 drunk

tide: 5 flood, surge; 7 current

tide it over: 4 wait

tidied up: 9 spruced up

tidings: 4 news, word; 6 advice; 7 message

tidy: 4 gimp, neat, trig, trim; 5 hefty, kempt, natty, smart

tidy sum: 3 lot, pot, wad; 4 deal, heap, mass, mess, mint, peck, pile, raft, slew; 5 batch; 6 plenty

tie: 3 wed; 4 bind, bond, link; 5 marry; 6 string; 7 connect

tiebeam: 6 girder

tied: 4 even; 5 laced; 7 trussed; 8 fastened

tie down: 4 bind

tie in: 4 link; 6 relate; 7 connect; 9 associate

tie one's hands: 6 hobble, lumber; 7 manacle, trammel; 8 handcuff

tier: 5 grade, level, range, stage

tiff: 3 ire; 4 feud, fume, fuss, spat; 5 snarl; 6 bicker; 7 dispute, quarrel

tiffin: 5 lunch

Tiflis: 7 Tbilisi; 16 capital of Georgia

tiger: 4 lion; 6 jockey; 14 Panthera tigris

tiger lily: 6 kentan

tight: 4 firm, high, mean, snug, taut; 5 close, stiff; 6 secure

tighten: 6 fasten, reduce; 7 stiffen; 8 strangle; 9 constrain

tightfistedness: 8 meanness; 9 closeness

tight hand: 8 iron rule

tight-laced: 4 prim; 6 prissy; 7 prudish; 8 priggish; 9 victorian

tightlipped: 5 close; 9 secretive

tights: 4 hose; 5 panty; 6 pantie

tightwad: 10 cheapskate

tike: 3 fry, kid; 5 child, churl, minor; 9 youngster

tile: 7 high hat, shingle, silk hat

tilefish: 10 blanquillo

Tilia cordata: 15 small-leaved lime

Tilia heterophylla: 10 cottonwood; 13 white basswood

Tilia tomentosa: 10 silver lime; 12 silver linden

tiling: 6 slates; 7 slating

till: 5 until; 6 tiller, trough; 7 cashbox

tillable: 6 arable; 10 cultivable; 12 cultivatable

tillage: 5 tilth; 7 farming

Tillandsia usneoides: 8 long moss; 9 black moss; 11 Spanish moss

tiller: 3 key; 4 helm, till; 5 blade, stool

tilt: 3 tip; 4 cant, dart, lean, list, rock, slip, sway, tent, trip; 5 angle, slant

tilt over: 6 topple

timber: 4 tone, wood; 5 woods; 6 forest, lumber

timbre: 4 tone; 10 intonation

time: 3 age, era; 4 span; 5 clock, meter, space; 6 period; 8 interval, occasion, sentence

time being: 5 nonce

time drawing on: 6 advent

time honored: 5 great; 8 immortal, emeritus; 9 venerable

time lag: 4 hold, wait; 5 delay; 12 postponement

timeless: 8 dateless, eternity; 9 intrusive

timely: 6 prompt; 7 apropos; 8 punctual

time measurement: 8 horology; 11 chronometry

time of life: 3 age
time of origin: 7 vintage
time of year: 6 season
time out: 5 break; **6** recess; **7** respite
timesaving: 11 expeditious
time-tested: 5 tried
timeworn: 9 hackneyed; **10** threadbare, antiquated
timid: 3 shy; **5** faint; **6** unsure; **7** bashful; **8**
cautious
timorous: 5 timid; **6** trepid; **7** fearful
timothy: 8 pin grass; **10** herd's grass
timpani: 5 bongo; **6** kettle
tin: 3 can, pot; **8** canister
tinamou: 9 partridge
tinct: 3 dye; **4** tint, wash; **5** stain, tinge, touch
tincture: 3 dye, hue, sop, sup; **4** cast, dash,
glow, tint, tone; **5** color, tinge
tinder: 8 kindling
tine: 5 yucca; **9** bear grass [U.S.]
tinea: 8 ringworm
tinea barbae: 11 barber's itch
tinea cruris: 8 jock itch
tined: 7 pronged
Tineola bisselliella: 11 webbing moth
tinge: 3 dye, hue, sop, sup; **4** cast, dash,
glow, tint, wash; **5** color
tingle: 4 itch, pant; **5** chill, creep, heave,
sting, throb; **6** quiver, shiver, thrill; **7** flutter
shudder, tremble
tinker: 6 fiddle; **7** bungler
tinker's root: 9 feverroot; **10** wild coffee; **12**
horse gentian
tinned: 6 canned
tinny: 5 cheap; **7** chintzy
tinsel: 7 spangle; sparkle
tint: 3 dye, hue; **4** cast, glow, tone, wash; **5**
color, flush, shade, stain, tinge, touch
tintinnabulation: 7 ringing
tin whistle: 7 catcall
tiny: 3 wee; **4** puny; **5** petit, petty; **6** bantam,
midget, petite
tip: 3 cap, nib, top; **4** lean, peak, tilt
tip over: 5 upset
tippet: 4 cape; **6** tabard; **7** mantlet
tipple: 5 drink
tipsiness: 9 inebriety
tipstaff: 7 bailiff
tipsy: 5 askew; **7** fuddled; **8** unsteady
tip-top: 5 prime
tipu: 8 tipu tree; **14** pride of Bolivia; **15** yellow jacaranda
tirade: 8 diatribe, harangue
tire: 4 bore, wear, jade; **5** weary; **7** exhaust,
fatigue
tiredly: 7 wearily
tiresome: 4 dull, slow; **6** boring; **7** tedious,
wearing
tissue: 3 web; **4** mesh; **7** netting
tissue layer: 8 membrane
titan: 5 giant; **8** behemoth, colossus; **11**
heavyweight

titanic: 5 giant; **8** colossal, gigantic
titillate: 5 tempt; **6** allure, tickle
titillating: 3 fun; **6** festal; **7** festive
titivate: 6 spruce; **7** smarten
title: 4 deed, head, name; **5** claim, right; **7**
holding; **9** privilege
titled: 8 nobility
title-holder: 5 champ; **8** champion; **10** proprietor
titter: 6 giggle; **7** snicker
tittle: 3 dab; **4** iota; **5** shred; **6** smidge
tittle-tattle: 6 gossip; **7** prattle
tizzy: 4 flap, fuss; **6** dither, pother
Tm: 7 thulium
to: 6 toward, versus
toad: 4 frog, snob, tool
to a certain extent: 6 sort of
toadshade: 11 red trillium
toadstool: 8 mushroom
to a fault: 7 too much; **11** excessively
to a greater extent: 4 more; **7** heavily
to and fro: 6 seesaw, zigzag
toast: 5 crisp, drink, parch, roast, singe; **6**
pledge, salute
tobacco: 5 baccy; **10** Indian weed; **12** fragrant weed
tobacco user: 6 smoker
tobacco wilt: 7 ring rot; **11** ring disease
toboggan: 4 luge
to boot: 4 else; **7** besides
tocopherol: 8 vitamin E
tocsin: 4 sign; **5** touch; **9** alarm bell
to date: 7 up to now
today: 3 now
toddle: 6 totter; **7** saunter
toddler: 3 tot; **4** tyke
toddy: 4 grog; **8** hot toddy
toddy palm: 6 lontar; **7** palmyra; **8** wine
palm; **10** longar palm; **11** palmyra palm
Todea barbara: 8 king fern
Todea superba: 9 crape fern
to-do: 4 fuss, stir; **6** bustle
toe: 4 hoof
toffee: 7 brittle
tofu: 8 bean curd
tog: 4 garb; **5** dress; **6** clothe; **7** apparel, garment
toga: 12 robes of state
together: 5 as one; **7** jointly; **9** assembled
togs: 4 duds; **7** threads
toilet: 3 can, pot; **4** head; **7** commode
toilet kit: 9 travel kit
toilet soap: 8 bath soap, face soap
toilet table: 6 vanity
toilette: 5 guise; **8** wardrobe; **9** trousseau
toilet water: 13 eau de toilette
toiling: 4 work; **5** labor; **6** effort
toilsome: 4 hard; **5** heavy; **7** arduous
token: 4 item, note; **5** relic; **7** memento; **8**
keepsake, souvenir

T

Tokyo: 3 Edo; **4** Yedo; **5** Tokio, Yeddo; **14** capital of Japan

told: 8 reported; **12** communicated

tolerable: 2 OK; **3** low; **4** fair; **7** average; **8** bearable, mediocre, passable

tolerance: 6 leeway, lenity, margin; **8** latitude

tolerant: 4 kind; **5** broad; **7** liberal

tolerate: 4 bear

to let: 7 for rent; **8** for lease

toll: 4 cost; **5** chime, price

Tolstoy: 10 Leo Tolstoy

tolu: 10 tolu balsam; **12** balsam of tolu

Tolypeutes tricinctus: 4 apar; **9** armadillo

tom: 6 tomcat; **7** gobbler; **9** tom turkey

tomahawk: 7 hatchet

tomatillo: 8 jamberry; **9** miltomate; **10** husk tomato

tomato: 9 love apple

tomato ketchup: 6 catsup

tomb: 3 pit; **5** grave; **9** sepulcher

tomboy: 6 hoyden

tome: 4 work; **6** volume; **7** writing

tomentum: 4 fuzz, hair

tomfoolery: 5 farce, folly

tommyrot: 7 foolery

tomography: 7 imaging

ton: 4 bulk; **5** vogue

tonal pattern: 6 melody

tone: 4 feel, form, note; **5** color; **7** quality

tongs: 6 pliers; **7** forceps, nippers, pincers

tongue: 5 lingo; **8** language

tongue fern: 8 felt fern

tongue-in-cheek: 8 jokingly; **9** facetious

tongueless: 4 mute; **8** unspoken, wordless; **9** voiceless

tongue of land: 9 peninsula

tongue-tied: 10 incoherent

tonic: 3 pop; **4** soda; **12** quinine water

tonka bean: 10 coumara nut

tonnage: 4 bulk

tonne: 9 metric ton

to no purpose: 8 futilely

tons: 4 gobs, lots, wads; **5** heaps, loads, piles

too: 3 and; **4** also; **6** as well

too big for one's breeches: 6 snooty, snotty, uppish

tool: 6 device

too large: 8 outsized, oversize

too little: 9 not enough; **10** inadequate; **12** insufficient

toot: 4 beep, honk

tooth: 4 tusk

tooth decay: 6 cavity

toothed: 6 jagged; **7** notched, serrate

toothed sword fern: 10 basket fern

toothed wheel: 8 roulette

toothless: 8 edentate

toothpaste: 10 dentifrice

tooth socket: 8 alveolus

toothsome: 8 luscious; **9** delicious

toothwort: 10 pepper root; **11** crinkle root, crinkleroot

toowomba canary grass: 12 Harding grass

top: 3 cap, tip; **4** apex, head, peak; **5** chief, crown, first

topaz: 3 tan

top banana: 6 bigwig; **7** kingpin

top dog: 4 head; **5** chief

top floor: 5 attic; **6** dormer

topgallant: 4 head; **5** polar; **7** capital

top grade: 5 prime

topi: 8 antelope

topic: 5 issue, theme; **6** matter

topical: 5 local

topless: 7 braless

top-level: 7 ranking

topminnow: 10 live-bearer

topnotch: 3 ace; **4** A-one, tops; **6** tiptop

topography: 9 geography

topple: 6 tumble; **8** fall over

top-quality: 6 finest

topsy-turvy: 5 chaos; **6** bedlam; **7** jumbled; **10** disorderly

TOPV: 3 OPV; **12** Sabin vaccine

toque: 6 turban

torch: 4 fuse, lamp

toreador: 11 bullfighter

torment: 6 teaser; **7** agonize, torture; **8** worrying

torn: 6 ripped

tornado: 7 twister

tornillo: 9 screw bean, screwbean

torn out: 7 removed

torpedo: 3 gun, sub; **4** hero; **5** hoagy, wedge; **6** bomber; **7** grinder

torpid: 4 dull, lazy; **9** apathetic

torrent: 4 rush; **5** flood; **6** deluge

Torreya californica: 9 nutmeg-yew

torrid: 5 fiery, sunny; **6** ardent, fervid, steamy, sultry

Torrid Zone: 7 tropics

torsion: 6 torque

torso: 4 body; **5** trunk

tort: 10 civil wrong

torticollis: 7 wryneck

tortious: 9 injurious

tortoise plant: 13 elephant's-foot

tortoiseshell: 9 calico cat

tortuous: 4 dark; **6** knotty, twisty; **7** crooked

torture: 4 rack; **5** agony; **7** agonize

toss: 5 chuck, fling, throw; **7** discard, dispose

tot: 4 tyke

total: 3 add, all, sum

total heat: 8 enthalpy

totalism: 7 tyranny; **10** absolutism

total recall: 13 perfect memory

tote: 3 lug; **5** carry

totter: 7 stagger

touch: 4 feel; **5** reach; **7** concern, contact

touch base: 7 connect

touching: 3 sad; **6** moving; **8** poignant

touch-me-not: 9 celandine, jewelweed; **10** shame plant; **11** action plant, humble plant
touch on: 5 refer; **6** relate; **7** pertain
touchstone: 8 standard; **9** criterion
touch the hat: 6 salute
touchwood: 4 punk
touchy: 5 cross, huffy, surly, testy; **6** crabby, feisty
tough: 3 bad; **4** hard; **5** rough, rowdy; **6** strong
tough guy: 7 bruiser
toughness: 6 temper; **7** stamina; **8** hardness
toupee: 3 rug
tour: 4 trip, road; **7** circuit; **9** excursion, traveling; **10** enlistment
tour de force: 8 strength; **9** ingenuity
tousle: 5 ravel; **6** ruffle; **8** dishevel
tout: 4 blow, brag; **5** boast
tow: 3 lug, tug; **4** drag, haul, pull
toward land: 6 ashore
towel: 5 cloth; **6** dry off
tower: 4 loom, soar; **6** castle, column, pillar
towering: 5 lofty; **6** mighty
tower mustard: 10 tower cress
towheaded: 9 ash-blonde
toxin: 6 poison
Toxostoma rufums: 11 brown thrush; **13** brown thrasher
toy: 4 play; **5** flirt, antic; **7** trinket
trace: 7 outline, remains
Trachurus symmetricus: 6 saurel; **8** mackerel
track: 3 tag; **4** hunt, path; **5** chase; **6** course; **7** raceway; **9** racetrack; **10** racecourse
track shoe: 7 sneaker
tract: 3 lot; **4** plot; **5** patch; **11** piece of land
tractability: 4 ease; **8** docility, obedient
traction: 4 grip
tractor trailer: 4 semi; **5** truck
trade: 4 deal, sell, swap; **5** craft; **6** barter, switch; **8** business
trademark: 7 earmark; **8** hallmark
trade mark: 5 brand
trader: 6 dealer, monger; **8** merchant, salesman
trade route: 6 seaway; **7** sea lane; **9** ship route
tradition: 6 custom, legend
traduce: 6 malign
traffic: 5 trade, wares, goods; **6** barter; **10** congestion, bottleneck
traffic circle: 6 rotary; **10** roundabout
traffic island: 10 safety zone
traffic signal: 9 stoplight
tragedy: 8 accident, casualty, disaster; **11** catastrophe
tragic: 7 ruinous
Tragopogon porrifolius: 7 salsify; **11** oyster plant
Tragopogon pratensis: 10 goatsbeard; **13** meadow salsify

trail: 3 tow; **4** drag, haul, hunt, tail; **5** chase; **7** dwindle
trailblazer: 7 pioneer
trailer: 10 mobile home
trailing: 6 behind
trailing arbutus: 9 mayflower
train: 3 tow; **4** drag, tail; **5** coach, groom, teach, tutor; **6** direct; **7** prepare, educate
traipse: 4 walk; **5** tramp; **6** wander
trait: 6 aspect; **7** feature, quality
traitor: 8 betrayer, turncoat
trajectory: 6 flight
tram: 7 ropeway, trolley; **9** streetcar
tammel: 6 hamper; **7** confine; **9** restraint
tramp: 3 bum; **4** hike
trampled: 7 trodden
trance: 4 coma; **5** spell; **8** entrance; **9** captivate, fascinate
tranquil: 4 calm; **5** quiet, still; **6** placid, serene
tranquilize: 5 abate, allay; **6** pacify, sedate, soothe; **7** appease, compose
transaction: 8 exchange, transfer
transcend: 4 pass, soar; **5** excel; **6** exceed; **7** surpass
transcendentalism: 12 spiritualis
transcribe: 5 adapt
transcript: 4 copy; **8** rescript
transfer: 4 move; **5** shift; **6** change; **8** transmit; **9** transport
transfix: 4 grip; **6** impale; **9** fascinate, spellbind
transfixed: 4 rapt; **7** riveted; **8** absorbed
transform: 5 shift; **7** convert
transgression: 6 breach; **7** offense; **8** trespass; **9** violating
transient: 7 passing; **8** temporal; **9** ephemeral
transit: 7 passage
translate: 9 interpret, transform
translocate: 9 displace
translucent: 10 semiopaque
transmit: 4 beam, pass, send; **6** convey, devise; **8** transfer; **9** broadcast,
transmute: 9 transform
transom: 8 traverse; **10** crosspiece
transparent: 5 clear
transpire: 5 occur; **7** develop
transplant: 8 relocate
transport: 4 send, move, ship; **6** convey, banish; **8** transfer
transpose: 4 swap; **6** switch; **7** commute; **8** transfer
Transvaal kafferboom: 10 kaffir boom
transversal: 5 cross
trap: 5 snare; **6** ambush, entrap
Trapa bicornis: 4 ling; **6** ling ko
trapdoor: 5 hatch
trappings: 9 dressings
trapshooting: 5 skeet

T

trash: 4 junk; 6 refuse; 7 discard, garbage, rubbish
trashiness: 7 poverty; 9 cheapness
trauma: 4 harm, hurt; 5 shock; 6 injury
travail: 4 work; 5 agony; 6 torment
travel: 4 move, trip; 6 course; 7 journey, commute
travel guidebook: 9 itinerary
travel plan: 9 itinerary
traverse: 4 span; 5 cross
travesty: 5 farce, spoof; 6 parody; 7 mockery; 8 satirize
trawl: 5 troll; 7 setline
treacherous: 9 faithless; 10 unreliable
treachery: 7 treason
treacle: 8 molasses; 11 golden syrup
tread: 4 step; 5 march
treadmill: 5 crank
treason: 8 betrayal; 9 treachery
treasure: 3 gem; 5 prize; 9 thesaurus; 10 appreciate
Treasure State: 7 Montana
treasury: 9 exchequer
treat: 4 deal; 5 goody; 6 handle; 9 negotiate
treated: 8 tempered
treatise: 5 theme; 7 account
treatment: 4 help; 6 remedy; 7 therapy
treaty: 4 pact; 6 accord; 8 Protocol
treble: 7 soprano; 9 threefold
tree: 7 gallows
tree clubmoss: 9 ground fir; 12 princess pine
tree farming: 13 arboriculture
tree fuchsia: 6 konini; 13 native fuchsia
tree heath: 5 briar, brier; 9 grass tree
tree-like: 6 ramose; 8 branched
tree mallow: 10 velvetleaf
tree tomato: 9 tamarillo
treetop: 5 crown
trefoil: 6 clover
trek: 6 course
trellis: 7 lattice; 10 interweave
tremble: 5 shake; 6 quiver, shiver
tremendous: 8 enormous; 9 monstrous
tremor: 5 quake
tremulous: 7 fidgety, jittery, nervous
trench: 5 ditch; 8 encroach
trend: 5 craze, style, vogue; 8 tendency
trendy: 4 chic, cool; 7 current, in vogue, stylish; 11 fashionable
Trenton: 18 capital of New Jersey
trepan: 5 snare
trepid: 7 fearful
trepidation: 4 fear; 6 tremor
trespass: 7 intrude; 8 infringe, overstep
tress: 5 braid
triad: 4 trey, trio; 5 three
Triaenodon obseus: 13 whitetip shark
trial: 4 test; 6 ordeal; 7 attempt
trial run: 8 practice
trials: 4 woes

triangle: 5 wedge; 8 three-way
tribe: 3 kin; 4 clan
tribulation: 6 misery
tribunal: 5 bench, court, forum
tributary: 6 feeder
tribute: 5 award; 8 accolade
trice: 6 secure; 7 instant
Trichophaga tapetzella: 10 carpet moth; 12 tapestry moth
Trichostema lanatum: 9 black sage
Trichostema lanceolatum: 11 camphorweed, vinegarweed
trick: 4 ruse, dupe; 5 feint; 8 maneuver
trickery: 9 deception
trickle: 4 drip
tricky: 3 sly; 4 foxy, wily; 5 dodgy, slick; 6 crafty; 7 cunning
tricycle: 5 trike; 10 velocipede
trident: 5 spear; 9 trinomial
tried: 6 tested
trifle: 3 toy; 5 dally, flirt; 8 slightly
trifoliate orange: 10 trifoliata, wild orange
Trifolium dubium: 8 shamrock; 9 hop clover
trigger: 3 key; 4 trip; 5 spark; 8 activate
trilateral: 8 three-way
trilby: 6 fedora; 7 felt hat
trill: 5 twirl; 6 quaver; 7 revolve, vibrato
trillium: 8 wood lily; 9 wake-robin
Trillium erectum: 9 birthroot
Trillium sessile: 9 toadshade
trim: 3 hem; 6 border, edging, fringe
trinket: 4 gaud; 5 jewel
trio: 9 threesome
Triostium perfoliatum: 9 feverroot; 10 wild coffee; 11 tinker's root; 12 horse gentian
trip: 3 hop; 4 fall, skip, slip; 6 travel
tripe: 7 stomach; 8 worthless
triple: 9 threefold; 11 three-bagger
triste: 6 dismal, gloomy, somber; 7 joyless
trite: 5 banal, stock, tired; 7 trivial
Triticum aestivum: 11 common wheat
Triticum aestivum spelta: 5 spelt
Triticum dicoccum: 5 emmer; 11 starch wheat; 13 two-grain spelt
Triticum durum: 5 durum; 9 hard wheat; 10 durum wheat; 14 maccaroni wheat
tritoma: 9 kniphofia; 11 flameflower
triturate: 9 granulate, pulverize
triumph: 3 win; 7 victory
trivial: 5 banal, petty, trite; 6 boring
troglodyte: 6 hermit; 7 caveman, recluse; 11 cave dweller
Troglodytes aedon: 9 house wren
Troglodytes troglodytes: 10 winter wren
troll: 4 roll, lure; 5 dwarf; 6 ramble
trolley: 4 tram; 9 streetcar
trombone: 5 bugle; 6 cornet; 7 clarion, trumpet
trompe-l'oeil: 12 eye-deceiving
trompillo: 12 prairie berry
troop: 5 flock; 6 parade; 8 military

trooper: 6 soldier; 7 officer; 10 cavalryman
Tropaeolum minus: 10 nasturtium
trope: 14 figure of speech
trophy: 3 cup; 5 award, prize
tropical: 5 sunny; 6 steamy, torrid
tropical rain forest: 6 jungle; 10 rain forest
trot: 3 jog; 5 hurry
troth: 3 vow; 5 trust, 6 pledge
troubadour: 8 minstrel
trouble: 3 irk, fuss; 5 worry; 6 bother, hassle; 7 disturb
trough: 5 basin, ditch; 6 gutter, trench
trounce: 4 beat, whip; 5 crush; 6 punish
troupe: 7 company
trousers: 5 pants; 8 overalls
trousseau: 8 wardrobe
trout: 5 brown, brook; 7 rainbow; 9 steel-head
trout lily: 9 amberbell
trowel: 5 ladle, spoon; 6 dipper, shovel; 7 spatula
truant: 4 awol; 6 absent; 11 hooky player
truce: 7 respite; 9 armistice, cease-fire
truck: 4 swap, haul; 6 barter, pick-up; 8 exchange
truck driver: 8 teamster
truckle: 6 submit
truculent: 5 cruel; 6 savage, deadly; 7 untamed
trudge: 5 tramp
true: 4 real; 5 loyal, right; 6 direct, honest, lawful
true frog: 5 ranid
truehearted: 5 loyal; 6 trusty
true laurel: 3 bay; 7 bay tree; 9 bay laurel
truelove: 6 steady; 7 sweetie; 10 sweetheart
true tulipwood: 9 tulipwood, whitewood; 11 white poplar; 12 yellow poplar
truffle: 8 earthnut; 9 earth-ball; 16 chocolate truffle
truly: 6 indeed, really; 7 exactly
Truman: 12 Harry S Truman
trump: 4 best; 5 outdo
trumped up: 5 phony, false; 6 tricky; 7 feigned
trumpery: 5 cheap, stuff, trash; 7 rubbish, useless
trumpet: 4 blow, horn; 5 bugle, sound
trumpeter: 5 crier; 6 herald; 7 marshal; 9 spokesman
trumpet flower: 9 cross vine, cupflower; 11 chalice vine, quartervine
trumpet tree: 7 imbauba; 9 snake wood; 11 trumpetwood
truncate: 6 deface, deform; 7 shorten; 8 mutilate
truncheon: 4 club; 5 baton
trundle: 4 roll, spin
trunk: 4 body; 5 torso; 7 luggage
trunkfish: 7 boxfish
trunks: 6 shorts
trunnel: 7 trenail

trunnion: 5 pivot
truss: 4 bind; 6 bracket
trust: 4 bank, hope, rely, sure; 5 faith
truth: 6 candor, verity; 7 honesty; 8 accuracy; 9 sincerity
try: 2 go; 4 test; 5 judge, prove; 7 attempt, venture; 8 endeavor
try hard: 4 push
trying: 5 weary; 9 stressful
try-on: 7 fitting
try one's luck: 6 raffle; 9 speculate
try one's temper: 7 provoke; 9 aggravate
tryst: 4 date; 10 rendezvous
tsar: 4 czar
tsarina: 7 czarina
tsetse fly: 6 tsetse, tzetze; 8 glossina; 9 tzetze fly
T-shirt: 6 jersey; 8 tee shirt
Tsuga canadensis: 10 spruce pine; 14 eastern hemlock; 15 Canadian hemlock
Tsuga mertensiana: 12 black hemlock; 15 mountain hemlock
tsunami: 9 tidal wave
tsutsugamushi disease: 11 scrub typhus
tub: 3 vat; 4 bath, pail; 6 bucket
tuba: 8 bass horn; 10 sousaphone
tuba root: 10 derris root
tubby: 5 dumpy, podgy, pudgy
tube: 2 TV; 4 pipe; 5 metro; 6 subway; 10 television; 11 underground
tube-nosed bat: 5 harpy; 8 harpy bat; 17 tube-nosed fruit bat
tubercle: 6 nodule
tuberculosis: 2 TB
tuberous vetch: 8 heath pea; 11 earthnut pea
tuck: 3 hem; 6 gather, insert
tucked away: 8 lay aside
tucker: 3 bib
tucker out: 4 beat; 7 exhaust
tufted pansy: 12 horned violet, Viola cornuta
tug: 4 drag, jerk, pull
tuition: 7 custody
tularaemia: 9 tularemia; 11 rabbit fever; 12 deer fly fever
Tulipa armena: 10 dwarf tulip
Tulipa clusiana: 9 lady tulip
tulip gentian: 8 bluebell; 14 prairie gentian
tulip poplar: 9 tulip tree; 12 yellow poplar
tulipwood: 9 whitewood; 11 white poplar; 12 yellow poplar; 13 true tulipwood
tumble: 4 fall, slip, trip; 5 spill; 6 topple
tumbledown: 9 crumbling; 10 ramshackle; 11 dilapidated
tumble grass: 10 witch grass
tumbler: 5 glass; 7 acrobat, gymnast
tumid: 5 large, puffy; 7 bloated, swollen
tummy: 3 pot; 5 belly; 7 stomach
tumult: 3 din; 4 riot; 5 furor; 6 clamor, ruckus

T

tumultuous: 7 chaotic
tumulus: 6 barrow
tun: 4 cask
tuna: 7 bluefin; **10** yellowtail
tune: 5 music, lyric; **6** melody
tuner: 5 radio; **8** receiver
tune up: 6 warm-up
Tunga penetrans: 6 chigoe; **7** chigger; **10** chigoe flea
tungsten: 7 wolfram
tuning: 11 calibration
Tunis: 16 capital of Tunisia
tunnel: 4 mine; **6** burrow
turban: 7 pillbox
Turbatrix aceti: 10 vinegar eel; **11** vinegar worm
turbid: 4 foul; **5** muddy, murky, thick
turbojet: 8 jet liner, jet plane
turbulent: 7 chaotic, riotous, roiling; **8** agitated, troubled; **9** clamorous, in turmoil; **10** disorderly
Turdus merula: 4 merl; **5** merle, ousel, ouzel; **9** blackbird
Turdus migratorius: 5 robin
Turdus philomelos: 5 mavis; **8** throstle; **10** song thrush
Turdus pilaris: 8 snowbird; **9** fieldfare
Turdus torquatus: 9 ring ouzel; **10** ring thrush; **13** ring blackbird
turf: 3 sod; **4** lawn, peat, plot
turgid: 5 large, tumid; **7** bloated; **8** swelling
turgidity: 7 bombast, pompous
turkey: 3 dud; **4** bomb; **5** joker
turkey oak: 11 bluejack oak, swamp red oak
turkey vulture: 7 buzzard; **13** turkey buzzard
Turkish bath: 5 sauna; **8** warm bath; **9** steam bath
turmeric: 6 ginger
turmeric root: 10 goldenseal, yellow root
turmoil: 4 stir; **6** tumult; **8** disorder, disquiet, upheaval; **9** agitation, commotion; **10** disruption
turn: 2 go; **3** say; **4** bend, spin, play; **5** curve, round; **7** convert, reverse
turn a deaf ear to: 6 ignore
turn against: 6 betray
turn back: 6 return, revert
turncoat: 7 traitor; **8** renegade, defector
turn down: 4 deny; **5** lower; **6** refuse, reject; **7** decline
turned: 4 sour
turned around: 8 inverted, reversed
turn in: 6 betray; **7** produce
turning point: 6 climax, summit; **7** fulcrum; **8** landmark
turn inside out: 6 search
turn into: 6 become
turnip cabbage: 8 kohlrabi, rutabaga; **13** rutabaga plant, Swedish turnip
turnkey: 5 ready; **8** complete

turn off: 4 bore; **7** dismiss, discharge; **8** suppress; **10** deactivate, disconnect
turn of events: 5 twist
turn on: 8 activate, energize
turn one's back upon: 6 slight
turn one's stomach: 7 disgust; **8** nauseate
turn-out: 4 gear; **5** getup; **9** equipment; **11** accessories
turn out: 3 end; **5** eject, expel
turnover: 6 volume
turn over: 6 rotate; **7** deliver; **9** surrender
turn red: 5 blush
turn signal: 7 blinker
turntable: 9 lazy Susan
turn the tables: 6 invert; **7** reverse
turn to: 4 go to; **7** address; **8** appeal to, call upon
turn up: 4 find; **6** appear; **7** discover
turpentine and beeswax: 9 burnisher
turpentine weed: 9 snakeweed; **10** rabbitweed
turpitude: 9 depravity
turquoise: 4 aqua; **8** sapphire; **10** aquamarine
turret: 5 spire; **7** steeple
turret ship: 3 ram
Turritis glabra: 10 tower cress; **12** Arabis glabra, tower mustard
turtleneck: 8 pullover
tusk: 5 tooth
Tussilago farfara: 9 coltsfoot
tussle: 7 scuffle
tussock: 4 tuft
tutelage: 12 guardianship
tutor: 5 coach, teach; **8** instruct
tutu: 11 ballet skirt
tux: 6 tuxedo; **8** black tie; **12** dinner jacket
tuyere: 6 heater
TV: 4 tube; **5** video; **10** television
twaddle: 6 babble
twain: 3 duo, two; **6** couple; **7** twosome
twang: 4 pang; **6** twinge
tweak: 4 pull; **5** pinch, pluck
tweed: 6 fabric; **7** flannel; **9** gabardine
tweet: 5 cheep, chirp
tweezer: 6 pincer
twelve: 5 dozen
twelve angry men: 4 jury
twelve noon: 6 midday
twenty: 5 score
twenty-dollar bill: 7 Jackson
twenty-five percent: 6 fourth; **7** quarter
twenty-four hours: 3 day; **8** solar day
twenty-one: 9 blackjack
twice: 6 double
twiddle: 5 twist; **6** fiddle
twig: 6 branch
twilight: 4 dusk; **9** nightfall
twill: 5 weave; **6** fabric
twin: 3 two; **4** mate, pair; **6** couple
twinberry: 8 boxberry
twine: 6 string

twinge: 4 pang; **5** pinch, sting; **6** flinch, twitch
twinkle: 4 wink; **5** blink, flash, gleam
twirl: 5 swirl, twist
twist: 4 bend, bias, coil, spin, turn, warp; **5** twirl; **6** deform, squirm; **7** distort
twister: 7 cruller, tornado
twit: 5 taunt
twitch: 4 jerk; **6** quiver
twitter: 6 giggle; **7** flutter
two: 4 twin; **5** deuce
two-bagger: 6 double
two bits: 7 quarter
two-channel: 6 stereo
two-dimensional: 4 flat
two-eyed violet: 10 heartsease
two-faced: 9 deceitful
twofold: 4 dual; **6** double
two-footed: 5 biped
two for the price of one: 7 half off
two-grain spelt: 5 emmer; **11** starch wheat
two-handed: 8 bimanual
two-party: 10 bipartisan
two-person bicycle: 6 tandem
two-piece: 6 bikini
twoscore: 5 forty
two-seater: 8 roadster, runabout
two-sided: 9 bilateral
twosome: 3 duo; **4** pair; **6** couple
two times: 5 twice; **7** twofold
two-timing: 8 cheating; **10** adulterous
two-way radio: 8 car radio, ham radio; **10** police band
two weeks: 9 fortnight

two-wheeler: 4 bike; **5** cycle; **7** bicycle
two-winged insects: 8 dipteran
two-year: 8 biennial
tycoon: 5 baron, mogul; **7** magnate; **12** top executive
tying up: 7 docking, mooring
tyke: 3 kid, tot; **5** child; **7** toddler; **9** youngster
Tylenchus tritici: 8 wheat eel; **9** wheatworm; **12** wheat eelworm
Tyler: 9 John Tyler
tympan: 4 drum
tympani: 6 kettle
tympanic cavity: 9 middle ear
tympanic membrane: 7 eardrum
Tympanuchus cupido cupido: 8 heath hen
tympanum: 6 kettle; **7** eardrum; **9** middle ear
type: 4 kind, sort; **5** model; **6** nature; **8** category; **9** character
typeface: 4 font
typesetter: 10 compositor; **11** typographer
type specimen: 8 holotype
typhoid: 12 enteric fever
typical: 5 usual, daily; **6** common, normal; **7** regular; **8** symbolic
typify: 7 signify; **9** epitomize, exemplify
typo: 5 error; **8** misprint
typographer: 10 compositor, typesetter
tyrant: 8 dictator; **9** oppressor
Tyto alba: 7 barn owl
tzar: 4 czar, tsar
tzetze: 6 tsetse; **8** glossina**

u

U: 7 uranium
U.S.: 3 U.S.A.; **7** America; **12** United States
U.S.A.: 2 U.S.; **7** America; **12** United States
U. S. Army Special Forces: 11 Green Berets; **13** Special Forces
U-2: 8 spy plane
U235: 15 enriched uranium
Ubermensch: 7 demigod; **8** superman
ubiquitous: 6 common; **11** commonplace, omnipresent
U-boat: 3 sub; **9** submarine; **12** undersea boat
udder: 3 bag; **8** pericarp; **12** mammary gland
UFO: 12 flying saucer
ugli: 7 tangelo; **9** ugli fruit
ugly: 4 vile; **5** surly; **7** baleful, ominous; **8** horrible, menacing, minatory, sinister,

unworthy; **9** atrocious, frightful, minacious; **10** despicable, forbidding, horrifying, uninviting, unpleasing; **11** threatening, unbeautiful; **12** unattractive
ugly customer: 4 hood; **5** brute, bully, rough, rowdy, tough; **6** meanie [jocular], mugger, savage, wretch; **7** caitiff, hoodlum, ruffian; **8** hooligan; **9** barbarian, desperado
uh: 2 um; **5** y'know; **7** you know
UK: 7 Britain; **12** Great Britain; **13** United Kingdom
ukase: 4 ukaz [Russ]; **5** edict; **6** decree, diktat; **7** dictate, mandate; **9** dictation
Ukraine: 8 Ukrayina
ukulele: 3 uke; **14** Hawaiian guitar
Ulan Bator: 11 Ulaanbaatar; **17** capital of Mongolia
ulcer: 4 sore; **10** ulceration
ulcerated: 8 ulcerous; **9** cankerous**

u

ulcer diet: 9 bland diet

ulema: 6 mullah

Ulex: 4 whin; **5** furze, gorse; **10** Irish gorse; **9** genus Ulex

ullage: 9 dead space; **10** empty space

Ulmaceae: 9 elm family; **14** family Ulmaceae

Ulmus: 3 elm; **7** wing elm; **8** Dutch elm; **8** dwarf elm; **10** genus Ulmus, Chinese elm; **11** slippery elm

ulster: 5 P-coat; **7** pea coat; **9** pea jacket; **11** dreadnaught, dreadnought

ulterior: 5 later; **6** future; **8** eventual; **12** subterranean

ulterior motive: 6 agenda; **12** hidden agenda

ultima ratio: 10 last resort

ultimate: 4 last; **5** final; **8** terminal; **9** elemental

ultimately: 6 at last; **7** finally, some day; **8** in the end; **10** at long last, eventually

ultima Thule: 5 Thule; **9** antipodes

ultimatum: 8 covenant; **10** obligation, sine qua non

ultra: 7 acutely, radical; **9** extremist, intensely; **11** exceedingly

ultraconservative: 11 reactionary; **11** rightwinger

ultrahigh frequency: 3 UHF

ultramarine: 4 blue

ultranationalism: 8 jingoism; **10** chauvinism; **15** superpatriotism

ultrasonic: 10 supersonic

ultraviolet: 2 UV; **6** purple, violet

ultraviolet radiation: 2 UV; **11** ultraviolet; **16** ultraviolet light

ultraviolet source: 6 UV lamp; **15** ultraviolet lamp

ululate: 3 cry; **4** howl, roar, wail, yawl

ululation: 3 baa, cry; **4** howl, wail; **6** crying, outcry; **7** howling, wailing, weeping

Ulvaceae: 16 sea-lettuce family

Ulysses: 8 Odysseus

um: 2 uh; **5** y'know; **7** you know

umbellate: 8 umbellar

Umbelliferae: 8 Apiaceae; **12** carrot family

umbelliferous plant: 10 umbellifer

umber: 6 coffee; **9** chocolate, deep brown; **10** burnt umber

umbilical: 5 axial, navel, focal; **7** abdomen, azygous; **10** concentric

umbilicus: 5 navel; **11** bellybutton

umbra: 5 shade; **6** shadow; **7** umbrage

umbrage: 4 gall, huff, miff; **5** pique, shade, umbra; **6** grudge, shadow, spleen; **7** offense; **8** acerbity, acrimony, asperity, rankling, soreness; **9** virulence; **10** bitterness

umbrella: 7 parasol

umlaut: 8 dieresis; **9** diaeresis

ump: 6 umpire

umpire: 3 ump; **7** referee

umpiring: 8 umpirage; **10** refereeing; **11** officiating, officiation

umpteenth: 8 umptieth, umteenth

UN: 13 United Nations

unabashed: 5 sassy, saucy; **6** unawed; **7** aweless; **8** impudent; **9** audacious, shameless, unalarmed, undaunted; **10** unappalled, unblanched, unblushing, undismayed; **11** unflinching; **13** unembarrassed

unabated: 12 undiminished, unrestricted

unable: 7 not able; **9** incapable; **11** incompetent, ineffective, ineffectual

unable to hear: 4 deaf

unable to help: 8 impotent, helpless

unaccented: 4 weak; **5** light; **6** atonic; **10** unstressed

unacceptable: 9 thankless, unpopular; **10** impossible, unaccepted; **12** insufferable

unaccommodating: 5 cross, rusty; **6** cussed [U.S.]; **7** froward; **9** invidious, ungallant, vexatious; **10** unobliging; **11** intractable

unaccompanied: 5 alone; **10** unattended

unaccredited: 10 unlicensed

unaccustomed: 7 strange, unusual; **8** uncommon

unacknowledged: 7 unnamed; **8** nameless, unavowed; **9** anonymous

unadorned: 4 bare; **7** prosaic; **9** untrimmed; **11** commonplace, undecorated, ungarnished; **12** unornamented

unadulterated: 4 pure; **9** unalloyed, uncolored, untainted

unaffected: 4 easy, lain, naif, pure; **5** attic, naive; **6** chaste, fluent, native, simple; **7** artless, flowing, natural, unmoved; **8** bona fide, graceful, readable, tripping; **9** classical, unexcited, unfeigned, unruffled, unspoiled, unstirred, untouched; **10** insensible, uninspired, unromantic; **11** undesigning, unimpressed; **12** uninfluenced

unaffectionate: 8 uncaring

unaffixed: 5 loose

unafflicted: 9 unworried, worriless; **10** unmolested

unafraid: 6 secure; **8** fearless; **10** untroubled

unaggressive: 13 nonaggressive

unaided: 8 unhelped; **10** unassisted; **11** unsupported

unalienable: 8 absolute; **10** inviolable, sacrosanct; **11** inalienable

unalike: 6 unlike; **8** not alike; **9** different, differing; **10** dissimilar; **15** distinguishable

unalleviated: 10 unrelieved

unallowable: 12 unreasonable; **13** unjustifiable, unwarrantable

unalterable: 9 immutable; **10** changeless; **11** inalterable; **12** unchangeable

unaltered: 9 unchanged; **10** unmodified

unambiguous: 8 univocal; **11** unequivocal; **12** unmistakable

unambiguously: 8 uniquely; 13 unequivocally

unambitious: 12 ambitionless

unamused: 9 mirthless

unanimous: 5 solid; 9 of one mind; 11 consentient; 13 consentaneous

unanimous agreement: 9 unanimity

unannexed: 4 free; 5 apart, loose; 7 asunder, insular; 8 discrete, separate; 9 disparate; 10 far between, unattached; 11 unconnected; 12 unassociated

unannounced: 10 unheralded; 11 unpredicted

unanswerable: 9 probative; 10 apodeictic, conclusive; 11 irrefutable, self-evident; 12 irrefragable, irresistible; 13 unaccountable

unanticipated: 10 surprising, unexpected, unforeseen

unappealing: 9 unlikable; 10 unlikeable; 13 unsympathetic

unappeasable: 4 grim; 5 stern; 10 headstrong, inexorable, relentless; 11 immitigable, unforgiving, unrelenting

unappreciated: 6 unsung; 8 unvalued; 9 thankless

unapproachable: 5 aloof; 6 remote; 8 fabulous; 9 ineffable, unreached; 11 unreachable

unappropriated: 7 unowned; 8 unculled

unarm: 6 disarm

unarmed: 8 harmless, sine ictu [Lat], vincible; 9 pregnable, untenable; 10 weaponless; 11 defenseless, unfortified; 12 indefensible

unashamedly: 11 barefacedly, shamelessly

unasked: 5 unbid; 8 unbidden, unwanted; 9 uninvited, unordered; 11 uncalled for, unrequested, unsolicited

unassailable: 6 secure, strong; 8 ironclad; 10 inviolable, unshakable, watertight; 11 impregnable, untouchable; 12 impenetrable

unassailed: 8 unforced; 9 undivided; 11 uncompelled; 13 unpartitioned

unassemble: 9 break down, take apart; 11 disassemble

unassisted: 7 unaided; 8 unbacked, unhelped; 10 unsuccored; 11 unsupported; 12 single-handed

unassisted eye: 8 naked eye

unassociated: 4 free; 5 apart, loose; 7 asunder, insular; 8 discrete, separate; 9 disparate, unannexed; 10 far between, unattached; 11 unconnected

unassuming: 4 meek; 8 retiring

unattached: 4 free; 5 apart, loose; 7 asunder, insular; 8 discrete, separate; 9 disparate, unannexed; 10 far between; 11 uncommitted, unconnected

unattempted: 8 unsought

unattended: 9 neglected; 13 unaccompanied

unattractive: 4 ugly; 8 unvalued; 9 undesired; 10 unalluring, uninviting, unpleasing, untempting

unattractiveness: 8 ugliness

unauthenticated: 10 unattested

unauthorized: 7 wildcat; 8 informal; 10 disallowed, unofficial; 12 unsanctioned

una voce: 6 to a man; 8 in chorus; 11 unanimously

unavoidable: 10 inevitable, inexorable; 11 inescapable, irrevocable; 12 irresistible; 14 uncontrollable

unavowed: 6 secret; 8 sneaking; 11 unconfessed

unaware: 4 dead [fig], numb; 7 out cold; 8 comatose, unwarned; 9 catatonic, senseless, unknowing, unwitting; 10 unapprised; 11 incognizant, unconscious

unawed: 9 unabashed, unalarmed, undaunted

unbalance: 7 derange; 9 imbalance; 11 derangement, instability

unbalanced: 3 mad; 4 sick; 5 crazy; 8 demented, unhinged; 9 disturbed; 10 asymmetric, distracted, imbalanced

unbeatable: 10 invincible

unbeaten: 6 untrod; 7 untried; 9 untrodden; 10 undefeated; 11 unconquered

unbelievable: 8 unlikely; 10 improbable, incredible, staggering

unbelievably: 10 improbably, incredibly; 11 implausibly

unbeliever: 5 cynic; 7 infidel, sceptic, skeptic; 11 disbeliever, nonbeliever

unbend: 5 relax, unlax; 6 uncurl, unfold, unwind, unwrap; 7 slacken; 8 loosen up, slow down; 10 decompress, straighten

unbendable: 4 firm; 6 steady; 9 steadfast; 10 unshakable, unwavering; 11 unfaltering

unbending: 4 ease; 5 rigid, stark; 8 relaxing, unlimber; 10 inflexible, unyielding

unblock: 4 free; 7 release; 8 unfreeze

unborn: 6 unmade; 8 in embryo; 10 unbegotten, unproduced; 11 unconceived

unbounded: 6 untold; 9 boundless, limitless, unlimited

unbroken: 4 kept; 5 uncut; 6 intact, unhurt; 7 unshorn; 8 unmarred, unplowed; 9 continued, uncropped, undivided, uninjured; 10 continuous

uncanny: 4 unco; 5 weird; 6 odious; 9 frightful, unearthly; 10 forbidding

uncaring: 9 unfeeling; 10 unthinking; 11 thoughtless

unceremonious: 5 loose; 6 casual; 7 natural, uncivil; 8 informal; 10 ungracious

uncertain: 6 fitful, unsure; 8 unsealed; 9 desultory, incertain, irregular, unsettled; 10 capricious, changeable, flickering, unpunctual

uncertainty: 5 doubt; 7 dubiety; 11 dubiousness, incertitude; 12 doubtfulness, irregularity

unchained: 4 free; 6 untied; 8 uncurbed;

u

9 unbridled, unmuzzled; **10** unfettered, unshackled

unchallenged: 8 absolute; **9** undoubted; **10** inviolable, sacrosanct, undisputed; **11** inalienable, unalienable; **12** indefeasible, unquestioned

unchanged: 7 regular; **8** unvaried; **9** unaltered

uncial: 5 Runic; **9** cuneiform

unciform bone: 6 hamate; **9** os hamatum; **10** hamate bone

uncivil: 4 rude

uncivilized: 4 wild; **6** savage; **8** barbaric; **9** barbarian

unclad: 8 ungarbed; **9** unattired, undressed; **11** unappareled, ungarmented

unclean: 5 dirty; **6** impure, soiled

uncleanly: 5 messy; **6** untidy; **8** slovenly

unclear: 7 obscure; **9** unobvious; **10** ill-defined, unreadable

unclog: 5 clear, unbar; **6** unbind, unbolt, uncork, unhand; **7** unchain, unclose, unleash; **9** unharness

unclothe: 5 strip; **6** uncase; **7** discase, disrobe, undress

unclutter: 5 clear

unco: 7 uncanny; **9** unusually; **10** remarkably; **13** outstandingly

uncoil: 6 unfold, unfurl, unroll, unwind; **7** untwist

uncoiled: 8 straight

uncolored: 9 colorless

uncomfortable: 6 uneasy

uncommitted: 9 available; **10** unattached

uncommon: 4 rare; **6** scarce; **7** strange, unusual; **8** unwonted; **11** exceptional, uncustomary; **12** unaccustomed

uncommunicative: 8 reserved, reticent; **10** buttoned up

uncomplicate: 8 simplify

uncomplicated: 6 simple; **10** elementary

uncompressed: 8 diffused

uncompromising: 5 rigid, sound; **6** strict; **7** austere, exigent; **8** exacting, obdurate, positive, rigorous; **9** demanding, hard-nosed, hard-shell [U.S.], searching, unsparing; **10** hard-headed, inexorable, inflexible

unconditional: 4 flat, free; **5** sheer; **7** regular; **9** categoric, unlimited; **10** consummate; **11** categorical, independent, unmitigated, unqualified; **12** unrestricted

unconditioned: 5 total; **6** innate; **8** absolute; **9** unlearned

unconnected: 4 free; **5** apart, loose, vague; **7** asunder, garbled, insular; **8** confused, discrete, separate; **9** disparate, illogical, scattered, separated, unannexed; **10** disjointed, disordered, unattached; **11** dissociated; **12** disconnected, unassociated

unconquerable: 10 dominating, invincible, resistless; **11** indomitable, insuperable

unconquered: 8 stubborn, unbeaten; **10** undefeated; **12** unvanquished

unconscionable: 5 steep; **8** swinging, usurious; **9** excessive; **10** exorbitant, immoderate, inordinate, outrageous; **11** extravagant; **12** extortionate, preposterous; **14** conscienceless

unconscious: 4 dead [fig], numb; **7** out cold, unaware; **8** comatose; **9** catatonic, senseless, unknowing, unwitting; **10** unapprised, unthinking

unconsciousness: 4 coma; **6** trance; **9** catatonia

unconsecrated: 7 profane; **12** unsanctified

unconsolable: 7 forlorn; **8** desolate; **11** comfortless, sick at heart; **12** disconsolate

uncontested: 9 undoubted; **10** undisputed; **12** unquestioned

uncontrollable: 6 unruly; **8** indocile; **10** inevitable, inexorable; **11** irrevocable, unavoidable; **12** irresistible, out of control, uncontrolled, ungovernable, unmanageable; **13** irrepressible, uncorrectable

unconventional: 8 improper, original, unlawful; **9** unheard of; **10** unfamiliar

uncooked: 3 raw; **6** coarse; **7** unblown; **8** unboiled, unformed

uncool: 3 out; **7** out of it; **9** unstylish; **13** unfashionable

uncoordinated: 5 jerky; **6** clumsy; **7** awkward, jerking, spastic, unhandy; **8** lubberly, separate; **9** maladroit; **11** floundering, heavy-handed, independent

uncork: 3 pop; **4** open; **5** unbar; **6** unclog

uncounted: 6 myriad, untold; **8** infinite; **9** countless; **10** innumerous, numberless, unnumbered; **11** innumerable

uncouple: 5 leave; **8** break off, break way; **9** disengage

uncouth: 5 harsh, stiff; **6** coarse, common, vulgar; **7** unkempt, untamed; **8** uncombed, ungainly; **9** barbarous, grotesque; **10** ungraceful, unpolished

uncover: 4 open; **6** devest, divest, expose, reveal, unfold, unseal, unveil; **7** lay open, pop open, unclose; **8** bring out

uncovering: 4 find; **6** baring; **7** husking, removal; **8** removing; **9** discovery, stripping, taking off, unveiling; **10** denudation, divestment

uncropped: 5 uncut; **6** intact; **7** unshorn; **8** unbroken; **9** undivided

unction: 4 glow; **5** grace, gusto, smarm; **6** warmth; **8** oiliness, piquance, piquancy; **9** inunction, vehemence; **10** smarminess; **11** consolation, edification, fulsomeness, inspiration

unctuous: 4 oily; **5** soapy; **6** smarmy; **7** buttery, canting, fulsome; **8** specious

uncultivated: 7 artless, lowbrow, out of it;

8 untaught, unversed; 9 lowbrowed, misguided, undrilled, unfledged, unhatched, untrained, untutored; 10 uncultured, uneducated, uninformed; 11 unexercised, uninitiated; 13 unenlightened

uncured: 5 green

uncut: 5 rough; 6 intact, unmown; 7 unshorn; 8 standing, unbroken; 9 uncropped, undivided, untrimmed; 10 full-length

undamaged: 8 harmless, unharmed; 9 uninjured, unscathed; 11 unblemished

undated: 8 dateless

undaunted: 6 unawed; 8 unshaken; 9 unabashed, unalarmed; 10 unappalled, unblanched, undismayed; 11 unflinching

undeceived: 9 disabused

undecided: 4 open; 7 untried; 9 unsettled; 10 on the fence, unresolved; 12 undetermined

undecipherable: 7 unclear; 10 unreadable; 14 indecipherable

undecorated: 9 unadorned

undefeated: 8 unbeaten; 11 unconquered; 12 unvanquished

undefended: 4 open; 10 assailable; 12 undefendable

undefiled: 4 pure; 6 decent, modest; 8 decorous, delicate; 10 immaculate; 11 uncorrupted

undefined: 5 vague; 7 shadowy; 10 indefinite

undeniable: 13 unimpeachable; 14 unquestionable

under: 5 below; 6 nether; 7 short of

underact: 9 underplay

underactive: 10 hypoactive

under age: 5 green, sappy, young; 6 callow, puisne; 7 budding; 8 juvenile, youthful; 9 beardless

underage: 5 minor; 7 nonaged

under anesthesia: 13 anaesthetized

under an illusion: 7 in error; 8 mistaken

under attack: 9 under fire

underbodice: 8 camisole

underbred: 3 cur; 4 rude; 5 mixed, scrub; 7 ill-bred, lowbred, mongrel; 8 yokelish; 10 bounderish

underbrush: 9 brushwood, underwood; 11 undergrowth

underclothed: 11 half-clothed; 12 scantily clad

underclothing: 9 underwear; 12 underclothes

undercoat: 5 prime; 6 ground, primer; 8 flat coat; 9 underseal; 11 priming coat

under control: 6 in hand; 7 in check; 10 controlled, restrained; 11 constrained, disciplined

undercover: 6 secret; 8 hush-hush; 10 on the quiet; 11 clandestine, underground; 13 surreptitious

undercover agent: 3 spy; 11 secret agent

undercover work: 6 spying

undercurrent: 4 eddy; 6 agenda, reflux, vortex; 8 head wind, overflow; 9 cross fire, Maelstrom, undertide, undertone, whirlpool

undercut: 9 undersell; 10 tenderloin

underdone: 9 half-baked; 10 half-cooked

underestimate: 7 lowball; 9 underrate; 10 undervalue

underfed: 6 ill-fed; 14 undernourished

underframe: 5 frame; 8 skeleton

undergird: 7 brace up

undergo: 3 get; 4 have, take; 5 enjoy; 6 submit, suffer; 7 receive; 9 encounter, go through; 10 experience

undergraduate: 9 undergrad

underground: 4 tube; 5 metro; 6 buried, secret, subway; 8 guerilla, hush-hush; 9 guerrilla, irregular, underhand; 10 resistance, undercover; 11 belowground, clandestine

underground railroad: 4 tube; 5 metro; 6 subway; 11 underground

underground water: 8 artesian; 11 ground water; 12 mineral water

undergrowth: 9 underwood; 10 underbrush; 11 ground cover, groundcover

underhanded: 6 sneaky, tricky; 8 underarm; 9 insidious, underhand; 13 surreptitious

underived: 6 simple

underlay: 4 slug; 5 scale, serif, shank; 6 rug pad; 8 shoulder; 9 carpet pad, sheet work, signature

underline: 9 emphasize; 10 accentuate, take note of, underscore

underling: 4 boor, lout; 5 churl; 6 menial; 9 subaltern; 10 subsidiary; 11 subordinate

underlying: 8 inherent; 10 implicit in; 11 fundamental, rudimentary

undermanned: 11 short-handed; 12 short-staffed, understaffed

undermentioned: 9 following

undermine: 3 sap; 5 shake; 6 burrow, tunnel, waylay, weaken; 7 break up, counter, stave in, subvert; 8 sabotage; 10 counteract; 11 countermine

undermost: 6 bottom; 10 nethermost

underneath: 7 beneath; 13 directly below

undernourished: 6 ill-fed; 8 underfed

underpants: 6 briefs, shorts; 8 breeches

underpin: 7 bear out, support; 11 corroborate

underprice: 4 dump

underrate: 10 undervalue; 13 underestimate

under sail: 8 under way; 10 under steam; 11 under canvas

underscore: 9 emphasize, underline

undersea: 9 submarine

undersea boat: 3 sub; 5 U-boat; 9 submarine

underseal: 9 undercoat

undersell: 8 undercut

u

underside: 6 bottom; 12 undersurface

underskirt: 4 slip; 9 petticoat

undersoil: 7 subsoil

understaffed: 11 short-handed, under-manned; 12 short-staffed

understand: 3 ken, see; 4 know, read, scan; 5 infer; 6 gather; 7 realize; 8 construe; 9 apprehend, be aware of, empathize, interpret, translate; 10 appreciate, comprehend, sympathize

understandable: 9 graspable; 11 perceivable; 12 intelligible; 13 apprehensible

understanding: 3 wit; 5 savvy; 6 reason; 7 knowing; 8 capacity, keenness, sympathy; 9 agreement, cognition, construal, intellect, realizing; 10 cognizance, conception; 11 discernment; 12 appreciating, apprehension, being aware of, intelligence, precognition; 13 comprehending, comprehension; 14 interpretation

understate: 8 minimize

understood: 5 known, tacit; 6 latent, silent; 7 implied; 8 admitted, implicit; 12 acknowledged

understrapper: 9 underling

understructure: 4 base, foot; 9 fundament; 10 foundation, groundwork; 12 substructure

understudy: 7 standby; 9 alternate

undersurface: 6 bottom; 9 underside

under suspicion: 9 suspected; 11 under a cloud

undertake: 6 engage, tackle, take on; 7 attempt, venture; 8 contract, endeavor, engage in, set about; 9 guarantee

undertaker: 9 mortician; 15 funeral director

undertaking: 4 task, word; 5 chore, labor; 6 effort, pledge; 7 project, promise, venture; 8 endeavor; 10 enterprise; 11 endeavoring

under the sun: 7 on earth; 8 existent

under the thumb of: 9 dominated

undertide: 12 undercurrent

undertone: 5 tinge; 6 breath; 12 undercurrent

underutilized: 9 underused

undervalue: 7 devalue; 9 devaluate, underrate; 10 depreciate; 13 underestimate

underwater: 9 submerged, submersed; 10 subaquatic, subaqueous

underwater diver: 5 diver; 7 frogman; 10 scuba diver

under way: 5 afoot; 7 en route, going on, running; 8 on course, on the way; 9 happening, in the fire, in transit, on one's way, on the road, on the wing, under sail; 10 en route for, in progress, under steam

underway: 5 afoot

underweight: 5 weedy; 6 skinny; 7 scraggy, scrawny

underworld: 3 Hel; 4 Hell; 5 Hades; 6 Scheol; 11 netherworld; 14 infernal region

underwrite: 5 cover; 6 accept, assure, clench, insure, ratify, secure; 7 confirm, indorse, warrant; 9 guarantee, subscribe

underwriter: 6 broker; 15 commission agent

undeserved: 8 unearned; 9 unmerited

undeserving: 10 unworthy of

undesirable: 8 unvalued, unwanted; 9 undesired, unwelcome; 10 unalluring, uncared for, uninviting, unsuitable; 12 unattractive

undetermined: 4 open; 5 loose, vague; 6 casual, chance; 7 untried; 8 uncaused; 9 ambiguous, causeless, undecided, unsettled; 10 accidental, contingent, fortuitous, incidental, unresolved; 12 adventitious; 13 indeterminate

undeterred: 13 undiscouraged

undeviating: 7 regular; 8 unturned, unvaried; 9 unchanged; 10 invariable, unchanging, unflagging, unswerving, unwavering; 11 undistorted, unfaltering, unflinching

undiluted: 4 pure; 7 unmixed

undiminished: 8 unabated; 10 unrelieved; 12 unrestricted

undiplomatic: 8 tactless; 9 impolitic, untactful

undirected: 5 stray; 6 adrift, afloat, zigzag; 7 aimless, erratic, vagrant; 8 indirect, planless, unguided; 10 circuitous, rudderless; 13 directionless

undisciplined: 10 ungoverned; 11 uncorrected

undisclosed: 8 held back, withheld; 10 unrevealed disclosed

undiscovered: 8 unsolved; 10 unexplored; 11 undeveloped, unexplained; 12 unrecognized

undisguised: 4 bare, open; 5 overt; 6 patent; 7 express, genuine, literal; 8 exoteric, explicit; 9 expressed; 11 undistorted

undisputed: 8 accepted; 9 undoubted; 11 uncontested; 12 unchallenged, unquestioned

undistinguished: 13 insignificant

undisturbed: 4 calm; 5 quiet; 7 unmoved; 9 unexcited, unruffled, unstirred; 10 deliberate, unagitated, unmolested; 11 unperturbed; 13 unimpassioned

undivided: 4 full, open; 5 solid, uncut; 6 intact, single; 7 unshorn; 8 unbroken, unfenced, wide open; 9 exclusive, uncropped; 10 unenclosed

undo: 4 dish, do in; 5 do for, untie; 6 unbind, unmake; 10 neutralize

undone: 4 lost, sunk; 6 broken, doomed, ruined; 7 decayed, devoted, done for, not done, unstuck; 8 accursed, stranded, washed-up

undress: 5 strip; 6 uncase; 7 discase, disrobe; 8 chastity, unclothe

undressed: 6 unclad; 8 undraped, ungarbed; 9 unattired; 11 unappareled, ungarmented

undue: 6 not due; 9 excessive; 10 inordinate; 11 unjustified, unwarranted; 12 unreasonable; 13 unjustifiable

undulant fever: 11 brucellosis

undulate: 4 flap, roll, wave; 6 riffle, ripple

undulation: 4 wave

undulatory theory: 10 wave theory

undutiful: 7 impious, naughty; 9 incorrect

undying: 8 immortal; 9 deathless; 12 imperishable; 13 incorruptible; 14 indestructible

unearned: 10 undeserved

unearth: 5 dig up; 6 dig out, exhume; 8 disinter; 12 bring to light

unearthly: 5 weird; 7 adopted, elected, elysian, ghostly, uncanny; 8 beatific, eldritch, heavenly, inspired, supernal; 9 celestial, converted, justified, spiritual; 10 sanctified; 11 consecrated, regenerated; 12 extramundane, paradisiacal, supernatural

unease: 5 worry; 7 anxiety, concern, malaise; 8 disquiet; 10 discomfort, inquietude, solicitude, uneasiness; 11 disquietude; 12 apprehension

uneasiness: 5 worry; 6 unease; 7 anxiety, concern, malaise; 8 disquiet, edginess; 10 inquietude, solicitude; 11 disquietude; 12 apprehension, restlessness

uneasy: 7 anxious, awkward, nervous, unquiet, worried; 8 restless; 9 concerned; 12 apprehensive; 13 uncomfortable

uneatable: 8 inedible

uneconomical: 8 wasteful

unedifying: 14 unenlightening

uneducated: 8 untaught; 9 unbookish, undrilled, unfledged, unhatched, unlearned, untrained, untutored; 10 uninformed, unlettered, unschooled; 11 unexercised; 12 uncultivated, uninstructed

unembarrassed: 6 degage [Fr]; 9 unabashed; 10 unburdened; 11 disburdened; 12 unencumbered

unembellished: 5 plain; 7 literal; 12 unornamented

unembodied: 8 bodiless, unbodied; 11 disembodied; 12 discorporate

unemotional: 8 reserved, reticent, soulless; 9 heartless, impassive; 10 restrained, spiritless; 11 emotionless, passionless

unemotional person: 5 stoic

unemployed: 6 unused; 7 jobless, not used; 9 unapplied; 10 unoccupied; 11 between jobs

unenclosed: 4 open; 8 unfenced, wide open; 9 free-range, undivided

unencumbered: 7 unbound; 10 unburdened

unending: 7 ageless, endless, eternal; 9 incessant, perpetual, unceasing; 11 everlasting

unengaged: 9 unpledged; 10 unpromised

unenlightened: 5 blunt, heavy; 6 obtuse, stolid, stupid, unwise; 7 doltish, out of it; 8 ignorant, nescient, ungifted, unversed; 9 misguided, unlearned; 10 uninformed, unlettered; 11 uninitiated; 12 uncultivated

unentertaining: 4 drab, dull, flat; 6 stodgy; 9 dry as dust; 13 unimaginative, uninteresting

unenviable: 6 sticky; 7 awkward; 12 embarrassing

unequal: 6 uneven, unlike; 7 partial; 8 one-sided; 9 disparate

unequaled: 5 alone; 6 unique; 10 unequalled; 12 unparalleled

unequivocal: 5 clear, stark; 7 decided, perfect; 8 absolute, decisive, definite, finished, positive, specific, univocal; 9 essential; 10 definitive; 11 ascertained, categorical, determinate, unambiguous; 12 unmistakable

unequivocally: 6 purely; 9 decidedly, downright, radically, seriously; 10 absolutely; 11 essentially; 13 fundamentally, unambiguously

unearned revenue: 14 unearned income

unerasable: 9 indelible

unergetic: 9 lethargic

unerring: 8 constant, faithful, inerrant; 9 inerrable, unspotted; 10 infallible; 11 unblemished

unethical: 4 base; 7 immoral; 12 dishonorable; 13 dishonourable

uneven: 5 scaly; 6 coarse, spotty, varied; 7 partial, unequal; 8 scabrous; 9 disparate, irregular; 10 mismatched, nonuniform; 11 diversified

unevenly: 8 raggedly; 9 unequally

unevenness: 8 imparity; 9 disparity, diversity, roughness; 11 variability; 12 irregularity; 13 nonuniformity

uneventful: 4 mere; 6 common

unexceptional: 6 normal; 7 default, natural; 12 run-of-the-mill

unexcitable: 13 imperturbable

unexcited: 7 unmoved; 9 unruffled, unstirred, untouched; 10 unaffected, uninspired; 11 undisturbed, unimpressed, unperturbed; 13 unimpassioned

unexciting: 13 unstimulating

unexclusive: 12 unrestricted

unexpected: 6 forced; 10 surprising, unforeseen, unhoped for; 11 unlooked for; 13 unanticipated

unexpectedly: 8 abruptly, by chance; 12 accidentally, surprisingly

unexplainable: 13 unaccountable

unexploited: 11 undeveloped

unexplored: 7 unknown; 8 unsifted; 9 unheard of, unstudied, untracked; 10 unexamined; 11 unexplained; 12 undiscovered

unfailing: 6 steady; 7 routine; 8 constant;

9 clockwork, continual, foolproof, incessant, perpetual, unceasing; **10** consistent, continuous, invariable, monotonous, unflagging

unfailingly: 6 always; **8** ever anon, steadily; **9** routinely; **10** at all times, constantly, invariably; **11** continually, incessantly, perpetually; **12** consistently, continuously

unfair: 6 unjust; **7** partial; **8** one-sided, uncandid; **11** inequitable

unfairness: 8 inequity, iniquity; **9** injustice

unfaithful: 5 false; **8** disloyal; **9** faithless; **10** of bad faith, traitorous

unfaltering: 4 firm; **6** steady; **9** steadfast; **10** unbendable, unflagging, unshakable, unswerving, unwavering; **11** undeviating, unflinching

unfamiliar: 8 original; **9** unheard of; **14** unconventional

unfashionable: 3 out; **6** uncool; **7** out of it; **9** unpopular, unstylish

unfastened: 4 open; **6** untied; **10** unbuttoned

unfastening: 7 undoing, untying

unfathomable: 8 infinite; **9** unplumbed; **10** fathomless, unfathomed, unknowable; **11** illimitable, innumerable; **12** immeasurable, incalculable, interminable; **13** inexhaustible, unaccountable

unfavorable: 7 unlucky; **8** untoward; **10** unfriendly; **11** unbefitting, unfortunate; **12** inauspicious, infelicitous, unfavourable, unpropitious

unfeeling: 7 unmoral; **8** uncaring; **9** senseless; **10** insensible; **11** hardhearted; **12** stonyhearted; **13** unsympathetic

unfenced: 4 open; **8** wide open; **9** undivided; **10** unenclosed

unfermented: 5 sweet

unfettered: 4 free; **6** untied; **8** uncurbed; **9** unbridled, unchained, unmuzzled; **10** ungoverned, unshackled

unfinished: 4 bare; **9** roughhewn; **10** unexecuted, unpolished, unsmoothed; **11** uncompleted, unperformed; **12** not completed, not fulfilled; **14** unaccomplished

unfinished business: 8 loose end

unfit: 3 bad; **5** cramp; **6** deaden, disarm, unmeet; **7** unhinge, unsound; **8** improper, unfitted; **9** indispose, unfitting; **10** disqualify, invalidate

unflagging: 8 tireless; **9** unfailing; **10** unswerving, unwavering, unwearying; **11** undeviating, unfaltering, unflinching; **13** indefatigable

unfledged: 7 newborn, unvaned; **8** immature, untaught; **9** fledgling, undrilled, unhatched, untrained, untutored; **10** uneducated; **11** unexercised; **12** uncultivated

unflinching: 6 unawed; **9** unabashed, unalarmed, undaunted; **10** unappalled,

unblanched, unblinking, undismayed, unflagging, unswerving, unwavering; **11** undeviating, unfaltering, unshrinking; **12** unhesitating; **13** unintimidated; **14** unapprehensive

unfluctuating: 4 firm; **6** steady

unfocused: 10 out of focus

unfold: 4 open; **6** extend, spread, unbend, uncoil, uncurl, unfurl, unroll, unseal, unveil, unwind, unwrap; **7** blossom, expound, stretch, uncover, untwist

unforeseeable: 5 dicey, risky; **6** chancy; **11** speculative; **13** unpredictable

unforeseen: 10 surprising, unexpected, unhoped for; **11** unlooked for; **13** unanticipated

unforgettable: 9 memorable

unforgettably: 9 memorably; **10** eventfully, stirringly

unforgivable: 11 inexcusable

unforgiving: 4 grim; **5** stern; **10** inexorable, relentless; **11** unrelenting; **12** unappeasable, uncharitable

unformed: 6 coarse; **7** unblown; **8** immature, unboiled, uncooked, unshaped, unshapen; **9** rough cast, rough hewn, unwrought; **10** unarranged, unpolished; **11** unconcocted

unforseeable: 13 unpredictable

unforseen: 11 unpredicted

unfortified: 7 unarmed; **8** harmless, vincible; **9** pregnable, unalloyed, untenable; **10** weaponless; **11** defenseless; **12** indefensible

unfortunate: 7 hapless, unhappy, unlucky; **8** hoodooed [U.S.], luckless, snakebit, untoward; **9** out of luck; **11** regrettable, unbefitting, unfavorable; **12** inauspicious, infelicitous, unpropitious

unfortunately: 4 alas; **9** unluckily; **11** regrettably

unfounded: 4 idle; **6** forged; **8** baseless, fabulous, invented; **10** fabricated, groundless; **11** unwarranted

unfreeze: 4 free, melt, thaw; **6** unthaw; **7** release, unblock

unfriendly: 6 chilly, unkind; **7** hostile; **8** inimical; **10** ungracious; **11** uncongenial, unfavorable

unfulfilled: 10 unexecuted, unrealized; **11** unperformed, unsatisfied

unfurl: 6 uncoil, unfold, unroll, unwind; **7** untwist

ungainly: 5 gawky, stiff; **6** clumsy, clunky; **7** awkward, uncouth; **8** ungentle, unwieldy; **10** bunglesome, ungraceful

unglamorous: 7 humdrum, prosaic; **11** commonplace

unglazed: 9 glassless

unglue: 7 unstick

ungodliness: 8 unbelief; **9** disbelief; **11** godlessness, incredulity, non-religion

ungodly: 6 sinful, unholy; 7 godless, impious; 10 iniquitous; 11 irreligious

ungovernable: 6 unruly; 8 indocile; 10 headstrong; 11 immitigable; 12 contumacious, incorrigible, unappeasable; 13 irrepressible; 14 uncontrollable

ungoverned: 8 uncurbed; 9 unbridled, unchained, unchecked, unmuzzled; 10 unfettered, unshackled; 13 undisciplined

ungraceful: 5 stiff; 7 awkward, cramped, uncouth; 8 ungainly; 9 graceless, inelegant; 10 unpolished

ungracious: 6 unkind; 7 uncivil; 10 unfriendly; 12 discourteous; 13 unceremonious

ungraded: 4 dirt; 8 unranked; 9 unordered

ungrammatical: 9 ill-formed; 10 solecistic; 11 incongruous

ungrateful: 9 thankless, unmindful; 10 unthankful

ungrateful person: 7 ingrate

ungrounded: 5 false; 6 unreal, untrue; 8 mistaken; 9 erroneous; 10 apocryphal, fallacious, groundless

unguarded: 6 unwary; 7 natural; 9 shiftless, unthrifty; 10 incautious, thriftless; 11 improvident, thoughtless, unprotected

unguent: 4 balm; 5 salve; 8 liniment, ointment

unguis: 4 claw

ungulate: 6 hoofed, hooved; 9 ungulated; 12 hoofed mammal

Unh: 11 unnilhexium

unhallowed: 6 impious, unholy; 7 profane

unhand me!: 7 let me go!

unhappily: 5 sadly

unhappiness: 4 pain; 5 dolor; 7 sadness; 9 suffering; 10 infelicity, mental pain, sufferance

unhappy: 3 sad; 7 hapless, unlucky; 8 luckless, snakebit; 9 dysphoric, out of luck, woe-begone; 10 distressed; 11 unfortunate

unharmed: 6 unhurt; 8 harmless; 9 undamaged, uninjured, unscathed

unhealthy: 3 ill; 4 sick; 6 ailing, unwell; 7 unsound; 8 diseased

unheard of: 7 unknown; 8 original; 10 unexplored, unfamiliar; 11 unexplained

unhesitating: 4 sure; 6 secure; 7 assured, certain; 8 cocksure, positive, resolute; 9 confident, convinced, satisfied; 11 unflinching

unhinged: 3 mad; 4 sick, wild; 5 crazy, giddy, rabid; 6 dashed, doting, raving; 7 berserk, crossed, frantic; 8 demented, frenetic, frenzied, rambling, unnerved, wild-eyed; 9 delirious, disturbed, insensate, possessed, wandering; 10 distracted, frustrated, incoherent, reasonless, unbalanced

unholy: 6 sinful, wicked; 7 demonic, godless, hellish, impious, satanic, ungodly; 8 diabolic, fiendish, infernal; 10 diabolical, unhallowed; 11 irreligious

unhorse: 5 light; 6 get off; 7 get down; 8 dismount

unhurt: 8 unbroken, unharmed, unmarred; 9 uninjured, unscathed; 10 unimpaired; 12 safe and sound

Uniate: 5 Uniat

unicycle: 9 monocycle

unidentified: 7 unknown, unnamed; 8 nameless

unidentified flying object: 3 UFO [acron]; 12 flying saucer

unidimensional: 6 linear; 14 one-dimensional

unification: 5 union; 6 fusing, fusion, merger; 7 uniting; 8 blending; 9 synthesis; 10 coalescing, embodiment; 11 coalescence; 12 amalgamation; 13 incorporation

unified: 6 merged; 10 integrated; 11 coordinated, incorporate; 12 incorporated; 14 interconnected

uniform: 4 even, neat, pure; 5 sheer; 6 livery, simple, single; 7 regular; 8 balanced, of a piece; 9 shipshape, unvarying; 10 consistent; 11 homogeneous, symmetrical

uniformity: 5 order; 9 constancy, even tenor; 10 regularity, steadiness; 11 consistency, homogeneity, orderliness

unify: 3 mix; 5 merge, unite; 6 mingle; 10 amalgamate

unilateral: 8 one-sided

unilluminated: 5 unlit; 9 lightless, unlighted

unimaginable: 9 unheard-of; 10 impossible; 11 unthinkable; 13 inconceivable

unimaginative: 4 drab, dull, flat; 5 trite; 6 stodgy; 7 sterile; 9 dry as dust; 10 uncreative, uninspired, unoriginal; 11 stereotyped, stereotypic, uninventive; 13 uninteresting

unimagined: 8 undreamt; 9 undreamed

unimpaired: 6 unhurt; 8 unbroken, unmarred; 9 uninjured

unimpassioned: 9 unexcited, unruffled, unstirred; 11 undisturbed, unperturbed

unimpeachable: 8 absolute; 9 blameless, estimable, plausible; 10 creditable, inculpable, inviolable, sacrosanct, undeniable; 11 inalienable, meritorious, unalienable

unimpressed: 7 unmoved; 9 unexcited, unruffled, unstirred, untouched; 10 unaffected, uninspired

unimproved: 10 unenhanced

uninfected: 5 clean

uninformed: 7 belated, out of it; 8 untaught, unversed; 9 benighted, misguided, unbookish, unlearned, untutored; 10 uneducated, unlettered, unschooled; 11 uninitiated; 12 uncultivated, uninstructed; 13 unenlightened

u

uninhabited: 7 forlorn; **8** deserted, desolate; **9** abandoned, unpeopled

uninitiated: 3 raw; **4** rank; **5** green; **8** unversed; **9** desperate, misguided; **10** uninformed; **12** uncultivated; **13** inexperienced, unenlightened

uninjured: 6 unhurt; **8** harmless, unbroken, unharmed, unmarred; **9** undamaged, unscathed, untainted; **10** unimpaired; **11** unblemished

uninspired: 5 trite; **7** sterile, unmoved; **9** unexcited, unruffled, unstirred, untouched; **10** unaffected, uncreative, unoriginal; **11** unimpressed, uninventive; **13** unimaginative

unintegrated: 10 segregated; **13** nonintegrated

unintellectual: 4 dull; **6** stupid, vacant; **7** earthly, no-brain, vacuous; **8** mindless; **9** airheaded, brainless, dim-witted; **10** uncultured, unoccupied, unthinking; **11** unreasoning

unintelligent: 4 dull; **5** petty; **6** stolid, stupid; **7** shallow, witless; **8** mindless; **9** airheaded, brainless, dim-witted; **10** dull minded; **11** unreasoning

unintelligible: 6 opaque; **16** incomprehensible

unintended: 8 not meant, unwilled; **9** unplanned, unwitting; **10** fortuitous, undesigned, unpurposed; **11** inadvertent

unintentional: 8 not meant, unwilled; **9** unplanned, unwitting; **10** fortuitous, undesigned, unintended, unpurposed; **11** inadvertent; **14** without purpose

uninterested: 5 blase, bored; **7** neutral; **9** apathetic, incurious, uncurious; **11** indifferent; **13** disinterested, uninquisitive

uninteresting: 3 dry; **4** arid, bald, drab, dull, flat; **6** boring, jejune, mortal, stodgy; **7** tedious; **13** unimaginative; **14** unentertaining

uninterrupted: 8 unbroken; **9** ceaseless, continued, incessant, unceasing, unvarying; **10** continuous; **12** interminable

unintimidated: 10 unblinking; **11** unflinching, unshrinking

uninventive: 5 trite; **7** sterile; **10** uncreative, uninspired, unoriginal; **13** unimaginative

uninvited: 7 unasked; **8** unwanted; **9** unordered, unvisited, unwelcome; **11** unrequested, unsolicited

uninviting: 4 ugly; **8** unwanted; **9** undesired, unwelcome; **10** unpleasing, untempting; **11** unbeautiful, undesirable; **12** unattractive

uninvolved: 6 degage; **8** detached

union: 3 bed, sum; **4** join; **5** match, unity; **6** fusing, fusion, mating, unison; **7** joinder [Law], pairing, uniting, wedlock; **8** blending, coupling, marriage; **9** matrimony, synthesis; **10** apposition, coalescing,

embodiment, federation, labor union, nuptial tie, trade union; **11** brotherhood, coalescence, conjugation, conjunction, parallelism, sexual union, trades union, unification; **12** amalgamation; **13** incorporation

Union: 5 North; **7** Federal

Union flag: 9 Union Jack

unionism: 13 trade unionism

unionist: 11 union member; **13** trade unionist

unionize: 8 organize

union member: 8 unionist; **13** trade unionist

Union of Soviet Socialist Republics: 4 USSR; **11** Soviet Union

Union soldier: 7 Federal; **9** Billy Yank; **14** Federal soldier

union suit: 13 long underwear

unique: 3 odd; **5** alone; **7** azygous; **8** singular; **9** unequaled, unmatched; **10** one-of-a-kind, unequalled; **12** first and last, unparalleled

uniqueness: 10 speciality; **11** singularity, specialness, specificity; **13** individuality, particularity; **14** individualness

unironed: 8 wrinkled

unison: 5 union, unity; **7** harmony; **9** homophony

unit: 5 whole; **6** system

Unitarian: 5 Deist; **6** theist

unitary: 3 one; **4** only, sole; **6** single; **8** solitary

unite: 4 fuse, join, link, meet; **5** blend, group, merge, unify; **6** absorb, concur, embody, rejoin; **7** blend in, combine, conjoin, connect; **8** coalesce, converge, dissolve; **9** cooperate; **10** amalgamate, centralize, fall in with; **11** act together, concentrate, consolidate, incorporate

united: 5 as one, joint; **6** joined; **8** agreeing, cemented, combined, conjunct, in accord; **9** concerted, congenial, in harmony; **10** concordant, federative, harmonious; **11** conjunctive, cooperative, harmonizing, unseparated; **12** confederated

United Arab Republic: 5 Egypt

United Kingdom: 2 UK; **7** Britain; **12** Great Britain

United Nations: 2 UN

United Nations Children's Fund: 6 UNICEF

United Nations Educational Scientific and Cultural Organization: 6 UNESCO

United Nations International Children's Emergency Fund: 6 UNICEF

United Parcel Service: 3 UPS

United Press International: 3 UPI

United States: 2 U.S.; **3** U.S.A.; **7** America; **21** United States of America

United States currency: 6 dollar; **9** greenback; **10** greenbacks [pl]

uniting: 5 union; **6** fusing, fusion, merger; **7** joinder [Law]; **8** blending, coupling; **9** synthesis; **10** coalescing, embodiment; **11** coalescence, conjugation, conjunction, unification; **12** amalgamation; **13** incorporation

unit of ammunition: 5 round; **7** one shot

unit of time: 4 span, time; **5** space; **6** period; **8** interval

unity: 5 union; **6** single, unison; **7** oneness; **9** wholeness

unity of time: 9 synchrony; **11** coexistence, isochronism, synchronism

univalve: 9 gastropod

universal: 7 general; **9** worldwide; **10** ecumenical

Universal Product Code: 7 bar code

universal time: 2 UT; **3** GMT, 13 Greenwich Time; **17** Greenwich Mean Time

universe: 5 world; **6** cosmos, nature; **8** creation; **9** existence, macrocosm

university student: 14 college student

univocal: 11 unambiguous, unequivocal

unjust: 6 unfair; **11** inequitable

unjustifiable: 5 undue; **11** unallowable, unjustified, unwarranted; **12** indefensible, unpardonable, unreasonable; **13** insupportable, unwarrantable

unkempt: 5 dowdy; **6** sloppy; **7** uncouth, untamed; **8** uncombed; **10** unpolished

unkennel: 6 unfold, unseal, unveil; **7** uncover, unhouse

unkind: 5 cruel, harsh; **6** brutal; **8** pitiless, rigorous; **10** unfriendly, ungracious

unknowing: 7 unaware; **8** ignorant; **9** nescience, unwitting; **10** unapprised; **11** unconscious

unknown: 5 alien; **6** unseen, unsung; **7** obscure, strange, unnamed; **8** nameless, stranger; **9** unheard of, unnoticed; **10** unapparent, unexplored, unperceive; **11** unexplained; **12** unidentified

unlace: 5 untie; **7** unbrace

unlade: 6 unload, unpack, unship; **7** offload; **9** discharge

unlamented: 5 hated; **7** unloved; **8** unvalued; **9** unbeloved, unmourned

unlatched: 8 unbarred, unbolted, unlocked; **9** unsecured

unlawful: 6 outlaw; **7** illegal, illicit, lawless; **8** improper, outlawed, wrongful; **12** illegitimate

unlearned: 6 innate; **7** belated; **8** ignorant, nescient, untaught; **9** benighted, unbookish, untutored; **10** uneducated, uninformed, unlettered, unschooled; **12** uninstructed; **13** unenlightened

unleash: 5 loose, unbar; **6** unbind, unclog, unhand; **7** unchain, unclose; **8** let loose; **9** unharness

unleavened bread: 5 matzo; **6** matzah, matzoh

unless: 7 without; **13** provisionally

unlettered: 7 belated; **8** ignorant, nescient, untaught; **9** benighted, unbookish, unlearned, untutored; **10** uneducated, unin-

formed, unschooled; **12** analphabetic, uninstructed; **13** unenlightened

unlicensed: 11 unwarranted; **12** unaccredited

unlike: 7 unalike, unequal; **8** not alike; **9** different, differing, disparate; **10** dissimilar; **15** distinguishable

unlikely: 10 improbable; **12** unbelievable, unconvincing

unlimber: 5 stark; **9** unbending; **10** unyielding

unlimited: 6 untold; **8** outright; **9** limitless, unbounded; **10** unmeasured, unnumbered; **11** straight-out, unmitigated; **12** unrestricted; **13** inexhaustible, unconditional

unlisted stock: 8 OTC stock

unload: 4 drop; **6** unlade, unpack, unship; **7** offload, put down, set down; **9** disburden

unlock: 5 crack; **7** unchain, unravel, unriddle; **9** crack open, unshackle

unlocked: 8 unbarred, unbolted; **9** unlatched, unsecured

unloose: 4 free; **5** clear, loose; **7** release; **8** liberate; **9** extricate

unloved: 5 hated; **8** unvalued; **9** unbeloved; **10** uncared for, undeplored, unlamented

unlubricated: 9 ungreased

unlucky: 6 doomed; **7** hapless, unhappy; **8** hoodooed [U.S.], ill-fated, luckless, sinister, snakebit, untoward; **9** ill-omened, out of luck; **10** ill-starred, mal a propos [Fr]; **11** unbefitting, unfavorable, unfortunate

unmake: 4 undo

unman: 4 damp, dash, dull, sink; **5** lower; **6** appall, deject; **7** cripple, unnerve; **8** castrate, enervate; **9** knock down, prostrate; **10** emasculate

unmanageable: 8 unwieldy; **10** refractory; **11** intractable; **13** uncorrectable; **14** uncontrollable

unmanned: 16 remote-controlled

unmannered: 4 rude; **8** impolite; **10** ill-behaved, unmannerly; **11** ill-mannered; **12** discourteous

unmapped: 9 chartless, uncharted

unmarked: 6 unseen; **7** unnoted; **8** unheeded; **9** unnoticed; **10** overlooked, uncared-for, unobserved, unremarked; **11** unperceived

unmarred: 6 unhurt; **8** unbroken; **9** uninjured, unscathed, untainted; **10** unimpaired; **11** unmutilated

unmarried: 6 single; **12** bachelorhood

unmarried parent: 12 single parent

unmarried woman: 4 maid; **12** bachelor girl, bachelor lady, girlbachelor

unmasking: 6 expose; **10** dismasking

unmatched: 3 odd, one; **6** unique; **7** unmated; **8** peerless, unpaired; **9** matchless, nonpareil, unrelated, unrivaled; **11** unmatchable; **12** unparalleled

unmeaning: 6 vacant; **9** senseless; **11** meaningless, nonsensical; **13** insignificant

unmeasured: 6 untold; **9** limitless, unbounded, unlimited, unsparing; **10** unnumbered; **11** illimitable, measureless

unmeditated: 9 improvise, unplanned; **10** improvised

unmentionable: 6 too bad; **7** private; **8** esoteric, infamous; **10** inviolable, scandalous; **12** confidential

unmindful: 6 blithe, casual; **8** careless, heedless, mindless; **9** forgetful, negligent, oblivious, unheeding; **10** neglectful, ungrateful, unthankful, unthinking; **11** unobservant, inattentive

unmistakable: 5 clear; **7** decided, evident, obvious; **8** decisive, definite, palpable, specific, striking; **10** pronounced; **11** ascertained, categorical, determinate, indubitable, self-evident, unambiguous, unequivocal

unmitigated: 4 free; **5** sheer; **7** regular; **9** unlimited; **10** consummate; **11** unqualified; **12** unrestricted; **13** unconditional

unmixed: 4 pure; **5** plain, sheer; **9** unblended, undiluted, unmingled; **10** uncombined; **12** uncompounded

unmodified: 7 vanilla; **9** unaltered, unchanged; **11** off-the-shelf; **12** plain vanilla

unmourned: 5 hated; **7** unloved; **8** unvalued; **9** unbeloved; **10** uncared for, undeplored, unlamented

unmoved: 6 in-situ; **9** unexcited, unruffled, unstirred, untouched; **10** unaffected, uninspired; **11** undisturbed, unimpressed; **12** uninfluenced

unmusical: 9 dissonant, unmelodic; **10** nonmusical; **11** unmelodious

unmuzzled: 8 uncurbed; **9** unbridled, unchained; **10** unfettered, unshackled

unnamed: 7 unknown; **8** nameless; **9** anonymous; **10** innominate; **12** unidentified; **14** unacknowledged

unnatural: 7 canting, stilted; **8** affected; **9** grotesque, insincere, monstrous, pretended; **10** artificial

unnecessary: 8 needless, unneeded; **9** not needed; **11** superfluous, uncalled for

unnerve: 4 faze; **5** unman; **8** enervate, unsettle

unnerving: 10 formidable; **11** redoubtable

unnilhexium: 3 Unh

unnilpentium: 3 Unp; **7** hahnium; **13** unnilquintium

unnilquadium: 2 Ku, Rf; **3** Unq; **12** kurchatovium; **13** rutherfordium

unnilseptium: 3 Uns

unnoticed: 6 unseen; **7** unknown; **8** unheeded, unmarked; **9** unhonored; **10** unapparent, uncared-for, unobserved, unperceive, unremarked; **11** unperceived

unnumbered: 6 myriad, untold; **8** infinite; **9** countless, unbounded, uncounted, unlimited; **10** innumerous, numberless, unmeasured; **11** innumerable, unnumerable; **12** unnumberable; **13** multitudinous

unobjectionable: 2 OK; **4** fair, so-so; **5** clean; **7** average; **8** bearable, mediocre, middling, ordinary, passable; **9** innocuous, tolerable; **10** acceptable, admissible; **11** indifferent; **12** satisfactory; **13** unimpeachable

unobstructed: 7 unbound; **8** uncaught, unloaded; **9** unchecked; **10** unbuttoned, unconfined, unhindered; **11** untrammeled; **12** uncontrolled, unrestrained; **13** unconstrained

unobtainable: 11 untouchable; **12** inaccessible, unattainable, unprocurable

unobtrusive: 4 meek; **10** unaspiring, unassuming

unoccupied: 4 void; **5** empty; **6** vacant; **7** nobrain, vacuous; **8** mindless; **10** unemployed, untenanted, unthinking; **11** thoughtless

unofficial: 8 informal; **12** unauthorized

unordered: 6 random; **7** unasked; **8** ungraded, unranked; **9** orderless, uninvited; **10** disordered, disorderly; **11** unrequested, unsolicited; **12** disorganized

unorganized: 7 unbegun; **9** untrimmed; **10** unequipped, unprovided; **11** unfurnished; **12** nonunionized

unoriginal: 5 trite; **7** sterile; **9** imitative; **10** derivative, uncreative, uninspired; **11** uninventive; **13** unimaginative

unorthodox: 8 maverick; **9** heretical, heterodox, irregular

Unp: 7 hahnium; **12** unnilpentium; **13** unnilquintium

unpack: 6 unlade, unload, unship; **7** offload, take out

unpaid: 3 due; **5** owing; **7** amateur, past due; **8** honorary, unbought; **9** volunteer; **10** delinquent; **11** outstanding; **12** recreational

unpaid worker: 9 volunteer

unpaired: 3 odd; **7** unmated; **9** unmatched

unpalatable: 6 bitter; **8** unsavory, bad taste; **11** distasteful

unparalleled: 5 alone; **6** unique; **9** unequaled, unmatched; **10** inimitable, unequalled, unexampled; **11** undescribed, unparagoned, unsurpassed; **13** unprecedented

unpatriotic: 8 disloyal; **10** antisocial; **12** misanthropic

unpatterned: 5 plain

unpeopled: 7 forlorn; **8** deserted, desolate;

9 abandoned; 10 tenantless, untenanted; 11 uninhabited, unpopulated

unperformed: 10 unexecuted, unfinished; 11 uncompleted, unfulfilled, unsatisfied; 14 unaccomplished

unpick: 6 unknot; 7 unravel; 8 untangle; 10 unscramble

unplanned: 5 ad lib; 8 not meant, unwilled; 9 ad libitem [Lat], improvise, unwitting; 10 fortuitous, improvised, off-the-cuff, undesigned, unintended, unpurposed, unscripted; 11 inadvertent, spontaneous, unmeditated, unrehearsed; 13 unintentional; 14 extemporaneous

unpleasant: 9 obnoxious; 10 unpleasing; 11 displeasing; 12 disagreeable; 13 objectionable

unpleated: 4 flat

unplug: 10 disconnect

unpolished: 6 coarse, gauche; 7 awkward, cramped, unblown, uncouth, unkempt, untamed; 8 unboiled, uncombed, uncooked, unformed; 9 graceless, inelegant, roughhewn, ungenteel, unwrought; 10 unfinished, ungraceful, unsmoothed; 11 uncivilized, unconcocted

unpopular: 9 thankless; 10 uncared for; 12 unacceptable; 13 unfashionable

unpopulated: 6 barren; 9 unpeopled

unprecedented: 10 unexampled; 11 undescribed; 12 unparalleled

unpredictable: 5 dicey, risky; 6 chancy; 9 irregular; 11 speculative; 13 unforeseeable

unpredicted: 10 surprising, unexpected, unforeseen, unheralded, unhoped for; 11 unannounced; 13 unanticipated

unprepared: 7 unready

unpretentious: 4 meek; 10 unaspiring, unassuming; 11 understated, unobtrusive

unprincipled: 4 vile; 5 wrong; 6 sinful, wicked; 7 immoral, lawless; 8 depraved, improper, scampish, unseemly; 10 disorderly, indecorous, iniquitous; 11 unrighteous

unprocessed: 3 raw; 5 crude; 7 natural; 9 unrefined

unprofitable: 4 vain; 7 inutile; 8 bootless, nugatory; 9 fruitless, pointless; 10 profitless

unpronounceable: 4 mute; 11 unutterable

unpropitious: 5 cross; 7 hostile, unlucky; 8 inimical, untoward; 10 mal a propos [Fr]; 11 unbefitting, unfavorable, unfortunate, unpromising

unprotected: 7 exposed; 9 unguarded; 10 unshielded, vulnerable

unprovoked: 6 wanton; 10 motiveless

unpublished: 6 untold; 9 unexposed; 10 unreported

Unq: 2 Ku, Rf; 12 kurchatovium, unnilquadium; 13 rutherfordium

unqualified: 4 free; 5 inapt, inept, sheer, unapt; 7 regular; 8 absolute, inhabile [Fr], positive; 9 incapable; 10 consummate, unentitled; 11 disentitled, incompetent, unchartered, unmitigated

unquenchable: 6 greedy; 7 craving; 8 covetous, grasping, ravenous; 9 insatiate; 10 avaricious, insatiable, quenchless; 11 acquisitive

unquestionable: 4 real, true; 7 genuine, regular; 8 bona fide; 9 authentic, veritable; 10 undeniable; 12 indisputable

unquestionably: 5 truly; 6 really; 7 no doubt; 8 of course; 9 assuredly, by all odds, decidedly, doubtless, genuinely; 10 definitely; 12 emphatically, indisputably

unraised: 4 flat

unranked: 7 undealt, unsized; 8 ungraded; 9 unalloted, ungrouped, unordered; 13 undistributed

unravel: 3 run; 4 card; 5 crack, ravel; 6 unknot, unlock, unpick; 7 untwine; 8 decipher, ravel out, unriddle, untangle; 9 crack open, extricate; 10 cut the knot, unscramble; 11 disentangle

unreactive: 5 inert; 12 unresponsive

unread: 4 rude; 5 empty, green; 7 shallow; 10 illiterate; 11 half-learned, superficial

unreadable: 7 unclear; 9 illegible

unreal: 5 false, ideal; 6 untrue; 7 virtual; 8 gossamer, illusory, mistaken; 9 erroneous, gossamery, potential; 10 apocryphal, artificial, fallacious, groundless, ungrounded; 11 incorporeal

unrealistic: 7 fanatic, flighty, utopian; 8 quixotic, romantic; 9 high flown; 11 extravagant

unreasonable: 4 dumb, fool, zany; 5 blind, false, goofy, sappy, silly, undue, wacky; 6 absurd, stupid, unwise; 7 asinine, foolish, invalid, unsound; 8 improper; 9 cockamamy, excessive, ill-judged, illogical; 10 cockamamie, exorbitant, ill-advised, ill-devised, inordinate; 11 extravagant, ill-imagined, incongruous, injudicious, unallowable, unreasoning; 12 extortionate; 13 unjustifiable, unwarrantable

unreasoning: 4 dull; 5 blind; 6 stupid; 7 witless; 8 mindless; 9 airheaded, brainless, dim-witted, fat witted, fat-headed, pig headed; 10 beef headed, dull minded, dull normal, dull witted, half witted, lean witted, weak headed, weak minded; 11 lack-brained, short witted; 12 beetle headed, feeble-minded, unreasonable; 13 blunder headed, unintelligent; 14 unintellectual

unrecognized: 6 unseen; 8 descried, unsolved; 9 discerned; 11 undeveloped, unexplained, unperceived; 12 undiscovered

u

unrecorded: 4 live; 9 unwritten; 12 unregistered

unrefined: 5 crude; 6 vulgar; 7 natural; 10 in bad taste; 11 unprocessed

unregistered: 7 unfiled; 9 unwritten; 10 unrecorded

unregulated: 9 arbitrary

unrehearsed: 5 ad lib; 7 offhand; 8 unguided; 9 ad libitem [Lat], extempore, offhanded, unplanned; 10 improvised, off-the-cuff, unprompted, unscripted; 11 extemporary, spontaneous; 14 extemporaneous

unrelated: 9 unmatched; 12 inharmonious

unrelenting: 4 grim; 5 stern; 10 inexorable, persistent, relentless; 11 unforgiving, unremitting; 12 unappeasable

unreliable: 11 treacherous; 12 undependable; 13 untrustworthy

unremarkable: 7 mundane, routine; 8 everyday, workaday; 9 quotidian

unremarked: 6 unseen; 8 unheeded, unmarked; 9 unnoticed; 10 uncared-for, unobserved; 11 unperceived

unremitting: 8 constant; 9 ceaseless, incessant, perpetual, unceasing; 11 never-ending, unrelenting

unreported: 6 untold; 9 unexposed, unwritten; 11 unpublished

unrequested: 7 unasked; 9 uninvited, unordered; 11 uncalled for, unsolicited

unreserved: 4 open; 5 frank; 6 candid; 7 sincere; 9 confiding, downright; 10 aboveboard

unresolved: 4 open; 8 unsolved; 9 dissonant, undecided; 12 undetermined

unrest: 7 ferment, fidgets; 8 disquiet; 9 agitation; 10 inquietude; 11 disquietude; 12 restlessness

unrestrained: 3 mad; 7 excited, frantic, unbound; 8 uncaught; 9 delirious, unchecked; 10 flamboyant, unbuttoned, unconfined, unhindered, untempered; 11 resplendent, untrammeled; 12 uncontrolled, unobstructed; 13 unconstrained

unrestricted: 8 unabated; 9 unlimited; 11 unexclusive, unmitigated; 12 nonsensitive, undiminished; 13 unconditional

unrhymed: 7 in prose, unrimed; 8 rimeless; 9 rhymeless

unrighteous: 4 vile; 5 wrong; 6 sinful, wicked; 7 immoral; 8 criminal, depraved; 10 iniquitous; 12 unprincipled

unripe: 5 green; 8 immature; 9 unripened

unrivaled: 8 peerless; 9 matchless, nonpareil, unmatched; 11 unmatchable

unroll: 6 uncoil, unfold, unfurl, unwind; 7 draw out, untwist, wind off; 8 bring out, set forth

unruffled: 4 calm; 5 quiet, still; 6 placid; 7

unmoved; 8 tranquil; 9 unexcited, unstirred, untouched; 10 unaffected, unflurried, uninspired; 11 undisturbed, unflustered, unimpressed, unperturbed; 13 unimpassioned

unruliness: 8 self-will; 9 balkiness, contumacy; 10 orneriness, perversity, wilfulness; 11 contrariety, restiveness, waywardness, willfulness; 12 contrariness

unruly: 5 balky, heady; 6 entete [Fr], ornery; 7 restive, wayward, willful; 8 contrary, indocile, perverse; 9 unbridled; 10 boisterous, headstrong, rebellious, refractory, robustious, self-willed, unquenched; 11 disobedient, rumbustious, unrepressed

Uns: 12 unnilseptium

unsaddle: 6 unseat; 9 offsaddle

unsafe: 5 risky; 7 parlous; 8 insecure, perilous; 9 dangerous, hazardous; 10 precarious

unsaid: 8 unspoken, unstated, unvoiced; 9 unuttered; 10 untalked of; 11 unexpressed; 12 unverbalized

unsanded: 3 raw; 5 rough

unsanitary: 10 insanitary; 11 unhealthful

unsatisfied: 7 unsated; 8 restless, unslaked; 10 unexecuted, unsatiated; 11 unfulfilled, ungratified, unperformed; 12 undischarged

unsatisfying: 13 disappointing

unsaved: 6 cursed, damned, doomed; 10 unredeemed

unsavory: 8 bad taste; 9 offensive, unsavoury; 11 distasteful, unpalatable

unscathed: 6 unhurt; 8 harmless, unharmed, unmarred; 9 undamaged, uninjured, untainted; 11 unblemished

unschooled: 8 untaught; 9 benighted, unbookish, unlearned, untutored; 10 uneducated, uninformed, unlettered; 12 uninstructed

unscramble: 6 decode, uncode, unknot, unpick; 7 decrypt, unravel; 8 decipher, untangle

unscripted: 5 ad lib; 9 ad libitem [Lat], unplanned; 10 improvised; 11 spontaneous, unrehearsed; 14 extemporaneous

unscrupulous: 9 dishonest; 12 dishonorable; 15 unconscientious

unseal: 4 open; 6 unfold, unveil; 7 uncover

unseasonable: 5 wrong; 8 ill timed, untimely

unseasoned: 7 untried; 8 unsalted, untested, unwonted; 9 untrained; 10 unleavened, unobserved; 12 unaccustomed

unseat: 8 unsaddle

unseemly: 7 lawless; 8 improper, indecent, scampish, uncomely, untoward; 9 unsightly; 10 disorderly, indecorous, unbecoming; 11 unbefitting; 12 unprincipled

unseen: 7 unknown; 8 descried, unheeded, unmarked; 9 discerned, unnoticed; 10 unapparent, uncared-for, unobserved,

unsegregated: **10** desegrated, integrated

unselected: **8** unchosen

unselfish: **4** free; **6** giving; **7** liberal; **8** generous, handsome, princely; **9** bounteous, bountiful; **10** altruistic, charitable

unsettle: **4** faze; **6** jumble, tumble; **7** disturb, embroil, trouble, unnerve; **8** enervate

unsettled: **7** unfixed; **8** immature, unplaced; **9** disturbed, uncertain, undecided; **10** changeable; **12** undetermined

unsex: **3** fix; **5** desex; **9** castrate, sterilize; **11** desexualize

unshackled: **4** free; **6** untied; **8** uncurbed, unlocked; **9** unbridled, unchained, unmuzzled; **10** unfettered, ungoverned

unshakable: **4** firm; **6** steady; **8** ironclad; **9** immovable, steadfast; **10** unbendable, unwavering, watertight; **11** unfaltering

unsheathed: **4** bare

unshielded: **7** exposed; **10** vulnerable; **11** unprotected

unship: **6** unlade, unload, unpack; **7** offload

unshorn: **5** uncut; **6** intact; **8** unbroken; **9** uncropped, undivided, unsheared

unskilled: **7** amateur; **8** inexpert; **10** amateurish, unskillful; **11** incompetent

unskillfulness: **9** ineptness; **10** ineptitude; **11** lack of skill, want of skill; **12** incompetence

unslaked lime: **4** calx, lime; **9** burnt lime, quicklime; **11** fluxing lime; **12** calcined lime, calcium oxide

unsocial: **9** reclusive; **10** antisocial, unsociable

unsoiled: **8** spotless; **9** unspotted, unstained, unsullied; **10** immaculate

unsold: **7** not sold; **8** unbought, unshared

unsolicited: **7** unasked; **8** unsought; **9** uninvited, unordered; **11** uncalled for, unrequested

unsolved: **10** unresolved; **11** undeveloped, unexplained; **12** undiscovered, unrecognized

unsophisticated: **4** hick; **5** naive; **6** callow, rustic; **9** bumpkinly, unalloyed, uncolored, untutored, unworldly; **13** inexperienced

unsound: **3** bad; **5** false, unfit; **6** faulty, flawed; **7** invalid, tainted; **8** unstable; **9** illogical, unhealthy; **10** bedraggled, broken-down, fallacious, ramshackle, tumbledown; **11** dilapidated; **12** unreasonable

unsparing: **6** lavish; **7** austere, exigent; **8** exacting, obdurate, prodigal, rigorous; **9** demanding, hard-nosed, searching, unstinted; **10** hard-headed, inexorable, inflexible, munificent, ungrudging, unmeasured, unstinting; **14** uncompromising

unspeakable: **5** awful; **7** painful; **8** dreadful, fabulous, terrible; **9** atrocious, ineffable; **10** abominable, unnameable, untellable; **11**

indefinable, unutterable; **13** indescribable, inexpressible

unspoiled: **4** good, lain, naif, pure; **5** naive; **6** native, simple; **7** artless, natural; **10** unaffected; **11** uncorrupted

unspoken: **4** mute; **6** unsaid; **8** unstated, unvoiced, wordless; **9** unuttered; **10** tongueless, untalked of; **11** unexpressed; **12** unverbalized

unsportsmanlike: **4** foul; **5** dirty; **8** cheating; **10** unsporting

unstable: **5** fluid; **7** unsound; **8** insecure, unsteady; **10** inconstant, precarious

unsteady: **5** jerky; **6** fickle, unfirm; **7** jerking; **8** shifting, unstable, wavering; **10** arrhythmic, inconstant; **11** vacillating

unstopped: **4** open; **8** unclosed, unvaried, wide open; **9** unrevoked

unstressed: **10** unaccented

unstructured: **9** amorphous

unstrung: **6** weakly

unstylish: **3** out; **6** uncool; **7** out of it; **9** styleless; **13** unfashionable

unsuccessful: **8** abortive; **9** stillborn; **10** unattained

unsuccessful person: **5** loser; **7** failure; **10** nonstarter

unsuitable: **5** wrong; **8** improper, unsuited; **11** undesirable; **12** inapplicable

unsuited: **8** mismated; **9** ill-sorted; **10** unsuitable; **12** incompatible

unsung: **7** obscure, unknown; **8** unvalued; **13** unappreciated

unsupported: **7** unaided; **8** unhelped; **10** unassisted, unsuccored

unsure: **3** shy; **5** timid; **9** diffident, incertain, uncertain

unsurpassed: **10** unequalled, unexceeded, unexcelled; **12** unparalleled

unswayed: **9** untouched; **12** uninfluenced

unswerving: **7** staunch; **8** unturned; **9** steadfast; **10** unflagging, unwavering; **11** undeviating, undistorted, unfaltering, unflinching

unsympathetic: **6** closed; **7** unmoral; **8** unkindly; **9** unfeeling, unlikable; **10** unlikeable; **11** unappealing; **12** disagreeable

untainted: **4** pure; **8** unmarred; **9** stainless, uninjured, unscathed, unstained, unsullied; **11** untarnished; **13** unadulterated

untamed: **4** fell, wild; **7** uncouth, unkempt; **8** tameless, uncombed; **9** truculent; **10** incendiary, unpolished; **12** semibarbaric

untangle: **6** unknot, unpick; **7** unravel; **9** extricate; **10** unscramble; **11** disencumber, disentangle

untarnished: **9** stainless, unstained, unsullied, untainted

untaught: **7** belated; **9** benighted, unbookish,

u

undrilled, unfledged, unhatched, unlearned, untrained, untutored; **10** uneducated, uninformed, unlettered, unschooled; **11** unexercised; **12** uncultivated, uninstructed

untaxed: 4 free; **6** gratis; **7** tax-free; **8** costless; **9** tax-exempt; **10** for nothing, gratuitous

untenable: 7 unarmed; **8** harmless, sine ictu [Lat], vincible; **9** pregnable; **10** weaponless; **11** defenseless, unfortified, unwarranted; **12** indefensible

untested: 7 untried; **8** unproven; **10** unseasoned, unverified; **11** speculative

unthaw: 4 melt, thaw; **8** unfreeze

unthinking: 6 blithe, casual, lumpen, vacant; **7** lumpish, no-brain, vacuous; **8** heedless, mindless, uncaring; **9** unheeding, unmindful, unwitting; **10** unoccupied; **11** thoughtless, unconscious, unobservant; **12** unreflective, unthinkingly, unthoughtful; **13** inconsiderate, thoughtlessly

untidy: 5 messy; **8** slovenly; **9** uncleanly

untie: 4 undo; **6** unbind, unlace; **7** unbrace

untied: 4 free; **7** unlaced; **9** unchained; **10** unfastened, unfettered, unshackled

untie the knot: 7 unravel; **9** extricate; **10** cut the knot; **11** disentangle

until: 4 till, up to; **6** before; **8** till then

until now: 3 yet; **5** as yet, so far; **6** til now; **7** thus far, till now, up to now; **8** hitherto; **10** heretofore

untimely: 4 late, slow; **5** tardy, wrong; **6** behind; **7** belated; **8** backward, ill timed; **9** premature; **10** behindhand, unpunctual; **11** prematurely; **12** unseasonable

untitled: 7 ignoble, obscure; **8** ungentle

untold: 9 unbounded, uncounted, unexposed, unlimited, unwritten; **10** unmeasured, unnumbered, unreported; **11** unpublished

untoward: 7 adverse, harmful, unlucky; **8** indecent, uncomely, unseemly; **10** disastrous, indecorous, mal a propos [Fr], unbecoming; **11** unbefitting, unfavorable, unfortunate; **12** inauspicious, infelicitous, unpropitious; **13** uncomfortable; **14** unsatisfactory

untrained: 8 untaught, unwonted; **9** undrilled, unfledged, untutored; **10** uneducated, unobserved, unseasoned; **11** unexercised; **12** unaccustomed, uncultivated

untried: 6 untrod; **8** unbeaten, untested; **9** undecided, untrodden; **10** unseasoned; **12** undetermined

untrimmed: 4 bare; **5** uncut; **7** unbegun; **9** unadorned; **10** unequipped, unprovided; **11** unfurnished, ungarnished, unorganized, unvarnished; **12** unornamented

untrue: 5 false, wrong; **6** unreal; **8** mistaken;

9 erroneous, out of true; **10** apocryphal, fallacious, groundless, ungrounded

untruth: 3 lie; **7** falsity; **9** falsehood, falseness

untying: 7 undoing; **11** unfastening

unused: 4 idle; **5** fresh; **7** not used; **9** unapplied; **10** unemployed; **12** unaccustomed

unusual: 7 strange; **8** uncommon, unwonted; **11** uncustomary; **12** unaccustomed

unusually: 4 unco; **6** mainly; **7** chiefly, notably; **8** signally; **9** curiously, pointedly; **10** peculiarly, remarkably, singularly, strikingly, uncommonly; **12** particularly; **13** outstandingly

unvaried: 3 dry; **7** harping, regular; **9** iterative, recursive, unchanged, unrevoked, unstopped, unvarying; **10** monotonous, unchanging; **11** undeviating; **13** undiversified

unvarnished: 4 bare; **5** plain; **7** prosaic; **9** unadorned, unalloyed, uncolored, unstained, untrimmed; **11** commonplace, ungarnished; **12** unornamented; **13** unadulterated

unveil: 6 reveal, unfold, unseal; **7** uncover; **8** bring out

unveiling: 5 debut, entry; **9** launching; **10** uncovering; **12** introduction

unwanted: 7 unasked; **9** undesired, uninvited, unwelcome; **10** uninviting; **11** undesirable

unwarranted: 4 idle; **5** undue; **8** baseless; **9** unfounded, untenable; **10** groundless, unlicensed; **11** unjustified; **12** indefensible; **13** insupportable, unjustifiable

unwary: 9 unguarded

unwavering: 4 firm; **5** level; **6** steady; **9** steadfast; **10** unbendable, unflagging, unshakable, unswerving; **11** undeviating, unfaltering, unflinching

unwelcome: 8 unwanted, unwished; **9** undesired, uninvited, unvisited; **10** uninviting; **11** undesirable

unwelcome guest: 7 crasher; **11** gatecrasher

unwelcome person: 15 persona non grata

unwell: 3 ill; **4** sick; **5** ill of; **6** ailing, peaked, poorly, sickly; **8** diseased; **9** unhealthy; **10** indisposed

unwieldy: 5 gaunt, gawky, hulky; **6** clumsy, clunky; **7** awkward, hulking, lumpish, massive; **8** cumbrous, lubberly, spanking, thumping, ungainly, whacking, whopping; **9** lumbering, walloping; **10** thundering; **12** unmanageable

unwind: 5 relax, unlax; **6** unbend, uncoil, unfold, unfurl, unroll; **7** untwist, wind off; **8** loosen up, slow down, unstrain; **10** decompress; **11** disentangle

unwise: 4 dumb; **5** blunt, heavy, silly; **6** obtuse, stolid, stupid; **7** asinine, doltish, foolish; **8** improper, ungifted; **9** ill-judged; **10** ill-advised

unwitting: 7 unaware; 8 ignorant, not meant, unwilled; 9 unknowing, unplanned; 10 fortuitous, unapprised, undesigned, unintended, unpurposed, unthinking; 11 inadvertent, unconscious; 13 unintentional

unworkable: 10 infeasible, unfeasible; 13 impracticable

unworried: 6 casual; 8 carefree; 9 easygoing, sans souci [Fr], worriless; 10 insouciant, nonchalant, phlegmatic, unmolested; 11 unafflicted, unconcerned

unworthy: 4 ugly, vile; 9 worthless; 10 despicable, unbecoming; 11 undeserving;

unwrap: 4 open; 6 unbend, uncurl, unfold

unwrinkled: 4 soft; 6 smooth; 11 wrinkleless

unwritten: 4 oral; 5 ad-lib; 6 untold; 7 lingual; 8 phonetic; 9 outspoken, unexposed; 10 unrecorded, unreported; 11 spontaneous, unpublished

unyielding: 4 dour; 5 stark; 6 dogged, flinty, steady; 7 bulldog; 8 constant, granitic, obdurate, stubborn, unlimber; 9 obstinate, steadfast, tenacious, unbending; 10 inflexible

up: 5 above, aloft, aloof, astir, on end; 6 frothy, high up, on high, upward; 7 up quark, upwards; 8 overhead, upwardly; 9 improving, sparkling; 12 effervescent

Upanishads: 4 Edda; 6 Purana

upbeat: 8 cheerful; 9 well-being

upbraid: 4 rate; 5 scold; 8 reproach; 9 objurgate

upbraiding: 6 earful; 7 chiding; 8 berating, scolding; 9 going-over; 10 bawling out, chewing out; 11 castigation; 12 dressing down

upbringing: 7 nurture, raising, rearing; 8 breeding; 9 fosterage, fostering, nurturing

upcoming: 4 soon; 6 at hand, coming, to come; 7 in store; 8 imminent; 9 impending; 11 approaching, forthcoming

upcountry: 7 midland; 8 interior

updated: 8 revamped; 9 renovated

upending: 9 inversion

up-front: 7 prepaid; 8 advanced

up-front money: 7 deposit, earnest, handsel; 11 down payment; 12 earnest money

upgrade: 4 rise; 5 climb, raise; 6 ascent; 7 advance, elevate, promote; 9 acclivity; 12 kick upstairs

upheaval: 6 uplift; 7 turmoil, upthrow; 8 upthrust; 9 agitation; 10 excitement, hullabaloo, turbulence

uphill: 5 stiff; 6 rising; 11 acclivitous

uphold: 4 prop; 6 bear on, hold up, ratify; 7 bear out, bolster, carry on, indorse, stand by, support, sustain, warrant; 8 continue, maintain, preserve, sanction; 11 corroborate

up in arms: 4 wild; 5 fiery; 6 fierce, savage;

7 furious; 9 embroiled, infuriate; 10 infuriated

upkeep: 4 care; 10 sustenance; 11 maintenance, safe-keeping, sustainment; 12 preservation, sustentation

upland: 8 highland, moorland

uplift: 5 elate; 6 lift up, pick up, uprear; 7 upheave, upraise, upthrow; 8 upheaval, upthrust; 10 intoxicate

upmost: 7 topmost; 9 uppermost

upper: 5 speed; 7 pep pill; 10 upper berth; 11 amphetamine

upper atmosphere: 12 stratosphere

uppercase letter: 4 caps [abbr]; 8 capitals [pl]; 9 majuscule; 13 capital letter

upper chamber: 6 senate

upper crust: 10 upper class

upper hand: 4 lead; 8 whip hand; 9 advantage

upper jawbone: 7 maxilla; 8 upper jaw

upper-level: 9 high-level; 11 high-ranking

upper limit: 7 maximum

upper side: 3 top; 6 upside; 7 top side

uppity: 8 arrogant; 12 presumptuous

upraise: 5 raise; 6 uplift, uprear; 7 upheave; 9 resurrect

uprear: 4 rise; 5 erect; 6 uplift; 7 upheave, upraise

upright: 4 good, just, pier; 5 erect, plumb; 6 column, normal, pillar, proper, unbent; 7 unbowed; 8 standing, straight, unsloped, vertical, virtuous; 9 honorable; 10 vertically; 11 bolt upright; 12 upright piano; 13 perpendicular

uprising: 6 revolt, rising; 8 outbreak; 9 rebellion; 10 insurgency; 12 insurrection

upriver: 8 upstream

uproar: 3 row; 4 fray, riot, to-do; 5 brawl, broil, furor, melee; 6 affray, clamor, fracas, racket, rumble, rumpus, squall, tumult; 7 howling, rioting, ruction, shindig, tempest, trouble; 8 brouhaha, scramble; 9 imbroglio, scrimmage; 10 convulsion, donnybrook, free-for-all; 11 embroilment

uproot: 6 pull up, root up; 7 root out; 8 displace; 9 eradicate, extirpate; 10 deracinate; 11 exterminate

upscale: 11 high quality

upset: 4 fell; 5 level, quell, swage, trump; 6 broken, untune; 7 disturb, nonplus, silence, subvert, tip over, trouble, worried; 8 bowl over, confound, confused, disorder, overturn, turn over, upturned; 9 checkmate, discomfit, disturbed, knock over, overthrow, prostrate, stalemate; 10 discompose, disconcert, disordered, disquieted, distressed, overturned; 11 disturbance; 12 perturbation

upset stomach: 9 dyspepsia; 11 indigestion

U

upshot: 5 issue; 6 effect, result; 7 outcome; 9 end result; 10 denouement, end product; 11 consequence

upside: 3 top; 7 top side; 9 upper side

upside down: 8 inverted; 10 overturned

upstanding: 5 erect, noble, solid; 6 worthy; 7 upright

upstart: 7 parvenu; 8 parvenue; 12 nouveau riche

upstream: 7 upriver

upsurge: 4 rush; 5 spate, surge

uptake: 6 intake; 9 ingestion; 11 consumption; 12 comprehension; 13 understanding

upthrow: 6 uplift; 8 upheaval, upthrust

uptight: 4 edgy; 5 jumpy, nervy; 7 jittery, nervous, restive; 10 high-strung, overstrung

up to: 4 till; 5 crack, until; 6 au fait, good at; 7 alive to, capable, equal to; 8 adequate; 9 au courant; 12 accomplished, thoroughbred

up to date: 3 mod; 4 last; 6 latest, modern, newest, with it; 9 in fashion; 10 present-day; 11 fashionable

up to one's eyes:

up to snuff: 5 canny, leery; 6 astute; 7 alive to, knowing

up to the minute: 6 with it; 8 up to date; 9 in fashion; 11 fashionable

up to this point: 3 yet; 5 so far; 7 as far as; 8 hereunto; 10 heretofore

upwards of: 6 plural; 7 at least; 8 multiple; 10 at a minimum, no less than

upwind: 7 leeward, weather; 11 into the wind

Urals: 13 Ural Mountains

Urania: 4 Muse

uraninite: 11 pitchblende

uranium: 1 U

uranologist: 9 stargazer; 10 astronomer

uranology: 9 astronomy; 11 uranography

urarthritis: 4 gout; 14 gouty arthritis

urban: 12 metropolitan

urban center: 4 city; 10 metropolis

urbane: 5 suave; 6 smooth, svelte; 7 gallant, refined; 8 polished, well-bred; 9 civilized; 10 cultivated; 11 gentlemanly; 13 gentlemanlike, sophisticated

urbanize: 13 industrialize

urban planning: 12 city planning, town planning

urchin: 3 elf; 4 brat, chit; 5 dwarf; 6 hornet; 7 butcher; 8 scorpion; 10 Liliputian; 11 spoiled brat; 14 enfant terrible [Fr]

urea: 9 carbamide

uremia: 7 uraemia; 8 azotemia; 9 azotaemia

urge: 3 dun, ply, tax; 4 boom, goad, itch, lash, spur, whip; 5 annoy, beset, cheer, drive, pep up, press; 6 exhort, madden, urge on; 7 barrack, impulse, inspire; 8 advocate, convulse, irritate; 9 aggravate, clamor for, importune, imprecate, infuriate,

recommend; 10 accelerate, exacerbate, exasperate

urgency: 5 haste, hurry; 6 stress; 8 pressure; 10 impatience; 11 needfulness; 12 essentiality

urgent: 6 crying; 7 exigent, instant; 8 critical, pressing; 9 absorbing, clamorous; 10 breathless; 11 hard pressed, importunate

urge on: 4 urge; 5 cheer, pep up, press; 6 exhort; 7 barrack, inspire

urn: 5 tazza; 6 patera, salver; 7 epergne, patella; 11 funerary urn

Urochordata: 8 Tunicata; 9 Urochorda

urochordate: 8 tunicate, urochord

Urocyon: 7 gray fox, grey fox; 12 genus Urocyon

Urocystis: 4 smut; 14 genus Urocystis

Ursa Major: 9 Great Bear

Ursa Minor: 10 Little Bear

Ursidae: 13 family Ursidae

ursine: 4 bear

Ursus: 4 bear; 5 bruin; 7 grizzly, ice bear; 9 black bear, brown bear, polar bear, silvertip, sloth bear; 10 genus Ursus

Urtica: 11 genus Urtica; 14 stinging nettle

Urticaceae: 12 nettle family; 16 family Urticaceae

urticaria: 5 hives; 10 nettle rash, urtication

Urubupunga Falls: 10 Urubupunga

urus: 7 aurochs

US: 3 U.S.A.; 7 America; 12 United States; 21 United States of America

USA: 2 U.S.; 7 America; 12 United States; 21 United States of America

usable: 5 of use; 6 useful; 7 useable; 8 operable; 9 available, of service; 10 functional; 11 operational, serviceable

usage: 3 use; 6 custom; 8 exercise, practice; 10 convention, employment, observance, prevalence; 11 utilisation, utilization

usance: 3 use; 5 usury; 8 interest; 11 consumption

Usbek: 5 Usbeg, Uzbak, Uzbeg, Uzbek

use: 4 role, wont; 5 apply, avail, habit, stead, usage, using; 6 custom, employ, expend, usance; 7 purpose, service, utilise, utilize; 8 exercise, function, practice; 9 enjoyment; 10 convention, employment, observance, prevalence; 11 application, consumption, utilization; 12 manipulation, prescription; 13 functionality

useable: 5 of use; 6 usable, useful; 8 operable; 9 available, of service; 10 functional; 11 operational, serviceable

used: 7 ill-used, put-upon; 8 employed, utilized; 9 exploited; 10 secondhand, victimized

used up: 5 blase; 6 done up, used-up; 7 drained, worn out; 8 consumed, depleted, expended, finished, flagging; 9 dulled out, exhausted, life-weary

useful: 5 of use, utile; 6 usable; 7 of value,

useable; **8** valuable; **9** of service; **11** serviceable, utilitarian

user: 7 end user, enjoyer; **8** consumer, drug user; **9** exploiter; **15** substance abuser

use up: 3 eat, sap; **4** take, tire; **5** eat up, spend; **6** expend, occupy; **7** consume, deplete, exhaust, run down, wipe out; **10** run through

use up all of: 5 drain, empty; **6** absorb, finish, tap out; **7** exhaust; **8** run out of; **9** swallow up; **10** impoverish

usher: 4 hail, show; **5** greet, guide; **7** receive; **9** attendant, pedagogue; **10** doorkeeper; **11** abecedarian; **12** schoolmaster

usher in: 4 head, lead; **6** herald, take in; **7** be first, premise; **8** announce; **9** come first, introduce; **10** inaugurate

using: 3 use; **4** with; **6** employ; **10** employment; **11** application, utilization; **12** exploitation; **13** victimisation, victimization

usquebaugh: 6 whisky; **11** uisquebaugh [Irish]

USSR: 11 Soviet Union

Ustilaginoidea: 4 smut; **19** genus Ustilaginoidea

usual: 6 common, normal, wonted; **7** nominal, typical; **8** everyday, familiar, habitual, ordinary, workaday; **9** customary; **12** conventional

usually: 8 commonly, normally; **9** generally, most often, typically; **10** ordinarily; **11** customarily; **12** unremarkably

Usumbura: 9 Bujumbura; **16** capital of Burundi

usurer: 5 miser; **9** loan shark, **11** moneylender

usurious: 5 steep, venal; **6** greedy; **8** covetous; **9** mercenary, rapacious; **10** avaricious, exorbitant, outrageous; **12** extortionate; **14** unconscionable

usurp: 5 exact; **6** assume, breach; **7** violate; **8** arrogate, encroach, infringe, take over

usurpation: 6 breach; **8** exaction; **9** breaching, violating, violation; **10** abdication, assumption, deposition, imposition, infraction; **11** domineering, presumption; **12** dethronement, encroachment, infringement; **13** transgression

usurper: 9 pretender; **10** supplanter

UT: 3 GMT, UT1; **13** Greenwich Time, universal time; **17** Greenwich Mean Time

ut: 2 do; **3** doh

UT1: 2 UT; **3** GMT; **13** Greenwich Time, universal time; **17** Greenwich Mean Time

utahraptor: 12 superslasher

utensil: 5 organ; **6** vessel; **7** scuttle; **9** implement; **10** instrument

uterus: 4 womb

Ute tribe: 4 Utes

utile: 6 useful

utilitarian: 6 humane, useful; **10** eudemonist; **11** cosmopolite; **12** cosmopolitan, humanitarian; **13** philanthropic

utility: 9 usability; **10** substitute, usefulness

utilization: 3 use; **5** usage, using; **6** employ; **8** exercise; **10** employment; **11** application

utilize: 3 use; **5** apply; **6** employ; **7** utilise; **9** implement

utmost: 4 last; **7** extreme, maximum, supreme; **8** farthest, foremost, furthest, greatest; **9** matchless, paramount, uttermost; **10** preeminent; **11** farthermost, furthermost

Utopia: 8 paradise; **10** perfection

utopian: 7 fanatic, flighty; **8** quixotic, romantic; **9** high flown; **11** extravagant, unrealistic

utricle: 3 pod; **4** cyst; **5** calyx; **7** bladder, capsule, vesicle; **8** cancelli; **9** utriculus

utter: 3 rat, say; **4** emit, pure, talk; **5** gross, issue, mouth, speak, stark; **6** arrant, broach, let out, retail, snitch, squeal, tattle; **7** breathe, deal out, deliver, express, perfect, sodding, staring; **8** announce, complete, let loose, vocalize; **9** pronounce, uttermost, verbalize; **10** articulate

utter failure: 6 fiasco

utterly: 5 fully, quite, stark; **6** in toto, wholly; **7** totally; **8** entirely, outright; **9** perfectly, sublimely; **10** absolutely, altogether, completely

uttermost: 5 utter; **6** utmost; **7** extreme, maximum; **8** farthest, furthest; **9** level best; **11** farthermost, furthermost

UV: 11 ultraviolet; **16** ultraviolet light

uvarovite: 6 garnet

uxorial: 6 wifely; **8** wifelike

uxorious: 4 fond; **6** ardent; **7** devoted; **8** motherly; **9** rapturous; **10** passionate

Uzbek: 5 Usbeg, Usbek, Uzbak, Uzbeg; **10** Uzbekistan, Uzbekiston

U

V

v: 4 five
V: 3 fin; 4 five, volt; 5 quint; 6 cinque, pentad; 7 quintet; 8 fivesome, vanadium; 10 quintuplet
V.P.: 13 vice president
V-1: 8 buzz bomb; 9 doodlebug, robot bomb; 10 flying bomb
V-2: 8 buzz bomb; 9 doodlebug, robot bomb; 10 flying bomb
vacancy: 4 void; 6 vacuum; 7 vacuity; 9 depletion, emptiness; 10 flaccidity; 11 vacuousness
vacant: 4 bare; 5 empty; 7 no-brain, vacuous; 8 mindless; 9 senseless, unmeaning; 10 unoccupied, unthinking; 11 meaningless, nonsensical, thoughtless; 13 inconsiderate; 14 unintellectual
vacate: 4 quit; 5 empty; 6 give up, resign; 7 abandon; 8 evacuate, renounce, withdraw
vacation: 7 holiday
vacation house: 5 dacha [Russ]; 11 summerhouse; 12 countryhouse
vacation spot: 6 resort; 10 playground
vaccinate: 8 immunize; 9 inoculate; 10 innoculate
vaccinia: 6 cowpox
Vaccinium: 9 blueberry, cranberry, deerberry; 11 huckleberry, lingonberry; 12 whortleberry; 14 genus Vaccinium
vacillate: 4 flit; 5 hover, shake, waver; 6 falter, totter; 7 flitter, flutter, shuffle, tremble; 8 hesitate; 9 fluctuate
vacillating: 6 fickle; 7 varying; 8 changing, hesitant, shifting, unsteady, wavering; 9 trembling, vacillant; 10 flittering, fluttering, inconstant; 11 fluctuating
vacuity: 4 void; 6 vacuum; 7 inanity, vacancy; 11 vacuousness; 12 mindlessness; 13 pointlessness, senselessness
vacuous: 5 empty, inane; 6 hollow, vacant; 7 asinine, fatuous, no-brain; 8 mindless; 10 unoccupied, unthinking; 11 thoughtless; 13 inconsiderate; 14 unintellectual
vacuum: 6 hoover; 7 vacancy, vacuity; 9 emptiness; 11 vacuum-clean; 13 vacuum-cleaner
vacuum bag: 7 dust bag
vacuum bottle: 7 thermos
vacuum-clean: 6 hoover, vacuum
vacuum flask: 7 thermos
vacuum tube: 4 tube; 12 electron tube
vade mecum: 6 manual, primer; 8 handbook; 9 rudiments
Vaduz: 22 capital of Liechtenstein
vagabond: 4 cast, jade, loon, roam, rove, swan; 5 drift, range, scrub, stray, tramp; 6 beggar, ramble, wander; 7 aimless, caitiff, outcast, tramper, vagrant; 8 drifting, floating, rootless; 10 panhandler, ragamuffin
vagary: 3 fad, fit; 4 bout, whim; 5 freak, prank, quirk; 6 maggot; 7 caprice, gambade, impulse, mummery; 8 crotchet, escapade, flimflam; 9 capriccio, poppycock; 10 tomfoolery
vagrancy: 6 vagary, roving
vagrant: 4 hobo [U.S.]; 5 stray, tramp; 6 roving, zigzag; 7 aimless, drifter, erratic, gadding, tramper, wayward; 8 drifting, floating, indirect, rambling, vagabond; 9 itinerant; 10 ambulatory, circuitous, discursive, undirected; 11 peripatetic
vague: 3 dim; 5 faint, loose, wispy; 7 general, obscure, shadowy, sketchy; 9 ambiguous, undefined; 11 unconnected; 12 undetermined; 13 indeterminate
vagus: 13 pneumogastric
vain: 6 futile; 7 flushed, swollen; 8 bootless, inflated, nugatory, puffed up; 9 conceited, egotistic, fruitless, high-flown, overblown, pointless; 10 profitless, sleeveless; 11 egotistical, overweening; 12 unprofitable, vainglorious; 13 self-conceited
vainglorious: 3 big; 4 high, vain; 5 blown, lofty; 6 mighty; 7 flushed, haughty, swelled, swollen; 8 boastful, inflated, puffed up; 9 conceited, high-flown, overblown
vainglory: 7 foppery, hauteur; 8 dandyism; 9 coxcombry; 11 foppishness, haughtiness, high notions; 12 boastfulness
Vaishnavism: 9 Vishnuism; 10 Vaisnavism
valance: 3 hem; 4 gimp, list, welt; 5 frill; 6 edging, fringe, pelmet; 7 cornice, flounce; 8 furbelow, selvedge, skirting, trimming
vale: 4 dale, dell, glen; 5 glade, grove, world; 6 bottom, valley
valediction: 4 ciao; 5 adieu, aloha; 7 goodbye; 8 farewell, sayonara; 10 dosvidanya [Russ]; 11 valedictory; 12 hasta la vista [Sp]; 14 auf wiedersehen [Ger]
valedictory: 8 farewell; 11 valediction; 18 valedictory address
valedictory speaker: 13 valedictorian
valentine: 7 tribute; 10 love letter
Valeriana: 8 valerian; 14 genus Valeriana
Valerianaceae: 14 valerian family
valeric acid: 13 pentanoic acid
valet: 4 page; 6 vassal; 7 servant
Valetta: 8 Valletta; 14 capital of Malta
valetudinarian: 4 sick, weak; 12 valetudinary
Valhalla: 8 paradise, Walhalla
valiance: 5 valor; 6 valour; 7 heroism; 8 valiancy; 9 gallantry
valiant: 8 valorous

valid: 4 good, hard; **5** hardy, solid, stout; **6** cogent, mighty, potent, robust, strong, sturdy; **8** faithful, forcible, in effect, powerful, puissant, tangible, vigorous; **9** competent, confirmed, effective; **10** adamantine, applicable; **11** substantial; **12** commensurate, satisfactory
validate: 9 formalize; **11** corroborate
validating: 5 proof; **7** proving; **9** verifying; **10** collateral, confirming, validation, validatory; **12** confirmative, confirmatory, verificatory; **13** corroborative, corroboratory
validation: 5 proof; **7** proving; **10** validating; **13** establishment
validity: 5 rigor; **6** rigour; **7** cogency; **9** authority, bona fides, validness; **11** genuineness; **12** authenticity; **13** applicability
valise: 3 bag; **4** grip; **8** suitcase; **12** traveling bag
Valium: 8 diazepam
Valletta: 7 Valetta; **14** capital of Malta
valley: 4 dale, dell, glen, vale; **5** glade, grove; **6** bottom
Vallisneria: 8 eelgrass; **9** tape grass; **10** wild celery; **16** genus Vallisneria
valor: 7 bravery, courage, heroism; **8** boldness, valiance, valiancy; **9** gallantry; **14** courageousness
valour: 5 valor; **7** heroism; **8** valiance, valiancy; **9** gallantry; **12** valorousness; **13** valourousness
valse: 5 waltz
valuable: 6 useful, worthy; **7** of value; **8** worthful; **9** estimable, valuables
valuableness: 5 merit, value; **8** goodness; **9** high value; **10** worthiness; **12** preciousness
valuation: 6 assize, rating; **9** appraisal; **10** assessment, estimation, evaluation; **12** appraisement, appreciation
valuator: 9 appraiser
value: 4 rate, tone; **5** merit, prise, prize, worth; **6** admire, assess, esteem, review; **7** care for, defer to, keeping, measure, respect; **8** appraise, estimate, evaluate, goodness, look up to, treasure; **10** appreciate, worthiness
value-added tax: 3 VAT; **12** ad valorem tax
valued at: 5 worth
valueless: 9 worthless
value-system: 5 ethic; **14** moral principle
valve: 6 faucet, spigot; **7** vent peg; **10** slide valve
valve rocker: 9 rocker arm
vamoose: 4 skip; **6** decamp, depart
vamp: 4 minx; **5** flirt, tease; **6** cobble, modify, revamp, tinker, vamp up, vamper; **7** retouch; **8** coquette
vampire: 6 undead; **8** verdulac, werdulac; **7** Dracula; **9** nosferatu; **11** bloodsucker
van: 3 bus; **7** caravan, minibus, minivan; **8** carriage, microbus, vanguard; **9** moving van; **10** avant garde; **12** advance guard

vanadium: 1 V
Van Buren: 14 Martin Van Buren
vancomycin: 8 Vancocin
Vandal: 9 barbarian
vandalism: 10 defacement; **11** destruction
Vandalism: 9 barbarism
Vandyke brown: 5 ocher, sepia
vane: 3 web; **4** cock; **5** blade; **8** wind sock, wind vane; **9** wind gauge; **11** weather vane, weathercock
van Gogh: 14 Vincent van Gogh
vanguard: 3 van; **9** forefront; **10** avant garde; **11** cutting edge; **12** advance guard
Vangueria: 6 medlar; **14** genus Vangueria
vanilla: 5 plain; **8** ordinary; **10** unmodified; **14** vanilla extract
vanish: 2 go; **3** fly; **4** fade, fell, flit, pass; **6** gallop, go away; **8** dissolve, fade away, melt away, pass away, vaporize; **9** disappear, evaporate
vanished: 4 gone, lost; **7** extinct; **8** departed; **9** exhausted
vanishing: 6 fading, flying; **10** fading away; **11** evaporating; **12** disappearing
vanishing cream: 9 cold cream, face cream
vanity: 7 conceit, egotism, inanity; **8** self-love; **9** emptiness; **10** self-esteem; **11** self-conceit, toilet table; **13** conceitedness, dressing table; **14** self-admiration
vanquish: 4 beat; **5** crush; **6** defeat; **7** beat out, conquer, trounce; **9** discomfit
vanquished: 6 beaten, routed; **8** overcome; **9** conquered; **10** overthrown; **11** overwhelmed
vanquisher: 9 conqueror
vantage: 9 advantage
vantage point: 5 angle; **6** aspect; **9** viewpoint; **11** perspective, point of view; **12** viewing angle
Vanuatu: 11 New Hebrides
vapid: 4 bald, fade, flat, mild, slow, tame, weak; **5** bland, stale; **6** feeble, jejune, meager, stupid; **7** humdrum, insipid, mawkish; **9** savorless; **10** flavorless, monotonous, wishy-washy; **11** flavourless
vapor: 3 air, fog, gas; **4** blow, haze, mist, puff; **5** cloud, crack, swell, vaunt; **6** vapour; **7** bluster, swagger, thin air, trumpet; **11** evaporation
vaporize: 2 go; **4** fade, pass; **6** aerify, gasify, vanish; **7** atomize; **8** dissolve, fade away, melt away; **9** disappear, evaporate; **10** volatilize
vaporizer: 6 mister
vaporous: 4 hazy; **5** filmy, foggy, gauzy, misty, sheer; **6** cloudy; **7** gaseous, miasmal, miasmic; **8** cobwebby, ethereal, gossamer, vaporish, volatile; **9** vaporific, vapourish, vapourous; **10** diaphanous, see-through, vapourific; **11** transparent

vaquero: 6 cowboy, drover; **7** grazier; **8** buckaroo, herdsman

var: 10 volt-ampere

var.: 4 form; **6** strain; **7** variant

Varanus: 7 monitor; **11** giant lizard; **12** dragon lizard, Komodo dragon, Komodo lizard, genus Varanus

variable: 7 mutable, varying; **9** checkered; **12** ever changing, unmethodical

variable resistor: 8 rheostat

variance: 7 variant, variety; **8** division, mismatch; **9** disparity, variation; **10** divergence; **11** discrepancy, variability; **12** disagreement

variant: 3 var.; **4** form; **5** plan B; **6** strain; **7** variate, version; **8** revision, variance; **9** expansion, expedient, extension, variation; **10** derivation, derivative; **11** alternative, discrepancy; **12** modification

variation: 4 form; **6** change; **7** variant, variety, version; **8** mutation, revision, variance; **9** expansion, extension; **10** alteration, derivation, derivative, divergence; **11** fluctuation; **12** modification

varicella: 10 chickenpox

varicolored: 4 pied; **6** motley; **7** painted, piebald; **10** multicolor, variegated; **11** culticolour; **12** multicolored

varied: 3 odd; **5** mixed; **6** divers, uneven; **7** altered, changed, diverse, mingled, various; **8** assorted, modified; **9** different, irregular; **10** dissimilar, nonuniform; **11** diversified, wide-ranging; **13** heterogeneous

variegate: 4 vary; **6** dapple, motley, streak, stripe; **7** checker, chequer

variegated: 6 mosaic, motley; **11** varicolored; **12** multicolored, varicoloured

variety: 4 form, kind, line, sort, type; **5** breed, class, stock; **6** change, motley, strain; **7** mixture, species; **8** category, division, variance; **9** diversity, potpourri, variation; **10** assortment, miscellany; **11** diverseness

variola: 8 smallpox

various: 3 odd; **5** mixed; **6** divers, sundry, varied; **7** diverse, mingled, several; **8** assorted; **9** different, versatile; **10** dissimilar, respective; **11** diversified; **13** heterogeneous

varlet: 4 page; **5** knave, rogue; **6** rascal; **8** scalawag; **9** scallywag

varmint: 4 pest; **6** rascal, vermin; **7** varment

varnish: 4 gild, seal, wash; **5** color, gloss, grain, japan, paint, stain; **6** enamel, mastic, polish; **7** dress up, furbish, garnish, lacquer, smarten; **9** embroider, gloss over, japanning, whitewash; **12** French polish, whitewashing

varsity: 9 first team

vary: 5 alter, shift, waver; **6** change, depart, differ, motley, mutate; **7** deviate, diverge, flicker; **8** flounder, mismatch, modulate; **9** fluctuate, variegate

varying hare: 12 snowshoe hare; **14** snowshoe rabbit

vas: 4 duct; **6** vessel

vascular: 8 spirited; **10** passionate

vascular plant: 12 tracheophyte

vasculum: 7 skippet

vasiform: 8 tubelike; **10** tube-shaped; **11** cylindrical

vasopressin: 3 ADH

vassal: 4 serf; **5** liege; **7** servant; **8** liegeman; **9** feudatory

vassalage: 7 serfdom; **8** serfhood; **9** villenage

vast: 4 huge; **5** vasty; **7** extreme, immense; **8** enormous; **9** humongous, world-wide; **10** widespread; **15** uncircumscribed

vat: 3 tub

VAT: 12 ad valorem tax; **13** value-added tax

vatic: 6 mantic; **7** vatical; **8** oracular, sibyllic; **9** prophetic, sibylline; **10** divinatory

Vatican: 7 Holy See; **13** Vatican Palace

vaticinate: 6 divine; **7** predict; **8** prophesy, soothsay; **12** tell fortunes

vaudeville: 9 music hall

vault: 3 hop; **4** arch, hold, jump, leap; **5** bound, crypt; **6** hurdle, jump up, spring; **8** overleap; **9** bank vault; **10** somersault; **11** burial vault

vaulted: 5 bowed, domed; **6** arched; **7** arclike, arcuate

vaulter: 11 pole vaulter

vaulting horse: 4 buck; **9** long horse

vault of heaven: 6 sphere, welkin; **7** heavens; **8** empyrean; **9** firmament

vaunt: 3 gas; **4** blow, brag, puff, tout; **5** boast, crack, swash, vapor; **7** bluster, swagger, trumpet; **9** gasconade

vaunter: 7 boaster; **8** blowhard, braggart

VDT: 7 monitor; **8** terminal

Veadar: 9 Adar Sheni

veal: 4 veau

vector: 5 array; **6** course; **7** bearing; **9** direction

vector sum: 9 resultant

vedalia: 5 onion; **7** ladybug

veer: 3 cut; **4** chop, slew, slue, tack, turn, warp; **5** curve, evert, sheer, shift, trend; **6** swerve; **7** deviate

veery: 13 Wilson's thrush

vegetable: 5 plant; **6** veggie; **7** vegetal; **10** vegetative; **11** couch potato

vegetable garden: 13 kitchen garden; **14** vegetable patch

vegetable kingdom: 5 flora; **7** verdure; **9** plant life

vegetable marrow: 6 marrow; **12** marrow squash

vegetable oyster: 7 salsify

vegetable silk: 5 kapok; **10** silk cotton

vegetable soup: 10 minestrone

vegetable sponge: 6 loofah
vegetate: 4 open; 8 put forth; 9 grow roots, pullulate; 10 burst forth; 11 pass the time
vegetation: 5 flora; 10 brain death
vegetative state: 10 brain death, vegetation; 14 vegetable state
veggie: 9 vegetable
veg out: 5 relax
vehemence: 4 fury, glow; 5 gusto; 6 fervor, warmth; 7 passion, unction; 8 emphasis, ferocity, violence, wildness; 10 fierceness; 11 furiousness
vehement: 4 rude, wild; 5 bluff, fiery, rough; 6 fervid, fierce, madcap, raging, savage; 7 excited, furious, tearing, violent; 8 ungentle; 9 ferocious; 10 blustering, boisterous, outrageous; 11 impassioned; 13 demonstrative
vehicle: 6 medium; 9 transport; 10 conveyance; 12 motor vehicle; 17 automotive vehicle; 20 motorized land vehicle; 27 wheeled motorized land vehicle
vehicle driver: 8 operator
vehicle motor: 6 engine
vehicle operator: 6 driver
veil: 4 caul; 5 blind, cloak, cloud, cover, gauze; 6 chador, screen, shroud; 7 curtain
veiled: 6 hidden; 7 covered; 8 obscured
veiling: 5 gauze; 7 netting
vein: 4 ease, lode, mine, mood, vena; 5 humor, strip; 6 animus, quarry, streak; 7 nervure; 8 attitude; 11 disposition, mineral vein
veined: 6 barred, venose; 8 striated, veinlike
veldt: 4 veld; 6 common; 7 prairie; 9 grassland
velleity: 11 inclination
vellum: 9 parchment
velocipede: 5 trike; 7 bicycle; 8 tricycle
velocity: 4 pace, rate; 5 speed; 12 rate of motion
velum: 10 soft palate
velvety: 5 downy; 6 fluffy, velvet, woolly; 10 flocculent
vena: 4 vein
vena jugularis: 7 jugular; 11 jugular vein
venal: 6 greedy; 7 corrupt; 8 bribable, covetous, usurious; 9 dishonest, mercenary, rapacious; 10 avaricious; 11 corruptible, purchasable; 12 extortionate
vena pulmonalis: 13 pulmonary vein
vend: 4 hawk, sell; 5 pitch; 6 monger, peddle
vendee: 5 buyer; 6 emptor; 9 purchaser
vendetta: 9 blood feud, death feud
vending: 4 sale, vent; 7 hawking, selling; 8 disposal, peddling; 9 vendition
vendor: 6 seller, vender; 10 trafficker
vendue: 6 outcry; 7 auction
veneer: 4 coat; 5 inlay, plate; 6 facing; 9 veneering

venerable: 6 august; 7 revered; 8 emeritus, time-worn; 10 antiquated, reverenced; 11 time-honored
venerate: 6 hallow, revere; 9 reverence
veneration: 3 awe; 8 devotion
venesection: 8 bleeding; 10 phlebotomy; 12 bloodletting
Venetian blinds: 6 louvre; 8 jalousie
Venezia: 6 Venice
vengeance: 7 revenge; 11 getting back, getting even, retribution
vengeful: 8 avenging, rigorous; 9 rancorous; 10 revengeful, vindictive
venial: 9 excusable; 10 defensible, forgivable, pardonable; 11 justifiable
Venice: 7 Venezia
venogram: 10 phlebogram
venom: 4 gall; 5 spite; 6 malice, rancor; 8 rankling; 9 virulence; 12 spitefulness; 13 maliciousness, rancorousness
venomous: 4 acid, sour; 5 acerb, acrid, sharp, short, taint; 6 biting, bitter, deadly; 7 acerbic, caustic, galling, vicious; 8 grinding, virulent; 9 envenomed, poisonous, sarcastic, sulfurous, trenchant, vitriolic; 10 blistering, maleficent
venous: 6 venose veined; 8 veinlike
vent: 3 air; 4 sale; 5 spout; 6 air out, crater, spread; 7 air vent, selling, vending, vent peg, volcano; 8 blowhole, disposal, give vent, spiracle, venthole; 9 ventilate
venter: 5 belly; 7 abdomen, stomach
ventilate: 3 air, fan; 4 vent; 6 air out; 8 give vent
ventilator: 3 fan; 5 lungs; 7 air pump, bellows; 8 blowpipe; 9 air blower
venting: 9 discharge
Ventolin: 9 albuterol, Proventil
ventral: 7 adaxial
ventricous: 7 swollen; 9 distended
ventriculus: 7 gizzard, stomach; 11 gastric mill
ventriloquism: 11 ventriloquy; 13 voice-throwing
venture: 3 try; 4 dare, risk; 5 brave, essay, guess, peril, stake, tempt; 6 danger, effort, embark, hazard, strive; 7 attempt; 8 endeavor, engage in, jeopardy, make bold; 9 adventure, put at risk, undertake; 10 coup d'essai [Fr], enterprise, insecurity, jeopardize; 11 speculation, undertaking
venture capital: 11 risk capital
venturesome: 4 bold; 5 risky; 6 daring; 9 audacious, hazardous, venturous
venturous: 5 risky; 6 daring; 9 audacious, hazardous; 11 venturesome
venue: 4 seat, site; 5 locus; 6 locale; 7 station; 11 whereabouts
Venus: 9 Aphrodite; 10 genus Venus; 11 Venus de Milo

V

veracious: 5 frank; 6 honest; 8 truthful; 9 veridical

veranda: 5 porch; 6 loggia, piazza; 7 gallery, portico; 8 verandah

verapamil: 5 Calan; 7 Isoptin

verbal: 7 literal

verbal intercourse: 4 talk; 6 speech; 7 talking; 8 colloquy, converse, locution, parlance, speaking; 9 discourse; 13 confabulation

verbalize: 4 talk; 5 mouth, speak, utter

Verbascum: 7 mullein; 14 genus Verbascum

verbatim: 3 sic; 6 direct; 7 mot a mot [Fr]; 9 literally, literatim [Lat]; 11 to the letter, word for word

verbena: 7 vervain

verbena family: 11 Verbenaceae

verbiage: 6 babble, hot air, jabber; 7 diction, wording; 8 phrasing; 9 mere words; 11 flow of words, phraseology

verbolatry: 11 word-worship; 13 grammatolatry

verbose: 5 windy, wordy; 7 copious, diffuse, lengthy, profuse, tedious; 9 expansive, exuberant, garrulous, talkative; 10 logorrheic, long-winded, loquacious, pleonastic

verb phrase: 9 predicate

verdancy: 7 verdure; 9 greenness

verdant: 9 verdurous

verdict: 6 decree; 8 decision, judgment

Verdun: 14 battle of Verdun

verdure: 5 flora [pl]; 8 greenery, verdancy; 9 greenness, plant life

verdurous: 7 verdant

verge: 3 dip; 4 bend, pale, tend, term, wand; 5 bourn, brink, trend; 6 bend to; 7 confine, dispose, enclave, incline, scepter, sceptre; 9 determine, threshold

Vergil: 6 Virgil; 20 Publius Vergilius Maro

veridical: 4 real; 7 genuine; 9 veracious

verification: 5 check, proof; 6 docket; 7 voucher, warrant; 9 probation; 11 certificate; 12 confirmation; 13 demonstration; 14 authentication, substantiation

verified: 6 proven; 12 corroborated; 13 substantiated

verify: 4 test; 5 prove, touch; 7 control; 8 make good; 9 establish; 10 make sure of; 12 authenticate, substantiate

verily: 6 indeed, really; 9 in reality

veritable: 4 true; 5 right; 7 correct, factual, regular; 8 bona fide; 9 authentic; 14 unquestionable

verity: 5 truth

vermiculate: 5 wormy; 9 worm-eaten; 10 vermicular; 12 vermiculated

vermiform: 7 serpent; 10 worm-shaped

vermifuge: 10 helminthic; 12 anthelmintic

vermilion: 7 cinibar, scarlet; 9 orange red; 10 vermillion

vermin: 3 bug; 4 flea, pest; 5 louse; 7 varmint; 8 riffraff

vernacular: 4 cant, home; 5 argot, lingo, slang, trite; 6 common, indoor, jargon, patois, vulgar; 7 current, general, regular; 8 domestic, familiar; 10 intramural; 11 naturalized, substandard; 12 domesticated

vernal: 8 youthful; 10 springlike

vernal equinox: 12 March equinox; 13 spring equinox

vernonia: 8 ironweed

veronica: 8 wishbone; 9 speedwell; 10 triskelion

Verrazano: 10 Verrazzano; 19 Giovanni da Verrazano; 20 Giovanni da Verrazzano

verruca: 4 wart

verrucose: 5 warty; 8 wartlike; 10 ventricose; 11 ventricular

versatile: 7 various; 8 variable

verse: 4 poem; 5 count, poesy, rhyme; 6 clause, poetry; 7 chapter, poetics, poetize, versify; 9 paragraph

versification: 7 rhyming, prosody; 12 making verses

versifier: 4 poet; 9 sonneteer

versify: 4 scan, sing; 5 rhyme, verse; 7 poetize

version: 5 light, sense; 7 edition, lection, reading, variant; 8 revision; 9 rendering, variation; 10 adaptation; 11 translation; 12 construction; 14 interpretation

vers libre: 9 free verse

verso: 7 reverse

versus: 2 to; 7 against; 9 counter to

vertebra: 5 spine; 8 backbone; 9 vertebrae

vertebral: 6 spinal

Vertebrata: 8 Craniata; 17 subphylum Craniata; 19 subphylum Vertebrata

vertebrate: 8 craniate

vertex: 3 top; 4 acme, apex, node, peak; 6 summit, zenith; 8 pinnacle, vertices [pl]

vertical: 5 erect, plumb; 6 normal; 7 upright; 8 straight; 13 perpendicular

vertical fin: 7 tailfin

vertical flute: 8 recorder

vertically: 7 upright

vertices: 4 node; 6 vertex

vertiginous: 5 dizzy, woozy; 6 rotary; 8 gyratory; 9 delirious, wandering; 10 incoherent, reasonless; 11 lightheaded

vertigo: 8 swimming; 9 dizziness, giddiness; 15 lightheadedness

vertu: 5 virtu; 15 connoisseurship

vervain: 7 verbena

vervain family: 11 Verbenaceae; 13 verbena family

verve: 4 elan, fire, gush, zeal, zest; 5 ardor, gusto; 6 fervor, spirit; 7 passion; 8 fervency, vitality; 10 enthusiasm

vervet monkey: 6 vervet

very: 4 real; 6 really; 8 rattling, selfsame, very much; 9 identical

very high frequency: 3 VHF [acron]
very important person: 3 VIP [acron]; 6 high-up; 7 big shot, his nibs; 8 big wheel; 9 dignitary; 10 panjandrum; 13 high muck-a-muck
very loudly: 10 fortissimo
very low frequency: 3 VLF
Very pistol: 8 flare gun
very softly: 10 pianissimo
very well: 2 OK; 4 fine; 7 alright; 8 all right, very true; 9 first-rate
Vesalius: 15 Andreas Vesalius
vesica: 7 bladder
vesicle: 3 pea, pod; 4 bulb, clew, cyst, drop, horn, knob, pill; 5 calyx; 6 bullet, marble, pellet, pommel; 7 bladder, blister, capsule, globule, utricle; 8 cancelli, envelope, spherule
Vespa: 10 genus Vespa; 11 giant hornet
vesperal: 8 evensong
vespertilionid: 3 bat
vespertine: 7 evening; 11 crepuscular
vespid: 4 wasp
Vespidae: 4 wasp; 14 family Vespidae
Vespucci: 15 Amerigo Vespucci; 17 Americus Vespucius
Vespula: 4 wasp; 6 hornet; 12 yellow jacket
vessel: 3 gut, vas; 4 boat, ship; 5 canal, craft; 6 bottom, tubule; 10 sea vehicle, watercraft; 12 water vehicle
vest: 3 rig; 4 robe; 5 array, drape, dress; 6 attire, clothe, enrobe, invest; 7 apparel, singlet; 8 enthrone, invest in; 9 waistcoat; 10 undershirt
vestal: 4 pure; 6 virgin; 8 virginal, virtuous
vested: 9 chartered, legalized; 14 constitutional
vestibule: 4 hall; 5 foyer, lobby; 6 wicket; 7 postern; 8 anteroom; 9 threshold; 11 antechamber; 12 entrance hall
vestige: 5 trace; 6 shadow; 7 remains
vestment: 7 vesture; 10 canonicals
vest-pocket park: 8 city park; 10 public park
vestry: 5 synod; 7 chapter; 8 conclave, sacristy; 10 consistory; 11 convocation
vesture: 4 wear; 7 apparel, clothes; 8 clothing, vestment
vesuvian: 4 fuse; 5 light, match, spill; 7 lucifer
Vesuvius: 11 Mt. Vesuvius; 13 Mount Vesuvius
vet: 7 veteran; 10 horse leech, veterinary; 11 horse doctor; 12 animal doctor, ex-serviceman, veterinarian
veteran: 3 vet; 7 old hand; 8 old timer, old-timer, seasoned, warhorse; 9 old person, old stager; 10 campaigner; 12 ex-serviceman
Veterans' Day: 12 Armistice Day
Veterans of Foreign Wars: 3 VFW
veteran soldier: 3 vet; 7 veteran

veterinarian: 3 vet; 10 horse leech, veterinary; 11 horse doctor; 12 animal doctor
veterinary doctor: 3 DVM [acron]
veto: 6 forbid; 8 disallow, negative, prohibit; 9 blackball, interdict, proscribe
vex: 3 bug, irk, rag; 4 faze, nark, rile, tire; 5 annoy, cross, devil, get at, get to, worry; 6 bother, gravel, nettle; 7 disturb, mortify, perplex, trouble; 8 disquiet, irritate; 9 disoblige, displease, incommode; 10 discomfort, discompose; 13 inconvenience
vexation: 4 stew; 5 chafe, worry; 6 bother, pother; 7 chagrin, concern; 8 annoying, headache, nuisance; 9 annoyance, esclandre [Fr], grievance, troubling; 10 harassment, irritation; 13 mortification
vexatious: 5 pesky; 6 plaguy, vexing; 7 galling, plaguey, teasing; 8 annoying; 9 invidious, pestering; 10 bothersome, irritating, nettlesome; 11 pestiferous
vexed: 5 tired; 6 teased; 7 annoyed, harried, plagued; 8 bothered, harassed, molested, pestered; 9 disturbed
vexing: 5 pesky; 6 plaguy; 7 galling, plaguey, teasing; 8 annoying; 9 maddening, pestering, vexatious; 10 bothersome, irritating, nettlesome; 11 infuriating, pestiferous; 12 exasperating
VI: 3 six; 4 sise; 5 hexad, sixer; 6 sestet, sextet; 9 sextuplet; 10 half a dozen
viable: 8 feasible, workable; 11 practicable
vial: 5 ampul, phial; 6 ampule; 7 ampoule
via lactea: 8 milky way; 9 ame no kawa [Jap: river of heaven]; 14 galactic circle, Milky Way galaxy
via media: 10 compromise
viands: 8 victuals; 9 provender; 10 provisions
vibes: 9 vibraharp; 10 vibraphone, vibrations
Vibramycin: 11 doxycycline
vibrancy: 7 ringing; 8 sonority; 9 plangency, resonance; 12 reverberance, sonorousness
vibrant: 7 booming; 8 sonorous; 9 deep-toned, vivacious; 12 deep-sounding
vibraphone: 5 vibes; 7 marimba; 9 vibraharp, xylophone; 12 glockenspiel
vibrate: 5 quake, shake; 6 quaver, quiver; 9 oscillate
vibration: 6 quiver, tremor; 7 shaking; 9 quivering, shakiness, trembling; 11 oscillation, palpitation
vibrion: 6 vibrio
vibrissa: 7 whisker; 11 sensory hair
Viburnum: 8 black haw; 9 arrow wood, twistwood; 13 cranberry bush, cranberry tree, genus Viburnum
vicar: 6 curate, parson, pastor, rector, regent; 9 rural dean
vicariate: 5 glebe, manse; 7 deanery, rectory;

V

8 vicarage; **9** parsonage, vicarship; **10** presbytery

Vicar of Christ: 4 pope; **7** pontiff; **10** Holy Father

vice: 4 vise; **6** acting; **7** frailty; **9** deputized, vice regal; **12** bad character, representing

vice president: 2 V.P.

vice regal: 4 vice; **6** acting; **9** deputized; **12** representing

viceregent: 6 regent

viceroy: 3 beg; **6** regent; **7** khedive; **8** palatine; **9** vicereine [female]

vice versa: 7 by turns; **10** in exchange

Vicia: 5 vetch; **9** broadbean; **10** genus Vicia

vicinage: 5 haunt; **8** confines, environs, precinct, vicinity; **9** precincts; **12** neighborhood

vicinity: 4 ward; **5** block, haunt; **6** barrio [Sp], corner, locale; **8** enceinte, environs, locality, precinct, vicinage; **9** precincts; **12** neighborhood

vicious: 4 evil, fell; **5** cruel; **6** brutal, savage; **8** depraved, venomous; **9** barbarous, poisonous, roughshod

viciousness: 6 infamy; **8** atrocity, savagery; **9** brutality, depravity, flagrancy; **10** savageness; **13** ferociousness

vicissitude: 10 succession; **11** fluctuation

Vicksburg: 16 siege of Vicksburg

victim: 4 dupe, prey; **6** pigeon; **8** casualty

victimization: 5 using; **12** exploitation

victimize: 2 do; **3** con, nab; **4** bilk, bite, scam; **5** cheat, pluck; **6** euchre, jockey, murder; **7** butcher, defraud, swindle

victimized: 4 used; **6** bilked; **7** cheated, crushed, ill-used, plucked, put-upon; **8** stricken, swindled; **9** defrauded, exploited

victimizer: 5 fraud; **8** bilkster, swindler

victor: 5 champ; **6** master, winner; **8** superior; **11** prizewinner

Victoria: 13 Victoria Falls; **19** capital of Seychelles

victorian: 4 prim; **6** prissy; **7** prudish; **8** priggish; **10** square-toed, tight-laced; **11** puritanical, straitlaced; **13** straightlaced

Victoria Nyanza: 12 Lake Victoria

victorious: 5 on top; **7** winning; **10** triumphant

victory: 3 win; **7** triumph

Victory Day: 4 V-day

victory in war: 8 conquest

victual: 5 cater; **6** edible, forage, purvey; **7** eatable, pabulum; **8** victuals; **9** provision; **10** comestible

victualer: 6 batman, feeder, sutler; **7** caterer; **8** purveyor; **10** commissary, victualler; **11** provisioner; **13** quartermaster

victuals: 4 food, grub; **6** edible, viands; **7** aliment, eatable, edibles, ingesta, pabulum,

victual; **8** eatables; **9** nutriment, provender; **10** comestible, provisions, sustenance; **11** comestibles, nourishment; **12** alimentation, sustentation

videlicet: 2 e.g. [abbr], i.e. [abbr]; **3** viz. [abbr]; **5** id est, to wit; **6** namely; **10** for example; **14** exemplia gratia [Lat]

video: 2 TV; **7** picture; **9** video tape; **10** television; **11** telecasting; **14** video recording

video camera: 8 TV camera

video capture board: 12 frame grabber

video casette: 9 videotape

videocassette recorder: 3 VCR

video display terminal: 3 VDT; **7** monitor

video game: 12 computer game

video image: 7 TV image; **9** televideo; **15** closed-circuit TV

video recording: 5 video; **9** video tape

videotape: 12 video casette

vie: 4 spar; **5** rival; **6** square, strive; **7** compete, contend, contest, emulate; **8** scramble, struggle; **9** square off

Vienna: 15 Austrian capital; **16** capital of Austria

Vienna sausage: 5 frank; **6** hot dog, wiener; **11** frankfurter

Vientiane: 13 capital of Laos

vietcong: 8 vietminh

Vietnam: 5 Annam; **7** Viet Nam

Vietnamese: 8 Annamese, Annamite

view: 3 ken, see, spy; **4** espy, look, mark, mind; **5** catch, image, scene, sight, vista, watch; **6** animus, aspect, gander, look at, notice, reckon, regard, remark, survey, take in; **7** eyeshot, horizon, observe, opinion, purview, thought, witness; **8** advert to, consider, discover, panorama, position, proposal, prospect; **9** coup d'oeil [Fr], recognize, sentiment; **10** appearance, persuasion

viewer: 7 watcher, witness; **9** spectator

viewers: 10 TV audience

viewing: 4 wake; **6** espial, seeing; **7** looking, showing; **9** beholding, observing, screening; **10** witnessing; **11** observation; **13** eyewitnessing

viewing angle: 5 angle; **6** aspect; **11** perspective

viewpoint: 5 stand; **7** posture; **8** attitude, position; **10** standpoint; **11** perspective

vigil: 5 watch; **7** look out

vigilance: 8 keenness; **9** alertness; **12** watchfulness

vigilant: 5 awake; **7** on watch, wakeful; **8** open-eyed, watchful; **9** argus-eyed

vigilantism: 6 mob law; **7** club law; **8** lynch law

Vigna: 4 gram; **6** cowpea; **8** moth bean, mung bean; **9** snail bean; **10** adzuki bean, genus Vigna; **12** black-eyed pea; **13** asparagus bean

vigneron: 10 wine grower; **13** viticulturist

vignette: 6 sketch; **9** tailpiece
vigor: 3 vim; **5** force, power; **6** energy, vigour; **8** haleness, strength; **9** hardiness, intensity, manliness; **10** robustness
vigorous: 4 hard; **5** brave, flush, hardy, stout, valid; **6** active, florid, mighty, potent, robust, stanch, strong, sturdy; **7** intense, nervous, staunch; **8** forcible, incisive, powerful, puissant; **9** energetic, trenchant; **10** adamantine, impressive
VII: 5 seven; **6** heptad, septet; **7** sevener
VIII: 5 eight, octad, octet; **6** ogdoad; **7** eighter; **8** octonary
viking: 6 pirate; **8** Norseman
Vila: 16 capital of Vanuatu
vile: 3 low; **4** base, foul, mean, ugly; **5** cheap, dirty, grave, gross, nasty, sorry, weedy, wrong; **6** abject, arrant, filthy, meager, scurvy, shabby, sinful, trashy, wicked; **7** heinous, ignoble, immoral, noisome, pitiful, scrubby; **8** beggarly, depraved, infamous, nauseous, shameful, sinister, trumpery, unworthy, wretched; **9** felonious, loathsome, miserable, nefarious, offensive, sickening, worthless; **10** despicable, iniquitous, nauseating, scandalous, villainous; **11** ignominious, unrighteous; **12** unprincipled
vilify: 4 rail; **6** insult, offend, revile; **7** affront, outrage; **9** bespatter
village: 3 ham; **5** kraal; **6** hamlet; **9** small town; **10** settlement
villain: 3 cad; **6** rascal; **7** bounder, villein; **9** scoundrel
villainous: 4 base, foul, vile; **5** black, grave, gross; **6** scurvy; **7** heinous; **8** infamous, shameful, sinister, wretched; **9** felonious, nefarious
villein: 4 serf; **5** helot; **7** villain
villous: 5 bushy; **6** hispid, shaggy; **7** bearded, shagged
Vilnius: 5 Vilna, Vilno; **18** capital of Lithuania
vim: 4 snap; **5** vigor; **6** energy, vigour; **8** vitality
vinaigrette: 8 dressing; **13** salad dressing
Vinca: 6 myrtle; **10** periwinkle
Vincent's infection: 11 trench mouth; **14** Vincent's angina
vincible: 7 unarmed; **8** beatable, harmless, sine ictu [Lat]; **9** pregnable, untenable; **10** weaponless; **11** defenseless, unfortified; **12** indefensible, vanquishable
vinculum: 4 bond, link; **7** linkage; **10** connection, connective
vindicate: 5 clear; **6** avenge; **7** absolve, justify, revenge; **9** exculpate, exonerate
vindication: 7 defence, defense, warrant; **9** whitewash; **11** exculpation, exoneration; **13** justification
vindicator: 7 avenger; **9** apologist, justifier
vindictive: 8 avenging, rigorous, spiteful,

vengeful; **9** rancorous; **10** despiteful, revengeful
vinegary: 7 acetose, acetous
vineyard: 6 vinery, winery
vingt-et-un: 9 blackjack, twenty-one
vinifera grape: 9 wine grape
vino: 4 wine
vinous: 9 vinaceous
vintage: 3 age; **11** viticulture
vintner: 9 winemaker
vinyl record: 4 disc; **6** record; **7** platter; **9** recording
vinyl resin: 7 polymer
Viocin: 8 viomycin
viol: 6 fiddle, violin; **11** viola d'amore; **12** kittenor viol
Violaceae: 12 violet family; **15** family Violaceae
viola clef: 8 alto clef
viola d'amore: 4 viol; **6** fiddle, violin; **12** kittenor viol
viola da gamba: 5 cello; **8** bass viol
violate: 4 rape; **5** abuse, break, usurp; **6** breach, offend, ravish; **7** despoil, infract, outrage, plunder, profane; **8** dishonor, infringe; **9** desecrate, dishonour; **10** transgress
violation: 4 rape; **6** breach; **7** assault, offence, offense; **8** exaction, trespass; **9** breaching, intrusion, violating; **10** assumption, imposition, infraction, ravishment, usurpation; **11** irreverence, misdemeanor, presumption; **12** encroachment, infringement, misdemeanour; **13** noncompliance, nonobservance, transgression
violator: 6 rapist; **8** ravisher; **9** debaucher; **10** lawbreaker
violence: 4 fury; **5** force; **8** ferocity, wildness; **9** vehemence; **10** fierceness; **11** furiousness
violent: 3 red; **4** rude, wild; **5** bluff, fiery, rough; **6** fierce, madcap, raging, savage; **7** crimson, excited, furious, tearing; **8** ungentle, vehement; **9** ferocious; **10** blustering, boisterous, outrageous; **11** impassioned; **13** demonstrative
violet: 6 purple; **8** purplish; **11** reddish blue, ultraviolet
violet family: 9 Violaceae; **15** family Violaceae
violin: 4 viol; **6** fiddle
violin bow: 11 fiddlestick
violinist: 7 fiddler
violoncello: 5 cello, tenor; **7** cremona
viomycin: 6 Viocin
VIP: 6 high-up; **7** big shot, his nibs; **8** big wheel; **9** dignitary
viper: 5 adder, snake; **7** reptile, serpent
Vipera: 3 asp; **5** adder, viper; **11** genus Vipera

V

Viperidae: 15 family Viperidae
virago: 5 scold, shrew, vixen; **6** amazon, dragon; **9** termagant
Vireonidae: 5 vireo; **16** family Vireonidae
Virgil: 6 Vergil; **20** Publius Vergilius Maro
Virgilia: 8 keurboom; **13** genus Virgilia
virgin: 4 maid, pure; **6** maiden, vestal; **8** virginal, virtuous; **9** unsullied
virginal: 4 pure; **6** vestal, virgin; **8** virtuous
virginals: 6 spinet
Virgin Birth: 8 Nativity
virgin forest: 9 old growth
Virginia creeper: 8 woodbine
Virginia fence: 9 rail fence
Virgin Mary: 4 Mary; **7** Madonna; **9** the Virgin
Virgo the Virgin: 5 Virgo
virgule: 5 slash; **6** stroke; **7** solidus; **8** diagonal
viridity: 5 green; **9** greenness
virile: 4 male; **5** manly; **6** manful, potent; **7** manlike; **9** masculine
virility: 7 manhood; **9** manliness; **10** manfulness
virtu: 9 objet d' art
virtual: 6 unreal; **9** potential, practical
virtually: 4 most, near, nigh; **5** about; **6** all but, almost, au fond, nearly; **8** at bottom, in effect, well-nigh; **9** just about, literally; **10** negatively; **11** practically; **13** substantially
virtue: 4 face, guts; **5** merit, shame, spunk; **7** ability, faculty, modesty, quality; **8** chastity, property; **9** attribute, endowment, fortitude, hardihood; **10** continence; **12** virtuousness; **13** qualification
virtuoso: 3 ace, wiz; **4** star, whiz; **5** adept, maven, whizz; **6** genius, wizard; **7** hotshot; **8** masterly; **9** masterful, sensation; **10** conoscente, consummate
virtuous: 4 good, just, pure; **6** honest, vestal, virgin; **7** upright
virtuously: 4 well; **5** nobly; **7** morally; **8** chastely; **11** righteously
virulence: 4 gall, huff, miff; **5** pique, venom; **6** rancor, spleen; **7** umbrage; **8** acerbity, acrimony, asperity, rankling, soreness; **10** bitterness; **13** rancorousness
virulent: 4 acid, sour; **5** acerb, acrid, harsh, sharp, short, taint; **6** biting, bitter, deadly; **7** acerbic, caustic, crabbed, doggish, mordant; **8** venomous; **9** corrosive, envenomed, rancorous, sarcastic, stringent, sulfurous, trenchant, vitriolic; **10** blistering, irritating, mordacious, sulphurous; **11** acrimonious; **12** contumelious
visage: 3 mug; **4** brow; **6** kisser, smiler; **8** forehead; **11** countenance
vis-a-vis: 4 as to; **6** calash; **8** love seat, sociable; **9** regarding, tete-a-tete; **10** concerning, face to face, in regard to; **11** counterpart

Viscaceae: 15 family Viscaceae, mistletoe family
viscacha: 11 chinchillon
viscera: 3 gut; **4** guts [pl]; **5** bowel; **6** bowels [pl], vitals [pl]; **7** innards; **8** entrails [pl]; **10** intestines [pl]
visceral: 9 glandular, intuitive; **10** splanchnic
viscid: 5 gluey, gummy, pasty, thick; **6** sticky; **7** viscous; **9** glutinous; **12** mucilaginous
Viscount St. Albans: 5 Bacon; **12** Baron Verulam, Francis Bacon
viscous: 5 gluey, gummy, pasty, thick; **6** sticky, syrupy, viscid; **9** glutinous; **12** mucilaginous
Viscum: 9 mistletoe; **11** genus Viscum
vise grip: 5 tongs; **6** pliers; **7** forceps, nippers, pincers; **8** clutches
visibility: 8 exposure; **11** visibleness; **14** perceptibility; **15** conspicuousness
visible: 6 in view, on hand; **7** in sight, obvious, seeable; **11** discernible, perceivable, perceptible
vision: 5 dream, ghost, shade, sight, spook; **6** seeing, shadow; **7** figment, specter; **8** eyesight, revenant; **10** apparition; **11** imagination
visionary: 4 airy, seer; **7** dreamer, shadowy; **8** fabulous, idealist, romancer, romantic, spectral; **9** fantastic
visionless: 5 blind; **9** sightless
visit: 3 see; **4** chat; **6** call on, claver, confab, impose; **7** sojourn, meeting; **8** travel to
visitation: 5 trial, visit, worry; **6** attack; **9** annoyance; **10** affliction, infliction, irritation; **11** tribulation
visiting card: 4 card; **11** address card, calling card
visitor: 5 guest; **6** caller; **8** visitant; **9** inspector
visor: 4 bill, mask, peak; **5** vizor; **6** domino; **8** eyeshade
vista: 4 view; **5** aisle, alley, glade, scene; **6** aspect; **7** horizon; **8** good view, panorama, prospect; **11** distant view, perspective
Vistula: 12 Vistula River
visual: 5 optic; **6** ocular; **7** optical
visual aid: 12 illustration
visualization: 5 image; **7** picture; **11** delineation, visual image, visualizing; **12** illustration
visualize: 3 see; **5** fancy, image; **6** figure; **7** picture, project; **8** envision
visualized: 8 pictured; **10** envisioned
visual sense: 5 sight; **6** vision
visual symbol: 13 graphic symbol
Vitaceae: 10 Vitidaceae; **15** grapevine family
vital: 6 lively; **7** radical; **8** cardinal, critical; **9** essential, paramount; **10** full of life, lifegiving
vitality: 3 vim; **4** life; **5** verve; **6** energy, liv-

ing; **8** strength; **9** animation, soundness, viability

vitally: 9 radically; **11** essentially

vital organ: 6 vitals

vitals: 3 gut; **4** guts [pl]; **5** bowel; **6** bowels [pl]; **7** viscera [pl]; **8** entrails [pl]; **10** intestines [pl], vital organ

vitamin A: 1 A; **7** retinol; **9** vitamin A1; **11** axerophthol

vitamin A2: 14 dehydroretinol

vitamin B: 1 B; **8** B complex

vitamin B1: 7 aneurin, thiamin; **8** thiamine; **12** antiberi-beri

vitamin B12: 9 cobalamin

vitamin B2: 8 vitamin G; **9** ovoflavin; **10** riboflavin; **11** lactoflavin; **12** hepato-flavin

vitamin B6: 7 adermin; **9** pyridoxal; **10** pyri-doxine; **12** pyridoxamine

vitamin Bc: 6 folate; **7** folacin; **8** vitamin M; **9** folic acid

vitamin C: 12 ascorbic acid

vitamin D: 1 D; **10** calciferol; **14** ergocalcif-erol

vitamin D3: 15 cholecarciferol

vitamin E: 1 E; **10** tocopherol

vitamin G: 10 riboflavin

vitamin H: 6 biotin

vitamin K1: 12 phytonadione; **13** phylloqui-none

vitamin P: 6 citrin; **12** bioflavinoid

vitiate: 3 mar; **4** void; **5** spoil; **6** debase, impair; **7** corrupt, debauch, deprave, per-vert, profane; **8** deflower; **9** misdirect; **10** demoralize, invalidate

viticulturist: 8 vigneron [Fr]

Vitidaceae: 8 Vitaceae; **14** family Vitaceae; **15** grapevine family

Vitis: 5 grape; **10** genus Vitis

vitreous: 6 glassy; **7** hyaline; **9** vitrified; **11** crystalline

vitreous silica: 6 quartz; **7** crystal; **11** quartz glass

vitrification: 12 ossification

vitrified: 6 glassy; **8** vitreous

vitrine: 8 showcase; **13** glass showcase

vitriol: 9 invective; **12** oil of vitriol

vitriolic: 4 acid; **5** acerb, acrid; **6** bitter; **7** acerbic, caustic, erosive; **8** venomous, viru-lent; **9** corrosive, sulfurous; **10** blistering, sulphurous

vituperate: 4 rail; **6** revile, vilify; **12** speak daggers

vituperation: 5 abuse; **7** vitriol; **9** contumely, invective; **11** fulmination, objurgation; **12** denunciation, vilification

vituperative: 4 acid; **7** abusive, searing; **8** scathing; **9** clamorous, scorching; **12** con-demnatory, contumelious, denunciatory

vivacious: 5 brisk; **6** active, lively, mobile; **7** vibrant; **8** animated, bustling, spirited; **10** expressive, mettlesome

703 **vitally / void**

vivacity: 4 dash, life; **6** energy, spirit; **8** alacrity; **9** animation

vivarium: 9 menagerie, terrarium

viva voce: 4 oral; **6** orally; **8** oral exam, ver-bally; **9** by talking; **10** by speaking; **11** word-of-mouth

Viverra: 5 civet; **12** genus Viverra

vivid: 4 deep, keen; **5** acute, brisk, sharp; **6** bright, lively, severe; **7** glowing, graphic, intense, shining; **8** deep-dyed, incisive, lifelike; **9** brilliant, pictorial, trenchant; **10** impressive; **11** thin-skinned

vividness: 5 color; **6** chroma, colour; **9** inten-sity; **10** saturation

vivify: 6 revive; **7** animate, quicken; **8** recre-ate, revivify; **9** reanimate

vixen: 3 fox; **5** harpy, scold, shrew; **6** dragon, virago; **7** hellcat, Reynard; **8** Xantippe; **9** termagant

viz: 2 e.g. [abbr], i.e. [abbr]; **5** id est; **6** namely; **9** videlicet; **10** for example; **11** that is to say; **14** exemplia gratia [Lat]

vizier: 8 minister; **11** grand vizier

vizor: 5 visor

vocable: 10 spoken word

vocabulary: 7 lexicon; **10** dictionary

vocal: 4 oral, sung; **6** spoken; **8** phonetic; **9** outspoken

vocalic: 8 syllabic

vocalist: 6 singer; **7** crooner, warbler; **8** melodist, songster

vocalize: 4 sing; **5** sound, utter, voice; **7** breathe; **8** vowelize; **9** enunciate; **10** articu-late

vocally: 6 in song

vocation: 4 walk; **6** career; **7** calling; **10** occupation, profession

vocational college: 6 vo-tech

vocational school: 11 trade school

vociferate: 6 clamor; **8** shout out

vociferation: 3 cry; **4** call, yell; **5** shout; **6** chorus, clamor, outcry, plaint, strain; **8** out-burst

vociferous: 7 blatant, clamant; **8** strident; **9** clamorous; **10** clamourous

vogue: 4 chic, mode, note, rage; **5** eclat, style, trend; **7** fashion; **8** currency; **9** celebrity, notoriety; **10** notability, popular-ity, sylishness

voice: 4 part, poll, vote, word; **5** sound; **6** bal-lot, phrase; **7** express; **8** election, suffrage, vocalize; **9** vox populi; **10** articulate, plebiscite; **12** articulation, spokesperson, vocalization

voice box: 6 larynx

voiceless: 4 surd; **8** unvoiced, wordless

voicelessness: 7 aphonia

voice-throwing: 13 ventriloquism

void: 3 nul; **4** null; **5** annul, avoid, empty, quash; **6** naught, nought; **7** nullify, nullity,

V

vacancy, vacuity, vitiate; **8** evacuate, nugatory; **9** eliminate, emptiness; **10** invalidate, unoccupied; **11** nothingness

voidance: 8 emptying; **10** evacuation

void of meaning: 6 vacant; **9** senseless, unmeaning; **11** meaningless, nonsensical

volatile: 4 taut; **5** cross, fiery, giddy, surly, tense, testy; **6** crabby, fickle, frothy, tetchy, touchy; **7** burning, crabbed; **8** volcanic; **9** excitable, explosive, frivolous, hot-headed, irascible, irritable, sensitive, simmering; **10** high-strung, sleeveless; **11** bad-tempered, hot-tempered, ill-tempered

volatile oil: 12 essential oil

volatilize: 8 vaporize, gasify; **9** evaporate

volcanic: 7 burning, igneous; **8** eruptive, meteoric, plutonic, volatile; **9** hot-headed, simmering

volcano: 4 vent; **6** crater

volcanology: 11 vulcanology

vole: 10 field mouse

Volga: 10 Volga River

Volgograd: 9 Tsaritsyn; **10** Stalingrad

volition: 4 will; **7** willing; **8** free will; **9** act of will; **10** discretion

volley: 5 blast, burst, cloud, salvo, storm; **6** blow up, firing, shower; **9** discharge, explosion, fusillade; **10** detonation

volt: 1 V

voltage: 3 emf

voltaic: 8 galvanic

Voltaire: 19 Francois-Marie Arouet

volt-ampere: 3 var

volte-face: 8 flip-flop, reversal; **9** about-face

voluble: 4 glib; **6** fluent; **8** flippant; **9** talkative

volume: 4 book, bulk, mass, tome, work; **7** writing; **8** capacity, loudness, turnover; **9** intensity

voluminous: 5 ample, bulky, massy; **7** massive; **8** numerous; **12** considerable

voluntary: 7 willing; **9** volunteer; **10** deliberate, gratuitous, volitional; **11** intentional, self-induced, spontaneous; **13** self-motivated

volunteer: 5 offer; **6** unpaid; **9** voluntary; **11** come forward

Volunteer State: 9 Tennessee

voluptuary: 8 hedonist, sybarite; **9** epicurean, sybaritic; **10** sensualist

voluptuous: 5 buxom, curvy, juicy; **6** red-hot, sonsie; **7** sensual; **8** luscious; **9** epicurean, luxurious, sybaritic; **10** curvaceous, voluptuary

volute: 4 coil, worm; **5** helix, whorl; **6** buckle, rundle, spiral; **7** coiling, helical, voluted, whorled; **9** corkscrew, spiraling, turbinate

Volvariella: 13 straw mushroom; **15** Chinese mushroom, genus Volvariella

vomit: 3 cat; **4** puke, sick, spew; **5** chuck, heave, retch; **6** be sick, cast up, emetic, puking; **7** bring up, chuck up, get sick, heaving, regorge, throw up, upchuck, vomit up, vomitus; **8** disgorge, nauseant, vomiting, vomitive; **11** regurgitate; **12** disgorgement; **13** regurgitation

vomiting agent: 6 emetic

voodoo: 4 juju; **6** fetich, fetish, hoodoo, vodoun; **7** bedevil, bewitch; **9** hoodooism, voodooism

voracious: 8 edacious, esurient, ravening, ravenous; **9** rapacious

voracity: 7 edacity; **8** gluttony, rapacity; **9** esurience; **12** ravenousness; **13** rapaciousness, voraciousness

vortex: 4 eddy, whir; **5** swirl, whirl; **6** reflux; **8** overflow; **9** Maelstrom, maelstrom, whirlpool; **11** convolution; **12** undercurrent; **13** regurgitation

votary: 3 fan; **4** buff; **5** lover; **7** amateur, devotee; **10** aficionado, dilettante, enthusiast

vote: 4 poll; **5** voice; **6** ballot, voting; **7** plumper; **8** election, suffrage; **9** balloting, vox populi

vote down: 4 kill; **6** defeat; **7** vote out

voteless: 13 disfranchised; **15** disenfranchised

vote out: 4 kill; **6** defeat; **8** vote down

voter: 7 elector

voting system: 15 electoral system

votive offering: 13 burnt offering

vouch: 4 avow; **6** assure, avouch; **7** certify, warrant; **9** guarantee; **10** asseverate

voucher: 6 coupon, docket; **7** warrant, witness; **11** certificate; **12** verification; **13** certification; **14** authentication

vouch for: 6 depose; **7** testify, witness; **11** bear witness

vouchsafe: 5 deign, grant; **6** accord; **7** concede

vow: 4 oath; **5** swear, troth; **6** depone, depose, parole, plight; **8** swearing; **10** consecrate; **11** word of honor

vowel rhyme: 9 assonance

vox populi: 4 poll, vote; **5** voice; **6** ballot; **7** opinion, plumper; **8** election, suffrage; **13** current belief, popular belief, public opinion

voyage: 4 sail; **6** cruise; **7** passage; **8** navigate; **9** ocean trip

voyager: 8 traveler, wayfarer; **9** itinerant

voyeur: 6 peeper; **10** Peeping Tom

Vulcan: 6 forger, smithy; **10** blacksmith, Hephaestus

vulcanism: 9 volcanism

vulcanite: 7 ebonite; **10** hard rubber

vulcanization: 13 vulcanisation

vulcanized: 5 cured

vulgar: 5 crude, gross; **6** coarse, common, earthy; **7** obscene, uncouth; **8** plebeian, unwashed; **9** low-minded, unrefined; **10** vernacular

vulgarism: 8 bad taste; **9** grossness, obscenity, vulgarity; **10** coarseness, commonness

vulgarity: 8 bad taste; **9** grossness, vulgarism; **10** coarseness, commonness

vulgar tongue: 10 vernacular

vulnerability: 8 exposure; **9** liability

vulnerable: 6 tender; **7** exposed; **10** unshielded; **11** unprotected

vulnerary: 8 liniment

Vulpes: 6 kit fox, red fox; **10** prairie fox; **11** genus Vulpes

vulpine: 4 foxy; **6** crafty, feline, subtle; **10** vulpecular

Vultur: 6 condor; **7** vulture, buzzard; **11** genus Vultur

vulture: 5 Draco, harpy; **7** buzzard; **8** marauder, predator

vulturine: 8 ravening; **9** predatory, rapacious, raptorial, vulturous

W

W: 4 watt, west; **7** due west, wolfram; **8** tungsten; **9** W particle

W.C.: 3 loo; **6** closet; **11** water closet

Wabash: 11 Wabash River

wacky: 4 bats, daft, fool, loco, nuts, zany; **5** balmy, barmy, batty, buggy, dotty, goofy, kooky, loony, loopy, nutty, sappy, silly; **6** fruity, kookie; **7** bonkers, cracked, haywire; **8** crackers; **9** cockamamy; **10** cockamamie

wad: 3 cud, jam, lot, pad, pot, ram; **4** chaw, chew, cram, deal, fill, heap, line, mass, mess, mint, pack, peck, pile, plug, quid, raft, slew, slug [U.S.]; **5** batch, flock, sight, spate, stack, stuff; **6** bundle, hatful, mickle, muckle, plenty; **7** chock up, compact, incrust, jampack, tidy sum; **8** good deal, whole lot; **9** great deal, whole slew; **10** wad of bills [U.S.], wad of money

wadding: 4 down; **7** filling, packing, padding; **8** stopping, stuffing

waddle: 4 halt, limp, slug; **6** coggle, dodder, hobble, paddle, slouch, toddle, totter; **7** shamble, shuffle, traipse

wade: 4 dive, skim

wadi: 4 wash; **5** gulch, gully; **6** arroyo; **11** dry river bed

wading bird: 5 wader; **9** water bird, shore bird

wads: 4 gobs, lots, tons; **5** heaps, loads, piles, rafts, scads, slews; **6** dozens, oodles, scores, stacks; **8** lashings

waffle: 4 bull, fake, trim; **5** demur, pause; **6** coquet, debate; **7** balance, shuffle; **8** straddle; **9** fluctuate

waft: 4 blow; **5** drift; **6** pennon; **7** pennant; **8** streamer

wafture: 4 wave; **6** waving

wag: 3 bob, wit; **4** beat, card, reel, sway, toss; **5** dance, dodge, lurch, quake, shake, swing; **6** quaver, quiver, seesaw, shiver, tumble, waddle, waggle, writhe; **7** shuffle, stagger, twitter; **8** humorist

wager: 3 bet; **5** stake; **6** gamble, stakes; **7** play for, risking, staking

wagerer: 6 better, bettor, punter

wages: 3 pay; **4** wage; **6** income, payoff, reward, salary; **8** earnings

wage war: 5 fight; **6** battle, combat; **8** do battle; **10** give battle

waggish: 6 jocose; **7** jocular; **8** humorous; **9** facetious, whimsical

waggle: 3 bob, wag; **4** reel, sway, toss; **5** quake, shake; **6** quaver, quiver, shiver, tumble, wamble, writhe; **7** shuffle, stagger, twitter

waggon: 5 wagon

Wagner: 13 Richard Wagner; **20** Wilhelm Richard Wagner

wagon: 4 cart, wain; **5** truck; **6** pick-up, wagon; **9** police van, road train; **10** beach wagon, black Maria, paddy wagon, streetcart; **11** beach waggon, patrol wagon, pick-up wagon, police wagon

wagoner: 6 carter; **8** waggoner; **9** postilion

wagon-lit: 7 sleeper; **10** Pullman car; **11** sleeping car

wagon train: 5 train; **7** caravan

wagonwright: 10 wainwright; **12** wagonwright

wahoo: 8 mackeral; **9** winged elm; **11** burning bush

Wahunsonacock: 8 Powhatan

waif: 5 stray; **9** found item, foundling

wail: 3 cry, sob; **4** howl, mewl, pipe, pule, roar, weep, yawl; **6** crying, lament, outcry, plaint; **7** blubber, ululate, wailing, weeping, whimper; **9** shed tears, ululation; **11** lamentation

wain: 5 wagon

wainscoted: 7 paneled

wainwright: 11 wagonwright; **12** wagonwright

waist: 5 shank; **6** middle; **7** midriff; **9** waistline

waistband: 4 sash; **6** girdle; **8** cincture; **10** waistcloth

waistcoat: 4 vest; **6** jacket

wait: 4 bide, hold, look, stay; **5** await, delay, pause, tarry; **6** expect; **7** hold off, respite, time lag, waiting; **8** hold back, take time; **9** lie in wait; **10** suspension; **11** adjournment

waiter: 6 server

waiter's assistant: 6 busboy

waiting area: 6 lounge; **11** waiting room

waiting line: 5 queue

wait on: 4 tend; **5** serve; **6** assist, attend, hang on; **8** attend to

waive: 5 forgo, spare; **6** give up, remand, render, retard; **7** abstain, adjourn, forbear, forfeit, lay over, neglect, not vote, suspend; **8** hold over, let alone, not touch; **9** do without, foreswear; **10** relinquish; **12** dispense with

waiver: 7 release; **9** discharge

wake: 4 rear, tail; **5** awake, queue, trail, train, waken; **6** arouse, awaken, wake up; **7** viewing; **8** backwash; **9** aftermath, come alive

Wake: 10 Wake Island

wakeful: 5 awake, light; **7** on watch; **8** openeyed, vigilant, watchful; **9** argus-eyed, sleepless, wide awake; **10** on the alert

wakeless: 5 heavy, sound; **8** profound

waken: 4 wake; **5** awake, rouse; **6** arouse, awaken, wake up; **9** come alive

wake-robin: 8 trillium

wake up: 4 wake; **5** awake, get up, rouse, waken; **6** arouse, awaken, blow up, call up; **7** light up, raise up; **8** summon up; **9** come alive

wake-up signal: 8 reveille

wale: 4 weal, welt; **5** ridge, wheal; **6** strake

Wales: 5 Cymru

Walhalla: 8 Valhalla

walk: 4 beat [of police], pass, race; **5** flags, march, paseo, range; **6** career, course, record; **7** calling, walking, walkway; **8** footpath, pavement, sidewalk, vocation; **10** profession, walk of life; **11** base on balls

walk around: 9 walk about; **11** perambulate; **14** circumambulate

walkaway: 4 romp; **6** shoo-in; **7** laugher, runaway

walk down the aisle: 3 wed; **4** join; **5** marry; **10** get hitched [U.S. slang], get married

walker: 6 footer, go-cart; **10** baby-walker, pedestrian

walk hand in hand with: 7 consort; **8** sort with; **13** associate with

walkie-talkie: 2 CB; **8** car radio, ham radio; **10** police band, walky-talky; **11** police radio, two-way radio; **12** amateur radio, citizen's band, handie-talkie; **13** airplane radio; **14** short-wave radio

walking on air: 5 bliss; **9** cloud nine; **12** blissfulness; **13** seventh heaven

walking papers: 4 sack; **8** pink slip

walkingstick: 11 stick insect; **12** walking stick

Walkman: 11 Sony Walkman

walk of life: 4 walk; **6** career; **7** calling; **8** vocation; **10** profession

walk-on: 4 mute; **5** extra; **11** nonspeaking; **14** general utility

walk on air: 5 exult; **10** jump for joy; **13** be on cloud nine

walk-on role: 5 cameo

walk out: 6 strike

walkout: 13 wildcat strike

walkover: 4 snap; **5** cinch; **6** picnic; **8** duck soup, pushover; **10** child's play

walk-up apartment: 6 walk-up

walkway: 4 walk; **5** paseo

wall: 4 side; **5** fence, hedge, sides, slope; **6** paries; **7** bulwark, fence in, rampart; **8** hedge row, palisade, surround

wallaby: 13 brush kangaroo

wallet: 8 billfold, notecase

walleye: 12 walleyed pike

wall in: 3 pen; **4** cage, coop; **5** hem in, pen in; **6** bolt in, coop up, rail in, wall up; **7** hedge in, impound

wall light: 11 wall fixture

wallop: 3 hit, jog; **4** beat, wham, whip, whop; **5** smite [biblical], whack; **6** buffet, hustle, joggle, jostle, jounce, strike

walloping: 5 gaunt, hulky; **7** debacle, hulking, lumpish; **8** drubbing, lubberly, spanking, thumping, unwieldy, whacking; **9** humongous, slaughter, thrashing, trouncing; **10** thundering

wallow: 5 revel; **6** billow, crouch, grovel, slouch, welter; **7** founder, rejoice, triumph

wall painting: 5 mural

wall plug: 6 outlet; **10** wall socket, receptacle

Walpole: 13 Robert Walpole; **16** Sir Robert Walpole

waltz: 5 valse

wamble: 4 flit, reel; **5** shake, shock; **6** rumble, totter, waggle; **7** disgust, flitter, flutter, shuffle, tremble; **8** nauseate; **9** vacillate

wampum: 5 money

WAN: 15 wide area network

wan: 3 dun; **4** ashy, cold, dead, dull, pale; **5** ashen, dingy, faint, muddy; **6** glassy, leaden, pallid, rueful, sallow; **7** ghastly; **9** long-faced; **10** cadaverous, lackluster

wand: 3 rod; **4** mace; **5** verge; **7** scepter, sceptre; **8** caduceus; **11** divining rod

wander: 4 cast, dote, rave, roam, rove, swan; **5** cheat, drift, range, stray; **6** betray, ramble; **7** cheat on, cuckold, digress; **8** divagate

wanderer: 5 rover; 6 roamer; 7 rambler; 8 vagabond; 9 straggler

wandering: 4 wild; 5 giddy, rabid, stray; 6 doting, mobile, raving, roving, wanton; 7 berserk, erratic, frantic, lawless, nomadic, roaming, wayward, winding; 8 frenetic, frenzied, informal, rambling; 9 delirious, insensate, peregrine, planetary, possessed; 10 incoherent, meandering, reasonless

wane: 3 ebb; 5 waste; 6 dodder, ebbing, go down, recede, shrink; 7 decline, dwindle, shrivel; 8 collapse, fall away, grow less

wangle: 4 cook, fake; 5 fudge; 6 manage; 7 falsify, finagle; 10 manipulate; 12 misrepresent

waning: 8 decrepit; 9 declining

Wankel engine: 12 rotary engine

wannabe: 7 hopeful; 8 aspirant, wannabee

wanness: 6 pallor; 8 lividity, paleness; 9 lividness, luridness; 10 achromasia, pallidness

want: 4 lack, miss, need, wish; 6 be poor, desire, have no, penury; 7 absence, poverty, require, wishing; 8 be void of, distress, exigency; 9 be empty of, indigence, necessity, neediness, pauperism, privation; 10 be indigent, deficiency; 11 deprivation, destitution

want ad: 5 job ad; 12 help wanted ad

wanted: 6 wished; 7 desired, invited; 8 precious; 9 cherished, treasured

wanted person: 8 fugitive

wanting: 4 soft, weak; 5 borne, sappy; 6 spoony, void of; 7 empty of, failing, lacking, missing, needing, shallow, wishing; 8 desiring; 9 defective, deficient; 11 nonexistent

wanton: 3 toy; 4 easy, wild; 5 feast, kinky [U.S.], light, loose, revel, sport, stray; 6 junket, lavish, madcap, piddle, trifle; 7 banquet, carouse, disport, lawless, profuse, rampant, replete, wayward; 8 fanciful, freakish, heedless, informal, overmuch, reckless, skittish, sluttish, unchaste; 9 debauched, dissolute, drown care, exuberant, fantastic, luxuriate, make merry, wandering; 10 inordinate, licentious, motiveless, particular, unprovoked

wapiti: 3 elk

wappentake: 5 lathe; 6 riding; 7 hundred, tithing

war: 6 combat; 7 warfare; 8 battling, conflict, fighting; 11 hostilities

war advocacy: 12 warmongering

War between the States: 8 Civil War

warble: 3 coo; 4 pipe, sing; 5 carol, chant, cheep, chirp, trill, tweet, yodel; 6 chaunt, cuckoo, intone, quaver; 7 chirrup, descant, twitter, whistle

warbler: 4 bird; 6 singer; 8 melodist, songster, vocalist

war cry: 3 cry; 8 war whoop; 9 battle cry; 11 rallying cry

ward: 4 care, keep; 5 block, cover, flank, guard; 6 barrio [Sp], charge, corner, locale, screen, shroud; 7 custody, protege [Fr], shelter; 8 enceinte, environs, locality, precinct, vicinity; 9 cellblock, precincts; 11 safekeeping; 12 hospital ward, neighborhood

warden: 6 archon, warder; 7 provost; 10 lieutenant

warder: 5 guard, probe, rimer, scoop; 6 beadle, chisel, custos [Lat], dibble, gaoler, gimlet, jailer, keeper, lancet, porter, ranger, trepan, warden; 7 doorman [male], terrier, turnkey; 8 cerberus, portress [female]; 9 custodian; 10 doorkeeper

ward-heeler: 4 hack; 9 party hack; 13 political hack

ward off: 5 avert, avoid, debar; 7 beat off, deflect, fend off, head off, keep off, obviate; 8 beat back, stave off

wardrobe: 4 trim; 5 guise, press; 6 closet, things, toilet

ware: 5 shirk, waste; 6 beware; 7 article, consume, product; 8 squander; 9 commodity, keep watch; 11 merchandise

warehouse: 10 storehouse

warehousing: 5 store; 7 storing; 10 repositing, reposition

wares: 5 goods; 7 effects, product; 11 merchandise

war games: 10 kriegspiel [Ger]; 11 Kriegsspiel [Ger]

warhead: 4 load; 7 payload

warhorse: 7 old hand, veteran; 8 old-timer

war horse: 7 charger; 8 destrier

warily: 10 stealthily

warlike: 7 martial; 9 bellicose, combative, unpacific; 11 belligerent

warlord: 14 military leader

warm: 3 cob, hot; 4 bang, fond, gild, glow, heat, trim, wipe; 5 acute, dress, quick, sharp, smart, swell, tepid; 6 ardent, caring, fervid, foment, foster, hearty, lively, strong, tender, warm up; 7 burning, cordial, cutting, glowing, make hot, well off; 8 incisive, lovesome, lukewarm, piercing, swelling, well to do; 9 dress down; 10 empathetic; 11 sympathetic, warm-hearted; 12 affectionate

warm bath: 5 sauna; 9 steam bath, vapor bath; 11 Russian bath, Turkish bath

warmed-over: 8 leftover, reheated; 10 cooked-over

warmer: 6 heater

warming: 4 thaw; 7 heating, melting, thawing

warmly: 8 heartily; 9 cordially

warmonger: 10 militarist

W

warmth: 4 glow, heat; 5 gusto; 7 passion, unction; 8 fondness, sympathy, warmness; 9 vehemence; 10 excitement, lovingness

warn: 7 caution; 8 admonish, forewarn; 10 discourage

warning: 6 caveat; 7 caution; 8 monitory; 9 exemplary; 10 admonition, admonitory, cautionary, cautioning; 11 premonitory

warning device: 5 alarm

warning light: 8 red light

warning signal: 5 alarm, alert; 6 alarum

war of words: 6 debate; 8 polemics; 9 wrangling

warp: 4 bias, boom, chop, pack, scud, stow, tack, turn, veer; 5 crook, crush, evert, heave, kedge, shift, shunt, twist; 6 buckle, crunch, garble, swerve; 7 contort, deviate, distort, falsify, purse up, shuffle, warping; 8 collapse; 9 cause bias, corrugate, crumple up, draw aside, prejudice, turn aside; 10 deflection, refraction

warrant: 4 avow; 5 order, vouch; 6 assure, avouch, brevet, coupon, docket, permit, ratify, secure, uphold; 7 bear out, certify, indorse, justify, license, support, voucher; 8 sanction, warranty; 9 authorize, debenture, guarantee, warrantee; 10 asseverate, imprimatur, underwrite; 11 certificate, corroborate, countenance, countersign, endorsement, exculpation, exoneration; 12 verification

warranted: 6 bonded; 7 secured; 10 guaranteed, privileged

warrantee: 6 assure; 7 warrant; 9 guarantee

warrantor: 6 surety; 9 guarantor

warranty: 6 pledge; 7 charter, warrant; 8 guaranty, sanction; 9 authority, guarantee; 10 accordance

warring: 8 fighting, militant; 9 war-ridden; 11 belligerent

Warsaw: 15 capital of Poland

warship: 7 gunboat; 8 man-of-war; 9 ship of war, war vessel; 10 battleship, combat ship

wart: 7 verruca; 9 pappiloma

War to End War: 8 Great War; 9 World War I; 13 First World War

war whoop: 6 war cry; 9 battle cry; 11 rallying cry

wary: 5 leery; 7 guarded; 8 cautious; 10 suspicious, untrusting; 11 mistrustful

wash: 3 dye; 4 buck, lave, mire, race, sump, tint; 5 bathe, grain, imbue, paint, rinse, stain, tinge; 6 dampen, slough; 7 bedizen, dry wash, ingrain, launder, laundry, moisten, varnish, wash-off, washing; 8 backwash, emblazon, quagmire, wash away

wash-and-wear: 7 drip-dry

washbasin: 6 lavabo; 8 lavatory, washbowl; 9 handbasin, washstand

washcloth: 7 flannel, washrag; 9 face cloth

washed-out: 5 faded, spent, washy; 6 fagged; 7 worn-out; 8 bleached, fatigued; 9 exhausted, played out

washed-up: 4 sunk; 6 ruined, undone; 7 done for

washing machine: 6 washer

washing soda: 4 soda; 7 sal soda, soda ash; 15 sodium carbonate

Washington: 7 Capitol; 14 Evergreen State; 15 American capital; 16 George Washington

wash one's hands of: 4 drop, quit; 6 abjure, forego, give up; 7 retract; 8 abnegate, break off, disclaim, forswear, leave off, renounce

washout: 3 dud; 4 flop

wash room: 8 restroom

washtub: 3 tub; 4 bath; 7 bathtub

washy: 4 weak, worn; 5 faded, seedy, wimpy; 6 rotten, trashy, wasted, watery; 7 decayed, laid low; 8 bleached, trumpery; 9 enervated, quibbling, twaddling, washed-out; 10 pulled down, wishy-washy; 11 languishing; 12 deteriorated

waspish: 3 hot; 5 hasty, quick; 6 abrupt; 7 bilious, bristly, brusque, peevish, peppery, prickly; 8 captious, choleric, shrewish, snappish; 9 fractious, overhasty, querulous, splenetic

wasp-waisted: 11 slim-waisted; 14 slender-waisted

wassail: 3 cup; 5 carol, revel; 6 bishop, racket; 8 carousal; 9 make happy, make merry

wassailer: 8 carouser

waste: 3 ebb, rot; 4 blow, bush, do in, wane, ware, wear, wild; 5 decay, scrap; 6 barren, desert, junked, ravage, run off, shrink; 7 cast-off, consume, despoil, dwindle, shrivel, wasting; 8 collapse, desolate, emaciate, fall away, grow less, knock off, languish, macerate, pine away, squander; 9 devastate, discarded, dissipate, liquidate, wasteland; 10 be prodigal, be wasteful, destroying, dilapidate, lay waste to, weary waste; 11 destruction, dissipation, godforsaken

wasted: 4 bony, worn; 5 gaunt, seedy, washy; 6 effete, otiose, rotten, ruined; 7 blasted, decayed, haggard, laid low, pinched, ravaged, starved, tainted; 8 blighted, cankered, desolate, skeletal; 9 atrophied, crumbling, desolated, emaciated, moldering, pointless; 10 cadaverous, devastated, diminished, pulled down, squandered, starveling, wasted away; 11 languishing, superfluous; 12 deteriorated

wasted away: 4 bony; 6 wasted; 7 starved; 9 emaciated; 10 starveling

wasteful: 6 lavish; 7 profuse; 8 prodigal; 9 unthrifty; 10 dissipated, profligate, thriftless; **11** extravagant, improvident, overliberal; **12** uneconomical

wasteland: 4 bush, wild; **5** waste; **6** barren

waste pipe: 5 drain; **9** drainpipe, waste line

waste removal: 12 trash removal; **13** garbage pick-up, refuse removal

waste time: 8 kill time, lose time; **11** consume time

wastewater: 6 sewage

wasting away: 7 atrophy

wasting time: 8 dawdling, trifling; **9** dalliance

wastrel: 6 waster; **8** prodigal; **9** foundling; **10** profligate, squanderer; **11** spendthrift

watch: 3 see; **4** tend, view; **5** abide, catch, check, learn, scout, shift, stint, vigil; **6** follow, look on, patrol, picket, sentry, take in, tend to, ticker; **7** find out, look out, lookout, monitor, observe; **8** sentinel, watch out, watching, watchman; **9** ascertain, determine, espionage, watch over; **10** espionnage [Fr], lookout man, mount guard, tour of duty; **14** reconnaissance

watchband: 8 bracelet; **9** wristband; **10** watchstrap

watch chain: 3 fob; **10** watch guard

watchdog: 8 guard dog

watchful: 5 alert, awake; **7** on watch, wakeful; **8** open eyed, vigilant

watchmaker: 9 horologer; **10** horologist

watchman: 5 watch; **7** watcher; **8** watchdog; **13** security agent, security guard

watchword: 3 mot [Fr]; **4** word; **5** motto; **6** byword, parole, slogan; **7** passkey; **8** password; **9** catchword; **10** pass-parole; **11** countersign

water: 3 wet; **5** sweat; **6** liquid; **8** irrigate; **9** soundings; **10** submersion; **11** body of water, water supply, water system

waterbird: 9 water bird, waterfowl

waterbuck: 7 defassa; **15** common waterbuck [Kobus ellipsiprymnus]

water buffalo: 7 water ox

water bug: 9 Croton bug; **13** water boatman; **15** German cockroach

water chestnut: 7 caltrop; **16** Eleocharis dulcis; **18** water chestnut plant; **20** Chinese water chestnut

water clock: 9 clepsydra; **10** water glass

water closet: 2 W.C.; **3** loo; **6** closet

water company: 10 waterworks

water contamination: 9 pollution

watercourse: 5 river; **6** stream; **8** waterway

watercraft: 6 vessel

watered down: 4 thin, weak; **6** dilute, watery; **7** diluted, watered

waterfall: 5 falls; **7** cascade; **8** cataract

water faucet: 3 tap; **6** spigot; **7** hydrant; **8** water tap

water finder: 6 dowser; **11** divining rod, waterfinder

water flea: 7 cyclops, daphnia

water gate: 8 head gate, penstock; **9** flood gate, floodgate; **10** sluicegate

Watergate: 15 Watergate affair

water gauge: 9 water gage; **10** water glass

water glass: 6 fresco; **9** clepsydra, water gage; **10** water clock, water gauge; **12** soluble glass; **14** sodium silicate

water gun: 9 squirt gun; **11** water pistol

water hen: 4 coot; **6** mud hen; **8** marsh hen, swamphen; **9** gallinule

watering hole: 3 spa; **5** oasis

waterjet: 3 jet; **5** spout, spurt; **6** squirt; **10** waterspout

waterless: 3 dry; **4** arid

water level: 9 waterline; **10** water table

water-lily family: 12 Nymphaeaceae

waterlogged: 5 soggy; **6** soaked; **9** saturated

waterman: 6 boater; **7** boatman; **8** bargeman, ferryman

watermark: 9 water line

watermelon-shaped: 7 prolate

water moccasin: 8 moccasin; **11** cottonmouth

water nymph: 5 naiad; **8** pond lily; **9** wood nymph; **11** water sprite

water ouzel: 5 ouzel; **6** dipper

water ox: 12 water buffalo

water pipe: 6 hookah, kalian; **8** narghile; **12** hubble-bubble, water conduit

water pistol: 8 water gun; **9** squirt gun

water plant: 10 hydrophyte

water-plantain family: 12 Alismataceae

waterproof: 8 raincoat; **9** rainproof; **12** weatherproof

water-repellent: 14 water-resistant

water right: 13 riparian right

watershed: 6 divide; **9** given time; **12** turning point, water parting

waters of oblivion: 13 waters of Lethe

water sport: 8 aquatics

waterspout: 3 jet; **5** spout, spurt; **6** deluge, soaker, squirt; **7** torrent; **8** downpour, waterjet; **10** cloudburst

water sprite: 10 water nymph

water table: 10 water level

water tank: 7 cistern

water tap: 3 tap; **6** spigot; **7** hydrant; **11** water faucet

water-target: 11 water-shield; **17** Brasenia schreberi

watertight: 8 ironclad; **9** leakproof; **10** unshakable, water proof; **12** unassailable

water travel: 9 seafaring

water vehicle: 4 boat, ship; **5** craft; **6** vessel

water witch: 6 dowser

waterworks: 12 water company

watery: 4 thin, weak; **5** washy; **6** dilute, liquid; **7** aquatic, aqueous, diluted, reeking, watered; **8** dripping, swimming; **11** watered down

WATS: 8 WATS line

watt: 1 W

wattage: 13 electric power

wattle: 5 plait; **6** lappet; **7** reticle, trellis

watt second: 1 J; **5** joule

wave: 3 sea; **4** curl, flap; **5** surge, swell; **6** beckon, billow, waving; **7** meander, wafture; **8** brandish, flourish, undulate; **10** undulation

waveform: 9 wave shape

wavelet: 6 riffle, ripple

wavelike: 4 wavy; **7** crinkly, rippled; **8** crinkled

waver: 4 vary; **5** shift, weave; **6** change, falter, quaver, quiver, swiver; **7** flicker, flitter, flutter; **8** flounder, hesitate; **9** faltering, fluctuate, vacillate; **10** hesitation; **11** be tentative, be undecided

wavering: 6 fickle, levity; **8** shifting, unsteady; **9** vacillant; **10** fickleness, hesitation, inconstant; **11** fluctuation, inconstancy, vacillating, vacillation

wave shape: 8 waveform

wavicle: 6 photon; **7** quantum

waving: 4 wave; **6** aflare, flying; **7** flaring, wafture; **10** fluttering

wax: 3 get; **4** full, grow, rise; **5** climb, mount; **6** mantle

wax bean: 10 yellow bean

wax figure: 7 waxwork

waxing: 7 priming; **8** painting; **10** lacquering; **11** shellacking

wax light: 5 taper; **6** candle

wax moth: 7 bee moth

wax-myrtle family: 10 Myricaceae

wax palm: 7 caranda; **8** caranday, carnauba

waxy: 5 waxen; **7** acharne, waxlike; **9** ceraceous

way: 2 MO; **4** mode, path, room, ways, wise, wont; **5** field, habit, means, range, route, scope, style, sweep, swing; **6** agency, course, manner, method, spread; **7** compass, fashion, process; **8** habitude, protocol; **9** direction, elbow room, expansion, mechanism, procedure, technique, way of life; **10** procedures, right smart; **12** thoroughfare

waybill: 12 bill of lading

wayfarer: 7 voyager; **8** traveler; **9** itinerant, journeyer

wayfaring: 6 travel; **7** traffic, wayworn; **9** traveling; **11** peripatetic

waylay: 4 lurk; **6** ambush; **7** scupper; **9** ambuscade, bushwhack, lie in wait, undermine

way-out: 5 kinky; **6** far-out, quirky; **7** offbeat

wayside: 8 roadside

wayward: 5 balky, heady, kinky [U.S.], stray; **6** unruly, wanton; **7** lawless, restive, vagrant, willful; **8** contrary, fanciful, freakish, informal, perverse, skittish; **9** fantastic, obstinate, wandering; **10** headstrong, particular, rebellious, refractory, self-willed

wayworn: 8 footsore; **9** wayfaring; **13** weather-beaten

Wb: 5 weber

WbN: 11 west by north

WbS: 11 west by south

weak: 3 bad, lax; **4** fade, high, mild, poor, soft, thin; **5** borne, frail, fusty, light, loose, sappy, stale, vapid, washy, wimpy; **6** dilute, effete, feeble, flimsy, infirm, spoony, watery, weakly; **7** diluted, fragile, gone bad, mawkish, sapless, shallow, touched, wanting, watered; **8** decrepit, delicate, fallible; **9** enervated, forceless, imperfect, powerless, sensitive; **10** effeminate, putrescent, unaccented, unforceful

weaken: 4 damp; **5** break, check, lower, relax, shake; **6** dampen, soften; **7** cut back, cut down, exhaust, shatter, subvert; **8** enervate, enfeeble, sabotage; **9** attenuate, extenuate, undermine; **10** counteract, de-escalate, debilitate, eviscerate

weakling: 4 wimp; **7** doormat

weakly: 4 weak; **6** feeble, infirm; **7** sapless; **8** decrepit, unstrung, weakened

weakness: 7 failing, frailty, pliancy; **8** softness; **10** pliability; **11** impuissance; **12** helplessness, imperfection, malleability

weak point: 4 flaw; **5** fault; **6** defect; **7** bad case; **10** deficiency

weak spot: 8 soft spot, weak part

weal: 4 wale, welt; **5** wheal; **6** behalf, behoof; **7** service; **8** interest; **10** commonweal

wealth: 5 lucre; **6** riches; **7** fortune; **8** opulence; **9** affluence

wealthy: 4 rich; **5** flush; **6** loaded, monied; **7** moneyed, opulent; **8** affluent

wealthy person: 6 monied, tycoon; **7** moneyed; **10** rich person; **11** millionaire; **12** moneyed class; **13** the upperclass, the uppercrust

wean: 7 convert, win over; **9** bring over; **10** bring round

weanling: 8 suckling, yearling; **9** nurseling

weapon: 3 arm, gun; **4** arms; **5** piece; **7** firearm; **8** ordnance; **9** artillery; **12** deadly weapon, weapon system

weaponless: 7 unarmed; **8** harmless, vincible; **9** pregnable, untenable; **11** unfortified

wear: 3 don, tax; **4** bear, bust, jade, task, tire; **5** break, decay, put on, waste, weary; **6** assume, endure, have on; **7** apparel, clothes, fatigue, get into, hold out, outwear, tire out, vesture, wear off, wear out, wearing; **8** clothing, wear down, wear thin, wear upon

wear away: 3 rot; 4 gnaw; 5 eat at, erode; 7 corrode

wearily: 7 tiredly

weariness: 7 fatigue; 9 tiredness

wearing: 4 wear; 6 tiring; 7 eroding, erosion; 8 tiresome, wearying; 9 wearisome; 10 exhausting

wearing apparel: 4 wear; 6 attire; 7 apparel, clothes, vesture; 8 clothing, garments

wearisome: 4 dull, slow; 5 ho-hum; 6 boring, tiring; 7 irksome, tedious, wearing; 8 tiresome, toilsome, wearying; 9 deadening; 11 troublesome

wear off: 4 wear; 7 wear out; 8 wear away, wear thin; 12 lose interest

wear out: 3 irk; 4 bust, flag, jade, tire, wear; 5 break, weary; 7 exhaust, fatigue, outwear, tire out

wear thin: 4 wear; 7 wear off, wear out

weary: 3 irk; 4 flag, jade, pall, tire, wear; 5 stale, tired; 6 aweary, trying; 7 exhaust, fatigue

weasel-worded: 6 hedged

weather: 5 brave; 6 endure, upwind; 8 brave out

weather-beaten: 7 wayworn; 8 footsore; 9 weathered; 11 weatherworn

weatherboard: 9 clapboard; 10 to windward; 11 weather side

weather bound: 8 ice bound; 9 wind bound

weather chart: 10 weather map

weathercock: 4 cock, vane; 8 wind sock; 9 wind gauge; 11 weather vane

weather deck: 11 shelter deck

weather forecast: 11 meteorology

weather forecaster: 10 weatherman; 13 weatherperson

weather gauge: 11 weather cock; 12 weather glass

weave: 4 wind; 5 twine, twist, waver; 6 thread, tissue; 7 entwine, meander, wreathe; 10 interweave

weaver: 10 weaverbird; 11 weaver finch

weaver's knot: 9 sheet bend; 10 becket bend; 12 weaver's hitch

weaving: 8 lurching; 9 stumbling; 10 staggering; 12 interweaving

web: 3 net, WWW; 4 mesh, vane; 5 grain; 6 plexus, tissue; 7 network; 8 meshwork; 12 entanglement, world wide web

webbed: 4 lacy; 5 webby; 6 netted; 7 netlike, weblike

web browser: 7 browser

weber: 2 Wb

Webster: 11 Noah Webster

wed: 3 tie; 4 join; 5 marry; 6 wedded; 7 conjoin, espouse, hitched [slang], married

Wed: 9 Wednesday

wedded: 3 wed; 7 marital; 8 conjugal; 9 connubial; 11 matrimonial

wedding: 6 bridal; 8 espousal, marriage, nuptials, spousals

wedding chest: 9 hope chest

wedding dress: 10 bridal gown; 11 wedding gown

wedding ring: 11 wedding band

wedge: 3 jam, sub, zep; 4 hero; 5 chock, force, hacek, hoagy, lodge, miter, stick; 6 bomber, cuneus, hoagie, rabbet; 7 deposit, grinder, mortise, poor boy, squeeze, torpedo; 8 dovetail, triangle; 9 submarine, wedge heel; 11 wedge-shaped; 12 hero sandwich

wedged: 8 impacted

wedge-shaped: 7 cuneate; 8 fusiform; 9 cuneiform

wedlock: 3 bed; 5 match, union; 8 marriage; 9 matrimony; 10 nuptial tie

Wednesday: 3 Wed

wee: 4 make, puny, tiny; 5 bitty, petit, petty, teeny, weeny; 6 bittie, petite, teensy, wee-wee, weensy; 7 teentsy; 9 miniature

weed: 3 pot; 4 cull, dope, gage, pick, sens, sess, sift; 5 ganja, grass, skunk, smoke; 6 winnow; 8 cannabis, Mary Jane, separate; 9 cigarette, eliminate, marihuana, marijuana

weeding: 7 sifting; 9 winnowing; 10 weeding out

weed killer: 9 herbicide

weed up: 6 grub up, rake up; 7 grub out, rake out

weedy: 5 gaunt, lanky; 6, skinny; 7 scraggy, scrawny

week: 8 hebdomad, workweek

weekday: 7 work day

weekend soldier: 9 auxiliary, guardsman; 10 life guards; 14 reserve soldier

weenie: 5 frank; 6 hotdog, wiener; 11 frankfurter, wienerwurst

weensy: 3 wee; 5 bitty, teeny, weeny; 6 bittie, teensy; 7 teentsy; 12 teensy-weensy

weep: 3 cry, sob; 4 melt, pipe, thaw, wail

weeper: 5 crier, cryer

weeping: 3 cry; 4 wail; 5 tears; 6 crying, outcry; 7 tearful, wailing; 8 dolorous; 9 dolourous, ululation; 10 lachrymose

weigh: 4 load, tell; 5 count, poise, press, study; 6 cumber, matter, ponder; 8 consider; 9 gravitate; 11 contemplate

weigh anchor: 8 shove off

weighing: 7 judging; 8 deciding; 10 advisement; 11 determining; 12 deliberation

weighing instrument: 5 scale; 6 scales; 15 weighing machine

weighing machine: 5 scale; 6 scales

weight: 4 bias; 5 angle, slant; 6 burden; 7 burthen, weights [pl]; 8 emphasis, pressure; 9 weighting; 10 body weight, partiality

weight down: 6 burden, weight

weightlift: 5 press

weights and measures: 9 metrology

W

weighty: 5 grave, heavy, obese; **6** cogent, rotund; **7** telling; **8** emphatic, grievous; **9** assertive, corpulent

weir: 3 dam; **8** penstock

weird: 6 mystic; **7** bizarre, uncanny; **8** fanciful; **9** fantastic, unearthly; **10** cabalistic, talismanic; **11** incantatory

weirdo: 5 crazy, creep, loony, spook; **6** looney, weirdy; **7** schmuck, weirdie; **13** nonconformist

weird sisters: 5 fates

weisenheimer: 7 wise guy; **8** wiseacre; **10** smart aleck; **11** wisenheimer

welcome: 2 hi; **3** ave; **4** hail, lief; **5** hello, howdy; **7** receive, well met; **9** reception

welcome mat: 7 doormat

weld: 4 fuse; **5** unite

welfare: 6 upbeat; **7** benefit; **9** welfarist, well-being; **10** prosperity

welfare worker: 10 caseworker; **12** social worker

welkin: 3 sky; **6** sphere; **7** heavens; **8** empyrean; **9** firmament

well: 3 pit, spa; **4** font, good, hale, most, much, roll; **5** a deal, fresh, green, nobly, shaft, sound, swell, whole; **6** aright, billow, crater, easily, hearty, hollow, indeed, spring, well up; **7** healthy, morally, no end of, well out; **8** fountain, in health, pump room; **9** favorably; **10** intimately, not a little, sanatorium, virtuously, wellspring; **11** comfortably, righteously

well-behaved: 5 civil; **6** polite; **8** mannerly; **9** courteous

well-being: 6 upbeat; **7** welfare; **10** prosperity

well-bred: 6 urbane; **7** gallant, refined; **8** polished; **9** civilized; **10** cultivated

well-built: 4 wiry; **6** brawny, sinewy; **8** gigantic, muscular, stalwart, well-knit, well-made; **9** strapping

well-defined: 5 clear, plain; **7** glaring, staring; **8** apparent, definite, distinct; **11** conspicuous

wellhead: 10 spring head, wellspring; **12** fountainhead

well-heeled: 4 easy; **7** well-off; **8** well-to-do; **9** well-fixed; **10** prosperous; **11** comfortable

well-informed: 4 keen; **8** well-read; **10** well-conned; **11** intelligent; **12** well educated, well grounded

Wellington: 19 capital of New Zealand

Wellington boot: 7 hessian; **8** jackboot; **10** Wellington; **11** Hessian boot

well-kept: 4 trim; **6** kept up; **9** shipshape; **10** maintained

well-known: 5 noted; **6** boring, common, old-hat; **7** trivial, typical; **8** everyday, frequent, ordinary; **9** household, notorious; **11** commonplace

well-nourished: 7 well-fed

well-off: 4 easy; **8** well-to-do; **9** well-fixed; **10** prosperous, well-heeled; **11** comfortable

well-proportioned: 4 even; **7** regular, uniform; **8** balanced

well-read: 7 knowing, learned; **8** lettered; **11** enlightened; **12** well-educated; **13** knowledgeable

well-rounded: 8 all-round; **9** all-around

well-timed: 6 timely; **7** apropos; **9** opportune, well timed; **10** seasonable, seasonably

well-trodden: 3 jog; **4** trot; **6** common; **7** typical; **8** everyday, frequent, ordinary, well-worn; **9** household, well-known; **11** commonplace

well up: 4 roll, well; **5** swell; **6** billow

well water: 11 ground water, spring water

wellwisher: 8 advocate, partisan; **11** sympathizer

well-worn: 5 banal, stock, tired, trite; **6** boring, old-hat; **7** trivial; **8** shopworn, time-worn; **9** hackneyed, well-known; **10** threadbare; **11** commonplace

Welsh rabbit: 7 rarebit; **12** Welsh rarebit

welt: 3 hem; **4** flog, lash, list, wale, weal, whip; **5** frill, slash, strap, wheal; **6** edging, fringe, lather; **7** flounce, trounce, valance; **8** furbelow, selvedge, skirting, trimming

weltanshauung: 7 outlook; **9** world view

welter: 6 jumble, muddle, wallow; **7** clutter, founder, smother, turmoil

Weltschmerz: 10 world-weary

wen: 4 cyst, wynn; **6** papula [Med], papule; **7** pustule

wench: 3 rig; **4** bird, dame, doll, drab, jade, minx, skit, slut; **5** bitch, chick, hussy, skirt; **7** baggage, demirep, trollop; **8** harridan, slattern

wend: 4 pace, plod, step; **5** march, tread; **6** direct, travel

werewolf: 7 wolfman; **11** lycanthrope

Wesley: 10 John Wesley

Wesleyan: 9 Methodist

west: 1 W

West: 8 occident

westbound: 8 westerly, westward

west by north: 3 WbN

west by south: 3 WbS

Western: 9 Hesperian; **10** horse opera, occidental

western: 4 folk; **7** country; **8** westerly; **9** hillbilly

Western Church: 11 Roman Church; **12** Church of Rome; **13** Roman Catholic

Western diamondback: 11 rattlesnake

western hemisphere: 8 New World, occident

West Indies: 9 the Indies

west northwest: 3 WNW

Weston cell: 11 cadmium cell

westward: 8 westerly; **9** westbound, westwards

wet: 4 damp; **5** moist, stiff, tight, tipsy, water; **6** blotto, dampen, loaded, soaked, soused, tiddly; **7** crocked, fuddled, moisten, slopped, sloshed, smashed, sozzled, squiffy, tiddley; **8** besotted, moisture; **9** lactating, pixilated, plastered

wet behind the ears: 3 new, raw; **5** green; **11** uninitiated; **13** inexperienced

wet blanket: 6 damper; **7** killjoy, marplot; **10** spoilsport; **11** party pooper

wetland: 5 marsh, swamp; **6** morass; **7** estuary

wet nurse: wet-nurse: **4** suck; **5** nurse; **6** suckle; **7** lactate; **10** breastfeed

whack: 3 pow, rap; **4** bang, belt, boom, clap, slam, swat, wham, whop; **5** blast, clack, clang, crack, knock, whang; **6** buffet, stroke, thwack, wallop

whale: 4 hulk; **5** giant; **8** cetacean; **9** leviathan

whalebone: 6 baleen

whalebone whale: 11 baleen whale

whaling ship: 6 whaler

wham: 3 pow; **4** bang, boom, clap, slam, whop; **5** blast, clack, clang, whack; **6** wallop

whap: 3 bop; **4** bash, bonk, pelt, plug, sock, whop; **5** punch, thump

wharf: 4 dock, port, quay, slip, yard; **5** basin; **6** harbor; **8** dockyard, shipyard, wharfage

wharf boat: 4 dhow

whatever: 3 any; **10** whatsoever

what is more: 8 moreover; **11** furthermore

whatnot: 5 curio; **6** bauble, gewgaw, trifle; **7** bibelot, novelty, trinket; **8** chotchke, gimcrack, kickshaw, nicknack

whatsoever: 3 any; **8** whatever

wheal: 4 wale, weal, welt

wheedle: 4 coax, lure; **5** charm, tempt; **6** cajole, cocker, cockle, coddle, cosset, seduce; **7** bewitch, blarney, palaver; **8** inveigle; **9** fascinate, sweet-talk

wheel: 3 wen; **4** bend, bike, rack, roll, turn; **5** cycle, pedal, twirl, whirl

wheelbarrow: 6 barrow; **8** lawn cart; **10** garden cart, hand barrow

wheeler dealer: 7 hustler; **8** operator

wheel horse: 7 wheeler

wheelhouse: 10 pilothouse

wheeling: 7 rolling, turning; **8** rotating; **9** revolving

wheelman: 6 driver; **7** cyclist, trucker; **8** helmsman; **11** truck driver

wheels: 3 car; **8** roadster; **9** sports car

wheelwork: 9 clockwork

wheeze: 3 gag, yak; **4** gasp, jape, jest, joke; **5** laugh; **7** snuffle, whistle

whelm: 4 glut, load; **5** gorge; **6** load up; **8** overcome, overtake; **9** overpower, overwhelm, sweep over

whelp: 3 cur, dog, lay, pup; **6** evolve; **7** mongrel

whence: 4 ergo, then, thus; **5** hence; **6** thence, thusly; **8** thence so; **9** therefore, wherefore, wherefrom; **10** propter hoc [Lat]; **11** accordingly

where: 7 where to, whither

whereabouts: 4 seat, site; **5** venue; **7** station

whereas: 3 for; **5** for as, since; **7** because; **10** ex concesso [Lat]; **11** considering

wherefore: 3 why; **4** ergo, then, thus; **5** hence; **6** thusly, whence; **7** how come; **8** thence so, wherefor; **9** therefore; **11** accordingly; **12** consequently

wherefrom: 6 whence

where to?: 8 whither?

wherewithal: 5 means; **7** needful; **8** resource, supplies; **9** resources, wherewith

wherry: 3 cog; **4** punt; **5** scull, shell; **7** rowboat

whet: 3 set; **4** bait, barb, dram, goad, nosh, spur, whip; **5** grind, point, strop; **6** fillip; **7** quicken, sharpen; **8** aculeate, junk food, stimulus; **9** incentive; **10** incitement; **11** provocation

whetstone: 10 grindstone

whicker: 5 neigh; **6** nicker, whinny

whiff: 4 gust, puff; **5** sniff; **6** zephyr; **7** whiffle; **9** strike out

while: 5 piece, spell; **6** during, whilst; **7** interim, pending; **12** intervention

while away time: 8 pass time

whilom: 6 former; **4** erst [Ger], over

whilst: 5 while; **6** during; **7** pending

whim: 4 salt; **5** fancy, humor, point; **6** esprit, maggot, notion, vagary, whimsy; **7** caprice, impulse

whimper: 3 sob; **4** mewl, pule, wail; **5** whine; **6** snivel; **7** grizzle, sobbing

whimsey: 4 whim; **6** notion, whimsy; **11** flightiness

whimsical: 5 fancy; **7** aimless, erratic, waggish; **8** fanciful, notional; **9** eccentric, impulsive; **10** capricious; **12** inconsistent

whin: 5 gorse

whine: 3 yap; **4** mewl, moan, pipe, pule, sigh, yawp; **5** groan; **6** murmur, mutter, plaint, snivel, squall, squeak, squeal, yammer; **7** grizzle, grumble, heaving, whimper; **9** complaint

whiner: 6 moaner; **7** crybaby; **8** grumbler, sniveler, squawker; **10** bellyacher, complainer

whinny: 5 neigh; **6** nicker; **7** whicker

whip: 3 jog, pip; **4** cane, comb, dram, flog, goad, lash, lick, spur, urge, welt, whet; **5** birch, knout, mop up, prick, slash, strap, thong, towel, whisk, worst; **6** buffet, fillip,

W

hustle, joggle, jostle, jounce, larrup, lather, rack up, switch, thrash, thresh, wallop; **7** blister, cowhide, scourge, trounce; **8** bullwhip, coachman, stimulus, whiplash; **9** bastinado, horsewhip, incentive; **10** flagellate, incitement; **11** provocation

whip hand: 4 lead; **9** advantage, upper hand

whiplike: 10 flagellate

whipper-snapper: 3 boy, lad; **7** youngun; **9** stripling

whipping boy: 9 scapegoat

whipping post: 6 stocks; **7** pillory

whippletree: 11 whiffletree

whippy: 4 live; **6** bouncy, lively; **7** springy; **9** resilient

whir: 4 birr, eddy, purr, whiz; **5** whirl, whirr, whizz; **6** vortex; **8** whirring; **9** whirlpool

whirl: 4 birl, eddy, pass, purl, reel, spin, whir; **5** crack, fling, gurge, offer, skirl, swirl, twirl, twist, wheel; **6** gyrate, tumble, vortex; **7** twiddle; **8** twisting; **9** commotion

whirligig: 3 top; **8** carousel, teetotum; **10** roundabout; **11** spinning top; **12** merry-go-round

whirlpool: 4 eddy, purl, whir; **5** gurge, swirl, whirl; **6** reflux, vortex; **8** overflow; **9** maelstrom

whirlwind: 7 tornado

whirlybird: 6 copter; **7** chopper; **9** eggbeater; **10** helicopter

whisk: 3 fly; **4** jerk, jolt, skim, tear, toss, whip, zoom; **5** brush, hitch, shoot, sweep, twirl; **6** swoosh, tumble; **7** cut away; **8** run a race, whisk off; **10** whiskbroom

whiskered: 7 barbate, bearded; **8** whiskery; **11** bewhiskered

whiskerless: 9 beardless

whiskers: 5 beard; **10** face fungus

whiskey: 3 rye; **6** whisky; **7** bourbon

whisper: 6 rustle; **8** rustling

whispering: 6 rustle; **7** whisper; **8** rustling; **9** murmuring

whist: 8 card game

whistle: 4 pipe, sing; **5** cheep, chirp, trill, tweet; **6** cuckoo, warble, wheeze; **7** catcall, chirrup, snuffle, twitter; **9** whistling; **10** tin whistle; **12** penny whistle, pennywhistle

whistler: 9 goldeneye

whistlestop: 9 barnstorm

whit: 3 dab; **4** iota; **5** every, shred; **6** smidge, tittle; **7** smidgen, smidgin, soupcon; **8** smidgeon; **9** scintilla

White: 9 Caucasian; **10** White River; **11** white person

white: 5 ashen, blank, clean, livid, snowy, tweed; **6** whiten, whites; **7** flannel; **8** blanched, white-hot, whitened; **9** bloodless, egg whites, gabardine, lily-white, whiteness; **10** achromatic

white Anglo-Saxon Protestant: 4 WASP

white ant: 7 termite

white as a sheet: 4 pale; **8** blanched

white bean: 8 navy bean

white birch: 9 gray birch; **10** paper birch

white blood cell: 9 leucocyte, leukocyte, white cell; **14** white corpuscle

white blood corpuscle: 9 leucocyte, leukocyte, white cell

white book: 10 white paper

white Burgundy: 7 Chablis

white cinnamon: 7 canella

white clover: 8 shamrock; **11** dutch clover

white-collar work: 10 office work

white-collar worker: 12 professional

white dove: 11 dove of peace

white dwarf star: 10 white dwarf; **11** neutron star

whiteface: 8 Hereford

white flag: 11 flag of truce

white fox: 9 arctic fox

White Friar: 9 Carmelite

white frost: 9 hoar frost

white-haired: 4 gray, grey, hoar; **5** hoary; **8** blue-eyed; **10** fair-haired, gray-haired, gray-headed, grey-haired, grey-headed

whitehead: 6 milium

white-hot: 5 white; **6** fervid

white lie: 3 fib; **9** half truth

white-livered: 6 yellow; **7** chicken; **11** lily-livered

white meat: 6 breast

whitener: 6 bleach

white out: 5 erase; **6** rub out; **7** blot out

white paper: 9 white book

white person: 9 Caucasian

white potato: 4 spud; **5** tater

white rice: 12 polished rice

white room: 9 clean room

White Russia: 7 Belarus; **8** Byelarus; **10** Belorussia; **11** Byelorussia

white sauce: 8 bechamel

white shark: 10 great white

white sheet: 6 shrift

whitetail: 4 deer

white-tailed sea eagle: 3 ern; **4** erne

white tie and tails: 5 tails; **6** tuxedo; **8** tailcoat, white tie; **9** dress suit, full dress

white trumpet lily: 10 Easter lily

whitewash: 4 bury, gild, sink; **5** grain, japan, paint; **6** enamel, hush up, polish, silver, stifle; **7** cover up, furbish, smarten, smother, varnish; **8** suppress

white water: 6 rapids; **7** torrent; **8** cataract

white whale: 6 beluga

white wolf: 10 Arctic wolf

whitewood: 9 tulipwood, tuliptree

whither: 3 for; **5** where; **7** where to

whiting: 10 silver hake

whitlow: 5 felon

Whitney: 12 Mount Whitney

Whitsunday: 9 Pentecost

Whitsuntide: 7 Whitsun; **8** Whitweek

whittle: 4 chip, pare; **5** shave; **8** penknife
whittle down: 8 wear away
whiz: 3 ace, wiz; **4** birr, purr, star, whir; **5** adept, maven, whirr, whizz; **6** genius, wizard; **7** hotshot; **8** virtuoso; **9** sensation
whiz-kid: 8 go-getter, whizz-kid; **10** ball of fire
whodunit: 7 mystery; **12** mystery story
whole: 3 all; **4** hale, unit, well; **5** fresh, green, total; **6** entire, hearty, wholly; **7** integer, totally; **8** ensemble, entirely, entirety, integral, totality; **10** altogether, completely
wholemeal: 7 wheaten; **10** whole-wheat
whole meal flour: 6 graham
whole name: 7 holonym
wholeness: 5 unity; **8** haleness; **9** integrity; **12** completeness
whole note: 9 semibreve
whole number: 7 integer
wholesale: 3 all; **7** en masse, in a body; **8** entirely, sweeping; **12** collectively
wholesale house: 13 discount house, discount store
wholesaler: 6 jobber; **9** middleman
wholesome: 7 healthy; **8** salutary; **9** healthful
whole tone: 4 step, tone; **9** whole step
whole to part relation: 8 holonymy
whole-wheat: 7 wheaten; **9** wholemeal
whole wheat bread: 9 dark bread; **10** brown bread
whole wheat flour: 6 graham; **11** graham flour
wholly: 3 all; **5** fully, quite, stark, whole, **6** in toto; **7** totally, utterly; **8** entirely, outright; **10** altogether, completely
whomp: 4 cuff
whoop: 4 bawl, hack, hoop, howl, roar, yell; **5** brawl, shout; **6** bellow, halloa, halloo, scream, shriek, shrill; **7** screech
whooping cough: 9 pertussis
whoop it up: 5 revel; **6** racket; **7** wassail
whoosh: 4 hiss
whop: 3 bop, hit; **4** bash, beat, bonk, sock, wham, whap; **5** smite [biblical], whack; **6** strike
whopper: 3 fib; **5** story
whopping: 5 gaunt, hulky; **7** hulking, lumpish; **8** lubberly, spanking, thumping, unwieldy, whacking; **9** humongous, walloping; **10** thundering
whore: 4 bawd, punk, tart; **6** harlot; **7** cocotte, cyprian, trollop; **8** strumpet; **10** prostitute
whorehouse: 7 brothel
whorl: 4 coil, curl, gyre, lock, roll; **5** helix; **6** scroll, spiral, volute; **7** ringlet; **8** curlicue
whortleberry: 9 blueberry
whump: 4 rump, bang; **5** thump
why: 5 marry; **6** i' faith, indeed; **7** how come; **9** wherefore
whydah: 6 whidah; **9** widow bird

wick: 5 taper
wicked: 4 evil, foul, vile; **5** wrong, yucky; **6** severe, sinful, unholy; **7** immoral, loathly; **8** criminal, depraved, terrible; **9** loathsome, repellant, repellent, revolting; **10** disgustful, disgusting, iniquitous; **11** distasteful, unrighteous; **12** unprincipled
wickedness: 3 sin; **4** evil; **8** iniquity, vileness; **9** evildoing; **10** immorality, sinfulness, wrongdoing
wicker: 6 caning; **10** wickerwork
wicket: 4 door, gate, hoop; **5** hatch; **6** grille; **7** lattice, postern; **8** trapdoor; **9** threshold, vestibule
wide: 4 full; **5** ample, broad, thick; **6** astray, widely; **7** blanket, wide-cut; **8** extended, panoptic, spacious; **9** extensive, round-eyed; **12** all-embracing, all-inclusive, encompassing
wide-angle lens: 11 fisheye lens
wide area network: 3 WAN
wide awake: 5 awake; **7** on watch, wakeful; **8** vigilant, watchful
wideband: 9 broadband
wide berth: 4 rope; **5** swing; **6** margin; **9** elbowroom
widely known: 5 noted; **8** received; **9** notorious, well-known
widen: 6 blow up, expand, extend, let out, rarefy, spread; **7** amplify, broaden, develop, distend, inflate, magnify, thicken; **9** spread out; **10** aggrandize
widened: 5 grown; **7** swollen; **8** enlarged, expanded, extended; **9** increased
wide open: 4 open; **6** gaping; **8** unclosed, unfenced; **9** cavernous, undivided, unstopped
widespread: 4 sown, vast; **8** far-famed, far-flung; **9** broadcast, extensive, world-wide
widget: 5 gizmo; **6** gadget; **9** appliance; **11** contraption, contrivance, convenience
widowman: 7 widower
widow woman: 5 widow
width: 7 breadth; **9** thickness
wield: 3 ply; **4** flap, work; **5** bandy, exert; **6** handle; **8** brandish, flourish, maintain; **10** manipulate
wieldy: 10 manageable
wiener: 5 frank; **6** hot dog, weenie; **11** frankfurter, wienerwurst
wierd: 4 zany; **6** madcap; **9** eccentric, screwball
wig: 7 wigging; **9** hairpiece
wigging: 3 wig; **6** blow up, rating; **7** lecture; **8** dressing, scolding, trimming
wiggle: 6 jiggle, joggle, squirm; **7** wriggle
wiggling: 6 wiggly; **7** wriggly; **8** twisting, writhing; **9** squirming, wriggling
wight: 8 creature, zoophyte
wild: 4 bush, fast, rude; **5** angry, bluff, fiery,

W

giddy, heavy, rabid, rough, waste; **6** desert, doting, far out, fierce, fuming, in a way, madcap, nature, raging, rakish, raving, savage, wanton; **7** berserk, excited, foolish, frantic, furious, in a fury, in a rage, natural, outback [Australia], the wild, untamed, violent; **8** barbaric, frenetic, frenzied, heedless, rambling, reckless, ungentle, unhinged, up in arms, vehement, wild-eyed; **9** barbarian, delirious, ferocious, in a taking, infuriate, insensate, possessed, rampantly, raving mad, wandering, wasteland; **10** blustering, boisterous, high-flying, incoherent, infuriated, out of sight, outrageous, outtasight, reasonless, wilderness; **11** dithyrambic, godforsaken, impassioned, tempestuous, uncivilized

wild apple: 9 crab apple

wild bergamot: 7 monarda

wild blue yonder: 4 blue; **7** blue air, blue sky

wild card: 5 trump

wild carrot: 14 Queen Anne's lace

wildcat: 4 lynx, wolf; **5** beast, brute; **6** cougar, ocelot, savage; **9** catamount 11 speculative, wildcat well; **12** experimental, unauthorized

wildcat strike: 7 walkout

wild celery: 8 eelgrass; **9** tape grass

wildebeest: 3 gnu

wilderness: 4 wild; **6** jungle; **7** the wild; **8** wildness

wild-eyed: 4 wild; **5** giddy, rabid; **6** doting, raving; **7** berserk, frantic; **8** frenetic, frenzied, quixotic, rambling, romantic, unhinged; **9** delirious, insensate, possessed, wandering; **10** incoherent, reasonless

wild indigo: 8 baptisia

wild leek: 4 ramp

wildly: 8 wantonly; **10** heedlessly, recklessly

wild man: 6 maniac; **7** berserk; **9** berserker

wild marjoram: 7 oregano

wild mustard: 8 chadlock, charlock

wildness: 4 fury; **7** abandon; **8** ferocity, violence; **9** vehemence; **10** fierceness, wilderness; **11** furiousness; **12** heedlessness, recklessness

wild pansy: 12 Johnny-jump-up

wild pig: 4 boar

wild rice: 10 Indian rice

wile: 4 bite; **5** blind, catch, cheat, craft, feint, fetch, guile, hocus, plant, reach, trick, while; **6** bubble, entice, juggle; **7** chicane, cunning; **8** subtlety, trickery, wiliness; **9** chicanery; **10** artfulness, craftiness, shenanigan, shrewdness

wilful: 7 willful

wiliness: 4 wile; **5** craft, guile; **7** cunning, slyness; **8** foxiness, subtlety; **10** artfulness, craftiness, shrewdness

will: 4 wish; **5** leave, shall; **6** decide; **7**

resolve; **8** bequeath, volition; **9** testament; **10** resolution; **12** resoluteness; **13** determination

willful: 5 balky, heady; **6** entete [Fr], unruly, wilful; **7** froward, knowing, restive, wayward; **8** contrary, perverse; **10** deliberate, headstrong, rebellious, refractory, self-willed; **11** intentional

willing: 4 fain; **6** minded; **7** bequest; **8** amenable, disposed, inclined, unforced, volition; **9** favorable, uncoerced; **10** bequeathal; **11** bequeathing

will-o'-the wisp: 3 nix; **5** nixie; **8** bad fairy; **11** ignis fatuus

willow family: 10 Salicaceae

willow herb: 8 fireweed

willowy: 6 pliant

willpower: 8 self-will; **11** self-command, self-control

willy-nilly: 6 random; **9** haphazard

Wilson: 13 Woodrow Wilson; **19** Thomas Woodrow Wilson

wilted: 4 limp; **5** faded, passe, stale; **6** frayed, shabby, shaken; **8** drooping; **10** secondhand, threadbare

wily: 3 sly; **4** foxy, slim; **5** dodgy, slick; **6** crafty, tricky; **7** cunning, knavish, tricksy; **8** guileful, stealthy

wimble: 5 auger, probe, rimer, scoop

wimp: 7 chicken, crybaby

wimpy: 4 weak; **5** washy; **7** wimpish; **9** enervated; **10** wishy-washy; **11** lilyhearted, weak-hearted; **12** fainthearted

win: 4 gain; **7** advance, profits, triumph, victory

wince: 3 shy; **4** fret, funk; **5** chafe, quail, start; **6** cringe, flinch, recoil, shrink; **7** squinch, wincing; **9** flinching

winch: 5 crank; **6** pinion; **7** capstan; **8** windlass

Winchester drive: 9 disc drive, disk drive, hard drive

wind: 3 tip; **4** hint, lead, lift, nose, roll, wrap; **5** curve, hoist, ravel, scent, steer, twine, twist, weave; **6** thread, wind up; **7** draught, entwine, meander, winding, wreathe; **8** entangle; **9** circulate; **11** nothingness, respiration

windbreaker: 5 parka; **6** anorak; **9** ski jacket; **11** windcheater

winded: 5 blown, pursy; **7** gasping, panting; **11** short-winded

winder: 3 key

windfall: 5 bonus, bunce, gravy; **7** bonanza, godsend, killing

windflower: 7 anemone

wind gauge: 4 vane; **8** wind sock; **10** anemometer; **11** weather vane, weathercock

wind generator: 8 windmill; **13** aerogenerator

wind harp: 11 aeolian harp

windhover: 7 kestrel

winding: 4 wind; 5 twist; 6 twisty; 7 twisted; 8 rambling, tortuous, twisting; 9 wandering; 10 meandering

winding-sheet: 4 pall; 6 shroud; 8 cerement; 14 winding-clothes

winding up: 6 finale, finish; 10 conclusion, denouement, wrapping up; 11 culmination; 12 consummation

windjammer: 4 ship; 6 sailer; 8 tall ship; 11 sailing ship

windlass: 4 haul; 5 hoist, winch; 7 capstan

window: 8 casement; 9 embrasure; 10 windowpane; 13 teller's window; 14 cashier's window

window dressing: 6 facade

windowpane: 6 window; 10 tattersall

windpipe: 7 trachea

wind scale: 13 Beaufort scale

windshield: 10 windscreen

windshield wipers: 5 wiper; 10 wiper blade

wind sleeve: 4 sock; 6 drogue; 7 air sock; 8 wind sock, windsock; 9 air sleeve

windup: 5 mop up; 7 closing; 10 completion; 11 culmination

wind vane: 4 vane; 11 weather vane, weathervane

windward: 8 downwind

windy: 5 blowy, wordy; 6 breezy, prolix; 7 blowing, gusting, tedious, verbose; 10 long-winded

Windy City: 7 Chicago

wine: 4 vino; 11 wine-colored

wine barrel: 4 cask

wine bucket: 10 wine cooler

wine cooler: 8 spritzer; 10 wine bucket

wine guzzler: 4 wino; 10 wine-bibber

wine lover: 9 oenophile; 11 oenophilist

winemaker: 7 vintner; 9 wine maker

winery: 6 vinery; 8 vineyard; 9 wine maker

wine steward: 9 sommelier; 10 wine waiter

wing: 3 arm, fly; 4 army, host, limb; 5 annex, corps, flank, jimmy, squad; 6 annexe, branch, column, fender, lobule, member, pinion, screen; 7 battery, brigade, company, lee wall, platoon, section; 8 division, garrison, offshoot, offstage, regiment, squadron; 9 backstage, battalion, extension, side scene; 10 detachment; 11 subdivision

winged: 8 electric; 9 mercurial; 11 eagle winged, telegraphic

wing it: 5 ad lib; 9 improvise; 11 extemporize

wing nut: 8 thumbnut; 9 wing screw

wingspan: 10 wingspread

wink: 4 leer; 5 blink, flash, jiffy, nudge, shrug, trice; 6 glance, winkle; 7 instant, nictate, twinkle; 9 blink away, nictitate, twinkling

winkle: 4 wink; 5 blink, flash; 7 twinkle; 9 winkle out; 10 periwinkle; 11 scintillate

winner: 5 champ; 6 victor; 7 success; 8 achiever; 11 prizewinner

winning: 6 taking; 7 winsome; 8 fetching; 9 seductive; 10 attractive, triumphant, victorious

winnings: 3 win; 5 prize; 7 innings, profits; 8 pickings

winnow: 3 fan; 4 bolt, cull, pick, sift, weed; 5 glean; 7 sifting; 9 eliminate, winnowing

wino: 10 wine-bibber; 11 wine guzzler

win over: 4 turn, wean; 6 disarm; 7 beguile, convert; 8 come over, convince, draw over, gain over, talk over; 9 bring over, reconcile

winsome: 5 bonny, buxom; 6 hearty; 7 winning

winter's bark family: 11 Winteraceae

wintergreen: 12 checkerberry

wintergreen family: 10 Pyrolaceae

winter melon: 6 casaba; 8 honeydew

wintry: 3 icy; 6 arctic, boreal, frigid, frosty, frozen; 7 glacial, wintery; 8 freezing, Siberian

wipe: 3 boo, cob, rub; 4 bang, gibe, hiss, hoot, jeer, jibe, quip, swab, trim, warm; 5 douse, dress, fling, flout, scoff, sneer, taunt; 6 efface, sponge; 8 flouting, pass over; 9 dress down; 10 obliterate

wiped out: 6 broken; 11 annihilated; 12 exterminated, impoverished

wipe off: 5 erase; 6 efface, rub off, rub out; 8 score out, wipe away

wipe out: 3 eat; 4 kill, raze; 5 eat up, erase, use up; 6 rub out; 7 blot out, consume, deplete, exhaust, expunge, take out, wash out; 8 carry off, decimate, white out; 9 cancel out, eliminate, eradicate, sweep away; 10 annihilate, extinguish, obliterate

wiper: 8 wiper arm; 10 contact arm, wiper blade

wipe up: 3 mop; 5 mop up

wire: 3 guy; 4 line; 5 cable, chain; 7 painter; 8 moorings, telegram; 9 electrify, telegraph

wired: 8 pumped up

wire grass: 9 yard grass

wirehaired terrier: 8 wirehair

wireless: 5 radio, tuner; 8 radio set, receiver

wire service: 10 news agency; 11 press agency

wiretap: 3 bug, tap; 9 intercept

wirework: 7 netting; 8 meshwork; 9 grillwork

wiry: 4 ropy; 6 sinewy; 7 stringy; 8 muscular, stalwart; 9 strapping

Wisconsin: 11 Badger State; 14 Wisconsin River

wisdom: 4 lore; 6 reason; 8 learning, sapience, wiseness; 9 knowledge, soundness; 11 information, rationality; 13 judiciousness

wise: 2 MO; 3 way; 4 mode, sage; 5 means;

6 manner, method, wise to; **7** fashion, knowing, process, sapient; **8** protocol, sensible; **9** judicious, mechanism, procedure, sagacious, technique; **10** considered, diplomatic

wisecrack: 4 quip; **5** crack, sally

wise guy: 8 smartass, wiseacre; **10** smart aleck; **11** wisenheimer; **12** weisenheimer

wisely: 6 sagely

wise man: 4 guru, sage; **6** mentor

Wise Men: 4 Magi

wisent: 7 aurochs; **12** Bison bonasus

wish: 3 bid; **4** care, like, list, mind, want, will; **6** choice, choose, decide, desire, regard; **7** wishing; **8** decision, pleasure, wish well; **9** determine; **11** compliments

wishful: 4 fain; **7** would-be; **8** aspirant, aspiring

wishing: 4 want, wish; **7** wanting; **8** desiring

wish-wash: 4 bosh; **5** trash, tripe; **7** rubbish; **8** trumpery; **9** moonshine; **10** applesauce; **12** fiddle-faddle

wishy-washy: 4 fade, mild, weak; **5** stale, vapid, washy, wimpy; **7** mawkish; **9** enervated, spineless

wisp: 4 tuft; **5** truss

wispy: 3 dim; **5** faint, vague; **7** shadowy

wistful: 6 sedate; **7** anxious, earnest, longing, pensive, sincere; **8** studious, yearning; **10** meditative, reflective, thoughtful; **11** speculative; **12** deliberative; **13** contemplative, introspective, philosophical

wit: 3 wag; **4** card, wits; **5** brain, humor; **6** reason; **8** capacity, humorist, keenness; **9** funniness, intellect, mentality, witticism, wittiness; **10** brainpower; **12** intelligence; **13** comprehension, understanding

witch: 3 hag, hex, pig; **4** jinx, seer; **5** crone; **6** wizard; **7** bewitch, enchant, glamour; **8** conjuror; **11** enchantress, necromancer

witchcraft: 8 witchery; **10** demonology; **12** demon-worship, devil-worship

witch doctor: 6 shaman

witchery: 5 charm; **7** amenity; **9** seduction; **10** amiability, bewitchery, witchcraft; **11** bewitchment, enchantment

witches' Sabbath: 6 sabbat

witch grass: 10 quack grass

witching hour: 6 midnight

wit-cracker: 7 wit-worm; **10** wit-snapper

with: 5 using, withe, withy; **6** withal; **9** by means of

withal: 3 yet; **4** with; **5** still; **6** enough, even so; **7** however; **8** adequacy; **10** competence; **11** nonetheless, sufficiency; **12** nevertheless

with child: 3 big; **5** great, heavy, large; **6** gravid; **8** enceinte; **9** expectant

with compassion: 8 with pity; **9** pityingly

with courtesy: 8 politely; **11** courteously

withdraw: 6 bow out, call in, recall, recede, remove, retire, shrink, vacate; **7** adjourn, back off, back out, retreat, seclude, swallow, take out; **8** back away, call back, draw back, move back, pull away, pull back, take away, take back, take from; **9** disengage

withdrawal: 7 removal; **8** backdown, coldness, coolness, removing; **9** aloofness, climb-down, defection, desertion, frigidity, going over, recession, secession; **10** detachment, remoteness, retirement

withdrawn: 6 remote; **7** indrawn, recluse, removed; **8** detached; **9** reclusive

withe: 4 with; **5** withy

with ease: 6 easily; **8** facilely

wither: 3 rot; **4** fade; **5** decay, go bad, go off, wizen; **6** molder, rankle, shrink; **7** shrivel

withered: 4 lame, sear, sere; **5** crazy, shaky, wizen; **6** broken, shaken; **7** dried-up, wizened; **8** shrunken

withering: 3 dry; **5** sharp; **6** biting, severe; **7** atrophy, cutting, cynical, haughty; **8** cavalier, hard upon, sardonic; **9** bumptious, sarcastic, satirical, trenchant; **10** desolating, desolation; **11** devastating

with glee: 7 happily; **8** joyfully

with happiness: 5 gayly; **7** happily, merrily; **8** blithely; **10** jubilantly, mirthfully

withheld: 4 held, kept; **8** retained; **10** unrevealed; **11** undisclosed

withhold: 4 keep; **5** limit; **6** deduct, recoup, retain; **7** conceal, not give, reserve; **8** hold back, hold onto, keep back, restrict

withholding: 7 reserve; **9** reticence; **10** deductions; **11** reservation, 11 tax withheld

within: 6 inside; **8** inwardly; **10** internally

within reach: 10 accessible, attainable, obtainable

within reason: 6 fairly; **8** middling, passably, somewhat; **10** moderately, reasonably

with it: 2 in; **6** trendy; **7** current, faddish, in vogue; **8** up to date; **9** in fashion, prevalent; **10** all the rage, prevailing; **11** fashionable

without: 4 save; **5** minus; **6** beside, except, unless; **7** barring, nowhere; **9** aside from, excepting

without accompaniment: 8 a capella

without a job: 7 jobless; **10** unemployed; **11** between jobs

without charge: 4 free; **6** gratis; **7** untaxed; **8** costless; **10** gratuitous

without effect: 4 vain; **9** fruitless, pointless; **10** bootlessly, of no effect, profitless; **11** pointlessly

without fail: 6 always; **8** ever anon, steadily; **9** routinely; **10** at all times, constantly, invariably; **11** continually, incessantly, perpetually, unfailingly; **12** consistently, continuously

with skill: 8 expertly; **10** skillfully; **11** competently; **12** proficiently

withstand: **4** defy, hold; **5** brave, stand; **6** hold up, resist
withy: **4** with; **5** withe
witless: **4** dull; **6** stupid; **7** foolish; **8** mindless; **9** airheaded, brainless, dim-witted, fat witted, fat-headed, nitwitted, pig headed, senseless
witloof: **6** endive
witness: **3** see; **4** find, view; **6** behold, depose, viewer; **7** testify, voucher, watcher; **8** beholder, looker-on, observer, onlooker, passer by, vouch for; **9** attestant, bystander, indicator, informant, spectator, testifier; **10** eyewitness
witnessing: **7** viewing; **9** beholding; **13** eye-witnessing
wits: **3** wit; **6** reason; **9** intellect
wittiness: **3** wit; **5** humor; **6** humour; **9** funniness, witticism
wittingly: **8** by design; **9** advisedly, expressly, knowingly, on purpose, purposely; **10** designedly, with intent; **11** puposefully; **12** deliberately; **13** intentionally
wiz: **3** ace; **4** star, whiz; **5** adept, maven, whizz; **6** genius, wizard; **7** hotshot; **8** virtuoso; **9** sensation
wizard: **3** ace, wiz; **4** seer, star, whiz; **5** adept, magic, maven, whizz, witch; **6** genius; **7** hotshot, magical; **8** charming, conjuror, magician, sorcerer, virtuoso, witching, wizardly; **9** sensation, sorcerous; **11** necromancer
wizen: **6** gullet, throat, wither; **7** wizened; **8** shrunken, withered; **9** lose flesh, shriveled; **10** shrivelled
wobble: **4** sway, tilt; **5** shift; **6** careen, coggle, shimmy; **8** nutation
wobbly: **5** shaky, wonky; **7** rickety
Woden: **4** Odin; **5** Wodan
woe: **5** grief, trial; **6** sorrow; **8** distress; **9** heartache, suffering; **10** affliction, woefulness
woebegone: **6** creaky, woeful; **7** run-down
woeful: **6** rueful; **8** mournful, pitiable, wretched; **9** execrable, miserable, woebegone; **10** deplorable, lamentable
woefully: **5** sadly; **6** sorely; **7** cruelly, grossly; **8** bitterly, horribly, terribly; fearfully, miserably, painfully, piteously; **10** deplorably, dreadfully, grievously, lamentably, shockingly; **11** frightfully
wolf: **5** beast, brute; **6** devour, masher, savage
wolf cub: **7** wolf pup
wolf down: **4** wolf; **8** bolt down, gulp down
wolfish: **8** edacious, esurient, ravening, ravenous, wolflike; **9** rapacious, voracious
wolfman: **8** werewolf; **11** lycanthrope
wolfram: **1** W; **8** tungsten
wolverine: **7** glutton; **8** carcajou, Gulo gulo; **9** skunk bear; **10** Gulo luscus

Wolverine State: **8** Michigan; **15** Great Lakes State
woman: **6** female; **11** adult female
woman's doctor: **12** gynecologist
woman's hat: **9** millinery
woman hater: **10** misogamist, misogynist
womanize: **9** philander
womb: **6** uterus; **10** birthplace
women's liberationist: **6** libber; **8** feminist
women's liberation movement: **8** feminism; **9** women's lib
wonder: **6** marvel; **7** inquire, miracle, prodigy; **8** question; **9** curiosity; **10** admiration, phenomenon
wonder boy: **9** golden boy
wonder child: **7** prodigy; **10** wunderkind
wonder drug: **10** antibiotic
wonderful: **5** great; **8**, terrific, wondrous; **9** fantastic, marvelous; **10** tremendous; **11** astonishing
wonderfully: **8** famously, superbly, wondrous; **9** amazingly, glaringly; **10** incredibly, strikingly, wondrously; **11** egregiously, marvelously, prominently; **12** astoundingly, emphatically, marvellously, stupendously, surprisingly, terrifically, tremendously; **13** astonishingly, extravagantly
wonk: **4** nerd, swot; **5** grind; **6** wombat
won over: **9** convinced, persuaded
wont: **3** apt, use, way; **5** habit; **8** habitude, inclined; **10** accustomed
woo: **5** court; **6** invite; **7** romance, solicit
wood: **5** woods; **6** forest, lumber, timber, wooden; **8** woodland, woodwind; **9** woodlands
wood alcohol: **8** methanol
wood anemone: **8** snowdrop
woodbine: **15** Virginia creeper
wood block: **7** woodcut; **9** engraving
woodchuck: **9** groundhog
wood coal: **8** charcoal
woodcutter: **8** forester, woodsman; **12** backwoodsman
wood ear: **7** tree ear
wooded: **5** woody; **6** sylvan, woodsy
wood engraving: **7** woodcut; **9** wood block; **10** xylography
wooden-head: **5** thick; **9** blockhead
wooden horse: **11** Trojan Horse
wooden leg: **6** pegleg
wood file: **4** rasp
wood frame house: **10** frame house
wood glue: **14** carpenter's glue
woodland: **4** wood; **6** forest, timber; **9** woodlands; **10** timberland
wood lithograph: **9** xylograph
wood nymph: **5** dryad
wood pussy: **5** skunk
woods: **4** wood; **6** forest, timber
woodsman: **7** woodman; **8** forester;

10 woodcutter, woodworker; **12** backwoodsman

wood spirit: 8 methanol; **11** wood alcohol; **13** methyl alcohol

wood sugar: 6 xylose

woodsy: 5 woody; **6** sylvan, wooded; **9** arboreous; **11** arboraceous

woodwind instrument: 3 sax; **4** oboe, wood, wind; **5** flute; **7** bassoon; **8** clarinet, woodwind; **9** saxophone

woodwork: 9 carpentry; **11** woodworking

woodworker: 9 carpenter

woody: 6 sylvan, wooded, woodsy; **9** arboreous, lignified; **11** arboraceous

wooer: 4 beau; **5** swain; **6** suitor; **8** follower; **9** inamorato; **10** sweetheart

woofer: 11 loudspeaker

wooing: 4 suit; **8** courting; **9** addresses, courtship; **10** lovemaking

wool: 6 fleece, woolen; **7** cambric, woollen

wool fat: 7 lanolin; **10** wool grease

woolgather: 5 dream; **8** daydream, stargaze

woolgatherer: 10 daydreamer

woolly: 5 downy, muzzy, wooly; **6** addled, fluffy, lanate; **7** muddled, velvety; **9** befuddled; **10** flocculent

wooly: 6 woolly

woozy: 5 dizzy, flush, giddy; **6** buzzed, mellow; **7** flushed; **11** vertiginous

word: 3 mot [Fr]; **4** news, term; **5** motto, voice; **6** advice, byword, parole, phrase, pledge, word it; **7** express, message, promise, tidings; **8** password; **9** formulate, watchword; **10** articulate, discussion, spoken word; **11** countersign, give words to, give-and-take, piece of news, undertaking, word of honor, written word

word accent: 10 word stress

word class: 12 part of speech

word division: 11 hyphenation

worded: 7 phrased; **9** expressed; **11** articulated

word for word: 3 sic; **7** mot a mot [Fr]; **8** verbatim; **9** literally, literatim [Lat]

wordiness: 9 prolixity, verbosity; **10** prolixness; **11** diffuseness, lengthiness, profuseness; **13** expansiveness; **14** long-windedness

wording: 5 style; **7** diction; **8** phrasing, verbiage; **11** phraseology

wordless: 4 mute; **8** unspoken; **9** voiceless; **10** breathless, speechless

word of advice: 7 warning; **10** admonition

word of honor: 3 vow; **4** word; **5** troth; **6** parole, plight

wordplay: 3 pun; **7** punning

words: 3 row; **5** lyric, run-in; **6** demele, dustup, speech; **7** quarrel, wrangle; **8** jangling, language; **9** bickering, wrangling; **10** squabbling

words per minute: 3 wpm

word-splitting: 13 hairsplitting

word square: 8 acrostic

word stress: 10 word accent

Wordsworth: 17 William Wordsworth

word-worship: 10 verbolatry; **13** grammatolatry

wordy: 5 windy; **7** copious, diffuse, lengthy, profuse, tedious, verbose; **9** expansive, exuberant, redundant; **10** long-winded

work: 2 be, do, go; **3** act, job, ply, run; **4** crop, deal, line, opus, play, task, toil; **5** avail, bring, chore [U.S.], cover, knead, labor, piece, solve, study, wield, wreak; **6** answer, do work, effort, follow, handle, living, number, office, squash, strain, thrift [Scot], volume, work on; **7** address, agendum, carry on, make for, operate, process, produce, toiling, working, writing; **8** business, exercise, function, laboring, practice; **9** cultivate, embroider, figure out, put to work, puzzle out, thing to do, workplace; **10** employment, line of work, livelihood, manipulate, occupation, production, take effect; **11** be effective, composition, maintenance, piece of work

workable: 6 viable; **7** ductile, plastic; **8** feasible, formable, shapable; **9** malleable, shapeable; **11** practicable

workaday: 5 usual; **6** common, normal; **7** mundane, nominal, prosaic, routine, typical; **8** everyday, habitual, ordinary; **9** quotidian; **12** businesslike, unremarkable

work against: 7 counter; **9** undermine; **11** countermine

workaholic: 12 overachiever

workbook: 12 exercise book

workbox: 7 workbag; **10** workbasket

work camp: 10 prison camp, prison farm

work done: 12 fait accompli [Fr], finished task; **14** accomplishment

worked up: 6 piqued; **7** labored, stirred, wrought; **9** elaborate, stirred up

worker: 4 doer; **7** laborer; **11** proletarian; **12** practitioner; **13** working person

workforce: 5 hands; **8** manpower; **9** work force

workhouse: 9 poorhouse [Br]

working: 4 toil, work; **5** force, labor; **6** acting, action, agency, at work, effort, on duty; **7** running, toiling; **8** employed, function, laboring, on the job, workings; **9** effectual, efficient, in harness, operation, operative, practical; **10** functional; **11** efficacious, functioning

working class: 5 labor; **6** labour; **10** blue-collar; **11** proletariat, wage-earning

working day: 7 weekday, work day, workday

working out: 7 workout; **8** exercise; **10** exercising; **11** elaboration

working person: 6 worker; **7** laborer

working stiff: 6 drudge; 7 laborer, workman; 10 workingman; 13 manual laborer

working together: 13 cooperativity

workman-like: 12 business-like

workmanship: 5 craft; 9 handiwork; 13 craftsmanship

work of art: 3 art; 4 opus; 7 artwork

workout: 8 exercise; 10 exercising, working out; 16 physical exercise, physical exertion

work out: 5 enact; 6 evolve, pan out; 9 elaborate

work party: 4 crew, gang

work permit: 10 work papers; 13 working papers

workplace: 4 shop, work; 8 workshop; 9 workhouse; 15 place of business

works: 4 opus; 5 deeds, plant; 7 factory

work stoppage: 6 strike

work together: 5 unite; 9 cooperate; 11 act together; 12 join together

work unit: 8 heat unit; 10 energy unit

work up: 4 stir; 5 build, get up, pique; 6 stir up; 7 build up; 8 progress

world: 5 earth, Earth, globe, terra; 6 cosmos, domain, global, humans, nature, public; 7 mankind, reality, society; 8 creation, humanity, populace, universe; 9 community, existence, great deal, human race, humankind, macrocosm, planetary, wide world, worldwide

World Bank: 4 IBRD

world-beater: 4 king; 8 champion

world beyond the grave: 9 afterlife, next world

World Health Organization: 3 WHO

worldliness: 11 materialism; 14 sophistication

worldly: 5 blase; 7 earthly, mundane, terrene; 8 temporal; 10 uncultured; 11 terrestrial, unspiritual

World Meteorological Organization: 3 WMO

world power: 5 power; 10 great power, major power, superpower

world-shaking: 12 earthshaking; 15 world-shattering

world traveler: 12 globetrotter

world view: 7 outlook; 13 weltanshauung [Ger]; 14 Weltanschauung

World War I: 8 Great War, World War ; 11 War to End War; 13 First World War

world-weariness: 11 Weltschmerz

world-weary: 5 bored

worldwide: 4 vast; 5 world; 6 common, global; 7 general; 8 far-famed; 9 extensive, planetary, universal; 10 ecumenical, widespread; 12 cosmopolitan

world wide web: 3 web, WWW

world wisdom: 11 savoir faire [Fr]

worm: 5 helix, louse, twist; 6 buckle, insect, rundle, spiral, squirm, volute, writhe; 7 wreathe, wrestle, wriggle; 9 corkscrew

WORM drive: 4 WORM

worm fence: 10 snake fence

worm-shaped: 9 vermiform

wormwood: 4 gall; 10 bitterness

wormy: 8 cringing, wormlike; 9 groveling, worm-eaten; 10 grovelling; 11 vermiculate

worn: 5 drawn, seedy, washy; 6 rotten, wasted; 7 abraded, decayed, haggard, laid low, raddled, scraped, worn out; 8 attrited, careworn, worn down; 10 pulled down; 11 languishing; 12 deteriorated

worn out: 4 worn; 5 spent; 6 used up; 7 worn-out; 8 fatigued, finished, flagging; 9 dulled out, exhausted

worried: 5 upset; 6 pained, uneasy; 7 anxious; 9 afflicted, concerned, disturbed; 10 disquieted, distressed; 12 apprehensive

worrier: 9 worrywart

worrisome: 8 worrying; 9 troubling; 10 disturbing, perturbing; 11 distressful, distressing; 12 unreassuring

worry: 3 bug, irk, vex; 4 bait, bore, care, faze, mind, tire; 5 abuse, annoy, beset, brood, cross, dwell, grind, harry, haunt, hound, tease; 6 badger, bother, harass, heckle, ill-use, infest, molest, occupy, pester, plague, pother, unease; 7 anxiety, concern, disturb, mortify, oppress, perplex, trouble; 8 bullirag, bullyrag, disquiet, distress, headache, ill-treat, interest, maltreat, mistreat, vexation; 9 annoyance, disoblige, displease, importune, incommode, persecute; 10 discomfort, discompose, infliction, inquietude, irritation, solicitude, uneasiness, visitation; 11 disquietude; 12 apprehension; 13 inconvenience

worrying: 6 biting; 7 carking, teasing, torment; 9 badgering, bothering, harassing, pestering, troubling, worrisome; 10 disturbing, perturbing, tormenting; 11 bedevilment, distressful, distressing, molestation

worry oneself: 4 fret; 5 chafe, wince

worsen: 7 decline, fall off; 9 aggravate; 10 degenerate, exacerbate, exasperate; 11 become worse, deteriorate

worsening: 4 harm; 5 decay; 6 damage, injury; 7 decline; 8 decaying; 9 declining, detriment, vitiation; 10 debasement, impairment; 11 aggravation, degradation, heightening; 12 degenerating, degeneration; 13 deteriorating, deterioration

worship: 5 adore; 6 aspire, homage, revere; 7 idolize; 8 devotion, lordship; 9 adoration, do service, pay homage; 10 aspiration

worshipper: 8 adherent, believer; 9 celebrant, worshiper; 11 communicant

worth: 5 merit, value; 6 credit, desert; 8 goodness, meriting, valued at; 9 deserving; 10 excellence

worthless: 4 mean, vile; 5 cheap, sorry,

W

weedy; **6** meager, scurvy, shabby, trashy; **7** scrubby; **8** beggarly, trumpery, unworthy, wretched; **9** miserable, valueless

worth one's salt: 7 gainful; **10** profitable; **12** remunerative

worthy: 5 noble, solid; **8** suitable, valuable; **9** deserving, desirable, dignitary, estimable, honest man; **10** upstanding; **11** meritorious

worthy of praise: 9 estimable, plausible; **10** creditable; **11** meritorious; **13** unimpeachable

would-be: 6 manque; **7** wishful; **8** aspirant, aspiring, assuming; **9** bumptious; **10** precocious; **11** pretentious; **12** preposterous

wound: 4 hurt, pain; **5** spite; **6** injure, injury, insult, lesion, offend; **8** embitter, open sore, puncture, wounding

wounded: 4 hurt; **6** maimed; **7** bruised

woven material: 5 weave

wow: 4 riot; **6** howler, scream; **10** belly laugh; **12** sidesplitter, thigh-slapper

W particle: 1 W

wpm: 14 words per minute

wrack: 4 rack; **5** wreck; **6** bust up; **7** sinking; **8** sea wrack; **9** shipwreck

wraith: 5 ghost, shade, spook; **7** specter

wrangle: 3 nag, row; **4** moot; **5** argue, brawl, run-in, words; **6** bicker, debate, dustup, haggle, jangle; **7** dispute, quarrel; **8** clashing, haggling, squabble; **9** bandy with, bickering, chop logic, wrangling; **10** bandy words; **14** bandy arguments, hold an argument; **16** misunderstanding; **17** carry on an argument; **18** try conclusions with

wrangler: 6 cowboy; **13** horse wrangler

wrangling: 5 words; **6** demele, haggle; **7** wrangle; **8** haggling, jangling, polemics; **9** bickering; **10** squabbling

wrap: 4 roll, wind; **6** enfold, enwrap, wrap up; **7** enclose, envelop, wrapper

wrapped: 4 rapt; **6** draped, intent; **7** cloaked, clothed, mantled; **8** absorbed; **9** engrossed, enwrapped

wrapper: 4 wrap; **9** dust cover; **10** book jacket, dust jacket

wrapping: 4 lint, wrap; **6** swathe; **7** bandage

wrapping up: 6 finale, finish; **9** winding up; **10** conclusion, denouement; **11** culmination; **12** consummation

wrap up: 4 seal, wrap; **5** cover, lap up; stamp; **6** clinch, finish, fold up, roll up, wind up

wrath: 3 ire, mad; **5** anger, angry, irate; **7** angered

wrathfully: 9 furiously

wrawl: 4 howl, yowl; **6** yammer

wreath: 3 lei; **4** knot, posy, sash; **5** braid, chain, cross; **6** fascia, fillet, flower, girdle; **7** baldric, bouquet, chaplet, coronal, festoon, garland, wreathe

wreck: 4 ruin; **5** crash, wrack; **6** bust up; **7** sinking; **9** honeycomb, mere wreck, shipwreck; **17** magni nominis umbra [Lat]

wrecked: 7 aground, swamped; **8** capsized, cast away, grounded, stranded; **9** foundered; **11** shipwrecked

wrecker: 8 saboteur; **9** destroyer; **12** diversionist

wrecking: 4 ruin; **6** razing; **7** ruining; **9** ruination; **11** laying waste

wrecking bar: 3 pry; **6** pry bar; **7** crowbar

wren: 9 jenny wren

wrench: 4 jerk, pull, rick, turn; **5** swoop, twist, wrick, wring; **6** clutch, sprain, twitch; **7** rupture, shatter, spanner

wrest: 8 pull away; **9** force away

wrestle: 4 worm; **5** twist; **6** rassle, squirm, writhe; **7** grapple, wriggle; **9** grappling, wrestling

wrestler: 6 matman; **7** athlete; **8** grappler

wretch: 4 hood; **5** brute, bully, rough, rowdy, tough; **6** meanie [jocular], mugger, savage; **7** caitiff, hoodlum, pug-ugly [U.S.], ruffian; **8** hooligan, plug-ugly, sufferer; **9** barbarian, desperado, poor devil; **10** mean mother; **11** bludgeon man; **12** ugly customer; **18** object of compassion

wretched: 3 sad; **4** mean, poor, vile; **5** sorry, weedy; **6** meager, scurvy, shabby, trashy, woeful; **7** hapless, in agony, piteous, pitiful, scrubby; **8** beggarly, grievous, pathetic, pitiable, trumpery; **9** agonizing, execrable, miserable, suffering

wretchedness: 6 misery; **7** poverty; **8** meanness, vileness; **9** cheapness; **10** desolation, meagerness, paltriness, shabbiness, trashiness

wriggle: 4 worm; **5** twist; **6** squirm, wiggle, writhe

wriggling: 6 wiggly; **7** wriggly; **8** twisting, wiggling, writhing; **9** squirming

wright: 5 maker; **9** artificer; **12** manufacturer

wring: 4 fret, rack; **5** crimp, gouge, grate, rinse; **6** deform, extort, harrow, indent, pierce, wrench; **7** agonize, contort, distort, scallop, squeeze; **8** convulse

wringing wet: 10 soaking wet

wring out: 10 squeeze out

wrinkle: 4 curl, line, seam; **5** crisp, purse, twill; **6** crease, furrow, ruckle, rumple; **7** crinkle, crumple, scrunch

wrist: 6 carpus

wristband: 4 cuff; **6** sleeve; **8** bracelet; **9** watchband; **10** watchstrap

wrist bone: 6 carpal; **10** carpal bone

wrist pin: 10 gudgeon pin

writ: 7 summons; **8** subpoena

write: 3 pen; **5** spell; **6** indite; **7** compose, publish; **9** drop a line

write by hand: 9 handwrite

write down: 7 get down, jot down, put down, set down; **8** note down, take down

write in code: 4 code; 6 cipher, cypher, encode; 7 encrypt; 8 encipher, inscribe
write-off: 12 tax deduction
write once read mostly memory: 4 WORM
write out: 3 cut; 5 issue; 7 make out, write up; 12 write out fair
write poetry: 4 scan, sing; 5 rhyme; 7 poetize, versify
writer: 6 author
write up: 5 story; 6 report; 7 account; 8 write out; 10 news report
writhe: 3 bob, wag; 4 reel, sway, toss, worm; 5 quake, twist; 6 flinch, quaver, quiver, shiver, squirm, tumble, twinge, twitch, waggle; 7 contort, shuffle, stagger, twitter, wrestle, wriggle
writing: 4 text, tome, work; 6 volume; 7 penning; 8 document; 10 authorship; 11 composition
writing in cipher: 12 cryptography
writing pad: 7 note pad; 8 legal pad; 10 message pad
writing paper: 10 stationery
writing style: 5 genre
writing table: 4 desk; 5 stand; 9 secretary; 10 escritoire, secretaire
written document: 6 papers
written record: 7 account

written text: 13 transcription
Wroclaw: 7 Breslau
wrong: 3 bad, ill; 4 awry, evil, harm, vile; 5 amiss; 6 damage, injury, sinful, untrue, wicked; 7 afflict, haywire, immoral, oppress, wrongly; 8 aggrieve, criminal, depraved, foul play, ill-timed, improper, untimely, wrongful; 9 incorrect, persecute; 10 iniquitous, unsuitable; 11 incorrectly, legal injury, unrighteous; 12 unprincipled, unseasonable, wrongfulness; 13 inappropriate
wrongdoer: 6 bad man; 8 offender; 9 miscreant
wrongful: 3 bad; 5 wrong; 8 unlawful
wrongness: 8 dishonor; 11 inrectitude; 13 incorrectness
wroth: 6 ireful; 8 wrathful, wrothful
wrought: 6 molded, shaped, worked; 8 worked up
wrought iron: 8 cast iron
wry: 3 dry; 4 awry; 5 askew; 6 ironic; 7 crooked; 8 ironical, sardonic
wryneck: 11 torticollis
WSW: 13 west southwest
Wurzburg: 9 Wuerzburg
WWW: 3 web; 12 world wide web

X

X: 3 ten; 6 decade, tenner
Xanax: 10 alprazolam
xanthophyll: 6 lutein; 10 xanthophyl
Xantippe: 5 scold, shrew, vixen; 6 dragon, virago; 9 termagant
XC: 6 ninety
Xe: 5 xenon
xenograft: 11 heterograft
xenon: 2 Xe
xerographic ink: 5 toner; 9 copier ink
xerography: 17 dry-process copying
xerophile: 9 xerophyte; 11 desert plant; 15 xerophytic plant
Xerophyllum: xerophyte; 9 xerophile; 11 desert plant; 15 xerophytic plant
xerox: 5 xerox; 7 xeroxer; 9 facsimile, photocopy, xerox copy; 11 xerox copier; 17 xerographic copier
Xian: 4 Sian; 5 Hsian; 6 Singan; 7 Changan
XII: 5 dozen; 6 twelve

XIII: 8 thirteen; 9 long dozen; 11 baker's dozen
Xiphias: 9 swordfish; 12 genus Xiphias
Xiphosura: 8 king crab; 13 horseshoe crab; 14 order Xiphosura
XL: 5 forty; 8 twoscore
Xmas: 9 Christmas
X-rated film: 9 skin flick; 10 porno flick; **X ray:** 10 X-radiation; 11 roentgen ray, X-ray picture; 13 roentgenogram; 14 X-ray photograph
XX: 6 twenty
XXX: 6 thirty
xylene: 5 xylol
Xylocaine: 9 lidocaine
xylograph: 14 wood lithograph
xylography: 13 wood engraving
xylophone: 7 marimba; 10 vibraphone; 12 glockenspiel
xylose: 9 wood sugar

X

Y

Y: 7 yttrium
yachting: 7 boating
yachting cap: 4 kepi
yacht race: 7 regatta; 8 boat race; 11 sailing-race
yack: 3 jaw, yak; 6 cackle; 7 chatter, yap away; 8 rattle on, yack away; 9 yakety-yak
Yagi aerial: 4 yagi
yahoo: 4 hick, rube; 5 yokel; 7 bumpkin, hayseed
Yahweh: 5 Yahve, Yahwe; 6 Jahvey, Jahweh, Wahvey, Yahveh; 7 Jehovah
yak: 3 gag; 4 jape, jest, joke, yack, zebu; 5 laugh; 6 cackle, wheeze; 7 chatter
Yale University: 4 Yale
yam: 8 yam plant; 11 sweet potato
yammer: 4 howl, yawp, yowl; 5 whine, wrawl; 7 grizzle
Yangtze: 5 Chang, Kiang; 12 Yangtze Kiang, Yangtze River
yang-yin: 7 yin-yang
yank: 4 jerk
Yankee: 4 Yank; 8 Uncle Sam; 10 Northerner; 12 New Englander, Yankee-Doodle
Yaounde: 17 capital of Cameroon
yap: 3 maw, yip; 4 hole, howl, pipe, pule, trap, yawl, yelp, yipe; 5 growl, snarl, whine; 6 baying, squall, squeak, squeal
yard: 1 G, K, M; 3 ell; 4 dock, foot, hand, inch, line, mews, mile, nail, pace, palm, pole, rood, slip, thou; 5 close, cubit, grand, rents, wharf; 6 fathom, league; 7 chiliad, furlong, grounds, passage; 8 dockyard, shipyard, thousand; 9 buildings, cubic yard; 11 one thousand, railway yard
yard goods: 10 piece goods
yard grass: 9 wire grass, yardgrass; 10 goose grass
yardmaster: 10 dispatcher; 11 trainmaster
yard measure: 9 yardstick
yard sale: 10 garage sale
yardstick: 11 yard measure
yarmulke: 8 skull cap, skullcap, yarmelke, yarmulka
yarn: 4 tale; 5 story; 6 fringe, thread; 7 recital; 8 tall tale; 9 fish story, narration, narrative; 10 embroidery, gooseberry
yarn-dye: 7 impress
yarrow: 7 milfoil; 9 sassafras
yashmak: 4 veil; 7 yashmac
yautia: 6 tannia; 7 malanga; 11 spoonflower
yawl: 3 yap, yip; 4 howl, roar, wail, yipe; 5 growl, snarl; 6 baying; 7 ululate; 9 jolly boat
yawn: 3 nod, yaw; 4 gape, open; 5 bilge; 8 get sleep
yawp: 4 bawl; 5 whine; 6 squall, squeak, squeal, yammer; 7 grizzle

yaws: 9 frambesia; 10 framboesia
Yb: 9 ytterbium
yea: 2 ay; 3 aye, yes; 4 even, yeah; 7 the most; 8 above all; 9 a fortiori, eminently, extremely, still more, supremely; 10 especially, peculiarly, surpassing, to crown all; 11 egregiously, exceedingly, of all things, principally, prominently; 12 particularly, preeminently, surpassingly
yeah: 3 yea
yearbook: 6 annual
yearling: 3 tot; 7 bambino, toddler; 8 suckling, weanling; 9 nurseling
yearly: 6 annual; 8 annually, each year; 9 every year
yearn: 3 yen; 4 ache, long, pine, sink; 5 droop; 6 hanker, repine; 8 languish
yearning: 5 flame, mercy; 7 longing, passion, rapture, wistful; 8 clemency, coveting, devotion, humanity, idolatry; 9 adoration, idolizing; 10 tenderness; 11 forbearance, idolization
years: 3 age; 4 days; 6 old age; 8 long time
yeast: 4 barm; 6 leaven; 7 ferment
Yeats: 18 William Butler Yeats
Yeddo: 3 Edo; 4 Yedo; 5 Tokio, Tokyo; 14 capital of Japan; 15 Japanese capital
yell: 3 cry; 4 bawl, call, hoop, howl, roar; 5 brawl, hollo, shout, whoop; 6 bellow, halloa, halloo, holler, outcry, scream, shriek, shrill, squall; 7 screech; 8 shout out
yelled: 7 shouted
yeller: 6 roarer; 7 shouter
yellow: 7 chicken; 8 yellowed; 9 jaundiced, yellowish; 10 yellowness; 11 lily-livered, yellow color; 12 white-livered; 13 yellow-bellied
yellow bile: 6 choler
yellowbird: 9 goldfinch; 13 golden warbler
yellow-brown: 5 amber
yellow cab: 3 cab; 6 hansom; 7 taxicab; 10 checker cab
yellowed skin: 8 jaundice
yellow-fever mosquito: 12 Aedes aegypti
yellowfin tuna: 9 yellowfin
yellow green: 8 pea green; 10 chartreuse
yellow hornet: 12 yellow jacket
yellow journalism: 7 tabloid; 14 sensationalism
yellow metal: 10 Muntz metal
yellow poplar: 9 tulip tree, tulipwood
yellow-shafted flicker: 12 yellowhammer
yellow streak: 8 cold feet [U.S.]
yellowwood: 10 gopherwood
yelp: 3 yap, yip; 5 growl, snarl
yen: 4 ache, long, pine; 5 yearn; 8 languish; 9 hankering
yeoman: 4 beau, chap; 5 blade, swain; 6 fel-

low, gaffer; **7** good man; **9** beefeater; **10** cultivator

yeoman of the guard: 6 yeoman; **9** beefeater

yes: 2 ay, OK; **3** aye, yea; **8** all right

yes-man: 4 toad, tool; **5** dweeb, toady; **6** flunky, stooge, sucker, suckup; **7** flunkey, sponger; **8** courtier, hanger on, parasite, truckler; **9** doughface [U.S.], sycophant, toad-eater; **10** boot-licker

yesteryear: 4 past, yore; **7** ages ago; **8** years ago; **9** past times

yet: 3 but; **4** even; **5** as yet, so far, still; **6** even so, in time, til now, withal; **7** already, as far as, however, thus far, up to now; **8** hereunto, hitherto, until now; **10** all the same, beforehand, by that time, eventually, heretofore; **11** nonetheless, prior to this; **12** nevertheless

yeti: 17 abominable snowman

yew family: 8 Taxaceae; **14** family Taxaceae

yield: 3 pay; **4** bear, bend, cede, cost, give, take; **5** admit, allow, fetch, fruit, grant, issue, let go, relax; **6** afford, ease up, give in, give up, output, payoff, relent, render, resign, result, return, soften, submit; **7** abandon, bring in, concede, defer to, give way, let slip, outcome, produce, product, sell for, succumb, takings; **8** abnegate, generate, move over, offshoot, proceeds; **9** aftermath, crop yield, resultant, surrender; **10** bring about, relinquish; **11** buckle under; **12** knuckle under

yield assent: 6 accede, assent; **7** consent

yip: 3 yap; **4** howl, yawl, yelp, yipe; **5** growl, snarl; **6** baying

Yisrael: 4 Zion; **6** Israel

ylang-ylang: 10 ilang-ilang; **12** custard apple

yobbo: 3 yob; **4** yoho; **5** bully, rowdy, tough; **7** ruffian; **8** hooligan; **9** roughneck

yodel: 6 warble; **7** descant

yogurt: 7 yoghurt; **8** yoghourt

yoke: 3 duo; **4** duad, duet, dyad, hook, link, lock, pair, span; **5** belay, brace, latch, leash, twain; **6** collar, couple; **7** bracket, couplet, distich, grapple, twosome; **8** coupling; **9** doubleton; **11** conjugation

yokel: 4 clod, hick, rube [U.S.]; **5** yahoo; **7** bumpkin, hayseed

Yom Kippur: 14 Day of Atonement

Yom Kippur War: 14 Arab-Israeli War

yonder: 3 yon; **6** abroad, beyond; **7** farther, further

yore: 4 past; **9** past times; **10** yesteryear

York: 11 House of York

Yoruba: 3 Aku

Yosemite: 13 Yosemite Falls

you: 4 thee, thou

you bet: 5 truly; **6** and how, indeed; **7** exactly; **9** certainly, precisely, you said it

young: 3 new; **4** baby; **5** green, sappy, youth; **6** callow, puisne; **7** budding; **8** immature, juvenile, under age, youthful; **9** beardless, offspring

younger: 2 jr.; **6** junior, little

young girl: 4 lass; **6** lassie; **10** jeune fille

young lady: 4 girl, miss; **5** fille, missy; **10** young woman

young love: 9 puppy love

young man: 4 beau; **5** swain, wooer; **6** fellow, suitor; **8** follower; **9** boyfriend; **10** sweetheart

young person: 5 minor, youth; **7** younker

youngster: 3 fry, kid; **4** tike, tyke; **5** bairn [Scot], child, minor, youth; **6** moppet, nipper, shaver; **7** tiddler; **8** children [pl], juvenile, nestling, small fry

young woman: 4 girl, miss; **5** fille, missy; **9** young lady

younker: 3 boy, lad; **5** youth; **7** youngun; **9** stripling; **11** young person; **14** whippersnapper

your: 3 thy

yours: 5 thine

yourself: 7 thyself

youth: 3 kid; **5** bairn [Scot], child, young; **6** moppet; **7** younker; **8** children [pl], juvenile, small fry; **9** early days, little one, youngster; **10** juvenility; **11** young person; **12** youthfulness

youthful: 5 green, sappy, young; **6** callow, puisne, vernal; **7** budding; **8** juvenile, under age

youth hostel: 6 hostel; **14** student lodging

youth movement: 12 youth crusade

yowl: 4 howl, roar; **5** holla, hollo, wrawl; **6** bellow, holler, holloa, yammer; **7** roaring, yowling; **9** bellowing, caterwaul, hollering

yr: 4 year; **11** twelvemonth

ytterbium: 2 Yb

yttrium: 1 Y

yuan: 4 kwai

Yucatan Peninsula: 7 Yucatan

yucca: 4 tine; **9** bear grass [U.S.]

yucky: 4 foul; **6** wicked; **7** loathly; **9** loathsome, offensive, repellant, repellent, revolting; **10** disgustful, disgusting, off-putting; **11** distasteful; **12** disagreeable

Yugoslav: 8 Jugoslav; **11** Jugoslavian, Yugoslavian

Yugoslavia: 10 Jugoslavia

Yukon: 10 Yukon River; **14** Yukon Territory

Yule: 4 Noel; **8** Yuletide; **9** Christmas; **13** Christmastide, Christmastime

yule log: 3 bat [U.S.], bum [U.S.]; **4** bust, tear; **5** randy; **7** blowout [U.S.], fish fry [U.S.], hoedown; **8** jamboree; **10** hullabaloo; **13** donation party [U.S.]

Yuletide: 4 Noel, Yule; **9** Christmas; **13** Christmastide, Christmastime

yummy: 8 luscious; **9** delicious, toothsome; **10** delectable; **11** scrumptious

Y

Z

Z: 5 omega; **9** Z particle
zabaglione: 7 sabayon
zaftig: 5 buxom, plump; **6** chubby, zoftig; **10** embonpoint
zag: 3 zig; **6** zigzag
Zaire: 12 Belgian Congo; **28** Democratic Republic of the Congo
Zalophus: 7 sea lion; **13** genus Zalophus
Zambezi: 12 Zambezi River
zaniness: 9 frivolity; **12** eccentricity; **13** frivolousness
Zantac: 10 ranitidine
zany: 4 fool, goof; **5** goofy, goose, sappy, silly, wacky, weird; **6** cuckoo, madcap; **7** fathead, jackass; **8** clownish; **9** clownlike, cockamamy, eccentric, screwball; **10** buffoonish, cockamamie, nincompoop; **12** unreasonable
zap: 3 zot; **4** nuke; **7** atomize; **9** micro-cook, microwave
Zaragoza: 9 Saragossa
Zarathustra: 9 Zoroaster
zeal: 4 elan, gush; **5** ardor, verve; **6** ardour, fervor; **7** passion; **8** fervency; **9** eagerness; **10** enthusiasm; **11** overanxiety, zealousness; **12** strong desire
zealot: 7 fanatic; **8** partisan
zealotry: 10 fanaticism
zealous: 4 avid; **5** eager, great; **6** gung ho; **7** fanatic, forward; **9** in earnest, strenuous; **10** breathless; **12** enterprising, enthusiastic
Zea mays: 4 corn; **5** maize; **10** Indian corn
Zea mays amylacea: 8 soft corn; **9** flour corn, squaw corn
Zea mays everta: 7 popcorn
Zea mays rugosa: 9 green corn, sugar corn, sweet corn
zed: 3 zee
zee: 3 zed
zeitgeist: 16 spirit of the times
Zen Buddhism: 3 Zen
Zend: 7 Avestan; **10** Zend-Avesta
zenith: 3 top; **4** apex, peak; **6** vertex; **8** pinnacle
zephyr: 3 air; **4** puff; **5** whiff; **6** breeze; **10** gentle wind
zeppelin: 9 dirigible; **12** Graf Zeppelin
zero: 3 nil, nix, zip; **4** nada; **5** aught, zilch; **6** cipher, cypher, naught, nought, zero in; **7** nothing, nullity; **8** goose egg
zero in: 4 zero; **6** home in; **7** range in
zero possibility: 8 no chance; **12** what cannot be; **13** impossibility, the impossible
zest: 3 nip; **4** elan, fire, tang; **5** gusto, spice, verve; **6** relish, spirit; **7** spice up; **8** piquance, piquancy; **9** tanginess
Zeus faber: 8 John dory

zidovudine: 3 AZT; **14** azidothymidine
zig: 3 zag; **6** zigzag
zilch: 3 nil, nix, zip [slang]; **4** nada, zero; **5** aught, zippo [slang]; **6** cipher, cypher, naught; **7** nothing; **8** goose egg
zillions: 8 billions, jillions, millions; **9** trillions
Zimbabwe: 8 Rhodesia
Zinacef: 6 Ceftin; **10** cefuroxime
zinc: 2 Zn
zinc plate: 11 zinc coating
zing: 5 oomph; **6** pizzaz; **7** pizzazz; **8** dynamism
Zingiber: 6 ginger; **13** genus Zingiber
Zingiberaceae: 12 ginger family
zinnia: 13 old maid flower
Zion: 6 Israel, Utopia; **7** Yisrael
zip: 3 nil, nix; **4** nada, zero; **5** aught, hurry, speed, zilch [slang], zip up, zippo [slang]; **6** cipher, cypher, naught, zipper; **7** nothing; **8** goose egg
zip code: 8 postcode; **10** postal code
zipper: 3 zip; **5** zip up; **11** zip-fastener
zippy: 5 brisk, merry, peppy; **6** bouncy, lively, snappy; **8** bouncing, rattling, spanking, spirited
zip up: 3 zip; **6** zipper
zirconia: 14 zirconium oxide
zirconium: 2 Zr
zirconium silicate: 6 zircon
zit: 4 mole; **6** pimple
zither: 6 cither; **7** zithern
Zizania: 12 genus Zizania
Zizania aquatica: 8 wild rice
Ziziphus: 6 jujube; **9** lotus tree; **10** jujube bush; **13** genus Ziziphus
Zn: 4 zinc
zodiac: 4 band, belt, girt; **5** clasp; **6** girdle; **7** baldric
zoftig: 5 buxom, plump; **6** chubby, zaftig; **10** embonpoint
Zola: 9 Emile Zola
zombie: 5 zombi; **10** living dead; **11** zombi spirit; **12** zombie spirit
zombi spirit: 5 zombi; **6** zombie; **12** zombie spirit
zone: 3 bed, orb; **4** band, belt; **5** clime, cycle, orbit; **6** cordon, course, rundle, sector; **7** climate, quarter, section; **8** district, division; **9** partition, subdivide
zonk out: 7 pass out; **8** black out
zoo: 9 menagerie
zooerastia: 9 zooerasty; **10** bestiality
zoolatry: 13 animal-worship
zoological: 6 animal
zoological garden: 3 zoo; **8** vivarium; **9** menagerie
zoological science: 7 zoology

zoologist: 15 animal scientist
zoom: 3 fly; 4 skim, soar, tear; 5 brush, shoot, surge, sweep, whisk, whizz; 6 soar up, swoosh; 7 cut away; 8 run a race; 9 zoom along; 10 rapid climb, whizz along; 11 rapid growth, soar upwards
zoom lens: 13 telephoto lens
zoophagous: 10 meat-eating; 11 flesh-eating
zoophyte: 5 beast, brute, wight; 6 animal; 7 critter [U.S. dialect]; 8 creature; 10 dumb animal
zori: 5 zoris; 6 pusher, sandal
Zoroaster: 11 Zarathustra
zoster: 8 shingles; 12 herpes zoster
Zosteraceae: 14 eelgrass family

zot: 3 zap
zouave: 7 trooper; 8 rifleman; 9 legionary; 10 skirmisher; 11 legionnaire, rank and file; 12 sharpshooter
Zovirax: 9 acyclovir
Zr: 9 zirconium
zucchini: 9 courgette
zwieback: 4 rusk; 15 Brussels biscuit, twice-baked bread
zwitterion: 10 dipolar ion
zygote: 6 hybrid
zymolysis: 7 ferment, zymosis; 10 fermenting; 12 fermentation
zymosis: 7 ferment; 9 zymolysis

Z

A

A&A	amniocentesis and abortion
AA	Alcoholics Anonymous
AAA	American Automobile Association
AAAS	American Association for the Advancement of Science
AACP	American Academy of Child Psychiatry
AAFP	American Academy of Family Physicians
AAHA	American Academy of Health Administration
AAM	air-to-air missile
AAME	American Academy of Medical Ethics
AAMFT	American Association for Marriage and Family Therapy
AANFP	American Academy of Natural Family Planning
AANP	American Academy of Nurse Practitioners
AANS	American Academy of Neurological Surgeons
AAP	American Academy of Pediatrics
AARP	American Association of Retired Persons
AAUN	American Association of the United Nations
AAUW	American Association of University Women
ABA	American Bar Association
ABA	American Booksellers' Association
ABC	American Baby Code
ABC	American Broadcasting Company
ABCL	American Birth Control League (later Planned Parenthood)
abd.	abdomen, abdominal
ABM	anti-ballistic missile
ABMS	American Board of Medical Specialties
ABOG	American Board of Obstetrics and Gynecology
abp.	archbishop
abr.	abridged
ABS	American Bible Society, able-bodied seaman
ABT	American Ballet Theatre
ACA	Americans for a Constitutional Amendment
acad.	academy
ACC	Atlantic Coast Conference
ACCL	American Citizens Concerned for Life
acct.	accountant, account
AC/DC	alternating current/direct current
ACE	American Council on Education
ACF	Americans for Constitutional Freedom
ACHR	American Convention on Human Rights
ACLU	American Civil Liberties Union
ACOG	American College of Obstetrics and Gynecology
ACOOG	American College of Osteopathic Obstetricians and Gynecologists
ACOP	American College of Osteopathic Pediatricians
ACP	American College of Physicians
ACS	American Cancer Society
ACS	American College of Surgeons
ACTH	adrenocorticotropic hormone
AD	anno Domini
ADA	Americans for Democratic Action
ADA	American Dental Association
ADC	Aid to Dependent Children
adj.	adjacent, adjective
adm.	admiral
admin.	administration
ADL	Anti-Defamation League (of B'nai B'rith)
ADRDA	Alzheimer's Disease and Related Disorders Association
adv.	adverb
AE	artificial embryonation
AEA	American Education Association
AEC	Atomic Energy Commission
AED	Academy for Educational Development
AEF	American Expeditionary Forces
AEI	American Enterprise Institute
aero.	aeronautical, aeronautics
AEU	American Ethical Union
AFAM	Ancient Free and Accepted Masons
AFB	air force base
AFC	American Football Conference
AFC	automatic flight control
AfDB	African Development Bank
AFDC	Aid for Families with Dependent Children
AFDC	American Family Defense Coalition
AFE	Americans for the Environment
Afg.	Afghanistan
AFGE	American Federation of Government Employees
Afgh.	Afghanistan
AFJ	Alliance for Justice

AFL-CIO	American Federation of Labor and Congress of Industrial Organizations	AL	Arab League
		Ala.	Alabama
		ALA	American Library Association
AFMCH	American Foundation for Maternal and Child Health	Alas.	Alaska
		Alb.	Albania
AFP	(maternal) alpha-feto protein	ALC	American Lutheran Church
Afr.	Africa, African	ALD	adrenoleukodystrophy
AFS	American Fertility Society	ALEC	American Legislative Exchange Council
AFSC	American Friends Service Committee	ALF	Animal Liberation Front
AFSCME	American Federation of State, County, and Municipal Employees	Alg.	Algeria, algebra
		ALI	American Law Institute
		ALI	American Liberties Institute
AFT	American Federation of Teachers	ALS	amyotrophic lateral sclerosis
AFTRA	American Federation of Television and Radio Artists	Alta.	Alberta
		alum.	aluminum
AG	Andean Group	AMA	American Medical Association
AG	attorney general	amb.	ambassador
AGA	American Genetic Association	Amer.	American
agcy.	agency	Amex.	American Stock Exchange
AGI	adjusted gross income	AMF	Arab Monetary Fund
AGPA	American Group Psychotherapy Association	AMFAR	American Foundation for AIDS Research
agri.	agriculture, agricultural	AMOS	assumptions are the mother of all screwups
AGS	American Geriatrics Society	amp.	amperage, ampere
AGS	American Gynecological Society	AMSLAN	American Sign Language
agt.	agent, agreement	amt.	amount
AHA	American Historical Association	AMU	Arab Maghreb Union
AHA	American Hospital Association	AMWA	American Medical Women's Association
AHA	American Humane Association		
AHA	American Humanist Association	ANA	American Nurses Association
AHEA	American Home Economics Association	anag.	anagram
		anat.	anatomy
AHST	Alaska-Hawaii Standard Time	ANC	African National Congress
AI	Amnesty International	Ang.	Angola
AI	artificial insemination, artificial intelligence	Angl.	Anglican
		ANM	auxiliary nurse-midwife
AIAA	Americans for International Aid and Adoption	anon.	anonymous
		ANSI	American National Standards Institute
AID	Agency for International Development	anth.	anthology
AID	artificial insemination (donor)	AOA	American Orthopsychiatric Association
AIDS	Acquired Immune Deficiency Syndrome		
		AOG	Assembly of God
AIFR	American Institute of Family Relations	AOH	Ancient Order of Hibernians
		AORN	American Association of Registered Nurses
AIH	artificial insemination (husband)		
AIM	Accuracy in Media	AP	Associated Press
AIM	American Indian Movement	APA	American Pharmaceutical Association
AIPOP	American Institute of Public Opinion Poll		
		APA	American Psychiatric Association
AIUM	American Institute of Ultrasound in Medicine		
		APA	American Psychoanalytic Association
AJC	American Jewish Congress		
AJOG	American Journal of Obstetrics and Gynecology	APA	American Psychological Association
AKA	also known as		
AKC	American Kennel Club	APB	all points bulletin

APC	American Parents Committee	ASPEN	American Society for Parenteral
APHA	American Public Health		and Enteral Nutrition
	Association	assn.	association
APO	army post office	asst.	assistant
apoc.	apocalypse, Apochrypha	AST	Atlantic Standard Time
apos.	apostrophe	AT&T	American Telephone and
Apr./APR	April, annual percentage rate		Telegraph
APS	artificial placentation system	ATC	air traffic control
APSH	Association for Persons with	ATF	Bureau of Alcohol, Tobacco, and
	Severe Handicaps		Firearms
APTN	American Public Television	Atl.	Atlantic
	Network	ATM	automatic teller machine
APWU	American Postal Workers Union	ATP	Adenosine triphosphate
Arab.	Arabian, Arabic	attn.	attention
ARC	American Red Cross	attny.	attorney
ARC	AIDS-related complex	ATV	all-terrain vehicle
arch.	archipelago, archaic, architecture,	at. wt.	atomic weight
	architect	AU	Angstrom unit
ARF	Animal Rights Front	Aug.	August
Arg.	Argentina	AUL	Americans United for Life
ARHO	Association of Reproductive	Aus.	Austria, Austrian
	Health Officials	Austral.	Australia
ARHP	Association of Reproductive	auth.	authority, author, authentic
	Health Professionals	aux.	auxiliary
Ariz.	Arizona	AVC	American Veterans Committee
Ark.	Arkansas	AVDA	American Venereal Disease
ARL	Americans for Religious Liberty		Association
ARP	Association for Retarded	avdp.	avoirdupois
	Persons	ave.	avenue
ARV	AIDS-related virus	AVES	Australian Voluntary Euthanasia
ASA	American Sociological		Society
	Association	avg.	average
ASAP	as soon as possible	AWACS	airborne warning and control
ASAT	anti-satellite weapons		system
asb.	asbestos	AWMA	American Women's Medical
ASC	American Security Council		Association
ASCAP	American Society of Composers,	AWOL	absent without leave
	Authors, and Publishers	AZT	Azidothymidine
ASCII	American Standard Code for		
	Information Interchange		**B**
AsDB	Asian Development Bank	BA	Bachelor of Arts
ASE	American Stock Exchange	Bapt.	Baptist
ASEAN	Association of Southeast Asian	bart.	baronet
	Nations	BATF	Bureau of Alcohol, Tobacco, and
ASHA	American Social Health		Firearms
	Association	Bav.	Bavaria, Bavarian
ASHG	American Society of Human	BB/BSA	Big Brothers/Big Sisters of
	Genetics		America
ASLM	American Society of Law and	BBA	Balanced Budget Amendment
	Medicine	BBB	Better Business Bureau
ASM	American Society of	BBC	British Broadcasting Corporation
	Mammologists	BBT	basal body temperature
ASMA	American Student Medical	BCFA	Birth Control Federation of
	Association		America
ASN	army service number	BCR	benefit-cost ratio
ASPCA	American Society for the	BD	Bachelor of Divinity
	Prevention of Cruelty to	BIDS	Birth Defects Information System
	Animals	Belg.	Belgium, Belgian

BEU	Benelux Economic Union	CAN	Cult Awareness Network
bev.	beverage	canc.	cancelled
BFA	Bachelor of Fine Arts	CAPD	continuous ambulatory peritoneal dialysis
B. Gen.	brigadier general		
BIA	Bureau of Indian Affairs	capt.	captain
bibl.	bibliography	CARE	Cooperative for American Relief to Everywhere
bio.	biography		
biol.	biological, biologist, biology	CARICOM	Caribbean Community and Common Market
BIP	basic infertile pattern		
BIS	Bank for International Settlements	Cath.	Catholic, cathedral
		cav.	cavalry
bldg.	building	CBC	Canadian Broadcasting Corporation
B.LIT	Bachelor of Letters		
BLS	Bureau of Labor Statistics	CBC	Congressional Black Caucus
BLT	bacon, lettuce, tomato	CBE	Center for Biomedical Ethics
blvd.	boulevard	CBPP	Center for Budget and Policy Priorities
BM	basal metabolism		
BMA	British Medical Association	CBS	Columbia Broadcasting System
BMI	Broadcast Music, Inc.	CBT	Chicago Board of Trade
BMOC	big man on campus	CBTV	Coalition for Better Television
BOHICA	bend over — here it comes again	CCA	Circuit Court of Appeals
Bol.	Bolivia, Bolivian	CCAR	Central Conference of American Rabbis
BOM	Billings Ovulation Method		
bor.	borough	CCBA	Coalition of Concerned Black Americans
bot.	botanical, botanist, botany		
BPOE	Benevolent and Protective Order of Elks	CCC	Civilian Conservation Corps
		CCEL	Christian Civic Education League
Braz.	Brazil, Brazilian	CCR	Center for Constitutional Rights
Brit.	Britain, British	CCR	Citizens for Congressional Reform
bro.	brother		
bros.	brothers	CCW	counterclockwise
BS	Bachelor of Science	CD	congressional district
BSA	Boy Scouts of America	CDB	Caribbean Development Bank
B.SC.	Bachelor of Science	CDC	Centers for Disease Control
BSEC	Black Sea Economic Cooperation Zone	CDF	Children's Defense Fund
		CDI	Center for Defense Information
BTU	British thermal unit	CDT	Central daylight time
Bul.	Bulgarian, Bulgaria	CE	Council of Europe
Bulg.	Bulgarian, Bulgaria	CEA	Council of Economic Advisors
bur.	bureau	CED	Committee for Economic Development
bus.	business		
BVI	British Virgin Islands	CEI	Central European Initiative
BVM	Blessed Virgin Mother	CEL	Celsius
BWS	Better World Society	cent.	central, center, centigrade, century, centime
BYOB	bring your own bottle		
		CEO	chief executive officer
	C	CEP	Council on Economic Priorities
C	(degrees) Celsius, commonwealth	CEP	Council on Environmental Quality
C-SPAN	Congressional Coverage Cable Network		
		cert.	certificate, certification, certifed, certify
CAB	Civil Aeronautics Board		
CACM	Central American Common Market	CETA	Comprehensive Employment and Training Act
		CFC	chlorofluorocarbon
CAD	computer assisted design	CFC	combined federal campaign
CAH	congenital adrenal hyperplasia	CFL	Canadian Football League
Cal(if).	California	CFM	cubic feet per minute
CAM	computer aided manufacturing	CFR	Code of Federal Regulations
Can.	Canada, Canadian		

CFS	cubic feet per second	C.O.D.	cash on delivery
CGD	chronic granulomatous disease	CODEL	coordination in development
CGI	computer generated imagery	COLA	cost-of-living adjustment
CHAP	Child Health Assurance Program	coll.	college, collegiate
CHCE	Center for Health Care Ethics	Colo.	Colorado
CHD	Campaign for Human Development	comm.	command, commander, commentary, commerce, commission, committee, common, commonwealth, communication, communist
chem.	chemical, chemist, chemistry		
Chin.	China, Chinese		
chm.	chairman, checkmate		
chol.	cholesterol	comp.	company, compare, compass, compensation, compilation, compiled, complete, composer, composition
chron.	chronicles		
CHSA	Consumer Health Service of America		
CIA	Central Intelligence Agency	comr.	commissioner
CIA	Culinary Institute of America	Con-Con	Constitutional Convention
CID	Criminal Investigation Department (Scotland Yard)	cond.	condensor, condensed, condition, conductor
CIF	Conservation International Foundation	conf.	confederation, confidential, conference
CIF	cost, insurance, and freight	cong.	congregation, congress, congressional
CIN	cervical intraepithelial neoplasia		
CIO	Congress of Industrial Organizations	conj.	conjugation, conjunction
		Conn.	Connecticut
CIOMS	Council for International Organizations of Medical Sciences	cont.	contents, continental, continued, contemporary, contract, control
		CONUS	Continental United States
cir.	circa, circle, circuit, circular, circulation, circumference	COPE	Committee on Political Education
		Cor.	Corinthians
circ.	circa, circle, circuit, circular, circulation, circumference	CORE	Congress of Racial Equality
		corp.	corporation, corporate
CISS	chromosomal in-situ suppression hybridization	COS	chief of staff, cosine
		COYOTE	cast off your old tired ethics
CIV	cultures, ideas, and values	CP	Colombo Plan
civ.	civilian	CP	communist party
CJ	chief justice	CPA	Center for Policy Alternatives
CJR	Citizens for Judicial Restraint	CPA	certified public accountant
CKW	clockwise	CPB	Corporation for Public Broadcasting
CLC	Clergy and Laity Concerned		
CLF	Conservation Law Foundation	CPC	Crisis Pregnancy Center
CLI	cost of living index	CPE	Council on Population and Environment
CM	Calendar method ("rhythm")		
CMA	Canadian Medical Association	CPGAF	Committee on Population Growth and the American Family
CM–BBT	cervical mucus–basal body temperature		
		CPI	consumer price index
cmdr.	commander	cpl.	corporal
CMEA	Council for Mutual Economic Assistance	CPM	Cesarian Prevention Movement
		CPO	chief petty officer
CMF	Cardinal Mindszenty Foundation	CPR	cardiopulmonary resuscitation
CNF	Conservation Network Foundation	CPS	contraceptive prevalence surveys, current population surveys
CN-M	certified nurse-midwife	CPU	central processing unit
CNN	Cable News Network	CPUSA	Communist Party of the United States of America
CNS	central nervous system		
CNS	Committee for National Security	CR	calendar rhythm
CO	conscientious objector	CRC	Civil Rights Commission
COBOL	Common Business Oriented Language	CREOG	Council on Resident Education in Obstetrics and Gynecology

CRF	Constitutional Rights Foundation	Dec.	December
crim.	criminal	decd.	deceased, declared, decreased
crit.	critical, criticism	DEF	defense, definition
CRT	cathode ray tube	deg.	degree
CS	Christian Science (practitioner)	DEIS	draft environmental impact statement
CSA	Confederate States of America		
CSC	Civil Service Commission	Del.	Delaware, delegate, delete
CSCPA	Committee for Social Change and Political Action	Dem.	Democrat, Democratic
		Den.	Denmark
CSII	continuous subcutaneous insulin infusion	dept.	department, deputy
		DES	diethylstilbestrol
CSOW	Commission on the Status of Women	Deut.	Deuteronomy
		DEW	distant early warning
CSP	Center for Security Policy	DFA	Development Fund for Africa
C-SPAN	Cable Satellite Public Affairs Network	DFC	Distinguished Flying Cross
		DG	Dei gratia (by the grace of God)
CSSP	Center for Studies of Suicide Prevention	DHEW	Department of Health Education and Welfare
CST	Central standard time	DHHS	Department of Health and Human Services
CT	certified teacher		
cts.	cents	DHS	demographic and health surveys
CTSA	Catholic Theological Society of America		
		DHT	dihydrotestosterone
CTW	Children's Television Network	diag.	diagonal, diagram
CU	Consumer's Union	diam.	diameter
CURE	Citizens United for Responsible Education	dict.	dictionary
		dif.	difference
CUSA	cavitron ultrasonic surgical aspirator	DINK	double-income; no kids
		dir.	director
CVA	Columbia Valley Authority	disc.	discharged, discontinue, discount, discovered
CVS	chorionic villi sampling		
CW	conventional wisdom	dist.	district, distance
CWA	Concerned Women for America	div.	dividend, division, divorced
CWLA	Child Welfare League of America	DIY	do-it-yourself
		DLC	Democratic Leadership Council
CWO	chief warrant officer	DLO	Dead Letter Office
CWU	Church Women United	DM	deutsche mark
CYO	Catholic Youth Organization	DMPA	depot-medroxyprogesterone acetate (Depo-Provera)

D

		DMV	Department of Motor Vehicles
D.A.	district attorney	DMZ	demilitarized zone
D&C	dilatation and curettage	DNA	deoxyribonucleic acid
D&E	dilatation and evacuation	DNC	Democratic National Committee
DAR	Daughters of the American Revolution	DNR	do not resuscitate
		D.O.A.	dead on arrival
DARE	Drug Abuse Resistance Education	doc.	doctor, document
DAT	digital audio tape	DOD	Department of Defense
DAV	Disabled American Veterans	DOE	Department of Energy
dbl.	double	dol.	dollar
DC	developed country	DOM	Deo optimo maximo (to God the best and greatest), domestic, dominion
DC	District of Columbia		
DC	Doctor of Chiropractic		
DCL	Doctor of Canon Law	DOS	disk operating system
DD	Doctor of Divinity	DOT	Department of Transportation
DDC	Dewey Decimal Classification	doz.	dozen
DDS	Doctor of Dental Surgery	DPA	durable power of attorney
DDT	dichlorodiphenyltrichloroethane	D.PH.	Doctor of Philosophy
DEA	Drug Enforcement Administration	DPW	Department of Public Works

DRG	diagnosis-related group	Ens.	ensign
DSC	Distinguished Service Cross	ENTA	norethindrone acetate
DSM	Diagnostic and Statistical Manual	EO	executive order
DSOC	Democratic Socialist Organizing Committee	EOE	equal opportunity employer
DSS	delayed shock syndrome	EPA	Environmental Protection Agency
DST	daylight saving time	EPC	Environmental Policy Center
D.TH.	Doctor of Theology	EPCOT	Experimental Prototype Community of Tomorrow
DV	Deo volente (God willing), Douay Version	Eph.	Ephesians
		epit.	epitaph
D.V.M.	Doctor of Veterinary Medicine	ERA	earned run average, Equal Rights Amendment
DWI	driving while intoxicated		
		ERC	Ethical Research Committee

E

EAB	ethics advisory board	ERIS	Exoatmospheric Reentry Intercept System
EAF	Environmental Action Foundation	ESA	European Space Agency
EC	European Community	ESF	economic support funds
eccl.	ecclesiastic, ecclesiastical	ESL	English as a second language
Eccles	Ecclesiastes	ESP	extra-sensory perception
ECG	electrocardiogram	esq.	esquire
ECMO	extracorporeal membrane oxygenation	est.	established, estimate, estimated
		EST	Eastern standard time
ECO	Economic Cooperation Organization	Estr.	Esther
		ET	embryo transfer
ecol.	ecology, ecological	ETA	estimated time of arrival
econ.	economic, economist, economy	etc.	et cetera
ECOSOC	Economic and Social Council (UN)	Eth	Ethiopia
		ETO	estimated time of ovulation
Ecua.	Ecuador	et seq	et sequens (and the following one)
EDF	Environmental Defense Fund		
EDT	Eastern daylight time	Eur.	Europe, European
educ.	education, educational	exec.	executive, execute
EE	engaged encounter	exp.	expense, experimental
EE2	ethinyl estradiol	Exod.	Exodus
EEC	European Economic Community	ext.	extension, exterior
EEG	electroencephalogram	Ezek.	Ezekiel
EEOC	Equal Employment Opportunity Commission		

F

EFM	electronic fetal monitoring	F	(degrees) Fahrenheit
EFT	electronic funds transfer	FAA	Federal Aviation Administration
EFTA	European Free Trade Association	FAA	Foreign Assistance Act
e.g.	exempli gratia (for example)	FACP	Fellow of the American College of Physicians
EGF	epidermal growth factor		
EIB	European Investment Bank	FACS	Fellow of the American College of Surgeons
EIFT	embryo intrafallopian transfer		
EIS	environmental impact statement	FACS	fluorescence-activated cell sorter
EKG	electrocardiogram	Fahr.	Fahrenheit
elec.	electric, electrical, electrician, electricity	FAM	fertility awareness method
		FAO	Food and Agricultural Organization
elem.	elementary, element		
elev.	elevation	FAS	Federation of American Scientists
ELISA	enzyme-linked immunosorbent assay	FAS	fetal alcohol syndrome
		FBI	Federal Bureau of Investigation
emb.	embassy	FCC	Federal Communications Commission
EMI	electromagnetic interference		
EMP	electromagnetic pulse	FDA	Food and Drug Administration
Eng.	English, England	FDIC	Federal Deposit Insurance Corp.
Engr.	engraver, engineer	Feb.	February

FEC   Federal Elections Commission
fed.   federal, federation
FEHB   Federal Employee's Health Benefits
fem.   female, feminine
FET   Federal Excise Tax
FEW   Federally Employed Women
FFP   Friends of Family Planning
FHA   Federal Housing Administration
FHA   Future Homemakers of America
FHI   Family Health International
FICA   Federal Insurance Contributions Act
Finn.   Finland, Finnish
Fla.   Florida
Flem.   Flemish
FISH   fluorescent in-situ hybridization
FNMA   Federal National Mortgage Association (Fannie Mae)
FOA   field operating activity
FOE   Fraternal Order of Eagles
FOIA   Freedom of Information Act
FORTRAN   formula translation
FPA   family planning associates
FPA   Family Protection Act
FRB   Federal Reserve Board
FRC   Family Research Council
FRCP   Fellow of the Royal College of Physicians London
FRCS   Fellow of the Royal College of Surgeons London
freq.   frequency
FRG   Federal Republic of Germany (former West Germany)
Fri.   Friday
FSA   Free Speech Advocates
FSH   follicle-stimulating hormone
FSP   fallopian tube sperm perfusion
FTA-Abs   fluorescent treponemal antibody-absorption
FTC   Federal Trade Commission
FUBAR   fouled up beyond all recognition
FY   fiscal year
FYI   for your information
FZ   Franc Zone

G

G   grand ($1,000)
G7   Group of Seven
G-77   Group of 77
Ga.   Georgia
gal.   gallon
GAO   General Accounting Office
GATT   General Agreement on Tariffs and Trade
GB   gigabyte
GDABM   Global Defense Against Ballistic Missiles

GDP   gross domestic product
GDR   German Democratic Republic (formerly East Germany)
GED   general equivalency diploma
Gen.   Genesis
genl.   general
geog.   geography, geographical
geol.   geology, geological
geom.   geometry
Ger.   Germany, German
glos.   glossary
GI   government issue
GIFT   gamete intra-fallopian transfer
GMC   General Medical Council
GM-CSF   granulocyte-macrophage colony-stimulating factor
GMT   Greenwich mean time
GNP   gross national product
GOBs   good old boys
GOMER   get out of my emergency room (a hopeless trauma case)
GOP   Grand Old Party (Republican)
GORK   God only really knows
govt.   government
GP   general practitioner
GPA   grade-point average
GPO   Government Printing Office
GRE   Graduate Record Examination
gro.   gross
GSA   General Services Administration
GSA   Genetics Society of America
GSA   Girl Scouts of America
Guat.   Guatamala

H

Hag.   Haggai
H.B.   house bill
HBO   Home Box Office
HCAP   handicap
HDBK   handbook
HDS   Human Development Services
HDTV   high-definition television
Heb.   Hebrews, Hebrew
HEW   Department of Health, Education, and Welfare
hgt.   height
hist.   history, historian
H.J.R.   House joint resolution
HATTS   test for syphilis
HC   Holy Communion
HC   House of Commons
HCFA   Health Care Financing Administration
HCG   human chorionic gonadotrophin
HCS   human chorionic somatomammotropin
HD   Huntington's disease
HDDA   Humane and Dignified Death Act

HDL	high-density lipoprotein (cholesterol)	ICC	International Chamber of Commerce
HEW	Department of Health Education and Welfare	ICC	Interstate Commerce Commission
HGP	Human Genome Project	ICD	intracervical device
HHS	Department of Health and Human Services	Ice.	Iceland
		ICFTU	International Confederation of Free Trade Unions
HIT	herd of independent thinkers (syndrome)	ICJ	International Court of Justice
HIV	human immunodeficiency virus	ICRC	International Committee of the Red Cross
HIV-Ag	human immunodeficiency virus antigen	ICU	intensive care unit
		IDA	International Development Association
HL	House of Lords		
HLA	Human Life Amendment	IDDS	Institute for Defense and Disarmament Studies
HMS	His or Her Majesty's Ship or Service	IEA	International Energy Agency
HMG	human menopausal gonadotrophin	IEC	institutional ethics committee
		IF	intellectual freedom
HMO	health maintenance organization	IFC	International Finance Corporation
hon.	honor, honorable, honorary	IFGR	International Foundation for Genetic Research (The Michael Fund)
Hond.	Honduras		
HOPE	Housing Opportunities for People Everywhere		
		IFN	interferon
hort.	horticulture	IGF	insulin-like growth factor
Hos.	Hosea	ign.	ignition
hosp.	hospital	IGY	International Geophysical Year
HOV	high-occupancy vehicle	IHM	(Servants of the) Immaculate Heart of Mary
HQ	headquarters		
HRH	His or Her Royal Highness	IHS	Indian Health Service
hrs.	hours	IIB	International Investment Bank
HRT	hormone replacement therapy	IIE	Institute of International Education
HSA	Health Systems Agencies		
HSLDA	Home School Legal Defense Association	IIED	International Institute for Environment and Development
HST	Hawaiian standard time		
HTLV	human T-cell lymphotropic virus	ILA	International Longshoreman's Association
hts.	heights		
HUAC	House Un-American Activities Committee	ILGWU	International Ladies' Garment Workers' Union
HUD	Department of Housing and Urban Development	Ill.	Illinois
		ILO	International Labor Organization
HUGO	Human Genome Organization	ILS	International Life Services
Hung.	Hungary	IME	Institute of Medical Ethics
HV	humanae vitae	IMF	International Monetary Fund
hwy.	highway	IMHO	in my humble opinion
		IMP	imprimatur (let it be printed)
I		Inc.	incorporated
IADB	Inter-American Development Bank	incl.	included, including, inclusive
IAEA	International Atomic Energy Agency	Ind.	Indiana, independent, included, inclusive
		info.	information
IBEC	International Bank for Economic Cooperation	init.	initial
ibid.	in the same place	INRI	Iesus Nazarenus Rex Iudaeorum (Jesus of Nazareth, King of the Jews)
IBM	International Business Machine		
ICAO	International Civil Aviation Organization	INS	Immigration and Naturalization Service
ICBM	intercontinental ballistic missile	insp.	inspector

inst.	institute, instructor, instrument, institution	IVH	intraventricular hemorrhage
int.	intelligence, interest	IVIG	intravenous immunoglobulin
INTELSAT	International Telecommunications Satellite Organization	IWHC	International Women's Health Coalition
intl.	international	IWO	Institute for World Order
INTERPOL	International Criminal Police Organization	IWW	Industrial Workers of the World
		IWY	International Women's Year
IOC	International Olympic Committee	IYC	International Year of the Child
IOOF	Independent Order of Odd Fellows	IYD	International Year of the Disabled

J

IOOF	International Order of Odd Fellows
IOU	I owe you
IPA	International Phonetic Alphabet
IPPF	International Planned Parenthood Federation
IPS	Institute for Policy Studies
IRA	individual retirement account
I.R.A.	Irish Republican Army
IRBM	intermediate range ballistic missile
IRC	International Red Cross
IRD	Institute for Resource Development, Westinghouse
Ire.	Ireland
irr.	irregular
IRS	Internal Revenue Service
Isa.	Isaiah
ISBC	International Small Business Consortium
ISBN	International Standard Book Number
isl.	island
ISO	International Organization for Standardization
Isr.	Israel
ISTI	International Science and Technology Institute, Inc.
ital.	italic, italicized
ITC	investment tax credit
ITOP	induced termination of pregnancy
IUB	intrauterine occlusion body
IUCD	intrauterine contraceptive device
IUD	intrauterine device
IUI	intrauterine insemination
IUP	intrauterine pregnancy
IUSSP	International Union for the Scientific Study of Population
IV	intravenous
IVD	intravas device
IVF	in-vitro fertilization
IVF-DE	IVF-donor embryo
IVF-DO	IVF-donor ova
IVF-DS	IVF-donor sperm
IVF-SET	IVF-surrogate embryo transfer

Jam.	Jamaica
JAMA	Journal of the American Medical Association
Jan.	January
Jap.	Japan, Japanese
JBS	John Birch Society
JCAH	Joint Commission on the Accreditation of Hospitals
JCB	Bachelor of Canon Law
JCHA	Joint Committee of Hospital Associations
JCL	Licentiate in Canon Law
JCS	joint chiefs of staff
jct.	junction
JD	Juris Doctor (Doctor of Law)
JDL	Jewish Defense League
Jer.	Jeremiah
JLC	Juvenile Law Center
JP	Justice of the Peace
JSD	Doctor of Juristic Science
Jul.	July
Jun.	June
JW	Jehovah's Witness

K

Kan(s).	Kansas
KB	kilobyte
KGB	Soviet State Security Committee
KI	karyopyknotic index
KIA	killed in action
KISS	keep it simple stupid
KJV	King James Version
KKK	Ku Klux Klan
K of C	Knights of Columbus
K of P	Knights of Pythias
KPH	kilometers per hour
KS	Kaposi's sarcoma
KWH	kilowatt-hour
Ky.	Kentucky

L

La.	Louisiana
L.A.	Latin America
Lab.	Labrador, laboratory
Lam.	Lamentations

lang.	language	Matt.	Matthew
LAPD	Los Angeles Police Department	max.	maximum
LAS	League of Arab States (Arab League)	MB	megabyte
		MBA	Master of Business Administration
LASER	light amplification by stimulated emission of radiation	MBS	Mutual Broadcasting System
Lat.	Latvia, latitude	MC	member of Congress
lav.	lavatory	Md.	Maryland
LAW	Legal Action for Women	MD	medical doctor
lbs.	pounds	MDA	Muscular Dystrophy Association
LC	Library of Congress	MDT	mountain daylight time
LCD	lowest common denominator, liquid crystal display	ME	marriage encounter
		ME	medical examiner
LCL	League of Catholic Laymen	Med.	Mediterranean, medicine, medical, medium
LD50	lethal dose 50%		
LDC	less-developed country	MEP	multiple exposure photography
LDL	low-density lipoprotein (cholesterol)	MeSH	medical subject headings
		Mex.	Mexico
LDS	Latter-Day Saints (Mormons)	mfd.	manufactured
Leb.	Lebanon	mfg.	manufacturing
LED	light-emitting diode	MG	Myasthenia Gravis
Lev.	Leviticus	MHD	magnetohydrodynamics
lgth.	length	MIA	missing in action
lieut.	lieutenant	MIC	maternal and infant care
LII	Life Issues Institute	Mic.	Micah
Lith.	Lithuania	Mich.	Michigan
LLB	Bachelor of Law	MICU	medical intensive care unit
LLD	Doctor of Law	mil.	million, military
LLDC	least developed country	min.	minor, minute
LLLI	La Leche League International	Minn.	Minnesota
LLM	Master of Law	MIRV	multiple independently-targeted reentry vehicles
loc.	location		
log.	logarithm	misc.	miscellaneous
long.	longitude	Miss.	Mississippi
LOOM	Loyal Order of Moose	MIT	Massachusetts Institute of Technology
LORAN	long-range navigation		
LORCS	League of Red Cross and Red Crescent Societies	Mlle.	mademoiselle
		MM	Maryknoll Missioners
LPGA	Ladies Professional Golf Association	Mme.	madame
		Mo.	Missouri
LPN	licensed practical nurse	MoD	March of Dimes
LRF	luteinizing releasing factor	Mon.	Monday
LSC	Legal Services Corporation	Mont.	Montana
LSD	lysergic acid; pounds sterling, shillings, pence	MP	member of parliament
		MPA	master of public administration, medroxyprogesterone acetate (Depo-Provera)
LSMT	life-sustaining medical treatment		
ltd.	limited		
LTL	laparoscopic tubal ligation	MPG	miles per gallon
Lux.	Luxembourg	MPH	master of public health, miles per hour
LWV	League of Women Voters		
		Mrs.	mistress
	M	MPS	mucopolysaccharidoses
		MS	Master of Science
MA	Master of Arts	MS	multiple sclerosis
MAD	mutual assured destruction	Msgr.	monsignor
maj.	major	M. Sgt.	master sergeant
MAR	mixed antiglobulin reaction	mss.	manuscript
MASH	mobile army surgical hospital	MST	mountain standard time
Mass.	Massachusetts		

MSW	Master of Social Work
MVP	most valuable player
MX	missile experimental
MYOB	mind your own business

N

NAACP	National Association for the Advancement of Colored People
NAB	National Association of Broadcasters
Nah.	Nahum
NAM	New Age movement
NAS	National Academy of Sciences
NAS	National Association of Scholars
NAS	National Audobon Society
NASA	National Aeronautics and Space Administration
NASCAR	National Association of Stock Car Auto Racing
NASDAQ	National Association of Securities Dealers Automated Quotations
NASW	National Association of Social Workers
NATO	North Atlantic Treaty Organization
naut.	nautical
NAWL	National Association of Women Lawyers
NAZI	Nationalen Socialisten (National Socialist Workers Party or Nazis)
NBA	National Basketball Association
NBC	National Broadcasting Company
NBFO	National Black Feminists Organization
NBS	National Bureau of Standards
N.C.	North Carolina
NCADV	National Coalition Against Domestic Violence
NCAA	National Collegiate Athletic Association
NCAN	National Coalition of American Nuns
NCC	National Catholic Coalition
NCC	National Council of Churches
NCCB	National Council of Catholic Bishops
NCCC	National Council of Catholic Charities
NCCJ	National Conference of Christians and Jews
NCCL	National Committee of Catholic Laymen
NCCL	National Coalition of Clergy and Laity
NCCM	National Council of Catholic Men
NCCW	National Council of Catholic Women

NCCY	National Committee for Children and Youth
NCHE	National Council on Higher Education
NCHS	National Center for Health Statistics
NCI	National Cancer Institute
NCO	non-commissioned officer
NCOG	National Council of Obstetrics and Gynecology
NCPAC	National Conservative Political Action Committee
NCSE	National Center for Science Education
NDA	National Dental Association
NDA	new drug application (for the Food and Drug Administration)
N. Dak.	North Dakota
NEA	National Education Association
NEA	National Endowment for the Arts
NEA	Nuclear Energy Agency
Neb(r).	Nebraska
neg.	negative
NEH	National Endowment for the Humanities
Neh.	Nehemiah
NEJM	New England Journal of Medicine
NEN	norethindrone acetate
NET	norethindrone
NET-EN	norethisterone enanthate
Neth.	Netherlands
Nev.	Nevada
NFL	National Football League
NGO	nongovernmental organization
NGU	nongonococcal urethritis
N.H.	New Hampshire
NHI	National Health Insurance (Britain)
NHL	National Hockey League
NHS	National Health Service
NIAAA	National Institute of Alcohol Abuse and Alcoholism
NIC	newly industrializing country
NIDA	National Institute on Drug Abuse
NIE	National Institute for Education
NIE	newly industrializing economy
NIH	National Institute of Health
NIMBY	not in my back yard
NIMH	National Institute of Mental Health
NIT	National Invitational Tournament
N.J.	New Jersey
NLF	National Liberation Front
NLG	National Lawyers Guild
NLRB	National Labor Relations Board
NMA	National Medical Association
N. Mex.	New Mexico

NMR	nuclear magnetic resonance (spectroscopy)
NOPE	National Optimum Population Effort
Nor.	Norway
NORAD	North American Air Defense Command
nos.	numbers
Nov.	November
NOW	National Organization for Women
NPC	National People's Congress
NPG	Negative Population Growth
NPR	National Public Radio
NRA	National Rifle Association
NRC	National Research Council
NRC	Nuclear Regulatory Commission
NRCA	Natural Resources Council of America
NRDA	Natural Resources Defense Association
NRDC	National Resource Defense Council
NSA	National Security Agency
NSC	National Security Council
NSF	National Science Foundation
NSNA	National Student Nurses Association
NSW	New South Wales
NT	New Testament
NTD	neural tube defect
NTSB	National Transportation and Safety Board
nt. wt.	net weight
NUL	National Urban League
num.	numbers
NWF	National Wildlife Federation
NWPC	National Women's Political Caucus
NWT	Northwest Territories
NYA	National Youth Administration
N.Y.	New York
NYC	New York City
NYSE	New York Stock Exchange

O

OAPEC	Organization of Arab Petroleum Exporting Countries
OAS	Organization of American States
OAU	Organization of African Unity
Obad.	Obadiah
O.B.E.	Officer of the Order of the British Empire
OB-GYN	obstetrics-gynecology
obit.	obituary
OBO	or best offer
OC	oral contraceptive
OC	Order of Cistercians
OCA	Office of Consumer Affairs

OCA	Orthodox Church of America
OCarm	Order of Carmelites
OCart	Order of Carthusians
OCI	ovum capture inhibitor
OCS	officer candidate school
Oct.	October
OEA	Office of Environmental Affairs
OEO	Office of Economic Opportunity
OES	Order of the Eastern Star
OGC	Office of General Council
OI	osteogenesis imperfecta
Okla.	Oklahoma
OM	ovulation method
OMB	Office of Management and Budget
ONI	Office of Naval Intelligence
Ont.	Ontario
OOB	off-off Broadway
op cit	opere citato (in the work cited)
OPEC	Organization of Petroleum Exporting Countries
OPM	Office of Personnel Management
Orch.	orchestra
Ore(g).	Oregon
org.	organization
orig.	original, origins
OSA	Order of St. Augustine
OSB	Order of St. Benedict (Benedictines)
OSF	Order of St. Francis
OSHA	Occupational Safety and Health Administration
OSS	Office of Strategic Services
OT	occupational therapy, Old Testament, ovum transfer
OTA	Office of Technology Assessment
OTB	off-track betting
OTC	over the counter
OTGH	Old-Time Gospel Hour
oz.	ounce, ounces

P

P.C.	politically correct
P.R.	public relations
Pa.	Pennsylvania
PA	physicians assistant, power of attorney, public address
PAC	Political action committee, Pacific
PAF	platelet-activating factor
PAHO	Pan American Health Organization
Pak.	Pakistan
Pan.	Panama
Par.	Paraguay
PAU	Pan American Union
PAW	People for the American Way
PBA	Professional Bowlers Association
PBK	Phi Beta Kappa

PBS	Public Broadcasting System
PC	personal computer, population communication
PCA	Permanent Court of Arbitration
PCA	Presbyterian Church in America
PCI	Population Communications International
PCO	polycystic ovary syndrome
pct.	percentage
PCUSA	Presbyterian Church of the USA
PD	peak day
PDA	Pregnancy Disability Act
PDQ	pretty damn quick
PDR	Physicians Desk Reference
PDT	Pacific daylight time
PECAM	platelet endothelial cell adhesion molecule
PEI	Prince Edward Island
PEN	(International Association of) Poets, Playwrights, Editors, Essayists, and Novelists
Penn.	Pennsylvania
Per.	Persia
PFC	private first class
PGA	Professional Golfers' Association
PHA	Public Housing Administration
phar.	pharmaceutical, pharmacy
Ph.D.	Philosophiae doctor (Doctor of Philosophy)
Phil.	Philippians
PHS	Public Health Service
PI	Pearl Index
PI	Population Institute
PI	private investigator (private eye)
PID	pelvic inflammatory disease
PIH	pyridoxal isonicotinoyl hydrazone
PIN	personal identification number
PIRG	Public Interest Research Group
PK	psychokinesis
PKU	phenylketonuria
PLO	Palestinian Liberation Organization
PMS	pre-menstrual syndrome
PND	prenatal diagnosis
PO	post office
POC	prisoners of conscience
POC	products of conception
Pol.	Poland
POM	public opinion message
pop.	population
Port.	Portugal
POV	point of view
POW	prisoner of war
PP	Planned Parenthood
PP5	placental protein 5
PPD	post-partum depression, postpaid, prepaid
PPFA	Planned Parenthood Federation of America

PPFC	Planned Parenthood Federation of Canada
PPNG	penicillinase-producing neisseria gonorrhea
PPP	Planned Parenthood Physicians
PPS	additional postscript
PRB	Population Reference Bureau
PRC	People's Republic of China
pres.	president
PRO	public relations officer, professional
prof.	professor
Prot.	Protestant
Prov.	Proverbs
PS	postscriptum (postscript)
PSA	public service announcement, Psalms
PSHA	Public Service Health Act
PSI	Population Services International
PST	Pacific standard time
PSYOPS	psychological operations
PTA	Parent-Teacher Association
PTO	Patent and Trademark Office
PTSD	post-traumatic stress disorder
PVS	persistent vegetative state
pvt.	private

Q

QALY	quality adjusted life years
QED	quod erat demonstrandum (proof of question)
QEF	which was to be done
QOL	quality of life

R

R	(degrees) Rankine
R&D	research and development
RAAF	Royal Australian Air Force
RAF	Royal Air Force
RAM	random access memory
RBI	runs batted in
RC	Roman Catholic
RCA	Reformed Church of America
RCAF	Royal Canadian Air Force
RCMP	Royal Canadian Mounted Police
RCP	Royal College of Physicians (England)
RCS	Royal College of Surgeons
rct.	receipt, recruit
RD	rural delivery
RDA	recommended daily allowance
REM	rapid eye movement
Rep.	Republican, representative, republic
req.	request
ret.	retired
Rev.	Revelations, reverend
RFD	rural free delivery

RFRA	Religious Freedom Restoration Act
RH	rhesus (positive or negative)
R.I.	Rhode Island
RICO	Racketeering-Influenced Corrupt Organizations Act
RIP	requiescat in pace (rest in peace)
RM	reichsmark (currency used in Nazi Germany)
rms.	rooms
RN	registered nurse
RNA	ribonucleic acid
RNC	Republican National Committee
ROC	Republic of China (Taiwan)
ROK	Republic of Korea (South Korea)
ROM	read-only memory, Roman, Romania, Romans
ROTC	Reserve Officers Training Corps
RPM	revolutions per minute
RSA	Republic of South Africa
RSV	Revised Standard Version
rte.	route
RU	Roussel-Uclaf
Russ.	Russia
RVN	Republic of Viet Nam
rwy.	railway

S

S&M	sadomasochism
SA	Salvation Army
SA	spontaneous abortion (miscarriage)
SAA	Society for Applied Anthropology
SAC	State Advisory Committee, Strategic Air Command
SAD	seasonal affective disorder
SADC	Southern African Development Community
SAG	Screen Actors Guild
SAIDS	simian (monkey) acquired immune deficiency syndrome
SALT	Strategic Arms Limitation Talks
SAM	Society for Adolescent Medicine
SAM	surface-to-air missle
SAMA	Student American Medical Association
Sask.	Saskatchewan
Sat.	Saturday
SAT	Scholastic Aptitude Test
SB	senate bill
SBA	Small Business Administration
SBC	School-based clinic
S.C.	South Carolina
SC	Sisters of Charity
Scand.	Scandinavia
ScD	Doctor of Science
sch.	school
sci.	science
sci-fi	science-fiction

SCLC	Southern Christian Leadership Conference
Scot.	Scotland
SCUBA	self-contained underwater breathing apparatus
SD	senile dementia, standard deviation
SD	Strategic Defense Development and Deployment
S. Dak.	South Dakota
SDAT	senile dementia, Alzheimer's type
SDC	Social Development Center
SDI	Strategic Defense Initiative
SDS	Students for a Democratic Society
SEAL	SeaAirLand (Navy)
SEATO	Southeast Asia Treaty Organization
SEC	Securities Exchange Commission
secy.	secretary
SEM	scanning electron microscope
sen.	senator, senate
Sept.	September
sess.	session
SFRY	Socialist Federal Republic of Yugoslavia
SG	surgeon general
sgd.	signed
sgt.	sergeant
SIDS	sudden infant death syndrome
SIFT	sperm intrafallopian transfer
SIG	special interest group
SIM	simian immunodeficiency virus
SJ	Society of Jesus (Jesuits)
SJD	Doctor of Juridical Science
SJR	Senate Joint Resolution
SLBM	submarine-launched ballistic missiles
SLC	Salt Lake City
SM	Society of Mary
SMP	Social Marketing Project
SMSA	Standard Metropolitan Statistical Area
SNAFU	situation normal (all fouled up)
SNCC	Student Non-Violent Coordinating Committee
soc.	society, socialist
SOMARC	Social Marketing for Change
SOP	standard operating procedure
SOR	Shield of Roses
SOS	distress signal
SP1	pregnancy-specific beta 1-glycoprotein
SPA-TP	staphylococcal protein A-IgG
SPC	South Pacific Commission
SPCA	Society for the Prevention of Cruelty to Animals
spec.	specialist, special, species, specification

SPF	South Pacific Forum	Thu(rs).	Thursday
SPHA	solid-phase hemadsorption assay	TKO	technical knockout
SPI	Sisters of Perpetual Indulgence	TLC	tender loving care
SPQR	senate and people of Rome	TM	transcendental meditation
SRA	Science Research Associates	TNT	trinitrotoluene
SRA	State's Rights Amendment	T.O.P.	(Dominican) Third Order of
Sra.	senora		Penance
SRD	Society for the Right to Die	topo.	topographical
SRO	single room occupancy, standing	TP	treponema pallidum
	room only	trig.	trigonometry
SRP	Short rib-polydactyly syndrome	Trin.	Trinidad
srta.	Senorita	TRO	temporary restraining order
SS	saints	TSC	Teachers Saving Children
SS	Schutzstaffel (elite Nazi Unit)	TSD	Tay-Sachs disease
SSA	Social Security Act	tsp.	teaspoon
SSA	Social Security Administration	Tue(s).	Tuesday
S. Sgt.	staff sergeant	Turk.	Turkey
SSN	social security number	TVA	Tennessee Valley Authority
SSS	Selective Service System	TWIMC	to whom it may concern
S-T	sympto-thermal (method)	TWP	township
START	strategic arms reduction treaty		
STD	standard		**U**
Ste.	saint (female)	UAE	United Arab Emirates
STM	sympto-thermal method	UAW	United Auto, Aircraft, and
STP	standard temperature and pressure		Agricultural Implements
subj.	subject		Workers of America
Sun.	Sunday	UCC	United Church of Christ
supt.	superintendent, support	UCLA	University of California at Los
surg.	surgery, surgeon		Angeles
SWAK	sealed with a kiss	UCMJ	Uniform Code of Military Justice
SUZI	sub-zonal insemination	UCS	Union of Concerned Scientists
SV	Soror Vitae (Sisters of Life)	UDDA	Uniform Determination of Death
SWAT	Special Weapons and Tactics		Act
Swed.	Sweden	UER	user effectiveness rate
SWS	Sociologists for Women in	UFO	unidentified flying object
	Society	UFT	United Federation of Teachers
SYL	Spartacus Youth League	UFW	United Farm Workers
syll.	syllable	UHF	ultra-high frequency
Syr.	Syria	UMC	United Methodist Church
sys.	system	UMW	United Mine Workers
		UN	United Nations
	T	UNCF	United Negro College Fund
TA	transabdominal	UNCTAD	United Nations Conference on
TANSTAAFL	there ain't no such thing as a		Trade and Development
	free lunch	UNDIESA	United Nations Department of
Tasm.	Tasmania		International Economic and
TBA	to be announced		Social Affairs
TBS	tablespoon	UNDP	United Nations Development
TC	transcervical		Program
TEF	The Environmental Fund	UNEP	United Nations Environment
tel.	telephone, telegram		Program
temp.	temperature, temporary, template	UNESCO	United Nations Educational,
Tenn.	Tennessee		Scientific, and Cultural
ter(r).	territory		Organization
Tex.	Texas	UNFAO	United Nations Food and
TFR	total fertility rate		Agricultural Organization
TGIF	thank God it's Friday	UNFPA	United Nations Fund for
ThD	Doctor of Theology		Population Activities

UNICEF	United Nations Children's Emergency Fund
UNIDO	United Nations International Development Organization
UNPROFOR	United Nations Protection Force
UNTSO	United Nations Truce Supervision Organization
UPC	Universal Product Code
UPI	United Press International
UPS	United Parcel Service
UPS	uterine progesterone system
UPU	Universal Postal Union
UPUSA	United Presbyterians USA
URC	University Research Corporation
Uru.	Uruguay
USA	United States of America
USA	United States Army
USAF	United States Air Force
USAID	United States Agency for International Development
USCC	United States Catholic Conference
USCG	United States Coast Guard
USCRC	United States Civil Rights Commission
USCSC	United States Civil Service Commission
USDA	United States Department of Agriculture
USGPO	United States Government Printing Office
USIA	United States Information Agency
USMA	United States Military Academy
USMC	United States Marine Corps
USN	United States Navy
USNA	United States Naval Academy
USNG	United States National Guard
USNR	United States Naval Reserve
USO	United Service Organizations
USOC	United States Olympic Committee
USPO	United States Patent Office
USPS	United States Postal Service
USS	United States ship
USSR	Union of Soviet Socialist Republics
USTA	United States Tennis Association
UTI	urinary tract infection
UUA	Unitarian Universalist Association
UWA	United Way of America

V

Va.	Virginia
VA	Veterans Administration
VAT	value-added tax
VBAC	vaginal birth after Cesarian (section)

VCR	videocassette recorder
VD	venereal disease
Ven.	Venezuela
ver.	verse, version
vert.	vertical
vet.	veteran, veterinarian
VFW	Veterans of Foreign Wars
VIP	very important person, voter identification project
visc.	viscount
VISTA	Volunteers in Service to America
VOA	Voice of America
vol.	volume, volunteer
VP	vice president
VSC	voluntary surgical contraception
Vt.	Vermont
VTOL	vertical takeoff and landing

W

WAAC	Women's Army Auxiliary Corps
WAAF	Women's Auxiliary Air Force
WAC	Women's Army Corps
WAF	Women in the Air Force
Wash.	Washington
WASP	white Anglo-Saxon Protestant
WATS	Wide Area Telephone System
WBA	World Boxing Association
WCC	World Council of Churches
WCL	World Confederation of Labor
Wed.	Wednesday
WEU	Western European Union
WFC	World Food Council
WFP	World Food Program
WFTU	World Federation of Trade Unions
WHCA	White House Conference on Aging
WHCCY	White House Conference on Children and Youth
WHCF	White House Conference on Families
WHCH	White House Conference on Hunger
WHO	World Health Organization
WIC	Women's International Conference
WIPO	World Intellectual Property Organization
Wis(c).	Wisconsin
wkly.	weekly
WLDF	Women's Legal Defense Fund
WLF	Washington Legal Foundation
WMA	Women's Medical Association
WMA	World Medical Association
WMO	World Meteorological Organization
WNBA	Women's National Basketball Association
WP	Warsaw Pact

WPA	Works Progress Administration	yds.	yards
WPC	World Population Council	yrs.	years
WPM	words per minute	YMCA	Young Men's Christian Association
WPS	World Population Society		
WRAF	Women's Royal Air Force	YMHA	Young Men's Hebrew Association
WRI	World Resources Institute	YWCA	Young Women's Christian Association
WTO	World Trade Organization		
W. Va	West Virginia	YWHA	Young Women's Hebrew Association
WWF	World Wildlife Fund		
WWI	Worldwatch Institute		
Wyo.	Wyoming		

X

xing. crossing

Y

YAF Young America Foundation
YAF Young Americans for Freedom
YCL Young Communist League

Z

ZACE zoapatle aqueous crude extract
ZDV zidovudine
Zech. Zechariah
Zeph. Zephaniah
ZIP zone improvement plan
ZOG Zionist Occupation Government
ZPG zero population growth

Academy Award Winners

1997
Best Picture: *Titanic*
Best Actress: Kate Winslet, *Titanic*
Best Actor: Jack Nicholson, *As Good as It Gets*
Best Supporting Actor: Robin Williams, *Good Will Hunting*
Best Supporting Actress: Kim Basinger, *L.A. Confidential*
Best Director: James Cameron, *Titanic*
Best Song: "My Heart Will Go On," *Titanic*

1996
Best Picture: *The English Patient*
Best Actress: Frances McDormand, *Fargo*
Best Actor: Geoffrey Rush, *Shine*
Best Supporting Actor: Cuba Gooding Jr., *Jerry Maguire*
Best Supporting Actress: Juliette Binoche, *The English Patient*
Best Director: Anthony Minghella, *The English Patient*
Best Song: "You Must Love Me," *Evita*

1995
Best Picture: *Braveheart*
Best Actress: Susan Sarandon, *Dead Man Walking*
Best Actor: Nicolas Cage, *Leaving Las Vegas*
Best Supporting Actor: Kevin Spacey, *The Usual Suspects*
Best Supporting Actress: Mira Sorvino, *Mighty Aphrodite*

Best Director: Mel Gibson, *Braveheart*
Best Song: "Colors of the Wind," *Pocahontas*

1994
Best Picture: *Forrest Gump*
Best Actress: Jessica Lange, *Blue Sky*
Best Actor: Tom Hanks, *Forrest Gump*
Best Supporting Actor: Martin Landau, *Ed Wood*
Best Supporting Actress: Dianne Wiest, *Bullets over Broadway*
Best Director: Robert Zemeckis, *Forrest Gump*
Best Song: "Can You Feel the Love Tonight," *The Lion King*

1993
Best Picture: *Schindler's List*
Best Actress: Holly Hunter, *The Piano*
Best Actor: Tom Hanks, *Philadelphia*
Best Supporting Actor: Tommy Lee Jones, *The Fugitive*
Best Supporting Actress: Anna Paquin, *The Piano*
Best Director: Steven Spielberg, *Schindler's List*
Best Song: "Streets of Philadelphia," *Philadelphia*

1992
Best Picture: *Unforgiven*
Best Actress: Emma Thompson, *Howards End*

Best Actor: Al Pacino, *Scent of a Woman*
Best Supporting Actor: Gene Hackman, *Unforgiven*
Best Supporting Actress: Marisa Tomei, *My Cousin Vinny*
Best Director: Clint Eastwood, *Unforgiven*
Best Song: "A Whole New World," *Aladdin*

1991
Best Picture: *The Silence of the Lambs*
Best Actress: Jodie Foster, *The Silence of the Lambs*
Best Actor: Anthony Hopkins, *The Silence of the Lambs*
Best Supporting Actor: Jack Palance, *City Slickers*
Best Supporting Actress: Mercedes Ruehl, *The Fisher King*
Best Director: Jonathan Demme, *The Silence of the Lambs*
Best Song: "Beauty and the Beast," *Beauty and the Beast*

1990
Best Picture: *Dances with Wolves*
Best Actress: Kathy Bates, *Misery*
Best Actor: Jeremy Irons, *Reversal of Fortune*
Best Supporting Actor: Joe Pesci, *Goodfellas*
Best Supporting Actress: Whoopi Goldberg, *Ghost*
Best Director: Kevin Costner, *Dances with Wolves*
Best Song: "Sooner or Later (I Always Get My Man)," *Dick Tracy*

1989
Best Picture: *Driving Miss Daisy*
Best Actress: Jessica Tandy, *Driving Miss Daisy*
Best Actor: Daniel Day-Lewis, *My Left Foot*
Best Supporting Actor: Denzel Washington, *Glory*
Best Supporting Actress: Brenda Fricker, *My Left Foot*
Best Director: Oliver Stone, *Born on the Fourth of July*
Best Song: "Under the Sea," *The Little Mermaid*

1988
Best Picture: *Rain Man*
Best Actress: Jodie Foster, *The Accused*
Best Actor: Dustin Hoffman, *Rain Man*
Best Supporting Actor: Kevin Kline, *A Fish Called Wanda*
Best Supporting Actress: Geena Davis, *The Accidental Tourist*

Best Director: Barry Levinson, *Rain Man*
Best Song: "Let the River Run," *Working Girl*

1987
Best Picture: *The Last Emperor*
Best Actress: Cher, *Moonstruck*
Best Actor: Michael Douglas, *Wall Street*
Best Supporting Actor: Sean Connery, *The Untouchables*
Best Supporting Actress: Olympia Dukakis, *Moonstruck*
Best Director: Bernardo Bertolucci, *The Last Emperor*
Best Song: "(I've Had) The Time of My Life," *Dirty Dancing*

1986
Best Picture: *Platoon*
Best Actress: Marlee Matlin, *Children of a Lesser God*
Best Actor: Paul Newman, *The Color of Money*
Best Supporting Actor: Michael Caine, *Hannah and Her Sisters*
Best Supporting Actress: Dianne Wiest, *Hannah and Her Sisters*
Best Director: Oliver Stone, *Platoon*
Best Song: "Take My Breath Away," *Top Gun*

1985
Best Picture: *Out of Africa*
Best Actress: Geraldine Page, *The Trip to Bountiful*
Best Actor: William Hurt, *Kiss of the Spider Woman*
Best Supporting Actor: Don Ameche, *Cocoon*
Best Supporting Actress: Anjelica Huston, *Prizzi's Honor*
Best Director: Sydney Pollack, *Out of Africa*
Best Song: "Say You, Say Me," *White Nights*

1984
Best Picture: *Amadeus*
Best Actress: Sally Field, *Places in the Heart*
Best Actor: F. Murray Abraham, *Amadeus*
Best Supporting Actor: Haing S. Ngor, *The Killing Fields*
Best Supporting Actress: Peggy Ashcroft, *A Passage to India*
Best Director: Milos Forman, *Amadeus*
Best Song: "I Just Called to Say I Love You," *The Woman in Red*

1983
Best Picture: *Terms of Endearment*
Best Actress: Shirley MacLaine, *Terms of Endearment*
Best Actor: Robert Duvall, *Tender Mercies*

Best Supporting Actor: Jack Nicholson, *Terms of Endearment*
Best Supporting Actress: Linda Hunt, *The Year of Living Dangerously*
Best Director: James L. Brooks, *Terms of Endearment*
Best Song: "Flashdance . . . What a Feeling," *Flashdance*

1982
Best Picture: *Gandhi*
Best Actress: Meryl Streep, *Sophie's Choice*
Best Actor: Ben Kingsley, *Gandhi*
Best Supporting Actor: Louis Gossett Jr., *An Officer and a Gentleman*
Best Supporting Actress: Jessica Lange, *Tootsie*
Best Director: Richard Attenborough, *Gandhi*
Best Song: "Up Where We Belong," *An Officer and a Gentleman*

1981
Best Picture: *Chariots of Fire*
Best Actress: Katharine Hepburn, *On Golden Pond*
Best Actor: Henry Fonda, *On Golden Pond*
Best Supporting Actor: John Gielgud, *Arthur*
Best Supporting Actress: Maureen Stapleton, *Reds*
Best Director: Warren Beatty, *Reds*
Best Song: "Arthur's Theme (Best That You Can Do)," *Arthur*

1980
Best Picture: *Ordinary People*
Best Actress: Sissy Spacek, *Coal Miner's Daughter*
Best Actor: Robert De Niro, *Raging Bull*
Best Supporting Actor: Timothy Hutton, *Ordinary People*
Best Supporting Actress: Mary Steenburgen, *Melvin and Howard*
Best Director: Robert Redford, *Ordinary People*
Best Song: "Fame," *Fame*

1979
Best Picture: *Kramer vs. Kramer*
Best Actress: Sally Field, *Norma Rae*
Best Actor: Dustin Hoffman, *Kramer vs. Kramer*
Best Supporting Actor: Melvyn Douglas, *Being There*
Best Supporting Actress: Meryl Streep, *Kramer vs. Kramer*
Best Director: Robert Benton, *Kramer vs. Kramer*
Best Song: "It Goes Like It Goes," *Norma Rae*

1978
Best Picture: *The Deer Hunter*
Best Actress: Jane Fonda, *Coming Home*
Best Actor: Jon Voight, *Coming Home*
Best Supporting Actor: Christopher Walken, *The Deer Hunter*
Best Supporting Actress: Maggie Smith, *California Suite*
Best Director: Michael Cimino, *The Deer Hunter*
Best Song: "Last Dance," *Thank God, It's Friday*

1977
Best Picture: *Annie Hall*
Best Actress: Diane Keaton, *Annie Hall*
Best Actor: Richard Dreyfuss, *The Goodbye Girl*
Best Supporting Actor: Jason Robards, *Julia*
Best Supporting Actress: Vanessa Redgrave, *Julia*
Best Director: Woody Allen, *Annie Hall*
Best Song: "You Light Up My Life," *You Light Up My Life*

1976
Best Picture: *Rocky*
Best Actress: Faye Dunaway, *Network*
Best Actor: Peter Finch (posthumously), *Network*
Best Supporting Actor: Jason Robards, *All the President's Men*
Best Supporting Actress: Beatrice Straight, *Network*
Best Director: John G. Avildsen, *Rocky*
Best Song: "Evergreen," *A Star Is Born*

1975
Best Picture: *One Flew over the Cuckoo's Nest*
Best Actress: Louise Fletcher, *One Flew over the Cuckoo's Nest*
Best Actor: Jack Nicholson, *One Flew over the Cuckoo's Nest*
Best Supporting Actor: George Burns, *The Sunshine Boys*
Best Supporting Actress: Lee Grant, *Shampoo*
Best Director: Milos Forman, *One Flew Over the Cuckoo's Nest*
Best Song: "I'm Easy," *Nashville*

1974
Best Picture: *The Godfather, Part II*
Best Actress: Ellen Burstyn, *Alice Doesn't Live Here Anymore*
Best Actor: Art Carney, *Harry and Tonto*

Best Supporting Actor: Robert De Niro, *The Godfather, Part II*
Best Supporting Actress: Ingrid Bergman, *Murder on the Orient Express*
Best Director: Francis Coppola, *The Godfather: Part II*
Best Song: "We May Never Love Like This Again," *The Towering Inferno*

1973
Best Picture: *The Sting*
Best Actress: Glenda Jackson, *A Touch of Class*
Best Actor: Jack Lemmon, *Save the Tiger*
Best Supporting Actor: John Houseman, *The Paper Chase*
Best Supporting Actress: Tatum O'Neal, *Paper Moon*
Best Director: George Roy Hill, *The Sting*
Best Song: "The Way We Were," *The Way We Were*

1972
Best Picture: *The Godfather*
Best Actress: Liza Minnelli, *Cabaret*
Best Actor: Marlon Brando (refused to accept the award), *The Godfather*
Best Supporting Actor: Joel Grey, *Cabaret*
Best Supporting Actress: Eileen Heckart, *Butterflies Are Free*
Best Director: Bob Fosse, *Cabaret*
Best Song: "The Morning After," *The Poseidon Adventure*

1971
Best Picture: *The French Connection*
Best Actress: Jane Fonda, *Klute*
Best Actor: Gene Hackman, *The French Connection*
Best Supporting Actor: Ben Johnson, *The Last Picture Show*
Best Supporting Actress: Cloris Leachman, *The Last Picture Show*
Best Director: William Friedkin, *The French Connection*
Best Song: "Theme from Shaft," *Shaft*

1970
Best Picture: *Patton*
Best Actress: Glenda Jackson, *Women in Love*
Best Actor: George C. Scott (refused to accept the award), *Patton*
Best Supporting Actor: John Mills, *Ryan's Daughter*
Best Supporting Actress: Helen Hayes, *Airport*
Best Director: Frank McCarthy, *Patton*

Best Song: "For All We Know," *Lovers and Other Strangers*

1969
Best Picture: *Midnight Cowboy*
Best Actress: Maggie Smith, *The Prime of Miss Jean Brodie*
Best Actor: John Wayne, *True Grit*
Best Supporting Actor: Gig Young, *They Shoot Horses, Don't They?*
Best Supporting Actress: Goldie Hawn, *Cactus Flower*
Best Director: John Schlesinger, *Midnight Cowboy*
Best Song: "Raindrops Keep Fallin' on My Head," *Butch Cassidy and the Sundance Kid*

1968
Best Picture: *Oliver*
Best Actress: Katharine Hepburn, *The Lion in Winter*
Best Actor: Cliff Robertson, *Charly*
Best Supporting Actor: Jack Albertson, *The Subject Was Roses*
Best Supporting Actress: Ruth Gordon, *Rosemary's Baby*
Best Director: Carol Reed, *Oliver*
Best Song: "The Windmills of Your Mind," *The Thomas Crown Affair*

1967
Best Picture: *In the Heat of the Night*
Best Actress: Katharine Hepburn, *Guess Who's Coming to Dinner*
Best Actor: Rod Steiger, *In the Heat of Night*
Best Supporting Actor: George Kennedy, *Cool Hand Luke*
Best Supporting Actress: Estelle Parsons, *Bonnie and Clyde*
Best Director: Mike Nichols, *The Graduate*
Best Song: "Talk to the Animals," *Dr. Doolittle*

1966
Best Picture: *A Man for All Seasons*
Best Actress: Elizabeth Taylor, *Who's Afraid of Virginia Woolf?*
Best Actor: Paul Scofield, *A Man for All Seasons*
Best Supporting Actor: Walter Matthau, *The Fortune Cookie*
Best Supporting Actress: Sandy Dennis, *Who's Afraid of Virginia Woolf?*
Best Director: Fred Zinnemann, *A Man for All Seasons*
Best Song: "Born Free," *Born Free*

1965

Best Picture: *The Sound of Music*
Best Actress: Julie Christie, *Darling*
Best Actor: Lee Marvin, *Cat Ballou*
Best Supporting Actor: Martin Balsam, *A Thousand Clowns*
Best Supporting Actress: Shelley Winters, *A Patch of Blue*
Best Director: Robert Wise, *The Sound of Music*
Best Song: "The Shadow of Your Smile," *The Sandpiper*

1964

Best Picture: *My Fair Lady*
Best Actress: Julie Andrews, *Mary Poppins*
Best Actor: Rex Harrison, *My Fair Lady*
Best Supporting Actor: Peter Ustinov, *Topkapi*
Best Supporting Actress: Lila Kedrova, *Alexis Zorbas*
Best Director: George Cukor, *My Fair Lady*
Best Song: "Chim Chim Cher-ee," *Mary Poppins*

1963

Best Picture: *Tom Jones*
Best Actress: Patricia Neal, *Hud*
Best Actor: Sidney Poitier, *Lilies of the Field*
Best Supporting Actor: Melvyn Douglas, *Hud*
Best Supporting Actress: Margaret Rutherford, *The V.I.P.s*
Best Director: Tony Richardson, *Tom Jones*
Best Song: "Call Me Irresponsible," *Papa's Delicate Condition*

1962

Best Picture: *Lawrence of Arabia*
Best Actress: Anne Bancroft, *The Miracle Worker*
Best Actor: Gregory Peck, *To Kill a Mockingbird*
Best Supporting Actor: Ed Begley, *Sweet Bird of Youth*
Best Supporting Actress: Patty Duke, *The Miracle Worker*
Best Director: David Lean, *Lawrence of Arabia*
Best Song: "Days of Wine and Roses," *Days of Wine and Roses*

1961

Best Picture: *West Side Story*
Best Actress: Sophia Loren, *La Ciociara*
Best Actor: Maximilian Schell, *Judgment at Nuremberg*

Best Supporting Actor: George Chakiris, *West Side Story*
Best Supporting Actress: Rita Moreno, *West Side Story*
Best Director: Robert Wise and Jerome Robbins, *West Side Story*
Best Song: "Moon River," *Breakfast at Tiffany's*

1960

Best Picture: *The Apartment*
Best Actress: Elizabeth Taylor, *Butterfield 8*
Best Actor: Burt Lancaster, *Elmer Gantry*
Best Supporting Actor: Peter Ustinov, *Spartacus*
Best Supporting Actress: Shirley Jones, *Elmer Gantry*
Best Director: Billy Wilder, *The Apartment*
Best Song: "Never on Sunday," *Pote tin Kyriaki*

1959

Best Picture: *Ben-Hur*
Best Actress: Simone Signoret, *Room at the Top*
Best Actor: Charlton Heston, *Ben-Hur*
Best Supporting Actor: Hugh Griffith, *Ben-Hur*
Best Supporting Actress: Shelley Winters, *The Diary of Anne Frank*
Best Director: William Wyler, *Ben-Hur*
Best Song: "High Hopes," *A Hole in the Head*

1958

Best Picture: *Gigi*
Best Actress: Susan Hayward, *I Want to Live!*
Best Actor: David Niven, *Separate Tables*
Best Supporting Actor: Burl Ives, *The Big Country*
Best Supporting Actress: Wendy Hiller, *Separate Tables*
Best Director: Vincente Minnelli, *Gigi*
Best Song: "Gigi," *Gigi*

1957

Best Picture: *The Bridge on the River Kwai*
Best Actress: Joanne Woodward, *The Three Faces of Eve*
Best Actor: Alec Guinness, *The Bridge on the River Kwai*
Best Supporting Actor: Red Buttons, *Sayonara*
Best Supporting Actress: Miyoshi Umeki, *Sayonara*
Best Director: David Lean, *The Bridge on the River Kwai*
Best Song: "All the Way," *The Joker Is Wild*

1956

Best Picture: *Around the World in 80 Days*
Best Actress: Ingrid Bergman, *Anastasia*
Best Actor: Yul Brynner, *The King and I*
Best Supporting Actor: Anthony Quinn, *Lust for Life*
Best Supporting Actress: Dorothy Malone, *Written on the Wind*
Best Director: George Stevens, *Giant*
Best Song: "Whatever Will Be, Will Be (Que Sera, Sera)," *The Man Who Knew Too Much*

1955

Best Picture: *Marty*
Best Actress: Anna Magnani, *The Rose Tattoo*
Best Actor: Ernest Borgnine, *Marty*
Best Supporting Actor: Jack Lemmon, *Mister Roberts*
Best Supporting Actress: Jo Van Fleet, *East of Eden*
Best Director: Delbert Mann, *Marty*
Best Song: "Love Is a Many-Splendored Thing," *Love Is a Many-Splendored Thing*

1954

Best Picture: *On the Waterfront*
Best Actress: Grace Kelly, *The Country Girl*
Best Actor: Marlon Brando, *On the Waterfront*
Best Supporting Actor: Edmond O'Brien, *The Barefoot Contessa*
Best Supporting Actress: Eva Marie Saint, *On the Waterfront*
Best Director: Elia Kazan, *On the Waterfront*
Best Song: "Three Coins in the Fountain," *Three Coins in the Fountain*

1953

Best Picture: *From Here to Eternity*
Best Actress: Audrey Hepburn, *Roman Holiday*
Best Actor: William Holden, *Stalag 17*
Best Supporting Actor: Frank Sinatra, *From Here to Eternity*
Best Supporting Actress: Donna Reed, *From Here to Eternity*
Best Director: Fred Zinnemann, *From Here to Eternity*
Best Song: "Secret Love," *Calamity Jane*

1952

Best Picture: *The Greatest Show on Earth*
Best Actress: Shirley Booth, *Come Back, Little Sheba*
Best Actor: Gary Cooper, *High Noon*

Best Supporting Actor: Anthony Quinn, *Viva Zapata!*
Best Supporting Actress: Gloria Grahame, *Bad and the Beautiful*
Best Director: John Ford, *The Quiet Man*
Best Song: "High Noon (Do Not Forsake Me, Oh My Darlin')," *High Noon*

1951

Best Picture: *An American in Paris*
Best Actress: Vivien Leigh, *A Streetcar Named Desire*
Best Actor: Humphrey Bogart, *The African Queen*
Best Supporting Actor: Karl Malden, *A Streetcar Named Desire*
Best Supporting Actress: Kim Hunter, *A Streetcar Named Desire*
Best Director: George Stevens, *A Place in the Sun*
Best Song: "In the Cool, Cool, Cool of the Evening," *Here Comes the Groom*

1950

Best Picture: *All About Eve*
Best Actress: Judy Holliday, *Born Yesterday*
Best Actor: José Ferrer, *Cyrano de Bergerac*
Best Supporting Actor: George Sanders, *All About Eve*
Best Supporting Actress: Josephine Hull, *Harvey*
Best Director: Joseph L. Mankiewicz, *All About Eve*
Best Song: "Mona Lisa," *Captain Carey, U.S.A.*

1949

Best Picture: *All the King's Men*
Best Actress: Olivia De Havilland, *The Heiress*
Best Actor: Broderick Crawford, *All the King's Men*
Best Supporting Actor: Dean Jagger, *Twelve O'Clock High*
Best Supporting Actress: Mercedes McCambridge, *All the King's Men*
Best Director: Joseph L. Mankiewicz, *A Letter to Three Wives*
Best Song: "Baby, It's Cold Outside," *Neptune's Daughter*

1948

Best Picture: *Hamlet*
Best Actress: Jane Wyman, *Johnny Belinda*
Best Actor: Laurence Olivier, *Hamlet*
Best Supporting Actor: Walter Huston, *Treasure of the Sierra Madre*

Best Supporting Actress: Claire Trevor, *Key Largo*
Best Director: John Huston, *Treasure of the Sierra Madre*
Best Song: "Buttons and Bows," *The Paleface*

1947
Best Picture: *Gentleman's Agreement*
Best Actress: Loretta Young, *Farmer's Daughter*
Best Actor: Ronald Colman, *A Double Life*
Best Supporting Actor: Edmund Gwenn, *Miracle on 34th Street*
Best Supporting Actress: Celeste Holm, *Gentleman's Agreement*
Best Director: Elia Kazan, *Gentleman's Agreement*
Best Song: "Zip-A-Dee-Doo-Dah," *Song of the South*

1946
Best Picture: *The Best Years of Our Lives*
Best Actress: Olivia De Havilland, *To Each His Own*
Best Actor: Fredric March, *The Best Years of Our Lives*
Best Supporting Actor: Harold Russell, *The Best Years of Our Lives*
Best Supporting Actress: Anne Baxter, *The Razor's Edge*
Best Director: William Wyler, *The Best Years of Our Lives*
Best Song: "On the Atchison, Topeka, and Santa Fe," *The Harvey Girls*

1945
Best Picture: *The Lost Weekend*
Best Actress: Joan Crawford, *Mildred Pierce*
Best Actor: Ray Milland, *The Lost Weekend*
Best Supporting Actor: James Dunn, *A Tree Grows in Brooklyn*
Best Supporting Actress: Anne Revere, *National Velvet*
Best Director: Billy Wilder, *The Lost Weekend*
Best Song: "It Might as Well Be Spring," *State Fair*

1944
Best Picture: *Going My Way*
Best Actress: Ingrid Bergman, *Gaslight*
Best Actor: Bing Crosby, *Going My Way*
Best Supporting Actor: Barry Fitzgerald, *Going My Way*
Best Supporting Actress: Ethel Barrymore, *None But the Lonely Heart*
Best Director: Leo McCarey, *Going My Way*

Best Song: "Swinging on a Star," *Going My Way*

1943
Best Picture: *Casablanca*
Best Actress: Jennifer Jones, *The Song of Bernadette*
Best Actor: Paul Lukas, *Watch on the Rhine*
Best Supporting Actor: Charles Coburn, *The More the Merrier*
Best Supporting Actress: Katina Paxinou, *For Whom the Bell Tolls*
Best Director: Michael Curtiz, *Casablanca*
Best Song: "Change of Heart," *Change of Heart*

1942
Best Picture: *Mrs. Miniver*
Best Actress: Greer Garson, *Mrs. Miniver*
Best Actor: James Cagney, *Yankee Doodle Dandy*
Best Supporting Actor: Van Heflin, *Johnny Eager*
Best Supporting Actress: Teresa Wright, *Mrs. Miniver*
Best Director: William Wyler, *Mrs. Miniver*
Best Song: "White Christmas," *Holiday Inn*

1941
Best Picture: *How Green Was My Valley*
Best Actress: Joan Fontaine, *Suspicion*
Best Actor: Gary Cooper, *Sergeant York*
Best Supporting Actor: Donald Crisp, *How Green Was My Valley*
Best Supporting Actress: Mary Astor, *The Great Lie*
Best Director: John Ford, *How Green Was My Valley*
Best Song: "The Last Time I Saw Paris," *Lady Be Good*

1940
Best Picture: *Rebecca*
Best Actress: Ginger Rogers, *Kitty Foyle*
Best Actor: James Stewart, *The Philadelphia Story*
Best Supporting Actor: Walter Brennan, *The Westerner*
Best Supporting Actress: Jane Darwell, *The Grapes of Wrath*
Best Director: John Ford, *The Grapes of Wrath*
Best Song: "When You Wish Upon a Star," *Pinocchio*

1939
Best Picture: *Gone With the Wind*
Best Actress: Vivien Leigh, *Gone With the Wind*

Best Actor: Robert Donat, *Goodbye, Mr. Chips*

Best Supporting Actor: Thomas Mitchell, *Stagecoach*

Best Supporting Actress: Hattie McDaniel, *Gone With the Wind*

Best Director: Victor Fleming, *Gone With the Wind*

Best Song: "Over the Rainbow," *The Wizard of Oz*

1938

Best Picture: *You Can't Take It with You*

Best Actress: Bette Davis, *Jezebel* (1938)

Best Actor: Spencer Tracy, *Boys Town*

Best Supporting Actor: Walter Brennan, *Kentucky*

Best Supporting Actress: Fay Bainter, *Jezebel*

Best Director: Frank Capra, *You Can't Take It with You*

Best Song: "Thanks for the Memory," *The Big Broadcast of 1938*

1937

Best Picture: *The Life of Émile Zola*

Best Actress: Luise Rainer, *The Good Earth*

Best Actor: Spencer Tracy, *Captains Courageous*

Best Supporting Actor: Joseph Schildkraut, *The Life of Émile Zola*

Best Supporting Actress: Alice Brady, *In Old Chicago*

Best Director: Leo McCarey, *The Awful Truth*

Best Song: "Sweet Leilani," *Waikiki Wedding*

1936

Best Picture: *The Great Ziegfeld*

Best Actress: Luise Rainer, *The Great Ziegfeld*

Best Actor: Paul Muni, *The Story of Louis Pasteur*

Best Supporting Actor: Walter Brennan, *Come and Get It*

Best Supporting Actress: Gale Sondergaard, *Anthony Adverse*

Best Director: Frank Capra, *Mr. Deeds Goes to Town*

Best Song: "The Way You Look Tonight," *Swing Time*

1935

Best Picture: *Mutiny on the Bounty*

Best Actress: Bette Davis, *Dangerous*

Best Actor: Victor McLaglen, *The Informer*

Best Director: John Ford, *The Informer*

Best Song: "Lullaby of Broadway," *The Gold Diggers of 1935*

1934

Best Picture: *It Happened One Night*

Best Actress: Claudette Colbert, *It Happened One Night*

Best Actor: Clark Gable, *It Happened One Night*

Best Director: Frank Capra, *It Happened One Night*

Best Song: "The Continental," *The Gay Divorcée*

1933

Best Picture: *Cavalcade*

Best Actress: Katharine Hepburn, *Morning Glory*

Best Actor: Charles Laughton, *The Private Life of Henry VIII*

Best Actor: Wallace Beery, *The Champ*

Best Director: Frank Lloyd, *Cavalcade*

1932

Best Picture: *Grand Hotel*

Best Actress: Helen Hayes, *The Sin of Madelon Claudet*

Best Actor: Fredric March, *Dr. Jekyll and Mr. Hyde*

Best Director: Frank Borzage, *Bad Girl*

1931

Best Picture: *Cimarron*

Best Actress: Marie Dressler, *Min and Bill*

Best Actor: Lionel Barrymore, *A Free Soul*

Best Director: Norman Taurog, *Skippy*

1930

Best Picture: *All Quiet on the Western Front*

Best Actress: Norma Shearer, *The Divorcée*

Best Actor: George Arliss, *Disraeli*

Best Director: Lewis Milestone, *All Quiet on the Western Front*

1929

Best Picture: *The Broadway Melody*

Best Actress: Mary Pickford, *Coquette*

Best Actor: Warner Baxter, *In Old Arizona*

Best Director: Frank Lloyd, *The Divine Lady*

1928

Best Picture (2): *Sunrise; Wings*

Best Actress: Janet Gaynor, *Seventh Heaven*

Best Actor: Emil Jannings, *The Way of All Flesh*

Best Director (2): Frank Borzage, *Seventh Heaven;* Lewis Milestone, *Two Arabian Nights*

The Animal Kingdom

I. Kingdom Protista
  A. Subkingdom Protozoa—single-celled "animals"
    1. Phylum Sarcomastigophora
      a. Subphylum Sarcodina—amebas (Amoeba)
      b. Subphylum Mastigophora—flagellates (Euglena)
    2. Phylum Ciliophora—ciliates (Paramecium)
    3. Phylum Apicomplexa (Plasmodium)

II. Kingdom Animalia
  A. Phylum Porifera- sponges
  B. Phylum Cnidaria
    1. Class Hydrozoa (Hydra, Obelia)
    2. Class Syphozoa—true jellyfish (Aurelia)
    3. Class Anthozoa—"flower" animals (sea anenome, corals)
  C. Phylum Platyhelminthes—flat "worms"
    1. Class Turbellaria (Planaria)
    2. Class Cestoda (tapeworms)
    3. Class Trematoda (flukes)
  D. Phylum Nematoda—round "worms" (Ascaris)
  E. Phylum Mollusca
    1. Class Bivalvia—"two valves" (clams, mussels)
    2. Class Gastropoda—"stomach foot" (snails, slugs)
    3. Class Cephalopoda—"head foot" (squid, octopus, nautilus)
  F. Phylum Annelida—segmented worms
    1. Class Polychaeta—"many hairs" (clamworms)
    2. Class Oligochaeta—"few hairs" (earthworms)
    3. Class Hirudinea (leeches)
  G. Phylum Arthropoda
    a. Subphylum Chelicerata
      1. Class Meristomata —"thigh mouth" (horseshoe crab)
      2. Class Arachnida (spiders, ticks, scorpions)
    b. Subphylum Crustacea (lobster, shrimp, crab, crayfish)
    c. Subphylum Uniramia
      1. Class Diplopoda (millipedes)
      2. Class Chilopoda (centipedes)
      3. Class Insecta (butterflies, ants, crickets, roaches)
  H. Phylum Echinodermata—"spine skin"
    1. Class Asteroidea (sea stars)
    2. Class Ophiuroidea (brittle stars)
    3. Class Holothuroidea (sea cucumbers)
    4. Class Echinoidea (sea urchins, sand dollars)
    5. Class Crinoidea (sea lilies, feather stars)
  I. Phylum Chordata
    1. Subphylum Urochordata—"tail cord" (tunicates)
    2. Subphylum Cephalochordata—"head cord" (Amphioxus)
    3. Subphylum Vertebrata—"backboned"
      a. Superclass Aganatha—"without jaws" (lamprey)
      b. Superclass Gnathostomata—"jawed mouth"
        1. Class Chondrichthyes—cartilaginous "fish" (sharks, rays)
        2. Class Osteichthyes—bony fish (perch)
        3. Class Amphibia—Orders: Anura, Caudata, Gymnophiona
        4. Class Reptilia—Orders: Squamata, Testudines, Crocodilia
        5. Class Aves—Birds—Orders: many
        6. Class Mammalia—Mammals—Orders: many, including primates

Insects

agrion	aphid	beetle, grain	beetle, wood
ant	assassin bug	beetle, grapevine	billbug
ant, army	bedbug	beetle, Japanese	blowfly
ant, black	bee	beetle, maul	bluebottle fly
ant, carpenter	beetle	beetle, scarab	boll weevil
ant, lion	beetle, amara	beetle, snout	borer
ant, red	beetle, dung	beetle, stag	botfly

Insects (continued)

bristletail
buffalo bug
butterfly
butterfly, admiral
butterfly, buckeye
butterfly, monarch
butterfly, swallowtail
butterfly, vanessa
butterfly, viceroy
chafer
chigger
chigoe
chinch bug
cicada
cockchafer
cockroach
corn-nose
cricket
cricket, mole
croton bug
curculio
damselfly
dobsonfly
dragonfly

drosophila
earwig
ephemerid
firebrat
firefly
flea
fly
fly, bee
fly, caddis
fly, crane
fly, deer
fly, fruit
fly, horn
fly, lantern
fly, robber
fly, scorpion
fly, shad
fly, shoemaker
fly, stone
fly, tsetse
gadfly
gallfly
glowworm
gnat

grasshopper
harlequin cabbage bug
hawk moth
hawker
hornet
horntail
horsefly
housefly
jigger, flea
june bug
katydid
kissing bug
lacewing
ladybug
leafhopper
locust
louse
mantis, praying
mayfly
mealworm
mealybug
midge
mosquito
moth

moth, cecropia
moth, codling
moth, Death's head
moth, tiger
no-see-um
pill bug
potato bug
punkie
roach
sawfly
silverfish
sow bug
springtail
squash bug
stink bug
termite
thrips
tick, deer
tick, wood
walking stick
wasp
waterbug
weevil
yellow jacket

Arachnids

black widow
brown recluse
scorpion

spider, black widow
spider, brown recluse
spider, brown widow

spider, funnel web
spider, trap door
spider, wolf

tarantula

Fish

albacore
alewife
amberjack
anchovy
angel fish
archerfish
barbel
barracuda
barramundi
bass
bass, black
bass, channel
bass, largemouth
bass, sea
bass, smallmouth
bass, striped
blackfish
bleak
blindfish
blowfish
bluefish
bluegill
bocaccio

bogue
bolina
bonefish
bonito
bordemer
bourgeois
bowfin
bream
bream, sea
buffalo fish
bullhead
burbot
butterfish
candlefish
capelin
carp
catfish
char
chimaera
chub
cichlic
cisco
cobia

cod
cod, ling
cod, rock
coelacanth
conger eel
cowfish
crappie
croaker
crooner
cutlass fish
dace
darter
devilfish
doctor fish
dogfish
dorado
dragon fish
drum
eel
eel, electric
eel, moray
eelpout
elver

filefish
flatfish
flounder
fluke
flying fish
flying gurnard
fourami
frostfish
fugu
gar
gemfish
ginko fish
globefish
goby
goosefish
grayling
grouper
grunion
grunt
guanchanco
gudgeon
guitarfish
gunnel

Fish (continued)

guppy
gurnards
haddock
hairtale
hake
halibut
harvestfish
herring
hobfish
hogfish
huss
jewfish
John Dory
kingfish
lamprey
lantern fish
ling
ling, Boston
loach
lung fish
mackerel
mahi-mahi
mango
mangrove
manta ray
marlin
menhaden
minnow
monkfish
mudfish
mullet
mulloway
muskellunge
nursehound
orange roughy

paddlefish
pandora
perch
peto
pickerel
pike
pike, Northern
pike, walleye
pilchard
pilot fish
piranha
plaice
pomfret
pompano
porbeagle
porgy
puffer
quin
rabbit fish
rajafish
rascasse
ray
ray, electric
ray, manta
ray, sting
redfin
redfish
ribbon fish
roach
rock cod
rockfish
rudderfish
sablefish
sailfish
salema

salmon
salmon, Atlantic
salmon, chinook
salmon, king
salmon, silver
sardine
sawfish
scabbard fish
scorpion fish
scup
sea bream
sea horse
sea robin
shad
shark
shark, angel
shark, blue
shark, great white
shark, hammerhead
shark, mako
shark, sand
shark, thresher
shark, tiger
sheepshead
shiner
skate
skipjack
smelt
snapper
snapper, red
snapper, yellow
snook
sole
spot
sprat

spur dog
stockfish
sturgeon
sucker
sunfish
swordfish
tarpon
tautog
tench
tetra
threadfins
tilapia
tilefish
toadfish
tope
torpedo fish
triggerfish
trout
trout, brook
trout, brown
trout, cutthroat
trout, golden
trout, lake
trout, rainbow
trout, sea
trout, speckled
trout, steelhead
tuna
turbot
wahoo
whitefish
whiting
wrasse
yellowtail

Other Marine Animals

abalone
anemone
barnacle
clam
clam, cherrystone
clam, littleneck
clam, razor
clam, steamer
clam, surf
cockle

conch
crab, Dungeness
crab, horseshoe
crab, king
crab, snow
crab, soft-shell
crab, spider
crab, stone
crayfish
crustaceans

dugong
geoduck
langosta
lobster
mollusk
mussel
octopus
oyster
prawn
quahog

scallop
sea cucumber
shellfish
shrimp
snail
squid
urchin

Amphibians

bullfrog
caecilian
eel
eel, congo
eel, lamprey

eel, moray
eft
frog
frog, bull
frog, grass

frog, green
frog, tree
frog, wood
hellbender
mud puppy

newt
salamander
siren
toad
toad, horned

Reptiles

agama
alligator
anole
basilisk
blindworm
caiman
chameleon
crocodile

gavial
gecko
gila monster
iguana
leatherback
lizard
lizard, beaded
lizard, sand

monitor
skink
terrapin
tortoise
tuatara
turtle
turtle, box
turtle, snapping

turtle, hawkbill
turtle, sea

Snakes

adder
anaconda
asp
black snake
blind snake
boa
boa constrictor
bull snake
bushmaster
cobra
cobra, king
cooter
copperhead
coral snake

corn snake
cottonmouth
daboia
fer-de-lance
garter
gopher snake
hamadryad
hognose snake
indigo snake
kerril
king snake
krait
mamba
massasauga

milk snake
moccasin
mole snake
naga
pine snake
puff adder
python
racer
rainbow snake
rat snake
rattlesnake
rattlesnake, Eastern
    diamondback
rattlesnake, horned

rattlesnake, timber
rattlesnake, Western
    diamondback
ribbon snake
shovel-nose snake
sidewinder
thunder snake
urutu
viper
viper, horned
water moccasin
water snake
worm snake

Birds

anhinga
ani
auk
auklet
avocet
bananaquit
bank swallow
becard
bittern
blackbird
blackbird, red-
    winged
bluebird
bluetail
bluethroat
bobolink
bobwhite
booby
brambling
budgerigar
bulbul
bullfinch
bunting
bunting, gray
bunting, snow
bushtit
caracara
cardinal
catbird
chaffinch

chickadee
condor
coot
cormorant
cowbird
crake
crane, common
crane, sandhill
crane, whooping
creeper
crossbill
crow
cuckoo
curlew
dickcissel
dipper
dotterel
dove, mourning
dove, rock
dovekie
dowitcher
duck
duck, black
duck, canvasback
duck, falcated
duck, gadwall
duck, mallard
duck, mottled
duck, muscovy
duck, ring-necked

duck, spot-billed
duck, tufted
duck, wood
dunlin
eagle, bald
eagle, golden
egret
eider
elaenia
falcon
falcon, peregrine
fieldfare
finch
flamingo
flicker
flycatcher
frigatebird
fulmar
gallinule
gannet
gnatcatcher
godwit
goldeneye
goldfinch
goose
goose, barnacle
goose, Canada
goose, emperor
goose, Ross's
goose, snow

goshawk
grackle
grassquit
greater pewee
grebe
greenfinch
greenshank
grosbeak
grouse, blue
grouse, ruffed
grouse, sage
grouse, sharp-tailed
grouse, spruce
guillemot
gull
gull, sea
harrier
hawfinch
hawk, Cooper's
hawk, red-tailed
heron
hoopoe
hummingbird
hummingbird, ruby-
    throated
ibis
jabiru
jacana
jackdaw
jaeger

jay, blue
jay, gray
junco
kestrel
kingbird
kingfisher
kinglet
kite
kittiwake
knot
lapwing
lark
limpkin
longspur
loon
magpie
mango
martin
merganser
mockingbird
moorhen
murre
murrelet
myna
needletail
nighthawk
nightjar
noddy
nutcracker
nuthatch
oriole
oriole, Baltimore
osprey
ovenbird
owl, barn
owl, great horned
owl, screech
owl, snowy

owl, spotted
oystercatcher
parakeet
parrot
partridge
parula
pauraque
pelican
petrel
petrel, storm
pewee
phalarope
pheasant
phoebe
pigeon
pigeon, passenger
pipit
plover
poorwill
pratincole
puffin
quail
rail
raven
razorbill
redpoll
redshank
redwing
roadrunner
robin
rubythroat
ruff
sanderling
sandpiper
sapsucker
sapsucker, yellow-
    bellied
scaup

shearwater
shrike
siskin
skua
smew
snipe
solitaire
sora
sparrow
sparrow, field
spoonbill
starling
stilt
stint
stonechat
stork
surfbird
swallow, barn
swallow, cave
swallow, cliff
swallow, tree
swan, mute
swan, trumpeter
swan, tundra
swift
tanager
tanager, scarlet
tattler
teal
tern
thrasher
thrush
thrush, wood
tit
titmouse
tityra
towhee
trogon

tropicbird
turkey, wild
turnstone
tyrannulet
veery
verdin
vireo
vulture
vulture, turkey
wagtail
warbler
waterthrush
waxwing
waxwing, cedar
wheatear
whimbrel
whip-poor-will
willet
woodcock
woodcock, Eurasian
woodpecker
woodpecker, great
    spotted
woodpecker, red-
    bellied
woodpecker, red-
    headed
wren
wren, canyon
wren, house
wren, marsh
wren, rock
wrentit
wryneck
yellowlegs
yellowthroat

Mammals

aardvark
addax
agouti
alpaca
angwantibo
anoa
anteater
antelope
antelope, sable
aoudad
ape
argali
armadillo
ass
aurochs
aye-aye

badger
bandicoot
bat
bat, vampire
bear, black
bear, brown
bear, cinnamon
bear, grizzly
bear, panda
bear, polar
beavers
binturong
bison
blind mole-rat
boar
boar, wild

bobcat
bottlenose
buffalo
buffalo, Cape
buffalo, Indian
buffalo, water
burro
bush baby
cachalot
camel
capucin
carabao
caracal
carcajou
caribou
cat, Chinese desert

cat, domestic
cat, jungle
cat, sand
cat, wild
catalo
catamount
cavy
chacma
chamois
cheetah
chimpanzee
chinchilla
chipmunk
civet cat
coatimundi
colobus

Mammals (continued)

cougar
cow
coyote
coypu
deer
deer, mule
deer, red
deer, spotted
deer, white-tailed
dhole
dingo
dog
dolphin
dolphin, bottle-nosed
donkey
dormouse
drill
dromedary
dugong
echidna
eland
elephant
elk
entellus
ermine
fennec
ferret
fitch
flying squirrel
fox, arctic
fox, flying
fox, gray
fox, kit
fox, red
fox, silver
galago
gazelle
gemsbok
gemsbuck
genet
gerbil
gibbon
giraffe
gnu
goat
goat, angora
goat, billy
goat, mountain
gopher
gopher, pocket
goral
gorilla
groundhog
gray, seal
grivet
guanaco
guenon
guinea pig

hamster
hanuman
hare
hare, arctic
hartebeest
hedgehog
hevonen
hippopotamus
hog
horse
howler
human
hyaena
hyrax
ibex
indri
jackal
jackass
jackrabbit
jaguar
jerboa
jird
kangaroo
karakul
kiang
kinkajou
koala
kudu
kulan
langur
lemming
lemur
leopard
lion
lion, mountain
llama
loris
lynx
macaque
man
manatee
mandrill
mangabey
mara
margay
markhor
marmoset
marmot
marten
mink
mole
mole, rat
mole, shrew
mole, voles
mongoose
monkey, proboscis
monkey, rhesus
monkey, spider

moose
mouse
mouse, deer
mouse, field
mouse, jumping
mouse, kangaroo
mule
muntjac
muskox
muskrat
narwhal
nutria
ocelot
okapi
onager
oont
opossum
orangutan
orca
oryx
otter
otter, sea
ox, domestic
ox, musk
ox, wild
panda bear
pangolin
panther
peccary
phalanger
pig
pika
platypus
polar bear
polecat
porcupine
porpoise
potto
prairie dog
pronghorn
puma
rabbit, cottontail
rabbit, snowshoe
raccoons
rat
rat, kangaroo
rat, Norway
rat, pack
rat, wharf
ratel
reindeer
rhesus monkey
rhinoceros
rhinoceros, black
rhinoceros, white
roebuck
sable
saiga

saki
sambar
sea cow
sea lion
seal
seal, harp
serows
serval
sheep
sheep, bighorn
sheep, mountain
shrew
siamang
sifaka
sika
skunk
skunk, striped
sloth
sloth, giant
sloth, three-toed
souslik
spider monkey
springbok
squirrel
squirrel, flying
squirrel, ground
squirrel, gray
squirrel, red
steenbok
swine
tahr
takin
talapoi
tamandua
tamarin
tapir
tarsier
tatouay
tiger
tur
uakari
urus
vole
wallaby
walrus
wapiti
warthog
water buffalo
waterbuck
weasel
whale, black right
whale, blue
whale, finner
whale, gray
whale, Greenland
  right
whale, humpback
whale, killer

Mammals (continued)

whale, piked
whale, pilot
whale, pollack
whale, white
whales, beaked
whales, bottle-nosed
whales, finback

whales, sperm
wildcat
wildebeest
wisent
wolf
wolf, brush
wolf, gray

wolf, prairie
wolf, timber
wolley
wolverine
wombat
woodchuck
yak

zebra
zebu
zokor
zoril

Cats

Abyssinian
American bobtail
American curl
American shorthair
American wirehair
Balinese
Bengal
Birman
Bombay
Brazilian shorthair
British shorthair
Burmese
California spangled
    cat

chantilly/tiffany
chartreux
colorpoint shorthair
Cornish rex
Devon rex
domestic, household
    pet (Nonpedigreed)
Egyptian mau
European shorthair
exotic shorthair
German rex
Havana brown
Himalayan
Japanese bobtail

Javanese
Korat
LaPerm
Maine coon cat
manx
Munchkin
Nebelung
Norwegian forest cat
ocicat
Oriental
Persian
pixiebob
ragdoll
Russian blue

Scottish fold
Selkirk rex
Siamese
Siberian
Singapura
snowshoe
Sokoke
Somali
sphynx
spotted mist
Tonkinese
Turkish angora
Turkish van

Dogs

afghan
Airedale
akita
Alaskan malamute
Alsatian
American Eskimo
Australian cattle dog
Australian shepherd
basenji
basset hound
beagle
Bernice mountain
    dog
bichon frise
bloodhound
boarhound
border collie
border terrier
borzoi
Boston bull
boxer
briard
Brittany
bulldog
bulldog, English
bulldog, French
bullmastiff
cairn terrier

chihuahua
chow
cocker spaniel
collie (rough and
    smooth)
dachshund
Dalmatian
doberman pinscher
elkhound
English bulldog
foxhound
German shepherd
German shorthaired
    pointer
giant schnauzer
golden retriever
Great Dane
greyhound
hairless
husky
Irish setter
Italian greyhound
Jack Russell terrier
keeshond
Kerry blue terrier
Labrador retriever
Lhasa apso
malamute

Maltese
mastiff
miniature
    schnauzer
mixed breeds (mutt)
Newfoundland
Old English mastiff
Old English sheep-
    dog
otter hound
Pekingese
pointer
Pomeranian
poodle, miniature,
    toy
pug
redbone coonhound
retriever, golden
    labrador
Rhodesian
    ridgeback
rottweiler
Saint Bernard
saluki
samoyed
schipperke
schnauzer
setter, Irish, English

shar pei
sheepdog, Old
    English, Belgian
Shetland sheepdog
Shiba inu
shih tzu
Siberian husky
spaniel, English,
    springer, cocker
spitz
staghound
standard poodle
standard schnauzer
terrier, bull, fox,
    Irish, Welsh,
    wire-haired,
    Yorkshire
toy poodle
Welsh corgi
West Highland
whippet
white terrier
wiemaraner
wolfhound
Yorkshire terrier

Primates

angwantibo	drill	langur	monkey, rhesus
ape	entellus	lemur	monkey, spider
aye-aye	gibbon	macaque	orangutan
capucin	gorilla	man	rhesus monkey
chacma	grivet	mandrill	saki
chimpanzee	guenon	marmoset	siamang
colobus	hanuman	monkey, proboscis	spider monkey

Cetaceans

beluga	orca	whale, Greenland	whale, white
bottlenose	porpoise	right	whales, beaked
cachalot	rorqual	whale, humpback	whales, bottle-nosed
dolphin	whale, baleen	whale, killer	whales, finback
dolphin, bottle-nosed	whale, black right	whale, piked	whale, sperm
finback	whale, blue	whale, pilot	
grampus	whale, finner	whale, pollack	
narwhal	whale, gray	whale, right	

International Most-Endangered Species List

Tiger (*Panthera tigris*)
Black rhino (*Diceros bicornis*)
Giant panda (*Ailuropoda melanoleuca*)
Asiatic black bear (*Ursus thibetanus*)
Himalayan yew (*Taxus wallichiana*)
Atlantic bluefin tuna (*Thunnus thynnus*)
Hawksbill sea turtle (*Eretmochelys imbricata*)
Saigo antelope (*Saiga tatarica*)

Egyptian tortoise (*Testudo kelinmanni*)
Red and blue lory (*Eos histrio*)
Golden-capped fruit bat (*Acerdon jubatus*)
American box turtle (*Terrapene spp.*)
Red panda (*Ailurus fulgens*)
African gray parrot (*Psittacus erithacus*)
American or big-leaf mahogany (*Swietenia macrophylla*)
Hippopotamus (*Hippopotamus amphibius*)

Endangered Mammals

Common Name: Bat, gray
  Historic Habitat: Central and southeastern U.S.A.
Common Name: Bat, Hawaiian hoary
  Historic Habitat: U.S.A. (HI)
Common Name: Bat, Mariana fruit
  Historic Habitat: Western Pacific — U.S.A. (Guam, Rota, Tinian, Saipan, Agiguan)
Common Name: Bat, Mexican long-nosed
  Historic Habitat: U.S.A. (NM, TX), Mexico, Central America
Common Name: Bat, Ozark big-eared
  Historic Habitat: U.S.A. (MO, OK, AR)
Common Name: Bat, Virginia big-eared
  Historic Habitat: U.S.A. (KY, NC, WV, VA)
Common Name: Bear, Louisiana black
  Historic Habitat: U.S.A. (LA, MS, TX)
Common Name: Caribou, woodland
  Historic Habitat: U.S.A. (AK, ID, ME, MI, MN, MT, NH, VT, WA, WI), Canada

Common Name: Deer, Columbian white-tailed
  Historic Habitat: U.S.A. (WA, OR)
Common Name: Deer, key
  Historic Habitat: U.S.A. (FL)
Common Name: Dugong
  Historic Habitat: East Africa to southern Japan, including U.S.A.
Common Name: Ferret, black-footed
  Historic Habitat : Western U.S.A., western Canada
Common Name: Fox, northern swift
  Historic Habitat: U.S.A. (northern plains), Canada
Common Name: Fox, San Joaquin kit
  Historic Habitat: U.S.A. (CA)
Common Name: Jaguar
  Historic Habitat: U.S.A. (AZ, NM, TX), Central and South America
Common Name: Jaguarundi
  Historic Habitat: U.S.A. (AZ, TX), Mexico

Endangered Mammals (continued)

Common Name: Kangaroo rat
Historic Habitat: U.S.A. (CA)
Common Name: Manatee, West Indian (or Florida)
Historic Habitat: southeastern U.S.A., Caribbean Sea, South America
Common Name: Margay
Historic Habitat: U.S.A. (TX), Central and South America
Common Name: Mountain beaver, Point Arena
Historic Habitat: U.S.A. (CA)
Common Name: Ocelot
Historic Habitat: U.S.A. (AZ, TX) to Central, South America
Common Name: Otter, southern sea
Historic Habitat: West Coast, U.S.A. (CA, OR, WA) south to Mexico
Common Name: Panther, Florida
Historic Habitat: U.S.A. (LA and AR east to SC and FL)
Common Name: Prairie dog, Utah
Historic Habitat: U.S.A. (UT)
Common Name: Pronghorn, Sonoran
Historic Habitat: U.S.A. (AZ), Mexico
Common Name: Sea-lion, Steller (=northern)
Historic Habitat: U.S.A. (AK, CA, OR, WA), Canada, Russia; North Pacific Ocean
Common Name: Seal, guadalupe fur
Historic Habitat: U.S.A. (Farallon Islands, CA) south to Mexico

Common Name: Seal, Hawaiian monk
Historic Habitat: U.S.A. (HI)
Common Name: Shrew, Dismal Swamp southeastern
Historic Habitat: U.S.A. (VA, NC)
Common Name: Squirrel, Carolina northern flying
Historic Habitat: U.S.A. (NC, TN)
Common Name: Squirrel, Delmarva Peninsula fox
Historic Habitat: U.S.A. (Delmarva Peninsula to southeastern PA)
Common Name: Squirrel, Mt. Graham red
Historic Habitat: U.S.A. (AZ)
Common Name: Squirrel, Virginia northern flying
Historic Habitat: U.S.A. (VA, WV)
Common Name: Vole, Amargosa
Historic Habitat: U.S.A. (CA)
Common Name: Vole, Florida salt marsh
Historic Habitat: U.S.A. (FL)
Common Name: Vole, Hualapai Mexican
Historic Habitat: U.S.A. (AZ)
Common Name: Wolf, red
Historic Habitat: U.S.A. (Southeastern U.S.A., west to central TX)
Common Name: Woodrat, Key Largo
Historic Habitat: U.S.A. (FL)

Endangered Birds

Common Name: Akepa, Hawaii (honeycreeper)
Historic Range: U.S.A. (HI)
Common Name: Akialoa, Kauai (honey-creeper)
Historic Range: U.S.A. (HI)
Common Name: Albatross, short-tailed
Historic Range: Japan, Russia, U.S.A. (AK, CA, HI, OR, WA)
Common Name: Blackbird, yellow-shouldered
Historic Range: U.S.A. (PR)
Common Name: Bobwhite, masked (quail)
Historic Range: U.S.A. (AZ), Mexico (Sonora)
Common Name: Broadbill, Guam
Historic Range: Western Pacific—U.S.A. (Guam)
Common Name: Caracara, Audubon's crested
Historic Range: U.S.A. (AZ, FL, LA, NM, TX) to Panama; Cuba
Common Name: Condor, California
Historic Range: U.S.A. (CA, OR), Mexico (Baja California)

Common Name: Coot, Hawaiian
Historic Range: U.S.A. (HI)
Common Name: Crane, Mississippi sandhill
Historic Range: U.S.A. (MS)
Common Name: Crane, whooping
Historic Range: Canada, U.S.A. (Rocky Mountains. to Carolinas), Mexico
Common Name: Creeper,
Historic Range: U.S.A. (HI)—Hawaii, Molokai, Oahu
Common Name: Crow, Hawaiian
Historic Range: U.S.A. (HI)
Common Name: Crow, Mariana
Historic Range: Western Pacific—U.S.A. (Guam, Rota)
Common Name: Crow, white-necked
Historic Range: U.S.A. (PR), Dominican Republic, Haiti
Common Name: Duck, Hawaiian
Historic Range: U.S.A. (HI)
Common Name: Duck, Laysan
Historic Range: U.S.A. (HI)
Common Name: Eider, spectacled
Historic Range: U.S.A. (AK), Russia

Common Name: Falcon, northern
aplomado
Historic Range: U.S.A. (AZ, NM, TX),
Mexico, Guatemala
Common Name: Finch, Laysan (honeycreeper)
Historic Range: U.S.A. (HI)
Common Name: Finch, Nihoa (honeycreeper)
Historic Range: U.S.A. (HI)
Common Name: Gnatcatcher, coastal
California
Historic Range: U.S.A. (CA), Mexico
Common Name: Goose, Aleutian Canada
Historic Range: U.S.A. (AK, CA, OR,
WA), Japan
Common Name: Goose, Hawaiian
Historic Range: U.S.A. (HI)
Common Name: Hawk, Hawaiian
Historic Range: U.S.A. (HI)
Common Name: Hawk, Puerto Rican broad-
winged
Historic Range: U.S.A. (PR)
Common Name: Hawk, Puerto Rican sharp-
shinned
Historic Range: U.S.A. (PR)
Common Name: Honeycreeper, crested
Historic Range: U.S.A. (HI)
Common Name: Jay, Florida scrub
Historic Range: U.S.A. (FL)
Common Name: Kingfisher, Guam
Historic Range: Western Pacific—U.S.A.
(Guam)
Common Name: Kite, Everglade snail
Historic Range: U.S.A. (FL), Cuba
Common Name: Mallard, Mariana
Historic Range: Western Pacific—U.S.A.
(Guam, Mariana Islands)
Common Name: Megapode, Micronesian
Historic Range: West Pacific—U.S.A.
(Palau Island, Mariana Islands)
Common Name: Millerbird, Nihoa
Historic Range: U.S.A. (HI)
Common Name: Monarch, Tinian
Historic Range: Western Pacific—Mariana
Islands
Common Name: Moorhen, Hawaiian
Historic Range: U.S.A. (HI)
Common Name: Moorhen, Mariana
Historic Range: Western Pacific—U.S.A.
(Guam, Tinian, Saipan, Pagan)
Common Name: Murrelet, marbled
Historic Range: U.S.A. (AK, CA, OR,
WA), Canada (B.C.)
Common Name: Nightjar, Puerto Rican
Historic Range: U.S.A. (PR)
Common Name: Nukupu`u (honeycreeper)
Historic Range: U.S.A. (HI)
Common Name: Oo, Kauai (honeyeater)
Historic Range: U.S.A. (HI)

Common Name: Ou (honeycreeper)
Historic Range: U.S.A. (HI)
Common Name: Owl, Mexican
spotted
Historic Range: U.S.A. (AZ, CO, NM, TX,
UT), Mexico
Common Name: Owl, northern spotted
Historic Range: U.S.A. (CA, OR, WA),
Canada (B.C.)
Common Name: Palila (honeycreeper)
Historic Range: U.S.A. (HI)
Common Name: Parrot, Puerto Rican
Historic Range: U.S.A. (PR)
Common Name: Parrot, thick-billed
Historic Range: Mexico, U.S.A. (AZ, NM)
Common Name: Parrotbill, Maui (honey-
creeper)
Historic Range: U.S.A. (HI)
Common Name: Pelican, brown
Historic Range: U.S.A (Carolinas to TX,
CA, OR, WA), West Indies, coastal
Central, South America
Common Name: Petrel, Hawaiian dark-
rumped
Historic Range: U.S.A. (HI)
Common Name: Pigeon, Puerto Rican plain
Historic Range: U.S.A. (PR)
Common Name: Plover, piping
Historic Range: U.S.A. (Great Lakes,
northern Great Plains, Atlantic and Gulf
coasts, PR, VI), Canada, Mexico, Bahamas,
West Indies
Common Name: Plover, western snowy
Historic Range: U.S.A. (AZ, CA, CO, KS,
NM, NV, OK, OR, TX, UT, WA), Mexico
Common Name: Po`ouli (honeycreeper)
Historic Range: U.S.A. (HI)
Common Name: Prairie-chicken, Attwater's
greater
Historic Range: U.S.A. (TX)
Common Name: Rail, California clapper
Historic Range: U.S.A. (CA)
Common Name: Rail, Guam
Historic Range: Western Pacific—U.S.A.
(Guam)
Common Name: Rail, Yuma clapper
Historic Range: Mexico, U.S.A. (AZ, CA)
Common Name: Shearwater, Newell's
Townsend's
Historic Range: U.S.A. (HI)
Common Name: Shrike, San Clemente log-
gerhead
Historic Range: U.S.A. (CA)
Common Name: Sparrow, Cape Sable
seaside
Historic Range: U.S.A. (FL)
Common Name: Sparrow, Florida grasshopper
Historic Range: U.S.A. (FL)

Common Name: Sparrow, San Clemente sage
Historic Range: U.S.A. (CA)
Common Name: Stilt, Hawaiian
Historic Range: U.S.A. (HI)
Common Name: Stork, wood
Historic Range: U.S.A., (CA, AZ, TX to Carolinas), Mexico, Central and South America
Common Name: Swiftlet, Mariana gray
Historic Range: Western Pacific—U.S.A. (Guam, Rota, Tinian, Saipan, Agiguan)
Common Name: Tern, California
Historic Range: Mexico, U.S.A. (CA)
Common Name: Thrush, large Kauai
Historic Range: U.S.A. (HI)
Common Name: Thrush, Molokai
Historic Range: U.S.A. (HI)
Common Name: Thrush, small Kauai
Historic Range: U.S.A. (HI)
Common Name: Towhee, Inyo California
Historic Range: U.S.A. (CA)
Common Name: Vireo, black-capped
Historic Range: U.S.A. (KS, LA, NE, OK, TX), Mexico

Common Name: Vireo, least Bell's
Historic Range: U.S.A. (CA), Mexico
Common Name: Warbler (wood), Bachman's
Historic Range: Southeastern U.S.A., Cuba
Common Name: Warbler (wood), golden-cheeked
Historic Range: U.S.A. (TX), Mexico, Guatemala, Honduras, Nicaragua, Belize
Common Name: Warbler (wood), Kirtland's
Historic Range: U.S.A. (principally MI), Canada, West Indies—Bahama Islands
Common Name: Warbler (Old World), nightingale reed
Historic Range: Western Pacific—U.S.A. (Guam, Alamagan, Saipan)
Common Name: White-eye, bridled
Historic Range: Western Pacific—U.S.A. (Guam)
Common Name: Woodpecker, ivory-billed
Historic Range: southcentral and southeastern U.S.A., Cuba
Common Name: Woodpecker, red-cockaded
Historic Range: southcentral and southeastern U.S.A.

Endangered Fishes

Ala balik (trout)
Ayumodoki (loach)
Blindcat, Mexican (catfish)
Bonytongue, Asian
Catfish
Catfish, giant
Cavefish
Chub, bonytail
Chub, Borax Lake
Chub, humpback
Chub, Mohave tui
Chub, Owens tui
Chub, Pahranagat roundtail
Chub, Virgin River
Chub, Yaqui
Cicek (minnow)
Cui-ui
Dace, Ash Meadows speckled
Dace, Clover Valley speckled
Dace, Independence Valley speckled
Dace, Kendall Warm Springs
Dace, Moapa
Darter, amber
Darter, boulder
Darter, duskytail
Darter, fountain
Darter, Maryland
Darter, Okaloosa
Darter, watercress
Gambusia, Big Bend

Gambusia, Clear Creek
Gambusia, Pecos
Gambusia, San Marcos
Logperch, Conasauga
Logperch, Roanoke
Madtom, pygmy
Madtom, Scioto
Madtom, Smoky
Nekogigi (catfish)
Poolfish, Pahrump
Pupfish, Ash Meadows Amargosa
Pupfish, Comanche Springs
Pupfish, desert
Pupfish, Devils Hole
Pupfish, Leon Springs
Pupfish, Owens
Pupfish, Warm Springs
Salmon, sockeye
Shiner, Cahaba
Shiner, Cape Fear
Shiner, Palezone
Spinedace, White River
Springfish, Hiko White River
Springfish, White River
Squawfish, Colorado
Stickleback, unarmored threespine
Sturgeon, pallid
Sturgeon, shortnose
Sucker, June
Sucker, Lost River

Sucker, Modoc
Sucker, razorback
Sucker, shortnose
Tango, Miyako (Tokyo bitterling)
Temoleh, Ikan (minnow)

Topminnow, Gila
Totoaba (seatrout or weakfish)
Trout, Gila
Woundfin

Endangered Reptiles

Common Name: Alligator, American
Historic Habitat: Southeast U.S.A.
Common Name: Anole, Culebra Island giant
Historic Habitat: U.S.A. (PR)
Common Name: Boa, Mona
Historic Habitat: U.S.A. (PR)
Common Name: Boa, Puerto Rican
Historic Habitat: U.S.A. (PR)
Common Name: Crocodile, American
Historic Habitat: U.S.A. (FL), Mexico,
Caribbean, Central, South America
Common Name: Crocodile, saltwater
Historic Habitat: Southeast Asia, South
Pacific
Common Name: Gecko, Monito
Historic Habitat: U.S.A. (PR)
Common Name: Iguana, Mona ground
Historic Habitat: U.S.A. (PR—Mona
Island)
Common Name: Lizard, blunt-nosed leopard
Historic Habitat: U.S.A. (CA)
Common Name: Lizard, Coachella Valley
fringe-toed
Historic Habitat: U.S.A. (CA)
Common Name: Lizard, Island night
Historic Habitat: U.S.A. (CA)
Common Name: Lizard, St. Croix ground
Historic Habitat: U.S.A. (VI)
Common Name: Rattlesnake, New Mexican
ridge-nosed
Historic Habitat: U.S.A. (NM), Mexico
Common Name: Skink, bluetail mole
Historic Habitat: U.S.A. (FL)

Common Name: Skink, sand
Historic Habitat: U.S.A. (FL)
Common Name: Snake, Atlantic salt marsh
Historic Habitat: U.S.A. (FL)
Common Name: Snake, Concho water
Historic Habitat: U.S.A. (TX)
Common Name: Snake, eastern indigo
Historic Habitat: U.S.A. (AL, FL, GA, MS,
SC)
Common Name: Snake, giant garter
Historic Habitat: U.S.A. (CA)
Common Name: Snake, San Francisco garter
Historic Habitat: U.S.A. (CA)
Common Name: Tortoise, desert
Historic Habitat: U.S.A. (AZ, CA, NV,
UT), Mexico
Common Name: Tortoise, desert
Historic Habitat: U.S.A. (AZ, CA, NV,
UT), Mexico
Common Name: Tortoise, gopher
Historic Habitat: U.S.A. (AL, FL, GA, LA,
MS, SC)
Common Name: Turtle, Alabama redbelly
Historic Habitat: U.S.A. (AL)
Common Name: Turtle, flattened musk
Historic Habitat: U.S.A. (AL)
Common Name: Turtle, Plymouth redbelly
Historic Habitat: U.S.A. (MA)
Common Name: Turtle, ringed map
Historic Habitat: U.S.A.
Common Name: Turtle, yellow-blotched map
Historic Habitat: U.S.A. (MS)

Prehistoric Creatures

Acrocanthosaurus	Aurochs	Cryolophosaurus	Eryopsid
Afrovenator	Baryonyx	Cryptoclidus	Gastonia
Albertosaurus	Brontops	Daspletosaurus	Giganotosaurus
Allosaurus	Brontosaurus	Dilophosaurus	Hadrosaur
Alxasaurus	Camarasaurus	Dimetrodon	Herrerasaurus
Amargasaurus	Carnotosaurus	Diplodocus	Hipsilophodont
Ammonite	Centrosaurus	Dipnoan	Hylaeosaurus
Anatosaurus	Ceratosaurus	Dromiceiomimus	Hypacrosaurus
Ankylosaurus	Chasmosaurus	Dryptosaur	Ichthyosaurus
Apatosaurus	Coelophysis	Edmontonia	Iguanodon
Archeaopteryx	Compsognathus	Edmontosaurus	Laelaps
Archelon	Corythosaurus	Elasmosaurus	Lambeosaurus
Argentinosaurus	Creodont	Eohippus	Lystrosaurus

Maiasaura	Oviraptor	Seismosaurus	Tiger, Saber-toothed
Mammoth, Wooly	Parasaurolophus	Sinosauropteryx	Troodon
Mastodon	Patagosaurus	Sloth, Giant	Tropeognathus
Megathere	Pelorosaurus	Smilodon	Tylosaurus
Merodus	Plesiosaurus	Stegoceras	Tyrannosaurus (Rex)
Miacis	Pleurocoelus	Stegosaurus	Urus
Monoclonius	Pteradactyl	Struthiomimus	Utahraptor
Mononykus	Pteranodon	Stygimoloch	Velociraptor
Mosasaurus	Quetzalcoatlus	Styracosaurus	Wooly Mammoth
Moshops	Revueltosaurus	Tenontosaurus	
Muttaburrasaurus	Rhamphorhynchus	Therizinosaurus	
Orodromeus	Sauropod	Thescelosaurus	

The Bible — King James

(Vulgate/Douay names in parentheses)

Old Testament

Genesis	Esther	Micah (Micheas)	Judith
Exodus	Job	Nahum	Esther (Additions to
Leviticus	Psalms	Habakkuk (Habacuc)	Esther)
Numbers	Proverbs	Zephaniah	Wisdom of
Deuteronomy	Ecclesiastes	(Sophonias)	Solomon
Joshua	Song of Solomon	Haggai (Aggeus)	Ecclesiasticus
Judges	(Canticle of	Zechariah	Sirach
Ruth	Canticles)	(Zacharias)	Baruch
1 Samuel (1 Kings)	Isaiah (Isaias)	Malachi (Malachias)	Letter of Jeremiah
2 Samuel (2 Kings)	Jeremiah (Jeremias)		Song of the Three
1 Kings (3 Kings)	Lamentations	**Apocrypha**	Holy Children
2 Kings (4 Kings)	Ezekiel (Ezechiel)	1 Esdras (3 Esdras)	Susanna
1 Chronicles (1	Daniel	2 Esdras (4 Esdras)	Bel and the Dragon
Paralipomenon)	Hosea (Osee)	1 Maccabees (1	Azariah
2 Chronicles (2	Joel	Machabees)	Manasseh Bel
Paralipomenon)	Amos	2 Maccabees (2	(Prayer of
Ezra (1 Esdras)	Obadiah (Abdias)	Machabees)	Manasses)
Nehemiah (2 Esdras)	Jonah (Jonas)	Tobit (Tobias)	

New Testament

Matthew	2 Corinthians	2 Timothy	2 John
Mark	Galatians	Titus	3 John
Luke	Ephesians	Philemon	Jude
John	Philippians	Hebrews	Revelation
Acts of the	Colossians	James	(Apocalypse)
Apostles	1 Thessalonians	1 Peter	
Romans	2 Thessalonians	2 Peter	
1 Corinthians	1 Timothy	1 John	

The Prophets

Amos	Ezra	Jeremiah	Moses
Daniel	Haggai	Joel	Nahum
Elisha	Hosea	Jonah	
Ezekiel	Isaiah	Micah	

Biblical Names

Male			Female
Aaron	Han	Nadab	Bilhah
Abednego	Haman	Nahbi	Dinah
Abel	Haran	Nahor	Eglah
Abiah	Herod	Noah	Esther
Abiel	Heth	Nun	Eve
Abraham	Hiram	Obal	Hagar
Adam	Hoham	Obed	Hamutal
Agag	Ibzan	Omar	Hannah
Ahab	Ira	Omri	Hoglah
Ahaz	Irad	Ophir	Jael
Ahira	Isaac	Oreb	Julia
Amasa	Ishmael	Ozem	Junia
Amos	Jacob	Peleg	Leah
Ananias	Jada	Rezon	Lydia
Annas	James	Sacar	Maacah
Ara	Japheth	Samson	Mahlah
Asa	Jarad	Saul	Mary
Boaz	Jared	Serug	Mary-Magdalene
Cain	Jehu	Seth	Merab
Caleb	Jephthah	Shadrach	Micah
Chuza	Joab	Shem	Miriam
Cush	Joram	Sodi	Naomi
Cyrus	Joshua	Solomon	Phoebe
Dan	Kish	Terah	Rachel
David	Laban	Ulam	Rahab
Doeg	Lamech	Unni	Rizpah
Eli	Levi	Uri	Ruth
Enoch	Lot	Uria	Sarah
Enos	Mash	Uriah	Salome
Esau	Massa	Zaham	Tamar
Gideon	Meshach		Vashti
Gog	Moab	**Female**	Zillah
Goliath	Moreh	Abigail	Zilpah
	Nabal	Adah	

Celestial Bodies

The Planets and Their Moons

KEY: **Planet** Moons			
Mercury	Thebe	Pandora	Bianca
	Leda	Titan	Umbriel
Venus	Himalia	Epimetheus	Cressida
	Lysithea	Hyperion	Desdemona
Earth	Io	Janus	Juliet
The Moon	Elara	Iapetus	Titania
	Ananke	Mimas	Portia
Mars	Carme	Phoebe	Rosalind
Phobos	Europa	Enceladus	Belinda
Deimos	Pasiphae	Tethys	Oberon
	Sinope	Telesto	Puck
	Ganymede	Calypso	Uranus Xvi
Jupiter		Dione	Uranus Xvii
Metis	**Saturn**	Helene	Miranda
Adrastea	Pan		Ariel
Amalthea	Atlas	**Uranus**	
Callisto	Rhea	Cordelia	**Neptune**
	Prometheus	Ophelia	Naiad

Thalassa	Galatea	Proteus	**Pluto**
Despina	Nereid		Charon
Triton	Larissa		

Asteroids

Amor	Apollo	Icarus	Vesta Asteroid
Amphitrite	Ceres	Toro Asteroid	

Comets

Arend-Roland Austin	Humason	Morehouse	Tempel 2 Comet
Brorsen-Metcalf	Iras-Araki-Alcock	Okazaki-Levy-	West Comet
Encke Halley's	Comet	Rudenko	
Giacobini-Zinner	Kohoutek	Schwassmann-	
Grigg-Skjellerup	Markos	Wachmann Comet	

Constellations

Andromeda	Circinus	Lacerta	Piscis Austrinus
Antlia	Columba	Leo	Puppis
Apus	Coma Berenices	Leo Minor	Pyxis
Aquarius	Corona Austrina	Lepus	Reticulum
Aquila	Corona Borealis	Libra	Sagitta
Ara	Corvus	Lupus	Sagittarius
Aries	Crater	Lynx	Scorpius
Auriga	Crux	Lyra	Sculptor
Boötes	Cygnus	Mensa	Scutum
Caelum	Delphinus	Microscopium	Serpens
Camelopardalis	Dorado	Monoceros	Sextans
Cancer	Draco	Musca	Taurus
Canes Venatici	Equuleus	Norma	Telescopium
Canis Major	Eridanus	Octans	Triangulum
Canis Minor	Fornax	Ophiuchus	Triangulum Australe
Capricornus	Gemini	Orion	Tucana
Carina	Grus	Pavo	Ursa Major
Cassiopeia	Hercules	Pegasus	Ursa Minor
Centaurus	Horologium	Perseus	Vela
Cepheus	Hydra	Phoenix	Virgo
Cetus	Hydrus	Pictor	Volans
Chamaeleon	Indus	Pisces	Vulpecula

Meteorites

Allendearoos	Ivuna	Odessa	Sikhote-Alin
Bondoc	Lazarev	Okhansk	Tonk
Bruderheim	Murchison	Orgueil	Tungusk
Harleton	Murray	Pribram	

Meteoroids

Aquarid	Draconid	Orionid	Taurid
Arietid	Geminid	Perseid	
Cyrillid	Leonid	Quadrantid	

Major Stars

Acamarachern-	Aldebaran	Alkaid	Alphekka
aracrux	Alderamin	Almaak	Alpheratz
Adara	Algenib	Alnair	Alshain
Agena	Algieba	Alnath	Altair
Albireo	Algol	Alnilam	Ankaa
Alcor	Alhena	Alnitak	Antares
Alcyone	Alioth	Alphard	Arcturus

Major Stars (continued)

Arneb	Etamin	Mirach	Sadalmelik
Bellatrix	Fomalhaut	Mirphak	Saiph
Betelgeuse	Hadar	Mizar	Scheat
Canopus	Hamal	Nihal	Shaula
Capella	Izar	Nunki	Shedir
Castor	Kaus Australis	Phad	Sirius
Cor Caroli	Kocab	Polaris	Spica
Deneb	Markab	Pollux	Tarazed
Denebola	Megrez	Procyon	Thuban
Diphda	Menkar	Rasalgethi	Unukalha
Dubhe	Merak	Rasalhague	Vega
Elnath	Mintaka	Regulus	Vindemiatrix
Enif	Mira	Rigel	

Order of Brightest Stars as Seen from Earth

Sun Irius	Procyon	Aldebaran	Deneb
Canopus Rigil	Achernar	Antares	Regulus
Kentaurusarc-	Betelgeuse	Spica	Adhara
turusvega	Hadar	Pollux	Castor
Capella	Acrux	Fomalhaut	Gacrux
Rigel	Altair	Becrux	Shaula

Other Celestial Bodies

Achondritesalais	Gum Nebula	Oberon	Supernova
Amalthea	Hercules Nova	Omicron Ceti Star	Supernovae
Andromeda Galaxy	Hyittis Chondrite	Orion Nebula	Tektites
Ariel	Hyperion	Phobos	Tethys
Asteroid Belts	Iapetus	Phoebe	Titan
Australites	Io	Planets	Titania
Black Holes	Janus	Pleiades Cluster	Triton
Blazars	Jupiter	Pluto	Umbriel
Brown Dwarf Stars	Kapoeta Achondrite	Pulsars	Uranus
Callisto	Maffei Galaxies	Quasars	Ureilites
Cassiopeia	Markarian Galaxies	R Coronae Borealis	Venus
Charon	Mars	Stars	Virgo Galactic Cluster
Chassignites	Mercury	Red Dwarf Stars	White Dwarf Stars
Chiron	Milky Way Galaxy	Red Giant Stars	White Holes
Crab Nebula	Mimas	Rhea	Wolf-Rayet Stars
Deimos	Miranda	Saturn	X-Ray Stars
Dione	Moon	Sigma Orionis	Zeta Aurigae Star
Eart	Nebulae	Spiral Galaxies	Zodiacal Dust
Enceladus	Nemesis	Star Clusters	
Europa	Neptune	Starburst Galaxies	
Ganymede	Nereid	Sun	

Chemical Elements

Sorted by Element Name

Element	Symbol	Atomic Number	Element	Symbol	Atomic Number
actinium	Ac	89	arsenic	As	33
aluminum	Al	13	astatine	At	85
americium	Am	95	barium	Ba	56
antimony	Sb	51	berkelium	Bk	97
argon	Ar	18	beryllium	Be	4

Elements Sorted by Name (continued)

Element	Symbol	Atomic Number	Element	Symbol	Atomic Number
bismuth	Bi	83	nickel	Ni	28
boron	B	5	niobium	Nb	41
bromine	Br	35	nitrogen	N	7
cadmium	Cd	48	nobelium	No	102
calcium	Ca	20	osmium	Os	76
californium	Cf	98	oxygen	O	8
carbon	C	6	palladium	Pd	46
cerium	Ce	58	phosphorus	P	15
cesium	Cs	55	platinum	Pt	78
chlorine	Cl	17	plutonium	Pu	94
chromium	Cr	24	polonium	Po	84
cobalt	Co	27	potassium	K	19
copper	Cu	29	praseodymium	Pr	59
curium	Cm	96	promethium	Pm	61
dysprosium	Dy	66	protactinium	Pa	91
einsteinium	Es	99	radium	Ra	88
erbium	Er	68	radon	Rn	86
europium	Eu	63	rhenium	Re	75
fermium	Fm	100	rhodium	Rh	45
fluorine	F	9	rubidium	Rb	37
francium	Fr	87	ruthenium	Ru	44
gadolinium	Gd	64	rutherfordium	Rf	104
gallium	Ga	31	samarium	Sm	62
germanium	Ge	32	scandium	Sc	21
gold	Au	79	selenium	Se	34
hafnium	Hf	72	silicon	Si	14
hahnium	Ha	105	silver	Ag	47
helium	He	2	sodium	Na	11
holmium	Ho	67	strontium	Sr	38
hydrogen	H	1	sulfur	S	16
indium	In	49	tantalum	Ta	73
iodine	I	53	technetium	Tc	43
iridium	Ir	77	tellurium	Te	52
iron	Fe	26	terbium	Tb	65
krypton	Kr	36	thallium	Tl	81
lanthanum	La	57	thorium	Th	90
lawrencium	Lr	103	thulium	Tm	69
lead	Pb	82	tin	Sn	50
lithium	Li	3	titanium	Ti	22
lutetium	Lu	71	tungsten	W	74
magnesium	Mg	12	uranium	U	92
manganese	Mn	25	vanadium	V	23
mendelevium	Md	101	xenon	Xe	54
mercury	Hg	80	ytterbium	Yb	70
molybdenum	Mo	42	yttrium	Y	39
neodymium	Nd	60	zinc	Zn	30
neon	Ne	10	zirconium	Zr	40
neptunium	Np	93			

Elements Sorted by Atomic Weight

Atomic Weight	Element Name	Symbol	Atomic Weight	Element Name	Symbol
1	hydrogen	H	6	carbon	C
2	helium	He	7	nitrogen	N
3	lithium	Li	8	oxygen	O
4	beryllium	Be	9	fluorine	F
5	boron	B	10	neon	Ne

Elements Sorted by Atomic Weight (continued)

Atomic Weight	Element Name	Symbol	Atomic Weight	Element Name	Symbol
11	sodium	Na	59	praseodymium	Pr
12	magnesium	Mg	60	neodymium	Nd
13	aluminum	Al	61	promethium	Pm
14	silicon	Si	62	samarium	Sm
15	phosphorus	P	63	europium	Eu
16	sulfur	S	64	gadolinium	Gd
17	chlorine	Cl	65	terbium	Tb
18	argon	Ar	66	dysprosium	Dy
19	potassium	K	67	holmium	Ho
20	calcium	Ca	68	erbium	Er
21	scandium	Sc	69	thulium	Tm
22	titanium	Ti	70	ytterbium	Yb
23	vanadium	V	71	lutetium	Lu
24	chromium	Cr	72	hafnium	Hf
25	manganese	Mn	73	tantalum	Ta
26	iron	Fe	74	tungsten	W
27	cobalt	Co	75	rhenium	Re
28	nickel	Ni	76	osmium	Os
29	copper	Cu	77	iridium	Ir
30	zinc	Zn	78	platinum	Pt
31	gallium	Ga	79	gold	Au
32	germanium	Ge	80	mercury	Hg
33	arsenic	As	81	thallium	Tl
34	selenium	Se	82	lead	Pb
35	bromine	Br	83	bismuth	Bi
36	krypton	Kr	84	polonium	Po
37	rubidium	Rb	85	astatine	At
38	strontium	Sr	86	radon	Rn
39	yttrium	Y	87	francium	Fr
40	zirconium	Zr	88	radium	Ra
41	niobium	Nb	89	actinium	Ac
42	molybdenum	Mo	90	thorium	Th
43	technetium	Tc	91	protactinium	Pa
44	ruthenium	Ru	92	uranium	U
45	rhodium	Rh	93	neptunium	Np
46	palladium	Pd	94	plutonium	Pu
47	silver	Ag	95	americium	Am
48	cadmium	Cd	96	curium	Cm
49	indium	In	97	berkelium	Bk
50	tin	Sn	98	californium	Cf
51	antimony	Sb	99	einsteinium	Es
52	tellurium	Te	100	fermium	Fm
53	iodine	I	101	mendelevium	Md
54	xenon	Xe	102	nobelium	No
55	cesium	Cs	103	lawrencium	Lr
56	barium	Ba	104	rutherfordium	Rf
57	lanthanum	La	105	hahnium	Ha
58	cerium	Ce			

Elements Sorted by Symbol

Symbol	Atomic Number	Element Name	Symbol	Atomic Number	Element Name
Ac	89	actinium	As	33	arsenic
Ag	47	silver	At	85	astatine
Al	13	aluminum	Au	79	gold
Am	95	americium	B	5	boron
Ar	18	argon	Ba	56	barium

Symbol	Atomic Number	Element Name	Symbol	Atomic Number	Element Name
Be	4	beryllium	Nd	60	neodymium
Bi	83	bismuth	Ne	10	neon
Bk	97	berkelium	Ni	28	nickel
Br	35	bromine	No	102	nobelium
C	6	carbon	Np	93	neptunium
Ca	20	calcium	O	8	oxygen
Cd	48	cadmium	Os	76	osmium
Ce	58	cerium	P	15	phosphorus
Cf	98	californium	Pa	91	protactinium
Cl	17	chlorine	Pb	82	lead
Cm	96	curium	Pd	46	palladium
Co	27	cobalt	Pm	61	promethium
Cr	24	chromium	Po	84	polonium
Cs	55	cesium	Pr	59	praseodymium
Cu	29	copper	Pt	78	platinum
Dy	66	dysprosium	Pu	94	plutonium
Er	68	erbium	Ra	88	radium
Es	99	einsteinium	Rb	37	rubidium
Eu	63	europium	Re	75	rhenium
F	9	fluorine	Rf	104	rutherfordium
Fe	26	iron	Rh	45	rhodium
Fm	100	fermium	Rn	86	radon
Fr	87	francium	Ru	44	ruthenium
Ga	31	gallium	S	16	sulfur
Gd	64	gadolinium	Sb	51	antimony
Ge	32	germanium	Sc	21	scandium
H	1	hydrogen	Se	34	selenium
Ha	105	hahnium	Si	14	silicon
He	2	helium	Sm	62	samarium
Hf	72	hafnium	Sn	50	tin
Hg	80	mercury	Sr	38	strontium
Ho	67	holmium	Ta	73	tantalum
I	53	iodine	Tb	65	terbium
In	49	indium	Tc	43	technetium
Ir	77	iridium	Te	52	tellurium
K	19	potassium	Th	90	thorium
Kr	36	krypton	Ti	22	titanium
La	57	lanthanum	Tl	81	thallium
Li	3	lithium	Tm	69	thulium
Lr	103	lawrencium	U	92	uranium
Lu	71	lutetium	V	23	vanadium
Md	101	mendelevium	W	74	tungsten
Mg	12	magnesium	Xe	54	xenon
Mn	25	manganese	Y	39	yttrium
Mo	42	molybdenum	Yb	70	ytterbium
N	7	nitrogen	Zn	30	zinc
Na	11	sodium	Zr	40	zirconium
Nb	41	niobium			

Gemstones and Precious Metals

Agate	Apatite	Calcite	Chrysoprase
Amber	Aventurine	Carnelian	Citrine
Amethyst	Azurite	Chrysanthemum	Copper
Ametrine	Bauzite	Stone	Coral
Andalusite	Beryl	Chrysoberyl	Corundum

Diamond	Iolite	Peridot	Spinel
Diopside	Jade, Green	Platinum	Sugilite
Dolomite	Jadeite, Green	Quartz	Sunstone
Emerald	Jasper	Rhodochrosite	Tanzanite
Fire Opal	Jasper Pyrite	Rhodonite	Thundereggs
Fluorite	Kornerupine	Ruby	Tigereye
Garnet	Labradorite	Sapphire	Tigeriron
Garnet, Pyrope	Lapis	Sapphire, Black	Topaz, Blue
Garnet, Rhodolite	Magnetite	Sapphire, Blue	Topaz, Imperial
Garnet, Rose	Malachite	Sapphire, Golden	Topaz, White
Garnet, Umba	Mica	Sapphire, Green	Tourmaline
Gold	Moonstone	Sapphire, Star	Turritella
Goldstone	Obsidian	Scapolite	Unakite
Hematite	Onyx	Silver	Zircon
Howlite	Opal	Sodalite	Zirconia

Lifestyle

Anniversaries

YEAR	TRADITIONAL	MODERN	YEAR	TRADITIONAL	MODERN
1st	Paper	Clock	15th	Crystal	Watches
2nd	Cotton	China	16th	—	Silverware
3rd	Leather	Crystal	17th	—	Furniture
4th	Fruit	Electrical Goods	18th	—	Porcelain
5th	Wood	Silverware	19th	—	Bronze
6th	Iron	Wood	20th	China	Platinum
7th	Wool	Pen/Pencil Sets	25th	Silver	Silver
8th	Bronze/Pottery	Linen	30th	Pearl	Diamond
9th	Pottery	Leather	35th	Coral	Jade
10th	Tin	Jewelry	40th	Ruby	Ruby
11th	Steel	Fashion Jewelry	45th	—	Sapphire
12th	Silk	Colored Gems	50th	Gold	Gold
13th	Lace	Textiles	55th	Emerald	Emerald
14th	Ivory	Gold Jewelry	60th	Diamond	Diamond

Birthstones by Month

MONTH	TRADITIONAL	MODERN	MONTH	TRADITIONAL	MODERN
January	Garnet	Garnet	August	Sardonyx	Peridot, Jade
February	Amethyst	Amethyst	September	Sapphire	Sapphire
March	Bloodstone	Aquamarine	October	Tourmaline	Opal
April	Diamond	Diamond	November	Citrine	Yellow Topaz
May	Emerald	Emerald	December	Zircon	Blue Topaz,
June	Alexandrite	Pearl			Turquoise
July	Ruby	Ruby			

Signs of the Zodiac

SIGN	NAME	SUN ENTERS	SIGN	NAME	SUN ENTERS
Aries	The Ram	March 21	Libra	The Scales	September 23
Taurus	The Bull	April 20	Scorpio	The Scorpion	October 24
Gemini	The Twins	May 21	Sagittarius	The Centaur	November 22
Cancer	The Crab	June 22	Capricorn	The Goat	December 22
Leo	The Lion	July 23	Aquarius	The Water Bearer	January 20
Virgo	The Virgin	August 23	Pisces	The Fish	February 19

Musical Terms and Styles

Absolute pitch: ability to identify pitches mentally

A cappella: sung without instrumental accompaniment

Accelerando: increase of speed in music

Accidentals: sharps, flats, or natural signs

Adagio: slow, leisurely

Air: song, melody

Allegretto: moderately fast; between Andante and Allegro

Allegro: lively, rapid

Allemande: a dance

Alto: lowest female vocal part

Andante: moderately slow, walking speed

Aria: opera or oratorio piece

Arpeggio: notes of a chord played consecutively

Atonal: music lacking a tonal center

Bagatelle: light musical piece

Ballad: song that tells a story

Baritone: voice between tenor and bass

Baroque: musical style and period, 1600 to 1750

Bass: lowest voice, below baritone

Bass clef: F clef

Berceuse: lullaby

Bitonal: two tonic centers at same time

Bow: drawn across strings to generate sound

Cacophony: discordant, dissonant sound

Cadence: resolution, or conclusion

Cadenza: extended solo passage

Cannon: melody repeated by a different voice, as in a round

Cantata: choral work

Canticle: nonmetrical hymn or song

C clef: represents C on staff

Cello: tenor string instrument

Chord: notes played simultaneously

Chromatic: by half steps

Classical: musical period and style, circa late 1700s to mid-1820s

Clef: indicates which lines and spaces represent which notes

Common time: 4/4 meter

Concerto: piece for soloist(s) and orchestra

Consonance: opposite of dissonance

Counterpoint: two or more melodic lines played against one another.

Crescendo: louder

Diatonic: notes or scale without sharps or flats

Diminished: lowered, reduced

Diminuendo: gradually growing softer

Diminution: shortened note values

Dirge: performed at funerals or memorial services

Dissonance: conflicting; opposite of consonance

Divertimento: instrumental piece

Dodecaphonic: 12-tone music

Dolce: sweetly, softly

Dynamics: degrees of loudness or softness in music

Eighth: octave

Elegy: melancholy piece

Ensemble: group of singers or musicians

Equal temperament: tuning system that divides octave into equal intervals

Etude: short song for instructional use

Expressionism: abstract early-twentieth-century musical style

Falsetto: voice used to sing above the normal register

Fermata: pause, stop, or interruption

Finale: last movement of a piece

Fine: end of musical piece

Flats: lowers a pitch one half-step

Forte: loud, strong

Fortissimo: very loud

Fugue: contrapuntal piece built in layers

Grand opera: large-scale

Grave: slow, heavy

Gregorian chant: Roman Catholic chants

Harmony: chord progression, or consonance

Hymn: religious song

Improvisation: spontaneous composition

Interlude: used to bridge two parts of a work

Interval: distance between two notes

Jazz: highly improvised music style with African-American roots

K: Kochel; number system used to designate the works of Mozart

Kapellmeister: music director for church or royalty

Key: tonal center

Key signature: sharps or flats indicating key of composition

Kyrie: "Lord"; first part of Mass

Largo: broad, slow, stately

Legato: smooth, connected

Leitmotif: musical phrase used to identify with a person, place, or thing

Lento: slow

Libretto: text of opera or oratorio

Lullaby: cradle song

Lyric: words to a song or choral work

Lyric Soprano: female singer with higher range than Dramatic Soprano

Lyric Tenor: male singer with higher range than Dramatic Tenor

Madrigal: unaccompanied Renaissance choral piece

Maestoso: majestic, dignified

March: marching music

Musical Terms and Styles (continued)

Mass: religious musical work

Meno: less

Mezzo forte: moderately loud

Mezzo piano: moderately soft

Mode: scale pattern with set intervals of whole and half steps; Aeolian, Dorian, Ionian, Locrian, Lydian, Mixolydian, Phrygian

Modern: twentieth-century, contemporary music

Modulation: to change keys

Molto, molta: much

Monophony: written in a single melodic line; opposite of polyphony

Motet: religious choral composition

Motif: short musical theme or idea

Movement: segment of a larger piece, e.g., sonatas, symphonies, concertos

Musicology: study of music, music history

Nachtmusik: "Night Music"

Natural: without sharps or flats

Nocturne: night-piece, serenade

Notation: written music

Octave: interval of eight diatonic steps

Octet: piece for eight parts; eight-member group

Opera: musical play

Operetta: light opera

Opus: a musical work

Oratorio: operatic work without staging, sets, or costumes.

Orchestration: arranging, writing, or scoring music

Ornament: melodic embellishment

Ostinato: repeated melodic or rhythmic fragment

Overture: introductory music for opera, ballet, or oratorio

Partita: set of variations or a suite

Perfect pitch: ability to identify any musical note

Phrase: single musical idea

Piano: softly

Pianissimo: very soft

Polonaise: Polish dance

Polyphony: "Many sounds"

Prelude: "Play before"; introductory movement or work

Presto: fast, rapid

Recitative: musical work in an opera or oratorio

Renaissance: musical period, from mid-fifteenth century through sixteenth century

Requiem: Mass to commemorate the dead

Resolution: from dissonance to consonance

Ritardando: gradually growing slower

Romantic: musical era, circa 1827–1900, characterized by emotional themes

Root: fundamental note of chord

Rubato: modification of strict rhythmical flow

Sanctus: "Holy"; part of a Requiem Mass

Scale: graduated series of tones arranged in a specified order

Scherzo: joke, jest; a sprightly movement

Serialism: form of music writing based on Twelve-Tone technique

Serenade: a love song or piece

Sforzando: explosively

Sharps: raises a pitch one half-step

Slur: notes connected smoothly without a break

Sonata: piece for solo or accompanied instrument

Song forms: sections in a song to contrast similar and different sections

Soprano: highest female vocal range, above alto

Sostenuto: sustained

Staccato: sounded in a short, detached manner

Staff: five horizontal lines upon which music is written

Subject: theme or motif that is the basis for a musical form

Symphony: piece for large orchestra; usually four movements

Syncopation: rhythmic result produced when a regularly accented beat is displaced onto an unaccented beat

Tempo: speed at which a musical composition is performed

Tenor: male voice between alto and baritone

Timbre: quality of musical tone that distinguishes one sound from another

Tonic: key center of scale or melody

Treble: highest voice, instrument, or part

Triad: three-note chord

Trill: ornament; rapid alternation between two pitches

Turn: ornament; four or five notes that move around a pitch

Tutto, Tutta: all, whole

Twelve-Tone: style in which given note not repeated until all other chromatic pitches have been used

Viola: alto instrument of violin family

Violin: treble instrument of string family

Vivace: spirited, bright, rapid, equal to or exceeding allegro

Votive: chant or hymn honoring a saint or the Virgin Mary

Mythology—Greek and Roman, Norse, and Egyptian

Roman-Greek Mythological Equivalents

Apollo	Apollo	god of the sun	Bacchus	Dionysus	god of revelry, wine
Diana	Artemis	goddess of the moon, huntress	Neptune	Poseidon	god of the sea
			Pluto	Hades	god of the Underworld
Faunus	Pan	god of woods, fields	Saturn	Cronus	god of harvest, father of Zeus
Gaea	Gaea	goddess of the earth			
Hercules	Heracles	hero, demigod	Ulysses	Odysseus	hero, king of Ithaca
Jupiter	Zeus	chief god	Venus	Aphrodite	goddess of love
Mars	Ares	god of war	Juno	Hera	queen of the gods
Mercury	Hermes	messenger of the gods	Ceres	Demeter	goddess of agriculture

Greek-Roman Mythology (Roman equivalents in parentheses)

Acheron: one of the Rivers of the Underworld

Achilles: Greek warrior, fought at Troy; killed by Paris, wounded in his vulnerable heel

Adonis: beautiful youth loved by Aphrodite

Aeacus: one of three judges of the dead in Hades; son of Zeus

Aeneas: Trojan; son of Anchises and Aphrodite

Aeolus: one of the Winds

Aether: personification of sky

Agamemnon: king of Mycenae; led Greeks against Troy; slain by Clytemnestra and Aegisthus

Agiaia: one of the Graces

Ajax: Greek warrior; killed himself at Troy

Alcmene: mother of Hercules by Zeus

Alcyone: one of the Pleiades

Alecto: one of the Furies

Amazons: female warriors

Amphitrite: sea goddess; wife of Poseidon

Andromeda: daughter of Cepheus; rescued by Perseus

Anteros: God who avenged unrequited love

Antigone: daughter of Oedipus

Aphrodite (Venus): goddess of love and beauty; daughter of Zeus; mother of Eros

Apollo: god of beauty, poetry, music; identified with Helios as Phoebus Apollo; son of Zeus and Leto

Aquilo: one of the Winds

Ares (Mars): god of war; son of Zeus and Hera

Argo: ship in which Jason and followers sailed to Colchis for Golden Fleece

Artemis (Diana): goddess of moon; huntress; twin sister of Apollo

Asclepius (Aesculapius): mortal son of Apollo; slain by Zeus for raising dead; later deified as god of medicine

Astarte: Phoenician goddess of love; variously identified with Aphrodite, Selene, and Artemis

Astraea: goddess of Justice; daughter of Zeus and Themis

Athena (Minerva): goddess of wisdom

Atlas: Titan; held world on his shoulders

Atreus: king of Mycenae; father of Menelaus and Agamemnon; brother of Thyestes, three of whose sons he slew and served to him at banquet; slain by Aegisthus

Atropos: one of the Fates

Auster: one of the Winds

Bellona: Roman goddess of war

Boreas: one of the Winds

Callisto: nymph loved by Zeus

Calliope: a Muse

Calypso: sea nymph; kept Odysseus on her island

Cassandra: prophetess who was never believed

Castor: twin brother of Pollux; sons of Leda and Zeus

Centaur: half man, half horse

Cerberus: three-headed dog guarding entrance to Hades

Chaos: formless void, first of gods

Charon: boatman on Styx who ferried souls of dead to Hades

Charybdis: female monster; whirlpool

Chimera: monster with head of lion, body of goat, tail of serpent

Chiron: famous centaur

Chronos: personification of time

Circe: sorceress; changed Odysseus's men into swine

Clio: one of the Muses

Clotho: one of the Fates

Clytemnestra: wife of Agamemnon

Cocytus: one of the Rivers of the Underworld

Greek-Roman Mythology (continued)

Creon: father of Jocasta; ordered burial alive of Antigone

Cronus (Saturn): Titan; god of harvest; son of Uranus and Gaea; dethroned by his son Zeus

Cyclopes: one-eyed giants (singular: Cyclops)

Daedalus: father of Icarus; devised wings attached with wax for himself and Icarus

Daphne: nymph; pursued by Apollo; changed to laurel tree

Decuma: one of the Fates

Demeter (Ceres): goddess of agriculture; mother of Persephone

Dido: queen of Carthage

Dione: Titan goddess; mother by Zeus of Aphrodite

Dionysus (Bacchus): god of wine; son of Zeus and Semele

Dryads: wood nymphs

Echo: nymph; fell hopelessly in love with Narcissus; faded away except for her voice

Electra: daughter of Agamemnon and Clytemnestra

Electra: one of the Pleiades

Elysium Fields: abode of blessed dead

Eos (Aurora): goddess of dawn

Erato: one of the Muses

Erebus: spirit of darkness; son of Chaos

Erinyes: one of the Furies

Eris: goddess of discord

Eros (Amor or Cupid): god of love; son of Aphrodite

Eumenides: Furies

Euphrosyne: one of the Graces

Eurus: one of the Winds

Eurydice: nymph; wife of Orpheus

Euterpe: one of the Muses

Fates: goddesses of destiny; Clotho (Spinner of thread of life), Lachesis (Determiner of length), and Atropos (Cutter of thread); also called Moirae. Identified by Romans with their goddesses of fate; Nona, Decuma, and Morta; also called Parcae

Fauns: Roman deities of woods and groves

Favonius: one of the Winds

Flora: Roman goddess of flowers

Fortuna: Roman goddess of fortune

Furies: avenging spirits; Alecto, Megaera, and Tisiphone; known also as Erinyes or Eumenides

Gaea: goddess of earth; daughter of Chaos; mother of Titans; known also as Ge, Gea, Gaia

Golden Fleece: fleece carried off by Jason

Gorgons: female monsters; Euryale, Medusa, and Stheno; snakes for hair; their gaze turned mortals to stone

Graces: goddesses; Aglaia (Brilliance), Euphrosyne (Joy), and Thalia (Bloom); daughters of Zeus

Hades (Pluto): brother of Zeus; realm of dead

Hamadryads: tree nymphs

Harpies: monsters with heads of women, bodies of birds

Hebe (Juventas): goddess of youth

Hecate: goddess of sorcery, witchcraft

Hector: son of Priam; slayer of Patroclus; slain by Achilles

Helen: world's most beautiful woman; daughter of Zeus and Leda; wife of Menelaus; carried to Troy by Paris, causing Trojan War

Helios (Sol): god of sun; later identified with Apollo

Hephaestus (Vulcan): god of fire; celestial blacksmith; son of Zeus and Hera; husband of Aphrodite

Hera (Juno): queen of heaven; wife of Zeus

Heracles (Hercules): hero and strong man

Hermes (Mercury): god of physicians and thieves; messenger of gods; son of Zeus and Maia

Hesperus: evening star

Hestia (Vesta): goddess of hearth; sister of Zeus

Hydra: nine-headed monster slain by Hercules

Hygeia: personification of health

Hyman: god of marriage

Hyperion: Titan; early sun god; father of Helios

Hypnos (Somnus): god of sleep

Icarus: flew too near sun with wax-attached wings, fell into sea and drowned

Iris: goddess of rainbow; messenger of Zeus and Hera

Janus: Roman god of gates and doors; represented with two opposite faces

Jason: brought back Golden Fleece.

Jocasta: mother of Oedipus; unwittingly became his wife; hanged herself

Lachesis: one of the Fates

Lares: Roman ancestral spirits protecting descendants and homes

Leander: swam Hellespont nightly to see Hero; drowned in storm

Lethe: one of the Rivers of the Underworld

Lucina: Roman goddess of childbirth

Maia: one of the Pleiades

Medea: sorceress; helped Jason obtain Golden Fleece

Medusa: a Gorgon with snakes for hair; slain by Perseus, who cut off her head

Megaera: one of the Furies

Melpomene: one of the Muses

Menelaus: king of Sparta; husband of Helen of Troy

Merope: one of the Pleiades

Midas: given gift of turning to gold all he touched

Minotaur: monster, half man, half beast, kept in Labyrinth in Crete; slain by Theseus

Mnemosyne: goddess of memory

Moirae: one of the Fates

Momus: god of ridicule

Morpheus: god of dreams

Morta: one of the Fates

Muses: goddesses presiding over arts and sciences; Calliope (epic poetry), Clio (history), Erato (lyric and love poetry), Euterpe (music), Melpomene (tragedy), Polymnia or Polyhymnia (sacred poetry), Terpsichore (choral dance and song), Thalia (comedy and bucolic poetry), Urania (astronomy); daughters of Zeus and Mnemosyne

Naiads: nymphs of waters, streams, and fountains

Napaeae: wood nymphs

Narcissus: beautiful youth loved by Echo; he was made to fall in love with his image reflected in pool; pined away and became flower

Nemesis: goddess of retribution

Nike: goddess of victory

Nona: one of the Fates

Notus: one of the Winds

Nymphs: beautiful maidens; inferior deities of nature

Nyx (Nox): goddess of night

Oceanids: ocean nymphs

Oceanus: Titan; god of waters

Odysseus (Ulysses): king of Ithaca; husband of Penelope; wandered ten years after fall of Troy before arriving home

Oedipus: king of Thebes; murdered his father, married his mother; tore his eyes out when relationship was discovered

Orion: hunter; slain by Artemis and made heavenly constellation

Orpheus: famed musician; husband of Eurydice

Pales: Roman goddess of shepherds and herdsmen

Pan (Faunus): god of woods and fields; part goat, part man; son of Hermes

Pandora: opened box containing human ills

Parcae: one of the Fates

Paris: son of Priam; slew Achilles at Troy

Pegasus: winged horse, sprang from Medusa's body at her death; ridden by Bellerophon when he slew Chimera

Penates: Roman household gods

Penelope: wife of Odysseus; waited faithfully for him for ten years

Persephone (Proserpine): queen of infernal regions; daughter of Zeus and Demeter; wife of Pluto

Perseus: slew Medusa; rescued Andromeda from monster and married her

Phlegethon: one of the Rivers of Underworld

Phosphor: morning star

Pleiades: Alcyone, Celaeno, Electra, Maia, Merope, Sterope or Asterope, Taygeta; seven daughters of Atlas; transformed into heavenly constellation, of which six stars are visible (Merope is said to have hidden in shame for loving a mortal)

Plutus: god of wealth

Pollux: twin brother of Castor

Polymnia: one of the Muses

Polyphemus: cyclops blinded by Odysseus

Pomona: Roman goddess of fruits

Poseidon (Neptune): god of sea; brother of Zeus

Priam: king of Troy

Priapus: god of regeneration

Prometheus: Titan; stole fire from heaven for man

Proteus: sea god

Pygmalion: king of Cyprus; carved ivory statue of maiden, which Aphrodite gave life as Galatea

Quirinus: Roman war god

Remus: brother of Romulus

Rhadamanthus: one of three judges of dead in Hades; son of Zeus and Europa

Rivers of the Underworld: Acheron (woe), Cocytus (wailing), Lethe (forgetfulness), Phlegethon (fire), Styx (across which souls of dead were ferried by Charon)

Romulus: founder of Rome; he and Remus suckled in infancy by she-wolf; slew Remus; deified by Romans

Satyrs: hoofed demigods of woods and fields

Scylla: female monster inhabiting rock opposite Charybdis; menaced passing sailors

Selene: goddess of moon

Silvanus: Roman god of woods and fields

Sirens: minor deities who lured sailors to destruction with their singing

Sisyphus: king of Corinth; condemned to roll huge stone to top of hill; it always rolled back down again

Sphinx: monster of Thebes; killed those who could not answer her riddle; slain by Oedipus.

Sterope: one of the Pleiades

Styx: one of the Rivers of the Underworld

Tartarus: underworld below Hades

Taygeta: one of the Pleiades

Telemachus: son of Odysseus

Tellus: Roman goddess of earth

Terminus: Roman god of boundaries and landmarks

Terpsichore: one of the Muses

Terra: Roman earth goddess

Thalia: one of the Graces

Theseus: slew Minotaur

Tisiphone: one of the Furies

Triton: demigod of sea; son of Poseidon

Urania: one of the Muses

Uranus: personification of Heaven; father of Titans

Vertumnus: Roman god of fruits and vegetables

Winds: Aeolus (keeper of winds), Boreas (Aquilo; north wind), Eurus (east wind), Notus (Auster; south wind), Zephyrus (Favonius; west wind)

Zephyrus: one of the Winds

Zeus (Jupiter): chief of Olympian gods; son of Cronus and Rhea; husband of Hera

Norse Mythology

Aegir: god of the sea

Aesir: the main Norse gods; lived in Asgard

Asgard: home of the gods

Balder: son of Odin and Freya, husband of Nanna, killed by Loki's mischief

Berserker: a berserker, transformed during battle into a wolf or bear

Bertha: goddess of spinning

Bragi: god of poetry and eloquence, married to the goddess Iduna

Brono: god of daylight, son of Balder

Bylgja: daughter of Aegir and Ran

Farbanti: a giant, ferried dead over waters to the underworld, father of Loki

Fenris: monstrous wolf of Loki; swallowed Odin; stabbed to death by Odin's son, Vidar

Freyr: Odin in another form, god of rain, sunshine, fruits; married Gredr

Frigg: goddess of sky; wife of Odin

Fulla: attendant to Frigg

Garm: hound that stands in front of Hel's home

Ginnunggap: the Yawning Void

Gioll: river that surrounded Hel, the underworld

Gladsheim: mansion in Asgard where the gods lived

Gold-comb: cock that crows when ragnarok comes

Gotterdammerung: end of the world

Gulltopr: horse of Heimdall

Gullveig: thrice-born, thrice-burnt virgin

Gungnir: Odin's spear

Heimdall: watchman of the bridge, Bifrost, leading to the underworld

Hel (Hela): goddess of the underworld

Hresvelgr: giant in the extreme north that causes wind and tempest

Hunin: raven of thought; sat with Munin upon Odin's shoulder and brought him news

Iduna: wife of Bragi, keeper of the golden apples that kept the gods young

Jormungandr: great dragon

Jotunheim: home of the giants

Kolga: daughter of Aegir and Ran

Loki: slayer of Balder; father of Jormungandr, the wolf Fenris, and Hela

Mimir: god of wisdom and knowledge

Munin: raven of memory that sat on Odin's shoulder with Hunin

Nastrand: worst region of hell

Nidhogg: dragon that devours the corpses of the evil

Njord: sea-god of fruitfulness

Norn: the three goddesses of fate: Urd, Verdandi, and Skuld

Norns: the three sisters responsible for the destiny of individuals and gods

Odin: chief god of Norse mythology

Ogres: creatures who make the storms

Outgard: abode of giants and monsters

Ragnarok: ultimate battle between good and evil from which a new order will emerge

Ran: wife of Aegir; draws sailors of sinking ships to their doom

Runes: letters of the ancient Norse alphabet

Runic wand: smooth willow wand inscribed with runes

Saga: goddess of poetry, Odin's daughter

Seidr: form of Norse magic used for harmful purposes

Skuld: Norn of the future

Sleipnir: Odin's swift horse

Surtr: giant who lived in the extreme south

Thiassi: giant who slew Thor

Thor: god of thunder

Troll: a race of giants.

Tyr: god of war, athletic sports; had one hand bitten off by the wolf Fenris

Ulle: god of the chase

Ullr: god of war and the chase

Urd: Norn of the past

Valhalla: paradise reserved for the souls of dead warriors

Verdandi: Norn of the present.Vingulf: mansion of the godesses in Asgard

Vithar: the god second in strength to Thor; killed the wolf Fenris

Woden: Anglo-Saxon name of Odin

Wotan: another name variation of Odin

Ymir: giant slain by Odin, Vili, and Ve.

Egyptian Mythology

Amaunet: female counterpart to Amon

Amon: king of the gods, god of fertility

Amon-re: sun god

Antaios: originally a double god, "the two falcons"

Anuket: associated with the gazelle

Apis: seen as a bull with a solar disk between its horns

Aton: also known as Aten

Atum: took form of a human and serpent

Bes: god of pleasure

Buto: serpent goddess

Hapi: the Nile as a god

Hathor: goddess of love, dance, alcohol; depicted as a cow; also goddess of the dead at Thebes

Horus: falcon or hawk headed, sky-god

Isis: mother of Horus and sister, consort of Osiris

Khnum: human with a ram's head

Khonsu: moon god, son of Amon and Mut

Min: God of fertility

Mut: consort of Amon

Nut: goddess of the sun, moon, and heavenly bodies

Osiris: god of the underworld

Ptah: worshipped in Memphis

Re: the sun god of Heliopolis

Sati: queen of the gods

Sekhmet: goddess of war and sickness

Serapis: god of lower regions

Seth (Set): god of the desert, evil

Shu: god of the air, bearer of heaven

Sobek: crocodile god

Thoth: god of sacred writings, wisdom, magic

Nations of the World

Afghanistan

Capital: Kabul

Location: Southwestern Asia

Mountains: Hindu Kush, Pamir, Himalayas, Khyber Pass, Nowshak, Sikaram, Koh-I-bab, Safed Koh

Rivers: Kabul, Amu-Darya, Panj, Kunar, Qonduz

Cities: Kandahar, Herat, Mazare Sharif, Heart, Tagob

People: Pushtuns (Pukhtuns), Pathan, Durrani, Ghilzais, Tajik, Hazar, Uzbek

Religions: Sunni Muslim, Shiite Muslim

Languages: Dari (Afghan Persian), Pashto (Pushtu), Uzbek

Currency: Afghani (Af) = 100 Puls

Albania

Capital: Tirane

Location: Europe

Seas: Adriatic

Rivers: Buene, Arta, Drin, Osum, Erzen, Seman, Shkumbi

Lakes: Ohrid, Prespa, Scutari

Cities: Durres, Elbasan, Shkoder, Vlore

People: Albanians, Geg (Gheg), Tosk

Religions: Muslims, Greek Orthodox, Roman Catholic

Languages: Albanian, Geg (Gheg), Tosk

Currency: Lek = 100 Quindars

Algeria

Capital: Algiers

Location: Northern Africa

Seas: Mediterranean

Mountains: Tell Atlas, Sahara Atlas

Deserts: Sahara, Great Western Erg, Great Eastern Erg

Rivers: Chelif, Shelif

Cities: Oran, Constantine, Annaba, Batna, Blida, Medea, Biskara

People: Arabs, Berbers

Religions: Sunni Muslim

Languages: Arabic, French

Currency: Dinar (DA) = 100 Centimes

American Samoa

Capital: Pago Pago

Government: United States Territory

Location: South Pacific Ocean

Islands: Tutuila, Aunu'u, Tau, Ofu, Olosega, Swain's Rose Island

People: Samoans, Polynesians

Religions: Christian

Languages: Samoan, English

Currency: US Dollar = 100 Cents

Andorra

Capital: Andorra La Vella
Location: Southwestern Europe
Mountains: Pyrenees, Coma Pedrosa
Rivers: Madriu, Valira
Cities: Les Escaldes
People: Spanish, Andorrans, French
Religions: Roman Catholic
Languages: Catalan, French, Spanish
Currency: French Franc (F) = 100 Centimes;
  Spanish Peseta (Pta) = 100 Centimos

Angola

Capital: Luanda
Location: Southern Africa
Oceans: Atlantic
Rivers: Congo, Zambezi, Cuito, Kasai,
  Cuanza, Kwango
Cities: Benguela, Malanje, Lubango
People: Bantu, Ovimbundu, Mbundu, Lunda,
  Chokwe, Nganguela
Religions: Roman Catholic, Protestant
Languages: Portuguese, Bantu
Currency: New Kwanza (NKz) = 100 Iwei

Antigua and Barbuda

Capital: St. John's
Location: Leeward Islands, Caribbean Sea
People: British, Portuguese
Religions: Anglican, Protestant
Languages: English
Currency: East Caribbean Dollar (ECD) =
  100 Cents

Argentina

Capital: Buenos Aires
Location: South America
Oceans: Atlantic
Regions: Pampas, Patagonia
Mountains: Andes, Mayo, Cachi, Laudo
  Pissis, Tincon, Tupungato, Maipo
Rivers: Parana, Uruguay, Paraguay,
  Colorado, Negro, La Plata, Atuel, Chico,
  Dulce, Negro, Quinto
Cities: Cordoba, Rosario, La Plata
People: Mestizo, Lule, Guarani
Religions: Roman Catholic
Languages: Spanish
Currency: Peso (P) (formerly Austral) = 100
  Centavos

Armenia

Capital: Yerevan
Location: Southwestern Asia
Mountains: Caucasus, Gukasian,
  Dzharakhetskii, Aragats
Rivers: Arak, Aras
Lakes: Sevan
Cities: Gyumri, Kirovakan
People: Armenians
Religions: Armenian Orthodox, Roman
  Catholic
Languages: Armenian
Currency: Dram (D) (formerly Ruble) = 100
  Lumas

Australia

Capital: Canberra
Location: Continent between Indian and
  South Pacific Oceans
States: Victoria, Tasmania, Queensland, New
  South Wales
Oceans: Pacific, Indian
Seas: Coral, Timor, Tasman, Arafura
Islands: Heard, Fraser, Ashmore, Cartier,
  Norfolk, Bathurst Kangaroo, Thursday,
  Christmas, Coral Sea
Deserts: Western Plateau, Gibson, Great
  Sandy, Great Victoria, Simpson
Mountains: Hamersley, Kimberley,
  Macdonnell, Musgrave, Petermann, Blue
  Mountains, Australian Alps, Snowy
  Mountains, Hale, Bruce, Bogong, Morgan,
  Kosciusko
Lakes: Eyre, Mackay Carnegie, Frome
Rivers: Murray, Darling, Murrumbidgee,
  Lachlan, Avon, Ord, Swan, Yarra, Bullo,
  Burdekin
Cities: Sydney, Melbourne, Brisbane, Perth,
  Adelaide, Newcastle
People: Europeans, Aborigines, Binghi
Religions: Protestant, Anglican, Roman
  Catholic
Languages: English
Currency: Dollar (AUD) = 100 Cents

Austria

Capital: Vienna
Location: South central Europe
Mountains: Alps, Hochfeiler, Wildspitze,
  Grossglockner, Allgau, Bavarian
Flower: Edelweiss
Rivers: Danube, Crava, Inn, Murz, Lech,
  Traun
Cities: Graz, Linz, Salzburg, Innsbruck
People: Austrians
Religions: Roman Catholic
Languages: German
Currency: Schilling (S) = 100 Groschen

Azerbaijani Republic

Capital: Baku
Location: Western Asia
Mountains: Greater Caucasus, Lesser
  Caucasus, Shakhdag, Karabakh,
  Murordg

Cities: Gyandzha (Kirovabad), Sumgait,
Mingechaur, Nakhickevan
People: Azerbaijanis, Azeri, Daghestani
Religions: Shiite Muslim
Languages: Azerbaijani
Currency: Manat (M) = 100 Gopik

Bahamas

Capital: Nassau
Location: West Atlantic Ocean
Oceanic Banks: Bahama, Great Bahama
Islands: Cat, Long, Abaco, Exuma, Grand
Turks, Bimini, Caicos, Acklins,
Mayaguana
Cities: Greater Nassau, Freeport/Lucaya
People: Lucayo
Religions: Baptist, Anglican, Roman Catholic
Language: English
Currency: Dollar (BD) = 100 Cents

Bahrain

Capital: Al Manamah
Location: Islands in Persian Gulf, Middle
East
Gulfs: Arabian, Persian
Islands: Bahrain, Muharraq, Sitrah, Umm al
Nassan, Jidda, Nabi Salih
Cities: Ar Rifa, Al Muharraq, Madinat Isa
People: Bahrainis, Asians, Arabs
Religions: Shiite Muslim, Sunni Muslim
Languages: Arabic
Currency: Dinar (BD) = 1000 Fils

Bangladesh

Capital: Dacca (Dhaka)
Location: Southern Asia
Rivers: Padma, Tista, Ganges, Jamuna
(Brahmaputra), Meghna
Mountains: Keokradong
Cities: Chittagong, Khulna, Rajshahi,
Mymensingh, Bogra
People: Bengalis, Biharis
Religions: Sunni Muslim
Languages: Bangla (Bengali)
Currency: Taka (Tk) = 100 Paisa

Barbados

Capital: Bridgetown
Location: Most easterly of Caribbean
Islands
Other Geology: Coral reef
Highest Point: Mt. Hillaby
Cities: Speightstown
People: Carib, Arawak
Religions: Anglican, Moravian Methodist,
Roman Catholic
Languages: English
Currency: Dollar (BDS) = 100 Cents

Belarus

Capital: Minsk
Location: Eastern Europe
Rivers: Dnieper, Zapadnaia, Dvina, Neman,
Bevezina, Dnepr, Pripyat (Pripet), Bug,
Sozh
Regions: Gomel, Brest, Grodno, Mogivlev
Cities: Gomel, Vitebsk, Mahilyou, Grodno,
Pinsk, Orsha
People: Belarussians, Russians, Polish,
Ukrainians
Religions: Orthodox Christian, Roman
Catholic
Languages: Belarussian
Currency: Ruble (R) = 100 Kopecks

Belgium

Capital: Brussels
Location: Northwestern Europe
Forests: Ardennes
Mountains: Botrange
Rivers: Meuse, Semois, Sambre, Ourthe,
Scheldt
Cities: Antwerp, Ghent, Charleroi, Liege,
Brugge, Bastogne, Waterloo, Ostend
People: Flemings, Walloons
Religions: Roman Catholic
Languages: Flemish (Dutch), French, German
Currency: Franc (BF) = 100 Centimes

Belize

Capital: Belmopan
Location: Eastern coast of Central America
Seas: Caribbean
Mountains: Maya, Victoria
Rivers: Belize, Sibun
Cities: Belize City, Orange Walk, San
Ignacio/Santa Elena, Corozal
People: Maya, Carib, Mestizo, Garifuna
Religions: Roman Catholic, Anglican
Languages: English, Spanish
Currency: Dollar (BZD) = 100 Cents

Benin

Capital: Porto Novo (Official), Cotonou
(Economic and Political)
Location: Western Africa
Gulfs: of Guinea
Lagoons: Cotonou, Ouidah, Grand Popo,
Porto Novo
Mountains: Atakora
Rivers: Niger, Queme, Mono, Mekrou,
Alibory, Sota, Pandjari
Cities: Cotonou, Djougou, Abomey, Calavi,
Parakou
People: Fons, Adjas, Baribas, Yorubas,
Fulanis, Dendis
Religions: Christian, Muslim

Languages: French, Fon, Adja, Bariba, Yoruba, Somba, Aizo
Currency: CFA Franc (Communaute Financiere Africaine/CFAF) = 100 Centimes

Bhutan

Capital: Thimphu
Location: Central Asia
Mountains: Himalayas, Black
Rivers: Kuru, Torsa, Sankosh
Cities: Phuntsholing
People: Bhote (Sharchops), Ngalops, Gurung, Rai, Limbu
Religions: Lamaistic Buddhist, Hindu
Languages: Dzongkha, Bumthangkha, Sharchopkha
Currency: Ngultrum (Nu) = 100 Chetrumu

Bolivia

Capital: Sucre (Judicial), La Paz (Administrative)
Location: Central South America
Plateaus: Altiplano
Mountains: Andes
Lakes: Titicaca, Poopo
Rivers: Beni, Itonomas, Paraguay, Guapore
Cities: La Paz, Santa Cruz, El Alto, Cochabamba, Oruro
People: Quechua, Aymara, Mestizo
Religions: Roman Catholic
Languages: Spanish, Aymara, Quechua, Guarani
Currency: Boliviano (Bs) = 100 Centavos

Bosnia-Herzegovina

Capital: Sarajevo
Location: Eastern Europe (former republic of socialist Yugoslavia)
Seas: Adriatic
Rivers: Sava, Neretva, Drina, Sara
Mountains: Dinaric Alps
Cities: Banja Luka, Zenica
People: Serbs, Muslims, Croats
Religions: Muslim; Croats—Roman Catholic; Serbs—Orthodox Christian
Languages: Serbo-Croatian (Bosnian)
Currency: Dinar (D) = 100 Paras

Botswana

Capital: Gaborone
Location: Southern Africa
Deserts: Kalahari
Other Geology: Makarikari Salt Pans, Okavango Swamps
Rivers: Okavango
Cities: Francistown, Selebi-Pikwe
People: Tswana (subtribes: Bakgatla, Bakwena, Bamalete, Bamangwato, Bangwaketsi, Batawana, Batalokwa, Barolong) Kalanga, Herero, Bushman (Sarwa)
Religions: Christian
Languages: English, Setswana, Tswana
Currency: Pula (P) = 100 Thebe

Brazil

Capital: Brasilia
Location: Eastern South America
Oceans: Atlantic Bays: Sao Marcos, Guanabara
Islands: Maraca, Mexiana
Mountains: Mar, Acarai, Orgaos, Parima, Roncador, Tombador
Rivers: Amazon, Sao Francisco, Paraguay, Parana, Uruguay, Negro, Verde, Xingu, Tapajos, Madeira, Parnaiba
Other Geography: Rain forest
Cities: Sao Paulo, Rio de Janeiro, Salvador, Belo Horizonte, Recife, Belem, Manaus, Santos, Pernambuco
People: Tupi, Ge, Carib, Arawak, Nambicuara, Anta, Arara, Arawak, Kayapo, Guarani
Religions: Roman Catholic, Protestant, Candomble, Macumba
Languages: Portuguese, Tupi, Ge, Garib, Arawak, Nambicuara
Currency: Real (R) = 100 Centavos

Brunei

Capital: Bandar Seri Begawan
Location: Southeastern Asia, northwest coast of Borneo
Seas: South China
Cities: Kuala Belait, Seria, Tutong
People: Malays, Chinese, Indians, Ibans, Dusans
Religions: Muslim, Buddhist, Christian
Languages: Malay
Currency: Dollar (BD) = 100 Cents (Sen)

Bulgaria

Capital: Sofia
Location: Southeastern Europe
Seas: Black Sea
Mountains: Balkans, Rhodope, Pirin
Rivers: Maritsa, Iskur, Yantra, Struma
Cities: Plovdiv, Varna, Burgas, Ruse
People: Slavs, Turks
Religions: Eastern Orthodox, Muslim
Languages: Bulgarian
Currency: Lev (plural; Leva) = 100 Stotinki

Burkina Faso

Capital: Ouagadougou
Location: Western Africa

Rivers: Black Volta, White Volta, Red Volta,
Niger
Lakes: Bama
Deserts: Sahara
Cities: Bobo-Dioulasso, Koudougou,
Ouahigouya
People: Mossi, Fulani, Gourma (Gurma),
Lobi-Dagar, Mande, Bobo, Senoufo,
Gourounsi
Religions: Sunni Muslim, Roman Catholic
Languages: French, More, Dioula,
Gourmantche
Currency: CFA Franc (Communaute
Financiere Africaine/CFAF) = 100
Centimes

Burundi
Capital: Bujumbura
Location: Central Africa
Lakes: Tanganyika, Rugwero, Cyohoha-Sud
Rivers: Ruzizi
Cities: Gitega, Ngozi
People: Hutu, Tutsi (Watutsi or Batutsi), Twa
Religions: Roman Catholic, Protestant
Languages: Rundi, French, Swahili
Currency: Franc (FBu) = 100 Centimes

Cambodia
Capital: Phnom Penh
Location: Southeastern Asia
Rivers: Mekong
Lakes: Tonle Sap
Cities: Batdambang, Kampong Cham, Pursat
People: Khmer, Vietnamese, Chinese
Religions: Buddhist
Languages: Khmer, French
Currency: New Riel = 100 Sen

Cameroon
Capital: Yaounde
Location: Central western Africa
Volcanoes: Mt. Cameroon
Rivers: Logone, Chari, Wouri, Sanaga,
Dibamba, Nyong
Other Geology: Gulf of Guinea, Lake Chad
Basin
Cities: Douala, Garoua, Maroua
People: Cameroon Highlanders, Bantu, Kirdi,
Fulani, Ibo, Ewe
Religions: Roman Catholic, Muslim,
Protestant
Languages: French, English
Currency: CFA Franc (Communaute
Financiere Africaine/CFAF) = 100
Centimes

Canada
Capital: Ottawa
Location: Northern North America

Provinces and Territories: Quebec, Alberta,
Ontario, Manitoba, Nova Scotia, New
Brunswick, Newfoundland, Saskatchewan,
British Columbia, Prince Edward Island,
Yukon, Northwest Territories
Oceans: Atlantic, Pacific, Arctic
Lakes: Great Lakes—Superior, Michigan,
Huron, Erie, Ontario; Winnipeg,
Athabasca, Winnipegosis, Manitoba
Islands: Vancouver, Queen Charlotte,
Newfoundland, Prince Edward, Cape
Breton, Grand Manan, Campobello,
Anticosti, Baffin, Banks, Ellesmere, Nova
Scotia
Rivers: Yukon, Mackenzie, North
Saskatchewan, South Saskatchewan,
Saskatchewan, Athabasca, Ottawa, St.
Lawrence
Mountains: Rocky, Mackenzie, Columbia,
Cascade, Selwyn, Logan, Laurentian,
Appalachian, Coastal
Other Geology: Canadian Shield, Arctic
Archipelago, Hudson Bay, James Bay,
Laurentian Plateau
Highest Point: Mt. Logan
Cities: Toronto, Montreal, Vancouver,
Edmonton, Calgary, Winnipeg, Quebec,
Hamilton, Regina, Banff, London, Halifax,
Victoria, Windsor, Thunder Bay, Saskatoon
People: Anglo-Canadians, French-Canadians,
Native Canadians, Inuit (Eskimo)
Religions: Roman Catholic, Protestant
Languages: French, English
Currency: Dollar (Can) = 100 Cents

Cape Verde
Capital: Praia
Location: Atlantic Ocean, off western coast
of Africa
Islands: Barlayento, Sotavento, Boa, Vista,
Maio, Sal
Cities: Mindelo, Sao Filipe
People: Creoles (Africans, Portuguese)
Religions: Roman Catholic
Languages: Portuguese, Crioulo
Currency: Escudo (CVEsc) = 100 Centavos

Cayman Islands
Capital: George Town
Location: Caribbean Sea
Islands: Grand Cayman, Little Cayman,
Cayman Brac
Religions: Christian
Languages: English
Currency: Dollar = 100 Cents

Central African Republic
Capital: Bangui
Location: Central Africa

Rivers: Chari, Ubangi
Cities: Bambari, Bouar, Berberati,
Bossangoa
People: Baya, Banda, Sara, Nabandi, Azande,
Mbaka
Religions: Christian, Muslim
Languages: French, Sangho (Sango)
Currency: CFA Franc (Communaute
Financiere Africaine/CFAF) = 100
Centimes

Chad

Capital: N'Djamena
Location: North central Africa
Deserts: Sahara
Lakes: Chad
Mountains and Plateaus: Ennedi Plateau,
Tibesti Ranges
Rivers: Logone, Chari
Cities: Moundou, Sarh, Abeche
People: Arab, Pagan, Kirdi, Sara, Bagirmi,
Kreish
Religions: Muslim, Roman Catholic,
Protestant
Languages: Arabic, French, Sara
Currency: CFA Franc (Communaute
Financiere Africaine/CFAF) = 100
Centimes

Chile

Capital: Santiago
Location: Southwestern coast of South
America
Oceans: Pacific
Mountains: Andes
Deserts: Atacama
Rivers: Loa, Huasco, Coquimbo, Limari,
Mapocho, Maule, Maipo, Bio-Bio
Other Geology: Andean Cordillera
Cities: Vina del Mar, Concepcion, Valparaiso,
Talcahuano
People: Mestizo, Mapuche, Araucanians
Religions: Roman Catholic, Protestant
Languages: Spanish, Araucan
Currency: Peso (P) = 100 Centavos

China, People's Republic of

Capital: Beijing (Peking)
Location: Central and eastern Asia
Seas: Yellow, East China, South China
Mountains: Omi, Omei, Tsins, Pamirs,
Everest, Himalayas, Altai
Other Geology: Tibetan Plateau, Manchurian
Plains, Sichuan Basin
Rivers: Yangtze, Yellow, Mekong, Pei, Wei,
Han, Amur, Hwang, Sikiang, Huang He
Lakes: Tung-ting, Qing Hai, Dongting

Regions: Anjui, Gansu, Hebei, Henan, Hubei,
Hunan, Jilin, Fukkien, Szechuan
Cities: Shanghai, Tianjin, Shenyang, Wuhan,
Canton, Harbin, Chengdu, Guangzhou,
Chongqing, Tsingtao, Hangchow,
Nanjing
People: Han, Chuang, Hui, Uigur, Yi, Miao,
Mangchu
Religions: Confucianist, Taoist, Buddhist
Languages: Putonghua, Mandarin,
Cantonese (Yue), Wu, Fuzhou, Hokkien,
Hakka
Currency: Yuan (Y) = 10 Jiao = 100 Fen

Colombia

Capital: Bogota
Location: Northern South America
Oceans: Pacific, Atlantic, Caribbean
Mountains: Cordillera Occidental, Cordillera
Central, Cordillera Oriental
Rivers: Cauca, Magdalena
Cities: Medellin, Cali, Barranquilla,
Cartagena
People: Mestizos
Religions: Roman Catholic
Languages: Spanish
Currency: Peso (P) = 100 Centavos

Comoros

Capital: Moroni
Location: Three islands in Mozambique
Channel
Islands: Grande Comore, Anjouan, Moheli
Volcanoes: Mount Kartala
Cities: Mutsamudu, Domoni, Fomboni
People: Antalaotra, Casre, Makoa,
Oimapasaha, Sakalava
Religions: Sunni Muslim
Languages: French, Arabic, Comorian
Currency: Franc (CF) = 100 Centimes

Congo, Democratic Republic of the (formerly Zaire)

Capital: Kinshasa
Location: South central Africa
Oceans: Atlantic
Mountains: Ngoma, Virunga, Ruwenzori,
Blue, Kundelunga, Marungu
Rivers: Zaire
Cities: Lubumbashi, Mbuji-Mayi, Kisangani,
Kananga
People: Bantu, Mongo, Kongo, Luba,
Mangbetu-Azande
Religions: Roman Catholic, Protestant
Languages: French, Bantu, Lingala, Swahili,
Kikongo, Tshiluba
Currency: New Zaire (NZ) = 100 Makuta
(singular; Likuta) = 10,000 Sengi

Congo, Republic of the
Capital: Brazzaville
Location: West central Africa
Oceans: Atlantic
Mountains: Mayombe
Rivers: Ogoove, Niari, Zaire
Cities: Pointe-Noire, Loubomo, Nkayi
People: Bantu, Negrillos, Kongo, Teke, Mboshi, Mbete
Religions: Roman Catholic, Protestant, African Christian
Languages: French, Kongo, Teke
Currency: CFA Franc (Communaute Financiere Africaine/CFAF) = 100 Centimes

Costa Rica
Capital: San Jose
Location: Central American Isthmus
Oceans: Pacific, Caribbean Sea
Rivers: Tempisque, San Juan, General Sixaola, San Jose, Grande de Tarcoles
Cities: Desamparados, Limon, Alajuela, Puntarenas
People: Chorotega-Mangues, Boruca, Talamanca, Bribi, Cabecares
Religions: Roman Catholic, Protestant
Languages: Spanish, Chibcha
Currency: Colon (C) = 100 Centimos

Croatia
Capital: Zagreb
Location: Eastern Europe
Seas: Adriatic
Mountains: Dinaric Alps
Rivers: Drava, Danube, Sava
Cities: Split, Rijeka, Osijel, Zadar
People: Croats, Serbs, Magyars (Hungarians)
Religions: Roman Catholic, Orthodox Christian
Languages: Croatian (Latin alphabet), Serbo-Croatian
Currency: Kuna (plural; Kune) (K) = 100 Lipa

Cuba
Capital: Havana
Location: Northern Caribbean Sea
Islands: Isla de la Juventud (Island of Youth)
Mountains: Central Escambray, Sierra de los Organos, Sierra Maestra
Rivers: Cauto
Cities: Santiago de Cuba, Camaguey, Holguin, Guantanamo
People: Cubans
Religions: Roman Catholic, Santeria
Languages: Spanish
Currency: Peso (CUP) = 100 Centavos

Cyprus
Capital: Nicosia (Lefkosia)
Location: Island in the Mediterranean Sea
Mountains: Troodos, Kyrenia
Cities: Limassol, Larnaca
People: Greeks, Turks
Religions: Greek Orthodox, Muslim (Turkish)
Languages: Greek, Turkish
Currency: Pound (CP) = 100 Cents

Czech Republic
Capital: Prague
Location: Central Europe
Mountains: Ore, Moravian Hills, Carpathian
Rivers: Danube, Morava
Cities: Brno, Ostrava, Plzen, Olomouc
People: Czechs, Moravians, Slovaks
Religions: Christian
Languages: Czech, German, Slovak
Currency: Czech Koruna (plural; Koruny) (Kc) = 100 Halura

Denmark
Capital: Copenhagen
Location: Northern Europe
Oceans: Atlantic
Seas: Baltic, North
Peninsulas: Jutland
Islands: Samso, Aero, Bornholm, Langeland, Als
Cities: Arhus, Odense, Alborg, Elsinore
People: Danes
Religions: Evangelical Lutheran
Languages: Danish
Currency: Krone (Dkr) (plural: Kroner) = 100 Ore

Djibouti
Capital: Djibouti
Location: Northeastern Africa
Gulfs: of Aden
Highest Point: Moussa Ali
Cities: Al Sabih, Tadjoura, Dikhil
People: Hamitic, Somalis (Issas), Afars
Religions: Sunni Muslim
Languages: French, Arabic, Somali, Afar
Currency: Franc (DF) = 100 Centimes

Dominica, Commonwealth of
Capital: Roseau
Location: Lesser Antilles, Caribbean Sea
Rivers: Clyde, Pagua, Rosalie, Roseau, Layou
Cities: Portsmouth, Marigot
People: Dominicans
Religions: Roman Catholic
Languages: English, French patois
Currency: East Caribbean Dollar (ECD) = 100 Cents

Dominican Republic

Capital: Santo Domingo
Location: Caribbean Sea, eastern two-thirds of the island of Hispaniola
Islands: Beata Catalina, Saona, Alto Velo, Catalinita
Oceans: Atlantic
Mountains: Cordillera Central, Cordillera Septentrional, Sierra de Neiba, Sierra de Baoruco
Lakes: Enriquillo
Cities: Santiago de los Caballeros, La Vega, San Pedro de Macoris
People: Dominicans
Religions: Roman Catholic
Languages: Spanish
Currency: Peso (P) = 100 Centavos

Ecuador

Capital: Quito
Location: Western South America
Oceans: Pacific
Mountains: Andes, Sierra, Andean Highlands, Cordillera Occidental, Cordillera Central, Cordillera Oriental
Volcanoes: Chimborazo, Cotopaxi, Cayambe, Antisana, Sangay
Rivers: Amazon
Islands: Galapagos
Cities: Guayaquil, Cuenca, Machala
People: Otavalos, Salasacas, Saraguros, Colorados, Cayapas, Jivaros, Aucas, Yumbos, Zaparos, Cofan
Religions: Roman Catholic
Languages: Spanish, Quechua
Currency: Sucre (S) = 100 Centavos

Egypt

Capital: Cairo
Location: Northeastern Africa
Seas: Red, Mediterranean
Deserts: Arabian, Sinai
Canals: Suez
Peninsulas: Sinai
Mountains: Sinai, Nugrus, Gharib
Rivers: Nile, Rosetta
Lakes: Nasser, Menzaleh, Brullos, Idku, Mariut
Cities: Alexandria, Al-Jizah, Giza, Suez, Luxor, Port Said, El Mansura
People: Arabs, Nubians, Hamitic
Religions: Sunni Muslim, Coptic
Languages: Arabic, Coptic, Nubian, Berber
Currency: Pound (EP) = 1,000 Milliemes = 100 Piastres = 5 Tallaris

El Salvador

Capital: San Salvador
Location: West coast of Central America
Oceans: Pacific
Mountains: Apeneca
Rivers: Lempa
Lakes: Guija, Coatepeque, Ilopango
Cities: Soyapango, Santa Ana, San Miguel, Mejicanos
People: Mestizo, Pipil, Lenca
Religions: Roman Catholic
Languages: Spanish, Pipil
Currency: Colon (C) = 100 Centavos

England (part of United Kingdom)

Capital: London
Location: Off northwestern coast of Europe
Oceans: Atlantic
Seas: North, Irish
Lakes: Windermere
Islands: Man, Wight
Channels: English, St. Georges
Rivers: Wye, Eden, Ouse, Severn, Thames, Humber, Tees, Tyne, Tweed, Avon, Exe, Mersey
Cities: Birmingham, Leeds, Manchester, Sheffield, Liverpool, Bristol, Oxford, Cambridge, Leicester, New Castle, Nottingham
Languages: English
Religions: Anglican, Roman Catholic
Currency: Pound Sterling (PdSt) = 100 New Pence

Eritrea

Capital: Asmera (Asmara)
Location: Northeastern Africa
Archipelagos: Dahlak
Seas: Red
Cities: Assab, Keren, Massawa, Mendefera
People: Tigrinya, Tigre, Kunama, Afar, Saho
Religions: Coptic Christian, Ethiopian Orthodox, Roman Catholic, Muslim
Languages: Tigrinya, Tigre, Afar-Saho, Bega (Beja), Arabic
Currency: Ethiopian Birr (Br) = 100 Cents

Estonia

Capital: Tallinn
Location: Eastern Europe
Seas: Baltic
Islands: Saarmaa, Hiiumaa
Rivers: Ema
Lakes: Peipus
Cities: Tartu, Narva, Kohtla-Jarve, Parnu
People: Estonians, Russians
Religions: Lutheran, Orthodox
Languages: Estonian
Currency: Kroon (EK) = 100 Senti

Ethiopia
Capital: Addis Ababa
Location: Northeastern Africa
Plateaus: Ethiopian, Somali
Mountains: Chercher, Aranna, Chelalo
Lakes: Zwai, Langano, Abiata, Shala, Awasa, Abaya, Chamo
Other Geology: Danakil Depression
Cities: Dire Dawa, Gonder, Nazret
People: Amhara, Galla, Tigrinya, Gurage, Falasha, Nilotic
Religions: Ethiopian Orthodox, Muslim
Languages: Amharic, Guraginya, Tigrinya, Orominga, Arabic
Currency: Birr (Br) = 100 Cents

Falkland Islands
Capital: Stanley
Location: Northeast of Cape Horn
Oceans: Atlantic
Highest Point: Mt. Usborne
People: Falkland Islanders (British)
Religions: Roman Catholic, United Free, Anglican
Languages: English
Currency: Falkland Pound = 100 Pence

Fiji
Capital: Suva
Location: South Pacific Ocean
Islands: Viti Levu, Vanua Levu
Rivers: Rewa, Sigatoka, Ba
Cities: Lautoka, Lami, Nadi, Ba
People: Fijians, Indians
Religions: Methodist, Roman Catholic, Hindu, Muslim
Languages: English, Bau
Currency: Dollar (FD) = 100 Cents

Finland
Capital: Helsinki
Location: Northern Europe
Gulfs: of Finland, of Bothnia
Other Geology: Punkaharju, Pyynikki, Pulkkila, Lapland, Saaristomeri
Rivers: Tornionjoki, Kemi, Oulu
Cities: Espo, Tampere, Vanta, Turku
People: Finns, Swedes, Lapps
Religions: Evangelical Lutheran
Languages: Finnish, Swedish, Lappish
Currency: Markka (Finmark/Fmk) = 100 Penni

France
Capital: Paris
Location: Western Europe
Islands: Corsica, Elba, Hyeres
Seas: Mediterranean
Oceans: Atlantic
Bays: Biscay
Channels: English Channel
Massifs: Hercynian Massifs, Ardennes, Vosges, Armorican
Mountains: Jura, Alps, Pyrenees, Mont Blanc, Auvergne, Vosge
Rivers: Loire, Garonne, Rhone, Rhine, Seine, Saar, Yser, Maine, Marne, Meuse, Saone, Gironde, Moselle, Charente
Cities: Marseille, Lyon, Toulouse, Nice, Strasbourg, Nantes, Aix, Metz, Caen, Canne, Arles, Dijon, Brest, Le Havre, Nime, Reims, Rouen, Tours, Calais, Le Mans, Toulon, Limoge, Orleans, Bordeaux
People: French (Celtic, Latin)
Religions: Roman Catholic
Languages: French, Provencal, Breton, Corsican, Basque
Currency: Franc (F) = 100 Centimes

French Guiana
Capital: Cayenne
Location: North coast of South America
Oceans: Atlantic
Mountains: Chaine Granitique, Sierra de Tumucumaque
Rivers: Amazon, Camopi, Inini, Ouaqui, Tampoc, Marowiny, Mana, Sinnamary, Comte, Approuague
Cities: Kourou
People: French, Carib, Arawak
Religions: Roman Catholic
Languages: French, Creole patois
Currency: French Franc (F) = 100 Centimes

French Polynesia
Capital: Papeete (Tahiti Island)
Location: South Pacific Ocean
Islands: Society (Tahiti, Bora-Bora), Tuamotu Archipelago, Gambier Archipelago, Marquesas, Austral
People: Polynesians, Polynesian-Europeans
Religions: Protestant, Roman Catholic
Languages: French, Tahitian
Currency: CFP Franc (Comptoire Francaise du Pacifique/CFPF) = 100 Centimes

Gabon
Capital: Libreville
Location: West coast of Africa
Oceans: Atlantic
Lagoons: N'Dogo, N'Goze, N'Komi
Mountains: Crystal
Rivers: Woleu, N'Tem, Ivindo, Ogooue, N'Gounie, Ivindo Rivers
Cities: Port Gentil, Franceville
People: Bantu, Fang, Eshira, M'bede,

Okande, Duma, Kanda, Seke, Mbete,
Bakele, Bongom, Pygmies
Religions: Roman Catholic
Languages: French, Fang, Myene, Bateke
Currency: CFA Franc (Communaute
Financiere Africaine/CFAF) = 100
Centimes

Gambia
Capital: Banjul
Location: West coast of Africa
Oceans: Atlantic
Rivers: Gambia
Cities: Greater Banjul, Serekunda, Brikama
People: Mandinka, Fulani, Wolof, Pyola,
Soninke
Religions: Sunni Muslim, Christian
Languages: English, Wolof, Fula, Madinka
Currency: Dalasi (D) = 100 Bututs

Georgia, Republic of
Capital: Tbilisi
Location: Western Asia
Seas: Black
Mountains: Greater Caucasus, Lesser
Caucasus, Armenian Highlands, Surami
Rivers: Kura, Rioni
Cities: Kutaisi, Rustavi, Batumi, Sukhumi
People: Georgians
Religions: Georgian and Armenian Orthodox
Languages: Georgian, Russian
Currency: Lari = 100 Tetri

Germany
Capital: Berlin
Location: North central Europe
Seas: Baltic, North
Mountains: Alps, Rhenish Slate, Harz
Forests: Schwarzwald (Black Forest)
Rivers: Danube, Ems, Weser, Moselle, Elbe,
Rhine, Oder, Main
Cities: Hamburg, Munich, Cologne,
Frankfurt, Essen, Dortmund, Stuttgart,
Dusseldorf, Bremen, Mannheim,
Nuremberg, Leigzig, Koln
People: Germans
Religions: Protestant, Roman Catholic
Languages: German
Currency: Deutsche Mark (DM) d = 100
Pfennig

Ghana
Capital: Accra
Location: Gulf of Guinea, western coast of
Africa
Other Geology: Accra Plains, Volta Delta,
Akan Lowlands, Ashanti Highlands
Mountains: Akwapim-Togo

Rivers: Volta, Pra, Ankobra, Tano Rivers
Cities: Kumasi, Tamale, Tema
People: Akan, Mossi, Ewe, Ga
Religions: Muslim, Christian
Languages: English, Twi-Fante, Ga, Ewe,
Dagbane, Grusi, Gurma
Currency: Cedi (C) = 100 Pesewas

Greece
Capital: Athens
Location: Southeastern Europe
Peninsulas: Balkan
Seas: Ionian, Aegean, Mediterranean
Islands: Crete, Euboea, Lesbos, Rhodes,
Khios, Kefallonia, Corfu, Limnos, Samos,
Naxos
Mountains: Pindhos, Dinaric Alps, Mt.
Olympus, Taiyetos, Parnon, Rhodope
Rivers: Mesta, Strimon, Arakhthos,
Akheloos, Aliakmon, Pinios, Alfios
Cities: Thessaloniki, Piraievs, Patrai
People: Greeks
Religions: Greek Orthodox
Languages: Greek
Currency: Drachma (Dr) (plural; Drachmae)
= 100 Lepta

Greenland
Capital: Nuuk
Location: Northeast of North America
Size: World's largest island
Cities: Thule
People: Ita, Greenlanders, Danish
Religions: Lutheran, Moravian
Languages: Greenlandic, Danish
Currency: Danish Krone = 100 Ore

Grenada
Capital: St. George's
Location: Windward Islands, Caribbean Sea
Islands: Grenada, Carriacou, Petit Martinique
Lakes: Grand Etang, Lake Antoine, Levera
Pond
Cities: Gouyave, Grenville
People: Grenadians
Religions: Roman Catholic, Protestant,
Anglican
Languages: English, French patois
Currency: East Caribbean Dollar (ECD) =
100 Cents

Guadeloupe
Capital: Basse-Terre
Location: Lesser Antilles, Caribbean Sea
Islands: Grande-Terre, Basse-Terre
Volcanoes: Grande Soufriere
Cities: Les Abymes, St. Martin, Pointe-a-
Pitre, Le Grosier

People: Creoles
Religions: Roman Catholic
Languages: French, French patois
Currency: French Franc (F) = 100 Centimes

Guatemala

Capital: Guatemala City
Location: Central America
Oceans: Pacific
Seas: Caribbean
Mountains: Sierra Madre, Sierra de Chaucus, Sierra de las Minas, Montanas del Mico, Sierra de los Chuchumatanes, Sierra de Chama
Rivers: Motagua, Polochic, Sarstun
Lakes: Atitlan, Amatitlan, Izabel, Peten Itza
Cities: Mixco, Villa Nueva, Chinautla, Amatitlan
People: Guatemalans, AmerIndians, Ladinos (all non-AmerIndians)
Religions: Roman Catholic, Protestant
Languages: Spanish, Quiche, Kelchi, Cakchiquel, Mam
Currency: Quetzal (Q) = 100 Centavos

Guinea

Capital: Conakry
Location: Western Africa
Oceans: Atlantic
Highlands: Fouta Djallon Massif, Guinea
Rivers: Niger, Rio Nunez, Fatala, Melikhoure, Konkoure, Rio Kapatchez
Cities: Kankan, N'zerekore, Kindia
People: Fulan, Malinke, Soussou (Susu), Kissi, Kpelle
Religions: Muslim
Languages: French, Poular, Malinke, Soussou, Kissi, Guerze, Toma, Coniagui, Bassari
Currency: Franc (GF) = 100 Cauris

Guinea, Republic of Equatorial

Capital: Malabo
Location: West central Africa
Oceans: Atlantic
Islands: Bioko, Fernando Po, Pigalu, Elobey Grande, Elobey Chico, Corisco
Mountains: Crystal
Rivers: Mbini, Rio Campo, Rio Muni
Cities: Malabo, Bata, Ela-Nguema
People: Fang (Fon), Ntumu Fang, Okak Fang, Kombe, Balengue, Bujebas, Bengas, Bubi, Fernandinos, Hausa, Ibo, Ibibo, Efik
Religions: Christian
Languages: Spanish, Fang, Pichinglis
Currency: CFA Franc (Communaute Financiere Africaine/CFAF) = 100 Centimes

Guinea-Bissau

Capital: Bissau
Location: Western Africa
Oceans: Atlantic
Rivers: Cacheu, Farim, Mansoa, Geba, Corubal, Rio Grande, Cacine
Cities: Bafata, Gabu
People: Balante, Fulani, Malinke, Mandyako, Pepel
Religions: Muslim
Languages: Portuguese, Creole patois, Niger-Congo
Currency: Peso (PG) = 100 Centavos

Guyana

Capital: Georgetown
Location: Northeast coast of South America
Oceans: Atlantic
Mountains: Pakaraima, Kaieteurian Plateau
Rivers: Corentyne, Berbice, Demerara, Essequibo, Georgetown, Linden, New Amsterdam
Cities: New Amsterdam, Mabaruma
People: Guyanese
Religions: Protestant, Roman Catholic, Hindu, Muslim
Languages: English
Currency: Dollar (GD) = 100 Cents

Haiti

Capital: Port-au-Prince
Location: Caribbean Sea, western one-third of the island of Hispaniola
Islands: Hispaniola
Oceans: Atlantic
Mountains: Massif du Nord, Montagnes Noires, Chaine de Mateaux, Seirra de Neiba
Rivers: Artibonite, Trois Rivieres, Grande Anse, Massacre (Rio Djabon), Pedernales
Cities: Carrefour, Delmas, Cap-Haitien
People: Haitians
Religions: Roman Catholic, Voodoo, Protestant
Languages: French, Haitian Creole
Currency: Gourde (G) = 100 Centimes

Honduras

Capital: Tegucigalpa
Location: Central America
Gulfs: of Honduras, of Fonseca
Islands: Bay, Swan, Tigre, Grand Zacate, Guegueensi
Oceans: Pacific
Mountains: Central American Cordillera
Rivers: Ulua, Aguan, Patuca, Guayape
Lakes: Yojoa, Laguna Caratasca

Cities: San Pedro Sula, La Ceiba, El
  Progreso, Choluteca
People: Ladinos (non-Indians), Mestizos
Religions: Roman Catholic
Languages: Spanish, Lenca, Xicaque, Chorti,
  Carib, Miskito, Sumo
Currency: Lempira (L) = 100 Centavos

Hong Kong

Capital: Victoria
Location: Southeastern coast of China
Seas: South China
Islands: Hong Kong, Lan Tau
Peninsulas: Kowloon
Cities: Kowloon, Tsuen Wan, Aberdeen
People: Chinese
Religions: Buddhist, Taoist
Languages: Mandarin, Cantonese, English
Currency: Hong Kong Dollar (HKD) = 100
  Cents; Chinese Yuan (Y) = 10 Jiao = 100
  Fen

Hungary

Capital: Budapest
Location: Central Europe
Mountains: Bakony, Vertes, Philis, Alps
Lakes: Balaton
Rivers: Danube, Tisza, Drava, Sava
Cities: Debrecen, Miskolc, Szeged, Pecs
People: Hungarians, Magyars
Religions: Roman Catholic
Languages: Hungarian (Magyar)
Currency: Forint (Ft) = 100 Filler

Iceland

Capital: Reykjavik
Location: Island between the Atlantic and
  Arctic Oceans
Seas: Greenland, Norwegian
Straits: of Denmark
Glaciers: Langjokull, Myrdalsjokull,
  Hofsjokull, Vatnajokull
Cities: Kopavogur, Hafnarfjordhur, Akureyri,
  Sudhurnesjabar
People: Icelanders
Religions: Evangelical Lutheran
Languages: Icelandic
Currency: Krona (ISK) (plural; Kronur) =
  100 Aurar

India

Capital: New Delhi
Location: Southern Asia
Bays: of Bengal
Oceans: Indian
Seas: Arabian
Islands: Andaman, Nicobar, Lakshadweep
Mountains: Himalaya, Ghats, Zaskar,
  Satpura, Hindu Kush, Kanchenjunga

Passes: Bolan, Khyber, Gumal
Rivers: Ganges, Indus, Brahmaputra, Jumna,
  Yamuna, Ghaghra, Gandak, Kosi, Chambi,
  Betwa, Son, Mahanadi, Godavari, Krishna,
  Cauvery, Narbada, Tapti, Ravi, Indravati
Cities: Mumbai (Bombay), Delhi, Calcutta,
  Madras, Bangalore, Hyperabad,
  Ahmadabad, Kanpur, Nagpur, Lucknow,
  Pune, New Delhi Patna, Allahabad, Jaipuir
People: Indo-Aryans, Dravidians, Parsis
Religions: Hindu, Muslim
Languages: Hindi, English
Currency: Rupee (Re) = 100 Paisa

Indonesia

Capital: Jakarta
Location: Southeastern Asia
Seas: South China
Oceans: Pacific, Indian
Rivers: Deli, Hari, Musi, Asahan, Kampar,
  Mahakam, Indragiri
Islands: Java, Sumatra, Sulawesi, Kalimantan,
  Irian Jaya, Borneo, Celebes, Bali, Sumba,
  Timor, Flores, Sumbawa, Sunda
Volcanoes: Krakatoa
Cities: Surabaya, Bandung, Medan,
  Semarang
People: Malay, Javanese, Sundanese,
  Madurese, Bahasa
Religions: Muslim
Languages: Bahasa Indonesian, Javanese,
  Sundanese, Madurese, Malay
Currency: Rupiah (Rp) = 100 Sen

Iran

Capital: Tehran
Location: Middle East
Seas: Caspian, Arabian
Gulfs: of Oman, Persian
Straits: of Hormuz
Mountains: Zagros, Elburz, Talish, Hindu Kush
Rivers: Karun, Atrek, Safid Karkheh
Lakes: Urmia (Rezaiyeh)
Cities: Mashhad, Esfahan, Tabriz, Shiraz,
  Qum, Qom
People: Persians (Farsi), Azerbaijanis
Religions: Shiite Muslim, Sunni Muslim
Languages: Persian (Farsi)
Currency: Rial (Rls)

Iraq

Capital: Baghdad
Location: Middle East
Gulfs: Persian
Mountains: Zagros
Rivers: Tigris, Euphrates
Deserts: Great Arabian, Syrian
Cities: Diyala, as-Sulaymaniyah, Irbil, Mosul

People: Arabs, Bedouins, Madans, Kurds
Religions: Shiite Muslim, Sunni Muslim
Languages: Arabic
Currency: Dinar (ID) = 20 Dirhams = 1,000
Fils

Ireland
Capital: Dublin
Location: Island in eastern North Atlantic
Ocean
Oceans: Atlantic
Seas: Irish
Other Geology: St. Georges Channel
Mountains: Mourne, Wicklow,
Macgillycuddy's Reek, Mayo, Donegal,
Connemara
Rivers: Shannon, Boyne, Barrow, Slaney,
Bann, Lagan, Foyle, Erne, Moy, Corib
Cities: Cork, Limerick, Galway, Waterford
People: Irish, Celtic
Religions: Roman Catholic
Languages: English, Gaelic
Currency: Irish Pound = 100 New Pence

Ireland, Northern
Capital: Belfast
Location: One-sixth of island of Ireland,
eastern North Atlantic Ocean
Oceans: Atlantic
Cities: Londonderry
Religions: Roman Catholic, Presbyterian,
Church of England, Methodist
Languages: English, Gaelic
Currency: Pound Sterling (PdSt) = 100 New
Pence

Israel
Capital: Jerusalem
Location: Middle East
Seas: Mediterranean, Dead
Mountains: Mt. Hermon, Upper Galilee,
Lower Galilee, Mt. Carmel
Valleys: Hula, Capernaum, Jordan, Jezreel
Deserts: Negev, Judean
Rivers: Jordan, Yarkon, Na'aman, Kishon,
Taninim, Alexander, Ga'aton
Cities: Jerusalem, Tel Aviv-Yafo, Haifa,
Holon, Petah Tiqwa, Bat Yam
People: Ashkenazim, Sephardim, Karaites,
Samaritans, Falashas, Palestinians, Arabs
Religions: Judaism, Muslim, Christian
Languages: Hebrew, Arabic
Currency: New Shekel (NIS) = 100 New
Agorot

Italy
Capital: Rome
Location: Southern Europe
Seas: Tyrrhenian, Ligurian, Adriatic, Ionian,
Mediterranean

Islands: Sardinia, Sicily, Capri, Elba, Lipari,
Stromboli
Mountains: Alps, Apennines, Mont Blanc
Plains: Po
Volcanoes: Vesuvius, Vulcano, Etna,
Stromboli
Rivers: Po, Tevere, Tiber, Arno, Volturno,
Liri, Adige, Ticino
Cities: Milan, Naples, Turin, Palermo,
Genoa, Bologna, Florence, Parma, Siena,
Venice, Trieste, Florence
People: Italians, Etruscans, Tyroleans, Greeks
Religions: Roman Catholic
Languages: Italian
Currency: Lira (L) (plural; Lire) = 100
Centesimi

Ivory Coast (Cote D'Ivoire)
Capital: Yamoussoukro
Location: Western Africa
Oceans: Atlantic
Rivers: Comoe, Bandama, Sassandra,
Cavally
Cities: Abidjan, Bouake, Daloa, Korhogo
People: Akan, Krou (Kru), Lagoon, Nuclear-
Mande, Peripheral-Mande, Senoufo
Religions: Muslim, Christian
Languages: French, Agni, Baoule, Senoufo,
Malinke-Bambara-Dioula
Currency: CFA Franc (Communaute
Financiere Africaine/CFAF) = 100
Centimes

Jamaica
Capital: Kingston
Location: Caribbean Sea
Mountains: New Mountain Range, Blue
Rivers: Plantain Garden Hope, Yallahs, Rio
Pedro, Rio Minho, Milk, Cabaritta, Rio
Grande, Wag Water, White, Martha Brae,
Montego, Great, Black
Cities: Spanish Town, Portmore, Montego Bay
People: Jamaicans
Religions: Christian
Languages: English, Jamaican English
Currency: Dollar (JD) = 100 Cents

Japan (Nippon)
Capital: Tokyo
Location: Islands off east coast of Asia
Seas: of Japan, East China, Okhotsk
Oceans: Pacific
Bays: Ise, Osaka, Suruga, Shimabara
Straits: Korea, La Perouse, Bungo, Tsugaru
Rivers: Sumida, Kiso, Tone, Tashio
Volcanoes: Aso, Fuji, Daisen, Ontake, Asama
Islands: Hokkaido, Honshu, Shikoku,
Kyushu

Mountains: Hida, Fuji, Kuju, Ontake
Cities: Yokohama, Osaka, Nagoya, Sapporo, Kobe, Kyoto, Nagasaki, Hiroshima
People: Japanese, Burakumin, Ainu, Koreans
Religions: Shinto, Buddhist
Languages, Writing: Japanese, Hondo, Nanto, Kanji, Hiragana, Katakana
Currency: Yen (Y)

Jordan

Capital: Amman
Location: Middle East
Seas: Dead
Rivers: Jordan
Cities: Az-Zarqa, Irbid, As-Salt, Ar-Rusayfah
People: Jordanians, Bedouins, Arabs, Palestinians
Religions: Sunni Muslim
Languages: Arabic
Currency: Dinar (JD) = 1,000 Filsbar

Kazakhstan

Capital: Almaty
Location: Central Asia
Seas: Caspian
Uplands: Kazakh
Mountains: Altai, Tarbagatai, Tian Shan
Cities: Karaganda, Chimkent, Semipalatinsk, Pavlodar
People: Kazakhs
Religions: Russian Orthodox, Sunni Muslim
Languages: Kazakh
Currency: Tenge (T)

Kenya

Capital: Nairobi
Location: Eastern Africa
Oceans: Indian
Deserts: Chalbi
Mountains: Mt. Kenya, Mt. Niandarawa, Mt. Elgon, Aberdare
Lakes: Naivasha, Elmenteita, Nakuri, Hannington, Bogoria, Magadi, Victoria
Rivers: Tana, Galana, Athi
Cities: Mombasa, Kisumu, Nakuru
People: Kikuyu, Luo, Luhya, Kamba, Kalenjin
Religions: Protestant, Roman Catholic
Languages: English, Swahili, Bantu
Currency: Shilling (KSh) = 100 Cents

Kiribati

Capital: Bairiki (Tarawa Atoll)
Location: Central Pacific Ocean
Islands: Banaba, Kiritimati, Teraina, Flint, Gilbert, Phoenix, Line, Christmas (world's largest coral atoll)
Cities: Tarawa

People: I-Kiribati, Micronesians
Religions: Christian
Languages: English, I-Kiribati, Micronesian
Currency: Australian Dollar (AUD) = 100 Cents

Korea, North (Democratic People's Republic of Korea)

Capital: Pyongyang
Location: Korean Peninsula, Eastern Asia
Seas: Yellow, of Japan
Mountains: Machollyong, Hamgyong, Pujol-Lyong, Nangnim, Myohyang, Chogu-Ryong, Mt. Paektu
Plains: Pyongyang, Unjon, Anju, Chaeryong, Yonbaek, Hamhung, Yongchon, Kilchu, Yonghung, Susong
Rivers: Yalu, Taedong
Cities: Hamhung, Chongjin, Nampo, Sunchon
People: Koreans, Tungusic
Religions: Buddhist, Confucianist
Languages: Korean, Choson Muntcha, Altaic
Currency: Won (W) = 100 Chon (Jun)

Korea, South (Republic of Korea)

Capital: Seoul
Location: Korean Peninsula, Eastern Asia
Seas: Yellow, of Japan
Straits: Korea, Cheju
Mountains: Taebaek, Sobaek
Rivers: Naktong, Han, Kum, Naktong, Somjin
Cities: Pusan, Taegu, Inchon, Kwangju
People: Koreans, Tungusic
Religions: Christian, Buddhist, Confucianist, Chondokyo
Languages: Korean, Choson Muntcha, Altaic
Currency: Won (W) = 100 Hwan = 10 Chun

Kuwait

Capital: Kuwait City
Location: Arabian Peninsula, Middle East
Gulfs: Persian
Islands: Faylakah, Bubiyan
Cities: Al-Jahra, As-Salimiyah, Hawalli, Al-farwaniyah
People: Kuwaitis, Arabs, Anaiza
Religions: Sunni Muslim, Shiite Muslim
Languages: Arabic
Currency: Dinar (KD) = 1,000 Fils

Kyrgyz

Capital: Bishkek
Location: Central Asia
Mountains: Tien Shan, Pamir-Alai
Lakes: Issyk Kul
Rivers: Naryn, Chu

Cities: Osh, Dzhalal-Abad, Tokmak, Przhevalsk
People: Kyrgyz, Russian, Uzbek
Religions: Sunni Muslim, Russian Orthodox
Languages: Kyrgyz, Russian
Currency: Som (S) = 100 Tyiyn

Laos
Capital: Vientiane
Location: Southeastern Asia
Mountains: Phou Bia, Eastern Annam Cordillera
Plateaus: Khammouane, Boloven
Rivers: Mekong
Cities: Savannakhet, Louangphrabang
People: Laotians, Lao Lum, Lao Theung, Lao Thai, Lao Soung
Religions: Buddhist
Languages: Lao
Currency: New Kip (KN) = 100 Ath

Latvia
Capital: Riga
Location: Eastern Europe
Seas: Baltic
Gulfs: Riga
Rivers: Daugava, Western Dvina
Cities: Daugavpils, Liepaja, Jelgava, Jurmala
People: Latvians, Russians
Religions: Lutheran, Orthodox Christian, Roman Catholic
Languages: Latvian
Currency: Lat (L) = 100 Santimi

Lebanon
Capital: Beirut
Location: Middle East
Seas: Mediterranean
Mountains: Lebano, Jabal ash Sharqi
Rivers: Orontes, Litani (Leontes)
Cities: Tripoli, Zahlah, Sayda (Sidon)
People: Lebanese Arabs, Palestinian Arabs
Religions: Sunni, Shiite, Druze Muslim; Christian
Languages: Arabic
Currency: Pound (LP) = 100 Piastres

Lesotho
Capital: Maseru
Location: Southern Africa
Mountains: Maluti, Thabana-Ntlenyana
Rivers: Orange, Caledon, Tugela
Cities: Maputsoe
People: Basotho, Bantus, Sotho, Zulu, Tembu, Fingo
Religions: Protestant, Roman Catholic
Languages: Sesotho, Southern Sotho
Currency: Loti (plural; Maloti) (M) = 100 Lisenti

Liberia
Capital: Monrovia
Location: Southwestern coast of Africa
Oceans: Atlantic
Mountains: Mt. Nimba, Wologisi, Bomi Hills, Niete
Rivers: Mano, Loffa, St. Paul, Farmington, St. John, Cess, Cavalla Monrovia, Harbel, Gbarnga, Buchanan, Yekepa
Cities: Buchanan, Greenville
People: Kpelle, Bassa, Gio, Kru, Grebo, Mano, Krahn, Gola, Gbandi, Loma, Kiffi, Vai, Di, Belle, Mandingo, Mende
Religions: Muslim, Christian
Languages: English, tribal dialects
Currency: Dollar (LD) = 100 Cents

Libya
Capital: Tripoli
Location: Mediterranean coast of North Africa
Deserts: Sahara, Tripoli, Banghazi, Misratah
Cities: Banghazi, Misratah, Tobruk
People: Arab-Berber, Harratin, Tebou
Religions: Sunni Muslim
Languages: Arabic, Berber
Currency: Dinar (LD) = 100 Dirhams

Liechtenstein
Capital: Vaduz
Location: Central Europe
Rivers: Rhine
Mountains: Alps, Grauspitz, Rhaetian, Schaan, Vaduz
Cities: Balzers, Schaan, Ruggell
People: Alemannic
Religions: Roman Catholic, Protestant
Languages: German, Alemannic dialect
Currency: Swiss Franc (SwF) = 100 Centimes

Lithuania
Capital: Vilnius
Location: Eastern Europe
Seas: Baltic
Rivers: Nemunas (Niemen)
Cities: Kaunas, Klaipeda
People: Lithuanians
Religions: Christian
Languages: Lithuanian
Currency: Litas (L) (plural; Litai) = 100 Centai

Luxembourg
Capital: Luxembourg
Location: Western Europe
Other Geology: Ardennes
Rivers: Sauer, Moselle

Cities: Esch-sur-Alzette, Dudelange,
Differdange, Schifflange
People: Luxembourgers
Religions: Roman Catholic
Languages: French, German
Currency: Franc (LuxF) = 100 Centimes

Macau
Capital: Mone de Deus De Macau
Location: Southern coast of China
Rivers: Pearl
Peninsulas: Macau
Islands: Taipa, Cologne
Cities: Macau
People: Chinese, Cantonese, Hakka,
Portuguese
Religions: Buddhist, Christian, Confucianist
Languages: Portuguese, Chinese (Cantonese)
Currency: Pataca (P) = 100 Avos

Macedonia
Capital: Skopje
Location: Southeastern Europe
Mountains: Skopska Tsrna Gora, Rhodope
Rivers: Vardar, Strumitsa
Lakes: Ohrid, Prespa
Cities: Bitolj, Prilep, Kumanovo, Tetovo
People: Macedonians
Religions: Orthodox Christian, Muslim
Languages: Macedonian, Albanian
Currency: Denar (De) (formerly Yugoslav
Dinar) (D) = 100 Paras

Madagascar
Capital: Antananarivo
Location: Island in the Indian Ocean
Mountains: Tsaratana, Ankaratra,
Andringingtra
Rivers: Sambirano, Betsiboka, Tsiribihina,
Mangoky, Omilahy, Menarandra,
Mandrare, Mananara, Mananjary,
Mangoro, Maningory
Cities: Toamasina, Antsirabe, Mahajanga,
Fianarantsoa, Tamatave
People: Malagasy tribes
Religions: Christian, Muslim
Languages: French, Malagasy
Currency: Franc (FMG) = 100 Centimes

Malawi
Capital: Lilongwe
Location: Southeastern Africa
Lakes: Nyasa (Malawi)
Mountains: Dedza, Zomba, Mulanje
Cities: Blantyre, Mzuzu
People: Chewa, Nyanja, Tumbuka, Yao,
Lomwe, Sena, Tongo, Ngoni

Religions: Christian, Muslim
Languages: Chichewa, English
Currency: Kwacha (MK) = 100 Tambala

Malaysia
Capital: Kuala Lumpur
Location: Southeastern Asia
Islands: Borneo
Seas: South China, Sulu
Rivers: Rajang, Baram, Lupar, Limbang,
Kinabatangan, Padas
Straits: of Malacca
Cities: Ipoh, Johor Baharu, Melaka, Petaling
Jaya
People: Maylays, Semang, Senoi, Jakun,
Ibans, Dayaks, Melanaus, Kayans,
Kenyahs, Kajangs, Muruts, Kelabits,
Kadazans, Bajans
Religions: Muslim, Buddhist, Confucianist
Languages: Bahasa Malay
Currency: Ringgit (R) = 100 Sen

Maldives
Capital: Male
Location: North central Indian Ocean
People: Sinhalese, Dravidians, Arabs,
Africans
Religions: Sunni Muslim
Languages: Divehi, Sinhalese
Currency: Rufiyaa (Rf) = 100 Laari

Mali
Capital: Bamako
Location: Western Africa
Mountains: Futa Djallon Highlands,
Manding, Hombori
Deserts: Sahara
Rivers: Senegal, Niger
Cities: Scgou, Mopti, Skasso
People: Mande, Bambara, Malinke, Sarakole,
Peul
Religions: Muslim
Languages: French, Bambara, Fulani,
Songhai
Currency: CFA Franc (Communaute
Financiere Africaine/CFAF) = 100
Centimes

Malta
Capital: Valletta
Location: Central Mediterranean Sea
Islands: Malta, Gozo, Comino, Cominotto
Filfa, St. Paul
Cities: Birkirkara, Qormi, Hamrun, Sliema
People: Maltese
Religions: Roman Catholic
Languages: Maltese, English
Currency: Lira (ML) = 100 Cents = 1,000
Mils

Marshall Islands

Capital: Majuro
Location: North Pacific Ocean
Cities: Ebeye
People: Marshallese (Micronesians)
Religions: Christian
Languages: English, Marshallese dialects
Currency: US Dollar (USD) = 100 Cents

Martinique

Capital: Fort-de-France
Location: Lesser Antilles, Caribbean Sea
Volcanoes: Mt. Pelée
Cities: Le Lamentin, Schoelcher, Sainte-Marie
People: Martiniquais
Religions: Roman Catholic
Languages: French, Creole
Currency: French Franc (F) = 100 Centimes

Mauritania

Capital: Nouakchott
Location: Northwestern Africa
Deserts: Sahara
Oceans: Atlantic
Rivers: Senegal
Cities: Nouadhibou, Kaedi, Kiffa, Rosso
People: Moor (Maure), Fulbe, Toucouleur, Soninke, Wolof, Bambara
Religions: Sunni Muslim
Languages: Arabic
Currency: Ouguiya (UM) = 5 Khoums

Mauritius

Capital: Port Louis
Location: Island in the southern Indian Ocean
Islands: Agalega, Rodrigues, St. Brandon
Mountains: Moka, Grande Port, Black River
Rivers: Grand
Cities: Beau Bassin, Vacoas Phoenix, Curepipe
People: Indo-Mauritian, Creole, Sino-Mauritian
Religions: Hindu, Christian, Muslim
Languages: English, Creole patois
Currency: Rupee (MauRs) = 100 Cents

Mexico

Capital: Mexico City
Location: Southern North America
Gulfs: California, Mexico
Oceans: Pacific
Mountains: Sierra Madre, Popocatepetl, Ixtacihuat, Orizaba
Deserts: Sonoran
Peninsulas: Yucatan, Baja California
Lakes: Chapala
Cities: Guadalajara, Monterrey, Puebla, Leon, Juarez, Tijuana, Jalapa, Durango, Merida, Oaxaca, Mazatlan, Culiacan, Vera Cruz, Chihuahua, Mexicali, Cancun, Acapulco, Puerto Vallarta
People: Mestizo, Maya, Aztec, Toltec, Nahuatl, Yaqui, Mixtec, Zacatec, Zapotec
Religions: Roman Catholic
Languages: Spanish, Maya, Nahuatl
Currency: New Peso (MexP) = 100 Centavos

Micronesia

Capital: Palikir on Pohnpei Island
Location: North Pacific Ocean
Islands: Pohnpei, Chuuk (formerly Truk), Kosrae, Yap
Cities: Weno, To, Kolonia
People: Melanesian, Carolinian
Religions: Christian
Languages: English, Malayo-Polynesian
Currency: US Dollar (USD) = 100 Cents

Moldova

Capital: Chisinau
Location: Eastern Europe
Rivers: Dnestr, Prut
Cities: Tiraspol, Balti, Tighina, Rabnita
People: Moldovans
Religions: Eastern Orthodox
Languages: Romanian, Russian
Currency: Leu (L) (plural; Lei) = 100 Bani

Monaco

Capital: Monaco-Ville
Location: Southwestern Europe, Mediterranean Sea
Size: Second smallest country in world
Cities: Monte Carlo
People: Monegasques (Rhaetians)
Religions: Roman Catholic
Languages: French, Monegasque
Currency: French Franc = 100 Centimes

Mongolia

Capital: Ulan Bator
Location: East central Asia
Mountains: Mongolian Altai, Khenti
Deserts: Gobi
Rivers: Kereulen, Orhon, Gol, Selenge Moron, Dzavhars Gol, Haraa Gol, Tuul Gol
Cities: Darhan, Erdenet, Choybalsan
People: Mongols, Khalka, Kazakh, Durbet, Dariganga, Turvins, Khotans
Religions: Lamaistic Buddhist
Languages: Khalka Mongolian
Currency: Tughrik (T) = 100 Mongo

Morocco

Capital: Rabat
Location: Northwestern Africa
Deserts: Sahara
Oceans: Mediterranean, Atlantic
Mountains: Rif, Atlas, Sarho, Dhara
Plateau
Plains: Gharb, Chaouia, Doukkala, Meseta,
Abda, Djebilet, Rehmana Plains
Rivers: Moulouya, Oumer Rebia, Sobou,
Bou, Regreg, Tensift, Draa, Sous
Cities: Casablanca, Fes
People: Berbers, Arabs
Religions: Sunni Muslim
Languages: Arabic, Berber
Currency: Dirham (DH) = 100 Francs

Mozambique

Capital: Maputo
Location: Southeast coast of Africa
Oceans: Indian
Highlands: Livingstone-Nyasa, Namuli
(Shire), Angonia, Tete
Mountains: Lebomo
Rivers: Zambezi
Lakes: Nyasa (Malawi), Chiuta, Shirwa
Cities: Beira, Nampula
People: Makua-Lomwe, Shona, Tsonga
Religions: Roman Catholic, Muslim
Languages: Portuguese, tribal languages
Currency: Metical (MT) (plural; Meticais) =
100 Centavos

Myanmar

Capital: Yangon
Location: Southeastern Asia
Seas: Andaman
Mountains: Dawna, Tenasserim, Arakan
Rivers: Irrawaddy, Chindwin, Sittang,
Salween
Bays: of Bengal
Cities: Rangoon, Mandalay, Moulmein,
Pegu, Bassein
People: Burmans, Karens, Shans
Religions: Theravada Buddhist
Languages: Burmese
Currency: Kyat (K) = 100 Pyas

Namibia

Capital: Windhoek
Location: Southwestern Africa
Oceans: Atlantic
Deserts: Namib, Kalahari
Mountains: Tsaris, Anas, Erongo
Rivers: Orange, Rio Okavango, Fish (Vis)
Cities: Swakopmund, Rundu, Rehoboth
People: Ovambo, Damara, Herero,
Okavango, Nama, East Caprivian,
Bushmen, Rehoboth Baster, Kaokovelder,
Tswana
Religions: Christian
Languages: English, German, Afrikaans,
Bantu
Currency: Namibian Dollar (ND) (formerly
South African Rand) (R) = 100 Cents

Nauru

Capital: Yaren
Location: Asia, west central Pacific Ocean
Size: Smallest nation in Asia
Lagoons: Buada
People: Micronesian, Melanesian,
Polynesian
Religions: Christian
Languages: English, Nauruan
Currency: Australian Dollar (AUD) = 100
Cents

Nepal

Capital: Kathmandu
Location: South central Asia
Mountains: Himalayas, Everest, Lhotse,
Makalu
Valleys: Kathmandu
Rivers: Kosi, Narayani (Gandak), Karnali,
Gogra
Cities: Biratnagar, Lalitpur, Pokhara,
Bhaktapur
People: Pahari, Newar, Tharu, Tarai, Tamang,
Rai, Limbu, Bhote, Sunwar, Magar, Gurung
Religions: Hindu
Languages: Nepali
Currency: Rupee (NRs) = 100 Paisa

Netherlands

Capital: Amsterdam
Location: Northwestern Europe
Seas: North
Rivers: Rhine, Waal, Maas, Ijssel, Schelde
Cities: Rotterdam, The Hague, Utrecht,
Eindhoven
People: Dutch
Religions: Christian
Languages: Dutch, Frisian
Currency: Guilder (NG) = 100 Cents

Netherlands Antilles

Capital: Willemstad
Location: Caribbean Sea
Islands: Curacao, Bonaire, St. Martin, St.
Eustatius, Saba
Cities: Westpunt, Kralendijk
People: Creoles
Religions: Roman Catholic, Protestant,
Jewish
Languages: Dutch, Papiamento

Currency: Antillean Guilder (NAG) = 100
Cents

New Caledonia
Capital: Noumea
Location: Islands in the South Pacific Ocean
Mountains: Mt. Panie
Cities: Mont-Dore, Dumbea, Paita
People: Melanesian Kanaks
Religions: Christian
Languages: French, Melanesian-Polynesian
dialects
Currency: CFP Franc (Comptoire Francaise
du Pacifique–CFPF) = 100 Centimes

New Zealand
Capital: Wellington
Location: South Pacific Ocean
Islands: North, South
Straits: Cook
Rivers: Waikato
Lakes: Taupo
Mountains: Southern Alps
Cities: Auckland, Christchurch, Manukau,
North Shore, Wellington
People: Maoris
Religions: Christian
Languages: English, Maori
Currency: Dollar (NZD) = 100 Cents

Nicaragua
Capital: Managua
Location: Central America
Oceans: Caribbean, Pacific
Lakes: Managua, Nicaragua
Cities: Leon, Masaya, Chinandega,
Matagalpa, Granada
People: Mestizo, Miskito, Sumu, Rama,
Carib, Matagalpa, Subtiaba, Monimbo
Religions: Roman Catholic
Languages: Spanish
Currency: Cordoba Oro (CO) = 100
Centavos

Niger
Capital: Niamey
Location: Western Africa
Mountains: Tamgak
Deserts: Tenere
Rivers: Niger
Cities: Zinder, Maradi, Tahoua, Agadez
People: Hausa, Songhai, Djerma, Fulani,
Beriberi-Manga, Tuareg
Religions: Sunni Muslim
Languages: French, Djerma, Hausa
Currency: CFA Franc (Communaute
Financiere Africaine/CFAF) = 100
Centimes

Nigeria
Capital: Abuja (formerly Lagos)
Location: Western Africa
Gulfs: of Guinea
Rivers: Niger, Benue
Cities: Lagos, Ibadan, Kano, Ogbomosho,
Oshogbo, Ilorin
People: Hausa, Fulani, Yoruba, Ibo
Religions: Muslim, Christian
Languages: English, Hausa, Yoruba, Ibo
Currency: Naira (N) = 100 Kobo

Norway
Capital: Oslo
Location: Northwestern Europe
Oceans: Arctic Ocean
Seas: Norwegian
Islands: Lofoten, Vesteralen, Senja, Soroya,
Ringvassoy, Hitra
Mountains: Kjolen, Dovrefjell, Jotunheim
Other Geology: Fjords
Lakes: Mjosa
Rivers: Glama, Dramselv, Lagen
Cities: Bergen, Trondheim, Stavanger, Baerum
People: Nordics, Sami (Lapps)
Religions: Evangelical Lutheran
Languages: Norwegian, Lappish
Currency: Krone (NKr) = 100 Ore

Oman
Capital: Muscat
Location: Southeastern Arabian Peninsula,
Middle East
Seas: Arabian
Gulfs: of Oman
Mountains: Ras al-Jabal, Hajar al-Sharqi, Qara
Islands: Al Masira
Cities: Nizwa, Samail
People: Arabs, Yamaniyah (Hinawi), Nizari
(Ghafiri)
Religions: Muslim
Languages: Arabic
Currency: Rial (RO) = 1,000 Baiza

Pakistan
Capital: Islamabad
Location: Southern Asia
Seas: Arabian
Mountains: Hindu Kush, K2, Safed Koh,
Toba Kakar, Ras Koh, Brahui, Kirthar,
Makran, Sulaiman
Other Geology: Khyber Pass
Rivers: Indus, Kabul, Gumal, Panjnad
Cities: Karachi, Lahore, Faisalabad,
Rawalpindi
People: Punjabis, Sindhi, Pushtuns, Baluchis,
Makranis, Mujahirs, Khos, Kafirs
Religions: Muslim

Languages: Punjabi , Urdu
Currency: Rupee (PRs) = 100 Paisa

Palau, Republic of

Capital: Koror
Location: West Pacific Ocean
Islands: Caroline, Babeldoab
People: Palauans, Micronesians
Religions: Christian
Languages: English, Palauan
Currency: US Dollar = 100 Cents

Panama

Capital: Panama City
Location: Central America
Seas: Caribbean
Oceans: Pacific, Atlantic
Other Geology: Isthmus of Panama, Central
   Isthmus, Panama Canal
Rivers: Tuira, Bayano, Chepo
Cities: San Miguel, David, Colon
People: Mestizo, Panameno, Guayami,
   Choco, Cuna
Religions: Roman Catholic
Languages: Spanish
Currency: Balboa (B) = 100 Centisimos

Papua New Guinea

Capital: Port Moresby
Location: South Pacific Ocean, eastern half
   of the island of New Guinea
Islands: Trobriand d'Entrecasteaux, New
   Britain, New Ireland, Bougainville
Gulfs: of Guinea
Seas: Coral, Solomon, Bismarck
Rivers: Sepik, Ramu, Markham, Fly, Purari,
   Kikori
Cities: Lae, Madang, Wewak, Goroka
People: Papuans, Melanesians
Religions: Christian
Languages: English, Pidgin
Currency: Kina (K) = 100 Toea

Paraguay

Capital: Asuncion
Location: Central South America
Rivers: Paraguay, Parana, Pilcomayo
Lakes: Ypoa, Ypacarai
Cities: Ciudad del Este, San Lorenzo,
   Lambare, Fernando de la Mora
People: Mestizos
Religions: Roman Catholic
Languages: Spanish, Guarani
Currency: Guarani (G) = 100 Centimos

Peru

Capital: Lima
Location: Western South America
Oceans: Pacific

Mountains: Andes, Huascaran
Deserts: Sechura, Cordillera Central and
   Oriental
Rivers: Amazon, Cuzco, Paita, Maranon,
   Huallaga, Ucayali, Tigre, Pastaza, Napo
Lakes: Titicaca
Cities: Ica, Arequipa, Callao, Trujillo,
   Chiclayo
People: Mestizos, Incas
Religions: Roman Catholic
Languages: Spanish, Quechua, Aymara
Currency: Nuevo Sol (NS) = 100 Centavos

Philippines

Capital: Manila
Location: Southeastern Asia
Seas: Philippines, South China, Sulu,
   Celebes
Islands: Luzon, Mindanao, Samar, Palawan,
   Mindoro, Panay, Negros, Cebu, Leyte,
   Masbate, Bohol
Rivers: Rio Grande de Cagayan, Agno, Abra,
   Bicol, Pampanga, Pasig, Agusan
Cities: Quezon City, Davao, Cebu, Caloocan,
   Zamboanga
People: Filipinos
Religions: Roman Catholic
Languages: Filipino, English
Currency: Peso (P) = 100 Centavos

Poland

Capital: Warsaw
Location: Central Europe
Seas: Baltic
Mountains: Carpathian, Sudetes
Rivers: Wisla (Vistula), Oder (Odra)
Cities: Lodz, Krakow
People: Slavs
Religions: Roman Catholic
Languages: Polish
Currency: Zloty (Zl) = 100 Groszybar

Portugal

Capital: Lisbon
Location: Southwestern Europe
Peninsulas: Iberian
Islands: Azores, Madeira, Porto Santo
Oceans: Atlantic
Mountains: Sierra da Estrela
Rivers: Tagus, Douro
Cities: Porto, Vila Nova de Gaia, Amadora
People: Portuguese
Religions: Roman Catholic
Languages: Portuguese
Currency: Escudo (Esc) = 100 Centavos

Puerto Rico, Commonwealth of

Capital: San Juan
Location: Greater Antilles, Caribbean Sea

Oceans: Atlantic
Seas: Caribbean
Mountains: Cordillera Central, Cerro de
Punta
Cities: Ponce, Caguas, Mayaguez, Arecibo
People: Puerto Ricans
Religions: Roman Catholic
Languages: Spanish
Currency: US Dollar (USD) = 100 Cents

Qatar

Capital: Doha
Location: East coast of the Arabian
Peninsula, Middle East
Gulfs: Persian
Other Geology: Sabkhah (salt flats)
Cities: Ar-Rayyan, Al-Wakrah
People: Qataris (Arabs, Pakistanis, Indians)
Religions: Wahhabi Muslim, Sunni Muslim
Languages: Arabic
Currency: Riyal (QR) = 100 Dirhams

Reunion

Capital: Saint-Denis
Location: Island in the Indian Ocean
Cities: Le Port, Le Tampon, Saint Andre,
Saint Pierre
People: Reunionese
Religions: Roman Catholic
Languages: French, Creole
Currency: French Franc (F) = 100 Centimes

Romania

Capital: Bucharest
Location: Balkan Peninsula, Southern
Europe
Seas: Black
Mountains: Carpathian
Rivers: Danube, Tisza, Mures, Prut, Siret, Olt
Rivers, Moldova
Cities: Constanta, Iasi, Timisoara, Galati,
Brasov
People: Romanians, Hungarians
Religions: Romanian Orthodox
Languages: Romanian
Currency: Leu (plural; Lei) = 100 Bani

Russian Federation

Capital: Moscow
Location: Eastern Europe and northern Asia
Seas: Barents, Black, Caspian, of Japan, of
Okhotsk, Bering, East Siberian, Chukchi,
Laptev, Kara
Oceans: Arctic
Rivers: Don, Ili, Ner, Oka, Ros, Ufa, Amur,
Duna, Kara, Lena, Neva, orel, Sura, Svir,
Ural, Dnepr, Dvina, Onega, Terek, Tobol,
Volga, Donets, Irtish, Irtysh, Dnieper

Mountains: Ural, Altai, Caucasus, Mt.
El'Brus, Pamirs
Islands: Kuril
Lakes: Aral, Neva, Sego, Elton, Ilmen,
Onega, Baikal
Cities: St. Petersburg, Gorki, Novosibirsk,
Yekaterinburg, Archangel, Smolensk,
Samara, Omsk, Kalinin, Kazan, Ufa,
Rostov, Vladimir, Novosibirsk,
Vladivostok
People: Russians, Ukrainians, Tartars
Religions: Russian Orthodox
Languages: Russian
Currency: Ruble (R) = 100 Kopecks

Rwanda

Capital: Kigali
Location: East central Africa
Lakes: Kivu
Mountains: Virunga
Lakes: Ruhondo, Muhazi, Mugasera, Ihema,
Rwanye, Burera, Rugwero, Cyohoha, Kivu
Rivers: Kagera, Ruzizi, Nyabarongo
Cities: Ruhengeri, Butare, Gisenyi
People: Hutu, Tutsi, Twa (Pygmies)
Religions: Christian, Muslim
Languages: French, Kinyarwanda (Rwandan)
Currency: Franc (RF) = 100 Centimes

Saint Kitts and Nevis

Capital: Basseterre
Location: Two leeward islands, Caribbean
Sea
Volcano, High Point: Mt. Misery (St. Kitts)
Cities: Basseterre, Charlestown
People: Kittsians, Nerisians
Religions: Christian
Languages: English, Creole-English
Currency: East Caribbean Dollar (ECD) =
100 Cents

Saint Lucia

Capital: Castries
Location: Windward islands, Caribbean Sea
Mountains: Mt. Gimie
Rivers: Dennery, Fond, Piaye, Doree,
Canaries, Roseau, Marquis
People: Saint Lucians
Religions: Christian
Languages: English, French patois
Currency: East Caribbean Dollar (ECD) =
100 Cents

Saint Vincent and the Grenadines

Capital: Kingstown
Location: Windward islands, Caribbean Sea
Mountains: (St. Vincent): Soufriere,
Richmond, Grand Bonhomme, St. Andrew

People: Caribs
Religions: Christian
Languages: English, French patois
Currency: East Caribbean Dollar (ECD) =
100 Cents

Samoa

Capital: Apia
Location: South Pacific Ocean
Islands: Upolu, Savaii
Straits: Apolima
Rivers: Sili, Faleate, Alia Senga,
Vaisingano
Cities: Mulifanua, Asau, Salelolga
People: Samoans, Polynesians
Religions: Christian
Languages: Samoan, English
Currency: Tala (T) = 100 Sene

San Marino

Capital: San Marino
Location: Southern Europe
Mountains: Mt. Titano
Rivers: Ausa
Cities: Serravalle, Borgo Maggiore, Murata
People: San Marinese
Religions: Roman Catholic
Languages: Italian
Currency: Italian Lira = 100 Centesimi

Sao Tome and Principe

Capital: Sao Tome
Location: Islands in the Gulf of Guinea,
Western Africa
Cities: Santa Cruz, Neves
People: Sao Tomeans
Religions: Roman Catholic
Languages: Portuguese-Creole
Currency: Dobra (Db) = 100 Centimos

Saudi Arabia

Capital: Riyadh
Location: Arabian Peninsula, Middle East
Seas: Red
Gulfs: Persian
Deserts: Dahana, Nafud, Rub al-Khali
(world's largest sand desert)
Cities: Jidda, Mecca
People: Arabs
Religions: Sunni Muslim, Shiite Muslim
Languages: Arabic
Currency: Riyal (SRls) = 100 Halalahs

Scotland

Capital: Edinburgh
Location: Off northwestern coast of Europe
Firth: Tay, Lock, Lorn, Clyde, Forth, Moray,
Linnhe, Cromarty

Islands: Iona, Arran, Orkney, Hebrides,
Shetland
Lakes: Lomond, Ness
Mountains: Ben Nevis, Grampians
Rivers: Ayr, Dee, don, Esk, Tay, Doon, Find,
Nith, Norn, Spey, Afton, Annan, Clyde,
North, Tweed, Teviot, Deveron
Cities: Ayr, Alloa, Leith, Perth, Troon,
Dundee, Glasgow, Grunock, Paisley,
Aberdeen, Stirling, Inverness, St. Andrews,
Kilmarnock
People: Scots
Religions: Presbyterian, Roman Catholic
Languages: English, Erse, Gaelic, Lallan,
Lalland
Currency: Pound Sterling (PdSt) = 100 New
Pence

Senegal

Capital: Dakar
Location: West coast of Africa
Oceans: Atlantic
Rivers: Senegal, Casamance, Sine, Saloum
Cities: Dakar, Thies, Kaolack, Ziguinchor, St.
Louis
People: Wolof, Fulani, Serer, Toucouleur,
Diola, Mandingo
Religions: Sunni Muslim
Languages: French, Wolof, Serer, Pulaar
Currency: CFA Franc (Communaute
Financiere Africaine/CFAF) = 100
Centimes

Seychelles

Capital: Victoria
Location: West Indian Ocean
Islands: Mahe, Praslin, La Digue, Silhouette
(4 largest)
People: Creoles
Religions: Christian
Languages: Creole, English
Currency: Rupee (SR) = 100 Cents

Sierra Leone

Capital: Freetown
Location: Western Africa
Oceans: Atlantic
Mountains: Loma
Islands: Sherbro
Rivers: Rokel, Gbangbar, Jong, Sewa,
Waanje, Great Scarcies, Little Scarcies,
Moa, Mano
Cities: Bo, Kenema, Makeni
People: Mende, Temne, Limba
Religions: Muslim
Languages: English, Krio, Mende,
Temne
Currency: Leone (Le) = 100 Cents

Singapore

Capital: Singapore
Location: Malay Peninsula, Southeastern Asia
Straits: Johore, of Malacca, of Singapore
Rivers: Singapore, Jurong, Kalang, Kranji, Seletar, Serangoon
Cities: Jurong, Changi
People: Chinese, Malays, Indians
Religions: Buddhist, Taoist, Muslim, Hindu, Christian
Languages: English, Chinese, Tamil, Malay
Currency: Dollar (SD) = 100 Cents

Slovak Republic

Capital: Bratislava
Location: Central Europe
Mountains: Carpathian, High Tatra, Gerlachovka, Ore
Rivers: Danube, Vah, Nitra, Hron
Cities: Kosice, Presov, Nitra, Zilina, Banska Bystrica
People: Slovaks, Moravians
Religions: Christian
Languages: Slovak, Magyar, Czech
Currency: Koruna (K) (plural; Koruny) = 100 Haleru

Slovenia

Capital: Ljubljana
Location: Central Europe
Gulfs: of Trieste
Mountains: Alps, Pohorije, Karawanken, Savinja, Julian, Triglav (highest point), Dinaric
Seas: Adriatic
Rivers: Sava, Drava
Cities: Maribor, Celje, Kranj, Velenje
People: Slovenes
Religions: Christian
Languages: Slovenian
Currency: Tolar (T) (formerly Yugoslav Dinar [D]) = 100 Stotin

Solomon Islands

Capital: Honiara
Location: Islands in the South Pacific Ocean
Islands: Choiseul, Guadalcanal, Malaita, New Georgia, San Cristobal, Santa Isabel
Cities: Aola, Gizo
People: Melanesians
Religions: Anglican, Roman Catholic, Baptist, Methodist
Languages: English, Pidgin, Melanesian
Currency: Dollar (SID) = 100 Cents

Somalia

Capital: Mogadishu
Location: On Horn of Africa, East Africa
Gulfs: Indian Ocean, of Aden
Rivers: Juba, Shebeli
Cities: Hargeysa, Kismaayo, Berbera
People: Hamitic, Bantu
Religions: Sunni Muslim
Languages: Somali
Currency: Shilling (SoSh) = 100 Cents

South Africa

Capital: Pretoria
Location: Southern tip of Africa
Oceans: Indian, Atlantic
Capes: of Good Hope, Agulhas
Mountains: Great Escarpment, Swartberg
Grasslands: Veldt (veld)
Rivers: Orange, Vaal, Caledon, Molopo, Limpopo
Cities: Cape Town, Johannesburg, Durban, Soweto, Germiston, Bloemfontein, Port Elizabeth
People: Nguni, Sotho, Bantu, Namas, Tswana, Pondo, Xhosa, Zulu, Bechuana
Religions: Dutch Reformed Church, Anglican, Roman Catholic
Languages: Afrikaans, English, Zulu, Xhosa, Swazi, Ndebele, Venda, Tsonga, Sotho, Taal
Currency: Rand (R) = 100 Cents

Spain

Capital: Madrid
Location: Iberian Peninsula, southwestern Europe
Islands: Balearic, Canary
Oceans: Atlantic
Seas: Mediterranean
Straits: of Gibraltar
Bays: of Biscay
Mountains: Asturian, Sierra Nevada, Cantabrian, Baetic, Andalusian, Iberian, Pyrenees, Cordillera Cantabrica
Rivers: Douro, Tajo, Guadiana, Ebro, Guadalquivir, Mino, Segura, Jucar, Tagus, Guadiana
Cities: Barcelona, Valencia, Seville, Zaragoza, Vigo, Bilbao, Malaga, Granada, Saragossa
People: Castilians, Basques, Catalans, Galicians
Religions: Roman Catholic
Languages: Castilian Spanish, Catalan, Galician, Basque
Currency: Peseta (Pta) = 100 Centimos

Sri Lanka

Capital: Colombo
Location: Island in the Indian Ocean
Straits: Palk
Plateaus: Hatton, Kandy

Rivers: Mahaweli Ganga, Aruvi Aru
Cities: Dehiwala, Moratuwa, Jaffna
People: Sinhalese, Tamil
Religions: Theravada Buddhist, Hindu
Languages: Sinhala, Tamil
Currency: Rupee (SLRs) = 100 Cents

Sudan

Capital: Khartoum
Location: Northeastern Africa
Seas: Red
Rivers: Blue Nile, White Nile
Deserts: Libyan, Nubian
Mountains: Nuba, Immatong, Dongotona
Cities: Omdurman, Port Sudan
People: Arabs, Nubians
Religions: Sunni Muslim
Languages: Arabic
Currency: Dinar (DSd) (formerly Pound)
(LSd) = 100 Piastres = 1,000 Milliemes

Suriname

Capital: Paramaribo
Location: Northern South America
Oceans: Atlantic
Rivers: Corantyne, Nickerie, Copename,
Saramacca, Suriname, Commewijne,
Marauijne
Cities: Nieuw Nickerie, Meerzorg,
Marienburg
People: Hindustani, Creole, Javanese
Religions: Roman Catholic, Moravian,
Hindu, Muslim
Languages: Dutch, Sranang Tongo, Taki-Taki
Currency: Guilder (Sf) = 100 Cents

Swaziland

Capital: Mbabane
Location: Southeastern Africa
Grasslands: Veldt (Veld)
Mountains: Lebombo
Rivers: Komati, Umbeluzi, Usutu,
Ngwavuma
Cities: Manzini, Nhlangano
People: Swazi, Zulu, Tsonga, Shangaan
Religions: Christian
Languages: English, Swazi, Nguni
Currency: Lilangeni (plural; Emalangeni)
(E) = 100 Cents

Sweden

Capital: Stockholm
Location: Scandinavian Peninsula, northern
Europe
Gulfs: of Bothnia
Seas: Baltic
Islands: Gotland, Oland
Lakes: Vanern, Vattern, Hjalmaren, Malaren

Cities: Goteborg, Malmo, Uppsala,
Linkoping
People: Swedes, Sami, Lapps
Religions: Evangelical Lutheran
Languages: Swedish
Currency: Krona (SKr) (plural; Kronor) =
100 Ore

Switzerland

Capital: Berne
Location: Central Europe
Mountains: Alps, Jura, Rigi, Rosa, Blanc,
Pennine, Matterhorn, St. Gotthard
Rivers: Rhone, Reuss, Ticino, Rhine, Aare,
Doubs, Inn
Lakes: Geneva, Lugano, Uri, Zug, Joux,
Thon, Leman, Bienne, Brienz, Sarnen,
Wallan, Zurich
Cities: Zurich, Basel, Geneva, Lausanne,
Montreux, Locarno
People: Swiss, German, French, Italian
Religions: Roman Catholic, Protestant
Languages: German, French, Italian,
Romansch
Currency: Franc (SwF) = 100 Centimes

Syria

Capital: Damascus
Location: Middle East
Seas: Mediterranean
Deserts: Hamad
Rivers: Euphrates, Orontes
Cities: Aleppo, Homs, Latakia
People: Arabs, Druze
Religions: Sunni Muslim, Shiite Muslim
Languages: Syrian Arabic
Currency: Pound (LS) = 100 Piastres

Taiwan

Capital: Taipei
Location: Off coast of mainland China
Islands: Taiwan, Pescadores, Lan Hsu, Lu Tao
Straits: Taiwan
Seas: South China, East China
Oceans: Pacific
Cities: Kaohsiung, Taichung, Tainan
People: Han Chinese
Religions: Buddhist, Taoist, Confucianist
Languages: Mandarin, Hokkien, Hakka
Currency: New Taiwan Dollar (NTD) = 100
Cents

Tajikistan

Capital: Dushanbe
Location: Central Asia
Valleys: Fergana, Gissar, Vakhsh
Mountains: Pamir, Turkmenistan, Zeravshan,
Gissar

Rivers: Amu-Darya (Pyandzh)
Lakes: Kara Kul
Cities: Khudzhand (Leninabad), Kulyab,
  Kurgan-Tyube, Ura-Tyube
People: Tajik, Uzbeks
Religions: Sunni Muslim
Languages: Tajik
Currency: Ruble (R) = 100 Kopecks

Tanzania

Capital: Dar-es-Salaam
Location: Eastern Africa
Islands: Mafia, Pemba, Zanzibar
Oceans: Indian
Mountains: Kondoa, Mbulu, Mpwapwa, Mt.
  Loolmalasin, Mt. Lengai, Mt. Kilimanjaro,
  Mt. Meru
Rivers: Pangani, Wami, Ruvu (Kingani),
  Rufiji, Kilombero, Mbaragandu, Matandu,
  Mbemkuru, Lewugu, Lukuledi, Ruvuma
Cities: Mwanza, Dodoma, Tanga, Zanzibar
People: Bantu, Nilotic, Khoisan, Iraqw
Religions: Muslim, Christian
Languages: Swahili
Currency: Shilling (TSh) = 100 Cents

Thailand

Capital: Bangkok
Location: Southeastern Asia
Seas: Andaman
Gulfs: of Thailand
Mountains: Phanom Dongrak, Phetchabun
Rivers: Chao Phraya
Cities: Nonthaburi, Nakhon Ratchasima,
  Chiang Mai
People: Thai
Religions: Buddhist (Theravada or Hinayana)
Languages: Thai
Currency: Baht (B) = 100 Satangs

Togo

Capital: Lome
Location: Western Africa
Gulfs: of Guinea
Rivers: Oti, Kara, Mo
Cities: Sokode, Kpalime
People: Hamitic, Ewe
Religions: Catholic, Muslim, Protestant
Languages: French, Evegbe (Ewe), Hausa,
  Twi, Dagomba, Tim, Cabrais, Fongbi
Currency: CFA Franc (Communaute
  Financiere Africaine/CFAF) = 100
  Centimes

Tonga

Capital: Nuku'alofa
Location: Archipelago in South Pacific
  Ocean
Cities: Mu'a, Neiafu

People: Tongans, Polynesians
Religions: Protestant, Roman Catholic
Languages: English, Tongan
Currency: Palanga (P) = 100 Seniti

Trinidad and Tobago

Capital: Port of Spain
Location: Lesser Antilles, Caribbean Sea
Rivers: Ortoire, Caron, Courland
People: Trinadadians, Tobagonians
Cities: Chaguanas, San Fernando, Arima,
  Point Fortin
Religions: Christian, Hindu, Muslim
Languages: English, English-Creole
Currency: Dollar (TTD) = 100 Cents

Tunisia

Capital: Tunis
Location: Northern Africa
Seas: Mediterranean
Mountains: Tell Atlas
Rivers: Medjerda
Deserts: Sahara
Gulfs: of Tunis
Cities: Safaqis, Aryanah, Ettadhamen
People: Arabs, Berbers
Religions: Sunni Muslim
Languages: Arabic
Currency: Dinar (D) = 1,000 Millimes

Turkey

Capital: Ankara
Location: Anatolian Peninsula, Asia
Seas: Aegean, Black, Mediterranean
Straits: Bosporus, Dardenelles
Plateaus: Anatolian Plateau
Mountains: Ararat
Rivers: Kizil Irma, Sakarya, Seyhan,
  Yesihrmak, Tigris, Euphrates, Gok, Mesta,
  Sarus, Delice
Cities: Istanbul, Izmir, Adana, Bursa
People: Turks, Kurds, Armenians
Religions: Sunni Muslim
Languages: Turkish
Currency: Lira (LT) = 100 Kurush

Turkmenistan

Capital: Ashgabat
Location: Central Asia
Seas: Caspian Sea
Deserts: Kara Kum
Mountains: Mt. Kopet
Rivers: Amu-Darya
Cities: Charjew, Dashhowuz, Mary, Nebit-Dag
People: Turkmen
Religions: Sunni Muslim
Languages: Turkmen
Currency: Manat (M)

Nations of the World (continued)

Tuvalu (formerly Ellice Islands)
Capital: Fongafale on Funafuti Atoll
Location: South Pacific Ocean
Islands: Funafuti, Nanumea, Nanumanga, Niulakita, Niuto, Nui, Nukufetau, Nukulailai, Vaitupu
People: Polynesians
Religions: Church of Tuvalu
Languages: English, Tuvaluan
Currency: Tuvalu Dollar (Tuv) = 100 Cents

Uganda
Capital: Kampala
Location: East central Africa
Mountains: Mufumbiro, Ruwenzori, Mt. Elgon
Lakes: George, Victoria
Rivers: Nile
Cities: Jinja, Mbale, Masaka
People: Bantu, Nilotic
Religions: Roman Catholic, Protestant, Muslim
Languages: Swahili
Currency: Shilling (USh) = 100 Cents

Ukraine
Capital: Kiev
Location: Eastern Europe
Seas: Black
Mountains: Carpathian
Marshes: Pripet
Rivers: Bug, Dnepr, Donets, Dnestr, Prut, Tisza
Cities: Kharkiv, Dnipropetrovsk, Donetsk, Odessa
People: Ukrainians
Religions: Christian
Languages: Ukrainian
Currency: Karbovanets (K)

United Arab Emirates
Capital: Abu Dhabi
Location: Arabian Peninsula
Emirates: Abu Dhabi, Ajman, Dubayy, Al Fujayrah, Ra's al Khaymah, Shariqah, Umm al Qaywayn
Gulfs: Persian
Salt Flats: Sabkha
Mountains: Hajar
Cities: Dubayy, al-Ayn
People: Emiris, Arabs
Religions: Muslim
Languages: Arabic
Currency: Dirham (Dh) = 100 Fils

United Kingdom *(See individual countries listed below)*
Capital: London
Location: Off northwestern coast of Europe
Countries: England, Scotland, Northern Ireland, Wales

United States of America *(See also individual states and territories)*
Capital: Washington, D.C.
Location: North America
Oceans: Atlantic, Pacific
Mountains: Appalachian, Catskill, Rocky, Blue Ridge, Smoky, Allegheny, White, Green, Sierra Nevada, Hood, Helena, Shasta, Rainier, Whitney, McKinley, Laurentian, Adirondack, Olympic
Lakes: Great Lakes—Superior, Michigan, Huron, Ontario, Erie; Great Salt, Lake of the Woods
Gulfs: of Mexico, of California
Plains: Great Plains
Islands: Hawaiian, Aleutian, Long, Staten, Keys, Catalina
Rivers: Mississippi, Hudson, Columbia, Missouri, Arkansas, Ohio, Colorado, St. Lawrence, Genesee, Susquehanna, Delaware, Potomac, Roanoake, Rio Grande, Yellowstone
Cities: New York, Los Angeles, Chicago, Houston, Philadelphia, San Diego, Phoenix, Dallas, San Antonio, Detroit
People: Americans
Religions: Christian, Jewish
Languages: English
Currency: Dollar (USD) = 100 Cents

Uruguay
Capital: Montevideo
Location: Southern South America
Oceans: Atlantic
Other Geology: Cuchilla Grande, Cuchilla de Haedo
Rivers: Rio Negro, Uruguay, Rio Yi, Rio Cebollati
Lakes: Laguna Merin
Cities: Salto, Paysandu, Las Piedras, Rivera
People: Uruguayans, Mestizos
Religions: Roman Catholic
Languages: Spanish
Currency: Peso (UrP) = 100 Centisimos

Uzbekistan
Capital: Tashkent
Location: Central Asia
Plateaus: Ustyurt
Deserts: Kyzyl Kum
Seas: Aral
Mountains: Pamir-Alai, Tien Shan, Alai
Rivers: Amu-Darya, Syr-Darya, Zeravshan
Cities: Samarkand, Namangan, Andizhan, Bukhara
People: Uzbeks
Religions: Sunni Muslim

Languages: Uzbek
Currency: Sum (plural; Sumy)

Vanuatu

Capital: Vila
Location: Islands in South Pacific Ocean
Islands: Espiritu Santo, Malekula, Efate, Tanna, Ambrym, Lopevi
Cities: Santo
People: Melanesian
Religions: Presbyterian, Roman Catholic, Anglican
Languages: English, French, Bislama
Currency: Vatu (VT) = 100 Centimes

Vatican City

Location: Rome, Italy
Basilicas: St. Peter's
Religions: Roman Catholic
Languages: Latin, Italian
Currency: Vatican City lira, Italian lira

Venezuela

Capital: Caracas
Location: Northern South America
Seas: Caribbean
Mountains: Andes
Lakes: Maracaibo (largest lake in South America)
Plains: Llanos
Rivers: Orinoco
Waterfalls: Angel
Cities: Maracaibo, Valencia, Barquisimeto, Maracay, Petare
People: Mestizos
Religions: Roman Catholic
Languages: Spanish
Currency: Bolivar (B) = 100 Centimos

Vietnam

Capital: Hanoi
Location: Southeastern Asia
Seas: South China
Rivers: Red, Mekong
Mountains: Annamite
Lakes: Ba-Be, HoTay, Hoan-Kiem
Cities: Ho Chi Minh City
People: Vietnamese, Annamese, Annamites
Religions: Buddhist (Mahayana and Theravada)
Languages: Vietnamese (Quoc-Ngu), French
Currency: Dong (D) = 100 Xu =10 Hao

Wales

Capital: Cardiff
Location: Off northwestern coast of Europe
Lakes: Bala

Rivers: Dee, Wye, Teme, Teifi, Conway, Severn
Mountains: Eryri, Berwyn, Snowdon, Cambrian
Cities: Amlweh, Bangor, Rhondda, Swansea, Hereford, Holyhead, Pembroke, Carnarvon, Worcester
People: Welsh, Cymry, Kymry
Religions: Protestant, Roman Catholic
Languages: Welsh, Cymric, Kymric, Cymraeg
Currency: Pound Sterling (PdSt) = 100 New Pence

Yemen

Capital: San'a
Location: Arabian Peninsula, Middle East
Seas: Red
Gulfs: of Aden
Islands: Socotra, Perim, Kamaran
Deserts: Rub al-Khali
Cities: Aden, Ta'izz, al-Hudaydah, al-Mukalla
People: Arabs, Qahtani, Adnani
Religions: Muslim
Languages: Arabic
Currency: Riyal (YRls) = 100 Fils

Yugoslavia

Capital: Belgrade
Location: Eastern Europe
Peninsulas: Balkan
Seas: Adriatic
Rivers: Sava, Danube, Kosovo Polje, Metonija, Zeta, Moraca
Mountains: Serbian
Lakes: Shkoder
Cities: Novi Sad, Nis, Kragujevac, Subotica
People: Serbs, Albanians, Magyar
Religions: Orthodox Church, Muslim
Languages: Serbo-Croatian (cyrillic alphabet)
Currency: New Dinar (D) = 100 Paras

Zambia

Capital: Lusaka
Location: Southern Africa
Valleys: Zambezi
Lakes: Mweru, Tanganyika
Rivers: Zambezi, Kabompo, Kafue, Luangwa
Cities: Ndola, Kitwe, Mufulira
People: Bantu
Religions: Christian, Hindu, Muslim
Languages: English, Bemba, Nyanja, Lozi, Luvale, Lunda, Tonga
Currency: Kwacha (K) = 100 Ngwee

Zimbabwe (formerly Rhodesia)
Capital: Harare (Salisbury)
Location: South central Africa
Grasslands: Veld (veldt)
Mountains: Mt. Inyangani
Rivers: Sabi, Lundi, Zambezi, Limpopo
Waterfalls: Victoria

Cities: Bulawayo, Chitungwiza, Mutare, Gweru
People: Shona, Ndebele
Religions: Christian, Muslim, Hindu
Languages: English, Shona, Ndebele, Bantu
Currency: Dollar (ZD) = 100 Cents

Nobel Prizes

Nobel Prizes by Year

Med/Phys = Medicine and Physiology
& = Shared Prize Among Collaborators
/ / = Denotes Split Prize

1997

Chemistry Paul D. Boyer & John E. Walker // Jens C. Skou
Economics Robert C. Merton & Myron S. Scholes
Literature Dario Fo
Med/Phys Stanley B. Prusiner
Peace International Campaign to Ban Landmines (ICBL) & Jody Williams
Physics Steven Chu, Claude Cohen-Tannoudji & William D. Phillips

1996

Chemistry Robert F. Curl Jr., Sir Harold W. Kroto, & Richard E. Smalley
Economics James A. Mirrlees & William Vickrey
Literature Wislawa Szymborska
Med/Phys Peter C. Doherty & Rolf M. Zinkernagel
Peace Carlos Felipe Ximenes Belo & Jose Ramos-Horta
Physics David M. Lee, Douglas D. Osheroff & Robert C. Richardson

1995

Chemistry Paul Crutzen, Mario Molina & F. Sherwood Rowland
Economics Robert Lucas
Literature Seamus Heaney
Med/Phys Edward B. Lewis, Christiane Nüsslein-Volhard & Eric F. Wieschaus
Peace Joseph Rotblat & Pugwash Conference on Science and World Affairs

Physics Martin L. Perl // Frederick Reines

1994

Chemistry George A. Olah
Economics John C. Harsanyi, John F. Nash & Reinhard Selten
Literature Kenzaburo Oe
Med/Phys Alfred G. Gilman & Martin Rodbell
Peace Yasser Arafat // Shimon Peres & Yitzhak Rabin
Physics Bertram N. Brockhouse // Clifford G. Shull

1993

Chemistry Kary B. Mullis // Michael Smith
Economics Robert W. Fogel and Douglass C. North
Literature Toni Morrison
Med/Phys Richard J. Roberts & Phillip A. Sharp
Peace Nelson Mandela // Fredrik Willem De Klerk
Physics Russell A. Hulse & Joseph H. Taylor Jr.

1992

Chemistry Rudolph A. Marcus
Economics Gary S. Becker
Literature Derek Walcott
Med/Phys Edmond H. Fischer & Edwin G. Krebs
Peace Rigoberta Menchu Tum
Physics Georges Charpak

1991

Chemistry Richard R. Ernst
Economics Ronald H. Coase
Literature Nadine Gordimer
Med/Phys Erwin Neher & Bert Sakmann

Peace Aung San Suu Kyi
Physics Pierre-Gilles De Gennes

1990
Chemistry Elias James Corey
Economics Harry M. Markowitz , Merton M. Miller & William F. Sharpe
Literature Octavio Paz
Med/Phys Joseph E. Murray & E. Donnall Thomas
Peace Mikhail Sergeyevich Gorbachev
Physics Jerome I. Friedman, Henry W. Kendall & Richard E. Taylor

1989
Chemistry Sidney Altman & Thomas R. Cech
Economics Trygve Haavelmo
Literature Camilo Jose Cela
Med/Phys J. Michael Bishop & Harold E. Varmus
Peace The Fourteenth Dalai Lama (Tenzin Gyatso)
Physics Norman F. Ramsey // Hans G. Dehmelt & Wolfgang Paul

1988
Chemistry Johann Deisenhofer, Robert Huber & Hartmut Michel
Economics Maurice Allais
Literature Naguib Mahfouz
Med/Phys Sir James W. Black, Gertrude B. Elion & George H. Hitchings
Peace United Nations Peace-Keeping Forces
Physics Leon M. Lederman, Melvin Schwartz & Jack Steinberger

1987
Chemistry Donald J. Cram, Jean-Marie Lehn & Charles J. Pedersen
Economics Robert M. Solow
Literature Joseph Brodsky
Med/Phys Susumu Tonegawa
Peace Oscar Arias Sanchez
Physics J. Georg Bednorz & K. Alexander Müller

1986
Chemistry Dudley R. Herschbach, Yuan T. Lee & John C. Polanyi
Economics James M. Buchanan Jr.
Literature Wole Soyinka
Med/Phys Stanley Cohen & Rita Levi-Montalcini
Peace Elie Wiesel
Physics Ernst Ruska Gerd Binnig & Heinrich Rohrer

1985
Chemistry Herbert A. Hauptman & Jerome Karle
Economics Franco Modigliani
Literature Claude Simon
Med/Phys Michael S. Brown & Joseph L. Goldstein
Peace International Physicians for the Prevention of Nuclear War
Physics Klaus Von Klitzing

1984
Chemistry Robert Bruce Merrifield
Economics Sir Richard Stone
Literature Jaroslav Siefert
Med/Phys Niels K. Jerne, Georges J. F. Köhler & César Milstein
Peace Desmond Mpilo Tutu
Physics Carlo Rubbia & Simon Van Der Meer

1983
Chemistry Henry Taube
Economics Gerard Debreu
Literature William Golding
Med/Phys Barbara McClintock
Peace Lech Walesa
Physics Subramanyan Chandrasekhar // William A. Fowler

1982
Chemistry Sir Aaron Klug
Economics George J. Stigler
Literature Gabriel García Márquez
Med/Phys Sune K. Bergström, Bengt I. Samuelsson & Sir John R. Vane
Peace Alva Myrdal & Alfonso García Robles
Physics Kenneth G. Wilson

1981
Chemistry Kenichi Fukui & Roald Hoffmann
Economics James Tobin
Literature Elias Canetti
Med/Phys Roger W. Sperry // David H. Hubel & Torsten N. Wiesel
Peace Office of the United Nations High Commissioner for Refugees
Physics Nicolaas Bloembergen & Arthur L. Schawlow // Kai M. Siegbahn

1980
Chemistry Paul Berg, Walter Gilbert & Frederick Sanger
Economics Lawrence R. Klein
Literature Czeslaw Milosz

Med/Phys Baruj Benacerraf, Jean Dausset & George D. Snell
Peace Dolfo Perez Esquivel
Physics James W. Cronin & Val L. Fitch

1979

Chemistry Herbert C. Brown & Georg Wittig
Economics Theodore W. Schultz & Sir Arthur Lewis
Literature Odysseus Elytis
Med/Phys Alan M. Cormack & Sir Godfrey N. Hounsfield
Peace Mother Teresa
Physics Sheldon L. Glashow, Abdus Salam & Steven Weinberg

1978

Chemistry Peter D. Mitchell
Economics Herbert A. Simon
Literature Isaac Bashevis Singer
Med/Phys Werner Arber, Daniel Nathans & Hamilton O. Smith
Peace Mohamed Anwar Al-Sadat // Menachem Begin
Physics Pyotr Leonidovich Kapitsa // Arno A. Penzias & Robert W. Wilson

1977

Chemistry Ilya Prigogine
Economics Bertil Ohlin & James E. Meade
Literature Vicente Aleixandre
Med/Phys Roger Guillemin & Andrew V. Schally // Rosalyn Yalow
Peace Amnesty International
Physics Philip W. Anderson, Sir Nevill F. Mott & John H. Van Vleck

1976

Chemistry William N. Lipscomb
Economics Milton Friedman
Literature Saul Bellow
Med/Phys Baruch S. Blumberg & D. Carleton Gajdusek
Peace Betty Williams & Mairead Corrigan
Physics Burton Richter & Samuel C. C. Ting

1975

Chemistry Sir John Warcup Cornforth // Vladimir Prelog
Economics Leonid Vitaliyevich Kantorovich & Tjalling C. Koopmans
Literature Eugenio Montale
Med/Phys David Baltimore, Renato Dulbecco & Howard Martin Temin

Peace Andrei Dmitrievich Sakharov
Physics Aage Bohr, Ben Mottelson & James Rainwater

1974

Chemistry Paul J. Flory
Economics Gunnar Myrdal & Friedrich August Von Hayek
Literature Eyvind Johnson
Med/Phys Albert Claude, Christian de Duve & George E. Palade
Peace Seán MacBride // Eisaku Sato
Physics Sir Martin Ryle & Antony Hewish

1973

Chemistry Ernst Otto Fischer & Sir Geoffrey Wilkinson
Economics Wassily Leontief
Literature Patrick White
Med/Phys Karl Von Frisch, Konrad Lorenz & Nikolaas Tinbergen
Peace Henry A. Kissinger // Le Duc Tho
Physics Leo Esaki & Ivar Giaever // Brian D. Josephson

1972

Chemistry Christian B. Anfinsen // Stanford Moore & William H. Stein
Economics Sir John R. Hicks & Kenneth J. Arrow
Literature Heinrich Böll
Med/Phys Gerald M. Edelman & Rodney R. Porter
Peace No Award
Physics John Bardeen, Leon N. Cooper & J. Robert Schrieffer

1971

Chemistry Gerhard Herzberg
Economics Simon Kuznets
Literature Pablo Neruda
Med/Phys Earl W. Sutherland Jr.
Peace Willy Brandt
Physics Dennis Gabor

1970

Chemistry Luis F. Leloir
Economics Paul A. Samuelson
Literature Aleksandr I. Solzhenitsyn
Med/Phys Sir Bernard Katz, Ulf Von Euler & Julius Axelrod
Peace Norman Borlaug
Physics Hannes Alfvén // Louis Néel

1969

Chemistry Sir Derek H. R. Barton & Odd Hassel

Economics Ragnar Frisch & Jan Tinbergen
Literature Samuel Beckett
Med/Phys Max Delbrück, Alfred D. Hershey
& Salvador E. Luria
Peace International Labour
Organization (ILO)
Physics Murray Gell-Mann

1968
Chemistry Lars Onsager
Literature Yasunari Kawabata
Med/Phys Robert W. Holley, Har Gobind
Khorana & Marshall W.
Nirenberg
Peace René Cassin
Physics Luis W. Alvarez

1967
Chemistry Manfred Eigen // Ronald George
Wreyford Norrish & Lord George
Porter
Literature Miguel Angel Asturias
Med/Phys Ragnar Granit, Haldan Keffer
Hartline & George Wald
Peace No Award
Physics Hans Albrecht Bethe

1966
Chemistry Robert S. Mulliken
Literature Nelly Sachs
Med/Phys Peyton Rous // Charles Brenton
Huggins
Peace No Award
Physics Alfred Kastler

1965
Chemistry Robert Burns Woodward
Literature Mikhail Sholokhov
Med/Phys François Jacob, André Lwoff &
Jacques Monod
Peace United Nations Children's Fund
(Unicef)
Physics Sin-Itiro Tomonaga, Julian
Schwinger & Richard P. Feynman

1964
Chemistry Dorothy Crowfoot Hodgkin
Literature Jean-Paul Sartre
Med/Phys Konrad Bloch & Feodor Lynen
Peace Martin Luther King Jr.
Physics Charles H. Townes // Nicolay
Gennadiyevich Basov &
Aleksandr Mikhailovich
Prokhorov

1963
Chemistry Karl Ziegler & Giulio Natt
Literature Giorgos Seferis

Med/Phys Sir John C. Eccles, Sir Alan L.
Hodgkin & Sir Andrew F. Huxley
Peace International Committee of the
Red Cross & League of Red
Cross Societies
Physics Eugene P. Wigner // Maria
Goeppert-Mayer & J. Hans D.
Jensen

1962
Chemistry Max Ferdinand Perutz & Sir John
Cowdery Kendrew
Literature John Steinbeck
Med/Phys Francis Crick, James D. Watson
& Maurice Wilkins
Peace Linus Carl Pauling
Physics Lev Davidovich Landau

1961
Chemistry Melvin Calvin
Literature Ivo Andric
Med/Phys Georg Von Békésy
Peace Dag Hjalmar Agne Carl
Hammarskjöld (Posthumously)
Physics Robert Hofstadter // Rudolf
Ludwig Mössbauer

1960
Chemistry Willard Frank Libby
Literature Saint-John Perse
Med/Phys Sir Frank Macfarlane Burnet &
Sir Peter Brian Medawar
Peace Albert John Lutuli
Physics Donald A. Glaser

1959
Chemistry Jaroslav Heyrovsky
Literature Salvatore Quasimodo
Med/Phys Severo Ochoa & Arthur Kornberg
Peace Philip J. Noel-Baker
Physics Emilio Gino Segrè & Owen
Chamberlain

1958
Chemistry Frederick Sanger
Literature Boris L. Pasternak
Med/Phys George Wells Beadle & Edward
Lawrie Tatum // Joshua Ederberg
Peace Georges Henri Pire
Physics Pavel Alekseyevich Cherenkov,
Il'ja Mikhailovich Frank &
Igoryevgenyevich Tamm

1957
Chemistry Lord Alexander R. Todd
Literature Albert Camus
Med/Phys Daniel Bovet
Peace Lester Bowles
Physics Chen Ning Yang & Tsung-Dao Lee

1956

Chemistry	Sir Cyril Norman Hinshelwood // Nikolaevich Semenov
Literature	Juan Ramón Jiménez
Med/Phys	André Frédéric Cournand, Werner Forssmann & Dickinson W. Richards
Peace	No Award
Physics	William Shockley, John Bardeen & Walter Houser Brattain

1955

Chemistry	Vincent du Vigneaud
Literature	Halldor K. Laxness
Med/Phys	Axel Hugo Theodor Theorell
Peace	No Award
Physics	Willis Eugene Lamb // Polykarp Kusch

1954

Chemistry	Linus Pauling
Literature	Ernest Hemingway
Med/Phys	John F. Enders, Thomas H. Weller & Frederick C. Robbins
Peace	Office of the United Nations High Commissioner for Refugees
Physics	Max Born // Walther Bothe

1953

Chemistry	Hermann Staudinger
Literature	Sir Winston Churchill
Med/Phys	Sir Hans Adolf Krebs // Fritz Albert Lipmann
Peace	George Catlett Marshall
Physics	Frits (Frederik) Zernike

1952

Chemistry	Archer John P. Martin & Richard Laurence // Millington Synge
Literature	François Mauriac
Med/Phys	Selman Abraham Waksman
Peace	Albert Schweitzer
Physics	Felix Bloch & Edward Mills Purcell

1951

Chemistry	Edwin Mattison McMillan & Glenn Theodore Seaborg
Literature	Pär F. Lagerkvist
Med/Phys	Max Theiler
Peace	Léon Jouhaux
Physics	Sir John Douglas Cockcroft & Ernest Thomas Sinton Walton

1950

Chemistry	Otto Paul Hermann Diels & Kurt Alder
Literature	Bertrand Russell
Med/Phys	Edward Calvin Kendall, Tadeus Reichstein & Philip Showalter
Peace	Ralph Bunche
Physics	Cecil Frank Powell

1949

Chemistry	William Francis Giauque
Literature	William Faulkner
Med/Phys	Walter Rudolf // Antonio Caetano de Abreu Freire Egas Moniz
Peace	Lord John Boyd Orr of Brechin
Physics	Hideki Yukawa

1948

Chemistry	Arne Wilhelm Kaurin Tiselius
Literature	T. S. Eliot
Med/Phys	Paul Hermann Müller
Peace	No Award
Physics	Lord Patrick Maynard Stuart Blackett

1947

Chemistry	Sir Robert Robinson
Literature	André Gide
Med/Phys	Carl F. Cori & Gerty T. Cori (Radnitz) // Bernardo Alberto Houssay
Peace	American Friends Service Committee & British Society of Friends Service Council (Quakers)
Physics	Sir Edward Victor Appleton

1946

Chemistry	James B. Sumner // John H. Northrop & Wendell Meredith Stanley
Literature	Hermann Hesse
Med/Phys	Hermann Joseph Muller
Peace	Emily Greene Balch // John Raleigh Mott
Physics	Percy Williams Bridgman

1945

Chemistry	Artturi Ilmari Virtanen
Literature	Gabriela Mistral
Med/Phys	Sir Alexander Fleming, Sir Ernst Boris Chain & Lord Howard Walter Florey
Peace	Cordell Hull
Physics	Wolfgang Pauli

1944

Chemistry	Otto Hahn
Literature	Johannes V. Jensen
Med/Phys	Joseph Erlanger & Herbert Spencer Gasser

Peace   International Committee of the
            Red Cross
Physics   Isidor Isaac Rabi

1943

Chemistry   George De Hevesy
Literature No Award
Med/Phys   Henrik Carl Peter Dam // Edward
            Adelbert
Peace   No Award
Physics   Otto Stern

1942–1940 No Awards Given

1939

Chemistry   Adolf Friedrich Johann
            Butenandt // Leopold Ruzicka
Literature Frans E. Sillanpaa
Med/Phys   Gerhard Domagk
Peace   No Award
Physics   Ernest Orlando Lawrence

1938

Chemistry   Richard Kuhn
Literature Pearl S. Buck
Med/Phys   Corneille Jean François
Peace   Nansen International Office for
            Refugees
Physics   Enrico Fermi

1937

Chemistry   Sir Walter Norman Haworth //
            Paul Karrer
Literature Roger Martin du Gard
Med/Phys   Albert Szent-Györgyi Von
Peace   Lord Edgar Algernon Robert
            Gascoyne Cecil
Physics   Clinton Joseph Davisson & Sir
            George Paget Thomson

1936

Chemistry   Petrus Josephus Wilhelmus
            Debye
Literature Eugene O'Neill
Med/Phys   Sir Henry Hallett Dale & Otto
            Loewi
Peace   Carlos Saavedra Lamas
Physics   Victor Franz Hess // Carl David
            Anderson

1935

Chemistry   Frederic Joliot & Irene Joliot-
            Curie
Literature No Award
Med/Phys   Hans Spemann

Peace   Carl Von Ossietzky
Physics   Sir James Chadwick

1934

Chemistry   Harold Clayton Urey
Literature Luigi Pirandello
Med/Phys   George Hoyt Whipple, George
            Richards Minot & William Parry
            Murphy
Peace   Arthur Henderson
Physics   No Award

1933

Chemistry   No Award
Literature Ivan A. Bunin
Med/Phys   Thomas Hunt Morgan
Peace   Sir Norman Angell (Ralph Lane)
Physics   Erwin Schrödinger & Paul Adrien
            Maurice Dirac

1932

Chemistry   Irving Langmuir
Literature John Galsworthy
Med/Phys   Sir Charles Scott Sherrington &
            Lord Edgar Douglas Adrian
Peace   No Award
Physics   Werner Heisenberg

1931

Chemistry   Carl Bosch & Friedrich Bergius
Literature Erik A. Karlfeldt
Med/Phys   Otto Heinrich Warburg
Peace   Jane Addams // Nicholas Murray
            Butler
Physics   No Award

1930

Chemistry   Hans Fischer
Literature Sinclair Lewis
Med/Phys   Karl Landsteiner
Peace   Lars Olof Nathan (Jonathan)
            Söderblom
Physics   Sir Chandrasekhara Venkata
            Raman

1929

Chemistry   Sir Arthur Harden & Hans K. A.
            Simon Von Euler-Chelpin
Literature Thomas Mann
Med/Phys   Christiaan Eijkman // Sir
            Frederick Gowland Hopkins
Peace   Frank Billings Kellogg
Physics   Prince Louis-Victor De Broglie

1928

Chemistry   Adolf Otto Reinhold Windaus
Literature Sigrid Undset
Med/Phys   Charles Jules Henri Nicolle

Peace   No Award
Physics   Sir Owen Willans Richardson

1927

Chemistry Heinrich Otto Wieland
Literature Henri Bergson
Med/Phys Julius Wagner-Jauregg
Peace   Ferdinand Buisson // Ludwig
           Quidde
Physics   Arthur Holly Compton // Charles
           Thomson Rees Wilson

1926

Chemistry The (Theodor) Svedberg
Literature Grazia Deledda
Med/Phys Johannes Andreas Grib Fibiger
Peace   Aristide Briand & Gustav
           Stresemann
Physics   Jean Baptiste Perrin

1925

Chemistry Richard Adolf Zsigmondy
Literature George Bernard Shaw
Med/Phys No Award
Peace   Sir Austen Chamberlain &
           Charles Gates
Physics   James Franck & Gustav Hertz

1924

Chemistry No Award
Literature Wladyslaw S. Reymont
Med/Phys Willem Einthoven
Peace   No Award
Physics   Karl Manne Georg Siegbahn

1923

Chemistry Fritz Pregl
Literature William B. Yeats
Med/Phys Sir Frederick Grant Banting &
           John James Richard Macleod
Peace   No Award
Physics   Robert Andrews Millikan

1922

Chemistry Francis William Aston
Literature Jacinto Benavente y Martinez
Med/Phys Sir Archibald Vivian Hill // Otto
           Fritz Meyerhof
Peace   Fridtjof Nansen
Physics   Niels Bohr

1921

Chemistry Frederick Soddy
Literature Anatole France
Med/Phys No Award
Peace   Karl Hjalmar Branting //
           Christian Louis Lange
Physics   Albert Einstein

1920

Chemistry Walther Hermann Nernst
Literature Knut Hamsun
Med/Phys Schack August Steenberger
           Krogh
Peace   Léon Victor Auguste Bourgeois
Physics   Charles Edouard Guillaume

1919

Chemistry No Award
Literature Carl F. G. Spitteler
Med/Phys Jules Bordet
Peace   (Thomas) Woodrow Wilson
Physics   Johannes Stark

1918

Chemistry Fritz Haber
Literature No Award
Med/Phys No Award
Peace   No Award
Physics   Max Planck

1917

Chemistry No Award
Literature Karl A. Gjellerup
Med/Phys No Award
Peace   International Committee of the
           Red Cross
Physics   Charles Glover Barkla

1916

Chemistry No Award
Literature Verner Von Heidenstamm
Med/Phys No Award
Peace   No Award
Physics   No Award

1915

Chemistry Richard Martin Willstätter
Literature Romain Rolland
Med/Phys No Award
Peace   No Award
Physics   Sir William Henry Bragg & Sir
           William Lawrence Bragg

1914

Chemistry Theodore William Richards
Literature No Award
Med/Phys Robert Bárány
Peace   No Award
Physics   Max Von Laue

1913

Chemistry Alfred Werner
Literature Rabindranath Tagore
Med/Phys Charles Robert Richet
Peace   Henri La Fontaine
Physics   Heike Kamerlingh-Onnes

1912

Chemistry	Victor Grignard // Paul Sabatier
Literature	Gerhart Hauptmann
Med/Phys	Alexis Carrel
Peace	Elihu Root
Physics	Nils Gustaf Dalén

1911

Chemistry	Marie Curie
Literature	Maurice Maeterlinck
Med/Phys	Allvar Gullstrand
Peace	Tobias Michael Carel Asser // Alfred Hermann Fried
Physics	Wilhelm Wiench

1910

Chemistry	Otto Wallach
Literature	Paul J. L. Heyse
Med/Phys	Albrecht Kossel
Peace	Permanent International Peace Bureau
Physics	Johannes Diderik Van Der Waalsy

1909

Chemistry	Wilhelm Ostwald
Literature	Selma Lagerlöf
Med/Phys	Emil Theodor Kocher
Peace	Auguste Marie François Beernaert // Paul Henribenjamin Balluet d'Estournelles de Constant, Baron de Constant de Rebecque
Physics	Guglielmo Marconi & Carl Ferdinand Braunch

1908

Chemistry	Lord Ernest Rutherford
Literature	Rudolph C. Eueken
Med/Phys	Ilya Ilyich Mechnikov & Paul Ehrlich
Peace	Klas Pontus Arnoldson & Fredrik Bajer
Physics	Gabriel Lippmann

1907

Chemistry	Eduard Buchner
Literature	Rudyard Kipling
Med/Phys	Charles Louis Alphonse Laveran
Peace	Ernesto Teodoro Moneta // Louis Renault
Physics	Albert Abraham Michelson

1906

Chemistry	Henri Moissan
Literature	Giosue Carducci
Med/Phys	Camillo Golgi & Santiago Ramon y Cajal
Peace	Theodore Roosevelt
Physics	Sir Joseph John Thomsonch

1905

Chemistry	Johann Friedrich Wilhelm Adolf von Baeyer
Literature	Henryk Sienkiewicz
Med/Phys	Robert Koch
Peace	Baroness Bertha Sophie Felicita von Suttner
Physics	Philipp Eduard Anton Lenard

1904

Chemistry	Sir William Ramsay
Literature	Frederic Mistral
Med/Phys	Ivan Petrovich Pavlov
Peace	Institute of International Law
Physics	Lord John William Strutt Rayleigh

1903

Chemistry	Svante August Arrhenius
Literature	Bjornsterne Björnson
Med/Phys	Niels Ryberg Finsen
Peace	Sir William Randal Cremer
Physics	Antoine Henri Becquerel // Pierre Curie & Marie Curie

1902

Chemistry	Hermann Emil Fischer
Literature	Theodor Mommsen
Med/Phys	Sir Ronald Ross
Peace	Élie Ducommun // Charles Albert Gobat
Physics	Hendrik Antoon Lorentz & Pieter Zeeman

1901

Chemistry	Jacobus Henricus Van't Hoff
Literature	René F. A. Sully-Prudhomme
Med/Phys	Emil Adolf von Behring
Peace	Jean Henri Dunant // Frédéric Passy
Physics	Wilhelm Conrad Röntgen

Nobel Prizewinners in Chemistry

NAME	YEAR	NAME	YEAR
Alder, Kurt	1950	Karrer, Paul	1937
Altman, Sidney	1989	Kendrew, Sir John Cowdery	1962
Anfinsen, Christian B.	1972	Klug, Sir Aaron	1982
Arrhenius, Svante August	1903	Kuhn, Richard	1938
Aston, Francis William	1922	Langmuir, Irving	1932
Baeyer, Johann Friedrich Wilhelm		Lee, Yuan T.	1986
Adolf von	1905	Lehn, Jean-Marie	1987
Barton, Sir Derek H. R.	1969	Leloir, Luis F.	1970
Berg, Paul	1980	Libby, Willard Frank	1960
Bergius, Friedrich	1931	Lipscomb, William N..	1976
Bosch, Carl	1931	Marcus, Rudolph A.	1992
Brown, Herbert C.	1979	Martin, Archer John Porter	1952
Buchner, Eduard	1907	McMillan, Edwin Mattison	1951
Butenandt, Adolf Friedrich Johann	1939	Merrifield, Robert Bruce	1984
Calvin, Melvin	1961	Michel, Hartmut	1988
Cech, Thomas R.	1989	Mitchell, Peter D.	1978
Corey, Elias James	1990	Moissan, Henri	1906
Cornforth, Sir John Warcup	1975	Molina, Mario	1995
Cram, Donald J.	1987	Moore, Stanford	1972
Crutzen, Paul	1995	Mulliken, Robert S.	1966
Curie, Marie	1911	Mullis, Kary B.	1993
Curl, Robert F. Jr.	1996	Natta, Giulio	1963
Debye, Petrus Josephus Wilhelmus	1936	Nernst, Walther Hermann	1920
De Hevesy, George	1943	Norrish, Ronald George Wreyford	1967
Deisenhofer, Johann	1988	Northrop, John Howard	1946
Diels, Otto Paul Hermann	1950	Olah, George A.	1994
Eigen, Manfred	1967	Onsager, Lars	1968
Ernst, Richard R.	1991	Ostwald, Wilhelm	1909
Euler-Chelpin, Hans Karl August		Pauling, Linus Carl	1954
Simon von	1929	Pedersen, Charles J.	1987
Fischer, Ernst Otto	1973	Perutz, Max Ferdinand	1962
Fischer, Hans	1930	Polanyi, John C.	1986
Fischer, Hermann Emil	1902	Porter, Lord George	1967
Flory, Paul J.	1974	Pregl, Fritz	1923
Fukui, Kenichi	1981	Prelog, Vladimir	1975
Giauque, William Francis	1949	Prigogine, Ilya	1977
Gilbert, Walter	1980	Ramsay, Sir William	1904
Grignard, Victor	1912	Richards, Theodore William	1914
Haber, Fritz	1918	Robinson, Sir Robert	1947
Hahn, Otto	1944	Rowland, F. Sherwood	1995
Harden, Sir Arthur	1929	Rutherford, Lord Ernest	1908
Hassel, Odd	1969	Ruzicka, Leopold	1939
Hauptman, Herbert A.	1985	Sabatier, Paul	1912
Haworth, Sir Walter Norman	1937	Sanger, Frederick	1958, 1980
Herschbach, Dudley R.	1986	Seaborg, Glenn Theodore	1951
Herzberg, Gerhard	1971	Semenov, Nikolay Nikolaevich	1956
Heyrovsky, Jaroslav	1959	Smith, Michael	1993
Hinshelwood, Sir Cyril Norman	1956	Smalley, Richard E.	1996
Hodgkin, Dorothy Crowfoot	1964	Soddy, Frederick	1921
Hoff, Jacobus Henricus Van't	1901	Stanley, Wendell Meredith	1946
Hoffmann, Roald	1981	Staudinger, Hermann	1953
Huber, Robert	1988	Stein, William H.	1972
Joliot-Curie, Irene	1935	Sumner, James Batcheller	1946
Joliot, Frederic	1935	Svedberg, The	1926
Karle, Jerome	1985	Synge, Richard Laurence Millington	1952

NAME	YEAR	NAME	YEAR
Taube, Henry	1983	Wieland, Heinrich Otto	1927
Tiselius, Arne Wilhelm Kaurin	1948	Wilkinson, Sir Geoffrey	1973
Todd, Lord Alexander R.	1957	Willstatter, Richard Martin	1915
Urey, Harold Clayton	1934	Windaus, Adolf Otto Reinhold	1928
Vigneaud, Vincent du	1955	Wittig, Georg	1979
Virtanen, Artturi Ilmari	1945	Woodward, Robert Burns	1965
Wallach, Otto	1910	Ziegler, Karl	1963
Werner, Alfred	1913	Zsigmondy, Richard Adolf	1925

Nobel Prizewinners in Economics

NAME	YEAR	NAME	YEAR
Allais, Maurice	1988	Markowitz, Harry M.	1990
Arrow, Kenneth J.	1972	Meade, James E	1977
Becker, Gary S.	1992	Miller, Merton M.	1990
Buchanan, James M. Jr.	1986	Mirrlees, James A.	1996
Coase, Ronald H.	1991	Modigliani, Franco	1985
Debreu, Gerard	1983	Myrdal, Gunnar	1974
Fogel, Robert W.	1993	Nash, John F.	1994
Friedman, Milton	1976	North, Douglass C.	1993
Frisch, Ragnar	1969	Ohlin, Bertil	1977
Haavelmo, Trygve	1989	Samuelson, Paul A	1970
Harsanyi, John C.	1994	Schultz, Theodore W.	1979
Hayek, Friedrich August Von	1974	Selten, Reinhard	1994
Hicks, Sir John R.	1972	Sharpe, William F.	1990
Kantorovich, Leonid Vitaliyevich	1975	Simon, Herbert A.	1978
Klein, Lawrence R.	1980	Solow, Robert M.	1987
Koopmans, Tjalling C.	1975	Stigler, George J.	1982
Kuznets, Simon	1971	Stone, Sir Richard	1984
Leontief, Wassily	1973	Tinbergen, Jan	1969
Lewis, Sir Arthur	1979	Tobin, James	1981
Lucas, Robert	1995	Vickrey, William	1996

Nobel Prizewinners in Literature

NAME	YEAR	NAME	YEAR
Agnon, Shmuel Yosef	1966	Churchill, Sir Winston Leonard	
Aleixandre, Vicente	1977	Spencer	1953
Andriic, Ivo	1961	Deledda, Grazia	1926
Asturias, Miguel Angel	1967	Eizaguirre, Jose Echegaray y	1904
Beckett, Samuel	1969	Eliot, Thomas Stearns	1948
Bellow, Saul	1976	Elytis, Odysseus	1979
Benavente, Jacinto	1922	Eucken, Rudolf Christoph	1908
Bergson, Henri	1927	Faulkner, William	1949
Bjornson, Bjornstjerne Martinus	1903	France, Anatole	1921
Böll, Heinrich	1972	Galsworthy, John	1932
Brodsky, Joseph	1987	Gard, Roger Martin du	1937
Buck, Pearl	1938	Gide, André	1947
Bunin, Ivan Alekseyevich	1933	Gjellerup, Karl Adolph	1917
Camus, Albert	1957	Golding, Sir William	1983
Canetti, Elias	1981	Gordimer, Nadine	1991
Carducci, Giosue	1906	Hamsun, Knut Pedersen	1920
Cela, Camilo Jose	1989	Hauptmann, Gerhart Johann Robert	1912

Name	Year	Name	Year
Heaney, Seamus	1995	Pasternak, Boris Leonidovich	1958
Heidenstam, Carl Gustaf Verner von	1916	Paz, Octavio	1990
Hemingway, Ernest	1954	Perse, Saint-John	1960
Hesse, Hermann	1946	Pirandello, Luigi	1934
Heyse, Paul Johann Ludwig	1910	Pontoppidan, Henrik	1917
Jensen, Johannes Vilhelm	1944	Prudhomme, Sully	1901
Jiménez, Juan Ramón	1956	Quasimodo, Salvatore	1959
Johnson, Eyvind	1974	Reymont, Wladyslaw Stanislaw	1924
Karlfeldt, Erik Axel	1931	Rolland, Romain	1915
Kawabata, Yasunari	1968	Russell, Earl Bertrand Arthur	
Kipling, Rudyard	1907	William	1950
Lagerkvist, Par Fabian	1951	Sachs, Nelly	1966
Lagerloef, Selma Ottilia Lovisa	1909	Sartre, Jean-Paul	1964
Laxness, Halldor Kiljan	1955	Seferis, Giorgos	1963
Lewis, Sinclair	1930	Seifert, Jaroslav	1984
Maeterlinck, Count Maurice Polidore		Shaw, George Bernard	1925
Marie Bernhard	1911	Sholokhov, Michail Aleksandrovich	1965
Mahfouz, Naguib	1988	Sienkiewicz, Henryk	1905
Mann, Thomas	1929	Sillanpaa, Frans Emil	1939
Márquez, Gabriel García	1982	Simon, Claude	1985
Martinson, Harry	1974	Singer, Isaac Bashevis	1978
Mauriac, François	1952	Solzhenitsyn, Aleksandr Isaevich	1970
Milosz, Czeslaw	1980	Soyinka, Wole	1986
Mistral, Frederic	1904	Spitteler, Carl Friedrich Georg	1919
Mistral, Gabriela	1945	Steinbeck, John	1962
Mommsen, Christian Matthias		Szymborska, Wislawa	1996
Theodor	1902	Tagore, Rabindranath	1913
Montale, Eugenio	1975	Undset, Sigrid	1928
Morrison, Toni	1993	Walcott, Derek	1992
Neruda, Pablo	1971	White, Patrick	1973
Oe, Kenzaburo	1994	Yeats, William Butler	1923
O'Neill, Eugene Gladstone	1936		

Nobel Prizewinners in Medicine and Physiology

Name	Year	Name	Year
Adrian, Lord Edgar Douglas	1932	Burnet, Sir Frank Macfarlane	1960
Arber, Werner	1978	Cajal, Santiago Ramon y	1906
Axelrod, Julius	1970	Carrel, Alexis	1912
Baltimore, David	1975	Chain, Sir Ernst Boris	1945
Banting, Sir Frederick Grant	1923	Claude, Albert	1974
Barany, Robert	1914	Cohen, Stanley	1986
Beadle, George Wells	1958	Cori, Carl Ferdinand	1947
Behring, Emil Adolf von	1901	Cori, Gerty Theresa	1947
Békésy, Georg von	1961	Cormack, Alan M.	1979
Benacerraf, Baruj	1980	Cournand, André Frédéric	1956
Bergström, Sune K.	1982	Crick, Francis Harry Compton	1962
Bishop, J. Michael	1989	Dale, Sir Henry Hallett	1936
Black, Sir James W.	1988	Dam, Henrik Carl Peter	1943
Bloch, Konrad	1964	Dausset, Jean	1980
Blumberg, Baruch S.	1976	De Duve, Christian	1974
Bordet, Jules	1919	Delbruck, Max	1969
Bovet, Daniel	1957	Doherty, Peter C.	1996
Brown, Michael S.	1985	Doisy, Edward Adelbert	1943

NAME	YEAR	NAME	YEAR
Domagk, Gerhard	1939	Laveran, Charles Louis	
Dulbecco, Renato	1975	Alphonse	1907
Eccles, Sir John Carew	1963	Lederberg, Joshua	1958
Edelman, Gerald M.	1972	Levi-Montalcini, Rita	1986
Ehrlich, Paul	1908	Lewis, Edward B.	1995
Eijkman, Christiaan	1929	Lipmann, Fritz Albert	1953
Einthoven, Willem	1924	Lorenz, Konrad	1973
Elion, Gertrude B.	1988	Luria, Salvador E.	1969
Enders, John Franklin	1954	Lwoff, André	1965
Erlanger, Joseph	1944	Lynen, Feodor	1964
Euler, Ulf von	1970	Macleod, John James Richard	1923
Fibiger, Johannes Andreas Grib	1926	McClintock, Barbara	1983
Finsen, Niels Ryberg	1903	Mechnikov, Ilya Ilyich	1908
Fischer, Edmond H.	1992	Medawar, Sir Peter Brian	1960
Fleming, Sir Alexander	1945	Meyerhof, Otto Fritz	1922
Florey, Lord Howard Walter	1945	Milstein, Cesar	1984
Forssmann, Werner	1956	Minot, George Richards	1934
Frisch, Karl von	1973	Moniz, Antonio Caetano de Abreu	
Gajdusek, D. Carleton	1976	Freire Egas	1949
Gasser, Herbert Spencer	1944	Monod, Jacoues	1965
Gilman, Alfred G.	1994	Morgan, Thomas Hunt	1933
Goldstein, Joseph L.	1985	Muller, Hermann Joseph	1946
Golgi, Camillo	1906	Muller, Paul Hermann	1948
Granit, Ragnar	1967	Murphy, William Parry	1934
Guillemin, Roger	1977	Murray, Joseph E.	1990
Gullstrand, Allvar	1911	Nagyrapolt, Albert Szent-	
Hartline, Haldan Keffer	1967	Gyorgyi von	1937
Hench, Philip Showalter	1950	Nathans, Daniel	1978
Hershey, Alfred D.	1969	Neher, Erwin	1991
Hess, Walter Rudolf	1949	Nicolle, Charles Jules Henri	1928
Heymans, Corneille Jean François	1938	Nirenberg, Marshall W.	1968
Hill, Sir Archibald Vivian	1922	Nüsslein-Volhard, Christiane	1995
Hitchings, George H.	1988	Ochoa, Severo	1959
Hodgkin, Sir Alan Lloyd	1963	Palade, George E.	1974
Holley, Robert W.	1968	Pavlov, Ivan Petrovich	1904
Hopkins, Sir Frederick Gowland	1929	Porter, Rodney R.	1972
Hounsfield, Sir Godfrey N.	1979	Prusiner, Stanley B.	1997
Houssay, Bernardo Alberto	1947	Reichstein, Tadeus	1950
Hubel, David H.	1981	Richards, Dickinson W.	1956
Huggins, Charles Brenton	1966	Richet, Charles Robert	1913
Huxley, Sir Andrew Fielding	1963	Robbins, Frederick Chapman	1954
Jacob, Francois	1965	Roberts, Richard J.	1993
Jerne, Niels K.	1984	Rodbell, Martin	1994
Katz, Sir Bernard	1970	Ross, Sir Ronald	1902
Kendall, Edward Calvin	1950	Rous, Peyton	1966
Khorana, Har Gobind	1968	Sakmann, Bert	1991
Koch, Robert	1905	Samuelsson, Bengt I.	1982
Kocher, Emil Theodor	1909	Schally, Andrew V.	1977
Koehler, Georges J. F.	1984	Sharp, Phillip A.	1993
Kornberg, Arthur	1959	Sherrington, Sir Charles Scott	1932
Kossel, Albrecht	1910	Smith, Hamilton O.	1978
Krebs, Edwin G.	1992	Snell, George D.	1980
Krebs, Sir Hans Adolf	1953	Spemann, Hans	1935
Krogh, Schack August		Sperry, Roger W.	1981
Steenberger	1920	Sutherland, Earl W. Jr.	1971
Landsteiner, Karl	1930	Tatum, Edward Lawrie	1958

NAME	YEAR	NAME	YEAR
Temin, Howard Martin	1975	Warburg, Otto Heinrich	1931
Theiler, Max	1951	Watson, James Dewey	1962
Theorell, Axel Hugo Theodor	1955	Weller, Thomas Huckle	1954
Thomas, E. Donnall	1990	Whipple, George Hoyt	1934
Tinbergen, Nikolaas	1973	Wieschaus, Eric F.	1995
Tonegawa, Susumu	1987	Wiesel, Torsten N.	1981
Vane, Sir John R.	1982	Wilkins, Maurice Hugh	
Varmus, Harold E.	1989	Frederick	1962
Wagner-Jauregg, Julius	1927	Yalow, Rosalyn	1977
Waksman, Selman Abraham	1952	Zinkernagel, Rolf M.	1996
Wald, George	1967		

Nobel Peace Prize Winners

NAME	YEAR	NAME	YEAR
Addams, Jane	1931	Fried, Alfred Hermann	1911
American Friends Service Committee	1947	Gobat, Charles Albert	1902
Amnesty International	1977	Gorbachev, Mikhail Sergeyevich	1990
Angell, Sir Norman	1933	Hammarskjöld, Dag Hjalmar	
Arafat, Yasser	1994	Agne Carl	1961
Arnoldson, Klas Pontus	1908	Henderson, Arthur	1934
Asser, Tobias Michael Carel	1911	Hull, Cordell	1945
Bajer, Fredrik	1908	Institute of International Law	1904
Balch, Emily Greene	1946	International Physicians for the	
Beernaert, Auguste Marie François	1909	Prevention of Nuclear War	1985
Begin, Menachem	1978	International Committee of	
Belo, Carlos Felipe Ximenes	1996	the Red Cross 1917, 1944, 1963	
Borlaug, Norman	1970	International Labour Organization	1969
Bourgeois, Léon Victor Auguste	1920	Jouhaux, Léon	1951
Brandt, Willy	1971	King, Martin Luther Jr.	1964
Branting, Karl Hjalmar	1921	Kellogg, Frank Billings	1929
Boyd Orr of Brechin, Lord John	1949	Kissinger, Henry A.	1973
Briand, Aristide	1926	Kyi, Aung San Suu	1991
British Society of Friends Service		Lamas, Carlos Saavedra	1936
Council	1947	Lange, Christian Lous	1921
Buisson, Ferdinand	1927	League of Red Cross Societies	1963
Bunche, Ralph	1950	Lutuli, Albert John	1960
Butler, Nicholas Murray	1931	MacBride, Sean	1974
Cassin, René	1968	Mandela, Nelson	1993
Cecil, Lord Edgar Algernon Robert		Marshall, George Catlett	1953
Gascoyne	1937	Moneta, Ernesto Teodoro	1907
Chamberlain, Sir Austen	1925	Mother Teresa	1979
Constant, Paul Henribenjamin Balluet		Mott, John Raleigh	1946
d'Estournelles de	1909	Myrdal, Alva	1982
Corrigan, Mairead	1976	Nansen, Fridtjof	1922
Cremer, Sir William Randal	1903	Noel-Baker, Philip J.	1959
Dalai Lama,		Office of the United Nations High	
Fourteenth	1989	Commissioner for Refugees 1954, 1981	
Dawes, Charles Gates	1925	Ossietzky, Carl von	1935
De Klerk, Fredrik Willem	1993	Passy, Frederic	1901
Ducommun, Elie	1902	Pauling, Linus Carl	1962
Dunant, Jean Henri	1901	Pearson, Lester Bowles	1957
Esquivel, Adolfo Perez	1980	Peres, Shimon	1994
Fontaine, Henri La	1913	Permanent International Peace Bureau	1910

NAME	YEAR	NAME	YEAR
Pire, Georges Henri	1958	Sato, Eisaku	1974
Pugwash Conferences on Science		Schweitzer, Albert	1952
and World Affairs	1995	Söderblom, Lars Olof Nathan	1930
Quidde, Ludwig	1927	Stresemann, Gustav	1926
Rabin, Yitzhak	1994	Suttner, Baroness Bertha Sophie	
Ramos-Horta, Jose	1996	Felicita von	1905
Refugees, Nansen International		Tho, Le Duc	1973
Office for	1938	Tum, Rigoberta Menchu	1992
Renault, Louis	1907	Tutu, Desmond Mpilo	1984
Robles, Alfonso Garcia	1982	United Nations Children's Fund	1965
Roosevelt, Theodore	1906	United Nations Peace-Keeping	
Root, Elihu	1912	Forces	1988
Rotblat, Joseph	1995	Walesa, Lech	1983
Sadat, Mohamed Anwar El	1978	Wiesel, Elie	1986
Sakharov, Andrei Dmitrievich	1975	Williams, Betty	1976
Sanchez, Oscar Arias	1987	Wilson, Thomas Woodrow	1919

Nobel Prizewinners in Physics

NAME	YEAR	NAME	YEAR
Alfven, Hannes	1970	Cooper, Leon N.	1972
Alvarez, Luis W.	1968	Curie, Marie	1903
Anderson, Carl David	1936	Curie, Pierre	1903
Anderson, Philip W.	1977	Dalen, Nils Gustaf	1912
Appleton, Sir Edward Victor	1947	Davisson, Clinton Joseph	1937
Bardeen, John	1956, 1972	De Broglie, Prince Louis-Victor	1929
Barkla, Charles Glover	1917	De Gennes, Pierre-Gilles	1991
Basov, Nicolay Gennadiyevich	1964	Dehmelt, Hans G.	1989
Becquerel, Antoine Henri	1903	Dirac, Paul Adrien Maurice	1933
Bednorz, J. Georg	1987	Einstein, Albert	1921
Bethe, Hans Albrecht	1967	Esaki, Leo	1973
Binnig, Gerd	1986	Fermi, Enrico	1938
Blackett, Lord Patrick Maynard		Feynman, Richard P.	1965
Stuart	1948	Fitch, Val L.	1980
Bloch, Felix	1952	Fowler, William A.	1983
Bloembergen, Nicolaas	1981	Franck, James	1925
Bohr, Aage	1975	Frank, Il'ja Mikhailovich	1958
Bohr, Niels	1922	Friedman, Jerome I.	1990
Born, Max	1954	Gabor, Dennis	1971
Bothe, Walther	1954	Gell-Mann, Murray	1969
Bragg, Sir William Henry	1915	Giaever, Ivar	1973
Bragg, Sir William Lawrence	1915	Glaser, Donald A.	1960
Brattain, Walter Houser	1956	Glashow, Sheldon L.	1979
Braun, Carl Ferdinand	1909	Goeppert-Mayer, Maria	1963
Bridgman, Percy Williams	1946	Guillaume, Charles Edouard	1920
Brockhouse, Bertram N.	1994	Heisenberg, Werner	1932
Chadwick, Sir James	1935	Hertz, Gustav	1925
Chamberlain, Owen	1959	Hess, Victor Franz	1936
Chandrasekhar, Subramanyan	1983	Hewish, Antony	1974
Charpak, Georges	1992	Hofstadter, Robert	1961
Cherenkov, Pavel Alekseyevich	1958	Hulse, Russell A.	1993
Cockcroft, Sir John Douglas	1951	James, W. Cronin	1980
Compton, Arthur Holly	1927	Jensen, J. Hans D.	1963

NAME	YEAR	NAME	YEAR
Josephson, Brian D.	1973	Richardson, Robert C.	1996
Taylor, Joseph H. Jr.	1993	Richardson, Sir Owen Willans	1928
Kamerlingh-Onnes, Heike	1913	Richter, Burton	1976
Kapitsa, Pyotr Leonidovich	1978	Röntgen, Wilhelm Conrad	1901
Kastler, Alfred	1966	Rohrer, Heinrich	1986
Kendall, Henry W.	1990	Rubbia, Carlo	1984
Klitzing, Klaus von	1985	Ruska, Ernst	1986
Kusch, Polykarp	1955	Ryle, Sir Martin	1974
Lamb, Willis Eugene	1955	Salam, Abdus	1979
Landau, Lev Davidovich	1962	Schawlow, Arthur L.	1981
Laue, Max von	1914	Schrieffer, J. Robert	1972
Lawrence, Ernest Orlando	1939	Schrödinger, Erwin	1933
Lederman, Leon M.	1988	Schwartz, Melvin	1988
Lee, David M.	1996	Schwinger, Julian	1965
Lee, Tsung-Dao	1957	Segrè, Emilio Gino	1959
Lenard, Philipp Eduard Anton	1905	Shockley, William	1956
Lippmann, Gabriel	1908	Shull, Clifford G.	1994
Lorentz, Hendrik Antoon	1902	Siegbahn, Kai M.	1981
Marconi, Guglielmo	1909	Siegbahn, Karl Manne Georg	1924
Meer, Simon Van Der	1984	Stark, Johannes	1919
Michelson, Albert Abraham	1907	Steinberger, Jack	1988
Millikan, Robert Andrews	1923	Stern, Otto	1943
Mössbauer, Rudolf Ludwig	1961	Tamm, Igor Yevgenyevich	1958
Mott, Sir Nevill F.	1977	Taylor, Richard E.	1990
Mottelson, Ben	1975	Thomson, Sir George Paget	1937
Muller, K. Alexander	1987	Thomson, Sir Joseph John	1906
Neel, Louis	1970	Ting, Samuel C. C.	1976
Osheroff, Douglas D.	1996	Tomonaga, Sin-Itiro	1965
Paul, Wolfgang	1989	Townes, Charles H.	1964
Pauli, Wolfgang	1945	Van Der Waals, Johannes Diderik	1910
Penzias, Arno A.	1978	Vleck, John H. Van	1977
Perl, Martin L.	1995	Walton, Ernest Thomas Sinton	1951
Perrin, Jean Baptiste	1926	Weinberg, Steven	1979
Planck, Max Karl Ernst Ludwig	1918	Wien, Wilhelm	1911
Powell, Cecil Frank	1950	Wigner, Eugene P.	1963
Prokhorov, Aleksandr Mikhailovich	1964	Wilson, Charles Thomson Rees	1927
Purcell, Edward Mills	1952	Wilson, Kenneth G.	1982
Rabi, Isidor Isaac	1944	Wilson, Robert W.	1978
Rainwater, James	1975	Yang, Chen Ning	1957
Raman, Sir Chandrasekhara Venkata	1930	Yukawa, Hideki	1949
Ramsey, Norman F.	1989	Zeeman, Pieter	1902
Rayleigh, Lord John William Strutt	1904	Zernike, Frits	1953
Reines, Frederick	1995		

North American Native Peoples

A'ani'	Anishinabe	Athabascan	Blackfoot
Abenaki	Apache	Athapascan	Blood
Acoma Pueblo	Arapahoe	Atsina	Brule
Akwesasne Mohawk	Arawak	Bannock	Caddo
Aleut	Arikara	Beaver	Cahuilla
Algonkin	Assiniboine	Bella Coola	Calusa
Algonquin	Assiniboine-Sioux	Beothuk	Carrier
Anishinaabe	Atakapa	Blackfeet	Catawa

Catawba
Cayuga
Cayuse
Chehalis
Chemehuevi
Cherokee
Cheyenne
Chickasaw
Chicora
Chilcotin
Chinook
Chipewyan
Chippewa
Chitimacha
Choctaw
Chumash
Cochimi
Cocopah
Coeur d'Alene
Coharie
Colorado River
Colville
Comanche
Commanceh
Conestoga
Conoy
Costanoan
Coushatta
Cree
Creek
Crow
Dakota
Delaware
Dene
Diguento
Dogrib
Edisto
Erie
Eskimo
Flathead
Fox
Gabrielino
Goshute
Guajiro
Haida
Haliwa-Saponi
Hare
Havasupai
Hawaiian Natives
Hidatsa
Hidatsas
Ho Chunk
(Winnebago)
Hoh
Hoopa
Hopi
Hualapi
Hupa

Huron
Illinois
Ingalik
Innu
Inuit
Inupiaq
Inupiat
Iowa
Iroquois
Isleta Pueblo
Jemez Pueblo
Jicarilla Apache
Kalispel
Kansa
Karankawa
Karok
Karuk
Kaska
Kaw
Kickapoo
Kiowa
Klallam
Klamath
Klikitat
Koyukan
Koyukon
Kutchin
Kwakiutl
Laguna Pueblo
Lakota
Luiseno
Lumbee
Lummi
Mahican
Maidu
Makah
Malecite
Maliseet
Mandan
Maricopa
Mascouten
Mashantucket Pequot
Mashpee
Massachusetts
Mattabesic
Mattaponi
Mee-Wuk
Meherrin
Menominee
Meskquakie
Mesquakie
Metis
Metoac
Mi'kmaq
Miami
Miccosukee
Mimbres
Missisauga

Missouri
Miwok
Modoc
Mohave
Mohawk
Mohegan
Mohican
Mono
Montagnais
Muckleshoot
Munsee
Muscogee
Narraganset
Naskapi
Natchez
Nauset
Navajo
Neutrals
Nez Perce
Niantic
Nipissing
Nipmuc
Nisqually
Nooksack
Nootka
Oglala
Ojibwe
Okanagan
Okanogan
Omaha
Oneida
Onondaga
Osage
Otoe
Otoe-Missouria
Otomi
Ottawa
Paiute
Paloos
Pasqua Yaqui
Passamaquoddy
Pawnee
Peigan
Pennacook
Penobscot
Penobscott
Peoria
Pequot
Pima
Pit River
Poarch Creek
Pocumtuc
Pomo
Ponca
Potawatomi
Powhatan
Powhattan
Pueblo

Puyallup
Quapaw
Quechan
Quileute
Quinault
Rappahannock
Saanich
Sac and Fox
Salish
Salish and Kootenai
Salteaux
San Juan Pueblo
Santa Clara Pueblo
Santee
Santo Domingo
Pueblo
Saponi
Sarsi
Sauk-Suiattle
Seminole
Seneca
Serrano
Shawnee
Shoalwater
Shoshone
Shuswap
Siksika
Siletz
Sioux
Skagit
Skitswish
Skokomish
Slave
Smith River
Sokoki
Spokane
Squawmish
Squaxin Island
Stillaguamish
Stockbridge Munsee
Suquamish
Susquehanna
Susquehannock
Swinomish
Tache
Tanaina
Tarascan
Teton
Tewa
Timucua
Tionontati
Tiwa
Tlingit
Tohono O'odham
(Papago)
Tolowa
Tonkawa
Tse-Shaht

Tsimshian	Waiguri	Winnebago	Yaqui
Tulalip	Wampanoag	Wintun	Yavapai
Tunica-Biloxi	Warm Springs	Wiyot	Yokut
Tuscarora	Wasco	Wyandot	Yuma
Umatilla	Washoe	Yakama	Yupik
Ute	Wenro	Yakima	Yurok
Waccamaw	Wichita	Yankton	Zuni Pueblo

Olympic Games

Olympic Games — Winter

Year	Number	Location	Year	Number	Location
1924	I	Chamonix, France	1964	IX	Innsbruck, Austria
1928	II	St. Moritz, Switzerland	1968	X	Grenoble, France
1932	III	Lake Placid, USA	1972	XI	Sapporo, Japan
1936	IV	Garmisch-Partenkirchen, Germany	1976	XII	Innsbruck, Austria
			1980	XIII	Lake Placid, USA
1940		Cancelled (World War II)	1984	XIV	Sarajevo, Yugoslavia
1944		Cancelled (World War II)	1988	XV	Calgary, Canada
1948	V	St. Moritz, Switzerland	1992	XVI	Albertville, France
1952	VI	Oslo, Norway	1994	XVII	Lillehammer, Norway
1956	VII	Cortina d'Ampezzo, Italy	1998	XVIII	Nagano, Japan
1960	VIII	Squaw Valley, USA	2002	XIX	Salt Lake City, USA

Olympic Games — Summer

Year	Number	Location	Year	Number	Location
1896	I	Athens, Greece	1952	XV	Helsinki, Finland
1900	II	Paris, France	1956	XVI	Melbourne, Australia
1904	III	St. Louis, USA	1960	XVII	Rome, Italy
1906	(none)	Athens, Greece	1964	XVIII	Tokyo, Japan
1908	IV	London, England	1968	XIX	Mexico City, Mexico
1912	V	Stockholm, Sweden	1972	XX	Munich, West Germany
1916	VI	Cancelled (World War I)	1976	XXI	Montreal, Canada
1920	VII	Antwerp, Belgium	1980	XXII	Moscow, USSR
1924	VIII	Paris, France	1984	XXIII	Los Angeles, USA
1928	IX	Amsterdam, Holland	1988	XXIV	Seoul, Korea
1932	X	Los Angeles, USA	1992	XXV	Barcelona, Spain
1936	XI	Berlin, Germany	1996	XXVI	Atlanta, USA
1940	XII	Cancelled (World War II)	2000	XXVII	Sydney, Australia
1944	XIII	Cancelled (World War II)	2004	XXVIII	Athens, Greece
1948	XIV	London, England			

Presidents of the United States

ORDER	NAME / FIRST LADY	TERM	VICE PRESIDENT(S)	STATE OF BIRTH	POLITICAL PARTY
1st	**George Washington** Martha Dandridge Custis Washington (1731–1802)	1789–1797	John Adams	Virginia	Federalist
2nd	**John Adams** Abigail Smith Adams (1744–1818)	1797–1801	Thomas Jefferson	Massachusetts	Federalist
3rd	**Thomas Jefferson** Martha Wayles Skelton Jefferson (1748–1782)	1801–1809	Aaron Burr, George Clinton	Virginia	Democratic-Republican
4th	**James Madison** Dolley Payne Todd Madison (1768–1849)	1809–1817	George Clinton, Elbridge Gerry	Virginia	Democratic-Republican
5th	**James Monroe** Elizabeth Kortright Monroe (1768–1830)	1817–1825	D. D. Tompkins	Virginia	Democratic-Republican
6th	**John Quincy Adams** Louisa Catherine Johnson Adams (1775–1852)	1825–1829	John C. Calhoun	Massachusetts	Democratic-Republican
7th	**Andrew Jackson** Rachel Donelson Jackson (1767–1828)	1829–1837	John C. Calhoun, Martin Van Buren	South Carolina	Democrat
8th	**Martin Van Buren** Hannah Hoes Van Buren (1783–1819)	1837–1841	Richard M. Johnson	New York	Democrat
9th	**William Henry Harrison** Anna Tuthill Symmes Harrison (1775–1864)	1841	John Tyler	Virginia	Whig
10th	**John Tyler** Letitia Christian Tyler (1790–1842), Julia Gardiner Tyler (1820–1889)	1841–1845	—	Virginia	Democrat
11th	**James Polk** Sarah Childress Polk (1803–1891)	1845–1849	George M. Dallas	North Carolina	Democrat
12th	**Zachary Taylor** Margaret Mackall Smith Taylor (1788–1852)	1849–1850	Millard Fillmore	Virginia	Whig
13th	**Millard Fillmore** Abigail Powers Fillmore (1798–1853)	1850–1853	—	New York	Whig
14th	**Franklin Pierce** Jane Means Appleton Pierce (1806–1863)	1853–1857	William R. D. King	New Hampshire	Democrat
15th	**James Buchanan** Harriet Lane (1830–1903)	1857–1861	John C. Breckinridge	Pennsylvania	Democrat

Presents of the United States (continued)

Order	Name First Lady	Term	Vice President(s)	State of Birth	Political Party
16th	**Abraham Lincoln** Mary Todd Lincoln (1818–1882)	1861–1865	Hannibal Hamlin, Andrew Johnson	Kentucky	Republican
17th	**Andrew Johnson** Eliza McCardle Johnson (1810–1876)	1865–1869	—	North Carolina	Democrat
18th	**Ulysses S. Grant** Julia Dent Grant (1826–1902)	1869–1877	Schuyler Colfax, Henry Wilson	Ohio	Republican
19th	**Rutherford B. Hayes** Lucy Ware Webb Hayes (1831–1889)	1877–1881	William A. Wheeler	Ohio	Republican
20th	**James A. Garfield** Lucretia Rudolph Garfield (1832–1918)	1881	Chester A. Arthur	Ohio	Republican
21st	**Chester A. Arthur** Ellen Lewis Herndon Arthur (1837–1880)	1881–1885	—	Vermont	Republican
22nd	**Grover Cleveland** Frances Folsom Cleveland (1864–1947)	1885–1889	Thomas A. Hendricks	New Jersey	Democrat
23rd	**Benjamin Harrison** Caroline Lavina Scott Harrison (1832–1892)	1889–1893	Levi P. Morton	Ohio	Republican
24th	**Grover Cleveland** Frances Folsom Cleveland (1864–1947)	1893–1897	Adlai Stevenson	New Jersey	Democrat
25th	**William McKinley** Ida Saxton McKinley (1847–1907)	1897–1901	Garret A. Hobart, Theodore Roosevelt	Ohio	Republican
26th	**Theodore Roosevelt** Edith Kermit Carow Roosevelt (1861–1948)	1901–1909	Charles W. Fairbanks	New York	Republican
27th	**William H. Taft** Helen Herron Taft (1861–1943)	1909–1913	James S. Sherman	Ohio	Republican
28th	**Woodrow Wilson** Ellen Louise Axson Wilson (1860–1914), Edith Bolling Galt Wilson (1872–1961)	1913–1921	Thomas Marshall	Virginia	Democrat
29th	**Warren Harding** Florence Kling Harding (1860–1924)	1921–1923	Calvin Coolidge	Ohio	Republican
30th	**Calvin Coolidge** Grace Anna Goodhue Coolidge (1879–1957)	1923–1929	Charles G. Dawes	Vermont	Republican
31st	**Herbert Hoover** Lou Henry Hoover (1874–1944)	1929–1933	Charles E. Curtis	Iowa	Republican

ORDER	NAME FIRST LADY	TERM	VICE PRESIDENT(S)	STATE OF BIRTH	POLITICAL PARTY
32nd	**Franklin D. Roosevelt** Anna Eleanor Roosevelt Roosevelt (1884–1962)	1933–1945	John Nance Garner, Henry A. Wallace, Harry S Truman	New York	Democrat
33rd	**Harry S Truman** Elizabeth Virginia Wallace Truman (1885–1982)	1945–1953	Alben W. Barkley	Missouri	Democrat
34th	**Dwight D. Eisenhower** Mamie Geneva Doud Eisenhower (1896–1979)	1953–1961	Richard M. Nixon	Texas	Republican
35th	**John F. Kennedy** Jacqueline Lee Bouvier Kennedy Onassis (1929–1994)	1961–1963	Lyndon B. Johnson	Massachusetts	Democrat
36th	**Lyndon B. Johnson** Claudia Taylor Johnson (1912–)	1963–1969	Hubert H. Humphrey	Texas	Democrat
37th	**Richard M. Nixon** Patricia Ryan Nixon (1912–1993)	1969–1974	Spiro T. Agnew, Gerald R. Ford	California	Republican
38th	**Gerald R. Ford** Elizabeth Bloomer Ford (1918–)	1974–1977	Nelson Rockefeller	Nebraska	Republican
39th	**Jimmy Carter** Rosalynn Smith Carter (1927–)	1977–1981	Walter Mondale	Georgia	Democrat
40th	**Ronald W. Reagan** Nancy Davis Reagan (1923–)	1981–1989	George Bush	Illinois	Republican
41st	**George Bush** Barbara Pierce Bush (1925–)	1989–1993	Dan Quayle	Massachusetts	Republican
42nd	**William J. Clinton** Hillary Rodham Clinton (1947–)	1993– Present	Albert Gore	Arkansas	Democrat

The Pulitzer Prize — Biography or Autobiography

1998 *Personal History,* Katharine Graham

1997 *Angela's Ashes,* Frank McCourt

1996 *God: A Biography,* Jack Miles

1995 *Harriet Beecher Stowe: A Life,* Joan D. Hedrick

1994 *W.E.B. DuBois: Biography of a Race, 1868–1919,* David Levering Lewis

1993 *Truman,* David McCullough

1992 *Fortunate Son: The Healing of a Vietnam Vet,* Lewis B. Puller Jr.

1991 *Jackson Pollock: An American Saga,* Steven Naifeh and Gregory White Smith

1990 *Machiavelli in Hell,* Sebastian de Grazia

1989 *Oscar Wilde,* Richard Ellmann

1988 *Look Homeward: A Life of Thomas Wolfe,* David Herbert Donald

1987 *Bearing the Cross: Martin Luther King, Jr. and the Southern Christian Leadership Conference,* David J. Garrow

1986 *Louise Bogan: A Portrait,* Elizabeth Frank

1985 *The Life and Times of Cotton Mather,* Kenneth Silverman

1984 *Booker T. Washington,* Louis R. Harlan

1983 *Growing Up,* Russell Baker

1982 *Grant: A Biography,* William S. McFeely

1981 *Peter the Great,* Robert K. Massie

1980 *The Rise of Theodore Roosevelt,* Edmund Morris

1979 *Days of Sorrow and Pain: Leo Baeck and the Berlin Jews,* Leonard Baker

1978 *Samuel Johnson,* Walter Jackson Bate

1977 *A Prince of Our Disorder,* John E. Mack

1976 *Edith Wharton: A Biography,* Richard W. B. Lewis

1975 *The Power Broker: Robert Moses and the Fall of New York,* Robert A. Caro

1974 *O'Neill, Son and Artist,* Louis Sheaffer

1973 *Luce and His Empire,* W. A. Swanberg

1972 *Eleanor and Franklin: The Story of Their Relationship, Based on Eleanor Roosevelt's Private Papers,* Joseph P. Lash

1971 *Robert Frost: The Years of Triumph, 1915–1938,* Lawrence Thompson

1970 *Huey Long,* T. Harry Williams

1969 *The Man from New York,* B. L. Reid

1968 *Memoirs, 1925–1950,* George F. Kennan

1967 *Mr. Clemens and Mark Twain,* Justin Kaplan

1966 *A Thousand Days,* Arthur M. Schlesinger, Jr.

1965 *Henry Adams (3 vols.),* Ernest Samuels

1964 *John Keats,* Walter Jackson Bate

1963 *Henry James: Vol. II, The Conquest of London, 1870–1881; Vol. III, The Middle Years, 1881–1895,* Leon Edel

1962 No award

1961 *Charles Sumner and the Coming of the Civil War,* David Donald

1960 *John Paul Jones,* Samuel Eliot Morison

1959 *Woodrow Wilson, American Prophet,* Arthur Walworth

1958 *George Washington,* Douglas Southall Freeman (vols. 1–6) and John Alexander Carroll and Mary Wells Ashworth (vol. 7)

1957 *Profiles in Courage,* John F. Kennedy

1956 *Benjamin Henry Latrobe,* Talbot F. Hamlin

1955 *The Taft Story,* William S. White

1954 *The Spirit of St. Louis,* Charles A. Lindbergh

1953 *Edmund Pendleton, 1721–1803,* David J. Mays

1952 *Charles Evans Hughes,* Merlo J. Pusey

1951 *John C. Calhoun: American Portrait,* Margaret Louise Coit

1950 *John Quincy Adams and the Foundations of American Foreign Policy,* Samuel Flagg Bemis

1949 *Roosevelt and Hopkins,* Robert E. Sherwood

1948 *Forgotten First Citizen: John Bigelow,* Margaret Clapp

1947 *The Autobiography of William Allen White,* William Allen White

1946 *Son of the Wilderness,* Linnie Marsh Wolfe

1945 *George Bancroft: Brahmin Rebel,* Russel Blaine Nye

1944 *The American Leonardo: The Life of Samuel F. B. Morse,* Carleton Mabee

1943 *Admiral of the Ocean Sea,* Samuel Eliot Morison

1942 *Crusader in Crinoline,* Forrest Wilson

1941 *Jonathan Edwards,* Ola E. Winslow

1940 *Woodrow Wilson: Life and Letters, vols. VII and VIII,* Ray Stannard Baker

1939 *Benjamin Franklin,* Carl Van Doren

1938 *Pedlar's Progress,* Odell Shepard

1937 *Hamilton Fish,* Allan Nevins

1936 *The Thought and Character of William James,* Ralph Barton Perry

1935 *R. E. Lee,* Douglas S. Freeman

1934 *John Hay,* Tyler Dennett

1933 *Grover Cleveland,* Allan Nevins

1932 *Charles W. Eliot,* Henry James

1931 *Theodore Roosevelt,* Henry F. Pringle

1930 *The Raven,* Marquis James

1929 *The Training of an American: The Earlier Life and Letters of Walter H. Page,* Burton J. Hendrick

1928 *The American Orchestra and Theodore Thomas,* Charles Edward Russell

1927 *Whitman,* Emory Holloway

1926 *The Life of Sir William Osler,* Harvey Cushing

1925 *Barrett Wendell and His Letters,* M. A. DeWolfe Howe

1924 *From Immigrant to Inventor,* Michael Idvorsky Pupin

1923 *The Life and Letters of Walter H. Page*, Burton J. Hendrick

1922 *A Daughter of the Middle Border*, Hamlin Garland

1921 *The Americanization of Edward Bok*, Edward Bok

1920 *The Life of John Marshall*, Albert J. Beveridge

1919 *The Education of Henry Adams*, Henry Adams

1918 *Benjamin Franklin, Self-Revealed*, William Cabell Bruce

1917 *Julia Ward Howe*, Laura E. Richards and Maude Howe Elliott, assisted by Florence Howe Hall

The Pulitzer Prize — Drama

1998 *How I Learned to Drive*, Paula Vogel

1997 No award

1996 *Rent*, Jonathan Larson

1995 *The Young Man from Atlanta*, Horton Foote

1994 *Three Tall Women*, Edward Albee

1993 *Angels in America: Millennium Approaches*, Tony Kushner

1992 *The Kentucky Cycle*, Robert Schenkkan

1991 *Lost in Yonkers*, Neil Simon

1990 *The Piano Lesson*, August Wilson

1989 *The Heidi Chronicles*, Wendy Wasserstein

1988 *Driving Miss Daisy*, Alfred Uhry

1987 *Fences*, August Wilson

1986 No award

1985 *Sunday in the Park with George*, Stephen Sondheim and James Lapine

1984 *Glengarry Glen Ross*, David Mamet

1983 *'Night, Mother*, Marsha Norman

1982 *A Soldier's Play*, Charles Fuller

1981 *Crimes of the Heart*, Beth Henley

1980 *Talley's Folly*, Lanford Wilson

1979 *Buried Child*, Sam Shepard

1978 *The Gin Game*, Donald L. Coburn

1977 *The Shadow Box*, Michael Cristofer

1976 *A Chorus Line*, conceived by Michael Bennett

1975 *Seascape*, Edward Albee

1974 No award

1973 *That Championship Season*, Jason Miller

1972 No award

1971 *The Effect of Gamma Rays on Man-in-the-Moon Marigolds*, Paul Zindel

1970 *No Place to Be Somebody*, Charles Gordone

1969 *The Great White Hope*, Howard Sackler

1968 No award

1967 *A Delicate Balance*, Edward Albee

1966 No award

1965 *The Subject Was Roses*, Frank D. Gilroy

1964 No award

1963 No award

1962 *How to Succeed in Business Without Really Trying*, Frank Loesser and Abe Burrows

1961 *All the Way Home*, Tad Mosel

1960 *Fiorello!*, George Abbott, Jerome Weidman, Jerry Bock and Sheldon Harnick

1959 *J.B.*, Archibald MacLeish

1958 *Look Homeward, Angel*, Ketti Frings

1957 *Long Day's Journey into Night*, Eugene O'Neill

1956 *The Diary of Anne Frank*, Frances Goodrich and Albert Hackett

1955 *Cat on a Hot Tin Roof*, Tennessee Williams

1954 *The Teahouse of the August Moon*, John Patrick

1953 *Picnic*, William Inge

1952 *The Shrike*, Joseph Kramm

1951 No award

1950 *South Pacific*, Richard Rodgers, Oscar Hammerstein II and Joshua Logan

1949 *Death of a Salesman*, Arthur Miller

1948 *A Streetcar Named Desire*, Tennessee Williams

1947 No award

1946 *State of the Union*, Russel Crouse and Howard Lindsay

1945 *Harvey*, Mary Chase

1944 No award

1943 *The Skin of Our Teeth*, Thornton Wilder

1942 No award

1941 *There Shall Be No Night*, Robert E. Sherwood

1940 *The Time of Your Life*, William Saroyan

1939 *Abe Lincoln in Illinois*, Robert E. Sherwood

Alison's House, Susan Glaspell

1938	*Our Town*, Thornton Wilder	1928	*Strange Interlude*, Eugene O'Neill
1937	*You Can't Take It With You*, Moss Hart and George S. Kaufman	1927	*In Abraham's Bosom*, Paul Green
		1926	*Craig's Wife*, George Kelly
1936	*Idiot's Delight*, Robert E. Sherwood	1925	*They Knew What They Wanted*, Sidney Howard
1935	*The Old Maid*, Zoe Akins		
1934	*Men in White*, Sidney Kingsley	1924	*Hell-Bent fer Heaven*, Hatcher Hughes
1933	*Both Your Houses*, Maxwell Anderson		
		1923	*Icebound*, Owen Davis
1932	*Of Thee I Sing*, George S. Kaufman, Morrie Ryskind and Ira Gershwin	1922	*Anna Christie*, Eugene O'Neill
		1921	*Miss Lulu Bett*, Zona Gale
1931	*Alison's House*, Susan Glaspell	1920	*Beyond the Horizon*, Eugene O'Neill
1930	*The Green Pastures*, Marc Connelly	1919	No award
1929	*Street Scene*, Elmer L. Rice	1918	*Why Marry?*, Jesse Lynch Williams

The Pulitzer Prize — Fiction

1998	*American Pastoral*, Philip Roth	1968	*The Confessions of Nat Turner*, William Styron
1997	*Martin Dressler: The Tale of an American Dreamer*, Steven Millhauser		
		1967	*The Fixer*, Bernard Malamud
		1966	*Collected Stories of Katherine Anne Porter*, Katherine Anne Porter
1996	*Independence Day*, Richard Ford		
1995	*Stone Diaries*, Carol Shields	1965	*The Keepers of the House*, Shirley Anne Grau
1994	*The Shipping News*, E. Annie Proulx		
1993	*A Good Scent from a Strange Mountain*, Robert Olen Butler	1964	No award
		1963	*The Reivers*, William Faulkner
1992	*Thousand Acres*, Jane Smiley	1962	*The Edge of Sadness*, Edwin O'Connor
1991	*Rabbit at Rest*, John Updike		
1990	*The Mambo Kings Play Songs of Love*, Oscar Hijuelos	1961	*To Kill a Mockingbird*, Harper Lee
		1960	*Advise and Consent*, Allen Drury
1989	*Breathing Lessons*, Anne Tyler	1959	*The Travels of Jamie McPheeters*, Robert Lewis Taylor
1988	*Beloved*, Toni Morrison		
1987	*A Summons to Memphis*, Peter Taylor	1958	*A Death in the Family*, James Agee
1986	*Lonesome Dove*, Larry McMurtry	1957	No award
1985	*Foreign Affairs*, Alison Lurie	1956	*Andersonville*, Mackinlay Kantor
1984	*Ironweed*, William Kennedy	1955	*A Fable*, William Faulkner
1983	*The Color Purple*, Alice Walker	1954	No award
1982	*Rabbit Is Rich*, John Updike	1953	*The Old Man and the Sea*, Ernest Hemingway
1981	*A Confederacy of Dunces*, John Kennedy Toole		
		1952	*The Caine Mutiny*, Herman Wouk
1980	*The Executioner's Song*, Norman Mailer	1951	*The Town*, Conrad Richter
		1950	*The Way West*, A. B. Guthrie
1979	*The Stories of John Cheever*, John Cheever	1949	*Guard of Honor*, James Gould Cozzens
1978	*Elbow Room*, James Alan McPherson	1948	*Tales of the South Pacific*, James A. Michener
1977	No award		
1976	*Humboldt's Gift*, Saul Bellow	1947	*All the King's Men*, Robert Penn Warren
1975	*The Killer Angels*, Michael Shaara		
1974	No award	1946	No award
1973	*The Optimist's Daughter*, Eudora Welty	1945	*A Bell for Adano*, John Hersey
		1944	*Journey in the Dark*, Martin Flavin
1972	*The Angle of Repose*, Wallace Stegner	1943	*Dragon's Teeth*, Upton Sinclair
		1942	*In This Our Life*, Ellen Glasgow
1971	No award	1941	No award
1970	*Collected Stories*, Jean Stafford	1940	*The Grapes of Wrath*, John Steinbeck
1969	*House Made of Dawn*, N. Scott Momaday	1939	*The Yearling*, Marjorie Kinnan Rawlings

1938	*The Late George Apley*, John Phillips Marquand	1928	*The Bridge of San Luis Rey*, Thornton Wilder
1937	*Gone with the Wind*, Margaret Mitchell	1927	*Early Autumn*, Louis Bromfield
1936	*Honey in the Horn*, Harold Davis	1926	*Arrowsmith*, Sinclair Lewis
1935	*Now in November*, Josephine Winslow Johnson	1925	*So Big*, Edna Ferber
		1924	*The Able McLaughlins*, Margaret Wilson
1934	*In His Bosom*, Caroline Miller Lamb	1923	*One of Ours*, Willa Cather
		1922	*Alice Adams*, Booth Tarkington
1933	*The Store*, T. S. Stribling	1921	*The Age of Innocence*, Edith Wharton
1932	*The Good Earth*, Pearl S. Buck	1920	No award
1931	*Barnes Years of Grace*, Margaret Ayer	1919	*The Magnificent Ambersons*, Booth Tarkington
1930	*Laughing Boy*, Oliver La Farge	1918	*His Family*, Ernest Poole
1929	*Scarlet Sister Mary*, Julia Peterkin		

The Pulitzer Prize — History of the United States

1998	*Summer for the Gods: The Scopes Trial and America's Continuing Debate Over Science and Religion*, Edward J. Larson	1985	*The Prophets of Regulation*, Thomas K. McCraw
		1984	No award
		1983	*The Transformation of Virginia, 1740–1790*, Rhys L. Isaac
1997	*Original Meanings: Politics and Ideas in the Making of the Constitution*, Jack N. Rakove	1982	*Mary Chestnut's Civil War*, C. Vann Woodward, editor
1996	*William Cooper's Town: Power and Persuasion on the Frontier of the Early American Republic*, Alan Taylor	1981	*American Education: The National Experience; 1783–1876*, Lawrence A. Cremin
		1980	*Been in the Storm So Long*, Leon F. Litwack
1995	*No Ordinary Time: Franklin and Eleanor Roosevelt: The Home Front in World War II*, Doris Kearns Goodwin	1979	*The Dred Scott Case: Its Significance in Law and Politics*, Don E. Fehrenbacher
1994	*The Disruption of American Democracy*, Roy Franklin Nichols	1978	*The Invisible Hand: The Managerial Revolution in American Business*, Alfred D. Chandler, Jr.
1993	*The Radicalism of the American Revolution*, Gordon S. Wood		
1992	*The Fate of Liberty: Abraham Lincoln and Civil Liberties*, Mark E. Neely Jr.	1977	*The Impending Crisis: 1841–1861*, David M. Potter (posthumous)
		1976	*Lamy of Santa Fe*, Paul Horgan
1991	*A Midwife's Tale: The Life of Martha Ballard, Based on Her Diary 1785–1812*, Laurel Thatcher Ulrich	1975	*Jefferson and His Time*, Dumas Malone
		1974	*The Americans: The Democratic Experience, Vol. 3*, Daniel J. Boorstin
1990	*In Our Image: America's Empire in the Philippines*, Stanley Karnow	1973	*People of Paradox: An Inquiry Concerning the Origin of American Civilization*, Michael Kammen
1989	*Parting the Waters*, Taylor Branch *Battle Cry of Freedom*, James M. McPherson	1972	*Neither Black Nor White: Slavery and Race Relations in Brazil and the United States*, Carl N. Degler
1988	*The Launching of Modern American Science 1846–1876*, Robert V. Bruce	1971	*Roosevelt: The Soldier of Freedom*, James McGregor Burns
1987	*Voyagers to the West: A Passage in the Peopling of America on the Eve of the Revolution*, Bernard Bailyn	1970	*Present at the Creation: My Years in the State Department*, Dean Acheson
1986	*. . . the Heavens and the Earth: A Political History of the Space Age*, Walter A. McDougall	1969	*Origins of the Fifth Amendment*, Leonard W. Levy

1968 *The Ideological Origins of the American Revolution,* Bernard Bailyn

1967 *Exploration and Empire: The Explorer and Scientist in the Winning of the American West,* William H. Goetzmann

1966 *Life of the Mind in America,* Perry Miller

1965 *The Greenback Era,* Irwin Unger

1964 *Puritan Village: The Formation of a New England Town,* Sumner Chilton Powell

1963 Washington, *Village and Capital, 1800–1878,* Constance McLaughlin Green

1962 *The Triumphant Empire, Thunder-Clouds Gather in the West,* Lawrence H. Gipson

1961 *Between War and Peace: The Potsdam Conference,* Herbert Feis

1960 *In the Days of McKinley,* Margaret Leech

1959 *The Republican Era: 1869–1901,* Leonard D. White, assisted by Jean Schneider

1958 *Banks and Politics in America: From the Revolution to the Civil War,* Bray Hammond

1957 *Russia Leaves the War: Soviet-American Relations, 1917–1920,* George F. Kennan

1956 *The Age of Reform,* Richard Hofstadter

1955 *Great River: The Rio Grande in North American History,* Paul Horgan

1954 *A Stillness at Appomattox,* Bruce Catton

1953 *The Era of Good Feelings,* George Dangerfield

1952 *The Uprooted,* Oscar Handlin

1951 *The Old Northwest, Pioneer Period 1815–1840,* R. Carlyle Buley

1950 *Art and Life in America,* Oliver W. Larkin

1949 *The Disruption of American Democracy,* Roy Franklin Nichols

1948 *Across the Wide Missouri,* Bernard DeVoto

1947 *Scientists Against Time,* James Phinney Baxter, III

1946 *The Age of Jackson,* Arthur M. Schlesinger, Jr.

1945 *Unfinished Business,* Stephen Bonsal

1944 *The Growth of American Thought,* Merle Curti

1943 *Paul Revere and the World He Lived In,* Esther Forbes

1942 *Reveille in Washington,* Margaret Leech

1941 *The Atlantic Migration, 1607–1860,* Marcus Lee Hansen

1940 *Abraham Lincoln: The War Years,* Carl Sandburg

1939 *A History of American Magazines,* Frank Luther Mott

1938 *The Road to Reunion, 1865–1900,* Paul Herman Buck

1937 *The Flowering of New England,* Van Wyck Brooks

1936 *The Constitutional History of the United States,* Andrew C. McLaughlin

1935 *The Colonial Period of American History,* Charles McLean Andrews

1934 *The People's Choice,* Herbert Agar

1933 *The Significance of Sections in American History,* Frederick J. Turner

1932 *My Experiences in the World War,* John J. Pershing

1931 *The Coming of the War: 1914,* Bernadotte E. Schmitt

1930 *The War of Independence,* Claude H. Van Tyne

1929 *The Organization and Administration of the Union Army, 1861–1865,* Fred Albert Shannon

1928 *Main Currents in American Thought,* Vernon Louis Parrington

1927 *Pinckney's Treaty,* Samuel Flagg Bemis

1926 *The History of the United States,* Edward Channing

1925 *A History of the American Frontier,* Frederic L. Paxson

1924 *The American Revolution— A Constitutional Interpretation,* Charles Howard McIlwain

1923 *The Supreme Court in United States History,* Charles Warren

1922 *The Founding of New England,* James Truslow Adams

1921 *The Victory at Sea,* William Sowden Sims in collaboration with Burton J. Hendrick

1920 *The War with Mexico,* Justin H. Smith

1919 No award

1918 *A History of the Civil War, 1861–1865,* James Ford Rhodes

1917 *With Americans of Past and Present Days,* J. J. Jusserand, ambassador of France to United States

The Pulitzer Prize — Nonfiction

1998   *Guns, Germs, and Steel: The Fates of Human Societies*, Jared Diamond

1997   *Ashes to Ashes: America's Hundred-Year Cigarette War, the Public Health, and the Unabashed Triumph of Philip Morris*, Richard Kluger

1996   *The Haunted Land: Facing Europe's Ghosts After Communism*, Tina Rosenberg

1995   *The Beak of the Finch: A Story of Evolution in Our Time*, Jonathan Weiner

1994   *Lenin's Tomb: The Last Days of the Soviet Empire*, David Remick

1993   *Lincoln at Gettysburg: The Words That Remade America*, Garry Wills

1992   *The Prize: The Epic Quest for Oil, Money and Power*, Daniel Yergin

1991   *The Ants*, Bert Holldobler and Edward O. Wilson

1990   *And Their Children After Them*, Dale Maharidge and Michael Williamson

1989   *A Bright Shining Lie*, Neil Sheehan

1988   *The Making of the Atomic Bomb*, Richard Rhodes

1987   *Arab and Jew: Wounded Spirits in a Promised Land*, David K. Shipler

1986   *Move Your Shadow: South Africa, Black and White*, Joseph Lelyveld

Common Ground: A Turbulent Decade in the Lives of Three American Families, J. Anthony Lukas

1985   *The Good War: An Oral History of World War II*, Studs Terkel

1984   *Social Transformation of American Medicine*, Paul Starr

1983   *Is There No Place on Earth for Me?*, Susan Sheehan

1982   *The Soul of a New Machine*, Tracy Kidder

1981   *Fin-de-Siecle Vienna: Politics and Culture*, Carl E. Schorske

1980   *Gödel, Escher, Bach: An Eternal Golden Braid*, Douglas R. Hofstadter

1979   *On Human Nature*, Edward O. Wilson

1978   *The Dragons of Eden*, Carl Sagan

1977   *Beautiful Swimmers: Watermen, Crabs and the Chesapeake Bay*, William W. Warner

1976   *Why Survive? Being Old in America*, Robert N. Butler

1975   *Pilgrim at Tinker Creek*, Annie Dillard

1974   *The Denial of Death*, Ernest Becker

1973   *Fire in the Lake: The Vietnamese and the Americans in Vietnam*, Frances FitzGerald

Children of Crisis (vols. 1 and 2), Robert M. Coles

1972   *Stilwell and the American Experience in China, 1911–1945*, Barbara W. Tuchman

1971   *The Rising Sun*, John Toland

1970   *Gandhi's Truth*, Erik H. Erikson

1969   *So Human an Animal*, René Jules Dubos

The Armies of the Night, Norman Mailer

1968   *Rousseau and Revolution*, Will and Ariel Durant

1967   *The Problem of Slavery in Western Culture*, David Brion Davis

1966   *Wandering Through Winter*, Edwin Way Teale

1965   *O Strange New World*, Howard Mumford Jones

1964   *Anti-Intellectualism in American Life*, Richard Hofstadter

1963   *The Guns of August*, Barbara W. Tuchman

1962   *The Making of the President, 1960*, Theodore H. White

Shakespeare's Plays

Comedies

All's Well That Ends Well

King of France
Duke of Florence
Bertram, Count of Rousillon
Lafeu
Parolles
Steward
Countess of Rousillon

Helena
Diana
Violeta
Mariana

As You Like It

Duke Senior
Duke Frederick

Amiens
Jaques
Le Beau
Charles
Oliver
Jaques (Jaques de Boys)
Orlando
Adam
Dennis
Touchstone
Sir Oliver Martext
Corin
Silvius
William
Hymen
Rosalind
Celia
Phebe
Audrey

The Comedy of Errors

Solinus
Aegeon
Antipholus of Ephesus
Antipholus of Syracuse
Dromio of Ephesus
Dromio of Syracuse
Balthazar
Angelo
Pinch
Aemilia
Adriana
Luciana
Luce

Cymbeline

Cymbeline
Cloten
Posthumus Leonatus
Belarius
Guiderius
Arviragus
Caius Lucius
Pisanio
Cornelius
Queen
Imogen
Helen

Love's Labour's Lost

Ferdinand
Biron
Longaville
Dumain
Boyet
Mercade
Don Adriano de Armado
Sir Nathaniel

Holofernes
Dull
Costard
Moth
Princess of France
Rosaline
Maria
Katharine
Jaquenetta

Measure for Measure

Duke Vincentio
Angelo
Escalus
Claudio
Lucio
Provost
Friar Peter
Friar Thomas
Varrius
Elbow
Froth
Pompey
Abhorson
Barnardine
Isabella
Mariana
Juliet
Francisca
Mistress Overdone

The Merchant of Venice

Duke of Venice
Prince of Morocco
Prince of Arragon
Antonio
Bassanio
Salanio
Salarino
Gratiano
Salerio
Lorenzo
Shylock
Tubal
Launcelot Gobbo
Old Gobbo
Leonardo
Balthasar
Stephano
Portia
Nerissa
Jessica

The Merry Wives of Windsor

Sir John Falstaff
Fenton
Shallow
Slender

Ford
Page
William Page
Sir Hugh Evans
Doctor Caius
Bardolph
Pistol
Nym
Robin
Simple
Rugby
Mistress Ford
Mistress Page
Anne Page
Mistress Quickly

A Midsummer Night's Dream

Theseus
Egeus
Lysander
Demetrius
Philostrate
Quince
Snug
Bottom
Flute
Snout
Starveling
Hippolyta
Hermia
Helena
Oberon
Titania
Puck (or Robin Goodfellow)
Peaseblossom
Cobweb
Moth
Mustardseed

Much Ado About Nothing

Don Pedro
Don John
Claudio
Benedick
Leonato
Antonio
Balthasar
Conrade
Borachio
Friar Francis
Dogberry
Verges
Hero
Beatrice
Margaret
Ursula

Pericles, Prince of Tyre

Antiochus
Pericles
Helicanus
Escanes
Simonides
Cleon
Lysimachus
Cerimon
Thaliard
Philemon
Leonine
Boult
Dionyza
Thaisa
Marina
Lychorida

The Taming of the Shrew

Baptista
Vincentio
Lucentio
Petruchio
Katharina
Gremio
Hortensio
Tranio
Biondello
Grumio
Curtis
Nathaniel
Nicholas
Joseph
Philip
Peter
Bianca

The Tempest

Alonso
Sebastian
Prospero
Antonio
Ferdinand
Gonzalo
Adrian
Francisco
Caliban
Trinculo
Stephano
Miranda
Ariel
Iris
Ceres
Juno

Troilus and Cressida

Priam
Hector

Troilus
Paris
Deiphobus
Helenus
Margarelon
Aeneas
Antenor
Calchas
Pandarus
Agamemnon
Menelaus
Achilles
Ajax
Ulysses
Nestor
Diomedes
Patroclus
Thersites
Alexander
Helen
Andromache
Cassandra
Cressida

Twelfth Night (What You Will)
Orsino
Sebastian
Antonio
Valentine
Curio
Sir Toby Belch
Sir Andrew Aguecheek
Malvolio
Fabian
Feste
Olivia

Viola
Maria

The Two Gentlemen of Verona
Duke of Milan
Valentine
Proteus
Antonio
Thurio
Eglamour
Host
Outlaws
Speed
Launce
Panthino
Julia
Silvia
Lucetta

The Winter's Tale
Leontes
Mamillius
Camillo
Antigonus
Cleomenes
Dion
Polixenes
Florizel
Archidamus
Clown
Autolycus
Hermione
Perdita
Paulina
Emilia
Mopsa
Dorcas

Tragedies

Antony and Cleopatra
Mark Antony
Octavius Caesar
Lepidus
Sextus Pompeius
Domitius Enobarbus
Ventidius
Eros
Scarus
Dercetas
Demetrius
Philo
Mecaenas
Agrippa
Dolabella
Proculeius

Thyreus
Gallus
Menas
Menecrates
Varrius
Taurus
Canidius
Silius
Euphronius
Alexas
Seleucus
Diomedes
Cleopatra
Octavia
Charmian
Iras

Coriolanus

Caius Marcius (Coriolanus)
Titus Lartius
Cominius
Menenius Agrippa
Sicinius Velutus
Junius Brutus
Marcus
Tullus Aufidius
Volumnia
Virgilia
Valeria

Hamlet

Claudius
Hamlet
Polonius
Horatio
Laertes
Lucianus
Voltimand
Cornelius
Rosencrantz
Guildenstern
Osric
Marcellus
Bernardo
Francisco
Reynaldo
Fortinbras
Gertrude
Ophelia

Julius Caesar

Julius Caesar
Octavius Caesar
Marcus Antonius
Lepidus
Cicero
Publius
Popilius Lena
Marcus Brutus
Cassius
Casca
Trebonius
Ligarius
Decius Brutus
Metellus Cimber
Cinna
Flavius
Marullus
Artemidorus
Cinna
Lucilius
Titinius
Messala
Cato
Volumnius

Varro
Clitus
Claudius
Strato
Lucius
Dardanius
Pindarus
Calpurnia
Portia

King Lear

King Lear
King of France
Duke of Burgundy
Duke of Cornwall
Duke of Albany
Earl of Kent
Earl of Gloucester
Edgar
Edmund
Curan
Oswald
Goneril
Regan
Cordelia

Macbeth

Duncan
Malcolm
Donalbain
Macbeth
Banquo
Macduff
Lennox
Ross
Menteith
Angus
Caithness
Fleance
Siward
Young Siward
Seyton
Lady Macbeth
Lady Macduff
Hecate

Othello

Duke of Venice
Brabantio
Gratiano
Lodovico
Othello
Cassio
Iago
Roderigo
Montano
Desdemona
Emilia
Bianca

Romeo and Juliet

Escalus, Prince of Verona
Paris
Montague
Capulet
Romeo
Mercutio
Benvolio
Tybalt
Friar Laurence
Friar John
Balthasar
Sampson
Gregory
Peter
Abraham
Lady Montague
Lady Capulet
Juliet
Nurse

Timon of Athens

Timon
Lucius
Lucullus
Sempronius
Ventidius
Alcibiades
Apemantus
Flavius
Flaminius

Lucilius
Servilius
Caphis
Philotus
Titus
Lucius
Hortensius
Phrynia
Timandra

Titus Andronicus

Saturninus
Bassianus
Titus Andronicus
Marcus Andronicus
Lucius
Quintus
Martius
Mutius
Lucius
Publius
Sempronius
Caius
Valentine
Aemilius
Alarbus
Demetrius
Chiron
Aaron
Tamora
Lavinia

Histories

King Henry IV, Part I

King Henry IV
Prince Henry
Prince John of Lancaster
Westmoreland
Sir Walter Blunt
Thomas Percy
Henry Percy
Hotspur
Edmund Mortimer
Richard Scroop
Archibald
Owen Glendower
Sir Richard Vernon
Sir John Falstaff
Sir Michael
Poins
Gadshill
Peto
Bardolph
Francis
Lady Percy
Lady Mortimer
Mistress Quickly

Henry IV, Part II

Rumour
King Henry IV
Prince Henry of Wales
Clarence
Prince Humphrey of Gloucester
Earl of Warwick
Earl of Westmoreland
Earl of Surrey
Gower
Harcourt
Blunt
Earl of Northumberland
Archbishop of York
Lord Mowbray
Lord Hastings
Lord Bardolph
Sir John Colevile
Travers
Morton
Sir John Falstaff
Page
Bardolph
Pistol

Poins
Peto
Shallow
Silence
Davy
Mouldy
Shadow
Wart
Feeble
Bullcalf
Fang
Snare
Lady Northumberland
Lady Percy
Mistress Quickly
Doll Tearsheet

Henry V

King Henry V
Duke of Gloucester
Duke of Bedford
Duke of Exeter
Duke of York
Earl of Salisbury
Earl of Westmoreland
Earl of Warwick
Bishop of Canterbury
Bishop of Ely
Earl of Cambridge
Lord Scroop
Sir Thomas Grey
Sir Thomas Erpingham
Gower
Fluellen
Macmorris
Jamy
Bates
Court
Williams
Pistol
Nym
Bardolph
Charles VI, King of France
Lewis the Dauphin
Duke of Burgundy
Duke of Orleans
Duke of Bourbon
Constable
Rambures
Grandpre
Governor
Montjoy
Queen Isabel of France
Katharine
Alice

Henry VI, Part I

King Henry VI
Duke of Gloucester

Duke of Bedford
Thomas Beaufort, Duke of Exeter
Henry Beaufort, Bishop of Winchester
John Beaufort, Duke of Somerset
Richard Plantagenet
Plantagenet, Duke of York
Earl of Warwick
Earl of Salisbury
Earl of Suffolk
Lord Talbot
John Talbot
Edmund Mortimer
Sir John Fastolfe
Sir William Lucy
Sir William Glansdale
Sir Thomas Gargrave
Mayor of London
Woodvile
Vernon
Basset
Charles
Reignier
Duke of Burgundy
Duke of Alencon
Bastard of Orleans
Margaret
Countess of Auvergne
Joan La Pucelle (Joan of Arc)

Henry VI, Part II

King Henry VI
Humphrey, Duke of Gloucester
Cardinal Beaufort
Richard Plantagenet, Duke of York
Edward
Richard
Duke of Somerset
Duke of Suffolk
Duke of Buckingham
Lord Clifford
Young Clifford
Earl of Salisbury
Earl of Warwick
Lord Scales
Lord Say
Sir Humphrey Stafford
William Stafford
Sir John Stanley
Vaux
Matthew Goffe
Walter Whitmore
John Hume
John Southwell
Bolingbroke
Thomas Horner
Peter
Clerk of Chatham
Mayor

Simpcox
Alexander Iden
Jack Cade
George Bevis
John Holland
Dick the Butcher
Smith the Weaver
Michael
Queen Margaret
Eleanor, Duchess of Gloucester
Margaret Jourdain

Henry VI, Part III

King Henry VI
Edward, Prince of Wales
King Louis XI
Duke of Somerset
Duke of Exeter
Earl of Oxford
Earl of Northumberland
Earl of Westmoreland
Lord Clifford
Richard Plantagenet, Duke of York
George
Richard III
Duke of Norfolk
Marquess of Montague
Earl of Warwick
Earl of Pembroke
Lord Hastings
Lord Stafford
Sir John Mortimer (John Mortimer)
Sir Hugh Mortimer (Hugh Mortimer)
Henry of Richmond
Lord Rivers
Sir William Stanley
Sir John Montgomery
Sir John Somerville
Queen Margaret
Lady Grey
Bona

Henry VIII

King Henry VIII
Cardinal Wolsey
Cardinal Campeius
Capucius
Cranmer
Duke of Norfolk
Duke of Buckingham
Duke of Suffolk
Earl of Surrey
Gardiner
Bishop of Lincoln
Lord Abergavenny
Lord Sands
Sir Henry Guildford

Sir Thomas Lovell
Sir Anthony Denny
Sir Nicholas Vaux
Cromwell
Griffith
Doctor Butts
Brandon
Queen Katharine
Anne Bullen
Patience

King John

King John
Prince Henry
Arthur
Earl of Pembroke
Earl of Essex
Earl of Salisbury
Bigot
Hubert de Burgh
Robert Faulconbridge
Philip the Bastard
James Gurney
Peter of Pomfret
Philip, King of France
Lewis
Lymoges
Cardinal Pandulph
Melun
Chatillon
Queen Elinor
Constance
Blanch of Spain
Lady Faulconbridge

Richard II

King Richard II
John of Gaunt
Edmund of Langley, Duke of York
Henry Bolingbroke
Duke of Aumerle
Thomas Mowbray
Duke of Surrey
Earl of Salisbury
Lord Berkeley
Bushy
Bagot
Green
Earl of Northumberland
Henry Percy
Hotspur
Lord Ross
Lord Willoughby
Lord Fitzwater
Bishop of Carlisle
Lord Marshal
Sir Stephen Scroop

Sir Pierce of Exton
Queen
Duchess of York
Duchess of Gloucester

King Richard III
King Edward IV
King Richard III
Henry, Earl of Richmond
Cardinal Bourchier
Thomas Rotherham, Archbishop of York
John Morton, Bishop of Ely
Duke of Buckingham
Duke of Norfolk
Earl of Surrey
Earl Rivers
Marquis of Dorset
Lord Grey

Earl of Oxford
Lord Hastings
Lord Stanley, Earl of Derby
Lord Lovel
Sir Thomas
Vaughan
Sir Richard Ratcliff
Sir William Catesby
Sir James Tyrrel
Sir James Blount
Sir Walter Herbert
Sir Robert Brakenbury
Christopher Urswick
Tressel
Berkeley
Elizabeth
Margaret
Lady Anne

Sports

National Basketball Association Champions (1947–1998)

1947	Philadelphia Warriors	1973	New York Knickerbockers
1948	Baltimore Bullets	1974	Boston Celtics
1949	Minneapolis Lakers	1975	Golden State Warriors
1950	Minneapolis Lakers	1976	Boston Celtics
1951	Rochester Royals	1977	Portland Trailblazers
1952	Minneapolis Lakers	1978	Washington Bullets
1953	Minneapolis Lakers	1979	Seattle Super Sonics
1954	Minneapolis Lakers	1980	Los Angeles Lakers
1955	Syracuse Nationals	1981	Boston Celtics
1956	Philadelphia Warriors	1982	Los Angeles Lakers
1957	Boston Celtics	1983	Philadelphia 76ers
1958	St. Louis Hawks	1984	Boston Celtics
1959	Boston Celtics	1985	Los Angeles Lakers
1960	Boston Celtics	1986	Boston Celtics
1961	Boston Celtics	1987	Los Angeles Lakers
1962	Boston Celtics	1988	Los Angeles Lakers
1963	Boston Celtics	1989	Detroit Pistons
1964	Boston Celtics	1990	Detroit Pistons
1965	Boston Celtics	1991	Chicago Bulls
1966	Boston Celtics	1992	Chicago Bulls
1967	Philadelphia 76ers	1993	Chicago Bulls
1968	Boston Celtics	1994	Houston Rockets
1969	Boston Celtics	1995	Houston Rockets
1970	New York Knickerbockers	1996	Chicago Bulls
1971	Milwaukee Bucks	1997	Chicago Bulls
1972	Los Angeles Lakers	1998	Chicago Bulls

World Series Champions (1903–1998)

1903	Boston Red Sox (AL)	1907	Chicago Cubs (NL)
1904	No series	1908	Chicago Cubs (NL)
1905	New York Giants (NL)	1909	Pittsburgh Pirates (NL)
1906	Chicago White Sox (AL)	1910	Philadelphia Athletics (AL)

1911	Philadelphia Athletics (AL)	1956	New York Yankees (AL)
1912	Boston Red Sox (AL)	1957	Milwaukee Braves (NL)
1913	Philadelphia Athletics (AL)	1958	New York Yankees (AL)
1914	Boston Braves (NL)	1959	Los Angeles Dodgers (NL)
1915	Boston Red Sox (AL)	1960	Pittsburgh Pirates (NL)
1916	Boston Red Sox (AL)	1961	New York Yankees (AL)
1917	Chicago White Sox (AL)	1962	New York Yankees (AL)
1918	Boston Red Sox (AL)	1963	Los Angeles Dodgers (NL)
1919	Cincinnati Reds (NL)	1964	St. Louis Cardinals (NL)
1920	Cleveland Indians (AL)	1965	Los Angeles Dodgers (NL)
1921	New York Giants (NL)	1966	Baltimore Orioles (AL)
1922	New York Giants (NL)	1967	St. Louis Cardinals (NL)
1923	New York Yankees (AL)	1968	Detroit Tigers (AL)
1924	Washington Senators (AL)	1969	New York Mets (NL)
1925	Pittsburgh Pirates (NL)	1970	Baltimore Orioles (AL)
1926	St. Louis Cardinals (NL)	1971	Pittsburgh Pirates (NL)
1927	New York Yankees (AL)	1972	Oakland Athletics (AL)
1928	New York Yankees (AL)	1973	Oakland Athletics (AL)
1929	Philadelphia Athletics (AL)	1974	Oakland Athletics (AL)
1930	Philadelphia Athletics (AL)	1975	Cincinnati Reds (NL)
1931	St. Louis Cardinals (NL)	1976	Cincinnati Reds (NL)
1932	New York Yankees (AL)	1977	New York Yankees (AL)
1933	New York Giants (NL)	1978	New York Yankees (AL)
1934	St. Louis Cardinals (NL)	1979	Pittsburgh Pirates (NL)
1935	Detroit Tigers (AL)	1980	Philadelphia Phillies (NL)
1936	New York Yankees (AL)	1981	Los Angeles Dodgers (NL)
1937	New York Yankees (AL)	1982	St. Louis Cardinals (NL)
1938	New York Yankees (AL)	1983	Baltimore Orioles (AL)
1939	New York Yankees (AL)	1983	Baltimore Orioles (AL)
1940	Cincinnati Reds (NL)	1984	Detroit Tigers (AL)
1941	New York Yankees (AL)	1985	Kansas City Royals (AL)
1942	St. Louis Cardinals (NL)	1986	New York Mets (NL)
1943	New York Yankees (AL)	1987	Minnesota Twins (AL)
1944	St. Louis Cardinals (NL)	1988	Los Angeles Dodgers (NL)
1945	Detroit Tigers (AL)	1989	Oakland Athletics (AL)
1946	St. Louis Cardinals (NL)	1990	Cincinnati Reds (NL)
1947	New York Yankees (AL)	1991	Minnesota Twins (AL)
1948	Cleveland Indians (AL)	1992	Toronto Blue Jays (AL)
1949	New York Yankees (AL)	1993	Toronto Blue Jays (AL)
1950	New York Yankees (AL)	1994	Cancelled
1951	New York Yankees (AL)	1995	Atlanta Braves (NL)
1952	New York Yankees (AL)	1996	New York Yankees (AL)
1953	New York Yankees (AL)	1997	Florida Marlins (NL)
1954	New York Giants (NL)	1998	New York Yankees (AL)
1955	Brooklyn Dodgers (NL)		

Super Bowl Champions (1967–1998)

I	1967	Green Bay Packers	XI	1977	Oakland Raiders
II	1968	Green Bay Packers	XII	1978	Dallas Cowboys
III	1969	New York Jets	XIII	1979	Pittsburgh Steelers
IV	1970	Kansas City Chiefs	XIV	1980	Pittsburgh Steelers
V	1971	Baltimore Colts	XV	1981	Oakland Raiders
VI	1972	Dallas Cowboys	XVI	1982	San Francisco 49ers
VII	1973	Miami Dolphins	XVII	1983	Washington Redskins
VIII	1974	Miami Dolphins	XVIII	1984	Los Angeles Raiders
IX	1975	Pittsburgh Steelers	XIX	1985	San Francisco 49ers
X	1976	Pittsburgh Steelers	XX	1986	Chicago Bears

XXI	1987	New York Giants	XXVII	1993	Dallas Cowboys
XXII	1988	Washington Redskins	XXVIII	1994	Dallas Cowboys
XXIII	1989	San Francisco 49ers	XXIX	1995	San Francisco 49ers
XXIV	1990	San Francisco 49ers	XXX	1996	Dallas Cowboys
XXV	1991	New York Giants	XXXI	1997	Green Bay Packers
XXVI	1992	Washington Redskins	XXXII	1998	Denver Broncos

NHL Stanley Cup Winners (1917–1998)

1917–18	Toronto Arenas	1957–58	Montreal Canadiens
1918–19	Cup not awarded: influenza epidemic	1958–59	Montreal Canadiens
		1959–60	Montreal Canadiens
1919–20	Ottawa Senators	1960–61	Chicago Blackhawks
1920–21	Ottawa Senators	1961–62	Toronto Maple Leafs
1921–22	Toronto St. Pats	1962–63	Toronto Maple Leafs
1922–23	Ottawa Senators	1963–64	Toronto Maple Leafs
1923–24	Montreal Canadiens	1964–65	Montreal Canadiens
1924–25	Victoria Cougars	1965–66	Montreal Canadiens
1925–26	Montreal Maroons	1966–67	Toronto Maple Leafs
1926–27	Ottawa Senators	1967–68	Montreal Canadiens
1927–28	New York Rangers	1968–69	Montreal Canadiens
1928–29	Boston Bruins	1969–70	Boston Bruins
1929–30	Montreal Canadiens	1970–71	Montreal Canadiens
1930–31	Montreal Canadiens	1971–72	Boston Bruins
1931–32	Toronto Maple Leafs	1972–73	Montreal Canadiens
1932–33	New York Rangers	1973–74	Philadelphia Flyers
1933–34	Chicago Blackhawks	1974–75	Philadelphia Flyers
1934–35	Montreal Maroons	1975–76	Montreal Canadiens
1935–36	Detroit Red Wings	1976–77	Montreal Canadiens
1936–37	Detroit Red Wings	1977–78	Montreal Canadiens
1937–38	Chicago Blackhawks	1978–79	Montreal Canadiens
1938–39	Boston Bruins	1979–80	New York Islanders
1939–40	New York Rangers	1980–81	New York Islanders
1940–41	Boston Bruins	1981–82	New York Islanders
1941–42	Toronto Maple Leafs	1982–83	New York Islanders
1942–43	Detroit Red Wings	1983–84	Edmonton Oilers
1943–44	Montreal Canadiens	1984–85	Edmonton Oilers
1944–45	Toronto Maple Leafs	1985–86	Montreal Canadiens
1945–46	Montreal Canadiens	1986–87	Edmonton Oilers
1946–47	Toronto Maple Leafs	1987–88	Edmonton Oilers
1947–48	Toronto Maple Leafs	1988–89	Calgary Flames
1948–49	Toronto Maple Leafs	1989–90	Edmonton Oilers
1949–50	Detroit Red Wings	1990–91	Pittsburgh Penguins
1950–51	Toronto Maple Leafs	1991–92	Pittsburgh Penguins
1951–52	Detroit Red Wings	1992–93	Montreal Canadiens
1952–53	Montreal Canadiens	1993–94	New York Rangers
1953–54	Detroit Red Wings	1994–95	New Jersey Devils
1954–55	Detroit Red Wings	1995–96	Colorado Avalanche
1955–56	Montreal Canadiens	1996–97	Detroit Red Wings
1956–57	Montreal Canadiens	1997–98	Detroit Red Wings

Kentucky Derby and Triple Crown Winners (1875–1998)

(** denotes Triple Crown Winner)		1879	Lard Murphy
1875	Aristides	1880	Fonso
1876	Vagrant	1881	Hindoo
1877	BadenBaden	1882	Apollo
1878	Day Star	1883	Leonatus

1884	Buchanan	1942	Shut Out
1885	Joe Cotton	1943	Count Fleet**
1886	Ben Ali	1944	Pensive
1887	Montrose	1945	Hoop Jr.
1888	Macbeth II	1946	Assault**
1889	Spokane	1947	Jet Pilot
1890	Riley	1948	Citation**
1891	Kingman	1949	Ponder
1892	Azra	1950	Middleground
1893	Lookout	1951	Count Turf
1894	Chant	1952	Hill Gail
1895	Halma	1953	Dark Star
1896	Ben Brush	1954	Determine
1897	Typhoon II	1955	Swaps
1898	Plaudit	1956	Needles
1899	Manuel	1957	Iron Liege
1900	Lieut. Gibson	1958	Tim Tam
1901	His Eminence	1959	Tomy Lee
1902	AlanADale	1960	Venetian Way
1903	Judge Himes	1961	Carry Back
1904	Elwood	1962	Decidedly
1905	Agile	1963	Chateaugay
1906	Sir Huon	1964	Northern Dancer
1907	Pink Star	1965	Lucky Debonair
1908	Stone Street	1966	Kauai King
1909	Wintergreen	1967	Proud Clarion
1910	Donau	1968	Forward Pass
1911	Meridian	1969	Majestic Prince
1912	Worth	1970	Dust Commander
1913	Donerail	1971	Canonero II
1914	Old Rosebud	1972	Riva Ridge
1915	Regret	1973	Secretariat**
1916	George Smith	1974	Cannonade
1917	Omar Khyyam	1975	Foolish Pleasure
1918	Exterminator	1976	Bold Forbes
1919	Sir Barton**	1977	Seattle Slew**
1920	Paul Jones	1978	Affirmed**
1921	Behave Yourself	1979	Spectacular Bid
1922	Morvich	1980	Genuine Risk
1923	Zev	1981	Pleasant Colony
1924	Black Gold	1982	Gato del Sol
1925	Flying Ebony	1983	Sunny's Halo
1926	Bubbling Over	1984	Swale
1927	Whiskery	1985	Spend a Buck
1928	Reigh Count	1986	Ferdinand
1929	Clyde Van Dusen	1987	Alysheba
1930	Gallant Fox**	1988	Winning Colors
1931	Twenty Grand	1989	Sunday Silence
1932	Burgoo King	1990	Unbridled
1933	Brokers Tip	1991	Strike the Gold
1934	Cavalcade	1992	Lil E Tee
1935	Omaha**	1993	Sea Hero
1936	Bold Venture	1994	Go for Gin
1937	War Admiral**	1995	Thunder Gulch
1938	Lawrin	1996	Grindstone
1939	Johnstown	1997	Silver Charm
1940	Gallahadion	1998	Real Quiet
1941	Whirlaway**		

1919	Sir Barton
1930	Gallant Fox
1935	Omaha
1937	War Admiral
1941	Whirlaway
1943	Count Fleet

1946	Assault
1948	Citation
1973	Secretariat
1977	Seattle Slew
1978	Affirmed

Sports — U.S. and Canadian Professional Teams

CITY, STATE/PROVINCE OR AREA	MAJOR LEAGUE BASEBALL (AL=AMERICAN LEAGUE, NL=NATIONAL LEAGUE)	FOOTBALL (NFL; CFL = CANADIAN FOOTBALL LEAGUE)	BASKETBALL (NBA)	HOCKEY (NHL)
Phoenix/ Arizona	Diamondbacks	Cardinals	Suns (Phoenix)	Coyotes
Atlanta	Braves	Falcons	Hawks	—
Baltimore	Orioles	Ravens	Bullets	—
Boston/ New England	Red Sox	Patriots (New England)	Celtics	Bruins
Buffalo	—	Bills	—	Sabres
Calgary	—	Stampeders (CFL)	—	Flames
Charlotte/ Carolina	—	Panthers	Hornets (Charlotte)	Hurricanes
Chicago	Cubs (NL), White Sox (AL)	Bears	Bulls	Blackhawks
Cincinnati	Reds	Bengals	—	—
Cleveland	Indians	Browns	Cavaliers	—
Dallas/Texas	Rangers (Texas)	Cowboys	Mavericks	Stars
Denver/ Colorado	Rockies (Colorado)	Broncos	Nuggets	Avalanche (Colorado)
Detroit	Tigers	Lions	Pistons	Red Wings
Edmonton	—	Eskimos (CFL)	—	Oilers
Houston	Astros	—	Rockets	—
Indianapolis/ Indiana	—	Colts	Pacers (Indiana)	—
Jacksonville/ Florida	—	Jaguars	—	—
Kansas City	Royals	Chiefs	—	—
Los Angeles/ Anaheim	Dodgers (Los Angeles, NL), Angels (Anaheim, AL)	—	Lakers, Clippers	Kings (Los Angeles), Mighty Ducks (Anaheim)
Miami/Florida	Marlins (Florida)	Dolphins	Heat	Panthers (Florida)
Milwaukee/ Green Bay	Brewers	Packers (Green Bay)	Bucks	—
Minnesota	Twins	Vikings	Timberwolves	—
Montreal	Expos	Alouettes (CFL)	—	Canadiens
Nashville/ Tennessee	—	Oilers (Tennessee)	—	Predators
New Jersey	—	—	Nets	Devils
New Orleans	—	Saints	—	—
New York	Mets (NL), Yankees (AL)	Giants (NFC), Jets (AFC)	Knicks	Rangers, Islanders
Orlando	—	—	Magic	

City, State/Province or Area	Major League Baseball (AL=American League, NL=National League)	Football (NFL; CFL = Canadian Football League)	Basketball (NBA)	Hockey (NHL)
Ottawa	—	Rough Riders (CFL)	—	Senators
Philadelphia	Phillies	Eagles	76ers	Flyers
Pittsburgh	Pirates	Steelers	—	Penguins
Portland	—	—	Trailblazers	—
Sacramento	—	—	Kings	—
San Antonio	—	—	Spurs	—
San Diego	Padres	Chargers	—	—
San Francisco/ San Jose/ Oakland/	Giants (San Francisco, NL), Athletics (Oakland, AL)	49ers, (San Francisco, NFC) Raiders (Oakland, AFC)	Warriors (Golden State)	Sharks (San Jose)
Seattle	Mariners	Seahawks	SuperSonics	—
St. Louis	Cardinals	Rams	—	Blues
Tampa Bay	Devil Rays	Buccaneers	—	Lightning
Tennessee	Oilers	—	—	Predators
Toronto	Blue Jays	Argonauts (CFL)	Raptors	Maple Leafs
Utah	—	—	Jazz	—
Vancouver/ British Columbia	—	Lions (British Columbia, CFL)	Grizzlies	Canucks
Washington, D.C.	—	Redskins	Wizards	Capitals

Supreme Court Chief Justices (1789–1998)

Chief Justice	Year Born	Year Appointed Chief Justice	President Who Appointed
John Jay	1745	1789	George Washington
John Rutledge	1739	1795	George Washington
Oliver Ellsworth	1745	1796	George Washington
John Marshall	1755	1801	John Adams
Roger B. Taney	1777	1836	Andrew Jackson
Salmon P. Chase	1808	1864	Abraham Lincoln
Morrison R. Waite	1816	1874	Ulysses S. Grant
Melville W. Fuller	1833	1888	Grover Cleveland
Edward D. White	1845	1910	William Taft
William H. Taft	1857	1921	Warren Harding
Charles E. Hughes	1862	1930	Herbert Hoover
Harlan F. Stone	1872	1941	Franklin D. Roosevelt
Fred M. Vinson	1890	1946	Harry Truman
Earl Warren	1891	1953	Dwight D. Eisenhower
Warren E. Burger	1907	1969	Richard Nixon
William Rehnquist	1924	1986	Ronald Reagan

The United States and Its Territories

State	Abbreviation	Capital	Nickname	Bird	Flower	Date Admitted	Order Admitted	Motto	Major Cities	Geography Facts
Alabama	AL	Montgomery	"Heart of Dixie"	Yellow-hammer	Camellia	December 14, 1819	22nd	"We dare to defend our rights"	Birmingham, Mobile, Montgomery	
Alaska	AK	Juneau	"Last Frontier"	Willow ptarmigan	Forget-me-not	January 3, 1959	49th	"North to the future"	Anchorage, Fairbanks, Juneau	*Glaciers:* Muir, Columbia *Islands:* Kodiak, Aleutians Mt. McKinley
Arizona	AZ	Phoenix	"Grand Canyon State"	Cactus wren	Saguaro cactus blossom	February 14, 1912	48th	"Ditat deus" (God enriches)	Phoenix, Tucson	Painted Desert *Lakes:* Mead, Powell Colorado River Grand Canyon
Arkansas	AR	Little Rock	"Land of Opportunity"	Mocking-bird	Apple blossom	June 15, 1836	25th	"Regnat populus" (Let the people rule)	Little Rock, Fort Smith, Fayetteville, Hot Springs	*Mountains:* Blue, Ozarks Mississippi River
California	CA	Sacramento	"Golden State"	California Valley quail	Golden poppy	September 9, 1850	31st	"Eureka" (I have found it)	Los Angeles, San Francisco, San Diego, Sacramento	*Deserts:* Mojave, Colorado *Islands:* Santa Cruz, Santa Catalina San Andreas Fault *Mountain Peaks:* Shasta, Whitney Yosemite National Park Death Valley
Colorado	CO	Denver	"Centennial State"	Lark bunting	Columbine	August 1, 1876	38th	"Nil sine numine" (Nothing without providence)	Denver, Colorado Springs	Pike's Peak *Rivers:* Rio Grande, Colorado, Arkansas

State	Abbr.	Capital	Nickname	State bird	State flower	Statehood	Order	Motto	Largest cities	Geographic features
Connecticut	CT	Hartford	"Constitution State"	American robin	Mountain laurel	January 9, 1788	5th	"Qui transtulit sustinet" (He who transplanted still sustains)	Bridgeport, Hartford, New Haven	Delaware River
Delaware	DE	Dover	"First State"	Blue hen chicken	Peach Blossom	December 7, 1787	1st	"Liberty and independence"	Wilmington, Dover, Newark, Milford	Delaware River
District of Columbia	DC	—	—	Wood thrush	American Beauty rose	December 1, 1800 (became nation's capital)	—	"Justitia omnibus" (Justice for all)	—	Potomac River
Florida	FL	Tallahassee	"Sunshine State"	Mockingbird	Orange blossom	March 3, 1845	27th	"In God we trust"	Miami, Jacksonville, Tampa, St. Petersburg, Orlando, Fort Lauderdale	Florida Keys, Key Largo, Lake Okeechobee
Georgia	GA	Atlanta	"Empire State of the South"	Brown thrasher	Cherokee rose	January 2, 1788	4th	"Wisdom, justice, moderation"	Atlanta, Columbus, Savannah, Macon, Athens, Augusta	St. Simon Island, Savannah River, *Mountains:* Blue Ridge, Appalachian
Hawaii	HI	Honolulu	"Aloha State"	Hawaiian goose	Yellow hibiscus	August 21, 1959	50th	"Ua mau ke ea o ka aina I ka pono" (The life of the land is perpetuated in righteousness)	Honolulu, Hilo, Kailua	*Islands:* Maui, Oahu, Kauai, Lanai, Hawaii, Niihau, Molokai, Kahoolawe, *Mountains, volcanoes:* Mauna Kea, Mauna Loa, Kilauea
Idaho	ID	Boise	"Gem State"	Mountain bluebird	Syringa	July 3, 1890	43rd	"Esto perpetua" (May it last forever)	Boise, Pocatello, Idaho Falls, Lewiston	Coeur d' Alene Lake, *Mountains:* Bitterroot, Rocky, Snake River
Illinois	IL	Springfield	"Prairie State"	Cardinal	Native violet	December 3, 1818	21st	"State sovereingty— national unity"	Chicago, Rockford, Peoria, Springfield	*Rivers:* Ohio, Wabash, Mississippi, Lake Michigan

The United States and Its Territories (continued)

State	Abbreviation	Capital	Nickname	Bird	Flower	Date Admitted	Order Admitted	Motto	Major Cities	Geography Facts
Indiana	IN	Indianapolis	"Hoosier State"	Cardinal	Peony	December 11, 1816	19th	"The crossroads of America"	Indianapolis, Fort Wayne, Evansville, Gary, South Bend	*Rivers:* Ohio, Wabash Lake Michigan
Iowa	IA	Des Moines	"Hawkeye State"	Eastern goldfinch	Wild rose	December 28, 1846	29th	"Our liberties we prize and our rights we will maintain"	Des Moines, Cedar Rapids, Davenport, Sioux City, Iowa City	*Rivers:* Mississippi, Missouri
Kansas	KS	Topeka	"Sunflower State"	Western meadowlark	Native sunflower	January 29, 1861	34th	"Ad astra per aspera" (To the stars through adversity)	Wichita, Kansas City, Topeka	Arkansaw River
Kentucky	KY	Frankfort	"Bluegrass State"	Cardinal	Goldenrod	June 1, 1792	15th	"United we stand, divided we fall"	Louisville, Lexington, Bowling Green	*Rivers:* Mississippi, Ohio, Tennessee
Louisiana	LA	Baton Rouge	"Pelican State"	Eastern brown pelican	Magnolia	April 30, 1812	18th	"Union, justice, confidence"	New Orleans, Baton Rouge, Shreveport, Lafayette	Mississippi River Lake Pontchartrain Mississippi Delta Bayous
Maine	ME	Augusta	"Pine Tree State"	Chickadee	Pine cone and tassel	March 15, 1820	23rd	"Dirigo" (I direct)	Portland, Lewiston, Bangor, Augusta	Kennebec River *Mountains:* Cadillac, Katahdin
Maryland	MD	Annapolis	"Old Line State"	Baltimore oriole	Black-eyed Susan	April 28, 1788	7th	"Fatti maschii, parole femine" (Manly deeds, womanly words)	Baltimore, Rockville, Frederick	Potomac River Chesapeake Bay
Massachusetts	MA	Boston	"Bay State"	Chickadee	Mayflower	February 6, 1788	6th	"Ense petit placidam sub libertate quietem" (By the sword we seek peace, but peace only under liberty)	Boston, Springfield, Worcester, Lowell, New Bedford	Connecticut River Cape Cod Berkshire Mountains

State		Capital	Nickname	Bird	Flower	Date admitted	Order	Motto	Cities	Geography
Michigan	MI	Lansing	"Wolverine State"	Robin	Apple blossom	January 26, 1837	26th	"If you are looking for a beautiful peninsula, look around you"	Detroit, Ann Arbor, Lansing, Grand Rapids, Dearborn	*Lakes:* Michigan, Superior, Huron, Erie, Winnebago; Curwood Mountain; Upper Peninsula; Mississippi River
Minnesota	MN	St. Paul	"North Star State"	Common loon	Showy lady's slipper	May 11, 1858	32nd	"L'etoile du nord" (The star of the North)	Minneapolis, St. Paul, Duluth, Rochester	*Lakes:* Superior, Lake of the Woods; *Rivers:* Mississippi, Red River of the North; Minnehaha Falls, Eagle Mt.
Mississippi	MS	Jackson	"Magnolia State"	Mocking-bird	Magnolia	December 10, 1817	20th	"Virtute et armis" (By virtue and arms)	Biloxi, Jackson, Hattiesburg, Gulfport	Mississippi River and Delta
Missouri	MO	Jefferson City	"Show Me State"	Bluebird	Hawthorn	August 10, 1821	24th	"Salus populi suprema lex esto" (The welfare of the people shall be the supreme law)	Kansas City, St. Louis, Independence, St. Joseph, Springfield	*Rivers:* Missouri, Mississippi; Lake of the Ozarks; *Hills:* Ozarks
Montana	MT	Helena	"Treasure State"	Western meadowlark	Bitterroot	November 8, 1889	41st	"Oro y plata" (Gold and silver)	Billings, Great Falls, Butte, Missoula, Bozeman, Helena	*Rivers:* Missouri, Yellowstone; *Mountains:* Bittersweet, Rocky. Granite Peak; *Lakes:* Fort Peck, Flathead
Nebraska	NE	Lincoln	"Cornhusker State"	Western meadowlark	Goldenrod	March 1, 1867	37th	"Equality before the law"	Omaha, Lincoln, Grand Island, Kearney	*Rivers:* Platte, Missouri
Nevada	NV	Carson City	"Silver State"	Mountain bluebird	Sagebrush	October 31, 1864	36th	"All for our country"	Las Vegas, Reno, Carson City	Colorado River; *Mountains:* Sierra Nevada, Butte, Carson; *Lakes:* Tahoe, Walker, Mead, Pyramid; Amargosa Desert
New Hampshire	NH	Concord	"Granite State"	Purple finch	Purple lilac	June 21, 1788	9th	"Live free or die"	Manchester, Nashua, Concord, Dover	*Rivers:* Connecticut, Merrimack; Lake Winnipesaukee; *Mountains:* White, Washington

The United States and Its Territories (continued)

State	Abbreviation	Capital	Nickname	Bird	Flower	Date Admitted	Order Admitted	Motto	Major Cities	Geography Facts
New Jersey	NJ	Trenton	"Garden State"	Eastern goldfinch	Purple violet	December 18, 1787	3rd	"Liberty and prosperity"	Newark, Jersey City, Trenton, Camden	*Rivers:* Hudson, Delaware *Mountains:* Ramapo, Kittatinny *Cape* May
New Mexico	NM	Santa Fe	"Land of Enchantment"	Roadrunner	Yucca	January 6, 1912	47th	"Crescit eundo" (It grows as it goes)	Albuquerque, Las Cruces, Santa Fe, Roswell	*Rivers:* Rio Grande, Pecos, Gila *Mountains:* Rocky, San Mateo, San Andres
New York	NY	Albany	"Empire State"	Bluebird	Rose	July 26, 1788	11th	"Excelsior" (Higher)	New York, Buffalo, Rochester, Syracuse, Albany, Utica, Schenectady	*Rivers:* Hudson, Delaware, St. Lawrence, Mohawk *Islands:* Long, Staten, Fisher's, Gardiner's, Thousand Islands *Lakes:* Erie, Ontario, Champlain, George, Finger Lakes, Placid, Saranac Erie Canal *Mountains:* Catskills, Adirondacks, Poconos
North Carolina	NC	Raleigh	"Tar Heel State"	Cardinal	Dogwood	November 21, 1789	12th	"Esse quam videri" (To be rather than to seem)	Charlotte, Greensboro, Raleigh, Winston-Salem	*Rivers:* Cape Fear, Roanoke *Mountains:* Blue Ridge, Great Smoky, Appalachian *Islands:* Roanoke, Outer Banks *Capes:* Hatteras, Lookout

State	Abbr.	Capital	Nickname	State Bird	State Flower	Statehood	Order	Motto	Major Cities	Geographic Features
North Dakota	ND	Bismarck	"Peace Garden State"	Western meadowlark	Wild prairie rose	November 2, 1889	39th	"Liberty and union, now and forever, one and inseparable"	Fargo, Grand Forks, Bismarck, Minot	*Rivers:* Missouri, James, Red River of the North White Butte Lake Sakakawea
Ohio	OH	Columbus	"Buckeye State"	Cardinal	Scarlet carnation	March 1, 1803	17th	"With God all things are possible"	Columbus, Cleveland, Cincinnati, Toledo, Akron, Dayton, Youngstown	*Rivers:* Ohio, Miami, Maumee *Mountains:* Allegheny Mountains Lake Erie
Oklahoma	OK	Oklahoma City	"Sooner State"	Scissortail flycatcher	Mistletoe	November 15, 1907	46th	"Labor omnia vincit" (Work overcomes all obstacles)	Oklahoma City, Tulsa, Norman, Lawton	*Rivers:* Arkansaw, Red *Mountains:* Ozark, Ouachita *Lakes:* Texoma, Eufaula
Oregon	OR	Salem	"Beaver State"	Western meadowlark	Oregon grape	February 14, 1859	33rd	"The Union"	Portland, Eugene, Salem, Medford, Corvallis	*Mountains:* Hood, Jefferson, Cascade, Klamath, Coastal *Lakes:* Crater Lake, Malheur *Rivers:* Columbia, Willamette, Hood
Pennsylvania	PA	Harrisburg	"Keystone State"	Ruffled grouse	Mountain laurel	December 12, 1787	2nd	"Virtue, liberty, and independence"	Philadelphia, Pittsburgh, Erie, Allentown, Scranton, Reading, Harrisburg	*Rivers:* Ohio, Monongahela, Allegheny, Susquehanna *Mountains:* Allegheny, Appalachian, Pocono Lake Erie
Rhode Island	RI	Providence	"Little Rhody"	Rhode Island Red	Violet	May 29, 1790	13th	"Hope"	Providence, Newport, Warwick, Pawtucket	*Islands:* Block, Prudence, Conanicut, Rhode Narraganset Bay
South Carolina	SC	Columbia	"Palmetto State"	Carolina wren	Yellow jessamine	May 23, 1788	8th	"Prepared in mind and deed?" "While I breathe I hope"	Columbia, Charleston, Greenville	*Mountains:* Blue Ridge, Sassafras Savannah River Lake Marion

The United States and Its Territories (continued)

State	Abbre-viation	Capital	Nickname	Bird	Flower	Date Admitted	Order Admitted	Motto	Major Cities	Geography Facts
South Dakota	SD	Pierre	"Coyote State"	Pheasant	Pasque-flower	November 2, 1889	40th	"Under God the people rule"	Sioux Falls, Rapid City, Aberdeen, Pierre	*Rivers:* Missouri, Cheyenne, James *Badlands* *Black Hills* *Lake Oahe*
Tennessee	TN	Nashville	"Volunteer State"	Mocking-bird	Iris	June 1, 1796	16th	"Agriculture and commerce"	Memphis, Knoxville, Nashville, Chattanooga	*Mountains:* Great Smoky, Appalachian, Blue Ridge, Lookout *Rivers:* Cumberland, Tennessee
Texas	TX	Austin	"Lone Star State"	Mocking-bird	Bluebonnet	December 29, 1845	28th	"Friendship"	Houston, Dallas, San Antonio, El Paso, Austin, Fort Worth	*Rivers:* Red, Pecos, Rio Grande, Brazos *Guadalupe Peak* *Islands:* Matagorda, San Jose, Padre *Gulf of Mexico,* *Galveston Bay*
Utah	UT	Salt Lake City	"Beehive State"	Seagull	Sego lily	January 4, 1896	45th	"Industry"	Salt Lake City, Provo, Ogden	*Rivers:* Snake, Colorado *Great Salt Lake* *Great Salt Lake Desert* *Kings Peak*
Vermont	VT	Montpelier	"Green Mountain State"	Hermit thrush	Red clover	March 4, 1791	14th	"Freedom and unity"	Burlington, Rutland, Montpelier	*Lake Champlain* *Connecticut River* *Green Mountains*
Virginia	VA	Richmond	"Old Dominion State"	Cardinal	Dogwood	June 25, 1788	10th	"Sic semper tyrannis" (Thus always to tyrants)	Virginia Beach, Norfolk, Richmond, Hampton, Lynchburg, Alexandria	*Rivers:* Potomac, Roanoke, Shenandoah, Rappahannock, James *Mountains:* Allegheny, Blue Ridge, Appalachian *Cumberland Gap* *Chesapeake Bay*

State	Abbr.	Capital	Nickname	State Bird	State Flower	Date	Order	Motto	Major Cities	Geography
Washington	WA	Olympia	"Evergreen State"	Willow goldfinch	Rhododendron	November 11, 1899	42nd	"Alki" (By and by)	Seattle, Spokane, Tacoma, Vancouver	*Rivers:* Columbia, Snake, Yakima, Spokane; *Mountains:* Cascade, Olympic, Rocky, Adams, Baker, Rainier, St. Helens, Glacier; Puget Sound; Olympic Peninsula
West Virginia	WV	Charleston	"Mountain State"	Cardinal	Big rhododendron	June 20, 1863	35th	"Montani semper liberi" (Mountaineers are always free)	Charleston, Huntington, Wheeling	*Rivers:* Ohio, Potomac; *Mountains:* Allegheny, Blue Ridge, Appalachian
Wisconsin	WI	Madison	"Badger State"	Robin	Wood violet	May 29, 1848	30th	"Forward"	Milwaukee, Madison, Green Bay, Racine	*Lakes:* Michigan, Superior, Winnebago, Mendota; *Rivers:* Mississippi, St. Croix, Wisconsin, Chippewa Green Bay
Wyoming	WY	Cheyenne	"Equality State"	Meadowlark	Indian paintbrush	July 10, 1890	44th	"Equal rights"	Cheyenne, Casper, Laramie	*Rivers:* Snake, Bighorn, North Platte, Powder; *Mountains:* Rocky, Teton, Bighorn, Granite, Sierra Madre, Laramie, Gannett Peak; Heart Lake; Devil's Tower

U. S. Territories

American Samoa
Canal Zone
Guam
Northern Mariana Islands
Puerto Rico
Trust Territory of the Pacific
Virgin Islands

Weights and Measures

International System
(Systeme International, SI) Units

Category	Name	Abbreviation	Other International System Units
Length	meter	m	farad (F): capacity to store electricity
Mass	kilogram	kg	hertz (Hz): frequency of a periodic phenome-
Time	second	s	non
Electric current	ampere	A	joule (J): work or energy
Temperature	kelvin	K	newton (N): force
Amount of substance	mole	mol	ohm (*): resistance of electrical conductor
Luminous intensity	candela	cd	pascal (Pa): pressure
			volt (V): electric potential
			watt (W): measure of power, rate of doing work

International System Prefixes

atto	femto	micro	tera
centi	giga	milli	yocto
deca	hecto	nano	yotta
deci	kilo	peta	zepto
exa	mega	pico	zetta

U.K. (Imperial) System of Measurements

Length

inch	yard	furlong
foot	chain	mile

Area

acre

Capacity

ounce	gallon
pint	

Volume

gills	quart
pint	gallon

Mass (Avoirdupois)

grain	stones
ounces	hundredweight (cwt)
pounds	ton

Troy Weights

grains	ounce
pennyweight	pound

Apothecaries' Measures

minim	ounce
scruple	pint
drachm	

Apothecaries' Weights

grain	ounce
scruple	pound
drachm	

U. S. System of Measurements

Length

inch	furlong
foot	rod
yard	mile

Area

square inch	square mile
square foot	acre
square yard	section
square rod	township

Capacity/Volume

ounce	peck
pint	bushel
quart	gallon
gills	

Mass

grain	stone
ounce	hundredweight (cwt)
pound	ton

Troy Weights

grain	ounce
pennyweight	pound

Apothecaries' Measures

minim	ounce
dram	pint

Apothecaries' Weights

grains	ounce
scruple	pound
drams	

Complete List of Units

acre
angstrom
are
atmosphere
bar
barleycorn
barrels (oil)
becquerel (Bq) (activity, ionizing radiations)
bel (power ratio)
British thermal unit
Btu
bushel
calorie
carat, metric
centigrade heat unit
centiliter
centimeter
centimeter of mercury or water
centimeter per minute, etc.
chains (surveyors')
circular inche
coulomb (C) (quantity of electricity)
cubic (+ any unit)
cubit
decibel (sound)
deciliter
denier
drex
dyne (force)
ells (UK)

em (pica)
erg (energy)
erg (torque)
fathom
feet
fluid ounce
foot pounds-force
furlong
gallon
gigajoule
gigawatt
grain
grain per gallon
gram
gram-force centimeter
gram per (any volume)
gram per area
gram per cm
gray (Gy) (absorbed dose)
hand
hectareshenry (H) (inductance)
hide
horsepower
horsepower hour
hundredweight
inch
joule
kilogram
kilojoule
kilojoule per hour, etc.
kilometers per hour, etc.

kilopascal
kilowatt
kilowatt hour
kip (force)
kip per square inch
knot
league
light-year
link (surveyors')
liter
lumen (light)
lux (light)
Mach number
meter
meters per second, etc.
mho (conductance)
micron (= micrometers)
mile
mile per gallon
mile per hour, etc.
millibar
newton
ohm (resistance)
ounce
parsec
pascal
perch (= rod or pole)
phot (illumination)
pica
pint
point (printers')
pound
poundal

poundal per square foot
pound per foot
pound per volume
quart
rad (radiation)
rem (radiation)
rhe (fluidity)
rood
siemens (conductance)
slug (or g-pounds)
sone (sound)
stone
square (+ any unit)
square (of timber)
sthene
tesla (T) (magnetic flux density, induction)
tex
therm
tonne
ton
torr (pressure)
township
troy
ounce
viscosity (poise)
volt (electromotive force)
watt
weber (electricity)
yard

Measurements of Length

angstrom
astronomical unit
aune (Belgium)
barleycorns
centimeter
chain (surveyors')
chih (China)
cubit
diraa (Egypt)
duim (Netherlands)
ell (UK)
em (pica)

fathom
feet (UK and US)
fod (Denmark)
fot (Russia)
furlong
fut (Russia)
hand
inch
ken (Japan)
kilometer
koss (India)

latro (Czech Republic)
league
light-year
link (surveyors')
meter (m)
micron (=micrometers)
mile (nautical)
mile (UK and US)
parsec
perch (=rods or poles)

pica (computer)
pica (printers')
picki (Greece)
pik (Egypt)
point (computer)
point (printers')
pole (UK)
rod (UK)
sun (Japan)
toise (France)
tsun (China)
yard

Measurements of Area

acre
are
cho (Japan)
chuo (China)
circular inch
hectare

hide
mou (China)
rai (Thailand)
rood
square (of timber)
square centimeter

square feet (UK and US)
square feet (US survey)
square inch
square kilometer

square meters
square miles
square millimeters
square rod (or pole)
square yard
township

Measurements of Volume or Capacity

aum (South Africa)	cubic inch	gallon, liquid (US)	oke (Cyprus)
barrel (oil)	cubic meter	hin (Israel)	pint (UK), dry (US)
bath (Israel)	cubic millimeter	immi (Swiss)	pint, liquid (US)
bushel (UK and US)	cubic yard	kan (Netherlands)	pot (Denmark)
cab (Israel)	deciliter	kela (Eqypt)	quart (UK)
centiliter	eimer (Germany)	koku (Japan)	quart, dry (US)
cor (Israel)	elle (Swiss)	kwan (Japan)	quart, liquid (US)
cubic centimeter	fluid ounce (UK and US)	liter (l or L)	sho (Japan)
cubic decameter		log (Israel)	tou (China)
cubic decimeter	gallon (UK)	milliter	vat (Netherlands)
cubic feet	gallon, dry (US)	mud (Netherlands)	zak (Netherlands)

Measurements of Weight / Mass

baht (Thailand)	hundredweight, long	obole (Greece)	pound
bat (Thailand)	hundredweight, short	ock (Turkey)	rio (Japan)
carat, metric	kati (Malaysia)	oka (Egypt)	slug (g-pounds)
catty (Malaysia)	kilogram (kg)	oke (Bulgaria)	stone
chee (Malaysia)	kin (Japan)	onca (Portugal)	tahil (Malaysia)
gin (Malaysia)	kon (Korea)	ons (Netherlands)	tan (China)
grain	libra (Portugal)	ounce, avoirdupois	tical (Thailand)
gram	lot (Germany)	ounce, troy	ton (UK or long)
hoon (Malaysia)	mna (Greece)	pood (Russia)	tonne

Measurements of Line Density

denier	drex	tex

Measurements of Energy or Work

British Thermal Unit (BTU)	calorie (food)	joule (J)	kilowatt hour (kWh)
	erg		

Measurements of Force

dyne	kip	newton	poundal

Measurements of Fuel Consumption

miles per gallon	miles per liter

Measurements of Power

horsepower (electric)	watts (W)	joules/hour

Measurements of Pressure or Stress

atmospheres	kg-force/square centimeter	kips/square inch	poundals/square foot
bars		pascals (Pa)	

Measurements of Speed

kilometers/hour	knots	Mach number	miles/hour

Measurement of Torque

dyne